COMPLETE PRONUNCIATION KEY

The pronunciation of each word is shown just after the word, in this way: **ab.bre.vi.ate** (ə.brē′vi.āt). The letters and signs used are pronounced as in the words below. The mark ′ is placed after a syllable with primary or strong accent, as in the example above. The mark ′ after a syllable shows a secondary or lighter accent, as in **ab.bre.vi.a.tion** (ə.brē′vi.ā′shən).

Some words, taken from foreign languages, are spoken with sounds that otherwise do not occur in English. Symbols for these sounds are given at the end of the table as "Foreign Sounds."

a	hat, cap	i	it, pin	s	say, yes
ā	age, face	ī	ice, five	sh	she, rush
ã	care, air			t	tell, it
ä	father, far	j	jam, enjoy	th	thin, both
		k	kind, seek	ŧħ	then, smooth
b	bad, rob	l	land, coal		
ch	child, much	m	me, am	u	cup, son
d	did, red	n	no, in	ů	put, book
		ng	long, bring	ü	rule, move
e	let, best	o	hot, rock	ū	use, music
ē	equal, see	ō	open, go		
èr	term, learn	ô	order, all	v	very, save
		oi	oil, toy	w	will, woman
f	fat, if	ou	out, now	y	you, yet
g	go, bag			z	zero, breeze
h	he, how	p	pet, cup	zh	measure,
		r	run, try		seizure

ə occurs only in unaccented syllables and represents the sound of *a* in *a*bout, *e* in tak*e*n, *i* in penc*i*l, *o* in lem*o*n, and *u* in circ*u*s.

FOREIGN SOUNDS

Y as in French *lune,* German *süss.* Pronounce ē as in *equal* with the lips rounded for ü as in *rule.*

œ as in French *deux,* German *könig.* Pronounce ā as in *age* with the lips rounded for ō as in *open.*

N as in French *bon.* The N is not pronounced, but shows that the vowel before it is nasalized.

H as in German *ach,* Scottish *loch.* Pronounce k without closing the breath passage.

COMMON SPELLINGS OF ENGLISH

The table below shows the different sounds of the English language and the commonest spellings for those sounds. After each symbol, the various spellings for that sound are boldface in each example. The spellings have been grouped into three sections to indicate position of occurrence of the sound (initial, medial, and terminal, but in some cases examples do not exist or are so rare as not to merit entry) and each of these sections is separated from the others after each symbol by a dash. This table will help the user who is unfamiliar with English spelling avoid errors in spelling and will help him find entries of whose spelling he is uncertain.

SYMBOL:	SPELLING:
a	at, almond, aunt — hat, plaid, half, salmon, laugh, meringue
ā	age, aid, ay, aye, eight, elite, éclair — came, maid, gaol, gauge, alcayde, break, vein, crepe, fete, regime, conveyance — brae, say, yea, weigh, they, attaché, dossier, bouquet
â	area, Aaron, aerial, air, ere, Eire, eyrie — care, chair, prayer, where, pear, their
ä	argue, aardvark, almond, alms, aunt, encore, ah — father, Afrikaans, half, calm, laugh, sergeant — bra, spa, baa
b	bad — rabid, rabbit — web, tube, ebb
ch	child — archer, Appalachian, scratchy, righteous, question, future — rich, avalanche, watch
d	did — ready, ladder — did, made, add, filled
e	any, aesthetic, elbow, émigré — many, said, says, let, bread, heifer, leopard, friend, assafoetida, bury
ē	Aesop, equal, eat, eel, either, eyrie, oesophagus — Caesar, meter, team, weak, week, receive, people, machine, believe, phoenix — algae, quay, tea, bee, key, Marie
ér	earth, ermine, err, irk, Irving, urn — pearl, stern, first, stirring, word, worry, journey, turn, burrow, myrtle — fir, shirr, entrepreneur, chauffeur, fur, burr
ər	polarize, advertise, avoirdupois, armory, acreage, apron — liar, mother, chauffeur, elixir, honor, honour, acre, augur, zephyr
f	fat, phrase — selfish, roofing, effort, gopher, telephone roof, carafe, off, giraffe, laugh, sylph
g	go, ghost, guest — eczema, auger, baggy, aghast, roguish — leg, egg, Pittsburgh, rogue
h	he, who — ahead
hw	wheat — awhile
i	Aeneas, England, it — cabbage, palaeography, pretty, been, bit, sieve, women, busy, build, hymn — Attlee, alley, Missouri, zombie, Annie, happy
ī	aisle, aye, ay, eider, either, eye, ice — height, geyser, nice, tied, higher, buyer, flying — assagai, alkali, lie, high, buy, sky, rye
j	gem, giaour, jam — lodging, soldier, adjoin, verdure, tragic, exaggerate, allegiance, Georgia, ajar — bridge, avenge
k	coat, chemistry, kind, queue — acre, account, Bacchus, anchor, bucket, acquire, okra, liquor — zinc, monarch, ache, back, sacque, park, folk, masque
l	land, llama, Lloyd — felt, bullet — control, boil, rule, tell, bagatelle, kiln

SYMBOL:	SPELLING:
m	me — drama, plumber, common — drachm, paradigm, calm, dream, home, climb, solemn
n	gnaw, knife, mnemonic, no — signing, many, manner — sign, cologne, pan, gone, Anne
ng	ink, finger, singer — long, tongue
o	odd — watch, hot
ō	open, oats, oh, own, owe — mauve, chauffeur, yeoman, sewing, bone, boat, goes, folk, brooch, soul — beau, sew, domino, Eskimo, whoa, cocoa, toe, though, low
ô	all, automobile, awe, awl, order, ought — warm, walk, taught, bawl, north, broad, reservoir, bought — Utah, Arkansas, Esau, law
oi	oil — boil, royal, buoyant — Illinois, Iroquois, boy, buoy
ou	out, owl — giaour, sauerkraut, house, powder — bough, now
p	play — maple, happy — cup, rope, hiccough
r	run, rhythm, wrong — pray, carry, catarrhal — car, care, parr, burr, catarrh
s	cent, psychology, say, scent, schism — acid, mercy, peaceful, most, descent — nice, gas, curse, acquiesce
sh	chauffeur, Chicago, pshaw, sure, schist, she — ocean, machine, special, insure, conscience, nauseous, ashes, tension, issue, mission, nation — douche, cash
t	ptomaine, tell, Thomas — meter, Esther, button — stopped, bought, yacht, cat, ate, Scott, dinette
th	thin — ethics — with, breath, absinthe
th	then — father — smooth, breathe
u	oven, up — come, does, flood, trouble, cup
ū	eugenic, Europe, ewe, ewer, use, you, yule — beauty, feud, pewter, cure, music — queue, few, adieu, view, emu, cue
ù	wolf, bosom, good, should, full
ü	ooze, ouzel, umiak — maneuver, Zeus, lewd, move, food, croup, rule, rueful, buhl, fruit, buoyant — threw, adieu, to, shoe, too, sou, through, gnu, blue, buoy, two, Sioux
v	very — liver, flivver — of, have
w	will — choir, quick, suite, awake
y	yes — azalea, opinion, hallelujah, canyon
z	Xerxes, zero — discern, easy, scissors, ozone, puzzle — has, rose, adz, adze, buzz
zh	jabot — regime, measure, division, azure, brazier — garage
ə	alone, effect, essential, oblige, occasion, upon — Isaac, abacus, fountain, moment, flageolet, pencil, complete, cautious, circus, ethyl — sofa, pariah, Missouri, kimono

THORNDIKE·BARNHART

Comprehensive Desk

Dictionary

EDITED BY

Clarence L. Barnhart

Editor of the Thorndike-Barnhart Dictionary Series,
The American College Dictionary,
The Dictionary of U.S. Army Terms and
The New Century Cyclopedia of Names

Volume I

A-K

DOUBLEDAY & COMPANY, INC.

Garden City, New York

PRINTED IN THE UNITED STATES OF AMERICA

TABLE OF CONTENTS

VOLUME ONE

General Editorial Advisory Committee............. vii-viii

Special Editors and Office Staff................. ix

Preface .... xi-xiii
    (Clarence L. Barnhart)

How to Use This Dictionary..................... xv-xxi

A Dictionary of the English Language: A-K........ 33-442

American English Grammar...................... xxv-xxix
    (Charles C. Fries and Aileen Traver Kitchin)

Punctuation .... xxxi-xxxiv
    (Albert H. Marckwardt)

Writing and Editing: Manuscript to Printed Page...... xxxv-xxxix
    (Ethel M. Ryan and W. D. Halsey)

Letter Writing: Business and Personal.............. xli-xlv
    (John A. Kouwenhoven)

VOLUME TWO

A Dictionary of the English Language: L-Z......... 443-896

GENERAL EDITORIAL ADVISORY COMMITTEE

Missouri Place Names and coauthor of *A Mark Twain Lexicon*]

ALLEN WALKER READ, Assistant Professor of English, Columbia University. [Managing editor of *American Speech;* president of the American Dialect Society; member of the Executive Committee of the Linguistic Society of America; assistant editor of *The Dictionary of American English*]

PAUL NORTH RICE, (formerly) Chief of Reference Department, New York Public Library.

ESTHER K. SHELDON, Assistant Professor of English, Queens College. [Member of the Advisory Committee of *American Speech;* author of "Pronouncing Systems in Eighteenth-Century Dictionaries" and "Walker's Influence on the Pronunciation of English"]

CHARLES K. THOMAS, Professor of Speech and Director of the Cornell University Speech Clinic, Cornell University. [Author of *An Introduction to the Phonetics of American English*]

CLAUDE M. WISE, Professor of Speech (Head of Department), Louisiana State University. [Former editor of *Quarterly Journal of Speech;* coauthor of *Foundations of Speech, Bases of Speech,* and *Modern Speech*]

SPECIAL EDITORS

PREFACE

To put the proper word in the proper place or to comprehend fully what you read is not easy. Even the well-informed speaker, writer, or reader often turns to reference books to determine the spelling or pronunciation of a word, to learn its meaning, or to clear up some point of usage. Facts about words and advice on their use are either scattered in many places—in grammars, books of synonyms, technical handbooks—or brought together only in the largest dictionaries, books that are cumbersome to use and expensive to buy. This handy-size dictionary is designed to bring within the covers of *one* compact book the essential information about the basic vocabulary necessary to carry on the daily affairs of the English-speaking world.

Over 80,000 words are entered; they have been selected on the basis of word counts of over 30,000,000 words of text in every field of general interest. These 80,000 words make up 99 per cent of the words used in newspapers and magazines, in current fiction and nonfiction; they include all except the very technical terms used in textbooks. An understanding of these 80,000 words will give you a vocabulary larger than that of many college professors or business executives—more than adequate for all daily needs. Some 300,000 facts about the spelling, pronunciation, meanings, origin, and use of these words are given. A careful reading of the very complete notes on pages xv to xxi, explaining point by point how to use this dictionary, will make these facts easily accessible to you.

The arrangement of information provides the greatest possible amount of help to the user at the least cost of time and effort to him. To treat 80,000 words, each in its most useful way, involves thousands of subtle and complex problems. It is not sufficient merely to present in one fashion or another the important facts about a word; these should be made readily available and comprehensible to the person who seeks the dictionary's help. Accordingly, we have put all entries in *one alphabetical list*, put common meanings first, clearly numbered the definitions, used clear, precise language in the definitions, and made frequent use of explanatory phrases and sentences to clarify them.

The reader most frequently uses a dictionary to find out the meaning of a hard word as used in a book or article. An efficient dictionary offers the greatest possible number of words and meanings without sacrificing full explanations of idiomatic uses and expressions. Space is at such a premium that information of little value to the users of the dictionary must be excluded, yet all relevant and needed information must be included. In the selection and arrangement of the definitions, *A Semantic Count of English Words* by Professor Irving Lorge and Professor E. L. Thorndike has been invaluable. In that study, every meaning in approximately 5,000,000 words of text in 29 different types of sources (such as the *Encyclopædia Britannica*, standard novels, and works of nonfiction) was counted and keyed to the meanings listed in the monumental *Oxford English Dictionary*. The value of such a count to a dictionary editor in selecting meanings, in allotting the amount of space for definitions and illustrative sentences, and in the arrangement of the definitions is evident. In addition, by using word counts of the general vocabulary, especially *The Teacher's Word Book of 30,000 Words* by Professor Thorndike and Professor Lorge, counts made of the vocabulary of various special technical and scientific subjects, and the glossaries and indexes of over 300 nonfiction books (five each in 60 different fields of knowledge), we have been able to include all but rare, archaic, obsolete, and excessively technical words and meanings.

The modern writer who has something to say, and takes some thought as to how he will say it, seeks effective control over a basic vocabulary of some 30,000 words (a vocabulary nearly twice as large as that used by Shakespeare). Many of these words —the so-called simple words, such as *set, run, off, about, from*—are extraordinarily complex, with many shades of meaning and numerous idiomatic uses which can be made clear only by the liberal use of explanatory sentences and phrases. Careful and full explanation of these words, the function words of the language, is usually sacrificed in dictionaries in order to include as many words as possible. In this dictionary we have paid special attention to the explanation of function words so that the writer may have at hand a catalogue of the rich variety of ways in which they are used.

Some writers and speakers affect the use of big words which often obscure the meaning of what they write and say. Certainly a writer or speaker who uses many words not in this dictionary can expect to be understood by only a limited few. If it is necessary to use such words—and it may be—they should be explained by the writer or speaker. Meanings labeled *Chem.*, *Physics*, *Biol.*, and *Law* are those used chiefly in these various fields and, unless the term is one used frequently in high-school texts, they will be understood readily only by chemists, physicists, biologists, and lawyers. Meanings labeled *Archaic*, *Obsolete*, or *Poetic* are inappropriate for a writer addressing modern English readers unless he wants to give an archaic or poetic flavor to his writing. Meanings labeled *Colloq.* are appropriate in all but formal writing. Before using a word with an unfamiliar meaning the writer should consider whether there is a restrictive label just after the definition number or the part of speech.

Writers, particularly beginning writers, frequently overuse favorite words. For such writers and others interested in developing a more varied vocabulary, we give over 5,000 synonym and antonym lists keyed to the proper definitions, so that they may, if they desire, choose a simpler or more fitting word or avoid overusing one word.

In addition to the synonym lists there are hundreds of notes describing in some detail cases of conflicting usage so that the person who consults the dictionary may decide which usage he prefers. Often the usage notes discuss general principles of style and language so that the writer, speaker, or reader has at his elbow a concise discussion of many of the most important results of a hundred years of linguistic study. These notes are by Professor Porter G. Perrin, whose *Writer's Guide and Index to English* is well known in the colleges and universities of this country.

In addition to the usage notes there are four special sections designed to give practical help to our users. The first section, written by Professor Charles C. Fries (author of the standard *American English Grammar*) and Professor Aileen Traver Kitchin, gives the fundamental principles of modern American English grammar and is based upon scientific studies of American English as it is used today. The second section, on punctuation, is written by Professor Albert H. Marckwardt of the University of Michigan, author of the *Scribner Handbook of English*, which is used in colleges and universities as a standard guide. The third section, describing the fundamental rules for the preparation of manuscript for the typesetter, has been prepared by a copy editor (Ethel M. Ryan of Doubleday) and an editor (W. D. Halsey, the managing editor for this dictionary) and will give many practical hints to writers. The fourth section, giving forms and styles for social and business letter-writing (the one form of composition we are all certain to practice), by Professor John A. Kouwenhoven of Barnard College, is authoritative and easy to follow. These special sections offer practical advice as well as a general discussion of principles and will be useful to anyone interested in the art of writing or speaking good English.

The speaker has one need over and above the needs of the writer: he must be furnished with acceptable pronunciations which can be used on all occasions in every part of the country. A dictionary, however, cannot be a substitute for the judgment and good taste of the speaker. He must decide the appropriateness to his purpose, his audience, and the occasion of the words and pronunciations that he uses. But a dictionary can be faithful in recording good present-day American English, and can set forth the more important variant pronunciations in use in the principal regions of the country. Professor Greet and Professor Hubbell, the special editors in charge of pronunciation, have ensured that these aims are carried out.

This dictionary employs a pronunciation key that is easy to learn and to remember. The symbols in the key are listed and explained on the inside of the front and back covers. Outside of the very frequent so-called short and long vowels (as in hat, let, it, hot, cup; āge, ēqual, īce, ōpen, ūse) there are only eight symbols for the user to learn (see the section How to Use This Dictionary, pages xv to xxi). One of these symbols, ə, is called *schwa* and is used to denote the neutral sound of a vowel in an unaccented syllable. It is the sound of *a* in about, *e* in taken, *i* in pencil, *o* in lemon, and *u* in circus. The use of only one symbol for this somewhat variable sound is the approved practice of modern phonetics. This special symbol (ə) for unaccented syllables has proved useful in radio as an aid in teaching broadcasters to avoid the overstressing of unaccented syllables which results in an unnatural or exaggerated pronunciation. It has also been employed in the widely used Thorndike-Century school-dictionary series for over fifteen years, with beneficial results in teaching pupils pronunciation.

A notion of the original meaning of a word will often give the reader a better understanding of it. This dictionary includes word origins generously and a reading of them may prove both profitable and interesting. To know that *acronym* is made up of Greek words meaning "tip name," that originally *abduct* meant "lead away," that *conduct* meant "lead to," that *assert* meant "join to" gives the reader, writer, or speaker an insight into the development of meaning and enables him to recognize familiar elements in new words. The word origins are concerned with the earliest form and meaning of a word, especially the meaning. They have been specially prepared by Professors Hall, Moulton, and Ward and have been carefully checked by Professor Kemp Malone. Users of this dictionary will find them readable and authoritative.

The contributions of America to the English language have not hitherto been recognized in dictionaries because the facts have not been available. For some years, however, Dr. M. M. Mathews has been compiling a historical dictionary of Americanisms (words American in origin), for the University of Chicago Press. We have carefully read the galleys of this scholarly work and have had the benefit of Dr. Mathews' advice in labeling all of the Americanisms in this dictionary. For the first time in a dictionary of this kind we label words and meanings that American English has contributed to the English vocabulary, such as *abalone, anesthesia, appendicitis, gangster, kitchenette, lowbrow, molasses, oscar, party line, phony,* and many others are evidence of the growth and vitality of American English.

The making of a reliable dictionary—a record of existing usage—is, or should be, the work of many scholars and editors working together. In framing the policies of this book we have had advice and help from twenty-eight scholars on the Editorial Advisory Committee. Many of them—those who were my associates on *The Thorndike-Century Senior Dictionary*—have worked with me for fifteen years. For their conscientious, helpful, and friendly advice I am much indebted, and especially to W. Cabell Greet, who, as its chairman, has given freely of his time and knowledge to the work of the committee.

The special editors (listed on page ix) have had charge of special sections of the book—pronunciation, etymology, Americanisms, new words, and usage notes— and have made these sections a convenient and authoritative guide to modern standard American usage. To Professor Lorge, I am indebted for the right to use the *English Semantic Count* which has been greatly expanded and brought up to date with a special count of the 570 commonest words, *here used for the first time*. Finally, I have had the right to use material from *The Thorndike-Century Senior Dictionary, The New Century Dictionary, The Dictionary of Americanisms,* and *The Dictionary of American English.* The selection and organization of material from these varied sources, the rewriting of definitions to make them more understandable, and the addition of modern words and meanings have been the work of the office staff and the special editors. We have tried to approach the language problems of this dictionary in the spirit of the late E. L. Thorndike, psychologist, and the late Leonard Bloomfield, linguist. I believe they would have been pleased to know that a permanent editorial staff has been set up to apply to dictionaries the results of scientific research on language and vocabulary. On behalf of all my associates I express the hope that the assemblage of such a wealth of material from so many sources will result in a reference tool of great value to the users of American English today.

Clarence L. Barnhart

HOW TO USE THIS DICTIONARY

1. The order in which information is given about a word (see **ability**, below) is as follows: (1) the word spelled in boldface type, (2) its pronunciation, (3) part of speech, (4) any irregular inflected forms (plural, past tense, etc.), (5) definitions of its meanings arranged under the appropriate parts of speech, (6) the origin of the word, or etymology, (7) synonyms keyed to the definitions, and (8) usage notes telling you about preferred forms of usage, awkward forms, good written style, and similar matters.

a·bil·i·ty (ə·bil′ə·ti), *n.*, *pl.* –ties. 1. power to do or act in any relation: *give according to your ability.* 2. skill: *mechanical ability.* 3. power to do some special thing; talent: *musical ability, natural abilities.* [< F < L. See ABLE.] —Syn. 1. capacity. 2. cleverness. 3. aptitude. ➤ Ability is followed by *to* and an infinitive rather than *of* (*ability to do,* not *of doing*) or *in* and a substantive: *ability to design buildings; ability in arithmetic.*

How to Find a Word

2. One Alphabetical List. You merely need to know the order of the letters of the alphabet to find a word in this dictionary. All main entries are in one long alphabetical list so that you have only one place to look to find a word. Look at column 1, page 33; words in the common vocabulary (A, a (the letter), a (the article), aardvark, abacá, aback, abacus, etc.), technical terms (abaft), proper names (Aachen, Aaron), chemical symbols (A), abbreviations (a., A.B.), and prefixes (a–¹, a–², ab–) are in one list.

3. Homographs (words spelled exactly alike but of different origin) have a small number raised a little above the line after each entry to remind you to look at the other entries spelled in the same way if you do not find the information you are seeking under the first one.

mail¹ (māl), *n.* 1. letters, papers, parcels, etc., sent by the postal system. 2. system by which they are sent, managed by the Post Office Department. —*v.* send by mail; put in a mailbox. —*adj.* of mail. [< OF *male* wallet < Gmc.] —mail′a·ble, *adj. Am.* —mail′er, *n.*
mail² (māl), *n.* 1. armor made of metal rings, or small loops of chain, linked together. 2. armor; protective covering. —*v.* cover or protect with mail. [< OF < L *macula* a mesh in network] —mailed, *adj.*

When looking up cross references as from **bore**³ to **bear**¹ be sure to look under the right homograph.

bore³ (bôr; bōr), *v.* pt. of bear¹.
bear¹ (bâr), *v.* bore or (*Archaic*) bare, borne or born, bear·ing. 1. carry: *bear a burden.* . . .
bear² (bâr), *n.*, *adj.*, *v.*, beared, bear·ing. —*n.* 1. a large, clumsy, quadruped animal. . . .

4. Main and Subordinate Entries. In this dictionary, main entries always appear on the left-hand margin in large boldface type. On page 33, the first four main entries in column 2 are **abandon, abandoned, abase, abash.** Both **abbrev.** and its variant **abbr.** are main entries; so is **abbreviation.** Subordinate entries on page 33 are idioms (**taken aback under aback),** derivatives or run-ons (**abbreviator under abbreviate),** inflected forms (–cat·ed,

–cat·ing under **abdicate).** Subordinate entries are put in a smaller-sized boldface type.

5. Derivatives (words formed from root words + suffixes) as Main Entries or Subordinate Entries. Note that derivative entries are sometimes entered as main entries and sometimes as subordinate entries. Derivatives formed with –*ly,* –*ness,* –*er,* –*able,* –*less,* –*like,* and less frequently –*tion,* –*ity,* and –*al,* are often printed in smaller boldface type at the very end of the definition of the word from which they are derived, because the meaning and the pronunciation can easily be obtained by combining the root with the suffix. Entries of this kind are called run-on entries. Sometimes, however, a derivative is very frequently used, has specialized meanings, or is hard to recognize as a derivative; in such cases the derivative is listed as a main entry (contrast **abbreviation,** a main entry, with **abbreviator,** a run-on entry).

6. Derivatives formed from root words + prefixes (*un–, non–,* etc.) are listed under the prefix without a definition if they are easy to understand by combining the meaning of the prefix with that of the root word. Certain common prefixes such as **non–, un–, over–,** and **re–** have long lists of such words. If a word beginning with one of the common prefixes is not in the list of words under the prefix, look in the proper place in the main entry list for it. Thus, **nonadhesive** can be found under **non–** (the meaning of the word is merely *not adhesive*). If further information is desired, **adhesive** may be looked up and "not" added to the beginning of each of its definitions. **Noncombatant,** however, has a specialized meaning and will be found in the main alphabetical list.

7. Idioms are phrases or expressions, such as *chip on one's shoulder,* that cannot be fully understood from the ordinary meanings of the words which combine to form them. Look for an idiom under its most important word. Thus, **feather in one's cap** is placed under the noun definitions of **feather;** **feather one's nest** is under the verb definitions of **feather.**

feath·er (feth′ər), *n.* 1. one of the light, thin growths that cover a bird's skin. 2. something like a feather in shape or lightness. 3. feather in one's cap, thing to be proud of. 4. in fine, good, or high feather, in good health, high spirits, etc. —*v.* 1. supply or cover with feathers. 2. grow like feathers. 3. move like feathers. 4. join by a tongue and groove. 5. turn the edge of a blade in the direction of movement. 6. feather one's nest, take advantage of chances to get rich. [OE *fether*] —feath′ered, *adj.* —feath′er·less, *adj.* —feath′er·like′, *adj.*

8. Guide Words are words printed at the top of each column in heavy black letters. The one at the top of the left column is the same as the first entry word on the page; the one at the top of the right column is the same as the last entry word on the page. All the main entries that fall alphabetically between the guide words can be found on that page. By using the guide words to see whether or not an entry is on a particular page you can save much time in locating desired entries.

How to Use This Dictionary for Spelling

9. Words of one syllable are printed solid (**each**); words of more than one syllable are separated into syllables by centered dots (**ab·di·cate, ea·ger, re·ly**). Syllabication of the printed or written word is determined partly by speech (but note that the syllables in the pronunciation sometimes, as in **double**, differ from those in the entry word), partly by the component parts (root + affixes) of which the word has been formed, and partly by the conventions of printers and writers. When more than one pronunciation is given for a word, the syllabication shown is ordinarily that of the first pronunciation.

reb·el (*n., adj.* reb′əl; *v.* ri-bel′), *n., adj., v.* . . . The dot in the entry word represents the point at which a word may normally be broken at the end of a written or printed line. In printed matter and formal writing, however, it is not considered good practice to break a word so that a single letter stands alone on one line (^a‑bed or l‑deologically or sleep‑y). Short words, such as **able**, should stand unbroken on one line or the other; long ones should be broken as near the middle as possible (**ideologi-cally**); hyphenated compounds (**double-cross**) are best broken only at the hyphen.

10. Variant Spellings. Often there are two or more ways of spelling the same word in English; both ways are current and in good use and it is merely a question of your preference or the preference (if you know it) of the person to or for whom you are writing. We record all of the common variant spellings. When two or more variants are close enough to be seen in the same eye-span they are entered together, and we put first the one that is simpler or is more common in American usage. If the variant spellings must be entered in different parts of the dictionary, we give them at the end of the preferred entry. Under the variant, we refer the user of the dictionary to the preferred form.

adz, adze (adz), *n.* . . .
la·bor, *esp. Brit.* **la·bour** (lā′bər), *n.* . . .
en·close (en-klōz′), *v.,* –closed, –clos·ing. **1.** shut in on all sides; surround. **2.** put a wall or fence around. **3.** put in an envelope along with a letter, etc. **4.** contain. Also, **inclose.**
in·close (in-klōz′), *v.,* –closed, –clos·ing. enclose.

11. Inflected Forms (the plurals of nouns, the forms of the verb, and the comparatives and superlatives of adjectives) are sometimes difficult to spell. All inflected forms in which there is any change in the root are given immediately after the pronunciation, so that the person seeking to determine their spelling or syllabication may find them quickly and easily. Notice the syllabication of inflected forms in the examples given.

ba·by (bā′bi), *n., pl.* –bies, *adj., v.,* –bied, –by·ing. . . .
need·y (nēd′i), *adj.,* need·i·er, need·i·est. . . .

How to Use the Pronunciations

12. The Standard for the Selection of Pronunciations. The system of indicating pronunciation used in this dictionary is intended to present as clearly as possible pronunciations customarily heard from educated speakers of English in the United States. You will use this dictionary, perhaps, for the purpose of finding what are the acceptable pronunciations of a certain word, or of finding whether the one which you have been using or hearing is one which is generally accepted or which prevails in a large section of the country. The purpose of this dictionary is to record social custom, with due regard for regional differences, not to impose the pronunciation of one section upon the whole country, or to prescribe or dictate innovations which some individuals might think desirable.

Since fashions in pronunciation change from time to time, it is not sufficient for a dictionary to establish a list of pronunciations and continue using them forever. Authorities have never agreed on all matters of pronunciation, nor can they be expected to agree as to the time when some new pronunciation may be considered to have established itself. For example, when the word *balcony* was borrowed into English from Italian, educated speakers accented the word on the second syllable; but English speakers who did not know Italian tended to treat the word as an English noun and accent it on the first syllable. Such a pronunciation was long considered vulgar, and was objected to by teachers and authors of textbooks. The question may now be considered settled for that particular word. It would be eccentric and indefensible pedantry to accent the word in English on the second syllable simply because such an accent was historically justified. Pronunciation is constantly changing. Some pronunciations that once were common, as (kun′i) for *cony*, are now rarely used. New pronunciations, as (ad·vėr′tiz·mənt) for *advertisement*, gradually come into wide use and often force older pronunciations into obscurity. This dictionary has included variant pronunciations, sometimes not recorded elsewhere, which its editors have reason to believe are now part of the language. Examples of changed or changing pronunciations that are recorded are:

dol·drum (dol′drəm; dōl′–)
hom·i·cide (hom′ə·sīd; hō′mə–)
ig·no·ra·mus (ig′nə·rā′məs; –ram′əs)
ja·bot (zha·bō′; zhab′ō; jab′ō)
pre·mo·ni·tion (prē′mə·nish′ən; prem′ə–)

In preparing the work on pronunciation, it was our purpose to have and to use the advice of the best available authorities of the past and present. For the first, the recommended pronunciations of the best existing dictionaries were consulted and compared. Only one who has worked on such a task can realize how widely good authorities may sometimes differ. To any naïve questioner who asks, "What does the dictionary say?" as if "the dictionary" were a sort of Olympian abstraction, an experienced lexicographer can only reply, "What dictionary, and which edition of it?" For the second, authorities to advise on the present state of pronunciation, a group of 28 were chosen. All the members of this committee are well known as scholars in their own professions. They represent all parts of the United States, and many different types of training and points of view. An experienced and skilled phonetician was entrusted with the task of carrying out the policies on pronunciation laid down by the group of advisers.

It is not possible to present in a dictionary all pronunciations that may be heard from cultivated speakers, but we have tried in each case to give the best-established American pronunciation and the commonest acceptable variants.

It is not even possible in a dictionary to give all the possible varying pronunciations used by the same speaker. A dictionary must present its material one word at a time, but we do not speak one word at a time. Even such a simple question as "How do you pronounce *the?*" can never have a single answer. One's pronunciation of this word and of other words depends on neighboring sounds, accent, speed of utterance, and, in many cases, on the style of discourse: formal, informal, colloquial, etc. The pronunciations are, as far as is possible when words must be treated in isolation, those of educated informal speech. The fact that a particular pronunciation is given first does not indicate that it is "more correct." We put the more frequent pronunciation first, wherever this can be ascertained, but usage is often rather evenly divided and in many instances the relative frequency of the variants can only be guessed at.

13. Regional Variations in Pronunciation. Although the United States is the most homogeneous speech community of comparable size in the world, there are nevertheless certain rather noticeable differences in the usage of different parts of the country. Educated speakers do not pronounce English in exactly the same way in Chicago, New York, Boston, and Atlanta. It is the task of special phonetic dictionaries to record these differences in minute detail; but even a general dictionary must include the more important regional variations in pronunciation. A careful use of symbols will make it unnecessary to enter some of these variants separately. For example, speakers from eastern New England and from the North Central states will not pronounce the key word *ärm* with the same vowels. But if each pronounces in every word respelled with (ä) the same vowel he uses in the key word, his pronunciation will be correct and appropriate to his own usage. In the more important instances where this device is not sufficient, as in the case of words like *forest* and *hoarse* (see below), the respellings include as many entries as are necessary to record the facts.

For our purposes here the various speech areas in the United States can be roughly grouped into five main areas—Northern (from western New England to, and including, the Midwest), Midland (from southern New Jersey and northern Delaware and Maryland westward to the Ohio Valley), Southern (from southern Delaware and Maryland southward and westward to Texas), Eastern New England, and Metropolitan New York. Little detailed information is available on pronunciation in the western part of the country.

a. Pronunciation of "r." In this dictionary (r) has been recorded in the pronunciations wherever *r* occurs in the spelling, as in far·ther (fär′thər), since a majority of the speakers of American English pronounce it in all positions. In eastern New England, metropolitan New York, and the many areas of the coastal South, however, (r) is often not pronounced when final or when followed by a consonant. If the reader is a native of one of these "r-less" regions, he should, of course, pronounce (r) only where it is natural for him.

b. Pronunciation of "o" in "log," "loft," "broth," "cost," "forest," "on," "prong." Before certain consonants, the pronunciation of a historical "short o" varies in American English between the limits of the (o) in *hot* and the (ô) in *law.* All words in which this variation occurs have been given two pronunciations, the first being the one which the editors consider more common in America as a whole.

log (lôg; log). . . .
loft (lôft; loft). . . .
doff (dof; dôf). . . .
broth (brôth; broth). . . .
cost (kôst; kost). . . .

for·est (fôr′ist; for′–). . . .
on (on; ôn). . . .
prong (prông; prong). . . .

A number of words spelled with *wa* or *ua* vary in the same fashion:

swamp (swomp; swômp). . . .
war·rant (wôr′ənt; wor′–). . . .
quar·rel (kwôr′əl; kwor′–). . . .

c. Pronunciation of "o" in "for" and "four." A distinction in the pronunciation of such pairs of words as *for* (fôr), *four* (fôr; fōr) and *horse* (hôrs), *hoarse* (hôrs; hōrs) is heard in some parts of the United States, particularly in eastern New England and the South. In other parts of the country, such pairs of words are more often pronounced identically, so that *horse* and *hoarse* are both (hôrs), rather than (hôrs) and (hōrs), respectively. Words in which such a distinction is made are recorded as follows:

mourn·ing (môr′ning; mōr′–). . . .

Compare this with the pronunciation for morning:

morn·ing (môr′ning). . . .

d. Pronunciation of "a" in "ask" and "command." The pronunciation of *a* in words like ask and command varies between (a) and (ä) and a vowel intermediate between the two (heard also in the eastern New England pronunciation of *barn, car,* etc.). In this dictionary such words are recorded as follows:

ask (ask; äsk). . . .
com·mand (kə·mand′; –mänd′). . . .

e. Pronunciation of "a" in "fat" and "man." The reader may find that he pronounces one vowel in fat and a much longer one of a different quality in man. There has been a tendency in many parts of the United States to lengthen an original "short *a*" before certain consonants and to change its quality. The longer vowel (in the speech of some breaking into a diphthong) has not been recorded in this dictionary because the facts about its occurrence are not yet fully known:

fat (fat). . . .
man (man). . . .

f. Pronunciation of "o" in "stop" and "lodge." The lengthening of "short *a*" referred to in paragraph e. above has been paralleled in some parts of America by a lengthening of an original "short *o*" under similar conditions, as in the word lodge. The result of this in the *"r-less"* parts of the South has been to make pairs of words like *lodge* and *large* identical in pronunciation. This longer vowel has not been separately recorded in this dictionary:

stop (stop). . . .
lodge (loj). . . .

g. Pronunciation of vowels before "r" as in "clear" and "poor." There is a variation in American speech in the pronunciation of long vowels before (r). Vowels followed by (r) tend to shorten, so that *ea* is pronounced (ē) in *clean,* but in *clear,* in the speech of many Americans, it becomes (i) or a vowel intermediate in quality between (ē) and (i). Words like *clear* may have the vowel of *beat* or of *bit,* and words like *poor* may have the vowel of *boot* or of *bush* in different sections of the country. Such words, in which the vowel is shortened by a following (r), have been recorded with the shortened vowel, but the variants with the longer vowel should be assumed to exist in all cases.

clear (klir). . . .
poor (pùr). . . .

h. Pronunciation of vowels before "r" in "dare" and "dairy." The exact quality of the vowel in words like dare and dairy varies considerably in cultivated American speech. Variation exists between vowels close to (e) or to (a) and a long vowel intermediate in quality between them. In New England and the coastal South words like dairy, which are not derived from forms in which the (r) is final, often have a vowel close to (ā), while in some parts of New England and the coastal South this type of pronunciation may even be heard in dare and hair. The symbol (â) is used in this dictionary to cover all these variants:

dare (dâr). . . .
dair·y (dâr′i). . . .

i. Pronunciation of "y" in "city" and "happy." In this dictionary we have shown (i) as the final vowel of words like city and happy, but a good many people pronounce a longer vowel approaching (ē) (in the speech of those who use the shorter vowel one would hear no distinction between pairs of words like candid and candied):

cit·y (sit′i). . . .
hap·py (hap′i). . . .

j. Pronunciation of "wh" in "whale" and "which." In the speech of many cultivated people no distinction is heard in pairs of words like whale, wail and which, witch, all of which are pronounced with a simple (w). In the pronunciations in this dictionary words spelled with wh have been recorded as (hw), but (w) should be assumed as an equally acceptable variant in each case:

whale (hwāl). . . .
which (hwich). . . .

The Pronunciation Key

14. Function of Letters of the Alphabet. The letters of the alphabet are directions to produce sounds: the letters used in bet direct us to utter a different set of sounds than are called for by the letters in sad. Since English spelling habits are very conservative and have not kept pace with the changes in pronunciation, the directions are often ambiguous: the ea in steak directs us to say ā and the ea in meat to say ē; the ei in receive directs us to say ē but the ei in vein to say ā. The 26 letters of the alphabet occur in over 200 different spelling combinations directing us to say some 40 English sounds.

15. Basis of the Pronunciation Key. The inconsistencies and conservatism of English spelling make necessary a system of giving clear directions to say the proper sounds. This can be done by assigning one sound only to a letter (a as in bat), combination of letters (ch as in much), or a letter modified by a diacritic (ā as in bate) to distinguish it from other sounds indicated by the same letter (â as in care, ä as in far). There are in the key 43 symbols to represent the speech sounds of English.

16. Diacritical Marks. The first step in learning to read the pronunciations is to learn the key. There are only 13 special symbols for English sounds; five of these are the so-called long vowels, ā, ē, ī, ō, ū; these symbols are well known and common to most dictionary systems and will cause little trouble. The "short" vowels, a, e, i, o, and u, left unmarked since they are approximately 40 per cent of all vowel sounds, occur chiefly in closed syllables (those with a consonant following a vowel, as in hat, bet, sit, hot, cut). There is no more reason to mark these common vowel symbols than there is to mark d or n or b with a diacritic.

17. The special symbols that must be learned are ä as in far, â as in care, ê as in her, ô as in order, tḥ as in then (contrast with th in thin), ů as in put, ü as in rule, and ə as in about (ə·bout′). These symbols are put in an abbreviated key at the bottom of every other page so that you may refer to them quickly and learn them easily. See also the full pronunciation key on the front and back end-sheets.

How to Find the Pronunciations

18. The pronunciation is entered in parentheses after the main entry.

ab·a·tis (ab′ə·tis). . . .

19. If there are two (or more) main entries, pronounced the same, the pronunciation follows the second (or last) variant spelling or form.

adz, adze (adz). . . .

20. If a variant form is pronounced differently from the main entry, the proper pronunciation follows directly after each word. In most cases, it is necessary to give only the differing part of the variant pronunciation.

bro·mine (brō′mēn; —min), **bro·min** (—min). . . .

21. If the words that make up a phrase are entered separately and pronunciations are given there, no pronunciation is entered for the phrase.

benefit of clergy. . . .

22. Difficult inflected forms are pronounced in the entry, unless they are separately entered.

for·mu·la (fôr′myə·lə), n., pl. —las, —lae (—lē). . . .
hoof (hůf; hüf), n., pl. hoofs or (Rare) hooves. **hooves** (hůvz; hüvz), n. Rare. pl. of hoof. . . .

23. Run-ons are pronounced when they involve a change in pronunciation from the main entry that is not clear from the syllabication and stress alone.

ge·om·e·try (ji·om′ə·tri), n. branch of mathematics that deals with lines, angles, surfaces, and solids. . . . —ge·o·met·ric (jē′ə·met′rik), adj.
cli·mate (klī′mit), n. 1. the kind of weather a place has. . . . —cli·mat·ic (klī·mat′ik), adj.

24. When a run-on has the variants of the entry word, and these are variants of stress, the run-on is entered with the stress of the first pronunciation, although either pronunciation is correct.

con·trite (kən·trīt′; kon′trīt). . . . —con·trite′ly, adv. —con·trite′ness, n.

25. Some words are differently pronounced depending on their grammatical function in a particular context. These pronunciations have been labeled in accordance with the parts of speech shown in the entry.

mod·er·ate (adj., n. mod′ər·it; v. mod′ər·āt). . . .

26. Foreign pronunciations, when considered helpful, are given with a label after the American pronunciation.

au grat·in (ō grat′ən, grä′tən; Fr. ō grä·taN′). . . .

Although it has been considered by some to be fashionable or "more correct" to retain foreign pronunciations, particularly those of French words, the best rule to follow on the pronunciation of foreign words is—if a good, usable Anglicized pronunciation exists, use it! In the pronunciation of foreign words and phrases in this dictionary, emphasis has been placed on providing the reader with a pronunciation he may use comfortably, as (ôr′ dĕrv′) for *hors d'oeuvre*. Where a foreign pronunciation is also commonly used, that, too, has been provided and labeled, as (*Fr.* dœ′vrə). See **Bund, concierge, debris.**

27. Accent is indicated in the pronunciations by the symbol ′ for the heavier or primary accent, and ′ for the lighter or secondary accent, placed *after* the syllable which is to be accented.

hes·i·ta·tion (hez′ə·tā′shən). . . .
Some words may be correctly accented in more than one way. Two (or more) pronunciations are given for such words.

ab·do·men (ab′də·mən; ab·dō′mən). . . .

How to Locate a Meaning

28. Order of Definitions. The meanings of words are arranged according to the frequency of their use. Meanings that are used most frequently are put first and those that are less frequent, such as archaic or technical meanings, come last.

If the meaning to be looked up is a common one the reader should scan the first few definitions of the entry. In neutral, *adj.*, the most common meanings are 1–4, and the less frequent chemical, electrical, and biological meanings are given later. This arrangement of definitions according to frequency enables the reader to find various meanings quickly and easily.

neu·tral (nū′trəl; nū′–), *adj.* **1.** on neither side in a quarrel or war. **2.** of or belonging to a neutral country or neutral zone: *a neutral port.* **3.** neither one thing nor the other; indefinite. **4.** having little or no color; grayish. **5.** *Chem.* neither acid nor alkaline. **6.** *Elect.* neither positive nor negative. **7.** *Biol.* neuter. . . .

29. Ways in Which Meanings Are Given. Meanings of words are given in one of the following four ways or some combination of them: descriptive statements (abatis), synonyms (abattoir), pictures (def. 2 of abdomen), explanatory examples (alive). Hard words or technical terms with only one or two meanings can be explained by using the first three methods; words with many meanings or closely related meanings require explanatory examples to clarify the meanings.

ab·a·tis (ab′ə·tis), *n., pl.* **ab·a·tis.** barricade of trees cut down and placed with their sharpened branches directed toward an enemy. . . .
ab·at·toir (ab′ə·twär; –twôr), *n.* slaughterhouse. . . .
ab·do·men (ab′də·mən; ab-dō′mən), *n.* **1.** *Anat., Zool.* the part of the body containing the stomach and other digestive organs; belly. **2.** *Zool.* the last of the three parts of the body of an insect or crustacean. . . .
a·live (ə·līv′), *adj.* **1.** living; not dead: *the man is alive.* **2.** in continued activity or operation: *keep the principles of liberty alive.* **3.** of all living: *happiest man alive.* . . .

Abdomen (def. 2)

HEAD
THORAX
ABDOMEN

30. Function of Explanatory Sentences. Many relation words (prepositions, adverbs, linking verbs) cannot be understood readily by merely giving a definition. Consider the importance of the explanatory examples in distinguishing the first two definitions of about: "of; concerned with" and "in connection with." These very frequent words with a complex network of meanings are difficult to use idiomatically, and great care is taken in this dictionary to make their various meanings clear.

a·bout (ə·bout′), *prep.* **1.** of; concerned with: *a book about bridges.* **2.** in connection with: *something queer about him.* . . .

31. Fitting the Definition into the Context. The best test of the adequacy of a definition is to fit the definition into a context in place of the hard word. If the definition makes the context clear to the reader, the dictionary has done its work well. Find the appropriate definition for the italicized word in the sentences containing the word *encore* at the end of this paragraph by running down the list of definitions for encore given below. Notice how the clear numbering of the definitions helps you to find the different senses quickly. "The singer tried hard to get an *encore.*" "Three *encores* are enough for any performer to give."

en·core (äng′kōr; –kôr; än′–), *interj., n., v.,* **–cored, –cor·ing.** —*interj.* once more; again. —*n.* **1.** demand by the audience for the repetition of a song, etc., or for another appearance of the performer or performers. **2.** repetition of a song, etc., in response to such a demand. **3.** an additional song, etc., given in response to such a demand. —*v.* make such a demand for (a performer, etc.) by applauding. [< F]

32. Special Constructions. A number of words are followed by certain prepositions (accede) and some have different meanings with different prepositions (abound). These prepositional usages should be learned as an integral part of the definition to avoid incorrect constructions in speech and writing. In this dictionary they are entered in italic type and enclosed in parentheses at the end of the definition.

ac·cede (ak·sēd′), *v.,* **–ced·ed, –ced·ing. 1.** give consent (*to*): *please accede to my request.* **2.** become a party (*to*): *our government acceded to the treaty.* **3.** attain (to an office or dignity); come (*to*): *the king's oldest son acceded to the throne.* . . .

a·bound (ə·bound′), *v.* **1.** be plentiful: *fish abound in the ocean.* **2.** be rich (*in*): *America abounds in oil.* **3.** be well supplied (*with*): *the ocean abounds with fish.* . . .

33. Definitions with Restrictive Labels. Not all words or meanings are used by every speaker or writer of English on every occasion. The great body of English is common to all users of the language but some meanings are used chiefly by members of certain trades and professions (subject labels), others are common only in certain geographical areas (*Dial., Am., Brit.*), still others are used only on certain occasions—in speaking and in informal, but not in formal, writing (*Colloq.*)—and others are the half-remembered common words of former generations (*Archaic, Obs., Poetic*) which are chiefly found in literary use or in old books. The chief labels are:

a. *Colloq.* = *Colloquial,* which merely means that the word or meaning is more common in speech than in writing. Colloquial English is good English as used in conversation and in those kinds of writing which resemble conversation, and is appropriate for all but the most formal occasions.

get·a·way (get′ə·wā′), *n. Colloq.* **1.** act of getting away; escape. **2.** start of a race.

b. *Slang* arises from a desire for novelty or for vivid emphasis or for unconventionality. Many slang words have short lives, but some prove more useful and become a part of the general colloquial and familiar vocabulary. Until they do, slang words and meanings should be avoided on formal occasions.

Veep (vēp), *n. Slang.* **1.** Vice-president of the United States. **2.** veep, any vice-president.

c. *Law, Elect., Bot., Physics, Electronics,* and similar labels are subject labels and indicate that the word or meaning is used chiefly by the members of a particular profession or trade.

an·dro·gen (an′drə·jən), *n. Biochem.* any substance that induces or strengthens masculine characteristics, as a male sex hormone. . . .

ad·i·a·bat·ic (ad′i·ə·bat′ik; ā′di–), *adj. Physics.* without transmission (gain or loss) of heat.

d. *Trademark* indicates that a word or meaning is a proprietary name owned by a particular company and valued by it as identifying its product. Sometimes a trademark by common use and wide application to related products becomes a part of the common vocabulary; **aspirin** was formerly a trademark. Great care has been taken to label trademarks but failure to include the label does not mean that the word is not a trademark.

Plex·i·glas (plek′sə·glas′; –gläs′), *n. Trademark.* a light, transparent thermoplastic, often used in place of glass. [< *pl(astic)* + *(fl)exi(ble)* + *glas(s)*]

as·pi·rin (as′pə·rin), *n.* drug for headaches, colds, etc., $C_9H_8O_4$. It is the acetate of salicylic acid. [from trademark]

ko·dak (kō′dak), *n., v.,* –daked, –dak·ing. *Am.* —*n.* **1.** a small camera with rolls of film on which photographs are taken. **2. Kodak,** *Trademark.* a small camera made by the Eastman Kodak Company. —*v.* take photographs with a kodak. —ko′dak·er, *n.*

e. *Dial.* = *Dialect.* A word or meaning used only in a certain geographical area or by a certain group.

a·nent (ə·nent′), *prep.* **1.** *Archaic or Scot.* concerning. **2.** *Brit. Dial.* beside. . . .

f. *Poetic.* A word or meaning found only in poetry or in prose that has some qualities of poetry.

ope (ōp), *v.,* oped, op·ing. *Poetic.* open.

g. *Archaic.* A word or meaning rare except in books written in, or in the style of, an earlier period.

a·vaunt (ə·vônt′; ə·vänt′), *interj. Archaic.* begone! get out! go away! . . .

h. *Obs.* = *Obsolete.* A word or meaning not used at all at the present time. It exists only in old books or books about the past.

cap·ti·vate (kap′tə·vāt), *v.,* –vat·ed, –vat·ing. **1.** hold captive by beauty or interest; charm; fascinate. **2.** *Obs.* capture. —cap′ti·va′tion, *n.* —cap′ti·va′tor, *n.* —Syn. **1.** enchant, entrance.

i. *Am.* = *Americanism.* A word or meaning originating in the United States, although its use may have spread throughout the English-speaking world.

a·board (ə·bêrd′; ə·bôrd′), *adv.* **1.** in or on a ship. **2.** *Am.* in or on a train, bus, airplane, etc. . . .

OK, O.K. (ō′kā′), *adj., adv., v.,* OK'd, OK'ing; O.K.'d, O.K.'ing; *n., pl.* OK's; O.K.'s. *Am., Colloq.* —*adj.* all right; correct; approved. —*v.* endorse; approve. —*n.* approval. . . .

j. *Am., S.W.* An Americanism which originated in and is chiefly used in the southwestern United States.

a·do·be (ə·dō′bē), *n. Am., S.W.* **1.** sun-dried clay or mud. **2.** a brick or bricklike piece of such material, used in building. —*adj.* built or made of sun-dried bricks: *an adobe house.* . . .

k. *Am., S.* An Americanism which originated in and is chiefly used in the southern United States.

pone (pōn), *n. Am., S.* **1.** bread made of corn meal. **2.** loaf or cake of this bread. . . .

l. *Am., W.* An Americanism which originated in and is chiefly used in the western United States.

ro·de·o (rō′di·ō; rō·dā′ō), *n., pl.* –de·os. *Am.* **1.** contest or exhibition of skill in roping cattle, riding horses, etc. **2.** *W.* the driving together of cattle. . . .

Both definitions 1 and 2 are Americanisms but definition 2 is used chiefly in the West.

m. *U.S.* A word used more commonly in the United States than in other parts of the English-speaking world, but which originated elsewhere than in the United States.

bowling alley, *U.S.* a long, narrow, enclosed floor for bowling.

n. *Brit.* = *Briticism.* A word or meaning more common in Great Britain and the British Empire than in the rest of the English-speaking world.

ac·cu·mu·la·tor (ə·kū′myə·lā′tər), *n.* **1.** one that accumulates. **2.** *Brit.* a storage battery.

o. Common non-English words from other languages used only or chiefly for special purposes, or by people familiar with other languages, are labeled with the name of the language before the definition.

gar·çon (gär·sôn′), *n., pl.* –çons (-sôn′). *French.* **1.** a young man; boy. **2.** servant. **3.** waiter.

ad in·fi·ni·tum (ad in′fə·nī′təm), *Latin.* without limit; forever.

Word Origins (Etymologies)

34. Selection of Word Origins. We give the origin for all root words when this origin is known. The origin of derivative words may be obtained by referring back to the root word. The origin of the word **accession** (from a Latin verb that breaks down into the component parts *ad-* to + *cedere* come) may be learned by referring to the root word **accede.**

35. Placement of Word Origins. The origin of a word is put immediately after all the definitions, in square brackets. Notice that only the ultimate form of the word is ordinarily given and that the various intermediate forms, of interest chiefly to the scholar, that a word acquired as it passed through various languages are ignored, so that a readable and concise history of the word can be given in a streamlined form, with essential information only, for the general reader.

accost . . . . [< F < Ital. < LL, < L *ad-* to + *costa* side, rib]

This word origin may be read "*accost* comes from a French word borrowed from an Italian word which came from a Late Latin word which in turn was formed from the Latin elements *ad-* meaning 'to' and *costa* meaning 'side' or 'rib.'" The sign < means "from" and may be variously read "comes from," "borrowed from," "taken from," "derived from," or "formed from." The etymologies can be easily read if you read the sign < as "from" and expand the abbreviation of the language. See the complete etymology key on the inside front cover for an explanation of the abbreviations and symbols used in the etymologies.

36. Omitted Forms. For those persons specially interested in the form of words in the various languages a comma is inserted after the abbreviation of the language to show that a form exists in that language which is either exactly or somewhat like the English form. Notice the comma after the *L* in the word origin for *ad-jacent*:

[< L, < *ad-* near + *jacere* to lie]

This word origin should be read *"adjacent* comes from a Latin word, somewhat similar in form to the English word *adjacent*. It was formed of two parts in Latin—*ad-* and *jacere* which meant 'to lie near.'" Or more simply it may be read *"adjacent* comes ultimately from the two Latin words *ad-* and *jacere*, meaning 'to lie near.'" Many dictionaries lay stress upon giving the actual language form in Latin but we have given rather the root or ultimate meaning in Latin, since the meaning of the parts in Latin may help the reader to understand the meaning in English and give the user of the dictionary some idea of the make-up or composition of the word. The plus sign (+) is used to unite the two parts of a word in these cases.

37. Breaking down Ultimate Form into Component Parts. Breaking down words into their component parts will often help the user to get a root or core meaning of the word and will enable him to understand other words. Consider the two word origins for reduce and produce:

reduce .... [< L, < *re-* back + *ducere* bring]
produce .... [< L, < *pro-* forth + *ducere* bring]

38. Cross References. Sometimes there is information entered elsewhere in the dictionary that the reader will find useful in reading and understanding a particular word origin. Cross references to such entries are given in small capital letters. For example, words formed from a foreign word and an English word element can be understood better if you understand the English word element. In such cases the word element is given in small capital letters.

biology .... [< Gk. *bios* life + –LOGY]
Often there is additional information in another etymology carrying the history of a word farther back. To avoid repetition, cross references in small capital letters are given to the entry where there is fuller information.

eleemosynary .... [< LL, < L *eleemosyna* ALMS]
alms .... [< VL < L < Gk. *eleemosyne* compassion < *eleos* mercy]
By cross-referring to **alms** from the etymology of eleemosynary, the reader finds that the Latin word *eleemosyna* meaning "alms" comes from the Greek word *eleemosyne* meaning "compassion," which was derived from the Greek word *eleos* meaning "mercy." Thus, the words *eleemosynary* and *alms* have their common derivation in the Greek word *eleos*.

39. Doublets. Because the English vocabulary has borrowed so widely from other languages, there are pairs of words, called doublets, which, though quite different in form in English, go back to the same earlier word.

fragile .... [< L *fragilis;* akin to *frangere* break. Doublet of FRAIL.]
frail .... [< OF < L *fragilis*. Doublet of FRAGILE.]

Thus, the Latin word *fragilis*, which came into English directly as *fragile*, but was altered in passing through Old French to give us *frail*, is the common ancestor of both these words.

40. Words of Scandinavian Origin. Words taken from the languages of the North and recorded in Old and Middle English are placed together under the generic term Scandinavian (Scand.), and, normally, the Old Norse form is cited. When no Old Norse form is recorded, the Scandinavian language in which the form cited occurs is indicated in parentheses.

skirt .... [< Scand. *skyrta* shirt]
skull .... [< Scand. (dial. Norw.) *skul* shell]

Synonyms

41. Synonyms are given for words which a speaker or writer may overuse, and for which a substitute word is therefore often desirable. They are also given in order to sharpen definitions and to help the reader distinguish between words which may look or sound alike but be very different in meaning (*council* and *counsel; accede* and *exceed*). These lists are keyed to specific definition numbers and parts of speech, since synonyms exist only for specific meanings of particular words. In able, below, *capable* may be used in place of *able* in the sense of "having ordinary power to do" but not strictly in the sense of "talented." For the second meaning of *able*, which is "talented, clever," either of the two synonyms may be substituted: *an expert lawyer, a skillful lawyer.* The third meaning is concerned with the manner or effect of something done, not with potentiality or present capacity: *an able speech, an effective speech.* By using care to choose synonyms that fit in the right contexts you will learn to use words more precisely and more effectively.

a·ble (ā′bəl), *adj.,* a·bler, a·blest. 1. having ordinary capacity, power, or means to do: *a man able to work.* 2. having more power or skill than most others have; talented; clever: *a supreme court justice should be an able lawyer.* 3. competently done: *an able speech.* [< OF < L *habilis* easily held or handled < *habere* hold] —Syn. 1. capable. 2. expert, skillful. 3. effective. —Ant. 1. incapable.

Usage Notes

42. Usage notes are given at the end of certain entries, and are preceded by a heavy black arrow. These discussions are concerned with such points as good idiomatic usage, substandard or awkward usage, problems of spelling, grammar, punctuation, literary style, and the nature of language. They are designed to help you make the best possible choice of two or more ways of expression.

con·tin·u·al (kən·tin′yū·əl), *adj.* 1. never stopping. . . . ➤ continual, continuous. *Continual* means "frequently or closely repeated": *Dancing requires continual practice. Continuous* means "without interruption": *a continuous procession of cars.*

A Dictionary
of the English
Language

A DICTIONARY
OF THE
ENGLISH LANGUAGE

A, a (ā), *n.*, *pl.* A's; a's. 1. the first letter of the alphabet. 2. *Music.* the sixth note in the scale of C major.

a (ə; *stressed* ā), *adj.* or *indefinite article.* 1. any: *a tree.* 2. one: *a pound of butter.* 3. a certain; a particular: *two at a time.* 4. to or for each: *ten dollars a day.* 5. a single: *not a one.* [var. of *an*¹] ➤ A is used before words pronounced with an initial consonant sound whether or not that consonant is shown by the spelling, as in *a* man, *a* year, *a* union, *a* hospital. Now we usually write *a* hotel or *a* historian but some people use *an* in such cases.

a–¹, *prefix.* not; without, as in *atonal*, without tone. [< Gk.; *a–* becomes *an–* before a vowel or *h*] ➤ a– is of Greek origin and is used in words taken directly, or through Latin, from Greek, as in *apathy.* It is also used as a naturalized English prefix in new formations, as in *achromatic.* a–, called alpha privative, corresponds to English *un–* and Latin *in–.*

a–², *prefix.* 1. in; on; to, as in *abed.* 2. in the act of ——ing, as in *a-fishing.* [OE *an*, *on*]

A, 1. *Physics.* angstrom unit. 2. *Chem.* argon.

a., 1. about. 2. acre; acres. 3. adjective.

A 1, *Colloq.* A one.

Aa·chen (ä'Hən), *n.* city in W Germany. French, Aix-la-Chapelle.

aard·vark (ärd'värk'), *n.* a burrowing African mammal that eats ants and termites. [< Afrikaans < Dutch *aarde* earth + *vark* pig]

Aardvark
(ab. 6 ft. long)

Aar·on (âr'ən), *n. Bible.* the brother of Moses and first high priest of the Jews.

ab–, *prefix.* from; away; off, as in *abnormal, abduct, abjure.* [< L *ab,* prep.; *ab–* appears as *a–* before *m* and *v,* and *abs–* before *c* and *t.* Akin to Greek *apo–* from, and English *of* and *off.*]

A.B., Bachelor of Arts. Also, B.A.

a·ba·cá (ä'bə·kä'), *n.* 1. hemp made from the fibers of a Philippine banana plant; Manila hemp. 2. the plant itself. [< Malay]

a·back (ə·bak'), *adv.* 1. toward the back. 2. **taken aback,** suddenly surprised.

ab·a·cus (ab'ə·kəs), *n., pl.* **–cus·es, –ci** (–sī). frame with rows of counters or beads that slide back and forth, used for calculating. [< L < Gk. *abax*]

a·baft (ə·baft'; ə·bäft'), *Naut.* —*prep.* back of; behind. —*adv.* toward or at the stern.

ab·a·lo·ne (ab'ə·lō'nē), *n. Am.* an edible mollusk, with a large, rather flat shell lined with mother-of-pearl. [< Am. Sp. *abulón* < Am. Ind. *aulun*]

a·ban·don¹ (ə·ban'dən), *v.* 1. give up entirely: *abandon a career.* 2. leave without intending to return to; desert: *abandon one's home.* 3. yield (oneself) completely (to a feeling, impulse, etc.): *abandon oneself to grief.* [< OF *a bandon* at liberty] —**a·ban'don·er,** *n.* —**a·ban'don·ment,** *n.* —Syn. 1. renounce, relinquish. 2. forsake. 3. succumb, surrender.

a·ban·don² (ə·ban'dən), *n.* freedom from conventional restraint. [< F]

a·ban·doned (ə·ban'dənd), *adj.* 1. deserted; forsaken. 2. shamelessly wicked. —**a·ban'doned·ly,** *adv.*

a·base (ə·bās'), *v.,* **a·based, a·bas·ing.** make lower in rank, condition, or character; degrade: *a traitor abases himself.* [< OF < LL, < L *ad–* + LL *bassus* low] —**a·base'ment,** *n.*

a·bash (ə·bash'), *v.* embarrass and confuse. [< OF *esbaïr* be astonished] —**a·bashed',** *adj.* —**a·bash'ment,** *n.* —Syn. disconcert, chagrin.

a·bate (ə·bāt'), *v.,* **a·bat·ed, a·bat·ing.** 1. make less: *the medicine abated his pain.* 2. become less: *the storm has abated.* 3. *Law.* put an end to (a nuisance, an action, or a writ). 4. deduct. 5. omit. [< OF *abatre* beat down] —**a·bat'a·ble,** *adj.* —**a·bate'ment,** *n.* —**a·bat'er,** *n.* —Syn. 1, 2. decrease, diminish.

ab·a·tis (ab'ə·tis), *n., pl.* **ab·a·tis.** barricade of trees cut down and placed with their sharpened branches directed toward an enemy. [< F]

ab·at·toir (ab'ə·twär; –twôr), *n.* slaughterhouse. [< F]

ab·ba·cy (ab'ə·sī), *n., pl.* **–cies.** 1. position, term of office, or district of an abbot. 2. an abbey. [< LL *abbatia.* See ABBOT.]

ab·bé (ab'ā; a·bā'), *n.* in France: 1. an abbot. 2. any clergyman, esp. a priest. [< F]

ab·bess (ab'is), *n.* woman at the head of a community of nuns. [< OF < LL *abbatissa*]

ab·bey (ab'ī), *n., pl.* **–beys.** 1. the building or buildings where monks or nuns live a religious life ruled by an abbot or abbess; a monastery or convent. 2. the monks or nuns as a group. 3. building that was once an abbey or a part of an abbey. [< OF < LL *abbatia*]

ab·bot (ab'ət), *n.* man at the head of an abbey of monks. [OE < LL < LGk. < Aramaic *abbā* father] —**ab'bot·ship,** *n.*

abbrev., abbr., abbreviation.

ab·bre·vi·ate (ə·brē'vi·āt), *v.,* **–at·ed, –at·ing.** 1. make (a word or phrase) shorter so that a part stands for the whole: *abbreviate "hour" to "hr."* 2. make briefer. [< L, < *ad–* + *brevis* short. Doublet of ABRIDGE.] —**ab·bre'vi·a'tor,** *n.* —Syn. 2. condense.

ab·bre·vi·a·tion (ə·brē'vi·ā'shən), *n.* 1. shortened form of a word or phrase standing for the whole: *"in." is an abbreviation of "inch."* 2. act of shortening; abridgment. ➤ **period with abbreviation.** Naturally a writer intends to use a period after an abbreviation and omitting it is a careless slip, but a pretty common careless slip. Some publishers do not use a period after an abbreviation that is to be followed by a colon (as *i.e.*:). There is a growing tendency today not to use a period after an abbreviation that ends with the last letter of the word abbreviated, that is, a word which really is a contraction: *Dr, Mr, Mrs, vs, Wm.* This is more common in British than in American usage.

ABC (ā'bē'sē'), *n., pl.* **ABC's.** 1. elementary principles. 2. ABC's, the alphabet.

ab·di·cate (ab'də·kāt), *v.,* **–cat·ed, –cat·ing.** 1. give up or renounce formally: *the king abdicated* his throne. 2. renounce office or power: *why did the king abdicate?* [< L, < ab– away + dicare proclaim] —**ab'di·ca'tion,** *n.* —**ab'di·ca'tor,** *n.*

ab·do·men (ab'də-mən; ab·dō'mən), *n.* 1. *Anat., Zool.* the part of the body containing the stomach and other digestive organs; belly. 2. *Zool.* the last of the three parts of the body of an insect or crustacean. [< L]

HEAD
THORAX
ABDOMEN
Abdomen (def. 2)

ab·dom·i·nal (ab·dom'ə-nəl), *adj.* of, in, or for the abdomen. —**ab·dom'i·nal·ly,** *adv.*

ab·duce (ab·dūs'; -dūs'), *v.,* –duced, –duc·ing. lead away; abduct.

ab·duct (ab·dukt'), *v.* 1. carry away (a person) unlawfully and by force; kidnap. 2. pull (a part of the body) away from its usual position. [< L, < ab– away + ducere lead] —**ab·duc'tion,** *n.* —**ab·duc'tor,** *n.* —Ant. 2. adduct.

a·beam (ə·bēm'), *adv.* directly opposite to the middle part of a ship's side.

a·bed (ə·bed'), *adv.* in bed.

A·bel (ā'bəl), *n. Bible.* second son of Adam and Eve, killed by his older brother Cain.

Ab·é·lard (ab'ə·lärd), *n.* Pierre, 1079–1142, French philosopher and teacher.

Ab·er·deen (ab'ər·dēn'), *n.* city in E Scotland. —**Ab·er·do·ni·an** (ab'ər·dō'ni·ən), *adj., n.*

ab·er·rant (ab·er'ənt), *adj.* deviating from what is regular, normal, or right. [< L, < ab– away + errare wander] —**ab·er'rance, ab·er'ran·cy,** *n.*

ab·er·ra·tion (ab'ər·ā'shən), *n.* 1. deviation from the right path or usual course of action. 2. deviation from a standard or type. 3. temporary mental disorder. 4. the failure of rays of light coming from one point to converge to one focus. —**ab'er·ra'tion·al,** *adj.*

a·bet (ə·bet'), *v.,* a·bet·ted, a·bet·ting. encourage or help, esp. in something wrong. [< OF abeter arouse < L ad– + Frankish bētan cause to bite] —**a·bet'ment,** *n.* —**a·bet'tor, a·bet'ter,** *n.* —Syn. support, assist.

a·bey·ance (ə·bā'əns), *n.* temporary inactivity: *hold the question in abeyance.* [< AF < OF abeance expectation < L ad– at + VL batare gape] —**a·bey'ant,** *adj.*

ab·hor (ab·hôr'), *v.,* –horred, –hor·ring. feel disgust or hate for; detest. [< L, < ab– from + horrere shrink] —**ab·hor'rer,** *n.* —Syn. loathe, abominate. —Ant. admire.

ab·hor·rence (ab·hôr'əns; –hor'–), *n.* 1. a feeling of loathing or hatred. 2. thing loathed or detested.

ab·hor·rent (ab·hôr'ənt; –hor'–), *adj.* 1. causing horror; disgusting; repugnant (*to*). 2. feeling disgust or hate (*of*). 3. remote in character (*from*). —**ab·hor'rent·ly,** *adv.*

a·bide (ə·bīd'), *v.,* a·bode or a·bid·ed, a·bid·ing. 1. continue to stay. 2. dwell. 3. put up with: *she cannot abide dirt.* 4. wait for. 5. endure. 6. abide by, a. accept and follow out. b. remain faithful to. [OE ābīdan stay on, and onbīdan wait for] —**a·bid'er,** *n.* —Syn. 3. bear, stand.

a·bid·ing (ə·bīd'ing), *adj.* continuing; lasting. —**a·bid'ing·ly,** *adv.* —**a·bid'ing·ness,** *n.*

a·bil·i·ty (ə·bil'ə·ti), *n., pl.* –ties. 1. power to do or act in any relation: *give according to your ability.* 2. skill: *mechanical ability.* 3. power to do some special thing; talent: *musical ability, natural abilities.* [< F < L. See ABLE.] —Syn. 1. capacity. 2. cleverness. 3. aptitude. ▶ **Ability** is followed by *to* and an infinitive rather than *of* (*ability to do,* not *of doing*) or in and a substantive: *ability to design buildings; ability in arithmetic.*

ab·ject (ab'jekt; ab·jekt'), *adj.* 1. wretched; miserable. 2. deserving contempt. [< L, < ab– down + jacere throw] —**ab·jec'tion,** *n.* —**ab·ject·ly** (ab'jekt·li; ab·jekt·li), *adv.* —**ab·ject'ness,** *n.* —Syn. 2. contemptible, despicable.

ab·jure (ab·jūr'), *v.,* –jured, –jur·ing. renounce on oath; repudiate. [< L, < ab– away + jurare swear] —**ab'ju·ra'tion,** *n.* —**ab·jur·a·**

to·ry (ab·jūr'ə·tô'ri; –tō'–), *adj.* —**ab·jur'er,** *n.* —Syn. forswear.

abl., ablative.

ab·la·tive (ab'lə·tiv), *n.* 1. the case in Latin expressing removal or separation. 2. a word or construction in this case. [< L ablativus < ab– away + ferre carry]

a·blaze (ə·blāz'), *adv., adj.* blazing.

a·ble (ā'bəl), *adj.,* a·bler, a·blest. 1. having ordinary capacity, power, or means to do: *a man able to work.* 2. having more power or skill than most others have; talented; clever: *a supreme court justice should be an able lawyer.* 3. competently done: *an able speech.* [< OF < L habilis easily held or handled < habere hold] —Syn. 1. capable. 2. expert, skillful. 3. effective. —Ant. 1. incapable.

–able, *suffix.* 1. that can be ——ed; able to be ——ed: *obtainable = that can be obtained.* 2. likely to or suitable for: *comfortable = suitable for comfort.* 3. inclined to: *peaceable = inclined to peace.* 4. deserving to be ——ed: *lovable = deserving to be loved.* See –ible. [< OF < L –abilis] ▶ The common and useful suffix –able appears in a number of words with the spelling –ible. –able is the living suffix and is much more frequent than –ible and should be used in coining occasional words like *jumpable.* –able is attached to verbs (*actable*), nouns (*actionable*), and even verbal phrases (*get-at-able*) to form adjectives.

a·ble-bod·ied (ā'bəl·bod'id), *adj.* physically fit and competent; strong and healthy.

Able Day, *Am.* day of the Bikini atom bomb test, June 30, 1946. Also, A-day. [< able, the signaler's word for the letter *a,* + day]

a·bloom (ə·blüm'), *adv., adj.* in bloom.

ab·lu·tion (ab·lü'shən), *n.* 1. a washing of one's person. 2. washing or cleansing as a religious ceremony of purification. 3. the liquid used. [< L, < ab– away + luere wash]

a·bly (ā'bli), *adv.* with skill or ability.

ab·ne·gate (ab'nə·gāt), *v.,* –gat·ed, –gat·ing. deny (anything) to oneself; renounce; give up. [< L, < ab– off, away + negare deny] —**ab'ne·ga'tion,** *n.* —**ab'ne·ga'tor,** *n.*

ab·nor·mal (ab·nôr'məl), *adj.* deviating from the normal, the standard, or a type; markedly irregular; unusual. [< AB– from + NORMAL] —**ab·nor'mal·ly,** *adv.* —**ab·nor'mal·ness,** *n.* —Syn. exceptional.

ab·nor·mal·i·ty (ab'nôr·mal'ə·ti), *n., pl.* –ties. 1. abnormal thing. 2. abnormal condition.

a·board (ə·bôrd'; ə·bōrd'), *adv.* 1. in or on a ship. 2. *Am.* in or on a train, bus, airplane, etc. 3. all aboard, everybody on (conductor's call directing passengers to enter a train, bus, etc.). 4. alongside. —*prep.* on board of.

a·bode (ə·bōd'), *n.* place to live in; dwelling. —*v.* pt. and pp. of abide. [OE ābād]

a·bol·ish (ə·bol'ish), *v.* do away with (a law, institution, or custom) completely: *abolish slavery.* [< F abolir < L abolere destroy] —**a·bol'ish·a·ble,** *adj.* —**a·bol'ish·er,** *n.* —**a·bol'ish·ment,** *n.* —Syn. suppress.

ab·o·li·tion (ab'ə·lish'ən), *n.* 1. act or fact of abolishing. 2. *Am., Hist.* suppression of Negro slavery. —**ab'o·li'tion·ism,** *n.* —**ab'o·li'tion·ist,** *n.*

ab·o·ma·sum (ab'ə·mā'səm), **ab·o·ma·sus** (–səs), *n.* the fourth stomach of cows, sheep, and other cud-chewing animals. [< L]

A-bomb (ā'bom'), *n.* the atomic bomb.

a·bom·i·na·ble (ə·bom'nə·bəl; ə·bom'ə·nə–), *adj.* 1. causing disgust; loathsome. 2. unpleasant. —**a·bom'i·na·ble·ness,** *n.* —**a·bom'i·na·bly,** *adv.* —Syn. 1. detestable, odious, revolting.

a·bom·i·nate (ə·bom'ə·nāt), *v.,* –nat·ed, –nat·ing. 1. feel disgust for; abhor; detest. 2. dislike. [< L, deplore as an ill omen, < ab– off + ominari prophesy < omen omen] —**a·bom'i·na'tor,** *n.* —Syn. 1. loathe, despise, hate.

a·bom·i·na·tion (ə·bom'ə·nā'shən), *n.* 1. a disgusting thing. 2. a shamefully wicked action or custom. 3. a feeling of disgust.

ab·o·rig·i·nal (ab'ə·rij'ə·nəl), *adj.* 1. existing from the beginning; first; original; native: *ab-*

original inhabitants. 2. of the earliest known inhabitants. —*n.* any one of the earliest known inhabitants. —**ab′o·rig′i·nal·ly,** *adv.*

ab·o·rig·i·nes (ab′ə·rij′ə·nēz), *n., pl.* of **aborigine.** 1. the earliest known inhabitants of a country. 2. the native animals and plants of a region. [< L, < *ab origine* from the beginning]

a·bort (ə·bôrt′), *v.* 1. miscarry. 2. fail to develop. 3. check the development of. [< L, < *ab–amiss + oriri* be born]

a·bor·tion (ə·bôr′shən), *n.* 1. birth that occurs before the embryo has developed enough to live; miscarriage. 2. something that has failed to develop properly. —**a·bor′tion·al,** *adj.*

a·bor·tion·ist (ə·bôr′shən·ist), *n.* Am. person who produces criminal abortions.

a·bor·tive (ə·bôr′tiv), *adj.* 1. coming to nothing; unsuccessful. 2. born before the right time. —**a·bor′tive·ly,** *adv.* —**a·bor′tive·ness,** *n.*

a·bound (ə·bound′), *v.* 1. be plentiful: *fish abound in the ocean.* 2. be rich (*in*): *America abounds in oil.* 3. be well supplied (*with*): *the ocean abounds with fish.* [< OF < L, < *ab–off + undare* rise in waves < *unda* a wave] —**a·bound′ing,** *adj.* —**a·bound′ing·ly,** *adv.*

a·bout (ə·bout′), *prep.* 1. of; concerned with: *a book about bridges.* 2. in connection with: *something queer about him.* 3. somewhere near: *he was about five miles from home.* 4. approximating; near: *about my size.* 5. on every side of; around: *a fence about the garden.* 6. on (one's person); with: *she has no money about her.* 7. on the point of; ready: *a plane about to take off.* 8. here and there in or on: *scatter papers about the room.* —*adv.* 1. nearly; almost: *about full.* 2. somewhere near: *loiter about.* 3. all around; in every direction: *the boy looked about.* 4. here and there: *scatter papers about.* 5. in the opposite direction: *face about.* 6. doing: *he knows what he is about.* 7. one after another; by turns: *turn about is fair play.* 5. on the outside of] ➤ **about (at about).** *At about* is a common colloquial doubling of prepositions: *I got there at about three o'clock.* In writing we should ordinarily choose the more accurate of the two: *I got there at three o'clock,* or *I got there about three o'clock. About* is usually the one intended.

a·bout-face (*n.* ə·bout′fās′; *v.* ə·bout′fās′), *n., v.,* -**faced,** -**fac·ing.** —*n.* a turning or going in the opposite direction. —*v.* turn or go in the opposite direction.

a·bove (ə·buv′), *adv.* 1. in or at a higher place; overhead: *the sky is above.* 2. on the upper side or on top: *leaves dark above and light below.* 3. higher in rank or power: *the courts above.* 4. in or from a direction thought of as higher: *there's good fishing above.* 5. earlier, in a book or article: *said above.* 6. in heaven. —*prep.* 1. in or to a higher place than: *birds fly above the earth.* 2. higher than; over: *a captain is above a sergeant.* 3. superior to: *above mean actions.* 4. more than: *the weight is above a ton.* 5. beyond: *the first corner above the school.* —*adj.* written above. —*n.* the above, something that is written above. [OE *abufan*] ➤ **Above** is primarily a preposition (*above the clouds*) or adverb (*the statements made above*—*above* modifying the verb *made*). Its common use as an adverb, as in *the story told above* (that is, on the same page or on a preceding page), would be avoided by most writers in favor of *the story I have told . . .* or some such expression. The use of *above* as an adjective (*the above statements*) or noun (*the above is confirmed . . .*) is better limited to business writing and reference works. This sentence shows how crude *above* as a noun may sound in an inappropriate context: *In answer to the above I would say that the children didn't grow up with the right parents.*

a·bove·board (ə·buv′bôrd′; -bōrd′), *adv., adj.* without tricks or concealment.

ab o·vo (ab ō′vō), *Latin.* from the beginning.

ab·ra·ca·dab·ra (ab′rə·kə·dab′rə), *n.* 1. a mystical word used in incantations, or as a charm to ward off diseases. 2. gibberish. [< L]

a·brade (ə·brād′), *v.,* **a·brad·ed, a·brad·ing.** wear away by rubbing; scrape off. [< L, < *ab–off + radere* scrape] —**a·brad′er,** *n.*

A·bra·ham (ā′brə·ham; -həm), *n. Bible.* the ancestor of the Hebrews. Gen. 12-25.

a·bra·sion (ə·brā′zhən), *n.* 1. place scraped or worn by rubbing. 2. act of abrading.

a·bra·sive (ə·brā′siv; -ziv), *n.* a substance used for grinding, smoothing, or polishing, as sandpaper. —*adj.* tending to abrade.

a·breast (ə·brest′), *adv., adj.* 1. side by side. 2. abreast of or with, up with; alongside of: *keep abreast of what is going on.*

a·bridge (ə·brij′), *v.,* **a·bridged, a·bridg·ing.** 1. make shorter by using fewer words. 2. make less: *abridge the rights of citizens.* 3. deprive (*of*): *abridge citizens of their rights.* [< OF *abregier* < L, < *ad– + brevis* short. Doublet of ABBREVIATE.] —**a·bridg′a·ble, a·bridge′a·ble,** *adj.* —**a·bridged′,** *adj.* —**a·bridg′er,** *n.*

a·bridg·ment, *occas. Brit.* **a·bridge·ment** (ə·brij′mənt), *n.* 1. condensed form of a book, long article, etc. 2. an abridging.

a·broad (ə·brôd′), *adv.* 1. in or to a foreign land or lands: *go abroad.* 2. out in the open air. 3. going around; current: *a rumor is abroad.* 4. far and wide. 5. in error.

ab·ro·gate (ab′rə·gāt), *v.,* -**gat·ed,** -**gat·ing.** 1. abolish or annul (a law or custom) by an authoritative act; repeal. 2. do away with. [< L, < *ab– away + rogare* demand] —**ab′ro·ga′tion,** *n.* —**ab′ro·ga′tor,** *n.*

a·brupt (ə·brupt′), *adj.* 1. sudden; unexpected: *an abrupt turn.* 2. very steep. 3. (of speech or manners) short or sudden; blunt. 4. (of style) disconnected. [< L *abruptus* < *ab– off + rumpere* break] —**a·brupt′ly,** *adv.* —**a·brupt′ness,** *n.* —Syn. 3. brusque, curt.

Ab·sa·lom (ab′sə·ləm), *n. Bible.* David's favorite son, who rebelled against him.

ab·scess (ab′ses; -sis), *n.* a collection of pus in the tissues of some part of the body. [< L *abscessus* < *ab– away + cedere* go] —**ab′scessed,** *adj.*

ab·scis·sa (ab·sis′ə), *n., pl.* -**scis·sas,** -**scis·sae** (-sis′ē). *Math.* line running from left to right on a graph that defines a point in a system of coördinates. [< L (*linea*) *abscissa* (line) cut off]

ab·scond (ab·skond′), *v.* go away suddenly and secretly; go off and hide. [< L, < *ab– away + condere* store] —**ab·scond′er,** *n.* —Syn. flee.

ab·sence (ab′səns), *n.* 1. a being away: *absence from work.* 2. time of being away: *an absence of two weeks.* 3. a being without; lack: *absence of light.* 4. absent-mindedness.

absence of mind, inattentiveness.

ab·sent (*adj.* ab′sənt; *v.* ab·sent′), *adj.* 1. not present (at a place); away: *John is absent today.* 2. not existing; lacking: *snow is absent in some countries.* 3. absent-minded. —*v.* take or keep (oneself) away: *absent oneself from class.* [< L *absens* < *ab– away + esse* to be] —**ab·sent′er,** *n.* —**ab′sent·ness,** *n.*

ab·sen·tee (ab′sən·tē′), *n.* one who is absent or remains absent. —*adj. Am.* of or for a voter or voters permitted to vote by mail. —**ab′sen·tee′ism,** *n.*

ab·sent·ly (ab′sənt·li), *adv.* absent-mindedly.

ab·sent-mind·ed (ab′sənt·mīn′did), *adj.* not paying attention to what is going on around one. —**ab′sent-mind′ed·ly,** *adv.* —**ab′sent-mind′ed·ness,** *n.* —Syn. inattentive.

ab·sinthe, ab·sinth (ab′sinth), *n.* a bitter, green liqueur flavored with wormwood and anise. [< F < L < Gk. *apsinthion* wormwood]

ab·so·lute (ab′sə·lūt), *adj.* 1. complete; entire: *absolute ignorance.* 2. not mixed with anything else; pure: *absolute alcohol.* 3. free from imperfection; perfect: *absolute purity.* 4. free from control or restrictions: *absolute liberty.* 5. not compared with anything else: *absolute velocity.* 6. real; actual. 7. certain; infallible: *absolute proof.* 8. *Gram.* forming a part of a sentence, but not connected with it grammatically. In "*The train being late, we missed the boat,*" *the*

āge, cãre, fär; ēqual, tėrm; īce; ōpen, ôrder; pùt, rüle, ūse; th, then; ə=a in about.

train being late is an absolute construction. —*n.* **the absolute,** that which is absolute. [< L *absolutus*, pp. See ABSOLVE.] —**ab'so·lute'ness,** *n.*

ab·so·lute·ly (ab'sə-lüt'li; *emphatic* ab'sə-lüt'li), *adv.* **1.** completely. **2.** *Am., Colloq.* positively. **3.** *U.S. Slang.* yes. ≯ In speech **absolutely** has become generalized to mean "very" or "quite": *he is absolutely the finest fellow I know* —and in slang means simply "yes." It is sometimes a useful word to put force into dialogue but would be out of place in most writing, except in its original meaning of "completely, unconditionally."

absolute zero, temperature at which substances would have no heat whatever; –273.13° centigrade or –459.72° Fahrenheit.

ab·so·lu·tion (ab'sə-lü'shən), *n.* **1.** remission of guilt and punishment for sin by a priest after the sinner confesses and does penance. **2.** act of declaring such remission. **3.** formula declaring remission of sin. **4.** release from consequences or penalties. —Syn. **1.** forgiveness.

ab·so·lut·ism (ab'sə-lüt-iz'əm), *n.* government whose ruler has unrestricted power; despotism. —**ab'so·lut·ist,** *n., adj.* —**ab'so·lut·is'tic,** *adj.*

ab·solve (ab·solv'; -zolv'), *v.,* -**solved,** -**solving. 1.** declare (a person) free from sin, guilt, or blame. **2.** set free (from a promise or duty). **3.** remit (sin). [< L, < *ab-* from + *solvere* loosen] —**ab·solv'a·ble,** *adj.* —**ab·sol'vent,** *adj., n.* —**ab·solv'er,** *n.* —Syn. **1.** exonerate, acquit. **2.** release, exempt. **3.** forgive.

ab·sorb (ab·sôrb'; -zôrb'), *v.* **1.** take in or suck up (liquids): *a blotter absorbs ink.* **2.** swallow up; assimilate. **3.** interest very much: *the circus absorbed the boys.* **4.** take up by chemical or molecular action: *charcoal absorbs gases.* **5.** take (digested food, oxygen, etc.) into the blood stream by osmosis. [< L, < *ab-* from + *sorbere* suck in] —**ab·sorb'a·ble,** *adj.* —**ab·sorb'a·bil'i·ty,** *n.* —**ab·sorb'er,** *n.*

ab·sorbed (ab·sôrbd'; -zôrbd'), *adj.* very much interested. —**ab·sorb·ed·ly** (ab·sôr'bid·li; -zôr'-), *adv.* —**ab·sorb'ed·ness,** *n.*

ab·sorb·ent (ab·sôr'bənt; -zôr'-), *adj.* absorbing or capable of absorbing. —*n.* any thing or substance that absorbs.

ab·sorb·ing (ab·sôr'bing; -zôr'-), *adj.* extremely interesting. —**ab·sorb'ing·ly,** *adv.*

ab·sorp·tion (ab·sôrp'shən; -zôrp'-), *n.* **1.** an absorbing. **2.** great interest (in something). **3.** process of taking digested food, oxygen, etc., into the blood stream by osmosis. —**ab·sorp'tive,** *adj.* —**ab·sorp'tive·ness,** *n.*

ab·stain (ab·stān'), *v.* do without something voluntarily; refrain (*from*): *abstain from smoking.* [< F, < L, < *ab-* off + *tenere* hold] —**ab·stain'er,** *n.* —Syn. forbear, cease.

ab·ste·mi·ous (ab·stē'mi·əs), *adj.* moderate in eating and drinking; temperate. [< L, < *ab-* off + unrecorded *temum* intoxicating drink] —**ab·ste'mi·ous·ly,** *adv.* —**ab·ste'mi·ous·ness,** *n.*

ab·sten·tion (ab·sten'shən), *n.* act of abstaining; abstinence. —**ab·sten'tious,** *adj.*

ab·sti·nence (ab'stə-nəns), *n.* **1.** partly or entirely giving up certain pleasures, food, drink, etc. **2.** act or practice of refraining (*from*): *abstinence from smoking.* **3.** total abstinence, a refraining from the use of any alcoholic liquor. —**ab'sti·nent,** *adj.* —**ab'sti·nent·ly,** *adv.* —Syn. **1, 2.** abstention.

ab·stract (*adj.* ab'strakt, ab·strakt'; *v.* ab·strakt' *for* **1, 3, 4,** ab'strakt *for* **2;** *n.* ab'strakt) *adj.* **1.** thought of apart from any particular object or real thing; not concrete: *an abstract number.* **2.** expressing a quality that is thought of apart from any particular object or real thing: *"goodness" is an abstract noun.* **3.** ideal; theoretical. **4.** hard to understand; difficult. **5.** pertaining to art that avoids the representation of realities and all ordinary conventional designs. —*v.* **1.** think of (a quality) apart from a particular object or real thing having that quality. **2.** make an abstract of; summarize. **3.** remove, esp. dishonestly. **4.** withdraw attention. —*n.* **1.** a short statement giving the main ideas of an article, book, etc.; summary. **2.** in the ab-

stract, in theory rather than in practice. [< L *abstractus* < *ab-* away + *trahere* draw] —**ab·stract'er,** *n.* —**ab'stract·ly,** *adv.* —**ab'stract·ness,** *n.* —Ant. *adj.* **1.** concrete.

ab·stract·ed (ab·strak'tid), *adj.* absent-minded. —**ab·stract'ed·ly,** *adv.* —**ab·stract'ed·ness,** *n.* —Syn. inattentive, preoccupied.

ab·strac·tion (ab·strak'shən), *n.* **1.** idea of a quality thought of apart from any particular object or real thing having that quality. **2.** formation of such an idea. **3.** removal. **4.** absence of mind. **5.** a work of abstract art.

ab·struse (ab·strüs'), *adj.* hard to understand. [< L *abstrusus* < *ab-* away + *trudere* thrust] —**ab·struse'ly,** *adv.* —**ab·struse'ness,** *n.* —Syn. profound, recondite. —Ant. obvious.

ab·surd (ab·sérd'; -zérd'), *adj.* plainly not true or sensible; foolish; ridiculous. [< L *absurdus* out of tune, senseless] —**ab·surd'ly,** *adv.* —**ab·surd'ness,** *n.*

ab·surd·i·ty (ab·sér'də·ti; -zér'-), *n., pl.* -**ties. 1.** something absurd. **2.** an absurd quality or condition; folly.

a·bun·dance (ə·bun'dəns), *n.* great plenty; full supply. [< OF < L. See ABOUND.] —Syn. profusion, superfluity.

a·bun·dant (ə·bun'dənt), *adj.* more than enough; very plentiful. —**a·bun'dant·ly,** *adv.*

a·buse (*v.* ə·būz'; *n.* ə·būs'), *v.,* a·bused, a·bus·ing, *n.* —*v.* **1.** put to a wrong or bad use; misuse: *abuse a privilege.* **2.** treat badly; mistreat: *abuse a child.* **3.** use harsh and insulting language to. —*n.* **1.** a wrong or improper use. **2.** harsh or severe treatment of a person. **3.** harsh and insulting language. **4.** a corrupt practice or custom. [< F < L *abusus* < *ab-* away + *uti* use] —**a·bus'er,** *n.* —Syn. *v.* **1.** misapply. **2.** maltreat. **3.** revile.

a·bu·sive (ə·bū'siv; -ziv), *adj.* **1.** using harsh or insulting language. **2.** containing abuse. —**a·bu'sive·ly,** *adv.* —**a·bu'sive·ness,** *n.*

a·but (ə·but'), *v.,* a·but·ted, a·but·ting. **1.** touch at one end or edge; end (*on* or *against*): *our house abuts on the street.* **2.** join at a boundary; border (*on* or *upon*): *his land abuts upon mine.* [< OF]

a·but·ment (ə·but'mənt), *n.* **1.** a support for an arch or bridge. **2.** the point or place where the support joins the thing supported.

a·but·ting (ə·but'ing), *adj.* adjacent.

a·bysm (ə·biz'əm), *n.* an abyss. [< OF *abisme*]

a·bys·mal (ə·biz'məl), *adj.* too deep to be measured; bottomless. —**a·bys'mal·ly,** *adv.*

Abutment: A, arch abutments; B, current abutments.

a·byss (ə·bis'), *n.* **1.** a bottomless or immeasurably deep space. **2.** the lowest depths of anything. **3.** the bottomless pit (hell). [< L < Gk., < *a-* without + *byssos* bottom] —Syn. **1.** chasm.

Ab·ys·sin·i·a (ab'ə·sin'i·ə), *n.* Ethiopia. —**Ab'ys·sin'i·an,** *adj., n.*

Ac, *Chem.* actinium.

A.C., a.c., *Elect.* alternating current.

a·ca·cia (ə·kā'shə), *n.* **1.** any of a genus of trees native to warm regions, several species of which yield gum arabic. **2.** *Am.* the locust tree of North America. [< L < Gk. *akakia* a thorny Egyptian tree]

ac·a·dem·ic (ak'ə·dem'ik), **ac·a·dem·i·cal** (-ə·kəl), *adj.* **1.** of or having to do with schools, colleges, and their studies. **2.** *Am.* concerned with general rather than commercial, technical, or professional education. **3.** scholarly. **4.** theoretical. **5.** following rules and traditions; formal. —**ac'a·dem'i·cal·ly,** *adv.*

academic freedom, *Am.* the freedom of a teacher to state the truth as he sees it without fear of losing his position or standing.

a·cad·e·mi·cian (ə·kad'ə·mish'ən; ak'ə·də-), *n.* member of a society for encouraging literature, science, or art.

a·cad·e·my (ə·kad'ə·mi), *n., pl.* -**mies. 1.** high school, esp. a private high school. **2.** school for instruction in a particular art or science: *a military academy.* **3.** society of authors, scholars, scientists, artists, etc., for encouraging literature, science, or art. [< L < Gk. *Akademeia* the grove where Plato taught]

A·ca·di·a (ə·kā'di·ə), *n.* a former French territory in SE Canada. —**A·ca'di·an**, *n., adj.*

a·can·thus (ə·kan'thəs), *n., pl.* **-thus·es, -thi** (-thī). **1.** a prickly plant with large, toothed leaves that grows in Mediterranean regions. **2.** an architectural ornament imitating these leaves. [< L < Gk., < *ake* thorn]

A, B

Acanthus: A, leaf of plant; B, ornament.

a cap·pel·la (ä' kə·pel'ə), *Music.* without instrumental accompaniment. [< Ital., in the manner of chapel (music)]

acc., **1.** account. **2.** accusative.

ac·cede (ak·sēd'), *v.,* **-ced·ed, -ced·ing. 1.** give consent (*to*): *please accede to my request.* **2.** become a party (*to*): *our government acceded to the treaty.* **3.** attain (to an office or dignity); come (*to*): *the king's oldest son acceded to the throne.* [< L, < *ad-* to + *cedere* come] —**ac·ced'ence,** *n.* —**ac·ced'er,** *n.* —**Syn. 1.** agree, assent.

ac·cel·er·an·do (ak·sel'ər·an'dō), *adv., adj. Music.* gradually increasing in speed. [< Ital.]

ac·cel·er·ate (ak·sel'ər·āt), *v.,* **-at·ed, -at·ing. 1.** go or cause to go faster. **2.** cause to happen sooner; hasten. **3.** *Physics.* change the speed or velocity of (a moving object). [< L, < *ad-* + *celer* swift] —**ac·cel'er·a'tive,** *adj.*

ac·cel·er·a·tion (ak·sel'ər·ā'shən), *n.* **1.** an accelerating or being accelerated. **2.** change in velocity, either a gradual increase (**positive acceleration**) or decrease (**negative acceleration**). **3.** rate of change in the velocity of a moving body.

ac·cel·er·a·tor (ak·sel'ər·ā'tər), *n.* **1.** thing that accelerates. **2.** a device for opening and closing the throttle of an automobile.

ac·cent (*n.* ak'sent; *v.* ak'sent, ak·sent'), *n.* **1.** special force or emphasis given to a syllable or a word in pronouncing it. **2.** a mark to indicate special force or emphasis. **3.** characteristic manner of pronunciation: *a foreign accent.* **4.** accents, tone of voice: *in soothing accents.* **5.** a mark to indicate vowel quality in foreign languages, as acute (´), grave (`), or circumflex (^). **6.** emphasis on certain words or syllables in a line of poetry to give them rhythm. **7.** *Music.* emphasis on certain notes or chords. —*v.* **1.** pronounce or mark with an accent. **2.** emphasize; accentuate. [< L *accentus* < *ad-* to + *canere* sing] ➤ accents. French words in English sometimes keep the accent marks with which they are spelled in their original language: *café, outré, attaché; crêpe, tête-à-tête; à la mode.* Words that are used frequently in English usually drop the accent marks after a time unless the marks are necessary to indicate pronunciation (as in *café, attaché*).

ac·cen·tu·al (ak·sen'chù·əl), *adj.* **1.** of or formed by accent. **2.** (of poetry) using stress instead of quantity. —**ac·cen'tu·al·ly,** *adv.*

ac·cen·tu·ate (ak·sen'chù·āt), *v.,* **-at·ed, -at·ing. 1.** emphasize. **2.** pronounce or mark with an accent. —**ac·cen'tu·a'tion,** *n.*

ac·cept (ak·sept'), *v.* **1.** take or receive (something offered): *accept a gift.* **2.** agree to; consent to: *accept a proposal.* **3.** take as true or satisfactory; believe: *accept an excuse.* **4.** receive (a thing or person) with favor; approve: *Einstein's new theory was widely accepted.* **5.** undertake as a responsibility: *accept a position as cashier.* **6.** *Com.* sign and promise to pay: *accept a note.* [< L *acceptare* < *ad-* to + *capere* take] —**ac·cept'er,** *esp. in Com.,* **ac·cep'tor,** *n.* —**Syn. 2.** accede, assent to. **3.** acknowledge, recognize. **5.** assume. ➤ See usage note under except.

ac·cept·a·ble (ak·sep'tə·bəl), *adj.* worth accepting; satisfactory. —**ac·cept'a·bil'i·ty,** ac-

cept'a·ble·ness, *n.* —**ac·cept'a·bly,** *adv.* —**Syn.** agreeable, welcome.

ac·cept·ance (ak·sep'təns), *n.* **1.** act of accepting. **2.** state of being accepted; favorable reception; approval. **3.** *Com.* **a.** agreement as to terms, esp. to pay a draft or bill of exchange when it is due. **b.** the draft or bill itself.

ac·cep·ta·tion (ak'sep·tā'shən), *n.* usual meaning; generally accepted meaning.

ac·cess (ak'ses), *n.* **1.** right to approach, enter, or use; admission: *access to the library.* **2.** condition of being easy or hard to reach: *access to the mountain town was difficult.* **3.** way or means of approach: *access to powerful men.* **4.** an attack (of disease). **5.** outburst (of anger). **6.** increase. [< L *accessus* < *ad-* to + *cedere* come]

ac·ces·sa·ry (ak·ses'ə·ri), *n., pl.* **-ries,** *adj. Esp. Law.* accessory. —**ac·ces'sa·ri·ly,** *adv.* —**ac·ces'sa·ri·ness,** *n.*

ac·ces·si·ble (ak·ses'ə·bəl), *adj.* **1.** that can be entered or reached. **2.** easy to get at; easy to reach. **3.** accessible to, capable of being influenced by. **4.** that can be obtained. —**ac·ces'si·bil'i·ty,** *n.* —**ac·ces'si·bly,** *adv.* —**Syn. 1.** approachable. **3.** susceptible. **4.** available.

ac·ces·sion (ak·sesh'ən), *n.* **1.** act of attaining to a right, office, etc. **2.** a yielding or agreeing (to a plan, opinion, demand, etc.); consent. **3.** an increase; addition. **4.** thing added. —**ac·ces'sion·al,** *adj.* —**Syn. 1.** attainment. **2.** assent.

ac·ces·so·ry (ak·ses'ə·ri), *n., pl.* **-ries,** *adj.* —*n.* **1.** an extra thing added to help something of more importance; subordinate part or detail. **2.** person who helps an offender against the law, without being present at the time of the offense, by encouraging the offender (**an accessory before the fact**) or shielding him (**an accessory after the fact**). —*adj.* **1.** helping something more important; subsidiary. **2.** *Law.* giving aid as an accessory. Also, *esp. Law,* accessary. —**ac·ces'so·ri·ly,** *adv.* —**ac·ces'so·ri·ness,** *n.* —**Syn.** *n.* **2.** accomplice.

ac·ci·dence (ak'sə·dəns), *n.* part of grammar dealing with word order and those changes in words that show case, number, tense, etc.

ac·ci·dent (ak'sə·dənt), *n.* **1.** an undesirable or unfortunate happening: *an automobile accident.* **2.** an unexpected or unintentional happening: *their meeting was an accident.* **3.** chance: *we met by accident.* **4.** a nonessential. [< L *accidens* < *ad-* to + *cadere* fall] —**Syn. 1.** misfortune, disaster.

ac·ci·den·tal (ak'sə·den'təl), *adj.* **1.** happening by chance; unexpected. **2.** nonessential; incidental. **3.** *Music.* of or having to do with an accidental. —*n. Music.* a sign used to show a change of pitch after the key signature and before the note to be changed. —**ac'ci·den'tal·ly,** *adv.* —**ac'ci·den'tal·ness,** *n.* —**Syn.** *adj.* **1.** fortuitous, unintentional, casual.

ac·claim (ə·klām'), *v.* **1.** show satisfaction and approval of by words or sounds; applaud. **2.** announce with signs of approval; hail. —*n.* shout or show of approval; applause. [< L, < *ad-* to + *clamare* cry out] —**ac·claim'er,** *n.*

ac·cla·ma·tion (ak'lə·mā'shən), *n.* **1.** shout of approval by a crowd; applause. **2.** oral vote.

ac·cli·mate (ə·klī'mit; ak'lə·māt), *v.,* **-mat·ed, -mat·ing.** *Esp. U.S.* accustom or become accustomed to a new climate or to new conditions. [< F *acclimater.* See CLIMATE.] —**ac·cli·mat·a·ble** (ə·klī'mit·ə·bəl), *adj.* —**ac·cli·ma·tion** (ak'lə·mā'shən), *n. Am.*

ac·cli·ma·tize (ə·klī'mə·tīz), *v.,* **-tized, -tizing.** *Esp. Brit.* acclimate. —**ac·cli'ma·tiz'a·ble,** *adj.* —**ac·cli'ma·ti·za'tion,** *n.* —**ac·cli'ma·tiz'er,** *n.*

ac·cliv·i·ty (ə·kliv'ə·ti), *n., pl.* **-ties.** an upward slope, as of ground. [< L, < *ad-* toward + *clivus* rising ground]

ac·co·lade (ak'ə·lād'; -läd'), *n.* **1.** a ceremony used in making a man a knight. **2.** honor; praise. [< F < Pg. *acolada* an embrace about the neck < L *ad-* to + *collum* neck]

ac·com·mo·date (ə·kom'ə·dāt), *v.,* **-dat·ed, -dat·ing. 1.** have room for; hold comfortably. **2.**

do a kindness or favor to; oblige. 3. furnish with lodging and sometimes with food as well. 4. supply; furnish. 5. *Am.* provide (a person) with (a loan of) money. 6. make fit; make suitable. 7. reconcile; adjust. [< L, < *ad-* + *com-* with + *modus* measure] —ac·com'mo·da'tor, *n.* —Syn. 4. provide, equip.

ac·com·mo·dat·ing (ə·kom'ə·dā'ting), *adj.* obliging. —ac·com'mo·dat'ing·ly, *adv.*

ac·com·mo·da·tion (ə·kom'ə·dā'shən), *n.* 1. lodging and sometimes food as well: *the hotel has accommodations for one hundred.* 2. help; favor; convenience. 3. *Am.* loan. 4. willingness to help out. 5. adjustment; adaptation. 6. settlement of differences; reconciliation.

accommodation train, *Am.* train that stops at all or nearly all stations.

ac·com·mo·da·tive (ə·kom'ə·dā'tiv), *adj.* obliging. —ac·com'mo·da'tive·ness, *n.*

ac·com·pa·ni·ment (ə·kum'pə·ni·mənt), *n.* 1. something incidental that goes along with something else. 2. *Music.* a supplementary part added to support the main part. —Syn. 1. adjunct.

ac·com·pa·nist (ə·kum'pə·nist), *n. Music.* one who plays an accompaniment.

ac·com·pa·ny (ə·kum'pə·ni), *v.,* –nied, –ny·ing. 1. go along with: *accompany a friend on a walk.* 2. be or happen in connection with: *fire is accompanied by heat.* 3. cause to be attended by; supplement (*with*): *accompany a speech with gestures.* 4. play or sing a musical accompaniment for or to. [< F *accompagner* < à to + *compagne* COMPANION] —ac·com'pa·ni·er, *n.* —Syn. 1. attend, escort. —Ant. 1. avoid.

ac·com·plice (ə·kom'plis), *n.* person who aids another in committing an unlawful act. [earlier *a complice* a confederate < F *complice* < L, < *com-* together with + *plicare* fold]

ac·com·plish (ə·kom'plish), *v.* 1. succeed in completing; carry out: *accomplish a purpose.* 2. finish; actually do: *accomplish nothing.* [< OF < LL, < *ad-* + *complere* fill up] —ac·com'plish·a·ble, *adj.* —ac·com'plish·er, *n.* —Syn. 1, 2. achieve, effect, complete, fulfill.

ac·com·plished (ə·kom'plisht), *adj.* 1. done; carried out; completed. 2. expert; skilled. 3. skilled in social arts and graces.

ac·com·plish·ment (ə·kom'plish·mənt), *n.* 1. an accomplishing or being accomplished. 2. thing accomplished; achievement. 3. skill in some social art or grace: *good manners are a desirable accomplishment.* —Syn. 1. completion. 2, 3. acquirement, attainment.

ac·cord (ə·kôrd'), *v.* 1. be in harmony; agree: *his report accords with yours.* 2. grant (a favor, request, etc.): *accord Tom praise for good work.* —n. 1. agreement; harmony: *opinions in accord.* 2. an informal agreement between nations. 3. harmony of color, pitch, or tone. 4. of one's own accord, without being asked. 5. with one accord, all together. [< OF < VL *acchordare* bring into harmony < L *ad-* to + *chorda* string] —ac·cord'a·ble, *adj.* —ac·cord'er, *n.* —Syn. *v.* 1. correspond, harmonize.

ac·cord·ance (ə·kôr'dəns), *n.* agreement; harmony: *in accordance with the plan.*

ac·cord·ant (ə·kôr'dənt), *adj.* agreeing; in harmony (*with* or *to*). —ac·cord'ant·ly, *adv.*

ac·cord·ing (ə·kôr'ding), *adv.* 1. according to, a. in agreement with: *according to his promise.* b. in proportion to: *spend according to your income.* c. on the authority of: *according to this book.* 2. according as, in proportion as. 3. accordingly. —*adj.* in harmony.

ac·cord·ing·ly (ə·kôr'ding·li), *adv.* 1. in agreement with something that has been stated; suitably. 2. for this reason; therefore.

ac·cor·di·on (ə·kôr'di·ən), *n.* a portable musical wind instrument with a bellows, metallic reeds, and keys. —*adj.* having folds like the

Boy playing an accordion

bellows of an accordion. [< G < Ital. *accordare* harmonize] —ac·cor'di·on·ist, *n.*

ac·cost (ə·kôst'; ə·kost'), *v.* approach and speak to first. [< F < Ital. < LL, < L *ad-* to + *costa* side, rib] —Syn. address, greet.

ac·couche·ment (ə·küsh'mənt; *Fr.* ä·küsh·mäN'), *n.* confinement for childbirth. [< F]

ac·count (ə·kount'), *n.* 1. detailed or explanatory statement: *please give an account of your trip.* 2. reason: *do not lie on any account.* 3. consideration: *take into account.* 4. value; worth: *of no account.* 5. regard; behalf: *don't wait on my account.* 6. profit; advantage: *turn to account.* 7. statement of money received and paid out. 8. a record of business dealings between a bank and a depositor. 9. a periodic record of purchases for which a customer is billed. 10. call to account, a. demand an explanation of. b. scold; reprimand. 11. on account, as part payment. 12. on account of, a. because of. b. for the sake of. 13. take account of, a. make allowance for; consider. b. make a note of; note. 14. take into account, make allowance for; consider. [< OF. See ACCOUNT, v.] —*v.* 1. give a statement of money received or paid out. 2. account for, a. give a reason for; explain. b. answer for. 3. hold to be; consider: *Solomon was accounted wise.* [< OF *aconter* count up < LL, < L *ad-* + *computare* compute] —Syn. *n.* 1. report, description, narrative.

ac·count·a·ble (ə·koun'tə·bəl), *adj.* 1. responsible. 2. explainable. —ac·count'a·bil'i·ty, *n.* —ac·count'a·ble·ness, *n.* —ac·count'a·bly, *adv.*

ac·count·an·cy (ə·koun'tən·si), *n.* the examining or keeping of business accounts.

ac·count·ant (ə·koun'tənt), *n.* person who examines or manages business accounts. —ac·count'ant·ship, *n.*

ac·count·ing (ə·koun'ting), *n.* theory or system of keeping, analyzing, and interpreting business accounts.

ac·cou·ter, *esp. Brit.* **ac·cou·tre** (ə·kü'tər), *v.,* –tered, –ter·ing; –tred, –tring. to outfit or equip; array. [< F *accoutrer*]

ac·cou·ter·ments, *esp. Brit.* **ac·cou·tre·ments** (ə·kü'tər·mənts), *n.pl.* 1. a soldier's equipment with the exception of his weapons and clothing. 2. personal equipment; outfit.

ac·cred·it (ə·kred'it), *v.* 1. give (a person) credit (for something): *accredit her with kindness.* 2. *Am.* consider (a thing) as belonging or due (to a person): *we accredit the invention of the telephone to Bell.* 3. accept as worth believing; trust: *Einstein is an accredited authority in mathematics.* 4. give authority to. 5. send or provide with credentials: *an accredited representative.* 6. recognize as coming up to an official standard: *an accredited high school.* [< F *accréditer*] —Syn. 1, 2. credit, attribute. 4. authorize.

ac·cre·tion (ə·krē'shən), *n.* 1. growth in size. 2. a growing together of separate things. 3. an increase in size by natural growth or gradual external addition. 4. thing added; addition. 5. a whole that results from such growths or additions. —ac·cre'tive, *adj.*

ac·cru·al (ə·krü'əl), *n.* 1. an accruing. 2. amount accrued or accruing.

ac·crue (ə·krü'), *v.,* –crued, –cru·ing. come as a natural product or result. [< F < L, < *ad-* to + *crescere* grow] —ac·crue'ment, *n.*

acct., 1. account. 2. accountant.

ac·cu·mu·late (ə·kü'myə·lāt), *v.,* –lat·ed, –lat·ing. 1. collect or heap up little by little: *accumulate a fortune.* 2. grow into a heap or mass. [< L, < *ad-* up + *cumulus* heap] —Syn. 1. gather, amass. 2. increase, accrue.

ac·cu·mu·la·tion (ə·kü'myə·lā'shən), *n.* 1. gradual collection. 2. material collected; mass.

ac·cu·mu·la·tive (ə·kü'myə·lā'tiv; –lə·tiv), *adj.* tending to accumulate; collective. —ac·cu'mu·la'tive·ly, *adv.* —ac·cu'mu·la'tive·ness, *n.*

ac·cu·mu·la·tor (ə·kü'myə·lā'tər), *n.* 1. one that accumulates. 2. *Brit.* a storage battery.

ac·cu·ra·cy (ak'yə·rə·si), *n.* condition of being without errors or mistakes. —Syn. correctness.

ac·cu·rate (ak′yə·rit), *adj.* **1.** making few or no errors: *an accurate observer.* **2.** without errors or mistakes; exact: *accurate measure.* [< L, < *ad*– to + *cura* care] —ac′cu·rate·ly, *adv.* —ac′cu·rate·ness, *n.* —Syn. **1.** careful, precise.

ac·curs·ed (ə·kêr′sid; ə·kerst′), **ac·curst** (ə·kêrst′), *adj.* **1.** detestable; abominable. **2.** under a curse. —ac·curs·ed·ly (ə·kêr′sid·li), *adv.*

accus., accusative.

ac·cu·sa·tion (ak′yụ·zā′shən), *n.* **1.** a charge of wrongdoing. **2.** the offense charged. **3.** act of accusing.

ac·cu·sa·tive (ə·kū′zə·tiv), *Gram.* —*n.* **1.** the objective case. **2.** word used as an object of a verb or preposition. —*adj.* showing the direct object; objective. —ac·cu′sa·tive·ly, *adv.*

ac·cu·sa·to·ry (ə·kū′zə·tô′ri; -tō′-), *adj.* containing an accusation; accusing.

ac·cuse (ə·kūz′), *v.,* –cused, –cus·ing. **1.** charge with some crime, offense, etc. **2.** find fault with; blame. [< OF < L *accusare* < *ad*– to + *causa* cause] —ac·cus′er, *n.* —ac·cus′ing·ly, *adv.* —Syn. **1.** denounce, arraign.

ac·cus·tom (ə·kus′təm), *v.* make familiar by use or habit; get used. [< OF *acostumer*] —Syn. habituate, familiarize.

ac·cus·tomed (ə·kus′təmd), *adj.* usual; customary. —ac·cus′tomed·ness, *n.*

ace (ās), *n.* **1.** a playing card, domino, or side of a die having a single spot. **2.** a single spot. **3.** a point won by a single stroke in tennis and certain other games. **4.** an expert. **5.** a combat pilot who has shot down five or more enemy planes. —*adj.* of very high quality; expert. [< OF *as* < L, smallest unit (of coinage, measure, etc.)]

a·cer·bi·ty (ə·sêr′bə·ti), *n., pl.* –ties. **1.** sharpness of taste; sourness. **2.** harshness of manner; severity. [< F < L, < *acerbus* bitter]

ac·e·tab·u·lum (as′ə·tab′yə·ləm), *n., pl.* –la (-lə). *Anat.* a socket. [< L, cup-shaped holder for vinegar, < *acetum* vinegar] —ac′e·tab′u·lar, *adj.*

ac·et·an·i·lid (as′ət·an′ə·lid), **ac·et·an·i·lide** (-ə·lid; -ə·lid), *n. Chem.* a white, crystalline drug, $C_6H_5NH·OC·CH_3$, used in medicines to relieve pain and lessen fever.

ac·e·tate (as′ə·tāt), *n. Chem.* any salt or ester of acetic acid. —ac′e·tat′ed, *adj.*

a·ce·tic (ə·sē′tik; ə·set′ik), *adj.* of or derived from vinegar or acetic acid. [< L *acetum* vinegar]

acetic acid, a very sour, colorless acid, CH_3COOH, present in vinegar.

a·cet·i·fy (ə·set′ə·fī), *v.,* –fied, –fy·ing. turn into vinegar. —a·cet′i·fi·ca′tion, *n.*

ac·e·tone (as′ə·tōn), *n.* a colorless, volatile, inflammable liquid, $CH_3·CO·CH_3$, used as a solvent and in making varnishes, etc.

ac·e·tyl·cho·line (as′ə·til·kō′lēn; -lin), *n.* chemical compound that transmits nerve impulses.

a·cet·y·lene (ə·set′ə·lēn; -lin), *n.* a colorless gas, C_2H_2, that burns with a bright light and very hot flame, used for lighting and, combined with oxygen, for welding metals.

ac·e·tyl·sal·i·cyl·ic acid (as′ə·til·sal′ə·sil′ik; ə·sē′təl-), aspirin.

A·chae·a (ə·kē′ə), **A·cha·ia** (ə·kā′ə), *n.* country in ancient Greece, in the S part. —A·chae′an, A·cha′ian, *adj., n.*

A·cha·tes (ə·kā′tēz), *n.* **1.** the faithful companion of Aeneas. **2.** a faithful companion.

ache (āk), *v.,* ached, ach·ing. —*v.* **1.** be in continued pain. **2.** *Colloq.* wish very much. —*n.* a dull, steady pain. [OE *acan*] —ach′ing·ly, *adv.* —Syn. *v.* **1.** hurt. **2.** long, yearn.

a·chene (ā·kēn′), *n. Bot.* any small, dry, hard fruit consisting of one seed with a thin outer covering that does not burst when ripe. Also, **akene.** [< NL < Gk., < *a*– not + *chainein* gape; because it ripens without bursting]

Ach·er·on (ak′ər·on), *n. Class. Myth.* **1.** river in Hades. **2.** the lower world; Hades.

a·chieve (ə·chēv′), *v.,* a·chieved, a·chiev·ing. **1.** bring to a successful end; accomplish: *achieve one's purpose.* **2.** get by effort: *achieve distinction.* [< OF, < (*venir*) a chief (come) to a head] —a·chiev′a·ble, *adj.* —a·chiev′er, *n.* —Syn. **1.**

finish, complete, effect. **2.** gain, attain. —Ant. **1.** fail.

a·chieve·ment (ə·chēv′mənt), *n.* **1.** thing achieved. **2.** act of achieving. —Syn. **1.** accomplishment, feat, exploit.

A·chil·les (ə·kil′ēz), *n. Gk. Legend.* hero of the Greeks at the siege of Troy. No weapon could injure Achilles anywhere, except in the heel. —Ach·il·le·an (ak′ə·lē′ən), *adj.*

ach·ro·mat·ic (ak′rə·mat′ik), *adj.* transmitting white light without breaking it up into the colors of the spectrum. [< Gk., < *a*– without + *chroma* color] —ach′ro·mat′i·cal·ly, *adv.*

ac·id (as′id), *n.* **1.** *Chem.* a compound that yields hydrogen ions when dissolved in water, usually reacts with a base to form salt and water, and turns blue litmus paper red. **2.** substance having a sour taste. —*adj.* **1.** *Chem.* of or having the properties of an acid. **2.** sour; sharp; biting. [< L *acidus* sour] —ac′id·ly, *adv.* —ac′id·ness, *n.*

a·cid·ic (ə·sid′ik), *adj.* forming acid.

a·cid·i·fy (ə·sid′ə·fī), *v.,* –fied, –fy·ing. **1.** make or become sour. **2.** change into an acid. —a·cid′i·fi·ca′tion, *n.* —a·cid′i·fi′er, *n.*

a·cid·i·ty (ə·sid′ə·ti), *n., pl.* –ties. acid quality or condition; sourness.

ac·i·do·sis (as′ə·dō′sis), *n.* a harmful condition in which the blood and tissues are less alkaline than is normal.

acid test, a thorough test.

a·cid·u·late (ə·sij′ə·lāt), *v.,* –lat·ed, –lat·ing. make slightly acid or sour. —a·cid′u·la′tion, *n.*

a·cid·u·lous (ə·sij′ə·ləs), *adj.* slightly acid or sour. —a·cid′u·lous·ly, *adv.* —a·cid′u·lous·ness, *n.*

ack-ack (ak′ak′), *n. Slang.* anti-aircraft fire. [British radio operator's code word for AA (anti-aircraft)]

ac·knowl·edge (ak·nol′ij), *v.,* –edged, –edg·ing. **1.** admit to be true. **2.** recognize the authority or claims of. **3.** express appreciation of: *acknowledge a letter.* **5.** recognize or certify in legal form: *acknowledge a deed.* [blend of obs. *acknow* admit + *knowledge,* v., admit] —ac·knowl′edge·a·ble, *adj.* —ac·knowl′edged·ly, *adv.* —ac·knowl′edg·er, *n.* —Syn. **1.** concede. **2.** accept. —Ant. **1.** deny. **2.** reject.

ac·knowl·edg·ment, *occas. Brit.* **ac·knowl·edge·ment** (ak·nol′ij·mənt), *n.* **1.** thing given or done to show that one has received a gift, favor, message, etc. **2.** act of admitting the existence or truth of anything. **3.** recognition of authority or claims. **4.** expression of thanks. **5.** official certificate in legal form. Syn. **2.** admission. **3.** acceptance.

ac·me (ak′mē), *n.* the highest point. [< Gk. *akme* point] —Syn. apex.

ac·ne (ak′nē), *n.* a skin disease in which the oil glands in the skin become clogged and inflamed, often causing pimples. [? < Gk. *akme* point]

ac·o·lyte (ak′ə·līt), *n.* **1.** altar boy. **2.** attendant; assistant. **3.** *Rom. Cath. Ch.* person ordained to the fourth and highest of the minor orders. [< Med.L < Gk. *akolouthos* follower]

ac·o·nite (ak′ə·nīt), *n.* **1.** any of a genus of poisonous plants, with blue, purple, or yellow flowers shaped like hoods, including wolf's-bane and monkshood. **2.** drug used to relieve inflammation and pain, obtained from one of these plants. [< F < L < Gk. *akoniton*]

a·corn (ā′kôrn; ā′kərn), *n.* the nut, or fruit, of an oak tree. [OE *æcern*]

a·cous·tic (ə·küs′tik), **a·cous·ti·cal** (-tə·kəl), *adj.* **1.** having to do with the sense or the organs of hearing. **2.** having to do with the science of sound. **3.** exploded by sound: *an acoustic mine.* [< F < Gk. *akoustikos* having to do with hearing < *akouein* hear] —a·cous′ti·cal·ly, *adv.*

a·cous·tics (ə·küs′tiks), *n.* **1.** (*pl. in use*) the qualities of a room, hall, auditorium, etc., that determine how well sounds can be heard in it;

acoustic qualities. 2. *Physics.* (*sing. in use*) science of sound.

ac·quaint (ə·kwānt'), *v.* 1. inform (a person about a thing): *acquaint him with your intention.* 2. make more or less familiar: *acquaint oneself with the facts.* 3. be acquainted with, have personal knowledge of: *he is acquainted with my father.* [< OF acointer < LL, < L ad- to + cognitus known < com with + gnoscere come to know] —Syn. 1. tell. 2. familiarize.

ac·quaint·ance (ə·kwān'təns), *n.* 1. person known to one, but not a close friend. 2. knowledge of persons or things gained from experience with them. —ac·quaint'ance·ship, *n.*

ac·qui·esce (ak'wi·es'), *v.*, -esced, -esc·ing. give consent by keeping silent; submit quietly: *we acquiesced in their plan.* [< F < L, < ad- to + quiescere to rest] —ac'qui·es'cing·ly, *adv.*

ac·qui·es·cence (ak'wi·es'əns), *n.* consent without making objections; submitting quietly.

ac·qui·es·cent (ak'wi·es'ənt), *adj.* submitting with apparent consent. —ac'qui·es'cent·ly, *adv.*

ac·quire (ə·kwīr'), *v.*, -quired, -quir·ing. 1. receive or get as one's own: *acquire land.* 2. get by one's own efforts or actions: *acquire an education.* [< L, < ad- to + quaerere seek] —ac·quir'a·ble, *adj.* —ac·quir'er, *n.* —Syn. 1. obtain. 2. gain, win.

ac·quire·ment (ə·kwīr'mənt), *n.* 1. act of acquiring. 2. something acquired; attainment.

ac·qui·si·tion (ak'wə·zish'ən), *n.* 1. act of acquiring. 2. thing acquired.

ac·quis·i·tive (ə·kwiz'ə·tiv), *adj.* fond of acquiring; likely to get and keep. —ac·quis'i·tive·ly, *adv.* —ac·quis'i·tive·ness, *n.*

ac·quit (ə·kwit'), *v.*, -quit·ted, -quit·ting. 1. declare (a person) not guilty (of an offense). 2. set free (from a duty, an obligation, etc.). 3. conduct (oneself): *the soldiers acquitted themselves well in battle.* 4. pay off or settle (a debt, claim, etc.). [< OF, < a– + quitte free < L quietus quiet] —ac·quit'ter, *n.* —Syn. 1. exonerate. 2. release. 3. behave. —Ant. 1. condemn.

ac·quit·tal (ə·kwit'əl), *n.* 1. a setting free by declaring not guilty; discharge; release. 2. performance (of a duty, obligation, etc.).

ac·quit·tance (ə·kwit'əns), *n.* 1. release from a debt or obligation. 2. payment of a debt. 3. a written acknowledgment.

a·cre (ā'kər), *n.* 1. a measure of land, 160 square rods or 43,560 square feet. 2. acres, lands; property. [OE æcer field]

A·cre (ä'kər; ā'kər), *n.* seaport in NW Palestine, important during the Crusades.

a·cre·age (ā'kər·ij), *n.* 1. number of acres. 2. piece of land sold by the acre.

ac·rid (ak'rid), *adj.* 1. sharp or stinging to the nose, mouth, or skin. 2. sharp or irritating in manner. [< L acer sharp] —a·crid·i·ty (ə·krid'ə·ti), ac·rid·ness, *n.* —ac·rid·ly, *adv.*

A·cri·lan (ak'rə·lan), *n. Trademark.* a synthetic, wrinkle-resistant fiber, resembling wool in texture.

ac·ri·mo·ni·ous (ak'rə·mō'ni·əs), *adj.* caustic and stinging; bitter. —ac'ri·mo'ni·ous·ly, *adv.* —ac'ri·mo'ni·ous·ness, *n.*

ac·ri·mo·ny (ak'rə·mō'ni), *n.*, *pl.* -nies. sharpness or bitterness in temper, language, or manner. [< L acrimonia < acer sharp]

ac·ro·bat (ak'rə·bat), *n.* person who can perform on a trapeze, a tightrope, etc. [< F < Gk., < akros tip (of the toes) + bainein to go] —ac'ro·bat'ic, *adj.* —ac'ro·bat'i·cal·ly, *adv.*

ac·ro·bat·ics (ak'rə·bat'iks), *n.pl.* 1. gymnastic feats. 2. feats like those of an acrobat.

ac·ro·gen (ak'rə·jən), *n. Bot.* plant growing only at the apex, such as the ferns and mosses. [< Gk. akros tip + -genes born] —ac·ro·gen·ic (ak'rə·jen'ik), ac·rog·e·nous (ə·kroj'ə·nəs), *adj.* —a·crog'e·nous·ly, *adv.*

ac·ro·meg·a·ly (ak'rō·meg'ə·li), *n.* a disease in which the head, hands, and feet become permanently enlarged. [< Gk. akros tip + megas big] —ac·ro·me·gal·ic (ak'rō·mə·gal'ik), *adj.*

ac·ro·nym (ak'rə·nim), *n.* word formed from the first letters or syllables of other words, as UNESCO. [< Gk. akros tip + onyma name]

a·crop·o·lis (ə·krop'ə·lis), *n.* the high, fortified part of an ancient Greek city, esp. the Acropolis of Athens. [< Gk., < akros highest part of + polis city]

a·cross (ə·krôs'; ə·kros'), *prep.* 1. from side to side of; over: *a bridge laid across a river.* 2. on or to the other side of; beyond: *across the sea.* 3. into contact with: *come across a new word.* 4. across the board, without any exceptions. —*adv.* 1. from one side to the other: *what is the distance across?* 2. from side to side; crosswise: *with arms across.* 3. on or to the other side: *when are you going across?* 4. come across, *U.S. Colloq.* a. pay up; hand over. b. own up; admit.

a·cros·tic (ə·krôs'tik; ə·kros'-), *n.* a composition in verse or an arrangement of words in which the first, last, or certain other letters of each line, taken in order, spell a word or phrase.—*adj.* of or forming an acrostic. [< L < Gk., < akros tip + stichos row] —a·cros'ti·cal·ly, *adv.*

North
East
West
South

Acrostic

ac·ry·lo·ni·trile (ak'rə·lō·ni'trəl), *n.* a colorless, inflammable, poisonous liquid, CH_2:CH·CN. It is used in making certain kinds of synthetic rubber, fabrics, etc.

act (akt), *n.* 1. thing done; deed: *an act of kindness.* 2. process of doing: *in the act of stealing.* 3. a main division of a play or opera. 4. one of several performances on a program: *the trained dog's act.* 5. a legislative decision; law: *an act of Congress.* 6. a legal document proving that something has been done. —*v.* 1. put forth effort: *act at once.* 2. perform specific duties or functions: *act as counsel for the committee.* 3. behave: *act tired.* 4. behave like: *act the fool.* 5. have an effect or influence: *yeast acts on dough.* 6. play a part; perform in a theater. 7. act as or for, take the place of; do the work of. 8. act up, *Am., Colloq.* a. behave badly. b. play tricks; make mischief. [< L actus a doing and actum (thing) done < agere do] —act'a·ble, *adj.* —Syn. *n.* 5. decree, statute. ►act. In the sense "to behave," act is a linking verb, so that its meaning can be completed by an adjective: *he acts old, he acts older than he is.*

ACTH, *n.* a hormone used in treating arthritis, rheumatic fever, etc.

act·ing (ak'ting), *adj.* 1. temporarily taking another's place and doing his duties. 2. that acts or functions. 3. arranged for the use of actors.

ac·tin·ic (ak·tin'ik), *adj.* 1. of actinism. 2. producing chemical changes by radiation. [< Gk. aktis ray]

ac·tin·ism (ak'tən·iz·əm), *n.* property in light that causes chemical changes.

ac·tin·i·um (ak·tin'i·əm), *n.* a radioactive chemical element, Ac, somewhat like radium, found in pitchblende.

ac·ti·no·zo·an (ak'tə·nə·zō'ən), *n. Zool.* sea animal belonging to the group that includes corals, sea anemones, etc.

ac·tion (ak'shən), *n.* 1. process of acting: *a machine in action.* 2. activity: *a soldier is a man of action.* 3. thing done; act. 4. actions, conduct; behavior. 5. exertion of power or force; influence: *the action of wind on a ship's sails.* 6. way of moving or working; movement: *a motor with an easy action.* 7. the working parts of a machine, instrument, etc. 8. a minor battle. 9. combat between military forces. 10. series of events in a story or play. 11. a lawsuit. 12. take action, a. become active. b. start working. c. start a lawsuit; sue. [< F < L actio. See ACT.] —ac'tion·less, *adj.*

ac·tion·a·ble (ak'shən·ə·bəl), *adj.* justifying a lawsuit. —ac'tion·a·bly, *adv.*

ac·ti·vate (ak'tə·vāt), *v.*, -vat·ed, -vat·ing. 1. make active. 2. *Physics.* make radioactive. 3. *Chem.* make capable of reacting or of speeding up a reaction. 4. purify (sewage) by treating it with air and bacteria. —ac'ti·va'tion, *n.* —ac'ti·va'tor, *n.*

ac·tive (ak'tiv), *adj.* 1. acting; working: *an active volcano.* 2. moving rather quickly; lively. 3. showing much or constant action: *an active market.* 4. real; effective: *take an active part.* 5. causing action or change. 6. *Gram.* showing the subject of a verb as acting. In "He broke the window," *broke* is in the active voice. —*n.* the active voice. [< F < L *activus.* See ACT.] —ac'·tive·ly, *adv.* —ac'tive·ness, *n.* —Syn. *adj.* 2. nimble, quick. 3. vigorous, energetic. ≫ A verb is in the active voice when its subject is the doer of the action: "Jimmy's father *gave* him a car" as contrasted with the passive verb in "Jimmy *was given* a car by his father."

active duty or **service, 1.** military service with full pay and regular duties. 2. service in the armed forces in time of war.

ac·tiv·i·ty (ak·tiv'ə·ti), *n., pl.* –ties. 1. state of being active: *mental activity.* 2. action; doing: *the activities of enemy spies.* 3. vigorous action; liveliness: *no activity in the market.* 4. thing to do; sphere of action: *outside activities.* 5. anything active; active force.

act of God, a sudden, unforeseeable, and uncontrollable action of natural forces, such as flood, storm, or earthquake.

ac·tor (ak'tər), *n.* 1. person who acts on the stage, in moving pictures, or in a broadcast. 2. person who acts; a doer.

ac·tress (ak'tris), *n.* a female actor.

Acts (akts), or **Acts of the Apostles,** *n.* the fifth book of the New Testament.

ac·tu·al (ak'chů·əl), *adj.* 1. existing as a fact; real: *the actual as opposed to the imaginary.* 2. now existing; present; current: *the actual state of affairs.* [< F < LL < L *actus* a doing. See ACT.] —ac'tu·al·ness, *n.* —Syn. 1. true, genuine.

ac·tu·al·i·ty (ak'chů·al'ə·ti), *n., pl.* –ties. 1. actual existence. 2. actual thing; fact.

ac·tu·al·ize (ak'chů·əl·iz), *v.,* –ized, –iz·ing. make actual. —ac'tu·al·i·za'tion, *n.*

ac·tu·al·ly (ak'chů·əl·i), *adv.* really; in fact.

ac·tu·ar·y (ak'chů·er'i), *n., pl.* –ar·ies. person whose work is figuring risks, rates, etc., for insurance companies. [< L *actuarius* account keeper. See ACT.] —ac·tu·ar·i·al (ak'chů·ãr'i·əl), *adj.* —ac'tu·ar'i·al·ly, *adv.*

ac·tu·ate (ak'chů·āt), *v.,* –at·ed, –at·ing. 1. put into action. 2. influence to act. [< L *actus* action] —ac'tu·a'tion, *n.* —ac'tu·a'tor, *n.*

a·cu·i·ty (ə·kū'ə·ti), *n.* sharpness; acuteness. [< Med.L < OF *aguteé* < *agu* sharp < L *acutus*]

a·cu·men (ə·kū'mən), *n.* sharpness and quickness in seeing and understanding; keen insight. [< L, < *acuere* sharpen]

a·cute (ə·kūt'), *adj.* 1. having a sharp point. 2. sharp and severe: *an acute fuel shortage.* 3. brief and severe: *an acute attack of appendicitis.* 4. keen: *an acute sense of smell.* 5. intense; poignant: *acute jealousy.* 6. (of sounds) high in pitch; shrill. 7. having the mark (´) over it. —*n.* acute accent. [< L, < *acuere* sharpen] —a·cute'ly, *adv.* —a·cute'ness, *n.*

acute accent, mark (´) used to show the quality of a vowel, as in French *abbé,* or to show stress, as in Spanish *adiós.*

acute angle, *Geom.* angle less than a right angle.

ad (ad), *n. Am., Colloq.* advertisement. ≫ Ad is the clipped form of *advertisement,* has only one *d,* and should not be followed by a period. Like other clipped words it belongs to informal and familiar speech and writing.

ad–, *prefix.* to; toward, as in *admit, administer, adverb, advert.* [< L *ad,* prep.; appears also, by assimilation to the following consonant, as *ac–, af–, ag–, al–, an–, ap–, ar–, as–, at–,* and, by reduction before *sc, sp, st,* as *a–*]

A.D., in the year of the Lord; since Christ was born: *Augustus lived from 63* B.C. *to 14* A.D. [for LL *anno domini*]

ad·age (ad'ij), *n.* a brief, familiar proverb; an old saying. [< F < L *adagium*]

a·da·gio (ə·dä'jō; –zhi·ō), *adv., adj., n., pl.* –gios. *Music.* —*adv.* slowly. —*adj.* slow. —*n.* a slow part in a piece of music. [< Ital. *ad agio* at ease]

Ad·am (ad'əm), *n. Bible.* the first man.

ad·a·mant (ad'ə·mant), *n.* substance too hard to be cut or broken. —*adj.* 1. too hard to be cut or broken. 2. unyielding; firm; immovable. [< OF *adamaunt* the hardest stone (= diamond) < L < Gk., < *a–* not + *damaein* subdue]

ad·a·man·tine (ad'ə·man'tin; –tēn; –tīn), *adj.* adamant; impenetrable; unyielding.

Ad·ams (ad'əmz), *n.* 1. John, 1735–1826, second president of the United States, 1797–1801. 2. John Quincy, 1767–1848, sixth president of the United States, 1825–29, son of John Adams.

Adam's apple, the lump in the front of the throat formed by the thyroid cartilage.

a·dapt (ə·dapt'), *v.* 1. make fit or suitable; adjust: *adapt oneself to a new job.* 2. modify or alter for a different use: *adapt a novel for the stage.* [< L, < *ad–* to + *aptare* fit] —a·dapt'·er, *n.* —Syn. 1. accommodate.

a·dapt·a·ble (ə·dap'tə·bəl), *adj.* 1. easily changed to fit different conditions. 2. changing easily to fit different conditions. —a·dapt'a·bil'i·ty, a·dapt'a·ble·ness, *n.*

ad·ap·ta·tion (ad'əp·tā'shən), *n.* 1. adjustment to new or different circumstances. 2. result of altering for a different use. 3. *Biol.* change in structure, form, or habits to fit different conditions. —ad'ap·ta'tion·al, *adj.*

a·dap·tive (ə·dap'tiv), *adj.* 1. that can adapt. 2. showing adaptation. —a·dap'tive·ly, *adv.* —a·dap'tive·ness, *n.*

A-day (ā'dā'), *n., adj. Am.* Able Day.

add (ad), *v.* 1. join (one thing to another); put together; put with: *add another stone to the pile.* 2. find the sum of: *add 8 and 2 and you have 10.* 3. make or form an addition; increase: *add to our pleasure.* 4. say further. [< L, < *ad–* to + *dare* put] —add'a·ble, add'i·ble, *adj.* —add'er, *n.*

ad·dax (ad'aks), *n.* a large antelope of Arabia and N Africa. [< L < an African word]

ad·den·dum (ə·den'dəm), *n., pl.* –da (–də). 1. thing to be added. 2. things added; appendix.

ad·der (ad'ər), *n.* 1. a small, poisonous snake of Europe. 2. a small, harmless snake of North America. 3. puff adder. [OE *nœdre;* in ME *a nadder* was taken as *an adder*]

ad·der's-tongue (ad'ərz·tung'), *n.* 1. a variety of small fern with a fruiting spike. 2. *Am.* the dogtooth violet.

ad·dict (*n.* ad'ikt; *v.* ə·dikt'), *n.* person who is a slave or devotee to a habit. —*v.* give (oneself) over, as to a habit. [< L, < *ad–* to + *dicere* say] —ad·dic'tion, *n.*

ad·dict·ed (ə·dik'tid), *adj.* slavishly following (a habit, practice); strongly inclined.

Ad·dis Ab·a·ba (ad'is ab'ə·bə), the capital of Ethiopia, in E Africa.

Ad·di·son (ad'ə·sən), *n.* Joseph, 1672–1719, English essayist, poet, and statesman. —Ad·di·so·ni·an (ad'ə·sō'ni·ən), *adj.*

ad·di·tion (ə·dish'ən), *n.* 1. act or process of adding. 2. result of adding; thing added. 3. *Am.* part added to a building. 4. *Am.* a. land added to existing holdings. b. recent extension of the residential section of a city. 5. **in addition to,** besides; also. [< F < L. See ADD.]

ad·di·tion·al (ə·dish'ən·əl), *adj.* added; supplementary. —ad·di'tion·al·ly, *adv.*

ad·di·tive (ad'ə·tiv), *adj.* 1. to be added. 2. *Gram.* linking and making equal two or more elements of a sentence. In "the dog and the cat," *and* is an additive element. —*n.* 1. an additive word or element. 2. a chemical compound or other substance added to anything to increase its effectiveness.

ad·dle (ad'əl), *v.,* –dled, –dling, *adj.* —*v.* 1. make or become confused. 2. make or become rotten. —*adj.* muddled; confused, as in **addle-brain, addleheaded,** etc. [OE *adela* liquid filth]

ad·dress (ə·dres'; *esp. for n. defs.* 3 *and* 4, ad'res), *n., v.* —*v.* –dressed or –drest, –dress·ing. —*n.* 1. a speech, esp. a formal one: *the President's inaugural address.* 2. an expression of views in writing transmitted to an authority: *an address from the colonists to the king, listing grievances.* 3. place at which a person, business,

āge, cãre, fär; ēqual, tėrm; īce; ōpen, ôrder; pút, rüle, ūse; th, then; ə=a in about.

etc., receives mail. 4. the writing on an envelope, package, etc., that shows where it is to be sent. 5. manner in conversation. 6. skill; adroitness. 7. addresses, attention paid in courtship. —v. 1. direct speech or writing to: *the President addressed the nation over the radio.* 2. use titles or other forms in speaking or writing to: *how do you address a mayor?* 3. direct to the attention: *address a warning to a friend.* 4. apply (oneself) in speech (to a person): *he addressed himself to the chairman.* 5. write on (a letter, package, etc.) where it is to be sent. 6. apply or devote (oneself); direct one's energies: *he addressed himself to the task of doing his homework.* [< F *adresser* direct to < OF < L, < *ad-* to + *directus* straight] —ad·dress′er, ad·dres′sor, *n.* ➤ addresses. When the various parts of a person's address are written on the same line, they are separated by commas: *Miss Louise Finney, 48 Adirondack View, Middlebury, Vermont; Mr. Davis was a native of Carroll County, Va., and a graduate of the College of William and Mary.*

ad·dress·ee (ə·dres·ē′; ad′res·ē′), *n. Am.* person to whom a letter, etc., is addressed.

ad·duce (ə·dūs′; ə·dūs′), *v.,* −duced, −duc·ing. offer as a reason; give as proof or evidence. [< L, < *ad-* to + *ducere* lead] —ad·duce′a·ble, ad·duc′i·ble, *adj.* —ad·duc′er, *n.*

ad·duct (ə·dukt′), *v. Physiol.* pull (a part of the body) inward toward the main axis. [< L *adductus,* pp. See ADDUCE.] —ad·duc′tive, *adj.* —ad·duc′tor, *n.* —Ant. abduct.

ad·duc·tion (ə·duk′shən), *n.* 1. an adducing; bringing forward statements. 2. *Physiol.* an adducting.

Ad·e·laide (ad′ə·lād), *n.* city in S Australia.

Ad·e·nau·er (ad′ə·nou′ər), *n.* Konrad, born 1876, German statesman; chancellor of West Germany since 1949.

ad·e·noid (ad′ə·noid), ad·e·noi·dal (ad′ə·noi′dəl), *adj.* 1. of the lymphatic glands. 2. glandular.

ad·e·noids (ad′ə·noidz), *n.pl.* growths of glandular tissue in the part of the throat behind the nose, that often interfere with natural breathing and speaking. [< Gk., < *aden* gland, acorn]

ad·ept (*n.* ad′ept, ə·dept′; *adj.* ə·dept′), *n.* a thoroughly skilled person; expert. —*adj.* thoroughly skilled. [< L *adeptus* < *ad-* to + *apisci* get] —a·dept′ly, *adv.* —a·dept′ness, *n.*

ad·e·qua·cy (ad′ə·kwə·si), *n.* as much as is needed for a particular purpose; sufficiency.

ad·e·quate (ad′ə·kwit), *adj.* 1. as much as is needed; fully sufficient: *means adequate to the object.* 2. suitable; competent: *an adequate person for the job.* [< L, < *ad-* to + *aequus* equal] —ad′e·quate·ly, *adv.* —ad′e·quate·ness, *n.* —Syn. 1. enough, requisite, needful.

ad·here (ad·hir′), *v.,* −hered, −her·ing. 1. stick fast (*to*): *mud adheres to your shoes.* 2. hold closely or firmly (*to*): *adhere to a plan.* 3. be devoted (*to*): *most people adhere to the church of their parents.* [< L, < *ad-* to + *haerere* stick]

ad·her·ence (ad·hir′əns), *n.* 1. steady attachment or loyalty (to a person, group, belief, etc.). 2. a holding to and following closely.

ad·her·ent (ad·hir′ənt), *n.* faithful supporter. —*adj.* adhering. —ad·her′ent·ly, *adv.*

ad·he·sion (ad·hē′zhən), *n.* 1. act or state of adhering; a sticking fast. 2. following and supporting; faithfulness. 3. agreement; assent. 4. *Physics.* the attraction that holds molecules together. 5. *Pathol.* the growing together of tissues that should be separate.

ad·he·sive (ad·hē′siv; −ziv), *adj.* 1. holding fast; adhering easily; sticky. 2. smeared with a sticky substance for holding (something) fast: *adhesive tape.* —*n. U.S.* gummed tape used to hold bandages in place. —ad·he′sive·ly, *adv.* —ad·he′sive·ness, *n.*

ad hoc (ad hok′), for a certain purpose; special. [< L, for this]

ad·i·a·bat·ic (ad′i·ə·bat′ik; ā′dī−), *adj. Physics.* without transmission (gain or loss) of heat. —ad′i·a·bat′i·cal·ly, *adv.*

a·dieu (ə·dū′; ə·dū̄′), *interj., n., pl.* a·dieus,

a·dieux (ə·dūz′; ə·dū̄z′). —*interj.* good-by; farewell. —*n.* a farewell. [< F *à dieu* to God]

ad in·fi·ni·tum (ad in′fə·nī′təm), *Latin.* without limit; forever.

ad in·te·rim (ad in′tə·rim), *Latin.* 1. in the meantime. 2. temporary.

a·di·os (ä′di·ōs′; ad′i−), *Am., S.W.* —*interj.* good-by. —*n.* a farewell. [< Sp. *a dios* to God]

ad·i·pose (ad′ə·pōs), *adj.* fatty. —*n.* animal fat. [< NL < L *adeps* fat] —ad′i·pose·ness, ad·i·pos·i·ty (ad′ə·pos′ə·ti), *n.*

Ad·i·ron·dacks (ad′ə·ron′daks), or Adi·rondack Mountains, *n.pl.* a mountain range in NE New York.

adj., 1. adjective. 2. adjunct. 3. adjustment.

ad·ja·cen·cy (ə·jā′sən·si), *n., pl.* −cies. 1. nearness. 2. that which is adjacent.

ad·ja·cent (ə·jā′sənt), *adj.* lying near or close; adjoining: *the garage is adjacent to our house.* [< L, < *ad-* near + *jacere* to lie] —ad·ja′cent·ly, *adv.* —Syn. bordering, neighboring. —Ant. distant.

adjacent angles, *Geom.* two angles that have the same vertex and the same line as one of their sides. In the diagram, ADB and BDC are adjacent angles.

ad·jec·ti·val (aj′ik·tī′vəl; aj′ik·ti·vəl), *adj.* of or used as an adjective. —ad′jec·ti′val·ly, *adv.*

ad·jec·tive (aj′ik·tiv), *Gram.* —*n.* a word used to qualify or limit a noun or pronoun. A descriptive adjective shows a quality or condition as belonging to the noun or pronoun named, as, a *blue* shirt, a *wrecked* car. A limiting adjective points out in some way the noun or pronoun named, or indicates quantity or number, as, *this* pencil, *his* book, *any* person, *twenty-five* cents. —*adj.* 1. of an adjective. 2. used as an adjective. [< L *adjectivus* that is added to < *ad-* to + *jacere* throw] —ad′jec·tive·ly, *adv.* ➤ adjective. 1. forms of adjectives. Many adjectives have come down from an early period of the language (*high, handsome, civil*) and many have been made and are still being made by adding a suffix to a noun or verb. Some suffixes that are still active are: *-able* (*-ible*), as in *translatable, dirigible; -ed,* as in *sugared,* and usually in adjectives that are compound words: *four-footed, well-lighted; -escent,* as in *florescent; -ese,* as in *Burmese, journalese; -ful,* as in *playful, soulful; -ish,* as in *babyish, cattish, womanish; -less,* as in *harmless, fearless; -like,* as in *birdlike; -y,* as in *cranky, dreamy, corny.* 2. position of adjectives. According to its position in a sentence, an adjective is either attributive or predicate: *Attributive adjectives* are placed next to their nouns, usually preceding as in the *tiny* brook, *horseless* carriages. *Predicate adjectives* come after some form of the verb *be* or some other linking verb (*taste, feel, turn, . . .*): *the day is warm,* the train was *crowded,* that pie smells *good,* for a while I felt *bad.* 3. comparison of adjectives. A greater degree of the quality named by an adjective is shown by adding *-er* or *-est* to the adjective or by placing *more* or *most* before it: *learned, more learned, most learned; warm, warmer* or *more warm, warmest* or *most warm.*

ad·join (ə·join′), *v.* 1. be next to; be in contact with: *Canada adjoins the United States.* 2. be next or close to each other; be in contact. [< OF *ajoindre* < L, < *ad-* to + *jungere* join] —ad·join′ing, *adj.*

ad·journ (ə·jėrn′), *v.* 1. put off until a later time: *the club adjourned consideration of the question.* 2. suspend the meeting of to a future time or to another place: *the judge adjourned the court for two hours.* 3. stop business or proceedings for a time: *the court adjourned from Friday until Monday.* 4. *Colloq.* go to another place. [< OF *ajorner* < *a-* for (< L *ad-*) + *jorn* day < L *diurnum,* ult. < L *dies* day]

ad·journ·ment (ə·jėrn′mənt), *n.* 1. act of adjourning. 2. time during which a court, law-making body, etc., is adjourned.

Adjt., Adjutant.

ad·judge (ə·juj′), *v.,* −judged, −judg·ing. 1. decree or declare by law: *the accused man was* adjudged guilty. 2. condemn or sentence by law: the thief was adjudged to prison for two years. 3. decide or settle by law; judge. 4. award or assign by law. [< OF ajugier < L, < ad- to + judicare judge. Doublet of ADJUDICATE.] —adjudge′a·ble, adj.

ad·ju·di·cate (ə·jü′də·kāt), v., -cat·ed, -cat·ing. 1. decide or settle by law. 2. act as judge. [< L adjudicatus, pp. Doublet of ADJUDGE.] —ad·ju′di·ca′tion, n. —ad·ju′di·ca′tive, adj. —ad·ju′di·ca′tor, n.

ad·junct (aj′ungkt), n. 1. something added that is less important or not necessary, but helpful. 2. a subordinate colleague. 3. Gram. word or phrase qualifying or modifying another word or phrase. [< L adjunctus, pp. of adjungere join to. See ADJOIN.] —ad·junc′tive, adj. —ad·junc′tive·ly, adv.

ad·jure (ə·júr′), v., -jured, -jur·ing. 1. command or charge (a person) on oath or under some penalty (to do something). 2. ask earnestly or solemnly. [< L, < ad- to + jurare swear] —ad·ju·ra·tion (aj′ù·rā′shən), n. —ad·jur·a·to·ry (ə·júr′ə·tô′ri, -tō′-), adj. —ad·jur′er, ad·ju′ror, n.

ad·just (ə·just′), v. 1. fit or adapt (one thing to another): adjust a seat to the height of a child. 2. regulate for use: adjust a radio dial. 3. arrange satisfactorily; settle: adjust a difference of opinion. 4. accommodate oneself; get used: adjust well to army life. [< F ajuster < a- (< L ad-) + juste right < L justus] —ad·just′a·ble, adj. —ad·just′a·bly, adv. —ad·just′ed, adj. —ad·just′er, ad·jus′tor, n.

ad·just·ment (ə·just′mənt), n. 1. act or process of adjusting. 2. orderly arrangement of parts or elements. 3. means of adjusting. 4. settlement of a dispute, a claim, etc.

ad·ju·tan·cy (aj′ə·tən·si), n., pl. -cies. rank or position of an adjutant in the army.

ad·ju·tant (aj′ə·tənt), n. 1. army officer who assists a commanding officer by sending out orders, writing letters, giving messages, etc. 2. helper; assistant. 3. a very large species of stork of India and Africa. —adj. helping. [< L adjutans, ult. < ad- to + juvare help] —ad′ju·tant·ship′, n.

adjutant general, pl. adjutants general. adjutant of a division or a larger military unit.

ad·lib (ad·lib′), v., -libbed, -lib·bing. Colloq. make up and insert as one speaks, performs, or acts; extemporize freely. [< L ad libitum at pleasure]

ad lib·i·tum (ad lib′ə·təm), Music. a direction to change, omit, or expand a passage as much as the player wishes. [< NL, at pleasure]

Adm., Admiral; Admiralty.

ad·min·is·ter (ad·min′əs·tər), v. 1. manage or conduct as chief agent or steward; direct: administer a government department. 2. put in force; dispense: administer relief. 3. supply or give: administer punishment to a person. 4. offer or tender (an oath). 5. Law. settle or take charge of (an estate). 6. act as administrator. 7. be helpful; add something; contribute. [< L, < ad- + ministrare serve < minister servant] —ad·min·is·tra·ble (ad·min′əs·trə·bəl), adj. —ad·min·is·trant (ad·min′əs·trənt), n.

ad·min·is·trate (ad·min′əs·trāt), v., -trat·ed, -trat·ing. U.S. administer.

ad·min·is·tra·tion (ad·min′əs·trā′shən), n. 1. management (of a business, public affairs, etc.). 2. the conducting of the governmental duties of a state, esp. its executive functions. 3. a. the officials charged with the execution of law and the management of public affairs. b. Am. the President of the United States and his Cabinet. 4. a. the period of office of these officials. b. Am. the term or terms during which a President holds office. 5. a giving out, applying, or dispensing (medicine, justice, etc.).

ad·min·is·tra·tive (ad·min′əs·trā′tiv), adj. executive. —ad·min′is·tra′tive·ly, adv.

ad·min·is·tra·tor (ad·min′əs·trā′tər), n. 1. person who administers. 2. Law. person appointed by a court to take charge of or settle an estate. —ad·min′is·tra′tor·ship, n. —Syn. 1. manager, director, executive.

ad·min·is·tra·trix (ad·min′əs·trā′triks), n. Law. woman administrator.

ad·mi·ra·ble (ad′mə·rə·bəl), adj. 1. worth admiring. 2. excellent; very good. —ad′mi·ra·ble·ness, n. —ad′mi·ra·bly, adv.

ad·mi·ral (ad′mə·rəl), n. 1. commander in chief of a fleet. 2. naval officer having the highest rank. 3. admiral, vice-admiral, or rear admiral. 4. flagship. [earlier amiral < OF < Ar. amīr al chief of the; akin to AMIR]

ad·mi·ral·ty (ad′mə·rəl·ti), n., pl. -ties. 1. law or court dealing with affairs of the sea and ships. 2. in England, the government department in charge of naval affairs. 3. the Admiralty, official building of the British commissioners for naval affairs, in London.

ad·mi·ra·tion (ad′mə·rā′shən), n. 1. a feeling of wonder, pleasure, and approval. 2. delight at something fine or beautiful. 3. one that is admired. 4. Archaic. wonder.

ad·mire (ad·mīr′), v., -mired, -mir·ing. 1. regard with wonder, approval, and delight. 2. feel or express admiration. 3. U.S. like. 4. Archaic. wonder at. [< L, < ad- at + mirari wonder]

ad·mir·er (ad·mīr′ər), n. 1. person who admires. 2. man who is in love with a woman.

ad·mir·ing (ad·mīr′ing), adj. full of admiration. —ad·mir′ing·ly, adv.

ad·mis·si·ble (ad·mis′ə·bəl), adj. 1. that can be permitted or considered; allowable. 2. Law. allowable as evidence. 3. having the right to enter or use. —ad·mis′si·bil′i·ty, ad·mis′si·ble·ness, n. —ad·mis′si·bly, adv.

ad·mis·sion (ad·mish′ən), n. 1. act of allowing (a person, animal, etc.) to enter: admission of aliens into a country. 2. power or right to enter or use an office, place, etc. 3. price paid for the right to enter. 4. acceptance into an office or position. 5. confession of an error or a crime. 6. an acknowledging; accepting as true or valid. 7. fact or point acknowledged; something accepted as true or valid. 8. Am. formal receiving of a State into the Union. 9. admission to the bar, Am. the granting of authority to practice as a lawyer.

ad·mis·sive (ad·mis′iv), adj. tending to admit.

ad·mit (ad·mit′), v., -mit·ted, -mit·ting. 1. acknowledge: admit a mistake. 2. accept as true or valid. 3. allow to enter or use; let in. 4. give the right to enter to. 5. allow; permit. 6. be capable (of): his answer admits of no reply. 7. have room for: the harbor admits three ships. 8. U.S. let attain to a position, privilege, etc. 9. Am. receive (a State) into the Union. 10. admit to the bar, Am. give authority to practice law. [< L, < ad- to + mittere let go] —ad·mit′ter, n. —Syn. 2. recognize.

ad·mit·tance (ad·mit′əns), n. 1. right to go in. 2. act of admitting. 3. actual entrance.

ad·mit·ted·ly (ad·mit′id·li), adv. without denial; by general consent.

ad·mix (ad·miks′), v. add in mixing; mix in.

ad·mix·ture (ad·miks′chər), n. 1. act of mixing; mixture. 2. anything added in mixing. [< L admixtus < ad- in addition + miscere mix]

ad·mon·ish (ad·mon′ish), v. 1. advise against something; warn: the policeman admonished him not to drive too fast. 2. reprove gently: admonish a student for careless work. 3. urge strongly; advise. 4. recall to a duty overlooked or forgotten; remind. [< admonition] —ad·mon′ish·er, n. —ad·mon′ish·ing·ly, adv. —ad·mon′ish·ment, n.

ad·mo·ni·tion (ad′mə·nish′ən), n. an admonishing; warning. [< L, < ad- to + monere warn]

ad·mon·i·to·ry (ad·mon′ə·tô′ri; -tō′-), adj. admonishing; warning.

a·do (ə·dü′), n. stir; bustle. [ME at do to do]

a·do·be (ə·dō′bē), Am., S.W. —n. 1. sun-dried clay or mud. 2. a brick or bricklike piece of such material, used in building. —adj. built or made of sun-dried bricks: an adobe house. [< Sp., < adobar to daub < Gmc.]

ad·o·les·cence (ad'ə·les'əns), *n.* **1.** growth from childhood to manhood (from 14 to 25) or womanhood (from 12 to 21). **2.** period or time of this growth; youth.

ad·o·les·cent (ad'ə·les'ənt), *n.* person from about 12 to about 22 years of age. —*adj.* **1.** growing up from childhood to maturity. **2.** of or characteristic of adolescents. [< L *adolescens* < *ad-* to + *alescere* grow]

A·don·is (ə·don'is; ə·dō'nis), *n.* **1.** *Class. Myth.* a handsome young man loved by Aphrodite (Venus). **2.** a handsome young man.

a·dopt (ə·dopt'), *v.* **1.** take for one's own. **2.** accept formally: *the legislature adopted the committee's report.* **3.** take (a child of other parents) and bring up as one's own. **4.** take (a person) into close relationship. [< L, < *ad-* to + *optare* choose] —**a·dopt'a·ble,** *adj.* —**a·dopt'- a·bil'i·ty,** *n.* —**a·dopt'er,** *n.* —**a·dop'tion,** *n.*

a·dop·tive (ə·dop'tiv), *adj.* **1.** tending to adopt. **2.** related by adoption. —**a·dop'tive·ly,** *adv.*

a·dor·a·ble (ə·dôr'ə·bəl; ə·dōr'-), *adj.* **1.** worthy of being adored. **2.** *Colloq.* lovely; delightful. —**a·dor'a·ble·ness, a·dor'a·bil'i·ty,** *n.* —**a·dor'a·bly,** *adv.*

ad·o·ra·tion (ad'ə·rā'shən), *n.* **1.** worship. **2.** highest respect; devoted love.

a·dore (ə·dôr'; ə·dōr'), *v.,* **a·dored, a·dor·ing. 1.** respect very highly; love very greatly. **2.** *Colloq.* like very much. **3.** worship. [< OF < L, < *ad-* to + *orare* pray] —**a·dor'er,** *n.* —**a·dor'- ing,** *adj.* —**a·dor'ing·ly,** *adv.* —**Syn. 1.** revere, idolize. **3.** venerate.

a·dorn (ə·dôrn'), *v.* **1.** add beauty to; make greater the splendor or honor of. **2.** put ornaments on; decorate. [< OF < L, < *ad-* + *ornare* fit out] —**a·dorn'er,** *n.* —**a·dorn'ing·ly,** *adv.*

a·dorn·ment (ə·dôrn'mənt), *n.* **1.** thing that adds beauty; decoration. **2.** act of adorning.

ad·re·nal (ə·drē'nəl), *Anat., Zool.* —*adj.* **1.** near or on the kidney. **2.** of or from the adrenal glands. —*n.* an adrenal gland. [< L *ad-* near + *renes* kidneys]

adrenal gland, *Anat., Zool.* one of the two endocrine glands above the kidneys; suprarenal gland.

ad·ren·al·in (ə·dren'əl·in), **ad·ren·al·ine** (-in; -ēn), *n.* **1.** hormone secreted by the adrenal glands. **2. Adrenalin,** *Trademark.* a white, crystalline drug prepared from this hormone, used to stimulate the heart and stop bleeding.

A·dri·at·ic Sea (ā'dri·at'ik), arm of the Mediterranean between Yugoslavia and Italy.

a·drift (ə·drift'), *adv., adj.* **1.** drifting. **2.** swayed by any chance impulse; at a loss.

a·droit (ə·droit'), *adj.* expert in the use of the hands or the mind; skillful: *a teacher adroit in asking questions.* [< F *à droit* rightly < L *ad-* to + *directus* straight] —**a·droit'ly,** *adv.* —**a·droit'ness,** *n.* —**Syn.** clever, dexterous, deft.

ad·sorb (ad·sôrb'; -zôrb'), *v.* gather (a gas, liquid, or dissolved substance) on a surface in a condensed layer. [< L *ad-* + *sorbere* suck in] —**ad·sorb'ent,** *adj., n.*

ad·sorp·tion (ad·sôrp'shən; -zôrp'-), *n.* an adsorbing or being adsorbed. —**ad·sorp'tive,** *adj.*

ad·u·late (aj'ə·lāt), *v.,* -**lat·ed,** -**lat·ing.** flatter excessively. [< L *adulatus*] —**ad'u·la'tion,** *n.* —**ad'u·la'tor,** *n.* —**ad·u·la·to·ry** (aj'ə·lə·tô'ri; -tō'-), *adj.*

a·dult (ə·dult'; ad'ult), *adj.* **1.** having reached full size and strength; grown-up. **2.** of or for adults. —*n.* **1.** grown-up person. **2.** a full-grown plant or animal. [< L *adultus* < *ad-* to + *alescere* grow up] —**a·dult'hood, a·dult'ness,** *n.*

a·dul·ter·ant (ə·dul'tər·ənt), *n.* substance used in adulterating. —*adj.* adulterating.

a·dul·ter·ate (ə·dul'tər·āt), *v.,* -**at·ed,** -**at- ing.** make lower in quality by adding inferior or impure materials: *adulterate milk with water.* [< L *adulteratus,* ult. < *ad-* + *alter* other, different] —**a·dul'ter·a'tion,** *n.* —**a·dul'ter·a'tor,** *n.* —**Syn.** debase.

a·dul·ter·er (ə·dul'tər·ər), *n.* person, esp. a man, guilty of adultery.

a·dul·ter·ess (ə·dul'tər·is; -tris), *n.* woman guilty of adultery.

a·dul·ter·y (ə·dul'tər·i), *n., pl.* -**ter·ies.** voluntary sexual relations of a married person with any other than the lawful mate. —**a·dul'ter·ous,** *adj.* —**a·dul'ter·ous·ly,** *adv.*

ad·um·brate (ad·um'brāt; ad'əm·brāt), *v.,* -**brat·ed,** -**brat·ing. 1.** foreshadow. **2.** conceal partially; overshadow. [< L, < *ad-* + *umbra* shade] —**ad'um·bra'tion,** *n.*

adv., 1. adverb. **2.** adverbial. **3.** advertisement.

ad va·lo·rem (ad və·lô'rəm; -lō'-), (of merchandise) in proportion to the value. [< Med.L]

ad·vance (ad·vans'; -väns'), *v.,* -**vanced,** -**vanc·ing,** *n., adj.* —*v.* **1.** move forward: *the troops advanced.* **2.** bring forward: *the troops were advanced.* **3.** make progress; improve: *we advance in knowledge.* **4.** help forward; further: *advance a cause.* **5.** raise to a higher rank; promote: *advance him from lieutenant to captain.* **6.** rise in rank; be promoted: *advance in one's profession.* **7.** raise (prices): *advance the price of milk.* **8.** rise in price: *the stock advanced three points.* **9.** make earlier; hasten: *advance the time of the meeting.* **10.** supply beforehand: *advance a salesman funds for expenses.* **11.** lend (money), esp. on security: *advance a loan.* **12.** put forward; suggest: *advance an opinion.* —*n.* **1.** movement forward. **2.** a step forward; progress. **3.** a rise in price. **4.** the furnishing of money or goods before they are due or as a loan. **5.** the money or goods furnished. **6. advances,** personal approaches toward another or others to settle a difference, to make an acquaintance, etc. **7.** a forward position. **8. in advance,** a. in front; ahead. b. ahead of time. —*adj.* **1.** going before. **2.** ahead of time. [< OF *avancier* < LL, < L *ab-* from + *ante* before] —**ad·vanc'er,** *n.* —**Syn.** *v.* **1.** progress. **12.** present, offer, propose.

ad·vanced (ad·vanst'; -vänst'), *adj.* **1.** in front of others; forward. **2.** *Am.* beyond most others. **3.** far along in life; very old.

ad·vance·ment (ad·vans'mənt; -väns'-), *n.* **1.** movement forward; advance. **2.** progress; improvement. **3.** promotion.

ad·van·tage (ad·van'tij; -vän'-), *n., v.,* -**taged,** -**tag·ing.** —*n.* **1.** any favorable condition, circumstance, or opportunity; means helpful in getting something desired. **2.** take advantage of, a. use to help or benefit oneself. b. impose upon. **3.** better or superior position. **4.** the result of a better position. **5. to advantage,** to a good effect; with a useful effect. **6.** the first point scored in a tennis game after deuce. —*v.* give an advantage to; help; benefit. [< OF, < *avant* before < LL. See ADVANCE.] —**Syn.** *n.* **3.** superiority, ascendancy. **4.** benefit, gain, profit.

ad·van·ta·geous (ad'vən·tā'jəs), *adj.* giving advantage; profitable. —**ad'van·ta'geous·ly,** *adv.* —**ad'van·ta'geous·ness,** *n.*

ad·vent (ad'vent), *n.* **1.** coming; arrival. **2. Advent,** a. the birth of Christ. b. the season of devotion including the four Sundays before Christmas. **3. Second Advent,** the coming of Christ at the Last Judgment. [< L, < *ad-* to + *venire* come]

Ad·vent·ism (ad'ven·tiz·əm; ad·ven'-), *n. Am.* belief that the second coming of Christ is near at hand. —**Ad'vent·ist,** *n. Am.*

ad·ven·ti·tious (ad'ven·tish'əs), *adj.* **1.** coming from outside. **2.** *Bot., Zool.* appearing in an unusual position or place. —**ad'ven·ti'tious·ly,** *adv.* —**ad'ven·ti'tious·ness,** *n.*

ad·ven·tive (ad·ven'tiv), *adj. Bot., Zool.* **1.** introduced into a new environment. **2.** not native, though growing with cultivation.

ad·ven·ture (ad·ven'chər), *n., v.,* -**tured,** -**tur·ing.** —*n.* **1.** an exciting or unusual experience. **2.** a bold and difficult undertaking, usually exciting and somewhat dangerous. **3.** seeking excitement or danger: *spirit of adventure.* **4.** business undertaking; commercial speculation. **5.** *Obs.* peril. —*v.* venture; dare. [< OF < L. See ADVENT.]

ad·ven·tur·er (ad·ven'chər·ər), *n.* **1.** person who seeks or has adventures. **2.** soldier who sold his services to the highest bidder. **3.** person who schemes to get money, social position, etc. **4.** speculator.

ad·ven·ture·some (ad·ven'chər·səm), *adj.* bold and daring; adventurous.

ad·ven·tur·ess (ad·ven'chər·is), *n.* 1. woman who schemes to get money, social position, etc. 2. woman adventurer.

ad·ven·tur·ous (ad·ven'chər·əs), *adj.* 1. fond of adventures; ready to take risks; daring. 2. full of risk; dangerous. —**ad·ven'tur·ous·ly,** *adv.* —**ad·ven'tur·ous·ness,** *n.*

ad·verb (ad'vėrb), *n. Gram.* word that extends or limits the meaning of verbs but is also used to qualify adjectives or other adverbs, esp. as to place, time, manner, or degree. *Soon, here, very, gladly,* and *not* are adverbs. [< L, < *ad–* to + *verbum* verb] —**ad·ver·bi·al** (ad·vėr'bi·əl), *adj.* —**ad·ver'bi·al·ly,** *adv.* ➤ **adverbs.** 1. forms. Some adverbs have forms that have developed from Old English forms without a special adverbial sign: *now, quite, since, then, there, where;* but most adverbs are adjectives or participles plus the ending *–ly:* he rowed *badly,* she was *deservedly* popular, *surely* you heard that. There are a number of adverbs with the same forms as adjectives, most of them going back to Old English adverbs that ended in *–e* (an ending which has disappeared) instead of to those that ended in *–lice* (which gives us the current *–ly*). Some of these are: *cheap, close, deep, even, first, high, loud, much, near, right, slow, smooth, tight, well, wrong.* Most of these adverbs also have forms in *–ly* too, so that we can write "He sang *loud*" or "He sang *loudly.*" The *–ly* forms are preferred in formal English although the shorter forms are frequently used in informal and familiar writing. 2. **comparison of adverbs.** A greater degree of the quality named by the adverb is shown by adding *–er* or *–est* to an adverb or by placing *more* or *most* before it: *hard, harder, hardest; slow, slower, slowest,* or *slowly, more slowly, most slowly.* Most adverbs of more than one syllable are compared with *more* and *most.*

ad·ver·sar·y (ad'vər·ser'i), *n., pl.* **–sar·ies.** 1. unfriendly opponent; enemy. 2. person or group on the other side in a contest. —**Syn.** 1. foe. 2. contestant, opponent, antagonist.

ad·ver·sa·tive (ad·vėr'sə·tiv), *adj.* (of words, etc.) expressing contrast or opposition. *But* and *yet* are adversative conjunctions.

ad·verse (ad·vėrs'; ad'vėrs), *adj.* 1. unfriendly in purpose; hostile: *adverse criticism.* 2. unfavorable; harmful. 3. acting in a contrary direction; opposing: *adverse winds.* [< L *adversus.* See ADVERT.] —**ad·verse'ly,** *adv.* —**ad·verse'ness,** *n.* —**Syn.** 1. inimical. —**Ant.** 2. favorable.

ad·ver·si·ty (ad·vėr'sə·ti), *n., pl.* **–ties.** 1. condition of unhappiness, misfortune, or distress. 2. stroke of misfortune.

ad·vert (ad·vėrt'), *v.* direct attention; refer (*to*): *advert to the need for more parks.* [< L, < *ad–* to + *vertere* turn] —**Syn.** allude.

ad·vert·ent (ad·vėr'tənt), *adj.* attentive; heedful. —**ad·vert'ence, ad·vert'en·cy,** *n.*

ad·ver·tise, *esp. Brit.* **ad·ver·tize** (ad'vėr·tīz; ad'vėr·tīz'), *v.,* **–tised, –tis·ing;** *esp. Brit.* **–tized, –tiz·ing.** 1. give public notice of: *advertise a house for sale.* 2. ask by public notice (*for*): *advertise for a job.* 3. make generally known. 4. inform. 5. praise the good qualities of (a product, etc.) in order to promote sales. 6. issue advertising: *it pays to advertise.* 7. call attention to (oneself). [< obs. F *advertir* < L. See ADVERT.] —**ad'ver·tis'er,** *esp. Brit.* **ad'ver·tiz'er,** *n.*

ad·ver·tise·ment, *esp. Brit.* **ad·ver·tize·ment** (ad'vėr·tīz'mənt; ad·vėr'tis·mənt; –tiz–), *n.* a public notice or announcement, as in a newspaper or magazine, or over the radio.

ad·ver·tis·ing, *esp. Brit.* **ad·ver·tiz·ing** (ad'vėr·tīz'ing), *n.* 1. business of preparing, publishing, or circulating advertisements. 2. advertisements.

ad·vice (ad·vīs'), *n.* 1. opinion about what should be done. 2. advices, information; news. [< obs. F *advis,* var. of *avis* < L *ad–* + *visum* thing seen] —**Syn.** 1. counsel. 2. report, word.

ad·vis·a·ble (ad·vīz'ə·bəl), *adj.* to be recommended; wise; sensible. —**ad·vis'a·bil'i·ty,** ad·vis'a·ble·ness, *n.* —**ad·vis'a·bly,** *adv.*

ad·vise (ad·vīz'), *v.,* **–vised, –vis·ing.** 1. give advice to; counsel: *advise him to be cautious.* 2. give advice: *I shall act as you advise.* 3. give notice; inform: *we were advised of the dangers.* 4. talk over plans; consult (*with*): *he advised with his friends.* [< OF *aviser* < *avis* opinion. See ADVICE.] —**Syn.** 1. caution, admonish, warn. 2. recommend. 3. notify, acquaint, tell. 4. confer.

ad·vised (ad·vīzd'), *adj.* planned and considered. —**ad·vis·ed·ness** (ad·vīz'id·nis), *n.*

ad·vis·ed·ly (ad·vīz'id·li), *adv.* after careful consideration; deliberately.

ad·vise·ment (ad·vīz'mənt), *n.* careful consideration: *take a case under advisement.*

ad·vis·er, ad·vi·sor (ad·vīz'ər), *n.* 1. person who gives advice. 2. teacher who is appointed to advise students. ➤ **Adviser** has been the more common spelling, but the *–or* form is being increasingly used. Either is correct.

ad·vi·so·ry (ad·vī'zə·ri), *adj.* 1. having power to advise. 2. containing advice.

ad·vo·ca·cy (ad'və·kə·si), *n.* speaking in favor; public recommendation; support.

ad·vo·cate (*v.* ad'və·kāt; *n.* ad'və·kit, –kāt), *v.,* **–cat·ed, –cat·ing,** *n.* —*v.* speak in favor of; recommend publicly: *he advocates building more schools.* —*n.* 1. person who pleads or argues for: *an advocate of peace.* 2. lawyer who pleads in a law court. [< L, < *ad–* to + *vocare* call] —**ad'vo·ca'tion,** *n.* —**ad'vo·ca'tor,** *n.*

adz, adze (adz), *n.* tool somewhat like an ax but with a blade set across the end of the handle and curving inward. [OE *adesa*]

AEC, A.E.C., Atomic Energy Commission.

ae·dile (ē'dīl), *n.* official in charge of public buildings, games, streets, and markets in ancient Rome. Also, **edile.** [< L, < *aedes* building]

A.E.F., American Expeditionary Forces.

Ae·ge·an Sea (i·jē'ən), arm of the Mediterranean between Asia Minor and Greece.

ae·gis (ē'jis), *n.* 1. *Gk. Myth.* the shield of Zeus, used also by Athena. 2. protection. 3. patronage. Also, **egis.** [< L < Gk. *aigis*]

Ae·ne·as (i·nē'əs), *n. Class. Legend.* Trojan hero who escaped from Troy and settled in Italy.

ae·o·li·an harp or **lyre** (ē·ō'li·ən), a boxlike stringed instrument that produces musical sounds when currents of air blow across it.

Ae·o·lus (ē'ə·ləs), *n. Gk. Myth.* god of the winds. —**Ae·o·li·an** (ē·ō'li·ən), *adj.*

ae·on (ē'ən; ē'on), *n.* an indefinitely long period of time. Also, **eon.** [< L < Gk. *aion*]

aer·ate (ãr'āt; ā'ər·āt), *v.,* **–at·ed, –at·ing.** 1. expose to air. 2. expose to and mix with air. 3. fill with a gas, esp. carbon dioxide. 4. expose to chemical action with oxygen. [< L *aer* < Gk., air] —**aer·a'tion,** *n.* —**aer'a·tor,** *n.*

aer·i·al (*adj.* ãr'i·əl, ā·ir'i·əl; *n.* ãr'i·əl), *adj.* 1. in the air. 2. of or pertaining to the air. 3. like air; thin and light as air. 4. ideal; imaginary. 5. growing in the air. 6. relating to aircraft in any way. —*n.* wire or wires used in radio or television for sending out or receiving electric waves. [< L *aerius* < Gk., < *aer* air] —**aer'i·al·ly,** *adv.*

aer·i·al·ist (ãr'i·əl·ist), *n.* performer on a trapeze; aerial acrobat.

aer·ie, aer·y (ãr'i; ir'i), *n., pl.* **aer·ies.** 1. the lofty nest of an eagle or other bird of prey. 2. young eagles or other birds of prey. 3. house, castle, etc., built in a high place. Also, **eyrie, eyry.** [< Med.L *aeria* < OF < L *area* AREA or *atrium* ATRIUM]

aer·i·fy (ãr'ə·fī; ā·ir'–), *v.,* **–fied, –fy·ing.** 1. convert into vapor. 2. aerate. —**aer'i·fi·ca'tion,** *n.*

X, Cooper's adz; Y, Carpenter's adz

aer·o (ãr′ō), *adj.* of or for aircraft.

aero-, *word element.* **1.** air; of the air. **2.** gas; of gas or gases. **3.** of or for aircraft. [< Gk. *aer* air]

aer·obe (ãr′ōb; ã′ər·ōb), *n.* any microörganism that lives in or grows on oxygen. [< NL < Gk. *aer* air + *bios* life] —**aer·o′bic**, *adj.* —**aer·o′bi·cal·ly**, *adv.*

aer·o·drome (ãr′ə·drōm), *n. Esp. Brit.* airdrome.

aer·o·dy·nam·ics (ãr′ō·dī·nam′iks; –dī–), *n.* the branch of physics that deals with the forces exerted by air or other gases in motion. —**aer′o·dy·nam′ic**, *adj.*

aer·o·lite (ãr′ə·līt), *n.* a stone meteorite. [< F, < Gk. *aer* air + *lithos* stone]

aer·o·me·chan·ics (ãr′ō·mə·kan′iks), *n.* science of the motion and equilibrium of air and other gases; aerodynamics and aerostatics. —**aer′o·me·chan′ic, aer′o·me·chan′i·cal**, *adj.*

aer·o·naut (ãr′ə·nôt), *n.* **1.** pilot of an airship or balloon; balloonist. **2.** person who travels in an airship or balloon. [< F, < Gk. *aer* air + *nautes* sailor]

aer·o·nau·tics (ãr′ə·nô′tiks), *n.* science or art having to do with the design, manufacture, and operation of aircraft. —**aer′o·nau′tic, aer′o·nau′ti·cal**, *adj.* —**aer′o·nau′ti·cal·ly**, *adv.*

aer·o·pause (ãr′ə·pôz), *n.* a region of the air beginning about 65 to 75 thousand feet above the earth's surface.

aer·o·plane (ãr′ə·plān), *n. Esp. Brit.* airplane. ❯ See airplane for usage note.

aer·o·pol·i·tics (ãr′ō·pol′ə·tiks), *n. Am.* political and social development as influencing, or as influenced by, the advance or application of aviation.

aer·o·stat (ãr′ə·stat), *n.* any lighter-than-air aircraft, as a balloon or dirigible. [< AERO- + Gk. *statos* standing]

aer·o·stat·ics (ãr′ə·stat′iks), *n.* branch of physics that deals with the equilibrium of air and other gases, and with the equilibrium of solid objects floating in air and other gases. —**aer′o·stat′ic, aer′o·stat′i·cal**, *adj.*

Aes·chy·lus (es′kə·ləs), *n.* 525–456 B.C., Greek tragic poet and dramatist.

Aes·cu·la·pi·us (es′kyə·lā′pi·əs), *n. Roman Myth.* god of medicine and healing. —**Aes′cu·la′pi·an**, *adj.*

Ae·sop (ē′səp; ē′sop), *n.* 620?–560? B.C., Greek writer of fables. —**Ae·so·pi·an** (ē·sō′pi·ən), *adj.*

aes·thete (es′thēt), *n.* **1.** person who pretends to care a great deal about beauty. **2.** person who is sensitive to or loves beauty. Also, **esthete.** [< Gk. *aisthetes* one who perceives]

aes·thet·ic (es·thet′ik), *adj.* **1.** Also, **aes·thet′i·cal.** having to do with the beautiful, as distinguished from the useful, scientific, etc. **2.** (of persons) sensitive to beauty. **3.** (of things) pleasing; artistic. Also, **esthetic.** —**aes·thet′i·cal·ly**, *adv.*

aes·thet·ics (es·thet′iks), *n.* study of beauty in art and nature; philosophy of beauty; theory of the fine arts. Also, **esthetics.**

aet., aetat., at the age of.

ae·ther (ē′thər), *n.* **1.** upper regions of space beyond the earth's atmosphere. **2.** invisible elastic substance formerly supposed to be distributed through all space and to conduct light waves, electric waves, etc. Also, **ether.** [< L < Gk.]

ae·the·re·al (i·thir′i·əl), *adj.* ethereal.

ae·ti·ol·o·gy (ē′ti·ol′ə·ji), *n.* etiology. —**ae·ti·o·log·i·cal** (ē′ti·ō′pi·ə·kəl), *adj.*

Aet·na (et′nə), *n.* Mount. See Etna, Mount.

AF, Anglo-French.

A.F., a.f., *Physics, Electronics.* audio frequency.

a·far (ə·fär′), *adv.* **1.** from a distance: *see from afar.* **2.** far away: *stand afar off.*

a·feard, a·feared (ə·fird′), *adj. Archaic* or *Dial.* frightened; afraid.

af·fa·ble (af′ə·bəl), *adj.* **1.** easy to speak to or approach; courteous, friendly, and pleasant. **2.** gracious; mild; benign. [< F < L *affabilis* easy to speak to < *ad-* to + *fari* speak] —**af′fa·bil′i·ty, af′fa·ble·ness**, *n.* —**af′fa·bly**, *adv.*

af·fair (ə·fãr′), *n.* **1.** anything done or to be done. **2.** affairs, matters of interest, esp. business matters. **3.** particular action or event (referred to in vague terms): *a jolly affair.* **4.** private concern: *that's my affair.* **5.** thing: *this machine is a complicated affair.* **6.** a romance. [< OF *a faire* to do < L *ad* to + *facere* do] —**Syn. 1.** activity. **3.** happening.

af·fect¹ (ə·fekt′), *v.* **1.** have an effect on; influence, esp. injuriously: *disease affects the body.* **2.** stir the emotions of. [< L *affectus* < *ad-* to + *facere* do] —**Syn. 2.** touch ❯ affect, effect. Since most people make no distinction in pronouncing the first vowel of these words, the spelling is likely to be confused. *Affect*, a rather formal word, is always a verb, meaning to "influence": *this will affect the lives of thousands. Effect* is most commonly a noun, meaning "result": *the effects of this will be felt by thousands. Effect* is also a verb in formal English, meaning to "bring about": *the change was effected peaceably.*

af·fect² (ə·fekt′), *v.* **1.** pretend to have or feel: *affect ignorance.* **2.** be fond of; like: *she affects old furniture.* **3.** assume, use, or frequent by preference: *he affects carelessness in dress.* **4.** (of animals and plants) inhabit naturally. [< F < L *affectare* strive for < *ad-* to + *facere* do] —**af·fect′er**, *n.* —**Syn. 1.** feign, simulate.

af·fec·ta·tion (af′ek·tā′shən; –ik–), *n.* **1.** behavior that is not natural. **2.** outward appearance; pretense.

af·fect·ed¹ (ə·fek′tid), *adj.* **1.** influenced. **2.** influenced injuriously. **3.** moved emotionally.

af·fect·ed² (ə·fek′tid), *adj.* **1.** put on for effect; unnatural. **2.** behaving, speaking, writing, etc., unnaturally for effect. —**af·fect′ed·ly**, *adv.* —**af·fect′ed·ness**, *n.* —**Syn. 1.** artificial.

af·fect·ing (ə·fek′ting), *adj.* causing emotion. —**af·fect′ing·ly**, *adv.*

af·fec·tion (ə·fek′shən), *n.* **1.** friendly feeling; tenderness; love. **2.** feeling; inclination. **3.** disease; unhealthy condition. **4.** *Archaic.* disposition; tendency. —**Syn. 1.** fondness.

af·fec·tion·ate (ə·fek′shən·it), *adj.* **1.** having affection; warmly attached. **2.** showing affection. —**af·fec′tion·ate·ly**, *adv.* —**af·fec′tion·ate·ness**, *n.* —**Syn. 1.** devoted, tender.

af·fec·tive (ə·fek′tiv), *adj.* of the feelings; emotional.

af·fer·ent (af′ər·ənt), *adj.* (of nerves or blood vessels) carrying inward to a central organ or point. [< L, < *ad-* to + *ferre* bring]

af·fi·ance (ə·fī′əns), *v.*, **–anced, –anc·ing**, *n.* —*v.* pledge solemnly, esp. in marriage; betroth. —*n.* **1.** the pledging of faith, esp. in marriage; betrothal. **2.** trust; confidence. [< OF *afiancer* betroth, ult. < L *ad-* to + *fidus* faithful]

af·fi·da·vit (af′ə·dā′vit), *n.* statement written down and sworn to be true. An affidavit is usually made before a judge or notary public. [< Med.L, he has stated on oath]

af·fil·i·ate (*v.* ə·fil′i·āt; *n.* ə·fil′i·it, –āt), *v.*, **–at·ed, –at·ing**, *n.* —*v.* **1.** *Am.* connect in close association: *affiliated clubs.* **2.** *Am.* associate oneself (*with*): *affiliate with a political party.* **3.** bring into relationship; adopt. —*n.* organization or group associated with other similar bodies. [< LL, < L *ad-* + *filius* son]

af·fil·i·a·tion (ə·fil′i·ā′shən), *n.* **1.** *Am.* association; relation. **2.** act of affiliating.

af·fin·i·ty (ə·fin′ə·ti), *n.*, *pl.* **–ties.** **1.** natural attraction to a person or liking for a thing: *an affinity for dancing.* **2.** person to whom one is especially attracted. **3.** relationship by marriage. **4.** relation; connection. **5.** resemblance; likeness. **6.** *Chem.* force that attracts certain chemical elements to others and keeps them combined. [< F < L, < *ad-* on + *finis* boundary]

af·firm (ə·fẽrm′), *v.* **1.** declare to be true; assert. **2.** confirm; ratify: *the higher court affirmed the lower court's decision.* **3.** *Law.* declare solemnly, but without taking an oath. [< OF < L, < *ad-* + *firmus* strong] —**af·firm′a·ble**, *adj.* —**af·firm′a·bly**, *adv.* —**af·firm′er**, *n.*

af·fir·ma·tion (af'ər·mā'shən), *n.* 1. *Law.* solemn declaration, equivalent to taking an oath, made by a person whose conscience forbids his taking an oath. 2. a positive statement; assertion. 3. act of confirming.

af·firm·a·tive (ə·fër'mə·tiv), *adj.* asserting that a fact is so. —*n.* 1. word or statement that gives assent or agrees. 2. **the affirmative**, the side arguing in favor of a question being debated. —af·firm'a·tive·ly, *adv.*

af·fix (*v.* ə·fiks'; *n.* af'iks), *v.* 1. make firm or fix (one thing to or on another). 2. add at the end. 3. make an impression of (a seal, etc.). 4. connect with; attach: *affix blame.* —*n.* 1. thing affixed. 2. a prefix, suffix, or infix. *Un-* and *-ly* are affixes. [< Med.L *affixare*, ult. < L *ad-* to + *figere* fix] —af·fix'er, *n.*

af·fla·tus (ə·flā'təs), *n.* divinely imparted knowledge; inspiration. [< L, < *ad-* on + *flare* blow]

af·flict (ə·flikt'), *v.* cause pain to; trouble greatly; distress. [< L *afflictus* < *ad-* upon + *fligere* dash] —af·flict'er, *n.* —Syn. torment.

af·flic·tion (ə·flik'shən), *n.* 1. state of pain or distress. 2. cause of pain, trouble, or distress. —Syn. 1. misery, wretchedness. 2. misfortune.

af·flu·ence (af'lü·əns), *n.* 1. wealth. 2. abundant supply. [< F < L, < *ad-* to + *fluere* flow]

af·flu·ent (af'lü·ənt), *adj.* 1. very wealthy. 2. abundant; plentiful. —*n.* stream flowing into a larger stream, etc. —af'flu·ent·ly, *adv.*

af·ford (ə·fôrd'; ə·fōrd'), *v.* 1. spare the money for: *we can't afford a new car.* 2. spare: *can you afford the time?* 3. manage: *I can't afford to take the chance.* 4. furnish from natural resources; yield: *some trees afford resin.* 5. yield or give as an effect or a result; provide: *reading affords pleasure.* [OE *geforthian* further, accomplish] —af·ford'a·ble, *adj.*

af·fray (ə·frā'), *n.* a noisy quarrel; fight in public; brawl. [< OF *affrei*, ult. < L *ex-* out of + unrecorded Frankish *frithu* peace]

af·front (ə·frunt'), *n.* 1. a word or act expressing openly intentional disrespect. 2. a slight or injury to one's dignity. —*v.* 1. insult openly; offend purposely. 2. confront. [< OF < VL < L *ad frontem* on the forehead] —af·front'er, *n.*

Af·ghan (af'gən; -gan), *n.* 1. native of Afghanistan. 2. **afghan**, blanket or shawl made of knitted or crocheted wool. —*adj.* of Afghanistan or its people.

Af·ghan·i·stan (af-gan'ə·stan), *n.* country in SW Asia.

a·fi·cio·na·do (ə·fē'syə·nä'dō), *n., pl.* -dos. 1. person who takes a very great interest in bullfighting, but who is never himself a bullfighter. 2. person who is very enthusiastic about anything. [< Sp., lit., fond of < *afición* affection < L *affectio* < *affectus*, pp. See AFFECT[2].]

a·field (ə·fēld'), *adv.* 1. on or in the field; to the field. 2. away from home; away. 3. out of the way; astray.

a·fire (ə·fīr'), *adv., adj.* on fire; burning.

A.F.L. or **A.F. of L.**, *Am.* American Federation of Labor, a group of trade unions.

a·flame (ə·flām'), *adv., adj.* on fire.

a·float (ə·flōt'), *adv., adj.* 1. floating. 2. on shipboard; at sea. 3. adrift. 4. flooded. 5. going around: *rumors of an outbreak were afloat.*

a·flut·ter (ə·flut'ər), *adv., adj.* fluttering.

a·foot (ə·fut'), *adv., adj.* 1. on foot; walking. 2. going on; in progress: *mischief afoot.*

a·fore (ə·fôr'; ə·fōr'), *adv., prep., conj. Archaic, Dial.,* or *Naut.* before.

a·fore·men·tioned (ə·fôr'men'shənd; ə·fōr'-), *adj.* spoken of before; mentioned above.

a·fore·said (ə·fôr'sed'; ə·fōr'-), *adj.* spoken of before; mentioned above.

a·fore·thought (ə·fôr'thôt'; ə·fōr'-), *adj.* thought of beforehand; deliberately planned.

a·fore·time (ə·fôr'tīm'; ə·fōr'-), *adv.* in time past; formerly. —*adj.* former.

a for·ti·o·ri (ā fôr'shi·ô'rī; -ō'-; -rī), *Latin.* for a still stronger reason; all the more.

a·foul (ə·foul'), *adv., adj.* 1. *Am.* in a tangle, in collision; entangled. 2. **run afoul of**, get into difficulties with.

a·fraid (ə·frād'), *adj.* feeling fear; frightened. [orig. pp. of archaic *v. affray* frighten]

af·reet, af·rit (af'rēt; ə·frēt'), *n.* in Arabian myths, a powerful evil demon or giant. [< Ar. *'ifrīt*]

a·fresh (ə·fresh'), *adv.* once more; again.

Af·ri·ca (af'rə·kə), *n.* continent south of Europe; the second largest continent.

Af·ri·can (af'rə·kən), *adj.* 1. of or from Africa. 2. of or belonging to the black race of Africa. —*n.* 1. a native of Africa. 2. a Negro.

Af·ri·kaans (af'rə·käns'; -känz'), *n.* variety of Dutch spoken in South Africa; South African Dutch.

Af·ri·kan·der (af'rə·kan'dər), *n.* a native, white South African, usually of Dutch or Huguenot descent.

aft (aft; äft), *adv. Naut.* at, near, or toward the stern; abaft. [OE *æftan* from behind]

af·ter (af'tər; äf'-), *prep.* 1. behind in place: *in line one after another.* 2. next to; following: *day after day.* 3. in pursuit of; in search of: *run after him.* 4. about; concerning: *your aunt asked after you.* 5. later in time than: *after supper.* 6. because of: *after the selfish way she acted, who could like her?* 7. in spite of: *after all her suffering she is still cheerful.* 8. imitating; in imitation of: *a fable after the manner of Aesop.* 9. lower in rank or importance: *a captain comes after a general.* 10. according to: *act after one's own ideas.* 11. for: *named after his cousin.* 12. **look after, see after, take care of.** —*adv.* 1. behind: *follow after.* 2. later: *three hours after.* —*adj.* 1. later; subsequent: *in after years he regretted the mistakes of his boyhood.* 2. *Naut.* nearer or toward the stern: *after sails.* —*conj.* later than the time that: *after he goes, we shall eat.* [OE *æfter* more to the rear, later]

af·ter·birth (af'tər·bėrth'; äf'-), *n.* placenta and membranes that enveloped the fetus, expelled from the uterus after childbirth.

af·ter·burn·er (af'tər·bér'nər; äf'-), *n.* (in the engine of a jet plane) a device which supplies additional fuel to the exhaust and reignites it, thus increasing the thrust of the plane so that bursts of very high speed can be obtained.

af·ter·deck (af'tər·dek'; äf'-), *n. Naut.* deck toward or at the stern of a ship.

af·ter·ef·fect (af'tər·i·fekt'; äf'-), *n.* result or effect that follows later.

af·ter·glow (af'tər·glō'; äf'-), *n.* 1. glow after something bright has gone. 2. glow in the sky after sunset.

af·ter·im·age (af'tər·im'ij; äf'-), *n.* sensation that persists or recurs after the stimulus is withdrawn.

af·ter·math (af'tər·math; äf'-), *n.* result; consequence. [< *after* + dial. *math* a mowing]

af·ter·most (af'tər·mōst; äf'-), *adj.* 1. *Naut.* nearest the stern. 2. hindmost; last.

af·ter·noon (*n.* af'tər·nün'; äf'-; *adj.* af'tər·nün', äf'-), *n.* the part of the day between noon and evening. —*adj.* of, in, or suitable for the afternoon.

af·ter·thought (af'tər·thôt'; äf'-), *n.* 1. thought that comes after the time when it could have been used. 2. later thought or explanation.

af·ter·ward (af'tər·wərd; äf'-), **af·ter·wards** (-wərdz), *adv.* later.

Ag, *Chem.* silver.

A.G., 1. Adjutant General. 2. Attorney General.

a·gain (ə·gen'; *esp. Brit.,* ə·gān'), *adv.* 1. once more; another time: *try again.* 2. in return; in reply: *answer again.* 3. to the same place or person: *bring us word again.* 4. moreover; besides: *again, I must say.* 5. on the other hand: *it might rain, and again it might not.* 6. again and again, often; frequently. 7. as much again, twice as much. [OE *ongegn* < *on-* on + *gegn* direct]

a·gainst (ə·genst′; *esp. Brit.* ə·gänst′), *prep.* 1. in an opposite direction to, so as to meet; upon; toward: *sail against the wind.* 2. in opposition to: *against reason.* 3. directly opposite to; facing: *over against the wall.* 4. in contrast to or with: *the ship appeared against the sky.* 5. in contact with: *lean against a wall.* 6. in preparation for: *against a rainy day.* 7. in defense from: *a fire is a protection against cold.* [see AGAIN]

Ag·a·mem·non (ag′ə·mem′non; -nən), *n.* Gk. Legend. king of Mycenae and leader of the Greeks in the Trojan War.

A·ga·ña (ä·gän′yə), *n.* capital of Guam.

a·gape (ə·gāp′; ə·gap′), *adv., adj.* with the mouth wide open, as in wonder or eagerness.

a·gar-a·gar (ä′gər-ä′gər; ag′ər-ag′ər), *n.* a gelatinlike extract obtained from certain seaweeds, used in making cultures for bacteria, fungi, etc. [< Malay]

ag·a·ric (ag′ə·rik; ə·gar′ik), *n.* any of several fungi, including mushrooms and toadstools. [< L < Gk., < *Agaria*, place name]

Ag·as·siz (ag′ə·si), *n.* (Jean) Louis (Rodolphe), 1807–1873, American naturalist, born in Switzerland.

ag·ate (ag′it), *n.* 1. a variety of quartz with variously colored stripes or clouded colors. 2. *Am.* a playing marble that looks like this. 3. *Am.* a size of printing type (5½ point). [< F < L < Gk. *achates*] —**ag′ate·like′**, *adj.*

a·ga·ve (ə·gā′vē), *n.* any of several North American desert plants (the century plant, sisal, etc.). Soap, alcoholic drinks, and rope are made from some kinds of agave. [< NL < Gk. *Agaue*, fem. proper name, noble]

age (āj), *n., v.,* aged, ag·ing or age·ing. —*n.* 1. length of life: *he died at the age of eighty.* 2. a period in life attained: *middle age.* 3. latter part of life: *the wisdom of age.* 4. of age, 21 years old or over and having full legal rights. 5. the full or average term of life: *the age of a horse is from 25 to 30 years.* 6. *Psychol.* the mental, physiological, emotional, etc., development of an individual as compared with the average development of individuals of his chronological age. 7. a period of history: *the golden age.* 8. generation: *ages yet unborn.* 9. *Colloq.* a long time: *I haven't seen you for an age.* —*v.* 1. grow old: *he ages rapidly.* 2. make old: *age wine.* [< OF *aage* < VL *aetaticum* < L *aetas* age] —Syn. *n.* 7. era, epoch.

-age, *suffix.* 1. act of, as in *breakage.* 2. collection of; group of, as in *baggage.* 3. condition of; rank of, as in *peerage.* 4. cost of, as in *postage.* 5. home of, as in *orphanage.* [< OF < L *-aticum* < Gk.]

a·ged (ā′jid *for 1 and 3;* ājd *for 2*), *adj.* 1. having lived a long time; old. 2. of the age of. 3. characteristic of old age. —**a′ged·ly**, *adv.* —**a′ged·ness**, *n.*

age·less (āj′lis), *adj.* never growing old.

age·long (āj′lông′; -long′), *adj.* lasting a long time.

a·gen·cy (ā′jən·si), *n., pl.* -cies. 1. means; action. 2. business of a person or company that has the authority to act for another. 3. office of such a person or company.

a·gen·da (ə·jen′də), *n.pl., sing.* -dum (-dəm). 1. things to be done. 2. (*sometimes sing. in use*) list of items of business to be considered, as at a meeting. [< L, things to be done]

a·gent (ā′jənt), *n.* 1. person or company that has the authority to act for another. 2. person who does things. 3. active power or cause that produces an effect. 4. means; instrument. 5. *Colloq.* a traveling salesman. 6. *Am.* a station agent or ticket agent. 7. *Chem.* substance that is capable of causing a reaction. [< L, < *agere* do] —**a·gen′tial** (ā·jen′shəl), *adj.* —Syn. 1. representative, intermediary.

ag·er·a·tum (aj′ər·ā′təm; ə·jer′ə-), *n.* any of several plants of the aster family with small, dense flower heads, usually blue. [< NL < Gk., < *a-* without + *geras* old age]

ag·glom·er·ate (*v.* ə·glom′ər·āt; *n., adj.*

ə·glom′ər·it, -āt), *v.,* -at·ed, -at·ing, *n., adj.* —*v.* gather together in a mass. —*n.* mass; collection; cluster. —*adj.* packed together in a mass. [< L, < *ad-* + *glomus* ball] —**ag·glom′er·a′tive,** *adj.*

ag·glom·er·a·tion (ə·glom′ər·ā′shən), *n.* 1. an agglomerating. 2. agglomerated condition. 3. mass of things gathered together.

ag·glu·ti·nate (*v.* ə·glü′tə·nāt; *adj.* ə·glü′tə·nit, -nāt), *v.,* -nat·ed, -nat·ing, *adj.* —*v.* 1. stick or join together, as with glue. 2. form (words) by joining words, or words and affixes, together. —*adj.* stuck or joined together: *"never-to-be-forgotten" is an agglutinate word.* [< L, < *ad-* to + *gluten* glue] —**ag·glu′ti·na′tion,** *n.* —**ag·glu′ti·na′tive,** *adj.*

ag·gran·dize (ə·gran′dīz; ag′rən·dīz), *v.,* -dized, -diz·ing. increase, as in power, wealth, rank, etc.; make greater. [< F *agrandir*, ult. < L *ad-* + *grandis* great] —**ag·gran·dize·ment** (ə·gran′diz·mənt), *n.* —**ag·gran′diz·er**, *n.*

ag·gra·vate (ag′rə·vāt), *v.,* -vat·ed, -vat·ing. 1. make worse or more severe. 2. *Colloq.* annoy; irritate; provoke. [< L, < *ad-* on, to + *gravis* heavy. Doublet of AGGRIEVE.] —**ag′gra·vat′ing,** *adj.* —**ag′gra·vat′ing·ly,** *adv.* —**ag′gra·va′tion,** *n.* —**ag′gra·va′tive·ly,** *adv.* —**ag′gra·va′tor,** *n.* —Syn. 1. intensify, increase.

ag·gre·gate (*v.* ag′rə·gāt; *n., adj.* ag′rə·git, -gāt), *v.,* -gat·ed, -gat·ing, *n., adj.* —*v.* 1. gather together in a mass or group; collect; unite. 2. *Colloq.* amount to. —*n.* 1. mass of separate things joined together; collection. 2. in the aggregate, together; as a whole. —*adj.* 1. gathered together in one mass or group. 2. total. [< L *aggregatus* < *ad-* + *grex* flock] —**ag′gre·gate·ly,** *adv.* —**ag′gre·ga′tive,** *adj.*

ag·gre·ga·tion (ag′rə·gā′shən), *n.* collection of separate things into one mass or whole.

ag·gres·sion (ə·gresh′ən), *n.* 1. first step in an attack or quarrel; an unprovoked attack. 2. practice of making assaults or attacks. [< L *aggressio* < *ad-* to + *gradi* to step]

ag·gres·sive (ə·gres′iv), *adj.* 1. beginning an attack or quarrel. 2. *U.S.* active; energetic. —**ag·gres′sive·ly,** *adv.* —**ag·gres′sive·ness,** *n.*

ag·gres·sor (ə·gres′ər), *n.* one that begins an attack or quarrel.

ag·grieve (ə·grēv′), *v.,* -grieved, -griev·ing. injure unjustly; cause grief or trouble to. [< OF *agrever* < L. Doublet of AGGRAVATE.]

a·ghast (ə·gast′; ə·gäst′), *adj.* filled with horror; frightened; terrified. [pp. of obs. *agast* terrify; akin to GHOST]

ag·ile (aj′əl), *adj.* moving quickly and easily; active; lively; nimble. [< L *agilis* < *agere* move] —**ag′ile·ly,** *adv.* —**ag′ile·ness,** *n.* —Syn. sprightly, spry, brisk, quick.

a·gil·i·ty (ə·jil′ə·ti), *n.* ability to move quickly and easily; nimbleness.

ag·i·tate (aj′ə·tāt), *v.,* -tat·ed, -tat·ing. 1. move or shake violently. 2. disturb; excite (the feelings or the thoughts). 3. argue about; discuss vigorously. 4. keep arguing and discussing to arouse public interest: *agitate for a shorter working day.* [< L *agitatus* < *agere* drive, move] —**ag′i·tat′ed·ly,** *adv.*

ag·i·ta·tion (aj′ə·tā′shən), *n.* 1. a violent moving or shaking. 2. disturbed, upset, or troubled state. 3. argument or discussion to arouse public interest. —Syn. 3. debate.

ag·i·ta·tor (aj′ə·tā′tər), *n.* 1. person who tries to make people discontented with things as they are. 2. device for shaking or stirring.

a·glow (ə·glō′), *adv., adj.* glowing.

ag·no·men (ag·nō′men), *n., pl.* -nom·i·na (-nom′ə·nə). 1. additional name given to a person by the ancient Romans in allusion to some quality or achievement. 2. any additional name. [< L, < *ad-* to + *nomen* name] —**ag·nom·i·nal** (ag·nom′ə·nəl), *adj.*

ag·nos·tic (ag·nos′tik), *n.* person who believes that nothing is known or can be known about the existence of God or about things outside of human experience. —*adj.* of agnostics or their beliefs. [< Gk., < *a-* not + *gnostos* (to be) known] —**ag·nos′ti·cal·ly,** *adv.*

ag·nos·ti·cism (ag·nos′tə·siz·əm), *n.* the belief or intellectual attitude of agnostics.

a·go (ə·gō′), *adj.* gone by; past (always after the noun): *a year ago.* —*adv.* in the past: *he went long ago.* [OE *āgān* gone by]

a·gog (ə·gog′), *adj.* eager; curious; excited. —*adv.* with eagerness, curiosity, or excitement. [? < F *en gogues* in happy mood]

a·gon·ic (ā·gon′ik; ə·gon′-), *adj.* not forming an angle. [< Gk., < *a*– without + *gonia* angle]

ag·o·nize (ag′ə·nīz), *v.*, **-nized, -niz·ing.** 1. feel very great pain. 2. pain very much; torture. 3. strive painfully; struggle. —**ag′o·niz′ing,** *adj.* —**ag′o·niz′ing·ly,** *adv.*

ag·o·ny (ag′ə·ni), *n.*, *pl.* **-nies.** 1. great pain or suffering. 2. intense mental suffering. 3. the struggle often preceding death. [< LL < Gk. *agonia* struggle] —**Syn.** 1, 2. anguish, torment.

ag·o·ra (ag′ə·rə), *n.*, *pl.* **-rae** (-rē). market place in an ancient Greek city. [< Gk.]

ag·o·ra·pho·bi·a (ag′ə·rə·fō′bi·ə), *n.* a morbid fear of open spaces.

a·gou·ti (ə·gü′ti), *n.*, *pl.* **-tis, -ties.** a rodent of tropical America related to the guinea pig, but having longer legs. [< F Sp. < native Indian name]

Agouti (18 in. long)

A·gra (ä′grə), *n.* city in N India; site of the Taj Mahal.

a·grar·i·an (ə·grār′i·ən), *adj.* 1. having to do with land, its use, or its ownership. 2. for the support and advancement of the interests of farmers. 3. agricultural. —*n.* person who favors a redistribution of land. [< L *agrarius* < *ager* field] —**a·grar′i·an·ism,** *n.*

a·gree (ə·grē′), *v.*, **a·greed, a·gree·ing.** 1. have the same opinion or opinions: *I agree with you.* 2. be in harmony; correspond (*with*): *your story agrees with mine.* 3. get along well together. 4. consent (*to*): *he agreed to accompany us.* 5. come to an understanding, esp. in settling a dispute. 6. have a good effect on; suit (*with*): *this food does not agree with me.* 7. *Gram.* have the same number, case, gender, person, etc. (*with*): *that verb agrees with its subject.* [< OF, < *a gre* to (one's) liking < L *ad*– to + *gratus* pleasing] —**Syn.** 2. coincide, match, tally. **≻** agree to, agree with. One agrees *to* a plan and agrees *with* a person.

a·gree·a·ble (ə·grē′ə·bəl), *adj.* 1. to one's liking; pleasing: *agreeable manners.* 2. ready to agree; willing to agree: *agreeable to a suggestion.* 3. in agreement; suitable (*to*): *music agreeable to the occasion.* —**a·gree′a·bil′i·ty, a·gree′a·ble·ness,** *n.* —**a·gree′a·bly,** *adv.*

a·greed (ə·grēd′), *adj.* fixed by common consent. 2. of like mind; agreeing.

a·gree·ment (ə·grē′mənt), *n.* 1. consent. 2. sameness of opinion. 3. harmony; correspondence. 4. an agreeing; an understanding reached by two or more nations, persons, or groups of persons among themselves. 5. *Gram.* correspondence of words with respect to number, case, gender, person, etc.

ag·ri·cul·tur·al (ag′rə·kul′chər·əl), *adj.* 1. having to do with farming; of agriculture. 2. *Am.* promoting the interests or the study of agriculture. —**ag′ri·cul′tur·al·ly,** *adv.*

ag·ri·cul·tur·al·ist (ag′rə·kul′chər·əl·ist), *n.* *U.S.* agriculturist.

ag·ri·cul·ture (ag′rə·kul′chər), *n.* farming; the raising of crops and livestock; science or art of cultivating the ground. [< L, < *ager* field + *cultura* cultivation]

ag·ri·cul·tur·ist (ag′rə·kul′chər·ist), *n.* 1. farmer. 2. an expert in farming.

ag·ri·mo·ny (ag′rə·mō′ni), *n.*, *pl.* **-nies.** plant with slender stalks of feathery leaves and yellow flowers, whose roots are used as an astringent. [< L < Gk. *argemone*]

ag·ro·nom·ics (ag′rə·nom′iks), *n.* art or science of managing farmland.

a·gron·o·my (ə·gron′ə·mi), *n.* branch of agriculture dealing with crop production; husbandry. [< Gk., < *agros* land + *nemein* manage] —**ag·ro·nom·ic** (ag′rə·nom′ik), **ag′ro·nom′i·cal,** *adj.* —**a·gron′o·mist,** *n.*

a·ground (ə·ground′), *adv., adj.* on the ground; on the bottom in shallow water.

agt., agent.

a·gue (ā′gū), *n.* 1. malarial fever characterized by intermittent fits of sweating and shivering. 2. fit of shivering; chill. [< OF < L *acuta* (*febris*) severe (fever)] —**a′gu·ish,** *adj.* —**a′gu·ish·ly,** *adv.*

ah (ä), *interj.* exclamation of pain, surprise, pity, joy, etc.

a·ha (ä·hä′), *interj.* exclamation of triumph, satisfaction, surprise, etc.

A·hab (ā′hab), *n. Bible.* king of Israel who was led into idolatry by his wife Jezebel.

a·head (ə·hed′), *adv.* 1. in front; before: *walk ahead of me.* 2. *Am., Colloq.* forward; onward: *go ahead with this work.* 3. *Am.* in an advanced or successful position or state. 4. *Am.* in advance: *ahead of his times.* 5. be ahead, *Am., Colloq.* be to the good. 6. get ahead, *Am., Colloq.* succeed. 7. get ahead of, surpass.

a·hem (ə·hem′), *interj.* a sound made to attract attention, express doubt, gain time, etc.

a·hoy (ə·hoi′), *interj.* a call used by sailors to hail persons at a distance.

ai (ī), *n.*, *pl.* **ais** (īz). a three-toed sloth of South America.

aid (ād), *v.* give support to; help: *the Red Cross aids flood victims.* —*n.* 1. help; support. 2. helper; assistant. 3. *U.S.* aide-de-camp. [< OF *aidier* < L, < *ad*– to + *juvare* help] —**aid′er,** *n.* —**aid′less,** *adj.* —**Syn.** *v.* assist.

aid-de-camp (ād′də·kamp′), *n.*, *pl.* **aids-de-camp.** *U.S.* an aide-de-camp.

aide (ād), *n. Am.* aide-de-camp.

aide-de-camp (ād′də·kamp′), *n.*, *pl.* **aides-de-camp.** army or navy officer who acts as an assistant to a superior officer. [< F]

ai·grette (ā′gret; ā·gret′), *n.* 1. tuft of feathers worn as an ornament on the head. 2. anything shaped or used like this. 3. egret. [< F. See EGRET.]

Aigrette
of feathers

ail (āl), *v.* 1. be the matter with; trouble: *what ails the man?* 2. be ill; feel sick: *he is ailing.* [OE *eglan*]

ai·lan·thus (ā·lan′thəs), *n.* an Asiatic tree with many leaflets and clusters of small, bad-smelling, greenish flowers. [< NL < Amboinan *aylanto* tree of heaven; form infl. by Gk. *anthos* flower]

ai·ler·on (ā′lər·on), *n.* a movable part of an airplane wing, usually part of the trailing edge, used primarily to maintain lateral balance while flying. [< F, dim. of *aile* < L *ala* wing]

ail·ment (āl′mənt), *n.* a slight sickness.

aim (ām), *v.* 1. point or direct (a gun, blow, etc.) in order to hit a target: *aim a gun.* 2. direct one's efforts: *man aims at happiness.* 3. *U.S.* intend: *I aim to go.* 4. *U.S.* try: *he aims to be helpful.* —*n.* 1. act of aiming. 2. direction aimed in; line of sighting. 3. mark aimed at; target. 4. purpose; intention. [< OF *esmer* < L *aestimare* appraise, and OF *aesmer* < VL *adaestimare*] —**aim′er,** *n.* —**Syn.** *n.* 4. intent, object.

aim·less (ām′lis), *adj.* without purpose. —**aim′less·ly,** *adv.* —**aim′less·ness,** *n.*

ain't (ānt), *Dial. or Illiterate.* contraction of the phrases: a. am not. b. are not; is not. c. have not; has not. **≻** Ain't is not acceptable in formal English. Even in informal English its use is subject to sharp criticism. Nevertheless it is often heard, usually in substandard speech, but sometimes from educated speakers tenacious of old ways and perhaps resentful of bookish authority. *Ain't I* or *an't I* is or would be a convenient contraction of *am not I.* (Compare *don't*

I, haven't I, etc.) It is surprising that neither is completely acceptable.

Ai·nu (ī′nū), *n.* member of a very primitive, light-skinned race in N Japan.

air (âr), *n.* 1. the mixture of gases that surrounds the earth; atmosphere. Air is a mixture of nitrogen, oxygen, argon, helium, and other inert gases. 2. space overhead; sky: *birds fly in the air.* 3. a light wind; breeze. 4. melody; tune. 5. public mention: *he gave air to his feelings.* 6. general character or appearance of anything: *an air of mystery.* 7. bearing; manner: *an air of importance.* 8. airs, unnatural or affected manners. 9. medium through which radio waves travel. 10. in the air, a. going around: *wild rumors were in the air.* b. uncertain. 11. on the air, broadcasting. 12. up in the air, a. uncertain. b. *Colloq.* very angry or excited. —*v.* 1. put out in the air; let air through: *air clothes.* 2. make known; mention publicly: *do not air your troubles.* —*adj.* 1. conducting or supplying air: *air duct.* 2. compressing or confining air: *air valve.* 3. using or worked by compressed air: *air drill.* 4. relating to aviation; done by means of aircraft: *air photography.* [< OF < L < Gk. *aer*] —Syn. *n.* 7. attitude. —*v.* 1. ventilate.

air-, *word element:* 1. air, as in *air-breathing.* 2. by air, as in *air-blown.* 3. of air, as in *air-phobia.* 4. against air, as in *airproof.*

air base, headquarters and airport for military airplanes.

air bladder, sac in most fishes and various animals and plants, filled with air.

air·borne (âr′bôrn′; -bōrn′), *adj.* 1. carried in airplanes or gliders: *air-borne troops.* 2. carried by air: *air-borne seeds.*

air brake, *Am.* brake operated by a piston or pistons worked by compressed air.

air brush, device operated by compressed air that is used to spray paint on a surface.

air·burst (âr′bèrst′), *n.* an exploding of a shell or bomb, now esp. an atomic bomb, in the air rather than on the ground or under water.

air castle, daydream.

air chamber, any compartment filled with air, esp. one in a hydraulic engine.

air coach, aircraft with low passenger rates, made possible by elimination of luxuries.

air-con·di·tion (âr′kən-dish′ən), *v. Am.* 1. supply with the equipment for air conditioning. 2. treat (air) by means of air conditioning.

air conditioning, *Am.* a means of treating air in buildings to free it from dust, etc., and to regulate its humidity and temperature.

air-cool (âr′kūl′), *v.* 1. remove heat produced in motor cylinders by combustion, friction, etc., by blowing air on. 2. remove heat in a room by blowing cool air in. —*air′-cooled′, adj.*

air·craft (âr′kraft′; -kräft′), *n., pl.* —craft. 1. machine for air navigation that is supported in air by buoyancy (such as a balloon) or by dynamic action (such as an airplane). 2. such machines collectively or as a class.

aircraft carrier, warship designed as a base for airplanes.

air·drome (âr′drōm′), *n.* airport. Also, *esp. Brit.* aerodrome. [< AIR- + Gk. *dromos* race course]

air drop, system of dropping food, supplies, etc., from aircraft, esp. to allies behind enemy lines, in occupied territory, etc.

Aire·dale (âr′dāl), *n.* a large terrier having a wiry brown or tan coat with dark markings. [< *Airedale* in Yorkshire, England]

air field, landing field of an airport.

air·foil (âr′foil′), *n.* any surface, such as a wing, rudder, etc., designed to help lift or control an aircraft.

air force, 1. branch of the military or naval forces that uses airplanes. 2. Air Force, a separate branch of the armed forces of the U.S. that includes aviation personnel, equipment, etc. 3. group of fliers for military aircraft.

air hole, 1. *Am.* open space in the ice on a river, pond, etc. 2. air pocket.

air·i·ly (âr′ə·li), *adv.* in an airy manner.

air·i·ness (âr′i·nis), *n.* airy quality.

air·ing (âr′ing), *n.* 1. exposure to air for drying, warming, etc. 2. a walk, ride, or drive in the open air.

air lane, a regular route used by aircraft.

air·less (âr′lis), *adj.* 1. without fresh air; stuffy. 2. without a breeze.

air lift, 1. system of using aircraft for passenger transportation and freight conveyance to a place when land approaches are closed. 2. something transported by such a system.

air line, *Am.* 1. system of transportation of people and things by aircraft. 2. company operating such a system. —*air′-line′, adj. Am.*

air liner, large airplane or airship for carrying many passengers.

air lock, an airtight compartment between places where there is a difference in air pressure. The pressure in an air lock can be raised or lowered.

air mail, *Am.* 1. system of sending mail by aircraft. 2. mail so sent. —*air′-mail′, adj. Am.*

air·man (âr′mən), *n., pl.* -men. 1. pilot of an airplane, airship, or balloon. 2. one of the crew of an aircraft.

air-mind·ed (âr′mīn′did), *adj.* 1. interested in aviation. 2. fond of traveling by air. —*air′-mind′ed·ness, n.*

air·plane (âr′plān′), *n.* a mechanically driven heavier-than-air aircraft supported in flight by the action of the air flowing past or thrusting upward on its fixed wings. Also, *esp. Brit.* aeroplane. ▶ airplane, aeroplane. For several years these two words competed for general usage, but in the United States at least *airplane* is both the official and popular form.

air pocket, a vertical current or condition in the air that causes a sudden drop in the altitude of an airplane.

air·port (âr′pôrt′; -pōrt′), *n.* tract of land or water where aircraft can land or take off, and where facilities for shelter and repair are supplied.

air pressure, pressure of the atmosphere.

air pump, apparatus for forcing air in or drawing air out of something.

air raid, attack by enemy aircraft.

air rifle, *Am.* gun worked by compressed air.

air sac, an air-filled space in the body of a bird, connected with the lungs.

air service, 1. transportation of people or things by aircraft. 2. branch of the military service that uses airplanes.

air·ship (âr′ship′), *n.* any aircraft that is lighter than air and self-propelled; dirigible.

air·sick (âr′sik′), *adj.* sick as a result of traveling by air. —*air′sick′ness, n.*

air speed, speed of an aircraft measured by its greater movement than that of the air.

air·strip (âr′strip′), *n.* a paved or cleared strip on which planes land and take off.

air·tight (âr′tīt′), *adj.* 1. so tight that no air or gas can get in or out. 2. having no weak points open to an opponent's attack.

air-to-air (âr′tū·âr′), *adj.* 1. launched from a flying aircraft, etc., to intercept and destroy another flying aircraft, etc.: *air-to-air rockets.* 2. between two flying aircraft: *air-to-air refueling.*

air·way (âr′wā′), *n.* 1. route for aircraft. 2. passage for air.

air·wor·thy (âr′wèr′thi), *adj.* fit or safe for service in the air. —*air′wor′thi·ness, n.*

air·y (âr′i), *adj.,* air·i·er, air·i·est. 1. like air; not solid or substantial. 2. light as air; graceful; delicate. 3. light in manner; light-hearted; gay. 4. open to currents of air; breezy. 5. reaching high into the air; lofty. 6. of air; in the air. 7. unnatural; affected.

aisle (īl), *n.* 1. passage between rows of seats in a hall, theater, school, etc. 2. any long or narrow passageway, as in a store. 3. part of a church at the side of the main part, separated from it by columns or piers. 4. nave. [< OF < L *ala* wing; infl. in form by *isle* and in meaning by *alley*] —*aisled* (īld), *adj.*

Aix-la-Cha·pelle (āks′lä·shä·pel′), *n.* French name of Aachen.

a·jar[1] (ə·jär′), *adj., adv.* partly opened. [ME *on char* on the turn; OE *cerr* turn]

a·jar[2] (ə·jär′), *adv., adj.* not in harmony. [< *a–* in + *jar* discord]

A·jax (ā′jaks), *n.* Gk. Legend. Greek hero at the siege of Troy.

a·kene (ā·kēn′), *n.* achene.

a·kim·bo (ə·kim′bō), *adj., adv.* with the hand on the hip and the elbow bent outward. [ME *in kene bowe,* appar., in keen bow, at a sharp angle]

Boy with arms akimbo

a·kin (ə·kin′), *adj.* 1. related by blood: *your cousins are akin to you.* 2. alike; similar. [for *of kin*]

Ak·ron (ak′rən), *n.* city in NE Ohio.

–al[1], *suffix.* of; like; having the nature of, as in *ornamental.* [< L *–alis, –ale* pertaining to]

–al[2], *suffix.* act of ——ing, as in *refusal.* [< L *–ale,* neut. of *–alis*]

Al, *Chem.* aluminum.

a la (ä′lə), *French* à la (ä lä), after; according to.

Ala., Alabama.

Al·a·bam·a (al′ə·bam′ə), *n. Am.* a Southern State of the United States. *Capital:* Montgomery. *Abbrev.:* Ala. —**Al′a·bam′an, Al·a·bam·i·an** (al′ə·bam′i·ən), *adj., n.*

al·a·bam·ine (al′ə·bam′ēn; –in), *n. Chem.* a rare, unisolated element. [< *Alabama*]

al·a·bas·ter (al′ə·bas′tər; –bäs′–), *n.* 1. a smooth, white, translucent variety of gypsum. 2. a variety of calcite, often banded like marble. —*adj.* Also, **al·a·bas·trine** (al′ə·bas′trin; –bäs′–). of or like alabaster. [< L < Gk. *alabast(r)os* an alabaster box]

à la carte (ä′ lə kärt′), with a stated price for each dish. [< F]

a·lack (ə·lak′), **a·lack·a·day** (ə·lak′ə·dā′), *interj. Archaic.* exclamation of sorrow or regret; alas.

a·lac·ri·ty (ə·lak′rə·ti), *n.* 1. brisk and eager action; liveliness. 2. cheerful willingness. [< L *alacer* brisk] —**a·lac′ri·tous,** *adj.* —Ant. 1. languor.

A·lad·din (ə·lad′ən), *n.* a youth in *The Arabian Nights,* who found a magic lamp and a magic ring.

à la king (ä′ lə king′), *Am.* creamed with pimiento or green pepper: *chicken à la king.*

Al·a·me·da (al′ə·mē′də; –mä′–), *n.* city in W California.

al·a·me·da (al′ə·mā′də), *n. Am., Esp. S.W.* promenade with trees, esp. poplars, on each side. [< Sp., < *alamo* poplar]

Al·a·mo (al′ə·mō), *n.* a mission in San Antonio, Texas. After a siege, the Mexicans finally captured it from the Americans on March 6, 1836.

à la mode, a la mode, a·la·mode (ä′ lə mōd′; al′ə–), *adv., adj.* 1. according to the prevailing fashion; in style. 2. *Cookery.* a. (of desserts) served with ice cream. b. (of beef) cooked with vegetables. [< F]

Al·a·ric (al′ə·rik), *n.* 370?–410 A.D., king of the Visigoths who captured Rome in 410 A.D.

a·larm (ə·lärm′), *n.* 1. sudden fear or fright. 2. a warning of approaching danger. 3. thing that gives such a warning. 4. call to arms or action. 5. a device that makes noise to warn or awaken people. —*v.* 1. fill with sudden fear. 2. warn (anyone) of approaching danger. 3. call to arms. [< OF < Ital., < *all'arme!* to arms!]

alarm clock, clock that can be set to make a noise at any desired time.

a·larm·ing (ə·lär′ming), *adj.* that alarms; frightening. —**a·larm′ing·ly,** *adv.*

a·larm·ist (ə·lär′mist), *n.* person who is easily alarmed or alarms others needlessly or on very slight grounds. —**a·larm′ism** (ə·lär′miz·əm), *n.*

a·lar·um (ə·lar′əm; ə·lär′–), *n. Archaic.* alarm.

a·las (ə·las′; ə·läs′), *interj.* exclamation of sorrow, grief, regret, pity, or dread. [< OF *a* ah + *las* miserable < L *lassus* weary]

Alas., Alaska.

A·las·ka (ə·las′kə), *n.* a territory in NW North America, belonging to the United States. *Capital:* Juneau. —**A·las′kan,** *adj., n.*

Alaska Highway, a highway that extends from Dawson Creek, British Columbia, Canada, to Fairbanks, Alaska.

a·late (ā′lāt), *adj.* having wings or winglike parts. [< L, < *ala* wing]

alb (alb), *n.* a white linen robe worn by Roman Catholic and some Anglican priests at the Eucharist. [< L (*vestis*) *alba* white (robe)]

al·ba·core (al′bə·kōr; –kôr), *n., pl.* –cores or (*esp. collectively*) –core. a long-finned, edible fish related to the tuna, found in the Atlantic. [< Pg. < Ar. *al–bakūra*]

Al·ba·ni·a (al·bā′ni·ə; –bān′yə), *n.* country in Europe, between Yugoslavia and Greece. —**Al·ba′ni·an,** *adj., n.*

Al·ba·ny (ôl′bə·ni), *n.* capital of New York State, on the Hudson River.

al·ba·tross (al′bə·trôs; –tros), *n.* any of various webfooted sea birds related to the petrel. [var. of obs. *alcatras* frigate bird < Sp. < Pg. < Ar. *al–qādus* the bucket < Gk. *kados* < Phoenician]

Albatross (30 in. long)

al·be·it (ôl·bē′it), *conj.* although; even though. [ME *al be it* although it be]

Al·ber·ta (al·bér′tə), *n.* province in W Canada.

al·bi·no (al·bī′nō), *n., pl.* –nos. 1. person who congenitally lacks pigmentation. Albinos have a pale, milky skin, very light hair, and pink eyes. 2. any animal or plant that has pale, defective coloring. [< Pg., < *albo* < L *albus* white] —**al·bin·ic** (al·bin′ik), *adj.* —**al·bi·nism** (al′bə·niz–əm), *n.*

Al·bi·on (al′bi·ən), *n. Poetic.* England.

al·bum (al′bəm), *n.* book with blank pages for holding pictures, stamps, autographs, etc. [< L, tablet, neut. of *albus* white]

al·bu·men (al·bū′mən), *n.* 1. white of an egg, consisting mostly of albumin dissolved in water. 2. *Chem.* albumin. 3. *Bot.* endosperm. [< L *albumen* < *albus* white]

al·bu·min (al·bū′mən), *n. Chem.* any of a class of proteins soluble in water and found in the white of egg and in many other animal and plant tissues and juices, esp. $C_{72}H_{112}N_{18}O_{22}S$. [< L. See ALBUMEN.]

al·bu·mi·nous (al·bū′mə·nəs), **al·bu·mi·nose** (–nōs), *adj.* of, like, or containing albumin.

Al·bu·quer·que (al′bə·kér′kē), *n.* city in central New Mexico.

al·caide, al·cayde (al·kād′), *n.* 1. governor of a Spanish fortress. 2. warden of a Spanish prison. [< Sp. < Ar. *al–qā'id* the commander]

Al·can Highway (al′kan), Alaska Highway.

Al·ca·traz (al′kə·traz), *n.* 1. a small island in San Francisco Bay. 2. a U.S. penitentiary there.

al·ca·zar (al′kə·zär; al·kaz′ər), *n.* palace of the Spanish Moors. [< Ar. *al–qasr* the castle < L *castrum* fort]

al·che·mist (al′kə·mist), *n.* in the Middle Ages, a man who studied alchemy. —**al′che·mis′tic, al′che·mis′ti·cal,** *adj.*

al·che·my (al′kə·mi), *n.* 1. medieval chemistry, esp. the search for a process by which baser metals could be turned into gold. 2. magic power or process for changing one thing into another. [< OF < Med.L < Ar. *al–kīmiyā′,* < LGk. *chymeia* < Gk. *chyma* molten metal] —**al·chem·ic** (al·kem′ik), **al·chem′i·cal,** *adj.* —**al·chem′i·cal·ly,** *adv.*

al·co·hol (al′kə·hôl; –hol), *n.* 1. the colorless liquid, C_2H_5OH, in wine, beer, whiskey, gin, etc., that makes them intoxicating; grain alcohol; ethyl alcohol. Alcohol is used in medicine, in manufacturing, and as a fuel. 2. any intoxicating liquor containing this liquid. 3. *Chem.* any of a group of similar organic compounds. Alcohols contain a hydroxyl group and react with organic acids to form esters. [< Med.L (orig., "fine powder," then "essence") < Ar. *al-kuḥl* powdered antimony]

al·co·hol·ic (al'kə·hôl'ik; -hol'-), *adj.* 1. of alcohol. 2. containing alcohol. 3. suffering from the excessive use of alcoholic liquors. —*n.* one addicted to excessive use of alcoholic liquors.

al·co·hol·ism (al'kə·hȯl·iz'əm; -hol-), *n.* diseased condition caused by drinking too much alcoholic liquor.

Al·co·ran (al'kō·rän'; -ran'), *n.* the Koran.

al·cove (al'kōv), *n.* 1. small room opening out of a larger room. 2. part in a wall set back from the rest. 3. summerhouse. [< F < Sp. < Ar. *al-qubba* the vaulted chamber]

Ald., Aldm., Alderman.

al·de·hyde (al'də·hīd), *n.* 1. a transparent, colorless liquid, CH₃CHO, with a suffocating smell, produced by the partial oxidation of ordinary alcohol. 2. any similar organic compound. —**al'de·hy'dic,** *adj.*

Al·den (ȯl'dən), *n.* John, 1599?–1687, one of the Pilgrims who settled at Plymouth, Mass.

al·der (ȯl'dər), *n.* any of several trees and shrubs that usually grow in wet land and have clusters of catkins. [OE *alor*]

al·der·man (ȯl'dər·mən), *n., pl.* -men. 1. *U.S.* member of a council that governs a city. An alderman is usually elected by the voters of a certain ward or district and represents them on the council. 2. in English and Irish cities, a member of a city or county council next in rank to the mayor. [see ELDER¹] —**al'der·man·cy,** al'der·man·ship', *n.* —**al'der·man·ic** (ȯl'dər·man'ik), *adj.*

Alder

Al·der·ney (ȯl'dər·ni), *n., pl.* -neys. 1. one of a group of British islands in the English Channel. 2. one of a breed of dairy cattle.

Al·drin (al'drin), *n.* Trademark. a very powerful organic insecticide, distantly related to DDT, effective against insects that infest the soil, as locusts, grasshoppers, etc.

ale (āl), *n.* a heavy, bitter beer, fermented from hops and malt. [OE *alu*]

a·lee (ə·lē'), *adv., adj. Naut.* on or toward the side of a ship that is away from the wind. [< Scand., < *ā* on + *hlē* shelter, lee]

ale·house (āl'hous'), *n.* place where ale or beer is sold; saloon.

A·le·mán (ä'lä·män'), *n.* Miguel, born 1902, president of Mexico 1946–1952.

a·lem·bic (ə·lem'bik), *n.* 1. a glass or metal container formerly used in distilling. 2. something that transforms or refines. [< Med.L < Ar. *al anbiq* the still < Gk. *ambix* cup]

A·len·çon (ä·län·sȯn' for 1; ə·len'sən, -son for 2), *n.* 1. city in NW France. 2. lace made there.

A·lep·po (ə·lep'ō), *n.* city in NW Syria.

a·lert (ə·lért'), *adj.* 1. watchful; wide-awake. 2. brisk; active; nimble. —*n.* 1. a signal warning of an air attack. 2. a signal to troops, etc., to be ready for action. 3. on the alert, on the lookout; watchful; wide-awake. —*v.* warn against and prepare for an approaching air attack. [< F < Ital. *all' erta* on the watch, ult. < L *erigere* raise up] —**a·lert'ly,** *adv.* —**a·lert'ness,** *n.* —Syn. *adj.* 1. attentive. —Ant. *adj.* 1. heedless.

Al·e·ut (al'i·üt), *n. Am.* an Eskimo native of the Aleutian Islands.

A·leu·tians (ə·lü'shənz), or **Aleutian Islands,** *n.pl.* chain of many small islands SW of Alaska, belonging to the United States.

ale·wife (āl'wīf'), *n., pl.* -wives. *Am.* a sea fish related to the herring and the shad.

Al·ex·an·der the Great (al'ig·zan'dər; -zän'-), 356–323 B.C., king of Macedonia from 336 to 323 B.C.

Al·ex·an·dri·a (al'ig·zan'dri·ə; -zän'-), *n.* seaport in N Egypt, on the Mediterranean.

Al·ex·an·dri·an (al'ig·zan'dri·ən; -zän'-),

adj. 1. of Alexandria. 2. of Alexander the Great. 3. of Alexandrine verse.

Al·ex·an·drine (al'ig·zan'drin; -drēn; -zän'-), *n.* line of poetry having six iambic feet, with a caesura (pause) after the third foot.

al·fal·fa (al·fal'fə), *n. Esp. U.S.* a plant of the pea family much grown in western United States for pasture and forage; lucerne. [< Sp. < Ar. *al-faṣ faṣah* the best kind of fodder]

Al·fred (al'frid), *n.* ("Alfred the Great") 849–899 A.D., king of the West Saxons, 871–899 A.D.

al·fres·co, al fres·co (al·fres'kō), *adv., adj.* in the open air; outdoors. [< Ital.]

alg., algebra.

al·ga (al'gə), *n., pl.* -gae (-jē). one of the algae. —**al·gal** (al'gəl), *adj.*

al·gae (al'jē), *n.pl.* group of plants that have chlorophyll but do not have true stems, roots, or leaves. Some algae are single-celled and form scum on rocks; others, such as the seaweeds, are very large. [< L, seaweed]

al·ge·bra (al'jə·brə), *n.* branch of mathematics in which quantities are denoted by letters, negative numbers as well as ordinary numbers are used, and problems are solved in the form of equations. [< Med.L < Ar. *al-jebr* the bone setting; hence, reduction] —**al·ge·bra·ic** (al'jə·brā'ik), al'ge·bra'i·cal, *adj.* —**al'ge·bra'i·cal·ly,** *adv.*

al·ge·bra·ist (al'jə·brā'ist), *n.* expert in algebra.

Al·ge·ri·a (al·jir'i·ə), *n.* French possession in N Africa, on the Mediterranean. —**Al·ge'ri·an,** Al·ge·rine (al'jə·rēn), *adj., n.*

Al·giers (al·jirz'), *n.* 1. capital of Algeria. 2. Algeria.

Al·gon·qui·an (al·gong'ki·ən; -kwi·ən), *n. Am.* 1. the most widespread linguistic stock of American Indians. 2. an Indian belonging to an Algonquian tribe. —*adj.* of or belonging to this linguistic stock.

Al·gon·quin (al·gong'kin; -kwin), **Al·gon·kin** (al·gong'kin), *n. Am.* 1. member of a family of tribes of the Algonquian linguistic stock. 2. the language of any of these tribes. 3. any Algonquian.

Al·ham·bra (al·ham'brə), *n.* palace of the Moorish kings at Granada, Spain.

a·li·as (ā'li·əs), *n., pl.* a·li·as·es, *adv.* —*n.* an assumed name. —*adv.* with the assumed name of. [< L, at another time]

al·i·bi (al'ə·bī), *n., pl.* -bis, *v.,* -bied, -bi·ing. —*n.* 1. *Law.* plea or fact that a person accused of a certain offense was somewhere else when the offense was committed. 2. *Am., Colloq.* an excuse. —*v. Am., Colloq.* make an excuse. [< L, elsewhere]

al·ien (āl'yən; ā'li·ən), *n.* 1. person who is not a citizen of the country in which he lives. 2. foreigner; stranger. —*adj.* 1. of another country; foreign. 2. opposed; hostile (to or from): *ideas alien to our way of thought.* 3. entirely different; not in agreement. [< L, < *alius* other]

al·ien·a·ble (āl'yən·ə·bəl; ā'li·ən-), *adj.* capable of being transferred to another owner. —**al'ien·a·bil'i·ty,** *n.*

al·ien·ate (āl'yən·āt; ā'li·ən-), *v.,* -at·ed, -at·ing. 1. turn away in feeling or affection; make unfriendly. 2. transfer the ownership of (property) to another. —**al'ien·a'tion,** *n.*

al·ien·ist (āl'yən·ist; ā'li·ən-), *n.* psychiatrist, esp. one who testifies in court. [< F < L *alienus* insane]

a·light¹ (ə·līt'), *v.,* a·light·ed or (Poetic) a·lit, a·light·ing. 1. get down; get off, as from horseback. 2. come down from the air and settle: *a bird alights on a tree.* 3. come upon by chance; happen to find. [OE *ālīhtan*] —Syn. 1. dismount.

a·light² (ə·līt'), *adv., adj.* lighted up: *her face was alight with joy.* [OE *ālīht* illuminated]

a·lign (ə·līn'), *v.* 1. bring into line; adjust to a line: *align the sights of a gun.* 2. form in line: *the troops aligned.* 3. join with others in or against a cause: *Germany was aligned with Japan in World War II.* Also, aline. [< F, < *a*- to + *ligner* < L, < *linea* line] —**a·lign'ment,** *n.*

a·like (ə·līk′), *adv.* **1.** in the same way. **2.** similarly; equally. —*adj.* like one another; similar. [OE *gelīc, onlīc*]

al·i·ment (al′ə·mənt), *n.* nourishment; food. [< L *alimentum* < *alere* nourish] —al·i·men·tal (al′ə·men′təl), *adj.* —al′i·men′tal·ly, *adv.*

al·i·men·ta·ry (al′ə·men′tə·ri; -men′tri), *adj.* **1.** having to do with food and nutrition. **2.** nourishing; nutritious. **3.** providing support.

alimentary canal, the digestive tract of any animal, extending from the mouth to the anus.

al·i·men·ta·tion (al′ə·men·tā′shən), *n.* **1.** nutrition. **2.** support. —al·i·men·ta·tive (al′ə·men′tə·tiv), *adj.*

al·i·mo·ny (al′ə·mō′ni), *n.* money that a man must pay his wife or ex-wife, legally separated from him. [< L *alimonia* < *alere* nourish]

a·line (ə·līn′), *v.,* a·lined, a·lin·ing. align. —a·line′ment, *n.* —a·lin′er, *n.*

al·i·quant (al′ə·kwənt), *adj. Math.* not dividing a number without a remainder: *5 is an aliquant part of 14.* [< L, < *alius* other + *quantus* how much]

al·i·quot (al′ə·kwət), *adj. Math.* dividing a number without a remainder: *3 is an aliquot part of 12.* [< L, < *alius* some + *quot* how many]

a·lit (ə·lit′), *v. Poetic* pt. and pp. of alight¹.

a·live (ə·līv′), *adj.* **1.** living; not dead: *the man is alive.* **2.** in continued activity or operation: *keep the principles of liberty alive.* **3.** of all living: *happiest man alive.* **4.** active; sprightly; lively. **5.** alive to, awake to; sensitive to. **6.** alive with, full of; swarming with; thronged with. **7.** look alive! hurry up! be quick! [OE *on līfe* in life] —a·live′ness, *n.*

a·liz·a·rin (ə·liz′ə·rin), **a·liz·a·rine** (-rin; -rēn), *n.* a red dye, $C_{14}H_8O_4$, prepared from coal tar, formerly obtained from madder. [< F, < *alizari* < Sp. < Ar. *al-'asāra* the extract]

al·ka·li (al′kə·lī), *n., pl.* -lis, -lies. **1.** *Chem.* any base or hydroxide that is soluble in water, neutralizes acids and forms salts with them, and turns red litmus blue. **2.** any salt or mixture of salts that neutralizes acids. Some desert soils contain much alkali. [< MF < Ar. *al-qalī* the ashes of saltwort (a genus of plants)]

al·ka·line (al′kə·līn; -lin), *adj.* **1.** of or like an alkali. **2.** *Am., W.* impregnated with alkali. —al·ka·lin·i·ty (al′kə·lin′ə·ti), *n.*

alkaline-earth metals, *Chem.* group of elements including calcium, strontium, barium, magnesium, and radium.

alkaline earths, *Chem.* oxides of the alkaline-earth metals.

al·ka·lize (al′kə·līz), *v.,* -lized, -liz·ing. make alkaline. —al′ka·li·za′tion, *n.*

al·ka·loid (al′kə·loid), *n. Chem.* any organic base containing nitrogen. Many alkaloids from plants are drugs, such as cocaine, strychnine, morphine, and quinine. —*adj.* noting or pertaining to an alkaloid. —al′ka·loi′dal, *adj.*

all (ôl), *adj.* **1.** the whole of: *all Europe.* **2.** every one of: *all men.* **3.** the greatest possible: *with all speed.* **4.** any; any whatever: *the prisoner denied all connection with the crime.* **5.** nothing but; only: *all words and no thought.* **6.** all in, *Am., Colloq.* weary; worn out. —*pron.* **1.** (*pl. in use*) the whole number; everyone: *all of us are going.* **2.** (*sing. in use*) the whole quantity; everything: *all that glitters is not gold.* —*n.* **1.** everything one has: *he lost his all in the fire.* **2.** above all, before everything else. **3.** after all, all things considered; nevertheless. **4.** all but, almost; nearly. **5.** all in all, a. everything. b. completely. **6.** at all, a. under any conditions. b. in any way. **7.** in all, altogether: *100 men in all.* —*adv.* **1.** wholly; entirely: *the cake is all gone.* **2.** each; apiece: *the score was one all.* **3.** all of, *Am., Colloq.* as much as; no less than. [OE *eall*] > **all** (of). Colloquially and familiarly *all* is followed by *of* in many constructions where the *of* is not necessary and would not be used in formal writing: *all* [of] *the milk was spilled. All of* is usual with a pronoun: *all of them went home.*

Al·lah (al′ə; ä′lə), *n.* the Mohammedan name of the Supreme Being.

all-A·mer·i·can (ôl′ə·mer′ə·kən), *Am.* —*adj.* **1.** representing the whole United States. **2.** made up entirely of Americans or American elements. **3.** selected as the best in the United States. —*n.* an all-American person, esp. a player on a team.

all-a·round (ôl′ə·round′), *adj. Am., Colloq.* able to do many things; useful in many ways. —all′-a·round′ness, *n. Am.*

al·lay (ə·lā′), *v.,* -layed, -lay·ing. **1.** put at rest; quiet: *his fears were allayed by the news of the safety of his family.* **2.** relieve; check: *her fever was allayed by the medicine.* **3.** make less. [OE *ālecgan*] —al·lay′er, *n.* —al·lay′ment, *n.* —Syn. **1.** pacify, calm.

all clear, signal indicating the end of an air raid or other danger. —all′-clear′, *adj.*

al·le·ga·tion (al′ə·gā′shən), *n.* **1.** assertion without proof. **2.** act of alleging; assertion: *the lawyer's allegation was proved.* **3.** assertion made as a plea or excuse.

al·lege (ə·lej′), *v.,* -leged, -leg·ing. **1.** assert without proof: *the alleged theft never happened.* **2.** state positively: *this man alleges that his watch has been stolen.* **3.** give or bring forward as a reason, etc. [< AF *alegier* < L *ex-* + *litigare* strive, sue; with sense of L *allegare* charge] —al·lege′a·ble, *adj.* —al·leg′er, *n.* —Syn. **2.** affirm. **3.** produce, cite.

al·leg·ed·ly (ə·lej′id·li), *adv.* according to what is or has been alleged.

Al·le·ghe·nies (al′ə·gā′niz; al′ə·gā′niz), or **Allegheny Mountains,** *n.pl.* a mountain range in Pennsylvania, Maryland, Virginia, and West Virginia. —Al·le·ghe·ni·an (al′ə·gā′ni·ən), *n., adj.*

al·le·giance (ə·lē′jəns), *n.* **1.** the loyalty owed by a citizen to his country or by a subject to his ruler. **2.** loyalty; faithfulness; devotion. [ME *ligeaunce* < OF, < *lige* liege]

al·le·gor·i·cal (al′ə·gôr′ə·kəl; -gor′-), **al·le·gor·ic** (-ik), *adj.* using allegory. —al′le·gor′i·cal·ly, *adv.* —al′le·gor′i·cal·ness, *n.*

al·le·go·rist (al′ə·gô′rist; -gō′-; al′ə·gə·rist), *n.* one who uses allegories.

al·le·go·rize (al′ə·gə·rīz), *v.,* -rized, -riz·ing. **1.** make into allegory. **2.** treat or interpret as an allegory. **3.** use allegory. —al·le·gor·i·za·tion (al′ə·gôr′ə·zā′shən; -gor′ə-), *n.* —al′le·go·riz′er, *n.*

al·le·go·ry (al′ə·gô′ri; -gō′-), *n., pl.* -ries. **1.** story which is told to explain or teach something: *Bunyan's "The Pilgrim's Progress" is an allegory.* **2.** emblem (def. 1). [< L < Gk., < *allos* other + *agoreuein* speak]

al·le·gro (ə·lā′grō; ə·leg′rō), *adj., adv., n., pl.* -gros. *Music.* —*adj.* quick; lively. —*adv.* in allegro time. —*n.* a movement in such time. [< Ital. < L *alacer* brisk]

al·le·lu·ia (al′ə·lü′yə), *interj.* liturgical form of hallelujah, meaning "praise ye the Lord." —*n.* hymn of praise to the Lord. [< L < Gk. < Heb. *hallĕlūjāh* praise ye Jehovah]

al·ler·gic (ə·lér′jik), *adj.* **1.** of allergy. **2.** having an allergy.

al·ler·gy (al′ər·ji), *n., pl.* -gies. unusual sensitiveness to a particular substance, as certain pollens and dusts. [< NL < Gk. *allos* different, strange + *ergon* action]

al·le·vi·ate (ə·lē′vi·āt), *v.,* -at·ed, -at·ing. make easier to endure (suffering of the body or mind). [< LL, < *al-* up + *levis* light] —al·le′vi·a′tion, *n.* —al·le′vi·a′tive, *adj., n.* —al·le′vi·a′tor, *n.* —Syn. allay, mitigate.

al·ley¹ (al′i), *n., pl.* -leys. **1.** *Am.* a narrow back street. **2.** *Brit.* a narrow street. **3.** path in a park or garden, bordered by trees. **4.** a long, narrow enclosed place for bowling. [< OF *alee* a going]

al·ley² (al′i), *n., pl.* -leys. a large, choice playing marble. [short for *alabaster*]

al·ley·way (al′i·wā′), *n. Am.* **1.** a narrow lane in a city or town. **2.** a narrow passageway.

All Fools' Day, April 1, April Fools' Day.

all fours, 1. all four legs of an animal. **2.** arms and legs of a person; hands and knees.

All·hal·lows (ôl′hal′ōz), *n.* Nov. 1, All Saints′ Day.

al·li·ance (ə·lī′əns), *n.* 1. union formed by agreement; joining of interests. An alliance may be a joining of family interests by marriage, a joining of national interests by treaty, etc. 2. nations, persons, etc., who belong to such a union. 3. association; connection. 4. similarity in structure or descent. [< OF, < *alier* unite < L, < *ad-* to + *ligare* bind]

al·lied (ə·līd′; al′īd), *adj.* 1. united by agreement or treaty: *allied nations.* 2. associated: *allied banks.* 3. connected by nature; akin: *allied animals.* 4. Allied, of the Allies.

Al·lies (al′īz; ə·līz′), *n.pl.* 1. nations that fought against Germany and Austria in World War I. 2. nations that fought against Germany, Italy, and Japan in World War II.

al·li·ga·tor (al′ə-gā′tər), *n.* 1. an American reptile, similar to the crocodile but having a shorter and flatter head. 2. leather prepared from its skin. 3. *Mil.* amphibian vehicle for carrying troops ashore, etc. [< Sp. *el lagarto* the lizard < L *lacertus* lizard]

Alligator (12 ft. long)

alligator pear, avocado.

al·lit·er·ate (ə·lit′ər·āt), *v.,* -at·ed, -at·ing. 1. begin with the same letter or sound. 2. use alliteration. [< L *ad-* + *litera* letter] —al·lit′er·a′tor, *n.*

al·lit·er·a·tion (ə·lit′ər·ā′shən), *n.* repetition of the same first letter or sound in a group of words or line of poetry; initial rhyme. *Example:* the sun sank slowly. —al·lit′er·a′tive, *adj.* —al·lit′er·a′tive·ly, *adv.* —al·lit′er·a′tive·ness, *n.*

al·lo·cate (al′ə-kāt), *v.,* -cat·ed, -cat·ing. 1. assign or allot, as a share, portion, etc. 2. locate. [< Med.L, < L *ad-* to, at + *locare* to place] —al′lo·ca′tion, *n.* —Syn. 1. distribute.

al·lo·path (al′ə-path), **al·lo·pa·thist** (ə·lop′ə·thist), *n.* 1. doctor who uses allopathy. 2. person who favors allopathy.

al·lop·a·thy (ə·lop′ə·thi), *n.* method of treating a disease by using remedies to produce effects different from those caused by the disease treated (opposite of *homeopathy*). [< G < Gk. *allos* other + -PATHY] —al·lo·path·ic (al′ə-path′ik), *adj.* —al′lo·path′i·cal·ly, *adv.*

al·lo·phone (al′ə-fōn), *n. Phonet.* one of the several individual sounds belonging to a single phoneme. The *t* in *take* and the *t* in *try* are allophones of the phoneme *t.* [< Gk. *allos* other + *phone* sound]

al·lot (ə·lot′), *v.,* -lot·ted, -lot·ting. 1. divide and distribute in parts or shares: *the profits have all been allotted.* 2. appropriate to a special purpose. 3. assign as a share: *the teacher allotted work to each student.* [< OF *aloter.* See LOT.] —al·lot′ta·ble, *adj.* —al·lot′ter, *n.*

al·lot·ment (ə·lot′mənt), *n.* 1. division and distribution in parts or shares. 2. share.

al·lo·trope (al′ə-trōp), *n.* an allotropic form.

al·lo·trop·ic (al′ə-trop′ik), **al·le·trop·i·cal** (-ə·kəl), *adj.* occurring in two or more forms that differ in physical and chemical properties but not in the kind of atoms of which they are composed. —al′lo·trop′i·cal·ly, *adv.*

al·lot·ro·py (ə·lot′rə·pi), **al·lot·ro·pism** (-piz·əm), *n.* the property or fact of being allotropic. [< Gk., < *allos* other + *tropos* way]

all-out (ôl′out′), *adj.* greatest possible.

al·low (ə·lou′), *v.* 1. permit: *smoking is not allowed.* 2. let have; give: *he is allowed two dollars a week.* 3. admit; acknowledge; recognize: *allow a claim.* 4. add or subtract to make up for something: *allow an extra hour for traveling time.* 5. permit to happen, esp. through carelessness or neglect: *allow a mine disaster.* 6. *U.S. Dial.* say or think. 7. allow for, take into consideration; provide for. [< OF *alouer* < L *allaudare* (< *ad-* + *laudare* praise) and *allo-*

care ALLOCATE] —al·low′er, *n.* —Syn. 1. let. 2. grant, yield, assign.

al·low·a·ble (ə·lou′ə·bəl), *adj.* 1. allowed by law or by a person in authority. 2. permitted by the rules of the game; not forbidden. —al·low′a·ble·ness, *n.* —al·low′a·bly, *adv.*

al·low·ance (ə·lou′əns), *n., v.,* -anced, -ancing. —*n.* 1. definite portion or amount given out: *a weekly allowance of $12.* 2. subtraction or addition to make up for something: *an allowance on a used car.* 3. an allowing: *allowance of a claim.* 4. tolerance: *allowance of slavery.* 5. make allowance for, take into consideration: *make allowance for a person′s youth.* —*v.* put upon an allowance; to limit (supplies, food, etc.) to a fixed, regular amount.

al·low·ed·ly (ə·lou′id·li), *adv.* admittedly.

al·loy (*n.* al′oi, ə·loi′; *v.* ə·loi′), *n.* 1. an inferior metal mixed with a more valuable one. 2. metal made by the fusion of two or more metals, or a metal and a nonmetal. 3. any injurious addition: *no happiness is without alloy.* —*v.* 1. make into an alloy. 2. lower in value by mixing with an inferior metal: *alloy gold with copper.* 3. make worse; debase: *happiness alloyed by misfortune.* [< OF *alei* < L, < *ad-* to + *ligare* bind. Doublet of ALLY.]

all-pur·pose (ôl′pėr′pəs), *adj.* that can be used for any end: *all-purpose thread.*

all right, 1. without error; correct. 2. yes. 3. certainly. 4. in good health. 5. satisfactory. ⟩ See alright for usage note.

all-round (ôl′round′), *adj. Colloq.* 1. all-around. 2. extending everywhere around.

All Saints′ Day, Nov. 1, a church festival honoring all the saints; Allhallows.

all·spice (ôl′spis′), *n.* 1. a spice supposed to have a flavor like a mixture of cinnamon, nutmeg, and cloves. 2. the berry of the West Indian pimento tree that it is made from.

all-star (ôl′stär′), *adj. Am.* composed of the best players or performers.

al·lude (ə·lüd′), *v.,* -lud·ed, -lud·ing. refer indirectly; mention slightly (*to*): *do not mention or even allude to his failure.* [< L, < *ad-* with + *ludere* play]

al·lure (ə·lůr′), *v.,* -lured, -lur·ing, *n.* —*v.* 1. fascinate; charm. 2. tempt by some advantage. —*n.* attractiveness. [< OF *alurer* LURE] —al·lure′ment, *n.* —al·lur′er, *n.*

al·lur·ing (ə·lůr′ing), *adj.* 1. tempting. 2. attractive. —al·lur′ing·ly, *adv.* —al·lur′ing·ness, *n.*

al·lu·sion (ə·lü′zhən), *n.* an indirect or casual reference; slight mention. ⟩ See illusion for usage note.

al·lu·sive (ə·lü′siv), *adj.* containing allusions. —al·lu′sive·ly, *adv.* —al·lu′sive·ness, *n.*

al·lu·vi·al (ə·lü′vi·əl), *adj.* consisting of or forming alluvium. —*n.* alluvial soil.

al·lu·vi·um (ə·lü′vi·əm), *n., pl.* -vi·ums, -vi·a (-vi·ə). sand, mud, etc., left by flowing water. [< L, < *ad-* up + *luere* wash]

al·ly (*v.* ə·lī′; *n.* al′ī, ə·lī′), *v.,* -lied, -ly·ing, *n., pl.* -lies. —*v.* 1. unite by formal agreement, as by marriage, treaty, or league (*to* or *with*): *France allied herself with England.* 2. connect by some relation, as of likeness, kinship, or friendship. 3. enter into an alliance. —*n.* 1. person or nation united with another for some special purpose. 2. a related animal, plant, or thing. 3. helper; supporter. See also Allies. [< OF *alier* < L, < *ad-* to + *ligare* bind. Doublet of ALLOY.]

al·ma ma·ter, Al·ma Ma·ter (al′mə mä′tər; äl′-; al′mə mā′tər), person′s school, college, or university. [< L, nourishing mother]

al·ma·nac (ôl′mə·nak), *n.* table or book of tables containing a calendar, astronomical data, etc. [< Med.L < Sp. < Ar. *almanākh,* appar. < LGk. *almenichiakon* calendar]

al·might·y (ôl·mīt′i), *adj.* 1. having supreme power; all-powerful. 2. *U.S. Colloq.* great; very. —*adv. U.S. Colloq.* exceedingly. —*n.* the Almighty, God. —al·might′i·ly, *adv.* —al·might′i·ness, *n.* —Syn. *adj.* 1. omnipotent.

almighty dollar, *Am., Colloq.* money thought of as all-powerful.

al·mond (ä′mənd; am′ənd), *n.* **1.** the nut, or seed, of a peachlike fruit growing in warm regions. **2.** tree that it grows on. [< OF *almande* < L < Gk. *amygdale*] —**al′mond·like′,** *adj.*

al·mon·er (al′mən·ər; ä′mən–), *n.* one who distributes alms for a king, monastery, etc. [< OF *almosnier* < VL *alemosynarius* of ALMS]

al·mon·ry (al′mən·ri; ä′mən–), *n., pl.* –ries. place where alms are distributed.

al·most (ôl′mōst; ôl·mōst′), *adv.* nearly. [OE *eal mǣst* nearly]

alms (ämz), *n.pl.* (*sometimes sing. in use*) money or gifts to help the poor. [< VL < L < Gk. *eleemosyne* compassion < *eleos* mercy]

alms·giv·ing (ämz′giv′ing), *n., adj.* giving help to the poor. —**alms′giv′er,** *n.*

alms·house (ämz′hous′), *n.* **1.** *Brit.* house endowed by private charity for the poor to live in. **2.** *U.S.* house maintained at public expense for the poor to live in.

al·oe (al′ō), *n., pl.* –oes. **1.** plant having a long spike of flowers and thick, narrow leaves, that grows in South Africa and other warm, dry climates. **2.** aloes (*sing. in use*), a bitter drug made from the leaves of this plant. **3.** *U.S.* the century plant. Cf. agave. [< L < Gk.]

a·loft (ə·lôft′; ə·loft′), *adv., adj.* **1.** far above the earth; high up. **2.** high above the deck of a ship. [< Scand. *ā lopti* in the air]

a·lo·ha (ə·lō′ə; ä·lō′hä), *n., interj. Hawaiian.* salutation meaning: **a.** welcome. **b.** good-by.

a·lone (ə·lōn′), *adj.* **1.** apart from other persons or things; solitary: *he was alone.* **2.** without anyone else; only: *he alone remained.* **3.** without anything more. **4.** unique. **5.** leave alone, not bother. **6.** let alone, **a.** not bother. **b.** not to mention. —*adv.* only; merely; exclusively. [ME *al one* all (completely) one] —**a·lone′ness,** *n.* —**Syn.** *adj.* **1.** lone, isolated.

a·long (ə·lông′; ə·long′), *prep.* on or by the whole length of; lengthwise of: *walk along a river.* —*adv.* **1.** lengthwise: *cars parked along by the stadium.* **2.** with progressive motion; onward: *let us walk along.* **3.** in company; together (*with*): *I'll go along with you.* **4.** *U.S.* going with one as a companion: *he took his dog along.* **5.** *Am., Colloq.* (of time) some way on. **6.** all along, all the time. **7.** be along, *Am., Colloq.* catch up with others. **8.** get along, **a.** *Am., Colloq.* manage with at least some success. **b.** agree. **c.** go away. **d.** advance. **e.** succeed; prosper. [OE *andlang*]

a·long·shore (ə·lông′shôr′; ə·long′–; –shôr′), *adv.* near or along the shore.

a·long·side (ə·lông′sīd′; ə·long′–), *adv.* at the side; side by side: *anchor alongside.* —*prep.* by the side of; beside: *alongside the wharf.*

a·loof (ə·lüf′), *adv.* at a distance; withdrawn; apart: *he stood aloof from the others.* —*adj.* unsympathetic; indifferent: *an aloof attitude.* [< *a*– on + *loof* windward, prob. < Du. *loef*] —**a·loof′ly,** *adv.* —**a·loof′ness,** *n.*

a·loud (ə·loud′), *adv.* **1.** loud enough to be heard; not in a whisper: *read aloud.* **2.** in a loud voice; loudly. —**Syn. 1.** audibly.

al·pac·a (al·pak′ə), *n.* **1.** a variety of llama with long, soft, silky hair or wool. **2.** its wool. **3.** cloth made from this wool. [< Sp. < Ar. *al* the + Peruvian *paco* alpaca]

al·pen·horn (al′pən·hôrn′), **alp·horn** (alp′-hôrn′), *n.* long, powerful horn used in Switzerland for military signals, etc. [< G]

al·pen·stock (al′pən·stok′), *n.* a strong staff with an iron point, used in climbing mountains. [< G]

al·pha (al′fə), *n.* **1.** the first letter of the Greek alphabet (Α, α). **2.** the first; beginning.

al·pha·bet (al′fə·bet), *n.* **1.** series of characters or signs representing sounds, used in writing a language. **2.** letters of a language arranged in the customary order. **3.** elementary principles. [< LL < Gk., < *alpha* A + *beta* B]

al·pha·bet·i·cal (al′fə·bet′ə·kəl), **al·pha·bet·ic** (–bet′ik), *adj.* **1.** arranged in the order of the alphabet. **2.** of the alphabet. **3.** using an alphabet. —**al′pha·bet′i·cal·ly,** *adv.*

al·pha·bet·ize (al′fə·bə·tīz), *v.,* –ized, –iz-

ing. **1.** arrange in alphabetical order. **2.** express by an alphabet. —**al·pha·bet·i·za·tion** (al′fə-bet′ə·zā′shən), *n.* —**al′pha·bet·iz′er,** *n.*

alpha particle, *Physics.* a positively charged particle consisting of two protons and two neutrons, released in the disintegration of radioactive substances, as radium.

alpha ray, *Physics.* stream of alpha particles.

Al·pine (al′pīn; –pin), *adj.* **1.** of the Alps. **2.** alpine, **a.** of high mountains. **b.** very high.

Alps (alps), *n.pl.* a mountain system in S Europe, famous for its beautiful scenery.

al·read·y (ôl·red′i), *adv.* before this time; by this time; even now: *the house is already full.* [for *all ready*] ▶ **All ready,** as distinguished from **already,** is used as an adjective phrase meaning "quite or completely ready": *the men were all ready to start their next job.*

al·right (ôl·rīt′), *adv.* all right. ▶ **All right** is the correct spelling of both the adjective phrase (*He is all right*) and the sentence adverb meaning, "Yes, certainly" (*All right, I'll come*). **Alright** is a natural analogy with *altogether* and *already,* but at present is found only in advertising, comic strips, familiar writing, etc.

Al·sace (al′sās; –sas; al·sās′), *n.* region in NE France. —**Al·sa·tian** (al·sā′shən), *adj., n.*

Al·sace-Lor·raine (al′sās·lə·rān′; al′sas–), *n.* Alsace and Lorraine, region in NE France; part of Germany, 1871–1919 and 1940–44.

al·so (ôl′sō), *adv.* in addition; too. [OE *ealswā* all so, quite so] —**Syn.** besides, likewise, furthermore. ▶ Also is a weak connective; ordinarily *and* will do its work better: *he came with tents, cooking things, and* [better than *also*] *about fifty pounds of photographic equipment.*

alt., **1.** alternate. **2.** altitude.

al·tar (ôl′tər), *n.* **1.** table or stand in the most sacred part of a church, synagogue, or temple. In Christian churches the altar is used in the Communion service or in celebrating Mass. **2.** an elevated structure on which sacrifices are offered to a deity. **3.** lead to the altar, marry. [< LL, < L *altus* high]

altar boy, person who helps a priest during certain religious services, esp. Mass.

al·tar·piece (ôl′tər·pēs′), *n.* a decorated panel or wall behind or above an altar.

al·ter (ôl′tər), *v.* **1.** make different in some respect without changing into something else: *alter a dress.* **2.** become different: *her whole outlook has altered.* **3.** *Am., Colloq.* castrate or spay (an animal). [< OF < LL, < L *alter* other]

alter., alteration.

al·ter·a·ble (ôl′tər·ə·bəl), *adj.* that can be altered. —**al′ter·a·bil′i·ty,** **al′ter·a·ble·ness,** *n.* —**al′ter·a·bly,** *adv.*

al·ter·a·tion (ôl′tər·ā′shən), *n.* **1.** result of altering; change. **2.** act of altering.

al·ter·a·tive (ôl′tər·ā′tiv), *adj.* **1.** causing change. **2.** *Med.* gradually restoring the healthy bodily functions. —*n. Med.* remedy that gradually restores health.

al·ter·cate (ôl′tər·kāt; al′–), *v.,* –cat·ed, –cating. dispute angrily; quarrel. [< L, < *alter* other]

al·ter·ca·tion (ôl′tər·kā′shən; al′–), *n.* an angry dispute; quarrel.

al·ter e·go (ôl′tər ē′gō; al′tər; eg′ō), **1.** another aspect of one's nature. **2.** a very intimate friend. [< L, trans. of Gk. *heteros ego*]

al·ter·nate (*v.* ôl′tər·nāt, al′–; *adj., n.* ôl′tər·nit, al′–), *v.,* –nat·ed, –nat·ing, *adj., n.* —*v.* **1.** occur by turns, first one and then the other; happen or be arranged by turns. **2.** arrange by turns; do by turns: *alternate work and pleasure.* **3.** take turns: *Lucy and her sister will alternate in setting the table.* **4.** interchange regularly. **5.** *Elect.* reverse direction at regular intervals. **6.** produce or be operated by such a current. —*adj.* **1.** placed or occurring by turns; first one and then the other. **2.** every other. **3.** reciprocal. **4.**

Alternate leaves

Bot. placed singly at different heights along a stem, as leaves. —*n. Am.* person appointed to take the place of another if necessary; substitute. [< L, < *alternus* every second < *alter* other] —al′ter·nate·ly, *adv.* —al′ter·nate·ness, *n.*

al·ter·nating current, electric current that reverses its direction at regular intervals.

al·ter·na·tion (ôl′tər·nā′shən; al′-), *n.* act of alternating; occurring by turns.

al·ter·na·tive (ôl·tėr′nə·tiv; al-), *adj.* **1.** giving or requiring a choice between only two things: *alternative results of two different actions.* **2.** (less strictly) giving a choice from among more than two things: *several alternative suggestions.* —*n.* **1.** choice between two things: *he had the alternative of going home or staying all night.* **2.** (less strictly) choice from among more than two things. **3.** one of the things to be chosen: *we have no alternative but to leave.* —al·ter′na·tive·ly, *adv.* —al·ter′na·tive·ness, *n.* —Syn. *n.* 1, 2. choice, selection. ➤ Alternative comes from the Latin *alternus,* "every second," i.e., "the second of two"; some formal writers, in deference to the word's origin, confine its meaning to "one of two possibilities," but it is commonly used to mean one of several possibilities.

al·ter·na·tor (ôl′tər·nā′tər; al′-), *n.* dynamo or generator for producing an alternating electric current.

al·the·a, al·thae·a (al·thē′ə), *n.* rose of Sharon, a shrub like the mallow. [< L < Gk. *althaia* wild mallow,? < *althainein* heal]

alt·horn (alt′hôrn′), *n.* a brass musical instrument similar to the French horn. Also, alto horn.

al·though, al·tho (ôl·thō′), *conj.* though. [ME *al thogh* even though] —Syn. despite, albeit. ➤ Altho is appropriate in familiar writing, but should not be used in formal writing.

al·tim·e·ter (al·tim′ə·tər; al′tə·mē′tər), *n.* any instrument for measuring altitudes, as a quadrant, sextant, or device for aircraft navigation (an aneroid barometer, radar, etc.).

al·ti·tude (al′tə·tūd; -tūd), *n.* **1.** the vertical height above sea level, the earth's surface, or some other reference plane. **2.** elevation or high place: *mountain altitude.* **3.** height. **4.** high position, power, etc. **5.** the vertical distance from the base of a geometrical figure to its highest point. **6.** the angular distance of a star, etc., above the horizon. [< L, < *altus* high]

al·to (al′tō), *n., pl.* **-tos,** *adj. Music.* —*n.* **1. a.** the lowest female voice; contralto. **b.** the highest male voice. **2.** singer with such a voice. **3.** an alto part. **4.** instrument playing such a part. —*adj.* of, sung by, or composed for an alto. [< Ital. < L *altus* high]

al·to·geth·er (ôl′tə·geth′ər), *adv.* **1.** wholly; entirely: *altogether wicked.* **2.** on the whole: *altogether, I'm sorry it happened.* **3.** all included: *altogether there were 14 books.* —*n.* a whole; general effect. [ME *altogeder*] —Syn. *adv.* 1. completely. ➤ **all together** as distinguished from altogether is used as an adjective phrase meaning "everyone in a group": *they went out all together.*

alto horn, althorn.

al·tru·ism (al′trü·iz·əm), *n.* unselfish devotion to the interests and welfare of others, esp. as a principle of action. [< F *altruisme* < Ital. *altrui* of or for others < L *alter* other] —al′tru·ist, *n.*

al·tru·is·tic (al′trü·is′tik), *adj.* having regard for the well-being and best interests of others; unselfish. —al′tru·is′ti·cal·ly, *adv.*

al·um (al′əm), *n.* **1.** an astringent crystalline substance, KAl(SO₄)₂·12H₂O, a double sulfate of aluminum and potassium, used in dyeing, medicine, etc. **2.** *Chem.* one of a class of double sulfates analogous to the potassium alum. **3.** aluminum sulfate, Al₂(SO₄)₃·18H₂O. [< OF < L *alumen*]

a·lu·mi·na (ə·lü′mə·nə), *n. Chem.* aluminum oxide, Al₂O₃, occurring in clay. [< NL < L *alumen* alum]

a·lu·mi·nous (ə·lü′mə·nəs), *adj.* **1.** of or containing alum. **2.** of or containing aluminum.

a·lu·mi·num (ə·lü′mə·nəm), esp. *Brit.* **al·u·min·i·um** (al′yə·min′yəm), *n.* a silver-white, very light, ductile metal that resists tarnish and is used for making utensils, instruments, etc. It is a metallic element that occurs in nature only in combination. [< ALUMINA]

a·lum·na (ə·lum′nə), *n., pl.* **-nae** (-nē). *Am.* a woman graduate or former student of a school, college, or university. Cf. alumnus.

a·lum·nus (ə·lum′nəs), *n., pl.* **-ni** (-nī). *Am.* **1.** graduate or former student of a school, college, or university. **2.** *Colloq.* a former member, as of a baseball team. [< L, foster child, < *alere* nourish]

al·ve·o·lar (al·vē′ə·lər), *adj.* **1.** *Anat., Zool.* **a.** of or pertaining to a socket, as of a tooth. **b.** of or pertaining to the air cells of the lungs. **2.** *Phonet.* formed by touching the tip of the tongue to or bringing it near the alveoli. English *t* and *d* are alveolar sounds.

al·ve·o·late (al·vē′ə·lit; -lāt), *adj.* deeply pitted. —al·ve′o·la′tion, *n.*

al·ve·o·li (al·vē′ə·lī), *n.pl.* **1.** *Phonet.* ridge behind and above the upper front teeth. **2.** pl. of alveolus.

al·ve·o·lus (al·vē′ə·ləs), *n., pl.* **-li** (-lī). *Anat., Zool.* **1.** a little cell or cavity, as the air cells of the lungs, etc. **2.** socket of a tooth. [< L, dim. of *alveus* cavity]

al·way (ôl′wā), *adv. Archaic.* always.

al·ways (ôl′wiz; -wāz), *adv.* **1.** all the time; continually: *mother is always cheerful.* **2.** every time; at all times: *he always comes home on Saturday.* [all + way] —Syn. **1.** forever, unceasingly, perpetually.

a·lys·sum (ə·lis′əm), *n.* **1.** a plant of the mustard family, having small white or yellow flowers. **2.** sweet alyssum. [< NL < Gk. *alysson,* name of a plant thought to cure rabies]

am (am; *unstressed* əm), *v.* the first person singular, present indicative of be. [OE *eom*]

Am, *Chem.* americium.

AM, A.M., amplitude modulation.

Am., 1. America; American. **2.** Americanism.

A.M., Master of Arts. Also, M.A.

a.m., A.M., 1. before noon. **2.** time from midnight to noon. [for L *ante meridiem*] ➤ A.m. and p.m. are usually written in small letters except in headlines and tables. In consecutive writing they are used only with figures for specific hours: *from 2 to 4 a.m.*

A.M.A., AMA, American Medical Association.

a·mah (ä′mə; am′ə), *n.* in India, etc., a nurse.

a·main (ə·mān′), *adv.* **1.** at full speed. **2.** with full force; violently. **3.** in haste.

a·mal·gam (ə·mal′gəm), *n.* **1.** an alloy of mercury with some other metal or metals, used for filling teeth, silvering mirrors, etc. **2.** mixture; blend. [< Med.L, appar. < L < Gk. *malagma* emollient < *malassein* soften]

a·mal·gam·ate (ə·mal′gə·māt), *v.,* **-at·ed, -at·ing. 1.** unite together; combine. **2.** alloy (one or more metals) with mercury. —a·mal·gam·a·ble (ə·mal′gəm·ə·bəl), *adj.* —a·mal′gam·a′tive, *adj.* —a·mal′gam·a′tor, *n.*

a·mal·gam·a·tion (ə·mal′gə·mā′shən), *n.* mixture; combination; blend; union.

a·man·u·en·sis (ə·man′yū·en′sis), *n., pl.* **-ses** (-sēz). person who writes what another says, or copies what another has written. [< L, < (servus) a manu secretary]

am·a·ranth (am′ə·ranth), *n.* **1.** *Poetic.* an imaginary flower that never fades. **2.** any of a large genus of plants, esp. some with colorful flowers. [< L < Gk. *amarantos* everlasting < not + *marainein* wither; infl. by Gk. *anthos* flower]

am·a·ran·thine (am′ə·ran′thin; -thīn), *adj.* **1.** of the amaranth. **2.** never-fading; undying. **3.** purplish-red.

Am·a·ril·lo (am′ə·ril′ō), *n.* city in NW Texas.

am·a·ryl·lis (am′ə·ril′is), *n.* a bulbous plant related to the lily, with large red, white, or purple flowers. See picture on next page. [< L < Gk., typical name of a country girl]

a·mass (ə·mas′), *v.* **1.** collect or accumulate

for oneself: *amass a fortune.* **2.** collect into a mass or heap. [< OF, < *a-* to + *masse* MASS] —a·mass′a·ble, *adj.* —a·mass′er, *n.* —a·mass′ment, *n.*

am·a·teur (am′ə·chûr; -chər; -tyûr; am′ə·tér′), *n.* **1.** person who does something for pleasure, not for money or as a profession. **2.** person who does something rather poorly. **3.** athlete who is not a professional. —*adj.* **1.** of amateurs; made or done by amateurs. **2.** being an amateur: *amateur pianist.* [< F < L *amator* < *amare* love] —am′a·teur′ish, *adj.* —am′a·teur′ish·ly, *adv.* —am′a·teur′ish·ness, *n.* —am′a·teur·ship′, *n.*

am·a·teur·ism (am′ə·chûr·iz′-əm; -chər-; -tyûr-; am′ə·tér′-iz-əm), *n.* **1.** amateurish way of doing things. **2.** position of an amateur.

Amaryllis
(2 to 4 ft. high)

am·a·to·ry (am′ə·tô′ri; -tō′-), *adj.* of love; causing love; having to do with making love or with lovers. [< L *amatorius* < *amare* love]

a·maze (ə·māz′), *v.*, **a·mazed, a·maz·ing,** *n.* —*v.* **1.** surprise greatly; strike with sudden wonder. **2.** *Obs.* stun; bewilder. —*n.* *Poetic.* amazement. [OE *āmasian*] —Syn. *v.* **1.** astonish, astound.

a·mazed (ə·māzd′), *adj.* greatly surprised. —a·maz·ed·ly (ə·māz′id·li), *adv.* —a·maz′ed·ness, *n.*

a·maze·ment (ə·māz′mənt), *n.* great surprise; sudden wonder; astonishment.

a·maz·ing (ə·māz′ing), *adj.* very surprising; wonderful; astonishing. —*adv.* Am., Colloq. wonderfully. —a·maz′ing·ly, *adv.*

Am·a·zon (am′ə·zon; -zən), *n.* **1.** the largest river in the world, flowing from the Andes Mountains in NW South America across Brazil to the Atlantic. **2.** *Gk. Legend.* one of a race of women warriors living near the Black Sea. **3.** **amazon,** a warlike or masculine woman. —Am·a·zo·ni·an (am′ə·zō′ni·ən), *adj.*

am·bas·sa·dor (am·bas′ə·dər; -dôr), *n.* **1.** the highest representative sent by one government or ruler to another who speaks and acts in behalf of his government. **2.** official messenger with a special errand. Also, **embassador.** [< F < Ital. *ambasciatore*] —am·bas·sa·do·ri·al (am·bas′ə·dô′ri·əl; -dō′-), *adj.* —am·bas′sa·dor·ship′, *n.*

am·bas·sa·dress (am·bas′ə·dris), *n.* **1.** a woman ambassador. **2.** wife of an ambassador.

am·ber (am′bər), *n.* **1.** a hard, translucent, yellow or yellowish-brown fossil resin of pine trees, used for jewelry, etc. **2.** color of amber. —*adj.* **1.** made of amber. **2.** yellow; yellowish-brown. [< OF < Ar. '*anbar* ambergris]

am·ber·gris (am′bər·grēs; -gris), *n.* a waxy intestinal concretion of the sperm whale, used esp. as a fixative in perfumes. [< F *ambre gris* gray amber]

ambi-, *prefix.* around; round about; on both sides, as in *ambidexterity.* [< L; also (before vowels) *amb-*; (before *p*) *am-*]

am·bi·dex·ter·i·ty (am′bə·deks·ter′ə·ti), *n.* **1.** ability to use both hands equally well. **2.** unusual skillfulness. **3.** deceitfulness.

am·bi·dex·trous (am′bə·dek′strəs), *adj.* **1.** able to use both hands equally well. **2.** very skillful. **3.** deceitful; double-dealing. [< LL < L *ambi-* both + *dexter* right] —am′bi·dex′trous·ly, *adv.* —am′bi·dex′trous·ness, *n.*

am·bi·ent (am′bi·ənt), *adj.* surrounding. [< L *ambiens* < *ambi-* around + *ire* go]

am·bi·gu·i·ty (am′bə·gū′ə·ti), *n.*, *pl.* -ties. **1.** possibility of two or more meanings. **2.** an ambiguous word or expression.

am·big·u·ous (am·big′yù·əs), *adj.* **1.** having more than one possible meaning. **2.** of uncertain meaning or nature. **3.** obscure. [< L *ambiguus* < *ambi-* in two ways + *agere* drive] —am·big′-u·ous·ly, *adv.* —am·big′u·ous·ness, *n.* —Syn. **1.** equivocal. **2.** puzzling. **3.** vague.

am·bi·tion (am·bish′ən), *n.* **1.** strong desire

for fame or honor; seeking after a high position or great power. 2. thing strongly desired or sought after. [< L *ambitio* a canvassing for votes < *ambi-* around + *ire* go] —am·bi′tion·less, *adj.* —Syn. **1.** aspiration, longing.

am·bi·tious (am·bish′əs), *adj.* **1.** having or guided by ambition. **2.** arising from or showing ambition. **3.** strongly desirous; eager (*of*): *ambitious of power.* **4.** showy; pretentious. —am·bi′-tious·ly, *adv.* —am·bi′tious·ness, *n.*

am·biv·a·lence (am·biv′ə·ləns), *n.* coexistence of contrary tendencies or feelings, as in the mind. —am·biv′a·lent, *adj.*

am·ble (am′bəl), *n.*, *v.*, **-bled, -bling.** —*n.* **1.** gait of a horse in which both legs on one side are moved at the same time. **2.** easy, slow pace in walking. —*v.* **1.** walk at a slow, easy pace. **2.** (of a horse) move at an amble. [< OF < L *ambulare* walk] —am′bler, *n.* —am′bling·ly, *adv.*

am·bro·sia (am·brō′zhə), *n.* **1.** *Class. Myth.* food of the ancient Greek and Roman gods. **2.** something especially pleasing to taste or smell. [< L < Gk., < *a-* not + *brotos* mortal] —am·bro′sial, am·bro′sian, *adj.* —am·bro′sial·ly, *adv.*

am·bu·lance (am′byə·ləns), *n.* a vehicle, boat, or airplane equipped to carry sick or wounded persons. [< F, < (*hôpital*) *ambulant* walking (hospital)]

am·bu·lant (am′byə·lənt), *adj.* walking.

am·bu·late (am′byə·lāt), *v.*, **-lat·ed, -lat·ing.** walk; move about. —am′bu·la′tion, *n.*

am·bu·la·to·ry (am′byə·lə·tô′ri; -tō′-), *adj.*, *n.*, *pl.* -ries. —*adj.* **1.** of or fitted for walking. **2.** moving from place to place. **3.** *Med.* able to walk. **4.** not permanent; changeable. —*n.* covered place for walking; cloister.

am·bus·cade (am′bəs·kād′), *n.*, *v.*, **-cad·ed, -cad·ing.** ambush. [< F < Ital. *imboscata* < *imboscare* AMBUSH] —am′bus·cad′er, *n.* Am.

am·bush (am′bùsh), *n.* **1.** soldiers or other enemies hidden to make a surprise attack. **2.** place where they are hidden. **3.** act or condition of lying in wait. —*v.* **1.** attack from an ambush. **2.** wait in hiding to make a surprise attack. **3.** put (soldiers or other persons) in hiding for a surprise attack. [< OF *embusche*, ult. < *en-* in + *busche* bush[1]] —am′bush·er, *n.* —am′bush-like′, *adj.* —am′bush·ment, *n.*

a·me·ba (ə·mē′bə), *n.*, *pl.* **-bas, -bae** (-bē). amoeba. —a·me′ba·like′, *adj.* —a·me′ban, *adj.*

a·me·bic (ə·mē′bik), *adj.* amoebic.

a·me·boid (ə·mē′boid), *adj.* amoeboid.

a·meer (ə·mir′), *n.* amir.

a·mel·io·ra·ble (ə·mēl′yə·rə·bəl; ə·mē′li·ə-), *adj.* that can be improved.

a·mel·io·rate (ə·mēl′yə·rāt; ə·mē′li·ə-), *v.*, **-rat·ed, -rat·ing.** make or become better; improve: *new housing ameliorated living conditions in the slums.* [< F *améliorer*, ult. < LL, < L *melior* better] —a·mel′io·ra′tion, *n.* —a·mel′io·ra′tive, *adj.* —a·mel′io·ra′tor, *n.*

a·men (ā′men′; ä′men′), *interj.* **1.** be it so; said after a prayer or wish and used as an expression of assent. **2.** *Colloq.* an expression of approval. —*n.* the word amen. [< L < Gk. < Heb., truth, certainty < *āman* strengthen]

a·me·na·ble (ə·mē′nə·bəl; ə·men′ə-), *adj.* **1.** open to suggestion or advice: *amenable to persuasion.* **2.** accountable; answerable: *amenable to the law.* [< AF, < *a-* to + *mener* lead < L *minare* drive] —a·me′na·bil′i·ty, a·me′na·ble·ness, *n.* —a·me′na·bly, *adv.*

amen corner, Am. **1.** a place in a church where formerly the deacons sat who led the responsive amens during the service. **2.** *Colloq.* any rallying place.

a·mend (ə·mend′), *v.* **1.** change the form of (a law, bill, or motion, etc.) by addition, omission, etc. **2.** change for the better; improve: *amend one's conduct.* **3.** free from faults; correct: *amend the spelling of a word.* **4.** to become better, as by reform or by regaining health. [< OF < L, < *ex-* out of + *mendum* fault] —a·mend′a·ble, *adj.* —a·mend′er, *n.*

a·mend·ment (ə·mend′mənt), *n.* **1.** change

āge, cāre, fär; ēqual, tèrm; īce; ōpen, ôrder; pùt, rüle, ūse; th, then; ə=a in about.

made in a law, bill, motion, etc. 2. change for the better; improvement. 3. change made to remove an error; correction. 4. *Am.* article added to the Constitution of the United States.

a·mends (ə·mendz′), *n.pl.* (*sometimes sing. in use*) compensation for a loss or injury.

a·men·i·ty (ə·men′ə·ti; ə·mē′nə–), *n., pl.* –ties. 1. amenities, pleasing manners or courteous acts that lead to agreeable social relations. 2. pleasant feature. 3. pleasantness; agreeableness. [< L, < *amoenus* pleasant]

am·ent (am′ənt; ā′mənt), *n. Bot.* a long, slender spike covered with rows of bracts having flowers of one sex and no petals; catkin. [< L *amentum* thong]

Amer., America; American.

a·merce (ə·mérs′), *v.,* a·merced, a·merc·ing. 1. punish by an arbitrary or discretionary fine. 2. punish by any penalty. [< AF, < *a merci* at the mercy (of)] —a·merce′a·ble, *adj.* —a·merce′ment, *n.* —a·merc′er, *n.*

A·mer·i·ca (ə·mer′ə·kə), *n.* 1. *Am.* the United States of America. 2. North America. 3. North America and South America; the Western Hemisphere. 4. South America.

A·mer·i·can (ə·mer′ə·kən), *adj.* 1. *Am.* of, having to do with, or in the United States: *an American citizen.* 2. of or in the Western Hemisphere: *the Amazon and other American rivers.* 3. *Am., Biol.* native only to the United States: *American eagle, American aloe.* —*n.* 1. *Am.* citizen of the United States, or of the earlier British colonies, not belonging to one of the aboriginal races. 2. native or inhabitant of the Western Hemisphere. 3. *Am.* American language.

A·mer·i·ca·na (ə·mer′ə·kä′nə; –kan′ə; –kä′nə), *n.pl.* collection of objects or documents about America, esp. its history.

A·mer·i·can·ism (ə·mer′ə·kən·iz′əm), *n. Am.* 1. devotion or loyalty to the United States, its customs, traditions, etc. 2. a word, phrase, or idiom originating in the United States, as *almighty dollar, amen corner.* 3. custom or trait peculiar to the United States. 4. thing considered typically American.

A·mer·i·can·ize (ə·mer′ə·kən·īz), *v.,* –ized, –iz·ing. *Am.* make or become American in habits, customs, or character. —A·mer′i·can·i·za′tion, A·mer′i·can·iz′ing, *n. Am.* —A·mer′i·can·ized, *adj. Am.*

American language, *Am.* English as used in the United States as distinct from British English.

American plan, *Am.* system used in hotels where one price covers room, board, and service (distinguished from *European plan*).

American Revolution, 1. war fought by the American colonies from 1775 to 1783 to gain their independence from England. 2. series of protests and acts of the American colonists from 1763 to 1783 against England's attempts to increase her power over them.

am·er·i·ci·um (am′ər·ish′i·əm), *n. Chem.* an artificial, radioactive metallic element, Am.

Am·er·ind (am′ər·ind), *n. Am.* the American Indian. —Am′er·in′di·an, *adj., n. Am.* —Am′er·in′dic, *adj.*

am·e·thyst (am′ə·thist), *n.* 1. a purple or violet variety of quartz, used as a precious stone. 2. violet-colored corundum, used for jewelry. [< OF < L < Gk. *amethystos* < *a*– not + *methy* wine; thought to prevent intoxication] —am′e·thyst·like′, *adj.*

a·mi·a·ble (ā′mi·ə·bəl), *adj.* good-natured and friendly; pleasant and agreeable: *an amiable disposition.* [< OF < LL *amicabilis* < L *amicus* friend. Doublet of AMICABLE.] —a′mi·a·bil′i·ty, a′mi·a·ble·ness, *n.* —a′mi·a·bly, *adv.*

am·i·ca·ble (am′ə·kə·bəl), *adj.* peaceable; friendly. [< LL *amicabilis* < L *amicus* friend. Doublet of AMIABLE.] —am′i·ca·bil′i·ty, am′i·ca·ble·ness, *n.* —am′i·ca·bly, *adv.*

am·ice (am′is), *n.* an oblong piece of linen covering the shoulders, worn by priests at Mass. [< OF < L *amictus* cloak]

a·mi·cus cu·ri·ae (ə·mī′kəs kyūr′i·ē; ə·mē′kəs kyūr′i·ī), *Law.* person with no interest in a

case who is called in to advise the judge. [< NL, friend of the court]

a·mid (ə·mid′), **a·midst** (ə·midst′), *prep.* in the midst or middle of; among.

am·ide (am′īd; –īd), **am·id** (–īd), *n. Chem.* a compound produced by replacing one or more of the hydrogen atoms of ammonia by univalent acid radicals. —a·mid·ic (ə·mid′ik), *adj.*

a·mid·ships (ə·mid′ships), **a·mid·ship** (–ship), *adv.* in or toward the middle of a ship; halfway between the bow and stern.

Am·i·ens (am′i·ənz; *Fr.* ä·myan′), *n.* city in N France, on the Somme River.

a·mi·go (ə·mē′gō), *n. Am., S.W.* a friend. [< Sp. < L *amicus*]

a·mine (ə·mēn′; am′in), **am·in** (am′in), *n. Chem.* a compound produced by replacing one or more of the hydrogen atoms of ammonia by univalent hydrocarbon radicals.

a·mi·no acids (ə·mē′nō; am′ə·nō), *Chem.* complex organic compounds of nitrogen that combine in various ways to form proteins.

a·mir (ə·mir′), *n.* in Mohammedan countries, a commander, ruler, or prince. Also, ameer. [< Ar., commander. Cf. ADMIRAL.]

Am·ish (am′ish; ä′mish), *n., pl.* Am·ish, *adj. Am.* —*n.* member of a strict Mennonite sect, founded in the 17th century. —*adj.* of this sect or its members. —Am′ish·man′, *n. Am.*

a·miss (ə·mis′), *adv.* 1. in a faulty manner; wrongly. 2. take amiss, be offended at. —*adj.* improper; wrong: *it is not amiss to ask advice.* [ME *a mis* by (way of) fault. See MISS[1].]

am·i·to·sis (am′ə·tō′sis), *n. Biol.* simple or direct method of cell division. —am·i·tot·ic (am′ə·tot′ik), *adj.* —am′i·tot′i·cal·ly, *adv.*

am·i·ty (am′ə·ti), *n., pl.* –ties. peace and friendship; friendly relations: *treaty of amity.* [< MF *amitié*, ult. < L *amicus* friend]

am·me·ter (am′mē′tər; am′ē′tər), *n. Elect.* instrument for measuring in amperes the strength of an electric current. [< *am(pere)* + –METER]

am·mo·nia (ə·mō′nyə; ə·mō′ni·ə), *n.* 1. a colorless, pungent gas, NH₃, consisting of nitrogen and hydrogen. 2. this gas dissolved in water, NH₄OH. [< NL; so named because obtained from sal *ammoniac*]

am·mo·ni·ac (ə·mō′ni·ak), *adj.* Also, am·mo·ni·a·cal (am′ə·nī′ə·kəl). of or like ammonia. —*n.* gum ammoniac. [< L < Gk. *ammoniakon*; applied to a salt obtained near the shrine of Ammon in Libya]

am·mo·nite (am′ə·nīt), *n.* one of the spiraled fossil shells of an extinct mollusk. [< NL *ammonites* < Med.L *cornu Ammonis* horn of Ammon (Egyptian god)]

Ammonite

am·mo·ni·um (ə·mō′ni·əm), *n. Chem.* the radical NH₄, which never appears in a free state by itself, but acts as a unit in chemical reactions.

ammonium chloride, NH₄Cl, colorless crystals or white powder used in medicine, in printing cloth, etc.; sal ammoniac.

ammonium hydroxide, alkali formed when ammonia gas dissolves in water, NH₄OH.

am·mu·ni·tion (am′yə·nish′ən), *n.* 1. bullets, shells, gunpowder, etc., for guns or other weapons. 2. thing or things that can be shot or thrown. 3. means of attack or defense. [< obs. F *amunition*, used for *munition*]

am·ne·sia (am·nē′zhə), *n.* loss of memory caused by injury to the brain, by disease, or by shock. [< NL < Gk., < *a*– not + *mnasthai* remember] —am·ne·sic (am·nē′sik; –zik), am·nes·tic (am·nes′tik), *adj.*

am·nes·ty (am′nəs·ti), *n., pl.* –ties, *v.,* –tied, –ty·ing. —*n.* a general pardon for past offenses against a government. —*v.* give amnesty to; pardon. [< L < Gk. *amnestia* < *a*– not + *mnasthai* remember]

am·ni·on (am′ni·ən), *n., pl.* –ni·ons, –ni·a (–ni·ə). *Zool.* a membrane lining the sac which encloses a fetus. [< Gk., dim. of *amnos* lamb] —am·ni·ot·ic (am′ni·ot′ik), *adj.*

a·moe·ba (ə·mē'bə), *n., pl.* **-bas, -bae** (-bē). *Zool.* microscopic one-celled animal that moves by forming temporary projections that are constantly changing. Also, **ameba**. [< Gk. *amoibe* change] —a·moe'ba-like', *adj.* —a·moe'ban, *adj.*

a·moe·bic (ə·mē'bik), *adj.* **1.** of or like an amoeba or amoebas. **2.** caused by amoebas. Also, **amebic**.

a·moe·boid (ə·mē'boid), *adj.* of or like an amoeba. Also, **ameboid**.

a·mok (ə·muk'; ə·mok'), *n.* a mental disturbance of the Malays, characterized by a period of depression followed by a murderous frenzy. —*adv.* amuck.

a·mong (ə·mung'), *prep.* **1.** in the number or class of: *that book is the best among modern novels.* **2.** by, with, or through the whole of: *political unrest among the people.* **3.** in contact or association with: *he fell among thieves.* **4.** surrounded by: *a house among the trees.* **5.** in comparison with: *one among many.* **6.** by or for distribution to; to each of: *divide the money among them.* **7.** by the mutual or reciprocal action of: *they fought among themselves.* **8.** by the combined action of: *settle it among yourselves.* [OE *amang* < *on* (*ge*)*mang* in a crowd] ➤ See between for usage note.

a·mongst (ə·mungst'), *prep.* among.

a·mor·al (ā·môr'əl; ā·mor'-; a-), *adj.* not involving any question of morality; nonmoral. [< *a*- not + *moral*] —a·mo·ral·i·ty (ā'mə·ral'ə·ti; am'ə-), *n.* —a·mor'al·ly, *adv.*

am·o·rous (am'ə·rəs), *adj.* **1.** inclined to love: *an amorous disposition.* **2.** in love. **3.** showing love; loving. **4.** having to do with love or courtship: *amorous poems.* [< OF, < *amour* love < L *amor*] —am'o·rous·ly, *adv.* —am'o·rous·ness, *n.* —Syn. **2.** enamored. **3.** fond, devoted.

a·mor·phism (ə·môr'fiz·əm), *n.* amorphous condition.

a·mor·phous (ə·môr'fəs), *adj.* **1.** *Chem.* not crystallized. Glass is amorphous; sugar is crystalline. **2.** of no particular kind or type. **3.** having no definite form; shapeless. [< Gk., < *a*- without + *morphe* shape] —a·mor'phous·ly, *adv.* —a·mor'phous·ness, *n.*

am·or·tize, *esp. Brit.* **am·or·tise** (am'ər·tiz; ə·môr'tiz), *v.,* **-tized, -tiz·ing;** *esp. Brit.* **-tised, -tis·ing.** set aside money regularly for future payment of (a debt, etc.). [< OF *amortir* deaden < *a*- to + *mort* death < L *mors*] —am'or·tiz'a·ble, *esp. Brit.* am'or·tis'a·ble, *adj.* —am·or·ti·za·tion *esp. Brit.* am·or·ti·sa·tion (am'ər·tə·zā'shən; ə·môr'-), a·mor·tize·ment, *esp. Brit.* a·mor·tise·ment (ə·môr'tiz·mənt), *n.*

A·mos (ā'məs), *n.* **1.** a Hebrew prophet who lived about 760 B.C. **2.** book of the Old Testament.

a·mount (ə·mount'), *n.* **1.** sum; total: *amount of the day's sales.* **2.** the full effect, value, or extent: *the amount of evidence against him is this.* **3.** quantity viewed as a whole: *a great amount of intelligence.* **4.** principal plus interest. —*v.* **1.** be equal; reach (*to*): *the debt amounted to $50.* **2.** be equivalent in quantity, value, force, effect, etc. (*to*): *his answer amounted to a threat.* [< OF, < *a mont* up; lit. to the mountain. See MOUNT².] ➤ **amount, number.** *Amount* is used of things viewed in the bulk, weight, or sums; *number* is used of things that can be counted: *an amount of milk* (but *a number of cans of milk*).

a·mour (ə·mŭr'), *n.* **1.** a love affair. **2.** an illicit love affair. [< OF, prob. < Pr. < L *amor* love]

A·moy (ä·moi'; ə-), *n.* **1.** seaport on an island near the SE coast of China. **2.** the island.

amp., *Elect.* **1.** amperage. **2.** ampere.

am·per·age (am'pər·ij; am·pir'-), *n.* Elect. strength of a current measured in amperes.

am·pere (am'pir; am·pir'), *n.* Elect. unit for measuring the strength of an electric current. It is the current one volt can send through a resistance of one ohm. [for A. M. *Ampère*, French physicist]

am·per·sand (am'pər·sand), *n.* the character &, meaning "and." [alter. of *and per se = and*, & by itself = and] ➤ Used chiefly in business

correspondence and reference works. In addressing firms, use the form they habitually use (. . . *and Company* or . . . *& Company*), and in quoting, follow your original carefully.

amphi-, *word element.* **1.** around; on both sides, as in *amphitheater.* **2.** in two ways; of two kinds, as in *amphibious.* [< Gk.]

Am·phib·i·a (am·fib'i·ə), *n.pl. Zool.* class of cold-blooded vertebrates with moist, scaleless skin, including frogs, toads, newts, salamanders, etc. Their young usually develop as tadpoles that have gills and live in water.

am·phib·i·an (am·fib'i·ən), *n.* **1.** animal that lives on land and in water. **2.** one of the Amphibia. **3.** plant that grows on land or in water. **4.** aircraft that can take off from and alight on land or water. **5.** *Mil.* tank for use both on land and in water. —*adj.* **1.** able to live both on land and in water. **2.** able to take off and alight on either land or water.

am·phib·i·ous (am·fib'i·əs), *adj.* **1.** able to live both on land and in water. **2.** suited for use on land or water: *an amphibious tank.* **3.** having two qualities, kinds, natures, or parts. **4.** by the combined action of land, water, and air forces: *amphibious attack.* [< L < Gk., < *amphi*- + *bios* life] —am·phib'i·ous·ly, *adv.* —am·phib'i·ous·ness, *n.*

am·phi·the·a·ter, *esp. Brit.* **am·phi·the·a·tre** (am'fə·thē'ə·tər), *n.* **1.** a circular or oval building with rows of seats rising around a central open space. **2.** something resembling an amphitheater in shape. [< L < Gk., < *amphi*- on all sides + *theatron* theater] —am·phi·the·at·ric (am'fə·thi·at'rik), am'phi·the·at'ri·cal, *adj.* —am'phi·the·at'ri·cal·ly, *adv.*

am·pho·ra (am'fə·rə), *n., pl.* **-rae** (-rē). tall two-handled jar, used by the ancient Greeks and Romans. [< L < Gk., < *amphi*- on both sides + *phoreus* bearer; with ref. to handles]

am·ple (am'pəl), *adj.,* **-pler, -plest. 1.** fully sufficient for any purpose: *ample food for the table.* **2.** large in extent or degree: *give ample praise.* **3.** large; big; roomy: *an ample room.* **4.** more than enough. [< F < L *amplus*] —am'ple·ness, *n.* —Syn. **1.** abundant, plentiful, copious, liberal. —Ant. **1.** insufficient.

am·plex·i·caul (am·plek'sə·kôl), *adj.* clasping the stem, as some leaves do at their bases. [< NL, < L *amplexus* an embrace + *caulis* stem]

am·pli·fi·ca·tion (am'plə·fə·kā'shən), *n.* **1.** act of amplifying; expansion. **2.** detail, example, etc., that amplifies a statement, narrative, etc. **3.** an expanded statement, etc. —am'pli·fi·ca'tive, am·plif·i·ca·to·ry (am·plif'ə·kə·tô'ri; -tō'-), *adj.*

am·pli·fi·er (am'plə·fī'ər), *n.* **1.** person or thing that amplifies. **2.** *Elect.* device for strengthening electrical impulses, as a radio vacuum tube.

am·pli·fy (am'plə·fī), *v.,* **-fied, -fy·ing. 1.** make fuller and more extensive; expand; enlarge. **2.** expand by giving details, examples, comparisons, etc.; develop fully: *amplify a theory.* **3.** *Elect.* increase the strength of (a sound or an electrical impulse). [< F < L, < *amplus* ample + *facere* make]

am·pli·tude (am'plə·tüd; -tūd), *n.* **1.** width; breadth; size. **2.** abundance; fullness, as of intelligence, understanding, etc. **3.** *Physics.* one half the range of symmetric vibrations. **4.** *Elect.* the peak strength of an alternating current in a given cycle. [< L *amplitudo.* See AMPLE.]

amplitude modulation, *Electronics.* purposeful alteration of the amplitude of radio waves. Ordinary broadcasting uses amplitude modulation. Cf. frequency modulation.

am·ply (am'pli), *adv.* in an ample manner; to an ample degree; liberally; sufficiently.

am·poule (am'pūl; -pūl), **am·pule** (am'pūl), *n.* small glass tube or bulb filled with a drug and hermetically sealed. [< F < L *ampulla* jar, dim. of *amphora*. See AMPHORA.]

am·pu·tate (am'pyə·tāt), *v.,* **-tat·ed, -tat·ing.** cut off (contrasted with *excise*). [< L, < *ambi*- about + *putare* prune] —am·pu·ta·tion, *n.* —am'pu·ta'tor, *n.*

am·pu·tee (am'pyə·tē'), *n.* one who has undergone an amputation, as of an arm or leg.

Am·ster·dam (am'stər·dam), *n.* important seaport and capital of the Netherlands.

amt., amount.

a·muck (ə·muk'), *adv.* **1.** in a murderous frenzy. **2.** run amuck, run about in a murderous frenzy. Also, **amok.** [< Malay *amoq*]

am·u·let (am'yə·lit), *n.* some object worn as a magic charm against evil or harm. [< L *amuletum*]

A·mur (ä·mūr'), *n.* river in NE Asia.

a·muse (ə·mūz'), *v.,* **a·mused, a·mus·ing. 1.** cause to laugh or smile: *amuse an audience.* **2.** keep pleasantly interested; entertain: *new toys amuse children.* [< OF *amuser* divert, < *a-* + *muser* stare] —**a·mus'a·ble,** *adj.* —**a·mus'er,** *n.*

a·mused (ə·mūzd'), *adj.* pleasantly entertained. —**a·mus·ed·ly** (ə·mūz'id·li), *adv.*

a·muse·ment (ə·mūz'mənt), *n.* **1.** condition of being amused. **2.** thing that amuses.

a·mus·ing (ə·mūz'ing), *adj.* **1.** entertaining. **2.** causing laughter, smiles, etc. —**a·mus'ing·ly,** *adv.* —**a·mus'ing·ness,** *n.*

Am·vets (am'vets'), *n. Am.* American Veterans of World War II, an organization founded in 1944.

am·yl (am'il), *n. Chem.* group of carbon and hydrogen atoms, $-C_5H_{11}$, that acts as a unit in forming compounds. [< L < Gk. *amylon* starch, orig., unground < *a-* not + *myle* mill] —**a·myl·ic** (ə·mil'ik), *adj.*

am·yl·ase (am'ə·lās), *n. Biochem.* enzyme in saliva, pancreatic juice, etc., or in parts of plants, that helps to change starch into sugar. [< *amyl*]

an¹ (an; *unstressed* ən), *adj.* or *indefinite article.* **1.** one; any: *an apple.* **2.** each; every: *twice an hour.* Cf. a. [OE (unstressed) *ān* (before vowels)] ➤ See **a** for usage note.

an², an' (an; *unstressed* ən), *conj.* **1.** *Dial.* or *Colloq.* and. **2.** *Archaic* or *Dial.* if. [var. of *and*]

an-, *prefix.* not; without, as in *anhydrous.* [var. of *a-¹* before vowels and *h*]

-an, *suffix.* **1.** of or having to do with, as in *republican.* **2.** native or inhabitant of, as in *American.* [< L *-ānus*]

An·a·bap·tist (an'ə·bap'tist), *n.* member of a Protestant sect opposing infant baptism and requiring adult baptism. —**An'a·bap'tism,** *n.*

a·nab·o·lism (ə·nab'ə·liz·əm), *n. Biol.* constructive metabolism in which matter is changed into the tissues of a living animal or plant (opposite of *catabolism*). [coined from *metabolism* by substitution of Gk. *ana-* up] —**an·a·bol·ic** (an'ə·bol'ik), *adj.*

a·nach·ro·nism (ə·nak'rə·niz·əm), *n.* **1.** act of putting a person, thing, or event in some time where it does not belong. It would be an anachronism to speak of Julius Caesar as telephoning. **2.** something placed or occurring out of its proper time. [< F < Gk., < *ana-* backwards + *chronos* time]

a·nach·ro·nis·tic (ə·nak'rə·nis'tik), *adj.* having or involving an anachronism.

a·nach·ro·nous (ə·nak'rə·nəs), *adj.* placed or occurring out of the proper time. —**a·nach'ro·nous·ly,** *adv.*

an·a·co·lu·thon (an'ə·kə·lü'thon), *n., pl.* **-tha** (-thə). change from one grammatical construction to another within the same sentence for greater force. [< LL < Gk., < *an-* not + *akolouthos* following] —**an'a·co·lu'thic,** *adj.*

an·a·con·da (an'ə·kon'də), *n.* **1.** a very large tropical snake that crushes its prey in its coils; water boa. **2.** any large snake that crushes its prey in its folds, such as the python.

a·nad·ro·mous (ə·nad'rə·məs), *adj. Zool.* going up rivers from the sea to spawn. [< LGk., < *ana-* up + *dromos* a running]

a·nae·mi·a (ə·nē'mi·ə), *n.* anemia. —**a·nae'mic,** *adj.*

an·aer·obe (an·ār'ōb; an·ā'ər·ōb), *n.* **1.** organism that cannot live in the presence of free oxygen. **2.** organism that can live without free oxygen. —**an'aer·o'bic,** *adj.* —**an'aer·o'bi·cal·ly,** *adv.*

an·aes·the·sia (an'əs·thē'zhə), *n. Am.* anesthesia.

an·aes·thet·ic (an'əs·thet'ik), *adj., n. Am.* anesthetic.

an·aes·the·tist (ə·nes'thə·tist), *n.* anesthetist.

an·aes·the·tize (ə·nes'thə·tīz), *v.,* **-tized, -tiz·ing.** anesthetize. —**an·aes·the·ti·za·tion** (ə·nes'thə·tə·zā'shən; an'əs·thet'ə-), *n.*

an·a·gram (an'ə·gram), *n.* **1.** word or phrase formed from another by transposing the letters. *Example:* lived—devil. **2. anagrams** (*sing. in use*), game in which players make words by changing and adding letters. [< NL < Gk. *anagrammatizein* transpose letters < *ana-* up or back + *gramma* letter]

a·nal (ā'nəl), *adj.* of or near the anus.

an·a·lects (an'ə·lekts), *n.pl.* literary extracts or fragments forming a collection. [< L < Gk. *analekta* < *ana-* up + *legein* pick]

an·al·ge·si·a (an'əl·jē'zi·ə; -si·ə; -zhə; -shə), *n.* insensibility to pain without losing consciousness. [< NL < Gk., < *an-* not + *algein* feel pain]

an·al·ge·sic (an'əl·jē'zik; -sik), *adj.* of or causing analgesia. —*n.* medicine or other agent that causes analgesia.

an·a·log·i·cal (an'ə·loj'ə·kəl), **an·a·log·ic** (-loj'ik), *adj.* using analogy; having to do with analogy. —**an'a·log'i·cal·ly,** *adv.*

a·nal·o·gize (ə·nal'ə·jīz), *v.,* **-gized, -giz·ing. 1.** explain by analogy. **2.** use analogy. —**a·nal·o·gist** (ə·nal'ə·jist), *n.*

a·nal·o·gous (ə·nal'ə·gəs), *adj.* **1.** corresponding in some way; similar; comparable. **2.** *Biol.* corresponding in function, but not in structure and origin. —**a·nal'o·gous·ly,** *adv.* —**a·nal'o·gous·ness,** *n.*

an·a·logue, an·a·log (an'ə·lôg; -log), *n.* something analogous.

analogue computer, a calculating machine or automatic control which deals directly with physical quantities (weights, voltages, etc.) rather than a numerical code.

a·nal·o·gy (ə·nal'ə·ji), *n., pl.* **-gies. 1.** likeness in some ways between things that are otherwise unlike; similarity. **2.** comparison of such things: *it is risky to argue by analogy.* **3.** *Biol.* correspondence in function but not in structure and origin. [< L < Gk. *analogia*] ➤ One says *analogy between* things, and that one thing has *analogy to* or *with* another. See also *metaphor.*

a·nal·y·sis (ə·nal'ə·sis), *n., pl.* **-ses** (-sēz). **1.** separation of a thing into parts; examination of a thing's parts to find out their essential features: *analysis of a book.* **2.** *Chem.* a. intentional separation of a substance into its ingredients or elements to determine their amount and nature. b. the determination of the kind or amount of one or more of the constituents of a substance, whether actually obtained in separate form or not. **3.** statement of the results of an analysis. [< Med.L < Gk., a breaking up, < *ana-* up + *lyein* loose]

an·a·lyst (an'ə·list), *n.* **1.** one who analyzes. **2.** one who practices psychoanalysis.

an·a·lyt·ic (an'ə·lit'ik), **an·a·lyt·i·cal** (-ə·kəl), *adj.* of or using analysis. —**an'a·lyt'i·cal·ly,** *adv.*

an·a·lyt·ics (an'ə·lit'iks), *n.* mathematical or algebraic analysis.

an·a·lyze, *esp. Brit.* **an·a·lyse** (an'ə·līz), *v.,* **-lyzed, -lyz·ing;** *esp. Brit.* **-lysed, -lys·ing. 1.** separate into its parts. **2.** examine the parts or elements of critically; find out the essential features of: *analyze an argument.* **3.** examine carefully and in detail. **4.** *Chem.* subject to analysis. —**an'a·lyz'a·ble,** *esp. Brit.* **an'a·lys'a·ble,** *adj.* —**an'a·ly·za'tion,** *esp. Brit.* **an'a·ly·sa'tion,** *n.* —**an'a·lyz'er,** *esp. Brit.* **an'a·lys'er,** *n.*

An·a·ni·as (an'ə·nī'əs), *n.* **1.** *Bible.* liar who was struck dead for this fault. Acts 5:1–10. **2.** *Colloq.* any liar.

an·a·pest, an·a·paest (an'ə·pest), *n.* measure or foot in poetry consisting of two unaccented syllables followed by an accented syllable. [< L < Gk. *anapaistos* < *ana-* back + *paiein* strike] —**an'a·pes'tic, an'a·paes'tic,** *adj., n.*

an·a·phor·ic pronoun (an'ə·fôr'ik; -for'-), *Gram.* word which refers to a previously mentioned word, phrase, etc. In "I couldn't get a large book, so I got two small ones," *ones* is an anaphoric pronoun.

an·ar·chism (an'ər·kiz·əm), *n.* 1. the political theory that all systems of government and law are harmful and prevent individuals from reaching their greatest development. 2. practice or support of this doctrine. 3. terrorism; lawlessness.

an·ar·chist (an'ər·kist), *n.* person who wants to overthrow established governments and have a world without rulers and laws. —**an'ar·chis'·tic**, *adj.*

an·ar·chy (an'ər·ki), *n.* 1. absence of a system of government and law. 2. confusion; lawlessness. [< Gk., < *an-* without + *archos* ruler] —**an·ar·chic** (an·är'kik), **an·ar'chi·cal**, *adj.* —**an·ar'chi·cal·ly**, *adv.*

anat., 1. anatomical. 2. anatomy.

a·nath·e·ma (ə·nath'ə·mə), *n., pl.* -**mas.** 1. a solemn curse by church authorities excommunicating some person from the church. 2. denouncing and condemning some person or thing as evil; curse. 3. person or thing accursed. 4. thing that is detested and condemned. [< L < Gk., thing devoted, esp. to evil, < *ana-* up + *tithenai* set]

a·nath·e·ma·tize (ə·nath'ə·mə·tīz), *v.,* -**tized**, -**tiz·ing.** denounce; curse. —**a·nath'e·ma·ti·za'tion**, *n.* —**a·nath'e·ma·tiz'er**, *n.*

An·a·to·li·a (an'ə·tō'li·ə), *n.* Asia Minor. —An'a·to'li·an, *adj., n.*

an·a·tom·i·cal (an'ə·tom'ə·kəl), **an·a·tom·ic** (-tom'ik), *adj.* of or having to do with anatomy. —**an·a·tom'i·cal·ly**, *adv.*

a·nat·o·mist (ə·nat'ə·mist), *n.* 1. an expert in anatomy. 2. person who dissects or analyzes.

a·nat·o·mize (ə·nat'ə·mīz), *v.,* -**mized**, -**miz·ing.** 1. divide into parts to study the structure; dissect. 2. examine the parts of; analyze. —**a·nat'o·mi·za'tion**, *n.*

a·nat·o·my (ə·nat'ə·mi), *n., pl.* -**mies.** 1. structure of an animal or plant. 2. science of the structure of animals and plants. 3. dissecting of animals or plants to study their structure. 4. examination of the parts or elements of a thing; analysis. [< LL < Gk., < *ana-* up + *tomos* cutting]

anc., ancient.

-ance, *suffix.* 1. act or fact of ——ing, as in *avoidance.* 2. quality or state of being ——ed, as in *annoyance.* 3. quality or state of being ——ant, as in *importance.* 4. thing that ——s, as in *conveyance.* 5. what is ——ed, as in *contrivance.* [< F < L *-antia, -entia*]

an·ces·tor (an'ses·tər), *n.* 1. person from whom one is descended (opposite of *descendant*). 2. *Biol.* early form from which the species or group in question has descended. 3. the precursor of a later type. [< OF *ancestre* < L *antecessor* < *ante* before + *cedere* go] —Syn. 1. forefather.

an·ces·tral (an·ses'trəl), *adj.* 1. of or pertaining to ancestors: *the ancestral home of the Pilgrims was England.* 2. inherited from ancestors. —**an·ces'tral·ly**, *adv.*

an·ces·tress (an'ses·tris), *n.* a woman ancestor.

an·ces·try (an'ses·tri), *n., pl.* -**tries.** 1. line of descent from ancestors; lineage. 2. honorable descent. 3. parents, grandparents, and other ancestors.

an·chor (ang'kər), *n.* 1. shaped piece of iron attached to a chain or rope and used to hold a ship in place. 2. thing for holding something else in place. 3. something that makes a person feel safe and secure.

Anchor

4. **at anchor**, held by an anchor. 5. **cast anchor**, drop the anchor. —*v.* 1. hold in place by an anchor: *anchor a ship.* 2. drop anchor; stop or stay in place by using an anchor. 3. hold in

place; fix firmly. [< L < Gk. *ankyra*] —**an'chor·less**, *adj.* —**an'chor·like'**, *adj.*

an·chor·age (ang'kər·ij), *n.* 1. place to anchor. 2. money paid for the right to anchor. 3. an anchoring or being anchored. 4. something to hold on to or depend on.

an·cho·ress (ang'kə·ris), *n.* a woman anchorite.

an·cho·rite (ang'kə·rīt), **an·cho·ret** (ang'kə·rit; -ret), *n.* 1. person who lives alone in a solitary place for religious meditation. 2. hermit. [< Med.L < LL < Gk. *anachoretes*, < *ana-* back + *choreein* withdraw] —**an·cho·rit·ic** (ang'kə·rit'ik), **an·cho·ret·ic** (-ret'ik), *adj.*

an·cho·vy (an'chō·vi; -chə·vi; an·chō'vi), *n., pl.* -**vies.** a very small fish that looks somewhat like a herring. Anchovies are pickled or made into a paste. [< Sp. and Pg. *anchova* < VL *apiuva* < Gk. *aphye*]

an·cienne no·blesse (äN·syen' nô·bles'), *French.* 1. the old nobility before the French Revolution. 2. the old nobility.

an·cien ré·gime (äN·syaN' rā·zhēm'), *French.* 1. the social and political structure of France before the Revolution of 1789. 2. the old order of things.

an·cient (ān'shənt), *adj.* 1. pertaining to the period of history before the fall of the Western Roman Empire (476 A.D.). 2. existing or occurring in time long past: *ancient records.* 3. of great age; very old: *an ancient city.* 4. having to do with the ancients. 5. old-fashioned; antique. —*n.* 1. a very old person. 2. **the ancients**, a. people who lived long ago, such as the Greeks and Romans. b. the classical authors of ancient times. [< OF *ancien* < LL, < L *ante* before] —**an'cient·ness**, *n.*

an·cient·ly (ān'shənt·li), *adv.* in ancient times.

an·cil·lar·y (an'sə·ler'i), *adj.* 1. subordinate. 2. assisting. [< L, < *ancilla* handmaid]

an·con (ang'kon), *n., pl.* **an·co·nes** (ang·kō'nēz). 1. elbow. 2. projection like a bracket, used to support a cornice. [< L < Gk. *ankon* bend] —**an·co·nal** (ang'kə·nəl), **an·co·ne·al** (ang·kō'ni·əl), *adj.*

-ancy, *suffix.* variant of **-ance**, as in *infancy.*

and (and; *unstressed* ənd, ən), *conj.* 1. as well as: *nice and cold.* 2. added to; with: *ham and eggs.* 3. as a result: *the sun came out and the grass dried.* 4. *Colloq.* to: *try and come.* [OE] ➤ **And** is a coördinating conjunction, that is, it connects words, phrases, or clauses of equal grammatical value.

An·da·lu·sia (an'də·lü'zhə; -shə), *n.* region in S Spain. —**An'da·lu'sian**, *adj., n.*

an·dan·te (an·dan'tē; än·dän'tā), *Music.* —*adj.* moderately slow. —*adv.* in andante time. —*n.* piece in andante time. [< Ital., < *andare* walk]

An·der·sen (an'dər·sən), *n.* Hans Christian, 1805–1875, Danish writer of fairy tales.

An·des (an'dēz), *n.pl.* mountain system in W South America. —**An·de·an** (an·dē'ən; an'di-), *adj., n.*

and·i·ron (and'ī'ərn), *n.* one of a pair of metal supports for wood burned in a fireplace. [< OF *andier*; *-iron* by association with *iron*]

and/or, both or either. ➤ **And/or** is primarily a business and legal locution. It is useful when three alternatives exist (both circumstances mentioned or either one of the two).

An·dor·ra (an·dôr'ə; -dor'ə), *n.* 1. a small country between France and Spain. 2. its capital.

An·drew (an'drü), *n. Bible.* one of Jesus' apostles.

an·dro·gen (an'drə·jən), *n. Biochem.* any substance that induces or strengthens masculine characteristics, as a male sex hormone. [< Gk. *aner* (*andr-*) male + *-genes* born, produced] —**an·dro·gen·ic** (an'drə·jen'ik), *adj.*

an·drog·y·nous (an·droj'ə·nəs), *adj.* 1. *Bot.* having male and female flowers in the same cluster. 2. hermaphroditic. [< L < Gk., < *aner* (*andr-*) man + *gyne* woman] —**an·drog'y·ny**, *n.*

An·drom·a·che (an·drom′ə·kē), *n. Gk. Leg-end.* the loyal wife of Hector.

an·ec·dot·age (an′ik·dōt′ij), *n.* **1.** anecdotes. **2.** talkative old age. [for def. 2, see DOTAGE]

an·ec·do·tal (an′ik·dō′təl; an′ik·dō′təl), *adj.* of anecdotes; containing anecdotes.

an·ec·dote (an′ik·dōt), *n.* short account of some interesting incident or event. [< Med.L < Gk. *anekdota* (things) unpublished < *an-* not + *ek-* out + *didonai* give] —**an·ec·dot·ic** (an′-ik·dot′ik), **an′ec·dot′i·cal,** *adj.*

a·ne·mi·a (ə·nē′mi·ə), *n.* deficiency of the blood; insufficiency of red corpuscles or hemoglobin in the blood. Also, **anaemia.** [< NL < Gk. *anaimia* lack of blood < *an-* not + *haima* blood] —**a·ne·mic** (ə·nē′mik), *adj.*

an·e·mom·e·ter (an′ə·mom′ə·tər), *n.* instrument for measuring the velocity or pressure of the wind. [< Gk. *anemos* wind + -METER] —**an·e·mo·met·ric** (an′ə·mō·met′rik), **an′e·mo·met′-ri·cal,** *adj.*

a·nem·o·ne (ə·nem′ə·nē), *n.* **1.** plant with small white flowers that blossoms early in the spring. **2.** plant of the same genus with much larger, bright-red, blue, or white flowers. **3.** sea anemone. [< L < Gk., wind flower, < *anemos* wind]

a·nent (ə·nent′), *prep.* **1.** *Archaic or Scot.* concerning. **2.** *Dial.* beside. [OE *on emn, on efn* on even (ground with)]

an·er·oid (an′ər·oid), *adj.* using no fluid. —*n.* an aneroid barometer. [< F *anéroïde* < Gk. *a-* without + LGk. *neros* water] *Sea anemone*

aneroid barometer, barometer that works by the pressure of air on the elastic lid of a box containing no air.

an·es·the·sia (an′əs·thē′zhə), *n. Am.* entire (**general**) or partial (**local**) loss of sensation by means of ether, chloroform, hypnotism, etc., or as the result of hysteria, paralysis, or disease. Also, **anaesthesia.** [< NL < Gk., < *an-* without + *aisthesis* sensation]

an·es·thet·ic (an′əs·thet′ik), *Am.* —*n.* substance that causes anesthesia, as ether. —*adj.* **1.** causing anesthesia. **2.** of or with anesthesia: *anesthetic effects.* Also, **anaesthetic.** —**an′es-thet′i·cal·ly,** *adv.*

an·es·the·tist (ə·nes′thə·tist), *n.* person whose work is giving anesthetics during operations, etc. Also, **anaesthetist.**

an·es·the·tize (ə·nes′thə·tīz), *v.,* **-tized, -tizing.** make unable to feel pain, touch, cold, etc.; make insensible. Also, **anaesthetize.** —**an·es·the·ti·za·tion** (ə·nes′thə·tə·zā′shən; an′əs·thet′ə-), *n.* —**an·es′the·tiz′er,** *n.*

an·eu·rysm, an·eu·rism (an′yə·riz·əm), *n. Pathol.* a permanent swelling of an artery, due to pressure of the blood on a part weakened by disease or injury. [< Gk. *aneurysma* dilatation, < *ana-* up + *eurys* wide] —**an′eu·rys′mal, an′-eu·ris′mal,** *adj.*

a·new (ə·nū′; ə·nū′), *adv.* **1.** once more; again: *to arm anew.* **2.** in a new form or way. [OE *of-niowe.* See NEW.]

an·gel (ān′jəl), *n.* **1.** *Theol.* one of an order of spiritual beings that are attendants and messengers of God. **2.** conventional representation of such a being. **3.** person as good or lovely as an angel. **4.** any spirit, either good or bad. **5.** *Am., Slang.* person who pays for producing a play. **6.** an old English coin in use between 1465 and 1634. [< L < Gk. *angelos* messenger]

angel cake, or **angel food cake,** *Am.* delicate, white, spongy cake made of the whites of eggs, sugar, and a little flour.

an·gel·fish (ān′jəl·fish′), *n., pl.* **-fish·es** or (*esp. collectively*) **-fish. 1.** shark with large pectoral fins that extend like wings. **2.** any of several showy tropical fish.

an·gel·ic (an·jel′ik), **an·gel·i·cal** (-ə·kəl), *adj.* **1.** of angels; heavenly. **2.** like an angel; pure; innocent; good and lovely. —**an·gel′i·cal·ly,** *adv.*

an·gel·i·ca (an·jel′ə·kə), *n.* perennial plant of the same family as the carrot, used in cooking, in medicine, etc. [< Med.L; named from its use as an antidote]

An·ge·li·co (an·jel′ə·kō), *n.* **Fra,** 1387–1455, Italian painter.

An·ge·lus (an′jə·ləs), *n.* **1.** prayer said by Roman Catholics in memory of Christ's assuming human form. **2.** bell rung at morning, noon, and night as a signal for Roman Catholics to say this prayer. [from first word in service]

an·ger (ang′gər), *n.* the feeling one has toward something that hurts, opposes, offends, or annoys; wrath. —*v.* **1.** make angry. **2.** become angry: *he angers easily.* [< Scand. *angr* grief] —**Syn.** *n.* fury, rage.

an·gi·na (an·jī′nə; *in Med. often* an′jə·nə), *n.* **1.** any inflammatory disease of the throat, such as quinsy, croup, or mumps. **2.** angina pectoris. [< L, quinsy, < *angere* choke]

angina pec·to·ris (pek′tə·ris), serious disease of the heart that causes sharp chest pains and a feeling of being suffocated.

an·gi·o·sperm (an′ji·ō·spėrm′), *n.* plant having its seeds enclosed in an ovary; a flowering plant. [< NL, < Gk. *angeion* vessel + *sperma* seed] —**an′gi·o·sper′mous,** *adj.*

an·gle¹ (ang′gəl), *n., v.,* **-gled, -gling.** —*n.* **1.** *Geom.* a space between two lines or surfaces that meet. **b.** figure formed by two such lines or surfaces. **c.** difference in direction between two such lines or surfaces. **2.** corner. **3.** point of view. **4.** one aspect of something; phase. —*v.* **1.** *Am.* move at an angle. **2.** turn or bend at an angle. **3.** present with bias or prejudice. [< F < L *angulus*] —**an′gled,** *adj.*

ACUTE   RIGHT   OBTUSE

an·gle² (ang′gəl), *v.,* **-gled, -gling. 1.** fish with a hook and line. **2.** scheme to get: *she angled for an invitation to his party by flattering him.* [OE *angel* fishhook] —**an′gler,** *n.*

angle iron, a triangular strip of iron or steel.

angle of incidence. See incidence, def. 3.

angle of reflection. See reflection, def. 8.

An·gles (ang′gəlz), *n.pl.* a Germanic tribe that settled in England in the fifth century A.D. —**An·gli·an** (ang′gli·ən), *adj., n.*

an·gle·worm (ang′gəl·wėrm′), *n.* earthworm.

An·gli·can (ang′glə·kən), *adj.* **1.** of or having to do with the Church of England or other churches of the same faith elsewhere. **2.** *Esp. U.S.* English. —*n.* member of an Anglican church. —**An′gli·can·ism,** *n.*

An·gli·cism (ang′glə·siz·əm), *n.* **1.** *U.S.* a Briticism. **2.** custom or trait peculiar to the English.

An·gli·cize, an·gli·cize (ang′glə·sīz), *v.,* **-cized, -ciz·ing.** make or become English in form, pronunciation, habits, customs, or character. *Chauffeur* and *garage* are French words that have been Anglicized. —**An′gli·ci·za′tion,** **an′gli·ci·za′tion,** *n.*

an·gling (ang′gling), *n.* act or art of fishing with a rod and line.

Anglo-, *word element.* **1.** English, as in *Anglo-Catholic church.* **2.** English and, as in *the Anglo-American alliance.*

An·glo-A·mer·i·can (ang′glō·ə·mer′ə·kən), *Am.* —*adj.* **1.** English and American. **2.** of Anglo-Americans. **3.** *S.W.* non-Spanish. —*n.* an American, esp. a U.S., citizen of English descent.

An·glo-E·gyp·tian Sudan (ang′glō·i·jip′-shən), country in NE Africa formerly under the control of Great Britain and Egypt. See Sudan.

An·glo-French (ang′glō-french′), *adj.* of or having to do with England and France together. —*n.* the dialect of French spoken by the Normans in England (esp. 1066–c1154); Anglo-Norman; Norman-French.

An·glo·ma·ni·a (ang′glə·mā′ni·ə), *n. Am.* craze for English institutions and customs, esp. for imitating them. —**An′glo·ma′ni·ac,** *n.*

An·glo-Nor·man (ang′glō-nôr′mən), *n.* **1.** one of the Normans who lived in England after its conquest in 1066. **2.** descendant of an English

Norman. 3. Anglo-French. —*adj.* English and Norman.

An·glo·phile (ang'glə·fīl), **An·glo·phil** (-fil), *n.* friend or admirer of England or the English.

An·glo-Sax·on (ang'glō·sak'sən), *n.* 1. member of the English-speaking world. 2. person of English descent. 3. plain English. 4. world English. 5. Englishman of the fifth to twelfth centuries. 6. his speech. —*adj.* 1. of the Anglo-Saxons. 2. of Anglo-Saxon.

An·go·ra (ang·gō'rə, -gō'-; *for 3, also* ang'-gə·rə), *n.* 1. variety of long-haired cat. 2. variety of goat with long, silky hair. 3. Ankara.

an·gos·tu·ra (ang'gəs·tûr'ə; -tyûr'ə), *n.* 1. the bitter bark of a South American tree. 2. Angostura, *Trademark.* a bitter tonic prepared from this bark. [for *Angostura*, Venezuela]

an·gry (ang'gri), *adj.,* –gri·er, –gri·est. 1. feeling or showing anger: *an angry reply.* 2. raging or stormy: *angry sky.* 3. moved by anger: *angry words.* 4. inflamed and sore: *an infected cut looks angry.* —an'gri·ly, *adv.* —an'gri·ness, *n.* —Syn. 1. furious, infuriated.

ang·strom unit (ang'strəm), or **angstrom**, *n. Physics.* one ten-millionth of a millimeter, a unit of measurement of the wave lengths of various radiations, as of light.

an·guish (ang'gwish), *n.* very great pain or grief. [< OF < L *angustia* tightness < *angustus* narrow] —Syn. agony, torment.

an·guished (ang'gwisht), *adj.* 1. suffering anguish. 2. full of anguish; showing anguish.

an·gu·lar (ang'gyə·lər), *adj.* 1. having angles; sharp-cornered. 2. measured by an angle. In the diagram, the angular distance of P from Q, when measured from O, is the angle X. 3. not plump; gaunt. 4. stiff and awkward. —an'gu·lar·ly, *adv.* —an'gu·lar·ness, *n.*

an·gu·lar·i·ty (ang'gyə·lar'ə·ti), *n., pl.* –ties. 1. angular quality or form. 2. an angular part; an angle.

an·hy·dride (an·hī'drīd; -drid), **an·hy·drid** (-drid), *n. Chem.* any oxide that unites with water to form an acid or base.

an·hy·drous (an·hī'drəs), *adj. Chem.* 1. without water. 2. containing no water of crystallization. [< Gk., < *an-* without + *hydor* water]

an·ile (an'īl; ā'nīl), *adj.* old-womanish. [< L < *anus* old woman]

an·i·line (an'ə·lin; -līn), **an·i·lin** (-lin), *n.* a colorless liquid, $C_6H_5NH_2$, obtained from coal tar and esp. from nitrobenzene ($C_6H_5NO_2$), used in making dyes, plastics, etc. —*adj.* made from aniline.

a·nil·i·ty (ə·nil'ə·ti), *n., pl.* –ties. 1. anile condition. 2. an anile act or notion.

an·i·mad·ver·sion (an'ə·mad·vér'zhən; -shən), *n.* 1. observation often implying reproof. 2. act of criticizing; censure; criticism.

an·i·mad·vert (an'ə·mad·vért'), *v.* make criticisms; express blame. [< L, < *animum* mind + *ad-* to + *vertere* turn] —an'i·mad·vert'er, *n.*

an·i·mal (an'ə·məl), *n.* 1. any living thing that is not a plant. Most animals can move about, while most plants cannot; most animals cannot make their own food from carbon dioxide, water, nitrogen, etc., while most plants can. 2. an inferior living being, as distinguished from man; brute; beast. 3. person like a brute or beast. —*adj.* 1. of animals. 2. like an animal; pertaining to the physical part of man's nature. [< L, < *anima* life, breath]

an·i·mal·cule (an'ə·mal'kūl), *n.* a minute or microscopic animal. [< NL *animalculum,* dim. of L *animal*] —an'i·mal·cu·lar, *adj.*

an·i·mal·ism (an'ə·məl·iz'əm), *n.* 1. animal existence, nature, or enjoyment. 2. doctrine that human beings are mere animals without souls. —an'i·mal·ist, *n.* —an'i·mal·is'tic, *adj.*

an·i·mal·i·ty (an'ə·mal'ə·ti), *n.* 1. animal nature or character in man. 2. animal life.

animal magnetism, hypnotism; mesmerism.
animal spirits, natural liveliness.

an·i·mate (*v.* an'ə·māt; *adj.* an'ə·mit), *v.,* -mat·ed, -mat·ing, *adj.* —*v.* 1. give life to; make alive. 2. make lively, gay, or vigorous. 3. inspire; encourage. 4. put into action; cause to act or work. —*adj.* 1. living; alive: *all plants and animals are animate.* 2. lively; gay; vigorous. [< L, < *anima* life, breath] —an'i·mate·ly, *adv.* —an'i·mat'er, *an* al'ma'tor, *n.* —an'i·ma'tion, *n.*

an·i·mat·ed (an'ə·māt'id), *adj.* 1. lively; gay. 2. living. —an'i·mat'ed·ly, *adv.*

animated cartoon, series of drawings arranged to be photographed and shown like a motion picture. Each drawing shows a slight change from the one before it.

an·i·mat·ing (an'ə·māt'ing), *adj.* giving life to; making lively; inspiring; encouraging. —an'i·mat'ing·ly, *adv.*

an·i·mism (an'ə·miz·əm), *n.* the belief that animals, trees, rocks, and other natural objects have souls. [< L *anima* life] —an'i·mist, *n.* —an'i·mis'tic, *adj.*

an·i·mos·i·ty (an'ə·mos'ə·ti), *n., pl.* –ties. violent hatred; active enmity.

an·i·mus (an'ə·məs), *n.* 1. violent hatred; ill will; active dislike or enmity. 2. moving spirit; intention. [< L, spirit]

an·i·on (an'ī'ən), *n. Physical Chem.* 1. a negatively charged ion that moves toward the positive pole in electrolysis. 2. atom or group of atoms having a negative charge. [< Gk., (thing) going up, < *ana-* up + *ienai* go]

an·ise (an'is), *n.* 1. plant of the carrot family grown for its fragrant seeds. 2. the seed. [< OF < L < Gk. *anison*]

an·i·seed (an'ə·sēd; an'is·sēd'), *n.* seed of anise, used as a flavoring or in medicine.

An·jou (an'jü), *n.* a former duchy in W France.

An·ka·ra (ang'kə·rə; äng'-), *n.* capital of Turkey since 1923. Also, Angora.

an·kle (ang'kəl), *n.* 1. joint that connects the foot and the leg. 2. part of the leg between this joint and the calf. [< Scand. Cf. Dan. *ankel.*]

an·kle·bone (ang'kəl·bōn'), *n. Anat.* talus.

an·klet (ang'klit), *n.* 1. a short sock. 2. band, often ornamental, worn around the ankle.

an·ky·lo·sis (ang'kə·lō'sis), *n.* 1. *Anat.* a growing together of bones as a result of disease or injury. 2. *Pathol.* stiffness of a joint caused by this. [< NL < Gk., < *ankyloein* stiffen < *ankylos* crooked] —an'ky·lot·ic (ang'kə·lot'ik), *adj.*

an·na (an'ə), *n.* in India: a. one-sixteenth of a rupee. b. a coin having this value.

an·nal·ist (an'əl·ist), *n.* writer of annals. —an'nal·is'tic, *adj.*

an·nals (an'əlz), *n.pl.* 1. a written account of events year by year. 2. historical records; history. [< L, < *annus* year]

An·nam (ə·nam'; an'am), *n.* a former French protectorate in Indo-China, now part of Viet-Nam. —An·na·mese (an'ə·mēz'; -mēs'), *adj., n.*

An·nap·o·lis (ə·nap'ə·lis), *n.* seaport and capital of Maryland, site of the U.S. Naval Academy.

Anne (an), *n.* 1665–1714, queen of Great Britain and Ireland, 1702–14.

an·neal (ə·nēl'), *v.* toughen (glass, metals, etc.) by heating and then cooling; temper. [OE *anǣlan* < *an-* on + *ǣlan* burn] —an·neal'er, *n.*

an·ne·lid (an'ə·lid), *Zool.* —*n.* one of the phylum of segmented worms, as the earthworms and leeches. —*adj.* of or having to do with annelids. [< F < F *annel* ring < L *anellus,* double dim. of *anus* ring] —an·nel·i·dan (ə·nel'ə·dən), *adj., n.*

an·nex (*v.* ə·neks'; *n.* an'eks), *v.* 1. to join or add to a larger thing: *the United States annexed Texas in 1845.* 2. attach as an attribute or consequence. 3. *Colloq.* take as one's own; appropriate. —*n.* 1. something annexed; an added part. 2. a supplementary building. [< Med. L, < L *annexus* < *ad-* to + *nectere* bind] —an·nex'a·ble, *adj.* —an·nex'ment, *n.*

an·nex·a·tion (an'ik·sā'shən; -ek-), *n.* 1. an

annexing or being annexed. **2.** something annexed. —**an′nex·a′tion·ist,** n.

An·nie Oak·ley (an′i ōk′li), *Am., Slang.* a free pass to a play, etc. Also, **Oakley.** [after Annie Oakley, 1860–1926, a noted woman marksman; in allusion to the resemblance between a punched pass and a small target used by her]

an·ni·hi·la·ble (ə·nī′ə·lə·bəl), n. that can be annihilated. —**an·ni′hi·la·bil′i·ty,** n.

an·ni·hi·late (ə·nī′ə·lāt), v., **-lat·ed, -lat·ing. 1.** destroy completely; wipe out of existence. **2.** bring to ruin or confusion. [< LL, < L ad- + nihil nothing] —**an·ni′hi·la′tion,** n. —**an·ni′hi·la′tive,** adj. —**an·ni′hi·la′tor,** n.

an·ni·ver·sa·ry (an′ə·vér′sə·ri), n., pl. **-ries,** adj. —n. **1.** the yearly return of a date: *a birthday is an anniversary.* **2.** celebration of the yearly return of a date. —adj. **1.** celebrated each year at the same date. **2.** having to do with an anniversary: *an anniversary gift.* [< L, returning annually, < annus year + vertere turn]

an·no Dom·i·ni (an′ō dom′ə·nī), in the year of our Lord; any year of the Christian Era. *Abbrev.:* A.D.

anon., anonymous.

an·no·tate (an′ō·tāt), v., **-tat·ed, -tat·ing. 1.** provide with explanatory notes or comments. **2.** make explanatory notes or comments. [< L, < ad- + nota note] —**an′no·ta′tor,** n.

an·no·ta·tion (an′ō·tā′shən), n. **1.** act of annotating. **2.** note of explanation.

an·nounce (ə·nouns′), v., **-nounced, -nounc·ing. 1.** give formal or public notice of: *announce a wedding in the papers.* **2.** make known; make evident. **3.** make known the presence or arrival of: *announce a guest.* [< OF < L, < ad- + nuntius messenger] —**an·nounce′ment,** n.

an·nounc·er (ə·noun′sər), n. person who announces, esp. on a radio or television broadcast.

an·noy (ə·noi′), v. **1.** make angry; disturb; trouble: *annoy by teasing.* **2.** hurt; harm; molest: *annoy the enemy by raids.* [< OF anuier < LL, < L in odio in hatred] —**an·noy′er,** n. —Syn. **1.** irritate, bother, vex, irk, tease.

an·noy·ance (ə·noi′əns), n. **1.** an annoying. **2.** a being annoyed. **3.** thing that annoys. —Syn. **3.** bother, pest.

an·noy·ing (ə·noi′ing), adj. disturbing. —**an·noy′ing·ly,** adv. —**an·noy′ing·ness,** n.

an·nu·al (an′yū·əl), adj. **1.** coming once a year: *annual celebration.* **2.** of or for a year; yearly: *an annual salary of $3,000.* **3.** accomplished during a year: *the earth's annual course around the sun.* **4.** Bot. living but one year or season. —n. **1.** an annual publication. **2.** plant that lives one year or season. [< OF < LL, < L annus year] —**an′nu·al·ly,** adv.

an·nu·i·tant (ə·nū′ə·tənt; -nū′-), n. person who receives an annuity.

an·nu·i·ty (ə·nū′ə·ti; -nū′-), n., pl. **-ties. 1.** sum of money paid every year. **2.** right to receive or duty to pay such a yearly sum. **3.** investment that provides a fixed yearly income. [< F < Med. L, < L annus year]

an·nul (ə·nul′), v., **-nulled, -nul·ling.** destroy the force of; make void: *annul a marriage.* [< LL, < L ad- + nullus none] —**an·nul′la·ble,** adj. —**an·nul′ler,** n. —**an·nul′ment,** n.

an·nu·lar (an′yə·lər), adj. ringlike; ring-shaped; ringed. [< L, < annulus ring] —**an·nu·lar·i·ty** (an′yə·lar′ə·ti), n. —**an′nu·lar·ly,** adv.

an·nu·let (an′yə·lit), n. **1.** a little ring. **2.** Archit. a ringlike molding of wood, stone, etc. [< L annulus ring]

an·nu·lus (an′yə·ləs), n., pl. **-li** (-lī), **-lus·es.** a ringlike part, band, or space. [< L annulus, dim. of anus ring]

an·num (an′əm), n. year.

an·nun·ci·ate (ə·nun′shi·āt; -si-), v., **-at·ed, -at·ing.** make known; announce. [< Med.L < L, < ad- to + nuntius messenger]

an·nun·ci·a·tion (ə·nun′ci·ā′shən; -shi-), n. **1.** announcement. **2.** the Annunciation, a. the angel Gabriel's announcement to the Virgin Mary that she was to be the mother of Christ. Luke 1:26–33. b. Lady Day.

an·nun·ci·a·tor (ə·nun′shi·ā′tər; -si-), n. Am. an electric signaling device or indicator.

A No. 1, *Am., Colloq.* A one.

an·ode (an′ōd), n. positive electrode. [< Gk., < ana- up + hodos way] —**an·od·ic** (an·od′ik), adj.

an·o·dyne (an′ə·dīn), n. anything that relieves pain. —adj. soothing. [< L < Gk., < an- without + odyne pain]

a·noint (ə·noint′), v. **1.** put oil on; rub with ointment; smear. **2.** consecrate by applying oil. [< OF enoint < L, < in- on + unguere smear] —**a·noint′er,** n. —**a·noint′ment,** n.

a·nom·a·lous (ə·nom′ə·ləs), adj. departing from the common rule; irregular; abnormal. [< LL < Gk., < an- not + homalos even] —**a·nom′a·lous·ly,** adv. —**a·nom′a·lous·ness,** n.

a·nom·a·ly (ə·nom′ə·li), n., pl. **-lies. 1.** departure from a common rule; irregularity. **2.** something abnormal. —**a·nom·a·lism** (ə·nom′ə·liz·əm), n.

a·non (ə·non′), adv. **1.** in a little while; soon. **2.** at another time; again. **3.** ever and anon, now and then. [OE on ān into one, on āne in one, at once]

anon., anonymous.

an·o·nym·i·ty (an′ə·nim′ə·ti), n. state of being anonymous.

a·non·y·mous (ə·non′ə·məs), adj. **1.** of unknown or unacknowledged authorship: *an anonymous letter, pamphlet, etc.* **2.** having no name; nameless. [< Gk., < an- without + dial. onyma name] —**a·non′y·mous·ly,** adv.

a·noph·e·les (ə·nof′ə·lēz), n., pl. **-les.** mosquito that can transmit malaria.

an·oth·er (ə·nuth′ər), adj. **1.** an additional; one more: *have another glass of milk.* **2.** different; not the same: *that is another matter entirely.* —pron. **1.** one more; an additional one: *have another.* **2.** a different one: *I don't like this book, give me another.* **3.** one of the same kind: *his father is a scholar, and he is another.* [for an other]

ans., answer; answered.

An·schluss (än′shlús), n. German. union, esp. that of Germany and Austria in 1938.

an·ser·ine (an′sər·īn; -in), **an·ser·ous** (—əs), adj. **1.** of, like, or pertaining to a goose or geese. **2.** stupid; foolish. [< L, < anser goose]

an·swer (an′sər; än′-), n. **1.** words spoken or written in reply to a question: *the boy gave a quick answer.* **2.** thing done in return: *a nod was her only answer.* **3.** solution to a problem, as in mathematics. —v. **1.** reply to: *he answered my question.* **2.** make answer; reply: *I asked him a question, but he would not answer.* **3.** reply or respond by act: *he knocked on the door, but no one answered.* **4.** act or move in response to: *she answered the doorbell.* **5.** serve: *his poor excuse will not answer.* **6.** be accountable or responsible: *you must answer for your mistakes.* **7.** correspond (to) : *this house answers to his description.* **8.** answer back, Colloq. make an insolent reply. [OE andswaru < and- against + swerian swear] —**an′swer·er,** n. —Syn. n. **1.** rejoinder, retort, return. —v. **1, 2.** retort, rejoin.

an·swer·a·ble (an′sər·ə·bəl; än′-), adj. **1.** responsible. **2.** that can be answered. **3.** Archaic. corresponding. —**an′swer·a·ble·ness,** n. —**an′swer·a·bly,** adv.

answering service, an agency that cuts in on the telephone circuits of its clients to answer calls, etc. in their absence.

ant (ant), n. any member of a family of small hymenopterous insects that live with others in colonies. [OE æmete] —**ant′like′,** adj.

-ant, suffix. **1.** ——ing, as in buoyant, compliant, triumphant. **2.** one that ——s, as in assistant. See also **-ent.** [< F < L -ans, -ens]

ant., **1.** antiquary. **2.** antonym.

Ant·a·buse (an′tə·būs), n. Trademark. drug used to combat alcoholism by making a person feel ill after drinking alcoholic liquor.

ant·ac·id (ant·as′id), adj. neutralizing acids; counteracting acidity. —n. substance that neutralizes acids, such as baking soda.

Ant. Line shows actual length.

an·tag·o·nism (an·tag'ə·niz·əm), *n.* active opposition; hostility.

an·tag·o·nist (an·tag'ə·nist), *n.* one who fights, struggles, or contends with another. —*Syn.* opponent, adversary, foe, enemy.

an·tag·o·nis·tic (an·tag'ə·nis'tik), *adj.* acting against each other. —**an·tag'o·nis'ti·cal·ly,** *adv.* —*Syn.* opposing, conflicting, hostile.

an·tag·o·nize (an·tag'ə·nīz), *v.,* -nized, -nizing. 1. make an enemy of; arouse dislike in. 2. oppose. [< Gk., < *anti-* against + *agon* contest] —an·tag'o·niz'er, *n.*

ant·arc·tic (ant·ärk'tik; -är'tik), *adj.* of or near the South Pole or the south polar region. —*n.* the south polar region.

Ant·arc·ti·ca (ant·ärk'tə·kə; -är'tə–), or **Ant·arctic Continent,** *n.* land around or near the South Pole.

Antarctic Circle, the imaginary boundary of the south polar region, running parallel to the equator at 23°30′ north of the South Pole.

Antarctic Ocean, ocean of the south polar region.

Antarctic Zone, region between the Antarctic Circle and the South Pole.

ant bear, 1. a large, shaggy, gray anteater of South America. 2. aardvark.

an·te (an'tē), *n., v.,* -ted or -teed, -te·ing. —*n. Am.* stake in the game of poker that every player must put up before receiving a hand or drawing new cards. —*v. Colloq.* 1. *Am.* put (one's stake) into the pool. 2. pay (one's share). [see ANTE-]

ante-, *prefix.* before, as in *antenatal, anteroom.* [< L]

ant·eat·er (ant'ēt'ər), *n.* a mammal with a long, slender, sticky tongue, such as the pangolin or ant bear, that feeds on ants.

an·te·bel·lum (an'ti·bel'əm), *adj.* 1. before the war. 2. *Am.* before the Civil War. [< L, before the war]

an·te·ced·ence (an'tə·sēd'əns), *n.* 1. a going before; precedence; priority. 2. apparent motion of a planet from east to west.

an·te·ced·ent (an'tə·sēd'ənt), *adj.* coming or happening before; preceding; previous: *an event antecedent to this one.* —*n.* 1. a previous thing or event. 2. antecedents, a. the past life or history. b. ancestors. 3. *Gram.* word, phrase, or clause that is referred to by a pronoun. In "The dog that killed the rat is brown," *dog* is the antecedent of *that.* 4. *Math.* the first term in any ratio; the first or third term in a proportion. [< L, < *ante-* before + *cedere* go] —**an'te·ced'ent·ly,** *adv.* —*Syn. adj.* prior, earlier.

an·te·cham·ber (an'ti·chām'bər), *n.* anteroom.

an·te·date (an'ti·dāt; an'ti·dāt'), *v.,* -dat·ed, -dat·ing, *n.* —*v.* 1. be or happen before. 2. give too early a date to. —*n.* 1. a prior date. 2. date earlier than the true date.

an·te·di·lu·vi·an (an'ti·di·lü'vi·ən), *adj.* 1. before the Flood. 2. very old; old-fashioned. —*n.* 1. person who lived before the Flood. 2. a very old person. 3. an old-fashioned person. [< ANTE- + L *diluvium* deluge]

an·te·lope (an'tə·lōp), *n., pl.* -lope, -lopes. 1. a cud-chewing, deerlike animal related to cattle, sheep, and goats. 2. *Am.* pronghorn. [< OF < Med.L < LGk. *antholops*]

an·te me·rid·i·em (an'tē mə·rid'i·əm), before noon. *Abbrev.:* a.m., A.M. [< L, before midday]

an·te·na·tal (an'ti·nā'təl), *adj.* before birth.

an·ten·na (an·ten'ə), *n., pl.* -ten·nae (-ten'ē) *for 1;* -ten·nas *for 2.* 1. *Zool.* one of two feelers on the head of an insect, lobster, etc. 2. *Radio, Television.* aerial. [< L, orig., sail yard]

an·te·nup·tial (an'ti·nup'shəl), *adj.* before marriage.

an·te·pe·nult (an'ti·pē'nult; -pi·nult'), *n.* the third syllable, counting back from the end of a word. In *an te ri or, te* is the antepenult.

an·te·pe·nul·ti·mate (an'ti·pi·nul'tə·mit), *adj.* third from the end. —*n.* antepenult.

an·te·ri·or (an·tir'i·ər), *adj.* 1. toward the front; fore. 2. going before; earlier; previous. [< L, comparative of *ante* before] —**an·te·ri·or·i·ty** (an·tir'i·ôr'ə·ti; -or'-), an·te'ri·or·ness, *n.*

an·te·room (an'ti·rüm'; -rum'), *n.* a small room leading to a larger one; a waiting room.

an·them (an'thəm), *n.* 1. song of praise, devotion, or patriotism: *the national anthem.* 2. piece of sacred music, usually with words from some passage in the Bible. [< VL < LL < Gk. *antiphona.* Doublet of ANTIPHON.]

an·ther (an'thər), *n. Bot.* part of the stamen that bears the pollen. [< NL < Gk., < *anthos* flower]

ANTHER

STAMEN

Anthers

an·ther·id·i·um (an'thər·id'i·əm), *n., pl.* -id·i·a (-id'i·ə). *Bot.* part of a fern, moss, etc., that produces male reproductive cells. —**an'ther·id'i·al,** *adj.*

an·thol·o·gy (an·thol'ə·ji), *n., pl.* -gies. 1. collection of poems or prose selections from various authors. 2. collection of epigrams from various authors. [< L < Gk., < *anthos* flower + *legein* gather] —**an·tho·log·i·cal** (an'thə·loj'ə·kəl), *adj.* —**an·thol'o·gist,** *n.*

an·tho·zo·an (an'thə·zō'ən), *n.* any sea anemone, coral, or other polyp with radial segments. —*adj.* of such polyps.

an·thra·cene (an'thrə·sēn), *n.* a colorless, crystalline compound, $C_{14}H_{10}$, used in making alizarin dyes.

an·thra·cite (an'thrə·sīt), *n.* coal that burns with very little smoke or flame; hard coal. [< L < Gk., name of a gem, < *anthrax* charcoal] —**an·thra·cit·ic** (an'thrə·sit'ik), *adj.*

an·thrax (an'thraks), *n., pl.* -thra·ces (-thrə·sēz). an infectious, often fatal, disease of cattle, sheep, etc., that may be transmitted to human beings. [< LL < Gk., carbuncle, live coal]

anthrop-, anthropological; anthropology.

anthropo-, *word element.* man; human being; human, as in *anthropology, anthropometry.* [< Gk. *anthropos*]

an·thro·poid (an'thrə·poid), *adj.* manlike; resembling man. —*n.* a manlike ape. Chimpanzees and gorillas are anthropoids. —**an'thro·poi'dal,** *adj.*

an·thro·pol·o·gy (an'thrə·pol'ə·ji), *n.* science that deals with the origin, development, races, customs, and beliefs of mankind. —**an·thro·po·log·i·cal** (an'thrə·pə·loj'ə·kəl), **an·thro·po·log·ic** (-ik), *adj.* —**an'thro·po·log'i·cal·ly,** *adv.* —**an'thro·pol'o·gist,** *n.*

an·thro·pom·e·try (an'thrə·pom'ə·tri), *n.* branch of anthropology that deals with the measurement of the human body. —**an·thro·po·met·ric** (an'thrə·pə·met'rik), **an'thro·po·met'ri·cal,** *adj.* —**an'thro·pom'e·trist,** *n.*

an·thro·po·mor·phic (an'thrə·pə·môr'fik), *adj.* attributing human form or qualities to gods or things. —**an'thro·po·mor'phi·cal·ly,** *adv.*

an·thro·po·mor·phism (an'thrə·pə·môr'fiz·əm), *n.* an attributing of human form or qualities to gods or things. —**an'thro·po·mor'phist,** *n.*

an·ti (an'tī; -ti), *n., pl.* -tis. *Colloq.* person opposed to some plan, idea, party, etc.

anti-, *prefix.* 1. against; opposed to, as in *anti-British.* 2. rival, as in *antipope.* 3. not; the opposite of, as in *antisocial.* 4. preventing or counteracting, as in *antirust.* 5. preventing, curing, or alleviating, as in *antituberculosis.* [< Gk.; also (before vowels and *h*), *ant-*] ▸ **Anti-** is hyphened only before root words beginning with *i* and before proper nouns: *anti-imperialistic, anti-intellectual, anti-British, anti-Semitic. Anti-* is pronounced an'ti or often, more emphatically, an'tī.

an·ti·air·craft (an'ti·ãr'kraft'; -kräft'), *adj.* used in defense against enemy aircraft.

an·ti·bi·ot·ic (an'ti·bī·ot'ik), *n.* product of an organism, as penicillin, that works against harmful microörganisms.

an·ti·bod·y (an'ti·bod'i), *n.*, *pl.* –bod·ies. one of a class of substances in the blood, etc., that destroy or weaken bacteria or neutralize toxins.

an·tic (an'tik), *n.*, *adj.*, *v.*, –ticked, –tick·ing. —*n.* 1. Often, antics. a grotesque gesture or action; a silly trick; caper. 2. Archaic. clown. —*adj.* Archaic. grotesque. —*v.* perform antics; caper. [< Ital. *antico* old (with sense of *grottesco* grotesque) < L *antiquus* ancient]

An·ti·christ (an'ti·krīst'), *n.* the great enemy or opponent of Christ.

an·tic·i·pate (an·tis'ə·pāt), *v.*, –pat·ed, –pat·ing. 1. look forward to; expect: *anticipate a good vacation*. 2. use or realize in advance; foresee: *anticipate the disaster*. 3. consider or mention before the proper time: *anticipate a point in his argument*. 4. take care of ahead of time: *anticipate a person's wishes*. 5. be before (another) in thinking, acting, etc. 6. cause to happen sooner; hasten. [< L *anticipatus* < *ante* before + *capere* take] —an·tic'i·pa'tor, *n.*

an·tic·i·pa·tion (an·tis'ə·pā'shən), *n.* 1. act of anticipating; foretaste; use, realization, or action in advance. 2. expectation.

an·tic·i·pa·tive (an·tis'ə·pā'tiv), *adj.* tending to anticipate; having anticipation (of).

an·tic·i·pa·to·ry (an·tis'ə·pə·tô'ri; –tō'–), *adj.* anticipating. —an·tic'i·pa·to'ri·ly, *adv.*

an·ti·cler·i·cal (an'ti·kler'ə·kəl), *adj.* opposed to the influence of the church and clergy in public affairs. —an'ti·cler'i·cal·ism, *n.*

an·ti·cli·max (an'ti·klī'maks), *n.* 1. an abrupt descent from the important to the trivial. 2. descent (in importance, interest, etc.) contrasting with a previous rise. —an·ti·cli·mac·tic (an'ti·klī·mak'tik), *adj.*

an·ti·cy·clone (an'ti·sī'klōn), *n.* winds moving around and away from a center of high pressure, which also moves. —an·ti·cy·clon·ic (an'ti·sī·klon'ik), *adj.*

an·ti·dote (an'ti·dōt), *n.* 1. medicine or remedy that counteracts a poison. 2. remedy for any evil. [< L < Gk. *antidoton* (thing) given against < *anti*– against + *didonai* give] —an'ti·dot'al, *adj.* —an'ti·dot'al·ly, *adv.*

An·tie·tam (an·tē'təm), *n.* small creek in Maryland near which a major battle of the Civil War was fought in 1862.

an·ti·freeze (an'ti·frēz'), *n. Am.* substance added to a liquid to prevent it from freezing. —an'ti·freeze', *adj.* —an'ti·freez'ing, *adj.*

an·ti·fric·tion (an'ti·frik'shən), *n.* prevention or reduction of friction.

an·ti·gen (an'tə·jən), *n.* any substance that stimulates the production of antibodies.

An·ti·gua (an·tē'gə; –gwə), *n.* island SE of Puerto Rico, in the British West Indies.

an·ti·his·ta·mine (an'ti·his'tə·mēn; –min), *n.* a chemical compound used against certain allergies and against symptoms of a cold.

an·ti·knock (an'ti·nok'), *n.* any material added to the fuel of an internal-combustion engine to reduce noise during its operation.

An·til·les (an·til'ēz), *n.pl.* chain of islands in the West Indies, including Cuba, Haiti, Puerto Rico, and smaller islands near by.

an·ti·log·a·rithm (an'ti·lôg'ə·rith·əm; –log'–), *n. Math.* number corresponding to a given logarithm.

an·ti·ma·cas·sar (an'ti·mə·kas'ər), *n.* a small covering to protect the back or arms of a chair, sofa, etc. [< *anti*– against + *macassar* a hair oil from Macassar]

an·ti·mo·ny (an'ti·mō'ni), *n. Chem.* a metallic, crystalline element, Sb, with a bluish-white luster, used chiefly in alloys and medicinal compounds. [< Med.L *antimonium*] —an'ti·mo'ni·al, *adj.*, *n.*

An·ti·och (an'ti·ok), *n.* city in Turkey, the former capital of ancient Syria.

an·ti·pas·to (än'tē·päs'tō), *n.*, *pl.* –tos. *Italian.* an appetizer consisting of fish, meats, etc.

an·tip·a·thet·ic (an·tip'ə·thet'ik; an'ti·pə–), **an·tip·a·thet·i·cal** (–ə·kəl), *adj.* contrary or opposed in nature or disposition. —an·tip'a·thet'i·cal·ly, *adv.*

an·tip·a·thy (an·tip'ə·thi), *n.*, *pl.* –thies. 1. intense or fixed dislike; a feeling against. 2. object of intense dislike. [< L < Gk., < *anti*– against + *pathos* feeling]

an·ti·per·son·nel (an'ti·pėr'sə·nel'), *adj. Mil.* used against individuals, rather than against mechanized equipment, supplies, etc.

an·ti·phon (an'tə·fon), *n.* verses sung or chanted by two groups alternately in a church service. [< L < Gk. *antiphona* sounding in response < *anti*– opposed to + *phone* sound. Doublet of ANTHEM.] —an·tiph·o·nal (an·tif'ə·nəl), *adj.* —an·tiph'o·nal·ly, *adv.*

an·tip·o·dal (an·tip'ə·dəl), *adj.* 1. on the opposite side of the earth. 2. directly opposite; exactly contrary: *antipodal ideas*.

an·ti·pode (an'ti·pōd), *n.* the direct opposite.

an·tip·o·des (an·tip'ə·dēz), *n.pl.* 1. two places on directly opposite sides of the earth. 2. (sometimes sing. in use) place on the opposite side of the earth. 3. persons who live on the opposite sides of the earth. 4. two opposites or contraries: *forgiveness and revenge are antipodes*. 5. (sometimes sing. in use) the direct opposite. [< L < Gk., < *anti*– opposite to + *pous* foot] —an·tip·o·de·an (an·tip'ə·dē'ən), *adj.*, *n.*

an·ti·pope (an'ti·pōp'), *n.* a rival pope.

an·ti·pro·ton, **an·ti·pro·ton** (an'ti·prō'ton), *n.* a tiny particle of the same mass as a proton, but negatively charged, created when a proton hits a neutron.

an·ti·py·ret·ic (an'ti·pī·ret'ik), *Med.* —*adj.* checking or preventing fever. —*n.* any medicine or remedy for checking or preventing fever.

an·ti·quar·i·an (an'tə·kwâr'i·ən), *adj.* having to do with antiques or antiquaries. —*n.* antiquary. —an'ti·quar'i·an·ism, *n.*

an·ti·quar·y (an'tə·kwer'i), *n.*, *pl.* –quar·ies. student or collector of antiques.

an·ti·quate (an'tə·kwāt), *v.*, –quat·ed, –quat·ing. make old-fashioned or out-of-date.

an·ti·quat·ed (an'tə·kwāt'id), *adj.* 1. old-fashioned; out-of-date. 2. old. —an'ti·quat'ed·ness, *n.*

an·tique (an·tēk'), *adj.* 1. old-fashioned; out-of-date. 2. of or belonging to ancient Greece or Rome. 3. of or from times long ago; ancient. 4. in the style of times long ago. —*n.* 1. something made long ago. 2. antique style, usually of Greek or Roman art. 3. *Printing.* style of type. This line is in antique. [< L *antiquus* < *ante* before] —an·tique'ly, *adv.* —an·tique'ness, *n.*

an·tiq·ui·ty (an·tik'wə·ti), *n.*, *pl.* –ties. 1. oldness; great age. 2. times long ago; early ages of history; the period from 5000 B.C. to 476 A.D. 3. people of long ago. 4. antiquities, a. things from times long ago. b. customs and life of olden times.

an·ti·ra·chit·ic (an'ti·rə·kit'ik), *adj.* preventing or curing rickets.

an·ti·sa·loon (an'ti·sə·lün'), *adj. Am.* opposed to the sale of intoxicating liquor.

an·ti·scor·bu·tic (an'ti·skôr·bū'tik), *Med.* —*adj.* preventing or curing scurvy. —*n.* remedy for scurvy.

an·ti·Sem·i·tism (an'ti·sem'ə·tiz·əm), *n.* dislike or hatred for Jews; prejudice against Jews. —an·ti·Sem·ite (an'ti·sem'īt; –sē'mīt), *n.* —an·ti·Se·mit·ic (an'ti·sə·mit'ik), *adj.* —an'ti·Sem'it·i·cal·ly, *adv.*

an·ti·sep·sis (an'tə·sep'sis), *n.* 1. prevention of infection. 2. method or medicine that prevents infection.

an·ti·sep·tic (an'tə·sep'tik), *adj.* preventing infection. —*n.* substance, as iodine, mercurochrome, etc., that prevents infection. —an'ti·sep'ti·cal·ly, *adv.*

an·ti·slav·er·y (an'ti·slāv'ər·i), *adj.* opposed to slavery; against slavery.

an·ti·so·cial (an'ti·sō'shəl), *adj.* 1. harmful to the public welfare; against the common good. 2. averse to social relations.

an·tis·tro·phe (an·tis'trə·fē), *n.* 1. part of an ancient Greek ode sung by the chorus when moving from left to right. 2. stanza following a strophe and usually in the same meter. [< LL

< Gk., < *anti-* against + *strephein* turn] —an-ti-stroph-ic (an'ti-strof'ik), *adj.*

an-ti-tank (an'ti-tangk'), *adj. Mil.* designed for use against armored vehicles, esp. tanks.

an-tith-e-sis (an-tith'ə-sis), *n., pl. -ses* (-sēz). 1. the direct opposite: *hate is the antithesis of love.* 2. contrast of ideas. 3. opposition; contrast (*of or between*): *antithesis of theory and fact.* [< L < Gk., < *anti-* against + *tithenai* set]

an-ti-thet-ic (an'tə-thet'ik), **an-ti-thet-i-cal** (-ə-kəl), *adj.* 1. of or using antithesis. 2. contrasted; opposite. —an'ti-thet'i-cal-ly, *adv.*

an-ti-tox-ic (an'ti-tok'sik), *adj.* 1. counteracting diseases or poisonings caused by toxins. 2. having to do with or like an antitoxin.

an-ti-tox-in (an'ti-tok'sən), **an-ti-tox-ine** (-sən, -sēn), *n.* 1. substance formed in the body to counteract a disease or poison. 2. a serum containing antitoxin.

an-ti-trades (an'ti-trādz'), *n.pl.* winds that blow in a direction opposite to the trade winds on a level above them and descend beyond the trade-wind belt.

an-ti-trust (an'ti-trust'), *adj. Am.* opposed to large corporations that control the trade practices of certain kinds of business.

ant-ler (ant'lər), *n.* 1. a branched horn of a deer or similar animal. 2. branch of such a horn. [< OF *antoillier* < L *ante* before + *oculus* eye]

ant lion, 1. insect whose larva digs a pit, where it lies in wait to catch ants, etc. 2. its larva.

An-toi-nette (an'twə-net'), *n.* Marie, 1755–1793, wife of Louis XVI of France.

An-to-ni-nus (an'tə-nī'nəs), *n.* Marcus Aurelius, 121–180 A.D., Roman emperor 161–180 A.D. and Stoic philosopher.

An-to-ni-us (an-tō'ni-əs), *n.* Marcus (*Mark Antony*), 83?–30 B.C., Roman general, friend of Julius Caesar, and rival of Augustus.

an-to-nym (an'tə-nim), *n.* word that means the opposite of another word (contrasted with *synonym*): *"hot" is the antonym of "cold."* [< Gk., < *anti-* opposite to + dial. *onyma* word]

Ant-werp (ant'wérp), *n.* seaport in NW Belgium.

A number 1, *Am., Colloq.* A one.

a-nus (ā'nəs), *n. Anat., Zool.* an opening at the lower end of the alimentary canal. [< L, orig., ring]

an-vil (an'vəl), *n., v., -viled, -vil-ing; esp. Brit. -villed, -vil-ling.* —*n.* 1. an iron or steel block on which metals are hammered and shaped. 2. *Anat.* incus. —*v.* form or shape on or as on an anvil. [OE *anfilt*]

anx-i-e-ty (ang-zī'ə-ti), *n., pl. -ties.* 1. anxious state or feeling; troubled, worried, or uneasy feeling. 2. eager desire: *anxiety to succeed.* —Syn. 1. apprehension, dread, misgiving.

anx-ious (angk'shəs; ang'-), *adj.* 1. uneasy because of thoughts or fears of what may happen; troubled; worried. 2. eagerly desiring; wishing very much. 3. attended by uneasiness or anxiety. [< L *anxius* troubled < *angere* choke, cause distress] —anx'ious-ly, *adv.* —anx'ious-ness, *n.* —Syn. 1. concerned, apprehensive, solicitous.

anxious seat or **bench,** 1. *Am.* seat near the pulpit at a revival meeting for those who are troubled about their religious life. 2. uneasy or troubled condition.

an-y (en'i), *adj.* 1. one (no matter which) out of many: *any book will do.* 2. some: *have you any fresh fruit?* 3. every: *any child knows that.* 4. even one; even a little; even one or two: *he was forbidden to go to any house.* 5. in no matter what quantity or number: *have you any sugar?* 6. enough to be noticed: *he had hardly any money.* —*pron.* 1. any person or thing; any part: *keep the cake; I don't want any.* 2. some: *have you any?* —*adv.* in some extent or degree; at all: *has the sick child improved any?* [OE *ǣnig*] ❯ **Any** is used primarily as an adjective (*any* member of the family, *any* dog is a good dog), but also as a pronoun (*any* will do). In comparison of things of the same class, idiom calls for *any other:* "This book is better than *any*

other on the subject"; but: "I think a movie is more entertaining than *any* book" (not the same class of things). See also *anyone.*

an-y-bod-y (en'i-bod'i), *pron., n., pl. -bod-ies.* 1. any person; anyone: *has anybody been here?* 2. an important person: *is he anybody?*

an-y-how (en'i-hou), *adv.* 1. in any way whatever. 2. in any case. 3. at least. 4. carelessly.

an-y-one (en'i-wun; -wən), *pron.* any person; anybody. ❯ **Anyone** is written as one word when the stress is on the *any,* and as two when the stress is on the *one: Anyone* (en'i-wun) *would know that. I'd like any one* (en-i wun') *of them.*

an-y-place (en'i-plās), *adv. Colloq.* anywhere.

an-y-thing (en'i-thing), *pron.* any thing. —*n.* a thing of any kind whatever. —*adv.* at all.

an-y-way (en'i-wā), *adv.* 1. in any way whatever. 2. in any case. 3. carelessly.

an-y-where (en'i-hwâr), *adv.* in, at, or to any place.

an-y-wise (en'i-wīz), *adv.* in any way; at all.

An-zac (an'zak), *n.* soldier from Australia or New Zealand.

AN-ZUS (an'zùs), *n.* Australia, New Zealand, and the U.S. acting collectively for the purpose of mutual defense in the Pacific.

A one (ā' wun'), *Colloq.* first-rate; first-class; excellent. Also, A 1; A No. 1 or A number 1, *Am.*

a-o-rist (ā'ə-rist), *n. Gram.* a tense of Greek verbs indicating simple past time. [< Gk. *aoristos* < *a-* not + *horizein* to limit < *horos* boundary]

a-or-ta (ā-ôr'tə), *n., pl. -tas, -tae* (-tē). *Anat.* the main artery that conveys blood from the left side of the heart to all parts of the body except the lungs. [< NL or Med.L < Gk. *aorte*] —a-or'-tic, a-or'tal, *adj.*

a-on-dad (ä'ù-dad), *n.* a wild sheep of northern Africa. [< F < Berber *audad*]

A.P., AP, *Am.* Associated Press.

a-pace (ə-pās'), *adv.* swiftly; quickly; fast.

A-pach-e (ə-pach'ē), *n., pl.* **A-pach-es, A-pach-e.** member of a tribe of warlike, nomadic Indians living in the SW United States.

a-pache (ə-pash'; ə-pash'), *n.* one of a band of roughs and criminals of Paris, Brussels, etc. [< F; special use of *Apache*]

ap-a-nage (ap'ə-nij), *n.* appanage.

ap-a-re-jo (ap'ə-rā'hō), *n., pl. -jos. Am., S.W.* a kind of packsaddle. [< Sp.]

a-part (ə-pärt'), *adv.* 1. to pieces; in pieces; in separate parts: *take the watch apart.* 2. away from each other: *keep the dogs apart.* 3. to one side; aside: *he stood apart from the others.* 4. separately; independently: *view each idea apart.* [< F *à part* to the side. See PART.] —a-part'ness, *n.*

a-part-heid (ä-pärt'hāt), *n. South African.* racial segregation. [Du., separateness < *apart* separate < F *à part*]

a-part-ment (ə-pärt'mənt), *n.* 1. *Am.* a set of rooms in a building for a single household. 2. *U.S.* a single room.

ap-a-thet-ic (ap'ə-thet'ik), **ap-a-thet-i-cal** (-ə-kəl), *adj.* 1. with little interest or desire for action; indifferent. 2. lacking in feeling. —ap'a-thet'i-cal-ly, *adv.*

ap-a-thy (ap'ə-thi), *n., pl. -thies.* 1. lack of interest or desire for activity; indifference. 2. lack of feeling. [< L < Gk., < *a-* without + *pathos* feeling]

ape (āp), *n., v.,* **aped, ap-ing.** —*n.* 1. any of various large, tailless monkeys that can stand almost erect and walk on two feet. Chimpanzees, gorillas, orang-utans, and gibbons are apes. 2. any monkey. 3. person who imitates or mimics. —*v.* imitate; mimic. [OE *apa*] —ape'like', *adj.*

Ap-en-nines (ap'ə-nīnz), *n.pl.* mountain system extending north and south in Italy.

a-pe-ri-ent (ə-pir'i-ənt), *Med.* —*adj.* laxative. —*n.* a mild laxative. [< L, < *aperire* open]

a-pe-ri-tif (ä-pā-rē-tēf'), *n. French.* 1. alcoholic drink taken as an appetizer. 2. appetizer.

ap-er-ture (ap'ər-chúr; -chər), *n.* 1. an opening; gap; hole. 2. in a telescope, camera, etc., the diameter of the exposed part of a lens. [< L *apertura* < *aperire* open. Doublet of OVERTURE.] —ap′er·tured, *adj.*

a·pet·al·ous (ā-pet′əl-əs), *adj. Bot.* having no petals.

a·pex (ā′peks), *n., pl.* a·pex·es, ap·i·ces. 1. the highest point; tip. 2. climax. [< L]

a·pha·sia (ə-fā′zhə), *n. Pathol.* loss of the ability to use or understand words. [< NL < Gk., < *a*- not + *phanai* speak] —a·pha·si·ac (ə-fā′zi-ak), *adj., n.* —a·pha·sic (ə-fā′zik; -sik), *adj., n.*

a·phe·li·on (ə-fē′li-ən; a–), *n., pl.* -li·a (-li-ə). *Astron.* point most distant from the sun, in the orbit of a planet or comet.[<NL < Gk. *apo*– away from + *helios* sun]

a·phid (ā′fid; af′id), a·phis (ā′fis; af′is), *n., pl.* a·phids; aph·i·des (af′ə-dēz). a very small insect that lives by sucking juices from plants; plant louse. [< NL *aphis*] —a·phid·i·an (ə-fid′i-ən), *adj., n.*

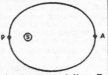

A, planet at aphelion; P, same planet at perihelion; S, sun.

aph·o·rism (af′ə-riz-əm), *n.* a short sentence stating a general truth; maxim; proverb. [< Med.L < Gk. *aphorismos* definition < *apo*- off + *horizein* to limit < *horos* boundary] —aph′o·rist, *n.* —aph′o·ris′tic, *adj.* —aph′o·ris′ti·cal·ly, *adv.*

aph·ro·dis·i·ac (af′rə-diz′i-ak), *Med.* —*adj.* exciting sexual desire; erotic. —*n.* an aphrodisiac drug or food.

Aph·ro·di·te (af′rə-dī′tē), *n.* the Greek goddess of love and beauty, identified by the Romans with Venus.

a·pi·ar·y (ā′pi-er′i), *n., pl.* -ar·ies. place where bees are kept. [< L, < *apis* bee] —a·pi·a·rist (ā′pi-ə-rist), *n.*

ap·i·cal (ap′ə-kəl; ā′pə-), *adj.* of or at the apex; forming the apex. —ap′i·cal·ly, *adv.*

ap·i·ces (ap′ə-sēz; ā′pə-), *n.* pl. of apex.

a·pi·cul·ture (ā′pə-kul′chər), *n.* the raising and caring for bees; beekeeping. [< L *apis* bee + E *culture*] —a′pi·cul′tur·al, *adj.* —a′pi·cul′tur·ist, *n.*

a·piece (ə-pēs′), *adv.* for each one; each.

ap·ish (āp′ish), *adj.* 1. like an ape. 2. senselessly imitative. 3. foolish; silly. —ap′ish·ly, *adv.* —ap′ish·ness, *n.*

a·plen·ty (ə-plen′ti), *adv. Colloq.* in plenty.

a·plomb (ə-plom′), *n.* self-possession; poise. [< F, < *à plomb* according to the plummet. See PLUMB.]

a·poc·a·lypse (ə-pok′ə-lips), *n.* 1. revelation. 2. the Apocalypse, last book of the New Testament. [< L < Gk., < *apo*- off, un- + *kalyptein* cover]

a·poc·a·lyp·tic (ə-pok′ə-lip′tik), a·poc·a·lyp·ti·cal (-tə-kəl), *adj.* 1. of the Apocalypse. 2. like a revelation; giving a revelation. —a·poc′-a·lyp′ti·cal·ly, *adv.*

a·poc·o·pe (ə-pok′ə-pē), *n.* the dropping out of the last sound, syllable, or letter in a word. *Th'* for *the* is an example of apocope. [< L < Gk., < *apo*- off + *koptein* cut]

A·poc·ry·pha (ə-pok′rə-fə), *n.pl.* 1. fourteen books included in the Roman Catholic Bible, but not accepted as genuine by Jews and Protestants. 2. apocrypha, writings or statements of doubtful authorship or authority.

a·poc·ry·phal (ə-pok′rə-fəl), *adj.* 1. of doubtful authorship or authority. 2. false; counterfeit; sham. 3. Apocryphal, of the Apocrypha. —a·poc′ry·phal·ly, *adv.* —a·poc′ry·phal·ness, *n.*

Orbit of the moon around the earth showing the apogee

ap·o·gee (ap′ə-jē), *n.* 1. furthermost point; highest point. 2. *Astron.* point most distant from the earth in the orbit of a planet, comet,

etc. [< F < Gk., < *apo*- away from + *ge* or *gaia* earth] —ap′o·ge′al, ap′o·ge′an, *adj.*

A·pol·lo (ə-pol′ō), *n., pl.* -los. 1. the Greek and Roman god of the sun, poetry, music, prophecy, and healing. 2. an extremely handsome young man.

A·pol·lyon (ə-pol′yən), *n. Bible.* the Devil.

a·pol·o·get·ic (ə-pol′ə-jet′ik), a·pol·o·get·i·cal (-ə-kəl), *adj.* 1. making an apology; expressing regret; acknowledging a fault; excusing failure. 2. defending by speech or writing. —a·pol′o·get′i·cal·ly, *adv.*

a·pol·o·get·ics (ə-pol′ə-jet′iks), *n.* branch of theology that deals with the defense of Christianity on the basis of reason.

ap·o·lo·gi·a (ap′ə-lō′ji-ə), *n.* statement in defense or justification; apology.

a·pol·o·gist (ə-pol′ə-jist), *n.* person who defends an idea, belief, religion, etc., in speech or writing; a defender.

a·pol·o·gize (ə-pol′ə-jīz), *v.* -gized, -giz·ing. 1. make an apology; express regret. 2. make a defense in speech or writing. —a·pol′o·giz′er, *n.*

ap·o·logue (ap′ə-lôg; -log), *n.* fable with a moral: *Aesop's fables are apologues.*

a·pol·o·gy (ə-pol′ə-ji), *n., pl.* -gies. 1. words of regret for an offense or accident. 2. defense in speech or writing: *an apology for the Christian religion.* 3. a poor substitute; makeshift. [< LL < Gk. *apologia* a speech in defense, ult. < *apo*- off + *legein* speak] —Syn. 2. justification.

ap·o·phthegm (ap′ə-them), *n.* apothegm. —ap·o·phtheg·mat·ic (ap′ə·theg·mat′ik), ap′-o·phtheg·mat′i·cal, *adj.*

ap·o·plec·tic (ap′ə-plek′tik), *adj.* Also, ap′o·plec′ti·cal. 1. of or causing apoplexy. 2. suffering from apoplexy. 3. showing symptoms of a tendency to apoplexy. —*n.* person who has or is likely to have apoplexy. —ap′o·plec′ti·cal·ly, *adv.*

ap·o·plex·y (ap′ə-plek′si), *n. Pathol.* sudden loss or impairment of the power to feel or think or move, caused by injury to the brain when a blood vessel breaks or the blood supply becomes obstructed. [< LL < Gk. *apoplexia*, < *apo*- off, from + *plessein* strike]

a·port (ə-pôrt′; ə-pōrt′), *adv. Naut.* to the port side; to the left.

a·pos·ta·sy (ə-pos′tə-si), *n., pl.* -sies. complete forsaking of one's religion, faith, principles, or political party. [< LL < Gk., < *apo*- away from + *stenai* stand]

a·pos·tate (ə-pos′tāt; -tit), *n.* person guilty of apostasy. —*adj.* guilty of apostasy; unfaithful.

a·pos·ta·tize (ə-pos′tə-tīz), *v.*, -tized, -tiz·ing. forsake completely one's religion, faith, principles, or political party.

a pos·te·ri·o·ri (ā pos-tir′i-ô′rī; -rī; -ō′-), 1. from particular cases to a general rule. 2. based on actual observation or experience. [< Med.L, from what comes after] —Ant. 1, 2, a priori.

a·pos·tle (ə-pos′əl), *n.* 1. Apostle, one of the twelve disciples chosen by Christ to go forth and preach the gospel to all the world. 2. any early Christian leader or missionary. 3. the first Christian missionary to any country or region. 4. leader of any reform movement or belief. 5. *Am.* one of the council of twelve officials of the Mormon Church who help administer the affairs of the church. [< L < Gk. *apostolos* messenger < *apo*- off + *stellein* send] —a·pos′tle·ship, *n.*

Apostles' Creed, statement of belief that contains the fundamental doctrines of Christianity.

ap·os·tol·ic (ap′əs-tol′ik), ap·os·tol·i·cal (-ə-kəl), *adj.* 1. of or having to do with apostles, esp. the twelve Apostles. 2. according to the beliefs and teachings of the Apostles. 3. of the Pope; papal. —ap′os·tol′i·cal·ly, *adv.* —ap·os·tol·i·cism (ap′əs·tol′ə·siz-əm), *n.* —a·pos·to·lic·i·ty (ə-pos′tə·lis′ə-ti), *n.*

Apostolic See, bishopric of the Pope.

a·pos·tro·phe¹ (ə-pos′trə-fē), *n.* sign (') used to show: a. omission of one or more letters, as in *o'er* for *over*, *thro'* for *through*. b. the possessive forms of nouns, as in *John's book*, *the lions' den.*

c. certain plurals, as in *two o's, four 9's in 9,999.* [< F < LL < Gk. *apostrophos* (*prosodia*) omission (mark) < *apostrephein* avert, get rid of. See APOSTROPHE[2].] ❯ The apostrophe is used: (1) to indicate genitive (possessive) case of nouns and of the indefinite pronouns (*anyone, nobody, someone*): *Dorothy's first picture, the companies' original charters, everybody's business;* (2) to show the omission of one or more letters in contractions: *can't, I'm, I'll, it's* [it is]; (3) in plurals of figures, letters of the alphabet, and words being discussed as words: *three e's, the 1920's, the first of the two that's* (there is a growing tendency to omit this apostrophe); (4) to show that certain sounds represented in the usual spelling were not spoken: *Good mornin'.*

a·pos·tro·phe² (ə·pos′trə·fē), *n.* words addressed to an absent person as if he were present or to a thing or idea as if it could appreciate them. [< LL < Gk., < *apo–* away from + *strephein* turn] —**ap·os·troph·ic** (ap′əs·trof′ik), *adj.*

a·pos·tro·phize (ə·pos′trə·fīz), *v.,* –phized, –phiz·ing. 1. stop in a speech, poem, etc., and address some person or thing, usually with emotion. 2. address an apostrophe to. 3. mark with an apostrophe.

apothecaries' measure, system of units used in the U.S. in compounding and dispensing liquid drugs.

apothecaries' weight, system of weights used in mixing drugs and filling prescriptions.

a·poth·e·car·y (ə·poth′ə·ker′i), *n., pl.* –car·ies. 1. druggist. 2. *Brit., Obs.* person who prescribed medicines and sold them. [< LL *apothecarius* warehouseman, < L *apotheca* storehouse < Gk., < *apo–* away + *tithenai* put]

ap·o·thegm (ap′ə·them), *n.* a short, forceful saying; maxim. Also, **apophthegm.** [< Gk. *apophthegma* < *apo–* forth + *phthengesthai* utter] —**ap·o·theg·mat·ic** (ap′ə·theg·mat′ik), **ap·o·theg·mat′i·cal,** *adj.* —**ap′o·theg·mat′i·cal·ly,** *adv.*

a·poth·e·o·sis (ə·poth′i·ō′sis; ap′ə·thē′ə·sis), *n., pl.* –ses (–sēz). 1. raising of a human being to the rank of a god; deification. 2. glorification; exaltation. 3. a glorified ideal. [< L < Gk., ult. < *apo–* + *theos* god]

a·poth·e·o·size (ə·poth′i·ə·sīz; ap′ə·thē′ə·sīz), *v.,* –sized, –siz·ing. 1. make a god of; deify. 2. glorify; exalt.

app., 1. apparent; apparently. 2. appendix.

Ap·pa·la·chi·ans (ap′ə·lā′chi·ənz, –lach′i-ənz; –lā′chənz, –lach′ənz), or **Appalachian Mountains,** *n.pl.* chief mountain system of E North America, extending from Quebec to Alabama.

ap·pall, ap·pal (ə·pôl′), *v.,* –palled, –pall·ing. fill with horror; dismay; terrify. [< OF *apallir* become or make pale < *a–* (< L *ad–*) + *pale* PALE[1]]

ap·pall·ing (ə·pôl′ing), *adj.* dismaying; terrifying; horrifying. —**ap·pall′ing·ly,** *adv.*

ap·pa·nage (ap′ə·nij), *n.* 1. land, property, or money set aside to support the younger children of kings, princes, etc. 2. person's assigned portion; rightful property. 3. a natural accompaniment; adjunct. Also, **apanage.** [< F, < *apaner* give bread to, ult. < L *ad–* to + *panis* bread]

ap·pa·ra·tus (ap′ə·rā′təs; –rat′əs), *n., pl.* –tus, –tus·es. 1. things necessary to carry out a purpose or for a particular use: *chemical apparatus.* 2. any complex appliance or piece of machinery for a particular purpose. [< L, preparation, < *ad–* + *parare* make ready]

ap·par·el (ə·par′əl), *n., v.,* –eled, –el·ing; esp. *Brit.* –elled, –el·ling. —*n.* 1. clothing; dress. 2. *Archaic.* equipment. —*v.* clothe; dress up. [< OF, < *apareiller* clothe, ult. < L *ad–* + *par* equal] —Syn. *n.* 1. raiment, garb, attire.

ap·par·ent (ə·par′ənt; ə·pãr′–), *adj.* 1. plain to see; so plain that one cannot help seeing it; easily understood. 2. according to appearances; seeming: *the apparent truth was really a lie.* 3. entitled to inherit a throne, title, etc.: *heir apparent.* 4. visible to the sight. [< OF < L, < *ad–* to + *parere* come in sight] —ap·par′ent-

ness, *n.* —Syn. 1. evident, unmistakable, certain, obvious.

ap·par·ent·ly (ə·par′ənt·li; ə·pãr′–), *adv.* 1. seemingly. 2. clearly; plainly; obviously.

ap·pa·ri·tion (ap′ə·rish′ən), *n.* 1. ghost; phantom. 2. appearance of something strange, remarkable, or unexpected. 3. act of appearing; appearance. —**ap′pa·ri′tion·al,** *adj.*

ap·peal (ə·pēl′), *n.* 1. attraction; interest. 2. an earnest request; call for help, favor, mercy, etc. 3. *Law.* a. a request to have a case heard again before a higher court or judge. b. right to have a case heard again. 4. a call to a recognized authority for proof or decision: *an appeal to truth.* —*v.* 1. be attractive, interesting, or enjoyable. 2. make an earnest request; apply for help, sympathy, etc. 3. *Law.* a. ask that a case be taken to a higher court or judge to be heard again. b. apply for a retrial of (a case) before a higher court. 4. call on a recognized authority for a decision. [< OF < L, *ad–* up + *pellare* call] —**ap·peal′a·ble,** *adj.* —**ap·peal′er,** *n.* —**ap·peal′ing,** *adj.* —**ap·peal′ing·ly,** *adv.* —**ap·peal′ing·ness,** *n.* —Syn. *n.* 2. plea, entreaty, petition, solicitation.

ap·pear (ə·pir′), *v.* 1. be seen; come in sight: *the sun appeared on the horizon.* 2. seem; look: *he appears very old.* 3. be published: *the book appeared in the autumn.* 4. present oneself publicly or formally: *appear on the stage.* 5. become known to the mind: *it appears that we must go.* 6. stand before an authority: *appear in court.* [< OF < L, < *ad–* + *parere* come in sight] —ap·pear′er, *n.*

ap·pear·ance (ə·pir′əns), *n.* 1. act of appearing. 2. the coming into court of a party to a law suit. 3. outward look; aspect. 4. outward show or seeming: *keep up appearances.* 5. apparition. —Syn. 3. air, mien, countenance. 4. semblance, guise.

ap·pease (ə·pēz′), *v.,* –peased, –peas·ing. 1. satisfy, as an appetite or desire: *appease one's hunger.* 2. make calm; quiet. 3. give in to the demands of (esp. a potential enemy): *Chamberlain appeased Hitler at Munich.* [< OF, < *a* to (< L *ad–*) + *pais* peace < L *pax*] —**ap·peas′a·ble,** *adj.* —**ap·pease′ment,** *n.* —**ap·peas′er,** *n.* —**ap·peas′ing·ly,** *adv.*

ap·pel·lant (ə·pel′ənt), *n.* person who appeals. —*adj.* appellate.

ap·pel·late (ə·pel′it), *adj.* 1. appealed to. 2. having the power to reëxamine and reverse the decisions of a lower court. [< L *appellatus,* pp. See APPEAL.]

ap·pel·la·tion (ap′ə·lā′shən), *n.* 1. name; title. 2. act or mode of naming.

ap·pel·la·tive (ə·pel′ə·tiv), *n.* 1. name; title. 2. a common noun. —*adj.* that names. —**ap·pel′la·tive·ly,** *adv.*

ap·pend (ə·pend′), *v.* add; attach. [< L, < *ad–* on + *pendere* hang]

ap·pend·age (ə·pen′dij), *n.* 1. thing attached; addition. 2. *Biol.* any of various external or subordinate parts, such as a leg, fin, tail, etc. —**ap·pend′aged,** *adj.*

ap·pend·ant, ap·pend·ent (ə·pen′dənt), *adj.* added; attached. —*n.* appendage; addition.

ap·pen·dec·to·my (ap′ən·dek′tə·mi), *n., pl.* –mies. *Am., Surg.* removal of the vermiform appendix by surgical operation.

ap·pen·di·ci·tis (ə·pen′də·sī′tis), *n. Am., Pathol.* inflammation of the vermiform appendix.

ap·pen·dix (ə·pen′diks), *n., pl.* –dix·es, –di·ces (–də·sēz). 1. addition at the end of a book or document. 2. outgrowth of some part of the body, esp. the vermiform appendix. [< L. See APPEND.] ❯ The English plural **appendixes** is rapidly overtaking the Latin **appendices** and is more frequent except in quite formal usage.

ap·per·cep·tion (ap′ər·sep′shən), *n.* 1. *Psychol.* assimilation of a new perception by means of a mass of ideas already in the mind. 2. clear perception; full understanding. [< F < NL. See PERCEPTION.] —**ap′per·cep′tive,** *adj.* —**ap′per·cep′tive·ly,** *adv.*

ap·per·tain (ap′ər·tān′), *v.* belong as a part;

ap·pe·tite (ap′ə·tīt), n. 1. desire for food. 2. desire to satisfy a need. [< OF < L *appetitus* < *ad-* + *petere* seek] —Syn. 1, 2. hunger, craving, longing.

ap·pe·tiz·er (ap′ə·tīz′ər), n. something that arouses the appetite or gives relish to food.

ap·pe·tiz·ing (ap′ə·tīz′ing), adj. exciting the appetite. —**ap′pe·tiz′ing·ly**, adv.

ap·plaud (ə·plôd′), v. 1. express approval by clapping hands, shouting, etc. 2. express approval of in this way. 3. approve; praise. [< L, < *ad-* + *plaudere* clap] —**ap·plaud′er**, n. —Syn. 2. acclaim.

ap·plause (ə·plôz′), n. 1. approval expressed by clapping the hands, shouting, etc. 2. approval; praise. —Syn. 2. commendation.

ap·ple (ap′əl), n. 1. the firm, fleshy fruit of a tree of the rose family widely grown in temperate regions. 2. the tree. 3. any of various other fruits or fruitlike products, as the oak apple. [OE *æppel*]

ap·ple·jack (ap′əl·jak′), n. Am. an intoxicating liquor distilled from apple cider.

ap·ple·sauce (ap′əl·sôs′), n. 1. Am. apples cut in pieces and cooked with sugar and water until soft. 2. Slang. nonsense.

ap·pli·ance (ə·plī′əns), n. 1. thing like a tool, small machine, etc., used in doing something; device. 2. an applying.

ap·pli·ca·ble (ap′lə·kə·bəl; ə·plik′ə-), adj. capable of being applied. —**ap′pli·ca·bil′i·ty, ap′pli·ca·ble·ness,** n. —**ap′pli·ca·bly,** adv. —Syn. appropriate, suitable, fitting.

ap·pli·cant (ap′lə·kənt), n. person who applies (for money, position, help, office, etc.).

ap·pli·ca·tion (ap′lə·kā′shən), n. 1. act of putting to use; use. 2. act of applying or putting on. 3. ways of using; reference; relevancy. 4. thing applied. 5. a making of a request. 6. a request. 7. continued effort; close attention. —**ap′pli·ca′tive, ap·pli·ca·to·ry** (ap′lə·kə·tô′ri; -tō′-), adj.

ap·plied (ə·plīd′), adj. put to practical use.

ap·pli·qué (ap′lə·kā′), n., v., -quéd, -qué·ing, adj. —n. ornaments made of one material sewed or otherwise fastened on another. —v. trim or ornament with appliqué. —adj. trimmed in this way. [< F, < *appliquer* APPLY]

ap·ply (ə·plī′), v., -plied, -ply·ing. 1. put: apply paint to a house. 2. put to practical use; fit: when does this rule apply? 4. use for a special purpose: apply a sum of money to charity. 5. make a request: apply for a job. 6. use (a word or words) appropriately with reference to a person or thing: apply a nickname. 7. set to work and stick to it: he applied himself to learning French. [< OF aplier < L, < *ad-* on + *plicare* fold, lay] —**ap·pli′er,** n. —Syn. 5. petition, solicit.

ap·pog·gia·tu·ra (ə·poj′ə·tūr′ə; -tyūr′ə), n. Music. grace note. [< Ital., < *appoggiare* lean, ult. < L *ad-* on + < *podium* PODIUM]

ap·point (ə·point′), v. 1. name for an office or position; choose: this man was appointed postmaster. 2. decide on; set: appoint a time for the meeting. 3. fix; prescribe: God appointed death as punishment for sin. 4. furnish; equip: a well-appointed office. [< OF apointer, ult. < L *ad-* to + *punctum* a POINT] —**ap·point′a·ble,** adj. —**ap·point′er,** n. —Syn. 1. designate. 4. supply.

ap·point·ee (ə·poin·tē′; ap′oin·tē′; ə·poin′tē), n. person appointed.

ap·poin·tive (ə·poin′tiv), adj. Am. filled by appointment. —**ap·poin′tive·ly,** adv.

ap·point·ment (ə·point′mənt), n. 1. act of naming for an office or position; choosing. 2. office or position. 3. act of ordaining. 4. engagement to be somewhere or to meet someone. 5. appointments, furniture; equipment. —Syn. 2. post.

Ap·po·mat·tox (ap′ə·mat′əks), n. village in C Virginia where Lee surrendered to Grant, April 9, 1865.

ap·por·tion (ə·pôr′shən; ə·pōr′-), v. divide and give out in fair shares; distribute according to some rule. [< obs. F, ult. < L *ad-* to + *portio* portion] —**ap·por′tion·er,** n. —**ap·por′tion·ment,** n.

ap·pose (ə·pōz′), v., -posed, -pos·ing. 1. put next; place side by side. 2. put (one thing to another). [< F, < *a-* to + *poser* put, POSE] —**ap·pos′a·ble,** adj.

ap·po·site (ap′ə·zit), adj. appropriate; suitable; apt. [< L *appositus* < *ad-* near + *ponere* place] —**ap′po·site·ly,** adv. —**ap′po·site·ness,** n.

ap·po·si·tion (ap′ə·zish′ən), n. 1. act of putting side by side. 2. Gram. a. a placing together in the same grammatical relation. b. relation of two words or phrases when the second is added to the first as an explanation. In "Mr. Brown, our neighbor, has a new car," Mr. Brown and neighbor are in apposition. 3. position side by side. —**ap′po·si′tion·al,** adj. —**ap′po·si′tion·al·ly,** adv.

ap·pos·i·tive (ə·poz′ə·tiv), Gram. —n. noun added to another noun as an explanation; phrase or clause in apposition. —adj. placed in apposition. —**ap·pos′i·tive·ly,** adv.

ap·prais·al (ə·prāz′əl), n. 1. an appraising. 2. estimate of the value.

ap·praise (ə·prāz′), v., -praised, -prais·ing. 1. estimate the value, amount, quality, etc., of. 2. set a price on; fix the value of. [< praise, ? after prize[3], apprize[2]] —**ap·prais′a·ble,** adj. —**ap·praise′ment,** n. —**ap·prais′er,** n. —**ap·prais′ing·ly,** adv.

ap·pre·ci·a·ble (ə·prē′shi·ə·bəl; -shə·bəl), adj. enough to be felt or estimated. —**ap·pre′ci·a·bly,** adv.

ap·pre·ci·ate (ə·prē′shi·āt), v., -at·ed, -at·ing. 1. recognize the worth or quality of; think highly of: appreciate good food. 2. be thankful for. 3. be sensitive to: a blind man cannot appreciate color. 4. make or form an estimate of the value or worth of: appreciate knowledge. 5. value or estimate correctly. 6. Am. raise (currency, property, etc.) in value. 7. Am. rise in value. [< L apretiatus appraised < *ad-* + *pretium* price. Doublet of APPRIZE[2].] —**ap·pre′ci·a′tor,** n. —**ap·pre·ci·a·to·ry** (ə·prē′shi·ə·tô′ri; -tō′-; -shə-), adj. —Syn. 1. esteem, prize. 3. appraise.

ap·pre·ci·a·tion (ə·prē′shi·ā′shən), n. 1. a valuing. 2. sympathetic understanding. 3. favorable criticism. 4. Am. a rise in value.

ap·pre·ci·a·tive (ə·prē′shi·ā′tiv; -shə·tiv), adj. having or showing appreciation. —**ap·pre′ci·a′tive·ly,** adv. —**ap·pre′ci·a′tive·ness,** n.

ap·pre·hend (ap′ri·hend′), v. 1. anticipate with fear; dread. 2. arrest. 3. understand. [< L, < *ad-* upon + *prehendere* seize]

ap·pre·hen·si·ble (ap′ri·hen′sə·bəl), adj. capable of being apprehended. —**ap′pre·hen′si·bil′i·ty,** n.

ap·pre·hen·sion (ap′ri·hen′shən), n. 1. expectation of evil; fear; dread. 2. arrest. 3. understanding. 4. opinion; notion.

ap·pre·hen·sive (ap′ri·hen′siv), adj. 1. afraid; anxious; worried. 2. quick to understand; able to learn. —**ap′pre·hen′sive·ly,** adv. —**ap′pre·hen′sive·ness,** n.

ap·pren·tice (ə·pren′tis), n., v., -ticed, -tic·ing. —n. 1. person learning a trade or art. In return for instruction the apprentice agrees to work for his master a certain length of time with little or no pay. 2. beginner; learner. —v. bind or take as an apprentice. [< OF aprentis < aprendre learn. See APPREHEND.] —**ap·pren′tice·ship,** n.

ap·prise[1], ap·prize[1] (ə·prīz′), v., -prised, -pris·ing; -prized, -priz·ing. inform; notify; advise. [< F appris, pp. of apprendre learn. See APPREHEND.]

ap·prize[2], ap·prise[2] (ə·prīz′), v., -prized, -priz·ing; -prised, -pris·ing. appraise. [< OF < L appretiare. Doublet of APPRECIATE.] —**ap·prize′ment, ap·prise′ment,** n. —**ap·priz′er, ap·pris′er,** n.

ap·proach (ə·prōch′), v. 1. come near or nearer to: approach the gate. 2. come near: winter ap-

proaches. **3.** come near in quality, character, or state: *approach manhood.* **4.** make advances or overtures to. **5.** *Am.* make overtures to (a person) in an effort to bribe or corrupt him. **6.** bring near to something. —*n.* **1.** act of coming near. **2.** way by which a place or a person can be reached; access. **3.** approximation; likeness. **4.** approach or approaches, a. advance; overture. b. *Am.* advance made to a person in an effort to influence his actions improperly. **5.** *Golf.* stroke toward the green. [< OF *aprochier* < LL, < L *ad-* to + *prope* near] —ap·proach′a·ble, *adj.* —ap·proach′a·bil′i·ty, ap·proach′a·ble·ness, *n.*

ap·pro·ba·tion (ap′rə·bā′shən), *n.* **1.** approval. **2.** sanction. [< L, < *approbare* APPROVE]

ap·pro·pri·ate (*adj.* ə·prō′pri·it; *v.* ə·prō′pri·āt), *adj.*, *v.*, -at·ed, -at·ing. —*adj.* suitable; proper: *clothes appropriate for school wear.* —*v.* **1.** set apart for some special use: *appropriate money for roads.* **2.** take for oneself. [< LL, < *ad-* to + *proprius* one's own] —ap·pro′pri·ate·ly, *adv.* —ap·pro′pri·ate·ness, *n.* —ap·pro′pri·a′tive, *adj.* —ap·pro′pri·a′tor, *n.* —Syn. *adj.* fitting, meet. —*v.* **1.** allot.

ap·pro·pri·a·tion (ə·prō′pri·ā′shən), *n.* **1.** sum of money or other thing appropriated. **2.** an appropriating. **3.** a being appropriated.

ap·prov·al (ə·prüv′əl), *n.* **1.** approving; favorable opinion. **2.** consent; sanction. **3.** on approval, with permission to return (an article purchased). —Syn. **1.** commendation.

ap·prove (ə·prüv′), *v.*, -proved, -prov·ing. **1.** think or speak well of; be pleased with. **2.** speak or think favorably (of); commend. **3.** sanction; consent to: *Congress approved the bill.* **4.** prove to be; show. [< OF < L, < *ad-* to + *probus* good] —ap·prov′a·ble, *adj.* —ap·prov′er, *n.* —ap·prov′ing·ly, *adv.* —Syn. **1.** praise, laud, like. **3.** authorize, endorse, ratify, uphold.

approx., approximately.

ap·prox·i·mate (*adj.* ə·prok′sə·mit; *v.* ə·prok′sə·māt), *adj.*, *v.*, -mat·ed, -mat·ing. —*adj.* **1.** nearly correct. **2.** very like. **3.** very near. —*v.* **1.** come near to; approach: *the crowd approximated a thousand people.* **2.** come near; be almost equal: *approximate the truth.* **3.** bring near. [< L, < *ad-* to + *proximus* nearest < *prope* near] —ap·prox′i·mate·ly, *adv.*

ap·prox·i·ma·tion (ə·prok′sə·mā′shən), *n.* **1.** an approximating; approach. **2.** nearly correct amount; close estimate.

ap·pur·te·nance (ə·pėr′tə·nəns), *n.* **1.** an added thing; accessory. **2.** a minor right or privilege. [< AF. See APPERTAIN.]

ap·pur·te·nant (ə·pėr′tə·nənt), *adj.* pertaining; belonging (to).

Apr., April.

a·pri·cot (ā′prə·kot; ap′rə-), *n.* **1.** a roundish, orange-colored fruit somewhat like both a peach and a plum. **2.** tree that it grows on. **3.** pale orange-yellow. [earlier *apricock* (< Pg. *albricoque*), later infl. by F *abricot* < Pg. < Sp. < Ar. < Gk. < L, < *prae* before + *coquere* cook, ripen]

A·pril (ā′prəl), *n.* the fourth month of the year, containing 30 days. [< L *aprilis*]

April fool, person who gets fooled on April 1.

April Fools′ Day, April 1, a day observed by fooling people with tricks and jokes.

a pri·o·ri (ā pri·ô′ri; ā pri·ō′rī; -ō′-), **1.** from a general rule to a particular case. **2.** based on opinion or theory rather than on actual observation or experience. [< Med.L, from (something) previous] —Ant. **1, 2.** a posteriori.

a·pron (ā′prən), *n.* **1.** garment worn over the front part of the body to cover or protect clothes. **2.** something resembling an apron in use or shape. [< OF *naperon*, dim. of *nape* < L *nappa* napkin; ME *a napron* taken as *an apron*]

ap·ro·pos (ap′rə·pō′), *adv.* **1.** fittingly; opportunely. **2.** apropos of, concerning; with regard to. —*adj.* fitting; suitable. [< F *à propos* to the purpose]

apse (aps), *n. Archit.* a semicircular or many-sided arched or vaulted recess in a church, usually at the east end. [< L < Gk. *hapsis* loop, arch < *haptein* fasten]

apt (apt), *adj.* **1.** fitted by nature; likely: *apt to make mistakes.* **2.** suitable; fitting: *an apt reply.* **3.** quick to learn: *an apt pupil.* [< L *aptus* joined, fitted] —apt′ly, *adv.* —apt′ness, *n.* —Syn. **1.** prone, inclined, liable. **2.** apposite, appropriate. **3.** clever, bright. ❯ See likely for usage note.

apt., *pl.* apts. apartment.

ap·ter·ous (ap′tər·əs), *adj. Zool.* wingless.

ap·ter·yx (ap′tər·iks), *n.*, *pl.* -ter·yx·es (-tər·ik·siz). any of several wingless birds of New Zealand with hairlike feathers, now almost extinct; kiwi. [< NL, < *a-* without + Gk. *pteryx* wing]

ap·ti·tude (ap′tə·tüd; -tūd), *n.* **1.** natural tendency; ability; capacity. **2.** readiness in learning; quickness to understand. **3.** special fitness. [< LL *aptitudo.* See APT.]

Aq., aq., water. [< L *aqua*]

aq·ua for·tis (ak′wə fôr′tis; ā′kwə), nitric acid. [< L, strong water]

aq·ua·lung (ak′wə·lung′), *n.* a diving device consisting of cylinders of compressed air strapped to the diver's back and a glass mask placed over the eyes and nose. The supply of air to the diver is regulated automatically by a valve.

aq·ua·ma·rine (ak′wə·mə·rēn′), *n.* **1.** a transparent, bluish-green precious stone, a variety of beryl. **2.** bluish green. [< F < L *aqua marina* sea water]

aq·ua·plane (ak′wə·plān′), *n.*, *v.*, -planed, -plan·ing. —*n.* a wide board on which a person rides for sport as he is towed by a speeding motorboat. —*v.* ride on such a board for sport. [< L *aqua* water + E *plane*]

aq·ua re·gi·a (ak′wə rē′ji·ə; ā′kwə), mixture of nitric acid and hydrochloric acid. [< NL, royal water; because it dissolves gold]

a·quar·i·um (ə·kwãr′i·əm), *n.*, *pl.* a·quar·i·ums, a·quar·i·a (ə·kwãr′i·ə). **1.** pond, tank, or glass bowl in which living fish, water animals, and water plants are kept. **2.** place where collections of living fish, etc., are exhibited. [< L, of water, < *aqua* water]

A·quar·i·us (ə·kwãr′i·əs), *n.*, *gen.* A·quar·i·i (ə·kwãr′i·ī). **1.** a northern constellation supposed to represent a man pouring water out of a vase. **2.** the 11th sign of the zodiac.

a·quat·ic (ə·kwat′ik; ə·kwot′-), *adj.* **1.** growing or living in water. **2.** taking place in or on water: *aquatic sports.* —*n.* **1.** plant or animal that lives in water. **2.** aquatics, sports that take place in or on water. —a·quat′i·cal·ly, *adv.*

aq·ua·tint (ak′wə·tint′), *n.* **1.** process in which spaces, not lines, are etched by acid. **2.** etching made by this process.

aq·ua vi·tae (ak′wə vī′tē; ā′kwə), **1.** alcohol. **2.** brandy; whiskey, etc. [< NL, water of life]

aq·ue·duct (ak′wə·dukt), *n.* **1.** an artificial channel or large pipe for bringing water from a distance. **2.** structure that supports such a channel or pipe. **3.** *Anat.* canal or passage in the body. [< L, < *aqua* water + *ducere* lead, convey]

a·que·ous (ā′kwi·əs; ak′wi-), *adj.* **1.** of water; like water; watery. **2.** containing water.

aqueous humor, watery liquid that fills the space in the eye between the cornea and the lens.

aq·ui·line (ak′wə·līn; -lin), *adj.* **1.** of or like an eagle. **2.** curved like an eagle's beak; hooked. [< L, < *aquila* eagle]

A·qui·nas (ə·kwī′nəs), *n.* Saint Thomas, 1225?–1274, Roman Catholic theologian and philosopher.

Aq·ui·taine (ak′wə·tān; ak′wə·tān′), *n.* region in SW France.

Ar, *Chem.* argon.

Ar., Arabic.

Ar·ab (ar′əb), *n.* **1.** native or inhabitant of Arabia; member of a Semitic race now widely scattered over SW and S Asia and N, E, and central Africa. **2.** one of a breed of swift, graceful horses. —*adj.* of the Arabs or Arabia.

ar·a·besque (ar′ə·besk′), *n.* an elaborate and fanciful design of flowers, leaves, geometrical figures, etc. —*adj.* **1.** carved or painted in arabesque. 2. elaborate; fanciful. [< F < Ital. *arabesco* < *Arabo* Arab]

A·ra·bi·a (ə·rā′bi·ə), *n.* a large peninsula in SW Asia. —**A·ra′bi·an,** *adj., n.*

Arabian Sea, part of the Indian Ocean between Arabia and India.

Ar·a·bic (ar′ə·bik), *adj.* of or coming from the Arabs; belonging to Arabia. —*n.* the Semitic language of the Arabs.

Arabic numerals or **figures,** figures 1, 2, 3, 4, 5, 6, 7, 8, 9, 0.

ar·a·ble (ar′ə·bəl), *adj.* fit for plowing: *arable land.* [< L, < *arare* plow]

Arab League, a loose confederation, since 1945, of Egypt, Iraq, Lebanon, Saudi Arabia, Syria, Transjordan, and Yemen.

a·rach·nid (ə·rak′nid), *n.* any of a large group of small arthropods including spiders, scorpions, mites, etc. [< Gk. *arachne* spider, web] —**a·rach′ni·dan** (ə·rak′nə·dən), *adj., n.*

Ar·a·gon (ar′ə·gon), *n.* region in NE Spain, formerly a kingdom.

Ar·al Sea (ar′əl), or **Lake Aral,** inland sea in W Asia, near the Caspian Sea.

Aram., Aramaic.

Ar·a·ma·ic (ar′ə·mā′ik), *n.* a Semitic language or group of dialects, including Syriac and the language spoken in Palestine at the time of Christ. —*adj.* of or in Aramaic.

Ar·a·rat (ar′ə·rat), *n.* mountain in E Turkey.

ar·ba·lest, ar·ba·list (är′bə·list), *n.* powerful crossbow with a steel bow. [< OF *arbaleste* < LL, < L *arcus* bow + *ballista* military engine, ult. < Gk. *ballein* throw] —**ar′ba·lest·er, ar′ba·list·er,** *n.*

Man using an arbalest

ar·bi·ter (är′bə·tər), *n.* 1. person chosen to decide a dispute. 2. person with full power to decide. [< L, orig., one who approaches (two disputants) < *ad*– to + *baetere* go] —Syn. 1. judge, umpire, arbitrator.

ar·bi·tra·ble (är′bə·trə·bəl), *adj.* capable of being decided by arbitration.

ar·bi·tra·ment (är·bit′rə·mənt), *n.* decision by an arbitrator or arbiter.

ar·bi·trar·y (är′bə·trer′i), *adj.* 1. based on one's own wishes, notions, or will; not going by rule or law. 2. capricious. 3. tyrannical. —**ar·bi·trar·i·ly** (är′bə·trer′ə·li; *emphatic* är′bə·trãr′ə·li), *adv.* —**ar′bi·trar′i·ness,** *n.* —Syn. 2. willful. 3. despotic, dictatorial.

ar·bi·trate (är′bə·trāt), *v.,* –trat·ed, –trat·ing. 1. give a decision in a dispute; act as arbiter. 2. settle by arbitration. 3. submit to arbitration. [< L, < *arbiter* ARBITER] —**ar′bi·tra′tive,** *adj.*

ar·bi·tra·tion (är′bə·trā′shən), *n.* settlement of a dispute by the decision of somebody chosen to be a judge, umpire, or arbiter. —**ar′bi·tra′tion·al,** *adj.*

ar·bi·tra·tor (är′bə·trā′tər), *n.* person chosen to decide a dispute. —**ar′bi·tra′tor·ship,** *n.* —Syn. judge, umpire.

ar·bi·tress (är′bə·tris), *n.* woman arbiter.

ar·bor[1], *esp. Brit.* **ar·bour** (är′bər), *n.* a shady place formed by trees or shrubs or by vines growing on latticework. [< AF *erber* < L, < *herba* plant]

ar·bor[2] (är′bər), *n.* the main shaft or axle of a machine. [< F *arbre*]

Arbor Day, *Am.* day observed in many States of the United States by planting trees.

ar·bo·re·al (är·bô′ri·əl; –bō′–), *adj.* 1. of or like trees. 2. living in or among trees: *an arboreal animal.*

ar·bo·res·cent (är′bə·res′ənt), *adj.* like a tree in structure or growth; branching.

ar·bo·re·tum (är′bə·rē′təm), *n., pl.* –tums, –ta (–tə). botanical garden of trees and shrubs. [< L]

ar·bor vi·tae (är′bər vī′tē), an evergreen tree of the pine family often planted for hedges. [< L, tree of life]

ar·bu·tus (är·bū′təs), *n.* 1. *Am.* plant that has clusters of fragrant pink or white flowers and grows in patches on the ground; Mayflower; trailing arbutus. 2. shrub or tree of the heath family, that has clusters of large white flowers and scarlet berries. [< L]

arc (ärk), *n., v.,* arced (ärkt), arc·ing (är′king), or arcked, arck·ing. —*n.* 1. any part of a circle or other curved line. 2. *Elect.* a curved stream of brilliant light or sparks formed as a current jumps from one conductor to another. —*v.* form an electric arc. [< L *arcus* bow]

Arc (ärk), *n.* Jeanne d'. See Joan of Arc.

Arcs of circles

ar·cade (är·kād′), *n.* 1. passageway with an arched roof. 2. any covered passageway. 3. row of arches supported by columns. [< F < Pr. *arcado* < OPr. *arca* ARCH[1]] —**ar·cad′ed,** *adj.*

Ar·ca·di·a (är·kā′di·ə), *n.* a mountain district in the S part of ancient Greece, famous for the simple, contented life of its people. —**Ar·ca′di·an,** *adj., n.*

Ar·ca·dy (är′kə·di), *n.* Poetic. Arcadia.

ar·ca·num (är·kā′nəm), *n., pl.* –nums, –na (–nə). a secret; mystery. [< L, (thing) hidden, < *arca* chest]

arch[1] (ärch), *n.* 1. a curved structure that bears the weight of the material above it. 2. monument forming an arch or arches. 3. archway. 4. instep. 5. something like an arch. —*v.* 1. bend into an arch; curve. 2. furnish with an arch. 3. form an arch over; span. [< OF, < VL *arca*, irreg. var. of L *arcus* bow] —arched, *adj.*

arch[2] (ärch), *adj.* 1. chief. 2. playfully mischievous. [< *arch*–] —**arch′ly,** *adv.* —**arch′ness,** *n.*

arch–, *prefix.* chief; principal, as in *archbishop, archduke, archfiend.* [< L < Gk. *arch*(e)–, *archi*– < *archein* be first, lead]

arch., 1. archaic; archaism. 2. Arch., Archbishop. 3. Also, **archit.** architecture.

ar·chae·ol·o·gy (är′ki·ol′ə·ji), *n.* study of the people, customs, and life of the remote past by excavating and classifying the remains of ancient cities, tools, monuments, etc. Also, archeology. [< Gk., < *archaios* ancient + *logos* discourse] —**ar·chae·o·log·i·cal** (är′ki·ə·loj′ə·kəl), **ar′chae·o·log′ic,** *adj.* —**ar′chae·o·log′i·cal·ly,** *adv.* —**ar′chae·ol′o·gist,** *n.*

ar·cha·ic (är·kā′ik), *adj.* 1. no longer in general use. 2. old-fashioned; out-of-date. 3. ancient. [< Gk. *archaikos,* ult. < *arche* beginning] —**ar·cha′i·cal·ly,** *adv.*

ar·cha·ism (är′ki·iz·əm; –kā–), *n.* 1. word or expression no longer in general use. *In sooth* is an archaism meaning *in truth.* 2. use of something out of date in language or art. —**ar′cha·ist,** *n.* —**ar′cha·is′tic,** *adj.*

arch·an·gel (ärk′ān′jəl), *n.* angel of a higher rank. [< L < Gk. See ARCH–, ANGEL.]

Arch·an·gel (ärk′ān′jəl), *n.* seaport in N Russia, on the White Sea.

arch·bish·op (ärch′bish′əp), *n.* bishop of the highest rank.

arch·bish·op·ric (ärch′bish′əp·rik), *n.* 1. church district governed by an archbishop. 2. position, rank, or dignity of an archbishop.

arch·dea·con (ärch′dē′kən), *n.* assistant to a bishop in the Church of England. —**arch·dea·con·ate** (ärch′dē′kən·it), *n.* —**arch′dea′con·ship,** *n.*

arch·dea·con·ry (ärch′dē′kən·ri), *n., pl.* –ries. position, rank, or residence of an archdeacon.

arch·di·o·cese (ärch′dī′ə·sis; –sēs), *n.* church district governed by an archbishop.

arch·du·cal (ärch′dü′kəl; –dū′–), *adj.* of an archduke or archduchy.

arch·duch·ess (ärch′duch′is), *n.* 1. wife or widow of an archduke. 2. princess of the former ruling house of Austria.

arch·duch·y (ärch′duch′i), *n., pl.* –duch·ies. territory under the rule of an archduke or archduchess.

arch·duke (ärch′dük′; -dük′), *n*. prince of the former ruling house of Austria.

ar·che·go·ni·um (är′kə·gō′ni·əm), *n.*, *pl.* **-ni·a** (-ni-ə). *Bot.* the female reproductive organ in ferns, mosses, etc. [< NL, ult. < Gk. *arche* beginning + *gonos* race] —**ar′che·go′ni·al**, *adj.* —**ar·che·go·ni·ate** (är′kə·gō′ni·it; -āt), *adj.*

ar·che·ol·o·gy (är′ki·ol′ə·ji), *n*. archaeology. —**ar·che·o·log·i·cal** (är′ki·ə·loj′ə·kəl), **ar′che·o·log′ic**, *adj.* —**ar′che·o·log′i·cal·ly**, *adv.* —**ar′-che·ol′o·gist**, *n*.

arch·er (är′chər), *n*. 1. person who shoots with a bow and arrows. 2. Archer, Sagittarius. [< AF < L, < *arcus* bow]

arch·er·y (är′chər·i), *n*. 1. practice or art of shooting with bows and arrows. 2. archers. 3. weapons of an archer.

ar·che·type (är′kə·tīp), *n*. an original model or pattern from which copies are made, or out of which later forms develop. [< L < Gk.] —**ar·che·typ·al** (är′kə·tīp′əl), **ar·che·typ·i·cal** (är′kə·tip′ə·kəl), *adj.*

arch·fiend (ärch′fēnd′), *n*. 1. chief fiend. 2. Satan.

ar·chi·e·pis·co·pal (är′ki·i·pis′kə·pəl), *adj.* of an archbishop.

ar·chi·e·pis·co·pate (är′ki·i·pis′kə·pit; -pāt), *n*. archbishopric.

Ar·chi·me·des (är′kə·mē′dēz), *n*. 287?-212 B.C., Greek mathematician, physicist, and inventor. —**Ar·chi·me·de·an** (är′kə·mē′di·ən; -mə·dē′ən), *adj.*

ar·chi·pel·a·go (är′kə·pel′ə·gō), *n.*, *pl.* **-gos**, **-goes**. 1. sea having many islands in it. 2. group of many islands. [< Ital., < *arci-* chief (ult. < Gk. *archi-*) + *pelago* sea (ult. < Gk. *pelagos*); orig., the Aegean]

archit., architecture.

ar·chi·tect (är′kə·tekt), *n*. 1. person whose profession is to design buildings and superintend their construction. 2. person skilled in architecture. 3. maker; creator. [< L < Gk., < *archi-* chief + *tekton* builder]

ar·chi·tec·ton·ic (är′kə·tek·ton′ik), *adj.* 1. having to do with architecture, construction, or design. 2. showing skill in construction or design. 3. directive.

ar·chi·tec·ture (är′kə·tek′chər), *n*. 1. science or art of building, including design, construction, and decorative treatment. 2. style or special manner of building: *Greek architecture made much use of columns.* 3. construction. 4. a building; structure. —**ar′chi·tec′tur·al**, *adj.* —**ar′-chi·tec′tur·al·ly**, *adv.* —Syn. 4. edifice.

ar·chi·trave (är′kə·trāv), *n*. 1. the main beam resting on the top of a column. See the diagram of entablature. 2. the molding around a door, window, etc. [< Ital., < *archi-* chief (ult. < Gk.) + *trave* beam (< L *trabs*)]

ar·chives (är′kīvz), *n.pl.* 1. place where public records or historical documents are kept. 2. public records or historical documents. [< F < L < Gk. *archeia* < *arche* government] —**ar·chi′val**, *adj.* —**ar·chi·vist** (är′kə·vist), *n*.

ar·chon (är′kon), *n*. chief magistrate in ancient Athens. —**ar′chon·ship**, *n*.

arch·priest (ärch′prēst′), *n*. 1. chief priest. 2. chief assistant to a bishop and dean of a cathedral chapter. —**arch′priest′hood**, *n*.

arch·way (ärch′wā′), *n*. 1. passageway with an arch above it. 2. an arch covering a passageway.

arc lamp or **light**, *Am.* lamp in which the light comes from an electric arc.

arc·tic (ärk′tik; är′tik), *adj.* 1. of or near the North Pole or the north polar region. 2. extremely cold; frigid. —*n*. 1. the north polar region. 2. arctics, *Am.* warm, waterproof overshoes. [< L < Gk. *arktikos* of the Bear (constellation) < *arktos* bear]

Arctic Circle, arctic circle, 1. imaginary boundary of the north polar region running parallel to the equator at 23°30′ south of the North Pole. 2. the polar region surrounded by this parallel.

Arctic Ocean, ocean of the north polar region.

Arctic Zone, region between the Arctic Circle and the North Pole.

Arc·tu·rus (ärk·tûr′əs; -tyûr′-), *n*. a very bright star in the northern sky.

ar·den·cy (är′dən·si), *n*. being ardent.

ar·dent (är′dənt), *adj.* 1. full of zeal; very enthusiastic; eager. 2. burning; fiery; hot. 3. glowing. [< F < L, < *ardere* burn] —**ar′dent·ly**, *adv.* —**ar′dent·ness**, *n*. —Syn. 1. fervent, keen. —Ant. 1. indifferent.

ar·dor, *esp. Brit.* **ar·dour** (är′dər), *n*. 1. warmth of emotion; great enthusiasm. 2. burning heat. [< L, < *ardere* burn] —Syn. 1. fervor, zeal. —Ant. 1. indifference.

ar·du·ous (är′jü·əs), *adj.* 1. hard to do; requiring much effort; difficult. 2. using up much energy; strenuous. 3. hard to climb; steep. [< L *arduus* steep] —**ar′du·ous·ly**, *adv.* —**ar′du·ous·ness**, *n*.

are[1] (är; *unstressed* ər), *v*. plural of the present indicative of **be**: *we are, you are, they are.* [OE (Northumbrian) *aron*]

are[2] (är; ār), *n*. in the metric system, a surface measure equal to 100 square meters, or 119.6 square yards. [< F < L *area* AREA]

ar·e·a (är′i·ə), *n*. 1. amount of surface; extent of surface: *an area of 600 square feet.* 2. extent; range; scope. 3. region: *the Rocky Mountain area.* 4. level space. 5. *Brit.* sunken space at the entrance of a cellar or basement. [< L, piece of level ground] —**ar′e·al**, *adj.* —Syn. 3. tract.

ar·e·a·way (är′i·ə·wā′), *n*. *Am.* area serving as a passageway between buildings.

a·re·na (ə·rē′nə), *n*. 1. space where contests or shows take place. 2. any place of conflict and trial. [< later var. of L *harena* sand; because floor of Roman arenas was sand]

ar·e·na·ceous (ar′ə·nā′shəs), *adj.* sandy.

aren't (ärnt), are not.

Ar·es (är′ēz), *n*. the Greek god of war, identified with the Roman god Mars.

ar·ga·li (är′gə·li), *n.*, *pl.* **-li**. 1. a large wild sheep of Asia with big curved horns. 2. the bighorn, or other wild sheep.

ar·gent (är′jənt), *n. Archaic or Poetic.* silver. —*adj.* silvery. [< F < L *argentum*]

Ar·gen·ti·na (är′jən·tē′nə), *n*. country in S South America. —**Ar·gen·tine** (är′jən·tēn; -tīn), *adj.*, *n*. —**Ar·gen·tin·e·an** (är′jən·tin′i·ən), *n.*, *adj.*

ar·gil (är′jil), *n*. clay, esp. potter's clay. [< F < L < Gk., < *argos* shining]

Ar·give (är′jīv; -gīv), *n.*, *adj.* Greek.

Ar·go (är′gō), *n. Gk. Legend.* ship in which Jason and his companions sailed in search of the Golden Fleece.

ar·gon (är′gon), *n. Chem.* a colorless, odorless, inert gas, A or Ar, an element that forms a very small part of the air. Argon is used in electric light bulbs and radio tubes. [< NL < Gk. *argos* idle < *a-* without + *ergon* work]

Ar·go·naut (är′gə·nôt), *n*. 1. *Gk. Legend.* one of the men who sailed with Jason in search of the Golden Fleece. 2. *Am.* person who went to California in 1849 in search of gold. —**Ar′go·nau′tic**, *adj.*

Ar·gonne (är′gon), *n*. forest in NE France; site of battles in World War I.

ar·go·sy (är′gə·si), *n.*, *pl.* **-sies**. 1. large merchant ship. 2. fleet of such ships. [< Ital. *Ragusea* ship of Ragusa, Italian port formerly trading extensively with England]

ar·got (är′gō; -gət), *n*. jargon or slang used by a group of persons: *argot of thieves.* [< F] —**ar·got·ic** (är·got′ik), *adj.*

ar·gue (är′gū), *v.*, **-gued**, **-gu·ing**. 1. discuss with someone who disagrees. 2. bring forward reasons for or against: *argue a question.* 3. persuade by giving reasons: *he argued me into going.* 4. try to prove by reasoning; maintain: *Columbus argued that the world was round.* 5. indicate; show; prove: *her rich clothes argue her to be wealthy.* 6. raise objections; dispute. [< OF

< L, < *arguere* make clear] —**ar′gu·a·ble**, *adj.* —**ar′gu·er**, *n.* —**Syn. 1.** debate. **5.** demonstrate, denote, imply.

ar·gu·ment (är′gyə·mənt), *n.* **1.** discussion by persons who disagree. **2.** process of reasoning. **3.** reason or statement intended to persuade or convince. **4.** short statement of what is in a book, poem, etc. —**Syn. 1.** debate.

ar·gu·men·ta·tion (är′gyə·men·tā′shən), *n.* **1.** process of arguing. **2.** discussion.

ar·gu·men·ta·tive (är′gyə·men′tə·tiv), *adj.* **1.** fond of arguing. **2.** controversial. —**ar′gu·men′ta·tive·ly**, *adv.* —**ar′gu·men′ta·tive·ness**, *n.*

Ar·gus (är′gəs), *n.* **1.** *Gk. Legend.* giant with a hundred eyes, killed by Hermes. **2.** a watchful guardian.

Ar·gus-eyed (är′gəs·īd′), *adj.* watchful.

a·ri·a (ä′ri·ə), *n.* air or melody; melody for a single voice with instrumental or vocal accompaniment. [< Ital. < L *aer* air < Gk.]

Ar·i·ad·ne (ar′i·ad′nē), *n. Gk. Legend.* daughter of a king of Crete, who gave Theseus a ball of thread to help him find his way out of the Labyrinth of the Minotaur.

Ar·i·an[1] (ãr′i·ən; ar′-), *adj.* of or pertaining to Arius or his doctrines. —*n.* believer in the doctrines of Arius. —**Ar′i·an·ism**, *n.*

Ar·i·an[2] (ãr′i·ən; ar′-), *adj., n.* Aryan.

ar·id (ar′id), *adj.* **1.** dry; barren: *desert lands are arid.* **2.** dull; uninteresting. [< L, < *arere* be dry] —**a·rid·i·ty** (ə·rid′ə·ti), **ar′id·ness**, *n.* —**ar′id·ly**, *adv.* —**Syn. 2.** lifeless.

Ar·ies (ãr′ēz; -i·ēz), *n., gen.* **A·ri·e·tis** (ə·rī′ə·tis). **1.** a northern constellation that was thought of as arranged in the shape of a ram. **2.** the first sign of the zodiac; the Ram.

a·right (ə·rīt′), *adv.* correctly; rightly.

ar·il (ar′il), *n. Bot.* accessory covering of certain seeds. [< NL < Med.L *arilli* raisins]

ar·il·late (ar′ə·lāt), *adj. Bot.* having an aril.

a·rise (ə·rīz′), *v.,* **a·rose, a·ris·en, a·ris·ing. 1.** rise up; get up: *the audience arose.* **2.** move upward: *vapors arose from the swamp.* **3.** come into being or action; come about; appear; begin: *a great wind arose, accidents arise from carelessness.* **4.** originate. **5.** rebel. [OE *ārīsan*] —**Syn. 2.** ascend, mount. ➤ See rise for usage note.

Ar·is·ti·des (ar′əs·tī′dēz), *n.* 530?–468? B.C., Athenian statesman and general.

ar·is·toc·ra·cy (ar′əs·tok′rə·si), *n., pl.* **-cies. 1.** a ruling body of nobles; nobility. **2.** any class that is superior because of birth, intelligence, culture, or wealth; upper class. **3.** government in which a privileged upper class rules. **4.** country or state having such a government. **5.** government by the best citizens. [< LL < Gk., < *aristos* best + *krateein* rule]

a·ris·to·crat (ə·ris′tə·krat; ar′is–), *n.* **1.** person who belongs to the aristocracy; noble. **2.** person who has the tastes, opinions, manners, etc., of the upper classes. **3.** person who favors government by an aristocracy.

a·ris·to·crat·ic (ə·ris′tə·krat′ik; ar′is–), **a·ris·to·crat·i·cal** (-ə·kəl), *adj.* **1.** belonging to the upper classes. **2.** like an aristocrat in manners; proud. **3.** having to do with an aristocracy. —**a·ris′to·crat′i·cal·ly**, *adv.*

Ar·is·toph·a·nes (ar′əs·tof′ə·nēz), *n.* 448?–385? B.C., Greek writer of comedies.

Ar·is·tot·le (ar′əs·tot′əl), *n.* 384–322 B.C., Greek philosopher. —**Ar·is·to·te·lian** (ar′is·tə·tēl′yən; -tē′li·ən), *adj., n.* —**Ar′is·to·te′lian·ism**, *n.*

arith., arithmetic; arithmetical.

a·rith·me·tic (ə·rith′mə·tik), *n.* **1.** science of positive, real numbers; art of computing with figures. **2.** textbook or handbook of arithmetic. [< L < Gk. *arithmetike* < *arithmos* number] —**ar·ith·met·i·cal** (ar′ith·met′ə·kəl), *adj.* —**ar′ith·met′i·cal·ly**, *adv.*

arithmetical progression. See progression (def. 2).

a·rith·me·ti·cian (ə·rith′mə·tish′ən; ar′ith–), *n.* expert in arithmetic.

Ar·i·us (ãr′i·əs; ə·rī′əs), *n.* d. 336 A.D., Alexan-

drian priest who asserted that Christ the Son was subordinate to God the Father.

Ariz., Arizona.

Ar·i·zo·na (ar′ə·zō′nə), *n.* a Southwestern State of the United States. *Capital:* Phoenix. *Abbrev.:* Ariz. —**Ar′i·zo′nan, Ar·i·zo·ni·an** (ar′-ə·zō′ni·ən), *adj., n.*

ark (ärk), *n.* **1.** *Bible.* the large boat in which Noah saved himself, his family, and a pair of each kind of animal from the Flood. **2.** *Colloq.* any large, clumsy boat. **3.** *Bible.* the repository of the Jewish tables of the law. [< L *arca* chest]

Ark., Arkansas.

Ar·kan·sas (är′kən·sô *for 1;* är′kən·sô, är-kan′zəs *for 2), n.* **1.** a Southern State of the United States. *Capital:* Little Rock. *Abbrev.:* Ark. **2.** river flowing from C Colorado SE into the Mississippi. —**Ar·kan·san** (är·kan′zən), *n., adj.*

Ar·ling·ton (är′ling·tən), *n.* the largest national cemetery in the United States, in NE Virginia.

arm[1] (ärm), *n.* **1.** part of the human body between the shoulder and the hand. **2.** forelimb of an animal. **3.** anything resembling an arm in shape or use: *the arm of a chair, an arm of the sea.* **4.** power; authority. **5.** arm in arm, with arms linked. **6. with open arms,** cordially. [OE *earm*] —**arm′less,** *adj.*

arm[2] (ärm), *n.* **1.** weapon. See arms. **2.** branch of the military service, such as the infantry, artillery, cavalry, etc. —*v.* **1.** supply with weapons. **2.** prepare for war. **3.** provide with a protective covering. [< F < L *arma,* pl.] —**arm′er,** *n.*

ar·ma·da (är·mä′də; -mā′–), *n.* **1.** fleet of warships. **2.** fleet of airplanes. **3. the Armada,** the Spanish fleet sent to attack England in 1588. [< Sp. < L *armata* < *armare* to arm. Doublet of ARMY.]

ar·ma·dil·lo (är′mə·dil′ō), *n., pl.* **-los.** any of several small burrowing animals of South America and southern North America, with an armorlike shell of bony plates. [< Sp., dim. of *armado* armed (one) < L, < *armare* arm]

Armadillo
(total length 2 ½ ft.)

Ar·ma·ged·don (är′mə·ged′ən), *n. Bible.* **1.** place of a great and final conflict between the forces of good and evil. Rev. 16:16. **2.** any great and final conflict.

ar·ma·ment (är′mə·mənt), *n.* **1.** war equipment and supplies. **2.** the army, navy, and other military forces of a nation. **3.** process of equipping or arming for war.

ar·ma·ture (är′mə·chùr; -chər), *n.* **1.** armor. **2.** a protective covering. **3.** wire wound round and round a cable. **4.** *Elect.* **a.** piece of soft iron placed in contact with the poles of a magnet. **b.** a revolving part of an electric motor or dynamo. **c.** a movable part of an electric relay, buzzer, etc. [< L *armatura* < *armare* arm. Doublet of ARMOR.]

arm·chair (ärm′châr′), *n.* chair with side pieces to support a person's arms or elbows.

Ar·me·ni·a (är·mē′ni·ə; -mēn′yə), *n.* a former country of W Asia, now divided among Turkey, Iran, and the Soviet Union. —**Ar·me′ni·an,** *adj., n.*

arm·ful (ärm′fùl), *n., pl.* **-fuls.** as much as one arm or both arms can hold.

arm·hole (ärm′hōl′), *n.* hole for the arm in a garment.

Ar·min·i·us (är·min′i·əs), *n.* 1560–1609, early Dutch Protestant theologian who denied Calvin's doctrine of predestination. —**Ar·min′i·an,** *adj., n.*

ar·mis·tice (är′mə·stis), *n.* temporary stop in fighting; truce. [< NL *armistitium* < L *arma* arms + *sistere* stop, stand]

Armistice Day, Nov. 11, the anniversary of the end of World War I. See Veterans Day.

arm·let (ärm′lit), *n.* **1.** an ornamental band for the upper arm. **2.** a small inlet.

ar·mor, *esp. Brit.* **ar·mour** (är′mər), *n.* **1.** a covering worn to protect the body in fighting. **2.** any kind of protective covering. **3.** *Am.* the steel or iron plates or other protective covering of a warship or fortification. —*v.* cover or protect with armor. [< OF *armeūre* < L *armatura* < *armare* arm. Doublet of ARMATURE.]

ar·mor-bear·er (är′mər-bâr′-ər), *n.* attendant who carried the armor or weapons of a warrior.

ar·mored, *esp. Brit.* **armoured** (är′mərd), *adj.* covered or protected with armor.

ar·mor·er, *esp. Brit.* **armour·er** (är′mər-ər), *n.* **1.** person who made or repaired armor. **2.** manufacturer of firearms. **3.** man in charge of firearms.

ar·mo·ri·al (är·mô′ri-əl; -mō′-), *adj.* of coats of arms or heraldry.

armorial bearings, the design of a coat of arms.

armor plate, steel or iron plating to protect warships, forts, etc. —**ar′mor-plat′ed,** *adj.*

ar·mor·y, *esp. Brit.* **armour·y** (är′mər-i), *n., pl.* —**mor·ies;** *esp. Brit.* —**mour·ies.** **1.** place where weapons are kept. **2.** *Am.* place where weapons are made. **3.** a building with a drill hall, offices, etc., for militia.

Armor: A, Helmet; B, Gorget; C, Gauntlet.

arm·pit (ärm′pit′), *n.* the hollow under the arm at the shoulder.

arms (ärmz), *n.pl.* **1.** weapons. **2.** fighting; war. **3.** symbols and designs used in heraldry or by governments. **4.** bear arms, serve as a soldier.

ar·my (är′mi), *n., pl.* —**mies. 1.** a large, organized group of soldiers trained and armed for war. **2.** Often, **Army.** the military organization of a nation, exclusive of its navy. **3.** any organized group of people: *the Salvation Army.* **4.** a very large number; multitude. [< OF < L *armata.* Doublet of ARMADA.] —Syn. **1.** troops. **4.** throng, host.

army worm, *Am.* caterpillar that travels in large numbers and is destructive to crops.

ar·ni·ca (är′nə-kə), *n.* **1.** a healing liquid used on bruises, sprains, etc., prepared from the dried flowers, leaves, or roots of a plant of the aster family. **2.** the plant itself. [< NL]

Ar·nold (är′nəld), *n.* Benedict, 1741–1801, American general in the Revolutionary War who turned traitor.

a·roint (ə·roint′), *interj. Archaic.* begone!

a·ro·ma (ə·rō′mə), *n.* **1.** fragrance; spicy odor. **2.** distinctive fragrance or flavor; subtle quality. [< L < Gk., spice]

ar·o·mat·ic (ar′ə·mat′ik), *adj.* fragrant. —*n.* fragrant plant or substance. —**ar′o·mat′i·cal·ly,** *adv.*

a·rose (ə·rōz′), *v.* pt. of arise.

a·round (ə·round′), *prep.* **1.** in a circle about: *travel around the world.* **2.** closely surrounding: *she had a coat around her shoulders.* **3.** on all sides of: *woods lay around the house.* **4.** *U.S. Colloq.* here and there in: *he leaves his books around the house.* **5.** *U.S. Colloq.* somewhere near: *play around the house.* **6.** *U.S. Colloq.* near in amount, number, etc., to: *that hat cost around five dollars.* **7.** on the far side of: *just around the corner.* **8.** around the clock, without stopping, closing, etc.: *work around the clock.* —*adv.* **1.** in a circle. **2.** in circumference: *the tree measures four feet around.* **3.** on all sides: *a dense fog lay around.* **4.** *U.S.* here and there: *we walked around to see the town.* **5.** *U.S. Colloq.* somewhere near: *wait around awhile.* **6.** in the opposite direction: *turn around.* ➤ See round for distinction in use between *around* and *round.*

a·rouse (ə·rouz′), *v.,* a·roused, a·rous·ing. **1.** awaken. **2.** stir to action; excite. —**a·rous·al** (ə·rouz′əl), *n.* —**a·rous′er,** *n.* —Syn. **2.** stimulate, kindle.

ar·peg·gi·o (är·pej′i·ō; -pej′ō), *n., pl.* —**gi·os.** *Music.* **a.** the sounding of the notes of a chord in rapid succession instead of together. **b.** chord

sounded in this way. [< Ital., < *arpa* harp < Gmc.]

ar·que·bus (är′kwə·bəs), *n.* harquebus.

ar·raign (ə·rān′), *v.* **1.** *Law.* bring before a court for trial. **2.** call in question; find fault with. [< AF *arainer* < VL, < L *ad-* to + *ratio* account] —**ar·raign′er,** *n.* —**ar·raign′ment,** *n.*

ar·range (ə·rānj′), *v.,* —ranged, —rang·ing. **1.** put in the proper order. **2.** settle (a dispute). **3.** come to an agreement. **4.** plan; prepare. **5.** adapt (a piece of music) to voices or instruments for which it was not written. [< OF, < *a* to + *rang* rank¹ < Gmc.] —**ar·range′a·ble,** *adj.* —**ar·rang′er,** *n.* —Syn. **1.** group, sort, classify, organize. **2.** adjust. **4.** devise. —Ant. **1.** jumble.

ar·range·ment (ə·rānj′mənt), *n.* **1.** a putting or being put in proper order. **2.** way or order in which things or persons are put. **3.** adjustment; settlement. **4.** Usually, **arrangements.** plan; preparation. **5.** something arranged in a particular way, as a piece of music.

ar·rant (ar′ənt), *adj.* thoroughgoing; downright. [var. of *errant*] —**ar′rant·ly,** *adv.*

ar·ras (ar′əs), *n.* kind of tapestry. [named for *Arras,* a city in France]

ar·ray (ə·rā′), *v.* **1.** arrange in order. **2.** dress in fine clothes; adorn. —*n.* **1.** order: *in battle array.* **2.** display of persons or things. **3.** military force; soldiers. **4.** clothes; dress: *bridal array.* [< OF *a* to + *rei* order < Gmc.] —**ar·ray′er,** *n.* —Syn. *v.* **1.** marshal. —*n.* **1.** formation. **3.** troops. **4.** attire.

ar·ray·al (ə·rā′əl), *n.* an arraying; array.

ar·rear·age (ə·rir′ij), *n.* debts; arrears.

ar·rears (ə·rirz′), *n.pl.* **1.** debts. **2.** unfinished work. **3.** in arrears, behind in payments, work, etc. [< OF *arere* < LL *ad retro* to the rear]

ar·rest (ə·rest′), *v.* **1.** seize by legal authority. **2.** catch and hold. **3.** stop; check. —*n.* **1.** a seizing by legal authority. **2.** a stopping; checking. **3.** any device for arresting motion in a mechanism. [< OF < VL, < L *ad-* + *re-* back + *stare* stand] —**ar·rest′er,** *n.* —**ar·rest′ment,** *n.* —Syn. *v.* **1.** apprehend. **2.** capture. **3.** halt.

ar·riv·al (ə·rīv′əl), *n.* **1.** act of arriving; a coming. **2.** person or thing that arrives.

ar·rive (ə·rīv′), *v.,* —rived, —riv·ing. **1.** reach the end of a journey; come to a place. **2.** reach a point in any course of action: *arrive at a decision.* **3.** be successful. **4.** come, as a time, opportunity, etc.; occur. [< OF *ar(r)iver* < VL, < L *ad ripam* to the shore] —Ant. **1.** depart. **3.** fail.

ar·ro·gance (ar′ə·gəns), *n.* overbearing pride; haughtiness.

ar·ro·gant (ar′ə·gənt), *adj.* too proud; haughty. [< L, < *ad-* to + *rogare* ask] —**ar′ro·gant·ly,** *adv.* —Syn. overbearing, presumptuous. —Ant. humble.

ar·ro·gate (ar′ə·gāt), *v.,* —gat·ed, —gat·ing. **1.** claim or take without right. **2.** attribute or assign without good reasons. [< L, < *ad-* to + *rogare* ask] —**ar′ro·ga′tion,** *n.* —**ar′ro·ga′tor,** *n.*

ar·ron·disse·ment (ä·rôn·dēs·män′), *n., pl.* —**ments** (-män′). in France, the largest administrative subdivision of a department.

ar·row (ar′ō), *n.* **1.** a slender, pointed shaft or stick for shooting from a bow. **2.** anything resembling an arrow in shape or speed. **3.** a sign (→) used to show direction or position. [OE *arwe*]

ar·row·head (ar′ō·hed′), *n.* **1.** head or tip of an arrow. **2.** plant with leaves shaped like arrowheads.

ar·row·root (ar′ō·rüt′; -rut′), *n. Am.* **1.** an easily digested starch made from the roots of a tropical American plant. **2.** the plant itself.

Indian arrowhead

ar·row·wood (ar′ō·wud′), *n. Am.* viburnum or other shrub with a tough, straight stem.

ar·roy·o (ə·roi′ō), *n., pl.* —**roy·os.** *Am., S.W.* **1.** the dry bed of a stream; gully. **2.** a small river. [< Sp., < L *arrugia* mine shaft]

ar·se·nal (är′sə·nəl), *n.* a building for storing

or manufacturing weapons and ammunition for an army or navy. [< Ital. < Ar. *dār aṣ-ṣinā'a* house (of) the manufacturing]

ar·se·nate (är′sə·nāt; -nĭt), *n. Chem.* a salt of arsenic acid. Arsenate of lead is a poison that is used to kill insects.

ar·se·nic (*n.* är′sə·nĭk; *adj.* är·sen′ĭk), *n.* **1.** a grayish-white chemical element, As, having a metallic luster and volatilizing when heated. **2.** a violent poison that is a compound of this element, As₂O₃, a white, tasteless powder. —*adj.* Also, ar·sen′i·cal. of or containing arsenic. [< L < Gk. *arsenikon* < Heb. < OPers., golden]

ar·son (är′sən), *n.* the crime of intentionally setting fire to a building or other property. [< OF < LL *arsio* a burning < L *ardere* burn]

art¹ (ärt), *n.* **1.** branch of learning appealing to the imagination, esp. drawing, painting, and sculpture, also architecture, poetry, music, dancing, etc. **2.** these branches of learning as a group. **3.** branch of learning that depends more on special practice than on general principles: *writing compositions is an art; grammar is a science.* **4.** branch or division of learning: *literature is one of the liberal arts.* **5.** skill. **6.** human skill. **7.** some kind of skill or practical application of skill: *cooking is a household art.* **8.** principles; methods. **9.** skillful act. **10.** trick. [< OF < L *ars*]

art² (ärt), *v. Archaic or Poetic.* are. "Thou art" means "You are." [OE *eart*]

art., **1.** article. **2.** artillery. **3.** artist.

Ar·te·mis (är′tə·mĭs), *n. Gk. Myth.* the goddess of the hunt, of the forests, of wild animals, and of the moon, identified by the Romans with Diana.

ar·te·ri·al (är·tir′i·əl), *adj.* **1.** *Anat.* pertaining to or resembling the arteries. **2.** *Physiol.* pertaining to the bright-red blood of the arteries. **3.** having a main channel with many branches. —ar·te′ri·al·ly, *adv.*

ar·te·ri·o·scle·ro·sis (är·tir′i·ō·sklə·rō′sis), *n.* a hardening of the walls of the arteries that makes circulation of the blood difficult.

ar·ter·y (är′tər·i), *n., pl.* -ter·ies. **1.** any of the blood vessels or tubes that carry blood from the heart to all parts of the body. **2.** a main road; important channel. [< L < Gk. *arteria*]

ar·te·sian well (är·tē′zhən), a deep-drilled well. [< F *artésien* of Artois, province where such wells first existed]

art·ful (ärt′fəl), *adj.* **1.** crafty; deceitful. **2.** skillful; clever. **3.** artificial. —art′ful·ly, *adv.* —art′ful·ness, *n.*

ar·thri·tis (är·thrī′tis), *n.* inflammation of a joint or joints. —ar·thrit·ic (är·thrit′ik), *adj.*

ar·thro·pod (är′thrə·pod), *n.* any of a phylum of invertebrate animals having segmented legs, such as the insects, arachnids, and crustaceans. —ar·throp·o·dous (är·throp′ə·dəs), *adj.*

Ar·thur (är′thər), *n.* **1.** a legendary king of ancient Britain who gathered about him a famous group of knights. **2. Chester A.,** 1830–1886, the 21st president of the U.S., 1881–1885.

Ar·thu·ri·an (är·thúr′i·ən; -thyúr′-), *adj.* of King Arthur and his knights.

ar·ti·choke (är′ti·chōk), *n.* **1.** a thistlelike plant whose flowering head is cooked and eaten. **2.** the flowering head. **3.** Jerusalem artichoke. [< Ital. < Provençal < Ar. *al-kharshûf*]

ar·ti·cle (är′ti·kəl), *n., v.,* -cled, -cling. —*n.* **1.** a literary composition, complete in itself, but forming part of a magazine, newspaper, or book. **2.** clause in a contract, treaty, statute, etc. **3.** particular thing; item: *bread is a main article of food.* **4.** one of the words *a, an,* or *the* or the corresponding words in certain other languages. *A* and *an* are indefinite articles; *the* is the definite article. —*v.* **1.** bind by contract: *an apprentice articled to serve for seven years.* **2.** bring charges; accuse. [< F < L *articulus,* dim. of *artus* joint]

ar·tic·u·lar (är·tik′yə·lər), *adj.* of the joints: *arthritis is an articular disease.*

ar·tic·u·late (är·tik′yə·lit; *v.* är·tik′yə·lāt), *adj., v.,* -lat·ed, -lat·ing. —*adj.* **1.** uttered in distinct syllables or words. **2.** capable of speaking. **3.** made up of distinct parts; distinct.

4. jointed; segmented. —*v.* **1.** speak distinctly. **2.** unite by joints. **3.** fit together in a joint. [< L *articulatus* divided into single joints. See ARTICLE.] —ar·tic′u·late·ly, *adv.* —ar·tic′u·late·ness, *n.* —ar·tic′u·la′tive, *adj.* —ar·tic′u·la′tor, *n.*

ar·tic·u·la·tion (är·tik′yə·lā′shən), *n.* **1.** way of speaking; enunciation. **2.** an articulate sound. **3.** joint. **4.** act or manner of connecting by a joint or joints.

ar·ti·fact, ar·te·fact (är′tə·fakt), *n.* **1.** anything made by human skill or work. **2.** an artificial product. [< L *ars* art + *factus* made]

ar·ti·fice (är′tə·fis), *n.* **1.** a clever stratagem or trick. **2.** trickery; craft. **3.** *Obs.* workmanship. [< F < L *artificium* < *arti-* art + *facere* make]

ar·tif·i·cer (är·tif′ə·sər), *n.* **1.** skilled workman; craftsman. **2.** maker.

ar·ti·fi·cial (är′tə·fish′əl), *adj.* **1.** made by human skill or labor; not natural. **2.** made as a substitute for or in imitation of; not real. **3.** assumed; false; affected. **4.** *Obs.* artful. —ar′ti·fi′cial·ly, *adv.* —ar′ti·fi′cial·ness, *n.*

ar·ti·fi·ci·al·i·ty (är′tə·fish′i·al′ə·ti), *n., pl.* -ties. **1.** artificial quality or condition. **2.** something unnatural or unreal.

ar·til·ler·y (är·til′ər·i), *n.* **1.** mounted guns; cannon, as distinguished from small arms. **2.** part of an army that uses and manages cannon. **3.** science of ballistics and gunnery. [< OF, < *artiller* equip, ult. < *a-* + *tire* order]

ar·til·ler·y·man (är·til′ər·i·mən), **ar·til·ler·ist** (-ər·ist), *n., pl.* -men; -ists. *U.S.* soldier who belongs to the artillery.

ar·ti·san (är′tə·zən), *n.* workman skilled in some industry or trade; craftsman. [< F < Ital. *artigiano* < L *ars* art] —Syn. mechanic.

art·ist (är′tist), *n.* **1.** person who paints pictures. **2.** person who is skilled in any of the fine arts, such as sculpture, music, or literature. **3.** person who does work with skill and good taste. [< F < Ital. *artista* < VL, < L *ars* art]

ar·tiste (är·tēst′), *n. French.* a very skillful performer or worker.

ar·tis·tic (är·tis′tik), **ar·tis·ti·cal** (-tə·kəl), *adj.* **1.** of art or artists. **2.** done with skill and good taste. **3.** having good color and design. **4.** having or showing appreciation of beauty. —ar·tis′ti·cal·ly, *adv.*

art·ist·ry (är′tis·tri), *n., pl.* -ries. artistic work; workmanship of an artist.

art·less (ärt′lis), *adj.* **1.** without any trickery or deceit; simple. **2.** natural. **3.** without art; unskilled; ignorant. —art′less·ly, *adv.* —art′less·ness, *n.*

art·y (är′ti), *adj.,* art·i·er, art·i·est. *Colloq.* trying to be artistic. —art′i·ness, *n.*

ar·um (âr′əm), *n.* **1.** a plant having heart-shaped or sword-shaped leaves and a partly hooded flower cluster. **2.** calla lily. [< L < Gk. *aron*]

-ary, *suffix.* **1.** place for ——, as in *library.* **2.** collection of ——, as in *statuary.* **3.** person or thing that is, does, belongs to, etc., ——, as in *commentary.* **4.** of or pertaining to ——, as in *legendary.* **5.** being; having the nature of ——, as in *supplementary.* **6.** characterized by ——, as in *honorary.* [< L *-arius* or (neut.) *-arium*]

Ar·y·an (âr′i·ən; ar′-), *n.* **1.** the assumed prehistoric language from which the Indo-European languages are derived. **2.** person who spoke this language. **3.** descendant of this prehistoric group of people. **4.** in Nazi use, a non-Jew. —*adj.* **1.** Indo-European. **2.** of the Aryans. Also, Arian.

as¹ (az; *unstressed* əz), *adv.* **1.** to the same degree or extent; equally: *as black as coal.* **2.** for example: *some animals, as dogs and cats, eat meat.* —*conj.* **1.** to the same degree or extent that: *she worked just so much as she was told to.* **2.** in the same way that: *run as I do.* **3.** during the time that; when; while: *she sang as she worked.* **4.** because: *he was well paid, as he had done the work well.* **5.** though: *brave as they were, the danger made them afraid.* **6.** that the result was: *the child so marked the picture as to spoil it.* **7.** as for, as to, about; concerning; referring to. **8.** as if, as though, as it would be if. **9. as yet,** up to this time; so far. —*prep. Am.* in the character of; doing the work of: *who will act as teacher?* —*pron.* **1.** a condition or fact that: *she is very careful, as her work shows.* **2.** that: *do the same thing as I do.* [OE (unstressed) *ealswā* quite so. See ALSO.] ▶ **1. as** to and as for are often clumsy substitutes for a single preposition, usually *about* or *of*. **2.** For the conflict between **as** and **like,** see **like¹. 3. As** occurs most commonly as a conjunction, introducing several kinds of clauses: Degree or Manner: *. . . as far as I could.* Time = While: *As I was coming, he was going out.* Attendant Circumstance: *He told stories as we went along.* Cause: *As it was getting dark, we made for home.* Such a handy word is of course much used in speech, which often prefers counter words to more exact ones. But the very variety of possible uses makes **as** a problem in written English. It is necessary in comparisons (*We went as far as he did*) and for attendant circumstance (*As we walked along he told us stories*) though *while* is preferable if the emphasis is on the time or the action (*While we were walking along he told us stories*). *As* is weak in the sense of *because.* Usually *since,* more exact and emphatic in the sentence given here, or *because,* most emphatic, a little formal, would be better in writing and certainly would be better in formal English: *As it was almost time to go, we were getting more and more exasperated.* ▶ See also because.

as² (as), *n., pl.* **as·ses** (as′ĭz). **1.** ancient Roman pound, equal to twelve ounces. **2.** ancient Roman coin, worth a few cents. [< L]

As, *Chem.* arsenic.

AS, A.S., Anglo-Saxon.

as·a·fet·i·da, as·a·foet·i·da (as′ə·fet′ə·də), *n.* gum resin with a garliclike odor, used in medicine to prevent spasms. Also, **assafetida, assafoetida.** [< Med.L, < *asa* (< Pers. *azā*) mastic + L *fetidus* stinking]

as·bes·tos, as·bes·tus (as·bes′təs; az–), *n.* **1.** a mineral, a silicate of calcium and magnesium, that does not burn or conduct heat, usually occurring in fibers. **2.** a fireproof fabric made of these fibers. [< OF < L < Gk. *asbestos* unquenchable (orig., of quicklime), < *a–* not + *sbennunai* quench]

as·cend (ə·send′), *v.* **1.** go up; rise; move upward. **2.** climb; go to or toward the top of. **3.** go toward the source or beginning. **4.** go back in time. **5.** slope upward. [< L *ascendere* < *ad–* up + *scandere* climb] —**as·cend′a·ble, as·cend′i·ble,** *adj.* —**as·cend′er,** *n.* —Syn. **2.** scale.

as·cend·ance, as·cend·ence (ə·sen′dəns), *n.* ascendancy.

as·cend·an·cy, as·cend·en·cy (ə·sen′dən·si), *n.* controlling influence.

as·cend·ant, as·cend·ent (ə·sen′dənt), *adj.* **1.** ascending; rising. **2.** superior; dominant; ruling; controlling. —*n.* position of power; controlling influence.

as·cen·sion (ə·sen′shən), *n.* **1.** act of ascending; ascent. **a.** Ascension, a. the bodily passing of Christ from earth to heaven. **b.** Also, **Ascension Day,** a church festival in honor of this on the fortieth day after Easter. —**as·cen′sion·al,** *adj.*

As·cen·sion (ə·sen′shən), *n.* a British island in the S Atlantic.

as·cent (ə·sent′), *n.* **1.** act of going up; a rising. **2.** a climbing; upward movement. **3.** a going back toward a source or beginning. **4.** place or way that slopes up.

as·cer·tain (as′ər·tān′), *v.* find out with certainty; determine. [< OF, < *a–* + *certain* CERTAIN] —**as′cer·tain′a·ble,** *adj.* —**as′cer·tain′a·ble·ness, as′cer·tain′a·bil′i·ty,** *n.* —**as′cer·tain′a·bly,** *adv.* —**as′cer·tain′ment,** *n.*

as·cet·ic (ə·set′ik), *n.* **1.** person who practices unusual self-denial and devotion, or severe discipline of self for religious reasons. **2.** person who refrains from pleasures and comforts. —*adj.* Also, **as·cet′i·cal.** refraining from pleasures and comforts; self-denying. [< Gk., < *askeein* exercise; hence, discipline] —**as·cet′i·cal·ly,** *adv.*

as·cet·i·cism (ə·set′ə·siz·əm), *n.* **1.** life or habits of an ascetic. **2.** doctrine that by abstinence and self-denial a person can train himself to be in conformity with God's will.

as·cid·i·an (ə·sid′i·ən), *n. Zool.* sea animal with a tough saclike covering.

as·cid·i·um (ə·sid′i·um), *n., pl.* **–cid·i·a** (–sid′i·ə). *Bot.* a baglike or pitcherlike part. [< NL < Gk. *askidion,* dim. of *askos* bag]

a·scor·bic acid (ā·skôr′bik; ə–), *Biochem.* vitamin C, $C_6H_8O_6$.

as·cot (as′kət; –kot), *n.* necktie with broad ends, tied so that the ends may be laid flat, one across the other.

Man wearing an ascot tie

as·cribe (əs·krīb′), *v.* **–cribed, –crib·ing. 1.** assign; attribute: *the police ascribed the automobile accident to fast driving.* **2.** consider as belonging: *men have ascribed their own characteristics to their gods.* [< OF < L, < *ad–* to + *scribere* write] —**as·crib′a·ble,** *adj.*

as·crip·tion (əs·krip′shən), *n.* **1.** act of ascribing. **2.** statement or words ascribing something.

a·sep·sis (ā·sep′sis; ā–), *n.* **1.** aseptic condition. **2.** aseptic methods or treatment.

a·sep·tic (ā·sep′tik; ā–), *adj.* free from germs causing infection. —**a·sep′ti·cal·ly,** *adv.*

a·sex·u·al (ā·sek′shŭ·əl), *adj. Biol.* **1.** having no sex. **2.** independent of sexual processes: *reproduction by spore formation is asexual.* —**a·sex·u·al·i·ty** (ā·sek′shŭ·al′ə·ti), *n.* —**a·sex′u·al·ly,** *adv.*

As·gard (as′gärd; az′–; äs′–), *n. Scand. Myth.* the home of the Norse gods and heroes.

ash¹ (ash), *n.* **1.** what remains of a thing after it has been thoroughly burned. **2.** powdered lava. [OE *æsce* ashes]

ash² (ash), *n.* **1.** timber or shade tree that has straight-grained wood. **2.** its tough, springy wood. [OE *æsc* the tree]

a·shamed (ə·shāmd′), *adj.* **1.** feeling shame. **2.** unwilling because of shame. —**a·sham·ed·ly** (ə·shām′id·li), *adv.* —**a·sham′ed·ness,** *n.*

ash·en¹ (ash′ən), *adj.* **1.** like ashes; pale as ashes. **2.** of ashes.

ash·en² (ash′ən), *adj.* **1.** of the ash tree. **2.** made from the wood of the ash tree.

ash·es (ash′iz), *n.pl.* **1.** what remains of a thing after it has been burned. **2.** remains; dead body.

ash·lar, ash·ler (ash′lər), *n.* **1.** a square stone used in building. **2.** masonry made of ashlars. [< OF < VL *axillarium* < *axis* plank]

a·shore (ə·shôr′; ə·shōr′), *adv., adj. Naut.* **1.** to the shore. **2.** on the shore.

Ash·to·reth (ash′tə·reth), *n.* Astarte.

Ash Wednesday, the first day of Lent.

ash·y (ash′i), *adj.,* **ash·i·er, ash·i·est. 1.** like ashes; pale as ashes. **2.** of ashes. **3.** covered with ashes.

A·sia (ā′zhə; ā′shə), *n.* the largest continent. China and India are in Asia.

Asia Minor, peninsula of W Asia, between the Black Sea and the Mediterranean. Also, **Anatolia.**

Asian flu or Asiatic flu, a kind of influenza caused by a new strain of virus, first identified in Hong Kong in early 1957.

A·si·at·ic (ā′zhi·at′ik; ā′shi–), *Asian* (ā′zhən; ā′shən), *adj.* of or having to do with Asia or its people. —*n.* native of Asia. —**A′si·at′i·cal·ly,** *adv.*

a·side (ə·sīd′), *adv.* **1.** on one side; to one side; away: *move the table aside.* **2.** *Am.* out of one's thoughts, consideration, etc.: *put one's troubles aside.* **3.** aside from, *Am.* a. apart from. b. *Colloq.* except for. —*n.* actor's remark that the other actors are not supposed to hear.

as·i·nine (as′ə·nīn), *adj.* **1.** like an ass. **2.** stupid; silly. [< L < *asinus* ass] —**as′i·nine·ly,** *adv.*

as·i·nin·i·ty (as′ə·nin′ə·ti), *n., pl.* **–ties.** stupidity; silliness.

ask (ask; äsk), *v.* **1.** try to find out by words; inquire: *why don't you ask?* **2.** seek the answer to: *ask any questions you wish, ask the way.* **3.** put a question to; inquire of: *ask him.* **4.** try to get by words; request: *ask a favor.* **5.** claim; demand: *ask too high a price for a house.* **6.** invite. **7.** need; require. **8.** *U.S. Colloq.* publish the banns of (a person or persons). [OE *āscian*] —ask′er, *n.* —Syn. **3.** query, question, interrogate. **4.** solicit. **5.** require, exact.

a·skance (ə·skans′), **a·skant** (ə·skant′), *adv.* **1.** with suspicion. **2.** sideways.

a·skew (ə·skū′), *adv., adj.* to one side; turned or twisted the wrong way.

a·slant (ə·slant′; ə·slänt′), *adv.* in a slanting direction. —*prep.* slantingly across. —*adj.* slanting.

a·sleep (ə·slēp′), *adj.* **1.** sleeping. **2.** in a condition of sleep. **3.** dull; inactive. **4.** numb: *my foot is asleep.* **5.** dead. —*adv.* into a condition of sleep.

a·slope (ə·slōp′), *adv., adj.* at a slant.

asp[1] (asp), *n.* **1.** any of several small, poisonous snakes of Africa, esp. the Egyptian cobra. **2.** a small, poisonous snake of Europe; adder. [< L < Gk. *aspis*]

asp[2] (asp), *n. Poetic.* aspen. [OE *æspe*]

as·par·a·gus (əs·par′ə·gəs), *n.* **1.** a perennial plant of the lily family having scalelike leaves and stems with many branches. **2.** the green tender shoots of one species, used as a vegetable. [< L < Gk. *asparagos*]

as·pect (as′pekt), *n.* **1.** look; appearance: *aspect of the countryside.* **2.** countenance; expression: *the solemn aspect of a judge.* **3.** one side or part or view (of a subject): *various aspects of a plan.* **4.** direction anything faces. **5.** side fronting in a given direction: *the southern aspect of a house.* **6.** relative position of planets as determining their supposed influence upon human affairs. [< L, < *ad-* at + *specere* look]

as·pen (as′pən), *n.* a poplar tree whose leaves tremble and rustle in the slightest breeze. —*adj.* **1.** of this tree. **2.** quivering; trembling. [earlier meaning "of the ASP[2]"]

as·per·i·ty (as·per′ə·ti), *n., pl.* -ties. roughness; harshness; severity. [< OF < L, < *asper* rough]

as·perse (əs·pėrs′), *v.,* -persed, -pers·ing. spread damaging or false reports about; slander. [< L *aspersus* < *ad-* on + *spargere* sprinkle] —as·pers′er, *n.*

as·per·sion (əs·pėr′zhən; -shən), *n.* damaging or false report; slander.

as·phalt (as′fôlt; -falt), **as·phal·tum** (as·fal′təm), *n.* **1.** a dark-colored substance, much like tar, found in various parts of the world or obtained by evaporating petroleum. **2.** mixture of this substance with crushed rock, used for pavements, roofs, etc. [< LL < Gk. *asphaltos* < Semitic] —as·phal′tic, *adj.*

as·pho·del (as′fə·del), *n.* **1.** plant of the lily family with spikes of white or yellow flowers. **2.** *Gk. Myth.* flower of the Greek paradise. **3.** *Poetic.* daffodil. [< L < Gk. *asphodelos*]

as·phyx·i·a (as·fik′si·ə), *n.* suffocation or unconscious condition caused by lack of oxygen and excess of carbon dioxide in the blood. [< NL < Gk., < *a-* without + *sphyxis* pulse < *sphyzein* throb]

as·phyx·i·ate (as·fik′si·āt), *v.,* -at·ed, -at·ing. suffocate because of lack of oxygen. —as·phyx′i·a′tion, *n.* —as·phyx′i·a′tor, *n.*

as·pic (as′pik), *n.* kind of jelly made from meat, tomato juice, etc. [< F]

as·pi·dis·tra (as′pə·dis′trə), *n.* plant with large, green leaves and very small flowers, used as a house plant. [< NL < Gk. *aspis* shield + *astron* star]

as·pir·ant (əs·pīr′ənt; as′pə·rənt), *n.* person who aspires; person who seeks a position of honor. —*adj.* aspiring.

as·pi·rate (*v.* as′pə·rāt; *adj., n.* as′pə·rit), *v.,* -rat·ed, -rat·ing, *adj., n. Phonet.* —*v.* pronounce with a breathing or *h*-sound. The *h* in *hot* is aspirated. —*adj.* pronounced with a breathing or

h-sound. —*n.* an aspirated sound. [< L *aspiratus.* See ASPIRE.]

as·pi·ra·tion (as′pə·rā′shən), *n.* **1.** earnest desire; longing. **2.** act of drawing air into the lungs; breathing. **3.** *Phonet.* **a.** an aspirating (of sounds). **b.** an aspirated sound. **4.** withdrawal by suction.

as·pi·ra·tor (as′pə·rā′tər), *n.* apparatus or device employing suction.

as·pire (əs·pīr′), *v.,* -pired, -pir·ing. **1.** have an ambition for something; desire earnestly. **2.** rise. [< L, < *ad-* toward + *spirare* breathe] —as·pir′er, *n.* —as·pir′ing·ly, *adv.*

as·pi·rin (as′pə·rin), *n.* drug for headaches, colds, etc., $C_9H_8O_4$. It is the acetate of salicylic acid. [from trademark]

a·squint (ə·skwint′), *adv., adj.* sideways.

ass (as), *n.* **1.** a long-eared mammal of the horse family, serving as a patient, sure-footed beast of burden when domesticated; donkey. **2.** stupid fool; silly person. [OE *assa* < OWelsh < L *asinus*]

as·sa·fet·i·da, as·sa·foet·i·da (as′ə·fet′ə·də), *n.* asafetida.

as·sa·gai, as·se·gai (as′ə·gī), *n., pl.* -gais. a slender spear or javelin of hard wood, used by some African tribes. [< Sp. < Ar. *az-zaghāyah* < Berber]

as·sail (ə·sāl′), *v.* **1.** set upon with violence; attack. **2.** set upon vigorously with arguments, abuse, etc. [< OF < VL < L *ad-* at + *salire* leap] —as·sail′a·ble, *adj.* —as·sail′er, *n.* —as·sail′ment, *n.*

as·sail·ant (ə·sāl′ənt), *n.* person who attacks. —*adj.* assailing.

as·sas·sin (ə·sas′ən), *n.* murderer, esp. one hired to murder. [< F < Ital. < Ar. *hashshāshīn* HASHISH eaters; with ref. to fanatics who murdered while under the influence of hashish]

as·sas·si·nate (ə·sas′ə·nāt), *v.,* -nat·ed, -nat·ing. kill by a sudden or secret attack; murder. —as·sas′si·na′tion, *n.* —as·sas′si·na′tor, *n.*

as·sault (ə·sôlt′), *n.* **1.** a sudden, vigorous attack; attack. **2.** *Law.* an attempt or offer to do violence to another. **3.** *Mil.* final phase of an attack; close hand-to-hand fighting. —*v.* make an assault on. [< OF, < L *ad-* at + *saltare* leap] —as·sault′a·ble, *adj.* —as·sault′er, *n.* —Syn. *n.* **1.** onslaught, charge.

as·say (*v.* ə·sā′; *n.* ə·sā′, as′ā), *v.* **1.** analyze (an ore, alloy, etc.) to find out the quantity of gold, silver, or other metal in it. **2.** try; test; examine. **3.** *Am.* (of ore) contain, as shown by analysis, a certain proportion of metal. **4.** *Archaic.* attempt. —*n.* **1.** analysis of an ore, alloy, etc., to find out the amount of metal in it. **2.** trial; test; examination. **3.** the substance analyzed or tested. **4.** a list of the results of assaying an ore, drug, etc. [< OF *a(s) sayer,* ult. < LL, < VL *exagere* weigh] —as·say′a·ble, *adj.* —as·say′er, *n.*

as·sem·blage (ə·sem′blij), *n.* **1.** group of persons gathered together; assembly. **2.** collection; group. **3.** a bringing or coming together; meeting. **4.** a putting or fitting together, as parts of a machine.

as·sem·ble (ə·sem′bəl), *v.,* -bled, -bling. **1.** gather or bring together. **2.** come together; meet. **3.** *Am.* put or fit together. [< OF *as(s)embler* < VL *assimulare* bring together < L, compare, ult. < *ad-* to + *similis* like, or *simul* together] —as·sem′bler, *n.* —Syn. **2.** congregate.

as·sem·bly (ə·sem′bli), *n., pl.* -blies. **1.** an assembling. **2.** a being assembled. **3.** group of people gathered together for some purpose; meeting. **4.** a reception. **5.** a ball. **6.** a lawmaking group. **7.** a putting or fitting together. **8.** signal on a bugle or drum for troops to form in ranks. **9.** Assembly, in some States, the lower branch of the State legislature. —Syn. **1.** gathering. **3.** convention, congregation. **6.** legislature.

assembly line, *Am.* row of workers and machines along which work is successively passed until the final product is made.

as·sem·bly·man, As·sem·bly·man (ə·sem′bli·mən), *n., pl.* -men. *U.S.* member of a lawmaking group.

as·sent (ə·sent′), *v.* express agreement; agree.

—*n.* acceptance of a proposal, statement, etc.; agreement. [< OF < L, < *ad-* along with + *sentire* feel, think] —as·sent′er, *n.* —as·sent′ing·ly, *adv.*

as·sert (ə·sèrt′), *v.* 1. state positively; declare. 2. insist on (a right, a claim, etc.); defend. 3. assert oneself, put oneself forward; refuse to be ignored. [< L, < *ad-* to + *serere* join] —as·sert′a·ble, as·sert′i·ble, *adj.* —as·sert′er, as·ser′tor, *n.* —Syn. 1. affirm, aver, maintain.

as·ser·tion (ə·sèr′shən), *n.* 1. positive statement; declaration. 2. act of asserting.

as·ser·tive (ə·sèr′tiv), *adj.* too confident and certain; positive. —as·ser′tive·ly, *adv.* —as·ser′tive·ness, *n.*

as·sess (ə·ses′), *v.* 1. estimate the value of (property or income) for taxation. 2. fix the amount of (a tax, fine, damages, etc.). 3. put a tax or fine on (a person, property, etc.). 4. portion out as a tax; apportion. [< OF < VL *assessare* fix a tax < L *assidere* < *ad-* by + *sedere* sit] —as·sess′a·ble, *adj.*

as·sess·ment (ə·ses′mənt), *n.* 1. act of assessing. 2. amount assessed.

as·ses·sor (ə·ses′ər), *n.* person who assesses taxes. —as·ses′sor·ship, *n.*

as·set (as′et), *n.* 1. something having value. 2. a single item of property.

as·sets (as′ets), *n.pl.* 1. things of value; property. 2. property that can be used to pay debts. [< OF *asez* enough < L *ad-* to + *satis* enough]

as·sev·er·ate (ə·sev′ər·āt), *v.,* -at·ed, -at·ing. declare solemnly; state positively. [< L, < *ad-* + *severus* serious] —as·sev′er·a′tion, *n.*

as·si·du·i·ty (as′ə·dü′ə·ti; -dū′ə-), *n.,* *pl.* -ties. careful and steady attention; diligence.

as·sid·u·ous (ə·sij′ù·əs), *adj.* careful and attentive; diligent. [< L, < *assidere* sit at. See ASSESS.] —as·sid′u·ous·ly, *adv.* —as·sid′u·ous·ness, *n.*

as·sign (ə·sīn′), *v.* 1. give as a share. 2. appoint, as to a post or duty. 3. name definitely; fix; set. 4. refer; ascribe; attribute. 5. transfer or hand over (property, a right, etc.) legally. —*n.* person to whom property, a right, etc., is legally transferred. [< OF < L, < *ad-* to, for + *signum* mark] —as·sign′a·ble, *adj.* —as·sign′a·bil′i·ty, *n.* —as·sign′a·bly, *adv.* —as·sign′er, *n.* —as·sign′or, *n.* —Syn. *v.* 1. allot. 3. designate.

as·sig·na·tion (as′ig·nā′shən), *n.* 1. appointment for a meeting. 2. illicit meeting of lovers. 3. legal transfer of property, a right, etc. 4. an allotting.

as·sign·ee (ə·sī·nē′; as′ə·nē′), *n.* person to whom some property, right, etc., is legally transferred.

as·sign·ment (ə·sīn′mənt), *n.* 1. something assigned. 2. *Am.* duty, task, position, etc., given to one to perform or fill. 3. an assigning. 4. legal transfer of some property, right, etc.

as·sign·or (ə·sī·nôr′; as′ə·nôr′), *n.* person who legally transfers to another some property, right, etc.

as·sim·i·la·ble (ə·sim′ə·lə·bəl), *adj.* that can be assimilated. —as·sim′i·la·bil′i·ty, *n.*

as·sim·i·late (ə·sim′ə·lāt), *v.,* -lat·ed, -lat·ing. 1. absorb; digest. 2. be absorbed. 3. make like. 4. liken; compare. 5. be like. [< L, < *ad-* to + *similis* like] —as·sim′i·la′tion, *n.* —as·sim′i·la′tor, *n.* —Syn. 1. incorporate.

as·sim·i·la·tive (ə·sim′ə·lā′tiv), *adj.* assimilating. —as·sim′i·la′tive·ness, *n.*

as·sist (ə·sist′), *v.* 1. help; aid. 2. be associated with as an assistant. —*n. Am., Baseball.* help given in putting a runner out. [< F < L, < *ad-* by + *sistere* take a stand] —as·sist′er, *Law* as·sis′tor, *n.*

as·sist·ance (ə·sis′təns), *n.* help; aid.

as·sist·ant (ə·sis′tənt), *n.* helper; aid. —*adj.* helping; assisting. —as·sist′ant·ship, *n.*

assistant professor, *Am.* teacher ranking below a professor.

as·size (ə·sīz′), *n.* 1. session of a law court. 2. verdict; judgment. 3. assizes, periodical sessions of court held in each county of England. [< OF

as(s)ise < *aseeir* < VL *assedere* sit at. See ASSESS.]

assn., Assn., association.

assoc., associate; association.

as·so·ci·ate (*v.* ə·sō′shi·āt; *n., adj.* ə·sō′shi·it, -āt), *v.,* -at·ed, -at·ing, *n., adj.* —*v.* 1. connect in thought. 2. join as a companion, partner, or friend. 3. join; combine; unite. 4. combine for a common purpose. 5. keep company (with). —*n.* 1. thing connected in thought with another. 2. companion; partner; friend. 3. member without full rights and privileges. —*adj.* 1. joined in companionship, interest, action, etc. 2. admitted to some, but not all, rights and privileges, etc. [< L, < *ad-* to + *socius* companion] —as·so′ci·ate·ship′, *n.* —as·so′ci·a′tor, *n.* —Syn. *n.* 2. ally, colleague, comrade. —*adj.* 1. allied.

as·so·ci·a·tion (ə·sō′si·ā′shən; -shi-), *n.* 1. an associating or being associated. 2. group of people joined together for some purpose; society. 3. companionship; partnership; friendship. 4. connection of ideas in thought. —as·so′ci·a′tion·al, *adj.* —Syn. 1. alliance. 2. club.

association football, soccer.

as·so·ci·a·tive (ə·sō′shi·ā′tiv), *adj.* 1. tending to associate. 2. pertaining to association. —as·so′ci·a′tive·ly, *adv.*

as·soil (ə·soil′), *v. Archaic.* 1. absolve. 2. atone for. [< F < L *absolvere* ABSOLVE]

as·so·nance (as′ə·nəns), *n.* 1. resemblance in sound. 2. a substitute for rhyme in which the vowels are alike but the consonants are different, as in *brave—vain, lone—show.* [< F < L, < *ad-* to + *sonare* sound] —as′so·nant, *adj., n.* —as·so·nan·tal (as′ə·nan′təl), *adj.*

as·sort (ə·sôrt′), *v.* 1. sort out; classify; arrange in sorts. 2. furnish with various sorts. 3. agree; suit; match. 4. associate. [< F, < *a-* to (< L *ad-*) + *sorte* SORT] —as·sort′er, *n.* —as·sort′ment, *n.*

as·sort·ed (ə·sôr′tid), *adj.* 1. selected so as to be of different kinds; various. 2. arranged by kinds; classified.

asst., Asst., assistant.

as·suage (ə·swāj′), *v.,* -suaged, -suag·ing. 1. make easier or milder: *assuage pain.* 2. grow easier or milder. 3. make less: *assuage thirst.* [< OF *assuagier,* ult. < L *ad-* + *suavis* sweet] —as·suage′ment, *n.* —as·suag′er, *n.*

as·sume (ə·süm′), *v.,* -sumed, -sum·ing. 1. take upon oneself; undertake. 2. take on; put on. 3. appropriate; usurp. 4. pretend. 5. take for granted; suppose. [< L, < *ad-* to + *sumere* take] —as·sum′a·ble, *adj.* —as·sum′a·bly, *adv.* —as·sum′ed·ly, *adv.* —as·sum′er, *n.* —Syn. 4. feign, simulate. 5. presume.

as·sum·ing (ə·süm′ing), *adj.* taking too much on oneself; presumptuous.

as·sump·tion (ə·sump′shən), *n.* 1. act of assuming. 2. thing assumed. 3. presumption; arrogance; unpleasant boldness. 4. the Assumption, a. the bodily taking of the Virgin Mary from earth to heaven after her death. b. a church festival in honor of this on August 15. —Syn. 2. hypothesis, conjecture.

as·sur·ance (ə·shùr′əns), *n.* 1. a making sure or certain. 2. positive declaration inspiring confidence. 3. security; certainty; confidence. 4. self-confidence. 5. impudence; too much boldness. 6. *Brit.* insurance. —Syn. 2. guarantee. 5. audacity, presumption.

as·sure (ə·shùr′), *v.,* -sured, -sur·ing. 1. make sure or certain. 2. make confident. 3. tell positively. 4. make safe; secure. 5. make safe against loss; insure. [< OF *aseürer* < VL < L *ad-* + *securus* safe, SECURE] —as·sur′a·ble, *adj.* —as·sur′er, *n.* —Syn. 1. ascertain. 2. encourage. 3. state. 4. ensure.

as·sured (ə·shùrd′), *adj.* 1. sure; certain. 2. confident; bold. 3. insured against loss. —*n.* 1. person who is the beneficiary of an insurance policy. 2. person whose life or property is insured. —as·sur·ed·ly (ə·shùr′id·li), *adv.* —as·sur′ed·ness, *n.*

As·syr·i·a (ə·sir′i·ə), *n.* an ancient country in SW Asia. —As·syr′i·an, *adj., n.*

āge, cāre, fär; ēqual, tèrm; īce; ōpen, ôrder; pùt, rüle, ūse; tħ, then; ə=a in about.

As·tar·te (as·tär′tē), *n.* Phoenician goddess of fertility and love. The Hebrews called her Ash-toreth.

as·ter (as′tər), *n.* **1.** *Bot.* any plant of a wide-spread genus whose daisylike blossoms are really compact heads of florets surrounded by small leaves or bracts. **2.** plant of some allied genus, as the China aster. [< L < Gk., star] —**as′ter·like′**, *adj.*

as·ter·isk (as′tər·isk), *n.* a star-shaped mark (*) used in printing and writing to call attention to a footnote, indicate an omission, etc. —*v.* mark with an asterisk. [< LL < Gk., dim. of *aster* star]

a·stern (ə·stérn′), *adv.* **1.** at or toward the rear of a ship. **2.** backward. **3.** behind.

as·ter·oid (as′tər·oid), *n.* **1.** any of the very numerous small planets revolving about the sun between the orbit of Mars and the orbit of Jupiter. **2.** any starfish. —**as′ter·oi′dal**, *adj.*

asth·ma (az′mə; as′-), *n.* a chronic disease that causes difficulty in breathing, a feeling of suffocation, and coughing. [< Gk., panting, < *azein* breathe hard]

asth·mat·ic (az·mat′ik; as-), *adj.* **1.** of or pertaining to asthma. **2.** suffering from asthma. —*n.* person suffering from asthma. —**asth·mat′i·cal·ly**, *adv.*

as·tig·mat·ic (as′tig·mat′ik), *adj.* **1.** having astigmatism. **2.** pertaining to astigmatism. **3.** correcting astigmatism. —**as′tig·mat′i·cal·ly**, *adv.*

a·stig·ma·tism (ə·stig′mə·tiz·əm), *n.* defect of the eye or of a lens whereby rays of light fail to converge to a focus, thus making objects look indistinct or imperfect. [< *a–* without + Gk. *stigma* point]

a·stir (ə·stér′), *adv., adj.* in motion.

as·ton·ish (əs·ton′ish), *v.* surprise greatly; amaze. [var. of *astoun* < OF *estoner* < VL *extonare.* Cf. L *attonare.*] —**as·ton′ished·ly**, *adv.* —**as·ton′ish·er**, *n.* —Syn. astound.

as·ton·ish·ing (əs·ton′ish·ing), *adj.* very surprising; amazing. —**as·ton′ish·ing·ly**, *adv.*

as·ton·ish·ment (əs·ton′ish·mənt), *n.* **1.** great surprise; amazement; sudden wonder. **2.** anything that causes great surprise.

as·tound (əs·tound′), *v.* surprise very greatly; amaze. [earlier *astoun,* var. of *astony* ASTONISH] —**as·tound′ing**, *adj.* —**as·tound′ing·ly**, *adv.*

a·strad·dle (ə·strad′əl), *adv., adj.* astride.

as·tra·gal (as′trə·gəl), *n.* *Archit.* a small, convex molding cut into the form of a string of beads.

as·trag·a·lus (as·trag′ə·ləs), *n., pl.* **-li** (-lī). *Anat.* the uppermost bone of the tarsus; anklebone; talus. [< L < Gk. *astragalos*]

as·tra·khan, as·tra·chan (as′trə·kən), *n.* **1.** the curly furlike wool on the skin of young lambs from Astrakhan, a district in E European Russia. **2.** a woolen cloth resembling it. [named for *Astrakhan*]

as·tral (as′trəl), *adj.* of the stars; starry. [< LL, < *astrum* star < Gk. *astron*]

a·stray (ə·strā′), *adj., adv.* out of the right way. —Syn. straying.

a·stride (ə·strīd′), *adj., adv.* **1.** with one leg on each side. **2.** with legs far apart. —*prep.* with one leg on each side of (something).

as·trin·gent (əs·trin′jənt), *adj.* **1.** having the property of shrinking or contracting. **2.** severe. —*n.* substance that shrinks tissues and checks the flow of blood by contracting blood vessels, as alum. [< L, < *ad–* to + *stringere* bind] —**as·trin′gen·cy** (əs·trin′jən·si), *n.* —**as·trin′gent·ly**, *adv.*

astrol., astrologer; astrology.

as·tro·labe (as′trə·lāb), *n.* an astronomical instrument formerly used for measuring the altitude of the sun or stars. [< OF < Med.L < Gk. *astrolabon,* orig., star-taking < *astron* star + *lambanein* take]

as·trol·o·ger (əs·trol′ə·jər), *n.* person who claims to interpret the influence of the stars and planets on persons, events, etc.

as·trol·o·gy (əs·trol′ə·ji), *n.* **1.** false science that claims to interpret the influence of the stars

and planets on persons, events, etc. **2.** *Archaic.* practical astronomy. —**as·tro·log·i·cal** (as′trə·loj′ə·kəl), as′tro·log′ic, *adj.* —**as′tro·log′i·cal·ly**, *adv.*

astron., astronomer; astronomical; astronomy.

as·tro·naut (as′trə·nôt), *n.* person who travels between planets, or advocates such travel.

as·tron·o·mer (əs·tron′ə·mər), *n.* expert in astronomy.

as·tro·nom·i·cal (as′trə·nom′ə·kəl), **as·tro·nom·ic** (-nom′ik), *adj.* **1.** of astronomy; having to do with astronomy. **2.** extremely large. —**as′tro·nom′i·cal·ly**, *adv.*

astronomical year, period of the earth's revolution around the sun; solar year.

as·tron·o·my (əs·tron′ə·mi), *n.* science of the sun, moon, planets, stars, and other heavenly bodies, their composition, motions, positions, distances, sizes, etc. [< L < Gk., < *astron* star + *nomos* distribution]

as·tro·phys·ics (as′trō·fiz′iks), *n.* branch of astronomy that deals with the physical and chemical characteristics of heavenly bodies. —**as′tro·phys′i·cal**, *adj.* —**as·tro·phys·i·cist** (as′trō·fiz′ə·sist), *n.*

as·tute (əs·tüt′; -tūt′), *adj.* sagacious; shrewd; crafty. [< L, < *astus* sagacity] —**as·tute′ly**, *adv.* —**as·tute′ness**, *n.*

A·sun·ción (ä·sün·syôn′), *n.* capital of Paraguay.

a·sun·der (ə·sun′dər), *adj.* apart; separate. —*adv.* in pieces; into separate parts.

a·sy·lum (ə·sī′ləm), *n.* **1.** institution for the support and care of the insane, blind, orphans, or other classes of unfortunate persons. **2.** an inviolable refuge, as formerly for debtors and criminals. [< L < Gk. *asylon* refuge < *a–* without + *syle* right of seizure] —Syn. **2.** sanctuary.

a·sym·me·try (ā·sim′ə·tri; a-), *n.* lack of symmetry. —**a·sym·met·ric** (ā′sə·met′rik; as′ə-), **a′sym·met′ri·cal**, *adj.* —**a′sym·met′ri·cal·ly**, *adv.*

as·ymp·tote (as′im·tōt), *n.* *Math.* a straight line that continually approaches a curve, but does not meet it within a finite distance. —**as·ymp·tot·ic** (as′im·tot′ik), **as′ymp·tot′i·cal**, *adj.* —**as′ymp·tot′i·cal·ly**, *adv.*

at (at; *unstressed* ət, it), *prep.* **1.** in; on; by; near: *at school, at the front door.* **2.** to; toward; in the direction of: *aim at the mark, look at me.* **3.** in a place or condition of: *at war.* **4.** on or near the time of: *at midnight.* **5.** through; by way of: *smoke came out at the chimney.* **6.** doing; trying to do: *at work.* **7.** because of; by reason of: *the shipwrecked sailors were happy at the arrival of the rescue ship.* **8.** for: *two books at a dollar each.* **9.** according to: *at will.* **10.** from: *the sick man got good treatment at the hands of his doctor.* [OE æt]

at., **1.** atmosphere. **2.** atomic.

At·a·brine (at′ə·brin; -brēn), *n.* *Trademark.* a synthetic compound used in treating malaria.

At·a·lan·ta (at′ə·lan′tə), *n.* *Gk. Legend.* a maiden famous for her beauty and her speed in running.

at·a·vism (at′ə·viz·əm), *n.* **1.** resemblance to a remote ancestor. **2.** reversion to a primitive type. [< L *atavus* ancestor] —**at′a·vist**, *n.* —**at′a·vis′tic**, *adj.* —**at′a·vis′ti·cal·ly**, *adv.*

a·tax·i·a (ə·tak′si·ə), *n.* inability to coördinate voluntary movements; irregularity in bodily functions or muscular movements. [< NL, Gk., < *a–* without + *taxis* order] —**a·tax′ic**, *adj.*

ate (āt), *v.* pt. of eat.

A·te (ā′tē), *n.* the Greek goddess of blind recklessness, later regarded as an avenging goddess.

–ate¹, *suffix.* **1.** of or pertaining to, as in *collegiate.* **2.** having; containing, as in *compassionate.* **3.** having the form of; like, as in *stellate.* **4.** become, as in *maturate.* **5.** cause to be, as in *alienate.* **6.** produce, as in *ulcerate.* **7.** supply or treat with, as in *aerate.* **8.** combine with, as in *oxygenate.* [< L *-atus, -atum,* pp. endings]

–ate², *suffix. Chem.* a salt formed by the action of an ——ic acid on a base, as in *sulfate.* [special use of *–ate¹*]

–ate³, *suffix.* office, rule, or condition of, as in *caliphate, magistrate.* [< L *-atus*, from 4th declension nouns]

at·el·ier (at'əl·yā), *n.* workshop; studio. [< F, orig., pile of chips, < OF *astele* chip, ult. < L *astula*]

Ath·a·na·sius (ath'ə·nā'shəs), *n.* Saint, 296?–373 A.D., bishop of Alexandria, one of the chief opponents of the Arian doctrine. —**Ath·a·na·sian** (ath'ə·nā'zhən), *adj.*

a·the·ism (ā'thi·iz·əm), *n.* 1. belief that there is no God. 2. godless living. [< F, < Gk. *atheos* denying the gods < *a-* without + *theos* a god] —**a'the·ist**, *n.*

a·the·is·tic (ā'thi·is'tik), **a·the·is·ti·cal** (-tə·kəl), *adj.* of atheism or atheists. —**a'the·is'ti·cal·ly**, *adv.*

A·the·na (ə·thē'nə), **A·the·ne** (-nē), *n.* the Greek goddess of wisdom, arts, industries, and prudent warfare, identified with the Roman goddess Minerva. Also, **Pallas, Pallas Athena.**

ath·e·nae·um, ath·e·ne·um (ath'ə·nē'əm), *n. Am.* 1. a scientific or literary club. 2. a reading room; library.

Ath·ens (ath'ənz), *n.* 1. capital of Greece, in the SE part. Athens was famous in ancient times for its art and literature. 2. *Am.* city compared to Athens because it is a center of art and literature. —**A·the·ni·an** (ə·thē'ni·ən), *adj., n.*

a·thirst (ə·thėrst'), *adj.* 1. thirsty. 2. eager.

ath·lete (ath'lēt), *n.* person trained in exercises of physical strength, speed, and skill. [< L < Gk., < *athlon* prize]

athlete's foot, *Am.* a contagious skin disease of the feet, caused by a fungus.

ath·let·ic (ath·let'ik), *adj.* 1. active and strong. 2. of, like, or suited to an athlete. 3. for athletes. 4. having to do with active games and sports. —**ath·let'i·cal·ly**, *adv.*

ath·let·i·cism (ath·let'ə·siz·əm), *n.* 1. the practice of athletics. 2. athletic quality or behavior.

ath·let·ics (ath·let'iks), *n.* 1. (*usually construed as pl.*) exercises of strength, speed, and skill; active games and sports: *athletics include baseball and basketball.* 2. (*usually construed as sing.*) the principles of athletic training: *athletics is recommended for every student.*

at·home (ət·hōm'), *n.* an informal reception, usually in the afternoon.

a·thwart (ə·thwôrt'), *adv.* crosswise; across from side to side. —*prep.* 1. across. 2. across the line or course of. 3. in opposition to; against.

a·tilt (ə·tilt'), *adj., adv.* tilted.

a·tin·gle (ə·ting'gəl), *adj.* tingling.

–ation, *suffix.* 1. act or state of ——ing, as in *admiration.* 2. condition or state of being ——ed, as in *agitation.* 3. result of ——ing, as in *civilization.* [< L *-atio*]

–ative, *suffix.* 1. tending to, as in *affirmative, talkative.* 2. having to do with, as in *qualitative.* [< L *-ativus*]

At·lan·ta (at·lan'tə), *n.* the capital of Georgia, in the N part.

At·lan·tic (at·lan'tik), *n.* ocean east of North and South America, extending to Europe and Africa. —*adj.* 1. of, on, or near the Atlantic Ocean. 2. *Am.* of or on the Atlantic coast of the U.S. 3. of or pertaining to the Atlas Mountains.

Atlantic Charter, the joint declaration of President Roosevelt and Prime Minister Churchill on August 14, 1941.

Atlantic City, a resort in SE New Jersey.

At·lan·tis (at·lan'tis), *n.* a legendary sunken island in the Atlantic.

at·las (at'ləs), *n.* 1. book of maps. 2. book of plates or tables illustrating any subject. 3. Atlas, *Gk. Legend.* giant who supported the heavens on his shoulders.

Atlas Mountains, mountain range in NW Africa.

at·mos·phere (at'məs·fir), *n.* 1. air that surrounds the earth; the air. 2. air in any given place: *a damp atmosphere.* 3. mass of gases that surrounds any heavenly body. 4. *Physics.* a unit of pressure equal to 14.69 pounds per square inch. 5. surrounding influence. [< NL < Gk. *atmos* vapor + *sphaira* sphere]

at·mos·pher·ic (at'məs·fer'ik), *adj.* Also, **at'mos·pher'i·cal.** 1. of, in, or having to do with the atmosphere. 2. caused, produced, or worked by the atmosphere. —*n.* **atmospherics,** radio static. —**at'mos·pher'i·cal·ly**, *adv.*

at. no., *Physics, Chem.* atomic number.

at·oll (at'ol; ə·tol'), *n.* a ring-shaped coral island enclosing or partly enclosing a lagoon. [? < Malayalam *aḍal* uniting]

Atoll

at·om (at'əm), *n.* 1. *Physics, Chem.* the smallest particle of a chemical element that can take part in a chemical reaction without being permanently changed. 2. a very small particle; tiny bit. [< L < Gk. *atomos* indivisible < *a-* not + *tomos* a cutting]

a·tom·ic (ə·tom'ik), **a·tom·i·cal** (-ə·kəl), *adj.* 1. of or having to do with atoms. 2. extremely small; minute. —**a·tom'i·cal·ly**, *adv.*

atomic age, era marked by the first use of atomic energy.

atomic bomb, atom bomb, bomb that uses the splitting of atoms to cause an explosion of tremendous force, accompanied by a blinding light. Also, **A-bomb.** —**atomic bombing, atom bombing,** *Am.*

atomic clock, a highly accurate clock, that is run by controlled radio waves.

atomic energy, energy generated through alteration of an atomic nucleus by fission, etc.

atomic furnace, *Nuclear Physics.* reactor.

atomic number, *Physics, Chem.* number used in describing an element and giving its relation to other elements. It is the number of positive charges on the nucleus of an atom of the element.

atomic pile. See reactor.

atomic theory or **hypothesis,** *Physics, Chem.* theory that all matter is composed of atoms, esp. the modern theory that an atom is made of a nucleus of neutrons and protons around which electrons speed.

atomic warfare, warfare using atomic bombs.

atomic weight, *Physics, Chem.* the relative weight of an atom of an element, using oxygen or hydrogen as a standard of comparison.

at·om·ize (at'əm·īz), *v.,* **-ized, -iz·ing.** 1. separate into atoms. 2. change (a liquid) into a fine spray. —**at'om·i·za'tion**, *n.* —**at'om·iz'er**, *n.*

a·ton·al (ā·tōn'əl), *adj. Music.* without tone. —**a·ton'al·ism**, *n.* —**a·ton'al·is'tic**, *adj.* —**a·to·nal·i·ty** (ā'tō·nal'ə·ti), *n.* —**a·ton'al·ly**, *adv.*

a·tone (ə·tōn'), *v.,* **a·toned, a·ton·ing.** make up; make amends (*for*). [< *atonement*] —**a·ton'er**, *n.*

a·tone·ment (ə·tōn'mənt), *n.* 1. giving satisfaction for a wrong, loss, or injury; amends. 2. the Atonement, reconciliation of God with sinners through the sufferings and death of Christ. [< *at onement* a being at one, i.e., in accord]

a·top (ə·top'), *adv.* on or at the top. —*prep.* on the top of.

at·ra·bil·ious (at'rə·bil'yəs), **at·ra·bil·iar** (-bil'yər), *adj.* 1. melancholy; hypochondriac. 2. bad-tempered. [< L *atra bilis* black bile]

a·tri·um (ā'tri·əm), *n., pl.* **a·tri·a** (ā'tri·ə). 1. the main room of an ancient Roman house. 2. hall; court. 3. *Anat.* auricle. [< L (def. 1) < Etruscan]

a·tro·cious (ə·trō'shəs), *adj.* 1. very wicked or cruel; very savage or brutal. 2. *Colloq.* very bad; abominable. —**a·tro'cious·ly**, *adv.* —**a·tro'cious·ness**, *n.*

a·troc·i·ty (ə·tros'ə·ti), *n., pl.* **-ties.** 1. very great wickedness or cruelty. 2. very cruel or brutal act. 3. *Colloq.* very bad blunder. [< L, < *atrox* fierce < *ater* dark]

at·ro·phy (at′rə·fi), *n., v.,* **-phied, -phy·ing.**
—*n.* a wasting away of a part or parts of the
body. —*v.* waste away. [< LL < Gk., < *a-* without
+ *trophe* nourishment] —**a·troph·ic** (ə·trof′ik),
adj. —**at′ro·phied,** *adj.*

at·ro·pine (at′rə·pēn; -pin), **at·ro·pin**
(-pin), *n.* a poisonous drug, $C_{17}H_{23}NO_3$, obtained
from belladonna and similar plants, that re-
laxes muscles and dilates the pupil of the eye.
[< NL *Atropa* belladonna < Gk. *Átropos* one of
the Fates]

at·tach (ə·tach′), *v.* 1. fasten (to). 2. join. 3.
assign; appoint. 4. affix: *attach one's signature
to a document.* 5. attribute. 6. fasten itself; belong: *the blame attaches to you.* 7. bind by affection. 8. take (person or property) by legal authority. [< OF *atachier* < L *ad-* to + Gmc.
ancestor of OF *tache* a fastening, a nail. See
TACK.] —**at·tach′a·ble,** *adj.* —**at·tached′,** *adj.*

at·ta·ché (at′ə·shā′; *esp. Brit.* ə·tash′ā), *n.*
person belonging to the official staff of an ambassador or minister to a foreign country. [< F.
See ATTACH.] —**at′ta·ché′ship,** *n.*

at·tach·ment (ə·tach′mənt), *n.* 1. an attaching. 2. a being attached. 3. thing attached. 4.
means of attaching; fastening. 5. bond arising
from affection and regard. 6. legal taking of a
person or property.

at·tack (ə·tak′), *v.* 1. use force or weapons on
to hurt. 2. talk or write against. 3. begin to work
vigorously on. 4. act harmfully on. 5. make an
attack. —*n.* 1. sudden occurrence of illness, discomfort, etc. 2. act or fact of attacking. [< F
< Ital. *attaccare.* See ATTACH.] —**at·tack′a·ble,**
adj. —**at·tack′er,** *n.* —Syn. *v.* 1. assail, assault,
beset. 2. criticize, blame.

at·tain (ə·tān′), *v.* 1. arrive at in due course;
reach, as by effort or progress. 2. gain; accomplish. 3. attain to, succeed in coming to or
getting. [< OF *ataindre* < VL, < *ad-* to + *tangere*
touch] —**at·tain′a·ble,** *adj.* —**at·tain′a·bil′i·ty,**
at·tain′a·ble·ness, *n.* —**at·tain′er,** *n.* —Syn. 2.
achieve.

at·tain·der (ə·tān′dər), *n.* loss of property
and civil rights as the result of being sentenced
to death or being outlawed. [< OF *ataindre*
attain; infl. by F *taindre* TAINT]

at·tain·ment (ə·tān′mənt), *n.* 1. act or fact
of attaining. 2. something attained. 3. accomplishment; ability.

at·taint (ə·tānt′), *v.* 1. condemn to death and
loss of property and civil rights. 2. disgrace. —*n.*
disgrace. [< OF *ataint,* pp. of *ataindre* ATTAIN]
—**at·taint′ment,** *n.*

at·tar (at′ər), *n.* perfume made from the petals
of roses or other flowers. [< Pers. < Ar. *'iṭr*]

at·tempt (ə·tempt′), *v.* 1. make an effort at;
try. 2. try to take or destroy (life, etc.). —*n.* 1.
a putting forth of effort to accomplish something, esp. something difficult. 2. an attack, as on
one's life. [< L, < *ad-* + *temptare* try] —**at·**
tempt′a·ble, *adj.* —**at·tempt′a·bil′i·ty,** *n.* —**at·**
tempt′er, *n.* —Syn. *v.* 1. essay, endeavor.

at·tend (ə·tend′), *v.* 1. be present at. 2. give
care and thought; pay attention. 3. apply oneself.
4. go with; accompany. 5. go with as a result.
6. wait on; care for; tend. 7. be ready; wait.
[< OF < L, < *ad-* toward + *tendere* stretch]
—**at·tend′er,** *n.* —Syn. 6. serve. —Ant. 2. disregard.

at·tend·ance (ə·ten′dəns), *n.* 1. act of attending. 2. persons attending.

at·tend·ant (ə·ten′dənt), *adj.* 1. waiting on
another to help or serve. 2. going with as a result; accompanying. 3. present: *attendant
hearers.* —*n.* 1. person who waits on another,
such as a servant. 2. accompanying thing or
event. 3. person who is present.

at·ten·tion (ə·ten′shən), *n.* 1. act or fact of
attending. 2. ability to give care and thought.
3. care and thought. 4. courtesy. 5. **attentions,**
acts of devotion of a suitor. 6. military attitude
of readiness. 7. **come to attention,** take a
straight and still position. 8. **stand at attention,**
stand straight and still. —*interj.* command to
soldiers to come to attention. [< L *attentio.* See
ATTEND.] —Syn. *n.* 3. application, concentration,
heed. 4. deference, civility.

at·ten·tive (ə·ten′tiv), *adj.* 1. giving attention.
2. courteous; polite. —**at·ten′tive·ly,** *adv.* —**at·**
ten′tive·ness, *n.*

at·ten·u·ate (ə·ten′yū·āt), *v.,* **-at·ed, -at·ing.**
1. make or become thin or slender. 2. weaken;
reduce. 3. make less dense; dilute. [< L, < *ad-* +
tenuis thin] —**at·ten′u·a′tion,** *n.*

at·test (ə·test′), *v.* 1. give proof or evidence of.
2. declare to be true or genuine; certify. 3. bear
witness; testify. [< L, < *ad-* to + *testis* witness]
—**at·tes·ta·tion** (at′es·tā′shən), *n.* —**at·test′er,**
at·tes′tor, *n.*

at·tic (at′ik), *n.* 1. space just below the roof in
a house. 2. a low story above an entablature or
main cornice of a building. [< F < L *Atticus*
Attic < Gk.]

At·tic (at′ik), *adj.* 1. of Attica; of Athens;
Athenian. 2. simple; elegant; refined.

At·ti·ca (at′ə·kə), *n.* district in ancient Greece
which included Athens.

At·ti·la (at′ə·lə), *n.* died 453 A.D., king of the
Huns from 433–453 A.D.

at·tire (ə·tīr′), *v.,* **-tired, -tir·ing,** *n.* dress;
array. [< OF *atirer* arrange < *a-* to (< L *ad-*) +
tire row < Gmc.] —**at·tire′ment,** *n.* —**at·tir′er,**
n.

at·ti·tude (at′ə·tūd; -tūd), *n.* 1. disposition or
manner toward a person or thing. 2. position of
the body appropriate to an action, purpose,
emotion, etc. [< F < Ital. < LL *aptitudo* APTITUDE]
—Syn. 2. posture, pose.

at·ti·tu·di·nize (at′ə·tū′də·nīz; -tū′-), *v.,*
-nized, -niz·ing. pose for effect. —**at′ti·tu′di·**
niz′er, *n.*

Att·lee (at′li), *n.* Clement Richard, born 1883,
British prime minister 1945–1951.

at·tor·ney (ə·tér′ni), *n., pl.* **-neys.** 1. person
who has power to act for another. 2. lawyer.
[< OF *atourné,* pp. of *atourner* assign, appoint
< *a-* to + *tourner* TURN] —**at·tor′ney·ship,** *n.*
—Syn. 1. agent.

attorney at law, lawyer.

attorney general, *n., pl.* **attorneys general,**
attorney generals. 1. the chief law officer of a
country. 2. *Am.* a. the chief law officer of the
United States. b. the chief law officer of a State
of the United States.

at·tract (ə·trakt′), *v.* 1. draw to oneself: *a
magnet attracts iron.* 2. be pleasing to; win the
attention and liking of. [< L *attractus* < *ad-* to
+ *trahere* draw] —**at·tract′a·ble,** *adj.* —**at·**
tract′a·bil′i·ty, *n.* —**at·trac′tor, at·tract′er,** *n.*
—Syn. 2. allure, fascinate.

at·trac·tion (ə·trak′shən), *n.* 1. act or power
of attracting. 2. thing that delights or attracts
people. 3. charm; fascination. 4. *Physics.* the
force exerted by molecules on one another, which
holds them together.

at·trac·tive (ə·trak′tiv), *adj.* 1. pleasing;
winning attention and liking. 2. attracting.
—**at·trac′tive·ly,** *adv.* —**at·trac′tive·ness,** *n.*
—Syn. 1. alluring. 2. magnetic.

at·trib·ute (*v.* ə·trib′ūt; *n.* at′rə·būt), *v.,*
-ut·ed, -ut·ing, *n.* —*v.* consider (something) as
belonging or appropriate (to a person or thing).
—*n.* 1. a quality considered as belonging to
a person or thing; a characteristic. 2. an object considered appropriate to a person, rank,
or office; symbol. 3. adjective; word or phrase
used as an adjective. [< L, < *ad-* to + *tribuere*
assign, orig., divide among the tribes < *tribus*
tribe] —**at·trib′ut·a·ble,** *adj.* —**at·trib′ut·er,**
at·trib′u·tor, *n.* —Syn. *v.* ascribe, credit. —*n.*
1. trait.

at·tri·bu·tion (at′rə·bū′shən), *n.* 1. act of
attributing. 2. thing attributed.

at·trib·u·tive (ə·trib′yə·tiv), *adj.* 1. expressing a quality or attribute. 2. that attributes. 3.
of or like an attribute. —*n.* an attributive word.
In the phrase "big brown dog," *big* and *brown*
are attributives. —**at·trib′u·tive·ly,** *adv.* —**at·**
trib′u·tive·ness, *n.* **▶** **attributive.** An adjective
that stands before its noun is attributive (a
blue shirt), as contrasted with a predicate adjective (the shirt is *blue*).

at·tri·tion (ə·trish′ən), *n.* 1. wearing away by
friction. 2. any gradual process of wearing

down: *war of attrition.* [< L *attritio* < *ad-* against + *terere* rub]

at·tune (ə·tün'; ə·tün'), *v.,* –tuned, –tun·ing. tune. —at·tune'ment, *n.*

at. wt., *Physics, Chem.* atomic weight.

Au, *Chem.* gold.

au·burn (ô'bərn), *n., adj.* reddish brown. [< OF *auborne* < L *alburnus* whitish < *albus* white; appar. confused with *brown*]

Auck·land (ôk'lənd), *n.* an important seaport in N New Zealand.

auc·tion (ôk'shən), *n.* 1. a public sale in which each thing is sold to the highest bidder. 2. auction bridge. —*v.* sell at an auction. [< L *auctio* < *augere* increase]

auction bridge, a variety of bridge in which the players bid for the privilege of declaring the trump or no trumps.

auc·tion·eer (ôk'shən·ir'), *n.* man who conducts auctions. —*v.* sell at an auction.

au·da·cious (ô·dā'shəs), *adj.* 1. bold; daring. 2. too bold; impudent. [< F, < *audace* daring (n.) < L *audacia,* ult. < *audere* dare] —au·da'cious·ly, *adv.* —au·da'cious·ness, *n.*

au·dac·i·ty (ô·das'ə·ti), *n., pl.* –ties. 1. boldness; reckless daring. 2. rude boldness.

au·di·ble (ô'də·bəl), *adj.* capable of being heard. [< Med.L, < L *audire* hear] —au'di·bil'i·ty, au'di·ble·ness, *n.* —au'di·bly, *adv.*

au·di·ence (ô'di·əns), *n.* 1. people gathered in a place to hear or see. 2. any person within hearing. 3. chance to be heard; hearing. 4. formal interview with a person of high rank. 5. act or fact of hearing. 6. *Am.* the readers of a book, newspaper, or magazine. [< OF < L *audientia* hearing < *audire* hear]

au·di·o (ô'di·ō), *adj.* having to do with electronic frequencies that are audible, as sound waves. [< L, I hear]

audio frequency, *Physics, Electronics.* frequency of sound vibrations from about 20 to about 20,000 cycles per second.

au·di·o·phile (ô'di·ə·fīl'), *n.* person who makes a hobby of high-fidelity sound reproduction.

au·dit (ô'dit), *n.* 1. an official examination and check of accounts. 2. statement of an account that has been examined and checked authoritatively. —*v.* 1. examine and check (accounts) officially. 2. *U.S.* attend (a course) as an auditor. [< L *auditus* a hearing < *audire* hear]

au·di·tion (ô·dish'ən), *n.* 1. act of hearing. 2. power or sense of hearing. 3. a hearing to test the voice of a singer, speaker, etc. —*v. U.S.* give (a person) an audition.

au·di·tor (ô'də·tər), *n.* 1. hearer; listener. 2. person who audits accounts. 3. *U.S.* one who attends a college course, but not for credit toward a degree. —au'di·tor·ship', *n.*

au·di·to·ri·um (ô'də·tô'ri·əm; –tō'–), *n., pl.* –to·ri·ums, –to·ri·a (–tô'ri·ə; –tō'–). 1. a large room for an audience in a church, theater, school, etc. 2. *Am.* a building especially designed for the giving of lectures, concerts, etc.

au·di·to·ry (ô'də·tô'ri; –tō'–), *adj., n., pl.* –ries. —*adj.* of or having to do with hearing, the sense of hearing, or the organs of hearing. —*n.* 1. audience. 2. auditorium.

Au·du·bon (ô'də·bon), *n.* **John James,** 1785–1851, American ornithologist and artist.

Aug., August.

au·ger (ô'gər), *n.* tool for boring holes in wood. [OE *nafugār,* orig., a nave borer < *nafu* nave of a wheel + *gār* spear; ME *a nauger* taken as *an auger*]

aught[1] (ôt), *n.* anything: *you may go for aught I care.* —*adv.* at all: *help came too late to avail aught.* [OE *āwiht* < *ā–* ever + *wiht* a thing]

aught[2] (ôt), *n.* zero; cipher; nothing. [see NAUGHT; *a naught* taken as *an aught*]

aug·ment (ôg·ment'), *v.* increase; enlarge. [< L, < *augere* increase] —aug·ment'a·ble, *adj.* —aug·men·ta'tion, *n.* —aug·ment'a·tive, *adj.* —aug·ment'er, *n.*

Augers

au grat·in (ō grat'ən, grä'tən; *Fr.* ō grä-tan'), *French.* cooked with crumbs or cheese, or both.

Augs·burg (ôgz'bėrg), *n.* city in SW Germany.

au·gur (ô'gər), *n.* 1. priest in ancient Rome who made predictions and gave advice. 2. prophet; fortuneteller. —*v.* 1. predict; foretell. 2. be a sign. [< L, appar. increase, growth (of crops), personified in ritual service, < *augere* increase]

au·gu·ry (ô'gyə·ri), *n., pl.* –ries. 1. art or practice of foretelling the future. 2. indication; sign; omen.

Au·gust (ô'gəst), *n.* the 8th month of the year, containing 31 days. [after *Augustus*]

au·gust (ô·gust'), *adj.* inspiring reverence and admiration; majestic; venerable. [< L, < unrecorded *augus* increase, power < *augere* to increase] —au·gust'ly, *adv.* —au·gust'ness, *n.*

Au·gus·ta (ô·gus'tə), *n.* capital of Maine, in the SW part.

Au·gus·tan age (ô·gus'tən), 1. period of Latin literature from 27 B.C. to 14 A.D. 2. period of English literature from 1700 to 1750.

Au·gus·tine (ô'gəs·tēn; ô·gus'tin), *n.* 1. **Saint,** 354–430 A.D., bishop of N Africa and one of the great leaders in the early Christian church. 2. **Saint,** died 604 A.D., Roman monk sent to preach Christianity in England in 597 A.D. —Au·gus·tin·i·an (ô'gəs·tin'i·ən), *adj., n.*

Au·gus·tus (ô·gus'təs), *n.* (*Augustus Caesar*), 63 B.C.–14 A.D., title of Gaius Octavianus (Octavian) as first emperor of Rome, 27 B.C.–14 A.D. —Au·gus'tan, *adj.*

auk (ôk), *n.* northern sea bird with short wings used only as paddles. [< Scand. *ālka*]

auk·let (ôk'lit), *n.* small kind of auk.

auld (ôld), *adj. Scot.* old.

auld lang syne (ôld' lang sīn'; zīn'), *Scot.* old times; long ago in one's life.

aunt (ant; änt), *n.* 1. sister of one's father or mother. 2. uncle's wife. [< OF < L *amita* father's sister]

au·ra (ô'rə), *n., pl.* au·ras, au·rae (ô'rē). something supposed to come from a person or thing and surround him or it as an atmosphere. [< L < Gk.]

au·ral (ô'rəl), *adj.* of the ear; having to do with hearing. —au'ral·ly, *adv.*

au·re·ate (ô'ri·it; –āt), *adj.* golden; gilded. [< L, < *aurum* gold]

Au·re·li·us (ô·rē'li·əs; ô·rēl'yəs), *n.* See Antoninus.

au·re·ole (ô'ri·ōl), **au·re·o·la** (ô·rē'ə·lə), *n.* 1. encircling radiance; halo. 2. a ring of light surrounding the sun. [< L *aureola* (*corona*) golden (crown) < *aurum* gold]

au·re·o·my·cin (ô'ri·ō·mī'sin), *n.* drug related to streptomycin, used to check or kill bacteria and viruses. [< L *aureus* golden + Gk. *mykes* fungus; from its color]

au re·voir (ō rə·vwär'), good-by; till I see you again. [< F; *revoir* < L, < *re–* again + *videre* see]

au·ri·cle (ô'rə·kəl), *n.* 1. *Anat.* a. chamber of the heart that receives the blood from the veins. b. outer part of the ear. 2. an earlike part. [< L *auricula,* dim. of *auris* ear] —au'ri·cled, *adj.*

au·ric·u·lar (ô·rik'yə·lər), *adj.* 1. of or near the ear. 2. said privately. 3. perceived by the sense of hearing. 4. shaped like an ear. 5. having to do with an auricle of the heart. —au·ric'u·lar·ly, *adv.*

au·rif·er·ous (ô·rif'ər·əs), *adj.* yielding gold. [< L, < *aurum* gold + *ferre* bear] —au·rif'er·ous·ly, *adv.*

au·rochs (ô'roks), *n., pl.* –rochs. 1. European bison, now almost extinct. 2. extinct wild ox. [< G *auerochs*]

Au·ro·ra (ô·rô'rə; –rō'–), *n.* 1. *Class. Myth.* goddess of the dawn. 2. **aurora,** a. dawn. b. streamers or bands of light appearing in the sky at night. —au·ro'ral, *adj.* —au·ro'ral·ly, *adv.*

aurora aus·tra·lis (ôs·trā'lis), streamers or bands of light appearing in the southern sky at night.

au·ro·ra bo·re·a·lis (bô′ri·al′is; -ā′lis; bō′-), streamers or bands of light appearing in the northern sky at night.

aus·pice (ôs′pis), *n.*, *pl.* **aus·pi·ces** (ôs′pə·siz). 1. divination or prophecy, esp. one made from the flight of birds. 2. omen; sign. 3. favorable circumstance; indication of success. 4. auspices, patronage. [< F < L *auspicium* < *avis* bird + *specere* look at. See def. 1.]

aus·pi·cious (ôs·pish′əs), *adj.* 1. with signs of success; favorable. 2. fortunate. —**aus·pi′cious·ly**, *adv.* —**aus·pi′cious·ness**, *n.*

Aus·ten (ôs′tən), *n.* Jane, 1775-1817, English novelist.

aus·tere (ôs·tir′), *adj.* 1. harsh to the feelings; stern in manner. 2. strict in self-discipline or in self-restraint. 3. severely simple. 4. sour. [< L < Gk. *austeros* < *auein* dry] —**aus·tere′ly**, *adv.*

aus·ter·i·ty (ôs·ter′ə·ti), *n.*, *pl.* -ties. 1. sternness; severity. 2. austerities, severe practices.

Aus·tin (ôs′tən), *n.* capital of Texas, in the C part.

aus·tral (ôs′trəl), *adj.* 1. southern. 2. Austral, a. Australian. b. Australasian. [< L, < *auster* the south wind; akin to EAST]

Aus·tral·a·sia (ôs′trəl·ā′zhə; -shə), *n.* Australia, Tasmania, New Zealand, and nearby islands. —**Aus′tral·a′sian**, *adj.*, *n.*

Aus·tral·ia (ôs·trāl′yə), *n.* 1. continent SE of Asia. 2. Commonwealth of, British dominion that includes this continent and Tasmania. —**Aus·tral′ian**, *adj.*, *n.*

Aus·tral·ian ballot, *Am.* ballot with the names of all candidates on it, which is marked secretly.

Aus·tri·a (ôs′tri·ə), *n.* country in central Europe. —**Aus′tri·an**, *adj.*, *n.*

Aus·tri·a-Hun·ga·ry (ôs′tri·ə·hung′gə·ri), *n.* a former monarchy in central Europe. —**Aus·tro-Hun·gar·i·an** (ôs′trō·hung·gãr′i·ən), *adj.*

au·tar·chy (ô′tär·ki), *n.*, *pl.* -chies. 1. autocracy. 2. autarky. —**au·tar′chic**, **au·tar′chi·cal**, *adj.*

au·tar·ky (ô′tär·ki), *n.*, *pl.* -kies. independence of imports from other nations. —**au·tar′ki·cal**, *adj.* —**au′tar·kist**, *n.*

au·then·tic (ô·then′tik), **au·then·ti·cal** (-tə·kəl), *adj.* 1. reliable: *an authentic count.* 2. genuine: *an authentic signature.* 3. authoritative. [< L < Gk., < *auto-* by oneself + *hentes* one who acts] —**au·then′ti·cal·ly**, *adv.*

au·then·ti·cate (ô·then′tə·kāt), *v.*, -**cat·ed**, -**cat·ing**. 1. establish the truth of. 2. establish the authorship of. —**au·then′ti·ca′tion**, *n.* —**au·then′ti·ca′tor**, *n.*

au·then·tic·i·ty (ô′then·tis′ə·ti), *n.* 1. reliability. 2. genuineness.

au·thor (ô′thər), *n.* 1. person who writes books, stories, or articles. 2. an author's publications: *have you read this author?* 3. person who creates or begins anything. [< OF < L *auctor* < *augere* increase] —**Syn.** 1. writer. 3. creator.

au·thor·ess (ô′thər·is), *n.* a woman author.

au·thor·i·tar·i·an (ə·thôr′ə·tãr′i·ən; -thor′-), *adj.* favoring obedience to authority instead of individual freedom. —*n.* person who supports authoritarian principles. —**au·thor′i·tar′i·an·ism**, *n.*

au·thor·i·ta·tive (ə·thôr′ə·tā′tiv; ə·thor′-), *adj.* 1. having authority; officially ordered. 2. commanding: *authoritative tones.* 3. that ought to be believed or obeyed. —**au·thor′i·ta′tive·ly**, *adv.* —**au·thor′i·ta′tive·ness**, *n.*

au·thor·i·ty (ə·thôr′ə·ti; ə·thor′-), *n.*, *pl.* -ties. 1. legal power to enforce obedience. 2. the authorities, a. officials of the government. b. persons in control. 3. influence that creates respect and confidence. 4. source of correct information or wise advice. 5. expert on some subject. [< F < L *auctoritas*] —**Syn.** 1. control, jurisdiction, dominion. 3. prestige.

au·thor·ize (ô′thər·īz), *v.*, -**ized**, -**iz·ing**. 1. give power or right to. 2. make legal; sanction. 3. give authority for; justify. —**au′thor·i·za′tion**, *n.* —**au′thor·iz′er**, *n.* —**Syn.** 1. empower.

au·thor·ized (ô′thər·īzd), *adj.* 1. having authority. 2. supported by authority.

Authorized Version, the English translation of the Bible published in 1611; the King James Version.

au·thor·ship (ô′thər·ship), *n.* 1. occupation of an author. 2. source; origin.

au·to (ô′tō), *n.*, *pl.* **au·tos**. *Am.* automobile.

auto-, *word element.* 1. self, as in *autobiography*, *auto-intoxication.* 2. automobile, as in *autobus.* [< Gk.; also (before vowels and *h*), *aut-*]

Au·to·bahn (ou′tō·bän′), *n.*, *pl.* -**bahn·nen** (-bä′nən). in Germany, a four-lane highway with no speed limit.

au·to·bi·og·ra·phy (ô′tə·bī·og′rə·fi; -bi-), *n.*, *pl.* -**phies**. story of a person's life written by himself. —**au′to·bi·og′ra·pher**, *n.* —**au′to·bi·o·graph·ic** (ô′tə·bī′ə·graf′ik), **au′to·bi′o·graph′i·cal**, *adj.* —**au′to·bi′o·graph′i·cal·ly**, *adv.* ➤ See biography for usage note.

au·to·clave (ô′tə·klāv), *n.* a strong, closed vessel used for sterilizing, cooking, etc. [< F, < *auto-* self + L *clavis* key]

auto court, *Am.* motel.

au·toc·ra·cy (ô·tok′rə·si), *n.*, *pl.* -**cies**. 1. government having absolute power over its citizens. 2. absolute authority; unlimited power over a group. —**au·to·crat·ic** (ô′tə·krat′ik), **au′to·crat′i·cal**, *adj.* —**au′to·crat′i·cal·ly**, *adv.*

au·to·crat (ô′tə·krat), *n.* 1. ruler having absolute power over his subjects. 2. person having unlimited power over a group of persons. [< Gk., < *auto-* self + *kratos* strength]

au·to·da·fé (ô′tō·də·fā′; ou′-), *n.*, *pl.* **au·tos·da·fé**. public ceremony accompanying the passing of sentence by the Spanish Inquisition. [< Pg., act of the faith, < L *actus* and *fides*]

au·to·gi·ro, au·to·gy·ro (ô′tə·ji′rō), *n.*, *pl.* -**ros**. 1. airplane with a horizontal propeller that enables the airplane to go straight up or down. 2. Autogiro, a trademark for this airplane. [< Sp. < Gk. *auto-* self + *gyros* circle]

au·to·graph (ô′tə·graf; -gräf), *n.* 1. person's signature. 2. something written in a person's own handwriting. —*v.* 1. write one's signature in or on. 2. write with one's own hand.

au·to·ist (ô′tō·ist), *n. Am., Colloq.* motorist.

au·to·mat (ô′tə·mat), *n.* restaurant in which food is obtained from compartments that open when coins are inserted in slots. [short for *automatic*]

au·to·mat·ic (ô′tə·mat′ik), *adj.* 1. moving or acting by itself: *automatic pump.* 2. *Physiol.* a. done unconsciously, as certain muscular reactions. b. independent of external stimuli, as the beating of the heart. 3. of a firearm, pistol, etc., utilizing the recoil, or part of the force of the explosions, to eject the cartridge shell, introduce a new cartridge, etc. —*n.* 1. a. any automatic gun. b. *Am.* an automatic pistol or rifle. 2. an automatic machine or device. [see AUTOMATON] —**au′to·mat′i·cal·ly**, *adv.*

au·to·ma·tion (ô′tə·mā′shən), *n.* method or technique of making a manufacturing process, a production line, etc., operate more automatically by the use of built-in or supplementary controls in a machine or number of machines. [< *autom(atic)* + *(oper)ation*]

au·tom·a·tism (ô·tom′ə·tiz·əm), *n.* 1. action not controlled by the will. 2. automatic quality.

au·tom·a·ton (ô·tom′ə·ton; -tən), *n.*, *pl.* -**tons**, -**ta** (-tə). 1. person or animal whose actions are purely mechanical. 2. machine that has its motive power concealed. 3. thing able to move itself. [< Gk., acting by one's self]

au·to·mo·bile (*n.* ô′tə·mə·bēl, ô′tə·mə·bēl′, -mō′bēl; *adj.* ô′tə·mō′bil, -bēl; *v.* ô′tə·mə·bēl′, -mō′bēl), *n.*, *adj.*, *v.*, -**biled**, -**bil·ing**. *Am.* —*n.* motorcar; car that carries its own engine. —*adj.* self-moving: *an automobile torpedo.* —*v.* travel by automobile. [< F. See MOBILE.]

au·to·mo·bil·ist (ô′tə·mə·bēl′ist; -mō′bil·ist), *n.* person who uses an automobile.

au·to·mo·tive (ô′tə·mō′tiv), *adj.* 1. of automobiles. 2. self-moving.

au·to·nom·ic (ô′tə·nom′ik), **au·to·nom·i·cal** (-ə·kəl), *adj.* autonomous.

autonomic system, the ganglia and nerves that control digestive and other involuntary reactions.

au·ton·o·mous (ô·ton′ə·məs), *adj.* 1. self-governing; independent. 2. *Biol.* reacting independently. 3. *Bot.* spontaneous. —au·ton′o·mous·ly, *adv.*

au·ton·o·my (ô·ton′ə·mi), *n., pl.* -mies. 1. power or right of self-government. 2. a self-governing community. [< Gk., < *auto*- of oneself + *nomos* law] —au·ton′o·mist, *n.*

au·top·sy (ô′top·si; ô′təp-), *n., pl.* -sies. medical examination of a dead body to find the cause of death. [< NL < Gk., < *auto*- for oneself + *opsis* a seeing]

au·to·sug·ges·tion (ô′tō·səg·jes′chən; -sə-jes′-), *n. Psychol.* suggestion to oneself of ideas that produce actual effects.

au·tumn (ô′təm), *n.* 1. season of the year between summer and winter. 2. season of maturity. —*adj.* of autumn; coming in autumn. [< L *autumnus*] —au·tum·nal (ô·tum′nəl), *adj.* —au·tum′nal·ly, *adv.*

autumnal equinox. See equinox.

aux·il·ia·ry (ôg·zil′yə·ri; -zil′ə-), *adj., n., pl.* -ries. —*adj.* 1. helping; assistant. 2. additional. —*n.* 1. helper; aid. 2. auxiliary verb. 3. auxiliaries, foreign or allied troops that help the army of a nation at war. [< L, < *auxilium* aid]

auxiliary verb, verb used to form the tenses, moods, or voices of other verbs, such as *be, can, do, have,* and *may*: I am going; he *will* go; they *are* lost; they *were* lost.

A.V., Authorized Version.

a·vail (ə·vāl′), *v.* 1. be of use or value to; help; benefit. 2. avail oneself of, take advantage of; make use of. —*n.* 1. help; benefit. 2. efficacy for a purpose; use. [appar. < *a*- to (< OF < L *ad*-) + *vail* < F < L *valere* be worth]

a·vail·a·ble (ə·vāl′ə·bəl), *adj.* 1. that can be used. 2. that can be had. 3. *Law.* efficacious; valid. —a·vail′a·bil′i·ty, a·vail′a·ble·ness, *n.* —a·vail′a·bly, *adv.*

av·a·lanche (av′ə·lanch; -länch), *n., v.,* -lanched, -lanch·ing. —*n.* 1. a large mass of snow and ice, or of dirt and rocks, sliding or falling down a mountainside. 2. anything like an avalanche. —*v.* slide down in or like an avalanche. [< F < Swiss F *lavenche,* infl. by F *avaler* go down < *à val* < L *ad vallem* to the valley]

a·vant-garde (ä·vän·gärd′), *n.* in art, literature, music, etc., those who are most experimental and inventive in a particular period. —*adj.* experimental and inventive. [< F < *avant* forward + *garde* guard] —a·vant′-gard′ist, *n.*

av·a·rice (av′ə·ris), *n.* greedy desire for money. [< OF < L, < *avarus* greedy] —av·a·ri·cious (av′ə·rish′əs), *adj.* —a·a·ri′cious·ly, *adv.* —av′a·ri′cious·ness, *n.* —Ant. generosity.

a·vast (ə·vast′; ə·väst′), *interj. Naut.* stop! stay! [prob. < Du. *houd vast* hold fast]

a·vaunt (ə·vônt′; ə·vänt′), *interj. Archaic.* go away! [< F < L *ab ante* forward, in front]

a·ve (ā′vā; ā′vē), *interj.* hail! farewell! —*n.* Ave, the prayer Ave Maria. [< L]

Ave., ave., avenue; avenue.

A·ve Ma·ri·a (ā′vā mə·rē′ə; ä′vē), **A·ve Mar·y** (ā′vē mār′i), 1. "Hail Mary!", the first words of the Latin form of a prayer of the Roman Catholic Church. 2. the prayer.

a·venge (ə·venj′), *v.,* -venged, a·veng·ing. 1. get revenge for. 2. get revenge on behalf of. 3. get revenge. [< OF, < *a*- to (< L *ad*-) + *vengier* < L *vindicare* punish < *vindex* champion] —a·venge′ment, *n.* —a·veng′er, *n.*

av·e·nue (av′ə·nü; -nū), *n.* 1. *Am.* wide or main street. 2. road or walk bordered by trees. 3. way of approach or departure; passage. 4. *Am.* a city thoroughfare, running at right angles to others properly called "streets." [< F, fem. pp. of *avenir* < L, < *ad*- to + *venire* come]

a·ver (ə·vér′), *v.,* a·verred, a·ver·ring. 1. state to be true; assert. 2. *Law.* prove; justify. [< OF, ult. < L *ad*- to + *verus* true] —a·ver′ment, *n.*

av·er·age (av′rij; av′ər·ij), *n., adj., v.,* -aged, -ag·ing. —*n.* 1. quantity found by dividing the sum of all the quantities by the number of quantities: *the average of 3, 5, and 10 is 6.* 2. usual kind or quality; ordinary amount or rate.

—*adj.* 1. obtained by averaging; being an average: *an average price.* 2. usual; ordinary: *average intelligence.* —*v.* 1. find the average of. 2. amount on an average to. 3. do on an average: *he averages six hours work a day.* 4. divide among several proportionately. [< F *avarie* damage to ship or cargo < Ar. *'awārīya* damage from sea water. In E extended to "equal distribution" (at first, "of loss").] —av′er·age·ly, *adv.* —av′er·ag·er, *n.*

A·ver·nus (ə·vér′nəs), *n. Rom. Myth.* the lower world; Hades. —A·ver′nal, *adj.*

a·verse (ə·vérs′), *adj.* opposed; unwilling. [< L *aversus.* See AVERT.] —a·verse′ly, *adv.* —a·verse′ness, *n.*

a·ver·sion (ə·vér′zhən; -shən), *n.* 1. strong or fixed dislike; antipathy. 2. object of dislike. 3. unwillingness.

a·vert (ə·vért′), *v.* 1. prevent; avoid. 2. turn away; turn aside. [< OF < LL, < L *ab*- from + *vertere* turn] —a·vert′ed·ly, *adv.* —a·vert′i·ble, a·vert′a·ble, *adj.* —a·vert′er, *n.*

A·ves (ā′vēz), *n.pl. Zool.* class of vertebrates comprising the birds. [< L]

A·ves·ta (ə·ves′tə), *n.* the sacred writings of the ancient Zoroastrianism. —A·ves′tan, *adj.*

a·vi·ar·y (ā′vi·er′i), *n., pl.* -ar·ies. place where many birds are kept. [< L, < *avis* bird] —a·vi·a·rist (ā′vi·ə·rist), *n.*

a·vi·a·tion (ā′vi·ā′shən; av′i-), *n.* flying in airplanes; art or science of navigating aircraft. [< F, < L *avis* bird]

a·vi·a·tor (ā′vi·ā′tər; av′i-), *n.* person who flies an airplane; airplane pilot.

a·vi·a·tress (ā′vi·ā′tris; av′i-), *n.* aviatrix.

a·vi·a·trix (ā′vi·ā′triks; av′i-), *n.* a woman aviator.

av·id (av′id), *adj.* eager; greedy. [< L *avidus* < *avere* desire eagerly] —a·vid·i·ty (ə·vid′ə·ti), *n.* —av′id·ly, *adv.*

A·vi·gnon (ä·vē·nyôn′), *n.* city in SE France; residence of the popes, 1309–1377.

av·o·ca·do (av′ə·kä′dō; ä′və-), *n., pl.* -dos. 1. *Am.* a pear-shaped tropical fruit with a dark-green skin; alligator pear. 2. tree that it grows on. [< Sp., var. of *aguacate* < Mexican *ahuacatl*]

av·o·ca·tion (av′ə·kā′shən), *n.* 1. minor occupation; hobby. 2. *Colloq.* regular business; occupation. [< L, < *ab*- away + *vocare* to call]

av·o·cet, av·o·set (av′ə·set), *n.* a web-footed wading bird. [< F < Ital. *avosetta*]

a·void (ə·void′), *v.* 1. keep out of the way of. 2. *Law.* make void; annul. [< AF var. of OF *esvuidier* empty, quit < *es*- out (< L *ex*-) + *vuidier* < VL *vocitare* empty] —a·void′a·ble, *adj.* —a·void′a·bly, *adv.* —a·void′ance, *n.* —a·void′er, *n.*

av·oir·du·pois (av′ər·də·poiz′), *n.* 1. avoirdupois weight. 2. *Am., Colloq.* a person's weight. [< OF *avoir de pois* (goods that) have weight < L *habere* have, *de* of, and *pensum* weight]

avoirdupois weight, system of weighing in which a pound containing sixteen ounces is used.

A·von (ā′von; av′on), *n.* river in C England.

a·vouch (ə·vouch′), *v.* 1. declare to be true. 2. guarantee. 3. acknowledge; affirm. [< OF *avochier* < *a*- + *vochier.* See VOUCH.]

a·vow (ə·vou′), *v.* declare frankly or openly; confess; admit; acknowledge. [< OF, < *a*- (< L *ad*- + *vouer* < VL *votare* vow] —a·vow′er, *n.*

a·vow·al (ə·vou′əl), *n.* frank or open declaration; confession; admission.

a·vowed (ə·voud′), *adj.* openly declared; admitted; acknowledged. —a·vow·ed·ly (ə·vou′id·li), *adv.* —a·vow′ed·ness, *n.*

a·vun·cu·lar (ə·vung′kyə·lər), *adj.* 1. of an uncle. 2. like an uncle. [< L *avunculus* mother's brother, dim. of *avus* grandfather]

a·wait (ə·wāt′), *v.* 1. wait for; look forward to. 2. be ready for; be in store for. 3. wait; be expectant. [< OF, < *a*- for (< L *ad*-) + *waitier* < Gmc.] —a·wait′er, *n.* —Syn. 1. expect.

a·wake (ə·wāk′), *v.,* a·woke or a·waked, a·wak·ing, *adj.* —*v.* wake up; arouse. —*adj.* not asleep; alert. [OE *āwacian* + OE *onwæcnan*]

a·wak·en (ə·wāk′ən), *v.* wake up; arouse. —a·wak′en·er, *n.*

a·wak·en·ing (ə·wāk′ən·ing), *adj.* arousing. —*n.* 1. act of awaking. 2. *Am.*, *Obs.* a religious revival.

a·ward (ə·wôrd′), *v.* 1. give after careful consideration; grant. 2. decide or settle by law; adjudge. —*n.* 1. something given after careful consideration; prize. 2. *Law.* decision by a judge. [< AF var. of OF *esguarder* observe, decide < L *ex-* from + *wardare* guard < Gmc.] —a·ward′·a·ble, *adj.* —a·ward′er, *n.*

a·ware (ə·wār′), *adj.* knowing; realizing; conscious. [OE *gewær*] —a·ware′ness, *n.*

a·wash (ə·wosh′; ə·wôsh′), *adv.*, *adj.* 1. just covered with water. 2. washed over. 3. floating.

a·way (ə·wā′), *adv.* 1. from a place; to a distance. 2. at a distance; far. 3. in another direction; aside: *turn away.* 4. out of one's possession: *he gave his boat away.* 5. out of existence: *the sounds died away.* 6. without stopping; continuously: *she worked away at her job.* 7. without hesitation; at once. 8. **away back,** *Am.*, *Colloq.* far back in space or time. 9. **away with,** a. take away. b. go away. 10. **do away with,** a. put an end to; get rid of. b. kill. —*adj.* 1. at a distance; far. 2. absent; gone. [OE *onweg*]

awe (ô), *n., v.,* awed, aw·ing. —*n.* great fear and wonder; fear and reverence. —*v.* 1. cause to feel awe; fill with awe. 2. influence or restrain by awe. [< Scand. *agi*] —aw′less, awe′less, *adj.*

a·weigh (ə·wā′), *adj. Naut.* raised off the bottom: *anchors aweigh.*

awe·some (ô′səm), *adj.* 1. causing awe. 2. showing awe; awed. —awe′some·ly, *adv.* —awe′·some·ness, *n.*

awe-struck (ô′struk′), **awe-strick·en** (ô′strik′ən), *adj.* filled with awe.

aw·ful (ô′fəl), *adj.* 1. dreadful; terrible: *an awful storm.* 2. *Colloq.* very bad, great, ugly, etc. 3. deserving great respect and reverence. 4. filling with awe; impressive. —*adv. Am., Colloq.* very: *he was awful mad.* [< *awe* + -*ful*] —aw′ful·ness, *n.* —Syn. *adj.* 1. fearful. 3. sublime, grand. 4. imposing. ▶ In formal English *awful* means "inspiring with awe." In familiar English it is a general utility word of disapproval: *awful manners.* As a result *awe-inspiring* has taken its place.

aw·ful·ly (ô′fli; ô′fəl·i), *adv.* 1. dreadfully; terribly. 2. *Colloq.* very.

a·while (ə·hwīl′), *adv.* for a short time.

awk·ward (ôk′wərd), *adj.* 1. clumsy; not graceful or skillful. 2. not well-suited to use. 3. not easy to manage or deal with. 4. embarrassing. [< obs. *awk* perversely, in the wrong way (< Scand. *öfugr* turned the wrong way) + -*ward*] —awk′ward·ly, *adv.* —awk′ward·ness, *n.* —Syn. 4. trying, disconcerting. —Ant. 2. handy.

awl (ôl), *n.* tool used for making small holes in leather or wood. [OE *æl*]

awn (ôn), *n. Bot.* one of the bristly hairs forming the beard on a head of barley, oats, etc. [< Scand. *ögn* chaff] —awned, *adj.* —awn′less, *adj.*

awn·ing (ôn′ing), *n.* a rooflike shelter of canvas, etc., over a door, window, porch, etc.

a·woke (ə·wōk′), *v.* pt. and pp. of awake.

A.W.O.L., a.w.o.l. (ā′wôl, *or pronounced as initials*), *Am., Mil.* absent without leave.

a·wry (ə·rī′), *adv., adj.* 1. with a twist or turn to one side. 2. wrong. [< *a* on, in + *wry*]

ax, axe (aks), *n., pl.* ax·es, *v.,* axed, ax·ing. —*n.* 1. tool with a bladed head on a handle, used for chopping, etc. 2. battle-ax. —*v.* cut or shape with an ax. [OE *æx*] —ax′like′, *adj.*

ax·es¹ (ak′sēz), *n.* pl. of axis.

ax·es² (ak′siz), *n.* pl. of ax.

ax·i·al (ak′si·əl), **ax·ile** (ak′sil; -sīl), *adj.* 1. of an axis; forming an axis. 2. on or around an axis. —ax′i·al·ly, *adv.*

ax·il (ak′sil), *n. Bot.* angle between the upper side of a leaf or stem and the supporting stem or branch. [< L *axilla* armpit]

ax·il·la (ak·sil′ə), *n., pl.* ax·il·lae (ak·sil′ē). 1. *Anat.* armpit. 2. *Bot.* axil. [< L]

ax·il·lar·y (ak′sə·ler′i), *adj.* 1. of or near the armpit. 2. *Bot.* in or growing from an axil.

ax·i·om (ak′si·əm), *n.* 1. statement seen to be true without proof; self-evident truth. 2. established principle. [< L < Gk., < *axios* worthy] —ax·i·o·mat·ic (ak′si·ə·mat′ik), ax′i·o·mat′i·cal, *adj.* —ax′i·o·mat′i·cal·ly, *adv.*

ax·is (ak′sis), *n., pl.* ax·es (ak′sēz). 1. imaginary or real line that passes through an object and about which the object turns or seems to turn. 2. central or principal line around which parts are arranged regularly. 3. central or principal structure extending lengthwise. 4. important line of relation: *the Berlin-Rome axis.* 5. **the Axis,** Germany, Italy, Japan, and their allies, before the end of World War II. [< L]

ax·le (ak′səl), *n.* 1. bar on which or with which a wheel turns. 2. axletree. [OE *eaxl* shoulder, *eax* axle; ? infl. by Scand. *öxl* axle] —ax′led, *adj.*

ax·le·tree (ak′səl·trē′), *n.* crossbar that connects two opposite wheels.

Ax·min·ster (aks′min·stər), *n.* a velvetlike carpet.

ay¹ (ā), *adv.* always; ever. Also, aye. [< Scand. *ei*]

ay² (ī), *adv., n.* yes. Also, aye.

a·yah (ä′yə), *n.* a native maid or nurse in India. [< Hind. < Pg. *aia* governess]

aye¹ (ā), *adv.* always; ever.

aye² (ī), *adv., n.* yes. [OE *gi* YEA]

aye-aye (ī′ī′), *n.* a squirrellike lemur of Madagascar.

a·zal·ea (ə·zāl′yə), *n.* 1. shrub with many showy flowers, resembling rhododendrons. 2. the flower. [< NL < Gk., dry, < *azein* parch]

az·i·muth (az′ə·məth), *n. Astron.* the angular distance east or west from the north point. The azimuth of the North Star is 0 degrees. [< F < Ar. *as-sumūt* the ways < *samt* way] —az·i·muth·al (az′ə·muth′əl; -mū′thəl), *adj.* —az′i·muth′al·ly, *adv.*

Aye-aye (total length 3 ft.; height 8 in.)

A·zores (ə·zôrz′, ə·zōrz′; ā′zôrz, ā′zōrz), *n.pl.* group of islands in the Atlantic west of and belonging to Portugal.

A·zov (ā·zôf′; ā′zov), *n.* **Sea of,** a small sea in S European Russia, connected with the Black Sea by a narrow channel.

Az·tec (az′tek), *n.* member of a highly civilized people who ruled Mexico before its conquest by the Spaniards in 1519. —*adj.* of the Aztecs. —Az′tec·an, *adj.*

az·ure (azh′ər), *adj.* 1. blue; sky blue. 2. the blue sky. 3. a blue pigment. —*adj.* blue; sky-blue. [< OF *l'azur* the azure < Ar. < Pers. *lajward* lapis lazuli]

az·u·rite (azh′ə·rīt), *n.* a blue copper ore. It is a basic carbonate of copper, $2CuCO_3 \cdot Cu(OH)_2$.

B

B, b (bē), *n., pl.* **B's; b's. 1.** the second letter of the alphabet. **2.** *Music.* the seventh note in the scale of C major.

B, *Chem.* boron.

B., 1. Bay. **2.** Bible. **3.** British.

b., 1. base. **2.** bass. **3.** bay. **4.** book. **5.** born.

Ba, *Chem.* barium.

B.A., Bachelor of Arts. Also, A.B.

baa (bä), *v.,* **baaed, baa·ing.** bleat.

Ba·al (bā′əl; bäl), *n., pl.* **Ba·al·im** (bā′əl·im). **1.** the chief god of the Canaanites and Phoenicians. **2.** a false god. —**Ba′al·ism,** *n.* —**Ba′al·ist, Ba·al·ite** (bā′əl·īt), *n.*

bab·bitt (bab′it), or **Babbitt metal,** *n. Am.* alloy of tin, antimony, and copper, used in bearings to lessen friction.

Bab·bitt (bab′it), *n. Am.* a self-satisfied businessman who readily conforms to middle-class ideas of respectability and business success. —**bab·bitt·ry** (bab′it·ri), *n.*

bab·ble (bab′əl), *v.,* **-bled, -bling,** *n.* —*v.* **1.** make indistinct sounds like a baby. **2.** talk or speak foolishly. **3.** talk too much; tell secrets. **4.** murmur. —*n.* **1.** talk that cannot be understood. **2.** foolish talk. **3.** murmur. [ME *babel,* imit.] —**bab′ble·ment,** *n.* —**bab′bler,** *n.* —**bab′bling·ly,** *adv.*

babe (bāb), *n.* **1.** baby. **2.** an innocent or inexperienced person.

Ba·bel (bā′bəl; bab′əl), *n.* **1.** Babylon, where, according to the Bible, the building of a lofty tower intended to reach heaven was begun and a confusion of the language of the people took place. Gen. 11:1–9. **2.** Also, **babel. a.** confusion of sounds; noise. **b.** place of noise and confusion. [< Heb.]

ba·bies'-breath, ba·by's-breath (bā′biz-breth′), *n.* a tall herb bearing numerous small, fragrant, white or pink flowers.

ba·boo, ba·bu (bä′bü), *n., pl.* **-boos; -bus. 1.** a Hindu title meaning "Mr." **2.** native of India with a smattering of English education. **3.** an Indian clerk who writes English. [< Hind. *babu*]

ba·boon (ba·bün′), *n.* any of various (usually) large, fierce monkeys of Arabia and Africa, with a doglike face and a short tail. [< OF *babouin* stupid person]

ba·by (bā′bi), *n., pl.* **-bies,** *adj., v.,* **-bied, -by·ing.** —*n.* **1.** a very young child. **2.** the youngest of a family or group. **3.** person who acts like a baby. **4.** something unusually small for its kind. **5.** *Am., Slang.* term of praise or approval applied to a person or thing. —*adj.* **1.** of or for a baby. **2.** young. **3.** small for its kind; small. **4.** childish. —*v.* treat as a baby; pamper. [ME *babi*] —**ba′by·hood,** *n.* —**ba′by·ish,** *adj.* —**ba′by·ish·ly,** *adv.* —**ba′by·ish·ness,** *n.* —**ba′by·like′,** *adj.*

Baboon (body 2 ft. high, 2 ft. long; tail 18 in.)

Bab·y·lon (bab′ə·lən; -lon), *n.* **1.** capital of ancient Babylonia, noted for its wealth, magnificence, and wickedness. **2.** any rich or wicked city.

Bab·y·lo·ni·a (bab′ə·lō′ni·ə), *n.* an ancient empire in SW Asia, from 2800 to 1000 B.C. —**Bab′y·lo′ni·an,** *adj., n.*

ba·by-sit (bā′bi·sit′), *v.,* **-sat, -sit·ting.** *Colloq.* take care of a child during the temporary absence of its parents. —**baby sitter.**

bac·ca·lau·re·ate (bak′ə·lô′ri·it), *n.* **1.** degree of bachelor given by a college or university. **2.** Also, **baccalaureate sermon.** *Am.* sermon delivered to a graduating class at commencement. [< Med.L, < *baccalarius*]

bac·ca·rat, bac·ca·ra (bak′ə·rä; bak′ə·rä′), *n.* kind of card game played for money. [< F]

bac·cha·nal (bak′ə·nəl; -nal), *adj.* having to do with Bacchus or his worship. —*n.* **1.** worshiper of Bacchus. **2.** a drunken reveler. **3.** a drunken revelry. **4.** Bacchanals, the Bacchanalia. [< L, < *Bacchus* god of wine < Gk. *Bakchos*]

Bac·cha·na·li·a (bak′ə·nā′li·ə), *n. pl.* **1.** a wild, noisy Roman festival in honor of Bacchus. **2.** bacchanalia, a drunken revelry; orgy. —**bac′cha·na′li·an,** *adj., n.*

bac·chant (bak′ənt), *n., pl.* **bac·chants, bac·chan·tes** (bə·kan′tēz). **1.** priest or worshiper of Bacchus. **2.** a drunken reveler. —**bac·chan·tic** (bə·kan′tik), *adj.*

bac·chan·te (bə·kan′tē; bə·kant′; bak′ənt), *n.* priestess or woman worshiper of Bacchus.

Bac·chic (bak′ik), *adj.* **1.** of Bacchus or his worship. **2.** Also, **bacchic.** drunken; riotous.

Bac·chus (bak′əs), *n. Class. Myth.* god of wine. The Greeks also called him Dionysus.

Bach (bäн), *n.* **Johann Sebastian,** 1685–1750, German composer of music and organist.

bach·e·lor (bach′ə·lər; bach′lər), *n.* **1.** man who has not married. **2.** person who has the first degree of a college or university. **3.** a young knight who served under the banner of another. [< OF < Med.L *baccalārius,* appar., small landowner] —**bach·e·lor·dom** (bach′ə·lər·dəm; bach′lər-), *n. Am.* —**bach′e·lor·hood′,** *n.* —**bach′e·lor·ship′,** *n.*

bach·e·lor-at-arms (bach′ə·lər·ət·ärmz′; bach′lər-), *n., pl.* **bach·e·lors-at-arms.** bachelor (def. 3).

bach·e·lor's-but·ton (bach′ə·lərz·but′ən; bach′lərz-), *n.* **1.** cornflower. **2.** any of several button-shaped flowers or the plants that bear them.

ba·cil·lus (bə·sil′əs), *n., pl.* **-cil·li** (-sil′ī). *Bacteriol.* **1.** any of the rod-shaped bacteria. **2.** any of the bacteria. [< LL, dim. of *baculus* rod]

back¹ (bak), *n.* **1.** part of a person's body opposite to his face or to the front part of his body. **2.** the upper part of an animal's body from the neck to the end of the backbone. **3.** the backbone. **4.** part opposite the front. **5.** part of a chair, couch, etc., that supports the back of a person sitting down. **6.** that part of a garment which covers any part of the body thought of as a back. **7.** the less used part: *the back of the hand.* **8.** player whose position is behind the front line in certain games. **9. behind one's back,** without one's knowing it. —*v.* **1.** support; help. **2.** move backward. **3.** endorse. **4.** bet on. **5.** get upon the back of; mount. **6.** make or be a back for. **7.** of the wind, move counterclockwise with respect to the compass. **8. back and fill, a.** move in a zigzag way. **b.** *U.S. Colloq.* keep changing one's mind. **9. back down,** give up; withdraw. **10. back out** or **out of,** *Colloq.* **a.** withdraw from an undertaking. **b.** break a promise. **11. back up, a.** *Am.* move backward. **b.** support; help. **12. back water,** *Am.* retreat; withdraw. —*adj.* **1.** opposite the front; away from one. **2.** at, in, to, or toward an earlier place, position, etc. **3.** belonging to the past. **4.** overdue. **5.** *Phonet.* pronounced at the back of the mouth. **6.** *Am.* in distant or frontier regions: *back country.* [OE *bæc*] —**back′less,** *adj.* —Syn. *v.* **3.** uphold, second. —*adj.* **1.** rear, hinder. —Ant. *v.* **3.** oppose.

back² (bak), *adv.* **1.** to or toward the rear; behind. **2.** in or toward the past. **3.** in return. **4.** in the place from which it (he, she, etc.) came: *put the books back.* **5.** in reserve. **6.** in check. **7. back of,** *U.S. Colloq.* **a.** in the rear of; behind. **b.** supporting; helping. **8. go back on,** *Colloq.* break a promise to. [var. of *aback*]

back·bite (bak′bīt′), *v.,* **-bit, -bit·ten** or

(*Colloq.*) –bit, –bit·ing. slander (an absent person). —back′bit′er, *n.* —back′bit′ing, *n.*

back·bone (bak′bōn′), *n.* 1. the main bone along the middle of the back in vertebrates; the spine. 2. anything resembling a backbone. 3. the most important part; chief support. 4. strength of character. —back′boned′, *adj.*

back·door (bak′dôr′; –dōr′), *adj.* secret; sly.

back·drop (bak′drop′), *n.* 1. curtain at the back of a stage. 2. background.

back·er (bak′ər), *n.* person who backs or supports another person, some plan or idea, etc.

back·field (bak′fēld′), *n. Am.* 1. *Football.* players behind the front line; quarterback, two halfbacks, and fullback. 2. *Baseball.* the outfield.

back·fire (bak′fīr′), *n.*, *v.*, –fired, –fir·ing. —*n.* 1. explosion of gas occurring too soon or in the wrong place in a gasoline engine, etc. 2. *Am.* fire set to check a forest or prairie fire by burning off the area in front of it. 3. an adverse reaction. —*v.* 1. explode prematurely. 2. *Am.* set a backfire. 3. have adverse results.

back formation, a word formed on analogy with other words and usually needed to serve as a different part of speech. *Typewrite* is a back formation from *typewriter.* ➤ A number of back formations, like *diagnose* from *diagnosis*, have made their way into the common vocabulary, but some modern ones are formed in fun, like *burgle*, and are used either in humor or in a derogatory sense, like *orate.*

back·gam·mon (bak′gam′ən; bak′gam′ən), *n.* game for two played on a special board, with pieces moved according to the throw of dice. [< *back*[1], adj. + *gammon* game; because the men are sometimes set back]

back·ground (bak′ground′), *n.* 1. part of a picture or scene toward the back. 2. surface against which things are seen or upon which things are made or placed. 3. earlier conditions or events that help to explain some later condition or event. 4. the past experience, knowledge, and training of a person. 5. the accompanying music or sound effects in a play, motion picture, etc. 6. **in the background**, not in clear view.

back·hand (bak′hand′), *n.* 1. stroke made with back of the hand turned outward. 2. handwriting in which the letters slope to the left. —*adj.* backhanded.

back·hand·ed (bak′han′did), *adj.* 1. done or made with the back of the hand turned outward. 2. slanting to the left. 3. awkward; clumsy. 4. indirect; insincere. —back′hand′ed·ly, *adv.*

back·ing (bak′ing), *n.* 1. support; help. 2. supporters; helpers. 3. back part supporting or strengthening something.

back·lash (bak′lash′), *n.* 1. the jarring reaction of a machine or mechanical device. 2. movement between worn or loosely fitting parts.

back·log (bak′lôg′; –log′), *n. Am.* 1. a large log at the back of a wood fire. 2. a reserve of orders, commitments, etc., that have not yet been filled.

back number, *Colloq.* 1. an old issue of a magazine or newspaper. 2. *Am.* an old-fashioned and out-of-date person or thing.

back seat, *Am.*, *Colloq.* place of inferiority or insignificance.

back·sheesh, back·shish (bak′shēsh), *n.* baksheesh.

back·side (bak′sīd′), *n.* 1. back. 2. rump.

back·slide (bak′slīd′), *v.*, –slid, –slid·den or –slid, –slid·ing. slide back into wrongdoing; lose one's enthusiasm for religion or the church. —back′slid′er, *n.*

back·stage (bak′stāj′), *adv.* 1. in the dressing rooms of a theater. 2. toward the rear of a stage. —*adj.* happening, located, etc., backstage.

back·stay (bak′stā′), *n.* 1. *Naut.* rope extending from the top of the mast to the ship's side. 2. *Mach.* a supporting or checking device.

back·stop (bak′stop′), *n.* 1. fence or screen used in various games to keep the ball from going too far away. 2. player who stops balls in various games.

back·stroke (bak′strōk′), *n.* 1. a swimming stroke made with the swimmer lying on his back. 2. a backhanded stroke.

back talk, *U.S. Colloq.* talking back; impudent answers.

back·track (bak′trak′), *v. Am.* 1. go back over a course or path. 2. withdraw from an undertaking, position, etc. —Syn. 1. return.

back·ward (bak′wərd), *adv.* Also, back′wards. 1. toward the back: *walk backward.* 2. with the back first. 3. toward the starting point. 4. opposite to the usual way; in the reverse way: *read backward.* 5. from better to worse. 6. toward the past. —*adj.* 1. directed toward the back: *a backward glance.* 2. with the back first. 3. reversed; returning. 4. done in reverse order. 5. from better to worse; retrogressive. 6. reaching back into the past. 7. slow in development; dull. 8. behind time; late. 9. shy; bashful. [ME *bakward* < *bak* BACK[1] + –WARD] —back′ward·ly, *adv.* —back′ward·ness, *n.*

back·wash (bak′wosh′; –wôsh′), *n.* 1. water thrown back by oars, paddle wheels, the passing of a ship, etc. 2. backward current.

back·wa·ter (bak′wô′tər; –wot′ər), *n.* 1. water held or pushed back. 2. a sluggish, stagnant condition; backward place. 3. backwash.

back·woods (bak′wủdz′), *n.pl. Am.* uncleared regions far away from towns. —*adj.* Also, back′wood′. 1. of the backwoods. 2. crude; rough. —back′woods′man, *n. Am.*

ba·con (bā′kən), *n.* salted and smoked meat from the back and sides of a hog. [< OF < Gmc.]

Ba·con (bā′kən), *n.* Francis, 1561–1626, English essayist, statesman, and philosopher. —Ba·co·ni·an (bā·kō′ni·ən), *adj.*, *n.*

bac·te·ri·a (bak·tir′i·ə), *n.pl.* microscopic vegetable organisms, usually single-celled and having no chlorophyll, multiplying by fission and spore formation. Various species of bacteria are concerned in fermentation and putrefaction, the production of disease, etc. —bac·te′ri·al, *adj.* —bac·te′ri·al·ly, *adv.*

SPHERE ROD SPIRAL
Bacteria

bac·te·ri·cide (bak·tir′ə·sīd), *n.* substance that destroys bacteria. [< *bacterium* + –*cide* < L –*cida* killer < *caedere* kill] —bac·te′ri·cid′al, *adj.*

bacteriol., bacteriology.

bac·te·ri·ol·o·gy (bak·tir′i·ol′ə·ji), *n.* science that deals with bacteria. [< *bacterium* + –LOGY] —bac·te·ri·o·log·i·cal (bak·tir′i·ə·loj′ə·kəl), *adj.* —bac·te′ri·ol′o·gist, *n.*

bac·te·ri·o·phage (bak·tir′i·ə·fāj), *n.* bactericide produced within the body and normally present in the intestines, urine, blood, etc. [< *bacterium* + –*phage* eating < Gk. *phagein* eat]

bac·te·ri·um (bak·tir′i·əm), *n.*, *pl.* –te·ri·a (–tir′i·ə). one of the bacteria. [< NL < Gk. *baktērion*, dim. of *baktron*]

Bac·tri·an camel (bak′tri·ən), camel with two humps.

bad[1] (bad), *adj.*, worse, worst, *n.*, *adv.* —*adj.* 1. not as it ought to be; not good. 2. evil; wicked. 3. disagreeable; painful. 4. harmful. 5. sick; injured. 6. unfavorable: *he came at a bad time.* 7. worthless; of no account. 8. incorrect; faulty. 9. not valid. 10. rotten; spoiled: *a bad egg.* 11. *Am.* hostile; dangerous; murderous. —*n.* 1. that which is bad; bad condition, quality, etc. 2. **be in bad**, *Am.*, *Slang.* be in disfavor (of or over). —*adv.* badly. [orig. pp. of OE *bæddan* defile] —bad′ness, *n.* —Syn. *adj.* 1. inferior, poor. 2. sinful. 4. injurious. 8. defective, imperfect. 11. vicious. ➤ *Bad* is usually the adjective, though *badly* is used in the predicate (either: I feel *bad* or I feel *badly*); *badly* is usually the adverb, but *bad* is colloquially used: He draws *badly* (colloq. *bad*). *Worse, worst,* the comparative and superlative of *bad,* were originally used in comparing *evil* and *ill;* when *bad* acquired the meaning of these words, *worse* and *worst* were used for it too.

bad[2] (bad), *v.* pt. of bid (defs. 1, 2).

bade (bad), *v.* pt. of bid.

badge (baj), n., v., badged, badg·ing. —n. 1. a token or device worn as a sign of occupation, authority, achievements, or membership. 2. symbol; sign. —v. furnish with a badge or as with a badge. [ME *bage*] —badge'less, adj.

badg·er (baj'ər), n. 1. any of various burrowing carnivorous mammals of Europe and America related to the weasels. 2. its fur. —v. keep on teasing or annoying; torment by nagging. [? < *badge*; with ref. to white spot on head]

bad·i·nage (bad'ə·näzh'; bad'ə·nij), n. joking; banter. [< F, < *badiner* banter < *badin* silly < VL *batāre* gape]

Bad Lands, Am. the rugged, barren region in SW South Dakota and NW Nebraska.

bad·ly (bad'li), adv. 1. in a bad manner. 2. *Colloq.* greatly; much.

bad·min·ton (bad'min·tən), n. game like tennis, but played with a feathered cork instead of a ball. [named for Duke of Beaufort's estate]

bad-tem·pered (bad'tem'pərd), adj. having a bad temper or disposition.

baf·fle (baf'əl), v., -fled, -fling, n. —v. 1. be too hard for (a person) to understand or solve. 2. hinder; thwart. 3. struggle without success. —n. a wall or screen for hindering or changing the flow of air, water, etc. —baf'fle·ment, n. —baf'fler, n. —baf'fling, adj.

bag (bag), n., v., bagged, bag·ging. —n. 1. container made of paper, cloth, leather, etc., that can be closed at the top. 2. sac in an animal's body. 3. something suggesting a bag by its use or shape, as a valise, suitcase, udder, etc. 4. game killed or caught by a hunter. 5. Am. a base in baseball. 6. **bag and baggage**, with all one's belongings; entirely. 7. **hold the bag**, *Colloq.* a. be left empty-handed. b. be left to take the blame, responsibility, etc. 8. **in the bag**, *Am., Colloq.* assured. —v. 1. put in a bag. 2. swell; bulge. 3. hang loosely. 4. kill or catch in hunting. 5. *Slang.* catch; take; steal. [< Scand. *baggi* pack] —Syn. n. 1. sack, pouch. —v. 4. capture.

ba·gasse (bə·gas'), n. Am. pulp of sugar cane after the juice has been extracted. [< F < Pr. *bagasso* husks]

bag·a·telle (bag'ə·tel'), n. 1. a mere trifle. 2. game somewhat like billiards. [< F < Ital. *bagatella*, dim. of *baga* berry]

Bag·dad, Bagh·dad (bag'dad), n. capital of Iraq, on the Tigris River.

bag·gage (bag'ij), n. 1. the trunks, bags, suitcases, etc., that a person takes with him when he travels. 2. *Brit.* the portable equipment of an army. 3. a lively young woman. 4. a worthless woman. [< OF, < *bagues* bundles]

bag·ging (bag'ing), n. material for making bags.

bag·gy (bag'i), adj., -gi·er, -gi·est. 1. swelling; bulging. 2. hanging loosely. —bag'gi·ly, adv. —bag'gi·ness, n.

bag·ni·o (ban'yō; bän'-), n., pl. bagn·ios. 1. prison. 2. house of prostitution; brothel. [< Ital. < L *balneum* < Gk. *balaneion* bath]

bag·pipe (bag'pīp'), n. Often, bagpipes. a shrill-toned musical instrument made of a windbag and pipes, now used chiefly in Scotland. —bag'pip'er, n.

ba·guette, ba·guet (ba·get'), n. gem that is cut in a narrow oblong shape. [< F < Ital., ult. < L *baculum* staff]

Scottish bagpipe

Ba·gui·o (bä·gi·ō), n. a mountain city in the N Philippines; summer capital.

Ba·ha·mas (bə·hä'məz; -hā'-), or **Bahama Islands**, n.pl. group of British islands in the West Indies.

Bah·rain, Bah·rein (bä·rān'), group of islands in the Persian Gulf, under British control.

bail¹ (bāl), n. 1. guarantee necessary to set a person free from arrest until he is to appear for trial. 2. amount guaranteed. 3. person or persons who stand ready to pay the money guaranteed. 4. **go bail for**, supply bail for. —v. obtain the freedom of (a person under arrest) by guaranteeing to pay bail. [< OF, custody, < *baillier* deliver < L *bajulāre* carry] —bail'a·ble, adj. —bail'ment, n.

bail² (bāl), n. 1. the arched handle of a kettle or pail. 2. a hooplike support. [prob. < Scand. *beygla*]

bail³ (bāl), n. scoop or pail used to throw water out of a boat. —v. 1. throw (water) out of a boat with a pail, a dipper, or any other container. 2. dip water from. 3. **bail out**, drop from an airplane in a parachute. [< F *baille* < L *bajulus* carrier] —bail'er, n.

bail⁴ (bāl), n. Cricket. either of two small bars that form the top of a wicket. [< OF, barrier]

bail·ie (bāl'i), n. official of a Scottish town or city corresponding to an English alderman. [< OF *bailli*, var. of *baillif* BAILIFF]

bail·iff (bāl'if), n. 1. assistant to a sheriff. 2. officer of a court who has charge of prisoners while they are in the courtroom. 3. overseer or steward of an estate. 4. in England, the chief magistrate in certain towns. [< OF *baillif* < *baillir* govern. See BAIL¹.]

bail·i·wick (bāl'i·wik), n. 1. district over which a bailiff or bailie has authority. 2. a person's field of knowledge, work, or authority. [< *bailie* + *wick* office < OE *wice*]

bails·man (bālz'mən), n., pl. -men. Law. person who gives bail.

bairn (bärn), n. Scot. child. [OE *bearn*]

bait (bāt), n. 1. anything, esp. food, used to attract fish or other animals so that they may be caught. 2. thing used to tempt or attract. —v. 1. put bait on (a hook) or in (a trap). 2. tempt; attract. 3. set dogs to attack and worry (a bull, bear, etc.) for sport. 4. torment or worry by unkind or annoying remarks. 5. stop and feed. [< Scand. *beita* cause to bite] —bait'er, n.

baize (bāz), n. a thick woolen cloth used for curtains, table covers, etc. [< F *baies*, pl. of *bai* chestnut-colored < L *badius*]

bake (bāk), v., baked, bak·ing, n. —v. 1. cook (food) by dry heat without exposing it directly to the fire. 2. dry or harden by heat. 3. become baked: *cookies bake quickly.* —n. 1. a baking. 2. Am. a social gathering at which a meal is served. [OE *bacan*]

Ba·ke·lite (bā'kə·līt), n. Trademark. an artificial material used to make beads, electric insulators, etc.

bak·er (bāk'ər), n. 1. person who makes or sells baked goods. 2. Am. a small portable oven.

Bak·er (bāk'ər), n. Mount. mountain in NW Washington.

Baker Day, Am. day of the second Bikini atom bomb test, July 25, 1946. [< *baker*, the signaler's word for the letter *b*, + *day*]

Baker Island, a small island in the Pacific near the equator, belonging to the U.S.

baker's dozen, thirteen.

bak·er·y (bāk'ər·i), n., pl. -er·ies. a baker's shop.

bak·ing (bāk'ing), n. 1. act or process of baking. 2. amount baked at one time; batch.

baking powder, Am. mixture of soda and cream of tartar, or of other substances, used instead of yeast to raise biscuits, cakes, etc.

baking soda, Am. sodium bicarbonate.

bak·sheesh, bak·shish (bak'shēsh), n. money given as a tip in Egypt, Turkey, India, etc. Also, **backsheesh, backshish**. [< Pers. *bakhshīsh* < *bakhshīdan* give]

Ba·ku (bä·kü'), n. seaport in S Soviet Union, on the Caspian Sea.

bal., balance.

Ba·laam (bā'ləm), n. Bible. a prophet who was rebuked by the ass he rode.

bal·a·lai·ka (bal'ə·lī'kə), n. a Russian musical instrument somewhat like a guitar. [< Russ.]

bal·ance (bal'əns), n., v., -anced, -anc·ing. —n. 1. instrument for weighing. 2. equality in weight, amount, force, effect, etc. 3. comparison as to weight, amount, importance, etc.; estimate.

āge, cāre, fär; ēqual, tėrm; īce; ōpen, ôrder; pŭt, rūle, ūse; th, then; ə=a in about.

4. harmony; proportion. 5. steady condition or position; steadiness. 6. anything that counteracts the effect, weight, etc., of something else. 7. difference between the debit and credit sides of an account. 8. *Am., Colloq.* part that is left over; remainder. 9. wheel that regulates the rate of movement of a clock or watch. 10. preponderating weight, amount, or power. 11. a balancing movement in dancing. 12. **in the balance,** undecided. —v. 1. weigh in a balance. 2. make or be equal in weight, amount, force, effect, etc. 3. compare the value, importance, etc., of. 4. make or be proportionate to. 5. bring into or keep in a steady condition or position. 6. counteract the effect, influence, etc., of; make up for. 7. make the debit and credit sides of (an account) equal. 8. be equal in the debit and credit sides of an account. 9. hesitate; waver. [< OF < LL *bilanx* two-scaled < *bi-* two + *lanx* scale²] —bal'ance·a·ble, *adj.* —bal'anc·er, *n.* —Syn. *n.* 1. scale, scales. 5. poise. 8. rest, surplus. —v. 5. steady. 6. offset.

balanced diet, diet having the correct amounts of all kinds of foods necessary for health.

balance of power, even distribution of power among nations or groups of nations.

balance of trade, difference in value between the imports and the exports of a country.

balance sheet, a written statement showing the profits and losses, the assets and liabilities, and the net worth of a business.

bal·a·ta (bal'ə·tə), *n.* 1. a tropical tree whose dried gumlike juice is used in making chewing gum, etc. 2. the juice. [< Sp.]

Bal·bo·a (bal·bō'ə), *n.* Vasco de, 1475?-1517, Spanish adventurer, discovered the Pacific, 1513.

bal·brig·gan (bal·brig'ən), *n.* a knitted cotton cloth, used for stockings, underwear, etc. [orig. made at *Balbriggan,* Ireland]

bal·co·ny (bal'kə·ni), *n., pl.* -nies. 1. a projecting platform with an entrance from an upper floor of a building. 2. a gallery in a theater or hall. [< Ital., < *balco* scaffold < OHG *balcho* beam] —bal'co·nied, *adj.*

bald (bôld), *adj.* 1. wholly or partly without hair on the head. 2. without its natural covering. 3. bare; plain. 4. undisguised. 5. having white on the head. [ME *balled,* appar. < obs. *ball* white spot] —bald'ly, *adv.* —bald'ness, *n.*

bald eagle, *Am.* a large, powerful eagle with white feathers on its head, neck, and tail.

Bal·der (bôl'dər), **Bal·dr** (bäl'dər), *n.* the Norse god of light, beauty, goodness, wisdom, and peace.

bal·der·dash (bôl'dər·dash), *n.* nonsense.

bald·pate (bôld'pāt'), *n.* 1. person who has a bald head. 2. *Am.* kind of duck. —bald'pat'ed, *adj.* —bald'pat'ed·ness, *n.*

bal·dric (bôl'drik), *n.* belt for a sword, horn, etc., hung from one shoulder to the opposite side of the body. [akin to MHG *balderich* girdle]

bale¹ (bāl), *n., v.,* baled, bal·ing. —n. a large bundle of merchandise securely wrapped or bound for shipping or storage: *a bale of cotton.* —v. make into bales. [prob. < Flem. < OF < OHG *balla* BALL¹] —bal'er, *n.*

BALDRIC

bale² (bāl), *n. Poetic or Archaic.* 1. evil; harm. 2. sorrow; pain. [OE *bealu*]

Bal·e·ar·ic Islands (bal'i·ar'ik; bə·lir'ik), a group of Spanish islands in the W Mediterranean.

bale·ful (bāl'fəl), *adj.* evil; harmful. —bale'ful·ly, *adv.* —bale'ful·ness, *n.*

Ba·li (bä'li), *n.* island in SE Indonesia, south of Borneo. —Ba·li·nese (bä'lə·nēz'; -nēs'), *adj., n.*

balk (bôk), *v.* 1. stop short and stubbornly refuse to go on. 2. thwart; hinder; check. 3. fail to use; let slip; miss. 4. *Am., Baseball.* make a balk. [< *n.*] —n. 1. hindrance; check; defeat. 2. blunder; mistake. 3. ridge between furrows; strip left unplowed. 4. a large beam or timber.

5. *Am., Baseball.* failure of a pitcher to complete a pitch he has started. Also, **baulk.** [OE *balca* ridge] —balk'er, *n.* —balk'ing, *n., adj.*

Bal·kan (bôl'kən), *adj.* 1. having to do with the Balkan Peninsula. 2. having to do with the Balkan States, or the people of these states. —n. **the Balkans,** the Balkan States.

Balkan Mountains, mountain range in the Balkan Peninsula.

Balkan Peninsula, peninsula in SE Europe.

Balkan States, Yugoslavia, Rumania, Bulgaria, Albania, Greece, and European Turkey.

balk·y (bôk'i), *adj.* balk·i·er, balk·i·est. 1. stopping short and stubbornly refusing to go on. 2. likely to balk. —Ant. 1. submissive.

ball¹ (bôl), *n.* 1. anything round or roundish. 2. game in which some kind of ball is thrown, hit, or kicked. 3. ball in motion: *a fast ball.* 4. baseball. 5. *Am.* baseball pitched too high, too low, or not over the plate, that the batter does not strike at. 6. bullet. 7. something that is somewhat like a ball. 8. globe; sphere; the earth. 9. **play ball,** *Colloq.* **a.** begin a game or start it again after stopping. **b.** get busy; get active. **c.** *Am.* work together; join in partnership. —v. make or form into a ball. [< Scand. *böllr*]

ball² (bôl), *n.* a large, formal party for dancing. [< F *bal* < *baler* dance < LL *ballāre*]

bal·lad (bal'əd), *n.* 1. a simple song. 2. a narrative poem, esp. one that tells a popular legend. [< OF < Pr. *balada* dancing song]

bal·last (bal'əst), *n.* 1. something heavy carried in a ship to steady it. 2. weight carried by a balloon or dirigible to control it. 3. anything which steadies a person or thing. 4. gravel or crushed rock used in making the bed for a road or railroad track. —v. 1. furnish with ballast. 2. give steadiness to. 3. load or weigh down. [appar. < Scand. (ODan.) *barlast* < *bar* bare + *last* load] —bal'last·er, *n.*

ball bearing, 1. bearing in which the shaft turns upon a number of loose metal balls to lessen friction. 2. one of the metal balls.

bal·le·ri·na (bal'ə·rē'nə), *n., pl.* -nas. a woman ballet dancer. [< Ital.]

bal·let (bal'ā; ba·lā'), *n.* 1. an elaborate dance by a group on a stage. 2. the dancers. [< F, dim. of *bal* dance. See BALL².]

bal·lis·ta (bə·lis'tə), *n., pl.* -tae (-tē). an ancient military machine for throwing stones and other missiles. [< L, < Gk. *ballein* throw]

Ballista

ballistic missile, projectile powered by a rocket engine or engines but reaching its target as a result of aim at the time of launching, used esp. as a long-range weapon of offense.

bal·lis·tics (bə·lis'tiks), *n.* science that deals with the motion of projectiles, such as bullets and shells. —bal·lis'tic, *adj.* —bal·lis'ti·cal·ly, *adv.* —bal·lis·ti·cian (bal'is·tish'ən), *n.*

bal·lo·net (bal'ə·net'), *n.* a small bag inside a balloon or airship that holds air or gas to regulate ascent or descent. [< F, dim. of *ballon* BALLOON]

bal·loon (bə·lün'), *n.* an airtight bag filled with some gas lighter than air, so that it will rise and float in the air. —v. 1. ride in a balloon. 2. swell out like a balloon. [< Ital. *ballone* < *balla* ball] —bal·loon'ist, *n.*

bal·lot (bal'ət), *n., v.,* -lot·ed, -lot·ing. —n. 1. piece of paper or other object used in voting. 2. the total number of votes cast. —v. vote by ballots. [< Ital. *ballotta,* dim. of *balla* BALL¹]

ballot box, *Am.* box into which voters put their ballots after they have voted.

ball·play·er (bôl'plā'ər), *n.* 1. a baseball player. 2. person who plays ball.

ball·room (bôl'rüm'; -rum'), *n.* a large room for dancing.

bal·ly·hoo (*n.* bal′i·hü; *v.* bal′i·hü, bal′i·hü′), *n., pl.* -hoos, *v.*, -hooed, -hoo·ing. *Slang.* —*n.* 1. *Am.* noisy advertising. 2. uproar; outcry. —*v. Am.* advertise noisily. —**bal′ly·hoo′er**, *n.*

balm (bäm), *n.* 1. a fragrant ointment or oil used in anointing or for healing or soothing. 2. anything that heals or soothes. 3. an aromatic fragrance; sweet odor. 4. a fragrant, oily, sticky substance obtained from certain kinds of trees. 5. a fragrant plant of the same family as mint. [< OF < L *balsamum* BALSAM]

balm of Gilead, 1. a fragrant ointment prepared from the resin of a small evergreen tree. 2. the tree itself. 3. *Am.* the balsam poplar. 4. *Am.* the balsam fir.

balm·y[1] (bäm′i), *adj.*, **balm·i·er, balm·i·est.** 1. mild and soothing. 2. fragrant. —**balm′i·ly,** *adv.* —**balm′i·ness,** *n.* —Syn. 1. bland, temperate.

balm·y[2] (bäm′i), *adj.*, **balm·i·er, balm·i·est.** *Brit. Slang.* silly; crazy. [var. of *barmy*] —**balm′i·ly,** *adv.* —**balm′i·ness,** *n.*

ba·lo·ney (bə·lō′ni), *n. Am., Slang.* nonsense. Also, **boloney.**

bal·sa (bôl′sə; bäl′-), *n.* 1. a tropical American tree with very lightweight wood. 2. the wood. 3. a raft or float. [< Sp., raft]

bal·sam (bôl′səm), *n.* 1. an ointment or preparation for healing or soothing. 2. a fragrant, oily, sticky substance obtained from certain kinds of trees. 3. tree that yields balsam; balsam fir. 4. a garden plant with seed vessels that burst open violently when ripe. 5. anything that heals or soothes. [< L < Gk. *balsamon*] —**bal·sam·ic** (bôl·sam′ik; bäl′-), *adj.* —**bal·sam′i·cal·ly,** *adv.*

balsam fir, *Am.* 1. an evergreen tree of North America that yields turpentine. 2. its wood.

balsam poplar, *Am.* a species of poplar grown as a shade tree.

Bal·tic (bôl′tik), *adj.* 1. of the Baltic Sea. 2. of the Baltic States.

Baltic Sea, sea in N Europe, north of Germany and southeast of Sweden.

Baltic States, Estonia, Latvia, Lithuania, and, sometimes, Finland.

Bal·ti·more (bôl′tə·môr; -mōr), *n.* city in N Maryland, on Chesapeake Bay.

Baltimore oriole, *Am.* a North American bird with orange and black feathers.

Ba·lu·chi·stan (bə·lü′chə·stän′; bə·lü′chə·stän), *n.* former country between India and Iran, on the Arabian Sea, now partly in Pakistan.

bal·us·ter (bal′əs·tər), *n.* a pillarlike support for a railing. [< F < Ital. < L < Gk. *balaustion* pomegranate blossom; from the shape]

Baluster and balustrade

bal·us·trade (bal′əs·trād′), *n.* row of balusters and the railing on them. [< F, < Ital. *balustro* BALUSTER] —**bal′us·trad′ed,** *adj.*

Bal·zac (bal′zak; bôl′-), *n.* Honoré de, 1799-1850, French novelist.

bam·bi·no (bam·bē′nō), *n., pl.* -ni (-ni). 1. baby; little child. 2. image or picture of the baby Jesus. [< Ital., dim. of *bambo* silly]

bam·boo (bam·bü′), *n., pl.* -boos. any of various woody or treelike tropical or semitropical grasses whose stiff, hollow stems are used for making canes, furniture, and even houses. [< Du. *bamboes*, prob. < Malay]

Bamboo Curtain, an imaginary wall, separating Communist China from the rest of the world, behind which strict censorship and secrecy are enforced.

bam·boo·zle (bam·bü′zəl), *v.*, -zled, -zling. *Colloq.* 1. impose upon; cheat; trick. 2. puzzle. —**bam·boo′zle·ment,** *n.* —**bam·boo′zler,** *n.*

ban (ban), *v.*, banned, ban·ning, *n.* —*v.* 1. prohibit; forbid. 2. place a ban on; pronounce a curse on. —*n.* 1. the forbidding of an act or speech by authority of the law, the church, or public opinion. 2. a solemn curse by the church. 3. sentence of outlawry. [< Scand. *banna* forbid]

ba·nal (bā′nəl; bə·nal′; -näl′; ban′əl), *adj.* commonplace; trite. [< F, < *ban* proclamation; < Gmc.; orig. sense, "of feudal service"; later, "open to the community"] —**ba·nal·i·ty** (bə·nal′ə·ti; bā-; ba-), *n.* —**ba·nal·ly,** *adv.* —Syn. hackneyed.

ba·nan·a (bə·nan′ə), *n.* 1. a slightly curved, yellow or red fruit with firm, creamy flesh. 2. a treelike tropical plant on which bananas grow in large clusters. [< Pg. or Sp.]

band[1] (band), *n.* 1. number of persons or animals joined or acting together. 2. group of musicians playing various instruments together. 3. *Am., W.* drove or flock of animals; herd. 4. a thin, flat strip of material for binding, trimming, or some other purpose. 5. stripe. 6. collar with two strips hanging in front, worn by certain clergymen. 7. *Radio.* a particular range of wave lengths in broadcasting. —*v.* 1. unite in a group. 2. put a band on. 3. mark with stripes. [< F *bande*, ult. < Gmc.] —Syn. *n.* 1. company, party, gang, group, crew.

band[2] (band), *n.* anything that ties, binds, or unites. [< Scand. *band* + F *bande* < Gmc.]

band·age (ban′dij), *n., v.*, -aged, -ag·ing. —*n.* strip of cloth or other material used in binding up and dressing a wound, injured leg or arm, etc. —*v.* bind, tie up, or dress with a bandage. [< F, < *bande* BAND[1]] —**band′ag·er,** *n.*

ban·dan·na, ban·dan·a (ban·dan′ə), *n.* a large, colored handkerchief. [prob. < Hind. *bāndhnū* tie-dyeing]

band·box (band′boks′), *n.* a light cardboard box to put hats, collars, etc., in.

ban·deau (ban·dō′; ban′dō), *n., pl.* -deaux (-dōz′; -dōz). 1. band worn about the head. 2. a narrow band. [< F *bandeau*, dim. of *bande* band[2], ult. < Gmc.]

ban·de·role, ban·de·rol (ban′də·rōl), *n.* a small flag. [< F < Ital., < *bandiera* BANNER]

ban·di·coot (ban′də·küt), *n.* 1. a very large rat of India, about two feet long. 2. a ratlike marsupial of Australia. [< Indian dial. *pandi·kokku* pig-rat]

ban·dit (ban′dit), *n., pl.* ban·dits, ban·dit·ti (ban·dit′i). highwayman; robber. [< Ital. *bandito,* pp. of *bandire* banish, proscribe, ult. < Gmc.; akin to BAN] —**ban′dit·ry,** *n.* —Syn. outlaw, brigand, desperado.

band·mas·ter (band′mas′tər; -mäs′-), *n.* leader of a band of musicians.

ban·do·leer, ban·do·lier (ban′də·lir′), *n.* a shoulder belt having loops for carrying cartridges. [< F < Sp., < *banda* BAND[1]]

bands·man (bandz′mən), *n., pl.* -men. member of a band of musicians.

band·stand (band′stand′), *n.* an outdoor platform, usually roofed, for band concerts.

band·wag·on (band′wag′ən), *n. Am.* 1. wagon that carries a musical band in a parade. 2. *Colloq.* the winning side in a political campaign.

ban·dy (ban′di), *v.*, -died, -dy·ing, *n., pl.* -dies, *adj.* —*v.* 1. throw back and forth; toss about. 2. give and take; exchange: *bandy words.* —*n. Esp. Brit.* the game of hockey. —*adj.* curved outward. [cf. F *bander* bandy, se *bander* band together]

ban·dy-leg·ged (ban′di·leg′id; -legd′), *adj.* having legs that curve outward; bowlegged.

bane (bān), *n.* 1. cause of death or harm. 2. thing that ruins or spoils. [OE *bana* murderer]

bane·ful (bān′fəl), *adj.* deadly; harmful. —**bane′ful·ly,** *adv.* —**bane′ful·ness,** *n.*

Banff (bamf), *n.* a resort in SW Canada.

bang[1] (bang), *n.* 1. a sudden, loud noise. 2. a violent, noisy blow. 3. vigor; impetus. 4. *U.S. Colloq.* kick; thrill. —*v.* 1. make a sudden loud noise. 2. hit with violent and noisy blows; strike noisily. 3. shut with noise; slam. 4. handle roughly. —*adv.* 1. suddenly and loudly. 2. violently and noisily. [? < Scand. *banga* to hammer]

bang[2] (bang), *Am.* —*n.* 1. fringe of banged hair. 2. bangs, hair cut straight over the forehead. —*v.* cut squarely across. [short for *bangtail* docked tail (of a horse)]

Bang·kok (bang′kok), *n.* capital of Siam.

ban·gle (bang'gəl), *n.* ring worn around the wrist, arm, or ankle. [< Hind. *bangri* glass bracelet]

ban·ian (ban'yən), *n.* 1. banyan. 2. a Hindu merchant of a caste that eats no meat. [< Pg., prob. < Ar. *banyān* < Gujarati (a language of western India), ult. < Skt. *vaṇij* merchant]

ban·ish (ban'ish), *v.* 1. condemn to leave a country; exile. 2. force to go away; send away; drive away. [< OF < LL *bannire* ban < Gmc.] —**ban'ish·er**, *n.* —**ban'ish·ment**, *n.* —Syn. 1. expel, outlaw.

ban·is·ter (ban'is·tər), *n.* 1. baluster. 2. banisters, balustrade of a staircase. Also, **bannister**. [var. of *baluster*]

ban·jo (ban'jō), *n., pl.* -jos, -joes. *Am.* a stringed musical instrument of the guitar class, played with the fingers or a plectrum. [alter. of *bandore* < Sp. < LL < Gk. *pandoura* 3-stringed instrument] —**ban'jo·ist**, *n.*

Man playing a banjo

bank¹ (bangk), *n.* 1. a long pile or heap. 2. ground bordering a river, lake, etc. 3. a shallow place in a body of water; shoal. 4. slope. 5. the lateral inclination of an airplane when making a turn. —*v.* 1. border with a bank or ridge. 2. form into a bank; pile or heap up. 3. slope. 4. make (an airplane) bank. 5. cover (a fire) with ashes or fresh fuel so that it will burn long and slowly. 6. *Am.* protect, esp. against the cold, by piling earth against. [prob. < Scand.] —**banked**, *adj.* —Syn. *n.* 1. ridge, mound. 3. bar.

bank² (bangk), *n.* 1. an institution for keeping, lending, exchanging, and issuing money. 2. the office of such an institution. 3. fund of money out of which the dealer or manager in gambling games pays his losses. 4. stock of pieces from which players draw in games. 5. any place where reserve supplies are kept, as of blood plasma for transfusions. —*v.* 1. keep a bank. 2. keep money in a bank. 3. put (money) in a bank. 4. bank on, *Am., Colloq.* depend on; be sure of. [< F < Ital. *banca*, orig., bench < Gmc.] —**bank'a·ble**, *adj.*

bank³ (bangk), *n.* 1. bench for rowers in a galley. 2. row or tier of oars. 3. row of keys on an organ, typewriter, etc. 4. row of things. —*v.* arrange in rows. [< OF < LL *bancus* < Gmc.; akin to BENCH] —**banked**, *adj.*

bank account, money in a bank that can be withdrawn by a depositor.

bank·book (bangk'bů k'), *n.* a depositor's book in which a bank keeps a record of his account.

bank·er (bangk'ər), *n.* 1. person or company that keeps a bank. 2. dealer in a gambling game.

bank·ing (bangk'ing), *n.* business of a bank.

bank note, note issued by a bank that must be paid on demand, circulating as money.

bank·rupt (bangk'rupt), *n.* person who is declared by a law court to be unable to pay his debts and whose property is distributed among his creditors. —*adj.* 1. declared legally unable to pay debts. 2. at the end of one's resources; destitute. 3. wanting; lacking. 4. of bankrupts. —*v.* make bankrupt. [< F < Ital. *bancarotta* bankruptcy < *banca* bank² + *rotta*, fem. pp. of *rompere* break < L *rumpere*]

bank·rupt·cy (bangk'rupt·si; -rəp·si), *n., pl.* -cies. bankrupt condition.

ban·ner (ban'ər), *n.* 1. flag. 2. piece of cloth with some design or words on it, attached by its upper edge to a pole or staff. —*adj. Am.* leading; foremost. [< OF *baniere* < LL *bandum* < Gmc.] —**ban'nered**, *adj.* —Syn. *n.* 1, 2. ensign, standard.

ban·nis·ter (ban'is·tər), *n.* banister.

banns (banz), *n.pl.* public notice, given three times in church, that a certain man and woman are to be married. [var. of *bans* proclamations]

ban·quet (bang'kwit), *n., v.,* -quet·ed, -quet·ing. —*n.* 1. feast. 2. a formal dinner with speeches. —*v.* 1. give a banquet to. 2. enjoy a banquet. [< F < Ital. *banchetto*, dim. of *banco* bench < Gmc.] —**ban'quet·er**, *n.*

ban·quette (bang·ket'), *n.* 1. platform along the inside of a parapet or trench for gunners. 2. *Am., Louisiana.* sidewalk. [< F]

ban·shee, ban·shie (ban'shē; ban·shē'), *n. Irish and Scot.* spirit whose wails mean that there will soon be a death in the family. [< Irish *bean sidhe* woman of the fairies]

ban·tam (ban'təm), *n.* 1. Often, Bantam. a small-sized kind of fowl. 2. a small person who is fond of fighting. —*adj.* light in weight; small. [prob. named for *Bantam*, city in Java]

ban·tam·weight (ban'təm·wāt'), *n.* boxer who weighs 118 pounds or less.

ban·ter (ban'tər), *n.* playful teasing; joking. —*v.* 1. tease playfully. 2. talk in a joking way. —**ban'ter·er**, *n.* —**ban'ter·ing·ly**, *adv.*

Ban·tu (ban'tü), *n., pl.* -tu, -tus, *adj.* —*n.* 1. member of a large group of Negroid tribes living in central and S Africa. 2. any of the languages of these tribes. —*adj.* of these tribes or their languages.

ban·yan (ban'yən), *n.* a fig tree of India whose branches have hanging roots that grow down to the ground and take root. Also, **banian**. [orig. a specific tree under which stood a banian pagoda]

ban·zai (bän'zī'), *interj.* a Japanese greeting or patriotic cheer. It means "May you live ten thousand years!"

Bap., Bapt., Baptist.

bap·tism (bap'tiz·əm), *n.* 1. rite or sacrament of dipping a person into water or sprinkling water on him, as a sign of the washing away of sin and of admission into the Christian church. 2. experience that cleanses a person or introduces him into a new kind of life. —**bap·tis·mal** (bap·tiz'məl), *adj.* —**bap·tis'mal·ly**, *adv.*

Bap·tist (bap'tist), *n.* 1. member of a Christian church that believes in baptism by dipping the whole person under water. 2. person who baptizes, as **John the Baptist**. —*adj.* of or having to do with the Baptists.

bap·tis·ter·y (bap'tis·tər·i; -tis·tri), **bap·tist·ry** (bap'tis·tri), *n., pl.* -ter·ies; -ries. a building, or a part of a church, in which baptism is administered.

bap·tize (bap·tīz'; bap'tīz), *v.,* -tized, -tiz·ing. 1. dip into water or sprinkle with water, in baptism. 2. purify; cleanse. 3. christen. [< OF < LL < Gk., < *baptein* dip] —**bap·tiz'er**, *n.*

bar (bär), *n., v.,* **barred, bar·ring,** *prep.* —*n.* 1. an evenly shaped piece of some solid, longer than it is wide or thick: *bar of soap.* 2. pole or rod put across a door, gate, window, etc., to fasten or shut off something. 3. anything that blocks the way or prevents progress. 4. band of color; stripe. 5. unit of rhythm in music. 6. line between two such units on a musical staff. 7. counter where drinks are served to customers. 8. place containing such a counter. 9. railing around the place where lawyers sit in a court. 10. profession of a lawyer. 11. lawyers as a group. 12. place where an accused person stands in a law court. 13. law court. 14. anything like a law court: *the bar of public opinion.* 15. *U.S.* metal part of a horse's bit. —*v.* 1. put bars across; fasten or shut off with a bar. 2. block; obstruct. 3. exclude; forbid. 4. mark with stripes or bands of color. —*prep.* except; excluding: *the best student, bar none.* [< OF < VL *barra* thick ends of bushes (collectively) < Celtic] —Syn. *n.* 3. barrier, obstacle, obstruction.

bar., 1. barometer; barometric. 2. barrel.

barb (bärb), *n.* 1. point projecting backward from the main point, as of a fishhook. 2. *Bot., Zool.* a beardlike growth or part. —*v.* furnish with barbs. [< F < L *barba* beard] —**barbed**, *adj.* —**barb'less**, *adj.*

BARBS

Bar·ba·dos (bär·bā'dōz; bär'bə·dōz), *n.* British island in the West Indies.

bar·bar·i·an (bär·bâr'i·ən), *n.* 1. person who is not civilized. 2. foreigner differing from the speaker or writer in language and customs. 3. person without sympathy for literary culture or art. —*adj.* 1. not civilized; barbarous. 2. differing from the speaker or writer in language and customs. —**bar·bar'i·an·ism**, *n.*

Barbs (def. 1)

bar·bar·ic (bär·bar′ik), *adj.* **1.** uncivilized; rough and rude. **2.** of or like that of barbarians. **3.** crudely rich or splendid. [< L < Gk. < *barbaros* foreign] **—bar·bar′i·cal·ly,** *adv.*

bar·ba·rism (bär′bə·riz·əm), *n.* **1.** condition of uncivilized people. **2.** a barbarous act, custom, or trait. **3.** use of a word or expression not in accepted use. **4.** word or expression not in accepted use, as "his'n" for *his.*

bar·bar·i·ty (bär·bar′ə·ti), *n., pl.* **-ties. 1.** brutal cruelty. **2.** act of cruelty. **3.** barbaric manner, taste, or style.

bar·ba·rize (bär′bə·riz), *v.,* **-rized, -riz·ing.** make or become barbarous. **—bar′ba·ri·za′tion,** *n.*

bar·ba·rous (bär′bə·rəs), *adj.* **1.** not civilized. **2.** rough; rude. **3.** savagely cruel; brutal. **4.** crude; harsh. **5.** differing from the language and customs of the speaker or writer. **6.** filled with words or expressions not in accepted use. [< L < Gk. *barbaros* foreign, appar. orig., stammering] **—bar′ba·rous·ly,** *adv.* **—bar′ba·rous·ness,** *n.* **—Syn. 1.** barbarian. **—Ant. 2.** cultured.

Bar·ba·ry (bär′bə·ri), *n.* the Mohammedan countries west of Egypt on the N coast of Africa.

Barbary ape, a tailless monkey that lives in N Africa and on the Rock of Gibraltar.

Barbary States, Morocco, Algeria, Tunis, and Tripoli.

bar·be·cue (bär′bə·kū), *n., v.,* **-cued, -cu·ing.** **—n. 1.** *Am.* **a.** a feast at which animals are roasted whole. **b.** food at such a feast. **c.** device on which the food is prepared. **2.** animal roasted whole. **3.** meat roasted before an open fire. **—v. 1.** roast (an animal) whole. **2.** roast (meat) before an open fire. **3.** cook (meat or fish) in a highly flavored sauce. [< Sp. < Haitian *barboka* framework of sticks]

barbed wire, or **barb·wire** (bärb′wīr′), *n. Am.* wire with sharp points on it every few inches, used for fences, etc.

bar·bel (bär′bəl), *n.* **1.** a long, thin growth hanging from the mouths of some fishes. **2.** fish having such growths. [< OF < LL *barbellus,* dim. of *barbus* a kind of fish < L *barba* beard]

BARBELS

bar·ber (bär′bər), *n.* person whose business is cutting hair, shaving men, and trimming beards. **—v.** cut the hair of; shave; trim the beard of. [< AF < L *barba* beard]

bar·ber·ry (bär′ber′i; -bər·i), *n., pl.* **-ries. 1.** shrub with sour red berries. **2.** the berry.

bar·ber·shop (bär′bər·shop′), *n. Am.* shop where barbers work.

bar·bi·can (bär′bə·kən), *n.* tower for defense built over a gate or bridge to a city or castle. [< OF < Med.L *barbicana*]

bar·bi·tal (bär′bə·tôl; -tal), *n.* a drug containing barbituric acid, used as a sedative or hypnotic.

bar·bi·tu·rate (bär·bich′ə·rāt, -rit; bär′bə·tūr′āt, -it, -tyūr′-), *n. Chem.* salt or ester of barbituric acid.

bar·bi·tu·ric acid (bär′bə·tūr′ik; -tyūr′-), *Chem.* an acid, $C_4H_4O_3N_2$, much used as the basis of sedatives and hypnotics.

bar·ca·role, bar·ca·rolle (bär′kə·rōl), *n.* **1.** a Venetian boat song. **2.** music imitating such a song. [< F < Ital. *barcarola* boatman's song < *barca* BARK³]

Bar·ce·lo·na (bär′sə·lō′nə), *n.* seaport in NE Spain.

bard (bärd), *n.* **1.** an ancient Celtic poet and singer. **2.** poet. [< Scotch Gaelic and Irish] **—bard′ic,** *adj.*

bare¹ (bär), *adj.,* **bar·er, bar·est,** *v.,* **bared, bar·ing.** **—adj. 1.** without covering; not clothed; naked. **2.** with the head uncovered. **3.** not concealed; not disguised; open. **4.** not furnished; empty. **5.** plain; unadorned. **6.** much worn; threadbare. **7.** just enough and no more; mere. **8.** lay bare, uncover; expose; reveal. **—v.** make bare; uncover; reveal. [OE *bær*] **—bare′ness,** *n.* **—bar′er,** *n.*

bare² (bär), *v. Archaic.* pt. of **bear¹.**

bare·back (bär′bak′), *adv., adj.* on a horse's bare back. **—bare′backed′,** *adj.*

bare·faced (bär′fāst′), *adj.* **1.** with the face bare. **2.** not disguised. **3.** shameless; impudent. **—bare·fac·ed·ly** (bär′fās′id·li; -fāst′li), *adv.* **—bare′fac′ed·ness,** *n.*

bare·foot (bär′fút′), *adj., adv.* without shoes and stockings. **—bare′foot′ed,** *adj.*

bare·hand·ed (bär′han′did), *adj.* **1.** without any covering on the hands. **2.** with empty hands.

bare·head·ed (bär′hed′id), *adj., adv.* wearing nothing on the head. **—bare′head′ed·ness,** *n.*

bare·leg·ged (bär′leg′id; -legd′), *adj.* without stockings.

bare·ly (bär′li), *adv.* **1.** only just; scarcely: *barely enough.* **2.** nakedly. **3.** openly; plainly.

bar·gain (bär′gin), *n.* **1.** agreement to trade or exchange. **2.** something offered for sale cheap or bought cheap. **3.** a good trade or exchange. **4. into the bargain,** besides; also. **—v. 1.** try to get good terms. **2.** make a bargain; come to terms. **3.** trade. **4. bargain for,** be ready for; expect. [< OF *bargaigne*] **—bar′gain·er,** *n.* **—Syn.** *n.* **1.** contract, transaction.

barge (bärj), *n., v.,* **barged, barg·ing. —n. 1.** a large, flat-bottomed boat for carrying freight. **2.** a large boat used for excursions, pageants, etc. **3.** a large motorboat or rowboat used by the commanding officer of a flagship. **4.** houseboat. **—v. 1.** carry by barge. **2.** move clumsily like a barge. **3.** *Colloq.* push oneself rudely. [< OF < L < Gk. *baris* boat used on Nile] **—barge′man,** *n.*

bar·ite (bär′īt; bar′-), *n.* native barium sulfate. Also, **barytes.**

bar·i·tone (bar′ə·tōn), *n.* **1.** a male voice between tenor and bass. **2.** part to be sung by such a voice. **3.** person who sings this part. **4.** a musical instrument that has the quality or range of this voice. **—adj.** of or for a baritone. Also, **barytone.** [< Gk., < *barys* deep + *tonos* pitch]

bar·i·um (bär′i·əm; bar′-), *n. Chem.* a soft, silvery-white metallic element, Ba. [< NL < Gk. *barytes* weight] **—bar′ic,** *adj.*

barium sulfate, a sulfate of barium, $BaSO_4$.

bark¹ (bärk), *n.* the tough outside covering of the trunk, branches, and roots of trees and plants **—v. 1.** strip the bark from (a tree, etc.). **2.** cover with bark. **3.** scrape the skin from (shins, knuckles, etc.). [< Scand. *börkr*] **—bark′er,** *n.* **—bark′less,** *adj.*

bark² (bärk), *n.* **1.** the short, sharp sound that a dog makes. **2.** a sound like this. **—v. 1.** make this sound or one like it. **2.** shout sharply; speak gruffly. **3.** *Colloq.* cough. **4.** *Am., Slang.* act as barker. [OE *beorcan*] **—Syn.** *n.* **1.** yelp, bay.

bark³ (bärk), *n.* **1.** ship with three masts, square-rigged on the first two masts and fore-and-aft-rigged on the other. **2.** *Poetic.* boat; ship. Also, **barque.** [< F < Ital. < LL *barca*]

bar·keep·er (bär′kēp′ər), *Am.* **bar·keep** (bär′kēp′), *n.* man who tends a bar where alcoholic drinks are sold.

bar·ken·tine, bar·kan·tine (bär′kən·tēn), *n. Am.* a three-masted ship with the foremast square-rigged and the other masts fore-and-aft-rigged. Also, **barquentine.** [< *bark³;* modeled on *brigantine*]

bark·er (bär′kər), *n.* **1.** one that barks. **2.** *U.S.* person who stands in front of a store, show, etc., urging people to go in.

Bark·ley (bärk′li), *n.* **Alben William,** born 1877, vice-president of the U.S. 1949–1953.

bar·ley (bär′li), *n.* **1.** the seed or grain of a cereal grass used for food and for making malt. **2.** plant yielding this grain. [OE *bærlic*]

Bar·ley·corn (bär′li·kôrn′), *n.* **John,** a name for intoxicating liquor.

barm (bärm), *n.* a foamy yeast that forms on malt liquors while they are fermenting. [OE *beorma*]

bar·maid (bär′mād′), *n.* woman who works in a bar, serving drinks to customers.

bar·man (bär′mən), *n., pl.* **–men.** barkeeper.

barm·y (bär′mi), *adj.,* **barm·i·er, barm·i·est.** 1. full of barm; fermenting. 2. *Colloq.* silly.

barn (bärn), *n.* 1. a building for storing hay, grain, etc. 2. *Am.* such a building which has the added use of sheltering cows, horses, etc. [OE *bœrn* < *bere* barley + *œrn* place]

bar·na·cle (bär′nə·kəl), *n.* a crustacean that attaches itself to rocks, the bottoms of ships, etc. [< OF *bernac*]

Barnacles
(2 to 6 in. long)

barn dance, *Am.* 1. dance held in a barn. 2. a lively dance resembling a polka.

barn·storm (bärn′stôrm′), *v. Am., Colloq.* act plays, make speeches, etc., in small towns and country districts. **—barn′-storm′er,** *n. Am.* **—barn′storm′ing,** *adj., n. Am.*

Bar·num (bär′nəm), *n.* Phineas Taylor, 1810–1891, American showman.

barn·yard (bärn′yärd′), *n. Am.* yard around a barn for livestock.

bar·o·graph (bar′ə·graf; –gräf), *n.* instrument that automatically records changes in air pressure. [< Gk. *baros* weight + –GRAPH] **—bar′o·graph′ic,** *adj.*

ba·rom·e·ter (bə·rom′ə·tər), *n.* 1. an instrument for measuring the pressure of the atmosphere, and thus determining the height above sea level, probable changes in the weather, etc. 2. something that indicates changes. [< Gk. *baros* weight + –METER] **—bar·o·met·ric** (bar′-ə·met′rik), **bar′o·met′ri·cal,** *adj.* **—bar′o·met′ri·cal·ly,** *adv.*

bar·on (bar′ən), *n.* 1. nobleman in Great Britain ranking next below a viscount. 2. nobleman in other countries having a similar rank. 3. *Am.* a powerful merchant or financier. [< OF < L *barō* man, fellow] **—ba·ro·ni·al** (bə·rō′ni·əl), *adj.*

bar·on·age (bar′ən·ij), *n.* 1. all the barons. 2. the nobility. 3. rank or title of a baron.

bar·on·ess (bar′ən·is), *n.* 1. wife or widow of a baron. 2. woman whose rank is equal to that of a baron.

bar·on·et (bar′ən·it; –et), *n.* 1. member of a hereditary order of honor in Great Britain ranking next below a baron and next above a knight. 2. title indicating this rank. **—bar′on·et·cy,** *n.*

bar·o·ny (bar′ə·ni), *n., pl.* **–nies.** 1. lands of a baron. 2. rank or title of a baron.

ba·roque (bə·rōk′; –rok′), *adj.* 1. artistically irregular; tastelessly odd; ornate; fantastic; grotesque. 2. irregular in shape. **—n.** *Art.* a. a baroque style. b. something in a baroque style. [< F < Pg. *barroco* irregular]

bar·o·scope (bar′ə·skōp), *n.* instrument for showing changes in the pressure or density of the air. [< Gk. *baros* weight + E –*scope* instrument for viewing < Gk. *skopein* look at] **—bar·o·scop·ic** (bar′ə·skop′ik), **bar′o·scop′i·cal,** *adj.*

ba·rouche (bə·rüsh′), *n.* a four-wheeled carriage with two seats facing each other and a folding top. [< dial. G < Ital. < L *birotus* two-wheeled < *bi–* two + *rota* wheel]

barque (bärk), *n.* bark³.

bar·quen·tine (bär′kən·tēn), *n.* barkentine.

bar·rack (bar′ək), *n.* Usually, **barracks.** 1. a building or group of buildings for soldiers to live in. 2. a large, plain building in which many people live. **—v.** lodge in barracks. [< F < Ital. *baracca*]

barracks bag, *Mil.* a cloth sack for holding clothing and equipment of military personnel.

bar·ra·cu·da (bar′ə·kü′də), *n., pl.* **–da, –das.** a large, voracious fish of the seas near the West Indies. [< Sp. < West Indian name]

bar·rage (bə·räzh′ *for n. 1 and v.;* bär′ij *for n. 2*), *n., v.,* **–raged, –rag·ing. —n.** 1. barrier of artillery fire to check the enemy or to protect one's own soldiers in advancing or retreating. 2. artificial bar in a river; dam. **—v.** fire at with artillery. [< F, < *barrer* BAR]

bar·ra·try (bar′ə·tri), *n.* fraud or gross negligence of a ship's officer or seaman against owners, insurers, etc. [< OF, < *barater* exchange, cheat] **—bar′ra·trous,** *adj.*

barred (bärd), *adj.* 1. having bars: *a barred window.* 2. marked with stripes.

bar·rel (bar′əl), *n., v.,* **–reled, –rel·ing;** *esp. Brit.* **–relled, –rel·ling. —n.** 1. container with round, flat top and bottom and slightly curved sides, usually made of thick boards held together by hoops. 2. amount that a barrel can hold. 3. something somewhat like a barrel: *the barrel of a drum.* 4. the metal tube of a gun. **—v.** put in barrels. [< OF *baril,* prob. < VL *barra* bar, stave] **—Syn.** *n.* 1. cask.

barrel organ, a hand organ.

bar·ren (bar′ən), *adj.* 1. not producing anything. 2. not able to bear offspring. 3. fruitless; unprofitable. 4. without interest; dull. **—n.** Usually, **barrens.** *Am.* barren stretch of land. [< OF *baraine*] **—bar′ren·ly,** *adv.* **—bar′ren·ness,** *n.* **—Syn.** *adj.* 1, 2. unproductive, sterile.

bar·rette (bə·ret′), *n.* a clasp, used by women or girls for holding the hair in place.

bar·ri·cade (bar′ə·kād′; bar′ə·kād), *n., v.,* **–cad·ed, –cad·ing. —n.** 1. a rough, hastily made barrier for defense. 2. any barrier or obstruction. **—v.** block or obstruct with a barricade. [< F, appar. < Pr. *barricada* < *barrica* cask; orig. made of casks. See BARREL.] **—bar′ri·cad′er,** *n.*

Bar·rie (bar′i), *n.* Sir James M., 1860–1937, Scottish writer of novels and plays.

bar·ri·er (bar′i·ər), *n.* 1. something that stands in the way; something stopping progress or preventing approach. 2. something that keeps apart. [< AF < LL, < *barra* bar]

bar·ring (bär′ing), *prep.* except; not including.

bar·ris·ter (bar′is·tər), *n.* lawyer in England who can plead in any court. [< *bar* + –*ster*] **—bar·ris·te·ri·al** (bar′is·tir′i·əl), *adj.*

bar·room (bär′rüm′; –rüm′), *n. Am.* room with a bar for the sale of alcoholic drinks.

bar·row¹ (bar′ō), *n.* 1. frame with two short shafts for handles at each end, used for carrying a load. 2. wheelbarrow. 3. handcart. [OE *bearwe;* akin to BEAR¹]

bar·row² (bar′ō), *n.* mound of earth or stones over an ancient grave. [OE *beorg*]

Bar·row (bar′ō), *n.* Point, northernmost point of land in Alaska.

bar sinister, supposed sign of illegitimacy.

Bart., Baronet.

bar·tend·er (bär′ten′dər), *n. Am.* man who serves alcoholic drinks to customers at a bar.

bar·ter (bär′tər), *v.* 1. trade by exchanging one kind of goods for other goods without using money. 2. exchange. **—n.** 1. act of bartering. 2. exchange. 3. something bartered. [< OF *barater* exchange; akin to BARRATRY] **—bar′ter·er,** *n.*

bar·ti·zan (bär′tə·zən; bär′tə·zan′), *n.* a small overhanging turret on a wall or tower. [alter. of *bratticing* < *brattice* parapet < OF, prob. < OE *brittisc* British (type of fortification)]

Bar·ton (bär′tən), *n.* Clara, 1821–1912, American woman who organized the American Red Cross in 1881.

ba·ry·tes (bə·rī′tēz), *n.* barite.

bar·y·tone (bar′ə·tōn), *n., adj.* baritone.

bas·al (bās′əl), *adj.* 1. of or at the base; forming the base. 2. fundamental; basic. **—bas′al·ly,** *adv.*

basal metabolism, *Physiol.* amount of energy used by an animal at rest.

ba·salt (bə·sôlt′; bas′ôlt), *n.* a hard, dark-colored rock of volcanic origin. [< LL *basaltēs,* a manuscript corruption of L *basanītēs* < Gk., < *basanos* touchstone]

bas·cule (bas′kūl), *n.* device that works like a seesaw. In a **bascule bridge** the rising part is counterbalanced by a weight. [< F, seesaw, ult. < *battre* beat (infl. by *bas* low) + *cul* posterior]

base¹ (bās), *n., v.,* **based, bas·ing. —n.** 1. part of a thing on which it rests; bottom. 2. a fundamental principle; basis. 3. the principal element; essential part. 4. a. part of a column on which the shaft rests. b. part at the bottom of a wall or monument. 5. *Bot.*, *Zool.* a. part of an animal or plant organ nearest its point of attachment. b. the point of attachment. 6. *Chem.* a compound that reacts with an acid to form a salt. Calcium hydroxide is a base. 7. station or goal in certain games, such as baseball. 8. starting place. 9. *Mil.* place from which an army, air force, or navy operates and from which supplies are obtained; headquarters. 10. *Math.* number that is a starting point for a system of numeration or logarithms. 11. *Geom.* line or surface forming that part of a figure on which it is supposed to stand. 12. *Surveying.* line used as the starting point. —*v.* 1. make or form a base or foundation for. 2. establish; found (on): *his large business was based on good service.* [< OF < L < Gk. *basis* base; lit., a step] —Syn. *n.* 2. groundwork.

Base (def. 5)

base² (bās), *adj.*, bas·er, bas·est, *n.* —*adj.* 1. morally low; mean; selfish; cowardly. 2. fit for an inferior person or thing; menial; unworthy. 3. *Archaic.* of humble birth or origin. 4. coarse in quality. 5. having little comparative value; inferior. 6. debased; counterfeit. 7. deep or grave in sound. —*n.* the lowest male voice; bass. [< OF < LL *bassus* low] —base′ly, *adv.* —base′ness, *n.* —Syn. *adj.* 1. abject, ignoble. 2. common.

base·ball (bās′bôl′), *n. Am.* 1. game played with bat and ball by two teams of nine players each on a field with four bases. 2. ball used in this game.

base·board (bās′bôrd′; –bōrd), *n. Am.* 1. line of boards around the walls of a room, next to the floor. 2. board forming the base of anything.

base·born (bās′bôrn′), *adj.* 1. born of humble parents. 2. illegitimate.

base hit, *Am.* successful hitting of the baseball by a batter so that he gets at least to first base without the help of an error.

Ba·sel (bä′zəl), *n.* city in NW Switzerland.

base·less (bās′lis), *adj.* groundless. —base′less·ness, *n.*

base line, 1. line used as a base. 2. *Am.* line between bases.

base·ment (bās′mənt), *n.* 1. story of a building partly or wholly below ground. 2. the lowest division of the wall of a building.

ba·ses¹ (bā′sēz), *n.* pl. of basis.

bas·es² (bās′iz), *n.* pl. of base¹.

bash (bash), *Dial. and Slang.* —*v.* strike with a smashing blow. —*n.* a smashing blow. [? imit.]

bash·ful (bash′fəl), *adj.* uneasy and awkward in the presence of strangers; shy. [< *bash*, v. (var. of *abash*) + *-ful*] —bash′ful·ly, *adv.* —bash′ful·ness, *n.* —Syn. timid.

bas·ic (bās′ik), *adj.* 1. of or at the base; forming the base; fundamental. 2. *Chem.* a. relating to, having the nature of, or containing a base. b. alkaline. —bas′i·cal·ly, *adv.*

Basic English, or Basic, *n.* a copyrighted system of simplified English having a vocabulary of 850 words used according to a simplified English grammar.

bas·il (baz′əl), *n. Am.* a sweet-smelling plant of the same family as mint, used in cooking. [< OF < L < Gk. *basilikon* royal]

bas·i·lar (bas′ə·lər), **bas·i·lar·y** (–ler′i), *adj.* at the base.

ba·sil·i·ca (bə·sil′ə·kə), *n.* 1. in ancient Rome, an oblong building with a broad nave separated from side aisles by rows of columns. 2. an early Christian church built in this form. [< L < Gk. *basilike* (*oikia*) royal (house) < *basileus* king] —ba·sil′i·can, *adj.*

bas·i·lisk (bas′ə·lisk; baz′–), *n.* 1. *Class. Legend.* a fabled reptile whose breath and look were thought to be fatal. 2. *Zool.* a crested lizard of tropical America. [< L < Gk. *basiliskos*, dim. of *basileus* king]

ba·sin (bā′sən), *n.* 1. a wide, shallow bowl; bowl. 2. an amount that a basin can hold. 3. a hollow place containing water. 4. a roundish valley or hollow. 5. all the land drained by a river and the streams that flow into it. [< OF *bacin* < LL *baccinum* < *bacca* water vessel] —ba′sined, *adj.* —ba′sin·like, *adj.*

ba·sis (bā′sis), *n.*, *pl.* -ses (-sēz). 1. main part; base. 2. a fundamental principle or set of principles; foundation. 3. the principal ingredient. 4. a starting point. [< L < Gk. See BASE¹.]

bask (bask; bäsk), *v.* warm oneself pleasantly. [< Scand. *bathask* bathe oneself] —bask′er, *n.*

bas·ket (bas′kit; bäs′–), *n.* 1. container made of twigs, grasses, fibers, strips of wood, etc., woven together. 2. amount that a basket holds. 3. anything resembling or shaped like a basket. 4. the structure beneath a balloon for carrying passengers or ballast. 5. *Am.* net shaped like a basket, used as a goal in basketball. 6. *Am.* score made in basketball by tossing the ball through a ring into the basket. —bas′ket·like, *adj.*

bas·ket·ball (bas′kit·bôl′; bäs′–), *n. Am.* 1. game played with a large, round leather ball by two teams of five players each. The players try to toss the ball through a ring into a net shaped like a basket. 2. the ball used.

bas·ket·ry (bas′kit·ri; bäs′–), *n.* 1. basketwork; baskets. 2. art of making baskets.

bas·ket·work (bas′kit·wėrk′; bäs′–), *n.* work woven like a basket; wickerwork.

Basque (bask), *n.* 1. member of a race living in the Pyrenees in S France and in N Spain. 2. their language. 3. basque, a woman's waist extending over the hips. —*adj.* having to do with the Basques or their language.

bas-re·lief (bä′ri·lēf′, bas′–; bä′ri·lēf, bas′–), *n.* carving or sculpture in which the figures project only slightly from the background. [< F < Ital. *basso-rilievo* low relief]

bass¹ (bās), *adj.* 1. low or deep in sound. 2. *Music.* of or for the lowest part. —*n. Music.* 1. the lowest male voice. 2. singer with such a voice. 3. lowest part in harmonized music. 4. instrument for such a part. [var. of *base²*; after Ital. *basso*]

bass² (bas), *n.*, *pl.* bass·es (*esp. collectively*) bass. any of various spiny-finned fishes, living in fresh water or in the ocean, as the black bass. [var. of *barse* perch; OE *bears*]

bass³ (bas), *n.* 1. basswood. 2. *Bot.* bast. [alter. of *bast*]

bass drum (bās), *Music.* a large drum that makes a deep, low sound when struck.

bas·set (bas′it), **or basset hound,** *n.* dog with short legs and a long body, like a dachshund, but larger and heavier. [< F, dim. of *bas* low]

bas·si·net (bas′ə·net′; bas′ə·net), *n.* 1. a basketlike cradle. 2. a baby carriage of similar shape. [< F, dim. of *bassin* BASIN]

bas·so (bas′ō; bäs′ō), *n.*, *pl.* -sos, -si (-si), *adj. Music.* —*n.* singer with a bass voice. —*adj.* bass¹. [< Ital. See BASS².]

bas·soon (bə·sün′; ba–), *n. Music.* a deep-toned wind instrument with a doubled wooden tube and a curved metal mouthpiece. [< F < Ital. *bassone* < *basso*] —bas·soon′ist, *n.*

bass viol (bās), *Music.* a deep-toned stringed instrument like a very large violin.

Man playing a bassoon

bass·wood (bas′wŏŏd′), *n.* 1. Also, basswood tree. a. *Am.* linden tree. b. the tulip tree. 2. *Am.* wood of either of these trees. —*adj. Am.* made of basswood.

bast (bast), *n.* 1. *Bot.* the inner layer of the bark that contains cells for carrying sap. 2. the tough fibers in this inner layer. [OE *bæst*]

bas·tard (bas′tərd), *n.* 1. child whose parents are not married to each other; illegitimate child. 2. anything inferior or spurious. —*adj.* 1. born of parents who are not married to each other. 2.

spurious; inferior. 3. irregular or unusual in shape, size, style, etc. [< OF < (*fils de*) *bast* packsaddle (child)] —bas′tar·dy, *n.*

baste[1] (bāst), *v.*, **bast·ed, bast·ing.** drip or pour melted fat or butter on (meat, etc.) while roasting.

baste[2] (bāst), *v.*, **bast·ed, bast·ing.** sew with long stitches to hold the cloth until the final sewing. [< OF *bastir*, < Gmc. Cf. OHG *bestan* tie up, sew with bast.] —bast′er, *n.*

baste[3] (bāst), *v.*, **bast·ed, bast·ing.** beat; thrash. [< Scand. *beysta*]

Bas·tille (bas·tēl′), *n.* **1.** an old fort in Paris used as a prison, destroyed by a mob on July 14, 1789. **2.** bastille, bastile, prison. [< F < LL *bastilia* < *bastire* build]

bas·ti·na·do (bas′tə·nā′dō), *n., pl.* -does, *v.,* -doed, -do·ing. —*n.* **1.** a beating with a stick, esp. on the soles of the feet. **2.** stick; cudgel. —*v.* beat or flog with a stick. [< Sp. *bastonada* < *baston* cudgel, ult. < Gmc.]

bast·ings (bās′tingz), *n.pl.* long, loose stitches to hold the cloth in place until the final sewing.

bas·tion (bas′chən; -ti·ən), *n.* **1.** a projecting part of a fortification. **2.** defense; fortification. [< F < Ital. *bastione* < *bastire* build. See BASTILLE.] —bas′tioned, *adj.*

Ba·su·to·land (bə·sü′tō·land′), *n.* territory in S Africa under British control.

bat[1] (bat), *n., v.,* **bat·ted, bat·ting.** —*n.* **1.** a stout wooden stick or club, used to hit the ball in baseball, etc. **2.** act of batting. **3.** turn at batting. **4.** *Colloq.* stroke; blow. **5.** *Slang.* a wild, gay time; spree. **6.** at bat, *Am.* in the batter's position. —*v.* **1.** hit with a bat; hit. **2.** *Am., Baseball.* hit safely balls served by the pitcher. [OE *batt*]

bat[2] (bat), *n.* a nocturnal flying mammal characterized by modified forelimbs which serve as wings. [< Scand. (Dan.) *-bakke*] —bat′like′, *adj.*

bat[3] (bat), *v.,* **bat·ted, bat·ting.** wink. [< OF < L *battuere* beat]

bat., batt., 1. battalion. **2.** battery.

Ba·taan (bə·tän′; -tan′), *n.* peninsula near Manila in the Philippines; surrender of U.S. troops to Japanese, 1942.

Ba·ta·vi·a (bə·tā′vi·ə), *n.* former name of Jakarta as capital of the Dutch East Indies.

batch (bach), *n.* **1.** quantity of bread made at one baking. **2.** quantity of anything made as one lot. **3.** number of persons or things taken together. [ME *bacche* < OE *bacan* bake]

bate (bāt), *v.,* **bat·ed, bat·ing. 1.** abate; lessen. **2. with bated breath,** holding the breath in great fear, awe, etc. [var. of *abate*]

ba·teau (ba·tō′), *n., pl.* -teaux (-tōz′). *Am.* a light boat with a flat bottom and tapering ends. [< F, ult. < OE *bāt* BOAT]

bath (bath; bäth), *n., pl.* **baths** (bathz; bäthz). **1.** a washing of the body. **2.** water, etc., for a bath. **3.** a tub, room, or other place for bathing. **4.** resort with baths for medical treatment. **5.** liquid in which something is washed or dipped. **6.** container holding the liquid. [OE *bæth*]

Bath (bath; bäth), *n.* city in SW England.

bathe (bāth), *v.,* **bathed, bath·ing. 1.** take a bath. **2.** give a bath to. **3.** apply water to; wash or moisten with any liquid. **4.** go in swimming. **5.** cover; surround. [OE *bathian*] —bath′er, *n.*

bath·house (bath′hous′; bäth′-), *n.* **1.** building fitted up for bathing. **2.** *Am.* building containing dressing rooms for swimmers.

ba·thos (bā′thos), *n.* **1.** a ludicrous descent from the lofty or elevated to the commonplace in writing or speech; anticlimax. **2.** excessive or insincere pathos. [< Gk., depth] —ba·thet·ic (bə·thet′ik), *adj.*

bath·robe (bath′rōb′; bäth′-), *n. Am.* a long, loose garment worn to and from the bath.

bath·room (bath′rüm′; -rum′; bäth′-), *n.* **1.** room fitted up for taking baths, etc. **2.** toilet.

bath·tub (bath′tub′; bäth′-), *n. Am.* tub to bathe in.

bath·y·sphere (bath′ə·sfir′), *n.* a watertight chamber with glass windows, in which men can go deep down in the sea to study animal and

plant life. [< Gk. *bathys* deep + E -*sphere* < Gk. *sphaira* sphere]

ba·tik (bə·tēk′; bat′ik), *n.* **1.** method of making designs on cloth by covering with wax the parts not to be dyed. **2.** cloth dyed in this way. **3.** design formed in this way. —*adj.* **1.** made by batik; made of batik. **2.** like batik; brightly or gaily colored. Also, **battik.** [< Malay]

ba·tiste (bə·tēst′), *n.* a fine, thin, cotton cloth. [< F *Baptiste*, prob. from name of maker]

ba·ton (ba·ton′; bə-), *n.* **1.** a staff or stick used as a symbol of office or authority. **2.** stick used by the leader of an orchestra or band for beating time to the music. [< F]

Bat·on Rouge (bat′ən rüzh′), capital of Louisiana, in the SE part, on the Mississippi.

ba·tra·chi·an (bə·trā′ki·ən), *Zool.* —*adj.* **1.** of or belonging to the division of vertebrates consisting of tailless amphibians, as frogs and toads. **2.** like frogs and toads. —*n.* a tailless amphibian. [< Gk. *batrachos* frog]

bat·tal·ion (bə·tal′yən), *n.* **1.** *U.S. Mil.* tactical unit comprising two or more companies, usually commanded by a major and forming part of a regiment. **2.** large part of an army organized to act together. **3.** army. **4.** organized group. **5. battalions, armies.** [< F < Ital. *bataglione*, dim. of *battaglia* BATTLE]

bat·ten[1] (bat′ən), *v.* **1.** grow fat. **2.** fatten. **3.** feed greedily. [< Scand. *batna* < *bati* improvement] —bat′ten·er, *n.*

bat·ten[2] (bat′ən), *n.* **1.** board used for flooring. **2.** strip of wood nailed across parallel boards to strengthen them, cover cracks, etc. —*v.* fasten or strengthen with strips of wood. [var. of *baton*]

bat·ter[1] (bat′ər), *v.* **1.** beat with repeated blows; pound. **2.** damage by hard use. [< *bat*[1]]

bat·ter[2] (bat′ər), *n.* mixture of flour, milk, eggs, etc., beaten together for use in cookery. [prob. < OF, < *batre* BAT[3]]

bat·ter[3] (bat′ər), *n.* player whose turn it is to bat in baseball, cricket, etc.

battering ram, 1. a military machine with a heavy horizontal beam used in ancient times for battering down walls, gates, etc. **2.** any heavy object similarly used.

bat·ter·y (bat′ər·i), *n., pl.* -ter·ies. **1.** set of similar or connected things. **2.** *Elect.* set of one or more cells that produce current. **3.** *Mil.* **a.** set of big guns for combined action in attack or defense. **b.** these guns together with the soldiers and equipment for them. **c.** platform or fortification equipped with big guns. **4.** *Am., Baseball.* the pitcher and catcher together. **5.** *Law.* the unlawful beating of another person. **6.** any act of beating or battering. [< F, < *battre* beat. See BAT[3], BATTLE.]

bat·tik (bat′ik), *n., adj.* batik.

bat·ting (bat′ing), *n. Am.* cotton or wool pressed into thin layers.

bat·tle (bat′əl), *n., v.,* -tled, -tling. —*n.* **1.** fight between armies or navies. **2.** fighting; war. **3.** fight; contest. —*v.* **1.** take part in a battle. **2.** fight; struggle; contend. [< OF < LL *battalia* < L *battuere* beat] —bat′tler, *n.*

bat·tle-ax, bat·tle-axe (bat′əl·aks′), *n.* ax used as a weapon in war.

battle cruiser, a large, fast warship, not so heavily armored as a battleship.

battle cry, 1. shout of soldiers in battle. **2.** motto or slogan in any contest.

bat·tle·dore (bat′əl·dôr; -dōr), *n.* a small racket used to hit a shuttlecock back and forth in the game of battledore and shuttlecock.

battle fatigue, neurosis from anxiety during combat.

bat·tle·field (bat′əl·fēld′), **bat·tle·ground** (bat′əl·ground′), *n.* place where a battle is fought or has been fought.

bat·tle·ment (bat′əl·mənt), *n.* **1.** wall with indentations for men to shoot through. **2.** *Archit.* wall built like this for ornament. [ult. < OF *bastiller* fortify]

Battlement for defense

bat·tle·ship (bat′əl·ship′), *n.* one of a class of the largest and most heavily armored warships.

bat·ty (bat′i), *adj.*, **–ti·er**, **–ti·est.** 1. batlike. 2. *U.S. Slang.* crazy; queer.

bau·ble (bô′bəl), *n.* a showy trifle having no real value. [< OF *babel* toy]

baulk (bôk), *v.*, *n.* balk.

baux·ite (bôk′sīt; bō′zīt), *n.* a claylike mineral from which aluminum is obtained. [from Les *Baux*, France]

Ba·var·i·a (bə·vâr′i·ə), *n.* a state in SW Germany. **—Ba·var′i·an**, *n.*, *adj.*

bawd (bôd), *n.* procurer; procuress; person who keeps a brothel. [< OF *baud* gay < Gmc.]

bawd·ry (bôd′ri), *n.* obscenity; lewdness.

bawd·y (bôd′i), *adj.*, **bawd·i·er**, **bawd·i·est.** lewd; obscene. **—bawd′i·ly**, *adv.* **—bawd′i·ness**, *n.*

bawl (bôl), *n.* 1. a noisy shout at the top of one's voice. 2. a loud crying. **—v.** 1. shout or cry out in a noisy way. 2. cry loudly. 3. **bawl out**, *Am.*, *Slang.* reprimand. [prob. < Med.L *baulare* bark] **—bawl′er**, *n.* **—Syn.** *v.* 2. weep.

bay¹ (bā), *n.* part of a sea or lake, extending into the land. [< OF *baie* < Gmc.]

bay² (bā), *n. Archit.* 1. space or division of a wall or building between columns, pillars, etc. 2. space with a window or set of windows in it, projecting out from a wall. 3. **bay window.** [< F *baie* opening < VL *batare* gape]

bay³ (bā), *n.* 1. the long, deep bark of a dog. 2. stand made by a hunted animal to face pursuers when escape is impossible. 3. similar stand made by a person against persecution, etc. 4. position of pursuers or enemy kept off. **—v.** bark; bark at. [< OF *bayer*, prob. < VL *batare* gape] **—bay′er**, *n.*

bay⁴ (bā), *n.* 1. a small evergreen tree with smooth, shiny leaves; laurel tree. 2. **bays**, a. laurel wreath worn by poets or victors. b. honor; renown; fame. [< OF *baie* < L *baca* berry]

bay⁵ (bā), *n.* 1. reddish brown. 2. a reddish-brown horse. **—adj.** reddish-brown. [< OF *bai* < L *badius*]

bay·ber·ry (bā′ber′i), *n.*, *pl.* **–ries.** 1. a. *Am.* a North American shrub with grayish-white berries coated with wax. b. one of the berries. 2. a tropical American tree whose leaves contain an oil used in bay rum.

bay·o·net (bā′ə·nit; –net), *n.*, *v.*, **–net·ed**, **–net·ing.** **—n.** blade for piercing or stabbing, attached to a gun. **—v.** pierce or stab with a bayonet. [< F *baïonnette*; named for *Bayonne*, France]

bay·ou (bī′ü), *n.*, *pl.* **–ous.** *Am.* a marshy inlet or outlet of a lake, river, or gulf in the southern United States. [< Louisiana F < Choctaw *bayuk* small stream]

bay rum, a fragrant liquid originally made from the leaves of a tree growing in the West Indies, used in medicine and cosmetics.

bay window, window or set of windows projecting out from a wall.

ba·zaar, **ba·zar** (bə·zär′), *n.* 1. street or streets full of shops. 2. place for the sale of many kinds of goods. 3. sale held for some charity, a worthy cause, etc. [< F < Ar. < Pers. *bāzār*]

ba·zoo·ka (bə·zü′kə), *n. Am.*, *Mil.* rocket gun used against tanks. [from resemblance to trombonelike instrument created and named by Bob Burns, American humorist]

B.B.C., British Broadcasting Corporation.

bbl., *pl.* **bbls.** barrel.

B-bop (bē′bop′), *n. Slang.* bebop.

B.C., 1. before Christ; before the birth of Christ. 350 B.C. is 100 years earlier than 250 B.C. 2. British Columbia.

bd., *pl.* **bds.** 1. board. 2. bond. 3. bound.

be (bē), *v.*, *pres. indic. sing.* am, are, is, *pl.* are; *pt. indic. sing.* was, were, was, *pl.* were; *pp.* been; *ppr.* be·ing. 1. have reality; exist; live. 2. take place; happen. 3. remain; continue. 4. equal; represent. 5. *Be* is used as a linking verb between a subject and a predicate modifier or to form infinitives and participial phrases: *you will be late, try to be just.* 6. *Be* is used as an auxiliary verb with: a. the present participle of another verb to form the progressive tense: *he is building a house.* b. the past participle of another verb to form the passive voice: *the date was fixed.* [OE *bēon*] ❯ Older usage of *be* survives in stock phrases, as "the powers that *be*," and in nonstandard spoken English, as in "You *ain't* (sometimes *be'n't*) going, *be* you?" Nonstandard spoken English also continues to use *was* in the plural, as in "*Was* the Adamses there?," which would have been good informal usage 200 years ago. ❯ a. **be** as **linking verb.** *Be* is the most common linking verb, linking, without adding specifically a meaning of its own, a subject and a predicate nominative or adjective: *Jerome was the secretary* [predicate nominative]. *She is sick* [predicate adjective]. b. as **auxiliary verb.** Forms of *be* are used with the present participles of other verbs to form the progressive tense form: *I am asking, he was asking, you will be asking.* Forms of *be* with past participles form the passive voice: *I am asked, you will be asked, he was asked.* c. as **verb of complete predication.** *Be* is a verb of complete predication when indicating states or positions: *I am tired, the fire was just across the street.*

be-, *prefix.* 1. thoroughly; all around, as in *bespatter.* 2. at; on; to; for; about; against, as in *bewail.* 3. make, as in *belittle.* 4. provide with, as in *bespangle.* [OE, unstressed form of *bī* by]

Be, *Chem.* beryllium.

B/E, **b.e.**, bill of exchange.

beach (bēch), *n.* the almost flat shore of sand or little stones at the edge of the sea, a river, or a large lake. **—v.** run or draw (a boat) ashore. **—beach′less**, *adj.* **—Syn.** *n.* strand, coast, seashore.

beach·comb·er (bēch′kōm′ər), *n.* 1. a vagrant or loafer on beaches. 2. *U.S.* a long wave rolling in from the ocean.

beach·head (bēch′hed′), *n. Mil.* the first position established by an invading army on a hostile shore.

bea·con (bē′kən), *n.* 1. fire or light used as a signal to guide or warn. 2. a radio signal for guiding aviators through fogs, storms, etc. 3. a tall tower for a signal; lighthouse. **—v.** 1. give light to; guide; warn. 2. shine brightly. 3. supply with beacons. [OE *bēacn*] **—bea′con·less**, *adj.*

bead (bēd), *n.* 1. a small ball or bit of glass, metal, etc., with a hole through it, so that it can be strung on a thread with others like it. 2. **beads**, a. string of beads. b. a rosary. 3. **say, tell,** or **count one's beads**, say prayers, using a rosary. 4. any small, round object like a drop or bubble: *beads of sweat.* 5. *Am.* the front sight of a rifle. 6. a narrow, semicircular molding. **—v.** 1. put beads on; ornament with beads. 2. form beads. [OE *bedu* prayer. See def. 2b.] **—bead′ed**, *adj.*

bead·ing (bēd′ing), *n.* 1. trimming made of beads threaded into patterns. 2. a narrow trimming. 3. pattern or edge on woodwork, silver, etc., made of small beads. 4. a narrow, semicircular molding.

bea·dle (bē′dəl), *n.* a minor officer in the Church of England. [OE *bydel*]

bead·y (bēd′i), *adj.*, **bead·i·er**, **bead·i·est.** 1. small, round, and shiny. 2. trimmed with beads. 3. covered with drops or bubbles.

bea·gle (bē′gəl), *n.* a small hunting dog with short legs and drooping ears. [ME *begle*]

beak (bēk), *n.* 1. a bird's bill, esp. one that is strong and hooked and useful in striking or tearing. 2. a similar part in other animals. 3. the projecting bow of an ancient warship. 4. a spout. [< OF < L *beccus* < Celtic] **—beaked** (bēkt; bēk′id), *adj.* **—beak′less**, *adj.* **—beak′like′**, *adj.*

beak·er (bēk′ər), *n.* 1. a large cup or drinking glass. 2. contents of a beaker. 3. a thin glass or metal cup used in laboratories. [< Scand. *bikarr*]

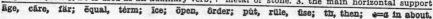
Beaker
(def. 3)

beam (bēm), *n.* 1. a large, long piece of timber, ready for use in building. 2. a similar piece of metal or stone. 3. the main horizontal support of a building or ship. 4. part of a plow by which it is pulled. 5. the crosswise bar of a balance, from the ends of which the scales or pans are suspended. 6. the balance itself. 7. ray or rays of light or heat; ray. 8. a bright look or smile. 9. a radio signal directed in a straight line, used to guide aviators, sailors, etc. 10. *Radio.* a. the maximum range at which a loudspeaker is effective. b. angle which gives the maximum performance to a microphone, amplifier, etc. 11. *Naut.* side of a ship, or the direction at right angles to the keel, with reference to wind, sea, etc. 12. the greatest width of a ship. 13. on her beam's ends, almost capsizing. 14. on the beam, a. of a ship, broadside. b. of an aircraft, in the right path by the directing signals. c. *Slang.* just right; exactly. —*v.* 1. send out rays of light; shine. 2. smile radiantly. 3. direct (a broadcast): *beam programs at Russia.* [OE *bēam* tree, piece of wood, ray of light] —beamed, *adj.* —beam'less, *adj.* —beam'like', *adj.*

beam·ing (bēm'ing), *adj.* 1. shining; bright. 2. smiling brightly. —beam'ing·ly, *adv.*

bean (bēn), *n.* 1. a smooth, kidney-shaped seed used as a vegetable. 2. the long pod containing such seeds. 3. plant that beans grow on. 4. any seed shaped somewhat like a bean. 5. *Am., Slang.* head. —*v. Am., Slang.* hit on the head. [OE *bēan*]

bean·ball (bēn'bôl'), *n. Am., Slang.* a baseball thrown by the pitcher so as to hit or attempt to hit the batter's head. —bean'ball'er, *n.*

bear[1] (bâr), *v.*, bore or (*Archaic*) bare, borne or born, bear·ing. 1. carry: *bear a burden.* 2. support: *bear the weight of the roof.* 3. put up with; endure: *he can't bear the noise.* 4. undergo; experience: *bear pain.* 5. produce; yield: *bear fruit.* 6. give birth to; have (offspring): *bear a child.* 7. have a connection or effect; relate: *his story does not bear on the question.* 8. behave; conduct. 9. bring forward; give: *bear witness to what happened.* 10. have; hold. 11. have as an identification or characteristic: *a coat bearing marks of hard wear.* 12. have as a duty, right, privilege, etc.: *bear sway over an empire.* 13. press; push. 14. move; go; tend in direction: *the ship bore north.* 15. lie; be situated: *the land bore due north of the ship.* 16. allow; permit: *the accident bears two explanations.* 17. bear down, a. put pressure on. b. approach; move toward. 18. bear out, support; prove. 19. bear up, keep one's courage; not lose hope or faith. 20. bear with, put up with; be patient with. [OE *beran*] —Syn. 1. bring, convey. 2. sustain. 3. abide, tolerate, brook. 10. cherish, harbor. 13. thrust, drive. ➤ See borne for usage note.

bear[2] (bâr), *n., adj., v.*, beared, bear·ing. —*n.* 1. a large, clumsy, quadruped animal that has coarse hair and a very short tail. 2. a gruff or surly person. 3. person who tries to lower prices in the stock market, etc. 4. Bear, *Astron.* one of two northern groups of stars; the Little Bear or the Great Bear. —*adj.* having to do with lowering prices in the stock market, etc. —*v.* operate for a decline in stocks, etc. [OE *bera*]

bear·a·ble (bâr'ə·bəl), *adj.* that can be borne; endurable. —bear'a·ble·ness, *n.* —bear'a·bly, *adv.*

beard (bird), *n.* 1. hair growing on a man's face. 2. something resembling or suggesting this, as the chin tuft of a goat. 3. hairs on the heads of plants like oats, barley, and wheat; awns. —*v.* face boldly; defy. [OE] —beard'ed, *adj.* —beard'less, *adj.* —beard'less·ness, *n.* —beard'like', *adj.*

bear·er (bâr'ər), *n.* 1. person or thing that carries. 2. person who holds or presents a check, draft, or note for payment. 3. tree or plant that produces fruit or flowers. 4. holder of a rank or office. 5. pallbearer.

A. bearded wheat; B, beardless wheat.

bear·ing (bâr'ing), *n.* 1. act of a person or thing that bears. 2. act, power, or season of bearing offspring or fruit. 3. way of standing, sitting, walking, etc.; manner: *a military bearing.* 4. reference; relation: *the question has no bearing on the problem.* 5. direction; position in relation to other things: *he got his bearings from*

the sun. 6. part of a machine on which another part turns or slides. 7. a supporting part. 8. a single device in a coat of arms. —Syn. 1. sustaining. 3. behavior, air, conduct.

bear·ish (bâr'ish), *adj.* 1. like a bear; rough; surly. 2. aiming at or tending to lower prices in the stock market, etc. —bear'ish·ly, *adv.* —bear'ish·ness, *n.*

bear·skin (bâr'skin'), *n.* fur of a bear.

beast (bēst), *n.* 1. any animal except man, esp. a four-footed animal. 2. a coarse, dirty, or brutal person. 3. the beastly nature in human beings. [< OF < LL *besta*] —beast'like', *adj.*

beast·ly (bēst'li), *adj.*, -li·er, -li·est, *adv.* —*adj.* 1. like a beast; brutal; coarse. 2. *Brit. Colloq.* annoying; irksome. —*adv. Brit. Colloq.* annoyingly. —beast'li·ness, *n.*

beat (bēt), *v.*, beat, beat·en or beat, beat·ing, *n., adj.* —*v.* 1. strike again and again; strike; whip; thrash. 2. throb: *her heart beats fast with joy.* 3. drive by blows; force by blows: *he beat off the savage dog.* 4. defeat; overcome. 5. *Colloq.* baffle. 6. *Am., Colloq.* cheat; swindle. 7. make flat; shape with a hammer: *beat gold into gold leaf.* 8. make flat by much walking; tread (a path). 9. mix by stirring; mix by striking with a fork, spoon, or other utensil: *beat eggs.* 10. move up and down; flap: *the bird beat its wings.* 11. make a sound by being struck: *the drums beat loudly.* 12. mark (time) with drumsticks or by tapping with hands or feet: *beat a tattoo.* 13. show musical beat by a stroke of the hand, etc. 14. go through in a hunt. 15. move against the wind by a zigzag course: *the sailboat beat along the coast.* 16. *Colloq.* win. 17. beat a retreat, a. run away; retreat. b. sound a retreat on a drum. 18. beat up, *Am., Colloq.* attack; thrash. —*n.* 1. stroke or blow made again and again: *the beat of a drum.* 2. *Music.* a. unit of time or accent: *three beats to a measure.* b. stroke of the hand, baton, etc., showing a musical beat. 3. a regular route or round made by a policeman or watchman. 4. *Am., Colloq.* person, thing, or event that wins. 5. *Am.* in journalism, the securing and publishing of news ahead of one's competitors. —*adj. Am., Colloq.* 1. exhausted. 2. overcome by astonishment; taken aback. [OE *bēatan*] —beat'er, *n.* —Syn. *v.* 1. smite, pommel, flog. 4. vanquish, conquer. 16. surpass, outdo.

beat·en (bēt'ən), *v.* pp. of beat. —*adj.* 1. whipped; thrashed. 2. shaped by blows of a hammer. 3. much walked on or traveled: *beaten path.* 4. defeated; overcome. 5. exhausted.

be·a·tif·ic (bē'ə·tif'ik), *adj.* making blessed; blissful. [< L *beatificus* < *beare* bless + *facere* make] —be'a·tif'i·cal·ly, *adv.*

be·at·i·fy (bi·at'ə·fī), *v.*, -fied, -fy·ing. 1. make supremely happy; bless. 2. declare (a dead person) by a decree of the Pope to be among the blessed in heaven. —be·at'i·fi·ca'tion, *n.*

beat·ing (bēt'ing), *n.* 1. act of one that beats. 2. whipping; thrashing. 3. defeat. 4. throbbing.

be·at·i·tude (bi·at'ə·tüd; -tūd), *n.* 1. supreme happiness; bliss. 2. blessing. 3. the Beatitudes, verses in the Bible beginning "Blessed are the poor in spirit." Matt. 5:3–12. [< L *beatitudo* < *beare* bless]

beat-up (bēt'up'), *adj. Am., Slang.* in very bad condition; showing evidence of hard use.

beau (bō), *n., pl.* beaus, beaux (bōz). 1. a suitor; lover. 2. dandy; fop. [< F, handsome, < L *bellus* fine] —beau'ish, *adj.* —Syn. 1. swain. 2. dude. ➤Beaux is the more formal plural form.

Beau·fort scale (bō'fərt), an internationally used scale of wind velocities, ranging from 0 (calm) to 12 (hurricane).

beau geste (bō zhest'), *pl.* beaux gestes (bō zhest'). 1. a graceful or kindly act. 2. *French.* pretense of kindness merely for effect.

beau·te·ous (bū'ti·əs), *adj. Esp. Poetic.* beautiful. —beau'te·ous·ly, *adv.* —beau'te·ous·ness, *n.*

beau·ti·ful (bū'tə·fəl), *adj.* very pleasing to see or hear; delighting the mind or senses. —beau'ti·ful·ly, *adv.* —beau'ti·ful·ness, *n.*

beau·ti·fy (bū'tə·fī), *v.*, -fied, -fy·ing. make or become beautiful or more beautiful. —beau'ti-fi·ca′tion, n. —beau′ti·fi′er, n. —Syn. ornament, decorate, adorn.

beau·ty (bū′ti), n., pl. –ties. 1. good looks. 2. quality that pleases in flowers, pictures, music, etc. 3. quality that pleases the intellect or moral sense. 4. a beautiful person, animal, or thing, esp. a beautiful woman. [< OF beauté < beau beautiful. See BEAU.] —Syn. 2. loveliness.

beauty parlor or shop, Am. place where women have their hair, skin, and fingernails cared for.

beaux-arts (bō-zär′), n.pl. French. fine arts; painting, sculpture, music, etc.

bea·ver¹ (bē′vər), n. 1. an amphibious rodent with a broad, flat tail, noted for its ingenuity in damming streams with mud, branches, etc. 2. its soft brown fur. 3. a man's high silk hat. [OE beofor] —bea′ver·like′, adj.

bea·ver² (bē′vər), n. 1. the movable lower part of a helmet. 2. visor of a helmet. 3. Slang. beard. [< OF bavière, orig., bib < bave saliva]

be·bop (bē′bop′), n. Slang. a fad in popular music, based on unusual rhythms, dissonance, and lack of formalism. Also, bop, B-bop.

B, beaver.

be·calm (bi·käm′), v. 1. prevent from moving by lack of wind. 2. make calm.

be·came (bi·kām′), v. pt. of become.

be·cause (bi·kôz′), conj. for the reason that; since. —adv. because of, by reason of; on account of: we did not go because of the rain. [ME bicause by cause] —Syn. conj. inasmuch as, for. ≻ Because introduces a subordinate clause, giving the reason for the independent statement: because we were late we hurried. Since and as can be used in such clauses, but they are less definite, more casual, and are more characteristic of easy speech than of writing. For, which also introduces reasons, is a more formal word and rather rare.

be·chance (bi·chans′; –chäns′), v., –chanced, –chanc·ing. happen; happen to; befall.

Bech·u·a·na·land (bech′ū·ä′nə·land′), n. district in S Africa under British control.

beck (bek), n. 1. motion of the head or hand meant as a call or command. 2. at one's beck and call, a. ready whenever wanted. b. under one's complete control. —v. beckon to. [< beck, v., short for beckon]

Beck·et (bek′it), n. Saint Thomas à, 1118?–1170, archbishop of Canterbury.

beck·on (bek′ən), v. signal (to a person) by a motion of the head or hand. —n. a beckoning gesture. [OE bēcnan] —beck′on·er, n. —beck′on·ing·ly, adv.

be·cloud (bi·kloud′), v. obscure.

be·come (bi·kum′), v., be·came, be·come, be·com·ing. 1. come to be; grow to be. 2. be suitable for; suit. 3. become of, happen to: what will become of her? [OE becuman] ≻ Become is primarily a linking verb with little meaning of its own, chiefly connecting a subject with a predicate adjective or noun: he became a doctor.

be·com·ing (bi·kum′ing), adj. 1. fitting; suitable; appropriate: becoming conduct for a gentleman. 2. that looks well: a becoming dress. —be·com′ing·ly, adv. —be·com′ing·ness, n. —Syn. 1. proper, meet, seemly.

Becque·rel rays (bek′rel), invisible rays given off by radioactive substances.

bed (bed), n., v., bed·ded, bed·ding. —n. 1. mattress. 2. bedstead. 3. anything to sleep or rest on. 4. the use of a bed: bed and board. 5. any place where people or animals rest or sleep. 6. flat base on which anything rests; foundation. 7. ground under a body of water: the bed of a river. 8. piece of ground in which plants are grown. 9. such a piece and the plants in it. 10. layer; stratum: a bed of coal. —v. 1. provide with a bed. 2. put to bed. 3. go to bed. 4. fix or set in a permanent position; embed. 5. plant in a garden bed. 6. form a compact layer. 7. lay flat; lay in order. [OE bedd] —bed′less, adj. —bed′like′, adj. —Syn. n. 3. couch, berth.

be·daze (bi·dāz′), v., –dazed, –daz·ing. stupefy.

be·daz·zle (bi·daz′əl), v., –zled, –zling. dazzle completely; confuse. —be·daz′zle·ment, n.

bed·bug (bed′bug′), n. a small, flat bloodsucking hemipterous insect.

bed·cham·ber (bed′chām′bər), n. bedroom.

bed·clothes (bed′klōz′; –klōthz′), n.pl. sheets, blankets, quilts, etc.

bed·ding (bed′ing), n. 1. sheets, blankets, quilts, etc.; bedclothes. 2. material for beds. 3. foundation; bottom layer.

be·deck (bi·dek′), v. adorn; decorate.

be·dev·il (bi·dev′əl), v., –iled, –il·ing; esp. Brit. –illed, –il·ling. 1. trouble greatly; torment. 2. confuse completely; muddle. 3. put under a spell; bewitch. —be·dev′il·ment, n.

be·dew (bi·dū′; –dū′), v. wet with dew or with drops like dew.

bed·fast (bed′fast′; –fäst′), adj. bedridden.

bed·fel·low (bed′fel′ō), n. 1. sharer of one's bed. 2. associate.

be·dight (bi·dīt′), v., –dight, –dight or –dighted, –dight·ing, adj. Archaic. —v. adorn; array. —adj. adorned; arrayed.

be·dim (bi·dim′), v., –dimmed, –dim·ming. make dim; darken; obscure. —Syn. overcast.

be·di·zen (bi·dī′zən; –diz′ən), v. ornament with showy finery. —be·di′zen·ment, n.

bed·lam (bed′ləm), n. 1. uproar; confusion. 2. insane asylum; madhouse. 3. Bedlam, insane asylum in London. [alter. of Bethlehem. See def. 3.]

Bed·ou·in (bed′u·in), n. 1. a wandering Arab who lives in the deserts of Arabia, Syria, or northern Africa. 2. wanderer; nomad.

bed·pan (bed′pan′), n. 1. Am. pan used as a toilet by sick people in bed. 2. pan filled with hot coals for warming a bed.

be·drag·gle (bi·drag′əl), v., –gled, –gling. make limp and soiled, as with dirt. —be·drag′gle·ment, n.

bed·rid·den (bed′rid′ən), bed·rid (–rid′), adj. confined to bed for a long time because of sickness or weakness.

bed·rock (bed′rok′), n. 1. Am. solid rock beneath the soil and looser rocks. 2. firm foundation. 3. the lowest level; bottom. 4. Am. fundamental or essential part.

bed·room (bed′rüm′; –rum′), n. room to sleep in.

bed·side (bed′sīd′), n. side of a bed.

bed·spread (bed′spred′), n. Am. cover for a bed, usually decorative.

bed·stead (bed′sted; –stid), n. the wooden or metal framework of a bed.

bed·time (bed′tim′), n. time to go to bed.

bee (bē), n. 1. any of various hymenopterous insects, esp. the common honeybee, producing honey and wax, and forming highly organized colonies. 2. any of various similar insects. 3. Am. a gathering for work or amusement: a husking bee. [OE bēo]

Worker honeybee (ab. ¾ actual size)

bee·bread (bē′bred′), n. a brownish, bitter substance consisting of pollen, or pollen mixed with honey, used by bees as food.

beech (bēch), n. 1. a tree with smooth, gray bark and glossy leaves that bears a sweet edible nut. 2. its wood. [OE bēce] —beech′en, adj.

beech·nut (bēch′nut′), n. the small, triangular nut of the beech tree.

beef (bēf), n., pl. beeves (bēvz) (for 2) or beefs (for 5), v. —n. 1. meat from a steer, cow, or bull. 2. steer, cow, or bull when full-grown and fattened for food. 3. Colloq. strength; muscle. 4. Colloq. weight. 5. Am., Colloq. complaint; grievance. —v. 1. Am., Slang. complain loudly. 2. beef up, Slang. strengthen: beef up defenses. [< OF boef < L bos ox] —beef′less, adj.

beef·steak (bēf′stāk′), *n.* slice of beef for broiling or frying.

beef·y (bēf′ĭ), *adj.*, beef·i·er, beef·i·est. strong; muscular; solid. —beef′i·ness, *n.*

bee·hive (bē′hīv′), *n.* 1. hive or house for bees. 2. a busy, swarming place.

bee·line (bē′līn′), *n. Am.* straightest way or line between two places.

Be·el·ze·bub (bi·el′zə·bub), *n.* 1. *Bible.* the Devil. 2. a devil.

been (bin; *rarely* bēn), *v.* pp. of be.

beer (bir), *n.* 1. an alcoholic drink made from malt and usually hops. 2. drink made from roots or plants, as root beer. [OE *bēor*]

Beer·she·ba (bir·shē′bə; bir′shi–), *n.* town near the S boundary of Arab Palestine.

beer·y (bir′ĭ), *adj.*, beer·i·er, beer·i·est. 1. of or like beer. 2. caused by beer. —beer′i·ness, *n.*

beest·ings (bēs′tingz), *n.pl.* the first milk from a cow after it has given birth to a calf. [OE *bȳsting* < *bēost* beestings]

bees·wax (bēz′waks′), *n.* wax given out by bees, from which they make their honeycomb. —*v.* rub, polish, or treat with beeswax.

beet (bēt), *n.* 1. thick root of a plant. Red beets are eaten as vegetables. Sugar is made from white beets. 2. the plant. The leaves are sometimes eaten as greens. [< L *beta*]

Bee·tho·ven (bā′tō·vən), *n.* Ludwig van, 1770-1827, German musical composer.

bee·tle[1] (bē′təl), *n.* 1. any of an order of insects with two hard, shiny cases to cover the wings when folded. 2. any similar insect. [OE *bitela* < *bītan* bite]

bee·tle[2] (bē′təl), *n.*, *v.*, -tled, -tling. —*n.* 1. a heavy wooden mallet. 2. a wooden household utensil for beating or mashing. —*v.* pound with a beetle. [OE *bietel* < *bēatan* beat]

bee·tle[3] (bē′təl), *v.*, -tled, -tling, *adj.* —*v.* project; overhang. —*adj.* projecting; overhanging. [< *beetle-browed*]

bee·tle-browed (bē′təl-broud′), *adj.* 1. having overhanging eyebrows. 2. scowling; sullen. [ME *bitel* biting + *brow*. See BEETLE[1].]

beeves (bēvz), *n.* pl. of beef (def. 2).

be·fall (bi·fôl′), *v.*, -fell, -fall·en, -fall·ing. 1. happen to. 2. happen. —Syn. 2. occur.

be·fit (bi·fit′), *v.*, -fit·ted, -fit·ting. be suitable for; be proper for; be suited to. —be·fit′ting, *adj.* —be·fit′ting·ly, *adv.*

be·fog (bi·fog′; -fôg′), *v.*, -fogged, -fog·ging. surround with fog; make foggy; obscure; confuse.

be·fore (bi·fôr′; -fōr′), *prep.* 1. in front of; in advance of; ahead of: *walk before me.* 2. earlier than: *come before five o'clock.* 3. rather than; sooner than: *I will die before giving in.* 4. in the presence or sight of: *stand before the king.* —*adv.* 1. in front; in advance; ahead: *go before.* 2. earlier: *come at five o'clock, not before.* 3. until now; in the past: *I didn't know that before.* —*conj.* 1. previously to the time when: *before she goes.* 2. rather than; sooner than: *I will die before I give in.* [OE *beforan*]

be·fore·hand (bi·fôr′hand′; -fōr′–), *adv.*, *adj.* ahead of time; in advance.

be·foul (bi·foul′), *v.* 1. make dirty; cover with filth. 2. entangle.

be·friend (bi·frend′), *v.* act as a friend to.

be·fud·dle (bi·fud′əl), *v.*, -dled, -dling. stupefy; confuse, esp. with alcoholic drink.

beg (beg), *v.*, begged, beg·ging. 1. ask for (food, money, clothes, etc.) as a charity. 2. ask help or charity. 3. ask earnestly or humbly. 4. ask formally and courteously. 5. **beg off,** get free by pleading. 6. **beg the question,** take for granted the very thing argued about. [OE *bedecian*] —Syn. 3. entreat, implore.

be·gan (bi·gan′), *v.* pt. of begin.

be·get (bi·get′), *v.*, be·got or (*Archaic*) be·gat, be·got·ten or be·got, be·get·ting. 1. become the father of. 2. cause to be; produce. —be·get′ter, *n.*

beg·gar (beg′ər), *n.* 1. person who lives by begging. 2. a very poor person. 3. fellow. —*v.* 1. bring to poverty. 2. make seem poor. —beg·gar·dom (beg′ər·dəm), beg′gar·hood, *n.*

beg·gar·ly (beg′ər·li), *adj.* fit for a beggar; poor. —beg′gar·li·ness, *n.*

beg·gar's-lice (beg′ərz·lis′), *n. Am.* 1. (*pl. in use*) burs or seeds of various plants that stick to clothes. 2. (*pl. or sing. in use*) weed on which such burs or seeds grow.

beg·gar's-ticks (beg′ərz·tiks′), **beg·gar-ticks** (beg′ər·tiks′), *n.* beggar's-lice.

beg·gar·y (beg′ər·i), *n.* very great poverty.

be·gin (bi·gin′), *v.*, be·gan, be·gun, be·gin·ning. 1. do the first part; do the first part of; start. 2. come into being; bring into being; originate. 3. be near; come near: *that suit doesn't even begin to fit you.* [OE *beginnan*] —Syn. 1. commence. 2. arise.

be·gin·ner (bi·gin′ər), *n.* 1. person who is doing something for the first time; person who lacks skill and experience. 2. person who begins anything. —Syn. 1. amateur, novice.

be·gin·ning (bi·gin′ing), *n.* 1. a commencing; start. 2. time when anything begins. 3. first part. 4. first cause; source; origin. —*adj.* that begins. —Syn. *n.* 1. initiation. —Ant. *n.* 1. end.

be·gird (bi·gėrd′), *v.*, -girt (-gėrt′) or -gird·ed, -gird·ing. surround; encircle.

be·gone (bi·gôn′; -gon′), *interj.*, *v.* be gone; go away; depart.

be·go·ni·a (bi·gō′ni·ə; -gōn′yə), *n.* a tropical plant with handsome leaves and waxy flowers. [from Michel *Bégon*, patron of botany]

be·got (bi·got′), *v.* pt. and pp. of beget.

be·got·ten (bi·got′ən), *v.* pp. of beget.

be·grime (bi·grīm′), *v.*, -grimed, -grim·ing. make grimy; make dirty.

be·grudge (bi·gruj′), *v.*, -grudged, -grudg·ing. envy (somebody) the possession of; be reluctant to give (something); grudge. —be·grudg′ing·ly, *adv.*

be·guile (bi·gīl′), *v.*, -guiled, -guil·ing. 1. deceive; cheat. 2. take away from deceitfully or cunningly. 3. entertain; amuse. 4. while away (time) pleasantly. —be·guil′er, *n.* —be·guil′ing·ly, *adv.* —Syn. 1. delude. 3. divert, charm.

be·gun (bi·gun′), *v.* pp. of begin.

be·half (bi·haf′; -häf′), *n.* 1. side; interest; favor: *his friends will act in his behalf.* 2. in behalf of, in the interest of; for. 3. on behalf of, a. as a representative of. b. in behalf of. [ME *behalve* beside, on the side of]

be·have (bi·hāv′), *v.*, -haved, -hav·ing. 1. act. 2. conduct (oneself or itself) in a certain way. 3. act well; do what is right.

be·hav·ior, *esp. Brit.* **be·hav·iour** (bi·hāv′yər), *n.* 1. way of acting; conduct; actions; acts. 2. manners; deportment. —Syn. 2. demeanor.

be·hav·ior·ism (bi·hāv′yər·iz·əm), *n.* doctrine that the objective acts of persons and animals are the chief or only subject matter of scientific psychology. —be·hav′ior·ist, *n.* —be·hav′ior·is′-tic, *adj.* —be·hav′ior·is′ti·cal·ly, *adv.*

be·head (bi·hed′), *v.* cut off the head of.

be·held (bi·held′), *v.* pt. and pp. of behold.

be·he·moth (bi·hē′məth; bē′ə–), *n. Bible.* a huge animal mentioned in Job 40:15-24. [< Heb. *b'hēmōth,* pl. of *b'hēmah* beast]

be·hest (bi·hest′), *n.* command; order. [OE *behǣs* promise]

be·hind (bi·hīnd′), *prep.* 1. at the back of; in the rear of: *behind the door.* 2. at or on the far side of: *behind the hill.* 3. concealed by: *vile treachery lurked behind his smooth manners.* 4. inferior to; less advanced than. 5. later than; after: *behind one's usual time.* 6. remaining after: *the dead man left a family behind him.* 7. in support of; supporting: *his friends are behind him.* —*adv.* 1. at or toward the back; in the rear. 2. farther back in place or time. 3. in reserve. 4. not on time; slow; late. [OE *behindan.* See BE-, HIND.]

be·hind·hand (bi·hīnd′hand′), *adv.*, *adj.* 1. behind time; late. 2. behind others in progress; backward; slow. 3. in debt.

be·hold (bi·hōld′), *v.*, be·held, be·hold·ing, *interj.* 1. see; look at. 2. look; take notice. [OE *behealdan*] —be·hold′er, *n.* —Syn. 1. observe.

be·hold·en (bi·hōl′dən), *adj.* indebted.

be·hoof (bi·hüf′), *n.* use; advantage; benefit. [OE *behōf* need]

be·hoove (bi·hüv′), *esp. Brit.* **be·hove** (bi·hōv′), *v.,* –hooved, –hoov·ing; –hoved, –hov·ing. 1. be necessary for. 2. be proper for. [OE *behōfian* to need]

beige (bāzh), *n., adj.* pale brown. [< F]

be·ing (bē′ing), *n.* 1. life; existence. 2. nature; constitution: *her whole being thrilled to the music.* 3. that which exists. 4. person; living creature. —*adj.* that is; present: *the time being.*

Bei·rut (bā′rüt; bā·rüt′), *n.* capital of Lebanon.

be·jew·el (bi·jü′əl), *v.,* –eled, –el·ing; *esp. Brit.* –elled, –el·ling. adorn with jewels.

be·la·bor, *esp. Brit.* **be·la·bour** (bi·lā′bər), *v.* 1. beat vigorously. 2. abuse; ridicule.

be·lat·ed (bi·lāt′id), *adj.* 1. delayed; too late. 2. overtaken by darkness. —**be·lat′ed·ly,** *adv.* —**be·lat′ed·ness,** *n.*

be·lay (bi·lā′), *v.,* be·layed, be·lay·ing. 1. *Naut.* fasten (a rope) by winding it around a pin or cleat. 2. *Colloq.* stop. [OE *belecgan.* See BE–, LAY¹.]

belaying pin, *Naut.* pin around which ropes can be wound and fastened.

belch (belch), *v.* 1. throw out gas from the stomach through the mouth. 2. throw out with force: *the volcano belched fire.* —*n.* act of belching. [cf. OE *bealcian*] —**belch′er,** *n.*

bel·dam (bel′dəm), **bel·dame** (–dəm; –dām′), *n.* 1. an old woman. 2. an ugly old woman. [< *bel–* grand– (< OF, < *belle* fair) + *dam* DAME]

be·lea·guer (bi·lē′gər), *v.* 1. besiege. 2. surround. [< Du. *belegeren* < *leger* camp] —**be·lea′-guered,** *adj.* —**be·lea′guer·er,** *n.* —**be·lea′guer-ment,** *n.*

Be·lém (bə·lem′), *n.* seaport in NE Brazil. Also, **Pará.**

Bel·fast (bel′fast; –fäst), *n.* seaport and capital of Northern Ireland.

bel·fry (bel′fri), *n., pl.* –fries. 1. tower for a bell or bells. 2. space for the bell in a tower. [< OF *berfrei* < Gmc.] —**bel·fried** (bel′frid), *adj.*

Belg., Belgium; Belgian.

Belgian Congo, Belgian colony in C Africa.

Bel·gium (bel′jəm), *n.* a small country in W Europe. —**Bel·gian** (bel′jən), *adj., n.*

Bel·grade (bel′grād; bel·grād′), *n.* capital of Yugoslavia, on the Danube River.

Be·li·al (bē′li·əl; bēl′yəl), *n.* the devil.

be·lie (bi·lī′), *v.,* –lied, –ly·ing. 1. give a false idea of; misrepresent. 2. show to be false; prove to be mistaken. 3. lie about. 4. be false to. —**be·li′er,** *n.*

be·lief (bi·lēf′), *n.* 1. what is held true; thing believed; opinion. 2. acceptance as true or real. 3. faith; trust: *he expressed his belief in the boy's honesty.* 4. religious faith. [ME *bileaje.* Cf. OE *gelēafa.*] —**Syn.** 1. conviction, view.

be·lieve (bi·lēv′), *v.,* –lieved, –liev·ing. 1. accept as true or real. 2. have faith in (a person or thing); trust. 3. think (somebody) tells the truth. 4. have religious belief. 5. think; suppose. [ME *bileve(n).* Cf. OE *gelīefan.*] —**be·liev′a·ble,** *adj.* —**be·liev′a·ble·ness,** *n.* —**be·liev′er,** *n.* —**be·liev′ing·ly,** *adv.*

be·lit·tle (bi·lit′əl), *v.,* –tled, –tling. *Am.* 1. cause to seem little, unimportant, or less important; speak slightingly of. 2. make small. —**be·lit′tle·ment,** *n.* —**be·lit′tler,** *n. Am.* —**Syn.** 1. depreciate, disparage.

bell (bel), *n.* 1. a hollow metal cup that makes a musical sound when struck by a clapper or hammer. 2. sound of a bell. 3. stroke of a bell every half hour to tell time on shipboard. —*v.* 1. put a bell on. 2. swell out like a bell. [OE *belle*] —**bell′less,** *adj.* —**bell′-like′,** *adj.*

Bell (bel), *n.* Alexander Graham, 1847–1922, American scientist who invented the telephone.

bel·la·don·na (bel′ə·don′ə), *n.* 1. a poisonous plant with black berries and red flowers. 2. drug made from this plant; atropine. [< Ital., fair lady]

bell·boy (bel′boi′), *n. Am.* man or boy whose work is carrying hand baggage and doing errands for the guests of a hotel or club.

bell buoy, *Naut.* buoy with a bell rung by the movement of the waves.

belle (bel), *n.* 1. a beautiful woman or girl. 2. the prettiest or most admired woman or girl. [< F, fem. of *beau.* See BEAU.]

belles-let·tres (bel′let′rə), *n.pl.* the finer forms of literature. [< F] —**bel·let·rist** (bel′let·rist), *n.* —**bel·le·tris·tic** (bel′le·tris′tik), *adj.*

bell·hop (bel′hop′), *n. Am., Colloq.* bellboy.

bel·li·cose (bel′ə·kōs), *adj.* warlike; fond of fighting. [< L *bellicosus* < *bellum* war] —**bel·li·cose′ly,** *adv.* —**bel·li·cos·i·ty** (bel′ə·kos′ə·ti), *n.*

bel·lig·er·ence (bə·lij′ər·əns), *n.* 1. fondness for fighting. 2. fighting; war.

bel·lig·er·en·cy (bə·lij′ər·ən·si), *n.* 1. state of being at war. 2. belligerence.

bel·lig·er·ent (bə·lij′ər·ənt), *adj.* 1. fond of fighting; warlike. 2. at war; engaged in war; fighting. 3. having to do with nations or persons at war. —*n.* nation or person at war. [< L, < *bellum* war + *gerere* wage] —**bel·lig′er·ent·ly,** *adv.* —**Syn.** *adj.* 1. hostile, pugnacious.

bel·low (bel′ō), *v.* 1. roar as a bull does. 2. shout loudly or angrily. 3. make a loud, deep noise; roar. —*n.* 1. such a roar. 2. any noise made by bellowing. [OE *bylgan*] —**bel′low·er,** *n.*

bel·lows (bel′ōz; –əs), *n. sing. or pl.* 1. instrument for producing a strong current of air, used for blowing fires or sounding an organ. 2. the folding part of a camera, behind the lens. [OE *belgas;* akin to BELLY]

bell·weth·er (bel′weth′ər), *n.* 1. a male sheep that wears a bell and leads the flock. 2. person or thing that leads a development, indicates a trend, etc.

bel·ly (bel′i), *n., pl.* –lies, *v.,* –lied, –ly·ing. 1. the lower part of the human body that contains the stomach and bowels; abdomen. 2. under part of an animal's body. 3. stomach. 4. the bulging part of anything; hollow space in a bulging part. —*v.* swell out; bulge. [OE *belg*]

be·long (bi·lông′; –long′), *v.* 1. have one's or its proper place: *that book belongs on this shelf.* 2. belong to, a. be the property of. b. be a part of; be connected with. c. be a member of. [ME *bilonge(n)* < *bi–* BE– + *longen* belong, ult. < OE *gelang* belonging to]

be·long·ing (bi·lông′ing; –long′–), *n.* 1. something that belongs. 2. belongings, things that belong to a person; possessions.

be·lov·ed (bi·luv′id; –luvd′), *adj.* dearly loved; dear. —*n.* person who is loved; darling.

be·low (bi·lō′), *adv.* 1. in a lower place; to a lower place. 2. in a lower rank; further down on a scale. 3. on a lower floor or deck; downstairs. 4. on earth. 5. in hell. 6. after in a book or article. —*prep.* 1. lower than; under: *below the third floor.* 2. less than; lower in rank or degree than: *four degrees below freezing.* 3. unworthy of: *below contempt.* [ME *bilooghe* by low]

belt (belt), *n.* 1. strip of leather, cloth, etc., worn around the body to hold in or support clothes or weapons. 2. any broad strip or band. 3. region having distinctive characteristics; zone: *the cotton belt.* 4. an endless band that moves the wheels and pulleys it passes over. 5. below the belt, a. foul; unfair. b. foully; unfairly. —*v.* 1. put a belt around. 2. fasten on with a belt. 3. beat with a belt. 4. hit. [OE, appar. ult. < L *balteus* girdle] —**belt′ed,** *adj.* —**belt′less,** *adj.*

belt·ing (bel′ting), *n.* 1. material for making belts. 2. belts.

be·mire (bi·mīr′), *v.,* –mired, –mir·ing. 1. make dirty with mud. 2. sink in mud.

be·moan (bi·mōn′), *v.* lament; bewail.

be·muse (bi·mūz′), *v.,* –mused, –mus·ing. confuse; bewilder; stupefy.

Ben·a·dryl (ben′ə·dril), *n. Trademark.* a synthetic drug used to relieve allergies such as hay fever, etc.

Be·na·res (bə·nä′riz), *n.* city in E India, on the Ganges; sacred city of the Hindus.

bench (bench), *n.* 1. a long seat, usually of wood or stone. 2. work table of a carpenter. 3. seat where judges sit in a law court. 4. judge or group of judges sitting in a law court. 5. position as a judge. 6. law court. 7. a raised level tract of land. 8. **on the bench**, **a.** sitting in a law court as a judge. **b.** sitting among the substitute players. —*v.* 1. furnish with benches. 2. assign a seat on a bench. 3. take (a player) out of a game. [OE *benc*] —**bench′less**, *adj.*

bench warrant, *Law.* a written order from a judge or law court to arrest a person.

bend (bend), *v.*, **bent** or (*Archaic*) **bend·ed**, **bend·ing**, *n.* —*v.* 1. make, be, or become curved or crooked. 2. stoop; bow. 3. force to submit. 4. submit. 5. turn in a certain direction; direct (mind or effort). 6. *Naut.* fasten (a sail, rope, etc.). —*n.* 1. part that is not straight; curve; turn. 2. stoop; bow. 3. knot for tying two ropes together or tying a rope to something else. 4. **the bends**, *U.S. Colloq.* cramps caused by changing too suddenly from high air pressure to ordinary air pressure. [OE *bendan* bind, band] —**bend′-a·ble**, *adj.* —**Syn.** *v.* 1. turn, twist, warp. 2. incline. 5. apply. —*n.* 1. crook, angle, twist.

bend·er (ben′dər), *n.* 1. person or thing that bends. 2. *Am., Slang.* a drinking spree.

be·neath (bi·nēth′), *adv.* below; underneath. —*prep.* 1. below; under; lower than. 2. unworthy of; worthy not even of: *beneath contempt.* [OE *beneothan* < *be-* by + *neothan* below]

ben·e·dic·i·te (ben′ə·dis′ə·tē), *interj.* Latin word that means *Bless you!* or *Bless us!* or *Bless me!* —*n.* 1. invocation of a blessing. 2. **Benedicite**, hymn of praise to God. [< L, < *bene* well + *dicere* say]

ben·e·dict (ben′ə·dikt), *n.* 1. a recently married man, esp. one who was a bachelor for a long time. 2. a married man. [< *Benedick*, character in Shakespeare's *Much Ado About Nothing*]

Ben·e·dict (ben′ə·dikt), *n.* Saint, 480?–543?, Italian founder of the Benedictine order.

Ben·e·dic·tine (ben′ə·dik′tin, –tēn, –tin *for n. 1 and adj.*; ben′ə·dik′tēn *for n. 2*), *n.* 1. monk or nun following the rules of Saint Benedict or the order founded by him. 2. a kind of liqueur. —*adj.* of Saint Benedict or a religious order following his rules.

ben·e·dic·tion (ben′ə·dik′shən), *n.* 1. the asking of God's blessings at the end of a church service. 2. blessing. [< L *benedictio*. See BENEDICITE.] —**ben′e·dic′tion·al**, *adj.* —**ben·e·dic·to·ry** (ben′ə·dik′tə·ri), *adj.*

ben·e·fac·tion (ben′ə·fak′shən), *n.* 1. a doing good; kind act. 2. benefit conferred.

ben·e·fac·tor (ben′ə·fak′tər; ben′ə·fak′–), *n.* person who has given money or kindly help. [< L, < *bene* well + *facere* do]

ben·e·fac·tress (ben′ə·fak′tris; ben′ə·fak′–), *n.* a woman benefactor.

ben·e·fice (ben′ə·fis), *n.* a permanent office or position created by proper ecclesiastical authority and consisting of a sacred duty and the income that goes with it. [< OF < L *beneficium* benefit. See BENEFACTOR.]

be·nef·i·cence (bə·nef′ə·səns), *n.* 1. kindness; doing good. 2. a kindly act; gift.

be·nef·i·cent (bə·nef′ə·sənt), *adj.* kind; doing good. —**be·nef′i·cent·ly**, *adv.*

ben·e·fi·cial (ben′ə·fish′əl), *adj.* helpful; productive of good: *sunshine and moisture are beneficial to plants.* —**ben′e·fi′cial·ly**, *adv.* —**ben′e·fi′cial·ness**, *n.*

ben·e·fi·ci·ar·y (ben′ə·fish′i·er′i; –fish′ər·i), *n., pl.* **-ar·ies**. 1. person who receives benefit. 2. person who receives money or property from an insurance policy, a will, etc.

ben·e·fit (ben′ə·fit), *n., v.* **-fit·ed**, **-fit·ing**. —*n.* 1. anything which is for the good of a person or thing; advantage. 2. act of kindness; favor. 3. money paid to the sick, disabled, etc. 4. performance at the theater, a game, etc., to raise money which goes to a worthy cause. —*v.* 1. give benefit

to; be good for. 2. receive good; profit. [< AF *benfet* < L *benefactum*. See BENEFACTOR.] —**ben′e·fit·er**, *n.* —**Syn.** *n.* 1. profit, help.

benefit of clergy, 1. privilege of being tried in church courts instead of regular courts. 2. services or approval of the church.

Ben·e·lux (ben′ə·luks), *n.* the economic union of Belgium, the Netherlands, and Luxembourg, since 1948.

be·nev·o·lence (bə·nev′ə·ləns), *n.* 1. good will; kindly feeling. 2. act of kindness; something good that is done; generous gift. [< OF < L, < *bene* well + *velle* wish]

be·nev·o·lent (bə·nev′ə·lənt), *adj.* kindly; charitable. —**be·nev′o·lent·ly**, *adv.* —**Syn.** generous, bountiful. —**Ant.** malevolent, unkind.

Ben·gal (ben·gôl′; beng–), *n.* 1. former province of NE India now divided into West Bengal (republic of India) and East Bengal (republic of Pakistan). 2. Bay of, bay between India and Burma.

Ben·ga·lese (ben′gə·lēz′; –lēs′; beng′–), *n., pl.* **-lese**, *adj.* —*n.* native of Bengal. —*adj.* of Bengal, its people, or their language.

be·night·ed (bi·nīt′id), *adj.* 1. not knowing right and wrong; ignorant. 2. overtaken by night. —**be·night′ed·ness**, *n.*

be·nign (bi·nīn′), *adj.* 1. gentle; kindly: *a benign old lady.* 2. favorable; mild: *a benign climate.* 3. *Med.* doing no harm; not dangerous: *a benign tumor.* [< OF < L *benignus* < *bene* well + *-gnus* born] —**be·nign′ly**, *adv.* —**Syn.** 1. gracious. 2. salutary. —**Ant.** 3. malignant.

be·nig·nant (bi·nig′nənt), *adj.* 1. kindly; gracious. 2. favorable; beneficial. —**be·nig·nan·cy** (bi·nig′nən·si), *n.* —**be·nig′nant·ly**, *adv.*

be·nig·ni·ty (bi·nig′nə·ti), *n., pl.* **-ties**. 1. kindliness; graciousness. 2. a kind act; favor.

ben·i·son (ben′ə·zən; –sən), *n.* blessing. [< OF *beneison* < L *benedictiō*]

Ben·ja·min (ben′jə·mən), *n.* 1. *Bible.* the youngest and favorite son of Jacob. 2. one of the twelve tribes of Israel.

ben·ny (ben′i), *n., pl.* **-nies**. *Am., Slang.* a pill of Benzedrine or some similar drug.

bent (bent), *v.* pt. and pp. of **bend**. —*adj.* 1. not straight; curved; crooked. 2. strongly inclined; determined. —*n.* 1. bent condition. 2. capacity of enduring. 3. inclination; tendency. —**Syn.** *adj.* 2. resolved, bound, set. —*n.* 3. bias.

bent[2] (bent), *n.* 1. Also, **bent grass**. a stiff, wiry grass that grows on sandy or waste land. 2. *Archaic.* heath; moor. [OE *beonet*]

Ben·tham (ben′thəm; –təm), *n.* Jeremy, 1748–1832, English philosopher and jurist.

Ben·ton (ben′tən), *n.* Thomas Hart, born 1889, American painter.

be·numb (bi·num′), *v.* 1. make numb. 2. stupefy; deaden.

Ben·ze·drine (ben′zə·drēn; –drin), *n. Trademark.* a drug, $C_9H_{13}N$, that causes wakefulness.

ben·zene (ben′zēn; ben·zēn′), *n. Chem.* a colorless, volatile, inflammable liquid, C_6H_6, obtained chiefly from coal tar and used for removing grease and in making dyes.

ben·zine (ben′zēn; ben·zēn′), *n.* a colorless, volatile, inflammable liquid consisting of a mixture of hydrocarbons obtained in distilling petroleum, used in cleaning, dyeing, etc.

ben·zo·ate (ben′zō·āt; –it), *n. Chem.* salt or ester of benzoic acid.

ben·zo·ic acid (ben·zō′ik), *Chem.* an acid, C_6H_5COOH, occurring in benzoin, cranberries, etc., used as an antiseptic or as a food preservative.

ben·zo·in (ben′zō·in; –zoin; ben·zō′in), *n.* 1. a fragrant resin obtained from certain species of trees of Java, Sumatra, etc., used in perfume and medicine. 2. substance somewhat like camphor made from this resin. [< F < Sp. or Pg. < Ar. *lubān jāwī* incense of Java]

ben·zol (ben′zōl; –zol), *n.* 1. benzene, C_6H_6. 2. liquid containing about 70 per cent of benzene and 20 to 30 per cent of toluene.

Be·o·wulf (bā′ə·wùlf), *n.* 1. an Old English epic poem, probably composed in England about 700 A.D. 2. hero of this poem.

be·queath (bi-kwēth′; -kwēth′), v. **1.** give or leave (property, etc.) by a will. **2.** hand down to posterity. [OE *becwethan* < *be-* to, for + *cwethan* say] —**be·queath′ment,** n.

be·queath·al (bi-kwēth′əl), n. a bequeathing.

be·quest (bi-kwest′), n. **1.** something bequeathed; legacy. **2.** act of bequeathing.

be·rate (bi-rāt′), v. -rat·ed, -rat·ing. scold sharply. —Syn. upbraid, reprimand.

Ber·ber (bér′bər), n. **1.** member of a race living in N Africa, west of Egypt. **2.** their language. —adj. of the Berbers or their language.

be·reave (bi-rēv′), v., be·reaved or be·reft (bi-reft′), be·reav·ing. **1.** deprive (of) ruthlessly; rob: *bereft of hope.* **2.** leave desolate. [OE *berēaflan* < *be-* away + *rēaflan* rob] —**be·reave′ment,** n. —**be·reav′er,** n.

be·ret (bə-rā′; ber′ā), n. a soft, round woolen cap. [< F. See BIRETTA.]

berg (bérg), n. iceberg.

ber·ga·mot (bér′gə-mot), n. **1.** a pear-shaped variety of orange. **2.** oil obtained from its rind, used in perfume. [< F < Ital., appar. < Turk. *begarmudi* prince's pear]

Man wearing a beret

Ber·gen (bér′gən), n. seaport in SW Norway.

Ber·ge·rac (bâr′zhə-räk), n. Cyrano de, 1619-1655, French dramatist and poet, hero of a famous play by Rostand.

Ber·i·a (ber′i-yä), n. Lavrentii Pavlovitch, 1899-1953, Soviet minister of the interior 1938-1953.

ber·i·ber·i (ber′i·ber′i), n. disease affecting the nerves, accompanied by weakness, loss of weight, and wasting away. [< Singhalese (the lang. of Ceylon), reduplication of *beri* weakness]

Ber·ing Sea (bir′ing; bâr′-), sea in the N Pacific, between Alaska and Siberia.

Bering Strait, strait between Bering Sea and the Arctic Ocean.

ber·ke·li·um (bér·kē′li·əm), n. Chem. a radioactive element, Bk, produced by the cyclotron at the University of California. [< *Berkeley,* California (site of the University)]

Berk·shires (bérk′shirz; -shərz), or **Berk·shire Hills,** n.pl. range of hills and mountains in W Massachusetts.

Ber·lin (bér·lin′), n. capital of East Germany and the former capital of Germany, in the N part.

berm (bérm), n. Am. **1.** bank of a canal opposite the towing path. **2.** the side of a road. [< F *berme* < MDu. and G]

Ber·mu·da (bər·mū′də), **Bermudas,** n. group of British islands in the Atlantic, 580 miles east of North Carolina. —**Ber·mu·di·an** (bər·mū′di·ən), adj., n.

Bermuda onion, a large, mild onion grown in Bermuda, Texas, and California.

Bern, Berne (bérn; bern), n. capital of Switzerland, in the W part.

Ber·nard (bér′nərd; bər·närd′), n. Saint, 1090-1153, French abbot.

Bern·hardt (bérn′härt), n. Sarah, 1845-1923, French actress.

ber·ry (ber′i), n., pl. -ries, v., -ried, -ry·ing. —n. **1.** a small, juicy fruit with many seeds, as the strawberry. **2.** a dry seed or kernel, as of wheat. **3.** Bot. a simple fruit with the seeds in the pulp and a skin or rind, as grapes or tomatoes. —v. **1.** gather or pick berries. **2.** produce berries. [OE *berie*]

ber·serk (bér·sérk; bér·sérk′), adj., adv. in a frenzy. [< Scand. *berserkr* wild warrior]

berth (bérth), n. **1.** Am. place to sleep on a ship, train, or airplane. **2.** a ship's place at a wharf. **3.** place for a ship to anchor conveniently or safely. **4.** appointment; position; job. **5.** give a wide berth to, keep well away from. —v. **1.** put in a berth; provide with a berth. **2.** have or occupy a berth. [? < *bear*[1]]

ber·tha (bér′thə), n. a woman's wide collar

that often extends over the shoulders. [named for *Berthe,* mother of Charlemagne]

Ber·til·lon system (bér′tə·lon), system of identifying persons, esp. criminals, by a record of individual measurements and physical peculiarities, esp. by fingerprinting. [from A. *Bertillon,* French anthropologist]

ber·yl (ber′əl), n. a very hard mineral, usually green or greenish-blue, a silicate of beryllium and aluminum. Emeralds and aquamarines are beryls. [< L < Gk. *beryllos*]

be·ryl·li·um (bə·ril′i·əm), n. Chem. a rare metallic element, Be; glucinum.

be·seech (bi·sēch′), v., -sought or -seeched, -seech·ing. ask earnestly; beg. [ME *biseche(n)* < *be-* thoroughly + *seche(n)* seek] —**be·seech′er,** n. —**be·seech′ing·ly,** adv. —Syn. entreat.

be·seem (bi·sēm′), v. **1.** be proper for; be fitting to. **2.** be seemly or fitting.

be·set (bi·set′), v., -set, -set·ting. **1.** attack on all sides; assail. **2.** surround; hem in. **3.** set; stud: *a bracelet beset with gems.* [OE *besettan* < *be-* around + *settan* set] —Syn. **1.** besiege. **2.** encompass.

be·set·ting (bi·set′ing), adj. habitually attacking: *laziness is her besetting sin.*

be·shrew (bi·shrū′), v. Archaic. call down evil upon; curse mildly.

be·side (bi·sīd′), prep. **1.** by the side of; near; close to: *we sat beside the fire.* **2.** in addition to: *other men beside ourselves.* **3.** compared with: *beside his efforts ours seem small.* **4.** away from; aside from: *beside the point.* **5.** beside oneself, out of one's senses. —adv. besides. [OE *be sidan* by side]

be·sides (bi·sīdz′), adv. **1.** moreover; further: *he didn't want to quarrel; besides, he had come to enjoy himself.* **2.** in addition: *we tried two other ways besides.* **3.** otherwise; else: *he is ignorant of politics, whatever he may know besides.* —prep. **1.** in addition to; over and above: *besides our own members.* **2.** except; other than: *we spoke of no one besides you.*

be·siege (bi·sēj′), v., -sieged, -sieg·ing. **1.** make a long-continued attempt to get possession of (a place) by armed force: *besiege a city.* **2.** crowd around. **3.** overwhelm with requests, questions, etc. —**be·siege′ment,** n. —**be·sieg′er,** n.

be·smear (bi·smir′), v. smear over.

be·smirch (bi·smérch′), v. make dirty; soil; sully. —**be·smirch′er,** n. —**be·smirch′ment,** n.

be·som (bē′zəm), n. **1.** broom made of twigs. **2.** the broom plant. [OE *besma*]

be·sot (bi·sot′), v., -sot·ted, -sot·ting. **1.** make foolish; stupefy. **2.** intoxicate. —**be·sot′ted·ly,** adv. —**be·sot′ted·ness,** n.

be·sought (bi·sôt′), v. pt. and pp. of beseech.

be·span·gle (bi·spang′gəl), v., -gled, -gling. adorn with or as with spangles.

be·spat·ter (bi·spat′ər), v. **1.** spatter all over; soil by spattering. **2.** slander. —**be·spat′ter·er,** n. —**be·spat′ter·ment,** n.

Besom

be·speak (bi·spēk′), v., -spoke or (Archaic) -spake, -spo·ken or -spoke, -speak·ing. **1.** engage in advance; order; reserve: *bespeak tickets for a play.* **2.** give evidence of; indicate: *a neat appearance bespeaks care.* **3.** Poetic. speak to.

be·spec·ta·cled (bi·spek′tə·kəld), adj. wearing glasses.

be·spread (bi·spred′), v., -spread, -spreading. spread over.

be·sprin·kle (bi·spring′kəl), v., -kled, -kling. sprinkle all over.

Bes·sa·ra·bi·a (bes′ə·rā′bi·ə), n. region in E Europe, under Russian control after World War II. —**Bes′sa·ra′bi·an,** adj., n.

Bes·se·mer process (bes′ə·mər), method of making steel by burning out carbon and impurities in molten iron with a blast of air.

best (best), adj. (superlative of *good*). **1.** the most desirable, valuable, superior, etc. **2.** of the greatest advantage, usefulness, etc.: *the best*

thing to do. **3.** largest: *the best part of the day.*
4. chief: *a best seller.* —*adv.* (*superlative of*
well[1]). **1.** in the most excellent way; most thoroughly. **2.** in the highest degree. **3.** had best,
should; ought to; will be wise to. —*n.* **1.** the best
thing or state. **2.** one's highest, finest, utmost,
etc.: *to look one's best.* **3.** at best, under the
most favorable circumstances. **4.** get the best
of, defeat. **5.** make the best of, do as well as
possible with. —*v.* outdo; defeat. [OE *betst*]
be·stead (bi·sted′), *v.,* –stead·ed, –stead·ed or
–stead, –stead·ing, *adj.* —*v.* help; assist; serve.
—*adj.* placed; situated. [< *be-* + *stead,* v., help]
bes·tial (bes′chəl; best′yəl), *adj.* **1.** beastly;
brutal; vile. **2.** of beasts. [< L, < *bestia*] —**bes-
ti·al·i·ty** (bes′chi·al′ə·ti; –ti·al′–), *n.* —**bes′tial-
ly,** *adv.* —**Syn. 1.** brutish.
be·stir (bi·stėr′), *v.,* –stirred, –stir·ring. stir
up; rouse to action; exert.
best man, chief attendant of the bridegroom
at a wedding.
be·stow (bi·stō′), *v.* **1.** give as a gift; give;
confer. **2.** make use of; apply. **3.** *Archaic.* put
safely; put; place. **4.** *Archaic.* find quarters for;
lodge. —**be·stow′a·ble,** *adj.* —**be·stow′al,** *n.*
be·strad·dle (bi·strad′əl), *v.,* –dled, –dling.
bestride; straddle.
be·strew (bi·strü′), *v.,* –strewed, –strewed or
–strewn, –strew·ing. **1.** strew. **2.** strew (things)
around; scatter about. **3.** lie scattered over.
be·stride (bi·strīd′), *v.,* –strode or –strid,
–strid·den or –strid, –strid·ing. **1.** get on, sit on,
or stand over with one leg on each side. **2.** stride
across; step over.
best seller, *Am.* **1.** anything, esp. a book, that
has a very large sale. **2.** author of such a book.
bet (bet), *v.,* bet or bet·ted, bet·ting, *n.* —*v.* **1.**
promise (money or a certain thing) to another if
he is right and you are wrong. **2.** make a bet. —*n.*
1. act of betting; wager. **2.** the money or thing
promised. **3.** thing to bet on. —**Syn.** *n.* **1.** stake.
be·ta (bā′tə; bē′–), *n.* **1.** the second letter of
the Greek alphabet (B, β). **2.** the second of a
series.
be·take (bi·tāk′), *v.* –took, –tak·en, –tak·ing.
betake oneself, **a.** go: *betake oneself to the
mountains.* **b.** apply oneself.
beta particle, *Physics.* an electron, esp. one
in a stream of electrons.
beta rays, *Physics.* stream of electrons from
radium and other radioactive substances.
be·ta·tron (bā′tə·tron; bē′–), *n.* apparatus in
which electrons are accelerated to high speeds.
be·tel (bē′təl), *n.* kind of pepper plant of the
East Indies, the leaves of which are chewed by
people in Asia. [< Pg. < Malayalam *veṭṭila*]
Be·tel·geuse (bē′təl·jūz; betⁱəl·jœz), *n.* a
very large reddish star in the constellation
Orion. [< F, ? < Ar. *bit-al-jāuza* shoulder of
the giant]
betel nut, the orange-colored nut of a tropical Asiatic palm tree.
betel palm, Asiatic palm tree on which the
betel nut grows.
bête noire (bāt′ nwär′), thing or person
dreaded or detested. [< F, black beast]
Beth·a·ny (beth′ə·ni), *n.* village in E Palestine, near Jerusalem.
Beth·el (beth′əl), *n.* ancient town in E Palestine, near Jerusalem.
beth·el (beth′əl), *n.* **1.** a holy place. **2.** church
or chapel for seamen. [< Heb., house of God]
be·think (bi·thingk′), *v.,* –thought, –thinking. **1.** think about; consider. **2.** remember.
Beth·le·hem (beth′li·əm; –lə·hem), *n.* birthplace of Jesus, six miles south of Jerusalem.
be·tide (bi·tīd′), *v.,* –tid·ed, –tid·ing. **1.** happen to. **2.** happen. [ME *betide(n)* < *be-* + *tiden*
happen]
be·times (bi·tīmz′), *adv.* **1.** early. **2.** soon. [ME
bitime by time]
be·to·ken (bi·tō′kən), *v.* be a sign or token of;
indicate; show. —**be·to′ken·er,** *n.*
be·took (bi·tùk′), *v.* pt. of betake.
be·tray (bi·trā′), *v.* **1.** give away to the enemy.
2. be unfaithful to. **3.** mislead; deceive. **4.** give

away (a secret); disclose unintentionally. **5.** reveal; show. **6.** seduce. [ME *bitraien* < *be-* (intensive) + *traie(n)* betray < OF < L *tradere* hand
over] —**be·tray′al,** *n.* —**be·tray′er,** *n.*
be·troth (bi·trôth′; –trōth′), *v.* promise in
marriage; engage. [ME *betrouthe(n),* var. of
betreuthien < *be-* + *treuthe,* OE *trēowth* pledge]
—**be·troth′ment,** *n.*
be·troth·al (bi·trôth′əl; –trōth′–), *n.* promise
of marriage; engagement.
be·trothed (bi·trôthd′; –trōtht′), *n.* person
engaged to be married.
bet·ter[1] (bet′ər), *adj.* (*comparative of good*).
1. more desirable, useful, etc., than another. **2.**
of superior quality. **3.** less sick. **4.** larger: *the
better part of a week.* —*adv.* (*comparative of
well*[1]). **1.** in a superior manner. **2.** in a higher
degree; more. **3.** better off, in better circumstances. **4.** had better, should; ought to; will be
wise to. **5.** think better of, think over and
change one's mind. —*n.* **1.** a better person, thing,
or state. **2.** advantage. **3.** betters, one's supe-
riors. **4.** get or have the better of, be superior
to; defeat. —*v.* **1.** make or become better; improve. **2.** do better than; surpass. [OE *betera*]
—**bet′ter·er,** *n.* —**Syn.** *v.* **1.** advance, ameliorate.
bet·ter[2], **bet·tor** (bet′ər), *n.* person who bets.
bet·ter·ment (bet′ər·mənt), *n.* **1.** improvement. **2.** Usually, **betterments,** *Am., Law.* an
improvement of real estate property.
be·tween (bi·twēn′), *prep.* **1.** in the space or
time separating (two points, objects, etc.): *between New York and Chicago.* **2.** in the range or
part separating: *shades between pink and red.*
3. from one to the other of; connecting: *relation
between ideas.* **4.** involving; having to do with:
war between two countries. **5.** by the combined
action of: *they caught twelve fish between them.*
6. in the combined possession of: *they own the
property between them.* —*adv.* **1.** in the intervening space or time. **2.** in an intermediate position or relation. [OE *betwēonum* < *be-* by +
twā two] ▸ **between, among.** *Among* implies
more than two objects: *They distributed food
among the survivors.* In its most exact use, *between* implies only two: *The banker divided the
books between Tom and Jim.* If *between* is used
of more than two it suggests the individuals involved more than the situation: *The family of
seven hadn't a pair of shoes between them.*
▸ **between you and me.** Since the object of a
preposition is grammatically in the accusative
case, the correct form is *between you and me,
for you and me, to you and me* (or when the
pronouns are objects of a verb, "He will take
you and me."). *Between you and I* is frequently
used—reversing the usual colloquial tendency to
use *me* (as in *It's me*), perhaps because the
speakers remember the prohibition against *It's
me* and carry over the taboo to a different construction.
be·twixt (bi·twikst′), *prep., adv.* **1.** between.
2. betwixt and between, neither one nor the
other. [OE *betweox*]
Bev (bev), *n. Am.* billion electron volts.
Bev·an (bev′ən), *n.* Aneurin, born 1897, the
leader of a faction of the British Labour Party.
—**Bev′an·ism,** *n.* —**Bev′an·ite,** *n.*
bev·a·tron (bev′ə·tron), *n. Am.* a high-energy
cyclotron.
bev·el (bev′əl), *n., v.,* –eled, –el·ing; *esp. Brit.*
–elled, –el·ling, *adj.* —*n.* **1.**
the angle that one line or
surface makes with another
when not at right angles. **2.**
instrument or tool for drawing angles, etc. —*v.* cut a
square edge to a sloping
edge; make slope. —*adj.*
slanting; oblique.

Bevel

bev·er·age (bev′ər·ij; bev′-
rij), *n.* a liquid used or prepared for drinking.
Milk, tea, coffee, beer, and wine are beverages.
[< OF *bevrage* < *bevre* drink < L *bibere*]
bev·y (bev′i), *n., pl.* bev·ies. **1.** a flock of birds.
2. a small group.
be·wail (bi·wāl′), *v.* mourn; lament. —**be·
wail′er,** *n.* —**be·wail′ing·ly,** *adv.*

be·ware (bi·wâr′), v. be on one's guard against; be careful. [< phrase be ware! See WARY.]

be·wil·der (bi·wil′dər), v. confuse completely; puzzle; perplex. —**be·wil′dered**, adj. —**be·wil′der·ed·ly**, adv. —**be·wil′der·ing**, adj. —**be·wil′der·ing·ly**, adv. —**be·wil′der·ment**, n.

be·witch (bi·wich′), v. 1. put under a spell. 2. charm; fascinate. —**be·witch′er**, n. —**be·witch′er·y**, n. —**be·witch′ing**, adj. —**be·witch′ing·ly**, adv. —**be·witch′ment**, n. —Syn. 2. enchant, captivate.

be·wray (bi·rā′), v. Archaic. 1. betray. 2. reveal. [ME bewreie(n) < be- + wreie(n) < OE wrēgan accuse]

bey (bā), n., pl. **beys**. 1. governor of a Turkish province. 2. Turkish title of respect. 3. native ruler of Tunis. [< Turk. beg]

be·yond (bi·yond′), prep. 1. on or to the farther side of: beyond the barn. 2. farther on than: beyond the hill. 3. later than: they stayed beyond the time set. 4. out of the reach, range, or understanding of: the dying man was beyond help. 5. more than; exceeding: a price beyond what I can pay. 6. in addition to; besides: I will pay nothing beyond the stated price. —adv. farther away: beyond were the hills. —n. the beyond, the great beyond, life after death. [OE begeondan < be- at, near + geondan beyond]

be·zique (bə·zēk′), n. card game somewhat like pinochle. [< F bésigue]

b.f., bf., boldface (type).

bg., pl. **bgs.,** bag.

bi-, prefix. 1. twice, as in biannual. 2. doubly, as in bipinnate. 3. two, as in bicuspid. 4. Chem. denoting the presence of two parts or equivalents of a constituent indicated, as in bicarbonate. [< L, < bis]

Bi, Chem. bismuth.

bi·an·nu·al (bī·an′yú·əl), adj. occurring twice a year. —**bi·an′nu·al·ly**, adv.

bi·as (bī′əs), n., adj., adv., v., bi·ased, bi·asing; esp. Brit. **bi·assed**, bi·as·sing. —n. 1. a slanting or oblique line. Cloth is cut on the bias when it is cut diagonally across the weave. 2. opinion before there is basis for it; prejudice; a leaning of the mind. —adj. slanting across the threads of cloth; oblique; diagonal. —adv. obliquely. —v. influence, usually not fairly. [< F biais slant < VL biaxius having a double axis] —Syn. n. 2. inclination, bent, partiality.

bi·ax·i·al (bī·ak′si·əl), adj. having two axes. —**bi·ax′i·al·ly**, adv.

bib (bib), n. 1. cloth worn under the chin by babies and small children to protect their clothing. 2. part of an apron above the waist. [< bib drink, ? < L bibere]

bi·be·lot (bib′lō; Fr. bē·blō′), n. a small object of curiosity, beauty, or rarity. [< F]

Bi·ble (bī′bəl), n. 1. the collection of sacred writings of the Christian religion, comprising the Old and New Testaments. 2. the Old Testament in the form received by the Jews. 3. the sacred writings of any religion. 4. bible, book accepted as an authority. [< Med.L < Gk. biblia, pl. dim. of biblos book] ≫ **Bible,** referring to the Christian scriptures, is capitalized but not italicized: "You will find it in the Bible." Bible in the sense of an authoritative book is not capitalized: "Gray's Manual, the botanist's bible, ..."

Bib·li·cal, bib·li·cal (bib′lə·kəl), adj. 1. of or in the Bible. 2. according to the Bible. —**Bib′li·cal·ly, bib′li·cal·ly**, adv.

bib·li·og·ra·phy (bib′li·og′rə·fi), n., pl. -phies. 1. list of books, articles, etc., about a subject or person. 2. list of books, articles, etc., by a certain author. 3. study of the authorship, editions, dates, etc., of books, articles, etc. [< Gk., < biblion book + graphein write] —**bib′li·og′ra·pher**, n. —**bib·li·o·graph·ic** (bib′li·ə·graf′ik), **bib′li·o·graph′i·cal**, adj. —**bib′li·o·graph′i·cal·ly**, adv.

bib·li·o·ma·ni·a (bib′li·ō·mā′ni·ə), n. craze for collecting books. —**bib·li·o·ma·ni·ac** (bib′li·ō·mā′ni·ak), n., adj.

bib·li·o·phile (bib′li·ə·fīl), **bib·li·o·phil**

(-fil), n. lover of books. [< F, < Gk. biblion book + philos loving]

bib·u·lous (bib′yə·ləs), adj. 1. fond of drinking alcoholic liquor. 2. absorbent. [< L bibulus < bibere drink] —**bib′u·lous·ly**, adv. —**bib′u·lous·ness**, n.

bi·cam·er·al (bī·kam′ər·əl), adj. having or consisting of two legislative assemblies. [< bi- two + L camera chamber. See CAMERA.]

bi·car·bo·nate (bī·kär′bə·nit; -nāt), n. salt of carbonic acid that contains a base and hydrogen. **bicarbonate of soda,** sodium bicarbonate.

bi·cen·te·nar·y (bī′sen′tə·ner′i; bī′sen·ten′-ər·i), adj., n., pl. -nar·ies. bicentennial.

bi·cen·ten·ni·al (bī′sen·ten′i·əl), adj. 1. having to do with a period of 200 years. 2. recurring every 200 years. —n. 1. a 200th anniversary. 2. its celebration.

bi·ceps (bī′seps), n. any muscle having two heads or origins, esp.: a. the large muscle in the front part of the upper arm. b. the large muscle in the back of the thigh. [< L, two-headed, < bi- two + caput head]

bi·chlo·ride (bī·klō′rīd; -rid; -klō′-), **bi·chlo·rid** (-rid), n. Chem. 1. compound containing two atoms of chlorine combined with another element or radical. 2. bichloride of mercury.

bichloride of mercury, an extremely poisonous, white substance, HgCl$_2$, used in solution as an antiseptic, in medicine, and in dyeing.

bick·er (bik′ər), v., n. quarrel. [ME biker(en)]

bi·cus·pid (bī·kus′pid), n. a double-pointed tooth. —adj. Also, **bi·cus·pi·date** (bī·kus′pə·dāt). having two points. [< bi- two + L cuspis point]

bi·cy·cle (bī′sə·kəl; -sik′əl), n., v., -cled, -cling. —n. a metal frame with two wheels, handles for steering, and a seat for the rider. —v. ride a bicycle. [< F. See BI-, CYCLE.] —**bi′cy·cler**, Am.; **bi′cy·clist**, n.

bid (bid), v., bade or bad (for 1, 2) or bid (for 3-10), bid·den or bid, bid·ding, n. —v. 1. command. 2. say; tell: bid him farewell. 3. Archaic. invite. 4. proclaim; declare. 5. bid fair, seem likely; have a good chance. 6. offer. 7. offer a price; state a price. 8. state as what one proposes to make or to win in some card game. 9. bid in, Am. buy at auction, to keep for the owner. 10. bid up, raise the price of by bidding more. —n. 1. a bidding. 2. an offer. 3. Am., Colloq. an invitation. 4. amount offered. 5. amount bid in a card game. 6. an attempt to secure, achieve, etc. 7. appeal: a bid for sympathy. [OE biddan ask; meaning infl. by OE bēodan offer] —**bid′da·ble**, adj. —**bid′der**, n. —Syn. v. 1. order, direct. 6. proffer, tender.

bid·ding (bid′ing), n. 1. command. 2. invitation. 3. offers at an auction. 4. in card games, bids collectively.

bid·dy (bid′i), n., pl. -dies. hen.

bide (bīd), v., bode or bid·ed, bid·ed, bid·ing. 1. Archaic or Dial. dwell; abide. 2. Archaic or Dial. continue; wait. 3. Archaic or Dial. bear; endure. 4. bide one's time, wait for a good chance. [OE bīdan] —**bid′er**, n.

bi·en·ni·al (bī·en′i·əl), adj. 1. occurring every two years. 2. Bot. lasting two years. —n. 1. event that occurs every two years. 2. Bot. plant that lives two years. [< L biennium < bi- two + annus year] —**bi·en′ni·al·ly**, adv.

bier (bir), n. movable stand on which a coffin or dead body is placed. [OE bēr < beran bear¹]

biff (bif), n., v. Am., Colloq. hit; slap.

bi·fid (bī′fid), adj. divided into two parts by a cleft. [< L bifidus < bi- two + findere cleave]

bi·fo·cal (bī·fō′kəl), adj. 1. having two focuses. 2. Am. (used of glasses) having two parts, the upper for far vision, the lower for near vision. —n. 1. Usually, bifocals, Am. pair of glasses having bifocal lenses. 2. bifocal lens.

bi·fur·cate (v., adj. bī′fər·kāt, bī·fėr′kāt; adj. also -kit), v., -cat·ed, -cat·ing, adj. —v. divide into two branches. —adj. divided into two branches; forked. [< Med.L, < L bi- two + furca fork] —**bi′fur·cate·ly**, adv. —**bi′fur·ca′tion**, n.

āge, câre, fär; ēqual, tėrm; īce; ōpen, ôrder; pút, rüle, ūse; th, then; ə=a in about.

big (big), *adj.*, **big·ger, big·gest**, *adv.* —*adj.* 1. great in extent, amount, size, etc.; large. 2. grown up. 3. *Am.*, *Colloq.* important; great. 4. full; loud: *a big voice*. 5. boastful: *big talk*. 6. pregnant. —*adv.* boastfully. [ME; orig. uncert.] —big′ly, *adv.* —big′ness, *n.* —Syn. *adj.* 1. huge.

big·a·my (big′ə·mi), *n.* having two wives or two husbands at the same time. [< F, < *bigame* < Med.L, < *bi-* twice + Gk. *gamos* married] —big′a·mist, *n.* —big′a·mous, *adj.* —big′a·mous·ly, *adv.*

Big Dipper, group of stars in the constellation of Ursa Major.

big game, 1. large animals sought by hunters, such as elephants, tigers, or lions. 2. very important thing that is sought.

big-heart·ed (big′här′tid), *adj.* kindly; generous.

big·horn (big′hôrn′), *n.*, *pl.* **-horn, -horns.** *Am.* a wild, grayish-brown sheep of the Rocky Mountains, with large, curved horns.

bight (bīt), *n.* 1. a long curve in a coastline. 2. bay¹. 3. bend; angle; corner. 4. the loop of a rope. 5. slack of rope between the fastened ends. [OE *byht*]

big·no·ni·a (big·nō′ni·ə), *n.* *Am.* vine with showy, trumpet-shaped orange flowers. [< NL; named for Abbé *Bignon*]

big·ot (big′ət), *n.* a bigoted person. [< F]

big·ot·ed (big′ət·id), *adj.* sticking to an opinion, belief, party, etc., without reason and not tolerating other views; intolerant. —big′ot·ed·ly, *adv.* —Syn. narrow-minded.

big·ot·ry (big′ət·ri), *n.*, *pl.* **-ries.** bigoted conduct or attitude; prejudice. —Syn. intolerance.

big top, *Am.* main tent of a circus.

big·wig (big′wig′), *n.* *Colloq.* an important person.

bi·jou (bē′zhū), *n.*, *pl.* **-joux** (-zhūz). 1. a jewel. 2. something small and fine. [< F]

bi·ju·gate (bī′jū·gāt; bi·jū′gāt), **bi·ju·gous** (bī′jū·gəs), *adj.* having two pairs of leaflets. [< *bi-* two + L *jugatus* yoked]

bike (bīk), *n.*, *v.*, **biked, bik·ing.** *Am.*, *Colloq.* bicycle.

Bi·ki·ni (bi·kē′ni), *n.* atoll in the Marshall Islands in the W Pacific, where atomic bomb tests took place.

bi·ki·ni (bi·kē′ni), *n.* a woman's very abbreviated bathing costume, in two pieces.

bi·la·bi·al (bī·lā′bi·əl), *adj.* 1. *Bot.* having two lips. 2. *Phonet.* formed by both lips. —*n.* sound formed by both lips, as *b, p, m,* and *w.*

bi·la·bi·ate (bī·lā′bi·āt; -it), *adj.* *Bot.* having an upper and a lower lip.

bi·lat·er·al (bī·lat′ər·əl), *adj.* 1. having two sides. 2. on two sides. 3. affecting or influencing two sides. —bi·lat′er·al·ism, bi·lat′er·al·ness, *n.* —bi·lat′er·al·ly, *adv.*

Bil·ba·o (bil·bä′ō), *n.* seaport in N Spain.

bil·ber·ry (bil′ber′i), *n.*, *pl.* **-ries.** 1. an edible berry much like a blueberry. 2. shrub that it grows on. [appar. alter. of Scand. (Dan.) *bölle·bær* after *berry*]

bil·bo (bil′bō), *n.*, *pl.* **-boes.** Usually **bilboes.** a long iron bar with sliding shackles and a lock.

bile (bīl), *n.* 1. a bitter, yellow or greenish liquid secreted by the liver and stored in the gall bladder to aid digestion. 2. ill humor; anger. [< F < L *bilis*]

bilge (bilj), *n.*, *v.*, **bilged, bilg·ing.** —*n.* 1. *Naut.* a. the lowest part of a ship's hold. b. bottom of a ship's hull. 2. bilge water. 3. the bulging part of a barrel. 4. *Colloq.* nonsense. —*v.* 1. spring a leak. 2. bulge; swell out.

bilge water, dirty water that collects in the bottom of a ship.

bil·i·ar·y (bil′i·er′i), *adj.* 1. of bile. 2. carrying bile. 3. bilious.

bi·lin·gual (bī·ling′gwəl), *adj.* 1. able to speak one's own language and another equally well. 2. containing or written in two languages. —bi·lin′gual·ism, *n.* —bi·lin′gual·ly, *adv.*

bil·ious (bil′yəs), *adj.* 1. having to do with bile. 2. suffering from or caused by some trouble with bile or the liver. 3. peevish; cross; bad-tempered. —bil′ious·ly, *adv.* —bil′ious·ness, *n.*

bilk (bilk), *v.* 1. avoid payment of; elude. 2. defraud; cheat; deceive. —*n.* 1. fraud; deception. 2. person who avoids paying his bills; swindler. —bilk′er, *n.*

bill¹ (bil), *n.* 1. account of money owed for work done or things supplied. 2. *U.S.* piece of paper money: *a dollar bill*. 3. a written or printed public notice; advertisement; poster; handbill. 4. a written or printed statement; list of items. 5. a theater program. 6. *Am.* entertainment in a theater. 7. a proposed law presented to a lawmaking body. 8. bill of exchange. 9. *Law.* a written request or complaint presented to a court. —*v.* 1. send a bill to. 2. enter in a bill. 3. *Am.* consign (freight) by rail to a destination. 4. announce by bills or public notice. 5. post bills in or on. 6. list on a theatrical program. [< Anglo-L *billa*, alter. of Med.L *bulla* document, seal, BULL²] —bill′a·ble, *adj.* —bill′er, *n.* —Syn. *n.* 1. invoice. 3. placard, circular, bulletin.

bill² (bil), *n.* 1. the horny mouth of a bird; beak. 2. anything shaped somewhat like a bird's bill. —*v.* 1. join beaks; touch bills. 2. show affection. [OE *bile*]

bill³ (bil), *n.* 1. spear with a hook-shaped blade. 2. Also, **billhook.** tool for pruning or cutting. [OE *bil*]

bil·la·bong (bil′ə·bong), *n.* *Australia.* a branch of a river flowing away from the main stream.

bill·board (bil′bôrd′; -bōrd′), *n.* *Am.* signboard for posting advertisements or notices.

bil·let¹ (bil′it), *n.*, *v.*, **-let·ed, -let·ing.** —*n.* 1. *Mil.* written order to provide board and lodging for a soldier. 2. place where a soldier is lodged. 3. job; position. —*v.* *Mil.* assign to quarters by billet. [< OF *billette*, dim. of *bille* bill¹]

bil·let² (bil′it), *n.* 1. a thick stick of wood. 2. bar of iron or steel. [< F *billette*, dim. of *bille* log, tree trunk]

bil·let-doux (bil′i·dū′; bil′ā-), *n.*, *pl.* **billets-doux** (bil′i·dūz′; bil′ā-). a love letter. [< F]

bill·fold (bil′fōld′), *n.* *Am.* a folding pocketbook for money.

bill·head (bil′hed′), *n.* name and business address printed at the top of a sheet of paper.

bill·hook (bil′hùk′), *n.* bill³ (def. 2).

bil·liard (bil′yərd), *adj.* of or for billiards. —*n.* point made by hitting the balls in billiards.

bil·liards (bil′yərdz), *n.* game played with balls on a special table. A long stick called a cue is used in hitting the balls. [< F *billard(s)*, dim. of *bille* log, tree trunk] —bil′liard·ist, *n.* *Am.*

bil·lings·gate (bil′ingz·gāt′; *esp. Brit.* bil′ingz·git), *n.* vulgar, abusive language.

bil·lion (bil′yən), *n.*, *adj.* 1. *Am.* in the United States and France, one thousand millions. 2. in Great Britain and Germany, one million millions. [< F, < *bi-* two (i.e., to the second power) + (*mi*)*llion* million] —bil′lionth, *adj.*, *n.*

bil·lion·aire (bil′yən·ãr′), *n.* *Am.* person who owns a billion dollars, francs, marks, etc.

bill of attainder, a legal act depriving a person of property and civil rights because of a sentence of death or outlawry.

bill of exchange, written order to pay a certain sum of money to a specified person.

bill of fare, list of the articles of food served or that can be served at a meal.

bill of health, certificate stating whether or not there are infectious diseases on a ship or in a port.

bill of lading, receipt given by a railroad, express agency, etc., showing a list of goods delivered to it for transportation.

bill of rights, 1. statement of the fundamental rights of the people of the nation. 2. **Bill of Rights**, *Am.* the first ten amendments to the Constitution of the United States.

bill of sale, written statement transferring ownership of something from seller to buyer.

bil·low (bil′ō), *n.* 1. a great wave or surge of the sea. 2. any great wave. —*v.* 1. rise or roll in big waves. 2. swell out; bulge. [< Scand. *bylgja*]

bil·low·y (bil′ō·i), *adj.*, **-low·i·er, -low·i·est.** 1. rising or rolling in big waves. 2. swelling out; bulging. —bil′low·i·ness, *n.*

bil·ly (bil′i), *n.*, *pl.* **-lies.** *Am.* club; stick.

billy goat, *Colloq.* a male goat.

bi·me·tal·lic (bī'mə·tal'ik), *adj.* **1.** using two metals. **2.** of or based on bimetallism.

bi·met·al·lism (bī·met'əl·iz·əm), *n.* use of both gold and silver at a fixed relative value as the basis of the money system of a nation. —bi·met'al·list, *n.*

bi·month·ly (bī·munth'li), *adj., n., pl.* –lies, *adv.* —*adj.* **1.** happening once every two months. **2.** happening twice a month. —*n.* magazine published bimonthly. —*adv.* **1.** once every two months. **2.** twice a month.

bin (bin), *n., v.,* binned, bin·ning. —*n.* box or enclosed place for holding grain, coal, etc. —*v.* store in a bin. [OE *binn*]

bi·na·ry (bī'nə·ri), *adj., n., pl.* –ries. —*adj.* consisting of two; involving two; dual. —*n.* a whole composed of two. [< L *binarius* < *bini* two at a time]

binary star, *Astron.* pair of stars that revolve around a common center of gravity.

bi·nate (bī'nāt), *adj. Bot.* growing in pairs; double. —bi'nate·ly, *adv.*

bind (bīnd), *v.,* bound, bind·ing, *n.* —*v.* **1.** tie together; hold together; fasten. **2.** stick together. **3.** hold by some force; restrain. **4.** hold by a promise, love, duty, etc.; oblige: *she was bound to help.* **5.** put under legal obligation: *bound to keep the peace.* **6.** put a bandage on. **7.** put a band or wreath around. **8.** fasten (sheets of paper) into a cover. **9.** constipate. —*n.* anything that binds or ties. [OE *bindan*] —Syn. *v.* **1.** connect, attach. **4.** obligate, constrain.

bind·er (bīn'dər), *n.* **1.** person or thing that binds. **2.** cover for holding loose sheets of paper together. **3.** *Am.* machine that cuts grain and ties it in bundles.

bind·er·y (bīn'dər·i), *n., pl.* –er·ies. *Am.* place where books are bound.

bind·ing (bīn'ding), *n.* **1.** a making fast, securing, or uniting. **2.** the covering of a book. **3.** strip protecting or ornamenting an edge. **4.** substance that binds. —*adj.* **1.** that binds, fastens, or connects. **2.** having force or power to hold to some agreement, pledge, etc.; obligatory. —bind'ing·ly, *adv.* —bind'ing·ness, *n.*

binding energy, *Nuclear Physics.* energy necessary to break a particular atomic nucleus into its smaller component parts.

bind·weed (bīnd'wēd'), *n.* plant that twines around the stems of other plants.

bin·go (bing'gō), *n.* a game derived from lotto.

bin·na·cle (bin'ə·kəl), *n.* box or stand that contains a ship's compass, placed near the man who is steering. [alter. of *bittacle* < Sp. or Pg. < L *habitaculum* dwelling place < *habitare* dwell]

bin·o·cle (bin'ə·kəl), *n.* binocular.

bi·noc·u·lar (bə·nok'yə·lər; bī–), *adj.* **1.** using both eyes. **2.** for both eyes. —*n.* Often, binoculars. a field glass or opera glass for both eyes. [< L *bini* two at a time + *oculi* eyes] —bi·noc'u·lar'i·ty, *n.* —bi·noc'u·lar·ly, *adv.*

bi·no·mi·al (bī·nō'mi·əl), *adj.* consisting of two terms. —*n.* expression or name consisting of two terms. **8a** + **2b** is a binomial. [< LL *binomius* having two names < *bi*– two + *nomen* name] —bi·no'mi·al·ly, *adv.*

biochem., biochemistry.

bi·o·chem·is·try (bī'ō·kem'is·tri), *n.* chemistry of living animals and plants; biological chemistry. [< Gk. *bios* life + E *chemistry*] —bi·o·chem·i·cal (bī'ō·kem'ə·kəl), bi'o·chem'ic, *adj.* —bi'o·chem'i·cal·ly, *adv.* —bi'o·chem'ist, *n.*

biog., biographer; biographical; biography.

bi·o·gen·e·sis (bī'ō·jen'ə·sis), biog·e·ny (bī·oj'ə·ni), *n. Biol.* theory that living things can be produced only by other living things. [< Gk. *bios* life + E *genesis*] —bi·o·ge·net·ic (bī'ō·jə·net'ik), *adj.* —bi'o·ge·net'i·cal·ly, *adv.*

bi·og·ra·phy (bī·og'rə·fi; bī–), *n., pl.* –phies. **1.** the written story of a person's life. **2.** part of literature that consists of biographies. [< L < Gk., < *bios* life + *graphein* write] —bi·og'ra-

pher, *n.* —bi·o·graph·i·cal (bī'ə·graf'ə·kəl), bi·o·graph'ic, *adj.* —bi'o·graph'i·cal·ly, *adv.* ➤ A biography is the life of a person written by someone else; an *autobiography* is the life of a person written by himself.

biol., biology.

bi·o·log·i·cal (bī'ə·loj'ə·kəl), **bi·o·log·ic** (–loj'ik), *adj.* **1.** of plant and animal life. **2.** having to do with biology. —bi'o·log'i·cal·ly, *adv.*

biological warfare, a waging of war by using disease germs, etc., against the enemy.

bi·ol·o·gy (bī·ol'ə·ji), *n.* science of life or living matter in all its forms and phenomena; study of the origin, reproduction, structure, etc., of plant and animal life. [< Gk. *bios* life + –LOGY] —bi·ol'o·gist, *n.*

bi·om·e·try (bī·om'ə·tri), *n.* **1.** measurement of life; calculation of the probable duration of human life. **2.** Also, **bi·o·met·rics** (bī'ə·met'riks). branch of biology that deals with living things by measurements and statistics. [< Gk. *bios* life + E –*metry* < Gk. *metron* measure] —bi·o·met·ric (bī'ə·met'rik), bi'o·met'ri·cal, *adj.* —bi'o·met'ri·cal·ly, *adv.*

bi·par·ti·san (bī·pär'tə·zən), *adj.* of or representing two political parties. —bi·par'ti·san·ship', *n.*

bi·par·tite (bī·pär'tīt), *adj.* **1.** having two parts. **2.** *Bot.* divided into two parts nearly to the base. —bi·par'tite·ly, *adv.* —bi·par·ti·tion (bī'pär·tish'ən), *n.*

bi·par·ty (bī'pär'ti), *adj.* combining two different political groups, etc.

bi·ped (bī'ped), *Zool.* —*n.* animal having two feet. —*adj.* having two feet. [< L, < *bi*– two + *pes* foot]

bi·pet·al·ous (bī·pet'əl·əs), *adj. Bot.* having two petals.

bi·pin·nate (bī·pin'āt), *adj. Bot.* doubly pinnate.

bi·plane (bī'plān'), *n.* airplane having two wings, one above the other.

birch (bėrch), *n.* **1.** tree whose smooth bark peels off in thin layers. **2.** its close-grained wood, often used in making furniture. **3.** bundle of birch twigs or a birch stick, used for whipping. —*v.* whip with a birch; flog. [OE *bierce*] —birch·en (bėr'chən), *adj.*

Bipinnate leaf

birch·bark (bėrch'bärk'), *n.* **1.** bark of a birch tree. **2.** Also, **birchbark canoe.** *Am.* canoe made of birchbark. —*adj.* made of or covered with birchbark.

bird (bėrd), *n.* **1.** any of a class of warm-blooded vertebrates having a body covered with feathers and the forelimbs modified to form wings by means of which most species fly. **2.** bird hunted for sport. **3.** *Am., Slang.* a fellow; guy. **4.** *Slang.* a hissing sound of disapproval. **5.** *Am., Slang.* a ballistic missile. [OE *bridd*, *bird*]

bird dog, *Am.* dog trained to find or bring back birds for hunters.

bird-dog (bėrd'dôg'), *v.,* –dogged, –dog·ging. *Am., Slang.* **1.** hunt or inquire closely and carefully into or about some problem. **2.** lead a buyer to a particular product, establishment, etc.

bird·ie (bėr'di), *n.* **1.** a little bird. **2.** *Am.* score of one stroke less than par for any hole on a golf course.

bird·lime (bėrd'līm'), *n.* a sticky substance smeared on twigs to catch small birds.

bird·man (bėrd'man'; –mən), *n., pl.* –men. *Colloq.* aviator.

bird of paradise, bird of New Guinea noted for its magnificent plumage.

bird of passage, 1. bird that migrates. **2.** *Colloq.* person who roams from place to place.

bird of prey, any of a group of flesh-eating birds, including eagles, hawks, vultures, etc.

bird's-eye (bėrdz'ī'), *adj.* **1.** seen from above or from a distance; general: *a bird's-eye view.* **2.** having markings somewhat like birds' eyes.

āge, cāre, fär; ēqual, tėrm; īce; ōpen, ôrder; pùt, rüle, ūse; tħ, then; ə=*a* in about.

bi·ret·ta (bə·ret′ə), *n.* a stiff, square cap with three upright projecting pieces, worn by Roman Catholic priests. [< Ital., ult. < LL *birretum* cap, dim. of *birrus* cloak]

birl (bérl), *v. Am.* among lumberjacks, to revolve a log in the water while standing on it.

Bir·ming·ham (bér′ming·əm *for 1;* bér′ming·ham *for 2), n.* 1. city in W England. 2. city in C Alabama.

birth (bérth), *n.* 1. coming into life; being born. 2. beginning; origin. 3. a bringing forth. 4. natural inheritance: *a musician by birth.* 5. descent; family: *he was a man of humble birth.* 6. noble family or descent. 7. that which is born. 8. **give birth to,** a. bear; bring forth. b. be the origin or cause of. [ME *birthe,* prob. < Scand. *byrth*] —Syn. 5. parentage, extraction.

birth·day (bérth′dā′), *n.* 1. day on which a person was born. 2. day on which a thing began. 3. anniversary of the day on which a person was born, or on which a thing began.

birth·mark (bérth′märk′), *n.* spot or mark on the skin that was there at birth.

birth·place (bérth′plās′), *n.* 1. place where a person was born. 2. place of origin.

birth rate, proportion of the number of births per year to the total population or to some other stated number.

birth·right (bérth′rīt′), *n.* right belonging to a person because of any fact about his birth.

birth·stone (bérth′stōn′), *n.* jewel associated with a certain month of the year.

Bis·cay (bis′kā; -ki), *n.* Bay of, bay N of Spain and W of France, part of the Atlantic.

bis·cuit (bis′kit), *n., pl.* -cuits, -cuit. 1. *Am.* a kind of bread in small soft cakes, made with baking powder, soda, etc. 2. *Brit.* cracker. 3. a pale brown. [< OF *bescuit* < *bes* twice < L *bis*) + *cuit,* pp. of *cuire* cook (< L *coquere*)]

bi·sect (bī·sekt′), *v.* 1. divide into two parts. 2. *Geom.* divide into two equal parts. [< *bi*– two + L *sectus,* pp. of *secare* cut] —**bi·sec′tion,** *n.* —**bi·sec′tion·al,** *adj.* —**bi·sec′tion·al·ly,** *adv.* —**bi·sec′tor,** *n.*

bish·op (bish′əp), *n.* 1. clergyman of high rank who has certain spiritual duties and who administers the affairs of a church district. 2. one of the pieces in the game of chess. [< VL (*e*)*biscopus,* var. of L *episcopus* < Gk. *episkopos* overseer < *epi* on, over + *skopos* watcher] —**bish′op·less,** *adj.*

bish·op·ric (bish′əp·rik), *n.* 1. position, office, or rank of bishop. 2. diocese.

Bis·marck (biz′märk), *n.* 1. Otto von, 1815-1898, German statesman. 2. capital of North Dakota, in the S part.

Bismarck Archipelago, group of islands NE of New Guinea, governed by Australia.

bis·muth (biz′məth), *n. Chem.* a brittle, reddish-white metallic element, Bi, used in medicine. [< G] —**bis′muth·al,** *adj.*

bi·son (bī′sən; -zən), *n., pl.* -son. 1. the American buffalo, a wild ox with a big, shaggy head and strong front legs. 2. the European buffalo, slightly larger than the American buffalo and now almost extinct. [< L < Gmc.]

bisque (bisk), *n.* a smooth, creamy soup. [< F]

bis·sex·tile (bi·seks′til), *n.* leap year. —*adj.* containing the extra day of leap year. [< L *bissextilis* (*annus*) leap (year) < *bis* twice + *sextus* sixth. The Julian calendar added an extra day after the *sixth* day before the calends of March.]

bis·ter, bis·tre (bis′tər), *n.* 1. a dark-brown coloring matter made from soot. 2. a dark brown. [< F *bistre*] —**bis′tered, bis′tred,** *adj.*

bi·sul·fate, bi·sul·phate (bī·sul′fāt), *n. Chem.* salt of sulfuric acid in which half of the hydrogen is replaced by a metal.

bi·sul·fide, bi·sul·phide (bī·sul′fīd; -fid), **bi·sul·fid, bi·sul·phid** (-fid), *n. Chem.* disulfide.

bit¹ (bit), *n., v.,* **bit·ted, bit·ting.** —*n.* 1. part of a bridle that goes in a horse's mouth. 2. anything that curbs or restrains. 3. the biting or cutting part of a tool. 4. tool for boring or drilling that usually fits into a handle called a brace. 5. part of a key that goes into a lock and makes it turn. —*v.* 1. put a bit in the mouth of; bridle. 2. curb; restrain. [OE *bite* a bite < *bītan* bite]

bit² (bit), *n.* 1. a small piece; small amount. 2. somewhat; a little. 3. *Colloq.* short time. 4. *Am. Colloq.* 12½ cents. 5. *Am., Slang.* a piece of stage business; routine. 6. **do one's bit,** do one's share. [OE *bita* < *bītan* bite] —Syn. 1. particle, speck.

bitch (bich), *n.* 1. a female dog, wolf, or fox. 2. vulgar term of contempt for a woman. [OE *bicce*]

bite (bīt), *n., v.,* **bit, bit·ten** (bit′ən) **or bit, bit·ing.** —*n.* 1. a piece bitten off; bit of food. 2. food. 3. act of biting. 4. result of a bite, wound, sting, etc. 5. a sharp, smarting pain. 6. tight hold. 7. action of acid in eating into a metal, etc. 8. *Am., Slang.* the amount or percentage of money, etc. taken from a total received, earned, etc.: *the tax bite.* —*v.* 1. seize, cut into, or cut off with the teeth. 2. cut; pierce. 3. wound with teeth, fangs, etc.; sting. 4. nip; snap: *a dog biting at fleas.* 5. cause a sharp, smarting pain to. 6. take a tight hold on; grip: *the wheels bite the rails.* 7. take a bait; be caught. 8. cheat; trick. 9. eat into: *acid bites metal.* 10. **bite the dust,** fall slain; be vanquished. [OE *bītan*] —**bit′er,** *n.*

bit·ing (bīt′ing), *adj.* 1. sharp; cutting. 2. sarcastic; sneering. —**bit′ing·ly,** *adv.*

bitt (bit), *Naut.* —*n.* a strong post on a ship's deck to which ropes, cables, etc., are fastened. —*v.* put (ropes, cables, etc.) around the bitts. [var. of *bit¹*]

bit·ter (bit′ər), *adj.* 1. having a sharp, harsh, unpleasant taste like quinine. 2. hard to admit or bear. 3. harsh or cutting, as words. 4. causing pain; sharp; severe. 5. of weather, very cold. 6. expressing grief, pain, misery, etc. —*n.* that which is bitter; bitterness. —*v.* make or become bitter. [OE *biter;* akin to BITE] —**bit′ter·ish,** *adj.* —**bit′ter·ly,** *adv.* —**bit′ter·ness,** *n.* —Syn. *adj.* 1. acrid. 2. painful, distressing. 3. caustic.

bit·tern (bit′ərn), *n.* a small kind of heron that lives in marshes and has a peculiar booming cry. [< OF *butor*]

bit·ter·root (bit′ər·rüt′; -rüt′), *n. Am.* a small plant with pink flowers, found in the northern Rocky Mountains.

bit·ters (bit′ərz), *n.pl.* a liquid, usually alcoholic, flavored with some bitter plant.

bit·ter·sweet (*n.* bit′ər·swēt′; *adj.* bit′ər·swēt′), *n.* 1. a climbing plant with purple flowers and poisonous, scarlet berries. 2. *Am.* a climbing shrub of North America, with greenish flowers, and scarlet arils growing from orange capsules. —*adj.* both bitter and sweet.

bi·tu·men (bi·tü′mən; -tū′-; bich′ü-), *n.* mineral that will burn, such as asphalt, petroleum, naphtha, etc. [< L] —**bi·tu·mi·noid** (bi·tü′mə·noid; -tū′-), *adj.* —**bi·tu′mi·nous,** *adj.*

bituminous coal, coal that burns with much smoke and a yellow flame; soft coal.

bi·va·lent (bī·vā′lənt; biv′ə-), *adj. Chem.* having a valence of two. [< *bi*– two + L *valens,* ppr. of *valere* be worth] —**bi·va·lence** (bī·vā′ləns; biv′ə-), **bi·va′len·cy,** *n.*

bi·valve (bī′valv′), *Zool.* —*n.* any mollusk whose shell consists of two parts hinged together, as oysters and clams. —*adj.* having two parts hinged together. —**bi′valved′, bi·val·vu·lar** (bī·val′vyə·lər), *adj.*

biv·ou·ac (biv′ù·ak; biv′wak), *n., v.,* **-acked, -ack·ing.** camp outdoors. [< F, prob. < Swiss G *biwache* < bi by + *wache* watch]

bi·week·ly (bī·wēk′li), *adj., n., pl.* -lies, *adv.* —*adj.* 1. happening once every two weeks. 2. happening twice a week; semiweekly. —*n.* newspaper or magazine published biweekly. —*adv.* 1. once every two weeks. 2. twice a week; semiweekly.

Biretta

The line DB bisects the angle ADC.

bi·zarre (bi·zär′), *adj.* odd; queer; fantastic; grotesque. [< F < Sp., brave, < Basque *bezar* beard] —**bi·zarre′ly,** *adv.* —**bi·zarre′ness,** *n.*

Bi·zet (bē·zā′), *n.* Georges, 1838–1875, French musical composer who wrote the opera *Carmen.*

Bi·zo·ni·a (bi·zō′ni·ə; bĭ–), **Bi·zone** (bī′zōn′), *n.* territory in W Germany occupied by British and American forces after World War II.

bk., 1. bank. 2. bark. 3. block. 4. book.

bl., 1. *pl.* **bls.** bale. 2. *pl.* **bls.** barrel.

blab (blab), *v.,* **blabbed, blab·bing,** *n.* —*v.* tell (secrets); talk too much. —*n.* 1. blabbing talk; chatter. 2. person who blabs. —**blab′ber,** *n.*

black (blak), *adj.* 1. opposite of white. 2. without any light; very dark. 3. clad in black. 4. having a dark skin. 5. Negro. 6. dirty; filthy. 7. dismal; gloomy. 8. sullen; angry. 9. evil; wicked. 10. calamitous; disastrous. 11. indicating blame or disgrace. —*n.* 1. opposite of white. 2. black coloring matter. 3. black clothes; mourning. 4. person who has dark skin. 5. Negro. —*v.* 1. make or become black. 2. put blacking on (shoes, etc.). 3. become temporarily blind or unconscious. [OE *blæc*] —**black′er,** *n.* —**black′ly,** *adv.* —**black′ness,** *n.* —Syn. *adj.* 2. dusky.

black·a·moor (blak′ə·mùr), *n.* 1. a Negro. 2. a dark-skinned person. [var. of *black Moor*]

black art, evil magic.

black·ball (black′bôl′), *v.* 1. vote against. 2. ostracize. —*n.* a vote against a person or thing. —**black′ball′er,** *n.*

black bass, *Am.* a North American game fish that lives in fresh water.

black bear, 1. a large American bear. 2. a large Asiatic bear.

black·ber·ry (blak′ber′ĭ), *n., pl.* **–ries,** *v.,* **–ried, –ry·ing.** —*n.* 1. a small, black or dark-purple, edible fruit of certain bushes and vines. 2. a thorny bush or vine that it grows on. —*v.* gather blackberries.

black·bird (blak′bėrd′), *n.* 1. *Am.* any American bird so named because the male is mostly black, as the red-winged blackbird. 2. any similar bird, as the European blackbird.

black·board (blak′-bôrd′; –bōrd′), *n.* a dark, smooth surface for writing or drawing on with chalk or crayon.

Red-winged blackbird (9 in. long)

Black Death, a violent plague that spread through Asia and Europe in the 14th century.

black·en (blak′ən), *v.,* **–ened, –en·ing.** 1. make or become black. 2. speak evil of. —**black′en·er,** *n.* —Syn. 1. darken. 2. slander, defame.

black eye, 1. bruise around an eye. 2. *Colloq.* cause of disgrace or discredit.

black-eyed Su·san (blak′īd′ sü′zən), *Am.* a yellow daisy with a black center.

black·face (blak′fās′), *n.* 1. *Am.* Negro minstrel; actor made up as a Negro. 2. *Am.* theatrical entertainment given by blackfaces. 3. make-up for Negro parts in a show, etc. 4. printing type with thick, heavy lines. —*adj.* having a black face.

Black·foot (blak′fùt′), *n., pl.* **–feet** (–fēt′), **–foot,** *adj. Am.* —*n.* 1. confederacy of Algonquian Indians of the northern plains and Canada. 2. their language. 3. an Algonquian Indian. —*adj.* of or having to do with the Blackfeet or their language.

Black Forest, mountains covered with forests in SW Germany.

black·guard (blag′ärd; –ərd), *n.* scoundrel. —*v.* abuse with vile language. [< *black* + *guard*] —**black′guard·ism,** *n.* —**black′guard·ly** (blag′-ərd·lĭ), *adj.*

Black Hand, *Am.* a secret society organized to commit blackmail and crimes of violence.

black·head (blak′hed′), *n.* 1. a small, black-tipped lump in a pore of the skin. 2. any of various birds that have a black head. 3. disease that attacks turkeys.

black-heart·ed (blak′här′tid), *adj.* evil.

Black Hills, mountains in W South Dakota and NE Wyoming.

black·ing (blak′ing), *n.* black polish used on shoes, stoves, etc.

black·ish (blak′ish), *adj.* somewhat black. —**black′ish·ly,** *adv.*

black·jack (blak′jak′), *n.* 1. *Am.* club with a flexible handle, used as a weapon. 2. a large drinking cup or jug. 3. the black flag of a pirate. —*v.* 1. *Am.* hit (a person) with a blackjack. 2. coerce. —**black′jack′,** *adj. Am.*

black knot, *Am.* a fungous disease of fruit trees and shrubs.

black lead, graphite.

black·leg (blak′leg′), *n.* 1. *Colloq.* swindler. 2. *Brit.* strikebreaker. 3. an infectious, usually fatal disease of cattle and sheep.

black letter, a printing type with thick, heavy lines. —**black′-let′ter,** *adj.*

black list, list of persons who are believed to deserve punishment, blame, suspicion, etc.

black-list (blak′list′), *v.* put on a black list.

black magic, evil magic.

black·mail (blak′māl′), *v.* get or try to get blackmail from. —*n.* 1. money obtained from a person by threatening to tell something bad about him. 2. act of blackmailing. [< *black* + *mail* rent, tribute, coin < OF *maille* < *mail, medaille* coin, medal] —**black′mail′er,** *n.*

Black Ma·ri·a (mə·rī′ə), *Am., Colloq.* police patrol wagon.

black mark, mark of criticism or punishment.

black market, the selling of goods at illegal prices or in illegal quantities. —**black′-mar′-ket·ing,** *n.*

black mar·ket·eer (mär′kə·tir′), one who deals on the black market.

black nightshade, plant with white flowers, poisonous, black berries, and poisonous leaves.

black oak, *Am.* 1. any of various American oaks, having dark bark and foliage. 2. its wood.

black·out (blak′out′), *n.* 1. a turning off of all the lights on the stage of a theater. 2. a turning out or concealing of all the lights of a city, district, etc., as a protection against an air raid. 3. *Aviation.* temporary blindness or unconsciousness experienced by a pilot, resulting from rapid changes in velocity or direction.

black out, 1. darken completely. 2. *Aviation.* experience a blackout.

black pepper, 1. a seasoning with a hot taste. It is made by grinding the berries of a plant. 2. the plant itself.

Black Sea, sea between Turkey and S Russia.

black sheep, a worthless member of a decent family; scoundrel.

Black Shirt, 1. an Italian Fascist. 2. member of any fascist organization, esp. one using black shirts as part of their uniforms.

black·smith (blak′smith′), *n.* man who works with iron. Blacksmiths mend tools and shoe horses. [with ref. to black metals, e.g., iron]

black·snake (blak′snāk′), *n. Am.* 1. a harmless, dark-colored snake of North America. 2. a heavy whip made of braided leather.

black spruce, 1. *Am.* a North American evergreen tree with dark-green foliage. 2. its light, soft wood.

Black·stone (blak′stōn; –stən), *n.* Sir William, 1723–1780, English legal writer and judge.

black·thorn (blak′thôrn′), *n.* a thorny European shrub of the peach family that has dark-purple, plumlike fruit called sloes.

black walnut, *Am.* 1. an oily nut that is good to eat. 2. the tall tree that it grows on. 3. its dark-brown wood, often used for furniture.

black widow, *Am.* a very poisonous spider, so called from its color and its habit of eating its mate.

blad·der (blad′ər), *n.* 1. *Anat., Zool.* a soft, thin bag in the body that secretes urine from the kidneys. 2. anything like this. [OE *blǣdre*] —**blad′der·like′,** *adj.* —**blad′der·y,** *adj.*

blad·der·wort (blad′ər·wėrt′), *n.* any of

various plants with yellow flowers. Some varieties float on the water; others take root in mud.

blade (blād), *n.* 1. the cutting part of anything like a knife or sword. 2. sword. 3. swordsman. 4. a smart or dashing fellow. 5. leaf of grass. 6. *Bot.* the flat, wide part of a leaf; leaf. 7. a flat, wide part of anything: *the blade of a paddle.* 8. the wide, flat part of a bone: *the shoulder blade.* 9. *Phonet.* the front, flat part of the tongue. [OE *blæd*] —blad′ed, *adj.* —blade′less, *adj.* —blade′like′, *adj.*

blain (blān), *n. Pathol.* an inflamed swelling or sore; blister; pustule. [OE *blegen*]

Blake (blāk), *n.* William, 1757–1827, English poet and artist.

blam·a·ble (blām′ə·bəl), *adj.* deserving blame. —blam′a·ble·ness, *n.* —blam′a·bly, *adv.*

blame (blām), *v.,* blamed, blam·ing, *n.* —*v.* 1. hold responsible (for something bad or wrong). 2. find fault with. 3. be to blame, deserve blame. —*n.* 1. responsibility for something bad or wrong. 2. fault. 3. finding fault. [< OF < L < Gk. *blasphemeein,* ? < *blapsis* harm + *-phemos* speaking] —blame′ful, *adj.* —blame′ful·ly, *adv.* —blame′ful·ness, *n.* —blame′less, *adj.* —blame′less·ly, *adv.* —blame′less·ness, *n.* —blam′er, *n.* —Syn. *v.* 1. accuse. 2. censure. *-n.* 1. guilt. 3. censure, condemnation, reproach. —Ant. *v.* 1. absolve. 2. praise.

blame·wor·thy (blām′wér′ŦHi), *adj.* deserving blame. —blame′wor′thi·ness, *n.*

blanch (blanch; blänch), *v.* 1. make white; bleach: *almonds are blanched.* 2. turn white or pale: *blanch with fear.* [< OF *blanchir* < *blanc* white, BLANK] —blanch′er, *n.*

blanc·mange (blə·mänzh′), *n.* a sweet dessert made of milk thickened with gelatin, cornstarch, etc. [< OF *blanc-manger* white food]

bland (bland), *adj.* 1. mild; gentle; soothing: *a bland spring breeze.* 2. agreeable; polite. [< L *blandus* soft] —bland′ly, *adv.* —bland′ness, *n.* —Syn. 1. soft, balmy. 2. suave, urbane.

blan·dish (blan′dish), *v.* coax; flatter. [< F < L *blandiri* flatter < *blandus* soft] —blan′dish·er, *n.* —blan′dish·ment, *n.*

blank (blangk), *n.* 1. space left empty or to be filled in: *leave a blank after each word.* 2. paper with spaces to be filled in: *an application blank.* 3. an empty or vacant place. 4. piece of metal prepared to be stamped or filed into a coin, key, or the like. —*adj.* 1. not written or printed on: *blank paper.* 2. with spaces to be filled in: *a blank check.* 3. empty; vacant. 4. without interest or meaning; dull. 5. complete; absolute: *blank stupidity.* 6. lacking some usual feature: *a blank cartridge.* [< F *blanc* white, shining < Gmc.] —blank′ly, *adv.* —blank′ness, *n.* —Syn. *adj.* 3. void, bare.

blank check, a signed check that allows the bearer to fill in the amount.

blan·ket (blang′kit), *n.* 1. a soft, heavy covering woven from wool or cotton, used to keep people or animals warm. 2. anything like a blanket. —*v.* 1. cover with a blanket. 2. cover; hinder; obscure. 3. apply to uniformly: *a law that blankets all commercial activities.* —*adj.* covering several or all: *a blanket insurance policy.* [< OF *blankete* < *blanc* white] —blan′ket·less, *adj.*

blank verse, 1. unrhymed poetry having five iambic feet in each line. 2. unrhymed poetry.

blare (blār), *v.,* blared, blar·ing, *n.* —*v.* 1. make a loud, harsh sound: *the trumpets blared.* 2. utter harshly or loudly. —*n.* 1. a loud, harsh sound. 2. brilliance of color; glare. [< MDu. *blaren*]

blar·ney (blär′ni), *n., v.,* -neyed, -ney·ing. —*n.* flattering, coaxing talk. —*v.* flatter; coax. [< *Blarney stone,* stone in a castle in Ireland, said to give skill in flattery to those who kiss it] —blar′ney·er, *n.*

bla·sé (blä·zā′; blä′zā), *adj.* tired of pleasures; bored. [< F, pp. of *blaser* exhaust with pleasure]

blas·pheme (blas·fēm′), *v.,* -phemed, -phem·ing. 1. speak about (God or sacred things) with abuse or contempt; utter blasphemy. 2. speak evil of. [< OF < L *blasphemare.* See BLAME.] —blas·phem′er, *n.*

blas·phe·my (blas′fə·mi), *n., pl.* -mies. abuse or contempt for God or sacred things. —blas′phe·mous, *adj.* —blas′phe·mous·ly, *adv.* —blas′phe·mous·ness, *n.* —Syn. profanity.

blast (blast; bläst), *n.* 1. a strong sudden rush of wind or air: *the icy blasts of winter.* 2. the blowing of a trumpet, horn, etc. 3. sound so made. 4. current of air used in smelting, etc. 5. charge of dynamite, gunpowder, etc., that blows up rocks, earth, etc. 6. a blasting; explosion. 7. cause of withering, blight, or ruin. 8. in full blast, in full operation. —*v.* 1. blow up (rocks, earth, etc.) with dynamite, gunpowder, etc. 2. wither; blight; ruin. [OE *blǣst*] —blast′er, *n.* —Syn. *v.* 2. destroy.

blast·ed (blas′tid; bläs′-), *adj.* 1. withered; blighted; ruined. 2. damned; cursed.

blast furnace, *Metall.* furnace in which ores are smelted by blowing a strong current of air into the furnace to make a very great heat.

blas·tu·la (blas′chù·lə), *n., pl.* -lae (-lē). *Embryol.* embryo of an animal. [< NL, dim. of Gk. *blastos* sprout, germ] —blas′tu·lar, *adj.*

blat (blat), *v.,* blat·ted, blat·ting. 1. cry like a calf or sheep; bleat. 2. *Colloq.* say loudly and foolishly; blurt out. [imit.]

bla·tant (blā′tənt), *adj.* 1. noisy; loudmouthed. 2. showy in dress, manner, etc. [coined by Spenser < L *blatire* babble] —bla′tan·cy, *n.* —bla′tant·ly, *adv.* —Syn. 1. clamorous.

blaze[1] (blāz), *n., v.,* blazed, blaz·ing. —*n.* 1. a bright flame or fire. 2. an intense light; glare. 3. bright display. 4. a violent outburst: *a blaze of temper.* —*v.* 1. burn with a bright flame; be on fire. 2. show bright colors or lights. 3. make a bright display. 4. burst out in anger or excitement. [OE *blæse*] —blaz′ing·ly, *adv.* —Syn. *n.* 1. conflagration. 2. brightness.

blaze[2] (blāz), *n., v.,* blazed, blaz·ing. —*n.* 1. mark made on a tree by chipping off a piece of bark. 2. a white spot on the face of a horse, cow, etc. —*v.* mark (a tree, trail, etc.) by chipping off a piece of the bark. [< LG *bläse*]

blaze[3] (blāz), *v.,* blazed, blaz·ing. make known; proclaim. [< MDu. *blasen*]

blaz·er (blāz′ər), *n.* a bright-colored jacket.

bla·zon (blā′zən), *v.* 1. make known; proclaim. 2. decorate; adorn. 3. describe or paint (a coat of arms). 4. display; show. —*n.* 1. coat of arms. 2. description or painting of a coat of arms. 3. display; show. [< OF *blason* shield] —bla′zon·er, *n.* —bla′zon·ment, bla′zon·ry, *n.*

Blazon

bldg., *pl.* bldgs. building.

bleach (blēch), *v.* 1. whiten by exposing to sunlight or by using chemicals. 2. turn white. —*n.* 1. chemical used in bleaching. 2. act of bleaching. [OE *blǣcean;* akin to BLEAK]

bleach·er (blēch′ər), *n.* 1. person who bleaches. 2. thing that bleaches or is used in bleaching. 3. bleachers, *Am.* low-priced, often roofless seats at outdoor sports.

bleak (blēk), *adj.* 1. swept by winds; bare. 2. chilly; cold. 3. dreary; dismal. [ME *bleke* pale. Cf. OE *blǣc, blāc.*] —bleak′ly, *adv.* —bleak′ness, *n.* —Syn. 1. desolate. 2. raw.

blear (blir), *adj.* dim; blurred. —*v.* make dim or blurred. [ME *blere(n)*]

blear-eyed (blir′īd′), *adj.* having blear eyes.

blear·y (blir′i), *adj.,* blear·i·er, blear·i·est. dim; blurred. —blear′i·ness, *n.*

bleat (blēt), *n.* cry made by a sheep, goat, or calf, or a sound like it. —*v.* make such a cry. [OE *blǣtan*] —bleat′er, *n.* —bleat′ing·ly, *adv.*

bleed (blēd), *v.,* bled (bled), bleed·ing. 1. lose blood. 2. shed one's blood; suffer wounds or death. 3. take blood from: *doctors used to bleed sick people.* 4. lose sap, juice, etc. 5. take sap, juice, etc., from. 6. feel pity, sorrow, or grief. 7. get money away from by extortion. [OE *blēdan* < *blōd* blood]

bleed·er (blēd′ər), *n.* person who bleeds very easily because the blood fails to clot.

blem·ish (blem′ish), *n.* stain; spot; scar: *a blemish on the skin.* —*v.* 1. stain; spot; scar. 2. injure; mar: *blemish one's reputation.* [< OF *ble(s)mir* make livid] —**blem′ish·er**, *n.* —Syn. *v.* 1. deface, disfigure. 2. tarnish, sully.

blench[1] (blench), *v.* draw back; shrink away. [appar. OE *blencan* deceive] —**blench′er**, *n.*

blench[2] (blench), *v.* 1. turn pale. 2. make white. [var. of *blanch*]

blend (blend), *v.*, **blend·ed** or **blent**, **blend·ing**, *n.* —*v.* 1. mix together thoroughly so that the things mixed cannot be distinguished. 2. make by mixing several kinds together. 3. shade into each other, little by little; merge. 4. go well together; harmonize. —*n.* 1. thorough mixture. 2. mixture of several kinds: *a blend of coffee.* 3. a word made by fusing two words, often with a syllable in common, as *cinemactress. Blotch* is a blend of *blot* and *botch.* [pt. of OE *blandan*] —**blend′er**, *n.* —Syn. *v.* 1. mingle, combine.

bless (bles), *v.*, **blessed** or **blest**, **bless·ing.** 1. make holy or sacred. 2. ask God's favor for. 3. wish good to. 4. make happy or successful. 5. praise; glorify. 6. guard; protect. 7. make the sign of the cross over. [OE *blētsian* consecrate (i.e., with blood) < *blōd* blood] —**bless′er**, *n.*

bless·ed (bles′id; blest), *adj.* 1. holy; sacred. 2. beatified. 3. happy; successful. 4. in heaven. 5. annoying; cursed. —**bless′ed·ly**, *adv.* —**bless′ed·ness**, *n.*

Blessed Virgin, the Virgin Mary.

bless·ing (bles′ing), *n.* 1. prayer asking God to show His favor. 2. giving of God's favor. 3. wish for happiness or success. 4. anything that makes one happy or contented. —Syn. 1. invocation.

blew (blü), *v.* pt. of **blow**[2].

blight (blīt), *n.* 1. any disease that causes plants to wither or decay. 2. insect or fungus that causes such a disease. 3. anything that causes destruction or ruin. —*v.* 1. cause to wither or decay. 2. destroy; ruin.

blimp (blimp), *n. Colloq.* a small, nonrigid dirigible airship. [appar. from Type *B limp*, designation for "limp dirigible"]

blind (blīnd), *adj.* 1. not able to see. 2. lacking discernment, understanding, or judgment. 3. not controlled by reason: *blind fury.* 4. made without thought or good sense: *a blind guess.* 5. covered; hidden. 6. without an opening: *a blind wall.* 7. with only one opening: *a blind alley.* 8. of or for blind persons. —*v.* 1. make unable to see temporarily or permanently. 2. darken; dim; cover; conceal. 3. rob of power to understand or judge. —*n.* 1. something that keeps out light or hinders sight. 2. anything that conceals an action or purpose. 3. *Am.* a hiding place for a hunter. 4. *Am.* any hiding place. [OE] —**blind′ing**, *adj.* —**blind′ing·ly**, *adv.* —**blind′ly**, *adv.* —**blind′ness**, *n.* —Syn. *adj.* 1. sightless. 4. heedless, oblivious, unmindful.

blind·er (blīn′dər), *n.* 1. one that blinds. 2. a blinker for a horse.

blind flying, directing an airplane by instruments only.

blind·fold (blīnd′fōld′), *v.* cover the eyes of. —*adj.* 1. with the eyes covered. 2. reckless. —*n.* thing covering the eyes. [OE *blindfellian* < *blind* blind + *fell*, var. of *fiell* fall; infl. by *fold*]

Blinders (def. 2)

blind spot, 1. *Anat.* a round spot on the retina of the eye that is not sensitive to light. 2. matter on which a person does not know that he is prejudiced or poorly informed. 3. *Radio.* an area of poor reception.

blink (blingk), *v.* 1. look with the eyes opening and shutting: *blink at a sudden light.* 2. wink: *blink one's eyes.* 3. shine with an unsteady light: *a lantern blinked in the darkness.* 4. blink at, look with indifference at; ignore. —*n.* 1. a blinking. 2. glimpse. [ME *blenken*] —**blink′ing·ly**, *adv.*

blink·er (blingk′ər), *n.* 1. a leather flap to keep a horse from seeing sidewise; blinder. 2. a warning signal with flashing lights.

blip (blip), *n.* image on a radar screen.

bliss (blis), *n.* 1. great happiness; perfect joy. 2. the joy of heaven; blessedness. [OE *blīths* < *blīthe* blithe] —**bliss′ful**, *adj.* —**bliss′ful·ly**, *adv.* —**bliss′ful·ness**, *n.* —Syn. 1. ecstasy, rapture.

blis·ter (blis′tər), *n.* 1. a little baglike place under the skin filled with watery matter, often caused by burns or rubbing. 2. a similar swelling on a surface. —*v.* 1. raise a blister on. 2. become covered with blisters. 3. attack with sharp words. [< OF *blestre* tumor, lump, prob. < Gmc.] —**blis′ter·y**, *adj.*

blithe (blīth; blīth), *adj.* gay; happy; cheerful. [OE *blīthe*] —**blithe′ly**, *adv.* —**blithe′ness**, *n.*

blithe·some (blīth′səm; blīth′-), *adj.* gay; happy; cheerful. —**blithe′some·ly**, *adv.* —**blithe′some·ness**, *n.*

blitz (blits), *n.* 1. blitzkreig. 2. a sudden, violent attack using many airplanes and tanks. 3. any sudden violent attack. —*v.* attack by blitz. [< G, lightning]

blitz·krieg (blits′krēg′), *n.* warfare in which the offensive is extremely rapid, violent, and hard to resist. [< G, lightning war]

bliz·zard (bliz′ərd), *n.* a violent, blinding snowstorm with a very strong wind and very great cold. [var. of *blizzer* blow, shot; orig., flash, blaze. Cf. OE *blysian* burn.]

bloat (blōt), *v.* swell up; puff up. [< *bloat*, adj., soft < Scand. *blautr*]

blob (blob), *n.* a small lump; bubble; drop.

bloc (blok), *n.* a member or members of a group combined for a purpose, esp. a number of legislators: *the farm bloc.* [< F. See BLOCK.]

block (blok), *n.* 1. a solid piece of wood, stone, metal, etc. 2. obstruction; hindrance. 3. *Sports.* a hindering of an opponent's play. 4. *Am.* part of a city enclosed by streets on each side. 5. length of one side of a city block. 6. *Am.* number of buildings close together. 7. group of things of the same kind: *a block of ten tickets for a play.* 8. a short section of railroad track with signals for spacing trains. 9. support for the neck of a person condemned to be beheaded. 10. platform where things are put up for sale at an auction. 11. pulley in a casing. 12. mold on which things are shaped. 13. piece of wood, etc., engraved for printing. —*v.* 1. fill so as to prevent passage or progress. 2. put things in the way of; obstruct; hinder. 3. mount on a block. 4. **block in** or **out**, plan roughly; outline. [< OF *bloc* < Gmc.] —**block′er**, *n.* —Syn. *v.* 2. bar, blockade.

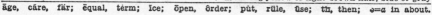

B, block (def. 11).

block·ade (blok·ād′), *n.*, *v.*, **-ad·ed**, **-ad·ing.** —*n.* 1. control of who or what goes into or out of a place by the use of an army or navy. 2. army or navy used to blockade a place. 3. anything that blocks up or obstructs. —*v.* 1. put under blockade. 2. obstruct. —**block·ad′er**, *n.*

blockade runner, *Am.* ship that tries to sneak into or out of a port that is being blockaded.

block and tackle, pulleys and ropes to lift or pull something.

block·bust·er (blok′bus′tər), *n. Colloq.* a very destructive aerial bomb that weighs two or more tons.

block·head (blok′hed′), *n.* a stupid person.

block·house (blok′hous′), *n.* 1. *Am.* house of square logs, often with a jutting second story, having holes for guns. 2. *Mil.* any small fortified building with ports for gunfire.

block·ish (blok′ish), *adj.* stupid; dull. —**block′ish·ly**, *adv.* —**block′ish·ness**, *n.*

block·y (blok′i), *adj.*, **block·i·er**, **block·i·est.** 1. like a block; chunky. 2. having patches of light and shade.

blond, blonde (blond), *adj.* 1. light-colored. 2. having yellow or light-brown hair, blue or gray eyes, and light skin. —*n.* person having such hair, eyes, and skin. A man is a blond; a woman is a blonde. [< F < Gmc.] —**blond′ness, blonde′ness,** *n.* —Syn. *adj.* 2. fair.

blood (blud), *n.* 1. the red liquid in the veins and arteries of the higher animals. 2. the corresponding liquid in lower animals. 3. juice; sap. 4. animal nature: *it stirred his blood.* 5. bloodshed; slaughter. 6. family; birth; relationship; parentage; descent. 7. high lineage, esp. royal lineage. 8. temper; state of mind: *there was bad blood between them.* 9. *Esp. Brit.* man of dash and spirit. 10. **in cold blood**, a. cruelly. b. on purpose. [OE *blōd*] —**blood′like′**, *adj.*

blood bank, 1. place for storage of blood. **2.** the blood kept in storage.

blood brother, 1. brother by birth. 2. person who goes through a ceremony of mixing some of his blood with another person's.

blood count, count of the number of red and white corpuscles in a sample of a person's blood to see if it is normal.

blood·cur·dling (blud′kėrd′ling), *adj.* terrifying; horrible.

blood·ed (blud′id), *adj.* 1. *Am.* of good stock or breed. 2. having a certain kind of blood.

blood group, blood type.

blood·hound (blud′hound′), *n.* 1. one of a breed of large, powerful dogs with a keen sense of smell. 2. *Slang.* detective.

blood·less (blud′lis), *adj.* 1. without blood; pale. 2. without bloodshed. 3. without energy; spiritless. 4. cold-hearted; cruel. —**blood′less·ly,** *adv.* —**blood′less·ness,** *n.*

blood·let·ting (blud′let′ing), *n.* act of opening a vein to take out blood.

blood money, 1. money paid to have somebody killed. 2. money paid to compensate for killing somebody.

blood poisoning, a diseased condition of blood caused by poisonous matter or germs.

blood pressure, pressure of the blood against the inner walls of the blood vessels, varying with exertion, excitement, health, age, etc.

blood relation or **relative,** person related by birth.

blood·root (blud′rüt′; -rùt′), *n. Am.* plant that has a red root, red sap, and a white flower.

blood·shed (blud′shed′), **blood·shed·ding** (-shed′ing), *n.* the shedding of blood.

blood·shot (blud′shot′), *adj.* of eyes, red and sore; tinged with blood.

blood·stained (blud′stānd′), *adj.* 1. stained with blood. 2. guilty of murder or bloodshed.

blood·stone (blud′stōn′), *n.* a semiprecious green stone with specks of red jasper scattered through it.

blood·suck·er (blud′suk′ər), *n.* 1. animal that sucks blood; leech. 2. person who gets all he can from others.

blood·thirst·y (blud′thėrs′ti), *adj.* eager for bloodshed; cruel; murderous. —**blood′thirst′i·ly,** *adv.* —**blood′thirst′i·ness,** *n.*

blood transfusion, injection of blood from one person or animal into another.

blood type, any one of four groups into which blood may be divided.

blood vessel, tube in the body through which the blood circulates, as an artery, vein, or capillary.

blood·y (blud′i), *adj.*, **blood·i·er, blood·i·est,** *v.*, **blood·ied, blood·y·ing.** —*adj.* 1. bleeding. 2. stained with blood. 3. with much bloodshed. 4. eager for bloodshed; cruel. 5. *Brit. Slang.* cursed; confounded. —*v.* 1. cause to bleed. 2. stain with blood. —**blood′i·ly,** *adv.* —**blood′i·ness,** *n.* —Syn. *adj.* 4. bloodthirsty, murderous.

bloom (blüm), *n.* 1. flower; blossom. 2. condition or time of flowering. 3. condition or time of greatest health, vigor, or beauty. 4. glow of health and beauty. 5. *Bot.* the powdery coating on some fruits and leaves. —*v.* 1. have flowers; open into flowers; blossom. 2. be in the condition or time of greatest health, vigor, or beauty. 3. glow with health and beauty. [< Scand. *blōm*] —**bloom′ing·ly,** *adv.*—Syn. *n.* 3. freshness, prime.

bloom·ers (blüm′ərz), *n.pl. Am.* **a.** loose trousers, gathered at the knee, worn by women and girls for physical training. **b.** underwear made like these. [first referred to in magazine published by Amelia J. *Bloomer,* 1851]

bloop·er (blüp′ər), *n. Am., Slang.* 1. a very foolish mistake; blunder. 2. *Baseball.* a ball hit high into the air.

blos·som (blos′əm), *n.* 1. flower, esp. of a plant that produces fruit. 2. condition or time of flowering. —*v.* 1. have flowers; open into flowers. 2. flourish; develop. [OE *blōstma*]

blot (blot), *v.*, **blot·ted, blot·ting,** *n.* —*v.* 1. spot with ink; stain. 2. dry (ink) with paper that soaks up ink. 3. blemish; disgrace. 4. **blot out,** a. hide; cover up. b. wipe out; destroy. —*n.* 1. spot of ink; stain of any kind. 2. blemish; disgrace. —**blot′less,** *adj.* —Syn. *v.* 3. sully.

blotch (bloch), *n.* 1. a large, irregular spot or stain. 2. place where the skin is red or broken out. —*v.* cover or mark with blotches. [blend of *blot* and *botch*] —**blotch′y,** *adj.*

blot·ter (blot′ər), *n.* 1. piece of blotting paper. 2. *Am.* book for writing down happenings, transactions, arrests, etc.

blotting paper, a soft paper used to dry writing by soaking up ink.

blouse (blous; blouz), *n.* 1. a loose shirtwaist worn by women and children. 2. loosely fitting garment for the upper part of the body: *sailors wear blouses.* 3. loosely fitting coat, worn as part of the undress uniform of the U.S. Army. 4. a kind of smock. [< F, < Pr., short (wool)] —**blouse′like′**, *adj.*

Blouse (def. 1)

blow¹ (blō), *n.* 1. a hard hit; knock; stroke. 2. a sudden happening that causes misfortune or loss; severe shock; misfortune. 3. a sudden attack or assault. [ME *blaw*] —Syn. 1. buffet. 2. calamity.

blow² (blō), *v.*, **blew, blown, blow·ing,** *n.* —*v.* 1. send forth a strong current of air. 2. move in a current; move rapidly or with power. 3. drive or carry by a current of air. 4. force a current of air into, through, or against. 5. clear or empty by forcing air through. 6. form or shape by air: *blow glass.* 7. make a sound by a current of air or steam: *the whistle blows at noon.* 8. puff up: *blown up with pride.* 9. swell with air: *to blow bubbles.* 10. break by an explosion. 11. be out of breath. 12. put out of breath. 13. exhale strongly. 14. *Colloq.* boast; brag. 15. of whales, spout air. 16. of flies, lay eggs in. 17. *Am., Slang.* spend (money, etc.) recklessly; squander. 18. melt (a fuse). 19. publish or spread (news). 20. **blow in,** *Am.* appear unexpectedly; drop in. 21. **blow up,** a. explode. b. fill with air. c. *Am., Colloq.* become very angry. d. *Colloq.* scold; abuse. e. arise; become stronger: *a storm suddenly blew up.* f. *Am., Colloq.* go to pieces, as from emotional stress. g. enlarge (a photograph). —*n.* 1. act or fact of forcing air into, through, or against something; blast. 2. a blowing. 3. gale of wind. [OE *blāwan*] —**blow′er,** *n.*

blow·fly (blō′flī′), *n., pl.* **-flies.** a two-winged fly that deposits its eggs on meat or in wounds.

blow·gun (blō′gun′), *n. Am.* tube through which a person blows arrows, darts, etc.

blow·hole (blō′hōl′), *n.* 1. hole where air or gas can escape. 2. hole for breathing, in the top of the head of whales and some other animals.

blown¹ (blōn), *adj.* 1. out of breath; exhausted. 2. tainted by flies; tainted; stale. 3. shaped by blowing. —*v.* pp. of blow².

blown² (blōn), *adj.* fully opened. [pp. of *blow* blossom, OE *blōwan*]

blow·out (blō′out′), *n.* 1. the bursting of the inner tube and casing of an automobile tire. 2. a sudden or violent escape of air, steam, etc. 3. the melting of an electric fuse caused by too much current. 4. *Slang.* big party or meal.

blow·pipe (blō′pīp′), *n.* 1. tube for blowing air or gas into a flame to increase the heat. 2. blowgun.

blow·torch (blō′tôrch′), *n. Am.* a small torch that shoots out a very hot flame.

blow·up (blō′up′), n. 1. explosion. 2. Colloq. outburst of anger. 3. Am. bankruptcy.

blow·y (blō′i), adj., blow·i·er, blow·i·est. windy. —**blow′i·ness,** n.

blowz·y (blouz′i), adj., blowz·i·er, blowz·i·est. 1. untidy; frowzy. 2. red-faced and coarse-looking. [< blowze wench, slattern]

blub·ber (blub′ər), n. 1. fat of whales and other sea animals. 2. noisy weeping. —v. weep noisily. —**blub′ber·er,** n. —**blub′ber·y,** adj.

bludg·eon (bluj′ən), n. short club with a heavy end. —v. 1. strike with a club. 2. bully; threaten. —**bludg′eon·er, bludg·eon·eer** (bluj′ən·ir′), n.

blue (blü), n., adj., blu·er, blu·est, v., blued, blu·ing or blue·ing. —n. 1. the color of the clear sky in daylight. 2. a lighter or darker shade of this color. 3. something having this color; blue coloring matter, dye, or pigment. 4. out of the blue, completely unexpected. 5. the blue, a. the sky. b. the sea. 6. the blues. See blues. —adj. 1. having the color of the clear sky in daylight. 2. wearing blue clothes. 3. livid: blue from cold. 4. sad; gloomy; discouraged. —v. 1. make blue. 2. use bluing on. [< OF bleu < Gmc.] —**blue′ly,** adv. —**blue′ness,** n. —Syn. adj. 4. depressed, despondent, dejected.

Blue·beard (blü′bird′), n. a cruel man in an old legend who murdered six of his wives.

blue·bell (blü′bel′), n. any of various plants with flowers shaped like bells.

blue·ber·ry (blü′ber′i; -bər·i), n., pl. -ries. Am. 1. a small, sweet, edible berry that has smaller seeds than the huckleberry. 2. the shrub that it grows on.

blue·bird (blü′bėrd′), n. Am. a small songbird of North America whose prevailing color is blue.

blue blood, aristocratic descent. —**blue′-blood′ed,** adj.

blue·bon·net (blü′bon′it), n. plant with blue flowers resembling sweet peas.

blue book, Am. book that lists socially promi-nent people.

blue·bot·tle (blü′bot′əl), n. 1. a large blowfly that has a blue abdomen and a hairy body. 2. any similar fly. 3. cornflower.

blue chip, 1. a poker chip of high value. 2. Colloq. anything of high value or quality. —**blue′-chip′,** adj.

blue·coat (blü′kōt′), n. 1. Am., Colloq. police-man. 2. Am. (formerly) soldier in the army of the United States. —**blue′-coat′ed,** adj.

blue·fish (blü′fish′), n., pl. -fish·es or (esp. collectively) -fish. a blue-and-silver salt-water edible fish of the Atlantic Coast.

blue·grass (blü′gras′; -gräs′), n. Am. any of various American grasses with bluish-green stems, esp. **Kentucky bluegrass.**

blue gum, eucalyptus.

blue·ing (blü′ing), n. bluing.

blue·ish (blü′ish), adj. bluish. —**blue′ish·ness,** n.

blue·jack·et (blü′jak′it), n. a sailor.

blue·jay (blü′jā′), n. Am. any of various North American jays, esp. a noisy, chattering bird with a crest and a blue back.

blue laws, Am. 1. severe laws for the regulation of re-ligious and personal conduct in the colonies of Connecticut and New Haven. 2. any very strict and puritanical laws.

blue·nose, Blue·nose (blü′nōz′), n. Am. an exces-sively puritanical or inquisi-tive person.

blue·pen·cil (blü′pen′səl), v., -ciled, -cil·ing; esp. Brit. -cilled, -cil·ling. change with a blue pencil; edit.

Bluejay (11 in. long)

blue·print (blü′print′), n. 1. photograph that shows white outlines on a blue background, used to make copies of building plans, maps, etc. 2. a detailed plan or outline of a project. —v. make a blueprint of.

blue ribbon, 1. first prize. 2. badge of a temperance society.

Blue Ridge, range of the Appalachian Moun-

tains, extending from E Pennsylvania to N Georgia.

blues (blüz), n.pl. Am. 1. depression of spirits; despondency. 2. a slow, melancholy jazz song.

blue-sky law (blü′skī′), Am., Colloq. law to prevent the sale of worthless stocks and bonds.

blue·stock·ing (blü′stok′ing), n. Colloq. woman who displays great interest in intellectual or literary subjects. [because blue stockings were affected by a group of such women in London c 1750] —**blue′stock′ing·ism,** n.

blue streak, Am., Colloq. with lightning speed: she talks a blue streak.

blu·et (blü′it), n. Am. small plant of the U.S., with pale bluish flowers.

bluff¹ (bluf), n. Am. a high, steep bank or cliff. —adj. 1. Am. rising with a straight, broad front. 2. abrupt, frank, and hearty in manner. [prob. < Du. blaf broad flat face] —**bluff′ly,** adv. —**bluff′ness,** n. —Syn. adj. 1. steep. 2. plain-spoken, unceremonious, blunt.

bluff² (bluf), n. 1. Am. show of pretended con-fidence, used to deceive or mislead. 2. threat that cannot be carried out. 3. person who bluffs. —v. Am. a. deceive by a show of pretended confidence. b. frighten with a threat that cannot be carried out. —**bluff′er,** n. Am.

blu·ing (blü′ing), n. Am. a blue liquid or powder put in water when rinsing clothes to keep white clothes from turning yellow. Also, blueing.

blu·ish (blü′ish), adj. somewhat blue. Also, blueish. —**blu′ish·ness,** n.

blun·der (blun′dər), v. 1. make a stupid mis-take. 2. do clumsily or wrongly; bungle. 3. move clumsily or blindly; stumble. 4. blurt out. —n. a stupid mistake. —**blun′der·er,** n. —**blun′der·ing·ly,** adv. —Syn. n. bungle, oversight, slip.

blun·der·buss (blun′dər·bus), n. 1. a short gun with a wide muzzle, now no longer used. 2. person who blunders. [alter. of Du. donderbus thunder box]

blunt (blunt), adj. 1. without a sharp edge or point; dull. 2. plain-spoken; outspoken; frank. 3. slow in perceiving or understanding. —v. make or become blunt. —**blunt′ly,** adv. —**blunt′ness,** n. —Syn. adj. 2. candid, brusque. 3. obtuse.

blur (blėr), v., blurred, blur·ring, n. 1. make confused in form or outline: mist blurred the hills. 2. dim: tears blurred my eyes. 3. become dim or indistinct. 4. smear; blot; stain. —n. 1. a blurred condition; dimness. 2. thing seen dimly or indistinctly. 3. smear; blot; stain. [? var. of blear] —**blur′ry,** adj.

blurb (blėrb), n. Am. advertisement or an-nouncement full of extremely high praise. [coined by Gelett Burgess, American humorist]

blurt (blėrt), v. say suddenly or without think-ing: blurt out a secret. [imit.]

blush (blush), n. 1. a reddening of the skin caused by shame, confusion, or excitement. 2. rosy color. —v. 1. become red because of shame, confusion, or excitement. 2. be ashamed. 3. be or become rosy. [ME blusche(n). Cf. OE blyscan be red.] —**blush′er,** n. —**blush′ful,** adj. —**blush′ing·ly,** adv.

blus·ter (blus′tər), v. 1. storm or blow noisily and violently. 2. talk noisily and violently. 3. do or say noisily and violently. 4. make or get by blustering. —n. 1. stormy noise and violence. 2. noisy and violent talk. —**blus′ter·er,** n. —**blus′-ter·ing·ly,** adv. —**blus′ter·y, blus′ter·ous,** adj.

blvd., boulevard.

bo·a (bō′ə), n., pl. bo·as. 1. any of various large tropical American snakes that kill their prey by squeezing with their coils. 2. a long scarf made of fur or feathers, worn around a woman's neck. [< L (def. 1)]

boa constrictor, a large tropical American boa.

boar (bôr; bōr), n. 1. a male pig or hog. 2. the wild boar. [OE bār]

board (bôrd; bōrd), n. 1. a broad, thin piece of wood ready for use in building, etc. 2. a flat piece of wood used for some special purpose: an iron-ing board. 3. pasteboard. 4. table to serve food on; table. 5. food served on a table. 6. meals provided for pay. 7. *Am.* blackboard. 8. *Am.* stock exchange. 9. group of persons managing something; council. 10. side of a ship. 11. border; edge. 12. **on board,** *Am.* on a ship, train, etc. 13. **the boards,** the stage of a theater. —*v.* 1. cover with boards. 2. provide with regular meals, or room and meals, for pay. 3. get meals, or room and meals, for pay. 4. get on a ship. 5. *Am.* go on or into a vehicle. 6. come alongside of or against (a ship). —*adj.* made of boards. [OE *bord*]

board·er (bôr'dər; bōr'-), *n.* 1. person who pays for meals, or for room and meals, at another's house. 2. one of the men assigned to board an enemy ship.

board foot, *Am.* unit of measure equal to a board 1 foot square and 1 inch thick; 144 cu. in.

board·ing (bôr'ding; bōr'-), *n.* 1. boards. 2. structure made of boards.

boarding house, house where meals, or room and meals, are provided for pay.

boarding school, school where pupils are lodged and fed.

board measure, system for measuring logs and lumber. The unit is the board foot.

board·walk (bôrd'wôk'; bōrd'-), *n.* *U.S.* promenade made of boards, esp. along a beach.

boast (bōst), *v.* 1. praise oneself; brag. 2. brag about. 3. be proud. 4. have and be proud of: *our town boasts many fine parks.* —*n.* 1. praising oneself; bragging. 2. thing to be proud of. —boast'er, *n.* —boast'ing·ly, *adv.*

boast·ful (bōst'fəl), *adj.* 1. boasting. 2. fond of boasting. —boast'ful·ly, *adv.* —boast'ful·ness, *n.*

boat (bōt), *n.* 1. a small, open vessel for traveling on water. 2. ship. 3. a boat-shaped dish for gravy, sauce, etc. —*v.* 1. go in a boat. 2. put or carry in a boat. [OE *bāt*]

boat·house (bōt'hous'), *n.* house or shed for sheltering a boat or boats.

boat·ing (bōt'ing), *n.* rowing; sailing.

boat·load (bōt'lōd'), *n.* 1. as much or as many as a boat can hold or carry. 2. load that a boat is carrying.

boat·man (bōt'mən), *n.*, *pl.* -men. man who manages or works on a boat.

boat·swain (bō'sən; *less often* bōt'swān'), *n.* a ship's officer in charge of anchors, ropes, rigging, etc. Also, bo's'n, bosun.

Bo·az (bō'az), *n. Bible.* the husband of Ruth.

bob¹ (bob), *n.*, *v.*, **bobbed, bob·bing.** —*n.* a short, quick motion up and down, or to and fro. —*v.* move up and down, or to and fro, with short, quick motions.

bob² (bob), *n.*, *v.*, **bobbed, bob·bing.** —*n.* 1. a short haircut. 2. a horse's docked tail. 3. weight on the end of a pendulum or plumb line. 4. a bait consisting of a knot of worms, rags, or the like. 5. float for a fishing line. —*v.* 1. cut (hair) short. 2. fish with a bob.

bob³ (bob), *n.*, *v.*, **bobbed, bob·bing.** —*n.* a light rap; tap. —*v.* rap lightly; tap.

bob⁴ (bob), *n.*, *pl.* **bob.** *Brit. Slang.* shilling.

bob·bin (bob'ən), *n.* reel or spool on which thread, yarn, etc., is wound. [< F *bobine*]

bob·by (bob'i), *n.*, *pl.* -bies. *Brit. Slang.* policeman. [for Sir *Robert* Peel, who improved the London police system]

bobby pin, metal hairpin whose prongs are close together.

bob·by·socks (bob'i·soks'), *n.pl. Colloq.* ankle-length socks, worn by young girls.

bob·by·sox·er (bob'i·sok'sər), *n. Colloq.* an adolescent girl, esp. one who enthusiastically follows every new fad.

bob·cat (bob'kat'), *n. Am.* wildcat; lynx.

bob·o·link (bob'ə·lingk), *n. Am.* an American songbird that lives in fields. [imit.]

bob·sled (bob'sled'), **bob·sleigh** (bob'slā'), *n.*, *v.*, -sled·ded, -sled·ding; -sleighed, -sleigh·ing. *Am.* —*n.* 1. two short sleds fastened together by a plank. 2. either of the short sleds. 3. sled for coasting made of two pairs of runners connected by a long board. —*v.* ride on a bobsled.

bob·stay (bob'stā'), *n.* rope or chain to hold a bowsprit down. See picture under **bowsprit.**

bob·tail (bob'tāl'), *n.* 1. a short tail; tail cut short. 2. animal having a bobtail. —*adj.* having a bobtail. —*v.* cut short the tail of.

bob·white (bob'hwit'), *n. Am.* 1. an American quail that has a grayish body with brown and white markings. 2. its call.

Boc·cac·ci·o (bō·kä'chi·ō), *n.* Giovanni, 1313-1375, Italian poet and storywriter.

bock beer (bok), or **bock,** *n. Am.* a strong, dark beer, usually brewed in the spring. [< G *Bockbier* for *Einbocker Bier* beer of Einbeck, city in Germany]

bode¹ (bōd), *v.*, bod·ed, bod·ing. be a sign of. [OE *bodian* < *boda* messenger] —bode'ment, *n.* —Syn. portend, foreshadow.

bode² (bōd), *v.* pt. of bide.

bod·ice (bod'is), *n.* 1. the close-fitting waist of a dress. 2. a wide girdle worn over a dress and laced up the front. [var. of pl. of *body*, part of a dress]

bod·i·ly (bod'ə·li), *adj.* of or in the body. —*adv.* 1. in person. 2. all together; as one group. —Syn. *adj.* corporeal, physical.

Bodice (def. 2)

bod·kin (bod'kin), *n.* 1. a large, blunt needle. 2. a long hairpin. 3. a pointed tool for making holes. [ME *boydekyn* dagger]

bod·y (bod'i), *n.*, *pl.* bod·ies, *v.*, bod·ied, bod·y·ing. —*n.* 1. the whole material part of a man, animal, or plant. 2. the main part or trunk of an animal, tree, etc. 3. the main part; larger part; bulk of anything. 4. a group of persons considered together; collection of persons or things: *a body of troops.* 5. *Colloq.* person. 6. dead person; corpse. 7. portion of matter; mass: *a lake is a body of water.* 8. matter; substance; density; substantial quality: *wine with an excellent body.* —*v.* 1. provide with a body; give substance to; embody. 2. **body forth,** a. give a real form to. b. be a sign of. [OE *bodig*] —bod'ied, *adj.*

bod·y·guard (bod'i·gärd'), *n.* 1. man or men who guard a person. 2. retinue; escort.

body politic, people forming a political group with an organized government.

Boe·o·tia (bē·ō'shə), *n.* district in ancient Greece, north of Athens. —Boe·o'tian, *adj.*, *n.*

Boer (bôr; bōr; bûr), *n.* person of Dutch descent living in South Africa. [< Du., farmer]

bog (bog; bôg), *n.*, *v.*, bogged, bog·ging. —*n.* soft, wet, spongy ground; marsh; swamp. —*v.* 1. sink or get stuck in a bog. 2. **bog down,** get stuck as if in mud. [< Irish or Scotch Gaelic *bogach* < *bog* soft] —bog'gish, *adj.* —bog'gy, *adj.* —bog'gi·ness, *n.*

bo·gey, bo·gie (bō'gi), *n.*, *pl.* -geys; -gies. 1. bogy. 2. *Golf.* a. par. b. one stroke over par on a hole. [var. of *Bogy*; from Colonel *Bogey*, imaginary partner]

bog·gle (bog'əl), *v.*, -gled, -gling, *n.* —*v.* 1. blunder; bungle; botch. 2. hold back; hesitate. 3. jump with fright; shy. 4. quibble; equivocate. —*n.* a boggling. —bog'gler, *n.*

Bo·go·tá (bō'gə·tä'), *n.* capital of Colombia.

bo·gus (bō'gəs), *adj. Am.* counterfeit; sham.

bo·gy (bō'gi), *n.*, *pl.* -gies. 1. goblin; specter; evil spirit. 2. person or thing that is feared; bugaboo. Also, bogey, bogie. [< obs. *bog*, var. of *bug* bugbear]

Bo·he·mi·a (bō·hē'mi·ə), *n.* a former country in C Europe, now part of Czechoslovakia.

Bo·he·mi·an (bō·hē'mi·ən; -hēm'yən), *adj.* 1. of Bohemia or Bohemians. 2. free and easy; unconventional. —*n.* 1. native or inhabitant of Bohemia. 2. Often, **bohemian.** artist, writer, etc., who lives in a free and easy, unconventional way. 3. gypsy. —Bo·he'mi·an·ism, *n.*

boil¹ (boil), *v.* 1. bubble up and give off vapor. 2. cause to boil. 3. cook by boiling. 4. of a container, have its contents boil. 5. clean or sterilize by boiling. 6. make by boiling: *a boiled dinner.* 7. be very excited or angry. 8. move violently. 9. **boil down,** a. reduce by boiling. b. reduce by getting rid of unimportant parts. 10. **boil over,** a.

come to the boiling point and overflow. b. show excitement or anger. —*n.* 1. a boiling. 2. boiling condition. [< OF < L *bullire* form bubbles] —Syn. *v.* 1. seethe, simmer.

boil² (boil), *n.* a painful, red swelling on the skin, formed by pus around a hard core. [OE *bȳl(e)*]

boil·er (boil′ər), *n.* 1. container for heating liquids. 2. tank for making steam to heat buildings or drive engines. 3. tank for holding hot water.

boiling point, temperature at which a liquid boils.

Boi·se (boi′zē; -sē), *n.* capital of Idaho, in the SW part.

bois·ter·ous (bois′tər·əs; -trəs), *adj.* 1. abounding in rough and noisily cheerful activity. 2. violent; rough. —**bois′ter·ous·ly,** *adv.* —**bois′ter·ous·ness,** *n.*

bo·la (bō′lə), **bo·las** (bō′ləs), *n.* weapon consisting of stone or metal balls tied to cords. [< Sp. and Pg., ball, < L *bulla* bubble]

bold (bōld), *adj.* 1. without fear; daring. 2. showing or requiring courage: *a bold act.* 3. too free in manners; impudent. 4. striking; vigorous; clear: *stand in bold outline against the sky.* 5. steep; abrupt. 6. **make bold,** take the liberty; dare. [OE *bald*] —**bold′ly,** *adv.* —**bold′ness,** *n.* —Syn. 1. fearless, courageous, brave. 3. forward, impertinent, saucy. —Ant. 1. timid.

bold·face (bōld′fās′), *n.* heavy type that stands out clearly. **This line is in boldface.**

bole (bōl), *n. Bot.* trunk of a tree. [< Scand. *bolr*]

bo·le·ro (bə·lãr′ō), *n., pl.* -ros. 1. a lively Spanish dance in ¾ time. 2. music for it. 3. a short, loose jacket. [< Sp.]

Bol·i·var (bol′ə·vər), *n.* Simon, 1783–1830, Venezuelan general and statesman.

Bo·liv·i·a (bə·liv′i·ə), *n.* country in W South America. —**Bo·liv′i·an,** *adj., n.*

Bolero (def. 3)

boll (bōl), *n. Bot.* a rounded seed pod or capsule, as of cotton or flax. [var. of *bowl*]

boll weevil, *Am.* a long-billed beetle whose larva damages young cotton bolls.

boll·worm (bōl′wẽrm), *n. Am.* larva that eats cotton bolls and the ears of corn.

bo·lo (bō′lō), *n., pl.* -los. a long, heavy knife, used in the Philippine Islands. [< Sp. < Philippine dial.]

Bo·lo·gna (bə·lōn′yə), *n.* city in N Italy.

bo·lo·gna sausage (bə·lō′ni; -nə), or **bologna,** *n.* a large sausage made of beef, veal, and pork.

bo·lo·ney (bə·lō′ni), *n.* 1. bologna sausage. 2. *Am., Slang.* baloney.

Bol·she·vik, bol·she·vik (bōl′shə·vik; bol′-), *n., pl.* -viks, -vi·ki (-vē′ki), *adj.* —*n.* 1. member of a radical political party in Russia that seized power in November, 1917. The Bolsheviks formed the Communist party in 1918. 2. an extreme radical. —*adj.* 1. of the Bolsheviks or Bolshevism. 2. extremely radical. [< Russ., < *bolshe* greater; with ref. to the majority of the party]

Bol·she·vism, bol·she·vism (bōl′shə·viz·əm; bol′-), *n.* 1. doctrines and methods of the Bolsheviks. 2. extreme radicalism.

Bol·she·vist, bol·she·vist (bōl′shə·vist; bol′-), *n., adj.* Bolshevik. —**Bol′she·vis′tic,** *adj.* —**Bol′she·vis′ti·cal·ly,** *adv.* bol′she·vis′ti·cal·ly, *adv.*

Bol·she·vize, bol·she·vize (bōl′shə·vīz; bol′-), *v.,* -vized, -viz·ing. make Bolshevik. —**Bol′she·vi·za′tion, bol′she·vi·za′tion,** *n.*

bol·ster (bōl′stər), *n., v.* 1. support with a bolster; support. 2. keep from falling; prop: *bolster up one's spirits.* —*n.* 1. a long pillow for a bed. 2. pad; cushion. [OE] —**bol′ster·er,** *n.*

bolt¹ (bōlt), *n.* 1. rod with a head on one end and a screw thread for a nut on the other.

2. a sliding fastener for a door. 3. part of a lock moved by a key. 4. short arrow with a thick head. 5. discharge of lightning. 6. sudden start; a running away. 7. roll of cloth or wallpaper. 8. *Am.* refusal to support a candidate, platform, etc., of one's political party. —*v.* 1. fasten with a bolt. 2. dash away; run away. 3. *Am.* break away from one's political party or its candidates. 4. swallow (one's food) without chewing. —*adv.* bolt upright, stiff and straight. [OE, arrow] —**bolt′er,** *n.* —**bolt′less,** *adj.* —**bolt′like′,** *adj.*

bolt² (bōlt), *v.* 1. sift through a cloth or sieve. 2. examine carefully; separate. [< OF *bulter*]

bomb (bom), *n.* 1. container filled with an explosive charge or a chemical substance, usually dropped by aircraft, and exploded by contact or a time mechanism. 2. a sudden, unexpected happening. —*v.* attack with bombs; drop bombs on. [< F < Ital. < L < Gk. *bombos* boom!]

bom·bard (bom·bärd′), *v.* 1. attack with heavy fire of shot and shell from big guns. 2. keep attacking vigorously. [< F *bombarder* < *bombarde* cannon. See BOMB.] —**bom·bard′er,** *n.* —**bom·bard′ment,** *n.*

bom·bar·dier (bom·bər·dir′), *n. Mil.* member of an airplane crew who operates the bombsight and the bomb-release mechanism.

bom·bast (bom′bast), *n.* fine-sounding language that is unsuitable. [< F < LL *bombax* cotton, var. of L *bombyx* silk < Gk.] —**bom·bas′tic, bom·bas′ti·cal,** *adj.* —**bom·bas′ti·cal·ly,** *adv.*

Bom·bay (bom·bā′), *n.* seaport in W India.

bomb bay, space in an airplane for bombs and from which they are dropped.

bomb·er (bom′ər), *n. Mil.* 1. a combat airplane used for dropping bombs on the enemy. 2. person who throws or drops bombs.

bomb·proof (bom′prüf′), *adj.* strong enough to be safe from bombs and shells.

bomb·shell (bom′shel′), *n.* 1. bomb. 2. a sudden unexpected happening; disturbing surprise.

bomb·sight (bom′sīt′), *n. Mil.* instrument used by a bombardier to aim bombs.

bo·na fide (bō′nə fīd; fī′dē), in good faith; genuine; without make-believe or fraud. [< L]

bo·nan·za (bə·nan′zə), *n. Am.* 1. accidental discovery of a rich mass of ore in a mine. 2. the mass itself. 3. *Colloq.* any rich source of profit. [< Sp., fair weather, prosperity, < L *bonus* good]

Bo·na·parte (bō′nə·pärt), *n.* Napoleon, 1769–1821, French general and emperor of France, 1804–1815. Also, **Napoleon I.**

Bo·na·part·ism (bō′nə·pärt′tiz·əm), *n.* rule of or adherence to the Bonapartes. —**Bo′na·part′ist,** *n.*

bon·bon (bon′bon′), *n.* piece of candy, often one with a fancy shape. [< F, good-good]

bond¹ (bond), *n.* 1. anything that ties, binds, or unites. 2. certificate issued by a government or company promising to pay back with interest the money borrowed. 3. written agreement by which a person says he will pay a certain sum of money if he, or another specified, does not perform certain duties properly. 4. person who acts as surety for another. 5. any agreement or binding engagement. 6. condition of goods placed in a warehouse until taxes are paid. 7. **bonds,** a. chains; shackles. b. imprisonment. —*v.* 1. *Am.* issue bonds on; mortgage. 2. convert into bonds: *bond a debt.* 3. *Am.* provide surety against financial loss by the act or default of: *bond an employee.* 4. put (goods) under bond. 5. bind or join firmly together. [var. of *band²*] —**bond′er,** *n.* —Syn. 1. link, tie. 4. security. 5. compact.

bond² (bond), *adj.* in slavery; captive; not free. [< Scand. *bōndi* peasant, orig., dweller]

bond·age (bon′dij), *n.* 1. lack of freedom; slavery. 2. condition of being under some power or influence. —Syn. 1. serfdom.

bond·ed (bon′did), *adj.* 1. secured by bonds. 2. put in a warehouse until taxes are paid.

bond·hold·er (bond′hōl′dər), *n.* person who owns bonds issued by a government or company. —**bond′hold′ing,** *n., adj.*

bond·man (bond′mən), *n., pl.* -men. 1. slave. 2. serf in the Middle Ages.

bonds·man (bondz′mən), *n., pl.* -men. person who becomes responsible for another by bond.

bond·wom·an (bond′wŭm′ən), *n., pl.* -wom-en. a woman slave.

bone (bōn), *n., v.,* boned, bon·ing. —*n.* 1. *Anat., Zool.* a. one of the pieces of the skeleton of an animal with a backbone. b. the hard substance of which bones are made. 2. any of various similar substances, as ivory. 3. bones, a. *U.S. Slang.* dice. b. wooden clappers used in keeping time to music. c. *Am.* end man in a minstrel show. d. skeleton. —*v.* 1. take bones out of. 2. *Am., Colloq.* study strenuously or diligently. [OE *bān*] —bone′less, *adj.* —bone′like′, *adj.*

bone-dry (bōn′drī′), *adj.* 1. dry as a bone; completely dry. 2. *Am.* with no intoxicating drink whatever.

bone·head (bōn′hed′), *n. Am., Slang.* 1. a very stupid person. 2. boner. —bone′head′ed, *adj.*

bon·er (bōn′ər), *n. Am., Slang.* a foolish mistake; stupid error; blunder.

bon·fire (bon′fīr′), *n.* fire built outdoors. [for *bone fire*]

bon·ho·mie (bon′ə·mē′), *n.* good nature; pleasant ways. [< F, < *bonhomme* good fellow]

bo·ni·to (bə·nē′tō), *n., pl.* -tos, -toes. type of salt-water mackerel with very red edible flesh. [< Sp., pretty, < L *bonus* good]

bon jour (bôn zhür′), *French.* good day.

bon mot (bôn mō′), *pl.* bons mots (bôn mōz′; *Fr.* mō′). *French.* clever saying; witty remark.

Bonn (bon; *Ger.* bôn), *n.* capital of West Germany, on the Rhine River.

bon·net (bon′it), *n.* 1. a head covering usually tied under the chin with strings or ribbons, worn by women and children. 2. cap worn by men and boys in Scotland. 3. headdress of feathers worn by American Indians. 4. a covering that protects a machine or chimney. —*v.* put a bonnet on. [< OF, orig., fabric for hats]

bon·ny, bon·nie (bon′i), *adj.,* -ni·er, -ni·est. 1. rosy and pretty; handsome. 2. fine; excellent. 3. healthy-looking. [ME *bonie,* appar. < OF *bon, bonne* good < L *bonus*] —bon′ni·ly, *adv.* —bon′ni·ness, *n.*

bon soir (bôn swär′), *French.* good evening.

bo·nus (bō′nəs), *n.* something extra; thing given in addition to what is due. [< L, good]

bon vo·yage (bôn vwä·yäzh′), *French.* good-by; good luck; pleasant trip.

bon·y (bōn′i), *adj.,* bon·i·er, bon·i·est. 1. of or like bone. 2. full of bones. 3. having big bones that stick out. 4. thin. —bon′i·ness, *n.*

boo (bü), *n., pl.* boos, *interj., v.,* booed, boo·ing. —*n., interj.* sound made to show dislike or contempt or to frighten. —*v.* 1. make such a sound. 2. cry "boo" at.

boob (büb), *n. Am.* a stupid person; fool; dunce. [see BOOBY]

boo·by (bü′bi), *n., pl.* -bies. 1. a stupid person; fool; dunce. 2. kind of large sea bird. 3. person who does the worst in a game or contest. [prob. < Sp. *bobo* (defs. 1, 3) < L *balbus* stammering] —boo′by·ish, *adj.*

Booby (30 in. long)

booby trap, 1. trick arranged to annoy some unsuspecting person. 2. *Mil.* bomb arranged to explode when an object is moved by an unwary person.

boo·dle (bü′dəl), *n., v.,* -dled, -dling. *Am., Slang.* —*n.* 1. lot; pack; crowd. 2. graft; money from bribes. —*v.* bribe. [< Du. *boedel* goods] —boo′dler, *n.*

boog·ie-woog·ie (bŭg′i·wŭg′i), *n. Music.* a form of instrumental blues characterized by bass obbligato contrasting with melodic variations.

boo·hoo (bü′hü′), *n., pl.* -hoos, *v.,* -hooed, -hoo·ing. —*n.* loud crying. —*v.* cry loudly.

book (bük), *n.* 1. a written or printed work of considerable length, esp. on sheets of paper bound together. 2. blank sheets bound together.

3. division of a literary work: *the books of the Bible.* 4. *Music.* words of an opera, operetta, etc.; libretto. 5. record of bets. 6. something fastened together like a book: *a book of tickets.* 7. trick or a number of tricks forming a set in a card game. 8. **bring to book,** a. demand an explanation from. b. rebuke. 9. **the Book,** the Bible. —*v.* 1. enter in a book or list. 2. engage (a place, passage, etc.): *they booked two staterooms on the steamship.* 3. engage; make engagements for. [OE *bōc*] —book′er, *n.* —book′less, *adj.* ➤ Book refers especially to the contents, volume to the physical appearance. A book may be in two or more *volumes.*

book agent, *Am.* a book salesman, esp. one who canvasses houses.

book·bind·er·y (bük′bīn′dər·i), *n., pl.* -er·ies. *Am.* establishment for binding books.

book·case (bük′kās′), *n.* piece of furniture with shelves for holding books.

book club, 1. group of persons who buy books to be circulated within the group. 2. a business organization that supplies certain books regularly to subscribers.

book end, something placed at the end of a row of books to hold them upright.

book·ie (bük′i), *n. Colloq.* bookmaker (def. 2).

book·ish (bük′ish), *adj.* 1. fond of reading or studying. 2. knowing books better than real life. 3. of books. 4. pedantic; formal. —book′ish·ly, *adv.* —book′ish·ness, *n.*

book·keep·er (bük′kēp′ər), *n.* person who keeps a record of business accounts.

book·keep·ing (bük′kēp′ing), *n.* work or art of keeping a record of business accounts.

book learning or **knowledge,** knowledge learned from books, not from real life. —book-learn·ed (bük′lér′nid), *adj.*

book·let (bük′lit), *n.* a little book; thin book.

book·lore (bük′lôr′; -lōr′), *n.* book learning.

book·mak·er (bük′māk′ər), *n.* 1. maker of books. 2. person who makes a business of betting other peoples' money on horse races. —book′mak′ing, *n.*

book·mark (bük′märk′), *n.* something put between the pages of a book to mark the place.

book·plate (bük′plāt′), *n.* a label with the owner's name or emblem on it, to paste in his books.

book·rack (bük′rak′), *n.* 1. rack for supporting an open book. 2. rack for holding a number of books.

book review, article written about a book, discussing its merits, faults, etc.

book·sell·er (bük′sel′ər), *n.* person whose business is selling books. —book′sell′ing, *n.*

book·stall (bük′stôl′), *n.* place where books (usually secondhand) are sold.

book·stand (bük′stand′), *n.* 1. bookrack. 2. *Am.* bookstall.

book·store (bük′stôr′; -stōr′), **book·shop** (-shop′), *n. Am.* store where books are sold.

book·worm (bük′wẽrm′), *n.* 1. insect larva that gnaws the bindings or leaves of books. 2. person very fond of reading and studying.

boom¹ (büm), *n.* 1. a deep hollow sound like the roar of cannon or of big waves. 2. *Am.* sudden activity and increase in business, prices, or values of property; rapid growth. 3. *Am.* a vigorous pushing or urging. —*v.* 1. *Am.* rush with force or vigor. 2. make a deep hollow sound: *the big guns boomed.* 3. utter with such a sound. 4. *Am.* increase suddenly in activity; grow rapidly. 5. *Am.* push or urge vigorously. —*adj. Am.* produced by a boom. [imit.]

boom² (büm), *n.* 1. *Naut.* a long pole or beam, used to extend the bottom of a sail or as the lifting pole of a derrick. 2. *Am.* chain, cable, or line of timbers that keeps logs from floating away. [< Du., tree, pole]

boom·er·ang (büm′ər·ang), *n.* 1. a curved piece of wood, used as a weapon by Australian natives, which can be so thrown that it returns to the thrower. 2. anything that recoils or reacts to harm the doer or user. [< dial. of New South Wales]

boom town, *Am.* town that has grown up suddenly.

boon[1] (bün), *n.* **1.** a blessing; great benefit. **2.** *Archaic.* something asked or granted as a favor. [< Scand. *bōn* petition] —**Syn. 1.** favor, gift.

boon[2] (bün), *adj.* **1.** jolly; gay; merry. **2.** *Poetic.* kindly. [< OF *bon* good < L *bonus*]

boon·docks (bün'doks), *n.pl. Am., Dial.* a desolate place or area, as a swamp, scrub forest, etc.

boon·dog·gle (bün'dog'əl), *v.,* -gled, -gling. *Am., Slang.* do useless work. —**boon'dog'gler,** *n. Am.* —**boon'dog'gling,** *n. Am.*

Boone (bün), *n.* Daniel, 1735–1820, American pioneer in Kentucky.

boor (bür), *n.* **1.** a rude, bad-mannered, or clumsy person. **2.** a farm laborer; peasant. [< LG *bur* or Du. *boer* farmer] —**boor'ish,** *adj.* —**boor'ish·ly,** *adv.* —**boor'ish·ness,** *n.*

boost (büst), *Am.* —*n.* a push or shove that helps a person in rising or advancing. —*v.* **1.** to lift or push from below or behind. **2.** speak favorably of. **3.** raise; increase: *boost prices.* **4.** cheer; hearten. [blend of *boom* and *hoist*]

boost·er (büs'tər), *n. Am., Slang.* one who or that which gives support to a person, cause, etc. —**boost'er·ism,** *n. Am.*

boot[1] (büt), *n.* **1.** a leather or rubber covering for the foot and leg. **2.** shoe that reaches above the ankle. **3.** a protecting apron or cover for the driver of an open carriage. **4.** kick. **5.** *Slang.* discharge; dismissal. **6.** *Slang.* a recruit in the U.S. Navy or Marines. —*v.* **1.** put boots on. **2.** kick. **3.** dismiss; discharge. [< OF *bote* < Gmc.]

boot[2] (büt), *n.* to boot, in addition; besides. [OE *bōt* advantage]

boot·black (büt'blak'), *n. Am.* person whose work is shining shoes and boots.

boot·ee (bü·tē'; *esp. for 1* büt'ē), *n. Am.* **1.** a baby's soft shoe. **2.** a woman's short boot.

booth (büth), *n., pl.* booths (büthz). **1.** place where goods are sold or shown at a fair, market, etc. **2.** a small, closed place for a telephone, motion-picture projector, etc. **3.** small, closed place for voting at elections. [< Scand. (ODan.) *bōth*]

Booth (büth), *n.,* William, 1829–1912, English clergyman who founded the Salvation Army.

boot·jack (büt'jak'), *n.* device to help in pulling off boots.

boot·leg (büt'leg'), *n., v.,* -legged, -leg·ging. *adj.* —*n. Am., Slang.* alcoholic liquor made or distributed illegally. —*v.* **1.** *Am.* sell or deal in illegally or secretly. **2.** *U.S.* transport goods secretly for illicit disposal. —*adj. Am.* made, transported, or sold illegally. [modern use from practice of smuggling liquor in boot legs] —**boot'leg'ger,** *n. Am.* —**boot'leg'ging,** *n. Am.*

boot·less (büt'lis), *adj.* useless. —**boot'less·ly,** *adv.* —**boot'less·ness,** *n.*

boot·lick (büt'lik'), *v. Am., Slang.* curry favor with (a person); be a toady. —**boot'lick'er,** *n. Am.* —**boot'lick'ing,** *n. Am.*

boo·ty (bü'tī), *n., pl.* -ties. **1.** things taken from the enemy in war. **2.** plunder. **3.** any valuable thing or things obtained; prize. [akin to *boot*[2]]

booze (büz), *n., v.,* boozed, booz·ing. *Colloq.* —*n.* **1.** intoxicating liquor. **2.** spree. —*v.* drink heavily. [prob. < MDu. *būzen* drink to excess] —**booz·y** (bü'zī), *adj.,* booz·i·er, booz·i·est. drunk.

bop (bop), *n. Am., Slang.* bebop.

bo·rac·ic (bə·ras'ik), *adj. Chem.* boric.

bor·age (bėr'ij; bor'-), *n.* plant, native to S Europe, with hairy leaves and blue or purplish flowers. [< AF *burage* < LL *burra* hair; with ref. to foliage]

bo·rate (*n.* bō'rāt, -rit, bō'-; *v.* bō'rāt, bō'-), *n., v.,* -rat·ed, -rat·ing. —*n. Chem.* salt or ester of boric acid. —*v.* treat with boric acid or borax.

bo·rax (bō'raks; -raks; bō'-), *n.* a white crystalline powder, Na₂B₄O₇·10H₂O, used as an antiseptic, in washing clothes, etc. [< OF < Med.L < Ar. < Pers. *bōrah*]

Bor·deaux (bôr·dō'), *n.* **1.** seaport in SW France. **2.** red or white wine made near Bordeaux.

bor·der (bôr'dər), *n.* **1.** a side, edge, or boundary of anything, or the part near it. **2.** frontier. **3.** strip on the edge of anything for strength or ornament. —*v.* **1.** form a border to; bound. **2.** put a border on; edge. **3.** border on or upon, a. be next to; adjoin. b. be close to; resemble. [< OF, < *bord* side < Gmc.] —**bor'dered,** *adj.* —**bor'der·less,** *adj.* —**Syn. n. 1.** margin, rim, brink.

bor·der·land (bôr'dər·land'), *n.* **1.** land forming, or next to, a border. **2.** uncertain district or space.

bor·der·line (bôr'dər·līn'), *adj.* **1.** on a border or boundary. **2.** uncertain; in between.

bore[1] (bôr; bōr), *v.,* bored, bor·ing, *n.* —*v.* **1.** make a hole by a tool that keeps turning, or as a worm does in fruit. **2.** make (a hole, passage, entrance, etc.) by pushing through or digging out. **3.** bore a hole in; hollow out evenly. —*n.* **1.** hole made by a revolving tool. **2.** a hollow space inside a pipe, tube, or gun barrel. **3.** distance across the inside of a hole or tube. [OE *borian*] —**bor'er,** *n.* —**Syn. v. 1.** pierce, perforate, drill.

bore[2] (bôr; bōr), *v.,* bored, bor·ing, *n.* —*v.* make weary by being dull or tiresome. —*n.* a dull, tiresome person or thing. —**Syn. v.** tire, fatigue.

bore[3] (bôr; bōr), *v.* pt. of bear[1].

bore[4] (bôr; bōr), *n.* a sudden, high tidal wave that rushes up a narrowing channel with great force. [< Scand. *bāra* wave]

bo·re·al (bō'ri·əl; bō'-), *adj.* **1.** northern. **2.** of Boreas.

Bo·re·as (bō'ri·əs; bō'-), *n.* the north wind. [< Gk.]

bore·dom (bôr'dəm; bōr'-), *n.* weariness caused by dull, tiresome people or events.

bore·some (bôr'səm; bōr'-), *adj.* dull; tiresome.

bo·ric (bō'rik; bō'-), *adj. Chem.* of or containing boron. Also, **boracic.**

boric acid, *Chem.* a white, crystalline substance, H₃BO₃, used as a mild antiseptic, to preserve food, etc.

born (bôrn), *adj.* **1.** brought into life; brought forth. **2.** by birth; by nature: *a born athlete.* —*v.* pp. of bear[1]. [pp. of *bear*[1]]

borne (bôrn; bōrn), *v.* pp. of bear[1]. ❯ **1.** Borne is the past participle of *bear* in most of its senses: *the ship was borne along by the breeze.* **2.** In the sense "give birth to," the past participle of *bear* is *borne* except in the very common passive when not followed by *by: She had borne five children. He was born in 1900.*

Bor·ne·o (bôr'ni·ō; bōr'-), *n.* island in the East Indies. Part of it is British, part is Indonesian.

bo·ron (bō'ron; bō'-), *n. Chem.* a nonmetallic element, B, found in borax. [blend of *borax* and *carbon*]

bor·ough (bėr'ō), *n.* **1.** *Am.* (in some States) an incorporated town smaller than a city. **2.** one of the five divisions of New York City. **3.** town in England with a municipal corporation and a charter that guarantees the right of local self-government. **4.** town in England that sends representatives to Parliament. [OE *burg*]

bor·row (bôr'ō; bor'ō), *v.* **1.** get (something) from another person with the understanding that it must be returned. **2.** take and use as one's own; take. **3.** *Math.* in subtraction, to take from one denomination to add to the next lower. [OE *borgian* < *borg* pledge, surety] —**bor'row·er,** *n.*

borsch (bôrsch), **borscht** (bôrsht), *n.* a Russian soup containing beets.

bos·cage (bos'kij), *n.* a small woods; thicket. [< OF, < *bosc* < Frankish *busk* woods]

bosh (bosh), *n., interj. Colloq.* nonsense.

bosk·y (bos'ki), *adj.* **1.** wooded. **2.** shady. —**bosk'i·ness,** *n.*

bo's'n (bō'sən), *n. Naut.* boatswain.

Bos·ni·a (boz'ni·ə), *n.* district in W Yugoslavia. —**Bos'ni·an,** *adj., n.*

bos·om (büz'əm; bü'zəm), *n.* **1.** the upper, front part of the human body; breast. **2.** part of a garment covering this. **3.** *Am.* a false shirt front; dickey. **4.** enclosure formed by the breast and arms. **5.** center or inmost part. **6.** heart, thought, affections, desires, etc. —*adj.* close; trusted: *a bosom friend.* —*v.* 1. embrace. 2. cherish. 3. keep in one's bosom; conceal. [OE *bōsm*]

Bos·po·rus (bos′pə·rəs), *n.* strait connecting the Black Sea and the Sea of Marmara.

boss[1] (bôs; bos), *Am., Colloq.* —*n.* 1. person who hires workers or watches over or directs them; foreman; manager. 2. person who controls a political organization. —*v.* 1. be the boss of; direct; control. 2. be too overbearing. —*adj.* master; chief. [< Du. *baas*]

boss[2] (bôs; bos), *n.* 1. *Bot., Zool.* a roundish protuberance on an animal or plant. 2. a raised ornament on a flat surface. 3. *Archit.* an ornamental projection or block. 4. any knoblike mass. —*v.* 1. decorate with bosses. 2. furnish with bosses. [< OF *boce*]

Boss (def. 2)

boss·ism (bôs′iz·əm; bos′-), *n. Am.* control by bosses, esp. political bosses.

boss·y[1] (bôs′i; bos′i), *adj.*, boss·i·er, boss·i·est. *Am., Colloq.* fond of telling others what to do and how to do it; domineering.

boss·y[2] (bôs′i; bos′i), *n., pl.* –sies. *Am., Colloq.* calf or cow. [cf. L *bos* ox]

Bos·ton (bôs′tən; bos′-), *n.* seaport and capital of Massachusetts, in the E part. —**Bos·to·ni·an** (bôs·tō′ni·ən; bos–), *adj., n.*

Boston terrier or **bull,** small, dark-brown dog with white markings and smooth, short hair.

bo·sun (bō′sən), *n.* boatswain.

Bos·well (boz′wel; –wəl), *n.* 1. James, 1740–1795, Scottish writer of a famous biography of Samuel Johnson. 2. any author of a biography of a close friend. —**Bos·well·i·an** (boz·wel′i·ən), *adj.*

bot (bot), *n.* larva of a botfly. It is a parasite of horses, cattle, and sheep. Also, **bott.**

bot., botany.

bo·tan·i·cal (bə·tan′ə·kəl), **bo·tan·ic** (–tan′ik), *adj.* 1. having to do with plants. 2. having to do with botany. [< Med.L < Gk., < *botane* plant] —**bo·tan′i·cal·ly,** *adv.*

bot·a·nize (bot′ə·nīz), *v.,* –nized, –niz·ing. 1. study plants where they grow. 2. collect plants for study. 3. explore the plant life of.

bot·a·ny (bot′ə·ni), *n., pl.* –nies. 1. science of plants; study of plants and plant life. 2. textbook or manual of this science. 3. botanical facts. [< *botanic*] —**bot·a·nist** (bot′ə·nist), *n.*

Botany Bay, bay on the SE coast of Australia, near Sydney, site of a former penal colony.

botch (boch), *v.* 1. spoil by poor work; bungle. 2. patch or mend clumsily. —*n.* a clumsy patch. —**botch′er,** *n.* —**botch′er·y,** *n.* —**botch′y,** *adj.* [appar. < Irish *bodhar* deaf] —**botch′er·er,** *n.* —Syn. *v.* 1. annoy, vex.

both·er·a·tion (both′ər·ā′shən), *n., interj. Colloq.* bother.

both·er·some (both′ər·səm), *adj.* causing worry or fuss; troublesome. —Syn. annoying.

bott (bot), *n.* bot.

Bot·ti·cel·li (bot′ə·chel′ē), *n.* Sandro, 1444?–1510, Italian painter.

bot·tle (bot′əl), *n., v.,* –tled, –tling. —*n.* 1. container for holding liquids that has a narrow neck that can be closed with a stopper, and is usually without handles. 2. contents of a bottle. 3. amount that a bottle can hold. 4. the bottle, intoxicating liquor. —*v.* 1. put into bottles. 2. hold in; keep back; control. 3. bottle up, hold in; control. [< OF < VL *butticula,* dim. of LL *buttis* butt[3]] —**bot′tler,** *n.*

bot·tle·neck (bot′əl·nek′), *n.* 1. a narrow thoroughfare. 2. *Am.* a. person or thing that hinders progress. b. situation in which progress is hindered.

bot·tom (bot′əm), *n.* 1. the lowest part; lowest rank. 2. part on which anything rests. 3. ground under water. 4. the low land along a river. 5. buttocks. 6. seat: *this chair needs a new bottom.* 7. power of endurance. 8. basis; foundation; origin. 9. keel or hull of a ship; ship. 10. at bottom, fundamentally. 11. be at the bottom of, be the cause of. —*v.* 1. put a seat on. 2. understand fully. 3. set upon a foundation; base; rest. —*adj.* 1. lowest; last. 2. underlying; fundamental. [OE *botm*] —**bot′tom·less,** *adj.* —Syn. *n.* 8. groundwork, base.

bot·u·lism (boch′ə·liz·əm), *n.* poisoning caused by a toxin formed in food that has been infected by certain bacteria. [< L *botulus* sausage; orig. attributed esp. to sausages]

bou·clé (bü·klā′), *n.* 1. a knitted cloth having a surface with tiny loops and curls. 2. yarn used in making such a surface. —*adj.* of cloth having such a surface. [< F, buckled]

bou·doir (bü′dwär; –dwôr; bü·dwär′; –dwôr′), *n.* a lady's private sitting room or dressing room. [< F, < *bouder* sulk]

bough (bou), *n.* 1. one of the main branches of a tree. 2. branch cut from a tree. [OE *bōg* bough, shoulder] —**bough′less,** *adj.*

bought (bôt), *v.* pt. and pp. of **buy.**

bought·en (bôt′ən), *adj. Dial.* bought; not homemade.

bouil·lon (bùl′yon; –yən), *n.* a clear, thin soup. [< F, < *bouillir* boil < L *bullire*]

boul·der (bōl′dər), *n.* a large, detached rock, esp. one rounded or worn by the action of water or weather. Also, **bowlder.** [for *boulderstone* < Scand. (Sw.) *bullersten* < *bullra* roar + *sten* stone]

Boulder Dam, Hoover Dam.

boul·e·vard (bùl′ə·värd; bùl′lə–), *n.* a broad street. [< F < Gmc. See BULWARK.]

bounce (bouns), *v.,* bounced, bounc·ing, *n.* —*v.* 1. bound like a ball. 2. cause to bounce. 3. spring suddenly. 4. burst noisily, angrily, etc. 5. *Colloq.* throw out. 6. *Am., Slang.* discharge from work or employment. —*n.* 1. a bound; a spring; a bouncing. 2. capacity to bound; resilience. 3. *Colloq.* liveliness. 4. a boasting; a bragging. 5. *Am., Slang.* discharge from work or employment. [cf. Du. *bonzen* thump] —**bounc′er,** *n.* —Syn. *v.* 3. leap.

bounc·ing (boun′sing), *adj.* 1. that bounces. 2. big; strong. 3. vigorous; healthy.

bound[1] (bound), *v.* pt. and pp. of **bind.** —*adj.* 1. put in covers: *a bound book.* 2. under obligation; obliged. 3. certain; sure. 4. determined; resolved. 5. **bound up in** or **with,** a. closely connected with. b. very devoted to. [pp. of *bind*]

bound[2] (bound), *v.* 1. leap; spring lightly along; jump: *bounding deer.* 2. leap or spring upward or onward. 3. spring back; bounce: *the ball bounded from the wall.* —*n.* 1. leap or spring upward or onward. 2. spring back; bounce. [< F *bondir* leap, orig., resound, ? < L *bombus.* See BOMB.]

bound[3] (bound), *n.* 1. Usually, **bounds.** boundary; limiting line; limit. 2. **bounds,** a. land on or near a boundary. b. area included within boundaries. —*v.* 1. limit as by bounds. 2. form the boundary or limit of. 3. name the boundaries of: *bound the State of Maine.* 4. have its boundary (*on*). [< OF < LL *butina*] —**bound′less,** *adj.* —**bound′less·ly,** *adv.* —**bound′less·ness,** *n.* —Syn. *n.* 1. border, confine.

bound[4] (bound), *adj.* ready or intending to go: *I am bound for home.* [< Scand. *būinn,* pp. of *būa* get ready]

bound·a·ry (boun′də·ri; -dri), *n.*, *pl.* **–ries.** a limiting line; limit; border.

bound·en (boun′dən), *adj.* 1. required; obligatory. 2. under obligation; obliged. [pp. of *bind*] —Syn. 1. indebted.

bound·er (boun′dər), *n. Esp. Brit. Colloq.* a rude, vulgar person; upstart; cad.

boun·te·ous (boun′ti-əs), *adj.* 1. generous; giving freely. 2. plentiful; abundant. —**boun′te·ous·ly,** *adv.* —**boun′te·ous·ness,** *n.* —Syn. 1. liberal. 2. copious, ample.

boun·ti·ful (boun′tə·fəl), *adj.* bounteous. —**boun′ti·ful·ly,** *adv.* —**boun′ti·ful·ness,** *n.*

boun·ty (boun′ti), *n.*, *pl.* **–ties.** 1. generosity. 2. a generous gift. 3. a reward. [< OF < L *bonitas* < *bonus* good] —Syn. 1. munificence, liberality.

bou·quet (bō·kā′, bū·kā′ for 2), *n.* 1. bunch of flowers. 2. characteristic fragrance; aroma. [< F, little wood, dim. of OF *bosc* wood. See BUSH[1].]

Bour·bon (bûr′bən, *occas.* bēr′- *for 1 and 2*; bēr′bən *for 3*), *n.* 1. member of a former royal family of France, Spain, Naples, and Sicily. 2. *Am.* an extreme conservative. 3. Also, **bourbon.** kind of whiskey. —**Bour′bon·ism,** *n.* —**Bour′bon·ist,** *n.*

bour·geois (bûr·zhwä′; bûr′zhwä), *n.*, *pl.* **-geois,** *adj.* —*n.* 1. person of the middle class. 2. any property owner. —*adj.* 1. of the middle class. 2. like the middle class; ordinary. [< F < LL *burgensis* < *burgus* fort < Gmc.]

bour·geoi·sie (bûr′zhwä·zē′), *n.* 1. people of the middle class. 2. the opposite of the proletariat.

bourn[1], bourne[1] (bōrn; bôrn), *n.* brook. [OE *burna*]

bourn[2], bourne[2] (bōrn; bôrn; bûrn), *n.* 1. *Archaic.* boundary; limit. 2. goal. [< F *borne.* Akin to BOUND[3].]

bourse (bûrs), *n.* stock exchange in Paris and other European cities. [< F, orig., purse, < LL *bursa* < Gk. *byrsa* hide]

bout (bout), *n.* 1. a trial of strength; contest. 2. a time of activity of any kind: *a long bout of house cleaning.* 3. a spell or fit of anything: *a bout of sickness.* [var. of *bought* a bending, turn; akin to BOW[1]]

bou·ton·niere, bou·ton·nière (bü′tə·nyâr′), *n.* flower or flowers worn in a buttonhole. [< F, buttonhole. See BUTTON.]

bo·vine (bō′vīn; -vin), *adj.* 1. of an ox or cow; like an ox or cow. 2. slow; stupid. 3. without emotion; stolid. —*n.* ox, cow, etc. [< LL *bovinus* < L *bos* ox, cow]

bow[1] (bou), *v.* 1. bend the head or body in greeting, respect, worship, or submission. 2. show by bowing: *bow one's thanks.* 3. bend; stoop. 4. submit; yield. —*n.* act of bowing. [OE *būgan*] —**bow′er,** *n.* —Syn. *v.* nod, curtsy.

bow[2] (bō), *n.* 1. weapon for shooting arrows, consisting of a strip of elastic wood bent by a string. 2. curve; bend. 3. a bowknot: *a bow of ribbon.* 4. a slender rod with horsehairs stretched on it, for playing a violin, etc. 5. something curved; curved part, as a rainbow. —*v.* 1. curve; bend. 2. play (a violin, etc.) with a bow. [OE *boga*] —**bow′less,** *adj.* —**bow′like′,** *adj.*

bow[3] (bou), *n.* the forward part of a ship, boat, or airship. [prob. < LG or Scand. orig.; akin to BOUGH]

bowd·ler·ize (boud′lər·īz), *v.*, **-ized, -iz·ing.** expurgate. [for Dr. T. *Bowdler*, who published an expurgated Shakespeare in 1818] —**bowd′ler·ism,** *n.* —**bowd′ler·i·za′tion,** *n.*

bow·el (bou′əl), *n.* 1. *Anat.* a. an intestine. b. Usually, **bowels.** tube in the body into which food passes from the stomach; intestines. 2. **bowels,** a. inner part: *the bowels of the earth.* b. *Archaic.* pity; tender feelings. [< OF < L *botellus,* dim. of *botulus* sausage]

bow·er[1] (bou′ər), *n.* 1. shelter of leafy branches. 2. summerhouse or arbor. 3. *Archaic.* bedroom. [OE *būr* dwelling] —**bow′er·like′,** *adj.*

bow·er[2] (bou′ər), *n. Am.* the high card in certain games. [< G *bauer* jack (in cards); peasant]

bow·er·y (bou′ər·i), *adj.* leafy; shady.

bow·fin (bō′fin′), *n. Am.* a North American fresh-water ganoid fish.

bow·ie knife (bō′i; bū′i), *Am.* a long, single-edged hunting knife carried in a sheath. [named for Col. J. *Bowie,* U.S. pioneer]

bow·knot (bō′not′), *n.* a looped slipknot, such as is made in tying shoelaces, usually with loops and two ends.

Single bowknot

bowl[1] (bōl), *n.* 1. a hollow, rounded dish. 2. amount that a bowl can hold. 3. a hollow, rounded part: *the bowl of a spoon or a pipe.* 4. a large drinking cup. 5. drink. 6. drinking. 7. formation or structure shaped like a bowl, as an amphitheater. [OE *bolla*] —**bowl′like′,** *adj.*

bowl[2] (bōl), *n.* 1. a wooden ball used in games. 2. a turn in the game of bowls. —*v.* 1. play the game of bowls; roll a ball in the game of bowls. 2. throw (the ball) to the batsman in the game of cricket. 3. roll or move along rapidly and smoothly. 4. **bowl down,** knock down. 5. **bowl over,** a. knock over. b. *Colloq.* make helpless and confused. [< F < L *bulla* ball, bubble] —**bowl′er,** *n.*

bowl·der (bōl′dər), *n.* boulder.

bow·leg (bō′leg′), *n.* an outward curve of the legs. —**bow·leg·ged** (bō′leg′id; -legd′), *adj.*

bow·line (bō′lən; -līn), *n.* 1. Also, **bowline knot.** knot used in making a loop. 2. *Naut.* rope to hold a sail steady when sailing into the wind.

Bowline knot

bowl·ing (bōl′ing), *n.* 1. game of bowls. 2. *U.S. and Canada.* tenpins. 3. playing the game of bowls.

bowling alley, *U.S.* a long, narrow, enclosed floor for bowling.

bowls (bōlz), *n.* 1. game played by rolling with a lopsided or weighted wooden ball toward a stationary ball. 2. ninepins or tenpins. [pl. of *bowl[2]*]

bow·man (bō′mən), *n.*, *pl.* **-men.** archer.

bow·shot (bō′shot′), *n.* distance that a bow will shoot an arrow.

bow·sprit (bou′sprit; bō′-), *n. Naut.* pole or spar projecting forward from the bow of a ship. Ropes from it help to steady sails and masts. [prob. < LG or Du. See BOW[3], SPRIT.]

BOWSPRIT

BOBSTAY

bow·string (bō′string′), *n.* 1. a strong cord stretched from the ends of a bow. 2. cord like this.

box[1] (boks), *n.* 1. container made of wood, metal, paper, etc., to pack or put things in. 2. amount that a box can hold. 3. a small boxlike space with chairs at a theater, etc. 4. an enclosed space for a jury, witnesses, etc. 5. a small shelter. 6. anything shaped or used like a box. 7. a hollow part that encloses or protects some piece of machinery. 8. the driver's seat on a coach, carriage, etc. 9. *Am., Baseball.* place where the batter, or sometimes the pitcher or coach, stands. 10. compartment for a horse in a stable or car. 11. space in a newspaper, magazine, etc. set off by enclosing lines. 12. a Christmas present; a present. 13. an awkward situation. 14. *Am.* cavity in a maple or pine for collecting sap or turpentine. 15. *Am.* receptacle in a post office for a subscriber's mail. —*v.* 1. pack in a box; put into a box. 2. provide with a box. 3. *Am.* make a box in a tree in which to collect sap or turpentine. 4. **box the compass,** a. name the points of the compass in order. b. go all the way around and end up where one started. 5. **box up,** shut in; keep from getting out. [specialization of meaning of *box[3]*] —**box′-like′,** *adj.* —Syn. *n.* 1. receptacle, chest, carton.

box[2] (boks), *n.* blow with the open hand or the fist, esp. on the ear. —*v.* 1. strike such a blow. 2. fight with the fists.

box[3] (boks), *n.* 1. shrub or small, bushy tree that stays green all winter, much used for hedges, etc. 2. its hard, durable wood. [< L < Gk. *pyxos*]

box·car (boks'kär'), *n. Am.* a railroad freight car enclosed on all sides.

box elder, *Am.* a maple tree of North America, often grown for shade or ornament.

box·er (bok'sər), *n.* 1. man who fights with his fists in padded gloves according to special rules. 2. a dog with a smooth brown coat, related to the bulldog and terrier.

box·ing (bok'sing), *n.* act of fighting with the fists.

boxing gloves, padded gloves worn when boxing.

box office, 1. place where tickets are sold in a theater, hall, etc. 2. money taken in at the box office.

box score, *Am.* tabular record of the plays of a baseball game arranged by the players.

box seat, a seat in a box of a theater, etc.

box·wood (boks'wŭd'), *n. Am.* box³.

boy (boi), *n.* 1. a male child from birth to about eighteen. 2. a male servant, esp. a native servant in India, China, etc. 3. a familiar term for a man. —Syn. 1. lad, youngster, youth.

boy·cott (boi'kot), *v.* 1. combine against and have nothing to do with (a person, business, nation, etc.) as a means of intimidation or coercion. 2. refuse to buy or use (a product, etc.). —*n.* a boycotting. [for Captain *Boycott*, first man so treated] —**boy'cott·er,** *n.*

boy friend, *Am., Colloq.* a girl's sweetheart or steady male companion.

boy·hood (boi'hŭd), *n.* 1. time or condition of being a boy. 2. boys as a group.

boy·ish (boi'ish), *adj.* 1. of a boy. 2. like a boy. 3. like a boy's. 4. fit for a boy. —**boy'ish·ly,** *adv.* —**boy'ish·ness,** *n.*

boy scout, member of the Boy Scouts.

Boy Scouts, organization for boys that develops manly qualities and usefulness to others.

boy·sen·ber·ry (boi'zən·ber'i), *n., pl.* **-ries.** *Am.* a purple berry like a blackberry in size and shape, and like a raspberry in flavor.

Br., *Chem.* bromine.

Br., Britain; British.

bra (brä), *n. Colloq.* brassière.

Bra·bant (brə·bant'; brä'bənt), *n.* region in the S Netherlands and N Belgium.

brace (brās), *n., v.,* **braced, brac·ing.** —*n.* 1. thing that holds parts together or in place, as a clamp, an iron frame to hold the ankle straight, etc. 2. anything that gives steadiness or rigidity. 3. pair; couple: *a brace of ducks.* 4. handle for a tool or drill used for boring. 5. either of these signs { } used to enclose words, figures, staves in music, etc. 6. **braces,** *Brit.* suspenders. 7. Often, **braces,** a metal wire used to straighten crooked teeth. [< v., but partly < OF *brace* the two arms] —*v.* 1. give strength or firmness to; support. 2. hold or fix firmly in place. 3. brace up, *Am., Colloq.* summon one's strength or courage. 4. stimulate: *the cold air braced him.* 5. furnish with braces. 6. make tight or taut. [< OF *bracier* embrace < *brace* the two arms < L *bracchia,* pl. < Gk. *brachion*]

brace·let (brās'lit), *n.* band or chain worn for ornament around the wrist or arm. [< OF, dim. of *bracel* < L *bracchium* arm < Gk. *brachion*] —**brace'let·ed,** *adj.*

brac·er (brās'ər), *n.* 1. one that braces. 2. *U.S. Colloq.* stimulating drink.

brach·i·o·pod (brak'i·ə·pod'; brā'ki-), *n. Zool.* sea animal with upper and lower shells and a pair of armlike tentacles, one on each side of its mouth. [< NL < Gk. *brachion* arm + *pous* foot]

brach·y·ce·phal·ic (brak'i·sə·fal'ik), **brach·y·ceph·a·lous** (brak'i·sef'ə·ləs), *adj.* having a short, broad head. [< Gk. *brachys* short + *kephale* head]

brac·ing (brās'ing), *adj.* giving strength and energy; refreshing. —*n.* brace or braces. —**brac'ing·ly,** *adv.*

brack·en (brak'ən), *n. Brit.* 1. a large fern. 2. growth of these ferns. [ME *braken,* appar. < Scand.]

brack·et (brak'it), *n.* 1. a flat piece of stone, wood, or metal projecting from a wall as a support for a shelf, a statue, etc. 2. support in the shape of a right triangle. 3. either of these signs [ ], used to enclose words or figures. 4. group thought of together or mentioned together: *in the low-income bracket.* —*v.* 1. support with brackets. 2. enclose within brackets. 3. think of together; mention together; group. [< F < Sp. *bragueta,* dim. of *braga* < L *bracae* breeches < Celtic] ▸ **Brackets [ ]** are rarely used in general writing and are not in the standard typewriter keyboard, but in much academic and professional writing they have specific and convenient uses. Brackets are primarily editorial marks, used to show where some explanation or comment has been added to the text, especially to quoted matter. In quoting material *sic* in brackets is sometimes used to indicate that an error was in the original: *"New Haven, Connecticut* [*sic*]*."* Or a correction may be inserted in brackets: *"When he was thirty-eight* [*Actually he was forty-three*] *he published his first novel."* In many of the usage notes in this dictionary, brackets are used in examples of faulty writing to enclose words that might better be left out, or to suggest an improved expression: *Throughout* [the course of] *the year I read such books as "Oliver Twist" and "Boots and Saddles." The continuously moving belt makes a noise similar to* [like] *a cement mixer.*

brack·ish (brak'ish), *adj.* 1. somewhat salty. 2. distasteful; unpleasant. —**brack'ish·ness,** *n.*

bract (brakt), *n. Bot.* a small leaf at the base of a flower or flower stalk. [< L *bractea* thin metal plate] —**brac·te·al** (brak'ti·əl), *adj.* —**bract'less,** *adj.*

brad (brad), *n.* a small, thin nail with a small head. [var. of *brod* < Scand. *broddr* spike]

brad·awl (brad'ôl'), *n.* awl with a cutting edge for making holes for brads, etc.

brae (brā), *n. Scot.* slope; hillside.

brag (brag), *n., v.,* **bragged, brag·ging.** —*n.* 1. boast. 2. boasting. —*v.* boast. [cf. Scand. *bragga sig* recover heart] —**brag'ger,** *n.*

brag·ga·do·ci·o (brag'ə·dō'shi·ō), *n., pl.* **-ci·os.** 1. boasting; bragging. 2. boaster; braggart. [coined by Spenser as name of character in his *Faerie Queene*]

brag·gart (brag'ərt), *n.* boaster. —*adj.* boastful. [< F *bragard* < *braguer* brag] —**brag'gart·ism,** *n.*

Brah·ma (brä'mə *for 1;* brä'mə, brä'mə *for 2*), *n.* 1. in Hindu theology: a. the god of creation. b. impersonal and absolute divinity. 2. *Am.* species of cattle, originally imported from India.

Brah·man (brä'mən), *n., pl.* **-mans.** member of the priestly caste, the highest caste or class in India. Also, **Brahmin.** —**Brah·man·ic** (brä·man'ik), **Brah·man'i·cal,** *adj.* —**Brah'man·ism,** *n.* —**Brah'man·ist,** *n.*

Brah·min (brä'mən), *n., pl.* **-min.** 1. Brahman. 2. a cultured, highly intellectual person, often snobbish. —**Brah·min·ic** (brä·min'ik), **Brah·min'i·cal,** *adj.* —**Brah'min·ism,** *n.* —**Brah'min·ist,** *n.*

Brahms (brämz), *n.* Johannes, 1833–1897, German composer of music.

braid (brād), *n.* 1. band formed by weaving together three or more strands of hair, ribbon, straw, etc. 2. a narrow band of fabric used to trim or bind clothing. —*v.* 1. form by weaving together three or more strands of hair, etc. 2. trim or bind with braid. [OE *bregdan*] —**braid'er,** *n.* —Syn. *v.* 1. plait, entwine.

Braille, braille (brāl), *n.* system of writing and printing for blind people. The letters in Braille are made of raised points and are read by touching them. [for Louis *Braille,* French teacher of the blind]

brain (brān), *n.* 1. mass of nerve tissue enclosed in the skull or head of vertebrate animals. The brain is used in feeling and thinking. 2. Usually, **brains.** mind; intelligence. —*v.* dash out the brains of. [OE *brægen*]

brain·less (brān'lis), *adj.* 1. without a brain.

2. stupid; foolish. —**brain′less·ly**, adv. —**brain′-less·ness**, n.

brain·pan (brān′pan′), n. cranium.

brain·sick (brān′sik′), adj. crazy; insane. —**brain′sick′ly**, adv. —**brain′sick′ness**, n.

brain storm, Colloq. a sudden inspired idea.

brain trust, Am. a group of experts acting as advisers to an administrator, a political leader, or an executive. —**brain truster**, Am.

brain·wash·ing (brān′wosh′ing; -wôsh′-), n. the process of purging the brain of one's previous historical and social convictions in order to accept different views (applied esp. to Communist indoctrination procedures in China).

brain·y (brān′i), adj., **brain·i·er**, **brain·i·est**. Colloq. intelligent; clever. —**brain′i·ness**, n.

braise (brāz), v., **braised**, **brais·ing**. brown (meat) quickly and then cook it long and slowly in a covered pan with very little water. [< F braiser < braise hot charcoal < Gmc.]

brake[1] (brāk), n., v., **braked**, **brak·ing**. —n. 1. anything used to check by pressing or scraping or by rubbing against. 2. tool or machine for breaking up flax or hemp into fibers. —v. 1. slow up or stop by using a brake. 2. use a brake on. 3. break up (flax or hemp) into fibers. [< MLG or ODu. braeke; akin to BREAK]

brake[2] (brāk), n. a thick growth of bushes; thicket. [cf. MLG brake]

brake[3] (brāk), n. large, coarse fern. [prob. var. of bracken]

brake[4] (brāk), v. Archaic. pt. of break.

brake·man (brāk′mən), n., pl. -men. Am. man who works brakes and helps the conductor of a railroad train.

bram·ble (bram′bəl), n. 1. a prickly shrub of the rose family, such as the blackberry or raspberry. 2. any rough, prickly shrub. [OE brēmel < brōm BROOM] —**bram′bly**, adj.

bran (bran), n. the broken covering of wheat, rye, etc., separated from the flour. [< OF]

branch (branch; bränch), n. 1. part of a tree growing out from the trunk; any woody part of a tree above the ground except the trunk; bough; twig. 2. any division that resembles a branch of a tree: a branch of a river. 3. division; part: history is a branch of learning. 4. a local office: a branch of a bank. 5. a line of family descent. —v. 1. put out branches; spread in branches. 2. divide into branches. 3. branch out, a. put out branches. b. extend business, interests, activities, etc. [< OF branche < LL branca paw]

brand (brand), n. 1. piece of wood that is burning or partly burned. 2. mark made by burning the skin with a hot iron. Cattle and horses on big ranches are marked with brands to show who owns them. 3. Am., Western. herd of cattle with a distinctive brand. 4. an iron stamp for burning a mark. 5. a certain kind, grade, or make as indicated by a stamp, trademark, etc.: a brand of coffee. 6. trademark. 7. mark of disgrace. 8. Archaic and Poetic. sword. —v. 1. mark by burning the skin with a hot iron. 2. put a mark of disgrace on. [OE] —**brand′er**, n.

Bran·den·burg (bran′dən·bėrg), n. 1. district in N Germany. 2. city in N Germany.

bran·died (bran′did), adj. prepared, mixed, or flavored with brandy.

bran·dish (bran′dish), v. wave or shake threateningly; flourish: brandish a sword. —n. threatening shake; flourish. [< OF brandir < brand sword < Gmc.] —**bran′dish·er**, n.

brand-new (brand′nü′; -nū′), **bran-new** (bran′nü′; -nū′), adj. very new; entirely new.

bran·dy (bran′di), n., pl. -dies, v., -died, -dy-ing. —n. 1. strong alcoholic liquor made from wine. 2. Am. similar alcoholic liquor made from fruit juice. —v. mix, flavor, or preserve with brandy. [< Du. brandewijn burnt (i.e., distilled) wine]

brant (brant), n., pl. brants or (esp. collectively) brant. a small, dark, wild goose.

brash (brash), adj. 1. hasty; rash. 2. impudent; saucy. —n. rush or dash. —**brash′y**, adj.

bra·sier (brā′zhər), n. brazier.

brass (bras; bräs), n. 1. yellow metal that is an alloy of copper and zinc. 2. thing made of brass. 3. Also, brasses. the brass winds. 4. Colloq. shamelessness; impudence. 5. Am., Slang. high-ranking military officers (in allusion to their gold braid). —adj. made of brass. [OE brœs]

bras·sard (bras′ärd), n. 1. band worn above the elbow as a badge. 2. Also, bras·sart (bras′ərt). armor for the upper part of the arm. [< F, < bras arm]

brass·ie, **brass·y** (bras′i; bräs′i), n., pl. brass·ies. golf club with a wooden head on the bottom of which is a metal plate.

bras·sière (brə·zir′), n. a bust support worn by women. [< F, bodice, < bras arm]

brass knuckles, Am. a protective metal device for the knuckles, used in fighting.

brass winds, metal musical instruments that are played by blowing, such as trumpets or trombones. —**brass′-wind′**, adj.

brass·y (bras′i; bräs′i), adj. brass·i·er, brass·i·est. 1. of or like brass. 2. loud and harsh. 3. Colloq. shameless; impudent. —**brass′i·ness**, n.

brat (brat), n. Contemptuous use. child. [cf. OE bratt cloak, covering]

bra·va·do (brə·vä′dō), n., pl. -does, -dos. a boastful defiance without much real desire to fight. [< Sp. bravada. See BRAVE.]

brave (brāv), adj., brav·er, brav·est, n., v., braved, brav·ing. —adj. 1. without fear; having courage. 2. making a fine appearance; showy. 3. Archaic. fine; excellent. —n. 1. a brave person. 2. Am. a North American Indian warrior. —v. 1. meet without fear. 2. dare; defy. [< F < Ital. bravo brave, bold < Sp., vicious (as applied to bulls), ? < L pravus] marauding —**brave′ly**, adv. —**brave′ness**, n. —Syn. adj. 1. fearless, courageous, valiant. —Ant. adj. 1. cowardly, fearful.

brav·er·y (brāv′ər·i), n., pl. -er·ies. 1. fearlessness; courage. 2. showy dress; finery. —Syn. 1. intrepidity, boldness, daring, pluck.

bra·vo (brä′vō), interj., n., pl. -vos. —interj. well done! fine! —n. cry of "bravo!" [< Ital. See BRAVE.]

bra·vu·ra (brə·vyŭr′ə), n. 1. Music. piece requiring skill and spirit in the performer. 2. display of daring; dash; spirit. [< Ital., bravery. See BRAVE.]

braw (brô; brä), adj. Scot. 1. making a fine appearance. 2. excellent; fine. [var. of brave]

brawl (brôl), n. noisy quarrel. —v. quarrel noisily. [ME brallen < brawl brawler]

brawn (brôn), n. muscle; firm, strong muscles; muscular strength. [< OF braon < Gmc.]

brawn·y (brôn′i), adj., brawn·i·er, brawn·i·est. strong; muscular. —**brawn′i·ness**, n. —Syn. sinewy, powerful.

bray (brā), n. 1. the loud, harsh sound made by a donkey. 2. noise like it. —v. 1. make a loud, harsh sound. 2. utter in a loud, harsh voice. [< F braire] —**bray′er**, n.

Braz., Brazil; Brazilian.

braze[1] (brāz), v., brazed, braz·ing. 1. cover or decorate with brass. 2. make like brass. [OE brasian < brœs brass]

braze[2] (brāz), v., brazed, braz·ing. solder with brass or other hard solder. [? < F braser < OF, burn]

bra·zen (brā′zən), adj. 1. made of brass. 2. like brass in color or strength. 3. loud and harsh. 4. shameless; impudent. —v. 1. make shameless or impudent. 2. brazen out or through, face boldly or shamelessly. [OE brœsen < brœs brass] —**bra′zen·ly**, adv. —**bra′zen·ness**, n.

bra·zier[1] (brā′zhər), n. a metal container to hold burning charcoal or coal, used for heating rooms. Also, **brasier**. [< F brasier < braise hot coals]

bra·zier[2] (brā′zhər), n. person who works with brass. Also, **brasier**. [< braze[1]]

Bra·zil (brə·zil′), n. the largest country in South America. —**Bra·zil·ian** (brə·zil′yən), adj., n.

Brazil nut, a large, triangular nut of a tree growing in Brazil.

āge, cāre, fär; ēqual, tėrm; īce; ōpen, ôrder; put, rüle, ūse; th, then; ə=a in about.

breach (brēch), *n.* 1. opening made by breaking down something solid; gap. 2. a broken or injured spot; break; rupture. 3. breaking (of a law, promise, duty, etc.); neglect. 4. breaking of friendly relations; quarrel. —*v.* break through; make an opening in. [< OF *breche* < Gmc.] —**Syn.** *n.* 1. fracture, crack, rent.

breach of promise, breaking of a promise to marry.

breach of the peace, public disturbance.

bread (bred), *n.* 1. food made of flour or meal mixed with milk or water and baked. 2. food; livelihood. 3. **break bread, a.** share a meal. **b.** take Communion. —*v.* cover with bread crumbs before cooking. [OE *brēad*] —**bread′less,** *adj.*

bread·board (bred′bôrd′; -bōrd′), *n.* 1. *Am.* board on which dough is kneaded, pastry is rolled, etc. 2. board on which bread is cut.

bread·fruit (bred′früt′), *n.* a large, round, starchy, tropical fruit of the Pacific Islands, much used, baked or roasted, for food.

bread line, *Am.* line of people waiting to get food given as charity or relief.

bread·stuff (bred′stuf′), *n. Am.* 1. grain, flour, or meal for making bread. 2. bread.

breadth (bredth; bretth), *n.* 1. how broad a thing is; distance across; width. 2. piece of a certain width: *a breadth of cloth.* 3. freedom from narrowness. 4. spaciousness; extent. [< OE *brǣdu* < *brād* broad] —**Syn.** 3. latitude, liberality, tolerance. 4. amplitude.

breadth·ways (bredth′wāz′; bretth′-), *adv.* in the direction of the breadth.

bread·win·ner (bred′win′ər), *n.* one who earns a living for those dependent on him.

break (brāk), *v.,* **broke** or (*Archaic*) **brake, bro·ken** or (*Archaic*) **broke, break·ing,** *n.* —*v.* 1. make come to pieces by a blow or pull; divide into two or more parts. 2. come apart; crack; burst. 3. bruise; abrade. 4. interrupt; disturb: *break silence.* 5. *Elect.* open (a circuit). 6. destroy evenness, wholeness, etc.: *break a five-dollar bill.* 7. injure; damage; ruin; destroy. 8. cause to be declared invalid: *break a will.* 9. make or become bankrupt; ruin financially. 10. fail to keep; act against: *break a law.* 11. force one's way: *break into a house.* 12. come suddenly. 13. change suddenly. 14. *Am.* of stocks, bonds, etc., decline suddenly and sharply in price. 15. fail suddenly in health. 16. of a voice or wind instrument, change in register or tone. 17. *Am., Baseball.* of a pitch, swerve or curve at or near the plate. 18. lessen the force of. 19. become weak; give way. 20. of the heart, be overcome by grief. 21. stop; put an end to. 22. reduce in rank. 23. train to obey; tame: *break a colt.* 24. train away from a habit or practice: *break a child of lying.* 25. go beyond; exceed: *break a record.* 26. dig or plow (ground). 27. make known; reveal. 28. *Am.* make a rush towards; dash; run (*for, to*). 29. **break down, a.** have an accident; fail to work. **b.** collapse; become weak; lose one's health. **c.** begin to cry. 30. **break in, a.** prepare for work or use; train. **b.** enter by force. **c.** interrupt. 31. **break out, a.** start; begin. **b.** have pimples, rashes, etc., on the skin. 32. **break up, a.** *Colloq.* a. scatter. **b.** stop; put an end to. **c.** upset; disturb greatly. —*n.* 1. act or fact of breaking. 2. a broken place; gap, crack. 3. interruption. 4. act of forcing one's way out. 5. an abrupt or marked change. 6. *Am.* a sudden sharp decline in the prices of stocks, etc. 7. sharp change in direction of a pitched or bowled ball. 8. *Am., Slang.* an awkward remark; mistake in manners. 9. *Am., Slang.* chance; opportunity. 10. opening in an electric circuit. [OE *brecan*] —**break′a·ble,** *adj.* —**Syn.** *v.* 1. shatter, burst, smash. 2. split, splinter. 10. violate, disobey. —*n.* 1. rupture, shattering.

break·age (brāk′ij), *n.* 1. act of breaking; break. 2. damage or loss caused by breaking. 3. allowance made for such damage or loss.

break·down (brāk′doun′), *n.* 1. failure to work. 2. loss of health; collapse. 3. *Am.* a noisy, lively dance. 4. analysis, as of a total.

break·er (brāk′ər), *n.* 1. wave that breaks into foam on the shore, rocks, etc. 2. machine for breaking things into smaller pieces.

break·fast (brek′fəst), *n.* the first meal of the day. —*v.* eat breakfast. [< *break* + *fast²*] —**break′fast·er,** *n.* —**break′fast·less,** *adj.*

break·neck (brāk′nek′), *adj.* likely to cause a broken neck; very dangerous.

break·through (brāk′thrü′), *n. Mil.* an offensive operation that pierces a defensive system and reaches the unorganized area behind it.

break·up (brāk′up′), *n.* 1. collapse; decay. 2. separation. 3. end.

break·wa·ter (brāk′wô′tər; -wot′ər), *n.* wall or barrier to break the force of waves.

bream (brēm), *n., pl.* **breams** or (*esp. collectively*) **bream.** 1. carp of inland European waters. 2. any of various related fishes. 3. *Am.* the common fresh-water sunfish. [< F *brème* < Gmc.]

breast (brest), *n.* 1. *Anat.* the upper, front part of the human body; chest. 2. *Zool.* the corresponding part in animals. 3. the upper, front part of a coat, dress, etc. 4. a front or forward part. 5. *Anat., Zool.* gland that gives milk. 6. heart; feelings. 7. **make a clean breast of,** confess completely. —*v. U.S.* struggle with; advance against; oppose; face. [OE *brēost*]

breast·bone (brest′bōn′), *n. Anat., Zool.* the thin, flat bone in the front of the chest to which the ribs are attached; sternum.

breast·pin (brest′pin′), *n. Am.* ornamental pin worn on the breast; brooch.

breast·plate (brest′plāt′), *n.* armor for the chest.

BREASTPLATE

breast·work (brest′wèrk′), *n.* a low, hastily built wall for defense.

breath (breth), *n.* 1. air drawn into and forced out of the lungs. 2. act of breathing. 3. moisture from breathing: *you can see your breath on a very cold day.* 4. ability to breathe easily: *out of breath.* 5. pause; respite. 6. a slight movement in the air; light breeze. 7. utterance; whisper. 8. life. 9. act of breathing out air without motion of the vocal cords, producing a hiss, puff, etc. 10. fragrance given off by flowers, etc. 11. **below** or **under one's breath,** in a whisper. [OE *brǣth* odor, steam]

breathe (brēth), *v.,* **breathed, breath·ing.** 1. draw (air) into the lungs and force it out. 2. stop for breath; rest; allow to rest and breathe. 3. put out of breath. 4. blow lightly. 5. say softly; whisper; utter. 6. be alive; live. 7. *Phonet.* utter with the breath and not with the voice. 8. draw into the lungs; inhale. 9. send out from the lungs; exhale. 10. send out; infuse: *breathe new life into tired soldiers.* 11. exhale an odor: *roses breathe fragrance.* 12. **breathe again** or **freely,** be relieved; feel easy. —**breath′a·ble,** *adj.*

breath·er (brēth′ər), *n.* 1. a short stop for breath; rest. 2. person or thing that breathes.

breath·ing (brēth′ing), *n.* 1. respiration. 2. a single breath. 3. time needed for a single breath. 4. remark; utterance. 5. a slight breeze. 6. aspiration; desire. 7. sound of the letter *h*.

breath·less (breth′lis), *adj.* 1. out of breath. 2. unable to breathe freely because of fear, interest, or excitement. 3. without breath; dead. 4. without a breeze. —**breath′less·ly,** *adv.* —**breath′less·ness,** *n.*

breath·tak·ing (breth′tāk′ing), *adj.* thrilling; exciting: *a breath-taking view.*

brec·ci·a (brech′i·ə; bresh′-), *n.* rock consisting of fragments of older rocks cemented together. [< Ital. < Gmc.; akin to BREAK]

bred (bred), *v.* pt. and pp. of **breed.**

breech (brēch), *n.* 1. the lower part; back part. 2. part of a gun behind the barrel. 3. rump; buttocks. [OE *brēc,* gen. and dat. of *brōc*]

breech·cloth (brēch′klôth′; -kloth′), **breech·clout** (-klout′), *n. Am.* cloth worn as a loincloth, esp. by Indians.

breech·es (brich′iz), *n.pl.* 1. short trousers reaching from the waist to the knees. 2. *Colloq.* trousers. [OE *brēc,* pl. of *brōc* BREECH]

breech·es buoy, *Naut.* pair of short canvas trousers fastened to a belt or life preserver. A breeches buoy slides along a rope on a pulley and is used to rescue people from sinking ships.

breech·ing (brich′ing; brēch′–), *n.* part of a harness that passes around a horse's rump.

breech·load·ing (brēch′lōd′ing), *adj.* of guns, loading from behind the barrel instead of at the mouth.

breed (brēd), *v.,* **bred, breed·ing,** *n.* —*v.* 1. produce (young). 2. raise (livestock, etc.). 3. produce; cause: *careless driving breeds accidents.* 4. be the native place or source of. 5. bring up; train. —*n.* 1. race; stock: *Jerseys and Guernseys are breeds of cattle.* 2. kind; sort. [OE *brēdan*] —**breed′er,** *n.* —**Syn.** *v.* 3. occasion. 5. educate, school.

breeder reactor or **pile,** *Nuclear Physics.* reactor which produces fissile material in excess of the amount required for the chain reaction.

breed·ing (brēd′ing), *n.* 1. producing offspring. 2. producing animals, esp. to get improved kinds. 3. bringing up; training; behavior; manners. 4. *Nuclear Physics.* the producing of a radioactive element at a rate exceeding the consumption of the original element used in the chain reaction.

breeze (brēz), *n., v.,* **breezed, breez·ing.** —*n.* a light wind. —*v. Am., Colloq.* proceed easily or briskly. [< OSp. and Pg. *briza* northeast wind] —**breeze′less,** *adj.*

breez·y (brēz′i), *adj.,* **breez·i·er, breez·i·est.** 1. with light winds blowing. 2. brisk; lively; jolly. —**breez′i·ly,** *adv.* —**breez′i·ness,** *n.*

Brem·en (brem′ən; brā′mən), *n.* city in NW Germany.

Bren·ner Pass (bren′ər), a mountain pass in the Alps between Austria and Italy.

Bres·lau (brez′lou; bres′–), *n.* German name of Wroclaw. The name still has fairly wide usage in western Europe and the United States.

Brest (brest), *n.* seaport in NW France.

Brest Li·tovsk (brest′ li·tôfsk′), city in W Russia.

breth·ren (breth′rən), *n.pl.* 1. brothers. 2. the fellow members of a church or society.

Bret·on (bret′ən), *n.* 1. native or inhabitant of Brittany. 2. language of Brittany. 3. Cape, the northeastern part of Nova Scotia. —*adj.* having to do with Brittany, its people, or their language.

breve (brēv), *n.* 1. curved mark (‿) put over a vowel or syllable to show that it is short. 2. *Music.* note equal to two whole notes. [< Ital. < L *brevis* short]

bre·vet (brə·vet′; *esp. Brit.* brev′it), *n., v.,* –**vet·ted,** –**vet·ting;** –**vet·ed,** –**vet·ing.** —*n.* commission promoting an army officer to a higher rank without an increase in pay. —*v.* give rank by a brevet. [< F, dim. of *bref* letter. See BRIEF.]

bre·vi·ar·y (brē′vi·er′i; brev′i–), *n., pl.* –**ar·ies.** book of prescribed prayers to be said daily by certain clergymen and religious of the Roman Catholic Church. [< L *breviarium* summary < *brevis* short]

brev·i·ty (brev′ə·ti), *n., pl.* –**ties.** shortness; briefness. [< L, < *brevis* short] —**Syn.** conciseness, terseness. —**Ant.** verbosity.

brew (brü), *v.* 1. make (beer, ale, etc.) by soaking, boiling, and fermenting. 2. make (a drink) by soaking, boiling, or mixing. 3. bring about; plan; plot: *boys brewing mischief.* 4. begin to form; gather: *a storm is brewing.* —*n.* 1. drink brewed. 2. quantity brewed at one time. [OE *brēowan*] —**brew′er,** *n.*

brew·er·y (brü′ər·i; brür′i), *n., pl.* –**er·ies.** place where beer, ale, etc., are brewed.

brew·ing (brü′ing), *n.* 1. preparing a brew. 2. amount brewed at one time.

bri·ar (brī′ər), *n.* brier. —**bri′ar·y,** *adj.*

bri·ar·wood (brī′ər·wùd′), *n.* brierwood.

bribe (brīb), *n., v.,* **bribed, brib·ing.** —*n.* 1. anything given or offered to get a person to do something that he thinks is wrong to do. 2. reward for doing something that a person does not want to do. —*v.* 1. offer a bribe to. 2. influence by giving a bribe. 3. give bribes. [? < OF, bit of

bread given to a beggar] —**brib′a·ble,** *adj.* —**brib′a·bil′i·ty,** *n.* —**brib′er,** *n.*

brib·er·y (brīb′ər·i), *n., pl.* –**er·ies.** 1. giving or offering a bribe. 2. taking a bribe.

bric-a-brac, bric-à-brac (brik′ə·brak′), *n.* interesting or curious knickknacks used as decorations. [< F]

brick (brik), *n.* 1. block of clay baked by sun or fire, used in building and paving. 2. bricks. 3. anything shaped like a brick. 4. *Slang.* a good fellow. —*adj.* made of bricks. —*v.* build or pave with bricks; wall in with bricks. [< F < MDu. *bricke*] —**brick′like′,** *adj.*

brick·bat (brik′bat′), *n.* 1. piece of broken brick. 2. *Colloq.* insult.

brick·lay·ing (brik′lā′ing), *n.* act or work of building with bricks. —**brick′lay′er,** *n.*

brick·work (brik′werk′), *n.* 1. thing made of bricks. 2. building with bricks; bricklaying.

brid·al (brīd′əl), *adj.* of a bride or a wedding. —*n.* wedding. [OE *brydealo* bride ale] —**brid′al·ly,** *adv.* —**Syn.** *adj.* nuptial.

bridal wreath, a kind of spiraea.

bride (brīd), *n.* woman just married or about to be married. [OE *bryd*]

bride·groom (brīd′grüm′; –grúm′), *n.* man just married or about to be married. [OE *brydguma* < *bryd* bride + *guma* man; infl. by *groom*]

brides·maid (brīdz′mād′), *n.* young, usually unmarried woman who attends the bride at a wedding.

bride·well (brīd′wel; –wəl), *n.* house of correction; jail.

bridge¹ (brij), *n., v.,* **bridged, bridg·ing.** —*n.* 1. structure built over a river, road, etc., so that people, trains, etc., can get across. 2. platform above the deck of a ship for the officer in command. 3. the upper, bony part of the nose. 4. mounting for false teeth fastened to real teeth near by. 5. a movable piece over which the strings of a violin, etc., are stretched. 6. any other thing like a bridge in form or use. —*v.* 1. build a bridge over. 2. extend over; span. 3. make a way over: *politeness will bridge many difficulties.* [OE *brycg*] —**bridge′a·ble,** *adj.* —**bridge′less,** *adj.*

bridge² (brij), *n.* 1. a card game for four players resembling whist, in which the dealer or his partner (the dummy) declares the trump, and the dealer plays both his own and his partner's hand. 2. auction bridge. 3. contract bridge.

bridge·head (brij′hed′), *n.* 1. fortification protecting the end of a bridge toward the enemy. 2. *Mil.* position obtained and held within enemy territory, used as a starting point for further attack. 3. either end of a bridge.

Bridge·port (brij′pôrt; –pōrt), *n.* city in SW Connecticut, on Long Island Sound.

bridge·work (brij′werk′), *n.* false teeth in a mounting fastened to real teeth near by.

bri·dle (brī′dəl), *n., v.,* –**dled, –dling.** —*n.* 1. head part of a horse's harness, used to hold back or control a horse. 2. anything that holds back or checks. —*v.* 1. put a bridle on. 2. hold back; check; control. 3. hold the head up high with the chin drawn back to express pride, vanity, scorn, or anger. [OE *bridel, brigdels* < *bregdan* braid] —**bri′dle·less,** *adj.* —**bri′dler,** *n.* —**Syn.** *v.* 2. curb, restrain.

Bridle

brief (brēf), *adj.* 1. lasting only a short time. 2. using few words. —*n.* 1. short statement; summary. 2. *Law.* a. a writ. b. statement of the facts and the points of law of a case to be pleaded in court. 3. **hold a brief for,** argue for; support; defend. 4. **in brief,** in few words. —*v.* 1. make a brief of; summarize. 2. furnish with a brief. 3. *Brit. Law.* retain as a lawyer or counsel. 4. give a briefing to. [< OF < L *brevis* short] —**brief′ly,** *adv.* —**brief′ness,** *n.* —**Syn.** *adj.* 1. fleeting, transitory. 2. concise, succinct, terse.

brief case, flat container for carrying loose papers, books, drawings, etc.

brief·ing (brēf′ing), *n.* a short summary of the details of a flight mission, given to the crew of a combat airplane just before it takes off.

bri·er[1] (brī′ər), *n.* a thorny or prickly bush, esp. the wild rose. Also, **briar.** [OE *brēr*]

bri·er[2] (brī′ər), *n.* 1. white heath bush. Its root is used in making tobacco pipes. 2. tobacco pipe made of this. Also, **briar.** [< F *bruyère* heath < Celtic] —**bri′er·y,** *adj.*

bri·er·wood (brī′ər·wúd′), *n.* roots of the brier tree, often carved into tobacco pipes. Also, **briarwood.**

brig (brig), *n. Naut.*
a. a square-rigged ship with two masts.
b. *U.S.* prison on a warship. [short for *brigantine*]

Brig

bri·gade (bri·gād′), *n., v.,* –gad·ed, –gad·ing. —*n.* 1. part of an army. It is usually made up of two or more regiments. 2. group of people organized for some purpose: *a fire brigade puts out fires.* —*v.* form into a brigade. [< F < Ital. *brigata,* ult. < *briga* strife < Celtic]

brig·a·dier (brig′ə·dir′), *n.* brigadier general.

brigadier general, *pl.* brigadier generals. *U.S. Mil.* officer commanding a brigade, a wing of the Air Force, or an equivalent unit, ranking above a colonel and below a major general.

brig·and (brig′ənd), *n.* man who robs travelers on the road; robber; bandit. [< OF < Ital. *brigante.* See BRIGADE.] —**brig′and·ish,** *adj.*

brig·and·age (brig′ən·dij), **brig·and·ism** (–diz–əm), *n.* robbery; plundering.

brig·an·tine (brig′ən·tēn; –tin), *n.* brig with the mainmast fore-and-aft-rigged. [< F < Ital. *brigantino.* See BRIGAND, BRIGADE.]

bright (brīt), *adj.* 1. giving much light; shining. 2. very light or clear. 3. quick-witted; clever. 4. intelligent. 5. vivid; glowing. 6. lively; gay; cheerful. 7. favorable. 8. famous; glorious. —*adv.* in a bright manner. [OE *briht, beorht*] —**bright′ly,** *adv.* —**bright′ness,** *n.* —Syn. *adj.* 1. beaming, gleaming, radiant. 3. smart, intelligent. 6. vivacious, animated. 7. promising. —Ant. *adj.* 1. dull, dim, dark.

bright·en (brīt′ən), *v.* 1. become bright or brighter. 2. make bright or brighter.

Bright's disease, *Pathol.* kidney disease characterized by albumin in the urine.

bril·liance (bril′yəns), **bril·lian·cy** (–yən·si), *n.* 1. great brightness; radiance; sparkle. 2. splendor; magnificence. 3. great ability.

bril·liant (bril′yənt), *adj.* 1. shining brightly; sparkling. 2. splendid; magnificent. 3. having great ability. —*n.* 1. diamond or other gem cut to sparkle brightly. 2. a very small size of type; 4 point. This line is set in brilliant. [< F *brillant,* ppr. of *briller* shine, ? < L *beryllus* beryl] —**bril′liant·ly,** *adv.* —**bril′liant·ness,** *n.*

bril·lian·tine (bril′yən·tēn), *n. Am.* an oily liquid used to make the hair glossy.

brim (brim), *n., v.,* **brimmed, brim·ming.** —*n.* 1. edge of a cup, bowl, etc.; rim. 2. the projecting edge of a hat. 3. edge bordering water. —*v.* fill to the brim; be full to the brim. [OE *brim* sea] —**brim′less,** *adj.*

brim·ful (brim′fúl′), *adj.* completely full.

brim·stone (brim′stōn′), *n.* sulfur. [ME *brinston* < *brinn–* burn + *ston* stone]

brin·dle (brin′dəl), *adj.* brindled. —*n.* 1. brindled color. 2. brindled animal. [< *brindled*]

brin·dled (brin′dəld), *adj.* gray, tan, or tawny with darker streaks and spots. [? akin to BRAND]

brine (brīn), *n.* 1. very salty water. 2. salt lake or sea; ocean. [OE *brȳne*] —**brin′ish,** *adj.*

bring (bring), *v.,* **brought, bring·ing.** 1. come with (some thing or person) from another place; take along to a place or person. 2. cause to come. 3. influence; lead. 4. *Law.* present before a court. 5. present (reasons, arguments, etc.); adduce. 6. sell for. 7. **bring about,** cause to happen. 8. **bring around or round, a.** restore to conscious-

ness. **b.** convince; persuade. 9. **bring forth, a.** give birth to; bear. **b.** reveal; show. 10. **bring out, a.** reveal; show. **b.** offer to the public. 11. **bring to, a.** restore to consciousness. **b.** stop; check. 12. **bring up, a.** care for in childhood. **b.** educate; train. **c.** suggest for action or discussion. **d.** stop suddenly. [OE *bringan*] —**bring′er,** *n.* —Syn. 1. convey, carry, bear.

bring·ing-up (bring′ing-up′), *n.* 1. care in childhood. 2. education; training.

brink (bringk), *n.* 1. edge at the top of a steep place. 2. **on the brink of,** very near. [ME; prob. < Scand.]

brin·y (brīn′i), *adj.,* **brin·i·er, brin·i·est.** of or like brine; salty. —**brin′i·ness,** *n.*

bri·quette, bri·quet (bri·ket′), *n.* a molded block, esp. of coal dust used for fuel. [< F, dim. of *brique* BRICK.]

Bris·bane (briz′bān; –bən), *n.* seaport in E Australia.

brisk (brisk), *adj.* 1. quick and active; lively. 2. keen; sharp. [? akin to BRUSQUE] —**brisk′ly,** *adv.* —**brisk′ness,** *n.* —Syn. 1. nimble, spry.

bris·ket (bris′kit), *n.* 1. meat from the breast of an animal. 2. breast of an animal. [< OF *bruschet* < Gmc.]

bris·tle (bris′əl), *n., v.,* –tled, –tling. —*n.* a short, stiff hair. —*v.* 1. stand up straight: *the angry dog's hair bristled.* 2. cause (hair) to stand up straight; ruffle. 3. have one's hair stand up straight: *the dog bristled.* 4. show that one is aroused and ready to fight. 5. be thickly set: *our path bristled with difficulties.* [ME *bristel*] —**bris′tly,** *adj.* —**bris′tli·ness,** *n.*

bris·tle·tail (bris′əl·tāl′), *n.* a wingless insect having long, bristlelike appendages.

Bris·tol (bris′təl), *n.* seaport in SW England.

Bristol Channel, an inlet of the Atlantic, between SW England and Wales.

Brit., 1. Britain; British. 2. Briticism.

Brit·ain (brit′ən), *n.* England, Scotland, and Wales; Great Britain.

Bri·tan·ni·a (bri·tan′i·ə; –tan′yə), *n.* 1. Britain; Great Britain. 2. the British Empire.

Bri·tan·nic (bri·tan′ik), *adj.* British.

Brit·i·cism (brit′ə·siz·əm), *n. Am.* word or phrase peculiar to the British. *Lift* meaning *elevator* is a Briticism. Also, *Am.* Britishism.

Brit·ish (brit′ish), *adj.* 1. of Great Britain, the British Empire, or its people. 2. of or pertaining to the ancient Britons. —*n.* 1. (*pl. in use*) people of Great Britain or the British Empire collectively. 2. their language. [OE *brittisc* < *Brittas* Britons < Celtic]

British America, *Am.* 1. Canada. 2. (formerly) the British part of North America.

British Columbia, province in W Canada.

British Commonwealth of Nations, United Kingdom of Great Britain and Northern Ireland and the self-governing dominions (Canada, Australia, New Zealand, Union of South Africa, Ceylon), the republics of India and Pakistan, and overseas colonies and dependencies, etc.; Commonwealth of Nations.

British East Africa, British territory in E Africa, including Kenya, Uganda, Tanganyika Territory, and the island of Zanzibar.

British Empire, 1. originally, all the countries and colonies owing allegiance to the British crown, including the dominions, colonies, dependencies, etc. 2. now, the colonies, dependencies, etc., exclusive of the dominions and other autonomous units. The term now has no official use.

Brit·ish·er (brit′ish·ər), *n. Am.* Englishman.

British Guiana, British colony in N South America.

British Honduras, British colony in Central America, SE of Mexico.

British India, all the territory in India formerly under British control or protection.

British Isles, Great Britain, Ireland, the Isle of Man, and other nearby islands.

Brit·ish·ism (brit′ish·iz·əm), *n. Am.* Briticism.

British thermal unit, amount of heat necessary to raise a pound of water one degree Fahrenheit at its maximum density.

British West Africa, British territory in W Africa, including Nigeria, the Gold Coast, etc.

British West Indies, British islands in the West Indies, including the Bahamas, Jamaica, Trinidad, etc.

Brit·on (brit′ən), *n.* **1.** native or inhabitant of Great Britain or the British Empire. **2.** member of a Celtic people who lived in S Britain long ago.

Brit·ta·ny (brit′ə·ni), *n.* region in NW France.

brit·tle (brit′əl), *adj.* very easily broken; breaking with a snap; apt to break. [ME *britel* < OE *brēotan* break] —**brit′tle·ly,** *adv.* —**brit′tle·ness,** *n.* —Syn. fragile, frail.

Br·no (ber′nō), *n.* city in central Czechoslovakia. Also, **Brünn.**

bro., Bro., *pl.* **bros., Bros.** brother.

broach (brōch), *n.* a pointed tool for making and shaping holes. —*v.* **1.** open by making a hole. **2.** begin to talk about: *broach a subject.* [< OF < L *broccus* projecting] —**broach′er,** *n.*

broad (brôd), *adj.* **1.** large across; wide. **2.** extensive: *a broad experience.* **3.** not limited; liberal; tolerant: *broad ideas.* **4.** main; general: *broad outlines.* **5.** clear; full: *broad daylight.* **6.** plain; plain-spoken. **7.** coarse; not refined: *broad jokes.* **8.** pronounced with the vocal passage open wide. The *a* in *father* is broad. —*n.* **1.** the broad part of anything. **2.** *Slang.* a woman. [OE *brād*] —**broad′ish,** *adj.* —**broad′ly,** *adv.* —Syn. *adj.* **2.** vast, ample. **7.** gross, indecent.

broad·ax, broad·axe (brôd′aks′), *n.,* *pl.* **-axes.** ax with a broad blade.

broad·cast (brôd′kast′; -käst′), *v.,* —**cast** or —**cast·ed, -cast·ing,** *n., adj., adv.* —*v.* **1.** send out by radio. **2.** scatter widely. —*n.* **1.** a sending out by radio. **2.** speech, music, etc., sent out by radio. **3.** a radio program. **4.** a scattering far and wide. —*adj.* **1.** sent out by radio. **2.** scattered widely. —*adv.* over a wide surface. —**broad′cast′er,** *n.*

broad·cloth (brôd′klôth′; -kloth′), *n.* **1.** a smooth, cotton or silk cloth, used in making shirts and dresses. **2.** a smooth, closely woven woolen cloth, used in making men's suits. [orig. 2 yards "broad"]

broad·en (brôd′ən), *v.* **1.** make broad or broader. **2.** become broad or broader.

broad·gauge (brôd′gāj′), **broad·gauged** (-gājd′), *adj.* **1.** having rails more than 56½ inches apart. **2.** *Am.* broad-minded; liberal.

broad·loom (brôd′lüm′), *adj.* woven on a wide loom in one color: *a broadloom carpet.*

broad·mind·ed (brôd′mīn′did), *adj.* liberal; tolerant; not prejudiced or bigoted. —**broad′-mind′ed·ly,** *adv.* —**broad′-mind′ed·ness,** *n.*

broad·side (brôd′sīd′), *n.* **1.** the whole side of a ship above the water line. **2.** all the guns that can be fired from one side of a ship. **3.** the firing of all these guns at the same time. **4.** *Colloq.* violent attack. **5.** Also, **broad·sheet** (brôd′shēt′). a large sheet of paper printed on one side only: *broadsides announcing a big sale.* —*adv.* with the side turned.

broad·sword (brôd′sôrd′; -sōrd′), *n.* sword with a broad, flat blade.

Broad·way (brôd′wā′), *n.* street running NE and SW through New York City.

Brob·ding·nag (brob′ding·nag), *n.* the land of giants in Swift's book *Gulliver's Travels.* —**Brob′ding·nag′i·an,** *adj., n.*

bro·cade (brō·kād′), *n., v.,* —**cad·ed, -cad·ing.** —*n.* an expensive cloth woven with raised designs on it. —*v.* weave or decorate with raised designs. [< Sp., Pg. *brocado,* pp. of *brocar* embroider; akin to BROACH] —**bro·cad′ed,** *adj.*

broc·co·li (brok′ə·li), *n.* variety of cauliflower whose green branching stems and flower heads are used as a vegetable. [< Ital. (pl.) sprouts < L *broccus* projecting]

bro·chure (brō·shúr′), *n.* pamphlet. [< F, < *brocher* stitch]

bro·gan (brō′gən), *n.* a coarse, strong shoe. [< Irish, Scotch Gaelic, dim. of *brog* shoe]

brogue¹ (brōg), *n.* **1.** Irish accent or pronunciation of English. **2.** accent or pronunciation peculiar to any dialect. [? specialization of meaning of *brogue²*]

brogue² (brōg), *n.* **1.** a coarse, strong shoe. **2.** shoe made for comfort and long wear. [< Irish, Scotch Gaelic *brōg* shoe]

broi·der (broi′dər), *v. Archaic.* embroider. [< OF *broder;* infl. by archaic E *broid* braid]

broil¹ (broil), *v.* **1.** cook by putting or holding near the fire. **2.** make very hot. **3.** be very hot. —*n.* **1.** a broiling. **2.** broiled meat, etc. [? < OF *bruillir* burn]

broil² (broil), *v.* engage in a broil; quarrel; fight. —*n.* an angry quarrel or struggle; brawl. [< F *brouiller* disorder]

broil·er (broil′ər), *n.* **1.** *Am.* pan or rack for broiling. **2.** a young chicken for broiling.

broke (brōk), *v.* **1.** pt. of break. **2.** *Archaic.* pp. of break. —*adj. Slang.* without money.

bro·ken (brō′kən), *v.* pp. of break. —*adj.* **1.** crushed; in pieces. **2.** destroyed. **3.** ruined. **4.** weakened. **5.** tamed. **6.** reduced to submission. **7.** violated. **8.** imperfectly spoken. **9.** interrupted. **10.** changing direction abruptly. —**bro′ken·ly,** *adv.* —**bro′ken·ness,** *n.*

bro·ken-heart·ed (brō′kən·här′tid), *adj.* crushed by sorrow or grief; heartbroken.

bro·ker (brō′kər), *n.* person who buys and sells stocks, bonds, grain, cotton, etc., for other people; agent. [< AF *brocour* tapster, retailer of wine; akin to BROACH]

bro·ker·age (brō′kər·ij), *n.* **1.** business of a broker. **2.** money charged by a broker for his services.

bro·mide (brō′mīd; -mid), *n.* **1.** Also, **bro·mid** (brō′mid). *Chem.* compound of bromine with another element or radical. **2.** potassium bromide, KBr, a drug used to calm nervousness, cause sleep, etc. **3.** *Am., Slang.* a trite remark. [def. 3 has ref. to the effect of the drug]

bro·mid·ic (brō·mid′ik), *adj. Am., Colloq.* like a bromide; commonplace; trite.

bro·mine (brō′mēn; -min), **bro·min** (-min), *n. Chem.* a nonmetallic element, Br, somewhat like chlorine and iodine. Bromine is a dark-brown liquid that gives off an irritating vapor.

bron·chi (brong′kī), *n.* pl. of bronchus. **1.** two main branches of the windpipe. **2.** the smaller, branching tubes in the lungs.

bron·chi·a (brong′ki·ə), *n.pl.* the bronchi, esp. their smaller branches.

bron·chi·al (brong′ki·əl), *adj.* of the bronchi.

bron·chi·tis (brong·kī′tis), *n.* inflammation of the lining of the bronchial tubes. —**bron·chit·ic** (brong·kit′ik), *adj.*

bron·chus (brong′kəs), *n., pl.* **-chi** (-kī). one of the bronchi. [< NL < Gk. *bronchos*]

bron·co, bron·cho (brong′kō), *n., pl.* **-cos; -chos.** *Am., Esp. W. and S.W.* pony of the western United States. Broncos are often wild or only half tame. [< Sp., rough, rude]

bron·co·bust·er (brong′kō·bus′tər), *n. Am., W. and S.W. Slang.* one who breaks broncos to the saddle.

bron·to·sau·rus (bron′tə·sôr′əs), *n.* a huge, extinct dinosaur of America. [< NL < Gk. *bronte* thunder + *sauros* lizard]

Bronx (brongks), *n.* The, northern borough of New York City.

Bronx cheer, *Am., Slang.* a contemptuous sound made by vibrating the tongue between the lips.

bronze (bronz), *n., adj., v.,* **bronzed, bronz·ing.** —*n.* **1.** a brown alloy of copper and tin. **2.** a similar alloy of copper with zinc or other metals. **3.** statue, medal, disk, etc., made of bronze. **4.** yellowish brown; reddish brown. —*adj.* **1.** made of bronze. **2.** yellowish-brown; reddish-brown. —*v.* make or become bronze in color. [< F < Ital. *bronzo* bell metal] —**bronz′y,** *adj.*

Bronze Age, period after the Stone Age when bronze tools, weapons, etc., were used.

brooch (brōch; brūch), n. an ornamental pin having the point secured by a catch. [var. of *broach*, n.]

brood (brūd), n. 1. young birds hatched at one time in the nest or cared for together. 2. young who are cared for. 3. breed; kind. —v. 1. sit on in order to hatch. 2. hover over; hang close over. 3. think a long time about some one thing. 4. dwell on in thought: *for years he brooded vengeance.* [OE *brōd*] —**brood'ing·ly**, adv. —**brood'y**, adj.

brood·er (brūd'ər), n. 1. Am. a closed place that can be heated, used in raising chicks, etc. 2. one that broods.

brook[1] (brůk), n. a small natural stream of water. [OE *brōc*] —**Syn.** creek, rivulet.

brook[2] (brůk), v. put up with; endure; tolerate: *her pride would not brook such insults.* [OE *brūcan* use]

brook·let (brůk'lit), n. a little brook.

Brook·lyn (brůk'lən), n. borough of New York City, on Long Island.

brook trout, Am. a fresh-water game fish of the E part of North America.

broom (brüm; brům), n. 1. shrub with slender branches, small leaves, and yellow flowers. 2. a long-handled brush for sweeping. [OE *brōm*]

broom·corn (brüm'kôrn'; brům'-), n. Am. a tall plant resembling corn, with flower clusters having long, stiff stems used for making brooms.

broom·stick (brüm'stik'; brům'-), n. the long handle of a broom.

broth (brôth; broth), n. water in which meat has been boiled; thin soup. [OE]

broth·el (broth'əl; broth'-; brôth'-), n. house of prostitution. [ME, < OE *brēothan* go to ruin]

broth·er (bruth'ər), n., pl. broth·ers, breth·ren, v. —n. 1. son of the same parents. 2. a close friend; companion; countryman. 3. a fellow member of a group or association, as a church, union, etc. 4. member of a religious order who is not a priest. —v. address or treat as a brother. [OE *brōthor*]

broth·er·hood (bruth'ər·hůd), n. 1. bond between brothers; feeling of brother for brother. 2. persons joined as brothers; association of men with some common aim, characteristic, belief, profession, etc.

broth·er·in·law (bruth'ər·in·lô'), n., pl. broth·ers·in·law. 1. brother of one's husband or wife. 2. husband of one's sister. 3. husband of the sister of one's wife or husband.

broth·er·ly (bruth'ər·li), adj. 1. of a brother. 2. like a brother. 3. friendly; kindly; affectionate. —adv. like a brother. —**broth'er·li·ness**, n.

brougham (brüm; brü'əm; brō'əm), n. a closed carriage or automobile having an outside seat for the driver. [for Lord H. P. *Brougham*]

brought (brôt), v. pt. and pp. of bring.

brow (brou), n. 1. forehead. 2. arch of hair over the eye; eyebrow. 3. facial expression. 4. edge of a steep place; top of a slope. [OE *brū*]

brow·beat (brou'bēt'), v., –beat, –beat·en, –beat·ing. frighten into doing something by overbearing looks or words; bully. —**brow'beat'-er**, n. —**Syn.** intimidate, domineer.

brown (broun), n. 1. color like that of toast, potato skins, and coffee. 2. paint or dye having this color. 3. something brown. —adj. 1. having this color. 2. dark-skinned; tanned. —v. make or become brown. [OE *brūn*] —**brown'ish**, adj. —**brown'ness**, n.

Brown (broun), n. John, 1800–1859, American abolitionist who attempted to incite a rebellion of the slaves but was captured at Harper's Ferry.

Brown·i·an movement or **motion** (broun'i·ən), Physics. a rapid oscillatory motion often observed in very minute particles suspended in water or other liquids.

brown·ie (broun'i), n. 1. a good-natured, helpful elf or fairy. 2. Am. a flat, sweet, chocolate cake with nuts, often in small squares.

Brown·ing (broun'ing), n. 1. Elizabeth Barrett, 1806–1861, English poet, wife of Robert Browning. 2. Robert, 1812–1889, English poet.

brown shirt, follower of Adolf Hitler; Nazi.

brown·stone (broun'stōn'), n. Am. reddish-brown sandstone, used as a building material.

brown study, condition of being absorbed in thought; serious reverie.

brown sugar, sugar that is not refined or only partly refined.

browse (brouz), v., browsed, brows·ing, n. —v. 1. feed; graze. 2. read here and there in a book, library, etc. [< n., or < F *brouster* feed on buds and shoots] —n. tender shoots of shrubs. [appar. < MF *broust* bud, shoot < Gmc.] —**brows'er**, n.

Bruce (brüs), n. Robert the, 1274–1329, king of Scotland, 1306–29.

bru·in (brü'ən), n. bear. [< MDu., brown]

bruise (brüz), v., bruised, bruis·ing, n. —v. 1. injure the outside of. 2. injure; hurt: *harsh words bruised her feelings.* 3. become bruised. 4. pound; crush. —n. 1. injury to the body, caused by a fall or a blow, that changes the color of the skin without breaking it. 2. injury to the outside of a fruit, vegetable, plant, etc. [fusion of OE *brȳsan* crush and OF *bruisier* break, shatter]

bruis·er (brü'zər), n. 1. prize fighter. 2. Colloq. a bully.

bruit (brüt), v. spread a report or rumor of. [< OF, < *bruire* roar]

bru·nette, bru·net (brü·net'), adj. 1. dark-colored; having an olive color. 2. having dark-brown or black hair, brown or black eyes, and a dark skin. —n. person having such hair, eyes, and skin. A man with this complexion is a brunet; a woman is a brunette. [< F, dim. of *brun* brown < Gmc.]

Brun·hild (brün'hild), n. the young queen in the *Nibelungenlied* whom Siegfried wins as a bride for King Gunther by means of magic.

Brünn (bryn), n. Brno.

Bruns·wick (brunz'wik), n. 1. city in NW Germany. 2. a state in NW Germany.

brunt (brunt), n. main force or violence; hardest part.

brush[1] (brush), n. 1. tool for cleaning, rubbing, painting, etc., made of bristles, hair, or wires set in a stiff back or fastened to a handle. 2. a brushing; a rub with a brush. 3. a light touch in passing. 4. a short, brisk fight or quarrel. 5. the bushy tail of an animal, esp. of a fox. 6. Elect. piece of carbon, copper, etc., used to connect the electricity from the revolving part of a motor or generator to the outside circuit. 7. art or skill of an artist. —v. 1. clean, rub, paint, etc., with a brush; use a brush on. 2. wipe away; remove: *brush the tears away.* 3. touch lightly in passing. 4. move quickly. 5. brush aside or away, refuse to consider. 6. brush up, refresh one's knowledge. [< OF *broisse* < Gmc.] —**brush'er**, n. —**brush'y**, adj.

brush[2] (brush), n. 1. a. U.S. branches broken or cut off. b. thick growth of shrubs, bushes, small trees, etc. 2. Am., S.W. a thinly settled country; backwoods. [< OF *broche*] —**brush'y**, adj.

brush·wood (brush'wůd'), n. brush[2] (def. 1).

brusque (brusk), adj. abrupt in manner or speech; blunt. [< F < Ital. *brusco* coarse < LL *bruscus*, blend of *ruscum* broom and Gaulish *brucus* broom] —**brusque'ly**, adv. —**brusque'-ness**, n.

Brus·sels (brus'əlz), n. capital of Belgium, in the central part.

Brussels sprouts, 1. variety of cabbage that has many small heads growing along a stalk. 2. heads of this plant, used as a vegetable.

bru·tal (brü'təl), adj. coarse and savage; like a brute; cruel. —**bru'tal·ly**, adv.

bru·tal·i·ty (brü·tal'ə·ti), n., pl. –ties. 1. cruelty; savageness; coarseness: *whipping a tired horse is brutality.* 2. a cruel, savage, or coarse act. —**Syn.** 1. inhumanity, barbarity.

bru·tal·ize (brü'təl·īz), v., –ized, –iz·ing. 1. make brutal: *war brutalizes many men.* 2. become brutal. —**bru'tal·i·za'tion**, n.

brute (brüt), n. 1. animal without power to reason. 2. a stupid, cruel, coarse, or sensual person. —adj. 1. without power to reason. 2. stupid; cruel; coarse; sensual. 3. unconscious: *the brute* *forces of nature.* [< F *brut* < L *brutus* heavy, dull]

brut·ish (brüt′ish), *adj.* stupid; coarse; savage; like a brute. —**brut′ish·ly,** *adv.* —**brut′ish·ness,** *n.*

Bru·tus (brü′təs), *n.* Marcus Junius, 85–42 B.C., Roman political leader and one of the men who killed Julius Caesar.

Bry·an (brī′ən), *n.* William Jennings, 1860–1925, American political leader and orator.

Bry·ant (brī′ənt), *n.* William Cullen, 1794–1878, American poet.

Bryn·hild (brin′hild), *n.* Brunhild.

bry·ol·o·gy (brī-ol′ə-ji), *n.* branch of botany that deals with mosses and liverworts. [< Gk. *bryon* moss + -LOGY] —**bry·o·log·i·cal** (brī′ə-loj′ə-kəl), *adj.* —**bry·ol′o·gist,** *n.*

bry·o·phyte (brī′ə-fīt), *n. Bot.* any of the mosses or liverworts. [< NL < Gk. *bryon* moss + *phyton* plant] —**bry·o·phyt·ic** (brī′ə-fit′ik), *adj.*

B.S., B.Sc., Bachelor of Science.

B.T.U., B.t.u., Btu, British thermal unit or units.

bu., bushel; bushels.

bub·ble (bub′əl), *n., v.,* -**bled,** -**bling.** —*n.* 1. a thin film of liquid enclosing air or gas. 2. a small globule of air in a solid or in a liquid. 3. act or process of bubbling; sound of bubbling. 4. plan or idea that looks good, but soon goes to pieces. —*v.* 1. have bubbles; make bubbles; look like water boiling. 2. make sounds like water boiling; gurgle. [ME *bobel*] —**bub′bling·ly,** *adv.* —**bub′bly,** *adj.*

bubble chamber, a small vessel filled with a superheated liquid, esp. pentane or hydrogen under pressure, through which subatomic particles make a bubbly track by means of which they may be isolated and identified.

bubble gum, a chewing gum which can be inflated so as to form a large bubble.

bu·bon·ic plague (bū-bon′ik), a very dangerous contagious disease, accompanied by fever, chills, and swelling of the lymphatic glands. It is carried to human beings by fleas from rats or squirrels. [< LL < Gk. *boubon* groin]

buc·cal (buk′əl), *adj. Anat.* 1. of the cheek. 2. of the sides of the mouth or the mouth. [< L *bucca* cheek, mouth]

buc·ca·neer (buk′ə-nir′), *n.* pirate; sea robber. [< F *boucanier* < *boucan* frame for curing meat, as done by the French in Haiti]

Bu·chan·an (bū-kan′ən; bə-), *n.* James, 1791–1868, 15th president of the U.S., 1857–61.

Bu·cha·rest (bū′kə-rest; bū′-), *n.* capital of Rumania, in the S part.

buck[1] (buk), *n.* 1. a male deer, goat, hare, rabbit, antelope, or sheep. 2. dandy. 3. *Colloq.* man. [coalescence of OE *buc* male deer and OE *bucca* male goat]

buck[2] (buk), *v.* 1. *Am., Colloq.* a. fight against; resist stubbornly. b. push or hit with the head; butt. c. rush at; charge against. 2. *Football.* charge into the opposing line with the ball. 3. *Am.* (of horses) jump into the air with back curved and come down with the front legs stiff. 4. **buck up,** *Colloq.* cheer up. —*n. Am.* a throw or attempt to throw by bucking. [special use of *buck*[1]] —**buck′er,** *n.*

buck[3] (buk), *n.* pass the buck, *Colloq.* shift the responsibility, work, etc., to someone else.

buck[4] (buk), *n., Am., Slang.* dollar.

buck·a·roo (buk′ə-rü; buk′ə-rü′), *n., pl.* -**roos.** *Am., S.W.* cowboy.

buck·board (buk′bôrd′; -bōrd′), *n. Am.* an open, four-wheeled carriage having the seat fastened to a platform of long, springy boards instead of a body and springs.

buck·et (buk′it), *n., v.,* -**et·ed,** -**et·ing.** —*n.* 1. pail made of wood or metal. 2. amount that a bucket can hold. 3. scoop of a dredging machine. 4. **kick the bucket,** *Slang.* die. —*v.* lift or carry in a bucket or buckets. [appar. < AF *buket* wash tub, milk pail < OE *būc* vessel, pitcher]

buck·et·ful (buk′it·fůl), *n., pl.* -**fuls.** amount that a bucket can hold.

buck·eye (buk′ī′), *n. Am.* tree or shrub of the same family as the horse chestnut with showy clusters of small flowers, large divided leaves, and large brown seeds. [< *buck*[1] + *eye;* with ref. to mark on the seed]

Buck·ing·ham Palace (buk′ing-əm), official London residence of the British sovereign.

buck·le (buk′əl), *n., v.,* -**led,** -**ling.** —*n.* 1. catch or clasp used to fasten together the ends of a belt, strap, etc. 2. metal ornament for a shoe. 3. bend; bulge; kink; wrinkle. —*v.* 1. fasten together with a buckle. 2. bend; bulge; kink; wrinkle. 3. **buckle down to,** *Am.* work hard at. [< F < L *buccula* cheek strap on helmet, dim. of *bucca* cheek]

buck·ler (buk′lər), *n.* 1. a small, round shield. 2. protection; defense.

buck private, *Am., Slang.* a common soldier below the rank of private first class.

buck·ram (buk′rəm), *n.* a coarse cloth made stiff with glue or something like glue. [? ult. named for *Bukhāra* in central Asia]

buck·saw (buk′sô′), *n. Am.* saw set in a light frame and held with both hands.

buck·shot (buk′shot′), *n. Am.* large lead shot used for shooting large game such as deer.

buck·skin (buk′skin′), *n.* 1. a strong, soft leather, yellowish or grayish in color, made from the skins of deer or sheep. 2. **buckskins,** breeches made of buckskin. 3. *Am.* horse the color of buckskin.

buck·thorn (buk′thôrn′), *n. U.S.* 1. a small thorny tree or shrub with clusters of black berries. 2. a low, thorny tree that grows in southern United States.

buck·tooth (buk′tüth′), *n., pl.* -**teeth.** a large, protruding front tooth.

buck·wheat (buk′hwēt′), *n.* 1. plant with brown, triangular seeds and fragrant white flowers. 2. the seeds, used as food for animals or ground into flour.

bu·col·ic (bū-kol′ik), *adj.* 1. of shepherds; pastoral. 2. rustic; rural. —*n.* poem about shepherds. [< L < Gk. *boukolikos* rustic < *boukolos* shepherd] —**bu·col′i·cal·ly,** *adv.*

bud (bud), *n., v.,* **bud·ded, bud·ding.** —*n.* 1. a small swelling on a plant that will develop into a flower, leaf, or branch. 2. a partly opened flower. 3. beginning stage. 4. *Anat.* a small organ or part, as a taste bud. 5. **nip in the bud,** stop at the very beginning. —*v.* 1. put forth buds. 2. graft (a bud) from one kind of plant into the stem of a different kind. 3. begin to grow or develop. —**bud′der,** *n.* —**bud′less,** *adj.*

Bu·da·pest (bū′də-pest), *n.* capital of Hungary, on the Danube River.

Bud·dha (būd′ə; bůd′ə), *n.* 563?–483? B.C., a great religious teacher of Asia. Also, Gautama.

Bud·dhism (būd′iz-əm; bůd′diz-), *n.* religion that originated in the sixth century B.C. in N India and spread widely over central, SE, and E Asia. —**Bud′dhist,** *n.* —**Bud·dhis′tic,** *adj.*

bud·dy (bud′i), *n., pl.* -**dies.** *Colloq.* 1. *Am.* comrade; pal. 2. a little boy.

budge (buj), *v.,* **budged, budg·ing.** move in the least: *he wouldn't budge from his chair.* [< F *bouger* stir < VL *bullicare* boil furiously < L *bullire* boil]

budg·et (buj′it), *n., v.,* -**et·ed,** -**et·ing.** —*n.* 1. estimate of the amount of money that can be spent, and the amounts to be spent for various purposes, in a given time. 2. stock or collection: *a budget of news.* —*v.* make a plan for spending. [< F *bougette,* dim. of *bouge* bag < L *bulga* < Celtic] —**budg·et·ar·y** (buj′ə-ter′i), *adj.*

Bue·nos Ai·res (bwā′nəs ī′riz; bō′nəs är′ēz), capital of Argentina, on the Plata River.

buff[1] (buf), *n.* 1. a strong, soft, dull-yellow leather having a fuzzy surface. 2. soldier's coat. 3. dull yellow. 4. a polishing wheel covered with buff. 5. *Colloq.* bare skin. —*adj.* 1. made of buff leather. 2. dull-yellow. —*v.* polish with a buff. [< F *buffle* BUFFALO]

buff² (buf), *n. Am., Colloq.* devotee; fan (usually qualified): *a model-train buff, football buff.*

buf·fa·lo (buf′ə·lō), *n., pl.* -loes, -los, or (*esp. collectively*) -lo, *v.,* -loed, -lo·ing. —*n.* 1. *Am.* the bison of America, a wild ox, the male of which has a big, shaggy head and strong front legs. 2. any of several kinds of oxen, as the tame water buffalo of India or the wild Cape buffalo of Africa. —*v. Am., Slang.* 1. intimidate or overawe. 2. puzzle; mystify. [< Ital. < L *bubalus* < Gk. *boubalos* wild ox]

Buf·fa·lo (buf′ə·lō), *n.* port in W New York State, on Lake Erie.

Buffalo Bill (*William F. Cody*), 1846–1917, American frontier scout and showman.

buffalo grass, *Am.* short grass of central and western North America.

buff·er¹ (buf′ər), *n.* anything that softens the shock of a blow. [< *buff* deaden force]

buff·er² (buf′ər), *n.* 1. person who polishes. 2. thing for polishing, covered with leather.

buffer state, a small country between two larger countries that are enemies or competitors.

buf·fet¹ (buf′it), *n., v.,* -fet·ed, -fet·ing. —*n.* 1. blow of the hand or fist. 2. knock; stroke; hurt. —*v.* 1. strike with the hand or fist. 2. knock about; strike; hurt. 3. fight; struggle. [< OF, dim. of *buffe* blow] —buf′fet·er, *n.*

buf·fet² (bu·fā′; bu–; bə–), *n.* 1. piece of dining-room furniture for holding dishes, silver, and table linen; sideboard. 2. counter where food and drinks are served. 3. restaurant with such a counter. [< F]

buffet supper or **lunch,** meal where the food is arranged on tables and buffet, and the guests serve themselves.

buf·foon (bu·fün′; bə–), *n.* person who amuses people with tricks, pranks, and jokes; clown. [< F < Ital. *buffone* < *buffa* jest] —buf·foon·er·y (bu·fün′ər·i; bə–), *n.* —buf·foon′ish, *adj.*

bug (bug), *n.* 1. crawling insect. 2. any insect or insectlike animal. 3. *Esp. Brit.* bedbug. 4. Often, **bugs,** *Am., Slang.* defect; fault. 5. *Am., Slang.* a small microphone used in wire tapping. 6. *Dial.* bugbear; bogy. [? < obs. Welsh *bwg* ghost]

bug·a·boo (bug′ə·bü), *n., pl.* -boos. imaginary thing feared. [< *bug* bogy + *boo,* interj.]

bug·bear (bug′bãr′), *n.* bugaboo. [< *bug* bogy + *bear²*]

bug·gy¹ (bug′i), *n., pl.* -gies. *Am.* a light carriage with one seat.

bug·gy² (bug′i), *adj.,* -gi·er, -gi·est. swarming with bugs.

bu·gle (bü′gəl), *n., v.,* -gled, -gling. —*n.* a musical instrument like a small trumpet, made of brass or copper, used in the army and navy for sounding calls and orders. —*v.* 1. blow a bugle. 2. direct or summon by blowing on a bugle. [< OF < L *buculus,* dim. of *bos* ox; with ref. to early hunting horns] —bu′gler, *n.*

Man blowing a bugle

buhl (bül), *n.* 1. wood inlaid with metal, tortoise shell, ivory, etc., in elaborate patterns. 2. furniture decorated with this. [< G spelling of F *Boule,* name of a cabinetmaker]

build (bild), *v.,* built or (*Archaic*) build·ed, build·ing, *n.* —*v.* 1. make by putting materials together; construct: *men build houses, dams, bridges, etc.* 2. form gradually; develop: *build a business.* 3. establish; base: *build a case on facts.* 4. rely; depend: *we can build on that man's honesty.* 5. make a structure: *he builds for a living.* —*n.* form, style, or manner of construction: *an elephant has a heavy build.* [OE *byldan* < *bold* dwelling] —Syn. *v.* 1. erect. 3. found.

build·er (bil′dər), *n.* 1. one who builds. 2. person whose business is building.

build·ing (bil′ding), *n.* 1. thing built, such as a house, factory, barn, etc. 2. business, art, or process of making houses, stores, ships, etc. —Syn. 1. edifice, structure.

build-up, build·up (bild′up′), *n.* 1. a building up; formation; development: *our build-up of military strength.* 2. *Colloq.* presentation of a person or thing with praise, fanfare, etc., esp. in advance of a performance or appearance.

built-in (bilt′in′), *adj.* built as part of the building: *a built-in bookcase.*

bulb (bulb), *n.* 1. *Bot.* a. a round, underground bud from which certain plants grow, as onions, tulips, and lilies. b. the thick part of an underground stem resembling a bulb; tuber: *a crocus bulb.* c. plant growing from a bulb. 2. *Elect.* a. the glass case of an incandescent lamp. b. an incandescent lamp. [< L < Gk. *bolbos* onion] —bulb·ar (bul′bər), *adj.* —bulb′less, *adj.*

bulb·ous (bul′bəs), *adj.* 1. having bulbs; growing from bulbs, as daffodils. 2. shaped like a bulb; rounded and swelling: *a bulbous nose.*

Bul·ga·nin (bül·gä′nin), *n.* Nikolai Alexandrovich, born 1895, Soviet premier since February, 1955.

Bul·gar (bul′gär; bül′–; –gər), *n.* Bulgarian.

Bul·gar·i·a (bul·gãr′i·ə; bül–), *n.* country in SE Europe.

Bul·gar·i·an (bul·gãr′i·ən; bül–), *adj.* of or having to do with Bulgaria, its people, or their language. —*n.* 1. a native or inhabitant of Bulgaria. 2. language of Bulgaria.

bulge (bulj), *v.,* bulged, bulg·ing, *n.* —*v.* 1. swell outward. 2. cause to swell outward. —*n.* 1. an outward swelling. 2. *Slang.* advantage. 3. *Naut.* bilge. [< OF < L *bulga* bag] —bulg′y, *adj.* —Syn. *v.* 1. protrude. —*n.* 1. protuberance.

bulk (bulk), *n.* 1. size; large size. 2. largest part; main mass. 3. heap; pile. 4. **in bulk,** a. loose, not in packages. b. in large quantities. —*v.* 1. have size; be of importance. 2. grow large; swell. 3. cause to swell out. 4. pile in heaps. [< Scand. *būlki* heap] —Syn. *n.* 1. volume, magnitude.

bulk·head (bulk′hed′), *n.* 1. *Naut.* one of the upright partitions dividing a ship into watertight compartments to prevent sinking. 2. wall or partition built to hold back water, earth, rocks, air, etc. 3. *Am.* a flat or slanting door over a cellar entrance.

bulk·y (bul′ki), *adj.,* bulk·i·er, bulk·i·est. 1. taking up much space; large. 2. hard to handle; clumsy. —bulk′i·ly, *adv.* —bulk′i·ness, *n.* —Syn. 1. massive, ponderous. 2. unwieldy.

bull¹ (bul), *n.* 1. the male of beef cattle. 2. male of the whale, elephant, seal, walrus, and other large animals. 3. person who tries to raise prices in the stock market, etc. 4. *Am., Slang.* policeman. 5. *Am., Slang.* foolish talk. 6. *Am.* a bulldog. 7. **Bull,** Taurus. —*adj.* 1. male. 2. like a bull; large; strong; roaring. 3. having to do with rising prices in the stock market, etc. [OE *bula;* akin to BULLOCK] —bull′ish, *adj.* —bull′ish·ly, *adv.* —bull′ish·ness, *n.*

bull² (bul), *n.* a formal announcement or official order from the Pope. [< Med.L *bulla* document, seal < L, bubble]

Bull (bul), *n.* John, England or its people.

bull·dog (bul′dôg′; –dog′), *n., adj., v.,* -dogged, -dog·ging. —*n.* a heavily built dog with a large head and short hair, that is very muscular and courageous. —*adj.* like a bulldog's. —*v. Am., W.* throw (a steer, etc.) by grasping its horns and twisting its neck.

bull·doze (bul′dōz′), *v.,* -dozed, -doz·ing. *Am., Colloq.* frighten by violence or threats; bully.

bull·doz·er (bul′dōz′ər), *n. Am.* 1. a very powerful scraper or pusher for grading, road-building, etc. 2. *Colloq.* one who bulldozes.

bul·let (bul′it), *n.* a shaped piece of lead, steel, or other metal to be shot from a gun. [< F *boulette,* dim. of *boule* ball]

bul·le·tin (bul′ə·tən), *n.* 1. a short statement of news. Newspapers publish bulletins about the latest happenings. 2. magazine or newspaper appearing regularly, esp. one published by a club or society for its members. [< F < Ital. *bullettino,* double dim. of *bulla* BULL²]

bulletin board, *Am.* board on which notices are posted.

bul·let·proof (bul′it·prüf′), *adj.* made so that a bullet cannot go through.

bull·fight (bul′fit′), *n.* fight between men and a bull in an enclosed arena. —bull′fight′er, *n.* —bull′fight′ing, *n.*

bull·finch (bul′finch′), *n.* a European songbird with handsome plumage and a short, stout bill. See p. 129 for picture.

bull·frog (bul'frog'; –frôg'), *n. Am.* a large frog of North America that makes a loud croaking noise.

bull·head (bul'hed'), *n. Am.* any of several American freshwater catfishes.

bull·head·ed (bul'hed'id), *adj.* stupidly stubborn; obstinate. —**bull'head'ed·ness**, *n.*

bul·lion (bul'yən), *n.* lumps, bars, etc., of gold or silver. [< AF *bullion* < *bouillir* boil; infl. by OF *billon* debased metal]

Bullfinch
(6 in. long)

bull·necked (bul'nekt'), *adj.* having a thick neck.

bull·ock (bul'ək), *n.* ox; steer.

bull pen, 1. pen for a bull or bulls. **2.** *Am., Colloq.* place in which prisoners, suspects, etc., are temporarily confined. **3.** *Baseball.* enclosure in which pitchers warm up during a game.

bull ring, an enclosed arena for bullfights.

bull's-eye (bulz'ī'), *n.* **1.** center of a target. **2.** shot that hits it. **3.** a lens shaped like a half-sphere to concentrate light. **4.** a small lantern with such a lens.

bull terrier, a strong, active, white dog, a cross between a bulldog and a terrier.

bull·whip (bul'hwip'), *n. Am., W.* whip made of rawhide, usually about 18 feet long.

bul·ly[1] (bul'i), *n., pl.* –**lies,** *v.,* –**lied,** –**ly·ing,** *adj., interj.* —*n.* person who teases, frightens, or hurts smaller or weaker people. —*v.* **1.** be a bully. **2.** tease; frighten; hurt. —*adj. Am., Colloq.* fine; good. —*interj. Am., Colloq.* bravo! well done!

bul·ly[2] (bul'i), or **bully beef,** *n.* canned or pickled beef. [? < F *bouilli* boiled beef]

bul·ly·rag (bul'i·rag'), *v.,* –**ragged,** –**rag·ging.** *Dial. and Colloq.* bully; tease; abuse.

bul·rush (bul'rush'), *n.* **1.** a tall, slender plant that grows in wet places. **2.** *Brit.* cattail.

bul·wark (bul'wərk), *n.* **1.** defense; protection. **2.** earthwork or other wall for defense against the enemy. **3.** Usually, **bulwarks,** *Naut.* a ship's side above the deck. —*v.* **1.** defend; protect. **2.** provide with a bulwark or bulwarks. [appar. < *bole* + *work*; akin to BOULEVARD]

bum (bum), *n., v.,* **bummed, bum·ming,** *adj.,* **bum·mer, bum·mest.** *Slang.* —*n.* **1.** *Am.* a. an idle or good-for-nothing person; tramp. b. a drunken loafer. **2.** spree. —*v.* **1.** loaf. **2.** drink heavily. **3.** sponge on others; beg. **4.** *Am.* get (something) by sponging on others. —*adj. Am.* of poor quality. —**bum'mer,** *n.*

bum·ble·bee (bum'bəl·bē'), *n.* a large bee with a thick, hairy body, usually banded with gold. Bumblebees live in colonies in nests in the ground. [< *bumble* buzz + *bee*]

Bumblebee (ab. ⅔ actual size)

bum·bling (bum'bling), *adj.* muddled; bungling. —**bum'bling·ly,** *adv.*

bump (bump), *v.* **1.** push, throw, or strike (against something fairly large or solid). **2.** move (along) with bumps. **3.** hit or come against with heavy blows. **4.** bump off, *Am., Slang.* kill; murder. —*n.* **1.** a heavy blow or knock. **2.** swelling caused by a bump. **3.** any swelling or lump. [imit.]

bump·er (bump'ər), *n.* **1.** *Am.* a bar or bars at the front or rear of a car or truck to keep it from being damaged if the vehicle is bumped. **2.** cup or glass filled to the brim. —*adj.* unusually large: *a bumper crop.*

bump·kin (bump'kin), *n.* an awkward person from the country. [? < MDu. *bommekyn* little barrel]

bump·tious (bump'shəs), *adj.* unpleasantly assertive or conceited. [< *bump*] —**bump'tious·ly,** *adv.* —**bump'tious·ness,** *n.*

bump·y (bump'i), *adj.,* **bump·i·er, bump·i·est.** having bumps; causing bumps; rough. —**bump'i·ly,** *adv.* —**bump'i·ness,** *n.*

bun (bun), *n.* a slightly sweet roll.

bu·na (bü'nə; bü'–), *n. Chem.* an artificial rubber made from butadiene.

bunch (bunch), *n.* **1.** group of things of the same kind growing or fastened together, placed together, or thought of together: *a bunch of grapes, a bunch of sheep.* **2.** *Colloq.* a group of people. —*v.* **1.** come together in one place. **2.** bring together and make into a bunch. ▸ Bunch, in formal English, is limited to objects that grow together or can be fastened together, as *a bunch of carrots or roses,* or *keys,* and to expressions like *a bunch of cattle.* Colloquial and informal English holds to the older usage of *bunch,* applying it to a small collection of anything—including people.

bunch·y (bun'chi), *adj.,* **bunch·i·er, bunch·i·est. 1.** having bunches. **2.** growing in bunches. —**bunch'i·ness,** *n.*

bun·co (bung'kō), *n., pl.* –**cos,** *v.,* –**coed,** –**co·ing.** *Am., Slang.* —*n.* **1.** a dice game. **2.** any swindling or confidence game. —*v.* swindle. Also, **bunko.** [short for *buncombe*]

bun·combe (bung'kəm), *n. Am.* insincere talk; humbug. Also, **bunkum.** [after *Buncombe* Co., N.C., whose congressman kept making pointless speeches "for Buncombe"]

Bund (bund; *Ger.* bunt), *n., pl.* **Bün·de** (byn'də). *German.* society; league; association.

Bun·des·rat (bun'dəs·rät'), *n.* the upper house of the legislature of West Germany.

Bun·des·tag (bun'dəs·täk'), *n.* the lower, popularly elected house of the legislature of West Germany.

bun·dle (bun'dəl), *n., v.,* –**dled,** –**dling.** —*n.* **1.** number of things tied or wrapped together. **2.** parcel; package. **3.** group; bunch. —*v.* **1.** wrap or tie together; make into a bundle. **2.** send or go in a hurry; hustle. **3.** conduct a courtship, fully dressed, in bed. **4. bundle up,** dress warmly. [cf. MDu. *bondel;* akin to BIND] —**bun'dler,** *n.*

bung (bung), *n.* **1.** stopper for closing the hole in the side or end of a barrel, keg, or cask. **2.** bunghole. —*v.* **1.** close (a bunghole) with a stopper. **2.** shut up in, or as in, a cask. **3.** *Slang.* bruise. [prob. < MDu. *bonghe*]

bun·ga·low (bung'gə·lō), *n.* a one-story house. [< Hind. *banglā* of Bengal]

bung·hole (bung'hōl'), *n.* hole in the side or end of a barrel, keg, or cask through which it is filled and emptied.

bun·gle (bung'gəl), *v.,* –**gled,** –**gling,** *n.* —*v.* do or make (something) in a clumsy, unskillful way. —*n.* a clumsy, unskillful performance. —**bun'gler,** *n.* —**bun'gling·ly,** *adv.*

bun·ion (bun'yən), *n. Pathol.* painful, inflamed swelling on the foot, esp. on the first joint of the big toe.

bunk[1] (bungk), *n.* **1.** a narrow bed set against a wall like a shelf. **2.** *Colloq.* any place to sleep. —*v.* **1.** *Colloq.* occupy a bunk. **2.** sleep in rough quarters. [? < Scand. (Dan.) *bunke* heap]

bunk[2] (bungk), *n. Am., Slang.* humbug. [short for *buncombe*]

bunk·er (bungk'ər), *n.* **1.** place or bin for coal on a ship. **2.** a sandy hollow or mound of earth on a golf course, used as an obstacle.

Bunker Hill, hill in Charlestown, Massachusetts. An early battle of the American Revolution was fought near there on June 17, 1775.

bunk·house (bungk'hous'), *n. Am.* a rough building with sleeping quarters for laborers.

bun·kum (bung'kəm), *n. Am., Colloq.* buncombe.

bun·ny (bun'i), *n., pl.* –**nies.** *Colloq.* a. rabbit. b. *U.S.* squirrel.

Bun·sen burner (bun'sən), a gas burner with a very hot, blue flame, used in laboratories.

bunt (bunt), *v.* **1.** strike with the head or horns, as a goat does. **2.** push; shove. **3.** *Am., Baseball.* hit (a pitch) lightly so that the ball goes to the ground and rolls only a short distance. —*n. Am., Baseball.* a. act of bunting. b. ball that is bunted. —**bunt'er,** *n.*

bun·ting[1] (bun'ting), *n.* **1.** a thin cloth used for flags. **2.** long pieces of cloth in flag colors and designs, used to decorate buildings and streets on holidays, etc.; flags.

bun·ting² (bun′ting), *n.* a small bird with a stout bill, somewhat like a sparrow.

Bun·yan (bun′yən), *n.* **1. John,** 1628–1688, English preacher and religious writer who wrote *Pilgrim's Progress.* **2. Paul,** imaginary hero of northwestern lumber camps.

buoy (boi; bü′i), *n. Naut.* **1.** a floating object anchored in a certain place on the water to warn or guide. It marks hidden rocks or shallows, shows the safe part of the channel, etc. **2.** life buoy. —*v.* **1.** *Naut.* furnish with buoys; mark with a buoy. **2.** keep from sinking. **3.** hold up; sustain; encourage. [< OF or MDu. < *boia* fetter]

buoy·an·cy (boi′ən·si; bü′yən–), *n.* **1.** power to float: *wood has more buoyancy than iron.* **2.** power to keep things afloat: *salt water has more buoyancy than fresh water.* **3.** tendency to rise. **4.** cheerfulness; hopefulness.

buoy·ant (boi′ənt; bü′yənt), *adj.* **1.** able to float. **2.** able to keep things afloat: *air is buoyant.* **3.** tending to rise. **4.** light-hearted; cheerful; hopeful. —**buoy′ant·ly,** *adv.*

bu·pres·tid beetle (bū·pres′tid), a beetle whose larvae poison cattle. [< L *buprestis* < Gk., poisonous beetle, lit., ox-burner]

bur (bėr), *n., v.,* **burred, bur·ring.** —*n.* **1.** a prickly, clinging seed case or flower. **2.** plant or weed bearing burs. **3.** person or thing that clings like a bur. —*v.* remove burs from. Also, **burr.** [prob. < Scand. (Dan.) *borre* burdock]

bur·bot (bėr′bət), *n., pl.* **-bots** or (*esp.* collectively) **-bot.** a fresh-water fish with a slender body, related to the cod. [< F *bourbotte* < L *barba* beard; infl. by F *bourbe* mud]

bur·den¹ (bėr′dən), *n.* **1.** what is carried; a load (of things, care, work, duty, or sorrow). **2.** thing hard to carry or bear; heavy load. **3.** quantity of freight that a ship can carry; weight of a ship's cargo. —*v.* **1.** put a burden on. **2.** load too heavily; oppress. Also, *Archaic,* **burthen.** [OE *byrthen;* akin to BEAR¹] —**Syn.** *n.* **2.** weight, oppression.

bur·den² (bėr′dən), *n.* **1.** main idea or message. **2.** repeated verse in a song; chorus; refrain. [< OF *bourdon* humming, drone of bagpipe < LL *burda* pipe]

burden of proof, *Esp. Law.* obligation of proving something said to be true.

bur·den·some (bėr′dən·səm), *adj.* hard to bear; very heavy; oppressive. —**bur′den·some·ly,** *adv.* —**Syn.** oppressing, onerous.

bur·dock (bėr′dok′), *n.* a coarse weed with prickly burs and broad leaves. [< *bur* + *dock*¹]

bu·reau (byūr′ō), *n., pl.* **bu·reaus, bu·reaux** (byūr′ōz). **1.** *Am.* chest of drawers for clothes, often one with a mirror. **2.** *Brit.* desk or writing table with drawers. **3.** office: *a travel bureau.* **4.** *Am.* subdivision of a government department: *the Weather Bureau.* [< F, desk (orig. clothcovered) < OF *burel,* dim. of *bure* coarse woolen cloth < LL *burra*]

bu·reauc·ra·cy (byu·rok′rə·si), *n., pl.* **-cies.** **1.** government by groups of officials. **2.** officials administering the government. **3.** concentration of power in administrative bureaus.

bu·reau·crat (byūr′ə·krat), *n.* **1.** official in a bureaucracy. **2.** a formal pretentious government official. [blend of *bureau* + (*auto*)*crat*] —**bu′reau·crat′ic,** **bu′reau·crat′i·cal,** *adj.* —**bu′reau·crat′i·cal·ly,** *adv.*

bu·rette, bu·ret (byu·ret′), *n.* a graduated glass tube with a valve at the bottom, for measuring out small amounts of a liquid or gas. [< F, dim. of *buire* vase]

burg (bėrg), *n. Am., Colloq.* town; city. [var. of *borough*]

bur·geon (bėr′jən), *v., n.* bud; sprout. [< OF *burjon,* appar. < Gmc.]

bur·gess (bėr′jis), *n.* **1.** citizen of a borough. **2.** *Am.* member of the lower house of the colonial legislature in Virginia or Maryland. [< OF < LL *burgensis* citizen. See BOURGEOIS.]

burgh (bėrg), *n.* a chartered town in Scotland; borough. [var. of *borough*] —**burgh′al,** *adj.*

burgh·er (bėr′gər), *n.* citizen of a burgh or town; citizen.

bur·glar (bėr′glər), *n.* person who breaks into a building at night to steal. [< Anglo-L *burglator,* ? partly < OE *burgbryce*]

bur·glar·i·ous (bėr·glâr′i·əs), *adj.* having to do with burglary. —**bur·glar′i·ous·ly,** *adv.*

bur·glar·ize (bėr′glər·īz), *v.,* **-ized, -iz·ing.** *Am., Colloq.* commit burglary in.

bur·glar·proof (bėr′glər·prüf′), *adj.* so strong or safe that burglars cannot break in.

bur·glar·y (bėr′glər·i), *n., pl.* **-glar·ies.** *Law.* **1.** act of breaking into a house, building, etc., at night to steal or commit some other crime. **2.** act of breaking into a building to steal.

bur·gle (bėr′gəl), *v.,* **-gled, -gling.** *Colloq.* burglarize.

bur·go·mas·ter (bėr′gə·mas′tər; -mäs′-), *n.* mayor of a town in the Netherlands, Flanders, or Germany. [< Du. *burgemeester* < *burg* borough + *meester* master]

Bur·gun·dy (bėr′gən·di), *n., pl.* **-dies. 1.** region in E France. **2.** a red or white wine made there. —**Bur·gun·di·an** (bėr·gun′di·ən), *adj., n.*

bur·i·al (ber′i·əl), *n.* a burying. —*adj.* having to do with burying: *a burial service.*

burial ground, graveyard; cemetery.

Burke (bėrk), *n.* **Edmund,** 1729–1797, British statesman and orator.

burl (bėrl), *n.* **1.** knot in wool, cloth, or wood. **2.** a hard, round growth on the trunks of certain trees. —*v.* remove knots from. [< OF < LL *burra* flock of wool] —**burled,** *adj.* —**burl′er,** *n.*

bur·lap (bėr′lap), *n.* a coarse fabric made from jute or hemp, used to make bags, curtains, etc.

bur·lesque (bėr·lesk′), *n., v.,* **-lesqued, -lesquing,** *adj.* —*n.* **1.** a literary or dramatic composition in which a serious subject is treated ridiculously, or with mock solemnity. **2.** *U.S.* a cheap, vulgar kind of vaudeville with dancing and horseplay. —*v.* imitate so as to ridicule. —*adj.* comical; making people laugh. [< F < Ital. *burlesco* < *burla* jest] —**bur·lesque′ly,** *adv.* —**bur·les′quer,** *n.* —**Syn.** *n.* **1.** parody, take-off.

bur·ley, Bur·ley (bėr′li), *n., pl.* **-leys.** *Am.* kind of thin-leaved tobacco grown widely in Kentucky. [from a proper name]

bur·ly (bėr′li), *adj.,* **-li·er, -li·est. 1.** strong; sturdy; big. **2.** bluff; rough. [OE *borlice* excellently] —**bur′li·ly,** *adv.* —**bur′li·ness,** *n.*

Bur·ma (bėr′mə), *n.* country in SE Asia, formerly a British dependency.

Burma Road, a highway from Burma to Chungking, China, used during World War II.

Bur·mese (bėr·mēz′; -mēs′), *n., pl.* **-mese,** *adj.* —*n.* **1.** native of Burma. **2.** language of Burma. —*adj.* of Burma, its people, or their language.

burn¹ (bėrn), *v.,* **burned** or **burnt, burn·ing,** *n.* —*v.* **1.** be on fire; be very hot; blaze; glow. **2.** set on fire; cause to burn. **3.** destroy or be destroyed by fire. **4.** injure or be injured by fire, heat, or an acid. **5.** make by fire, by a heated tool, etc.: *his cigar burned a hole in the rug.* **6.** feel hot; give a feeling of heat to. **7.** be very excited or eager. **8.** inflame or be inflamed with anger, passion, etc. **9.** give light: *lamps were burning in every room.* **10.** sunburn; tan. **11.** produce, harden, glaze, etc., by fire or heat: *burn bricks, burn lime.* **12.** *Chem.* undergo or cause to undergo combustion; oxidize. **13.** cauterize. —*n.* **1.** injury caused by fire, heat, or an acid. **2.** a burned place. [coalescence of OE *beornan* be on fire and OE *bærnan* consume with fire] —**burn′a·ble,** *adj.* —**Syn.** *v.* **1.** flame. **2.** ignite, char.

burn² (bėrn), *n. Scot.* and *N.Eng.* a small stream; brook. [OE *burna*]

burn·er (bėr′nər), *n.* **1.** part of a lamp, stove, etc., where flame is produced. **2.** thing that burns. **3.** man whose work is burning something.

burn·ing (bėr′ning), *adj.* glowing; hot. —**burn′ing·ly,** *adv.*

Burette

bur·nish (bėr′nish), v., n. polish; shine. [< OF burnir make brown, polish < brun BROWN]

bur·noose, bur·nous (bėr·nüs′, bėr′nüs), n. cloak with a hood, worn by Moors and Arabs. [< F < Ar. burnus]

Burns (bėrnz), n. Robert, 1759–1796, Scottish poet.

burn·sides, Burn·sides (bėrn′sīdz′), n.pl. Am. growth of hair on cheeks but not on the chin. [for Gen. A. E. Burnside, American Civil War general]

burnt (bėrnt), v. pt. and pp. of burn[1].

burp gun (bėrp), a small, air-cooled, automatic machine gun, usually, of smaller caliber and having a higher rate of fire than a Thompson submachine gun.

burr[1] (bėr), n. 1. bur. 2. a rough ridge or edge left by a tool on metal, wood, etc., after cutting or drilling it. 3. tool that resembles a burr: dentists use tiny burrs. 4. a rounded growth, as on a tree. —v. bur. [var. of bur]

burr[2] (bėr), n. 1. rough pronunciation of r. 2. rough pronunciation: a Scotch burr. 3. a whirring sound. —v. 1. pronounce r roughly. 2. pronounce roughly. 3. make a whirring sound. [prob. imit.]

Burr (bėr), n. Aaron, 1756–1836, vice-president of the United States, 1801–05.

bur·ro (bėr′o; bùr′ō), n., pl. -ros. Am., S.W. donkey. [< Sp., < burrico small horse < LL burricus]

bur·row (bėr′ō), n. 1. hole dug in the ground by an animal for refuge or shelter. 2. similar dwelling or refuge. —v. 1. dig a hole in the ground. 2. live in burrows. 3. hide. 4. dig. 5. search: burrow in the library for a book. [cf. OE beorg; akin to BOROUGH, BURY] —bur′row·er, n.

bur·sa (bėr′sə), n., pl. -sae (-sē), -sas. Anat., Zool. sac, esp. one containing a lubricating fluid; pouch; cavity. [< LL < Gk. byrsa wineskin] —bur′sal, adj.

bur·sar (bėr′sər; -sär), n. treasurer of a college. [< Med.L bursarius < LL bursa purse]

bur·si·tis (bėr·sī′tis), n. inflammation of a bursa.

burst (bėrst), v., burst, burst·ing, n. —v. 1. break open; break out; fly apart suddenly with force; explode: the bomb burst. 2. break or give way because of grief or shock: her heart almost burst with sadness. 3. be very full: after the harvest the barns were bursting with grain. 4. go, come, do, etc., by force or suddenly: he burst into the room. 5. open or be opened suddenly or violently: the trees burst into bloom. 6. act or change suddenly in a way suggesting a break or explosion: she burst into loud laughter. 7. cause to break open or into pieces; shatter. —n. 1. bursting; split; explosion. 2. outbreak. 3. sudden and violent issuing forth. 4. sudden display of activity or energy: a burst of speed. 5. Mil. a. series of shots fired by one pressure of the trigger of an automatic weapon. b. explosion of a projectile in the air or when it strikes the ground or target. [OE berstan] —burst′er, n.

bur·then (bėr′tħən), n., v. Archaic. burden[1].

bur·y (ber′i), v., bur·ied, bur·y·ing. 1. put (a dead body) in the earth, a tomb, etc. 2. perform a funeral service for. 3. cover up; hide. 4. plunge; sink. [OE byrgan] —bur′i·er, n. —Syn. 1. inter, entomb. 3. conceal, secrete.

bus (bus), n., pl. bus·es, bus·ses. automobile that carries passengers along a certain route; omnibus. [short for omnibus]

bus boy or girl, Am. waiter's assistant, who fills glasses, carries off dishes, etc.

bus·by (buz′bi), n., pl. -bies. a tall fur hat, worn by hussars in the British army.

bush[1] (bùsh), n. 1. a woody plant smaller than a tree, often with many separate branches starting from or near the ground. 2. something that resembles or suggests a bush. 3. Am. open forest; uncleared land: take to the bush. —v. 1. spread out like a

Busby

bush; grow thickly. 2. set (ground) with bushes; cover with bushes. [ME busch, busk]

bush[2] (bùsh), n. a bushing. —v. put a bushing in. [< MDu. busse BOX[1]]

bushed (bùsht), adj. Am., Colloq. worn-out.

bush·el[1] (bùsh′əl), n. 1. measure for grain, fruit, vegetables, and other dry things, equal to 4 pecks or 32 quarts. 2. container that holds a bushel. [< OF boissiel, dim. of boisse a measure]

bush·el[2] (bùsh′əl), v., -eled, -el·ing; esp. Brit. -elled, -el·ling. Am. repair or alter (clothing). —bush′el·er, esp. Brit. bush′el·ler, n.

Bu·shi·do, bu·shi·do (bü′shē·dō), n. moral code of feudal Japan; Japanese chivalry.

bush·ing (bùsh′ing), n. 1. a metal lining. 2. a removable metal lining used as a bearing.

bush·man (bùsh′mən), n., pl. -men. 1. settler in the Australian bush. 2. person who knows much about life in the bush. 3. Bushman, member of a South African tribe of roving hunters.

bush·mas·ter (bùsh′mas′tər; -mäs′-), n. a large, poisonous snake of tropical America.

bush pilot, Am. pilot who flies a small plane over relatively unsettled country, as Alaska.

bush·whack·er (bùsh′hwak′ər), n. Am. 1. frontiersman. 2. guerrilla fighter. —bush′whack′ing, n.

bush·y (bùsh′i), adj., bush·i·er, bush·i·est. 1. spreading out like a bush; growing thickly. 2. overgrown with bushes. —bush′i·ness, n.

bus·i·ly (biz′ə·li), adv. in a busy manner.

busi·ness (biz′nis), n. 1. thing that one is busy at; work; occupation. 2. matter; affair. 3. activities of buying and selling; trade; commercial dealings. 4. commercial enterprise; industrial establishment: a bakery business. 5. right to act; concern: that's not your business. 6. action in a play; thing done to make a play seem like real life. [< busy + -ness] —Syn. 1. trade, profession.

business college or school, Am. school that gives training in shorthand, typewriting, bookkeeping, and other business subjects.

busi·ness·like (biz′nis·līk′), adj. having system and method; well-managed; practical.

busi·ness·man (biz′nis·man′), n., pl. -men. 1. man in business. 2. man who runs a business.

busi·ness·wom·an (biz′nis·wùm′ən), n., pl. -wom·en. Am. 1. woman in business. 2. woman who runs a business.

bus·kin (bus′kin), n. 1. high shoe with a very thick sole, worn by Greek and Roman actors of tragedies. 2. tragedy; tragic drama. [cf. OF brousequin] —bus′kined, adj.

bus·man's holiday (bus′mənz), holiday spent in doing what one does at one's daily work.

buss (bus), v., n. Archaic. or Dial. kiss.

bus·ses (bus′iz), n. pl. of bus.

bust[1] (bust), n. 1. statue of a person's head, shoulders, and chest. 2. the upper, front part of the body. 3. a woman's bosom. [< F < Ital. < L bustum funeral monument]

bust[2] (bust), n. 1. Substandard. burst. 2. Am., Slang. total failure; bankruptcy. 3. Am., Colloq. spree. —v. 1. Substandard. burst. 2. Slang. bankrupt; ruin. 3. Am., Slang. fail financially; become bankrupt. 4. Colloq. lower in rank. 5. Colloq. punch; hit. 6. train to obey; tame. 7. break up (a trust) into smaller companies. [var. of burst] ▶ Bust is the substandard form of burst in the sense of "exploding" or "breaking out." It is slang in the sense of "going broke" but is good English in busting a bronco or busting a trust.

bus·tard (bus′tərd), n. a large game bird of Africa, Europe, and Asia. [blend of OF bistarde and oustarde, both < L avis tarda slow bird]

bus·tle[1] (bus′əl), v., -tled, -tling, n. —v. 1. be noisily busy and in a hurry. 2. make (others) hurry or work hard. —n. noisy or excited activity. [? imit.] —bus′tler, n. —bus′tling·ly, adv. —Syn. n. stir, commotion, ado.

bus·tle[2] (bus′əl), n. pad used to puff out the upper back part of a woman's skirts. [? special use of bustle[1]]

bus·y (biz′i), adj., bus·i·er, bus·i·est, v., bus-ied, bus·y·ing. —adj. 1. working; active. 2. of a telephone line, in use. 3. full of work or activity. 4. prying into other people's affairs; meddling. —v. make busy; keep busy. [OE bisig] —bus'y·ness, n. —Syn. adj. 1. employed, occupied.

bus·y·bod·y (biz'i·bod'i), n., pl. -bod·ies. person who pries into other people's affairs.

but (but; unstressed bət), conj. 1. on the other hand; yet: it rained, but I went anyway. 2. if not; unless; except that: it never rains but it pours. 3. other than; otherwise than: we cannot choose but hear. 4. that: I don't doubt but he will come. 5. that not: he is not so sick but he can eat. 6. who not; which not: none sought his aid but were helped. —prep. with the exception of: he works every day but Sunday. —adv. 1. only; merely: he is but a boy. 2. all but, nearly; almost. —n. objection: not so many buts, please. [OE būtan without, unless < be- + ūtan outside < ūt OUT] ▶ But is the natural coördinating conjunction to connect two contrasted (adversative) statements of equal grammatical rank. It is more natural than the heavy and formal however or yet: He worked fast but accurately. Two clauses separated by but should ordinarily be separated by a comma. The contrast in idea suggests the use of punctuation even when the clauses are relatively short: I couldn't get the license number, but it was a New York plate.

bu·ta·di·ene (bū'tə·di'ēn; -di·ēn'), n. Chem. 1. a colorless gas, C₄H₆, used in making artificial rubber and as an anesthetic. 2. its isomeric hydrocarbon.

bu·tane (bū'tān; bū·tān'), n. Chem. either of two isomeric hydrocarbons, C₄H₁₀, of the methane series. Both are inflammable gases.

butch·er (bůch'ər), n. 1. man whose work is killing animals for food. 2. man who sells meat. 3. a brutal killer; murderer. 4. Am. vender; peddler, esp. a man who goes through trains selling magazines, candy, etc. —v. 1. kill (animals) for food. 2. kill wholesale, needlessly, or cruelly. 3. kill brutally; murder. 4. spoil by poor work. [< OF bocher < boc he-goat, BUCK¹ < Gmc.] —butch'er·er, n.

butch·er·y (bůch'ər·i), n., pl. -er·ies. 1. brutal killing; wholesale murder. 2. slaughterhouse; butcher shop.

but·ler (but'lər), n. manservant in charge of the pantry and table service in a household; head servant. [< AF var. of OF bouteillier < bouteille BOTTLE] —but'ler·ship, n.

butler's pantry, a small room between the kitchen and dining room, for use by a butler, serving maid, etc.

butt¹ (but), n. 1. the thicker end of anything, as a tool, weapon, ham, etc. 2. end that is left; stub; stump. [akin to BUTTOCKS]

butt² (but), n. 1. target. 2. object of ridicule or scorn. 3. an embankment of earth on which targets are placed for shooting practice. 4. the butts, place to practice shooting. —v. join end to end; abut. [< F bout end < Gmc.]

butt³ (but), v. 1. push or hit with the head. 2. butt in, Am., Colloq. meddle; interfere. —n. push or hit with the head. [< OF bouter thrust < bout end < Gmc.] —butt'er, n.

butt⁴ (but), n. 1. a large barrel for wine or beer. 2. a liquid measure equal to 126 gallons. [< OF < LL butta]

butte (būt), n. Am., W. a steep hill standing alone.

but·ter (but'ər), n. 1. the solid yellowish fat obtained from cream by churning. 2. something like butter, as apple butter. —v. 1. put butter on. 2. Colloq. flatter. [< L < Gk. boutyron] —but'ter·less, adj.

but·ter·cup (but'ər·kup'), n. plant with bright-yellow flowers shaped like cups.

but·ter·fat (but'ər·fat'), n. fat in milk.

but·ter·fin·gers (but'ər·fing'gərz), n. Colloq. a careless or clumsy person.

but·ter·fish (but'ər·fish'), n., pl. -fish·es or (esp. collectively) -fish. a small, silvery fish, used for food.

but·ter·fly (but'ər·flī'), n., pl. -flies. 1. insect with a slender body and four large, usually

bright-colored, wings. 2. person who suggests a butterfly by delicate beauty, bright clothes, fickleness, etc. [OE buterflēoge. See BUTTER, FLY¹.]

but·ter·milk (but'ər·milk'), n. an acid beverage obtained when butter is churned from cream.

but·ter·nut (but'ər·nut'), n. Am. 1. an oily kind of walnut. 2. tree that bears butternuts.

but·ter·scotch (but'ər·skoch'), n. candy made from brown sugar and butter. —adj. flavored with brown sugar and butter.

but·ter·y¹ (but'ər·i), adj. 1. like butter. 2. containing butter; spread with butter.

but·ter·y² (but'ər·i; but'ri), n., pl. -ter·ies. 1. storeroom, esp. for wines and liquors. 2. pantry. [< OF, < botte BUTT⁴]

but·tocks (but'əks), n.pl. rump. [ME buttok. Cf. OE buttuc end, small piece of land]

but·ton (but'ən), n. 1. knob or round piece fastened to clothing and other things to close them, decorate them, etc. 2. anything that resembles or suggests a button, as the knob or disk pressed to ring an electric bell. 3. buttons, Brit. Colloq. bellboy or page. —v. fasten with buttons; close with buttons. [< OF boton < bouter thrust. See BUTT³.] —but'ton·er, n. —but'ton·less, adj. —but'ton·like', adj.

but·ton·hole (but'ən·hōl'), n., v., -holed, -hol·ing. —n. slit or loop through which a button is passed. —v. 1. make buttonholes in. 2. hold in conversation; force to listen.

but·ton·wood (but'ən·wood'), n. Am. 1. a tall plane tree with button-shaped fruit. 2. its wood.

but·tress (but'ris), n. 1. support built against a wall or building to strengthen it. See the picture under flying buttress. 2. support; prop. —v. 1. strengthen with a buttress. 2. support; prop. [< OF bouterez (pl.) < bouter thrust against. See BUTT³.]

bu·tyr·ic (bū·tir'ik), adj. Chem. of or derived from butyric acid. [< L butyrum butter]

butyric acid, Chem. colorless liquid, C₄H₈O₂, that has an unpleasant odor. It is formed by fermentation in rancid butter, cheese, etc.

bux·om (buk'səm), adj. plump and good to look at; healthy and cheerful. [ME buhsum, ? < OE būgan bend] —bux'om·ly, adv. —bux'om·ness, n.

buy (bī), v., bought, buy·ing, n. —v. 1. get by paying a price. 2. buy things. 3. get by sacrifice: buy peace by surrender. 4. bribe. 5. buy off, get rid of by paying money to. 6. buy out, buy all the shares, rights, etc., of. 7. buy up, buy all that one can of; buy. —n. 1. Colloq. thing bought; a purchase. 2. Am., Colloq. a bargain. [OE bycgan]

buy·er (bī'ər), n. 1. person who buys. 2. person whose work is buying goods for a department store or other business.

buyer's strike, a combined refusal of consumers to buy in protest against high prices.

buzz (buz), n. 1. a humming sound made by flies, mosquitoes, or bees. 2. a low, confused sound of many people talking quietly. 3. whisper; rumor. —v. 1. hum loudly. 2. sound in a low, confused way. 3. talk excitedly. 4. utter or express by buzzing. 5. whisper; rumor. 6. fly a plane very fast and low over. 7. buzz about, move about busily. 8. buzz off, a. ring off on the telephone. b. Brit. Colloq. go away; leave. [imit.]

buz·zard (buz'ərd), n. 1. any of various more or less heavily built diurnal birds of prey of the hawk family. 2. turkey buzzard. [< OF busart, ult. < L buteo hawk]

buzz bomb, Mil. an aerial projectile that can be guided to a target where it explodes; robot bomb.

buzz·er (buz'ər), n. 1. thing that buzzes. 2. electrical device that makes a buzzing sound as a signal.

buzz saw, Am. a circular saw.

bx., pl. bxs. box.

by (bī), prep. 1. near; beside: by the house. 2. along; over; through: go by the bridge. 3. through the act of; through the means, use, or efficacy of: travel by airplane. 4. combined with in multiplication or relative dimensions: a room ten by twenty feet. 5. in the measure of: eggs by the dozen. 6. to the extent of: larger by half. 7.

according to: *work by rule.* 8. in relation to: *she did well by her children.* 9. separately with: *two by two.* 10. during: *by day.* 11. not later than: *by six o'clock.* 12. toward: *the island lies south by east from here.* —*adv.* 1. at hand: *near by.* 2. past (in space): *a car dashed by.* 3. past (in time): *days gone by.* 4. aside or away: *to put something by.* 5. *Am., Colloq. Southern.* at, in, or into another's house when passing: *please come by and eat with me.* 6. by and by, after a while. 7. b. and large, *Am.* in every way or aspect. —*n.* bye. [OE *bī,* unstressed *be*]

by-, *prefix.* 1. secondary; minor; less important, as in *by-product.* 2. near by, as in *bystander.*

bye (bī), *n.* 1. odd man or condition of being the odd player in games where players are grouped in pairs. 2. by the bye, incidentally. —*adj.* 1. aside from the main point, subject, etc. 2. secondary. 3. incidental. [var. of *by,* prep.]

bye-bye (bī′bī′), *interj. Colloq.* good-by.

bye-e-lec-tion (bī′i·lek′shən), *n.* a special election, not held at the time of the regular elections.

by-gone (bī′gôn′; -gon′), *adj.* past; former. —*n.* 1. something in the past. 2. the past.

by-law (bī′lô′), *n.* 1. law made by a city, company, club, etc., for the control of its own affairs. 2. a secondary law or rule; not one of the main rules. [< Scand. (Dan.) *bylov* < *by* town + *lov* LAW; meaning infl. by BY-]

by-line (bī′līn′), *n. Am.* line at the beginning of a newspaper or magazine article giving the name of the writer.

by-name (bī′nām′), *n.* 1. second name; surname. 2. nickname.

by-pass (bī′pas′; -päs′), *n.* 1. road, channel, pipe, etc., providing a secondary passage to be used instead of the main passage. 2. *Elect.* a shunt. —*v.* 1. provide a secondary passage for. 2. go around. 3. pass over the head of (a superior, etc.) to a higher authority. 4. set aside or ignore (regulations, etc.) in order to reach a desired objective. 5. get away from; avoid; escape: *by-pass a question.* 6. *Mil.* flank.

by-path (bī′path′; -päth′), *n.* a side path.

by-play (bī′plā′), *n.* action that is not part of the main action, esp. on the stage.

by-prod-uct (bī′prod′əkt), *n.* something produced in making or doing something else; not the main product.

by-road (bī′rōd′), *n.* a side road.

By-ron (bī′rən), *n.* George Gordon, Lord, 1788–1824, English poet. —**By-ron-ic** (bī·ron′ik), *adj.* —**By-ron′i-cal-ly,** *adv.*

by-stand-er (bī′stan′dər), *n.* person standing near or by; looker-on.

by-street (bī′strēt′), *n.* a side street.

by-word (bī′wẽrd′), *n.* 1. object of contempt; thing scorned. 2. common saying; proverb.

Byz-an-tine (biz′ən·tēn; -tīn; bi·zan′tin), *adj.* having to do with Byzantium or a style of architecture developed there that uses round arches, crosses, circles, domes, and mosaics. —*n.* native or inhabitant of Byzantium.

Byzantine Empire, eastern part of the Roman Empire from 395 A.D. to 1453.

By-zan-ti-um (bi·zan′shi·əm; -ti·əm), *n.* ancient city where Istanbul now is.

C

C, c (sē), *n., pl.* **C's; c's.** 1. the third letter of the alphabet. 2. the first note of the musical scale of C major. 3. Roman numeral for 100.

C, 1. *Chem.* carbon. 2. central. 3. *Am., Colloq.* a hundred-dollar bill.

C., 1. Cape. 2. Catholic. 3. centigrade.

c., 1. carton; cartons. 2. case. 3. *Baseball.* catcher. 4. cent; cents. 5. center. 6. centimeter. 7. Also, *ca.* approximately. [L *circa* or *circum*] 8. copyright. 9. cubic.

Ca, *Chem.* calcium.

CAA, Civil Aeronautics Administration.

Caa-ba (kä′bə), *n.* Kaaba.

cab (kab), *n.* 1. taxicab. 2. carriage that can be hired, pulled by one horse. 3. *Am.* the covered part of a locomotive where the engineer and fireman sit. 4. an enclosed seat on a truck for the driver. [for *cabriolet*]

ca-bal (kə·bal′), *n., v.,* **-balled, -bal-ling.** —*n.* 1. a small group of people working or plotting in secret. 2. a secret scheme of such a group. —*v.* form such a group; conspire. [see CABALA] —Syn. *n.* 1. faction, junto, conspiracy.

cab-a-la (kab′ə·lə; kə·bä′-), *n.* 1. a secret religious philosophy of the Jewish rabbis, based on a mystical interpretation of the Scriptures. 2. a mystical belief. Also, cabbala. [< Med.L < Heb. *qabbalah* tradition] —**cab-a-lism** (kab′-ə·liz·əm), *n.* —**cab′a-list,** *n.*

cab-a-lis-tic (kab′ə·lis′tik), **cab-a-lis-ti-cal** (-tə·kəl), *adj.* having a mystical meaning; secret. —**cab′a-lis′ti-cal-ly,** *adv.*

cab-al-le-ro (kab′əl·yãr′ō), *n., pl.* **-ros.** 1. *Am., W.* gentleman or gallant. 2. escort. [< Sp. < L *caballarius* horseman < *caballus* horse]

ca-ba-ña (kə·bä′nyə; -ban′ə), *n. Am., Orig. S.W.* 1. cabin (def. 1). 2. bathhouse. [< Sp. < LL *capanna.* Doublet of CABIN.]

cab-a-ret (kab′ə·rā′; kab′ə·rā), *n.* 1. restaurant where an entertainment of singing and dancing is provided. 2. the entertainment. [< F]

cab-bage (kab′ij), *n., v.,* **-baged, -bag-ing.** —*n.* vegetable whose leaves are closely folded into a round head that grows from a short stem. —*v.* form a head like a cabbage. [< F < Pr., ult. < L *caput* head]

cab-ba-la (kab′ə·lə; kə·bä′-), *n.* cabala.

cab-by (kab′i), *n., pl.* **-bies.** *Colloq.* cabman.

cab-in (kab′ən), *n.* 1. a small, roughly built house; hut. 2. room in a ship. 3. place for passengers in an airplane or airship. —*v.* 1. live in a cabin. 2. confine; cramp. [< F < LL *capanna.* Doublet of CABAÑA.] —Syn. *n.* 1. shanty, shack.

cabin boy, boy whose work is waiting on the officers and passengers in a ship.

cab-i-net (kab′ə·nit), *n.* 1. piece of furniture with shelves or drawers for holding dishes, etc. 2. group of advisers chosen by the head of a nation to help him with the administration of the government. 3. the Cabinet, *Am.* the cabinet of the President of the United States. 4. a small, private room. —*adj.* 1. of or having to do with a political cabinet. 2. private. 3. of such value, beauty, or size as to be suited for a private room or for keeping in a case. [< F < Ital. *gabinetto,* ult. < LL *cavea* CAGE]

cab-i-net-mak-er (kab′ə·nit·māk′ər), *n.* man who makes fine furniture and woodwork. —**cab′i-net-mak′ing,** *n.*

cab-i-net-work (kab′ə·nit·wẽrk′), *n.* 1. beautifully made furniture and woodwork. 2. the making of such furniture and woodwork.

ca-ble (kā′bəl), *n., v.,* **-bled, -bling.** —*n.* 1. a strong, thick rope, usually made of wires twisted together. 2. cable's length. 3. *Elect.* a protected bundle of wires to carry current. 4. *Am.* cablegram. —*v.* 1. tie or fasten with a cable. 2. send a message under the ocean by cable. [< F < Pr. < L *capulum* halter]

Cable (def. 1)

cable car, *Am.* car pulled by a moving cable operated by a stationary engine.

ca-ble-gram (kā′bəl·gram), *n. Am.* telegram sent by cable.

cable's length, unit of measurement at sea, 720 ft. (U.S.); 607.56 ft. (British navy).

cab-man (kab′mən), *n., pl.* **-men.** a cab driver.

ca-boo-dle (kə·bü′dəl), *n. Am., Colloq.* group of people or things.

ca·boose (kə·büs'), *n.* 1. *Am.* a small car on a freight train in which the trainmen can rest and sleep. 2. kitchen on the deck of a ship. [< MLG *kabuse* cabin]

Cab·ot (kab'ət), *n.* **John**, 1450?-1498, Italian navigator who explored for England. He discovered the North American continent in 1497.

cab·ri·o·let (kab'ri·ə·lā'), *n.* 1. automobile somewhat like a coupé, but having a folding top. 2. a one-horse carriage with two wheels, and often with a folding top. [< F, < *cabrioler* leap < Ital. < L *caper* goat; from bouncing motion]

ca·ca·o (kə·kā'ō; -kä'ō), *n., pl.* **-ca·os.** 1. seeds from which cocoa and chocolate are made. 2. the tropical American tree they grow on. [< Sp. < Mex. *caca-uatl*]

cach·a·lot (kash'ə·lot; -lō), *n.* sperm whale. [< F < Pg. < L *caccabus* pot]

cache (kash), *n., v.,* **cached, cach·ing.** —*n.* 1. a hiding place to store food or supplies. 2. a hidden store of food or supplies. —*v.* put in a cache; hide. [< F, < *cacher* hide]

ca·chet (ka·shā'; kash'ā), *n.* 1. a private seal or stamp. 2. a distinguishing mark of quality or genuineness. [< F, < *cacher* hide]

cach·in·nate (kak'ə·nāt), *v.,* **-nat·ed, -nat·ing.** laugh loudly. [< L *cachinnatus*] —**cach'in·na'tion,** *n.*

ca·cique (kə·sēk'), *n.* 1. a native chief in the West Indies, Mexico, etc. 2. *Am., S.W.* a pompous political leader. [< Sp. < Haitian]

cack·le (kak'əl), *v.,* **-led, -ling,** *n.* —*v.* 1. make a shrill, broken sound. 2. laugh shrilly, harshly, and brokenly. 3. chatter. —*n.* 1. the shrill, broken sound that a hen makes after laying an egg. 2. shrill, harsh, broken laughter. 3. noisy chatter; silly talk. [ME *cakelen*; imit.]

ca·coph·o·ny (kə·kof'ə·ni), *n., pl.* **-nies.** harsh, clashing sound; dissonance; discord. [< Gk., < *kakos* bad + *phone* sound] —**ca·coph'o·nous,** *adj.* —**ca·coph'o·nous·ly,** *adv.*

cac·tus (kak'təs), *n., pl.* **-tus·es, -ti** (-tī). plant whose thick, fleshy stems have spines but usually have no leaves. Most cactuses grow in very hot, dry regions. [< L < Gk. *kaktos*]

Common cactus

cad (kad), *n.* an ill-bred person. [< *caddie*]

ca·dav·er (kə·dav'ər; -dā'vər), *n.* dead body; corpse. [< L] —**ca·dav'er·ic,** *adj.*

ca·dav·er·ous (kə·dav'ər·əs), *adj.* 1. of or like a cadaver. 2. pale and ghastly. 3. thin and worn. —**ca·dav'er·ous·ly,** *adv.* —**ca·dav'er·ous·ness,** *n.*

cad·die (kad'i), *n., v.,* **-died, -dy·ing.** —*n.* person who carries a golf player's clubs, etc. —*v.* help a golf player in this way. Also, **caddy.** [< F *cadet* CADET]

cad·dis fly (kad'is), a mothlike insect whose larvae (caddis worms) live under water in cocoons that are coated with sand, gravel, etc.

cad·dish (kad'ish), *adj.* ungentlemanly; ill-bred. —**cad'dish·ly,** *adv.* —**cad'dish·ness,** *n.*

cad·dy[1] (kad'i), *n., pl.* **-dies.** a small box, can, or chest. [< Malay *kati* a small weight]

cad·dy[2] (kad'i), *n., pl.* **-dies,** *v.,* **-died, -dy·ing.** caddie.

ca·dence (kā'dəns), **ca·den·cy** (-dən·si), *n., pl.* **-den·ces; -cies.** 1. rhythm. 2. measure or beat of any rhythmical movement. 3. fall of the voice. 4. rising and falling sound; modulation. 5. *Music.* series of chords, a trill, etc., that brings part of a piece of music to an end. [< F < Ital. See CADENZA.] —**ca'denced,** *adj.*

ca·den·za (kə·den'zə), *n. Music.* an elaborate flourish or showy passage near the end of an aria, concerto, etc. [< Ital. < L *cadentia* < *cadere* fall]

ca·det (kə·det'), *n.* 1. a young man who is training to be an officer in the army or navy. 2. a younger son or brother. [< F < Gascon *capdet* < L *capitellum,* dim. of *caput* head] —**ca·det'ship,** **ca·det·cy** (kə·det'si), *n.*

cadge (kaj), *v.,* **cadged, cadg·ing.** 1. *Dial.* peddle. 2. *Colloq.* beg. —**cadg'er,** *n.*

ca·di (kä'di; kā'-), *n., pl.* **-dis.** a minor Mohammedan judge. Also, **kadi.** [< Ar. *qāḍī* judge]

Cá·diz (kə·diz'; kā'diz), *n.* seaport in SW Spain.

cad·mi·um (kad'mi·əm), *n. Chem.* a bluish-white, ductile metallic element, Cd, resembling tin, used in making certain alloys. [< NL < L *cadmia* zinc ore < Gk. *kadmeia*] —**cad'mic,** *adj.*

Cad·mus (kad'məs), *n. Gk. Legend.* the founder of Thebes. —**Cad·me·an** (kad·mē'ən), *adj.*

ca·dre (kä'dər; *Mil.* kad'rē), *n.* 1. framework. 2. a permanent skeleton organization, esp. of officers of a military unit, that can be filled out as needed. [< F < Ital. < L *quadrum* square]

ca·du·ce·us (kə·dū'si·əs; -dū'-), *n., pl.* **-ce·i** (-si·ī). staff carried by the god Hermes and by heralds in ancient Greece and Rome, now often used as an emblem of the medical profession. [< L < dial. Gk. *karykeion* herald's staff] —**ca·du'ce·an,** *adj.*

cae·cum (sē'kəm), *n., pl.* **-ca** (-kə). *Anat.* a cavity closed at one end, esp. the first part of the large intestine. [< L, blind (thing)] —**cae'cal,** *adj.*

Cae·sar (sē'zər), *n.* 1. **Gaius Julius,** 102?-44 B.C., Roman general, statesman, and historian, conqueror of Gaul. 2. a title of the Roman emperors from Augustus to Hadrian. 3. an emperor. 4. dictator; tyrant.

Cae·sar·e·an, Cae·sar·i·an (si·zâr'i·ən), *adj.* of Julius Caesar or the Caesars. —*n.* a Caesarean operation. Also, **Cesarean, Cesarian.**

Caesarean operation or **section,** operation by which a baby is removed from the uterus by cutting through the abdominal wall.

cae·si·um (sē'zi·əm), *n.* cesium.

cae·su·ra (si·zhur'ə; -zyur'ə), *n., pl.* **-sur·as, -sur·ae** (-zhur'ē; -zyur'ē). 1. a break, esp. a sense pause, near the middle of a line in English poetry and in the middle of a foot in Greek and Latin poetry. 2. a break. Also, **cesura.** [< L, cutting, < *caedere* cut] —**cae·sur'al,** *adj.*

ca·fé (ka·fā'; kə-), *n.* 1. restaurant. 2. coffee. 3. *Am.* barroom. [< F. See COFFEE.]

caf·e·te·ri·a (kaf'ə·tir'i·ə), *n. Am.* restaurant where people wait on themselves. [< Mex. Sp., coffee shop]

caf·feine, caf·fein (kaf'ēn; kaf'i·in), *n.* a stimulating drug, $C_8H_{10}N_4O_2$, found in coffee and tea. [< F, < *café* coffee]

caf·tan (kaf'tən; käf·tän'), *n.* a long tunic with a girdle, worn under the coat in Turkey, Egypt, etc. Also, **kaftan.** [< Turk.]

cage (kāj), *n., v.,* **caged, cag·ing.** —*n.* 1. frame or place closed in with wires, bars, etc., for confining birds, wild animals, etc. 2. thing shaped like a cage, as the closed platform of an elevator. 3. prison. —*v.* put or keep in a cage. [< F < L *cavea* cell < *cavus* hollow]

cage·ling (kāj'ling), *n.* bird kept in a cage.

cage·y (kāj'i), *adj.* **cag·i·er, cag·i·est.** *Am., Slang.* shrewd; sharp. —**cag'i·ly,** *adv.* —**cag'i·ness,** *n.*

ca·hoot (kə·hüt'), *n. Am., Slang.* 1. in cahoot or cahoots, in partnership, company or league. 2. go cahoots, go into partnership.

cai·man (kā'mən), *n., pl.* **-mans.** cayman.

Cain (kān), *n.* 1. the oldest son of Adam and Eve, who killed his brother Abel. 2. murderer. 3. **raise Cain,** *Am., Colloq.* make a great disturbance.

ca·ique (kä·ēk'), *n.* a long, narrow Turkish rowboat, much used on the Bosporus.

cairn (kârn), *n.* pile of stones heaped up as a memorial, tomb, or landmark. [< Scotch Gaelic *carn* heap of stones] —**cairned** (kârnd), *adj.*

Cai·ro (kī'rō), *n.* capital of Egypt, in the NE part.

cais·son (kā'sən; -son), *n.* 1. box for ammunition. 2. wagon to carry ammunition. 3. a watertight box or chamber in which men can work under water. 4. a watertight float used in raising sunken ships. [< F, < *caisse* chest < L *capsa* box]

caisson disease, *Am.* the bends.

cai·tiff (kā′tif), *n.* a mean, bad person; coward. —*adj.* vile; cowardly; mean. [< OF < L *captivus* captive]

ca·jole (kə·jōl′), *v.*, -joled, -jol·ing. persuade by pleasant words, flattery, or false promises; coax. [< F *cajoler*] —ca·jol′er, *n.* —Syn. beguile.

ca·jol·er·y (kə·jōl′ər·i), *n.*, *pl.* -er·ies. persuasion by smooth, deceitful words; flattery; coaxing.

cake (kāk), *n.*, *v.*, caked, cak·ing. —*n.* 1. a baked mixture of flour, sugar, eggs, flavoring, and other things. 2. a flat, thin mass of dough baked or fried. 3. any small, flat mass of food fried on both sides: *a fish cake.* 4. a shaped mass: *a cake of soap.* —*v.* form into a solid mass. [prob. < Scand. *kaka*]

cakes and ale, pleasures of life.

cake·walk (kāk′wôk′), *Am. n.* a march or dance to music of American Negro origin, to see who could do the most graceful or eccentric steps. —*v.* do a cakewalk. —cake′walk′er, *n. Am.*

Cal., California.

cal·a·bash (kal′ə·bash), *n.* 1. gourd or fruit whose dried shell is used to make bottles, bowls, drums, rattles, etc. 2. a tropical plant or tree that it grows on. 3. bottle, bowl, etc., made from such a dried shell. [< F < Sp., prob. < Pers. *kharbuz* melon]

cal·a·boose (kal′ə·büs; kal′ə·büs′), *n. Am., Esp. Southern Colloq.* jail; prison. [< Sp. *calabozo* dungeon]

ca·la·di·um (kə·lā′di·əm), *n.* a tropical plant with large leaves. [< Malay *kelady*]

Cal·ais (ka·lā′; kal′ā), *n.* seaport in N France that is nearest England.

cal·a·mine (kal′ə·mīn; -min), *n.* native hydrous zinc silicate, (ZnOH)₂SiO₃. [< F < Med.L *calamina* < L *cadmia*. See CADMIUM.]

ca·lam·i·tous (kə·lam′ə·təs), *adj.* causing calamity; accompanied by calamity; disastrous. —ca·lam′i·tous·ly, *adv.* —ca·lam′i·tous·ness, *n.* —Syn. dire, deplorable, grievous.

ca·lam·i·ty (kə·lam′ə·ti), *n.*, *pl.* -ties. 1. a great misfortune. 2. serious trouble; misery. [< L *calamitas*] —Syn. 1. disaster, catastrophe.

cal·a·mus (kal′ə·məs), *n.*, *pl.* -mi (-mī). 1. sweet flag. 2. its fragrant root. [< L < Gk. *kalamos* reed]

ca·lash (kə·lash′), *n.* 1. a light, low carriage that usually has a folding top. 2. a folding top or hood. 3. a kind of silk hood or bonnet formerly worn by women. [< F < Slavic]

Calash

cal·car·e·ous (kal·kãr′i·əs), *adj.* 1. of or containing lime or limestone. 2. of or containing calcium. [< L, < *calx* lime]

cal·ces (kal′sēz), *n. pl.* of calx.

cal·cif·er·ous (kal·sif′ər·əs), *adj. Chem.* containing calcite.

cal·ci·fy (kal′sə·fī), *v.*, -fied, -fy·ing. harden by the deposit of lime. [< L *calx* lime] —cal′ci·fi·ca′tion, *n.*

cal·ci·mine (kal′sə·mīn; -min), *n.*, *v.*, -mined, -min·ing. —*n.* a white or colored liquid consisting of a mixture of water, coloring matter, glue, etc., used on ceilings and walls. —*v.* cover with calcimine. Also, kalsomine.

cal·cine (kal′sīn; -sin), *v.*, -cined, -cin·ing. 1. change to lime by heating. 2. burn to ashes or powder. —cal·ci·na·tion (kal′sə·nā′shən), *n.* —cal·cin·a·to·ry (kal·sin′ə·tô′ri; -tō′-; kal′-sin-), *adj.*, *n.*

cal·cite (kal′sīt), *n.* mineral composed of calcium carbonate, CaCO₃. It occurs as limestone, chalk, marble, etc.

cal·ci·um (kal′si·əm), *n. Chem.* a soft, silvery-white metallic element, Ca. It is a part of limestone, milk, bones, etc. [< L *calx* lime]

calcium carbide, *Chem.* a heavy gray substance, CaC₂, that reacts with water to form acetylene gas.

calcium carbonate, *Chem.* mineral, CaCO₃, occurring in rocks as marble and limestone and in animals as bones, shells, teeth, etc.

calcium chloride, *Chem.* compound of calcium and chlorine, CaCl₂, used in making artificial ice and chlorine.

cal·cu·la·ble (kal′kyə·lə·bəl), *adj.* 1. that can be calculated. 2. reliable. —cal′cu·la·bly, *adv.*

cal·cu·late (kal′kyə·lāt), *v.*, -lat·ed, -lat·ing. 1. find out by adding, subtracting, multiplying, or dividing; figure; compute. 2. find out beforehand by any process of reasoning; estimate. 3. *Am., Colloq.* rely; depend; count. 4. *Am., Colloq.* or *Dial.* plan; intend. 5. *Am., Colloq.* or *Dial.* think; believe; suppose. [< L, < *calculus* stone, used in counting, dim. of *calx* stone] —cal′cu·la′tor, *n.* ▷ Calculate, guess, and reckon are localisms for the *think*, *suppose*, *expect* of standard English.

calculated risk, venture or undertaking whose outcome can be estimated with some degree of confidence but not with certainty.

cal·cu·lat·ing (kal′kyə·lāt′ing), *adj.* 1. that calculates. 2. shrewd; careful. 3. scheming; selfish. —Syn. 2. crafty, astute.

cal·cu·la·tion (kal′kyə·lā′shən), *n.* 1. act of calculating. 2. result found by calculating. 3. careful thinking; deliberate planning. —cal′cu·la′tive, *adj.* —Syn. 3. forethought, prudence.

cal·cu·lus (kal′kyə·ləs), *n.*, *pl.* -li (-lī), -lus·es. 1. a method of calculation in higher mathematics. 2. a stone that has formed in the body because of a diseased condition. Gallstones are calculi. [see CALCULATE]

Cal·cut·ta (kal·kut′ə), *n.* seaport in E India.

cal·dron (kôl′drən), *n.* a large kettle or boiler. Also, cauldron. [< OF < L *caldus* hot]

Cal·e·do·ni·a (kal′ə·dō′ni·ə), *n. Poetic.* Scotland. —Cal′e·do′ni·an, *adj.*

cal·en·dar (kal′ən·dər), *n.* 1. table showing the months, weeks, and days of the year. 2. system by which the beginning, length, and divisions of the year are fixed. 3. list; record; schedule: *a court calendar.* —*v.* enter in a calendar or list. [< AF < L *calendarium* account book < *calendae* calends (day bills were due)]

calendar day, the 24 hours from one midnight to the next midnight.

calendar month, month.

calendar year, period of 365 days (or in leap year, 366 days) that begins on January 1 and ends on December 31.

cal·en·der (kal′ən·dər), *n.* machine in which cloth, paper, etc., is smoothed and glazed by pressing between rollers. —*v.* make smooth and glossy by pressing in a calender. [< F < L < Gk. *kylindros* cylinder] —cal′en·der·er, *n.*

cal·ends (kal′əndz), *n.pl.* the first day of the month in the ancient Roman calendar. Also, kalends. [< L *calendae*]

ca·len·du·la (kə·len′jə·lə), *n.* kind of marigold with yellow or orange flowers. [< NL, dim. of *calendae* the calends]

calf¹ (kaf; käf), *n.*, *pl.* calves. 1. a young cow or bull. 2. a young elephant, whale, seal, etc. 3. leather made from the skin of a calf. 4. *Colloq.* a silly boy. [OE *cealf*]

calf² (kaf; käf), *n.*, *pl.* calves. the thick, fleshy part of the back of the leg below the knee. [< Scand. *kálfi*]

calf·skin (kaf′skin′; käf′-), *n.* 1. skin of a calf. 2. leather made from it.

cal·i·ber, *esp. Brit.* **cal·i·bre** (kal′ə·bər), *n.* 1. diameter, esp. inside diameter. A .45-caliber revolver has a barrel with an inside diameter of 45/100 of an inch. 2. amount of ability. 3. amount of merit or importance. [< F < Ar. *qālib* mold]

cal·i·brate (kal′ə·brāt), *v.*, -brat·ed, -brat·ing. 1. determine, check, or rectify the scale of (a thermometer, gauge, or other measuring instrument). 2. find the caliber of. —cal′i·bra′tion, *n.* —cal′i·bra′tor, *n.*

cal·i·co (kal′ə·kō), *n.*, *pl.* -coes, -cos, *adj.* —*n.* *Am.* a cotton cloth, usually with colored patterns printed on one side. —*adj.* 1. made of calico. 2. spotted in colors. [after *Calicut*, India]

Cal·i·cut (kal′ə-kut), *n.* seaport in SW India.

ca·lif (kā′lif; kal′if), *n.* caliph.

Calif., official abbreviation of California.

cal·if·ate (kal′ə-fāt; –fit; kā′lə-), *n.* caliphate.

Cal·i·for·nia (kal′ə-fôr′nyə; –fôr′ni-ə), *n.* 1. a Western State of the United States, on the Pacific coast. *Capital:* Sacramento. *Abbrev.:* Calif. 2. Gulf of, gulf east of Lower California. —Cal′i·for′nian, *adj., n.*

California poppy, *Am.* 1. a small poppy with finely divided leaves and colorful flowers. 2. its flower.

cal·i·for·ni·um (kal′ə-fôr′ni-əm), *n. Chem.* a radioactive element, Cf, produced by the bombardment of curium in the cyclotron at the University of California; the heaviest of known elements. [< *California*]

cal·i·per (kal′ə-pər), *n.* Usually, calipers. instrument used to measure the diameter or thickness of something. Also, calliper. [var. of *caliber*]

Calipers

ca·liph (kā′lif; kal′if), *n.* the head of a Moslem state. Also, calif, khalif. [< OF < Med.L < Ar. *khalīfa* successor, vicar]

cal·iph·ate (kal′ə-fāt; –fit; kā′lə-), *n.* rank, reign, government, or territory of a caliph. Also, califate.

cal·is·then·ic (kal′əs-then′ik), **cal·is·then·i·cal** (-ə-kəl), *adj.* of calisthenics. Also, callisthenic, callisthenical.

cal·is·then·ics (kal′əs-then′iks), *n.* 1. (*sing. in use*) the practice or art of calisthenic exercises. 2. (*pl. in use*) exercises to develop a strong and graceful body. Also, callisthenics. [< Gk. *kallos* beauty + *sthenos* strength]

calk¹ (kôk), *v.* fill up (a seam, crack, or joint) so that it will not leak; make watertight, as with oakum and tar. Also, caulk. [< OF < L *calcare* tread, press in] —calk′er, *n.*

calk² (kôk), *n.* 1. a projecting piece on a horseshoe to prevent slipping. 2. *Am.* a sharp, projecting piece of metal on the bottom of a shoe to prevent slipping. —*v.* put calks on. [< L *calx* heel or *calcar* spur] —calk′er, *n.*

call (kôl), *v.* 1. speak loudly; cry; shout: *he called from downstairs.* 2. (of a bird or animal) utter its cry. 3. signal: *the bugle called the men to assemble.* 4. rouse; waken: *call me in the morning.* 5. invite; command; summon: *obey when duty calls.* 6. ask to come; cause to come: *call off your dog, the assembly was called to order.* 7. get; bring: *call forth a reply.* 8. give a name to; term: *they called the baby John.* 9. consider; estimate: *they called the play a big hit.* 10. make a short visit or stop: *they called on us at home.* 11. read over: *the teacher called the roll.* 12. telephone (to). 13. demand payment of. 14. *Am.* demand for payment. 15. *Am.* demand a show of hands in poker. 16. *Am., Baseball.* a. declare (a game) ended: *the game was called on account of rain.* b. pronounce (a pitch) a strike or ball. 17. **call back**, a. recall. b. revoke. c. telephone to someone who has called previously. 18. **call down**, a. invoke. b. *Am., Colloq.* scold. 19. **call for**, go and get; stop and get. 20. **call off**, *Am.*, enumerate. 21. **call up**, a. bring to mind; bring back. b. telephone to. —*n.* 1. a shout; a cry. 2. the characteristic sound of a bird or other animal. 3. signal given by sound. 4. invitation; request; command; summons. 5. claim; demand: *a doctor is on call at all hours.* 6. need; occasion: *you have no call to meddle.* 7. a short visit or stop. 8. *Am.* demand for payment. 9. act of calling. 10. **on call**, *Am.* a. subject to payment on demand. b. ready. [OE. Cf. West Saxon *ceallian.*] —call′a·ble, *adj.* —Syn. *v.* 1. yell, shriek, scream. 5. bid. 8. designate.

cal·la (kal′ə), *n.* 1. calla lily. plant with a large, petallike, white leaf around a thick spike of yellow florets. 2. a marsh plant with heart-shaped leaves. [< NL]

call·boy (kôl′boi′), *n.* 1. bellboy in a hotel, ship, etc. 2. boy who calls actors when they are supposed to go on the stage.

call·er (kôl′ər), *n.* 1. person who makes a short visit. 2. person who calls.

cal·lig·ra·phy (kə-lig′rə-fi), *n.* 1. handwriting. 2. beautiful handwriting. [< Gk., < *kallos* beauty + *graphein* write] —cal·lig′ra·pher, *n.* —cal·li·graph·ic (kal′ə-graf′ik), *adj.*

call·ing (kôl′ing), *n.* 1. business; occupation; profession. 2. invitation; command; summons.

calling card, *Am.* a small card with a person's name on it. It is used when visiting someone, to acknowledge gifts, etc.

cal·li·o·pe (kə-lī′ə-pē; *for 1, also* kal′i-ōp), *n.* 1. *Am.* musical instrument having a series of steam whistles played by pushing keys. 2. Calliope, the Muse of eloquence and heroic poetry. [< L, < Gk. *kalliope* beautiful-voiced < *kallos* beauty + *ops* voice]

cal·li·per (kal′ə-pər), *n.* caliper.

cal·lis·then·ic (kal′əs-then′ik), **cal·lis·then·i·cal** (-ə-kəl), *adj.* calisthenic.

cal·lis·then·ics (kal′əs-then′iks), *n.* calisthenics.

call loan, *Am.* loan repayable on demand.

call money, money borrowed that must be paid back on demand.

cal·los·i·ty (kə-los′ə-ti), *n., pl.* –ties. 1. a hard thickening of the skin; callus. 2. lack of feeling; hardness of heart.

cal·lous (kal′əs), *adj.* 1. hard; hardened, as portions of the skin exposed to friction. 2. unfeeling; not sensitive. [< L, < *callus* hard skin] —cal′lous·ly, *adv.* —cal′lous·ness, *n.* —Syn. 2. insensible, unsusceptible. —Ant. 2. sensitive.

cal·low (kal′ō), *adj.* 1. young and inexperienced. 2. not fully developed. 3. (of birds) without feathers sufficiently developed for flight. [OE *calu* bald] —cal′low·ness, *n.* —Syn. 1. green.

cal·lus (kal′əs), *n., pl.* –lus·es. 1. a hard, thickened place on the skin. 2. a new growth to unite the ends of a broken bone. [see CALLOUS]

calm (käm), *adj.* 1. not stormy or windy; quiet; still; not moving. 2. peaceful; not excited. —*n.* 1. absence of motion or wind; quietness; stillness. 2. absence of excitement; peacefulness. —*v.* make or become calm. [< OF < Ital. < VL < Gk. *kauma* heat of the day; hence, time for rest, stillness] —calm′ly, *adv.* —calm′ness, *n.* —Syn. *adj.* 1. motionless, smooth, placid. 2. undisturbed, composed. —Ant. *adj.* 1. stormy. 2. excited.

cal·o·mel (kal′ə-mel; –məl), *n.* mercurous chloride, Hg_2Cl_2, a white, tasteless, crystalline powder, used in medicine as a cathartic, etc.

ca·lor·ic (kə-lôr′ik; –lor′-), *n.* heat. —*adj.* having to do with heat. —cal·o·ric·i·ty (kal′ə-ris′ə-ti), *n.*

cal·o·rie, cal·o·ry (kal′ə-ri), *n., pl.* –ries. 1. *Physics.* unit of heat. The quantity of heat necessary to raise the temperature of a gram of water one degree centigrade is a **small calorie**. The quantity of heat necessary to raise the temperature of a kilogram of water one degree centigrade is a **large calorie**. 2. *Physiol.* a. unit of the energy supplied by food. It corresponds to a large calorie. An ounce of sugar will produce about a hundred such calories. b. quantity of food capable of producing such an amount of energy. [< F < L *calor* heat]

cal·o·rif·ic (kal′ə-rif′ik), *adj.* producing heat.

cal·o·rim·e·ter (kal′ə-rim′ə-tər), *n. Physics.* apparatus for measuring the quantity of heat.

cal·o·rim·e·try (kal′ə-rim′ə-tri), *n.* measurement of heat. —cal·o·ri·met·ric (kal′ə·rə-met′-rik; kə-lôr′-; –lor′-), cal′o·ri·met′ri·cal, *adj.*

cal·u·met (kal′yə-met; kal′yə-met′), *n. Am.* a long, ornamented tobacco pipe smoked by the American Indians in ceremonies as a symbol of peace. [< F, ult. < L *calamus* < Gk. *kalamos* reed]

ca·lum·ni·ate (kə-lum′ni-āt), *v.*, –at·ed, –at·ing. say false and injurious things about; slander. —ca·lum′ni·a′tor, *n.*

ca·lum·ni·a·tion (kə-lum′ni-ā′shən), *n.* slander; calumny.

ca·lum·ni·ous (kə-lum′ni-əs), *adj.* slanderous. —ca·lum′ni·ous·ly, *adv.*

cal·um·ny (kal′əm-ni), *n., pl.* –nies. false statement made to injure someone's reputation; slander. [< L *calumnia*] —Syn. defamation.

Cal·va·ry (kal′və·ri), *n.* place near Jerusalem where Jesus died on the cross. Luke 23:33. [< L *calvaria* skull, trans. of Aram. *Gogoltha* Golgotha]

calve (kav; käv), *v.*, **calved**, **calv·ing.** give birth to a calf. [OE *calfian* < *calf* calf¹]

calves (kavz; kävz), *n.* pl. of **calf**¹ and **calf**².

Cal·vin (kal′vən), *n.* **John**, 1509–1564, French Protestant religious leader at Geneva.

Cal·vin·ism (kal′vən·iz·əm), *n.* religious teachings of Calvin and his followers. —**Cal′vin·ist**, *n.* —**Cal′vin·is′tic**, **Cal′vin·is′ti·cal**, *adj.*

calx (kalks), *n.*, pl. **calx·es**, **cal·ces** (kal′sēz). an ashy substance left after a metal or a mineral has been thoroughly roasted, burned, etc. [< L *calx* lime]

Cal·y·don (kal′ə·don), *n.* ancient city in W Greece. —**Cal·y·do·ni·an** (kal′ə·dō′ni·ən), *adj.*

Ca·lyp·so (kə·lip′sō), *n.* Gk. Legend. sea nymph who detained Odysseus on her island for seven years.

ca·lyp·so (kə·lip′sō), *n.* a type of improvised song that originated in the British West Indies.

ca·lyx (kā′liks; kal′iks), *n.*, pl. **ca·lyx·es**, **cal·y·ces** (kal′ə·sēz; kā′lə-). **1.** Bot. the outer part of a flower that is a holder for the petals; the sepals. **2.** Anat., Zool. a cuplike part. [< L < Gk. *kalyx* covering]

cam (kam), *n.* projection on a wheel or shaft that changes a regular circular motion into an irregular circular motion or into a back-and-forth motion. [< Du. *kam* cog, comb]

Cam: A, open; B, closed.

ca·ma·ra·de·rie (kä′mə·rä′də·ri), *n.* comradeship. [< F. See COMRADE.]

cam·a·ril·la (kam′ə·ril′ə), *n.* cabal; clique. [< Sp., dim. of *cámara* chamber]

cam·ass, cam·as (kam′as), *n.* Am. plant of the lily family growing in the W United States. [< Am. Ind.]

cam·ber (kam′bər), *v.* arch slightly. —*n.* **1.** a slight arch. **2.** a slightly arching piece of timber. **3.** the rise and fall of the curve of an airfoil. [< F *cambre* bent < L *camur* crooked]

cam·bi·um (kam′bi·əm), *n.* Bot. layer of soft, growing tissue between the bark and the wood of trees and shrubs. [< LL *cambium* exchange]

Cam·bo·di·a (kam·bō′di·ə), *n.* country in SE Asia, formerly under French influence.

Cam·bri·a (kam′bri·ə), *n.* old name of Wales.

Cam·bri·an (kam′bri·ən), *adj.* **1.** Welsh. **2.** having to do with an early geological period or group of rocks. —*n.* **1.** Welshman. **2.** an early geological period or group of rocks.

cam·bric (kām′brik), *n.* a fine, thin linen or cotton cloth. [after *Cambrai*, France]

cambric tea, Am. drink made of hot water, milk, sugar, and sometimes a little tea.

Cam·bridge (kām′brij), *n.* **1.** city in SE England. **2.** city in E Massachusetts, near Boston.

Cam·den (kam′dən), *n.* city in SW New Jersey.

came (kām), *v.* pt. of **come**.

cam·el (kam′əl), *n.* a large animal with one or two humps on its back, used as a beast of burden. The Arabian camel, or dromedary, has one hump; the Bactrian camel of southern Asia has two humps. [< L < Gk. *kamelos*; of Semitic orig.]

ca·mel·lia (kə·mēl′yə; -mē′li·ə), *n.* **1.** shrub or tree with glossy leaves and waxy white or red flowers shaped like roses. **2.** the flower. [for G. J. *Kamel*, missionary in Luzon]

ca·mel·o·pard (kə·mel′ə·pärd), *n.* a giraffe.

Cam·e·lot (kam′ə·lot), *n.* a legendary place in England where King Arthur had his palace.

camel's hair, **1.** hair of a camel, used in making cloth, paintbrushes, etc. **2.** cloth made of this hair or something like it.

Cam·em·bert (kam′əm·bâr), *n.* a rich, soft cheese.

cam·e·o (kam′i·ō), *n.*, pl. **-e·os.** a precious or semiprecious stone carved so that there is a raised part on a background. [< Ital.]

cam·er·a (kam′ər·ə; kam′rə), *n.*, pl. **-er·as** for 1, **-er·ae** (-ər·ē) for 2. **1.** an apparatus in which photographic film or plates are exposed, the image being formed by means of a lens. **2.** Television. part of the transmitter which converts images into electronic impulses for transmitting. **3.** a judge's private office. **4. in camera, a.** in a judge's private office. **b.** privately. [< L, arched chamber, arch < Gk. *kamara*. Doublet of CHAMBER.]

Cameo

cam·er·a·man (kam′ər·ə·man′; kam′rə-), *n.*, pl. **-men.** man who operates a camera, esp. a motion-picture camera.

Cam·er·oons (kam′ə·rünz′), *n.* **1.** a former German possession in W Africa, divided into French and British mandates after World War I, since 1946 trust territories under the United Nations. **2.** the British trust territory.

Ca·me·roun (kam·rün′), *n.* a French trust territory in W Africa, part of Cameroons (def. 1).

cam·i·sole (kam′ə·sōl), *n.* **1.** a woman's underwaist. **2.** a loose jacket worn by women as a dressing gown. **3.** a kind of strait jacket. [< F < Sp., < *camisa* shirt; akin to CHEMISE]

cam·o·mile (kam′ə·mil), *n.* plant of the aster family with daisylike flowers. Its flowers and leaves are sometimes dried and used in medicine. Also, **chamomile.** [< L < Gk. *chamaimēlon* earth apple]

Ca·mor·ra (kə·môr′ə; -mor′ə), *n.* **1.** a powerful secret political society formed in Naples, Italy, about 1820 that later was associated with blackmail, robbery, etc. **2.** camorra, a similar secret society. —**Ca·mor′rism**, *n.* —**Ca·mor′rist**, *n.*

cam·ou·flage (kam′ə·fläzh), *n.*, *v.*, **-flaged**, **-flag·ing.** —*n.* **1.** disguise; deception. **2.** in warfare, giving things a false appearance to deceive the enemy. —*v.* give a false appearance to in order to conceal; disguise. [< F, < *camoufler* disguise] —**cam′ou·flag′er**, *n.*

camp (kamp), *n.* **1.** group of tents, huts, or other shelters where people live for a time. **2.** a place where a camp is. **3.** people living in a camp. **4.** Am. one or more buildings, usually near a lake or in the woods, forming a temporary residence, esp. in summer. **5.** living an outdoor life with very simple shelter; camping. **6.** group of people who agree or work together. **7.** military life. —*v.* **1.** make a camp. **2.** live in a camp for a time. **3.** live simply without comforts for a time. **4. camp out**, Am. **a.** spend the night outdoors. **b.** live in the open in a tent or camp. [< F < L *campus* field] —**camp′er**, *n.*

cam·paign (kam·pān′), *n.* **1.** series of related military operations for some special purpose. **2.** series of connected activities to do or get something; planned course of action for some special purpose: *a campaign to raise money*. **3.** Am. organized action in influencing voters in an election: *a political campaign*. —*v.* **1.** take part in or serve in a campaign. **2.** Am. conduct a political campaign. [< F *campagne* open country, ult. < L *campus* field] —**cam·paign′er**, *n.*

cam·pa·ni·le (kam′pə·nē′lē), *n.*, pl. **-ni·les**, **-ni·li** (-nē′lē), a bell tower. [< Ital., ult. < LL *campana* bell]

cam·pan·u·la (kam·pan′yə·lə), *n.* bluebell, Canterbury bell, or other similar plant with bell-shaped flowers. [< LL, dim. of *campana* bell]

camp chair, a lightweight, folding chair.

camp·fire (kamp′fir′), *n.* **1.** fire in a camp for warmth or cooking. **2.** social gathering of soldiers, scouts, etc.

camp·ground (kamp′ground′), *n.* Am. **1.** place where a camp is. **2.** place where a camp meeting is held.

cam·phor (kam′fər), *n.* **1.** a white, crystalline substance with a strong odor and a bitter taste, $C_{10}H_{16}O$, used in medicine, to protect clothes from moths, in the manufacture of celluloid, etc.

age, cãre, fär; ēqual, tėrm; īce; ōpen, ôrder; půt, rüle, ũse; th, then; ə=a in about.

2. *Am.* camphor in alcohol; spirits of camphor. [< Med.L < Ar., ult. < Malay *kapur*] —**cam·phor·ic** (kam·fôr′ik; -for′-), *adj.*

cam·phor·ate (kam′fər·āt), *v.,* -at·ed, -at·ing. impregnate with camphor. —**cam′phor·at′ed,** *adj.*

camphor ball, a small ball made of camphor, naphthalene, etc., used to keep moths out of clothes, furniture, etc.

cam·pi·on (kam′pi·ən), *n.* plant with red or white flowers of the same family as the pink. [< L *campus* field]

camp meeting, *Am.* religious meeting held outdoors or in a tent, usually lasting several days.

camp·stool (kamp′stül′), *n.* a lightweight, folding seat.

cam·pus (kam′pəs), *n. Am.* grounds of a college, university, or school. [< L, field, plain]

can¹ (kan; *unstressed* kən), *v., pres. sing.* 1 can, 2 can *or* (*Archaic*) canst, 3 can; *pt.* could. **1.** be able to. **2.** know how to. **3.** have the right to. **4.** *Colloq.* be allowed to. **5.** feel inclined to. [OE *can(n)* know, know how, can] ≫ **can, may. 1.** In formal English careful distinction is kept between the auxiliary *can* with the meaning of ability, "being able to," and *may,* with the meaning of permission: *You may go now. He can walk with crutches. You can't go now. May I if you can. May* also indicates possibility: *He may have been the one.* **2.** In informal and colloquial English *may* occurs rather rarely except in the sense of possibility: *It may be all right for her, but not for me. Can* is generally used for both permission and ability: *Can I go now? You can if you want to. I can go 80 miles an hour with my car.* This is in such general usage that it should be regarded as good English in speaking and in informal writing.

can² (kan), *n., v.,* canned, can·ning. —*n.* **1.** *Am.* a metal container: *a milk can.* **2.** contents of a can. **3.** drinking cup. **4.** *Am.* a glass jar for canning at home. —*v.* **1.** *Am.* preserve by putting in airtight cans or jars. **2.** *Am., Slang.* dismiss from a job. [OE *canne*]

Can., Canada; Canadian.

Ca·naan (kā′nən), *n.* **1.** region in Palestine between the Jordan River and the Mediterranean. **2.** land of promise.

Ca·naan·ite (kā′nən·īt), *n.* inhabitant of Canaan before its conquest by the Hebrews.

Can·a·da (kan′ə·də), *n.* a British dominion, north of the United States.

Canada goose, the common wild goose of North America.

Ca·na·di·an (kə·nā′di·ən), *adj.* of Canada or its people. —*n.* native or inhabitant of Canada.

ca·naille (kə·nāl′; ka·nī′), *n.* rabble; riffraff. [< F < Ital. *canaglia,* ult. < L *canis* dog]

ca·nal (kə·nal′), *n., v.,* -nalled, -nal·ling; -naled, -nal·ing. —*n.* **1.** waterway dug across land for navigation. **2.** tube in the body or in a plant for carrying food, liquid, or air. **3.** *Am., S.W.* a large irrigation ditch. **4.** *Am.* a long arm of a large body of water. —*v.* **1.** *Am.* make a canal through. **2.** furnish with canals. [< L *canalis* trench, pipe. Doublet of CHANNEL.]

canal boat, a long, narrow boat used on canals.

ca·nal·i·za·tion (kə·nal′ə·zā′shən; kan′ə·lə-), *n.* **1.** act of canalizing. **2.** system of canals.

ca·nal·ize (kə·nal′īz; kan′ə·līz), *v.,* -ized, -iz·ing. **1.** make a canal or canals through. **2.** make into or like a canal.

Canal Zone, *Am.* Panama Canal and the land five miles on each side, governed by the U.S.

can·a·pé (kan′ə·pā; -pē), *n.* a cracker, thin piece of bread, etc., spread with a seasoned mixture of fish, cheese, etc. [< F, orig., a couch covered with mosquito netting. See CANOPY.]

ca·nard (kə·närd′), *n.* a false rumor; exaggerated report; hoax. [< F *canard* duck]

Ca·nar·ies (kə·när′iz), *or* **Canary Islands,** *n.pl.* group of Spanish islands in the Atlantic.

ca·nar·y (kə·när′i), *n., pl.* -nar·ies. **1.** Also, **canary bird.** small, yellow songbird. Canaries

are often kept in cages. **2.** Also, **canary yellow.** light yellow. **3.** wine from the Canary Islands. —*adj.* light-yellow. [after the islands]

ca·nas·ta (kə·nas′tə), *n.* a card game.

Can·ber·ra (kan′ber·ə; -ber·ə), *n.* capital of Australia, in the SE part.

can·can (kan′kan), *n.* a dance by women marked by extravagant kicking. [< F]

can·cel (kan′səl), *v.,* -celed, -cel·ing; *esp. Brit.* -celled, -cel·ling, *n.* —*v.* **1.** cross out; mark (something) so that it cannot be used. **2.** cross out the same factor from the numerator and denominator of a fraction, or from the two sides of an equation. **3.** do away with; abolish: *he canceled his order.* **4.** make up for; balance. —*n.* **1.** a canceling. **2.** a canceled part. [< L *cancellare* cross out with latticed lines < *cancelli* cross bars] —**can′cel·a·ble,** *esp. Brit.* **can′cel·la·ble,** *adj.* —**can′cel·er,** *esp. Brit.* **can′cel·ler,** *n.* —Syn. *v.* **3.** annul, nullify, revoke.

can·cel·la·tion (kan′sə·lā′shən), *n.* **1.** a canceling or being canceled. **2.** marks made where something is canceled or crossed out.

can·cer (kan′sər), *n.* **1.** very harmful growth in the body; malignant tumor. Cancer tends to spread and destroy the healthy tissues and organs of the body. **2.** evil or harmful thing that tends to spread. **3.** Cancer, a. tropic of Cancer. **b.** a northern constellation that was thought of as arranged in the shape of a crab. **c.** the fourth sign of the zodiac. [< L *cancer* crab, tumor] —**can′cer·ous,** *adj.*

can·cer·o·gen·ic (kan′sər·ə·jen′ik), *adj.* carcinogenic.

can·de·la·bra (kan′də·lä′brə; -lä′-), *n.* **1.** pl. of **candelabrum. 2.** (*pl. but taken as sing. with pl.* -bras) candelabrum.

can·de·la·brum (kan′də·lä′brəm; -lä′-), *n., pl.* -bra (-brə) or -brums. an ornamental candlestick with several branches for candles. [< L, < *candela* candle]

Candelabrum

can·des·cent (kan·des′ənt), *adj.* glowing with heat; incandescent.[< L *candescens* beginning to glow] —**can·des′cence,** *n.* —**can·des′cent·ly,** *adv.*

can·did (kan′did), *adj.* **1.** frank; sincere. **2.** fair; impartial. **3.** *Obs.* white. **4.** clear; pure. [< L *candidus* white] —**can′did·ly,** *adv.* —**can′did·ness,** *n.* —Syn. **1.** truthful, straightforward.

can·di·da·cy (kan′də·də·si), *n.* being a candidate: *please support my candidacy for treasurer.*

can·di·date (kan′də·dāt; -dit), *n.* person who seeks, or is proposed for, some office or honor. [< L *candidatus* clothed in white (toga)] —**can′di·date·ship′,** *n.*

can·di·da·ture (kan′də·də·chər; -dā′chər), *n. Brit.* candidacy.

candid camera, small camera with a fast lens for photographing persons unposed and often unaware.

can·died (kan′did), *adj.* **1.** turned into sugar: *candied honey.* **2.** cooked in sugar; covered with sugar. **3.** made sweet or agreeable.

can·dle (kan′dəl), *n., v.,* -dled, -dling. —*n.* **1.** stick of wax or tallow with a wick in it, burned to give light. **2.** anything shaped or used like a candle. **3.** unit for measuring the strength of a light. **4. burn the candle at both ends,** use up one's strength and resources rapidly. **5. not hold a candle to,** not compare with. —*v.* test (eggs) for freshness by holding them in front of a light. [< L *candela < candere* shine] —**can′dler,** *n.*

can·dle·ber·ry (kan′dəl·ber′i), *n., pl.* -ries. *Am.* **1.** wax myrtle or bayberry. **2.** its fruit.

can·dle·fish (kan′dəl·fish′), *n. Am.* an edible fish of the northwestern coast of America.

can·dle·light (kan′dəl·līt′), *n.* **1.** light of a candle or candles. **2.** time when candles are lighted; dusk; twilight; nightfall.

Can·dle·mas (kan′dəl·məs), *n.* February 2, a church festival in honor of the purification of the Virgin Mary. [OE *candelmæsse*]

candle power, light given by a standard candle, used as a unit for measuring light.

can·dle·stick (kan'dəl·stik'), **can·dle·hold·er** (-hōl'dər), *n.* holder for a candle, to make it stand up straight.

can·dor, *esp. Brit.* **can·dour** (kan'dər), *n.* 1. speaking openly what one really thinks; honesty in giving one's view or opinion. 2. fairness; impartiality. [< L, whiteness, purity < *candere* shine] —Syn. 1. frankness, sincerity.

can·dy (kan'di), *n., pl.* **-dies,** *v.,* **-died, -dy·ing.** —*n.* 1. sugar or syrup, cooked and flavored, then cooled and made into small pieces for eating. Chocolate, butter, milk, nuts, fruits, etc., are often added. 2. piece of this. —*v.* 1. turn into sugar. 2. cook in sugar; preserve by boiling in sugar. 3. make sweet or agreeable. [< F < Pers. *qand* sugar] —Syn. *n.* 1. confection, bonbon.

can·dy·tuft (kan'di·tuft'), *n.* plant with clusters of white, purple, or pink flowers.

cane (kān), *n., v.,* **caned, can·ing.** —*n.* 1. stick to help a person in walking; walking stick. 2. stick used to beat with. 3. a long, jointed stem, such as that of the bamboo. 4. plant having such stems. Sugar cane and bamboo are canes. 5. material made of such stems, used for furniture, chair seats, etc. 6. a slender stalk or stem. —*v.* 1. beat with a cane. 2. make or provide with cane. [< F < L < Gk. *kanna* reed]

cane·brake (kān'brāk'), *n. Am., Southern.* thicket or region of cane plants.

cane sugar, sugar made from sugar cane.

ca·nine (kā'nīn), *n.* 1. dog. 2. canine tooth. —*adj.* 1. of a dog; like a dog. 2. belonging to a group of meat-eating animals including dogs, foxes, and wolves. [< L, < *canis* dog]

canine tooth, one of the four pointed teeth next to the incisors.

Ca·nis Ma·jor (kā'nis mā'jər), group of stars SE of Orion that contains Sirius, the brightest of the stars.

Ca·nis Mi·nor (kā'nis mī'nər), group of stars SE of Orion, separated from Canis Major by the Milky Way.

can·is·ter (kan'is·tər), *n.* 1. a small box or can. 2. can filled with bullets that is shot from a cannon. [< L < Gk. *kanastron* basket]

can·ker (kang'kər), *n.* 1. a spreading sore, esp. one in the mouth. 2. disease of plants that causes slow decay. 3. anything that causes decay, rotting, or gradual eating away. —*v.* 1. infect or be infected with canker. 2. become malignant; decay. [< L *cancer* crab, gangrene]

can·ker·worm (kang'kər·wėrm'), *n. Am.* caterpillar that eats away the leaves of trees and plants.

can·na (kan'ə), *n.* 1. plant with large, pointed leaves and large, red, pink, or yellow flowers. 2. the flower. [< L, reed. See CANE.]

canned (kand), *adj. Am.* 1. put up and sealed for preservation. 2. *Slang.* recorded, as music.

can·nel (kan'əl), or **cannel coal,** *n.* soft coal in large lumps that burns with a bright flame. [appar. var. of *candle*]

can·ner (kan'ər), *n. Am.* person who cans food.

can·ner·y (kan'ər·i), *n., pl.* **-ner·ies.** *Am.* factory where meat, fish, fruit, vegetables, etc., are canned.

can·ni·bal (kan'ə·bəl), *n.* 1. person who eats human flesh. 2. animal that eats others of its own kind. —*adj.* of or like cannibals. [< Sp. *Caníbal < Caribe* Carib]

can·ni·bal·ism (kan'ə·bəl·iz'əm), *n.* practice of eating the flesh of one's own kind. —**can'ni·bal·is'tic,** *adj.* —**can'ni·bal·is'ti·cal·ly,** *adv.*

can·ni·bal·ize (kan'ə·bəl·īz), *v.,* **-ized, -iz·ing.** 1. assemble or repair (a vehicle, piece of machinery, etc.) by using parts from others which are useless as a whole. 2. take usable parts from (a vehicle, piece of machinery, etc.) to assemble or repair another.

can·ni·kin (kan'ə·kin), *n.* a small can; cup. [< *can*[1] + *-kin*]

can·ning (kan'ing), *n. Am.* the process or business of preserving food by putting it in airtight cans or jars.

can·non (kan'ən), *n., pl.* **-nons** or (*esp. collectively*) **-non,** *v.* —*n.* 1. big mounted gun or

guns. 2. *Zool.* cannon bone. 3. the part of a bit that goes inside a horse's mouth; a smooth round bit. 4. *Brit.* carom. —*v.* 1. discharge cannon. 2. strike and rebound. 3. collide violently. 4. *Brit.* make a carom. [< F *canon* < Ital. < L < Gk. *kanna* reed]

can·non·ade (kan'ən·ād'), *n., v.,* **-ad·ed, -ad·ing.** —*n.* continued firing of cannons. —*v.* attack with cannons.

cannon ball, a large, iron or steel ball, formerly fired from cannons.

cannon bone, *Zool.* bone between the hock and fetlock.

can·non·eer (kan'ən·ir'), *n.* gunner.

can·non·ry (kan'ən·ri), *n., pl.* **-ries.** 1. continuous firing of cannons. 2. artillery.

can·not (kan'ot; ka·not'; kə-), *v.* can not.

can·ny (kan'i), *adj.,* **-ni·er, -ni·est.** *Scot.* 1. shrewd; cautious. 2. thrifty. [< *can*[1]] —**can'ni·ly,** *adv.* —**can'ni·ness,** *n.*

ca·noe (kə·nü'), *n., v.,* **ca·noed, ca·noe·ing.** —*n.* light boat moved with paddles. —*v. Am.* paddle a canoe; go in a canoe. [< F < Sp. < Carib *kanoa*] —**ca·noe'ing,** *n. Am.*

can·on[1] (kan'ən), *n.* 1. law of a church; body of church law. 2. rule by which a thing is judged. 3. the official list of the books contained in the Bible; books of the Bible accepted by the church. 4. list of saints. 5. an official list. 6. part of the Mass coming after the offertory. 7. *Music.* a kind of composition in which the different participants begin the same melody one after another at regular intervals. [< L < Gk. *kanon*]

can·on[2] (kan'ən), *n.* 1. *Esp. Brit.* member of a group of clergymen belonging to a cathedral or collegiate church. 2. *Rom. Cath. Ch.* member of a group of clergymen living according to a certain rule. [< OF < L *canonicus* canonical < *canon* canon[1]]

ca·ñon (kan'yən), *n. Am., S.W.* canyon.

ca·non·i·cal (kə·non'ə·kəl), *adj.* Also, **ca·non'ic.** 1. according to or prescribed by the laws of a church. 2. in the canon of the Bible. 3. authorized; accepted. —*n.* **canonicals,** clothes worn by a clergyman at a church service. —**ca·non'i·cal·ly,** *adv.* —**ca·non'i·cal·ness,** *n.*

canonical hours, the seven periods of the day for prayer and worship.

can·on·ize (kan'ən·īz), *v.,* **-ized, -iz·ing.** 1. declare (a dead person) to be a saint; place in the official list of the saints. 2. treat as a saint; glorify. 3. make or recognize as canonical. 4. authorize. —**can'on·i·za'tion,** *n.*

canon law, laws of a church governing ecclesiastical affairs.

can·on·ry (kan'ən·ri), *n., pl.* **-ries.** office or benefice of a canon.

can·o·py (kan'ə·pi), *n., pl.* **-pies,** *v.,* **-pied, -py·ing.** —*n.* 1. a covering fixed over a bed, throne, entrance, etc., or held over a person. 2. a rooflike covering; shelter; shade. 3. sky. —*v.* cover with a canopy. [< F < L < Gk. *konopeion* mosquito net < *konops* gnat]

canst (kanst), *v. Archaic.* 2nd pers. sing. present of *can*.

cant[1] (kant), *n.* 1. insincere talk; moral and religious statements that many people make, but few really believe or follow out. 2. whining or singsong speech like that of beggars. 3. peculiar language of a special group, using many strange words: *thieves' cant.* —*adj.* peculiar to a special group. —*v.* use cant. [< L *cantus* song]

cant[2] (kant), *n., v.* 1. slant; slope; bevel. 2. tip; tilt. 3. pitch; toss; throw with a sudden jerk. [prob. < MDu., MLG < OF < L *cant(h)us* corner, side < Celtic]

can't (kant; känt), cannot. ➤ *can't, mayn't. Can't* almost universally takes the place of the awkward *mayn't: Can't I go now?* ➤ *can't help* (but). This idiom illustrates differences between various levels of usage: Formal: *I cannot but feel sorry for him.* Informal: *I can't help feeling sorry for him.* Familiar, substandard: *I can't* *help but feel* sorry for him. The last is so commonly used in speaking and writing that perhaps it should be regarded as good English.

can·ta·bi·le (kän·tä′bĭ·lā), *Music.* —*adj.* in a smooth and flowing style; songlike. —*n.* a cantabile style, passage, or piece. [< Ital. < L *cantare* sing]

can·ta·loupe, can·ta·loup (kan′tə·lōp), *n.* a sweet, juicy melon with a hard, rough rind; muskmelon. [< F < Ital. *Cantalupo* place where first cultivated]

can·tan·ker·ous (kan·tang′kər·əs), *adj.* hard to get along with because ready to make trouble and oppose anything suggested; ill-natured. —**can·tan′ker·ous·ly,** *adv.* —**can·tan′ker·ous·ness,** *n.*

can·ta·ta (kən·tä′tə), *n.* story or play set to music to be sung by a chorus, but not acted. [< Ital. < L *cantare* sing]

can·teen (kan·tēn′), *n.* 1. a small container for carrying water or other drinks. 2. a military store where food, drinks, etc., are sold to soldiers and sailors. 3. box of cooking utensils for use in camp. [< F < Ital. *cantina* cellar < LL *canthus* side]

Canteen

can·ter (kan′tər), *n.* gentle gallop. —*v.* gallop gently. [for *Canterbury gallop,* pace of pilgrims to Canterbury]

Can·ter·bur·y (kan′tər·ber′ĭ), *n.* city in SE England.

Canterbury bell, plant with tall stalks of bell-shaped flowers, usually purplish-blue or white.

cant hook, *U.S.* pole with a movable hook at one end, used to grip and turn over logs.

can·ti·cle (kan′tə·kəl), *n.* a short song, hymn, or chant used in church services. [< L *canticulum* little song < *cantus* song]

can·ti·lev·er (kan′tə·lev′ər; -lē′vər), *n.* a large, projecting bracket or beam that is fastened at one end only.

cantilever bridge, bridge made of two cantilevers whose projecting ends meet but do not support each other.

can·tle (kan′təl), *n.* part of a saddle that sticks up at the back. [< OF < Med.L *cantellus* little corner]

can·to (kan′tō), *n., pl. -tos.* one of the main divisions of a long poem. A canto of a poem corresponds to a chapter of a novel. [< Ital. < L *cantus* song]

can·ton (kan′tən, -ton, kan·ton′ *for n. and v.* 1; kan·ton′, -tōn′, *esp. Brit.* -tün′ *for v.* 2), *n.* small part or political division of a country. Switzerland is made up of 22 cantons. —*v.* 1. divide into cantons. 2. allot quarters to. [< OF *canton* corner, portion. See CANT².]

Can·ton (kan·ton′ *for* 1; kan′tən *for* 2), *n.* 1. city in S China. 2. city in NE Ohio.

Can·ton·ese (kan′tən·ēz′; -ēs′), *n., pl. -ese.* 1. native or inhabitant of Canton, China. 2. Chinese dialect spoken in or near Canton, China. —*adj.* of Canton, China, its people, or their dialect.

Canton flannel (kan′tən), a strong cotton cloth that is soft and fleecy on one side.

can·ton·ment (kan·ton′mənt; -tōn′-; *esp. Brit.* -tün′-), *n.* place where soldiers live; quarters. [< F]

can·tor (kan′tər; -tôr), *n.* 1. man who leads the singing of a choir or congregation. 2. soloist in a synagogue. [< L, singer, < *canere* sing]

Ca·nuck (kə·nuk′), *n., adj. Am., Slang.* 1. Canadian. 2. French Canadian.

can·vas (kan′vəs), *n.* 1. a strong cloth made of cotton, flax, or hemp, used to make tents and sails. 2. something made of canvas. 3. sail or sails. 4. piece of canvas on which an oil painting is painted. 5. an oil painting. 6. under canvas, a. in tents. b. with sails spread. —*adj.* made of canvas. [< OF < L *cannabis* hemp]

can·vas·back (kan′vəs·bak′), or **canvasback duck,** *n. Am.* a wild duck of North America with grayish feathers on its back.

can·vass (kan′vəs), *v.* 1. examine carefully; examine. 2. discuss. 3. *Am.* go through (a city, district, etc.) asking for votes, orders, etc. 4. *Am.* ask for votes, orders, etc. 5. *Am.* examine and count the votes cast in an election. —*n.* 1. act, fact, or process of canvassing. 2. *Am.* an official scrutiny of votes. 3. *Am.* personal visiting of homes or stores in a district to sell something. 4. *Am.* a survey to determine sentiment for or against a candidate or a cause. [< *canvas,* orig., toss (someone) in a sheet, later, shake out, discuss] —**can′vass·er,** *n.*

can·yon (kan′yən), *n. Am., S.W.* a narrow valley with high, steep sides, usually with a stream at the bottom. Also, *cañon.* [< Sp. *cañón* tube, ult. < L *canna* cane]

caou·tchouc (kŭ′chŭk; kou·chük′), *n.* the gummy, coagulated juice of various tropical plants; rubber. [< F < Sp. < S Am.Ind.]

cap (kap), *n., v.,* capped, cap·ping. —*n.* 1. a close-fitting covering for the head with little or no brim. 2. a special head covering worn to show rank, occupation, etc.: *a nurse's cap.* 3. anything like a cap. 4. the highest part; top. 5. a small quantity of explosive in a wrapper or covering. 6. set one's cap for, *Colloq.* try to get for a husband. —*v.* 1. put a cap on. 2. put a top on; cover the top of. 3. do or follow with something as good or better: *each clown capped the other's last joke.* [< LL *cappa.* Cf. L *caput* head.]

cap., 1. capacity. 2. capital. 3. capitalize. 4. *pl.* **caps.** capital letter. 5. chapter.

ca·pa·bil·i·ty (kā′pə·bil′ə·tĭ), *n., pl. -ties.* ability; power; fitness; capacity.

ca·pa·ble (kā′pə·bəl), *adj.* 1. having capacity or qualifications to meet ordinary requirements; competent: *a capable teacher.* 2. capable of, a. having ability, power, or fitness for: *capable of criticizing music.* b. open to; ready for: *a statement capable of many interpretations.* [< LL *capabilis* < L *capere* take] —**ca′pa·ble·ness,** *n.* —**ca′pa·bly,** *adv.* —**Syn.** 1. proficient, qualified, fitted.

ca·pa·cious (kə·pā′shəs), *adj.* able to hold much; roomy; large. —**ca·pa′cious·ly,** *adv.* —**ca·pa′cious·ness,** *n.* —**Syn.** spacious.

ca·pac·i·ty (kə·pas′ə·tĭ), *n., pl. -ties.* 1. amount of room or space inside; largest amount that can be held by a container. 2. power of receiving and holding: *the theater has a capacity of 400.* 3. power of delivering electric current, power, etc. 4. ability; power; fitness: *a great capacity for learning.* 5. legal qualification. 6. position; relation: *he acted in the capacity of guardian.* [< L *capacitas* < *capere* take] —**Syn.** 1. volume. 4. competency. 6. character.

cap·a·pie, cap·à·pie (kap′ə·pē′), *adv.* from head to foot; completely. [< F]

ca·par·i·son (kə·par′ə·sən), *n.* 1. ornamental covering for a horse. 2. rich dress; outfit. —*v.* dress richly; fit out. [< F < Pr. *capa* cape]

cape¹ (kāp), *n.* an outer garment, or part of one, without sleeves, worn falling loosely from the shoulders. [< F < Sp. < LL *cappa* cap]

cape² (kāp), *n.* 1. point of land extending into the water. 2. the Cape, the Cape of Good Hope. [< F < Pr. < L *caput* head]

Cape buffalo, a large, savage buffalo of southern Africa.

cap·e·lin (kap′ə·lin), *n.* a small fish of the N Atlantic, used as bait for cod. [< F < Pr. *capelan* chaplain]

ca·per¹ (kā′pər), *n.* 1. a playful leap or jump. 2. prank; trick. —*v.* leap or jump about playfully. [< L *caper* he-goat] —**ca′per·er,** *n.* —**Syn.** *v.* skip, spring, gambol.

ca·per² (kā′pər), *n.* 1. a prickly shrub of the Mediterranean region. 2. capers, the green flower buds of this shrub, pickled and used for seasoning. [< L < Gk. *kapparis*]

cap·er·cail·lie (kap′ər·kāl′yĭ), **cap·er·cail·zie** (-kāl′yĭ; -kāl′zĭ), *n.* a large European grouse. [< Scotch Gaelic *capullcoille*]

Ca·per·na·um (kə·pėr′nā·əm; -nĭ-), *n.* ancient town in Palestine, on the Sea of Galilee.

Ca·pet (kā′pĭt; kap′ĭt), *n.* Hugh, 938?–996 A.D., king of France from 987 to 996 A.D. —**Ca·pe·tian** (kə·pē′shən), *adj., n.*

Cape Town, Cape·town (kāp′toun′), seaport near the S tip of Africa. The legislature for the Union of South Africa meets there.

Cape Verde (kāp′ vẽrd′), 1. cape in extreme W Africa. 2. Cape Verde Islands, group of islands west of this cape, belonging to Portugal.

cap·ful (kap′fŭl), *n., pl.* –fuls. as much as a cap will hold.

ca·pi·as (kā′pĭ·əs; kap′ĭ–), *n. Law.* writ ordering an officer to arrest a certain person. [< L *capias* you may take]

cap·il·lar·i·ty (kap′ə·lar′ə·ti), *n.* 1. capillary attraction or repulsion. 2. quality of having or causing capillary attraction or repulsion.

cap·il·lar·y (kap′ə·ler′ĭ), *adj., n., pl.* –lar·ies. —*adj.* 1. hairlike; very slender. 2. of, by means of, or in a tube of fine bore. —*n.* Also, **capillary tube**. tube with a very slender, hairlike opening or bore. Capillaries join the end of an artery to the beginning of a vein. [< L *capillaris* of hair, hairlike < *capillus* hair]

capillary attraction, 1. force that raises the part of the surface of a liquid that is in contact with a solid. 2. ability of a porous substance to soak up a liquid. A blotter absorbs ink by means of capillary attraction.

cap·i·tal[1] (kap′ə·təl), *n.* 1. city where the government of a country or state is located. 2. A, B, C, D, or any similar large letter. 3. amount of money or property that a company or a person uses in carrying on a business. 4. source of power or advantage. 5. capitalists as a group. 6. **make capital of**, take advantage of; use to one's own advantage. —*adj.* 1. of or having to do with capital. 2. important; leading. 3. main; chief. 4. of the best kind; excellent. 5. (of letters) of the large kind used at the beginning of a sentence, or as the first letter of a proper name. 6. involving death; punishable by death. [< L *capitalis* chief, pertaining to the head < *caput* head] —**Syn.** *adj.* 2. foremost. 3. principal. 4. splendid. ▶ **Capital letters.** Certain uses of capitals, as at the beginning of sentences or for proper names, are conventions followed by everyone; certain others show divided usage or are matters of taste. In general, formal English tends to use more capitals than informal English. The principal uses of capitals in current writing are:

1. **Sentence Capitals.** The first word of a sentence is capitalized. In quotations, the first word of a quoted sentence or part of sentence is capitalized, but when the quotation is broken, the second quoted part of a sentence is not capitalized: *"The first time I came this way," he said, "almost none of the roads were hard surfaced."*

2. **Proper Names.** Proper names and abbreviations of proper names are capitalized: names of people, places, races (*Indian, Negro, Caucasian*), languages (*French, Latin*), days of the week, months, companies, ships, institutions, fraternities, religious bodies, historical events (*the Revolutionary War*), documents (*the Constitution*).

3. **Lines of Poetry.** The first letter of a line of poetry is capitalized unless it was originally written without a capital.

4. **Titles of Articles, Books, etc.** The usual convention in English is to capitalize the first word, all nouns, pronouns, verbs, adjectives, and adverbs as well as prepositions that stand last or contain more than four (sometimes five) letters: *With Malice Toward Some; The Book of a Naturalist.*

5. **The Pronoun *I* Is Capitalized** (not from any sort of egotism, but simply because a small *i* is likely to be lost or to become attached to other words).

6. **Names of Relatives, Individuals.** Names of members of one's family (*my Father, my Brother Wren*—or *my father, my brother Wren*) are often capitalized in familiar writing as a mark of courtesy. A title and also nouns standing for

the name of a person in a high position are capitalized: *The President spoke.*

7. **References to Deity.** *God, Jesus,* nouns such as *Saviour,* and pronouns referring directly to a sacred figure are capitalized—though practice is divided on the pronouns.

8. **Street, River, Park, etc.** Usage is divided over capitalizing such words as *street, river, park, hotel, church* when they follow a proper name. Typically, books and conservative magazines would use capitals; more informal writing, in many magazines and most newspapers, would not: Formal: *the Mississippi River;* informal: *the Mississippi river.*

9. **Abstract Nouns.** Abstract nouns are likely to be capitalized, more in formal writing than in informal, when they are personified or when they refer to ideals or institutions: *the State has nothing to do with the Church, nor the Church with the State.*

cap·i·tal[2] (kap′ə·təl), *n.* the top part of a column, pillar, etc. [< L *capitellum,* dim. of *caput* head]

Capital

cap·i·tal·ism (kap′ə·təl·ĭz′-əm), *n.* 1. economic system based on private property, competition, and the production of goods for profit. 2. concentration of wealth with its power and influence in the hands of a few people. 3. possession of capital.

cap·i·tal·ist (kap′ə·təl·ĭst), *n.* 1. person whose money and property are used in carrying on business. 2. a wealthy person. 3. person who favors or supports capitalism. —*adj.* capitalistic.

cap·i·tal·is·tic (kap′ə·təl·ĭs′tĭk), *adj.* 1. Am. of or having to do with capitalism or capitalists. 2. favoring or supporting capitalism. —**cap′i·tal·is′ti·cal·ly,** *adv.*

cap·i·tal·ize (kap′ə·təl·īz), *v.,* –ized, –iz·ing. 1. Am. write or print with a capital letter. 2. Am. invest in or provide with capital. 3. set the capital of (a company) at a certain amount. 4. turn into capital; use as capital. 5. Am. take advantage of; use to one's own advantage. —**cap′i·tal·i·za′tion,** *n.*

cap·i·tal·ly (kap′ə·təl·ĭ), *adv.* 1. very well; excellently. 2. chiefly.

capital ship, a large warship; battleship.

cap·i·ta·tion (kap′ə·tā′shən), *n.* tax, fee, or charge of the same amount for every person.

Cap·i·tol (kap′ə·təl), *n.* 1. Am. the building at Washington, D.C., in which Congress meets. 2. Often, **capitol**, Am. the building in which a State legislature meets. 3. the ancient temple of Jupiter in Rome. [< L *Capitolium* chief temple (of Jupiter) < *caput* head]

ca·pit·u·late (kə·pĭch′ə·lāt), *v.,* –lat·ed, –lat·ing. surrender on certain terms or conditions: *the men in the fort capitulated upon the condition that they should go away unharmed.* [< Med.L, < *capitulare* draw up under separate heads, arrange in chapters < L *caput* head]

ca·pit·u·la·tion (kə·pĭch′ə·lā′shən), *n.* 1. a surrender on certain terms or conditions. 2. agreement; condition. 3. statement of the main facts of a subject; summary.

ca·pon (kā′pon; –pən), *n.* rooster specially raised to be eaten. It is castrated and fattened. [< OF < L *capo*]

ca·pote (kə·pōt′), *n.* 1. Am. a long cloak with a hood. 2. a close-fitting bonnet with strings. [< F]

Cap·pa·do·cia (kap′ə·dō′shə), *n.* ancient Roman province in E Asia Minor.

Ca·pri (kä′prĭ; kə·prē′), *n.* a small island in the Bay of Naples, Italy.

ca·pric·ci·o (kə·prē′chĭ·ō), *n., pl.* –ci·os. 1. caper; prank; caprice. 2. a lively piece of music in a free, irregular style. [< Ital., < *capro* goat < L *caper*]

ca·price (kə·prēs′), *n.* 1. sudden change of mind without reason; unreasonable notion or desire. 2. tendency to change suddenly and without reason. 3. *Music.* capriccio (def. 2). [< F

āge, cáre, fär; ēqual, tèrm; īce; ōpen, ôrder; pùt, rüle, ūse; th, then; ə=a in about.

< Ital. *capriccio.* See CAPRICCIO.] —Syn. **1.** whimsy, whim, humor, fancy.

ca·pri·cious (kə·prish′əs; -prē′shəs), *adj.* guided by one's fancy; changeable; fickle. —**ca·pri′cious·ly,** *adv.* —**ca·pri′cious·ness,** *n.*

Cap·ri·corn (kap′rə·kôrn), *n.* **1.** tropic of Capricorn. **2.** a southern constellation that was thought of as arranged in the shape of a goat. **3.** the 10th sign of the zodiac.

ca·pri·ole (kap′ri·ōl), *n., v.,* -oled, -ol·ing. —*n.* **1.** high leap made by a horse without moving forward. **2.** a leap; caper. —*v.* **1.** of a horse, make a high leap. **2.** to leap; caper. [< F < Ital. *capriola,* ult. < *capro* goat. See CAPRICCIO.]

caps., capital letters.

cap·si·cum (kap′sə·kəm), *n.* **1.** any of several plants with red or green pods containing seeds that usually have a hot, peppery taste. Green peppers, chillies, and pimientos are pods of different kinds of capsicum. **2.** such pods prepared for seasoning or medicine. [< NL < L *capsa* box]

cap·size (kap·sīz′; kap′sīz), *v.,* -sized, -siz·ing. turn bottom side up; upset; overturn.

cap·stan (kap′stən), *n.* machine for lifting or pulling that stands upright. [< Pr. < L *capistrum* halter, < *capere* take]

capstan bar, pole used to turn a capstan.

cap·stone (kap′stōn), *n.* top stone of a wall or other structure.

cap·su·lar (kap′sə·lər; -syə-), *adj.* **1.** of or like a capsule. **2.** in a capsule.

cap·sule (kap′səl; -sŭl), *n.* **1.** a small gelatin case for enclosing a dose of medicine. **2.** a dry seedcase that opens when ripe. **3.** *Anat.* a membrane enclosing an organ; membranous bag or sac. [< L *capsula,* dim. of *capsa* box]

Capsule

Capt., Captain.

cap·tain (kap′tən), *n.* **1.** leader; chief. **2.** an army officer ranking next below a major and next above a lieutenant. **3.** a navy officer ranking next below a commodore and next above a commander. **4.** commander of a ship. **5.** leader of a team in sports. —*v.* lead or command as captain. [< OF < LL *capitaneus* chief < L *caput* head] —**cap′tain·cy,** *n.*

cap·tain·ship (kap′tən·ship), *n.* **1.** rank, position, or authority of a captain. **2.** ability as a captain; leadership.

cap·tan (kap′tan), *n.* powder used in solution on plants as a fungicide.

cap·tion (kap′shən), *n.* **1.** *Am.* title or heading at the head of a page, article, chapter, etc., or under a picture. **2.** a taking; a seizing. —*v. Am.* put a caption on. [< L *captio* a taking < *capere* take]

cap·tious (kap′shəs), *adj.* hard to please; faultfinding. [< L *captiosus,* ult. < *capere* take] —**cap′tious·ly,** *adv.* —**cap′tious·ness,** *n.* —Syn. carping, contentious.

cap·ti·vate (kap′tə·vāt), *v.,* -vat·ed, -vat·ing. **1.** hold captive by beauty or interest; charm; fascinate. **2.** *Obs.* capture. —**cap′ti·vat′ing·ly,** *adv.* —**cap′ti·va′tion,** *n.* —**cap′ti·va′tor,** *n.* —Syn. **1.** enchant, entrance.

cap·tive (kap′tiv), *n.* prisoner. —*adj.* **1.** held as a prisoner; made a prisoner. **2.** captivated. [< L *captivus,* ult. < *capere* take]

captive audience, *Am.* group of persons who may be involuntarily subjected to an advertising appeal or other message, as passengers on a bus, etc.

cap·tiv·i·ty (kap·tiv′ə·ti), *n., pl.* -ties. **1.** a being in prison. **2.** a being held or detained anywhere against one's will. —Syn. **2.** bondage.

cap·tor (kap′tər), *n.* person who captures.

cap·ture (kap′chər), *v.,* -tured, -tur·ing, *n.* —*v.* make a prisoner of; take by force, skill, or trick; seize. [< n.] —*n.* **1.** person or thing taken in this way. **2.** act of capturing; fact of capturing or being captured. [< F < L *captura* taking < *capere* take] —**cap′tur·er,** *n.* —Syn. *v.* catch, apprehend. —*n.* **2.** seizure, arrest.

cap·u·chin (kap′yù·chin; -shin), *n.* **1.** a South American monkey with black hair on its head that looks like a hood. See the picture in col. 2. **2.** a hooded cloak for women. **3. Capuchin,**

Franciscan monk belonging to an order that wears a long, pointed hood or cowl.

ca·put (kā′pət; kap′ət), *n., pl.* **cap·i·ta** (kap′ə·tə). *Anat.* head. [< L]

car (kär), *n.* **1.** vehicle moving on wheels. **2.** automobile. **3.** *Am.* railroad vehicle for freight or passengers. **4.** vehicle running on rails. **5.** the closed platform of an elevator, balloon, etc., for carrying passengers. **6.** *Poetic.* chariot. [< OF < L *carrus* two-wheeled cart] ▶ **Car is a satisfactory and economical solution of the contest** between *automobile, auto, motor car,* and other terms for a "gasoline-propelled pleasure vehicle."

Capuchin (body 1½ ft. long)

car·a·ba·o (kä′rə·bä′ō), *n., pl.* -ba·os. water buffalo of the Philippine Islands. [< Sp. < Malay *karbau*]

car·a·bi·neer, car·a·bi·nier (kar′ə·bə·nir′), *n.* cavalry soldier armed with a carbine. Also, **carbineer.**

ca·ra·ca·ra (kä′rə·kä′rə), *n.* a vulturelike bird of South America.

Ca·rac·as (kə·rak′əs; -rä′kəs), *n.* capital of Venezuela.

car·a·cole (kar′ə·kōl), **car·a·col** (-kol), *n., v.,* -coled, -col·ing; -colled, -col·ling. —*n.* a half turn to the right or left, made by a horse and rider. —*v.* prance from side to side. [< F < Ital. < Sp. *caracol* spiral shell]

car·a·cul (kar′ə·kəl), *n.* the flat, loose, curly fur made from the skin of newborn lambs. Also, **karakul.** [< *Kara Kul,* lake in Turkestan]

ca·rafe (kə·raf′; -räf′), *n.* a glass water bottle. [< F < Ital. < Sp. < Ar. *gharráf* drinking vessel]

car·a·mel (kar′ə·məl; -mel; kär′mel′), *n.* **1.** burnt sugar used for coloring and flavoring. **2.** a small block of chewy candy. [< F < Sp. *caramelo*]

car·a·pace (kar′ə·pās), *n.* shell on the back of a turtle, lobster, crab, etc. [< F < Sp. *carapacho*]

car·at (kar′ət), *n.* **1.** unit of weight for precious stones, equal to ⅕ gram. **2.** one 24th part. Also, **karat.** [< F < Ital. < Ar. < Gk. *keration* small horn-shaped bean used as a weight, dim. of *keras* horn]

car·a·van (kar′ə·van), *n.* **1.** group of merchants, pilgrims, tourists, etc., traveling together for safety through a desert or a dangerous country. **2.** a large, covered wagon for people or goods. **3.** *Brit.* house on wheels. **4.** van. [< F < Pers. *kārwān*]

car·a·van·sa·ry (kar′ə·van′sə·ri), **car·a·van·se·rai** (-rī; -rā), *n., pl.* -ries; -rais. **1.** inn or hotel where caravans rest in the Orient. **2.** *Am.* large inn or hotel. [< Pers., < *kārwān* caravan + *serāi* inn]

car·a·vel (kar′ə·vel), *n.* a small, fast ship of former times. Also, **carvel.** [< F *caravelle* < Ital. < LL *carabus* < Gk. *karabos* kind of light ship < ancient Macedonian]

car·a·way (kar′ə·wā), *n.* **1.** plant yielding fragrant, spicy seeds used to flavor bread, rolls, cakes, etc. **2.** its seeds. [< Med.L < Ar. *karawyā*]

car·bide (kär′bīd; -bid), *n. Chem.* **1.** compound of carbon with a more electropositive element or radical. **2.** calcium carbide.

car·bine (kär′bīn; -bēn), *n.* a short rifle or musket. [< F]

car·bi·neer (kär′bə·nir′), *n.* carabineer.

car·bo·hy·drate (kär′bō·hī′drāt), *n.* substance composed of carbon, hydrogen, and oxygen. Sugar and starch are carbohydrates. Carbohydrates are made from carbon dioxide and water by green plants in sunlight. [< *carbo(n)* + *hydrate*]

car·bo·lat·ed (kär′bō·lāt′id), *adj.* containing carbolic acid.

car·bol·ic acid (kär·bol′ik), *adj.* a very poisonous, corrosive, white, crystalline substance, C_6H_5OH, used in solution as a disinfectant and antiseptic; phenol.

car·bon (kär′bən), *n.* **1.** *Chem.* a very common nonmetallic element, C. Diamonds and graphite are pure carbon; coal and charcoal are impure carbon. 2. *Elect.* piece of carbon used in batteries, arc lamps, etc. 3. piece of carbon paper. 4. copy made with carbon paper. [< F < L *carbo* coal]

carbon 14, a radioactive form of carbon. The extent of its decay in wood, bone, etc. is evidence of the age of archaeological finds or geological formations in which organic matter occurs.

car·bo·na·ceous (kär'bə·nā'shəs), *adj.* of, like, or containing coal.

car·bon·ate (*n.* kär'bən·āt, –ĭt; *v.* kär'bən·āt), *n., v.,* –at·ed, –at·ing. *n. Chem.* a salt or ester of carbonic acid. —*v.* 1. change into a carbonate. 2. charge with carbon dioxide. Soda water is carbonated to make it fizz. —**car'bon·a'tion,** *n.*

carbon dioxide, a heavy, colorless, odorless gas, CO_2, present in the atmosphere.

car·bon·ic acid (kär·bon'ik), acid made when carbon dioxide is dissolved in water, H_2CO_3.

carbonic-acid gas, carbon dioxide.

Car·bon·if·er·ous (kär'bən·if'ər·əs), *n.* 1. period when the warm, moist climate produced great forests, whose remains form the great coal beds. 2. rock and coal beds formed during this period. —*adj.* **carboniferous,** containing coal.

car·bon·ize (kär'bən·īz), *v.,* –ized, –iz·ing. 1. change into carbon by burning. 2. cover or combine with carbon. —**car'bon·i·za'tion,** *n.*

carbon monoxide, a colorless, odorless, very poisonous gas, CO, formed when carbon burns with an insufficient supply of air.

carbon paper, thin paper having a preparation of carbon or other inky substance on one surface, used for making copies of letters, etc.

carbon tet·ra·chlo·ride (tet'rə·klô'rīd; –rĭd; –klŏr–), a colorless, noninflammable liquid, CCl_4, often used in cleaning fluids.

car·bo·run·dum (kär'bə·run'dəm), *n. Am.* 1. an extremely hard compound of carbon and silicon, SiC, used for grinding, polishing, etc. 2. Carborundum, trademark for this abrasive. [< *carbo(n)* + (co)*rundum*]

car·boy (kär'boi), *n.* a very large, glass bottle, usually enclosed in basketwork or in a wooden box or crate to keep it from being broken. [< Pers. *qarābah* large flagon]

car·bun·cle (kär'bung·kəl), *n.* 1. a very painful, inflamed swelling under the skin. 2. a smooth, round garnet or other deep-red jewel. [< L *carbunculus* < *carbo* coal] —**car'bun·cled,** *adj.* —car·bun·cu·lar (kär·bung'kyə·lər), *adj.*

car·bu·ret (kär'bə·rāt, –byə·ret), *v.,* –ret·ed, –ret·ing; *esp. Brit.* –ret·ted, –ret·ting. 1. mix (air or gas) with carbon compounds, such as gasoline, etc. 2. combine with carbon. —**car·bu·re·tion** (kär'bə·rā'shən; –byə·ret'ən), *n.*

car·bu·re·tor (kär'bə·rā'tər; –byə·ret'ər), *esp. Brit.* **car·bu·ret·tor** (kär'byə·ret'ər), *n.* device for mixing air with gasoline to make an explosive mixture.

car·ca·jou (kär'kə·jü; –zhü), *n. Am.* 1. the wolverine (animal). 2. American badger. [< Canadian F < Algonquian]

car·cass, car·case (kär'kəs), *n.* 1. dead body of an animal or, contemptuously, of a human being. 2. *Contemptuously.* a living body. 3. an unfinished framework or skeleton. [< F < Ital. *carcassa*]

car·cin·o·gen (kär·sin'ə·jən), *n.* any substance or agent that produces cancer.

car·cin·o·gen·ic (kär·sin'ə·jen'ik), *adj.* 1. tending to cause cancer. 2. caused by cancer. Also, **cancerogenic.**

car·ci·no·ma (kär'sə·nō'mə), *n., pl.* –mas, –ma·ta (–mə·tə). cancer. [< L < Gk. *karkinoma*]

card¹ (kärd), *n.* 1. piece of stiff paper or thin cardboard, usually small and rectangular. 2. one of a pack of cards used in playing games. 3. **cards,** a game played with such a pack. 4. *Colloq.* a queer or amusing person. 5. **in** or **on the cards,** likely to happen; possible. —*v.* 1. provide with a card. 2. put on a card. [< F *carte* < L *charta.* Doublet of CHART.]

card² (kärd), *n.* a toothed tool or wire brush. —*v.* clean or comb with such a tool. [< F < Pr.

< L *carrere* to card; infl. by L *carduus* thistle] —**card'er,** *n.*

car·da·mom, car·da·mum (kär'də·məm), or **car·da·mon** (–mən), *n.* 1. a spicy seed used as seasoning and in medicine. 2. the Asiatic plant that it grows on. [< L < Gk. *kardamomon*]

card·board (kärd'bôrd'; –bōrd'), *n.* a stiff material made of paper, used to make cards and boxes.

card catalogue, *Am.* catalogue, esp. one for library books, made out on cards.

car·di·ac (kär'di·ak), *adj.* 1. of or having to do with the heart. 2. having to do with the upper part of the stomach. —*n.* medicine that stimulates the heart. [< L < Gk. *kardiakos* < *kardia* heart]

Car·diff (kär'dif), *n.* seaport in SE Wales.

car·di·gan (kär'də·gən), *n.* a knitted woolen jacket. [named for the Earl of *Cardigan* (1797–1868)]

car·di·nal (kär'də·nəl), *adj.* 1. of first importance; main. 2. bright-red. —*n.* 1. bright red. 2. one of the princes, or high officials, of the Roman Catholic Church, appointed by the Pope. 3. *Am.* cardinal bird. 4. cardinal number. [< L *cardinalis* chief, pertaining to a hinge < *cardo* hinge] —**car'di·nal·ly,** *adv.* —**car'di·nal·ship',** *n.* —Syn. *n.* 1. chief, principal.

car·di·nal·ate (kär'də·nəl·āt), *n.* position or rank of cardinal.

cardinal bird or **grosbeak,** or **cardinal,** *n. Am.* an American songbird that has bright-red feathers marked with black. It is a kind of finch.

cardinal flower, *Am.* 1. the bright-red flower of a North American plant. 2. the plant it grows on; the scarlet lobelia.

cardinal number or **numeral,** number that shows how many are meant. ➤ **Cardinal numbers,** like three, ten, 246, 9371, are the numbers used in counting and are contrasted with ordinal numbers, like 1st, 2nd, 24th, etc., which are used to indicate order or succession.

cardinal points, the four main directions of the compass; north, south, east, and west.

card index, *Am.* file of cards arranged systematically.

card·ing (kär'ding), *n.* preparation of the fibers of wool, cotton, flax, etc., for spinning by combing them.

car·di·o·graph (kär'di·ə·graf'; –gräf'), *n.* instrument that records the strength and nature of movements of the heart. [< Gk. *kardia* heart + –GRAPH] —**car'di·o·graph'ic,** *adj.* —**car·di·og·ra·phy** (kär'di·og'rə·fi), *n.*

card·play·ing (kärd'plā'ing), *n.* act, practice, or conventions of playing card games. —**card'play'er,** *n.*

cards (kärdz), *n.pl.* See card¹ (*n.* def. 3).

card·sharp (kärd'shärp'), **card·sharp·er** (kärd'shärp'ər), *n.* a dishonest professional cardplayer. —**card'sharp'ing,** *n.*

care (kär), *n., v.,* cared, car·ing. —*n.* 1. burden of thought; worry. 2. serious attention; caution. 3. object of concern or attention. 4. watchful oversight; charge. 5. food, shelter, and protection. 6. **have a care,** be careful. 7. **take care,** be careful. 8. **take care of,** a. attend to; provide for. b. be careful of. c. *Colloq.* deal with. —*v.* 1. be concerned; feel an interest. 2. like; want; wish. 3. **care for,** a. be fond of; like. b. want; wish: *I don't care for any dessert tonight.* c. attend to; provide for. [OE *caru*] —**car'er,** *n.* —Syn. *n.* 1. anxiety, concern. 2. heed, regard. 4. custody, management.

CARE, Cooperative for American Remittances to Europe, Inc.

ca·reen (kə·rēn'), *v.* 1. lean to one side; tilt; tip. 2. lay (a ship) over on one side for cleaning, painting, repairing, etc. [< F < L *carina* keel] —**ca·reen'er,** *n.*

ca·reer (kə·rir'), *n.* 1. general course of action or progress through life. 2. way of living; occupation; profession. 3. speed; full speed. —*v.* rush along wildly; dash. —*adj. Am.* having to do with someone who has seriously followed a profession: *a career diplomat.* [< F *carrière* race course < L *carrus* wagon] —**ca·reer′ist,** *n.*

care·free (kār′frē′), *adj.* without worry; happy; gay.

care·ful (kār′fəl), *adj.* 1. thinking what one says; watching what one does; cautious. 2. done with thought or pains; exact; thorough. 3. *Archaic.* anxious; worried. —**care′ful·ly,** *adv.* —**care′ful·ness,** *n.* —**Syn.** 1. heedful, mindful, guarded. 2. painstaking, particular.

care·less (kār′lis), *adj.* 1. not thinking what one says; not watching what one does. 2. done without enough thought or pains; not exact or thorough. 3. not troubling oneself. 4. *Archaic.* without worry. —**care′less·ly,** *adv.* —**care′less·ness,** *n.* —**Syn.** 1. inattentive. thoughtless. 2. inaccurate, negligent. 3. indifferent, unconcerned.

ca·ress (kə·res′), *n.* a touch or stroke to show affection; embrace; kiss. —*v.* touch or stroke to show affection; embrace; kiss. [< F < Ital. *carezza,* ult. < L *carus* dear] —**ca·ress′a·ble,** *adj.* —**ca·ress′er,** *n.* —**ca·ress′ing·ly,** *adv.*

car·et (kar′ət), *n.* mark (∧) to show where something should be put in, used in writing and in correcting proof. See proofreading marks on page 27 for example. [< L, there is wanting]

care·tak·er (kār′tāk′ər), *n.* person who takes care of a person, place, or thing.

care·worn (kār′wôrn′; -wōrn′), *adj.* showing signs of worry; tired; weary.

car·fare (kär′fār′), *n.* money to pay for riding on a streetcar, bus, etc.

car·go (kär′gō), *n., pl.* -goes, -gos. load of goods carried on a ship. [< Sp., < *cargar* load, ult. < L *carrus* wagon]

Car·ib (kar′ib), *n.* 1. member of an Indian tribe of NE South America. 2. a language family found primarily in NE South America, and to a lesser extent in Central America and the West Indies. —**Car′ib·an,** *adj.*

Car·ib·be·an (kar′ə·bē′ən; kə·rib′i–), *n.* Also, **Caribbean Sea.** sea between Central America, the West Indies, and South America. —*adj.* 1. of this sea or the islands in it. 2. of the Caribs.

car·i·bou (kar′ə·bü), *n., pl.* -bous or (*esp. collectively*) -bou. *Am.* North American reindeer. [< Canadian F < Algonquian *xalibu* pawer]

car·i·ca·ture (kar′i·kə·chür; -chər), *n., v.,* -tured, -tur·ing. —*n.* 1. picture, cartoon, description, etc., that ridiculously exaggerates the peculiarities or defects of a person or thing. 2. art of making such pictures or descriptions. 3. a very inferior imitation. —*v.* make a caricature of. [< F < Ital., < *caricare* overload] —**car·i·ca·tur·al** (kar′i·kə·chür′əl; -chər-; kar′i·kə·chür′əl), *adj.* —**car′i·ca·tur′ist,** *n.* —**Syn.** *n.* 1. burlesque.

car·ies (kār′ēz; -i·ēz), *n.* decay of teeth, bones, or tissues. [< L]

car·il·lon (kar′ə·lon; -lən; kə·ril′yən), *n., v.,* -lonned, -lon·ning. —*n.* 1. set of bells arranged for playing melodies. 2. melody played on such bells. 3. part of an organ imitating the sound of bells. —*v.* play a carillon. [< F, ult. < L *quattuor* four; orig. consisted of four bells]

car·il·lon·neur (kar′ə·lə·nér′), *n.* person who plays a carillon.

car·i·ole (kar′i·ōl), *n.* 1. a small carriage drawn by one horse. 2. a covered cart. Also, **carriole.** [< F < Ital. < L *carrus* wagon]

car·i·ous (kār′i·əs), *adj.* having caries; decayed. [< L *cariosus* < *caries* decay] —**car·i·os·i·ty** (kār′i·os′ə·ti), **car′i·ous·ness,** *n.*

car·load (kär′lōd′), *n.* as much as a car, esp. a railroad freight car, can hold or carry. —*adj. Am.* bought and sold by the carload.

Carls·bad Caverns (kärlz′bad), national park in SE New Mexico, famous for its huge limestone caverns.

Car·lyle (kär·līl′), *n.* Thomas, 1795–1881, British essayist and historian.

car·man (kär′mən), *n., pl.* -men. motorman or conductor of a streetcar.

Car·mel·ite (kär′məl·īt), *n.* a mendicant friar or nun of a religious order founded in the 12th century. —*adj.* of this order.

car·min·a·tive (kär·min′ə·tiv; kär′mə·nā′-tiv), *adj.* expelling gas from the stomach and intestines. —*n.* medicine that does this. [< L *carminatus* carded]

car·mine (kär′min; -mīn), *n.* 1. deep red with a tinge of purple. 2. light crimson. 3. crimson coloring matter found in cochineal. —*adj.* 1. deep-red with a tinge of purple. 2. light-crimson. [< Med.L < Sp. *carmesi* CRIMSON]

car·nage (kär′nij), *n.* slaughter of a great number of people. [< F < Ital. *carnaggio* < L *caro* flesh]

car·nal (kär′nəl), *adj.* 1. worldly; not spiritual. 2. bodily; sensual. [< L *carnalis* < *caro* flesh] —**car·nal·i·ty** (kär·nal′ə·ti), *n.* —**car′nal·ly,** *adv.*

car·na·tion (kär·nā′shən), *n.* 1. a red, white, or pink flower with a spicy fragrance. 2. the plant that it grows on. 3. rosy pink. —*adj.* rosy-pink. [< F < Ital. *carnagione* flesh color. See CARNAGE.]

car·nel·ian (kär·nēl′yən), *n.* a red stone used in jewelry. Also, **cornelian.** [alter. of *cornelian;* infl. by L *caro* flesh]

car·ni·val (kär′nə·vəl), *n.* 1. place of amusement or traveling show having merry-go-rounds, side shows, etc. 2. feasting and merrymaking. 3. time of feasting and merrymaking just before Lent. [< Ital. < Med.L < L *carnem levare* putting away of flesh]

Car·niv·o·ra (kär·niv′ə·rə), *n.pl. Zool.* a large group of flesh-eating animals, including cats, dogs, lions, tigers, and bears.

car·ni·vore (kär′nə·vôr; -vōr), *n. Zool.* a flesh-eating animal. —**car·niv·o·ral** (kär·niv′ə·rəl), *adj.*

car·niv·o·rous (kär·niv′ə·rəs), *adj.* 1. flesh-eating: *carnivorous animals.* 2. of or having to do with the Carnivora. [< L *carnivorus* < *caro* flesh + *vorare* devour] —**car·niv′o·rous·ly,** *adv.* —**car·niv′o·rous·ness,** *n.*

car·ol (kar′əl), *n., v.,* -oled, -ol·ing; *esp. Brit.* -olled, -ol·ling. —*n.* 1. song of joy. 2. hymn: *Christmas carols.* —*v.* sing; sing joyously; praise with carols. [< OF *carole,* ? < L < Gk. *choraules* flute player] —**car′ol·er,** *esp. Brit.* **car′ol·ler,** *n.*

Car·o·li·na (kar′ə·lī′nə), *n.* 1. an early American colony on the Atlantic coast. 2. either North Carolina or South Carolina. 3. **the Carolinas,** *Am.* North Carolina and South Carolina. —**Car·o·lin·i·an** (kar′ə·lin′i·ən), *adj., n.*

Car·o·line Islands (kar′ə·līn; -lin), group of over 500 islands in the W Pacific, near the equator; now under U.S. administration.

car·om (kar′əm), *n.* 1. *Billiards.* shot in which the ball struck with the cue hits two balls, one after the other. 2. a hitting and bouncing off. —*v.* 1. make a carom. 2. *Am.* hit and bounce off. Also, **carrom.** [< F < Sp. *carambola,* ? < Malay *carambil* name of fruit]

ca·rot·id (kə·rot′id), *Anat.* —*n.* either of two large arteries, one on each side of the neck, that carry blood to the head. —*adj.* having to do with these arteries. [< Gk. *karotides* < *karos* stupor (state produced by compression of carotids)]

ca·rous·al (kə·rouz′əl), *n.* 1. noisy revelry. 2. a drinking party.

ca·rouse (kə·rouz′), *n., v.,* -roused, -rous·ing. —*n.* a noisy feast; drinking party. —*v.* drink heavily; take part in noisy feasts or revels. [< obs. adv. < G *gar aus*(*trinken*) (drink) all up] —**ca·rous′er,** *n.*

car·ou·sel (kar′ə·sel′; -zel′), *n.* carrousel.

carp¹ (kärp), *v.* find fault with; complain. [< Scand. *karpa* wrangle] —**carp′er,** *n.* —**carp′ing·ly,** *adv.* —**Syn.** cavil.

carp² (kärp), *n., pl.* **carps** or (*esp. collectively*) **carp.** 1. a fresh-water fish containing many bones that feeds mostly on plants. 2. any of a group of similar fishes, including goldfish, min-

Caribou (4 ft. high at the shoulder)

nows, chub, and dace. [< OF < Pr. < LL *carpa* < Gmc.]

carp., carpenter; carpentry.

car·pal (kär′pəl), *Anat.* —*adj.* of the carpus. —*n.* bone of the carpus. [< NL < Gk. *karpos* wrist]

Car·pa·thi·an Mountains (kär·pā′thi·ən), or **Carpathians,** *n.pl.* mountain system in E and C Europe, chiefly in Czechoslovakia and Poland.

car·pel (kär′pəl), *n. Bot.* a modified leaf from which a pistil of a flower is formed. [< Gk. *karpos* fruit] —car·pel·lar·y (kär′pə·ler′i), *adj.*

car·pen·ter (kär′pən·tər), *n.* man whose work is building with wood. —*v.* do such work. [< OF < LL *carpentarius* wagonmaker < L *carpentum* wagon]

car·pen·try (kär′pən·tri), *n.* work of a carpenter.

car·pet (kär′pit), *n.* **1.** a heavy, woven fabric for covering floors and stairs. **2.** a covering made of this fabric. **3.** anything like a carpet. **4. on the carpet,** *Colloq.* being scolded or rebuked. —*v.* cover with a carpet. [< Med.L *carpeta* < L *carpere* card (wool)] —car′pet·less, *adj.*

car·pet·bag (kär′pit·bag′), *n.* traveling bag made of carpet.

car·pet·bag·ger (kär′pit·bag′ər), *n. Am.* Northerner who went to the South to get political or other advantages after the Civil War.

car·pet·ing (kär′pit·ing), *n.* **1.** fabric for carpets. **2.** carpets.

car·port (kär′pôrt′; -pōrt′), *n.* a roofed shelter for one or more automobiles, usually attached to a house and open on at least one side.

car·pus (kär′pəs), *n., pl.* -pi (-pī). *Anat.* **1.** wrist. **2.** bones of the wrist. [< NL < Gk. *karpos* wrist]

car·rack (kar′ək), *n. Archaic.* galleon. [< OF < Sp. < Ar. *qarāqir* (pl.)]

car·riage (kar′ij; *for* 7, *also* kar′i·ij), *n.* **1.** vehicle moving on wheels, for carrying persons. **2.** a wheeled passenger vehicle pulled by horses. **3.** frame on wheels supporting a gun. **4.** a moving part of a machine that supports some other part. **5.** manner of holding the head and body; bearing. **6.** act of carrying or transporting. **7.** cost or price of carrying. **8.** management; handling. [< OF *cariage* < *carier* CARRY]

car·ri·er (kar′i·ər), *n.* **1.** person or thing that carries something: *mail carrier.* **2.** thing to carry something in or on. **3.** person or thing that carries or transmits a disease. **4.** *Elect.* radio wave whose intensity is decreased or increased and whose frequency is regulated in transmitting a signal. **5.** an aircraft carrier.

carrier pigeon, 1. *Colloq.* homing pigeon. **2.** in technical use, one of a breed of large, heavy domestic pigeons.

car·ri·ole (kar′i·ōl), *n.* cariole.

car·ri·on (kar′i·ən), *n.* **1.** dead and decaying flesh. **2.** rottenness; filth. —*adj.* **1.** dead and decaying. **2.** feeding on dead and decaying flesh. **3.** rotten. [< OF *caroigne* < VL < L *caries* decay]

Car·roll (kar′əl), *n.* Lewis, 1832–1898, English writer and mathematician. His real name was Charles L. Dodgson.

car·rom (kar′əm), *n., v.* carom.

car·rot (kar′ət), *n.* **1.** plant that has a long, tapering, orange-red root eaten as a vegetable. **2.** its root. [< F < L < Gk. *karoton*]

car·rot·y (kar′ət·i), *adj.* **1.** like a carrot in color; orange-red. **2.** red-haired.

car·rou·sel (kar′ə·sel′; -zel′), *n.* **1.** *Am.* merry-go-round. **2.** a kind of tournament to which dances, etc., were sometimes added. Also, **carousel.** [< F < Ital. *carosello* < L *carrus* cart]

car·ry (kar′i), *v.,* -ried, -ry·ing, *n., pl.* -ries. —*v.* **1.** take from one place to another: *carry goods in a ship.* **2.** transfer in any manner; take or bring: *the ship carries goods to market.* **3.** bear the weight of; hold up; support; sustain: *those columns carry the roof.* **4.** hold (one's body and head) in a certain way. **5.** capture; win. **6.**

get (a motion or bill) passed or adopted. **7.** continue; extend: *carry a road into the mountains.* **8.** cover or reach to a certain distance: *his voice carries well.* **9.** have the power of throwing or driving: *our guns could only carry ten miles.* **10.** influence greatly; lead: *his acting carried the audience.* **11.** have as a result; involve: *his judgment carries great weight.* **12.** *Am.* **a.** keep in stock. **b.** keep on the account books of a business. **13.** *Am.* extend credit to. **14.** *Am.* sustain or perform (a melody or musical part): *carry the tune.* **15.** *Southern U.S.* take; accompany: *carry Aunt Therese to the station.* **16.** carry away, arouse strong feeling in. **17.** carry off, **a.** win (a prize, honor, etc.). **b.** succeed with; pass off. **18.** carry on, **a.** do; manage; conduct. **b.** go on with after being stopped. **c.** keep going; continue. **d.** *U.S. Colloq.* behave wildly or foolishly. **19.** carry out, do; get done; accomplish; complete. —*n.* **1.** distance covered; distance that something goes. **2.** *Am.* a portage. [< OF < LL *carricare* < L *carrus* wagon, cart. Doublet of CHARGE.] —Syn. *v.* 1, 2, convey, transport, bring.

car·ry·all (kar′i·ôl′), *n. Am.* a lightweight covered carriage. [alter. of *cariole*]

car·ry·back, car·ry·back (kar′i·bak′), *n.* a credit on income tax in a given year as a result of previous overpayment or earlier losses not accounted for in computing the tax.

car·ry·o·ver (kar′i·ō′vər), *n.* part left over.

car·sick (kär′sik′), *adj.* nauseated by traveling in a car, train, etc.

Car·son City (kär′sən), capital of Nevada.

cart (kärt), *n.* **1.** vehicle with two wheels, for carrying heavy loads. **2.** a light wagon, used to deliver goods, etc. **3.** a small vehicle on wheels, moved by hand. —*v.* carry in a cart. [OE *cræt* or < Scand. *kartr*] —cart′er, *n.*

cart·age (kärt′ij), *n.* **1.** cost or price of carting. **2.** act of carting.

carte blanche (kärt′ blänsh′), *French.* full authority; freedom to use one's own judgment.

car·tel (kär·tel′; kär′təl), *n.* **1.** a large group of businesses that agree to fix prices and production. **2.** a written agreement between countries at war for the exchange of prisoners or some other purpose. **3.** a written challenge to a duel. [< F < Ital. *cartello* little CARD[1]]

Car·te·sian (kär·tē′zhən), *adj.* having to do with Descartes, or with his doctrines or methods. [< NL, < *Cartesius*, Latinized form of *Descartes*]

Car·thage (kär′thij), *n.* a powerful ancient city and seaport in N Africa, founded by the Phoenicians, destroyed by the Romans in 146 B.C. —Car·tha·gin·i·an (kär′thə·jin′i·ən), *adj., n.*

Car·thu·sian (kär·thü′zhən), *n.* member of an order of monks founded in 1086. —*adj.* of this order. [< *Chatrousse*, village where the first monastery of the order was]

car·ti·lage (kär′tə·lij), *n. Anat., Zool.* **1.** the firm, tough, elastic, flexible substance forming parts of a skeleton; gristle. **2.** part formed of this substance. The nose is supported by cartilages. [< F < L *cartilago*]

car·ti·lag·i·nous (kär′tə·laj′ə·nəs), *adj.* **1.** of or like cartilage; gristly. **2.** *Zool.* having the skeleton formed mostly of cartilage.

cart·load (kärt′lōd′), *n.* as much as a cart can hold or carry.

car·tog·ra·phy (kär·tog′rə·fi), *n.* the making of maps or charts. [< Med.L *carta* chart, map + E -*graphy* drawing < Gk. *graphein* draw, write] —car·tog′ra·pher, *n.* —car·to·graph·ic (kär′tə·graf′ik), car′to·graph′i·cal, *adj.* —car′to·graph′i·cal·ly, *adv.*

car·ton (kär′tən), *n.* box made of pasteboard. [< F *carton* pasteboard < Ital., < *carta.* See CARD[1].]

car·toon (kär·tün′), *n.* **1.** sketch or drawing that interests or amuses by showing persons, things, political events, etc., in an exaggerated way. **2.** a full-size drawing of a design or painting, for a fresco, mosaic, tapestry, etc. **3.** comic strip. **4.** animated cartoon. —*v. Am.* make a cartoon of. [var. of *carton*; because drawn on paper] —car·toon′ing, *n. Am.* —car·toon′ist, *n.*

car·tridge (kär′trij), *n.* **1.** case made of metal or cardboard for holding gunpowder. **2.** roll of camera film. [alter. of *cartouche* (< F) a roll of paper]

cart wheel, 1. wheel of a cart. **2.** a sidewise handspring or somersault.

carve (kärv), *v.,* **carved, carv·ing. 1.** cut into slices or pieces. **2.** cut; make by cutting. **3.** decorate with figures or designs cut on the surface. [OE *ceorfan*] —**carv′er,** *n.*

car·vel (kär′vəl), *n.* caravel.

carv·en (kär′vən), *adj. Poetic.* carved.

carv·ing (kär′ving), *n.* **1.** act or art of one that carves. **2.** carved work: *a wood carving.*

car·y·at·id (kar′i·at′id), *n., pl.* **-ids, -i·des** (-ə·dēz). statue of a woman used as a column. [< L < Gk. *Karyatides* women of Caryae] —**car′y·at′i·dal,** *adj.*

ca·sa·ba (kə·sä′bə), or **ca·saba melon,** *n. Am.* kind of muskmelon with a yellow rind. Also, **cassaba.** [after *Kasaba* near Smyrna, Asia Minor]

Caryatids

Cas·a·blan·ca (kas′ə·blang′kə; kä′sə·bläng′kə), *n.* seaport in NW Morocco.

Cas·a·no·va (kaz′ə·nō′və; kas′-), *n.* Giovanni Jacopo, 1725–1798, Italian adventurer.

cas·cade (kas·kād′), *n., v.,* **-cad·ed, -cad·ing.** —*n.* **1.** a small waterfall. **2.** anything like this. —*v.* fall in a cascade. [< F < Ital. *cascata* < L *cadere* fall]

Cascade Range, mountain range in NW United States, extending from N California to British Columbia.

cas·car·a (kas·kär′ə), *n. Am.* laxative made from the dried bark of a species of buckthorn. [< Sp., bark]

case[1] (kās), *n.* **1.** instance; example: *a case of poor work.* **2.** condition; situation; state: *a case of poverty.* **3.** actual condition; real situation; true state: *that is the case.* **4.** instance of a disease or injury: *a case of measles.* **5.** person who has a disease or injury; patient. **6.** *Law.* **a.** matter for a law court to decide. **b.** statement of facts for a law court to consider. **7.** a convincing argument. **8.** *Gram.* **a.** one of the forms of a noun, pronoun, or adjective used to show its relation to other words. **b.** relation shown by such a form. *I* is in the nominative case. **9.** *Am., Slang.* a queer or unusual person. **10.** in any case, under any circumstances; anyhow. **11.** in case, if it should happen that; if; supposing. **12.** in case of, in the event of. **13.** in no case, under no circumstances. [< OF < L *casus* a falling, chance < *cadere* fall] ▶ Some of the commonest bits of deadwood in writing are various locutions with case. They are wordy and keep the real person or situation or thing (whatever the "case" stands for) one construction away from the reader: *Drinking went on moderately except in a few scattered cases.* [This was written of a convention. The "cases" would be delegates?]

case[2] (kās), *n., v.,* **cased, cas·ing.** —*n.* **1.** thing to hold or cover something. **2.** covering; sheath. **3.** box. **4.** quantity in a box. **5.** frame: *a window fits in a case.* **6.** tray for printing type, with a space for each letter. —*v.* put in a case; cover with a case. [< OF < L *capsa* box < *capere* hold]

case·hard·en (kās′här′dən), *v.* **1.** *Metall.* harden (iron or steel) on the surface. **2.** render callous; make unfeeling.

ca·se·in (kā′si·in; -sēn), *n. Biochem.* protein present in milk. Cheese is mostly casein. [< L *caseus* cheese]

case knife, 1. knife carried in a case. **2.** table knife.

case·mate (kās′māt), *n.* **1.** a shellproof vault; bombproof room. A casemate in the wall of a fort has holes for big guns to shoot through. **2.** an armored enclosure protecting guns on a warship. [< F < Ital. *casamatta,* orig., round house < L *casa* hut + *matta* round, spinning] —**case′mat·ed,** *adj.*

case·ment (kās′mənt), *n.* **1.** a window opening on hinges like a door. **2.** *Poetic.* any window. **3.** casing; covering; frame. —**case′ment·ed,** *adj.*

ca·se·ous (kā′si·əs), *adj.* of or like cheese. [< L *caseus* cheese]

ca·sern, ca·serne (kə·zėrn′), *n.* place for soldiers to live in a fortified town; barrack. [< F < Sp. *caserna* < L *casa* house]

cash[1] (kash), *n.* **1.** ready money; coins and bills. **2.** money, or an equivalent, as a check, paid at the time of buying something. —*v.* **1.** get cash for. **2.** give cash for. **3. cash in,** *Am., Colloq.* **a.** in poker, etc., change (chips, etc.) into cash. **b.** pass away; die. **4. cash in on,** *U.S. Colloq.* **a.** make a profit from. **b.** use to advantage. [< F *caisse* < Pr. < L *capsa* box, coffer]

cash[2] (kash), *n., pl.* **cash.** coin of small value, used in China, India, etc. [< Tamil *kasu*]

cash·book (kash′bůk′), *n.* book in which a record is kept of money received and paid out.

cash·ew (kash′ü; kə·shü′), *n.* **1.** a small kidney-shaped nut. **2.** the tropical American tree that it grows on. [< F < Brazilian Pg. *acajú* < Tupi]

cash·ier[1] (kash·ir′), *n.* person who has charge of money in a bank or business. [< F *caissier* treasurer. See CASH[1].]

cash·ier[2] (kash·ir′), *v.* dismiss from service; discharge in disgrace. [< Du. < F < L *quassare* shatter and LL *cassare* annul]

cash·mere (kash′mir), *n.* **1.** a fine, soft wool from goats. **2.** a costly kind of shawl made of this wool. **3.** a fine, soft wool from sheep. **4.** a fine, soft woolen cloth. [after *Kashmir*]

Cash·mere (kash·mir′; kash′mir), *n.* Kashmir.

cash register, *Am.* machine which records and shows the amount of a sale, usually with a drawer to hold money.

cas·ing (kās′ing), *n.* **1.** thing put around something; covering; case. **2.** *Am.* the part of a tire that encloses the inner tube. **3.** *Am.* framework around a door or window.

ca·si·no (kə·sē′nō), *n., pl.* **-nos. 1.** a building or room for dancing, gambling, etc. **2.** cassino. [< Ital., dim. of *casa* house < L *casa*]

cask (kask; käsk), *n.* **1.** barrel. A cask may be large or small, and is usually made to hold liquids. **2.** amount that a cask holds. [< Sp. *casco* skull, cask of wine, ult. < L *quassare* break]

cas·ket (kas′kit; käs′-), *n.* **1.** a small box to hold jewels, letters, etc. **2.** *Am.* coffin.

Cas·pi·an Sea (kas′pi·ən), an inland salt sea between Europe and Asia.

cas·sa·ba (kə·sä′bə), *n.* casaba.

Cas·san·dra (kə·san′drə), *n.* **1.** *Gk. Legend.* a prophetess of ancient Troy, who was fated never to be believed. **2.** person who prophesies misfortune, but is not believed.

cas·sa·va (kə·sä′və), *n.* **1.** a tropical plant with starchy roots. **2.** a nutritious starch from its roots; manioc. Tapioca is made from cassava. [< F < Sp. < Haitian *cacábi*]

cas·se·role (kas′ə·rōl), *n.* **1.** a covered baking dish in which food can be both cooked and served. **2.** food cooked and served in such a dish. [< F, < *casse* pan < VL *cattia* < Gk. *kyathion,* dim. of *kyathos* cup]

cas·sia (kash′ə; kas′i·ə), *n.* **1.** an inferior kind of cinnamon. **2.** the tree that produces it. **3.** plant from whose leaves and pods the drug senna is obtained. **4.** the pods or their pulp. [< L < Gk. < Heb. *q'tsi'āh*]

cas·si·mere (kas′ə·mir), *n.* a soft, lightweight, woolen cloth, sometimes used for men's suits. [var. of *cashmere*]

cas·si·no (kə·sē′nō), *n.* a card game. Also, ca·sino. [var. of *casino*]

Cas·si·o·pei·a (kas′i·ə·pē′ə), *n.* **1.** *Gk. Legend.* mother of an Ethiopian princess who was rescued from a sea monster by Perseus. **2.** a northern constellation fancied to resemble Cassiopeia sitting in a chair.

cas·sock (kas′ək), *n.* a long outer garment, usually black, worn by a clergyman. [< Ital. *casacca*] —**cas′socked,** *adj.*

cas·so·war·y (kas′ə·wer′ĭ), n., pl. -war·ies. a large bird of Australia and New Guinea, like an ostrich, but smaller. [< Malay *kasuari*]

cast (kast; käst), v., cast, cast·ing, n., adj. —v. 1. throw: *cast a fishing line.* 2. throw off; let fall: *the snake cast its skin.* 3. direct; turn: *he cast me a look.* 4. shape by pouring or squeezing into a mold to harden. 5. arrange (actors and parts in a play). 6. add; calculate. 7. cast a ballot, vote. 8. cast about, a. search; look. b. make plans. 9. cast down, a. turn downward; lower. b. make sad or discouraged. 10. cast out, drive away; banish; expel. 11. cast up, a. turn upward; raise. b. add up; find the sum of. —n. 1. act of throwing. 2. thing made by casting. 3. mold used in casting; mold. 4. actors in a play. 5. form; look; appearance. 6. kind; sort. 7. a slight amount of color; tinge. 8. a slight squint. —adj. (of a play) having all the actors chosen. [< Scand. *kasta* throw]

cas·ta·net (kas′tə·net′), n. a pair, or one of a pair, of instruments of hard wood or ivory like little cymbals, held in the hand and clicked together to beat time for dancing or music. [< Sp. *castaneta* < L *castanea* CHESTNUT]

cast·a·way (kast′ə·wā′; käst′-), adj. 1. thrown away; cast adrift. 2. outcast. —n. 1. shipwrecked person. 2. outcast.

caste (kast; käst), n. 1. any of the hereditary social classes into which the Hindus are divided. 2. an exclusive social group; distinct class. 3. a social system having class distinctions based on rank, wealth, position, etc. 4. lose caste, lose social rank or position. [< Sp. < Pg. *casta* race < L *castus* pure]

cas·tel·lat·ed (kas′tə·lāt′ĭd), adj. having turrets and battlements. —cas′tel·la′tion, n.

cast·er (kas′tər; käs′-), n. 1. person or thing that casts. 2. Also, **castor.** a. a small wheel on a piece of furniture to make it easier to move. b. bottle containing salt, mustard, vinegar, or other seasoning for table use. c. Am. stand or rack for such bottles.

cas·ti·gate (kas′tə·gāt), v., -gat·ed, -gat·ing. criticize severely; punish. [< L *castigatus*, ult. < *castus* pure] —cas′ti·ga′tion, n. —cas′ti·ga′tor, n.

Cas·tile (kas·tēl′), n. 1. region in N and central Spain, formerly a kingdom. 2. Castile soap.

Cas·tile soap (kas′tēl), a pure, hard soap made from olive oil.

Cas·til·ian (kas·til′yən), adj. of Castile, its people, or their language. —n. 1. Castilian Spanish, the accepted standard form of Spanish. 2. native or inhabitant of Castile.

cast·ing (kas′ting; käs′-), n. thing shaped by being poured into a mold to harden.

cast iron, a hard, brittle form of iron made by casting.

cast-i·ron (kast′ī′ərn; käst′-), adj. 1. made of cast iron. 2. hard; not yielding. 3. hardy; strong.

cas·tle (kas′əl; käs′-), n., v., -tled, -tling. —n. 1. a building or group of buildings with thick walls, towers, and other defenses against attack. 2. palace that once had defenses against attack. 3. a large and imposing residence. 4. piece in the game of chess, shaped like a tower. —v. Chess. move the king two squares toward a castle and bring that castle to the square the king has passed over. [< L *castellum*, dim. of *castrum* fort. Doublet of CHATEAU.] —cas′tled, adj. —Syn. n. 1. fortress, citadel, stronghold. 3. mansion, château.

castle in the air, something imagined but not likely to come true; daydream.

cast-off (kast′ôf′; -of′; käst′-), adj. thrown away; abandoned. —n. person or thing that has been cast off.

cas·tor¹ (kas′tər; käs′-), n. caster (def. 2).

cas·tor² (kas′tər; käs′-), n. 1. a hat made of beaver fur. 2. an oily substance with a strong odor, secreted by beavers. It is used in making perfume and in medicines. [< L < Gk. *kastor* beaver]

Cas·tor (kas′tər; käs′-), n. 1. Class. Myth. the mortal twin brother of Pollux. 2. the fainter star of the two bright stars in the constellation called Gemini.

castor bean, Am. seed of the castor-oil plant.

castor oil, yellow oil obtained from castor beans, used as a cathartic, a lubricant, etc.

cas·tor-oil plant (kas′tər·oil′; käs′-), a tall tropical plant from whose seeds castor oil is obtained.

cas·trate (kas′trāt), v., -trat·ed, -trat·ing. 1. remove the male glands of. 2. mutilate; expurgate. [< L *castratus*] —cas·tra′tion, n.

cas·u·al (kazh′ū·əl), adj. 1. happening by chance; not planned or expected; accidental. 2. without plan or method. 3. careless; unconcerned; offhand. 4. uncertain; indefinite; vague. 5. occasional; irregular. A casual laborer does any kind of work that he can get. —n. 1. a casual laborer. 2. person occasionally receiving charity. 3. soldier temporarily separated from his unit. [< L *casualis* < *casus* chance] —cas′u·al·ly, adv. —cas′u·al·ness, n. —Syn. adj. 1. chance, fortuitous, unexpected. —Ant. adj. 1. expected. 2. planned; intentional.

cas·u·al·ty (kazh′ū·əl·ti), n., pl. -ties. 1. accident. 2. an unfortunate accident; mishap. 3. soldier or sailor who has been wounded, killed, or lost. 4. person injured or killed in an accident.

cas·u·ist (kazh′ū·ist), n. 1. person who decides questions of right and wrong in regard to conduct, duty, etc. 2. person who reasons cleverly but falsely. [< F *casuiste* < L *casus* case]

cas·u·is·tic (kazh′ū·is′tik), **cas·u·is·ti·cal** (-tə·kəl), adj. 1. of or like casuistry. 2. too subtle; sophistical. —cas′u·is′ti·cal·ly, adv.

cas·u·ist·ry (kazh′ū·is·tri), n., pl. -ries. 1. act or process of deciding questions of right and wrong in regard to conduct, duty, etc. 2. clever but false reasoning.

cat (kat), n., v., cat·ted, cat·ting. —n. 1. a small animal often kept as a pet or for catching mice. 2. any animal of the group including cats, lions, tigers, leopards, etc. 3. Am. lynx. 4. animal something like a cat. 5. Am. catfish. 6. a mean, spiteful woman. 7. Slang. person devoted to swing music and to the cant that pertains to it. 8. cat-o′-nine-tails. 9. Naut. tackle for hoisting. —v. hoist (an anchor) and fasten it to a beam on the ship's side. [OE *catt* (male), *catte* (fem.), prob. < LL *cattus, catta*] —cat′like′, adj.

cat., 1. catalogue. 2. catechism.

ca·tab·o·lism (kə·tab′ə·liz·əm), n. process of breaking down living tissues into simpler substances or waste matter, thereby producing energy. [prob. < *metabolism*, by substitution of *cata-* down] —cat·a·bol·ic (kat′ə·bol′ik), adj. —cat′a·bol′i·cal·ly, adv.

cat·a·chre·sis (kat′ə·krē′sis), n., pl. -ses (-sēz). misuse of words. [< L < Gk. *katachresis* misuse < *kata-* amiss + *chresthai* use] —cat·a·chres·tic (kat′ə·kres′tik), adj. —cat′a·chres′ti·cal·ly, adv.

cat·a·clysm (kat′ə·kliz·əm), n. 1. a flood, earthquake, or any sudden, violent change in the earth. 2. any violent change. [< L < Gk. *kataklysmos* flood < *kata-* down + *klyzein* wash]

cat·a·clys·mic (kat′ə·kliz′mik), **cat·a·clys·mal** (-məl), adj. of or like a cataclysm; extremely sudden and violent. —cat′a·clys′mi·cal·ly, adv.

cat·a·comb (kat′ə·kōm), n. Usually, catacombs. an underground gallery forming a burial place. [< LL *catacumbae* < *cata* (< Gk.) *tumbas* among the tombs. See TOMB.]

cat·a·falque (kat′ə·falk), n. stand or frame to support the coffin in which a dead person lies. [< F < Ital. *catafalco* < LL, < L *cata-* down + *fala* tower]

Cat·a·lan (kat′ə·lan; -lən), adj. of Catalonia, its people, or their language. —n. 1. native or inhabitant of Catalonia. 2. dialect spoken in Catalonia.

cat·a·lep·sy (kat′ə·lep′si), **cat·a·lep·sis** (kat′ə·lep′sis), n. kind of fit during which a person loses consciousness and power to feel and his

Caster (def. 2a)

muscles become rigid. [< LL < Gk. *katalepsis* seizure < *kata-* down + *lambanein* seize] —cat'a·lep'tic, *adj., n.*

Cat·a·li·na (kat'ə·lē'nə), *n.* Santa Catalina.

cat·a·logue, cat·a·log (kat'ə·lôg; -log), *n., v.,* -logued, -logu·ing; -loged, -log·ing. —*n.* 1. a list, esp. a list arranged in alphabetical or other methodical order, with brief particulars concerning the names, articles, etc., listed. 2. *Am.* volume or booklet issued by a college or university listing rules, courses to be given, etc. —*v.* make a catalogue of; put in a catalogue. [< F < LL < Gk. *katalogos* list < *kata-* down + *legein* count] —cat'a·logu'er, cat'a·logu'ist; cat'a·log'er, cat'a·log'ist, *n.* ▶ catalogue, catalog. The spelling is divided, with the shorter form gaining. Nearly half the colleges now use *catalog* as the name of their annual bulletin of announcements.

Cat·a·lo·ni·a (kat'ə·lō'ni·ə), *n.* region in NE Spain.

ca·tal·pa (kə·tal'pə), *n. Am.* tree with large, heart-shaped leaves, bell-shaped flowers, and long pods. [< NL < Am.Ind. (Creek) *kutuhlpa*]

ca·tal·y·sis (kə·tal'ə·sis), *n., pl.* -ses (-sēz). *Chem.* the causing or speeding up of a chemical reaction by the presence of a substance that does not itself change. [< NL < Gk. *katalysis* dissolution < *kata-* down + *lyein* to loose] —cat·a·lyt·ic (kat'ə·lit'ik), *adj.* —cat'a·lyt'i·cal·ly, *adv.*

cat·a·lyst (kat'ə·list), *n.* substance that causes catalysis.

cat·a·lyze (kat'ə·līz), *v.,* -lyzed, -lyz·ing. act upon by catalysis. —cat'a·lyz'er, *n.*

cat·a·ma·ran (kat'ə·mə·ran'), *n. Am.* 1. boat with two hulls side by side. 2. raft made of pieces of wood lashed together. [< Tamil *katta-maram* tied tree]

Catamaran

cat·a·mount (kat'ə·mount'), *n. Am.* wildcat, such as a puma or lynx. [short for *catamountain* cat of (the) mountain]

Ca·ta·nia (kə·tän'yə; kä·tä'nyä), *n.* seaport in E Sicily.

cat·a·pult (kat'ə·pult), *n.* 1. an ancient weapon for shooting stones, arrows, etc. 2. *Brit.* slingshot. 3. device for launching an airplane from the deck of a ship. —*v.* shoot from a catapult; throw; hurl. [< L < Gk. *katapeltes*, prob. < *kata-* down + *pallein* hurl]

cat·a·ract (kat'ə·rakt), *n.* 1. a large, steep waterfall. 2. a violent rush or downpour of water; flood. 3. an opaque region in the lens or capsule of the eye that causes partial or total blindness. [< L < Gk. *kataraktes* < *kata-* down + *arassein* dash]

ca·tarrh (kə·tär'), *n.* an inflamed condition of a mucous membrane, usually that of the nose or throat, causing a discharge of mucus. [< F < L < Gk. *katarrhous* < *kata-* down + *rheein* flow] —ca·tarrh'al, *adj.*

ca·tas·tro·phe (kə·tas'trə·fē), *n.* 1. a sudden, widespread, or extraordinary disaster; great calamity or misfortune. 2. outcome; unhappy ending. 3. disastrous end; ruin. 4. sudden violent disturbance, esp. of the earth's surface. [< Gk. *katastrophe* overturning < *kata-* down + *strophein* turn] —cat·a·stroph·ic (kat'ə·strof'ik), *adj.* —Syn. 4. cataclysm.

Ca·taw·ba (kə·tô'bə), *n., pl.* -bas. *Am.* 1. a light-red grape. 2. a light wine made from it.

cat·bird (kat'bėrd'), *n. Am.* a slate-gray, American songbird that makes a sound like a cat mewing.

cat·boat (kat'bōt'), *n.* sailboat with one mast set far forward. It has no bowsprit or jib.

cat·call (kat'kôl'), *n.* a shrill cry or whistle to express disapproval. —*v.* 1. make catcalls. 2. attack with catcalls.

catch (kach), *v.,* caught, catch·ing, *n., adj.* —*v.* 1. take and hold; seize; capture. 2. take; get. 3. become caught. 4. become lighted; burn: *tinder catches easily.* 5. come on suddenly; surprise. 6.

Am. act as catcher in baseball. 7. **catch on,** *Am., Colloq.* a. understand; get the idea. b. become popular; be widely used or accepted. 8. **catch up,** a. come up even with a person or thing; overtake. b. pick up suddenly; snatch; grab. c. interrupt and annoy with criticisms or questions; heckle. d. hold up in loops. —*n.* 1. act of catching. 2. thing that catches. A fastener for a door or window is a catch. 3. thing caught. 4. *Colloq.* a good person to marry. 5. game of throwing and catching a ball. 6. *Music.* a short song sung by several persons or groups, beginning one after another. 7. *Am., Colloq.* a hidden or veiled condition in a plan, etc. —*adj.* 1. getting one's attention; arousing one's interest: *a catch phrase.* 2. tricky; deceptive: *a catch question.* [< OF *cachier* < LL *captiare* < L *capere* take. Doublet of CHASE¹.] —catch'a·ble, *adj.* —Syn. v. 1. grip, grasp, clutch, nab.

catch·all (kach'ôl'), *n. Am.* container for odds and ends.

catch·er (kach'ər), *n.* 1. person or thing that catches. 2. *Am.* a baseball player who stands behind the batter to catch the ball thrown by the pitcher.

catch·ing (kach'ing), *adj.* 1. contagious; infectious. 2. attractive; fascinating.

catch·pen·ny (kach'pen'i), *adj., n., pl.* -nies. —*adj.* showy but worthless or useless; made to sell quickly. —*n.* a catchpenny article.

catch·up (kech'əp; kach'-), *n. Now U.S.* sauce to use with meat, fish, etc. Tomato catchup is made of tomatoes, onions, salt, sugar, and spices. Also, **catsup, ketchup.**

catch·word (kach'wėrd'), *n.* 1. word or phrase used again and again for effect; slogan. 2. word so placed as to catch attention.

catch·y (kach'i), *adj.,* catch·i·er, catch·i·est. 1. easy to remember; attractive. 2. tricky; misleading; deceptive.

cat·e·chism (kat'ə·kiz·əm), *n.* 1. book of questions and answers about religion, used for teaching religious doctrine. 2. set of questions and answers about any subject. 3. a long or formal set of questions. —cat'e·chis'mal, *adj.*

cat·e·chist (kat'ə·kist), *n.* person who catechizes. —cat·e·chis·tic, cat'e·chis'ti·cal, *adj.* —cat'e·chis'ti·cal·ly, *adv.*

cat·e·chize, cat·e·chise (kat'ə·kīz), *v.,* -chized, -chiz·ing; -chised, -chis·ing. 1. teach by questions and answers. 2. question closely. [< L < Gk. *katechizein* teach orally < *kata-* thoroughly + *echeein* sound] —cat'e·chi·za'tion, cat'e·chi·sa'tion, *n.* —cat'e·chiz'er, cat'e·chis'er, *n.*

cat·e·chu·men (kat'ə·kū'mən), *n.* person who is being taught the elementary facts of Christianity. [< LL < Gk. *katechoumenos* one being instructed. See CATECHIZE.] —cat'e·chu'me·nal, *adj.*

cat·e·gor·i·cal (kat'ə·gôr'ə·kəl; -gor'-), *adj.* 1. without conditions or qualifications; positive. 2. of or in a category. —cat'e·gor'i·cal·ly, *adv.* —cat'e·gor'i·cal·ness, *n.*

cat·e·go·ry (kat'ə·gō'ri; -gō'-), *n., pl.* -ries. group or division in a general system of classification; class. [< L < Gk. *kategoria* assertion < *kata-* down + *agoreuein* speak]

cat·e·nate (kat'ə·nāt), *v.,* -nat·ed, -nat·ing. connect in a series. [< L, < *catena* chain] —cat'e·na'tion, *n.*

ca·ter (kā'tər), *v.* 1. provide food or supplies. 2. supply means of enjoyment. [verbal use of *cater, n.,* ME *acatour* buyer of provisions < F, < *acater* < LL *accaptare* acquire]

cat·er·cor·nered (kat'ər·kôr'nərd), *adj.* diagonal. —*adv.* diagonally. [< *cater* diagonally (< F *quatre* four) + *cornered*]

ca·ter·er (kā'tər·ər), *n.* person who provides food or supplies for parties, etc.

Caterpillar
(⅓ actual size)

cat·er·pil·lar (kat'ər·pil'ər), *n.* 1. wormlike form or larva of a butterfly or moth. 2. Also, **caterpillar tractor.** *Am.* tractor that can travel

over very rough ground on its two endless belts.
3. **Caterpillar**, trademark for this tractor. [cf.
OF *chatepelose* hairy cat]

cat·er·waul (kat'ər·wôl), v. howl like a cat;
screech. —n. Also, **cat'er·waul'ing**. such a howl
or screech. [ME *caterwrawe* < *cater*, appar., cat
+ *wrawe* wail, howl]

cat·fish (kat'fish'), n., pl. **-fish·es** or (esp. collectively) **-fish**. a scaleless fish with long, slender feelers around the mouth.

cat·gut (kat'gut'), n. a tough string made from
the dried and twisted intestines of sheep or other
animals, used for violin strings, etc.

Cath., 1. Also, **cath**. Cathedral. 2. Catholic.

ca·thar·sis (kə·thär'sis), n. 1. *Med*. a purging.
2. an emotional purification or relief. [< NL
< Gk. *katharsis*, ult. < *katharos* clean]

ca·thar·tic (kə·thär'tik), n. a strong laxative.
Epsom salts and castor oil are cathartics. —adj.
Also, **ca·thar'ti·cal**. strongly laxative.

Ca·thay (ka·thā'), n. *Poetic or Archaic*. China.

ca·the·dral (kə·thē'drəl), n. 1. the official
church of a bishop. 2. a large or important
church. —adj. 1. having a bishop's throne. 2. of
or like a cathedral. 3. authoritative. [< Med.L
< L < Gk. *kathedra* seat]

Catherine the Great, 1729–1796, empress of
Russia from 1762 to 1796.

cath·e·ter (kath'ə·tər), n. *Med*. a slender metal
or rubber tube to be inserted into a duct of the
body. [< LL < Gk. *katheter* < *kata-* down +
hienai send]

cath·ode (kath'ōd), n. negative electrode. The
zinc coating of a dry cell and the filament of a radio
tube are cathodes. [< Gk. *kathodos* a way down
< *kata-* down + *hodos* a way] —**ca·thod·ic** (kə·
thod'ik), **ca·thod'i·cal**, adj.

cathode rays, invisible streams of electrons
from the cathode in a vacuum tube. When cathode rays strike a solid substance, they produce
X rays.

cath·o·lic (kath'ə·lik; kath'lik), adj. 1. of interest or use to all people; including all; universal. 2. having sympathies with all; broad-
minded; liberal. 3. of the whole Christian church.
[< L < Gk. *katholikos* < *kata-* in respect to +
holos whole] —**ca·thol·i·cal·ly** (kə·thol'ik·li),
adv. —Syn. 1. all-embracing, general. 2. tolerant.

Cath·o·lic (kath'ə·lik; kath'lik), adj. 1. of the
Christian church governed by the Pope; Roman
Catholic. 2. of the ancient undivided Christian
church, or of its present representatives. —n.
member of either of these churches.

Ca·thol·i·cism (kə·thol'ə·siz·əm), **Cath·o·
lic·i·ty** (kath'ə·lis'ə·ti), n. faith, doctrine, organization, and methods of the Roman Catholic
Church.

cath·o·lic·i·ty (kath'ə·lis'ə·ti), **ca·thol·i·
cism** (kə·thol'ə·siz·əm), n. 1. universality; wide
prevalence. 2. broad-mindedness; liberalness.

ca·thol·i·cize (kə·thol'ə·sīz), v., **-cized, -ciz-
ing**. make or become catholic; universalize.

cat·i·on (kat'ī'ən), n. positive ion. During electrolysis, cations move toward the cathode.
[< Gk. *kation* going down < *kata-* down + *ienai*
go]

cat·kin (kat'kin), n. the downy or
scaly spike of flowers that grows on
willows, birches, etc.; ament. [< Du.
katteken little cat]

cat·mint (kat'mint'), n. *Brit*. catnip.

cat·nap (kat'nap'), n., v., **-napped,
-nap·ping**. —n. doze. —v. sleep or
doze for a little while.

cat·nip (kat'nip'), n. *Am*. kind of
mint of which cats are fond. Also,
Brit. **catmint**. [< *cat* + *nip*, var. of
nep catnip < L *nepeta*]

Catkin

Ca·to (kā'tō), n. 1. **Marcus Porcius**, 234–149 B.C.,
Roman statesman and patriot. 2. his great-
grandson, **Marcus Porcius**, 95–46 B.C., Roman
statesman, soldier, and Stoic philosopher.

cat-o'-nine-tails (kat'ə·nīn'tālz'), n., pl.
-tails. whip consisting of nine pieces of knotted
cord fastened to a handle.

Cats·kills (kats'kilz), or **Catskill Mountains**, n.pl. a low mountain range in SE New
York State.

cat's-paw, cats'paw (kats'pô'), n. 1. person
used by another to do something unpleasant or
dangerous. 2. a light breeze that ruffles a small
stretch of water.

cat·sup (kech'əp; kat'səp), n. catchup.

cat·tail (kat'tāl'), n. 1. tall marsh plant with
flowers in long, round, furry, brown spikes. 2.
Bot. ament; catkin.

cat·tish (kat'ish), adj. 1. catlike. 2. catty.
—**cat'tish·ly**, adv. —**cat'tish·ness**, n.

cat·tle (kat'əl), n. 1. *U.S.* cows, bulls, and
steers; oxen. 2. farm animals; livestock. 3. low,
worthless people. [< OF *catel* < L *capitale* property, CAPITAL[1]. Doublet of CHATTEL.]

cat·tle·man (kat'əl·mən), n., pl. **-men**. *Am*.
man who raises or takes care of cattle.

cat·ty (kat'i), adj., **-ti·er, -ti·est**. 1. mean;
spiteful. 2. catlike. 3. of cats. —**cat'ti·ly**, adv.
—**cat'ti·ness**, n.

Ca·tul·lus (kə·tul'əs), n. **Gaius Valerius**, 87?–
54? B.C., Roman lyric poet.

cat·walk (kat'wôk'), n. narrow place for walking on a bridge or in an airship.

Cau·ca·sia (kô·kā'zhə; -shə), n. region in S
Russia, between the Black and Caspian Seas.
Also, **Caucasus**.

Cau·ca·sian (kô·kā'zhən; -shən; -kazh'ən;
-kash'ən), n. 1. member of the so-called white
race, including the chief peoples of Europe,
southwestern Asia, and northern Africa. 2. native of Caucasia. —adj. 1. of or having to do
with the so-called white race. 2. of or having to
do with Caucasia or its inhabitants.

Cau·ca·sus (kô'kə·səs), n. 1. mountain range
in S Russia, between the Black and Caspian seas.
2. Caucasia.

cau·cus (kô'kəs), n. *Am*. a meeting of members
or leaders of a political party to make plans,
choose candidates, decide how to vote, etc. —v.
hold a caucus. [? < Med.L *caucus* < Med.Gk.
kaukos, a drinking vessel; "in allusion to the
convivial feature" of the Caucus Club, a political
club of the 18th century]

cau·dal (kô'dəl), adj. *Zool*. a. of, at, or near the
tail. b. taillike. [< NL *caudalis* < L *cauda* tail]
—**cau'dal·ly**, adv.

cau·date (kô'dāt), **cau·dat·ed** (-dāt·id),
adj. having a tail.

cau·dle (kô'dəl), n. a warm drink for sick people; gruel sweetened and flavored with wine, ale,
spices, etc. [< OF < L *calidus* warm]

caught (kôt), v. pt. and pp. of **catch**.

caul (kôl), n. membrane sometimes covering the
head of a child at birth. [< OF *cale* a kind of
little cap]

caul·dron (kôl'drən), n. caldron.

cau·li·flow·er (kô'lə·flou'ər; kol'i-), n. vegetable having a solid, white head with a few leaves
around it. [half-trans. of NL *cauliflora* < *caulis*
cabbage + *flos* flower]

cauliflower ear, *Am*. ear that has been mis-
shapen by injuries received in boxing, etc.

caulk (kôk), v. calk[1]. —**caulk'er**, n.

caus·al (kôz'əl), adj. 1. of a cause; being a
cause. 2. having to do with cause and effect. 3.
showing a cause or reason. —**caus'al·ly**, adv.

cau·sal·i·ty (kô·zal'ə·ti), n., pl. **-ties**. 1. relation of cause and effect; principle that nothing
can happen or exist without a cause. 2. causal
quality or agency.

cau·sa·tion (kô·zā'shən), n. 1. a causing or
being caused. 2. whatever produces an effect;
cause or causes. 3. relation of cause and effect;
principle that nothing can happen or exist without a cause.

caus·a·tive (kôz'ə·tiv), adj. 1. being a cause;
productive. 2. expressing causation. —**caus'a·
tive·ly**, adv. —**caus'a·tive·ness**, n.

cause (kôz), n., v., **caused, caus·ing**. —n. 1.
whatever produces an effect; person or thing that
makes something happen: *the earthquake was
the cause of much damage*. 2. occasion for ac-

tion; reason; ground; motive: *cause for celebration.* 3. good reason; reason enough: *he was angry without cause.* 4. subject or movement in which many people are interested and to which they give their support. 5. matter for a law court to decide; lawsuit. 6. **make common cause with,** join efforts with; side with. —*v.* produce as an effect; make happen; bring about. [< L *causa*] —**caus′a·ble,** *adj.* —**cause′less,** *adj.* —**caus′er,** *n.* —**Syn.** *n.* 2. incentive, inducement. —*v.* prompt, induce, occasion, effect.

cause cé·lè·bre (kōz sā·leb′rə), *French.* famous case (in law).

cau·se·rie (kō′zə·rē′), *n.* 1. an informal talk or discussion; chat. 2. short written article. [< F, < *causer* talk]

cause·way (kôz′wā′), *n.* 1. a raised road or path, usually built across wet ground, shallow water, etc. 2. a paved road; highway. —*v.* 1. provide with a causeway. 2. pave with cobbles or pebbles. [var. of *causey(way)* < OF < LL *calciata* paved way < L *calx* limestone]

caus·tic (kôs′tik), *n.* substance that burns or destroys flesh; corrosive substance. —*adj.* 1. that burns or destroys flesh; corrosive. 2. sarcastic; stinging; biting. [< L < Gk. *kaustikos*] —**caus′-ti·cal·ly,** *adv.* —**Syn.** *adj.* 2. satirical, cutting.

caustic soda, sodium hydroxide, NaOH.

cau·ter·ize (kô′tər·īz), *v.* —**ized, -iz·ing.** burn with a hot iron or a caustic substance, esp. to prevent infection. —**cau′ter·i·za′tion,** *n.*

cau·ter·y (kô′tər·i), *n., pl.* **-ter·ies.** 1. a cauterizing. 2. instrument or substance used in cauterizing. [< L < Gk. *kauterion,* dim. of *kauter* branding iron]

cau·tion (kô′shən), *n.* 1. cautious behavior. 2. a warning. 3. *Am., Colloq.* a very unusual person or thing. —*v.* warn; urge to be careful. [< L *cautio* < *cavere* beware] —**Syn.** *n.* 1. prudence, wariness. 2. admonition, advice, counsel.

cau·tion·ar·y (kô′shən·er′i), *adj.* warning; urging to be careful.

cau·tious (kô′shəs), *adj.* very careful; taking care to be safe; never taking chances. —**cau′-tious·ly,** *adv.* —**cau′tious·ness,** *n.* —**Syn.** prudent, wary. —**Ant.** heedless, careless.

cav·al·cade (kav′əl·kād′; kav′əl·kād), *n.* procession of persons riding on horses or in carriages. [< F < Ital., < *cavalcare* ride horseback < LL, < L *caballus* horse]

cav·a·lier (kav′ə·lir′), *n.* 1. a courteous gentleman. 2. a courteous escort for a lady. 3. horseman; mounted soldier; knight. 4. **Cavalier,** person who supported Charles I of England in his struggle with Parliament from 1641 to 1649. —*adj.* 1. proud and scornful; haughty; arrogant. 2. free and easy; offhand. 3. **Cavalier,** of the Cavaliers. [< F < Ital. *cavaliere* < *cavallo* horse < L *caballus*] —**cav′a·lier′ly,** *adv.*

cav·al·ry (kav′əl·ri), *n., pl.* **-ries.** 1. soldiers who fight on horseback. 2. horsemen, horses, etc., collectively. [< F < Ital. *cavalleria* knighthood. See CAVALIER.] —**cav′al·ry·man** (kav′əl·ri·mən), *n.*

cave (kāv), *n., v.,* **caved, cav·ing.** —*n.* hollow space underground. —*v.* **cave in,** a. fall in; sink. b. cause to fall in; smash. c. *Colloq.* give in; yield; submit. [< F < L *cava* hollow (places)] —**Syn.** *n.* cavern, grotto, den.

ca·ve·at (kā′vi·at), *n.* 1. a warning. 2. *Law.* legal notice given to a law officer or some legal authority not to do something until the person giving notice can be heard. [< L *caveat* let him beware]

cave-in (kāv′in′), *n. Colloq.* 1. a caving in. 2. place where something has caved in.

cave man, 1. Also, **cave dweller.** man who lived in caves in prehistoric times. 2. a rough, crude man.

cav·ern (kav′ərn), *n.* a large cave. [< F < L *caverna* < *cavus* hollow]

cav·ern·ous (kav′ər·nəs), *adj.* 1. like a cavern; large and hollow. 2. full of caverns. —**cav′ern·ous·ly,** *adv.*

cav·i·ar, cav·i·are (kav′i·är; kä′vi-), *n.* 1. a salty relish made from the eggs of sturgeon or other large fish. 2. **caviar to the general,** too

good a thing to be appreciated by ordinary people. [< F < Ital. < Turk. *khaviar*]

cav·il (kav′əl), *v.,* **-iled, -il·ing;** *esp. Brit.* **-illed, -il·ling,** *n.* —*v.* find fault unnecessarily; raise trivial objections. —*n.* a petty objection. [< F < L *cavillari* jeer] —**cav′il·er,** *esp. Brit.* **cav′il·ler,** *n.* —**Syn.** *v.* carp, criticize.

cav·i·ty (kav′ə·ti), *n., pl.* **-ties.** 1. hole; hollow place: *a cavity in a tooth.* 2. *Anat.* enclosed space inside the body: *the abdominal cavity.* [< F < LL *cavitas* < L *cavus* hollow]

ca·vort (kə·vôrt′), *v. Am., Colloq.* prance about; jump around. [orig. unknown] —**ca·vort′er,** *n. Am.* —**ca·vort′ing,** *n., adj. Am.*

ca·vy (kā′vi), *n., pl.* **-vies.** a South American rodent of the family which includes the guinea pig.

caw (kô), *n.* 1. the harsh cry made by a crow or raven. —*v.* make this cry. [imit.]

Cawn·pore (kôn′pôr; -pōr), **Cawn·pur** (-pur), *n.* city in C India, on the Ganges River.

Cax·ton (kak′stən), *n.* **William,** 1422?–1491, first English printer.

cay (kā; kē), *n.* low island; reef; key.

cay·enne (kī·en′; kā–), or **cayenne pepper,** *n.* red pepper; very hot, biting powder made from seeds or fruit of a pepper plant. [after *Cayenne,* French Guiana]

cay·man (kā′mən), *n., pl.* **-mans.** a large alligator of tropical America. Also, **caiman.**

Ca·yu·ga (kā·ū′gə; kī–), *n., pl.* **-ga, -gas.** *Am.* member of a tribe of Iroquois Indians formerly living in W New York State.

cay·use (kī·ūs′), *n. Am., W.* 1. an Indian pony. 2. *Colloq.* any horse. [for the *Cayuse* Indians]

Cb, *Chem.* columbium.

cc., c.c., cubic centimeter; cubic centimeters.

Cd, *Chem.* cadmium.

Ce, *Chem.* cerium.

cease (sēs), *v.,* **ceased, ceas·ing.** 1. come to an end. 2. put an end or stop to. [< F < L *cessare*] —**Syn.** 1. discontinue, stop, quit, pause, desist.

cease-fire (sēs′fīr′), *n.* a halt in military operations, esp. for the purpose of discussing peace.

cease·less (sēs′lis), *adj.* never stopping; going on all the time; continual. —**cease′less·ly,** *adv.* —**Syn.** uninterrupted, unending, constant.

Ce·cro·pi·a moth (si·krō′pi·ə), *Am.* a large silkworm moth of the eastern United States.

ce·dar (sē′dər), *n.* 1. an evergreen tree with wide-spreading branches and fragrant, durable wood. 2. any of several trees with similar wood. 3. wood of any of these trees. —*adj. Am.* made of cedar. [< L < Gk. *kedros*]

ce·dar·bird (sē′dər·bėrd′), **cedar waxwing,** *n. Am.* a small American bird with a crest and small, red markings on its wings; waxwing.

Cedarbird (7 in. long)

cede (sēd), *v.,* **ced·ed, ced·ing.** give up; surrender; hand over to another. [< L *cedere* yield, go] —**Syn.** yield, relinquish, deliver. —**Ant.** keep, hold.

ce·dil·la (si·dil′ə), *n.* mark somewhat like a comma (ç) put under *c* in certain words to show that it has the sound of *s* before *a, o,* or *u. Example:* façade. [< Sp. < VL, dim. of L *zeta* < Gk., the letter *z*]

ceil (sēl), *v.* 1. put a ceiling in. 2. cover the ceiling of. [? < F *ciel* canopy, sky < L *caelum* heaven]

ceil·ing (sēl′ing), *n.* 1. the inside, top covering of a room; surface opposite to the floor. 2. a. greatest height to which an airplane or airship can go under certain conditions. b. distance from the earth of the lowest clouds. 3. greatest height to which prices, wages, etc., are permitted to go. [< *ceil*]

cel·an·dine (sel′ən·dīn), *n.* plant with yellow flowers. [< OF < L < Gk., < *chelidon* swallow²]

Cel·a·nese (sel′ə·nēz′), *n. Trademark.* an acetate rayon material.

Cel·e·bes (sel′ə·bēz), *n.* a large island in E Indonesia.

cel·e·brant (sel′ə·brənt), *n.* 1. person who performs a ceremony or rite. 2. priest who performs Mass.

cel·e·brate (sel′ə·brāt), *v.*, **-brat·ed, -brat·ing.** 1. observe with the proper ceremonies or festivities. 2. perform publicly with the proper ceremonies and rites: *a priest celebrates Mass in church.* 3. make known publicly; proclaim. 4. praise; honor. 5. observe a festival or event with ceremonies or festivities. 6. *Colloq.* have a gay time. [< L *celebratus*] **—cel′e·bra′tor,** *n.* **—Syn.** 1, 2. solemnize. 4. laud. 5. commemorate.

cel·e·brat·ed (sel′ə·brāt′id), *adj.* famous; well-known. **—Syn.** noted, renowned, eminent.

cel·e·bra·tion (sel′ə·brā′shən), *n.* 1. act of celebrating. 2. whatever is done to celebrate something.

ce·leb·ri·ty (sə·leb′rə·ti), *n., pl.* **-ties.** 1. a famous person. 2. fame; being well known or much talked about.

ce·ler·i·ty (sə·ler′ə·ti), *n.* swiftness; speed. [< L, *< celer* swift]

cel·er·y (sel′ər·i; sel′ri), *n.* vegetable whose long stalks can be whitened by keeping them covered. Celery is usually eaten raw. [< F < dial. Ital. < L *< Gk. selinon* parsley]

ce·les·tial (sə·les′chəl), *adj.* 1. of the sky; having to do with the heavens. The sun, moon, planets, and stars are celestial bodies. 2. heavenly; divine. 3. **Celestial,** Chinese. **—n. Celestial,** a Chinese. [< OF < L *caelestis* heavenly *< caelum* heaven] **—ce·les′tial·ly,** *adv.*

ce·li·ac (sē′li·ak), *adj. Anat.* coeliac.

cel·i·ba·cy (sel′ə·bə·si), *n., pl.* **-cies.** unmarried state; single life.

cel·i·bate (sel′ə·bit; -bāt), *n.* an unmarried person; person who takes a vow to lead a single life. **—adj.** unmarried; single. [< L *caelibatus < caelebs* unmarried]

cell (sel), *n.* 1. a small room in a prison, convent, etc. 2. a small, hollow place. Bees store honey in the cells of a honeycomb. 3. unit of living matter. Most cells have a nucleus near the center and are enclosed by a **cell wall** or **membrane.** 4. container holding materials for producing electricity by chemical action. 5. a small group that acts as a political, social, or religious unit for a larger, sometimes revolutionary, organization. [< L *cella* small room]

cel·lar (sel′ər), *n.* 1. an underground room or rooms, usually under a building and often used for storing food or fuel. 2. cellar for wines. 3. supply of wines. [< F < L *cellarium < cella* small room]

cel·lar·age (sel′ər·ij), *n.* 1. space in a cellar. 2. cellars. 3. charge for storage in a cellar.

cel·lar·er (sel′ər·ər), *n.* person who takes care of a cellar and the food or wines in it.

Cel·li·ni (chə·lē′ni), *n.* Benvenuto, 1500–1571, Italian artist.

cel·list, 'cel·list (chel′ist), *n.* person who plays the cello. Also, **violoncellist.**

cel·lo, 'cel·lo (chel′ō), *n., pl.* **-los.** instrument like a violin, but very much larger; bass violin. Also, **violoncello.**

cel·lo·phane (sel′ə·fān), *n.* 1. a transparent substance made from cellulose, used as a wrapping to keep food, candy, tobacco, etc., fresh and clean. 2. **Cellophane,** trademark for this substance. [< *cell(ul)o(se)* + Gk. *phanein* appear]

cel·lu·lar (sel′yə·lər), *adj.* 1. having to do with cells. 2. consisting of cells.

cel·lule (sel′ūl), *n.* a tiny cell. [< L *cellula,* dim. of *cella* small room]

cel·lu·loid (sel′yə·loid), *Am.* **—n.** 1. a hard, transparent substance made from cellulose and camphor. 2. **Celluloid,** trademark for this substance. **—adj.** pertaining to motion pictures.

cel·lu·lose (sel′yə·lōs), *n. Chem.* substance that forms the walls of plant cells; woody part of trees and plants. Cellulose is used to make paper, artificial silk, explosives, etc. [L *cellula* small cell]

Celt (selt; *esp. Brit.* kelt), *n.* member of a people to which the Irish, Highland Scotch, Welsh, and Bretons belong. The ancient Gauls and Britons were Celts. Also, **Kelt.**

Celt·ic (sel′tik; *esp. Brit.* kel′tik), *adj.* of the Celts or their language. **—n.** the group of languages spoken by the Celts, including Irish, Gaelic, Welsh, and Breton. Also, **Keltic.**

ce·ment (si·ment′), *n.* 1. substance made by burning clay and limestone. 2. this substance mixed with sand and water to make sidewalks, streets, floors, and walls and to hold stones or bricks together in building. 3. any soft substance that hardens and holds things together. 4. anything that joins together or unites. **—v.** 1. hold together with cement. 2. cover with cement. 3. join together; unite. [< OF < L *caementum* chippings of stone *< caedere* cut] **—ce·ment′er,** *n.*

cem·e·ter·y (sem′ə·ter′i), *n., pl.* **-ter·ies.** place for burying the dead; graveyard. [< LL < Gk. *koimeterion < koimaein* lull to sleep]

ce·no·bite (sē′nə·bīt; sen′ə-), *n.* member of a religious group living in a monastery or convent. [< LL *coenobita < Gk., < koinos* common + *bios* life] **—ce·no·bit·ic** (sē′nə·bit′ik; sen′ə-), **ce′no·bit′i·cal,** *adj.*

cen·o·taph (sen′ə·taf; -täf), *n.* monument erected in memory of a dead person whose body is elsewhere. [< L < Gk., *< kenos* empty + *taphos* tomb] **—cen′o·taph′ic,** *adj.*

cen·ser (sen′sər), *n.* container in which incense is burned. [< OF *(en)censier,* ult. < L *incensum* incense]

cen·sor (sen′sər), *n.* 1. person who examines and, if necessary, changes books, plays, motion pictures, etc., so as to make them satisfactory to the government or to the organization that employs him. 2. a Roman magistrate who took the census and told people how to behave. 3. person who tells others how they ought to behave. 4. person who likes to find fault. **—v.** act as censor; make changes in; take out part of (letters, etc.). [< L, *< censere* appraise] **—cen·so·ri·al** (sen·sô′ri·əl; -sō′-), *adj.*

cen·so·ri·ous (sen·sô′ri·əs; -sō′-), *adj.* too severely critical. **—cen·so′ri·ous·ly,** *adv.* **—cen·so′ri·ous·ness,** *n.* **—Syn.** hypercritical, carping.

cen·sor·ship (sen′sər·ship), *n.* 1. act or system of censoring. 2. position or work of a censor.

cen·sur·a·ble (sen′shər·ə·bəl), *adj.* worthy of censure. **—cen′sur·a·ble·ness, cen′sur·a·bil′i·ty,** *n.* **—cen′sur·a·bly,** *adv.*

cen·sure (sen′shər), *n., v.,* **-sured, -sur·ing. —n.** act or fact of blaming; expression of disapproval; criticism. **—v.** express disapproval of; blame; criticize. [< L *censura < censere* appraise] **—cen′sur·er,** *n.* **—Syn.** *n.* faultfinding, reproof, rebuke. **-v.** reprove, rebuke, reprimand.

cen·sus (sen′səs), *n.* an official count of the people of a country, with details as to age, sex, pursuits, etc. [< L, *< censere* appraise]

cent (sent), *n.* a coin, usually copper, of the United States and Canada, equal to the hundredth part of a dollar. [? < L *centesimus* hundredth]

cent., 1. centigrade. 2. central. 3. century.

cen·taur (sen′tôr), *n. Gk. Legend.* a monster that is half man and half horse. [< L < Gk. *kentauros*]

cen·ta·vo (sen·tä′vō), *n., pl.* **-vos.** a small coin used in Mexico, Cuba, the Philippines, etc., equal to the hundredth part of a peso. [< Am.Sp. See CENT.]

cen·te·nar·i·an (sen′tə·nār′i·ən), *n.* person who is 100 years old or more.

cen·te·nar·y (sen′tə·ner′i; sen′tə·nār′i; *esp. Brit.* sen·tē′nə·ri), *n., pl.* **-nar·ies.** 1. period of 100 years. 2. 100th anniversary. [< L *centenarius* relating to a number *< centum* hundred]

cen·ten·ni·al (sen·ten′i·əl), *adj.* of or having to do with 100 years or the 100th anniversary. **—n.** 100th anniversary. [< L *centum* hundred + E *(bi)ennial*] **—cen·ten′ni·al·ly,** *adv.*

cen·ter (sen′tər), *n.* 1. a point within a circle or sphere equally distant from all of the circumference or surface. 2. the middle point, place, or part. 3. person, thing, or group in a middle position. 4. point toward which people or things go, or from which they come; main point. 5. player in the center of the line in football. 6. *Am.* player who starts play in basketball. 7. the political groups of a legislature having moderate opinions. —*v.* 1. place in or at the center. 2. collect at a center. 3. be at a center. Also, *esp. Brit.* **centre.** [< OF < L < Gk. *kentron* sharp point] ≫ **Center around** (or **about**) (the story *centers around* the theft of a necklace) is a colloquial idiom. The formal idiom is *center on* or *upon.*

center field, *Am., Baseball.* section of the outfield behind second base.

center of gravity, point in something around which its weight is evenly balanced.

cen·ter·piece (sen′tər·pēs′), *n.* an ornamental piece for the center of a dining table. Also, *esp. Brit.* centrepiece.

cen·tes·i·mal (sen·tes′ə·məl), *adj.* 1. 100th. 2. divided into 100ths. [< L *centesimus* hundredth] —**cen·tes′i·mal·ly,** *adv.*

centi-, *word element.* 1. 100. 2. 100th part of. [< L *centum* hundred]

cen·ti·grade (sen′tə·grād), *adj.* 1. divided into 100 degrees. 2. of or according to a centigrade thermometer. [< F < L *centum* hundred + *gradus* degree]

centigrade thermometer, thermometer having 0 for the temperature at which ice melts and 100 for the temperature at which water boils.

cen·ti·gram, *esp. Brit.* **cen·ti·gramme** (sen′tə·gram), *n.* ¹⁄₁₀₀ of a gram. [< F]

cen·ti·li·ter, *esp. Brit.* **cen·ti·li·tre** (sen′tə·lē′tər), *n.* ¹⁄₁₀₀ of a liter. [< F]

cen·time (sän′tēm), *n.* ¹⁄₁₀₀ of a franc. [< F < L *centesimus* hundredth]

cen·ti·me·ter, *esp. Brit.* **cen·ti·me·tre** (sen′tə·mē′tər), *n.* ¹⁄₁₀₀ of a meter. [< F]

cen·ti·pede (sen′tə·pēd), *n.* a small wormlike animal with many pairs of legs. [< L *centipeda* < *centum* hundred + *pes* foot]

cen·tral (sen′trəl), *adj.* 1. of or being the center. 2. at or near the center. 3. from the center. 4. equally distant from all points; easy to get to or from. 5. main; chief. —*n. Am.* 1. a telephone exchange. 2. a telephone operator. [< L *centralis.* See CENTER.] —**cen′tral·ly,** *adv.* —**cen′tral·ness,** *n.* —**Syn.** *adj.* 5. leading, principal.

Centi- pede (1 in. long)

Central America, that part of North America between Mexico and South America. —**Central American.**

cen·tral·ize (sen′trəl·īz), *v.,* -ized, -iz·ing. 1. collect at a center; gather together. 2. bring or come under one control. —**cen′tral·i·za′tion,** *n.* —**cen′tral·iz′er,** *n.*

cen·tre (sen′tər), *n., v.,* -tred, -tring. *Esp. Brit.* center.

cen·tre·piece (sen′tər·pēs′), *n. Esp. Brit.* centerpiece.

cen·tric (sen′trik), **cen·tri·cal** (-trə·kəl), *adj.* central. —**cen′tri·cal·ly,** *adv.* —**cen·tric·i·ty** (sen·tris′ə·ti), *n.*

cen·trif·u·gal (sen·trif′yə·gəl; -trif′ə-), *adj.* 1. moving away from the center. 2. making use of or acted upon by centrifugal force. [< NL, < E *centri-* center + L *fugere* flee] —**cen·trif′u·gal·ly,** *adv.*

centrifugal force or **action,** inertia of a body rotated around a center, tending to move it away from the center.

cen·tri·fuge (sen′trə·fūj), *n.* machine for separating cream from milk, bacteria from a fluid, etc., by means of centrifugal force. [< F]

cen·trip·e·tal (sen·trip′ə·təl), *adj.* 1. moving toward the center. 2. making use of or acted upon by centripetal force. [< NL, < E *centri-* center + L *petere* seek] —**cen·trip′e·tal·ly,** *adv.*

centripetal force or **action,** force that tends to move things toward the center around which they are turning.

cen·tu·ple (sen′tə·pəl; -tyə-), *adj., v.,* -pled,

-pling. —*adj.* 100 times as much or as many; hundredfold. —*v.* make 100 times as much or as many. [< F < LL *centuplus* hundredfold]

cen·tu·ri·on (sen·tûr′i·ən; -tyûr′-), *n.* commander of a group of about 100 soldiers in the ancient Roman army. [< L, < *centuria* CENTURY]

cen·tu·ry (sen′chə·ri), *n., pl.* -ries. 1. each 100 years, counting from some special time, such as the birth of Christ. 2. period of 100 years. 3. group of 100 people or things. 4. body of soldiers in the ancient Roman army. [< L *centuria* a division of a hundred units < *centum* hundred] ≫ Remember that the fifth century A.D. ran from the beginning of the year 401 to the end of the year 500, the nineteenth century from January 1, 1801, through December 31, 1900. That is, to name the century correctly, add one to the number of its hundred. Dates before Christ are figured like those after: the first century B.C. runs back from the birth of Christ through 100, the second century from 101 through 200, the fifth century from 401 through 500, and so on.

century plant, *Am.* a large, thick-leaved plant growing in Mexico and SW United States.

ce·phal·ic (sə·fal′ik), *adj.* 1. of the head. 2. near, on, or in the head. 3. toward the head. [< L < Gk., < *kephale* head]

ceph·a·lo·pod (sef′ə·lə·pod′), *n.* sea mollusk that has long, armlike tentacles around the mouth, a soft body, a pair of large eyes, and a sharp, birdlike beak. Cuttlefish and squids are cephalopods. —**ceph·a·lop·o·dan** (sef′ə·lop′ə·dən), *adj.*

ce·ram·ic (sə·ram′ik), *adj.* having to do with pottery, earthenware, porcelain, etc., or with making them. [< Gk., < *keramos* potter's clay]

ce·ram·ics (sə·ram′iks), *n.* 1. (*sing. in use*) art of making pottery, earthenware, porcelain, etc. 2. (*pl. in use*) articles made of pottery, earthenware, porcelain, etc. —**cer·a·mist** (ser′ə·mist), *n.*

Cer·be·rus (sér′bər·əs), *n.* 1. *Gk. and Roman Legend.* three-headed dog that guarded the entrance to Hades. 2. surly, watchful guard.

ce·re·al (sir′i·əl), *n.* 1. any grass that produces a grain used as food, as wheat, rice, oats, etc. 2. the grain. 3. a food made from the grain, as oatmeal and corn meal. —*adj.* of or having to do with grain or the grasses producing it. [< L *Cerealis* pertaining to Ceres]

cer·e·bel·lum (ser′ə·bel′əm), *n., pl.* -bellums, -bel·la (-el′ə). *Anat., Zool.* part of the brain that controls the coördination of the muscles. [< L, dim. of *cerebrum* brain] —**cer′e·bel′lar,** *adj.*

cer·e·bral (ser′ə·brəl; se·rē′brəl), *adj.* 1. of the brain. 2. of the cerebrum. [< L *cerebrum* brain]

cerebral palsy, paralysis due to a lesion of the brain.

cer·e·brate (ser′ə·brāt), *v.,* -brat·ed, -brat·ing. use the brain; think. —**cer′e·bra′tion,** *n.*

cer·e·brum (ser′ə·brəm), *n., pl.* -brums, -bra (-brə). 1. *Anat.* part of the human brain that controls thought and voluntary muscular movements. 2. *Zool.* the corresponding part (anatomically) of the brain of any vertebrate. [< L]

cere·ment (sir′mənt), *n.* Usually, cerements. cloth or garment in which a dead person is wrapped for burial.

cer·e·mo·ni·al (ser′ə·mō′ni·əl), *adj.* 1. formal. 2. of or having to do with ceremony. —*n.* formal actions proper to an occasion. —**cer′e·mo′ni·al·ism,** *n.* —**cer′e·mo′ni·al·ist,** *n.* —**cer′e·mo′ni·al·ly,** *adv.*

cer·e·mo·ni·ous (ser′ə·mō′ni·əs), *adj.* 1. full of ceremony. 2. very formal; extremely polite. —**cer′e·mo′ni·ous·ly,** *adv.* —**cer′e·mo′ni·ous·ness,** *n.* —**Syn.** 2. stiff, precise.

cer·e·mo·ny (ser′ə·mō′ni), *n., pl.* -nies. 1. a special form or set of acts to be done on special occasions such as weddings, funerals, graduations, Christmas, or Easter. 2. any usage of politeness or civility. 3. very polite conduct. 4. a meaningless formality. 5. formality; formalities. [< L *caerimonia* rite]

Ce·res (sir'ēz), *n.* Roman goddess of agriculture, identified with the Greek goddess Demeter.

ce·rise (sə·rēz'; -rēs'), *n., adj.* bright, pinkish red. [< F *cerise* cherry < VL < LGk. *kerasia* < Gk. *kerasos* cherry tree]

ce·ri·um (sir'i·əm), *n. Chem.* a grayish metallic element, Ce. [< NL, from the asteroid *Ceres*]

cer·tain (sér'tən), *adj.* 1. sure: *certain to happen.* 2. settled; fixed: *at a certain hour.* 3. reliable; dependable. 4. definite but not named; some; one: *certain persons.* —*n.* for certain, surely; without a doubt. [< OF, ult. < L *certus* sure] —cer'tain·ness, *n.* —Syn. *adj.* 3. trustworthy, unfailing. 4. particular.

cer·tain·ly (sér'tən·li), *adv.* surely; without a doubt. —*interj.* surely! of course!

cer·tain·ty (sér'tən·ti), *n., pl.* -ties. 1. freedom from doubt. 2. a sure fact.

cer·tif·i·cate (*n.* sər·tif'ə·kit; *v.* sər·tif'ə·kāt), *n., v.,* -cat·ed, -cat·ing. —*n.* 1. a written or printed statement that declares something to be a fact. 2. such a statement legally attested. —*v.* 1. give a certificate to. 2. authorize by a certificate. [< Med.L *certificatum.* See CERTIFY.] —cer·ti·fi·ca·tion (sér'tə·fə·kā'shən; sər·tif'ə-), *n.*

cer·ti·fy (sér'tə·fī), *v.,* -fied, -fy·ing. 1. declare (something) true or correct by spoken, written, or printed statement. 2. guarantee the quality or value of. 3. assure; make certain. [< Med.L *certificare* < L *certus* sure + *facere* make] —cer'ti·fi'a·ble, *adj.* —cer'ti·fi'er, *n.*

cer·ti·o·ra·ri (sér'shi·ə·rār'ī; -rār'ī), *n. Law.* order from a higher court to a lower one, calling for the record of a case for review. [< LL, be informed. See CERTAIN.]

cer·ti·tude (sér'tə·tūd; -tūd), *n.* certainty; sureness. [< LL *certitudo.* See CERTAIN.]

ce·ru·le·an (sə·rü'li·ən), *adj., n.* sky-blue. [< L *caeruleus* dark blue]

Cer·van·tes (sér·van'tēz), *n.* Miguel de, 1547–1616, Spanish author who wrote *Don Quixote.*

cer·vi·cal (sér'və·kəl), *adj.* of the neck.

cer·vine (sér'vīn; -vin), *adj.* of or like a deer. [< L, < *cervus* deer]

cer·vix (sér'viks), *n., pl.* cer·vix·es, cer·vi·ces (sər·vī'sēz). 1. the neck, esp. the back of the neck. 2. a necklike part. [< L]

Ce·sar·e·an, Ce·sar·i·an (si·zãr'i·ən), *adj., n.* Caesarean.

ce·si·um (sē'zi·əm), *n. Chem.* a silvery metallic element, Cs. Also, caesium. [< NL, < L *caesius* bluish-gray]

ces·sa·tion (se·sā'shən), *n.* a ceasing or stopping. [< L, < *cessare* cease] —Syn. pause, lull.

ces·sion (sesh'ən), *n.* a handing over to another; ceding; giving up; surrendering. [< L *cessio* < *cedere* yield]

cess·pool (ses'pül'), *n.* 1. pool or pit for house drains to empty into. 2. filthy place.

ce·su·ra (sə·zhür'ə; -zyür'ə), *n.* caesura. —ce·su'ral, *adj.*

ce·ta·cean (sə·tā'shən), *adj.* Also, ce·ta'ceous. of or belonging to a group of mammals living in the water, including whales, dolphins, and porpoises. —*n.* animal that belongs to this group.

Cey·lon (si·lon'), *n.* island in the Indian Ocean, just off S India, a dominion in the British Commonwealth of Nations since 1948. —Cey·lo·nese (sē'lə·nēz'; -nēs'), *adj., n.*

Cé·zanne (sā·zan'; -zän'), *n.* Paul, 1839–1906, French painter.

cf., compare.

cg., centigram; centigrams.

ch., Ch., 1. chapter. 2. church.

cha-cha (chä'chä'), *n.* a ballroom dance that originated in Haiti.

Chad (chad), *n.* Lake, lake in N Africa.

chafe (chāf), *v.,* chafed, chaf·ing, *n.* —*v.* 1. rub to make warm. 2. wear or be worn away by rubbing. 3. make or become sore by rubbing. 4. make angry. 5. become angry. —*n.* a chafing; irritation. [< OF *chaufer*, ult. < L, < *calere* be warm + *facere* make] —Syn. *v.* 4. irritate, gall.

chaf·er (chāf'ər), *n. Esp. Brit.* any of a group of beetles. [OE *ceafor*]

chaff[1] (chaf; chäf), *n.* 1. husks of wheat, oats, rye, etc., separated from grain by threshing. 2. worthless stuff; rubbish. [OE *ceaf*] —chaff'y, *adj.*

chaff[2] (chaf; chäf), *v.* banter; tease. —*n.* banter. —chaff'er, *n.*

chaf·fer (chaf'ər), *v.* dispute about a price; bargain. —*n.* bargaining. [ME *chaffare* < OE *cēap* bargain + *faru* journey] —chaf'fer·er, *n.*

chaf·finch (chaf'inch), *n.* a European songbird with a pleasant, short song, often kept as a cage bird. [OE *ceaffinc.* See CHAFF[1], FINCH.]

chaf·ing dish (chāf'ing), *Am.* pan with a heater under it, used to cook food at the table or to keep it warm.

cha·grin (shə·grin'), *n.* a feeling of disappointment, failure, or humiliation. —*v.* cause to feel chagrin. [< F, < OF *graignier* < *graim* sad, sorrowful] —Syn. *n.* mortification, dismay.

chain (chān), *n.* 1. series of links joined together. 2. series of things joined or linked together: *a mountain chain, a chain of happenings.* 3. anything that binds or restrains. 4. a measuring instrument like a chain. A surveyor's chain is 66 feet long; an engineer's chain is 100 feet long. 5. *Am.* number of similar restaurants, theaters, etc., owned and operated by one person or company. 6. **chains,** a. bonds; fetters. b. imprisonment; bondage. 7. *Chem.* a number of atoms of the same element linked together like a chain. —*v.* 1. join together or fasten with a chain. 2. bind; restrain. 3. keep in prison; make a slave of. [< OF *chaeine* < L *catena* chain]

chain gang, *Am.* gang of convicts, etc., chained together while at work outdoors.

chain mail, flexible armor made of metal rings linked together.

chain reaction, 1. *Physics.* process marked by an explosive release of atomic energy, as in the bombardment of unstable uranium nuclei by plutonium neutrons in the explosion of an atomic bomb, each uranium nucleus releasing a number of plutonium neutrons, which in turn split other uranium nuclei. 2. any series of events or happenings, each being the preceding one or ones. —chain'-re·act'ing, *adj.*

chain-smoke (chān'smōk'), *v.* smoke incessantly or heavily; smoke by lighting a cigarette or cigar from the one just smoked. —chain'-smok'er, *n.*

chain stitch, kind of sewing or crocheting in which each stitch makes a loop through which the next stitch is taken.

chain store, *Am.* one of a group of retail stores owned and operated by one company.

chair (chãr), *n.* 1. seat for one person that has a back and, sometimes, arms. 2. seat of position, dignity, or authority. 3. position or authority of a person who has such a seat. 4. chairman. 5. *Am.* electric chair. 6. **take the chair,** a. begin a meeting. b. be in charge of or preside at a meeting. —*v.* 1. put or carry in a chair. 2. put in a position of authority. [< OF *chaiere* < L < Gk. *kathedra* seat]

chair·man (chãr'mən), *n., pl.* -men. 1. person who presides at or is in charge of a meeting. 2. head of a committee. —chair'man·ship, *n.*

chair·wom·an (chãr'wùm'ən), *n., pl.* -women. a woman chairman.

chaise (shāz), *n.* a lightweight carriage, often one with a folding top. [< F *chaise* chair, var. of *chaire* CHAIR]

chaise longue (shāz' lông'; long'), chair with a long seat and a back at one end, somewhat like a couch. [< F, long chair]

chal·ced·o·ny (kal·sed'ə·ni; kal'sə·dō'ni), *n., pl.* -nies. variety of quartz that has a waxy luster and occurs in various colors and forms. [< L < Gk. *chalkedon*]

Chal·da·ic (kal·dā'ik), *adj., n.* Chaldean.

Chal·de·a (kal·dē′ə), *n.* ancient region in SW Asia, on the Tigris and Euphrates rivers. —Chal-de′an, *adj., n.*

Chal·dee (kal·dē′; kal′dē), *adj., n.* Chaldean.

cha·let (sha·lā′; shal′ā), *n.* 1. a house or villa with wide, overhanging eaves. 2. a herdsman's hut or cabin in the Swiss mountains. [< Swiss F]

chal·ice (chal′is), *n.* 1. cup. 2. cup that holds the wine used in the Communion service. 3. a cup-shaped flower. [< OF < L *calix* cup] —chal′iced (chal′ist), *adj.*

chalk (chôk), *n.* 1. soft limestone, made up mostly of very small fossil sea shells. 2. substance like chalk, used for writing or drawing on a blackboard. 3. piece of this substance. 4. a record of credit given. —*v.* 1. mark, write, or draw with chalk. 2. mix or rub with chalk; whiten with chalk. 3. score; record. 4. **chalk up,** a. *Am.* increase a price, score, etc.; mark up. b. write down; record. [< L *calx* lime] —chalk′-like′, *adj.* —chalk′y, *adj.* —chalk′i·ness, *n.*

Chalice (def. 2)

chal·lenge (chal′inj), *v.,* -lenged, -leng·ing, *n.* —*v.* 1. call to fight, esp. call to fight in a duel. 2. invite or summon to a game or contest. 3. call on (a person, etc.) to answer and explain. 4. call in question; doubt; dispute. 5. object to (a juror, vote, etc.). 6. *Am.* object to (a certain person's vote) as illegal. 7. claim; demand: *a problem that challenges everyone's attention.* b. make a challenge. —*n.* 1. call to fight, esp. in a duel. 2. call to a game or contest. 3. a demand to answer and explain: *"Who goes there?" is the guard's challenge.* 4. objection made, as to a juror or a vote. 5. *Am.* an objection that a voter is not qualified to vote. [< OF < L *calumnia* CALUMNY] —chal′lenge·a·ble, *adj.* —chal′leng-er, *n.*

chal·lis, chal·lie (shal′i), *n.* a lightweight plain or printed cloth, used for dresses.

cham·ber (chām′bər), *n.* 1. a room (in a house). 2. bedroom. 3. hall where a legislature or a governing body meets. 4. a legislative, judicial, or other like body. 5. a cavity: *the heart has four chambers.* 6. that part of the barrel of a gun which receives the charge. 7. place for a cartridge in the cylinder of a revolver. 8. **chambers,** a. *Brit.* set of rooms in a building to live in or use as offices. b. office of a lawyer or judge. —*v.* provide with a chamber. [< OF < L < Gk. *kamara* vaulted place. Doublet of CAMERA.] —cham′bered, *adj.*

cham·ber·lain (chām′bər·lin), *n.* 1. person who manages the household of a king or lord; steward. 2. a high official of a king's court. 3. treasurer: *city chamberlain.* [< OF < L *camera* vault + Gmc. *-ling*]

cham·ber·maid (chām′bər·mād′), *n.* maid who makes the beds, cleans the bedrooms, etc.

chamber music, music suited to a room or small hall; music for a trio, quartet, etc.

chamber of commerce, group of people organized to protect and promote business interests of a city, state, etc.

cham·bray (sham′brā), *n. Am.* a fine variety of gingham. [var. of *cambric*]

cha·me·le·on (kə·mē′li·ən; -mēl′yən), *n.* 1. lizard that can change the color of its body. 2. a changeable or fickle person. [< L < Gk., lit., ground lion, < *chamai* on the ground, dwarf + *leon* lion] —cha·me·le·on·ic (kə·mē′li·on′ik), *adj.*

cham·ois (sham′i), *n., pl.* -ois. 1. a small, goat-like antelope that lives in the high mountains of Europe and SW Asia. 2. Also, cham′my. a soft leather made from the skin of sheep, goats, deer, etc. [< F < LL *camox*]

Chamois (2 ft. high at the shoulder)

cham·o·mile (kam′ə·mīl), *n.* camomile.

champ[1] (champ), *v.* 1. bite and chew noisily. 2. bite on impatiently. [? akin to *chap* CHOP[2]]

champ[2] (champ), *n. Am., Slang.* champion.

cham·pagne (sham·pān′), *n.* 1. a sparkling, bubbling wine. 2. pale, brownish yellow.

cham·paign (sham·pān′), *n.* a wide plain; level, open country. —*adj.* level and open. [< OF *champaigne.* See CAMPAIGN.]

cham·pi·on (cham′pi·ən), *n.* 1. person, animal, or thing that wins first place in a game or contest. 2. person who fights or speaks for another; defender; supporter. —*adj.* having won first place; ahead of all others. —*v.* fight or speak in behalf of; defend; support. [< OF < LL *campio* < *campus* field (i.e., of battle)] —cham′pi·on·less, *adj.* —Syn. *n.* 2. protector. —*v.* advocate.

cham·pi·on·ship (cham′pi·ən·ship′), *n.* 1. position of a champion; first place. 2. defense; support.

Cham·plain (sham·plān′), *n.* Lake, a long, narrow lake between New York and Vermont.

chance (chans; chäns), *n., v.,* chanced, chanc-ing, *adj.* —*n.* 1. opportunity: *the chance to go to college.* 2. possibility: *there's a chance he may go to college.* 3. probability: *the chances are that he will have enough money.* 4. fate; luck. 5. a risk. 6. a happening. 7. **by chance,** accidentally. —*v.* 1. happen. 2. *Colloq.* take the risk of; risk. —*adj.* not expected or planned; accidental; casual. [< OF < L *cadentia* a falling < *cadere* fall] —Syn. *n.* 3. likelihood. —*adj.* fortuitous, offhand, unexpected.

chan·cel (chan′səl; chän′-), *n.* space around the altar of a church, usually enclosed, used by the clergy and the choir. [< F < L *cancelli* a grating]

chan·cel·ler·y (chan′sə·lər·i; -slər·i; chän′-), *n., pl.* -ler·ies. 1. position of a chancellor. 2. office of a chancellor.

chan·cel·lor (chan′sə·lər; -slər; chän′-), *n.* 1. the title, esp. in Great Britain, of various high officials: *Chancellor of the Exchequer.* 2. *Am.* the chief judge of a court of chancery or equity in some States. 3. formerly, the prime minister in Germany or Austria. 4. the chief secretary of an embassy. 5. title of the president in certain universities. [< AF < L *cancellarius* officer stationed at tribunal. See CHANCEL.] —chan′cel·lor·ship′, *n.*

chan·cer·y (chan′sər·i; chän′-), *n., pl.* -cer·ies. 1. court of equity. 2. equity. 3. office where public records are kept. 4. office of a chancellor. 5. **in chancery,** a. in a court of equity. b. in a helpless position. [var. of CHANCELLERY]

chan·cre (shang′kər), *n.* ulcer or sore with a hard base. [< F. See CANKER.] —chan′crous, *adj.*

chan·de·lier (shan′də·lir′), *n.* fixture with branches for lights. [< F < VL *candelarius* < L *candela* CANDLE]

chan·dler (chan′dlər; chän′-), *n.* 1. maker or seller of candles. 2. dealer in groceries and supplies: *a ship chandler.* [< AF *chaundeler* < VL *candelarius* < L *candela* CANDLE]

Chang·chun (chäng′chún′), *n.* city in Manchuria.

change (chānj), *v.,* changed, chang·ing, *n.* —*v.* 1. make or become different. 2. put (something) in place of another; substitute. 3. take in place of. 4. give or get (money of a different sort) for. 5. take a different train, bus, etc. 6. put on other clothes. 7. put other clothing or covering on: *change a bed.* 8. give and take; exchange. 9. **change hands,** a. pass from one owner to another. b. substitute one hand for the other. —*n.* 1. act or fact of changing. 2. a changed condition or appearance. 3. *Music.* change of key; modulation. 4. variety; difference. 5. thing to be used in place of another of the same kind. 6. a second set of clothes. 7. money returned to a person when he has given an amount larger than the price of what he buys. 8. smaller pieces of money given in place of a large piece of money. 9. small coins. 10. Also, 'change. exchange; place for trading in securities or commodities. 11. **changes,** different ways in which a set of bells can be rung. [< OF < LL *cambiare*] —change′ful, *adj.* —change′ful·ly, *adv.* —change′ful·ness, *n.* —chang′er, *n.* —Syn. *v.* 1. alter, transform, transmute. —*n.* 1. altera-

ation. 2. transformation. 4. diversity. 5. substitute.

change·a·ble (chān'jə-bəl), *adj.* 1. that can change; likely to change: *a changeable person.* 2. that can be changed; likely to be changed. 3. having a color or appearance that changes. —**change'a·bil'i·ty, change'a·ble·ness,** *n.* —**change'a·bly,** *adv.* —Syn. 1. inconstant. 2. alterable, variable, unstable, uncertain.

change·less (chānj'lis), *adj.* not changing; not likely to change; constant; steadfast. —**change'less·ly,** *adv.* —**change'less·ness,** *n.*

change·ling (chānj'ling), *n.* child secretly substituted for another.

change of venue, change of the place of a trial.

change·o·ver (chānj'ō'vər), *n.* a planned shift from one procedure of operation, manufacture, etc. to another.

chan·nel (chan'əl), *n., v.,* -neled, -nel·ing; *esp. Brit.* -nelled, -nel·ling. —*n.* 1. bed of a stream, river, etc. 2. body of water joining two larger bodies of water: *the English Channel.* 3. the deeper part of a waterway. 4. passage for liquids; groove. 5. means by which something is carried: *secret channels.* 6. *Radio.* a narrow band of frequencies. 7. course of action; line of doing things: *useful channels.* —*v.* form a channel in; cut out as a channel. [< OF < L *canalis* CANAL. Doublet of CANAL.]

Channel Islands, British islands near the NW coast of France; Alderney, Guernsey, Jersey, and Sark.

chant (chant; chänt), *n.* 1. song. 2. a short, simple song in which several syllables or words are sung in one tone, used in a church service. 3. psalm, prayer, or other song for chanting. 4. a singsong way of talking. —*v.* 1. sing. 2. sing to, or in the manner of, a chant. A choir chants psalms or prayers. 3. celebrate in song. 4. keep talking about; say over and over again. [< OF < L *cantare* < *canere* sing] —**chant'er,** *n.*

chant·ey, chant·y (shan'ti; chan'-), *n., pl.* -eys; -ies. song sung by sailors, in rhythm with the motions made during their work. Also, **shanty.** [alter. of F *chanter* sing. See CHANT.]

chan·ti·cleer (chan'tə·klir), *n.* rooster. [< OF, < *chanter* sing + *cler* clear]

cha·os (kā'os), *n.* 1. great confusion; complete disorder. 2. infinite space or formless matter before the universe existed. [< L < Gk.] —Syn. 1. disorganization, anarchy.

cha·ot·ic (kā·ot'ik), *adj.* in great confusion; very confused; completely disordered. —**cha·ot'i·cal·ly,** *adv.*

chap¹ (chap), *v.,* chapped, chap·ping, *n.* —*v.* crack open; make or become rough: *a person's lips often chap in cold weather.* —*n.* a place where the skin is chapped. [ME *chappe(n)* cut]

chap² (chap), *n. Colloq.* fellow; man; boy. [short for *chapman* a peddler; OE *cēapman* < *cēap* trade + *man* man]

chap³ (chap), *n.* chop (def. 2).

chap., 1. chapel. 2. chaplain. 3. chapter.

cha·pa·ra·jos (chä'pə·rä'hōs), **cha·pa·re·jos** (-rā'hōs), *n.pl. Am., S.W.* chaps. [< Mex. Sp.]

chap·ar·ral (chap'ə·ral'), *n. Am., S.W.* thicket of low shrubs, thorny bushes, etc. [< Sp., < *chaparro* evergreen oak]

chap·book (chap'bûk'), *n.* a small book or pamphlet of popular tales, ballads, etc., formerly sold on the streets.

chap·el (chap'əl), *n.* 1. a building for Christian worship, not so large as a church. 2. a small place for worship in a larger building. 3. room or building for worship in a palace, school, etc. 4. a religious service in a chapel. 5. *Brit.* a place for worship used by people who do not belong to an established church. [< OF < LL *cappella* orig., a shrine in which was preserved the *cappa* or cape of St. Martin]

chap·er·on, chap·er·one (shap'ər·ōn), *n., v.,* -oned, -on·ing. —*n.* a married woman or an older woman who accompanies a young unmarried woman in public for the sake of good form

and protection. —*v.* act as a chaperone to. [< F *chaperon* hood, protector. See CAPE¹.] —**chap·er·on·age** (shap'ər·ōn'ij), *n.*

chap·fall·en (chop'fôl'ən; chap'-), *adj.* dejected; discouraged. Also, **chopfallen.**

chap·lain (chap'lin), *n.* clergyman officially authorized to perform religious functions for a family, court, society, public institution, regiment, or warship. [< OF < LL *capellanus* < *cappella* CHAPEL] —**chap'lain·cy, chap'lain·ship,** *n.*

chap·let (chap'lit), *n.* 1. wreath worn on the head. 2. string of beads. 3. string of beads for keeping count in saying prayers, one third as long as a rosary. 4. prayers said with such beads. [< OF *chapelet,* dim. of *chapel* headdress. See CAP.] —**chap'let·ed,** *adj.*

chaps (chaps; shaps), *n.pl. Am., S. W.* strong leather trousers without a back, worn over other trousers, esp. by cowboys. Also, **chaparajos, chaparejos.**

chap·ter (chap'tər), *n.* 1. a main division of a book or other writing. 2. anything like a chapter; part; section. 3. *Am.* a local division of an organization; branch of a club, society, etc. 4. group of clergymen usually attached to a cathedral. 5. meeting of such a group. —*v.* divide into chapters; arrange in chapters. [< OF < L *capitulum,* dim. of *caput* head]

Cha·pul·te·pec (chə·pul'tə·pek), *n.* fort near Mexico City, scene of battle in Mexican War (1847) and site of international conference (1945) in World War II.

char¹ (chär), *v.,* charred, char·ring. 1. burn to charcoal. 2. scorch. [< *charcoal*]

char² (chär), *n., v.,* charred, char·ring. *Esp. Brit.* —*n.* an odd job; chore. —*v.* 1. do odd jobs or chores. 2. do housework by the day or hour. Also, **chare.** [OE *cerr* turn, occasion]

char·ac·ter (kar'ik·tər), *n.* 1. all qualities or features possessed; kind; sort; nature. 2. moral strength or weakness; special way in which any person feels, thinks, and acts. 3. good character. 4. reputation. 5. good reputation. 6. special thing or quality that makes one person, animal, thing, or group different from others. 7. position; condition: *the treasurer of the club also serves in the character of secretary.* 8. person in a play or book. 9. *Colloq.* person who attracts attention because he is different or queer. 10. description of a person's qualities. 11. letter, mark, or sign used in writing or printing. A, a, +, −, 1, 2, and 3 are characters. —*v.* 1. inscribe; engrave. 2. describe. [< F < L < Gk. *charaktēr* instrument for marking < *charassein* engrave] —Syn. *n.* 2. personality, individuality, nature, temperament.

char·ac·ter·is·tic (kar'ik·tər·is'tik), *adj.* distinguishing from others; special. —*n.* a special quality or feature; whatever distinguishes one person or thing from others. —**char'ac·ter·is'ti·cal·ly,** *adv.* —Syn. *n.* attribute, trait.

char·ac·ter·ize (kar'ik·tər·īz), *v.,* -ized, -iz·ing. 1. describe the special qualities or features of (a person or thing); describe. 2. be a characteristic of; distinguish. 3. give character to. —**char'ac·ter·i·za'tion,** *n.* —**char'ac·ter·iz'er,** *n.* —Syn. 1. portray.

char·ac·ter·less (kar'ik·tər·lis), *adj.* 1. without a character. 2. without distinction; uninteresting.

cha·rade (shə·rād'), *n.* game of guessing a word from the descriptive or dramatic representation of each syllable or part, and of the whole. [< F < Pr. *charrada* < *charra* chatter]

char·coal (chär'kōl'), *n.* 1. black substance made by partly burning wood or bones in a place from which the air is shut out. 2. pencil made of charcoal for drawing. 3. drawing made with such a pencil. [ME *charcole*]

chare (chär), *n., v.,* chared, char·ing. *Esp. Brit.* char².

charge (chärj), *v.,* charged, charg·ing, *n.* —*v.* 1. load; fill: *a gun is charged with powder and*

āge, câre, fär; ēqual, tèrm; īce; ōpen, ôrder; pùt, rüle, ūse; tʜ, then; ə=a in about.

shot. **2.** restore the capacity of (an electric storage battery) by sending a direct current through it. **3.** give a task, duty, or responsibility to. **4.** give an order or command to; direct. **5.** accuse: *the driver was charged with speeding.* **6.** ask as a price; put on a price of. **7.** put down as a debt to be paid. **8.** make a violent final rush: *the soldiers charged the enemy.* **9. charge off, a.** subtract as a loss. **b.** put down as belonging: *a bad mistake must be charged off to experience.* —*n.* **1.** quantity needed to load or fill something, esp. the explosive used in firing a gun. **2.** task; duty; responsibility. **3.** care; management: *doctors and nurses have charge of sick people.* **4.** person, persons, or thing under the care or management of someone. **5.** order; command; direction. **6.** formal instruction or exhortation: *a judge's charge to the jury.* **7.** formal statement accusing a person of having broken the law, violated a rule, etc. **8.** price asked for or put on something. **9.** a debt to be paid. **10.** the violent final rush in an attack or assault. **11.** the military signal for attack. **12. in charge,** having the care or management. [< F < LL *carricare* load < L *carrus* wagon. Doublet of CARRY.] —**Syn.** *v.* **5.** indict, arraign. **8.** assault. —*n.* **3.** custody. **7.** indictment, complaint. **10.** assault, onset.

charge·a·ble (chär′jə·bəl), *adj.* **1.** that can be charged. **2.** liable to become a public charge.

char·gé d'af·faires (shär·zhā′ də·fār′), *pl.* **char·gés d'af·faires** (shär·zhāz′ də·fār′). *French.* deputy of a diplomat.

charg·er[1] (chär′jər), *n.* **1.** war horse. **2.** person or thing that charges.

charg·er[2] (chär′jər), *n. Archaic.* a large, flat dish; platter. [< OF, < *charger* CHARGE]

char·i·ly (chār′ə·li), *adv.* carefully; warily.

char·i·ness (chār′i·nis), *n.* chary quality.

char·i·ot (char′i·ət), *n.* **1.** a two-wheeled car pulled by horses, used in ancient times in fighting, racing, and processions. **2.** a four-wheeled carriage or coach. [< OF, < *char* CAR]

char·i·ot·eer (char′i·ət·ir′), *n.* person who drives a chariot.

char·i·ta·ble (char′ə·tə·bəl), *adj.* **1.** of charity. **2.** generous in giving help to poor or suffering people. **3.** kindly in judging people and their actions. —**char′i·ta·ble·ness,** *n.* —**char′i·ta·bly,** *adv.* —**Syn.** **2.** liberal, bountiful. **3.** tolerant.

char·i·ty (char′ə·ti), *n., pl.* **-ties. 1.** help given to the poor or suffering. **2.** act or work of charity. **3.** fund, institution, or organization for helping the poor or suffering. **4.** Christian love of one's fellow men. **5.** kindness in judging people. [< OF < L *caritas* dearness < *carus* dear] —**Syn.** **1.** philanthropy, beneficence.

char·la·tan (shär′lə·tən), *n.* person who pretends to have more knowledge or skill than he really has; quack. [< F < Ital. *ciarlatano*, ult. < Mongolian *dzar* proclaim, tell lies] —**Syn.** impostor, cheat.

char·la·tan·ism (shär′lə·tən·iz′əm), **char·la·tan·ry** (-tən·ri), *n.* quackery.

Char·le·magne (shär′lə·mān), *n.* 742?–814 A.D., king of the Franks from 768 to 814 A.D. and emperor of the Holy Roman Empire 800–814 A.D.

Charles I, 1. 1600–1649, king of England from 1625, executed in 1649. **2.** Charlemagne.

Charles II, 1630–1685, king of England from 1660 to 1685, son of Charles I.

Charles·ton (chärlz′tən), *n.* **1.** capital of West Virginia, in the W part. **2.** seaport in SE South Carolina.

char·ley horse (chär′li), *Am., Colloq.* stiffness caused by straining a muscle.

Char·lotte (shär′lət), *n.* city in S North Carolina.

Char·lot·te A·ma·li·e (shär·lot′ə ə·mä′li·ə), seaport and capital of the Virgin Islands.

char·lotte russe (shär′lət rüs′), dessert made of a mold of sponge cake filled with whipped cream or custard. [< F, Russian charlotte (a type of dessert)]

Char·lottes·ville (shär′ləts·vil), *n.* city in C Virginia.

charm (chärm), *n.* **1.** power of delighting or fascinating; attractiveness. **2.** a very pleasing quality or feature. **3.** a small ornament or trinket worn on a watch chain, bracelet, etc. **4.** word, verse, act, or thing supposed to have magic power to help or harm people. —*v.* **1.** please greatly; delight; fascinate; attract. **2.** act on as if by magic: *laughter charmed away his troubles.* **3.** give magic power to; protect as by a charm. [< OF < L *carmen* song, enchantment < *canere* sing] —**charm′er,** *n.* —**charm′less,** *adj.* —**Syn.** *n.* **1.** allurement. —*v.* **1.** captivate, entrance.

charm·ing (chär′ming), *adj.* very pleasing; delightful; fascinating; attractive. —**charm′ing·ly,** *adv.* —**charm′ing·ness,** *n.*

char·nel house (chär′nəl), place where dead bodies or bones are laid. [< OF < LL *carnale.* See CARNAL.]

Char·on (kãr′ən), *n. Gk. Myth.* boatman who ferried the spirits of the dead across the river Styx to Hades.

chart (chärt), *n.* **1.** map, esp. a hydrographic or marine map. **2.** an outline map showing special conditions or facts: *a weather chart.* **3.** sheet giving information in lists, pictures, tables, or diagrams. **4.** such a list, table, picture, or diagram. —*v.* make a chart of; show on a chart. [< F < L *charta* < Gk. *chartes* leaf of paper. Doublet of CARD.] —**chart′less,** *adj.*

char·ter (chär′tər), *n.* **1.** a written grant of certain rights or privileges, esp. one by a ruler to his subjects, or by a legislature to a city or company, telling how it is to be organized and what it can do. **2.** a written order from the authorities of a society, giving to a group of persons the right to organize a new chapter, branch, or lodge. —*v.* **1.** give a charter to. **2.** hire; rent. [< OF < L *chartula,* dim. of *charta.* See CHART.] —**char′ter·er,** *n.* —**char′ter·less,** *adj.*

char·treuse (shär·trœz′; *for 2, also* shär·trüz′, -trüs′), *n.* **1.** a green, yellow, or white liqueur first made by Carthusian monks. **2.** a light, yellowish green. [< F, Carthusian]

char·wom·an (chär′wüm′ən), *n., pl.* **-wom·en.** woman whose work is doing odd jobs by the day, esp. cleaning. [see CHAR[2]]

char·y (chãr′i), *adj.,* **char·i·er, char·i·est. 1.** careful. **2.** shy. **3.** sparing; stingy. [OE *cearig* < *caru* care] —**Syn.** **1.** wary, cautious. **3.** frugal.

Cha·ryb·dis (kə·rib′dis), *n.* whirlpool in the strait between Sicily and Italy, opposite the rock Scylla. Charybdis sucked down ships.

chase[1] (chās), *v.,* **chased, chas·ing,** *n.* —*v.* **1.** run after to catch or kill. **2.** drive; drive away. **3.** hunt. **4.** follow; pursue. **5.** rush; hurry. —*n.* **1.** chasing. **2.** hunting as a sport. **3.** a hunted animal. **4.** give chase, run after; chase. [< OF *chacier* < LL *captiare.* Doublet of CATCH.] —**chas′er,** *n.*

chase[2] (chās), *v.,* **chased, chas·ing.** engrave; emboss. [var. of *enchase*] —**chas′er,** *n.*

chase[3] (chās), *n.* **1.** groove; furrow; trench. **2.** iron frame to hold type that is ready to print or make plates from. [< F < L *capsa* box]

chasm (kaz′əm), *n.* **1.** a deep opening or crack in the earth; gap. **2.** wide difference of feelings or interests between people or groups. [< L < Gk. *chasma*] —**chas·mal** (kaz′məl), *adj.* —**Syn.** **1.** fissure, gorge, cleft, breach, abyss.

chas·sis (shas′i; chas′i), *n., pl.* **chas·sis** (shas′iz; chas′-). **1.** frame, wheels, and machinery of a motor vehicle. **2.** main landing gear of an aircraft. [< F < VL *capsiceum* < L *capsa.* See CHASE[3].]

chaste (chāst), *adj.* **1.** pure; virtuous. **2.** decent; modest. **3.** simple in taste or style. [< OF < L *castus* pure] —**chaste′ly,** *adv.* —**chaste′ness,** *n.* —**Syn.** **1.** innocent. **3.** classic, refined. —**Ant.** **1.** immoral.

chas·ten (chās′ən), *v.* **1.** punish to improve. **2.** restrain from excess or crudeness. [< obs. *chaste* < F < L *castigare* make pure < *castus* pure] —**chas′ten·er,** *n.* —**Syn.** **1.** discipline.

chas·tise (chas·tīz′), *v.,* **-tised, -tis·ing.** punish by beating or thrashing. [< obs. *chaste* CHASTEN + *-ise*] —**chas·tise·ment** (chas′tiz·mənt; chas·tīz′-), *n.* —**chas·tis′er,** *n.*

chas·ti·ty (chas′tə·ti), *n.* **1.** purity; virtue.

2. decency; modesty. 3. simplicity of style or taste; absence of too much decoration.

chas·u·ble (chaz′yə-bəl; chas′-), *n.* a sleeveless outer vestment covering all other vestments, worn by the priest at Mass. [< F < LL *casubula* < L *casa* house; akin to CASSOCK]

chat (chat), *n., v.,* chat·ted, chat·ting. —*n.* 1. easy, familiar talk. 2. any of several birds with a chattering cry. —*v.* talk in an easy, familiar way. [short for *chatter*]

châ·teau (sha·tō′), *n., pl.* -teaux (-tōz′). in France: 1. a castle. 2. a large country house. [< F < L *castellum* CASTLE. Doublet of CASTLE.]

Châ·teau-Thier·ry (sha·tō′tyär′i; -tē′ə·ri), *n.* town in N France, on the Marne River; site of several battles in World War I.

chat·e·laine (shat′ə·lān), *n.* 1. mistress or lady of a castle. 2. clasp to which keys, a purse, etc., may be attached. [< F, ult. < L *castellum* CASTLE]

Chat·ta·noo·ga (chat′ə·nü′gə), *n.* city in SE Tennessee, on the Tennessee River.

chat·tel (chat′əl), *n.* movable possession; piece of property that is not real estate. Furniture, automobiles, slaves, and animals are chattels. [< OF *chatel.* Doublet of CATTLE.]

chat·ter (chat′ər), *v.* 1. talk constantly, rapidly, and foolishly. 2. make quick, indistinct sounds: *monkeys chatter.* 3. utter rapidly or uselessly. 4. rattle together. —*n.* 1. quick, foolish talk. 2. quick, indistinct sounds. [imit.] —chat′ter·er, *n.*

chat·ter·box (chat′ər·boks′), *n.* person who talks all the time.

chat·ty (chat′i), *adj.,* -ti·er, -ti·est. 1. fond of friendly, familiar talk. 2. conversational. —chat′ti·ly, *adv.* —chat′ti·ness, *n.*

Chau·cer (chô′sər), *n.* Geoffrey, 1340?-1400, English poet, author of *The Canterbury Tales.* —Chau·ce·ri·an (chô·sir′i·ən), *adj.*

chauf·feur (shō′fər; shō·fėr′), *n.* man whose work is driving an automobile. —*v.* act as a chauffeur to. [< F, stoker < *chauffer* to heat; term from days of steam automobiles]

chaunt (chônt; chänt), *n., v.* Archaic. chant.

chau·tau·qua, Chau·tau·qua (shə·tô′kwə), *n. Am.* assembly for education and entertainment by lectures, concerts, etc. —chau·tau′quan, Chau·tau′quan, *n., adj. Am.*

chau·vin·ism (shō′vən·iz·əm), *n.* boastful, warlike patriotism. [< F *chauvinisme;* after Nicolas *Chauvin,* overenthusiastic patriot] —chau′vin·ist, *n., adj.* —chau·vin·is′tic, *adj.* —chau′vin·is′ti·cal·ly, *adv.*

cheap (chēp), *adj.* 1. costing little. 2. costing less than it is worth. 3. charging low prices: *a cheap market.* 4. easily obtained. 5. of low value; common. 6. feel cheap, feel inferior and ashamed. —*adv.* at a low price; at small cost. [short for *good cheap* a good bargain; OE *cēap* price, bargain] —cheap′ly, *adv.* —cheap′ness, *n.* —Syn. *adj.* 1. inexpensive, low-priced. 5. poor, mean, inferior, paltry, worthless.

cheap·en (chēp′ən), *v.* make or become cheap. —cheap′en·er, *n.*

cheat (chēt), *v.* 1. deceive or trick; play or do business in a way that is not honest. 2. beguile. 3. elude. —*n.* 1. person who is not honest and does things to deceive and trick others. 2. fraud; trick. [var. of *escheat*] —cheat′er, *n.* —cheat′ing·ly, *adv.* —Syn. *v.* 1. swindle, dupe, defraud, fool. —*n.* 1. swindler, impostor, deceiver. 2. swindle, deception, hoax.

check (chek), *v.* 1. stop suddenly. 2. hold back; control; restrain. 3. control to prevent error, fraud, etc. 4. rebuff; repulse; reverse. 5. examine or compare to prove true or right. 6. *Am.* agree or be similar in every detail on comparison: *the two accounts check.* 7. *Am.* get a check for; put a check on. 8. *Am.* write a check; draw a check. 9. mark in a pattern of squares. 10. crack; split. 11. *Am.* send (baggage identified by means of a check) to a given destination. 12. in chess, have (an opponent's king) in check. 13. check in, a. arrive and register at a hotel, etc. b. *Am., Slang.* die. 14. check off, mark as checked and found true or right. 15. check out, a. pay one's bill at a hotel and leave. b. *Slang.* die. 16. check up, *Am.* examine or compare to prove true or correct. —*n.* 1. a sudden stop. 2. a holding back; control; restraint. 3. means of preventing error, fraud, etc. 4. any person, thing, or event that controls or holds back action. 5. rebuff; repulse; reverse. 6. an examination or comparison to prove something true or right. 7. mark to show that something has been checked and found true or right. 8. ticket or metal piece given in return for a coat, hat, baggage, package, etc., to show ownership. 9. *Am.* bill for a meal, etc. 10. Also, *Brit.* cheque. a written order directing a bank to pay money to the person named on it. 11. pattern of squares. 12. one of these squares. 13. fabric marked in squares. 14. crack; split. 15. in chess, position of an opponent's king when it is in danger and must be moved. 16. in check, held back; controlled. —*adj.* 1. used in checking. 2. marked in a pattern of squares. —*interj.* a call in the game of chess warning that an opponent's king is in danger and must be moved. [< OF *eschec* a check at chess < Pers. *shāh* king, king at chess] —check′a·ble, *adj.* —check′er, *n.* —Syn. *v.* 1. halt, block. 2. repress, curb, bridle. —*n.* 1. stoppage, repulse. 4. restriction, curb, bridle, obstruction, ocstacle, hindrance. 8. tag, token, coupon. ➤ check, cheque. *Cheque* is a British spelling and its use in the United States is likely to seem pretentious.

check·book (chek′búk′), *n.* book of blank checks on a bank.

check·er (chek′ər), *v.* 1. mark in a pattern of squares of different colors. 2. mark off with patches different from one another. 3. have ups and downs; change; vary. —*n.* 1. pattern of squares. 2. one of these squares. 3. one of the flat, round pieces used in the game of checkers. Also, *Brit.* chequer. [< OF *escheker* chessboard]

check·er·board (chek′ər·bôrd′; -bôrd′), *n.* board marked in a pattern of 64 squares of two alternating colors, used in playing checkers or chess. Also, *Brit.* chequerboard.

check·ered (chek′ərd), *adj.* 1. marked in a pattern of many-colored squares. 2. marked in patches. 3. often changing; varied. Also, *Brit.* chequered.

check·ers (chek′ərz), *n.* game played on a checkerboard by two people. Each player has 12 round, flat pieces to move. Also, *Brit.* chequers.

checking account, *Am.* bank account against which checks may be drawn.

check·mate (chek′māt′), *v.,* -mat·ed, -mat·ing, *n.* —*v.* 1. make a move in chess that wins the game. 2. defeat completely. —*n.* 1. in chess, a move that ends the game by putting the opponent's king in inescapable check. 2. a complete defeat. [< OF *echec mat* < Ar. *shāh māt* the king is dead]

check-off (chek′ôf′; -of′), *n. Am.* system of collecting union dues through wage deductions made by the employer.

check point, a gate, sentry box, etc. at which persons are stopped so that their passports or other documents, baggage, etc. may be examined.

check·rein (chek′rān′), *n.* a short rein to keep a horse from lowering its head.

check·up (chek′up′), *n.* 1. *Am.* a careful examination. 2. a thorough physical examination.

cheek (chēk), *n.* 1. side of the face below either eye. 2. anything suggesting the human cheek in form or position. 3. *Colloq.* saucy talk or behavior; impudence. [OE *cēce*]

cheek·bone (chēk′bōn′), *n.* bone just below either eye.

cheek·y (chēk′i), *adj.,* cheek·i·er, cheek·i·est. *Colloq.* saucy; impudent. —cheek′i·ly, *adv.* —cheek′i·ness, *n.*

cheep (chēp), *v.* make a short, sharp sound like

a young bird; chirp; peep. —*n.* such a sound. [imit.] —**cheep′er,** *n.*

cheer (chir), *n.* **1.** joy; gladness; comfort; encouragement. **2.** shout of encouragement, approval, praise, etc. **3.** food. **4.** state of mind; condition of feeling: *"Be of good cheer,"* said the priest. **5.** Archaic. expression of face. —*v.* **1.** fill with cheer; give joy to; gladden; comfort; encourage. **2.** shout encouragement, approval, praise, etc. **3.** urge on with cheers. **4.** greet or welcome with cheers. **5. cheer up,** don't be sad; be glad. [< F < LL *cara* face < Gk. *kara* head, face] —**cheer′er,** *n.* —Syn. *n.* **2.** acclamation, shouting, applause. -*v.* **1.** enliven, console. **2.** applaud, acclaim.

cheer·ful (chir′fəl), *adj.* **1.** full of cheer; joyful; glad: *a smiling, cheerful person.* **2.** filling with cheer; pleasant; bright: *a cheerful, sunny room.* **3.** willing: *a cheerful giver.* —**cheer′-ful·ly,** *adv.* —**cheer′ful·ness,** *n.* —Syn. **1.** cheery, joyous, gay, blithe. —Ant. **1.** sad, depressed.

cheer·i·o (chir′i·ō), *interj., n., pl.* -i·os. *Esp. Brit. Colloq.* **1.** hello! **2.** good-by! **3.** hurrah!

cheer·less (chir′lis), *adj.* without joy or comfort; gloomy; dreary. —**cheer′less·ly,** *adv.* —**cheer′less·ness,** *n.* —Syn. dismal, sad.

cheer·y (chir′i), *adj.,* cheer·i·er, cheer·i·est. cheerful; pleasant; bright; gay. —**cheer′i·ly,** *adv.* —**cheer′i·ness,** *n.*

cheese[1] (chēz), *n.* **1.** solid food made from the thick part of milk. **2.** mass of this pressed into shape. [< L *caseus*]

cheese[2] (chēz), *v.,* cheesed, chees·ing. *Slang.* **1.** stop; leave off. **2. cheese it,** look out! run away! [alter. of *cease*]

cheese cake, 1. dessert made of cheese, eggs, sugar, etc., baked together. **2.** *Slang.* **a.** the photographing of a woman or women in such a fashion as to emphasize or reveal physical charms. **b.** such photographs.

cheese·cloth (chēz′klôth′; -kloth′), *n.* a thin, loosely woven cotton cloth.

chees·y (chēz′i), *adj.,* chees·i·er, chees·i·est. **1.** of or like cheese. **2.** *U.S. Slang.* poorly made; inferior. —**chees′i·ness,** *n.*

chee·tah (chē′tə), *n.* animal somewhat like a leopard, found in S Asia and Africa. Also, **chetah.** [< Hind. *chītā*]

chef (shef), *n.* **1.** head cook. **2.** cook. [< F. Doublet of CHIEF.]

Che·khov (chek′ôf; -of), *n.* Anton, 1860–1904, Russian dramatist and novelist.

che·la (kē′lə), *n., pl.* -lae (-lē). claw of a lobster, crab, scorpion, etc. It is like a pincer. [< L < Gk. *chele* claw]

Chel·sea (chel′si), *n.* borough in SW London.

chem., chemical; chemist; chemistry.

chem·i·cal (kem′ə·kəl), *adj.* **1.** of chemistry. **2.** made by or used in chemistry. —*n.* substance obtained by or used in a chemical process. Oxygen, sulfuric acid, bicarbonate of soda, borax, etc., are chemicals. —**chem′i·cal·ly,** *adv.*

che·mise (shə·mēz′), *n.* a loose, shirtlike undergarment worn by women and girls. [< F < LL *camisia* shirt < Celtic]

chem·ist (kem′ist), *n.* **1.** expert in chemistry. **2.** *Brit.* druggist. [var. of *alchemist*]

chem·is·try (kem′is·tri), *n., pl.* -tries. **1.** science that deals with the characteristics of elements or simple substances, the changes that take place when they combine to form other substances, and the laws of their combination and behavior under various conditions. **2.** application of this to a certain subject. [< *chemist*]

chem·ur·gy (kem′ér·ji), *n.* branch of applied chemistry that deals with the use of organic raw materials, such as casein and cornstalks, otherwise than for food, and especially in manufacturing.

che·nille (shə·nēl′), *n.* **1.** a velvety cord, used in embroidery, fringe, etc. **2.** fabric woven from this cord, used for rugs and curtains. [< F *chenille* caterpillar < L *canicula* little dog; from its furry look]

Che·ops (kē′ops), *n.* Egyptian king who lived about 2900 B.C., builder of a great pyramid. Also, **Khufu.**

cheque (chek), *n. Brit.* check (def. 10).

cheq·uer (chek′ər), *v., n. Brit.* checker.

cheq·uer·board (chek′ər·bôrd′; -bōrd′), *n. Brit.* checkerboard.

cheq·uered (chek′ərd), *adj. Brit.* checkered.

cheq·uers (chek′ərz), *n. Brit.* checkers.

Cheq·uers (chek′ərz), *n.* the official country residence of the prime minister of Great Britain, NW of London.

Cher·bourg (shãr′bùrg), *n.* seaport in NW France.

cher·ish (cher′ish), *v.* **1.** hold dear; treat with affection. **2.** care for tenderly. **3.** keep in mind; cling to. [< F *chérir* < *cher* dear < L *carus*] —**cher′ish·er,** *n.* —**cher′ish·ing·ly,** *adv.*

Cher·o·kee (cher′ə·kē; cher′ə·kē′), *n., pl.* -kee, -kees. *Am.* **1.** member of a tribe of American Indians, now living mostly in Oklahoma. **2.** their language.

che·root (shə·rüt′), *n.* cigar cut off square at both ends. [< F < Tamil *shuruttu* roll]

cher·ry (cher′i), *n., pl.* -ries, *adj.* —*n.* **1.** a small, round, juicy fruit with a stone or pit in it. **2.** tree that it grows on. **3.** its wood. **4.** bright red. —*adj.* **1.** made of this wood. **2.** bright-red. [OE *ciris* < VL *cerisia* < Gk. *kerasia* < Gk. *kerasos* cherry tree. See CERISE.]

cher·ub (cher′əb), *n., pl.* **cher·u·bim** (cher′ə-bim; -yů·bim) *for 1 and 2,* **cher·ubs** *for 3 and 4.* **1.** one of the second highest order of angels. **2.** picture or statue of a child with wings, or of a child's head with wings. **3.** beautiful, innocent, or good child. **4.** person with a chubby, innocent face. [< Heb. *kerūb*] —**che·ru·bic** (chə·rü′bik), *adj.* —**che·ru′bi·cal·ly,** *adv.*

Cherub

Ches·a·peake Bay (ches′ə·pēk), bay of the Atlantic in Maryland and Virginia.

Chesh·ire (chesh′ər; -ir), *n.* county in W England. Also, **Chester.**

chess (ches), *n.* game played on a chessboard by two people. Each player has 16 pieces to move in different ways. [< OF *esches* (pl.). See CHECK.]

chess·board (ches′bôrd′; -bōrd′), *n.* board marked in a pattern of 64 squares of two different colors, used in playing chess.

chess·man (ches′man′; -mən), *n., pl.* -men (-men′; -mən). one of the pieces used in playing chess.

chest (chest), *n.* **1.** part of the body enclosed by ribs. **2.** a large box with a lid, used for holding things: *a linen chest.* **3.** piece of furniture with drawers. **4.** place where money is kept; treasury. **5.** the money itself. [< L < Gk. *kiste* box]

Ches·ter (ches′tər), *n.* **1.** city in W England. **2.** Cheshire.

Ches·ter·field (ches′tər·fēld′), *n.* **1.** 4th Earl of, 1694–1773, English statesman who wrote witty and instructive letters to his son. **2. chesterfield,** a single-breasted overcoat with the buttons hidden.

chest·nut (ches′nut; -nət), *n.* **1.** large tree belonging to the same family as the beech, that bears sweet edible nuts in prickly burs. **2.** nut of this tree. **3.** wood of this tree. **4.** horse chestnut. **5.** reddish brown. **6.** reddish-brown horse. **7.** *Am., Colloq.* stale joke or story. —*adj.* reddish-brown. [< obs. *chesten* chestnut (< L < Gk. *kastanea* chestnut) + *nut*]

chest·y (ches′ti), *adj.,* chest·i·er, chest·i·est. *Am., Slang.* pompous or self-assertive; conceited.

che·tah (chē′tə), *n.* cheetah.

chet·nik (chet′nik), *n., pl.* **chet·ni·ci** (chet-nē′tsē) -niks. one of a Yugoslav guerrilla force, most of which was active against the Nazis during the second World War. [< Serbian, < *cheta* band]

chev·a·lier (shev′ə·lir′), *n.* **1.** Archaic. knight. **2.** member of the lowest rank in the Legion of Honor of France. **3.** in the old French nobility, a younger son. [< F, < *cheval* horse < L *caballus*. See CAVALIER.]

Chev·i·ot (chev′i·ət, chē′vi- *for 1;* shev′i·ət *for 2*), *n.* **1.** breed of sheep that originated in the Cheviot Hills. **2.** **cheviot, a.** a rough, woolen cloth. **b.** a cotton cloth like it.

Cheviot Hills, hills on the boundary between England and Scotland.

chev·ron (shev′rən), *n.* **1.** a cloth design consisting of stripes meeting at an angle, worn on the sleeve as an indication of rank (by non-commissioned officers, policemen, etc.) or of service or wounds in war. **2.** design shaped like an inverted V, used in coats of arms and in architecture. [< F, rafter, < *chèvre* goat < L *capra*]

chev·y (chev′i), *n., pl.* **chev·ies,** *v.,* **chev·ied, chev·y·ing.** *Brit.* —*n.* **1.** a hunting cry. **2.** hunt; chase. —*v.* **1.** hunt; chase. **2.** scamper; race. **3.** worry; harass. Also, *Brit.* **chivy, chivvy.**

chew (chü), *v.* **1.** crush or grind with the teeth. **2.** think over; consider. —*n.* **1.** chewing. **2.** thing chewed; piece for chewing. [OE *cēowan*] —**chew′er,** *n.* —Syn. *v.* **1.** munch, crunch, champ.

chewing gum, *Am.* gum prepared for chewing, usually sweetened and flavored chicle.

che·wink (chi·wingk′), *Am.* finch of eastern and central North America whose cry sounds somewhat like its name. [imit.]

Chey·enne (shī·en′; -an′), *n.* capital of Wyoming, in the SE part.

Chey·enne (shī·en′), *n., pl.* **-enne, -ennes,** *adj.* —*n.* **1.** *Am.* member of an Algonquian tribe of American Indians, now living in Montana and Oklahoma. **2.** *Am.* this tribe. —*adj.* of this tribe.

chi (kī), *n.* the 22nd letter of the Greek alphabet (X, χ), written as *ch* in English, but sounded like *k.*

Chiang Kai-shek (chyäng′ kī′shek′; chyang′), born 1886, Chinese general and political leader.

Chi·an·ti (kī·än′ti; -an′-), *n.* a dry, red Italian wine.

chi·a·ro·scu·ro (ki·ä′rə·skyur′ō), **chi·a·ro·os·cu·ro** (ki·ä′rə·ō·skyur′ō), *n., pl.* **-ros.** **1.** treatment of light and shade in a picture. **2.** art using only light and shade in pictures. **3.** a sketch in black and white. [< Ital., clear-dark] —**chi·a′ro·scu′rist,** *n.*

chic (shēk; shik), *n.* style. —*adj.* **1.** stylish. **2.** *Am., Colloq.* clever; neat. [< F]

Chi·ca·go (shə·kô′gō; -kä′-), *n.* city in NE Illinois, on Lake Michigan; the second largest city in the United States. —**Chi·ca′go·an,** *n.*

chi·can·er·y (shi·kān′ər·i), *n., pl.* **-er·ies.** low trickery; unfair practice; quibbling. —Syn. deception, sophistry.

chic·co·ry (chik′ə·ri), *n., pl.* **-ries.** chicory.

chick (chik), *n.* **1.** young chicken. **2.** young bird. **3.** child. [var. of *chicken*]

chick·a·dee (chik′ə·dē), *n.* *Am.* a small bird with black, white, and gray feathers. [imit.]

Chickadee (5 in. long)

chick·en (chik′ən), *n.* **1.** the young of domestic fowl. **2.** *Am.* a domestic or barnyard fowl of any age. **3.** flesh of a chicken used for food. **4.** a young bird of certain other kinds. **5.** *U.S. Slang.* young or immature woman; young person. —*adj.* young; small. [OE *cīcen*]

chick·en-heart·ed (chik′ən·här′tid), *adj.* timid; cowardly.

chicken pox, a mild contagious disease of children accompanied by a rash on the skin.

chick·weed (chik′wēd′), *n.* a common weed whose leaves and seeds are eaten by birds.

chic·le (chik′əl), or **chicle gum,** *n.* *Am.* a tasteless, gumlike substance used in making chewing gum. It is the dried milky juice of a sapodilla tree of tropical America. [< Am.Sp. < Mex. *jiktli*]

chic·o·ry (chik′ə·ri), *n., pl.* **-ries. 1.** plant with bright-blue flowers whose leaves are used for salad. **2.** its root, roasted and used as a sub-

stitute for coffee. Also, **chiccory.** [< F < L < Gk. *kichoreion*]

chide (chīd), *v.,* **chid·ed** or **chid** or **chid** (chid); **chid·ed, chid,** or **chid·den** (chid′ən); **chid·ing.** reproach; blame; scold. [OE *cīdan*] —**chid′er,** *n.* —**chid′ing·ly,** *adv.* —Syn. rebuke, reprove.

chief (chēf), *n.* **1.** person highest in rank or authority; head of a group; leader. **2.** head of a tribe or clan. **3.** *Archaic.* the most important part; best part. **4. in chief,** at the head; of the highest rank or authority. —*adj.* **1.** highest in rank or authority; at the head; leading. **2.** most important; main. [< OF < L *caput* head. Doublet of CHEF.] —**chief′less,** *adj.* —Syn. *adj.* **2.** prime, essential, cardinal.

chief·ly (chēf′li), *adv.* **1.** mainly; mostly. **2.** first of all; above all.

chief·tain (chēf′tən), *n.* **1.** chief of a tribe or clan. **2.** leader; head of a group. [< OF < LL *capitanus.* See CAPTAIN.] —**chief′tain·cy, chief′-tain·ship,** *n.*

chif·fon (shi·fon′; shif′on), *n.* **1.** a very thin silk or rayon cloth, used for dresses. **2.** bit of ribbon, lace, or other feminine finery. [< F, < *chiffe* rag]

chif·fo·nier, chif·fon·nier (shif′ə·nir′), *n.* a high bureau or chest of drawers, often one with a mirror. [< F. See CHIFFON.]

chig·ger (chig′ər), *n.* **1.** *Am.* mite whose larvae stick to the skin and cause severe itching. **2.** chigoe. [alter. of *chigoe*]

chi·gnon (shēn′yon; *Fr.* shē·nyôN′), *n.* a roll of hair worn by women at the back of the head or on the nape of the neck. [< F]

chig·oe, chig·o (chig′ō), *n.* flea of the West Indies and South America. The female burrows under the skin of people and animals, where it causes severe itching and sores. [< WInd.]

Chi·hua·hua (chi·wä′wä), *n.* **1.** state in N Mexico. **2.** Also, **chihuahua,** *Am.* a very small dog of ancient Mexican breed.

chil·blain (chil′blān′), *n.* Usually, **chilblains.** an itching sore or redness on the hands or feet caused by cold. [< *chill* + *blain*] —**chil′blained′,** *adj.*

child (chīld), *n., pl.* **chil·dren** (chil′drən). **1.** baby; infant. **2.** boy or girl. **3.** son or daughter. **4.** descendant. **5.** person like a child in nearness, affection, interest, etc. **6.** an immature or childish person. **7.** result; product. **8. with child,** pregnant. [OE *cild*] —**child′less,** *adj.*

child·bear·ing (chīld′bār′ing), *n.* giving birth to children.

child·bed (chīld′bed′), *n.* condition of a woman giving birth to a child.

child·birth (chīld′bėrth′), *n.* giving birth to a child.

child·hood (chīld′hud), *n.* condition or time of being a child.

child·ish (chīl′dish), *adj.* **1.** of a child. **2.** like a child. **3.** not suitable for a grown person; weak; silly; foolish. —**child′ish·ly,** *adv.* —**child′ish·ness,** *n.* —Syn. **2.** immature, infantile, babyish.

child·like (chīld′līk′), *adj.* **1.** like a child; innocent; frank; simple. **2.** suitable for a child.

chil·dren (chil′drən), *n.* pl. of child.

child's play, something very easy to do.

Chil·e (chil′ē), *n.* country in SW South America. —**Chil′e·an,** *adj., n.*

chil·e con car·ne, chil·i con car·ne (chil′ē kon kär′nē), *Am.* meat cooked with red peppers and, usually, beans. [< Sp., chili with meat]

Chile saltpeter, sodium nitrate, $NaNO_3$.

chil·i, chil·e, or **chil·li** (chil′ē), *n., pl.* **chil·ies; chil·es; chil·lies. 1.** *Am.* a hot-tasting pod of red pepper, used for seasoning. **2.** plant that it grows on, a tropical American shrub grown in the S part of the United States. **3.** *Am.* chile con carne. [< Sp. < Mex. *chilli*]

chili sauce, chilli sauce, *Am.* sauce made of red peppers, tomatoes, and spices, used on meat, fish, etc.

chill (chil), *n.* **1.** unpleasant coldness. **2.** sudden coldness of the body with shivering. **3.** unfriendliness; lack of heartiness. **4.** depressing influence; discouraging feeling. **5.** feeling cold; shivering. —*adj.* **1.** unpleasantly cold. **2.** cold in manner; unfriendly. **3.** depressing; discouraging. —*v.* **1.** make cold. **2.** become cold; feel cold. **3.** harden (metal) on the surface by sudden cooling. **4.** depress; dispirit. [OE *ciele*] —chill′er, *n.* —chill′ing·ly, *adv.* —chill′ness, *n.*

chill·y (chil′i), *adj.*, **chill·i·er, chill·i·est. 1.** unpleasantly cool; rather cold. **2.** cold in manner; unfriendly. —chill′i·ly, *adv.* —chill′i·ness, *n.* —Syn. **1.** chill, raw.

chime (chim), *n., v.,* **chimed, chim·ing.** —*n.* **1.** set of tuned bells to make musical sounds. **2.** musical sound made by a set of tuned bells. **3.** agreement; harmony. —*v.* **1.** make musical sounds on (a set of tuned bells). **2.** ring out musically: *the bells chimed midnight.* **3.** agree; be in harmony. **4.** say or utter in cadence or singsong. **5.** chime in, a. be in harmony; agree. **b.** *Colloq.* join in. [< L < Gk. *kymbalon* CYMBAL]

chi·me·ra, chi·mae·ra (kə·mir′ə; kī–), *n., pl.* –ras. **1.** Often, **Chimera.** *Gk. Legend.* monster with a lion's head, a goat's body, and a serpent's tail, supposed to breathe out fire. **2.** a horrible creature of the imagination. **3.** an absurd idea; impossible notion; wild fancy. [< L < Gk. *chimaira* she-goat]

chi·mer·i·cal (kə·mer′ə·kəl; –mir′–; kī–), **chi·mer·ic** (–ik), *adj.* **1.** unreal; imaginary. **2.** absurd; impossible. **3.** wildly fanciful; visionary.

chim·ney (chim′ni), *n., pl.* –neys. **1.** an upright structure to make a draft and carry away smoke. **2.** part of this that rises above a roof. **3.** glass tube put around the flame of a lamp. **4.** crack or opening in a rock, mountain, volcano, etc. [< OF < LL *caminata* < L *caminus* oven < Gk. *kaminos*] —chim′ney·less, *adj.*

chimney corner, corner or side of a fireplace; place near the fire.

chimney sweep or **sweeper,** person whose work is cleaning out chimneys.

chimney swift, *Am.* bird of North America that often builds its nest in unused chimneys.

chim·pan·zee (chim′pan·zē′; chim·pan′zē), *n.* African manlike ape, smaller than a gorilla. [from native West African name]

chin (chin), *n., v.,* **chinned, chin·ning.** —*n.* **1.** the front of the lower jaw below the mouth. **2.** *Am., Slang.* talk. —*v.* **1. chin oneself,** *Am.* hang by the hands from a bar and pull oneself up until one's chin is even with the bar. **2.** *Am., Slang.* talk; gossip. [OE *cin*]

Chi·na (chī′nə), *n.* a large country in E Asia.

chi·na (chī′nə), *n.* **1.** a fine, white ware made of clay baked by a special process, first used in China. **2.** dishes, vases, ornaments, etc., made of china. **3.** dishes of any kind. —*adj.* made of china.

chi·na·ber·ry (chī′nə·ber′i), **china tree,** *Am.* **1.** an ornamental tree with purple flowers and yellow fruit, especially used as a shade tree in the South. **2.** soapberry of the S United States, Mexico, and the West Indies.

Chi·na·man (chī′nə·mən), *n., pl.* –men. **1.** native or inhabitant of China. **2.** person of Chinese descent. ➤ See **Chinese** for usage note.

China Sea, part of the Pacific E and SE of Asia. Formosa divides it into **South China Sea** and **East China Sea.**

Chi·na·town (chī′nə·toun′), *n. Am.* section of a city where Chinese live.

chi·na·ware (chī′nə·wãr′), *n.* **1.** dishes, vases, ornaments, etc., made of china. **2.** dishes of any kind.

chin·ca·pin (ching′kə·pin), *n.* chinquapin.

chinch bug (chinch), *Am.* a small, black-and-white bug that does much damage to grain in dry weather. [< Sp. < L *cimex* bedbug]

Chinchilla (total length 15 in.)

chin·chil·la (chin·chil′ə), *n.* **1.** a South American rodent that looks somewhat like a squirrel. **2.** its very valuable soft, whitish-gray fur. **3.** a thick woolen fabric woven in small,

closely set tufts, used for overcoats. [< Sp., dim. of *chinche* CHINCH BUG]

chine (chīn), *n.* **1.** backbone; spine. **2.** piece of an animal's backbone with the meat on it, for cooking. [< OF *eschine* < Gmc.]

Chi·nese (chī·nēz′; –nēs′), *n., pl.* –nese, *adj.* —*n.* **1.** native or inhabitant of China. **2.** person of Chinese descent. **3.** language of China. —*adj.* of China, its people, or their language. ➤ **Chinese** is preferred by natives of China (and others) to *Chinaman, Chinamen,* because of the belittling connotations of those words. Say *a Chinese, the Chinese.*

chink¹ (chingk), *n.* narrow opening; crack. —*v.* **1.** fill up the chinks in. **2.** make chinks in.

chink² (chingk), *n.* a short, sharp, ringing sound like coins or glasses hitting together. —*v.* **1.** make such a sound. **2.** cause to make such a sound. [imit.]

chin·ka·pin (ching′kə·pin), *n.* chinquapin.

Chi·nook (chi·nûk′; –nûk′), *n., pl.* –nook, –nooks. *Am.* **1.** member of a group of American Indian tribes living along the Columbia River in NW United States. **2.** dialect of Indian, French, and English. **3. chinook, a.** *Am.* a warm, moist wind blowing from the sea to land in winter and spring in NW United States. **b.** *U.S.* a warm, dry wind that comes down from the Rocky Mountains.

chin·qua·pin (ching′kə·pin), *Am.* **1.** a dwarf chestnut tree, whose nuts are good to eat. **2.** an evergreen tree of California and Oregon that has a similar nut. **3.** nut of either tree. Also, **chincapin, chinkapin.** [< Am.Ind. (Algonquian)]

chintz (chints), *n.* a cotton cloth printed in patterns of various colors and often glazed. [orig. pl., < Hind. *chint* < Skt. *citra* variegated]

chip (chip), *n., v.,* **chipped, chip·ping.** —*n.* **1.** a small, thin piece cut or broken off. **2.** place where a small, thin piece has been cut or broken off. **3.** a small, thin piece of food or candy, as potato chips. **4.** a round, flat piece used for counting in games. **5.** strip of wood, palm leaf, or straw used in making baskets or hats. **6.** piece of dried dung. **7. chip on one's shoulder,** *Am., Colloq.* readiness to quarrel or fight. **8. dry as a chip,** very dry. —*v.* **1.** cut or break off in small, thin pieces. **2.** shape by cutting at the surface or edge with an ax or chisel. **3. chip in,** *Colloq.* **a.** *Am.* give (money or help). **b.** put in (a remark) when others are talking. [OE (*for*) *cippian*]

chip·munk (chip′mungk), *n. Am.* a small, striped American squirrel. [< Ojibwa *achitamo* squirrel]

chip·per (chip′ər), *adj. U.S. Colloq.* lively; cheerful.

Chip·pe·wa (chip′ə·wä; –wã; –wə), *n., pl.* –wa, –was, *adj. Am.* Ojibwa.

chipping sparrow, a small sparrow of E and C North America.

chirk (chérk), *U.S. Colloq.* —*adj.* cheerful. —*v.* be or become cheerful. [OE *circian* roar]

chi·rog·ra·phy (kī·rog′rə·fi), *n.* handwriting. [< Gk. *cheir* hand + E –*graphy* writing < Gk. *graphein* write] —chi·rog′ra·pher, *n.* —chi·ro·graph·ic (kī′rə·graf′ik), chi′ro·graph′i·cal, *adj.*

chi·rop·o·dist (kə·rop′ə·dist; kī–), *n.* person who removes corns and treats other troubles of the feet.

chi·rop·o·dy (kə·rop′ə·di; kī–), *n.* work of a chiropodist. [< Gk. *cheir* hand + *pous* foot; orig. treatment of hands and feet]

chi·ro·prac·tic (kī′rə·prak′tik), *n.* **1.** *Am.* treatment of diseases by manipulating the spine. **2.** chiropractor. —*adj. Am.* having to do with the treatment of diseases by manipulating the spine. [< Gk. *cheir* hand + *praktikos* practical]

chi·ro·prac·tor (kī′rə·prak′tər), *n. Am.* person who treats diseases by manipulating the spine.

chirp (chérp), *v.* **1.** make a short, sharp sound such as some small birds and insects make. **2.** utter with a chirp. —*n.* such a sound. [? var. of *chirk*] —chirp′er, *n.*

chirr (chér), *v.* make a shrill, trilling sound. —*n.* such a sound. Also, **churr.** [imit.]

chir·rup (chir′əp; cher′-), v., **-ruped, -rup-ing.** chirp; chirp again and again. [< chirp]

chis·el (chiz′əl), n., v., **-eled, -el·ing;** esp. Brit. **-elled, -el·ling.** —n. a cutting tool with a sharp edge at the end of a strong blade, used to cut or shape wood, stone, or metal. —v. 1. cut or shape with a chisel. 2. U.S. Slang. use unfair practices; swindle. [< OF, ult. < L caesus < caedere cut]

chis·el·er, esp. Brit. **chis·el·ler** (chiz′əl·ər), n. 1. one that chisels. 2. Slang. a cheat.

chit[1] (chit), n. 1. child. 2. a saucy, forward girl. [akin to KITTEN. Cf. dial. chit puss.]

chit[2] (chit), n. voucher of a debt, as for food. [< Hind. chitthi]

chit-chat (chit′chat′), n. 1. friendly, informal talk; chat. 2. gossip. [< chat]

chi·tin (kī′tin), n. a horny substance forming the hard outer covering of beetles, lobsters, crabs, etc. [< F < Gk. chiton tunic]

chit·ter·ling (chit′ər·ling), n. Usually, chit-terlings. part of the small intestine of pigs, cooked as food.

chiv·al·ric (shiv′əl·rik; shi·val′rik), adj. 1. having to do with chivalry. 2. chivalrous.

chiv·al·rous (shiv′əl·rəs), adj. 1. having the qualities of an ideal knight. 2. having to do with chivalry. —**chiv′al·rous·ly,** adv. —**chiv′al·rous·ness,** n. —Syn. 1. gallant, courteous, considerate.

chiv·al·ry (shiv′əl·ri), n. 1. qualities of an ideal knight, including bravery, honor, courtesy, respect for women, protection of the weak, generosity, and fairness to enemies. 2. rules and customs of knights in the Middle Ages; system of knighthood. 3. knights as a group. 4. gallant warriors or gentlemen. [< OF. See CHEVALIER.]

chive (chīv), or **chive garlic,** n. plant of the same family as the onion, with long, slender leaves used as seasoning. [< L caepa onion]

chiv·vy, chiv·y (chiv′i), n., pl. **chiv·vies;** v., **chiv·vied, chiv·vy·ing; chiv·ied, chiv·y·ing.** Brit. chevy.

chlo·ral (klô′rəl; klō′-), n. Chem. 1. a colorless liquid, CCl₃CHO, made from chlorine and alcohol. 2. chloral hydrate.

chloral hydrate, Chem. a white, crystalline drug, CCl₃CH (OH)₂, that causes sleep.

chlo·rate (klô′rāt; -rit; klō′-), n. Chem. salt of chloric acid.

chlo·ric (klô′rik; klō′-), adj. Chem. of or containing chlorine.

chloric acid, Chem. acid, HClO₃, existing only as salts and in solution.

chlo·ride (klô′rīd; -rid; klō′-), **chlo·rid** (-rid), n. compound of chlorine with another element or radical; salt of hydrochloric acid.

chlo·rin·ate (klô′rə·nāt; klō′-), v., **-at·ed, -at·ing.** 1. combine or treat with chlorine. 2. disinfect with chlorine. —**chlo′rin·a′tion,** n.

chlo·rine (klô′rēn; -rin; klō′-), **chlo·rin** (-rin), n. Chem. a poisonous, greenish-yellow, gaseous chemical element, Cl, used in bleaching and disinfecting. It is very irritating to the nose, throat, and lungs. [< Gk. chloros green]

chlo·ro·form (klô′rə·fôrm; klō′-), n. Chem. CHCl₃, a colorless liquid with a sweetish smell, used as an anesthetic and to dissolve rubber, resin, wax, and many other substances. —v. 1. make unable to feel pain by giving chloroform. 2. kill with chloroform.

chlo·ro·my·ce·tin (klô′rə·mī′sə·tin; klō′-), n. an antibiotic drug, used chiefly against typhoid fever and certain types of pneumonia. [< chloro- green (< Gk. chloros) + Gk. mykes, -etos fungus]

chlo·ro·phyll, chlo·ro·phyl (klô′rə·fil; klō′-), n. the green coloring matter of plants. In the presence of light it makes carbohydrates, such as starch, from carbon dioxide and water. [< Gk. chloros green + E -phyll leaf < Gk. phyllon]

chm., 1. Also, **chmn.** chairman. 2. checkmate.

chock (chok), n. 1. block; wedge. 2. Naut. a. block with two arms curving inward for a rope to pass through. b. one of the pieces of wood on

which a boat rests. —v. 1. provide or fasten with chocks. 2. Naut. put (a boat) on chocks. —adv. as close or as tight as can be; quite. [appar. < OF choque log]

chock-full (chok′fŭl′), adj. as full as can be. Also, **chuck-full, choke-full.**

choc·o·late (chôk′lit; chok′-; chôk′ə·lit; chok′ə-), n. 1. preparation made by roasting and grinding cacao seeds. 2. drink made of chocolate with hot milk or water and sugar. 3. candy made of chocolate. 4. dark brown. —adj. 1. made of chocolate. 2. dark-brown. [< Sp. < Mex. chocolatl]

Choc·taw (chok′tô), n., pl. **-taw, -taws,** adj. —n. Am. member of a tribe of American Indians, now living mostly in Oklahoma. —adj. of this tribe.

choice (chois), n., adj., **choic·er, choic·est.** —n. 1. act of choosing: make your choice. 2. care in selecting: her library showed choice and good taste. 3. preference: his choice was to stay at home. 4. person or thing chosen. 5. power or chance to choose. 6. quantity and variety to choose from. 7. the best part. —adj. carefully chosen; of fine quality; excellent; superior. [< OF chois < Gmc.] —**choice′ly,** adv. —**choice′ness,** n. —Syn. n. 1. selection. 5. alternative, option. —adj. select, exquisite, fine, elegant.

choir (kwīr), n. 1. group of singers used in a church service. 2. part of a church set apart for such a group. 3. any group of singers. —v. sing all together at the same time. [< OF < L chorus CHORUS]

choke (chōk), v., **choked, chok·ing,** n. —v. 1. keep from breathing by squeezing or blocking up the throat. 2. be unable to breathe. 3. check or extinguish by cutting off the supply of air. 4. control; hold; suppress. 5. block; fill; clog. 6. choke off, put an end to; get rid of; stop. —n. 1. act or sound of choking. 2. valve that cuts off the supply of air in a gasoline engine. [var. of OE āceōcian] —Syn. v. 1, 2. suffocate, stifle.

choke-damp (chōk′damp′), n. a heavy, suffocating gas, mainly carbon dioxide, that gathers in mines, old wells, etc.

choke-full (chōk′fŭl′), adj. chock-full.

chok·er (chōk′ər), n. 1. one that chokes. 2. Colloq. a. a high collar. b. a tight necklace.

chol·er (kol′ər), n. irritable disposition; anger. [< L < Gk. cholera cholera, appar. < chole bile]

chol·er·a (kol′ər·ə), n. an acute disease of the stomach and intestines, characterized by vomiting, cramps, and diarrhea. Summer cholera is not infectious. Asiatic cholera is infectious and often causes death. [< L < Gk. See CHOLER.]

chol·er·ic (kol′ər·ik), adj. easily made angry.

cho·les·ter·ol (kə·les′tər·ōl; -ol), n. Biochem. a white, crystalline substance, C₂₇H₄₅OH, a constituent of all animal fats, bile, gallstones, egg yolk, etc. It is important in metabolism.

choose (chüz), v., **chose, cho·sen** or (Obs.) **chose, choos·ing.** 1. make a choice: you must choose. 2. pick out; select from a number: he chose a book from the library. 3. prefer and decide; think fit: he did not choose to go. 4. cannot choose but, cannot do otherwise than. [OE cēosan] —**choos′er,** n. —Syn. 2. elect, prefer.

chop[1] (chop), v., **chopped, chop·ping,** n. —v. 1. cut by hitting with something sharp. 2. cut into small pieces. 3. make quick, sharp movements; jerk. 4. make by cutting. —n. 1. a cutting stroke. 2. slice of lamb, pork, veal, etc. There are rib, loin, and shoulder chops. 3. a short, irregular, broken motion of waves. [ME choppe(n)] —**chop′per,** n. —Syn. v. 1. hew, hack. 2. mince.

chop[2] (chop), n. 1. Usually, chops. jaw. 2. cheek. Also, **chap.** [< chop[1]]

chop[3] (chop), v., **chopped, chop·ping.** change suddenly; shift quickly. [? akin to cheap change. See CHEAP.]

chop·fall·en (chop′fôl′ən), adj. chapfallen.

chop·house (chop′hous′), n. restaurant that makes a specialty of serving chops, steaks, etc.

Cho·pin (shō′pan), n. Frédéric François, 1809-1849, Polish pianist and composer in France.

chop·py (chop′i), adj., **-pi·er, -pi·est.** 1. making

quick, sharp movements; jerky. 2. moving in short, irregular, broken waves. [< *chop*[1]]

chop·stick (chop'stik'), *n.* one of the small sticks used to raise food to the mouth by the Chinese. [< Chinese Pidgin English *chop* quick + E *stick*[1]]

chop su·ey or **soo·y** (chop' sü'i), *Am.* fried or stewed meat and vegetables cut up and cooked together in a sauce. [alter. of Chinese word meaning "mixed pieces"]

cho·ral (adj. kô'rəl, kō'-; *n.* kô·ral', -räl', kō-, kô'rəl, kō'-), *adj.* 1. of a choir or chorus. 2. sung by a choir or chorus. —*n.* Also, **chorale. a.** a hymn tune. **b.** a simple hymn tune sung by the choir and congregation together. —**cho'ral·ly,** *adv.*

chord[1] (kôrd), *n.* combination of three or more musical notes sounded together in harmony. [var. of *cord*, var. of *accord*, *n.*]

chord[2] (kôrd), *n.* 1. a straight line connecting two points on a circumference. 2. *Anat.* cord (def. 4). 3. string of a harp or other musical instrument. 4. a feeling; emotion: *touch a sympathetic chord.* [< L < Gk. *chorde* gut, string of a musical instrument. Doublet of CORD.] —**chord'al,** *adj.*

AB and AC are chords.

chore (chôr; chōr), *n. U.S.* 1. an odd job; small task. 2. a difficult or disagreeable thing to do. [OE *cyrr*, var. of *cierr, cerr* turn, business]

cho·re·a (kô·rē'ə; kō-), *n.* a nervous disease characterized by involuntary twitching of the muscles; St. Vitus's dance. [< NL < Gk. *choreia* dance]

cho·re·og·ra·phy (kô'ri·og'rə·fi; kō'-), *esp. Brit.* **cho·reg·ra·phy** (kə·reg'rə·fi), *n.* 1. art of planning the dances in a ballet. 2. dancing; ballet dancing. [< Gk. *choreia* dance + E *-graphy* writing < Gk. *graphein* write] —**cho·re·og·raph·ic** (kô'ri·ə·graf'ik; kō-), *adj.* —**cho're·og'ra·pher,** *n.*

cho·ric (kô'rik), *adj.* of or for a chorus.

chor·is·ter (kôr'is·tər; kor'-), *n.* 1. singer in a choir. 2. boy who sings in a choir. 3. *Am.* leader of a choir. [< Med.L *chorista* chorister < L *chorus* CHORUS]

chor·tle (chôr'təl), *v.*, **-tled, -tling,** *n.* —*v.* chuckle or snort with glee. —*n.* a gleeful chuckle or snort. [blend of *chuckle* and *snort*; coined by Lewis Carroll] —**chor'tler,** *n.*

cho·rus (kô'rəs; kō'-), *n., pl.* **-rus·es,** *v.,* **-rused, -rus·ing.** —*n.* 1. group of singers who sing together, such as a choir. 2. song sung by many singers together. 3. a musical composition to be sung by all singers together. 4. the repeated part of a song coming after each stanza. 5. a saying by many at the same time: *a chorus of noes.* 6. group of singers and dancers. 7. in chorus, all together at the same time. —*v.* sing or speak all at the same time. [< L < Gk. *choros* dance, band of dancers]

chose (chōz), *v.* pt. of choose.

cho·sen (chō'zən), *v.* pp. of choose. —*adj.* picked out; selected from a group.

Cho·sen (chō'sen'), *n.* Japanese name of Korea.

Chou En-lai (chou' en'lī'), born 1898, premier of the Chinese Communist government since 1949.

chow (chou), *n.* 1. a medium-sized Chinese breed of dog with short, compact body, large head, and thick coat of one color, usually brown or black. 2. *Am., Slang.* food. [short for Chinese Pidgin English *chow-chow*]

Chow

chow·der (chou'dər), *n. Am.* a thick soup or stew usually made of clams or fish with potatoes, onions, etc. [appar. < F *chaudière* pot, ult. < L *calidus* hot]

chow mein (chou' mān'), *Am.* fried noodles served with a thickened stew of onions, celery, meat, etc. [< Chinese, fried flour]

chres·tom·a·thy (kres·tom'ə·thi), *n., pl.* **-thies.** collection of passages from literature or a foreign language. [< Gk., < *chrestos* useful + *-matheia* learning]

chrism (kriz'əm), *n.* consecrated oil, used by some churches in baptism and other sacred rites. [< L < Gk. *chrisma* < *chriein* anoint]

Christ (krīst), *n.* Jesus, the founder of the Christian religion. [< L < Gk. *christos* anointed]

chris·ten (kris'ən), *v.* 1. admit to a Christian church by baptism; baptize. 2. give a first name to at baptism. 3. give a name to. 4. *Colloq.* make the first use of. [OE *christnian* make Christian < *cristen* Christian < L *christianus*]

Chris·ten·dom (kris'ən·dəm), *n.* 1. the Christian part of the world. 2. all Christians.

chris·ten·ing (kris'ən·ing; kris'ning), *n.* act or ceremony of baptizing and naming; baptism.

Chris·tian (kris'chən), *adj.* 1. of Christ or His teachings. 2. believing in Christ; belonging to the religion founded by Him. 3. of Christians or Christianity. 4. showing a gentle, humble, helpful spirit: *Christian charity.* 5. human; not animal. 6. *Colloq.* decent; respectable. —*n.* 1. believer in Christ; follower of His example or teachings; member of the religion founded by Him. 2. *Colloq.* a decent person. —**Chris'tian·ly,** *adj., adv.*

Christian Era, time since the birth of Christ.

Chris·ti·a·ni·a (kris'chi·an'i·ə; kris'ti·ä'-ni·ə), *n.* former name of Oslo.

Chris·ti·an·i·ty (kris'chi·an'ə·ti), *n., pl.* **-ties.** 1. religion taught by Christ and His followers; Christian religion. 2. Christian beliefs or faith; Christian spirit or character. 3. a particular Christian religious system.

Chris·tian·ize (kris'chən·īz), *v.*, **-ized, -iz·ing.** make Christian; convert to Christianity. —**Chris'tian·i·za'tion,** *n.* —**Chris'tian·iz'er,** *n.*

Christian name, first name; given name.

Christian Science, *Am.* religion and system of healing founded by Mary Baker Eddy in 1866. —**Christian Scientist,** *Am.*

Christ·like (krīst'līk'), *adj.* like Christ; like that of Christ; showing the spirit of Christ. —**Christ'like'ness,** *n.*

Christ·ly (krīst'li), *adj.* of Christ; Christlike. —**Christ'li·ness,** *n.*

Christ·mas (kris'məs), *n.* the yearly celebration of the birth of Christ; December 25. [OE *Christes mæsse* Christ's MASS] —**Christ'mas·y, Christ'mas·sy,** *adj.*

Christmas Eve, the evening before Christmas.

Christ·mas·tide (kris'məs·tīd'), *n.* Christmas time.

chro·mate (krō'māt), *n. Chem.* salt of chromic acid.

chro·mat·ic (krō·mat'ik), *adj.* 1. of color or colors. 2. *Music.* progressing by half tones instead of by the regular intervals of the scale. [< L < Gk., < *chroma* color (in musical sense)] —**chro·mat'i·cal·ly,** *adv.*

chro·mat·ics (krō·mat'iks), **chro·ma·tol·o·gy** (krō'mə·tol'ə·ji), *n.* branch of science that deals with colors. —**chro·ma·tist** (krō'mə·tist), *n.*

chromatic scale, *Music.* scale divided equally into twelve half tones.

chro·ma·tin (krō'mə·tin), *n. Biol.* that part of the nucleus of an animal or plant cell which absorbs stains readily and comprises the chromosomes.

chrome (krōm), *n.* chromium, esp. as the source of various pigments (chrome green, chrome red, chrome yellow, etc.). [< F < Gk. *chroma* color]

chrome steel, chromium steel, a very hard, strong steel containing chromium.

chro·mic (krō'mik), *adj. Chem.* of or containing chromium.

chromic acid, acid, H_2CrO_4, existing only as salts and in solution.

chro·mi·um (krō'mi·əm), *n. Chem.* a shiny, hard, brittle metallic element, Cr, that does not rust or become dull easily when exposed to air. [< Gk. *chroma* color]

chro·mo·lith·o·graph (krō'mō·lith'ə·graf; -gräf), *n.* a colored picture printed from a series of stones or plates. —**chro·mo·li·thog·ra·pher** (krō'mō·li·thog'rə·fər), *n.* —**chro'mo·lith'o·graph'ic,** *adj.*

chro·mo·some (krō'mə·sōm), *n. Biol.* any of the microscopic filaments composed of chromatin that appear in an animal or plant cell during mitosis or division. Chromosomes are derived from the parents and carry the genes that determine heredity. [< Gk. *chroma* color + E -*some* body < Gk. *soma*]

chro·mo·sphere (krō'mə·sfir), *n.* a scarlet layer of gas around the sun.

Chron., *Bible.* Chronicles.

chron·ic (kron'ik), **chron·i·cal** (-ə·kəl), *adj.* 1. continuing a long time. 2. constant. 3. having had a disease, habit, etc., for a long time: *a chronic liar.* [< L < Gk., < *chronos* time] —**chron'i·cal·ly,** *adv.* —**Syn.** 3. habitual, veterate, confirmed, hardened.

chron·i·cle (kron'ə·kəl), *n., v.,* -**cled,** -**cling.** —*n.* record of happenings in the order in which they happened. —*v.* record in a chronicle; write the history of; tell the story of. [< AF < L < Gk. *chronika* annals. See CHRONIC.] —**chron'i·cler,** *n.* —Syn. *n.* history, annals.

Chron·i·cles (kron'ə·kəlz), *n.pl.* two books of the Old Testament, called I and II Chronicles.

chron·o·log·i·cal (kron'ə·loj'ə·kəl), **chron·o·log·ic** (-loj'ik), *adj.* arranged in the order in which the events happened. —**chron'o·log'i·cal·ly,** *adv.*

chro·nol·o·gy (krə·nol'ə·ji), *n., pl.* -**gies.** 1. arrangement of time in periods; giving the exact dates of events arranged in the order in which they happened. 2. table or list that gives the exact dates of events arranged in the order in which they happened. —**chro·nol'o·gist,** **chro·nol'o·ger,** *n.*

chro·nom·e·ter (krə·nom'ə·tər), *n.* clock or watch that keeps very accurate time. —**chron·o·met·ric** (kron'ə·met'rik), **chron'o·met'ri·cal,** *adj.* —**chron'o·met'ri·cal·ly,** *adv.*

chrys·a·lid (kris'ə·lid), *n.* chrysalis. —*adj.* of a chrysalis.

chrys·a·lis (kris'ə·lis), *n., pl.* **chrys·a·lis·es,** **chry·sal·i·des** (kri·sal'ə·dēz). 1. form of an insect when it is in a case; pupa. 2. the case; cocoon. 3. stage of development or change. [< L < Gk. *chrysallis* golden sheath < *chrysos* gold]

chry·san·the·mum (kri·san'thə·məm), *n.* 1. any of several cultivated plants of the aster family, which have showy, ball-shaped flowers in the autumn. 2. one of these flowers. [< L < Gk., < *chrysos* gold + *anthemon* flower]

chrys·o·lite (kris'ə·līt), *n.* a green or yellow semiprecious stone. [< L < Gk., < *chrysos* gold + *lithos* stone]

chub (chub), *n., pl.* **chubs** or (*esp. collectively*) **chub.** 1. a thick fresh-water fish, related to the carp. 2. *Am., Local.* any of various American fishes, such as the tautog, black bass, etc. [ME *chubbe*]

chub·by (chub'i), *adj.,* -**bi·er,** -**bi·est.** round and plump. —**chub'bi·ness,** *n.*

chuck¹ (chuk), *n., v.* 1. pat; tap. 2. throw; toss. [prob. imit.]

chuck² (chuk), *n.* 1. clamp. A chuck holds a tool or piece of work in a lathe. 2. cut of beef between the neck and the shoulder. [var. of *chock*]

chuck-full (chuk'fúl'), *adj.* chock-full.

chuck·le (chuk'əl), *v.,* -**led,** -**ling,** *n.* —*v.* 1. laugh to oneself. 2. cluck. —*n.* 1. a soft, quiet laugh. 2. cluck. [< *chuck* cluck, laugh; imit.] —**chuck'ler,** *n.*

chuck wagon, *Am., W.* wagon carrying provisions and cooking equipment for cowboys.

chug (chug), *n., v.,* **chugged, chug·ging.** —*n. Am.* a short, loud, explosive sound: *the chug of an engine's exhaust.* —*v.* 1. make such sounds. 2. *Am., Colloq.* move with such sounds. [imit.]

chuk·ker, chuk·kar (chuk'ər), *n.* one of the periods of play in polo. [< Hind. *chakar*]

chum (chum), *n., v.,* **chummed, chum·ming.** *Colloq.* —*n.* 1. a very close friend. 2. roommate. —*v.* 1. be very close friends. 2. room together. [? abbr. of *chambermate*]

chum·my (chum'i), *adj.,* -**mi·er,** -**mi·est.** *Colloq.* like a chum; very friendly. —**chum'mi·ly,** *adv.*

chump (chump), *n.* 1. *Colloq.* a foolish or stupid person; blockhead. 2. a short, thick block of wood. 3. a thick, blunt end. 4. *Slang.* the head.

Chung·king (chŭng'king'), *n.* city in C China, on the Yangtze River.

chunk (chungk), *n. Colloq.* 1. a thick piece or lump. 2. a stocky person, etc. [var. of *chuck²*]

chunk·y (chungk'i), *adj.,* **chunk·i·er, chunk·i·est.** *Colloq.* 1. like a chunk; short and thick. 2. stocky. —**chunk'i·ly,** *adv.* —**chunk'i·ness,** *n.*

church (chérch), *n.* 1. a building for public Christian worship or religious services. 2. public Christian worship or religious service in a church. 3. all Christians. 4. group of Christians with the same beliefs and under the same authority: *the Methodist Church.* 5. organization of a church; ecclesiastical authority or power. 6. profession of a clergyman. 7. any building, group, or congregation like a church. —*adj.* of a church. [< Gk. *kyriakon* (*doma*) (house) of the Lord < *kyrios* lord < *kyros* power] —**church'less,** *adj.* —**church'like',** *adj.* —Syn. *n.* 1. cathedral, temple, chapel. 4. denomination, sect.

church·go·er (chérch'gō'ər), *n.* person who goes to church regularly. —**church'go'ing,** *n.*

Church·ill (chérch'il; -əl), *n.* Sir Winston, born 1874, English statesman and writer, prime minister of England 1940–45 and 1951–55.

church·ly (chérch'li), *adj.* 1. of a church. 2. suitable for a church. —**church'li·ness,** *n.*

church·man (chérch'mən), *n., pl.* -**men.** 1. clergyman. 2. member of a church. —**church'man·ly,** *adv.* —**church'man·ship,** *n.*

Church of England, the Christian church in England that is recognized as a national institution by the government. Its head is the king.

Church of Jesus Christ of Latter-day Saints, official name of the Mormon Church.

church·ward·en (chérch'wôr'dən), *n.* 1. a lay official in the Church of England or the Episcopal Church who manages the business, property, and money of a church. 2. *Colloq.* a clay tobacco pipe with a very long stem.

church·yard (chérch'yärd'), *n.* ground around a church, sometimes used as a burial ground.

churl (chérl), *n.* 1. a rude, surly person. 2. person of low birth; peasant. [OE *ceorl* freeman (of low rank)]

churl·ish (chér'lish), *adj.* rude; surly. —**churl'ish·ly,** *adv.* —**churl'ish·ness,** *n.*

churn (chérn), *n.* 1. container or machine in which cream or milk is made into butter by beating and shaking. 2. act or fact of stirring violently. —*v.* 1. stir or shake (cream or milk) in a churn. 2. make (butter) by using a churn. 3. stir violently; make or become foamy. 4. move as if beaten and shaken. [OE *cyrn*] —**churn'er,** *n.*

churr (chér), *v., n.* chirr.

chute (shüt), *n.* 1. *Am.* an inclined trough, tube, etc., for sliding or dropping things down to a lower level. 2. *Am.* rapids in a river. 3. a steep slope. 4. *Colloq.* parachute. [appar. blend of F *chute* fall (of water) and E *shoot*]

chut·ney, chut·nee (chut'ni), *n., pl.* -**neys;** -**nees.** a spicy sauce or relish made of fruits, herbs, pepper, etc. [< Hind. *chatni*]

chyle (kīl), *n.* a milky liquid composed of digested fat and lymph, formed from the chyme in the small intestine and carried from there into the veins. [< Med.L < Gk. *chylos* < *cheein* pour]

chyme (kīm), *n.* a pulpy, semiliquid mass into which food is changed by the action of the stomach. [< Med.L < Gk. *chymos* < *cheein* pour]

CIA, C.I.A., Central Intelligence Agency.

ci·bo·ri·um (si·bô'ri·əm; -bō'-), *n., pl.* -**bo-**

ri·a (-bōʹri·ə; -bōʹ-). 1. vessel used to hold the consecrated bread of the Eucharist. 2. a dome-shaped canopy over an altar. [< Med.L, < L, drinking cup, < Gk. *kiborion* cuplike seed vessel]

C.I.C., Counter Intelligence Corps.

ci·ca·da (si·kāʹdə; -kāʹ-), *n., pl.* **-das, -dae** (-dē). a large insect with transparent wings. The male makes a shrill sound in hot, dry weather. [< L]

Cicada
(ab. ½ actual size)

cic·a·trix (sikʹə·triks; si·kāʹ-), **cic·a·trice** (sikʹə·tris), *n., pl.* **cic·a·tri·ces** (sikʹə·trīʹsēz). 1. scar left by a healed wound. 2. *Bot.* scar left on a tree or plant by a fallen leaf, seed, etc. [< L]

cic·a·trize (sikʹə·trīz), *v.,* **-trized, -triz·ing.** heal by forming a scar.

Cic·e·ro (sisʹə·rō), *n.* Marcus Tullius, 106–43 B.C., Roman orator, writer, and statesman. —**Cic·e·ro·ni·an** (sisʹə·rōʹni·ən), *adj.*

cic·e·ro·ne (sisʹə·rōʹne; chichʹə-), *n., pl.* **-ni** (-nē), **-nes** (-nēz). person who acts as a guide for sightseers. [< Ital. < L *Cicero* Cicero]

ci·der (sīʹdər), *n.* 1. juice pressed out of apples, used as a drink and in making vinegar. 2. juice pressed from other fruits. [< OF < LL < Gk. < Heb. *shēkār* liquor]

ci·gar (si·gärʹ), *n.* a tight roll of tobacco leaves for smoking. [< Sp. *cigarro*]

cig·a·rette, cig·a·ret (sigʹə·retʹ; sigʹə·ret), *n. Am.* a small roll of finely cut tobacco enclosed in a thin sheet of paper for smoking. [< F, dim. of *cigare* CIGAR]

cil·i·a (silʹi·ə), *n.pl., sing.* **cil·i·um** (silʹi·əm). 1. eyelashes. 2. *Zool.* very small hairlike projections. Some microscopic animals use cilia to move themselves or to set up currents in the surrounding water. [< L]

cil·i·ar·y (silʹi·erʹi), *adj.* of or resembling cilia.

Cim·me·ri·an (si·mirʹi·ən), *n.* one of a mythical people said to live in perpetual mists and darkness. —*adj.* very dark and gloomy.

cinch (sinch), *Am.* —*n.* 1. a strong girth for fastening a saddle or pack on a horse. 2. *Colloq.* a firm hold or grip. 3. *Slang.* something sure and easy. —*v.* 1. fasten on with a cinch; bind firmly. 2. *Slang.* get a firm hold or grip on. [< Sp. < L *cincta* girdle < *cingere* bind]

cin·cho·na (sin·kōʹnə), *n.* 1. a small tree that grows in South America, the East Indies, India, and Java. 2. its bitter bark, from which quinine is obtained; Peruvian bark. [< NL; named for Countess *Chinchón,* wife of a Spanish viceroy of Peru] —**cin·chon·ic** (sin·konʹik), *adj.*

Cin·cin·nat·i (sinʹsə·natʹi; -natʹə), *n.* city in SW Ohio, on the Ohio River.

cinc·ture (singkʹchər), *n.* 1. belt; girdle. 2. border; enclosure. [< L *cinctura* < *cingere* bind, gird]

cin·der (sinʹdər), *n.* 1. cinders, wood or coal partly burned and no longer flaming. 2. piece of burned-up wood or coal. [OE *sinder*]

Cin·der·el·la (sinʹdər·elʹə), *n.* 1. heroine of a famous fairy tale. 2. person whose real worth or beauty is not recognized.

cin·e·ma (sinʹə·mə), *n.* 1. a motion picture. 2. a motion-picture theater. 3. the cinema, motion pictures. [short for *cinematograph*] —**cin·e·mat·ic** (sinʹə·matʹik), *adj.* —**cin·e·mat·i·cal·ly,** *adv.*

Cin·e·ma·Scope (sinʹə·mə·skōp), *n. Trademark.* a motion-picture medium in which the use of a special lens on both a standard camera and projector gives the images greater depth when projected on a curved screen about 2½ times larger than an ordinary screen. [< *cinema* + -*scope* < NL, < Gk. -*skopion* instrument for observing < Gk. *skopeein* look at]

cin·e·mat·o·graph (sinʹə·matʹə·graf; -gräf), *n.* 1. *Brit.* machine for projecting moving pictures on a screen. 2. camera for taking moving pictures. Also, **kinematograph.** [< Gk. *kinema* motion + -GRAPH] —**cin·e·ma·tog·ra·phy,** *n.*

Cin·er·a·ma (sinʹər·ämʹə), *n. Trademark.* a motion-picture medium that uses a camera with three lenses and a large curved screen to produce the illusion of three dimensions and a system whereby sound is reproduced from the direction of its original source. [< *cine(ma)* + (*pano*)*rama*]

cin·e·rar·i·um (sinʹə·rārʹi·əm), *n., pl.* **-rar·i·a** (-rārʹi·ə). place for keeping the ashes of cremated bodies. [< L]

cin·na·bar (sinʹə·bär), *n.* 1. a reddish mineral that is the chief source of mercury; native mercuric sulfide. 2. artificial mercuric sulfide, used as a red pigment in making paints, dyes, etc. 3. bright red; vermilion. [< L < Gk. *kinnabari;* of Oriental orig.]

cin·na·mon (sinʹə·mən), *n.* 1. spice made from the dried, reddish-brown inner bark of a laurel tree or shrub of the East Indies. 2. this bark. 3. tree or shrub yielding this bark. 4. a light, reddish brown. —*adj.* 1. flavored with cinnamon. 2. light reddish-brown. [< F < LL < Gk. *kinnamon;* of Semitic orig.]

cinque·foil (singkʹfoilʹ), *n.* 1. plant having small, yellow flowers and leaves divided into five parts. 2. ornament in architecture, made of five connected semicircles or part circles. [< OF < L, < *quinque* five + *folium* leaf]

Cinquefoil

CIO, C.I.O., *Am.* Congress of Industrial Organizations.

ci·on (sīʹən), *n.* scion (def. 2).

Ci·pan·go (si·pangʹgō), *n. Poetic.* Japan.

ci·pher (sīʹfər), *n.* 1. zero; 0. 2. person or thing of no importance. 3. any Arabic numeral. 4. method of secret writing which transposes the letters of a message according to a set pattern, or replaces the proper letters with substitutes called for in the system used, or combines both methods. 5. something in secret writing. 6. key to a method of secret writing. 7. monogram. —*v.* 1. do arithmetic. 2. work by arithmetic. Also, **cypher.** [< Med.L < Ar. *ṣifr* empty. Doublet of ZERO.]

cir·ca (sėrʹkə), *adv., prep.* about: *Mohammed was born circa 570 A.D.* [< L]

Cir·cas·sia (sėr·kashʹə), *n.* region in S Russia, on the NE shore of the Black Sea. —**Cir·cas·sian,** *adj., n.*

Cir·ce (sėrʹsē), *n. Gk. Legend.* an enchantress who changed men into swine. —**Cir·ce·an** (sėr·sēʹən), *adj.*

cir·cle (sėrʹkəl), *n., v.,* **-cled, -cling.** —*n.* 1. line every point of which is equally distant from a point within called the center. 2. a plane figure bounded by such a line. 3. circlet, halo, crown, or anything shaped like a circle or part of one. 4. a ring. 5. set of seats in the balcony of a theater. 6. a complete series or course; period; cycle. 7. orbit of a heavenly body. 8. period of revolution of a heavenly body. 9. group of people held together by the same interests: *the family circle.* 10. sphere of influence, action, etc. —*v.* 1. go around in a circle; revolve around. 2. form a circle around; surround; encircle. [< F < L *circulus,* dim. of *circus* ring] —**cirʹcler,** *n.*

Circle

cir·clet (sėrʹklit), *n.* 1. a small circle. 2. a round ornament worn on the head, neck, arm, or finger.

cir·cuit (sėrʹkit), *n.* 1. a going around; a trip around. 2. way over which a person or group makes repeated journeys at certain times. Some judges make a circuit. 3. part of the country through which such circuits are made. 4. district under the jurisdiction of a circuit court. 5. distance around any space. 6. line enclosing any space. 7. space enclosed. 8. path over which an electric current flows. —*v.* make a circuit of; go in a circuit. [< L *circuitus* a going round < *circum* around + *ire* go] —Syn. *n.* 2. route, course.

circuit court, court whose judges regularly hold court at certain places in a district.

cir·cu·i·tous (sėr·kūʹi·təs), *adj.* roundabout; not direct. —**cir·cuʹi·tous·ly,** *adv.* —**cir·cuʹi·tous·ness,** *n.* —Syn. indirect, devious.

circuit rider, *Am.* a Methodist minister who rides from place to place over a circuit to preach.

cir·cu·lar (sér′kyə-lər), *adj.* **1.** round like a circle. **2.** moving in a circle; going around a circle. **3.** having to do with a circle. **4.** sent to each of a number of people: *a circular letter.* **5.** roundabout; indirect. —*n.* letter, notice, or advertisement sent to each of a number of people. [< L *circularis.* See CIRCLE.] —**cir·cu·lar·i·ty** (sér′kyə-lar′ə·ti), *n.* —**cir′cu·lar·ly,** *adv.*

cir·cu·lar·ize (sér′kyə·lər·īz), *v.,* –ized, –izing. **1.** send circulars to. **2.** make circular or round. —**cir′cu·lar·i·za′tion,** *n.* —**cir′cu·lar·iz′-er,** *n.*

circular saw, a thin disk with teeth in its edge, turned at high speed by machines.

cir·cu·late (sér′kyə·lāt), *v.,* –lat·ed, –lat·ing. **1.** move in a circle or circuit; go around: *money circulates.* **2.** send around from person to person or place to place. [< L *circulatus.* See CIRCLE.] —**cir′cu·la′tive,** *adj.* —**cir′cu·la′tor,** *n.* —**cir·cu·la·to·ry** (sér′kyə·lə·tô′ri; –tō′–), *adj.*

cir·cu·la·tion (sér′kyə·lā′shən), *n.* **1.** a going around; a circulating. **2.** movement of blood from the heart through the body and back to the heart. **3.** a sending around of books, papers, news, etc., from person to person or place to place. **4.** number of copies of a book, newspaper, magazine, etc., that are sent out during a certain time. **5.** coins, notes, bills, etc., in use as money.

circum–, *prefix.* **1.** round about; on all sides, as in *circumstance.* **2.** in a circle; around, as in *circumnavigate.* [< L]

cir·cum·am·bi·ent (sér′kəm·am′bi·ənt), *adj.* surrounding; encircling. —**cir′cum·am′bi·ence,** **cir′cum·am′bi·en·cy,** *n.*

cir·cum·cise (sér′kəm·sīz), *v.,* –cised, –cis·ing. cut off the foreskin or internal labia of. [< L *circumcisus* < *circum* around + *caedere* cut] —**cir′cum·cis′er,** *n.* —**cir·cum·ci·sion** (sér′kəm·sizh′ən), *n.*

cir·cum·fer·ence (sər·kum′fər·əns), *n.* **1.** the boundary line of a circle or of certain other surfaces. **2.** the distance around. [< L *circumferentia* < *circum* around + *ferre* bear] —**cir·cum·fer·en·tial** (sər·kum′fər·en′shəl), *adj.*

cir·cum·flex (sér′kəm·fleks), *n.* a circumflex accent. —*adj.* **1.** of or having a circumflex accent. **2.** bent, bending, or winding around. [< L *circumflexus* bent around < *circum* around + *flectere* bend] —**cir·cum·flex·ion** (sér′kəm·flek′shən), *n.*

circumflex accent, mark (∧ or ∩) placed over a vowel to tell something about its pronunciation, as in the French words *fête* and *goût.*

cir·cum·flu·ent (sər·kum′flü·ənt), *adj.* flowing around; surrounding. [< L, < *circum* around + *fluere* flow]

cir·cum·fuse (sér′kəm·fūz′), *v.,* –fused, –fus·ing. **1.** pour or spread around. **2.** surround; suffuse. [< L *circumfusus* < *circum* around + *fundere* pour] —**cir′cum·fu′sion,** *n.*

cir·cum·lo·cu·tion (sér′kəm·lō·kū′shən), *n.* a roundabout way of speaking. [< L *circumlocutio* < *circum* around + *loqui* speak] —**cir·cum·loc·u·to·ry** (sér′kəm·lok′yə·tô′ri; –tō′–), *adj.*

cir·cum·nav·i·gate (sér′kəm·nav′ə·gāt), *v.,* –gat·ed, –gat·ing. sail around. —**cir′cum·nav′-i·ga′tion,** *n.* —**cir′cum·nav′i·ga′tor,** *n.*

cir·cum·scribe (sér′kəm·skrīb′), *v.,* –scribed, –scrib·ing. **1.** draw a line around; mark the boundaries of. **2.** surround. **3.** limit; restrict. **4.** *Geom.* **a.** draw (a figure) around another figure so as to touch as many points as possible. **b.** be so drawn around. [< L, < *circum* around + *scribere* write] —**cir′cum·scrib′er,** *n.* —Syn. **3.** confine.

cir·cum·scrip·tion (sér′kəm·skrip′shən), *n.* **1.** a circumscribing or being circumscribed. **2.** thing that circumscribes. **3.** inscription around a coin, medal, etc. **4.** outline; boundary. **5.** space circumscribed. **6.** limitation; restriction.

cir·cum·spect (sér′kəm·spekt), *adj.* careful; cautious; prudent. [< L, < *circum* around + *specere* look] —**cir′cum·spec′tion,** *n.* —**cir′-cum·spec′tive,** *adj.* —**cir′cum·spect′ly,** *adv.* —**cir′cum·spect′ness,** *n.* —Syn. watchful, wary.

cir·cum·stance (sér′kəm·stans), *n.* **1.** condition of an act or event. **2.** fact or event, esp. in relation to others. **3.** a particular or detail. **4.** incident; occurrence. **5.** circumstances, condition of affairs: *a rich person is in easy circumstances.* **6. under no circumstances,** never; no matter what the conditions are. **7. under the circumstances,** because of conditions; things being as they are or were. **8.** *Archaic.* ceremony; display: *pomp and circumstance.* [< L *circumstantia* surrounding condition < *circum* around + *stare* stand] —**cir′cum·stanced,** *adj.*

cir·cum·stan·tial (sér′kəm·stan′shəl), *adj.* **1.** depending on circumstances: *circumstantial evidence.* **2.** incidental; not essential; not important. **3.** giving full and exact details; complete: *a circumstantial report.* —**cir·cum·stan·ti·al·i·ty** (sér′kəm·stan′shi·al′ə·ti), **cir′cum·stan′tial-ness,** *n.* —**cir′cum·stan′tial·ly,** *adv.*

cir·cum·stan·ti·ate (sér′kəm·stan′shi·āt), *v.,* –at·ed, –at·ing. give the circumstances of; support or prove with details. —**cir′cum·stan′-ti·a′tion,** *n.*

cir·cum·vent (sér′kəm·vent′), *v.* **1.** get the better of; defeat by trickery. **2.** go around. **3.** catch in a trap. [< L, < *circum* around + *venire* come] —**cir′cum·vent′er,** **cir′cum·ven′tor,** *n.* —**cir′cum·ven′tion,** *n.* —**cir′cum·ven′tive,** *adj.*

cir·cus (sér′kəs), *n.* **1.** a traveling show of acrobats, clowns, horses, riders, and wild animals. **2.** *Colloq.* an amusing person, thing, or event. **3.** in ancient Rome, a round or oval space with rows of seats around it, one row above the other. [< L, ring]

cir·rho·sis (si·rō′sis), *n.* a diseased condition of the liver, kidneys, etc., due to excessive formation of connective tissue. [< NL < Gk. *kirrhos* orange-yellow] —**cir·rhot·ic** (si·rhot′ik), *adj.*

cir·rus (sir′əs), *n., pl.* **cir·ri** (sir′ī). **1.** a thin, fleecy cloud very high in the air. **2.** *Bot.* a tendril. **3.** *Zool.* a slender appendage. [< L *cirrus* curl]

cis·co (sis′kō), *n., pl.* –coes, –cos. *Am.* a whitefish or herring of the Great Lakes. [< Am.Ind.]

Cis·ter·cian (sis·tér′shən), *n.* member of a Benedictine order of monks and nuns founded in France in 1098. —*adj.* of this order.

cis·tern (sis′tərn), *n.* **1.** reservoir or tank for storing water. **2.** *Anat.* vessel or cavity of the body. [< L *cisterna* < *cista* box]

cit·a·del (sit′ə·del; –del), *n.* **1.** fortress commanding a city. **2.** a strongly fortified place; stronghold. **3.** a strong, safe place; refuge. [< F < Ital. *cittadella,* dim. of *città* CITY]

ci·ta·tion (sī·tā′shən), *n.* **1.** quotation or reference, esp. given as an authority for facts, opinions, etc. **2.** specific mention in an official dispatch. **3.** *Am.* public commendation or decoration for unusual achievement or gallant action, esp. in time of war. **4.** summons to appear before a law court. —**ci·ta·to·ry** (sī′tə·tô′ri; –tō′–), *adj.*

cite (sīt), *v.,* cit·ed, cit·ing. **1.** quote (a passage, book, or author), esp. as an authority. **2.** refer to; mention as an example. **3.** mention for bravery in war. **4.** summon to appear before a law court. **5.** arouse to action; summon. [< L *citare* summon < *ciere* set in motion]

cith·a·ra (sith′ə·rə), *n.* an ancient musical instrument somewhat like a lyre. [< L < Gk. *kithara.* Doublet of GUITAR and ZITHER.]

cith·er (sith′ər), *n.* **1.** cithara. **2.** cithern.

cith·ern (sith′ərn), *n.* a musical instrument somewhat like a guitar, popular in the 16th and 17th centuries. Also, cittern. [see CITTERN]

cit·i·zen (sit′ə·zən; –sən), *n.* **1.** person who by birth or by choice is a member of a state or nation. **2.** person who is not a soldier, policeman, etc.; civilian. **3.** inhabitant of a city or town. [< AF *citisein* < OF *cite* CITY] —Syn. **1.** national, subject. **3.** resident.

cit·i·zen·ry (sit′ə·zən·ri; –sən–), *n., pl.* –ries. citizens as a group.

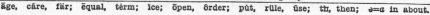

Girl playing a cithara

cit·i·zen·ship (sit′ə·zən·ship′; –sən–), n. 1. condition of being a citizen. 2. duties, rights, and privileges of a citizen.

cit·rate (sit′rāt; sī′trāt), n. Chem. salt or ester of citric acid.

cit·ric (sit′rik), adj. of or from fruits such as lemons, limes, oranges, etc.

citric acid, Chem. acid, $C_6H_8O_7$, from such fruits as lemons, limes, etc., used as a flavoring, as a medicine, and in making dyes.

cit·ron (sit′rən), n. 1. a pale-yellow fruit somewhat like a lemon but larger, less acid, and with a thicker rind. 2. the candied rind of this fruit, used in fruit cakes, plum pudding, candies, etc. 3. shrub or small tree that this fruit grows on. [< F < Ital. citrone < L citrus citrus tree]

cit·ron·el·la (sit′rən·el′ə), n. oil used in making perfume, soap, liniment, etc., and for keeping mosquitoes away. [< NL]

cit·rous (sit′rəs), adj. pertaining to fruits such as lemons, grapefruit, limes, oranges, etc.

cit·rus (sit′rəs), n. 1. any tree bearing lemons, limes, oranges, or similar fruit. 2. Also, Am., citrus fruit. fruit of such a tree. —adj. of such trees. [< L]

cit·tern (sit′ərn), n. cithern. [blend of L cithara CITHARA + E gittern]

cit·y (sit′i), n., pl. cit·ies, adj. —n. 1. a large and important town. 2. division of local government in the United States having a charter from the State that fixes its boundaries and powers, usually governed by a mayor and a board of aldermen or councilmen. 3. division of local government in Canada of the highest class. 4. people living in a city. —adj. 1. of a city. 2. in a city. [< OF < L civitas citizenship, state, city < civis citizen]

cit·y·bust·er (sit′i·bus′tər), n. Colloq. an atomic or hydrogen bomb.

city hall, Am. a building containing offices for the officials, bureaus, etc., of a city government.

city manager, Am. person appointed by a city council or commission to manage the government of a city. He is not elected by the people.

cit·y·state (sit′i·stāt′), n. an independent state consisting of a city and the territories depending on it.

Ciu·dad Tru·jil·lo (sü·thäth′ trü·hē′yō), n. capital of the Dominican Republic. Formerly called **Santo Domingo.**

civ·et (siv′it), n. 1. a yellowish secretion of certain glands of the civet cock. It has a musky odor and is used in making perfume. 2. Also, civet cat. a. a small, spotted animal of Africa, Europe, and Asia having glands that secrete a yellowish substance with a musky odor. b. any of certain similar animals. [< F < Ital. < Ar. zabād]

civ·ic (siv′ik), adj. 1. of a city. 2. of or having to do with citizenship. 3. of citizens. [< L civicus < civis citizen] —civ′i·cal·ly, adv.

civ·ics (siv′iks), n. Am. study of the duties, rights, and privileges of citizens.

civ·il (siv′əl), adj. 1. of a citizen or citizens; having to do with citizens. 2. of or having to do with the government, state, or nation: civil servants. 3. not military, naval, or connected with the church. Post offices are part of the civil service of the government. 4. polite; courteous. 5. pertaining to the private rights of individuals and to legal proceedings connected with these rights. [< L civilis < civis citizen] —Syn. 4. respectful, gracious, affable.

civil disobedience, refusal to obey the laws of the state, esp. by not paying taxes.

civil engineering, the planning and directing of the construction of bridges, roads, harbors, etc. —**civil engineer.**

ci·vil·ian (sə·vil′yən), n. person who is not a soldier or sailor. —adj. of civilians; not military or naval.

ci·vil·i·ty (sə·vil′ə·ti), n., pl. –ties. 1. politeness; courtesy. 2. act of politeness or courtesy. 3. Archaic. civilization.

civ·i·li·za·tion (siv′ə·lə·zā′shən), n. 1. act of civilizing. 2. process of becoming civilized; improvement in culture. 3. civilized condition; advanced stage in social development. 4. nations and peoples that have reached advanced stages in social development. 5. the culture and ways of living of a race, nation, etc.: Chinese civilization.

civ·i·lize (siv′ə·līz), v., –lized, –liz·ing. 1. bring out of a savage or barbarian condition; train in culture, science, and art. 2. improve in culture and good manners; refine. [< Med.L civilizare. See CIVIL, –IZE.] —civ′i·liz′a·ble, adj. —civ′i·liz′er, n.

civ·i·lized (siv′ə·līzd), adj. 1. trained in culture, art, and science. 2. of civilized nations or persons. 3. showing culture and good manners; refined.

civil law, law that regulates and protects private rights and is controlled and used by civil courts, not military courts.

civil liberty, right of a person to do and say what he pleases as long as he does not harm anyone else.

civ·il·ly (siv′ə·li), adv. 1. politely; courteously. 2. according to the civil law.

civil rights, Am. the rights of a citizen, esp. the rights guaranteed to citizens of the United States, irrespective of race or color, by the 13th and 14th amendments to the Constitution.

civil service, public service concerned with affairs not military, naval, legislative, or judicial. —**civil servant.**

civil war, 1. war between two groups of citizens of one nation. 2. Civil War, a. Am. war between the Northern and Southern States of the United States from 1861 to 1865. b. war between Charles I of England and Parliament, living from 1642 to 1646 and from 1648 to 1652.

Cl, Chem. chlorine.

cl., 1. centiliter. 2. class. 3. clause.

clab·ber (klab′ər), n. thick, sour milk. —v. become thick in souring; curdle. [< Irish clabar curds, short for bainne clabair bonnyclabber (curdled milk)]

clack (klak), v. 1. make or cause to make a short, sharp sound. 2. chatter. —n. 1. short, sharp sound. 2. chatter. [imit.] —clack′er, n.

clad (klad), v. pt. and pp. of clothe.

claim (klām), v. 1. demand as one's own or one's right. 2. say one has and demand that others recognize (a right, title, possession, etc.); assert one's right to. 3. declare as a fact; say strongly; maintain. 4. require; call for; deserve. —n. 1. demand for something due; assertion of a right. 2. right or title to something. 3. something that is claimed. 4. Am. piece of public land that a settler or prospector marks out for himself. 5. assertion of something as a fact. [< OF < L clamare call, proclaim] —claim′a·ble, adj. —claim′er, n. —Syn. v. 2. exact.

claim·ant (klām′ənt), n. one who makes a claim.

clair·voy·ance (klār·voi′əns), n. 1. power of knowing about things that are out of sight. 2. exceptional insight. [< F, < clair clear + voyant seeing] —clair·voy′ant, adj., n.

clam (klam), n., v., clammed, clam·ming. —n. 1. mollusk somewhat like an oyster, with a shell in two halves. 2. Am., Slang. a close-mouthed or dull person. —v. Am. go out after clams; dig for clams. [appar. special use of clam pair of pincers; OE clamm fetter]

clam·ber (klam′bər), v. climb, using both hands and feet; climb awkwardly or with difficulty; scramble. —n. an awkward or difficult climb. [ME clambre(n)] —clam′ber·er, n.

clam·my (klam′i), adj., –mi·er, –mi·est. cold and damp. —clam′mi·ly, adv. —clam′mi·ness, n.

clam·or, esp. Brit. **clam·our** (klam′ər), n. 1. a loud noise; continual uproar; shouting. 2. a noisy demand or complaint. —v. 1. make a loud noise or continual uproar; shout. 2. demand or complain noisily. [< OF < L, < clamare cry out] —clam′or·er, esp. Brit. clam′our·er, n. —Syn. n. 1. outcry.

clam·or·ous (klam′ər·əs), adj. 1. noisy; shouting. 2. making noisy demands or complaints. —clam′or·ous·ly, adv. —clam′or·ous·ness, n.

clamp (klamp), n. 1. brace, band, wedge, or other device for holding things tightly together.

2. instrument for holding things tightly together temporarily. —*v.* fasten together with a clamp; put in a clamp; strengthen with a clamp. [< MDu. *klampe*]

clan (klan), *n.* **1.** group of related families that claim to be descended from a common ancestor. **2.** group of people closely joined together by some common interest. [< Scotch Gaelic *clann* family]

clan·des·tine (klan·des′tən), *adj.* secret; concealed; underhand. [< L *clandestinus*, ult. < *clam* secretly] —**clandes′tine·ly**, *adv.* —**clan·des′tine·ness,** *n.* —**Syn.** hidden, furtive, covert.

Clamp

clang (klang), *n.* a loud, harsh, ringing sound, as of metal being hit. —*v.* **1.** make a clang. **2.** strike together with a clang. [imit.]

clan·gor, *esp. Brit.* **clan·gour** (klang′gər; klang′ər), *n.* **1.** continued clanging. **2.** clang. —*v.* clang. [< L, < *clangere* clang] —**clan′gor·ous,** *adj.* —**clan′gor·ous·ly,** *adv.*

clank (klangk), *n.* a sharp, harsh sound like the rattle of a heavy chain. —*v.* **1.** make such a sound. **2.** cause to clank. [? < Du. *klank*]

clan·nish (klan′ish), *adj.* **1.** pertaining to a clan. **2.** closely united; not liking outsiders. —**clan′nish·ly,** *adv.* —**clan′nish·ness,** *n.*

clans·man (klanz′mən), *n., pl.* -men. member of a clan.

clap (klap), *n., v.,* clapped, clap·ping. —*n.* **1.** a sudden noise, such as a single burst of thunder, the sound of the hands struck together, or the sound of a loud slap. **2.** applause. —*v.* **1.** strike together loudly. **2.** applaud by striking the hands together. **3.** strike with a quick blow. **4.** put or place quickly and effectively. **5.** *Now Colloq.* make or arrange hastily. [OE *clæppan*]

clap·board (klab′ərd; klap′bôrd; -bōrd), *Am.* —*n.* a thin board, thicker along one edge than along the other, used to cover the outer walls of wooden buildings. —*v.* cover with clapboards.

clap·per (klap′ər), *n.* **1.** one that claps. **2.** part that strikes a bell. **3.** device for making noise.

clap·trap (klap′trap′), *n.* empty talk; an insincere remark. —*adj.* cheap and showy.

claque (klak), *n.* **1.** group of persons hired to applaud in a theater. **2.** group that applauds or follows another person for selfish reasons. [< F, < *claquer* clap]

clar·et (klar′ət), *n.* **1.** kind of red wine. **2.** a dark, purplish red. —*adj.* dark purplish-red. [< OF, light colored, < *cler* CLEAR]

clar·i·fy (klar′ə·fī), *v.,* -fied, -fy·ing. **1.** make or become clear; purify: *clarify fat by straining it.* **2.** make clearer; explain. [< OF < LL *clarificare* < L *clarus* clear + *facere* make] —**clar′i·fi·ca′tion,** *n.* —**clar′i·fi′er,** *n.*

clar·i·net (klar′ə·net′), *n.* a wooden wind instrument played by means of holes and keys. [< F *clarinette,* dim. of *clarine* bell < L *clarus* clear] —**clar′i·net′ist, clar′i·net′tist,** *n.*

clar·i·on (klar′i·ən), *adj.* clear and shrill. —*n.* **1.** a kind of trumpet with clear, shrill tones. **2.** a clear, shrill sound. [< Med.L *clario* < L *clarus* clear]

clar·i·ty (klar′ə·ti), *n.* clearness.

Man playing a clarinet

clash (klash), *n.* **1.** a loud, harsh sound like that of two things running into each other, of striking metal, or of bells rung together but not in tune. **2.** strong disagreement; conflict. —*v.* **1.** strike with a clash. **2.** throw, shut, etc., with a clash. **3.** disagree strongly; conflict. [imit.] —**Syn.** *n.* **2.** discord.

clasp (klasp; kläsp), *n.* **1.** thing to fasten two parts or pieces together. **2.** a close hold with the arms or hands. **3.** a firm grip with the hand. —*v.* **1.** fasten together with a clasp. **2.** hold closely with the arms or hands. **3.** grip firmly with the hand. [ME *claspe(n)*] —**clasp′er,** *n.* —**Syn.** *v.* **1.** hook. **2.** embrace, hug. **3.** grasp, clutch.

class (klas; kläs), *n.* **1.** group of persons or things alike in some way; kind; sort. **2.** group of students taught together. **3.** a meeting of such

a group. **4.** *Am.* group of pupils entering a school together and graduating in the same year. **5.** rank or division of society: *the middle class.* **6.** system of ranks or divisions in society. **7.** *Mil.* group of draftees of the same age. **8.** high rank in society. **9.** grade; quality: *first class is the best way to travel.* **10.** *Slang.* excellence; style. **11.** group of animals or plants ranking below a phylum or subkingdom and above an order. —*v.* put or be in a class or group. [< L *classis* class, collection, fleet] —**class′a·ble,** *adj.* —**class′er,** *n.*

class., 1. classic; classical. 2. classified.

clas·sic (klas′ik), *adj.* **1.** of the highest grade or quality; excellent; first-class. **2.** of the literature, art, and life of ancient Greece and Rome. **3.** like this literature and art; simple, regular, and restrained. **4.** famous in literature or history. —*n.* **1.** work of literature or art of the highest quality. **2.** author or artist of acknowledged excellence. **3. the classics,** the literature of ancient Greece and Rome. [< L *classicus* < *classis* CLASS]

clas·si·cal (klas′ə·kəl), *adj.* **1.** classic. **2.** knowing the classics well. **3.** devoted to the classics. **4.** based on the classics. **5.** orthodox and sound, but not quite up to date: *classical physics.* **6.** *Music.* of high quality and enjoyed especially by serious students of music. —**clas′si·cal′i·ty,** *n.* —**clas′si·cal·ly,** *adv.* —**clas′si·cal·ness,** *n.*

clas·si·cism (klas′ə·siz·əm), **clas·si·cal·ism** (-kəl·iz′əm), *n.* **1.** principles of the literature and art of ancient Greece and Rome. **2.** adherence to these principles. **3.** knowledge of the literature of ancient Greece and Rome; classical scholarship. **4.** idiom or form from Greek or Latin introduced into another language.

clas·si·cist (klas′ə·sist), **clas·si·cal·ist** (-kəl·ist), *n.* **1.** follower of the principles of classicism in literature and art. **2.** expert in the literature of ancient Greece and Rome. **3.** person who urges the study of Greek and Latin.

clas·si·fi·ca·tion (klas′ə·fə·kā′shən), *n.* arrangement in classes or groups; a grouping according to some system. —**clas·si·fi·ca·to·ry** (klas′ə·fə·kə·tô′ri; -tō′-), *adj.*

clas·si·fied (klas′ə·fīd), *adj.* **1.** of certain public documents of the U.S., having a classification as secret, confidential, or restricted. **2.** *Slang.* secret.

classified ad, *Am.* want ad.

clas·si·fy (klas′ə·fī), *v.,* -fied, -fy·ing. arrange in classes or groups; group according to some system. —**clas′si·fi′a·ble,** *adj.* —**clas′si·fi′er,** *n.*

class·mate (klas′māt′; kläs′-), *n. Am.* member of the same class in school.

class·room (klas′rüm′; -rům′; kläs′-), *n.* room where classes meet in school; schoolroom.

clat·ter (klat′ər), *n.* **1.** a confused noise like that of many plates being struck together. **2.** noisy talk. —*v.* **1.** move or fall with confused noise; make a confused noise. **2.** talk fast and noisily. **3.** cause to clatter. [OE *clatrian*] —**clat′ter·er,** *n.* —**clat′ter·ing·ly,** *adv.*

clause (klôz), *n.* **1.** part of a sentence having a subject and predicate. In "He came before we left," "He came" is a **main clause,** and "before we left" is a **subordinate clause.** **2.** a single provision of a law, treaty, or any other written agreement. [< Med.L *clausa* for L *clausula* close of a period < *claudere* close] —**claus′al,** *adj.*

▶ A clause is a part of a compound or complex sentence that ordinarily has a subject and a finite verb. Compound sentences have two coördinate clauses, of grammatically equal value, connected usually by *and, but, for,* or another coördinating conjunction: [First clause] *The drive for funds went well* [second clause] *and a large amount of money was accumulated.* Complex sentences have at least one main clause, grammatically capable of standing alone, and one or more subordinate clauses, joined to the main clause or clauses by *as, because, since, when,* or some other subordinating conjunction, or by a relative pronoun, *that, who, which:* [Main clause] *There are differences of opinion on the matter* [subordinate clause] *which cause a great deal of disharmony.*

claus·tro·pho·bi·a (klôs′trə·fō′bi·ə), *n.* morbid fear of enclosed spaces. [< NL, < L *claustrum* closed place + E *-phobia* fear (< Gk.)]

clave (klāv), *v. Archaic.* pt. of cleave².

clav·i·chord (klav′ə·kôrd), *n.* a stringed musical instrument with a keyboard. The piano developed from it. [< Med.L < L *clavis* key + *chorda* string]

clav·i·cle (klav′ə·kəl), *n. Anat., Zool.* collarbone. [< L *clavicula* bolt, dim. of *clavis* key]
—**cla·vic·u·lar** (klə·vik′yə·lər), *adj.*

cla·vier (klə·vir′), *n.* any musical instrument with a keyboard, as the harpsichord and clavichord. [< G < F < L *clavis* key]

claw (klô), *n.* **1.** a sharp, hooked nail on a bird's or animal's foot. **2.** foot with such sharp, hooked nails. **3.** pincers of lobsters, crabs, etc. **4.** anything like a claw. **5.** act of clawing. —*v.* scratch, tear, seize, or pull with claws or hands. [OE *clawu*]

clay (klā), *n.* **1.** a stiff, sticky kind of earth, that can be easily shaped when wet and hardens after drying or baking. **2.** earth. **3.** human body. [OE *clæg*] —**clay·ey** (klā′i), **clay′ish,** *adj.*

Clay (klā), *n.* Henry, 1777–1852, American statesman.

Claws of a bird

clay·more (klā′môr; -mōr), *n.* a heavy, two-edged sword, formerly used by Scottish Highlanders. [< Scotch Gaelic *claidheamh mor* great sword]

clean (klēn), *adj.* **1.** free from dirt or filth; not soiled or stained. **2.** pure; innocent. **3.** having clean habits. **4.** fit for food. **5.** free from anything that mars or impedes; clear: *clean copy.* **6.** even; regular: *a clean cut.* **7.** well-shaped; trim. **8.** clever; skillful. **9.** complete; entire; total. —*adv.* **1.** completely; entirely; totally. **2.** in a clean manner. —*v.* **1.** make clean. **2.** perform or undergo a process of cleaning. **3.** remove in the process of cleaning. [OE *clǣne*] —**clean′a·ble,** *adj.* —**clean′ness,** *n.* —**Syn.** *adj.* **1.** unstained, unsoiled. **2.** chaste, virtuous. **5.** spotless, immaculate. —*v.* **1.** cleanse, scour, scrub, wash.

clean-cut (klēn′kut′), *adj.* **1.** having clear, sharp outlines. **2.** well-shaped. **3.** clear; definite; distinct. **4.** having a clear, definite character or a distinct personality.

clean·er (klēn′ər), *n.* **1.** person whose work is keeping buildings, windows, or other objects clean. **2.** tool or machine for cleaning. **3.** anything that removes dirt, grease, or stains.

clean·ly (*adj.* klen′li; *adv.* klēn′li), *adj.,* -li·er, -li·est, *adv.* —*adj.* clean; habitually clean. —*adv.* in a clean manner. —**clean·li·ly** (klēn′lə·li), *adv.* —**clean·li·ness** (klēn′li·nis), *n.*

cleanse (klenz), *v.,* cleansed, cleans·ing. **1.** make clean. **2.** make pure. [OE *clǣnsian* < *clǣne* clean] —**cleans′a·ble,** *adj.* —**cleans′er,** *n.* —**Syn.** **1.** clean. **2.** purify.

clean·up (klēn′up′), *n.* **1.** a cleaning up. **2.** *Slang.* money made; profit.

clear (klir), *adj.* **1.** not cloudy; bright; light. **2.** transparent: *clear glass.* **3.** having a pure, even color: *a clear blue.* **4.** without stain or blemish. **5.** that perceives distinctly: *a clear mind.* **6.** easily seen, heard, or understood. **7.** sure; certain. **8.** not blocked or obstructed; open. **9.** without touching; without being caught. **10.** free from blame or guilt; innocent. **11.** free from debts or charges. **12.** without limitation; complete. —*v.* **1.** make or become clear; get clear. **2.** remove to leave a space. **3.** pass by or over without touching or being caught. **4.** make free from blame or guilt; prove to be innocent. **5.** make as profit free from debts or charges. **6.** get (a ship or cargo) free by meeting requirements on entering or leaving a port. **7.** leave a port after doing this. **8.** exchange (checks and bills) and settle accounts between different banks. **9.** clear up, **a.** make or become clear. **b.** put in order by clearing. **c.** explain. **d.** become clear after a storm. —*adv.* **1.** in a clear manner. **2.** completely; entirely. —*n.* **in the clear, a.** between the outside parts. **b.** free. **c.** in plain text;

not in cipher or code. [< OF < L *clarus* clear] —**clear′a·ble,** *adj.* —**clear′er,** *n.* —**clear′ly,** *adv.* —**clear′ness,** *n.* —**Syn.** *adj.* **6.** plain, distinct, evident, obvious, manifest, apparent, patent. —*v.* **4.** absolve, acquit. —**Ant.** *adj.* **1.** cloudy, dim. **2.** opaque. **6.** abstruse, ambiguous, unintelligible.

clear·ance (klir′əns), *n.* **1.** act of making clear. **2.** a clear space between two objects. **3.** papers permitting a ship or aircraft to leave on a voyage or flight. **4.** the settling of accounts between different banks.

clear-cut (klir′kut′), *adj.* **1.** having clear, sharp outlines. **2.** clear; definite; distinct.

clear-head·ed (klir′hed′id), *adj.* having or showing a clear understanding. —**clear′-head′-ed·ly,** *adv.* —**clear′-head′ed·ness,** *n.*

clear·ing (klir′ing), *n. Am.* an open space of cleared land in a forest.

clearing house, place where banks exchange checks and bills and settle their accounts.

clear-sight·ed (klir′sīt′id), *adj.* **1.** able to see clearly. **2.** able to understand or think clearly. —**clear′-sight′ed·ly,** *adv.* —**clear′-sight′ed·ness,** *n.*

clear·sto·ry (klir′stô′ri; -stō′-), *n., pl.* -ries. clerestory.

cleat (klēt), *n.* **1.** strip of wood or iron fastened across anything for support or for sure footing. **2.** *Naut.* **a.** a small, wedge-shaped block fastened to a spar, etc., as a support, check, etc. **b.** piece of wood or metal used for securing ropes or lines. —*v.* fasten to or with a cleat. [ME *cleete*]

cleav·age (klēv′ij), *n.* **1.** split; division. **2.** way in which something splits or divides. **3.** *Biol.* any of the series of divisions by which a fertilized egg develops into an embryo.

cleave[1] (klēv), *v.,* cleft or cleaved or clove, cleft or cleaved or clo·ven, cleav·ing. **1.** split; divide. **2.** pass through; pierce; penetrate. **3.** make by cutting. [OE *clēofan*] —**cleav′a·ble,** *adj.*

cleave[2] (klēv), *v.,* cleaved or (*Archaic*) clave, cleaved, cleav·ing. stick; cling; be faithful. [OE *cleofian*]

cleav·er (klēv′ər), *n.* **1.** one that cleaves. **2.** cutting tool with a heavy blade and a short handle.

clef (klef), *n. Music.* symbol indicating the pitch of the notes on a staff. [< F < L *clavis* key]

cleft (kleft), *v.* pt. and pp. of cleave[1]. —*adj.* split; divided. —*n.* a space or opening made by splitting; crack. [OE *geclyft*] —**Syn.** *n.* fissure, crevice, chink.

clem·a·tis (klem′ə·tis), *n.* vine with clusters of fragrant white or purple flowers. [< L < Gk., < *klema* vine branch]

Clem·en·ceau (klem′ən·sō′), *n.* Georges, 1841–1929, premier of France, 1906–09, 1917–20.

Clem·ens (klem′ənz), *n.* Samuel Langhorne, 1835–1910, the real name of Mark Twain.

clem·ent (klem′ənt), *adj.* **1.** merciful. **2.** mild. [< L *clemens*] —**clem′en·cy,** *n.* —**clem′ent·ly,** *adv.*

clench (klench), *v.* **1.** close tightly together; *clench one's fists in anger.* **2.** grasp firmly; grip tightly. **3.** clinch (a nail, etc.). —*n.* firm grasp; tight grip. [OE *(be)clencan* hold fast] —**clench′er,** *n.*

Cle·o·pat·ra (klē′ə·pat′rə; -pä′trə; -pā′trə), *n.* 69?–30 B.C., last queen of ancient Egypt, 47–30 B.C.

clere·sto·ry (klir′stô′ri; -stō′-), *n., pl.* -ries. **1.** the upper part of the wall of a church, having windows in it above the roofs of the aisles. **2.** a similar structure in any building. Also, *clear-story.* [appar. < *clere* clear + *story*²]

cler·gy (klėr′ji), *n., pl.* -gies. persons ordained for religious work; ministers, pastors, and priests. [< OF *clergie*, ult. < LL *clericus* CLERIC]

cler·gy·man (klėr′ji·mən), *n., pl.* -men. member of the clergy; minister; pastor; priest.

cler·ic (kler′ik), *n.* clergyman. —*adj.* of a clergyman or the clergy. [< LL < Gk., < *klēros* clergy, orig., lot, allotment. Doublet of CLERK.]

cler·i·cal (kler′ə·kəl), *adj.* **1.** of a clerk or clerks; for clerks. **2.** of a clergyman or the clergy. **3.** supporting the power or influence of the clergy in politics. —*n.* **1.** clergyman. **2.** supporter of the power or influence of the clergy in politics. —**cler′i·cal·ly,** *adv.*

cler·i·cal·ism (kler′ə·kəl·iz′em), *n.* power or influence of the clergy in politics. —**cler′i·cal·ist,** *n.*

clerk (klėrk; *Brit.* klärk), *n.* **1.** *Am.* person whose work is waiting on customers and selling goods in a store; salesman or saleswoman. **2.** person whose work is keeping records or accounts, copying letters, etc., in an office. **3.** official who keeps records and takes care of regular business in a law court, legislature, etc. **4.** layman who has minor church duties. **5.** *Esp. Law.* clergyman. **6.** *Archaic,* a scholar. —*v.* work as a clerk. [< LL *clericus.* Doublet of .CLERIC.] —**clerk′ly,** *adv.* —**clerk′li·ness,** *n.* —**clerk′ship,** *n.*

Cleve·land (klēv′lənd), *n.* **1.** city in NE Ohio, on Lake Erie. **2.** (Stephen) Grover, 1837–1908, the 22nd and 24th president of the United States 1885–89, 1893–97.

clev·er (klev′ər), *adj.* **1.** having a quick mind; bright; intelligent. **2.** skillful or expert in doing some particular thing. **3.** showing skill or intelligence. [ME *cliver*] —**clev′er·ly,** *adv.* —**clev′er·ness,** *n.* —**Syn. 1.** ingenious, smart. **2.** adroit. —Ant. **1.** stupid. **2.** clumsy.

clev·is (klev′is), *n.* a U-shaped piece of metal with a bolt or pin through the ends. [akin to CLEAVE¹]

clew (klū), *n.* **1.** clue. **2.** ball of thread or yarn. —*v.* coil into a ball. [OE *cleowen*]

cli·ché (klē·shā′), *n.* a worn-out idea or trite expression. [< F, pp. of *clicher* stereotype]

click (klik), *n.* **1.** a light, sharp sound like that of a key turning in a lock. **2.** sound made by withdrawing the tongue from contact with some part of the mouth. **3.** pawl. —*v.* **1.** make a light, sharp sound. **2.** cause to make such a sound. **3.** *Slang.* be a success. [imit.] —**click′er,** *n.*

cli·ent (klī′ənt), *n.* **1.** person for whom a lawyer acts. **2.** customer. [< L *cliens;* akin to *–clinare* lean] —**cli·en·tal** (klī·en′təl, klī′ən·təl), *adj.* —**cli′ent·less,** *adj.*

cli·en·tele (klī′ən·tel′), *n.* **1.** clients; customers. **2.** number of clients. [< L *clientela*]

cliff (klif), *n.* a high, steep rock. [OE *clif*]

cli·mac·ter·ic (klī·mak′tər·ik; klī′mak·ter′ik), *n.* time when some important event occurs; crucial period. —*adj.* Also, **cli·mac·ter·i·cal** (klī′mak·ter′ə·kəl). of or like such a period; crucial [< L < Gk., < *klimakter* rung of a ladder < *klimax* ladder]

cli·mac·tic (klī·mak′tik), **cli·mac·ti·cal** (-tə·kəl), *adj.* of or forming a climax.

cli·mate (klī′mit), *n.* **1.** the kind of weather a place has, including conditions of heat and cold, moisture and dryness, clearness and cloudiness, wind and calm. **2.** intellectual and moral atmosphere. [< L < Gk. *klima* slope (of the earth) < *klinein* incline] —**cli·mat·ic** (klī·mat′ik), *adj.* —**cli·mat′i·cal·ly,** *adv.* —**Syn. 1.** clime.

cli·ma·tol·o·gy (klī′mə·tol′ə·ji), *n.* science that deals with climate. —**cli·ma·to·log·ic** (klī′mə·tə·loj′ik), **cli′ma·to·log′i·cal,** *adj.* **cli′ma·tol′o·gist,** *n.*

cli·max (klī′maks), *n.* **1.** the highest point; point of greatest interest; most exciting part. **2.** arrangement of ideas in a rising scale of force and interest. —*v.* bring or come to a climax. [< LL < Gk. *klimax* ladder] —**Syn. n. 1.** peak, zenith, culmination.

climb (klīm), *v.,* **climbed** or (*Archaic*) **clomb, climb·ing,** *n.* —*v.* **1.** go up by using the hands or feet; ascend: *climb a ladder.* **2.** rise slowly with steady effort: *climb from poverty to wealth.* **3.** grow upward by holding on or twining around: *some vines climb.* **4. climb down, a.** go down by using the hands and feet. **b.** *Colloq.* give in; back down. —*n.* **1.** a climbing; ascent. **2.** place to be climbed. [OE *climban*] —**climb′a·ble,** *adj.* —**climb′er,** *n.* —**Syn. v. 1.** mount, scale.

clime (klīm), *n. Poetic.* **1.** country; region. **2.** climate. [< L *clima.* See CLIMATE.]

clinch (klinch), *v.* **1.** fasten (a driven nail, a bolt, etc.) firmly by bending over the part that projects. **2.** fasten (things) together in this way. **3.** fix firmly; settle decisively: *clinch a bargain.* **4.** *Am.* grasp tightly in fighting or wrestling. —*n.* **1.** a clinching. **2.** a tight grasp in fighting or wrestling. [var. of *clench*]

clinch·er (klin′chər), *n.* **1.** nail or bolt that is clinched. **2.** *Colloq.* argument, statement, etc., that is decisive.

cling (kling), *v.,* **clung, cling·ing,** *n.* —*v.* **1.** stick; hold fast. **2.** keep near. **3.** grasp; embrace. —*n.* act of clinging. [OE *clingan*] —**cling′er,** *n.* —**cling′ing·ly,** *adv.* —**cling′y,** *adj.*

cling·stone (kling′stōn′), *n. Am.* peach whose stone clings to the fleshy part.

clin·ic (klin′ik), *n.* **1.** place, usually connected with a hospital or medical school, where outpatients can receive medical treatment. **2.** practical instruction of medical students by examining or treating patients in the students' presence. [< L < Gk. *klinikos* of a bed < *kline* bed]

clin·i·cal (klin′ə·kəl), *adj.* **1.** of or having to do with a clinic. **2.** used or performed in a sickroom. **3.** having to do with the study of disease by observation of the patient. —**clin′i·cal·ly,** *adv.*

clink (klingk), *n.* **1.** a light, sharp, ringing sound like that of glasses hitting together. **2.** rhyme. —*v.* **1.** make a clink. **2.** cause to clink. [ME *clinke(n),* ? < Du. *klinken*]

clink·er (klingk′ər), *n.* **1.** a large, rough cinder. **2.** a very hard brick. —*v.* form clinkers. [< Du. *klinker* brick < *klinken* ring]

cli·nom·e·ter (klī·nom′ə·tər; klī–), *n.* instrument for measuring deviation from the horizontal. [< L *–clinare* incline + –METER]

Cli·o (klī′ō), *n.* Gk. *Myth.* the Muse of history.

clip¹ (klip), *v.,* **clipped, clip·ping,** *n.* —*v.* **1.** trim with shears or scissors; cut. **2.** cut the hair or fleece of. **3.** omit sounds in pronouncing. **4.** cut short; curtail. **5.** *Colloq.* move fast. **6.** *Colloq.* hit or punch sharply. **7.** cut pieces from a magazine, newspaper, etc. —*n.* **1.** act of clipping. **2.** anything clipped off. **3.** fast motion. **4.** *Colloq.* a sharp blow, etc. **5.** *Am., Colloq.* one time: *at one clip.* [ME *clippe(n),* prob. < Scand. *klippa*]

clip² (klip), *v.,* **clipped, clip·ping,** *n.* —*v.* hold tight; fasten. —*n.* **1.** thing used for clipping (things) together. **2.** a metal holder for cartridges on some firearms. [OE *clyppan* embrace]

clipped word, a shortened form made by dropping a syllable or more, as *ad* for *advertisement.* ▶ Clipped words are typical of shoptalk and familiar speech and often find their way into the general vocabulary. Many, like *gent* or *prof,* are out of place in writing.

clip·per (klip′ər), *n.* **1.** person who clips or cuts. **2.** Often, **clippers.** tool for cutting. **3.** *Am.* a sailing ship built and rigged for speed. **4.** a large, fast aircraft.

clip·ping (klip′ing), *n. Am.* piece cut out of a newspaper, magazine, etc.

clique (klēk; klik), *n.* a small, exclusive set or snobbish group of people. [< F, < *cliquer* click] —**cli′quish,** *adj.* —**cli′quish·ly,** *adv.* —**cli′quish·ness,** *n.*

cli·to·ris (klī′tə·ris; klit′ə–), *n. Anat.* in most mammals, a small organ of the female homologous to the penis of the male. [< NL < Gk., < *kleiein* shut]

clo·a·ca (klō·ā′kə), *n., pl.* **-cae** (-sē). **1.** sewer. **2.** privy. **3.** receptacle of moral filth. **4.** *Zool.* cavity in the body of birds, reptiles, amphibians, etc., into which the intestinal, urinary, and generative canals open. [< L, prob. < *cluere* purge] —**clo·a′cal,** *adj.*

cloak (klōk), *n.* **1.** a loose outer garment with or without sleeves. **2.** anything that hides or conceals. —*v.* **1.** cover with a cloak. **2.** hide. [< OF < LL *clocca,* orig., bell, < OIrish *cloc*]

cloak-and-dag·ger (klōk′ənd·dag′ər), *adj. Colloq.* associated or done with secrecy and violence.

cloak·room (klōk′rüm′; -rŭm′), *n.* room where coats, hats, etc., can be left for a time.

clob·ber (klob′ər), *v. Am., Slang.* 1. attack violently. 2. *Sports.* defeat severely.

cloche (klōsh), *n.* a close-fitting hat for women. [< F, bell, ult. < LL *clocca.* See CLOCK[1].]

clock[1] (klok), *n.* instrument for measuring and showing time, esp. one that is not carried around like a watch. —*v.* 1. measure the time of. 2. record the time of. [< MDu. *clocke* < OF *cloque* or LL *clocca* < OIrish *cloc*] —clock′er, *n.*

clock[2] (klok), *n.* an ornamental pattern sewn or woven on the side of a stocking, extending up from the ankle. —*v.* ornament with clocks.

clock·wise (klok′wīz′), *adv., adj.* in the direction in which the hands of a clock move.

clock·work (klok′wėrk′), *n.* 1. machinery used to run a clock. 2. machinery like this. 3. like clockwork, with great regularity.

clod (klod), *n.* 1. lump of earth; lump. 2. earth; soil. 3. anything earthy. 4. a stupid person; blockhead. [OE *clod*] —clod′dy, *adj.*

clod·hop·per (klod′hop′ər), *n.* 1. a clumsy boor. 2. a large, heavy shoe.

clog (klog), *v.,* clogged, clog·ging, *n.* —*v.* 1. fill up; choke up. 2. become filled or choked up. 3. hinder; interfere; hold back. 4. dance by beating a heavy rhythm on the floor. —*n.* 1. thing that hinders or interferes. 2. a heavy shoe with a wooden sole. 3. a lighter shoe with a wooden sole, used in dancing. 4. dance in which wooden-soled shoes are worn. [ME *clogge* block]

clois·ter (klois′tər), *n.* 1. a covered walk along the wall of a building, with a row of pillars on the open side. 2. place of religious retirement; convent or monastery. 3. a quiet place shut away from the world. —*v.* shut away in a quiet place. [< OF < L *claustrum* closed place, lock < *claudere* close] —clois·tral (klois′trəl), *adj.*

clomb (klōm), *v. Archaic,* pt. and pp. of climb.

close[1] (klōz), *v.,* closed, clos·ing, *n.* —*v.* 1. shut. 2. stop up; fill; block: *close a gap.* 3. bring or come together: *close the ranks of troops.* 4. grapple. 5. surround; enclose. 6. come to terms; agree. 7. end; finish: *close a debate.* 8. close down, *Am.* shut completely. 9. close in, come near and shut in on all sides. 10. close out, *Am.* sell to get rid of. 11. close up, a. shut completely. b. bring or come nearer together. c. heal. d. *Am.* finish off; wind up. —*n.* end; finish. [< OF *clore* < L *claudere* close] —Syn. *v.* 7. conclude.

close[2] (klōs), *adj.,* clos·er, clos·est, *adv.* —*adj.* 1. with very little in between; near together; near. 2. fitting tightly; tight; narrow: *close quarters.* 3. having its parts near together; compact. 4. intimate; dear. 5. careful; exact: *a close translation.* 6. thorough; strict: *close attention.* 7. having little fresh air: *a close room.* 8. hard to breathe. 9. not fond of talking; keeping quiet about oneself. 10. secret; hidden. 11. strictly guarded; confined. 12. restricted; limited. 13. stingy. 14. hard to get; scarce. 15. nearly equal; almost even. 16. closed; shut; not open. 17. pronounced with the mouth or lips partly shut. —*adv.* in a close manner. [< OF *clos* < L *clausum* closed place < *claudere* close] —close′ly, *adv.* —close′ness, *n.* —Syn. *adj.* 3. dense.

close call (klōs), *Am., Colloq.* narrow escape.

closed-cir·cuit (klōzd′sėr′kit), *adj.* denoting television broadcasting that is limited to a certain audience, as in a group of classrooms, etc.

closed shop, *Am.* factory or business that employs only members of labor unions.

close-fist·ed (klōs′fis′tid), *adj.* stingy. —close′-fist′ed·ly, *adv.* —close′-fist′ed·ness, *n.*

close-hauled (klōs′hôld′), *adj.* having sails set for sailing as nearly as possible in the direction from which the wind is blowing.

close-mouthed (klōs′mouthd′; -mouth′t′), *adj.* not fond of talking; reticent.

clos·et (kloz′it), *n.* 1. a small room used for storing clothes or household supplies. 2. a small, private room for prayer, study, or interviews. 3. a water closet; toilet. —*adj.* 1. private; secluded. 2. unpractical. —*v.* shut up in a private room for a secret talk. [< OF, dim. of *clos* < L *clausum* closed place < *claudere* close]

close-up (klōs′up′), *n. Am.* 1. picture taken at close range. 2. a close view.

clo·sure (klō′zhər), *n.* 1. a closing. 2. a closed condition. 3. thing that closes. 4. end; finish; conclusion. 5. Also, *U.S.* cloture. way of ending a debate and getting an immediate vote on the question being discussed. [< OF < LL *clausura* < L *claudere* close]

clot (klot), *n., v.,* clot·ted, clot·ting. —*n.* a half-solid lump; thickened mass, as of coagulated blood. —*v.* form into clots. [OE *clott*]

cloth (klôth; kloth), *n., pl.* cloths (klôthz; klothz; klôths; kloths), *adj.* —*n.* 1. material made from wool, cotton, silk, linen, hair, etc., by weaving, knitting, or rolling and pressing. 2. piece of this material for some purpose, as a tablecloth. 3. the cloth, clergymen; the clergy. —*adj.* made of cloth. [OE *clāth*]

clothe (klōth), *v.,* clothed or clad, cloth·ing. 1. put clothes on; cover with clothes; dress. 2. provide with clothes. 3. cover. 4. provide; furnish; equip: *clothed with authority.* [OE *clāthian* < *clāth* cloth] —Syn. 1. attire, array, invest, robe, vest, garb. —Ant. 1. undress.

clothes (klōz; klōthz), *n.pl.* 1. covering for a person's body. 2. coverings for a bed. —Syn. 1. apparel, clothing, attire, garb.

clothes·horse (klōz′hôrs′; klōthz′-), *n.* frame to hang clothes on to dry or air them.

clothes·line (klōz′līn′; klōthz′-), *n.* rope or wire to hang clothes on to dry or air them.

clothes·pin (klōz′pin′; klōthz′-), *n. Am.* a wooden clip to hold clothes on a clothesline.

clothes tree, an upright pole with branches on which to hang coats and hats.

cloth·ier (klōth′yər; -i-ər), *n.* 1. seller or maker of clothing. 2. seller of cloth.

cloth·ing (klōth′ing), *n.* 1. clothes. 2. covering.

Clo·tho (klō′thō), *n. Gk. Myth.* one of the three Fates. Clotho spins the thread of life.

clo·ture (klō′chər), *n. U.S.* closure (def. 5). [< F < VL *clausitura.* See CLOSURE.]

cloud (kloud), *n.* 1. a white, gray, or almost black mass in the sky, made up of tiny drops of water. 2. mass of smoke or dust. 3. a great number of things moving close together: *a cloud of arrows.* 4. streak; spot. 5. anything that darkens or dims; cause of gloom, trouble, suspicion, or disgrace. 6. in the clouds, a. far above the earth. b. fanciful; theoretical. c. daydreaming; absent-minded. 7. under a cloud, a. under suspicion; in disgrace. b. in gloom or trouble. —*v.* 1. cover with a cloud or clouds. 2. grow cloudy. 3. streak; spot: *clouded marble.* 4. make or become gloomy, troubled, suspected, or disgraced. [OE *clūd* rock, hill] —cloud′less, *adj.*

cloud·burst (kloud′bėrst′), *n. Am.* a sudden, violent rainfall.

cloud chamber, a large vessel filled with a vapor, esp. a vapor of hydrogen and methyl alcohol, through which subatomic particles may be caused to move and thus permit themselves to be isolated and identified.

cloud seeding, the scattering of particles of carbon dioxide or certain other chemicals in clouds to produce rain.

cloud·y (kloud′i), *adj.,* cloud·i·er, cloud·i·est. 1. covered with clouds; having clouds in it. 2. of or like clouds. 3. not clear: *a cloudy liquid.* 4. streaked; spotted: *cloudy marble.* 5. confused; indistinct: *a cloudy notion.* 6. gloomy; frowning. —cloud′i·ly, *adv.* —cloud′i·ness, *n.*

clout (klout), *n. Colloq.* or *Dial.* —*n.* a blow, esp. with the hand. —*v.* strike, esp. with the hand; cuff. [OE *clūt* small piece of cloth or metal]

clove[1] (klōv), *n.* 1. a strong, fragrant spice obtained from the dried flower buds of a tropical tree. 2. the dried flower bud. 3. the tree. [ME *cloue* < OF *clou* < L *clavus* nail]

clove[2] (klōv), *n.* a small, separate section of a bulb: *a clove of garlic.* [OE *clufu*]

clove[3] (klōv), *v.* pt. of cleave[1].

clo·ven (klō′vən), *v.* pp. of cleave[1]. —*adj.* split; divided.

clo·ven-foot·ed (klō′vən·fût′id), *adj.* 1. having cloven feet. 2. devilish.

clo·ven-hoofed (klō′vən·hûft′; -hûft′), *adj.* 1. having cloven hoofs. 2. devilish.

clo·ver (klō′vər), *n.* a low plant with leaves in three small parts and rounded heads of small red, white, or purple flowers, grown as food for horses and cattle. [OE *clāfre*]

clown (kloun), *n.* 1. man whose business is to amuse others by tricks and jokes. 2. a bad-mannered, awkward person. —*v.* act like a clown; play tricks and jokes; act silly. —**clown′-ish,** *adj.* —**clown′ish·ly,** *adv.* —**clown′ish·ness,** *n.*

clown·er·y (kloun′ər·i), *n., pl.* -er·ies. tricks and jokes of a clown; clownish act.

cloy (kloi), *v.* 1. weary by too much, too sweet, or too rich food. 2. weary by too much of anything pleasant. [< MF *encloyer* < *clou* < L *clavus* nail] —**cloy′ing·ly,** *adv.* —**cloy′ing·ness,** *n.* —Syn. 2. surfeit, pall.

club (klub), *n., v.,* **clubbed, club·bing.** —*n.* 1. a heavy stick of wood, thicker at one end, used as a weapon. 2. stick or bat used to hit a ball in games. 3. group of people joined together for some special purpose: *a tennis club.* 4. a building or rooms used by a club. 5. a playing card with one or more black designs on it shaped like this: ♣. 6. **clubs,** the suit of cards marked with this design. —*v.* 1. beat or hit with a club. 2. join; unite; combine. [< Scand. *klubba*] —Syn. *n.* 1. cudgel. 3. association, society.

club·foot (klub′fůt′), *n., pl.* -feet. 1. a deformed foot. 2. deformity of the foot caused by faulty development before birth. —**club′foot′ed,** *adj.*

club·house (klub′hous′), *n.* a building used by a club.

cluck (kluk), *n.* sound made by a hen calling her chickens. —*v.* make such a sound. [imit.]

clue (klü), *n.* guide to the solving of a mystery or problem. Also, **clew.** [var. of *clew;* OE *cliwen*]

clump (klump), *n.* 1. cluster: *a clump of trees.* 2. lump: *a clump of earth.* 3. sound of heavy, clumsy walking. —*v.* walk heavily and clumsily. [var. of OE *clympre* lump of metal] —**clump′y,** **clump′ish,** *adj.*

clum·sy (klum′zi), *adj.,* -si·er, -si·est. 1. not graceful or skillful; awkward. 2. not well-shaped or well-made. [< *clumse* be numb with cold, prob. < Scand.] —**clum′si·ly,** *adv.* —**clum′si·ness,** *n.* —Syn. 1. ungraceful, ungainly.

clung (klung), *v.* pt. and pp. of **cling.**

clus·ter (klus′tər), *n.* number of things of the same kind growing or grouped together. —*v.* form into a cluster; gather in clusters; group together closely. [OE] —**clus′ter·y,** *adj.*

clutch (kluch), *n.* 1. a tight grasp. 2. a grasping claw, paw, hand, etc. 3. Usually, **clutches.** control; power. 4. device in a machine for connecting or disconnecting the engine or motor that makes it go. 5. lever or pedal that operates this device. —*v.* 1. grasp tightly. 2. seize eagerly; snatch. [var. of OE *clyccan* bend, clench]

clut·ter (klut′ər), *n.* 1. a litter; confusion; disorder. 2. a loud clatter. —*v.* 1. litter with things. 2. clatter loudly. [< CLOT]

Cly·tem·nes·tra (klī′təm·nes′trə), *n.* Gk. *Legend.* wife of Agamemnon. She killed her husband and was killed by her son, Orestes.

Cm, *Chem.* curium.

cm., cm, centimeter; centimeters.

Cnos·sus (nos′əs), *n.* Knossos.

co-, *prefix.* 1. with; together: *coöperate = act with or together.* 2. joint; fellow: *coauthor = joint or fellow author.* 3. equally: *coextensive = equally extensive.* [< L, var. of *com-*]

Co, *Chem.* cobalt.

Co., co., 1. Company. 2. County.

C.O., 1. Commanding Officer. 2. *Colloq.* conscientious objector.

c.o., c/o, 1. in care of. 2. carried over.

coach (kōch), *n.* 1. a large, closed carriage with seats inside and often on top. 2. *Am.* a passenger car of a railroad train. 3. a closed automobile like a sedan. 4. *Am.* bus. 5. person who teaches or trains athletic teams, etc. 6. a private teacher who helps a student prepare for a special test. —*v.* 1. teach; train. 2. help to prepare for a

special test. [< Hung. *kocsi*] ⊳ **Coach** as a verb is used either with persons (teams) or with the name of the sport as object: *he coaches baseball; he coached a winning team that fall.*

coach-and-four (kōch′ən·fôr′; -fōr′), *n.* coach pulled by four horses.

coach dog, Dalmatian.

coach·man (kōch′mən), *n., pl.* -men. man whose work is driving a coach or carriage.

co·ad·ju·tor (kō·aj′ə·tər; kō′ə·jü′tər), *n.* 1. assistant; helper. 2. bishop appointed to assist a bishop.

co·ag·u·late (kō·ag′yə·lāt), *v.,* -lat·ed, -lat·ing. change from a liquid into a thickened mass; thicken. [< L, < *coagulum* means of curdling < *co-* together + *agere* drive] —**co·ag′u·la′tion,** *n.* —**co·ag′u·la′tive,** *adj.* —**co·ag′u·la′tor,** *n.*

coal (kōl), *n.* 1. a black mineral that burns and gives off heat, composed mostly of carbon. It is formed from partly decayed vegetable matter under great pressure in the earth. 2. piece of this mineral. 3. piece of wood, coal, etc., burning, partly burned, or all burned. 4. charcoal. —*v.* 1. supply with coal. 2. take in a supply of coal. [OE *col* (def. 3)]

co·a·lesce (kō′ə·les′), *v.,* -lesced, -lesc·ing. 1. grow together. 2. unite into one body, mass, party, etc.; combine. [< L, < *co-* together + *alescere* grow] —**co′a·les′cence,** *n.* —**co′a·les′cent,** *adj.*

coal gas, 1. gas made from coal, used for heating and lighting. 2. gas given off by burning coal.

co·a·li·tion (kō′ə·lish′ən), *n.* 1. union; combination. 2. a temporary alliance of statesmen, political parties, etc., for some special purpose. [< Med.L *coalitio* < L *coalescere.* See COALESCE.]

coal oil, *Am.* 1. kerosene. 2. petroleum.

coal tar, a black, sticky residue left after soft coal has been distilled to make coal gas. Coal tar is distilled to make aniline dyes, flavorings, perfumes, benzene, etc.

coam·ing (kōm′ing), *n.* a raised edge around a hatch in the deck of a ship, a skylight, etc., to prevent water from running down below.

coarse (kôrs; kōrs), *adj.,* coars·er, coars·est. 1. made up of fairly large parts; not fine: *coarse sand.* 2. rough: *coarse cloth.* 3. common; poor; inferior: *coarse food.* 4. not delicate or refined; crude; vulgar: *coarse manners.* [adjectival use of *course,* n., meaning "ordinary"] —**coarse′ly,** *adv.* —**coarse′ness,** *n.* —Syn. 4. gross, low.

coarse-grained (kôrs′grānd′; kōrs′-), *adj.* 1. having a coarse texture. 2. crude.

coars·en (kôr′sən; kōr′-), *v.* make or become coarse.

coast (kōst), *n.* 1. land along the sea; seashore. 2. region near a coast. 3. **the Coast,** *U.S.* the region along the Pacific. 4. *Am.* ride or slide down a hill without using power. —*v.* 1. go along or near the coast of. 2. sail along a coast. 3. sail from port to port of a coast. 4. *Am.* ride or slide down a hill without using power. [< OF < L *costa* side] —**coast′al,** *adj.* —Syn. *n.* 1. seaboard, shore, strand.

coast·er (kōs′tər), *n.* 1. person or thing that coasts. 2. ship trading along a coast. 3. *Am.* sled to coast on. 4. a little tray to hold a glass or bottle.

coaster brake, *Am.* brake on the rear wheel of a bicycle, worked by pushing back on the pedals.

coast guard, 1. group of men whose work is saving lives and preventing smuggling along the coast of a country. 2. member of this group.

coast·land (kōst′land′), *n.* land along a coast.

coast·line (kōst′līn′), *n.* outline of a coast; coast.

coast·ward (kōst′wərd), *adv., adj.* toward the coast.

coast·ways (kōst′wāz′), *adv.* coastwise.

coast·wise (kōst′wīz′), *adv., adj.* along the coast.

coat (kōt), *n.* 1. an outer garment with sleeves. 2. an outer covering: *a dog's coat of hair.* 3. layer covering a surface: *a coat of paint.* —*v.*

1. provide with a coat. **2.** cover with a layer. [< OF *cote* < Gmc.] —**coat′less,** *adj.*

co·a·ti (kō·ä′ti), *n., pl.* -**tis.** a small animal somewhat like a raccoon, living in Central and South America. [< Brazilian (Tupi)]

coat·ing (kōt′ing), *n.* **1.** layer covering a surface. **2.** cloth for making coats.

coat of arms, shield, or drawing of a shield, with pictures and designs on it. Each family of noble rank has its own special coat of arms.

coat of mail, *pl.* **coats of mail.** garment made of metal rings or plates, worn as armor.

co·au·thor (kō·ô′thər), *n.* a joint author.

coax (kōks), *v.* **1.** persuade by soft words; influence by pleasant ways. **2.** get by coaxing. [< obs. *cokes* a fool] —**coax′er,** *n.* —**coax′ing·ly,** *adv.* —Syn. **1.** wheedle, cajole, beguile, inveigle.

co·ax·i·al (kō·ak′si·əl), **co·ax·al** (-ak′səl), *adj.* having a common axis.

coaxial cable, an insulated connecting cable containing conducting materials surrounding a central conductor, used for transmitting telegraph, telephone, and television impulses.

cob (kob), *n.* **1.** *Am.* the center part of an ear of corn, on which the kernels grow. **2.** a strong horse with short legs. [ME]

co·balt (kō′bôlt), *n.* **1.** *Chem.* a silver-white metallic element, Co, with a pinkish tint, used in making steel, paints, etc. **2.** dark-blue coloring matter made from cobalt. **3.** dark blue. —*adj.* dark-blue. [< G *kobalt,* var. of *kobold* goblin] —**co·bal′tic,** *adj.* —**co·bal′tous,** *adj.*

cobalt bomb, 1. a hydrogen bomb encased in a shell of cobalt instead of steel. It is potentially, because of the wide dispersal of radioactive cobalt dust, the most dangerous atomic weapon thus far conceived. **2. cobalt-60 bomb,** radioactive cobalt (**cobalt 60**) enclosed in a lead case, used in the treatment of cancer.

cob·ble¹ (kob′əl), *v.,* -**bled,** -**bling. 1.** mend (shoes, etc.). **2.** put together clumsily.

cob·ble² (kob′əl), *n.* cobblestone.

cob·bler (kob′lər), *n.* **1.** man whose work is mending shoes. **2.** *Am.* a fruit pie baked in a deep dish.

cob·ble·stone (kob′əl·stōn′), *n.* a rounded stone that was formerly much used in paving.

co·bel·lig·er·ent (kō′bə·lij′ər·ənt), *n.* nation that helps another nation carry on a war.

co·bra (kō′brə), *n.* a very poisonous snake of southern Asia and Africa. [short for Pg. *cobra de capello* snake with a hood]

cob·web (kob′web′), *n.* **1.** a spider's web or the stuff it is made of. **2.** anything thin and slight or entangling like a spider's web. [OE (ātor) *coppe* spider + *web*] —**cob′web′by,** *adj.*

co·ca (kō′kə), *n.* **1.** a small tropical shrub growing in South America whose dried leaves are used to make cocaine and other alkaloids. **2.** its dried leaves. [< Peruvian *cuca*]

co·caine, co·cain (kō·kān′; kō′kān), *n.* drug used to deaden pain and as a stimulant.

coc·cus (kok′əs), *n., pl.* **coc·ci** (kok′sī). bacterium shaped like a sphere. [< NL < Gk. *kokkos* seed]

coc·cyx (kok′siks), *n., pl.* **coc·cy·ges** (kok·sī′jēz). a small triangular bone at the lower end of the spinal column. [< L < Gk. *kokkyx,* orig., cuckoo; because shaped like cuckoo's bill]

coch·i·neal (koch′ə·nēl′; koch′ə·nēl), *n.* a bright-red dye made from the dried bodies of the females of a scale insect that lives on cactus plants of tropical America. [< F < Sp. *cochinilla,* ult. < L *coccinus* scarlet < Gk.]

coch·le·a (kok′li·ə), *n., pl.* -**le·ae** (-li·ē). a spiral-shaped cavity of the inner ear, containing the sensory ends of the auditory nerve. [< L < Gk. *kochlias* snail] —**coch′le·ar,** *adj.*

cock¹ (kok), *n.* **1.** a male chicken; rooster. **2.** the male of other birds. **3.** faucet used to turn the flow of a liquid or gas on or off. **4.** hammer of a gun. **5.** position of the hammer of a gun when it is pulled back, ready to fire. **6.** weathercock. —*v.* pull back the hammer of (a gun), ready to fire. [OE *cocc*]

cock² (kok), *v.* turn up jauntily; stick up defiantly. —*n.* an upward turn, as of the brim of a hat. [appar. < *cock¹*]

cock³ (kok), *n.* a small, cone-shaped pile of hay in a field. —*v.* pile in cocks. [ME]

cock·ade (kok·ād′), *n.* knot of ribbon or a rosette worn on the hat as a badge. [alter. of *cockard* < F, < *coq* cock] —**cock·ad′ed,** *adj.*

cock·a·too (kok′ə·tü′; kok′ə·tü), *n., pl.* -**toos.** a large, brightly colored parrot of Australia, East Indies, etc. [< Du. < Malay *kakatua*]

cock·a·trice (kok′ə·tris), *n.* a fabled serpent whose look was supposed to cause death. [< OF *cocatris* < L *calcare* tread]

cock·boat (kok′bōt′), *n.* a small rowboat.

cock·chaf·er (kok′chāf′ər), *n.* a large European beetle that destroys plants.

cock·crow (kok′krō′), *n.* dawn.

cocked hat, 1. hat with the brim turned up. **2.** hat pointed in front and in back.

cock·er·el (kok′ər·əl; kok′rəl), *n.* a young rooster, not more than one year old.

cock·er spaniel (kok′ər), or **cocker,** *n.* any of a breed of small dogs with long, silky hair and drooping ears.

cock·eyed (kok′īd′), *adj.* **1.** cross-eyed. **2.** *Slang.* tilted or twisted to one side. **3.** *Slang.* foolish; silly.

Cocker spaniel (11 in. tall)

cock·fight (kok′fit′), *n.* fight between roosters or gamecocks armed with steel spurs. —**cock′fight′ing,** *n.*

cock·horse (kok′hôrs′), *n.* a child's hobbyhorse.

cock·le (kok′əl), *n., v.,* -**led,** -**ling.** —*n.* **1.** a salt-water mollusk with two ridged shells that are somewhat heart-shaped. **2.** cockleshell. **3.** bulge on the surface. **4. cockles of one's heart,** the inmost part of one's heart or feelings. —*v.* wrinkle; pucker. [< F *coquille,* blend of F *coque* shell and L *conchylium* < Gk. *konchylion,* dim. of *konche* conch]

cock·le·bur (kok′əl·bėr′), *n. Am.* any of several weeds with spiny burs.

cock·le·shell (kok′əl·shel′), *n.* **1.** shell of the cockle. **2.** a small, light, shallow boat.

cock·ney (kok′ni), *n., pl.* -**neys,** *adj.* —*n.* **1.** native or inhabitant of the poorer section of London who speaks a particular dialect of English. **2.** this dialect. —*adj.* **1.** of or like this dialect. **2.** of or like cockneys. [ME *cokeney*]

cock·pit (kok′pit′), *n.* **1.** a small, open place in an airplane, boat, etc., where the pilot or passengers sit. **2.** an enclosed place for cockfights.

cock·roach (kok′rōch′), *n.* any of a family of insects, esp. a small brownish or yellowish species found in kitchens, around water pipes, etc. [alter. of Sp. *cucaracha*]

cocks·comb (koks′kōm′), *n.* **1.** the fleshy, red part on the head of a rooster. **2.** coxcomb. **3.** plant with crested or feathery clusters of red or yellow flowers.

Cockscomb

cock·sure (kok′shůr′), *adj.* **1.** perfectly sure; absolutely certain. **2.** too sure. —*adv.* in a cocksure manner. —**cock′sure′ness,** *n.*

cock·swain (kok′sən; -swān′), *n.* coxswain.

cock·tail (kok′tāl′), *n.* **1.** *Am.* an iced drink, often composed of gin or whiskey, mixed with bitters, vermouth, fruit juices, etc. **2.** appetizer: *a tomato-juice cocktail.* **3.** shellfish served in a small glass with a highly seasoned sauce. **4.** mixed fruits served in a glass.

cock·y (kok′i), *adj.,* **cock·i·er, cock·i·est,** *Colloq.* conceited; swaggering. —**cock′i·ly,** *adv.* —**cock′i·ness,** *n.*

co·co (kō′kō), *n., pl.* **co·cos. 1.** a tall palm tree on which coconuts grow. **2.** its fruit or seed. Also, **cocoa.** [< Pg. *coco* grinning face]

co·coa¹ (kō′kō), *n.* **1.** powder made by roasting and grinding cacao seeds. **2.** drink made of this powder with milk or water and sugar. **3.** dull brown. —*adj.* of or having to do with cocoa. [var. of *cacao*]

co·coa[2] (kō′kō), n. coco.

co·co·nut, co·coa·nut (kō′kə·nut′; -nət), n. a large, round, brown, hard-shelled fruit of the coco palm. Coconuts have a white, edible lining and a white liquid called **coconut milk**.

co·coon (kə·kün′), n. a silky case spun by the larva of an insect to live in while it is a pupa. [< F cocon < coque shell]

cod (kod), n., pl. **cods** or (esp. collectively) **cod**. an important food fish found in the cold parts of the N Atlantic. [ME]

Cod (kod), n. Cape, a hook-shaped peninsula in SE Massachusetts.

C.O.D., c.o.d., Am. cash on delivery; collect on delivery.

cod·dle (kod′əl), v., -dled, -dling. 1. treat tenderly; pamper. 2. cook in hot water without boiling: a coddled egg. [var. of caudle, n., gruel < OF < L calidus hot] —Syn. 1. humor, indulge.

code (kōd), n., v., **cod·ed, cod·ing.** —n. 1. a collection of the laws of a country arranged in a clear way so that they can be understood and used. 2. any set of rules. 3. system of signals for sending messages by telegraph flags, etc. 4. arrangement of words, figures, etc., to keep a message short or secret. —v. 1. change or translate into a code. 2. arrange in a code. [< F < L codex CODEX]

co·deine (kō′dēn; -di·ēn), **co·de·in** (kō′di·in), n. a white, crystalline drug obtained from opium, used to relieve pain and cause sleep. [< Gk. kodeia poppy head]

co·dex (kō′deks), n., pl. **co·di·ces** (kō′də·sēz; kod′ə-). volume of manuscripts, esp. of the Scriptures. [< L, var. of caudex tree trunk, book]

cod·fish (kod′fish′), n., pl. **-fish·es** or (esp. collectively) **-fish**. cod.

codg·er (koj′ər), n. Colloq. a queer or odd person.

cod·i·cil (kod′ə·səl), n. 1. something added to a will to change it, add to it, or explain it. 2. anything added to change or explain something. [< L codicillus, dim. of codex CODEX]

cod·i·fy (kod′ə·fī; kō′də-), v., -fied, -fy·ing. arrange (laws, etc.) according to a system. —cod′i·fi·ca′tion, n. —cod′i·fi′er, n.

cod·ling (kod′ling), **cod·lin** (-lin), n. an unripe apple.

codling moth, codlin moth, a small moth whose larvae destroy apples, pears, etc.

cod-liv·er oil (kod′liv′ər), oil extracted from the liver of cod, used as a medicine. It is rich in vitamins A and D.

Co·dy (kō′di), n. William F. ("Buffalo Bill"), 1846–1917, American frontier scout and showman.

co·ed, co-ed (kō′ed′), n. Am., Colloq. a girl or woman student at a coeducational college or school.

co·ed·u·ca·tion (kō′ej·ù·kā′shən), n. Am. education of boys and girls or men and women together in the same school or classes. —co′ed·u·ca′tion·al, adj. —co′ed·u·ca′tion·al·ly, adv.

co·ef·fi·cient (kō′ə·fish′ənt), n. 1. Math. a number or symbol put before and multiplying another. In 3x, 3 is the coefficient of x. 2. Physics. a ratio used as a multiplier to calculate the behavior of a substance under different conditions of heat, light, etc.

coe·la·canth (sē′lə·kanth), n. any of a group of fishes having rounded scales and lobed fins, formerly considered extinct. A coelacanth is similar to the primitive sea vertebrates which gave rise to all land vertebrates. [< NL, < Gk. koilos hollow + akantha thorn, spine]

coe·len·ter·ate (si·len′tər·āt; -it), Zool. —n. one of a group of salt-water animals with saclike bodies. —adj. belonging to this group. Hydras, jellyfish, corals, etc., are coelenterates. [< NL < Gk. koilos hollow + enteron intestine]

coe·li·ac (sē′li·ak), adj. Anat. of or in the abdominal cavity. Also, celiac.

co·e·qual (kō·ē′kwəl), adj. equal in rank, degree, etc. —n. one that is coequal. —co·e·qual·i·ty (kō′i·kwol′ə·ti), n. —co·e′qual·ly, adv.

co·erce (kō·ėrs′), v., **co·erced, co·erc·ing.** 1.

compel; force. 2. control or restrain by force. [< L coercere < co- together + arcere restrain] —co·erc′er, n. —co·er′ci·ble, adj. —co·er′cive, adj. —co·er′cive·ly, adv. —co·er′cive·ness, n.

co·er·cion (kō·ėr′shən), n. 1. use of force; compulsion; constraint. 2. government by force. —co·er′cion·ist, n.

co·e·val (kō·ē′vəl), adj. 1. of the same age, date, or duration. 2. contemporary. —n. a contemporary. [< LL, < co- equal + aevum age]

co·ex·ec·u·tor (kō′ig·zek′yə·tər), n. person who is an executor of a will along with another.

co·ex·ist (kō′ig·zist′), v. exist together or at the same time. —co′ex·ist′ence, n. —co′ex·ist′ent, adj.

co·ex·tend (kō′iks·tend′), v. extend equally or to the same limits. —co·ex·ten·sion (kō′iks·ten′shən), n. —co′ex·ten′sive, adj.

cof·fee (kôf′i; kof′i), n. 1. a dark-brown drink, first used in Europe about 1600. 2. the seeds from which the drink is made. 3. a tall, tropical shrub on which the seeds grow. 4. a social gathering, often in the morning, at which coffee is served. 5. the color of coffee. [< Turk. qahveh < Ar. qahwa]

coffee bean, seed of the coffee shrub. Coffee beans are roasted and ground to make coffee.

cof·fer (kôf′ər; kof′-), n. 1. box, chest, or trunk, esp. one used to hold money or other valuable things. 2. coffers, treasury; funds. [< OF < L cophinus basket. See COFFIN.]

cof·fin (kôf′in; kof′-), n. box into which a dead person is put to be buried. —v. put into a coffin. [< OF < L Gk. kophinos basket]

cog (kog), n. 1. one of a series of teeth on the edge of a wheel that transfers motion by locking into the teeth of another wheel of the same kind. 2. wheel with such a row of teeth on it. [< Scand. (Sw.) kugge) —cogged (kogd), adj.

co·gent (kō′jənt), adj. forcible; convincing: cogent arguments. [< L cogens, ult. < co- together + agere drive] —co′gen·cy, n. —co′gent·ly, adv. —Syn. potent, compelling.

cog·i·tate (koj′ə·tāt), v., -tat·ed, -tat·ing. think over; consider with care; meditate; ponder. [< L, < co- (intensive) + agitare consider < agere discuss] —cog′i·ta′tion, n. —cog′i·ta′tive, adj. —cog′i·ta′tive·ly, adv. —cog′i·ta′tive·ness, n. —cog′i·ta′tor, n.

co·gnac (kōn′yak; kon′-), n. kind of French brandy. [< F]

cog·nate (kog′nāt), adj. related by family, origin, nature, or quality: English, Dutch, and German are cognate languages. —n. person, word, or thing so related to another. German Wasser and English water are cognates. [< L, < co- together + gnatus born]

cog·ni·tion (kog·nish′ən), n. 1. act of knowing; perception; awareness. 2. thing known, perceived, or recognized. [< L cognitio, < co- (intensive) + gnoscere know] —cog·ni′tion·al, adj.

cog·ni·zance (kog′nə·zəns; kon′ə-), n. 1. knowledge; perception; awareness. 2. Law. a. an official notice. b. right or power to deal with judicially. [< OF conoissance < conoistre know < L cognoscere. See COGNITION.]

cog·ni·zant (kog′nə·zənt; kon′ə-), adj. aware.

cog·no·men (kog·nō′mən), n. 1. surname; family name; last name. 2. any name. 3. nickname. [< L, < co- with + nomen name; form infl. by cognoscere recognize] —cog·nom·i·nal (kog·nom′ə·nəl; -nō′mə-), adj.

cog·wheel (kog′hwēl′), n. wheel with teeth projecting from the rim for transmitting or receiving motion.

Cogwheels

co·hab·it (kō·hab′it), v. 1. live together as husband and wife do. 2. live together. —co·hab·i·tant (kō·hab′ə·tənt), n. —co·hab′i·ta′tion, n.

co·here (kō·hir′), v., -hered, -her·ing. 1. stick together; hold together. 2. be connected logically; be consistent. [< L, < co- together + haerere cleave] —Syn. 1. cleave, adhere.

co·her·ence (kō·hir′əns), **co·her·en·cy**

(–ən·si), *n.* **1.** logical connection; consistency. **2.** a sticking together; cohesion. —Syn. **1.** congruity.

co·her·ent (kō·hir′ənt), *adj.* **1.** sticking together; holding together. **2.** logically connected; consistent. —**co·her′ent·ly**, *adv.*

co·he·sion (kō·hē′zhən), *n.* **1.** a sticking together; tendency to hold together. **2.** *Physics.* attraction between molecules of the same kind. —**co·he′sive**, *adj.* —**co·he′sive·ly**, *adv.* —**co·he′sive·ness**, *n.*

co·hort (kō′hôrt), *n.* **1.** one of the ten infantry divisions of an ancient Roman legion. **2.** group of soldiers. **3.** any group or company. [< L *cohors* court, enclosure. Doublet of COURT.]

coif (koif), *n.* cap or hood that fits closely around the head. —*v.* cover with a coif or something like a coif. [< OF < LL *cofia* < Gmc.]

coif·fure (kwä·fyùr′), *n.* **1.** style of arranging the hair. **2.** headdress. [< F < *coiffer* COIF, v.]

coign of vantage (koin), good location for watching or doing something.

coil (koil), *v.* **1.** wind around and around in circular or spiral shape. **2.** move in a winding course. —*n.* **1.** anything wound around and around in this way. **2.** one wind or turn of a coil. **3.** series of connected pipes arranged in a coil or row, as in a radiator. **4.** a spiral of wire for conducting electricity. **5.** twist of hair. [< OF < L *colligere* COLLECT] —coil′er, *n.*

Coil (def. 1)

coin (koin), *n.* **1.** piece of metal stamped by the government for use as money. **2.** metal money. —*v.* **1.** make (money) by stamping metal. **2.** make (metal) into money. **3.** make up; invent: *the word "blurb" was coined by Gelett Burgess.* **4.** coin money, *Colloq.* become rich. [< F, corner, < L *cuneus* wedge] —coin′er, *n.*

coin·age (koin′ij), *n.* **1.** the making of coins. **2.** coins; metal money. **3.** system of coins. **4.** right of coining money. **5.** act or process of making up; inventing. **6.** word, phrase, etc., invented.

co·in·cide (kō′in·sīd′), *v.*, **-cid·ed**, **-cid·ing**. **1.** occupy the same place in space. **2.** occupy the same time. **3.** correspond exactly; agree. [< Med.L *coincidere* < L *co-* together + *in* upon + *cadere* fall] —Syn. **3.** concur, harmonize, tally.

co·in·ci·dence (kō·in′sə·dəns), *n.* **1.** exact correspondence; agreement, esp. the chance occurrence of two things at such a time as to seem remarkable, fitting, etc. **2.** a coinciding; act or fact of occupying the same time or place.

co·in·ci·dent (kō·in′sə·dənt), *adj.* **1.** happening at the same time. **2.** occupying the same place or position. —**co·in′ci·dent·ly**, *adv.*

co·in·ci·den·tal (kō·in′sə·den′təl), *adj.* **1.** coincident. **2.** showing coincidence. —**co·in′ci·den′tal·ly**, *adv.*

co·i·tion (kō·ish′ən), **co·i·tus** (kō′ə·təs), *n.* sexual intercourse. [< L *coitio* < *co-* together + *ire* go]

coke¹ (kōk), *n.*, *v.*, **coked**, **cok·ing**. —*n.* fuel made from coal by heating it in a closed oven until the gases have been removed. Coke burns with much heat and little smoke, and is used in furnaces, for melting metal, etc. —*v.* change into coke. [? var. of *colk* core]

coke² (kōk), *n. Am., Colloq.* a dark-colored, carbonated soft drink. [short for *Coca-Cola*, a trademark]

Col., **1.** Colonel. **2.** Colorado (official abbrev., Colo.).

col., column.

co·la (kō′lə), *n.* kola.

col·an·der (kul′ən·dər; kol′–), *n.* vessel or dish full of small holes for draining off liquids. [< VL *colator* or Med.L *colatorium* < L *colare* strain]

cold (kōld), *adj.* **1.** much less warm than the body. **2.** having a relatively low temperature. **3.** not warm enough for comfort. **4.** dead. **5.** unconscious. **6.** lacking in feeling; unfriendly: *a cold greeting.* **7.** lacking in feeling, passion, or enthusiasm; indifferent: *a cold nature.* **8.** failing to excite interest. **9.** depressing. **10.** faint; weak: *a cold scent.* **11.** blue, green, or gray; not red or yellow. —*n.* **1.** lack of heat or warmth; low tem-

perature. **2.** cold weather. **3.** sensation produced by contact with anything cold. **4.** sickness that causes running at the nose, sore throat, sneezing, etc. **5.** catch cold, become sick with a cold. **6.** in the cold, all alone; neglected. [OE *cald*] —cold′ish, *adj.* —cold′ly, *adv.* —cold′ness, *n.* —Syn. *adj.* **1.** chill, chilly, frosty, wintry. **2.** cool.

cold-blood·ed (kōld′blud′id), *adj.* **1.** having blood whose temperature varies with that of the surroundings. **2.** feeling the cold because of poor circulation. **3.** lacking in feeling; cruel. —**cold′-blood′ed·ly**, *adv.* —**cold′-blood′ed·ness**, *n.*

cold cream, a creamy, soothing salve for the skin.

cold-heart·ed (kōld′här′tid), *adj.* lacking in feeling; unsympathetic; unkind. —**cold′-heart′ed·ly**, *adv.* —**cold′-heart′ed·ness**, *n.*

cold rubber, a tough synthetic rubber formed at a low temperature.

cold shoulder, *Colloq.* deliberately unfriendly or indifferent treatment; neglect.

cold-shoul·der (kōld′shōl′dər), *v. Colloq.* treat in an unfriendly or indifferent way.

cold sore, blister in or on the mouth, often accompanying a cold or a fever.

cold war, a prolonged contest for national advantage, conducted by diplomatic, economic, and psychological rather than military means.

cold wave, a kind of permanent hair waving using a setting solution that does not need to be heated.

cole (kōl), or **cole·wort** (kōl′wert′), *n.* any of various plants belonging to the same family as the cabbage, esp. rape. [< L *caulis* cabbage]

co·le·op·ter·ous (kō′li·op′tər·əs; kol′i–), *adj.* belonging to a group of insects including beetles and weevils. [< Gk., < *koleos* sheath + *pteron* wing]

Cole·ridge (kōl′rij), *n.* Samuel Taylor, 1772–1834, English poet, critic, and philosopher.

cole·slaw (kōl′slô′), *n. Am.* salad made of sliced raw cabbage. [< Du. *kool sla* cabbage salad]

col·ic (kol′ik), *n.* severe pains in the abdomen. —*adj.* of or pertaining to the colon. [< LL < Gk. *kolikos* of the COLON²] —**col′ick·y** (kol′ik·i), *adj.*

col·i·se·um (kol′ə·sē′əm), *n.* a large building or stadium for games, contests, etc. [< Med.L var. of *colosseum*]

co·li·tis (kō·lī′tis; kə–), *n.* inflammation of the colon, often causing severe pain in the abdomen.

coll., **1.** collect. **2.** college; collegiate.

col·lab·o·rate (kə·lab′ə·rāt), *v.*, **-rat·ed**, **-rat·ing**. **1.** work together. **2.** aid or coöperate traitorously. [< L, < *com-* with + *laborare* work] —**col·lab′o·ra′tion**, *n.* —**col·lab′o·ra′tive**, *adj.* —**col·lab′o·ra′tor**, **col·lab′o·ra′tion·ist**, *n.*

col·lapse (kə·laps′), *v.*, **-lapsed**, **-laps·ing**, *n.* —*v.* **1.** fall in; shrink together suddenly. **2.** break down; fail suddenly. **3.** *Am.* fold or push together: *collapse a telescope.* **4.** lose courage, strength, etc., suddenly. —*n.* **1.** a falling in; a sudden shrinking together. **2.** breakdown; failure. [< L *collapsus* < *com-* completely + *labi* fall] —**col·laps′i·ble**, **col·laps′a·ble**, *adj.*

col·lar (kol′ər), *n.* **1.** a straight or turned-over neckband of a coat, a dress, or a shirt. **2.** a separate band of linen, lace, or other material worn around the neck. **3.** a leather or metal band for a dog's neck. **4.** a leather roll for a horse's neck to bear the weight of the loads he pulls. —*v.* **1.** put a collar on. **2.** seize by the collar; capture. **3.** *Colloq.* seize; take. [< L *collare* < *collum* neck]

col·lar·bone (kol′ər·bōn′), *n.* bone connecting the breastbone and the shoulder blade; clavicle.

col·late (kə·lāt′; kol′āt), *v.*, **-lat·ed**, **-lat·ing**. **1.** compare carefully. **2.** check (pages, sheets, etc.) for correct arrangement. [< L, < *com-* together + *latus*, pp. of *ferre* bring] —**col·la′tor**, *n.*

col·lat·er·al (kə·lat′ər·əl), *adj.* **1.** situated at the side. **2.** parallel; side by side. **3.** related but less important; secondary; indirect. **4.** descended from the same ancestors, but in a different line. **5.** additional. **6.** accompanying. **7.** secured by stocks, bonds, etc. —*n.* **1.** a collateral relative. **2.** *Am.* stocks, bonds, etc., pledged as security for a loan. [< Med.L, < *com*- + L *lateralis* lateral] —col·lat'er·al·ly, *adv.*

col·la·tion (kə·lā'shən), *n.* 1. a light meal. 2. a collating. 3. a careful comparison.

col·league (kol'ēg), *n.* an associate; fellow worker. [< F < L *collega* < *com*- together + *legare* send or choose as deputy] —col'league-ship, *n.*

col·lect (*v., adj., adv.* kə·lekt'; *n.* kol'ekt), *v.* 1. bring or come together; gather together. 2. gather together for a set: *collect stamps for a hobby.* 3. ask and receive pay for (bills, debts, dues, taxes, etc.). 4. regain control of (oneself). —*n.* a short prayer used in certain church services. —*adj., adv.* Am. to be paid for at the place of delivery: *telephone collect.* [< L *col·lectus* < *com*- together + *legere* gather] —col·lect'a·ble, col·lect'i·ble, *adj.*

col·lect·ed (kə·lek'tid), *adj.* 1. brought together; gathered together. 2. under control; not confused or disturbed; calm. —col·lect'ed·ly, *adv.* —col·lect'ed·ness, *n.*

col·lec·tion (kə·lek'shən), *n.* 1. act or practice of collecting. 2. group of things gathered from many places and belonging together. 3. money collected. 4. mass; heap.

col·lec·tive (kə·lek'tiv), *adj.* 1. of a group; as a group; taken all together. 2. singular in form, but plural in meaning. *Crowd, people, troop,* and *herd* are collective nouns. 3. formed by collecting. 4. forming a collection. —*n.* 1. noun whose singular form names a group of objects or persons. 2. farm, factory, or other organization with collectivistic management. ➤ collective noun. When a writer means the group as a whole, the noun takes a singular verb and a singular pronoun; when he means the individuals of the group, the noun takes a plural verb or pronoun: *The first couple on the floor was Tom and Janet. We drove near the place where the old couple were living.* There is often a temptation to use a collective noun and try to keep it singular when the meaning really calls for a plural construction. Often the writer slips unconsciously from singular to plural in such a passage: *Into the church troops the entire town, seats itself on the uncomfortable wooden benches and there remains for a good two hours, while an aged curé preaches to them* [consistency demands it] *of their* [its] *wicked lives and awful sins.* [This might better have started *Into the church troop all the people, seat themselves. . . .*] Obviously a collective should not be treated as *both* singular and plural in the same context: *The company was* organized and immediately sent out *its* [not *their*] representatives.

collective bargaining, negotiation about wages, hours, and other working conditions between workers organized as a group and their employer or employers.

col·lec·tive·ly (kə·lek'tiv·li), *adv.* 1. as a group; all together. 2. in a singular form, but with a plural meaning.

col·lec·tiv·ism (kə·lek'tiv·iz·əm), *n.* control of the production of goods and services and the distribution of wealth by people as a group or by the government. —col·lec'tiv·ist, *n.* —col·lec'tiv·is'tic, *adj.*

col·lec·tor (kə·lek'tər), *n.* 1. person or thing that collects. 2. person hired to collect money owed. —col·lec'tor·ship, *n.*

col·leen (kol'ēn; kə·lēn'), *n. Irish.* girl.

col·lege (kol'ij), *n.* 1. institution of higher learning that gives degrees. 2. *Am.* the academic department of a university for general instruction, as distinguished from the special, professional, or graduate schools. 3. *Am.* school for special or professional instruction, as in medicine, pharmacy, agriculture, or music. 4. an organized association of persons having certain powers, rights, duties, and purposes. 5. building or buildings used by a college. [< OF < L *collegium* < *collega* COLLEAGUE]

College of Cardinals, Sacred College.

col·le·gian (kə·lē'jən; -ji·ən), *n.* a college student.

col·le·giate (kə·lē'jit; -ji·it), *adj.* of or like a college or college students.

col·lide (kə·līd'), *v.,* -lid·ed, -lid·ing. 1. come violently into contact; run into with force; crash. 2. clash; conflict. [< L *collidere* < *com*- together + *laedere,* orig., to strike]

col·lie (kol'i), *n.* a large, intelligent, long-haired breed of dog used for tending sheep and as a pet.

Collie (ab. 2 ft. high at the shoulder)

col·lier (kol'yər), *n. Esp. Brit.* 1. ship for carrying coal. 2. a coal miner. [ME *colier* < col COAL]

col·lier·y (kol'yər·i), *n., pl.* -lier·ies. coal mine and its buildings and equipment.

col·li·mate (kol'ə·māt), *v.,* -mat·ed, -mat·ing. 1. bring into line; make parallel. 2. adjust accurately the line of sight of (a surveying instrument, telescope, etc.). [< L *collimatus,* misread for *collineatus,* ult. < *com*- together + *linea* line] —col'li·ma'tion, *n.*

col·li·sion (kə·lizh'ən), *n.* 1. a violent rushing against; hitting or striking violently together. 2. clash; conflict. —Syn. 1. impact.

col·lo·cate (kol'ō·kāt), *v.,* -cat·ed, -cat·ing. 1. place together. 2. arrange. [< L, < *com*- together + *locare* place] —col'lo·ca'tion, *n.*

col·lo·di·on (kə·lō'di·ən), *n.* a gluelike liquid that dries very rapidly and leaves a tough, waterproof, transparent film. [< Gk. *kollodes* gluey < *kolla* glue]

col·loid (kol'oid), *n. Physics, Chem.* substance composed of particles that are extremely small but larger than most molecules. Colloids do not actually dissolve, but remain suspended in a suitable gas, liquid, or solid. —*adj.* colloidal. [< Gk. *kolla* glue]

col·loi·dal (kə·loi'dəl), *adj.* being, containing, or like a colloid. —col·loid·al·i·ty (kol'oi·dal'ə·ti), *n.*

col·lop (kol'əp), *n.* 1. a small slice, esp. of meat. 2. fold of flesh or skin on the body. [ME *colope*]

colloq., colloquial; colloquialism.

col·lo·qui·al (kə·lō'kwi·əl), *adj.* used in everyday, informal talk, but not in formal speech or writing. —col·lo'qui·al·ly, *adv.* —col·lo'qui·al·ness, *n.* —Syn. conversational, familiar, informal. ➤ Colloquial means conversational, used in speaking. Since the speech of people varies with their education, work, and social status, there are obviously many different types of colloquial English. Since the bulk of conversation is informal, *colloquial* suggests informal rather than formal English. It need not, however, mean the speech of uneducated people, and in this book applies to the language spoken by people of some education and social standing, to language that can be safely used except on decidedly formal occasions.

col·lo·qui·al·ism (kə·lō'kwi·əl·iz'əm), *n.* 1. a colloquial word or phrase. 2. a colloquial style or usage.

col·lo·quist (kol'ə·kwist), *n.* interlocutor.

col·lo·quy (kol'ə·kwi), *n., pl.* -quies. 1. a talking together; conversation. 2. conference. [< L, < *com*- with + *loqui* speak]

col·lude (kə·lüd'), *v.,* -lud·ed, -lud·ing. act together through a secret understanding; conspire in a fraud. [< L, < *com*- with + *ludere* play]

col·lu·sion (kə·lü'zhən), *n.* a secret agreement for some wrong purpose; conspiracy. —col·lu'sive, *adj.* —col·lu'sive·ly, *adv.* —col·lu'sive·ness, *n.*

Colo., Colorado (official abbrev.).

co·logne (kə·lōn'), *n. Am.* a fragrant liquid, not so strong as perfume. [for *eau de Cologne,* a trademark meaning water of *Cologne*]

Co·logne (kə·lōn'), *n.* city in W Germany, on the Rhine.

Co·lom·bi·a (kə·lum'bi·ə), *n.* country in NW South America. —Co·lom'bi·an, *adj., n.*

Co·lom·bo (kə·lum′bō), *n.* seaport and capital of Ceylon.

co·lon[1] (kō′lən), *n.* mark (:) of punctuation used before a series of items, explanations, long quotations, etc., to set them off from the rest of the sentence. [< L < Gk. *kolon* limb, clause]
> The colon is a mark of anticipation, directing attention to what follows. (Contrast the semicolon, which is a stop.) The colon is a formal mark and usually emphatic. The principal uses of the colon are:
1. After introductory phrases, as in the preceding line, and after the salutation of formal letters: *Dear Sir:* [contrast the comma in informal letters: *Dear Fritz,*].
2. Between two clauses of a compound sentence when the second is either an illustration of the first, a restatement in different terms, or sometimes an amplification of the first: *They obtained the information by careful digging: they examined old files, read through unpublished manuscripts, and checked thousands of reports.*
3. In a few conventional uses, although even these vary:
(a) Between hours and minutes expressed in figures: *11:42 a.m., 3:28 p.m.* [or: *11.42 a.m., 3.28 p.m.*].
(b) In formal bibliographies and formal citations of books: between author and title—Stuart Chase: *Men and Machines;* between place of publication and publisher—New York: Holt, 1930; between volume and page—*The Atlantic Monthly,* 160: 129–40. In these three positions a comma would often and perhaps usually be found.
4. Followed by either a capital or a small letter. The capital is more usual when the matter following the colon is in the form of a complete sentence, a small letter when it is a phrase.
5. Following an abbreviation. The period of the abbreviation is often omitted (*i.e:* rather than *i.e.:*).

co·lon[2] (kō′lən), *n.*, *pl.* **co·lons, co·la** (kō′lə). *Anat.* the lower part of the large intestine. [< L < Gk. *kolon*] —**co·lon·ic** (kə·lon′ik), *adj.*

Co·lón (kō·lon′; -lōn′), *n.* seaport in N Panama near the Atlantic end of the Panama Canal.

colo·nel (kér′nəl), *n.* an army officer ranking next below a brigadier general and next above a lieutenant colonel. He usually commands a regiment. [earlier *coronel,* < F *coronel,* now *colonel* < Ital. *colonnello* < *colonna* COLUMN] —**colo′nel·cy, colo′nel·ship,** *n.* > Colonel is a good example of a spelling that has survived a change of pronunciation. The word, from the French, had two parallel forms, *colonel, coronel,* each pronounced in three syllables. For 150 years the word has been pronounced (kér′nəl), from the *coronel* form, but spelling has kept *colonel.*

co·lo·ni·al (kə·lō′ni·əl), *adj.* 1. of a colony; having to do with colonies. 2. of or having to do with the thirteen British colonies that became the United States. —*n.* person living in a colony. —**co·lo′ni·al·ly,** *adv.*

col·o·nist (kol′ə·nist), *n.* 1. person who helps to found a colony; settler. 2. person living in a colony.

col·o·nize (kol′ə·nīz), *v.,* -nized, -niz·ing. 1. establish a colony or colonies in. 2. establish (persons) in a colony; settle in a colony. 3. form a colony. —**col′o·ni·za′tion,** *n.* —**col′o·niz′er,** *n.*

col·on·nade (kol′ə·nād′), *n. Archit.* series of columns set the same distance apart. [< F < Ital. *colonnata* < *colonna* COLUMN] —**col′on·nad′ed,** *adj.*

col·o·ny (kol′ə·ni), *n., pl.* -nies. 1. group of people who leave their own country and go to settle in another land, but who still remain citizens of their own country. 2. settlement made by such a group of people. 3. territory distant from the country that governs it. 4. group of people from the same country or with the same occupation, living in a certain part of a city: *a colony of artists.* 5. group of animals or plants of the same kind, living or growing together: *a colony of ants.* 6. an aggregation of bacteria in a culture. 7. the Colonies, the

thirteen British colonies that became the United States of America. [< L, < *colonus* cultivator, settler < *colere* cultivate] —Syn. 3. possession.

col·o·phon (kol′ə·fon; -fən), *n.* words or inscription placed at the end of a book, telling the name of the publisher, etc. [< LL < Gk. *kolophon* summit, final touch]

col·or (kul′ər), *n.* 1. sensation produced by the effect of waves of light striking the retina of the eye. 2. red, yellow, green, blue, purple, etc., or any combination of these: *she never wears colors, but always dresses in black, white, or gray.* 3. paint; dye; pigment. 4. redness of face; ruddy complexion. 5. flush caused by blushing. 6. the skin color of any race that is not white. 7. an outward appearance; show: *his lies had some color of truth.* 8. effect of adding realistic details to a description. 9. distinguishing quality; vividness. 10. any hue adopted for distinction, as for a badge. 11. change color, a. turn pale. b. blush. 12. colors, badge, ribbon, dress, etc., worn to shown allegiance. 13. give or lend color to, cause to seem true or likely. 14. lose color, turn pale. 15. show one's colors, a. show oneself as one really is. b. declare one's opinions or plans. 16. the colors, a. the flag of a nation, regiment, etc.: *salute the colors.* b. the ceremony of raising the flag in the morning and lowering it in the evening. c. the army or navy. —*v.* 1. give color to; put color on; change the color of. 2. become red in the face; blush. 3. change to give a wrong idea: *to color a report of a battle.* 4. give a distinguishing quality to. Also, *esp. Brit.* colour. [< L] —**col′or·er,** *n.* —Syn. *v.* 1. paint, dye, stain, tint, tinge. 2. flush.

col·or·a·ble (kul′ər·ə·bəl), *adj.* 1. capable of being colored. 2. plausible. 3. pretended; deceptive. Also, *esp. Brit.* colourable. —**col′or·a·bil′i·ty, col′or·a·ble·ness,** *n.* —**col′or·a·bly,** *adv.*

Col·o·rad·o (kol′ə·rad′ō; -rä′dō), *n.* 1. a Western State of the United States. *Capital:* Denver. *Abbrev.:* Colo. 2. river flowing from N Colorado to the Gulf of California. —**Col′o·rad′an,** *adj., n.*

col·or·a·tion (kul′ər·ā′shən), *n.* coloring. Also, *esp. Brit.* colouration.

col·o·ra·tu·ra (kul′ə·rə·tür′ə; -tyür′ə), *n.* 1. ornamental passages in music, such as trills, runs, etc. 2. a soprano who sings such passages. —*adj.* fit for singing such passages: *a coloratura soprano.* [< Ital., < L *color* color]

col·or·blind (kul′ər·blīnd′), *adj.* unable to tell certain colors apart; unable to see certain colors. —**color blindness.**

col·or·cast (kul′ər·kast′; -käst′), *n.* television broadcast in color. —*v.* broadcast (a television program) in color.

col·ored (kul′ərd), *adj.* 1. having color; not black or white. 2. having a certain kind of color. 3. of the Negro race or other race than white. 4. influenced; influenced unfairly. Also, *esp. Brit.* coloured.

col·or·ful (kul′ər·fəl), *adj.* 1. abounding in color. 2. vivid. Also, *esp. Brit.* colourful. —**col′or·ful·ly,** *adv.* —**col′or·ful·ness,** *n.*

col·or·ing (kul′ər·ing), *n.* 1. way in which a person or thing is colored. 2. substance used to color; pigment. 3. false appearance. Also, *esp. Brit.* colouring.

col·or·ist (kul′ər·ist), *n.* 1. artist who is skillful in painting with colors. 2. user of color. Also, *esp. Brit.* colourist. —**col′or·is′tic,** *adj.*

col·or·less (kul′ər·lis), *adj.* 1. without color. 2. without excitement or variety; uninteresting. Also, *esp. Brit.* colourless. —**col′or·less·ly,** *adv.* —**col′or·less·ness,** *n.*

color line, *Am.* difference in social, economic, or political privileges between members of the white race and of the colored races.

co·los·sal (kə·los′əl), *adj.* huge; gigantic; vast. —**co·los′sal·ly,** *adv.*

Col·os·se·um (kol′ə·sē′əm), *n.* a large, outdoor theater at Rome, completed in 80 A.D. The Colosseum was used for games and contests. [< LL, neut. of L *colosseus* gigantic < *colossus* < Gk.]

Co·los·sians (kə·losh′ənz), *n.* book of the New Testament, written by the apostle Paul to the

Christian people of Colossae, an ancient city of Asia Minor.

co·los·sus (kə·los′əs), *n.*, *pl.* **-los·si** (-los′ī), **-los·sus·es.** 1. a huge statue. 2. anything huge; gigantic person or thing. [< L < Gk. *kolossos*]

Colossus of Rhodes, huge statue of Apollo made at Rhodes about 280 B.C. It was one of the seven wonders of the ancient world.

col·our (kul′ər), *n.*, *v. Esp. Brit.* color. **—col′-our·a·ble,** *adj.* **—col′our·a′tion,** *n.* **—col′oured,** *adj.* **—col′our·er,** *n.* **—col′our·ful,** *adj.* **—col′our·ing,** *n.* **—col′our·ist,** *n.* **—col′our·less,** *adj.*

colt (kōlt), *n.* 1. a young horse, donkey, etc. A male horse until it is four or five years old is a colt. 2. a young or inexperienced person. [OE]

col·ter (kōl′tər), *n.* a sharp blade or disk on a plow to cut the earth ahead of the plowshare. Also, **coulter.** [< L *culter* knife]

colt·ish (kōl′tish), *adj.* lively and frisky.

colts·foot (kōlts′fút′), *n.* plant of the aster family with yellow flowers and large, heart-shaped leaves which were formerly much used in medicine.

Co·lum·bi·a (kə·lum′bi·ə), *n.* 1. capital of South Carolina, in the C part. 2. river flowing from British Columbia through E Washington and Oregon into the Pacific. 3. *Am.* a name for the United States of America. **—Co·lum′bi·an,** *adj.*, *n.*

col·um·bine (kol′əm·bīn), *n.* plant whose flowers have petals shaped like hollow spurs. [< LL *columbina* < L, fem., dovelike < *columba* dove]

co·lum·bi·um (kə·lum′bi·əm), *n. Chem.* a steel-gray, rare metallic element, Cb, that resembles tantalum in its chemical properties. Also, **niobium.** [< NL, < *Columbia*]

Co·lum·bus (kə·lum′bəs), *n.* 1. Christopher, 1446?-1506, Italian navigator in the service of Spain who discovered America in 1492. 2. capital of Ohio, in the C part.

Columbus Day, *Am.* October 12, the anniversary of Columbus's discovery of America.

col·umn (kol′əm), *n.* 1. *Archit.* a slender, upright structure, usually used as support or ornament to a building; pillar. 2. anything that seems slender and upright like a column: *a column of figures; the spinal column is the backbone.* 3. arrangement of soldiers in several short rows one behind another. 4. line of ships, one behind another. 5. a narrow division of a page reading from top to bottom, kept separate by lines or by blank spaces. A newspaper often has eight columns on a page. 6. part of a newspaper used for a special subject or written by a special writer. [< L *columna*] **—col·umned** (kol′əmd), *adj.*

co·lum·nar (kə·lum′nər), *adj.* 1. like a column. 2. made of columns. 3. written or printed in columns.

col·um·nist (kol′əm·nist; -əm·ist), *n. Am.* journalist who comments on people, events, etc., in a special, regular column in a newspaper.

com-, *prefix.* with; together; altogether: *commingle = mingle with one another; compress = press together.* [< L; also (by assimilation to the following consonant) col-, con-, cor-]

Com., 1. Commander. 2. Committee.

com., commerce.

co·ma¹ (kō′mə), *n.*, *pl.* **co·mas.** a prolonged unconsciousness caused by disease, injury, or poison; stupor. [< Gk. *koma*]

co·ma² (kō′mə), *n.*, *pl.* **co·mae** (kō′mē). *Astron.* a cloudlike mass around the nucleus of a comet. [< L < Gk. *kome* hair] **—co′mal,** *adj.*

Co·man·che (kə·man′chē), *n.*, *pl.* **-ches.** *Am.* member of a tribe of American Indians that formerly roamed from Wyoming to northern Mexico, now living in Oklahoma.

com·a·tose (kom′ə·tōs; kō′mə-), *adj.* 1. unconscious. 2. lethargic. **—com′a·tose·ly,** *adv.*

comb (kōm), *n.* 1. a narrow, short piece of metal, rubber, celluloid, etc., with teeth, used to arrange or clean the hair or to hold it in place. 2. anything shaped or used like a comb. One kind of comb cleans and takes out the tangles in wool or flax. 3. currycomb. 4. the thick, red, fleshy piece on the top of the head in some fowls. 5. honeycomb. 6. top of a wave rolling over or breaking. **—v.** 1. arrange, clean, or take out tangles in, with a comb. 2. *Am.* search through; look everywhere in. 3. *Am.* (of waves) roll over or break at the top. [OE]

com·bat (*v.*, *n.* kom′bat; *v.* also kəm·bat′), *v.*, **-bat·ed, -bat·ing;** *esp. Brit.* **-bat·ted, -bat·ting,** *n.* **—v.** 1. fight (*with* or *against*); contend. 2. oppose vigorously. **—n.** 1. a fight, esp. between two. 2. a struggle; a conflict; a battle. [< F *combattre* < LL < L com- (intensive) + *battuere* beat] **—com·bat·a·ble** (kom′bat·ə·bəl; kəm·bat′-), *adj.* **—com′bat·er,** *n.* **—Syn.** *n.* 1. duel, engagement.

com·bat·ant (kəm·bat′ənt; kom′bə·tənt), *n.* fighter. **—adj.** 1. fighting. 2. ready to fight.

com·bat·ive (kəm·bat′iv; kom′bə·tiv), *adj.* ready to fight or oppose; fond of fighting. **—com·bat′ive·ly,** *adv.* **—com·bat′ive·ness,** *n.*

combat team, a self-sustaining tactical group combining elements of infantry, artillery, tank, and air forces in the army, and submarines, air forces, etc., as well as surface craft in the navy.

comb·er (kōm′ər), *n.* 1. one that combs. 2. *Am.* wave that rolls over or breaks at the top.

com·bi·na·tion (kom′bə·nā′shən), *n.* 1. a combining or being combined. 2. thing made by combining. 3. group of persons or parties joined together for some common purpose. 4. *Math.* a. arrangement of individuals in groups so that each group has a certain number of individuals. b. the groups thus formed. 5. *Am.* series of numbers or letters used in opening or closing a certain kind of lock. 6. suit of underwear having the shirt and drawers in one piece. **—com′bi·na′tion·al,** *adj.* **—Syn.** 3. league, combine, cooperative.

com·bine (*v.* kəm·bīn′; *n.* 1 kom′bīn, kəm·bīn′; *n.* 2 kom′bīn), *v.*, **-bined, -bin·ing,** *n.* **—v.** 1. join together; unite. 2. *Chem.* unite to form a compound. **—n.** 1. *Am.*, *Colloq.* combination (def. 3). 2. *Am.* machine for harvesting and threshing grain. [< LL *combinare* < com- together + *bini* two by two] **—com·bin′a·ble,** *adj.* **—com·bin′er,** *n.* **—Syn.** *v.* 1. merge, associate. 2. blend, mix. ▶ **Combine** is not in good use in the abstract senses of *combination*, but is good colloquial English for a group of people joined together for business or political gain and usually implies either shady or forceful activities.

combining form, a word element.

com·bus·ti·ble (kəm·bus′tə·bəl), *adj.* 1. capable of taking fire and burning; easy to burn. 2. easily excited; fiery. **—n.** a combustible substance. **—com·bus′ti·bil′i·ty, com·bus′ti·ble·ness,** *n.* **—com·bus′ti·bly,** *adv.*

com·bus·tion (kəm·bus′chən), *n.* 1. act or process of burning. 2. rapid oxidation accompanied by high temperature and usually by light. 3. slow oxidation not accompanied by high temperature and light. 4. violent excitement; tumult. [< L *combustio* < com- up + *urere* burn] **—com·bus′tive,** *adj.*

come (kum), *v.*, **came, come, com·ing.** 1. move toward the speaker or the place where he is or will be; approach: *come this way.* 2. arrive: *he came to the city yesterday.* 3. appear: *light comes and goes.* 4. reach; extend. 5. happen; take place; occur: *what will come, let come.* 6. be caused; result. 7. be born. 8. get to be; turn out to be; become. 9. be brought; pass; enter. 10. occur to the mind. 11. be available. 12. be equal; amount: *the total comes to $100.* 13. here! look! stop! behave! 14. come about, a. happen; take place; occur. b. turn around; change direction. 15. come around, come round, a. return to consciousness or health; recover. b. give in; yield; agree. c. turn around; change direction. 16. come down, a. lose position, rank, money, etc. b. be handed down or passed along. **c.** *Am.*, *Colloq.* become ill (*with*). **17.** **come out, a.** be revealed or shown. **b.** be offered to the public. **c.** do one's part; leave an activity. **d.** be introduced to society; make a debut. **18. come to, a.** return to consciousness. **b.** anchor; stop. [OE *cuman*] —com′er, *n.*

come·back (kum′bak′), *n.* **1.** *Colloq.* return to a former condition or position. **2.** *Am.*, *Slang.* clever answer.

co·me·di·an (kə·mē′di·ən), *n.* **1.** actor in comedies. **2.** writer of comedies. **3.** person who amuses others with his funny talk and actions.

co·me·di·enne (kə·mē′di·en′), *n.* actress in comedies; actress of comic parts.

come·down (kum′doun′), *n.* *Colloq.* loss of position, rank, money, etc.

com·e·dy (kom′ə·di), *n.*, *pl.* **–dies. 1.** amusing play or show having a happy ending. **2.** branch of drama concerned with such plays. **3.** the comic element of drama, of literature in general, or of life. **4.** an amusing happening; funny incident. [< L < Gk., < *komoidos* comedian < *komos* merrymaking + *aoidos* singer]

come·ly (kum′li), *adj.*, **–li·er**, **–li·est. 1.** having a pleasant appearance; attractive. **2.** *Archaic.* fitting; suitable; proper. [OE *cȳmlic*] —come′li·ness, *n.* —*Ant.* **1.** ugly, homely, plain.

co·mes·ti·ble (kə·mes′tə·bəl), *adj.* eatable. —*n.* Usually, **comestibles.** things to eat.

com·et (kom′it), *n.* a bright heavenly body with a starlike center and often with a cloudy tail of light, moving around the sun in a long, oval course. [< L < Gk. *kometes* wearing long hair < *kome* hair] —**co·met·ic** (kə·met′ik), *adj.*

com·fit (kum′fit; kom′–), *n.* piece of candy. [< OF < L *confectus* prepared < *com–* + *facere* make]

com·fort (kum′fərt), *v.* **1.** ease the grief or sorrow of; cheer. **2.** give ease to. —*n.* **1.** anything that makes trouble or sorrow easier to bear. **2.** freedom from pain or hardship; ease. **3.** person or thing that makes life easier or takes away hardship. [< OF < LL *confortare* strengthen < *com–* + *fortis* strong] —com′fort·ing, *adj.* —com′fort·ing·ly, *adv.* —com′fort·less, *adj.* —*Syn. v.* **1.** soothe, solace, console.

com·fort·a·ble (kumf′tə·bəl; kum′fər·tə·bəl), *adj.* **1.** giving comfort. **2.** in comfort. **3.** at ease; contented. **4.** *Colloq.* enough for one's needs. —com′fort·a·ble·ness, *n.* —com′fort·a·bly, *adv.*

com·fort·er (kum′fər·tər), *n.* **1.** person or thing that gives comfort. **2.** *Am.* a padded or quilted covering for a bed.

com·ic (kom′ik), *adj.* **1.** of comedy. **2.** amusing; funny. —*n.* **1.** the amusing or funny side of literature, life, etc. **2.** *Colloq.* a comic book. **3.** comics, *Am.* comic strips. [< L < Gk. *komikos.* See COMEDY.]

com·i·cal (kom′ə·kəl), *adj.* amusing; funny. —com′i·cal·ly, *adv.* —com′i·cal·ness, *n.*

comic book, *Am.* magazine with comic strips.

comic opera, amusing opera having a happy ending.

comic strip, *Am.* series of drawings, sometimes humorous, presenting an adventure.

Com·in·form (kom′in·fôrm), *n.* an international Communist propaganda organization formed in 1947.

com·ing (kum′ing), *n.* arrival. —*adj.* **1.** next. **2.** *Colloq.* on the way to importance or fame.

Com·in·tern (kom′in·têrn), *n.* the Third Communist International, an organization founded at Moscow in 1919 to spread communism, and dissolved in 1943.

com·i·ty (kom′ə·ti), *n.*, *pl.* **–ties.** courtesy; civility. [< L, < *comis* friendly]

com·ma (kom′ə), *n.* mark (,) of punctuation, used to show the smallest interruptions in the thought or in the grammatical structure of a sentence. [< L < Gk. *komma* piece cut off < *koptein* to cut] ➤ **comma (,).** As a general thing writers use more commas than are required by the simple material and direct movement of the average sentence. Most textbooks and most teachers have tended to encourage close punctuation, and students for this reason sometimes

give their writing a slow movement that it doesn't deserve. The boy who wrote this sentence was taking no chances: *Naturally, the first thing he does, after his interest is aroused, is to attempt to construct a small receiving set of his own.* No one of those commas is wrong but no one of them is necessary either, and without them the sentence moves more easily—and more appropriately to a simple account of experiences in amateur radio: *Naturally the first thing he does after his interest is aroused is to attempt to construct a small receiving set of his own.* The general advice of this book, then, is to use commas where the reader will expect them, but beyond this to use them only when they actually contribute to the understandability of the sentence. Where choice is possible, the final decision will often depend on fitness to other factors of style: the formal writer will always tend to use more commas than the informal. Partly because the use of commas depends on the movement of a passage, it is better not to pause in writing the first draft to decide about putting in a comma. Commas should be attended to in revision, when the context can help decide questions of appropriateness. The following sections are intended to help you decide how and where to use the comma.

1. Between Clauses. (a) BETWEEN COORDINATE CLAUSES. A comma is used when clauses are long and when it is desirable to emphasize their distinctness from each other: *The frozen steel edges shrieked as they bit into the ice-covered turns, and the driving sleet slashed against their goggles and jackets with such force that it was impossible to keep clear vision, to say nothing of protection for their bodies.*
A comma is generally used between two coördinate locutions joined by *but* or *not,* to emphasize the contrast: *I told him that I was ready to pay my half of the bill, but that didn't satisfy him. The sympathizers with these plans are to be pitied, not blamed.*
A comma is generally used between clauses connected by the conjunction *for,* to avoid confusion with the preposition *for:* Conjunction: *They are obviously mistaken, for all intercollegiate sports are competitive.* Preposition: *The English teacher had assigned us "Treasure Island"* [ ] *for a book report.*
(b) AFTER A SUBORDINATE CLAUSE (OR LONG PHRASE) THAT PRECEDES THE MAIN CLAUSE OF THE SENTENCE. If a clause or phrase preceding the main clause of the sentence is long or if it is not closely connected with the main clause, it should be followed by a comma: *Although willing to use his athletic ability, he wouldn't study hard enough to become eligible.*
(c) BEFORE A SUBORDINATE CLAUSE THAT FOLLOWS THE MAIN CLAUSE. A comma usually stands before a subordinate clause that follows the main clause if it is not closely related in thought to the main clause. If the subordinate clause is an essential modifier of the main statement, the comma is often omitted. The writer's sense of the closeness of the connection between the two statements should guide him unless actual misunderstanding could arise from omitting the comma: *Last spring the best miler in college failed to run* [,] *because he was too lazy to practice.*
2. In Lists and Series. The comma is the natural mark to use between the units of:
(a) ENUMERATIONS, LISTS, SERIES: *Among the numerous guests were socialites, artists, chorus girls, and even two university professors.* Usage is divided on the comma before the last member of a series: *celery, onions, and olives* [or] *celery, onions and olives.* Traditional formal usage calls for the comma, but newspaper and business writers quite generally omit it.
(b) ADJECTIVES IN SERIES. In the sentence *When the long, cold, lonesome evenings would come, we gathered about the old wood stove and ate the chestnuts,* there are commas between *long—cold—lonesome* because each stands in the same relation to the noun *evenings.* There is no comma between *old* and *wood* because *old* modifies *wood stove* rather than just *stove.* A comma following *old* would throw more emphasis upon *wood* and might sometimes be wanted.

3. With Nonrestrictive Modifiers. Modifiers which do not limit the meaning of a noun or verb but add a descriptive detail are nonrestrictive and are set off by a comma or commas. The material in italics is nonrestrictive: They had on old tattered overalls, *over which they were wearing a variety of differently colored sweaters.* However, a restrictive modifier, which is essential to a correct understanding of the material it modifies, is not set off by punctuation: Wouldn't it be as just to remove from his suffering a person *who has committed no crime* as to make suffer one *who has committed a crime?*

4. With Interrupting and Parenthetical Words and Phrases. (a) INTERRUPTING CONSTRUCTIONS. A phrase or clause that interrupts the direct movement of the sentence should be set off by commas: *did intelligent people, he asked himself, do things like that?* Usage is divided over setting off short parenthetical words and phrases like *incidentally* and *of course.* Setting them off with commas is more characteristic of formal than of informal writing, though there is often a difference in emphasis according to whether or not commas are used: *These early attempts, of course, brought no results. These early attempts of course brought no results.*

(b) CONNECTIVES. When a conjunctive adverb stands after the first phrase of its clause, as it often does, it is usually set off by commas, and often it is set off when it stands first in the clause: *The next morning, however, they all set out as though nothing had happened. However, the next morning they all set out as though nothing had happened.*

5. For Emphasis and Contrast. (a) The pause indicated by a comma tends to keep distinct the constructions it separates and to emphasize slightly the construction that follows the mark: *Temporarily the wine industry was all but ruined, and farmers turned to dairying, and to coöperation to give them a market.*

(b) This is especially true when a connective is omitted: *And afterwards I told her how I felt, how I kept feeling about her.*

(c) In the idiom *the more . . . the greater,* formal usage tends to have a comma, informal not: *The more he pursued the subject* [,] *the larger its scope seemed to be.*

6. For Clearness. Often a comma can guide a reader in interpreting a sentence and make it unnecessary for him to go back over it for meaning. In material that is likely to be read aloud, the writer should give special heed to this device. Two such constructions are especially helped by commas:

(a) When a word has two possible functions. *For* or *but* may be either a conjunction or a preposition, and confusion may be avoided by using a comma before either when it is used as a conjunction: *The surgeon's face showed no emotion, but anxiety and a little nervousness must be seething behind that impassive mask* [to avoid reading "no emotion but anxiety"].

(b) When a noun might be mistaken for the object of a verb: *When the boll weevil struck, the credit system collapsed and ruined a great part of the landowners and tenants* [not: "When the boll weevil struck the credit system . . ."].

(c) Sometimes a faulty interpretation of word grouping can be prevented: *The only way that you can develop honestly is to discover how you write now, and then write naturally in everything you hand in* [avoiding "now and then"].

(d) Ordinarily when the same word occurs twice consecutively a comma should be used: *What the trouble really is, is of no interest to him.*

7. Conventional Uses. (a) IN DATES, to separate the day of the month from the year: *May 26, 1939.* When the day of the month is not given, a comma may or may not be used: *in May 1939* or *in May, 1939.* The less formal use is without the comma.

(b) IN ADDRESSES, to separate town from state or country when they are written on the same line: *Chicago, Illinois; Berne, Switzerland.*

(c) AFTER SALUTATIONS in informal letters: *Dear Len,.*

(d) IN FIGURES, to separate thousands, millions, etc: *4,672,342.*

(e) TO SEPARATE DEGREES and titles from names: *Elihu Root, Esq.; Charles Evans Hughes, Jr.; Ronald C. MacKenzie, Ph.D.*

com·mand (kə·mand′; -mänd′), *v.* 1. give an order to; direct. 2. give orders. 3. have authority or power over; be in control of. 4. be commander. 5. have a position of control over; overlook. 6. be able to have and use. 7. deserve and get; force to be given: *command respect.* —*n.* 1. order; direction. 2. authority; power; control. 3. position of a person who has the right to command. 4. soldiers, ships, district, etc., under a person who has the right to command them. 5. mastery or control by position. 6. outlook over. 7. ability to use; mastery: *he has a good command of French.* [< OF < LL, < L *com-* + *mandare* commit, command] —Syn. *v.* 1. charge, enjoin, instruct. 3. govern, rule. 7. exact, secure. —*n.* 1. charge, injunction, mandate.

com·man·dant (kom′ən·dant′; -dänt′), *n.* officer in command of a fort, navy yard, etc.

com·man·deer (kom′ən·dir′), *v.* 1. seize (private property) for military or public use. 2. force (men) into military service. 3. *Colloq.* take by force. [< Afrikaans < F *commander*]

com·mand·er (kə·man′dər; -män′-), *n.* 1. person who commands. 2. officer in charge of an army or a part of an army. 3. a navy officer ranking next below a captain and next above a lieutenant commander. —**com·mand′er·ship,** *n.*

commander in chief, *pl.* **commanders in chief.** 1. person who has complete command of the army and navy of a country. 2. officer in command of part of an army or navy.

com·mand·ing (kə·man′ding; -män′-), *adj.* 1. in command. 2. controlling; powerful. 3. authoritative; impressive. 4. having a position of control. —**com·mand′ing·ly,** *adv.*

com·mand·ment (kə·mand′mənt; -mänd′-), *n.* 1. order; direction; law. 2. one of the ten laws that, according to the Bible, God gave to Moses. Exod. 20:2–17; Deut. 5:6–21.

com·man·do (kə·man′dō; -män′-), *n., pl.* -dos, -does. 1. Commando, *Esp. Brit.* soldier who makes brief, daring raids upon enemy territory. 2. an armed force raised for service against marauders, rebellious natives, etc. [< Afrikaans < Pg.]

com·mem·o·rate (kə·mem′ə·rāt), *v.,* -rat·ed, -rat·ing. 1. preserve the memory of. 2. honor the memory of. [< L, < *com-* + *memorare* relate] —**com·mem·o·ra·ble** (kə·mem′ə·rə·bəl), *adj.* —**com·mem·o·ra′tion,** *n.* —**com·mem′o·ra·tive,** *adj.* —**com·mem′o·ra·tive·ly,** *adv.* —**com·mem′o·ra·tor,** *n.* —**com·mem·o·ra·to·ry** (kə·mem′ə·rə·tô′ri; -tō′-), *adj.*

com·mence (kə·mens′), *v.,* -menced, -menc·ing. begin; start. [< OF *comencer* < VL < L *com-* + *initiare* begin. See INITIATE.] —**com·menc′er,** *n.*

com·mence·ment (kə·mens′mənt), *n.* 1. a beginning; start. 2. day when a school or college gives diplomas or degrees to students who have completed the required course of study; day of graduation. 3. ceremonies on this day.

com·mend (kə·mend′), *v.* 1. praise. 2. mention favorably; recommend. 3. hand over for safekeeping. [< L *commendare*. See COMMAND.] —**com·mend′a·ble,** *adj.* —**com·mend′a·bly,** *adv.*

com·men·da·tion (kom′ən·dā′shən), *n.* 1. praise; approval. 2. favorable mention. 3. a handing over to another for safekeeping; entrusting.

com·mend·a·to·ry (kə·men′də·tô′ri; -tō′-), *adj.* approving; mentioning favorably.

com·men·su·ra·ble (kə·men′shə·rə·bəl; -sə-rə-), *adj.* measurable by the same set of units. —**com·men′su·ra·bil′i·ty, com·men′su·ra·ble·ness,** *n.* —**com·men′su·ra·bly,** *adv.*

com·men·su·rate (kə·men′shə·rit; -sə-), *adj.* 1. in the proper proportion; proportionate. 2. of the same size, extent, etc.; equal. 3. measurable by the same set of units. [< LL *commensuratus.* See COM-, MENSURATION.] —**com·men′su·rate·ly,**

adv. —com·men'su·rate·ness, *n.* —com·men'-su·ra'tion, *n.*

com·ment (kom'ent), *n.* **1.** a short statement, note, or remark that explains, praises, or criticizes something that has been written, said, or done. **2.** remark. **3.** talk; gossip. —*v.* **1.** make a comment or comments. **2.** talk; gossip. [< L *commentum* < *commentus*, pp. of *comminisci* < *com-* up + *-minisci* think]

com·men·tar·y (kom'ən·ter'i), *n., pl.* -tar·ies. **1.** series of notes for explaining the hard parts of a book; explanation. **2.** an explanatory essay or treatise.

com·men·ta·tor (kom'ən·tā'tər), *n.* person who makes comments, as on the radio, explaining or criticizing books, concerts, recent events, etc.

com·merce (kom'ərs; -ērs), *n.* buying and selling in large amounts between different places; trade; business. [< F < L *commercium*, ult. < *com-* with + *merx* wares] —Syn. dealings, traffic.

com·mer·cial (kə·mėr'shəl), *adj.* **1.** having to do with commerce. **2.** made to be sold. **3.** manufactured, or capable of being produced, in sizable quantities. **4.** supported or subsidized by an advertiser: *a commercial radio program.* —*n.* a radio or television program, or the part of a program, that advertises something. —com·mer'cial·ly, *adv.*

com·mer·cial·ism (kə·mėr'shəl·iz·əm), *n.* **1.** methods and spirit of commerce. **2.** business custom; expression used in business.

com·mer·cial·ize (kə·mėr'shəl·īz), *v.,* -ized, -iz·ing. apply the methods and spirit of commerce to; make a matter of business or trade. —com·mer'cial·i·za'tion, *n.*

com·min·gle (kə·ming'gəl), *v.,* -gled, -gling. mingle together; blend.

com·mi·nute (kom'ə·nūt; -nūt), *v.,* -nut·ed, -nut·ing. pulverize. [< L, < *com-* + *minuere* make smaller < *minus* less] —com'mi·nu'tion, *n.*

com·mis·er·ate (kə·miz'ər·āt), *v.,* -at·ed, -at·ing. feel or express sorrow for; sympathize with; pity. —com·mis'er·a'tion, *n.*

com·mis·sar (kom'ə·sär), *n.* head of a government department in Soviet Russia.

com·mis·sar·i·at (kom'ə·sãr'i·ət; -at), *n.* **1.** department of an army that supplies food, etc. **2.** a government department in Soviet Russia. [< F, < Med.L *commissarius*. See COMMISSARY.]

com·mis·sar·y (kom'ə·ser'i), *n., pl.* -sar·ies. **1.** *Am.* store handling food and supplies in a mining camp, lumber camp, army camp, etc. **2.** an army officer in charge of food and daily supplies for soldiers. **3.** deputy; representative. [< Med.L *commissarius* < L *commissus*, pp., entrusted. See COMMIT.]

com·mis·sion (kə·mish'ən), *n.* **1.** a written paper giving certain powers, privileges, and duties. **2.** a written order giving military or naval rank and authority. **3.** rank and authority given by such an order. **4.** a giving of authority. **5.** authority, power, or right given. **6.** thing for which authority is given; thing trusted to a person to do. **7.** group of people appointed or elected with authority to do certain things. **8.** doing; performance. **9.** pay based on a percentage of the amount of business done. **10. in commission, a.** in service; in use. **b.** in working order. **11. out of commission, a.** not in service or use. **b.** not in working order. —*v.* **1.** give a commission to. **2.** give authority to; give (a person) the right or power (to do something). **3.** put in service or use; make ready for service or use. —Syn. *n.* **5.** warrant, license. -*v.* **2.** license, authorize, empower.

com·mis·sion·er (kə·mish'ən·ər), *n.* **1.** member of a commission. **2.** official in charge of some department of a government: *police commissioner.* **3.** one of a group of persons elected or appointed to govern a city or a county. —com·mis'sion·er·ship', *n.*

com·mit (kə·mit'), *v.,* -mit·ted, -mit·ting. **1.** hand over for safekeeping; deliver. **2.** confine officially: *commit to prison.* **3.** refer to a committee for consideration. **4.** do or perform (usually something wrong). **5.** involve; pledge. **6.**

commit to memory, learn by heart. [< L < *com-* with + *mittere*, send, put] —com·mit'ta·ble, *adj.* —Syn. **1.** commend, entrust, confide.

com·mit·ment (kə·mit'mənt), **com·mit·tal** (-mit'əl), *n.* **1.** a committing or being committed. **2.** a sending to prison or an asylum. **3.** order sending a person to prison or to an asylum. **4.** pledge; promise.

com·mit·tee (kə·mit'i), *n.* group of persons appointed or elected to do certain things. ➤ Committee is a collective noun, to be construed as singular or plural according as the group or the individuals are meant. The singular would usually be the form desired: *the committee meets today at four; the committee get together with difficulty.* [< AF, committed. See COMMIT.]

com·mit·tee·man (kə·mit'i·mən; -man'), *n., pl.* -men (-mən; -men'). member of a committee.

com·mode (kə·mōd'), *n.* **1.** chest of drawers. **2.** washstand (def. 2). [< F < L *commodus* convenient < *com-* with + *modus* measure]

com·mo·di·ous (kə·mō'di·əs), *adj.* **1.** roomy. **2.** convenient; handy. [< Med.L *commodiosus*. See COMMODE.] —com·mo'di·ous·ly, *adv.*

com·mod·i·ty (kə·mod'ə·ti), *n., pl.* -ties. **1.** anything that is bought and sold. **2.** useful thing.

com·mo·dore (kom'ə·dôr; -dōr), *n.* **1.** an officer in the U.S. Navy ranking next below a rear admiral and next above a captain. **2.** captain in the British navy in temporary command of a squadron. **3.** title of honor given to the president or head of a yacht club. [earlier *commandore*; ? < Du. < F, < *commander* to command]

com·mon (kom'ən), *adj.* **1.** belonging equally to each or all. **2.** of all; from or by all; to all; general: *common knowledge, common nuisance.* **3.** belonging to the community at large; public: *a common council.* **4.** often met with; usual; familiar. **5.** generally known, used, etc. **6.** notorious. **7.** without rank. **8.** below ordinary; inferior; low; vulgar. **9.** applicable to any individual of a class. **10.** belonging equally to two or more quantities: *a common factor.* —*n.* **1.** land owned or used by all the people of a town, village, etc. **2. in common,** equally with another or others; owned, used, done, etc., by both or all. [< OF < L *communis* < *com-* together + *munia* duties] —com'mon·ly, *adv.* —com'mon·ness, *n.* —Syn. *adj.* **1.** joint. **2.** popular, universal. **8.** cheap.

com·mon·al·ty (kom'ən·əl·ti), *n., pl.* -ties. **1.** the common people. **2.** people as a group. **3.** members of a corporation.

common carrier, person or company whose business is conveying goods or people for pay.

com·mon·er (kom'ən·ər), *n.* one of the common people; person who is not a nobleman.

common law, the unwritten law based on custom and usage and confirmed by the decisions of judges, as distinct from statute law.

common noun, name for any one of a class. *Boy, city,* and *dog* are common nouns. *John, Boston,* and *Rover* are proper nouns.

com·mon·place (kom'ən·plās'), *n.* **1.** common or everyday thing. **2.** ordinary or obvious remark. —*adj.* not new or interesting; everyday; ordinary. —com'mon·place'ness, *n.*

com·mons (kom'ənz), *n.pl.* **1.** the common people. **2.** a dining hall or building where food is served to a large group at common tables. **3.** the food served. **4.** food. **5. the Commons,** House of Commons.

common sense, good sense in everyday affairs; practical intelligence. —com'mon-sense', *adj.*

com·mon·weal (kom'ən·wēl'), **common weal,** *n.* general welfare; public good.

com·mon·wealth (kom'ən·welth'), *n.* **1.** group of people who make up a nation; citizens of a state. **2.** a democratic state; republic. **3.** *Am.* one of the States of the United States. **4.** group of persons, nations, etc., united by some common interest.

Commonwealth of Nations, British Commonwealth of Nations.

com·mo·tion (kə·mō'shən), *n.* violent movement; confusion; disturbance; tumult.

com·mu·nal (kom′yə·nəl; kə·mū′nəl), *adj.* **1.** of a community; public. **2.** owned jointly by all; used or participated in by all members of a group or community. **3.** of a commune. —**com′mu·nal·ly,** *adv.*

com·mune[1] (*v.* kə·mūn′; *n.* kom′ūn), *v.,* –**muned,** –**mun·ing,** *n.* —*v.* **1.** talk intimately. **2.** receive Holy Communion. —*n.* intimate talk; communion. [< OF, < *comun* COMMON]

com·mune[2] (kom′ūn), *n.* the smallest division for local government in France, Belgium, and several other European countries. [< F, fem. of *commun* COMMON]

com·mu·ni·ca·ble (kə·mū′nə·kə·bəl), *adj.* that can be communicated. —**com′mu′ni·ca·bil′i·ty, com·mu′ni·ca·ble·ness,** *n.* —**com·mu′ni·ca·bly,** *adv.*

com·mu·ni·cant (kə·mū′nə·kənt), *n.* **1.** person who receives Holy Communion. **2.** person who gives information by talking, writing, etc.

com·mu·ni·cate (kə·mū′nə·kāt), *v.,* –**cat·ed,** –**cat·ing. 1.** pass along; transfer: *a stove communicates heat to a room.* **2.** give (information) by talking, writing, etc.; talk, write, telephone, telegraph, etc.; send and receive messages. **3.** be connected. **4.** receive Holy Communion. [< L *communicatus* < *communis* COMMON] —**com·mu′ni·ca′tor,** *n.* —**Syn. 1.** convey. **2.** impart.

com·mu·ni·ca·tion (kə·mū′nə·kā′shən), *n.* **1.** act or fact of passing along; transfer. **2.** a giving of information by talking, writing, etc. **3.** information given in this way. **4.** letter, message, etc., that gives information. **5.** means of going from one place to the other; connection; passage. **6. communications,** a system of communicating by telephone, radio, etc.

com·mu·ni·ca·tive (kə·mū′nə·kā′tiv; –kə·tiv), *adj.* **1.** ready to give information; talkative. **2.** pertaining to communication. —**com·mu′ni·ca′tive·ly,** *adv.* —**com·mu′ni·ca′tive·ness,** *n.*

com·mun·ion (kə·mūn′yən), *n.* **1.** act of sharing; a having in common. **2.** exchange of thoughts and feelings; intimate talk; fellowship. **3.** close spiritual relationship. **4.** group of people having the same religious beliefs. **5. Communion, a.** act of sharing in the Lord's Supper as a part of church worship. **b.** celebration of the Lord's Supper. See COMMON.] [< L *communio*]

com·mu·ni·qué (kə·mū′nə·kā′; kə·mū′nə·kā), *n.* an official bulletin, statement, etc.

com·mu·nism (kom′yə·niz·əm), *n.* system by which the means of production and distribution are owned and managed by the government, and the goods produced are shared by all citizens. [< F *communisme* < *commun* COMMON]

com·mu·nist (kom′yə·nist), *n.* **1.** person who favors and supports communism. **2. Communist,** member of a political party advocating communism. —**com′mu·nis′tic, com′mu·nis′ti·cal,** *adj.*

Communist Party, political party that supports communism.

com·mu·ni·ty (kə·mū′nə·ti), *n., pl.* –**ties. 1.** a number of people having common ties or interests and living in the same locality. **2.** group of people living together: *a community of monks.* **3.** the public. **4.** ownership together; sharing together. **5.** group of animals or plants living together. **6.** likeness; similarity; identity. [< OF < L *communitas.* See COMMON.]

community center, *Am.* a building where the people of a community meet for recreation, social purposes, etc.

com·mu·tate (kom′yə·tāt), *v.,* –**tat·ed,** –**tat·ing.** *Elect.* reverse the direction of (an electric current). —**com′mu·ta′tor,** *n.*

com·mu·ta·tion (kom′yə·tā′shən), *n.* **1.** exchange; substitution. **2.** reduction (of an obligation, penalty, etc.) to a less severe one. **3.** regular, daily travel back and forth to work by train.

commutation ticket, *Am.* ticket sold at a reduced rate, entitling the holder to travel over a given route a certain number of times or during a certain period.

com·mute (kə·mūt′), *v.,* –**mut·ed,** –**mut·ing. 1.** exchange; substitute. **2.** change (an obligation,

penalty, etc.) to an easier one. **3.** *Am.* travel regularly back and forth to work by train; use a commutation ticket. [< L, < *com*– + *mutare* change]

com·mut·er (kə·mūt′ər), *n. Am.* person who travels regularly back and forth from his home in a suburb to his work in a city.

com·pact[1] (*adj., v.* kəm·pakt′; *n.* kom′pakt), *adj.* **1.** firmly packed together; closely joined. **2.** composed or made (*of*). **3.** using few words; brief. —*v.* **1.** pack firmly together; join closely. **2.** make by putting together firmly. **3.** condense. —*n.* a small case containing face powder and often rouge. [< L *compactus* < *com*– together + *pangere* fasten] —**com·pact′ly,** *adv.* —**com·pact′ness,** *n.*

com·pact[2] (kom′pakt), *n.* agreement. [< L *compactum* agreement < *com*– + *pacisci* contract]

com·pan·ion (kəm·pan′yən), *n.* **1.** person who goes along with another; person who shares in what another is doing. **2.** anything that matches or goes with another in kind, size, color, etc. **3.** person paid to live or travel with another as a friend and helper. —*v.* be a companion to; go along with. [< OF < LL *companio* < *com*– together + *panis* bread] —**com·pan′ion·less,** *adj.* —**com·pan′ion·ship,** *n.* —**Syn. n. 1.** comrade, associate.

com·pan·ion·a·ble (kəm·pan′yən·ə·bəl), *adj.* fitted to be a companion; pleasant; agreeable; sociable. —**com·pan′ion·a·bil′i·ty, com·pan′ion·a·ble·ness,** *n.* —**com·pan′ion·a·bly,** *adv.*

com·pan·ion·ate (kəm·pan′yən·it), *adj.* of companions; of companionship.

com·pan·ion·way (kəm·pan′yən·wā′), *n. Naut.* stairway from the deck of a ship down to the rooms below.

Companionway

com·pa·ny (kum′pə·ni), *n., pl.* –**nies,** *v.,* –**nied,** –**ny·ing.** —*n.* **1.** group of people. **2.** group of persons joined together for some purpose: *a business company, a company of actors.* **3.** a gathering of persons for social purposes. **4.** companion or companions. **5.** association as companions. **6.** *Colloq.* guest or guests; visitor or visitors. **7.** *Mil.* part of an army commanded by a captain. **8.** *Naut.* a ship's crew; officers and sailors of a ship. **9. part company, a.** go separate ways. **b.** end companionship. —*v.* associate. [< OF, < *compagne* COMPANION] —**Syn.** *n.* **5.** fellowship.

compar., comparative.

com·pa·ra·ble (kom′pə·rə·bəl), *adj.* **1.** able to be compared. **2.** fit to be compared. —**com′pa·ra·ble·ness,** *n.* —**com′pa·ra·bly,** *adv.*

com·par·a·tive (kəm·par′ə·tiv), *adj.* **1.** that compares. **2.** measured by comparison with something else. **3.** showing the comparative degree. —*n.* **1.** the second degree of comparison of an adjective or adverb. **2.** form or combination of words that shows this degree. *Fairer* is the comparative of *fair.* —**com·par′a·tive·ly,** *adv.*

com·pare (kəm·pâr′), *v.,* –**pared,** –**par·ing,** *n.* —*v.* **1.** find out or point out the likenesses or differences of. **2.** consider as similar; liken. **3.** bear comparison; be considered like or equal. **4.** change the form of (an adjective or adverb) to show the comparative and superlative degree. —*n.* **1.** comparison. **2. beyond compare,** without an equal. [< F < L, < *com*– with + *par* equal] —**com·par′er,** *n.* —**Syn.** *v.* **3.** approach, rival, parallel. ▶ **compare, contrast.** *Compare* is commonly used in two senses: (1) to point out likenesses (used with *to*); (2) to examine two or more objects to find likenesses or differences (used with *with*). *Comparing* in the second sense may discover *differences* as well as *likenesses.* *Contrast* always means difference: *He compared my stories to Maupassant's* [said they were like his]; *he compared my stories with Maupassant's* [pointed out like and unlike traits]. *He contrasted my work with* (sometimes *to*) *Maupassant's.*

com·par·i·son (kəm·par′ə·sən), *n.* **1.** act or process of comparing; finding the likenesses and differences. **2.** likeness; similarity. **3.** change in an adjective or adverb to show degrees. The three degrees of comparison are positive, comparative, and superlative. *Example:* good, better, best; cold, colder, coldest; helpful, more helpful, most helpful. **4. in comparison with,** compared with. ❯ See adjective and adverb for usage notes.

com·part·ment (kəm·pärt′mənt), *n.* a separate division or section; part of an enclosed space set off by walls or partitions. [< F < Ital. *compartimento* < *compartire* divide < LL, < L *com-* with + *partiri* share]

com·pass (kum′pəs), *n.* **1.** instrument for showing directions, consisting of a needle that points to the N Magnetic Pole. **2.** boundary; circumference. **3.** space within limits; extent; range. **4.** range of a voice or musical instrument. **5.** circuit; going around. **6.** Usually, **compasses.** instrument for drawing circles and measuring distances. —*v.* **1.** make a circuit of; go around. **2.** form a circle around; surround. **3.** do; accomplish; get. [< OF, < *compasser* divide equally < VL < L *com-* with + *passus* step] —Syn. *n.* **3.** reach, scope.

Compass (def. 6)

com·pas·sion (kəm·pash′ən), *n.* feeling for another's sorrow or hardship that leads to help; sympathy; pity. [< L *compassio* < *com-* with + *pati* suffer]

com·pas·sion·ate (*adj.* kəm·pash′ən·it; *v.* kəm·pash′ən·āt), *adj., v.,* -at·ed, -at·ing. —*adj.* desiring to relieve another's suffering; deeply sympathetic; pitying. —*v.* take pity on. —**com·pas′sion·ate·ly,** *adv.* —**com·pas′sion·ate·ness,** *n.*

com·pat·i·ble (kəm·pat′ə·bəl), *adj.* able to exist together; that can get on well together; agreeing; in harmony. [< Med.L *compatibilis.* See COMPASSION.] —**com·pat′i·bil′i·ty,** com·pat′·i·ble·ness, *n.* —**com·pat′i·bly,** *adv.*

com·pa·tri·ot (kəm·pā′tri·ət; *esp. Brit.* kəm·pat′ri·ət), *n.* a fellow countryman.

com·peer (kəm·pir′; kom′pir), *n.* **1.** equal. **2.** comrade. [< OF < L, < *com-* with + *par* equal]

com·pel (kəm·pel′), *v.,* -pelled, -pel·ling. **1.** force. **2.** cause or get by force. [< L, < *com-* + *pellere* drive] —**com·pel′la·ble,** *adj.* —**com·pel′ler,** *n.* —Syn. **1.** constrain, oblige.

com·pen·di·ous (kəm·pen′di·əs), *adj.* brief but comprehensive; concise. —**com·pen′di·ous·ly,** *adv.* —**com·pen′di·ous·ness,** *n.*

com·pen·di·um (kəm·pen′di·əm), *n., pl.* -di·ums, -di·a (-di·ə). summary that gives much information in little space; concise treatise. [< L, a saving, shortening, < *com-* in addition + *pendere* weigh]

com·pen·sate (kom′pən·sāt), *v.,* -sat·ed, -sat·ing. **1.** make an equal return to; give an equivalent to. **2.** balance by equal weight, power, etc.; make up (*for*). **3.** *Econ.* stabilize the buying power of (money) to meet varying price levels by changing gold content or backing. **4.** pay. [< L, < *com-* with + *pensare* weigh < *pendere*] —**com′pen·sa′tor,** *n.* —**com·pen·sa·to·ry** (kəm·pen′sə·tô′ri; -tō′-), *adj.* —Syn. **2.** offset. **4.** recompense, reward.

com·pen·sa·tion (kom′pən·sā′shən), *n.* **1.** something given as an equivalent; something given to make up for a loss, injury, etc. **2.** a balancing by equal power, weight, etc. **3.** *Am.* pay. **4.** increased activity of one part to make up for loss or weakness of another. **5.** any act, instance, or principle of compensating. —**com′pen·sa′tion·al,** *adj.*

com·pete (kəm·pēt′), *v.,* -pet·ed, -pet·ing. **1.** try hard to obtain something wanted by others; be rivals; contend. **2.** take part (in a contest). [< L, < *com-* together + *petere* seek]

com·pe·tence (kom′pə·təns), **com·pe·ten·cy** (-tən·si), *n.* **1.** ability; fitness. **2.** enough money or property to provide a comfortable living.

com·pe·tent (kom′pə·tənt), *adj.* **1.** able; fit. **2.** legally qualified. [< L, being fit, < *competere* meet. See COMPETE.] —**com′pe·tent·ly,** .*adv.* —Syn. **1.** capable.

com·pe·ti·tion (kom′pə·tish′ən), *n.* **1.** effort to obtain something wanted by others; rivalry. **2.** contest.

com·pet·i·tive (kəm·pet′ə·tiv), *adj.* of or having competition; based on or decided by competition. —**com·pet′i·tive·ly,** *adv.* —**com·pet′i·tive·ness,** *n.*

com·pet·i·tor (kəm·pet′ə·tər), *n.* person who competes; rival.

com·pile (kəm·pīl′), *v.,* -piled, -pil·ing. **1.** collect and bring together in one list or account. **2.** make (a book, report, etc.) out of various materials. [< F < L *compilare* steal, orig., pile up < *com-* together + *pilare* press] —**com·pi·la·tion** (kom′pə·lā′shən), *n.* —**com·pil′er,** *n.*

com·pla·cen·cy (kəm·plā′sən·si), **com·pla·cence** (-səns), *n., pl.* -cies; -ces. **1.** being pleased with oneself; self-satisfaction. **2.** contentment.

com·pla·cent (kəm·plā′sənt), *adj.* pleased with oneself; self-satisfied. [< L, < *com-* + *placere* please] —**com·pla′cent·ly,** *adv.*

com·plain (kəm·plān′), *v.* **1.** say that something is wrong; find fault. **2.** talk about one's pains, troubles, etc. **3.** make an accusation or charge. [< OF < VL, bewail, < L *com-* + *plangere* lament] —**com·plain′er,** *n.* —**com·plain′ing·ly,** *adv.* —Syn. **1.** grumble, growl.

com·plain·ant (kəm·plān′ənt), *n.* **1.** person who complains. **2.** plaintiff.

com·plaint (kəm·plānt′), *n.* **1.** a complaining; a finding fault. **2.** a cause for complaining. **3.** accusation; charge. **4.** sickness; ailment.

com·plai·sant (kəm·plā′zənt; kom′plə·zant), *adj.* **1.** obliging; gracious; courteous. **2.** compliant. [< F, < *complaire* acquiesce < L, < *com-* + *placere* please] —**com·plai′sance,** *n.* —**com·plai′sant·ly,** *adv.*

com·ple·ment (*n.* kom′plə·mənt; *v.* kom′plə·ment), *n.* **1.** something that completes or makes perfect. **2.** number required to fill. **3.** either of two parts or things needed to complete each other. **4.** full quantity. **5.** word or group of words completing a predicate. In "The man is good" *good* is a complement. **6.** *Geom.* amount needed to make an angle or an arc equal to 90 degrees. —*v.* supply a lack of any kind; complete. [< L *complementum* < *complere* to COMPLETE] ❯ complement, compliment. *Complement* means a number or amount that makes a whole, or an allotment (related to *complete*): *she has her full complement of good looks. Compliment* has to do with politeness and praise: *their progress deserved his compliment.*

The arc BD is the complement of the arc AB and the angle BCD is the complement of the angle ACB.

com·ple·men·tal (kom′plə·men′təl), *adj.* complementary. —**com·ple·men′tal·ly,** *adv.*

com·ple·men·ta·ry (kom′plə·men′tə·ri; -tri), *adj.* forming a complement; completing.

com·plete (kəm·plēt′), *adj., v.,* -plet·ed, -plet·ing. —*adj.* **1.** with all the parts; whole; entire. **2.** perfect; thorough. **3.** ended; finished; done. —*v.* **1.** make up all the parts of; make whole or entire. **2.** make perfect or thorough. **3.** get done; end; finish. [< L *completus* < *com-* up + *plere* fill] —**com·plete′ly,** *adv.* —**com·plete′ness,** *n.* —**com·plet′er,** *n.* —**com·ple′tive,** *adj.* —Syn. *adj.* **1.** total, full, intact. —*v.* **1.** complement.

com·ple·tion (kəm·plē′shən), *n.* **1.** act of completing. **2.** condition of being completed.

com·plex (*adj.* kəm·pleks′, kom′pleks; *n.* kom′pleks), *adj.* **1.** made up of a number of parts. **2.** complicated. —*n.* **1.** a complicated whole. **2.** idea or group of ideas associated with emotional disturbance so as to influence a person's behavior to an abnormal degree. **3.** *Colloq.* an unreasonable prejudice; strong dislike. [< L *complexus* embracing < *com-* together + *plecti* twine] —**com·plex′ly,** *adv.* —**com·plex′ness,** *n.* —Syn. *adj.* **1.** composite, compound. **2.** intricate, involved.

com·plex·ion (kəm·plek′shən), n. 1. color, quality, and general appearance of the skin, particularly of the face. 2. general appearance; nature; character. [< LL *complexio* constitution < L, combination. See COMPLEX.] —com·plex′ion·al, adj.

com·plex·i·ty (kəm·plek′sə·ti), n., pl. –ties. 1. a complex quality, condition, or structure. 2. something complex; complication.

complex sentence, sentence having one main clause and one or more subordinate clauses. ➤ See clause for usage note.

com·pli·a·ble (kəm·plī′ə·bəl), adj. complying. —com·pli′a·ble·ness, n. —com·pli′a·bly, adv.

com·pli·ance (kəm·plī′əns), **com·pli·an·cy** (–ən·si), n. 1. act of complying; act of doing as another wishes; act of yielding to a request or command. 2. tendency to yield to others. —Syn. 1. assent, consent, submission.

com·pli·ant (kəm·plī′ənt), adj. complying; yielding; obliging. —com·pli′ant·ly, adv.

com·pli·cate (v. kom′plə·kāt; adj. kom′plə·kit), v., –cat·ed, –cat·ing, adj. —v. 1. make hard to understand, settle, cure, etc.; mix up; confuse. 2. make worse or more mixed up. —adj. complex; involved. [< L, < com– together + plicare fold]

com·pli·cat·ed (kom′plə·kāt′id), adj. made up of many parts; intricate. —com′pli·cat′ed·ly, adv. —com′pli·cat′ed·ness, n.

com·pli·ca·tion (kom′plə·kā′shən), n. 1. a complex or confused state of affairs. 2. something causing such a state of affairs. 3. a complicating element in a plot. 4. act or process of complicating. 5. Pathol. a secondary disease or condition occurring in the course of a primary disease.

com·plic·i·ty (kəm·plis′ə·ti), n., pl. –ties. partnership in wrongdoing. [< complice confederate < L complex < com– together + plicare fold]

com·pli·ment (n. kom′plə·mənt; v. kom′plə·ment), n. something good said about one; something said in praise of one's work. —v. pay a compliment to; congratulate. [< F < Ital. < Sp. cumplimiento. Var. of COMPLEMENT.] —Syn. n. commendation, tribute. –v. commend. ➤ See complement for usage note.

com·pli·men·ta·ry (kom′plə·men′tə·ri; –tri), adj. 1. like or containing a compliment; praising. 2. U.S. given free. —com′pli·men′ta·ri·ly, adv.

com·ply (kəm·plī′), v., –plied, –ply·ing. act in agreement with a request or a command. [< Ital. < Sp. < L complere complete; infl. by ply¹] —com·pli′er, n.

com·po·nent (kəm·pō′nənt), adj. constituent. —n. an essential part; part. [< L, < com– together + ponere put]

com·port (kəm·pôrt′; –pōrt′), v. 1. behave: comport oneself with dignity. 2. agree; suit. [< F < L, < com– together + portare carry] —com·port′ment, n.

com·pose (kəm·pōz′), v., –posed, –pos·ing. 1. make up. 2. make or form by uniting the parts of. 3. be the parts of. 4. get (oneself) ready; make up one's mind. 5. make calm (oneself or one's features). 6. settle; arrange: compose a dispute. 7. write music, books, etc. [< OF, < com– (< L) together + poser place (see POSE)]

com·posed (kəm·pōzd′), adj. calm; tranquil. —com·pos·ed·ly (kəm·pōz′id·li), adv.

com·pos·er (kəm·pōz′ər), n. person who composes, esp. a writer of music.

com·pos·ite (kəm·poz′it), adj. 1. made up of various parts; compound. 2. Bot. belonging to a group of plants, as the aster, daisy, etc., in which the florets are borne in dense heads. —n. 1. Bot. composite plant. 2. any composite thing. [< L compositus < com– together + ponere put] —com·pos′ite·ly, adv.

com·po·si·tion (kom′pə·zish′ən), n. 1. make-up of anything; what is in it. 2. a putting together of a whole. 3. thing composed. 4. act or art of composing prose or verse or a musical work. 5. a short essay written as a school exercise. 6. Art. arrangement of parts to produce an esthetically satisfying whole. 7. mixture of substances. 8. agreement; settlement.

com·pos·i·tor (kəm·poz′ə·tər), n. typesetter.

com·post (kom′pōst), n. mixture of leaves, manure, etc., for fertilizing land. [< OF. See COMPOSITE.]

com·po·sure (kəm·pō′zhər), n. calmness; self-control.

com·pote (kom′pōt), n. 1. Am. dish with a supporting stem for fruit, etc. 2. stewed fruit. [< F. See COMPOSITE.]

com·pound¹ (adj. kom′pound, kom·pound′; n. kom′pound; v. kom·pound′, kəm–), adj. having more than one part. Steamship is a compound word. [< v.] —n. 1. something made by combining parts. 2. compound word. 3. Chem. substance formed by chemical combination of two or more substances. [< adj.] —v. 1. mix; combine. 2. make by combining parts. 3. settle (a quarrel or a debt) by a yielding on both sides. 4. compound a felony, accept money not to prosecute a crime, etc. [< OF < L, < com– together + ponere put] —com·pound′a·ble, adj. —com·pound′er, n.

com·pound² (kom′pound), n. an enclosed yard with buildings in it, occupied by foreigners. [prob. < Malay kampong]

Compound E, cortisone.

Compound F, hydrocortisone.

compound interest, interest paid on both the original sum of money borrowed and on the unpaid interest added to it.

compound sentence, sentence made up of coördinate independent clauses. Example: He went out but she came. ➤ See clause for usage note.

com·pre·hend (kom′pri·hend′), v. 1. understand. 2. include; contain. [< L, < com– + prehendere seize] —com′pre·hend′i·ble, adj. —com′pre·hend′ing·ly, adv. —Syn. 1. apprehend, grasp, perceive. 2. comprise, embrace.

com·pre·hen·si·ble (kom′pri·hen′sə·bəl), adj. understandable. —com′pre·hen′si·bil′i·ty, com′pre·hen′si·ble·ness, n. —com′pre·hen′si·bly, adv.

com·pre·hen·sion (kom′pri·hen′shən), n. 1. act or power of understanding; ability to get the meaning. 2. act or fact of including. 3. comprehensiveness.

com·pre·hen·sive (kom′pri·hen′siv), adj. 1. including; including much. 2. comprehending. —com′pre·hen′sive·ly, adv. —com′pre·hen′sive·ness, n. —Syn. 1. inclusive, broad, wide, extensive. 2. understanding.

com·press (v. kəm·pres′; n. kom′pres), v. squeeze together; make smaller by pressure. —n. pad of wet cloth applied to some part of the body to create pressure or to reduce inflammation. [< L compressare, ult. < com– together + premere press] —com·pressed′, adj. —com·pres′sion, n. —com·pres′sive, adj.

com·press·i·ble (kəm·pres′ə·bəl), adj. that can be compressed. —com·press′i·bil′i·ty, n.

com·pres·sor (kəm·pres′ər), n. 1. one that compresses. 2. in surgery, an instrument for compressing a part of the body. 3. machine for compressing air, gas, etc.

com·pris·al, com·priz·al (kəm·prīz′əl), n. comprehension; inclusion.

com·prise, com·prize (kəm·prīz′), v., –prised, –pris·ing; –prized, –priz·ing. consist of; include. [< F compris, pp. of comprendre < L comprehendere. See COMPREHEND.] —com·pris′a·ble, com·priz′a·ble, adj. —Syn. embrace.

com·pro·mise (kom′prə·mīz), v., –mised, –mis·ing, n. —v. 1. settle (a dispute) by agreeing that each will give up a part of what he demands. 2. put under suspicion; put in danger. —n. 1. settlement of a dispute by a partial yielding on both sides. 2. result of such a settlement. 3. anything halfway between two different things. 4. a putting under suspicion. [< F < L compromissum. See COMPROMISE.] —com′pro·mis′er, n.

comp·trol·ler (kən·trōl′ər), n. controller (def. 1). —comp·trol′ler·ship, n.

com·pul·sion (kəm·pul′shən), n. 1. act of compelling; use of force; force. 2. state of being compelled. —com·pul′sive, adj. —com·pul′sive·ly, adv. —Syn. 1. coercion. 2. obligation.

com·pul·so·ry (kəm·pul′sə·ri), *adj.* **1.** required. **2.** using force. —**com·pul′so·ri·ly,** *adv.* —**com·pul′so·ri·ness,** *n.*

com·punc·tion (kəm·pungk′shən), *n.* the pricking of conscience; regret; remorse. [< LL *compunctio* < L, < *com-* + *pungere* prick]

com·pute (kəm·pūt′), *v.,* –put·ed, –put·ing. do by arithmetical work; reckon; calculate. [< L, < *com-* up + *putare* reckon. Doublet of COUNT1.] —**com·put′a·ble,** *adj.* —**com·put′a·bil′i·ty,** *n.* —**com·pu·ta·tion** (kom′pyə·tā′shən), *n.* —**com·put′er,** *n.*

com·rade (kom′rad), *n.* **1.** companion and friend; partner. **2.** a fellow member of a union, political party, etc. [< F < Sp. *camarada* roommate, ult. < L *camera* CHAMBER] —**com′rade·ship,** *n.* —**Syn. 1.** chum, pal.

con1 (kon), *adv.* against a proposition, opinion, etc. —*n.* reason, person, etc., against. [short for L *contra* against]

con2 (kon), *v.,* **conned, con·ning.** learn well enough to remember; study. [var. of *can*1]

con3 (kon), *adj., v.,* **conned, con·ning.** *Am., Slang.* —*adj.* confidence, as in con game, con man. —*v.* to swindle. [short for *confidence*]

con·cat·e·na·tion (kon′kat·ə·nā′shən), *n.* **1.** a linking together or being linked together. **2.** a connected series. [< L, < *com-* together + *catena* chain]

con·cave (*adj., v.* kon·kāv′, kon′kāv, kong′–; *n.* kon′kāv, kong′–), *adj., n., v.,* –caved, –cav·ing. —*adj.* hollow and curved like the inside of a circle or sphere. —*n.* a concave surface or thing. —*v.* make concave. [< L, < *com-* + *cavus* hollow] —**con·cave′ly,** *adv.* —**con·cave′ness,** *n.*

con·cav·i·ty (kon·kav′ə·ti), *n., pl.* –ties. **1.** a concave condition or quality. **2.** a concave surface or thing.

Concave lenses

con·ceal (kən·sēl′), *v.* **1.** hide. **2.** keep secret. [< OF < L, < *com-* + *celare* hide] —**con·ceal′a·ble,** *adj.* —**con·ceal′er,** *n.* —**con·ceal′ment,** *n.* —**Syn. 1.** shroud, veil, cloak, mask. —**Ant. 1.** display, expose. **2.** uncover.

con·cede (kən·sēd′), *v.,* –ced·ed, –ced·ing. **1.** admit as true; admit. **2.** give (what is asked or claimed); grant; yield. [< L, < *com-* + *cedere* yield] —**con·ced′ed·ly,** *adv.* —**con·ced′er,** *n.*

con·ceit (kən·sēt′), *n.* **1.** too high an opinion of oneself or of one's ability, importance, etc. **2.** a fanciful notion; witty thought or expression. **3.** a personal opinion. **4.** a favorable opinion. **5.** imagination; fancy. **6.** thought. —*v.* **1.** flatter. **2.** imagine.

con·ceit·ed (kən·sēt′id), *adj.* having too high an opinion of oneself or one's ability, importance, etc.; vain. —**con·ceit′ed·ly,** *adv.* —**con·ceit′ed·ness,** *n.* —**Syn.** egotistical, proud, self-satisfied.

con·ceiv·a·ble (kən·sēv′ə·bəl), *adj.* that can be conceived or thought of; imaginable. —**con·ceiv′a·bil′i·ty, con·ceiv′a·ble·ness,** *n.* —**con·ceiv′a·bly,** *adv.*

con·ceive (kən·sēv′), *v.,* –ceived, –ceiv·ing. **1.** form in the mind; think up; imagine. **2.** have an idea or feeling; think. **3.** put in words; express. **4.** become pregnant. **5.** become pregnant with. [< OF < L *concipere* take in < *com-* + *capere* take] —**con·ceiv′er,** *n.*

con·cen·trate (kon′sən·trāt), *v.,* –trat·ed, –trat·ing, *n.* —*v.* **1.** bring or come together to one place. **2.** pay close attention; focus the mind. **3.** make stronger, purer, or more intense; condense. —*n.* something that has been concentrated. [< L *com-* + *centrum* CENTER] —**con′cen·tra′tor,** *n.* —**Syn. *v.* 1.** gather, collect, assemble, focus. **3.** intensify. —**Ant. *v.* 1.** disperse. **3.** dilute.

con·cen·tra·tion (kon′sən·trā′shən), *n.* **1.** a concentrating or being concentrated. **2.** close attention. **3.** something that has been concentrated. —**Syn. 1.** collection, gathering.

concentration camp, camp where political enemies, prisoners of war, and interned foreigners are held.

con·cen·tric (kən·sen′trik), *adj.* having the same center. —**con·cen′tri·cal,** *adj.* —**con·cen′tri·cal·ly,** *adv.* —**con·cen·tric·i·ty** (kon′sən·tris′ə·ti), *n.*

Concentric circles

con·cept (kon′sept), *n.* general notion; idea of a class of objects; idea. [< L *conceptus,* pp. of *concipere* CONCEIVE]

con·cep·tion (kən·sep′shən), *n.* **1.** act or power of conceiving. **2.** a being conceived. **3.** a becoming pregnant. **4.** idea; impression. **5.** design; plan. —**con·cep′tive,** *adj.*

con·cep·tu·al (kən·sep′chü·əl), *adj.* having to do with concepts or general ideas. —**con·cep′tu·al·ly,** *adv.*

con·cern (kən·sérn′), *v.* **1.** have to do with; have an interest for; be the business or affair of. **2.** concern oneself, **a.** take an interest; be busy. **b.** be troubled or worried; be anxious or uneasy. —*n.* **1.** whatever has to do with a person or thing; important matter; business affair. **2.** interest. **3.** a troubled state of mind; worry; anxiety; uneasiness. **4.** a business company; firm. **5.** relation; reference. [< Med.L, relate to, < L *com-* together + *cernere* sift] —**Syn. *v.* 1.** affect, touch.

con·cern·ing (kən·sér′ning), *prep.* having to do with; regarding; relating to; about.

con·cern·ment (kən·sérn′mənt), *n.* **1.** importance. **2.** worry; anxiety. **3.** affair.

con·cert (*n., adj.* kon′sért, –sərt; *v.* kən·sért′), *n.* **1.** a musical performance in which several musicians or singers take part. **2.** agreement; harmony; union. **3. in concert,** all together. —*adj.* used in concerts; for concerts. —*v.* arrange by agreement; plan or make together. [< F < Ital. *concerto* CONCERTO]

con·cert·ed (kən·sér′tid), *adj.* arranged by agreement; planned or made together; combined.

con·cer·ti·na (kon′sər·tē′nə), *n.* a small musical instrument somewhat like an accordion.

con·cer·to (kən·cher′tō), *n., pl.* –tos. a long musical composition for one or more principal instruments, such as a violin, piano, etc., accompanied by an orchestra. [< Ital. < L *concentus* symphony, harmony, ult. < *com-* together + *canere* sing]

con·ces·sion (kən·sesh′ən), *n.* **1.** a conceding. **2.** anything conceded or yielded; admission; acknowledgment. **3.** something conceded or granted by a government or controlling authority; grant. **4.** *Am.* place rented for a small business, as a newsstand, etc. —**Syn. 3.** franchise.

conch (kongk; konch), *n., pl.* **conchs** (kongks), **con·ches** (kon′chiz). a large, spiral sea shell. [< L < Gk. *konche*]

con·ci·erge (kon′si·ėrzh′; *Fr.* kôN·syerzh′), *n.* **1.** doorkeeper. **2.** janitor. [< F]

con·cil·i·ate (kən·sil′i·āt), *v.,* –at·ed, –at·ing. **1.** win over; soothe. **2.** gain (good will, regard, favor, etc.) by friendly acts. **3.** reconcile; bring into harmony. [< L *conciliatus* < *concilium* COUNCIL] —**con·cil′i·a′tion,** *n.* —**con·cil′i·a′tor,** *n.*

con·cil·i·a·to·ry (kən·sil′i·ə·tô′ri; –tō′–), **con·cil·i·a·tive** (–i·ā′tiv), *adj.* tending to win over, soothe, or reconcile. —**con·cil′i·a·to′ri·ly,** *adv.* —**con·cil′i·a·to′ri·ness,** *n.*

con·cise (kən·sīs′), *adj.* expressing much in few words; brief but full of meaning. [< L *concisus* < *com-* + *caedere* cut] —**con·cise′ly,** *adv.* —**con·cise′ness,** *n.*

con·clave (kon′klāv; kong′–), *n.* **1.** a private meeting. **2.** a meeting of the cardinals for the election of a pope. **3.** rooms where the cardinals meet in private for this purpose. [< L, < *com-* with + *clavis* key]

con·clude (kən·klüd′), *v.,* –clud·ed, –clud·ing. **1.** end; finish. **2.** say in ending. **3.** arrange; settle. **4.** find out by thinking; reach (certain facts or opinions) as a result of reasoning; infer. **5.** decide; resolve. [< L *concludere* < *com-* up + *claudere* close] —**con·clud′er,** *n.* —**Syn. 1.** terminate. **4.** deduce.

con·clu·sion (kən·klü′zhən), *n.* **1.** end. **2.** the last main division of a speech, essay, etc. **3.** a final result; outcome. **4.** arrangement; settlement. **5.** decision, judgment, or opinion reached by reasoning. **6.** in conclusion, finally; lastly; to conclude. —**Syn. 1.** termination. **5.** inference.

con·clu·sive (kən·klū′siv), *adj.* decisive; convincing; final. —**con·clu′sive·ness,** *n.*

con·coct (kon·kokt′; kən-), *v.* prepare; make up. [< L *concoctus* < *com*- together + *coquere* cook] —**con·coct′er,** *n.* —**con·coc′tion,** *n.*

con·com·i·tant (kon·kom′ə·tənt; kən-), *adj.* accompanying; attending. —*n.* an accompanying thing, quality, or circumstance; accompaniment. [< L, < *com*- + *comitari* accompany]

con·cord (kon′kôrd; kong′-), *n.* **1.** agreement; harmony; peace. **2.** a harmonious combination of tones sounded together. **3.** treaty. **4.** *Gram.* agreement in number, person, case, or gender of a word or element with another word or element, usually within the same sentence. In "he walk," the elements are not in concord; in "he walks," the elements are in concord. [< F < L *concordia,* ult. < *com*- together + *cor* heart]

Con·cord (kong′kərd), *n.* **1.** town in E Massachusetts; the second battle of the American Revolution, April 19, 1775. **2.** capital of New Hampshire, in the S part.

con·cord·ance (kon·kôr′dəns; kən-), *n.* **1.** agreement; harmony. **2.** an alphabetical list of the principal words of a book with references to the passages in which they occur.

con·cord·ant (kon·kôr′dənt; kən-), *adj.* agreeing; harmonious. —**con·cord′ant·ly,** *adv.*

con·cor·dat (kon·kôr′dat), *n.* **1.** agreement; compact. **2.** a formal agreement between the pope and a government about church affairs. [< F < LL *concordatum,* pp. of *concordare* make harmonious]

con·course (kon′kôrs; kong′-; -kōrs), *n.* **1.** a running, flowing, or coming together. **2.** crowd. **3.** *Am.* place where crowds come. **4.** *Am.* an open space in a railroad station. **5.** driveway; boulevard. [< OF < L *concursus* < *com*- together + *currere* run]

con·crete (*adj., n., and v.* 1 kon′krēt, kon-krēt′; *v.* 2 kon·krēt′), *adj., n., v.,* -cret·ed, -cret·ing. —*adj.* **1.** existing of itself in the material world, not merely in idea or as a quality; real. **2.** not abstract or general; specific; particular. **3.** naming a thing, esp. something perceived by the senses. *Sugar* is a concrete noun; *sweetness* is an abstract noun. **4.** made of concrete. **5.** formed into a mass; solid; hardened. —*n.* mixture of crushed stone or gravel, sand, cement, and water that hardens as it dries. —*v.* **1.** cover with concrete. **2.** form or mix into a mass; harden into a mass. [< L *concretus* < *com*- together + *crescere* grow] —**con·crete′ness,** *n.*

con·cre·tion (kon·krē′shən), *n.* **1.** a forming into a mass; a solidifying. **2.** a solidified mass; hard formation.

con·cu·bine (kong′kyə·bīn; kon′-), *n.* **1.** woman who lives with a man without being legally married to him. **2.** wife who has an inferior rank, rights, etc. [< L, < *com*- with + *cubare* lie] —**con·cu·bi·nage** (kon·kū′bə·nij), *n.*

con·cu·pis·cent (kon·kū′pə·sənt), *adj.* **1.** eagerly desirous. **2.** lustful; sensual. [< L *concupiscens,* ult. < *com*- (intensive) + *cupere* desire] —**con·cu′pis·cence,** *n.*

con·cur (kən·kėr′), *v.,* -curred, -cur·ring. **1.** be of the same opinion; agree. **2.** work together. **3.** come together; happen at the same time. [< L, < *com*- together + *currere* run]

con·cur·rence (kən·kėr′əns), **con·cur·ren·cy** (-ən·si), *n.* **1.** having the same opinion; agreement. **2.** a working together. **3.** a happening at the same time. **4.** a coming together.

con·cur·rent (kən·kėr′ənt), *adj.* **1.** existing side by side; happening at the same time. **2.** coöperating. **3.** having equal authority or jurisdiction; coördinate. **4.** agreeing; consistent; harmonious. **5.** coming together; meeting in a point. —**con·cur′rent·ly,** *adv.*

con·cus·sion (kən·kush′ən), *n.* **1.** a sudden, violent shaking; shock. **2.** injury to the brain, spine, etc., caused by a blow, fall, or other shock. [< L *concussio* < *concutere* shake violently

< *com*- (intensive) + *quatere* shake]

con·demn (kən·dem′), *v.* **1.** express strong disapproval of. **2.** pronounce guilty of a crime or wrong. **3.** doom: *condemned to death.* **4.** declare not sound or suitable for use. **5.** *Am.* take for public use under special provision of the law. [< OF < L, < *com*- + *damnare* cause loss to, condemn] —**con·dem·na·ble** (kən·dem′nə·bəl), *adj.* —**con·dem·na·to·ry** (kən·dem′nə·tô′ri; -tō′-), *adj.* —**con·demn·er** (kən·dem′ər), *n.* —**con·demn′ing·ly,** *adv.* —**Syn. 1.** denounce, damn. **2.** convict. —**Ant. 1.** commend. **2.** acquit.

con·dem·na·tion (kon′dem·nā′shən; -dəm-), *n.* **1.** a condemning or being condemned. **2.** cause or reason for condemning.

con·den·sa·tion (kon′den·sā′shən), *n.* **1.** a condensing or being condensed. **2.** something condensed; condensed mass. **3.** act of changing a gas or vapor to a liquid.

con·dense (kən·dens′), *v.,* -densed, -dens·ing. **1.** make or become denser or more compact. **2.** make stronger; concentrate. **3.** change from a gas or vapor to a liquid. **4.** put into fewer words; express briefly. [< L, < *com*- + *densus* thick] —**con·den′sa·ble, con·den′si·ble,** *adj.* —**con·den·sa·bil·i·ty, con·den·si·bil·i·ty,** *n.* —**Syn. 1.** compress. **4.** reduce, contract, shorten.

con·dens·er (kən·den′sər), *n.* **1.** person or thing that condenses something. **2.** *Elect.* device for receiving and holding a charge of electricity. **3.** apparatus for changing gas or vapor into a liquid. **4.** strong lens or lenses for concentrating light upon a small area.

con·de·scend (kon′di·send′), *v.* come down willingly or graciously to the level of one's inferiors in rank. [< LL *condescendere.* See COM-, DESCEND.] —**con′de·scen′sion,** *n.* —**Syn.** deign, stoop, vouchsafe.

con·dign (kən·dīn′), *adj.* deserved; adequate; fitting: *condign punishment.* [< F < L *condignus* very worthy < *com*- completely + *dignus* worthy] ► Because **condign** is so often coupled with *punishment,* it is sometimes misunderstood and used as a synonym for *severe.*

con·di·ment (kon′də·mənt), *n.* something used to give flavor and relish to food, such as pepper and spices. [< L *condimentum* spice < *condire* put up, preserve]

con·di·tion (kən·dish′ən), *n.* **1.** state in which a person or thing is. **2.** good condition: *keep in condition.* **3.** rank; social position. **4.** thing on which something else depends. **5.** something demanded as an essential part of an agreement. **6.** a restricting or limiting circumstance. **7. on condition that, if.** —*v.* **1.** put in good condition. **2.** be a condition of. **3.** subject to a condition. **4.** make conditions; make it a condition. **5.** adapt or modify by shifting a response to a different stimulus. [< L *condicio* agreement < *com*- together + *dicere* say] —**con·di′tion·er,** *n.*

con·di·tion·al (kən·dish′ən·əl), *adj.* **1.** depending on something else; not absolute; limited. **2.** expressing or containing a condition. —**con·di′tion·al·i·ty,** *n.* —**con·di′tion·al·ly,** *adv.*

con·dole (kən·dōl′), *v.,* -doled, -dol·ing. express sympathy; sympathize. [< L, < *com*- with + *dolere* grieve, suffer] —**con·do′lence, con·dole′ment,** *n.* —**con·dol′er,** *n.* —**con·dol′ing·ly,** *adv.*

con·done (kən·dōn′), *v.,* -doned, -don·ing. forgive; overlook. [< L, < *com*- up + *donare* give] —**con·do·na·tion** (kon′dō·nā′shən), *n.* —**con·don′er,** *n.*

con·dor (kon′dər), *n.* a large American vulture with a bare neck and head. [< Sp. < Peruvian *cuntur*]

Condor (4 ft. long; wingspread 9 ft.)

con·duce (kən·dūs′; -dūs′), *v.,* -duced, -duc·ing. lead; contribute; be favorable. [< L, < *com*- together + *ducere* lead] —**con·duc′er,** *n.* —**con·du′cive,** *adj.* —**con·du′cive·ness,** *n.*

con·duct (*n.* kon′dukt; *v.* kən·dukt′), *n.* **1.** behavior; way of acting. **2.** direction; management.

3. leading; guidance. [< v.] —v. **1.** act in a certain way; behave: *she always conducts herself like a lady.* **2.** direct; manage. **3.** direct (an orchestra, etc.) as leader. **4.** lead; guide. **5.** transmit (heat, electricity, etc.); be a channel for. [< L *conductus* < *com-* together + *ducere* lead] —con·duct′i·ble, *adj.* —con·duct′i·bil′i·ty, *n.* —con·duc′tive, *adj.* —**Syn.** *n.* **1.** deportment.

con·duct·ance (kən·duk′təns), *n.* *Elect.* power of conducting electricity as affected by the shape, length, etc., of the conductor.

con·duc·tion (kən·duk′shən), *n.* **1.** transmission of heat, electricity, etc., by the transferring of energy from one particle to another. **2.** a conveying: *conduction of water in a pipe.*

con·duc·tiv·i·ty (kon′duk·tiv′ə·ti), *n.* power of conducting heat, electricity, etc.

con·duc·tor (kən·duk′tər), *n.* **1.** person who conducts; director; manager; leader; guide. **2.** director of an orchestra, chorus, etc. **3.** person in charge of a streetcar, bus, railroad train, etc. **4.** thing that transmits heat, electricity, light, sound, etc. **5.** *Am.* a lightning rod.

con·duit (kon′dit; -dū·it), *n.* **1.** channel or pipe for carrying liquids long distances. **2.** tube or underground passage for electric wires. [< OF < Med.L *conductus* a leading, a pipe < L, contraction < *com-* together + *ducere* draw]

cone (kōn), *n.*, *v.*, **coned, con·ing.** —n. **1.** solid with a flat, round base that tapers evenly to a point at the top. **2.** *Geom.* surface traced by a moving straight line, one point of which is fixed, that constantly touches a fixed curve. **3.** anything shaped like a cone. **4.** *Am.* a cone-shaped, edible shell filled with ice cream. **5.** *Bot.* part that bears the seeds on pine, cedar, fir, and other evergreen trees. **6.** in machines, a cone-shaped part. —v. shape like a cone. [< L < Gk. *konos* pine cone, cone]

Cone

Con·el·rad (kon′əl·rad), *n.* a system for broadcasting instructions, etc., over radio stations by shifting frequencies, going on and off the air irregularly, etc., while keeping enemy airplanes from utilizing the beams of the station for navigation. [short for Con(trol) (of) El(ectromagnetic) Rad(iation)]

co·ney (kō′ni), *n.*, *pl.* **co·neys.** cony.

con·fab·u·late (kən·fab′yə·lāt), *v.*, **-lat·ed, -lat·ing.** talk together informally and intimately; chat. [< L, ult. < *com-* together + *fabula* fable] —con·fab′u·la′tion, *n.*

con·fec·tion (kən·fek′shən), *n.* piece of candy, candied fruit, sugared nut, jam, etc. [< L *confectio* < *com-* up + *facere* make]

con·fec·tion·er (kən·fek′shən·ər), *n.* person who makes and sells candies, ice cream, etc.

con·fec·tion·er·y (kən·fek′shən·er′i), *n.*, *pl.* **-er·ies.** **1.** candies, sweets, etc.; confections. **2.** business of making or selling confections. **3.** *Am.* place where confections, ice cream, etc., are made or sold; candy shop.

con·fed·er·a·cy (kən·fed′ər·ə·si), *n.*, *pl.* **-cies.** **1.** union of countries or states; group of people joined together for a special purpose. **2.** league; alliance. **3.** conspiracy. **4. the Confederacy,** *Am.* group of eleven Southern States that seceded from the United States in 1860 and 1861. —**Syn.** **1.** confederation, federation.

con·fed·er·ate (adj., *n.* kən·fed′ər·it; *v.* kən·fed′ər·āt), *adj.*, *n.*, *v.*, **-at·ed, -at·ing.** —adj. **1.** joined together for a special purpose; allied. **2. Confederate,** of or belonging to the Confederacy. —n. **1.** country, person, etc., joined with another for a special purpose; ally; companion. **2.** accomplice; partner in crime. **3. Confederate,** *Am.* person who lived in and supported the Confederacy. —v. join (countries, people, etc.) together for a special purpose; ally. [< L, < *com-* together + *foedus* league] —**Syn.** *n.* **2.** accessory.

con·fed·er·a·tion (kən·fed′ər·ā′shən), *n.* **1.** a joining or being together in a league; federation. **2.** group of countries, states, etc., joined together for a special purpose; league. **3. the Confederation,** *Am.* the confederation of the American States from 1781 to 1789.

con·fer (kən·fėr′), *v.*, **-ferred, -fer·ring. 1.** consult together; exchange ideas; talk things over. **2.** give; bestow: *confer a medal.* [< L, < *com-* together + *ferre* bring] —con·fer′ment, *n.*

con·fer·ee (kon′fər·ē′), *n.* *Am.* person who takes part in a conference.

con·fer·ence (kon′fər·əns), *n.* **1.** a meeting of interested persons to discuss a particular subject. **2.** consultation with a person or a group of persons. **3.** association of schools, churches, etc., joined together for some special purpose. **4.** act of bestowing; conferment.

con·fess (kən·fes′), *v.* **1.** acknowledge; admit; own up. **2.** admit one's guilt. **3.** tell (one's sins) to a priest in order to obtain forgiveness. **4.** acknowledge one's belief in or adherence to. [< LL *confessare*, ult. < *com-* + *fateri* confess] —con·fess′ed·ly, *adv.* —con·fess′er, *n.*

con·fes·sion (kən·fesh′ən), *n.* **1.** acknowledgment; admission; owning up. **2.** admission of guilt. **3.** the telling of one's sins to a priest in order to obtain forgiveness. **4.** thing confessed. **5.** acknowledgment of belief; profession of faith. **6.** belief acknowledged; creed.

con·fes·sion·al (kən·fesh′ən·əl), *n.* a small booth where a priest hears confessions. —adj. of or having to do with confession.

con·fes·sor (kən·fes′ər), *n.* **1.** person who confesses. **2.** priest who has the authority to hear confessions.

con·fet·ti (kən·fet′i), *n.* **1.** bits of colored paper thrown about at carnivals, weddings, etc. **2.** candies. [< Ital., pl., comfits. See CONFECTION.]

con·fi·dant (kon′fə·dant′; kon′fə·dant), *n.* person trusted with one's secrets, private affairs, etc.; close friend.

con·fi·dante (kon′fə·dant′; kon′fə·dant), *n.* woman confidant.

con·fide (kən·fīd′), *v.*, **-fid·ed, -fid·ing. 1.** tell as a secret. **2.** entrust secrets, private affairs, etc. **3.** hand over (a task, person, etc.) in trust; give to another for safekeeping. **4.** put trust; have faith. [< L, < *com-* completely + *fidere* trust]

con·fi·dence (kon′fə·dəns), *n.* **1.** firm belief; trust. **2.** firm belief in oneself and one's abilities. **3.** boldness; too much boldness. **4.** a feeling of trust; assurance that a person will not tell others what is said. **5.** thing told as a secret. —adj. *Am.* having to do with swindling that takes advantage of the victim's confidence. —**Syn.** *n.* **1.** conviction. **2.** assurance, self-reliance. **3.** presumption.

confidence game, *Am.* fraud in which the swindler persuades his victim to trust him.

confidence man, *Am.* swindler who persuades his victim to trust him.

con·fi·dent (kon′fə·dənt), *adj.* **1.** firmly believing; certain; sure. **2.** sure of oneself and one's abilities. **3.** too bold; too sure. —n. close, trusted friend; confidant. —con′fi·dent·ly, *adv.*

con·fi·den·tial (kon′fə·den′shəl), *adj.* **1.** told or written as a secret. **2.** showing confidence. **3.** trusted with secrets, private affairs, etc. —con′fi·den′tial·ly, *adv.* —con′fi·den′tial·ness, *n.*

con·fig·u·ra·tion (kən·fig′yə·rā′shən), *n.* **1.** the relative position of parts; manner of arrangement. **2.** form; shape; outline. —con·fig′u·ra′tion·al, *adj.*

con·fine (v. kən·fīn′; *n.* kon′fīn), *v.*, **-fined, -fin·ing,** *n.* —v. **1.** keep within limits; restrict. **2.** keep indoors; shut in. **3.** imprison. **4.** be confined, give birth to a child. —n. Usually, confines. boundary; border; limit. [< F, < *confins,* pl., bounds < L *confinium,* ult. < *com-* together + *finis* end, border] —con·fine′ment, *n.*

con·firm (kən·fėrm′), *v.* **1.** prove to be true or correct; make certain. **2.** approve by formal consent; approve; consent to. **3.** strengthen; make firmer. **4.** admit to full membership in a church after required study and preparation. [< OF < L, < *com-* + *firmus* firm] —con·firm′a·ble, *adj.* —**Syn.** **1.** verify. **2.** ratify.

con·fir·ma·tion (kon′fər·mā′shən), *n.* **1.** a confirming. **2.** thing that confirms; proof. **3.** ceremony of admitting a person to full membership in a church after required study and preparation.

con·firm·a·to·ry (kən·fër'mə·tô'ri; -tō'-),
con·firm·a·tive (-mə·tiv), *adj.* confirming.
con·firmed (kən·fërmd'), *adj.* 1. firmly established; proved. 2. habitual; constant; chronic:
a confirmed invalid. —con·firm·ed·ly (kən·fër'-
mid·li), *adv.* —con·firm'ed·ness, *n.*
con·fis·cate (kon'fis·kāt), *v.*, -cat·ed, -cat·ing.
1. seize for the public treasury. 2. seize by
authority; take and keep. [< L, orig., lay away
in a chest, < com- + *fiscus* chest, public treas-
ury] —con'fis·ca'tion, *n.* —con'fis·ca'tor, *n.*
—Syn. 1, 2. appropriate.
con·fis·ca·to·ry (kən·fis'kə·tô'ri; -tō'-), *adj.*
1. of or like confiscation; tending to confiscate.
2. confiscating.
con·fla·gra·tion (kon'flə·grā'shən), *n.* a big
fire. [< L *conflagratio* < *com-* up + *flagrare*
burn]
con·flict (*v.* kən·flikt'; *n.* kon'flikt), *v.* 1. fight;
struggle. 2. be directly opposed; disagree; clash.
—*n.* 1. fight; struggle. 2. direct opposition; disagreement; clash. [< L *conflictus* < *com-* together + *fligere* strike] —con·flic'tion, *n.* —con-
flic'tive, *adj.* —Syn. *n.* 1. strife. 2. collision.
con·flu·ence (kon'flù·əns), *n.* 1. a flowing together, as of two rivers. 2. a coming together of
people or things; throng. [< L, < *com-* together
+ *fluere* flow] —con'flu·ent, *adj.*
con·flux (kon'fluks), *n.* confluence.
con·form (kən·fôrm'), *v.* 1. act according to
law or rule; be in agreement with generally
accepted standards of business, law, conduct, or
worship. 2. become the same in form; correspond
in form or character. 3. make similar. 4. adapt.
[< OF < L, < *com-* + *formare* shape < *forma* a
shape] —con·form'er, *n.* —Syn. 4. adjust, accommodate, suit.
con·form·a·ble (kən·fôr'mə·bəl), *adj.* 1. similar. 2. adapted; suited. 3. in agreement; agreeable; harmonious. 4. obedient; submissive. —conform'a·ble·ness, *n.* —con·form'a·bly, *adv.*
con·form·ance (kən·fôr'məns), *n.* conformity.
con·for·ma·tion (kon'fôr·mā'shən), *n.* 1.
structure; shape; form of a thing resulting from
the arrangement of its parts. 2. a symmetrical
arrangement of the parts of a thing. 3. a conforming; adaptation.
con·form·ist (kən·fôr'mist), *n.* person who
conforms.
con·form·i·ty (kən·fôr'mə·ti), *n.*, *pl.* -ties. 1.
similarity; corresponding; agreement. 2. action
in agreement with generally accepted standards
of business, law, conduct, or worship; fitting
oneself and one's actions to the ideas of others;
compliance. 3. submission.
con·found (kon·found', kən- *for 1-3;* kon'-
found' *for 4*), *v.* 1. confuse; mix up. 2. be unable
to tell apart. 3. surprise and puzzle. 4. damn.
Confound is used as a mild oath. [< OF < L, <
com- together + *fundere* pour] —con·found'er,
n.
con·found·ed (kon'foun'did; kən-), *adj.* 1.
damned. *Confounded* is used as a mild oath. 2.
hateful; detestable. —con·found'ed·ly, *adv.*
con·frere (kon'frâr), *n.* a fellow member; colleague. [< F < OF < Med.L *confrater* < L *com-*
together + *frater* brother]
con·front (kən·frunt'), *v.* 1. meet face to face;
stand facing. 2. face boldly; oppose. 3. bring face
to face; place before. [< F < Med.L, < L *com-*
together + *frons* forehead] —con·fron·ta·tion
(kon'frun·tā'shən), con·front'ment, *n.*
Con·fu·cius (kən·fū'shəs), *n.* 551?–478 B.C.,
Chinese philosopher and moral teacher. He
taught that the chief virtues are respect for
parents and ancestors, kindliness, faithfulness,
intelligence, and proper behavior. —Con·fu'cian,
adj., *n.* —Con·fu'cian·ism, *n.* —Con·fu'cian-
ist, *n.*
con·fuse (kən·fūz'), *v.*, -fused, -fus·ing. 1. mix
up; throw into disorder. 2. bewilder. 3. be unable
to tell apart; mistake (one thing for another).
4. make uneasy and ashamed; embarrass. [< F
< L *confusus*, pp. of *confundere*. See CONFOUND.]
—con·fus·ed·ly (kən·fūz'id·li; -fūzd'li), *adv.*
—con·fus'ed·ness, *n.* —con·fus'ing·ly, *adv.*

—Syn. 2. puzzle, perplex. 3. confound. 4. disconcert. —Ant. 3. distinguish.
con·fu·sion (kən·fū'zhən), *n.* 1. act or fact
of confusing. 2. confused condition; disorder. 3.
failure to distinguish clearly. 4. bewilderment.
5. uneasiness and shame. —con·fu'sion·al, *adj.*
—Syn. 4. perplexity. 5. embarrassment.
con·fute (kən·fūt'), *v.*, -fut·ed, -fut·ing. 1.
prove (an argument, testimony, etc.) to be false
or incorrect. 2. prove (a person) to be wrong;
overcome by argument. 3. make useless. [< L
confutare] —con·fu·ta·tion (kon'fyù·tā'shən),
n. —con·fut'er, *n.*
Cong., Congress; Congressional.
con·ga (kong'gə), *n.* a Cuban dance.
con·geal (kən·jēl'), *v.* 1. freeze. 2. thicken;
stiffen. [< OF < L, < *com-* up + *gelare* freeze]
—con·geal'a·ble, *adj.* —con·geal'er, *n.* —con-
geal'ment, *n.*
con·gen·ial (kən·jēn'yəl), *adj.* 1. having
similar tastes and interests; getting on well together. 2. agreeable; suitable: *he seeks more
congenial work.* [< L, < *com-* together + *genialis*
< *genius* spirit] —con·ge·ni·al·i·ty (kən·jē'-
ni·al'ə·ti; -jēn'yal'-), *n.* —con·gen'ial·ly, *adv.*
—Syn. 1. sympathetic.
con·gen·i·tal (kən·jen'ə·təl), *adj.* present at
birth. [< L *congenitus* born with. See GENITAL.]
—con·gen'i·tal·ly, *adv.*
con·ger (kong'gər), or **conger eel,** *n.* a large
ocean eel that is caught for food along the
coasts of Europe. [< OF < L < Gk. *gongros*]
con·gest (kən·jest'), *v.* 1. fill too full; over-
crowd. 2. *Pathol.* cause too much blood to gather
in (one part of the body). 3. become too full of
blood. [< L *congestus* < *com-* together + *gerere*
carry] —con·ges'tion, *n.* —con·ges'tive, *adj.*
con·glom·er·ate (*v.* kən·glom'ər·āt; *adj.*, *n.*
kən·glom'ər·it), *v.*, -at·ed, -at·ing, *adj.*, *n.* —*v.*
gather in a rounded mass. —*adj.* 1. gathered
into a rounded mass; clustered. 2. made up of
miscellaneous materials gathered from various
sources. —*n.* 1. mass formed of fragments. 2.
rock consisting of pebbles, gravel, etc., held together by a cementing material. [< L, < *com-*
+ *glomus* ball] —con·glom'er·a'tion, *n.*
Con·go (kong'gō), *n.* river in C Africa, flowing
from SE Belgian Congo to the Atlantic.
congo snake or **eel,** *Am.* an eellike amphibian
that has very small, weak legs.
con·grat·u·late (kən·grach'ə·lāt), *v.*, -lat·ed,
-lat·ing. express one's pleasure at the happiness
or good fortune of. [< L, < *com-* + *gratulari*
show joy] —con·grat'u·la'tor, *n.* —con·grat-
u·la·to·ry (kən·grach'ə·lə·tô'ri; -tō'-), *adj.*
con·grat·u·la·tion (kən·grach'ə·lā'shən), *n.*
1. act of congratulating. 2. Usually, congrat-
ulations. expression of pleasure at another's
happiness or good fortune.
con·gre·gate (kong'grə·gāt), *v.*, -gat·ed, -gat-
ing, *adj.* —*v.* come together into a crowd or
mass. —*adj.* assembled; collected. [< L *congre-
gatus* < *com-* together + *grex* flock] —con'-
gre·ga'tive, *adj.* —con'gre·ga'tor, *n.*
con·gre·ga·tion (kong'grə·gā'shən), *n.* 1. act
of congregating. 2. a gathering of people or
things; assembly. 3. group of people gathered
together for religious worship. 4. a religious
community or order with a common rule but
not under solemn vows.
con·gre·ga·tion·al (kong'grə·gā'shən·əl),
adj. 1. of a congregation; done by a congregation.
2. Congregational, of or belonging to Congregationalism or Congregationalists.
con·gre·ga·tion·al·ism (kong'grə·gā'shən-
əl·iz'əm), *n.* 1. system of church government in
which each individual church governs itself. 2.
Congregationalism, principles and system of
organization of a Protestant denomination in
which each individual church governs itself.
—con'gre·ga'tion·al·ist, Con'gre·ga'tion·al·ist,
n., *adj.*
con·gress (kong'gris), *n.* 1. the lawmaking
body of a nation, esp. of a republic. 2. Congress,
Am. a. the national lawmaking body of the
United States, consisting of the Senate and

House of Representatives. **b.** the body of senators and representatives for each term of two years for which representatives are elected. **3.** a formal meeting of representatives to discuss some subject. —*v.* meet in congress. [< L *congressus* < *com-* together + *gradī* go]

con·gres·sion·al (kən-gresh′ən-əl), *adj. Am.* **1.** of a congress. **2.** Congressional, of Congress.

con·gress·man (kong′gris-mən), *n.*, *pl.* **-men.** Often, **Congressman.** *Am.* **1.** member of Congress. **2.** member of the House of Representatives.

con·gress·wom·an (kong′gris-wùm′ən), *n.*, *pl.* **-wom·en.** *Am.* a woman congressman.

con·gru·ent (kong′grü-ənt), *adj.* **1.** agreeing; harmonious. **2.** *Geom.* exactly coinciding. [< L, < *congruere* agree] —**con′gru·ence, con′gru·en·cy,** *n.* —**con′gru·ent·ly,** *adv.*

con·gru·i·ty (kən-grü′ə-ti), *n.*, *pl.* **-ties. 1.** agreement; harmony. **2.** *Geom.* the exact coincidence of lines, angles, figures, etc. **3.** point of agreement.

con·gru·ous (kong′grü-əs), *adj.* **1.** agreeing; harmonious. **2.** fitting; appropriate. **3.** *Geom.* exactly coinciding. —**con′gru·ous·ly,** *adv.* —**con′-gru·ous·ness,** *n.* —**Ant.** 1. disagreeing.

con·ic (kon′ik), **con·i·cal** (-ə-kəl), *adj.* **1.** cone-shaped; like a cone. **2.** of a cone. —**con′i·cal·ly,** *adv.*

co·ni·fer (kō′nə-fər; kon′ə-), *n.* any of a large group of trees and shrubs, most of which are evergreen and bear cones. [< L, < *conus* cone (< Gk. *konos*) + *ferre* to bear] —**co·nif·er·ous** (kō-nif′ər-əs), *adj.*

conj., **1.** conjugation. **2.** conjunction.

con·jec·tur·al (kən-jek′chər-əl), *adj.* **1.** involving conjecture. **2.** inclined to conjecture. —**con·jec′tur·al·ly,** *adv.*

con·jec·ture (kən-jek′chər), *n.*, *v.*, **-tured, -tur·ing.** —*n.* **1.** formation of an opinion without sufficient evidence for proof; guessing. **2.** a guess. —*v.* guess. [< L *conjectura* < *com-* together + *jacere* throw] —**con·jec′tur·a·ble,** *adj.* —**con·jec′tur·a·bly,** *adv.* —**con·jec′tur·er,** *n.* —**Syn.** *n.* 2. supposition. —*v.* suppose.

con·join (kən-join′), *v.* unite. —**con·join′er,** *n.*

con·joint (kən-joint′; kon′joint), *adj.* **1.** joined together; united. **2.** joint. —**con·joint′ly,** *adv.*

con·ju·gal (kon′jə-gəl), *adj.* of marriage; having to do with marriage. [< L *conjugalis* < *com-* with + *jugum* yoke] —**con′ju·gal·ly,** *adv.*

con·ju·gate (*v.* kon′jə-gāt; *adj.*, *n.* kon′jə-git, -gāt), *v.*, **-gat·ed, -gat·ing,** *adj.*, *n.* —*v.* **1.** give the forms of (a verb) according to a systematic arrangement. **2.** join together; couple. —*adj.* joined together; coupled. —*n.* word derived from the same root as another. [< L, < *com-* with + *jugum* yoke] —**con′ju·ga′tive,** *adj.* —**con′ju·ga′tor,** *n.*

con·ju·ga·tion (kon′jə-gā′shən), *n.* **1.** systematic arrangement of the forms of a verb. **2.** group of verbs having similar forms in such an arrangement. **3.** act of giving the forms of a verb according to such an arrangement. **4.** a joining together; a coupling.

con·junc·tion (kən-jungk′shən), *n.* **1.** act of joining together; union; combination. **2.** word that connects words, phrases, clauses, or sentences. **3.** *Astron.* the apparent nearness of two or more heavenly bodies. [< L *conjunctio* < *com-* with + *jungere* join] ❯ **Conjunctions** introduce and tie clauses together and tie together series of words and phrases. **1.** ACCURATE CONJUNCTIONS. The fitting together of clauses by an exact use of conjunctions is a mark of mature, practiced writing. In everyday speech we get along with a relatively small number of conjunctions—*and, as, but, so, when, while,* and a few others. We don't bother to emphasize shades of meaning and exact relationships, which are suggested by pauses, tones of voice, gestures. In writing, accurate connectives go a long way toward making up for the loss of these oral means of holding ideas together. Some conjunctions vary in definiteness of meaning: *as* means *because,* but *means* it very weakly; *while* may mean *although* or *whereas,* but the core of its meaning relates to time, and careful writers restrict it to that. **2.**

WEIGHT. It is important for the conjunctions to be appropriate to other traits of style. Their weight should fit with the weight of other words and with the formality or informality of constructions. The chief fault in weight of conjunctions has to do with the conjunctive adverbs (*however, therefore, consequently* . . .) in ordinary, informal writing. These words are heavy and fit best in rather formal writing. *But* and *however,* for example, both connect statements in opposition, but one cannot always be substituted for the other. *But* fits in all levels, but *however* is often too formal or too heavy for informal writing: *The entrance and registration desk didn't strike me as beautiful. From here, however, I went upstairs and then I could see what they meant* [but from here . . .]. English has a number of long connecting phrases that are often used in place of shorter conjunctions: Football was distinctively a military pastime in Rome *in the same manner in which* [as] polo is among the soldiers today.

con·junc·ti·va (kon′jungk·tī′və), *n.*, *pl.* **-vas, -vae** (-vē). *Anat.* the mucous membrane that covers the inner surface of the eyelids.

con·junc·tive (kən-jungk′tiv), *adj.* **1.** joining together. **2.** joined together; joint. **3.** like a conjunction. *When* is a conjunctive adverb. —*n.* a conjunctive word; conjunction. —**con·junc′tive·ly,** *adv.* ❯ **conjunctive adverbs. 1.** A number of words which are primarily adverbs are used also as connectives. They are called conjunctive adverbs (or relative adverbs). Their adverbial meaning remains rather prominent, so that they are relatively weak connectives and need special discussion. Except for *when* and *where* and so they are coördinating conjunctions and make compound sentences. The most common are: *accordingly, also, anyhow, anyway* (colloquial), *besides, consequently, furthermore, hence, however, indeed, likewise, moreover, namely, nevertheless, so, still, then, therefore, when, where, yet. However* [adverb] *the election goes, the public will lose. The results were disappointing; however* [conjunction], *we were not surprised. The lights were not yet* [adverb] *turned on. He had been appointed by the governor, yet* [conjunction] *he did not support him.* **2. Weight and Use.** The important fact about the conjunctive adverbs is that most of them are relatively heavy connectives. Except for *so, when,* and *where* they are most appropriate in formal writing. **3. Position.** Conjunctive adverbs are often placed within their clauses instead of at the beginning. This helps take the initial stress from them and gives it to more important words. When they are so placed, they are usually set off by commas as in the sentences in paragraph 1 above. **4. Punctuation.** The conventional rule is that a clause introduced by a conjunctive adverb is preceded by a semicolon. This is generally true but the semicolon is used not because of the conjunctive adverb but because the clauses are rather heavy and the connecting force of the conjunctive adverb relatively weak. With the lighter conjunctive adverbs, especially with *so, then,* and *yet,* a comma is often sufficient: *The morning had been a bore, so we wanted to make sure that we had a good time after lunch.*

con·junc·ti·vi·tis (kən-jungk′tə-vī′tis), *n. Pathol.* inflammation of the conjunctiva.

con·ju·ra·tion (kon′jū-rā′shən), *n.* **1.** act of invoking by a sacred name. **2.** magic form of words used in conjuring; magic spell.

con·jure (kun′jər; kon′-), *v.*, **-jured, -jur·ing. 1.** compel (a spirit, devil, etc.) to appear or disappear by magic words. **2.** summon a devil, spirit, etc. **3.** cause to be or happen by magic. **4.** practice magic. **5. conjure up, a.** cause to appear in a magic way. **b.** cause to appear in the mind. [< OF < L *conjurare* make a compact < *com-* together + *jurare* swear] —**con′jur·er, con′-jur·or,** *n.*

conk (kongk), *Slang.* —*n.* **1.** hit. —*v.* **1.** hit. **2. conk out, break down.** [dial. < *conk*(er) a blow on the nose < *conk* nose < *conch* shell]

Conn., Connecticut.

con·nect (kə-nekt′), *v.* **1.** join (one thing to

another); link (two things together). 2. join in some business or interest. 3. associate in the mind. 4. *Am.* run so that passengers can change from one train, bus, etc., to another without delay. [< L, < *com–* together + *nectere* tie] —con·nect′ed·ly, *adv.* —con·nect′er, con·nec′tor, *n.* ➤ Connected with and in connection with are wordy locutions, usually for *in* or *with*: *the environment in connection with a fraternity* (in a fraternity).

Con·nect·i·cut (kə·net′ə·kət), *n.* one of the New England States in NE United States. *Capital:* Hartford. *Abbrev.:* Conn.

con·nec·tion, *esp. Brit.* **con·nex·ion** (kə·nek′shən), *n.* 1. act of connecting. 2. condition of being joined together or connected; union. 3. thing that connects. 4. any kind of practical relation with another thing. 5. group of people associated in some way. 6. thinking of persons or things together. 7. *Am.* meeting of trains, ships, etc., so that passengers can change from one to the other without delay. 8. a relative. —con·nec′tion·al, *esp. Brit.* con·nex′ion·al, *adj.* —Syn. 2. junction. 3. bond, tie, link. 8. kin, kinsman.

con·nec·tive (kə·nek′tiv), *adj.* that connects. —*n.* 1. thing that connects. 2. word used to connect words, phrases, and clauses. Conjunctions and relative pronouns are connectives. —con·nec′tive·ly, *adv.* —con·nec·tiv·i·ty (kon′ek·tiv′ə·ti), *n.*

conn·ing tower (kon′ing), 1. an armored shelter on the deck of a warship. 2. a small tower on the deck of a submarine, used as an entrance and as a place for observation.

con·niv·ance (kə·nīv′əns), **con·niv·an·cy** (–ən·si), *n.* 1. act of conniving. 2. *Law.* pretended ignorance or secret encouragement of wrongdoing.

con·nive (kə·nīv′), *v.,* –nived, –niv·ing. 1. give aid to wrongdoing by not telling of it, or by helping it secretly. 2. coöperate secretly. [< L *connivere* shut the eyes, wink < *com–* together + *niv–* press] —con·niv′er, *n.*

con·nois·seur (kon′ə·sér′), *n.* expert; critical judge. [< F, ult. < L, < *co–* + *gnoscere* recognize]

con·no·ta·tion (kon′ə·tā′shən), *n.* 1. a connoting. 2. what is suggested in addition to the simple meaning. —con·no·ta·tive (kon′ə·tā′tiv; kə·nō′tə–), *adj.* —con′no·ta′tive·ly, *adv.*

con·note (kə·nōt′), *v.,* –not·ed, –not·ing. suggest in addition to the literal meaning; imply. [< Med.L, < L *com–* with + *notare* to NOTE]

con·nu·bi·al (kə·nü′bi·əl; –nū′–), *adj.* of or having to do with marriage. [< L, < *com–* + *nubere* marry] —con·nu′bi·al′i·ty, *n.* —con·nu′bi·al·ly, *adv.*

con·quer (kong′kər), *v.* 1. get by fighting; win in war. 2. overcome by force; defeat. 3. be victorious. [< OF < L, < *com–* + *quaerere* seek] —con′quer·a·ble, *adj.* —con′quer·ing, *adj.* —con′quer·ing·ly, *adv.* —con′quer·or, *n.* —Syn. 2. vanquish, subdue.

con·quest (kon′kwest; kong′–), *n.* 1. act of conquering. 2. thing conquered; land, people, etc., conquered. 3. person whose love or favor has been won. [< OF, < *conquerre* CONQUER] —Syn. 1. victory, triumph. —Ant. 1. defeat.

con·quis·ta·dor (kon·kwis′tə·dôr), *n., pl.* –dors, –dores. 1. a Spanish conqueror in North or South America during the 16th century. 2. conqueror. [< Sp., < *conquistar* CONQUER]

Con·rad (kon′rad), *n.* Joseph, 1857–1924, English novelist, born in Poland.

con·san·guin·e·ous (kon′sang·gwin′i·əs), *adj.* descended from the same parent or ancestor. [< L, < *com–* together + *sanguis* blood] —con′san·guin′e·ous·ly, *adv.* —con′san·guin′i·ty, *n.*

con·science (kon′shəns), *n.* 1. ideas and feelings within a person that warn him of what is wrong. 2. conscientiousness. [< OF < L *con·scientia* < *com–* + *scire* know] —con′science·less, *adj.*

con·sci·en·tious (kon′shi·en′shəs), *adj.* 1.

careful to do what one knows is right; controlled by conscience. 2. done with care to make it right. —con′sci·en′tious·ly, *adv.* —con′sci·en′tious·ness, *n.* —Syn. 1. upright, honorable. 2. particular, painstaking. —Ant. 1. unscrupulous. 2. careless, negligent.

conscientious objector, person whose beliefs forbid him to take an active part in warfare.

con·scion·a·ble (kon′shən·ə·bəl), *adj.* according to conscience; just. —con′scion·a·bly, *adv.*

con·scious (kon′shəs), *adj.* 1. aware; knowing. 2. able to feel. 3. known to oneself; felt: *conscious guilt.* 4. meant; intended: *a conscious lie.* 5. self-conscious; shy; embarrassed. [< L *conscius* < *com–* + *scire* know] —con′scious·ly, *adv.* —Syn. 4. deliberate.

con·scious·ness (kon′shəs·nis), *n.* 1. state of being conscious; awareness. 2. all the thoughts and feelings of a person. 3. awareness of what is going on about one.

con·script (*v.* kən·skript′; *adj., n.* kon′-skript), *v.* 1. *Am.* compel by law to enlist in the army or navy; draft. 2. take for government use. —*adj.* conscripted; drafted. —*n.* a conscripted soldier or sailor. [< L *conscriptus* < *com–* down + *scribere* write] —con·scrip′tion, *n.*

con·se·crate (kon′sə·krāt), *v.,* –crat·ed, –crating, *adj.* —*v.* 1. set apart as sacred; make holy: *a church is consecrated to worship.* 2. devote to a purpose. —*adj. Archaic.* consecrated. [< L *consecratus* < *com–* + *sacer* sacred] —con′se·cra′tion, *n.* —con′se·cra′tor, *n.* —Syn. *v.* 1. sanctify. 2. dedicate.

con·sec·u·tive (kən·sek′yə·tiv), *adj.* 1. following without interruption; successive. 2. made up of parts that follow each other in logical order. [< F, < L *consecutus* following closely < *com–* up + *sequi* follow] —con·sec′u·tive·ly, *adv.* —con·sec′u·tive·ness, *n.*

con·sen·sus (kən·sen′səs), *n.* general agreement. [< L, < *consentire* CONSENT]

con·sent (kən·sent′), *v.* agree; give approval or permission. —*n.* 1. agreement; permission. 2. harmony; accord. [< OF < L, < *com–* together + *sentire* feel, think] —con·sent′er, *n.* —Syn. *v.* assent, comply. —*n.* 1. approval, assent. —Ant. *v.* refuse, disapprove.

con·se·quence (kon′sə·kwens; –kwəns), *n.* 1. act or fact of following something as its effect. 2. result; effect. 3. a logical result; deduction; inference. 4. importance. —Syn. 2. outcome, issue.

con·se·quent (kon′sə·kwent; –kwənt), *adj.* 1. following as an effect; resulting. 2. following as a logical conclusion. 3. logically consistent. —*n.* thing that follows something else; result; effect. [< L *consequens,* ppr. of *consequi.* See CONSEQUITIVE.]

con·se·quen·tial (kon′sə·kwen′shəl), *adj.* 1. following as an effect; resulting. 2. important. 3. self-important; pompous. —con·se·quen·ti·al·i·ty (kon′sə·kwen′shi·al′ə·ti), *n.* —con′se·quen′tial·ly, *adv.* —con′se·quen′tial·ness, *n.*

con·se·quent·ly (kon′sə·kwent′li; –kwənt–), *adv.* as a result; therefore.

con·ser·va·tion (kon′sər·vā′shən), *n.* 1. a protecting from harm, loss, or from being used up. 2. the official protection and care of forests, rivers, etc. 3. forest, etc., under official protection and care. —con′ser·va′tion·al, *adj.* —con′-ser·va′tion·ist, *n.*

conservation of energy, principle that the total amount of energy in the universe does not vary.

con·ser·va·tive (kən·sér′və·tiv), *adj.* 1. inclined to keep things as they are; opposed to change. 2. Often, Conservative. of or belonging to a political party that opposes changes in national institutions. 3. cautious; moderate. —*n.* 1. a conservative person. 2. Often, Conservative. member of a conservative political party. 3. means of preserving. —con·ser′va·tism, *n.* —con·serv′a·tive·ly, *adv.* —con·serv′a·tive·ness, *n.*

con·serv·a·to·ry (kən·sér′və·tô′ri; –tō′–), *n.,*

pl. **-ries. 1.** greenhouse or glass-enclosed room for growing and displaying plants and flowers. **2.** *U.S.* school for instruction in music, art, or oratory. **3.** preservative.

con·serve (*v.* kən·sėrv′; *n.* kon′sėrv, kən·sėrv′), *v.,* -served, -serv·ing, *n.* —*v.* **1.** protect from harm, loss, or from being used up. **2.** preserve (fruit) with sugar. [< L, < *com*– + *servare* preserve] —*n.* Often, conserves. fruit preserved in sugar; jam. [< F, < *conserver.* See v.] —con·serv′a·ble, *adj.* —con·serv′er, *n.*

con·sid·er (kən·sid′ər), *v.* **1.** think about in order to decide. **2.** think to be; think of as. **3.** allow for; take into account. **4.** be thoughtful of (others and their feelings). **5.** think carefully; reflect. [< L *considerare,* orig., examine the stars, < *com*– + *sidus* star] —Syn. **1.** study, weigh, contemplate. **2.** deem, judge. **4.** respect, regard. **5.** deliberate, ponder.

con·sid·er·a·ble (kən·sid′ər·ə·bəl), *adj.* **1.** worth thinking about; important. **2.** not a little; much. —*n.* *U.S. Colloq.* not a little; much. —con·sid′er·a·bly, *adv.* ➤ considerable, considerably. In speech there is a tendency to use *considerable* as an adverb as well as an adjective: *the night crew was considerable help* (adj.); *the night crew helped considerably* or in informal speech *the night crew helped considerable* (adv.).

con·sid·er·ate (kən·sid′ər·it), *adj.* **1.** thoughtful of others and their feelings. **2.** deliberate. —con·sid′er·ate·ly, *adv.* —con·sid′er·ate·ness, *n.*

con·sid·er·a·tion (kən·sid′ər·ā′shən), *n.* **1.** act of thinking about in order to decide. **2.** something thought of as a reason. **3.** money or other payment. **4.** thoughtfulness for others and their feelings. **5.** sympathetic regard or respect. **6.** importance. —Syn. **1.** attention, deliberation. **3.** compensation, recompense. **5.** esteem.

con·sid·er·ing (kən·sid′ər·ing), *prep.* taking into account; making allowance for. —*adv.* taking everything into account: *he does very well, considering.*

con·sign (kən·sīn′), *v.* **1.** hand over; deliver. **2.** transmit; send. **3.** set apart; assign. **4.** *Com.* transmit, as by public carrier, esp. for safekeeping or sale. [< F < L *consignare* furnish with a seal < *com*– + *signum* seal] —con·sign′a·ble, *adj.* —con·sign·ee (kon′sī·nē′; -sī·nē′), *n.* —con·sign·or (kən·sīn′ər; kon′sī·nôr′; kon′si-), con·sign·er (kən·sīn′ər), *n.*

con·sign·ment (kən·sīn′mənt), *n.* **1.** act of consigning. **2.** shipment sent to a person or company for safekeeping or sale.

con·sist (kən·sist′), *v.* **1.** be made up; be formed. **2.** agree; be in harmony. **3.** consist in, be contained in; be made up of. [< L, come to a stand, exist, consist, < *com*– + *sistere* stand] —Syn. **1.** comprise.

con·sist·en·cy (kən·sis′tən·si), **con·sist·ence** (-təns), *n., pl.* -cies; -ces. **1.** firmness; stiffness. **2.** degree of firmness or stiffness. **3.** a keeping to the same principles, course of action, etc. **4.** harmony; agreement.

con·sist·ent (kən·sis′tənt), *adj.* **1.** keeping or inclined to keep to the same principles, course of action, etc. **2.** in agreement; in accord. **3.** cohering. —con·sist′ent·ly, *adv.*

con·sis·to·ry (kən·sis′tə·ri), *n., pl.* -ries. **1.** a church council or court. **2.** place where it meets.

con·so·la·tion (kon′sə·lā′shən), *n.* **1.** comfort. **2.** a comforting person, thing, or event. —con·sol·a·to·ry (kən·sol′ə·tô′ri; -tō′-), *adj.*

con·sole¹ (kən·sōl′), *v.,* -soled, -sol·ing. comfort. [< L, < *com*– + *solari* soothe] —con·sol′a·ble, *adj.* —con·sol′er, *n.*

con·sole² (kon′sōl), *n.* **1.** the desk-like part of an organ containing the keyboard, stops, and pedals. **2.** a radio cabinet made to stand on the floor. **3.** a heavy, ornamental bracket. **4.** console table. [< F]

Console (def. 3)

con·sole table (kon′sōl), a narrow table, usually placed against a wall.

con·sol·i·date (kən·sol′ə·dāt), *v.,* -dat·ed, -dat·ing. **1.** unite; combine; merge. **2.** make or

become solid. **3.** *Mil.* organize and strengthen (a newly captured position) so that it can be used against the enemy. [< L, < *com*– + *solidus* solid] —con·sol′i·da′tion, *n.*

con·sol·ing (kən·sōl′ing), *adj.* that consoles. —con·sol′ing·ly, *adv.*

con·som·mé (kon′sə·mā′), *n.* a clear soup made by boiling meat in water. [< F, pp. of *consommer* CONSUMMATE]

con·so·nant (kon′sə·nənt), *n.* **1.** *Phonet.* a sound during the articulation of which the breath stream is impeded to a greater or lesser degree, as the sound of *b* in *boy* or the sound of *f* in *fast*. **2.** a letter representing such a sound. —*adj.* **1.** harmonious; in agreement; in accord. **2.** agreeing in sound. **3.** consonantal. [< L, < *com*– together + *sonare* sound] —con′so·nance, *n.* —con′so·nant·ly, *adv.*

con·so·nan·tal (kon′sə·nan′təl), *adj.* having to do with a consonant or its sound.

con·sort (*n.* kon′sôrt; *v.* kən·sôrt′), *n.* **1.** husband or wife. **2.** an associate. **3.** ship accompanying another. —*v.* **1.** associate. **2.** agree; accord. [< F < L, sharer, < *com*– with + *sors* lot]

con·sor·ti·um (kən·sôr′shi·əm), *n., pl.* -ti·a (-shi·ə). an agreement among bankers of several nations to give financial aid to another nation. [< L, partnership]

con·spic·u·ous (kən·spik′yù·əs), *adj.* **1.** easily seen. **2.** worthy of notice; remarkable. [< L *conspicuus* visible < *com*– + *specere* look at] —con·spic′u·ous·ly, *adv.* —con·spic′u·ous·ness, *n.* —Syn. **1.** prominent, noticeable. **2.** notable, noteworthy. —Ant. **1.** obscure.

con·spir·a·cy (kən·spir′ə·si), *n., pl.* -cies. **1.** secret planning with others to do something wrong. **2.** plot. —con·spir′a·tor, *n.* —Syn. **1.** intrigue.

con·spire (kən·spīr′), *v.,* -spired, -spir·ing. **1.** plan secretly with others to do something wrong; plot. **2.** act together. [< L, < *com*– together + *spirare* breathe] —con·spir·a·to·ri·al (kən·spir′ə·tô′ri·əl; -tō′-), *adj.* —con·spir′er, *n.*

con·sta·ble (kon′stə·bəl; kun′-), *n.* a police officer; policeman. [< OF < LL *comes stabuli* count of the stable; later, chief household officer] —con′sta·ble·ship′, *n.*

con·stab·u·lar·y (kən·stab′yə·ler′i), *n., pl.* -lar·ies. **1.** constables of a district. **2.** police force organized like an army; state police.

con·stant (kon′stənt), *adj.* **1.** always the same; not changing. **2.** never stopping. **3.** happening often or again and again. **4.** faithful; loyal; steadfast. —*n.* **1.** thing that is always the same. **2.** *Math.* quantity assumed to be invariable throughout a given discussion. [< L, < *com*– (intensive) + *stare* stand] —con′stan·cy, *n.* —Syn. *adj.* **1.** unchanged, steady. **2.** ceaseless, continuous. **4.** true, stanch. —Ant. *adj.* **1.** variable, varying. **4.** false, fickle.

Con·stan·tine the Great (kon′stən·tīn; -tēn), or **Constantine I**, 288?–337 A.D., Roman emperor from 324 to 337 A.D., who established the city of Constantinople.

Con·stan·ti·no·ple (kon′stan·tə·nō′pəl), *n.* former name of Istanbul.

con·stant·ly (kon′stənt·li), *adv.* **1.** without change. **2.** without stopping. **3.** often.

con·stel·la·tion (kon′stə·lā′shən), *n.* **1.** a group of stars: *the Big Dipper is the easiest constellation to locate.* **2.** division of the heavens occupied by such a group. [< LL, < L *com*– together + *stella* star]

con·ster·na·tion (kon′stər·nā′shən), *n.* great dismay; paralyzing terror. [< L, < *consternare* terrify, var. of *consternere* lay low < *com*– + *sternere* strew]

con·sti·pate (kon′stə·pāt), *v.,* -pat·ed, -pat·ing. cause constipation in. [< L, < *com*– together + *stipare* press] —con′sti·pat′ed, *adj.*

con·sti·pa·tion (kon′stə·pā′shən), *n.* sluggish condition of the bowels.

con·stit·u·en·cy (kən·stich′ù·ən·si), *n., pl.* -cies. **1.** voters in a district. **2.** the district; the people living there.

con·stit·u·ent (kən·stich′ù·ənt), *adj.* **1.** forming a necessary part; that composes. **2.** appointing; electing. 3. having the power to make or change a political constitution. —*n.* 1. a necessary part of a whole; component. 2. person who votes or appoints; voter.

con·sti·tute (kon'stə·tüt; -tūt), *v.*, -tut·ed, -tut·ing. 1. make up; form. 2. appoint; elect. 3. set up; establish. 4. give legal form to. [< L *constitutus* < *com-* + *statuere* set up] —Syn. 1. compose, comprise.

con·sti·tu·tion (kon'stə·tü'shən; -tū'-), *n.* 1. way in which a person or thing is organized; nature; make-up: *a healthy constitution.* 2. system of fundamental principles according to which a nation, state, or group is governed. 3. document stating these principles. 4. appointing; making. 5. **Constitution,** *Am.* the constitution by which the United States is governed. It was drawn up in 1787 and became effective in 1788. Since then 21 amendments have been added to it.

con·sti·tu·tion·al (kon'stə·tü'shən·əl; -tū'-), *adj.* 1. of or in the constitution of a person or thing. 2. of, in, or according to the constitution of a nation, state, or group. 3. for one's health. —*n. Colloq.* walk or other exercise taken for one's health. —con'sti·tu'tion·al·ly, *adv.* —Syn. *adj.* 1. inherent.

con·sti·tu·tion·al·i·ty (kon'stə·tü'shən·al'ə·ti; -tū'-), *n.* quality of being constitutional.

con·strain (kən·strān'), *v.* 1. force; compel. 2. confine; imprison. 3. repress; restrain. [< OF *constreindre* < L, < *com-* together + *stringere* pull tightly] —con·strain'a·ble, *adj.* —con·strain'er, *n.*

con·strained (kən·strānd'), *adj.* forced. —con·strain·ed·ly (kən·strān'id·li), *adv.*

con·straint (kən·strānt'), *n.* 1. confinement. 2. restraint. 3. forced or unnatural manner. 4. force; compulsion. [< OF, < *constreindre* CONSTRAIN]

con·strict (kən·strikt'), *v.* draw together; contract; compress. [< L *constrictus*, pp. of *constringere* CONSTRAIN] —con·stric'tion, *n.* —con·stric'tive, *adj.*

con·stric·tor (kən·strik'tər), *n.* 1. snake that kills its prey by squeezing it with its coils. 2. person or thing that constricts.

con·struct (*v.* kən·strukt'; *n.* kon'strukt), *v.* 1. put together; build. 2. *Geom.* draw (a figure, etc.) so as to fulfill given conditions. —*n.* thing constructed. [< L *constructus* < *com-* up + *struere* pile] —con·struc'tor, con·struct'er, *n.*

con·struc·tion (kən·struk'shən), *n.* 1. act of constructing. 2. way in which a thing is constructed. 3. thing constructed; a building. 4. meaning; explanation; interpretation. 5. arrangement of words in a sentence, clause, phrase, etc. —con·struc'tion·al, *adj.*

con·struc·tive (kən·struk'tiv), *adj.* 1. tending to construct; building up; helpful. 2. structural. 3. not directly expressed; inferred. —con·struc'tive·ly, *adv.* —con·struc'tive·ness, *n.*

con·strue (kən·strü'), *v.*, -strued, -stru·ing. 1. show the meaning of; explain; interpret. 2. translate. 3. analyze the arrangement and connection of words in (a sentence, clause, phrase, etc.). [< L *construere* CONSTRUCT] —con·stru'a·ble, *adj.* —con·stru'er, *n.*

con·sul (kon'səl), *n.* 1. official appointed by a government to live in a foreign city to look after the business interests of his own country and to protect citizens of his country who are traveling or living there. 2. either of the two chief magistrates of the ancient Roman republic. [< L, prob. orig., one who consults the senate] —con'su·lar, *adj.* —con'sul·ship, *n.*

con·su·late (kon'sə·lit), *n.* 1. the duties, authority, and position of a consul. 2. a consul's term of office. 3. an official residence or offices of a consul.

consul general, *pl.* **consuls general.** consul of the highest rank.

con·sult (kən·sult'), *v.* 1. seek information or advice from; refer to. 2. exchange ideas; talk things over. 3. take into consideration; have regard for. [< L, < *consulere* take counsel, consult] —con·sult'a·ble, *adj.* —Syn. 2. confer.

con·sult·ant (kən·sul'tənt), *n.* 1. person who consults another. 2. person who gives professional or technical advice.

con·sul·ta·tion (kon'səl·tā'shən), *n.* 1. act of consulting. 2. a meeting to exchange ideas or talk things over.

con·sume (kən·süm'), *v.*, -sumed, -sum·ing. 1. use up. 2. eat or drink up. 3. destroy; burn up. 4. waste away; be destroyed. 5. spend; waste (time, money, etc.). [< L, < *com-* + *sumere* take up] —con·sum'a·ble, *adj.* —Syn. 1. expend, exhaust. 5. squander. —Ant. 1. conserve.

con·sum·er (kən·süm'ər), *n.* 1. person or thing that consumes. 2. person who uses food, clothing, or anything grown or made by producers.

con·sum·mate (*v.* kon'sə·māt; *adj.* kən·sum'it), *v.*, -mat·ed, -mat·ing, *adj.* —*v.* 1. complete; fulfill. 2. complete (a marriage) by sexual intercourse. —*adj.* complete; perfect; in the highest degree. [< L, < *consummare* bring to a peak < *com-* + *summa* highest degree] —con·sum'mate·ly, *adv.* —con'sum·ma'tor, *n.*

con·sum·ma·tion (kon'sə·mā'shən), *n.* completion; fulfillment.

con·sump·tion (kən·sump'shən), *n.* 1. act of using up; use. 2. amount used up. 3. destruction. 4. a wasting disease of the lungs or of some other part of the body; tuberculosis of the lungs.

con·sump·tive (kən·sump'tiv), *adj.* 1. having or likely to have tuberculosis of the lungs. 2. of tuberculosis of the lungs. 3. tending to consume; destructive; wasteful. —*n.* person who has tuberculosis of the lungs. —con·sump'tive·ly, *adv.* —con·sump'tive·ness, *n.*

cont., 1. containing. 2. continued.

con·tact (kon'takt), *n.* 1. condition of touching; touch. 2. connection. 3. *Elect.* connection between two conductors of electricity through which a current passes. 4. device for producing such a connection. —*adj. Am.* in aeronautics, within sight of the ground: *contact flying.* —*v. Am., Colloq.* get in touch with; make a connection with. [< L *contactus* a touching < *com-* + *tangere* touch] ▸ Contact as a verb meaning "to get in touch with a person" is a use of the word by salesmen, and many people have unpleasant associations with being "contacted." Others object to using business terms in other contexts. The word in this sense is primarily commercial and familiar and should therefore be used infrequently in other circumstances.

contact lens, a plastic lens which covers the front of the eyeball by fitting under the eyelids and corrects defects in vision.

con·ta·gion (kən·tā'jən), *n.* 1. the spreading of disease by contact. 2. disease spread in this way; contagious disease. 3. means by which disease is spread. 4. the spreading of any influence from one person to another. [< L *contagio* touching. See CONTACT.]

con·ta·gious (kən·tā'jəs), *adj.* 1. spread by contact: *scarlet fever is a contagious disease.* 2. causing contagious diseases. —con·ta'gious·ly, *adv.* —con·ta'gious·ness, *n.*

con·tain (kən·tān'), *v.* 1. have within itself; hold as contents; include. 2. be capable of holding. 3. be equal to: *a pound contains 16 ounces.* 4. control; hold back; restrain: *the Western powers hope to contain Russian military strength.* 5. *Math.* be divisible by without a remainder: *12 contains 2, 3, 4, and 6.* [< OF < L, < *com-* in + *tenere* hold] —con·tain'a·ble, *adj.* —Syn. 1. enclose. 2. accommodate. 3. comprise. 4. repress.

con·tain·er (kən·tān'ər), *n.* box, can, jar, etc., used to hold something.

con·tain·ment (kən·tān'mənt), *n. International Relations,* the confinement of a hostile or potentially hostile political or military force within existing geographical boundaries.

con·tam·i·nate (kən·tam'ə·nāt), *v.*, -nat·ed, -nat·ing. make impure by contact. [< L *contaminatus* < *com-* + *tag-* touch. See CONTACT.] —con·tam'i·na'tion, *n.* —con·tam'i·na'tive, *adj.* —con·tam'i·na'tor, *n.* —Syn. taint, corrupt.

contd., continued.

con·temn (kən·tem′), v. treat with contempt; despise; scorn. [< L, < com- + temnere disdain, orig., cut] —**con·temn·er** (kən·tem′ər), **con·tem·nor** (kən·tem′nər), n.

con·tem·plate (kon′təm·plāt), v., -plat·ed, -plat·ing. 1. look at for a long time; gaze at. 2. think about for a long time; study carefully. 3. meditate. 4. expect; intend. [< L, < contemplari survey < com- + templum restricted area marked off for the taking of auguries] —**con·tem·pla·tive** (kon′təm·plā′tiv; kən·tem′plə-), adj. —**con′tem·pla′tor**, n. —Syn. 1. survey, regard.

con·tem·pla·tion (kon′təm·plā′shən), n. 1. act of looking at or thinking about something for a long time. 2. deep thought; meditation. 3. expectation; intention.

con·tem·po·ra·ne·ous (kən·tem′pə·rā′ni·əs), adj. belonging to the same period of time. —**con·tem′po·ra·ne·ous·ly**, adv. —**con·tem′po·ra′ne·ous·ness**, n.

con·tem·po·rar·y (kən·tem′pə·rer′i), adj., n., pl. -rar·ies. —adj. 1. belonging to or living in the same period of time. 2. of the same age or date. —n. 1. person who belongs to the same period of time as another or others. 2. person, magazine, etc., of the same age or date. [< L com- + temporarius < tempus time]

con·tempt (kən·tempt′), n. 1. the feeling that a person, act, or thing is mean, low, or worthless; scorn; a despising. 2. condition of being scorned or despised; disgrace. 3. Law. disobedience to or open disrespect for the rules or decisions of a law court, a lawmaking body, etc. [< L contemptus. See CONTEMN.] —Syn. 1. disdain.

con·tempt·i·ble (kən·temp′tə·bəl), adj. deserving contempt or scorn. —**con·tempt′i·bil′i·ty**, **con·tempt′i·ble·ness**, n. —**con·tempt′i·bly**, adv.

con·temp·tu·ous (kən·temp′chü·əs), adj. showing contempt; scornful. —**con·temp′tu·ous·ly**, adv. —**con·temp′tu·ous·ness**, n.

con·tend (kən·tend′), v. 1. fight; struggle. 2. take part in a contest; compete. 3. argue; dispute. 4. declare to be a fact; maintain as true. [< L, < com- (intensive) + tendere stretch] —**con·tend′er**, n. —Syn. 1. cope, wrestle, combat, battle. 3. wrangle. 4. affirm, assert.

con·tent[1] (kon′tent), n. 1. Usually, contents. what is contained. 2. facts and ideas stated, as in a book or speech. 3. power of containing; capacity. 4. amount contained; volume. [< L contentum, pp. of continere CONTAIN] —Syn. 1. substance, matter. ▶ content, contents. Content is used more as an abstract term (the content of the course) and in amounts (the moisture content); contents is rather more concrete (the contents of the box).

con·tent[2] (kən·tent′), v. satisfy; please; make easy in mind. —adj. 1. satisfied; pleased. 2. easy in mind. 3. willing; ready. —n. contentment. [< F < L contentus, pp., restrained. See CONTAIN.] —Syn. v. gratify, appease. —n. satisfaction, gratification.

con·tent·ed (kən·ten′tid), adj. satisfied; pleased; easy in mind. —**con·tent′ed·ly**, adv. —**con·tent′ed·ness**, n.

con·ten·tion (kən·ten′shən), n. 1. argument; dispute; quarrel. 2. statement or point that one has argued for. 3. an arguing; disputing; quarreling. 4. struggle; contest. —Syn. 3. dissension.

con·ten·tious (kən·ten′shəs), adj. 1. quarrelsome. 2. characterized by contention. —**con·ten′tious·ly**, adv. —**con·ten′tious·ness**, n.

con·tent·ment (kən·tent′mənt), n. satisfaction; being pleased; ease of mind.

con·ter·mi·nous (kən·tér′mə·nəs), adj. 1. having a common boundary; bordering; meeting at their ends. 2. having the same boundaries or limits; coextensive. Also, **coterminous**.

con·test (n. kon′test; v. kən·test′), n. 1. trial to see which can win; competition. 2. fight; struggle. 3. argument; dispute. [< v.] —v. 1. try to win. 2. fight for; struggle for. 3. argue against; dispute about. 4. take part in a contest. [< F < L contestari call to witness < com- + testis witness] —**con·test′a·ble**, adj. —**con·test′er**, n. —Syn. n. 1. match. -v. 4. compete.

con·test·ant (kən·tes′tənt), n. 1. person who takes part in a contest. 2. person who contests, as election returns, etc.

con·text (kon′tekst), n. parts directly before and after a word, sentence, etc., that influence its meaning. [< L, < com- + texere weave] —**con·tex·tu·al** (kən·teks′chü·əl), adj. —**con·tex′tu·al·ly**, adv.

con·ti·gu·i·ty (kon′tə·gū′ə·ti), n., pl. -ties. condition of being contiguous.

con·tig·u·ous (kən·tig′yü·əs), adj. 1. in actual contact; touching. 2. adjoining; near. [< L contiguus < com- + tag- touch. See CONTACT.] —**con·tig′u·ous·ly**, adv. —**con·tig′u·ous·ness**, n.

con·ti·nence (kon′tə·nəns), **con·ti·nen·cy** (-nən·si), n., pl. -ces; -cies. 1. self-control; self-restraint; moderation. 2. chastity.

con·ti·nent[1] (kon′tə·nənt), n. 1. one of the seven great masses of land on the earth; North America, South America, Europe, Africa, Asia, Australia, or Antarctica. 2. mainland. 3. the Continent, the mainland of Europe. [< L, < continere CONTAIN]

con·ti·nent[2] (kon′tə·nənt), adj. 1. showing restraint with regard to the desires or passions. 2. chaste. [see CONTINENT[1]] —**con′ti·nent·ly**, adv.

con·ti·nen·tal (kon′tə·nen′təl), adj. 1. of or characteristic of a continent. 2. Usually, Continental. belonging to or characteristic of the mainland of Europe. 3. Continental, of or having to do with the American colonies at the time of the American Revolution. —n. 1. Continental, Am. soldier of the American army during the American Revolution. 2. Am. piece of American paper money issued during the American Revolution. 3. Usually, Continental. person living on the Continent.

Continental Congress, Am. either of two legislative assemblies representing the American colonies from 1774 to 1781. The Second Continental Congress adopted the Declaration of Independence in 1776.

con·tin·gen·cy (kən·tin′jən·si), n., pl. -cies. 1. uncertainty of occurrence; dependence on chance. 2. an accidental happening; unexpected event; chance. 3. a happening or event depending on something that is uncertain; possibility.

con·tin·gent (kən·tin′jənt), adj. 1. conditional; depending on something not certain. 2. liable to happen or not to happen; possible; uncertain. 3. happening by chance; accidental; unexpected. —n. 1. share of soldiers, laborers, etc., furnished as an addition to a larger force from other sources. 2. group that is part of a larger group. 3. accidental or unexpected event. [< L contingens touching < com- + tangere to touch] —**con·tin′gent·ly**, adv.

con·tin·u·al (kən·tin′yü·əl), adj. 1. never stopping. 2. repeated many times; very frequent. —**con·tin′u·al·ly**, adv. ▶ continual, continuous. Continual means "frequently or closely repeated": Dancing requires continual practice. Continuous means "without interruption": a continuous procession of cars.

con·tin·u·ance (kən·tin′yü·əns), n. 1. continuation. 2. Law. adjournment or postponement until a future time.

con·tin·u·a·tion (kən·tin′yü·ā′shən), n. 1. act of going on with a thing after stopping. 2. a being continued. 3. anything by which a thing is continued; added part. 4. act or fact of not stopping.

con·tin·ue (kən·tin′ū), v., -tin·ued, -tin·u·ing. 1. keep up; keep on; go on; go on with. 2. go on or go on with after stopping; begin again. 3. last; endure. 4. cause to last. 5. stay. 6. cause to stay. 7. put off until a later time; postpone; adjourn. [< L continuare < continere hold together. See CONTAIN.] —**con·tin′u·a·ble**, adj. —**con·tin′u·er**, n. —Syn. 1. prolong, extend.

con·ti·nu·i·ty (kon′tə·nū′ə·ti; -nū′-), n., pl. -ties. 1. state or quality of being continuous. 2. a continuous or connected whole. 3. Am. the detailed plan of a motion picture. 4. connecting comments or announcements between the parts of a radio program.

con·tin·u·ous (kən·tin′yü·əs), adj. without a

stop or break; connected; unbroken. **—con·tin'-u·ous·ly,** *adv.* **—con·tin'u·ous·ness,** *n.* **—Syn.** ceaseless, incessant, perpetual. ➤ See **continual** for usage note.

con·tin·u·um (kən·tin'yū·əm), *n., pl.* **-tin·u·a** (-tin'yū·ə). continuous quantity, series, etc. [< L]

con·tort (kən·tôrt'), *v.* twist or bend out of shape; distort. [< L *contortus* < *com-* + *torquere* twist] **—con·tor'tion,** *n.* **—con·tor'tive,** *adj.*

con·tor·tion·ist (kən·tôr'shən·ist), *n.* person who can twist or bend his body into odd and unnatural positions.

con·tour (kon'tūr), *n.* outline of a figure. *—v.* mark with lines showing the contour of. *—adj.* **1.** showing topographical outlines, as hills, valleys, etc.: *a contour map.* **2.** following natural ridges and furrows or general contour to avoid erosion: *contour planting.* [< F < Ital. *contorno,* ult. < L *com-* + *tornus* turning lathe < Gk. *tornos*]

contra-, *prefix.* in opposition; against, as in *contradistinction.* [< L *contra*]

con·tra·band (kon'trə·band), *adj.* against the law; prohibited: *contraband trade.* *—n.* **1.** goods imported or exported contrary to law; smuggled goods. **2.** trading contrary to law; smuggling. **3.** contraband of war (see below). [< Sp. < Ital., < *contra-* against (< L) + *bando* < LL *bandum* ban < Gmc.]

contraband of war, goods supplied by neutral nations to any country at war with another, that either warring country has a right to seize.

con·tra·bass (kon'trə·bās'), *Music.* *—n.* **1.** the lowest bass voice or instrument. **2.** large stringed instrument shaped like a cello and having a very low bass tone; double bass. *—adj.* having to do with such instruments.

con·tra·cep·tion (kon'trə·sep'shən), *n.* prevention of conception. [< *contra-* + (con)cep tion] **—con'tra·cep'tive,** *adj., n.*

con·tract (*v.* kən·trakt' *for 1–3,* kon'trakt, kən·trakt' *for 4; n.* kon'trakt), *v.* **1.** draw together; shrink. **2.** shorten (a word, etc.) by omitting some of the letters or sounds. **3.** get; acquire. **4.** make a contract; agree by contract. *—n.* **1.** agreement. **2.** a written agreement that can be enforced by law. **3.** a formal agreement of marriage. [< L *contractus* < *com-* together + *trahere* draw] **—con·tract'ed,** *adj.* **—con·tract'-i·ble,** *adj.* **—con·trac'tive,** *adj.*

con·tract bridge (kon'trakt), a card game played by four people divided into two opposing pairs. The highest bidder can score toward a game only as many points as he promised to make in his bid.

con·trac·tile (kən·trak'təl), *adj.* **1.** capable of contracting. **2.** producing contraction. **—con·trac·til·i·ty** (kon'trak·til'ə·ti), *n.*

con·trac·tion (kən·trak'shən), *n.* **1.** process of contracting. **2.** state of being contracted. **3.** something contracted; shortened form. *Can't* is a contraction of *cannot.*

con·trac·tor (kon'trak·tər; kən·trak'tər), *n.* person who agrees to furnish materials or to do a piece of work for a certain price.

con·trac·tu·al (kən·trak'chū·əl), *adj.* of, or having the nature of, a contract.

con·tra·dict (kon'trə·dikt'), *v.* **1.** deny (a statement, rumor, etc.). **2.** deny the words of (a person). **3.** be contrary to; disagree with. [< L *contradictus* < *contra* in opposition + *dicere* say] **—con'tra·dict'a·ble,** *adj.* **—con'tra·dict'er, con'tra·dic'tor,** *n.*

con·tra·dic·tion (kon'trə·dik'shən), *n.* **1.** act of denying what has been said. **2.** statement that contradicts another; denial. **3.** disagreement; opposition. **4.** inconsistency.

con·tra·dic·to·ry (kon'trə·dik'tə·ri), *adj.* **1.** contradicting; contrary; in disagreement. **2.** inclined to contradict.

con·tra·dis·tinc·tion (kon'trə·dis·tingk'-shən), *n.* distinction by opposition or contrast.

con·trail (kon'trāl), *n.* vapor trail left by a plane flying at a high altitude.

con·tral·to (kən·tral'tō), *n., pl.* **-tos,** *adj. Music.* *—n.* **1.** the lowest woman's voice. **2.** part

to be sung by the lowest woman's voice. **3.** person who sings this part. **4.** formerly, the highest male voice. *—adj.* of or for a contralto. [< Ital., < *contra-* counter to (< L) + *alto* high < L *altus*]

con·trap·tion (kən·trap'shən), *n. Colloq.* contrivance; device; gadget.

con·tra·pun·tal (kon'trə·pun'təl), *adj.* **1.** of or having to do with counterpoint. **2.** according to the rules of counterpoint. [< Ital. *contra- punto* COUNTERPOINT]

con·tra·ri·wise (kon'trer·i·wīz'; *for 3, also* kən·trãr'i·wīz'), *adv.* **1.** in the opposite way or direction. **2.** on the contrary. **3.** perversely.

con·tra·ry (kon'trer·i; *for adj. 4, also* kən·trãr'i), *adj., n., pl.* **-ries,** *adv.* *—adj.* **1.** opposed; opposite; completely different. **2.** opposite in direction, position, etc. **3.** unfavorable: *a contrary wind.* **4.** opposing others; stubborn; perverse. *—n.* fact or quality that is the opposite of something else; the opposite. *—adv.* in opposition. [< AF < L *contrarius* < *contra* against] **—con'tra·ri·ly,** *adv.* **—con'tra·ri·ness,** *n.* **—Syn.** *adj.* **2.** counter. **4.** obstinate.

con·trast (*n.* kon'trast; *v.* kən·trast'), *n.* **1.** a striking difference. **2.** person, thing, event, etc., that shows differences when put side by side with another. *—v.* **1.** compare (two things) so as to show their differences. **2.** show differences when compared or put side by side. **3.** form a contrast to; set off. **4.** put close together to heighten an effect by emphasizing differences. [< F < Ital. < LL, < L *contra-* against + *stare* stand] **—con·trast'a·ble,** *adj.* **—Syn.** *n.* **1.** distinction. ➤ See **compare** for usage note.

con·tra·vene (kon'trə·vēn'), *v.,* **-vened, -ven·ing. 1.** conflict with; oppose. **2.** violate; infringe. [< LL, < L *contra-* against + *venire* come] **—con'tra·ven'er,** *n.* **—con·tra·ven·tion** (kon'-trə·ven'shən), *n.*

con·trib·ute (kən·trib'yūt), *v.,* **-ut·ed, -ut·ing. 1.** give (money, help, etc.) along with others. **2.** write (articles, stories, etc.) for a newspaper or magazine. **3.** contribute to, help bring about. [< L, bring together, collect, < *com-* together + *tribuere* bestow] **—con·trib'ut·a·ble,** *adj.* **—con·trib'u·tive, con·trib'u·to·ry** (kən·trib'yə·tô'ri; -tō'-), *adj.* **—con·trib'u·tive·ly,** *adv.* **—con·trib'u·tor,** *n.*

con·tri·bu·tion (kon'trə·bū'shən), *n.* **1.** act of giving money, help, etc., along with others. **2.** money, help, etc., given; gift. **3.** article, story, etc., written for a newspaper or magazine. **4.** tax; levy.

con·trite (kən·trīt'; kon'trīt), *adj.* **1.** broken in spirit by a sense of guilt; penitent. **2.** showing deep regret and sorrow. [< L *contritus* crushed < *com-* (intensive) + *terere* rub, grind] **—con·trite'ly,** *adv.* **—con·trite'ness, con·tri·tion** (kən·trish'ən), *n.*

con·triv·ance (kən·trīv'əns), *n.* **1.** thing invented; mechanical device. **2.** act or manner of contriving. **3.** power or ability of contriving.

con·trive (kən·trīv'), *v.,* **-trived, -triv·ing. 1.** invent; design. **2.** plan; scheme; plot. **3.** manage. **4.** bring about. [< OF, < *con-* (< L *com-*) + *trover* find < VL, start, rouse, < L *turbare* stir up < *turba* commotion] **—con·triv'er,** *n.* **—Syn. 1.** devise.

con·trol (kən·trōl'), *n., v.,* **-trolled, -trol·ling.** *—n.* **1.** power; authority; direction. **2.** a holding back; a keeping down; restraint: *he lost control of his temper.* **3.** means of restraint; check. **4.** device that controls a machine. **5.** standard of comparison for testing the results of scientific experiments. *—v.* **1.** have power or authority over; direct. **2.** hold back; keep down; restrain. **3.** regulate. [< F *contrôler,* ult. < OF *contrerolle* register < *contre* against (< L *contra*) + *rôle* ROLL] **—con·trol'la·ble,** *adj.* **—con·trol'la·bil'-i·ty,** *n.* **—con·trol'ment,** *n.* **—Syn.** *n.* **1.** regulation, management.

con·trol·ler (kən·trōl'ər), *n.* **1.** Also, **comptroller.** person employed to supervise expenditures, etc. **2.** person who controls. **3.** device that controls or regulates. **—con·trol'ler·ship,** *n.*

con·tro·ver·sial (kon'trə·vėr'shəl), *adj.* **1.**

of controversy. 2. open to controversy; debatable. 3. fond of controversy. —con'tro·ver'sial·ist, *n.* —con'tro·ver'sial·ly, *adv.*

con·tro·ver·sy (kon'trə·vėr'si), *n., pl.* –sies. 1. debate; dispute. 2. quarrel; wrangle. [< L, < *contro-* against + *versus*, pp. of *vertere* turn]

con·tro·vert (kon'trə·vėrt; kon'trə·vėrt'), *v.* 1. dispute; deny. 2. discuss; debate.

con·tu·ma·cious (kon'tū·mā'shəs; -tyū-), *adj.* stubbornly rebellious; obstinately disobedient. [< L, < *contumax* insolent < *tumere* swell up] —con'tu·ma'cious·ly, *adv.* —con'tu·ma'cious·ness, con·tu·ma·cy (kon'tū·mə·si, -tyū-; kən·tü'mə·si, -tū'-), *n.*

con·tu·me·ly (kon'tū·mə·li, -tyū-; kən·tü'mə·li, -tū'-), *n., pl.* –lies. 1. insulting words or actions; humiliating treatment. 2. a humiliating insult. [< L *contumelia*, orig., insolent action < *tumere* swell up]

con·tuse (kən·tūz'; -tūz'), *v.,* –tused, –tus·ing. bruise. [< L *contusus* < *com-* (intensive) + *tundere* to pound]

con·tu·sion (kən·tū'zhən; -tū'-), *n.* a bruise.

co·nun·drum (kə·nun'drəm), *n.* 1. riddle whose answer involves a pun or play on words. 2. any puzzling problem.

con·va·lesce (kon'və·les'), *v.,* –lesced, –lesc·ing. make progress toward health. [< L *convalescere* < *com-* + *valere* be strong]

con·va·les·cence (kon'və·les'əns), *n.* 1. a gradual recovery of health and strength after illness. 2. time during which one is convalescing. —con'va·les'cent, *adj., n.*

con·vec·tion (kən·vek'shən), *n.* 1. act of conveying. 2. *Physics.* the transfer of heat from one place to another by the circulation of heated particles of a gas or liquid. [< L *convectio* < *com-* together + *vehere* carry] —con·vec'tion·al, *adj.* —con·vec'tive, *adj.*

con·vene (kən·vēn'), *v.,* –vened, –ven·ing. meet for some purpose; assemble. [< L, < *com-* together + *venire* come] —con·ven'er, *n.*

con·ven·ience (kən·vēn'yəns), *n.* 1. fact or quality of being convenient. 2. a convenient condition or time. 3. comfort; advantage. 4. anything handy or easy to use; thing that saves trouble or work.

con·ven·ient (kən·vēn'yənt), *adj.* 1. saving trouble; well arranged; easy to reach or use; handy. 2. easily done; not troublesome. 3. convenient to, *Colloq.* near. [< L *conveniens*, ppr. of *convenire* meet, agree, be suitable. See CONVENE.] —con·ven'ient·ly, *adv.*

con·vent (kon'vent), *n.* 1. community of nuns; group of women living together who devote their lives to religion. 2. building or buildings in which they live. [< AF < L *conventus* assembly < *convenire* CONVENE] —Syn. 2. cloister, abbey.

con·ven·ti·cle (kən·ven'tə·kəl), *n.* 1. a secret meeting, esp. for religious reasons. 2. place of such a meeting. [< L *conventiculum*, dim. of *conventus* meeting. See CONVENT.]

con·ven·tion (kən·ven'shən), *n.* 1. a meeting for some purpose; gathering; assembly. 2. delegates to a meeting or assembly. 3. agreement. 4. general agreement; common consent; custom. 5. custom approved by general agreement; rule based on common consent. [< L *conventio* < *convenire* CONVENE] —Syn. 1. conference. 3. compact. 5. usage, etiquette.

con·ven·tion·al (kən·ven'shən·əl), *adj.* 1. depending on conventions; customary. 2. established by general consent. 3. formal; not natural; not original. 4. *Art.* following custom rather than nature. —con·ven'tion·al·ism, *n.* —con·ven'tion·al·ly, *adv.*

con·ven·tion·al·i·ty (kən·ven'shən·al'ə·ti), *n., pl.* –ties. 1. conventional quality or character. 2. conventional behavior; adherence to custom. 3. a conventional custom or rule.

con·ven·tion·al·ize (kən·ven'shən·əl·īz), *v.,* –ized, –iz·ing. 1. make conventional. 2. draw in a conventional manner. —con·ven'tion·al·i·za'tion, *n.*

con·verge (kən·vėrj'), *v.,* –verged, –verg·ing. 1. tend to meet in a point. 2. cause to converge. [< LL, < L *com-* together + *vergere* incline]

con·ver·gence (kən·vėr'jəns), con·ver·gen·cy (-jən·si), *n., pl.* –ces; –cies. 1. act, process, or fact of converging. 2. tendency to meet in a point. 3. point of meeting. —con·ver'gent, *adj.*

con·ver·sant (kən·vėr'sənt; kon'vər-), *adj.* 1. familiar by use or study. 2. intimately associated. —con·ver'sant·ly, *adv.*

con·ver·sa·tion (kon'vər·sā'shən), *n.* exchange of thoughts by talking informally.

con·ver·sa·tion·al (kon'vər·sā'shən·əl), *adj.* 1. of or having to do with conversation. 2. fond of conversation; good at conversation. —con'ver·sa'tion·al·ly, *adv.*

con·ver·sa·tion·al·ist (kon'vər·sā'shən·əl·ist), *n.* person who is fond of or good at conversation.

con·verse¹ (*v.* kən·vėrs'; *n.* kon'vėrs), *v.,* –versed, –vers·ing, *n.* —*v.* talk informally together. —*n.* conversation. [< OF < L, live with < *com-* with + *versari* live, be busy < *verti* to turn] —con·vers'er, *n.* —Syn. *v.* chat.

con·verse² (*adj.* kən·vėrs'; kon'vėrs; *n.* kon'vėrs), *adj.* 1. opposite; contrary. 2. reversed in order; turned about. —*n.* 1. thing that is opposite or contrary. 2. thing that is turned around. [< L *conversus* turned around, pp. of *convertere* CONVERT] —con·verse'ly, *adv.*

con·ver·sion (kən·vėr'zhən; -shən), *n.* act of converting. —con·ver'sion·al, *adj.*

con·vert (*v.* kən·vėrt'; *n.* kon'vėrt), *v.* 1. change; turn. 2. change from unbelief to faith; change from one religion, party, etc., to another. 3. take and use unlawfully. 4. turn the other way around; invert; transpose. 5. exchange for an equivalent: *convert bank notes into gold.* —*n.* person who has been converted. [< L, < *com-* around + *vertere* turn] —Syn. *v.* 1. transform.

con·vert·er, con·ver·tor (kən·vėr'tər), *n.* 1. person or thing that converts. 2. machine for changing the form of an electric current. 3. furnace in which pig iron is changed into steel.

con·vert·i·ble (kən·vėr'tə·bəl), *adj.* 1. capable of being converted. 2. of an automobile, having a top that may be folded down. —*n.* automobile with a folding top. —con·vert'i·bil'i·ty, *n.* —con·vert'i·bly, *adv.*

con·vert·i·plane (kən·vėr'tə·plān'), *n.* an aircraft that operates like a conventional airplane in level flight, but which takes off and lands like a helicopter. [< *converti(ble)* + *(air) plane*]

con·vex (*adj.* kon·veks', kon-, kon'veks; *n.* kon'veks), *adj.* curved out. —*n.* a convex surface, part, or thing. [< L *convexus* vaulted, prob. < *com-* around + *vac-* bend] —con·vex'i·ty, *n.* —con·vex'ly, *adv.*

con·vey (kən·vā'), *v.* 1. carry; transport. 2. transmit; conduct. 3. express; make known; communicate. 4. *Law.* transfer the ownership of (property) from one person to another. [< OF *conveier* < VL, set on the road, accompany < L *com-* with + *via* road. Doublet of CONVOY.] —con·vey'a·ble, *adj.*

Convex lenses

con·vey·ance (kən·vā'əns), *n.* 1. act of carrying. 2. thing that carries people and goods; vehicle. 3. *Law.* transfer of the ownership of property from one person to another.

con·vey·er, con·vey·or (kən·vā'ər), *n.* 1. person or thing that conveys. 2. device that carries things from one place to another.

con·vict (*v.* kən·vikt'; *n.* kon'vikt), *v.* 1. prove guilty. 2. declare guilty. —*n.* 1. person convicted by a court. 2. person serving a prison sentence. [< L *convictus*, pp. of *convincere*. See CONVINCE.]

con·vic·tion (kən·vik'shən), *n.* 1. act of proving or declaring guilty. 2. state of being proved or declared guilty. 3. act of convincing (a person). 4. a being convinced. 5. firm belief. —con·vic'tion·al, *adj.* —Syn. 1, 2. condemnation.

con·vince (kən·vins'), *v.,* –vinced, –vinc·ing. persuade by argument or proof. [< L, < *com-* + *vincere* overcome] —con·vinc'er, *n.* —con·vin'ci·ble, *adj.*

con·vinc·ing (kən·vin'sing), *adj.* that convinces. —con·vinc'ing·ly, *adv.* —con·vinc'ing·ness, *n.* —Syn. persuasive, cogent.

con·viv·i·al (kən·viv′i·əl), *adj.* **1.** fond of eating and drinking with friends. **2.** of or suitable for a feast or banquet. [< LL, < *convivium* feast < *com–* with + *vivere* live] —**con·viv′i·al′i·ty**, *n.* —**con·viv′i·al·ly**, *adv.*

con·vo·ca·tion (kon′və·kā′shən), *n.* **1.** a calling together. **2.** an assembly. —**con′vo·ca′tion·al**, *adj.*

con·voke (kən·vōk′), *v.*, -**voked**, -**vok·ing**. call together; summon to assemble. [< L, < *com–* together + *vocare* call] —**con·vok′er**, *n.*

con·vo·lute (kon′və·lüt), *adj.*, *v.*, -**lut·ed**, -**lut·ing.** —*adj.* coiled. —*v.* to coil. [< L *convolutus* < *com–* up + *volvere* roll] —**con′vo·lute′ly**, *adv.*

con·vo·lu·tion (kon′və·lü′shən), *n.* **1.** a coiling, winding, or twisting together. **2.** coil; winding; twist. **3.** an irregular fold or ridge on the surface of the brain.

con·voy (*v.* kon·voi′, kon′voi; *n.* kon′voi), *v.* accompany in order to protect. —*n.* **1.** act of convoying. **2.** an escort; protection. **3.** warships, soldiers, etc., that convoy; protecting escort. **4.** fleet, supplies, etc., accompanied by a protecting escort. [< F *convoyer*. Doublet of CONVEY.]

con·vulse (kən·vuls′), *v.*, -**vulsed**, -**vuls·ing.** **1.** shake violently. **2.** throw into a fit of laughter; cause to shake with laughter. [< L *convulsus* < *com–* (intensive) + *vellere* tear]

con·vul·sion (kən·vul′shən), *n.* **1.** a violent, involuntary contracting and relaxing of the muscles; spasm. **2.** fit of laughter. **3.** a violent disturbance. —**con·vul′sive**, *adj.* —**con·vul′sive·ly**, *adv.*

co·ny (kō′ni), *n.*, *pl.* -**nies. 1.** rabbit fur. **2.** *Archaic.* rabbit. Also, **coney.** [< OF *conil* < L *cuniculus* rabbit < Iberian]

coo (kü), *n.*, *v.*, **cooed, coo·ing.** —*n.* a soft, murmuring sound made by doves or pigeons. —*v.* **1.** make this sound. **2.** murmur softly; speak in a soft, loving manner. [imit.] —**coo′er**, *n.*

coo·ee, coo·ey (kü′i; kü′ē), *n.*, *pl.* -**ees**, -**eys;** *interj.*, *v.*, -**eed**, -**ee·ing;** -**eyed, -ey·ing.** —*n.*, *interj.* long, shrill cry or call. —*v.* utter "cooee."

cook (kůk), *v.* **1.** prepare (food) by using heat. **2.** undergo cooking; be cooked. **3.** act as cook; work as cook. **4.** subject (anything) to the action of heat. **5.** *Colloq.* tamper with. [< *n.*] —*n.* person who cooks. [< LL *cocus* < L *coquus*]

cook·book (kůk′bůk′), *n.* *Am.* book of recipes containing directions for cooking.

cook·er (kůk′ər), *n.* apparatus or container for cook things in.

cook·er·y (kůk′ər·i), *n.*, *pl.* -**er·ies. 1.** art of cooking. **2.** room or place for cooking.

cook·out (kůk′out′), *n.* cooking and eating of a meal out-of-doors.

cook·y, cook·ie (kůk′i), *n.*, *pl.* -**ies.** *Am.* small, flat cake. [< Du. *koekje* little cake]

cool (kül), *adj.* **1.** somewhat cold; more cold than hot. **2.** allowing or giving a cool feeling: *cool clothes.* **3.** not excited; calm. **4.** having little enthusiasm or interest. **5.** bold; impudent. **6.** *Colloq.* without exaggeration or qualification: *a cool million dollars.* —*n.* something cool; cool part, place, or time: *the cool of the evening.* —*v.* **1.** become cool. **2.** make cool. **3.** cool one's heels, *Colloq.* be kept waiting for a long time. [OE *cōl*] —**cool′ish**, *adj.* —**cool′ly**, *adv.* —**cool′ness**, *n.* —**Syn.** *adj.* **3.** unmoved, composed. **4.** indifferent. —**Ant.** *adj.* **1.** warm. **3.** excited, disturbed.

cool·ant (kül′ənt), *n.* a cooling medium, used for machinery, etc.

cool·er (kül′ər), *n.* **1.** apparatus or container that cools foods or drinks, or keeps them cool. **2.** anything that cools. **3.** *Am., Slang.* jail.

Cool·idge (kül′ij), *n.* **Calvin,** 1872–1933, the 30th president of the United States, 1923–1929.

coo·lie, coo·ly (kül′li), *n.*, *pl.* -**lies.** an unskilled, native laborer in China, India, etc. [prob. < Tamil *kuli* hire, hired servant]

coon (kün), *n.* *Colloq.* raccoon.

coop (küp; kůp), *n.* **1.** a small cage or pen for chickens, rabbits, etc. **2.** any small confining structure. **3.** *Slang.* jail. —*v.* **1.** keep or put in a coop. **2.** confine in a very small space. [ME *coupe* basket < L *cupa* cask]

co·öp (kō′op; kō·op′), *n. Colloq.* a coöperative store.

coop·er (küp′ər; kůp′–), *n.* man who makes or repairs barrels, casks, etc. —*v.* make or repair (barrels, casks, etc.). [? < MDu., MLG *kuper* < L *cuparius* < *cupa* cask]

Coo·per (kü′pər; kůp′ər), *n.* **James Fenimore,** 1789–1851, American novelist.

coop·er·age (küp′ər·ij; kůp′–), *n.* **1.** work done by a cooper. **2.** shop of a cooper.

co·öp·er·ate, co·op·er·ate, or **co·op·er·ate** (kō·op′ər·āt), *v.*, -**at·ed**, -**at·ing.** work together. [< LL, < *co–* together + *operari* to work] —**co·öp′er·a′tor**, *n.*

co·öp·er·a·tion, co·op·er·a·tion, or **co·op·er·a·tion** (kō·op′ər·ā′shən), *n.* **1.** act of working together; united effort or labor. **2.** combination of persons for purposes of production, purchase, or distribution for their joint benefit.

co·öp·er·a·tive, co·op·er·a·tive, or **co·op·er·a·tive** (kō·op′ər·ā′tiv; -op′rə·tiv), *adj.* **1.** wanting or willing to work together with others. **2.** of, having to do with, or being a coöperative. —*n.* organization in which the profits and losses are shared by all members. —**co·öp′er·a′tive·ly**, *adv.* —**co·öp′er·a′tive·ness**, *n.*

coöperative store, store managed by an organization whose members share in the profits and losses according to the amount they buy.

co·ör·di·nate, co·or·di·nate, or **co·or·di·nate** (*adj.* *n.* kō·ôr′də·nit, -nāt; *v.* kō·ôr′də·nāt), *adj.*, *n.*, *v.*, -**nat·ed**, -**nat·ing.** —*adj.* **1.** equal in importance; of equal rank. **2.** made up of coördinate parts. **3.** joining words, phrases, or clauses of equal grammatical importance. *And* and *but* are coördinate conjunctions. —*n.* **1.** a coördinate person or thing. **2.** *Math.* any of two or more magnitudes that define the position of a point, line, or plane by reference to a fixed figure, system of lines, etc. —*v.* **1.** make coördinate; make equal in importance. **2.** arrange in proper order or relation; harmonize; adjust [< L *co–* with + *ordinatus*, pp. of *ordinare* regulate] —**co·ör′di·nate·ly**, *adv.* —**co·ör′di·nate·ness**, *n.* —**co·ör′di·na′tive**, *adj.* —**co·ör′di·na′tor**, *n.*

co·ör·di·na·tion (kō·ôr′də·nā′shən), *n.* act of coördinating.

European coot
(18 in. long)

coot (küt), *n.* **1.** a wading and swimming bird with short wings and lobate toes. **2.** *Colloq.* fool; simpleton. [? < Du. *koet*]

coot·ie (küt′i), *n. Slang.* louse.

cop (kop), *n.*, *v.*, **copped, cop·ping.** —*n. Colloq.* policeman. —*v. Slang.* steal. [OE *coppian*]

co·part·ner (kō·pärt′nər), *n.* a fellow partner; associate. —**co·part′ner·ship**, *n.*

cope[1] (kōp), *v.*, **coped, cop·ing.** struggle or contend (*with*), esp. on even terms or successfully. [< F *couper* strike < *coup* COUP]

cope[2] (kōp), *n.*, *v.*, **coped, cop·ing.** —*n.* **1.** a long cape worn by priests during certain religious rites. **2.** anything like a cope, such as a canopy, the sky, etc. —*v.* cover with a cope. [< Med.L *capa* cloak, var. of LL *cappa* hood]

co·peck (kō′pek), *n.* kopeck.

Co·pen·ha·gen (kō′pən·hā′gən; -hä′–), *n.* capital of Denmark.

Co·per·ni·cus (kə·pér′nə·kəs), *n.* **Nikolaus,** 1473–1543, Polish astronomer. —**Co·per′ni·can**, *adj.*

cope·stone (kōp′stōn′), *n.* **1.** the top stone of a wall. **2.** a finishing touch. [< *cope*[2] + *stone*]

cop·i·er (kop′i·ər), *n.* **1.** imitator. **2.** copyist.

co·pi·lot (kō′pī′lət), *n.* the assistant or second pilot in an aircraft.

cop·ing (kōp′ing), *n.* the top layer of a brick or stone wall, usually sloping. [< *cope*[2]]

coping saw, a narrow saw in a U-shaped frame, used to cut curves.

co·pi·ous (kō′pi·əs), *adj.* **1.** plentiful; abundant. **2.** containing much matter. **3.** containing many words. [< L, < *copia* plenty] —co'pi-ous·ly, *adv.* —co'pi·ous·ness, *n.* —Syn. 1. ample.

cop·per (kop'ər), *n.* 1. *Chem.* a tough, reddish-brown metallic element, Cu, that is easily shaped into thin sheets or fine wire and resists rust. 2. thing made of copper. 3. *Am.* coin made of copper or bronze; penny. 4. a reddish brown. —*v.* cover with copper. —*adj.* 1. of copper. 2. reddish-brown. [< L *cuprum*, for earlier *aes Cyprium* metal of Cyprus] —cop'per·y, *adj.*

cop·per·as (kop'ər-əs), *n.* ferrous sulfate, $FeSO_4 7H_2O$, used in dyeing, inkmaking, medicine, and photography. [< F < Med.L (*aqua*) *cuprosa* (water) of COPPER]

cop·per·head (kop'ər-hed'), *n. Am.* 1. a poisonous North American snake related to the water moccasin and the rattlesnake. 2. Copperhead, *Am.* a Northerner sympathetic with the South during the Civil War.

cop·per·plate (kop'ər-plāt'), *n.* 1. a thin, flat piece of copper on which a design, writing, etc., is engraved or etched. 2. an engraving, picture, or print made from a copperplate. 3. copperplate printing or engraving.

cop·ra (kop'rə), *n.* the dried meat of coconuts. [< Pg. < Malayalam *koppara*]

copse (kops), cop·pice (kop'is), *n.* a thicket of small trees, bushes, etc. [< OF *coupeiz* a cut-over forest < *couper* cut. See COUP.]

Copt (kopt), *n.* native of Egypt, descended from the ancient Egyptians.

Cop·tic (kop'tik), *n.* the former language of the Copts. —*adj.* of or by the Copts.

cop·u·la (kop'yə-lə), *n., pl.* -las, -lae (-lē). 1. verb that connects the subject and the predicate, usually some form of *be.* 2. something that connects. [< L, bond, < *co-* together + *apere* fasten. Doublet of COUPLE.] —cop'u·lar, *adj.*

cop·u·late (kop'yə-lāt), *v.* -lat·ed, -lat·ing. have sexual intercourse. [< L *copulatus,* pp. of *copulare.* See COPULA.] —cop'u·la'tion, *n.*

cop·u·la·tive (kop'yə-lā'tiv; -lə-), *n.* copulative word. —*adj.* 1. connecting. *Be* is a copulative verb; *and* is a copulative conjunction. 2. pertaining to copulation. [< L *copulativus*] —cop'u·la'tive·ly, *adv.*

cop·y (kop'i), *n., pl.* cop·ies, *v.,* cop·ied, cop·y·ing. —*n.* 1. thing made like another. 2. thing made to be followed as a pattern or model. 3. one of a number of books, newspapers, magazines, pictures, etc., made at the same printing. 4. material ready to be set in type. —*v.* follow as a pattern or model; imitate. [< F < Med.L *copia* transcript < L, plenty] —Syn. *n.* 1. duplicate, transcript, reproduction, imitation. —*v.* duplicate, reproduce. —Ant. *n.* 1. original.

cop·y·book (kop'i·bùk'), *n.* book with models of handwriting to be copied. —*adj.* commonplace; conventional; ordinary.

copy desk, a central desk in a newspaper office, where stories, etc., undergo final preparation for publication.

cop·y·ist (kop'i·ist), *n.* 1. person who makes written copies. 2. imitator.

cop·y·right (kop'i·rīt'), *n.* the exclusive right to make and sell a certain book, picture, etc. —*adj.* protected by copyright. —*v.* protect by getting a copyright. —cop'y·right'a·ble, *adj.* —cop'y·right'er, *n.*

co·quet (kō·ket'), *v.,* -quet·ted, -quet·ting. 1. flirt. 2. trifle. [< F, < *coquet,* dim. of *coq* cock] —co·quet·ry (kō'kə·tri; kō·ket'ri), *n.*

co·quette (kō·ket'), *n.* woman who tries to attract men merely to please her vanity; flirt. [< F. See COQUET.] —co·quet'tish, *adj.* —co·quet'tish·ly, *adv.* —co·quet'tish·ness, *n.*

cor·a·cle (kôr'ə-kəl; kor'-), *n.* a small, light boat made by covering a wooden frame with waterproof material. [< Welsh < *corwg*]

cor·al (kôr'əl; kor'-), *n.* 1. a stony substance consisting of the skeletons of very small sea animals called polyps. 2. polyp that secretes a skeleton of coral and forms large, branching colonies by budding. 3. a deep pink; red. —*adj.* 1. made of coral. 2. deep-pink; red. [< OF < L < Gk. *koral(l)ion*]

coral reef, reef consisting mainly of coral.

Coral Sea, part of the Pacific at the NE Australian coast.

coral snake, *Am.* any of several species of small, poisonous American snakes, most of which are banded with alternating rings of red, yellow, and black.

cor·bel (kôr'bəl), *n., v.,* -beled, -bel·ing; *esp. Brit.* -belled, -bel·ling. —*n.* bracket of stone, etc., on a wall. —*v.* furnish with corbels; support by corbels. [< OF, dim. of *corp* raven < L *corvus*]

CORBEL

cord (kôrd), *n.* 1. a thick string; very thin rope. 2. influence that binds or restrains. 3. *Elect.* a pair of covered wires with fittings to connect an iron, lamp, etc., with a socket. 4. Also, chord. *Anat.* structure in an animal body that is somewhat like a cord: *the spinal cord.* 5. ridge on cloth. 6. cloth with ridges on it; corduroy. 7. cords, corduroy breeches or trousers. 8. measure of cut wood; 128 cubic feet. —*v.* 1. fasten or tie with a cord. 2. pile (wood) in cords. [< OF < L < Gk. *chorde* gut. Doublet of CHORD².] —cord'ed, *adj.* —cord'er, *n.*

cord·age (kôr'dij), *n.* 1. cords; ropes. The cordage of a ship is its rigging. 2. quantity of wood measured in cords.

cor·date (kôr'dāt), *adj.* heart-shaped. [< NL, < L *cor* heart] —cor'date·ly, *adv.*

cor·dial (kôr'jəl), *n.* 1. food, drink, or medicine that makes the heart beat faster. 2. liqueur. —*adj.* 1. sincere; hearty; warm; friendly. 2. stimulating. [< Med.L, < L *cor* heart] —cor'dial·ly, *adv.* —cor'dial·ness, *n.*

cor·dial·i·ty (kôr·jal'ə·ti; -ji·al'-), *n., pl.* -ties. cordial quality or feeling; heartiness; friendliness.

cor·dil·le·ra (kôr'dəl·yâr'ə; kôr·dil'ər·ə), *n. Am., W.* a long mountain range. [< Sp., ult. < L *chorda* rope, CORD] —cor'dil·le'ran, *adj.*

cord·ite (kôr'dīt), *n.* a smokeless gunpowder composed chiefly of nitroglycerin and guncotton. [< *cord, n.* + -*ite²*]

cor·don (kôr'dən), *n.* 1. line or circle of people or things placed at intervals as a guard. 2. cord, braid, or ribbon worn as an ornament or badge of honor. [< F, < *corde* CORD]

cor·do·van (kôr'də·vən; kôr·dō'vən), *n.* kind of soft, fine-grained leather. —*adj.* of or having to do with this leather.

cor·du·roy (kôr'də·roi; kôr'də·roi'), *n.* 1. a thick cotton cloth with close, velvetlike ridges. 2. corduroys, corduroy trousers. —*adj.* 1. made of corduroy. 2. *Am.* pertaining to a road, etc., made of logs or poles placed crosswise, as across muddy or swampy sections. [appar. < F *corde du roi* king's cord]

cord·wood (kôrd'wùd'), *n.* 1. wood sold or piled in cords. 2. wood cut in 4-foot lengths.

core (kôr; kōr), *n., v.,* cored, cor·ing. —*n.* 1. the central part, containing the seeds, of fruits like apples and pears. 2. the central or most important part: *the core of an argument.* 3. *Elect.* bar of soft iron forming the center of an electromagnet or of an induction coil. —*v.* take out the core. [ME] —Syn. *n.* 2. heart, nucleus.

co·re·op·sis (kō'ri·op'sis; kō'-), *n. Am.* plant with yellow, red-and-yellow, or reddish flowers shaped like daisies. [< NL, < Gk. *koris* bedbug + *opsis* appearance; from the shape of the seed]

co·re·spond·ent (kō'ri·spon'dənt; kôr'i-; kor'-), *n. Law.* person accused of adultery with a husband or wife being sued for divorce.

co·ri·an·der (kō'ri·an'dər; kō'-), *n.* 1. plant whose aromatic, seedlike fruits are used in cooking and in medicine. 2. the fruit. [< F < L < Gk. *koriandron,* var. of *koriannon*]

Cor·inth (kôr'inth; kor'-), *n.* seaport in S Greece. In ancient times, Corinth was a center of commerce, art, and luxury.

Co·rin·thi·an (kə·rin'thi·ən), *adj.* 1. of or having to do with Corinth or its people. 2. noting or pertaining to the most elaborate of the three types of Greek architecture. The capital of a Corinthian

Corinthian capital

column is adorned with acanthus leaves. 3. luxurious. —*n.* 1. native or inhabitant of Corinth. 2. **Corinthians,** either of two books of the New Testament, written by the Apostle Paul to the Christians of Corinth.

cork (kôrk), *n.* 1. a light, thick, outer bark of a kind of oak, used for bottle stoppers, floats for fishing lines, etc. 2. Also, **cork oak.** the tree. 3. shaped piece of cork. 4. any stopper for a bottle, etc. 5. *Bot.* the protective outer bark of woody plants. —*v.* 1. stop up with a cork. 2. restrain. 3. blacken with burnt cork. —*adj.* of cork. [< Sp. *alcorque* < Ar. < L *quercus* oak] —**cork′y,** *adj.*

Cork (kôrk), *n.* seaport in S Eire.

cork·screw (kôrk′skrü′), *n.* tool for removing corks from bottles. —*v.* move or advance in a spiral or zigzag course. —*adj.* spiral.

corm (kôrm), *n.* a bulblike underground stem. [< NL < Gk. *kormos* stripped tree trunk < *keirein* shear]

Cork-screw

cor·mo·rant (kôr′mə·rənt), *n.* 1. a large, greedy sea bird with a pouch under its beak. 2. a greedy person. —*adj.* greedy. [< OF *cormareng* < *corp* raven (< L *corvus*) + *marenc* of the sea < L *mare*]

corn[1] (kôrn), *n.* 1. *Am.* kind of grain that grows on large ears; maize; Indian corn. 2. plant that it grows on. 3. in England, grain in general, esp. wheat. 4. in Scotland and Ireland, oats. 5. Also, **corn whiskey,** *Am., Colloq.* whiskey made from corn. —*v.* preserve (meat) with strong salt water or by dry salt. [OE] —**corned** (kôrnd), *adj.*

corn[2] (kôrn), *n.* a hardening of the skin, usually on a toe. [< OF, horn, < L *cornu*]

corn bread, *Am.* bread made of corn meal.

corn·cob (kôrn′kob′), *n. Am.* 1. the central, woody part of an ear of corn. 2. *Colloq.* a tobacco pipe with a bowl hollowed out of a piece of dried corncob.

cor·ne·a (kôr′ni·ə), *n. Anat.* the transparent part of the outer coat of the eyeball. The cornea covers the iris and the pupil. [< Med.L *cornea* (*tela*) horny (web) < L *cornu* horn] —**cor′ne·al,** *adj.*

cor·nel (kôr′nəl), *n.* 1. in Europe, a shrub or small tree with yellow flowers. 2. in the United States, the flowering dogwood. [< G < Med.L *cornolius* < L *cornus*]

cor·ner (kôr′nər), *n.* 1. the point or place where lines or surfaces meet. 2. space between two lines or surfaces near where they meet; angle. 3. the place where two streets meet. 4. piece to protect or decorate a corner. 5. place away from crowds. 6. place that is far away; region. 7. an awkward or difficult position; place from which escape is impossible. 8. *Am.* a buying up of the available supply of some stock or article to raise its price. 9. cut corners, a. *Am.* shorten the way by going across corners. b. save money, effort, time, etc., by cutting down. —*adj.* 1. at a corner. 2. for a corner. —*v.* 1. *Am.* put or drive into a corner. 2. *Am., Colloq.* force into a difficult position. 3. *Am.* buy up all or nearly all that can be had of (something) to raise its price. 4. *Am.* meet at a corner. 5. *Slang.* (of an automobile) round sharp curves at relatively high speeds without sway, etc. [< AF var. of OF *cornere* < L *cornu* horn, tip] —Syn. *n.* 5. nook.

cor·ner·stone (kôr′nər·stōn′), *n.* 1. stone at the corner of two walls that holds them together. 2. main part on which something rests; basis.

cor·ner·wise (kôr′nər·wīz′), **cor·ner·ways** (−wāz′), *adv.* 1. with the corner in front; forming a corner. 2. diagonally.

cor·net (kôr·net′ *for* 1; kôr′nit, kôr·net′ *for* 2), *n.* 1. *Music.* a wind instrument somewhat like a trumpet, usually made of brass. 2. piece of paper rolled into a cone and twisted at one end, used to hold candy, nuts, etc. [< OF, < L *cornu* horn] —**cor·net′tist, cor·net′ist,** *n.*

corn·flow·er (kôrn′flou′ər), *n.* plant with blue, pink, white, or purple flowers; bachelor's-button.

corn·husk (kôrn′husk′), *n. Am.* husk of an ear of corn. —**corn′husk′ing,** *n. Am.*

cor·nice (kôr′nis), *n., v.* —**niced, −nic·ing.** —*n.* a projecting ornamental molding along the top of a wall, pillar, building, etc. See the diagram under entablature. —*v.* furnish or finish with a cornice. [< F < Ital. < Med.Gk. *koronis* copestone < Gk., something bent]

Cor·nish (kôr′nish), *adj.* of or having to do with Cornwall, its people, or their former language. —*n.* the ancient Celtic language of Cornwall. —**Cor·nish·man** (kôr′nish·mən), *n.*

corn meal, *Am.* meal made from Indian corn ground up.

corn pone, *Am., S.* a flat, usually rectangular loaf of corn meal shaped by hand.

corn silk, *Am.* the glossy threads or styles at the end of an ear of corn.

corn·stalk (kôrn′stôk′), *n. Am.* stalk of Indian corn.

corn·starch (kôrn′stärch′), *n. Am.* a starchy flour made from Indian corn, used to thicken puddings, etc.

cor·nu·co·pi·a (kôr′nə·kō′pi·ə), *n.* 1. a horn-shaped container or ornament. 2. horn of plenty, overflowing with fruits and flowers. [< LL, for L *cornu copiae* horn of plenty]

Corn·wall (kôrn′wôl; −wəl), *n.* county in SW England.

Corn·wal·lis (kôrn·wôl′is; −wol′is), *n.* **Charles,** 1738−1805, British general who surrendered to Washington at Yorktown, 1781.

corn·y (kôr′ni), *adj.,* **corn·i·er, corn·i·est.** *Am., Slang.* 1. trite; of poor quality. 2. of music, having an unsophisticated or overly sentimental style.

co·rol·la (kə·rol′ə), *n. Bot.* the internal envelope or floral leaves of a flower; the petals. [< L, garland, dim. of *corona* crown]

cor·ol·lar·y (kôr′ə·ler′i; kor′−), *n., pl.* −lar·ies. 1. an additional proposition that can be easily inferred from a proved proposition. 2. inference. 3. a natural consequence or result. [< LL *corollarium* < L, gift, < *corolla* garland. See COROLLA.]

co·ro·na (kə·rō′nə), *n., pl.* −nas, −nae (−nē). 1. ring of light or halo seen around the sun or moon. 2. *Anat.* the top of the head. 3. *Bot.* the appendage on the inner side of the corolla of some plants. 4. *Elect.* discharge on the surface of a conductor. [< L, crown. Doublet of CROWN.] —**co·ro·nal** (kə·rō′nəl; kôr′ə·nəl; kor′−), *adj.*

Co·ro·na·do (kôr′ə·nä′dō; kor′−), *n.* **Francisco Vásquez de,** 1500?−1554?, Spanish soldier and explorer.

cor·o·nar·y (kôr′ə·ner′i; kor′−), *adj.* 1. pertaining to or resembling a crown. 2. *Anat.* of or designating either or both of the two arteries that supply blood to the muscular tissue of the heart. [< L *coronarius* encircling < *corona* crown]

coronary thrombosis, thrombosis of the heart, involving a coronary artery.

cor·o·na·tion (kôr′ə·nā′shən; kor′−), *n.* ceremony of crowning a king, emperor, etc.

cor·o·ner (kôr′ə·nər; kor′−), *n.* 1. a local official who investigates before a jury any unnatural death. 2. coroner's jury, group of persons chosen to witness the investigation. [< AF *corouner* officer of the crown < *coroune* CROWN] —**cor′o·ner·ship′,** *n.*

cor·o·net (kôr′ə·nit; −net; kor′−), *n.* 1. a small crown worn as a mark of high rank. 2. circlet of anything worn around the head as an ornament. [< OF *coronet,* dim. of *corone* CROWN] —**cor′o·net·ed,** *adj.*

Co·rot (kə·rō′), *n.* **Jean Baptiste Camille,** 1796−1875, French landscape painter.

Corp., corp., 1. Corporal. 2. Corporation.

cor·po·ral[1] (kôr′pə·rəl), *adj.* of the body: *corporal punishment.* [< L *corporalis* < *corpus* body] —**cor·po·ral·i·ty,** *n.* —**cor′po·ral·ly,** *adv.*

cor·po·ral[2] (kôr′pə·rəl), *n.* the lowest noncommissioned army officer, next below a sergeant and next above a private. [< F < Ital. *caporale* < *capo* head < L *caput*] —**cor′po·ral·ship′,** *n.*

cor·po·rate (kôr′pə·rit), *adj.* **1.** of or forming a corporation; incorporated. **2.** combined. [< L, < *corporare* form into a body < *corpus* body] —cor′po·rate·ly, *adv.*

cor·po·ra·tion (kôr′pə·rā′shən), *n.* **1.** group of persons who under a charter giving them as a group certain legal rights and privileges distinct from those of the individual members of the group. **2.** group of persons with authority to act as a single person. **3.** *Colloq.* prominent abdomen.

cor·po·re·al (kôr·pô′ri·əl; -pō′-), *adj.* **1.** of or for the body; bodily. **2.** material; tangible. [< L *corporeus* < *corpus* body] —cor·po′re·al′i·ty, cor·po′re·al·ness, *n.* —cor·po′re·al·ly, *adv.*

corps (kôr; kōr), *n.*, *pl.* **corps** (kôrz; kōrz). **1.** branch of specialized military service, such as the Signal Corps. **2.** *Mil.* a tactical unit usually consisting of two or more divisions, and smaller than an army. **3.** group of people organized for working together. [< F. See CORPSE.]

corpse (kôrps), *n.* a dead human body. [< OF < L *corpus* body]

cor·pu·lence (kôr′pyə·ləns), **cor·pu·len·cy** (-lən·si), *n.* fatness. —cor′pu·lent, *adj.* —cor′pu·lent·ly, *adv.* [< L, < *corpus* body]

cor·pus (kôr′pəs), *n.*, *pl.* **-po·ra** (-pə·rə). **1.** a body. **2.** a complete collection of writings, laws, etc. [< L, body]

Cor·pus Chris·ti (kôr′pəs kris′ti; kris′tī), feast in honor of the Eucharist, held on the first Thursday after Trinity Sunday.

cor·pus·cle (kôr′pəs·əl; -pus-), *n.* any of the cells that float in the blood, lymph, etc., carrying oxygen and carbon dioxide or destroying disease germs. [< L *corpusculum*, dim. of *corpus* body] —cor·pus·cu·lar (kôr·pus′kyə·lər), *adj.*

cor·pus de·lic·ti (kôr′pəs di·lik′tī), *Law.* **a.** the actual facts that prove a crime or offense has been committed. **b.** body of a murdered person. [< L, body of the crime]

cor·ral (kə·ral′), *n.*, *v.*, **-ralled**, **-ral·ling.** *Am.* —*n.* an enclosed space for keeping or for capturing horses, cattle, etc. —*v.* **1.** drive into or keep in a corral. **2.** surround; capture. [< Sp., < *corro* ring]

cor·rect (kə·rekt′), *adj.* **1.** free from mistakes or faults; right. **2.** in good taste; proper. —*v.* **1.** change to what is right; remove mistakes from. **2.** alter to agree with some standard: *correct the reading of a barometer.* **3.** mark the errors of. **4.** find fault with to improve; punish. **5.** counteract (something hurtful); cure. [< L *correctus*, pp. of *corrigere* make straight < *com-* + *regere* direct] —cor·rect′ly, *adv.* —cor·rect′ness, *n.* —cor·rec′tor, *n.* —**Syn.** *adj.* **1.** accurate, exact, precise. —*v.* **1.** amend. **4.** admonish, discipline. **5.** remedy. —**Ant.** *adj.* **1.** erroneous.

cor·rec·tion (kə·rek′shən), *n.* **1.** act of correcting. **2.** thing put in place of an error or mistake. **3.** punishment; rebuke; scolding. —cor·rec′tion·al, *adj.*

cor·rec·tive (kə·rek′tiv), *adj.* tending to correct; making better. —*n.* something that tends to correct anything that is wrong or hurtful. —cor·rec′tive·ly, *adv.*

Cor·reg·i·dor (kə·reg′ə·dôr), *n.* a fortified island at the entrance to Manila Bay, Philippines; surrendered to the Japanese in 1942.

cor·re·late (kôr′ə·lāt; kôr′-), *v.*, **-lat·ed**, **-lat·ing**, *adj.*, *n.* —*v.* **1.** have a mutual relation. **2.** bring into proper relation with one another. —*adj.* correlated. —*n.* either of two related things. [< *com-* + *relate*]

cor·re·la·tion (kôr′ə·lā′shən; kôr′-), *n.* **1.** the mutual relation of two or more things. **2.** a correlating or being correlated.

cor·rel·a·tive (kə·rel′ə·tiv), *adj.* **1.** mutually dependent; each implying the other. **2.** having a mutual relation and commonly used together. Conjunctions used in pairs, such as *either . . . or* and *both . . . and,* are correlative words. —*n.* either of two closely related things. —cor·rel′a·tive·ly, *adv.*

cor·re·spond (kôr′ə·spond′; kor′-), *v.* **1.** be in harmony; agree. **2.** be similar: *the arms of a man correspond to the wings of a bird.* **3.** ex-

change letters. [< Med.L, < L *com-* together, with + *respondere* answer] —cor′re·spond′ing, *adj.* —cor′re·spond′ing·ly, *adv.* —**Syn.** **1.** harmonize, match. **2.** parallel.

cor·re·spond·ence (kôr′ə·spon′dəns; kor′-), *n.* **1.** agreement; harmony. **2.** similarity in structure or function. **3.** exchange of letters; letter writing. **4.** letters.

correspondence school, school that gives lessons by mail.

cor·re·spond·ent (kôr′ə·spon′dənt; kor′-), *n.* **1.** person who exchanges letters with another. **2.** person employed by a newspaper or magazine to send news from a distant place. **3.** thing that corresponds to something else. —*adj.* corresponding; in agreement. —cor′re·spond′ent·ly, *adv.*

cor·ri·dor (kôr′ə·dər; -dôr; kor′-), *n.* **1.** a long hallway. **2.** a narrow strip of land connecting two parts of a country or an inland country with a seaport. [< F < Pr. *corredor* < *correr* run < L *currere*] —**Syn.** **1.** passageway, hall.

cor·ri·gi·ble (kôr′ə·jə·bəl; kor′-), *adj.* **1.** that can be corrected. **2.** open to correction. [< LL, < L *corrigere* CORRECT] —cor′ri·gi·bil′i·ty, *n.* —cor′ri·gi·bly, *adv.*

cor·rob·o·rate (kə·rob′ə·rāt), *v.*, **-rat·ed**, **-rat·ing.** make more certain; confirm. [< L, < *corroborare* strengthen < *com-* + *robur* oak] —cor·rob·o·ra′tion, *n.* —cor·rob′o·ra′tor, *n.*

cor·rob·o·ra·tive (kə·rob′ə·rā′tiv; -rə·tiv), *adj.* confirming. —cor·rob′o·ra′tive·ly, *adv.*

cor·rode (kə·rōd′), *v.*, **-rod·ed**, **-rod·ing.** **1.** eat away gradually. **2.** become corroded. [< L, < *com-* + *rodere* gnaw] —cor·rod′i·ble, *adj.*

cor·ro·sion (kə·rō′zhən), *n.* **1.** act or process of corroding. **2.** a corroded condition. **3.** product of corroding.

cor·ro·sive (kə·rō′siv), *adj.* producing corrosion; corroding; eating away. —*n.* substance that corrodes. —cor·ro′sive·ly, *adv.* —cor·ro′sive·ness, *n.*

corrosive sublimate, bichloride of mercury, $HgCl_2$, a poisonous, white crystalline substance.

cor·ru·gate (v. kôr′ə·gāt, kor′-; *adj.* kôr′ə·git, -gāt, kor′-), *v.*, **-gat·ed**, **-gat·ing**, *adj.* —*v.* **1.** bend or shape into a row of wavelike folds. **2.** wrinkle; furrow. —*adj.* wrinkled; furrowed. [< L, < *com-* + *ruga* wrinkle]

cor·ru·ga·tion (kôr′ə·gā′shən; kor′-), *n.* **1.** a corrugating. **2.** a being corrugated. **3.** one of a series of wavelike ridges.

cor·rupt (kə·rupt′), *adj.* **1.** evil; wicked. **2.** influenced by bribes; dishonest. **3. a.** incorrect because of alterations, as a text. **b.** considered inferior by some because of change in meaning or form, or deviation from standard usage, as a language, dialect, form, etc. **4.** rotten; decayed. —*v.* **1.** make evil or wicked. **2.** bribe. **3. a.** make incorrect by changing, as a text. **b.** cause to differ from standard usage, as a form, meaning, dialect, etc. **4.** rot; decay. **5.** become corrupt. [< L *corruptus* < *com-* + *rumpere* break] —cor·rupt′er, *n.* —cor·rupt′ing·ly, *adv.* —cor·rupt′ly, *adv.* —cor·rupt′ness, *n.* —**Syn.** *v.* **1.** pervert; deprave. **4.** taint, spoil.

cor·rupt·i·ble (kə·rup′tə·bəl), *adj.* **1.** that can be corrupted; that can be bribed. **2.** liable to be corrupted; perishable. —cor·rupt′i·bil′i·ty, cor·rupt′i·ble·ness, *n.* —cor·rupt′i·bly, *adv.*

cor·rup·tion (kə·rup′shən), *n.* **1.** a making or being made evil or wicked. **2.** evil conduct; wickedness. **3.** bribery; dishonesty. **4. a.** a making incorrect by changing, as a text. **b.** a causing to differ from standard usage, as a form, meaning, dialect, etc. **c.** an instance of this: *a corrupt form of a word.* **5.** rot; decay. **6.** thing that causes corruption.

cor·sage (kôr·säzh′), *n.* **1.** *Am.* bouquet to be worn at a woman's waist or her shoulder, etc. **2.** the upper part of a woman's dress. [< F, < OF *cors* body < L *corpus*]

cor·sair (kôr′sâr), *n.* **1.** pirate. **2.** a pirate ship. **3.** privateer. [< F < Ital. < VL *cursarius* runner < L *cursus* a run]

corse·let (kôrs′lit *for 1;* kôr′sə·let′ *for 2), n.* **1.**

Also, **cors′let**. armor for the body. **2.** a woman's undergarment somewhat like a corset. [< F, double dim. of OF *cors* body < L *corpus*]

cor·set (kôr′sĭt), *n.* Often, **corsets**. a woman's stiff, close-fitting undergarment, worn about the waist and hips to support or shape the body. [< F, dim. of OF *cors* body < L *corpus*]

Cor·si·ca (kôr′sə·kə), *n.* French island in the Mediterranean, SE of France. —**Cor′si·can**, *adj., n.*

cor·tege, **cor·tège** (kôr·tãzh′; -tezh′), *n.* **1.** procession. **2.** group of followers, attendants, etc.; retinue. [< F < Ital. *corteggio* < *corte* COURT]

Cor·tés, Cor·tez (kôr·tez′), *n.* Hernando, 1485–1547, Spanish soldier who conquered Mexico.

cor·tex (kôr′teks), *n., pl.* **-ti·ces** (-tə·sēz). **1.** *Bot.* bark. **2.** *Anat., Zool.* **a.** the outer layers of an internal organ, as of the kidney. **b.** layer of gray matter that covers most of the surface of the brain. [< L, bark] —**cor·ti·cal** (kôr′tə·kəl), *adj.* —**cor′ti·cal·ly**, *adv.*

cor·ti·sone (kôr′tə·zōn), *n.* hormone derived from the cortex of the adrenal gland, used experimentally in controlling arthritis. Also, Compound E.

co·run·dum (kə·run′dəm), *n.* an extremely hard mineral consisting of aluminum oxide, Al₂O₃, used as an abrasive. [< Tamil *kurundam*. Cf. Skt. *kuruvinda* ruby.]

cor·us·cate (kôr′əs·kāt; kor′-), *v.*, **-cat·ed**, **-cat·ing**. give off flashes of light; sparkle. [< L, < *coruscus* darting, flashing] —**cor′us·ca′tion**, *n.*

cor·vette, **cor·vet** (kôr·vet′), *n.* **1.** warship with sails and only one tier of guns. **2.** gunboat used in antisubmarine convoy work. [prob. < MDu. *korf* a kind of ship < *corbis* basket]

cor·ymb (kôr′imb; -im; kor′-), *n. Bot.* a flat cluster of flowers in which the outer flowers blossom first. [< L < Gk. *korymbos* top, cluster] —**co·rym·bose** (kə·rim′bōs), *adj.* —**co·rym′bose·ly**, *adv.*

Corymb

cor·y·phée (kôr′ə·fā′; kor′-), *n.* **1.** dancer who leads a ballet. **2.** a ballet dancer. [< F < L < Gk. *koryphaios* leader < *koryphe* head]

co·ry·za (kə·rī′zə), *n. Med.* cold in the head. [< L < Gk. *koryza* catarrh]

cos (kos; kôs), *n.* kind of lettuce. [from the island of *Cos* in the Aegean]

co·se·cant (kō·sē′kənt; -kant), *n. Trigon.* the secant of the complement of a given angle or arc.

co·sig·na·to·ry (kō·sig′nə·tô′ri; -tō′-), *adj., n., pl.* **-ries.** —*adj.* signing along with another or others. —*n.* one who so signs.

co·sine (kō′sīn), *n. Trigon.* sine of the complement of a given angle or arc.

cos·met·ic (koz·met′ik), *n.* preparation for beautifying the skin, etc. —*adj.* beautifying. [< Gk. *kosmetikos* of order, adornment < *kosmos* order]

cos·mic (koz′mik), *adj.* **1.** of or belonging to the cosmos; having to do with the whole universe. **2.** vast. [< Gk. *kosmikos* < *kosmos* order, world] —**cos′mi·cal·ly**, *adv.*

cosmic dust, fine particles of matter falling upon the earth from outer space.

cosmic rays, *Am.* rays of very short wave lengths and very great penetration, coming to the earth from interstellar space.

cos·mog·o·ny (koz·mog′ə·ni), *n., pl.* **-nies. 1.** origin of the universe. **2.** theory of its origin. [< Gk. *kosmogonia* < *kosmos* world + *gignesthai* be born]

cos·mog·ra·phy (koz·mog′rə·fi), *n., pl.* **-phies.** science that deals with the general appearance and structure of the universe. [< Gk., < *kosmos* world + *graphein* write]

cos·mol·o·gy (koz·mol′ə·ji), *n.* science or theory of the universe, its parts, and laws. —**cos·mo·log·i·cal** (koz′mə·loj′ə·kəl), *adj.*

cos·mo·pol·i·tan (koz′mə·pol′ə·tən), *adj.* **1.** belonging to all parts of the world; widely spread. **2.** free from national or local prejudices; feeling at home in any part of the world. —*n.* a cosmopolitan person or thing.

cos·mop·o·lite (koz·mop′ə·līt), *n.* **1.** a cosmopolitan person. **2.** animal or plant found in all or many parts of the world. [< Gk., < *kosmos* world + *polites* citizen < *polis* city]

cos·mos (koz′məs; -mos), *n.* **1.** the universe thought of as an orderly, harmonious system. **2.** any complete system that is orderly and harmonious. **3.** plant with white, pink, or purple flowers, that blooms in the fall. [< NL < Gk. *kosmos* order, world] —**Ant. 1.** chaos.

cos·mo·tron (koz′mə·tron), *n.* an atomic accelerator at Brookhaven National Laboratory, Upton, N.Y., designed to produce particles with energy of over two billion electron volts. [appar. < *cosm*(ic) + (*cycl*)*otron*]

Cos·sack (kos′ak; -ək), *n.* one of a people living in S Russia, noted as horsemen.

cos·set (kos′it), *n.* a pet lamb; a pet. [< *v.*] —*v.* treat as a pet; pamper. [< unrecorded OE *cossettan* to kiss < *coss* a kiss]

cost (kôst; kost), *n., v., cost, cost·ing.* —*n.* **1.** price paid. **2.** loss; sacrifice. **3. at all costs** or **at any cost,** by all means; no matter what must be done. **4. costs,** *Law.* expenses of a lawsuit or case in court. —*v.* be obtained at the price of; require. [< OF, < *coster* < L, < *com-* + *stare* stand] —**Syn.** *n.* **1.** charge, expense, outlay.

cos·tal (kos′təl), *adj.* **1.** of or pertaining to a rib or ribs. **2.** bearing ribs. [< Med.L, < L *costa* rib]

Cos·ta Ri·ca (kos′tə rē′kə; kôs′-; kōs′-), country in Central America. —**Costa Rican.**

cos·ter (kos′tər; kôs′-), or **cos·ter·mon·ger** (-mung′gər; -mong′-), *n. Esp. Brit.* person who sells fruit, vegetables, fish, etc., in the street. [< *costard* a kind of English apple]

cos·tive (kos′tiv; kôs′-), *adj.* constipated. [< OF < L *constipatus*, pp. See CONSTIPATE.] —**cos′tive·ly**, *adv.* —**cos′tive·ness**, *n.*

cost·ly (kôst′li; kost′-), *adj.,* **-li·er, -li·est. 1.** of great value. **2.** costing much. **3.** *Archaic.* costing too much. —**cost′li·ness**, *n.* —**Syn. 1.** precious, valuable, sumptuous, rich. **2.** expensive, dear. —**Ant. 1.** cheap. **2.** inexpensive.

cos·tume (*n.* kos′tūm, -tūm; *v.* kos·tūm′, -tūm′), *n., v.,* **-tumed, -tum·ing.** —*n.* **1.** style of dress, etc., including the way the hair is worn, kind of jewelry, etc. **2.** dress belonging to another time or place, worn on the stage, etc. **3.** a complete set of outer garments. —*v.* provide a costume for; dress. [< F < Ital. < VL *consuetumen* custom. Doublet of CUSTOM.]

cos·tum·er (kos·tūm′ər; -tūm′-), **cos·tum·i·er** (-tūm′i·ər; -tūm′-), *n.* person who makes, sells, or rents costumes or dresses.

co·sy (kō′zi), *adj.,* **co·si·er, co·si·est,** *n., pl.* **co·sies.** cozy. —**co′si·ly**, *adv.* —**co′si·ness**, *n.*

cot[1] (kot), *n.* **1.** a narrow, portable bed, esp. one made of canvas. **2.** *Brit.* crib. [< Anglo-Ind. < Hind. *khat.* Cf. Skt. *khatvā.*]

cot[2] (kot), *n.* **1.** cottage. **2.** something small built for cover or protection. [OE]

co·tan·gent (kō·tan′jənt), *n. Trigon.* tangent of the complement of a given angle or arc. —**co·tan·gen·tial** (kō′tan·jen′shəl), *adj.*

cote (kōt), *n.* **1.** shelter or shed for small animals, etc. **2.** *Brit.* cottage. [OE. See COT[2].]

co·te·rie (kō′tə·ri), *n.* set or circle of acquaintances; group of people who often meet socially. [< F, association for holding land, < *cotier* COT-TER[2]] —**Syn.** clique, ring.

co·ter·mi·nous (kō·tér′mə·nəs), *adj.* conterminous.

co·til·lion (kə·til′yən), *n. Esp. U.S.* a dance with complicated steps and much changing of partners. It is led by one couple. [< F, orig., petticoat, dim. of *cotte* COAT]

cot·tage (kot′ij), *n.* **1.** a small house. **2.** *Am.* house at a summer resort. [see COT[2], -AGE]

cottage cheese, *Am.* a soft, white cheese made from the curds of sour milk.

cot·tag·er (kot′ij·ər), *n.* **1.** person who lives in a cottage. **2.** *Am.* person who lives in a cottage at a resort.

cot·ter[1] (kot′ər), *n.* **1.** pin that is inserted through a slot to hold small parts of machinery, etc., together. **2.** cotter pin.

cot·ter[2], **cot·tar** (kot′ər), *n.* a Scottish peasant who works for a farmer and is allowed to use a small cottage and a plot of land. [< Med.L *cotarius* < *cota* < OE *cot* cor[2]]

cotter pin, split pin with bent ends, used as a cotter.

cot·ton (kot′ən), *n.* **1.** soft, white fibers in a fluffy mass around the seeds of a plant of the mallow family. **2.** plant or plants that produce these fibers. **3.** thread of cotton fibers. **4.** cloth made of cotton thread. —*adj.* made of cotton. —*v. Colloq.* take a liking. [< OF < Ital. < Ar. *quṭn*] —**cot′ton·y,** *adj.*

cotton batting, soft, fluffy cotton pressed into thin layers.

cotton gin, *Am.* machine for separating the fibers of cotton from the seeds.

cot·ton·mouth (kot′ən·mouth′), *n. Am.* water moccasin.

cot·ton·seed (kot′ən·sēd′), *n., pl.* –seeds or (*esp. collectively*) –seed. seed of cotton, used for making cottonseed oil, fertilizer, cattle food, etc.

cottonseed oil, *Am.* oil pressed from cottonseed, used for cooking, for making soap, etc.

cot·ton·tail (kot′ən·tāl′), *n. Am.* a common American wild rabbit.

cot·ton·wood (kot′ən·wůd′), *n.* **1.** an American poplar tree having cottonlike tufts on the seeds. **2.** its soft wood.

cotton wool, 1. raw cotton, before or after picking. **2.** cotton batting.

cot·y·le·don (kot′ə·lē′dən), *n. Bot.* an embryo leaf in the seed of a plant; the first leaf, or one of the first pair of leaves, growing from a seed. [< L < Gk. *kotylēdōn* cup-shaped hollow < *kotylē* small vessel] —**cot′y·le′don·al,** *adj.* —**cot′y·le′don·ous,** *adj.*

C, cotyledon.

couch (kouch), *n.* **1.** thing made to sleep or rest on. **2.** place to sleep or rest in: *a grassy couch.* —*v.* **1.** lay on a couch. **2.** lie down on a couch. **3.** put in words; express. **4.** lower; bring down. **5.** put in a level position ready to attack. **6.** lie hidden ready to attack. **7.** crouch; cower; stoop. [< OF, < *coucher* lay in place < L, < *com-* + *locare* place < *locus* a place] —**couch′er,** *n.*

couch·ant (kouch′ənt), *adj.* lying down, but with the head raised. [< F, ppr. See COUCH.]

cou·gar (kü′gər), *n.* a large, tawny American wildcat; puma; mountain lion. [< F < NL < Tupi-Guarani]

Cougar (total length 8 ft.)

cough (kôf; kof), *v.* **1.** force air from the lungs with sudden effort and noise. **2.** cough up, **a.** expel from the throat by coughing. **b.** *Am., Slang.* give; bring out; produce. —*n.* **1.** act of coughing. **2.** repeated acts of coughing. **3.** a diseased condition of the lungs, etc., that causes coughing. [ME *coghen* < OE *cohhetan*]

could (kůd), *v.* pt. of can. ➤ **could, might.** *Could,* the past of *can,* and *might,* originally the past of *may,* are now used chiefly to convey a shade of doubt, or a smaller degree of possibility: *it might be all right for her, but it wasn't for me; perhaps I could write a poem, but I doubt it.*

cou·lee (kü′li), *n.* **1.** *Am.* a deep ravine or gulch. A coulee is usually dry in summer. **2.** stream of lava. [< F, < *couler* flow < L *colare* strain]

cou·lomb (kü·lom′), *n.* quantity of electricity furnished by one current of one ampere in one second. [for C. A. de *Coulomb,* French physicist]

coul·ter (kōl′tər), *n.* colter.

coun·cil (koun′səl), *n.* **1.** group of people called together to give advice, talk things over, or settle questions. **2.** a small group of people elected by citizens to make laws for and govern a city or town. **3.** an ecclesiastical assembly for deciding matters of doctrine or discipline. [< OF < L *concilium* < *com-* together + *calare* call] —Syn. **1.** assembly, meeting, conference.

coun·cil·man (koun′səl·mən), *n., pl.* -men. member of the council of a city or town.

council of war, conference to talk over and decide on matters of importance.

coun·ci·lor, *esp. Brit.* **coun·cil·lor** (koun′sə·lər), *n.* a council member. —**coun′ci·lor·ship′,** *esp. Brit.* **coun′cil·lor·ship′,** *n.*

coun·sel (koun′səl), *n., v.,* -seled, -sel·ing; *esp. Brit.* -selled, -sel·ling. —*n.* **1.** act of exchanging ideas; act of talking things over. **2.** advice. **3.** person or group that gives advice about the law; lawyer or group of lawyers. **4.** design; plan. —*v.* **1.** give advice to; advise. **2.** recommend. **3.** exchange ideas; consult together; deliberate. [< OF < L *consilium* < *consulere* consult, orig., convoke < *com-* together + *sel-* take] —Syn. *n.* **1.** consultation, deliberation. **2.** recommendation. **3.** counselor. –*v.* **1.** admonish.

coun·se·lor, *esp. Brit.* **coun·sel·lor** (koun′sə·lər), *n.* **1.** person who gives advice; adviser. **2.** lawyer. —**coun′se·lor·ship′,** *esp. Brit.* **coun′sel·lor·ship′,** *n.*

count[1] (kount), *v.* **1.** name numbers in order; name the numbers up to: *wait till I count ten.* **2.** add; find how many. **3.** include in counting; take into account. **4.** depend; rely. **5.** count out, *Am.* **a.** fail to consider or include. **b.** defeat by counting ballots wrongly. **c.** declare (a fallen boxer) the loser when he fails to rise after 10 seconds. **6.** be included in counting; be taken into account. **7.** have an influence; be of value. **8.** consider. —*n.* **1.** an adding up; a finding out how many. **2.** the total number; amount. **3.** an accounting. **4.** ten seconds counted to give a fallen boxer time to rise. **5.** *Law.* each charge in a formal accusation. [< OF < L *com-* up + *putare* reckon. Doublet of COMPUTE.] —**count′a·ble,** *adj.*

count[2] (kount), *n.* a European nobleman having a rank about the same as that of an English earl. [< OF < L *comes* companion < *com-* with + *ire* go]

coun·te·nance (koun′tə·nəns), *n., v.,* -nanced, -nanc·ing. —*n.* **1.** expression of the face. **2.** face; features. **3.** approval; encouragement. **4.** calmness; composure. **5.** put out of countenance, embarrass and confuse; make uneasy and ashamed. —*v.* approve; encourage. [< OF < Med.L *continentia* demeanor < L, self-control. See CONTINENT[2].] —Syn. *n.* **2.** visage. **3.** support.

count·er[1] (koun′tər), *n.* **1.** a piece of wood, metal, etc., used to count, as in card games. **2.** an imitation coin. **3.** *Esp. U.S.* a long table in a store, bank, restaurant, etc. [< OF, < *conter* COUNT[1]]

count·er[2] (koun′tər), *n.* **1.** person who counts. **2.** a machine for counting.

coun·ter[3] (koun′tər), *adv.* in the opposite direction; opposed; contrary. —*adj.* opposite; contrary. —*v.* **1.** go or act counter to; oppose. **2.** give a blow in boxing in return for another. —*n.* **1.** that which is opposite or contrary to something else. **2.** blow given in boxing in return for another. **3.** a stiff piece inside the back of a shoe around the heel. **4.** part of a ship's stern from the water line to the end of the curved part. [< F < L *contra* against]

counter-, *word element.* **1.** against; in opposition to, as in *counteract.* **2.** in return, as in *counterattack.* **3.** that corresponds; so as to correspond, as in *counterpart.* [see COUNTER[3]]

coun·ter·act (koun′tər·akt′), *v.* act against; neutralize the action or effect of; hinder. —**coun′ter·ac′tion,** *n.* —**coun′ter·ac′tive,** *adj.,n.*

coun·ter·at·tack (*n.* koun′tər·ə·tak′; *v.* koun′tər·ə·tak′), *n.* attack made to counteract an attack. —*v.* attack in return.

coun·ter·bal·ance (*n.* koun′tər·bal′əns; *v.* koun′tər·bal′əns), *n., v.,* -anced, -anc·ing. —*n.* **1.** weight balancing another weight. **2.** influence, power, etc., balancing another. —*v.* act as a counterbalance to; offset.

coun·ter·claim (*n.* koun′tər·klām′; *v.* koun′-

tər·klăm′), *n.* an opposing claim; claim made by a person to offset a claim made against him. —*v.* make a counterclaim.

coun·ter·clock·wise (koun′tər·klok′wīz′), *adv., adj.* in the direction opposite to that in which the hands of a clock go.

coun·ter·es·pi·o·nage (koun′tər·es′pi·ə·nij; -näzh′), *n.* measures taken to prevent or confuse enemy espionage.

coun·ter·feit (koun′tər·fĭt), *v.* 1. copy (money, handwriting, pictures, etc.) in order to deceive or defraud. 2. resemble closely. 3. pretend; dissemble. —*n.* copy made to deceive or defraud and passed as genuine. —*adj.* made to deceive or defraud. [< OF *contrefait* imitated < *contre-* against (< L *contra-*) + *faire* make < L *facere*] —**coun′ter·feit′er,** *n.* —**Syn.** *adj.* forged, fraudulent. —**Ant.** *adj.* genuine, real.

coun·ter·ir·ri·tant (koun′tər·ir′ə·tənt), *n.* something used to produce irritation in one place in order to relieve irritation elsewhere.

coun·ter·mand (*v.* koun′tər·mand′, -mänd′; *n.* koun′tər·mand, -mänd), *v.* 1. withdraw or cancel (an order, command, etc.). 2. recall or stop by a contrary order. —*n.* command, etc., that revokes a previous one. [< OF, < L *contra-* against + *mandare* order]

coun·ter·of·fen·sive (koun′tər·ə·fen′siv), *n. Mil.* aggressive action on a large scale undertaken by a defending force to seize the initiative from the attacking force.

coun·ter·pane (koun′tər·pān′), *n.* quilt; coverlet. [alter. of *counterpoint* quilt < OF]

coun·ter·part (koun′tər·pärt′), *n.* 1. copy; duplicate. 2. person or thing closely resembling another. 3. person or thing that complements another.

coun·ter·plot (*n., v.* koun′tər·plot′; *v. also* koun′tər·plot′), *n., v.,* -plot·ted, -plot·ting. —*n.* plot to defeat another plot. —*v.* devise a counterplot.

coun·ter·point (koun′tər·point′), *n. Music.* 1. melody added to another as an accompaniment. 2. art of adding melodies to a given melody according to fixed rules.

coun·ter·poise (koun′tər·poiz′), *n., v.,* -poised, -pois·ing. —*n.* 1. weight balancing another weight. 2. influence, power, etc., balancing or offsetting another. —*v.* act as a counterpoise to; offset. [< OF *countrepeis* < *contre-* against (< L *contra-*) + *peis* weight < L *pensum*]

coun·ter·rev·o·lu·tion (koun′tər·rev′ə·lū′-shən), *n.* revolution against a government established by a previous revolution. —**coun·ter·rev·o·lu·tion·ar·y** (koun′tər·rev′ə·lū′shən·er′i), *adj., n.* —**coun′ter·rev′o·lu′tion·ist,** *n.*

coun·ter·shaft (koun′tər·shaft′; -shäft′), *n.* shaft that transmits motion from the main shaft to the working part of a machine.

coun·ter·sign (*n., v.* koun′tər·sīn′; *v. also* koun′tər·sīn′), *n.* 1. *Mil.* password given in answer to the challenge of a sentinel. 2. signature added to another signature to confirm it. —*v.* sign (something already signed by another) to confirm it.

coun·ter·sink (*v., n.* koun′tər·singk′; *v. also* koun′tər·singk′), *v.,* -sunk, -sink·ing, —*v.* 1. enlarge the upper part of (a hole) to make room for the head of a screw, bolt, etc. 2. sink the head of (a screw, bolt, etc.) into such a hole so that it is even with or below the surface. —*n.* 1. a countersunk hole. 2. tool for countersinking holes.

coun·ter·weight (koun′tər·wāt′), *n.* weight that balances another weight.

counter word, word that is used more frequently than its exact meaning warrants. In "we had a lousy time at the party," *lousy* is a counter word meaning "unpleasant."

count·ess (koun′tis), *n.* 1. wife or widow of an earl or a count. 2. woman whose rank is equal to that of an earl or a count.

counting house or **room,** building or office used for keeping accounts and doing business.

count·less (kount′lis), *adj.* too many to count; very many; innumerable.

coun·tri·fied, coun·try·fied (kun′tri·fīd), *adj.* like the country; rural.

coun·try (kun′tri), *n., pl.* -tries, *adj.* —*n.* 1. land; region; district. 2. all the land of a nation. 3. people of a nation. 4. land where a person was born or is a citizen. 5. land without many houses; rural district. —*adj.* 1. of the country; rural. 2. rustic. [< OF < VL *contrata* what lies opposite < L *contra* against]

country club, *Am.* club in the country near a city.

coun·try·dance (kun′tri·dans′; -däns′), *n.* dance in which partners face each other in two long lines.

coun·try·man (kun′tri·mən), *n., pl.* -men. 1. man of one's own country. 2. man who lives in the country.

coun·try·seat (kun′tri·sēt′), *n.* residence or estate in the country.

coun·try·side (kun′tri·sīd′), *n.* 1. rural district; country. 2. certain section of the country. 3. its people.

coun·try·wom·an (kun′tri·wùm′ən), *n., pl.* -wom·en. 1. woman of one's own country. 2. woman living in the country.

coun·ty (koun′ti), *n., pl.* -ties. 1. *Am.* in the United States, the political unit next below the State. 2. one of the chief districts into which a state or country, as Great Britain and Ireland, is divided. 3. people of a county. [< AF *counté* < *counte* COUNT²]

county seat, *Am.* town or city where the county government is located.

coup (kü), *n., pl.* **coups** (küz). a sudden, brilliant action. [< F < L < Gk. *kolaphos*]

coup de grâce (kü′ də gräs′), 1. action that gives a merciful death to a suffering animal or person. 2. the finishing stroke. [< F, lit., stroke of grace]

coup d'é·tat (kü′ dā·tä′), a sudden and decisive measure in politics, esp. one affecting a change of government illegally or by force. [< F, lit., stroke of state]

cou·pé (kü·pā′; *for 1, also* küp), *n.* 1. a closed, two-door automobile seating two to five people. 2. a closed carriage with a seat for the driver outside. [< F, pp. of *couper* cut. See COUP.]

cou·ple (kup′əl), *n., v.,* -pled, -pling. —*n.* 1. two things of the same kind that go together; pair. 2. man and woman who are married, engaged, or partners in a dance. —*v.* join together; join together in pairs. [< OF *cople* < L *copula* bond. Doublet of COPULA.] —**cou′pler,** *n.* —**Syn.** *n.* 1. mates. —*v.* unite.

cou·plet (kup′lit), *n.* 1. two successive lines of poetry, esp. two that rhyme and are equally long. 2. couple; pair.

cou·pling (kup′ling), *n.* 1. act or process of joining together. 2. device for joining together parts of machinery. 3. device used to join together two railroad cars. 4. *Elect.* device or arrangement for transferring electrical energy from one circuit to another.

cou·pon (kü′pon; kū′-), *n.* 1. a printed statement of interest due on a bond, which can be cut from the bond and presented for payment. 2. part of a ticket, advertisement, ration book, etc., that gives the person who holds it certain rights. [< F, < *couper* cut. See COUP.]

cour·age (kėr′ij), *n.* bravery; fearlessness. [< OF *corage* < *cuer* heart < L *cor*] —**Syn.** valor, pluck, heroism, daring.

cou·ra·geous (kə·rā′jəs), *adj.* full of courage; brave; fearless. —**cou·ra′geous·ly,** *adv.* —**cou·ra′geous·ness,** *n.*

cour·i·er (kėr′i·ər; kùr′-), *n.* 1. messenger sent in haste. 2. person who goes with travelers and takes care of hotel reservations, tickets, etc. [< F *courrier* < Ital. < L *currere* run]

course (kōrs; kôrs), *n., v.,* coursed, cours·ing. —*n.* 1. onward movement. 2. direction taken. 3. line of action; way of doing. 4. way; path; track; channel. 5. group of similar things arranged in some regular order. 6. regular order. 7. series of studies in a school, college, or university. 8. one of the studies. 9. part of a meal served at one time. **10.** place for races or games. **11.** layer of bricks, stones, shingles, etc.; row. **12.** in due course, at the proper or usual time; after a while. **13.** in the course of, during; in the process of. **14.** of course, a. surely; certainly. **b.** naturally; as should be expected. —*v.* **1.** race; run. **2.** hunt with dogs. **3.** cause (dogs) to pursue game. [< F *cours* < L *cursus*, a running and < F *course* < Ital. *corsa* a running < L *currere* run] —**Syn.** *n.* **1.** progress, career. **3.** process, method, manner, mode, procedure. **4.** road, passage. **6.** sequence, succession.

cours·er (kôr′sər; kōr′-), *n. Poetic.* a swift horse.

court (kôrt; kōrt), *n.* **1.** space partly or wholly enclosed by walls or buildings. **2.** a short street. **3.** area marked off for a game, as for tennis. **4.** one of the divisions of such an area. **5.** building or buildings surrounded by a clear space; a stately dwelling. **6.** residence where a king, queen, or other sovereign lives; royal palace. **7.** family, household, or followers of a sovereign. **8.** sovereign and his advisers as a ruling power. **9.** a formal assembly held by a sovereign. **10.** *Law.* **a.** place where justice is administered. **b.** persons who are chosen to administer justice; judge or judges. **c.** assembly of such persons to administer justice. **11.** attention paid to get favor; effort to please. **12.** act of making love; act of wooing. —*v.* **1.** pay attention to (a person) to get his favor; try to please. **2.** make love to; woo. **3.** try to get; act so as to get; seek: *court danger.* [< OF < L *cohors* enclosure, retinue. Doublet of COHORT.] —**Syn.** *n.* **1.** yard. –*v.* **3.** invite, solicit.

cour·te·ous (kér′ti·əs), *adj.* polite; thoughtful of others. [< OF *corteis* < *cort* COURT] —**cour′te·ous·ly,** *adv.* —**cour′te·ous·ness,** *n.* —**Syn.** civil, attentive.

cour·te·san, cour·te·zan (kôr′tə·zən; kōr′-; kér′-), *n.* a prostitute. [< F < Ital. *cortigiana* woman of the court < *corte* COURT]

cour·te·sy (kér′tə·si), *n., pl.* -**sies.** **1.** polite behavior; thoughtfulness for others. **2.** polite act; thoughtful act; favor. **3.** curtsy. [< OF *cortesie* < *corteis* COURTEOUS] —**Syn.** **1.** politeness, civility.

court·house (kôrt′hous′; kōrt′-), *n.* **1.** a building where law courts are held. **2.** *Am.* a building used for the government of a county.

cour·ti·er (kôr′ti·ər; kōr′-), *n.* **1.** person often present at the court of a king, prince, etc. **2.** person who tries to win the favor of another.

court·ly (kôrt′li; kōrt′-), *adj.,* -**li·er,** -**li·est.** **1.** suitable for a king's court; elegant. **2.** trying hard to please one's superior; flattering. —**court′li·ness,** *n.*

court-mar·tial (kôrt′mär′shəl; kōrt′-), *n., pl.* **courts-mar·tial,** *v.,* -**tialed,** -**tial·ing;** *esp. Brit.* -**tialled,** -**tial·ling.** —*n.* **1.** court of army or navy officers for trying offenders against military or naval laws. **2.** trial by such a court. —*v.* try by such a court.

Court of St. James's, court of the British sovereign.

court·room (kôrt′rüm′; -rům′; kōrt′-), *n.* room where a law court is held.

court·ship (kôrt′ship; kōrt′-), *n.* making love; wooing.

court·yard (kôrt′yärd′; kōrt′-), *n.* space enclosed by walls, in or near a large building.

cous·in (kuz′ən), *n.* **1.** son or daughter of one's uncle or aunt. **2.** a distant relative. **3.** term used by one sovereign in speaking to another sovereign or to a great nobleman. [< F < L *consobrinus* mother's sister's child < *com-* together + *soror* sister] —**cous′in·ly,** *adj., adv.* —**cous′in·ship,** *n.*

cous·in-ger·man (kuz′ən·jér′mən), *n., pl.* **cous·ins-ger·man.** son or daughter of one's uncle or aunt; first cousin.

cou·tu·ri·er (kü·tür′i·ər; *Fr.* kü·ty·ryā′), *n.* a man dressmaker. [< F]

cove (kōv), *n., v.,* **coved, cov·ing.** —*n.* **1.** a small, sheltered bay; inlet on the shore. **2.** sheltered nook. —*v.* arch; arch over. [OE *cofa* chamber]

COVE

cov·e·nant (kuv′ə·nənt), *n.* **1.** a solemn agreement between two or more persons or groups to do or not to do a certain thing; compact. **2.** in the Bible, the solemn promises of God to man. **3.** *Law.* a legal contract; formal agreement that is legal. —*v.* solemnly agree. [< OF, < *covenir* < L *convenire*. See CONVENE.] —**cov′e·nant·er,** *n.*

Cov·en·try (kuv′ən·tri; kov′-), *n.* city in C England.

cov·er (kuv′ər), *v.* **1.** put something over. **2.** be over; occupy the surface of; spread over. **3.** clothe; wrap up. **4.** be thick over. **5.** hide; conceal. **6.** protect; shelter. **7.** go over; travel. **8.** include; make up. **9.** be enough for; provide for. **10.** aim straight at. **11.** have within range. **12.** put one's hat or cap on. **13.** *Am.* act as a reporter or photographer of: *to cover a fire for a newspaper.* **14.** deposit the equivalent of (money deposited in betting); accept the conditions of (a bet). **15.** *Am.* buy (commodities, securities, etc.) for future delivery as a protection against loss. **16.** brood or sit on (eggs or chicks). —*n.* **1.** thing that covers. **2.** protection; shelter. **3.** place for one person at a table, set with a plate, knife, fork, spoon, napkin, etc. **4.** break cover, come out in the open. **5.** under cover, a. hidden; secret; disguised. **b.** secretly. [< OF < L, < *co-* up + *operire* cover] —**cov′er·er,** *n.* —**cov′er·less,** *adj.* —**Syn.** *v.* **3.** envelop. **5.** screen, cloak, shroud. –*n.* **1.** lid, top, case, envelope, wrapping. **2.** refuge, retreat.

cov·er·age (kuv′ər·ij), *n.* **1.** amount covered by something. **2.** *Am.* risks covered by an insurance policy.

cover charge, *Am.* in some restaurants, a charge made for service, music, etc.

covered wagon, *Am.* a wagon having a removable canvas cover.

cov·er·ing (kuv′ər·ing), *n.* thing that covers.

cov·er·let (kuv′ər·lit), **cov·er·lid** (–lid), *n.* **1.** an outer covering for a bed; bedspread. **2.** any covering.

cov·ert (kuv′ərt; *for 4* kō′vərt, kuv′ərt), *adj.* **1.** covered; sheltered. **2.** secret; hidden; disguised: *covert glances.* —*n.* **1.** shelter; hiding place. **2.** thicket in which animals hide. **3.** coverts, the smaller and weaker feathers that cover the bases of the large feathers of a bird's wings and tail. **4.** covert cloth. [< OF, pp. of *covrir* COVER] —**cov′ert·ly,** *adv.* —**cov′ert·ness,** *n.*

co·vert cloth (kō′vərt; kuv′ərt), cloth, of wool, silk and wool, or rayon, usually brownish, used for coats.

cov·et (kuv′it), *v.* desire eagerly (esp. something that belongs to another). [< OF *covetier*, ult. < L *cupere* desire] —**cov′et·a·ble,** *adj.* —**cov′et·er,** *n.*

cov·et·ous (kuv′ə·təs), *adj.* overly desirous (esp. of things that belong to others). —**cov′et·ous·ly,** *adv.* —**cov′et·ous·ness,** *n.* —**Syn.** greedy, avaricious.

cov·ey (kuv′i), *n., pl.* -**eys.** **1.** brood of partridges, quail, etc. **2.** small flock; group. [< OF, < *cover* incubate < L *cubare* lie]

cow[1] (kou), *n., pl.* **cows,** (*Archaic* or *Dial.*) **kine** (kīn). **1.** female of a bovine family, esp. of the domestic species that furnishes milk. **2.** female of various other large animals: *an elephant cow.* [OE *cū*]

cow[2] (kou), *v.* make afraid; frighten. [< Scand. *kūga*] —**Syn.** scare, bully.

cow·ard (kou′ərd), *n.* person who lacks courage or is afraid. —*adj.* **1.** lacking courage; cowardly. **2.** showing fear. [< OF *coart* < *coe* tail < L *cauda*]

cow·ard·ice (kou′ər·dis), *n.* lack of courage; being easily made afraid.

cow·ard·ly (kou′ərd·li), *adj.* **1.** lacking courage. **2.** of a coward. —*adv.* fit for a coward. —**cow′ard·li·ness,** *n.*

cow·boy (kou′boi′), *n. Am.* man who looks after cattle on a ranch and rides horseback to do most of his work.

cow·catch·er (kou′kach′ər), *n. Am.* a metal frame on the front of a locomotive, streetcar, etc., for clearing the tracks.

cow·er (kou′ər), *v.* **1.** crouch in fear or shame.

2. draw back tremblingly from another's threats, blows, etc. [< Scand. *kūra* sit moping]

cow·girl (kou′gėrl′), *n. Am.* woman who works on a ranch, at rodeos, etc.

cow hand, *Am.* person who works on a cattle ranch.

cow·herd (kou′hėrd′), *n.* person whose work is looking after cattle.

cow·hide (kou′hīd′), *n., v.,* –hid·ed, –hid·ing. —*n.* 1. hide of a cow. 2. leather made from it. 3. *Am.* strong leather whip. —*v. Am.* whip with a cowhide; flog.

cowl (koul), *n.* 1. a monk's cloak with a hood. 2. the hood itself. 3. anything shaped like a cowl. 4. the narrow part of an automobile body that includes the windshield and the dashboard. 5. metal covering over an airplane engine. 6. a covering for the top of a chimney to increase the draft. —*v.* 1. put a monk's cowl on. 2. cover with a cowl or something resembling a cowl. [< LL *cuculla,* var. of L *cucullus* hood] —**cowled** (kould), *adj.*

Cowl

cow·lick (kou′lik′), *n.* a small tuft of hair that will not lie flat.

cowl·ing (kou′ling), *n.* metal covering over the engine of an airplane.

cow·man (kou′mən), *n., pl.* –men. *Am.* an owner of cattle; ranchman.

co·work·er (kō·wér′kər), *n.* person who works with another.

cow·pea (kou′pē′), *n. Am.* 1. plant that has very long pods, used as food for cattle, fertilizer, etc. 2. seed of this plant.

cow·pox (kou′poks′), *n.* disease of cows causing small pustules on cows' udders. Vaccine for smallpox is obtained from cows that have cowpox.

cow·punch·er (kou′pun′chər), *n. Am., Colloq.* cowboy.

cow·rie, cow·ry (kou′rĭ), *n., pl.* –ries. a yellow shell used as money in some parts of Africa and Asia. [< Hind. *kaurī*]

cow·slip (kou′slip′), *n.* 1. *Am.* a wild plant with yellow flowers; marsh marigold. 2. an English primrose. [OE, < *cū* cow + *slyppe* slime]

cox (koks), *n. Colloq.* coxswain.

cox·comb (koks′kōm′), *n.* 1. a vain, empty-headed man; conceited dandy. 2. *Bot.* cockscomb. 3. a cap resembling a cock's comb, worn by clowns or jesters. [var. of *cock's comb*]

cox·swain (kok′sən; –swān′), *n.* person who steers a boat, racing shell, etc. Also, **cockswain.**

coy (koi), *adj.* 1. shy; modest; bashful. 2. pretending to be shy. [< F *coi* < L *quietus* at rest. Doublet of QUIET[1] and QUIT, *adj.*] —**coy′ly,** *adv.* —**coy′ness,** *n.*

coy·o·te (kī·ō′tē; kī′ōt), *n., pl.* –tes *or* (esp. *collectively*) –te. *Am.* a prairie wolf of W North America. [< Mex.Sp. < Nahuatl *koyotl*]

coy·pu (koi′pū), *n., pl.* –pus *or* (esp. *collectively*) –pu. a large ratlike water animal of South America. Its fur is called nutria. [< Sp. < Araucanian (S Am. Ind. linguistic stock) *koypu*]

coz·en (kuz′ən), *v.* cheat. —**coz′en·er,** *n.*

co·zy (kō′zĭ), *adj.,* co·zi·er, co·zi·est, *n., pl.* co·zies. —*adj.* warm and comfortable; snug. —*n.* padded cloth cover to keep a teapot warm. Also, **cosy.** [< Scand. (Norw.) *koselig*] —**co′zi·ly,** *adv.* —**co′zi·ness,** *n.*

cp., 1. compare. 2. coupon.

C.P.A., *Am.* Certified Public Accountant.

Cpl., cpl., Corporal.

Cr, *Chem.* chromium.

cr., credit; creditor.

crab[1] (krab), *n., v.,* crabbed, crab·bing. —*n.* 1. a shellfish that has a short, broad body with the abdomen or tail folded under, four pairs of legs, and one pair of pincers. 2. machine for raising heavy weights. 3. a cross, ill-natured person. 4. Crab, Cancer, a constellation of the zodiac. —*v.* catch crabs for eating. [OE *crabba*] —**crab′ber,** *n.*

crab[2] (krab), *n.* crab apple.

crab[3] (krab), *v.,* crabbed, crab·bing. *Colloq.* find fault (with); criticize. [cf. MDu. *krabben* scratch, quarrel]

crab apple, 1. any of various small, very sour apples, used for making jelly. 2. tree that bears crab apples.

crab·bed (krab′id), *adj.* 1. Also, crab′by. peevish; ill-natured; cross. 2. hard to understand. 3. hard to read or decipher. [< *crab*[1]]

crab grass, *Am.* a coarse grass that spreads rapidly and spoils lawns, etc.

crack (krak), *n.* 1. place, line, surface, or opening made by breaking without separating into parts. 2. a sudden, sharp noise, as of a whip. 3. *Colloq.* blow that makes a sudden, sharp noise. 4. a narrow opening. 5. instant; moment. 6. *Slang.* try; effort. 7. *Am., Slang.* joke. —*v.* 1. break without separating into parts. 2. break with a sudden, sharp noise. 3. make or cause to make a sudden, sharp noise. 4. *Colloq.* hit with a sudden, sharp noise. 5. make or become harsh and shrill: *his voice cracked.* 6. *Slang.* give way; break down. 7. tell (a joke, etc.). 8. break into: *crack a safe.* 9. **crack down,** *Am., Slang.* take stern measures. 10. **crack up, a.** suffer a mental collapse. **b.** crash; go to pieces. **c.** *Colloq.* praise. [OE *cracian*] —Syn. *n.* 1. cleft, fissure, crevice. 2. clap, report. 4. chink. —*v.* 1. split, fracture. 3. snap, pop.

crack-brained (krak′brānd′), *adj.* crazy; insane.

crack-down (krak′doun′), *n. Am.* taking sudden and stern measures to end a practice, activity, etc.

cracked (krakt), *adj.* 1. broken without separating into parts. 2. harsh and shrill. 3. *Colloq.* crazy; insane.

crack·er (krak′ər), *n.* 1. a thin, crisp biscuit. 2. firecracker. 3. a small, paper roll used as a party favor, containing candy, a motto, a paper cap, etc. It explodes when it is pulled at both ends. 4. *Am.* a poor white person living in the hills and backwoods regions of Georgia, Florida, etc. 5. person or instrument that cracks.

crack·er·jack (krak′ər·jak′), *Am.* —*n.* 1. *Colloq.* person or thing especially fine of its kind. 2. Crackerjack, *Trademark.* a kind of candied popcorn. —*adj. Colloq.* of superior ability or quality.

crack·ing (krak′ing), *n.* process of changing certain hydrocarbons in petroleum and other oils into lighter hydrocarbons by heat and pressure.

crack·le (krak′əl), *v.,* –led, –ling, *n.* —*v.* make slight, sharp sounds. —*n.* 1. a slight, sharp sound, such as paper makes when crushed. 2. surface containing very small cracks on some kinds of china, glass, etc. [< *crack*]

crack·ling (krak′ling), *n.* 1. the crisp, browned skin of roasted pork. 2. Usually, crack·lings. *Dial.* crisp part left after lard has been fried out of hog's fat.

crack-up (krak′up′), *n.* 1. crash; smash. 2. *Colloq.* a mental or physical collapse.

Cra·cow (krak′ou; krä′kō), *n.* city in S Poland.

cra·dle (krā′dəl), *n., v.,* –dled, –dling. —*n.* 1. a baby's little bed, usually on rockers. 2. place where a thing begins its growth. 3. frame to support a ship, aircraft, or other large object while it is being built, repaired, lifted, etc. 4. *Am.* box on rockers to wash gold from earth. 5. frame attached to a scythe for laying grain evenly as it is cut. —*v.* 1. put or rock in a cradle; hold as in a cradle. 2. shelter or train in early life. 3. support in a cradle. 4. *Am.* wash in a cradle. 5. cut with a cradle scythe. [OE *cradol*]

craft (kraft; kräft), *n.* 1. special skill. 2. trade or work requiring special skill. 3. members of a trade requiring special skill. Carpenters are a craft. 4. skill in deceiving others; slyness; trickiness. 5. (*pl. in use*) boats, ships, or aircraft. 6. a boat, ship, or aircraft. [OE *cræft*] —Syn. 4. cunning, guile, wile.

crafts·man (krafts′mən; kräfts′–), *n., pl.* –men. 1. a skilled workman. 2. artist. —**crafts′-man·ship,** *n.*

craft·y (kraf′ti; kräf′–), *adj.*, **craft·i·er, craft·i·est.** skillful in deceiving others; sly; tricky. —**craft′i·ly,** *adv.* —**craft′i·ness,** *n.* —**Syn.** cunning.

crag (krag), *n.* a steep, rugged rock rising above others. [< Celtic] —**crag′gy, crag·ged** (krag′id), *adj.* —**crag′gi·ness,** *n.*

cram (kram), *v.*, **crammed, cram·ming. 1.** force; stuff. **2.** fill too full. **3.** eat too fast or too much. **4.** *Colloq.* stuff with knowledge or information, esp. for an examination. **5.** *Slang.* tell lies or exaggerated stories to. **6.** *Colloq.* learn hurriedly. [OE *crammian* < *crimman* insert] —**cram′mer,** *n.*

cramp¹ (kramp), *n.* **1.** a metal bar bent at both ends, used for holding together blocks of stone, timbers, etc. **2.** clamp. **3.** something that confines or hinders; limitation; restriction. —*v.* **1.** fasten together with a cramp. **2.** confine in a small space; limit; restrict. —*adj.* **1.** confined; limited; restricted. **2.** hard to read; difficult to understand. [< MDu. *cramp(e)*, MLG *krampe*]

cramp² (kramp), *n.* **1.** a sudden, painful contracting of muscles from chill, strain, etc. **2.** a paralytic affection of particular muscles. **3.** cramps, very sharp pains in the abdomen. —*v.* cause to have a cramp. [< MDu. See CRAMP¹.]

cran·ber·ry (kran′ber′i; –bər·i), *n.*, *pl.* **–ries.** *Am.* **1.** a firm, sour, dark-red berry, used for jelly, sauce, etc. **2.** a small shrub that the berries grow on. [< LG *kraanbere*]

crane (krān), *n.*, *v.*, **craned, cran·ing.** —*n.* **1.** machine with a long, swinging arm, for lifting and moving heavy weights. **2.** a swinging metal arm in a fireplace, used to hold a kettle over the fire. **3.** a large wading bird with very long legs and a long neck. **4.** any of various herons, esp. the great blue heron. —*v.* **1.** move by, or as if by, a crane. **2.** stretch out (one's neck). [OE *cran*]

crane fly, any of several insects which have long legs; the daddy-longlegs of Great Britain.

cra·ni·ol·o·gy (krā′ni·ol′ə·ji), *n.* science that deals with the size, shape, and other characteristics of skulls. —**cra·ni·o·log·i·cal** (krā′ni·ə·loj′ə·kəl), *adj.* —**cra′ni·o·log′i·cal·ly,** *adv.* —**cra′ni·ol′o·gist,** *n.*

cra·ni·om·e·try (krā′ni·om′ə·tri), *n.* science of measuring skulls; measurement of skulls. —**cra·ni·o·met·ric** (krā′ni·ə·met′rik), *adj.* —**cra′ni·o·met′ri·cal·ly,** *adv.* —**cra′ni·om′e·trist,** *n.*

cra·ni·um (krā′ni·əm), *n.*, *pl.* **–ni·ums, –ni·a** (–ni·ə). the skull. [< LL < Gk. *kranion*] —**cra′ni·al,** *adj.*

crank (krangk), *n.* **1.** part or handle of a machine connected at right angles to another part to transmit motion. **2.** turn of speech or thought. **3.** a queer notion or act. **4.** *Am.*, *Colloq.* person with queer notions or habits. **5.** *Colloq.* a cross or ill-tempered person. —*v.* **1.** work or start by means of a crank. **2.** bend into the shape of a crank. [OE *cranc*]

crank·case (krangk′kās′), *n.* a heavy, metal case enclosing the crankshaft, connecting rods, etc., of an internal-combustion engine.

crank·shaft (krangk′shaft′; –shäft′), *n.* shaft turned by cranks operated by the movement of the pistons in a gasoline engine.

crank·y (krang′ki), *adj.*, **crank·i·er, crank·i·est. 1.** cross; irritable; ill-natured. **2.** odd; queer. **3.** liable to capsize; loose; shaky. —**crank′i·ly,** *adv.* —**crank′i·ness,** *n.*

cran·ny (kran′i), *n.*, *pl.* **–nies.** a small, narrow opening; crack; crevice. [< F *cran* fissure < Med.L *crena* notch] —**cran′nied,** *adj.*

crape (krāp), *n.* crepe.

crap·pie (krap′i), *n.* *Am.* a small fresh-water fish, used for food.

craps (kraps), *n.* *Am.* a gambling game played with two dice.

crap·shoot·er (krap′shüt′ər), *n.* *Am.* person who plays craps.

crash¹ (krash), *n.* **1.** a sudden, loud noise. **2.** a falling, hitting, or breaking with force and a loud noise. **3.** sudden ruin; severe failure in business. **4.** of an airplane, a fall to the earth or a bad

landing. —*v.* **1.** make a sudden, loud noise. **2.** fall, hit, or break with force and a loud noise. **3.** move or go with force and a loud noise. **4.** be suddenly ruined; fail in business. **5.** land in such a way as to damage or wreck an aircraft; make a very bad landing. **6.** cause (an aircraft) to land in such a way. **7.** *Am.*, *Slang.* go to (a party, etc.) although not invited. —*adj.* of or naming something which protects from a crash or is used to rescue persons involved in a crash: *a crash boat.* [blend of *craze* shatter and *mash*] —**crash′er,** *n.* —**Syn.** *n.* **2.** smash. **3.** collapse, bankruptcy. —*v.* **2.** smash.

crash² (krash), *n.* a coarse linen cloth, used for towels, curtains, upholstering, etc. [prob. < Russ.; cf. Russ. *krashenina* colored linen]

crash program, plan of action involving maximum effort and speed.

crass (kras), *adj.* **1.** gross; stupid. **2.** thick; coarse. [< L *crassus* thick] —**crass′ly,** *adv.* —**crass′ness,** *n.*

crate (krāt), *n.*, *v.*, **crat·ed, crat·ing.** —*n.* a large frame, box, basket, etc., used to pack glass, fruit, etc., for shipping or storage. —*v.* *Am.* pack in a crate. [< L *cratis* wickerwork] —**crat′er,** *n.*

cra·ter (krā′tər), *n.* **1.** depression around the opening of a volcano. **2.** a bowl-shaped hole. [< L < Gk. *krater* bowl < *kra–* mix]

cra·vat (krə·vat′), *n.* **1.** necktie. **2.** neckcloth; scarf. [< F *cravate*, special use of *Cravate* Croat]

crave (krāv), *v.*, **craved, crav·ing. 1.** long for; yearn for; desire strongly. **2.** ask earnestly; beg. [OE *crafian* demand]

cra·ven (krā′vən), *adj.* cowardly. —*n.* coward. —**cra′ven·ly,** *adv.* —**cra′ven·ness,** *n.*

crav·ing (krā′ving), *n.* strong desire; longing.

craw (krô), *n.* **1.** crop of a bird or insect. **2.** stomach of any animal. [ME *crawe*]

craw·fish (krô′fish′), *n.*, *pl.* **–fish·es** or (*esp. collectively*) **–fish,** *v.* *Am.* —*n.* Also, *esp. Brit.* crayfish). any of numerous crustaceans much like small lobsters. —*v.* *Colloq.* back out of something; retreat. [var. of *crayfish*]

crawl (krôl), *v.* **1.** move slowly, pulling the body along the ground: *worms and snakes crawl.* **2.** move slowly on hands and knees. **3.** move slowly. **4.** swarm with crawling things. **5.** feel creepy. —*n.* **1.** a crawling; slow movement. **2.** a fast way of swimming by overarm strokes. [appar. < Scand. (Dan.) *kravle*]—**crawl′er,** *n.* —**crawl′ing·ly,** *adv.*

Crawfish (3 to 6 in. long)

crawl·y (krôl′i), *adj.* *Colloq.* creepy.

cray·fish (krā′fish′), *n.*, *pl.* **–fish·es** or (*esp. collectively*) **–fish.** *Esp. Brit.* crawfish. [< OF *crevice* < Gmc.; akin to CRAB¹]

cray·on (krā′on; –ən), *n.*, *v.*, **–oned, –on·ing.** —*n.* **1.** stick of white or colored chalk or wax or charcoal used for drawing or writing. **2.** drawing made with crayons. —*v.* draw with a crayon or crayons. [< F, < *craie* chalk < L *creta*]

craze (krāz), *n.*, *v.*, **crazed, craz·ing.** —*n.* **1.** something everybody is very much interested in for a short time; fad. **2.** a tiny crack in the glaze of pottery, etc. —*v.* **1.** make or become crazy. **2.** make tiny cracks all over the surface of (a dish, etc.). **3.** become minutely cracked. [appar. < Scand. (Sw.) *krasa* break in pieces] —**crazed,** *adj.*

cra·zy (krā′zi), *adj.*, **–zi·er, –zi·est. 1.** having a diseased mind; insane. **2.** showing insanity. **3.** *Colloq.* unreasonably eager or enthusiastic. **4.** not strong or sound; frail. —**cra′zi·ly,** *adv.* —**cra′zi·ness,** *n.* —**Syn.** **1.** mad, lunatic. —**Ant.** **1.** sane.

crazy quilt, *Am.* patchwork quilt.

creak (krēk), *v.* squeak loudly. —*n.* a creaking noise. [ME *creken* < OE *crœcettan* croak]

creak·y (krēk′i), *adj.*, **creak·i·er, creak·i·est.** likely to creak; creaking. —**creak′i·ly,** *adv.* —**creak′i·ness,** *n.*

cream (krēm), *n.* **1.** the oily, yellowish part of milk. **2.** food made of cream; food like cream. **3.** an oily preparation put on the skin to make it smooth and soft. **4.** a yellowish white. **5.** the best part. —*v.* **1.** put cream in. **2.** take cream from. **3.** form like cream on the top; foam; froth. **4.** cook with cream. **5.** make into a smooth mix-

ture like cream. —*adj.* **1.** containing cream:
cream soup. **2.** yellowish-white. [< OF *cresme* <
LL *crama* cream < Gaulish, and < Eccl.L *chrisma*
ointment < Gk., < *chriein* anoint]

cream cheese, a soft, bland, white cheese.

cream·er (krēm′ər), *n.* **1.** *Am.* a small pitcher.
2. apparatus for separating cream from milk.

cream·er·y (krēm′ər·i), *n.,* *pl.* -er·ies. **1.** *Am.*
place where butter and cheese are made. **2.** place
where cream, milk, and butter are sold or bought.

cream of tartar, a very sour, white powder,
KHC₄H₄O₆, used in cooking and in medicine.

crease[1] (krēs), *n.,* *v.,* **creased, creas·ing.** —*n.*
line or mark made by folding; fold; wrinkle. —*v.*
1. make a crease or creases in. **2.** become creased.
—**creas′er,** *n.*

crease[2] (krēs), *n.* creese.

cre·ate (krē·āt′), *v.,* -at·ed, -at·ing. **1.** cause to
be; bring into being; make. **2.** make by giving
a new character, function, or status to. **3.** be the
first to represent (a role in a play, or the like).
4. give rise to; cause. [< L, < *creare*] —Syn. **1.**
originate, produce, invent. **4.** occasion.

cre·a·tion (krē·ā′shən), *n.* **1.** a creating or being created. **2.** all things created; the universe.
3. thing created. **4.** an artistic product. **5.** the
Creation, the creating of the universe by God.
—**cre·a′tion·al,** *adj.*

cre·a·tive (krē·ā′tiv), *adj.* having the power to
create; inventive; productive. —**cre·a′tive·ly,**
adv. —**cre·a′tive·ness,** *n.*

cre·a·tor (krē·ā′tər), *n.* **1.** person who creates.
2. the Creator, God. —**cre·a′tor·ship,** *n.*

cre·a·ture (krē′chər), *n.* **1.** a living being. **2.** a
farm animal. **3.** person who is completely under
the influence of another. **4.** result; product. [< L
creatura. See CREATE.]

crèche (kresh; krâsh), *n.* **1.** place where children are taken care of while their mothers are
at work. **2.** model of the Christ child in the manger with attendant figures, often displayed at
Christmas.

cre·dence (krē′dəns), *n.* belief. [< Med.L, < L
credere believe]

cre·den·tial (kri·den′shəl), *n.* **1.** that which
gives a title to credit or confidence. **2.** Usually,
credentials. letters of introduction; references.

cred·i·ble (kred′ə·bəl), *adj.* believable; reliable;
trustworthy. [< L, < *credere* believe] —**cred′i-
bil′i·ty, cred′i·ble·ness,** *n.* —**cred′i·bly,** *adv.*

cred·it (kred′it), *n.* **1.** belief; faith; trust. **2.**
trust in a person's ability and intention to pay. **3.**
money in a person's bank account, etc. **4.** entry
of money paid on account. **5.** the right-hand side
of an account where such entries are made. **6.**
delayed payment; time allowed for delayed payment. **7.** *Am.* unit of academic work counting toward graduation. **8.** reputation in money matters.
9. good reputation. **10.** honor; praise. **11.** person
or thing that brings honor or praise. —*v.* **1.** believe; have faith in; trust. **2.** give credit in a bank
account, etc. **3.** enter on the credit side of an account. **4.** put an academic credit on the record of.
[< F < Ital. < L *creditum* a loan < *credere* trust,
entrust] —Syn. *n.* **9.** repute, standing.

cred·it·a·ble (kred′it·ə·bəl), *adj.* bringing
honor or praise. —**cred′it·a·ble·ness, cred′it·a-
bil′i·ty,** *n.* —**cred′it·a·bly,** *adv.*

cred·i·tor (kred′i·tər), *n.* **1.** person who gives
credit. **2.** person to whom a debt is owed.

cre·do (krē′dō; krā′dō), *n.,* *pl.* -dos. creed. [<
L, I believe]

cre·du·li·ty (krə·dü′lə·ti; -dū′-), *n.* a too
great readiness to believe.

cred·u·lous (krej′ə·ləs), *adj.* **1.** too ready to
believe; easily deceived. **2.** characterized by credulity. **3.** caused by credulity. —**cred′u·lous·ly,**
adv. —**cred′u·lous·ness,** *n.*

creed (krēd), *n.* **1.** a brief statement of the essential points of religious belief as approved by
some church. **2.** any statement of faith, principles, opinions, etc. [< L *credo* I believe]

creek (krēk; krik), *n.* **1.** *Am.* a small stream. **2.**
Esp. Brit. a narrow bay, running inland. [appar.
< MDu. *crēke,* and/or Scand. *kriki* nook]

creel (krēl), *n.* basket for holding fish. [? < F
creil, ult. < L *cratis* wickerwork]

creep (krēp), *v.,* **crept, creep·ing,** *n.* —*v.* **1.**
move with the body close to the ground or floor.
2. move slowly. **3.** grow along the ground or over
a wall by means of clinging stems, as ivy. **4.** feel
as if things were creeping over the skin. **5.** move
in a timid, stealthy, or servile manner. **6.** slip
slightly out of place. —*n.* **1.** a creeping. **2.** the
creeps, Colloq. a feeling as if things were creeping over one's skin. [OE *crēopan*]

creep·er (krēp′ər), *n.* **1.** person or thing that
creeps. **2.** Bot. any plant that grows along a
surface, sending out rootlets from the stem. **3.**
creepers, garment combining waist and pants,
worn by babies.

creep·ie-peep·ie (krēp′i·pēp′i), *n.* a portable
television camera weighing about four pounds. It
is powered by batteries. [< *creep* + *peep*[1],
modeled on *walkie-talkie*]

creep·y (krēp′i), *adj.,* creep·i·er, creep·i·est. **1.**
having a feeling as if things were creeping over
one's skin; frightened. **2.** causing such a feeling.

creese (krēs), *n.* dagger with a wavy blade, used
by the Malays. Also, **crease, kris.** [< Malay *kris*]

cre·mate (krē′māt; kri·māt′), *v.,* -mat·ed,
-mat·ing. burn (a dead body) to ashes. [< L,
cremare burn] —**cre·ma′tion,** *n.* —**cre·ma′tor,** *n.*

cre·ma·to·ry (krē′mə·tô′ri; -tō′-; krem′ə-),
n., *pl.* -ries, *adj.* —*n.* **1.** furnace for cremating. **2.**
building that has a furnace for cremating. —*adj.*
of or having to do with cremating.

cre·nate (krē′nāt), *adj.* with a scalloped edge.
[< NL, < Med.L *crena* notch] —**cre′nate·ly,** *adv.*

cren·el·ate, esp. Brit. cren·el·late (kren′əl-
āt), *v.,* -at·ed, -at·ing; *esp. Brit.* -lat·ed, -lat-
ing. furnish with battlements. [< F *créneler*
< *crenel* notch, ult. < Med.L *crena*]

Cre·ole (krē′ōl), *n.* **1.** *Am.* a white person who is
a descendant of the French who settled in Louisiana. **2.** a French or Spanish person born in
Spanish America or the West Indies. —*adj.* of
or having to do with the Creoles. [< F < Sp.
< Pg. *crioulo* < *criar* bring up < L *creare* create]

cre·o·sote (krē′ə·sōt), *n.,* *v.,* -sot·ed, -sot·ing.
—*n.* **1.** an oily liquid with a penetrating odor, obtained by distilling wood tar, used as a preservative, etc. **2.** a similar substance obtained
from coal tar. —*v.* treat with creosote. [orig.,
meat preservative; < Gk. *kreo-* (for *kreas* flesh)
+ *soter* savior < *sozein* save]

crepe, crêpe (krāp), *n.* **1.** a thin silk, cotton,
rayon, or woolen cloth with a crinkled surface.
2. Also, **crepe paper.** tissue paper that looks like
crepe. **3.** piece of black crepe worn as a sign of
mourning. Also, **crape.** [< F < L *crispa* curled]

crep·i·tate (krep′ə·tāt), *v.,* -tat·ed, -tat·ing.
crackle; rattle. [< L, < *crepitare* crackle <
crepare crack] —**crep′i·ta′tion,** *n.*

crept (krept), *v.* pt. and pp. of creep.

cre·pus·cu·lar (kri·pus′kyə·lər), *adj.* **1.** of
twilight; resembling twilight; dim; indistinct. **2.**
Zool. appearing or flying by twilight. [< L *cre-
pusculum* twilight]

cre·scen·do (krə·shen′dō), *n.,* *pl.* -dos, *adj.,*
adv. —*n.* a gradual increase in force or loudness.
—*adj., adv.* gradually increasing in force or loudness. [< Ital., ppr. of *crescere* increase < L]

cres·cent (kres′ənt), *n.* **1.** shape of the moon in
its first or last quarter. **2.** anything having this
or a similar shape. —*adj.* **1.** shaped like the moon
in its first or last quarter. **2.** growing; increasing.
[< L, ppr. of *crescere* grow]

cre·sol (krē′sōl; -sol), *n.* oily liquid, C₇H₈O, obtained from tar, used
as a disinfectant.

cress (kres), *n.* plant whose leaves
have a peppery taste. [OE *cresse*]

cres·set (kres′it), *n.* a metal container for burning oil, wood, etc., to
give light. [< OF]

crest (krest), *n.* **1.** comb, tuft, etc.,
on the head of a bird or animal. **2.** decoration,
plumes, etc., on the top of a helmet. **3.** decoration at the top of a coat of arms. **4.** an ornamental part which surmounts a wall, the ridge of

Crest
(def. 2)

a roof, etc. 5. the top part; top of a hill, wave, etc.; ridge; peak; summit. 6. the highest or best of its kind. —v. 1. furnish with a crest. 2. form into a crest. [< OF < L *crista* tuft] —crest'ed, *adj.* —crest'less, *adj.*

crest·fall·en (krest'fôl'ən), *adj.* with bowed head; dejected; discouraged. —crest'fall'en·ly, *adv.* —crest'fall'en·ness, *n.*

cre·ta·ceous (kri·tā'shəs), *adj.* like chalk; containing chalk. [< L, < *creta* chalk]

Crete (krēt), *n.* a Greek island in the Mediterranean, SE of Greece. —Cre'tan, *adj.*, *n.*

cre·tin (krē'tən), *n.* a deformed idiot. [< F < Swiss dial. < L *Christianus* Christian; came to mean "man," then "fellow," then "poor fellow'']

cre·tin·ism (krē'tən·iz·əm), *n.* a chronic, congenital disease due to a deficiency in the thyroid gland, often resulting in deformity and idiocy.

cre·tonne (kri·ton'; krē'ton), *n.* a strong cotton cloth with printed designs, used for curtains, etc. [< F, prob. < *Creton*, village in Normandy]

cre·vasse (krə·vas'), *n.*, *v.*, -vassed, -vass·ing. —*n.* 1. a deep crack or crevice in the ice of a glacier. 2. *Am.* break in a levee. —*v.* fissure with crevasses. [< F, CREVICE]

crev·ice (krev'is), *n.* a narrow split or crack. [< OF *crevace* < VL *crepacia* < L *crepare* crack] —crev'iced, *adj.*

crew[1] (krü), *n.* 1. men needed to do work on a ship, or to row a boat. 2. group of people working or acting together. 3. crowd; gang. [< OF *creüe* increase, recruit < *creistre* grow < L *crescere*]

crew[2] (krü), *v.* pt. of CROW[1].

crew cut, a kind of very short haircut.

crib (krib), *n.*, *v.*, cribbed, crib·bing. —*n.* 1. a small bed with high sides to keep a baby from falling out. 2. rack or manger for horses and cows to eat from. 3. building or box for storing grain, salt, etc. 4. framework of logs or timbers used in building. 5. *Colloq.* use of another's words or ideas as one's own. 6. *Slang.* notes or helps that are unfair to use in doing schoolwork. 7. a small room or house. —*v.* 1. provide with a crib. 2. *Colloq.* use (another's words or ideas) as one's own. 3. *Slang.* use notes unfairly in doing schoolwork. 4. shut up in a small space. [OE *cribb*] —crib'ber, *n.*

crib·bage (krib'ij), *n.* a card game for two, three, or four people.

crick (krik), *n.* a sudden, painful muscular cramp. —*v.* cause a crick in.

Cricket (1 in. long)

crick·et[1] (krik'it), *n.* a black insect of the grasshopper family. [< OF *criquet*; imit.]

crick·et[2] (krik'it), *n.* 1. an outdoor game played by two teams of eleven players each, with ball, bats, and wickets. 2. *Colloq.* fair play; good sportsmanship. —*v.* play this game. [< OF *criquet* goal post, stick, prob. < MDu. *cricke* stick to lean on] —crick'et·er, *n.*

crick·et[3] (krik'it), *n.* a small stool.

cri·er (krī'ər), *n.* 1. official who shouts out public announcements. 2. person who shouts out announcements of goods for sale. 3. person who cries.

crime (krīm), *n.* 1. a wrong act that is against the law. 2. violation of law. 3. a wrong act; sin. [< OF < L *crimen* < *cernere* judge, decide] —Syn. 1. offense, trespass.

Cri·me·a (krī·mē'ə; kri-), *n.* peninsula in SW Soviet Union, on the N coast of the Black Sea. Cri·me'an, *adj.*

crim·i·nal (krim'ə·nəl), *n.* person guilty of a crime. —*adj.* 1. guilty of crime. 2. having to do with crime. 3. like crime; wrong; sinful. —crim'i·nal'i·ty, *n.* —crim'i·nal·ly, *adv.*

crim·i·nol·o·gy (krim'ə·nol'ə·ji), *n.* study of crimes and criminals. —crim·i·no·log·ic (krim'ə·nə·loj'ik), crim'i·no·log'i·cal, *adj.* —crim'i·nol'o·gist, *n.*

crimp (krimp), *v.* press into small, narrow folds; make wavy. —*n.* 1. a crimping. 2. something crimped; fold; wave. 3. a waved or curled lock of hair. 4. put a crimp in, *Slang.* hinder. [OE *gecrympan*] —crimp'er, *n.* —crimp'y, *adj.*

crim·son (krim'zən), *n.* a deep red. —*adj.* deep-red. —*v.* turn deep red. [< Ital. or Sp. < Ar. *qirmizi* < Skt. *kṛmi-* insect]

cringe (krinj), *v.*, cringed, cring·ing, *n.* —*v.* 1. shrink or crouch in fear. 2. try to get favor or attention by servile behavior. —*n.* a cringing. [ME *crengen* < OE *cringan* give way] —cring'er, *n.*

crin·kle (kring'kəl), *v.*, -kled, -kling, *n.* —*v.* 1. wrinkle; ripple. 2. rustle: *paper crinkles when it is crushed.* —*n.* 1. wrinkle; ripple. 2. rustle. [ME *crenkle(n)* < OE *crincan* bend] —crin'kly, *adv.*

cri·noid (krī'noid; krin'oid), *n.* a flower-shaped sea animal, usually anchored by a stalk. —*adj.* of or like a crinoid. [< Gk., < *krinon* lily]

crin·o·line (krin'ə·lin; -lēn), *n.* 1. a stiff cloth used as a lining. 2. petticoat of crinoline to hold a skirt out. 3. a hoop skirt. [< F < Ital., < *crino* horsehair (< L *crinia* hair) + *lino* thread (< L *linum*)]

crip·ple (krip'əl), *n.*, *v.*, -pled, -pling. —*n.* a lame person or animal; one that cannot use his legs, arms, or body properly. —*v.* 1. make a cripple of. 2. damage; disable; weaken. [OE *crypel*; akin to CREEP] —crip'pler, *n.* —Syn. *v.* 1. lame, maim. 2. impair.

cri·sis (krī'sis), *n.*, pl. -ses (-sēz). 1. the turning point in a disease, toward life or death. 2. the deciding event in the course of anything. 3. time of danger or anxious waiting. [< L < Gk., < *krinein* decide]

crisp (krisp), *adj.* 1. hard and thin; breaking easily with a snap. 2. fresh; sharp and clear; bracing: *crisp winter air.* 3. clear-cut; decisive. —*v.* make or become crisp. [< L *crispus* curled] —crisp'ly, *adv.* —crisp'ness, *n.* —Syn. *adj.* 1. brittle. 2. brisk.

crisp·y (kris'pi), *adj.*, crisp·i·er, crisp·i·est. crisp.

criss·cross (kris'krôs'; -kros'), *adj.* made or marked with crossed lines; crossed. —*adv.* crosswise. —*v.* mark or cover with crossed lines. —*n.* mark or pattern made of crossed lines. [alter. of *Christ's cross*]

Cris·to·bal (kris·tō'bəl), *n.* seaport in the Canal Zone, at the Atlantic end of the Panama Canal, near Colón.

cri·te·ri·on (krī·tir'i·ən), *n.*, pl. -te·ri·a (-tir'i·ə), -te·ri·ons. rule or standard for making a judgment; test. [< Gk., < *krinein* judge]

crit·ic (krit'ik), *n.* 1. person who makes judgments of the merits and faults of books, music, plays, etc. 2. person whose profession is writing such judgments for a newspaper, etc. 3. person who finds fault. [< L < Gk. *kritikos* critical < *krinein* judge]

crit·i·cal (krit'ə·kəl), *adj.* 1. inclined to find fault or disapprove. 2. skilled as a critic. 3. coming from one who is skilled as a critic: *a critical judgment.* 4. belonging to the work of a critic. 5. of a crisis: *the critical moment.* 6. full of danger or difficulty. 7. of supplies, labor, or resources, essential for the work or project but existing in inadequate supply. —crit'i·cal·ly, *adv.* —crit'i·cal·ness, *n.*

crit·i·cism (krit'ə·siz·əm), *n.* 1. disapproval; faultfinding. 2. the making of judgments; analysis of merits and faults. 3. a critical comment, essay, review, etc.

crit·i·cize (krit'ə·sīz), *v.*, -cized, -ciz·ing; *esp. Brit.* crit·i·cise (krit'ə·sīz), *v.*, -cised, -cis·ing. 1. disapprove; find fault with. 2. judge or speak as a critic. —crit'i·ciz'a·ble, *esp. Brit.* crit'i·cis'a·ble, *adj.* —crit'i·ciz'er, *esp. Brit.* crit'i·cis'er, *n.*

cri·tique (kri·tēk'), *n.* 1. art of criticism. 2. a critical essay or review. [< F < Gk. *kritike* (*techne*) the critical art. See CRITIC.]

croak (krōk), *n.* a deep, hoarse cry, as of a frog, crow, or raven. —*v.* 1. make such a sound. 2. utter in a deep, hoarse voice. 3. be always prophesying misfortune; grumble. 4. *Slang.* die. [< OE *cræcettan*]

croak·er (krōk'ər), *n.* 1. one that croaks. 2. *Am.* any of various fishes that make a croaking or grunting noise.

Cro·a·tia (krō·ā′shə), *n.* district in NW Yugoslavia. —**Cro·at** (krō′at), *n.* —**Cro·a′tian**, *adj.*, *n.*

cro·chet (krō·shā′), *v.*, –**cheted** (–shād′), –**chet·ing** (–shā′ing), *n.* —*v.* knit (sweaters, lace, etc.) with a single needle having a hook at one end. —*n.* knitting done in this way. [< F, dim. of *croc* hook < Gmc.]

crock (krok), *n.* pot or jar made of baked clay. [OE *crocc*(a)]

crock·er·y (krok′ər·i), *n.* dishes, jars, etc., made of baked clay; earthenware.

Crock·ett (krok′it), *n.* David, 1786–1836, American pioneer, killed at the Alamo.

Crocodile (14 ft. long)

croc·o·dile (krok′ə·dīl), *n.* a large, lizardlike reptile with a thick skin, long narrow head, and webbed feet. [< OF < L < Gk. *krokodeilos*, earlier, lizard]

crocodile tears, false or insincere grief.

croc·o·dil·i·an (krok′ə·dil′i·ən), *adj.* of or like a crocodile. —*n.* any of a group of reptiles that includes crocodiles, alligators, etc.

cro·cus (krō′kəs), *n., pl.* **cro·cus·es, cro·ci** (–sī). 1. a small flowering plant that grows from a bulblike stem, usually blooming very early in the spring. 2. the flower. [< L < Gk. *krokos* < Semitic]

Croe·sus (krē′səs), *n.* 1. a very rich king of Lydia from 560 to 546 B.C. 2. a very rich person.

croft (krôft; kroft), *n.* 1. *Brit.* a small enclosed field. 2. a very small rented farm. [OE] —**croft′·er,** *n.*

croix de guerre (krwä′ də gâr′), a French medal given to soldiers for bravery under fire.

Cro-Mag·non (krō·mag′non), *adj.* belonging to a group of prehistoric people who lived in SW Europe.

crom·lech (krom′lek), *n.* 1. circle of upright stones built in prehistoric times. 2. a dolmen. [< Welsh, < *crom* bent + *llech* flat stone]

Crom·well (krom′wel; –wəl), *n.* Oliver, 1599–1658, English general, Puritan leader, and lord protector of the Commonwealth, 1653–1658.

crone (krōn), *n.* a shrunken old woman. [< MDu. < F *carogne* carcass, hag. See CARRION.]

cro·ny (krō′ni), *n., pl.* –**nies.** a very close friend; chum.

crook (krúk), *v.* hook; bend; curve. —*n.* 1. hook; bend; curve. 2. a hooked, curved, or bent part. 3. a shepherd's staff. 4. *Am., Colloq.* a dishonest person; thief; swindler. [appar. < Scand. *krōkr*]

crook·ed (krúk′id *for* 1 *and* 2; krúkt *for* 3), *adj.* 1. not straight; bent; curved; twisted. 2. *Am., Colloq.* dishonest. 3. having a crook. —**crook′·ed·ly,** *adv.* —**crook′ed·ness,** *n.*

croon (krün), *v.* 1. hum, sing, or murmur in a low tone. 2. sing in a low voice with exaggerated emotion. —*n.* low humming, singing, or murmuring. [< Scand. *krauna* murmur] —**croon′er,** *n.*

crop (krop), *n., v.,* **cropped, crop·ping.** —*n.* 1. product grown or gathered for use, esp. for use as food. 2. the whole amount (of the produce of any plant or tree) that is borne in one season. 3. the yield of any product in a season: *a large ice crop.* 4. group; collection. 5. clipped hair; a short haircut. 6. mark produced by clipping the ears. 7. a baglike swelling of a bird's food passage where food is prepared for digestion. 8. a short whip with a loop instead of a lash. 9. handle of a whip. —*v.* 1. plant and cultivate a crop. 2. cut or bite off the top of. 3. clip; cut short. 4. **crop out** or **up,** a. appear; come to the surface. b. be shown unexpectedly. [OE *cropp* sprout, craw]

crop·per (krop′ər), *n.* 1. person or thing that crops. 2. one who raises a crop, esp. on shares. 3. *Colloq.* a heavy fall. 4. *Colloq.* failure; collapse.

cro·quet (krō·kā′), *n.* an outdoor game played by knocking wooden balls through small wire arches with mallets. [< F, dial. var. of *crochet*. See CROCHET.]

cro·quette (krō·ket′), *n.* a small mass of chopped meat, fish, etc., coated with crumbs and fried. [< F, < *croquer* crunch]

cro·sier (krō′zhər), *n.* an ornamental staff carried by or before bishops or certain abbots. Also, **crozier.** [< F, crook bearer, < VL *croccia* crook < Gmc.]

cross (krôs; kros), *n.* 1. stick or post with another across it. 2. **the Cross,** a. the cross on which Christ died. b. Christ's sufferings and death; the Atonement. c. the Christian religion. 3. the symbol (†) of the Christian religion. 4. two intersecting lines (× +). A person who cannot sign his name makes a cross instead. 5. thing, design, or mark shaped like a cross. 6. burden of duty; suffering; trouble. 7. a mixing of kins, breeds, or races. 8. result of such mixing. —*v.* 1. mark with a cross. 2. draw a line across. 3. put or lay across. 4. lie across; be in the form of a cross. 5. go across; move across. 6. meet and pass: *my letter to her and hers to me crossed.* 7. make the sign of the cross on or over. 8. oppose; hinder. 9. cause (different kinds, breeds, races, etc.) to interbreed. —*adj.* 1. crossing; lying or going across. 2. opposing; counter. 3. in a bad temper. 4. mixed in kind, breed, or race. [< OIrish *cros* < L *crux.* Doublet of CRUX.] —**cross′ly,** *adv.* —**cross′ness,** *n.* —Syn. *n.* 6. trial, affliction. 8. hybrid. —*v.* 2. cancel. 8. thwart, frustrate. —*adj.* 3. irritable. 4. hybrid.

cross·bar (krôs′bär′; kros′–), *n.* bar, line, or stripe going crosswise.

cross·beam (krôs′bēm′; kros′–), *n.* a large beam that crosses another or extends from wall to wall.

cross·bones (krôs′bōnz′; kros′–), *n.pl.* two large bones placed crosswise, symbolizing death.

cross·bow (krôs′bō′; kros′–), *n.* a medieval weapon with a bow and a grooved stock in the middle to direct the arrows, stones, etc. —**cross′bow′man,** *n.*

cross·bred (krôs′bred′; kros′–), *adj.* produced by crossbreeding. —*n.* a crossbreed.

cross·breed (krôs′brēd′; kros′–), *v.,* –**bred,** –**breed·ing,** *n.* —*v.* breed by mixing kinds, breeds, or races. —*n.* individual or breed produced by crossbreeding.

cross bun, bun marked with a cross on the top, often eaten on Good Friday.

cross·coun·try (krôs′kun′tri; kros′–), *adj.* across open country instead of by road.

cross·cut (krôs′kut′; kros′–), *adj., n., v.,* –**cut,** –**cut·ting.** —*adj.* 1. used or made for cutting across. 2. cut across. —*n.* 1. a cut across. 2. short cut. —*v.* cut across.

cross·ex·am·ine (krôs′ig·zam′ən; kros′–), *v.,* –**ined,** –**in·ing.** 1. *Law.* question (a witness for the opposing side) closely to test the truth of his evidence. 2. examine closely or severely. —**cross′ex·am′i·na′tion,** *n.* —**cross′ex·am′in·er,** *n.*

cross·eye (krôs′ī′; kros′–), *n.* strabismus, esp. the form in which both eyes turn toward the nose. —**cross′-eyed′,** *adj.*

cross·fer·ti·li·za·tion (krôs′fér′tə·lə·zā′shən; kros′–), *n. Bot.* fertilization of one flower by pollen from another.

cross·fer·ti·lize (krôs′fér′tə·līz; kros′–), *v.,* –**lized,** –**liz·ing.** cause the cross-fertilization of.

cross·grained (krôs′grānd′; kros′–), *adj.* having the grain running across the regular grain.

cross·hatch (krôs′hach′; kros′–), *v.* mark or shade with two sets of parallel lines crossing each other.

cross·ing (krôs′ing; kros′–), *n.* 1. place where things cross each other. 2. place at which a street, river, etc., may be crossed. 3. act of crossing. 4. voyage across water.

cross·patch (krôs′pach′; kros′–), *n. Colloq.* a cross, bad-tempered person.

cross·piece (krôs′pēs′; kros′–), *n.* piece that is placed across something.

cross·pol·li·nate (krôs′pol′ə·nāt; kros′–), *v.,* –**nat·ed,** –**nat·ing.** cause cross-fertilization in. —**cross′·pol′li·na′tion,** *n.*

cross-pur-pose (krôs′pér′pəs; kros′-), *n.* **1.** opposing or contrary purpose. **2. at cross-purposes,** a. misunderstanding each other's purpose. b. acting under such a misunderstanding.

cross-ques-tion (krôs′kwes′chən; kros′-), *v.* cross-examine.

cross-re-fer (krôs′ri-fér′; kros′-), *v.,* **-ferred, -fer-ring. 1.** refer from one part to another. **2.** make a cross reference.

cross reference, reference from one part of a book, index, etc., to another.

cross-road (krôs′rōd′; kros′-), *n.* **1.** road that crosses another. **2.** road connecting main roads. **3.** Often, **crossroads** (*sing. in use*). a. place where roads cross. b. a meeting place, esp. for people living far apart.

cross section, 1. act of cutting anything across. **2.** piece cut in this way. **3.** a representative sample.

cross-stitch (krôs′stich′; kros′-), *n.* **1.** one stitch crossed over another, forming an X. **2.** embroidery made with this stitch. —*v.* embroider or sew with this stitch.

cross trees, *Naut.* two horizontal bars of wood near the top of a mast.

cross-wise (krôs′wīz′; kros′-), **cross-ways** (-wāz′), *adv.* **1.** so as to cross; across. **2.** in the form of a cross. **3.** opposite to what is required; wrongly.

cross-word puzzle (krôs′wérd′; kros′-), puzzle with sets of squares to be filled in with words, one letter to each square. Synonyms or definitions of the words are given with numbers corresponding to numbers in the squares.

crotch (kroch), *n.* **1.** a forked piece or part. **2.** place where the body divides into the two legs. [var. of *crutch*] —**crotched** (krocht), *adj.*

crotch-et (kroch′it), *n.* **1.** an odd notion; unreasonable whim. **2.** a small hook or hooklike part. **3.** *Esp. Brit., Music.* a quarter note. [< OF *crochet*. See CROCHET.]

crotch-et-y (kroch′ə-ti), *adj.* **1.** full of odd notions or unreasonable whims. **2.** of the nature of a crotchet. —**crotch′et-i-ness,** *n.*

cro-ton (krō′tən), *n.* a tropical shrub or tree of Asia with a strong odor. The seeds of a croton tree yield an oil (**croton oil**) used in medicine. [< NL < Gk. *krotōn* tick?]

croton bug, *Am.* a small cockroach.

crouch (krouch), *v.* **1.** stoop low with bent legs like an animal ready to spring, or in hiding, or shrinking in fear. **2.** bow down in a timid or slavish manner. **3.** bend low. —*n.* **1.** act or state of crouching. **2.** a crouching position. [< OF *crochir* < *croc* hook < Gmc.]

croup[1] (krüp), *n.* inflammation or diseased condition of the throat and windpipe characterized by a hoarse cough and difficult breathing. [? < *croup, v.,* blend of *croak* and *whoop*] —**croup′y,** *adj.*

croup[2] (krüp), *n.* rump of a horse, etc. [< F *croupe* < Gmc.]

crou-pi-er (krü′pi-ər), *n.* attendant at a gambling table who rakes in the money and pays the winners. [< F, < *croupe* CROUP[2]; orig., one who rides behind]

crou-ton (krü′ton), *n.* a small piece of toasted or fried bread, often served in soup. [< F, < *croûte* CRUST]

crow[1] (krō), *n., v.,* **crowed (or crew** for 2), **crowed, crow-ing.** —*n.* **1.** a loud cry made by a rooster. **2.** a happy sound made by a baby. —*v.* **1.** make the happy sound of a baby. **2.** make the cry of a cock. **3.** show happiness and pride; boast. [OE *crāwan;* imit.]

crow[2] (krō), *n.* **1.** a large, glossy-black bird that has a harsh cry or caw. **2.** any similar bird, such as ravens, magpies, jays, etc. **3.** crow-bar. **4. as the crow flies,** in a straight line; in or by the shortest way. **5. eat crow,** *Am., Colloq.* be forced to do something very disagreeable and humiliating. [OE *crāwe*]

Man using a crowbar

Crow (krō), *n. Am.* member of a tribe of American Indians living in Montana.

crow-bar (krō′bär′), *n. Am.* a strong iron or steel bar, used as a lever.

crowd (kroud), *n.* **1.** a large number of people together. **2.** people in general; the masses. **3.** *Am., Colloq.* group; set. **4.** large numbers of things together. [< v.] —*v.* **1.** collect in large numbers. **2.** fill; fill too full. **3.** push; shove. **4.** press forward; force one's way. **5.** force into a small space. **6.** *Am., Colloq.* press; urge; dun. [OE *crūdan* press] —**crowd′ed,** *adj.* —Syn. *n.* **1.** throng, multitude, host, horde, swarm, mob, crush. —*v.* **1.** throng, swarm. **2.** cram, pack.

crow-foot (krō′fut′), *n., pl.* **-foots.** buttercup or other plant with leaves shaped somewhat like a crow's foot.

crown (kroun), *n.* **1.** head covering for a king, queen, etc. **2.** power and authority of a king, queen, etc.; royal power. **3.** a king, queen, etc. **4.** design or thing shaped like a crown. **5.** wreath for the head. **6.** honor; reward. **7.** head. **8.** the highest part; top. **9.** the highest state or quality of anything. **10.** part of a tooth above the gum. **11.** an artificial substitute for this part. **12.** a British silver coin, worth 5 shillings or about $.70 (1950). **13.** *Naut.* end of an anchor between the arms. **14. the Crown,** royal power. —*v.* **1.** make king, queen, etc. **2.** honor; reward. **3.** be on top of; cover the highest part of: *a fort crowns the hill.* **4.** make perfect or complete; add the finishing touch to. **5.** put a crown on. **6.** make a king of (a checker that has been moved across the checkerboard). [< AF < L *corona* garland, wreath. Doublet of CORONA.] —**crown′er,** *n.*

crown glass, very clear glass used in optical instruments.

crown prince, the oldest living son of a king, queen, etc.; heir apparent to a kingdom.

crown princess, 1. wife of a crown prince. **2.** girl or woman who is heir apparent to a kingdom.

crow's-foot (krōz′fut′), *n., pl.* **-feet.** Usually, **crow's-feet.** wrinkle at the outer corner of the eye.

crow's-nest (krōz′nest′), *n. Naut.* **1.** a small, enclosed platform near the top of a mast, used by the lookout. **2.** any similar platform ashore.

Croy-don (kroi′dən), *n.* city in SE England, near London, containing a great airport.

cro-zier (krō′zhər), *n.* crosier.

cru-cial (krü′shəl), *adj.* **1.** very important; critical; decisive. **2.** very trying; severe. [< NL (medical) < L *crux* cross] —**cru′cial-ly,** *adv.*

cru-ci-ble (krü′sə-bəl), *n.* **1.** container in which metals, ores, etc., can be melted. **2.** a severe test or trial. [< Med.L *crucibulum,* orig., night lamp]

cru-ci-fix (krü′sə-fiks), *n.* **1.** a cross with the figure of Christ crucified on it. **2.** a cross. [< LL *crucifixus* fixed to a cross < *crux* cross + *fixus,* pp. of *figere* fasten]

cru-ci-fix-ion (krü′sə-fik′shən), *n.* **1.** act of crucifying. **2. Crucifixion,** a. the putting to death of Christ on the cross. b. picture, statue, etc., of this.

cru-ci-form (krü′sə-fôrm), *adj.* shaped like a cross. —**cru′ci-form′ly,** *adv.*

cru-ci-fy (krü′sə-fī), *v.,* **-fied, -fy-ing. 1.** put to death by nailing or binding the hands and feet to a cross. **2.** treat severely; torture. [< OF < LL *crucifigere.* See CRUCIFIX.] —**cru′ci-fi′er,** *n.*

crude (krüd), *adj.,* **crud-er, crud-est. 1.** in a natural or raw state; unrefined. **2.** not mature; unripe. **3.** rough; coarse: *a crude log cabin.* **4.** lacking finish, grace, taste, or refinement: *crude manners.* [< L *crudus* raw] —**crude′ly,** *adv.* —**crude′ness, cru′di-ty,** *n.* —Syn. **1.** unfinished. **2.** green. **4.** rude. —Ant. **4.** cultivated, refined.

cru-el (krü′əl), *adj.* **1.** fond of causing pain to others and delighting in their suffering. **2.** showing a cruel nature: *cruel acts.* **3.** causing pain and suffering: *a cruel war.* [< F < L *crudelis* rough. See CRUDE.] —**cru′el-ly,** *adv.* —**cru′el-ness,** *n.* —Syn. **1.** brutal, savage, barbarous, ruthless, pitiless, merciless. —Ant. **1.** kindly.

cru-el-ty (krü′əl-ti), *n., pl.* **-ties. 1.** readiness to give pain to others or to delight in their suffering. **2.** a cruel act.

cru·et (krü′it), *n.* a glass bottle to hold vinegar, oil, etc., for the table. [< OF, dim. of *cruie* pot < Gmc.]

cruise (krüz), *v.,* **cruised, cruis·ing,** *n.* —*v.* 1. sail about from place to place on pleasure or business; sail over or about. 2. journey or travel from place to place. 3. fly in an airplane at the speed of maximum efficiency. —*n.* a cruising voyage. [< Du. *kruisen* < *kruis* < L *crux* cross]

cruis·er (krüz′ər), *n.* 1. warship with less armor and more speed than a battleship. 2. airplane, taxi, etc., that cruises. 3. *Am.* a police car connected with headquarters by radio.

crul·ler (krul′ər), *n. Am.* a twisted doughnut. [appar. < *krullen* curl]

crumb (krum), *n.* 1. a very small piece of bread, cake, etc., broken from a larger piece. 2. the soft inside part of bread. 3. a little bit: *a crumb of comfort.* —*v.* 1. break into crumbs. 2. cover with crumbs for frying or baking. 3. *Colloq.* brush or wipe the crumbs from (a tablecloth, etc.). [OE *cruma*] —**crumb′y,** *adj.*

crum·ble (krum′bəl), *v.,* **-bled, -bling.** 1. break into very small pieces or crumbs. 2. fall into pieces; decay. [earlier *crimble* < OE *gecrymman* < *cruma* crumb]

crum·bly (krum′bli), *adj.,* **-bli·er, -bli·est.** easily crumbled. —**crum′bli·ness,** *n.*

crum·pet (krum′pit), *n. Esp. Brit.* cake baked on a griddle, that is thicker than a pancake and is usually toasted after being baked. [OE *crompeht* a cake]

crum·ple (krum′pəl), *v.,* **-pled, -pling,** *n.* —*v.* 1. crush together; wrinkle. 2. *Colloq.* collapse. —*n.* wrinkle made by crushing something together. [< OE *crump* bent]

crunch (krunch), *v.* 1. crush noisily with the teeth. 2. crush or grind noisily. —*n.* act or sound of crunching.

crup·per (krup′ər), *n.* strap attached to the back of a harness and passing under a horse's tail. [< OF *cropiere* < *crope* CROUP²]

cru·sade (krü·sād′), *n., v.,* **-sad·ed, -sad·ing.** —*n.* 1. Often, **Crusade.** any one of the Christian military expeditions between the years 1096 and 1272 to recover the Holy Land from the Mohammedans. 2. war having a religious purpose and approved by the church. 3. a vigorous campaign against a public evil or in favor of some new idea. —*v.* take part in a crusade. [blend of earlier *crusado* (< Sp. *cruzada*) and *croisade* (< F < Pr., from a verb meaning "take the cross"). See CROSS.] —**cru·sad′er,** *n.*

cruse (krüz; krüs), *n.* jug, pot, or bottle made of earthenware. [< MDu. *croes*]

crush (krush), *v.* 1. squeeze together violently so as to break or bruise. 2. wrinkle or crease by wear or rough handling. 3. break into fine pieces by grinding or pounding or pressing. 4. flatten by heavy pressure. 5. subdue; conquer. 6. drink: *to crush a goblet of wine.* —*n.* 1. a violent pressure like grinding or pounding. 2. *Am.* mass of people crowded close together. 3. *Am., Slang.* a. a sudden or ardent infatuation. b. object of a sudden or ardent infatuation. [appar. < OF *croissir* < Gmc.] —**crush′er,** *n.*

Cru·soe (krü′sō), *n.* **Robinson,** shipwrecked hero of a book of the same name by Daniel Defoe.

crust (krust), *n.* 1. the hard, outside part of bread. 2. piece of this; any hard, dry piece of bread. 3. the baked outside covering of a pie. 4. any hard outside covering. 5. the solid outside part of the earth. —*v.* 1. cover or become covered with a crust. 2. form or collect into a crust. [< L *crusta* rind]

crus·ta·cean (krus·tā′shən), *n.* any of a group of water animals with hard shells, jointed bodies and appendages, and gills for breathing, including crabs, lobsters, shrimps, etc. —*adj.* of or belonging to this group. [< NL, < L *crusta* shell, rind]

crust·y (krus′ti), *adj.,* **crust·i·er, crust·i·est.** 1. having a crust; hard; crustlike. 2. harsh in manner, speech, etc. —**crust′i·ly,** *adv.* —**crust′i·ness,** *n.*

crutch (kruch), *n.* 1. stick with a crosspiece at the top that fits under a lame person's arm and supports part of his weight in walking. 2. a forked support or part. 3. anything like a crutch in shape or use; support; prop. —*v.* support with or as with a crutch; prop or sustain. [OE *crycc*]

crux (kruks), *n.* 1. the essential part; the most important point. 2. a puzzling or perplexing question. [< L, cross. Doublet of CROSS.]

cry (krī), *v.,* **cried, cry·ing,** *n., pl.* **cries.** —*v.* 1. make sounds showing pain, fear, sorrow, etc. 2. shed tears; weep. 3. (of animals) give forth characteristic calls. 4. call loudly; shout. 5. **cry down,** make little of; speak of as unimportant or less valuable; deprecate. 6. announce in public. 7. **cry for,** a. ask earnestly for; beg for. b. need very much. —*n.* 1. sound made by a person or animal that shows some strong feeling, such as pain, fear, anger, or sorrow. 2. fit of weeping. 3. noise or call of an animal: *the cry of the crow.* 4. the yelping of hounds in the chase. 5. a loud call; shout: *a cry for help.* 6. general opinion; public report. 7. call to action; slogan. 8. **a far cry,** a. a long way. b. a great difference. [< OF < L *quiritare*]

cry·ing (krī′ing), *adj.* 1. that cries. 2. demanding attention; very bad.

crypt (kript), *n.* an underground room or vault. The crypt beneath the main floor of a church was formerly often used as a burial place. [< L < Gk. *kryptos* hidden. Doublet of GROTTO.]

cryp·tic (krip′tik), **cryp·ti·cal** (-tə·kəl), *adj.* having a hidden meaning; secret; mysterious. [< LL < Gk., < *kryptos* hidden] —**cryp′ti·cal·ly,** *adv.*

cryp·to·gam (krip′tə·gam), *n. Bot.* plant having no stamens and pistils, and therefore no flowers and seeds, as ferns and mosses. [< NL < Gk. *kryptos* hidden + *gamos* marriage] —**cryp′to·gam′ic, cryp·tog·a·mous** (krip·tog′ə·məs), *adj.*

cryp·to·gram (krip′tə·gram), *n.* something written in secret code or cipher.

cryp·to·graph (krip′tə·graf; -gräf), *n.* 1. cryptogram. 2. a system of secret writing. —**cryp′to·graph′ic, cryp′to·graph′i·cal,** *adj.*

cryp·tog·ra·phy (krip·tog′rə·fi), *n.* process or art of writing in secret characters. —**cryp·tog′ra·pher,** *n.*

crys·tal (kris′təl), *n.* 1. a clear, transparent mineral, a kind of quartz, that looks like ice. 2. piece of crystal cut to form an ornament. 3. very transparent glass. 4. glass over the face of a watch. 5. a regularly shaped piece with angles and flat surfaces into which a substance solidifies. 6. *Radio.* piece of quartz used in radio. —*adj.* 1. made of crystal. 2. clear and transparent like crystal. [< OF < L < Gk. *krystallos* clear ice]

Crystal shapes

crystal detector, device consisting of a crystal embedded in soft metal, sometimes used in a radio instead of vacuum tubes.

crys·tal·line (kris′təl·in; -ēn; -īn), *adj.* 1. consisting of crystals; solidified in the form of crystals. 2. made of crystal. 3. clear and transparent like crystal.

crys·tal·lize (kris′təl·īz), *v.,* **-lized, -liz·ing.** 1. form into crystals; solidify into crystals. 2. form into definite shape. 3. coat with sugar. —**crys′tal·liz′a·ble,** *adj.* —**crys′tal·li·za′tion,** *n.*

crys·tal·log·ra·phy (kris′tə·log′rə·fi), *n.* science that deals with the form, structure, and properties of crystals. —**crys′tal·log′ra·pher,** *n.*

crys·tal·loid (kris′təl·oid), *adj.* like crystal. —*n.* substance (usually capable of crystallization) that, when dissolved in a liquid, will diffuse readily through vegetable or animal membranes. —**crys′tal·loi′dal,** *adj.*

crystal set, radio that uses a crystal detector instead of vacuum tubes.

Cs, *Chem.* cesium.

C.S.T., CST, or **c.s.t.,** *Am.* Central Standard Time.

Cu, *Chem.* copper.

cu., cubic.

cub (kub), *n.* **1.** a young bear, fox, lion, etc. **2.** an inexperienced or awkward boy.

Cu·ba (kū'bə), *n.* country on the largest island in the West Indies, S of Florida. —**Cu'ban,** *adj., n.*

cub·by (kub'i), or **cub·by·hole** (–hōl'), *n.* a small, enclosed space.

cube (kūb), *n., v.,* **cubed, cub·ing.** —*n.* **1.** solid with six equal, square sides. **2.** product obtained when a number is cubed: *the cube of 4 is 64.* —*v.* **1.** make or form into the shape of a cube. **2.** use (a number) three times as a factor: *5 cubed is 125.* [< L < Gk. *kybos* cube, die]

cu·beb (kū'beb), *n.* a dried, unripe berry of a tropical shrub, used in medicine. [< F < Ar. *kabāba*]

cube root, number used as the factor of a cube: *the cube root of 125 is 5.*

cu·bic (kū'bik), **cu·bi·cal** (–bə·kəl), *adj.* **1.** shaped like a cube. **2.** having length, breadth, and thickness. **3.** having to do with or involving the cubes of numbers. —**cu'bi·cal·ly,** *adv.*

cu·bi·cle (kū'bə·kəl), *n.* a very small room or compartment. [< L *cubiculum* bedroom < *cubare* lie]

cubic measure, system of measurement of volume in cubic units. 1728 cubic inches = 1 cubic foot.

cub·ism (kūb'iz·əm), *n.* method of painting, drawing, and sculpture in which objects are represented by cubes and other geometrical figures rather than by realistic details. —**cub'ist,** *n.* —**cu·bis'tic,** *adj.*

cu·bit (kū'bit), *n.* an ancient measure of length, about 18 to 22 inches. [< L *cubitum* elbow, cubit]

cub reporter, *Am.* a young, inexperienced newspaper reporter.

cuck·old (kuk'əld), *n.* husband of an unfaithful wife. —*v.* make a cuckold of. [< OF *cucuault* < *coucou* cuckoo]

cuck·oo (kuk'ü; *esp. for adj.* kū'kü), *n., pl.* **–oos,** *adj.* —*n.* **1.** bird whose call sounds much like its name. The common European cuckoo lays its eggs in the nests of other birds instead of hatching them itself. **2.** *Am.* the American cuckoo, which builds its own nest. **3.** call of the cuckoo. —*adj. U.S. Slang.* crazy; silly. [imit.]

cu·cum·ber (kū'kum·bər), *n.* **1.** vegetable that has a green skin with firm flesh inside, used in salads and for pickles. **2.** vine that it grows on. [< OF < L *cucumis*]

cud (kud), *n.* mouthful of food that cattle and similar animals bring back into the mouth from the first stomach for a slow, second chewing. [OE *cudu,* var. of *cwidu*]

cud·dle (kud'əl), *v.,* **–dled, –dling,** *n.* —*v.* **1.** hold closely and lovingly in one's arms or lap. **2.** lie close and snug; curl up. **3.** hug. —*n.* hug. —**cud'dly,** *adj.*

cudg·el (kuj'əl), *n., v.,* **–eled, –el·ing;** *esp. Brit.* **–elled, –el·ling.** —*n.* **1.** a short, thick stick used as a weapon; club. **2. take up the cudgels for,** defend strongly. —*v.* **1.** beat with a cudgel. **2. cudgel one's brains,** try very hard to think. [OE *cycgel*]

cue[1] (kū), *n.* **1.** hint or suggestion as to what to do or when to act. **2.** in a play, the last word or words of one actor's speech that is the signal for another to come on the stage, begin speaking, etc. **3.** part one is to play; course of action. **4.** frame of mind; mood. [prob. < F *queue* tail, end; with ref. to the end of a preceding actor's speech. See QUEUE.]

cue[2] (kū), *n.* **1.** queue. **2.** a long, tapering stick used for striking the ball in billiards, pool, etc. [var. of *queue*]

cuff[1] (kuf), *n.* **1.** band around the wrist, either attached to a sleeve or separate. **2.** turned-up fold around the bottom of the legs of trousers. **3.** handcuff. [ME *cuffe* glove]

cuff[2] (kuf), *v., n.* hit with the hand; slap. [cf. Sw. *kuffa* push]

cui bo·no (kwē' bō'nō; kī'), *Latin.* **1.** for whose benefit? **2.** of what good?

cui·rass (kwi·ras'), *n.* **1.** piece of armor for the body made of a breastplate and a plate for the back fastened together. **2.** the breastplate alone. [< F *cuirasse* < Ital. < VL < LL *coriacea (vestis)* (garment) of leather < L *corium* leather; form infl. by F *cuir* leather < L *corium*]

cui·sine (kwi·zēn'), *n.* **1.** style of cooking or preparing food. **2.** food. **3.** kitchen. [< F < L *cocina,* var. of *coquina* < *coquus* a cook]

cuisse (kwis), *n.* piece of armor to protect the thigh. [< F, thigh, < L *coxa* hip]

cul-de-sac (kul'də·sak'; kŭl'–), *n.* street or passage open at only one end; blind alley. [< F, bottom of the sack]

cu·lex (kū'leks), *n., pl.* **–li·ces** (–lə·sēz). the most common mosquito of North America and Europe. [< L, gnat]

cu·li·nar·y (kū'lə·ner'i; kul'ə–), *adj.* **1.** having to do with cooking. **2.** used in cooking. [< L, < *culina* kitchen]

cull (kul), *v.* **1.** pick out; select. **2.** pick over; make selections from. —*n.* something picked out as being inferior or worthless. [< OF < L *colligere* COLLECT]

culm[1] (kulm), *n.* **1.** coal dust. **2.** hard coal of poor quality. [? akin to COAL]

culm[2] (kulm), *n.* the jointed stem of grasses, usually hollow. [< L *culmus* stalk]

cul·mi·nate (kul'mə·nāt), *v.,* **–nat·ed, –nat·ing.** reach its highest point; reach a climax. [< LL *culminatus* < L *culmen,* earlier *columen* top]

cul·mi·na·tion (kul'mə·nā'shən), *n.* **1.** the highest point; climax. **2.** a reaching the highest point. —Syn. **1.** acme, zenith, peak.

cul·pa·ble (kul'pə·bəl), *adj.* deserving blame. [< F < L < *culpa* fault] —**cul'pa·bil'i·ty, cul'pa·ble·ness,** *n.* —**cul'pa·bly,** *adv.*

cul·prit (kul'prit), *n.* **1.** person guilty of a fault or crime; offender. **2.** prisoner in court accused of a crime.

cult (kult), *n.* **1.** system of religious worship. **2.** great admiration for a person, thing, idea, etc.; worship. **3.** group showing such admiration; worshipers. [< L *cultus* worship < *colere* cultivate]

cul·ti·va·ble (kul'tə·və·bəl), **cul·ti·vat·a·ble** (–vāt'ə·bəl), *adj.* that can be cultivated. —**cul'ti·va·bil'i·ty,** *n.*

cul·ti·vate (kul'tə·vāt), *v.,* **–vat·ed, –vat·ing.** **1.** prepare and use (land) to raise crops by plowing it, planting seeds, and taking care of the growing plants. **2.** loosen the ground around (growing plants) to kill weeds, etc. **3.** improve; develop, as by education. **4.** give time, thought, and effort to. **5.** seek better acquaintance with. [< Med.L, < *cultivare* < *cultivus* under cultivation < L *cultus* pp. of *colere* till] —**cul'ti·vat'ed,** *adj.*

cul·ti·va·tion (kul'tə·vā'shən), *n.* **1.** act of cultivating. **2.** improvement; development. **3.** the giving of time and thought to improving and developing (the body, mind, or manners). **4.** culture. —Syn. **4.** refinement, enlightenment.

cul·ti·va·tor (kul'tə·vā'tər), *n.* **1.** person or thing that cultivates. **2.** a tool or machine used to loosen the ground and destroy weeds.

cul·tur·al (kul'chər·əl), *adj.* of or having to do with culture. —**cul'tur·al·ly,** *adv.*

cul·ture (kul'chər), *n., v.,* **–tured, –tur·ing.** —*n.* **1.** fineness of feelings, thoughts, tastes, manners, etc. **2.** civilization of a given race or nation at a given time. **3.** development of the mind or body by education, training, etc. **4.** preparation of land to raise crops by plowing, planting, and necessary care; cultivation. **5.** proper care given to the raising of animals or plants. **6.** *Biol.* colony or growth of germs of a given kind that has been carefully made for a special purpose. —*v.* cultivate. [< F < L *cultura* a tending. See CULT.] —Syn. *n.* **1.** breeding, refinement.

cul·tured (kul'chərd), *adj.* **1.** having or showing culture; refined. **2.** produced or raised by culture.

cul·vert (kul'vərt), *n.* a small channel for water crossing under a road, railroad, canal, etc.

cum·ber (kum'bər), *v.* **1.** burden; trouble. **2.** hinder; hamper. —*n.* hindrance. [prob. < OF *combrer* impede < *combre* barrier < Celtic]

Cum·ber·land (kum'bər·lənd), *n.* river flowing through Kentucky and Tennessee into the Ohio River.

cum·ber·some (kum'bər·səm), **cum·brous** (-brəs), *adj.* 1. clumsy; unwieldy. 2. burdensome. —**cum'ber·some·ly, cum'brous·ly,** *adv.* —**cum'ber·some·ness, cum'brous·ness,** *n.*

cum lau·de (kŭm lou'dē; kŭm lô'dē), *Am.* with praise or honor. [< L]

cum·quat (kum'kwot), *n.* kumquat.

cu·mu·late (*v.* kū'myə·lāt; *adj.* kū'myə·lit, -lāt), *v.,* -**lat·ed,** -**lat·ing,** *adj.* —*v.* heap up; accumulate. —*adj.* heaped up. [< L, < *cumulus* heap] —**cu'mu·la'tion,** *n.*

cu·mu·la·tive (kū'myə·lā'tiv; -lə·tiv), *adj.* 1. increasing or growing in amount, force, etc., by additions. 2. of a dividend that must be added to future dividends if not paid when due. —**cu'mu·la'tive·ly,** *adv.* —**cu'mu·la'tive·ness,** *n.*

cu·mu·lus (kū'myə·ləs), *n., pl.* -**li** (-lī). 1. cloud made up of rounded heaps with a flat bottom. 2. heap. [< L, heap] —**cu'mu·lous,** *adj.*

cu·ne·ate (kū'ni·it; -āt), *adj.* wedge-shaped. [< L, < *cuneus* wedge]

cu·ne·i·form (kū·nē'ə·fôrm; kū'ni·ə·fôrm'), **cu·ni·form** (kū'nə·fôrm), *adj.* wedge-shaped. —*n.* cuneiform writing of ancient Babylonia, Assyria, Persia, etc. [< L *cuneus* wedge + -FORM]

Y	NUMERAL 9
◁	10
Ⅎ	TAP
⋈	BE
⊁	ME

Cuneiform characters

cun·ning (kun'ing), *adj.* 1. clever in deceiving; sly. 2. skillful; clever. 3. *Am., Colloq.* pretty and dear; attractive. —*n.* 1. slyness in getting what one wants. 2. skill; cleverness. [OE *cunnung* < *cunnan* know (how). See CAN¹.] —**cun'ning·ly,** *adv.* —**cun'ning·ness,** *n.* —**Syn.** *n.* 1. shrewdness. 2. expertness, ability.

cup (kup), *n., v.,* **cupped, cup·ping.** —*n.* 1. dish to drink from. 2. as much as a cup holds; cupful. 3. a cup with its contents. 4. in cooking, a half pint. 5. thing shaped like a cup. The petals of some flowers form a cup. 6. ornamental cup, vase, etc., given to the winner of a contest. 7. the containing part of a goblet or wineglass. 8. drink; mixture: *a claret cup.* 9. cup used in Communion. 10. wine used in Communion. 11. thing to be endured or experienced; fate. 12. in golf, the hole. 13. **in one's cups,** drunk. —*v.* 1. shape like a cup. 2. take or put in a cup. [< LL *cuppa;* cf. L *cupa* tub]

cup·bear·er (kup'bãr'ər), *n.* person who fills and passes around the cups in which drinks are served.

cup·board (kub'ərd), *n.* 1. closet or cabinet with shelves for dishes, food, etc. 2. *Esp. Brit.* any small closet.

cup·cake (kup'kāk'), *n. Am.* a small cake baked in a cup-shaped tin.

cup·ful (kup'fŭl), *n., pl.* -**fuls.** as much as a cup holds.

Cu·pid (kū'pid), *n.* 1. the Roman god of love, son of Venus, identified with the Greek god Eros. 2. cupid, a winged baby used as a symbol of love.

cu·pid·i·ty (kū·pid'ə·ti), *n.* eager desire; greed. [< L, < *cupidus* desirous < *cupere* long for, desire] —**Syn.** avarice.

cu·po·la (kū'pə·lə), *n.* 1. a rounded roof; dome. 2. a small dome or tower on a roof. [< Ital. < LL *cupula,* dim. of L *cupa* tub]

cup·ping (kup'ing), *n.* use of a glass cup to create a partial vacuum to draw blood to or through the skin.

cu·pre·ous (kū'pri·əs), *adj.* 1. of or containing copper. 2. copper-colored.

cu·pric (kū'prik), *adj. Chem.* of or containing divalent copper.

cu·prous (kū'prəs), *adj. Chem.* of or containing monovalent copper.

cu·prum (kū'prəm), *n.* copper. [< L. See COPPER.]

cur (kėr), *n.* 1. a worthless dog; mongrel. 2. an ill-bred, worthless person. [ME *curre*]

cur·a·ble (kyŭr'ə·bəl), *adj.* that can be cured.

cur·a·bil·i·ty, cur·a·ble·ness, *n.* —**cur'a·bly,** *adv.*

Cu·ra·cao (kyŭr'ə·sō'; kū'rä·sou'), *n.* 1. group of Dutch islands in the West Indies. 2. the largest island of this group. 3. curaçao, liqueur or cordial flavored with orange peel.

cu·ra·cy (kyŭr'ə·si), *n., pl.* -**cies.** the position, rank, or work of a curate.

cu·ra·re, cu·ra·ri (kyu·rä'rē), *n.* a poisonous, resinlike substance obtained from a tropical vine. [< Carib *kurare*]

cu·rate (kyŭr'it), *n. Esp. Brit.* clergyman who is an assistant to a pastor, rector, or vicar. [< Med.L, < *cura* cure (def. 5) < L, care]

cur·a·tive (kyŭr'ə·tiv), *adj.* having the power to cure; curing; tending to cure. —*n.* means of curing.

cu·ra·tor (kyu·rā'tər), *n.* person in charge of all or part of a museum, library, etc. [< L, < *curare* care for < *cura* care] —**cu·ra·to·ri·al** (kyŭr'ə·tô'ri·əl; -tō'-), *adj.* —**cu·ra'tor·ship,** *n.*

curb (kėrb), *n.* 1. chain or strap fastened to a horse's bit and passing under its lower jaw, used to restrain the horse. 2. check; restraint. 3. a raised border of concrete, stone, or wood along the edge of a pavement, etc. 4. *Am.* market that deals in stocks and bonds not listed on the regular stock exchange. —*v.* 1. hold in check; restrain. 2. provide with a curb. [< F < L *curvus* bent]

curb bit, a horse's bit having a curb.

curb·ing (kėrb'ing), *n.* 1. material for making a curb. 2. a raised border of concrete, etc.; curb.

curb·stone (kėrb'stōn'), *n.* stone or stones forming a curb.

cur·cu·li·o (kėr·kū'li·ō), *n., pl.* -**li·os.** a snout beetle, esp. one that destroys fruit. [< L]

curd (kėrd), *n.* Often, **curds.** the thick part of milk that separates from the watery part when milk sours. —*v.* form into curds; curdle. [ME *curd, crud*] —**curd'y,** *adj.*

cur·dle (kėr'dəl), *v.,* -**dled,** -**dling.** 1. form into curds. 2. thicken. 3. curdle the blood, horrify; terrify. [< *curd*]

cure (kyŭr), *v.,* **cured, cur·ing,** *n.* —*v.* 1. make well; bring back to health. 2. get rid of. 3. preserve (meat) by drying and salting. —*n.* 1. act or fact of curing. 2. means of curing; treatment that brings a person back to health. 3. medicine that is a means of curing; remedy. 4. way of curing meat. 5. spiritual charge; religious care. [< F < L *cura* care, concern] —**cure'less,** *adj.* —**cur'er,** *n.* —**Syn.** *v.* 1. heal, restore. 2. relieve.

cu·ré (kyu·rā'), *n.* a parish priest. [< F. See CURATE.]

cure-all (kyŭr'ôl'), *n. Am.* remedy supposed to cure all diseases or evils.

cur·few (kėr'fū), *n.* 1. a ringing of a bell at a fixed time every evening as a signal, as for children to come off the streets. 2. bell ringing such a signal: *"the curfew tolls the knell of parting day."* 3. time when it is rung. 4. in the Middle Ages, a signal to put out lights and cover fires. [< AF, < *covrir* cover + *feu* fire < L *focus* hearth]

cu·ri·a (kyŭr'i·ə), *n., pl.* cu·ri·ae (kyŭr'i·ē). group of high officials who assist the Pope in the government and administration of the Roman Catholic Church.

Cu·rie (kyŭr'ē; kyū·rē'), *n.* 1. Marie, 1867–1934, French physicist and chemist, born in Poland. She and her husband, Pierre, discovered radium in 1898. 2. Pierre, 1859–1906, French physicist and chemist.

cu·rie (kyŭr'ē; kyū·rē'), *n. Chem., Physics.* unit of radioactivity. [for Mme. *Curie*]

cu·ri·o (kyŭr'i·ō), *n., pl.* cu·ri·os. object valued as a curiosity. [short for *curiosity*]

cu·ri·os·i·ty (kyŭr'i·os'ə·ti), *n., pl.* -**ties.** 1. an eager desire to know. 2. a strange, rare, or novel object. 3. an interesting quality, as from strangeness.

cu·ri·ous (kyŭr'i·əs), *adj.* 1. eager to know. 2. too eager to know; prying. 3. interesting because strange, unusual, etc. 4. very careful; exact. 5. *Colloq.* very odd; eccentric. [< OF < L *curiosus* inquisitive, full of care, ult. < *cura* care] —cu'ri·ous·ly, *adv.* —cu'ri·ous·ness, *n.* —Syn. 1. inquisitive. 3. singular, rare, novel.

cu·ri·um (kyūr'i·əm), *n. Chem.* an element, Cm, produced by bombardment of plutonium and uranium by helium ions. [for Mme. *Curie*]

curl (kėrl), *v.* 1. twist into rings; roll into coils. 2. twist out of shape; bend into a curve. —*n.* 1. a curled lock of hair. 2. anything like it. 3. a curling or being curled. [ME *curle(n)*, *crulle(n)* < *crul* curly]

curl·er (kėr'lər), *n.* 1. person or thing that curls. 2. a device on which hair is twisted to make it curl.

cur·lew (kėr'lū), *n.*, *pl.* -lews or (*esp. collectively*) -lew. a wading bird with a long, thin bill. [< OF *courlieu;* imit.]

Curlew (from 1 to 2 ft. long)

curl·i·cue (kėr'li·kū), *n.* a fancy twist, curl, flourish, etc.

curl·ing (kėr'ling), *n.* game played on the ice in which large, smooth stones are slid at a target.

curl·y (kėr'li), *adj.*, curl·i·er, curl·i·est. 1. curling; wavy. 2. having curls. —curl'i·ly, *adv.* —curl'i·ness, *n.*

cur·mudg·eon (kər·muj'ən), *n.* a rude, stingy, bad-tempered person; miser. —cur·mudg'eon·ly, *adv.*

cur·rant (kėr'ənt), *n.* 1. a small, seedless raisin, used in cakes, etc. 2. a small, sour, edible berry that grows in bunches on certain shrubs. 3. bush that bears currants. [< AF (*raisins de*) *Corauntz* raisins of Corinth]

cur·ren·cy (kėr'ən·si), *n.*, *pl.* -cies. 1. *Am.* money in actual use in a country. 2. a passing from person to person; circulation: *people who spread a rumor give it currency.* 3. general use or acceptance; common occurrence.

cur·rent (kėr'ənt), *n.* 1. a flow. 2. flow of electricity along a wire, etc. 3. course; movement; general direction. —*adj.* 1. going around; passing from person to person. 2. generally used or accepted; commonly occurring. 3. of the present time: *the current issue of a magazine.* [< L *currens*, ppr. of *currere* run] —cur'rent·ly, *adv.* —Syn. *adj.* 2. prevalent, widespread.

cur·ric·u·lar (kə·rik'yə·lər), *adj.* having to do with a curriculum.

cur·ric·u·lum (kə·rik'yə·ləm), *n.*, *pl.* -lums, -la (-lə). course of study or set of courses of study in a school, college, etc. [< L, race course, chariot, dim. of *currus* chariot < *currere* run]

cur·ry¹ (kėr'i), *v.*, -ried, -ry·ing. 1. rub and clean (a horse, etc.) with a brush or currycomb. 2. prepare (tanned leather) for use by soaking, scraping, beating, coloring, etc. 3. curry favor, seek a person's favor by insincere flattery, constant attentions, etc. [< OF *correier* put in order < *con-* (< L *com-*) + *reier* arrange < Gmc.] —cur'ri·er, *n.*

cur·ry², **cur·rie** (kėr'i), *n.*, *pl.* -ries, *v.*, -ried, -ry·ing. —*n.* 1. a peppery sauce or powder containing a mixture of spices, seeds, vegetables, etc., much used in India. 2. stew flavored with curry. —*v.* prepare or flavor with curry. [< Tamil *kari*]

cur·ry·comb (kėr'i·kōm'), *n.* brush with metal teeth for rubbing and cleaning a horse. —*v.* use a currycomb on.

curse (kėrs), *v.*, cursed or curst, curs·ing, *n.* —*v.* 1. ask God to bring evil or harm on. 2. bring evil or harm on. 3. swear; swear at; blaspheme. —*n.* 1. the words that a person says when he asks God to curse someone or something. 2. something that is cursed. 3. harm or evil that comes as if in answer to a curse. 4. cause of evil or harm. 5. word or words used in swearing. [OE *cūrs*, *n.*, *cūrsian*, *v.*] —curs'er, *n.* —Syn. *v.* 3. damn. —*n.* 5. oath.

curs·ed (kėr'sid; kėrst), *adj.* 1. under a curse. 2. deserving a curse; evil; hateful; damnable. —curs'ed·ly, *adv.* —curs'ed·ness, *n.*

cur·sive (kėr'siv), *adj.* written with the letters

joined together: *ordinary handwriting is cursive.* —*n.* 1. letter made to join other letters. 2. type imitating handwriting. [< Med.L, < *cursus*, pp. of L *currere* run] —cur'sive·ly, *adv.*

cur·so·ry (kėr'sə·ri), *adj.* hasty and superficial; without attention to details. [< LL *cursorius* of a race < *currere* run] —cur'so·ri·ly, *adv.* —cur'so·ri·ness, *n.* —Syn. rapid, careless.

curt (kėrt), *adj.* 1. short; brief. 2. rudely brief; abrupt: *a curt way of talking.* [< L *curtus* cut short] —curt'ly, *adv.* —curt'ness, *n.*

cur·tail (kėr·tāl'), *v.* cut short; cut off part of; reduce; lessen. [< *curtal*, adj., cut short (esp. of tails) < OF < L *curtus*; infl. by *tail*] —cur·tail'er, *n.* —cur·tail'ment, *n.*

cur·tain (kėr'tən), *n.* 1. piece of material hung to shut off, cover, hide, or decorate something. 2. thing that covers or hides. —*v.* 1. provide with a curtain; shut off with a curtain; decorate with a curtain. 2. cover; hide. [< OF < LL *cortina*] —Syn. *n.* 1. hanging, drapery.

curtain call, call for an actor, musician, etc., to return to the stage and acknowledge the applause of the audience.

curt·sy, **curt·sey** (kėrt'si), *n.*, *pl.* -sies; -seys; *v.*, -sied, -sy·ing; -seyed, -sey·ing. —*n.* bow of respect or greeting by women, consisting of bending the knees and lowering the body slightly. —*v.* make a curtsy. [var. of *courtesy*]

cur·va·ture (kėr'və·chər; -chūr), *n.* 1. a curving. 2. a curved piece or part; curve.

curve (kėrv), *n.*, *v.*, curved, curv·ing, *adj.* —*n.* 1. line that has no straight part. 2. something having the shape of a curve; bend: *curves in a road.* 3. *Am.* baseball thrown so as to curve just before it reaches the batter. 4. *Math.* a line or lines that can be defined by an equation or equations. —*v.* 1. bend so as to form a curve. 2. move in the course of a curve. —*adj.* curved. [< L *curvus* bending]

cur·vet (*n.* kėr'vit; *v.* kėr·vet', kėr'vit), *n.*, *v.*, -vet·ed, -vet·ing; -vet·ted, -vet·ting. —*n.* leap in the air made by a horse, in which all the legs are off the ground for a second. —*v.* 1. make such a leap. 2. make (a horse) leap in this way. [< Ital. *corvetta*, dim. of *corvo* CURVE]

cur·vi·lin·e·ar (kėr'və·lin'i·ər), **cur·vi·lin·e·al** (-i·əl), *adj.* consisting of or enclosed by curved lines.

cush·ion (kush'ən), *n.* 1. a soft pillow or pad used to sit, lie, or kneel on. 2. anything used or shaped like a cushion. 3. the elastic lining of the sides of a billiard table. 4. something to counteract a sudden shock, jar, or jolt. —*v.* 1. put or seat on a cushion; support with cushions. 2. supply with a cushion. 3. protect from sudden shocks or jars with a cushion, esp. a cushion of steam. [< OF *coussin*, prob. < VL *coxinum* < L *coxa* hip]

cusp (kusp), *n.* 1. a pointed end; point. A crescent has two cusps. 2. a blunt or pointed protuberance of the crown of a tooth. [< L *cuspis*]

cus·pid (kus'pid), *n.* tooth having one cusp; canine tooth. —cus'pi·dal, *adj.*

cus·pi·date (kus'pə·dāt), **cus·pi·dat·ed** (-dāt'id), *adj.* having a sharp, pointed end.

cus·pi·dor (kus'pə·dôr), *n. Am.* container to spit into; spittoon. [< Pg., spitter, < *cuspir* spit < L *conspuere*]

cuss (kus), *Colloq.* —*n.* 1. curse. 2. *Am.* an insignificant or troublesome person or animal. —*v.* curse. [var. of *curse*]

cus·tard (kus'tərd), *n.* a baked or boiled pudding made of eggs, sugar, milk, etc. [var. of *crustade* < F < Pr. *croustado* pasty < L *crustare* encrust < *crusta* crust]

Cus·ter (kus'tər), *n.* George Armstrong, 1839-1876, American general in many Indian wars.

cus·to·di·an (kus·tō'di·ən), *n.* person in charge; caretaker: *the custodian of a museum.* —cus·to'di·an·ship', *n.*

cus·to·dy (kus'tə·di), *n.*, *pl.* -dies. 1. keeping; care. 2. a being confined or detained; imprisonment. 3. in custody, in the care of the police; in prison. 4. take into custody, arrest. [< L, < *custos* guardian] —cus·to·di·al (kus·tō'di·al) *adj.*

cus·tom (kus′təm), *n.* 1. a usual action; habit. 2. habit maintained for so long that it has almost the force of law. 3. habits or usages collectively. 4. the regular business given by a customer. 5. tax or service regularly due from feudal tenants to their lord. 6. **customs,** a. taxes paid to the government on things brought in from a foreign country. b. department of the government that collects these taxes. —*adj.* 1. made specially for individuals; made to order; not ready-made. 2. making things to order. [< OF < VL *consuetumen* < L *com-* + *suescere* accustom. Doublet of COSTUME.] —Syn. *n.* 1. usage.

cus·tom·a·ry (kus′təm·er′ĭ), *adj., n., pl.* -ar·ies. —*adj.* 1. according to custom; as a habit; usual. 2. holding or held by custom; pertaining to or established by custom, as distinguished from law. —*n.* 1. **customaries,** a body of legal customs, or customary laws of a manor, city, province, etc. 2. book or document containing them. —**cus·tom·ar·i·ly** (kus′təm·er′ə·lĭ; *emphatic* kus′təm·âr′ə·lĭ), *adv.* —**cus′tom·ar′i·ness,** *n.* —Syn. *adj.* 1. habitual, accustomed.

cus·tom-built (kus′təm·bilt′), *adj.* built to order; not ready-made.

cus·tom·er (kus′təm·ər), *n.* 1. person who buys. 2. *Colloq.* person; fellow.

custom house, a building where taxes on things brought into a country are collected.

cus·tom-made (kus′təm·mād′), *adj. Am.* made to order; not ready-made.

cut (kut), *v.,* cut, cut·ting, *adj., n.* —*v.* 1. separate, open, or remove with something sharp: *cut meat, timber, grass, one's nails, etc.* 2. make by cutting. 3. be cut; admit of being cut. 4. wound with a knife, saw, etc. 5. reduce; decrease. 6. pass; go; come: *he cut through the woods to get home.* 7. go across; divide by crossing: *a brook cuts that field.* 8. hit or strike sharply. 9. *Sports.* hit with a slicing stroke: *he cut the ball so that it bounded almost backward.* 10. hurt the feelings of. 11. *Colloq.* refuse to recognize socially (a class, lecture, etc.). 13. make less sticky or stiff; dissolve: *gasoline cuts grease and tar.* 14. divide (a pack of cards) at random. 15. *Colloq.* do; perform; make. 16. **cut across,** go straight across or through. 17. **cut back,** a. *Football.* go back suddenly. b. shorten by cutting off the end. 18. **cut in,** a. go in suddenly. b. break in; interrupt and replace. c. *Am.* interrupt a dancing couple to take the place of one of them. 19. **cut off,** a. remove by cutting. b. shut off. c. stop suddenly. d. break; interrupt. 20. **cut out,** a. remove by cutting. b. take out; leave out. c. take the place of; get the better of. d. make by cutting; make; form. e. *Am., Slang.* stop doing something. 21. **cut teeth,** have teeth grow through the gums. 22. **cut up,** a. cut to pieces. b. *Colloq.* hurt. c. *Am., Slang.* show off; play tricks. —*adj.* 1. that has been cut. 2. shaped or formed by cutting. 3. reduced: *cut prices.* 4. **cut and dried,** a. ready for use; arranged in advance. b. dead; dull; uninteresting. —*n.* 1. wound or opening made by cutting. 2. passage, channel, etc., made by cutting or digging. 3. piece cut off or cut out. 4. way in which a thing is cut; style; fashion. 5. *Am.* a decrease; reduction. 6. way straight across or through; short cut. 7. a sharp blow or stroke. 8. a slicing stroke. 9. action or speech that hurts the feelings. 10. *Colloq.* refusal to recognize socially. 11. *Am., Colloq.* absence from a class, lecture, etc. 12. block or plate with a picture engraved on it, used in printing. 13. picture made from such a block or plate. 14. *Am., Slang.* share of booty, etc. [ME *cutte*(n)] —Syn. *v.* 1. chop, hew, slash.

cu·ta·ne·ous (kū·tā′nĭ·əs), *adj.* of or having to do with the skin. [< Med.L, < L *cutis* skin]

cut·a·way (kut′ə·wā′), *n.* coat having the lower part cut back in a curve from the waist.

cut·back (kut′bak′), *n. Colloq.* 1. a scheduled slowing down of any industrial operation: *a cutback in steel production.* 2. reduction: *a cutback in the defense budget.*

cute (kūt), *adj.,* cut·er, cut·est. *Colloq.* 1. *Am.* pleasing or attractive because pretty, dear,

dainty, etc. 2. clever; shrewd. [var. of *acute*] —**cute′ly,** *adv.* —**cute′ness,** *n.*

cut glass, glass shaped or decorated by grinding and polishing. —**cut′-glass′,** *adj.*

cu·ti·cle (kū′tə·kəl), *n.* 1. outer skin. 2. the hardened skin around the edges of the fingernail or toenail. [< L *cuticula,* dim. of *cutis* skin]

cut·lass, cut·las (kut′ləs), *n.* a short, heavy, slightly curved sword. [< F *coutelas* < L *culter* knife]

CUTLASS

cut·ler (kut′lər), *n.* person who makes, sells, or repairs knives, scissors, and other cutting instruments. [< F, < *coutel* small knife < L *cultellus,* dim. of *culter* knife]

cut·ler·y (kut′lər·ĭ), *n.* 1. knives, scissors, and other cutting instruments. 2. knives, forks, spoons, etc., for table use. 3. business of a cutler.

cut·let (kut′lit), *n.* 1. slice of meat for broiling or frying. 2. a flat, fried cake of chopped meat or fish. [< F *côtelette,* ult. < L *costa* rib]

cut·off (kut′ôf′; -of′), *n.* 1. a short way across or through. 2. a stopping of the passage of steam or working fluid to the cylinder of an engine. 3. mechanism or device that does this.

cut·out (kut′out′), *n.* 1. *Am.* shape or design to be cut out: *some books have cutouts.* 2. device for disconnecting an engine from its muffler. 3. device for breaking an electric current.

cut·purse (kut′pèrs′), *n.* pickpocket.

cut rate, price lower than the usual price: *buy appliances at a cut rate.*

cut·ter (kut′ər), *n.* 1. person who cuts. 2. tool or machine for cutting: *a meat cutter.* 3. *Am.* a small, light sleigh, usually pulled by one horse. 4. a small sailboat with one mast. 5. boat belonging to a warship, used to carry people and supplies to and from the ship. 6. a small, armed ship used by the coast guard.

cut·throat (kut′thrōt′), *n.* murderer. —*adj.* 1. murderous. 2. *Am.* relentless; merciless; severe.

cut·ting (kut′ing), *n.* 1. thing cut off or cut out. 2. a small shoot cut from a plant to grow a new plant. 3. a newspaper or magazine clipping. 4. act of one that cuts. —*adj.* 1. that cuts; sharp. 2. hurting the feelings; sarcastic. —**cut′ting·ly,** *adv.*

cut·tle·fish (kut′əl·fish′), or **cut·tle** (kut′əl), *n., pl.* -fish·es or (*esp. collectively*) -fish; -tles. a saltwater mollusk with ten sucker-bearing arms and a hard, internal shell. One kind of cuttlefish squirts out an inky fluid when frightened. [OE *cudele* cuttlefish]

Cuttlefish (8 in. long)

cut·up (kut′up′), *n. Am., Slang.* person who shows off or plays tricks.

cut·wa·ter (kut′wô′tər; -wot′ər), *n.* the front part of a ship's prow.

cut·worm (kut′wèrm′), *n.* caterpillar that cuts off the stalks of young plants near the ground.

cwt., hundredweight.

-cy, *suffix.* 1. office, position, or rank of, as in *captaincy.* 2. quality, state, condition, or fact of being, as in *bankruptcy.* [< F *-cie,* < L *-cia,* Gk. *-kia*]

cy·an·ic (sī·an′ik), *adj.* 1. of cyanogen; containing cyanogen. 2. blue.

cyanic acid, *Chem.* a colorless, poisonous liquid, HOCN.

cy·a·nide (sī′ə·nīd; -nid), **cy·a·nid** (-nid), *n.* 1. salt of hydrocyanic acid. 2. potassium cyanide, KCN, a powerful poison.

cy·an·o·gen (sī·an′ə·jən), *n.* 1. a colorless, poisonous, inflammable gas, C_2N_2, with the odor of bitter almonds. 2. a univalent radical, CN, consisting of one atom of carbon and one of nitrogen.

cy·a·no·sis (sī′ə·nō′sis), *n. Pathol.* blueness or lividness of the skin, caused by lack of oxygen in the blood. [< NL < Gk. *kyanosis* dark-blue color] —**cy·a·not·ic** (sī′ə·not′ik), *adj.*

cy·ber·net·ics (sī'bər·net'iks), *n. Am.* comparative study of complex calculating machines and the human nervous system in order to understand better the functioning of the brain.

cy·cad (sī'kad), *n.* a large, tropical, palmlike plant with a cluster of long, fernlike leaves at the top. [< NL < Gk. *kykas*, scribal mistake for the pl. of *koiz* palm]

cyc·la·men (sik'lə·mən; -men), *n.* plant of the same family as the primrose, with heart-shaped leaves and snowy white, purple, pink, or crimson flowers, whose five petals bend backwards. [< NL < L < Gk. *kyklaminos*]

cy·cle (sī'kəl), *n., v.,* **-cled, -cling.** —*n.* 1. period of time or complete process of growth or action that repeats itself in the same order. Spring, summer, autumn, and winter make a cycle. 2. a complete set or series. 3. all the stories, poems, legends, etc., about a great hero or event. 4. a very long period of time; age. 5. bicycle, tricycle, etc. 6. *Physics.* a complete or double alteration or reversal of an alternating electric current. —*v.* 1. pass through a cycle; occur over and over again in the same order. 2. ride a bicycle, tricycle, etc. [< LL < Gk. *kyklos*] —cy'cler, *n.*

cy·clic (sī'klik; sik'lik), **cy·cli·cal** (sī'klə·kəl; sik'lə-), *adj.* 1. of a cycle. 2. moving or occurring in cycles. 3. arranged in a ring. 4. containing a ring of atoms. 5. of or pertaining to an arrangement of atoms in a ring or closed chain.

cy·clist (sī'klist), *n. Esp. Brit.* rider of a bicycle, tricycle, etc.

cy·clom·e·ter (sī·klom'ə·tər), *n.* instrument that measures the distance that a wheel travels by recording the revolutions that it makes.

cy·clone (sī'klōn), *n.* 1. a very violent windstorm; tornado. 2. storm moving around and toward a calm center of low pressure, which also moves. [< Gk. *kyklon*, ppr. of *kyklōein* move around in a circle] —**cy·clon·ic** (sī·klon'ik), **cy·clon'i·cal**, *adj.* —**cy·clon'i·cal·ly**, *adv.*

cy·clo·pe·di·a, cy·clo·pae·di·a (sī'klə·pē'di·ə), *n.* an encyclopedia. [shortened form of *encyclopedia*] —**cy'clo·pe'dic, cy'clo·pae'dic,** *adj.* —**cy'clo·pe'dist, cy'clo·pae'dist,** *n.*

Cy·clops (sī'klops), *n., pl.* **Cy·clo·pes** (sī·klō'pēz). *Gk. Legend.* one of a group of one-eyed giants. [< L < Gk., < *kyklos* circle + *ops* eye] —**Cy·clo·pe·an** (sī'klə·pē'ən; sī·klō'pi·ən), *adj.*

cy·clo·ram·a (sī'klə·ram'ə; -rä'mə), *n.* a large picture of a landscape, battle, etc., on the wall of a circular room. [< Gk. *kyklos* circle + *horama* spectacle] —**cy'clo·ram'ic,** *adj.*

cy·clo·tron (sī'klə·tron), *n. Physics.* a powerful apparatus that sends out electrons at very high velocities, and so can disintegrate atoms and cause radioactivity. [< Gk. *kyklos* circle + E *-tron* (as in *neutron*)]

cyg·net (sig'nit), *n.* a young swan.

cyl·in·der (sil'ən·dər), *n.* 1. *Geom.* a solid bounded by two equal, parallel circles and a curved surface formed by moving a straight line of fixed length so that its ends always lie on the two parallel circles. 2. volume of such a solid. 3. any long, round object, solid or hollow, with flat ends. 4. *Am.* part of a revolver that contains chambers for cartridges. 5. the piston chamber of an engine. [< L < Gk., < *kylindein* to roll]

Cylinder

cy·lin·dri·cal (sə·lin'drə·kəl), **cy·lin·dric** (-drik), *adj.* shaped like a cylinder; having the form of a cylinder. —**cy·lin'dri·cal·i·ty,** *n.* —**cy·lin'dri·cal·ly,** *adv.*

cym·bal (sim'bəl), *n.* one of a pair of brass plates, used as a musical instrument. When cymbals are struck together, they make a loud, ringing sound. [< L < Gk., < *kymbe* hollow of a vessel] —**cym'bal·ist,** *n.*

cyme (sīm), *n.* a flower cluster in which there is a flower at the top of the main stem and of

each branch of the cluster. [< L < Gk. *kyma* something swollen, sprout] —**cy·mose** (sī'mōs; sī·mōs'), *adj.*

Cym·ry (kim'ri), *n.* the Welsh people. —**Cym·ric** (kim'rik; sim'-), *adj., n.*

cyn·ic (sin'ik), *n.* 1. person inclined to believe that the motives for people's actions are insincere and selfish. 2. a sneering, sarcastic person. 3. **Cynic,** member of a group of ancient Greek philosophers who taught that self-control is the essential part of virtue, and despised pleasure, money, and personal comfort. —*adj.* 1. cynical. 2. **Cynic,** of or having to do with the Cynics or their doctrines. [< L < Gk. *kynikos* doglike < *kyon* dog]

cyn·i·cal (sin'ə·kəl), *adj.* 1. doubting the worth of life. 2. sneering; sarcastic. —**cyn'i·cal·ly,** *adv.* —**cyn'i·cal·ness,** *n.*

cyn·i·cism (sin'ə·siz·əm), *n.* 1. cynical quality or disposition. 2. a cynical remark.

cy·no·sure (sī'nə·shūr; sin'ə-), *n.* 1. center of attraction, interest, or attention. 2. something used for guidance or direction. [< L < Gk. *kynosoura* dog's tail < *kyon* dog + *oura* tail]

cy·pher (sī'fər), *n., v.* cipher.

cy·press (sī'prəs), *n.* 1. an evergreen tree of the South, with hard wood and dark leaves. 2. its wood. 3. any of various similar plants such as the European "true" cypress, and the "standing cypress" of the United States. [< OF < L *cypressus* < Gk. *kyparissos*]

cyp·ri·noid (sip'rə·noid), *n.* any of a large group of fresh-water fishes, including the carps, suckers, goldfishes, breams, most fresh-water minnows, etc. —*adj.* of or belonging to this group. [< L *cyprinus* carp (< Gk.) + -OID]

Cyp·ri·ot (sip'ri·ət), *adj.* of Cyprus. —*n.* a native or inhabitant of Cyprus.

Cy·prus (sī'prəs), *n.* an island and British colony in the E Mediterranean, S of Turkey.

Cy·rus (sī'rəs), *n.* died 529 B.C., king of Persia from 558? to 529 B.C.

cyst (sist), *n.* 1. an abnormal, saclike growth in animals or plants. Cysts usually contain liquid and diseased matter. 2. a saclike structure in animals or plants. [< NL < Gk. *kystis* pouch, bladder] —**cyst'ic,** *adj.*

Cyth·er·e·a (sith'ər·ē'ə), *n. Gk. Myth.* Aphrodite. —**Cyth'er·e'an,** *adj.*

cy·tol·o·gy (sī·tol'ə·ji), *n.* branch of biology that deals with the formation, structure, and function of the cells of animals and plants. [< Gk. *kytos* receptacle, cell + -LOGY] —**cy·tol'o·gist,** *n.*

cy·to·plasm (sī'tə·plaz·əm), **cy·to·plast** (-plast), *n. Biol.* the living substance or protoplasm of a cell, exclusive of the nucleus. —**cy'to·plas'mic,** *adj.*

C.Z., Canal Zone.

czar (zär), *n.* 1. emperor. It was the title of the emperors of Russia. 2. autocrat; person with absolute power. Also, **tsar, tzar, tzar.** [< Russ. *tsar* < Old Church Slavic < Gothic < L *Caesar* Caesar]

czar·e·vitch (zär'ə·vich), *n.* 1. the eldest son of a Russian czar. 2. son of a Russian czar. Also, **tsarevitch, tzarevitch.**

cza·ri·na (zä·rē'nə), *n.* wife of a czar; Russian empress. Also, **tsarina, tzarina.**

czar·ism (zär'iz·əm), *n.* autocracy.

Czech (chek), *n.* 1. member of the most westerly branch of the Slavs. Bohemians, Moravians, and Silesians are Czechs. 2. their language; Bohemian. —*adj.* of or having to do with Czechoslovakia, its language, or its people. —**Czech'ic, Czech'ish,** *adj.*

Czech·o·slo·vak, Czech·o·Slo·vak (chek'ə·slō'vak; -väk), *adj.* of or having to do with Czechoslovakia, its people, or their language. —*n.* 1. native or inhabitant of Czechoslovakia. 2. their language.

Czech·o·slo·va·ki·a, Czech·o·Slo·va·ki·a (chek'ə·slō·vä'ki·ə; -vak'i·ə), *n.* country in C Europe. —**Czech'o·slo·va'ki·an, Czech'o·Slo·va'ki·an,** *adj., n.*

D

D, d (dē), *n., pl.* **D's; d's. 1.** the fourth letter of the alphabet. **2.** the second note or tone of the musical scale of C major. **3.** the Roman numeral for 500.

D, *Chem.* deuterium.

D., 1. December. **2.** Democrat; Democratic. **3.** Dutch.

d., 1. day. **2.** dead. **3.** degree. **4.** delete. **5.** died. **6.** dollar. **7.** dose. **8.** English penny; pence.

D.A., District Attorney.

dab (dab), *v.,* **dabbed, dab·bing,** *n.* —*v.* **1.** touch lightly; pat with something soft or moist; tap. **2.** put on with light strokes. —*n.* **1.** a quick, light touch or blow; a pat; a tap. **2.** a small, soft or moist mass. **3.** a little bit. [ME] —**dab′ber,** *n.*

dab·ble (dab′əl), *v.,* **-bled, -bling. 1.** dip (hands, feet, etc.) in and out of water; splash. **2.** do superficially; work a little: *dabble at painting.* [< Flem. *dabbelen*] —**dab′bler,** *n.*

dace (dās), *n., pl.* **dac·es** or (*esp. collectively*) **dace.** any of several small fresh-water fish. [ME *darse* < OF *dars* DART]

Dach·au (däʜ′ou), *n.* a former Nazi concentration camp located in S Germany.

dachs·hund (däks′húnd′; -húnt′; daks′-; dash′-), *n.* dog of a German breed that is small, with a long body and very short legs. [< G, < *dachs* badger + *hund* dog]

Da·cron (dā′kron), *n. Trademark.* a synthetic wrinkle- and abrasion-resistant fiber used for shirts, suits, etc.

dac·tyl (dak′təl), *n.* a metrical foot of three syllables (– ◡ ◡), one accented followed by two unaccented, or, in classical verse, one long followed by two short. [< L < Gk. *daktylos* finger] —**dac·tyl·ic** (dak·til′ik), *adj., n.*

dad (dad), *n. Colloq.* father.

dad·dy (dad′i), *n., pl.* **-dies.** *Colloq.* father.

dad·dy-long-legs (dad′i-lông′legz′; -long′-), *n., pl.* **-legs.** *U.S.* **1.** animal similar to a spider, with a small body and very long, thin legs. **2.** crane fly.

Daddy-longlegs

da·do (dā′dō), *n., pl.* **-does, -dos. 1.** the lower part of the wall of a room when it is decorated differently from the upper part. **2.** part of a pedestal between the base and the cap. [< Ital., DIE²]

Daed·a·lus (ded′ə-ləs), *n. Gk. Legend.* a skillful worker who made wings for flying and built the labyrinth in Crete.

dae·mon (dē′mən), *n.* **1.** *Gk. Myth.* **a.** a supernatural being. **b.** an inferior deity. **2.** demon. [< L < Gk. *daimon*] —**dae·mon·ic** (dē·mon′ik), *adj.*

daf·fo·dil (daf′ə·dil), *n.* **1.** narcissus with yellow flowers and long, slender leaves. **2.** the flower. **3.** yellow. [var. of *affodill* < VL < L < Gk. *asphodelos*]

daff·y (daf′i), *adj.,* **daff·i·er, daff·i·est.** *Colloq.* foolish; silly; crazy.

daft (daft; däft), *adj.* **1.** silly; foolish. **2.** crazy. [cf. OE *gedœfte* gentle] —**daft′ness,** *n.*

da Gam·a (də gam′ə), Vasco, 1469?–1524, Portuguese navigator.

dag·ger (dag′ər), *n.* **1.** a small weapon with a short, pointed blade, used for stabbing. **2.** sign (†) used in printing to refer the reader to a footnote, etc. [prob. < obs. *dag* slash]

da·guerre·o·type (də·ger′ə·tīp; -i·ə·tīp), *n., v.,* **-typed, -typ·ing.** —*n.* **1.** an early method of photography in which the pictures were made on silvered metal plates. **2.** picture made in this way. —*v.* photograph by this process. [for L. J. M. *Daguerre,* inventor]

dahl·ia (dal′yə; däl′yə; *esp. Brit.* dāl′yə), *n.* **1.** a tall plant of the aster family that has large, showy flowers in the autumn. **2.** the flower. [< NL; named for A. *Dahl,* botanist]

Da·ho·mey (də·hō′mi), *n.* territory in French West Africa.

Dail Eir·eann (dôl âr′ən; doil), or **Dail,** *n.* the lower house of parliament of the Irish Republic.

dai·ly (dā′li), *adj., n., pl.* **-lies,** *adv.* —*adj.* done, happening, or appearing every day, or every day but Sunday. —*n. Am.* newspaper appearing every day, or every day but Sunday. —*adv.* every day; day by day.

dain·ty (dān′ti), *adj.,* **-ti·er, -ti·est,** *n., pl.* **-ties.** —*adj.* **1.** having delicate beauty; fresh and pretty. **2.** having or showing delicate tastes and feeling; particular. **3.** good to eat; delicious. **4.** too particular; overnice. [< n.] —*n.* something very good to eat; a delicious bit of food. [< OF < L *dignitas* worthiness < *dignus* worthy] —**dain′ti·ly,** *adv.* —**dain′ti·ness,** *n.* —Syn. *adj.* **2.** fastidious. **4.** squeamish.

dair·y (dâr′i), *n., pl.* **dair·ies. 1.** room or building where milk and cream are kept and made into butter and cheese. **2.** farm where milk and cream are produced and butter and cheese made. **3.** store or company that sells milk, butter, etc. **4.** business of producing milk, butter, etc. [ME *deierie* < *deie* maid (OE *dæge* breadmaker)]

dair·y·man (dâr′i·mən), *n., pl.* **-men. 1.** man who works in a dairy. **2.** man who owns or manages a dairy. **3.** man who sells milk, butter, etc.

da·is (dā′is; dās), *n.* a raised platform in a hall or large room for a throne, seats of honor, etc. [< OF < L *discus* quoit, DISH]

dai·sy (dā′zi), *n., pl.* **-sies,** *adj.* —*n.* **1.** plant of the aster family whose flowers or petals are usually white or pink around a yellow center. **2.** *Am.* a tall plant of the same family whose flower heads have a yellow disk and white rays; the common "white daisy" of the U.S. **3.** *Slang.* something fine or first-rate. —*adj. Slang.* first-rate. [OE *dæges eage* day's eye] —**dai′sied,** *adj.*

Da·kar (dä·kär′), *n.* seaport and capital of French West Africa.

Da·lai La·ma (dä·lī′ lä′mə), the chief priest of the religion of Lamaism in Tibet and Mongolia. Also, **Grand Lama.**

dale (dāl), *n.* valley. [OE *dœl*]

Da·li (dä′lē), *n.* Salvador, born 1904, Spanish surrealist painter.

Dal·las (dal′əs), *n.* city in NE Texas.

dal·li·ance (dal′i·əns), *n.* **1.** flirtation. **2.** a playing; trifling.

dal·ly (dal′i), *v.,* **-lied, -ly·ing. 1.** act in a playful manner. **2.** flirt (with danger, temptation, a person, etc.). **3.** trifle. **3.** be idle; loiter. **4.** waste (time). [< OF *dalier* chat] —**dal′li·er,** *n.*

Dal·ma·tian (dal·mā′shən), *n.* a large, short-haired dog, usually white with black spots; coach dog.

Dalmatian (20 in. high at the shoulder)

dam¹ (dam), *n., v.,* **dammed, dam·ming.** —*n.* **1.** wall built to hold back flowing water. **2.** water held back by a dam. **3.** anything resembling a dam. —*v.* **1.** provide with a dam; hold back (water, etc.) by means of a dam. **2.** hold back; block up. [ME]

dam² (dam), *n.* **1.** the female parent of four-footed animals. **2.** mother. [var. of *dame*]

dam·age (dam′ij), *n., v.,* **-aged, -ag·ing.** —*n.* **1.** harm or injury that lessens value or usefulness. **2.** *Slang.* cost; price. **3.** **damages,** money necessary to make up for some harm done to a person or his property. —*v.* harm or injure so as to lessen value or usefulness; to harm; to hurt. [< OF, < *dam* < L *damnum* loss, hurt] —**dam′age·a·ble,** *adj.* —**dam′ag·ing·ly,** *adv.* —Syn. *n.* **1.** detriment, impairment. —*v.* impair, disfigure.

dam·a·scene (dam′ə·sēn; dam′ə·sēn′), v., -scened, -scen·ing, adj., n. —v. ornament (metal) with inlaid gold or silver or with a wavy design. —adj. of or like such an ornament. —n. the ornament or design itself. [< L < Gk. *Damaskenos* of Damascus]

Da·mas·cus (də·mas′kəs), n. capital of Syria, a very ancient trading center.

dam·ask (dam′əsk), n. 1. silk woven with an elaborate pattern. 2. linen with woven designs. 3. damascened metal. 4. a rose color; pink. —v. make damask. —adj. 1. of or named after the city of Damascus. 2. made of damask. 3. pink; rose-colored. [< L < Gk. *Damaskos* Damascus]

damask steel, Damascus steel, ornamented steel, used in making swords, etc.

dame (dām), n. 1. an elderly woman. 2. *Slang.* woman. 3. in Great Britain, a. title given to a woman who has received an honorable rank corresponding to that of a knight. b. the legal title of the wife or widow of a knight or baronet (in ordinary use, Lady). [< OF < L *domina* mistress]

damn (dam), v. 1. declare (something) to be bad or inferior; condemn. 2. cause to fail; ruin. 3. doom to eternal punishment; condemn to hell. 4. swear or swear at by saying "damn"; curse. —n. a saying of "damn"; curse. [< OF < L *damnare* condemn < *damnum* loss] —damn′er, n. —Syn. v. 1. denounce, proscribe, execrate.

dam·na·ble (dam′nə·bəl), adj. 1. abominable; outrageous; detestable. 2. deserving damnation. —dam′na·ble·ness, n. —dam′na·bly, adv.

dam·na·tion (dam·nā′shən), n. 1. a damning or being damned; condemnation. 2. condemnation to eternal punishment. 3. curse. —dam·na·to·ry (dam′nə·tô′ri; -tō′-), adj.

damned (damd), adj. 1. condemned as bad or inferior. 2. doomed to eternal punishment. 3. cursed; abominable. —n. the damned, the souls in hell. —adv. very.

Dam·o·cles (dam′ə·klēz), n. flatterer and courtier of Dionysius, king of Syracuse, who enjoyed a banquet given by Dionysius until he saw a sword hung by a single hair above his head.

Da·mon (dā′mən), n. Rom. Legend. a man who pledged his life for his friend Pythias, who was sentenced to death.

damp (damp), adj. slightly wet; moist. —n. 1. moisture. 2. thing that checks or deadens. 3. dejection; discouragement. 4. any harmful gas that collects in mines, such as chokedamp or firedamp. —v. 1. make moist or slightly wet. 2. check; deaden. 3. stifle; suffocate. 4. extinguish. [< MDu. or MLG] —damp′ly, adv. —damp′ness, n.

damp·en (dam′pən), v. 1. moisten. 2. depress; discourage. 3. *Radio.* eliminate extraneous sounds or echoes in a studio by using special wall coverings. —damp′en·er, n.

damp·er (dam′pər), n. 1. person or thing that depresses. 2. a movable plate to control the draft in a stove or furnace. 3. device for checking vibration, as of piano strings.

dam·sel (dam′zəl), n. girl; maiden. [< OF *dameisele*, ult. < L *domina* DAME]

dam·son (dam′zən), n. 1. a small, dark-purple plum. 2. tree that it grows on. [< L (*prunum*) *damascenum* (plum) of Damascus]

Dan (dan), n. 1. a Hebrew tribe that migrated to N Palestine. 2. city in N Palestine. 3. from Dan to Beersheba, from one end of a place to the other.

Dan., Danish.

Da·na·i·des (də·nā′ə·dēz), n.pl. Gk. Legend. the fifty daughters of Danaüs (dan′i·əs), a Greek king. All but one killed their husbands on their wedding night, and were condemned to draw water with a sieve forever in Hades.

dance (dans; däns), v., danced, danc·ing, n., adj. —v. 1. move in rhythm, usually in time with music. 2. do or take part in (a dance). 3. jump up and down; move in a lively way. 4. bob up and down. —n. 1. movement in rhythm, usually in time with music. 2. some special group of steps, etc. 3. one round of dancing. 4. piece of music for dancing. 5. party where people dance. 6. movement up and down; lively move-

ment. —adj. of or for dancing. [< OF *danser*, prob. < Gmc.] —danc′er, n. —danc′ing·ly, adv.

dance hall, Am. a public hall or room in which dances are held.

dan·de·li·on (dan′də·lī′ən), n. weed with deeply notched leaves and bright-yellow flowers. [< F *dent de lion* lion's tooth; from toothed leaves]

dan·der (dan′dər), n. *Colloq.* 1. temper; anger. 2. get one's dander up, get angry.

dan·di·fy (dan′də·fī), v., -fied, -fy·ing. make dandylike or foppish. —dan′di·fi·ca′tion, n.

dan·dle (dan′dəl), v., -dled, -dling. 1. move (a child) up and down on one's knees or in one's arms. 2. pet; pamper. —dan′dler, n.

dan·druff (dan′drəf), n. small, whitish scales that form on the scalp.

dan·dy (dan′di), n., pl. -dies, adj., -di·er, -di·est. —n. 1. man who is too careful of his dress and appearance. 2. *Slang.* an excellent or first-rate thing. —adj. 1. of a dandy; too carefully dressed. 2. *Slang.* excellent; first-rate. —dan′dy·ism, n. —Syn. n. 1. fop. —adj. 1. foppish.

Dane (dān), n. 1. native or inhabitant of Denmark. 2. person of Danish descent.

Dane·law (dān′lô′), n. 1. set of laws enforced by the Danes when they held NE England in the 9th and 10th centuries A.D. 2. part of England under these laws.

dan·ger (dān′jər), n. 1. chance of harm; nearness to harm; risk; peril. 2. thing that may cause harm. [< OF *dangier* < L *dominium* sovereignty < *dominus* master] —Syn. 1. hazard, jeopardy. 2. menace, threat. —Ant. 1. safety.

dan·ger·ous (dān′jər·əs), adj. likely to cause harm; not safe; risky. —dan′ger·ous·ly, adv. —dan′ger·ous·ness, n. —Syn. perilous, precarious, unsafe.

dan·gle (dang′gəl), v., -gled, -gling, n. —v. 1. hang and swing loosely. 2. hold or carry (a thing) so that it swings loosely. 3. hang about; follow. 4. cause to dangle. —n. 1. act or fact of dangling. 2. something that dangles. [< Scand. (Dan.)] —dan′gler, n.

Dan·iel (dan′yəl), n. 1. *Bible.* a Hebrew prophet. 2. book of the Bible that tells about him.

Dan·ish (dān′ish), adj. of or having to do with the Danes, their language, or Denmark. —n. language of the Danes.

dank (dangk), adj. unpleasantly damp; moist; wet. —dank′ly, adv. —dank′ness, n.

dan·seuse (dän·sœz′), n., pl. -seuses (-sœz′). a woman dancer in a ballet. [< F]

Dan·te (dan′tē; dän′tā), n. 1265–1321, Italian poet, author of the *Divine Comedy.*

Dan·ube (dan′ūb), n. river flowing from SW Germany into the Black Sea. —Dan·u·bi·an (dan·ū′bi·ən), adj.

Dan·zig (dant′sig; dänt′-; dan′zig), n. 1. seaport in N Poland, on the Baltic Sea. 2. Bay of, an inlet of the Baltic Sea.

Daph·ne (daf′nē), n. Gk. Legend. nymph pursued by Apollo, whom she escaped by being changed into a laurel tree.

dap·per (dap′ər), adj. 1. neat; trim; spruce. 2. small and active. [cf. MDu. *dapper* agile, strong] —dap′per·ly, adv. —dap′per·ness, n.

dap·ple (dap′əl), adj., n., v., -pled, -pling. —adj. spotted: a dapple horse. —n. 1. a spotted appearance or condition. 2. animal with a spotted or mottled skin. —v. mark or become marked with spots. [cf. Scand. *depill* spot]

D.A.R., Am. Daughters of the American Revolution.

Dar·da·nelles (där′də·nelz′), n. strait between Europe and Asia, connecting the Sea of Marmara with the Aegean Sea. In ancient times it was called the Hellespont.

dare (dār), v., dared or durst, dared, dar·ing, n. —v. 1. have courage; be bold; be bold enough. 2. have courage for; not be afraid of; be bold enough for. 3. meet and resist; face and defy. 4. challenge. —n. a challenge. [OE *dearr* (inf., *durran*)] —dar′er, n. —Syn. v. 2. venture. 3. brave.

dare·dev·il (dār′dev′əl), n. a reckless person. —adj. reckless.

Dar·i·en (dār′i·en; dâr′i·en′), *n.* **1.** Isthmus of, a former name of the Isthmus of Panama. **2.** Gulf of, gulf of the Caribbean Sea, between Panama and Colombia.

dar·ing (dâr′ing), *n.* courage to take risks; boldness. —*adj.* courageous; bold. —**dar′ing·ly,** *adv.* —**dar′ing·ness,** *n.*

Da·ri·us I (də·rī′əs), 558?–486? B.C., king of Persia from 521 to 486? B.C.

dark (därk), *adj.* **1.** without light; with very little light. **2.** not light-colored: *a dark complexion.* **3.** nearly black. **4.** hard to understand or explain. **5.** secret; hidden. **6.** ignorant. **7.** evil; wicked. **8.** gloomy; dull; dismal. **9.** sad; sullen; frowning. **10.** of radio stations, not broadcasting. **11. keep dark,** keep silent; not tell about. —*n.* **1.** absence of light. **2.** night; nightfall. **3.** a dark color. **4.** obscurity. **5.** secrecy. **6.** ignorance. **7.** in the dark, without knowledge or information. [OE *deorc*] —**dark′ish,** *adj.* —**dark′ish·ness,** *n.* —**dark′ly,** *adv.* —**dark′ness,** *n.*

Dark Ages, the early part of the Middle Ages, from about 500 A.D. to about 1000 A.D.

dark·en (där′kən), *v.* make or become dark or darker. —**dark′en·er,** *n.*

dark horse, an unexpected winner that little is known about.

dark lantern, lantern whose light can be hidden by a cover or dark glass.

dark·ling (därk′ling), *adv., adj.* in the dark.

dark·room (därk′rüm′; -rum′), *n.* room arranged for developing photographs.

dar·ling (där′ling), *n.* person very dear to another; person much loved. —*adj.* very dear; much loved. [OE *dēorling < dēore* DEAR]

darn[1] (därn), *v.* mend by making rows of stitches back and forth across a hole, torn place, etc. —*n.* **1.** act of darning. **2.** place so mended. [< dial. F *darner* mend < *darne* piece < Breton *darn*] —**darn′er,** *n.*

darn[2] (därn), *v. Colloq.* damn; curse. —*n.* **not give a darn,** be completely indifferent. [< *damn*; infl. by *tarnal* (colloq. for *eternal*)] —**darned,** *adj.,* *adv.*

dart (därt), *n.* **1.** a slender, pointed weapon to be thrown or shot. **2.** a sudden, swift movement. **3.** stinger of an insect. **4.** seam to make a garment fit better. —*v.* **1.** throw or shoot suddenly and swiftly. **2.** move suddenly and swiftly. **3.** send suddenly. [< OF < Gmc.] —Syn. *n.* **2.** dash. —*v.* **1.** hurl, launch. **2.** dash, bolt.

Dart

dart·er (där′tər), *n.* **1.** animal or person that moves suddenly and swiftly. **2.** *Am.* a small fresh-water fish, somewhat like a perch, that darts away very rapidly. **3.** *Am.* a swimming bird that has a long neck and darts at its prey.

Dar·win (där′wən), *n.* **Charles,** 1809–1882, English scientist, famous for his theory of evolution. —**Dar·win·i·an** (där·win′i·ən), *adj., n.*

Dar·win·ism (där′wən·iz·əm), *n.* doctrine maintained by Charles Darwin respecting the origin of species as derived by descent, with variation, from parent forms through the natural selection of those best adapted to survive in the struggle for existence. —**Dar′win·ist,** *n., adj.*

dash (dash), *v.* **1.** throw. **2.** splash. **3.** apply roughly as by splashing. **4.** rush. **5.** strike violently against something. **6.** smash. **7.** ruin: *our hopes were dashed.* **8.** depress; discourage; abash. **9.** adulterate; dilute. **10.** mix with a small amount of something else. **11. dash off,** do, make, write, etc., quickly. —*n.* **1.** a splash. **2.** a rush. **3.** a smash. **4.** thing that depresses or discourages; check. **5.** a small amount. **6.** *Am.* a short race. **7.** a blow; a stroke. **8.** mark (—) used in writing or printing to show a break in sense, parenthetical material, omitted letters or words, etc. **9.** a long sound used in sending messages by telegraph or radiotelegraph. **10.** energy; spirit; liveliness. **11.** showy appearance

or behavior. **12.** dashboard. [ME *dasche(n)*] —**dash′er,** *n.* —Syn. *n.* **5.** spot, touch, tinge, smack, trace. ➤ **dash** (-, —, ——). Three dashes of varying lengths are used in printing: - (en dash), — (em dash, the usual mark), and —— (2-em dash). On the typewriter use a hyphen for the first, two hyphens not spaced away from the neighboring words for the usual dash, and four hyphens for the long dash. The em dash, the one we have in mind when we say just *dash,* has aroused more discussion and more violent feeling than punctuation seems to deserve. Some textbooks and some publishers forbid its use generally, while others specify minute shades of meaning which they believe it indicates. Some writers rarely use it. Others, especially in matter not intended for publication, use it at the expense of other marks. A dash is roughly equivalent to a comma, that is, it separates small units within a sentence, but if used sparingly it suggests a definite tone, usually a note of surprise, an emotional emphasis. From a strictly logical point of view some other mark could always be substituted for a dash, but there would be a difference in movement and suggestiveness in the sentence. At its best it is a rather abrupt and emphatic mark.

1. The most typical use of the dash is to mark a sharp turn in the thought or construction of a sentence: *Of course, there is one place safe from salesmen—in heaven.*

2. A dash is often used before an interpolated or added phrase, usually either one that summarizes what has just been said or that gives contrasting or emphasizing details of what has been said, or often a striking apposition. This dash has the force of a more vigorous comma: *The waiting, the watching, the hundreds of small necessary acts about the sickroom—all this was past.*

3. A dash is often used between two compound clauses of a sentence, for abrupt separation: *Ideally, the student listens carefully, the teacher provides many examples—comprehension is at a maximum, not thwarted by professorial vagueness.*

4. A dash is sometimes used to enclose parenthetical statements that are more informal than a parenthesis would be, separating the expression from the context more than a comma but less definitely than parentheses would: *The general feeling among the men—most of them union members—was that the speaker avoided the central issue.*

5. Formerly a dash was often combined with other marks, especially with a comma or a colon, but recently this use has declined. The dash adds nothing in the salutation of a letter (*Dear Sir:—* means no more than *Dear Sir:*) and adds a displeasing mark to the page. Within sentences the old comma-dash combination has very generally disappeared also, so that now we find either a comma, or if emphasis makes it useful, a dash alone.

dash·board (dash′bôrd′; -bōrd′), *n.* **1.** the panel with instruments and gauges in an automobile, airplane, etc. **2.** protection on the front of a boat, etc., that prevents mud or water from being splashed into it.

dash·ing (dash′ing), *adj.* **1.** full of energy and spirit; lively. **2.** stylish; showy. —**dash′ing·ly,** *adv.*

dash·y (dash′i), *adj.,* **dash·i·er, dash·i·est.** dashing.

das·tard (das′tərd), *n.* a mean coward; sneak. —*adj.* mean and cowardly; sneaking. [ME, orig., a dullard, appar. < *dased,* pp. of DAZE] —**das′tard·ly,** *adj.* —**das′tard·li·ness,** *n.*

dat., dative.

da·ta (dā′tə; dat′ə; dä′tə), *n.* **1.** pl. of **da·tum. 2.** *Am.* things known or granted; facts. ➤ data. **1.** pronounced dā′tə, sometimes dat′ə, or (affecting Latin) dä′tə. **2.** Strictly, **data** is a plural, with a little-used singular *datum.* Its meaning is actually collective and may sometimes stress a group of facts as a unit and so be used with a singular verb. Sometimes, referring to individual facts, *data* is used with a plural: *The actual* *data of history consists of contemporary facts* (sing.). *Our task is to analyze when the data have been secured* (pl.). The singular verb can be safely used in any but the most formal writing.

date[1] (dāt), *n., v.,* **dat·ed, dat·ing.** —*n.* **1.** time when something happens. **2.** statement of time. **3.** period of time. **4.** *Am., Colloq.* appointment for a certain time. **5.** *Am., Colloq.* person of the opposite sex with whom an appointment is made. **6. to date,** till now; yet. —*v.* **1.** mark with a date; put a date on. **2.** find out the date of; give a date to. **3.** be dated; have a date on it. **4.** belong to a certain period of time; have its origin: *that house dates from the 18th century.* **5.** *Am., Colloq.* make a social appointment with (a person of the opposite sex). [< F < Med.L *data,* pp. fem. of L *dare* give] ➤ **dates.** Unless you have good reason for some other form, write dates in the common method: *November 27, 1938; June 16, 1940.* If saving space is important, as in business or reference writing, months having more than four letters should be abbreviated: *Jan., Feb., Mar., Apr., Aug., Sept., Oct., Nov., Dec.* In familiar and informal writing, figures are convenient: *11/27/38, 6/16/40.* In England and other countries the day of the month is usually put first, but that is confusing in the United States, unless Roman numerals are used for the month: *8-vii-38 (July 8, 1938).* Better style now usually omits the *st, nd, th* from the day of the month: *May 1* rather than *May 1st, September 17* rather than *September 17th.* In rather formal style the day of the month may be written in words when the year is not given: *September seventeen* or *September seventeenth.*

date[2] (dāt), *n.* **1.** the sweet fruit of a kind of palm tree. **2.** date palm. [(< OF < L < Gk. *daktylos* date, finger]

dat·ed (dāt′id), *adj.* **1.** marked with a date; showing a date on it. **2.** out-of-date.

date·less (dāt′lis), *adj.* **1.** without a date; not dated. **2.** endless; unlimited. **3.** so old that it cannot be given a date. **4.** old but still interesting.

date line, 1. an imaginary line agreed upon as the place where each calendar day first begins. It runs north and south through the Pacific, mostly along the 180th meridian. **2.** *Am.* line in a letter, newspaper, etc., giving the date when it was written or issued.

date palm, a palm tree on which dates grow.

da·tive (dā′tiv), *adj.* showing the indirect object of a verb. In "Give me the book," *me* is in the dative case. In Latin *Puero librum dedit,* "He gave the boy a book," *puero* is in the dative case. —*n.* **1.** the dative case. **2.** word in this case. [< L *dativus* of giving < *datus,* pp. of *dare* give] —**da′tive·ly,** *adv.* ➤ **dative case.** A noun or pronoun in the dative case either has the same form as the accusative or appears in a phrase made with *to* or *for* or *on.* If both a dative and accusative object are used with the same verb, the dative usually precedes if it is the simple form and follows if it is the prepositional form: *They gave him three dollars. They gave the man three dollars. They gave three dollars to him* [*to the man*]. The dative indicates that the action is for the advantage or disadvantage of the person or object it names or that the act in some way refers to the person or object. Such a noun or pronoun is called an "indirect object."

da·tum (dā′təm; dat′əm; dä′təm), *n., pl.* **da·ta.** fact from which conclusions can be drawn. [< L, (thing) given, pp. of *dare*]

daub (dôb), *v.* **1.** coat or cover with plaster, clay, mud, etc. **2.** make dirty; soil; stain. **3.** paint unskillfully. —*n.* **1.** anything daubed on. **2.** act of daubing. **3.** a badly painted picture. [< F < L, < *de-* + *albus* white] —**daub′er,** *n.*

daugh·ter (dô′tər), *n.* **1.** a female child. **2.** a female descendant. **3.** girl or woman related in the same way that a child is related to its parents. **4.** anything thought of as a daughter in relation to its origin. [OE *dohtor*] —**daugh′ter·ly,** *adj.*

daughter element, *Nuclear Physics.* element produced by the decay of a radioactive element.

daugh·ter-in-law (dô′tər·in·lô′), *n., pl.* **daugh·ters-in-law.** wife of one's son.

daunt (dônt; dänt), *v.* **1.** frighten. **2.** discourage. [< OF *danter* < L *domitare* < *domare* tame] —**Syn. 1.** intimidate, scare. **2.** dismay, dishearten.

daunt·less (dônt′lis; dänt′-), *adj.* not to be frightened or discouraged; brave. —**daunt′less·ly,** *adv.* —**daunt′less·ness,** *n.*

dau·phin (dô′fən), *n.* title of the oldest son of the king of France, from 1349 to 1830. [< F, orig. a family name]

dav·en·port (dav′ən·pôrt; -pōrt), *n. Am.* a long couch with back and ends. Some davenports can be made into beds. [prob. from the maker's name]

Da·vid (dā′vid), *n.* the second king of Israel.

da Vin·ci (də vin′chi), Leonardo, 1452–1519, Italian painter, architect, and scientist.

Da·vis (dā′vis), *n.* Jefferson, 1808–1889, president of the Confederate States, 1861 to 1865.

dav·it (dav′it; dā′vit), *n.* a curved arm at the side of a ship, used to hold or lower a small boat, anchor, etc. [< AF *daviot*]

Da·vy (dā′vi), *n.* Sir Humphry, 1778–1829, English Chemist.

Da·vy Jones (dā′vi jōnz′), *Naut.* the sailor's devil.

Da·vy Jones's locker, grave of those who die at sea; bottom of the ocean.

daw (dô), *n.* a jackdaw. [ME *dawe*]

daw·dle (dô′dəl), *v.,* **-dled, -dling.** waste time; idle; loiter. —**daw′dler,** *n.*

dawn (dôn), *n.* **1.** the first light in the east; daybreak. **2.** beginning. —*v.* **1.** grow bright or clear. **2.** grow clear to the eye or mind. **3.** begin; appear: *a new era is dawning.* [< *dawning,* prob. < Scand. (Dan.) *dagning*]

Daw·son (dô′sən), *n.* city in NW Canada, in Yukon Territory.

day (dā), *n.* **1.** time between sunrise and sunset. **2.** light of day; daylight. **3.** the 24 hours of day and night (called a **mean solar day**). **4.** a certain day set aside for a particular purpose or for celebration, as Christmas Day. **5.** hours for work: *an eight-hour day.* **6.** *Astron.* time taken by some specified heavenly body to make one complete turn on its axis: *the moon's day.* **7.** time; period: *in days of old.* **8.** period of life, activity, power, or influence: *he has had his day.* **9.** conflict; contest. **10.** victory. [OE *dæg*]

day bed, day·bed (dā′bed′), *n. Esp. U.S.* bed, usually narrow, with low head and foot boards of equal height, used as a couch by day.

day book, *Bookkeeping.* book in which a record is kept of each day's business.

day·break (dā′brāk′), *n.* time when it first begins to get light in the morning.

day coach, *Am.* an ordinary passenger car of a railroad train.

day·dream (dā′drēm′), *n.* **1.** dreamy thought about pleasant things. **2.** a pleasant plan or fancy, unlikely to come true. —*v.* think dreamily about pleasant things. —**day′dream′er,** *n.*

day laborer, an unskilled or manual worker who is paid by the day.

day letter, *Esp. U.S.* telegram sent during the day, usually slower and cheaper than a regular telegram.

day·light (dā′līt′), *n.* **1.** light of day. **2.** daytime. **3.** dawn; daybreak. **4.** publicity; openness.

day·light-sav·ing time (dā′līt′sāv′ing), time that is one hour faster than standard time, usually used during the summer to give more daylight after working hours.

day nursery, *Am.* nursery for the care of small children during the day.

Day of Atonement, Yom Kippur.

day school, 1. school held in the daytime. **2.** a private school for students who live at home.

day·time (dā′tim′), *n.* time when it is day.

Day·ton (dā′tən), *n.* city in SW Ohio.

daze (dāz), *v.,* **dazed, daz·ing.** —*v.* **1.** confuse and bewilder; cause to feel stupid; stun. **2.** dazzle. —*n.* a dazed condition; bewilderment;

stupor. [ME *dase(n)*. Cf. Scand. *dasa* make tired.] —daz′ed·ly, *adv.*

daz·zle (daz′əl), *v.*, -zled, -zling, *n.* —*v.* 1. hurt (the eyes) with too bright light or with quick-moving lights. 2. overcome (the sight or the mind) by brightness, display, etc. —*n.* act or fact of dazzling; bewildering brightness. [< *daze*] —daz′zler, *n.* —daz′zling·ly, *adv.*

D.C., 1. Also, d.c. direct current. 2. District of Columbia.

D-day (dē′dā′), *n. Mil.* day on which a previously planned attack is to be made, or on which an operation is to be started.

DDT, D.D.T., the symbol for a kind of odorless and very powerful insecticide.

de-, *prefix.* 1. do the opposite of, as in *decentralize, demobilize.* 2. down, as in *depress, descend.* 3. away; off, as in *deport.* 4. entirely; completely, as in *despoil.* [< L *de* from, away]

dea·con (dē′kən), *n.* 1. officer of a church who helps the minister in church duties not connected with the preaching. 2. member of the clergy next below a priest in rank. [< L < Gk. *diakonos* servant] —dea′con·ry, dea′con·ship, *n.*

dea·con·ess (dē′kən·is), *n.* 1. woman who is an official assistant in church work, esp. in caring for the sick and poor. 2. a female deacon.

dead (ded), *adj.* 1. no longer living; that has died. 2. without life. 3. like death. 4. not active; dull; quiet. 5. without force, power, spirit, or feeling. 6. lacking its characteristic quality: *a dead electric circuit.* 7. not productive: *dead capital.* 8. no longer in use. 9. not to be used as it is. 10. out of play; not in the game. 11. *Colloq.* very tired; worn-out. 12. sure; certain. 13. complete; absolute. —*adv.* 1. completely; absolutely. 2. directly; straight. 3. precisely; exactly. —*n.* 1. dead person or persons. 2. time of greatest darkness, cold, etc.: *the dead of night.* [OE *dēad*] —dead′ness, *n.* —Syn. *adj.* 1. deceased, defunct, late. 2. lifeless, inanimate, inert. —Ant. *adj.* 1. alive, living.

dead beat, *Am., Slang.* 1. person who avoids paying for what he gets. 2. loafer.

dead center, position of the crank and connecting rod in an engine, at which the connecting rod has no power to turn the crank.

dead·en (ded′ən), *v.* 1. make dull or weak; lessen the intenseness or force of: *some drugs deaden pain.* 2. make soundproof. —dead′en·er, *n.*

dead end, street, passage, etc., closed at one end. —dead′-end′, *adj.*

dead·head (ded′hed′), *n. Am., Colloq.* person who rides on a bus, sees a game, etc., without paying.

dead letter, 1. an unclaimed letter; letter that cannot be delivered. 2. law, rule, etc., that is not enforced.

dead·line (ded′līn′), *n. Am.* 1. the latest possible time to do something. 2. line or boundary that must not be crossed.

dead·lock (ded′lok′), *n.* a complete standstill. —*v.* bring or come to a deadlock.

dead·ly (ded′li), *adj.*, -li·er, -li·est, *adv.* —*adj.* 1. causing death; liable to cause death; fatal. 2. like death. 3. like death's. 4. until death: *deadly enemies.* 5. causing death of the spirit: *deadly sin.* 6. *Colloq.* extreme; intense. —*adv.* 1. *Colloq.* extremely. 2. like death. 3. as if dead. —dead′li·ness, *n.* —Syn. *adj.* 1. mortal, lethal.

dead pan, *Am., Slang.* an expressionless face.

dead reckoning, finding one's position by means of a compass and calculations based on speed, time elapsed, and direction from a known position.

Dead Sea, a salt lake on the E boundary of Palestine.

dead·wood (ded′wud′), *n.* 1. dead branches or trees. 2. *Am.* useless people or things. 3. a conventional word or phrase that adds nothing to the meaning of a sentence.

deaf (def), *adj.* 1. not able to hear. 2. not able to hear well. 3. not willing to hear; heedless: *deaf to all requests.* 4. deaf and dumb, unable

to hear and speak. [OE *dēaf*] —deaf′ly, *adv.* —deaf′ness, *n.*

deaf·en (def′ən), *v.* 1. make deaf. 2. stun with noise. 3. drown out by a louder sound. 4. make soundproof. —deaf′en·ing·ly, *adv.*

deaf-mute (def′mūt′), *n.* person who is deaf and dumb.

deal¹ (dēl), *v.*, dealt (delt), deal·ing, *n.* —*v.* 1. have to do: *arithmetic deals with numbers.* 2. occupy oneself; take action. 3. act; behave. 4. do business; buy and sell: *a butcher deals in meat.* 5. give: *one fighter dealt the other a blow.* 6. give a share or to each; distribute. 7. distribute (playing cards). —*n.* 1. *Am., Colloq.* a business arrangement. 2. *Colloq.* distribution; arrangement; plan. 3. in cardplaying, the distribution of cards. 4. a player's turn to deal. 5. time during which one deal of cards is being played. 6. quantity; amount. [OE *dǣlan*] —deal′er, *n.*

deal² (dēl), *n.* board of pine or fir wood. [< MLG or MDu. *dele*]

deal·ing (dēl′ing), *n.* Usually, dealings. a. business relations. b. friendly relations.

dean (dēn), *n.* 1. *Am.* member of the faculty of a college or university who has charge of the studies of the students. 2. head of a division or school in a college or university. 3. a high official of a church, often one in charge of a cathedral. 4. member who has belonged to a group longest. [< OF < LL *decanus* master of ten < *decem* ten] —dean′ship, *n.*

dean·er·y (dēn′ər·i), *n.*, *pl.* -er·ies. 1. position or authority of a dean. 2. residence of a dean.

dear (dir), *adj.* 1. much loved; precious. 2. (as a form of address at the beginning of letters) much valued; highly esteemed. 3. high-priced; costly. —*n.* a dear one. —*adv.* 1. with affection; fondly. 2. at a high price. —*interj.* exclamation of surprise. [OE *dēore*] —dear′ly, *adv.* —dear′ness, *n.* —Syn. *adj.* 1. beloved. 3. expensive.

dearth (dėrth), *n.* 1. scarcity; lack. 2. scarcity of food; famine. [ME *derthe* < *dere* hard]

death (deth), *n.* 1. the ending of any form of life. 2. Often, Death. power that destroys life, often represented as a skeleton. 3. any ending that is like dying. 4. being dead. 5. any condition like being dead. 6. cause of death. 7. bloodshed; murder. [OE *dēath*] —death′like′, *adj.*

death·bed (deth′bed′), *n.* 1. bed on which a person dies. 2. the last hours of life. —*adj.* during the last hours of life: *a deathbed confession.*

death·blow (deth′blō′), *n.* 1. blow that kills. 2. thing that puts an end (to something).

death cup, a poisonous mushroom that has a cuplike enlargement at the base of the stem.

death house, *U.S.* place where condemned prisoners are kept until put to death.

death·less (deth′lis), *adj.* never dying; living forever; immortal; eternal. —death′less·ly, *adv.* —death′less·ness, *n.*

death·ly (deth′li), *adj.* 1. like that of death. 2. causing death; deadly. 3. *Poetic.* of death. —*adv.* 1. as if dead. 2. extremely.

death rate, proportion of the number of deaths per year to the total population or to some other stated number.

death sand, *Mil.* radioactive dust that may be scattered over vast areas. It would kill all, or most, of the life it touched.

death's-head (deths′hed′), *n.* a human skull used as a symbol of death.

death·trap (deth′trap′), *n. Am.* an unsafe building or structure where the fire risk is great.

Death Valley, valley in E California; the lowest land in the Western Hemisphere, 276 ft. below sea level.

death·watch (deth′woch′; -wôch′), *n.* 1. watch kept beside a dying or dead person. 2. guard for a person about to be put to death.

de·ba·cle (də-bä′kəl; dĭ-; dā′bä′kəl), *n.* 1. disaster; overthrow; downfall. 2. the breaking up of ice in a river. 3. a violent rush of waters carrying debris. [< F, < *dé-* + *bâcler* to bar]

de·bar (di·bär′), *v.*, -barred, -bar·ring. bar out; shut out; prevent. —de·bar′ment, *n.*

āge, câre, fär; ēqual, tėrm; īce; ōpen, ôrder; pút, rüle, ūse; th, then; ə=a in about.

de·bark (di·bärk′), v. go or put ashore from a ship or aircraft; disembark. [< F, < dé- + barque BARK³] —**de·bar·ka·tion** (dē′bär·kā′shən), n.

de·base (di·bās′), v., -based, -bas·ing. make low or lower; lessen the value of. [< de- + (a)base] —**de·base′ment**, n. —**de·bas′er**, n.

de·bate (di·bāt′), v., -bat·ed, -bat·ing, n. —v. 1. discuss reasons for and against (something); consider. 2. argue about (a question, topic, etc.) in a public meeting. 3. Obs. quarrel. —n. 1. discussion of reasons for and against. 2. a public argument for and against a question in a meeting. [< OF, < de- + batre BEAT] —**de·bat′a·ble**, adj. —**de·bat′er**, n. —Syn. v. 1. deliberate.

de·bauch (di·bôch′), v. 1. corrupt morally; seduce. 2. corrupt; pervert; deprave. —n. excessive indulgence in sensual pleasures. [< F débaucher entice from duty] —**de·bauch′ed·ly**, adv. —**de·bauch′er**, n. —**de·bauch′ment**, n.

deb·au·chee (deb′ô·chē′; -shē′), n. a corrupt, dissipated, or depraved person.

de·bauch·er·y (di·bôch′ər·i), n., pl. -er·ies. 1. excessive indulgence in sensual pleasures. 2. seduction from duty, virtue, or morality.

de·ben·ture (di·ben′chər), n. a written acknowledgment of a debt. [< L debentur there are owing. See DEBIT.]

de·bil·i·tate (di·bil′ə·tāt), v., -tat·ed, -tat·ing. weaken. —**de·bil′i·tat′ed**, adj. —**de·bil′i·ta′tion**, n. —**de·bil′i·ta′tive**, adj.

de·bil·i·ty (di·bil′ə·ti), n., pl. -ties. weakness. [< L, < debilis weak]

deb·it (deb′it), n. 1. entry of something owed in an account. 2. the left-hand side of an account where such entries are made. —v. 1. enter on the debit side of an account. 2. charge with a debt. [< L debitum (thing) owed, pp. of debere]

deb·o·nair, deb·o·naire, or **deb·on·naire** (deb′ə·nār′), adj. 1. gay; cheerful. 2. pleasant; courteous. [< OF, < de bon aire of good disposition] —**deb′o·nair′ness**, n.

de·bouch (di·būsh′), v. come out from a narrow or confined place into open country. [< F, < dé- + bouche mouth < L bucca] —**de·bouch′ment**, n.

de·bris, dé·bris (də·brē′; dā′brē; esp. Brit. deb′rē), n. 1. scattered fragments; ruins; rubbish. 2. mass of stones, fragments of rocks, etc. [< F, < OF, < de- + brisier break]

Debs (debz), n. Eugene Victor, 1855–1926, American Socialist and labor leader.

debt (det), n. 1. something owed to another. 2. liability or obligation to pay or render something. 3. sin. [< OF dete < L debitum (thing) owed, pp. of debere] —Syn. 2. indebtedness.

debt·or (det′ər), n. person who is in debt.

de·bunk (di·bungk′), v. Am., Slang. remove nonsense or sentimentality from. —**de·bunk′er**, n.

De·bus·sy (də·bū′si; Fr. də·by·sē′), n. Claude A., 1862–1918, French composer.

de·but, dé·but (dā′bū; dā·bū′; di-), n. 1. a first public appearance, as on the stage. 2. a first formal appearance in society. [< F débuter make the first stroke < dé- + but goal]

deb·u·tante, dé·bu·tante (deb′yə·tänt; -tant; deb′yə·tänt′), n. 1. girl during her first season in society. 2. woman making a debut.

Dec., December.

dec., 1. deceased. 2. decimeter.

deca-, prefix. ten, as in decagram. [< Gk. deka]

dec·ade (dek′ād), n. 1. ten years. 2. group of ten. [< F < LL < Gk. dekas group of ten < deka ten]

de·ca·dence (di·kā′dəns; dek′ə·dəns), **de·ca·den·cy** (-dən·si), n. a falling off; decline; decay. [< F < Med.L, < L de- + cadere fall]

de·ca·dent (di·kā′dənt; dek′ə·dənt), adj. falling off; declining; growing worse. —n. a decadent person. —**de·ca′dent·ly**, adv.

dec·a·gon (dek′ə·gon), n. Geom. a plane figure having 10 angles and 10 sides. —**de·cag·o·nal** (di·kag′ə·nəl), adj.

dec·a·gram, esp. Brit. **dec·a·gramme** (dek′ə·gram), n. weight equal to 10 grams.

dec·a·he·dron (dek′ə·hē′drən), n., pl. -drons, -dra (-drə). Geom. a solid figure having 10 surfaces. —**dec·a·he·dral** (dek′ə·hē′drəl), adj.

de·cal·co·ma·ni·a (di·kal′kə·mā′ni·ə), or **de·cal** (dē′kal; di·kal′), n. 1. design or picture treated so that it will stick fast to glass, wood, etc. 2. process of applying these designs or pictures. [< F décalcomanie, < décalquer transfer a tracing + manie MANIA]

dec·a·li·ter, esp. Brit. **dec·a·li·tre** (dek′ə·lē′tər), n. measure of volume equal to 10 liters.

Dec·a·logue, Dec·a·log (dek′ə·lôg; -log), n. 1. the Ten Commandments. Exod. 20:2–17. 2. decalogue, decalog, any set of ten commandments.

dec·a·me·ter, esp. Brit. **dec·a·me·tre** (dek′ə·mē′tər), n. measure of length equal to 10 meters.

de·camp (di·kamp′), v. 1. depart quickly or secretly. 2. leave a camp. —**de·camp′ment**, n.

de·cant (di·kant′), v. pour off (liquor or a solution) gently without disturbing the sediment. [< Med.L, < de- + canthus lip < Gk. kanthos corner of the eye] —**de·can·ta·tion** (dē′kan·tā′shən), n.

de·cant·er (di·kan′tər), n. 1. a bottle used to decant. 2. a glass bottle used for serving wine or liquor.

de·cap·i·tate (di·kap′ə·tāt), v., -tat·ed, -tat·ing. behead. [< LL < de- + L caput head] —**de·cap′i·ta′tion**, n.

dec·a·pod (dek′ə·pod), n. 1. crustacean having ten legs or arms, such as lobsters and crabs. 2. mollusk having ten legs or arms, such as squid. —adj. having ten legs or arms.

Decanter

dec·a·syl·la·ble (dek′ə·sil′ə·bəl), n. line of poetry having ten syllables. —**dec·a·syl·lab·ic** (dek′ə·sə·lab′ik), adj.

de·cath·lon (di·kath′lon), n. an athletic contest having ten parts, such as racing, jumping, etc., won by the person having the highest total score. [< DECA- + Gk. athlon contest]

de·cay (di·kā′), v. 1. rot. 2. grow less in power, strength, beauty, etc. —n. 1. process of rotting. 2. loss of power, strength, beauty, etc. 3. Nuclear Physics. loss in quantity of a radioactive substance through disintegration of its component nuclei. [< OF, < de- + cair < L cadere fall] —Syn. v. 1. decompose, putrefy. 2. deteriorate, decline.

Dec·can (dek′ən; de·kan′), n. peninsula in S India.

de·cease (di·sēs′), n., v., -ceased, -ceas·ing. —n. death. —v. die. [< F < L decessus < de- + cedere go]

de·ceased (di·sēst′), adj. dead. —n. the deceased, a dead person.

de·ce·dent (di·sē′dənt), n. Law. a dead person.

de·ceit (di·sēt′), n. 1. act or fact of deceiving, lying, or cheating. 2. a dishonest trick. 3. deceitful quality; deceitfulness. —Syn. 1. hypocrisy, guile. 2. deception, fraud.

de·ceit·ful (di·sēt′fəl), adj. 1. ready or willing to deceive or lie. 2. deceiving; fraudulent. —**de·ceit′ful·ly**, adv. —**de·ceit′ful·ness**, n.

de·ceive (di·sēv′), v., -ceived, -ceiv·ing. 1. make (a person) believe as true something that is false; mislead. 2. use dishonest tricks. [< OF decevoir < L, < de- + capere take] —**de·ceiv′er**, n. —**de·ceiv′ing·ly**, adv. —Syn. 1. delude, beguile.

de·cel·er·ate (dē·sel′ər·āt), v., -at·ed, -at·ing. decrease the velocity of; slow down. [< de- + (ac)celerate] —**de·cel′er·a′tion**, n. —**de·cel′er·a′tor**, n.

De·cem·ber (di·sem′bər), n. the 12th and last month of the year. It has 31 days. [< L, < decem ten; from the order of the early Roman calendar]

de·cen·cy (dē′sən·si), n., pl. -cies. 1. state or quality of being decent. 2. propriety of behavior. 3. a proper regard for modesty or delicacy. 4. decencies, a. suitable acts. b. things required for a proper standard of living.

de·cen·ni·al (di·sen′i·əl), *adj.* 1. of or for ten years. 2. happening every ten years. —*n. Am.* tenth anniversary. [< L *decennium* decade < *decem* ten + *annus* year] —**de·cen′ni·al·ly**, *adv.*

de·cent (dē′sənt), *adj.* 1. proper and right. 2. conforming to the standard of good taste. 3. respectable. 4. good enough; fairly good. 5. suitable to one's position; adequate. 6. not severe; rather kind. [< L *decens* becoming, fitting, ppr. of *decere*] —**de′cent·ly**, *adv.* —**de′cent·ness**, *n.* —Syn. 1. suitable, appropriate. 4. tolerable.

de·cen·tral·ize (dē·sen′trəl·īz), *v.*, **-ized**, **-iz·ing.** spread or distribute (authority, power, etc.).

de·cep·tion (di·sep′shən), *n.* 1. act of deceiving. 2. state of being deceived. 3. thing that deceives; illusion. 4. fraud; sham. —Syn. 1. imposture, subterfuge, trickery. 4. hoax, ruse.

de·cep·tive (di·sep′tiv), *adj.* apt or tending to deceive. —**de·cep′tive·ly**, *adv.* —**de·cep′tive·ness**, *n.*

deci-, *prefix.* one tenth of, as in *decigram.* [< L *decem* ten, *decimus* tenth]

dec·i·bel (des′ə·bel), *n.* unit for measuring the loudness of sounds.

de·cide (di·sīd′), *v.*, **-cid·ed**, **-cid·ing.** 1. settle (a question, dispute, etc.) by giving victory to one side. 2. make up one's mind; resolve. 3. cause (a person) to reach a decision. [< L *decidere* cut off < *de-* + *caedere* cut] —Syn. 2. determine.

de·cid·ed (di·sīd′id), *adj.* 1. clear; definite; unquestionable. 2. firm; determined. —**de·cid′ed·ly**, *adv.* —**de·cid′ed·ness**, *n.*

de·cid·u·ous (di·sij′ū·əs), *adj.* 1. falling off at a particular season or stage of growth, as horns. 2. shedding leaves annually. [< L, < *de-* + *cadere* fall] —**de·cid′u·ous·ly**, *adv.* —**de·cid′u·ous·ness**, *n.*

dec·i·gram, *esp. Brit.* **dec·i·gramme** (des′ə·gram), *n.* weight equal to ¹⁄₁₀ of a gram.

dec·i·li·ter, *esp. Brit.* **dec·i·li·tre** (des′ə·lē′tər), *n.* measure of volume equal to ¹⁄₁₀ of a liter.

dec·i·mal (des′ə·məl), *adj.* based upon ten or tenths; increasing by tens, as the metric system. —*n.* a decimal fraction. [< L *decimus* tenth] —**dec′i·mal·ly**, *adv.*

decimal fraction, fraction whose denominator is ten or some power of ten.

decimal point, period placed before a fraction expressed in decimal figures, as in 2.03, .623.

dec·i·mate (des′ə·māt), *v.*, **-mat·ed**, **-mat·ing.** 1. destroy much of; kill a large part of. 2. select by lot and execute every tenth man of. [< L *decimatus*, pp. of *decimare* take a tenth, ult. < *decem* ten] —**dec′i·ma′tion**, *n.* —**dec′i·ma′tor**, *n.*

dec·i·me·ter, *esp. Brit.* **dec·i·me·tre** (des′ə·mē′tər), *n.* measure of length equal to ¹⁄₁₀ of a meter.

de·ci·pher (di·sī′fər), *v.* 1. make out the meaning of (bad writing, an unknown language, or anything puzzling). 2. translate (a message in code) into plain language by using a key. —**de·ci′pher·a·ble**, *adj.* —**de·ci′pher·ment**, *n.*

de·ci·sion (di·sizh′ən), *n.* 1. the deciding or settling of a question, dispute, etc. 2. judgment reached or given, as by a court. 3. a making up of one's mind. 4. firmness; determination. —Syn. 2. verdict, decree.

de·ci·sive (di·sī′siv), *adj.* 1. having or giving a clear result. 2. having or showing decision. —**de·ci′sive·ly**, *adv.* —**de·ci′sive·ness**, *n.*

deck (dek), *n.* 1. floor or platform extending from side to side of a ship. 2. part or floor resembling it: *the deck of an airplane.* 3. pack of playing cards. 4. **on deck,** *Am., Colloq.* present; on hand. —*v.* cover; dress. [< MDu. *dec* roof]

deck hand, *Am.* sailor who works on deck.

deck·le edge (dek′əl), 1. the rough edge of untrimmed paper. 2. an imitation of it. [< G *deckel*, dim. of *decke* cover]

de·claim (di·klām′), *v.* 1. recite in public; make a formal speech. 2. speak or write for effect. [< L, < *de-* + *clamare* cry]

dec·la·ma·tion (dek′lə·mā′shən), *n.* 1. act or art of reciting in public. 2. selection of poetry, prose, etc., for reciting. 3. a speaking or writing for effect. —**de·clam·a·to·ry** (di·klam′ə·tô′ri; -tō′-), *adj.*

dec·la·ra·tion (dek′lə·rā′shən), *n.* 1. act of declaring. 2. thing declared. 3. statement of goods, etc., for taxation. 4. a formal announcement. 5. *Bridge.* a bid, esp. the winning bid.

Declaration of Independence, *Am.* a public statement adopted by the Continental Congress on July 4, 1776, in which the American colonies were declared free and independent of Great Britain.

de·clare (di·klār′), *v.*, **-clared**, **-clar·ing.** 1. announce publicly or formally; make known; proclaim: *declare a dividend.* 2. say openly or strongly. 3. make a declaration; proclaim oneself. 4. make a statement of (goods, etc.) for taxation. 5. in bridge, announce (what suit) will be played as trumps. [< L, < *de-* + *clarus* clear] —**de·clar·a·tive** (di·klar′ə·tiv), **de·clar·a·to·ry** (di·klar′ə·tô′ri; -tō′-), *adj.* —**de·clar′er**, *n.*

de·clas·si·fy (dē′klas′ə·fī), *v.*, **-fied**, **-fy·ing.** remove (documents, codes, etc.) from the list of restricted, confidential, or secret information.

de·clen·sion (di·klen′shən), *n.* 1. the giving of the different endings to nouns, pronouns, and adjectives according to their case. 2. group of words whose endings for the different cases are alike. 3. a downward movement, bend, or slope. 4. a sinking into a lower or inferior condition; decline. 5. deviation from a standard. 6. a polite refusal. —**de·clen′sion·al**, *adj.*

dec·li·na·tion (dek′lə·nā′shən), *n.* 1. a downward bend or slope. 2. decline; deterioration. 3. a polite refusal. 4. difference in direction between true north and magnetic north at any given point. 5. the angular distance of a star, planet, etc., from the celestial equator.

CP, celestial poles; CE, celestial equator; DS, declination of the star S.

de·cline (di·klīn′), *v.*, **-clined**, **-clin·ing.** —*v.* 1. refuse. 2. refuse politely. 3. bend or slope down. 4. grow less in strength, power, value, etc.; grow worse; decay. 5. give the different cases or case endings of (a noun, pronoun, or adjective). —*n.* 1. a falling; a sinking: *a decline in prices.* 2. a downward slope. 3. a losing of strength, power, value, etc.; a growing worse. 4. the last part of anything. [< L, < *de-* + *clinare* bend] —**de·clin′a·ble**, *adj.* —**de·clin′er**, *n.* —Syn. *v.* 1. reject. 4. deteriorate. —*n.* 3. decay.

de·cliv·i·ty (di·kliv′ə·ti), *n., pl.* **-ties.** a downward slope. [< L, < *de-* + *clivus* slope]

de·coct (di·kokt′), *v.* extract desired substances from (herbs, etc.) by boiling. [< L *decoctus* < *de-* + *coquere* cook] —**de·coc·tion** (di·kok′shən), *n.*

de·code (dē·kōd′), *v.*, **-cod·ed**, **-cod·ing.** translate (secret writing) from code into ordinary language. —**de·cod′er**, *n.*

dé·colle·té (dā′kol·tā′; -kol·ə·tā′), *adj.* 1. low-necked. 2. wearing a low-necked gown. [< F]

de·com·pose (dē′kəm·pōz′), *v.*, **-posed**, **-pos·ing.** 1. decay; rot. 2. separate (a substance) into what it is made of. —**de′com·pos′a·ble**, *adj.* —**de·com·po·si·tion** (dē′kom·pə·zish′ən), *n.*

de·con·tam·i·nate (dē′kən·tam′ə·nāt), *v.*, **-nat·ed**, **-nat·ing.** 1. free from poison gas or harmful radioactive agents. 2. free from any sort of contamination. —**de′con·tam′i·na′tion**, *n.*

de·con·trol (dē′kən·trōl′), *v.*, **-trolled**, **-trol·ling.** —*v.* remove controls from: *decontrol prices.* —*n.* removing of controls.

dé·cor (dā·kôr′), *n.* 1. decoration. 2. scenery on a stage. [< F, < *décorer* DECORATE]

dec·o·rate (dek′ə·rāt), *v.*, **-rat·ed**, **-rat·ing.** 1. make beautiful; adorn. 2. paint or paper (a room, etc.). 3. give a medal, ribbon, etc., to (a person) as an honor. [< L *decoratus* < *decus* adornment] —**dec·o·ra·tive** (dek′ə·rā′tiv; -rə·tiv), *adj.* —**dec′o·ra′tive·ly**, *adv.* —**dec′o·ra′tive·ness**, *n.* —**dec′o·ra′tor**, *n.*

dec·o·ra·tion (dek'ə·rā'shən), n. 1. act of decorating. 2. thing used to decorate; ornament. 3. medal, ribbon, etc. given as an honor.

Decoration Day, Am. Memorial Day.

dec·o·rous (dek'ə·rəs; di·kô'rəs; -kō'-), adj. well-behaved; acting properly. —dec'o·rous·ly, adv. —dec'o·rous·ness, n.

de·co·rum (di·kô'rəm; -kō'-), n. 1. propriety of action, speech, dress, etc. 2. observance or requirement of polite society. [< L, (that which is) seemly]

de·coy (v. di·koi'; n. dē'koi, di·koi'), v. 1. lure (wild birds, animals, etc.) into a trap or within gunshot. 2. lead or tempt into danger. —n. 1. an artificial bird used to lure birds into a trap or within gunshot. 2. place into which wild birds or animals are lured. 3. any person or thing used to lead or tempt into danger. [< Du. de kooi the cage < L cavea cave] —de·coy'er, n.

de·crease (v. di·krēs'; n. dē'krēs, di·krēs'), v., -creased, -creas·ing, n. —v. become or make less. —n. 1. a becoming less. 2. amount by which a thing becomes or is made less. [< OF < L, < de- + crescere grow] —de·creas'ing·ly, adv. —Syn. v. diminish, dwindle, abate, wane, shrink, reduce. —Ant. v. increase, expand.

de·cree (di·krē'), n., v., -creed, -cree·ing. —n. something ordered or settled by authority. —v. order or settle by authority. [< OF < L decretum < de- + cernere decide]

de·crep·it (di·krep'it), adj. broken down or weakened by old age. [< L decrepitus broken down < de- + crepare creak] —de·crep'it·ly, adv.

de·crep·i·tude (di·krep'ə·tūd; -tūd), n. feebleness, usually from old age; decrepit condition.

de·cre·scen·do (dē'krə·shen'dō; dā'-), n., pl. -dos, adj., adv. —n. a gradual decrease in force or loudness; diminuendo. —adj., adv. with a gradual decrease in force or loudness. [< Ital.]

de·cre·tal (di·krē'təl), n. decree or reply by the pope settling some question of doctrine or ecclesiastical law.

de·cry (di·krī'), v., -cried, -cry·ing. 1. condemn. 2. make little of; try to lower the value of. [< OF décrier. See DE-, CRY.] —de·cri'al, n. —de·cri'er, n.

de·cum·bent (di·kum'bənt), adj. 1. reclining. 2. Bot. lying or trailing on the ground with the end tending to climb. [< L decumbens, ppr. of decumbere lie down]

ded·i·cate (ded'ə·kāt), v., -cat·ed, -cat·ing. 1. set apart for a sacred or solemn purpose. 2. give up wholly or earnestly, as to some person or end. 3. address (a book, poem, etc.) to a friend or patron as a mark of affection, gratitude, etc. [< L, < de- + dicare proclaim] —ded'i·ca'tive, ded·i·ca·to·ry (ded'ə·kə·tô'ri; -tō'-), adj.

ded·i·ca·tion (ded'ə·kā'shən), n. 1. a setting apart or being set apart for a sacred or solemn purpose. 2. words dedicating a book.

de·duce (di·dūs'; -dūs'), v., -duced, -duc·ing. 1. infer from a general rule or principle. 2. trace the course, descent, or origin of. [< L, < de- + ducere lead] —de·duc'i·ble, adj.

de·duct (di·dukt'), v. take away; subtract. [< L deductus, pp. See DEDUCE.] —de·duct'i·ble, adj.

de·duc·tion (di·duk'shən), n. 1. act of taking away; subtraction. 2. amount deducted. 3. a logical inference from a general rule or principle. —de·duc'tive, adj. —de·duc'tive·ly, adv.

deed (dēd), n. 1. thing done; act. 2. a brave, skillful, or unusual act. 3. action; doing; performance. 4. Law. a written or printed agreement legally transferring ownership, esp. of real estate. —v. Am. transfer by a deed. [OE dēd] —Syn. n. 2. feat, exploit.

deem (dēm), v. think; believe; consider. [OE dēman < dōm judgment]

deep (dēp), adj. 1. going far down or back. 2. from far down or back. 3. far down or back. 4. far on. 5. in depth. 6. low in pitch. 7. strong and dark in color. 8. strong; great; intense; extreme. 9. going below the surface. 10. hard to understand. 11. with the mind fully taken up. 12.
wise; shrewd. 13. sly; crafty. —adv. 1. far down or back. 2. of time, far on. —n. 1. a deep place. 2. the most intense part: the deep of winter. 3. the deep, the sea. [OE dēop] —deep'ly, adv. —deep'ness, n. —Syn. adj. 8. heartfelt, profound. 10. abstruse. 11. absorbed. 12. astute.

deep·en (dēp'ən), v. make or become deeper.

deep-freeze (dēp'frēz'), n., v., -froze or -freezed, -fro·zen or -freezed, -freez·ing. —n. Deep-freeze, Trademark. container for freezing and storing food. —v. use a Deep-freeze.

deep-root·ed (dēp'rüt'id; -rüt'-), adj. 1. deeply rooted. 2. firmly fixed.

deep-seat·ed (dēp'sēt'id), adj. 1. far below the surface. 2. firmly fixed.

deep-set (dēp'set'), adj. 1. set deeply. 2. firmly fixed.

deer (dir), n., pl. deer, deers. 1. a swift, graceful animal of a group that have hoofs and chew the cud. A male deer has horns or antlers, which are shed and grow again every year. 2. any of a group of animals including deer, elk, moose, and caribou. [OE dēor animal]

deer·hound (dir'hound'), n. hound with a shaggy coat, related to the greyhound.

deer·skin (dir'skin'), n. 1. skin of a deer. 2. leather made from it.

def., definition.

de·face (di·fās'), v., -faced, -fac·ing. spoil the appearance of; mar. [< obs. F defacer. See DIS-, FACE.] —de·face'a·ble, adj. —de·face'ment, n. —de·fac'er, n.

de fac·to (dē fak'tō), in fact; in reality. [< L, from the fact]

de·fal·cate (di·fal'kāt; -fôl'-), v., -cat·ed, -cat·ing. steal or misuse money trusted to one's care. [< L defalcatus < de- + falx sickle] —de·fal·ca·tion (dē'fal·kā'shən; -fôl-), n. —de·fal'ca·tor, n.

de·fame (di·fām'), v., -famed, -fam·ing. attack the good name of; harm the reputation of; speak evil of; slander. [< OF < L, < de- + fama rumor] —def·a·ma·tion (def'ə·mā'shən; dē'fə-), n. —de·fam·a·to·ry (di·fam'ə·tô'ri; -tō'-), adj. —de·fam'er, n.

de·fault (di·fôlt'), n. 1. failure to do something or to appear somewhere when due; neglect. 2. in sports, failure to compete in a scheduled match. 3. failure to pay when due. —v. 1. fail to do something or appear somewhere when due. 2. fail to pay when due. [< OF defaute < defaillir. See FAULT.] —de·fault'er, n.

de·feat (di·fēt'), v. 1. win a victory over; overcome. 2. frustrate; thwart. 3. make useless. —n. a defeating or being defeated. [< OF < LL, < dis- un- + facere do] —de·feat'er, n. —Syn. v. 1. vanquish, conquer, beat. 2. foil, outwit, baffle.

de·feat·ism (di·fēt'iz·əm), n. attitude or behavior of a person who expects, wishes for, or admits the defeat of his country, cause, party, etc. —de·feat'ist, n.

def·e·cate (def'ə·kāt), v., -cat·ed, -cat·ing. have a movement of the bowels. [< L, < de- from + faeces, pl., dregs] —def'e·ca'tion, n.

de·fect (di·fekt'; dē'fekt), n. 1. fault; blemish; imperfection. 2. lack of something essential to completeness; a falling short. —v. forsake one's own country, group, etc. for another, esp. another that is opposed to it in political or social doctrine. [< L defectus want < deficere fail. See DEFICIENT.] —de·fec'tor, n. —Syn. n. 1. flaw. 2. want, deficiency.

de·fec·tion (di·fek'shən), n. 1. a falling away from loyalty, duty, religion, etc.; desertion. 2. failure.

de·fec·tive (di·fek'tiv), adj. 1. having a flaw or blemish; not perfect. 2. Psychol. subnormal in behavior or intelligence. 3. Gram. lacking one or more of the usual forms of grammatical inflection. —n. person who has some defect of body or mind. —de·fec'tive·ly, adv. —de·fec'tive·ness, n. —Syn. adj. 1. faulty, imperfect.

de·fence (di·fens'), n. Brit. defense. —de·fence'less, adj. —de·fence'less·ly, adv. —defence'less·ness, n.

de·fend (di·fend'), v. 1. guard from attack or harm. 2. act, speak, or write in favor of. 3. contest (a lawsuit). 4. *Law.* make a defense. [< L *defendere* ward off] —de·fend′a·ble, *adj.* —de·fend′er, *n.* —Syn. 1. protect. 2. uphold.

de·fend·ant (di·fen′dənt), *n. Law.* person accused or sued in a law court.

de·fense (di·fens′), *n.* 1. act of defending or protecting. 2. thing that defends or protects. 3. act of defending oneself, as in boxing or fencing. 4. team or players defending a goal in a game. 5. action, speech, or writing in favor of something. 6. answer of a defendant to an accusation or lawsuit against him. 7. a defendant and his lawyers. Also, *Brit.* defence. [< OF < L *defensa* < *defendere* DEFEND] —de·fense′less, *adj.* —de·fense′less·ly, *adv.* —de·fense′less·ness, *n.* —de·fen′si·ble, *adj.* —de·fen′si·bil′i·ty, de·fen′si·ble·ness, *n.* —de·fen′si·bly, *adv.*

defense in depth, *Mil.* system of mutually supporting positions designed to break up and absorb an attack.

de·fen·sive (di·fen′siv), *adj.* 1. ready to defend; defending. 2. for defense. 3. of defense. —*n.* 1. position or attitude of defense. 2. thing that defends. —de·fen′sive·ly, *adv.* —de·fen′sive·ness, *n.*

de·fer¹ (di·fėr′), *v.,* -ferred, -fer·ring. put off; delay. [< L *differre.* See DIFFER.] —de·fer′ment, *n.* —de·fer′rer, *n.* —Syn. postpone.

de·fer² (di·fėr′), *v.,* -ferred, -fer·ring. yield in judgment or opinion; submit courteously. [< F < L, < *de-* down + *ferre* carry] —de·fer′rer, *n.*

def·er·ence (def′ər·əns), *n.* 1. a yielding to the judgment or opinion of another; courteous submission. 2. great respect.

def·er·en·tial (def′ər·en′shəl), *adj.* showing deference; respectful. —def′er·en′tial·ly, *adv.*

de·fi·ance (di·fī′əns), *n.* 1. a standing up against authority and refusing to recognize or obey it; open resistance. 2. challenge to meet in a contest, to do something, or to prove something. [< OF. See DEFY.]

de·fi·ant (di·fī′ənt), *adj.* showing defiance; challenging; openly resisting. —de·fi′ant·ly, *adv.* —de·fi′ant·ness, *n.*

de·fi·cien·cy (di·fish′ən·si), *n., pl.* -cies. 1. lack or absence of something needed or required; incompleteness. 2. amount by which something falls short or is too small.

de·fi·cient (di·fish′ənt), *adj.* 1. incomplete; defective. 2. not sufficient in quantity, force, etc. [< L *deficiens* failing < *de-* + *facere* do] —de·fi′cient·ly, *adv.*

def·i·cit (def′ə·sit), *n.* amount by which a sum of money falls short; shortage. [< L, it is wanting. See DEFICIENT.]

de·fi·er (di·fī′ər), *n.* person who defies.

de·file¹ (di·fīl′), *v.,* -filed, -fil·ing. 1. make filthy or dirty; make disgusting in any way. 2. destroy the purity or cleanness of; corrupt. [alter. of *defoul* (< OF *defouler* trample down, violate) after obs. *file* befoul < OE *fȳlan* < *fūl* foul] —de·file′ment, *n.* —de·fil′er, *n.*

de·file² (di·fīl′; dē′fīl), *v.,* -filed, -fil·ing, —*v.* march in a line. —*n.* a narrow way or passage, esp. a steep and narrow valley. [< F, special use of pp. of *défiler* march by files < *dé-* off + *file* FILE¹]

de·fine (di·fīn′), *v.,* -fined, -fin·ing. 1. make clear the meaning of; explain. 2. make clear; make distinct. 3. fix; settle. 4. settle the limits of. [< F < L *definire* to limit < *de-* + *finis* end] —de·fin′a·ble, *adj.* —de·fin′a·bly, *adv.* —de·fin′er, *n.*

def·i·nite (def′ə·nit), *adj.* 1. clear; exact; not vague. 2. limited; restricted. 3. limiting; restricting. The English definite article is *the.* —def′i·nite·ness, *n.*

def·i·nite·ly (def′ə·nit·li), *adv.* 1. in a definite manner. 2. certainly. ▶ **Definitely** is one of the most frequently misspelled words. Remember there is no *a* in it and associate def 1 *nite* with def 1 *nite* ly. At present *definitely* is overused as a counter word to give emphasis or in the sense of "certainly, quite" (*I will not do it, definitely; he was definitely worse than usual; she definitely disapproves of those methods*) in-

stead of in its exact sense of "in a definite manner."

def·i·ni·tion (def′ə·nish′ən), *n.* 1. act of defining. 2. statement that makes clear the meaning of a word; explanation. 3. capacity of a lens to give a clear, distinct image. 4. *Radio.* accuracy with which sound is reproduced by a receiver. 5. clearness.

de·fin·i·tive (di·fin′ə·tiv), *adj.* 1. conclusive; final. 2. limiting; defining. —*n.* word that limits or defines a noun. *The, this, all, none,* etc., are definitives. —de·fin′i·tive·ly, *adv.* —de·fin′i·tive·ness, *n.*

de·flate (di·flāt′), *v.,* -flat·ed, -flat·ing. 1. let air or gas out of (a balloon, tire, football, etc.). 2. reduce the amount of; reduce. [< L, < *de-* off + *flare* blow] —de·fla′tor, *n.*

de·fla·tion (di·flā′shən), *n.* 1. act of letting the air or gas out; the *deflation of a tire.* 2. reduction. 3. reduction of the amount of available money in circulation. 4. increase in the value of money so that prices go down. —de·fla·tion·ar·y (di·flā′shən·er′i), *adj.*

de·flect (di·flekt′), *v.* bend or turn aside; change the direction of. [< L, < *de-* away + *flectere* bend] —de·flec′tion, *n.* —de·flec′tive, *adj.* —de·flec′tor, *n.*

de·flow·er (dē·flou′ər), *v.* 1. strip flowers from. 2. deprive of virginity; ravish. 3. spoil; ruin.

De·foe (di·fō′), *n.* Daniel, 1661?-1731, English author.

de·for·est (dē·fôr′ist; -for′-), *v.* clear of trees. —de·for′est·a′tion, *n.* —de·for′est·er, *n.*

de·form (di·fôrm′), *v.* 1. spoil the form or shape of. 2. make ugly. 3. change the form of; transform. —de·for·ma·tion (dē′fôr·mā′shən; def′ər-), *n.* —de·formed′, *adj.*

de·form·i·ty (di·fôr′mə·ti), *n., pl.* -ties. 1. part that is not properly formed. 2. condition of being improperly formed. 3. an improperly formed person or thing. 4. ugliness.

de·fraud (di·frôd′), *v.* take money, rights, etc., away from by fraud; cheat. [< L *defraudare.* See DE-, FRAUD.]

de·fray (di·frā′), *v.* pay (costs or expenses). [< F, < *dé-* + *frai* cost] —de·fray′a·ble, *adj.* —de·fray′al, de·fray′ment, *n.* —de·fray′er, *n.*

de·frost (dē·frôst′; -frost′), *v.* remove frost or ice from. —de·frost′er, *n.*

deft (deft), *adj.* skillful; nimble. [var. of *daft*] —deft′ly, *adv.* —deft′ness, *n.*

de·funct (di·fungkt′), *adj.* dead; extinct. [< L *defunctus* finished < *de-* + *fungi* perform] —de·funct′ness, *n.*

de·fy (di·fī′), *v.,* -fied, -fy·ing. 1. resist boldly or openly. 2. withstand; resist. 3. challenge (a person) to do or prove something. [< OF *desfier* < VL, < L *dis-* + *fīdus* faithful] —Syn. 1. brave.

De·gas (də·gä′; də-; -gäs′), *n.* Hilaire Germaine Edgard, 1834-1917, French painter.

De Gaulle (də gōl′), Charles André Joseph Marie, born 1890, French army officer and political leader.

de·gauss (di·gous′; -gôs′), *v.* equip (a steel ship) with a device preventing the explosion of magnetic mines. [< Karl F. *Gauss* (1777-1855), German mathematician]

de·gen·er·a·cy (di·jen′ər·ə·si), *n.* degenerate condition.

de·gen·er·ate (*v.* di·jen′ər·āt; *adj., n.* di·jen′-ər·it), *v.,* -at·ed, -at·ing, *adj., n.* —*v.* 1. decline in physical, mental, or moral qualities; grow worse. 2. *Biol.* sink to a lower or less organized type. —*adj.* showing a decline in physical, mental, or moral qualities. —*n.* person having an evil and unwholesome character. [< L, ult. < *de-* + *genus* race, kind] —de·gen′er·ate·ly, *adv.* —de·gen′er·ate·ness, *n.* —de·gen′er·a′tion, *n.* —de·gen′er·a′tive, *adj.*

de·grade (di·grād′), *v.,* -grad·ed, -grad·ing. 1. reduce to a lower rank; take away a position, an honor, etc., from. 2. make worse; lower. 3. wear down by erosion. [< Eccl.L < L *de-* + *gradus* step, grade] —deg·ra·da·tion (deg′rə-dā′shən), *n.* —de·grad′er, *n.*

de·gree (di·grē′), *n.* 1. stage or step in a scale

or process. 2. step in direct line of descent. 3. amount; extent. 4. unit for measuring temperature. 5. unit for measuring angles or arcs. A degree is ¹⁄₃₆₀ of the circumference of a circle. 6. rank. 7. rank or title given by a college or university to a student whose work fulfills certain requirements, or to a person as an honor: *an A.B. degree.* 8. one of the three stages in the comparison of adjectives or adverbs. *Fastest* is the superlative degree of *fast.* 9. *Algebra.* rank as determined by an exponent or sum of exponents. 10. relative condition, manner, way, or respect. 11. *Law.* the relative measure of guilt: *murder in the first degree.* 12. interval between any note of the scale and the next note. 13. by degrees, gradually. 14. to a degree, a. to a large amount; to a great extent. b. somewhat; rather. [< OF *degre* < VL, < *degradare* divide into steps < LL, DEGRADE] ≫ degrees. Ordinarily a person's academic degrees are not given with his name except in college publications, reference works, etc. When used, they are separated from the name by a comma, and in campus publications are often followed by the year of granting: *Harvey J. Preble, A.B.; James T. Thomson, M.A.; Harvey J. Preble, A.B. '08; James T. Thomson, A.B. '21, A.M. '24; James T. Thomson, Ph.D., M.D.* As a rule, except in reference lists, only a person's highest degree in each academic or professional field need be mentioned. If the institution granting the degree is named, the following forms are usual: *George H. Cook, A.B. (Grinnell), A.M. (Indiana), Ph.D. (Chicago).*

de·his·cence (di·his'əns), *n.* a bursting open, esp. of seed capsules, etc., to scatter the seeds. [< L *dehiscens,* ult. < *de-* + *hiare* gape] —**de·his'cent,** *adj.*

de·hy·drate (dē·hī'drāt), *v.,* –drat·ed, –drat·ing. 1. deprive (a chemical compound) of water or the elements of water. 2. take moisture from. 3. lose water or moisture. —**de'hy·dra'tion,** *n.*

de·i·cer (dē·īs'ər), *n.* device to prevent or remove ice formation.

de·i·fy (dē'ə·fī), *v.,* –fied, –fy·ing. 1. make a god of. 2. worship or regard as a god. [< OF < LL *deificare* < *deus* god + *facere* make] —**de·i·fi·ca·tion** (dē'ə·fə·kā'shən), *n.* —**de'i·fi'er,** *n.*

deign (dān), *v.* 1. condescend. 2. condescend to give (an answer, a reply, etc.). [< OF < L, < *dignus* worthy]

de·ism (dē'iz·əm), *n.* 1. belief that God exists entirely apart from our world and does not influence the lives of human beings. 2. belief in God without accepting any particular religion. [< L *deus* god] —**de'ist,** *n.* —**de·is'tic, de·is'ti·cal,** *adj.* —**de·is'ti·cal·ly,** *adv.*

de·i·ty (dē'ə·ti), *n., pl.* –ties. 1. god or goddess. 2. divine nature; being a god. 3. the Deity, God. [< F < L *deitas* < *deus* god]

de·ject·ed (di·jek'tid), *adj.* in low spirits; sad; discouraged. —**de·ject'ed·ly,** *adv.* —**de·ject'ed·ness,** *n.*

de·jec·tion (di·jek'shən), *n.* lowness of spirits; sadness; discouragement. [< L *dejectio* < *de-* down + *jacere* throw]

de ju·re (dē jūr'ē), *Latin.* by right.

Del., Delaware.

Del·a·ware (del'ə·wār), *n.* 1. an Eastern State of the United States. *Capital:* Dover. *Abbrev.:* Del. 2. river flowing from S New York State between Pennsylvania and New Jersey into the Atlantic. —**Del·a·war·e·an** (del'ə·wār'i·ən), *adj., n.*

de·lay (di·lā'), *v.* 1. put off till a later time. 2. make late; keep waiting; hinder. 3. be late; wait; go slowly. —*n.* 1. act of delaying. 2. fact of being delayed. [< OF, < *de-* + *laier* leave, let, prob. < Celtic] —**de·lay'er,** *n.* —Syn. *v.* 1. postpone, defer. 2. retard.

de·le (dē'lē), *v.,* –led, –le·ing. cross out; delete. [< L, imperative of *delere* delete]

de·lec·ta·ble (di·lek'tə·bəl), *adj.* very pleasing; delightful. [< OF < L, < *delectare* DELIGHT] —**de·lec'ta·ble·ness,** *n.* —**de·lec'ta·bly,** *adv.*

de·lec·ta·tion (dē'lek·tā'shən), *n.* delight.

del·e·gate (*n.* del'ə·gāt, –git; *v.* del'ə·gāt), *n., v.,* –gat·ed, –gat·ing. —*n.* 1. person given power or authority to act for others; representative. 2. representative of a Territory in the United States House of Representatives. 3. member of the lower branch of the legislature in Maryland, Virginia, and West Virginia. —*v.* 1. appoint or send (a person) as a delegate. 2. give over (one's power or authority) to another as agent or deputy. [< L, < *de-* + *legare* send with a commission]

del·e·ga·tion (del'ə·gā'shən), *n.* 1. act of delegating. 2. fact of being delegated. 3. group of delegates.

de·lete (di·lēt'), *v.,* –let·ed, –let·ing. strike out or take out (anything written or printed). [< L, pp. of *delere* destroy] —**de·le'tion,** *n.*

del·e·te·ri·ous (del'ə·tir'i·əs), *adj.* harmful; injurious. [< NL < Gk. *deleterios,* ult. < *deleesthai* hurt] —**del'e·te'ri·ous·ly,** *adv.*

delft (delft), **delf** (delf), or **delft·ware** (delft'wār'), *n.* kind of glazed earthenware made in Holland, often decorated in blue.

Del·hi (del'i), *n.* 1. city in N India, a former capital of the Mogul empire. 2. New Delhi.

Delft

de·lib·er·ate (*adj.* di·lib'ər·it; *v.* di·lib'ər·āt), *adj., v.,* –at·ed, –at·ing. —*adj.* 1. carefully thought out; made or done on purpose. 2. slow and careful in deciding what to do. 3. not hurried; slow. —*v.* 1. think over carefully; consider. 2. discuss reasons for and against something; debate. [< L, < *de-* + *librare* weigh] —**de·lib'er·ate·ly,** *adv.* —**de·lib'er·ate·ness,** *n.* —**de·lib'er·a'tor,** *n.* —Syn. *adj.* 1. premeditated, intentional. 2. thoughtful, cautious. 3. unhurried. –*v.* 1. ponder.

de·lib·er·a·tion (di·lib'ər·ā'shən), *n.* 1. careful thought. 2. discussion of reasons for and against something; debate: *the deliberations of Congress.* 3. slowness and care.

de·lib·er·a·tive (di·lib'ər·ā'tiv), *adj.* 1. for deliberation; having to do with deliberation: *Congress is a deliberative body.* 2. characterized by deliberation. —**de·lib'er·a'tive·ly,** *adv.* —**de·lib'er·a'tive·ness,** *n.*

del·i·ca·cy (del'ə·kə·si), *n., pl.* –cies. 1. delicate quality or nature; slightness and grace. 2. subtle quality. 3. fineness of feeling for small differences; sensitiveness. 4. need of care, skill, or tact. 5. thought or regard for the feelings of others. 6. a shrinking from what is offensive or not modest. 7. susceptibility to illness; weakness. 8. a choice kind of food; a dainty.

del·i·cate (del'ə·kit), *adj.* 1. pleasing to the taste; lightly flavored; mild; soft: *delicate foods.* 2. of fine weave, quality, or make; easily torn; thin. 3. requiring careful handling: *a delicate situation.* 4. very rapidly responding to slight changes of condition: *delicate instruments.* 5. easily hurt or made ill: *a delicate child.* 6. hard to appreciate. 7. subtle. 8. careful of the feelings of others; considerate. 9. avoiding anything that is offensive or immodest. [< L *delicatus* pampered] —**del'i·cate·ly,** *adv.* —**del'i·cate·ness,** *n.* —Syn. 1. exquisite, dainty. 2. fragile. 3. critical. 5. frail, weakly, sickly. 8. tactful.

del·i·ca·tes·sen (del'ə·kə·tes'ən), *n. Am.* 1. (*sing. in use*) store that sells prepared foods, such as cooked meats, salads, relishes, etc. 2. (*pl. in use*) the foods. [< G, pl. of *delikatesse* delicacy < F]

de·li·cious (di·lish'əs), *adj.* 1. very pleasing to taste or smell. 2. very pleasing; delightful. [< OF < LL, < *deliciae* a delight < *delicere* entice. See DELIGHT.] —**de·li'cious·ly,** *adv.* —**de·li'cious·ness,** *n.* —Syn. 1. luscious.

de·light (di·līt'), *n.* 1. great pleasure; joy. 2. thing that gives great pleasure. —*v.* 1. please greatly. 2. have great pleasure. [< OF *delit,* ult. < L *delectare* to charm < *delicere* entice < *de-* + *lacere* entice] —**de·light'ed,** *adj.* —**de·light'ed·ly,** *adv.* —**de·light'ed·ness,** *n.* —**de·light'er,** *n.* —Syn. *n.* 1. ecstasy, rapture. –*v.* 1. gladden. —Ant. *v.* 1. grieve, depress.

de·light·ful (dĭ-līt′fəl), *adj.* very pleasing; giving joy. —**de·light′ful·ly**, *adv.* —**de·light′-ful·ness**, *n.* —**Syn.** enjoyable, pleasurable.

De·li·lah (dĭ-lī′lə), *n.* 1. woman who betrayed Samson, her lover, to the Philistines. Judges 16. 2. a false, treacherous woman; temptress.

de·lim·it (dĭ-lĭm′ĭt), *v.* fix the limits of; mark the boundaries of. —**de·lim′i·ta′tion**, *n.* —**de·lim′i·ta′tive**, *adj.*

de·lin·e·ate (dĭ-lĭn′ĭ-āt), *v.,* -at·ed, -at·ing. 1. trace the outline of. 2. draw; sketch. 3. describe in words. [< L, < *de-* + *linea* line] —**de·lin′e·a′tion**, *n.* —**de·lin′e·a′tor**, *n.*

de·lin·quen·cy (dĭ-lĭng′kwən-sĭ), *n., pl.* -cies. 1. failure to do what is required by law or duty; guilt. 2. fault; offense.

de·lin·quent (dĭ-lĭng′kwənt), *adj.* 1. failing to do what is required by law or duty. 2. having to do with delinquents. —*n.* a delinquent person; offender; criminal. [< L, < *de-* + *linquere* leave] —**de·lin′quent·ly**, *adv.*

del·i·quesce (del′ə-kwes′), *v.,* -quesced, -quesc·ing. become liquid by absorbing moisture from the air. [< L, < *de-* + *liquere* be liquid] —**del′i·ques′cence**, *n.* —**del′i·ques′cent**, *adj.*

de·lir·i·ous (dĭ-lĭr′ĭ-əs), *adj.* 1. temporarily out of one's senses. 2. wildly excited. 3. caused by delirium. —**de·lir′i·ous·ly**, *adv.* —**de·lir′i·ous·ness**, *n.*

de·lir·i·um (dĭ-lĭr′ĭ-əm), *n., pl.* -lir·i·ums, -lir·i·a (-lĭr′ĭ-ə). 1. a temporary disorder of the mind, as during fevers, characterized by wild excitement, irrational talk, and hallucinations. 2. any wild excitement that cannot be controlled. [< L, < *delirare* rave, be crazy < *de lira (ire)* (go) out of the furrow (in plowing)]

delirium tre·mens (trē′mənz), delirium caused by excessive drinking of alcoholic liquor. [< NL, trembling delirium]

de·liv·er (dĭ-lĭv′ər), *v.* 1. carry and give out; distribute: *the postman delivers letters.* 2. give up; hand over. 3. give forth in words: *the jury delivered its verdict.* 4. strike; throw: *deliver a blow.* 5. set free; rescue. 6. help (a woman) give birth to a child. 7. deliver oneself of, speak; give out. [< F < L *deliberare* set free < *de-* + *liber* free] —**de·liv′er·a·ble**, *adj.* —**de·liv′er·er**, *n.* —**Syn.** 2. cede, surrender. 3. utter. 5. liberate.

de·liv·er·ance (dĭ-lĭv′ər-əns), *n.* 1. act of setting free or state of being set free. 2. a formal expression of opinion or judgment.

de·liv·er·y (dĭ-lĭv′ər-ĭ; -lĭv′rĭ), *n., pl.* -er·ies. 1. act or fact of delivering or distributing; *parcel-post delivery.* 2. a giving up; handing over. 3. way of giving a speech, lecture, etc. 4. act or way of striking, throwing, etc. 5. rescue; release. 6. giving birth to a child; childbirth. 7. anything that is delivered. —**Syn.** 2. surrender.

dell (del), *n.* a small, sheltered glen or valley, usually with trees in it. [OE]

de·louse (dē-lous′; -louz′), *v.,* -loused, -lous·ing. remove lice from.

Del·phi (del′fī), *n.* town in ancient Greece where an oracle of Apollo was located. —**Del·phic** (del′fĭk), **Del·phi·an** (del′fĭ-ən), *adj.*

Delphic oracle, oracle of Apollo at Delphi.

del·phin·i·um (del-fĭn′ĭ-əm), *n.* larkspur. [< NL < Gk., < *delphin* dolphin; from shape of nectar gland]

del·ta (del′tə), *n.* 1. deposit of earth and sand that collects at the mouths of some rivers and is usually three-sided. 2. the fourth letter of the Greek alphabet (Δ or δ).

Delta of the Mississippi River

Del·ta-wing, del·ta-wing (del′tə-wing′), *adj.* of a jet plane, having wings in the shape of a Greek delta or triangle.

del·toid (del′toid), *adj.* triangular. —*n.* a large, triangular muscle of the shoulder.

de·lude (dĭ-lüd′), *v.,* -lud·ed, -lud·ing. mislead; deceive. [< L, < *de-* (to the detriment of) + *ludere* play] —**de·lud′er**, *n.*

del·uge (del′ūj), *n., v.,* -uged, -ug·ing. —*n.* 1. a great flood. 2. a heavy fall of rain. 3. any overwhelming rush. 4. **the Deluge,** *Bible.* the great flood in the days of Noah. Gen. 7. —*v.* 1. to flood. 2. overwhelm. [< OF < L *diluvium* < *dis-* away + *luere* wash]

de·lu·sion (dĭ-lü′zhən), *n.* 1. a deluding or being deluded. 2. a false notion or belief. 3. *Psychiatry.* a fixed belief maintained in the face of indisputable evidence to the contrary.

de·lu·sive (dĭ-lü′sĭv), *adj.* deceptive; false; unreal. —**de·lu′sive·ly**, *adv.* —**de·lu′sive·ness**, *n.*

de·lu·so·ry (dĭ-lü′sə·rĭ), *adj.* delusive; deceptive.

de luxe, de·luxe (də-lúks′; -luks′), *adj.* of exceptionally good quality; elegant. [< F]

delve (delv), *v.,* delved, delv·ing. 1. *Archaic* or *Dial.* dig. 2. search carefully for information. [OE *delfan*] —**delv′er**, *n.*

Dem., Democrat; Democratic.

de·mag·net·ize (dē-mag′nə-tīz), *v.,* -ized, -iz·ing. deprive of magnetism. —**de′mag·net·i·za′tion**, *n.* —**de·mag′net·iz′er**, *n.*

dem·a·gog·ic (dem′ə-goj′ĭk; -gog′ĭk), **dem·a·gog·i·cal** (-ə-kəl), *adj.* of or like a demagogue. —**dem′a·gog′i·cal·ly**, *adv.*

dem·a·gogue, dem·a·gog (dem′ə-gôg; -gog), *n.* a popular leader who stirs up the people in order to get something for himself. [< Gk., < *demos* people + *agogos* leader < *agein* lead] —**dem′a·gog′er·y** (dem′ə-gôg′ər·ĭ; -gog′-), *n. Am.* methods or principles of a demagogue.

dem·a·go·gy (dem′ə-gō′jĭ; -gôg′ĭ; -gog′ĭ), *n. Esp. Brit.* 1. demagoguery. 2. character of a demagogue.

de·mand (dĭ-mand′; -mänd′), *v.* 1. ask for as a right. 2. ask for with authority. 3. ask to know or be told. 4. call for; require; need. 5. summon (to court). —*n.* 1. act of demanding. 2. thing demanded. 3. claim; requirement. 4. desire and ability to buy. 5. inquiry. [< L, < *de-* + *mandare* to order] —**de·mand′a·ble**, *adj.* —**de·mand′er**, *n.* —**Syn.** *v.* 1. claim. 2. requisition.

de·mar·ca·tion, de·mar·ka·tion (dē′mär-kā′shən), *n.* 1. act of setting and marking the limits. 2. separation; distinction. [< Sp., < *de-* off + *marcar* mark]

de·mean[1] (dĭ-mēn′), *v.* lower in dignity or standing; humble. [< *de-* + *mean*[2]; formed after *debase*]

de·mean[2] (dĭ-mēn′), *v.* behave or conduct (oneself). [< OF, < *de-* + *mener* lead < L *minare* drive]

de·mean·or, *esp. Brit.* **de·mean·our** (dĭ-mēn′ər), *n.* way a person looks and acts; behavior. [ME *demenure* < *demenen* behave]

de·ment·ed (dĭ-men′tĭd), *adj.* insane; crazy. [< L, < *de-* out of + *mens* mind] —**de·ment′ed·ly**, *adv.* —**de·ment′ed·ness**, *n.*

de·men·tia (dĭ-men′shə), *n.* a partial or complete loss of mind.

dementia prae·cox (prē′koks), insanity that usually occurs or begins in late adolescence. [< L, precocious insanity]

de·mer·it (dē-mer′ĭt), *n.* 1. fault; defect. 2. mark against a person's record for poor work or unsatisfactory behavior.

de·mesne (dĭ-mān′; -mēn′), *n.* 1. *Law.* the possession of land as one's own. 2. land or land and buildings possessed as one's own. 3. house and land belonging to a lord and used by him. 4. domain; realm. 5. region. [< AF *demeyne* DOMAIN]

De·me·ter (dĭ-mē′tər), *n. Gk. Myth.* the Greek goddess of agriculture and of the fruitful earth, identified with the Roman goddess Ceres.

demi-, *prefix.* half, as in *demigod.* [< F *demi* half < VL < L, < *dis-* apart + *medius* middle]

dem·i·god (dem′ĭ·god′), *n.* 1. god that is partly human. 2. a minor or lesser god. —**dem·i·god·dess** (dem′ĭ·god′ĭs), *n.* a female demigod.

dem·i·john (dem′ĭ·jon), *n.* a large bottle of earthenware enclosed in wicker.

Demijohn

de·mil·i·tar·ize (dē·mil′ə·tə·rīz), v., –rized, –riz·ing. free from military control. —de·mil′i·ta·ri·za′tion, n.

dem·i·monde (dem′i·mond; dem′i·mond′), n. class of women whose reputation and morals are doubtful. [< F, half-world]

de·mise (di·mīz′), n., v., –mised, –mis·ing. —n. 1. death. 2. Law. transfer of an estate by a will or lease. 3. transfer of royal power by death or abdication. —v. 1. Law. transfer (an estate) by a will or lease. 2. transfer (royal power) by death or abdication. [appar. < AF, pp. of desmettre put away < des- away (< L dis-) + mettre put < L mittere let go, send] —de·mis′a·ble, adj.

dem·i·sem·i·qua·ver (dem′i·sem′i·kwā′vər), n. Music. a thirty-second note.

dem·i·tasse (dem′i·tas′; –täs′), n. a very small cup of coffee. [< F, half-cup]

de·mo·bi·lize (dē·mō′bə·līz), v., –lized, –liz·ing. disband (troops, etc.). —de·mo′bi·li·za′tion, n.

de·moc·ra·cy (di·mok′rə·si), n., pl. –cies. 1. government that is run directly or indirectly by the people who live under it. 2. country, state, or community having such a government. 3. treatment of others as one's equals. 4. Democracy, Am. a. the principles of the Democratic Party. b. its members collectively. [< F < Gk., < demos people + kratos rule]

dem·o·crat (dem′ə·krat), n. 1. person who believes that a government should be run by the people who live under it. 2. person who holds or acts on the belief that all people are his equals. 3. Democrat, Am. member of the Democratic Party.

dem·o·crat·ic (dem′ə·krat′ik), **dem·o·crat·i·cal** (–ə·kəl), adj. 1. of a democracy; like a democracy. 2. treating all classes of people as one's equals. 3. Democratic, Am. of the Democratic Party.

Democratic Party, Am. one of the two main political parties in the United States.

de·moc·ra·tize (di·mok′rə·tīz), v., –tized, –tiz·ing. make or become democratic. —de·moc′ra·ti·za′tion, n.

de·mog·ra·phy (di·mog′rə·fi), n. science dealing with statistics of births, deaths, diseases, etc., of a community. —de·mog′ra·pher, n.

de·mol·ish (di·mol′ish), v. pull or tear down; destroy. [< F < L demoliri tear down < de- + moles mass] —de·mol′ish·er, n. —de·mol′ish·ment, n.

dem·o·li·tion (dem′ə·lish′ən; dē′mə-), n. destruction; ruin.

demolition bomb, Mil. a bomb with a relatively large explosive charge designed to destroy buildings, etc.

de·mon (dē′mən), n. 1. an evil spirit; devil; fiend. 2. a very wicked or cruel person. 3. an evil influence. 4. person who has great energy or vigor. 5. an attendant or guiding spirit. 6. daemon. [(defs. 1–5) < L < Gk. daimonion divine (thing), in Christian writings, evil spirit; (def. 6) see DAEMON]

de·mon·e·tize (dē·mon′ə·tīz; –mun′-), v., –tized, –tiz·ing. deprive of its standard value as money. —de·mon′e·ti·za′tion, n.

de·mo·ni·ac (di·mō′ni·ak), adj. Also, de·mo·ni·a·cal (dē′mə·nī′ə·kəl). 1. of demons. 2. devilish; fiendish. 3. raging; frantic. —n. person supposed to be possessed by an evil spirit. —de·mo·ni·a·cal·ly (dē′mə·nī′ik·li), adv.

de·mon·ic (di·mon′ik), adj. 1. of or caused by evil spirits. 2. influenced by a guiding spirit.

de·mon·ol·o·gy (dē′mən·ol′ə·ji), n. study of demons or of beliefs about demons. —de·mon·ol′o·gist, n.

de·mon·stra·ble (di·mon′strə·bəl; dem′ən-), adj. capable of being proved. —de·mon′stra·bil′i·ty, n. —de·mon′stra·bly, adv.

dem·on·strate (dem′ən·strāt), v., –strat·ed, –strat·ing. 1. establish the truth of; prove. 2. explain by using examples, experiments, etc. 3. show or advertise the merits of (a thing for sale). 4. show openly; exhibit. 5. show feeling by a parade, meeting, etc. 6. display military

strength to frighten or deceive an enemy. [< L, < de- + monstrare show] —dem′on·stra′tor, n. —Syn. 1. attest.

dem·on·stra·tion (dem′ən·strā′shən), n. 1. clear proof. 2. explanation with the use of examples, experiments, etc. 3. a showing of the merits of a thing for sale; advertising or making known some new product or process in a public place. 4. an open show or exhibition, as of feeling, ability, etc. 5. show of feeling by a parade, meeting, etc. 6. display of military strength to frighten or deceive an enemy.

de·mon·stra·tive (di·mon′strə·tiv), adj. 1. expressing one's affections freely and openly. 2. showing clearly; explanatory. 3. giving proof; conclusive. 4. pointing out. This and that are demonstrative pronouns and also demonstrative adjectives. —n. pronoun or adjective that points out. —de·mon′stra·tive·ly, adv. —de·mon′stra·tive·ness, n. ⟩ This, that, these, those are called demonstrative adjectives or pronouns according to their use in a sentence: This car we bought in May (adj.). This costs a good bit more than those (pron.).

de·mor·al·ize (di·môr′əl·īz; –mor′-), v., –ized, –iz·ing. Am. 1. corrupt the morals of. 2. weaken the spirit, courage, or discipline of; dishearten. 3. throw into confusion or disorder. —de·mor′al·i·za′tion, n. —de·mor′al·iz′er, n. Am.

De·mos·the·nes (di·mos′thə·nēz), n. 384?–322 B.C., the most famous orator of ancient Greece.

de·mote (di·mōt′), v., –mot·ed, –mot·ing. Am. put back to a lower grade; reduce in rank. [< de- + (pro)mote] —de·mo′tion, n. Am.

de·mul·cent (di·mul′sənt), adj. soothing. —n. a soothing ointment or medicine. [< L, < de- + mulcere soothe]

de·mur (di·mėr′), v., –murred, –mur·ring, n. —v. 1. object. 2. Law. interpose a demurrer. —n. an objection. [< OF < L, < de- + morari delay]

de·mure (di·myûr′), adj., –mur·er, –mur·est. 1. falsely proper; unnaturally modest; coy. 2. serious; sober. [< obs. mure, adj., demure < OF < L maturus mature] —de·mure′ly, adv.

de·mur·rage (di·mér′ij), n. 1. failure to load or unload a ship, railroad car, etc., within the time specified. 2. payment made for this.

de·mur·rer (di·mér′ər), n. 1. person who objects. 2. objection. 3. Law. a legal plea that a lawsuit be dismissed, even if the facts are as alleged by the opposite party, because the facts do not sustain his claim.

den (den), n., v., denned, den·ning. —n. 1. place where a wild animal lives. 2. place where thieves or the like have their headquarters. 3. a small and cozy private room. —v. inhabit a den. [OE denn]

de·nar·i·us (di·nār′i·əs), n., pl. –nar·i·i (–när′i·ī). 1. an ancient Roman silver coin. 2. an ancient Roman gold coin. [< L, containing ten (here, ten times the value of an as²) < deni ten at a time]

de·na·tion·al·ize (dē·nash′ən·əl·īz; –nash′nəl–), v., –ized, –iz·ing. deprive of national rights, scope, etc. —de·na′tion·al·i·za′tion, n.

de·nat·u·ral·ize (dē·nach′ə·rəl·īz; –nach′rəl–), v., –ized, –iz·ing. make unnatural. —de·nat′u·ral·i·za′tion, n.

de·na·ture (dē·nā′chər), v., –tured, –tur·ing. 1. change the nature of. 2. make (alcohol, food, etc.) unfit for drinking or eating without destroying for other purposes. —de·na′tur·a′tion, n.

de·na·zi·fy (dē·nät′sə·fī; –nat′-), v., –fied, –fy·ing. get rid of Nazi doctrines or Nazi influences. —de·na′zi·fi·ca′tion, n. Am.

den·drite (den′drīt), n. Anat. the branching part at the receiving end of a nerve cell. [< Gk., < dendron tree]

de·neu·tral·ize (dē·nü′trəl·īz; –nū′-), v., –ized, –iz·ing. abolish the neutral status of (a country, territory, etc.). —de·neu′tral·i·za′tion, n.

den·gue (deng′gā; –gi), n. Am. an infectious fever with skin rash and severe pain in the joints and muscles. [< Sp., < Swahili (lang. of C Africa) kidinga popo]

de·ni·al (di·nī′əl), n. 1. act of saying that something is not true. 2. act of saying that one does not hold to or accept: *a public denial of communism.* **3.** a refusing. **4.** a refusing to acknowledge. **5.** self-denial.

de·ni·er¹ (di·nī′ər), *n.* person who denies.

de·ni·er² (den′yər; də·nir′), *n.* unit of weight used to express the fineness of silk, rayon, or nylon yarn. [< OF < L *denarius* DENARIUS]

den·im (den′əm), *n. Am.* a heavy, coarse cotton cloth for overalls, etc. [short for F *serge de Nîmes* serge of Nîmes]

den·i·zen (den′ə·zən), *n.* **1.** inhabitant; occupant. **2.** a foreign word, plant, animal, etc., that has been adopted. —*v.* make (one) a denizen; naturalize. [< OF *denzein* < *denz* within < LL < L *de* from + *intus* within]

Den·mark (den′märk), *n.* a small country in N Europe.

de·nom·i·nate (*v.* di·nom′ə·nāt; *adj.* di·nom′ə·nit, -nāt), *v.,* -nat·ed, -nat·ing, *adj.* —*v.* give a name to; name. —*adj.* called by a specific name. [< L, < *de-* + *nomen* name]

de·nom·i·na·tion (di·nom′ə·nā′shən), *n.* **1.** name for a group or class of things. **2.** a religious group or sect. **3.** class or kind of units: *a coin of low denomination.*

de·nom·i·na·tion·al (di·nom′ə·nā′shən·əl; -nāsh′nəl), *adj.* having to do with some religious denomination or denominations; controlled by a religious denomination. —**de·nom′i·na′tion·al·ly,** *adv.*

de·nom·i·na·tion·al·ism (di·nom′ə·nā′shən·əl·iz′əm; -nāsh′nəl-), *n.* **1.** denominational principles. **2.** division into denominations.

de·nom·i·na·tive (di·nom′ə·nā′tiv; -nə·tiv), *adj.* **1.** giving a distinctive name; naming. **2.** formed from a noun or an adjective. *To center* is a denominative verb. —*n.* a denominative word. —**de·nom′i·na′tive·ly,** *adv.*

de·nom·i·na·tor (di·nom′ə·nā′tər), *n.* **1.** number below the line in a fraction, stating the size of the parts in their relation to the whole. **2.** person or thing that names.

de·no·ta·tion (dē′nō·tā′shən), *n.* **1.** meaning, esp. the exact, literal meaning. The denotation of *home* is "place where one lives," but it has many connotations. **2.** indication; denoting.

de·note (di·nōt′), *v.,* -not·ed, -not·ing. **1.** be the sign of; indicate. **2.** be a name for; mean. [< F < L, < *de-* + *notare* note < *nota* mark]

de·noue·ment, dé·noue·ment (dā′nü·mäN′), *n.* solution of a plot in a play, a story, etc.; outcome; end. [< F, < *dénouer* untie < L *dis-* + *nodus* knot]

de·nounce (di·nouns′), *v.,* -nounced, -nouncing. **1.** condemn publicly; express strong disapproval of. **2.** inform against; accuse. **3.** give formal notice of the termination of (a treaty, etc.). [< OF < L, < *de-* + *nuntiare* announce < *nuntius* messenger] —**de·nounce′ment,** *n.*

de no·vo (dē nō′vō), *Latin.* anew; afresh.

dense (dens), *adj.,* dens·er, dens·est. **1.** closely packed together; thick. **2.** stupid. [< L *densus*] —**dense′ly,** *adv.* —**dense′ness,** *n.* —**Syn. 1.** compact.

den·si·ty (den′sə·ti), *n., pl.* -ties. **1.** dense condition or quality; compactness; thickness. **2.** stupidity. **3.** *Physics.* quantity of matter in a unit of volume. **4.** specific gravity.

dent (dent), *n.* hollow made by a blow or pressure. —*v.* **1.** make a dent in. **2.** become dented. [ME *dente,* var. of *dint*]

den·tal (den′təl), *adj.* **1.** of or for the teeth. **2.** of or for a dentist's work. **3.** *Phonet.* produced by placing the tip of the tongue against or near the upper front teeth. —*n.* a dental sound. [< L *dens* tooth]

den·tate (den′tāt), *adj. Bot., Zool.* having toothlike projections; toothed; notched. —**den′tate·ly,** *adv.*

den·ti·frice (den′tə·fris), *n.* paste, powder, or liquid for cleaning the teeth. [< F < L, < *dens* tooth + *fricare* rub]

den·tine (den′tēn; -tin), **den·tin** (-tin), *n.* the hard, bony material that forms the main part of a tooth.

Dentate leaf

den·tist (den′tist) *n.* doctor who cleans and extracts teeth, fills cavities in them, and supplies artificial teeth.

den·tist·ry (den′tis·tri), *n.* work, art, or occupation of a dentist.

den·ti·tion (den·tish′ən), *n.* **1.** growth of teeth; teething. **2.** kind, number, and arrangement of the teeth.

den·ture (den′chər), *n.* **1.** set of artificial teeth. **2.** set of teeth.

de·nude (di·nüd′; -nūd′), *v.,* -nud·ed, -nud·ing. **1.** make bare; strip. **2.** lay (a rock, etc.) bare by removing what lies above. —**de·nu·da·tion** (dē′nü·dā′shən; -nū-; den′yu-), *n.*

de·nun·ci·a·tion (di·nun′si·ā′shən; -shi-), *n.* **1.** strong, public disapproval. **2.** act of informing against; accusation. **3.** formal notice of the intention to end a treaty, etc. **4.** a warning; threat.

de·nun·ci·a·to·ry (di·nun′si·ə·tô′ri; -shi-; -tō′-), *adj.* condemning; accusing.

Den·ver (den′vər), *n.* capital of Colorado, in the central part.

de·ny (di·nī′), *v.,* -nied, -ny·ing. **1.** declare (something) is not true. **2.** say that one does not hold to or accept. **3.** refuse. **4.** refuse to acknowledge; disown. **5.** deny oneself, do without the things one wants. [< F < L, < *de-* + *negare* say no] —**Syn. 1.** contradict, dispute. **4.** repudiate, disclaim. —**Ant. 1.** admit, concede.

de·o·dor·ant (dē·ō′dər·ənt), *n.* preparation that destroys odors. —*adj.* that destroys odors.

de·o·dor·ize (dē·ō′dər·īz), *v.,* -ized, -iz·ing. destroy the odor of. —**de·o′dor·i·za′tion,** *n.* —**de·o′dor·iz′er,** *n.*

dep., **1.** department. **2.** deputy.

de·part (di·pärt′), *v.* **1.** go away; leave. **2.** turn away; change *(from).* **3.** die. [< OF, < LL *departire* divide < L *de-* + *partire* < *pars* part] —**Syn. 1.** quit, retire. **2.** diverge, deviate. —**Ant. 1.** arrive, come.

de·part·ed (di·pär′tid), *n.* dead person or persons. —*adj.* **1.** dead. **2.** gone; past.

de·part·ment (di·pärt′mənt), *n.* **1.** separate part; division: *the fire department.* **2.** one of the administrative districts into which France is divided. **3.** a chief division of governmental administration. —**de·part·men·tal** (dē′pärt·men′təl), *adj.* —**de′part·men′tal·ly,** *adv.*

department store, *Am.* store that sells many kinds of articles arranged in separate departments.

de·par·ture (di·pär′chər), *n.* **1.** act of going away; act of leaving. **2.** a turning away; change. **3.** *Archaic.* death.

de·pend (di·pend′), *v.* **1.** rely; trust. **2.** rely for support or help. **3.** be controlled or influenced by something else. **4.** depend on, be controlled or influenced by. [< OF < L, < *de-* from + *pendere* hang]

de·pend·a·ble (di·pen′də·bəl), *adj.* reliable; trustworthy. —**de·pend′a·bil′i·ty, de·pend′a·ble·ness,** *n.* —**de·pend′a·bly,** *adv.*

de·pend·ence (di·pen′dəns), *n.* **1.** reliance on another for support or help. **2.** reliance; trust. **3.** fact of being controlled or influenced by something else: *the dependence of crops on the weather.* **4.** person or thing relied on.

de·pend·en·cy (di·pen′dən·si), *n., pl.* -cies. **1.** country or territory controlled by another country. **2.** dependence. **3.** thing that depends on another for existence, support, or help.

de·pend·ent (di·pen′dənt), *adj.* **1.** relying on another for support or help. **2.** controlled or influenced by something else. **3.** hanging down. —*n.* person who relies on another for support or help. —**Syn.** *adj.* **2.** contingent, conditional. ►A **dependent clause** modifies or supports in some way a word or sentence element: *The house that stood on the other side* was even more dilapidated. [Clause modifies *house.*] Ordinarily a dependent clause does not stand by itself but is part of a complex sentence.

de·pict (di·pikt′), *v.* represent by drawing, painting, or describing; show; picture; portray. [< L *depictus* < *de-* + *pingere* paint] —**de·pict′er,** *n.* —**de·pic′tion,** *n.*

de·pil·a·to·ry (di·pil′ə·tô′ri; -tō′-), *adj.*, *n.*, *pl.* -ries. —*adj.* capable of removing hair. —*n.* paste, liquid, or other preparation for removing hair. [< L, < *de-* + *pilus* hair]

de·plete (di·plēt′), *v.*, -plet·ed, -plet·ing. empty; exhaust. [< L *depletus* empty < *de-* + *-plere* fill] —de·ple′tion, *n.* —de·ple′tive, *adj.*

de·plor·a·ble (di·plôr′ə·bəl; -plōr′-), *adj.* 1. to be deplored; lamentable. 2. wretched; miserable. —de·plor′a·bly, *adv.*

de·plore (di·plôr′; -plōr′), *v.*, -plored, -plor·ing. be very sorry about; lament. [< L, < *de-* + *plorare* weep] —Syn. bewail, bemoan.

de·ploy (di·ploi′), *v. Mil.* spread out from a column into a long battle line. [< F, < *dé-* (< L *dis-*) + *ployer* < L *plicare* fold] —de·ploy′ment, *n.*

de·po·nent (di·pō′nənt), *n.* 1. *Law.* person who testifies in writing under oath. 2. in Greek and Latin grammar, verb passive in form but active in meaning. —*adj.* having passive form but active meaning. [< L, < *de-* away, down + *ponere* put]

de·pop·u·late (dē·pop′yə·lāt), *v.*, -lat·ed, -lat·ing. deprive of inhabitants. —de′pop·u·la′tion, *n.* —de·pop′u·la′tor, *n.*

de·port (di·pôrt′; -pōrt′), *v.* 1. banish; expel; remove. 2. behave or conduct (oneself) in a particular manner. [< F < L, < *de-* away + *portare* carry]

de·por·ta·tion (dē′pôr·tā′shən; -pōr-), *n.* expulsion, as of undesirable aliens; banishment.

de·port·ment (di·pôrt′mənt; -pōrt′-), *n.* way a person acts; behavior; conduct.

de·pose (di·pōz′), *v.*, -posed, -pos·ing. 1. put out of office or a position of authority: *depose a government.* 2. declare under oath; testify. [< OF, < *de-* down + *poser* POSE] —de·pos′a·ble, *adj.* —de·pos′al, *n.*

de·pos·it (di·poz′it), *v.* 1. put down; lay down; leave lying. 2. put in a place for safekeeping. 3. pay as a pledge to do something or to pay more later. —*n.* 1. something laid down or left lying. 2. thing put in a place for safekeeping. 3. money put in a bank. 4. money paid as a pledge to do something or to pay more later. 5. mass of some mineral in rock or in the ground. [< L *depositus* < *de-* away + *ponere* put]

de·pos·i·tar·y (di·poz′ə·ter′i), *n.*, *pl.* -tar·ies. 1. person or company that receives something for safekeeping; trustee. 2. depository.

dep·o·si·tion (dep′ə·zish′ən; dē′pə-), *n.* 1. act of deposing. 2. *Law.* a. testimony. b. a sworn statement in writing; deposit. 3. act of depositing. 4. thing deposited; deposit.

de·pos·i·tor (di·poz′ə·tər), *n.* 1. person who deposits. 2. person who deposits money in a bank.

de·pos·i·to·ry (di·poz′ə·tô′ri; -tō′-), *n.*, *pl.* -ries. 1. place where a thing is put for safekeeping; storehouse. 2. trustee.

de·pot (dē′pō; *Mil. and Brit.* dep′ō), *n.* 1. *Am.* a railroad station. 2. storehouse; warehouse. 3. place where military supplies are stored. 4. place where recruits are brought together and trained. [< F < L *depositum.* See DEPOSIT.]

de·prave (di·prāv′), *v.*, -praved, -prav·ing. make bad; corrupt. [< L, < *de-* + *pravus* crooked, wrong] —de·prav′er, *n.*

de·prav·i·ty (di·prav′ə·ti), *n.*, *pl.* -ties. 1. wickedness; corruption. 2. a corrupt act; bad practice.

dep·re·cate (dep′rə·kāt), *v.*, -cat·ed, -cat·ing. express strong disapproval of; protest against. [< L, plead in excuse, avert by prayer < *de-* + *precari* pray] —dep′re·cat′ing·ly, *adv.* —dep′re·ca′tion, *n.* —dep′re·ca′tor, *n.*

dep·re·ca·to·ry (dep′rə·kə·tô′ri; -tō′-), *adj.* 1. deprecating. 2. apologetic. —dep′re·ca·to′ri·ly, *adv.* —dep′re·ca·to′ri·ness, *n.*

de·pre·ci·ate (di·prē′shi·āt), *v.*, -at·ed, -at·ing. 1. lessen the value or price of. 2. *Am.* lessen in value, as money. 3. speak slightingly of; belittle. [< L, < *de-* + *pretium* price] —de·pre′ci·a′tor, *n.*

de·pre·ci·a·tion (di·prē′shi·ā′shən), *n.* 1. *Am.* a lessening or lowering in value. 2. a speaking slightingly of; a belittling.

de·pre·ci·a·to·ry (di·prē′shi·ə·tô′ri; -tō′-), *adj.* tending to depreciate, disparage, or undervalue.

dep·re·da·tion (dep′rə·dā′shən), *n.* act of plundering; robbery; a ravaging. [< L, < *de-* + *praeda* booty]

de·press (di·pres′), *v.* 1. press down; push down; lower. 2. lower in pitch. 3. lower in amount or value. 4. reduce the activity of; weaken. 5. make sad or gloomy; cause to have low spirits. [< OF, < L *depressus* < *de-* + *premere* press] —de·press′ing·ly, *adv.* —Syn. 5. deject, sadden.

de·pres·sant (di·pres′ənt), *Med.* —*adj.* decreasing the rate of vital activities. —*n.* medicine that lessens pain or excitement; sedative.

de·pressed (di·prest′), *adj.* 1. sad; gloomy; low-spirited. 2. pressed down; lowered. 3. *Bot., Zool.* flattened down; broader than high.

de·pres·sion (di·presh′ən), *n.* 1. act of pressing down. 2. depressed condition. 3. a low place; hollow. 4. sadness; gloominess; low spirits. 5. reduction of activity; dullness of trade. 6. the angular distance of an object below the horizon. —de·pres′sive, *adj.* —de·pres′sive·ly, *adv.* —Syn. 4. dejection, melancholy.

dep·ri·va·tion (dep′rə·vā′shən), *n.* act of depriving; state of being deprived.

de·prive (di·prīv′), *v.*, -prived, -priv·ing. 1. take away from by force. 2. keep from having or doing. [< OF, < *de-* (< L *de-*) + *priver* deprive < L, orig., exempt] —Syn. dispossess, divest. 2. debar.

dept., 1. department. 2. deputy.

depth (depth), *n.* 1. quality of being deep; deepness. 2. distance from top to bottom. 3. distance from front to back. 4. a deep place. 5. the deepest part: *in the depths of the earth.* 6. the most central part: *in the depth of the forest.* 7. profound penetration: *depth of mind.* 8. deep tone; intensity. [ME, < OE *dēop* deep]

depth charge or **bomb**, an explosive charge dropped from a ship or airplane and arranged to explode at a certain depth under water.

dep·u·ta·tion (dep′yə·tā′shən), *n.* 1. act of deputing. 2. group of persons appointed to act for others.

de·pute (di·pūt′), *v.*, -put·ed, -put·ing. 1. appoint to do one's work or to act in one's place. 2. give (work, power, etc.) to another. [< F < LL, assign < L, consider as < *de-* + *putare* think, count]

dep·u·tize (dep′yə·tīz), *v.*, -tized, -tiz·ing. 1. appoint as deputy. 2. act as deputy.

dep·u·ty (dep′yə·ti), *n.*, *pl.* -ties, *adj.* —*n.* 1. person appointed to do the work or to act in the place of another: *a sheriff's deputy.* 2. representative in certain lawmaking assemblies. —*adj.* acting as a deputy. —Syn. *n.* 1. proxy, delegate.

De Quin·cey (di kwin′si), Thomas, 1785–1859, English essayist.

der., derivation; derivative; derived.

de·rail (dē·rāl′), *v.* 1. cause (a train, etc.) to run off the rails. 2. run off the rails. —de·rail′-ment, *n.*

de·range (di·rānj′), *v.*, -ranged, -rang·ing. 1. disturb the order or arrangement of. 2. make insane. [< F *déranger.* See DE-, RANGE.] —de·ranged′, *adj.* —de·range′ment, *n.*

Der·by (dėr′bi; *Brit.* där′bi), *n.*, *pl.* -bies. 1. a horse race in England run every year at Epsom Downs. 2. a horse race of similar importance: *the Kentucky Derby.* 3. an important race, as of automobiles or airplanes. 4. derby, *Am.* a stiff hat with a rounded crown and narrow brim.

der·e·lict (der′ə·likt), *adj.* 1. abandoned; deserted; forsaken. 2. *Am.* failing in one's duty; negligent. —*n.* 1. ship abandoned at sea. 2. any worthless, deserted person or thing. [< L *derelictus* < *de-* wholly + *re-* behind + *linquere* leave]

der·e·lic·tion (der′ə·lik′shən), *n.* 1. failure in one's duty; negligence. 2. abandonment; desertion; forsaking.

de·ride (di·rīd′), *v.*, -rid·ed, -rid·ing. laugh at in scorn; ridicule. [< L, < *de-* at + *ridere* laugh] —de·rid′er, *n.* —de·rid′ing·ly, *adv.* —Syn. jeer, scoff, mock.

de ri·gueur (də rē·gœr'), *French.* required by etiquette; according to custom; proper.

de·ri·sion (di·rizh'ən), *n.* 1. scornful laughter; ridicule; contempt. 2. an object of ridicule.

de·ri·sive (di·rī'siv), **de·ri·so·ry** (-sə·ri), *adj.* mocking; ridiculing. —**de·ri'sive·ly**, *adv.*

deriv., derivation; derivative.

der·i·va·tion (der'ə·vā'shən), *n.* 1. act or fact of deriving. 2. state of being derived. 3. source; origin. 4. theory of the development or origin of a word. —**der'i·va'tion·al**, *adj.*

de·riv·a·tive (di·riv'ə·tiv), *adj.* derived; not original. —*n.* 1. something derived. 2. a word formed by adding a prefix or suffix to another word. 3. *Chem.* substance obtained from another by substituting a different element.

de·rive (di·rīv'), *v.,* –rived, –riv·ing. 1. get; receive; obtain. 2. obtain from a source or origin. *Decimal* and *December* are derived from the Latin word *decem,* which means "ten." 3. come from a source or origin; originate. 4. trace (a word, custom, etc.) from or to a source or origin. 5. obtain by reasoning. 6. *Chem.* obtain (a compound) from another by substituting a different element. [< F < L *derivare* lead off, draw off < *de-* + *rivus* stream] —**de·riv'a·ble**, *adj.* —**de·riv'er**, *n.*

der·ma (der'mə), *n.* 1. the sensitive layer of skin beneath the epidermis. 2. skin. [< Gk., skin] —**der'mal**, *adj.*

der·ma·tol·o·gy (der'mə·tol'ə·ji), *n.* science that deals with the skin and its diseases. —**der·ma·to·log·i·cal** (der'mə·tə·loj'ə·kəl), *adj.* —**der'ma·tol'o·gist**, *n.*

der·mis (der'mis), *n.* derma. —**der'mic**, *adj.*

der·o·gate (der'ə·gāt), *v.,* –gat·ed, –gat·ing. 1. take away; detract. 2. become worse; degenerate. [< L, < *de-* away from + *rogare* ask] —**der'o·ga'tion**, *n.*

de·rog·a·to·ry (di·rog'ə·tô'ri; –tō'-), **de·rog·a·tive** (-ə·tiv), *adj.* 1. disparaging; belittling. 2. lessening the value; detracting. —**de·rog'a·to'ri·ly**, **de·rog'a·tive·ly**, *adv.*

der·rick (der'ik), *n.* 1. machine with a long arm for lifting and moving heavy objects. 2. *Am.* a towerlike framework over an oil well, gas well, etc. [for *Derrick,* a hangman at Tyburn, London]

der·ring-do (der'ing·dü'), *n. Archaic.* daring deeds. [alter. of ME *dorryng don* daring to do]

der·ring·er (der'ən·jər), *n. Am.* a short pistol that has a large caliber. [for the inventor]

der·vish (der'vish), *n.* a member of any of various Mohammedan orders. [< Turk. < Pers. *darvīsh*]

des·cant (*v.* des·kant', dis–; *n.* des'kant), *v.* 1. talk at great length; discourse. 2. *Music.* sing or play a melody with another melody. —*n. Music.* a. part music. b. melody to be played or sung with another melody. [< OF < Med.L, < L *dis-* + *cantus* song < *canere* sing]

Des·cartes (dā·kärt'), *n.* René, 1596–1650, French philosopher and mathematician.

de·scend (di·send'), *v.* 1. go or come down from a higher place to a lower place. 2. go from earlier to later time. 3. go from greater to less. 4. go from more important to less important matters. 5. go from general to particular matters. 6. go from higher to lower standards; lower oneself; stoop. 7. slope downward. 8. be handed down from parent to child. 9. make a sudden attack. 10. *Astron.* move toward the horizon. [< OF < L, < *de-* + *scandere* climb] —**de·scend'a·ble**, *adj.*

de·scend·ant (di·sen'dənt), *n.* 1. person born of a certain family or group. 2. offspring; child. —*adj.* Also, **de·scend'ent**, descending. ➤ Descendant is used both as adjective and noun; descendent, only as adjective. Obviously, to be on the safe side, use descendant: Noun: *He claims to be a descendant of Benjamin Franklin.* Adjective: *Nearly all the people of the town are descendant from* [more usual, *descended from*] *these first settlers.*

de·scent (di·sent'), *n.* 1. a coming down or going down from a higher to a lower place. 2. a downward slope. 3. way or passage down; means

of descending. 4. family line; ancestry. 5. a lowering of oneself. 6. a sudden attack.

de·scribe (di·skrīb'), *v.,* –scribed, –scrib·ing. 1. tell or write about. 2. give a picture or account of in words. 3. draw the outline of; trace. [< L, < *de-* + *scribere* write] —**de·scrib'a·ble**, *adj.* —**de·scrib'er**, *n.* —Syn. 1. recount, relate. 2. depict.

de·scrip·tion (di·skrip'shən), *n.* 1. act of describing. 2. composition or account that describes or gives a picture in words. 3. kind; sort: *people of every description.* 4. act of drawing in outline.

de·scrip·tive (di·skrip'tiv), *adj.* describing; using description. —**de·scrip'tive·ly**, *adv.* —**de·scrip'tive·ness**, *n.*

de·scry (di·skrī'), *v.,* –scried, –scry·ing. catch sight of; be able to see; make out. [< OF *descrier* proclaim. See DIS-, CRY.]

des·e·crate (des'ə·krāt), *v.,* –crat·ed, –crating. disregard the sacredness of. [< *de-* + (*con*)*secrate*] —**des'e·crat'er**, **des'e·cra'tor**, *n.* —**des'e·cra'tion**, *n.*

de·seg·re·ga·tion (dē·seg'rə·gā'shən), *n.* abolishment of the practice of segregating Negroes from whites, esp. in the U.S. public schools.

de·sen·si·tize (dē·sen'sə·tīz), *v.,* –tized, –tizing. make less sensitive. —**de·sen'si·ti·za'tion**, *n.* —**de·sen'si·tiz'er**, *n.*

des·ert[1] (dez'ərt), *n.* 1. a dry, barren region, usually sandy and without trees. 2. region that is not inhabited or cultivated; wilderness. —*adj.* 1. dry; barren. 2. not inhabited or cultivated; wild. [< OF < Eccl.L *desertum,* (thing) abandoned, pp. See DESERT[2].]

de·sert[2] (di·zért'), *v.* 1. go away and leave; abandon; forsake. 2. run away from duty. 3. leave military service without permission. [< F < LL *desertare* < L *deserere* abandon < *de-* DIS- + *serere* join] —**de·sert'er**, *n.*

de·sert[3] (di·zért'), *n.* what is deserved; suitable reward or punishment: *the robber got his just deserts; he was sentenced to five years in prison.* [< OF *deserte,* pp. of *deservir* DESERVE] —Syn. merit, due, meed.

de·ser·tion (di·zér'shən), *n.* 1. a deserting, esp. in violation of duty or obligation. 2. state of being deserted.

de·serve (di·zérv'), *v.,* –served, –serv·ing. have a claim or right to; be worthy of. [< F < L *deservire* serve well < *de-* + *servire* serve] —**de·serv'er**, *n.* —Syn. merit.

de·serv·ed·ly (di·zér'vid·li), *adv.* justly.

de·serv·ing (di·zér'ving), *adj.* 1. that deserves; worthy (of something). 2. worth helping.

des·ha·bille (dez'ə·bēl'), *n.* dishabille.

des·ic·cate (des'ə·kāt), *v.,* –cat·ed, –cat·ing. 1. dry thoroughly. 2. preserve by drying thoroughly. [< L, < *de-* out + *siccus* dry] —**des'ic·ca'tion**, *n.* —**des'ic·ca'tive**, *adj.*

de·sid·er·a·tum (di·sid'ər·ā'təm; –ä'təm), *n., pl.* –ta (-tə). something desired or needed. [< L, pp. of *desiderare* long for]

de·sign (di·zīn'), *n.* 1. a drawing, plan, or sketch made to serve as a pattern from which to work: *design for a machine.* 2. arrangement of detail, form, and color in painting, etc.: *a wallpaper design.* 3. art of making designs: *school of design.* 4. piece of artistic work. 5. a plan in mind to be carried out. 6. scheme of attack; evil plan. 7. purpose; intention. —*v.* 1. make a first sketch of; plan out. 2. make drawings, sketches, plans, etc. 3. plan out; form in the mind; contrive. 4. have in mind to do. [< F < L, < *de-* + *signum* mark]

des·ig·nate (*v.* dez'ig·nāt; *adj.* dez'ig·nit, –nāt), *v.,* –nat·ed, –nat·ing, *adj.* —*v.* 1. point out; indicate definitely. 2. name; entitle. 3. select for duty, office, etc.; appoint. —*adj.* appointed; selected. [< L *designatus,* pp. See DESIGN.] —**des'ig·na'tive**, *adj.* —**des'ig·na'tor**, *n.*

des·ig·na·tion (dez'ig·nā'shən), *n.* 1. act of designating. 2. a descriptive title; name. 3. appointment; selection.

de·sign·ed·ly (di·zīn'id·li), *adv.* purposely.

de·sign·er (di-zīn′ər), *n.* **1.** person who designs: *a dress designer.* **2.** plotter; schemer.

de·sign·ing (di-zīn′ing), *adj.* **1.** scheming; plotting. **2.** showing plan or forethought. —*n.* art of making designs. —**de·sign′ing·ly,** *adv.*

de·sir·a·ble (di-zīr′ə-bəl), *adj.* worth wishing for; worth having. —**de·sir′a·bil′i·ty, de·sir′-a·ble·ness,** *n.* —**de·sir′a·bly,** *adv.*

de·sire (di-zīr′), *v.,* -**sired,** -**sir·ing,** *n.* —*v.* **1.** wish for; wish strongly for. **2.** express a wish for; ask for. **3.** crave sexually. —*n.* **1.** wish; strong wish. **2.** an expressed wish; request. **3.** thing desired. **4.** sexual craving; lust. [< OF < L *desiderare* long for] —**Syn.** *v.* **1.** long, yearn, crave. —*n.* **1.** longing, yearning.

de·sir·ous (di-zīr′əs), *adj.* having or showing desire; full of desire; desiring.

de·sist (di-zist′), *v.* stop; cease. [< OF < L *de-* + *sistere* stop]

desk (desk), *n.* **1.** piece of furniture with a flat or sloping top on which to write or to rest books for reading. **2.** lectern; pulpit. [< Med.L *desca* < Ital. *desco* < L *discus* quoit, DISH < Gk. *diskos*]

Des Moines (də moin′), capital of Iowa, in the central part.

des·o·late (*adj.* des′ə-lit; *v.* des′ə-lāt), *adj., v.,* -**lat·ed,** -**lat·ing.** —*adj.* **1.** laid waste; devastated; barren. **2.** not lived in; deserted. **3.** left alone; solitary; lonely. **4.** unhappy; wretched; forlorn. **5.** dreary; dismal. —*v.* **1.** make unfit to live in; lay waste. **2.** deprive of inhabitants. **3.** make lonely, unhappy, or forlorn. [< L, < *de-* + *solus* alone] —**des′o·late·ly,** *adv.* —**des′o·late·ness,** *n.* —**des′o·lat′er, des′o·la′tor,** *n.* —**Syn.** *adj.* **1.** ravaged. **3.** forsaken.

des·o·la·tion (des′ə-lā′shən), *n.* **1.** act of making desolate. **2.** a lonely or deserted condition. **3.** desolate place. **4.** sadness; sorrow.

De So·to (di sō′tō), Hernando, 1500?-1542, Spanish explorer in America.

de·spair (di-spār′), *n.* **1.** loss of hope; hopelessness. **2.** person or thing that causes despair. —*v.* lose hope; be without hope. [< OF < L, < *de-* + *sperare* to hope] —**de·spair′ing,** *adj.* —**de·spair′ing·ly,** *adv.* —**de·spair′ing·ness,** *n.*

des·patch (dis-pach′), *v., n.* dispatch.

des·per·a·do (des′pər·ā′dō; -ä′dō), *n., pl.* -**does,** -**dos.** a bold, reckless criminal. [< OSp. See DESPERATE.]

des·per·ate (des′pər·it), *adj.* **1.** reckless because of despair. **2.** showing recklessness caused by despair. **3.** with little or no hope of improvement; very serious. **4.** hopeless. [< L *desperatus,* pp. See DESPAIR.] —**des′per·ate·ly,** *adv.* —**des′-per·ate·ness,** *n.*

des·per·a·tion (des′pər·ā′shən), *n.* act or fact of despairing; despair.

des·pi·ca·ble (des′pi·kə·bəl; des·pik′ə·bəl), *adj.* to be despised; contemptible. —**des′pi·ca-ble·ness,** *n.* —**des′pi·ca·bly,** *adv.*

de·spise (di-spīz′), *v.,* -**spised,** -**spis·ing.** look down on; feel contempt for. [< OF < L, < *de-* down + *specere* look at] —**de·spis′er,** *n.* —**Syn.** scorn. —**Ant.** admire.

de·spite (di-spīt′), *n., v.,* -**spit·ed,** -**spit·ing,** *prep.* —*n.* **1.** malice; spite. **2.** contempt; scorn. **3.** insult; injury. **4.** in **despite of,** in spite of. —*v.* treat with contempt. —*prep.* in spite of. [< OF < L *despectus* a looking down upon < *de-* + *specere* look at]

de·spoil (di-spoil′), *v.* rob; plunder. [< OF < L, < *de-* + *spoliare* strip < *spolium* armor, booty] —**de·spoil′er,** *n.* —**de·spoil′ment, de·spo·li·a-tion** (di-spō′li·ā′shən), *n.*

de·spond (di-spond′), *v.* lose heart, courage, or hope. —*n. Archaic.* despondency. [< L, < *de-* + *spondere* lose heart] —**de·spond′ing,** *adj.* —**de·spond′ing·ly,** *adv.*

de·spond·en·cy (di-spon′dən·si), **de·spond·ence** (-dəns), *n., pl.* -**cies; -ces.** loss of courage or hope. —**de·spond′ent,** *adj.*

des·pot (des′pət; -pot), *n.* **1.** tyrant; oppressor. **2.** monarch having unlimited power; absolute ruler. [< OF < Med.Gk. *despotes* master < Gk.]

des·pot·ic (des·pot′ik), *adj.* of a despot; tyrannical. —**des·pot′i·cal·ly,** *adv.*

des·pot·ism (des′pət·iz·əm), *n.* **1.** tyranny; oppression. **2.** government by a monarch having unlimited power.

des·sert (di-zėrt′), *n.* a course served at the end of a meal, such as pie, cake, ice cream, etc. [< F, < *desservir* clear the table < *des-* (< L *dis-*) + *servir* serve < L]

de·sta·lin·i·za·tion (dē·stä′lin·ə·zā′shən), *n.* elimination or alteration by a Communist government of policies, doctrines, etc. originated by or associated with Stalin.

des·ti·na·tion (des′tə·nā′shən), *n.* **1.** place to which a person or thing is going or is being sent. **2.** a setting apart for a particular purpose.

des·tine (des′tən), *v.,* -**tined,** -**tin·ing.** **1.** set apart for a particular purpose or use; intend. **2.** cause by fate. **3.** **destined for, a.** intended for. **b.** bound for: *ships destined for England.* [< OF < L *destinare* make fast, < *de-* + *stare* stand]

des·ti·ny (des′tə·ni), *n., pl.* -**nies.** **1.** what becomes of a person or thing in the end; one's lot or fortune. **2.** what will happen in spite of all efforts to change or prevent it. **3.** fate.

des·ti·tute (des′tə·tüt; -tūt), *adj.* **1.** lacking necessary things such as food, clothing, and shelter. **2.** destitute of, having no; without [< L, < *destituere* forsake < *de-* away + *statuere* put, place] —**Syn.** **1.** needy, indigent. **2.** deprived.

des·ti·tu·tion (des′tə·tü′shən; -tū′-), *n.* **1.** destitute condition; extreme poverty. **2.** lack.

de·stroy (di-stroi′), *v.* **1.** break to pieces; make useless; ruin; spoil. **2.** put an end to; do away with. **3.** deprive of life; kill. **4.** counteract the effect of; make void. [< OF < VL < L, < *de-* un- + *struere* pile, build] —**de·stroy′a·ble,** *adj.* —**Syn.** **1.** demolish, raze. **2.** abolish, extinguish.

de·stroy·er (di-stroi′ər), *n.* **1.** person or thing that destroys. **2.** a relatively small, very fast warship used to attack submarines, for escort duty, etc.

destroyer escort, a warship which is smaller and slower than a destroyer, but larger than a corvette (def.2).

de·struct·i·ble (di-struk′tə·bəl), *adj.* capable of being destroyed. —**de·struct′i·bil′i·ty,** *n.*

de·struc·tion (di-struk′shən), *n.* **1.** act of destroying. **2.** state of being destroyed. **3.** cause or means of destroying.

de·struc·tive (di-strukt′iv), *adj.* **1.** tending to destroy. **2.** causing destruction. **3.** tearing down; not helpful. —**de·struc′tive·ly,** *adv.* —**de·struc′-tive·ness,** *n.* —**Syn.** **1.** ruinous.

des·ue·tude (des′wə·tüd; -tūd), *n.* disuse. [< F < L *desuetudo* < *de-* dis- + *suescere* accustom]

des·ul·to·ry (des′əl·tô′ri; -tō′-), *adj.* **1.** jumping from one thing to another; unconnected. **2.** without aim or method. [< L *desultorius* of a leaper, ult. < *de-* down + *salire* leap] —**des′-ul·to′ri·ly,** *adv.* —**des′ul·to′ri·ness,** *n.*

de·tach (di-tach′), *v.* **1.** loosen and remove; unfasten; separate. **2.** send away on special duty. [< F, formed with *dé-* (< L *dis-*) after *at-tacher* ATTACH] —**de·tach′a·ble,** *adj.* —**de·tach′-er,** *n.*

de·tached (di-tacht′), *adj.* **1.** separate from others; isolated. **2.** not influenced by others or by one's own interests and prejudices.

de·tach·ment (di-tach′mənt), *n.* **1.** separation. **2.** group of soldiers or ships sent on some special duty. **3.** a standing apart; aloofness. **4.** freedom from prejudice or bias; impartiality.

de·tail (*n.* di-tāl′, dē′tāl; *v.* di-tāl′), *n.* **1.** a small or unimportant part. **2.** a dealing with small things one by one. **3.** a minute account. **4.** a minor decoration or subordinate part in a building, picture, machine, etc. **5.** a small group selected for or sent on some special duty. **6.** in **detail,** part by part. —*v.* **1.** tell fully; give the particulars of. **2.** select for or send on special duty. [< F, < *détailler* cut in pieces < *de-* + *tailler* cut] —**Syn.** *n.* **1.** item, trifle. **5.** squad, detachment, party. ▶ **detail,** *n.* The formal pronunciation is di-tāl′; informal usage is divided but the pronunciation is likely to be dē′tāl.

de·tain (di-tān′), *v.* **1.** hold back; keep from going; delay. **2.** keep in custody; confine. **3.** withhold. [< OF < L, < *de-* + *tenere* hold] —**de·tain′er,** *n.* —**de·tain′ment,** *n.* —**Syn.** **1.** retard.

de·tect (di·tekt'), v. 1. find out; discover. 2. discover the existence of. 3. change (the alternating currents in a radio set) by a detector. [< L *detectus* < *de-* un- + *tegere* cover]—**de·tect'a·ble**, **de·tect'i·ble**, adj.

de·tec·tion (di·tek'shən), n. 1. a finding out; discovery. 2. a being found out or discovered. 3. change of alternating currents in a radio set.

de·tec·tive (di·tek'tiv), n. policeman or other person whose work is finding information secretly, discovering who committed a crime, etc. —adj. pertaining to detectives and their work.

de·tec·tor (di·tek'tər), n. 1. person or thing that detects. 2. a vacuum tube or crystal in a radio that helps in the change of radio waves into sound waves.

de·ten·tion (di·ten'shən), n. 1. act of detaining. 2. state of being detained; delay. 3. confinement.

de·ter (di·tér'), v., **-terred**, **-ter·ring**. discourage; keep back; hinder. [< L, < *de-* from + *terrere* frighten]—**de·ter'ment**, n.

de·ter·gent (di·tér'jənt), adj. cleansing. —n. a detergent substance. [< L, < *de-* off + *tergere* wipe]

de·te·ri·o·rate (di·tir'i·ə·rāt), v., **-rat·ed**, **-rat·ing**. make or become worse; depreciate. [< L, < *deterior* worse]—**de·te'ri·o·ra'tion**, n. —**de·te'ri·o·ra'tive**, adj.

de·ter·mi·na·ble (di·tér'mə·nə·bəl), adj. capable of being settled or decided.

de·ter·mi·nant (di·tér'mə·nənt), n. thing that determines. —adj. determining.

de·ter·mi·nate (di·tér'mə·nit), adj. 1. with exact limits; fixed; definite. 2. settled; positive. 3. determined; resolute. 4. Bot. having the primary and each secondary axis ending in a flower or bud. —**de·ter'mi·nate·ly**, adv. —**de·ter'mi·nate·ness**, n.

de·ter·mi·na·tion (di·tér'mə·nā'shən), n. 1. act of settling beforehand. 2. finding out the exact amount or kind, by weighing, measuring, or calculating. 3. result of finding out exactly; conclusion. 4. state of being determined; settlement; decision. 5. great firmness in carrying out a purpose. 6. a fixed direction or tendency.

de·ter·mi·na·tive (di·tér'mə·nā'tiv; -nə·tiv), adj. determining. —n. thing that determines. —**de·ter'mi·na'tive·ly**, adv. —**de·ter'mi·na'tive·ness**, n.

de·ter·mine (di·tér'mən), v., **-mined**, **-min·ing**. 1. make up one's mind firmly; resolve. 2. settle; decide. 3. find out exactly; fix. 4. fix the geometrical position of. 5. be the deciding factor in reaching a certain result. 6. fix or settle beforehand. 7. give an aim to; direct; impel. 8. limit; define. [< OF < L *determinare* set limits to < *de-* + *terminus* end] —**de·ter'min·er**, n. —Syn. 3. ascertain, establish. 5. influence.

de·ter·mined (di·tér'mənd), adj. firm; resolute. —**de·ter'mined·ly**, adv. —**de·ter'mined·ness**, n.

de·ter·min·ism (di·tér'mən·iz·əm), n. doctrine that human actions and all events are the necessary results of antecedent causes. —**de·ter'min·ist**, n., adj.

de·ter·rent (di·tér'ənt; -ter'-), adj. deterring; restraining. —n. something that deters. —**de·ter'rence**, n.

de·test (di·test'), v. dislike very much; hate. [< F < L *detestari* curse while calling the gods to witness < *de-* + *testis* witness] —**de·test'a·ble**, adj. —**de·test'a·bil'i·ty**, **de·test'a·ble·ness**, n. —**de·test'a·bly**, adv. —**de·test'er**, n. —Syn. abhor, loathe. —Ant. love.

de·tes·ta·tion (dē'tes·tā'shən), n. 1. very strong dislike; hatred. 2. a detested person or thing.

de·throne (dē·thrōn'), v., **-throned**, **-thron·ing**. deprive of the power to rule; remove from a throne; depose. —**de·throne'ment**, n. —**de·thron'er**, n.

det·o·nate (det'ə·nāt), v., **-nat·ed**, **-nat·ing**. explode with a loud noise. [< L, < *de-* (intensive) + *tonare* thunder] —**det'o·na'tion**, n. —**det'o·na'tor**, n.

de·tour (dē'tůr; di·tůr'), n. 1. road that is used when the main or direct road cannot be traveled. 2. a roundabout way. —v. 1. use a detour. 2. cause to use a detour. [< F, < *détourner* turn aside < *dé-* (< L *dis-*) + *tourner* turn]

de·tract (di·trakt'), v. take away. [< L *detractus* < *de-* away + *trahere* draw] —**de·trac'tion**, n. —**de·trac'tive**, adj. —**de·trac'tor**, n.

det·ri·ment (det'rə·mənt), n. 1. damage; injury; harm. 2. something that causes damage or harm. [< L *detrimentum* < *de-* away + *terere* wear]

det·ri·men·tal (det'rə·men'təl), adj. damaging; injurious; harmful. —**det'ri·men'tal·ly**, adv.

de·tri·tus (di·trī'təs), n. Geol. particles of rock or other material worn away from a mass. [< L, a rubbing away]

De·troit (di·troit'), n. city in SE Michigan.

deuce[1] (dūs; dūs), n. 1. in a game of cards or dice, two. 2. a playing card marked with a 2. 3. the side with two spots in dice. 4. Tennis. a tie score at 40 each in a game, or 5 games each in a set. [< OF *deus* two < L *duos*, accus. of *duo* two]

deuce[2] (dūs; dūs), interj. Colloq. exclamation of annoyance meaning "bad luck," "the mischief," "the devil." [prob. < LG *duus* DEUCE[1], an unlucky throw at dice]

deu·ced (dū'sid, dū'-; dūst, dūst), adj. Colloq. devilish; excessive. —adv. devilishly; excessively. —**deu'ced·ly**, adv.

Deut., Deuteronomy.

deu·te·ri·um (dū·tir'i·əm; dū-), n. Chem. an isotope of hydrogen, D, whose molecules weigh twice as much as those of ordinary hydrogen; heavy hydrogen. [< NL < Gk. *deutereion*, neut., having second place < *deuteros* second]

deu·ter·on (dū'tər·on; dū'-), n. Physics. the nucleus of deuterium, consisting of one proton and one neutron that have parallel spins. [< Gk. *deuteron*, neut. of *deuteros* second (with ref. to deuterium as H[2])]

Deu·ter·on·o·my (dū'tər·on'ə·mi; dū'-), n. the fifth book of the Old Testament. [< L < Gk., < *deuteros* second + *nomos* law]

De Va·le·ra (dā' və·lâr'ə; dev'ə-; -lir'ə), Eamon, born 1882, Irish statesman.

de·val·u·ate (dē·val'yů·āt), v., **-at·ed**, **-at·ing**. lessen the value of. —**de·val'u·a'tion**, n.

dev·as·tate (dev'əs·tāt), v., **-tat·ed**, **-tat·ing**. make desolate; destroy; ravage. [< L, < *de-* + *vastus* waste] —**dev'as·tat'ing·ly**, adv. —**dev'as·ta'tion**, n. —**dev'as·ta'tor**, n.

de·vel·op (di·vel'əp), v. 1. bring or come into being or activity; grow. 2. make or become bigger, better, fuller, more useful, etc. 3. Music. elaborate (a theme) by changes of rhythm, melody, or harmony. 4. display; show. 5. make or become known; reveal. 6. treat or be treated with chemicals to bring out an image, as a photograph. [< F *développer* unwrap] —**de·vel'op·a·ble**, adj. —Syn. 1. generate, evolve, unfold. 2. mature, expand. 5. disclose.

de·vel·op·er (di·vel'əp·ər), n. 1. person or thing that develops. 2. a chemical used to bring out the picture on a photographic film, plate, print, etc.

de·vel·op·ment (di·vel'əp·mənt), n. 1. a developing. 2. a developed stage, state, or result. —**de·vel'op·men'tal**, adj.

de·vi·ate (dē'vi·āt), v., **-at·ed**, **-at·ing**. turn aside (from a way, course, rule, truth, etc.); diverge. [< LL, < *de-* aside + *via* way] —**de'vi·a'tion**, n. —**de'vi·a'tor**, n.

de·vice (di·vīs'), n. 1. a mechanical invention used for a special purpose; machine; apparatus. 2. plan; scheme; trick. 3. a drawing or figure used in a pattern or as an ornament. 4. picture or design on a coat of arms, often accompanied by a motto. 5. motto. 6. leave to one's own devices, leave to do as one thinks best. [fusion of ME *devis* separation, talk + *devise* design, emblem, plan; both < OF < L *divisus*, pp. of *dividere* DIVIDE] —Syn. 1. contrivance. 2. ruse, wile.

dev·il (dev'əl), n., v., **-iled**, **-il·ing**; esp. Brit.

-illed, -il·ling, *interj.* —*n.* 1. a. an evil spirit; fiend; demon. b. the Devil, Satan. 2. a wicked or cruel person. 3. a very clever, energetic, or reckless person. 4. an unfortunate or wretched person. 5. an evil influence or power. 6. the errand boy in a printing office; printer's apprentice. 7. the devil to pay, much trouble ahead. —*v.* 1. *Am., Colloq.* bother; tease; torment. 2. prepare (food) with hot seasoning. —*interj.* exclamation of disgust, anger, etc. [< L < Gk. *diabolos* slanderer < *dia-* across, against + *ballein* throw]

dev·iled, *esp. Brit.* **devilled** (dev'əld), *adj.* highly seasoned: *deviled ham.*

dev·il·fish (dev'əl·fish'), *n., pl.* -fish·es or (*esp. collectively*) -fish. 1. a large, odd-shaped fish related to the shark; giant ray. 2. octopus.

Devilfish (ab. 20 ft. across)

dev·il·ish (dev'əl·ish; dev'lish), *adj.* 1. like a devil. 2. mischievous; daring. 3. *Colloq.* very great; extreme. —*adv. Colloq.* extremely. —**dev'il·ish·ly**, *adv.* —**dev'il·ish·ness**, *n.*

dev·il·ment (dev'əl·mənt), *n.* devilish behavior.

dev·il·try (dev'əl·tri), *n., pl.* -tries. *U.S.* 1. wicked behavior. 2. daring behavior; mischief. 3. great cruelty or wickedness.

de·vi·ous (dē'vi·əs), *adj.* 1. winding; twisting. 2. straying from the right course; not straightforward. [< L, < *de-* out of + *via* the way] —**de'vi·ous·ly**, *adv.* —**de'vi·ous·ness**, *n.*

de·vise (di·vīz'), *v.,* -vised, -vis·ing. —*v.* 1. think out; plan; contrive; invent. 2. *Law.* give or leave (land, buildings, etc.) by a will. —*n. Law.* a. a giving or leaving of land, buildings, etc., by a will. b. a will or part of a will doing this. c. land, buildings, etc., given or left in this way. [< OF *deviser* dispose in portions, arrange, ult. < L *dividere* DIVIDE] —**de·vis'a·ble**, *adj.* —**de·vis'er**, *esp. Law.* **de·vi'sor**, *n.*

de·vis·ee (di·vīz'ē'; dev'ə·zē'), *n. Law.* person to whom land, etc., is devised.

de·vi·tal·ize (dē·vī'təl·īz), *v.,* -ized, -iz·ing. take the life or vitality of. —**de·vi'tal·i·za'tion**, *n.*

de·void (di·void'), *adj.* lacking (*of*): *devoid of sense.* [< OF, < *des-* (< L *dis-*) + *voidier* VOID]

de·voir (də·vwär'; dev'wär), *n.* 1. act of courtesy or respect. 2. duty. [< F < L *debere* owe]

de·volve (di·volv'), *v.,* -volved, -volv·ing. 1. transfer (duty, work, etc.) to someone else. 2. be handed down to someone else; be transferred. [< L, < *de-* down + *volvere* roll] —**dev·o·lu'tion** (dev'ə·lü'shən), **de·volve'ment**, *n.*

Dev·on (dev'ən), or **Dev·on·shire** (-shir; -shər), *n.* county in SW England.

de·vote (di·vōt'), *v.,* -vot·ed, -vot·ing. 1. give up (oneself, one's money, time, or efforts) to some person, purpose, or service. 2. dedicate; consecrate. [< L *devotus* < *de-* entirely + *vovere* vow] —**de·vote'ment**, *n.* —**Syn.** 1. apply, appropriate, assign.

de·vot·ed (di·vōt'id), *adj.* 1. loyal; faithful. 2. dedicated; consecrated. —**de·vot'ed·ly**, *adv.* —**de·vot'ed·ness**, *n.*

dev·o·tee (dev'ə·tē'), *n.* person deeply devoted to something, such as a religion.

de·vo·tion (di·vō'shən), *n.* 1. deep, steady affection; loyalty; faithfulness. 2. act of devoting or state of being devoted. 3. earnestness in religion; devoutness. 4. a religious observance. 5. devotions, religious worship; prayers. —**de·vo'tion·al**, *adj.* —**de·vo'tion·al·ly**, *adv.*

de·vour (di·vour'), *v.* 1. eat (usually said of animals). 2. eat like an animal; eat hungrily. 3. consume; waste; destroy: *a devouring disease.* 4. swallow up; engulf. 5. take in with eyes or ears in a hungry, greedy way: *devour a book.* [< OF < L, < *de-* down + *vorare* gulp] —**de·vour'er**, *n.* —**de·vour'ing·ly**, *adv.*

de·vout (di·vout'), *adj.* 1. active in worship and prayer; religious. 2. devoted; earnest; sincere. [< OF < L *devotus*, pp. See DEVOTE.] —**de·vout'ly**, *adv.* —**de·vout'ness**, *n.* —**Syn.** 1. pious.

dew (dū; dōō), *n.* 1. moisture from the air that condenses and collects in small drops on cool surfaces during the night. 2. moisture in small drops, as perspiration. 3. anything fresh or refreshing like dew. —*v.* wet with dew; moisten. [OE *dēaw*] —**dew'less**, *adj.*

dew·ber·ry (dū'ber'i; dū'-), *n., pl.* -ries. 1. a blackberry vine that grows along the ground. 2. fruit of one of these vines.

dew·drop (dū'drop'; dū'-), *n.* a drop of dew.

Dew·ey (dū'i; dū'-), *n.* 1. George, 1837–1917, American admiral. 2. John, 1859–1952, American philosopher and educator. 3. Thomas Edmund, born 1902, American lawyer and political leader.

dew·lap (dū'lap'; dū'-), *n.* a loose fold of skin under the throat of cattle and some other animals. [< *dew* (orig. and meaning uncert.) + *lap* < OE *læppa* pendulous piece]

DEW line, D.E.W. line, the Distant Early Warning line, a chain of radar stations stretching across northern Canada, north of the Arctic Circle, designed to give the earliest possible warning of an attack on the United States or Canada by bombing planes over the north polar region.

dew point, temperature of the air at which dew begins to form.

dew·y (dū'i; dū'i), *adj.,* dew·i·er, dew·i·est. 1. wet with dew. 2. of dew. 3. like dew; refreshing. —**dew'i·ness**, *n.*

Dex·e·drine (deks'ə·drēn; -drin), *n. Trademark.* drug, $(C_9H_{13}N)_2 \cdot H_2SO_4$, that causes wakefulness and loss of appetite.

dex·ter (deks'tər), *adj.* of or on the right-hand side. [< L, right]

dex·ter·i·ty (deks·ter'ə·ti), *n.* 1. skill in using the hands. 2. skill in using the mind; cleverness.

dex·ter·ous (deks'tər·əs; -trəs), *adj.* 1. having or showing skill in using the hands. 2. having or showing skill in using the mind; clever. Also, dextrous. —**dex'ter·ous·ly**, *adv.* —**dex'ter·ous·ness**, *n.*

dex·tral (deks'trəl), *adj.* right; right-hand. —**dex·tral'i·ty**, *n.* —**dex'tral·ly**, *adv.*

dex·trin (deks'trin), **dex·trine** (-trin; -trēn), *n.* a gummy substance obtained from starch, used as an adhesive, for sizing paper, etc. [< F *dextrine*]

dex·trose (deks'trōs), *n.* a sugar, $C_6H_{12}O_6$, less sweet than cane sugar; a form of glucose.

dex·trous (deks'trəs), *adj.* dexterous. —**dex'trous·ly**, *adv.* —**dex'trous·ness**, *n.*

di (dē), *n.* tone of the musical scale, intermediate between do and re.

di–, *prefix.* twice; double; twofold, as in dioxide. [< Gk. *dis*]

di·a·be·tes (dī'ə·bē'tis; -tēz), *n.* disease in which the digestive system is unable to absorb normal amounts of sugar and starch. [< NL < Gk., a passer-through < *dia-* through + *bainein* go] —**di·a·bet·ic** (dī'ə·bet'ik; -bē'tik), *adj., n.*

di·a·bol·ic (dī'ə·bol'ik), **di·a·bol·i·cal** (-ə·kəl), *adj.* 1. like the Devil; very cruel or wicked. 2. having to do with the Devil or devils. [< LL < Gk. *diabolikos.* See DEVIL.] —**di·a·bol'i·cal·ly**, *adv.*

di·a·crit·ic (dī'ə·krit'ik), *adj.* diacritical. —*n.* a diacritical mark. [< Gk. *diakritikos* < *dia-* apart + *krinein* separate]

di·a·crit·i·cal (dī'ə·krit'ə·kəl), *adj.* used to distinguish. —**di·a·crit'i·cal·ly**, *adv.*

diacritical mark, mark like — ·· ^ ⁄ or ⁀ placed over or under a letter to indicate pronunciation, etc.

di·a·dem (dī'ə·dem), *n.* crown. [< L < Gk. *diadema* < *dia-* across + *deein* bind]

di·aer·e·sis (dī·er'ə·sis), *n., pl.* -ses (-sēz). dieresis.

di·ag·nose (dī'əg·nōs'; -nōz'), *v.,* -nosed, -nos·ing. make a diagnosis of.

di·ag·no·sis (dī'əg·nō'sis), *n., pl.* -ses (-sēz). 1. act or process of finding out what disease a person or animal has by examination and careful study of the symptoms. X rays and blood tests are used in diagnosis. 2. careful study of the facts about something to find out its essential features, faults, etc. 3. decision reached after a careful study of symptoms or facts. [< NL < Gk., < *dia-* apart + *gignoskein* learn to know] **—di·ag·nos·tic** (dī'əg-nos'tik), *adj.* **—di·ag·nos·ti·cian** (dī'əg-nos·tish'ən), *n.*

di·ag·o·nal (dī·ag'ə-nəl), *n.* **1.** a straight line that cuts across in a slanting direction, often from corner to corner. **2.** any slanting line, row, course, etc. **—adj. 1.** taking the direction of a diagonal; slanting; oblique. **2.** having slanting lines, ridges, etc. **3.** connecting two corners that are not next to each other. [< L, < Gk. *diagonios* from angle to angle < *dia-* across + *gonia* angle] **—di·ag'o·nal·ly,** *adv.*

Line AB is a diagonal.

di·a·gram (dī'ə-gram), *n.*, *v.*, **-gramed, -gram·ing;** *esp. Brit.* **-grammed, -gram·ming.** **—n.** an outline, a plan, a drawing, a figure, a chart, or a combination of any of these made to show clearly what a thing is or how it works. **—v.** make a diagram of. [< L < Gk. *diagramma* < *dia-* apart, out + *graphein* mark] **—di·a·gram·mat·ic** (dī'ə-grə-mat'ik), **di·a·gram·mat'i·cal,** *adj.* **—di'a·gram·mat'i·cal·ly,** *adv.*

di·al (dī'əl), *n.*, *v.*, **-aled, -al·ing;** *esp. Brit.* **-alled, -al·ling.** **—n. 1.** a marked surface on which time is shown by a moving pointer or shadows. **2.** disk with numbers, etc., on which the amount of water, pressure, etc., is shown by a pointer. **3.** plate, disk, etc., of a radio with numbers, letters, etc., on it for tuning in to a radio station. **4.** part of an automatic telephone used in making telephone calls. **—v. 1.** show on a telephone dial. **2.** call by means of a telephone dial. [appar. < Med.L (*rota*) *dialis* daily (wheel) < L *dies* day]

dial., dialectal; dialectal.

di·a·lect (dī'ə-lekt), *n.* **1.** form of speech characteristic of a fairly definite region: *the Scottish dialect.* **2.** words and pronunciations used by certain professions, classes of people, etc. **3.** one of a group of closely related languages. Some of the dialects descended from the Latin language are French, Italian, Spanish, and Portuguese. [< L < Gk. *dialektos,* ult. < *dia-* between + *legein* speak] ▶ A **dialect** is the speech (words, sounds, stress, phrasing, grammatical habits) that does not attract attention to itself among the residents of a region. Dialects exist because of the separation of groups of speakers and are not peculiar to backward regions, for the "Oxford accent" forms a minor dialect, and the people of Boston and of New York speak differently from their neighbors. Nor do dialects depend upon education or social standing. An educated, as well as an uneducated, westerner will speak somewhat differently from a southerner or New Englander of a similar degree and quality of education. Regional differences in the United States are not so conspicuous as are the differences between other kinds of usage (between formal and informal English, for example), but characteristic differences in vocabulary and, even more noticeably, in pronunciation are found.

di·a·lec·tal (dī'ə-lek'təl), *adj.* of a dialect; like that of a dialect. **—di'a·lec'tal·ly,** *adv.*

di·a·lec·tic (dī'ə-lek'tik), *n.* **1.** art or practice of logical discussion. **2.** Also, **dialectics.** the principles of logic. **—adj. 1.** pertaining to logical discussion. **2.** dialectical.

di·a·lec·ti·cian (dī'ə-lek·tish'ən), *n.* person skilled in dialectic or dialectics; logician.

di·a·logue, di·a·log (dī'ə-lôg; -log), *n.* **1.** conversation. **2.** a literary work in the form of a conversation. **3.** conversation in a play, story, etc. [< L < Gk., < *dia-* between + *logos* speech] **—di'a·logu'er,** *n.*

di·al·y·sis (dī·al'ə-sis), *n.*, *pl.* **-ses** (-sēz). separation of crystalloids from colloids in solution by diffusion through a membrane. [< Gk., < *dia-* apart + *lyein* loose] **—di·a·lyt·ic** (dī'ə-lit'ik), *adj.*

diam., diameter.

di·a·mag·net·ic (dī'ə-mag-net'ik), *adj.* re-

pelled by a magnet. **—di'a·mag·net'i·cal·ly,** *adv.* **—di·a·mag·net·ism** (dī'ə-mag'nə-tiz-əm), *n.*

di·am·e·ter (dī·am'ə-tər), *n.* **1.** a straight line passing from one side to the other through the center of a circle, sphere, etc. **2.** the length of such a line; width; thickness. [< OF < L < Gk., < *dia-* across + *metron* measure]

Line AB is a diameter.

di·a·met·ric (dī'ə-met'rik), **di·a·met·ri·cal** (-rə-kəl), *adj.* **1.** of or along a diameter. **2.** exactly opposite. **—di'a·met'ri·cal·ly,** *adv.*

dia·mond (dī'mənd; dī'ə-), *n.* **1.** a form of pure carbon in crystals, the hardest known substance, used as a precious stone. **2.** tool having a diamond tip for cutting glass. **3.** a plane figure shaped like this ◇. **4.** a playing card with one or more red designs like a diamond on it. **5.** diamonds, the complete suit. **6.** *Am.* space inside the lines that connect the bases in baseball. **7.** a very small size of type; 4½ point. **—adj.** made of diamonds. **—v.** adorn with diamonds or as with diamonds. [< OF < Med.L *diamas,* alter. of L *adamas* ADAMANT]

dia·mond·back (dī'mənd-bak'; dī'ə-), *n. Am.* **1.** any rattlesnake with diamond-shaped markings on its back. **2.** Also, **diamondback terrapin.** turtle that has diamond-shaped markings on its shell.

Di·an·a (dī·an'ə), *n.* the Roman goddess of the hunt and of the moon and protectress of women, identified with the Greek goddess Artemis.

di·a·net·ics (dī'ə-net'iks), *n.* system of mental treatment that seeks to alleviate certain apparently physical ailments that are supposedly caused primarily by a mental attitude, etc.

di·a·pa·son (dī'ə-pā'zən; -sən), *n. Music.* **1.** melody; strain. **2.** the whole range of a voice or instrument. **3.** either of two principal stops in an organ: **a.** open diapason, a stop giving full, majestic tones. **b.** stopped diapason, a stop giving powerful flutelike tones. [< L < Gk., < *dia pason* (*chordon*) across all (the notes of the scale)]

di·a·per (dī'ə-pər; dī'pər), *n.* a small piece of cloth used as part of a baby's underclothing. **—v.** put a diaper on. [< OF < Med.Gk. *diaspros* < *dia-* (intensive) + *aspros* white]

di·aph·a·nous (dī·af'ə-nəs), *adj.* transparent. [< Med.L < Gk., < *dia-* through + *phainein* show] **—di·aph'a·nous·ly,** *adv.*

di·a·phragm (dī'ə-fram), *n.* **1.** *Anat.* a partition of muscles and tendons separating the cavity of the chest from the cavity of the abdomen. **2.** a vibrating disk in a telephone. **3.** device for controlling the light entering a camera, microscope, etc. **—v. 1.** furnish with a diaphragm. **2.** act upon by a diaphragm. [< LL < Gk. *diaphragma* < *dia-* across + *phrassein* fence] **—di·a·phrag·mat·ic** (dī'ə-frag-mat'ik), *adj.*

di·ar·rhe·a, di·ar·rhoe·a (dī'ə-rē'ə), *n.* too many and too loose movements of the bowels. [< L < Gk., < *dia-* through + *rhein* flow]

di·a·ry (dī'ə-ri), *n.*, *pl.* **-ries. 1.** account written down each day, of what one has done, thought, etc. **2.** book for keeping such an account, with a blank space for each day of the year. [< L *diarium* < *dies* day] **—di·a·rist** (dī'ə-rist), *n.*

di·a·stase (dī'ə-stās), *n.* enzyme that changes starch into dextrin and maltose during digestion, germination of seeds, etc. [< F < Gk. *diastasis* separation < *dia-* apart + *sta-* stand] **—di·a·stat·ic** (dī'ə-stat'ik), *adj.*

di·as·to·le (dī·as'tə-lē), *n.* **1.** the normal, rhythmical dilation of the heart, esp. that of the ventricles. **2.** the lengthening of a syllable which is regularly short. [< LL < Gk., expansion < *dia-* apart + *stellein* send] **—di·as·tol·ic** (dī'əs-tol'ik), *adj.*

di·as·tro·phism (dī·as'trə-fiz-əm), *n. Geol.* action of the forces which have caused the deformation of the earth's crust, producing continents, mountains, etc. [< Gk. *diastrophe* distortion < *dia-* apart + *strephein* twist] **—di·a·stroph·ic** (dī'ə-strof'ik), *adj.*

di·a·ther·my (dī'ə-ther'mi), *n.* **1.** method of treating diseases by heating the tissues beneath the skin with an electric current. 2. apparatus for doing this. [< F < Gk. *dia-* through + *therme* heat] —di'a·ther'mic, *adj.*

di·a·ton·ic (dī'ə·ton'ik), *adj. Music.* of or using the tones of a standard major or minor scale. [< L < Gk., < *dia-* through + *tonos* tone]

di·a·tribe (dī'ə·trīb), *n.* a bitter and violent denunciation of some person or thing. [< L < Gk. *diatribe* pastime, study, discourse < *dia-* away + *tribein* wear]

Dí·az, Dí·az (dē'äs), *n.* Porfirio, 1830–1915, president of Mexico, 1877–1880, 1884–1911.

di·ba·sic (dī·bā'sik), *adj. Chem.* having two hydrogen atoms that can be replaced by two atoms or radicals of a base in forming salts.

dib·ble (dib'əl), *n., v.,* –bled, –bling. —*n.* a pointed tool for making holes in the ground for seeds, young plants, etc. —*v.* make a hole in (the ground) with or as with a dibble. —dib'bler, *n.*

dice (dīs), *n.pl., sing.* die, *v.,* diced, dic·ing. —*n.* 1. small cubes with a different number of spots (one to six) on each side, used in playing games and gambling. 2. game played with dice. 3. small cubes. —*v.* 1. play dice. 2. cut into small cubes. —dic'er, *n.*

di·chot·o·my (dī·kot'ə·mi), *n., pl.* –mies. 1. division into two parts. 2. branching by repeated divisions into two parts. [< L < Gk. *dichotomos* cut in half < *dicha* in two + *temnein* cut] —di·chot'o·mous, di·chot·om·ic (dī'kō·tom'ik), *adj.*

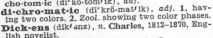

Dichotomy (def. 2)

di·chro·mat·ic (dī'krō·mat'ik), *adj.* 1. having two colors. 2. *Zool.* showing two color phases.

Dick·ens (dik'ənz), *n.* Charles, 1812–1870, English novelist.

dick·ens (dik'ənz), *n., interj.* devil.

dick·er (dik'ər), *Am.* —*v.* trade by barter or by petty bargaining; haggle. —*n.* a petty bargain. [< *dicker,* n., a lot of ten hides]

dick·ey, dick·y, or **dick·ie** (dik'i), *n., pl.* dick·eys; dick·ies; dick·ies. a shirt front that can be detached.

Dick·in·son (dik'ən·sən), *n.* Emily, 1830–1886, American poet.

di·cot·y·le·don (dī·kot'ə·lē'dən; dī'kot-), *n.* a flowering plant that has two seed leaves. —di·cot'y·le'don·ous, *adj.*

dict., 1. dictator. 2. dictionary.

dic·ta (dik'tə), *n. pl.* of dictum.

Dic·ta·phone (dik'tə·fōn), *n. Trademark.* instrument that records and reproduces words that are spoken into it. [< *dicta(te)* + –*phone*]

dic·tate (*v.* dik'tāt, dik·tāt'; *n.* dik'tāt), *v.,* –tat·ed, –tat·ing, *n.* —*v.* 1. say or read (something) aloud for another person or other persons to write down. 2. command with authority; give orders that must be obeyed. —*n.* direction or order that is to be carried out or obeyed. [< L *dictatus,* pp. of *dictare* say often < *dicere* tell, say] —Syn. *v.* 2. order, decree. —*n.* command.

dic·ta·tion (dik·tā'shən), *n.* 1. act of saying or reading (something) aloud for another person or persons to write down. 2. words said or read aloud to be written down. 3. act of commanding with authority. —dic·ta'tion·al, *adj.*

dic·ta·tor (dik'tā·tər; dik·tā'-), *n.* 1. person exercising absolute authority, esp. over a country. 2. one who dictates. —dic'ta·tor·ship', *n.*

dic·ta·to·ri·al (dik'tə·tô'ri·əl; –tō'-), *adj.* 1. of or like that of a dictator. 2. imperious; domineering; overbearing. —dic'ta·to'ri·al·ly, *adv.*

dic·tion (dik'shən), *n.* 1. manner of expressing ideas in words; style of speaking or writing. 2. manner of using the voice in speaking; the utterance or enunciation of words. ➤ Good *diction* means that the words of an article, book, speech, etc., seem to the reader or listener well chosen to convey the meanings or attitudes the writer or speaker wishes; faulty *diction,* that the words either fail to convey the meaning fully or accurately or do not satisfy the reader's or listener's expectation in some other way.

dic·tion·ar·y (dik'shən·er'i), *n., pl.* –ar·ies. book containing a selection of the words of a language or of some special subject, arranged alphabetically, with explanations of their meanings and other information about them. ➤ **dictionaries.** The most useful tool for a writer, in or out of a composition course, is a good dictionary. Nowhere else can he find so much information about words and their use and nowhere else, if he is really interested in his language, can he find so much curious, incidental, and even amusing information about words. The more he refers to his dictionary and browses in it, the more his powers of communication can grow. But dictionaries are primarily for reference. They answer questions about the meaning of words so that the student can read with more understanding. They settle doubts (or arguments) over single words. And they help a writer decide on the most accurate and effective word or phrase to use. A writer will use his dictionary most in the revision state and should get the habit of turning to it frequently while revising a paper and preparing the final copy. Obviously to get the most out of a dictionary, its owner needs to know what various matters it includes. He should look through its table of contents to see what units of material there are besides the main alphabetical list of words. He should read a page or two consecutively to see how words and phrases are handled, and he should try pronouncing some familiar words to see how the pronunciation key works. A few pains taken to learn a particular dictionary will be more than repaid by its increased usefulness.

Dic·to·graph (dik'tə·graf; –gräf), *n. Trademark.* telephone with a transmitter so sensitive that no mouthpiece is needed, used in secretly listening to or recording conversation.

dic·tum (dik'təm), *n., pl.* –tums, –ta (–tə). 1. a formal comment; authoritative opinion. 2. maxim; saying. [< L, (thing) said, pp. of *dicere* say]

did (did), *v.* pt. of do[1].

di·dac·tic (dī·dak'tik; di–), **di·dac·ti·cal** (–tə·kəl), *adj.* 1. intended to instruct. 2. inclined to instruct others; teacherlike. [< Gk. *didaktikos* < *didaskein* teach] —di·dac'ti·cal·ly, *adv.* —di·dac'ti·cism, *n.*

did·dle (did'əl), *v.,* –dled, –dling. *Colloq.* waste (time). —did'dler, *n.*

did·n't (did'ənt), did not.

Di·do (dī'dō), *n.* the legendary founder and queen of Carthage who killed herself when Aeneas left her.

di·do (dī'dō), *n., pl.* –dos, –does. *U.S. Colloq.* prank; trick.

didst (didst), *v. Archaic or Poetic.* did. "Thou didst" means "You did."

die[1] (dī), *v.,* died, dy·ing. 1. cease to live; stop living; become dead. 2. come to an end; lose force or strength; stop. 3. lose spiritual life. 4. suffer as if dying. 5. want very much; be very desirous. 6. die away or down, stop or end little by little; lose force or strength gradually. 7. die out, a. lose force or strength gradually. b. cease or end completely. [OE *diegan*]

die[2] (dī), *n., pl. dice for 1, dies for 2, v.,* died, die·ing. —*n.* 1. one of a set of dice. 2. any tool or apparatus for shaping, cutting, or stamping things. —*v.* to shape with a die. [< OF < L *datum* (thing) given (i.e., by fortune), pp. of *dare* give]

di·e·cious (dī·ē'shəs), *adj.* dioecious. —di·e'cious·ly, *adv.*

die-hard, die·hard (dī'härd'), *adj.* resisting to the very end; refusing to give in. —*n.* person who resists vigorously to the end.

di·e·lec·tric (dī'i·lek'trik), *adj.* conveying electricity otherwise than by conduction; nonconducting: *dry air is dielectric.* —*n.* a dielectric substance, such as glass, rubber, or wood. —di·e·lec'tri·cal·ly, *adv.*

Dien·bien·phu, Dien Bien Phu (dyen'-byen'fü'), *n.* a fortified town in E Indo-China, in N Viet-Nam, taken by Communist Viet Minh soldiers in May, 1954 from the French.

di·er·e·sis (dī·er'ə·sis), *n., pl.* –ses (–sēz). two dots (··) placed over the second of two consecutive vowels to indicate that the second vowel is to be pronounced in a separate syllable, as in coöperate. Also, diaeresis. [< LL < Gk. *diairesis* separation, division < *dia-* apart + *hairein* take] —di·e·ret·ic (dī′ə·ret′ik), adj. ≫ dieresis. A hyphen is often used instead of a dieresis to indicate that the vowels are to be kept separate, especially in words with *re-* (*re-enlist*). There is a tendency now not to use either dieresis or hyphen in the more commonly used words, so that *cooperation, zoology* are now common.

Die·sel engine or motor (dē′zəl; -səl), an internal-combustion engine that burns oil with heat caused by the compression of air.

die·sink·er (dī′singk′ər), n. person who makes dies for shaping or stamping. —die′-sink′ing, n.

Di·es I·rae (dī′ēz ī′rē; dē′ās ē′rī), a medieval Latin hymn describing the judgment day. [< L, day of wrath]

di·et¹ (dī′ət), n., v., -et·ed, -et·ing. —n. 1. the usual food and drink for a person or animal. 2. a special selection of food and drink eaten during sickness, or to gain or lose weight. —v. keep to a diet. [< OF < L < Gk. *diaita* way of life] —di′et·er, n.

di·et² (dī′ət), n. 1. a formal assembly. 2. the national lawmaking body in certain countries. [< Med.L *dieta* day's work, session of councilors, ult. identical with *diet¹* but infl. by L *dies* day]

di·e·tar·y (dī′ə·ter′i), adj., n., pl. -tar·ies. —adj. having to do with diet. —n. system of diet.

di·e·tet·ic (dī′ə·tet′ik), di·e·tet·i·cal (-ə·kəl), adj. having to do with diet. —di′e·tet′i·cal·ly, adv.

di·e·tet·ics (dī′ə·tet′iks), n. science that deals with the amount and kinds of food needed by the body.

di·e·ti·tian, di·e·ti·cian (dī′ə·tish′ən), n. person trained to plan meals that have the proper proportion of various kinds of food.

dif·fer (dif′ər), v. 1. be unlike; be different. 2. have or express a different opinion; disagree. 3. differ from, a. be unlike; disagree. b. vary. [< F < L *differre* set apart, differ < *dis-* apart + *ferre* carry] —Syn. 2. dissent. —Ant. 2. agree, concur.

dif·fer·ence (dif′ər·əns; dif′rəns), n., v., -enced, -enc·ing. —n. 1. condition of being different. 2. way of being different; point in which people or things are different. 3. amount by which one quantity is different from another. 4. condition of having a different opinion; disagreement. 5. dispute. —v. make different. —Syn. n. 1. variance, disparity, distinction.

dif·fer·ent (dif′ər·ənt; dif′rənt), adj. 1. not alike; not like. 2. not the same; separate; distinct. 3. not like others or most others; unusual. —dif′fer·ent·ly, adv. —Syn. 1. dissimilar, unlike. ≫ different. The correct American idiom with *different* is *from*: His second book was entirely different from his first. Informal usage is *different than*, especially when the object is a clause.

dif·fer·en·tial (dif′ər·en′shəl), adj. 1. of a difference; showing a difference; depending on a difference. 2. distinguishing; distinctive. 3. pertaining to distinguishing characteristics or specific differences. 4. Math. pertaining to or involving differentials: *differential calculus*. 5. Physics. concerning the difference of two or more motions, pressures, etc. —n. 1. a differential duty or rate; the difference involved. 2. Math. an infinitesimal difference between consecutive values of a variable quantity. 3. arrangement of gears in an automobile that allows one of the rear wheels to turn faster than the other in going round a corner or curve. —dif′fer·en′tial·ly, adv.

dif·fer·en·ti·ate (dif′ər·en′shi·āt), v., -at·ed, -at·ing. 1. make different. 2. become different. 3. perceive the difference in; make a distinction between. 4. note differences. 5. Math. obtain the differential of. —dif′fer·en′ti·a′tion, n. —dif′fer·en′ti·a′tor, n.

dif·fi·cult (dif′ə·kult; -kəlt), adj. 1. hard to understand. 2. hard to deal with, get along with, or please. —dif′fi·cult·ly, adv. —Syn. 1. arduous. 2. trying. —Ant. 1. easy, simple.

dif·fi·cul·ty (dif′ə·kul′ti; -kəl·ti), n., pl. -ties. 1. fact or condition of being difficult. 2. hard work; much effort. 3. trouble. 4. financial trouble. 5. thing that is difficult; thing in the way; obstacle. 6. disagreement; quarrel. [< L *difficultas* < *difficilis* hard < *dis-* + *facilis* easy] —Syn. 3. hardship, dilemma, predicament. 5. hindrance. 6. controversy.

dif·fi·dent (dif′ə·dənt), adj. lacking in self-confidence; shy. —dif′fi·dence, n. —dif′fi·dent·ly, adv. [< L, ult. < *dis-* + *fidere* trust]

dif·fract (di·frakt′), v. break up by diffraction. [< L *diffractus* < *dis-* up + *frangere* break]

dif·frac·tion (di·frak′shən), n. Physics. 1. a breaking up of a ray of light into a series of light and dark bands or into colored bands of the spectrum. 2. a similar breaking up of sound waves, electricity, etc.

dif·frac·tive (di·frak′tiv), adj. causing or pertaining to diffraction. —dif·frac′tive·ly, adv. —dif·frac′tive·ness, n.

dif·fuse (v. di·fūz′; adj. di·fūs′), v., -fused, -fus·ing, adj. —v. 1. spread out so as to cover a larger space or surface; scatter widely. 2. mix together by spreading into one another, as gases and liquids do. —adj. 1. not drawn together at a single point; spread out. 2. using many words where a few would do. [< L *diffusus* < *dis-* in every direction + *fundere* pour] —dif·fuse·ly (di·fūs′li), adv. —dif·fuse′ness, n. —dif·fus·er, dif·fu·sor (di·fūz′ər), n. —Syn. v. 1. disseminate, disperse. —adj. 1. widespread, scattered, dispersed. 2. wordy. —Ant. adj. 1. compact.

dif·fu·sion (di·fū′zhən), n. 1. act or fact of diffusing. 2. a being widely spread or scattered; diffused condition. 3. a mixing together of the molecules of gases, etc. by spreading into one another. 4. use of too many words; wordiness.

dif·fu·sive (di·fū′siv), adj. 1. tending to diffuse. 2. showing diffusion. 3. using too many words; wordy. —dif·fu′sive·ly, adv. —dif·fu′sive·ness, n.

dig (dig), v., dug or (Archaic) digged, dig·ging, n. —v. 1. use a shovel, spade, hands, claws, or snout in making a hole or in turning over the ground. 2. break up and turn over (ground) with a spade, etc. 3. make (a hole, cellar, etc.) by removing material. 4. make a way by digging. 5. get by digging: *dig clams*. 6. make a careful search or inquiry (for information or into some author). 7. Am., Colloq. study hard. 8. Am., Slang. understand; comprehend. 9. dig in, Colloq. a. dig trenches for protection. b. Am. work hard. 10. dig into, Colloq. work hard at. 11. dig up, a. Am., Colloq. bring to light; produce. b. excavate. —n. 1. act of digging. 2. a thrust or poke; a sarcastic remark. [ME *dygge(n)*, prob. < F *diguer* < Gmc.] —Syn. v. 1. delve, spade, grub.

di·gest (v. də·jest′, dī-; n. dī′jest), v. 1. change (food) in the stomach and intestines so that the body can absorb it. 2. undergo this process. 3. promote such change in (food). 4. understand and absorb mentally; make part of one's thoughts. 5. condense and arrange according to some system; summarize. 6. Chem. soften by heat or moisture; dissolve. —n. information condensed and arranged according to some system; summary: *a digest of law*. [< L *digestus*, pp. of *digerere* separate, dissolve < *dis-* apart + *gerere* carry] —di·gest′er, n. —Syn. v. 4. assimilate.

di·gest·i·ble (də·jes′tə·bəl; dī-), adj. capable of being digested; easily digested. —di·gest′i·bil′i·ty, n.

di·ges·tion (də·jes′chən; dī-), n. 1. the digesting of food. 2. ability to digest. 3. act of digesting.

di·ges·tive (də·jes′tiv; dī-), adj. 1. of or for digestion. 2. helping digestion. —n. something that aids digestion.

dig·ger (dig′ər), n. 1. person that digs. 2. the part of a machine that turns up the ground. 3. any tool for digging.

dig·gings (dig'ingz), *n.pl.* **1.** mine or place where digging is being done. **2.** *Esp. Brit. Colloq.* place to live.

dig·it (dij'it), *n.* **1.** finger or toe. **2.** any of the figures 0, 1, 2, 3, 4, 5, 6, 7, 8, 9. Sometimes 0 is not called a digit. [< L *digitus* finger]

dig·it·al (dij'ə·təl), *adj.* of a digit or digits. —*n.* key of an organ, piano, etc., played with the fingers. —**dig'it·al·ly,** *adv.*

digital computer, a calculating machine which uses numbers, esp. simple numbers on a binary basis, to solve problems capable of expression in mathematical terms.

dig·it·al·is (dij'ə·tal'is; -tā'lis), *n.* **1.** medicine used for stimulating the heart, obtained from the leaves and seeds of the foxglove. **2.** foxglove. [< L, < *digitus* finger; from shape of corolla]

dig·i·tate (dij'ə·tāt), **dig·i·tat·ed** (-tāt'id), *adj.* **1.** having fingers or toes. **2.** having radiating divisions like fingers. —**dig'i·tate·ly,** *adv.*

dig·ni·fied (dig'nə·fīd), *adj.* having dignity; noble; stately. —**dig'ni·fied'ly,** *adv.*

dig·ni·fy (dig'nə·fī), *v.,* —**fied, -fy·ing. 1.** give dignity to; make noble, worth-while, or worthy. **2.** give a high-sounding name to. [< OF < L, < *dignus* worthy + *facere* make]

dig·ni·tar·y (dig'nə·ter'i), *n., pl.* **-tar·ies.** person who has a position of honor.

dig·ni·ty (dig'nə·ti), *n., pl.* **-ties. 1.** proud and self-respecting character or manner; stateliness. **2.** degree of worth, honor, or importance. **3.** a high office, rank, or title. **4.** person of high office, rank, or title. **5.** such persons as a group. **6.** worth; nobleness. [< OF < L, < *dignus* worthy]

di·graph (dī'graf; -gräf), *n.* two letters used together to spell a single sound, as *ea* in *each* or *head.* —**di·graph'ic,** *adj.*

di·gress (də·gres'; dī-), *v.* turn aside; get off the main subject in talking or writing. [< L *digressus* < *dis-* aside + *gradi* to step]

di·gres·sion (də·gresh'ən; dī-), *n.* a turning aside; a getting off the main subject in talking or writing. —**di·gres'sion·al,** *adj.*

di·gres·sive (də·gres'iv; dī-), *adj.* tending to digress; digressing. —**di·gres'sive·ly,** *adv.* —**di·gres'sive·ness,** *n.*

di·he·dral (dī·hē'drəl), *adj.* **1.** having two plane surfaces. **2.** formed by two plane surfaces. **3.** making a dihedral angle. **4.** of an airplane, having important nonhorizontal surfaces. —*n.* the figure formed by two intersecting plane surfaces. [< Gk. *di-* two + *hedra* seat] —**di·he'dral·ly,** *adv.*

A dihedral angle is included between the planes ABCD and ABMN.

dike (dīk), *n., v.,* **diked, dik·ing.** —*n.* **1.** a bank of earth or a dam built as a defense against flooding by a river or the sea. **2.** ditch or channel for water. **3.** bank of earth thrown up in digging. **4.** a low wall of earth or stone; causeway. **5.** *Geol.* a fissure in a stratum filled with deposited matter. —*v.* **1.** provide with dikes. **2.** drain with a ditch or channel for water. Also, **dyke.** [< Scand. *dīk;* akin to DITCH] —**dik'er,** *n.*

di·lan·tin (dī·lan'tin), or **dilantin so·dium,** *n.* a white, powdery drug, $C_{15}H_{11}N_2O_2Na$, used in controlling epilepsy.

di·lap·i·dat·ed (də·lap'ə·dāt'id), *adj.* falling to pieces; partly ruined or decayed through neglect. [< L *dilapidatus,* pp. of *dilapidare* lay low (with stones) < *dis-* (intensive) + *lapidare* to stone < *lapis* stone]

di·lap·i·da·tion (də·lap'ə·dā'shən), *n.* a falling to pieces; decayed condition.

dil·a·ta·tion (dil'ə·tā'shən; dī'lə-), *n.* dilation.

di·late (dī·lāt'; də-), *v.,* **-lat·ed, -lat·ing. 1.** make or become larger or wider. **2.** speak or write in a very complete or detailed manner. **3.** set forth at length. [< L, < *dis-* apart + *latus* wide] —**di·lat'a·ble,** *adj.* —**di·la'tor,** *n.*

di·la·tion (dī·lā'shən; də-), *n.* **1.** act of dilating; enlargement; widening. **2.** dilated condition. **3.** a dilated part.

dil·a·to·ry (dil'ə·tô'ri; -tō'-), *adj.* **1.** tending to delay; not prompt. **2.** causing delay. —**dil'a·to'ri·ly,** *adv.* —**dil'a·to'ri·ness,** *n.*

di·lem·ma (də·lem'ə; dī-), *n.* **1.** situation requiring a choice between two evils. **2.** any perplexing situation; a difficult choice. **3.** argument forcing an opponent to choose one of two alternatives equally unfavorable to him. [< LL < Gk., < *di-* two + *lemma* premise]

dil·et·tan·te (dil'ə·tan'tē; -tänt'), *n., pl.* **-tes, -ti** (-tē), *adj.* —*n.* **1.** lover of the fine arts. **2.** person who follows some art or science as an amusement or in a trifling way. **3.** trifler. —*adj.* having to do with dilettantes. [< Ital., < *dilet.tare* DELIGHT] —**dil'et·tant'ish,** *adj.* —**dil'et·tant'ism,** *n.*

dil·i·gence[1] (dil'ə·jəns), *n.* a working hard; careful effort; being diligent; industry. [< F < L *diligentia.* See DILIGENT.]

dil·i·gence[2] (dil'ə·jəns), *n.* a public stage-coach formerly used in some parts of Europe. [special use of *diligence*[1]]

dil·i·gent (dil'ə·jənt), *adj.* **1.** hard-working; industrious. **2.** careful and steady. [< L *diligens,* ppr. of *diligere* value highly, love < *dis-* apart + *legere* choose] —**dil'i·gent·ly,** *adv.*

dill (dil), *n.* **1.** spicy seeds or leaves used to flavor pickles. **2.** plant that they grow on. [OE *dile*]

dill pickle, *Am.* a cucumber pickle flavored with dill.

dil·ly·dal·ly (dil'i·dal'i), *v.,* **-lied, -ly·ing.** waste time; loiter; trifle.

di·lute (də·lüt'; dī-), *v.,* **-lut·ed, -lut·ing,** *adj.* —*v.* **1.** make weaker or thinner by adding water or some other liquid. **2.** weaken; lessen. **3.** become diluted. —*adj.* weakened or thinned by the addition of water or other liquid. [< L, < *dis-* apart + *luere* wash] —**di·lute'ness,** *n.*

di·lu·tion (də·lü'shən; dī-), *n.* **1.** act of diluting. **2.** fact or state of being diluted. **3.** something diluted.

di·lu·vi·al (də·lü'vi·əl; dī-), **di·lu·vi·an** (-ən), *adj.* of, having to do with, or caused by a flood. [< L, < *diluvium* DELUGE]

dim (dim), *adj.,* **dim·mer, dim·mest,** *v.,* **dimmed, dim·ming.** —*adj.* **1.** not bright; not clear; not distinct. **2.** not clearly seen, heard, or understood. **3.** not seeing, hearing, or understanding clearly. —*v.* make or become dim. [OE *dimm*] —**dim'ly,** *adv.* —**dim'ness,** *n.*

dim., dimin., 1. diminuendo. **2.** diminutive.

dime (dīm), *n. Am.* a silver coin of the United States and of Canada, worth 10 cents. [< OF < L *decima (pars)* tenth (part) < *decem* ten]

dime novel, *Am.* a sensational story that has no literary merit.

di·men·sion (də·men'shən), *n.* **1.** measurement of length, breadth, or thickness. **2.** size; extent. [< F < L *dimensio* < *dis-* out + *metiri* measure] —**di·men'sion·al,** *adj.* —**di·men'sion·less,** *adj.*

dime store, *Am.* store handling a large variety of low-priced commodities.

di·min·ish (də·min'ish), *v.* **1.** make or become smaller in size, amount, or importance; lessen; reduce. **2.** lessen in esteem; degrade. **3.** cause to taper. **4.** *Music.* lessen (an interval) by a half step. [blend of *diminue* (< L, < *dis-* (intensive) + *minuere* lessen) and *minish* (< OF < VL *minutiare,* ult. < L *minutus* small)] —**di·min'ish·a·ble,** *adj.*

di·min·u·en·do (də·min'yü·en'dō), *n., pl.* **-dos,** *adj., adv. Music.* —*n.* **1.** a gradual lessening of loudness. **2.** passage to be played or sung with a diminuendo. —*adj., adv.* with a diminuendo. [< Ital., ppr. of *diminuire* diminish]

dim·i·nu·tion (dim'ə·nü'shən; -nū'-), *n.* a diminishing; a lessening; decrease.

di·min·u·tive (də·min'yə·tiv), *adj.* **1.** small; tiny. **2.** *Gram.* expressing smallness or affection. —*n.* **1.** a small person or thing. **2.** *Gram.* word or part of a word expressing smallness. The suffixes *-let* and *-kin* are diminutives. —**di·min'u·tive·ly,** *adv.* —**di·min'u·tive·ness,** *n.*

dim·i·ty (dim'ə·ti), *n., pl.* **-ties.** a thin cotton cloth woven with heavy threads at intervals in striped or crossbarred arrangement, used for dresses, curtains, etc. [< Ital. < Gk. *dimitos* of double thread < *di-* double + *mitos* warp thread]

dim·mer (dim′ər), *n.* **1.** person or thing that dims. **2.** device that dims an electric light or automobile headlight.

dim·out (dim′out′), *n.* a lessening or concealment of light at night.

dim·ple (dim′pəl), *n., v.,* **-pled, -pling.** *—n.* **1.** a small hollow, usually in the cheek or chin. **2.** any small, hollow place. *—v.* **1.** make or show dimples in. **2.** form dimples. [ME *dympull*]

din (din), *n., v.,* **dinned, din·ning.** *—n.* a loud, confused noise that lasts. *—v.* **1.** make a din. **2.** strike with din. **3.** say over and over. [OE *dynn*]

dine (dīn), *v.,* **dined, din·ing. 1.** eat dinner. **2.** give a dinner to or for. **3. dine out,** eat dinner away from home. [< F *dîner* < VL *disjejunare* to breakfast < *dis-* + *jejunium* fast]

din·er (dīn′ər), *n.* **1.** person who is eating dinner. **2.** *Am.* a railroad car in which meals are served. **3.** *Am.* restaurant shaped like such a car.

di·nette (dī·net′), *n. Am.* a small dining room.

ding (ding), *v.* **1.** make a sound like a bell; ring continuously. **2.** *Colloq.* say over and over. *—n.* sound made by a bell. [imit.]

ding-dong (ding′dông′; -dong′), *n.* sound made by a bell or anything like a bell; continuous ringing. [imit.]

din·ghy, din·gey, or **din·gy** (ding′gi), *n., pl.* **-ghies; -geys; -gies. 1.** a small rowboat. **2.** a small boat used as a tender by a large boat. [< Hind. *dingi*]

din·gy (din′ji), *adj.,* **-gi·er, -gi·est.** dirty-looking; not bright and fresh; dull. **—din′gi·ly,** *adv.* **—din′gi·ness,** *n.*

dining car, *Am.* a railroad car in which meals are served.

dining room, room in which meals are served.

dink·ey (dingk′i), *n., pl.* **dink·eys.** *Am.* a small locomotive, used for pulling freight cars, hauling logs, etc.

dink·y (dingk′i), *adj.,* **dink·i·er, dink·i·est.** *Slang.* small; insignificant.

din·ner (din′ər), *n.* **1.** the main meal of the day. **2.** a formal meal in honor of some person or occasion. [< F *dîner* dine; inf. used as n.]

di·no·saur (dī′nə·sôr), *n.* any of a group of extinct reptiles. [< NL < Gk. *deinos* terrible + *sauros* lizard]

dint (dint), *n.* **1.** force. **2.** dent. *—v.* dent. [OE *dynt*] **—dint′less,** *adj.*

di·oc·e·san (dī·os′ə·sən; dī′ə·sē′sən), *adj.* of or having to do with a diocese. *—n.* bishop of a diocese.

di·o·cese (dī′ə·sis; -sēs), *n.* district over which a bishop has authority. [< OF < LL < L < Gk. *dioikesis* province, diocese]

di·oe·cious (dī·ē′shəs), *adj. Biol.* having male and female flowers in separate plants. Also, **diecious.** [< NL *dioecia* < Gk. *di-* double + *oikos* house] **—di·oe′cious·ly,** *adv.*

Di·og·e·nes (dī·oj′ə·nēz), *n.* 412?-323 B.C., Greek Cynic philosopher.

Di·o·ny·si·us (dī′ə·nish′i·əs; -nis′i-), *n.* 430?-367 B.C., ruler of the ancient Greek city of Syracuse.

Di·o·ny·sus, Di·o·ny·sos (dī′ə·nī′səs), *n.* Greek god of wine; Bacchus. **—Di·o·ny·sian** (dī′ə·nish′ən; -nis′i·ən), *adj.*

di·o·ra·ma (dī′ə·ram′ə; -rä′mə), *n.* picture that is usually looked at through a small opening. It is lighted in such a way as to be very realistic. [< F < Gk. *dia-* through + *horama* sight]

di·ox·ide (dī·ok′sīd; -sid), **di·ox·id** (-sid), *n. Chem.* oxide containing two atoms of oxygen and one of a metal or other element.

dip (dip), *v.,* **dipped** or **dipt, dip·ping,** *n.* *—v.* **1.** put under water or any liquid and lift quickly out again. **2.** go under water and come quickly out again. **3.** dye in a liquid. **4.** make wet; immerse. **5.** make (a candle) by putting a wick into hot tallow or wax. **6.** take up in the hollow

of the hand or with a pail, pan, or other container. **7.** put (one's hand, a spoon, etc.) into to take out something. **8.** lower and raise again quickly: *the flag is dipped as a kind of salute.* **9.** make a curtsy. **10.** sink or drop down: *a bird dips in its flight.* **11.** sink or drop down but rise again soon. **12.** slope downward. **13.** dip into, read or look at for a short time; glance at. *—n.* **1.** a dipping of any kind, esp. a plunge into and out of a tub of water, the sea, etc. **2.** mixture in which to dip something. **3.** candle made by dipping. **4.** that which is taken out or up by dipping. **5.** a sudden drop. **6.** a sudden drop followed by a rise. **7.** amount of slope down; angle made with a horizontal plane. **8.** *Slang.* pickpocket. [OE *dyppan*]

diph·the·ri·a (dif·thir′i·ə; dip-), *n.* a dangerous, infectious disease of the throat, usually accompanied by a high fever and formation of membranes that hinder breathing. [< F < Gk. *diphthera* hide]

diph·the·rit·ic (dif′thə·rit′ik; dip′-), **diph·the·ri·al** (-thir′i·əl), *adj.* **1.** of diphtheria; like diphtheria. **2.** suffering from diphtheria.

diph·thong (dif′thông; -thong; dip′-), *n.* a vowel sound made up of two identifiable vowel sounds in immediate sequence and pronounced in one syllable, as *oi* in point. [< F < LL < Gk., < *di-* double + *phthongos* sound] **—diph·thong′al,** *adj.* ➤ Sometimes a diphthong is represented by only one letter, as *i* in ice. The commonest English diphthongs are: ī (ä + ĭ), oi (ô + ĭ), ou (ä + ŭ), and ū (ĭ[y] + ŭ).

di·plo·ma (di·plō′mə), *n., pl.* **-mas, -ma·ta** (-mə·tə). **1.** certificate given by a school, college, or university to its graduating students. **2.** any certificate that bestows certain rights, privileges, honors, etc. [< L < Gk., paper folded double, ult. < *diploos* double]

di·plo·ma·cy (di·plō′mə·si), *n., pl.* **-cies. 1.** management of relations between nations. **2.** skill in managing such relations. **3.** skill in dealing with others; tact. [< F, < *diplomate* diplomat]

dip·lo·mat (dip′lə·mat), *esp. Brit.* **di·plo·ma·tist** (di·plō′mə·tist), *n.* **1.** representative of a nation who is located in a foreign country to look after the interests of his own nation in the foreign country. **2.** a tactful person.

dip·lo·mat·ic (dip′lə·mat′ik), *adj.* **1.** of or having to do with diplomacy. **2.** skillful in dealing with others; tactful. **—dip′lo·mat′i·cal·ly,** *adv.*

dip·per (dip′ər), *n.* **1.** person or thing that dips. **2.** *Am.* a long-handled cup or larger vessel for dipping water or other liquids. **3. Dipper,** *Am.* either of two groups of stars in the northern sky somewhat resembling the shape of a dipper; Big Dipper or Little Dipper.

dip·so·ma·ni·a (dip′sə·mā′ni·ə), *n.* an abnormal, uncontrollable craving for alcoholic liquor. [< NL < Gk. *dipsa* thirst + *mania* mania]

dip·so·ma·ni·ac (dip′sə·mā′ni·ak), *n.* person who has dipsomania.

dipt (dipt), *v.* pt. and pp. of dip.

dip·ter·ous (dip′tər·əs), *adj.* **1.** *Bot.* having two winglike parts. **2.** belonging to the order including mosquitoes, gnats, and houseflies, characterized by one pair of membranous wings. [< L < Gk., < *di-* two + *pteron* wing]

dire (dīr), *adj.,* **dir·er, dir·est.** causing great fear or suffering; dreadful. [< L *dirus*] **—dire′ly,** *adv.* **—dire′ness,** *n.*

di·rect (də·rekt′; dī-), *v.* **1.** manage; control; guide. **2.** give orders; order; command. **3.** tell or show the way; give information about where to go, what to do, etc. **4.** point (to); aim (at). **5.** put the address on (a letter, package, etc.). **6.** address (words, etc.) to a person. **7.** turn (a thing) straight to. *—adj.* **1.** proceeding in a straight line; straight. **2.** in an unbroken line of descent. **3.** immediate. **4.** without anyone or anything in between; not through others: *a direct tax.* **5.** straightforward; frank; plain; truthful. **6.** exact; absolute: *the direct opposite.* *—adv.* directly. [< L *directus,* pp. of *dirigere* set straight < *dis-* apart + *regere* guide] **—di·rect′-**

ness, *n.* ➤ **direct address.** The name or descriptive term by which a person or persons are addressed in speaking, reading, or writing: *My friends, I wish you would forget this night. That's all right, Mrs. Williams, you may come in.* As these examples show, the person or persons addressed are separated from the rest of the sentence by a comma, or if it is in the midst of the sentence, by two commas.

direct current, *Elect.* a steady current that flows in one direction.

di·rec·tion (də·rek′shən; dī–), *n.* **1.** guidance; management; control: *the direction of a play or movie.* **2.** order; command. **3.** a knowing or telling what to do, how to do, where to go, etc.; instruction. **4.** address on a letter or package. **5.** course taken by a moving body, such as a ball or a bullet. **6.** any way in which one may face or point. **7.** line of action; tendency.

di·rec·tion·al (də·rek′shən·əl; dī–), *adj.* **1.** of or having to do with direction in space. **2.** fitted for determining the direction from which signals come, or for sending signals in one direction only.

di·rect·ly (də·rekt′li; dī–), *adv.* **1.** in a direct line or manner; straight. **2.** *Esp. Brit.* immediately; at once.

direct object, a grammatical term denoting the person or thing upon which the verb directly acts.

di·rec·tor (də·rek′tər; dī–), *n.* **1.** person who directs, esp. one who directs the production of a play or motion picture. **2.** one of the persons chosen to direct the affairs of a company or institution. —**di·rec·to·ri·al** (di·rek′tô′ri·əl; –tô′–; dī′rek–), *adj.* —**di·rec′tor·ship,** *n.*

di·rec·tor·ate (də·rek′tər·it; dī–), *n.* **1.** position of a director. **2.** group of directors.

di·rec·to·ry (də·rek′tə·ri; –tri; dī–), *n., pl.* –ries, *adj.* —*n.* **1.** book of names and addresses. **2.** book of rules or instructions. **3.** group of directors; directorate. —*adj.* directing; advisory.

direct primary, election in which the voters of a political party choose the candidates of their party for office.

direct tax, tax demanded of the very persons who must pay it, as a poll tax, income tax, etc.

dire·ful (dīr′fəl), *adj.* dire; dreadful; terrible. —**dire′ful·ly,** *adv.* —**dire′ful·ness,** *n.*

dirge (dėrj), *n.* a funeral song or tune. [contraction of L *dirige* DIRECT (imperative of *dirigere*), first word in office for the dead]

dir·i·gi·ble (dir′ə·jə·bəl; də·rij′ə–), *n.* balloon that can be steered. —*adj.* capable of being directed. [< L *dirigere* to DIRECT] —**dir′i·gi·bil′i·ty,** *n.*

dirk (dėrk), *n.* dagger. —*v.* stab with a dirk.

dirn·dl (dėrn′dəl), *n.* **1.** an Alpine peasant girl's costume consisting of a blouse, a tight bodice, and a full skirt. **2.** dress imitating it. [< South G dial., girl, dim. of *dirne* maid]

dirt (dėrt), *n.* **1.** mud, dust, earth, or anything like them. **2.** loose earth; soil. **3.** *Mining.* earth, gravel, or other refuse. **4.** unclean action, thought, or speech. **5.** uncleanness; meanness. [ME *drit,* ? short for OE *dríting* excrement]

dirt-cheap (dėrt′chēp′), *adj.* very cheap.

dirt farmer, *Am., Colloq.* person who has practical experience in doing his own farming.

dirt·y (dėr′ti), *adj.,* dirt·i·er, dirt·i·est, *v.,* dirt·ied, dirt·y·ing. —*adj.* **1.** soiled by dirt; unclean. **2.** not clear or pure in color; clouded. **3.** low; mean; vile. **4.** unclean in action, thought, or speech. **5.** stormy; windy. —*v.* make dirty; soil. —**dirt′i·ly,** *adv.* —**dirt′i·ness,** *n.*

Dis (dis), *n. Roman Myth.* **1.** god of the lower world, identified with the Greek god Pluto. **2.** the lower world; Hades.

dis-, *prefix.* **1.** opposite of, as in *discontent.* **2.** reverse of, as in *disentangle.* **3.** apart; away, as in *dispel.* [< L; also, *di–, dif–*]

dis·a·bil·i·ty (dis′ə·bil′ə·ti), *n., pl.* –ties. **1.** a disabled condition. **2.** something that disables. **3.** something that disqualifies.

dis·a·ble (dis·ā′bəl), *v.,* –bled, –bling. **1.** deprive of ability or power; make useless; cripple. **2.** disqualify legally. —**dis·a′ble·ment,** *n.*

dis·a·buse (dis′ə·būz′), *v.,* –bused, –bus·ing. free from deception or error.

dis·ad·van·tage (dis′əd·van′tij; –vän′–), *n., v.,* –taged, –tag·ing. —*n.* **1.** lack of advantage; unfavorable condition: *a deaf person is at a disadvantage in school.* **2.** loss; injury. —*v.* subject to a disadvantage.

dis·ad·van·ta·geous (dis·ad′vən·tā′jəs; dis′ad–), *adj.* causing disadvantage; unfavorable. —**dis·ad′van·ta′geous·ly,** *adv.* —**dis·ad′van·ta′geous·ness,** *n.*

dis·af·fect (dis′ə·fekt′), *v.* make unfriendly, disloyal, or discontented. —**dis·af·fec′tion,** *n.*

dis·af·fect·ed (dis′ə·fek′tid), *adj.* unfriendly; disloyal; discontented.

dis·a·gree (dis′ə·grē′), *v.,* –greed, –gree·ing. **1.** fail to agree; differ. **2.** quarrel; dispute. **3.** have a bad effect; be harmful.

dis·a·gree·a·ble (dis′ə·grē′ə·bəl), *adj.* **1.** not to one's liking; unpleasant. **2.** bad-tempered; cross. —**dis·a·gree′a·ble·ness,** *n.* —**dis·a·gree′a·bly,** *adv.*

dis·a·gree·ment (dis′ə·grē′mənt), *n.* **1.** failure to agree; difference of opinion. **2.** quarrel; dispute. **3.** difference; unlikeness.

dis·al·low (dis′ə·lou′), *v.* refuse to allow; deny the truth or value of; reject. —**dis·al·low′ance,** *n.*

dis·ap·pear (dis′ə·pir′), *v.* **1.** pass from sight. **2.** pass from existence; be lost. —**dis′ap·pear′ance,** *n.*

dis·ap·point (dis′ə·point′), *v.* **1.** fail to satisfy or please; leave (one) wanting or expecting something. **2.** fail to keep a promise to. **3.** keep from happening; oppose and defeat.

dis·ap·point·ment (dis′ə·point′mənt), *n.* **1.** state of being or feeling disappointed. **2.** person or thing that causes disappointment. **3.** act or fact of disappointing.

dis·ap·pro·ba·tion (dis′ap·rə·bā′shən), *n.* disapproval.

dis·ap·prov·al (dis′ə·prüv′əl), *n.* **1.** opinion or feeling against; expression of an opinion against; dislike. **2.** refusal to consent; rejection.

dis·ap·prove (dis′ə·prüv′), *v.,* –proved, –proving. **1.** have or express an opinion against. **2.** show dislike (*of*). **3.** refuse consent to; reject. —**dis′ap·prov′ing·ly,** *adv.*

dis·arm (dis·ärm′), *v.* **1.** take weapons away from. **2.** stop having an army and navy; reduce or limit the size of an army, navy, etc. **3.** remove suspicion from; make friendly; calm the anger of. **4.** make harmless.

dis·ar·ma·ment (dis·är′mə·mənt), *n.* **1.** act of disarming. **2.** reduction or limitation of armies, navies, and their equipment.

dis·ar·range (dis′ə·rānj′), *v.,* –ranged, –ranging. disturb the arrangement of; put out of order. —**dis′ar·range′ment,** *n.*

dis·ar·ray (dis′ə·rā′), *n.* **1.** disorder; confusion. **2.** disorder of clothing. —*v.* **1.** put into disorder or confusion. **2.** undress; strip.

dis·as·sem·ble (dis′ə·sem′bəl), *v.,* –bled, –bling. take apart. —**dis′as·sem′bly,** *n.*

dis·as·ter (di·zas′tər; –zäs′–), *n.* event that causes much suffering or loss; great misfortune. [< F < Ital. < L *dis–* without + *astrum* star < Gk. *astron*]

dis·as·trous (di·zas′trəs; –zäs′–), *adj.* bringing disaster; causing great danger, suffering, loss, etc. —**dis·as′trous·ly,** *adv.*

dis·a·vow (dis′ə·vou′), *v.* deny that one knows about, approves of, or is responsible for; disclaim. —**dis·a·vow′al,** *n.* —**dis·a·vow′er,** *n.*

dis·band (dis·band′), *v.* **1.** disperse; scatter. **2.** dismiss from service. —**dis·band′ment,** *n.*

dis·bar (dis·bär′), *v.,* –barred, –bar·ring. *Law.* deprive (a lawyer) of the right to practice law. —**dis·bar′ment,** *n.*

dis·be·lief (dis′bi·lēf′), *n.* lack of belief; refusal to believe.

dis·be·lieve (dis′bi·lēv′), *v.,* –lieved, –liev·ing. have no belief in. —**dis′be·liev′er,** *n.*

dis·bur·den (dis·bėr′dən), *v.* **1.** relieve of a burden. **2.** get rid of (a burden). —**dis·bur′den·ment,** *n.*

dis·burse (dis·bėrs′), *v.,* –bursed, –burs·ing. pay out; expend. [< OF, < *des–* (< L *dis–*) +

bourse purse < LL *bursa* < Gk. *byrsa* leather, wineskin] —**dis·burs′a·ble**, *adj.* —**dis·burse′-ment**, *n.* —**dis·burs′er**, *n.*

disc (disk), *n.* disk.

dis·card (*v.* dis·kärd′; *n.* dis′kärd), *v.* **1.** give up as useless or worn out; throw aside. **2.** get rid of (useless or unwanted playing cards) by throwing them aside or playing them. **3.** throw out an unwanted card. —*n.* **1.** act of throwing aside as useless. **2.** thing thrown aside as useless or not wanted. **3.** unwanted cards thrown aside; card played as useless. [see DIS–, CARD]

dis·cern (di·zėrn′; –sėrn′), *v.* **1.** perceive; see clearly. **2.** recognize as distinct or different; distinguish. [< F < L, < *dis–* off + *cernere* separate] —**dis·cern′er**, *n.* —**dis·cern′i·ble**, *adj.* —**dis·cern′i·bly**, *adv.*

dis·cern·ing (di·zėr′ning; –sėr′–), *adj.* shrewd; acute; discriminating. —**dis·cern′ing·ly**, *adv.*

dis·cern·ment (di·zėrn′mənt; –sėrn′–), *n.* **1.** keenness in perceiving and understanding; good judgment; shrewdness. **2.** act of discerning.

dis·charge (*v.* dis·chärj′; *n.* also dis′chärj), *v.*, –**charged**, –**charg·ing.** —*v.* **1.** unload (a ship); unload (cargo) from a ship; unload. **2.** fire; shoot: *discharge a gun.* **3.** release; let go; dismiss; get rid of: *discharge a servant.* **4.** come or pour forth. **5.** rid of an electric charge; withdraw electricity from. **6.** pay (a debt, etc.). **7.** perform (a duty). **8.** *Law.* cancel or set aside (a court order). —*n.* **1.** an unloading. **2.** a firing off of a gun, a blast, etc. **3.** a release; a letting go; a dismissing. **4.** writing that shows a person's release or dismissal; certificate of release: *a soldier's discharge.* **5.** a giving off; a letting out. **6.** thing given off or let out. **7.** rate of flow. **8.** transference of electricity between two charged bodies when placed in contact or near each other. **9.** payment. **10.** performance. [see DIS–, CHARGE] —**dis·charge′a·ble**, *adj.* —**dis·charg′er**, *n.*

dis·ci·ple (di·sī′pəl), *n.*, *v.*, –**pled**, –**pling.** —*n.* **1.** believer in the thought and teaching of a leader; follower. **2.** one of the followers of Jesus. —*v.* cause to become a follower. [< L *discipulus* pupil < unrecorded *discipere* grasp, apprehend] —**dis·ci′ple·ship**, *n.*

dis·ci·pli·nar·i·an (dis′ə·plə·nãr′i·ən), *n.* person who enforces discipline or who believes in strict discipline. —*adj.* disciplinary.

dis·ci·pli·nar·y (dis′ə·plə·ner′i), *adj.* **1.** having to do with discipline. **2.** for discipline.

dis·ci·pline (dis′ə·plin), *n.*, *v.*, –**plined**, –**plin·ing.** —*n.* **1.** training; esp. training of the mind or character. **2.** the training effect of experience, adversity, etc. **3.** trained condition of order and obedience. **4.** order among school pupils, soldiers, or members of any group. **5.** a particular system of rules for conduct. **6.** methods or rules for regulating the conduct of members of a church. **7.** punishment; chastisement. **8.** branch of instruction or education. —*v.* **1.** train; bring to a condition of order and obedience; bring under control. **2.** punish. [< L *disciplina.* See DISCIPLE.] —**dis′ci·plin·er**, *n.*

dis·claim (dis·klām′), *v.* **1.** refuse to recognize as one's own; deny connection with. **2.** give up all claim to.

dis·claim·er (dis·klām′ər), *n.* **1.** a disclaiming. **2.** person who disclaims.

dis·close (dis·klōz′), *v.*, –**closed**, –**clos·ing.** **1.** open to view; uncover. **2.** make known; reveal. —**dis·clos′er**, *n.*

dis·clo·sure (dis·klō′zhər), *n.* **1.** act of disclosing. **2.** thing disclosed.

dis·coid (dis′koid), *adj.* flat and circular; disklike.

dis·col·or, *esp. Brit.* **dis·col·our** (dis·kul′ər), *v.* **1.** change or spoil the color of; stain. **2.** become changed in color. —**dis′col·or·a′tion,** dis·col′or·ment; *esp. Brit.* dis′col·our·a′tion, dis·col′our·ment, *n.*

dis·com·fit (dis·kum′fit), *v.* **1.** overthrow completely; defeat; rout. **2.** defeat the plans or hopes of; frustrate. **3.** embarrass greatly; confuse; disconcert. [< OF, ult. < L *dis–* + *conficere* accomplish] —**Syn.** **1.** vanquish. **3.** baffle, abash.

dis·com·fi·ture (dis·kum′fi·chər), *n.* **1.** a complete overthrow; defeat; rout. **2.** defeat of plans or hopes; frustration. **3.** confusion.

dis·com·fort (dis·kum′fərt), *v.* **1.** disturb the comfort of. **2.** distress; sadden. **3.** make uncomfortable or uneasy. —*n.* **1.** thing that causes discomfort. **2.** lack of comfort; uneasiness.

dis·com·mode (dis′kə·mōd′), *v.*, –**mod·ed**, –**mod·ing.** disturb; trouble; inconvenience.

dis·com·pose (dis′kəm·pōz′), *v.*, –**posed**, –**pos·ing.** disturb the self-possession of; make uneasy; bring into disorder. —**dis′com·pos′ed·ly**, *adv.* —**dis′com·pos′ing·ly**, *adv.*

dis·com·po·sure (dis′kəm·pō′zhər), *n.* state of being disturbed; uneasiness; embarrassment.

dis·con·cert (dis′kən·sėrt′), *v.* **1.** disturb the self-possession of; confuse. **2.** upset; disorder. —**dis′con·cert′ing·ly**, *adv.* —**dis′con·cer′tion**, *n.* —**Syn. 1.** embarrass.

dis·con·cert·ed (dis′kən·sėrt′id), *adj.* disturbed; confused. —**dis′con·cert′ed·ly**, *adv.*

dis·con·nect (dis′kə·nekt′), *v.* undo or break the connection of; unfasten. —**dis′con·nec′tion,** *esp. Brit.* **dis′con·nex′ion,** *n.* —**Syn.** separate.

dis·con·nect·ed (dis′kə·nek′tid), *adj.* **1.** not connected; separate. **2.** incoherent; broken. —**dis′con·nect′ed·ly**, *adv.* —**dis′con·nect′ed·ness**, *n.*

dis·con·so·late (dis·kon′sə·lit), *adj.* **1.** without hope; forlorn. **2.** unhappy; cheerless. [< Med.L, < L *dis–* + *consolatus*, pp. of *consolari* CONSOLE¹] —**dis·con′so·late·ly**, *adv.* —**dis·con·so·la·tion** (dis′kon·sə·lā′shən), dis·con′so·late·ness, *n.* —**Syn. 2.** dejected, sad.

dis·con·tent (dis′kən·tent′), *adj.* not content; dissatisfied. —*n.* Also, **dis′con·tent′ment.** dislike of what one has and a desire for something different; feeling not satisfied; uneasiness; restlessness. —*v.* dissatisfy; displease.

dis·con·tent·ed (dis′kən·ten′tid), *adj.* not contented; not satisfied. —**dis′con·tent′ed·ly**, *adv.* —**dis′con·tent′ed·ness**, *n.* —**Syn.** dissatisfied, displeased.

dis·con·tin·ue (dis′kən·tin′ū), *v.*, –**tin·ued**, –**tin·u·ing. 1.** cause to cease; put an end or stop to. **2.** cease from; cease to take, use, etc. **3.** *Law.* terminate (a suit) by request of the plaintiff or by his failing to continue it. —**dis′con·tin′u·ance,** *esp.* **dis′con·tin′u·a′tion,** *n.* —**dis′con·tin′u·er**, *n.* —**Syn. 2.** stop, quit.

dis·con·tin·u·ous (dis′kən·tin′ū·əs), *adj.* not continuous; broken; interrupted. —**dis′con·ti·nu·i·ty** (dis′kon·tə·nü′ə·ti; –nū′–), dis′con·tin′u·ous·ness, *n.* —**dis′con·tin′u·ous·ly**, *adv.*

dis·cord (*n.* dis′kôrd; *v.* dis·kôrd′), *n.* **1.** difference of opinion; disagreement. **2.** *Music.* a lack of harmony in notes sounded at the same time. **3.** harsh, clashing sounds. —*v.* be out of harmony; disagree. [< OF < *discors* discordant < *dis–* apart + *cor* heart] —**Syn.** *n.* **1.** dissension.

dis·cord·ant (dis·kôr′dənt), *adj.* **1.** not in harmony: *a discordant note in music.* **2.** not in agreement; not fitting together. **3.** harsh; clashing. —**dis·cord′ance,** dis·cord′an·cy, *n.*

dis·count (*v.* dis′kount, dis·kount′; *n.* dis′kount), *v.* **1.** deduct (a certain percentage) of the amount or cost. **2.** allow for exaggeration, prejudice, or inaccuracy in; believe only part of. **3.** leave out of account; disregard. **4.** make less effective by anticipation. **5.** buy, sell, or lend money on (a note, bill of exchange, etc.), deducting a certain percentage to allow for unpaid interest. **6.** lend money, deducting the interest in advance. —*n.* **1.** deduction from the amount or cost. **2.** percentage charged for doing this. **3.** interest deducted in advance. [< OF, < *des–* (< L *dis–*) + *conter* COUNT¹] —**dis′count·a·ble,** *adj.* —**dis′count·er**, *n.*

dis·coun·te·nance (dis·koun′tə·nəns), *v.*, –**nanced**, –**nanc·ing. 1.** refuse to approve; discourage. **2.** abash.

discount house, store or distributor that regularly sells merchandise at prices lower than the manufacturers' list prices.

dis·cour·age (dis·kėr′ij), *v.*, –**aged**, –**ag·ing. 1.** take away the courage of; lessen the hope or confidence of. 2. try to prevent by disapproving; frown upon. 3. prevent; hinder. [< OF, < *des-* (< L *dis-*) + *corage* COURAGE] —**dis·cour′age·ment**, *n.* —**dis·cour′ag·er**, *n.* —**dis·cour′ag·ing·ly**, *adv.* —Syn. 1. dishearten, depress, daunt.

dis·course (*n.* dis′kôrs, -kōrs, dis·kôrs′, -kōrs′; *v.* dis·kôrs′, -kōrs′), *n.*, *v.*, -**coursed**, -**cours·ing.** —*n.* 1. a formal speech or writing: *a lecture is a discourse.* 2. conversation; talk. —*v.* 1. speak or write formally. 2. converse; talk. [< F < Med.L, < L, < *dis-* in different directions + *currere* run] —**dis·cours′er**, *n.*

dis·cour·te·ous (dis·kér′ti·əs), *adj.* not courteous; rude; impolite. —**dis·cour′te·ous·ly**, *adv.* —**dis·cour′te·ous·ness**, *n.* —Syn. uncivil, disrespectful.

dis·cour·te·sy (dis·kér′tə·si), *n.*, *pl.* -**sies.** 1. lack of courtesy; rudeness; impoliteness. 2. a rude or impolite act.

dis·cov·er (dis·kuv′ər), *v.* 1. see or learn of for the first time; find out. 2. *Archaic.* make known; reveal. [< OF, < *des-* (< L *dis-*) + *covrir* COVER] —**dis·cov′er·a·ble**, *adj.* —**dis·cov′er·er**, *n.*

dis·cov·er·y (dis·kuv′ər·i; -kuv′ri), *n.*, *pl.* -**er·ies.** 1. act of discovering. 2. thing discovered.

dis·cred·it (dis·kred′it), *v.* 1. cast doubt on; destroy belief, faith, or trust in. 2. refuse to believe; decline to trust or have faith in. —*n.* 1. loss of belief, faith, or trust; doubt. 2. loss of good name or standing; disgrace. 3. thing that causes loss of good name or standing; disgrace. —Syn. *v.* 2. dishonor.

dis·cred·it·a·ble (dis·kred′it·ə·bəl), *adj.* bringing discredit. —**dis·cred′it·a·bly**, *adv.* —Syn. disgraceful, dishonorable.

dis·creet (dis·krēt′), *adj.* careful and sensible in speech and action; wisely cautious. [< OF < Med.L < L *discretus*, pp., separated. See DISCERN.] —**dis·creet′ly**, *adv.* —**dis·creet′ness**, *n.* —Syn. prudent, wary.

dis·crep·an·cy (dis·krep′ən·si), *n.*, *pl.* -**cies.** 1. lack of consistency; difference; disagreement. 2. an example of inconsistency.

dis·crep·ant (dis·krep′ənt), *adj.* disagreeing; different; inconsistent. [< L, < *dis-* differently + *crepare* sound] —**dis·crep′ant·ly**, *adv.*

dis·crete (dis·krēt′), *adj.* 1. separate; distinct. 2. consisting of distinct parts. [< L *discretus*, separated, pp. See DISCERN.] —**dis·crete′ly**, *adv.* —**dis·crete′ness**, *n.*

dis·cre·tion (dis·kresh′ən), *n.* 1. freedom to judge or choose. 2. good judgment; carefulness in speech or action; wise caution. —Syn. 1. choice, liberty.

dis·cre·tion·ar·y (dis·kresh′ən·er′i), *adj.* left to one's own judgment.

dis·crim·i·nate (*v.* dis·krim′ə·nāt; *adj.* dis·krim′ə·nit), *v.*, -**nat·ed**, -**nat·ing**, *adj.* —*v.* 1. make or see a difference. 2. make a distinction. 3. make or see a difference between; distinguish. 4. constitute a distinction in or between; differentiate. —*adj.* having discrimination; making nice distinctions. [< L *discriminatus* distinguished < *discernen* separation < *discernere* DISCERN] —**dis·crim′i·nate·ly**, *adv.* —**dis·crim′i·nat′ing**, *adj.* —**dis·crim′i·nat′ing·ly**, *adv.* —**dis·crim′i·na′tor**, *n.*

dis·crim·i·na·tion (dis·krim′ə·nā′shən), *n.* 1. act of making or recognizing differences and distinctions. 2. ability to make fine distinctions. 3. the making of a difference in favor of or against. —Syn. 2. discernment, insight, acumen.

dis·crim·i·na·tive (dis·krim′ə·nā′tiv), **dis·crim·i·na·to·ry** (-ə·nə·tô′ri; -tō′-), *adj.* 1. discriminating. 2. showing discrimination. —**dis·crim′i·na′tive·ly**, *adv.*

dis·cur·sive (dis·kér′siv), *adj.* wandering or shifting from one subject to another; rambling. —**dis·cur′sive·ly**, *adv.* —**dis·cur′sive·ness**, *n.*

dis·cus (dis′kəs), *n.* a heavy, circular plate of stone or metal, used in athletic games as a test of skill and strength in throwing. [< L < Gk. *diskos*]

dis·cuss (dis·kus′), *v.* consider from various points of view; talk over. [< L *discussus* < *dis-* apart + *quatere* shake] —Syn. argue, debate.

dis·cus·sion (dis·kush′ən), *n.* a going over the reasons for and against; discussing things.

dis·dain (dis·dān′), *v.* look down on; consider beneath oneself; scorn. —*n.* act of disdaining; feeling of scorn. [< OF, < *des-* (< L *dis-*) + *deignier* DEIGN] —Syn. *v.* despise, spurn.

dis·dain·ful (dis·dān′fəl), *adj.* feeling or showing disdain. —**dis·dain′ful·ly**, *adv.* —**dis·dain′ful·ness**, *n.* —Syn. contemptuous, scornful.

dis·ease (di·zēz′), *n.*, *v.*, -**eased**, -**eas·ing.** —*n.* 1. sickness; illness. 2. any particular illness. 3. unhealthy condition of a plant or a product: *the diseases of grains.* 4. disordered or bad condition of mind, morals, public affairs, etc. —*v.* 1. affect with disease. 2. disorder. [< OF, < *des-* (< L *dis-*) + *aise* EASE] —**dis·eased′**, *adj.* —Syn. *n.* 1. malady, ailment.

dis·em·bark (dis′em·bärk′), *v.* go or put ashore from a ship; land from a ship. —**dis·em·bar·ka·tion** (dis′em·bär·kā′shən), **dis′em·bark′·ment**, *n.*

dis·em·bar·rass (dis′em·bar′əs), *v.* 1. disengage. 2. free from embarrassment or uneasiness.

dis·em·bod·y (dis′em·bod′i), *v.*, -**bod·ied**, -**bod·y·ing.** separate (a soul, spirit, etc.) from the body. —**dis′em·bod′i·ment**, *n.*

dis·em·bow·el (dis′em·bou′əl), *v.*, -**eled**, -**el·ing**; *esp. Brit.* -**elled**, -**el·ling.** take or rip out the bowels of. —**dis′em·bow′el·ment**, *n.*

dis·en·chant (dis′en·chant′; -chänt′), *v.* free from a magic spell or illusion. —**dis′en·chant′er**, *n.* —**dis′en·chant′ment**, *n.*

dis·en·cum·ber (dis′en·kum′bər), *v.* free from a burden, annoyance, or trouble.

dis·en·fran·chise (dis′en·fran′chīz), *v.*, -**chised**, -**chis·ing.** disfranchise. —**dis·en·fran·chise·ment** (dis′en·fran′chiz·mənt), *n.*

dis·en·gage (dis′en·gāj′), *v.*, -**gaged**, -**gag·ing.** 1. free from an engagement, pledge, obligation, etc. 2. detach; loosen. —**dis′en·gage′ment**, *n.* —Syn. 1. release, liberate.

dis·en·tan·gle (dis′en·tang′gəl), *v.*, -**tan·gled**, -**tan·gling.** free from tangles or complications; untangle. —**dis′en·tan′gle·ment**, *n.*

dis·es·tab·lish (dis′es·tab′lish), *v.* deprive of the character of being established, esp. to withdraw state recognition or support from (a church). —**dis′es·tab′lish·ment**, *n.*

dis·es·teem (dis′es·tēm′), *v.*, *n.* scorn; dislike.

dis·fa·vor (dis·fā′vər), *n.* 1. dislike; disapproval. 2. state of being regarded with dislike or disapproval. —*v.* regard with dislike; disapprove. —Syn. *n.* 2. disgrace.

dis·fig·ure (dis·fig′yər), *v.*, -**ured**, -**ur·ing.** spoil the appearance of; hurt the beauty of. —**dis·fig′ure·ment**, *n.* —**dis·fig′ur·er**, *n.* —Syn. deface.

dis·fran·chise (dis·fran′chīz), *v.*, -**chised**, -**chis·ing.** 1. take the rights of citizenship away from. 2. take a right or privilege from. —**dis·fran·chise·ment** (dis·fran′chiz·mənt), *n.* —**dis·fran·chis·er** (dis·fran′chīz·ər), *n.*

dis·gorge (dis·gôrj′), *v.*, -**gorged**, -**gorg·ing.** 1. throw up what has been swallowed. 2. pour forth; discharge. 3. give up unwillingly.

dis·grace (dis·grās′), *n.*, *v.*, -**graced**, -**grac·ing.** —*n.* 1. loss of honor or respect; shame. 2. cause of disgrace. 3. loss of favor or trust. —*v.* 1. cause disgrace to. 2. dismiss in disgrace. [< F < Ital. *disgrazia.* See DIS-, GRACE.] —**dis·grac′er**, *n.* —Syn. *n.* 1. dishonor, disrepute, discredit.

dis·grace·ful (dis·grās′fəl), *adj.* causing loss of honor or respect; shameful. —**dis·grace′ful·ly**, *adv.* —**dis·grace′ful·ness**, *n.*

dis·grun·tle (dis·grun′təl), *v.*, -**tled**, -**tling.** fill with bad humor or discontent. [< *dis-* + obs. *gruntle* to grunt, grumble] —**dis·grun′tle·ment**, *n.* —Syn. disgust, displease.

dis·guise (dis·gīz′), *v.*, -**guised**, -**guis·ing.** —*v.* 1. make a change in clothes and appearance to hide who one really is or to look like someone else. 2. hide what (a thing) really is; make (a thing) seem like something else. —*n.* 1. use of a changed or unusual dress and appearance in order not to be known. 2. clothes, actions, etc., used to hide who one really is or to make a person look like someone else. 3. a false or misleading appearance; deception; conceal-

ment. [< OF, < *des-* (< L *dis-*) + *guise* GUISE]
—dis·guis'er, *n.*

dis·gust (dis·gust'), *n.* strong dislike; sickening dislike. —*v.* arouse disgust in. [< early modern F, < *des-* (< L *dis-*) + *goust* taste < L *gustus*] —dis·gust'ing·ly, *adv.* —Syn. *n.* distaste, loathing, repugnance.

dis·gust·ed (dis·gus'tid), *adj.* filled with disgust. —dis·gust'ed·ly, *adv.* —dis·gust'ed·ness, *n.*

dish (dish), *n.* 1. anything to serve food in, such as a plate, platter, bowl, cup, or saucer. 2. amount of food served in a dish. 3. the food served. 4. thing shaped like a dish. —*v.* 1. serve (food) by putting it in a dish. 2. make concave. [< L *discus* dish, DISCUS]

dis·ha·bille (dis'ə·bēl'), *n.* 1. informal, careless dress. 2. garment or costume worn in dishabille; negligee. 3. condition of being only partly dressed. Also, deshabille. [< F *déshabillé*, pp. < *dés-* (< L *dis-*) + *habiller* dress]

dis·har·mo·ny (dis·här'mə·ni), *n., pl.* -nies. lack of harmony; discord.

dish·cloth (dish'klôth'; -kloth'), *n.* cloth to wash dishes with.

dis·heart·en (dis·här'tən), *v.* discourage; depress. —dis·heart'en·ing·ly, *adv.* —dis·heart'en·ment, *n.*

di·shev·eled, *esp. Brit.* di·shev·elled (dishev'əld), *adj.* 1. rumpled; mussed; disordered; untidy. 2. hanging loosely or in disorder: *disheveled hair.*

dis·hon·est (dis·on'ist), *adj.* not honest: *lying, stealing, and cheating are dishonest acts.* —dis·hon'est·ly, *adv.* —Syn. corrupt, fraudulent.

dis·hon·es·ty (dis·on'əs·ti), *n., pl.* -ties. 1. lack of honesty. 2. a dishonest act.

dis·hon·or, *esp. Brit.* dis·hon·our (dison'ər), *n.* 1. loss of honor or reputation; shame; disgrace. 2. cause of dishonor. 3. refusal or failure to pay a check, bill, etc. —*v.* 1. cause or bring dishonor to. 2. refuse or fail to pay (a check, bill, etc.).

dis·hon·or·a·ble, *esp. Brit.* dis·hon·our·a·ble (dis·on'ər·ə·bəl), *adj.* 1. causing loss of honor; shameful; disgraceful. 2. without honor. —dis·hon'or·a·ble·ness, *esp. Brit.* dis·hon'our·a·ble·ness, *n.* —dis·hon'or·a·bly, *esp. Brit.* dis·hon'our·a·bly, *adv.*

dish·pan (dish'pan'), *n. Am.* pan in which to wash dishes.

dis·il·lu·sion (dis'i·lü'zhən), *v.* free from illusion. —*n.* a freeing or being freed from illusion. —dis'il·lu'sion·ment, *n.* —dis·il·lu·sive (dis'i·lü'siv), *adj.*

dis·in·cli·na·tion (dis'in·klə·nā'shən), *n.* unwillingness.

dis·in·cline (dis'in·klīn'), *v.,* -clined, -clining. make or be unwilling.

dis·in·fect (dis'in·fekt'), *v.* destroy the disease germs in. —dis'in·fec'tion, *n.* —dis'in·fec'tor, *n.*

dis·in·fect·ant (dis'in·fek'tənt), *n.* means for destroying disease germs. Alcohol, iodine, and carbolic acid are disinfectants. —*adj.* destroying disease germs.

dis·in·gen·u·ous (dis'in·jen'yü·əs), *adj.* not frank; insincere. —dis'in·gen'u·ous·ly, *adv.* —dis'in·gen'u·ous·ness, *n.*

dis·in·her·it (dis'in·her'it), *v.* prevent from inheriting; deprive of an inheritance. —dis'in·her'it·ance, *n.*

dis·in·te·grate (dis·in'tə·grāt), *v.,* -grat·ed, -grat·ing. 1. separate into small parts or bits. 2. *Physics.* change in nuclear structure through bombardment by charged particles. —dis·in·te·gra·ble (dis·in'tə·grə·bəl), *adj.* —dis·in·te·gra'tion, *n.* —dis·in'te·gra'tor, *n.*

dis·in·ter (dis'in·tėr'), *v.,* -terred, -ter·ring. 1. take out of a grave or tomb; dig up. 2. discover and reveal. —dis·in·ter'ment, *n.*

dis·in·ter·est (dis·in'tər·ist; -trist), *n.* lack of interest; indifference.

dis·in·ter·est·ed (dis·in'tər·is·tid; -tris·tid; -tər·es'tid), *adj.* 1. free from selfish motives; impartial; fair. 2. *U.S. Colloq.* not interested.

—dis·in'ter·est·ed·ly, *adv.* —dis·in'ter·est·ed·ness, *n.* ≯ See interested for usage note.

dis·join (dis·join'), *v.* separate.

dis·joint (dis·joint'), *v.* 1. take apart at the joints. 2. break up; disconnect; put out of order. 3. put out of joint; dislocate. 4. come apart; be put out of joint. —dis·joint'ed, *adj.* —dis·joint'ed·ly, *adv.* —dis·joint'ed·ness, *n.*

dis·junc·tion (dis·jungk'shən), *n.* a disjoining or being disjoined; separation.

dis·junc·tive (dis·jungk'tiv), *adj.* 1. causing separation; separating. 2. showing a choice or contrast between two ideas, words, etc. *But, yet, either . . . or,* etc., are disjunctive conjunctions. *Otherwise, else,* etc., are disjunctive adverbs. 3. involving alternatives. A disjunctive proposition asserts that one or the other of two things is true. —*n.* 1. statement involving alternatives. 2. a disjunctive conjunction. —dis·junc'tive·ly, *adv.*

disk (disk), *n.* 1. a round, flat, thin object. 2. a round, flat surface, or an apparently round, flat surface: *the sun's disk.* 3. *Bot., Zool.* a roundish, flat part in a plant or animal. 4. anything resembling a disk. 5. a phonograph record. 6. discus. Also, disc. [< L *discus* DISCUS] —disk'like', *adj.*

Disk

disk harrow, *Am.* harrow with a row of sharp, revolving disks used in preparing ground for planting or sowing.

disk jockey, *Slang.* announcer for a radio program consisting chiefly of recorded music.

dis·like (dis·līk'), *n., v.,* -liked, -lik·ing. —*n.* a feeling of not liking; a feeling against. —*v.* not like; object to; have a feeling against. —dis·lik'a·ble, *adj.* —Syn. *n.* distaste, aversion.

dis·lo·cate (dis'lō·kāt), *v.,* -cat·ed, -cat·ing. 1. put out of joint. 2. put out of order; disturb; upset. —dis'lo·ca'tion, *n.*

dis·lodge (dis·loj'), *v.,* -lodged, -lodg·ing. drive or force out of a place, position, etc. —dis·lodg'ment, *n.*

dis·loy·al (dis·loi'əl), *adj.* not loyal; unfaithful. —dis·loy'al·ly, *adv.* —Syn. false, traitorous.

dis·loy·al·ty (dis·loi'əl·ti), *n., pl.* -ties. 1. lack of loyalty. 2. a disloyal act.

dis·mal (diz'məl), *adj.* 1. dark; gloomy. 2. dreary; miserable. —dis'mal·ly, *adv.* —dis'mal·ness, *n.* —Syn. 1. somber. 2. cheerless, sad.

dis·man·tle (dis·man'təl), *v.,* -tled, -tling. 1. strip of covering, equipment, furniture, guns, rigging, etc. 2. pull down; take apart. [< OF *desmanteler.* See DIS-, MANTLE.] —dis·man'tle·ment, *n.*

dis·may (dis·mā'), *n.* loss of courage because of fear of what is about to happen. —*v.* trouble greatly; make afraid. [ME *desmayen* < AF < VL, deprive of strength < L *ex-* + unrecorded Frankish *magan* have strength] —Syn. *n.* consternation, fear, apprehension.

dis·mem·ber (dis·mem'bər), *v.* 1. separate or divide into parts. 2. cut or tear the limbs from. —dis·mem'ber·ment, *n.*

dis·miss (dis·mis'), *v.* 1. send away; allow to go. 2. remove from office or service. 3. put out of mind; stop thinking about. 4. refuse to consider (a complaint, plea, etc.) in a law court. [< L *dismissus,* var. of *dimissus* < *dis-* away + *mittere* send] —dis·miss'al, *n.* —Syn. 2. discharge, oust.

dis·mount (dis·mount'), *v.* 1. get off a horse, bicycle, etc. 2. throw or bring down from a horse; unhorse. 3. take (a thing) from its setting or support. 4. take apart; take to pieces. —dis·mount'a·ble, *adj.*

dis·o·be·di·ent (dis'ō·bē'di·ənt), *adj.* refusing or failing to obey. —dis'o·be'di·ence, *n.* —dis'o·be'di·ent·ly, *adv.*

dis·o·bey (dis'ō·bā'), *v.* refuse or fail to obey. —dis'o·bey'er, *n.* —Syn. defy.

dis·o·blige (dis'ō·blīj'), *v.,* -bliged, -blig·ing. 1. refuse or fail to oblige. 2. give offense to. —dis'o·blig'ing, *adj.* —dis'o·blig'ing·ly, *adv.*

dis·or·der (dis·ôr'dər), *n.* 1. lack of order; confusion. 2. public disturbance; riot. 3. sickness; disease. —v. **1.** destroy the order of; throw into confusion. **2.** cause sickness in. —Syn. n. **1.** jumble. **2.** commotion, tumult.

dis·or·der·ly (dis·ôr'dər·li), adj. **1.** not orderly; in confusion. **2.** causing disorder; unruly. **3.** Law. contrary to good morals or decency. —adv. in a disorderly manner. —dis·or'der·li·ness, n.

dis·or·gan·ize (dis·ôr'gən·īz), v., -ized, -iz·ing. throw into confusion and disorder. —dis·or'gan·i·za'tion, n. —dis·or'gan·iz'er, n.

dis·own (dis·ōn'), v. refuse to recognize as one's own.

dis·par·age (dis·par'ij), v., -aged, -ag·ing. **1.** speak slightingly of; belittle. **2.** lower the reputation of; discredit. [< OF desparagier match unequally < des- (< L dis-) + parage rank, lineage < L par equal. See PEER¹.] —dis·par'age·ment, n. —dis·par'ag·er, n. —dis·par'ag·ing·ly, adv. —Syn. **1.** depreciate.

dis·pa·rate (dis'pə·rit), adj. essentially different; unlike. [< L, < dis- apart + parare get] —dis'pa·rate·ly, adv. —dis'pa·rate·ness, n.

dis·par·i·ty (dis·par'ə·ti), n., pl. -ties. inequality; difference.

dis·pas·sion (dis·pash'ən), n. freedom from emotion or prejudice; impartiality.

dis·pas·sion·ate (dis·pash'ən·it), adj. free from emotion or prejudice; calm; impartial. —dis·pas'sion·ate·ly, adv. —dis·pas'sion·ate·ness, n.

dis·patch (dis·pach'), v. **1.** send off to some place or for some purpose. **2.** get (something) done promptly or speedily. **3.** give the death blow to; kill. —n. **1.** a sending off (of a letter, a messenger, etc.). **2.** a written message, such as special news or government business. **3.** promptness; speed. **4.** a putting to death; a killing. Also, despatch. [< Ital. dispacciare hasten or Sp. despachar] —dis·patch'er, n.

dis·pel (dis·pel'), v., -pelled, -pel·ling. drive away and scatter; disperse. [< L, < dis- away + pellere drive] —dis·pel'ler, n.

dis·pen·sa·ble (dis·pen'sə·bəl), adj. **1.** that may be done without; unimportant. **2.** that may be forgiven, condoned, or declared not binding. **3.** capable of being dispensed or administered. —dis·pen'sa·bil'i·ty, dis·pen'sa·ble·ness, n.

dis·pen·sa·ry (dis·pen'sə·ri), n., pl. -ries. place where medicines and medical advice are given free or for a very small charge.

dis·pen·sa·tion (dis'pən·sā'shən; -pen-), n. **1.** act of distributing: the dispensation of charity to the poor. **2.** thing given out or distributed: the dispensations of Providence. **3.** rule; management: England under the dispensation of Elizabeth. **4.** management or ordering of the affairs of the world by Providence or Nature. **5.** a religious system: the Christian dispensation, the Jewish dispensation. **6.** official permission to disregard a rule. —dis'pen·sa'tion·al, adj. —dis'pen·sa'tor, n.

dis·pen·sa·to·ry (dis·pen'sə·tô'ri; -tō'-), n., pl. -ries. **1.** book that tells how to prepare and use medicines. **2.** dispensary.

dis·pense (dis·pens'), v., -pensed, -pens·ing. **1.** give out; distribute. **2.** carry out; put in force; apply. **3.** prepare and give out: a druggist dispenses medicines. **4.** release; excuse. **5.** dispense with, a. do away with. b. get along without. [< OF < L dispensare weigh out < dis- out + pendere weigh] —dis·pens'er, n. —Syn. **1.** allot, apportion.

dis·perse (dis·pèrs'), v., -persed, -pers·ing. **1.** spread in different directions; scatter. **2.** distribute; diffuse; disseminate. **3.** dispel; dissipate. **4.** be dispelled; disappear. **5.** divide (white light) into its colored rays. [< F < L dispersus < dis- in every direction + spargere scatter] —dis·pers'ed·ly, adv. —dis·pers'er, n. —dis·pers'i·ble, adj. —dis·pers'ive, adj.

dis·per·sion (dis·pèr'zhən; -shən), n. **1.** Also, dis·per'sal. a. a dispersing. b. a being dispersed. **2.** the separation of light into its different colors, as by a prism.

dis·pir·it (dis·pir'it), v. depress; discourage. —dis·pir'it·ed, adj. —dis·pir'it·ed·ly, adv.

dis·place (dis·plās'), v., -placed, -plac·ing. **1.** put something else in the place of. **2.** remove from a position of authority. **3.** move from its usual place or position.

displaced person, a European or other person forced out of his native country by war or threat of captivity.

dis·place·ment (dis·plās'mənt), n. **1.** act of displacing. **2.** a being displaced. **3.** weight of the volume of water displaced by a ship or other floating object.

dis·play (dis·plā'), v. **1.** expose to view; show. **2.** show in a special way, so as to attract attention. **3.** let appear; reveal. **4.** spread out; unfold. —n. **1.** a displaying; exhibition. **2.** Printing. the choice and arrangement of type so as to make certain words, etc., prominent. **3.** printed matter so chosen and arranged. **4.** a showing off; ostentation. [< OF < L displicare scatter. See DEPLOY.] —dis·play'er, n. —Syn. n. **1.** show, exhibit.

dis·please (dis·plēz'), v., -pleased, -pleas·ing. not please; offend; annoy. —Syn. anger.

dis·pleas·ure (dis·plezh'ər), n. **1.** the feeling of being displeased; slight anger; annoyance. **2.** Archaic. discomfort. **3.** Archaic. offense.

dis·port (dis·pôrt'; -pōrt'), v. amuse (oneself); sport; play. —n. Archaic. pastime; amusement. [< OF, < des- (< L dis-) away from + porter carry < L portare]

dis·pos·a·ble (dis·pōz'ə·bəl), adj. **1.** capable of being disposed of. **2.** at one's disposal.

dis·pos·al (dis·pōz'əl), n. **1.** act of getting rid (of something). **2.** act of giving away. **3.** sale. **4.** an arranging of matters; a settling of affairs. **5.** act of putting in a certain order or position; arrangement. **6.** at or in one's disposal, ready for one's use or service at any time.

dis·pose (dis·pōz'), v., -posed, -pos·ing, n. —v. **1.** put in a certain order or position; arrange. **2.** arrange (matters). **3.** make ready or willing. **4.** make liable or subject. **5.** arrange or decide matters; make terms. **6.** dispose of, a. get rid of. b. give away. c. sell. —n. Archaic. disposition. [< OF, < dis- (< L) variously + poser place (see POSE)] —dis·pos'er, n.

dis·po·si·tion (dis'pə·zish'ən), n. **1.** one's natural way of acting toward others or of thinking about things; nature: a cheerful disposition. **2.** tendency; inclination: a disposition to argue. **3.** act of putting in order or position; arrangement: the disposition of soldiers in battle. **4.** management; settlement. **5.** disposal.

dis·pos·sess (dis'pə·zes'), v. force to give up the possession of a house, land, etc.; oust. —dis'pos·ses'sion, n. —dis'pos·ses'sor, n. —Syn. evict, remove.

dis·praise (dis·prāz'), v., -praised, -prais·ing, n. —v. express disapproval of; blame. —n. expression of disapproval; blame.

dis·proof (dis·prüf'), n. **1.** a disproving; refutation. **2.** fact, reason, etc., that disproves something.

dis·pro·por·tion (dis'prə·pôr'shən; -pōr'-), n. lack of proper proportion; lack of symmetry. —v. make disproportionate.

dis·pro·por·tion·al (dis'prə·pôr'shən·əl; -pōr'-), adj. disproportionate. —dis'pro·por'tion·al·ly, adv.

dis·pro·por·tion·ate (dis'prə·pôr'shən·it; -pōr'-), adj. out of proportion; lacking in proper proportion. —dis'pro·por'tion·ate·ly, adv. —dis'pro·por'tion·ate·ness, n.

dis·prove (dis·prüv'), v., -proved, -prov·ing. prove false or incorrect; refute. —dis·prov'a·ble, adj.

dis·put·a·ble (dis·pūt'ə·bəl; dis'pyū·tə·bəl), adj. liable to be disputed; uncertain. —dis·put'a·bil'i·ty, n. —dis·put'a·bly, adv.

dis·pu·tant (dis'pyū·tənt; dis·pū'-), adj. engaged in argument or controversy. —n. person who takes part in a dispute or debate.

dis·pu·ta·tion (dis'pyū·tā'shən), n. **1.** debate; controversy. **2.** dispute.

dis·pu·ta·tious (dis'pyū·tā'shəs), **dis·put·a·tive** (dis·pūt'ə·tiv), adj. fond of disputing; inclined to argue. —dis'pu·ta'tious·ly, adv. —dis'pu·ta'tious·ness, n. —Syn. quarrelsome.

dis·pute (dis·pūt′), v., –put·ed, –put·ing, n. —v. 1. discuss; argue; debate. 2. quarrel. 3. disagree with (a statement); declare not true; call in question. 4. fight against; oppose; resist. 5. fight for; fight over. 6. contend for; try to win. —n. 1. argument; debate. 2. a quarrel. [< L, ex- amine, discuss, argue < dis- item by item + putare calculate] —dis·put′er, n.

dis·qual·i·fi·ca·tion (dis′kwol·ə·fə·kā′shən), n. 1. a disqualifying. 2. a being disqualified. 3. something that disqualifies.

dis·qual·i·fy (dis·kwol′ə·fī), v., –fied, –fy·ing. 1. make unable to do something. 2. declare unfit or unable to do something.

dis·qui·et (dis·kwī′ət), v. make uneasy or anx- ious; disturb. —n. uneasiness; anxiety.

dis·qui·e·tude (dis·kwī′ə·tüd; –tūd), n. anxi- ety.

dis·qui·si·tion (dis′kwə·zish′ən), n. a long or formal speech or writing about a subject. [< L disquisitio, ult. < dis- (intensive) + quaerere seek]

Dis·rae·li (diz·rā′li), n. Benjamin (Earl of Beaconsfield), 1804–1881, English statesman and novelist.

dis·re·gard (dis′ri·gärd′), v. 1. pay no atten- tion to; take no notice of. 2. treat without proper regard or respect; slight. —n. 1. lack of attention; neglect. 2. lack of proper regard or re- spect. —dis′re·gard′ful, adj. —Syn. v. 1. ignore, overlook, neglect.

dis·re·pair (dis′ri·pār′), n. bad condition.

dis·rep·u·ta·ble (dis·rep′yə·tə·bəl), adj. 1. having a bad reputation. 2. not respectable. —dis·rep′u·ta·bil′i·ty, n. —dis·rep′u·ta·bly, adv.

dis·re·pute (dis′ri·pūt′), n. disgrace; dis- credit; disfavor.

dis·re·spect (dis′ri·spekt′), n. lack of respect. —v. treat or consider with a lack of respect. —dis′re·spect′ful, adj. —dis′re·spect′ful·ly, adv. —dis′re·spect′ful·ness, n. —Syn. n. dis- courtesy, impoliteness, rudeness.

dis·robe (dis·rōb′), v., –robed, –rob·ing. un- dress. —dis·robe′ment, n. —dis·rob′er, n.

dis·rupt (dis·rupt′), v. break up; split. [< L disruptus < dis- apart + rumpere break] —dis· rupt′er, n. —dis·rup′tion, n. —dis·rup′tive, adj.

dis·sat·is·fac·tion (dis′sat·is·fak′shən), n. discontent; displeasure.

dis·sat·is·fac·to·ry (dis′sat·is·fak′tə·ri), adj. causing discontent; unsatisfactory.

dis·sat·is·fy (dis·sat′is·fī), v., –fied, –fy·ing. fail to satisfy; displease.

dis·sect (di·sekt′; dī–), v. 1. separate or divide the parts of (an animal, plant, etc.) in order to examine or study the structure. 2. examine care- fully part by part; analyze. [< L, < dis- apart + secare cut] —dis·sec′tion, n. —dis·sec′tor, n.

dis·sect·ed (di·sek′tid; dī–), adj. 1. cut or di- vided into many parts. 2. Bot. deeply cut into numerous segments. 3. Geol. cut up by irregular valleys.

dis·sem·ble (di·sem′bəl), v., –bled, –bling. 1. disguise or hide (one's real feelings, thoughts, plans, etc.). 2. conceal one's motives, etc.; be a hypocrite. 3. pretend; feign. 4. disregard; ignore. [alter., after resemble, of obs. dissimule dissimu- late] —dis·sem′bler, n.

dis·sem·i·nate (di·sem′ə·nāt), v., –nat·ed, –nat·ing. scatter widely; spread abroad. [< L, < dis- in every direction + semen seed] —dis· sem′i·na′tion, n. —dis·sem′i·na′tive, adj. —dis·sem′i·na′tor, n.

dis·sen·sion (di·sen′shən), n. 1. a disputing; a quarreling. 2. hard feeling caused by a differ- ence in opinion. —Syn. 1. disagreement, conten- tion.

dis·sent (di·sent′), v. 1. differ in opinion; dis- agree. 2. refuse to conform to the rules and be- liefs of an established church. —n. 1. difference of opinion; disagreement. 2. refusal to conform to the rules and beliefs of an established church. [< L, < dis- differently + sentire think, feel] —dis·sent′er, n.

dis·sen·tient (di·sen′shənt), adj. dissenting. —n. person who dissents. —dis·sen′tience, n.

dis·ser·ta·tion (dis′ər·tā′shən), n. a formal discussion of a subject; treatise. [< L dissertatio < dis- + serere join words]

dis·serv·ice (dis·sér′vis), n. harm; injury.

dis·sev·er (di·sev′ər), v. sever; separate. —dis·sev′er·ance, n.

dis·si·dent (dis′ə·dənt), adj. disagreeing; dis- senting. —n. person who disagrees or dissents. —dis′si·dence, n.

dis·sim·i·lar (di·sim′ə·lər), adj. not similar; unlike; different. —dis·sim·i·lar·i·ty (di·sim′ə- lar′ə·ti), n. —dis·sim′i·lar·ly, adv.

dis·si·mil·i·tude (dis′si·mil′ə·tüd; –tūd), n. unlikeness; difference.

dis·sim·u·late (di·sim′yə·lāt), v., –lat·ed, –lat·ing. disguise; dissemble. —dis·sim′u·la′· tion, n. —dis·sim′u·la′tor, n.

dis·si·pate (dis′ə·pāt), v., –pat·ed, –pat·ing. 1. spread in different directions; scatter. 2. disap- pear or cause to disappear; dispel. 3. spend fool- ishly. 4. indulge too much in evil or foolish pleas- ures. [< L, < dis- in different directions + sipare throw] —dis′si·pat′er, dis′si·pa′tor, n. —dis′· si·pa′tive, adj. —Syn. 3. squander, waste.

dis·si·pat·ed (dis′ə·pāt′id), adj. 1. indulging too much in evil or foolish pleasures; dissolute. 2. scattered. 3. wasted. —dis′si·pat′ed·ly, adv. —dis′si·pat′ed·ness, n.

dis·si·pa·tion (dis′ə·pā′shən), n. 1. a dissi- pating or being dissipated. 2. amusement; diver- sion, esp. harmful amusements. 3. too much in- dulgence in evil or foolish pleasures.

dis·so·ci·ate (di·sō′shi·āt), v., –at·ed, –at·ing. 1. break the connection or association with; sep- arate. 2. Chem. separate or decompose by disso- ciation. [< L, < dis- apart + socius ally]

dis·so·ci·a·tion (di·sō′si·ā′shən; –shi·ā′–), n. 1. act of dissociating or state of being disso- ciated. 2. Chem. separation or decomposition of a substance into simpler constituents. —dis·so- ci·a·tive (di·sō′shi·ā′tiv), adj.

dis·sol·u·ble (di·sol′yə·bəl), adj. capable of being dissolved. —dis·sol′u·bil′i·ty, dis·sol′u- ble·ness, n.

dis·so·lute (dis′ə·lüt), adj. living an evil life; very wicked; lewd; immoral. [< L dissolutus, pp. of dissolvere DISSOLVE] —dis′so·lute·ly, adv. —dis′so·lute·ness, n. —Syn. dissipated.

dis·so·lu·tion (dis′ə·lü′shən), n. 1. a break- ing up into parts. 2. the ending of a business partnership. 3. the breaking up of an assembly by ending its session. 4. ruin; destruction. 5. death.

dis·solve (di·zolv′), v., –solved, –solv·ing, n. —v. 1. make or become liquid, esp. by putting or being put into a liquid. 2. break up; end: dissolve a partnership. 3. fade away. 4. separate into parts; decompose. —n. Am. in movies and tele- vision, the gradual disappearing of the figures of a scene while those of a succeeding scene slowly take their place. [< L, < dis- (intensive) + solvere loose] —dis·solv′a·ble, adj. —dis·solv′er, n. —Syn. v. 1. melt, thaw.

dis·so·nance (dis′ə·nəns), **dis·so·nan·cy** (–nən·si), n., pl. –nan·ces; –cies. 1. combination of sounds that is not harmonious; discord. 2. Music. a chord in a state of unrest and needing completion. [< L, < dis- differently + sonare to sound]

dis·so·nant (dis′ə·nənt), adj. 1. harsh in sound. 2. out of harmony. —dis′so·nant·ly, adv.

dis·suade (di·swād′), v., –suad·ed, –suad·ing. persuade not to do something. [< L, < dis- against + suadere to urge] —dis·suad′er, n. —dis·sua·sion (di·swā′zhən), n. —dis·sua·sive (di·swā′siv), adj.

dis·syl·la·ble (dis′sil′ə·bəl; di·sil′–), n. word having two syllables. [< F < L < Gk., < di- two + syllabe SYLLABLE] —dis·syl·lab·ic (dis′si·lab′- ik; dis′l–), adj.

dist., 1. distance. 2. district.

dis·taff (dis′taf; –täf), n. 1. a split stick that holds the wool, flax, etc., for spinning. See the picture on the next page. 2. woman's work

āge, cāre, fär; ēqual, tėrm; īce; ōpen, ôrder; put, rüle, ūse; th, then; ə=a in about.

or affairs. **3.** the female sex; woman or women. [OE, < *dis-* (see DIZEN) + *stœf* staff]

dis·taff side, the mother's side of a family.

dis·tance (dis′təns), *n., v.,* -tanced, -tanc·ing. —*n.* **1.** space in between. **2.** a being far away. **3.** place far away. **4.** time in between; interval. **5.** *Music.* the interval or difference between two tones. **6.** lack of friendliness or familiarity; reserve. —*v.* leave far behind; do much better than.

dis·tant (dis′tənt), *adj.* **1.** far away in space. **2.** away. **3.** far apart in time, relationship, etc.; not close. **4.** not friendly. [< F < L *distans* < *dis-* off + *stare* stand] —**dis′tant·ly,** *adv.* —**Syn. 1.** remote, far. **4.** aloof, reserved.

dis·taste (dis·tāst′), *n.* dislike.

dis·taste·ful (dis·tāst′fəl), *adj.* unpleasant; disagreeable; offensive. —**dis·taste′ful·ly,** *adv.* —**dis·taste′ful·ness,** *n.*

dis·tem·per[1] (dis·tem′pər), *n.* **1.** an infectious disease of dogs and other animals, accompanied by a short, dry cough and a loss of strength. **2.** sickness of the mind or body; disorder; disease. **3.** disturbance. [< v.] —*v.* **1.** disturb; disorder. **2.** *Archaic.* trouble. [< LL *distemperare* mix improperly. See DIS-, TEMPER.]

dis·tem·per[2] (dis·tem′pər), *n.* **1.** paint made by mixing the colors with eggs or glue instead of oil. **2.** method of painting with such a mixture. —*v.* paint with such a mixture. [< OF *destemprer* < Med.L, soak, < LL, mix thoroughly. See DIS-, TEMPER.]

dis·tend (dis·tend′), *v.* stretch out; expand. [< L, < *dis-* apart + *tendere* stretch] —**dis·ten·si·ble** (dis·ten′sə·bəl), *adj.* —**dis·ten′si·bil′i·ty,** *n.* —**dis·ten′tion,** *n.*

dis·tich (dis′tik), *n., pl.* -tichs. two lines of verse together that make complete sense; couplet. [< L < Gk., < *di-* two + *stichos* line]

dis·till, *esp. Brit.* **dis·til** (dis·til′), *v.,* -tilled, -till·ing. **1.** heat (a liquid, or other substance) and condense the vapor given off. **2.** obtain by distilling. **3.** extract; refine. **4.** fall or let fall in drops; drip. [< L, < *de-* down + *stillare* to drop < *stilla* drop] —**dis·till′a·ble,** *adj.*

dis·til·late (dis′tə·lit; -lāt), *n.* a distilled liquid; something obtained by distilling.

dis·til·la·tion (dis′tə·lā′shən), *n.* **1.** a distilling. **2.** something distilled; extract; essence.

dis·till·er (dis·til′ər), *n.* **1.** person or thing that distills. **2.** person or corporation that makes whiskey, rum, brandy, etc.

dis·till·er·y (dis·til′ər·i), *n., pl.* -er·ies. place where distilling is done.

dis·tinct (dis·tingkt′), *adj.* **1.** not the same; separate. **2.** not alike; not like; different. **3.** clear; plain. **4.** unmistakable; definite; decided. [< L *distinctus,* pp. of *distinguere* DISTINGUISH] —**dis·tinct′ness,** *n.* —**Syn. 1.** different, dissimilar. **3.** obvious.

dis·tinc·tion (dis·tingk′shən), *n.* **1.** act of distinguishing; making a difference: *he gave every servant 10 dollars without distinction.* **2.** difference. **3.** point of difference; special quality or feature. **4.** honor: *the soldier served with distinction.* **5.** mark or sign of honor. **6.** excellence; superiority.

dis·tinc·tive (dis·tingk′tiv), *adj.* distinguishing from others; special; characteristic. —**dis·tinc′tive·ly,** *adv.* —**dis·tinc′tive·ness,** *n.*

dis·tin·gué (dis′tang·gā′; dis·tang′gā), *adj.* looking important or superior; distinguished.

dis·tin·guish (dis·ting′gwish), *v.* **1.** tell apart; see or show the difference in. **2.** see or show the difference. **3.** see or hear clearly. **4.** be a special quality or feature of. **5.** make famous or well-known. **6.** separate into different groups. [< L, < *dis-* between + *stinguere* to prick] —**dis·tin′guish·a·ble,** *adj.* —**dis·tin′guish·a·bly,** *adv.*

dis·tin·guished (dis·ting′gwisht), *adj.* **1.** famous; well-known. **2.** having the appearance of an important person.

dis·tort (dis·tôrt′), *v.* **1.** pull or twist out of shape. **2.** change from the truth. [< L *distortus* < *dis-* (intensive) + *torquere* twist] —**dis·tort′ed,** *adj.* —**dis·tort′ed·ly,** *adv.* —**dis·tort′ed·ness,** *n.* —**dis·tort′er,** *n.* —**dis·tor′tion,** *n.* —**dis·tor′tion·al,** *adj.* —**Syn. 1.** contort. **2.** misrepresent, falsify.

dis·tract (dis·trakt′), *v.* **1.** draw away (the mind, attention, etc.). **2.** confuse; disturb; bewilder. **3.** put out of one's mind; make insane. [< L *distractus* < *dis-* away + *trahere* draw] —**dis·tract′ed,** *adj.* —**dis·tract′ed·ly,** *adv.* —**dis·tract′er,** *n.* —**dis·tract′ing,** *adj.* —**dis·tract′ing·ly,** *adv.* —**dis·trac′tive,** *adj.*

dis·trac·tion (dis·trak′shən), *n.* **1.** act of distracting. **2.** thing that distracts. **3.** confusion of mind; disturbance of thought. **4.** insanity; madness. **5.** confusion; perplexity. **6.** relief from continued thought, grief, or effort.

dis·train (dis·trān′), *v.* seize (goods) for unpaid rent or other debts. [< OF < L, < *dis-* apart + *stringere* draw] —**dis·train′a·ble,** *adj.* —**dis·train′er, dis·train′or,** *n.* —**dis·train′ment,** *n.*

dis·trait (dis·trā′), *adj.* not paying attention; absent-minded. [< F, pp. of *distraire* DISTRACT]

dis·traught (dis·trôt′), *adj.* **1.** distracted. **2.** crazed. [var. of obs. *distract,* adj. See DISTRACT.]

dis·tress (dis·tres′), *n.* **1.** great pain or sorrow; anxiety; trouble. **2.** something that causes distress; misfortune. **3.** dangerous condition; difficult situation: *ship in distress.* **4.** a legal seizure of the goods of another as security or satisfaction for debt, etc. **5.** the thing so seized. —*v.* cause pain, grief, or suffering to. [< OF *distrece,* ult. < L *districtus* < *dis-* apart + *stringere* draw] —**dis·tress′ful,** *adj.* —**dis·tress′ful·ly,** *adv.* —**dis·tress′ing,** *adj.* —**dis·tress′ing·ly,** *adv.* —**Syn.** *n.* **1.** grief, agony, anguish.

dis·trib·ute (dis·trib′yùt), *v.,* -ut·ed, -ut·ing. **1.** divide and give out in shares. **2.** spread; scatter. **3.** divide into parts. **4.** arrange; classify. [< L, < *dis-* individually + *tribuere* assign] —**dis·trib′ut·a·ble,** *adj.* —**Syn. 1.** deal, dispense, allot. **4.** sort, group.

dis·tri·bu·tion (dis′trə·bū′shən), *n.* **1.** act of distributing. **2.** way of being distributed. **3.** thing distributed. **4.** the distributing to consumers of goods grown or made by producers. —**dis′tri·bu′tion·al,** *adj.*

dis·trib·u·tive (dis·trib′yə·tiv), *adj.* **1.** of or having to do with distribution; distributing. **2.** referring to each individual of a group considered separately. *Each, every, either,* and *neither* are distributive words. —*n.* a distributive word. —**dis·trib′u·tive·ly,** *adv.* —**dis·trib′u·tive·ness,** *n.*

dis·trib·u·tor, dis·trib·ut·er (dis·trib′yə·tər), *n.* **1.** person or thing that distributes. **2.** person or company that distributes to consumers the goods grown or made by producers. **3.** part of a gasoline engine that distributes electric current to the spark plugs.

dis·trict (dis′trikt), *n.* **1.** portion of a country; region. **2.** *Am.* portion of a country, state, or city serving as a unit for policing, fire prevention, political representation, etc. —*v. Am.* divide into districts. [< LL *districtus* district < L *distringere.* See DISTRESS.]

district attorney, *Am.* lawyer who handles cases for the government for a certain district.

District of Columbia, *Am.* district in the E United States belonging to the federal government. It is entirely occupied by the capital, Washington, and is governed by Congress. *Abbrev.:* D.C.

dis·trust (dis·trust′), *v.* have no confidence in; be suspicious of. —*n.* lack of trust or confidence; suspicion. —**dis·trust′ful,** *adj.* —**dis·trust′ful·ly,** *adv.* —**Syn.** *n.* doubt, mistrust.

dis·turb (dis·tèrb′), *v.* **1.** destroy the peace, quiet, or rest of. **2.** break in upon with noise or change. **3.** put out of order. **4.** make uneasy; trouble. [< L < *dis-* (intensive) + *turbare* agitate < *turba* commotion] —**dis·turb′er,** *n.* —**dis·turb′ing·ly,** *adv.* —**Syn. 1.** agitate, perturb.

dis·turb·ance (dis·tèr′bəns), *n.* **1.** a disturbing or being disturbed. **2.** thing that disturbs. **3.** confusion; disorder.

di·sul·fide, di·sul·phide (dī-sulʹfīd; –fĭd), **di·sul·fid,** or **di·sul·phid** (–fĭd), *n.* compound consisting of two atoms of sulfur combined with another element or radical; bisulfide.

dis·un·ion (dis-ūnʹyən), *n.* **1.** separation; division. **2.** lack of unity; disagreement.

dis·u·nite (disʹyū-nītʹ), *v.,* –nit·ed, –nit·ing. **1.** separate; divide. **2.** destroy the unity of. —**dis·u·ni·ty** (dis-ūʹnə-tĭ), *n.*

dis·use (*n.* dis-ūsʹ; *v.* dis-ūzʹ), *n., v.,* –used, –us·ing. —*n.* lack of use. —*v.* stop using.

ditch (dich), *n.* a long, narrow place dug in the earth, usually used to carry off water. —*v.* **1.** dig a ditch in. **2.** *Slang.* get rid of. [OE *dīc*] —ditchʹer, *n.*

dith·er (dĭthʹər), *n.* **1.** a tremble; shiver; quiver. **2.** *Colloq.* a confused, excited condition.

dith·y·ramb (dĭthʹə-ram; –ramb), *n.* **1.** a Greek choral song in honor of Dionysus. **2.** poem that is full of wild emotion, enthusiasm, etc. **3.** any speech or writing like this. [< L < Gk. *dithyrambos*] —**dith·y·ram·bic** (dĭthʹə-ramʹbĭk), *adj.*

dit·to (dĭtʹō), *n., pl.* –tos, *v.,* –toed, –to·ing, *adv.* —*n.* **1.** the same as was said before; the same. **2.** mark (″) or abbreviation (do.) that stands for ditto. **3.** a copy; duplicate. —*v.* to copy; duplicate. —*adv.* as said before; likewise. [< Ital., said, < L *dictus,* pp. of *dicere* say] ▶ Ditto marks are used with lists and tabulations in reference works instead of repeating words that fall directly underneath. Ditto marks are not used in consecutive writing, nor are they used now in footnotes and bibliographies. In general they are much less used than formerly.

dit·ty (dĭtʹĭ), *n., pl.* –ties. a short, simple song or poem. [< OF *ditié* < L *dictatum* (thing) dictated, pp. of *dictare* DICTATE]

ditty bag, a small bag used by sailors to hold needles, thread, buttons, etc.

di·u·ret·ic (dīʹyū-retʹĭk), *Med.* —*adj.* causing an increase in the flow of urine. —*n.* drug that does this. [< LL < Gk., < *dia-* through + *oureein* urinate]

di·ur·nal (dī-érʹnəl), *adj.* **1.** occurring every day; daily. **2.** of or belonging to the daytime. **3.** lasting a day. [< LL *diurnalis* < L *dies* day. Doublet of JOURNAL.] —**di·urʹnal·ly,** *adv.*

div., **1.** divide; divided. **2.** dividend. **3.** division.

di·va (dēʹvə), *n., pl.* –vas. a prima donna. [< Ital. < L, goddess]

di·va·lent (dī-vāʹlənt), *adj. Chem.* having a valence of two.

di·van (dīʹvan, dī-vanʹ), *n.* a long, low, soft couch or sofa. [< Turk. < Pers. *dēvān*]

dive (dīv), *v.,* dived or (*U.S. Colloq. and Brit. Dial.*) dove, dived, div·ing, *n.* —*v.* **1.** plunge head first into water. **2.** go down or out of sight suddenly. **3.** (of an airplane) plunge downward at a steep angle. —*n.* **1.** act of diving. **2.** the downward plunge of an airplane. **3.** *Am., Colloq.* a low, cheap place for drinking and gambling. [OE *dūfan*] —divʹer, *n.*

dive bomber, airplane used to bomb a target by making an almost vertical dive straight at it. —dive bombing.

di·verge (də-vérjʹ; dī-), *v.,* –verged, –verg·ing. **1.** move or lie in different directions from the same point. **2.** differ; vary; deviate. [< LL, < *dis-* in different directions + *vergere* slope] —di·verʹgence, di·verʹgen·cy, *n.* —di·verʹgent, *adj.* —di·verʹgent·ly, *adv.*

di·vers (dīʹvərz), *adj.* **1.** several different; various. **2.** *Obs.* diverse. [< OF < L *diversus,* pp. of *divertere* DIVERT]

di·verse (də-vérsʹ; dī-), *adj.* **1.** different; unlike. **2.** varied: *a person of diverse interests.* [var. of *divers;* now regarded as immediately from L] —di·verseʹly, *adv.* —di·verseʹness, *n.*

di·ver·si·fy (də-vérʹsə-fī; dī-), *v.,* –fied, –fy·ing. give variety to; vary. —di·verʹsi·fi·caʹtion, *n.* —di·verʹsi·fiʹer, *n.*

di·ver·sion (də-vérʹzhən; –shən; dī-), *n.* **1.** a turning aside. **2.** amusement; entertainment; pastime. —**Syn.** **1.** deviation. **2.** sport, recreation.

di·ver·sion·ar·y (də-vérʹzhən·erʹĭ; –shən–, dī–), *adj. Esp. Brit.* of or like a diversion or feint, esp. in military tactics.

di·ver·si·ty (də-vérʹsə-tĭ; dī–), *n., pl.* –ties. **1.** complete difference. **2.** variety.

di·vert (də-vértʹ; dī–), *v.* **1.** turn aside. **2.** amuse; entertain. [< F < L, < *dis-* aside + *vertere* turn] —di·vertʹer, *n.* —di·verʹtive, *adj.*

di·ver·tisse·ment (dē-ver-tēs-mänʹ), *n.* amusement; entertainment. [< F]

di·vest (də-vestʹ; dī–), *v.* **1.** strip; rid; free. **2.** force to give up; deprive. [< Med.L *divestire* < OF, < *des-* away (< L *dis-*) + *vestir* < L *vestire* clothe]

di·vide (də-vīdʹ), *v.,* –vid·ed, –vid·ing, *n.* —*v.* **1.** separate into parts: *a brook divides the field.* **2.** separate into equal parts: *divide 8 by 2, and you get 4.* **3.** mark off or arrange regular steps, stages, or degrees on. **4.** find a quotient by mathematical procedures. **5.** give some of to each; share: *the children divided the candy among them.* **6.** disagree or cause to disagree; differ or cause to differ in feeling, opinion, etc.: *the school divided on the choice of a motto; jealousy divided us.* **7.** separate into two groups in voting. —*n. Am.* ridge of land between two regions drained by different river systems. [< L *dividere*] —di·vidʹa·ble, *adj.* —di·vidʹer, *n.* —**Syn.** *v.* **1.** sever, split, part.

di·vid·ed (də-vīdʹĭd), *adj.* **1.** separated. **2.** *Bot.* (of a leaf) cut to the base so as to form distinct portions. ▶ **divided usage.** Usage is said to be *divided* when two or more forms exist in the language, both in reputable use in the same dialect or style. *Divided usage* is not applied, for example, to localisms, like *sack, bag, poke,* or to differences like *ain't* and *isn't* which belong to separate styles of the language. It applies to spellings, pronunciations, or constructions on which speakers and writers of similar education might differ. The two pronunciations of *either* (ēʹthər and īʹthər), the two spellings of *catalogue* (*catalog* and *catalogue*), and the two past tenses of *sing* (*sang* and *sung*) are examples of divided usage.

div·i·dend (divʹə-dend), *n.* **1.** number or quantity to be divided by another: *in 8 + 2, 8 is the dividend.* **2.** money to be shared by those to whom it belongs. If a company makes a profit, it declares a dividend to the owners of the company. **3.** share of anything that is divided. [< L, (thing) to be divided]

di·vid·er (də-vīdʹər), *n.* **1.** person or thing that divides. **2.** Usually, **dividers.** instrument for dividing lines, etc.; compasses.

div·i·na·tion (divʹə-nāʹshən), *n.* **1.** act of foreseeing the future or foretelling the unknown. **2.** a skillful guess or prediction. —di·vin·a·to·ry (də-vinʹə-tôʹrĭ; –tōʹ–), *adj.*

di·vine (də-vīnʹ), *adj., n., v.,* –vined, –vin·ing. —*adj.* **1.** of God or a god. **2.** by or from God. **3.** to or for God; sacred; holy. **4.** like God or a god; heavenly. **5.** very excellent. —*n.* clergyman; minister; priest. —*v.* find out or foretell. [< OF < L *divinus* of a deity < *divus* deity] —di·vineʹly, *adv.* —di·vineʹness, *n.* —di·vinʹer, *n.*

diving bell, a large, hollow container filled with air. People can work in it under water.

divining rod, a forked stick supposed to be useful in locating water, oil, metal, and other things underground.

Diving bell

di·vin·i·ty (də-vinʹə-tĭ), *n., pl.* –ties. **1.** a divine being; a god. **2.** the Divinity, God; the Deity. **3.** divine nature or quality. **4.** study of God, religion, and divine things; theology. **5.** godlike character or attribute. **6.** creamy fudge.

di·vis·i·ble (də-vizʹə-bəl), *adj.* **1.** capable of being divided. **2.** capable of being divided without leaving a remainder: *any even number is divisible by 2.* —di·visʹi·bilʹi·ty, *n.* —di·visʹi·bly, *adv.*

di·vi·sion (də·vizh′ən), *n.* **1.** a dividing or being divided. **2.** act of giving some to each; a sharing. **3.** process of dividing one number by another. **4.** thing that divides. **5.** part; group; section. **6.** part of an army consisting of two or three brigades of infantry and a certain amount of cavalry, artillery, etc., usually commanded by a major general. **7.** difference of opinion, thought, or feeling; disagreement. **8.** separation of a legislature, parliament, etc., into two groups in taking a vote. —di·vi′sion·al, *adj.* —Syn. **2.** allotment, distribution, apportionment. ❧ **division of words.** When necessary in manuscript or print, a word is divided at the end of a line by a hyphen ("division hyphen"). In preparing manuscript if you will leave a reasonable right-hand margin, you will not be forced to divide so many words as you will if you crowd to the end of the line. A good habit is not to divide words unless the lines will be conspicuously uneven if the last word is completely written or completely carried over to the next line. In manuscript for publication most publishers prefer an uneven right margin to divided words. When it is necessary to divide a word, break it between syllables. Both the divided parts should be pronounceable; that is, words of one syllable, like *matched, said, thought,* should not be divided at all. English syllables are difficult to determine but in general they follow pronunciation groups: *auto-cratic* would be divided into syllables *au to crat ic,* but *autocracy* is *au toc ra cy.* The following words are divided to show typical syllables: *mar gin, hi lar i ous, hy phen, ac com-plished, long ing, pitch er.* Double consonants are usually separable: *ef fi cient, com mit tee, bat ted.* A single letter is not allowed to stand by itself; that is, do not divide at the end of lines words like *enough* (which would leave a lone *e* at the end of a line) or *many* (which would put a lone *y* at the beginning of a line). Words spelled with a hyphen (*half-hearted, well-disposed*) should be divided only at the point of the hyphen to avoid the awkwardness of two hyphens in the same word.

division of labor, a dividing up of work so that each person has a certain part to do.

di·vi·sor (də·vī′zər), *n.* number or quantity by which another is divided: *in 8 ÷ 2, 2 is the divisor.*

di·vorce (də·vôrs′), *n., v.,* -vorced, -vorc·ing. —*n.* **1.** the legal ending of a marriage. **2.** a complete separation. —*v.* **1.** end legally a marriage between. **2.** separate from by divorce: *Mrs. Smith divorced her husband.* **3.** separate. [< OF < L *divortium* separation < *divertere* DIVERT]

di·vor·cee (də·vôr′sē′; -vōr′-), *n.* a divorced woman.

div·ot (div′ət), *n.* a small piece of turf or earth dug up by a golf club in making a stroke.

di·vulge (də·vulj′), *v.,* -vulged, -vulg·ing. make known; make public; tell; reveal: *the traitor divulged secret plans to the enemy.* [< L *divulgare* make common < *dis-* + *vulgus* common people] —di·vulge′ment, *n.* —di·vulg′er, *n.* —Syn. disclose.

Dix·ie (dik′si), or **Dixie Land,** *n. Am.* the Southern States of the United States.

Dix·ie·crat (dik′si·krat), *n. Am.* one of those Democrats who opposed first the civil rights program of the Truman Administration and later the civil rights plank of the 1948 platform of the Democratic Party. Also, States' Rights Democrat. [< *Dixie* + (*demo*)*crat*]

diz·en (diz′ən; dī′zən), *v.* dress gaudily. [cf. MDu. *disen* wind up flax, MLG *dise* bunch of flax on distaff]

diz·zy (diz′i), *adj.,* -zi·er, -zi·est, *v.,* -zied, -zy·ing. —*adj.* **1.** disposed to fall, stagger, or spin around; not steady. **2.** confused; bewildered. **3.** causing dizziness: *a dizzy height.* **4.** *Colloq.* foolish; stupid. —*v.* make dizzy. [OE *dysig* foolish] —diz′zi·ly, *adv.* —diz′zi·ness, *n.*

DNB, D.N.B., a German news agency.

Dne·pro·pe·trovsk (dnye′prō·pye·trôfsk′), *n.* city in SW Soviet Union, on the Dnieper.

Dnie·per (nē′pər), *n.* river flowing from W Soviet Union into the Black Sea.

do[1] (dü), *v., pres. sing.* **1** do, **2** (*Archaic*) do·est or dost, **3** does or (*Archaic*) do·eth or doth; *pl.* do; *pt.* did; *pp.* done; *ppr.* do·ing; *n.* —*v.* **1.** carry out; perform: *do your work.* **2.** act; work: *do or die.* **3.** complete; finish; end: *that's done!* **4.** make; produce: *Walt Disney did a movie about the seven dwarfs.* **5.** be the cause of; bring about: *your work does you credit.* **6.** act; behave: *do wisely.* **7.** render: *do homage.* **8.** deal with as the case may require; put in order: *do the dishes.* **9.** get along; manage; fare: *how do you do?* **10.** be satisfactory; be enough; serve: *this hat will do.* **11.** work out; solve. **12.** cook: *the roast will be done in an hour.* **13.** cover; traverse: *we did 80 miles in an hour.* **14.** *Colloq.* cheat; trick. **15.** *Do* has special uses where it has no definite meaning: **a.** in asking questions: *do you like milk?* **b.** in emphasizing a verb: *I do want to go.* **c.** in standing for a verb already used: *my dog goes where I do.* **d.** in expressions that contain *not: people talk; animals do not.* **e.** in inverted constructions after the adverbs *rarely, hardly, little,* etc.: *rarely did she laugh.* **16.** do away with, **a.** abolish. **b.** kill. **17.** do by, act or behave toward; treat. **18.** do in, **a.** cheat. **b.** ruin. **c.** *Slang.* kill. **19.** do up, **a.** wrap up. **b.** clean and get ready for use. **c.** comb (one's hair). **d.** *Colloq.* wear out; exhaust. —*n. Colloq.* a festive party. [OE *dōn*] —Syn. *v.* **1.** execute, effect. **9.** prosper. **10.** suffice, answer.

do[2] (dō), *n.* the first and last of a series of syllables that are used for the eight tones of a musical scale. [substituted for *ut.* See GAMUT.]

do., ditto.

do·a·ble (dü′ə·bəl), *adj.* that can be done.

dob·bin (dob′ən), *n.* a slow, gentle horse.

Do·ber·man pin·scher (dō′bər·mən pin′shər), a medium-sized dog with short, dark hair.

Doberman pinscher (ab. 2 ft. high at the shoulder)

doc·ile (dos′əl), *adj.* **1.** easily managed; obedient. **2.** easily taught; willing to learn. [< F < L *docilis* < *docere* teach] —doc′-ile·ly, *adv.* —do·cil·i·ty (dō·sil′ə·ti; do-), *n.*

dock[1] (dok), *n.* **1.** *Am.* platform built on the shore or out from the shore; wharf; pier. **2.** water between two piers. **3.** place where a ship may be repaired, often built watertight so that the water may be kept high or pumped out. —*v.* **1.** bring (a ship) to a dock. **2.** come into a dock. [< MDu. or MLG *docke*]

dock[2] (dok), *n.* the solid, fleshy part of an animal's tail. —*v.* **1.** cut short; cut the end off. **2.** cut down; reduce: *dock wages for lateness.* [OE -*docca,* as in *finger-docca* finger muscle]

dock[3] (dok), *n.* place where an accused person stands in a law court. [cf. Flem. *dok* pen]

dock[4] (dok), *n.* a large weed with sour or bitter leaves. [OE *docce*]

dock·age (dok′ij), *n.* **1.** place to dock ship. **2.** charge for using a dock. **3.** the docking of ships.

dock·et (dok′it), *n., v.,* -et·ed, -et·ing. —*n.* **1.** *Am.* list of lawsuits to be tried by a court. **2.** *U.S.* any list of matters to be considered by some group of people. **3.** label or ticket giving the contents of a package, document, etc. —*v.* **1.** *Am.* enter on a docket. **2.** make a summary or list of. **3.** mark with a docket.

dock·yard (dok′yärd′), *n.* place where ships are built, equipped, and repaired.

doc·tor (dok′tər), *n.* **1.** person licensed to treat diseases or physical disorders; physician or surgeon. **2.** any person who treats diseases: *a witch doctor.* **3.** person who has received one of the highest degrees given by a university: *a Doctor of Philosophy.* **4.** the academic degree held by such a person. **5.** *Archaic.* a learned man; teacher. —*v.* **1.** *Colloq.* be a doctor; practice medicine. **2.** treat diseases in (a person, animal, etc.). **3.** take medicine. **4.** repair; mend. **5.** *Colloq.* tamper with. [< OF < L, teacher, < *docere* teach] —doc′tor·al, *adj.*

doc·tor·ate (dok′tər·it), *n.* degree of doctor given by a university.

doc·tri·naire (dok′trə·nâr′), **doc·tri·nar·i·an** (–nâr′i·ən), *n.* an impractical theorist; person who tries to apply a theory without considering the actual circumstances.

doc·trine (dok′trən), *n.* 1. what is taught as the belief of a church, nation, etc. 2. what is taught; teachings. [< F < L *doctrina* < *doctor* DOCTOR] —doc′tri·nal, *adj.* —doc′tri·nal·ly, *adv.*

doc·u·ment (*n.* dok′yə·mənt; *v.* dok′yə·ment), *n.* 1. something written, printed, etc., that gives information or proof of some fact. 2. a printed or woven material or wallpaper. —*v.* 1. provide with documents. 2. prove or support by means of documents. [< L *documentum* example, proof < *docere* show] —doc′u·men·ta′tion, *n.*

doc·u·men·ta·ry (dok′yə·men′tə·ri), *adj.*, *n.*, *pl.* –ries. —*adj.* 1. of, pertaining to, or like a document or documents. 2. verified in writing. 3. presenting or recording factual information in an artistic fashion: *a documentary film.* —*n.* a documentary motion picture.

dod·der (dod′ər), *v.* shake; tremble; totter.

Do·dec·a·nese Islands (dō′dek·ə·nēs′; –nēz′; dō·dek′ə–), group of Greek islands in the Aegean Sea, off SW Turkey.

dodge (doj), *v.*, dodged, dodg·ing, *n.* —*v.* 1. move quickly to one side. 2. move quickly in order to get away from (a person, a blow, or something thrown). 3. get away from by some trick. —*n.* 1. sudden movement to one side. 2. *Colloq.* a clever trick or ruse. —**Syn.** *v.* 3. evade, equivocate.

dodg·er (doj′ər), *n.* 1. person who dodges. 2. a shifty or dishonest person. 3. *Am.* a small handbill. 4. *Am.* kind of corn bread.

Dodg·son (doj′sən), *n.* Charles L., 1832–1898, English mathematician who wrote *Alice in Wonderland.* His pen name was Lewis Carroll.

do·do (dō′dō), *n., pl.* –dos, –does. a large, clumsy bird unable to fly. Dodoes are now extinct. [< Pg. *doudo* fool]

Dodo (4 ft. long)

doe (dō), *n.* a female deer, antelope, rabbit, or hare. [OE *dā*]

Doe (dō), *n.* John, name used in legal documents, etc., to mean anyone.

do·er (dü′ər), *n.* person who does something.

does (duz), *v.* third pers. sing., pres. indic. of do[1].

doe·skin (dō′skin′), *n.* 1. skin of a female deer. 2. leather made from it. 3. a smooth, soft woolen cloth.

does·n't (duz′ənt), does not.

do·est (dü′ist), *v. Archaic.* do.

do·eth (dü′ith), *v. Archaic.* does.

doff (dof; dôf), *v.* take off; remove, as a hat. [contraction of *do off*]

dog (dôg; dog), *n., v.*, dogged, dog·ging. —*n.* 1. a domesticated carnivorous animal (of the genus *Canis*), kept as a pet, for hunting, etc. Two varieties are the cocker spaniel and the greyhound. 2. any animal of the family that includes wolves, foxes, and jackals. 3. a male dog, fox, wolf, etc. 4. any of various animals somewhat like a dog, such as the prairie dog. 5. a low, worthless man. 6. man; fellow. 7. *Am., Slang.* outward show. 8. thing that holds or grips. 9. andiron. 10. go to the dogs, be ruined. —*v.* hunt or follow like a dog. [OE *docga*]

dog·cart (dôg′kärt′; dog′–), *n.* 1. a small cart pulled by dogs. 2. a small, open carriage with two seats that are back to back.

dog days, period of very hot and uncomfortable weather during July and August.

doge (dōj), *n.* the chief magistrate of Venice or Genoa when they were republics. [< Venetian Ital. < L *dux* leader. Doublet of DUCE, DUKE.]

dog-ear (dôg′ir′; dog′–), *n.* a folded-down corner of a page in a book. —*v.* fold down the corner of (the page or pages of a book). Also, dog's-ear. —dog′-eared′, *adj.*

dog·fight (dôg′fīt′; dog′–), *n. Colloq.* an engagement of fighter planes at close quarters with the enemy. —dog′fight′, *v.*

dog·fish (dôg′fish′; dog′–), *n., pl.* –fish·es or (*esp. collectively*) –fish. any of several kinds of small shark, as the spiny dogfish of the North Atlantic coast.

dog·ged (dôg′id; dog′–), *adj.* stubborn: *dogged determination.* —dog′ged·ly, *adv.* —dog′ged·ness, *n.* —**Syn.** obstinate, headstrong.

dog·ger·el (dôg′ər·əl; dog′–), **dog·grel** (dôg′rəl; dog′–), *n.* very poor poetry that is not artistic in form or meaning. —*adj.* of or like doggerel; not artistic; poor.

dog·gy (dôg′i; dog′i), *adj.*, –gi·er, –gi·est. 1. like a dog. 2. *Am., Colloq.* outwardly showy.

dog·house (dôg′hous′; dog′–), *n.* 1. a small house or shelter for a dog. 2. in the doghouse, *Am., Slang.* out of favor.

do·gie (dō′gi), *n. Am., W.* a motherless calf on the range or in a range herd.

dog·ma (dôg′mə; dog′–), *n., pl.* –mas, –ma·ta (–mə·tə). 1. belief taught or held as true, esp. by a church. 2. doctrine. 3. opinion asserted in a positive manner as if it were authoritative. [< L < Gk., opinion, < *dokeein* think]

dog·mat·ic (dôg·mat′ik; dog–), **dog·mat·i·cal** (–ə·kəl), *adj.* 1. having to do with dogma. 2. asserting opinions as if one were the highest authority; positive; overbearing. 3. asserted without proof. —dog·mat′i·cal·ly, *adv.* —dog·mat′i·cal·ness, *n.*

dog·ma·tism (dôg′mə·tiz·əm; dog′–), *n.* positive or authoritative assertion of opinion. —dog′ma·tist, *n.*

dog·ma·tize (dôg′mə·tīz; dog′–), *v.*, –tized, –tiz·ing. speak or write in a dogmatic way. —dog′ma·ti·za′tion, *n.* —dog′ma·tiz′er, *n.*

do-good·er (dü′gůd′ər), *n.* a person who is overly eager to correct or set things right.

dog's-ear (dôgz′ir′; dogz′–), *n., v.* dog-ear.

Dog Star, 1. Sirius. 2. Procyon.

dogtooth violet, dog's-tooth violet, a small plant of the lily family that has yellow, white, or purple flowers; adder's-tongue.

dog·trot (dôg′trot′; dog′–), *n.* a gentle trot.

dog·watch (dôg′woch′; –wôch′; dog′–), *n.* one of the two two-hour periods of work on a ship, from 4 to 6 P.M. and from 6 to 8 P.M.

dog·wood (dôg′wůd′; dog′–), *n.* 1. tree with pink or white flowers that bloom in the spring. 2. its hard wood.

doi·ly (doi′li), *n., pl.* –lies. a small piece of linen, lace, paper, etc., used under plates, vases, etc. [after a London dry-goods dealer]

do·ing (dü′ing), *n.* 1. action. 2. doings, *Am.* a. things done; actions. b. behavior; conduct.

dol·drum (dol′drəm; dōl′–), *n.* 1. a calm, windless region of the ocean near the equator. 2. doldrums, dullness; low spirits.

dole[1] (dōl), *n., v.*, doled, dol·ing. —*n.* 1. portion of money, food, etc., given in charity. 2. a small portion. 3. relief money given by a government to unemployed workers. —*v.* 1. deal out in portions to the poor. 2. give in small portions. [OE *dāl* part; akin to DEAL[1]]

dole[2] (dōl), *n. Archaic.* sorrow; grief. [< OF *doel* < VL *dolus* grief, < L *dolere* grieve]

dole·ful (dōl′fəl), *adj.* sad; mournful; dreary; dismal. —dole′ful·ly, *adv.* —dole′ful·ness, *n.* —**Syn.** sorrowful, woeful, plaintive.

doll (dol), *n.* 1. a child's plaything made to look like a baby, child, or grown person. 2. a pretty girl or woman without much intelligence. —*v. Slang.* dress (*up* or *out*) in a stylish or showy way. [pet name for *Dorothy*]

dol·lar (dol′ər), *n.* 1. *Am.* a unit of money in the United States, equivalent to 100 cents. 2. a similar unit of money in Canada, Mexico, etc.

Dogtooth violet

3. *Am.* a silver coin or piece of paper money worth one dollar. [earlier *daler* < LG; corresponds to HG *Joachimsthaler* coin of St. Joachim's valley (in Bohemia)]

dollar crisis, condition resulting when a country reduces its supply of dollars through failure to balance its imports from the United States by its exports.

dollar gap, the shortage of dollars (for exchange) in a country suffering from a dollar crisis.

dollar imperialism, the extending of control and authority into foreign countries through the buying power of the dollar. —**dollar imperialist.**

doll·y (dol′i), *n., pl.* **doll·ies.** **1.** a child's name for a doll. **2.** a small, low frame with wheels, used to move heavy things.

dol·man (dol′mən), *n., pl.* **-mans.** a woman's coat with capelike flaps instead of sleeves. [ult. < Turk. *dōlāmān*]

dol·men (dol′men), *n.* a prehistoric tomb made by laying a large, flat stone across several upright stones. [< F]

dol·o·mite (dol′ə·mīt), *n.* a rock consisting of calcium and magnesium carbonate. [for M. *Dolomieu,* geologist]

do·lor, *Brit.* do·lour (dō′lər), *n. Poetic.* sorrow; grief. [< OF < L *dolor*]

dol·or·ous (dol′ər·əs; dō′lər-), *adj.* **1.** mournful; sorrowful. **2.** grievous; painful. —**dol′or·ous·ly,** *adv.* —**dol′or·ous·ness,** *n.*

dol·phin (dol′fən), *n.* **1.** a small whale that has a beaklike snout. **2.** post or buoy to which to moor a vessel. [< OF *daulphin* < L < Gk. *delphis*]

Dolphin (6 to 10 ft. long)

dolt (dōlt), *n.* a dull, stupid person.

dolt·ish (dōl′tish), *adj.* dull and stupid. —**dolt′ish·ly,** *adv.* —**dolt′ish·ness,** *n.*

-dom, *suffix.* **1.** position, rank, or realm of a ——, as in *kingdom.* **2.** condition of being ——, as in *martyrdom.* **3.** all those who are ——, as in *heathendom.* [OE *-dōm*]

do·main (dō·mān′), *n.* **1.** territory under the control of one ruler or government. **2.** land owned by one person; estate. **3.** field of thought, action, etc. [< F *domaine* < L, < *dominus* lord, master]

dome (dōm), *n., v.,* **domed, dom·ing.** —*n.* **1.** a large, rounded roof on a circular or many-sided base. **2.** something high and rounded: *the dome of the sky.* —*v.* **1.** cover with a dome. **2.** shape like a dome. **3.** rise or swell as a dome does. [< F < Pr. < LL, roof, house, < Gk. *doma*]

do·mes·tic (də·mes′tik), *adj.* **1.** of the home, household, or family affairs. **2.** fond of home and family life. **3.** not wild; tame. **4.** of one's own country; native. **5.** made in one's own country; not foreign. —*n.* servant in a household. [< L, ult. < *domus* house] —**do·mes′ti·cal·ly,** *adv.*

do·mes·ti·cate (də·mes′tə·kāt), *v.,* **-cat·ed, -cat·ing.** **1.** change (animals, savages, or plants) from a wild to a tame state; tame. **2.** make fond of home and family life. **3.** naturalize. —**do·mes′ti·ca′tion,** *n.*

do·mes·tic·i·ty (dō′mes·tis′ə·ti), *n., pl.* **-ties.** **1.** home and family life. **2.** fondness for home and family life.

dom·i·cile (dom′ə·səl; -sīl), *n., v.,* **-ciled, -cil·ing.** —*n.* **1.** house; home; residence. **2.** place of permanent residence. —*v.* **1.** settle in a domicile. **2.** dwell; reside. [< F < L *domicilium* < *domus* house + *colere* dwell] —**dom·i·cil·i·ar·y** (dom′ə·sil′i·er′i), *adj.*

dom·i·cil·i·ate (dom′ə·sil′i·āt), *v.,* **-at·ed, -at·ing.** domicile. —**dom′i·cil′i·a′tion,** *n.*

dom·i·nance (dom′ə·nəns), **dom·i·nan·cy** (-nən·si), *n., pl.* **-ces, -cies.** a being dominant; rule; control.

dom·i·nant (dom′ə·nənt), *adj.* **1.** most influential; ruling. **2.** occupying a commanding position. **3.** *Music.* based on or pertaining to the dominant. **4.** *Biol.* of a characteristic that reappears in a larger number of offspring than a contrasting characteristic. —*n. Music.* the fifth

note in a scale. —**dom′i·nant·ly,** *adv.* —**Syn.** *adj.* **1.** governing, controlling.

dom·i·nate (dom′ə·nāt), *v.,* **-nat·ed, -nat·ing.** **1.** control or rule by strength or power. **2.** rise high above; hold a commanding position over. [< L, < *dominus* lord, master] —**dom′i·na′tive,** *adj.* —**dom′i·na′tor,** *n.*

dom·i·na·tion (dom′ə·nā′shən), *n.* act or fact of dominating; control; rule.

dom·i·neer (dom′ə·nir′), *v.* rule (over) at one's own will; tyrannize. [< Du. < F < L *dominari.* See DOMINATE.]

dom·i·neer·ing (dom′ə·nir′ing), *adj.* inclined to domineer; arrogant. —**dom′i·neer′ing·ly,** *adv.* —**dom′i·neer′ing·ness,** *n.*

Dom·i·nic (dom′ə·nik), *n.* Saint, 1170–1221, Spanish priest who founded an order called the Dominican order.

Do·min·i·can (də·min′ə·kən), *adj.* **1.** of Saint Dominic or the religious order founded by him. **2.** of the Dominican Republic. —*n.* **1.** friar or nun belonging to the Dominican order. **2.** native or inhabitant of the Dominican Republic.

Dominican Republic, republic in the E part of the island of Hispaniola (Haiti), in the West Indies. Also, **Santo Domingo.**

dom·i·nie (dom′ə·ni; *for 2, also* dō′mə·ni), *n.* **1.** *Esp. Scot.* schoolmaster. **2.** clergyman. [< L *domine* (vocative) lord, master]

do·min·ion (də·min′yən), *n.* **1.** supreme authority; rule; control. **2.** territory under the control of one ruler or government. **3.** a self-governing territory. [< obs. F < Med.L *dominio,* alter. of L *dominium* ownership]

Dominion Day, July 1, a national holiday in Canada in honor of the establishment of the Dominion of Canada in 1867.

dom·i·no[1] (dom′ə·nō), *n., pl.* **-noes, -nos.** a loose cloak with a small mask covering the upper part of the face, worn esp. at masquerades. [< F < L *dominus* lord, master]

dom·i·no[2] (dom′ə·nō), *n., pl.* **-noes.** **1.** dominoes (*sing. in use*), game played with flat, oblong pieces having dots marked on one side. **2.** one of these pieces.

don[1] (don), *n.* **1.** Don, Mr.; Sir (a Spanish title). **2.** a Spanish lord or gentleman. **3.** a distinguished person. **4.** *Colloq.* head, fellow, or tutor of a college at Oxford or Cambridge University. [< Sp. < L *dominus* lord, master]

don[2] (don), *v.,* **donned, don·ning.** put on (clothing, etc.). [contraction of *do on*]

Don (don), *n.* river flowing from C Soviet Union into the Sea of Azov.

Do·ña (dō′nyä), *n.* **1.** Lady; Madam (a Spanish title). **2.** doña, a Spanish lady. [< Sp. < L *domina* mistress]

do·nate (dō′nāt), *v.,* **-nat·ed, -nat·ing.** *Am.* give; contribute. [< L, < *donum* gift]

do·na·tion (dō·nā′shən), *n.* **1.** act of giving or contributing. **2.** gift; contribution.

done (dun), *adj.* **1.** completed; finished; ended. **2.** *Colloq.* worn out; exhausted. **3.** cooked enough. —*v.* pp. of *do*.

Do·nets (dō·nets′), *n.* river in S Soviet Union that flows into the Don.

don·jon (dun′jən; don′-), *n.* a large, strongly fortified tower of a castle. [var. of *dungeon*]

Don Juan (don′ wän′; jü′ən), **1.** a legendary Spanish nobleman who led a dissolute life. **2.** person leading an immoral life.

don·key (dong′ki; dung′-), *n., pl.* **-keys. 1.** a small animal somewhat like a horse but with longer ears, a shorter mane, and a tuft of hair on the end of its tail. **2.** a stubborn person. **3.** a silly or stupid person.

donkey engine, a small steam engine.

don·na (don′ə), *n.* **1.** a lady. **2.** Donna, title of respect; Madam. [< Ital. < L *domina* mistress]

Donne (dun), *n.* John, 1573–1631, English poet.

do·nor (dō′nər), *n.* person who contributes; giver. [< AF < L *donator* < *donare* DONATE] —**do′nor·ship,** *n.*

Don Qui·xo·te (don′ ki·hō′tē; kwik′sət), **1.** story by Cervantes that satirized chivalric romances. It was published in two parts in 1605 and 1615. **2.** its hero.

don't (dōnt), do not. ► Don't is universally used in conversation and often in informal writing when *do not* would seem too emphatic or when rhythm seems more comfortable with the shorter form. In substandard usage *don't* = *doesn't*, and the usage often finds its way into familiar speech and even into casual writing: *he don't look as well as he used to.* Educated speakers and writers avoid it.

doo·dad (dü′dad), *n. Am., Colloq.* a fancy, trifling ornament.

doo·dle (dü′dəl), *v.,* –dled, –dling, *n. Am.* —*v.* make drawings, etc., while talking or thinking. —*n.* 1. a meaningless drawing or mark. 2. a silly person; simpleton.

doo·dle·bug[1] (dü′dəl·bug′), *n. Am.* larva of the ant lion.

doo·dle·bug[2] (dü′dəl·bug′), *n.* 1. *Am., Colloq.* any of various devices with which it is claimed mineral and oil deposits can be located. 2. *Colloq.* buzz bomb.

doom (düm), *n.* 1. fate. 2. an unhappy or terrible fate; ruin; death. 3. judgment; sentence. —*v.* 1. fate. 2. destine to an unhappy or terrible fate. 3. ordain or fix as a sentence or fate: *the emperor will doom her death.* [OE *dōm* law, judgment] —**Syn.** *n.* 1. destiny, lot, portion.

dooms·day (dümz′dā′), *n.* end of the world; day of God's final judgment of mankind.

door (dôr; dōr), *n.* 1. a movable part to close an opening in a wall. A door turns on hinges or slides open and shut. 2. any movable part that suggests a door. 3. an opening where a door is; doorway. 4. room, house, or building to which a door belongs: *his house is three doors down the street.* 5. way to get something. [OE *duru*]

door·bell (dôr′bel′; dōr′–), *n.* bell to be rung on the outside of a door as a signal that someone wishes to have the door opened.

door·jamb (dôr′jam′; dōr′–), **door·post** (–pōst′), *n.* the upright piece forming the side of a doorway.

door·keep·er (dôr′kēp′ər; dōr′–), *n.* 1. person who guards a door or entrance. 2. doorman.

door·knob (dôr′nob′; dōr′–), *n.* handle on a door.

door·man (dôr′mən; –man′; dōr′–), *n., pl.* –men. 1. man whose work is opening the door of a hotel, store, apartment house, etc., for people going in or out. 2. man who guards a door.

door·nail (dôr′nāl′; dōr′–), *n.* 1. nail with a large head. 2. dead as a doornail, entirely dead.

door·sill (dôr′sil′; dōr′–), *n.* threshold.

door·step (dôr′step′; dōr′–), *n.* step leading from an outside door to the ground.

door·way (dôr′wā′; dōr′–), *n.* an opening in a wall where a door is.

door·yard (dôr′yärd′; dōr′–), *n. Am.* yard near the door of a house; yard around a house.

dope (dōp), *n., v.,* doped, dop·ing. —*n.* 1. *Am., Slang.* a. a harmful, narcotic drug, such as opium, morphine, etc. b. a drug addict. 2. oil, grease, etc., used to make machinery run smoothly. 3. varnish put on the cloth parts of an airplane to make them stronger, waterproof, and airtight. 4. *Racing Slang.* drug, e.g. Adrenalin, given to a horse to stimulate it. 5. *Am., Slang.* information; forecast; prediction. 6. *U.S. Slang.* a very stupid person. —*v.* 1. *Am., Slang.* apply or give dope to. 2. use dope. 3. *Am., Slang.* work out; forecast; predict. [< Du. *doop* dipping sauce < *doopen* dip] —*dop′er, n. Slang.*

Do·ré (dô·rā′), *n.* Paul Gustave, 1832?–1883, French illustrator, painter, and sculptor.

Dor·ic (dôr′ik; dor′–), *adj.* of or having to do with the oldest or simplest of the Greek kinds of architecture.

Doric capital

dorm (dôrm), *n. Am., Colloq.* dormitory.

dor·man·cy (dôr′mən·si), *n.* dormant state.

dor·mant (dôr′mənt), *adj.* 1. sleeping. 2. quiet as if asleep. 3. inactive. Plant bulbs stay dormant during the cold of winter. [< OF, ppr. of *dormir* sleep < L *dormire*]

dor·mer (dôr′mər), *n.* 1. Also, dormer window. an upright window that projects from a sloping roof. 2. the projecting part of a roof that contains such a window. [< OF < L *dormitorium* DORMITORY]

dor·mi·to·ry (dôr′mə·tō′ri; –tô′–), *n., pl.* –ries. 1. *U.S.* a building with many sleeping rooms. 2. a sleeping room containing several beds. [< L, < *dormire* sleep]

dor·mouse (dôr′mous′), *n., pl.* –mice. a small animal that looks somewhat like a squirrel and sleeps all winter.

dor·sal (dôr′səl), *adj.* of, on, or near the back. [< LL < L *dorsum* back] —*dor′sal·ly, adv.*

Dor·set (dôr′sit), or **Dor·set·shire** (–shir; –shər), *n.* county in S England.

Dort·mund (dôrt′múnt), *n.* city in W Germany.

do·ry (dô′ri; dō′–), *n., pl.* –ries. *Am.* rowboat with a flat bottom and high sides. [< Central Am. Ind.]

dos·age (dōs′ij), *n.* 1. amount of a medicine to be taken at one time. 2. the giving of medicine in doses.

dose (dōs), *n., v.,* dosed, dos·ing. —*n.* 1. amount of a medicine to be given or taken at one time. 2. amount of anything given at one time as a remedy, treatment, etc. —*v.* give medicine to in doses; treat with medicine. [< F < L < Gk. *dosis* a giving < *didonai* give] —*dos′er, n.*

dos·si·er (dos′i·ā; –i·ər), *n.* collection of documents about some subject. [< F]

dost (dust), *v. Archaic.* do.

Dos·to·ev·ski (dos′tə·yef′ski), *n.* Feodor, 1821–1881, Russian novelist.

dot[1] (dot), *n., v.,* dot·ted, dot·ting. —*n.* 1. a tiny round mark; very small spot; point. 2. a small spot. 3. *Music.* a point after a note or rest that makes it half again as long. 4. a short sound used in sending messages by telegraph or radio. 5. on the dot, *Colloq.* at exactly the right time. —*v.* 1. mark with a dot or dots. 2. be here and there in. [OE *dott* head of a boil] —*dot′ter, n.*

dot[2] (dot), *n. Law.* dowry. [< F < L *dos*] —*do·tal* (dō′təl), *adj.*

dot·age (dōt′ij), *n.* weak-minded and childish condition caused by old age. [< *dote*]

do·tard (dō′tərd), *n.* person who is weak-minded and childish because of old age. [< *dote*]

dote (dōt), *v.,* dot·ed, dot·ing. 1. be weak-minded and childish because of old age. 2. dote on or upon, be foolishly fond of. [ME *doten*] —*dot′er, n.* —*dot′ing, adj.* —*dot′ing·ly, adv.*

doth (duth), *v. Archaic.* does.

dot·ty (dot′i), *adj.,* –ti·er, –ti·est. 1. *Esp. Brit. Colloq.* half-witted; partly insane. 2. *Colloq.* unsteady; shaky; feeble. 3. full of dots.

Dou·ai, Dou·ay (dü·ā′), *n.* town in N France.

Douay Bible or **Version,** an English translation of the Latin Vulgate Bible, made by a group of Roman Catholics. The New Testament was published at Reims in 1582, the Old Testament at Douai in 1609–1610.

dou·ble (dub′əl), *adj., adv., n., v.,* –bled, –bling. —*adj.* 1. twice as much, as many, as large, as strong, etc. 2. for two. 3. made of two like parts: *double doors.* 4. *Music.* having two beats (or some multiple of two) to the measure. 5. made of two unlike parts; combining two in one. *Bear* has a double meaning: *carry* and *animal.* 6. insincere; deceitful; false. 7. *Bot.* having more than one set of petals. —*adv.* 1. twice. 2. two together. —*n.* 1. number or amount that is twice as much. 2. person or thing just like another. 3. in motion pictures, a person who acts in the place of a leading actor or actress. 4. a fold; bend. 5. a sharp backward bend or turn; shift. 6. the next quickest step to a run. 7. *Am.* hit by which a batter gets to second base in baseball. 8. act of doubling a bid in bridge. 9. doubles, game with two players on each side. 10. on the double, a. quickly. b. *Mil.* in double time. —*v.* 1. make twice as much or twice as many. 2. become twice as much or as many. 3. be used for another; be the double of. 4. serve two purposes; play two parts: *the maid doubled as cook.* 5. fold; bend:

he *doubled his fists in anger.* **6.** bend or turn sharply backward. **7.** go around: *the ship doubled the Cape.* **8.** increase the points or penalties of (an opponent's bid) in bridge. [< OF < L *duplus*] —**dou′ble·ness,** *n.* —**dou′bler,** *n.* —Syn. *adj.* **3.** paired.

double bass, a musical instrument shaped like a cello but much larger, with a very low bass tone; bass viol.

double bassoon, a large bassoon, an octave lower in pitch than the ordinary bassoon.

double boiler, *Am.* pair of cooking pans, one of which fits down into the other.

dou·ble-breast·ed (dub′əl-bres′tid), *adj.* overlapping enough to make two thicknesses across the breast and having two rows of buttons.

dou·ble-cross (dub′əl-krôs′; -kros′), *v. Slang.* promise to do one thing and then do another; be treacherous to. —**dou′ble-cross′er,** *n.*

double cross, act of treachery.

double dagger, mark (‡) used to refer the reader to another section or to a note in a book.

dou·ble-deal·ing (dub′əl-dēl′ing), *n., adj.* pretending to do one thing and then doing another; deceiving. —**dou′ble-deal′er,** *n.*

dou·ble-en·ten·dre (dü·bläN·täN′dra), *n.* word or expression with two meanings. One meaning is often improper. [< obs. F, lit., to be taken two ways]

double entry, system of bookkeeping in which each transaction is written down twice, once on the credit side of the account and once on the debit side.

dou·ble-faced (dub′əl-fāst′), *adj.* **1.** pretending to be what one is not; hypocritical; deceitful. **2.** having two faces or aspects.

dou·ble-head·er (dub′əl-hed′ər), *n. Am.* in baseball, two games on the same day in immediate succession.

dou·ble-park (dub′əl-pärk′), *v. Am.* park (a car, etc.) beside another car which is occupying the area specified for parking. —**dou′ble-park′ing,** *n. Am.*

dou·ble-quick (dub′əl-kwik′), *n.* the next quickest step to a run in marching. —*adj.* very quick. —*adv.* in double-quick time. —*v.* march in double-quick step.

dou·blet (dub′lit), *n.* **1.** a man's close-fitting jacket. **2.** pair of two similar or equal things. **3.** one of a pair. **4.** one of two words in a language, derived from the same original but coming through different routes, as *guard* and *ward.*

Doublet

double talk, speech that is purposely incoherent, but that is made to seem serious by mixing in normal words, intonations, etc.

double time, 1. in the U.S. army, a rate of marching in which 180 paces, each of 3 feet, are taken in a minute. **2.** double-quick.

dou·ble-tree (dub′əl-trē′), *n.* crossbar on a carriage, wagon, plow, etc.

dou·bloon (dub-lün′), *n.* a former Spanish gold coin. [< F *doublon* or < Sp. *doblón* < *doble* DOUBLE]

dou·bly (dub′li), *adv.* **1.** twice; twice as. **2.** two at a time.

doubt (dout), *v.* **1.** not believe; not be sure of; feel uncertain about. **2.** be uncertain. **3.** *Archaic.* be afraid; fear. —*n.* **1.** lack of belief or sureness; uncertainty. **2.** *Obs.* fear; apprehension. **3.** no doubt, a. surely; certainly. b. probably. [< OF *douter* < L *dubitare*] —**doubt′a·ble,** *adj.* —**doubt′er,** *n.* —**doubt′ing·ly,** *adv.* —Syn. *v.* **1.** mistrust, question. —*n.* **1.** misgiving, mistrust. ▶ doubt. The idioms with *doubt* are: **1.** negative (where there is no real doubt), *doubt that: I do not doubt that he means well.* **2.** positive (when doubt exists), *doubt that, whether* (in formal use): *I doubt whether he meant it that way; I doubt that he meant it that way* (indicating unbelief really more than doubt); *if* (in informal use): *I doubt if he meant it that way.*

doubt·ful (dout′fəl), *adj.* **1.** in doubt; not sure; uncertain. **2.** causing doubt; open to question or suspicion. —**doubt′ful·ly,** *adv.* —**doubt′ful-**

ness, *n.* —Syn. **1.** indefinite. **2.** questionable. —Ant. **1.** sure, certain.

doubt·less (dout′lis), *adv.* **1.** surely; certainly. **2.** probably. —*adj.* sure; certain. —**doubt′less·ly,** *adv.* —**doubt′less·ness,** *n.*

douche (düsh), *n., v.,* **douched, douch·ing.** —*n.* **1.** jet of water applied on or into any part of the body. **2.** application of a douche. **3.** spray, syringe, or other device for applying a douche. —*v.* **1.** apply a douche to. **2.** take a douche. [< F < Ital. *doccia,* ult. < L *ducere* lead]

dough (dō), *n.* **1.** a soft, thick mixture of flour, liquid, and other materials for baking. **2.** any soft, thick mass like this. **3.** *Am., Slang.* money. [OE *dāg*]

dough·boy (dō′boi′), *n. Am., Colloq.* an infantryman in the U.S. army.

dough·nut (dō′nut′), *n.* a small, brown cake, usually ring-shaped, cooked in deep fat.

dough·ty (dou′ti), *adj.,* **-ti·er, -ti·est.** *Archaic or Humorous.* brave; valiant; strong. [OE *dohtig* < *dugan* be good] —**dough′ti·ly,** *adv.* —**dough′ti·ness,** *n.*

dough·y (dō′i), *adj.,* **dough·i·er, dough·i·est.** of or like dough.

Doug·las (dug′ləs), *n.* **1.** Stephen A., 1813–1861, American statesman and political leader. **2.** William Orville, born 1898, associate justice of the United States Supreme Court from 1939.

Douglas fir, *Am.* a very tall evergreen tree common in the western United States.

Doug·lass (dug′ləs), *n.* Frederick, 1817–1895, American Negro leader who opposed slavery.

dour (dür; dour), *adj.* **1.** gloomy; sullen. **2.** *Scot.* stern; severe. **3.** *Scot.* stubborn. [< L *durus* hard, stern]

douse (dous), *v.,* **doused, dous·ing. 1.** plunge into water or any other liquid. **2.** throw water over; extinguish. **3.** *Colloq.* put out (a light); extinguish. **4.** *Colloq.* take off; doff. **5.** lower or slacken (a sail) in haste. **6.** close (a porthole). —**dous′er,** *n.*

dove[1] (duv), *n.* **1.** bird with a thick body, short legs, and a beak enlarged at the tip; pigeon. **2.** Dove, the Holy Ghost. **3.** an innocent, gentle, or loving person. [OE *dufe–;* akin to DIVE]

dove[2] (dōv), *n. U.S. Colloq. and Brit. Dial.* pt. of dive.

dove·cote (duv′kōt′), **dove·cot** (-kot′), *n.* a small shelter for doves or pigeons.

Do·ver (dō′vər), *n.* **1.** seaport in SE England, the nearest English port to France. **2.** Strait of, a narrow channel or strait between N France and SE England. **3.** capital of Delaware.

dove·tail (duv′tāl′), *n.* **1.** projection at the end of a piece of wood, metal, etc., that can be fitted into a corresponding opening at the end of another piece to form a joint. **2.** the joint formed in this way. —*v.* **1.** fasten, join, or fit together with projections that fit into openings. **2.** fit together exactly.

dow·a·ger (dou′ə·jər), *n.* **1.** widow who holds some title or property from her dead husband. **2.** *Colloq.* a dignified, elderly lady. [< OF *douagere* (def. 1) < *douage* DOWER]

dow·dy (dou′di), *adj.,* **-di·er, -di·est,** *n., pl.* **-dies.** —*adj.* poorly dressed; not neat; not stylish; shabby. —*n.* woman whose clothes are dowdy. —**dow′di·ly,** *adv.* —**dow′di·ness,** *n.*

DOWEL

dow·el (dou′əl), *n., v.,* **-eled, -el·ing;** *esp. Brit.* **-elled, -el·ling.** —*n.* peg on a piece of wood, metal, etc., to fit into a corresponding hole on another piece, and so form a joint. —*v.* fasten with dowels.

dow·er (dou′ər), *n.* **1.** a widow's share for life of her dead husband's property. **2.** dowry. **3.** a natural gift, talent, or quality; endowment. —*v.* provide with a dower; endow. [< OF < Med.L *dotarium,* < LL *dotare* endow < L *dos* dowry]

down[1] (doun), *adv.* **1.** from a higher to a lower place or condition. **2.** in a lower place or condition. **3.** to a place or condition thought of as lower: *down South.* **4.** to a position or condition that is difficult, dangerous, etc.: *the dogs ran down the fox.* **5.** from an earlier to a later time or person: *hand down a house.* **6.** from a larger to a smaller amount, degree, etc. **7.** actually; really: *get down to work.* **8.** on paper; in writing: *take down what I say.* **9.** when bought: *you can pay part of the price down and the rest later.* —*prep.* down along, through, or into: *walk down a street.* —*adj.* **1.** in a lower place or condition. **2.** going or pointed down. **3.** sick; ill: *she is down with a cold.* **4.** sad; discouraged: *he felt down about his failure.* **5.** of a football; no longer in play. **6.** behind an opponent by a certain number. —*v.* **1.** put down; get down: *he downed the medicine at one swallow.* **2.** lie down: *down, Fido!* —*n.* **1.** a downward movement. **2.** piece of bad luck. **3.** chance to move a football forward: *a team has four downs to make ten yards.* [var. of *adown*]

down² (doun), *n.* soft feathers or hair; fluff. [< Scand. *dünn*]

down³ (doun), *n.* **1.** mound or ridge of sand heaped up by the wind; dune. **2.** Usually, **downs.** rolling, grassy land. [OE *dūn* hill]

down·cast (doun′kast′; -kȧst′), *adj.* **1.** directed downward. **2.** dejected; sad; discouraged. —*n.* **1.** a downcast look. **2.** a casting down; overthrow; ruin. **3. a.** a drawing or forcing down, esp. of air for ventilation in a mine or the like. **b.** shaft used for this.

down·fall (doun′fôl′), *n.* **1.** overthrow; ruin. **2.** a heavy rain or snow. **3.** a kind of trap in which a weight or missile falls upon the prey. —**down′fall′en,** *adj.*

down·grade (doun′grād′), *n., adj., adv., v.,* -grad·ed, -grad·ing. —*n. Am.* a downward slope. —*adj., adv.* downward. —*v. Am.* move to a lower position with a smaller salary. —**down′grad′ing,** *adj., n. Am.*

down·heart·ed (doun′här′tid), *adj.* dejected. —**down′heart′ed·ly,** *adv.* —**down′heart′ed·ness,** *n.*

down·hill (doun′hil′), *adv.* down the slope of a hill; downward. —*adj.* **1.** sloping downward; tending downward. **2.** worse.

Down·ing Street (doun′ing), **1.** street in London where several important offices of the British government are located. **2.** the British government.

down·pour (doun′pôr′; -pōr′), *n.* a heavy rain.

down·right (doun′rīt′), *adj.* **1.** thorough; complete. **2.** plain; positive. **3.** directed straight downward. —*adv.* **1.** thoroughly; completely. **2.** straight down. —**down′right′ly,** *adv.* —**down′right′ness,** *n.*

down·stairs (doun′stärz′), *adv.* **1.** down the stairs. **2.** on a lower floor. —*adj.* on a lower floor. —*n.* lower floor or floors.

down·stream (doun′strēm′), *adv., adj.* with the current of a stream; down a stream.

down·town, *Am.* the commercial section or main district of a town.

down·town (doun′toun′), *adv., adj.* **1.** to, toward, or in the lower part of a town. **2.** *Am.* to or in the main part of a town.

down·trod·den (doun′trod′ən), **down·trod** (-trod′), *adj.* **1.** oppressed. **2.** trodden down.

down·ward (doun′wərd), *adv.* Also, **down′wards.** toward a lower place or condition. —*adj.* moving or tending toward a lower place or condition. —**down′ward·ly,** *adv.* —**down′ward·ness,** *n.*

down·y (doun′i), *adj.,* down·i·er, down·i·est. **1.** of soft feathers or hair. **2.** covered with soft feathers or hair. **3.** like down; soft; fluffy. —**down′i·ness,** *n.*

dow·ry (dou′ri), *n., pl.* -ries. **1.** money, property, etc., that a woman brings to her husband when she marries him. **2.** a natural gift, talent, or quality. Also, **dower.** [< AF *dowarie*]

dowse (douz), *v.,* dowsed, dows·ing. use a divining rod to locate water, etc. —**dows′er,** *n.*

dox·ol·o·gy (doks·ol′ə·ji), *n., pl.* -gies. hymn or statement praising God. Three of the best-known doxologies begin: "Glory to God in the highest," "Glory be to the Father and to the Son and to the Holy Ghost," and "Praise God from whom all blessings flow." [< Med.L. < Gk., <

doxa glory, praise + -*logos* speaking] —**dox·o·log·i·cal** (dok′sə·loj′ə·kəl), *adj.* —**dox′o·log′i·cal·ly,** *adv.*

Doyle (doil), *n.* Sir Arthur Conan, 1859–1930, English writer of detective stories.

doz., dozen; dozens.

doze (dōz), *v.,* dozed, doz·ing, *n.* —*v.* **1.** sleep lightly; be half asleep. **2.** doze off, fall into a doze. —*n.* a light sleep; a nap. [cf. Dan. *döse* make dull] —**doz′er,** *n.*

doz·en (duz′ən), *n., pl.* -ens or (*after a number*) -en. group of 12. [< OF *dozeine* < *douse* twelve < L *duodecim*] —**doz′enth,** *adj.*

Dr., Dr, Doctor.

dr., 1. debtor. **2.** dram; drams.

drab¹ (drab), *n., adj.* drab·ber, drab·best. —*n.* a dull, brownish gray. —*adj.* **1.** dull; monotonous; unattractive. **2.** dull brownish-gray. [appar. var. of *drap* cloth < F. See DRAPE.] —**drab′ly,** *adv.* —**drab′ness,** *n.*

drab² (drab), *n., v.,* drabbed, drab·bing. —*n.* **1.** a dirty, untidy woman. **2.** prostitute. —*v.* keep company with drabs. [cf. Irish *drabog* slattern]

drachm (dram), *n.* **1.** *Brit.* dram. **2.** drachma.

drach·ma (drak′mə), *n., pl.* -mas, -mae (-mē). **1.** a unit of Greek money. **2.** an ancient Greek silver coin, varying in value. [< L < Gk. *drachme* handful < *drassesthai* grasp]

draft (draft; dräft), *n.* **1.** current of air. **2.** device for regulating a current of air: *the draft of a furnace.* **3.** a plan; a sketch. **4.** a rough copy: *a draft of a speech.* **5.** selection of persons for some special purpose: *in time of war men are often supplied to the army and navy by draft.* **6.** persons selected for some special purpose. **7.** act of pulling loads. **8.** the quantity pulled. **9.** Usually, **draught.** **a.** the pulling in of a net to catch fish. **b.** quantity of fish caught in a net. **10.** a written order from one person or bank to another, requiring the payment of a stated amount of money. **11.** a heavy demand or drain on anything. **12.** Usually, **draught.** depth of water that a ship needs for floating. **13.** Usually, **draught. a.** act of drinking: *he emptied the glass at one draft.* **b.** amount taken in one drink. **c.** breathing in of air, smoke, etc. **d.** air, smoke, etc., breathed in. **e.** drawing beer, ale, etc., from a barrel when ordered. —*v.* **1.** make a plan or sketch of. **2.** write out a rough copy of. **3.** select for some special purpose. —*adj.* **1.** for pulling loads: *a big, strong horse or ox is a draft animal.* **2.** Usually, **draught.** drawn from a barrel when ordered. [var. of *draught*] —**draft′er,** *n.* ➤ See **draught** for usage note.

draft·ee (draf·tē′; dräf-), *n. Am.* person who is drafted for military service.

drafts (drafts; dräfts), *n.pl. U.S.* spelling of **draughts.**

drafts·man (drafts′mən; dräfts′-), *n., pl.* -men. **1.** person who makes plans or sketches, as of buildings and machines. **2.** person who writes out rough copies of documents, speeches, etc. Also, **draughtsman.** —**drafts′man·ship,** *n.*

draft·y (draf′ti; dräf′-), *adj.,* draft·i·er, draft·i·est. **1.** in a current of air. **2.** having many currents of air. **3.** causing a current of air. —**draft′i·ly,** *adv.* —**draft′i·ness,** *n.*

drag (drag), *v.,* dragged, drag·ging, *n.* —*v.* **1.** pull or move along heavily or slowly. **2.** go too slowly. **3.** pull a net, hook, harrow, etc., over or along for some purpose. **4.** be drawn or hauled along; trail on the ground. —*n.* **1.** net, hook, etc., used in dragging. **2.** act of dragging. **3.** thing dragged. **4.** anything that holds back; hindrance. **5.** a low, strong sled for carrying heavy loads. **6.** a heavy harrow to break up ground. **7.** *Am., Slang.* influence. [ME *dragge*(*n*)] —**Syn.** *v.* **1.** haul, tug, trail. —*n.* **4.** impediment, obstruction.

drag·gle (drag′əl), *v.,* -gled, -gling. make or become wet or dirty by dragging through mud, water, dust, etc.

drag·net (drag′net′), *n.* **1.** net pulled over the bottom of a river, pond, etc., or along the ground. **2.** means of catching criminals.

drag·o·man (drag′ə·mən), *n., pl.* -mans,

āge, cāre, fär; ēqual, tėrm; īce; ōpen, ôrder; pūt, rūle, ūse; тн, then; ə=a in about.

—men. in the Orient, an interpreter. [< F < Ital. < Med.Gk. < Ar. < Aram. < Assyrian-Babylonian *targumânu*]

drag·on (drag′ən), *n.* 1. a huge, fierce animal supposed to look like a snake with wings and claws, often breathing out fire and smoke. 2. a very strict and watchful woman, esp. a stern chaperon. [< OF < L < Gk. *drakon*]

drag·on·fly (drag′ən·flī′), *n., pl.* –flies. a large, harmless insect, with a long, slender body and two pairs of gauzy wings, that catches flies, mosquitoes, etc.

Dragonfly (½ to 4 in. long)

dra·goon (drə·gün′), *n.* soldier who fights on horseback. —*v.* 1. oppress or persecute by dragoons. 2. compel by oppression or persecution. [< F *dragon* DRAGON, pistol, (later) soldier]

drag race, *Am., Slang.* a race to test acceleration, in which two cars compete over a measured distance (**drag strip**), usually a quarter of a mile. —**drag′·rac′er,** *n.*

drain (drān), *v.* 1. draw off or flow off slowly. 2. empty or dry by draining. 3. use up little by little; deprive. —*n.* 1. channel or pipe for carrying off water or other liquid. 2. anything that drains. 3. a slow leaking away. [OE *drēahnian;* akin to DRY] —**drain′a·ble,** *adj.* —**drain′er,** *n.*

drain·age (drān′ij), *n.* 1. act or process of draining. 2. system of channels or pipes for carrying off water or waste of any kind. 3. what is drained off. 4. area that is drained.

drainage basin, *Am.* area that is drained by a river and its tributaries.

drain·pipe (drān′pīp′), *n.* pipe for carrying off water or other liquid.

drake (drāk), *n.* a male duck. [ME]

Drake (drāk), *n.* Sir Francis, 1540?–1596, English admiral.

dram (dram), *n.* 1. a small weight. In apothecaries′ weight, 8 drams make one ounce; in avoirdupois weight, 16 drams make one ounce. 2. a fluid dram. 3. *Esp. Brit.* a small drink of intoxicating liquor. 4. *Esp. Brit.* a small amount of anything. Also, *Brit.* **drachm.** [< OF < L *drachma* DRACHMA]

dra·ma (drä′mə; dram′ə), *n.* 1. story written to be acted out by actors on a stage. 2. series of happenings that seem like those of a play. 3. the drama, the art of writing, acting, or producing plays. [< LL < Gk., play, deed < *draein* do]

Dram·a·mine (dram′ə·mēn), *n. Trademark.* drug used as a remedy for seasickness, etc.

dra·mat·ic (drə·mat′ik), *adj.* 1. of drama; having to do with plays. 2. seeming like a drama or play; exciting. —**dra·mat′i·cal·ly,** *adv.*

dra·mat·ics (drə·mat′iks), *n.* 1. (*sing. or pl. in use*) art of acting or producing plays. 2. (*pl. in use*) plays given by amateurs.

dram·a·tis per·so·nae (dram′ə·tis pər·sō′nē), characters or actors in a play. [< L]

dram·a·tist (dram′ə·tist), *n.* writer of plays; playwright.

dram·a·tize (dram′ə·tīz), *v.,* –tized, –tiz·ing. 1. make a drama of; arrange in the form of a play. 2. show or express in a dramatic way. —**dram′a·ti·za′tion,** *n.* —**dram′a·tiz′er,** *n.*

dram·a·tur·gy (dram′ə·tėr′ji), *n.* art of writing or producing dramas. [< Gk. *dramatourgia* < *drama* DRAMA + –*ourgos* making < *ergon* work] —**dram′a·tur′gic,** **dram′a·tur′gi·cal,** *adj.* —**dram′a·tur′gist,** *n.*

dram·shop (dram′shop′), *n. Esp. Brit.* place where intoxicating liquor is sold; saloon.

drank (drangk), *v.* pt. of drink.

drape (drāp), *v.,* draped, drap·ing, *n.* —*v.* 1. cover or hang with cloth falling loosely in folds. 2. arrange (clothes, hangings, etc.) in graceful folds. 3. fall in folds. —*n.* cloth hung in graceful folds; hanging. [< F < drap cloth < LL *drappus* cloth]

drap·er (drāp′ər), *n.* 1. *Esp Brit.* dealer in cloth or dry goods. 2. person that drapes.

dra·per·y (drā′pər·i), *n., pl.* –per·ies. 1. clothing or hangings arranged in graceful folds. 2. graceful arrangement of hangings or clothing. 3. cloth or fabric.

dras·tic (dras′tik), *adj.* acting with force or violence; extreme. [< Gk. *drastikos* effective < *draein* do] —**dras′ti·cal·ly,** *adv.*

draught (draft; dräft), *n., v., adj.* draft. [ME *draht* < OE *dragan* draw] —**draught′er,** *n.* ▶

draft, draught. The spelling of *draught* (from the Old English *dragan,* to draw) has gradually come to represent its pronunciation (draft). *Draft* is always the spelling for a *bank draft,* the *military draft,* a *draft of a composition,* a *draft of air;* usage is divided on the word in the sense of a maker of drawings — *draftsman* or *draughtsman; draught* is more common for a *ship's draught,* a *draught of fish,* and for a *draught of ale* or *beer on draught* — though *draft* is rapidly gaining in this last sense.

draughts (drafts; dräfts), *n.pl. Brit.* (*sing. in use*) game of checkers.

draughts·man (drafts′mən; dräfts′–), *n., pl.* –men. draftsman. —**draughts′man·ship,** *n.*

drave (drāv), *v. Archaic.* pt. of drive.

Dra·vid·i·an (drə·vid′i·ən), *adj.* of or having to do with the non-Aryan races in southern India and in Ceylon. —*n.* 1. member of any of these races. 2. languages spoken by them.

draw (drô), *v.,* drew, drawn, draw·ing, *n.* —*v.* 1. pull; drag: *a horse draws a wagon.* 2. pull out; pull up; pull back: *he drew his hand from his pocket.* 3. bring out; take out; get out: *draw a pail of water from the well.* 4. take out a pistol, sword, etc., for action. 5. take; get; receive: *I drew another idea from the story.* 6. make; cause; bring: *your actions draw praise or blame on yourself.* 7. move; come; go: *we drew near the fire to get warm.* 8. attract: *a parade draws a crowd.* 9. make a picture or likeness of with pencil, pen, chalk, crayon, etc.; represent by lines. 10. write out in proper form; frame; draft. 11. write (an order to pay money). 12. make a demand; be a drain. 13. make a current of air to carry off smoke: *a chimney draws.* 14. breathe in; inhale; take in. 15. utter: *draw a sigh.* 16. make the same score in; finish with neither side winning. 17. make or become longer; stretch. 18. make or become smaller; shrink. 19. make (wire) by pulling a rod of metal through a succession of holes of decreasing diameter. 20. (of a ship) need for floating; sink to a depth of. 21. take out the insides of. 22. make (tea) by extracting the essence. 23. steep: *the tea is drawing.* 24. draw up, a. arrange in order. b. write out. c. stop. —*n.* 1. act of drawing. 2. thing that attracts. 3. a tie in a game. 4. *Am.* part of a drawbridge that can be moved. 5. a drawing of lots. 6. the lot drawn. 7. a land basin into or through which water drains; valley. [OE *dragan*] —**Syn.** *v.* 1. haul, tug. 3. extract. 5. obtain, derive, infer. 8. entice, allure. 9. trace, sketch, depict. 10. formulate. 17. lengthen, prolong.

draw·back (drô′bak′), *n.* 1. something unfavorable or unpleasant; disadvantage; hindrance. 2. *Am.* money paid back from a charge made.

draw·bridge (drô′brij′), *n.* bridge that can be wholly or partly lifted, lowered, or moved to one side.

draw·ee (drô·ē′), *n.* person for whom an order to pay money is written.

drawer (drôr *for* 1; drô′ər *for* 2 *and* 3), *n.* 1. box that slides in and out of a chest, desk, table, etc. 2. person or thing that draws. 3. person who writes an order to pay money. 4. **drawers** (drôrz), undergarment fitting over the legs and around the waist.

draw·ing (drô′ing), *n.* 1. picture or likeness made with pencil, pen, chalk, crayon, etc.; lines representing a person or thing. 2. the making of such pictures or likenesses. 3. act of a person or thing that draws anything.

drawing room, 1. room for receiving or entertaining guests; parlor. 2. *Am.* a private compartment in a Pullman car. [for *withdrawing room*]

draw·knife (drô′nīf′), or **drawing knife,** *n., pl.* –knives. blade with a handle at each end, used to shave off surfaces. Also, **drawshave.**

drawl (drôl), *v.* talk in a slow, lazy way. —*n.* a slow, lazy way of talking. [appar. akin to DRAW] —**drawl′er,** *n.* —**drawl′ing·ly,** *adv.*

drawn (drôn), *v.* pp. of **draw**.

drawn work, ornamental work done by drawing threads from a fabric, the remaining portions usually being formed into patterns by needlework.

draw·shave (drô'shāv'), *n.* drawknife.

dray (drā), *n.* a low, strong cart for hauling heavy loads. —*v.* transport or carry on a cart. [OE *dræg-* drag < *dragan* draw]

dray·age (drā'ij), *n.* 1. act of hauling a load on a dray. 2. *Am.* charge for hauling a load on a dray.

dray·man (drā'mən), *n., pl.* **-men.** man who drives a dray.

dread (dred), *v.* look forward to with fear. —*n.* 1. fear, esp. fear of something that will happen or may happen. 2. person or thing inspiring fear. 3. awe. —*adj.* 1. dreaded; dreadful. 2. held in awe; awe-inspiring. [OE *drǣdan*] —Syn. *v.* apprehend.

dread·ful (dred'fəl), *adj.* 1. causing dread; awe-inspiring. 2. *Colloq.* very bad; very unpleasant. —**dread'ful·ly,** *adv.* —**dread'ful·ness,** *n.* —Syn. 1. fearful, terrible, dire.

dread·nought, dread·naught (dred'nôt'), *n.* a big, powerful battleship with heavy armor and large guns.

dream (drēm), *n., v.,* **dreamed** or **dreamt** (dremt), **dream·ing.** —*n.* 1. something thought, felt, seen, or heard during sleep. 2. something as unreal as a dream. 3. state in which a person has dreams. 4. something having great beauty or charm. —*v.* 1. have dreams. 2. think of (something) as possible; imagine. 3. spend in dreaming. 4. dream up, *Colloq.* create (an invention, etc.) mentally. [OE *drēam* joy, music] —**dream'er,** *n.* —**dream'ing·ly,** *adv.* —**dream'less,** *adj.* —Syn. *n.* 2. vision, fantasy.

dream·y (drēm'i), *adj.,* **dream·i·er, dream·i·est.** 1. full of dreams. 2. like a dream; vague; dim: *a dreamy recollection.* 3. impractical: *a dreamy person.* 4. causing dreams; soothing. —**dream'i·ly,** *adv.* —**dream'i·ness,** *n.*

drear (drir), *adj. Poetic.* dreary.

drear·y (drir'i), *adj.,* **drear·i·er, drear·i·est.** 1. dull; gloomy; cheerless; depressing. 2. *Archaic.* sad; sorrowful. [OE *drēorig*] —**drear'i·ly,** *adv.* —**drear'i·ness,** *n.* —Syn. 1. tedious, tiresome, dismal.

dredge¹ (drej), *n., v.,* **dredged, dredg·ing.** —*n.* 1. machine with a scoop or series of buckets for removing mud, sand, or other materials from the bottom of a river, harbor, etc. 2. apparatus with a net, used for gathering oysters, etc. —*v.* 1. clean out or deepen (a channel, harbor, etc.) with a dredge. 2. bring up or gather with a dredge. [ME *dreg;* akin to DRAG] —**dredg'er,** *n.*

dredge² (drej), *v.,* **dredged, dredg·ing.** sprinkle: *dredge meat with flour.* [appar. < *dredge,* n., grain mixture] —**dredg'er,** *n.*

dreg (dreg), *n.* Usually, **dregs.** 1. solid bits of matter that settle to the bottom of a liquid. 2. the most worthless part. [< Scand. *dreggjar*] —**dreg'gy,** *adj.*

Drei·ser (drī'sər; -zər), *n.* Theodore, 1871-1945, American novelist.

drench (drench), *v.* wet thoroughly; soak. —*n.* 1. a thorough wetting; a soaking. 2. something that drenches. 3. solution for soaking. [OE *drencan < drincan* drink] —**drench'er,** *n.*

Dres·den (drez'dən), *n.* city in C Germany, on the Elbe River.

dress (dres), *n., adj., v.,* **dressed** or **drest, dress·ing.** —*n.* 1. the outer garment worn by women, girls, and babies. 2. an outer covering. 3. clothes. 4. formal clothes. [< v.] —*adj.* 1. of or for a dress. 2. of formal dress; characterized by formal dress. [< v.] —*v.* 1. put clothes on. 2. put formal clothes on. 3. decorate; trim; adorn. 4. make ready for use; prepare. 5. cultivate (land). 6. comb, brush, and arrange (hair). 7. put a medicine, bandage, etc., on (a wound or sore). 8. form in a straight line: *the captain ordered the soldiers to dress their ranks.* 9. smooth; finish: *dress leather.* 10. dress down, a. scold; rebuke. b. beat; thrash. 11. dress up, a. put best

clothes on. b. put formal clothes on. [< OF *dresser* arrange, ult. < L *directus* straight. See DIRECT.] —Syn. *n.* 1. frock, gown. 3. clothing, attire, apparel, garments, garb, raiment. —*v.* 1. attire, garb, clothe.

dress·er¹ (dres'ər), *n.* person who dresses (himself, another person, a shop window, or a wound).

dress·er² (dres'ər), *n.* 1. *Am.* piece of furniture with a mirror and drawers for clothes; bureau. 2. piece of furniture with shelves for dishes. 3. table on which to get food ready for serving. [< early F *dresseur.* See DRESS.]

dress·ing (dres'ing), *n.* 1. what is put on or in something to get it ready for use. 2. sauce for salads, fish, meat, etc. 3. a stuffing of bread crumbs, seasoning, etc., for chicken, turkey, etc. 4. medicine, bandage, etc., put on a wound or sore. 5. fertilizer. 6. *Colloq.* a scolding or beating. 7. any act or process of dressing.

dress·ing-down (dres'ing-doun'), *n. Colloq.* 1. a scolding; rebuke. 2. a beating; a thrashing.

dressing gown, a loose robe worn while dressing or resting.

dress·mak·er (dres'māk'ər), *n.* person whose work is making dresses, etc. —*adj.* of women's apparel, characterized by delicate or flowing lines and decoration. —**dress'mak'ing,** *n.*

dress parade, a formal parade of soldiers or sailors in dress uniform.

dress rehearsal, rehearsal of a play with costumes and scenery just as for a regular performance.

dress suit, a formal suit worn by men in the evening.

dress·y (dres'i), *adj.,* **dress·i·er, dress·i·est.** *Colloq.* 1. fond of wearing showy clothes. 2. stylish; fashionable. —**dress'i·ness,** *n.*

drest (drest), *v.* pt. and pp. of **dress**.

drew (drü), *v.* pt. of **draw**.

Drey·fus (drā'fəs; drī'-), *n.* Alfred, 1859-1935, French army officer of Jewish birth who was convicted of treason in 1894 but was proved innocent in 1906.

drib·ble (drib'əl), *v.,* **-bled, -bling,** *n.* —*v.* 1. flow or let flow in drops, small amounts, etc.; trickle. 2. let saliva run from the mouth. 3. move (a ball) along by bouncing it or giving it short kicks. —*n.* 1. a dropping; dripping; trickle. 2. a very light rain. 3. act of dribbling a ball. [< *drib,* var. of *drip*] —**drib'bler,** *n.*

drib·let, drib·blet (drib'lit), *n.* a small amount.

dried (drīd), *v.* pt. and pp. of **dry**.

dri·er (drī'ər), *adj.* comparative of **dry**. —*n.* 1. person or thing that dries. 2. Also, **dryer.** a. device or machine that removes water by heat, air, etc. b. substance put in paint, varnish, etc., to make it dry more quickly.

drift (drift), *v.* 1. carry or be carried along, as by currents of water or air: *the wind drifted the boat onto the rocks.* 2. go along without knowing or caring where one is going. 3. heap or be heaped up, as by the wind: *the snow is drifting badly, the wind is so strong it's drifting the snow.* [< n.] —*n.* 1. a drifting. 2. direction of drifting. 3. tendency; trend. 4. direction of thought; meaning. 5. snow, sand, etc., heaped up by the wind. 6. current of water or air caused by the wind. 7. a driving movement or force. 8. current; flow. 9. distance that a ship or aircraft is off its course because of currents. 10. sand, gravel, rocks, etc., moved from one place and left in another by a river, glacier, etc. 11. an almost horizontal passageway in a mine along a vein of ore, coal, etc. [ME, a driving, < OE *drīfan* DRIVE] —Syn. *v.* 1. float. —*n.* 4. intent. 7. impulse, impetus, pressure.

drift·age (drif'tij), *n.* 1. a drifting. 2. the distance drifted. 3. what has drifted.

drift·wood (drift'wůd'), *n.* wood drifting in the water or washed ashore by water.

Drill
(def. 1)

drill¹ (dril), *n.* **1.** tool or machine for boring holes. See picture on p. 253. **2.** method of teaching or training by having the learners do a thing over and over again. **3.** group instruction and training in physical exercises or in marching, handling a gun, etc. **4.** *Am.* snail that bores into and destroys oysters. —*v.* **1.** bore a hole in; pierce with a drill. **2.** teach by having learners do a thing over and over again. **3.** do or cause to do military or physical exercises. [< Du. *dril* = *drillen* to bore] —drill′er, *n.* —Syn. *n.* 2. exercise, practice.

drill² (dril), *n.* **1.** machine for planting seeds in rows. **2.** a small furrow to plant seeds in. **3.** row of planted seeds. —*v.* plant in small furrows. —drill′er, *n.*

drill³ (dril), *n.* a strong, twilled cotton or linen cloth, used for overalls, linings, etc. [short for *drilling* < G *drillich* < L *trilix* of three threads < *tri-* three + *licium* thread]

drill⁴ (dril), *n.* baboon of western Africa, smaller than the mandrill. [prob. < African name]

drill·mas·ter (dril′mas′tər; -mäs′-), *n.* **1.** officer who drills soldiers in marching, handling guns, etc. **2.** person who drills others in anything.

dri·ly (drī′li), *adv.* dryly.

drink (dringk), *v.,* **drank** or (*formerly*) **drunk**; **drunk** or (*formerly as pred. adj.*) **drunk·en**; **drink·ing.** —*v.* **1.** swallow (liquid). **2.** take and hold; absorb: *the dry ground drank up the rain.* **3.** drink alcoholic liquor. **4.** drink in honor of. **5.** drink to, drink in honor of. —*n.* **1.** liquid swallowed or to be swallowed. **2.** alcoholic liquor. **3.** too much drinking of alcoholic liquor. [OE *drincan*] —drink′a·ble, *adj., n.* —drink′er, *n.*

Drink·wa·ter (dringk′wô′tər; -wot′ər), *n.* John, 1882–1937, English dramatist and critic.

drip (drip), *v.,* **dripped** or **dript** (dript), **drip·ping,** *n.* —*v.* **1.** fall or let fall in drops. **2.** be so wet that drops fall. —*n.* **1.** a falling in drops. **2.** liquid that falls in drops. **3.** part that projects to keep water off the parts below. [OE *dryppan* < *dropa* a drop]

drip·ping (drip′ing), *n.* **1.** function of a thing which drips. **2.** drippings, **a.** liquids that have dripped down. **b.** melted fat and juices that drip down from meat while roasting.

drive (drīv), *v.,* **drove** or (*Archaic*) **drave,** **driv·en, driv·ing,** *n.* —*v.* **1.** make go: *grief drove her insane.* **2.** force (into or out of some place, condition, act, etc.): *hunger drove him to steal.* **3.** direct the movement of (an automobile, vehicle drawn by a horse, etc.). **4.** go or carry in an automobile, carriage, etc. **5.** work hard or compel to work hard. **6.** dash or rush with force. **7.** carry out with vigor; bring about: *drive a bargain.* **8.** hit very hard and fast: *drive a golf ball.* **9.** aim; strike. **10.** get or make by drilling, boring, etc.: *drive a well.* **11.** drive at, mean; intend. —*n.* **1.** trip in an automobile, carriage, etc. **2.** road to drive on. **3.** vigor; energy. **4.** an impelling force; pressure: *the craving for approval is a strong drive in mankind.* **5.** a special effort of a group for some purpose: *the town had a drive to get money for charity.* **6.** a very hard, fast hit. **7.** *Mil.* an attack. **8.** a driving. **9.** thing or things driven: *a drive of logs.* **10.** the driving mechanism for an automobile, machine, etc. [OE *drīfan*] —Syn. *v.* 2. impel, push, compel. 3. steer.

drive-in (drīv′in′), *n. Am.* place where customers may make purchases, eat, attend movies, etc., while seated in their cars.

driv·el (driv′əl), *v.,* **-eled, -el·ing;** *esp. Brit.* **-elled, -el·ling,** *n.* —*v.* **1.** let saliva run from the mouth. **2.** flow like saliva running from the mouth. **3.** talk or say in a stupid, foolish manner; talk silly nonsense. **4.** waste (time, energy, etc.) in a stupid, foolish way. —*n.* **1.** saliva running from the mouth. **2.** stupid, foolish talk; silly nonsense. [OE *dreflian*] —driv′el·er, *esp. Brit.* driv′el·ler, *n.*

driv·en (driv′ən), *v.* pp. of **drive.** —*adj.* carried along and gathered into heaps by the wind.

driv·er (drīv′ər), *n.* **1.** person or thing that drives. **2.** person who directs the movement of an engine, automobile, horses, etc. **3.** person who

makes the people under him work very hard. **4.** a golf club with a wooden head, used in hitting the ball from the tee. **5.** any of several tools used in forcing things in, on, out, or through. **6.** in machinery, a part that transmits force or motion.

drive·way (drīv′wā′), *n.* a private road that leads from a house to the street.

driz·zle (driz′əl), *v.,* **-zled, -zling.** *n.* rain in very small drops like mist. [? < ME *drese* to fall < OE *drēosan*] —driz′zly, *adj.*

drogue (drōg), *n.* a device shaped like a large funnel at the end of the hose used to refuel planes in flight. The pilot of the plane being refueled guides the nose of his plane into the drogue. [appar. < F, cord game in which the loser wears clothespins on his nose; orig., a drug] —droll (drōl), *adj.* amusingly odd; humorously quaint. [< F *drôle* (orig. n.) good fellow < Du. *drol* little fat fellow]

droll·er·y (drōl′ər·i), *n., pl.* **-er·ies. 1.** laughable trick. **2.** quaint humor. **3.** jesting.

drom·e·dar·y (drom′ə·der′i; drum′-), *n., pl.* **-dar·ies.** a swift camel for riding, usually the one-humped camel of Arabia. [< LL *dromedarius* < Gk. *dromas kamelos* running camel < *dromos* a running]

drone¹ (drōn), *n.* **1.** a male honeybee. **2.** person not willing to work; idler; loafer. [OE *drān*]

drone² (drōn), *v.,* **droned, dron·ing,** *n.* —*v.* **1.** make a deep, continuous, humming sound. **2.** talk or say in a monotonous voice. —*n.* **1.** a deep, continuous, humming sound: *the continuous, humming sound: the drone of airplane motors.* **2.** the bass pipe of a bagpipe. [akin to DRONE¹]

Drone (life size)

drool (drül), *v.* **1.** let saliva run from the mouth as a baby does. **2.** *Slang.* talk or say foolishly. —*n.* **1.** saliva running from the mouth. **2.** *Am., Slang.* foolish talk. [contraction of DRIVEL]

droop (drüp), *v.* **1.** hang down; bend down. **2.** become weak; lose strength and energy. **3.** become discouraged or depressed; be sad and gloomy. —*n.* a bending position; hanging down. [< Scand. *drūpa*] —droop′ing·ly, *adv.* —droop′y, *adj.* —Syn. *v.* 2. fade, wilt, flag, fail.

drop (drop), *n., v.,* **dropped** or **dropt, drop·ping.** —*n.* **1.** a small amount of liquid in a roundish shape. **2.** a very small amount of liquid. **3.** anything roundish like a drop. **4.** a sudden fall. **5.** distance down; length of a fall: *from the top of the cliff to the water is a drop of 200 feet.* **6.** anything arranged to fall, as a trapdoor, curtain, etc. **7.** a drop kick. **8.** drops, liquid medicine given in drops. —*v.* **1.** fall or let fall in drops. **2.** fall suddenly; let fall suddenly. **3.** fall or cause to fall. **4.** fall dead, wounded, or tired out. **5.** cause to fall dead; kill. **6.** go or make lower; sink. **7.** pass into a less active or a worse condition: *she finally dropped off to sleep.* **8.** let go; dismiss. **9.** leave behind: *our fast car soon dropped its pursuers.* **10.** leave out; omit. **11.** stop; end: *let a matter drop.* **12.** send (a letter, etc.). **13.** come casually or unexpectedly. **14.** give or express casually: *drop a hint.* **15.** go along gently with the current or tide. **16.** in cooking, poach. **17.** set down from a ship, automobile, carriage, etc. **18.** of animals: **a.** give birth to. **b.** be born. **19.** drop off, **a.** go away; disappear. **b.** go to sleep. [OE *dropa*]

drop-forge (drop′fôrj′; -fôrj′), *v.,* **-forged, -forg·ing.** beat (hot metal) into shape with a very heavy hammer or weight. —drop′-forg′er, *n.* —drop forging.

drop hammer, a very heavy weight lifted by machinery and then dropped on the metal to be beaten into shape.

drop kick, kick given to a football as it touches the ground after being dropped.

drop-kick (drop′kik′), *v.* give (a football) a drop kick. —drop′-kick′er, *n.*

drop·let (drop′lit), *n.* a tiny drop.

drop·per (drop′ər), *n.* **1.** person or thing that drops. **2.** a glass tube with a hollow rubber cap at one end and a small opening at the other end from which a liquid can be made to fall in drops.

drop·si·cal (drop′sə·kəl), *adj.* **1.** of or like dropsy. **2.** having dropsy. —drop′si·cal·ly, *adv.*

drop·sy (drop'sĭ), n. Pathol. an abnormal accumulation of watery fluid in certain tissues or cavities of the body. [var. of hydropsy < OF < L hydropisis, ult. < Gk. hydrops < hydor water]

dropt (dropt), v. pt. and pp. of drop.

drosh·ky (drosh'kĭ), **dros·ki, dros·ky** (dros'kĭ), n., pl. -kies. a low, four-wheeled, open carriage used in Russia. [< Russ. drozhki, dim. of drogi wagon]

dro·soph·i·la (drō·sof'ə·lə), n., pl. -lae (-lē). a small fly whose larvae feed on fruit and decaying plants; fruit fly. [< NL < Gk. drosos dew + philos loving]

dross (drôs; dros), n. 1. waste or scum that comes to the surface of melting metals. 2. waste material; rubbish. [OE drōs]

drought (drout), **drouth** (drouth), n. 1. a long period of dry weather; continued lack of rain. 2. lack of moisture; dryness. [OE drūgath; akin to DRY] —**drought'y, drouth'y,** adj. ≫ drought, drouth. Both forms are in good use, drought probably more common in formal English, drouth in informal and colloquial. Newspaper accounts of the unusually dry seasons of the mid-1930's did much to give drouth increased currency.

drove¹ (drōv), v. pt. of drive.

drove² (drōv), n., v., droved, drov·ing. —n. 1. group of cattle, sheep, hogs, etc., moving or driven along together; herd; flock. 2. many people moving along together; crowd. —v. 1. drive (cattle) to market. 2. deal in (cattle). [OE drāf]

dro·ver (drō'vər), n. 1. man who drives cattle, sheep, hogs, etc., to market. 2. dealer in cattle.

drown (droun), v. 1. die under water or other liquid because of lack of air to breathe. 2. kill by keeping under water or other liquid. 3. cover with water; flood. 4. be stronger or louder than. 5. get rid of; suppress. [OE druncnian; akin to DRINK] —**drown'er,** n.

drowse (drouz), v., drowsed, drows·ing, n. —v. 1. be sleepy; be half asleep. 2. make sleepy. 3. pass (time) in drowsing. —n. being half asleep; sleepiness. [OE drūs(i)an sink, become slow]

drow·sy (drou'zĭ), adj., -si·er, -si·est. 1. half asleep; sleepy. 2. causing sleepiness; lulling. 3. caused by sleepiness. —**drow'si·ly,** adv. —**drow'si·ness,** n.

drub (drub), v., drubbed, drub·bing, n. —v. 1. beat with a stick; whip soundly. 2. defeat by a large margin in a fight, game, contest, etc. 3. stamp (the feet). —n. a blow; thump; knock. [? < Ar. ḍaraba beat] —**drub'ber,** n. —Syn. v. 1. thrash, cudgel.

drub·bing (drub'ing), n. 1. a beating. 2. a thorough defeat.

drudge (druj), n., v., drudged, drudg·ing. —n. person who does hard, tiresome, or disagreeable work. —v. do such work. [ME drugge(n); cf. OE drēogan work, suffer] —**drudg'er,** n.

drudg·er·y (druj'ər·ĭ), n., pl. -er·ies. hard, uninteresting, or disagreeable work.

drug (drug), n., v., drugged, drug·ging. —n. 1. substance (other than food) that, when taken into the body, produces a change in it. If the change helps the body, the drug is a medicine; if the change harms the body, the drug is a poison. 2. drug on the market, article that is too abundant, is no longer in demand, or has too slow a sale. —v. 1. give harmful drugs to. 2. put a harmful or poisonous drug in (food or drink). 3. affect or overcome (the body or senses) in a way not natural: the wine had drugged him. [< OF drogue, ? < Du. drog, akin to E DRY] —**drug'less,** adj.

drug·gist (drug'ist), n. 1. person who sells drugs, medicines, etc. 2. U.S. person licensed to fill prescriptions; pharmacist.

drug·store (drug'stôr'; -stōr'), n. Am. pharmacy, often also selling soft drinks, cosmetics, magazines, etc., as well as drugs.

Dru·id (drü'id), n. Often, druid. member of a religious order of priests, prophets, poets, etc., among the ancient Celts of Britain, Ireland, and France. —**dru·id'ic, dru·id'i·cal,** adj. —**dru'id·ism,** n.

drum (drum), n., v., drummed, drum·ming. —n. 1. a musical instrument that makes a sound when it is beaten. A drum is hollow with a covering stretched tightly over the ends. 2. sound made when a drum is beaten; sound like this. 3. anything shaped somewhat like a drum. 4. part around which something is wound in a machine. 5. drum-shaped container to hold oil, food, etc. 6. membrane covering the hollow part of the ear. 7. the hollow part of the middle ear. —v. 1. beat or play a drum. 2. beat, tap, or strike again and again. 3. force into one's mind by repeating over and over. [< drumslade drummer < Du. or LG trommelslag drumbeat]

drum·beat (drum'bēt'), n. sound made when a drum is beaten.

drum·head (drum'hed'), n. 1. parchment or membrane stretched tightly over the end of a drum. 2. eardrum. 3. the top part of a capstan.

drum·lin (drum'lən), n. Geol. ridge or oval hill formed by deposit from a glacier. [for drumling, dim. of drum ridge < Scotch Gaelic and Irish druim ridge]

drum major, leader or director of a marching band.

drum·mer (drum'ər), n. 1. person who plays a drum. 2. U.S. Colloq. a traveling salesman.

drum·stick (drum'stik'), n. 1. stick for beating a drum. 2. the lower half of the leg of a cooked chicken, turkey, etc.

drunk (drungk), adj. 1. overcome with alcoholic liquor; intoxicated. 2. very much excited or affected. —n. Colloq. 1. person who is drunk. 2. spell of drinking alcoholic liquor. —v. 1. pp. of drink. 2. Archaic. pt. of drink. ≫ drunk. It seems to take courage to use this natural word. We either go formal—intoxicated; or grasp at respectability through euphemisms—under the influence of liquor or indulged to excess; or make a weak attempt at humor with one of the dozen slang phrases like get plastered. But drunk is the word.

drunk·ard (drungk'ərd), n. person who is often drunk.

drunk·en (drungk'ən), adj. 1. drunk. 2. caused by or resulting from being drunk. 3. often drinking too much alcoholic liquor. —v. Archaic. pp. of drink. —**drunk'en·ly,** adv. —**drunk'en·ness,** n. —Syn. adj. 1. intoxicated.

dru·pa·ceous (drü·pā'shəs), adj. Bot. 1. like a drupe. 2. producing drupes.

drupe (drüp), n. Bot. fruit whose seed is contained in a hard pit or stone surrounded by soft, pulpy flesh, as cherries, peaches, etc. [< NL < L druppa very ripe olive < Gk. drypepa, accus. of drypeps ripening on the tree]

drupe·let (drüp'lit), n. Bot. a small drupe. A raspberry or blackberry is a mass of drupelets.

dry (drī), adj., dri·er, dri·est, v., dried, dry·ing, n., pl. drys. —adj. 1. not wet; not moist. 2. having little or no rain. 3. not giving milk. 4. having no water in it. 5. not shedding tears; not accompanied by tears. 6. wanting a drink; thirsty. 7. causing thirst: dry work. 8. not liquid; solid: dry measure. 9. showing no feeling: dry humor. 10. not interesting; dull. 11. without butter: dry toast. 12. without mucus: a dry cough. 13. without bloodshed: a dry fight. 14. not using live ammunition: dry fire. 15. free from sweetness or fruity flavor: dry wine. 16. Am., Colloq. having or favoring laws against making and selling alcoholic drinks. 17. not covered with water: dry land. —v. 1. make or become dry. 2. dry up, Slang. a. make or become completely dry. b. Am. stop talking. —n. Am., Colloq. person who favors laws against making and selling alcoholic drinks. [OE drȳge] —Syn. adj. 1. arid. 2. droughty. -v. 1. evaporate.

dry·ad, Dry·ad (drī'əd; -ad), n., pl. -ads, -a·des (-ə·dēz). Gk. Myth. nymph that lives in a tree; wood nymph. [< L < Gk. Dryades, pl., < drys tree] —**dry·ad'ic** (drī·ad'ik), adj.

dry battery, Elect. a. set of dry cells connected to produce electric current. b. dry cell.

dry cell, a small, portable device that produces electric current. It is an electric cell made with absorbent material so that its contents cannot spill.

dry-clean (drī'klēn'), v. clean (clothes, etc.) with naphtha, benzine, etc., instead of water. —**dry cleaner.** —**dry cleaning.**

Dry·den (drī'dən), n. **John,** 1631-1700, English poet, dramatist, and critic.

dry dock, dock from which the water can be pumped out. Dry docks are used for building or repairing ships.

dry-dock (drī'dok'), v. 1. place in a dry dock. 2. go into dry dock.

dry·er (drī'ər), n. drier (def. 2).

dry farming, way of farming land in regions where there is no irrigation and little rain.

dry goods, cloth, ribbon, lace, etc.

Dry Ice, Trademark. a very cold, white solid formed when carbon dioxide is greatly compressed and then cooled, used as a refrigerant.

dry law, law prohibiting the making and selling of alcoholic liquor.

dry·ly (drī'li), adv. in a dry manner. Also, **drily.**

dry measure, 1. system for measuring such things as grain, vegetables, or fruit. In the United States: 2 pints = 1 quart; 8 quarts = 1 peck; 4 pecks = 1 bushel. 2. measurement of dry things.

dry·ness (drī'nis), n. a being dry; dry quality.

dry nurse, nurse who takes care of a baby, but does not suckle it.

dry-nurse (drī'nèrs'), v., -nursed, -nurs·ing. act as dry nurse to.

dry point, 1. picture made from a copper plate into which lines have been engraved with a hard needle without using acid. 2. the needle used. 3. this method of engraving.

dry rot, decay of seasoned wood, causing it to crumble to a dry powder, due to various fungi.

dry run, 1. a practice test or session. 2. Mil. simulated firing practice, bombing approach, etc., without use of ammunition.

Ds, Chem. dysprosium. Also, **Dy.**

D.S., D. Sc., Doctor of Science.

d.s., daylight saving.

D.S.C., Distinguished Service Cross.

D.S.T., Daylight Saving Time.

d.t., d.t.'s, Colloq. delirium tremens.

du·al (dü'əl; dū'-), adj. 1. of two; showing two. 2. consisting of two parts; double; twofold. 3. Gram. signifying or implying two persons or things. —n. the dual number. [< L dualis < duo two] —**du'al·ly,** adv.

du·al·ism (dü'əl·iz·əm; dū'-), n. 1. dual condition. 2. Philos. doctrine that all the phenomena of the universe can be explained by two separate and distinct substances or principles, such as mind and matter. —**du'al·ist,** n. —**du'al·is'tic,** adj.

du·al·i·ty (dü·al'ə·ti; dū-), n., pl. -ties. dual condition or quality.

dub[1] (dub), v., **dubbed, dub·bing.** 1. make (a man) a knight by striking his shoulder lightly with a sword. 2. give a title to; call; name. 3. smooth by cutting, rubbing, scraping, etc. [OE dubbian]

dub[2] (dub), n. Slang. an awkward, clumsy player. [? akin to DUB[1]]

dub[3] (dub), v., **dubbed, dub·bing,** n. —v. add or alter sounds on a motion-picture film. —n. the sounds thus added or altered. [short for double]

Du Bar·ry (dü bar'i; dū), Comtesse, 1746?-1793, mistress of Louis XV of France who had great political influence.

du·bi·e·ty (dü·bī'ə·ti; dū-), n., pl. -ties. 1. doubtfulness; uncertainty. 2. something which is doubtful.

du·bi·ous (dü'bi·əs; dū'-), adj. 1. doubtful; uncertain. 2. of questionable character; probably bad. [< L dubiosus < dubius doubtful < du- two] —**du'bi·ous·ly,** adv. —**du'bi·ous·ness,** n.

Dub·lin (dub'lən), n. capital of the Republic of Ireland.

du·cal (dü'kəl; dū'-), adj. of a duke or dukedom. —**du'cal·ly,** adv.

duc·at (duk'ət), n. 1. a gold or silver coin formerly used in some European countries. Its value varied, being at most about $2.30. 2. Slang. a ticket. [< F < Ital. ducato < Med.L < L dux leader]

du·ce (dü'chā), n. Italian. 1. leader. 2. il Duce, title given to Mussolini. [< Ital. < L dux leader. Doublet of DOGE, DUKE.]

duch·ess (duch'is), n. 1. wife or widow of a duke. 2. lady with a rank equal to a duke's.

duch·y (duch'i), n., pl. duch·ies. territory under the rule of a duke or duchess; dukedom.

duck[1] (duk), n. 1. a wild or tame swimming bird with a short neck, short legs, and webbed feet. Most ducks have broad, flat bills. 2. the female duck. 3. flesh of a duck used for food. 4. Colloq. darling; pet. 5. Am., Slang. a fellow; chap. 6. **play ducks and drakes with,** handle recklessly; squander foolishly. [OE dūce; akin to DUCK[2]]

Pintail duck (2 ft. long)

duck[2] (duk), v. 1. dip or plunge suddenly under water and out again. 2. lower the head or bend the body suddenly to keep from being hit, seen, etc. 3. lower (the head) or bend (the body) suddenly. 4. Am., Colloq. get or keep away from by ducking; avoid. —n. 1. a sudden dip or plunge under water and out again. 2. a sudden lowering of the head or bending of the body to keep from being hit, seen, etc. [ME duke(n)]

duck[3] (duk), n. 1. a strong, cotton or linen cloth with a lighter and finer weave than canvas, used for sails, tents, etc. 2. **ducks,** trousers made of duck. [< Du. doek cloth]

duck[4] (duk), n. an amphibious army truck of World War II, used to carry supplies or troops over water. [for DUKW, code name]

duck·bill (duk'bil'), or **duck-billed platypus,** n. a small water mammal that lays eggs and has webbed feet and a beak like a duck. Also, **platypus.**

Duckbill (ab. 1½ ft. long)

duck·ling (duk'ling), n. a young duck.

duck·weed (duk'wēd'), n. a very small flowering plant that grows in water.

duct (dukt), n. 1. tube, pipe, or channel for carrying liquid, air, wires, etc. 2. tube in the body for carrying a bodily fluid: tear ducts. [< L, < ducere lead] —**duct'less,** adj.

duc·tile (duk'təl), adj. 1. capable of being hammered out thin or drawn out into a wire, as gold or copper. 2. easily molded or shaped, as wax. 3. easily managed or influenced; docile. —**duc·til·i·ty,** n.

ductless gland, Anat., Zool. gland without a duct whose secretion passes directly into the blood or lymph circulating through it. The thyroid and the spleen are ductless glands.

dud (dud), n. Colloq. 1. an article of clothing. 2. **duds,** a. clothes. b. belongings. 3. Mil. shell or bomb that did not explode. 4. Slang. failure.

dude (düd; dūd), n. Am. 1. man who pays too much attention to his clothes; dandy. 2. W. an Easterner or city-bred person, esp. one who vacations on a ranch. —**dud'ish,** adj.

dude ranch, Am. ranch that is run as a tourist resort.

dudg·eon (duj'ən), n. 1. anger; resentment. 2. **in high dudgeon,** very angry; resentful.

due (dü; dū), adj. 1. owed as a debt; to be paid as a right. 2. proper; suitable; rightful: due reward. 3. as much as needed; enough. 4. promised to come; to be ready, be paid, etc.; expected. 5. **due to,** caused by. —n. 1. thing owed as a debt or to be paid as a right. 2. **dues,** a. amount of money owed or to be paid. b. amount of money owed or to be paid to a club, etc., by a member. —adv. straight; directly; exactly: the wind is due east. [< OF deü, pp. of devoir owe < L debere] —Syn. adj. 1. payable. 2. appropriate, fitting. 3. adequate, sufficient. —n. 2 a, b. fee. ➤ **Due to** in the sense of because of has long been used popularly as a preposition. Advocates of strict usage have set themselves sternly against it. *Due* was originally an adjective and is still most strictly used as one: *the epidemic was due to the brown rat*, in which *due* modifies *epidemic*. But the prepositional use is convenient and has been increasingly common in print: *due to the danger of war, we have had to increase military expenditures*. Opinion of *due to* as a preposition is then divided. A writer should consider whether or not it is appropriate to his style: if he is rather formal, he should not use *due to* as a preposition; if he is less formal he doesn't need to worry—except perhaps in writing for readers known to be formal. A person may not care to use *due* to himself, but in view of actual usage today he hardly has the right to deny it to others.

du·el (dū′əl; dū′-), *n., v.,* **-eled, -el·ing;** *esp. Brit.* **-elled, -el·ling.** —*n.* 1. a formal fight between two people armed with swords or firearms, arranged to settle a quarrel, etc. 2. any fight or contest between two opponents: *duel of wits.* —*v.* fight a duel. [< F < Med.L *duellum* < L (archaistic for *bellum*) war] —du′el·er, *esp. Brit.* du′el·ler, *n.* —du′el·ist, *esp. Brit.* du′el·list, *n.*

du·en·na (dū·en′ə; dū-), *n.* 1. (in Spain and Portugal) an elderly woman who is the governess and chaperon of a young girl. 2. governess; chaperon. [< Sp. < L *domina* mistress. See DOMINATE.]

du·et (dū·et′; dū-), *n.* 1. piece of music to be sung or played by two people. 2. two singers or players performing together. [< Ital. *duetto,* dim. of *duo* DUO]

duff (duf), *n.* a flour pudding boiled in a cloth bag. [var. of *dough*]

duf·fel (duf′əl), *n. Am.* camping equipment. [< Du.; named for town near Antwerp]

duffel bag, duffle bag, 1. a bag of stout material. 2. a small canvas bag used by soldiers for carrying personal effects.

duff·er (duf′ər), *n. Brit. Colloq.* a useless, clumsy, or stupid person.

dug[1] (dug), *v.* pt. and pp. of dig.

dug[2] (dug), *n.* nipple; teat. [< Scand. Cf. Dan. *dægge,* Sw. *dägga* suckle.]

du·gong (dū′gong), *n.* a large, fish-shaped mammal of tropical seas with flipperlike forelimbs and a crescent-shaped tail. [< Malay *dūyong*]

dug·out (dug′out′), *n. Am.* 1. a rough shelter made by digging into the side of a hill, trench, etc. 2. *Baseball.* a small shelter at the side of a field, used by players who are not at bat or not in the game. 3. boat made by hollowing out a large log.

Dugong (10 ft. long)

Duis·burg-Ham·born (dys′bûrk·häm′börn), *n.* city in W Germany, on the Rhine River.

duke (dūk; dūk), *n.* 1. nobleman ranking next below a prince. 2. prince who rules a small state or country called a duchy. 3. dukes, *Slang.* fists. [< OF < L *dux* leader. Doublet of DOGE, DUCE.] —duke′dom, *n.*

dul·cet (dul′sit), *adj.* soothing, esp. to the ear; sweet; pleasing. [< F *doucet,* dim. of *doux* sweet < L *dulcis*]

dul·ci·mer (dul′sə·mər), *n. Music.* instrument with strings, played by striking the strings with two hammers. [< OF < L *dulcis* sweet + *melos* song (< Gk.)]

dull (dul), *adj.* 1. not sharp or pointed. 2. not bright or clear. 3. slow in understanding; stupid. 4. having little feeling; insensitive. 5. not interesting; tiresome; boring. 6. having little life, energy, or spirit; not active. 7. not felt sharply: *a dull pain.* —*v.* 1. make dull. 2. become dull. [ME *dul*] —dull′ness, dul′ness, *n.* —dul′ly, *adv.* —Syn. *adj.* 1. blunt. 2. dim, clouded, dingy. 3. dense, slow. 5. uninteresting, colorless. 6. lifeless, sluggish. —Ant. *adj.* 1. sharp. 3. acute, quick, smart. 6. keen, eager.

dull·ard (dul′ərd), *n.* a stupid person who learns very slowly.

dull·ish (dul′ish), *adj.* somewhat dull.

dulse (duls), *n.* any of several coarse, edible seaweeds that have red fronds. [< Irish and Scotch Gaelic *duileasg*]

Du·luth (də·lūth′; dū-), *n.* city in E Minnesota, on Lake Superior.

du·ly (dū′li; dū′-), *adv.* 1. according to what is due; as due; properly; suitably; rightfully. 2. as much as is needed; enough. 3. when due; at the proper time.

Du·mas (dū·mä′, dū-; dü′mä, dū′-), *n.* 1. Alexandre, 1802-1870, French novelist and dramatist. 2. his son, Alexandre, 1824-1895, French dramatist and novelist.

dumb (dum), *adj.* 1. not able to speak: *dumb animals.* 2. silenced for the moment by fear, surprise, shyness, etc. 3. that does not speak; silent. 4. *Am., Colloq.* stupid; dull. 5. lacking some usual property or characteristic. [(defs. 1-3, 5) OE; (def. 4) < G *dumm* stupid] —dumb′ly, *adv.* —dumb′ness, *n.* —Syn. 1. mute. 2. speechless.

dumb·bell (dum′bel′), *n.* 1. a short bar of wood or iron with large, heavy, round ends, used to exercise the muscles of the arms, back, etc. 2. *Am., Slang.* a very stupid person.

dumb show, gestures without words; pantomime.

dumb·wait·er (dum′wāt′ər), *n.* 1. *Am.* a small box with shelves, pulled up and down a shaft to send dishes, food, rubbish, etc., from one floor to another. 2. a small stand placed near a dining table, for holding dishes, etc.

dum·dum (dum′dum), or **dumdum bullet,** *n.* bullet that spreads out when it strikes, causing a serious wound. [after *Dum Dum,* India]

dum·found, dumb·found (dum′found′), *v.* amaze and make unable to speak; bewilder; confuse. [< *dumb* + (con)*found*] —dum′found′er, dumb′found′er, *n.*

dum·my (dum′i), *n., pl.* **-mies,** *adj.* —*n.* 1. figure of a person, used to display clothing in store windows, to shoot at in rifle practice, to tackle in football, etc. 2. *Am., Colloq.* a stupid person; blockhead. 3. an imitation; counterfeit. 4. person supposedly acting for himself, but really acting for another. 5. in card games, a. player whose cards are laid face up on the table and played by his partner. b. hand of cards played in this way. 6. *Am.* a kind of locomotive with a silent exhaust. —*adj.* 1. imitation; counterfeit; sham. 2. acting for another while supposedly acting for oneself.

dump (dump), *v.* 1. empty out; throw down; unload in a mass. 2. unload rubbish. 3. *Am.* put (goods) on the market in large quantities and at a low price. —*n.* 1. *Am.* place for unloading rubbish. 2. heap of rubbish. 3. *Mil.* place for storing ammunition or other supplies. [? < Scand. (Dan.) *dumpe* fall with a thud] —dump′er, *n.*

dump·ling (dump′ling), *n.* 1. a rounded piece of dough, boiled or steamed and served with meat. 2. a small pudding made by enclosing fruit in a piece of dough and baking or steaming it.

dumps (dumps), *n.pl. Colloq.* low spirits.

dump·y (dump′i), *adj.,* **dump·i·er, dump·i·est.** short and fat.—dump′i·ly, *adv.*—dump′i·ness, *n.*

dun[1] (dun), *v.,* **dunned, dun·ning.** —*v.* demand payment of a debt from, again and again. —*n.* 1. demand for payment of a debt. 2. person constantly demanding payment of a debt. [appar. < obs. *dun* make a DIN < Scand. *duna* to thunder]

dun[2] (dun), *n.* a dull, grayish brown. —*adj.* dull grayish-brown. [OE *dunn,* ? < Celtic]

dunce (duns), *n.* 1. child slow at learning his lessons in school. 2. a stupid person. [< *Duns*(*man*), name applied by attackers to any follower of *Duns Scotus,* theologian]

dunce cap, dunce's cap, a tall, cone-shaped cap formerly worn as a punishment by a child who was slow in learning his lessons in school.

Dun·dee (dun-dē′), *n.* seaport in E Scotland.

dun·der·head (dun′dər·hed′), *n.* a stupid, foolish person; dunce; blockhead.

dune (dün; dūn), *n.* mound or ridge of loose sand heaped up by the wind. [< F < MDu. *düne;* akin to DOWN³]

dung (dung), *n.* waste matter from animals; manure. —*v.* put dung on as a fertilizer. [OE] —dung′y, *adj.*

dun·ga·ree (dung′gə·rē′), *n.* **1.** a coarse cotton cloth, used for work clothes, sails, etc. **2.** dungarees, trousers or clothing made of this cloth. [< Hind. *dungri*]

dun·geon (dun′jən), *n.* **1.** a dark underground room to keep prisoners in. **2.** donjon. —*v.* confine in a dungeon; imprison. [< OF *donjon* < Gmc.]

dung·hill (dung′hil′), *n.* **1.** heap of dung. **2.** a vile place or person.

dunk (dungk), *v. Am., Colloq.* dip (something to eat) into a liquid: *dunk doughnuts into coffee.* [< LG *dunken* dip] —dunk′er, *n.*

Dun·kirk (dun′kērk; dun·kērk′), *n.* seaport in N France; evacuation of British forces, 1940.

dun·lin (dun′lən), *n.,* *pl.* -lins or (*esp. collectively*) -lin. a small wading bird that has a broad black stripe across the abdomen during the breeding season. [dim. of *dun²*]

Dunlin (8 to 9 in. long)

dun·nage (dun′ij), *n.* **1.** baggage or clothes. **2.** *Naut.* branches, mats, etc., placed around a cargo to protect it from damage by water or chafing.

du·o (dü′ō; dū′ō), *n.* duet. [< Ital. < L, two]

du·o·dec·i·mal (dü′ō·des′ə·məl; dū′-), *adj.* pertaining to twelfths or to twelve; proceeding by twelves. —*n.* **1.** one twelfth. **2.** one of a system of numerals, the base of which is twelve instead of ten. **3.** duodecimals, system of counting by twelves.

du·o·dec·i·mo (dü′ō·des′ə·mō; dū′-), *n., pl.* -mos. **1.** the page size of a book in which each leaf is one twelfth of a whole sheet of paper, or about 5 by 7½ inches. **2.** book having pages of this size. [< L *in duodecimo* in a twelfth]

du·o·de·num (dü′ō·dē′nəm; dū′-), *n., pl.* -na (-nə). *Anat., Zool.* the first part of the small intestine, just below the stomach. [< Med.L < L *duodeni* twelve each; with ref. to its length, about twelve finger breadths] —du′o·de′nal, *adj.*

dup., duplicate.

dupe (düp, dūp), *n., v.,* duped, dup·ing. —*n.* person easily deceived or tricked. —*v.* deceive; trick. [< F < L *upupa* hoopoe (a bird)] —dup′-er, *n.*

du·ple (dü′pəl; dū′-), *adj.* **1.** double. **2.** *Music.* having two or a multiple of two beats to the measure. [< L *duplus* double]

du·plet (dü′plit; dū′-), *n.* **1.** *Nuclear Physics.* pair of charged particles. **2.** *Chem.* pair of electrons which is shared by two atoms.

duple time, *Music.* two-part time.

du·plex (dü′pleks; dū′-), *adj.* double; twofold. —*n.* a duplex house or duplex apartment. [< L, < *du-* two + *plicare* fold] —du·plex′i·ty, *n.*

duplex apartment, an apartment having rooms on two floors.

duplex house, *Am.* a house accommodating two families.

du·pli·cate (*adj., n.* dü′plə·kit, dū′-; *v.* dü′plə·kāt, dū′-), *adj., n., v.,* -cat·ed, -cat·ing. —*adj.* **1.** exactly like something else; corresponding to something else. **2.** double. **3.** having two corresponding parts; twofold. **4.** of card games, so arranged that the same hands are played by different players. —*n.* **1.** one of two things exactly alike; an exact copy. **2.** in duplicate, in two forms exactly alike. —*v.* make an exact copy of; repeat exactly. [< L, < *duplicare* double. See DUPLEX.] —du′pli·ca′tion, *n.*

du·pli·ca·tor (dü′plə·kā′tər; dū′-), *n.* ma-

chine for making many exact copies of anything written or typed.

du·plic·i·ty (dü·plis′ə·ti; dū-), *n., pl.* -ties. deceitfulness in speech or action; treachery.

du·ra·ble (dùr′ə·bəl; dyùr′-), *adj.* lasting a long time; not soon injured or worn out. [< F < L, < *durare* to last, harden < *durus* hard] —du′-ra·bil′i·ty, du′ra·ble·ness, *n.* —du′ra·bly, *adv.* —Syn. permanent, stable, enduring, strong. —Ant. fragile, frail, weak.

Du·ral·u·min (dù·ral′yə·min; dyù-), *n. Trademark.* a light, strong, hard metal that is an alloy of aluminum, containing copper, manganese, and sometimes magnesium. [< *dur(able)* + *alumin(um)*]

du·rance (dùr′əns; dyùr′-), *n.* imprisonment.

du·ra·tion (dù·rā′shən; dyù-), *n.* **1.** length of time; time during which anything continues. **2.** for the duration, until the end, esp. of a war.

Dur·ban (dėr′bən; dėr·ban′), *n.* seaport in the SE part of the Union of South Africa.

dur·bar (dėr′bär), *n.* **1.** an official court or reception held by a native prince of India or by a British king, viceroy, governor, etc., in India. **2.** hall where a durbar is held.

Dü·rer (dy′rər), *n.* Albrecht, 1471–1528, German artist noted for his engravings.

du·ress (dù·res′, dyù-; dùr′es, dyùr′-), *n.* **1.** compulsion. **2.** imprisonment. [< OF < L *duritia* hardness < *durus* hard]

dur·ing (dùr′ing; dyùr′-), *prep.* **1.** through the whole time of. **2.** at some time in; in the course of. [ppr. of obs. *dure* ENDURE]

dur·ra (dùr′ə), *n.* kind of sorghum with slender stalks that produces grain. [< Ar. *dhura*]

durst (dėrst), *v.* pt. of dare.

du·rum (dùr′əm; dyùr′-), or **durum wheat,** *n.* a hard wheat from which the flour used in macaroni, spaghetti, etc., is made.

Du·se (dü′zā), *n.* Eleonora, 1859–1924, Italian actress.

dusk (dusk), *n.* **1.** time just before dark. **2.** shade; gloom. —*adj.* dark-colored; dusky. —*v.* make or become dusky. [var. of OE *dux* dark] —Syn. n. **1.** twilight.

dusk·y (dus′ki), *adj.,* dusk·i·er, dusk·i·est. **1.** somewhat dark; dark-colored. **2.** dim; obscure. **3.** sad; gloomy. —dusk′i·ly, *adv.* —dusk′i·ness, *n.* —Syn. **1.** swarthy.

Düs·sel·dorf (düs′əl·dôrf, dùs′-; *Ger.* dYs′-), *n.* city in W Germany, on the Rhine River.

dust (dust), *n.* **1.** fine, dry earth; any fine powder. **2.** earth; ground. **3.** what is left of a dead body after decay. **4.** cloud of dust in the air. **5.** turmoil; disturbance. **6.** low or humble condition. **7.** a worthless thing. **8.** *Am.* gold dust. **9.** *Slang.* money. —*v.* **1.** brush or wipe the dust from; get dust off. **2.** get dust on; soil with dust. **3.** sprinkle (with dust, powder, etc.). [OE *düst*] —dust′less, *adj.*

dust bowl, *Am.* area, esp. in the W part of the United States, where dust storms are frequent and violent.

dust·er (dus′tər), *n.* **1.** person or thing that dusts. **2.** cloth, brush, etc., used to get dust off things. **3.** *Am.* a long, lightweight coat worn over the clothes to keep dust off them. **4.** *Am., Colloq.* a dust storm.

dust jacket, *Am.* the jacket of a book.

dust·pan (dust′pan′), *n.* a flat, broad pan to sweep dust into from the floor.

dust storm, a strong wind carrying clouds of dust across or from a dry region.

dust·y (dus′ti), *adj.,* dust·i·er, dust·i·est. **1.** covered with dust; filled with dust. **2.** like dust; dry and powdery. **3.** having the color of dust; grayish. —dust′i·ly, *adv.* —dust′i·ness, *n.*

Dutch (duch), *adj.* **1.** of or having to do with the Netherlands, its people, or their language. **2.** *Slang.* German. **3.** go Dutch, *Colloq.* have each person pay for himself. —*n.* **1.** the Dutch, a. the people of the Netherlands. b. *Slang.* the people of Germany. The ancestors of the Pennsylvania Dutch came from Germany, not from the Netherlands. **2.** language of the Netherlands. **3.** *Slang.* the German language. **4.** in Dutch, *Am., Slang.* a. in disgrace. b. in trouble.

Dutch East Indies, islands in the East Indies formerly belonging to the Netherlands, now mostly in Indonesia. Also, **Netherlands Indies.**

Dutch Guiana, Surinam.

Dutch Harbor, a U.S. naval station in the Aleutian Islands.

Dutch·man (duch'mən), *n., pl.* -men. 1. native or inhabitant of the Netherlands. 2. *Slang.* German.

Dutch·man's-breech·es (duch'mənz-brich'iz), *n. sing. and pl. Am.* 1. a spring wild flower shaped somewhat like breeches. 2. the plant that bears it.

Dutch oven, 1. a metal box that opens in front, used for roasting meat, etc., before an open fire or on top of a stove. 2. a heavy iron kettle with a close-fitting cover.

Dutch treat, *Am., Colloq.* meal or entertainment in which each person pays for himself.

Dutch uncle, *Colloq.* person who sternly or severely criticizes or scolds another.

Dutch West Indies, Surinam and six islands off South America belonging to the Netherlands. Also, **Netherlands West Indies.**

du·te·ous (dū'ti-əs; dū'-), *adj.* dutiful; obedient. —**du'te·ous·ly,** *adv.* —**du'te·ous·ness,** *n.*

du·ti·a·ble (dū'ti-ə-bəl; dū'-), *adj.* on which a duty or tax must be paid.

du·ti·ful (dū'ti-fəl; dū'-), *adj.* 1. performing the duties one owes; obedient. 2. required by duty; proceeding from or expressing a sense of duty. —**du'ti·ful·ly,** *adv.* —**du'ti·ful·ness,** *n.*

du·ty (dū'ti; dū'-), *n., pl.* -ties. 1. thing that a person ought to do; thing that is right to do. 2. the binding force of what is right: *sense of duty.* 3. thing that a person has to do in his work; action required by one's occupation or position. 4. proper behavior owed to an older or superior person; obedience; respect. 5. tax on articles brought into or taken out of a country, made, sold, etc. 6. **off duty,** not at one's work. 7. **on duty,** at one's work. [< AF *dueté* < *du* DUE] —**Syn.** 1, 2. obligation. 3. responsibility, office, function. 4. deference, homage. 5. customs.

du·ve·tyn, du·ve·tyne, or **du·ve·tine** (dū'və-tēn), *n.* a soft, closely woven cloth having a velvety finish. [< *duvet* down quilt < F]

D.V., God willing. [< L *Deo volente*]

Dvo·řák (dvôr'zhäk), *n.* Anton, 1841–1904, Czech composer.

dwarf (dwôrf), *n.* 1. person, animal, or plant much smaller than the usual size for its kind. 2. in fairy tales, an ugly little man with magic power. —*adj.* much smaller than the usual size of its kind; checked in growth. —*v.* 1. keep from growing large; check in growth. 2. cause to seem small by contrast or by distance: *that tall building dwarfs the other.* [OE *dweorg*] —**dwarf'ness,** *n.* —**Syn.** *v.* 1. stunt.

dwarf·ish (dwôr'fish), *adj.* like a dwarf; smaller than usual. —**dwarf'ish·ly,** *adv.* —**dwarf'ish·ness,** *n.*

dwell (dwel), *v.,* dwelt (dwelt) or dwelled, dwell·ing. 1. make one's home; live. 2. dwell on, a. think, write, or speak about for a long time. b. put stress on. [OE *dwellan* delay] —**dwell'er,** *n.* —**Syn.** reside, abide.

dwell·ing (dwel'ing), or **dwelling place,** *n.* house to live in; place in which one lives. —**Syn.** residence, abode, habitation.

dwin·dle (dwin'dəl), *v.,* -dled, -dling. become smaller and smaller; shrink; diminish. [dim. of obs. *dwine* < OE *dwinan* waste away] —**Syn.** lessen, decrease, decline, wane.

dwt., pennyweight; pennyweights.

Dy, *Chem.* dysprosium. Also, **Ds.**

dye (dī), *n., v.,* dyed, dye·ing. —*n.* 1. a coloring

matter used to color cloth, hair, etc.; liquid containing this. 2. color produced by such coloring matter; tint; hue. —*v.* 1. color (cloth, hair, etc.) by putting in a liquid containing coloring matter. 2. color; stain. [OE *dēag*]

dyed-in-the-wool (dīd'in·thə·wùl'), *adj.* 1. dyed before being woven into cloth. 2. *Am.* thoroughgoing, esp. in a political sense; complete.

dye·ing (dī'ing), *n.* the coloring of fabrics with dye.

dy·er (dī'ər), *n.* person whose business is dyeing fabrics.

dye·stuff (dī'stuf'), *n.* substance yielding a dye or used as a dye, as indigo.

dy·ing (dī'ing), *adj.* 1. about to die. 2. coming to an end. 3. of death; at death. —*n.* death.

dyke (dīk), *n., v.,* dyked, dyk·ing. dike.

dy·nam·ic (dī·nam'ik), **dy·nam·i·cal** (-ə-kəl), *adj.* 1. having to do with energy or force in motion. 2. having to do with dynamics. 3. active; energetic; forceful. [< Gk. *dynamikos* < *dynamis* power < *dynasthai* be powerful] —**dy·nam'i·cal·ly,** *adv.*

dy·nam·ics (dī·nam'iks), *n.* 1. (*sing. in use*) branch of physics dealing with the action of force on bodies either at motion or at rest. Dynamics includes kinematics, kinetics, and statics. 2. (*pl. in use*) forces, physical or moral, at work in any field.

dy·na·mite (dī'nə·mīt), *n., v.,* -mit·ed, -mit·ing. —*n.* a powerful explosive used in blasting rock, tree stumps, etc. —*v.* blow up or destroy with dynamite. —**dy'na·mit'er,** *n.*

dy·na·mo (dī'nə·mō), *n., pl.* -mos. machine that changes mechanical energy into electric energy and produces electric current.

dy·na·mo·e·lec·tric (dī'nə·mō·i·lek'trik), *adj.* pertaining to the transformation of mechanical energy into electric energy, or vice versa.

dy·na·mom·e·ter (dī'nə·mom'ə·tər), *n.* apparatus to measure force.

dy·na·mo·tor (dī'nə·mō'tər), *n.* a combined electric motor and dynamo for changing the voltage of an electric current.

dy·nast (dī'nast; -nəst), *n.* 1. member of a dynasty; hereditary ruler. 2. any ruler. [< L < Gk., < *dynasthai* be powerful]

dy·nas·ty (dī'nəs·ti; *esp. Brit.* din'əs-), *n., pl.* -ties. 1. series of rulers who belong to the same family. 2. period of time during which a dynasty rules. —**dy·nas·tic** (dī·nas'tik; dī-), **dy·nas'ti·cal,** *adj.* —**dy·nas'ti·cal·ly,** *adv.*

dyne (dīn), *n. Physics.* amount of force that, acting on a mass of one gram for one second, gives it a velocity of one centimeter per second. [< F < Gk. *dynamis* power < *dynasthai* be powerful]

Dy·nel (dī·nel'), *n. Trademark.* a synthetic fiber resembling wool, resistant to fire, mildew, etc.

dys·en·ter·y (dis'ən·ter'i), *n.* a painful disease of the intestines, producing diarrhea with blood and mucus. [< OF < L < Gk., < *dys-* bad + *entera* intestines] —**dys'en·ter'ic,** *adj.*

dys·pep·si·a (dis·pep'si·ə; -shə), *n.* poor digestion; indigestion. [< L < Gk., < *dys-* bad + *pep-* cook, digest]

dys·pep·tic (dis·pep'tik), **dys·pep·ti·cal** (-tə·kəl), *adj.* 1. pertaining to dyspepsia. 2. suffering from dyspepsia. 3. gloomy; pessimistic. —*n.* person who has dyspepsia. —**dys·pep'ti·cal·ly,** *adv.*

dys·pro·si·um (dis·prō'si·əm; -shi-), *n. Chem.* a rare element, Dy or Ds, the most magnetic substance known. [< NL < Gk. *dysprositos* hard to get at]

dz., dozen; dozens.

E

E, e (ē), *n., pl.* E's; e's. 1. the fifth letter of the alphabet. 2. *Music.* the third tone of the scale of C major.

E, E., 1. East; east; Eastern; eastern. 2. English.

ea., each.

each (ēch), *adj.* every one of two or more con-

āge, cāre, fär; ēqual, tėrm; īce; ōpen, ôrder; pùt, rüle, ūse; th. then; ə=a in about.

sidered separately or one by one: *each dog has a name.* —*pron.* each one: *each went his way.* —*adv.* for each; to each; apiece: *these pencils are a penny each.* [OE *ēlc* < *ā* ever + *gelīc* alike]
➤ **each. 1.** As a pronoun, *each* is singular: *Each of the three has a different instructor.* **2.** As an adjective, *each* does not affect the number of a verb; when the subject modified by *each* is plural, the verb is plural: *Each applicant has to fill out the blanks* (sing.). *Three students, also from this country, each receive a scholarship* (pl.).

each other, 1. each the other: *they struck each other,* that is, they struck, *each striking the other.* **2.** one another: *they struck at each other.* ➤ **each other, one another.** By some grammarians *each other* is restricted to cases in which only two are concerned, *one another* being used of the greater number.

ea·ger (ē′gər), *adj.* **1.** wanting very much; desiring strongly; anxious to do or get something. **2.** ardent in desire or feeling. **3.** characterized by intensity of desire or feeling: *eager looks, an eager contest.* [< OF < L *acer* keen] —**ea′ger·ly,** *adv.* —**ea′ger·ness,** *n.* —Syn. **2.** keen, fervent.

ea·gle (ē′gəl), *n.* **1.** a large bird of prey that has keen eyes and powerful wings. **2.** picture of an eagle, or object shaped like an eagle, used as an emblem on a flag, stamp, etc. **3.** standard bearing the figure of an eagle as an emblem. **4.** *Am.* a former gold coin of the United States, worth $10. **5.** *Golf.* two strokes less than par for any hole. [< OF < L *aquila*]

Eagle (3 ft. from head to tail)

ea·gle-eyed (ē′gəl·īd′), *adj.* able to see far and clearly.

ea·glet (ē′glit), *n.* a young eagle.

ear¹ (ir), *n.* **1.** part of the body by which human beings and animals hear; organ of hearing. **2.** the external ear; visible part of the ear. **3.** sense of hearing. **4.** ability to distinguish small differences in sounds. **5.** favorable attention; listening. **6.** thing shaped like the external part of an ear. **7. be all ears,** *Colloq.* listen eagerly; pay careful attention. **8. fall on deaf ears,** not be listened to; receive no attention. **9. have or keep an ear to the ground,** *Am.* pay attention to what people are thinking and saying so that one can act accordingly. **10. up to the ears,** *Colloq.* thoroughly involved; almost overcome. [OE *ēare*]

ear² (ir), *n.* part of certain plants, such as corn, wheat, etc., that contains the grains. —*v.* grow ears; form ears. [OE *ēar*]

ear·ache (ir′āk′), *n.* pain in the ear.

ear·drum (ir′drum′), *n.* a thin membrane across the middle ear that vibrates when sound waves strike it; tympanic membrane.

earl (ėrl), *n.* a British nobleman ranking below a marquis and above a viscount. [OE *eorl*] —**earl′dom, earl′ship,** *n.*

ear·ly (ėr′li), *adv., adj.,* –li·er, –li·est. —*adv.* **1.** in the first part. **2.** before the usual time: *call me early.* **3.** long ago; in ancient times. **4.** before very long; soon. —*adj.* **1.** of or occurring in the first part: *in early life.* **2.** occurring before the usual or expected time: *have an early dinner.* **3.** occurring far back in time: *in early times.* **4.** occurring in the near future: *an early reply.* [OE, < *ǣr* ere + –*līce* -LY¹] —**ear′li·ness,** *n.*

early bird, person who gets up or arrives early; one who gains by acting promptly.

ear·mark (ir′märk′), *n.* **1.** mark made on the ear of an animal to show who owns it. **2.** a special mark, quality, or feature that gives information about a person or thing; sign. —*v.* **1.** make an earmark on; identify or give information about. **2.** set aside for some special purpose.

ear·muffs (ir′mufs′), *n.pl. Am.* pair of coverings to put over the ears to keep them warm.

earn (ėrn), *v.* **1.** receive for work or service; be paid. **2.** do enough work for; deserve; be worth. **3.** bring or get as deserved. [OE *earnian*] —**earn′er,** *n.*

ear·nest¹ (ėr′nist), *adj.* **1.** sincerely zealous; firm in purpose; serious. **2.** important: *"Life is*

real, *life is earnest."* —*n.* **in earnest,** sincerely zealous; serious. [OE *eornost*] —**ear′nest·ly,** *adv.* —**ear′nest·ness,** *n.* —Syn. *adj.* **1.** sincere, diligent, eager.

ear·nest² (ėr′nist), *n.* part given or done in advance as a pledge for the rest, or to bind a bargain. [ME *ernes,* appar. alter (by assoc. with –NESS) of *erres* < OF, pl. < L *arra* < Gk. *arrhabon* < Heb. *'ērābōn*]

earn·ing (ėr′ing), *n.* **1.** act of gaining. **2.** earnings, money earned; wages; profits.

ear·phone (ir′fōn′), *n.* receiver that is fastened over the ear; headphone.

ear·ring (ir′ring′), *n.* ornament for the ear.

ear·shot (ir′shot′), *n.* distance a sound can be heard; range of hearing: *he was out of earshot and could not hear our shouts.*

earth (ėrth), *n.* **1.** planet on which we live; the third planet from the sun, and the fifth in size. **2.** inhabitants of this planet. **3.** this world (often in contrast to heaven and hell). **4.** dry land. **5.** ground; soil; dirt. **6.** hole of a fox or other burrowing animal. **7.** worldly matters. **8.** *Chem.* a metallic oxide from which it is hard to remove the oxygen, such as alumina. **9.** connection of an electrical conductor with the earth. **10. come back to earth,** stop dreaming and get back to practical matters. **11. run to earth,** hunt until found. —*v.* **1.** of an animal, hide underground. **2.** drive (a fox, etc.) to its hole. **3.** cover with earth. [OE *eorthe*]

earth·en (ėr′thən), *adj.* **1.** made of earth. **2.** made of baked clay.

earth·en·ware (ėr′thən·wãr′), *n.* **1.** coarse baked clay dishes, containers, etc. **2.** baked clay. —*adj.* of earthenware.

earth·ly (ėrth′li), *adj.,* –li·er, –li·est. **1.** having to do with the earth, not with heaven. **2.** possible; conceivable. —**earth′li·ness,** *n.*

earth·nut (ėrth′nut′), *n.* an underground part of certain plants, such as a root, tuber, etc.

earth·quake (ėrth′kwāk′), *n.* a shaking of the earth, caused by the sudden movement of rock masses or by changes beneath the surface.

earth satellite, a satellite of the earth, esp. a metal sphere or other structure launched by rockets into an orbit around the earth.

earth·ward (ėrth′wərd), *adv.* Also, **earth′wards.** toward the earth. —*adj.* at or toward the earth.

earth·work (ėrth′werk′), *n.* **1.** bank of earth piled up for a fortification. **2.** a moving of earth in engineering operations.

earth·worm (ėrth′wẽrm′), *n.* a reddish-brown worm that lives in the soil; angleworm.

earth·y (ėr′thi), *adj.,* earth·i·er, earth·i·est. **1.** of or like earth or soil. **2.** not spiritual; worldly. **3.** not refined; coarse. —**earth′i·ness.** *n.*

ear trumpet, a trumpet-shaped instrument held to the ear as an aid in hearing.

ear·wax (ir′waks′), *n.* the sticky, yellowish substance in the canal of the outer ear.

ear·wig (ir′wig′), *n., v.,* –wigged, –wig·ging. —*n.* a beetlelike insect. Supposedly it creeps into the ear. —*v.* make private insinuations to. [OE, < *ēare* ear + *wicga* beetle, worm]

ease (ēz), *n., v.,* eased, eas·ing. —*n.* **1.** freedom from pain or trouble; comfort. **2.** freedom from trying hard; lack of effort; readiness: *he writes with ease.* **3.** freedom from constraint; natural or easy manner. **4. at ease, a.** free from pain or trouble; comfortable. **b.** *Mil.* with the body relaxed and the feet apart but quiet and stationary in position. —*v.* **1.** make free from pain or trouble; give relief or comfort to. **2.** lessen; lighten: *some medicines ease pain.* **3.** release from tension; make easy; loosen: *ease a rudder, rope,* or *sail.* **4.** move slowly and carefully: *he eased the big box through the narrow door.* **5. ease off** or **up,** a. lessen; lighten. **b.** loosen. [< OF *aise* comfort, opportunity < VL *adjacens* neighborhood < L, ADJACENT] —**eas′er,** *n.* —Syn. *n.* **1.** tranquility, contentment, rest. —*v.* **1.** relieve, soothe.

ea·sel (ē′zəl), *n.* a support or upright frame for a picture, blackboard, etc. [< Du. *ezel* easel, lit., ass < L *asinus*]

ease·ment (ēz′mənt), *n. Law.* a right held by one person in land owned by another.

eas·i·ly (ēz′ə·li), *adv.* in an easy manner.

eas·i·ness (ēz′i·nis), *n.* **1.** quality, condition, or state of being easy. **2.** carelessness; indifference.

east (ēst), *n.* **1.** direction of the sunrise; direction just opposite west. **2.** Also, **East.** part of any country toward the east. **3.** **the East**, the Orient. **4.** **East**, *Am.* region from Maine through Maryland in the United States. **5.** **down East**, *Am.* **a.** New England. **b.** the E part of New England. —*adj.* **1.** lying toward or situated in the east. **2.** originating in or coming from the east: *an east wind.* —*adv.* **1.** toward the east. **2.** in the east. [OE *ēast*]

East China Sea. See China Sea.

East·er (ēs′tər), *n.* day for celebrating Christ's rising from the dead, observed on the first Sunday after the first full moon after March 21. [OE *ēastre*, orig., name of dawn goddess < *ēast* EAST]

Easter Island, island in the S Pacific, 2000 miles W of Chile, and belonging to it.

east·er·ly (ēs′tər·li), *adj., adv.* **1.** toward the east. **2.** from the east. —**east′er·li·ness,** *n.*

east·ern (ēs′tərn), *adj.* **1.** toward the east. **2.** from the east. **3.** of or in the east. **4.** **Eastern**, *Am.* of or in the E part of the United States. **5.** Usually, **Eastern**, of or in the countries in Asia; Oriental. —**east·ern·most** (ēs′tərn·mōst), *adj.*

Eastern Church, **1.** group of Christian churches in E Europe, W Asia, and Egypt that do not recognize the Pope as spiritual leader but follow the ceremonies used by the patriarch of Constantinople. **2.** the Orthodox Church.

east·ern·er (ēs′tər·nər), *n.* **1.** native or inhabitant of the east. **2.** **Easterner**, *Am.* native or inhabitant of the E part of the United States.

Eastern Hemisphere, the half of the world that includes Europe, Asia, Africa, and Australia.

East·er·tide (ēs′tər·tīd′), *n.* the Easter season.

East Germany, area of Germany under Communist control.

East Indies, 1. the collective name given to India, Indo-China, and the Malay Archipelago. **2.** the islands of the Malay Archipelago. —**East Indian.**

East Prussia, region on the SE Baltic coast, divided after World War II between Poland and Russia.

east·ward (ēst′wərd), *adv.* Also, **east′wards.** toward the east. —*adj.* **1.** toward the east. **2.** east.

East Zone, Eastern Zone, the E portion of Germany, including part of Berlin, under Russian military control.

eas·y (ēz′i), *adj.,* **eas·i·er, eas·i·est,** *adv.* —*adj.* **1.** requiring little effort; not hard: *easy work.* **2.** free from pain, discomfort, trouble, or worry: *easy circumstances.* **3.** giving comfort or rest: *an easy chair.* **4.** fond of comfort or rest; lazy. **5.** not harsh; not severe; not strict: *easy terms, an easy master.* **6.** not hard to influence; ready to agree with, believe in, or help anyone. **7.** smooth and pleasant: *an easy literary style.* **8.** not tight; loose: *an easy fit.* **9.** not fast; slow: *an easy pace.* **10.** not much in demand; not hard to get. **11.** **on easy street,** *Am.* in comfortable circumstances. —*adv.* **1.** with little effort. **2.** *Colloq.* easily. [< OF *aisié*, pp. of *aaisier* set at ease < *a*– (< L *ad*–) + *aise* at EASE] —Syn. *adj.* **2.** tranquil, comfortable, contented.

eas·y·go·ing (ēz′i·gō′ing), *adj.* taking matters easily; not worrying.

easy mark, *Am., Colloq.* person who is easily imposed on.

eat (ēt), *v.,* **ate, eat·en** (ēt′ən), **eat·ing** (see usage note below). **1.** chew and swallow (food). **2.** have a meal. **3.** bite into and destroy: *acid eats metal.* **4.** destroy as if by eating; use up; wear away; waste away. **5.** make by eating. **6.** eat one's words, take back what one has said; retract. **7.** **eat out, a.** eat away from home. **b.** *Colloq.* admonish; castigate. **8.** **eat up, a.** eat all of. **b.** use up; waste away: *extravagance ate up*

his inheritance. [OE *etan*] —**eat′er,** *n.* —Syn. **4.** consume, waste. ≽ **eat.** The principal parts of *eat* are: in formal and informal usage, *eat* (ēt), *ate, eaten, eating;* in local and substandard usage, *eat, eat* (et or ēt), *eat* (ēt or et), *eating. Eat* is more common as the past tense in British than in American speech and writing and is pronounced *et.*

eat·a·ble (ēt′ə·bəl), *adj.* fit to eat. —*n.* Usually, **eatables.** things fit to eat; edibles.

eau de Co·logne (ō′ də kə·lōn′), *Trademark.* cologne. [< F, water of Cologne]

eaves (ēvz), *n.pl.* the lower edge of a roof that projects beyond a wall. [OE *efes*]

eaves·drop (ēvz′drop′), *v.,* **-dropped, -dropping.** listen to what one is not supposed to hear; listen secretly to private conversation. —**eaves′drop′per,** *n.* —**eaves′drop′ping,** *n.*

ebb (eb), *n.* **1.** a flowing of the tide away from the shore; fall of the tide. **2.** a growing less or weaker; decline. **3.** point of decline. —*v.* **1.** flow out; fall. **2.** grow less or weaker; decline. [OE *ebba*] —Syn. *v.* **2.** wane, decrease.

eb·on (eb′ən), *n.* ebony. —*adj. Poetic.* **1.** made of ebony. **2.** dark; black.

eb·on·ite (eb′ən·īt), *n.* vulcanite.

eb·on·y (eb′ən·i), *n., pl.* **-on·ies,** *adj.* —*n.* **1.** a hard, heavy, durable wood, used for the black keys of a piano, the backs and handles of brushes, ornamental woodwork, etc. **2.** a tropical tree that yields this wood. —*adj.* **1.** made of ebony. **2.** like ebony; black; dark. [< L < Gk., < *ebenos* ebony < Egypt. *hebni*]

e·bul·lient (i·bul′yənt), *adj.* **1.** overflowing with enthusiasm, liveliness, etc. **2.** boiling; bubbling. [< L, < *ex*– out + *bullire* boil] —**e·bul′lience, e·bul′lien·cy,** *n.* —**e·bul′lient·ly,** *adv.*

eb·ul·li·tion (eb′ə·lish′ən), *n.* **1.** a boiling; a bubbling up. **2.** outburst (of feeling, etc.).

ECA, E.C.A., Economic Coöperation Administration.

é·car·té (ā′kär·tā′), *n.* a card game for two people, played with 32 cards. [< F, pp. of *écarter* discard < *é*– (< L *ex*–) out + *carte* CARD[1]]

ec·ce ho·mo (ek′sē hō′mō; ek′e), *Latin.* behold the man.

ec·cen·tric (ik·sen′trik), *adj.* **1.** out of the ordinary; odd; peculiar. **2.** not having the same center. **3.** not moving in a circle. **4.** off center; having its axis set off center. **5.** *Astron.* not circular in form. —*n.* **1.** an eccentric person. **2.** disk or wheel set off center so that it can change circular motion into back-and-forth motion. [< Med.L < L *eccentrus* < Gk., < *ex*– out + *kentron* center] —**ec·cen′tri·cal·ly,** *adv.* —Syn. *adj.* **1.** irregular, queer, strange.

ec·cen·tric·i·ty (ek′sən·tris′ə·ti; –sen–), *n., pl.* **-ties. 1.** eccentric quality or condition. **2.** something queer or out of the ordinary; oddity; peculiarity.

eccl., ecclesiastical.

Ec·cle·si·as·tes (i·klē′zi·as′tēz), *n.* book of the Old Testament. [< LL < Gk. *ekklesiastes* preacher, ult. < *ex*– out + *kaleein* call]

ec·cle·si·as·tic (i·klē′zi·as′tik), *n.* clergyman. —*adj.* ecclesiastical.

ec·cle·si·as·ti·cal (i·klē′zi·as′tə·kəl), *adj.* of or having to do with the church or the clergy. —**ec·cle′si·as′ti·cal·ly,** *adv.*

ech·e·lon (esh′ə·lon), *n.* **1.** a steplike arrangement of troops, ships, etc. **2.** *Mil.* level of command. —*v.* form into a steplike arrangement. [< F, round of a ladder < *échelle* ladder < L *scala*]

e·chid·na (i·kid′nə), *n., pl.* **-nas, -nae** (-nē). a small, egg-laying, ant-eating animal of Australia with a covering of spines and a long, slender snout. [< L < Gk., viper]

e·chi·no·derm (i·kī′nə·dėrm; ek′i·nə–), *n.* starfish, sea urchin, or other similar small sea animal with a stony shell and a body whose parts are arranged radially. [< NL, < Gk. *echinos,* sea urchin, orig., hedgehog + *derma* skin]

ech·o (ek′ō), *n., pl.* **ech·oes,** *v.,* **ech·oed, ech·o·ing.** —*n.* **1.** a sounding again; a repeating of a sound. **2.** person who repeats the words or imitates the feelings, acts, etc., of another. **3.**

imitation of the feelings, acts, etc., of another. 4. a sympathetic response. —v. 1. sound again; repeat or be repeated in sound; reflect sounds. 2. repeat (the words) or imitate (the feelings, acts, etc.) of another. [< L < Gk.] —ech'o·er, n. —Syn. v. 1. resound.

Ech·o (ek'ō), n. Gk. Legend. a nymph who pined away with love for Narcissus until only her voice was left.

é·clair (ā·klãr'), n. an oblong puff or piece of pastry filled with whipped cream or custard and covered with icing. [< F, lightning, ult. < L ex- clarare lighten < ex- out + clarus clear]

é·clat (ā·klä'), n. 1. a brilliant success. 2. fame; glory. 3. burst of applause or approval. [< F, < éclater burst out]

ec·lec·tic (ek·lek'tik), adj. 1. selecting and using what seems best from various sources. 2. from various sources. —n. follower of an eclectic method. [< Gk. eklektikos < ex- out + legein pick] —ec·lec'ti·cism, n.

e·clipse (i·klips'), n., v., e·clipsed, e·clips·ing. —n. 1. a darkening of the sun, moon, etc., when some other heavenly body is in a position that cuts off its light. A solar eclipse occurs when the moon is between the sun and the earth. 2. loss of importance or reputation; failure for a time. —v. 1. cut off or obscure the light from; darken. 2. cut off or obscure the importance of; make less outstanding by comparison; surpass. [< OF < L < Gk. ekleipsis < ex- out + leipein leave] —Syn. v. 2. outshine, excel.

e·clip·tic (i·klip'tik), n. path that the sun appears to travel in one year. It is the great circle of the celestial sphere, cut by the plane containing the orbit of the earth. —adj. Also, e·clip'ti·cal. 1. of this circle. 2. having to do with eclipses.

ABCD, orbit of the earth; A₁B₁C₁D₁, ecliptic; S, sun.

ec·logue (ek'lôg; -log), n. a short poem about country life, esp. a dialogue between shepherds. [< L < Gk. ekloge a selection. See ECLECTIC.]

e·col·o·gy (ē·kol'ə·ji), n. branch of biology that deals with the relation of living things to their environment and to each other. [< Gk. oikos house + -LOGY] —ec·o·log·ic (ek'ə·loj'ik; ē'kə-), ec'o·log'i·cal, adj. —ec'o·log'i·cal·ly, adv. —e·col'o·gist, n.

econ., economic; economics; economy.

e·co·nom·ic (ē'kə·nom'ik; ek'ə-), adj. 1. of or pertaining to economics. Economic problems have to do with the production, distribution, and consumption of wealth. 2. having to do with the management of the income, supplies, and expenses of a household, community, government, etc.

e·co·nom·i·cal (ē'kə·nom'ə·kəl; ek'ə-), adj. 1. avoiding waste; saving: an efficient engine is economical of fuel. 2. having to do with economics. —e'co·nom'i·cal·ly, adv. —Syn. 1. frugal, thrifty.

Economic Coöperation Administration, governmental agency of the United States in charge of economic aid granted to foreign nations, abolished in December, 1951.

e·co·nom·ics (ē'kə·nom'iks; ek'ə-), n. science of the production, distribution, and consumption of wealth. Economics deals with the material welfare of mankind and the problems of capital, labor, wages, prices, tariffs, taxes, etc.

e·con·o·mist (i·kon'ə·mist), n. 1. an expert in economics. 2. person who is economical.

e·con·o·mize (i·kon'ə·mīz), v., -mized, -mizing. 1. manage so as to avoid waste; use to the best advantage. 2. cut down expenses. —e·con'o·miz'er, n. —Syn. 2. retrench.

e·con·o·my (i·kon'ə·mi), n., pl. -mies. 1. a making the most of what one has; freedom from waste in the use of anything; thrift. 2. instance of this. 3. managing affairs and resources so as to avoid waste; management. 4. efficient arrangement of parts; organization; system. 5. system of managing the production, distribution, and consumption of goods: feudal economy. [< L < Gk. oikonomia < oikos house + nemein manage]

ec·ru, é·cru (ek'rü; ā'krü), n., adj. pale brown; light tan. [< F, raw, unbleached, var. of cru raw < L crudus]

ec·sta·sy (ek'stə·si), n., pl. -sies. 1. state of great joy; thrilling or overwhelming delight; rapture. 2. any strong feeling that completely absorbs the mind; uncontrollable emotion. 3. trance. [< L < Gk. ekstasis trance, distraction < ex- out + histanai to place]

ec·stat·ic (ik·stat'ik), adj. Also, ec·stat'i·cal. 1. full of or tending to show ecstasy. 2. caused by ecstasy. —n. 1. one subject to fits of ecstasy. 2. ecstatics, fits of ecstasy; raptures. —ec·stat'i·cal·ly, adv.

ec·to·derm (ek'tə·dèrm), n. the outer layer of cells formed during the development of the embryos of animals. —ec'to·der'mal, ec'to·der'mic, adj.

ec·to·plasm (ek'tə·plaz·əm), n. 1. the outer portion of the cytoplasm of a cell. 2. an alleged emanation from the body of a medium in a trance. —ec'to·plas'mic, adj.

Ec·ua·dor (ek'wə·dôr), n. country in NW South America. —Ec'ua·do'ri·an, adj., n.

ec·u·men·i·cal (ek'yū·men'ə·kəl), ec·u·men·ic (-men'ik), adj. 1. general; universal. 2. of or representing the whole Christian Church. Also, Brit. oecumenical, oecumenic. [< L oecumenicus < Gk., < oikoumene (ge) inhabited (world), ult. < oikos dwelling] —ec'u·men'i·cal·ly, adv.

ec·ze·ma (ek'sə·mə; ig·zē'-), n. a skin inflammation characterized by itching and the formation of patches of red scales. [< NL < Gk. ekzema < ex- out + zeein boil]

-ed, suffix. 1. forming the past tense. 2. forming the past participle. 3. with various meanings: a. having; supplied with, as in bearded, long-legged, pale-faced, tender-hearted. b. having the characteristics of, as in honeyed. [OE]

ed., 1. edited; edition; editor. 2. educated.

E·dam cheese (ē'dam; ē'dəm), or Edam, n. a round, yellow cheese made in Holland, usually colored red on the outside. [after village in Holland]

EDC, E.D.C., European Defense Community.

Ed·da (ed'ə), n., pl. Ed·das. either of two books written in Old Icelandic.

Ed·ding·ton (ed'ing·tən), n. Sir Arthur Stanley, born 1882, English astronomer and physicist.

ed·dy (ed'i), n., pl. -dies, v., -died, -dy·ing. —n. water, air, etc., moving against the main current and having a whirling motion; small whirlpool or whirlwind. —v. 1. move against the main current in a whirling motion; whirl. 2. move in circles. [? < OE ed- turning + ēa stream]

Ed·dy (ed'i), n. Mary Baker, 1821–1910, founder of the Christian Science Church.

e·del·weiss (ā'dəl·vīs), n. a small Alpine plant having yellow flowers covered with white fuzz. [< G, < edel noble + weiss white]

e·de·ma (i·dē'mə), n., pl. -ma·ta (-mə·tə). a watery swelling in the tissues of the body. [< NL < Gk., < oidos tumor]

E·den (ē'dən), n. 1. garden where Adam and Eve lived at first. 2. a delightful spot; paradise.

E·den (ē'dən), n. Anthony, born 1897, English statesman, prime minister since April, 1955.

e·den·tate (ē·den'tāt), adj. toothless. —n. one of a group of animals that are toothless or lack front teeth, as anteaters, armadillos, and sloths. [< L, < ex- without + dens tooth]

edge (ej), n., v., edged, edg·ing. —n. 1. line or place where something ends; part farthest from the middle; side. 2. brink; verge. 3. a thin, sharp side that cuts. 4. sharpness; keenness. 5. Colloq. advantage. 6. on edge, a. disturbed; excited; uncomfortable. b. eager; anxious; impatient. 7. take the edge off, deprive of force, strength, or enjoyment. —v. 1. put an edge on; form an edge on. 2. move in a sidewise manner or little by little. 3. border. 4. edge in, manage to get in. [OE ecg] —edged, adj. —Syn. n. 1. margin, border. 2. rim.

edge·ways (ej'wāz'), **edge·wise** (-wīz'), adv. 1. with the edge forward; in the direction of the edge. 2. **get a word in edgeways,** manage to say a few words.

edg·ing (ej'ing), *n.* border or trimming on or for an edge.

edg·y (ej'i), *adj.,* edg·i·er, edg·i·est. 1. having a sharp edge. 2. impatient; irritable.

ed·i·ble (ed'ə·bəl), *adj.* fit to eat. —*n.* Usually, **edibles.** things fit or intended for eating. [< LL, < L *edere* eat] —ed'i·bil'i·ty, ed'i·ble·ness, *n.*

e·dict (ē'dikt), *n.* a public order or command by some authority; decree. [< L, < *ex*- out + *dicere* say] —Syn. proclamation.

ed·i·fi·ca·tion (ed'ə·fə·kā'shən), *n.* moral improvement; spiritual benefit; instruction.

ed·i·fice (ed'ə·fis), *n.* a building, esp. a large or imposing building. [< F < L *aedificium* < *aedis* temple (pl., house) + *facere* make]

ed·i·fy (ed'ə·fī), *v.,* -fied, -fy·ing. 1. improve morally; benefit spiritually; instruct. 2. build; construct. [< F < L *aedificare* build (up). See EDIFICE.] —ed'i·fi'er, *n.*

e·dile (ē'dīl), *n.* aedile.

Ed·in·burgh (ed'ən·bér'ō; *Brit.* ed'ən·brə, -bə·rə), *n.* capital of Scotland.

Ed·i·son (ed'ə·sən), *n.* Thomas Alva, 1847-1931, American inventor.

ed·it (ed'it), *v.* 1. prepare (another person's writings) for publication. 2. have charge of (a newspaper, magazine, etc.) and decide what shall be printed. [< L *editus* < *ex*- out + *dare* give; partly < *editor*]

edit., edited; edition; editor.

e·di·tion (i·dish'ən), *n.* 1. all the copies of a book, newspaper, etc., issued about the same time. 2. form in which a book is printed or published: *a three-volume edition.*

ed·i·tor (ed'ə·tər), *n.* 1. person who edits. 2. person who writes editorials. [< L. See EDIT.] —ed'i·tor·ship', *n.*

ed·i·to·ri·al (ed'ə·tô'ri·əl; -tō'-), *adj.* of or having to do with an editor; by an editor. —*n. Am.* article in a newspaper or magazine written by the editor or under his direction, giving an opinion or attitude of the paper. —ed'i·to'ri·al·ly, *adv.*

ed·i·to·ri·al·ize (ed'ə·tô'ri·əl·īz; -tō'-), *v.,* -ized, -iz·ing. 1. write an editorial. 2. express one's opinions publicly, esp. in a newspaper. 3. *Am.* write news articles as if they were editorials.

Ed·mon·ton (ed'mən·tən), *n.* city in SW Canada; the capital of Alberta.

E·dom (ē'dəm), *n.* region in Palestine S of the Dead Sea. —**E·dom·ite** (ē'dəm·īt), *n.*

E.D.T., e.d.t., Eastern daylight time.

ed·u·ca·ble (ej'ù·kə·bəl), *adj. Am.* capable of being educated.

ed·u·cate (ej'ù·kāt), *v.,* -cat·ed, -cat·ing. 1. develop in knowledge, skill, ability, or character by training, study, etc. 2. send to school. [< L *educatus,* pp. of *educare* bring up, raise, akin to *educere* EDUCE] —Syn. 1. train, teach, instruct.

ed·u·ca·tion (ej'ù·kā'shən), *n.* 1. development in knowledge, skill, ability, or character by teaching, training, study, or experience. 2. knowledge, skill, ability, or character developed by teaching, training, study, or experience. 3. science or art that deals with the principles, problems, etc., of teaching and learning. —ed'u·ca'tor, *n.*

ed·u·ca·tion·al (ej'ù·kā'shən·əl), *adj.* 1. of or having to do with education. 2. giving education; tending to educate. —ed'u·ca'tion·al·ist, ed'u·ca'tion·ist, *n.* —ed'u·ca'tion·al·ly, *adv.*

ed·u·ca·tive (ej'ù·kā'tiv), *adj.* that educates.

e·duce (i·düs'; i·dūs'), *v.,* e·duced, e·duc·ing. bring out; draw forth; elicit; develop. [< L, < *ex*- out + *ducere* lead] —e·duc'i·ble, *adj.* —e·duc·tion (i·duk'shən), *n.*

Ed·ward (ed'wərd), 1. VI, 1537-1553, king of England 1547-1553, son of Henry VIII. 2. VII, 1841-1910, king of England 1901-1910, son of Queen Victoria. 3. VIII, born 1894, king of England in 1936, son of George V. He abdicated and received the title of Duke of Windsor.

Ed·wards (ed'wərdz), *n.* Jonathan, 1703-1758, American theologian and metaphysician.

Edward the Confessor, 1004?-1066, king of England from 1042 to 1066.

-ee, *suffix.* 1. person who is ——, as in *absentee.* 2. person who is ——ed, as in *appointee.* 3. person to whom something is ——ed, as in *mortgagee.* [< F -*é,* masc. pp. ending]

E.E., Electrical Engineer.

eel (ēl), *n.* a long, slippery fish shaped like a snake and lacking ventral fins. [OE *ǣl*] —eel'like', *adj.*

eel·grass (ēl'gras'; -gräs'), *n. Am.* a North Atlantic sea plant with long, narrow leaves.

eel·pout (ēl'pout'), *n.* 1. a small, eellike saltwater fish. 2. the burbot.

e'en (ēn), *adv.* Poetic. even.

e'er (âr), *adv.* Poetic. ever.

-eer, *suffix.* 1. one who is concerned or deals with, as in *auctioneer, charioteer.* 2. person who produces, as in *pamphleteer, sonneteer.* 3. be concerned or deal with, as in *electioneer.* [< F -*ier*]

ee·rie, ee·ry (ir'i), *adj.,* -ri·er, -ri·est. 1. causing fear; strange; weird. 2. timid because of superstition. [ME *eri,* var. of *erg,* OE *earg* cowardly] —ee'ri·ly, *adv.* —ee'ri·ness, *n.*

ef·face (i·fās'), *v.,* -faced, -fac·ing. 1. rub out; blot out; do away with; destroy; wipe out. 2. keep (oneself) from being noticed; make inconspicuous. [< F, < *es*- (< L *ex*-) away + face FACE] —ef·face'a·ble, *adj.* —ef·face'ment, *n.* —ef·fac'er, *n.*

ef·fect (i·fekt'), *n.* 1. whatever is produced by a cause; something made to happen by a person or thing; result. 2. power to produce results; force; validity. 3. influence. 4. impression produced. 5. combination of color or form in a picture, etc. 6. purport; intent; meaning. 7. effects, a. personal property; belongings; goods. b. *Brit.* imitation: *tweed effects.* 8. **for effect,** for show; to impress or influence others. 9. **in effect,** a. in result; in fact; really. b. in operation; active. 10. **into effect,** in operation; in action; in force. 11. **take effect,** begin to operate; become active. 12. **to the effect,** with the meaning or purpose. —*v.* produce as a result; make happen; get done; bring about. [< L *effectus* < *ex*- + *facere* make] —ef·fect'er, *n.* —ef·fect'i·ble, *adj.* —Syn. *n.* 1. outcome, consequence. —*v.* accomplish, achieve, realize. ➤ See affect for usage note.

ef·fec·tive (i·fek'tiv), *adj.* 1. producing the desired effect. 2. in operation; active. 3. striking; impressive. —*n. Mil.* soldier or sailor equipped and available for fighting. —ef·fec'tive·ly, *adv.* —ef·fec'tive·ness, *n.*

ef·fec·tu·al (i·fek'chù·əl), *adj.* 1. producing the effect desired; capable of producing the effect desired: *quinine is an effectual preventive for malaria.* 2. valid. —ef·fec'tu·al'i·ty, *n.* —ef·fec'tu·al·ly, *adv.*

ef·fec·tu·ate (i·fek'chù·āt), *v.,* -at·ed, -at·ing. cause; make happen; bring about; accomplish. —ef·fec'tu·a'tion, *n.*

ef·fem·i·nate (i·fem'ə·nit), *adj.* lacking in manly qualities; showing unmanly weakness or delicacy; womanish. [< L, < *ex*- + *femina* woman] —ef·fem'i·na·cy (i·fem'ə·nə·si), *n.* —ef·fem'i·nate·ly, *adv.* —ef·fem'i·nate·ness, *n.*

ef·fen·di (i·fen'di), *n., pl.* -dis. 1. a former Turkish title of respect equivalent to "Sir" or "Master." 2. person having this title; Turkish doctor, official, scholar, etc. [< Turk. < Gk. *authentes* master, doer. See AUTHENTIC.]

ef·fer·ent (ef'ər·ənt), *adj.* conveying outward from a central organ or point. Efferent nerves carry impulses from the brain to the muscles. —*n.* an efferent nerve or blood vessel. [< L, < *ex*- out + *ferre* carry]

ef·fer·vesce (ef'ər·ves'), *v.,* -vesced, -vesc·ing. 1. give off bubbles of gas; bubble. 2. be lively and gay; be excited. [< L *effervescere* boil up < *ex*- out + *fervere* be hot] —ef'fer·ves'cence, ef'fer·ves'cen·cy, *n.* —ef'fer·ves'cent, *adj.*

ef·fete (i·fēt'), *adj.* unable to produce; worn out; exhausted. [< L *effetus* worn out by bearing < *ex*- out + *fe*- breed, bear] —ef·fete'ness, *n.*

ef·fi·ca·cious (ef'ə·kā'shəs), *adj.* producing

 āge, câre, fär; ēqual, térm; īce; ōpen, ôrder; pùt, rüle, ūse; th, then; ə=a in about.

the desired results; effective. —**ef'fi·ca'cious·ly**, *adv.* —**ef'fi·ca'cious·ness**, *n.*

ef·fi·ca·cy (ef'ə·kə·si), *n.*, *pl.* –**cies.** power to produce a desired effect or result; effectiveness. [< L, < *efficere* accomplish. See EFFICIENT.]

ef·fi·cien·cy (i·fish'ən·si), *n.*, *pl.* –**cies.** 1. ability to produce the effect wanted without waste of time, energy, etc. 2. efficient operation.

efficiency expert, *Am.* person whose profession is to devise more effective, economical methods of doing things.

ef·fi·cient (i·fish'ənt), *adj.* 1. able to produce the effect wanted without waste of time, energy, etc. 2. producing an effect. [< L *efficiens* < *ex-* + *facere* do, make] —**ef·fi'cient·ly**, *adv.* —**Syn.** 1. competent, capable.

ef·fi·gy (ef'ə·ji), *n.*, *pl.* –**gies.** 1. statue, etc., of a person; image. 2. burn or hang in effigy, burn or hang a stuffed image of a person to show hatred or contempt. [< F < L *effigies* < *ex-* out + *fingere* form] —**ef·fi·gi·al** (e·fij'i·əl), *adj.*

ef·flo·resce (ef'lō·res'; –lō–), *v.*, –**resced**, –**resc·ing.** 1. burst into bloom. 2. change from crystals to powder by loss of water. 3. become covered with a crusty deposit when water evaporates. [< L *efflorescere* < *ex-* out + *flos* flower]

ef·flo·res·cence (ef'lō·res'əns; –lō–), **ef·flo·res·cen·cy** (–ən·si), *n.*, *pl.* –**cen·ces;** –**cies.** 1. a blooming; a flowering. 2. mass of flowers or anything resembling it. 3. a change in which crystals lose water and become powder. 4. powder formed in this way. 5. eruption on the skin; rash. 6. a crusty deposit formed when water evaporates from a solution. —**ef'flo·res'cent**, *adj.*

ef·flu·ent (ef'lü·ənt), *adj.* flowing out or forth. —*n.* Often, **ef'flu·ence.** 1. that which flows out or forth; outflow. 2. stream flowing out of another stream, lake, etc. [< L, < *ex-* out + *fluere* flow]

ef·flu·vi·um (i·flü'vi·əm), *n.*, *pl.* –**vi·a** (–vi·ə), –**vi·ums.** vapor or odor. [< L. See EFFLUENT.] —**ef·flu'vi·al**, *adj.*

ef·fort (ef'ərt), *n.* 1. exertion of power, physical or mental; use of energy and strength to do something; trying hard. 2. hard try; strong attempt. 3. result of effort; thing done with effort; achievement. [< F < OF, < *esforcier* force, exert < L *ex-* out + *fortis* strong] —**ef'fort·less**, *adj.* —**ef'fort·less·ly**, *adv.* —**ef'fort·less·ness**, *n.*

ef·fron·ter·y (i·frun'tər·i), *n.*, *pl.* –**ter·ies.** shameless boldness; impudence. [< F < OF *esfront* shameless < L *ex-* out + *frons* brow] —**Syn.** presumption, insolence.

ef·ful·gent (i·ful'jənt), *adj.* shining brightly; radiant. [< L, < *ex* forth + *fulgere* shine] —**ef·ful'gence**, *n.* —**ef·ful'gent·ly**, *adv.*

ef·fuse (*v.* i·fūz'; *adj.* i·fūs'), *v.*, –**fused**, –**fus·ing**, *adj.* —*v.* pour out; spill; shed. —*adj.* 1. *Bot.* spread out. 2. profuse. [< L *effusus* < *ex-* out + *fundere* pour]

ef·fu·sion (i·fū'zhən), *n.* 1. a pouring out. 2. unrestrained expression of feeling, etc., in talking or writing.

ef·fu·sive (i·fū'siv), *adj.* showing too much feeling; too emotional. —**ef·fu'sive·ly**, *adv.* —**ef·fu'sive·ness**, *n.*

eft¹ (eft), *n.* *U.S.* a small newt. [OE *efete*. See NEWT.]

eft² (eft), *adv.* *Obs.* again.

eft·soon (eft·sün'), **eft·soons** (–sünz'), *adv.* *Archaic.* 1. soon afterward. 2. again. [OE, < *eft* again + *sōna* at once]

e.g., for example. [< L *exempli gratia*] ➤ **E.g.** is not usually italicized. In formal style or in a long, rather complicated sentence, it would usually be preceded by a semicolon.

egg¹ (eg), *n.* 1. a roundish body covered with a shell or membrane that is laid by the female of birds, reptiles, and fishes. Their offspring come from these eggs. 2. anything shaped like a hen's egg. 3. a female germ cell. —*v.* 1. prepare (food) with eggs. 2. *Colloq.* pelt with eggs. [< Scand.]

egg² (eg), *v.* urge; encourage: *the boys egged him on to fight.* [< Scand. *eggja* < *egg* edge]

egg cell, the reproductive cell produced by a female plant or animal.

egg·head (eg'hed'), *n.* *Am. Colloq.* an intellectual.

egg·nog (eg'nog'), *n.* *Am.* drink made of eggs,

milk, and sugar, often containing whiskey, brandy, or wine. [< *egg¹* + *nog* strong ale]

egg·plant (eg'plant'; –plänt'), *n.* 1. plant with a large, oval, purple-skinned fruit. 2. the fruit, used as a vegetable.

egg·shell (eg'shel'), *n.* shell covering an egg. —*adj.* like an eggshell; very thin and delicate.

e·gis (ē'jis), *n.* aegis.

eg·lan·tine (eg'lən·tīn; –tēn), *n.* a wild rose with pink flowers; sweetbrier. [< F, dim. of OF *aiglent* < VL *aculentus* < L *acus* needle]

e·go (ē'gō; eg'ō), *n.*, *pl.* **e·gos.** 1. the individual as a whole in his capacity to think, feel, and act; self. 2. *Colloq.* conceit. [< L, I]

e·go·ism (ē'gō·iz·əm; eg'ō–), *n.* 1. seeking the welfare of oneself only; selfishness. 2. talking too much about oneself; conceit. —**e'go·ist**, *n.*

e·go·is·tic (ē'gō·is'tik; eg'ō–), **e·go·is·ti·cal** (–tə·kəl), *adj.* 1. seeking the welfare of oneself only; selfish. 2. talking too much about oneself; conceited. —**e'go·is'ti·cal·ly**, *adv.*

e·go·tism (ē'gə·tiz·əm; eg'ə–), *n.* 1. excessive use of *I*, *my*, and *me*; habit of thinking, talking or writing too much of oneself. 2. selfishness. —**e'go·tist**, *n.* —**Syn.** 1. self-conceit, vanity.

e·go·tis·tic (ē'gə·tis'tik; eg'ə–), **e·go·tis·ti·cal** (–tə·kəl), *adj.* 1. characterized by egotism; conceited. 2. selfish. —**e'go·tis'ti·cal·ly**, *adv.*

e·gre·gious (i·grē'jəs), *adj.* 1. outrageous; flagrant. 2. remarkable; extraordinary. [< L *egregius* < *ex-* out + *grex* herd, flock] —**e·gre'gious·ly**, *adv.* —**e·gre'gious·ness**, *n.*

e·gress (ē'gres), *n.* 1. a going out. 2. way out; exit. 3. right to go out. [< L *egressus* < *ex-* out + *gradi* step, go]

e·gret (ē'gret; eg'ret), *n.* 1. heron with tufts of beautiful, long plumes. 2. one of its plumes; aigrette. 3. snowy egret, the North American egret. [< F *aigrette*]

E·gypt (ē'jipt), *n.* country in NE Africa.

E·gyp·tian (i·jip'shən), *adj.* 1. of or having to do with Egypt or its people. 2. Gypsy. —*n.* 1. native or inhabitant of Egypt. 2. language of the ancient Egyptians. 3. Gypsy.

E·gyp·tol·o·gy (ē'jip·tol'ə·ji), *n.* science or study of the history, language, etc., of ancient Egypt. —**E·gyp·to·log·i·cal** (i·jip'tə·loj'ə·kəl), *adj.* —**E'gyp·tol'o·gist**, *n.*

Ehr·lich (ār'liн), *n.* Paul, 1854–1915, German physician and bacteriologist.

ei·der (ī'dər), *n.* 1. eider duck. 2. its down. [< Scand. *œthr*]

eider down, 1. the soft feathers of the eider duck, used as stuffing. 2. quilt stuffed with these feathers. [< Scand. *œthar-dūn*]

eider duck, a large, northern sea duck with very soft feathers on its breast.

Eif·fel Tower (ī'fəl), a lofty tower in Paris.

eight (āt), *n.* 1. a cardinal number, one more than seven. 2. symbol of this number; 8. 3. crew of eight rowers. —*adj.* one more than seven; 8. [OE *eahta*]

Eider duck
(2 ft. long)

eight ball, 1. *Pool.* a black-colored ball carrying the number 8. 2. **behind the eight ball**, *Am.* in a difficult situation.

eight·een (ā'tēn'), *n.* 1. a cardinal number, eight more than ten. 2. symbol of this number; 18. —*adj.* eight more than ten; 18. —**eight·eenth** (ā'tēnth'), *adj.*, *n.*

eight·fold (āt'fōld'), *adj.* 1. eight times as much or as many. 2. having eight parts. —*adv.* eight times as much or as many.

eighth (ātth), *adj.* 1. next after the seventh; last in a series of 8. 2. being one of 8 equal parts. —*n.* 1. next after the seventh; last in a series of 8. 2. one of 8 equal parts. 3. *Music.* one octave.

eighth note, *Music.* a short note; one eighth of a whole note; quaver. See picture on next page.

eight·y (ā′ti), *n., pl.* **eight·ies,** *adj.* —*n.*
1. a cardinal number, eight times ten. 2.
symbol of this number; 80. —*adj.* eight times
ten; 80. —**eight·i·eth** (ā′ti·ith),
adj., n.

ei·kon (ī′kon), *n.* icon.

Ein·stein (īn′stīn), *n.* Albert,
1879-1955, American physicist,
born in Germany, who developed
the theory of relativity.   Eighth note

ein·stein·i·um (īn·stīn′i·əm), *n.* a rare, radioactive, artificial element, E, produced as a by-
product of nuclear fission. [named for Albert
Einstein]

Eir·e (ãr′ə), *n.* the Republic of Ireland.

Ei·sen·how·er (ī′zən·hou′ər), *n.* Dwight D.,
born 1890, American general, the 34th president
of the United States, since 1953.

ei·ther (ē′thər; ī′–), *adj.* 1. one or the other of
two: *either hat is becoming.* 2. each of two: *take
seats on either side.* —*pron.* one or the other of
two: *either of the hats is becoming.* —*adv.* any
more than another: *if you do not go, I shall not
go either.* —*conj.* one or the other of two: *either
come in or go out.* [OE *ægther < æghwœther*
each of two < *ā* always + *gehwœther* each of
two. See WHETHER.] ➤ **either.** 1. The pronunciation ī′thər has not made so much progress in the
United States as in England, and outside some
communities in New England and a few families
or circles that radiate from New England it is
usually an affectation. 2. *Either* means primarily
"one or the other of two," as adjective (*either
way you look at it*), or pronoun (*bring me either*). For emphasis the pronoun is usually supported by *one* (*bring me either one*). Used of
three or more objects (*either of the corners*) it is
loose and rare; *any one of the corners* is the
more usual idiom. *Either* is construed as singular.
3. *Either* meaning "each" is definitely formal:
broil the fish on either side. Each or both would
be more common in such expressions.

e·jac·u·late (i·jak′yə·lāt), *v.,* –**lat·ed,** –**lat·ing.**
1. say suddenly and briefly; exclaim. 2. eject;
discharge. [< L, < *ex*- out + *jaculum* javelin
< *jacere* throw] —**e·jac′u·la·tive,** *adj.* —**e·jac′-
u·la′tor,** *n.*

e·jac·u·la·tion (i·jak′yə·lā′shən), *n.* 1. something said suddenly and briefly; exclamation. 2.
ejection; discharge.

e·jac·u·la·to·ry (i·jak′yə·lə·tô′ri, –tō′–), *adj.*
1. said suddenly and briefly; containing exclamations. 2. ejecting; discharging.

e·ject (i·jekt′), *v.* throw out; force out; expel.
[< L *ejectare,* ult. < *ex*- out + *jacere* throw]
—**e·jec′tion,** **e·ject′ment,** *n.* —**e·jec′tive,** *adj.*
—**e·jec′tor,** *n.*

eke¹ (ēk), *v.,* **eked, ek·ing.** 1. *Archaic and Dial.*
increase; enlarge; lengthen. 2. eke out, a. supply what is lacking; supplement. b. barely
make (a living). [dial. var. of obs. *eche* to augment < OE *ēcan* < OE *ēaca* addition]

eke² (ēk), *adv., conj. Archaic.* also. [OE *ēac*]

el (el), *n.* 1. ell¹. 2. ell². 3. *Colloq.* an elevated
railroad.

e·lab·o·rate (*adj.* i·lab′ə·rit; *v.* i·lab′ə·rāt),
adj., v., –**rat·ed,** –**rat·ing.** —*adj.* 1. worked out
with great care; having many details; complicated. —*v.* 1. work out with great care; add details to. 2. talk, write, etc., in great detail; give
added details. 3. make with labor; produce. [< L,
< *ex*- out + *labor* work] —**e·lab′o·rate·ly,** *adv.*
—**e·lab′o·rate·ness,** *n.* —**e·lab′o·ra′tive,** *adj.*
—**e·lab′o·ra′tor,** *n.* —**Syn.** *adj.* detailed, minute.

e·lab·o·ra·tion (i·lab′ə·rā′shən), *n.* 1. an
elaborating. 2. a being elaborated. 3. something
elaborated.

El A·la·mein (el ä′lə·mān′; al′ə–), a coastal
town in N Egypt; scene of a decisive British
victory over the Germans in 1942.

E·lam (ē′ləm), *n.* an ancient country in what is
now W Iran, E of ancient Babylonia. —**E·lam-
ite** (ē′ləm·īt), *n.* —**E·lam·it·ic** (ē′ləm·it′ik), *adj.*

é·lan (ā·län′), *n.* enthusiasm; liveliness. [< F,
< *élancer* to dart]

e·land (ē′lənd), *n.* a large African antelope
with twisted horns. [< Du., elk]

e·lapse (i·laps′), *v.,* **e·lapsed, e·laps·ing.** slip
away; glide by; pass. [< L *elapsus* < *ex*- away +
labi glide]

e·las·mo·branch (i·las′mə·brangk; i·laz′–),
n. fish whose skeleton is formed of cartilage and
whose gills are thin and platelike. [< NL < Gk.
elasmos metal plate + *branchia* gills]

e·las·tic (i·las′tik), *adj.* 1. having the quality
of springing back to its original size, shape, or
position after being stretched, squeezed, etc. 2.
springing back; springy: *an elastic step.* 3. re-
covering quickly from low spirits, etc.; buoyant.
4. easily altered to suit changed conditions; flexible; adaptable. —*n.* 1. tape, cloth, etc., woven
partly of rubber. 2. a rubber band. [< NL < Gk.
elastikos driving, propulsive < *elaunein* drive]
—**e·las′ti·cal·ly,** *adv.* —**e·las·tic·i·ty** (i·las′tis′-
ə·ti; ē′las–), *n.* —**Syn.** *adj.* 2. rebounding, flexible.

e·late (i·lāt′), *v.,* **e·lat·ed, e·lat·ing.** put in
high spirits; make joyful or proud. [< L, < *ex*-
out, away + *latus,* pp. to *ferre* carry] —**e·lat′er,**
n.

e·lat·ed (i·lāt′id), *adj.* in high spirits; joyful;
proud. —**e·lat′ed·ly,** *adv.*

e·la·tion (i·lā′shən), *n.* high spirits; joyous
pride; exultant gladness.

El·ba (el′bə), *n.* an Italian island between Italy
and Corsica. Napoleon I was in exile there from
1814 to 1815.

El·be (el′bə), *n.* river flowing from Czechoslovakia through C Germany into the North Sea.

el·bow (el′bō), *n.* 1. joint between the upper
and lower arm. 2. anything resembling a bent
elbow. 3. up to the elbows, a. very busy. b.
deeply involved. —*v.* push with the elbow or
elbows. [OE *elnboga.* See ELL¹, BOW².]

elbow room, el·bow·room (el′bō·rüm′,
–rüm′), *n. Am.* plenty of room; enough space to
move or work in.

El·brus, El·bruz (el′brüs; –brüz; ãl′–), *n.*
Mount, the highest mountain in Europe, located
in S Russia, in the Caucasus Mountains.

El Cha·co (el chä′kō), region divided between
Bolivia and Paraguay in 1938.

eld (eld), *n. Archaic.* 1. old age. 2. old times;
former times. [OE *ældu < ald* old]

eld·er¹ (el′dər), *adj.* 1. born, produced, or
formed before something else; older; senior: *my
elder brother.* 2. prior in rank, validity, etc.: *an
elder title to an estate.* 3. earlier; former: *in
elder times.* —*n.* 1. an older person. 2. an aged
person. 3. ancestor. 4. one of the older and more
influential men of a tribe or community; chief,
ruler, etc. 5. any of various important officers in
certain churches. [OE *eldra,* comp. of *ald* old]
➤ **elder, eldest.** These archaic forms of *old*
survive in formal English and they are used,
when speaking of persons, only of members of
the same family: *the elder brother; our eldest
daughter.*

eld·er² (el′dər), *n.* elderberry. [OE *ellærn*]

el·der·ber·ry (el′dər·ber′i), *n., pl.* –**ries.** 1.
shrub or tree with black or red berries, sometimes used in making wine. 2. berry of this plant.

eld·er·ly (el′dər·li), *adj.* somewhat old; beyond
middle age; near old age. —**eld′er·li·ness,** *n.*

eld·er·ship (el′dər·ship), *n.* 1. office or position
of an elder in a church. 2. group or court of
elders; presbytery.

eld·est (el′dist), *adj.* oldest (of brothers and
sisters or of a group). [OE, superl. of *ald* old]
➤ See **elder** for usage note.

El·do·ra·do (el′də·rä′dō; –rä′–), **El Do-
ra·do,** *n., pl.* –**dos.** 1. a legendary city of great
wealth. 2. any fabulously wealthy place.

e·lect (i·lekt′), *v.* 1. choose or select for an office
by voting. 2. choose. —*adj.* 1. elected but not yet
in office. 2. chosen; selected. 3. chosen by God for
salvation and eternal life. —*n.* the elect, a. people selected or chosen by God for salvation and
eternal life. b. people who belong to a group with
special rights and privileges. [< L *electus < ex*-
out + *legere* choose] —**Syn.** *v.* 2. select, pick.

elect., elec., electric; electrical; electricity.

e·lec·tion (i·lek′shən), *n.* 1. choice. 2. a choosing by vote. 3. selection by God for salvation. —Syn. 1. selection, preference.

e·lec·tion·eer (i·lek′shən·ir′), *v. Am.* work for the success of a candidate or party in an election. —*n. Esp. Brit.* a political campaigner. —e·lec′tion·eer′er, *n.* —e·lec′tion·eer′ing, *n.*

e·lec·tive (i·lek′tiv), *adj.* 1. chosen by an election: *elective officials.* 2. filled by an election: *an elective office.* 3. having the right to vote in an election. 4. open to choice; not required. —*n.* course of study that may be taken, but is not required. —e·lec′tive·ly, *adv.* —e·lec′tive·ness, *n.*

e·lec·tor (i·lek′tər), *n.* 1. one having the right to vote in an election. 2. *Am.* member of the electoral college. 3. one of the princes who had the right to elect the emperor of the Holy Roman Empire. —e·lec′tor·al, *adj.*

electoral college, *Am.* group of people chosen by the voters to elect the president and vice-president of the United States.

e·lec·tor·ate (i·lek′tər·it), *n.* 1. the persons having the right to vote in an election. 2. territory under the rule of an elector of the Holy Roman Empire.

E·lec·tra (i·lek′trə), *n. Gk. Legend.* daughter of Agamemnon and Clytemnestra.

e·lec·tric (i·lek′trik), *adj.* Also, **e·lec′tri·cal.** 1. of electricity; having to do with electricity. 2. charged with electricity. 3. producing electricity. 4. run by electricity. 5. exciting; thrilling. —*n. Am., Colloq.* car or railroad run by electricity. [< NL *electricus* < L < Gk. *elektron* amber (which, under friction, has the property of attracting)] —e·lec′tri·cal·ly, *adv.* —Syn. *adj.* 5. stimulating, stirring.

electrical transcription, 1. radio broadcasting from a special phonograph record. 2. a special phonograph record used in radio broadcasting.

electric brain, electronic brain.

electric chair, *Am.* chair used in electrocuting criminals.

electric eel, a large, eellike fish of South America that can give strong electric shocks.

electric eye, a photoelectric cell. An electric eye can operate a mechanism so as to open a door when its invisible beam is interrupted.

electric heater, 1. a portable device furnishing heat by means of small electric coils. 2. in England, a radiator.

e·lec·tri·cian (i·lek′trish′ən; ē′lek-), *n. Am.* person whose work is installing or repairing electric wires, lights, motors, etc.

e·lec·tric·i·ty (i·lek′tris′ə·ti; ē′lek-), *n.* 1. form of energy that can produce light, heat, magnetism, and chemical changes, and which can be generated by friction, induction, or chemical changes. 2. an electric current; flow of electrons. 3. branch of physics that deals with electricity.

e·lec·tri·fy (i·lek′trə·fī), *v.,* -fied, -fy·ing. 1. charge with electricity. 2. equip to use electricity. 3. give an electric shock to. 4. excite; thrill. —e·lec′tri·fi·ca′tion, *n.* —e·lec′tri·fi′er, *n.*

electro-, *word element.* 1. electric, as in *electromagnet.* 2. electrically, as in *electropositive.* 3. electricity. [< Gk. *elektron* amber]

e·lec·tro·chem·is·try (i·lek′trō·kem′is·tri), *n.* branch of chemistry that deals with chemical changes produced by electricity and the production of electricity by chemical changes. —e·lec·tro·chem·i·cal (i·lek′trō·kem′ə·kəl), *adj.*

e·lec·tro·cute (i·lek′trə·küt), *v.,* -cut·ed, -cut·ing. *Am.* kill by electricity. [< *electro-* + (*exe*) *cute*] —e·lec′tro·cu′tion, *n. Am.*

e·lec·trode (i·lek′trōd), *n.* either of the two terminals of a battery or any other source of electricity. [< *electro-* + Gk. *hodos* way]

e·lec·tro·dy·nam·ics (i·lek′trō·dī·nam′iks), *n.* branch of physics that deals with the action of electricity or with electric currents. —e·lec′tro·dy·nam′ic, e·lec′tro·dy·nam′i·cal, *adj.*

e·lec·tro·lier (i·lek′trə·lir′), *n.* chandelier or other support for electric lights. [< *electro-* + (*chande*) *lier*]

e·lec·trol·y·sis (i·lek′trol′ə·sis; ē′lek-), *n.* 1. decomposition of a chemical compound into ions

by the passage of an electric current through a solution of it. 2. removal of excess hair, moles, etc., by destruction with an electrified needle.

e·lec·tro·lyte (i·lek′trə·līt), *n.* 1. *Elect.* solution that will conduct a current. 2. *Chem.* compound whose solution is a conductor. [< *electro-* + Gk. *lytos* dissoluble < *lyein* loose] —e·lec·tro·lyt·ic (i·lek′trə·lit′ik), e·lec′tro·lyt′i·cal, *adj.* —e·lec′tro·lyt′i·cal·ly, *adv.*

e·lec·tro·lyze (i·lek′trə·līz), *v.,* -lyzed, -lyz·ing. decompose by electrolysis. —e·lec′tro·ly·za′tion, *n.* —e·lec′tro·lyz′er, *n.*

e·lec·tro·mag·net (i·lek′trō·mag′nit), *n.* piece of iron that becomes a strong magnet when electricity passes through wire coiled around it. —e·lec·tro·mag·net·ic (i·lek′trō·mag·net′ik), *adj.*

e·lec·tro·mag·net·ism (i·lek′trō·mag′nə·tiz·əm), *n.* 1. magnetism as produced by electric currents. 2. branch of physics that deals with this.

e·lec·trom·e·ter (i·lek′trom′ə·tər; ē′lek-), *n.* instrument for measuring differences in electrical charge or potential.

e·lec·tro·mo·tive (i·lek′trə·mō′tiv), *adj.* of or producing a flow of electricity.

electromotive force, force that causes an electric current to flow, produced by differences in electrical charge or potential.

e·lec·tro·mo·tor (i·lek′trə·mō′tər), *n.* 1. machine producing electric current. 2. motor run by electricity.

e·lec·tron (i·lek′tron), *n.* unit charge of negative electricity. All atoms are composed of electrons and protons. [< *electric* + -*on* (as in *ion,* etc.)] —e·lec·tron·ic (i·lek′tron′ik; ē′lek-), *adj.*

e·lec·tro·neg·a·tive (i·lek′trō·neg′ə·tiv), *adj.* 1. charged with negative electricity. 2. assuming negative potential in contacting a dissimilar substance. 3. nonmetallic; acid.

electron gun, device that guides the flow and greatly increases the speed of atomic particles. Electron guns are being developed for use in oil refining and various other industries.

electronic brain, a complex electric calculating machine, as UNIVAC. Also, **electric brain.**

e·lec·tron·ics (i·lek′tron′iks; ē′lek-), *n.* branch of physics that treats of electrons.

electron microscope, microscope that uses beams of electrons instead of beams of light, and has much higher power than any ordinary microscope.

electron tube, *Electronics.* vacuum tube.

e·lec·troph·o·rus (i·lek′trof′ə·rəs; ē′lek-), *n., pl.* -ri (-rī). a simple device for producing charges of electricity by means of induction. [< NL, < *electro-* + Gk. -*phoros* bearing]

e·lec·tro·plate (i·lek′trə·plāt′), *v.,* -plat·ed, -plat·ing, *n.* —*v.* cover with a coating of metal by means of electrolysis. —*n.* silverware, etc., covered in this way. —e·lec′tro·plat′er, *n.*

e·lec·tro·pos·i·tive (i·lek′trō·poz′ə·tiv), *adj.* 1. charged with positive electricity. 2. assuming positive potential when contacting another substance. 3. metallic; basic.

e·lec·tro·scope (i·lek′trə·skōp), *n.* device that indicates the presence of minute charges of electricity and shows whether they are positive or negative. —e·lec·tro·scop·ic (i·lek′trə·skop′ik), *adj.*

e·lec·tro·stat·ics (i·lek′trə·stat′iks), *n.* branch of physics dealing with objects charged with electricity. —e·lec′tro·stat′ic, *adj.*

Electroscope

e·lec·tro·ther·a·py (i·lek′trō·ther′ə·pi), *n.* treatment of disease by electricity. —e·lec′tro·ther′a·pist, *n.*

e·lec·tro·type (i·lek′trə·tīp), *n., v.,* -typed, -typ·ing. —*n.* a copy of a page of type, an engraving, etc., used in printing, consisting of a thin shell of metal deposited by electrolytic action in a wax mold of the original and backed with type metal. —*v.* make such a plate or plates of. —e·lec′tro·typ′er, *n.*

e·lec·trum (i·lek′trəm), *n.* a pale-yellow alloy of gold and silver, used by the ancients. [< L < Gk. *elektron*]

el·ee·mos·y·nar·y (el'ə·mos'ə·ner'i; el'i·ə-), *adj.* **1.** of or for charity; charitable. **2.** provided by charity; free. **3.** dependent on charity; supported by charity. [< LL, < L *eleemosyna* ALMS]

el·e·gance (el'ə·gəns), **el·e·gan·cy** (-gən·si), *n., pl.* **-ganc·es; -cies. 1.** refined grace and richness; luxury free from showiness. **2.** something elegant. —Syn. **1.** fineness, choiceness.

el·e·gant (el'ə·gənt), *adj.* **1.** having or showing good taste; gracefully and richly refined. **2.** expressed with taste; correct and polished in expression or arrangement. **3.** *Colloq.* fine; excellent; superior. [< L *elegans*] —el'e·gant·ly, *adv.*

el·e·gi·ac (el'ə·ji'ak; -ək; i·lē'ji·ak), *adj.* Also, **el'e·gi'a·cal. 1.** of or suitable for an elegy. **2.** sad; mournful; melancholy. **3.** written in elegiacs. —*n.* a dactylic hexameter couplet, the second line having only an accented syllable in the third and sixth feet.

el·e·gize (el'ə·jīz), *v.,* **-gized, -giz·ing. 1.** compose an elegy. **2.** lament in an elegy.

el·e·gy (el'ə·ji), *n. pl.* **-gies. 1.** a mournful or melancholy poem; poem that is a lament for the dead. **2.** poem written in elegiac verses. [< F < L < Gk. *elegeia,* ult. < *elegos* mournful poem]

elem., element; elementary; elements.

el·e·ment (el'ə·mənt), *n.* **1.** one of the simple substances, such as gold, hydrogen, etc., that cannot as yet be separated into simpler parts by ordinary means; substance composed of atoms that are chemically alike. **2.** one of the parts of which anything is made up. **3.** one of the four substances—earth, water, air, and fire—that were once thought to make up all other things. **4.** natural or suitable surroundings. **5.** *Mil.* any unit or part of a larger group, formation, or maneuver. **6.** *U.S. Air Force.* group of two or three fighter planes flying in formation. **7.** the **elements, a.** the simple, necessary parts to be learned first; the first principles. **b.** the atmospheric forces: *the storm seemed a war of the elements.* **c.** bread and wine used in the Eucharist. [< L *elementum* rudiment, first principle]

el·e·men·tal (el'ə·men'təl), *adj.* **1.** of the four elements—earth, water, air, and fire. **2.** of the forces of nature. **3.** as found in nature; simple but powerful: *hunger is an elemental feeling.* **4.** being a necessary or essential part. **5.** elementary. —el'e·men'tal·ly, *adv.*

el·e·men·ta·ry (el'ə·men'tə·ri; -tri), *adj.* **1.** of or dealing with the simple, necessary parts to be learned first; introductory. **2.** made up of only one chemical element; not a compound. **3.** having to do with a chemical element or elements. **4.** elemental. —el'e·men'ta·ri·ly, *adv.* —el'e·men'ta·ri·ness, *n.* —Syn. **1.** rudimentary.

elementary school, 1. school of six grades followed by junior high school. **2.** school of eight grades, followed by a four-year high school.

el·e·phant (el'ə·fənt), *n., pl.* **-phants** or (*esp. collectively*) **-phant.** a huge, heavy mammal, with a long trunk and ivory tusks, that is the largest four-footed animal now living. [< OF < L < Gk. *elephas* elephant, ivory, prob. < Egypt.]

el·e·phan·ti·a·sis (el'ə·fən·ti'ə·sis; -fan-), *n.* disease in which parts of the body, usually the legs, become greatly enlarged, caused by parasitic worms that block the flow of lymph.

el·e·phan·tine (el'ə·fan'tin; -tīn; -tēn), *adj.* **1.** like an elephant; huge; heavy; clumsy; slow. **2.** of elephants.

E·leu·sis (i·lü'sis), *n.* city in ancient Greece, near Athens, site of yearly secret religious ceremonies in honor of the goddesses Demeter and Persephone. —El·eu·sin·i·an (el'yū·sin'i·ən), *adj.*

el·e·vate (el'ə·vāt), *v.,* **-vat·ed, -vat·ing. 1.** lift up; raise. **2.** raise in rank or station. **3.** raise in quality. **4.** put in high spirits; make joyful or proud. [< L, < *ex-* out + *levare* lighten, raise] —Syn. **1.** hoist. **2.** promote, advance. **4.** cheer.

el·e·vat·ed (el'ə·vāt'id), *adj.* **1.** lifted up; raised; high. **2.** dignified; lofty; noble. **3.** in high spirits; joyful; proud. —*n. Am., Colloq.* a street railway raised above the ground.

el·e·va·tion (el'ə·vā'shən), *n.* **1.** a raised place; high place. **2.** height above the earth's surface or above sea level. **3.** a raising or being raised. **4.** loftiness; nobility. **5.** a drawing showing how the front, rear, or side of something looks from the outside.

el·e·va·tor (el'ə·vā'tər), *n.* **1.** thing that raises or lifts up. **2.** *Am.* a moving platform or cage to carry people and things up and down in a building, mine, etc. **3.** *Am.* a building for storing grain. **4.** an adjustable surface that causes an airplane to go up or down.

elevator shaft, *Am.* a verticle chute or passageway for an elevator.

e·lev·en (i·lev'ən), *n.* **1.** a cardinal number, one more than ten. **2.** symbol of this number; 11. **3.** team of eleven players. —*adj.* one more than ten; 11. [OE *endleofan* one left (over ten)] —e·lev'enth, *adj., n.*

eleventh hour, the latest possible moment.

elf (elf), *n., pl.* **elves. 1.** a tiny, mischievous fairy. **2.** a small, mischievous person. [OE *œlf*] —elf'like', *adj.*

elf·in (el'fən), *adj.* of or suitable for elves; like an elf's. —*n.* elf.

elf·ish (el'fish), *adj.* elflike; elfin; mischievous. —elf'ish·ly, *adv.* —elf'ish·ness, *n.*

elf·lock (elf'lok'), *n.* a tangled lock of hair.

El Gre·co (el grek'ō; grä'kō), 1548?–1614, painter of religious pictures in Spain and Italy, who was born in Crete.

E·li·a (ē'li·ə), *n.* pen name of Charles Lamb.

e·lic·it (i·lis'it), *v.* draw forth: *elicit a reply, elicit applause.* [< L *elicitus* < *ex-* out + *lacere* entice] —e·lic'i·ta'tion, *n.* —e·lic'i·tor, *n.*

e·lide (i·līd'), *v.,* **e·lid·ed, e·lid·ing. 1.** omit or slur over in pronunciation. The *e* in *the* is elided in "th' inevitable hour." **2.** *Law.* annul. [< L, < *ex-* out + *laedere* dash] —e·lid'i·ble, *adj.*

e·li·gi·bil·i·ty (el'ə·jə·bil'ə·ti), *n., pl.* **-ties.** fitness; qualification; desirability.

el·i·gi·ble (el'ə·jə·bəl), *adj.* fit to be chosen; properly qualified; desirable. —*n.* an eligible person. [< F < LL < L *eligere* pick out, choose. See ELECT.] —el'i·gi·bly, *adv.*

E·li·jah (i·lī'jə), *n.* a great Hebrew prophet who lived in the ninth century B.C. I Kings 17–19; II Kings 2:1–11.

e·lim·i·nate (i·lim'ə·nāt), *v.,* **-nat·ed, -nat·ing. 1.** get rid of; remove. **2.** pay no attention to; leave out of consideration; omit. **3.** *Math.* get rid of (an unknown quantity) by combining algebraic equations. **4.** *Physiol.* to void. **5.** execute. [< L, < *ex-* off + *limen* threshold] —e·lim'i·na'tion, *n.* —e·lim'i·na'tive, *adj.* —e·lim'i·na'tor, *n.* —Syn. **2.** exclude, except.

El·i·ot (el'i·ət; el'yət), *n.* **1.** Charles W., 1834–1926, American educator, president of Harvard University from 1869 to 1909. **2.** George, 1819–1880, pen name of Mary Ann Evans, an English novelist. **3.** T(homas) S(tearns), born 1888, British poet, essayist, and critic, born in the United States.

E·lis (ē'lis), *n.* an ancient division of W Greece. Olympic games were held on the plains of Olympia in Elis.

E·li·sha (i·lī'shə), *n.* Hebrew prophet who was taught by Elijah. II Kings 2.

e·li·sion (i·lizh'ən), *n.* suppression of a vowel or a syllable. In poetry it generally consists in omitting a final vowel when the next word has an initial vowel.

e·lite, é·lite (i·lēt'; ā-), *n.* the choice or distinguished part; the best people. [< F, fem. pp. of *élire* pick out < L *eligere.* See ELECT.]

e·lix·ir (i·lik'sər), *n.* **1.** substance allegedly having the power of changing lead, iron, etc., into gold or of lengthening life indefinitely. **2.** a universal remedy; cure-all. **3.** medicine made of more than one base, usually of drugs or herbs mixed with alcohol and syrup. [< Med.L < Ar. *al-iksir* (def. 1), prob. < Gk. *xerion* drying powder used on wounds < *xeros* dry]

E·liz·a·beth (i·liz'ə·bəth), *n.* **1.** 1533–1603, Queen Elizabeth, ruler of England from 1558 to

1603, daughter of Henry VIII. **2.** born 1926, queen of Great Britain and Northern Ireland, and head of the British Commonwealth of Nations, daughter of George VI. **3.** *Bible.* cousin of the Virgin Mary. **4.** city in NE New Jersey.

E·liz·a·be·than (i·liz´ə·bē´thən; –beth´ən), *adj.* of the time of Queen Elizabeth. —*n.* person, esp. a writer, of the time of Queen Elizabeth.

Elizabethan sonnet, type of sonnet written by Shakespeare and many other Elizabethans. It has the rhyme scheme *abab cdcd efef gg.*

elk (elk), *n., pl.* **elks** or (*esp.* collectively) **elk. 1.** a large deer of N Europe and Asia. It has antlers like a moose. **2.** a large, reddish deer of North America; wapiti. [appar. < AF form of OE *eolh*]

ell[1] (el), *n.* an old measure of length, chiefly used in measuring cloth. In England it was equal to 45 inches. Also, **el.** [OE *eln* length of lower arm]

ell[2] (el), *n.* **1.** something shaped like an L. **2.** an extension of a building at right angles to it. Also, **el.**

el·lipse (i·lips´), *n. Geom.* a plane curve, the path of a point that moves so that the sum of its distances from two fixed points remains the same. [< L *ellipsis* ELLIPSIS]

el·lip·sis (i·lip´sis), *n., pl.* **–ses** (–sēz). **1.** omission of a word or words needed to complete the grammatical construction of a sentence. *Example:* She is as tall as her brother (is tall), if not taller (than her brother is tall). **2.** marks (. . . or ***) used to show an omission in writing or printing. [< L < Gk., < *elleipein* come short, leave out]

el·lip·ti·cal (i·lip´tə·kəl), **el·lip·tic** (–tik), *adj.* **1.** like an ellipse; of an ellipse. **2.** showing ellipsis; having a word or words omitted. —**el·lip´ti·cal·ly,** *adv.*

El·lis Is·land (el´is), a small island in New York harbor where immigrants were examined, until 1954, before entering the United States.

elm (elm), *n.* **1.** a tall, graceful shade tree. **2.** its hard, heavy wood. [OE]

el·o·cu·tion (el´ə·kū´shən), *n.* **1.** art of speaking or reading clearly and effectively in public; art of public speaking. **2.** manner of speaking or reading in public. [< L *elocutio* < *ex–* out + *loqui* speak] —**el·o·cu·tion·ar·y** (el´ə·kū´shən·er´i), *adj.* —**el´o·cu´tion·ist,** *n.*

e·lon·gate (i·lông´gāt; i·long´–), *v.,* **–gat·ed, –gat·ing,** *adj.* —*v.* lengthen; extend; stretch. —*adj.* **1.** lengthened. **2.** long and thin: *the elongate leaf of the willow.* [< L, < *ex–* out + *longus* long] —**e·lon·ga·tion** (i·lông´gā´shən, i·long´–; ē´lông–, ē´long–), *n.*

E, elongate; O, oblong.

Leaves:

e·lope (i·lōp´), *v.,* **e·loped, e·lop·ing. 1.** run away with a lover. **2.** run away; escape. [< AF *aloper* < ME *lope(n)* run. See LOPE.] —**e·lope´ment,** *n.* —**e·lop´er,** *n.*

el·o·quence (el´ə·kwens), *n.* **1.** flow of speech that has grace and force. **2.** power to win by speaking; art of speaking so as to stir the feelings. [< L *eloquentia* < *ex–* out + *loqui* speak] —Syn. **1.** elocution. **2.** oratory, rhetoric.

el·o·quent (el´ə·kwənt), *adj.* **1.** having eloquence. **2.** very expressive. —**el´o·quent·ly,** *adv.* —Syn. **1.** voluble, fluent, glib. **2.** significant.

El Pas·o (el pas´ō), city in W Texas, on the Rio Grande.

El Sal·va·dor (el sal´və·dôr), country in W Central America.

else (els), *adj.* **1.** other; different. **2.** in addition. —*adv.* **1.** instead. **2.** differently. **3.** otherwise; if not. [OE *elles*] ▶ Because else follows the word (usually a pronoun) it modifies, it takes the sign of the possessive: *he finally decided the book was somebody else's.*

else·where (els´hwâr), **else·whith·er** (–hwith´ər), *adv.* somewhere else; in or to some other place.

e·lu·ci·date (i·lū´sə·dāt), *v.,* **–dat·ed, –dat·ing.** make clear; explain. [< LL, < L *ex–* out + *lucidus* bright] —**e·lu´ci·da´tion,** *n.* —**e·lu´ci·da´tive,** *adj.* —**e·lu´ci·da´tor,** *n.*

e·lude (i·lūd´), *v.,* **e·lud·ed, e·lud·ing. 1.** slip away from; escape by cleverness, quickness, etc. **2.** escape discovery by; baffle. [< L, < *ex–* out + *ludere* play] —**e·lud´er,** *n.* —**e·lu·sion** (i·lū´zhən), *n.* —Syn. **1.** avoid, evade, shun. **2.** foil, frustrate.

e·lu·sive (i·lū´siv), *adj.* **e·lu·so·ry** (–sə·ri), *adj.* **1.** hard to describe or understand; baffling. **2.** tending to elude. —**e·lu´sive·ly,** *adv.* —**e·lu´sive·ness,** *n.*

elves (elvz), *n.* pl. of elf.

elv·ish (el´vish), *adj.* elfish; elflike. —**elv´ish·ly,** *adv.*

E·ly·si·um (i·lizh´i·əm; i·liz´–; i·lizh´əm), *n.* **1.** *Gk. Myth.* place where heroes and virtuous people lived after death. **2.** any place or condition of perfect happiness; paradise. —**E·ly·sian** (i·lizh´ən), *adj.*

em (em), *n., pl.* **ems. 1.** the letter M, m. **2.** unit for measuring the amount of print in a line, page, etc.

e·ma·ci·ate (i·mā´shi·āt), *v.,* **–at·ed, –at·ing.** make unnaturally thin; cause to lose flesh or waste away. [< L, ult. < *ex–* + *macies* leanness] —**e·ma·ci·a·tion** (i·mā´shi·ā´shən; –si–), *n.*

em·a·nate (em´ə·nāt), *v.,* **–nat·ed, –nat·ing.** come forth. [< L, < *ex–* out + *manare* flow] —**em·a·na·tion,** *n.* —**em´a·na´tive,** *adj.*

e·man·ci·pate (i·man´sə·pāt), *v.,* **–pat·ed, –pat·ing.** release from slavery or restraint; set free. [< L *emancipatus* < *ex–* away + *manceps* purchaser < *manus* hand + *capere* take] —**e·man´ci·pa´tion,** *n.* —**e·man´ci·pa´tive,** *adj.* —**e·man´ci·pa´tor,** *n.*

e·mas·cu·late (*v.* i·mas´kyə·lāt; *adj.* i·mas´kyə·lit; –lāt), *v.,* **–lat·ed, –lat·ing,** *adj.* —*v.* **1.** remove the male glands of; castrate. **2.** destroy the force of; weaken. —*adj.* deprived of vigor; weakened; effeminate. [< L *emasculatus* < *ex–* away + *masculus* male] —**e·mas´cu·la´tion,** *n.* —**e·mas´cu·la´tor,** *n.*

em·balm (em·bäm´), *v.* **1.** treat (a dead body) with drugs, chemicals, etc., to keep it from decaying. **2.** keep in memory; preserve. **3.** fill with sweet scent; perfume. —**em·balm´er,** *n.* —**em·balm´ment,** *n.*

em·bank (em·bangk´), *v.* protect, enclose, or confine with a raised bank of earth, stones, etc.

em·bank·ment (em·bangk´mənt), *n.* **1.** a raised bank of earth, stones, etc., used to hold back water, support a roadway, etc. **2.** an embanking.

em·bar·go (em·bär´gō), *n., pl.* **–goes,** *v.,* **–goed, –go·ing.** —*n.* **1.** order of a government forbidding ships to enter or leave its ports. **2.** any restriction put on commerce by law. **3.** restriction; restraint; hindrance. —*v.* lay an embargo on; forbid to enter or leave port. [< Sp., < *embargar* restrain < VL *in–* in + *barra* BAR]

em·bark (em·bärk´), *v.* **1.** go on board ship. **2.** put on board ship. **3.** set out; start. **4.** involve (a person) in an enterprise; invest (money) in an enterprise. [< F *embarquer*. See EN–, BARK[3].] —**em´bar·ka´tion, em·bar·ca´tion,** *n.* —**em·bark´ment,** *n.*

em·bar·rass (em·bar´əs), *v.* **1.** disturb (a person); make self-conscious. **2.** complicate; mix up. **3.** involve in difficulties; hinder. **4.** burden with debt; involve in financial difficulties. [< F, lit., to block < Ital., < *imbarrare* to bar < VL *barra* BAR] —**em·bar´rass·ing,** *adj.* —**em·bar´rass·ing·ly,** *adv.* —**em·bar´rass·ment,** *n.* —Syn. **1.** discomfit, disconcert, abash, confuse. **3.** hamper, impede, obstruct.

em·bas·sa·dor (em·bas´ə·dər; –dôr), *n.* ambassador.

em·bas·sy (em´bə·si), *n., pl.* **–sies. 1.** ambassador and his staff of assistants. **2.** the official residence, offices, etc., of an ambassador in a foreign country. **3.** position or duties of an ambassador. **4.** person or group officially sent as ambassadors. **5.** a special errand; important mission; official message. [< OF < Ital. < Pr. < Gothic *andbahti* service, ult. < Gaulish *ambactus*]

em·bat·tle[1] (em·bat´əl), *v.,* **–tled, –tling.** prepare for battle; form into battle order. [see EN–, BATTLE]

em·bat·tle[2] (em-bat′əl), v., -tled, -tling. provide with battlements; fortify. [< en- + obs. battle, v., furnish with battlements]

em·bed (em-bed′), v., -bed·ded, -bed·ding. 1. put in a bed. 2. fix or enclose in a surrounding mass. Also, imbed.

em·bel·lish (em-bel′ish), v. 1. decorate; adorn; ornament. 2. make more interesting by adding real or imaginary details; elaborate. [< OF embellir < en- in (< L in-) + bel handsome < L bellus] —em·bel′lish·er, n. —em·bel′lish·ment, n. —Syn. 1. beautify.

em·ber (em′bər), n. piece of wood or coal still glowing in the ashes of a fire. [OE æmerge]

Ember days, three days set apart in each season for fasting and prayer by the Roman Catholic, Anglican, and some other churches.

em·bez·zle (em-bez′əl), v., -zled, -zling. steal (money, securities, etc., entrusted to one's care). [< AF enbesiler < en- + beseler destroy] —embez′zle·ment, n. —em·bez′zler, n.

em·bit·ter (em-bit′ər), v. make bitter; make more bitter.

em·bla·zon (em-blā′zən), v. 1. display conspicuously; picture in bright colors. 2. decorate; adorn. 3. praise highly; honor publicly; make known the fame of. —em·bla′zon·er, n. —em·bla′zon·ment, em·bla′zon·ry, n.

em·blem (em′bləm), n. 1. representation of an invisible quality, idea, etc., by some connection of thought; symbol. The dove is an emblem of peace. 2. a heraldic device. [< L, inlaid work < Gk. emblema insertion < en- in + ballein throw] —Syn. 1. token, sign, badge.

em·blem·at·ic (em′blə·mat′ik), **em·blem·at·i·cal** (-ə-kəl), adj. used as an emblem; symbolical. The Cross is emblematic of Christianity. —em′blem·at′i·cal·ly, adv.

em·bod·y (em-bod′i), v., -bod·ied, -bod·y·ing. 1. put into visible form; express in definite form. 2. bring together and include in a book, system, etc.; organize. 3. make part of an organized book, law, system, etc.; incorporate. —em·bod′i·ment, n. —Syn. 1. incarnate, materialize, externalize. 3. include, combine.

em·bold·en (em-bōl′dən), v. make bold; encourage.

em·bo·lism (em′bə-liz-əm), n. Med. obstruction of a blood vessel by a clot, a bit of fat, or other obstacle. [< L < Gk. embolismos. See EM-BLEM.] —em′bo·lis′mic, adj.

em·bo·lus (em′bə-ləs), n., pl. -li (-lī). a solid material in the vascular system.

em·bos·om (em-buz′əm; -bū′zəm), v. 1. surround; enclose; envelop. 2. embrace; cherish.

em·boss (em-bôs′; -bos′), v. decorate with a design, pattern, etc., that stands out from the surface. [see EN-, BOSS[2]] —em·boss′er, n. —emboss′ment, n.

em·bou·chure (äm′bu-shur′), n. 1. mouth of a river or valley. 2. mouthpiece of a wind instrument. [< F, < emboucher put into or discharge from a mouth < en- in (< L in-) + bouche mouth < L bucca]

em·bow·er (em-bou′ər), v. enclose in a shelter of leafy branches.

em·brace (em-brās′), v., -braced, -brac·ing. n. —v. 1. clasp or hold in the arms to show love or friendship; hug. 2. hug one another. 3. take up; take for oneself; accept: embrace the Christian religion. 4. include; contain. 5. surround; enclose. —n. an embracing; a hug. [< OF < VL < L in- in + brachium arm] —em·brace′a·ble, adj. —em·brace′ment, n. —em·brac′er, n. —Syn. v. 3. adopt, espouse. 4. comprise. —Ant. v. 3. spurn, reject. 4. exclude, eliminate.

em·bra·sure (em-brā′zhər), n. 1. an opening in a wall for a gun, with sides that spread outward. 2. a slanting off of the wall at an oblique angle on the inner sides of a window or door. [< F, < embraser widen an opening]

em·bro·cate (em′brō-kāt), v., -cat·ed, -cat·ing. bathe and rub with liniment or lotion. [< LL embrocatus < embroch(a)a < Gk. embroche lotion] —em′bro·ca′tion, n.

em·broi·der (em-broi′dər), v. 1. ornament

(cloth, leather, etc.) with a design, pattern, etc., of stitches. 2. make or put (a design, pattern, etc.) on cloth, leather, etc., with stitches. 3. do embroidery. 4. add imaginary details to; exaggerate. [see EN-, BROIDER] —em·broi′der·er, n. —Syn. 1. embellish, beautify, decorate.

em·broi·der·y (em-broi′dər-i), n., pl. -deries. 1. art of working raised and ornamental designs in cloth, leather, etc., with a needle; embroidering. 2. embroidered work or material.

em·broil (em-broil′), v. 1. involve (a person, country, etc.) in a quarrel. 2. throw (affairs, etc.) into a state of confusion. —em·broil′er, n. —em·broil′ment, n.

em·brown (em-broun′), v. tan; darken.

em·bry·o (em′bri-ō), n., pl. -bry·os, adj. —n. 1. animal during the period of its growth from the fertilized egg until its organs have developed so that it can live independently. 2. Bot. an undeveloped plant within a seed. —adj. embryonic; undeveloped; not mature. [< Med.L < Gk. embryon, < en- in + bryein swell]

embryol., embryology.

em·bry·ol·o·gy (em′bri-ol′ə-ji), n. Biol. study of the formation and development of embryos. —em·bry·o·log·i·cal (em′bri-ə-loj′ə-kəl), em′bry·o·log′ic, adj. —em′bry·ol′o·gist, n.

Embryo (def. 2) — ENDOSPERM, EMBRYO

em·bry·on·ic (em′bri-on′ik), adj. 1. of the embryo. 2. undeveloped; not mature.

em·cee (em′sē′), n., v., -ceed, -cee·ing. U.S. —n. master of ceremonies. —v. act as master of ceremonies of. Also, M.C.

e·meer (ə-mir′), n. emir.

e·mend (i-mend′), **e·men·date** (ē′men-dāt), v., e·mend·ed, e·mend·ing; e·men·dat·ed, e·men·dat·ing. suggest changes to free (a faulty text, document, etc.) from errors; correct; improve. [< L, < ex- away + menda fault] —e·mend′a·ble, adj. —e·men·da·tion (ē′men-dā′shən; em′en-), n. —e·men·da·to·ry (i-men′də-tō′ri; -tô′-), adj.

em·er·ald (em′ər·əld; em′rəld), n. a bright-green precious stone; transparent green beryl. —adj. bright-green. [< OF esmeralde < L < Gk. smaragdos]

e·merge (i-mérj′), v., e·merged, e·merg·ing. come out; come into view. [< L, < ex- out + mergere dip] —e·mer′gence, n. —e·mer′gent, adj.

e·mer·gen·cy (i-mér′jən-si), n., pl. -cies, adj. —n. a sudden need for immediate action. —adj. for use in time of sudden need. —Syn. n. crisis.

e·mer·i·tus (i-mer′ə-təs), adj. honorably discharged; retired from active service, but still holding one's rank and title. [< L, < ex- to the end + merere serve]

e·mer·sion (i-mér′zhən; -shən), n. an emerging.

Em·er·son (em′ər-sən), n. Ralph Waldo, 1803–1882, American essayist, poet, and philosopher.

em·er·y (em′ər-i), n. a hard, dark mineral, an impure corundum, used for grinding, smoothing, and polishing. [< F < Ital. < Gk smericulum < Med.Gk. smeris < Gk. smyris abrasive powder]

e·met·ic (i-met′ik), adj. causing vomiting. —n. medicine or treatment that causes vomiting. [< L < Gk. emetikos < emeein vomit]

E.M.F., e.m.f., or **emf,** electromotive force.

em·i·grant (em′ə-grənt), n. person who leaves his own country or region to settle in another. —adj. leaving one's own country or region to settle in another.

em·i·grate (em′ə-grāt), v., -grat·ed, -grat·ing. leave one's own country or region to settle in another. [< L, < ex- out + migrare to move. See MIGRATE.] —em′i·gra′tion, n. ► **emigrate, immigrate.** Emigrate means to move out of a country or region, immigrate to move into a country. An emigrant from Norway would be an immigrant to the United States.

é·mi·gré (em'ə·grā), n., pl. **-grés** (-grāz). 1. emigrant. 2. member of a refugee group. [< F]

em·i·nence (em'ə·nəns), n. 1. rank or position above all or most others; high standing; fame. 2. a high place; lofty hill. 3. Eminence, title of honor given to a cardinal in the Roman Catholic Church. [< L eminentia < ex- out + minere jut] —Syn. 1. distinction, prominence, renown.

em·i·nent (em'ə·nənt), adj. 1. distinguished; exalted. 2. conspicuous; noteworthy. 3. high; lofty. 4. projecting. —em'i·nent·ly, adv.

eminent domain, right of government to take private property for public use. The owner must be paid for the property taken.

e·mir (ə·mir'), n. 1. an Arabian chief, prince, or military leader. 2. title of the descendants of Mohammed. 3. title of certain Turkish officials. Also, emeer. [< Ar. amir commander]

em·is·sar·y (em'ə·ser'i), n., pl. -sar·ies, adj. —n. 1. person sent on a mission or errand. 2. a secret agent; spy. —adj. of, or acting as, an emissary. [< L emissarius. See EMIT.]

e·mis·sion (i·mish'ən), n. 1. act or fact of emitting. 2. thing emitted. —e·mis'sive, adj.

e·mit (i·mit'), v., e·mit·ted, e·mit·ting. 1. give off; send out. 2. put into circulation; issue. 3. utter; voice. [< L, < ex- out + mittere send] —e·mit'ter, n. —Syn. 1. exude, expel, eject.

Em·man·u·el (i·man'yū·əl), n. Immanuel.

Em·my (em'i), n., pl. -mies. Am. a small statuette awarded annually by the Academy of Television Arts and Sciences for achievements of outstanding excellence in television.

e·mol·lient (i·mol'yənt), adj. softening; soothing. —n. something that softens and soothes. [< L < emollire soften < ex- + mollis soft]

e·mol·u·ment (i·mol'yə·mənt), n. profit from an office or position; fee [< L, profit, ult. < ex- out + molere grind]

e·mote (i·mōt'), v., e·mot·ed, e·mot·ing. Am. 1. act, esp. in an exaggerated manner. 2. show emotion. —e·mo'tive, adj. —e·mo·tiv·i·ty (ē'mō·tiv'ə·ti), n.

e·mo·tion (i·mō'shən), n. a strong feeling, as of fear, anger, love, joy, etc. [< F, (after motion) < émouvoir stir up < L, < ex- out + movere move] —e·mo'tion·al, adj. —e·mo'tion·al·i·ty, n. —e·mo'tion·al·ly, adv. —e·mo'tion·less, adj. —Syn. sentiment, sensation, passion.

e·mo·tion·al·ism (i·mō'shən·əl·iz'əm), n. 1. emotional quality or character. 2. an appealing to the emotions. 3. tendency to display emotion too easily.

em·pan·el (em·pan'əl), v., -eled, -el·ing; esp. Brit. -elled, -el·ling. impanel.

em·pa·thy (em'pə·thi), n. the complete understanding of another's feelings, motives, etc. [< Gk., < en- in + pathos feeling] —em·path·ic (em·path'ik), adj.

em·per·or (em'pər·ər), n. man who is the ruler of an empire. [< OF < L imperator commander < in- in + parare to order] —em'per·or·ship', n. —Syn. kaiser, czar.

em·pha·sis (em'fə·sis), n., pl. -ses (-sēz). 1. special force; stress; importance. 2. special force given to particular syllables, words, or phrases. [< L < Gk., < emphainein indicate < en- in + phainein show] —Syn. 2. accent, accentuation.

em·pha·size (em'fə·sīz), v., -sized, -siz·ing. give special force to; stress.

em·phat·ic (em·fat'ik), adj. 1. spoken or done with force or stress; strongly expressed. 2. speaking with force or stress; expressing oneself strongly. 3. attracting attention; striking. —em·phat'i·cal·ly, adv. —Syn. 1. forcible.

em·pire (em'pir), n. 1. group of countries or states under the same ruler or government: the British Empire. 2. country ruled by an emperor or empress: the Japanese Empire. 3. absolute power; supreme authority. [< OF < L imperium. See EMPEROR.] —Syn. 1. realm.

em·pir·ic (em·pir'ik), n. 1. person who lacks theoretical or scientific knowledge and relies entirely on practical experience. 2. person without regular or proper training; quack. —adj. empirical. [< L < Gk. empeirikos < en- in + peira experience, experiment]

em·pir·i·cal (em·pir'ə·kəl), adj. 1. based on experiment and observation. 2. based entirely on practical experience. —em·pir'i·cal·ly, adv.

em·pir·i·cism (em·pir'ə·siz·əm), n. 1. use of methods based on experiment and observation. 2. undue reliance upon experience; unscientific practice; quackery. —em·pir'i·cist, n.

em·place·ment (em·plās'mənt), n. 1. space or platform for a heavy gun or guns. 2. an assigning to a place; locating.

em·ploy (em·ploi'), v. 1. use the services of; give work and pay to. 2. use. 3. engage the attention of; keep busy; occupy. —n. a being employed; service for pay; employment. [< F < L, < in- in + plicare fold] —em·ploy'a·ble, adj. —Syn. v. 1. engage, hire.

em·ploy·ee, em·ploy·e, or **em·ploy·é** (em·ploi'ē; em'ploi·ē'), n. person who works for some person or firm for pay.

em·ploy·er (em·ploi'ər), n. 1. person or firm that employs one or more persons. 2. user.

em·ploy·ment (em·ploi'mənt), n. 1. an employing or being employed. 2. what a person is doing; business. 3. use. —Syn. 2. occupation, work, trade, profession, vocation.

em·po·ri·um (em·pô'ri·əm; -pō'-), n., pl. -po·ri·ums, -po·ri·a (-pô'ri·ə; -pō'-), 1. center of trade; market place. 2. a large store selling many different things. [< L < Gk. emporion < emporos merchant, traveler < en- on + poros voyage]

em·pow·er (em·pou'ər), v. 1. give power to. 2. enable; permit. Also, impower. —em·pow'er·ment, n. —Syn. 1. authorize, commission.

em·press (em'pris), n. 1. wife of an emperor. 2. woman who is the ruler of an empire.

emp·ty (emp'ti), adj., -ti·er, -ti·est, v., -tied, -ty·ing, n., pl. -ties. —adj. 1. with nothing or no one in it. 2. not real; meaningless: an empty threat has no force. 3. Colloq. hungry. 4. empty of, having no. —v. 1. pour out or take out the contents of; make empty. 2. become empty. 3. flow out; discharge. —n. Colloq. something with nothing or no one in it. [OE ǣmtig < ǣmetta leisure] —emp'ti·ly, adv. —emp'ti·ness, n. —Syn. adj. 1. vacant, unoccupied, unfilled. 2. hollow, unsubstantial. —v. 1. unload, unburden, evacuate.

em·pur·pled (em·pėr'pəld), adj. made purple; colored with purple.

em·pyr·e·al (em·pir'i·əl; em'pə·rē'əl, -pī-), adj. 1. of the empyrean; celestial; heavenly. 2. formed of pure fire or light.

em·py·re·an (em'pə·rē'ən; -pī-), n. 1. the highest heaven; region of pure light. 2. sky; firmament. —adj. empyreal. [< LL < Gk. empyrios, empyros < en- in + pyr fire]

e·mu (ē'mū), n. a large, flightless Australian bird resembling an ostrich but smaller. [< Moluccan emeu]

em·u·late (em'yə·lāt), v., -lat·ed, -lat·ing. try to equal or excel. [< L, < aemulus striving to equal] —em'u·la'tion, n. —em'u·la'tive, adj.

em·u·lous (em'yə·ləs), adj. 1. wishing to equal or excel. 2. arising from or pertaining to emulation. —em'u·lous·ly, adv. —em'u·lous·ness, n.

e·mul·si·fy (i·mul'sə·fī), v., -fied, -fy·ing. make into an emulsion. —e·mul'si·fi·ca'tion, n. —e·mul'si·fi'er, n.

e·mul·sion (i·mul'shən), n. 1. liquid that is a mixture of liquids that do not dissolve in each other. 2. a coating on a camera film, plate, etc., that is sensitive to light. [< NL emulsio < L ex- out + mulgere milk]

en (en), n. 1. the letter N, n. 2. half the width of an em in printing.

en–, prefix. 1. cause to be; make, as in enable, enfeeble. 2. put in; put on, as in encircle, enthrone. 3. other meanings, as in enact, encourage, entwine. En– often changes the meaning of a verb little or not at all. [< OF < L in–; before b, p, or m the form becomes em–] ► en–, im–. In– is either a native English prefix or a prefix of Latin origin; en– is the same Latin prefix modified in French. (Em– and im– are variant forms.) In several common words, usage is divided, though usually one form is more common. We tend to use in– more than the British do but en– is often preferred in formal usage.

In the following examples of divided usage, the preferred form is put first: *enclose—inclose* (gaining); *endorse—indorse; ensure—insure* (but *insure* is preferred in the financial sense).

–en, *suffix.* 1. cause to be; make, as in *blacken, sharpen.* 2. cause to have, as in *heighten, strengthen.* 3. become, as in *sicken, soften.* 4. come to have; gain, as in *lengthen.* 5. made of, as in *silken, wooden.* 6. *–en* is used to form past participles of strong verbs, as in *fallen, shaken.* 7. *–en* is used to form the plural of a few nouns, as in *children, oxen.* [OE]

en·a·ble (en·ā′bəl), *v.,* **–bled, –bling.** give ability, power, or means to; make able. —**Syn.** empower, permit, authorize, warrant.

en·act (en·akt′), *v.* 1. pass (a bill) giving it validity as law; make into a law. 2. decree; order. 3. play the part of; act out; play. —**Syn.** 2. ordain, adjudge.

en·act·ment (en·akt′mənt), *n.* 1. an enacting. 2. a being enacted. 3. law.

en·am·el (i·nam′əl), *n., v.,* **–eled, –el·ing;** *esp.* *Brit.* **–elled, –el·ling.** —*n.* 1. a glasslike substance melted and then cooled to make a smooth, hard surface. 2. paint or varnish used to make a smooth, hard, glossy surface. 3. a coating applied to the skin to simulate a beautiful complexion. 4. the smooth, hard, glossy outer layer of the teeth. 5. thing covered or decorated with enamel. 6. any smooth, hard coating or surface that shines. [< v.] —*v.* cover or decorate with enamel. [< AF *enamayller* < *en-* on (< L *in-*) + *amayl* (OF *esmail*) enamel < Gmc.] —**en·am′el·er,** *esp. Brit.* **en·am′el·ler,** *n.* —**en·am′el·work′,** *n.*

en·am·or, *esp. Brit.* **en·am·our** (en·am′ər), *v.* arouse to love; charm: *her beauty enamored the prince.* [< OF *enamourer* < *en-* in (< L *in-*) + *amour* love < L *amor*] —**en·am′ored,** *esp. Brit.* **en·am′oured,** *adj.*

en bloc (en blok′; än), all together; in one lump. [< F]

en·camp (en·kamp′), *v.* 1. make a camp. 2. stay in a camp. 3. put in a camp. —**en·camp′ment,** *n.*

en·case (en·kās′), *v.,* **–cased, –cas·ing.** incase.

–ence, *suffix.* 1. act, fact, quality, or state of ——ing, as in *abhorrence, indulgence.* 2. quality or state of being ——ent, as in *absence, confidence, competence, prudence.* [< L *-entia*]

en·ceph·a·li·tis (en·sef′ə·lī′tis), *n.* inflammation of the brain caused by injury, infection, poison, etc. —**en·ceph·a·lit·ic** (en·sef′ə·lit′ik), *adj.*

en·ceph·a·lon (en·sef′ə·lon), *n.* the brain. [< NL < Gk., < *en-* in + *kephale* head] —**en·ce·phal·ic** (en′sə·fal′ik), *adj.*

en·chain (en·chān′), *v.* 1. put in chains; fetter. 2. attract and fix firmly; hold fast. —**en·chain′ment,** *n.*

en·chant (en·chant′; –chänt′), *v.* 1. use magic on; put under a spell. 2. delight greatly; charm. [< F < L < *in-* against + *cantare* chant] —**Syn.** 2. fascinate, captivate, enrapture.

en·chant·er (en·chan′tər; –chän′-), *n.* one that enchants.

en·chant·ing (en·chan′ting; –chän′-), *adj.* 1. very delightful; charming. 2. bewitching. —**en·chant′ing·ly,** *adv.*

en·chant·ment (en·chant′mənt; –chänt′-), *n.* 1. an enchanting or being enchanted. 2. something that enchants.

en·chan·tress (en·chan′tris; –chän′-), *n.* woman who enchants.

en·cir·cle (en·sér′kəl), *v.,* **–cled, –cling.** 1. form a circle around; surround. 2. go in a circle around. —**en·cir′cle·ment,** *n.* —**Syn.** 1. encompass, gird, circumscribe.

en·clave (en′klāv), *n.* country or district surrounded by a foreign territory. [< F, < *enclaver* enclose]

en·close (en·klōz′), *v.,* **–closed, –clos·ing.** 1. shut in on all sides; surround. 2. put a wall or fence around. 3. put in an envelope along with a letter. 4. contain. Also, **inclose.**

en·clo·sure (en·klō′zhər), *n.* 1. an enclosing

or being enclosed. 2. an enclosed place. 3. thing that encloses. 4. thing enclosed. Also, **inclosure.**

en·co·mi·ast (en·kō′mi·ast), *n.* writer or speaker of encomiums; eulogist.

en·co·mi·um (en·kō′mi·əm), *n., pl.* **–mi·ums, –mi·a** (–mi·ə). an elaborate expression of praise; high praise; eulogy. [< LL < Gk. *enkomion,* neut., laudatory < *en-* in + *komos* revelry]

en·com·pass (en·kum′pəs), *v.* 1. surround completely; shut in on all sides; encircle. 2. enclose; contain. —**en·com′pass·ment,** *n.*

en·core (äng′kôr; –kōr; än′-), *interj., n., v.,* **–cored, –cor·ing.** —*interj.* once more; again. —*n.* 1. demand by the audience for the repetition of a song, etc., or for another appearance of the performer or performers. 2. repetition of a song, etc., in response to such a demand. 3. an additional song, etc., given in response to such a demand. —*v.* make such a demand for (a performer, etc.) by applauding. [< F]

en·coun·ter (en·koun′tər), *v.* 1. meet unexpectedly. 2. meet with (difficulties, opposition, etc.). 3. meet as an enemy; meet in a fight or battle. —*n.* 1. a meeting, esp. an unexpected one. 2. a meeting of enemies; fight; battle. [< OF < VL, < L *in-* in + *contra* against] —**Syn.** *n.* 2. conflict, combat, skirmish.

en·cour·age (en·kér′ij), *v.,* **–aged, –ag·ing.** 1. give courage to; increase the hope or confidence of; urge on. 2. be favorable to; help; support. [< OF, < *en-* in + *corage* COURAGE] —**en·cour′ag·er,** *n.* —**en·cour′ag·ing·ly,** *adv.* —**Syn.** 1. hearten, inspirit, animate. 2. promote, advance.

en·cour·age·ment (en·kér′ij·mənt), *n.* 1. an encouraging. 2. a being encouraged. 3. thing that encourages.

en·croach (en·krōch′), *v.* 1. go beyond proper or usual limits. 2. trespass upon the property or rights of another; intrude. [< OF, < *en-* in (< L *in-*) + *croc* hook < Gmc.] —**en·croach′er,** *n.* —**en·croach′ment,** *n.*

en·crust (en·krust′), *v.* incrust. —**en′crus·ta′-tion,** *n.*

en·cum·ber (en·kum′bər), *v.* 1. hold back (from running, doing, etc.); hinder; hamper. 2. make difficult to use; fill; obstruct. 3. weigh down; burden. Also, **incumber.** [< OF, < *en* in + *combre* barrier, prob. < Celtic]

en·cum·brance (en·kum′brəns), *n.* 1. anything that encumbers; hindrance; obstruction; burden. 2. a dependent person; child. 3. claim, mortgage, etc., on property. Also, **incumbrance.**

–ency, *suffix.* 1. act, fact, quality, or state of ——ing, as in *dependency.* 2. quality or state of being ——ent, as in *frequency.* 3. other meanings, as in *agency, currency.* [< L *-entia*]

en·cyc·li·cal (en·sik′lə·kəl; –sī′klə-), **en·cyc·lic** (–lik), *n.* letter about the general welfare of the church from the pope to his clergy. —*adj.* intended for wide circulation. [< LL *encyclicus* < Gk., < *en-* in + *kyklos* circle]

en·cy·clo·pe·di·a, en·cy·clo·pae·di·a (en·sī′klə·pē′di·ə), *n.* book or series of books giving information, arranged alphabetically, on all branches of knowledge. [< LL < Gk. *enkyklopaideia,* for *enkyklios paideia* well-rounded education] —**en·cy′clo·pe′dic, en·cy′clo·pae′dic,** *adj.* —**en·cy′clo·pe′dist, en·cy′clo·pae′dist,** *n.*

en·cyst (en·sist′), *v.* enclose or become enclosed in a cyst or sac. —**en·cyst′ment,** *n.*

end (end), *n.* 1. the last part; conclusion. 2. place where a thing stops. 3. purpose; object. 4. result; outcome. 5. death; destruction. 6. part left over; remnant; fragment. 7. *Am.* player at either end of the line in football. —*v.* 1. bring or come to an end; stop; finish. 2. destroy; kill. 3. form the end of; be the end of. [OE *ende*] —**end′er,** *n.* —**Syn.** *n.* 1. termination, close, finish, expiration. 3. intention, design, goal, aim. 4. issue, consequence. 5. extermination, annihilation. 6. remainder. —*v.* 1. conclude, terminate, cease.

en·dan·ger (en·dān′jər), *v.* cause danger to; expose to loss or injury. —**en·dan′ger·ment,** *n.*

en·dear (en·dir′), *v.* make dear. —**en·dear′ing·ly,** *adv.*

en·dear·ment (en·dir′mənt), *n.* 1. an endearing. **2.** thing that endears. **3.** act or word showing love or affection; caress.

en·deav·or, *esp. Brit.* **en·deav·our** (en-dev′ər), *v.* try hard; attempt earnestly; make an effort; strive. —*n.* an earnest attempt; effort. [< *en-* + F *devoir* duty] —en·deav′or·er, *esp. Brit.* en·deav′our·er, *n.* —Syn. *v.* struggle, labor, essay. –*n.* exertion, struggle.

en·dem·ic (en·dem′ik), *adj.* Also, **en·dem′i·cal.** regularly found in a particular people or locality. —*n.* an endemic disease. [< Gk. *endemos* native < *en-* in + *demos* people] —en·dem′i·cal·ly, *adv.*

end·ing (en′ding), *n.* **1.** the last part; end. **2.** death. **3.** letter or syllable added to a word or stem to change its meaning or to show its relationship to other words; inflection. The common plural ending in English is *s* or *es*.

en·dive (en′dīv; än′dēv), *n. U.S.* **1.** kind of chicory with finely divided, curly leaves, used for salads. **2.** kind of chicory that looks like very smooth white celery, also used for salads. [< OF < Med.L < Med.Gk. < L *intibum*]

end·less (end′lis), *adj.* **1.** having no end; never stopping; lasting or going on forever. **2.** with the ends joined for continuous action: *an endless chain.* —end′less·ly, *adv.* —end′less·ness, *n.* —Syn. **1.** boundless, limitless, immeasurable, interminable, incessant, unceasing, continual, perpetual, eternal. —Ant. **1.** limited, finite, brief, transient, temporary.

end·most (end′mōst), *adj.* nearest to the end; last; farthest.

endo-, *word element.* within; inside; inner, as in *endocarp, endoplasm.* [< Gk.]

en·do·carp (en′dō·kärp), *n. Bot.* the inner layer of a ripened ovary of a plant.

en·do·crine (en′dō·krīn; –krin), *adj.* of or having to do with the endocrine glands. —*n.* **1.** an endocrine gland. **2.** its secretion. [< *endo-* + Gk. *krinein* separate]

endocrine gland, any of various glands that produce secretions that pass directly into the blood stream instead of into a duct, as the thyroid gland.

E, endocarp of a peach.

en·dog·e·nous (en·doj′ə·nəs), *adj.* growing from the inside; originating within. —en·dog′e·nous·ly, *adv.*

en·do·plasm (en′dō·plaz·əm), *n. Biol.* the inner portion of the cytoplasm of a cell. —en′do·plas′mic, *adj.*

en·dorse (en·dôrs′), *v.,* –dorsed, –dors·ing. **1.** write one's name, comment, etc., on the back of (a check or other document). **2.** approve; support. Also, **indorse.** [alter. of ME *endosse(n)* < OF, < *en-* on + *dos* back < L *dorsum*] —dors′a·ble, *adj.* —en·dor·see (en·dôr′sē′; en′-dôr–), *n.* —en·dors′ment, *n.* —en·dors′er, *n.*

en·do·sperm (en′dō·spérm), *n.* nourishment for the embryo enclosed with it in the seed of a plant. See the picture under **embryo.**

en·dow (en·dou′), *v.* **1.** give money or property to provide an income for. **2.** provide with some ability, quality, or talent: *nature endowed her with both beauty and brains.* **3.** *Archaic.* provide with a dower. [< OF, < *en-* (< L *in-*) + *douer* endow < L *dotare*] —en·dow′er, *n.* —Syn. **2.** furnish, equip, invest.

en·dow·ment (en·dou′mənt), *n.* **1.** an endowing. **2.** money or property given to provide an income. **3.** Usually, **endowments.** talent, esp. a natural, inborn talent; ability.

end product, 1. portion remaining after something is processed; the result of a processing. **2.** *Nuclear Physics.* the last stable member of a series of isotopes, each produced by the radioactive decay of the preceding isotope.

end stop, a mark of punctuation used at the end of a sentence, usually a period, exclamation mark, or question mark.

en·due (en·dü′; –dū′), *v.,* –dued, –du·ing. provide with a quality or power. Also, **indue.**

en·dur·ance (en·dür′əns; –dyür′–), *n.* **1.** power to last or keep on. **2.** power to put up with, bear, or stand. **3.** act or instance of enduring pain, hardship, etc. **4.** duration. —Syn. **2.** fortitude, patience, forbearance, tolerance.

en·dure (en·dür′; –dyür′), *v.,* –dured, –dur·ing. **1.** remain; last. **2.** undergo; bear; tolerate. [< OF < LL < L, make hard < *in-* + *durus* hard] —en·dur′a·ble, *adj.* —en·dur′a·bly, *adv.* —Syn. **1.** continue, remain. **2.** suffer, stand, experience.

en·dur·ing (en·dür′ing; –dyür′–), *adj.* lasting; permanent. —en·dur′ing·ly, *adv.* —en·dur′ing·ness, *n.* —Syn. abiding, unchangeable.

end use, the particular function which a manufactured product serves or is limited to.

end·ways (end′wāz′), **end·wise** (–wīz′), *adv.* **1.** on end; upright. **2.** with the end forward; in the direction of the end. **3.** lengthwise. **4.** end to end.

en·e·ma (en′ə·mə), *n., pl.* en·e·mas, e·nem·a·ta (i·nem′ə·tə). injection of liquid into the rectum to flush the bowels. [< Gk., < *en-* in + *hienai* send]

en·e·my (en′ə·mi), *n., pl.* –mies, *adj.* —*n.* **1.** person or group that hates and tries to harm another. **2.** a hostile force, nation, army, fleet, or air force; person, ship, etc., of a hostile nation. **3.** anything harmful: *frost is an enemy of plants.* —*adj.* of an enemy. [< OF < L, < *in-* not + *amicus* friendly] —Syn. *n.* **1, 2.** adversary, opponent, foe.

en·er·get·ic (en′ər·jet′ik), *adj.* full of energy; eager to work; full of force; active. —en′er·get′i·cal·ly, *adv.* —Syn. vigorous, strenuous, forcible.

en·er·gize (en′ər·jīz), *v.,* –gized, –giz·ing. give energy to. —en′er·giz′er, *n.*

en·er·gy (en′ər·ji), *n., pl.* –gies. **1.** active strength or force; healthy power; vigor. **2.** strength; force; power. **3.** *Physics.* capacity for doing work. [< LL < Gk., < *energos* active < *en-* in + *ergon* work] —Syn. **1.** potency, push, zeal.

en·er·vate (en′ər·vāt), *v.,* –vat·ed, –vat·ing. lessen the vigor or strength of; weaken. [< L, < *ex-* away + *nervus* sinew, nerve] —en′er·va′tion, *n.* —en′er·va′tor, *n.*

en fa·mille (än fä·mē′yə), *French.* with one's family; at home; informally.

en·fant ter·ri·ble (än·fän te·rē′blə), *French.* **1.** child whose behavior, questions, remarks, etc., embarrass older people. **2.** person who is indiscreet or lacks a sense of responsibility.

en·fee·ble (en·fē′bəl), *v.,* –bled, –bling. make feeble; weaken. —en·fee′ble·ment, *n.* —en·fee′bler, *n.*

en·fi·lade (en′fə·lād′), *n., v.,* –lad·ed, –lad·ing. *Am.* —*n.* **1.** gunfire directed from the side at a line of troops or a position held by them. **2.** situation exposed to such raking gunfire. —*v.* fire guns at (a line of troops or the position held by them) from the side. [< F, < *enfiler* thread, pierce < *en-* on (< L *in-*) + *fil* thread < L *filum*]

en·fold (en·fōld′), *v.* infold. —en·fold′er, *n.* —en·fold′ment, *n.*

en·force (en·fôrs′; –fōrs′), *v.,* –forced, –forc·ing. **1.** force obedience to; put into force: *policemen and judges enforce the laws.* **2.** force; compel: *the bandits enforced obedience to their demand by threats of violence.* **3.** urge with force: *the teacher enforced the principle by examples.* **4.** produce or effect by force. **5.** obtain (payment, obedience, etc.) by force. **6.** *Obs.* use force upon. [< OF, ult. < L *in-* + *fortis* strong] —en·force′a·ble, *adj.* —en·forc·ed·ly (en·fôr′-sid·li; –fōr′–), *adv.* —en·force′ment, *n.* —en·forc′er, *n.* —Syn. **1.** execute, administer.

en·fran·chise (en·fran′chīz), *v.,* –chised, –chis·ing. **1.** give the right to vote. **2.** set free; release from slavery or restraint. —en·fran·chise·ment (en·fran′chiz·mənt), *n.* —en·fran′chis·er, *n.*

Eng., England; English.

eng., **1.** engineer; engineering. **2.** engraved; engraving.

en·gage (en·gāj′), *v.,* –gaged, –gag·ing. **1.** bind by a pledge; bind oneself; promise; pledge. **2.** promise or pledge to marry. **3.** keep busy; occupy. **4.** keep oneself busy; be occupied; be active. **5.** hire; employ; take for use or work; reserve (seats, rooms, a cab, etc.). **6.** catch and hold; attract. **7.** fit into; lock together: *gears that engage.* **8.** start a battle with; attack. [< F, < *en gage* under pledge] —en·gag′er, *n.*

en·gaged (en·gājd′), *adj.* **1.** promised or

pledged to marry. 2. busy; occupied. 3. taken for use or work; hired. 4. fitted together. 5. involved in a fight or battle. —*Syn.* 1. betrothed, affianced.

en·gage·ment (en-gāj′mənt), *n.* 1. act of engaging. 2. fact or condition of being engaged. 3. promise; pledge. 4. promise to marry. 5. a meeting with someone at a certain time; appointment. 6. period of being hired; time of use or work. 7. fight; battle. 8. the interlocking of mechanical parts. —*Syn.* 3. contract, agreement. 4. betrothal. 7. encounter, combat, conflict.

en·gag·ing (en-gāj′ing), *adj.* attractive; pleasing; charming. —**en·gag′ing·ly,** *adv.* —**en·gag′-ing·ness,** *n.*

En·gels (eng′gəlz; *Ger.* eng′əls), *n.* Friedrich, 1820–1895, German socialist writer in England, collaborator with Karl Marx.

en·gen·der (en-jen′dər), *v.* bring into existence; produce; cause. [< OF < L, < *in* + *generare* create] —**en·gen′der·er,** *n.* —**en·gen′-der·ment,** *n.*

en·gine (en′jən), *n.* 1. machine that applies power to some work, esp. a machine that can start others moving. 2. machine that pulls a railroad train. 3. machine; device; instrument: *big guns are engines of war.* [< OF < L *ingenium* inborn qualities, talent < *in–* in + *gen–* create]

en·gi·neer (en′jə-nir′), *n.* 1. man who runs an engine. 2. person who plans, builds, or manages engines, machines, roads, bridges, canals, railroads, forts, etc.; expert in engineering. 3. member of a group of men who do engineering work in the army or navy. —*v.* 1. plan, build, direct, or work as an engineer. 2. *Am.* manage cleverly; guide skillfully.

en·gi·neer·ing (en′jə-nir′ing), *n.* science, work, or profession of an engineer; planning, building, or managing engines, machines, roads, bridges, canals, railroads, forts, etc.

Eng·land (ing′glənd), *n.* the largest division of Great Britain, in the S part.

Eng·lish (ing′glish), *adj.* of or having to do with England, its people, or their language. —*n.* 1. the people of England collectively. 2. the English language, including Old English or Anglo-Saxon (before 1100), Middle English (about 1100–1500), and Modern English (from about 1500). 3. the English used in a certain locality or by a certain group. 4. Sometimes, **english,** *Am., Sports.* a spinning motion imparted to a ball. —*v.* translate into English; express in plain English. [OE *Englisc* < *Engle* the English people] ▶ English is a member of the Germanic branch of Indo-European languages, which also includes the Scandinavian languages, German, and Dutch. The Germanic branch comprises the following:

				Swedish
Germanic {	North (Scandinavian) {		{	Danish
				Norwegian
				Icelandic
	East (Gothic—extinct)			
	West {		{	German
				Dutch
				Flemish
				Frisian
				English

A brief selection of facts about the different periods of our language will show some of the roots of the richness—and confusion—of modern English.

1. **Old English, Before 1100.** The Angles, Saxons, and Jutes brought to England from their old homes in northwestern Europe somewhat differing Germanic dialects. They pushed back the native Celts from the parts of the island they conquered, so that Celtic speech contributed almost nothing to English, but survived in Welsh, Cornish, and Highland Scotch. The conquerors' languages developed into several main dialects—Northumbrian, Mercian, Kentish, West Saxon—which together are known as Old English (or Anglo-Saxon). These dialects still leave their marks in the substandard speech of various parts of England. They had many points in common, and were gradually brought

together, each making some contribution, but East Midland, a descendant of Mercian, contributed the most to what now after seven or eight hundred years we know as English. Somewhat less than a quarter of the present English vocabulary goes back to the words of Old English. The modern descendants of Old English words are often changed in meaning and almost always in pronunciation—according to regular processes: Old English *stān* becomes Modern English *stone, bān* becomes *bone,* etc. Our common verbs (*go, sit, eat, fight, whistle*), many of our most common nouns (*meat, house, breakfast, land, water*), and adjectives like *fast, slow, high* go back to Old English words, so that though less than a fourth of the dictionary words are of this "native" origin, they play a part in our speech out of proportion to their number.

Furthermore, most of the machinery of our language is from Old English: the articles *a, an, the,* most of the connecting words (*at, by, for, from, in, out, under . . . as, like, since, when*); most of the pronouns (*I, we, us . . .*); the inflectional endings of nouns (*house—houses, boy—boys—boy's*) and of adjectives and adverbs (*merry—merrier—merriest* or *more merry—most merry;* harshly, kindly); the forms of verbs (*pass, passes, passed, passing*). These endings are applied to words borrowed from other languages (*indict-ed, political-ly*), so that although three quarters of the vocabulary may come from Romance or other languages the borrowed words are built into an English pattern. And when we consider word order we see that the texture of English is Germanic and it must be regarded as a Germanic language.

Within the Old English period the practice of absorbing words from other languages was already strong. A number of Latin words, some of them originally Greek, were taken in, most of them pertaining to the church (*abbot, priest, school*), though there was still a tendency to translate the elements of the Latin words into Old English elements, so that we have *gospel* from *gōd spel,* "good tidings," which is a translation of the Greek-Latin *evangelium.*

In the ninth century the east and north of England was conquered by the Danes, whose language left a large number of words and forms, partly because it was a closely related language, partly because of the intimacy between the two peoples. The *sk* words are likely to date from this mixture (*sky, skin, scream, skirt*—a cousin of the Old English *shirt,* both related to *short*), place names ending in *–by* and *–thorp,* and a number of common words like *odd, anger, egg.* Nearly five per cent of our words are Scandinavian.

A number of the most conspicuous irregularities of Modern English existed already in Old English: *be, is, are, was* as forms of the verb "to be"; *may, might, shall, should, ought,* and the other "auxiliaries"; the pronouns *I, my, me, we, our, us, he, she, it.* These words are in such common use that they have never been brought into any consistent grammatical pattern. Here and there we have remnants of Old English forms that generally lost out in the development of the language, as the plurals *children, oxen, men, geese,* instead of the regular plural in *–s.* There is a considerable body of writing from the Old English period. It includes poems, sermons, riddles, history, translations from Latin, and most conspicuously the *Anglo-Saxon Chronicles, Beowulf,* and the large group of writings and translations in West Saxon made by or at the court of Alfred the Great, King of the West Saxons, 871–899. Some 30,000 different words are found in this literature.

2. **Middle English, 1100–1500.** The conquest of England by the Normans in 1066 was the most far-reaching single historical event influencing our language. The speakers of Old English in the main became serfs, servants, everything but leaders in affairs. Their language was seldom used in official proceedings and rarely written. One result was the loss of the more elevated

Old English words that had been used in poetry and that would correspond to the rather archaic vocabulary of our formal literature.

A far-reaching development of this period was the decline and in some instances complete loss of the inflectional endings that Old English had used. The definite article was no longer declined (our *the* is the sole descendant of eight forms in Old English); *-n* disappeared from the infinitive of most verbs, and other endings, since they were in unstressed syllables and did not receive full pronunciation, dropped away. This process went far to make English one of the least inflected languages.

On the other hand the language of the invaders was making its way. The words for the acts of the ruling class—war, government, law, social activity—were Anglo-French (a dialect of Old French) and they have generally come down to Modern English: *siege, soldier, judge, jury, suit, servant.* Over a fourth of our current English words are from Anglo-French. The majority of the Anglo-French words were ultimately from Latin, though considerably changed in form. For many notions Modern English has two roughly synonymous words, one Anglo-French, one Old English: *dress—clothes, aid—help, royal —kingly.* Some French spellings made their way into English, like *gu* for hard *g* (*guest, guess*) and *qu* for *cw* (*queen* for Old English *cwēn*).

In 1362 English was restored as the language of the law courts, an official recognition that it was reasserting itself again after conquest. The speech of the region around London was now the basis for future development. How far the fusion of Old English and Anglo-French resources had gone can be seen from a few lines by Chaucer, written in the 1380's. The Anglo-French words are in italics:

"What folk ben ye, that at myn hoomcominge
Perturben so my *feste* with *crynge?*"
Quod Theseus, "have ye so greet *envye*
Of myn *honour*, that thus *compleyne* and *crye?*
Or who hath yow misboden, or *offended?*
And telleth me if it may been *amended;*
And why that ye ben clothed thus in blak?"

Geoffrey Chaucer, "The Knightes Tale"

Except for the Old English *misboden* ("insulted"), all of these words, both native and French, are in use today, and in spite of some differences in spelling, the passage can be read by anyone. Many of the words show inflectional endings that have since been dropped or changed: *ben* for *are* or *be*, perturben, telle*th*, and the final *e* of nouns.

3. **Early Modern English, 1500–1700.** In this period we have the beginnings of conscious concern for the language and actual or attempted "improvement" by manipulation of words and constructions, "school-mastering the speech." The early printers, from 1476 on, felt the need for uniformity, especially in spelling and choice of word forms, and began the domination of these traits that ever since in the written language has been exercised by publishers. Translators and writers believed the language was rough, unpolished, incapable of doing what Latin and Greek had done and what Italian could do. They set about enlarging the vocabulary, chiefly by transliterating words from Greek and Latin. More than twenty-five per cent of modern English words are pretty directly from classical languages and very often we have two words that go back to the same Latin original, one brought in by the Normans and one taken in directly later: *paint—picture, certainty—certitude.* Latin was the language of the Church at the beginning of this period, though after the Reformation the Book of Common Prayer and the King James translation of the Bible became tremendous forces for elevated English. Most books of the learned world were in Latin—and college classes were conducted in Latin, even in the United States, until a century and a half ago.

The spoken language was vigorous and was written down in some popular literature but most literature that has survived was from the hands of university men and conscious stylists. Shakespeare shows the complete range, from formal,

Latinized lines to rough and tumble lines, often combining the elevated and the simple in a single speech.

Prose style lagged behind poetic, especially in sentence sense, producing "sentence heaps" running to hundreds of words. In the sixteen hundreds the wealth of experiment of the preceding century was analyzed and many words and phrases were disposed of. The less useful and more ponderous of the Latin importations were dropped, and interest in native words increased the proportion of Saxon words in use. Prose style especially developed in directness and sureness until in Dryden modern English prose is usually said to be established.

4. **Modern English, 1700—.** By 1700 English had become substantially the language we now know and use. The vocabulary has been enlarged in the last two centuries chiefly from two sources: borrowings from India and America and from all peoples touched by British and American traders; and through scientific coinages, chiefly from Greek and Latin roots. There has been, especially in recent years, a tendency toward shorter and more direct sentences. The paragraph has become a more distinct unit in written expression. The most important point for study in this period has probably been the different levels of usage, and different traditions of style, especially formal and informal style and the relations between them. Today the language of England and the British Empire and of the United States is spoken by considerably over 200,000,000 people—perhaps the largest group of people who can easily understand each other. The result of this varied history is a language full of anomalies, with exceptions to every rule, but of unusual range.

English Channel, strait between England and France.

English horn, a wooden musical instrument resembling an oboe, but larger and having a lower tone.

English ivy, ivy (def. 1).

Eng·lish·man (ing′glish·mən), *n., pl.* –men. 1. native or inhabitant of England. 2. one whose ancestry is English. Canadians and Australians sometimes call themselves Englishmen.

English sparrow, a small, brownish-gray bird, now very common in America.

Eng·lish·wom·an (ing′glish·wum′ən), *n., pl.* –wom·en. 1. woman who is a native or inhabitant of England. 2. woman whose ancestry is English.

engr., 1. engineer. 2. engraved; engraver.

en·graft (en·graft′; –gräft′), *v.* insert or graft (a shoot from one tree or plant) into or on another. Also, **ingraft.**

en·grave (en·grāv′), *v.*, –graved, –grav·ing. 1. carve artistically; decorate by engraving. 2. cut in lines on a metal plate, block of wood, etc., for printing. 3. print from such a plate, block, etc. 4. impress deeply. [< *en-* + *grave³*] —en·grav′er, *n.* —Syn. 1. chisel, carve, cut.

en·grav·ing (en·grāv′ing), *n.* 1. art of an engraver; cutting lines in metal plates, blocks of wood, etc., for printing. 2. picture printed from an engraved plate, block, etc. 3. an engraved plate, block, etc.; engraved design or pattern.

en·gross (en·grōs′), *v.* 1. occupy wholly; take up all the attention of. 2. copy or write in large letters; write a beautiful copy of. 3. write out in formal style; express in legal form. 4. buy all or much of (the supply of some commodity) so as to control prices. [(defs. 1, 4) < *in gross* < F *en gros* in a lump; (defs. 2, 3) < AF, < *en-* in + *grosse* large writing, document. See GROSS.] —en·gross′er, *n.* —en·gross′ing, *adj.* —en·gross′ment, *n.*

en·gulf (en·gulf′), *v.* swallow up; overwhelm; submerge. Also, **ingulf.**

en·hance (en·hans′; –häns′), *v.*, –hanced, –hanc·ing. make greater; add to; heighten. [< AF var. of OF *enhaucier* < *en-* on, up + *haucier* raise. See HAWSER.] —en·hance′ment, *n.* —en·hanc′er, *n.* —Syn. increase, intensify, augment.

EN·I·AC (en′i·ak), *n.* Am., *Trademark.* an electronic brain used by the U.S. Army. [< E (*lec-*

tronic) *N(umerical) I(ntegrator) A(nd) C(om-puter)*]

e·nig·ma (i·nig′mə), *n.* 1. a puzzling statement; riddle. 2. a baffling or puzzling problem, situation, person, etc. [< L < Gk. *ainigma* < *ainissesthai* speak darkly < *ainos* fable] —en·ig·mat·i·cal (en′ig·mat′ə·kəl; ē′nig-), en′ig·mat′ic, *adj.* —en′ig·mat′i·cal·ly, *adv.*

En·i·we·tok (en′i·wē′tok), *n.* atoll in the Marshall Islands, site of U.S. atomic bomb tests which started in 1948.

en·join (en·join′), *v.* 1. order; direct; urge. 2. forbid; prohibit: *the judge enjoined him from infringing on the rights of his neighbors.* [< OF *enjoindre* < L. attack, charge < *in-* on + *jungere* join] —en·join′er, *n.* —Syn. 1. prescribe, command, charge, bid.

en·joy (en·joi′), *v.* 1. have or use with joy; be happy with; take pleasure in. 2. have as an advantage or benefit. [< OF, < *en-* + *joir* enjoy < L *gaudere*] —en·joy′a·ble, *adj.* —en·joy′a·ble·ness, *n.* —en·joy′a·bly, *adv.* —en·joy′er, *n.*

en·joy·ment (en·joi′mənt), *n.* 1. an enjoying. 2. thing enjoyed. 3. joy; happiness; pleasure. —Syn. 3. delight, felicity, satisfaction.

en·kin·dle (en·kin′dəl), *v.*, -dled, -dling. light up; brighten. —en·kin′dler, *n.*

en·lace (en·lās′), *v.*, -laced, -lac·ing. 1. wind about; encircle; infold. 2. twine together; interlace. —en·lace′ment, *n.*

en·large (en·lärj′), *v.*, -larged, -larg·ing. make or become larger; increase in size. —en·larg′er, *n.* —Syn. augment, broaden, extend, expand.

en·large·ment (en·lärj′mənt), *n.* 1. an enlarging or being enlarged. 2. anything that is an enlarged form of something else. An enlargement is often made from a small photograph. 3. thing that enlarges something else; addition.

en·light·en (en·līt′ən), *v.* give the light of truth and knowledge to; free from prejudice, ignorance, etc. —en·light′en·er, *n.* —en·light′en·ment, *n.* —Syn. instruct, teach, inform, edify.

en·list (en·list′), *v.* 1. enroll in some branch of the military service. 2. induce to join in some cause or undertaking; secure the help or support of. —en·list′er, *n.* —Syn. 1. register.

enlisted man, *Esp. U.S.* member of the armed forces who is not a commissioned officer or cadet.

en·list·ment (en·list′mənt), *n.* 1. an enlisting. 2. a being enlisted. 3. time for which a person enlists.

en·liv·en (en·līv′ən), *v.* make lively, active, gay, or cheerful. —en·liv′en·er, *n.* —en·liv′en·ment, *n.*

en masse (en mas′; än mäs′), in a group; all together. [< F]

en·mesh (en·mesh′), *v.* catch in a net; enclose in meshes; entangle.

en·mi·ty (en′mə·ti), *n., pl.* -ties. the feeling that enemies have for each other; hate. [< OF *ennemistie* < VL < L *inimicus* ENEMY] —Syn. hostility, hatred, animosity, ill-will, antipathy.

en·no·ble (en·nō′bəl), *v.*, -bled, -bling. 1. give a title or rank of nobility to. 2. raise in the respect of others; dignify; exalt. —en·no′ble·ment, *n.* —en·no′bler, *n.* —Syn. 2. elevate.

en·nui (än′wē), *n.* a feeling of weariness and discontent from lack of occupation or interest; boredom. [< F. See ANNOY.]

e·nor·mi·ty (i·nôr′mə·ti), *n., pl.* -ties. 1. extreme wickedness; outrageousness. 2. an extremely wicked crime; outrageous offense.

e·nor·mous (i·nôr′məs), *adj.* 1. extremely large; huge. 2. extremely wicked; outrageous. [< L, *ex-* out of + *norma* pattern] —e·nor′mous·ly, *adv.* —e·nor′mous·ness, *n.* —Syn. 1. immense, colossal, gigantic, vast, mammoth, prodigious, stupendous. 2. abominable, atrocious.

e·nough (i·nuf′), *adj.* adequate for the need or want. —*n.* an adequate quantity or number. —*adv.* 1. sufficiently; adequately. 2. quite; fully: *he is willing enough to take a tip.* —*interj.* stop! no more! [OE *genōg*] —Syn. *adj.* sufficient, ample. —*n.* sufficiency, plenty.

en·quire (en·kwīr′), *v.*, -quired, -quir·ing. inquire. —en·quir·y (en·kwīr′i; en′kwə·ri), *n.*

en·rage (en·rāj′), *v.*, -raged, -rag·ing. put into a rage; make very angry. —en·rage′ment, *n.* —Syn. infuriate, exasperate, incense, anger.

en rap·port (än rä·pôr′), *French.* in sympathy; in agreement.

en·rap·ture (en·rap′chər), *v.*, -tured, -tur·ing. fill with great delight; entrance.

en·rich (en·rich′), *v.* 1. make rich or richer: *an education enriches your mind, fertilizer enriches soil.* 2. raise the nutritive value of (a food) by adding vitamins and minerals in processing. —en·riched′, *adj.*

en·roll, en·rol (en·rōl′), *v.*, -rolled, -roll·ing. 1. write in a list. 2. have one's name written in a list. 3. make a member. 4. become a member. 5. enlist. —en·roll′er, *n.* —Syn. 1. register, record. 4. enter.

en·roll·ment, en·rol·ment (en·rōl′mənt), *n.* 1. an enrolling. 2. number enrolled.

en route (än rüt′), on the way. [< F]

Ens., Ensign.

en·sconce (en·skons′), *v.*, -sconced, -sconc·ing. 1. shelter safely; hide. 2. settle comfortably and firmly. [< *en-* + *sconce* fortification, prob. < Du. *schans*]

en·sem·ble (än·säm′bəl), *n.* 1. all the parts of a thing considered together; general effect. 2. a united performance of the full number of singers, musicians, etc. 3. group of musicians or the musical instruments used in taking part in such a performance. 4. a complete, harmonious costume. [< F, < VL < L *in-* + *simul* at the same time]

en·shrine (en·shrīn′), *v.*, -shrined, -shrining. 1. enclose in a shrine. 2. keep sacred; cherish. —en·shrine′ment, *n.*

en·shroud (en·shroud′), *v.* cover with, or as with, a shroud; hide; veil: *fog enshrouded the ship.*

en·sign (en′sən; en′sīn, *esp. for* 1, 3, *and* 4), *n.* 1. flag; banner: *the ensign of the United States is the Stars and Stripes.* 2. *Am.* the lowest commissioned officer in the navy. 3. a former British army officer whose duty was carrying the flag. 4. sign of one's rank, position, or power; symbol of authority. [< OF < L *insignia* INSIGNIA] —en′sign·ship, en′sign·cy, *n.*

en·si·lage (en′sə·lij), *n., v.*, -laged, -lag·ing. —*n.* 1. preservation of green fodder by packing it in a silo or pit. 2. fodder preserved in this way. Ensilage is used to feed cattle in winter. —*v.* preserve in a silo. [< F]

en·slave (en·slāv′), *v.*, -slaved, -slav·ing. make a slave or slaves of; take away freedom from. —en·slave′ment, *n.* —en·slav′er, *n.*

en·snare (en·snār′), *v.*, -snared, -snar·ing. catch in a snare; trap. Also, insnare. —en·snare′ment, *n.* —en·snar′er, *n.*

en·sue (en·sü′), *v.*, -sued, -su·ing. come after; happen as a result; follow. The ensuing year means the next year. [< OF *ensivre* < L, < *in-* upon + *sequi* follow] —Syn. succeed, result.

en·sure (en·shūr′), *v.*, -sured, -sur·ing. 1. make sure or certain. 2. make sure of getting; secure. 3. make safe; protect. 4. *Obs.* assure; convince. [< AF, < *en-* (< L *in-*) + *seūr* SURE]

-ent, *suffix.* 1. —ing, as in *absorbent, indulgent, coincident.* 2. one that —s, as in *correspondent, president, superintendent.* 3. other meanings, as in *competent, confident.* [< L -*ens* (-*ent-*)]

CORNICE FRIEZE ARCHITRAVE ENTABLATURE

en·tab·la·ture (en·tab′lə·chər), *n.* part of a building resting on the top of columns. [< Ital. *intavolatura* < *in-* on (< L *in-*) + *tavola* board, tablet < L *tabula*]

en·tail (en·tāl′), *v.* 1. impose; require. 2. limit the inheritance of (property, etc.) to a specified line of heirs so that it cannot be left to anyone else. —*n.* 1. an entailing. 2. an entailed inheritance. 3. order of descent specified for an entailed estate. —en·tail′ment, *n.*

en·tan·gle (en·tang′gəl), *v.*, -gled, -gling. 1.

get twisted up and caught; tangle. **2.** get into difficulty; involve. **3.** perplex; confuse. —**en·tan'-gle·ment,** *n.* —Syn. **1.** snarl, knot, mat. **2.** implicate, ensnare. **3.** bewilder, embarrass.

en·tente (än·tänt'), *n.* **1.** an understanding; agreement between two or more governments. **2.** parties to an understanding; governments that have made an agreement. [< F]

en·tente cor·diale (än·tänt' kôr·dyäl'), *French.* a friendly understanding or agreement.

en·ter (en'tər), *v.* **1.** go into; come into. **2.** go in; come in. **3.** become a part or member of; join. **4.** cause to join or enter; obtain admission for. **5.** begin; start. **6.** write or put in a book, list, etc. **7.** put in regular form; record: *the injured man entered a complaint in court.* **8.** report (a ship or its cargoes) at the custom house. [< OF < L *intrare* < *intro* inwards, *intra* within] —**en'-ter·a·ble,** *adj.*

en·ter·ic (en·ter'ik), *adj.* intestinal. [< Gk., < *entera* intestines]

en·ter·prise (en'tər·prīz), *n.* **1.** an important, difficult, or dangerous undertaking. **2.** an undertaking; project: *a business enterprise.* **3.** readiness to start projects; courage and energy in starting projects. [< OF, < *entre-* between (< L *inter-*) + *prendre* take < L *prehendere*] —Syn. **2.** plan, venture. **3.** boldness.

en·ter·pris·ing (en'tər·prīz'ing), *adj.* courageous and energetic in starting projects. —**en'-ter·pris'ing·ly,** *adv.* —Syn. bold, venturesome.

en·ter·tain (en'tər·tān'), *v.* **1.** interest; please; amuse. **2.** have as a guest. **3.** have guests; provide entertainment for guests. **4.** take into the mind; consider. [< F, < *entre-* among (< L *inter-*) + *tenir* hold < L *tenere*] —**en'ter·tain'-er,** *n.* —Syn. **1.** divert, beguile, delight. **4.** harbor.

en·ter·tain·ing (en'tər·tān'ing), *adj.* interesting; pleasing; amusing. —**en'ter·tain'ing·ly,** *adv.* —**en'ter·tain'ing·ness,** *n.*

en·ter·tain·ment (en'tər·tān'mənt), *n.* **1.** an entertaining. **2.** a being entertained. **3.** thing that interests, pleases, or amuses. —Syn. **3.** amusement, diversion, recreation, pastime.

en·thrall, en·thral (en·thrôl'), *v.,* -thralled, -thral·ling. **1.** captivate; fascinate; charm. **2.** make a slave of; enslave. Also, **inthrall, inthral.** —**en·thrall'er,** *n.* —**en·thrall'-ing,** *adj.* —**en·thrall'ing·ly,** *adv.* —**en·thrall'-ment, en·thral'ment,** *n.*

en·throne (en·thrōn'), *v.,* -throned, -thron-ing. **1.** set on a throne. **2.** invest with authority, esp. as a sovereign or as a bishop. Also, **inthrone.** —**en·throne'ment,** *n.*

en·thuse (en·thüz'), *v.,* -thused, -thus·ing. *Am.* **1.** become enthusiastic; show enthusiasm. **2.** fill with enthusiasm. [< *enthusiasm*] ► Many people object to **enthuse** and most dictionaries label it colloquial, but *enthuse* seems to be an improvement over the only locution we have for the idea, the clumsy *be enthusiastic over* or *about.* It is now in fairly general use.

en·thu·si·asm (en·thü'zi·az·əm), *n.* **1.** eager interest; zeal. **2.** extreme religious emotion; ecstasy. [< LL < Gk., < *entheos* god-possessed < *en-* in + *theos* god] —Syn. **1.** eagerness, warmth, ardor, fervor. —Ant. **1.** indifference, apathy.

en·thu·si·ast (en·thü'zi·ast), *n.* **1.** person who is filled with enthusiasm. **2.** person who is carried away by his feelings for a cause. —Syn. **2.** zealot, fanatic, devotee.

en·thu·si·as·tic (en·thü'zi·as'tik), *adj.* full of enthusiasm; eagerly interested. —**en·thu'si·as'ti·cal·ly,** *adv.* —Syn. zealous, eager, ardent.

en·tice (en·tīs'), *v.,* -ticed, -tic·ing. tempt by arousing hopes or desires; attract by offering some pleasure or reward. [< OF *enticier* stir up, incite < *en-* in (< L *in-*) + L *titio* firebrand] —**en·tice'ment,** *n.* —**en·tic'er,** *n.* —**en·tic'ing·ly,** *adv.* —Syn. lure, inveigle, decoy.

en·tire (en·tīr'), *adj.* **1.** having all the parts or elements; whole; complete. **2.** not broken; having an unbroken outline. **3.** *Bot.* of leaves, not indented. **4.** of animals, not gelded. [< OF < L *integer* < *in-* not + *tag-* touch] —**en·tire'ly,** *adv.* —**en·tire'ness,** *n.* —Syn. **1.** total, full. **2.** intact, unimpaired.

en·tire·ty (en·tīr'ti), *n., pl.* -ties. **1.** whole-

ness; completeness. **2.** a complete thing; the whole. **3.** in its entirety, wholly; completely.

en·ti·tle (en·tī'təl), *v.,* -tled, -tling. **1.** give the title of; call by the name of. **2.** give a claim or right to. Also, **intitle.** —Syn. **1.** name, denominate, designate. **2.** empower, qualify, enable.

en·ti·ty (en'tə·ti), *n., pl.* -ties. **1.** something that has a real and separate existence either actually or in the mind. **2.** being; existence. [< LL *entitas* < L *ens,* ppr. of *esse* be]

en·tomb (en·tüm'), *v.* place in a tomb; bury. Also, **intomb.** —**en·tomb'ment,** *n.*

en·to·mo·log·i·cal (en'tə·mə·loj'ə·kəl), **en·to·mo·log·ic** (-loj'ik), *adj.* of or pertaining to entomology. —**en'to·mo·log'i·cal·ly,** *adv.*

en·to·mol·o·gy (en'tə·mol'ə·ji), *n.* branch of zoölogy that deals with insects. [< Gk. *entomon* insect + -LOGY] —**en'to·mol'o·gist,** *n.*

en·tou·rage (än'tù·räzh'), *n.* **1.** environment, esp. social environment. **2.** family, servants, attendants, and others accompanying a person. [< F, < *entourer* surround]

en·tr'acte (än·trakt'), *n.* **1.** interval between two acts of a play. **2.** music, dancing, or any entertainment performed during this interval. [< F, between-act]

en·trails (en'trālz; -trəlz), *n.pl.* **1.** the inner parts of a man or animal. **2.** intestines; bowels. **3.** any inner parts. [< OF < LL *intralia* < L *interanea* < *inter* within]

en·train (en·trān'), *v.* **1.** get on a train. **2.** put on a train. —**en·train'ment,** *n.*

en·trance¹ (en'trəns), *n.* **1.** act of entering. **2.** place by which to enter; door, passageway, etc. **3.** freedom or right to enter; permission to enter. [< OF, < *entrer* ENTER] —Syn. **1.** entry, ingress. **2.** opening, inlet, gate, portal.

en·trance² (en·trans'; -träns'), *v.,* -tranced, -tranc·ing. **1.** put into a trance. **2.** fill with joy; delight; charm. —**en·trance'ment,** *n.* —**en·tranc'ing,** *adj.* —**en·tranc'ing·ly,** *adv.*

en·trant (en'trənt), *n.* person who enters.

en·trap (en·trap'), *v.,* -trapped, -trap·ping. **1.** catch in a trap. **2.** bring into difficulty or danger; deceive; trick. —**en·trap'ment,** *n.*

en·treat (en·trēt'), *v.* ask earnestly; beg and pray; implore. Also, **intreat.** [< OF, < *en-* (< L *in-*) + *traiter* TREAT] —**en·treat'ing·ly,** *adv.* —**en·treat'ment,** *n.* —Syn. beseech, supplicate.

en·treat·y (en·trēt'i), *n., pl.* -treat·ies. an earnest request; prayer. —Syn. supplication, appeal, solicitation, suit, petition.

en·tree, en·trée (än'trā), *n.* **1.** freedom or right to enter; access. **2.** *U.S.* the main dish of food at dinner or lunch. **3.** dish of food served before the roast or between the main courses at dinner. [< F, fem. pp. of *entrer* ENTER]

en·trench (en·trench'), *v.* **1.** surround with a trench; fortify with trenches. **2.** establish firmly. **3.** trespass; encroach; infringe. Also, **intrench.** —**en·trench'ment,** *n.*

en·tre nous (än'trə nü'), *French.* between ourselves; confidentially.

en·tre·pre·neur (än'trə·prə·nér'), *n.* person who organizes and manages a business or industrial enterprise, taking the risk of loss and getting the profit when there is one. [< F, < *entreprendre* undertake. See ENTERPRISE.]

en·trust (en·trust'), *v.* **1.** charge with a trust; trust. **2.** give the care of; hand over for safekeeping. Also, **intrust.**

en·try (en'tri), *n., pl.* -tries. **1.** act of entering. **2.** place by which to enter; way to enter: *a vestibule is an entry.* **3.** thing written or printed in a book, list, etc. Each word explained in a dictionary is an entry. **4.** person or thing that takes part in a contest. **5.** *Law.* the act of taking possession of lands or buildings by entering or setting foot on them. [< OF, < *entrer* ENTER]

en·twine (en·twīn'), *v.,* -twined, -twin·ing. **1.** twine together. **2.** twine around. —**en·twine'-ment,** *n.*

e·nu·mer·ate (i·nü'mər·āt; -nū'-), *v.,* -at·ed, -at·ing. **1.** name one by one; give a list of. **2.** count. —**e·nu'mer·a'tion,** *n.* —**e·nu'mer·a'tive,** *adj.* —**e·nu'mer·a'tor,** *n.* —Syn. **1.** recapitulate, recount, rehearse, detail.

e·nun·ci·ate (i·nun′si·āt; –shi–), *v.*, –at·ed, –at·ing. **1.** pronounce (words): *a well-trained actor enunciates very distinctly.* **2.** state definitely; announce: *after many experiments the scientist enunciated a new theory.* [< L, < *ex-* out + *nuntius* messenger] —e·nun′ci·a′tion, *n.* —e·nun′ci·a′tive, *adj.* —e·nun′ci·a′tor, *n.*

en·vel·op (en·vel′əp), *v.*, –oped, –op·ing, *n.* —*v.* **1.** wrap; cover. **2.** surround: *our soldiers enveloped the enemy.* **3.** hide; conceal: *fog enveloped the village.* —*n.* envelope. [< OF, < *en-* in (< L *in-*) + *voloper* wrap] —en·vel′op·er, *n.* —Syn. *v.* **1.** infold. **2.** encompass, encircle.

en·ve·lope (en′və·lōp; än′–), *n.* **1.** a folded and gummed paper cover in which a letter or anything flat can be mailed. **2.** a covering; wrapper. **3.** bag that holds the gas in a balloon. [< F *enveloppe* < *envelopper* ENVELOP]

en·vel·op·ment (en·vel′əp·mənt), *n.* **1.** an enveloping. **2.** a being enveloped. **3.** thing that envelops; wrapping; covering.

en·ven·om (en·ven′əm), *v.* **1.** make poisonous. **2.** fill with bitterness, hate, etc.

en·vi·a·ble (en′vi·ə·bəl), *adj.* to be envied; desirable; worth having. —en′vi·a·ble·ness, *n.* —en′vi·a·bly, *adv.*

en·vi·ous (en′vi·əs), *adj.* full of envy; feeling or showing envy. —en′vi·ous·ly, *adv.* —en′vi·ous·ness, *n.*

en·vi·ron (en·vī′rən), *v.* surround; enclose. [< OF *environner* < *environ* around < *en-* in (< L *in-*) + *viron* circle]

en·vi·ron·ment (en·vī′rən·mənt), *n.* **1.** act or fact of surrounding. **2.** surroundings. **3.** all of the surrounding conditions and influences that affect the development of a living thing. —en·vi′ron·men′tal, *adj.*

en·vi·rons (en·vī′rənz), *n.pl.* surrounding districts; suburbs.

en·vis·age (en·viz′ij), *v.*, –aged, –ag·ing. **1.** look in the face of. **2.** contemplate. **3.** form a mental picture of. [< F *envisager*. See EN-, VISAGE.]

en·voy (en′voi), *n.* **1.** messenger. **2.** diplomat ranking next below an ambassador and next above a minister. [< OF, < *envoier* send < VL, < L *in via* on the way]

en·vy (en′vi), *n.*, *pl.* –vies, *v.*, –vied, –vy·ing. —*n.* **1.** discontent or ill will at another's good fortune because one wishes it had been his. **2.** the object of such feeling. —*v.* feel envy for or because of. [< OF *envie* < L *invidia*, ult. < *invidere* look with enmity at < *in-* against + *videre* see] —en′vi·er, *n.* —en′vy·ing·ly, *adv.*

en·wrap (en·rap′), *v.*, –wrapped, –wrap·ping. wrap. Also, **inwrap.**

en·wrought (en·rôt′), *adj.* inwrought.

en·zyme (en′zīm; –zim), *n.* a chemical substance, produced in living cells, that can cause changes in other substances without being changed itself. Pepsin is an enzyme. [< Med.Gk. *enzymos* leavened < *en-* in + *zyme* leaven] —en·zy·mat·ic (en′zi·mat′ik; –zi–), *adj.*

E·O·K·A (ē·ō′kä′ä; ē·ō′kə), *n.* the anti-British terrorist organization on the island of Cyprus.

E·o·li·an (ē·ō′li·ən), *adj.* Aeolian.

e·o·lith·ic (ē′ə·lith′ik), *adj.* pertaining to an early stage of human culture, characterized by the use of very primitive stone instruments. [< Gk. *eos* dawn + *lithos* stone]

e·on (ē′ən; ē′on), *n.* aeon.

E·os (ē′os), *n.* the Greek goddess of the dawn, identified with the Roman goddess Aurora.

E·pam·i·non·das (i·pam′ə·non′dəs), *n.* 418?–362 B.C., Greek general and statesman.

ep·au·let, ep·au·lette (ep′ə·let), *n.* ornament on the shoulder of a uniform. [< F, dim. of *épaule* shoulder]

Eph., Ephesians.

e·phah (ē′fə), *n.* a Hebrew dry measure equal to a little more than a bushel. [< Heb.]

Epaulet

e·phed·rine (i·fed′rin; *Chem.*, also ef′ə·drēn,

–drin), **e·phed·rin** (i·fed′rin; *Chem.*, also ef′ə·drin), *n.* drug, $C_{10}H_{15}ON$, used to relieve hay fever, asthma, head colds, etc. [< NL *ephedra* < L, horsetail (a plant) < Gk.]

e·phem·er·al (i·fem′ər·əl), *adj.* lasting for only a day; lasting for only a very short time; very short-lived. [< Gk. *ephemeros* liable to be cut short < *epi-* subject to + *hemera* the day (of destiny)] —e·phem′er·al·ly, *adv.*

e·phem·er·id (i·fem′ər·id), *n.* May fly.

E·phe·sian (i·fē′zhən), *adj.* of Ephesus or its people. —*n.* **1.** native or inhabitant of Ephesus. **2.** Ephesians, book of the New Testament written in the name of the Apostle Paul to the Christians at Ephesus.

Eph·e·sus (ef′ə·səs), *n.* an ancient Greek city in W Asia Minor.

eph·od (ef′od; ē′fod), *n.* an official vestment worn by Hebrew priests in ancient times. [< Heb.]

E·phra·im (ē′fri·əm), *n.* **1.** in the Bible, the younger son of Joseph. **2.** tribe of Hebrews descended from him. **3.** kingdom of Israel.

ep·ic (ep′ik), *n.* a long poem that tells of the adventures of one or more great heroes. An epic is written in a dignified, majestic style, and often gives expression to the ideals of a nation or race. The *Iliad*, the *Aeneid*, and *Paradise Lost* are epics. —*adj.* Also, **ep′i·cal.** **1.** of or having to do with an epic. **2.** like an epic; grand in style; heroic. [< L < Gk. *epikos* < *epos* word, story] —ep′i·cal·ly, *adv.*

ep·i·ca·lyx (ep′ə·kā′liks; –kal′iks), *n. Bot.* ring of bracts at the base of a flower that looks like an outer calyx.

ep·i·carp (ep′ə·kärp), *n.* the outer layer of a fruit or ripened ovary of a plant. The skin of a pear is its epicarp.

ep·i·cen·ter (ep′ə·sen′tər), *n. Geol.* point of focus for the vibrations of an earthquake.

ep·i·cure (ep′ə·kyūr), *n.* person who has a refined taste in eating and drinking and cares much about foods and drinks. [Anglicized var. of *Epicurus*] —Syn. gourmet.

ep·i·cu·re·an (ep′ə·kyū·rē′ən), *adj.* **1.** like an epicure; fond of pleasure and luxury. **2.** fit for an epicure. **3.** Epicurean, of Epicurus or his philosophy. —*n.* **1.** person fond of pleasure and luxury; epicure. **2.** believer in the philosophy of Epicurus.

Ep·i·cu·re·an·ism (ep′ə·kyū·rē′ən·iz·əm), *n.* **1.** philosophy or principles of Epicurus or his followers. **2.** Also, **epicureanism.** belief or practice of this philosophy.

Ep·i·cu·rus (ep′ə·kyūr′əs), *n.* 342?–270 B.C., Greek philosopher who taught that happiness is the highest good and that virtue alone produces happiness.

ep·i·dem·ic (ep′ə·dem′ik), *n.* **1.** the rapid spreading of a disease so that many people have it at the same time. **2.** the rapid spread of an idea, fashion, etc. —*adj.* Also, **ep′i·dem′i·cal.** affecting many people at the same time; widespread. [< F *épidémie* < Med.L < Gk., < *epi-* among + *demos* people] —ep′i·dem′i·cal·ly, *adv.* —ep·i·de·mic·i·ty (ep′ə·də·mis′ə·ti), *n.*

ep·i·der·mis (ep′ə·der′mis), *n.* **1.** the outer layer of the skin. **2.** the outer covering on the shells of many mollusks. **3.** any of various other outer layers of invertebrates. **4.** a skinlike layer of cells in seed plants and ferns. [< LL < Gk., < *epi-* on + *derma* skin] —ep′i·der′mal, ep′i·der′mic, *adj.*

ep·i·der·moid (ep′ə·der′moid), **ep·i·der·moi·dal** (–der·moi′dəl), *adj.* resembling epidermis.

ep·i·glot·tis (ep′ə·glot′is), *n.* a thin, triangular plate of cartilage that covers the entrance to the windpipe during swallowing, so that food, etc., does not get into the lungs. [< LL < Gk., < *epi-* on + *glotta* tongue]

ep·i·gram (ep′ə·gram), *n.* **1.** a short, pointed

āge, cāre, fär; ēqual, tèrm; īce; ōpen, ôrder; pùt, rüle, ūse; tʜ, then; ə=a in about.

or witty saying. 2. a short poem ending in a witty or clever turn of thought. [< L < Gk., < *epi-* on + *graphein* write] —ep·i·gram·mat·ic (ep′ə·grə·mat′ik), ep′i·gram·mat′i·cal, *adj.* —ep′i·gram·mat′i·cal·ly, *adv.* ➤ **Epigrams.** An *epigram* is a short, pithy statement, usually with a touch of wit, in either verse or prose. In prose this means really a detached or detachable and "quotable" sentence. *Epigrams* are the chief stock in trade of columnists and newspaper "paragraphers" (writers of the one- or two-sentence remarks that come at the end of the editorial columns in some dailies). In consecutive prose, *epigrams* sometimes become too prominent, attract too much attention to themselves, or suggest straining for effect. But they can be really useful for focusing attention or for putting a fact or opinion so that a reader can remember (and perhaps repeat) it. Example: *It's no disgrace to be poor, but it might as well be.* A special type of epigram is the *paradox,* which makes a statement that as it stands contradicts fact or common sense or itself, and yet suggests a truth or at least a half truth: *All generalizations are false, including this one.*

ep·i·gram·ma·tize (ep′ə·gram′ə·tīz), *v.,* -tized, -tiz·ing. 1. express by epigrams. 2. make epigrams.

e·pig·ra·phy (i.pig′rə·fi), *n.* 1. inscriptions. 2. branch of knowledge that deals with the deciphering and interpretation of inscriptions. —e·pig′ra·phist, e·pig′ra·pher, *n.*

ep·i·lep·sy (ep′ə·lep′si), *n.* a chronic nervous disease whose attacks cause convulsions and unconsciousness. [< LL < Gk. *epilepsia* seizure, ult. < *epi-* on + *lambanein* take]

ep·i·lep·tic (ep′ə·lep′tik), *adj.* 1. of or having to do with epilepsy. 2. having epilepsy. —*n.* person who has epilepsy.

ep·i·logue, ep·i·log (ep′ə·lôg; -log), *n.* 1. the concluding part of a novel, poem, etc. 2. speech or poem after the end of a play. It is addressed to the audience and is spoken by one of the actors. [< F < L < Gk., ult. < *epi-* in addition + *legein* speak]

E·piph·a·ny (i.pif′ə·ni), *n.* January 6, the anniversary of the coming of the Wise Men to Christ at Bethlehem.

ep·i·phyte (ep′ə·fīt), *n.* plant that grows on another plant for support, but not for nourishment. Many mosses, lichens, and orchids are epiphytes. [< Gk. *epi-* on + *phyton* plant] —ep·i·phyt·ic (ep′ə·fit′ik), ep′i·phyt′i·cal, *adj.* —ep′i·phyt′i·cal·ly, *adv.*

e·pis·co·pa·cy (i.pis′kə·pə·si), *n., pl.* -cies. 1. government of a church by bishops. 2. bishops as a group. 3. position, rank, or term of office of a bishop; episcopate.

e·pis·co·pal (i.pis′kə·pəl), *adj.* 1. of or having to do with bishops. 2. governed by bishops. 3. Episcopal, of or having to do with the Church of England, or certain Protestant churches of the United States, such as the Protestant Episcopal Church. [< LL, < L *episcopus* BISHOP] —e·pis′co·pal·ly, *adv.*

E·pis·co·pa·lian (i.pis′kə·pāl′yən; -pā′li·ən), *n.* member of the Protestant Episcopal church. —*adj.* Episcopal.

e·pis·co·pate (i.pis′kə·pit; -pāt), *n.* 1. position, rank, or term of office of a bishop. 2. district under the charge of a bishop; bishopric. 3. bishops as a group.

ep·i·sode (ep′ə·sōd), *n.* a single happening or group of happenings in real life or a story. [< Gk. *episodion,* neut., coming in besides, ult. < *epi-* on + *eis* into + *hodos* way] —ep·i·sod·ic (ep′ə·sod′ik), ep′i·sod′i·cal, *adj.* —ep′i·sod′i·cal·ly, *adv.*

e·pis·te·mol·o·gy (i.pis′tə·mol′ə·ji), *n.* part of philosophy that deals with the origin, nature, and limits of knowledge. [< Gk. *episteme,* knowledge + -LOGY] —e·pis·te·mo·log·i·cal (i.pis′tə·mə·loj′ə·kəl), *adj.* —e·pis′te·mo·log′i·cal·ly, *adv.* —e·pis′te·mol′o·gist, *n.*

e·pis·tle (i.pis′əl), *n.* 1. letter, usually a long, instructive letter written in formal or elegant language. 2. Epistle, a. letter written by one of Christ's Apostles. The Epistles make up 21 books

of the New Testament. b. selection from one of these, read as part of Mass or of the Anglican service of Holy Communion. [< L < Gk. *epistole,* ult. < *epi-* to + *stellein* send]

e·pis·to·lar·y (i.pis′tə·ler′i), *adj.* 1. carried on by letters; contained in letters. 2. of letters; suitable for writing letters.

ep·i·taph (ep′ə·taf; -täf), *n.* a short statement in memory of a dead person, usually put on his tombstone. [< L < Gk. *epitaphion* funeral oration < *epi-* at + *taphos* tomb] —ep′i·taph′ic, *adj.* —ep′i·taph′ist, *n.*

ep·i·the·li·um (ep′ə·thē′li·əm), *n., pl.* -li·ums, -li·a (-li·ə). *Biol.* a thin layer of cells forming a tissue that covers surfaces and lines hollow organs. [< NL, < Gk. *epi-* on + *thele* nipple] —ep′i·the′li·al, *adj.*

ep·i·thet (ep′ə·thet), *n.* a descriptive expression; adjective or noun expressing some quality or attribute, as in "Richard the Lion-Hearted." [< L < Gk. *epitheton* added < *epi-* on + *tithenai* place] —ep′e·thet′ic, ep′i·thet′i·cal, *adj.*

e·pit·o·me (i.pit′ə·mē), *n.* 1. a condensed account; summary. 2. a condensed representation of something; some thing or part that is typical or representative of the whole. [< L < Gk., < *epi-* into + *temnein* cut] —e·pit·o·mist (i.pit′ə·mist), *n.*

e·pit·o·mize (i.pit′ə·mīz), *v.,* -mized, -miz·ing. make an epitome of; summarize. —e·pit′o·miz′er, *n.* —Syn. abridge, condense, reduce.

ep·i·zo·öt·ic (ep′ə·zō·ot′ik), *adj.* temporarily prevalent among animals. —*n.* an epizoötic disease. [< Gk. *epi-* among + *zoion* animal]

e plu·ri·bus u·num (ē plūr′ə·bəs ū′nəm), *Latin.* out of many, one (the motto of the United States).

ep·och (ep′ək; *esp. Brit.* ē′pok), *n.* 1. period of time; era. 2. period of time in which striking things happened. 3. the starting point of such a period. 4. *Astron.* an arbitrarily fixed instant of time used as a reference point. 5. the dividing line between geological periods. [< Med.L < Gk. *epoche* a stopping, fixed point in time < *epi-* up + *echein* hold] —ep′och·al, *adj.* —Syn. 1. age.

ep·ode (ep′ōd), *n.* 1. a lyric poem in which a long line is followed by a shorter one. 2. part of a lyric ode following the strophe and antistrophe. [< F < L < Gk. *epoidos* < *epi-* after + *aidein* sing]

ep·on·y·mous (ep·on′ə·məs), *adj.* giving one's name to a nation, tribe, place, etc. Romulus is the eponymous hero of Rome. [< Gk., < *epi-* to + *onyma* (dial.) name]

ep·si·lon (ep′sə·lon; -lən), *n.* the fifth letter of the Greek alphabet (E, ε).

Ep·som (ep′səm), *n.* 1. town in SE England, near London. 2. Epsom Downs, track where England's famous horse race, the Derby, is run.

Epsom salt or salts, hydrated magnesium sulfate, $MgSO_4 \cdot 7H_2O$, a bitter, white, crystalline powder taken in water to move the bowels.

Ep·stein (ep′stīn), *n.* Jacob, born 1880, English sculptor born in the United States.

E.P.T., EPT, excess-profits tax.

eq., 1. equal. 2. equation. 3. equivalent.

eq·ua·ble (ek′wə·bəl; ē′kwə-), *adj.* changing little; uniform; even; tranquil. [< L, < *aequare* make uniform < *aequus* even, just] —eq′ua·bil′i·ty, eq′ua·ble·ness, *n.* —eq′ua·bly, *adv.* —Syn. unvarying, steady, smooth.

e·qual (ē′kwəl), *adj., n., v.,* equaled, e·qual·ing; *esp. Brit.* e·qualled, e·qual·ling. —*adj.* 1. the same in amount, size, number, value, degree, rank, etc.; as much; neither more nor less. 2. the same throughout; even; uniform. 3. equal to; able to; strong enough for; brave enough for; etc. —*n.* person or thing that is equal. —*v.* 1. be equal to. 2. make or do something equal to. [< L, < *aequus* even, just] —Syn. *adj.* 1. equivalent. —*n.* peer, equivalent, match.

e·qual·i·ty (i.kwol′ə·ti), *n., pl.* -ties. a being equal; sameness in amount, size, number, value, degree, rank, etc.

e·qual·ize (ē′kwəl·īz), *v.,* -ized, -iz·ing. 1. make equal. 2. make even or uniform. —e′qual·i·za′tion, *n.* —e′qual·iz′er, *n.*

e·qual·ly (ē′kwəl·i), *adv.* in an equal manner; in or to an equal degree; so as to be equal.

e·qua·nim·i·ty (ē′kwə·nim′ə·ti; ek′wə-), *n.* evenness of mind or temper; calmness. [< L, < *aequus* even + *animus* mind, temper] —**Syn.** composure.

e·quate (i·kwāt′), *v.*, **e·quat·ed, e·quat·ing. 1.** state to be equal; put in the form of an equation. **2.** consider, treat, or represent as equal. **3.** make equal. [< L *aequatus* made equal < *aequus* equal]

e·qua·tion (i·kwā′zhən; -shən), *n.* **1.** statement of equality between two quantities. *Examples:* (4×8) + 12 = 44. C = 2πr. **2.** expression using chemical formulas and symbols showing the substances used and produced in a chemical change. *Example:* HCl + NaOH = NaCl + H_2O. **3.** an equating or being equated.

e·qua·tor (i·kwā′tər), *n.* **1.** an imaginary circle around the middle of the earth, halfway between the North Pole and the South Pole. **2.** a similarly situated circle on any heavenly or spherical body. **3.** an imaginary circle in the sky corresponding to that of the earth. [< LL *aequator* (*diei et noctis*) equalizer (of day and night). See **EQUAL**.] —**e·qua·to·ri·al** (ē′kwə·tô′ri·əl; -tō′-; ek′wə-), *adj.* —**e′qua·to′ri·al·ly,** *adv.*

eq·uer·ry (ek′wər·i), *n., pl.* **-ries. 1.** officer of a household who has charge of the horses or who accompanies his master's carriage. **2.** attendant on a royal or noble person. [< F *écurie* stable < Gmc.; infl. by L *equus* horse]

e·ques·tri·an (i·kwes′tri·ən), *adj.* **1.** of horsemen or horsemanship; having to do with horseback riding. **2.** on horseback; mounted on horseback. —*n.* rider or performer on horseback. [< L *equestris* of a horseman < *equus* horse]

e·ques·tri·enne (i·kwes′tri·en′), *n.* a woman rider or performer on horseback. [< F]

equi-, *word element.* **1.** equal, as in *equivalence.* **2.** equally, as in *equidistant.* [< L *aequus* equal]

e·qui·an·gu·lar (ē′kwi·ang′gyə·lər), *adj.* having all angles equal, as a square.

e·qui·dis·tant (ē′kwə·dis′tənt), *adj.* equally distant. —**e′qui·dis′tance,** *n.* —**e′qui·dis′tant·ly,** *adv.*

e·qui·lat·er·al (ē′kwə·lat′ər·əl), *adj.* having all sides equal. —*n.* figure having all sides equal. —**e′qui·lat′er·al·ly,** *adv.*

e·quil·i·brant (i·kwil′ə·brənt), *n.* force able to balance a specified force or set of forces.

Equilateral triangle

e·quil·i·brate (ē′kwə·lī′brāt; i·kwil′ə-), *v.*, **-brat·ed, -brat·ing.** balance. —**e·qui·li·bra′tion** (ē′kwə·lə·brā′shən; i·kwil′ə-), *n.*

e·qui·lib·ri·um (ē′kwə·lib′ri·əm), *n.* **1.** state of balance; condition in which opposing forces exactly balance or equal each other. **2.** mental poise. [< L, ult. < *aequus* equal + *libra* balance]

e·quine (ē′kwīn), *adj.* of horses; like a horse; like that of a horse. —*n.* a horse. [< L, < *equus* horse]

e·qui·noc·tial (ē′kwə·nok′shəl), *adj.* **1.** having to do with either equinox. **2.** occurring at or near the equinox: *equinoctial gales.* **3.** at or near the earth's equator. —*n.* the equinoctial line.

equinoctial line, an imaginary circle in the sky corresponding to the earth's equator.

e·qui·nox (ē′kwə·noks), *n.* either of the two times in the year when the center of the sun crosses the celestial equator, and day and night are of equal length all over the earth, occurring about March 21 (**vernal equinox**) and Sept. 22 (**autumnal equinox**). [< Med.L < L, < *aequus* equal + *nox* night]

e·quip (i·kwip′), *v.*, **e·quipped, e·quip·ping. 1.** furnish with all that is needed; fit out; provide. **2.** fit up; array. [< F *équipper* < OF *esquiper* < Scand. *skipa* to man (a ship)]

eq·ui·page (ek′wə·pij), *n.* **1.** carriage. **2.** carriage with its horses, driver, and servants. **3.** equipment; outfit.

e·quip·ment (i·kwip′mənt), *n.* **1.** act of equipping. **2.** state of being equipped. **3.** anything used in or provided for equipping; outfit. **4.** knowledge or skill; ability.

e·qui·poise (ē′kwə·poiz; ek′wə-), *n.* **1.** state of balance. **2.** a balancing force; counterbalance.

eq·ui·se·tum (ek′wə·sē′təm), *n., pl.* **-tums, -ta** (-tə). **1.** genus of plants with hard, rough, unbranched stems. **2.** horsetail. [< NL < L, < *equus* horse + *saeta* (coarse) hair]

eq·ui·ta·ble (ek′wə·tə·bəl), *adj.* **1.** fair; just. **2.** *Law.* pertaining to or dependent upon equity; valid in equity, as distinguished from common law and statute law. —**eq′ui·ta·ble·ness,** *n.* —**eq′ui·ta·bly,** *adv.*

eq·ui·ty (ek′wə·ti), *n., pl.* **-ties. 1.** fairness; justice. **2.** what is fair and just. **3.** system of rules and principles based on fairness and justice. Equity supplements common law and statute law by covering cases in which fairness and justice require a settlement not covered by law. In the U.S., law and equity are usually administered by the same court. **4.** interest of a shareholder. **5.** amount that a property is worth beyond what is owed on it. [< L, < *aequus* even, just]

e·quiv·a·lence (i·kwiv′ə·ləns), **e·quiv·a·len·cy** (-lən·si), *n., pl.* **-len·ces; -cies.** a being equivalent; equality in value, force, significance, etc.

e·quiv·a·lent (i·kwiv′ə·lənt), *adj.* **1.** equal in value, area, force, effect, meaning, etc. **2.** having the same extent. A triangle and a square of equal area are equivalent. —*n.* **1.** something equivalent. **2.** *Chem.* the number of parts by weight in which an element will combine with or displace 8 parts of oxygen or 1 part of hydrogen. [< LL, < L *aequus* equal + *valere* be worth] —**e·quiv′a·lent·ly,** *adv.*

e·quiv·o·cal (i·kwiv′ə·kəl), *adj.* **1.** having two or more meanings; intentionally vague or ambiguous. **2.** undecided; uncertain. **3.** questionable; suspicious. [< LL *aequivocus* ambiguous < L *aequus* equal + *vocare* call] —**e·quiv′o·cal·ly,** *adv.* —**e·quiv′o·cal·ness,** *n.* —**Syn. 1.** doubtful. —**Ant. 1.** certain, evident, definite.

e·quiv·o·cate (i·kwiv′ə·kāt), *v.*, **-cat·ed, -cat·ing.** use expressions of double meaning in order to mislead. —**e·quiv′o·ca′tion,** *n.* —**e·quiv′o·ca′tor,** *n.*

-er[1], *suffix.* **1.** person or thing that ——s, as in *admirer, burner.* **2.** person living in ——, as in *New Yorker, villager.* **3.** person that makes or works with ——, as in *hatter, tiler, tinner.* **4.** person or thing that is or has ——, as in *six-footer, three-master, fiver.* [OE *-ere*] ≯ **-er, -or.** Names of persons performing an act (nouns of agent) and some other nouns are freely formed in English by adding *-er* to a verb (*doer, killer, painter, thinker*), but many, chiefly nouns taken in from Latin or French (*assessor, prevaricator*), end in *-or.* Since the two endings are pronounced the same (ər), it is hard to tell whether *-er* or *-or* should be written. Here are a few as samples; a dictionary will have to settle most questions. With *-er:* *advertiser, adviser* (now shifting to *advisor*), *debater, manufacturer, subscriber.* With *-or:* *administrator, competitor, conductor, distributor, inventor* (or sometimes *inventer*), *objector, supervisor.*

-er[2], *suffix forming the comparative degree.* **1.** of adjectives, as in *softer, smoother.* **2.** of adverbs, as in *slower.* [OE *-ra, -re*]

Er, *Chem.* erbium.

e·ra (ir′ə; ē′rə), *n.* **1.** a historical period distinguished by certain important or significant happenings. **2.** period of time starting from some important or significant happening, date, etc. **3.** system of reckoning time from some important or significant happening, given date, etc. The Christian era is the period of time reckoned from about four years after the birth of Christ. **4.** a point of time from which succeeding years are numbered. **5.** one of five very extensive periods of time in geological history. [< LL, var. of *aera* number, epoch, prob. same word as L *aera* counters (for reckoning), pl. of *aes* brass]

ERA, E.R.A., Emergency Relief Administration.

e·rad·i·ca·ble (i·rad′ə·kə·bəl), *adj.* that can be eradicated.

e·rad·i·cate (i·rad′ə·kāt), v., -cat·ed, -cat-ing. 1. get entirely rid of; destroy completely. 2. pull out by the roots. [< L, < ex- out + radix root] —e·rad′i·ca′tion, n. —e·rad′i·ca′tive, adj. —e·rad′i·ca′tor, n.

e·rase (i·rās′), v., e·rased, e·ras·ing. 1. rub out; scrape out. 2. remove all trace of; blot out. [< L erasus < ex- out + radere scrape] —e·ras′a·ble, adj. —Syn. 2. efface, obliterate, delete.

e·ras·er (i·rās′ər), n. thing for erasing marks made with pencil, ink, chalk, etc.

E·ras·mus (i·raz′məs), n. 1466?-1536, Dutch scholar and humanist, a leader of the Renaissance movement.

e·ra·sure (i·rā′shər; -zhər), n. 1. an erasing. 2. an erased word, letter, etc. 3. place where a word, letter, etc., has been erased.

er·bi·um (ėr′bi·əm), n. Chem. a rare metallic element, Er, of the yttrium group. [< NL, < (Ytt)erb(y), Swedish place name]

ere (ār), prep. before. —conj. 1. sooner than; rather than. 2. before. [OE ǣr]

e·rect (i·rekt′), adj. 1. straight up; upright. 2. raised; bristling. —v. 1. put straight up; set upright. 2. build; form. 3. in geometry, draw; construct. 4. put together; set up. 5. Archaic. establish. [< L erectus < ex- up + regere direct] —e·rect′er, e·rec′tor, n. —e·rec′tion, n. —e·rect′ly, adv. —e·rect′ness, n. —Syn. adj. 1. perpendicular, vertical, standing.

e·rec·tile (i·rek′təl), adj. 1. capable of being erected. 2. that can become distended and rigid: erectile tissues in animals. —e·rec·til·i·ty (i·rek′til′ə·ti; ē′rek-), n.

ere·long (ār′lông′; -long′), adv. before long; soon.

er·e·mite (er′ə·mīt), n. hermit. [< L < Gk. eremites < eremos uninhabited] —er·e·mit·ic (er′ə·mit′ik), er′e·mit′i·cal, adj.

erg (ėrg), n. unit for measuring work or energy. It is the amount of work done by one dyne acting through a distance of one centimeter. [< Gk. ergon work]

er·go (ėr′gō), adv., conj. therefore. [< L]

er·got (ėr′gət; -got), n. 1. disease of rye caused by a fungus. 2. a hard, dark body produced by this disease. 3. medicine made from this body, used to stop bleeding and to contract unstriped muscles. [< F < OF argot cock's spur]

er·i·ca·ceous (er′ə·kā′shəs), adj. belonging to the heath family. Heather, azalea, and rhododendron are ericaceous plants.

Er·ic·son (er′ik·sən), n. Leif, Viking chieftain and son of Eric the Red. He probably discovered North America about 1000 A.D.

Er·ic the Red (er′ik), born 950? A.D., Viking chief who discovered Greenland about 982 A.D.

E·rie (ir′i), n. 1. Lake, one of the five Great Lakes, between the United States and Canada. 2. city in NW Pennsylvania on Lake Erie. 3. Am. member of a tribe of American Indians formerly living along the S and E shores of Lake Erie.

Erie Canal, Am. canal in New York State between Buffalo and Albany. Parts of it are now abandoned, but most of it is included in the New York State Barge Canal system.

Er·in (er′ən; ir′-), n. Poetic. Ireland.

E·ris (ir′is; er′-), n. the Greek goddess of strife and discord.

Er·i·tre·a (er′ə·trē′ə), n. a former Italian colony on the Red Sea in NE Africa.

erl·king (ėrl′king′), n. in Teutonic legend, spirit or personification of a natural force, such as cold, storm, etc., that does harm, esp. to children. [< G erlkönig alder-king, a mistrans. of Dan. ellerkonge king of the elves]

er·mine (ėr′mən), n., pl. -mines or (esp. collectively) -mine. 1. weasel of northern climates. It is brown in summer, but white with a black-tipped tail in winter. 2. its soft, white fur, used for women's coats, trimming, etc. The official robes of English judges are trimmed with ermine as a symbol of purity and fairness. 3. position, rank, or duties of a judge. Few attain the ermine before they are fifty. [< OF < Gmc.]

erne, ern (ėrn), n. eagle that lives near the sea. [OE earn]

e·rode (i·rōd′), v., e·rod·ed, e·rod·ing. 1. eat into; eat or wear away gradually. 2. form by a gradual eating or wearing away. [< L, < ex- away + rodere gnaw]

E·ros (ir′os; er′-), n. the Greek god of love, the son of Aphrodite, identified by the Romans with Cupid.

e·rose (i·rōs′), adj. 1. shaped unevenly. 2. Bot. having an irregularly incised margin.

e·ro·sion (i·rō′zhən), n. 1. a gradual eating or wearing away. 2. a being eaten or worn away. —e·ro′sive, adj.

e·rot·ic (i·rot′ik), **e·rot·i·cal** (-ə·kəl), adj. of or having to do with sexual love. [< Gk. erotikos of Eros] —e·rot′i·cal·ly, adv. —e·rot′i-cism, n.

ERP, E.R.P., European Recovery Program.

err (ėr; er), v. 1. go wrong; make mistakes. 2. be wrong; be mistaken or incorrect. 3. do wrong; sin. [< OF < L errare wander] —err′ing, adj. —err′ing·ly, adv. —Syn. 1. stray, deviate, blunder. ▸ err. Usually pronounced ėr; but there is a growing tendency to pronounce it er, from analogy with error (er′ər).

er·rand (er′ənd), n. 1. a trip to do something. 2. what one is sent to do. 3. purpose or object of a trip. [OE ǣrende]

er·rant (er′ənt), adj. 1. traveling in search of adventure; wandering; roving. 2. wrong; mistaken; incorrect. [< F, ppr. of OF errer travel (< VL iterare < L iter journey), blended with F errant, ppr. of errer err] —er′rant·ly, adv.

er·rant·ry (er′ənt·ri), n., pl. -ries. conduct or action of a knight-errant.

er·rat·ic (i·rat′ik), adj. 1. not steady; uncertain; irregular. 2. queer; odd: erratic behavior. [< L, < errare err] —er·rat′i·cal·ly, adv. —Syn. 2. eccentric.

er·ra·tum (i·rā′təm; i·rä′-), n., pl. -ta (-tə). error or mistake in writing or printing. [< L, neut. pp. of errare err]

er·ro·ne·ous (ə·rō′ni·əs; e-), adj. incorrect. —er·ro′ne·ous·ly, adv. —er·ro′ne·ous·ness, n.

er·ror (er′ər), n. 1. something wrong; what is incorrect; mistake. 2. condition of being wrong, mistaken, or incorrect. 3. wrongdoing; sin. 4. Am., Baseball. a faulty play that gives the side at bat some added advantage. [< OF < L. See ERR.] —Syn. 1. blunder, slip, inaccuracy.

er·satz (er′zäts), adj., n. substitute: ersatz rubber. [< G]

Erse (ėrs), n. 1. Scotch Gaelic. 2. the Celtic language of Ireland. —adj. of either of these languages. [Scot. var. of Irish]

erst (ėrst), adv. Archaic. formerly; long ago. [OE ǣrst, superl. of ǣr]

erst·while (ėrst′hwīl′), adv. some time ago; in time past; formerly. —adj. former; past. ▸ Erstwhile is often only affected for former.

e·ruct (i·rukt′), v. belch. [< L, < ex- out + ructare belch]

e·ruc·tate (i·ruk′tāt), v., -tat·ed, -tat·ing. belch. —e·ruc·ta·tion (i·ruk′tā′shən; ē′ruk-), n. —e·ruc′ta·tive, adj.

er·u·dite (er′ù·dīt; er′yù-), adj. scholarly; learned. [< L eruditus instructed < ex- away + rudis rude] —er′u·dite′ly, adv. —er′u·dite′-ness, n.

er·u·di·tion (er′ù·dish′ən; er′yù-), n. acquired knowledge; scholarship; learning. —er′-u·di′tion·al, adj.

e·rupt (i·rupt′), v. 1. burst forth. 2. throw forth. 3. break out in a rash. The skin erupts during measles. [< L eruptus < ex- out + rumpere burst]

e·rup·tion (i·rup′shən), n. 1. a bursting forth. 2. a throwing forth of lava, etc., from a volcano or of hot water from a geyser. 3. a breaking out in a rash. 4. red spots on the skin; rash. —e·rup′tive, adj.

-ery, suffix. 1. place for ——ing, as in cannery, hatchery. 2. place for ——s, as in nunnery. 3. occupation or business of a ——, as in cookery. 4. state or condition of a——, as in slavery. 5. qualities, actions, etc., of a ——, as in knavery. 6. ——s as a group, as in machinery. [< OF -erie]

er·y·sip·e·las (er′ə·sip′ə·ləs; ir′ə-), *n.* an acute infectious disease caused by streptococcus bacteria and characterized by a high fever and a deep-red inflammation of the skin. [< Gk.]

e·ryth·ro·my·cin (i·rith′rō·mī′sin), *n.* drug related to streptomycin, used against certain bacterial infections. [< Gk. *erythros* red + *mykes* fungus]

E·sau (ē′sô), *n. Bible.* older son of Isaac and Rebecca, who sold his birthright to his brother Jacob. Gen. 25:21–34.

es·ca·drille (es′kə·dril′), *n.* a small fleet of airplanes or warships. [< F, dim. of *escadre* SQUADRON; form infl. by Sp. *escuadrilla*, dim. of *escuadra*]

es·ca·lade (es′kə·lād′), *n., v.* -lad·ed, -lad·ing. —*n.* climbing the walls of a fortified place by ladders. —*v.* climb thus. [< F < Ital. *scalata*, ult. < L *scala* ladder]

es·ca·la·tor (es′kə·lā′tər), *n. Am.* 1. a moving stairway. 2. Escalator, *Trademark.* a moving stairway built by the Otis Elevator Company. [blend of *escalade* and *elevator*]

escalator clause, provision in a contract allowing an increase or decrease in wages under specified conditions.

es·cal·lop, es·cal·op (es·kol′əp; -kal′-), *v.* bake in a cream sauce or with bread crumbs. —*n.* scallop. [(orig. n.) < OF *escalope* shell < Gmc.] —es·cal′loped, *adj. Am.*

es·ca·pade (es′kə·pād; es′kə·pād′), *n.* a breaking loose from rules or restraint; wild adventure or prank. [< F < Ital., < *scappare* ESCAPE]

es·cape (es·kāp′), *v.* -caped, -cap·ing, *n., adj.* —*v.* 1. get free; get out and away. 2. get free from. 3. keep free or safe from; avoid. 4. avoid capture, trouble, etc. 5. come out of without being intended: *a cry escaped her lips.* 6. fail to be noticed or remembered by: *his name escapes me.* —*n.* 1. an escaping. 2. way of escaping. 3. *Psychol.* an avoiding of reality. 4. outflow or leakage of gas, water, etc. —*adj.* providing a way of escape or avoidance. [< OF *escaper*, ult. < L *ex-* out of + *cappa* cloak] —es·cap′er, *n.* —Syn. v. 1. flee, abscond. 3. evade, elude, shun.

es·ca·pee (es′kə·pē′; es·kāp′ē), *n.* person who has escaped; esp. one who has escaped from an area under Communist control.

es·cape·ment (es·kāp′mənt), *n.* 1. device in a timepiece by which the motion of the wheels and of the pendulum or balance wheel are accommodated to each other. One tooth of the wheel escapes at each swing of the pendulum. 2. mechanism that controls the movement of a typewriter carriage.

Two forms of escapement

es·cap·ism (es·kāp′iz·əm), *n.* a habitual avoidance of unpleasant realities by recourse to imagination and fiction. —es·cap′ist, *n.*

es·ca·role (es′kə·rōl), *n.* a broad-leaved kind of endive, used for salads.

es·carp·ment (es·kärp′mənt), *n.* 1. a steep slope; cliff. 2. ground made into a steep slope in a fortification. [< F < Ital. *scarpa* < Gmc.]

es·cheat (es·chēt′), *Law.* —*n.* 1. a reverting of the ownership of property to the legal state or the lord of a manor when there are no legal heirs. 2. property whose ownership has so reverted. —*v.* revert thus. [< OF *eschete*, ult. < L *ex-* out + *cadere* fall] —es·cheat′a·ble, *adj.*

es·chew (es·chü′), *v.* avoid as bad or harmful; shun. [< OF *eschiver* < Gmc.]

es·cort (*n.* es′kôrt; *v.* es·kôrt′), *n.* 1. one or a group going with another to give protection, show honor, etc. 2. act of going with another as an escort. —*v.* go with as an escort. [< F < Ital. *scorta* < *scorgere* guide < L *ex-* + *corrigere* CORRECT] —Syn. v. accompany, conduct, attend.

es·cri·toire (es′kri·twär′), *n.* a writing desk. [< F < LL *scriptorium* < *scribere* write]

es·crow (es′krō; es·krō′), *n.* deed, bond, or other written agreement put in charge of a third person until certain conditions are fulfilled. [< AF var. of OF *escroue* scrap, scroll < Gmc.]

es·cu·do (es·kü′dō), *n., pl.* -dos. 1. a unit of

Portuguese gold money. 2. a former gold or silver coin of Spain, Portugal, etc. [< Sp., Pg. < L *scutum* shield]

es·cu·lent (es′kyə·lənt), *adj.* suitable for food; edible. [< L, < *esca* food]

es·cutch·eon (es·kuch′ən), *n.* shield or shield-shaped surface on which a coat of arms is put. [< OF *escuchon*, < L *scutum* shield]

Es·dras (ez′drəs), *n.* 1. either of the first two books of the Protestant Apocrypha. 2. two books in the Douay Bible, called Ezra and Nehemiah in the Protestant and Jewish Bibles.

-ese, *suffix.* 1. of or pertaining to, as in Japanese art. 2. native or inhabitant of, as in Portuguese. 3. language of, as in Chinese. [< OF *-eis* < L *-ensis*]

Es·ki·mo (es′kə·mō), *n., pl.* -mos, -mo, *adj.* —*n.* member of a race living on the arctic shores of North America and NE Asia. Eskimos are short and stocky, and have broad, flat faces, yellowish skin, and black hair. —*adj.* of or having to do with the Eskimos or their language. [< Dan. < F < Algonquian *eskimantsis* raw-flesh-eaters]

Eskimo dog, a strong dog used by the Eskimos to pull sledges.

e·soph·a·gus (ē·sof′ə·gəs), *n., pl.* -gi (-jī). passage for food from the mouth to the stomach; gullet. Also, oesophagus. [< NL < Gk., < *oiso-* carry + *phagein* eat]

es·o·ter·ic (es′ə·ter′ik), *adj.* 1. understood only by the select few; intended for an inner circle of disciples, scholars, etc. 2. secret; confidential. [< Gk. *esoterikos*, ult. < *eso* within] —es′o·ter′i·cal·ly, *adv.*

ESP, extrasensory perception.

esp., especially.

es·pal·ier (es·pal′yər), *n.* 1. framework upon which trees and shrubs grow. 2. tree or shrub trained to grow this way.

es·pe·cial (es·pesh′əl), *adj.* 1. special; particular. 2. exceptional in amount or degree. [< OF < L *specialis* SPECIAL]

es·pe·cial·ly (es·pesh′əl·i), *adv.* particularly; chiefly. —Syn. mostly, principally, primarily.

Es·pe·ran·to (es′pə·rän′tō; -ran′-), *n.* a simple artificial language for international use.

es·pi·al (es·pī′əl), *n.* 1. act of spying. 2. act of watching. 3. discovery.

es·pi·o·nage (es′pi·ə·nij; es′pi·ə·näzh), *n.* use of spies; spying. [< F, < *espion* spy < Ital. *spione* < *spia* spy]

es·pla·nade (es′plə·nād′; -näd′), *n.* 1. an open, level space used for public walks or drives. 2. an open space separating a fortress from the houses of a town. [< F < Sp., ult. < L *ex-* out + *planus* level]

es·pous·al (es·pouz′əl), *n.* 1. an espousing; adoption of a cause, etc.). 2. ceremony of becoming engaged or married.

es·pouse (es·pouz′), *v.* -poused, -pous·ing. 1. marry. 2. take up or make one's own: *espouse a new religion.* [< OF < L *sponsare* < *sponsus* betrothed, pp. of *spondere* betroth] —es·pous′er, *n.*

es·prit (es·prē′), *n.* lively wit; spirit. [< F < L *spiritus* SPIRIT]

es·prit de corps (es·prē′ də kôr′), *French.* a sense of union and of common interests and responsibilities to some group.

es·py (es·pī′), *v.* -pied, -py·ing. see; spy. [< OF *espier* < Gmc.] ► Usually espy suggests that a thing is hard to see because it is far away, etc.

Esq., Esqr., Esquire. ► Esq., Esquire. Written following a man's name in the inside and outside address of a letter, *Esq.* or *Esquire* is formal, with archaic or British suggestion, and in the United States is not often used except to professional men, chiefly to lawyers. No other title (such as *Mr., Dr., Hon.*) should be used with the word: *Harry A. Kinne, Esq.*

-esque, *suffix.* 1. in the —— style; resembling the —— style, as in *Romanesque.* 2. like a ——; like that of a ——, as in *statuesque.* [< F < Ital. *-esco*]

es·quire (es·kwīr′; es′kwīr), *n., v.* -quired,

āge, câre, fär; ēqual, tėrm; īce; ōpen, ôrder; pút, rüle, ūse; TH, then; ə=a in about.

-quir·ing. —*n.* **1.** in the Middle Ages, a young man of noble family who attended a knight until he himself was made a knight. **2.** Englishman ranking next below a knight. **3. Esquire,** title of respect placed after a man's last name. —*v.* **1.** raise to the rank of esquire. **2.** address as esquire. **3.** escort (a lady). [< OF < L *scutarius* shieldbearer < *scutum* shield] ➤ See Esq. for usage note.

-ess, *suffix.* female, as in *heiress, hostess, lioness.* [< F -*esse* < L -*issa* < Gk.]

es·say (*n. 1* es'ā; *n. 2* es'ā, e·sā'; *v.* e·sā'), *n.* **1.** a literary composition on a certain subject. An essay is usually shorter and less methodical than a treatise. **2.** try; attempt. —*v.* try; attempt. [< OF < L *exagium* a weighing] —essay'er, *n.* —Syn. *n.* **2.** effort, endeavor.

es·say·ist (es'ā·ist), *n.* writer of essays.

Es·sen (es'ən), *n.* city in W Germany.

es·sence (es'əns), *n.* **1.** that which makes a thing what it is; necessary part or parts; important feature or features. **2.** substance. **3.** entity, esp. a spiritual entity. **4.** any concentrated substance that has the characteristic flavor, fragrance, or effect of the plant, fruit, etc., from which it is obtained. **5.** solution of such a substance in alcohol. **6.** perfume. [< L, < *esse* be]

es·sen·tial (ə·sen'shəl), *adj.* **1.** needed to make a thing what it is; necessary; very important. **2.** of, like, or constituting the essence of a substance. **3.** of the highest sort; in the highest sense: *essential happiness.* —*n.* an absolutely necessary element or quality; fundamental feature. [< Med.L *essentialis.* See ESSENCE.] —essen'tial·ly, *adv.* —es·sen'tial·ness, *n.* —Syn. *adj.* **1.** indispensable, requisite, vital.

essential oil, a volatile oil that gives a plant, fruit, etc., its characteristic flavor, fragrance, or effect.

-est, *suffix* forming the superlative degree. **1.** of adjectives, as in *warmest.* **2.** of adverbs, as in *slowest.*

E.S.T., EST, or **e.s.t.,** *Am.* Eastern Standard Time.

es·tab·lish (es·tab'lish), *v.* **1.** set up permanently: *establish a business.* **2.** settle in a position; set up in business. **3.** bring about permanently; cause to be accepted: *establish a custom.* **4.** show beyond dispute; prove: *establish a fact.* **5.** make (a church) a national institution recognized and supported by the government. [< OF *establir* < L *stabilire* make STABLE²] —es·tab'lish·er, *n.* —Syn. **4.** verify, substantiate.

established church, church that is a national institution recognized and supported by the government.

es·tab·lish·ment (es·tab'lish·mənt), *n.* **1.** an establishing. **2.** a being established. **3.** thing established. **4.** recognition by the state of a church as the official church. **5.** an institution. A household, business, church, or army is an establishment.

es·tate (es·tāt'), *n.* **1.** a large piece of land belonging to a person; landed property. **2.** that which a person owns; property; possessions. **3.** interest, ownership, or property in land or other things. **4.** condition or stage in life. **5.** social status or rank; high rank. **6.** class or group of people in a nation. [< OF < L *status* state]

es·teem (es·tēm'), *v.* **1.** have a favorable opinion of; regard highly. **2.** value; rate. **3.** think; consider. —*n.* a very favorable opinion; high regard. [< OF < L *aestimare* value] —Syn. *n.* estimation, favor, respect. —Ant. *n.* contempt.

es·ter (es'tər), *n.* **1.** *Chem.* compound in which the acid hydrogen of an acid is replaced by the organic radical of an alcohol. Animal and vegetable fats and oils are esters. **2.** any salt containing a hydrocarbon radical.

Es·ther (es'tər), *n.* **1.** the Jewish wife of a Persian king, who saved her people from massacre. **2.** book of the Old Testament that tells her story.

es·thete (es'thēt), *n.* aesthete. —**es·thet·ic** (es·thet'ik), *adj.* —**es·thet'i·cal,** *adj.* —**es·thet'i·cal·ly,** *adv.*

es·thet·ics (es·thet'iks), *n.* aesthetics.

Es·tho·ni·a (es·thō'ni·ə; -thō'-), *n.* Estonia. —**Es·tho'ni·an,** *adj., n.*

es·ti·ma·ble (es'tə·mə·bəl), *adj.* **1.** worthy of esteem; deserving high regard. **2.** capable of being estimated or calculated. —**es'ti·ma·ble·ness,** *n.* —**es'ti·ma·bly,** *adv.*

es·ti·mate (*n.* es'tə·mit; -māt; *v.* es'tə·māt), *n., v.,* -**mat·ed,** -**mat·ing.** —*n.* **1.** judgment or opinion about how much, how many, how good, etc. **2.** statement of what certain work will cost, made by one willing to do the work. —*v.* **1.** have an opinion of. **2.** fix the worth, size, amount, etc., esp. in a rough way; calculate approximately. [< L *aestimatus,* pp. of *aestimare* value] —**es'ti·ma'tive,** *adj.* —**es'ti·ma'tor,** *n.* —Syn. *v.* **1.** judge. **2.** reckon, gauge.

es·ti·ma·tion (es'tə·mā'shən), *n.* **1.** judgment; opinion. **2.** esteem; respect. **3.** act or process of estimating.

Es·to·ni·a (es·tō'ni·ə), *n.* country in N Europe, on the Baltic Sea, now under the Soviet Union. Also, Esthonia. —**Es·to'ni·an,** *adj., n.*

es·top (es·top'), *v.,* -**topped,** -**top·ping.** **1.** *Law.* prevent from asserting or doing something contrary to a previous assertion or act. **2.** stop; bar; obstruct. [< OF, < *estoupe* tow < L *stuppa*]

es·trange (es·trānj'), *v.,* -**tranged,** -**trang·ing.** **1.** turn (a person) from affection to indifference, dislike, or hatred; make unfriendly; separate: *a quarrel had estranged him from his family.* **2.** keep apart; keep away. [< OF < L, < *extraneus* STRANGE] —**es·trange'ment,** *n.* —**es·trang'er,** *n.* —Syn. **1.** alienate.

es·tro·gen (es'trə·jən), *n.* any of various hormones which induce a series of physiological changes in females, esp. in the reproductive or sexual organs. —**es·tro·gen·ic** (es'trə·jen'ik), *adj.*

es·tu·ar·y (es'chů·er'i), *n., pl.* -**ar·ies.** **1.** a broad mouth of a river into which the tide flows. **2.** inlet of the sea. [< L, < *aestus* tide] —**es·tu·ar·i·al** (es'chů·ãr'i·əl), *adj.*

-et, *suffix.* little, as in *owlet, islet.* This meaning has disappeared in most words formed by adding -*et.* [< OF]

e·ta (ā'tə; ē'tə), *n.* the seventh letter of the Greek alphabet (H, η).

et al., **1.** and elsewhere. **2.** and others. [(def.1) < L *et alibi;* (def. 2) < L *et alii*]

etc., et cetera. ➤ etc., et cetera. *Etc.,* usually read *and so forth,* is sometimes a convenient way to end a series that samples rather than completes an enumeration, but it belongs primarily to reference and business usage: *The case is suitable for prints, maps, blueprints, etc.* Its inappropriateness can be seen in a sentence like this: *A student's professors can be of immense aid to him because of their knowledge of boys and their habits, customs, needs, ideals, etc.* Writing out *et cetera* now seems an affectation. In consecutive writing most people would probably use the English "and so forth." It is better to avoid these end tags (which really take away from emphasis by putting a catchall at the end of a clause or sentence) by rephrasing the list, preceding it by *such as* or some other warning that the list you have given is not exhaustive. *And etc.* shows the writer doesn't realize that the *et* of *etc.* means *and,* so that he is really writing *and and so forth.*

et cet·er·a (et set'ər·ə; set'rə), and others; and the rest; and so forth; and so on; and the like. [< L] ➤ See etc. for usage note.

etch (ech), *v.* **1.** engrave (a drawing or design) on metal, glass, etc., by means of acid. When filled with ink, the lines of the design will reproduce a copy on paper. **2.** engrave a drawing or design on by means of acid. **3.** make drawings or designs by this method. [< Du. < G *ätzen;* akin to EAT] —**etch'er,** *n.*

etch·ing (ech'ing), *n.* **1.** picture or design printed from an etched plate. **2.** an etched plate; etched drawing or design. **3.** art of an etcher; process of engraving a drawing or design on metal, glass, etc., by means of acid.

e·ter·nal (i·tėr'nəl), *adj.* **1.** without beginning or ending; lasting throughout all time. **2.** always and forever the same. **3.** seeming to go on forever; occurring very frequently. —*n.* the Eternal, God. [< L *aeternalis*, ult. < *aevum* age] —e·ter'nal·ly, *adv.* —e·ter'nal·ness, *n.* —Syn. *adj.* 1. everlasting, perpetual, immortal.

Eternal City, the, Rome.

e·ter·ni·ty (i·ter'nə·ti), *n., pl.* –ties. 1. time without beginning or ending; all time. 2. eternal quality; endlessness. 3. the endless period after death; future life. 4. a seemingly endless period of time.

e·ter·nize (i·ter'nīz), *v.,* –nized, –niz·ing. make eternal; perpetuate; immortalize.

eth·ane (eth'ān), *n. Chem.* a colorless, odorless, inflammable gas, C₂H₆. It is a hydrocarbon present in natural gas and illuminating gas.

e·ther (ē'thər), *n.* 1. *Chem.* a colorless, strong-smelling liquid, (C₂H₅)₂O, that burns and evaporates readily. Its fumes cause unconsciousness when deeply inhaled. Ether is used as a solvent for fats and resins. 2. Also, **aether.** a. the upper regions of space beyond the earth's atmosphere; clear sky. b. the invisible, elastic substance supposed to be distributed evenly through all space and to conduct light waves, electric waves, etc. [< L < Gk. *aither* upper air]

e·the·re·al (i·thir'i·əl), *adj.* 1. light; airy; delicate: *ethereal beauty.* 2. not of the earth; heavenly. 3. of or pertaining to the upper regions of space. 4. of or pertaining to the ether diffused through space. Also, **aethereal.** —e·the're·al'i·ty, *n.* —e·the're·al·ly, *adv.* —e·the're·al·ness, *n.* —Syn. 1. intangible, tenuous.

e·the·re·al·ize (i·thir'i·əl·īz), *v.,* –ized, –iz·ing. make ethereal. —e·the're·al·i·za'tion, *n.*

e·ther·ize (ē'thər·īz), *v.,* –ized, –iz·ing. *Am.* 1. make unconscious with ether fumes. 2. change into ether. —e'ther·i·za'tion, *n.* —e'ther·iz'er, *n.*

eth·ic (eth'ik), *adj.* ethical. —*n.* ethics; system of ethics. [< L < Gk., < *ethos* moral character]

eth·i·cal (eth'ə·kəl), *adj.* 1. having to do with standards of right and wrong; of ethics or morality. 2. in accordance with formal or professional rules of right and wrong. —eth'i·cal'i·ty, *n.* —eth'i·cal·ly, *adv.* —eth'i·cal·ness, *n.*

eth·ics (eth'iks), *n.* 1. (*sing. in use*) study of standards of right and wrong; that part of science and philosophy dealing with moral conduct, duty, and judgment. 2. (*sing. in use*) book about ethics. 3. (*pl. in use*) formal or professional rules of right and wrong; system of conduct or behavior.

E·thi·o·pi·a (ē'thi·ō'pi·ə), *n.* 1. an ancient region in NE Africa, S of Egypt. 2. country in E Africa; Abyssinia.

E·thi·o·pi·an (ē'thi·ō'pi·ən), **E·thi·op** (ē'thi·op), *adj.* 1. of or having to do with Ethiopia or its people. 2. Negro. —*n.* 1. native or inhabitant of Ethiopia. 2. Negro.

E·thi·op·ic (ē'thi·op'ik; –ō'pik), *adj.* of or having to do with the ancient language of Ethiopia or the church using this language. —*n.* the ancient language of Ethiopia.

eth·nic (eth'nik), **eth·ni·cal** (–nə·kəl), *adj.* 1. having to do with the various races of people and the characteristics and customs they have in common; racial. 2. heathen; pagan; not Christian; not Jewish. [< L < Gk., < *ethnos* nation] —eth'ni·cal·ly, *adv.*

eth·nog·ra·phy (eth·nog'rə·fi), *n.* the scientific description and classification of the various races of people. —eth·nog'ra·pher, *n.* —eth·no·graph·ic (eth'nə·graf'ik), **eth'no·graph'i·cal,** *adj.* —eth'no·graph'i·cal·ly, *adv.*

eth·nol·o·gy (eth·nol'ə·ji), *n.* science that deals with the various races of people, their origin, distribution, characteristics, customs, institutions, and culture. —eth·no·log·ic (eth'nə·loj'ik), **eth'no·log'i·cal,** *adj.* —eth'no·log'i·cal·ly, *adv.* —eth·nol'o·gist, *n.*

eth·yl (eth'əl), *n.* 1. *Chem.* a univalent radical, –C₂H₅, in many organic compounds. Ordinary alcohol contains ethyl. 2. Ethyl, *Trademark.* a poisonous, colorless lead compound, Pb (C₂H₅)₄, used in gasoline to reduce knocking.

ethyl alcohol, ordinary alcohol, C₂H₅OH, made by the fermentation of grain, sugar, etc.

eth·yl·ene (eth'ə·lēn), *n.* a colorless, inflammable gas, C₂H₄, with an unpleasant odor, used as a fuel and anesthetic, and for coloring and ripening citrus fruits.

e·ti·ol·o·gy (ē'ti·ol'ə·ji), *n.* 1. an assigning of a cause. 2. science that deals with origins or causes. 3. theory of the causes of disease. Also, **aetiology.** [< L < Gk., < *aitia* cause + –*logos* treating of] —e·ti·o·log·i·cal (ē'ti·ə·loj'ə·kəl), *adj.* —e'ti·o·log'i·cal·ly, *adv.* —e'ti·ol'o·gist, *n.*

et·i·quette (et'ə·ket), *n.* 1. conventional rules for conduct or behavior in polite society. 2. formal rules or conventions governing conduct in a profession, official ceremony, etc.: *medical etiquette.* [< F < Gmc.]

Et·na (et'nə), *n.* Mount, volcano in NE Sicily. Also, Aetna, Mount.

E·tru·ri·a (i·trūr'i·ə), *n.* an ancient country in W Italy.

E·trus·can (i·trus'kən), **E·tru·ri·an** (i·trūr'i·ən), *adj.* of or having to do with Etruria, its people, their language, art, or customs. —*n.* 1. native or inhabitant of Etruria. 2. language of Etruria.

et seq., and the following; and that which follows. [< L et *sequens*]

–ette, *suffix.* 1. little, as in *kitchenette, statuette.* 2. female, as in *farmerette, suffragette.* 3. substitute for, as in *leatherette.* [< F, fem. of –*et* –ET]

é·tude (ā·tüd'; ā·tūd'), *n.* 1. study. 2. piece of music intended to develop skill in technique. [< F, study]

et·y·mol·o·gy (et'ə·mol'ə·ji), *n., pl.* –gies. 1. account or explanation of the origin and history of a word. 2. a historical study dealing with linguistic changes, esp. a study dealing with individual word origins. [< L < Gk., < *etymon* the original sense or form of a word (neut. of *etymos* true, real) + –*logos* treating of] —et·y·mo·log·i·cal (et'ə·mo·loj'ə·kəl), *adj.* —et'y·mo·log'i·cal·ly, *adv.* —et'y·mol'o·gist, *n.*

eu–, *prefix.* good; well, as in *eulogy, euphony.* [< Gk.]

Eu, *Chem.* europium.

Eu·boe·a (ū·bē'ə), *n.* the largest island in the Aegean Sea, near Greece and belonging to it. —Eu·boe'an, *n., adj.*

eu·ca·lyp·tus (ū'kə·lip'təs), *n., pl.* –tus·es, –ti (–tī) a very tall tree that originated in Australia. It is valued for its timber and for an oil made from its leaves. [< NL, < Gk. *eu*– well + *kalyptos* covered; with ref. to bud covering]

Eu·cha·rist (ū'kə·rist), *n.* 1. sacrament of the Lord's Supper; Holy Communion. 2. the consecrated bread and wine used in this sacrament. [< LL < Gk. *eucharistia* thankfulness, the Eucharist] —Eu'cha·ris'tic, Eu'cha·ris'ti·cal, *adj.*

eu·chre (ū'kər), *n., v.,* –chred, –chring. —*n. Am.* a simple card game for two, three, or four players, using the 32 (or 28, or 24) highest cards. —*v.* 1. defeat (the side that declared the trump) at euchre. 2. *Am., Colloq.* outwit.

Eu·clid (ū'klid), *n.* Greek mathematician who wrote a book on geometry about 300 B.C.

Eu·clid·e·an, Eu·clid·i·an (ū·klid'i·ən), *adj.* of Euclid or his principles of geometry.

eu·gen·ic (ū·jen'ik), **eu·gen·i·cal** (–ə·kəl), *adj.* 1. having to do with improvement of the race; improving the offspring produced; improving the race. 2. possessing good inherited characteristics. [< Gk. *eugenes* well-born < *eu*– well + *genos* birth] —eu·gen'i·cal·ly, *adv.*

eu·gen·ics (ū·jen'iks), *n.* science of improving the human race. Eugenics would apply the same principles to human beings that have long been applied to animals and plants, and develop healthier, more intelligent, and better children.

Eu·gé·nie (œ·zhā·nē'), *n.* 1826–1920, wife of Napoleon III and empress of the French.

eu·lo·gist (ū'lə·jist), *n.* person who eulogizes.

eu·lo·gis·tic (ū'lə·jis'tik), **eu·lo·gis·ti·cal** (–tə·kəl), *adj.* praising highly. —eu'lo·gis'ti·cal·ly, *adv.*

eu·lo·gi·um (ū·lō'ji·əm), *n., pl.* –gi·ums, –gi·a (–ji·ə). eulogy; praise.

āge, cãre, fär; ēqual, tèrm; īce; ōpen, ôrder; pùt, rüle, ūse; th, then; ə=a in about.

eu·lo·gize (ū′lə·jīz), v., –gized, –giz·ing. praise very highly. —eu′lo·giz′er, n.

eu·lo·gy (ū′lə·ji), n., pl. –gies. speech or writing in praise of a person, action, etc.; high praise. [< Gk. *eulogia* < *eu-* well + *legein* speak]

eu·nuch (ū′nək), n. 1. a castrated man. 2. a castrated man in charge of a harem or the household of an Oriental ruler. [< L < Gk., < *eune* bed + *echein* keep]

eu·pep·sia (ū·pep′shə; –si·ə), n. good digestion. [< NL < Gk. See EU–, DYSPEPSIA.] —eu·pep·tic (ū·pep′tik), adj.

eu·phe·mism (ū′fə·miz·əm), n. 1. use of a mild or indirect expression instead of one that is harsh or unpleasantly direct. 2. a mild or indirect expression used in this way. "Pass away" is a common euphemism for "die." [< Gk., < *eu-* good + *pheme* speaking] —eu′phe·mist, n. —eu′phe·mis′tic, adj. —eu′phe·mis′ti·cal·ly, adv. ➤ The most excusable euphemisms are those intended to soften the misfortunes of life, as *laid to rest* for *buried*. The largest group of euphemisms consists of substitutes for many short abrupt words, the names of physical functions and social unpleasantness. For years *sweat* was taboo and was replaced by *perspire* and *perspiration*.

eu·phe·mize (ū′fə·mīz), v., –mized, –miz·ing. 1. employ euphemism. 2. express by euphemism. —eu′phe·miz′er, n.

eu·phon·ic (ū·fon′ik), **eu·phon·i·cal** (–ə·kəl), adj. 1. having to do with euphony. 2. euphonious. —eu·phon′i·cal·ly, adv. —eu·phon′i·cal·ness, n.

eu·pho·ni·ous (ū·fō′ni·əs), adj. sounding well; pleasing to the ear; harmonious. —eu·pho′ni·ous·ly, adv. —eu·pho′ni·ous·ness, n.

eu·pho·ni·um (ū·fō′ni·əm), n. a brass musical instrument like a tuba, having a loud, deep tone.

eu·pho·ny (ū′fə·ni), n., pl. –nies. 1. agreeableness of sound; pleasing effect to the ear; agreeableness of speech sounds as uttered or combined in utterance. 2. tendency to change sounds so as to favor ease of utterance. [< LL < Gk., < *eu-* good + *phone* sound]

eu·phor·bi·a (ū·fôr′bi·ə), n. any of a genus of plants with acrid, milky juice and small, inconspicuous flowers; spurge. Some euphorbias resemble cacti. [< L, < *Euphorbus*, a Greek physician]

eu·pho·ri·a (ū·fō′ri·ə; –fō′–), n. 1. *Psychol.* sense of well-being and expansiveness. 2. *Med.* physical soundness; good health. [< NL < Gk., < *eu* well + *pherein* to bear]

Eu·phra·tes (ū·frā′tēz), n. river in SW Asia, flowing from E Turkey into the Persian Gulf. It joins the Tigris River in Iraq.

eu·phu·ism (ū′fū·iz·əm), n. 1. an affected style of speaking and writing English that was fashionable around 1600, characterized by long series of antitheses, frequent similes, and alliteration. 2. any affected, elegant style of writing; flowery, artificial language. [< *Euphues*, main character in two works of John Lyly, English dramatist]

eu·phu·is·tic (ū′fū·is′tik), **eu·phu·is·ti·cal** (–tə·kəl), adj. using or containing euphuism; like euphuism. —eu′phu·is′ti·cal·ly, adv.

Eur., Europe; European.

Eur·a·sia (yŭr·ā′zhə; –shə), n. Europe and Asia. —Eur·a′sian, adj., n.

Eur·at·om (yŭr·at′əm), n. a proposed grouping of six European countries (France, West Germany, Italy, Belgium, the Netherlands, and Luxembourg) for atomic research on a coöperative basis.

eu·re·ka (yū·rē′kə), interj. I have found it! (the motto of California). [< Gk.]

Eu·rip·i·des (yū·rip′ə·dēz), n. 480?–406? B.C., Greek tragic poet.

Eu·rope (yŭr′əp), n. continent W of Asia.

Eu·ro·pe·an (yŭr′ə·pē′ən), adj. of or having to do with Europe or its people. —n. native or inhabitant of Europe.

Eu·ro·pe·an·ize (yŭr′ə·pē′ən·īz), v., –ized, –iz·ing. make European in appearance, habit, way of life, etc.

European plan, *Am.* system of charges to guests in a hotel by which the price covers the room, but not the meals (distinguished from American plan).

European Recovery Program, plan adopted by the United States for giving financial aid to European nations after World War II.

eu·ro·pi·um (yū·rō′pi·əm), n. *Chem.* a rare metallic element, Eu, of the same group as cerium. [< NL, < L *Europa* Europe < Gk.]

Eu·ryd·i·ce (yū·rid′ə·sē), n. *Gk. Myth.* the wife of Orpheus, who freed her from Hades by the charm of his music, but lost her again because he disobeyed orders and turned back to see whether she was following.

Eu·sta·chi·an tube (ū·stā′ki·ən; –stā′shən), *Anat.* a slender canal between the pharynx and the middle ear. It equalizes the air pressure on the two sides of the eardrum.

Eu·ter·pe (ū·tér′pē), n. the Greek Muse of music and lyric song.

eu·tha·na·sia (ū′thə·nā′zhə), n. 1. easy, painless death. 2. a painless killing, esp. to end a painful and incurable disease. [< Gk., < *eu-* easy + *thanatos* death]

eu·then·ics (ū·then′iks), n. *Am.* science or art of improving living conditions. [< Gk. *euthenia* well-being] —eu·then·ist (ū′thən·ist), n. *Am.*

Eux·ine Sea (ūk′sin), an ancient name for the Black Sea.

e·vac·u·ate (i·vak′yū·āt), v., –at·ed, –at·ing. 1. leave empty; withdraw from: *after surrendering, the soldiers evacuated the fort.* 2. withdraw; remove: *efforts were made to evacuate all foreign residents from the war zone.* 3. make empty: *evacuate the bowels.* [< L, < *ex-* out + *vacuus* empty] —e·vac′u·a′tion, n. —e·vac′u·a′tor, n.

e·vac·u·ee (i·vak′yū·ē; i·vak′yū·ē′), n. one who is removed to a place of greater safety.

e·vade (i·vād′), v., e·vad·ed, e·vad·ing. 1. get away from by trickery; avoid by cleverness. 2. elude. [< L, < *ex-* away + *vadere* go] —e·vad′a·ble, e·vad′i·ble, adj. —e·vad′er, n. —e·vad′ing·ly, adv. —Syn. 2. avoid, escape, dodge.

e·val·u·ate (i·val′yū·āt), v., –at·ed, –at·ing. find the value or the amount of; fix the value of. —e·val′u·a′tion, n.

ev·a·nesce (ev′ə·nes′), v., –nesced, –nes·cing. disappear; fade away; vanish. [< L *evanescere* < *ex-* out + *vanus* insubstantial] —ev′a·nes′cence, n.

ev·a·nes·cent (ev′ə·nes′ənt), adj. tending to disappear or fade away; able to last only a short time. —ev′a·nes′cent·ly, adv. —Syn. fleeting.

e·van·gel (i·van′jəl), n. 1. good news of the saving of mankind through Christ. 2. good news. 3. evangelist. 4. **Evangel,** one of the four gospels; Matthew, Mark, Luke, or John. [< LL < Gk. *euangelion* good tidings, ult. < *eu-* good + *angellein* announce]

e·van·gel·i·cal (ē′van·jel′ə·kəl; ev′ən–), adj. Also, **e′van·gel′ic.** 1. of, concerning, or according to the four Gospels or the New Testament. 2. of or having to do with the Protestant churches that emphasize Christ's atonement and salvation by faith as the most important parts of Christianity, as the Methodists and Baptists. 3. evangelistic. —n. 1. an adherent of evangelical doctrines. 2. member of an evangelical church. —e′van·gel′i·cal·ism, n. —e′van·gel′i·cal·ly, adv.

e·van·ge·lism (i·van′jə·liz·əm), n. 1. a preaching of the Gospel; earnest effort for the spread of the Gospel. 2. work of an evangelist. 3. belief in the doctrines of an evangelical church or party.

e·van·ge·list (i·van′jə·list), n. 1. preacher of the Gospel. 2. a traveling preacher who stirs up religious feeling in revival services or camp meetings. 3. **Evangelist,** any of the writers of the four Gospels; Matthew, Mark, Luke, or John. —e·van′ge·lis′tic, e·van′ge·lis′ti·cal, adj. —e·van′ge·lis′ti·cal·ly, adv.

e·van·ge·lize (i·van′jə·līz), v., –lized, –liz·ing. 1. preach the Gospel to. 2. convert to Christianity by preaching. —e·van′ge·li·za′tion, n. —e·van′ge·liz′er, n.

Ev·ans (ev′ənz), n. Mary Ann, 1819–1880, English novelist whose pen name was George Eliot.

Ev·ans·ville (ev′ənz·vil), n. city in SW Indiana, on the Ohio River.

e·vap·o·rate (i·vap′ə·rāt), v., –rat·ed, –rat·ing. 1. change from a liquid or solid into a vapor. 2. remove water or other liquid from: *heat is used to evaporate milk.* 3. give off moisture. 4. vanish; disappear. [< L, < *ex-* out + *vapor* VAPOR] —e·vap′o·ra′tion, n. —e·vap′o·ra′tive, adj. —e·vap′o·ra′tor, n.

evaporated milk, Am. a thick, unsweetened, canned milk, prepared by evaporating some of the water from ordinary milk.

e·va·sion (i·vā′zhən), n. 1. a getting away from something by trickery; an avoiding by cleverness. 2. an attempt to escape an argument, a charge, a question, etc. 3. means of evading; trick or excuse used to avoid something.

e·va·sive (i·vā′siv; –ziv), adj. tending or trying to evade. "Perhaps" is an evasive answer. —e·va′sive·ly, adv. —e·va′sive·ness, n. —Syn. shifty, misleading.

eve (ēv), n. 1. evening or day before a holiday or some other special day: *Christmas Eve.* 2. time just before. 3. *Poetic.* evening. [var. of *even*²]

Eve (ēv), n. *Bible.* the first woman, Adam's wife.

e·ven¹ (ē′vən), adj. 1. level; flat; smooth. 2. at the same level; in the same plane or line. 3. always the same; regular; uniform. 4. equal. 5. leaving no remainder when divided by 2. 6. neither more nor less; exact. 7. owing nothing. 8. not easily disturbed or angered; calm. 9. not favoring one more than another; fair. —v. make even; make level; make equal. —adv. 1. evenly. 2. just; exactly. 3. indeed. 4. fully; quite: *he was faithful even unto death.* 5. though one would not expect it; as one would not expect: *even the least noise disturbs her.* 6. still; yet. 7. break even, have equal gains and losses. 8. get even, a. owe nothing. b. Am. have revenge. [OE *efen*] —e′ven·er, n. —e′ven·ly, adv. —e′ven·ness, n. —Syn. adj. 1. plane. 8. equable, unruffled.

e·ven² (ē′vən), n. *Poetic.* evening. [OE *ǣfen*]

e·ven-hand·ed (ē′vən·han′did), adj. impartial; fair; just.

eve·ning (ēv′ning), n. 1. the last part of day and early part of night; time between sunset and bedtime. 2. *Southern U.S.* afternoon. 3. the last part: *old age is the evening of life.* —adj. in the evening; of the evening; for the evening. [OE *ǣfnung* < *ǣfnian* become evening < *ǣfen* evening]

evening primrose, a tall plant with spikes of fragrant yellow or white flowers that open in the evening.

evening star, a bright planet seen in the western sky after sunset.

e·ven·song (ē′vən·sông′; –song′), n. a church service said or sung in the late afternoon or early evening; vespers.

e·vent (i·vent′), n. 1. a happening. 2. result; outcome. 3. item or contest in a program of sports. [< L, < *ex-* out + *venire* come] —Syn. 1. occurrence, episode, affair. 2. consequence.

e·ven-tem·pered (i·ven′·tem′pərd), adj. not easily disturbed or angered; calm.

e·vent·ful (i·vent′fəl), adj. 1. full of events; having many unusual events. 2. having important results; important. —e·vent′ful·ly, adv. —e·vent′ful·ness, n.

e·ven·tide (ē′vən·tīd′), n. *Poetic.* evening.

e·ven·tu·al (i·ven′chū·əl), adj. 1. coming in the end; final. 2. depending on uncertain events; possible. —e·ven′tu·al·ly, adv.

e·ven·tu·al·i·ty (i·ven′chū·al′ə·ti), n., pl. –ties. a possible occurrence or condition; possibility.

e·ven·tu·ate (i·ven′chū·āt), v., –at·ed, –at·ing. come out in the end; happen finally; result. —e·ven′tu·a′tion, n.

ev·er (ev′ər), adv. 1. at any time: *was there ever a man with such bad luck.* 2. at all times: *ever at your service.* 3. continuously: *ever since.* 4. at all; by any chance; in any case. [OE *ǣfre*] —Syn. 2. always, forever. 3. constantly.

Ev·er·est (ev′ər·ist), n. **Mount,** peak in the Himalayas in S Tibet, the highest in the world.

ev·er·glade (ev′ər·glād′), n. Am. 1. a large

tract of low, wet ground partly covered with tall grass; large swamp or marsh. 2. **Everglades,** a swampy region in S Florida.

ev·er·green (ev′ər·grēn′), adj. having green leaves all the year. —n. 1. an evergreen plant, as pine, spruce, cedar, ivy, etc. 2. evergreens, evergreen twigs or branches used for decoration, esp. at Christmas.

ev·er·last·ing (ev′ər·las′ting; –läs′–), adj. 1. lasting forever; never ending or stopping. 2. lasting a long time. 3. lasting too long; repeated too often; tiresome. —n. 1. eternity. 2. flower that keeps its shape and color when dried. 3. the Everlasting, God. —ev′er·last′ing·ly, adv. —ev′er·last′ing·ness, n.

ev·er·more (ev′ər·môr′; –mōr′), adv., n. always; forever.

e·ver·sion (i·vér′zhən; –shən), n. a turning of an organ, structure, etc., inside out; being turned inside out. —e·ver·si·ble (i·vér′sə·bəl), adj.

e·vert (i·vèrt′), v. turn inside out. [< L, < *ex-* out + *vertere* turn]

eve·ry (ev′ri), adj. 1. all, regarded singly or separately; each and all. 2. all possible: *we showed him every consideration.* 3. every other, each first, third, fifth, etc., or second, fourth, sixth, etc. [< OE *ǣfre* ever + *ǣlc* each]

eve·ry·bod·y (ev′ri·bod′i), pron. every person; everyone: *everybody likes the new minister.*

eve·ry·day (ev′ri·dā′), adj. 1. of every day; daily. 2. for every ordinary day; not for Sundays or holidays. 3. not exciting; usual.

eve·ry·one (ev′ri·wun; –wən), pron. every person; everybody: *everyone took his purchases home.* **every one,**

eve·ry·thing (ev′ri·thing), pron. every thing; all things. —n. something extremely important; very important thing.

eve·ry·where (ev′ri·hwâr), adv. in every place; in all places.

e·vict (i·vikt′), v. expel by a legal process from land, a building, etc.; eject (a tenant). [< L *evictus* < *ex-* out + *vincere* conquer] —e·vic′tion, n. —e·vic′tor, n.

ev·i·dence (ev′ə·dəns), n., v., –denced, –dencing. —n. 1. whatever makes clear the truth or falsehood of something. 2. *Law.* facts established and accepted in a court of law. 3. person who gives testimony in a court of law; witness: *state's evidence.* 4. indication; sign. 5. in evidence, easily seen or noticed. —v. make easy to see or understand; show clearly; prove. [< L, < *ex-* out + *vertere* turn] —Syn. n. 1. proof. 2. testimony.

ev·i·dent (ev′ə·dənt), adj. easy to see or understand; clear; plain. —ev·i·den·tial (ev′ə·den′shəl), adj. —ev·i·dent·ly (ev′ə·dənt·li; –dent′–), adv. —Syn. obvious, manifest, apparent.

e·vil (ē′vəl), adj. 1. bad; wrong; sinful; wicked. 2. causing harm or injury. 3. unfortunate. 4. due to bad character or conduct: *an evil reputation.* —n. 1. something bad; sin; wickedness. 2. thing that causes harm or injury. —adv. badly. [OE *yfel*] —e′vil·ly, adv. —e′vil·ness, n. —Syn. adj. 1. depraved, vicious, corrupt. 2. harmful, pernicious.

e·vil·do·er (ē′vəl·dū′ər), n. person who does evil. —e′vil·do′ing, n.

evil eye, the supposed power of causing harm or bringing bad luck to others by looking at them.

e·vil-mind·ed (ē′vəl·mīn′did), adj. having an evil mind; wicked; malicious.

e·vince (i·vins′), v., e·vinced, e·vinc·ing. 1. show clearly; reveal. 2. show that one has (a quality, trait, etc.). [< L, < *ex-* out + *vincere* conquer] —e·vin′ci·ble, e·vin′cive, adj.

e·vis·cer·ate (i·vis′ər·āt), v., –at·ed, –at·ing. 1. remove the bowels from; disembowel. 2. deprive of something essential. [< L, < *ex-* out + *viscera* VISCERA] —e·vis′cer·a′tion, n.

e·voke (i·vōk′), v., e·voked, e·vok·ing. call forth; bring out. [< L, < *ex-* out + *vocare* call] —ev·o·ca·tion (ev′ō·kā′shən), n. —e·vok′er, n.

ev·o·lu·tion (ev′ə·lū′shən), n. 1. any process

of formation or growth; gradual development: *the evolution of the modern steamship from the first boat.* 2. something evolved; product of development; not a sudden discovery or creation. 3. *Biol.* theory that all living things developed from a few simple forms of life. 4. movement of ships or soldiers, planned beforehand. 5. movement that is a part of a definite plan, design, or series. 6. a releasing; giving off; setting free: *the evolution of heat from burning coal.* —**ev·o·lu·tion·ar·y** (ev′ə-lü′shən-er′ĭ), **ev′o·lu′tion·al,** *adj.* —**ev′o·lu′tion·al·ly,** *adv.*

ev·o·lu·tion·ist (ev′ə-lü′shən-ĭst), *n.* student of, or believer in, the theory of evolution.

e·volve (ĭ-volv′), *v.,* **e·volved, e·volv·ing.** 1. develop gradually; work out. 2. *Biol.* develop by a process of growth and change to a more highly organized condition. 3. release; give off; set free. [< L, < *ex*- out + *volvere* roll] —**e·volv′er,** *n.*

ewe (ū), *n.* a female sheep. [OE *ēowu*]

ew·er (ū′ər), *n.* a wide-mouthed water pitcher. [< AF < VL *aquaria* < L *aquarius* for drawing water < *aqua* water]

Ewer and basin

ex (eks), *prep.* 1. out of. "Ex elevator" means free of charges until the time of removal out of the elevator. 2. without; not including. Ex-dividend stocks are stocks on which the purchaser will not receive the next dividend to be paid. [< L]

ex-, *prefix.* 1. out of; from; out, as in *exclude, exit, export.* 2. utterly; thoroughly, as in *excruciating, exasperate.* 3. former; formerly, as in *ex-member, ex-president, ex-soldier.* [< L *ex*- out of, without; also, *e*- (before *b, d, g, h, l, m, n, r, v*), and *ef*- (before *f*)]

Ex., Exodus.

ex., 1. example. 2. except.

ex·act (ĭg-zakt′), *adj.* 1. without any error or mistake; strictly correct. 2. strict; severe; rigorous. 3. characterized by or using strict accuracy. —*v.* 1. demand and get; force to be paid. 2. call for; need; require. [< L *exactus,* pp. of *exigere* weigh accurately < *ex*- out + *agere* weigh] —**ex·act′a·ble,** *adj.* —**ex·act′er,** or **ex·ac′tor,** *n.* —**ex·act′ness,** *n.* —Syn. *adj.* 1. accurate, precise.

ex·act·ing (ĭg-zak′ting), *adj.* 1. requiring much; making severe demands; hard to please. 2. requiring effort, care, or attention. —**ex·act′ing·ly,** *adv.* —**ex·act′ing·ness,** *n.*

ex·ac·tion (ĭg-zak′shən), *n.* 1. an exacting. 2. thing exacted, as taxes, fees, etc.

ex·act·i·tude (ĭg-zak′tə-tüd; -tūd), *n.* exactness.

ex·act·ly (ĭg-zakt′lĭ), *adv.* 1. in an exact manner; accurately; precisely. 2. just so; quite right.

ex·ag·ger·ate (ĭg-zaj′ər-āt), *v.,* **-at·ed, -at·ing.** 1. make (something) greater than it is; overstate: *exaggerate a misfortune.* 2. increase or enlarge abnormally. 3. say or think something is greater than it is. [< L, < *ex*- out, up + *agger* heap] —**ex·ag′ger·at′ed,** *adj.* —**ex·ag′ger·a′tion,** *n.* —**ex·ag′ger·a′tor,** *n.* —Syn. 1. stretch, magnify.

ex·alt (ĭg-zôlt′), *v.* 1. raise in rank, honor, power, character, quality, etc. 2. fill with pride, joy, or noble feeling. 3. praise; honor; glorify. 4. intensify; heighten. [< L, < *ex*- out, up + *altus* high] —**ex·alt′ed·ly,** *adv.* —**ex·alt′er,** *n.* —Syn. 1. elevate, promote, ennoble.

ex·al·ta·tion (eg′zôl-tā′shən), *n.* 1. an exalting. 2. a being exalted. 3. lofty emotion; rapture.

ex·am (ĭg-zam′), *n. Colloq.* examination.

ex·am·i·na·tion (ĭg-zam′ə-nā′shən), *n.* 1. an examining or being examined. 2. test of knowledge or qualifications; list of questions. 3. answers given in such a test. 4. *Law.* a formal interrogation.

ex·am·ine (ĭg-zam′ĭn), *v.,* **-ined, -in·ing.** 1. look at closely and carefully. 2. test the knowledge or qualifications of; ask questions of. [< L *examinare* < *examen* a weighing. See EXACT.] —**ex·am′in·a·ble,** *adj.* —**ex·am′in·er,** *n.* —Syn. 1. scrutinize, investigate. 2. interrogate.

ex·am·i·nee (ĭg-zam′ə-nē′), *n.* person who is being examined.

ex·am·ple (ĭg-zam′pəl; -zäm′-), *n., v.,* **-pled, -pling.** —*n.* 1. one taken to show what others are like; case that shows something; sample. 2. a parallel case; precedent. 3. person or thing to be imitated; model; pattern. 4. problem in arithmetic, etc. 5. warning to others: *the captain made an example of the soldiers who shirked by making them clean up the camp.* —*v.* 1. be an example of; exemplify. 2. set an example to. [< OF < L *exemplum.* See EXEMPT.] —Syn. *n.* 1. specimen. 3. paragon, ideal.

ex·as·per·ate (ĭg-zas′pər-āt; -zäs′-), *v.,* **-at·ed, -at·ing.** 1. irritate very much; annoy extremely; make angry. 2. increase the intensity or violence of. [< L, < *ex*- thoroughly + *asper* rough] —**ex·as′per·at′er,** *n.* —**ex·as′per·at′ing·ly,** *adv.* —Syn. 1. incense, anger, nettle, vex, provoke.

ex·as·per·a·tion (ĭg-zas′pər-ā′shən; -zäs′-), *n.* extreme annoyance; irritation; anger.

Exc., Excellency.

Ex·cal·i·bur (eks-kal′ə-bər), *n.* the magic sword of King Arthur.

ex ca·the·dra (eks kə-thē′drə; kath′ə-), *Latin.* with authority; from the seat of authority.

ex·ca·vate (eks′kə-vāt), *v.,* **-vat·ed, -vat·ing.** 1. make hollow; hollow out. 2. make by digging; dig. 3. dig out; scoop out. 4. get or uncover by digging. [< L, < *ex*- out + *cavus* hollow] —**ex′ca·va′tion,** *n.* —**ex′ca·va′tor,** *n.*

ex·ceed (ĭk-sēd′), *v.* 1. go beyond; overstep. 2. be more or greater than others; surpass. [< F < L, < *ex*- out + *cedere* go] —**ex·ceed′er,** *n.* —Syn. 1. transcend. 2. excel.

ex·ceed·ing (ĭk-sēd′ing), *adj.* surpassing; very great; unusual; extreme.

ex·cel (ĭk-sel′), *v.,* **-celled, -cel·ling.** 1. be better than; do better than. 2. be better than others; do better than others. [< F < L *excellere*] —Syn. 1. surpass, outstrip, eclipse.

ex·cel·lence (ek′sə-ləns), *n.* 1. a being better than others; superiority. 2. an excellent quality or feature. —Syn. 1. preëminence, transcendence. 2. merit, worth, virtue.

ex·cel·len·cy (ek′sə-lən-sĭ), *n., pl.* **-cies.** 1. excellence. 2. Excellency, title of honor used in speaking to or of a president, governor, ambassador, bishop, etc.

ex·cel·lent (ek′sə-lənt), *adj.* unusually good; better than others. —**ex′cel·lent·ly,** *adv.* —Syn. superior, meritorious, worthy, estimable, choice.

ex·cel·si·or (*adj.* ĭk-sel′sĭ-ôr; *n.* ĭk-sel′si-ər), *Am., adj.* ever upward; higher. —*n.* short, thin, curled shavings of soft wood. [< L, comparative of *excelsus* high, pp. of *excellere* excel]

ex·cept (ĭk-sept′), *prep.* Also, **ex·cept′ing.** leaving out; other than. —*v.* 1. take out; leave out; exclude: *present company excepted.* 2. make objection. —*conj. Archaic.* unless. [< L *exceptus* < *ex*- out + *capere* take] ⯈ **except, accept.** *Except,* as a verb, means to "leave out, exclude": *He excepted those who had done the assignment from the extra reading.* It is decidedly formal, and *excused* or even *exempted* would be more natural in the sentence given. *Accept* means to *get or receive* and is slightly formal: *I accept with pleasure. He accepted the position.* Confusing the two words in writing, practically always due to carelessness rather than to ignorance, comes from the fact that we see and write the preposition *except* (*everyone except you*) so much oftener than we do either of the verbs.

ex·cep·tion (ĭk-sep′shən), *n.* 1. a leaving out. 2. person or thing left out. 3. an unusual instance; case that does not follow the rule. 4. objection. ⯈ **exception.** "And this was no exception" is a colorless and often wordy way of combining a particular and a general statement: *Most young actors experience numerous difficulties in their early appearances. I was no exception.* Better: *Like most young actors, I experienced. . . .*

ex·cep·tion·a·ble (ĭk-sep′shən-ə-bəl), *adj.* objectionable. —**ex·cep′tion·a·bly,** *adv.*

ex·cep·tion·al (ĭk-sep′shən-əl), *adj.* out of the ordinary; unusual. —**ex·cep′tion·al·ly,** *adv.* —Syn. uncommon, singular, extraordinary.

ex·cerpt (*n.* ek′sėrpt; *v.* ĭk-sėrpt′), *n.* a selected passage; quotation. —*v.* take out; select (a passage) from; quote. [< L *excerptum* < *ex-* out + *carpere* pluck]

ex·cess (*n.* ik·ses´; *adj.* ek´ses, ik·ses´), *n.* 1. more than enough; part that is too much. 2. amount or degree by which one thing is more than another. 3. action that goes beyond what is necessary or just. 4. eating or drinking too much; overindulgence; intemperance. —*adj.* extra: *excess baggage.* [< L *excessus* < *ex-* out + *cedere* go; akin to EXCEED] —Syn. *n.* 1. surplus, superfluity. 4. dissipation, immoderation. —Ant. *n.* 1. dearth, deficiency, lack.

ex·ces·sive (ik·ses´iv), *adj.* too much; too great; going beyond what is necessary or right. —ex·ces´sive·ly, *adv.* —ex·ces´sive·ness, *n.* —Syn. superfluous, immoderate, inordinate, extreme.

ex·change (iks·chānj´), *v.*, –changed, –changing, *n.* —*v.* 1. give (for something else). 2. give and take (one thing in return for another); change for another. 3. be taken in a trade. —*n.* 1. an exchanging. 2. what is exchanged. 3. place where things are exchanged. Stocks are bought, sold, and traded in a stock exchange. 4. a central office. A telephone exchange handles telephone calls. 5. system of settling accounts in different places by exchanging bills of exchange that represent money instead of exchanging money itself. 6. changing the money of one country into the money of another. 7. fee charged for settling accounts or changing money. 8. rate of exchange; varying rate or sum in one currency given for a fixed sum in another currency. [< OF < VL, < *ex-* out + *cambiare* change < Celtic] —ex·change´a·ble, *adj.* —ex·change´a·bil´i·ty, *n.* —ex·chang´er, *n.* —Syn. *v.* 2. interchange, trade.

exchange reaction, *Nuclear Physics.* ejection of a subatomic particle by a nucleus when penetrated by another such particle.

ex·cheq·uer (iks·chek´ər; eks´chek·ər), *n.* 1. treasury of a state or nation. 2. treasury. 3. *Colloq.* finances; funds. 4. Exchequer, department of the British government in charge of its finances and the public revenues. [< OF *eschequier* chessboard; because accounts were kept on a table marked in squares]

ex·cise¹ (ek´sīz; -sīs; ik·sīz´), *n.* tax on the manufacture, sale, or use of certain articles made, sold, or used within a country. [appar. < MDu. < OF *acceis* tax, ult. < L *ad-* to + *census* tax]

ex·cise² (ik·sīz´), *v.*, –cised, –cis·ing. cut out; remove. [< L *excisus* < *ex-* out + *caedere* cut] —ex·cis´a·ble, *adj.* —ex·ci·sion (ik·sizh´ən), *n.*

ex·cit·a·ble (ik·sīt´ə·bəl), *adj.* capable of being excited; easily excited. —ex·cit´a·bil´i·ty, ex·cit´a·ble·ness, *n.* —ex·cit´a·bly, *adv.* —Syn. emotional. —Ant. impassive, imperturbable.

ex·ci·ta·tion (ek´sī·tā´shən), *n.* 1. an exciting. 2. a being excited.

ex·cite (ik·sīt´), *v.*, –cit·ed, –cit·ing. 1. stir up the feelings of. 2. arouse. 3. stir to action; stimulate. [< L *excitare*, ult. < *ex-* out + *ciere* set in motion] —ex·cit´ed, *adj.* —ex·cit´ed·ly, *adv.* —ex·cit´er, *n.* —Syn. 1. rouse, animate, kindle.

excited atom, *Nuclear Physics.* atom having a higher energy level than is normal.

ex·cite·ment (ik·sīt´mənt), *n.* 1. an exciting; arousing. 2. state of being excited. 3. thing that excites. —Syn. 2. agitation, perturbation, commotion, ado, tumult.

ex·cit·ing (ik·sīt´ing), *adj.* arousing; stirring. —ex·cit´ing·ly, *adv.*

ex·claim (iks·klām´), *v.* say or speak suddenly in surprise or strong feeling; cry out. [< F < L, < *ex-* + *clamare* cry out] —ex·claim´er, *n.* —Syn. shout, ejaculate.

ex·cla·ma·tion (eks´klə·mā´shən), *n.* 1. an exclaiming. 2. thing exclaimed. *Ah!* and *oh!* are exclamations. —ex·clam·a·to·ry (iks·klam´ə·tô´rī; -tō´-), *adj.* ≽ **exclamation mark** (!). An *exclamation mark* (or *point*) is used after an emphatic interjection and after a phrase, clause, or sentence that is genuinely exclamatory. Clearcut exclamations offer no problem: *Oh! Ouch!*

No, no, no! But many interjections are weak and deserve no more than a comma: *Well, well, so you're in college now.*

ex·clude (iks·klüd´), *v.*, –clud·ed, –clud·ing. 1. shut out; keep out. 2. drive out and keep out; expel. [< L *excludere* < *ex-* out + *claudere* shut] —ex·clud´a·ble, *adj.* —ex·clud´er, *n.* —ex·clu·sion (iks·klü´zhən), *n.* —Syn. 1. eliminate, reject. 2. eject, exile.

ex·clu·sive (iks·klü´siv; -ziv), *adj.* 1. shutting out all others. 2. shutting out all or most: *an exclusive school.* 3. each shutting out the other: *exclusive terms.* 4. not divided or shared with others; single; sole: *an exclusive right.* 5. very particular about choosing friends, members, patrons, etc.: *an exclusive club.* —ex·clu´sive·ly, *adv.* —ex·clu´sive·ness, *n.* —Syn. 4. undivided. 5. select, clannish, snobbish.

ex·com·mu·ni·cate (eks´kə·mū´nə·kāt), *v.*, –cat·ed, –cat·ing. cut off from membership in a church; expel formally from the fellowship of a church; prohibit from participating in any of the rites of a church. —ex´com·mu´ni·ca´tion, *n.* —ex´com·mu´ni·ca´tor, *n.*

ex·co·ri·ate (iks·kô´ri·āt; -kō´-), *v.*, –at·ed, –at·ing. 1. strip or rub off the skin of; make raw and sore. 2. denounce violently. [< L, < *ex-* off + *corium* hide, skin] —ex·co´ri·a´tion, *n.*

ex·cre·ment (eks´krə·mənt), *n.* waste matter discharged from the bowels. [< L *excrementum*, ult. < *ex-* out + *cernere* sift] —ex´cre·men´tal, *adj.*

ex·cres·cence (iks·kres´əns), **ex·cres·cen·cy** (–ən·si), *n., pl.* –cen·ces; –cies. 1. an unnatural growth; disfiguring addition, as a wart. 2. a natural outgrowth, as a fingernail. [< L, < *ex-* out + *crescere* grow] —ex·cres´cent, *adj.*

ex·cre·ta (iks·krē´tə), *n.pl.* waste matter discharged from the body. —ex·cre´tal, *adj.*

ex·crete (iks·krēt´), *v.*, –cret·ed, –cret·ing. discharge (waste matter) from the body; separate (waste matter) from the blood or tissues. [< L *excretus*, pp. See EXCREMENT.] —ex·cre´tion, *n.* —ex·cre´tive, ex·cre·to·ry (eks´krə·tô´ri; -tō´-), *adj.*

ex·cru·ci·ate (iks·krü´shi·āt), *v.*, –at·ed, –at·ing. crucify; torture. [< L *excruciatus* < *ex-* utterly + *cruciare* to torture < *crux* cross] —ex·cru´ci·at´ing, *adj.* —ex·cru´ci·at´ing·ly, *adv.*

ex·cul·pate (eks´kul·pāt; iks·kul´-), *v.*, –pat·ed, –pat·ing. free from blame; prove innocent. [< L *ex-* out + *culpa* guilt] —ex´cul·pa´tion, *n.*

ex·cur·sion (iks·kér´zhən; -shən), *n.* 1. a short journey made with the intention of returning; pleasure trip. 2. trip on a train, ship, etc., at lower fares than are usually charged. 3. group of people who go on an excursion. 4. sally; raid. 5. a wandering from the subject; deviation; digression. [< L *excursio* < *ex-* out + *currere* run] —ex·cur´sion·ist, *n.* —Syn. 1. expedition, tour, jaunt.

ex·cur·sive (iks·kér´siv), *adj.* off the subject; wandering; rambling. —ex·cur´sive·ly, *adv.* —ex·cur´sive·ness, *n.*

ex·cuse (*v.* iks·kūz´; *n.* iks·kūs´), *v.*, –cused, –cus·ing, *n.* —*v.* 1. overlook (a fault, etc.); pardon; forgive. 2. give a reason or apology for; try to clear of blame. 3. be a reason or explanation for; clear of blame. 4. free from duty or obligation; let off. 5. seek exemption or release for. —*n.* 1. a real or pretended reason or explanation. 2. apology. 3. act of excusing. [< OF < L *excusare* < *ex-* away + *causa* cause] —ex·cus´a·ble, *adj.* —ex·cus´a·bly, *adv.* —ex·cus´er, *n.* —Syn. *v.* 1. condone, absolve, exculpate. 3. justify, extenuate. —*n.* 1. justification. ≽ **excuse, pardon.** Small slips are *excused*, more considerable faults (and crimes) are *pardoned*. "Pardon me" is sometimes incorrectly considered more elegant than "Excuse me" in upper-class social situations. *Excuse* has also the special meaning of "give permission to leave."

exec, *n.* executive; executor.

ex·e·cra·ble (ek´sə·krə·bəl), *adj.* abominable; detestable. —ex´e·cra·bly, *adv.*

ex·e·crate (ek´sə·krāt), *v.*, –crat·ed, –crat·ing. 1. abhor; loathe; detest. 2. curse. [< L *execratus*, ult. < *ex-* completely + *sacer* accursed] —ex'e-cra'tion, *n.* —ex'e·cra'tive, *adj.* —ex'e·cra'tor, *n.*

ex·e·cute (ek'sə·kūt), *v.,* –cut·ed, –cut·ing. 1. carry out; do. 2. put into effect; enforce. 3. put to death according to law. 4. make according to a plan or design. 5. *Law.* make (a deed, contract, etc.) legal by signing, sealing, or doing whatever is necessary. [< Med.L *executare,* ult. < L *ex-* out + *sequi* follow] —ex'e·cut'a·ble, *adj.* —ex'e-cut'er, *n.* —Syn. 1. perform, accomplish, fulfill, complete. 3. kill, hang, electrocute.

ex·e·cu·tion (ek'sə·kū'shən), *n.* 1. an executing. 2. a being executed. 3. mode or style of performance. 4. infliction of capital punishment. 5. effective action.

ex·e·cu·tion·er (ek'sə·kū'shən·ər), *n.* person who puts criminals to death according to law.

ex·ec·u·tive (ig·zek'yə·tiv), *adj.* 1. having to do with carrying out or managing affairs. 2. having the duty and power of putting the laws into effect. —*n.* 1. person who carries out or manages affairs. 2. person, group, or branch of government that has the duty and power of putting the laws into effect. 3. Usually, Executive. *Am.* the President of the United States. —ex·ec'u·tive·ly, *adv.*

Executive Mansion, *Am.* 1. the official residence of the President of the United States; the White House in Washington, D.C. 2. the official residence of the governor of a State.

ex·ec·u·tor (ig·zek'yə·tər *for 1;* ek'sə·kū'tər *for 2), n.* 1. *Law.* person named in a will to carry out the provisions of the will. 2. person who executes plans, laws, etc. —ex·ec·u·to·ri·al (ig·zek'-yə·tō'ri·əl; –tô'–), *adj.*

ex·ec·u·trix (ig·zek'yə·triks), *n., pl.* **ex·ec·u-tri·ces** (ig·zek'yə·trī'sēz), **ex·ec·u·trix·es.** a woman executor.

ex·e·ge·sis (ek'sə·jē'sis), *n., pl.* –ses (–sēz). 1. a scholarly explanation or interpretation of the Bible. 2. an explanatory note. [< Gk., < *ex-* out + *hegeesthai* lead, guide] —ex·e·get·ic (ek'sə·jet'ik), ex'e·get'i·cal, *adj.* —ex'e·get'i·cal·ly, *adv.*

ex·em·plar (ig·zem'plər; –plär), *n.* 1. model; pattern. 2. a typical case; example.

ex·em·pla·ry (ig·zem'plə·ri; eg'zəm·pler'i), *adj.* 1. worth imitating; being a good model or pattern: *exemplary conduct.* 2. serving as a warning to others: *exemplary punishment.* 3. serving as an example; typical. [< L *exemplaris.* See EXAMPLE.] —ex·em'pla·ri·ly, *adv.* —ex·em'-pla·ri·ness, *n.*

ex·em·pli·fy (ig·zem'plə·fī), *v.,* –fied, –fy·ing. 1. show by example; be an example of. 2. make an attested copy of under seal. —ex·em'pli·fi·ca'tion, *n.*

ex·em·pli gra·ti·a (ig·zem'plī grā'shi·ə), *Latin.* for instance.

ex·empt (ig·zempt'), *v.* free from a duty, obligation, rule, etc., to which others are subject; release. —*adj.* freed from a duty, obligation, rule, etc.; released. —*n.* an exempt person. [< L *exemptus* < *ex-* out + *emere* take] —ex·empt'-i·ble, *adj.* —ex·emp'tion, *n.*

ex·er·cise (ek'sər·sīz), *n., v.,* –cised, –cis·ing. —*n.* 1. active use to give practice and training or to cause improvement. 2. thing that gives practice and training or causes improvement. 3. active use. 4. Often, exercises. *Am.* ceremony. —*v.* 1. give exercise to; train. 2. take exercise. 3. use actively. 4. carry out in action; perform. 5. have as an effect. 6. occupy the attention of. 7. make uneasy; worry; trouble; annoy. [< OF < L *exer-citium* < *exercere* not allow to rest < *ex-* + *arcere* keep away] —ex'er·cis'a·ble, *adj.* —ex'-er·cis'er, *n.* —Syn. *n.* 1. discipline, drilling, drill. 3. employment, application. —*v.* 1. discipline, drill. 3. employ, apply.

ex·ert (ig·zėrt'), *v.* use actively; put into action. [< L, thrust out, < *ex-* out + *serere* attach] —ex·er'tive, *n.*

ex·er·tion (ig·zėr'shən), *n.* 1. effort. 2. a putting into action; active use; use. —Syn. 1. endeavor, struggle, attempt.

Ex·e·ter (ek'sə·tər), *n.* city in SW England.

ex·e·unt (ek'si·ənt), *v. Latin.* they go out (stage direction for actors to leave the stage).

ex·hale (eks·hāl'), *v.,* –haled, –hal·ing. 1. breathe out. 2. give off (air, vapor, smoke, odor, etc.). 3. pass off as vapor; rise like vapor. 4. change into vapor; evaporate. [< F < L, < *ex-* out + *halare* breathe] —ex·ha·la·tion (eks'hə-lā'shən), *n.*

ex·haust (ig·zôst'), *v.* 1. empty completely. 2. use up. 3. tire very much. 4. drain of strength, resources, etc. 5. draw off: *exhaust the air in a jar.* 6. create a vacuum in. 7. leave nothing important to be found out or said about; study or treat thoroughly. 8. be discharged; go forth. —*n.* 1. the escape of used steam, gasoline, etc., from a machine. 2. means or way for used steam, gasoline, etc., to escape from an engine. 3. the used steam, gasoline, etc., that escapes. [< L *exhaustus* < *ex-* out, off + *haurire* draw] —ex·haust'er, *n.* —ex·haust'i·ble, *adj.* —ex·haust'-i·bil'i·ty, *n.* —Syn. *v.* 1. drain, deplete. 2. consume. 3. fatigue, enervate.

ex·haus·tion (ig·zôs'chən), *n.* 1. an exhausting. 2. a being exhausted. 3. extreme fatigue. —Syn. 3. weariness, lassitude, languor.

ex·haus·tive (ig·zôs'tiv), *adj.* leaving out nothing important; thorough; comprehensive. —ex·haus'tive·ly, *adv.* —ex·haus'tive·ness, *n.*

ex·hib·it (ig·zib'it), *v.* 1. show; display. 2. show publicly. 3. *Law.* show in court as evidence; submit for consideration or inspection. —*n.* 1. show; display. 2. thing or things shown publicly. 3. a public show. 4. *Law.* thing shown in court as evidence. [< L *exhibitus* < *ex-* out + *habere* hold] —ex·hib'i·tor, ex·hib'it·er, *n.* —Syn. *v.* 1. manifest, evince, reveal, disclose.

ex·hi·bi·tion (ek'sə·bish'ən), *n.* 1. a showing; display: *an exhibition of bad manners.* 2. a public show. 3. thing or things shown publicly; exhibit. —Syn. 2. exposition.

ex·hi·bi·tion·ism (ek'sə·bish'ən·iz·əm), *n.* 1. an excessive tendency to show off one's abilities. 2. tendency to show what should not be shown. —ex'hi·bi'tion·ist, *n.*

ex·hil·a·rate (ig·zil'ə·rāt), *v.,* –rat·ed, –rat·ing. make merry or lively; put into high spirits; stimulate. [< L, < *ex-* thoroughly + *hilaris* merry] —ex·hil'a·rat'ing, *adj.* —ex·hil'a·rat'-ing·ly, *adv.* —ex·hil'a·ra'tion, *n.*

ex·hort (ig·zôrt'), *v.* urge strongly; advise or warn earnestly. [< L, < *ex-* + *hortari* urge strongly] —ex·hor·ta·tion (eg'zôr·tā'shən; ek'-sôr–), *n.* —ex·hor'ta·tive, ex·hor·ta·to·ry (ig-zôr'tə·tô'ri, –tō'–), *adj.* —ex·hort'er, *n.*

ex·hume (eks·hūm'; ig·zūm'), *v.,* –humed, –hum·ing. 1. take out of a grave or the ground; dig up. 2. reveal. [< Med.L, < L *ex-* out of + *humus* ground] —ex·hu·ma·tion (eks'hyû·mā'-shən), *n.*

ex·i·gen·cy (ek'sə·jən·si), *n., pl.* –cies; **ex·i·gence** (–jəns), *n., pl.* –gen·ces. 1. Usually, exigencies. an urgent need; demand for immediate action or attention. 2. situation demanding immediate action or attention; emergency.

ex·i·gent (ek'sə·jənt), *adj.* 1. demanding immediate action or attention; urgent. 2. demanding a great deal; exacting. [< L *exigens,* ppr. of *exigere* EXACT]

ex·ig·u·ous (ig·zig'yù·əs; ik·sig'–), *adj.* scanty; small. [< L *exiguus*] —ex·i·gu·i·ty (ek'-sə·gū'ə·ti), *n.*

ex·ile (eg'zīl; ek'sīl), *v.,* –iled, –il·ing, *n.* —*v.* force (a person) to leave his country or home; banish. —*n.* 1. a being exiled; banishment. 2. an exiled person. 3. any prolonged absence from one's own country. [< OF < L *exilium*] —ex·il·ic (eg·zil'ik; ek·sil'–), *adj.* —Syn. *v.* expel, expatriate. —*n.* 1. expulsion, expatriation.

ex·ist (ig·zist'), *v.* 1. have actual existence; be; be real. 2. continue to be; live; have life. 3. be present; occur. [< F < L, < *ex-* forth + *sistere* stand] —ex·ist'ent, *adj.*

ex·ist·ence (ig·zis'təns), *n.* 1. real or actual being; being. 2. continued being; living; life. 3. occurrence; presence. 4. all that exists. 5. thing that exists.

ex·is·ten·tial·ism (eg'zis·ten'shəl·iz·əm; ek'-sis–), *n.* philosophy stressing the need for personal decision in a world lacking purpose. —ex'-is·ten'tial·ist, *n.*

ex·it (eg′zit; ek′sit), *n.* **1.** way out. **2.** a going out; departure. **3.** act of leaving the stage. —*v.* goes out; departs; leaves (stage direction for an actor to leave the stage). [< L, goes out; also < L *exitus* a going out < *ex-* out + *ire* go]

ex li·bris (eks lī′bris; lē′-), *Latin.* from the library (of).

Exod., Exodus.

ex·o·dus (ek′sə-dəs), *n.* **1.** a going out; departure. **2.** Often, **Exodus.** departure of the Israelites from Egypt. **3. Exodus,** second book of the Old Testament. [< L < Gk., < *ex-* out + *hodos* way]

ex of·fi·ci·o (eks ə-fish′i-ō), because of one's office. [< L] —**ex′-of-fi′ci·o,** *adj.*

ex·og·e·nous (eks-oj′ə-nəs), *adj.* **1.** *Bot.* having stems that grow by the addition of layers of wood on the outside under the bark. **2.** originating from the outside. [< NL *exogenus* growing on the outside < Gk. *exo-* outside + *gen-* bear, produce] —**ex·og′e·nous·ly,** *adv.*

ex·on·er·ate (ig-zon′ər-āt), *v.,* -at·ed, -at·ing. free from blame. [< L, < *ex-* off + *onus* burden] —**ex·on′er·a′tion,** *n.* —**ex·on′er·a′tive,** *adj.*

ex·or·bi·tant (ig-zôr′bə-tənt), *adj.* exceeding what is customary, proper, or reasonable; very excessive. [< L, < *ex-* out of + *orbita* track. See ORBIT.] —**ex·or′bi·tance, ex·or′bi·tan·cy,** *n.* —**ex·or′bi·tant·ly,** *adv.*

ex·or·cise, ex·or·cize (ek′sôr-sīz), *v.,* -cised, -cis·ing; -cized, -ciz·ing. **1.** drive out (an evil spirit) by prayers, ceremonies, etc. **2.** free (a person or place) from an evil spirit. [< LL < Gk. *exorkizein* bind by oath < *ex-* + *horkos* oath] —**ex′or·cis′er, ex′or·ciz′er,** *n.*

ex·or·cism (ek′sôr-siz-əm), *n.* **1.** an exorcising. **2.** prayers, ceremonies, etc., used in exorcising. —**ex′or·cist,** *n.*

ex·or·di·um (ig-zôr′di-əm; ik-sôr′-), *n., pl.* -di·ums, -di·a (-di-ə). **1.** the beginning. **2.** the introductory part of a speech, treatise, etc. [< L, < *ex-* + *ordiri* begin, orig. begin a web] —**ex·or′di·al,** *adj.*

ex·ot·ic (ig-zot′ik), *adj.* foreign; strange; rare: *exotic plants.* —*n.* anything exotic. [< L < Gk. *exotikos* < *exo* outside < *ex-* out of] —**ex·ot′i·cal·ly,** *adv.*

ex·pand (iks-pand′), *v.* **1.** increase in size; enlarge; swell. **2.** spread out; open out; unfold; extend. **3.** express in fuller form or greater detail. [< L, < *ex-* out + *pandere* spread. Doublet of SPAWN.] —**ex·pand′er,** *n.* —**Syn. 1.** dilate, distend. **2.** unfurl.

ex·panse (iks-pans′), *n.* a large, unbroken space or stretch; wide, spreading surface.

ex·pan·si·ble (iks-pan′sə-bəl), *adj.* capable of being expanded. —**ex·pan′si·bil′i·ty,** *n.*

ex·pan·sion (iks-pan′shən), *n.* **1.** an expanding. **2.** being expanded; increase in size, volume, etc. **3.** amount or degree of expansion. **4.** an expanded part or form.

ex·pan·sive (iks-pan′siv), *adj.* **1.** capable of expanding; tending to expand. **2.** wide; spreading. **3.** taking in much or many things; broad; extensive. **4.** showing one's feelings freely and openly; effusive. —**ex·pan′sive·ly,** *adv.* —**ex·pan′sive·ness,** *n.*

ex·pa·ti·ate (iks-pā′shi-āt), *v.,* -at·ed, -at·ing. write or talk much. [< L, < *exspatiari* walk about < *ex-* out + *spatium* space] —**ex·pa′ti·a′tion,** *n.* —**ex·pa′ti·a′tor,** *n.*

ex·pa·tri·ate (v. eks-pā′tri-āt; *adj., n.* eks-pā′tri-it, -āt), *v.,* -at·ed, -at·ing, *adj., n.* —*v.* banish; exile. —*adj.* expatriated. —*n.* an expatriated person; exile. [< LL, < *ex-* out of + *patria* fatherland] —**ex·pa′tri·a′tion,** *n.*

ex·pect (iks-pekt′), *v.* **1.** look forward to; think likely to come or happen. **2.** look forward to with reason or confidence; desire and feel sure of getting. **3.** *Colloq.* think; suppose; guess. [< L, < *ex-* out + *specere* look] —**Syn. 1.** anticipate. **2.** hope.

ex·pect·an·cy (iks-pek′tən-si), **ex·pect·ance** (-təns), *n., pl.* -cies; -anc·es. expectation.

ex·pect·ant (iks-pek′tənt), *adj.* **1.** having expectations; expecting. **2.** showing expectation.

3. pregnant. —*n.* person who expects something. —**ex·pect′ant·ly,** *adv.*

ex·pec·ta·tion (eks′pek-tā′shən), *n.* **1.** an expecting or being expected; anticipation. **2.** thing expected. **3.** ground for expecting something; prospect. —**Syn. 1.** expectancy, hope.

ex·pec·to·rant (iks-pek′tə-rənt), *Med.* —*adj.* causing or helping the discharge of phlegm, etc. —*n.* an expectorant medicine.

ex·pec·to·rate (iks-pek′tə-rāt), *v.,* -rat·ed, -rat·ing. cough up and spit out (phlegm, etc.); spit. [< L, < *ex-* out of + *pectus* breast] —**ex·pec′to·ra′tion,** *n.*

ex·pe·di·en·cy (iks-pē′di-ən-si), **ex·pe·di·ence** (-əns), *n., pl.* -cies; -enc·es. **1.** suitability for bringing about a desired result; desirability or fitness under the circumstances. **2.** personal advantage; self-interest.

ex·pe·di·ent (iks-pē′di-ənt), *adj.* **1.** fit for bringing about a desired result; desirable or suitable under the circumstances. **2.** giving or seeking personal advantage; based on self-interest. —*n.* a useful means of bringing about a desired result. [< L *expediens,* ppr. of *expedire* to free from a net, set right < *ex-* out + *pes* foot] —**ex·pe′di·ent·ly,** *adv.* —**Syn.** *adj.* **1.** advantageous, profitable, advisable, wise. —*n.* resort, resource, shift, device.

ex·pe·dite (eks′pə-dīt), *v.,* -dit·ed, -dit·ing. **1.** make easy and quick; speed up. **2.** do quickly. **3.** issue officially. [< L *expeditus.* See EXPEDIENT.]

ex·pe·dit·er (eks′pə-dīt′ər), *n.* **1.** person who is responsible for supplying raw materials or delivering finished products on schedule. **2.** person who issues official statements and decisions. **3.** any person who supplies something.

ex·pe·di·tion (eks′pə-dish′ən), *n.* **1.** journey for some special purpose. **2.** group of people, ships, etc., that make such a journey. **3.** efficient and prompt action. —**Syn. 1.** voyage, trip, excursion. **3.** promptness, haste, quickness, speed.

ex·pe·di·tion·ar·y (eks′pə-dish′ən-er′i), *adj.* of or making up an expedition.

ex·pe·di·tious (eks′pə-dish′əs), *adj.* efficient and prompt. —**ex′pe·di′tious·ly,** *adv.*

ex·pel (iks-pel′), *v.,* -pelled, -pel·ling. **1.** force out; force to leave. **2.** put out; dismiss permanently. [< L, < *ex-* out + *pellere* drive] —**ex·pel′la·ble,** *adj.* —**ex·pel′ler,** *n.* —**Syn. 1.** banish.

ex·pend (iks-pend′), *v.* spend; use up. [< L, < *ex-* out + *pendere* weigh, pay. Doublet of SPEND.] —**ex·pend′er,** *n.* —**Syn.** disburse, consume.

ex·pend·a·ble (iks-pen′də-bəl), *adj.* **1.** that can be expended. **2.** *Mil.* worth giving up or sacrificing to the enemy or to destruction for strategic reasons. —*n.* Usually, **expendables.** expendable persons or things.

ex·pend·i·ture (iks-pen′di-chər; -chur), *n.* **1.** act of expending. **2.** cost; expense.

ex·pense (iks-pens′), *n.* **1.** an expending; paying out money; outlay. **2.** cost; charge. **3.** cause of spending. **4.** loss; sacrifice. [< AF < LL *expensa.* See EXPEND.] —**Syn. 1.** expenditure, disbursement. **2.** price.

ex·pen·sive (iks-pen′siv), *adj.* costly; highpriced. —**ex·pen′sive·ly,** *adv.* —**ex·pen′sive·ness,** *n.* —**Syn.** dear.

ex·pe·ri·ence (iks-pir′i-əns), *n., v.,* -enced, -enc·ing. —*n.* **1.** what has happened to one; anything or everything observed, done, or lived through. **2.** an observing, doing, or living through things: *people learn by experience.* **3.** skill, practical knowledge, or wisdom gained by observing, doing, or living through things. —*v.* have happen to one. [< OF < L, < *experiri* test < *ex-* out + *peri-* try] —**Syn.** *v.* undergo, endure, suffer, bear.

ex·pe·ri·enced (iks-pir′i-ənst), *adj.* **1.** having had experience. **2.** taught by experience. **3.** skillful or wise because of experience. —**Syn. 1.** skilled, expert, practiced, veteran.

ex·per·i·ment (v. iks-per′ə-ment; *n.* iks-per′ə-mənt), *v.* try in order to find out; make trials or tests: *that man is experimenting with dyes to get the color he wants.* —*n.* **1.** test or trial to find out something: *a cooking experiment.* **2.** a conducting of such tests or trials: *scientists test out theories by experiments.* [< L *experimentum.* See EXPERIENCE.] —ex·per'i·ment'er, *n.* —Syn. *n.* 1. examination.

ex·per·i·men·tal (iks·per'ə·men'təl), *adj.* 1. based on experiments: *chemistry is an experimental science.* 2. used for experiments. 3. based on experience, not on theory or authority. —ex·per'i·men'tal·ly, *adv.*

ex·per·i·men·ta·tion (iks·per'ə·men·tā'shən), *n.* an experimenting.

ex·pert (*n.* eks'pėrt; *adj.* iks·pėrt', eks'pėrt), *n.* person who knows a great deal about some special thing. —*adj.* 1. very skillful; knowing a great deal about some special thing. 2. from an expert; requiring or showing knowledge about some special thing. [< L *expertus,* pp. of *experiri* test. See EXPERIENCE.] —ex·pert'ly, *adv.* —ex·pert'ness, *n.* —Syn. *n.* authority, specialist. *-adj.* 1. experienced, practiced, skilled. —Ant. *n.* novice, beginner, amateur.

ex·pi·ate (eks'pi·āt), *v.,* -at·ed, -at·ing. make amends for (a wrong, sin, etc.); atone for. [< L, < *ex-* completely + *piare* appease < *pius* devout] —ex·pi·a·ble (eks'pi·ə·bəl), *adj.* —ex'pi·a'tion, *n.* —ex'pi·a'tor, *n.*

ex·pi·a·to·ry (eks'pi·ə·tô'ri; -tō'-), *adj.* intended to expiate; expiating; atoning.

ex·pi·ra·tion (ek'spə·rā'shən), *n.* 1. a coming to an end. 2. a breathing out. —ex·pir·a·to·ry (ik·spīr'ə·tô'ri; -tō'-), *adj.*

ex·pire (ik·spīr'), *v.,* -pired, -pir·ing. 1. come to an end. 2. die. 3. breathe out: *used air is expired from the lungs.* 4. Obs. emit. [< L, < *ex-* out + *spirare* breathe] —ex·pir'er, *n.* —Syn. 2. perish, decease.

ex·plain (iks·plān'), *v.* 1. make plain or clear; tell how to do. 2. tell the meaning of; interpret. 3. give reasons for; account for. [< L, < *ex-* out +*planus* flat] —ex·plain'a·ble, *adj.* —ex·plain'er, *n.* —ex·plan·a·to·ry (iks·plan'ə·tô'ri; -tō'-), *adj.* —ex·plan'a·to'ri·ly, *adv.* —Syn. 1. elucidate, expound.

ex·pla·na·tion (eks'plə·nā'shən), *n.* 1. an explaining. 2. thing that explains. 3. interpretation. —Syn. 1. elucidation, exposition, definition.

ex·ple·tive (eks'plə·tiv), *adj.* filling out a sentence or line; completing. —*n.* 1. something that fills out a sentence or line. 2. oath or meaningless exclamation. [< LL *expletivus* < *ex-* out + *plere* fill] —ex'ple·tive·ly, *adv.*

ex·pli·ca·ble (eks'plə·kə·bəl; iks·plik'ə-), *adj.* capable of being explained.

ex·pli·cate (eks'plə·kāt), *v.,* -cat·ed, -cat·ing. 1. develop (a principle, doctrine, etc.). 2. explain. —ex'pli·ca'tion, *n.*

ex·plic·it (iks·plis'it), *adj.* 1. clearly expressed; distinctly stated; definite. 2. not reserved; frank; outspoken. [< L, < *ex-* un- + *plicare* fold] —ex·plic'it·ly, *adv.* —ex·plic'it·ness, *n.* —Syn. 1. precise, exact, unequivocal. —Ant. 1. vague, indefinite, ambiguous.

ex·plode (iks·plōd'), *v.,* -plod·ed, -plod·ing. 1. blow up; burst with a loud noise. 2. cause to explode. 3. burst forth noisily: *explode with laughter.* 4. cause to be rejected; destroy belief in. [< L *explodere* drive out by clapping < *ex-* out + *plaudere* clap] —ex·plod'er, *n.* —Syn. 1. detonate. 4. discredit, disprove.

ex·ploit (*n.* eks'ploit, iks·ploit'; *v.* iks·ploit'), *n.* a bold, unusual act; daring deed. —*v.* 1. make use of; turn to practical account. 2. make unfair use of; use selfishly for one's own advantage. [< OF < VL *explicitum* achievement < L, pp. neut. of *explicare* unfold, settle. See EXPLICIT.] —ex·ploit'a·ble, *adj.* —ex'ploi·ta'tion, *n.* —ex·ploit'a·tive (iks·ploit'ə·tiv), *adj.* —ex·ploit'er, *n.* —Syn. *n.* feat, achievement.

ex·plore (iks·plôr'; -plōr'), *v.,* -plored, -plor·ing. 1. travel in (little known lands or seas) for the purpose of discovery. 2. go over carefully; look into closely; examine. [< L *explorare* spy out, orig., cry out (at sight of game or enemy) < *ex-* out + *plorare* weep] —ex'plo·ra'tion, *n.* —ex·plor·a·to·ry (iks·plôr'ə·tô'ri; iks·plōr'ə·tô'-ri), ex·plor'a·tive, *adj.* —ex·plor'er, *n.* —Syn. 2. search, investigate, scrutinize.

ex·plo·sion (iks·plō'zhən), *n.* 1. a blowing up; a bursting with a loud noise. 2. loud noise caused by this. 3. a noisy bursting forth; outbreak: *explosions of anger.*

ex·plo·sive (iks·plō'siv; -ziv), *adj.* 1. of or for explosion; tending to explode. 2. tending to burst forth noisily. —*n.* an explosive substance. —ex·plo'sive·ly, *adv.* —ex·plo'sive·ness, *n.*

ex·po·nent (iks·pō'nənt), *n.* 1. person or thing that explains, interprets, etc. 2. person or thing that stands as an example, type or symbol of something: *Lincoln is a famous exponent of self-education.* 3. index or small number written above and to the right of an algebraic symbol or a quantity to show how many times the symbol or quantity is to be used as a factor, as in a^3. [< L *exponens.* See EXPOUND.] —ex·po·nen·tial (eks'pō·nen'shəl), *adj.* —ex'po·nen'tial·ly, *adv.*

ex·port (*v.* iks·pôrt', -pōrt', eks'pôrt, -pōrt; *n.* eks'pôrt, -pōrt), *v.* send (goods) out of one country for sale and use in another. —*n.* 1. article exported. 2. an exporting; exportation. [< L, < *ex-* away + *portare* carry] —ex·port'a·ble, *adj.* —ex'por·ta'tion, *n.* —ex·port'er, *n.*

ex·pose (iks·pōz'), *v.,* -posed, -pos·ing. 1. lay open; leave unprotected; uncover. 2. show openly; display: *goods are exposed for sale in a store.* 3. make known; show up; reveal: *he exposed the plot.* 4. allow light to reach and act on (a photographic film or plate). [< OF, < *ex-* forth + *poser* put, POSE] —ex·pos'er, *n.* —Syn. 2. exhibit. 3. disclose.

ex·po·sé (eks'pō·zā'), *n.* a showing up of crime, dishonesty, etc. [< F. See EXPOSE.]

ex·po·si·tion (eks'pə·zish'ən), *n.* 1. a public show or exhibition. 2. a detailed explanation. 3. speech or writing explaining a process or idea. —Syn. 1. display, fair. 2. elucidation.

ex·pos·i·tor (iks·poz'ə·tər), *n.* person or thing that explains; expounder, interpreter.

ex·pos·i·to·ry (iks·poz'ə·tô'ri; -tō'-), ex·pos·i·tive (-ə·tiv), *adj.* explaining; serving or helping to explain.

ex post fac·to (eks' pōst' fak'tō), made or done after something, but applying to it. [< Med.L *ex postfacto* from what is done afterward]

ex·pos·tu·late (iks·pos'chə·lāt), *v.,* -lat·ed, -lat·ing. reason earnestly with a person, protesting against something he means to do or has done; remonstrate. [< L, < *ex-* (intensive) + *postulare* demand] —ex·pos'tu·la'tion, *n.* —ex·pos'tu·la'tor, *n.* —ex·pos·tu·la·to·ry (iks·pos'chə·lə·tô'ri; -tō'-), *adj.*

ex·po·sure (iks·pō'zhər), *n.* 1. an exposing. 2. a being exposed. 3. position in relation to the sun and wind: *a southern exposure.* 4. time during which light reaches and acts on a photographic film or plate. 5. a putting off without shelter; abandoning.

ex·pound (iks·pound'), *v.* 1. make clear; explain; interpret. 2. set forth or state in detail. [< OF < L, < *ex-* forth + *ponere* put] —ex·pound'er, *n.*

ex·press (iks·pres'), *v.* 1. put into words: *your thoughts are well expressed.* 2. show by look, voice, or action; reveal: *express feeling in one's tone.* 3. show by a sign, figure, etc.; indicate. 4. *Am.* send by express. 5. press out; squeeze out: *express the juice of grapes.* —*adj.* 1. clear; definite. 2. for a particular purpose; special. 3. exact. 4. having to do with express. 5. traveling fast and making few stops: *an express train.* 6. for fast traveling: *an express highway.* —*n.* 1. message sent for a particular purpose. 2. a quick or direct means of sending things. 3. *Am.* system or company for sending parcels, money, etc. 4. *Am.* things sent by express. 5. train, bus, elevator, etc., traveling fast and making few stops. —*adv.* by express; directly. [< L *expressus* < *ex-* out + *premere* press] —ex·press'er, *n.* —ex·press'i·ble, *adj.* —Syn. *v.* 1. utter, declare, state, say. 3. signify.

ex·press·age (iks·pres'ij), *n. Am.* 1. business of carrying parcels, money, etc., by express. 2. charge for carrying parcels, etc., by express.

ex·pres·sion (iks·presh'ən), *n.* 1. a putting into words. 2. word or group of words used as a unit. 3. a showing by look, voice, or action.

indication of feeling, spirit, etc.; look that shows feeling. 5. a bringing out the meaning or beauty of something read, sung, etc. 6. a showing or expressing by a sign, figure, etc. 7. symbol or group of symbols expressing some mathematical fact. 8. a pressing out. —ex·pres′sion·less, adj. —expres′sion·less·ness, n. —Syn. 1. utterance, declaration. 4. sign, token.

ex·pres·sive (iks·pres′iv), adj. 1. serving as a sign or indication; expressing. 2. full of expression; having much feeling, meaning, etc. —ex·pres′sive·ly, adv. —ex·pres′sive·ness, n. —Syn. 1. indicative, significant.

ex·press·ly (iks·pres′li), adv. 1. clearly; plainly; definitely. 2. on purpose.

ex·press·man (iks·pres′mən), n., pl. -men. Am. person who works in the express business.

ex·press·way (iks·pres′wā′), n. an express highway.

ex·pro·pri·ate (eks·prō′pri·āt), v., -at·ed, -at·ing. 1. take (land, etc.) out of the owner's possession, esp. for public use. 2. put (a person) out of possession; dispossess. [< Med.L, < ex- away from + proprius one's own] —ex·pro′pri·a′tion, n. —ex·pro′pri·a′tor, n.

ex·pul·sion (iks·pul′shən), n. 1. an expelling; forcing out. 2. a being expelled or forced out: expulsion from school. —ex·pul′sive, adj.

ex·punge (iks·punj′), v., -punged, -pung·ing. remove completely; blot out; erase. [< L, < ex- out + pungere prick] —ex·pung′er, n.

ex·pur·gate (eks′pər·gāt), v., -gat·ed, -gat·ing. remove objectionable passages or words from (a book, letter, etc.); purify. [< L, < ex- out + purgare purge] —ex′pur·ga′tion, n. —ex′pur·ga′tor, n.

ex·qui·site (eks′kwi·zit; iks·kwiz′it), adj. 1. very lovely; delicate. 2. sharp; intense. 3. of highest excellence; most admirable: exquisite taste and manners. 4. keenly sensitive. —n. person who is overnice in dress; a dandy. [< L exquisitus < ex- out + quaerere seek] —ex′qui·site·ly, adv. —ex′qui·site·ness, n. —Syn. adj. 1. dainty, fine, beautiful. 2. acute, keen.

ex·tant (eks′tənt; iks·tant′), adj. still in existence. [< L exstans < ex- out, forth + stare stand]

ex·tem·po·ra·ne·ous (iks·tem′pə·rā′ni·əs), **ex·tem·po·ra·ry** (-tem′pə·rer′i), adj. 1. spoken or done without preparation; offhand: an extemporaneous speech. 2. made for the occasion: an extemporaneous shelter against a storm. [< LL, < L ex tempore according to the moment] —ex·tem′po·ra′ne·ous·ly, ex·tem·po·rar·i·ly (iks·tem′pə·rer′ə·li; emphatic iks·tem′pə·rãr′ə·li), adv. —ex·tem′po·ra′ne·ous·ness, ex·tem′po·rar′i·ness, n.

ex·tem·po·re (iks·tem′pə·rē), adv. on the spur of the moment; without preparation; offhand. —adj. extemporaneous. [< L]

ex·tem·po·rize (iks·tem′pə·rīz), v., -rized, -riz·ing. 1. speak, play, sing, or dance, composing as one proceeds. 2. compose offhand; make for the occasion. —ex·tem′po·ri·za′tion, n. —ex·tem′po·riz′er, n.

ex·tend (iks·tend′), v. 1. stretch out. 2. straighten out. 3. lengthen. 4. widen; enlarge. 5. give; grant. [< L, < ex- out + tendere stretch] —ex·tend′ed, adj. —ex·tend′ed·ly, adv. —extend′i·ble, adj. —Syn. 3. prolong, protract.

ex·ten·si·ble (iks·ten′sə·bəl), adj. capable of being extended. —ex·ten′si·bil′i·ty, ex·ten′si·ble·ness, n.

ex·ten·sion (iks·ten′shən), n. 1. an extending. 2. a being extended. 3. an extended part; addition. 4. range; extent. 5. Physics. that property of a body by which it occupies a portion of space. —ex·ten′sion·al, adj. —Syn. 1. stretching, expansion, enlargement. 3. projection.

ex·ten·sive (iks·ten′siv), adj. 1. of great extent. 2. affecting many things; comprehensive. 3. depending on the use of large areas: extensive agriculture. —ex·ten′sive·ly, adv. —ex·ten′sive·ness, n. —Syn. 1. extended, broad, large, ample.

ex·ten·sor (iks·ten′sər; -sôr), n. muscle that extends or straightens out a limb or other part of the body.

ex·tent (iks·tent′), n. 1. size, space, length, amount, or degree to which a thing extends. 2. something extended; extended space. —Syn. 1. magnitude, area, scope, compass, range.

ex·ten·u·ate (iks·ten′yū·āt), v., -at·ed, -at·ing. 1. make (guilt, a fault, offense, etc.) seem less; excuse in part. 2. make thin or weak; diminish. [< L, < ex- out + tenuis thin] —ex·ten′u·a′tion, n. —ex·ten′u·a′tive, adj. —ex·ten′u·a′tor, n.

ex·te·ri·or (iks·tir′i·ər), n. 1. an outer surface or part; outward appearance; outside: a harsh exterior but a kind heart. 2. exteriors, externals. —adj. 1. on the outside; outer. 2. coming from without; happening outside. [< L, < exterus outside < ex out of] —ex·te′ri·or·ly, adv. —Syn. adj. 1. outward, outlying, external.

ex·ter·mi·nate (iks·tėr′mə·nāt), v., -nat·ed, -nat·ing. destroy completely. [< LL, < L, drive out < ex- out of + terminus boundary] —ex·ter′mi·na′tion, n. —ex·ter′mi·na′tor, n.

ex·ter·nal (iks·tėr′nəl), adj. 1. on the outside; outer. 2. to be used on the outside of the body. 3. entirely outside; coming from without. 4. having existence outside one's mind. 5. having to do with outward appearance or show; superficial. 6. having to do with international affairs; foreign. —n. 1. an outer surface or part; outside. 2. externals, clothing, manners, outward acts, or appearances. [< L externus outside < exterus outside < ex out of] —ex·ter′nal·ly, adv. —Syn. adj. 1. outward, exterior.

ex·tinct (iks·tingkt′), adj. 1. no longer in existence. 2. no longer active; extinguished: an extinct volcano. [< L exstinctus, pp. of exstinguere. See EXTINGUISH.] —Syn. 1. dead.

ex·tinc·tion (iks·tingk′shən), n. 1. an extinguishing. 2. a being extinguished; extinct condition. 3. a doing away with completely; wiping out; destruction.

ex·tin·guish (iks·ting′gwish), v. 1. put out; quench. 2. put an end to; do away with; wipe out; destroy. 3. eclipse or obscure by superior brilliancy. [< L, < ex- out + stinguere quench] —ex·tin′guish·a·ble, adj. —ex·tin′guish·a·bly, adv. —ex·tin′guish·er, n. —ex·tin′guish·ment, n.

ex·tir·pate (eks′tər·pāt; iks·tėr′pāt), v., -pat·ed, -pat·ing. 1. remove completely; destroy totally. 2. tear up by the roots. [< L, < ex- out + stirps root] —ex′tir·pa′tion, n. —ex′tir·pa′tive, adj. —ex′tir·pa′tor, n.

ex·tol, ex·toll (iks·tōl′; -tol′), v., -tolled, -tol·ling. praise highly. [< L, < ex- up + tollere raise] —ex·tol′ler, n. —ex·tol′ment, ex·toll′ment, n. —Syn. commend, laud, eulogize.

ex·tort (iks·tôrt′), v. obtain (money, a promise, etc.) by threats, force, fraud, or illegal use of authority. [< L extortus < ex- out + torquere twist] —ex·tort′er, n. —ex·tor′tive, adj.

ex·tor·tion (iks·tôr′shən), n. 1. act of extorting. 2. anything obtained by extortion.

ex·tor·tion·ar·y (iks·tôr′shən·er′i), adj. characterized by or given to extortion.

ex·tor·tion·ate (iks·tôr′shən·it), adj. characterized by extortion. —ex·tor′tion·ate·ly, adv.

ex·tor·tion·er (iks·tôr′shən·ər), ex·tor·tion·ist (-ist), n. person who is guilty of extortion.

ex·tra (eks′trə), adj. more, greater, or better than what is usual, expected, or needed. —n. 1. something in addition to what is usual, expected, or needed. 2. an additional charge. 3. Am. a special edition of a newspaper. 4. Am. person who is employed by the day to play minor parts in motion pictures. 5. an additional worker. —adv. more than usually. [prob. short for extraordinary] —Syn. adj. additional, supplemental, supplementary.

extra-, prefix. outside; beyond; besides, as in extraordinary. [< L]

ex·tra·bold (eks′trə·bōld′), n. a very heavy boldface.

ex·tract (v. iks·trakt′; n. eks′trakt), v. 1. pull out or draw out, usually with some effort: extract a tooth, extract a confession. 2. obtain by pressure, suction, etc.: oil is extracted from olives. **3.** deduce: *extract a principle from a collection of facts.* **4.** derive: *extract pleasure from a situation.* **5.** take out; select (a passage) from a book, speech, etc. **6.** calculate or find (the root of a number). —*n.* **1.** something drawn out or taken out; passage taken from a book, speech, etc. **2.** a concentrated preparation of a substance: *vanilla extract.* [< L *extractus* < *ex-* out + *trahere* draw] —ex·tract′a·ble, ex·tract′i·ble, *adj.* —ex·trac′tive, *adj.*, *n.* —ex·trac′tor, *n.* —Syn. *v.* **1.** elicit, exact, extort, wrest, separate. —*n.* **1.** excerpt, citation, quotation, selection.

ex·trac·tion (iks·trak′shən), *n.* **1.** an extracting. **2.** a being extracted. **3.** descent; origin.

ex·tra·cur·ric·u·lar (eks′trə·kə·rik′yə·lər), *adj.* outside the regular course of study: *football is an extracurricular activity.*

ex·tra·dite (eks′trə·dīt), *v.*, –dit·ed, –dit·ing. **1.** give up or deliver (a fugitive or prisoner) to another nation or legal authority for trial or punishment. **2.** obtain the extradition of (such a person). [< *extradition*] —ex′tra·dit′a·ble, *adj.*

ex·tra·di·tion (eks′trə·dish′ən), *n.* surrender of a fugitive or prisoner by one state, nation, or legal authority to another for trial or punishment. [< L, < *ex-* out + *tradere* trade]

ex·tra·ne·ous (iks·trā′ni·əs), *adj.* from outside; not belonging; foreign. [< L, < *extra* outside < *ex-* out of. Doublet of STRANGE.] —ex·tra′ne·ous·ly, *adv.* —ex·tra′ne·ous·ness, *n.*

ex·traor·di·nar·y (iks·trôr′də·ner′i; *esp. for* 2 eks′trə·ôr′-), *adj.* **1.** beyond what is ordinary; most unusual; very remarkable. **2.** outside of, additional to, or ranking below the regular class of officials; special. [< L, < *extra ordinem* out of the (usual) order] —ex·traor′di·nar′i·ly, *adv.* —ex·traor′di·nar′i·ness, *n.* —Syn. uncommon, exceptional, singular.

ex·tra·sen·so·ry (eks′trə·sen′sə·ri), *adj.* not within ordinary sense perception.

extrasensory perception, the perceiving of thoughts, actions, etc., in other than a normal fashion; mental telepathy.

ex·tra·ter·ri·to·ri·al (eks′trə·ter′ə·tô′ri·əl; -tō′-), *adj.* beyond territorial limits or jurisdiction, as persons resident in a country but not subject to its laws. Any ambassador to the United States has certain extraterritorial privileges. —ex′tra·ter′ri·to′ri·al′i·ty, *n.* —ex′tra·ter′ri·to′ri·al·ly, *adv.*

ex·trav·a·gance (iks·trav′ə·gəns), *n.* **1.** careless and lavish spending; wastefulness. **2.** a going beyond the bounds of reason; excess. —Syn. **1.** dissipation, profusion. —Ant. **1.** thrift.

ex·trav·a·gant (iks·trav′ə·gənt), *adj.* **1.** spending carelessly and lavishly; wasteful. **2.** beyond the bounds of reason; excessive; exorbitant. [< Med.L, < L *extra-* outside + *vagari* wander] —ex·trav′a·gant·ly, *adv.* —Syn. **1.** prodigal, lavish. **2.** immoderate, inordinate.

ex·trav·a·gan·za (iks·trav′ə·gan′zə), *n.* a fantastic play, piece of music, etc. [blend of Ital. *stravaganza* peculiar behavior, and E *extra*]

ex·treme (iks·trēm′), *adj.*, –trem·er, –trem·est, *n.* —*adj.* **1.** much more than usual; very great; very strong. **2.** very severe; very violent. **3.** at the very end; farthest possible; last. —*n.* **1.** something extreme; one of two things as far or as different as possible from each other. **2.** an extreme degree. **3.** *Math.* the first or last term in a proportion or series. **4.** go to extremes, do or say too much. [< L *extremus*, superl. of *exterus* outer] —ex·treme′ly, *adv.* —ex·treme′ness, *n.* —Syn. *adj.* **1.** immoderate, excessive, radical, fanatical. **3.** outermost, utmost, final.

extreme unction, sacrament of the Roman Catholic Church, given by a priest to a dying person or one in danger of death.

ex·trem·ist (iks·trēm′ist), *n.* **1.** person who goes to extremes. **2.** person who has extreme ideas or favors extreme measures.

ex·trem·i·ty (iks·trem′ə·ti), *n.*, *pl.* –ties. **1.** the very end; farthest possible place; last part or point. **2.** extreme need, danger, suffering, etc. **3.** an extreme degree. **4.** an extreme action. **5.** extremities, hands and feet. —Syn. **1.** termination, verge, limit.

ex·tri·cate (eks′trə·kāt), *v.*, –cat·ed, –cat·ing. set free (from entanglements, difficulties, embarrassing situations, etc.); release. [< L, < *ex-* out of + *tricae* perplexities] —ex·tri·ca·ble (eks′trə·kə·bəl), *adj.* —ex′tri·ca·bil′i·ty, *n.* —ex′tri·ca·bly, *adv.* —ex′tri·ca′tion, *n.*

ex·trin·sic (eks·trin′sik), *adj.* **1.** not essential or inherent; caused by external circumstances. **2.** being outside of a thing; coming from without; external. [< later L *extrinsecus* outer < earlier L, from outside, < unrecorded OL *extrim* from outside + *secus* following] —ex·trin′si·cal·ly, *adv.*

ex·tro·vert (eks′trə·vėrt), *n.* person more interested in what is going on around him than in his own thoughts and feelings. [< *extro-* (var. of *extra-* outside) + L *vertere* turn]

ex·trude (iks·trüd′), *v.*, –trud·ed, –trud·ing. **1.** thrust out; push out. **2.** stick out; protrude. [< L, < *ex-* out + *trudere* thrust] —ex·tru·sion (iks·trü′zhən), *n.* —ex·tru·sive (iks·trü′siv), *adj.*

ex·u·ber·ance (ig·zü′bər·əns), ex·u·ber·an·cy (–ən·si), *n.* fact, quality, state, or condition of being exuberant. [< L, < *exuberare* grow luxuriantly < *ex-* thoroughly + *uber* fertile]

ex·u·ber·ant (ig·zü′bər·ənt), *adj.* **1.** very abundant; overflowing; lavish. **2.** profuse in growth; luxuriant. —ex·u′ber·ant·ly, *adv.*

ex·ude (ig·züd′; ik·süd′), *v.*, –ud·ed, –ud·ing. **1.** ooze. **2.** give forth. [< L, < *ex-* out + *sudare* to sweat] —ex·u·da·tion (eks′yù·dā′shən), *n.*

ex·ult (ig·zult′), *v.* **1.** be very glad; rejoice greatly. **2.** *Obs.* leap for joy. [< L *exsultare* < *ex-* forth + *salire* leap] —ex·ul·ta·tion (eg′zul·tā′shən; ek′sul–), *n.* —ex·ult′ing·ly, *adv.*

ex·ult·ant (ig·zul′tənt), *adj.* rejoicing greatly; exulting. —ex·ult′ant·ly, *adv.*

ex·ur·ban·ite (eks′ėr′bən·īt), *n.* person who lives in the exurbs. [< *ex-* (def. 1, ? also def. 3) + (sub)*urbanite*]

ex·ur·bi·a (eks′ėr′bi·ə), *n.* the exurbs.

ex·urbs (eks′ėrbz), *n.pl.* region outside a large city, between the suburbs and the country, inhabited largely by people who have moved out from the city and whose way of life is a mixture of urban and rural elements. [< *ex-* + (sub)*urbs*]

-ey, *suffix.* full of; containing; like, as in *clayey*, *skyey.* [var. of -*y*[1]]

eye (ī), *n.*, *v.*, eyed, ey·ing or eye·ing. —*n.* **1.** organ of the body by which people and animals see; organ of sight. **2.** the colored part of the eye; iris. **3.** region surrounding the eye: *the blow gave him a black eye.* **4.** any organ that is sensitive to light. **5.** sense of seeing; vision; sight. **6.** ability to see small differences in things: *an eye for color.* **7.** look; glance. **8.** a watchful look. **9.** way of thinking or considering; view; opinion: *in the eye of the law.* **10.** thing shaped like, resembling, or suggesting an eye. —*v.* **1.** look at; watch: *the dog eyed the stranger.* [OE *ēage*]

eye·ball (ī′bôl′), *n.* the ball-shaped part of the eye, without the lids and bony socket.

eye·brow (ī′brou′), *n.* **1.** arch of hair above the eye. **2.** the bony ridge that it grows on.

eye·glass (ī′glas′; ī′gläs′), *n.* **1.** a glass lens to aid poor vision. **2.** eyepiece. **3.** eyeglasses, pair of glass lenses to help vision.

eye·hole (ī′hōl′), *n.* **1.** the bony socket for the eyeball. **2.** hole to look through. **3.** a round opening for a pin, hook, rope, etc., to go through.

eye·lash (ī′lash′), *n.* one of the hairs on the edge of the eyelid.

eye·less (ī′lis), *adj.* without eyes; blind.

eye·let (ī′lit), *n.* **1.** a small, round hole for a lace or cord to go through. **2.** a metal ring around such a hole to strengthen it.

eye·lid (ī′lid′), *n.* the movable fold of skin over the eye.

eye·piece (ī′pēs′), *n.* lens nearest to the eye of the user in a telescope, microscope, etc.

eye·shot (ī′shot′), *n.* range of vision.

eye·sight (ī′sīt′), *n.* **1.** power of seeing; sight. **2.** range of vision; view.

eye·sore (ī′sôr′; ī′sōr′), *n.* thing unpleasant to look at.

eye·strain (ī′strān′), *n.* a tired or weak condition of the eyes caused by using them too much, reading in a dim light, etc.

eye·tooth (ī′tüth′), *n.*, *pl.* –teeth. an upper canine tooth.

eye·wash (ī′wosh′; ī′wôsh′), *n.* a liquid preparation to clean or heal the eyes.

eye·wink·er (ī′wingk′ər), *n.* eyelash.

eye·wit·ness (ī′wit′nis), *n.* person who actually sees or has seen some act or happening.

ey·rie, ey·ry (âr′i; ir′i), *n.*, *pl.* –ries. aerie.

E·ze·ki·el (i-zē′ki-əl; i-zēk′yəl), *n.* 1. a Hebrew prophet in the sixth century B.C. 2. book of the Old Testament.

Ez·ra (ez′rə), *n.* 1. a Hebrew scribe who led a revival of the religion of Judaism. 2. a book of chronicles in the Old Testament.

F

F, f (ef), *n.*, *pl.* **F's; f's.** 1. the sixth letter of the alphabet. 2. *Music.* the fourth note of the scale of C major.

F, 1. *Chem.* fluorine. Also, Fl. 2. French.

F., 1. Fahrenheit. 2. February. 3. Friday.

f., 1. feminine. 2. folio. 3. following.

fa (fä), *n. Music.* the fourth note of the scale. [see GAMUT]

Fa·bi·an (fā′bi-ən), *adj.* using stratagem and delay to wear out an opponent; cautious; slow.

fa·ble (fā′bəl), *n.*, *v.*, –bled, –bling. —*n.* 1. story made up to teach a lesson. 2. an untrue story; falsehood. 3. legend; myth. —*v.* 1. tell or write fables. 2. lie. [< OF < L *fabula* < *fari* speak] —fa′bled, *adj.* —fa′bler, *n.*

fab·ric (fab′rik), *n.* 1. woven or knitted material; cloth. 2. construction; texture. 3. thing constructed of combined parts; framework. [< F < L *fabrica* workshop. Doublet of FORGE¹.]

fab·ri·cate (fab′rə-kāt), *v.*, –cat·ed, –cat·ing. 1. build; construct; manufacture. 2. make by fitting together standardized parts. 3. make up; invent (stories, lies, excuses, etc.). —fab′ri·ca′-tion, *n.* —fab′ri·ca′tor, *n.*

fab·u·list (fab′yə-list), *n.* 1. person who tells, writes, or makes up fables. 2. liar.

fab·u·lous (fab′yə-ləs), *adj.* 1. like a fable. 2. not believable; amazing. 3. of or belonging to a fable; imaginary. [< L *fabula* FABLE] —fab′u-lous·ly, *adv.* —fab′u·lous·ness, *n.* —Syn. 2. incredible, astonishing. 3. legendary, mythical.

fa·çade (fə·säd′), *n.* the front part or principal side of a building. [< F, < *face* FACE]

face (fās), *n.*, *v.*, faced, fac·ing. —*n.* 1. the front part of the head. 2. look; expression. 3. an ugly or peculiar look made by distorting the face. 4. outward appearance. 5. show; pretense. 6. the front part; right side; surface: *the face of a clock.* 7. the working surface of an implement. 8. the principal side of a building; front. 9. the printing side of a plate or piece of type. 10. *Colloq.* boldness; impudence. 11. personal importance; dignity; self-respect: *face is very important to Oriental peoples.* 12. the stated value. 13. face to face, a. with faces toward each other. b. in the actual presence. 14. in the face of, a. in the presence of. b. in spite of. —*v.* 1. have the face (toward); be opposite (to). 2. turn the face (toward). 3. cause to face. 4. meet face to face; stand before. 5. meet bravely or boldly; oppose and resist. 6. present itself to: *a crisis faced us.* 7. cover or line with a different material. 8. smooth the surface of (stone, etc.). 9. turn face up: *face a card.* [< F, ult. < L *facies* form] —face′a·ble, *adj.* —face′less, *adj.* —Syn. *n.* 1. visage, countenance, physiognomy, features. 3. grimace. 10. assurance, effrontery, audacity. —*v.* 4. front, confront. 5. brave, defy, oppose.

face card, *Cards.* king, queen, or jack.

fac·et (fas′it), *n.*, *v.*, –et·ed, –et·ing; *esp. Brit.* –et·ted, –et·ting. —*n.* 1. any one of the small, polished surfaces of a cut gem. 2. thing like the facet of a gem. —*v.* cut facets on. [< F *facette*, dim. of *face* FACE]

Cut gem showing facets

fa·ce·tious (fə-sē′shəs), *adj.* 1. having the habit of joking. 2. said in fun; not to be taken seriously. [< L *facetia* jest < *facetus* witty] —fa·ce′tious·ly, *adv.* —fa·ce′tious·ness, *n.*

face value, 1. value stated on a bond, check, note, etc. 2. apparent worth, meaning, etc.

fa·cial (fā′shəl), *adj.* 1. of the face. 2. for the face. —*n. Colloq.* massage or treatment of the face. —fa′cial·ly, *adv.*

fac·ile (fas′əl), *adj.* 1. easily done, used, etc.: *a facile task.* 2. moving, acting, working, etc., with ease: *a facile pen.* 3. of easy manners or temper; agreeable; yielding: *a facile nature.* [< L *facilis* easy < *facere* do] —fac′ile·ly, *adv.* —fac′ile·ness, *n.*

fa·cil·i·tate (fə-sil′ə·tāt), *v.*, –tat·ed, –tat·ing. make easy; lessen the labor of; assist. —fa·cil′i-ta′tion, *n.* —Syn. help, expedite, promote.

fa·cil·i·ty (fə-sil′ə·ti), *n.*, *pl.* –ties. 1. absence of difficulty; ease. 2. power to do anything easily, quickly, and smoothly. 3. something that makes an action easy; aid; convenience. 4. easy-going quality; tendency to yield to others. —Syn. 1. easiness. 2. knack, readiness.

fac·ing (fās′ing), *n.* 1. a covering of different material for ornament, protection, etc. 2. material put around the edge of cloth to protect or trim it.

fac·sim·i·le (fak-sim′ə-lē), *n.*, *v.*, –led, –le·ing, *adj.* —*n.* 1. an exact copy or likeness; perfect reproduction. 2. process for transmitting printed matter and photographs by radio and reproducing them on paper at the receiving set. —*v.* make a facsimile of. —*adj.* of a facsimile. [< L *fac* make! + *simile* like]

fact (fakt), *n.* 1. thing known to be true or to have really happened. 2. what is true or has really happened; truth; reality. 3. thing said or supposed to be true or to have really happened: *we doubted his facts.* 4. deed; act. [< L *factum* (thing) done, pp. of *facere* do. Doublet of FEAT.] —Syn. 2. actuality. ► fact (the fact that). *The fact that* is very often a circumlocution for which *that* alone would do as well: *He was quite conscious [of the fact] that his visitor had come other reason for coming.*

fac·tion (fak′shən), *n.* 1. group of people in a political party, church, club, etc., acting together or having a common end in view. 2. strife among the members of a political party, church, club, etc.; discord. [< L *factio* party, orig., a doing < *facere* do. Doublet of FASHION.] —fac′-tion·al, *adj.* —fac′tion·al·ism, *n.* —Syn. 1. party, group, clique, cabal. 2. dissension, division.

fac·tious (fak′shəs), *adj.* 1. fond of causing faction. 2. of or caused by faction. —fac′tious·ly, *adv.* —fac′tious·ness, *n.*

fac·ti·tious (fak-tish′əs), *adj.* developed by effort; not natural; forced; artificial. [< L *facticius* artificial] —fac·ti′tious·ly, *adv.* —fac·ti′-tious·ness, *n.*

fac·tor (fak′tər), *n.* 1. element, condition, quality, etc., that helps to bring about a result. 2. *Math.* any of the numbers, algebraic expressions, etc., that form a product when multiplied together. 3. person who does business for another; agent. —*v. Math.* separate into factors. —fac′tor·ship, *n.*

fac·to·ry (fak′tə·ri; –tri), *n.*, *pl.* –ries. a building or group of buildings where things are manufactured. —fac′to·ry·like′, *adj.* —Syn. mill, shop.

fac·to·tum (fak-tō′təm), *n.* person employed to do all kinds of work. [< Med.L, < L *fac* do! + *totum* the whole]

fac·tu·al (fak′chù·əl), *adj.* concerned with fact; consisting of facts. —fac′tu·al·ly, *adv.*

fac·ul·ty (fak′əl·ti), *n.*, *pl.* –ties. 1. power of the mind or body; ability. 2. power to do some special thing, esp. a power of the mind. 3. power

āge, câre, fär; ēqual, tėrm; īce; ōpen, ôrder; put, rūle, ūse; tħ, then; ə=a in about.

or privilege conferred; license; authorization. **4.**
a. *Am.* teachers of a school, college, or university.
b. department of learning: *faculty of theology*.
5. members of a profession. [< L *facultas* <
facilis FACILE] **—Syn. 1.** capacity, capability.

fad (fad), *n.* **1.** something everybody is very
much interested in for a short time; craze; rage.
2. hobby. **—fad′dish,** *adj.* **—fad′dist,** *n.*

fade (fād), *v.,* **fad·ed, fad·ing. 1.** lose color or
brightness. **2.** lose freshness or strength; wither.
3. die away; disappear. **4.** cause to fade. **5.** *Am.*
in motion pictures and television: **a.** fade in,
appear slowly. **b.** fade out, disappear slowly.
[< OF, < *fade* VAPID] **—Syn. 1.** blanch, bleach,
pale. **2.** droop, languish.

fade-out (fād′out′), *n.* **1.** *Am.* scene in a motion picture that slowly disappears. **2.** a gradual
disappearance.

fae·ces (fē′sēz), *n.pl.* feces. **—fae·cal** (fē′kəl),
adj.

fa·er·ie, fa·er·y (fā′ər·i; fār′i), *n., pl.* -er·ies,
adj. Archaic. **—n. 1.** fairyland. **2.** fairy. **—adj.**
fairy.

fag[1] (fag), *v.,* **fagged, fag·ging,** *n.* **—v. 1.** work
hard or until wearied. **2.** tire by work. **—n. 1.**
Brit. hard, uninteresting work. **2.** person who
does hard work; drudge.

fag[2] (fag), *n. Esp. Brit. Slang.* cigarette.

fag end, 1. the last and poorest part of anything; remnant. **2.** an untwisted end of rope.

fag·ot, *esp. Brit.* **fag·got** (fag′ət), *n.* bundle
of sticks or twigs tied together. **—v.** tie or fasten
together into bundles; make
into a fagot. [< OF]

fag·ot·ing, *esp. Brit.* **fag-
got·ing** (fag′ət·ing), *n.* an
ornamental stitch made with
the threads of a piece of cloth.

Fahr·en·heit (far′ən·hīt),
adj. of, based on, or according to a scale for
measuring temperature on which 32 degrees
marks the freezing point of water and 212 degrees the boiling point. [after G. D. *Fahrenheit,*
physicist]

Fagoting

fail (fāl), *v.* **1.** not succeed; be unable to do or
become; come out badly. **2.** not do; neglect. **3.** be
of no use or help to. **4.** be lacking or absent; be
not enough. **5.** lose strength; become weak; die
away. **6.** be unable to pay what one owes. **7.** be
unsuccessful in an examination, etc.; receive
a mark of failure. **8.** *Colloq.* give the mark of
failure to (a student). **—n.** failure. [< OF *faillir,*
ult. < L *fallere* deceive] **—Syn.** *v.* **5.** decline, sink,
wane, dwindle, deteriorate.

fail·ing (fāl′ing), *n.* **1.** failure. **2.** fault; defect.
—prep. in the absence of; lacking. **—adj.** that
fails. **—fail′ing·ly,** *adv.*

faille (fīl; fāl), *n.* a soft, ribbed silk or rayon
cloth. [< F]

fail·ure (fāl′yər), *n.* **1.** a being unable to do or
become; failing. **2.** not doing; neglecting. **3.** a
being lacking or absent; being not enough; falling short. **4.** losing strength; becoming weak;
dying away. **5.** a being unable to pay what one
owes. **6.** person or thing that has failed. **—Syn.**
4. decline, decay, deterioration. **5.** bankruptcy.

fain (fān), *Archaic and Poetic.* **—adv.** by choice;
gladly; willingly. **—adj.** **1.** willing, but not eager;
forced by circumstances. **2.** glad; willing. **3.**
eager; desirous. [OE *fægen*]

faint (fānt), *adj.* **1.** not clear or plain; dim. **2.**
weak; feeble. **3.** timid. **4.** done feebly or without
zest. **5.** ready to faint; about to faint. **—v.** lose
consciousness temporarily. **—n.** condition in
which a person lies for a time as if asleep and
does not know what is going on around him.
[< OF, pp. of *faindre* FEIGN] **—faint′er,** *n.*
—faint′ish, *adj.* **—faint′ly,** *adv.* **—faint′ness,**
n. **—Syn.** *adj.* **1.** indistinct, faded, dull. **2.** faltering, languid, wearied. **3.** irresolute.

faint-heart·ed (fānt′här′tid), *adj.* lacking
courage; cowardly; timid. **—faint′-heart′ed·ly,**
adv. **—faint′-heart′ed·ness,** *n.*

fair[1] (fār), *adj.* **1.** not favoring one more than
the other or others; just; honest. **2.** according
to the rules. **3.** pretty good; average. **4.** favorable;
promising. **5.** not dark; light. **6.** not cloudy or
stormy; clear; sunny. **7.** pleasing to see; beauti-

ful. **8.** civil; courteous. **9.** without spots or stains;
clean: *a person's fair name.* **10.** easily read;
plain. **11.** not blocked up; open. **—adv. 1.** in a
fair manner. **2.** directly; straight: *the stone
hit him fair in the head.* **—n.** *Archaic.* woman;
sweetheart. [OE *fæger*] **—fair′ish,** *adj.* **—fair′-
ness,** *n.* **—Syn.** *adj.* **1.** impartial, unprejudiced,
unbiased. **2.** middling, passable, tolerable. **4.** pro-
pitious, likely. **5.** blond, white. **7.** pretty, comely,
attractive. **9.** spotless, untarnished, pure.

fair[2] (fār), *n.* **1.** display of goods, products, etc.
2. a gathering of people to buy and sell, often
held in a certain place at regular times during
the year: *a county fair.* **3.** *Am.* a combined
entertainment and sale of articles for charity,
a church, etc. [< OF < LL *feria* holiday]

fair ball, *Am., Baseball.* ball hit to or over the
legal playing area.

fair·ly (fār′li), *adv.* **1.** in a fair manner. **2.** to
a fair degree. **3.** justly; honestly. **4.** rather;
somewhat. **5.** actually. **6.** clearly. **—Syn. 2.**
tolerably. **3.** impartially. **5.** positively, absolutely.
6. legibly, distinctly, plainly.

fair-mind·ed (fār′mīn′did), *adj.* not prejudiced; just; impartial. **—fair′-mind′ed·ness,** *n.*

fair-spo·ken (fār′spō′kən), *adj.* speaking
smoothly and pleasantly; courteous.

fair trade agreement, agreement which
permits U.S. manufacturers to set minimum
price levels on products, to which retailers must
adhere in States that have legalized the practice.

fair·way (fār′wā′), *n.* **1.** an unobstructed passage or way. **2.** *Golf.* the mowed and tended area
between the tee and putting green.

fair-weath·er (fār′weth′ər), *adj.* of or fitted
for fair weather; weakening or failing in time
of need.

fair·y (fār′i), *n., pl.* **fair·ies,** *adj.* **—n.** a tiny
supernatural being, very lovely and delicate,
supposed to help or harm human beings. **—adj.**
1. of fairies. **2.** like a fairy; lovely; delicate.
[< OF *faerie* < *fae* FAY] **—fair′y·like′,** *adj.*
—Syn. *n.* elf, fay, sprite, brownie.

fair·y·land (fār′i·land′), *n.* **1.** the imaginary
place where the fairies live. **2.** an enchanting and
pleasant place.

fait ac·com·pli (fe·tä·kôn·plē′), *French.*
thing done and no longer worth opposing.

faith (fāth), *n.* **1.** a believing without proof;
trust. **2.** belief in God, religion, or spiritual
things. **3.** what is believed. **4.** religion. **5.** a being
faithful; loyalty. **—interj.** truly; indeed. [< OF
feit < L *fides*] **—Syn.** *n.* **1.** confidence, reliance.
3. doctrine, tenet, creed, belief. **5.** fidelity, constancy, faithfulness. **—Ant. 1.** doubt.

faith·ful (fāth′fəl), *adj.* **1.** worthy of trust;
doing one's duty; keeping one's promise; loyal.
2. true; accurate. **3.** full of faith. **—n.** the faithful, **a.** the true believers. **b.** loyal followers or
supporters. **—faith′ful·ly,** *adv.* **—faith′ful·ness,**
n. **—Syn.** *adj.* **1.** devoted, constant. **2.** precise,
exact.

faith·less (fāth′lis), *adj.* **1.** unworthy of trust;
failing in one's duty; breaking one's promise;
not loyal. **2.** not reliable. **3.** without faith; unbelieving. **—faith′less·ly,** *adv.* **—faith′less·ness,**
n. **—Syn. 1.** disloyal, false, inconstant, fickle.
3. doubting, skeptical.

fake (fāk), *v.,* **faked, fak·ing,** *n., adj.* **—v.** make
to seem satisfactory; falsify; counterfeit. **—n.**
1. fraud; deception. **2.** *Am.* one who fakes. **—adj.**
Am. intended to deceive; false. **—fak′er,** *n.*

fa·kir, fa·keer (fə·kir′; fā′kər), *n.* **1.** a Mohammedan holy man who lives by begging. **2.** a
Hindu ascetic. [< Ar. *faqir* poor]

Fa·lan·gist (fə·lan′jist), *n.* member of the
Falange, a Spanish fascist group. **—Fa·lan′-
gism,** *n.*

fal·cate (fal′kāt), *adj.* curved like a sickle;
hooked. [< L, < *falx* sickle]

fal·chion (fôl′chən), *n.* **1.** a broad, short
sword with an edge that curves to a point.
2. *Poetic.* any sword. [< OF < Ital. *falcione,*
ult. < L *falx* sickle]

fal·con (fôl′kən; fô′kən), *n.* **1.** hawk trained to
hunt and kill birds and small game. **2.** a swift-
flying hawk having a short, curved, notched bill.
See picture on next page. [< OF < LL *falco*]

fal·con·ry (fôl′kən·ri; fô′kən-), *n.* **1.** sport of hunting with falcons. **2.** the training of falcons to hunt. —**fal′con·er**, *n.*

fal·de·ral (fal′də·ral), **fal-de·rol** (-rol), *n.* **1.** a flimsy thing; trifle. **2.** nonsense. **3.** a meaningless refrain in songs. Also, **folderol**.

Falk·land Islands (fôk′-lənd), group of islands in the S Atlantic, E of the Strait of Magellan, administered by Great Britain but claimed also by Argentina.

Falcon (17 in. long)

fall (fôl), *v.*, **fell**, **fall·en**, **fall·ing**, *n.* —*v.* **1.** drop or come down from a higher place: *the snow falls fast.* **2.** come down suddenly from an erect position. **3.** hang down: *her curls fell upon her shoulders.* **4.** droop: *she blushed and her eyes fell.* **5.** become bad or worse: *he was tempted and fell.* **6.** lose position, dignity, etc.; be taken by any evil. **7.** be captured or destroyed. **8.** drop wounded or dead; be killed. **9.** pass into a certain condition: *he fell asleep.* **10.** come as if by dropping: *when night falls, the stars appear.* **11.** come by chance or lot: *our choice fell on him.* **12.** come to pass; happen; occur: *Christmas falls on Sunday this year.* **13.** come by right: *the money fell to the only son.* **14.** be put properly: *the accent of "farmer" falls on the first syllable.* **15.** become lower or less: *prices fell sharply.* **16.** be divided: *the story falls into five parts.* **17.** look sad or disappointed: *his face fell at the bad news.* **18.** slope downward: *the land falls gradually to the beach.* **19.** be directed: *the light falls on my book.* **20.** fall away, a. withdraw support or allegiance. b. become bad or worse. c. be overthrown or destroyed. d. become thin. **21.** fall back, go toward the rear; retreat. **22.** fall in, a. *Mil.* take a place in a formation and come to a position of attention. b. meet. c. agree. **23.** fall on, attack. **24.** fall out, a. *Mil.* leave a place in a formation. b. stop being friends; quarrel. c. turn out; happen. **25.** fall through, fail. **26.** fall under, belong under; be classified as. —*n.* **1.** a dropping from a higher place. **2.** amount that falls: *a heavy fall of snow.* **3.** distance that anything falls. **4.** a coming down suddenly from an erect position. **5.** a hanging down; dropping. **6.** a becoming bad or worse. **7.** capture; destruction. **8.** a lowering; becoming less. **9.** a downward slope. **10.** *Esp. U.S.* season of the year between summer and winter; autumn. **11.** in wrestling, a being thrown on one's back. **12.** Usually, **falls.** waterfall; cataract; cascade. **13.** the Fall, the sin of Adam and Eve in yielding to temptation and eating the forbidden fruit. [OE *feallan*] —Syn. *v.* **1.** descend, sink. —*n.* **1.** drop, descent. ▶ Falls is plural in form but really singular (or collective) in meaning. In informal and colloquial usage people speak of *a falls;* formal usage keeps *falls* strictly plural.

fal·la·cious (fə·lā′shəs), *adj.* **1.** deceptive; misleading. **2.** logically unsound; erroneous. —**fal·la′cious·ly**, *adv.* —**fal·la′cious·ness**, *n.*

fal·la·cy (fal′ə·si), *n., pl.* **-cies.** **1.** a false idea; mistaken belief; error. **2.** mistake in reasoning; misleading or unsound argument. [< L, ult. < *fallere* deceive]

fall·en (fôl′ən), *v.* pp. of **fall.** —*adj.* **1.** dropped. **2.** on the ground; down flat. **3.** degraded. **4.** overthrown; destroyed. **5.** dead. —Syn. *adj.* **1.** decreased, depreciated. **3.** debased. **4.** ruined.

fall guy, *Am., Slang.* person left in a difficult situation.

fal·li·ble (fal′ə·bəl), *adj.* **1.** liable to be deceived or mistaken; liable to err. **2.** liable to be erroneous, inaccurate, or false. [< Med.L, < L *fallere* deceive] —**fal′li·bil′i·ty**, **fal′li·ble·ness**, *n.* —**fal′li·bly**, *adv.*

falling sickness, epilepsy.

falling star, meteor.

Fal·lo·pi·an tubes (fə·lō′pi·ən), *Anat., Zool.* pair of slender tubes through which ova from the ovaries pass to the uterus.

fall-out (fôl′out′), *n.* the radioactive particles or dust that fall to the earth after an atomic explosion.

fal·low¹ (fal′ō), *adj.* plowed and left unseeded for a season or more; uncultivated; inactive. —*n.* **1.** land plowed and left unseeded for a season or more. **2.** the plowing of land without seeding it for a season in order to destroy weeds, improve the soil, etc. —*v.* plow and harrow (land) without seeding. [OE *fealg*]

fal·low² (fal′ō), *adj.* pale yellowish-brown. [OE *fealu*]

fallow deer, a small European deer with a yellowish coat that is spotted with white in the summer.

Fall River, city in SE Massachusetts.

Fallow deer (3 ft. high at the shoulder)

false (fôls), *adj.*, **fals·er**, **fals·est**, *adv.* —*adj.* **1.** not true; not correct; wrong. **2.** not truthful; lying. **3.** not loyal; not faithful. **4.** used to deceive; deceiving: *false weights.* **5.** substitute; supplementary. **6.** not true in pitch. **7.** not real; artificial. **8.** *Biol.* improperly called or named. The false acacia is really a locust tree. —*adv.* in a false manner. [< L *falsus* < *fallere* deceive] —**false′ly**, *adv.* —**false′ness**, *n.* —Syn. *adj.* **1.** erroneous, mistaken, incorrect. **2.** untruthful, mendacious. **3.** disloyal, unfaithful, inconstant, treacherous, traitorous. **4.** misleading, deceptive, fallacious. **7.** spurious, bogus, counterfeit, sham.

false·hood (fôls′hůd), *n.* **1.** quality of being false. **2.** something false. **3.** a making of false statements; lying. **4.** a false statement; lie. —Syn. **1.** falseness, untruthfulness, mendacity. **4.** untruth, fib.

fal·set·to (fôl·set′ō), *n., pl.* **-tos,** *adj., adv.* —*n.* an unnaturally high-pitched voice, esp. in a man. —*adj.* that sings in a falsetto. —*adv.* in a falsetto. [< Ital., dim. of *falso* FALSE]

fal·si·fy (fôl′sə·fī), *v.*, **-fied**, **-fy·ing.** **1.** make false; change in order to deceive; misrepresent. **2.** make false statements; lie. **3.** prove to be false; disprove. —**fal′si·fi·ca′tion**, *n.* —**fal′si·fi′er**, *n.*

fal·si·ty (fôl′sə·ti), *n., pl.* **-ties.** **1.** a being false; incorrectness. **2.** untruthfulness; deceitfulness. **3.** that which is false.

Fal·staff (fôl′staf; -stäf), *n.* a fat, jolly, swaggering soldier, brazen and without scruples, in three of Shakespeare's plays. —**Fal·staff·i·an** (fôl·staf′i·ən; -stäf′-), *adj.*

fal·ter (fôl′tər), *v.* **1.** lose courage; draw back; hesitate; waver. **2.** move unsteadily; stumble; totter. **3.** speak in hesitating, broken words; stammer. **4.** come forth in hesitating, broken sounds. —*n.* act of faltering; faltering sound. [cf. Scand. *faltrask* be cumbered] —**fal′ter·er**, *n.* —**fal′ter·ing·ly**, *adv.* —Syn. *v.* **1.** vacillate. **2.** stagger, tremble. **3.** stutter.

fame (fām), *n., v.*, **famed**, **fam·ing.** —*n.* **1.** a being very well known; having much said or written about one. **2.** what is said about one; reputation. **3.** *Archaic.* rumor. —*v.* make famous. [< obs. F < L *fama* < *fari* speak] —Syn. *n.* **1.** notoriety, celebrity, renown, eminence.

famed (fāmd), *adj.* made famous; celebrated; well-known. ▶ *famed.* When *famed* is used for *famous* or *well-known,* it usually suggests a journalese style or a staccato one: *famed Nobel prize winner.* It is often a sign of amateur writing to label as *famed* (or as *famous,* for that matter) really well-known people.

fa·mil·iar (fə·mil′yər), *adj.* **1.** well-known. **2.** widely used. **3.** well-acquainted. **4.** close; personal; intimate. **5.** not formal; friendly. **6.** too friendly; presuming; forward. —*n.* **1.** a familiar friend or acquaintance. **2.** spirit or demon supposed to serve a particular person. [< OF < L *familiaris.* See FAMILY.] —**fa·mil′iar·ly**, *adv.* —Syn. *adj.* **3.** conversant, versed. **4.** confidential. **5.** unceremonious, informal.

➤ **Familiar English** is the way we speak and write for ourselves—as in diaries and notes for future work—and with or for our friends. In such informal circumstances we know that we are not going to be judged by our language, as in part we are when we speak or write for strangers, and we can therefore use our natural, easy speech—with contractions, clipped words and abbreviated sentences, and allusions to our common background that might puzzle an outsider. In more formal circumstances we have to approach the standards set for the language used in carrying on public affairs.

fa·mil·iar·i·ty (fə·mil′yar′ə·ti), *n.*, *pl.* –ties. 1. close acquaintance. 2. freedom of behavior suitable only to friends; lack of formality or ceremony. 3. instance of such behavior. —Syn. 1. intimacy, friendship, fellowship. 2. informality, unconstraint.

fa·mil·iar·ize (fə·mil′yər·īz), *v.*, –ized, –iz·ing. 1. make well acquainted. 2. make well known. —fa·mil′iar·i·za′tion, *n.*

fam·i·ly (fam′ə·li; fam′li), *n.*, *pl.* –lies. 1. father, mother, and their children. 2. children of a father and mother. 3. group of people living in the same house. 4. all of a person's relatives. 5. group of related people; tribe. 6. *Esp. Brit.* good or noble descent. 7. group of related or similar things. 8. *Biol.* group of related animals or plants ranking below an order and above a genus. [< L *familia* household < *famulus* servant] —Syn. 5. clan, race. 6. ancestry, stock, lineage.

family name, the last name of all the members of a certain family; surname.

fam·ine (fam′ən), *n.* 1. starvation. 2. lack of food in a place; time of starving. 3. a very great lack of anything. [< F, ult. < L *fames* hunger] —Syn. 3. scarcity, insufficiency, deficiency.

fam·ish (fam′ish), *v.* be or make extremely hungry; starve. —fam′ish·ment, *n.*

fa·mous (fā′məs), *adj.* 1. very well known; noted. 2. *Colloq.* first-rate; excellent. [< AF < L, < *fama* FAME] —fa′mous·ly, *adv.* —fa′mous·ness, *n.* —Syn. 1. celebrated, renowned, distinguished, illustrious, eminent. —Ant. 1. obscure, unknown. ➤ See **notorious** for usage note.

fan¹ (fan), *n.*, *v.*, **fanned, fan·ning.** —*n.* 1. instrument or device to make a current of air. It causes a cooling breeze, blows dust away, etc. 2. thing spread out like an open fan. 3. a winnowing machine. 4. *Baseball.* a striking out. —*v.* 1. make a current of (air) with a fan, etc. 2. direct a current of air toward with a fan, etc. 3. drive away with a fan, etc. 4. stir up; arouse: *bad treatment fanned their dislike into hate.* 5. spread out like an open fan. 6. winnow. 7. *Am., Baseball.* strike out. [< L *vannus* fan for winnowing grain] —fan′ner, *n.*

fan² (fan), *n. Am., Colloq.* 1. an enthusiastic devotee or follower of a sport, hobby, etc.: *a baseball fan.* 2. admirer of an actor, writer, etc. [short for *fanatic*]

fa·nat·ic (fə·nat′ik), *n.* person who is carried away beyond reason by his beliefs. —*adj.* enthusiastic or zealous beyond reason. [< L, < *fanum* temple] —fa·nat′i·cism, *n.*

fa·nat·i·cal (fə·nat′ə·kəl), *adj.* unreasonably enthusiastic; extremely zealous. —fa·nat′i·cal·ly, *adv.*

fan·cied (fan′sid), *adj.* imagined; imaginary.

fan·ci·er (fan′si·ər), *n.* person who is especially interested in something, as dogs, etc.

fan·ci·ful (fan′si·fəl), *adj.* 1. showing fancy; quaint; odd. 2. influenced by fancy; imaginative. 3. suggested by fancy; imaginary; unreal. —fan′ci·ful·ly, *adv.* —fan′ci·ful·ness, *n.*

fan·cy (fan′si), *n.*, *pl.* –cies, *v.*, –cied, –cy·ing, *adj.*, –ci·er, –ci·est. —*n.* 1. power to imagine; imagination. 2. thing imagined. 3. thing supposed; idea; notion. 4. a personal taste or judgment. 5. a liking; fondness. —*v.* 1. imagine. 2. have an idea or belief; suppose. 3. be fond of; like. —*adj.* 1. made or arranged specially to please; valued for beauty rather than use. 2. decorated; ornamental. 3. requiring much skill: *fancy skating.* 4. costing extra to please the fancy or one's special taste, etc.: *fancy fruit.* 5. bred for special excellence. [contraction of *fan-*

tasy] —Syn. *n.* 1. fantasy. 3. conception, whim, caprice. –*v.* 1. conceive, picture. 2. presume, conjecture. –*adj.* 1. fine, elegant.

fan·cy-free (fan′si·frē′), *adj.* free from influence; not in love.

fan·cy·work (fan′si·wèrk′), *n.* ornamental needlework; embroidery, crocheting, etc.

fan·dan·go (fan·dang′gō), *n.*, *pl.* –gos. a lively Spanish dance in three-quarter time. [< Sp.]

fane (fān), *n. Archaic and Poetic.* temple; church. [< L *fanum* temple]

fan·fare (fan′fār), *n.* 1. a short tune or call sounded by trumpets, bugles, etc. 2. a loud show of activity, talk, etc.; showy flourish. [< F, < *fanfarer*, v., < Sp. < Ar.]

fang (fang), *n.* 1. a long, pointed tooth of a dog, wolf, snake, etc. 2. a long, slender, tapering part of anything. [OE] —fanged (fangd), *adj.* —fang′-less, *adj.* —fang′like′, *adj.*

Fangs of a snake

fan·light (fan′līt′), *n.* 1. a semicircular window with bars spread out like an open fan. 2. any semicircular or other window over a door.

fan·tail (fan′tāl′), *n.* 1. tail, end, or part spread out like an open fan. 2. pigeon whose tail spreads out like an open fan.

fan·tan (fan′tan′), *n.* 1. a Chinese gambling game. 2. *Cards.* game in which the player who gets rid of his cards first wins the game. [< Chinese *fan t'an* repeated divisions]

fan·ta·si·a (fan·tā′zhi·ə; –zhə; –zi·ə), *n. Music.* 1. composition following no fixed form or style. 2. medley of well-known airs. [< Ital. See FANTASY.]

fan·tas·tic (fan·tas′tik), **fan·tas·ti·cal** (–tə·kəl), *adj.* 1. very odd or queer; wild and strange in shape; showing unrestrained fancy: *weird, fantastic shadows.* 2. very fanciful; capricious; eccentric; irrational: *a fantastic idea.* 3. existing only in the imagination; unreal: *superstition causes fantastic fears.* —fan·tas′ti·cal·ly, *adv.* —fan·tas′ti·cal·ness, fan·tas′ti·cal′i·ty, *n.* —Syn. 1. freakish, bizarre, grotesque.

fan·ta·sy (fan′tə·si; –zi), *n.*, *pl.* –sies. 1. play of the mind; imagination; fancy. 2. a wild, strange fancy. 3. caprice; whim. 4. daydream. 5. *Music.* fantasia. Also, **phantasy.** [< OF < L < Gk. *phantasia* appearance, image, ult. < *phainein* show] —Syn. 2. illusion, hallucination.

far (fär), *adj.*, far·ther, far·thest, *adv.* —*adj.* 1. distant; not near: *a far country.* 2. more distant: *the far side of the hill.* —*adv.* 1. a long way off in time or space. 2. very much. 3. as far as, to the distance, point, or degree that. 4. by far, very much. 5. far and away, very much. 6. far and near, everywhere. 7. far and wide, everywhere; even in distant parts. 8. far be it from me, I do not dare or want. 9. go far, a. last long. b. tend very much. c. get ahead. 10. how far, to what distance, point, or degree. 11. in so far as, to the extent that. 12. so far, a. to this or that point. b. until now or then. 13. so far as, to the extent that. 14. so far so good, until now everything has been safe or satisfactory. [OE *feorr*] —Syn. *adj.* 1. remote.

far·ad (far′əd), *n. Elect.* a unit of capacity. It is the capacity of a condenser that, when charged with one coulomb, gives a pressure of one volt. [for Michael *Faraday*]

Far·a·day (far′ə·dā; –di), *n.* Michael, 1791-1867, English physicist and chemist.

far·a·way (fär′ə·wā′), *adj.* 1. distant. 2. dreamy.

farce (färs), *n.*, *v.*, farced, farc·ing. —*n.* 1. play intended merely to make people laugh, full of ridiculous happenings, absurd actions, etc. 2. kind of humor found in such plays; broad humor. 3. ridiculous mockery; absurd pretense. —*v.* season (a speech or writing), as with jokes and allusions. [< F, lit., stuffing, ult. < L *farcire* stuff] —far·cial (fär′shəl), *adj.*

far·ci·cal (fär′sə·kəl), *adj.* of or like a farce; absurd; improbable. —far′ci·cal′i·ty, far′ci·cal·ness, *n.* —far′ci·cal·ly, *adv.*

fare (fār), *n.*, *v.*, fared, far·ing. —*n.* 1. sum

of money paid to ride in a train, car, bus, etc.
2. passenger on a train, car, bus, etc. 3. food.
[blend of OE *faer* and *faru*] —v. 1. eat food; be
fed. 2. get along; do. 3. turn out; happen. 4. go;
travel. [OE *faran*] —**far'er,** *n.*

Far East, China, Japan, and other parts of E
Asia.

fare·well (fãr'wel'), *interj.* good-by; good
luck. —*n.* 1. expression of good wishes at parting;
good-by. 2. departure; leave-taking. —*adj.* of
farewell; parting; last.

far-fetched (fär'fecht'), *adj.* not coming
naturally; forced; strained.

far-flung (fär'flung'), *adj.* widely spread; covering a large area.

fa·ri·na (fə·rē'nə), *n.* flour or meal made from
grain, potatoes, beans, nuts, etc. [< L, < *far*
grits]

far·i·na·ceous (far'ə·nā'shəs), *adj.* consisting of flour or meal; starchy; mealy.

far·kle·ber·ry (fär'kəl·ber'i), *n., pl.* -ries.
Am. shrub or small tree that has small black
berries.

farm (färm), *n.* 1. piece of land used to raise
crops or animals. 2. thing like a farm. A sheet of
water for cultivating oysters is an oyster farm.
3. *Am., Baseball.* a minor-league team belonging
to or associated with a major-league club.
—*v.* 1. raise crops or animals on a farm. 2. cultivate (land). 3. take proceeds or profits of (a tax,
undertaking, etc.) on paying a fixed sum. 4. let
out (taxes, revenues, an enterprise, etc.) to another for a fixed sum or percentage. 5. let the
labor or services of (a person) for hire. 6. be a
farmer. 7. farm out, *Baseball.* assign to a minor-
league team. [< F, ult. < L *firmus* firm]

farm·er (fär'mər), *n.* 1. person who raises
crops or animals on a farm; person who runs a
farm. 2. person who takes a contract for the
collection of taxes by agreeing to pay a certain
sum to the government. —*Syn.* 1. agriculturist,
husbandman, granger.

farm hand, man who works on a farm.

farm-house (färm'hous'), *n.* house on a farm.

farm·ing (fär'ming), *n.* 1. business of raising
crops or animals on a farm; agriculture. 2. practice of letting out the collection of public revenue. 3. condition of being let out at a fixed rate.
—*adj.* of or pertaining to farms. —*Syn. n.* 1.
husbandry, tillage, agronomy.

farm·stead (färm'sted), **farm·stead·ing**
(-sted·ing), *n. Esp. Brit.* farm with its buildings.

farm·yard (färm'yärd'), *n.* yard connected
with the farm buildings or enclosed by them.

far·o (fãr'ō), *n.* a gambling game played by betting on the order in which certain cards will
appear. [appar. alter. of *Pharaoh*]

far-off (fär'ôf', -of'), *adj.* distant.

Fa·rouk I (fä·rük'), born 1920, king of Egypt
1936-1952.

far·ra·go (fə·rā'gō; -rä'-), *n., pl.* -goes. a confused mixture; hodgepodge; jumble. [< L, mixed
fodder, ult. < *far* grits]

far-reach·ing (fär'rēch'ing), *adj.* having a
wide influence or effect; extending far.

far·ri·er (far'i·ər), *n. Esp. Brit.* 1. blacksmith
who shoes horses. 2. a horse doctor; veterinarian.
[< OF < L, < *ferrum* iron]

far·ri·er·y (far'i·ər·i), *n., pl.* -er·ies. *Esp. Brit.*
1. work of a farrier. 2. place where a farrier
works.

far·row (far'ō), *n.* litter of pigs. —*v.* 1. give
birth to a litter of pigs. 2. give birth to (pigs).
[OE *fearh*]

far-see·ing (fär'sē'ing), *adj.* 1. able to see
far. 2. looking ahead; planning wisely for the
future.

far-sight·ed (fär'sit'id), *adj.* 1. able to see
far. 2. seeing distant things more clearly than
near ones. 3. looking ahead; planning wisely for
the future. —**far'-sight'ed·ly,** *adv.* —**far'-
sight'ed·ness,** *n.*

far·ther (fär'thər), *comparative of* far. —*adj.*
1. more distant. 2. more; additional: *do you need
farther help?* —*adv.* 1. at or to a greater distance. 2. at or to a more advanced point. 3. in

addition; also. [ME *ferther*] ≯ **farther, further.**
In formal English some people make a distinction between *farther* and *further,* confining the
first to expression of physical distance and the
second to abstract relationships of degree or
quantity: *We went on twenty miles farther. He
went farther than I but neither of us reached
the town. He carries that sort of thing further
than I would. He went further into his family
history. He got further and further into debt.* In
colloquial and informal English the distinction
is not kept and there seems to be a rather definite tendency for *further* to be used in all senses.

far·ther·most (fär'thər·mōst), *adj.* most distant; farthest.

far·thest (fär'thist), *superlative of* far. —*adj.*
1. most distant. 2. longest. —*adv.* 1. to or at the
greatest distance. 2. most. [ME *ferthest*]

far·thing (fär'thing), *n.* a British coin, worth
a fourth of a British penny. [OE
fēorthung < *fēortha* fourth]

far·thin·gale (fär'thing·gāl), *n.*
a hoop skirt worn in England from
about 1550 to about 1650. [< F <
Sp., < *verdugo* rod]

fas·ces (fas'ēz), *n.pl., sing.* fascis (fas'is). bundle of rods or sticks
containing an ax with the blade
projecting, carried before a Roman
magistrate as a symbol of authority. [< L, pl. of *fascis* bundle]

fas·ci·cle (fas'ə·kəl), *n.* 1. a small
bundle. 2. *Bot.* a close cluster of
flowers, leaves, etc. 3. a single part
of a printed work issued in sections.
[< L *fasciculus,* dim. of *fascis* bundle] —**fas'ci·
cled,** *adj.*

Ancient Ro-
man holding
fasces

fas·ci·nate (fas'ə·nāt), *v.,* -nat·ed, -nat·ing.
1. attract very strongly; enchant by charming
qualities. 2. hold motionless by strange power,
terror, etc. Snakes are said to fascinate small
birds. 3. *Obs.* bewitch. [< L, < *fascinum* spell]
—**fas'ci·nat'ed·ly,** *adv.* —**fas'ci·nat'ing,** *adj.*
—**fas'ci·nat'ing·ly,** *adv.* —**fas'ci·na'tor,** *n.*
—*Syn.* 1. charm, entrance, enrapture, captivate.

fas·ci·na·tion (fas'ə·nā'shən), *n.* 1. a fascinating or being fascinated. 2. very strong attraction; charm; enchantment.

fas·cism (fash'iz·əm), *n.* 1. Fascism, a strongly
nationalistic movement in favor of government
control of business. Fascism seized control of the
Italian government in 1922 under the leadership
of Mussolini. 2. any system of government
in which property is privately owned, but all
industry and business is regulated by a strong
national government. [< Ital., < *fascio* bundle
(as political emblem) < L *fascis*] ≯ fascism,
fascist. Pronounced fash'iz·əm, fash'ist; rarely
fas'iz·əm, fas'ist. *Fascism, Fascist* are capitalized when they refer to Italian politics, as
we capitalize *Republican* and *Democrat* in this
country. When the word refers to a movement in
another country in which the party has a different name, it need not be capitalized but often is.
When it refers to the general idea of fascist politics, or an unorganized tendency, as in the
United States, it is not capitalized. *Fascisti*
(singular, *Fascista*) has also been Anglicized in
pronunciation: fə·shis'ti; Italian pronunciation
fä·shē'stē. *Fascismo* (fä·shēz'mō) is rarely used
in English, *Fascism* being the translation. Compare *Nazi.*

fas·cist (fash'ist), *n.* 1. person who favors and
supports fascism. 2. Fascist, person who favored
and supported Fascism in Italy. —*adj.* of or
having to do with fascism or fascists. ≯ See
fascism for usage note.

fash·ion (fash'ən), *n.* 1. manner; way. 2. the
prevailing style; current use in clothes, manners,
speech, etc. 3. a particular make; kind; sort;
form; shape. 4. polite society; fashionable people. 5. after or in a fashion, in some way or
other; not very well. —*v.* make; shape; form.
[< OF < L *factio* a doing or making. Doublet of
FACTION.] —**fash'ion·er,** *n.* —*Syn. n.* 1. mode,
practice, custom. 2. vogue, fad, rage. -*v.* frame,
construct.

fash·ion·a·ble (fash′ən·ə·bəl; fash′nə·bəl), *adj.* 1. following the fashion; in fashion; stylish. 2. of, like, or used by people of fashion. —**fash′ion·a·ble·ness,** *n.* —**fash′ion·a·bly,** *adv.* —Syn. 1. modish, smart.

fast[1] (fast; fäst), *adj.* 1. quick; rapid; swift. 2. facilitating the rapid motion of something: *a fast race track.* 3. indicating a time ahead of the correct time. 4. not restrained in pleasures; too gay; wild. 5. firm; secure; tight: *a fast hold on a rope, roots fast in the ground.* 6. loyal; faithful. 7. that will not fade easily. —*adv.* 1. quickly; rapidly; swiftly. 2. firmly; securely; tightly. 3. thoroughly; completely; soundly: *he was fast asleep.* 4. **play fast and loose,** say one thing and do another; be tricky, insincere, or unreliable. [OE *fæst*] —Syn. *adj.* 1. fleet, speedy, hasty. 4. dissipated, dissolute, profligate, immoral. 5. fixed, immovable, tenacious, adhesive.

fast[2] (fast; fäst), *v.* go without food; eat little or nothing; go without certain kinds of food. —*n.* 1. a fasting. 2. day or time of fasting. [OE *fæstan*]

fast day, day observed by fasting, esp. a day regularly set apart by a church.

fas·ten (fas′ən; fäs′-), *v.* 1. fix firmly in place; tie; lock; shut. 2. attach; connect: *he tried to fasten the blame upon his companions.* 3. direct; fix: *the dog fastened his eyes on the stranger.* 4. become fast. 5. become fastened. [OE *fæstnian* < *fæst* fast[1]] —**fas′ten·er,** *n.* —Syn. 1. link, hook, clasp, clamp, secure, bind, moor, latch.

fas·ten·ing (fas′ən·ing; fäs′ning; fäs′-), *n.* thing used to fasten something, as a lock, bolt, clasp, hook, button, etc.

fas·tid·i·ous (fas·tid′i·əs), *adj.* hard to please; extremely refined or critical; easily disgusted. [< L, < *fastidium* loathing] —**fas·tid′i·ous·ly,** *adv.* —**fas·tid′i·ous·ness,** *n.*

fast·ness (fast′nis; fäst′-), *n.* 1. a strong, safe place; stronghold. 2. a being fast.

fat (fat), *n.*, *adj.*, **fat·ter, fat·test,** *v.*, **fat·ted, fat·ting.** —*n.* 1. a white or yellow, oily substance formed in the bodies of animals. 2. animal tissue containing this substance. 3. *Chem.* any of a class of organic compounds of which the natural fats are usually mixtures. 4. the richest or best part. —*adj.* 1. consisting of or containing fat; oily: *fat meat.* 2. abounding in some element; fertile: *fat land.* 3. yielding much money; profitable: *a fat office.* 4. affording good opportunities. 5. plentifully supplied; plentiful. 6. fleshy; plump; well-fed. 7. thick; broad. 8. dull; stupid. 9. too fat; corpulent; obese. —*v.* make fat; become fat. [OE *fætt,* orig. pp., fatted] —**fat′ly,** *adv.* —**fat′ness,** *n.* —Syn. *adj.* 1. greasy, unctuous. 3. lucrative, remunerative. 9. stout.

fa·tal (fā′təl), *adj.* 1. causing death. 2. causing destruction or ruin. 3. important; decisive; fateful. [< L, < *fatum* FATE] —**fa′tal·ly,** *adv.* —**fa′tal·ness,** *n.* —Syn. 1. mortal, deadly. 3. destructive, disastrous, ruinous.

fa·tal·ism (fā′təl·iz·əm), *n.* 1. belief that fate controls everything that happens. 2. submission to everything that happens as inevitable. —**fa′tal·ist,** *n.* —**fa′tal·is′tic,** *adj.* —**fa′tal·is′ti·cal·ly,** *adv.*

fa·tal·i·ty (fā·tal′ə·ti; fə-), *n.*, *pl.* **-ties.** 1. a fatal accident or happening; death. 2. a fatal influence or effect. 3. liability to disaster. 4. a being controlled by fate; inevitable necessity: *doctrine of fatality.*

fate (fāt), *n.*, *v.*, **fat·ed, fat·ing.** —*n.* 1. power supposed to fix beforehand and control everything that happens. 2. what is caused by fate. 3. what becomes of a person or thing. 4. death; ruin. —*v.* destine. [< L *fatum* (thing) spoken (i.e., by the gods), pp. of *fari* speak] —Syn. *n.* 1. destiny, lot, fortune, doom.

fat·ed (fāt′id), *adj.* determined by fate.

fate·ful (fāt′fəl), *adj.* 1. controlled by fate. 2. determining what is to happen; important; decisive. 3. showing what fate decrees; prophetic. 4. causing death, destruction, or ruin; disastrous. —**fate′ful·ly,** *adv.* —**fate′ful·ness,** *n.*

Fates (fāts), *n.pl. Gk. and Roman Myth.* the three goddesses supposed to control human life.

fa·ther (fä′thər), *n.* 1. a male parent. 2. person who is like a father. 3. a male ancestor; forefather. 4. person who helped to make something; founder; inventor; author. 5. title of respect used in addressing priests or other clergymen. 6. clergyman having this title. 7. senator of ancient Rome. 8. the Father, God. 9. **the fathers,** the chief writers and teachers of the Christian Church during the first six centuries A.D. —*v.* 1. be the father of. 2. take care of as a father does; act as a father to. 3. make; originate. [OE *fæder*] —**fa′ther·hood,** *n.* —**fa′ther·less,** *adj.* —**fa′ther·less·ness,** *n.*

fa·ther-in-law (fä′thər·in·lô′), *n.*, *pl.* **fathers-in-law.** 1. father of one's husband or wife. 2. *Colloq.* stepfather.

fa·ther·land (fä′thər·land′), *n.* one's native country; land of one's ancestors.

fa·ther·ly (fä′thər·li), *adj.* 1. of a father. 2. like a father; kindly. —*adv.* in the manner of a father. —**fa′ther·li·ness,** *n.*

fath·om (fath′əm), *n.*, *pl.* **fath·oms** or (*esp. collectively*) **fath·om,** *v.* —*n.* a unit of measure equal to 6 feet, used mostly in measuring the depth of water and the length of ships' ropes, cables, etc. —*v.* 1. measure the depth of. 2. get to the bottom of; understand fully. [OE *fæthm* width of the outstretched arms] —**fath′om·a·ble,** *adj.* —**fath′om·er,** *n.* —**fath′om·less,** *adj.* —**fath′om·less·ly,** *adv.*

fa·tigue (fə·tēg′), *n.*, *v.*, **-tigued, -ti·guing,** *adj.* —*n.* 1. weariness. 2. hard work; effort. 3. a weakening (of metal) caused by long-continued use or strain. 4. *Mil.* fatigue duty. 5. **fatigues,** *Mil.* work clothes. —*v.* 1. cause fatigue in; weary. 2. weaken by much use or strain. —*adj.* pertaining to fatigue. [< F, ult. < L *fatigare* tire] —**fa·tigue′less,** *adj.* —Syn. *n.* 1. lassitude, languor, exhaustion. *-v.* 1. tire, exhaust.

fatigue duty, *Mil.* nonmilitary work done by soldiers, as cleaning up the camp, etc.

Fa·ti·ma (fə·tē′mə; fat′i·mə), *n.* 606?-632 A.D., only daughter of Mohammed.

fat·ling (fat′ling), *n.* calf, lamb, kid, or pig fattened to be killed for food.

fat·ten (fat′ən), *v.* make fat; become fat. —**fat′ten·er,** *n.*

fat·tish (fat′ish), *adj.* somewhat fat. —**fat′tish·ness,** *n.*

fat·ty (fat′i), *adj.*, **-ti·er, -ti·est.** 1. of fat; containing fat. 2. like fat; oily; greasy. —**fat′ti·ly,** *adv.* —**fat′ti·ness,** *n.*

fa·tu·i·ty (fə·tū′ə·ti; -tū′-), *n.*, *pl.* **-ties.** self-satisfied stupidity; silliness.

fat·u·ous (fach′ù·əs), *adj.* 1. stupid but self-satisfied; foolish; silly. 2. unreal; illusory. [< L *fatuus* foolish] —**fat′u·ous·ly,** *adv.* —**fat′u·ous·ness,** *n.*

fau·ces (fô′sēz), *n.pl. Anat.* cavity at the back of the mouth, leading into the pharynx. [< L] —**fau·cal** (fô′kəl), **fau·cial** (fô′shəl), *adj.*

fau·cet (fô′sit), *n.* device containing a valve for controlling the flow of water or other liquid from a pipe, tank, barrel, etc. [< F *fausset* < *fausser* bore through]

fault (fôlt), *n.* 1. something that is not as it should be. 2. mistake. 3. cause for blame. 4. *Geol.* a break in a rock or vein with part pushed up or down. 5. failure to serve the ball into the right place in tennis and similar games. 6. **at fault,** a. deserving blame; wrong. b. puzzled; perplexed. 7. **find fault,** pick out faults; complain. 8. **find fault with,** object to; criticize. 9. **in fault,** deserving blame; wrong. 10. **to a fault,** too much; very. —*v. Geol.* suffer or cause a fault. [< OF *faute,* ult. < L *fallere* deceive] —Syn. *n.* 1. defect, flaw, imperfection. 2. error, slip, lapse.

fault·find·ing (fôlt′fīn′ding), *n.*, *adj.* finding fault; complaining; pointing out faults. —**fault′find′er,** *n.*

fault·less (fôlt′lis), *adj.* without a single fault; free from blemish or error; perfect. —**fault′less·ly,** *adv.* —**fault′less·ness,** *n.*

fault·y (fôl′ti), *adj.*, **fault·i·er, fault·i·est.** 1. having faults; containing blemishes or errors; wrong; imperfect. 2. blamable. —**fault′i·ly,** *adv.* —**fault′i·ness,** *n.* —Syn. 1. defective, incomplete. 2. culpable, reprehensible.

faun (fôn), *n. Roman Myth.* deity that helped

farmers and shepherds, represented as looking like a man, but with the ears, horns, tail, and sometimes the legs, of a goat. [< L *Faunus* a pastoral deity]

fau·na (fô′nə), *n.* animals of a given region or time. [< NL, orig. (in LL) name of a rural goddess]

Faun

Faust (foust), *n.* man who sold his soul to the devil in return for having everything that he wanted on earth.

faux pas (fō′ pä′), *pl.* faux pas (fō′ päz′), slip in speech, conduct, manners, etc.; breach of etiquette; blunder. [< F]

fa·vor, *esp. Brit.* **fa·vour** (fā′vər), *n.* 1. kindness. 2. liking; approval. 3. condition of being liked or approved: *in favor, out of favor.* 4. indulgence. 5. pardon. 6. permission. 7. more than fair treatment; too great kindness. 8. gift; token. 9. in favor of, a. on the side of; supporting. b. to the advantage of; helping. c. to be paid to: *write a check in favor of the bank.* —*v.* 1. show kindness to. 2. like; approve. 3. give more than fair treatment to. 4. be on the side of; support. 5. be to the advantage of; help. 6. treat gently: *the dog favors his sore foot.* 7. look like: *the girl favors her mother.* [< OF < L, < *favere* show kindness to] —fa′vored, *esp. Brit.* fa′voured, *adj.* —fa′vor·er, *esp. Brit.* fa′vour·er, *n.* —fa′vor·ing·ly, *esp. Brit.* fa′vour·ing·ly, *adv.* —Syn. *n.* 2. good will, grace, countenance, patronage. —*v.* 1. patronize, befriend.

fa·vor·a·ble, *esp. Brit.* **fa·vour·a·ble** (fā′vər·ə·bəl; fāv′rə-), *adj.* 1. favoring; approving. 2. being to one's advantage; helping: *a favorable wind.* 3. granting what is desired. 4. boding well; promising. —fa′vor·a·ble·ness, *esp. Brit.* fa′vour·a·ble·ness, *n.* —fa′vor·a·bly, *esp. Brit.* fa′vour·a·bly, *adv.* —Syn. 1. well-disposed, commendatory, friendly. 2. advantageous, helpful.

fa·vor·ite, *esp. Brit.* **fa·vour·ite** (fā′vər·it; fāv′rit), *adj.* liked better than others; liked very much. —*n.* 1. one liked better than others; person or thing liked very much. 2. person treated with special favor. 3. one expected to win a contest.

fa·vor·it·ism, *esp. Brit.* **fa·vour·it·ism** (fā′vər·ə·tiz′əm; fāv′rə-), *n.* 1. a favoring of one or some more than others; having favorites. 2. state of being a favorite.

fawn¹ (fôn), *n.* 1. deer less than a year old. 2. a light, yellowish brown. —*adj.* light yellowish-brown. [< OF *faon,* ult. < L *fetus* fetus]

fawn² (fôn), *v.* 1. cringe and bow; act slavishly. 2. (of dogs, etc.) show fondness by crouching, wagging the tail, licking the hand, etc. [OE *fagnian* < *fægen* fain] —fawn′er, *n.* —fawn′ing·ly, *adv.* —Syn. 1. shrink, cower, truckle.

fay (fā), *n.* fairy. [< OF, ult. < L *fatum* FATE]

faze (fāz), *v.,* fazed, faz·ing. *U.S. Colloq.* disturb; worry; bother. [var. of *feeze,* OE *fēsian* drive] ▷ Faze is a word which has worked its way from dialect to good American colloquial and informal usage. It is almost always used negatively (*the rebuke did not faze him*). Do not confuse this word with *phase,* meaning "aspect."

FBI, *Am.* Federal Bureau of Investigation.

F.C.C., FCC, Federal Communications Commission.

F clef, the bass clef in music.

Fe, *Chem.* iron. [< L *ferrum*]

fe·al·ty (fē′əl·ti), *n., pl.* -ties. 1. loyalty and duty owed by a vassal to his feudal lord. 2. loyalty; faithfulness; allegiance. [< OF < L *fidelitas.* Doublet of FIDELITY.]

fear (fir), *n.* 1. a being afraid; feeling that danger or evil is near; dread. 2. cause for fear; danger: *there is no fear of our losing.* 3. an uneasy feeling; anxious thought. 4. awe; reverence. 5. **for fear of** (a thing), in order to prevent (that thing) from occurring. 6. **without fear or favor,** impartially; justly. —*v.* 1. feel fear. 2. feel fear of. 3. have an uneasy feeling or anxious thought; feel concern. 4. have awe or reverence for. [OE *fǣr* peril] —fear′er, *n.* —fear′less, *adj.* —fear′-

less·ly, *adv.* —fear′less·ness, *n.* —Syn. *n.* 1. terror, fright, alarm. —*v.* 2. dread, apprehend.

fear·ful (fir′fəl), *adj.* 1. causing fear; terrible; dreadful. 2. full of fear; afraid. 3. showing fear; caused by fear. 4. *Colloq.* very bad, unpleasant, ugly, etc. —fear′ful·ly, *adv.* —fear′ful·ness, *n.* —Syn. 1. awful, frightful, horrible, appalling, dire. 2. frightened, alarmed.

fear·some (fir′səm), *adj.* 1. causing fear; frightful. 2. timid; afraid. —fear′some·ly, *adv.* —fear′some·ness, *n.*

fea·si·ble (fē′zə·bəl), *adj.* 1. capable of being done or carried out easily. 2. likely; probable. 3. suitable; convenient. [< OF *faisable,* ult. < L *facere* do] —fea′si·bil′i·ty, fea′si·ble·ness, *n.* —fea′si·bly, *adv.*

feast (fēst), *n.* 1. an elaborate meal prepared for some special occasion and for a number of guests. 2. an unusually delicious or abundant meal. 3. thing that gives pleasure or joy. 4. a religious festival or celebration. —*v.* 1. have a feast. 2. provide with a feast. 3. give pleasure or joy to. [< OF < L *festa* festal ceremonies] —feast′er, *n.* —Syn. *n.* 1. banquet.

feat (fēt), *n.* a great or unusual deed; act showing great skill, strength, etc. [< OF < L *factum* (thing) done. Doublet of FACT.] —Syn. achievement, exploit, stunt.

feath·er (feth′ər), *n.* 1. one of the light, thin growths that cover a bird's skin. 2. something like a feather in shape or lightness. 3. feather in one's cap, thing to be proud of. 4. in fine, good, or high feather, in good health, high spirits, etc. —*v.* 1. supply or cover with feathers. 2. grow like feathers. 3. move like feathers. 4. join by a tongue and groove. 5. turn the edge of a blade in the direction of movement. 6. feather one's nest, take advantage of chances to get rich. [OE *fether*] —feath′ered, *adj.* —feath′er·less, *adj.* —feath′er·like′, *adj.*

feath·er-bed·ding (feth′ər·bed′ing), *n. Am.* the practice on the part of unions of forcing employers to hire more men than are needed for a particular job.

feath·er·brain (feth′ər·brān′), *n.* a silly, foolish, weak-minded person. —feath′er-brained′, *adj.*

feath·er·edge (feth′ər·ej′), *n.* a very thin edge. —feath′er·edged′, *adj.*

feath·er·weight (feth′ər·wāt′), *n.* 1. a very light thing or person. 2. boxer who weighs less than 126 pounds and more than 118 pounds. —*adj.* very light.

feath·er·y (feth′ər·i), *adj.* 1. having feathers; covered with feathers. 2. like feathers. 3. light; flimsy. —feath′er·i·ness, *n.*

fea·ture (fē′chər), *n., v.,* -tured, -tur·ing. —*n.* 1. part of the face. The nose, mouth, chin, and forehead are features. 2. features, the face. 3. a distinct part or quality; thing that stands out and attracts attention. 4. a long motion picture. 5. a special article, comic strip, etc., in a newspaper. —*v.* 1. be a feature of. 2. make a feature of. 3. show the features of. [< OF < L *factura* < *facere* do] —fea′ture·less, *adj.* —Syn. *n.* 3. characteristic, attribute, property, mark, trait.

fea·tured (fē′chərd), *adj.* 1. made a feature of; given prominence to. 2. having a certain kind of features: *hard-featured.*

Feb., February.

feb·ri·fuge (feb′rə·fūj), *adj.* that cures or lessens fever. —*n.* medicine to reduce fever. [< F < L, < *febris* fever + *fugare* drive away] —fe·brif·u·gal (fē·brif′yə·gəl; feb′rə·fū′gəl), *adj.*

fe·brile (fē′brəl; feb′rəl), *adj.* 1. of fever; feverish. 2. caused by fever. [< Med.L *febrilis.* See FEVER.]

Feb·ru·ar·y (feb′rü·er′i; feb′yu̇-), *n., pl.* -ar·ies. the second month of the year. It has 28 days except in leap years, when it has 29. [< L, < *februa,* pl., the feast of purification celebrated on Feb. 15]

fe·ces (fē′sēz), *n.pl.* 1. waste matter discharged from the intestines. 2. dregs; sediment. Also, faeces. [< L *faeces,* pl., dregs] —fe·cal (fē′kəl), *adj.*

āge, cāre, fär; ēqual, tėrm; īce; ōpen, ôrder; pu̇t, rüle, ūse; ŧɦ, then; ə=a in about.

feck·less (fek′lis), *adj.* 1. futile; ineffective. 2. weak; helpless. [< *feck* vigor, var. of *fect* < *effect*] —**feck′less·ly**, *adv.* —**feck′less·ness**, *n.*

fe·cund (fē′kənd; fek′ənd), *adj.* fruitful; productive; fertile. [< F < L *fecundus*] —**fe·cun·di·ty** (fi·kun′də·ti), *n.*

fed (fed), *v.* pt. and pp. of feed.

fed·er·al (fed′ər·əl; fed′rəl), *adj.* 1. formed by an agreement between groups establishing a central regulating organization. 2. of or having to do with the central government formed in this way. 3. Federal, a. of or having to do with the central government of the United States. b. supporting the Constitution. c. supporting the central government of the United States during the Civil War. —*n.* Federal, *Am.* supporter or soldier of the central government of the United States during the Civil War. [< L *foedus* compact] —**fed′er·al·ly**, *adv.*

Federal Bureau of Investigation, *Am.* bureau of the Department of Justice established to investigate Federal crimes and safeguard national security.

fed·er·al·ism (fed′ər·əl·iz′əm; fed′rəl–), *n.* 1. federal principles of government. 2. Federalism, principles of the Federalist Party in the United States.

fed·er·al·ist (fed′ər·əl·ist; fed′rəl–), *n.* 1. Federalist, *Am.* member of the Federalist Party in the United States. 2. *Am.* advocate of a federal union among the colonies during and after the War of Independence. 3. federalist, person who favors the federal principle of government. —*adj. Am.* of federalism or the Federalists. —**fed′er·al·is′tic**, *adj.*

Federalist Party, *Am.* a political party in the United States that favored the adoption of the Constitution and a strong central government. It existed from about 1791 to about 1816.

fed·er·al·ize (fed′ər·əl·īz; fed′rəl–), *v.*, –ized, –iz·ing. 1. unite into a federal union. 2. bring under control of the federal government. —**fed′er·al·i·za′tion**, *n.*

fed·er·ate (*v.* fed′ər·āt; *adj.* fed′ər·it, fed′rit), *v.*, –at·ed, –at·ing, *adj.* —*v.* form into a federation. —*adj.* federated. [< L *foederatus* leagued together. See FEDERAL.]

fed·er·a·tion (fed′ər·ā′shən), *n.* 1. formation of a political unity out of a number of separate states, etc. 2. union by agreement, often a union of states or nations. —**fed′er·a′tive**, *adj.* —**fed′er·a′tive·ly**, *adv.*

fe·do·ra (fi·dô′rə; –dō′–), *n. Am.* a man's soft felt hat with a curved brim.

fee (fē), *n., v.,* feed, fee·ing. —*n.* 1. sum of money asked or paid for a service or privilege; charge. Doctors and lawyers get fees for their services. 2. a present of money; tip. 3. right to keep and use land; fief. 4. *Law.* an inherited estate in land. 5. ownership. —*v.* give a fee to. [< AF *fieu* < Gmc.] —**Syn.** *n.* 1. pay, compensation, payment.

fee·ble (fē′bəl), *adj.,* –bler, –blest. weak; ineffective: *a feeble old man, a feeble mind, a feeble attempt.* [< OF < L *flebilis* lamentable < *flere* weep] —**fee′ble·ness**, *n.* —**fee′blish**, *adj.* —**fee′bly**, *adv.* —**Syn.** infirm, frail, sickly, doddering.

fee·ble-mind·ed (fē′bəl·mīn′did), *adj.* weak in mind; lacking normal intelligence. —**fee′ble·mind′ed·ly**, *adv.* —**fee′ble-mind′ed·ness**, *n.*

feed (fēd), *v.,* fed, feed·ing, *n.* —*v.* 1. give food to. 2. eat. 3. supply with material: *feed a machine.* 4. satisfy; gratify: *praise fed his vanity.* 5. nourish: *he fed his anger with thoughts of revenge.* —*n.* 1. food for animals; allowance of food for an animal. 2. *Am., Colloq.* meal for a person. 3. a supplying with material. 4. the material supplied. 5. part of a machine that supplies material. [OE *fēdan* < *fōda* food] —**feed′er**, *n.* —**Syn.** *v.* 5. sustain. –*n.* 1. fodder, provender, forage.

feel (fēl), *v.,* felt, feel·ing, *n.* —*v.* 1. touch: *feel this cloth.* 2. try to touch; try to find by touching: *feel in all your pockets.* 3. find out by touching: *feel how cold my hands are.* 4. be aware of: *feel the cool breeze.* 5. have the feeling of being; be: *she feels sure.* 6. give the feeling of

being; seem: *the air feels cold.* 7. have in one's mind; experience: *he feels joy.* 8. have pity or sympathy: *she feels for all who suffer.* 9. be influenced or affected by: *the ship feels her helm.* 10. think; believe; consider: *I feel that we shall win.* —*n.* 1. touch: *I like the feel of silk.* 2. a feeling: *a feel of frost in the air.* 3. the sense of touch. [OE *fēlan*] —**Syn.** *v.* 1. handle. 2. grope. 6. appear.

FEELERS
LEGS

feel·er (fēl′ər), *n.* 1. person or thing that feels. 2. *Zool.* a special part of an animal's body for touching, as an insect's antenna. 3. suggestion, remark, hint, question, etc., made to find out what others are thinking or planning.

feel·ing (fēl′ing), *n.* 1. act or condition of one that feels. 2. sense of touch. 3. a being conscious; awareness. 4. emotion. 5. pity; sympathy. 6. opinion; sentiment. 7. quality felt to belong to something. 8. impression made by a work of art. 9. emotional insight. 10. feelings, sympathies; susceptibilities: *hurt one's feelings.* —*adj.* 1. sensitive; emotional. 2. showing emotion. —**feel′ing·ly**, *adv.* —**Syn.** *n.* 3. sensation, impression. 4. passion.

feet (fēt), *n.* pl. of foot.

feign (fān), *v.* 1. put on a false appearance of; make believe; pretend. 2. make up to deceive; invent falsely: *feign an excuse.* [< OF *feindre* (*feign–*) < L *fingere* form] —**feigned**, *adj.* —**feign·ed·ly** (fān′id·li), *adv.* —**feign′er**, *n.* —**feign′ing·ly**, *adv.* —**Syn.** 1. assume, affect, simulate.

feint (fānt), *n.* 1. false appearance; pretense. 2. movement intended to deceive; pretended blow; sham attack. —*v.* make a pretended blow or sham attack. [< F, < *feindre* FEIGN]

feld·spar (feld′spär; fel′–), *n.* any of several crystalline minerals composed mostly of aluminum silicates. Also, felspar. [< *feld*– (< G *feldspat,* lit. field spar) + *spar*³] —**feld·spath·ic** (feld·spath′ik; fel–), *adj.*

fe·lic·i·tate (fə·lis′ə·tāt), *v.,* –tat·ed, –tat·ing. formally express good wishes to; congratulate. [< LL, < *felix* happy] —**fe·lic′i·ta′tion**, *n.*

fe·lic·i·tous (fə·lis′ə·təs), *adj.* 1. well chosen for the occasion; unusually appropriate. 2. having a gift for apt speech. —**fe·lic′i·tous·ly**, *adv.* —**fe·lic′i·tous·ness**, *n.*

fe·lic·i·ty (fə·lis′ə·ti), *n.,* pl. –ties. 1. happiness; bliss. 2. good fortune; blessing. 3. a pleasing aptness in expression; appropriateness; grace. 4. a happy turn of thought; well-chosen phrase.

fe·line (fē′līn), *adj.* 1. of or belonging to the cat family. 2. catlike; stealthy. —*n.* any animal belonging to the cat family, such as lions, tigers, leopards, and panthers. [< L *felis* cat] —**fe′line·ly**, *adv.* —**fe′line·ness, fe·lin·i·ty** (fi·lin′ə·ti), *n.*

fell¹ (fel), *v.* pt. of fall.

fell² (fel), *v.* 1. cause to fall; knock down. 2. cut down (a tree). 3. turn down and stitch one edge of (a seam) over the other. —*n.* 1. all the trees cut down in one season. 2. seam made by felling. [OE *fellan* < *feallan* fall] —**fell′a·ble,** *adj.* —**fell′er,** *n.*

fell³ (fel), *adj.* 1. cruel; fierce; terrible: *a fell blow.* 2. deadly; destructive: *a fell disease.* [< OF < VL *fello.* See FELON¹.] —**fell′ness,** *n.*

fell⁴ (fel), *n.* skin or hide of an animal. [OE; SPOKE akin to FILM]

fel·loe (fel′ō), *n.* the circular rim of a wheel into which the outer ends of the spokes are inserted. Also, felly. [var. of *felly*]

HUB
AXLE
SPOKE
RIM
FELLOE

fel·low (fel′ō), *n.* 1. man; boy. 2. *Colloq.* a young man courting a young woman; beau. 3. companion; comrade; associate. 4. *Colloq.* person. 5. one of the same class or rank; equal: *the world has not his fellow.* 6. the other one of a pair. 7. a graduate student who has a fellowship in a university or college. **8.** an honored member of a learned society. —*adj.* belonging to the same class; united by the same work, aims, etc.; being in the same or a like condition: *fellow citizens, fellow workers.* —*v.* produce an equal to; match. [< Scand. *fēlagi* partner (lit., fee-layer)] ▶ **Fellow** is colloquial and informal when used to mean "person"; formal in sense of "associate." Most commonly used in writing as adjective: *his fellow sufferers, a fellow feeling.*

fel·low·ship (fel′ō·ship), *n., v.,* –shiped, –ship·ing; *esp. Brit.* –shipped, –ship·ping. —*n.* **1.** condition or relation of being a fellow. **2.** companionship. **3.** a taking part with others; sharing. **4.** group of people having similar tastes, interests, etc.; brotherhood. **5.** position or sum of money given to a graduate student in a university or college to enable him to go on with his studies. —*v.* **1.** admit to fellowship. **2.** join in fellowship. —Syn. *n.* **2.** comradeship, friendship.

fellow traveler, one sympathizing with a political movement or party but who is a non-member.

fel·ly (fel′i), *n., pl.* –lies. felloe. [OE *felg*]

fel·on[1] (fel′ən), *n. Law.* person who has committed a serious crime. —*adj.* wicked; cruel. [< OF, ult. < L *fellare* suck (obscene)]

fel·on[2] (fel′ən), *n. Pathol.* a very painful infection on a finger or toe, usually near the nail.

fe·lo·ni·ous (fə·lō′ni·əs), *adj.* **1.** *Law.* that is a felony; criminal. **2.** very wicked; villainous. —fe·lo′ni·ous·ly, *adv.* —fe·lo′ni·ous·ness, *n.*

fel·o·ny (fel′ə·ni), *n., pl.* –nies. *Law.* crime more serious than a misdemeanor. Murder and burglary are felonies.

fel·spar (fel′spär′), *n.* feldspar.

felt[1] (felt), *v.* pt. and pp. of feel.

felt[2] (felt), *n.* cloth made by rolling and pressing together wool, hair, or fur, used to make hats, slippers, etc. —*adj.* made of felt. —*v.* **1.** make into felt. **2.** cover with felt. [OE]

fem., feminine.

fe·male (fē′māl), *n.* **1.** woman or girl. **2.** animal belonging to the sex that brings forth young. **3.** *Bot.* plant having a pistil and no stamens. —*adj.* **1.** of or pertaining to women or girls. **2.** belonging to the sex that brings forth young. **3.** *Bot.* having pistils. **4.** designating some part of a machine, connection, etc., into which a corresponding part fits. [< OF < L < *femella,* dim. of *femina* woman; form infl. by *male*] —fe·mal·i·ty (fi·mal′ə·ti), *n.* ▶ **female.** Usage now restricts *female* to designations of sex, usually in scientific contexts, leaving English without a single word for female-human-being-regardless-of-age.

fem·i·nine (fem′ə·nin), *adj.* **1.** of women or girls. **2.** like a woman; womanly. **3.** like that of a woman; not suited to a man. **4.** of or belonging to the female sex. **5.** *Gram.* of the gender to which names of females belong. *Actress, queen,* and *cow* are feminine nouns. —*n. Gram.* a. the feminine gender. b. word or form in the feminine gender. [< OF < L < *femina* woman] —fem′i·nine·ly, *adv.* —fem·i·nin·i·ty (fem′ə·nin′ə·ti), fem′i·nine·ness, *n.*

fem·i·nism (fem′ə·niz·əm), *n.* **1.** doctrine that favors more rights and activities for women. **2.** feminine nature or character. —fem′i·nist, *n.* —fem′i·nis′tic, *adj.*

femme fa·tale (fam fä·täl′), *French.* a dangerously fascinating or alluring woman; siren.

fe·mur (fē′mər), *n., pl.* fe·murs, fem·o·ra (fem′ə·rə). *Anat.* the thighbone. [< L, thigh] —fem·o·ral (fem′ə·rəl), *adj.*

fen (fen), *n. Brit.* marsh; swamp; bog. [OE *fenn*]

fence (fens), *n., v.,* fenced, fenc·ing. —*n.* **1.** railing, wall, or other means of enclosing a yard, garden, field, farm, etc., to show where it ends or to keep people or animals out or in. **2.** skill or adroitness in argument or repartee. **3.** person who buys and sells stolen goods. **4.** place where stolen goods are bought and sold. **5. on the fence,** *Am., Colloq.* not having made up one's mind which side to take; doubtful; hesitating.

—*v.* **1.** put a fence around; enclose. **2.** fight with swords or foils. **3.** parry; evade. **4.** defend. [var. of *defence*] —fence′less, *adj.* —fence′less·ness, *n.* —fence′like′, *adj.* —fenc′er, *n.*

fenc·ing (fen′sing), *n.* **1.** art of fighting with swords or foils. **2.** *Am.* material for fences.

fend (fend), *v.* **1.** defend; resist. **2. fend for oneself,** *Colloq.* provide for oneself; get along by one's own efforts. [var. of *defend*]

fend·er (fen′dər), *n.* **1.** anything that keeps or wards something off. **2.** *Am.* guard or protection over the wheel of an automobile, motorcycle, etc.; mudguard. **3.** *Am.* a metal frame on the front of a locomotive, streetcar, etc., to catch or thrust aside anything in the way; cowcatcher. **4.** *Am.* a metal guard, frame, or screen in front of a fireplace to keep hot coals and sparks from the room. [var. of *defender*]

Fe·ni·an (fē′ni·ən; fēn′yən), *Am.* —*n.* member of an Irish secret organization founded in the United States about 1858 for the purpose of overthrowing English rule in Ireland. —*adj.* of or having to do with the Fenians. —Fe′ni·an·ism, *n.*

fen·nel (fen′əl), *n. Bot.* a tall plant with yellow flowers, used in medicine and cooking. [< VL *fenuclum,* ult. < L *fenum* hay]

fen·ny (fen′i), *adj. Brit.* marshy; swampy.

fe·off (n. fēf; v. fef, fēf), *n.* fief. —*v.* invest with a fief. —feoff·ment (fef′mənt; fēf′–), *n.* —feoff′or, feoff′fer, *n.*

FEPC, Fair Employment Practices Committee.

fe·ral (fir′əl), *adj.* **1.** wild; untamed. **2.** brutal; savage. [< L *fera* beast]

fer-de-lance (fer·də·läns′), *n.* a large, poisonous snake of tropical America. [< F, iron (tip) of a lance]

Fer·di·nand V of Castile (fer′də·nand), 1452–1516, Spanish king 1474–1516. His queen, Isabella, encouraged Christopher Columbus in his voyages.

fer·ment (*v.* fər·ment′; *n.* fer′ment), *v.* **1.** undergo a gradual chemical change, becoming sour or alcoholic and giving off bubbles of gas. **2.** cause this chemical change in. **3.** cause unrest in; excite; agitate. **4.** be excited; seethe with agitation or unrest. —*n.* **1.** substance causing fermentation: *yeast is a ferment.* **2.** excitement; agitation; unrest: *national ferment.* [< L *fermentum* < *fervere* boil] —ferment′a·ble, *adj.*

fer·men·ta·tion (fer′men·tā′shən), *n.* **1.** act or process of fermenting. **2.** excitement; agitation; unrest. **3.** *Chem.* a change, as becoming sour or alcoholic and giving off bubbles of gas, caused by a ferment.

Fer·mi (fer′mē), *n.* Enrico, 1901–1954, American physicist, born in Italy, director of first nuclear reactor.

fer·mi·um (fer′mi·əm), *n.* a rare, radioactive, artificial element, Fm, produced as a by-product of nuclear fission. [named for Enrico *Fermi*]

fern (fern), *n. Bot.* plant that has roots, stems, and leaves, but no flowers, and reproduces by spores instead of seeds. [OE *fearn*] —fern′like′, *adj.* —fern′y, *adj.*

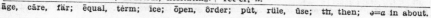

Fern

fern·er·y (fer′nər·i), *n., pl.* –er·ies. **1.** place where ferns grow. **2.** container in which ferns are grown for ornament.

fe·ro·cious (fə·rō′shəs), *adj.* savagely cruel; fierce. [< L, < *ferox* fierce] —fe·ro′cious·ly, *adv.* —fe·roc·i·ty (fə·ros′ə·ti), fe·ro′cious·ness, *n.* —Syn. ruthless, brutal, murderous.

fer·ret (fer′it), *n.* a white or yellowish-white weasel used for killing rats, hunting rabbits, etc. —*v.* **1.** hunt with ferrets. **2.** hunt; search. [< OF *fuiret,* ult. < L *fur* thief] —fer′ret·er, *n.*

Ferret (total length ab. 1½ ft.)

fer·ric (fer'ik), *adj. Chem.* a. of or containing iron. b. containing trivalent iron. [< L *ferrum* iron]

Fer·ris wheel (fer'is), *Am.* a large, revolving wheel with seats hanging from its rim, used in carnivals, amusement parks, etc. [for G. W. G. Ferris, its inventor]

fer·rous (fer'əs), *adj. Chem.* a. of or containing iron. b. containing divalent iron.

fer·ru·gi·nous (fə·rü'jə·nəs), *adj.* 1. of or containing iron; like that of iron. 2. reddish-brown like rust. [< L, < *ferrugo* iron rust < *ferrum* iron]

fer·rule (fer'əl; -ül), *n., v.,* -ruled, -rul·ing. —*n.* 1. a metal ring or cap put around the end of a cane, umbrella, etc. 2. a metal ring or short tube. —*v.* supply with a ferrule. Also, **ferule**. [< OF, ult. < L *viriola*, dim. of *viriae* bracelets]

fer·ry (fer'i), *n., pl.* -ries, *v.,* -ried, -ry·ing. —*n.* 1. place where boats carry people and goods across a river or narrow stretch of water. 2. the boat used; ferryboat. 3. system for flying airplanes to a destination for delivery. [< v.] —*v.* 1. carry (people and goods) back and forth across a river or narrow stretch of water. 2. go across in a ferryboat. 3. carry back and forth across a wide stretch of water in an airplane. 4. fly an airplane to a destination for delivery. [OE *ferian* < *fœr* fare]

fer·ry·boat (fer'i·bōt'), *n.* boat used for ferrying.

fer·ry·man (fer'i·mən), *n., pl.* -men. man who owns or has charge of a ferry.

fer·tile (fėr'təl), *adj.* 1. able to produce much; rich in things that aid growth, development, etc. 2. *Obs.* abundant. 3. capable of reproduction; able to produce seeds, fruit, young, etc. 4. *Biol.* capable of developing into a new individual; fertilized. [< L *fertilis* < *ferre* bear] —**fer'tile·ly,** *adv.* —**fer'tile·ness,** *n.*

fer·til·i·ty (fėr·til'ə·ti), *n.* a being fertile.

fer·til·ize (fėr'tə·līz), *v.,* -lized, -liz·ing. 1. make fertile; make able to produce much. 2. put fertilizer on. 3. *Biol.* unite with (an egg cell) in fertilization; impregnate. —**fer'ti·liz'a·ble,** *adj.* —**fer'ti·li·za'tion,** *n.*

fer·til·iz·er (fėr'tə·līz'ər), *n.* substance put on land to make it able to produce more, as manure.

fer·ule[1] (fer'əl; -ül), *n., v.,* -uled, -ul·ing. —*n.* stick or ruler used for punishing children by striking them on the hand. —*v.* punish with a stick or ruler. [< L *ferula* rod]

fer·ule[2] (fer'əl; -ül), *n., v.,* -uled, -ul·ing. ferrule.

fer·vent (fėr'vənt), *adj.* 1. showing warmth of feeling; very earnest. 2. hot; glowing. [< F < L *fervens* boiling] —**fer'ven·cy, fer'vent·ness,** *n.* —**fer'vent·ly,** *adv.* —**Syn.** 1. ardent, zealous, passionate.

fer·vid (fėr'vid), *adj.* 1. showing great warmth of feeling; intensely emotional. 2. intensely hot. [< L, < *fervere* boil] —**fer'vid·ly,** *adv.* —**fer'vid·ness,** *n.*

fer·vor, *esp. Brit.* **fer·vour** (fėr'vər), *n.* 1. great warmth of feeling; intense emotion. 2. intense heat. [< OF < L. See FERVENT.] —**Syn.** 1. zeal, ardor.

fes·cue (fes'kū), *n.* a tough grass used for pasture. [< OF, ult. < L *festuca*]

fess, fesse (fes), *n.* in heraldry, a wide, horizontal band across the middle of a shield. [< OF < L *fascia* band]

fes·tal (fes'təl), *adj.* of a feast, festival, or holiday; gay; joyous; festive. [< OF < LL < L *festum* feast] —**fes'tal·ly,** *adv.*

fes·ter (fes'tər), *v.* 1. form pus. 2. cause pus to form. 3. cause soreness or pain; rankle. 4. decay; rot. [< n.] —*n.* sore that forms pus; small ulcer. [< OF < L *fistula* pipe, ulcer]

fes·ti·val (fes'tə·vəl), *n.* 1. day or special time of rejoicing or feasting, often in memory of some great happening. 2. celebration; entertainment: *a music festival.* 3. merrymaking; revelry. —*adj.* having to do with a festival. [< Med.L, ult. < L *festum* feast]

fes·tive (fes'tiv), *adj.* of or for a feast, festival, or holiday; joyous; merry. —**fes'tive·ly,** *adv.* —**fes'tive·ness,** *n.*

fes·tiv·i·ty (fes·tiv'ə·ti), *n., pl.* -ties. 1. festive activity; thing done to celebrate. 2. gaiety; merriment. 3. festivities, festive proceedings.

fes·toon (fes·tün'), *n.* a hanging curve of flowers, leaves, ribbons, etc. —*v.* 1. decorate with festoons. 2. form into festoons; hang in curves. [< F < Ital. *festone* < *festa* festival, feast]

Festoon

fe·tal (fē'təl), *adj.* 1. of a fetus. 2. like that of a fetus. Also, foetal.

fetch (fech), *v.* 1. go and get; bring. 2. cause to come; succeed in bringing. 3. be sold for. 4. *Colloq.* attract; charm. 5. *Colloq.* hit; strike. 6. give (a groan, sigh, etc.). 7. take a course (said chiefly of ships); move; go. —*n.* act of fetching. [OE *feccan*] —**fetch'er,** *n.*

fetch·ing (fech'ing), *adj. Colloq.* attractive; charming. —**fetch'ing·ly,** *adv.*

fete, fête (fāt), *n., v.,* fet·ed, fet·ing; fêt·ed, fêt·ing. —*n.* festival; entertainment; party. —*v.* honor with a fete; entertain: *the engaged couple were feted by their friends.* [< F, feast]

fet·id (fet'id; fē'tid), *adj.* smelling very bad; stinking. [< L *foetidus* < *foetere* to smell] —**fet'id·ly,** *adv.* —**fet'id·ness, fe·tid'i·ty,** *n.*

fe·tish, fe·tich (fē'tish; fet'ish), *n.* 1. any material thing supposed to have magic power. 2. anything regarded with unreasoning reverence or devotion. [< F < Pg. *feitiço* charm < L *facticius* artificial] —**fe'tish·like', fe'tich·like',** *adj.*

fe·tish·ism, fe·tich·ism (fē'tish·iz·əm; fet'ish-), *n.* 1. belief in fetishes; worship of fetishes. 2. *Psychiatry.* an abnormal attachment of erotic feeling to some inanimate object. —**fe'tish·ist, fe'tich·ist,** *n.* —**fe'tish·is'tic, fe'tich·is'tic,** *adj.*

fet·lock (fet'lok), *n.* 1. tuft of hair above a horse's hoof on the back part of the leg. See the picture under cannon bone. 2. part of a horse's leg where this tuft grows. [ME *fetlok*]

fet·ter (fet'ər), *n.* 1. chain or shackle for the feet to prevent escape. 2. Usually, fetters. anything that shackles or binds; restraint. —*v.* 1. bind with fetters; chain the feet of. 2. bind; restrain. [OE *feter*; akin to FOOT] —**Syn.** *v.* 2. confine, hamper, impede.

fet·tle (fet'əl), *n.* condition; trim: *the horse is in fine fettle.* [? < ME *fettel(en)* gird up, < OE *fetel* belt]

fe·tus (fē'təs), *n.* an animal embryo during the later stages of its development. Also, foetus. [< L]

feud[1] (fūd), *n.* 1. a long and deadly quarrel between families, often passed down from generation to generation. 2. bitter hatred between two persons, groups, etc. 3. quarrel. [var. of ME *fede* < OF < OHG *fehida* enmity] —**feu'dal,** *adj.* —**Syn.** 2. hostility, enmity.

feud[2] (fūd), *n.* a feudal estate; fief. [< Med.L *feudum* < Gmc.]

feu·dal (fū'dəl), *adj.* 1. of or having to do with feudalism. 2. of or having to do with feuds or fiefs. [< Med.L *feudalis*. See FEUD[2].] —**feu'dal·ly,** *adv.*

feu·dal·ism (fū'dəl·iz·əm), *n.* the feudal system or its principles and practices. —**feu'dal·ist,** *n.* —**feu'dal·is'tic,** *adj.*

feudal system, the social, economic, and political system of Europe in the Middle Ages, under which vassals held land on condition of giving military and other services to the lord owning it in return for the protection and the use of the land.

feu·da·to·ry (fū'də·tô'ri; -tō'-), *adj., n., pl.* -ries. —*adj.* 1. owing feudal services to a lord. 2. holding or held as a feudal estate or fief. —*n.* 1. a feudal vassal: *the duke summoned his feudatories to aid him in war.* 2. a feudal estate; fief. **feud·ist** (fūd'ist), *n. Am.* person engaging in a feud.

fe·ver (fē'vər), *n.* 1. an unhealthy condition of

the body in which the temperature is higher than normal. 2. any of various diseases that cause fever, such as scarlet fever and typhoid fever. 3. an excited, restless condition. —v. 1. affect with fever; heat. 2. become feverish. [< L *febris*] —**fe′vered**, *adj.* —**fe′ver·less**, *adj.*

fe·ver·few (fē′vər·fū), *n.* a perennial plant of the aster family with small, white, daisylike flowers. [< LL *febrifug(i)a* FEBRIFUGE]

fe·ver·ish (fē′vər·ish), *adj.* 1. having fever. 2. having a slight degree of fever. 3. causing fever. 4. infested with fever. 5. excited; restless. —**fe′ver·ish·ly**, *adv.* —**fe′ver·ish·ness**, *n.*

fe·ver·ous (fē′vər·əs), *adj.* feverish. —**fe′ver·ous·ly**, *adv.*

fe·ver·root (fē′vər·rüt′; -rút′), *n. Am.* a coarse plant sometimes used for medicine.

fever sore, a cold sore.

few (fū), *adj.* not many. —*n.* 1. a small number. 2. the few, the minority. 3. quite a few, *Colloq.* a good many. [OE *fēawe*] —**few′ness**, *n.* ≻ **fewer**, **less.** Fewer refers only to number and things that are counted: *Fewer cars were on the road. There were fewer than sixty present.* In formal usage *less* refers only to amount or quantity and things measured: *There was a good deal less tardiness in the second term* [amount]. *There was even less hay than the summer before.* In general usage it refers also to number: *In the making of the present book no less than 100,000 words were critically examined.*

fez (fez), *n., pl.* **fez·zes.** a felt cap, usually red, ornamented with a long, black tassel, formerly worn by Turkish men. [< Turk.; named after *Fez*, Morocco]

ff., and the following; and what follows.

fi·an·cé (fē′än·sā′; fē′än·sā), *n.* man engaged to be married. [< F, betrothed] ≻ **fiancé, fiancée.** About a century ago the simple English *betrothed* was replaced by the French word (probably by "society" journalists), and now we are cursed not only with accent marks but with separate forms for the man (*fiancé*) and the woman (*fiancée*). Pronunciation for both is fē′än·sā′, with a strong informal tendency to fē′än·sā. The plurals are *fiancés, fiancées.* In newspapers and much informal writing the accent mark is dropped and probably it will soon disappear generally.

fi·an·cée (fē′än·sā′; fē′än·sā), *n.* woman engaged to be married. [< F]

fi·as·co (fi·as′kō), *n., pl.* **-cos, -coes.** failure; breakdown. [< F < Ital., flask]

fi·at (fī′ət; -at), *n.* 1. an authoritative order or command; decree. 2. sanction. [< L, let it be done]

fiat money, *Am.* paper currency made legal tender by the decree of the government, but not based on or convertible into coin.

fib (fib), *n., v.,* **fibbed, fib·bing.** lie about some small matter. [? < *fibble-fable* < *fable*] —**fib′ber**, *n.*

fi·ber, **fi·bre** (fī′bər), *n.* 1. a threadlike part; thread: *a muscle is made up of many fibers.* 2. substance made up of threads or threadlike parts. Hemp fiber can be spun into rope or woven into a coarse cloth. 3. texture: *cloth of coarse fiber.* 4. character; nature. 5. a threadlike root of a plant. [< F < L *fibra*]

fi·ber·board (fī′bər·bôrd′; -bōrd′), *n.* a building material made by compressing fibers, esp. of wood, into flat sheets.

Fi·ber·glas (fī′bər·glas′; -gläs′), *n. Trademark.* a very fine, flexible glass fiber that can be made into insulating material or even into fabrics.

fi·bril (fī′brəl), *n.* a small fiber.

fi·brin (fī′brən), *n.* 1. a tough, elastic, yellowish protein formed when blood clots. 2. *Bot.* gluten in plants. —**fi·brin·ous** (fī′brə·nəs), *adj.*

fi·broid (fī′broid), *adj.* composed of fibers. —*n. Pathol.* tumor composed of fibers or fibrous tissue.

fi·brous (fī′brəs), *adj.* composed of fibers; having fibers; like fiber.

fib·u·la (fib′yə·lə), *n., pl.* **-lae** (-lē), **-las.** 1. *Anat.* the outer and thinner of the two bones in the human lower leg. It extends from knee to ankle. 2. *Zool.* a similar bone in the hind leg of animals. [< L, clasp, brooch] —**fib′u·lar**, *adj.*

fich·u (fish′ū), *n.* a three-cornered piece of muslin, lace, or other soft material worn by women about the neck, with the ends drawn together or crossed on the breast. [< F]

Fichu

fick·le (fik′əl), *adj.* likely to change without reason; changing; not constant. [OE *ficol*] —**Syn.** unstable, unsteady. —**Ant.** constant, steadfast, unchanging.

fic·tion (fik′shən), *n.* 1. novels, short stories, and other prose writings that tell about imaginary people and happenings. 2. what is imagined or made up. 3. an imaginary account or statement; made-up story. 4. an inventing of imaginary accounts, stories, etc. 5. thing acted upon as a fact, in spite of its possible falsity. It is a legal fiction that a corporation is a person. [< L *fictio < fingere* to form, fashion] —**fic′tion·al**, *adj.* —**fic′tion·al·ly**, *adv.*

fic·ti·tious (fik·tish′əs), *adj.* 1. not real; imaginary; made-up: *characters in novels are usually fictitious.* 2. assumed in order to deceive; false: *the criminal used a fictitious name.* —**fic·ti′tious·ly**, *adv.* —**fic·ti′tious·ness**, *n.* —**Syn.** 2. counterfeit, sham, feigned.

fid·dle (fid′əl), *n., v.,* **-dled, -dling.** —*n.* 1. *Colloq.* violin. 2. **play second fiddle**, take a secondary part. —*v.* 1. *Colloq.* play on a violin. 2. make aimless movements; play nervously. 3. trifle: *he fiddled away the whole day doing absolutely nothing.* [OE *fithele* (recorded in *fithelere* fiddler); prob. akin to *viol*] —**fid′dler**, *n.*

fid·dle·stick (fid′əl·stik′), *n.* 1. a violin bow. 2. a mere nothing; trifle.

fid·dle·sticks (fid′əl·stiks′), *interj.* nonsense! rubbish!

fi·del·i·ty (fi·del′ə·ti; fə-), *n., pl.* **-ties.** 1. faithfulness to a trust or vow; steadfast faithfulness. 2. accuracy; exactness. [< L *fidelitas*, ult. < *fides* faith. Doublet of FEALTY.] —**Syn.** 1. constancy, loyalty.

fidg·et (fij′it), *v.* 1. move about restlessly; be uneasy: *a child fidgets if he has to sit still a long time.* 2. make uneasy. —*n.* 1. condition of being restless or uneasy. 2. person who moves about restlessly. 3. **the fidgets**, fit of restlessness or uneasiness. [< obs. *fidge* move restlessly] —**fidg′et·y**, *adj.* —**fidg′et·i·ness**, *n.*

fi·du·ci·ar·y (fi·dū′shi·er′i; -dū′-), *adj., n., pl.* **-ar·ies.** —*adj.* 1. held in trust: *fiduciary estates.* 2. *Law.* holding in trust. A fiduciary possessor is legally responsible for what belongs to another. 3. of a trustee; of trust and confidence. 4. depending upon public trust and confidence for its value. Paper money that cannot be redeemed in gold or silver is fiduciary currency. —*n. Law.* trustee. [< L, < *fiducia* trust]

fie (fī), *interj.* for shame! shame! [< OF]

fief (fēf), *n.* 1. piece of land held on condition of giving military and other services to the lord owning it in return for protection and the use of the land; feudal estate. 2. the land or territory so held. Also, **feoff.** [< F < Gmc.]

field (fēld), *n.* 1. land with few or no trees. 2. piece of land used for crops or pasture. 3. piece of land used for some special purpose, esp. one used for sports or contests. 4. land yielding some product: *a coal field.* 5. place where a battle is or has been fought. 6. battle. 7. region where military or other operations are carried on. 8. a flat space; broad surface: *a field of ice.* 9. surface on which something is pictured or painted: *the field of a coat of arms.* 10. range of opportunity or interest; sphere of activity or operation. 11. *Physics.* space throughout which a force operates. A magnet has a magnetic field around it. 12. *Television.* the entire screen area occupied by an image. 13. all those in a game, contest, or outdoor sport. **14.** take the field, begin a battle, campaign, game, etc. —*v.* **1.** stop or catch and return (a ball) in baseball, cricket, etc. **2.** act as a fielder in baseball, cricket, etc. —*adj.* **1.** of or pertaining to fields. **2.** growing or living in fields. **3.** performed on a field, not on a track. [OE *feld*]

field·er (fēl'dər), *n.* **1.** *Baseball.* player who is stationed around or outside the diamond to stop the ball and throw it in. **2.** a similar player in a game of cricket.

field glass, a small binocular telescope.

field goal, *Am.* **1.** *Football.* a goal counting 3 points made by a drop kick. **2.** *Basketball.* a toss into the basket made during regular play, not as a result of a foul.

field grade, *Mil.* classification of officers above captain and below brigadier general.

Field·ing (fēl'ding), *n.* Henry, 1707–1754, English novelist, author of the novel *Tom Jones*.

field marshal, an army officer ranking next to the commander in chief in the British, German, and some other armies.

field of fire, *Mil.* area that a gun or battery covers effectively.

field·piece (fēld'pēs'), *n. Mil.* cannon mounted on a carriage for use in the field.

field work, scientific or technical work done in the field by surveyors, geologists, etc. —**field'work·er,** *n.*

field·work (fēld'werk'), *n.* a temporary fortification for defense made by soldiers in the field.

fiend (fēnd), *n.* **1.** an evil spirit; devil. **2.** a very wicked or cruel person. **3.** *Colloq.* person who gives himself up to some habit, practice, game, etc.; devotee. **4. the Fiend,** the Devil. [OE *fēond*] —**fiend'like',** *adj.*

fiend·ish (fēn'dish), *adj.* very cruel or wicked; devilish. —**fiend'ish·ly,** *adv.* —**fiend'ish·ness,** *n.*

fierce (firs), *adj.*, **fierc·er, fierc·est. 1.** savage; wild: *a fierce lion.* **2.** raging; violent: *a fierce wind.* **3.** very eager or active; ardent: *fierce efforts.* **4.** *Slang.* very bad, unpleasant, etc. [< OF < L *ferus* wild] —**fierce'ly,** *adv.* —**fierce'ness,** *n.* —**Syn. 1.** cruel, ferocious. —**Ant. 1.** tame, gentle.

fier·y (fīr'i; fī'ər·i), *adj.*, **fier·i·er, fier·i·est. 1.** containing fire; burning; flaming. **2.** like fire; very hot; flashing; glowing. **3.** full of feeling or spirit; ardent: *a fiery speech.* **4.** easily aroused or excited: *a fiery temper.* **5.** inflamed: *a fiery sore.* —**fier'i·ly,** *adv.* —**fier'i·ness,** *n.* —**Syn. 3.** fervent, fervid, spirited.

fi·es·ta (fi·es'tə), *n.* **1.** a religious festival; saint's day. **2.** holiday; festivity. [< Sp., FEAST]

fife (fīf), *n., v.,* **fifed, fif·ing.** —*n.* a small, shrill musical instrument like a flute. —*v.* play on a fife. [< G *pfeife* pipe] —**fif'er,** *n.*

fif·teen (fif'tēn'), *n.* **1.** a cardinal number, five more than ten. **2.** symbol of this number; 15. —*adj.* five more than ten; 15. —**fif·teenth** (fif'tēnth'), *adj., n.*

fifth (fifth), *adj.* **1.** next after the fourth; last in a series of 5. **2.** being one of 5 equal parts. —*n.* **1.** next after the fourth; last in a series of 5. **2.** one of 5 equal parts. **3. a.** one fifth of a gallon (U.S.), a measure used for alcoholic beverages. **b.** bottle or container holding a fifth. —**fifth'ly,** *adv.*

fifth column, persons within a country who secretly aid its enemies. —**fifth columnist.**

fif·ty (fif'ti), *n., pl.* **-ties,** *adj.* —*n.* **1.** a cardinal number, five times ten. **2.** symbol of this number; 50. —*adj.* five times ten; 50. —**fif'ti·eth,** *adj., n.*

fif·ty-fif·ty (fif'ti-fif'ti), *adv., adj. Slang.* in or with equal shares.

fig (fig), *n.* **1.** a small, soft, sweet fruit that grows in warm regions, eaten fresh or dried like dates and raisins. **2.** tree that figs grow on. **3.** very small amount: *I don't care a fig for your opinion.* [< OF < Pr., ult. < L *ficus* fig tree]

Figs

fig., **1.** figurative; figuratively. **2.** figure; figures.

fig·eat·er (fig'ēt'ər), *n. Am., S.* a large, green-

and-red beetle that feeds on ripe fruit; southern June bug.

fight (fīt), *n., v.,* **fought, fight·ing.** —*n.* **1.** struggle; battle; conflict. **2.** an angry dispute. **3.** power or will to fight. [< v.] —*v.* **1.** take part in a fight. **2.** take part in a fight against; war against. **3.** carry on (a fight, conflict, etc.). **4.** get or make by fighting. **5.** cause to fight. **6.** maneuver (ships, guns, etc.) in battle. **7. fight shy of,** keep away from; avoid. [OE *feohtan*] —**fight'a·ble,** *adj.* —**Syn.** *n.* **1.** combat, contest, engagement.

fight·er (fīt'ər), *n.* **1.** one who or that which fights. **2.** a professional boxer. **3.** Also, **fighter plane.** *Mil.* a highly maneuverable and heavily armed airplane used mainly for attacking enemy airplanes or strafing ground forces.

fig·ment (fig'mənt), *n.* something imagined; made-up story. [< L *figmentum* < *fingere* to form, fashion]

fig·u·ra·tion (fig'yər·ā'shən), *n.* **1.** form; shape. **2.** a forming; shaping. **3.** representation by a likeness or symbol.

fig·ur·a·tive (fig'yər·ə·tiv), *adj.* **1.** using words out of their literal meaning to add beauty or force. **2.** having many figures of speech. **3.** representing by a likeness or symbol. —**fig'ur·a·tive·ly,** *adv.* —**fig'ur·a·tive·ness,** *n.*

fig·ure (fig'yər), *n., v.,* **-ured, -ur·ing.** —*n.* **1.** symbol for a number, as 1, 2, 3, 4, etc. **2. figures,** arithmetic. **3.** amount or value given in figures. **4.** form; shape: *she saw dim figures moving.* **5.** form enclosing a surface or space. Circles, triangles, squares, cubes, and spheres are geometrical figures. **6.** person; character: *a great figure in history.* **7.** human form. **8.** way in which a person looks or appears: *the poor old woman was a figure of distress.* **9.** image; likeness. **10.** emblem; type. **11.** picture; drawing; diagram; illustration. **12.** design; pattern. **13.** outline traced by movements: *figures made by an airplane.* **14.** set of movements in dancing or skating. **15.** expression in which words are used out of their ordinary meaning to add beauty or force; figure of speech. **16.** *Music.* a brief succession of notes which produces a single, complete, and distinct impression. —*v.* **1.** use figures to find the answer to a problem; reckon; compute. **2.** *Colloq.* conclude; judge. **3.** show by a figure; represent in a diagram. **4.** make; shape. **5.** decorate with a figure or pattern. **6.** be conspicuous; appear: *the names of great leaders figure in the story of human progress.* **7. figure on,** *Am., Colloq.* **a.** depend on; rely on. **b.** consider as part of a plan or undertaking. [< F < L *figura* < *fingere* form] —**fig'ur·er,** *n.* —**Syn.** *n.* **4.** conformation, outline. **9.** effigy, statue. **10.** symbol. —*v.* **1.** calculate, cipher.

fig·ured (fig'yərd), *adj.* **1.** decorated with a design or pattern; not plain. **2.** formed; shaped.

fig·ure·head (fig'yər·hed'), *n.* **1.** statue or carving put on the front of a ship to decorate it. **2.** person who is the head in name only, and has no real authority or responsibility.

figure of speech, expression in which words are used out of their literal meaning or out of their ordinary use to add beauty or force. Similes and metaphors are figures of speech.

fig·ur·ine (fig'yər·ēn'), *n.* a small ornamental figure made of stone, pottery, metal, etc.; statuette. [< F < Ital. *figurina*]

fig·wort (fig'wert'), *n.* **1.** a tall, coarse plant with small, greenish-purple or yellow flowers that have a disagreeable odor. **2.** any similar plant.

Fi·ji (fē'jē), *n.* **1.** Fiji Islands. **2.** native of these islands. **3.** a British colony including these islands. —**Fi·ji·an** (fē'ji·ən; fi·jē'ən), *adj., n.*

Fiji Islands, group of British islands in the S Pacific, N of New Zealand.

fil·a·gree (fil'ə·grē), *n., v.,* **-greed, -gree·ing,** *adj.* filigree.

fil·a·ment (fil'ə·mənt), *n.* **1.** a very fine thread; very slender, threadlike part. **2.** *Elect.* wire that gives off light in an electric-light bulb. **3.** *Bot.* the stalklike part of a stamen that supports the anther. [< LL, < L *filum* thread] —**fil·a·men-**

◀FILAMENT

ta·ry (fil'ə·men'tə·ri), **fil·a·men·tous** (fil'ə-men'təs), *adj.*

fil·bert (fil'bərt), *n.* a cultivated hazelnut. [for St. *Philibert,* because the nuts ripen about the time of his day]

filch (filch), *v.* steal in small quantities; pilfer. —**filch'er,** *n.*

file[1] (fil), *n., v.,* **filed, fil·ing.** —*n.* 1. place for keeping papers in order. 2. set of papers kept in order. 3. line of people or things one behind another. 4. *Mil.* a small detachment of soldiers. 5. on file, in a file; put away and kept in order. —*v.* 1. put away in order. 2. march or move in a file. 3. make application. [< F *fil* thread (< L *filum*) and F *file* row (ult. < LL *filare* spin a thread)] —**fil'er,** *n.*

file[2] (fil), *n., v.,* **filed, fil·ing.** —*n.* a steel tool with many small ridges or teeth on it. Its rough surface is used to smooth or wear away hard substances. —*v.* smooth or wear away with a file. [OE *fil*] —**fil'er,** *n.*

file·fish (fil'fish'), *n., pl.* **-fish·es** or (*esp. collectively*) **-fish.** fish whose skin is covered with many very small spines instead of scales.

fi·let (fi·lā'; fil'ā), *n.* 1. net or lace having a square mesh. 2. fillet (def. 3). —*v.* fillet (def. 2). [< F. See FILLET.]

fil·i·al (fil'i·əl), *adj.* 1. of a son or daughter; due from a son or daughter. 2. *Genetics.* of any generation following that of the parents. [< LL, < L *filius* son, *filia* daughter] —**fil'i·al·ly,** *adv.*

fil·i·bus·ter (fil'ə·bus'tər), *n.* 1. *Am.* a. member of a legislature who deliberately hinders the passage of a bill by long speeches or other means of delay. b. the deliberate hindering of the passage of a bill by such means. 2. person who fights against another country without the authorization of his government; pirate. —*v.* 1. *Am.* deliberately hinder the passage of a bill by long speeches or other means of delay. 2. fight against another country without the authorization of one's government; act as a pirate. [< Sp. < Du. *vrijbuiter* freebooter] —**fil'i·bus'ter·er,** *n.*

fil·i·gree (fil'ə·grē), *n., v.,* **-greed, -gree·ing,** *adj.* —*n.* 1. very delicate, lacelike ornamental work of gold or silver wire. 2. anything very delicate or fanciful. —*v.* ornament with filigree. —*adj.* Also, fil'i-greed'. ornamented with filigree; made into filigree. Also, **filagree, fillagree.** [for *filigrane* < F < Ital. < L *filum* thread + *granum* grain]

Filigree around a gem

fil·ings (fil'ingz), *n.pl.* small pieces removed by a file.

Fil·i·pine (fil'ə·pēn), *adj.* Philippine.

Fil·i·pi·no (fil'ə·pē'nō), *n., pl.* **-nos.** native of the Philippines. —*adj.* Philippine.

fill (fil), *v.* 1. put into until there is room for no more; make full: *fill a cup.* 2. become full: *the hall filled rapidly.* 3. take up all the space in: *the crowd filled the hall.* 4. satisfy hunger or appetite. 5. supply what is needed for: *a store fills orders, prescriptions, etc.* 6. stop up or close by putting something in: *a dentist fills decayed teeth.* 7. hold and do the duties of (a position, office, etc.). 8. supply a person for or appoint a person to (a position, office, etc.). 9. fill in, a. fill with something; put in. b. complete by filling. c. put in to complete something. 10. fill out, a. make larger; grow larger; swell. b. make rounder; grow rounder. c. complete by filling. 11. fill up, fill; fill completely. —*n.* 1. enough to fill something. 2. all that is needed or wanted. 3. something that fills. [OE *fyllan* < *full* full] —**Syn.** *v.* 3. pervade, permeate. 7. occupy. 10a. inflate, expand, distend.

fil·la·gree (fil'ə·grē), *n., v.,* **-greed, -gree·ing,** *adj.* filagree.

fill·er (fil'ər), *n.* 1. person or thing that fills. 2. thing put in to fill something.

fil·let (fil'it; *n.* 3 *and v.* 2, *usually* fi·lā', fil'ā), *n.* 1. a narrow band, ribbon, etc., put around the head to keep the hair in place or as an ornament. 2. a narrow band or strip of any material.

3. Also, **filet.** slice of fish, meat, etc., without bones or fat. 4. *Bookbinding.* line impressed upon the cover of a book as a decoration. —*v.* 1. bind or decorate with a narrow band, ribbon, strip, etc. 2. Also, **filet.** cut (fish, meat, etc.) into fillets. [< F, dim. of *fil* < L *filum* thread]

fill·ing (fil'ing), *n.* thing put in to fill something.

filling station, *Am.* place where gasoline and oil for automobiles are sold.

fil·lip (fil'əp), *v.* 1. strike with the fingernail as it is snapped quickly from the end of the thumb. 2. rouse; revive; stimulate. —*n.* 1. act of filliping. 2. thing that rouses, revives, or stimulates. [prob. imit.]

Fill·more (fil'môr; -mōr), *n.* Millard, 1800–74, the 13th president of the United States, 1850–53.

fil·ly (fil'i), *n., pl.* **-lies.** 1. a female colt; young mare. 2. *Slang.* a lively girl. [? < Scand. *fylja;* akin to FOAL]

film (film), *n.* 1. a very thin layer, sheet, surface, or coating. 2. roll or sheet of thin, flexible material, such as cellulose nitrate or cellulose acetate, used in making photographs. This roll or sheet is coated with an emulsion that is sensitive to light. 3. a motion picture. 4. a delicate web of fine threads; a single fine thread. —*v.* 1. cover or become covered with a film: *her eyes filmed with tears.* 2. make a motion picture of. 3. photograph or be photographed for motion pictures. [OE *filmen;* akin to FELL[4]]

film·y (fil'mi), *adj.,* **film·i·er, film·i·est.** 1. of or like a film; very thin. 2. covered with a film. —**film'i·ly,** *adv.* —**film'i·ness,** *n.*

fil·ter (fil'tər), *n.* 1. device for straining out substances from a liquid or gas by passing it slowly through felt, paper, sand, charcoal, etc. 2. felt, paper, sand, charcoal, or other porous material used in such a device. 3. device for controlling certain light rays, electric currents, etc. —*v.* 1. pass through a filter; strain. 2. act as a filter for. 3. pass or flow very slowly. 4. remove or control by a filter. [< Med.L *filtrum* felt < Gmc.] —**fil'ter·er,** *n.*

fil·ter·a·ble (fil'tər·ə·bəl), **fil·tra·ble** (-trə-bəl), *adj.* 1. that can be filtered. 2. that passes through a filter. —**fil'ter·a·bil'i·ty, fil'ter·a·ble-ness; fil'tra·bil'i·ty, fil'tra·ble·ness,** *n.*

filth (filth), *n.* 1. foul, disgusting dirt. 2. obscene words or thoughts; vileness; moral corruption. [OE *fylth* < *ful* foul]

filth·y (fil'thi), *adj.,* **filth·i·er, filth·i·est.** 1. disgustingly dirty; foul. 2. vile. —**filth'i·ly,** *adv.* —**filth'i·ness,** *n.* —**Syn.** 1. squalid, nasty. 2. obscene, corrupt, indecent.

fil·trate (fil'trāt), *n., v.,* **-trat·ed, -trat·ing.** —*n.* liquid that has been passed through a filter. —*v.* pass through a filter. —**fil·tra'tion,** *n.*

fin (fin), *n., v.,* **finned, fin·ning.** —*n.* 1. a movable winglike part of a fish's body. 2. thing shaped or used like a fin. —*v.* 1. cut off the fins from. 2. move the fins. 3. lash the water with the fins or tail. [OE *finn*] —**fin'less,** *adj.* —**fin'like',** *adj.*

fi·na·gle (fə·nā'gəl), *v.,* **-gled, -gling.** 1. manage craftily or cleverly. 2. cheat. —**fi·na'gler,** *n.*

fi·nal (fi'nəl), *adj.* 1. at the end; last; with no more after it. 2. settling the question; not to be changed: *a decision of the Supreme Court is final.* 3. having to do with purpose. —*n.* 1. something final. 2. finals, the last or deciding set in a series of contests, examinations, etc. [< L, < *finis* end] —**Syn.** *adj.* 1. ultimate, eventual, terminal. 2. definitive.

fi·na·le (fi·nä'lē), *n.* 1. the last part of a piece of music or a play. 2. the last part; end. [< Ital., FINAL]

fi·nal·ist (fi'nəl·ist), *n.* person who takes part in the last or deciding set in a series of contests.

fi·nal·i·ty (fi·nal'ə·ti), *n., pl.* **-ties.** 1. a being final, finished, or settled. 2. something final; final act, speech, etc.

fi·nal·ly (fi'nəl·i), *adv.* 1. at the end; at last. 2. so as to decide or settle the question.

fi·nance (fə·nans′; fī–; fī′nans), n., v., –nanced, –nanc·ing. —n. 1. money matters. 2. management of large sums of government revenue and expenditure. 3. finances, money matters; money; funds; revenues. —v. 1. provide money for. 2. manage the finances of. [< OF, ending, settlement of a debt, ult. < fin end < L finis; akin to FINE²]

fi·nan·cial (fə·nan′shəl; fī–), adj. 1. having to do with money matters. 2. having to do with the management of large sums of money. —fi·nan′cial·ly, adv.

fin·an·cier (fin′ən·sir′; fī′nən–), n. 1. person skilled in finance. 2. person who is active in matters involving large sums of money.

fin·back (fin′bak′), n. kind of whale having a fin on its back.

finch (finch), n. a small songbird having a cone-shaped bill, as sparrows, buntings, and canaries. [OE finc]

House finch
(6 in. long)

find (find), v., found, find·ing, n. —v. 1. come upon; happen on; meet with: find a splinter in the sugar. 2. look for and get; obtain: find favor with the public. 3. discover: an astronomer finds a new star, find conditions satisfactory. 4. see; know; feel; perceive: he found himself growing sleepy. 5. perceive by trial to be: we found him honest. 6. get the use of: can you find time to do this? 7. arrive at; reach: water finds its level. 8. decide and declare: the jury found the accused man guilty. 9. provide; supply: find food and lodging for a friend. 10. find oneself, learn one's abilities and how to make good use of them. 11. find out, learn about; come to know; discover. —n. 1. a finding. 2. thing found. [OE findan] —find′a·ble, adj.

find·er (fin′dər), n. 1. person or thing that finds. 2. a small extra lens on the outside of a camera that shows what is being photographed. 3. Astron. a small telescope attached to a larger one to help find objects more easily.

fin de siè·cle (faⁿ də syä′klə), French. end of the century.

find·ing (fin′ding), n. 1. discovery. 2. thing found. 3. Law. decision reached after an examination or inquiry; the verdict of a jury.

fine¹ (fīn), adj., fin·er, fin·est, adv. —adj. 1. of very high quality; very good; excellent: a fine sermon, a fine view, a fine scholar. 2. very small or thin: fine wire. 3. sharp: a tool with a fine edge. 4. not coarse or heavy; delicate: fine linen. 5. refined; elegant: fine manners. 6. subtle: the law makes fine distinctions. 7. too highly decorated; showy: fine language or writing. 8. good-looking. 9. clear; bright: fine weather. 10. without impurities. 11. having a stated proportion of gold or silver in it. —adv. Colloq. very well; excellently. [< OF fin, ult. < L finire finish] —fine′ly, adv. —fine′ness, n. —Syn. adj. 1. choice, rare, splendid. 2. slender, minute. 4. dainty. 8. handsome. ▶ Fine is a counter word of general approval, slightly more vigorous than nice, but of little value in writing and better omitted: Spring football practice has one aim, to weld eleven men into a [fine,] coördinate team.

fine² (fīn), n., v., fined, fin·ing. —n. 1. sum of money paid as a punishment. 2. in fine, a. finally. b. in a few words; briefly. —v. cause to pay a fine. [< OF < L finis end; in Med.L, settlement, payment]

fine arts, arts depending upon taste and appealing to the sense of beauty; painting, drawing, sculpture, and architecture. Literature, music, dancing, and acting are also often included in the fine arts.

fine-drawn (fīn′drôn′), adj. 1. drawn out until very small or thin. 2. very subtle.

fine-grained (fīn′grānd′), adj. having a fine, close grain.

fin·er·y (fīn′ər·i), n., pl. –er·ies. showy clothes, ornaments, etc.

fine-spun (fīn′spun′), adj. 1. spun or drawn out until very small or thin. 2. very subtle.

fi·nesse (fə·nes′), n., v., –nessed, –ness·ing. —n. 1. delicacy of execution; skill. 2. the skillful handling of a delicate situation to one's advantage; craft; stratagem. 3. Cards. attempt to take a trick in bridge, whist, etc., with a low card while holding a higher card in the same hand. —v. 1. use finesse. 2. bring or change by finesse. 3. make a finesse with (a card). [< F, < fin FINE¹] —Syn. n. 2. artifice, subterfuge, strategy.

fin·ger (fing′gər), n. 1. one of the five end parts of the hand, esp. the four besides the thumb. 2. part of a glove that covers a finger. 3. anything shaped or used like a finger. 4. breadth of a finger; ¾ inch. 5. length of a finger; 4½ inches. 6. put one's finger on, point out exactly. —v. touch or handle with the fingers; use the fingers on. [OE] —fin′ger·er, n. —fin′ger·less, adj.

finger bowl, a small bowl to hold water for rinsing the fingers after or during a meal.

fin·ger·ing (fing′gər·ing), n. 1. a touching or handling with the fingers; using the fingers. 2. Music. signs marked on a piece to show how the fingers are to be used in playing it.

fin·ger·nail (fing′gər·nāl′), n. a hard layer of horn at the end of a finger.

fin·ger·print (fing′gər·print′), n. impression of the markings on the inner surface of the last joint of a finger or thumb. —v. take the fingerprints of.

fin·i·al (fin′i·əl; fī′ni–), n. Archit. ornament on top of a roof or lamp, end of a pew in church, etc. [< Med.L finium final settlement (prob. orig., end) < L finis]

fin·i·cal (fin′ə·kəl), **fin·ick·y** (–ə·ki), adj. too dainty or particular; too precise; fussy. [appar. < fine¹] —fin′i·cal′i·ty, fin′i·cal·ness, n. —fin′i·cal·ly, adv. —Syn. overnice, fastidious, squeamish.

fi·nis (fī′nis; fin′is), n. end. [< L]

fin·ish (fin′ish), v. 1. bring (action, speech, etc.) to an end; end. 2. bring (work, affairs, etc.) to completion; complete: he started the race but did not finish it. 3. use up completely: finish a spool of thread. 4. overcome completely: my answer finished him. 5. destroy; kill: finish a wounded animal. 6. perfect; polish. 7. prepare the surface of in some way: finish cloth with nap. —n. 1. end. 2. polished condition or quality; perfection. 3. way in which the surface is prepared. 4. thing used to finish something. [< OF fenir < L finire] —fin′ished, adj. —fin′ish·er, n.

finishing school, a private school that prepares young women for social life rather than for business or a profession.

fi·nite (fī′nīt), adj. 1. having limits or bounds; not infinite: death ends man's finite existence. 2. having definite grammatical person and number; not an infinitive or participle. —n. what is finite; something finite. [< L finitus finished] —fi′nite·ly, adv. —fi′nite·ness, n. ▶ finite verbs. A finite verb form is one that indicates person (by one of the pronouns or by a subject), or time (by a tense form: had gone), or number (singular or plural). These are contrasted with the "infinite" forms, the infinitives (go, to go, to have gone), participles (going, gone), and verbal nouns (going) which do not indicate person or number. Finite verbs can be main verbs in clauses and sentences (I had gone before he came); infinite forms ordinarily cannot (before coming, gone with the wind).

fink (fingk), n. Slang. 1. informer. 2. Am. strikebreaker.

Fin·land (fin′lənd), n. 1. country in N Europe. 2. Gulf of, part of the Baltic Sea, south of Finland. —Fin′land·er, Finn (fin), n.

fin·nan had·die (fin′ən had′i) or **had·dock** (had′ək), smoked haddock. [for Findhorn haddock; from name of town in Scotland]

Finn·ish (fin′ish), adj. of or having to do with Finland, its people, or their language. —n. language of Finland.

fiord (fyôrd; fyōrd), n. a long, narrow bay of the sea between high banks or cliffs. Also, fjord. [< Norw., earlier fjorthr; akin to FIRTH]

fir (fèr), n. 1. tree somewhat like a pine. 2. its wood. [OE fyrh]

fire (fīr), *n., v.,* **fired, fir·ing. —*n.* 1.** flame, heat, and light caused by burning. **2.** something burning. **3.** destruction by burning. **4.** preparation that will burn: *red fire is used in signaling.* **5.** fuel burning or arranged so that it will burn quickly. **6.** something that suggests a fire because it is hot, glowing, brilliant, or light: *the fire in a diamond.* **7.** any feeling that suggests fire; passion, fervor, excitement, etc. **8.** burning pain; fever; inflammation: *the fire of a wound.* **9.** severe trial or trouble. **10.** the shooting or discharge of guns, etc. **11. on fire, a.** burning. **b.** full of a feeling or spirit like fire. **12. under fire, a.** exposed to shooting from the enemy's guns. **b.** attacked; blamed. —*v.* **1.** cause to burn. **2.** begin to burn; burst into flame. **3.** supply with fuel; tend the fire of: *fire a furnace.* **4.** dry with heat; bake. Bricks are fired to make them hard. **5.** grow or make hot, red, glowing, etc. **6.** arouse; excite; inflame. **7.** become inflamed, excited, or aroused. **8.** discharge (gun, bomb, gas mine, etc.). **9.** shoot. **10.** *Colloq.* throw. **11.** *Am., Colloq.* dismiss from a job, etc. [OE *fўr*] —**fir′er**, *n.* —**Syn.** *n.* **1.** blaze, combustion, conflagration. **7.** ardor, enthusiasm, vehemence.

fire·arm (fīr′ärm′), *n.* gun, pistol, or other weapon to shoot with.

fire·ball (fīr′bôl′), *n.* **1.** the great billowing mass of fire produced by an atomic explosion. **2.** a very fast pitch to the batter in baseball.

fire·box (fīr′boks′), *n.* place for the fire in a furnace, boiler, etc.

fire·brand (fīr′brand′), *n.* **1.** piece of burning wood. **2.** person who arouses strife or angry feeling in others.

fire·brick (fīr′brik′), *n.* brick that can stand great heat, used to line furnaces and fireplaces.

fire·bug (fīr′bug′), *n. Am., Colloq.* person who purposely sets houses or property on fire.

fire clay, clay capable of resisting high temperatures, used for making firebricks, etc.

fire·crack·er (fīr′krak′ər), *n. Am.* a paper roll containing gunpowder and a fuse.

fire·damp (fīr′damp′), *n.* methane, a gas formed in coal mines, dangerously explosive when mixed with certain proportions of air.

fire·dog (fīr′dôg′; -dog′), *n.* andiron.

fire engine, machine for throwing water, chemicals, etc., to put out fires.

fire escape, stairway, ladder, etc., in or on a building, to use in case of fire.

fire extinguisher, container filled with chemicals which, when sprayed upon fire, extinguish it.

fire·fly (fīr′flī′), *n., pl.* **-flies.** a small beetle that gives off flashes of light when it flies at night; lightning bug.

Firefly
(½ in. long)

fire·man (fīr′mən), *n., pl.* **-men. 1.** man whose work is putting out fires. **2.** man whose work is taking care of the fire in a furnace, boiler, locomotive, etc.

fire·place (fīr′plās′), *n.* place built in the wall of a room or outdoors to hold a fire.

fire·pow·er (fīr′pou′ər), *n.* the total number of bullets, directed missiles, etc., that can be fired at an enemy or target in a given instant.

fire·proof (fīr′prüf′), *adj.* that will not burn; almost impossible to burn. —*v.* make fireproof.

fire·side (fīr′sīd′), *n.* **1.** space around a fireplace or hearth. **2.** home. **3.** home life. —*adj.* beside the fire: *fireside comfort.*

fire·trap (fīr′trap′), *n.* **1.** a building hard to get out of when it is on fire. **2.** a building that will burn very easily.

fire·wa·ter (fīr′wô′tər; -wot′-), *n. Am.* strong alcoholic drink. The American Indians called whiskey, gin, rum, etc., firewater.

fire·weed (fīr′wēd′), *n.* any of various weeds which grow on land that has been burned over.

fire·wood (fīr′wùd′), *n.* wood to make a fire.

fire·works (fīr′wėrks′), *n.pl.* **1.** firecrackers, bombs, rockets, etc., that make a loud noise or a beautiful, fiery display at night. **2.** display of these.

fir·kin (fėr′kən), *n.* **1.** quarter of a barrel, used as a measure of capacity. **2.** a small wooden cask for butter, etc. [ME *ferdekyn* < MDu. *verdelkijn,* dim. of *verdel,* lit., fourth part]

firm¹ (fėrm), *adj.* **1.** not yielding easily to pressure or force; solid; hard: *firm ground.* **2.** not easily moved or shaken; tightly fastened or fixed: *a candle firm in its socket.* **3.** not easily changed; determined; resolute; positive: *a firm purpose.* **4.** not changing; staying the same; steady: *a firm price.* —*v.* **1.** make or become firm. **2.** *Archaic.* establish; confirm. [< L *firmus*] —**firm′ly,** *adv.* —**firm′ness,** *n.* —**Syn.** *adj.* **1.** compact, impenetrable, rigid. **2.** fast, secure, immovable. **4.** enduring, constant, steadfast.

firm² (fėrm), *n.* a business company or partnership. [< Ital. < Sp., Pg. *firma* signature, ult. < L *firmus* firm¹]

fir·ma·ment (fėr′mə·mənt), *n.* arch of the heavens; sky. [< L, ult. < *firmus* firm¹]

first (fėrst), *adj.* **1.** before all others; before anything else. **2.** most important. **3.** *Music.* **a.** highest in pitch. **b.** playing or singing the part highest in pitch. —*adv.* **1.** before all others; before anything else: *the good die first.* **2.** in the first place. **3.** before some other thing or event: *first bring me the chalk.* **4.** for the first time. **5.** rather; sooner: *I'll go to jail first.* —*n.* **1.** person, thing, place, etc., that is first. **2.** *Sports.* the winning position in a race, etc. **3.** beginning. [OE *fyrst*] —**Syn.** *adj.* **1.** earliest, original, initial. **2.** chief, foremost, principal, leading. ▸ **first, last, latest.** *First, last* refer to items in a series, usually of more than two: *The first president had set up a very informal organization. His last act was to advise his family on their future. Latest* refers to the current item of a series that is still continuing (*the latest fashions*). *Last* refers either to the final item of a completed series (*their last attempt was successful*) or to the most recently completed or past item of a continuing series (*the last election, last week*).

first aid, emergency treatment given to an injured person before a doctor comes. —**first′-aid′,** *adj.*

first base, *Am., Baseball.* **1.** the first of the bases from the home plate. **2.** player stationed there.

first-born (fėrst′bôrn′), *adj.* born first; oldest. —*n.* the first-born child.

first-class (fėrst′klas′; -kläs′), *adj.* of the highest class or best quality; excellent. —*adv.* on a first-class ship, train, etc.

first-hand (fėrst′hand′), *adj., adv.* from the original source; direct.

first lady, *Am.* the wife of the president of the United States.

first lieutenant, *U.S. Army.* officer ranking below a captain and above a second lieutenant.

first·ling (fėrst′ling), *n.* **1.** the first of its kind. **2.** the first product or result. **3.** the first offspring of an animal.

first·ly (fėrst′li), *adv.* in the first place; first.

first person, *Gram.* form of a pronoun or verb used to refer to the speaker. *I, me, my,* and *we, us, our* are pronouns of the first person.

first-rate (fėrst′rāt′), *adj.* **1.** of the highest class. **2.** excellent; very good. —*adv. Colloq.* excellently; very well.

first sergeant, *U.S. Army.* a master sergeant in direct charge of a company or similar unit under the commissioned officer in command.

firth (fėrth), *n. Esp. Scot.* a narrow arm of the sea; estuary of a river. [< Scand. *firthir,* pl. of *fjörthr*; akin to FIORD]

fis·cal (fis′kəl), *adj.* **1.** financial. **2.** having to do with a treasury or exchequer. [< L, < *fiscus* purse] —**fis′cal·ly,** *adv.*

fish (fish), *n., pl.* **fish·es** or (*esp. collectively*) **fish,** *v.* —*n.* **1.** a vertebrate animal that lives in water and has gills instead of lungs for breathing. Fish are usually covered with scales and have fins for swimming. In popular use, whales and dolphins are called fish, and certain invertebrates are called shellfish. 2. flesh of fish used for food. 3. *Colloq.* person; fellow. 4. **Fishes**, Pisces. —*v.* 1. catch fish; try to catch fish. 2. try to catch fish in. 3. search. 4. find and pull: *he fished the map from the back of the drawer.* —*adj.* of or pertaining to fishes, fishing, or the sale of fish. [OE *fisc*] —**fish′a·ble**, *adj.* —**fish′less**, *adj.* —**fish′like′**, *adj.*

fish·er (fish′ər), *n.* 1. fisherman. 2. *Am.* a slender animal like a weasel but larger.

fish·er·man (fish′ər·mən), *n., pl.* -men. 1. man who fishes for a living or for pleasure. 2. ship used in fishing.

fish·er·y (fish′ər·i), *n., pl.* -er·ies. 1. business or industry of catching fish. 2. place for catching fish. 3. right of fishing in certain waters in certain ways.

fish hawk, large bird that feeds on fish; osprey.

fish·hook (fish′hŭk′), *n.* hook used for catching fish.

fish·ing (fish′ing), *n.* the catching of fish for a living or for pleasure.

fishing rod, a long pole with a line attached to it, used in catching fish.

fish·mon·ger (fish′mung′gər; -mong′-), *n. Esp. Brit.* dealer in fish.

fish·wife (fish′wīf′), *n., pl.* -wives. woman who sells fish.

fish·y (fish′i), *adj.*, fish·i·er, fish·i·est. 1. like a fish in smell, taste, or shape. 2. of fish. 3. full of fish. 4. *Colloq.* doubtful; unlikely; suspicious. 5. dull. —**fish′i·ly**, *adv.* —**fish′i·ness**, *n.*

fis·sile (fis′əl), *adj.* 1. easily split. 2. capable of nuclear fission. [< L *fissilis* < *findere* cleave]

fis·sion (fish′ən), *n.* 1. a splitting apart; division into parts. 2. *Biol.* method of reproduction in which the body of the parent divides to form two or more independent individuals. 3. *Physics, Chem.* the splitting that occurs when the nucleus of an atom under bombardment absorbs a neutron. Nuclear fission releases tremendous amounts of energy when heavy elements, esp. plutonium and uranium, are involved. [< L *fissio*. See FISSILE.]

fis·sion·a·ble (fish′ən·ə·bəl), *adj.* capable of nuclear fission: *fissionable material.*

fission bomb, atomic bomb that derives its force solely from the splitting of atoms. The original atomic bombs were fission bombs; the newer hydrogen bombs are fusion bombs.

fis·sure (fish′ər), *n., v.,* -sured, -sur·ing. —*n.* 1. split or crack; long, narrow opening. 2. a splitting apart; division into parts. —*v.* split apart; divide into parts.

fist (fist), *n.* 1. hand closed tightly. 2. *Colloq.* hand. 3. *Colloq.* handwriting. 4. symbol (☞) used in printing. [OE *fȳst*]

fist·ic (fis′tik), *adj.* having to do with fighting with the fists; done with the fists.

fist·i·cuff (fis′tə·kuf′), *n.* 1. blow with the fist. 2. fisticuffs, a. fight with the fists. b. blows with the fists. —**fist′i·cuff′er**, *n.*

fis·tu·la (fis′chů·lə), *n., pl.* -las, -lae (-lē). 1. tube or pipe. 2. *Pathol.* a tubelike sore. [< L, pipe, ulcer] —**fis·tu·lous** (fis′chů·ləs), **fis′tu·lar**, *adj.*

fit¹ (fit), *adj.*, fit·ter, fit·test, *v.*, fit·ted, fit·ting, *n.* —*adj.* 1. having the necessary qualities; suitable. 2. right; proper. 3. ready; prepared: *fit for active service.* 4. in good health; in good physical condition. —*v.* 1. be fit; be fit for. 2. have the right size or shape; have the right size or shape for. 3. cause to fit; make fit. 4. make ready; prepare. 5. supply with what is needed; equip. —*n.* 1. manner in which one thing fits another: *a tight fit.* 2. process of fitting. 3. thing that fits: *this coat is a good fit.* [ME *fyt*] —**fit′ly**, *adv.* —**fit′ness**, *n.* —**fit′ter**, *n.* —Syn. *adj.* 1. appropriate, qualified. 2. seemly. —*v.* 5. furnish.

fit² (fit), *n.* 1. a sudden, sharp attack of disease: *a fit of colic.* 2. a sudden attack characterized by loss of consciousness or by convulsions: *a fainting fit, fit of epilepsy.* 3. a sudden, sharp attack: *in a fit of anger he hit his friend.* 4. a short period of doing one thing. [OE *fitt* conflict]

fitch (fich), **fitch·et** (fich′it), or **fitch·ew** (fich′ū), *n.* 1. polecat of Europe. 2. its fur, yellowish with dark markings. [? < MDu. *vitsche*]

fit·ful (fit′fəl), *adj.* going on and then stopping awhile; irregular. —**fit′ful·ly**, *adv.* —**fit′ful·ness**, *n.* —Syn. spasmodic, variable, intermittent.

Fitch
(body ab. 17 in. long)

fit·ting (fit′ing), *adj.* right; proper; suitable. —*n.* 1. a making fit. 2. a trying on unfinished clothes to see if they will fit. 3. **fittings**, furnishings; fixtures. —**fit′ting·ly**, *adv.* —**fit′ting·ness**, *n.*

Fiu·me (fū′mā), *n.* the Italian name of Rieka, a seaport in NW Yugoslavia.

five (fīv), *n.* 1. a cardinal number, one more than four. 2. symbol for this number; 5. 3. *Sports.* team of five players. —*adj.* one more than four; 5. [OE *fīf*]

five·fold (fīv′fōld′), *adj.* 1. five times as much or as many. 2. having five parts. —*adv.* five times as much or as many.

Five Nations, *Am.* confederacy of Iroquois Indian tribes, consisting of the Mohawks, Oneidas, Onondagas, Cayugas, and Senecas.

five percenter, person who obtains government contracts for others in return for a 5% fee.

fix (fiks), *v.*, fixed or fixt, fix·ing, *n.* —*v.* 1. make firm; become firm; fasten tightly; be fastened tightly: *fix a post in the ground.* 2. settle; set: *fix the price at one dollar.* 3. direct or hold (eyes, attention, etc.) steadily; be directed or held steadily. 4. make or become rigid. 5. put definitely: *fix the blame on the leader.* 6. treat to keep from changing or fading. 7. treat (organisms or parts of organisms) to preserve them for future study. 8. mend; repair. 9. *U.S. Colloq.* put in order; arrange; prepare. 10. *Colloq.* put in a condition or position favorable to oneself or unfavorable to one's opponents. 11. *Colloq.* get revenge upon; get even with; punish. 12. *Chem.* make (nitrogen) into a compound that can be used. 13. **fix up**, *Esp. U.S. Colloq.* a. mend; repair. b. put in order; arrange. —*n.* 1. *Colloq.* position hard to get out of; awkward state of affairs. 2. point on a map or chart at which two lines of position cross one another. [< F, ult. < L *fixus* fixed] —**fix′a·ble**, *adj.* —**fix′er**, *n.* —Syn. *v.* 2. determine, confirm.

fix·a·tion (fiks·ā′shən), *n.* 1. act of fixing or condition of being fixed. 2. treatment to keep something from changing or fading: *fixation of a photographic film.* 3. *Chem.* process of combining nitrogen with hydrogen under high pressure to form ammonia, used in making fertilizers and explosives. 4. *Psychol.* a morbid attachment or prejudice.

fix·a·tive (fik′sə·tiv), *adj.* that prevents fading or change. —*n.* substance used to keep something from fading or changing.

fixed (fikst), *adj.* 1. not movable; firm. 2. settled; set; definite. 3. steady; not moving. 4. made stiff or rigid. 5. not volatile; permanent. 6. put into order. 7. *Colloq.* prearranged privately or dishonestly. —**fix·ed·ly** (fik′sid·li), *adv.* —**fix′ed·ness**, *n.* —Syn. 1. stationary. 2. established.

fixed star, *Astron.* star whose position in relation to other stars appears not to change.

fix·ing (fik′sing), *n.* 1. act of one who or that which fixes. 2. **fixings**, *Am.*, *Colloq.* trimmings.

fix·i·ty (fik′sə·ti), *n., pl.* -ties. 1. fixed condition or quality; permanence; steadiness; firmness. 2. something fixed.

fixt (fikst), *v.* pt. and pp. of fix.

fix·ture (fiks′chər), *n.* 1. thing put in place to stay: *electric-light fixtures.* 2. person or thing that stays in one place, job, etc.

fiz (fiz), *v.*, fizzed, fiz·zing, *n.* fizz.

fizz (fiz), *v.* make a hissing sound. —*n.* 1. a hissing sound. 2. a bubbling drink, such as champagne, soda water, etc. —**fizz′er**, *n.*

fiz·zle (fiz′əl), *v.*, -zled, -zling, *n.* —*v.* 1. hiss or sputter weakly. 2. *Colloq.* fail. —*n.* 1. a hissing; sputtering. 2. *Colloq.* failure.

fizz·y (fiz′i), *adj.*, fizz·i·er, fizz·i·est. that fizzes.

fjord (fyôrd; fyord), n. flord.

Fl, Chem. fluorine. Also, **F.**

fl., 1. flourished. 2. fluid.

Fla., Florida.

flab·ber·gast (flab′ər·gast), v. Colloq. make speechless with surprise; astonish greatly; amaze. [? blend of flap or flabby + aghast]

flab·by (flab′ĭ), adj., –bi·er, –bi·est. lacking firmness or force; soft. [var. of earlier flappy < flap] —flab′bi·ly, adv. —flab′bi·ness, n.

flac·cid (flak′sĭd), adj. limp; weak: flaccid muscles, a flaccid will. [< L, <flaccus flabby] —flac·cid′i·ty, flac′cid·ness, n. —flac′cid·ly, adv.

fla·con (flä·kôn′), n. a small bottle with a stopper, used for perfume, smelling salts, etc. [< F. See FLAGON.]

flag[1] (flag), n., v., flagged, flag·ging. —n. 1. piece of cloth with a color or pattern that stands for some country, city, party, club, etc., or which gives some information or signal. 2. something that suggests a flag. 3. flags, a. feathers on the second joint of a bird's wing. b. long feathers on the lower parts of certain birds' legs. —v. 1. put a flag or flags over or on; decorate with flags. 2. stop or signal by a flag: flag a train. 3. communicate by a flag: flag a message. [? < flag[3]] —Syn. n. 1. ensign, standard, banner.

flag[2] (flag), n. 1. iris with blue, purple, yellow, or white flowers and sword-shaped leaves. 2. the sweet flag. [cf. Dan. flœg]

flag[3] (flag), v., flagged, flag·ging. get tired; grow weak; droop. [cf. earlier Du. vlaggheren flutter] —Syn. decline, languish, fail.

flag[4] (flag), n., v., flagged, flag·ging. —n. flagstone. —v. pave with flagstones. [var. of flake]

Flag Day, Am. June 14, the anniversary of the day in 1777 when the flag of the United States was adopted.

flag·el·lant (flaj′ə·lənt; flə·jel′ənt), n. 1. person who whips. 2. a religious fanatic who whips himself for religious discipline or for penance. —adj. having the habit of whipping.

flag·el·late (flaj′ə·lāt), v., –lat·ed, –lat·ing, adj. —v. whip; flog. —adj. Also, flag′el·lat′ed. 1. shaped like a whiplash. 2. having flagella. [< L, flagellum whip] —flag′el·la′tion, n. —flag′el·la′tor, n.

fla·gel·lum (flə·jel′əm), n., pl. –la (–lə) –lums. 1. Biol. a long, whiplike tail or part, which is an organ of locomotion in certain cells, bacteria, protozoa, etc. 2. whip. 3. Bot. runner of a plant. [< L, whip]

flag·eo·let (flaj′ə·let′), n. a wind instrument somewhat like a flute, with a mouthpiece at one end, six main finger holes, and sometimes keys. [< F, dim. of OF flajol flute, ult. < L flare blow]

flag·ging[1] (flag′ing), adj. drooping; tired; weak. —flag′ging·ly, adv.

flag·ging[2] (flag′ing), n. 1. flagstones. 2. pavement made of flagstones.

fla·gi·tious (flə·jish′əs), adj. scandalously wicked; shamefully vile. [< L, ult. < flagitium shame] —fla·gi′tious·ly, adv. —fla·gi′tious·ness, n.

flag·on (flag′ən), n. 1. container for liquids, usually having a handle and a spout, and often a cover. 2. a large bottle, holding about two quarts. 3. contents of a flagon. [< OF flascon. Cf. FLASK.]

flag·pole (flag′pōl′), n. **flag·staff** (-staf′; -stäf′), n. pole from which a flag is flown.

fla·gran·cy (flā′grən·sĭ), **fla·grance** (-grəns), n. flagrant nature or quality.

fla·grant (flā′grənt), adj. 1. notorious; outrageous; scandalous. 2. Archaic. blazing; burning; glowing. [< L flagrans burning] —fla′grant·ly, adv. —Syn. 1. glaring.

flag·ship (flag′ship′), n. ship that carries the officer in command of a fleet or squadron and displays his flag.

flag·stone (flag′stōn′), n. a large, flat stone, used for paving walks, etc.

flail (flāl), n. instrument for threshing grain by hand. —v. 1. strike with a flail. 2. beat; thrash. [< LL flagellum < L, whip]

flair (flâr), n. 1. keen perception: a flair for bargains. 2. talent: a flair for making clever rhymes. [< F, scent < flairer smell < L fragrare]

flak (flak), n. fire from anti-aircraft guns. [for Fl.A.K., G abbrev. of flieger-abwehrkanone anti-aircraft cannon]

flake (flāk), n., v., flaked, flak·ing. —n. 1. a small, light mass; soft, loose bit: a flake of snow. 2. a thin, flat piece or layer: flakes of rust. —v. 1. come off in flakes; take off, chip, or peel in flakes. 2. break or separate into flakes. 3. cover or mark with flakes; spot. 4. form into flakes. [? < Scand. (Dan.) (sne) flage (snow) flake]

flak·y (flāk′ĭ), adj., flak·i·er, flak·i·est. 1. consisting of flakes. 2. easily broken or separated into flakes. —flak′i·ly, adv. —flak′i·ness, n.

flam·beau (flam′bō), n., pl. –beaus (-bōz), -beaus. a flaming torch. [< F, < OF flambe flame, ult. < L flamma]

flam·boy·ant (flam-boi′ənt), adj. 1. gorgeously brilliant; flaming. 2. very ornate. 3. having wavy lines or flamelike curves. [< F, flaming. See FLAMBEAU.] —flam·boy′ance, flam·boy′an·cy, n. —flam·boy′ant·ly, adv.

flame (flām), n. v., flamed, flam·ing. —n. 1. one of the glowing, red or yellow tongues of light that shoot out from a blazing fire. 2. a burning gas or vapor. 3. a burning with flames; blaze. 4. thing or condition that suggests flame. 5. a bright light. 6. a burning feeling. 7. Slang. sweetheart. —v. 1. burn with flame; blaze. 2. grow hot, red, etc. 3. shine brightly; give out a bright light. 4. have or show a burning feeling. 5. burst out quickly and hotly; be or act like a flame. [< OF < L flamma] —flame′less, adj. —flam′er, n. —Syn. v. 1. flare, glow, flash.

fla·men·co (flə·meng′kō), n. gypsy dancing, music, etc., of a style characteristic of Andalusia. [< Sp.]

flame·out (flām′out′), n. the sudden failure of a jet engine to function, esp. while the aircraft containing it is in flight.

flame thrower, Mil. weapon that throws a spray of oil that ignites in the air.

flam·ing (flām′ing), adj. 1. burning with flames. 2. like a flame; very bright; brilliant. 3. violent; vehement. —flam′ing·ly, adv.

fla·min·go (flə·ming′gō), n., pl. –gos, –goes. a tropical wading bird with very long legs and feathers that vary from pink to scarlet. [< Pg. < Sp. < Pr. flamenc < flama FLAME]

flam·ma·ble (flam′ə·bəl), adj. inflammable.

Flan·ders (flan′dərz; flän′-), n. district in W Belgium, N France, and SW Netherlands.

flange (flanj), n., v., flanged, flang-ing. —n. a projecting edge, rim, collar, etc., on an object for keeping it in place, attaching it to another object, strengthening it, etc. —v. provide with a flange. [var. of flanch, n., < flanch, v., < OF flanchir bend; akin to flank]

Flanges

flank (flangk), n. 1. side of an animal or person between the ribs and the hip. 2. piece of beef cut from this part. 3. side. 4. Mil. a. the far right or left side of an army, fleet, etc. b. part of a fortification that defends another part by gunfire along the outside of the latter's parapet. —v. 1. be at the side of: high buildings flanked the dark, narrow alley. 2. get around the far right or left side of. 3. attack from or on the side. [< OF flanc <Gmc.] —flank′er, n.

flan·nel (flan′əl), n. 1. a soft, warm woolen cloth. 2. flannelet. 3. flannels, a. clothes made of flannel. b. woolen underwear.

flan·nel·et, flan·nel·ette (flan′əl·et′), n. a soft, warm cotton cloth with a fuzzy nap.

flap (flap), v., flapped, flap·ping, n. —v. 1. swing or sway about loosely and with more or less noise: curtains flapped in the open windows. 2. move (wings, arms, etc.) up and down. 3. fly by moving wings up and down: the large bird flapped away. 4. strike noisily with something broad and flat. —*n.* **1.** a flapping motion. **2.** noise caused by flapping. **3.** blow from something broad and flat. **4.** a broad, flat piece, usually hanging or fastened at one edge only. **5.** an extra hinged section on an airfoil of an airplane, esp. a wing, which can be moved to assist a take-off or a landing. [prob. imit.]

flap·jack (flap′jak′), *n.* a griddlecake.

flap·per (flap′ər), *n.* **1.** a flap (def. 4). **2.** *Colloq.* a young girl who is rather forward and unconventional.

flare (flâr), *v.*, **flared, flar·ing,** *n.* —*v.* **1.** flame up briefly or unsteadily, sometimes with smoke. **2.** spread out in the shape of a bell: *the sides of a ship flare from the keel to the deck.* **3.** flare up or out, flame up; burst into anger, violence, etc. —*n.* **1.** a bright, unsteady light or blaze that lasts only a short time. **2.** a dazzling light that burns for a short time, used for signaling. **3.** a sudden outburst. **4.** a spreading out into a bell shape. **5.** part that spreads out. [cf. Norw. *flara* blaze]

flare-up (flâr′up′), *n.* **1.** outburst of flame. **2.** *Colloq.* a sudden outburst of anger, violence, etc.

flar·ing (flâr′ing), *adj.* **1.** flaming. **2.** gaudy. **3.** spreading gradually outward in form.

flash (flash), *n.* **1.** a sudden, brief light or flame: *a flash of lightning.* **2.** a sudden, brief feeling or display: *a flash of hope, a flash of wit.* **3.** a very brief time; instant. **4.** *Am.* a brief news report, usually received by telegraph or teletype. **5.** a showy display. —*v.* **1.** give out a sudden, brief light or flame. **2.** come suddenly; pass quickly. **3.** cause to flash. **4.** give out or send out like a flash. **5.** communicate by flashes; send by telegraph, radio, etc. **6.** *Colloq.* show off. [appar. imit.] —**flash′er,** *n.* —**flash′ing·ly,** *adv.*

flash burn, a severe burn caused by instantaneous thermal radiation, as from an atomic bomb.

flash flood, a very sudden, violent flooding of a river, stream, etc.

flash gun, bulb, or **lamp,** a portable electric device used to make bright flashes for taking photographs indoors or at night.

flash·light (flash′līt′), *n.* **1.** light that flashes, used in a lighthouse or for signaling. **2.** *Am.* a portable electric light, operated by batteries. **3.** a flash gun.

flash·y (flash′i), *adj.*, **flash·i·er, flash·i·est. 1.** very bright for a short time; flashing. **2.** showy; gaudy. —**flash′i·ly,** *adv.* —**flash′i·ness,** *n.* —Syn. **1.** glittering, dazzling. **2.** tawdry.

flask (flask; fläsk), *n.* **1.** any bottle-shaped container. **2.** a small bottle with flat sides, made to be carried in the pocket. [OE *flasce.* Cf. LL *flasca* < Gmc.]

Flask

flat[1] (flat), *adj.*, **flat·ter, flat·test,** *n., adv., v.,* **flat·ted, flat·ting.** —*adj.* **1.** smooth and level; even: *flat land.* **2.** spread out; at full length. **3.** not very deep or thick: *a plate is flat.* **4.** with little air in it: *a flat tire.* **5.** not to be changed; positive: *a flat refusal.* **6.** without much life, interest, flavor, etc.: *flat food.* **7.** not shiny or glossy: *a flat yellow.* **8.** not clear or sharp in sound. **9.** *Music.* **a.** below the true pitch. **b.** one half step or half note below natural pitch. **10.** *Phonet.* having the sound of *a* in *hat.* **11.** *Gram.* not having a characteristic ending or sign. **12.** *Am.* of times, exact or within a fifth of a second. —*n.* **1.** something flat. **2.** a flat part. **3.** *Am.* flat land. **4.** land covered with shallow water; marsh; swamp. **5.** *Music.* sign (♭) that lowers a tone or note one half step below natural pitch. **6.** *Colloq.* tire with little air in it. —*adv.* **1.** *Music.* below the true pitch. **2.** in a flat manner. **3.** in a flat position. **4.** fall flat, fail completely; have no effect or interest. —*v.* make or become flat. [< Scand. *flatr*] —**flat′ly,** *adv.* —**flat′ness,** *n.* —**flat′tish,** *adj.* —Syn. *adj.* **1.** plane. **2.** prostrate, prone, supine. **5.** downright, absolute. **6.** dull, monotonous.

flat[2] (flat), *n.* apartment or set of rooms on one floor. [alter. of *flet,* OE *flett*]

flat·boat (flat′bōt′), *n.* a large boat with a flat bottom, often used on a river or canal.

flat·car (flat′kär′), *n. Am., Colloq.* a railroad freight car without a roof or sides.

flat·fish (flat′fish′), *n., pl.* **-fish·es** or (*esp. collectively*) **-fish.** fish with a flat body, and with both eyes on the side kept uppermost when lying flat.

flat·foot (flat′fut′), *n., pl.* **-feet. 1.** *Pathol.* **a.** foot with a flattened arch. **b.** condition in which the feet have flattened arches. **2.** *Slang.* policeman.

flat·foot·ed (flat′fut′id), *adj.* **1.** having feet with flattened arches. **2.** *Am.* not to be changed or influenced; firm; uncompromising. —**flat′-foot′ed·ly,** *adv.* —**flat′-foot′ed·ness,** *n.*

flat·i·ron (flat′ī′ərn), *n.* iron with a flat surface, used for pressing cloth.

flat silver, *Am.* silver knives, forks, etc.

flat·ten (flat′ən), *v.* make or become flat. —**flat′ten·er,** *n.*

flat·ter (flat′ər), *v.* **1.** praise too much or beyond what is true; praise insincerely. **2.** show to be better looking than what is true: *this picture flatters her.* **3.** try to please or win over by flattering. **4.** cause to be pleased or feel honored. **5.** flatter oneself, be pleased to know or think. [? extended use of ME *flateren* float, FLUTTER] —**flat′ter·er,** *n.* —**flat′ter·ing·ly,** *adv.* —Syn. **1.** compliment. **3.** cajole, blandish.

flat·ter·y (flat′ər·i), *n., pl.* **-ter·ies. 1.** act of flattering. **2.** words of praise, usually untrue or overstated.

flat·top (flat′top′), *n. U.S.* an aircraft carrier.

flat·u·lent (flach′ə·lənt), *adj.* **1.** having gas in the stomach or intestines. **2.** causing gas in the stomach or intestines. **3.** pompous in speech or behavior; vain; empty. [< F < L *flatus* a blowing] —**flat′u·lence, flat′u·len·cy,** *n.* —**flat′u·lent·ly,** *adv.*

flat·worm (flat′wėrm′), *n.* worm with a flat body, that lives in water or as a parasite on some animal.

Flau·bert (flō·bâr′), *n.* Gustave, 1821–1880, French novelist.

flaunt (fônt; flänt), *v.* **1.** show off: *the ill-bred woman flaunted her riches in public.* **2.** wave proudly: *banners flaunting in the breeze.* —*n.* a flaunting. [? < Scand. *Norw. flanta* gad about] —**flaunt′er,** *n.* —**flaunt′ing·ly,** *adv.* —**flaunt′y,** *adj.* ➤ **flaunt, flout.** *Flaunt* (fônt; flänt), to "show off," and *flout* (flout), to "treat with contempt or scorn," are sometimes confused.

flau·tist (flô′tist), *n.* flutist.

fla·vor, *esp. Brit.* **fla·vour** (flā′vər), *n.* **1.** taste, esp. a characteristic taste: *chocolate and vanilla have different flavors.* **2.** thing used to give a certain taste to food or drink; flavoring. **3.** a characteristic quality: *stories that have a flavor of the sea.* **4.** aroma; odor. —*v.* **1.** give an added taste to; season. **2.** give a characteristic quality to. [< OF *flaur,* ult. < L *fragrare* emit odor] —**fla′vor·er,** *esp. Brit.* **fla′vour·er,** *n.* —**fla′vor·less,** *esp. Brit.* **fla′vour·less,** *adj.* —Syn. *n.* **1.** savor, smack, tang, relish.

fla·vor·ing, *esp. Brit.* **fla·vour·ing** (flā′vər·ing; flāv′ring), *n.* thing used to give a certain taste to food or drink.

flaw[1] (flô), *n.* **1.** a defective place; crack. **2.** fault; defect. —*v.* make or become defective; crack. [< Scand. (Sw.) *flaga*] —Syn. *n.* **1.** chink, rent, breach. **2.** imperfection, blemish.

flaw[2] (flô), *n.* **1.** a sudden gust; brief windstorm. **2.** a short period of rough weather. [cf. Scand. (Sw.) *flaga* gust]

flaw·less (flô′lis), *adj.* without a flaw. —**flaw′less·ly,** *adv.* —**flaw′less·ness,** *n.*

flax (flaks), *n.* **1.** plant with small, narrow leaves, blue flowers, and slender stems about two feet tall. Linseed oil is made from its seeds. **2.** the threadlike fibers of this plant, spun into linen thread. [OE *fleax*]

flax·en (flak′sən), **flax·y** (flak′si), *adj.* **1.** made of flax. **2.** like the color of flax; pale-yellow: *flaxen hair.*

flax·seed (flaks′sēd′), *n.* seeds of flax.

flay (flā), *v.* **1.** strip off the skin or outer covering of. **2.** scold severely; criticize without pity or mercy. **3.** rob; cheat. [OE *flēan*] —**flay′er,** *n.*

flea (flē), *n.* a small, wingless, jumping insect that lives as a parasite on animals, sucking their blood. [OE *flēah*]

flea·bane (flē'bān'), *n.* plant supposed to drive away fleas.

fleck (flek), *n.* **1.** spot or patch of color, light, etc. **2.** a small particle; flake. —*v.* sprinkle with spots or patches of color, light, etc.; speckle. [? < Scand. *flekkr*] —**flecked** (flekt), *adj.*

Flea. Line shows actual length.

flec·tion (flek'shən), *n.* **1.** a bending. **2.** a bent part; bend. Also, *esp. Brit.* flexion. [< L *flexio* < *flectere* bend] —**flec'tion·al**, *adj.*

fledge (flej), *v.*, **fledged, fledg·ing. 1.** grow the feathers needed for flying. **2.** bring up (a young bird) until it is able to fly. **3.** provide or cover with feathers. [cf. OE *unflicge* unfledged, unfit to fly]

fledg·ling, *esp. Brit.* **fledge·ling** (flej'ling), *n.* **1.** a young bird just able to fly. **2.** a young, inexperienced person.

flee (flē), *v.*, **fled** (fled), **flee·ing. 1.** run away; try to get away by running. **2.** run away from. **3.** go quickly; move swiftly. **4.** pass away; cease; vanish. [OE *flēon*] —**fle'er,** *n.* —Syn. **2.** escape.

fleece (flēs), *n.*, *v.*, **fleeced, fleec·ing. —n. 1.** wool that covers a sheep or similar animal. **2.** quantity of wool cut from a sheep at one time. **3.** something like a fleece. **4.** cloth having a soft nap or pile. —*v.* **1.** cut the fleece from. **2.** strip of money or belongings; rob; cheat; swindle. [OE *flēos*] —**fleeced** (flēst), *adj.* —**fleece'less,** *adj.* —**fleec'er,** *n.*

fleec·y (flēs'i), *adj.*, **fleec·i·er, fleec·i·est. 1.** like a fleece; soft and white. **2.** covered with fleece. **3.** made of fleece. —**fleec'i·ly,** *adv.* —**fleec'i·ness,** *n.*

fleer (flir), *v.*, *n.* sneer; gibe. —**fleer'ing·ly,** *adv.*

fleet¹ (flēt), *n.* **1.** group of warships under one command; navy. **2.** any group of boats sailing together. **3.** group of airplanes, automobiles, etc., moving or working together. [OE *flēot* < *flēotan* float]

fleet² (flēt), *adj.* swift; rapid. [< v.] —*v.* pass swiftly; move rapidly. [OE *flēotan* float] —**fleet'ly,** *adv.* —**fleet'ness,** *n.*

fleet·ing (flēt'ing), *adj.* passing swiftly; moving rapidly; soon gone. —**fleet'ing·ly,** *adv.* —**fleet'ing·ness,** *n.* —Syn. transitory, momentary, temporary.

Flem., Flemish.

Flem·ing (flem'ing), *n.* **1.** native of Flanders. **2.** a Belgian whose native language is Flemish.

Flem·ish (flem'ish), *adj.* of or having to do with Flanders, its people, or their language. —*n.* **1.** the people of Flanders. **2.** their language.

flesh (flesh), *n.* **1.** a soft substance of the body that covers the bones and is covered by skin. Flesh consists mostly of muscles and fat. **2.** tissue of muscles. **3.** fatness. **4.** meat. **5.** body, not the soul or spirit. **6.** the bad side of human nature. **7.** the human race; people as a group. **8.** all living creatures. **9.** family or relatives by birth. **10.** *Bot.* the soft part of fruits or vegetables; the part of fruits that can be eaten. **11.** a pinkish white with a little yellow. **12.** in the flesh, a. alive. b. in person. [OE *flǣsc*] —**flesh'less,** *adj.*

flesh-col·ored (flesh'kul'ərd), *adj.* pinkish-white with a tinge of yellow.

flesh·ly (flesh'li), *adj.*, **-li·er, -li·est. 1.** of the flesh; bodily. **2.** sensual. —**flesh'li·ness,** *n.*

flesh·pot (flesh'pot'), *n.* **1.** pot for cooking meat. **2.** fleshpots, good food and living; luxuries.

flesh·y (flesh'i), *adj.*, **flesh·i·er, flesh·i·est. 1.** having much flesh; fat. **2.** of or like flesh. **3.** *Bot.* pulpy. —**flesh'i·ness,** *n.*

fleur-de-lis (flėr'də·lē'; -lēs'), *n.*, *pl.* **fleurs-de-lis** (flėr'də·lēz'). **1.** design or device used in heraldry. See the picture in the next column. **2.** the royal coat of arms of France. **3.** the iris flower or plant. [< F, lily flower]

flew (flü), *v.* pt. of **fly².**

flex (fleks), *v.* bend. [< L *flexus* bent]

flex·i·ble (flek'sə·bəl), *adj.* **1.** easily bent; not stiff; bending without breaking. Leather, rubber, and wire are flexible. **2.** easily adapted to fit various uses, purposes, etc.: *the actor's flexible voice.* **3.** easily managed; willing to yield to influence or persuasion. [< F < L *flexibilis.* See FLEX.] —**flex'i·bil'i·ty, flex'i·ble·ness,** *n.* —**flex'i·bly,** *adv.* —Syn. **1.** pliable, pliant, supple, limber. **3.** compliant, yielding, tractable.

flex·ion (flek'shən), *n. Esp. Brit.* flection. [var. of *flection*] —**flex'ion·al,** *adj.*

flex·or (flek'sər), *n. Anat.* any muscle that bends some part of the body.

flex·ure (flek'shər), *n.* **1.** a bending; curving. **2.** bend; curve. —**flex'ur·al,** *adj.*

flib·ber·ti·gib·bet (flib'ər·ti·jib'it), *n.* **1.** a frivolous, flighty person. **2.** a chatterbox.

flic (flik; *Fr.* flēk), *n.* French Slang. policeman.

flick (flik), *n.* **1.** a quick, light blow; sudden, snapping stroke. **2.** the light, snapping sound of such a blow or stroke. **3.** streak; splash; fleck. —*v.* **1.** strike lightly with a quick, snapping blow. **2.** make a sudden, snapping stroke with: *the boys flicked wet towels at each other.* **3.** flutter; move quickly and lightly. [prob. imit.] —**flick'er,** *n.*

flick·er¹ (flik'ər), *v.* **1.** shine with a wavering light; burn with an unsteady flame. **2.** move quickly and lightly in and out or back and forth: *the tongue of a snake flickers.* —*n.* **1.** a wavering, unsteady light or flame. **2.** a brief flame; spark. **3.** a quick, light movement. [OE *flicorian*] —**flick'er·ing·ly,** *adv.*

flick·er² (flik'ər), *n. Am.* woodpecker of North America with golden-yellow feathers on the underside of the wings. [? imit. of its note]

fli·er (flī'ər), *n.* **1.** person or thing that flies. **2.** an aviator. **3.** a very fast train, ship, bus, etc. **4.** *Am.*, *Colloq.* a risky financial venture. Also, flyer.

Flicker (ab. 12 in. long)

flight¹ (flīt), *n.* **1.** act or manner of flying. **2.** distance a bird, bullet, airplane, etc., can fly. **3.** group of things flying through the air together. **4.** *U.S. Air Force.* a tactical unit consisting of two or more airplanes, but frequently two or three elements flying together. **5.** trip in an airplane or airship. **6.** a swift movement. **7.** a soaring above or beyond what is ordinary. **8.** set of stairs or steps between landings or stories of a building. [OE *flyht*; akin to FLY²]

flight² (flīt), *n.* act of fleeing; running away. [ME *fliht* < OE *flēon* flee]

flight·less (flīt'lis), *adj.* unable to fly.

flight·y (flīt'i), *adj.*, **flight·i·er, flight·i·est. 1.** likely to have sudden fancies; full of whims; frivolous. **2.** slightly crazy; light-headed. —**flight'i·ly,** *adv.* —**flight'i·ness,** *n.*

flim·sy (flim'zi), *adj.*, **-si·er, -si·est,** *n.* —*adj.* **1.** slight and thin; frail. **2.** lacking seriousness or sense; trivial: *a flimsy excuse.* —*n.* **1.** a thin paper used by reporters. **2.** a newspaper report on this paper. [? < alter. of *film*] —**flim'si·ly,** *adv.* —**flim'si·ness,** *n.* —Syn. *adj.* **2.** shallow, feeble, weak.

flinch (flinch), *v.* draw back from difficulty, danger, or pain; shrink. —*n.* **1.** a drawing back. **2.** game played with cards bearing numbers from 1 to 14. [prob. < OF *flenchir* < unrecorded Frankish *hlankian* bend. Cf. G *lenken*.] —**flinch'er,** *n.* —**flinch'ing·ly,** *adv.* —Syn. *v.* wince, quail, recoil.

flin·der (flin'dər), *n.* a small piece; fragment; splinter: *smashed to flinders.* [cf. Norw. *flindra*]

fling (fling), *v.*, **flung, fling·ing,** *n.* —*v.* **1.** throw with force; throw: *fling a stone.* **2.** rush; dash. **3.** plunge; kick. **4.** put suddenly or violently:

fling him into jail. —*n.* **1.** a sudden throw. **2.** plunge; kick. **3.** time of doing as one pleases. **4.** a lively Scottish dance. **5.** have a fling at, a. try; attempt. b. make scornful remarks about. [? akin to Scand. *flengja* flog] —**fling′er,** *n.*

flint (flint), *n.* **1.** a very hard, gray or brown stone that makes a spark when struck against steel. **2.** piece of this used with steel to light fires, explode gunpowder, etc. **3.** anything very hard or unyielding. [OE]

Flint (flint), *n.* city in SE Michigan.

flint glass, a brilliant glass containing lead, potassium or sodium, and silicon.

FLINT STEEL
TRIGGER PRIMING-PAN
Gun showing flintlock

flint·lock (flint′lok′), *n.* **1.** gunlock in which a flint striking against steel makes sparks that explode the gunpowder. **2.** an old-fashioned gun with such a gunlock.

flint·y (flin′ti), *adj.,* **flint·i·er, flint·i·est. 1.** consisting of flint; containing flint. **2.** like flint; very hard; unyielding. —**flint′i·ly,** *adv.* —**flint′i·ness,** *n.*

flip¹ (flip), *v.,* flipped, flip·ping, *n., adj.,* flip·per, flip·pest. —*v.* **1.** toss or move with a snap of a finger and thumb. **2.** jerk: *the branch flipped back.* **3.** flick. —*n.* **1.** a smart tap; snap. **2.** a sudden jerk. —*adj. Colloq.* flippant. [prob. imit.]

flip² (flip), *n.* a hot drink containing beer, ale, cider, or the like, with sugar and spice. [n. use of *flip¹,* v.]

flip·pan·cy (flip′ən·si), *n., pl.* -cies. a being flippant.

flip·pant (flip′ənt), *adj.* smart or pert in speech; not respectful. [cf. Scand. *fleipa* babble] —**flip′pant·ly,** *adv.* —**flip′pant·ness,** *n.* —Syn. impertinent, saucy.

flip·per (flip′ər), *n.* a broad, flat limb esp. adapted for swimming. Seals have flippers.

flirt (flėrt), *v.* **1.** make love without meaning it. **2.** trifle; toy: *he flirted with the idea of going to Europe.* **3.** move quickly; flutter. **4.** toss; jerk. —*n.* **1.** person who makes love without meaning it. **2.** a quick movement or flutter. **3.** toss; jerk. [imit.] —**flirt′er,** *n.* —**flirt′ing·ly,** *adv.*

flir·ta·tion (flėr·tā′shən), *n.* **1.** a making love without meaning it. **2.** a love affair that is not serious. —**flir·ta′tious,** *adj.* —**flir·ta′tious·ly,** *adv.* —**flir·ta′tious·ness,** *n.* —Syn. **1.** dalliance.

flit (flit), *v.,* flit·ted, flit·ting, *n.* —*v.* **1.** fly lightly and quickly; flutter. **2.** pass quickly. —*n.* a light, quick movement. [? < Scand. *flytjask*] —**flit′ter,** *n.*

flitch (flich), *n.* side of a hog salted and cured; side of bacon. [OE *flicce*]

flit·ter (flit′ər), *v.,* n. flutter.

fliv·ver (fliv′ər), *n. Am., Slang.* a small, cheap automobile.

float (flōt), *v.* **1.** stay on top of or be held up by air, water, or other liquid; drift: *the boat floated out to sea.* **2.** move with a moving liquid; drift. **3.** rest or move in a liquid, the air, etc. **4.** move around gently. **5.** be unattached; be unstable. **6.** cause to float. **7.** cover with liquid; flood. **8.** set going as a company. **9.** sell (securities): *float an issue of stock.* —*n.* **1.** anything that stays up or holds up something else in water. **2.** a raft. **3.** a cork on a fish line. **4.** a low, flat car that carries something to be shown in a parade. [OE *flotian*] —**float′a·ble,** *adj.*

float·a·tion (flō·tā′shən), *n. Brit.* flotation.

float·er (flōt′ər), *n.* **1.** person or thing that floats. **2.** *Am., Colloq.* person who often changes his place of living, working, etc. **3.** *Am.* person who votes illegally in several places.

float·ing (flōt′ing), *adj.* **1.** that floats. **2.** not fixed; not staying in one place; moving around. **3.** in use or circulation; not permanently invested. **4.** *Com.* not funded; changing. —**float′ing·ly,** *adv.*

floating ribs, *Anat.* ribs not attached to the breastbone; last two pairs of ribs.

floc·cu·lent (flok′yə·lənt), *adj.* **1.** like bits of wool. **2.** made up of soft, woolly masses. [< L *floccus* tuft of wool] —**floc′cu·lence,** *n.* —**floc′cu·lent·ly,** *adv.*

flock¹ (flok), *n.* **1.** group of animals of one kind keeping, feeding, or herded together, esp. of sheep, goats, or birds. **2.** a large group; crowd. **3.** people of the same church group. —*v.* go or gather in a flock; come crowding. [OE *flocc*] —Syn. *n.* **1.** herd, drove. **2.** throng, multitude.

flock² (flok), *n.* **1.** tuft of wool. **2.** waste wool or cotton used for stuffing furniture, etc. **3.** a tiny woolly flake. [< OF < L *floccus*]

floe (flō), *n.* **1.** field or sheet of floating ice. **2.** a floating piece broken off from such a field or sheet. [< Scand. (Norw.) *flo*]

flog (flog; flôg), *v.,* flogged, flog·ging. whip very hard; beat with a whip, stick, etc. —**flog′ger,** *n.*

flood (flud), *n.* **1.** flow of water over what is usually dry land. **2.** a large amount of water; ocean, lake, etc. **3.** a great outpouring of anything: *flood of light, flood of words.* **4.** a flowing of the tide toward the shore; rise of the tide. **5.** the Flood, the water that covered the earth in the time of Noah. Gen. 7. —*v.* **1.** flow over. **2.** fill much fuller than usual. **3.** put much water on. **4.** pour out or stream like a flood. **5.** fill, cover, or overcome like a flood. **6.** flow like a flood. [OE *flōd*] —**flood′a·ble,** *adj.* —**flood′er,** *n.* —**flood′less,** *adj.*

flood control, control of rivers that tend to overflow by the use of dams, levees, dikes, extra outlets, reforestation, etc.

flood·gate (flud′gāt′), *n.* **1.** gate in a canal, river, stream, etc., to control the flow of water. **2.** thing that controls any flow or passage.

flood·light (flud′līt′), *n.* **1.** lamp that gives a broad beam of light. **2.** a broad beam of light from such a lamp. —*v.* illuminate by such a lamp.

floor (flôr; flōr), *n.* **1.** the inside bottom covering of a room. **2.** story of a building. **3.** a flat surface at the bottom. **4.** part of a room or hall where members of a lawmaking body, etc., sit and from which they speak. **5.** right or privilege to speak in a lawmaking body, etc. The chairman decides who has the floor. **6.** the main part of an exchange, where buying and selling of stocks, bonds, etc., is done. **7.** *Colloq.* of prices, amounts, etc., the lowest level. —*v.* **1.** put a floor in or over. **2.** knock down. **3.** *Colloq.* defeat. **4.** *Colloq.* confuse; puzzle. [OE *flōr*] —**floor′less,** *adj.*

floor·ing (flôr′ing; flōr′-), *n.* **1.** floor. **2.** floors. **3.** material for making floors.

floor leader, *Am.* member of a lawmaking body chosen to direct the members who belong to his political party.

floor show, *Am.* an entertainment presented at a night club.

floor·walk·er (flôr′wôk′ər; flōr′-), *n. Am.* person employed in a large store to oversee sales, direct customers, etc.

flop (flop), *v.,* flopped, flop·ping, *n.* —*v.* **1.** move loosely or heavily; flap around clumsily. **2.** fall, throw, or move heavily. **3.** change or turn suddenly. **4.** fail. —*n.* **1.** a flopping. **2.** sound made by flopping. **3.** failure. [imit. var. of *flap*] —**flop′per,** *n.*

flop·py (flop′i), *adj.,* -pi·er, -pi·est. *Colloq.* flopping; tending to flop. —**flop′pi·ly,** *adv.* —**flop′pi·ness,** *n.*

flo·ra (flô′rə; flō′-), *n.* plants of a particular region or time. [< L]

flo·ral (flô′rəl; flō′-), *adj.* **1.** of flowers; having to do with flowers. **2.** resembling flowers. —**flo′ral·ly,** *adv.*

Flor·ence (flôr′əns; flor′-), *n.* city in C Italy. —**Flor·en·tine** (flôr′ən·tēn; flor′-), *adj., n.*

flo·res·cence (flō·res′əns; flô-), *n.* **1.** act of blossoming. **2.** condition of blossoming. **3.** period of blossoming. [< NL *florescentia,* ult. < L *florere* flourish] —**flo·res′cent,** *adj.*

flo·ret (flô′rit; flō′-), *n.* **1.** a small flower. **2.** *Bot.* one of the small flowers in a flower head of a composite plant.

flo·ri·cul·ture (flô′rə·kul′chər; flō′-), *n.* cultivation of flowers. —**flo′ri·cul′tur·al,** *adj.* —**flo′ri·cul′tur·al·ist,** *n.* —**flo′ri·cul′tur·al·ly,** *adv.*

flor·id (flôr'id; flor'-), *adj.* **1.** highly colored; ruddy: *a florid complexion.* **2.** elaborately ornamented; flowery; showy; ornate. [< L *floridus* < *flos* flower] **—flo·rid·i·ty** (flō·rid'ə·ti; flō-flo-), *flor'id·ness, n.* **—flor'id·ly,** *adv.*

Flor·i·da (flôr'ə·də; flor'-), *n.* a State in the extreme SE part of the United States. *Capital:* Tallahassee. *Abbrev.:* Fla. **—Flo·rid·i·an** (flō-rid'i·ən; flō-; flor'-), **Flor'i·dan,** *adj., n. Am.*

flor·in (flôr'ən; flor'-), *n.* **1.** an English silver coin worth 2 shillings. **2.** a gold coin issued at Florence in 1252. **3.** any of various gold or silver coins used in different countries of Europe since then. [< F < Ital. *fiorino* Florentine coin marked with a lily, ult. < L *flos* flower]

flo·rist (flō'rist; flôr'-; flor'ist), *n.* person who raises or sells flowers.

floss (flôs; flos), or **floss silk,** *n.* **1.** short loose silk fibers. **2.** a shiny, untwisted silk thread made from such fibers. **3.** soft, silky fluff or fibers.

floss·y (flôs'i; flos'i), *adj.,* **floss·i·er, floss·i·est.** **1.** of floss. **2.** like floss.

flo·ta·tion (flō·tā'shən), *n.* **1.** a floating or launching. **2.** a selling or putting on sale. Also, *Brit.* floatation.

flo·til·la (flō·til'ə), *n.* **1.** a small fleet. **2.** fleet of small ships. [< Sp., dim. of *flota* fleet]

flot·sam (flot'səm), *n.* **1.** wreckage of a ship or its cargo found floating on the sea. **2.** person or thing that is adrift. [< AF *floteson* < *floter* float < OE]

flounce¹ (flouns), *v.,* **flounced, flounc·ing,** *n.* **—v. 1.** go with an angry or impatient fling of the body: *she flounced out of the room in a rage.* **2.** twist; turn; jerk. **—n. 1.** an angry or impatient fling of the body. **2.** twist; turn; jerk. [< Scand. (Sw.) *flunsa* plunge]

flounce² (flouns), *n., v.,* **flounced, flounc·ing. —n.** a wide ruffle used to trim a dress, skirt, etc. **—v.** trim with a flounce or flounces. [var. of *frounce* < OF *fronce* wrinkle]

floun·der¹ (floun'dər), *v.* **1.** struggle awkwardly without making much progress; plunge about. **2.** be clumsy or confused and make mistakes. **—n.** a floundering. **—floun'der·ing·ly,** *adv.*

Dress with flounces

floun·der² (floun'dər), *n., pl.* **-ders** or (*esp. collectively*) **-der.** flatfish that has a large mouth. [< AF *flo(u)ndre* < Scand. (Norw.) *flundra*]

flour (flour), *n.* **1.** a fine, powdery substance made by grinding and sifting wheat or other grain. **2.** any fine, soft powder. **—v. 1.** cover with flour. **2.** make (grain) into flour. [special use of *flower* (i.e., the flower of the meal)] **—flour'less,** *adj.* **—flour'y,** *adj.*

flour·ish (flér'ish), *v.* **1.** grow or develop with vigor; thrive; do well. **2.** be in the best time of life or activity. **3.** wave (a sword, arm, etc.) in the air. **4.** make a showy display. **5.** make fanciful strokes with a pen; embellish by such strokes. **6.** parade, flaunt, or display ostentatiously. **—n. 1.** a waving in the air. **2.** a showy decoration in writing. **3.** *Music.* a showy trill or passage. **4.** a showy display. [< OF *florir,* ult. < L *flos* flower] **—flour'ish·er,** *n.* **—flour'ish·ing,** *adj.* **—flour'ish·ing·ly,** *adv.* **—Syn.** *v.* **1.** succeed, prosper. **3.** brandish.

Flourishes in handwriting

R.E.Avery

flout (flout), *v.* **1.** treat with contempt or scorn; mock; scoff at. **2.** show contempt or scorn; scoff. **—n.** contemptuous speech or act; insult; mockery; scoffing. [var. of *flute,* v.] **—flout'er,** *n.* **—flout'ing·ly,** *adv.* **—Syn.** *v.* **1.** jeer, taunt. ➤ See **flaunt** for usage note.

flow (flō), *v.* **1.** run like water; circulate. **2.** pour out; pour along. **3.** move easily or smoothly; glide. **4.** hang loose and waving. **5.** be plentiful; be full and overflowing. **6.** flow in; rise. **7.** flood.

—n. 1. act of flowing. **2.** any continuous movement like that of water in a river. **3.** way of flowing. **4.** rate of flowing. **5.** thing that flows; current; stream. **6.** the flowing of the tide toward the shore; rise of the tide. [OE *flōwan*]

flow·er (flou'ər), *n.* **1.** part of a plant that produces the seed; blossom; bloom. **2.** plant grown for its blossoms. **3.** *Bot.* any of several kinds of reproductive structures in lower plants, such as the mosses. **4.** the finest part. **5.** time of being at one's best. **6.** flowers, *Chem.* substance in the form of a fine powder. **7. in flower,** flowering. **—v. 1.** have flowers; produce flowers. **2.** cover or decorate with flowers. **3.** be at one's best. [< OF < L *flos*]

flow·ered (flou'ərd), *adj.* **1.** having flowers. **2.** covered or decorated with flowers.

flow·er·et (flou'ər·it), *n.* a small flower; floret.

flow·er·ing (flou'ər·ing), *adj.* having flowers.

flow·er·pot (flou'ər·pot'), *n.* pot to hold dirt for a plant to grow in.

flow·er·y (flou'ər·i), *adj.,* **-er·i·er, -er·i·est. 1.** having many flowers. **2.** containing many fine words and fanciful expressions. **—flow'er·i·ly,** *adv.* **—flow'er·i·ness,** *n.* ➤ Flowery language originally meant too figurative language, but is now loosely used for any high-flown writing.

flown (flōn), *v.* pp. of **fly²**.

flu (flü), *n. Colloq.* influenza.

flub (flub), *v.,* **flubbed, flub·bing.** *Colloq.* do (something) very clumsily; make a mess of.

fluc·tu·ate (fluk'chū·āt), *v.,* **-at·ed, -at·ing. 1.** rise and fall; change continually; vary irregularly. **2.** move in waves. [< L, < *fluctus* wave] **—fluc'tu·a'tion,** *n.* **—Syn. 1.** oscillate, vacillate.

flue (flü), *n.* **1.** tube, pipe, or other enclosed passage for conveying smoke, hot air, etc. **2.** a flue pipe in an organ. **3.** the air passage in such a pipe.

flu·ent (flü'ənt), *adj.* **1.** flowing. **2.** flowing smoothly or easily: *speak fluent French.* **3.** speaking or writing easily and rapidly. [< L *fluens* flowing] **—flu'en·cy, flu'ent·ness,** *n.* **—flu'ent·ly,** *adv.* **—Syn. 3.** voluble, glib.

flue pipe, an organ pipe in which the sound is made by a current of air striking the mouth or opening in the pipe.

fluff (fluf), *n.* **1.** soft, light, downy particles. **2.** a downy mass: *a fluff of fur.* **—v. 1.** shake or puff out (hair, feathers, etc.) into a soft, light mass. **2.** become fluffy. **—fluff'er,** *n.*

fluff·y (fluf'i), *adj.,* **fluff·i·er, fluff·i·est. 1.** soft and light like fluff: *whipped cream is fluffy.* **2.** covered with fluff; downy: *fluffy baby chicks.* **—fluff'i·ly,** *adv.* **—fluff'i·ness,** *n.*

flu·id (flü'id), *n.* any liquid or gas; any substance that flows. Water, mercury, air, and oxygen are fluids. **—adj. 1.** in the state of a fluid; like a fluid; flowing. **2.** of or having to do with fluids. **3.** changing easily; not fixed. [< L, < *fluere* flow] **—flu·id'ic,** *adj.* **—flu·id'i·ty, flu'id·ness,** *n.* **flu'id·ly,** *adv.*

fluid dram, one eighth of a fluid ounce.

fluid ounce, measure for liquids. In the United States, 16 fluid ounces = 1 pint.

fluke¹ (flük), *n.* **1.** either of the two points of an anchor. **2.** *Am.* the barbed head or barb of an arrow, harpoon, etc. [? special use of *fluke³*]

fluke² (flük), *n.* **1.** a lucky shot in billiards or pool. **2.** a lucky chance; fortunate accident.

fluke³ (flük), *n.* flatfish. [OE *flōc*]

fluk·y, fluk·ey (flük'i), *adj.,* **fluk·i·er, fluk·i·est.** *Colloq.* obtained by chance rather than by skill.

flume (flüm), *n.* **1.** a deep, narrow valley with a stream running through it. **2.** a large, inclined trough or chute for carrying water. [< OF < L *flumen* river < *fluere* flow]

flum·mer·y (flum'ər·i), *n., pl.* **-mer·ies. 1.** oatmeal or flour boiled with water, etc., until thick. **2.** silly talk; nonsense. [< Welsh *llymru*]

flung (flung), *v.* pt. and pp. of **fling.**

flunk (flungk), *Am., Colloq.* **—v. 1.** fail in school work. **2.** cause to fail. **3.** mark or grade as having failed. **4.** give up; back out. **—n.** failure.

flunk·y, flunk·ey (flungk'i), *n., pl.* **flunk·ies;**

flunk·eys. 1. a man servant who wears livery; footman. **2.** a flattering, fawning person.

flu·o·resce (flü′ə·res′), *v.,* –resced, –resc·ing. give off light by fluorescence.

flu·o·res·cence (flü′ə·res′əns), *n. Physics, Chem.* **1.** a giving off of light by a substance when it is exposed to certain rays (X rays and ultraviolet rays). **2.** property of a substance that causes this. **3.** light given off in this way. —**flu·o·res′cent,** *adj.*

fluorescent lamp, an electric lamp usually comprised of a cathode-ray tube containing a gas or vapor which produces light (**fluorescent light**) when electric current is introduced. —**fluorescent lighting.**

fluor·i·date (flür′ə·dāt; flü′ə·rə–), *v.,* –dat·ed, –dat·ing. add small amounts of fluorine to drinking water, esp. to decrease tooth decay in children. [< *fluoridation*]

fluor·i·da·tion (flür′ə·dā′shən; flü′ə·rə–), *n.* act or process of fluoridating. [< *fluoride*]

flu·o·ride (flü′ə·rīd; –rid), **flu·o·rid** (–rid), *n. Chem.* compound of fluorine and another element or radical.

flu·o·rine (flü′ə·rēn; –rin), **flu·o·rin** (–rin), *n. Chem.* a poisonous, greenish-yellow gas, F or Fl, that is a very active element similar to chlorine. —**flu·or·ic** (flü·ôr′ik; –or′–), *adj.*

flu·o·rite (flü′ə·rīt), **flu·or·spar** (flü′ôr·spär′; –ər′–), *n.* calcium fluoride, CaF₂, a transparent, crystalline mineral that occurs in many colors.

fluor·o·scope (flür′ə·skōp; flü′ə·rə–), *n. Am.* device containing a fluorescent screen for examining objects exposed to X rays, etc.

flur·ry (flėr′i), *n., pl.* –ries, *v.,* –ried, –ry·ing. —*n.* **1.** a sudden gust. **2.** *Am.* a sudden, gusty shower or snowfall. **3.** sudden excitement, confusion, or commotion. —*v.* excite; confuse; disturb.

flush¹ (flush), *v.* **1.** blush; glow. **2.** cause to blush or glow. **3.** rush suddenly; flow rapidly: *embarrassment caused the blood to flush to her cheeks.* **4.** wash or cleanse with a rapid flow of water. **5.** make joyful and proud; excite. —*n.* **1.** blush; glow. **2.** a sudden rush; rapid flow. **3.** an excited condition or feeling; sudden rush of joyous pride, etc. **4.** a sudden, fresh growth. **5.** glowing vigor; freshness: *the first flush of youth.* **6.** fit of feeling very hot. [? connected with *flash, blush*]

flush² (flush), *adj.* **1.** even; level. **2.** well supplied; having plenty: *flush with money.* **3.** abundant; plentiful. **4.** glowing; ruddy. **5.** vigorous. —*adv.* **1.** so as to be level; evenly. **2.** directly; squarely. —*v.* make even; level. [? extended use of *flush¹*]

flush³ (flush), *v.* **1.** fly or start up suddenly, as a bird. **2.** cause to fly or start up suddenly.

flush⁴ (flush), *n. Cards.* a hand all of one suit. [cf. F *flus, flux* < L *fluxus* flow]

flus·ter (flus′tər), *v.* make or become nervous and excited; confuse. —*n.* nervous excitement; confusion. [cf. Scand. *flaustr* bustle and *flaustra* be flustered] —**flus′ter·a′tion, flus·tra′tion,** *n.* —Syn. *v.* agitate, embarrass, disconcert.

flute (flüt), *n., v.,* flut·ed, flut·ing. —*n.* **1.** *Music.* a long, slender, pipelike instrument with a series of finger holes or keys along the side. It is played by blowing across a hole near one end. **2.** a long, round groove, as in cloth, a column, etc. —*v.* **1.** play on a flute. **2.** sing or whistle so as to sound like a flute. **3.** make long, round grooves in. [< OF < Pr. *flauta,* ult. < L *flatus* blown] —**flut′ed,** *adj.* —**flute′like′,** *adj.*

flut·ing (flüt′ing), *n.* **1.** decoration made of flutes. **2.** act of playing a flute.

flut·ist (flüt′ist), *n.* person who plays a flute. Also, **flautist.**

flut·ter (flut′ər), *v.* **1.** wave back and forth quickly and lightly. **2.** flap the wings; flap. **3.** come or go with a fluttering motion. **4.** move restlessly. **5.** move quickly and unevenly; tremble: *her heart fluttered.* **6.** beat feebly and irregularly: *her pulse fluttered.* **7.** confuse; excite. —*n.* **1.** a fluttering. **2.** confused or excited condition. Also, **flitter.** [OE *flotorian* < *flēotan* float] —**flut′-**

Fluting

ter·er, *n.* —**flut′ter·ing·ly,** *adv.* —Syn. *v.* **3.** hover, flicker, flit.

flux (fluks), *n.* **1.** a flow; flowing. **2.** a flowing in of the tide. **3.** continuous change. **4.** *Physiol.* an unnatural discharge of blood or liquid matter from the body. **5.** substance used to help metals or minerals melt together. **6.** rate of flow of a fluid, heat, etc., across a certain surface or area. —*v.* **1.** cause a discharge in; purge. **2.** melt together. [< L *fluxus* < *fluere* flow]

flux·ion (fluk′shən), *n.* **1.** a flowing; flow. **2.** discharge.

fly¹ (flī), *n., pl.* flies. **1.** a housefly. **2.** any of a large group of insects that have two wings, including houseflies, mosquitoes, gnats, etc. **3.** any insect with transparent wings, such as a May fly. **4.** fishhook with feathers, silk, tinsel, etc., on it to make it look like an insect. [OE *flēoge*]

fly² (flī), *v.,* flew, flown, fly·ing for 1–9; flied, fly·ing for 10; *n., pl.* flies. —*v.* **1.** move through the air with wings. **2.** float or wave in the air. **3.** cause to fly. **4.** travel through the air in an airplane or airship. **5.** travel over in an airplane or airship. **6.** manage (an airplane or airship). **7.** carry in an airplane or airship. **8.** move swiftly; go rapidly. **9.** run away; flee; flee from; shun. **10.** *Am., Baseball.* hit a ball high in the air. —*n.* **1.** flap to cover buttons on clothing. **2.** flap forming the door of a tent. **3.** a light, public carriage for passengers. **4.** *Am., Baseball.* ball hit high in the air with a bat. [OE *flēogan*] —Syn. *v.* **9.** abscond, decamp.

fly·blown (flī′blōn′), *adj.* **1.** tainted by the eggs or larvae of flies. **2.** spoiled.

fly-by-night (flī′bī·nīt′), *adj.* not reliable; not to be trusted.

fly·catch·er (flī′kach′ər), *n.* any of a family of songless, perching birds having small, weak feet, short necks, and large heads with broad, flattened bills hooked at the tip.

fly·er (flī′ər), *n.* flier.

fly·fish (flī′fish′), *v.* fish with flies as bait. —**fly′-fish′er,** *n.* —**fly′-fish′ing,** *n.*

fly·ing (flī′ing), *adj.* **1.** that flies; moving through the air. **2.** floating or waving in the air. **3.** swift. **4.** short and quick; hasty.

flying boat, airplane that can float on water; seaplane.

flying buttress, *Archit.* an arched support or brace built against the wall of a building to resist outward pressure.

FLYING BUTTRESS

flying colors, success; victory.

flying fish, a tropical fish that has winglike fins and can leap through the air.

flying jib, *Naut.* a small, triangular sail set in front of the regular jib.

flying machine, 1. airplane. **2.** airship.

flying saucer or disk, any of various mysterious disklike objects reportedly seen flying over the United States and Mexico, since 1947.

flying spot, *Television.* a moving beam of light which produces a succession of thin lines against a surface containing an image.

fly·leaf (flī′lēf′), *n., pl.* –leaves. a blank sheet of paper at the beginning or end of a book, pamphlet, etc.

fly·o·ver (flī′ō′vər), *n.* a mass flight of aircraft over a city, reviewing stand, etc., usually as a display of air power.

fly·past (flī′past′; –päst′), *n. Brit.* flyover.

fly·speck (flī′spek′), *n.* a tiny spot left by a fly. —*v.* make flyspecks on.

fly·weight (flī′wāt′), *n.* boxer who weighs not more than 112 pounds.

fly·wheel (flī′hwēl′), *n.* a heavy wheel attached to machinery to keep the speed even.

Fm, fermium.

FM, F.M., frequency modulation.

foal (fōl), *n.* a young horse, donkey, etc.; colt or filly. —*v.* give birth to (a foal). [OE *fola*]

foam (fōm), *n.* mass of very small bubbles. —*v.* **1.** form or gather foam. **2.** cause to foam. **3.** break into foam. [OE *fām*] —**foam′less,** *adj.*

foam rubber, rubber processed so that it is soft and porous, used for cushions, etc.

foam·y (fōm′i), *adj.*, **foam·i·er**, **foam·i·est**. **1.** covered with foam; foaming. **2.** made of foam. **3.** like foam. —**foam′i·ly**, *adv.* —**foam′i·ness**, *n.*

fob (fob), *n.* **1.** a small pocket in trousers or breeches to hold a watch, etc. **2.** *Am.* **a.** a short watch chain, ribbon, etc., that hangs out of a watch pocket. **b.** ornament worn at the end of such a chain, ribbon, etc. [cf. dial. HG *fuppe* pocket]

f.o.b., F.O.B., free on board. The price $850, f.o.b. Detroit, means that the $850 does not pay for freight or other expenses after the article has been put on board a freight car at Detroit.

fo·cal (fō′kəl), *adj.* of a focus; having to do with a focus. —**fo′cal·ly**, *adv.*

focal distance or **length**, distance of the focus from the optical center of a lens.

fo·cal·ize (fō′kəl·īz), *v.*, **-ized**, **-iz·ing**. **1.** focus. **2.** bring into focus. —**fo′cal·i·za′tion**, *n.*

fo·cus (fō′kəs), *n.*, *pl.* **-cus·es**, **-ci** (-sī), *v.*, **-cused**, **-cus·ing**; *esp. Brit.* **-cussed**, **-cus·sing**. —*n.* **1.** point where rays of light, heat, etc., meet, appear to meet, or should meet after being bent by a lens, curved mirror, etc. **2.** distance of this point from the lens, curved mirror, etc.; focal distance. **3.** correct adjustment of a lens, the eye, etc., to make a clear image. **4.** the central point of attention, activity, disturbance, etc. **5.** **in focus**, clear; distinct. **6.** **out of focus**, blurred; indistinct. —*v.* **1.** bring (rays of light, heat, etc.) to a point. **2.** adjust (a lens, the eye, etc.) to make a clear image. **3.** make (an image, etc.) clear by adjusting a lens, the eye, etc. **4.** concentrate: *when studying, he focused his mind on his lessons.* [< L, hearth] —**fo′cus·er**, *n.*

Rays of light brought to a focus at F by the lens, L.

fod·der (fod′ər), *n.* coarse food for horses, cattle, etc. [OE *fōdor* < *fōda* food]

foe (fō), *n.* enemy. [OE *fāh* hostile]

foe·man (fō′mən), *n.*, *pl.* **-men**. *Archaic.* enemy.

foe·tus (fē′təs), *n.* fetus. —**foe′tal**, *adj.*

fog (fog; fôg), *n.*, *v.*, **fogged**, **fog·ging**. —*n.* **1.** cloud of fine drops of water just above the earth's surface; thick mist. **2.** a darkened condition; dim, blurred state. **3.** a confused or puzzled condition. —*v.* **1.** cover with fog. **2.** darken; dim; blur. **3.** confuse; puzzle. [< *foggy*]

fog bank, a dense mass of fog.

fog·gy (fog′i; fôg′i), *adj.*, **-gi·er**, **-gi·est**. **1.** having much fog; misty. **2.** not clear; dim; blurred. **3.** confused; puzzled. [< *fog* long grass; orig., marshy] —**fog′gi·ly**, *adv.* —**fog′gi·ness**, *n.*

fog·horn (fog′hôrn′; fôg′-), *n.* horn that warns ships in foggy weather.

fo·gy, fo·gey (fō′gi), *n.*, *pl.* **-gies**, **-geys**. **1.** person who lacks enterprise. **2.** person who is behind the times. —**fo′gy·ish, fo′gey·ish**, *adj.*

foi·ble (foi′bəl), *n.* a weak point; weakness. [< F, older form of modern *faible* FEEBLE] —Syn. failing, fault, frailty.

foil¹ (foil), *v.* prevent from carrying out (plans, attempts, etc.); turn aside or hinder. [< OF *fuler* trample, full (cloth). See FULLER.]

foil² (foil), *n.* **1.** metal beaten, hammered, or rolled into a very thin sheet. **2.** anything that makes something else look or seem better by contrast. **3.** a very thin layer of polished metal, placed under a gem to give it more color or sparkle. **4.** *Archit.* a leaflike ornament. —*v.* **1.** cover or back with metal foil. **2.** set off by contrast. **3.** ornament with foils. [< F < L *folia* leaves]

foil³ (foil), *n.* a long, narrow sword with a knob or button on the point to prevent injury, used in fencing.

foist (foist), *v.* **1.** palm off as genuine; impose slyly. **2.** insert secretly or slyly. [prob. < dial. Du. *vuisten* take in hand < *vuist* fist]

fold¹ (fōld), *v.* **1.** bend or double over on itself. **2.** bring together with the parts in or around one another. **3.** bring close to the body. **4.** put the arms around and hold tenderly. **5.** wrap; enclose. **6.** fail. —*n.* **1.** layer of something folded. **2.** a hollow place made by folding. **3.** a doubling; bending. **4.** *Geol.* bend in rock after its stratification. [OE *fealdan*]

fold² (fōld), *n.* **1.** pen to keep sheep in. **2.** sheep kept in a pen. **3.** church group; church. —*v.* put or keep (sheep) in a pen. [OE *falod*]

-fold, *suffix.* **1.** times as many; times as great, as in *tenfold*. **2.** formed or divided into ——parts, as in *manifold*. [OE *-feald*]

fold·er (fōl′dər), *n.* **1.** person or thing that folds. **2.** holder for papers, made by folding a piece of stiff paper. **3.** a small book made of one or more folded sheets.

fol·de·rol (fol′də·rol), *n.* falderal.

fo·li·a·ceous (fō′li·ā′shəs), *adj.* **1.** leaflike; leafy. **2.** made of leaflike plates or thin layers. [< L, < *folia* leaves]

fo·li·age (fō′li·ij), *n.* **1.** leaves. **2.** decoration made of carved or painted leaves, flowers, etc. [alter. of F *feuillage*, ult. < L *folia* leaves]

fo·li·ate (*adj.* fō′li·it, -āt; *v.* fō′li·āt), *adj.*, *v.*, **-at·ed**, **-at·ing**. —*adj.* having leaves; covered with leaves. —*v.* put forth leaves.

fo·li·a·tion (fō′li·ā′shən), *n.* **1.** a growing of leaves; putting forth of leaves. **2.** a being in leaf. **3.** decoration with leaflike ornaments. **4.** the arrangement of leaves within the bud. **5.** the consecutive numbering of leaves of a book.

fo·li·o (fō′li·ō), *n.*, *pl.* **-li·os**, *adj.*, *v.*, **-li·oed**, **-li·o·ing**. —*n.* **1.** a large sheet of paper folded once to make two leaves, or four pages, of a book, etc. **2.** book of the largest size, having pages made by folding large sheets of paper once. **3.** any book more than 11 inches in height. **4.** in printing, a page number of a book, etc. **5.** leaf of a book, manuscript, etc., numbered on the front side only. **6.** **in folio**, of folio size or form. —*adj.* of the largest size; made of large sheets of paper folded once. —*v.* number the leaves of a book, pamphlet, etc. [< L, abl. of *folium* leaf]

folk (fōk), *n.*, *pl.* **folk, folks**, *adj.* —*n.* **1.** people. **2.** tribe; nation. **3.** **folks**, **a.** people. **b.** members of one's own family. —*adj.* of or having to do with the common people, their beliefs, legends, customs, etc. [OE *folc*] ▸ **folk, folks.** Formal English, and some local speech, uses *folk* as the plural; informal usually has *folks*, esp. in the sense of "members of one's family."

folk dance, **1.** dance originating and handed down among the common people. **2.** music for it.

folk·lore (fōk′lôr′; -lōr′), *n.* beliefs, legends, customs, etc., of a people, tribe, etc. —**folk′lor·ist**, *n.* —**folk′lor·is′tic**, *adj.*

folk music, music originating and handed down among the common people.

folk song, folk-song (fōk′sông′; -song′), *n.* **1.** song originating and handed down among the common people. **2.** song imitating this.

folk·sy (fōk′si), *adj.*, **-si·er**, **-si·est**. *Colloq.* **1.** appealing to ordinary people; informal. **2.** sociable.

folk tale or **story**, story or legend originating and handed down among the common people.

folk·way (fōk′wā′), *n.* custom or habit that has grown up within a social group and is common among the members of this group.

fol·li·cle (fol′ə·kəl), *n.* **1.** *Anat.* a small cavity, sac, or gland. Hair grows from follicles. **2.** *Bot.* a dry, one-celled seed vessel. Milkweed pods are follicles. [< L *folliculus*, dim of *follis* bellows] —**fol·lic·u·lar** (fə·lik′yə·lər), *adj.*

fol·low (fol′ō), *v.* **1.** go or come after. **2.** result from; result. **3.** go along. **4.** go along with; accompany. **5.** pursue. **6.** act according to; take as a guide; use; obey. **7.** keep the eyes or attention on. **8.** keep the mind on; keep up with and understand. **9.** take as one's work; be concerned with. **10.** **follow out**, carry out to the end. **11.** **follow through**, continue a stroke or motion through to the end. **12.** **follow up**, **a.** follow closely and steadily. **b.** carry out to the end. **c.** increase the effect of by further action. —*n.* act of following. [OE *folgian*] —**fol′low·a·ble**, *adj.* —Syn. *v.* **2.** ensue. **4.** attend.

Follicles (def. 2)

fol·low·er (fol′ō·ər), *n.* 1. person or thing that follows. 2. person who follows the ideas or beliefs of another. 3. attendant; servant. 4. a male admirer; beau. —**Syn.** 2. adherent, disciple.

fol·low·ing (fol′ō·ing), *n.* 1. followers; attendants. 2. the following, persons, things, items, etc., now to be named, related, described, etc. —*adj.* that follows; next after.

fol·ly (fol′i), *n.*, *pl.* -lies. 1. being foolish; lack of sense; unwise conduct. 2. a foolish act, practice, or idea; something silly. 3. a costly but foolish undertaking. [< OF, < *fol* foolish. See FOOL.]

fo·ment (fō·ment′), *v.* 1. promote; foster (trouble, rebellion, etc.). 2. apply warm water, hot cloths, etc., to (a hurt or pain). [< LL *fomentare*, ult. < L *fovere* to warm] —**fo′men·ta′tion,** *n.* —**fo·ment′er,** *n.*

fond (fond), *adj.* 1. liking: *fond of children.* 2. loving: *a fond look.* 3. loving foolishly or too much. 4. cherished. 5. *Archaic.* foolish. [ME *fonned*, pp. of *fonne(n)* be foolish] —**fond′ly,** *adv.* —**fond′ness,** *n.* —**Syn.** 2. affectionate, amorous.

fon·dant (fon′dənt), *n.* a creamy sugar candy used as a filling or coating of other candies. [< F, lit., melting]

fon·dle (fon′dəl), *v.*, -dled, -dling. pet; caress. [< *fond*, v., special use of *fond*, adj.] —**fond′-dler,** *n.*

fon·due (fon′dü; fon·dü′), *n.* a combination of melted cheese, eggs, and butter. [< F, fem. pp. of *fondre* melt]

font¹ (font), *n.* 1. basin holding water for baptism. 2. basin for holy water. 3. fountain; source. [< L *fons* spring]

font² (font), *n.* in printing, a complete set of type of one size and style. Also, *esp. Brit.* fount. [< F *fonte* < *fondre* melt]

Fon·taine·bleau (fon′tən·blō; fon′tən·blō′), *n.* town, in a forest of the same name, near Paris, France. It contains a palace long used by the rulers of France.

Foo·chow (fü′chou′), *n.* seaport in SE China.

food (füd), *n.* 1. what an animal or plant takes in to enable it to live and grow. 2. what is eaten: *give food to the hungry.* 3. a particular kind or article of food. 4. what sustains or serves for consumption in any way: *food for thought.* [OE *fōda*] —**food′less,** *adj.* —**Syn.** 1. nourishment, sustenance, aliment.

food·stuff (füd′stuf′), *n.* material for food.

fool (fül), *n.* 1. person without sense; unwise or silly person. 2. clown formerly kept by a king or lord to amuse people; jester. 3. person who has been deceived or tricked; dupe. —*v.* 1. act like a fool for fun; play; joke. 2. make a fool of; deceive; trick. 3. fool around, *Am., Colloq.* waste time foolishly. 4. fool away, *Colloq.* waste foolishly. 5. fool with, *Colloq.* meddle foolishly with. [< OF *fol* madman, prob. < LL *follis* empty-headed < L, bag, bellows] —**Syn.** *n.* 1. simpleton, dunce.

fool·er·y (fül′ər·i), *n.*, *pl.* -er·ies. foolish action or behavior.

fool·har·dy (fül′här′di), *adj.*, -di·er, -di·est. foolishly bold; rash. —**fool′har′di·ly,** *adv.* —**fool′har′di·ness,** *n.*

fool·ish (fül′ish), *adj.* 1. like a fool; without sense; unwise; silly. 2. ridiculous. 3. trifling. —**fool′ish·ly,** *adv.* —**fool′ish·ness,** *n.*

fool·proof (fül′prüf′), *adj. Am., Colloq.* so safe or simple that even a fool can use or do it.

fools·cap (fülz′kap′), *n.* writing paper in sheets from 12 to 13½ inches wide and 15 to 17 inches long. [from the watermark]

fool's gold, mineral that looks like gold; iron pyrites or copper pyrites.

foot (fut), *n.*, *pl.* feet, *v.* —*n.* 1. the end part of a leg; part that a person, animal, or thing stands on. 2. part near the feet; end toward which the feet are put. 3. the lowest part; bottom; base. 4. part that covers the foot. 5. soldiers that go on foot; infantry. 6. measure of length, twelve inches. 7. one of the parts into which a line of poetry is divided. This line has four feet: "The boy|stood on|the burn|ing deck." —*v.* 1. make or

renew the foot of (a stocking, etc.). 2. walk; step; pace. 3. dance. 4. add. 5. *Colloq.* pay (a bill, etc.). [OE *fōt*]

foot·age (fut′ij), *n.* length in feet.

foot-and-mouth disease, a dangerous, contagious disease of cattle and some other animals, characterized by blisters in the mouth and around the hoofs.

foot·ball (fut′bôl′), *n.* 1. game played with a large, inflated leather ball by two teams of eleven players each on a field with a goal at each end. 2. ball used in this game. 3. any game or ball like this.

foot·board (fut′bôrd′; -bōrd′), *n.* 1. board or small platform to be used as a support for the feet. 2. an upright piece across the foot of a bed.

foot·bridge (fut′brij′), *n.* bridge for people on foot only.

foot·can·dle (fut′kan′dəl), *n.* unit for measuring illumination. It is the amount of light produced by a standard candle at a distance of one foot.

foot·ed (fut′id), *adj.* having a certain kind or number of feet: *a four-footed animal.*

foot·fall (fut′fôl′), *n.* sound of steps coming or going; footstep.

foot·hill (fut′hil′), *n.* a low hill at the base of a mountain or mountain range.

foot·hold (fut′hōld′), *n.* 1. place to put the feet; support for the feet; surface to stand on. 2. a firm footing or position.

foot·ing (fut′ing), *n.* 1. a firm placing or position of the feet. 2. place to put the feet; support for the feet; surface to stand on. 3. a firm place or position. 4. condition; position; relationship: *the United States and Canada are on a friendly footing.* 5. an adding.

foot·lights (fut′līts′), *n.pl.* 1. row of lights at the front of a stage. 2. profession of acting; stage; theater.

foot·loose (fut′lüs′), *adj. Colloq.* free to go anywhere or do anything.

foot·man (fut′mən), *n.*, *pl.* -men. a male servant who answers the bell, waits on the table, etc.

foot·note (fut′nōt′), *n.* note at the bottom of a page about something on the page.

foot·pad (fut′pad′), *n.* a highway robber who goes on foot only.

foot·path (fut′path′; -päth′), *n.* path for people on foot only.

foot·pound (fut′pound′), *n.* quantity of energy needed to raise a weight of one pound to a height of one foot.

foot·print (fut′print′), *n.* mark made by a foot.

foot soldier, soldier who fights on foot; infantryman.

foot·sore (fut′sôr′; -sōr′), *adj.* having sore feet from much walking.

foot·step (fut′step′), *n.* 1. sound of steps coming or going. 2. mark made by a foot; footprint. 3. distance covered in one step. 4. step on which to go up or down.

foot·stool (fut′stül′), *n.* a low stool to put the feet on when sitting.

foot·wear (fut′wâr′), *n.* shoes, slippers, stockings, gaiters, etc.

foot·work (fut′wėrk′), *n. Sports, etc.* way of using the feet.

foo·zle (fü′zəl), *v.*, -zled, -zling, *n.* —*v.* do clumsily; bungle (a stroke in golf, etc.). —*n.* a foozling.

fop (fop), *n.* a vain man who is very fond of fine clothes and has affected manners; empty-headed dandy. —**fop′per·y,** *n.* —**fop′pish,** *adj.* —**fop′-pish·ly,** *adv.* —**fop′pish·ness,** *n.*

for (fôr; *unstressed* fər), *prep.* 1. in place of: *we used boxes for chairs.* 2. in support of; in favor of: *he voted for Roosevelt.* 3. representing; in the interest of: *a lawyer acts for his client.* 4. in consideration of: *these apples are twelve for a dollar.* 5. with the object or purpose of: *he went for a walk.* 6. in order to become, have, keep, etc.: *the navy trains men for sailors, he ran for his life.* 7. in search of: *she is hunting for her cat.* 8. in order to get to: *he has just left for New York.* 9. meant to belong to or be used with;

suited to: *books for children.* 10. because of; by reason of: *he was punished for stealing.* 11. in honor of: *a party was given for her.* 12. with a feeling toward: *we longed for home.* 13. with respect or regard to: *eating too much is bad for one's health.* 14. as far or as long as; throughout; during: *we worked for an hour.* 15. as being: *they know it for a fact.* 16. in spite of: *for all his faults, we like him still.* 17. in proportion to: *for one poisonous snake there are many harmless ones.* 18. to the amount of: *his father gave him a check for $20.* —*conj.* because: *we can't go, for it is raining.* [OE] ➤ **for.** See the usage note under **because.** A comma is usually needed between two coördinate clauses joined by *for;* without it the *for* might be read as a preposition: *He was glad to go, for Mrs. Crane had been especially good to him.* [Not: *He was glad to go for Mrs. Crane.* . . .]

for·age (fôr′ij; for′–), *n., v.,* –aged, –ag·ing. —*n.* 1. food for horses, cattle, etc. 2. a hunting or searching for food. —*v.* 1. supply with food; feed. 2. hunt or search for food. 3. get by hunting or searching about. 4. hunt; search about. 5. get or take food from. 6. plunder. [< F, < OF *fuerre* fodder < Gmc.] —**for′ag·er,** *n.*

fo·ram·i·nif·er·a (fō–ram′ə-nif′ər-ə; fō–), *n.pl.* group of tiny, one-celled sea animals, most of which have shells with tiny holes in them. [< NL, < L *foramen* a small opening + *ferre* to bear] —**fo·ram′i·nif′er·al, fo·ram′i·nif′er·ous,** *adj.*

for·as·much as (fôr′əz-much′ az), in view of the fact that; since; because.

for·ay (fôr′ā; for′ā), *n.* a raid for plunder. —*v.* plunder; lay waste; pillage. [akin to FORAGE. Cf. OF *forrer* forage.] —**for′ay·er,** *n.*

for·bear¹ (fôr-bãr′), *v.,* –bore, –borne, –bear·ing. 1. hold back; keep from doing, saying, using, etc. 2. be patient; control oneself. [OE *forberan*] —**for·bear′er,** *n.* —**for·bear′ing·ly,** *adv.* —Syn. 1. refrain, abstain.

for·bear² (fôr′bãr), *n.* forebear; ancestor.

for·bear·ance (fôr-bãr′əns), *n.* 1. act of forbearing. 2. patience; self-control.

for·bid (fər-bid′), *v.,* –bade (–bad′) or –bad (–bad′), –bid·den or –bid, –bid·ding. 1. order (one) not to do something; make a rule against; prohibit. 2. rule against the appearance or use of; exclude. 3. keep from happening; prevent: *God forbid!* 4. command to keep away from; exclude from: *I forbid you the house.* [OE *forbēodan*] —**for·bid′der,** *n.* —Syn. 1. interdict, proscribe.

for·bid·ding (fər-bid′ing), *adj.* causing fear or dislike; looking dangerous or unpleasant. —**for·bid′ding·ly,** *adv.* —**for·bid′ding·ness,** *n.* —Syn. disagreeable, displeasing, grim.

force (fôrs; fōrs), *n., v.,* forced, forc·ing. —*n.* 1. strength; power. 2. strength used against a person or thing; violence. 3. power to control, influence, persuade, convince, etc.; effectiveness. 4. *Am.* group of people working or acting together: *our office force.* 5. group of soldiers, sailors, policemen, etc. 6. *Physics.* cause that produces, changes, or stops the motion of a body. 7. meaning. 8. **forces,** army, navy, etc. 9. **in force,** a. in effect or operation; binding; valid. b. with full strength. —*v.* 1. use force on 2. compel. 3. *Cards.* a. compel (an opponent) to play a trump or to indicate the strength of his hand. b. compel to play (a particular card). 4. *Am., Baseball.* compel a player to leave one base and try in vain to reach the next. 5. make or drive by force. 6. get or take by force. 7. put by force. 8. break open or through by force. 9. ravish; violate. 10. urge to violent effort. 11. make by an unusual or unnatural effort; strain. 12. hurry the growth or development of. [< F, ult. < L *fortis* strong] —**force′a·ble,** *adj.* —**force′less,** *adj.* —**for′cer,** *n.* —Syn. *n.* 1. might, vigor, energy. 2. coercion, compulsion, constraint. 7. significance, import.

forced (fôrst; fōrst), *adj.* 1. made, compelled, or driven by force: *forced labor.* 2. made by an unusual or unnatural effort: *a forced smile.* —Syn. 1. compulsory, enforced. 2. strained.

forced march, an unusually long, fast march.

force·ful (fôrs′fəl; fōrs′–), *adj.* full of force; strong; powerful; vigorous; effective. —**force′ful·ly,** *adv.* —**force′ful·ness,** *n.*

force·meat (fôrs′mēt′; fōrs′–), *n.* chopped and seasoned meat, used for stuffing, etc.

for·ceps (fôr′seps; –səps), *n.* small pincers or tongs used by surgeons, dentists, etc., for seizing, holding, and pulling. [< L, < *formus* hot + *capere* take]

force pump, pump with a valveless piston whose action forces liquid through a pipe; any pump which delivers liquid under pressure.

for·ci·ble (fôr′sə-bəl; fōr′–), *adj.* 1. made or done by force; using force: *a forcible entrance into a house.* 2. having or showing force; strong; powerful; effective; convincing: *a forcible speaker.* —**for′ci·ble·ness,** *n.* —**for′ci·bly,** *adv.*

ford (fôrd; fōrd), *n.* place where a river or other body of water is not too deep to cross by walking through the water. —*v.* cross by a ford. [OE] —**ford′a·ble,** *adj.* —**ford′less,** *adj.*

fore (fôr; fōr), *adj., adv.* at the front; toward the beginning or front; forward. [adj. use of *fore–*] —*n.* the forward part; front. [< adj.] —*interj. Golf.* shout of warning to persons ahead who are liable to be struck by the ball.

fore–, *prefix.* 1. front; in front; at or near the front, as in *foredeck, foremast.* 2. before; beforehand, as in *foreknow, foresee.* [OE *for(e)*]

fore-and-aft (fôr′ənd-aft′; fōr′–; –äft′), *adj. Naut.* lengthwise on a ship; from bow to stern; placed lengthwise.

fore and aft, *Naut.* 1. at or toward both bow and stern of a ship. 2. lengthwise on a ship; from bow to stern; placed lengthwise.

fore·arm¹ (fôr′ärm′; fōr′–), *n.* that part of the arm between the elbow and wrist.

fore·arm² (fôr-ärm′; fōr–), *v.* prepare for trouble ahead of time; arm beforehand.

fore·bear (fôr′bãr; fōr′–), *n.* ancestor; forefather. Also, *forbear.*

fore·bode (fôr-bōd′; fōr–), *v.,* –bod·ed, –bod·ing. 1. give warning of; predict. 2. have a feeling that something bad is going to happen. —**fore·bod′er,** *n.* —**fore·bod′ing,** *n., adj.* —**fore·bod′ing·ly,** *adv.* —Syn. 1. foretell.

fore·brain (fôr′brān′; fōr′–), *n.* the front section of the brain.

fore·cast (fôr′kast′; fōr′–; –käst′), *v.,* –cast or –cast·ed, –cast·ing, *n.* —*v.* 1. prophesy; predict. 2. be a prophecy or prediction of. 3. foresee; plan ahead. —*n.* 1. prophecy; prediction. 2. a planning ahead; foresight. —**fore′cast′er,** *n.*

fore·cas·tle (fōk′səl; fôr′– kas′əl; fōr′–; –käs′–), *n. Naut.* 1. the upper deck in front of the foremast. 2. sailors' quarters in a merchant ship, formerly in the forward part of the ship.

FORECASTLE, DECK
FORECASTLE
MAIN DECK
LOWER DECK

fore·close (fôr-klōz′; fōr–), *v.,* –closed, –clos·ing. 1. shut out; prevent; exclude. 2. *Law.* take away the right to redeem (a mortgage). [< OF *forclos* excluded < *for–* out (< Frankish *fora–* and L *foris*) + *clore* shut < L *claudere*] —**fore·clos′a·ble,** *adj.*

fore·clo·sure (fôr-klō′zhər; fōr–), *n.* the foreclosing of a mortgage.

fore·done (fôr-dun′; fōr–), *adj., v. Archaic.* exhausted.

fore·doom (fôr-düm′; fōr–), *v.* doom beforehand.

fore·fa·ther (fôr′fä′thər; fōr′–), *n.* ancestor.

fore·fin·ger (fôr′fing′gər; fōr′–), *n.* finger next to the thumb; first finger; index finger.

fore·foot (fôr′fût′; fōr′–), *n., pl.* –feet. 1. one of the front feet of an animal having four or more feet. 2. *Naut.* the forward end of a ship's keel.

fore·front (fôr′frunt′; fōr′–), *n.* place of greatest importance, activity, etc.; foremost part.

fore·gath·er (fôr-gath′ər; fōr–), *v.* forgather.

fore·go¹ (fôr·gō′; fôr-), v., -went, -gone, -going. forgo. —fore·go′er, n.

fore·go² (fôr·gō′; fôr-), v., -went, -gone, -going. precede; go before. —fore·go′er, n.

fore·go·ing (fôr′gō·ing, fôr′-; fôr′gō′ing, fôr′-), adj. preceding; previous.

fore·gone (fôr·gôn′, fôr-, -gon′; fôr′gôn, fôr′-, -gon), adj. that has gone before; previous.

foregone conclusion, fact that was almost surely known beforehand.

fore·ground (fôr′ground′; fôr′-), n. part of a picture or scene nearest the observer; part toward the front.

fore·hand (fôr′hand′; fôr′-), adj. 1. foremost. 2. Tennis, etc. made with the palm of the hand turned forward. —n. 1. Tennis, etc. a forehand stroke. 2. position in front or above; advantage.

fore·hand·ed (fôr′han′did; fôr′-), adj. 1. providing for the future; prudent; thrifty. 2. done beforehand; early. —fore′hand′ed·ness, n.

fore·head (fôr′id; for′id; fôr′hed′), n. 1. part of the face above the eyes. 2. a front part.

for·eign (fôr′ən; for′-), adj. 1. outside one's own country. 2. of, characteristic of, or coming from outside one's own country: foreign money. 3. having to do with other countries; carried on or dealing with other countries: foreign trade. 4. not belonging; not related: sitting still is foreign to a boy's nature. 5. not belonging naturally to the place where found: a foreign substance in the blood. [< OF forain, ult. < L foras outside] —for′eign·ness, n. —Syn. 4. unfamiliar, strange.

foreign affairs, a country's relations with other countries.

for·eign-born (fôr′ən-bôrn′; for′-), adj. born in another country.

for·eign·er (fôr′ən·ər; for′-), n. person from another country; alien.

foreign office, Brit. the government department in charge of foreign affairs.

fore·judge (fôr·juj′; fôr-), v., -judged, -judging. judge beforehand.

fore·know (fôr·nō′; fôr-), v., -knew, -known, -know·ing. know beforehand. —fore·know′a·ble, adj. —fore·knowl·edge (fôr′nol′ij, fôr′-; fôr·nol′ij, fôr-), n.

fore·land (fôr′land′; fôr′-), n. cape; headland; promontory.

fore·leg (fôr′leg′; fôr′-), n. one of the front legs of an animal having four or more legs.

fore·lock (fôr′lok′; fôr′-), n. lock of hair that grows just above the forehead.

fore·man (fôr′mən; fôr′-), n., pl. -men. 1. man in charge of a gang of workers or of some part of a factory. 2. Law. chairman of a jury.

fore·mast (fôr′mast′; fôr′-; -mäst′; Naut. -məst), n. Naut. mast nearest the bow of a ship.

fore·most (fôr′mōst, fôr′-), adj. first in rank, order, place, etc. —adv. first: he stumbled and fell head foremost.

fore·noon (fôr·nün′; fôr-), n. time between early morning and noon.

fo·ren·sic (fə·ren′sik), adj. of or suitable for a law court or public debate. —n. a spoken or written exercise in argumentation, as in a college or high-school class in speech or rhetoric. [< L forensic < forum forum]

fore·or·dain (fôr′ôr·dān′; fôr′-), v. ordain beforehand; predestine. —fore′or·dain′ment, fore·or·di·na·tion (fôr·ôr·də·nā′shən; fôr′-), n. —Syn. predetermine.

fore·paw (fôr′pô′; fôr′-), n. a front paw.

fore·quar·ter (fôr′kwôr′tər; fôr′-), n. a front leg, shoulder, and nearby ribs of beef, lamb, pork, etc.; front quarter.

fore·run (fôr·run′; fôr-), v., -ran, -run, -running. 1. precede. 2. be a sign or warning of (something to come). 3. forestall.

fore·run·ner (fôr′run′ər, fôr′-; fôr·run′ər, fôr-), n. 1. person that goes before or is sent before; herald. 2. sign or warning of something to come. 3. predecessor; ancestor. —Syn. 2. harbinger.

fore·sail (fôr′sāl′; fôr′-; Naut. -səl), n. 1. the principal sail on the foremast of a schooner. 2.
the lowest sail on the foremast of a square-rigged ship.

fore·see (fôr·sē′; fôr-), v., -saw, -seen, -seeing. see or know beforehand. —fore·see′a·ble, adj. —fore·se′er, n. —Syn. anticipate, divine.

fore·shad·ow (fôr·shad′ō; fôr-), v. indicate beforehand; be a warning of. —fore·shad′ow·er, n.

fore·sheet (fôr′shēt′; fôr′-), n. one of the ropes used to hold a foresail in place.

fore·shore (fôr′shôr′; fôr′shōr′), n. part of the shore between the high-water mark and low-water mark.

fore·short·en (fôr·shôr′tən; fôr-), v. represent (lines, etc.) as of less than true length in order to give the proper impression to the eye.

Foreshortening of lines in a cube

fore·show (fôr·shō′; fôr-), v., -showed, -shown, -show·ing. show beforehand; foreshadow.

fore·sight (fôr′sīt′; fôr′-), n. 1. power to see or realize beforehand what is likely to happen. 2. careful thought for the future; prudence. 3. a looking ahead; view into the future. —fore′sight′ed, adj. —fore′sight′ed·ness, n.

fore·skin (fôr′skin′; fôr′-), n. Anat. fold of skin that covers the end of the penis; prepuce.

for·est (fôr′ist; for′-), n. 1. a large area of land covered with trees; thick woods; woodland. 2. the trees themselves. —v. plant with trees; change into a forest. [< OF, ult. < L foris out of doors] —for′est·ed, adj. —for′est·less, adj. —for′est·like′, adj.

fore·stall (fôr·stôl′; fôr-), v. 1. prevent by acting first. 2. deal with (a thing) in advance; anticipate; be ahead of. [ME forstalle(n) < OE foresteall prevention] —fore·stall′er, n. —fore·stall′ment, fore·stal′ment, n.

for·est·a·tion (fôr′is·tā′shən; for′-), n. the planting or taking care of forests.

fore·stay (fôr′stā′; fôr′-), n. Naut. rope or cable reaching from the foremast to the bowsprit.

for·est·er (fôr′is·tər; for′-), n. 1. person in charge of a forest who looks after the trees and guards against fires. 2. person who lives in a forest.

forest preserve, forest protected by the government from wasteful cutting, fires, etc.

for·est·ry (fôr′is·tri; for′-), n. 1. science of planting and taking care of forests. 2. art of making and managing forests. 3. forest land.

fore·taste (n. fôr′tāst′, fôr′-; v. fôr·tāst′, fôr-), n., v., -tast·ed, -tast·ing. —n. a preliminary taste; anticipation. —v. taste beforehand; anticipate.

fore·tell (fôr·tel′; fôr-), v., -told, -tell·ing. tell or show beforehand; predict; prophesy. —fore·tell′er, n. —Syn. forecast.

fore·thought (fôr′thôt′; fôr′-), n. 1. previous thought or consideration; planning. 2. careful thought for the future; prudence.

fore·to·ken (v. fôr·tō′kən, fôr-; n. fôr′tō′kən, fôr′-), v. indicate beforehand; be an omen of. —n. indication of something to come; omen.

fore·top (fôr′top′; fôr′-; Naut. -təp), n. Naut. platform at the top of the foremast.

fore·top·gal·lant (fôr′top·gal′ənt; fôr′-; Naut. -tə·gal′ənt), adj. Naut. next above the fore-topmast.

fore·top·mast (fôr′top′mast′; fôr′-; -mäst′; Naut. -məst), n. Naut. mast next above the foremast.

fore·top·sail (fôr′top′sāl′; fôr′-; Naut. -səl), n. Naut. sail set on the fore-topmast and next above the foresail.

for·ev·er (fər·ev′ər), adv. 1. for always; without ever coming to an end. 2. all the time; always. —Syn. 1. ever, evermore, eternally, everlastingly. 2. continually.

for·ev·er·more (fər·ev′ər·môr′; -mōr′), adv. forever.

fore·warn (fôr·wôrn′; fôr-), v. warn beforehand.

fore·went (fôr·went′; fôr-), v. pt. of forego.

fore·word (fôr′wėrd′; fôr′-), n. introduction; preface.

for·feit (fôr′fit), v. lose or have to give up as a penalty for some act, neglect, fault, etc. —n. 1. thing lost or given up because of some act, neglect, or fault; penalty; fine. 2. loss or giving up of something as a penalty. —adj. lost or given up as a penalty. [< OF forfait < forfaire transgress < for- wrongly (< Frankish for- and L foris outside) + faire do < L facere] —for′feit·a·ble, adj. —for′feit·er, n.

for·fei·ture (fôr′fi·chər), n. 1. a forfeiting. 2. thing forfeited; penalty; fine.

for·gat (fər·gat′), v. Archaic. pt. of forget.

for·gath·er (fôr·gaᵗʰ′ər), v. 1. gather together; assemble; meet. 2. meet by accident. 3. be friendly; associate. Also, foregather.

for·gave (fər·gāv′), v. pt. of forgive.

forge¹ (fôrj; fōrj), n., v., forged, forg·ing. —n. 1. place with fire where metal is heated very hot and then hammered into shape. 2. a blacksmith's shop; smithy. 3. place where iron or other metal is melted and refined. —v. 1. heat (metal) very hot and then hammer into shape. 2. make; shape; form. 3. make or write (something false). 4. sign (another's name) falsely to deceive. [< OF, ult. < L fabrica workshop. Doublet of FABRIC.] —forge′a·ble, adj. —forg′er, n. —Syn. v. 3. counterfeit, falsify.

forge² (fôrj; fōrj), v., forged, forg·ing. move forward slowly but steadily.

for·ger·y (fôr′jər·i; fōr′-), n., pl. -ger·ies. 1. act of forging a signature, etc. 2. something made or written falsely to deceive.

for·get (fər·get′), v., -got or (Archaic) -gat, -got·ten or -got, -get·ting. 1. let go out of the mind; fail to remember; be unable to remember. 2. omit or neglect without meaning to. [OE forgietan]

for·get·ful (fər·get′fəl), adj. 1. apt to forget; having a poor memory. 2. heedless. 3. causing to forget. —for·get′ful·ly, adv. —for·get′ful·ness, n.

for·get-me-not (fər·get′mē-not′), n. any of several small plants with hairy leaves and clusters of small blue or white flowers.

for·give (fər·giv′), v., -gave, -giv·en, -giv·ing. 1. give up the wish to punish or get even with; pardon; excuse. 2. give up all claim to; not demand payment for: forgive a debt. [OE forgiefan] —for·giv′a·ble, adj. —for·giv′er, n. —Syn. 1. absolve.

for·give·ness (fər·giv′nis), n. 1. act of forgiving; pardon. 2. willingness to forgive.

for·giv·ing (fər·giv′ing), adj. that forgives; willing to forgive. —for·giv′ing·ly, adv. —for·giv′ing·ness, n.

for·go (fôr·gō′), v., -went, -gone, -go·ing. 1. do without; give up. 2. refrain; forbear. Also, forego. [OE forgān] —for·go′er, n. —Syn. 1. surrender, relinquish, yield.

for·got (fər·got′), v. pt. and pp. of forget.

for·got·ten (fər·got′ən), v. pp. of forget.

fork (fôrk), n. 1. instrument with a handle and two or more long, pointed parts at one end. 2. anything shaped like a fork, as the place where a tree, road, or stream divides into branches. 3. one of the branches into which anything is divided. —v. 1. lift, throw, or dig with a fork. 2. make in the shape or form of a fork. 3. have a fork or forks; divide into branches. 4. fork over, Am., Slang. hand over; pay out. [< L furca] —fork′less, adj. —fork′like′, adj.

forked (fôrkt; Archaic and Poetic fôr′kid), adj. 1. having a fork or forks. 2. zigzag: forked lightning. —fork·ed·ly (fôr′kid·li), adv. —fork′ed·ness, n.

for·lorn (fôr·lôrn′), adj. 1. left alone; neglected; deserted. 2. wretched in feeling or looks; unhappy. 3. hopeless; desperate. 4. bereft (of). [OE forloren lost, pp. of forlēosan] —for·lorn′ly, adv. —for·lorn′ness, n. —Syn. 1. abandoned, forsaken. 2. miserable.

form (fôrm), n. 1. appearance apart from color or materials; shape. 2. shape of body; body of a person or animal. 3. thing that gives shape to something. A mold is a form. 4. an orderly arrangement of parts. The effect of a work of literature, art, or music comes from its form as well as its content. 5. way of doing something; manner; method: he is a fast runner, but his form in running is bad. 6. a set way of doing something; set way of behaving according to custom or rule; formality; ceremony. 7. a set order of words; formula. 8. document with printing or writing on it and blank spaces to be filled in. 9. way in which a thing exists, takes shape, or shows itself; condition; character. 10. kind; sort; variety: heat, light, and electricity are forms of energy. 11. Philos. that which determines the mode in which a thing exists or is perceived. 12. good condition of body or mind: athletes exercise to keep in form. 13. Gram. any of the various shapes a word has to express different relationships, etc. Boys is the plural form of boy, saw is the past form of see. 14. Brit. class in school. 15. in printing, type fastened in a frame ready for printing or making plates. —v. 1. give shape to; make. 2. be formed; take shape: clouds form in the sky. 3. become: water forms ice when it freezes. 4. make up; compose. 5. organize; establish: we formed a club. 6. develop: form good habits while you are young. 7. arrange in some order: the soldiers formed themselves into lines. [< OF < L forma form, mold] —Syn. n. 1. contour, outline. 6. conventionality. —v. 1. fashion, shape, mold.

-form, suffix. 1. shaped, as in cruciform. 2. (number of) forms, as in multiform. [< L -formis]

for·mal (fôr′məl), adj. 1. with strict attention to outward forms and ceremonies; not familiar and homelike. 2. according to set customs or rules; conventional. 3. done with the proper forms; clear and definite: a contract is a formal agreement. 4. very regular; symmetrical; rigorously methodical; orderly. 5. of language, conforming to established convention in grammar, syntax, and pronunciation. 6. Philos. having to do with the form, not the content. 7. observant of forms; devoted to ceremony. [< L formalis. See FORM.] —for′mal·ly, adv. —for′mal·ness, n. —Syn. 1. stiff, ceremonious. 4. systematic.

form·al·de·hyde (fôr·mal′də·hīd), n. Chem. a colorless gas, CH₂O, with a sharp, irritating odor. It is used in solution as a disinfectant and preservative.

for·mal·ism (fôr′məl·iz·əm), n. strict attention to outward forms and ceremonies. —for′mal·ist, n. —for′mal·is′tic, adj.

for·mal·i·ty (fôr·mal′ə·ti), n., pl. -ties. 1. procedure required by custom or rule; outward form; ceremony. 2. attention to forms and customs. 3. stiffness of manner, behavior, or arrangement. 4. something done merely for form's sake.

for·mal·ize (fôr′məl·īz), v., -ized, -iz·ing. 1. make formal. 2. give a definite form to. —for′mal·i·za′tion, n. —for′mal·iz′er, n.

for·mat (fôr′mat), n. shape, size, and general arrangement of a book, magazine, etc. [< F < L (liber) formatus (book) formed (in a special way)]

for·ma·tion (fôr·mā′shən), n. 1. a forming or being formed. 2. way in which a thing is arranged; arrangement; order: troops in battle formation. 3. thing formed. 4. Geol. series of layers or deposits of the same kind of rock or mineral.

form·a·tive (fôr′mə·tiv), adj. 1. having to do with formation or development; forming; molding. 2. Gram. used to form words. The suffixes –ly and –ness are formative endings. —n. Gram. a formative element. —form′a·tive·ly, adv. —form′a·tive·ness, n.

for·mer¹ (fôr′mər), adj. 1. first of two. 2. earlier; past; long past. [ME formere, a comparative patterned after formest foremost] —Syn. 2. prior, bygone.

form·er² (fôr′mər), n. person or thing that forms.

for·mer·ly (fôr′mər·li), adv. in the past; some time ago. —Syn. previously, once.

for·mic acid (fôr′mik), Chem. a colorless liquid, CH₂O₂, that is irritating to the skin. It occurs in ants, spiders, nettles, etc. [< L *formica* ant]

for·mi·da·ble (fôr′mə·də·bəl), *adj.* hard to overcome; hard to deal with; to be dreaded. [< L, < *formidare* dread] —**for′mi·da·ble·ness,** **for′mi·da·bil′i·ty,** *n.* —**for′mi·da·bly,** *adv.* —Syn. dread, appalling, fearful.

form·less (fôrm′lis), *adj.* without definite or regular form; shapeless. —**form′less·ly,** *adv.* —**form′less·ness,** *n.*

form letter, *Am.* letter so phrased that it may be sent to many different people.

For·mo·sa (fôr·mō′sə), *n.* island off SE China, the seat after 1949 of the Chinese nationalist government.

for·mu·la (fôr′myə·lə), *n., pl.* **-las, -lae** (-lē). 1. a set form of words, esp. one which by much use has partly lost its meaning. "How do you do?" is a polite formula. 2. statement of religious belief or doctrine. 3. rule for doing something, esp. as used by those who do not know the reason on which it is based. 4. recipe; prescription: *formula for making soap.* 5. *Chem.* expression showing by chemical symbols the composition of a compound. The formula for water is H₂O. 6. *Math.* expression showing by algebraic symbols a rule, principle, etc. [< L, dim. of *forma* form]

for·mu·lar·y (fôr′myə·ler′i), *n., pl.* **-lar·ies,** *adj.* —*n.* 1. collection of formulas. 2. a set form of words; formula. —*adj.* having to do with formulas.

for·mu·late (fôr′myə·lāt), *v.,* **-lat·ed, -lat·ing.** 1. state definitely; express in systematic form. 2. express in a formula; reduce to a formula. —**for′mu·la′tion,** *n.* —**for′mu·la′tor,** *n.*

for·ni·cate (fôr′nə·kāt), *v.,* **-cat·ed, -cat·ing.** commit fornication. [< Eccl.L, < *fornix* brothel] —**for′ni·ca′tor,** *n.*

for·ni·ca·tion (fôr′nə·kā′shən), *n.* a sexual act between unmarried persons.

for·sake (fôr·sāk′), *v.,* **-sook** (-sŭk′), **-sak·en, -sak·ing.** give up; leave alone; leave. [OE, < *for-* + *sacan* dispute, deny] —Syn. abandon, desert.

for·sak·en (fôr·sāk′ən), *v.* pp. of forsake. —*adj.* deserted; abandoned; forlorn. —**for·sak′en·ly,** *adv.*

for·sooth (fôr·süth′), *adv. Archaic.* in truth; indeed. [OE *forsōth*]

for·spent (fôr·spent′), *adj. Archaic.* worn out or exhausted with effort, work, etc.

for·swear (fôr·swâr′), *v.,* **-swore, -sworn, -swear·ing.** 1. renounce on oath; swear or promise solemnly to give up. 2. deny solemnly or on oath. 3. be untrue to one's sworn word or promise; perjure (oneself). —**for·swear′er,** *n.*

for·syth·i·a (fôr·sith′i·ə; -sī′thi·ə), *n. Am.* shrub having many bell-shaped, yellow flowers in early spring before its leaves come out. [< NL; named for W. *Forsyth,* horticulturist]

fort (fôrt; fōrt), *n.* a strong building or place that can be defended against an enemy. [< F < L *fortis* strong]

forte¹ (fôrt; fōrt), *n.* something a person does very well; strong point. [< F *fort* < L *fortis* strong]

for·te² (fôr′tā), *adj., adv. Music.* loud. [< Ital., strong, < L *fortis*]

forth (fôrth; fōrth), *adv.* 1. forward; onward. 2. into view or consideration; out. 3. away. [OE]

Forth (fôrth; fōrth), *n.* river in S Scotland.

forth·com·ing (fôrth′kum′ing; fōrth′-), *adj.* 1. about to appear; approaching. 2. ready when wanted: *she needed help, but none was forthcoming.* —*n.* appearance; approach.

forth·right (fôrth′rīt′, fôrth′-; fôrth′rīt′, fōrth′-), *adj.* frank and outspoken; straightforward; direct: *forthright criticism.* —*adv.* 1. straight ahead; directly forward. 2. at once; immediately. —**forth′right′ness,** *n.*

forth·with (fôrth′with′; fōrth′-; -with′), *adv.* at once; immediately.

for·ti·fi·ca·tion (fôr′tə·fə·kā′shən), *n.* 1. a fortifying. 2. fort, wall, ditch, etc., used in fortifying. 3. a fortified place. 4. the enriching of foods, as with vitamins.

for·ti·fy (fôr′tə·fī), *v.,* **-fied, -fy·ing.** 1. build

forts, walls, etc.; strengthen against attack; provide with forts, walls, etc. 2. give support to; strengthen. 3. strengthen with alcohol. 4. enrich (def. 2). 5. confirm: *a claim fortified by facts.* [< F < LL, ult. < L *fortis* strong + *facere* make] —**for′ti·fi′a·ble,** *adj.* —**for′ti·fi′er,** *n.*

for·tis·si·mo (fôr·tis′ə·mō), *adj., adv. Music.* very loud. [< Ital., superlative of *forte* strong]

for·ti·tude (fôr′tə·tüd; -tūd), *n.* courage in facing pain, danger, or trouble; firmness of spirit. [< L, < *fortis* strong] —Syn. endurance, bravery, resolution.

fort·night (fôrt′nīt; -nit), *n.* two weeks.

fort·night·ly (fôrt′nīt·li), *adv., adj., n., pl.* **-lies.** —*adv.* once in every two weeks. —*adj.* appearing or happening once in every two weeks. —*n.* periodical published every two weeks.

for·tress (fôr′tris), *n.* a fortified place; fort. —Syn. citadel, stronghold.

for·tu·i·tous (fôr·tü′ə·təs; -tū′-), *adj.* happening by chance; accidental: *a fortuitous meeting.* [< L *fortuitus,* ult. < *fors* chance] —**for·tu′i·tous·ly,** *adv.* —**for·tu′i·tous·ness,** *n.*

for·tu·i·ty (fôr·tü′ə·ti; -tū′-), *n., pl.* **-ties.** chance; accident.

for·tu·nate (fôr′chə·nit), *adj.* 1. having good luck; lucky. 2. bringing good luck; having favorable results. [< L, < *fortuna* fortune] —**for′tu·nate·ly,** *adv.* —**for′tu·nate·ness,** *n.*

for·tune (fôr′chən), *n., v.,* **-tuned, -tun·ing.** —*n.* 1. good luck; prosperity. 2. what is going to happen to a person; fate. 3. what happens; luck; chance. 4. a great deal of money or property; riches; wealth. 5. amount of wealth. 6. position in life. —*v.* happen; chance. [< OF < L *fortuna*] —**for′tune·less,** *adj.* —Syn. *n.* 1. success. 2. destiny, lot.

for·tune·tell·er (fôr′chən·tel′ər), *n.* person who claims to be able to tell what will happen to people. —**for′tune·tell′ing,** *adj., n.*

Fort Wayne (wān), city in NE Indiana.

Fort Worth (wêrth), city in N Texas.

for·ty (fôr′ti), *n., pl.* **-ties,** *adj.* —*n.* 1. a cardinal number, four times ten. 2. symbol of this number; 40. —*adj.* four times ten; 40. [OE *fēowertig*] —**for′ti·eth,** *adj., n.*

for·ty-nin·er (fôr′ti·nīn′ər), *n. Am.* person who went to California to seek gold in 1849, soon after its discovery there in 1848.

fo·rum (fô′rəm; fō′-), *n., pl.* **fo·rums, fo·ra** (fô′rə; fō′-). 1. the public square or market place of an ancient Roman town. 2. assembly for discussing questions of public interest. 3. a law court; tribunal. [< L]

for·ward (fôr′wərd), *adv.* Also, **for′wards.** 1. ahead; onward: *run forward.* 2. toward the front. —*adj.* 1. toward the front: *the forward part of a ship.* 2. of or pertaining to the future: *forward buying.* 3. far ahead; advanced: *a child of four years that can read is forward for his age.* 4. radical; extreme. 5. ready; eager: *he knew his lesson and was forward with his answers.* 6. pert; bold. —*v.* 1. send on further: *please forward my mail to my new address.* 2. help along. —*n. Sports.* a. a player whose position is in the front line in certain games. b. a forward pass. [OE *forweard*] —**for′ward·er,** *n.* —**for′ward·ly,** *adv.* —**for′ward·ness,** *n.* —Syn. *adj.* 3. precocious. 6. impertinent, presumptuous.

forward pass, *Am.* in football, a pass in the direction of the opponents' goal.

for·went (fôr·went′), *v.* pt. of forgo.

fos·sa (fos′ə), *n., pl.* **fos·sae** (fos′ē). *Anat.* a shallow depression or pit in a bone, etc. [< L, ditch]

fosse, foss (fôs; fos), *n.* ditch; trench; canal; moat. [< F < L *fossa* ditch]

fos·sil (fos′əl), *n.* 1. the hardened remains or traces of animals or plants. 2. a very old-fashioned person, set in his ways. —*adj.* 1. forming a fossil; of the nature of a fossil. 2. belonging to the outworn past: *fossil ideas.* [< F < L *fossilis* dug up < *fodere* dig] —**fos′sil-like′,** *adj.*

Fossil arthropod

fos·sil·if·er·ous (fos′ə·lif′ər·əs), *adj.* containing fossils.

fos·sil·ize (fos′ə·līz), v., -ized, -iz·ing. 1. change into a fossil; turn into stone. 2. make or become antiquated, set, stiff, or rigid. 3. search for fossils. —fos′sil·i·za′tion, n.

fos·ter (fôs′tər; fos′-), v. 1. help the growth or development of. 2. care for fondly; cherish. 3. bring up; rear. —adj. in the same family, but not related by birth: a foster brother. [OE fōstrian nourish, fōster nourishment; akin to FOOD] —fos′ter·er, n. —Syn. v. 1. promote, further. 3. nourish, support.

Fos·ter (fôs′tər; fos′-), n. Stephen Collins, 1826–1864, American composer.

fought (fôt), v. pt. and pp. of **fight**.

foul (foul), adj. 1. containing filth; covered with filth; very dirty; nasty; smelly. 2. very wicked; vile. 3. against the rules; unfair. 4. hitting against: one boat was foul of the other. 5. tangled up; caught: the sailor cut the foul rope. 6. clogged up: the fire will not burn because the chimney is foul. 7. unfavorable; stormy: foul weather delayed the ship. 8. contrary: a foul wind. 9. very unpleasant or objectionable. 10. Am., Baseball. pertaining to a ball not hit within the legal playing area: a foul ball. —v. 1. make or become dirty; soil; defile; disgrace. 2. make a foul; make a foul against. 3. Am., Baseball. hit a ball so that it falls outside the base lines. 4. Naut. hit against: one boat fouled the other. 5. get tangled up with; catch: the rope fouled the anchor chain. 6. clog up. 7. Naut. cover (a ship's bottom) with seaweed, barnacles, etc. —n. 1. thing done contrary to the rules; unfair play. 2. Am., Baseball. ball hit so that it falls outside the base lines. —adv. go, fall, or run foul of, a. hit against and get tangled up with. b. get into trouble or difficulties with. [OE fūl] —foul′ly, adv. —foul′ness, n. —Syn. adj. 1. soiled, polluted, unclean.

fou·lard (fü·lärd′; fə-), n. a soft, thin fabric made of silk, rayon, or cotton, used for neckties, dresses, etc. [< F < Swiss F foulat cloth that has been cleansed and thickened]

foul line, Am., Baseball. either the line from home to first base, or from home to third base, with their unmarked extensions.

found[1] (found), v. pt. and pp. of **find**.

found[2] (found), v. 1. establish; set up: the Pilgrims founded a colony at Plymouth. 2. rest for support; base: he founded his claim on facts. 3. be founded or based. [< OF < L, < fundus bottom] —Syn. 1. settle, plant.

found[3] (found), v. melt and mold (metal); make of molten metal; cast. [< F < L fundere pour]

foun·da·tion (foun·dā′shən), n. 1. part on which the other parts rest for support; base. 2. basis; ground. 3. a founding or establishing. 4. a being founded or established. 5. institution founded and endowed. 6. fund given to support an institution. —foun·da′tion·al, adj.

foun·der[1] (foun′dər), v. 1. fill with water and sink. 2. break down; go lame; stumble. 3. become worn out; fail. 4. cause (a horse) to break down, fall lame, etc. [< OF foundrer, ult. < L fundus bottom]

found·er[2] (foun′dər), n. person who founds or establishes something.

found·er[3] (foun′dər), n. person who casts metals.

found·ling (found′ling), n. baby or child found deserted. [ME fundeling; akin to FIND]

found·ry (foun′dri), n., pl. -ries. 1. place where metal is melted and molded; place where things are made of molten metal. 2. the melting and molding of metal; making things of molten metal.

fount[1] (fount), n. 1. fountain. 2. source. [< L fons spring]

fount[2] (fount; font), n. Esp. Brit. font[2].

foun·tain (foun′tən), n. 1. stream of water rising into the air. 2. pipes through which the water is forced and the basin that receives it. 3. spring of water. 4. place to get a drink. 5. source; origin. 6. container to hold a steady supply of ink, oil, etc. [< OF < LL fontana of a

spring < L fons spring] —foun′tain·less, adj. —foun′tain·like′, adj.

foun·tain·head (foun′tən·hed′), n. 1. source of a stream. 2. original source.

fountain pen, pen for writing that has a reservoir to give a steady supply of ink.

four (fôr; fōr), n. 1. a cardinal number, one more than three. 2. symbol for this number; 4. —adj. one more than three; 4. [OE fēower]

four-flush·er (fôr′flush′ər; fōr′-), n. Am., Slang. person who pretends to be more or other than he really is; bluffer.

four·fold (fôr′fōld′; fōr′-), adj. 1. four times as much or as many. 2. having four parts. —adv. four times as much or as many.

four-foot·ed (fôr′fut′id; fōr′-), adj. having four feet.

four freedoms, freedom of speech, freedom of worship, freedom from want, and freedom from fear; set forth by Franklin D. Roosevelt in 1941.

four hundred, the most fashionable or exclusive social set.

four-in-hand (fôr′in·hand′; fōr′-), n. 1. necktie tied in a slip knot with the ends left hanging. 2. Am. carriage pulled by four horses driven by one person. 3. team of four horses. —adj. 1. tied in a slip knot. 2. pulled by four horses.

four·pence (fôr′pəns; fōr′-), n. 1. four British pennies. 2. a former British silver coin worth four British pennies.

four·pen·ny (fôr′pen′i; fōr′-; -pən·i), n., pl. -nies, adj. —n. fourpence. —adj. worth fourpence; costing fourpence.

four-post·er (fôr′pōs′tər; fōr′-), n. bed with four tall corner posts for supporting curtains.

four·score (fôr′skōr′; fōr′skôr′), adj., n. four times twenty; 80.

four·some (fôr′səm; fōr′-), n. 1. in golf, a game played by four people, two on each side. 2. the players. 3. group of four people.

four-square (adj. fôr′skwär′, fōr′-; n. fôr′skwär′, fōr′-), adj. 1. square. 2. frank; outspoken. 3. not yielding; firm. —n. a square. —four′square′ly, adv. —four′square′ness, n.

four·teen (fôr′tēn′; fōr′-), n. 1. a cardinal number, four more than ten. 2. symbol of this number; 14. —adj. four more than ten; 14. —four′teenth′, adj., n.

fourth (fôrth; fōrth), adj. 1. next after the third; last in a series of 4. 2. being one of 4 equal parts. —n. 1. next after the third; last in a series of 4. 2. one of 4 equal parts. 3. Music. a. tone on the 4th degree from a given tone that is counted as the 1st. b. interval between such tones. c. combination of such tones. —fourth′ly, adv.

fourth dimension, dimension in addition to length, width, and thickness. Time can be thought of as a fourth dimension. —fourth′-di·men′sion·al, adj.

fourth estate, newspapers or newspaper workers; journalism or journalists.

Fourth of July, Am. holiday in honor of the adoption of the Declaration of Independence on July 4, 1776; Independence Day.

fowl (foul), n., pl. fowls or (esp. collectively) fowl, v. —n. 1. any bird. 2. any of several kinds of large birds used for food, such as the hen, rooster, and turkey. 3. flesh of a fowl used for food. —v. hunt wild fowl. [OE fugol] —fowl′er, n.

fowling piece, a light gun for shooting wild birds.

fox (foks), n. 1. a wild animal somewhat like a dog. 2. its fur. 3. a sly, crafty person. —v. 1. Colloq. trick by being sly and crafty. 2. become discolored; cause to become discolored. [OE] —fox′like′, adj.

Red fox
(total length ab. 3½ ft.)

fox·glove (foks′gluv′), n. plant with tall stalks having many bell-shaped flowers.

āge, cāre, fär; ēqual, tėrm; īce; ōpen, ôrder; pút, rüle, ūse; tu, then; ə=a in about.

fox·hole (foks'hōl'), *n. Mil.* hole in the ground for protection against enemy fire.

fox·hound (foks'hound'), *n.* hound with a keen sense of smell, bred and trained to hunt foxes.

fox·tail (foks'tāl'), *n.* 1. tail of a fox. 2. grass with brushlike spikes of flowers.

fox terrier, a small, active dog of a breed once trained to drive foxes from their holes.

fox trot, *Am.* 1. dance with short, quick steps. 2. music for it. 3. pace of a horse between a walk and a trot.

fox-trot (foks'trot'), *v.,* **–trot·ted, –trot·ting.** 1. *Am.* dance the fox trot. 2. (of a horse) go at a pace between a walk and a trot.

fox·y (fok'si), *adj.,* **fox·i·er, fox·i·est.** 1. like a fox; sly; crafty. 2. discolored; stained. **—fox'i·ly,** *adv.* **—fox'i·ness,** *n.*

foy·er (foi'ər; foi'ā), *n.* 1. an entrance hall used as a lounging room in a theater or hotel; lobby. 2. an entrance hall. [< F, ult. < L *focus* hearth]

Fr, *Chem.* francium.

Fr., 1. Father. 2. French. 3. Friday.

fr., 1. fragment. 2. *pl.* **fr., frs.** franc. 3. from.

Fra (frä), *n.* Brother. It is used as the title of a monk or friar.

fra·cas (frā'kəs), *n.* a noisy quarrel or fight; disturbance; brawl. [< F < Ital. *fracasso* < *fracassare* smash]

frac·tion (frak'shən), *n.* 1. *Math.* one or more of the equal parts of a whole. 2. a part: *he got only a fraction of what he wanted.* 3. a very small part, amount, etc.; fragment. [< LL *fractio* < L *frangere* break] **—frac'tion·al,** *adj.* **—frac'tion·al·ly,** *adv.*

frac·tious (frak'shəs), *adj.* 1. cross; fretful; peevish. 2. hard to manage; unruly. **—frac'tious·ly,** *adv.* **—frac'tious·ness,** *n.* **—Syn.** 1. irritable, snappish. 2. refractory, intractable.

frac·ture (frak'chər), *v.,* **–tured, –tur·ing,** *n.* *—v.* break; crack. *—n.* 1. break; crack. 2. a breaking or being broken. 3. a breaking of a bone or cartilage. 4. *Geol.* surface of a freshly broken mineral. [< F < L *fractura* < *frangere* break] **—frac'tur·al,** *adj.*

frae (frā), *Scot.* **—prep.** from. **—adv.** fro.

frag·ile (fraj'əl), *adj.* easily broken, damaged, or destroyed; delicate; frail. [< L *fragilis;* akin to *frangere* break. Doublet of FRAIL.] **—frag'ile·ly,** *adv.* **—fra·gil·i·ty** (frə·jil'ə·ti), **frag'ile·ness,** *n.* **—Syn.** breakable, weak. **—Ant.** tough, strong, elastic.

frag·ment (frag'mənt), *n.* 1. a broken piece; part broken off. 2. an incomplete or disconnected part. 3. part of an incomplete or unfinished work. [< L *fragmentum* < *frangere* break] **—frag·men'tal,** *adj.* **—Syn.** 1. chip, scrap, bit.

frag·men·tar·y (frag'mən·ter'i), *adj.* made up of fragments; incomplete; disconnected. **—frag'men·tar'i·ly,** *adv.* **—frag'men·tar'i·ness,** *n.*

frag·men·ta·tion (frag'mən·tā'shən), *adj.* denoting a bomb, grenade, etc., that scatters pieces of its casing or contents widely upon explosion.

fra·grance (frā'grəns), **fra·gran·cy** (-grən·si), *n., pl.* **–granc·es; –cies.** a sweet smell; pleasing odor.

fra·grant (frā'grənt), *adj.* having a pleasing odor; sweet-smelling. [< L *fragrans* smelling, emitting odor] **—fra'grant·ly,** *adv.*

frail (frāl), *adj.* 1. slender and not very strong; weak. 2. easily broken, damaged, or destroyed. 3. morally weak; liable to yield to temptation. [< OF < L *fragilis.* Doublet of FRAGILE.] **—frail'ly,** *adv.* **—frail'ness,** *n.* **—Syn.** 1. delicate. 2. brittle, fragile.

frail·ty (frāl'ti), *n., pl.* **–ties.** 1. a being frail. 2. moral weakness; liability to yield to temptation. 3. fault or sin caused by moral weakness.

frame (frām), *n., v.,* **framed, fram·ing.** *—n.* 1. support over which something is stretched or built: *frame of a house.* 2. framework. 3. body. 4. skeleton. 5. way in which a thing is put together. 6. an established order; plan; system. 7. shape; form. 8. border in which a thing is set:

a picture frame. 9. one of the individual pictures on a strip of motion-picture film. 10. a triangular form used to set up the balls in the game of pool. 11. one turn at bowling. [< v.] *—v.* 1. shape; form. 2. take shape. 3. put together; plan; make. 4. put a border around. 5. be a border for. 6. *Am., Slang.* prearrange falsely; make seem guilty. [OE *framian* to profit < *fram* forth] **—frame'less,** *adj.* **—fram'er,** *n.* **—Syn. v.** 1. fashion. 3. devise, fabricate, concoct.

frame of mind, way of thinking or feeling; disposition; mood.

frame-up (frām'up'), *n. Am., Slang.* 1. a secret and dishonest arrangement made beforehand. 2. arrangement made to have a person falsely accused.

Part of the frame of a house

frame·work (frām'wėrk'), *n.* 1. support over which a thing is stretched or built; stiff part that gives shape to a thing. 2. way in which a thing is put together; structure.

franc (frangk), *n.* 1. unit of money in France, Belgium, and Switzerland. 2. coin worth one franc. [< OF < *Francorum Rex* king of the Franks, on early coins]

France (frans; fräns), *n.* country in W Europe.

fran·chise (fran'chīz), *n.* 1. privilege or right granted by a government: *a franchise to operate buses on the city streets.* 2. right to vote. [< OF, < *franc* free; akin to FRANK] **—fran'chised,** *adj.* **—fran·chise·ment** (fran'chiz·mənt), *n.*

Fran·cis (fran'sis; frän'-), *n.* Saint, 1181?–1226, the Italian founder of the Franciscan order.

Fran·cis·can (fran·sis'kən), *n.* member of a religious order founded by Saint Francis in 1209. **—adj.** of this religious order.

fran·ci·um (fran'si·əm), *n. Chem.* a rare radioactive element. **—Fr.**

Franck (frängk), *n.* César, 1822–1890, French composer, born in Belgium.

Fran·co (frang'kō), *n.* Francisco, born 1892, Spanish military leader and politician.

fran·gi·ble (fran'jə·bəl), *adj.* breakable. [< OF < L *frangere* break] **—fran'gi·bil'i·ty, fran'gi·ble·ness,** *n.*

frank (frangk), *adj.* 1. free in expressing one's real thoughts, opinions, and feelings; not afraid to say what one thinks. 2. clearly manifest; undisguised; plain: *frank mutiny.* *—v.* send (a letter, package, etc.) without charge. *—n.* 1. mark to show that a letter, package, etc., is to be sent without charge. 2. right to send letters, packages, etc., without charge. 3. letter, package, etc., sent without charge. [< OF, free, sincere (orig., a Frank) < Gmc.] **—frank'a·ble,** *adj.* **—frank'er,** *n.* **—frank'ly,** *adv.* **—frank'ness,** *n.* **—Syn. adj.** 1. open, sincere, straightforward, outspoken. **—Ant. adj.** 1. insincere, hypocritical, deceitful.

Frank (frangk), *n.* 1. member of a group of German tribes that conquered northern Gaul in the sixth century A.D. 2. a Greek and Mohammedan name for any European.

Frank·en·stein (frangk'ən·stīn), *n.* 1. man in a story, who creates a monster that he cannot control. 2. thing that causes the ruin of its creator. [from novel by Mary Shelley]

Frank·fort (frangk'fərt), *n.* capital of Kentucky, in the N part.

Frankfort on the Main (mān), city in W Germany, on the Main River, headquarters of the American occupation forces after World War II.

Frankfort on the O·der (ō'dər), city in E Germany, on the Oder River.

frank·furt·er (frangk'fər·tər), **frank·furt** (-fərt), *n. Am.* a reddish sausage made of beef and pork. [< G, of Frankfort]

frank·in·cense (frangk'in·sens), *n.* a fragrant resin from certain Asiatic or African trees. [< OF *franc encens* pure incense]

Frank·ish (frangk'ish), *adj.* of or having to do with the Franks. *—n.* the language of the Franks (def. 1).

Frank·lin (frangk'lən), n. Benjamin, 1706–1790, American statesman, author, and scientist.

frank·lin (frangk'lən), n. in the 14th and 15th centuries, an English landowner of free birth who ranked next below the gentry. [ME *francoleyn*, ult. < Med.L *francus* free. See FRANK.]

fran·tic (fran'tik), adj. 1. very much excited. 2. *Archaic.* insane. [< OF < L < Gk. *phrenitikos* < *phrenitis* FRENZY. Doublet of PHRENETIC.] —fran'ti·cal·ly, fran'tic·ly, adv. —fran'tic·ness, n. —Syn. 1. mad, distracted, raving, raging.

frap·pé (fra·pā'), *Am.* —adj. iced; cooled. —n. 1. fruit juice sweetened and frozen. 2. any frozen or iced food or drink. [< F, chilled, beaten]

fra·ter·nal (frə·tér'nəl), adj. 1. brotherly. 2. having to do with a fraternal order. [< L *fraternus* brotherly < *frater* brother] —fra·ter'nal·ism, n. —fra·ter'nal·ly, adv.

fraternal order, group organized for mutual aid and fellowship; secret society.

fra·ter·ni·ty (frə·tér'nə·ti), n., pl. -ties. 1. *Am.* group of men or boys joined together for fellowship or for some other purpose. 2. group having the same interests, kind of work, etc. 3. a fraternal feeling; brotherhood.

frat·er·nize (frat'ər·nīz), v., -nized, -niz·ing. 1. associate in a brotherly way; be friendly. 2. associate intimately with the citizens of a hostile nation during occupation of their territory. —frat'er·ni·za'tion, n. —frat'er·niz'er, n.

frat·ri·cide[1] (frat'rə·sīd; frā'trə-), n. act of killing one's own brother or sister. [< L, < *frater* brother + *cidium* act of killing] —frat'ri·cid'al, adj.

frat·ri·cide[2] (frat'rə·sīd; frā'trə-), n. person who kills his own brother or sister. [< L, < *frater* brother + -*cida* killer]

Frau (frou), n., pl. Fraus (frouz), Ger. Frau·en (frou'ən). German. 1. Mrs. 2. wife.

fraud (frôd), n. 1. deceit; cheating; dishonesty. 2. a dishonest act, statement, etc.; something done to deceive or cheat; trick. 3. *Esp. U.S. Colloq.* person who is not what he pretends to be. [< OF < L *fraus* cheating] —Syn. 2. dodge, sham, fake. 3. cheat, impostor, humbug.

fraud·u·lent (frô'jə·lənt; frôd'yu-), adj. 1. deceitful; cheating; dishonest. 2. intended to deceive. 3. done by fraud. —fraud'u·lence, fraud'u·len·cy, n. —fraud'u·lent·ly, adv.

fraught (fôrt), adj. loaded; filled. [< MDu. or MLG *vracht* freight]

Fräu·lein (froi'līn), n., pl. Fräu·leins, Ger. Fräu·lein. German. 1. Miss. 2. an unmarried woman; young lady.

fray[1] (frā), n. a noisy quarrel; fight. [var. of *affray*]

fray[2] (frā), v. 1. separate into threads; make or become ragged or worn along the edge. 2. wear away; rub. [< F *frayer* < L *fricare* rub]

fraz·zle (fraz'əl), v., -zled, -zling, n. *Esp. U.S.* —v. 1. tear to shreds; fray; wear out. 2. tire out; weary. —n. *Colloq.* frazzled condition.

F.R.B., FRB, Federal Reserve Board.

freak (frēk), n. 1. something very queer or unusual. 2. a sudden change of mind without reason; odd notion or fancy. —adj. very queer or unusual. [cf. OE *frician* dance] —freak'ish, adj. —freak'ish·ly, adv. —freak'ish·ness, n. —Syn. n. 2. whim, vagary, caprice.

freck·le (frek'əl), n., v., -led, -ling. —n. a small, light-brown spot on the skin. —v. 1. cover with freckles. 2. become marked or spotted with freckles. [prob. alter. of *frecken* < Scand. *freknur*, pl.] —freck'led, freck'ly, adj.

Fred·er·ick the Great (fred'rick; fred'ər·ik), (*Frederick II*), 1712–1786, second king of Prussia, from 1740 to 1786.

Fred·er·ic·ton (fred'rik·tən; fred'ər·ik-), n. capital of New Brunswick, Canada.

free (frē), adj., fre·er, free·est, adv., v., freed, free·ing. —adj. 1. not under another's control; having liberty; able to do, act, or think as one pleases. 2. showing liberty; caused by liberty. 3. not held back, fastened, or shut up; released; loose. 4. not hindered. 5. clear; open. 6. open to all: *a free port.* 7. without cost, payment, or return. 8. without paying a tax or duty. 9. giving or using much. 10. abundant. 11. not following rules, forms, or words exactly; not strict. 12. saying what one thinks; frank. 13. not restrained enough by manners or morals. 14. not combined with something else: *oxygen exists free in air.* —adv. 1. without cost, payment, or return. 2. freely. —v. 1. relieve from any kind of burden, bondage, or slavery; make free. 2. let loose; release. 3. clear. [OE *frēo*, *frīo*] —free'ly, adv. —free'ness, n. —Syn. 1. independent. 3. movable, unfastened. 9. generous, liberal, lavish. —v. 1. liberate, emancipate. —Ant. adj. 1. subject, bound, restrained. 3. firm, fastened, tied.

free·board (frē'bôrd'; -bōrd'), n. *Naut.* part of a ship's side between the water line and the deck or gunwale.

free·boot·er (frē'büt'ər), n. pirate; buccaneer. [< Du. *vrijbuiter* < *vrij* free + *buit* booty]

free·born (frē'bôrn'), adj. 1. born free, not in slavery. 2. of or suitable for people born free.

free city, city forming an independent state.

freed·man (frēd'mən), n., pl. -men. man freed from slavery.

free·dom (frē'dəm), n. 1. state or condition of being free. 2. not being under another's control; power to do, say, or think as one pleases; liberty. 3. right of enjoying all privileges accompanying citizenship, membership, etc. 4. release from ties, obligations, control, etc. 5. exemption; immunity. 6. free use: *we give a guest the freedom of our home.* 7. lack of restraint; frankness. 8. undue familiarity. 9. ease of movement or action.

freed·wom·an (frēd'wùm'ən), n., pl. -women. woman freed from slavery.

free·hand (frē'hand'), adj. done by hand without using instruments, measurements, etc.

free·hand·ed (frē'han'did), adj. 1. generous; liberal. 2. having the hands free.

free·hold (frē'hōld'), n. *Law.* 1. piece of land held for life or with the right to transfer it to one's heirs. 2. the holding of land in this way. —free'hold'er, n.

free lance, 1. writer, artist, etc., who sells his work to anyone who will buy it. 2. soldier in the Middle Ages who fought for any person, group, or state that would pay him. 3. person who fights or works for any cause that he chooses.

free-lance (frē'lans'; -läns'), v., -lanced, -lanc·ing. work as a free lance.

free·man (frē'mən), n., pl. -men. 1. person who is not a slave or a serf. 2. person who has civil or political freedom; citizen.

Free·ma·son (frē'mā'sən), n. member of a world-wide secret society; Mason. The purpose of the society of Freemasons is mutual aid and fellowship. —free·ma·son·ic (frē'mə·son'ik), adj.

Free·ma·son·ry (frē'mā'sən·ri), n. 1. principles or doctrines of the society of Freemasons. 2. freemasonry, natural fellowship.

free on board, *Com.* delivered free of charge on a train, ship, etc.

free-piston engine, an internal-combustion engine in which each cylinder contains two opposed pistons which are driven apart by the explosion of the fuel so as to force air out of the cylinder and against the blades of a turbine.

free press, *Am.* a press not censored or controlled by the government.

free silver, *Am.* the free coinage of silver; making silver into coins for anybody who brings it to the mint.

free-soil (frē'soil'), adj. *Am., Hist.* pertaining to or in favor of the nonextension of slavery into the Territories, or those parts of the country not yet erected into States. —free'-soil'er, n. *Am.*

free-spo·ken (frē'spō'kən), adj. speaking freely; saying what one thinks; frank. —free'-spo'ken·ly, adv. —free'-spo·ken·ness, n.

free·stone (frē'stōn'), n. 1. stone, such as limestone or sandstone, that can easily be cut without splitting. 2. fruit having a stone that is easily separated from the pulp. —adj. having a fruit stone that is easily separated from the pulp.

free·think·er (frē′thingk′ər), *n.* person who forms his religious opinions independently of authority or tradition. —free′think′ing, *n., adj.* —free thought.

free trade, trade unrestricted by taxes, imposts, or differences of treatment; esp. international trade free from protective tariffs, subject only to tariff for revenue. —free′trad′er, *n.*

free verse, poetry not restricted by the usual rules about meter, rhyme, etc.

free·way (frē′wā′), *n.* a high-speed highway for which no tolls are charged.

free·will (frē′wil′), *adj.* of one's own accord; voluntary: *a freewill offering.*

free will, will free from outside restraints; voluntary choice; freedom of decision.

free world, Free World, the non-Communist nations. —free′world′, *adj.*

freeze (frēz), *v.,* froze, fro·zen, freez·ing, *n.* —*v.* 1. turn into ice; harden by cold. 2. make very cold. 3. become very cold. 4. kill or injure by frost. 5. be killed or injured by frost. 6. cover or become covered with ice; clog with ice. 7. fix or become fixed to something by freezing. 8. make or become stiff and unfriendly. 9. chill or be chilled with fear, etc. 10. become motionless. 11. *Am.* fix a price at a definite amount, usually by governmental decree. 12. *Finance.* make (funds, bank balances, etc.) unusable and inaccessible by governmental decree. 13. freeze out, *Am., Colloq.* force out; get rid of. —*n.* 1. a freezing or being frozen. 2. period during which there is freezing weather. [OE *frēosan*]

freez·er (frēz′ər), *n.* 1. machine to freeze ice cream. 2. a refrigerator cabinet (for frozen foods, ice cream, etc.) within which a temperature below the freezing point is maintained.

freezing point, temperature at which a liquid freezes. The freezing point of water is 32 degrees F. or 0 degrees C.

freight (frāt), *n.* 1. load of goods carried on a train, ship, etc. 2. the carrying of goods on a train, ship, etc. 3. charge for this. 4. train for carrying goods. 5. load; burden. —*v.* 1. load with freight. 2. carry as freight. 3. send as freight. 4. load; burden. [< MDu. or MLG *vrecht*] —freight′less, *adj.*

freight·age (frāt′ij), *n.* 1. the carrying of goods on a train, ship, etc. 2. charge for this. 3. freight; cargo.

freight·er (frāt′ər), *n. Am.* ship for carrying freight.

French (french), *adj.* of or having to do with France, its people, or their language. —*n.* 1. people of France. 2. their language. —French′man, *n.*

French chalk, talc used for marking lines on cloth or removing grease.

French Guiana, a French colony in N South America.

French Guinea, a French colony in W Africa.

French horn, a brass wind instrument that has a mellow tone.

French·i·fy (fren′chə-fī), *v.,* -fied, -fy·ing. make French or like the French.

French Indo-China, territory in SE Asia, S of China, formerly a French colonial possession but since 1949 divided into separate states.

Man playing a French horn

French leave, act of leaving without ceremony, permission, or notice; secret or hurried departure.

French Revolution, revolution in France from 1789 to 1799, which changed France from a monarchy to a republic.

French toast, slices of bread dipped in a mixture of egg and milk and then fried.

French Union, federation of the republic of France and its overseas territories, etc.

French West Africa, group of French colonies in W Africa, reorganized in 1946 as a territory in the French Union.

fre·net·ic (frə·net′ik), *adj.* frantic; frenzied. Also, **phrenetic.** [var. of *phrenetic*] —fre·net′i·cal·ly, *adv.*

fren·zy (fren′zi), *n., pl.* -zies, *v.,* -zied, -zy·ing. —*n.* brief fury; almost madness; very great excitement. —*v.* make frantic. [< OF < L *phrenesis,* ult. < Gk. *phren* mind] —fren′zied, *adj.* —Syn. *n.* rage, raving.

fre·quen·cy (frē′kwən·si), *n., pl.* -cies. 1. Also, **frequence,** a frequent occurrence. 2. rate of occurrence. 3. *Physics.* number of complete cycles per second of an alternating current.

frequency modulation, *Electronics.* 1. a deliberate modulation of the frequency of the transmitting wave in broadcasting. 2. a broadcasting system, relatively free of static, using this method of modulation. Cf. amplitude modulation.

fre·quent (*adj.* frē′kwənt; *v.* fri·kwent′), *adj.* 1. occurring often, near together, or every little while. 2. doing (the act specified) often; regular; habitual. —*v.* go often to; be often in. [< L *frequens* crowded] —fre·quent′er, *n.* —fre′quent·ly, *adv.* —Syn. *v.* haunt, infest.

fre·quen·ta·tive (fri·kwen′tə·tiv), *Gram.* —*adj.* expressing frequent repetition of an action. —*n.* a frequentative verb.

fres·co (fres′kō), *n., pl.* -coes, -cos, *v.,* -coed, -co·ing. —*n.* 1. act or art of painting with water colors on damp, fresh plaster. 2. picture or design so painted. 3. in fresco, with water colors on damp, fresh plaster. —*v.* paint in fresco. [< Ital., cool, fresh] —fres′co·er, *n.*

fresh (fresh), *adj.* 1. newly made, arrived, or obtained: *fresh footprints.* 2. not known, seen, or used before; new; recent. 3. additional; further; another: *a fresh start.* 4. not salty. 5. not spoiled; not stale. 6. not artificially preserved. 7. not wearied; vigorous; lively. 8. not faded or worn; bright. 9. looking healthy or young. 10. pure; cool; refreshing: *a fresh breeze.* 11. *Meteorol.* fairly strong; brisk: *a fresh wind.* 12. not experienced. 13. *Am., Slang.* too bold; impudent. —*n.* 1. the early part. 2. spring, pool, or stream of fresh water. 3. flood. —*adv.* freshly. [OE *fersc;* but infl. in form by OF *freis,* fem. *fresche* < Gmc.] —fresh′ness, *n.* —Syn. *adj.* 2. novel. 12. untrained.

fresh·en (fresh′ən), *v.* make fresh; become fresh. —fresh′en·er, *n.*

fresh·et (fresh′it), *n.* 1. flood caused by heavy rains or melted snow. 2. rush of fresh water flowing into the sea.

fresh·ly (fresh′li), *adv.* in a fresh manner.

fresh·man (fresh′mən), *n., pl.* -men, *adj.* —*n.* 1. *Am.* student in the first year of high school or college. 2. beginner. —*adj.* of these students.

fresh·wa·ter (fresh′wô′tər; -wot′ər), *adj.* of or living in water that is not salty.

fret[1] (fret), *v.,* fret·ted, fret·ting, *n.* —*v.* 1. be peevish, unhappy, discontented, or worried. 2. make peevish, unhappy, discontented, or worried. 3. eat away; wear; rub. 4. roughen; disturb. —*n.* peevish complaining; worry; discontented condition. [OE *fretan* eat] —fret′ter, *n.* —Syn. *v.* 2. harass, vex, provoke, irritate.

fret[2] (fret), *n., v.,* fret·ted, fret·ting. —*n.* an ornamental pattern made of straight lines bent or combined at angles. —*v.* decorate with fretwork. [? < OF *frete*]

fret[3] (fret), *n., v.,* fret·ted, fret·ting. —*n.* any of a series of ridges of wood, ivory, or metal on a guitar, banjo, etc., to show where to put the fingers in order to produce certain tones. —*v.* provide with frets. —fret′ted, *adj.*

fret·ful (fret′fəl), *adj.* apt to fret; peevish. —fret′ful·ly, *adv.* —fret′ful·ness, *n.*

fret·work (fret′wérk′), *n.* 1. ornamental openwork or carving. 2. anything patterned like fretwork.

Fretwork

Freud (froid), *n.* Sigmund, 1856-1939, Austrian physician who developed a theory and technique of psychoanalysis. —Freud·i·an (froid′i·ən), *adj., n.* —Freud′i·an·ism, *n.*

Fri., Friday.

fri·a·ble (frī′ə·bəl), *adj.* easily crumbled. [< L

< *friare* crumble] —fri′a·bil′i·ty, fri′a·ble·ness, *n.*

fri·ar (frī′ər), *n.* member of certain religious orders of the Roman Catholic Church. [< OF < L *frater* brother]

fri·ar·y (frī′ər·i), *n.*, *pl.* -ar·ies. 1. a building or buildings where friars live; monastery. 2. brotherhood of friars.

fric·as·see (frik′ə·sē′), *n.*, *v.*, -seed, -see·ing. —*n.* meat cut up, stewed, and served in a sauce made with its own gravy. —*v.* prepare (meat) in this way. [< F, < *fricasser* mince and cook in sauce]

fric·a·tive (frik′ə·tiv), *Phonet.* —*adj.* pronounced by forcing the breath through a narrow opening formed by placing the tongue or lips near or against the palate, teeth, etc.; spirant. F, v, s, and z are fricative consonants. —*n.* a fricative consonant.

fric·tion (frik′shən), *n.* 1. a rubbing of one object against another; rubbing. 2. resistance to motion or surfaces that touch. 3. conflict of differing ideas, opinions, etc.; disagreement. [< L, < *fricare* rub] —fric′tion·al, *adj.* —fric′tion·al·ly, *adv.* —fric′tion·less, *adj.*

Fri·day (frī′di; -dā), *n.* 1. the sixth day of the week, following Thursday. 2. servant of Robinson Crusoe. 3. any faithful servant or devoted follower.

fried (frīd), *adj.* cooked in hot fat. —*v.* pt. and pp. of fry[1].

fried·cake (frīd′kāk′), *n. Am.* doughnut or cruller.

friend (frend), *n.* 1. person who knows and likes another. 2. person who favors and supports. 3. person who belongs to the same side or group. 4. Friend, member of the Society of Friends, a religious group opposed to war and to taking oaths; Quaker. [OE *frēond*] —friend′ed, *adj.* —friend′less, *adj.* —friend′less·ness, *n.* —Syn. 1. comrade, chum, crony, companion. 2. favorer, supporter, patron, advocate.

friend at court, person who can help one with others; influential friend.

friend·ly (frend′li), *adj.*, -li·er, -li·est, *adv.* —*adj.* 1. of a friend; having the attitude of a friend. 2. like a friend; like a friend's. 3. on good terms; not hostile. 4. wanting to be a friend: *a friendly dog.* 5. favoring and supporting; favorable. —*adv.* in a friendly manner; as a friend. —friend′li·ly, *adv.* —friend′li·ness, *n.*

friend·ship (frend′ship), *n.* 1. state of being friends. 2. the liking between friends. 3. friendly feeling or behavior.

Fries·land (frēz′lənd), *n.* district in N Netherlands.

frieze[1] (frēz), *n. Archit.* 1. a horizontal band of decoration around a room, building, mantel, etc. 2. a horizontal band, often ornamented with sculpture, between the cornice and architrave of a building. See the diagram under entablature. [< F *frise*]

frieze[2] (frēz), *n.* a thick woolen cloth with a shaggy nap on one side. [< F < MDu.]

frig·ate (frig′it), *n.* a three-masted, sailing warship of medium size. [< F < Ital. *fregata*]

frigate bird, a strong-flying, tropical sea bird that steals other birds' food.

fright (frīt), *n.* 1. sudden fear; sudden terror. 2. *Colloq.* person or thing that is ugly, shocking, or ridiculous. —*v. Poetic.* frighten. [OE *fryhto*] —Syn. *n.* 1. dismay, consternation, alarm.

fright·en (frīt′ən), *v.* 1. fill with fright; make afraid; scare. 2. become afraid. 3. drive (away, off, etc.) by scaring. —fright′en·er, *n.* —fright′en·ing·ly, *adv.* —Syn. 1. alarm, dismay, terrify.

fright·ful (frīt′fəl), *adj.* 1. that should cause fright; dreadful; terrible. 2. ugly; shocking. 3. *Colloq.* disagreeable; unpleasant. 4. *Colloq.* very great. —fright′ful·ly, *adv.* —fright′ful·ness, *n.*

frig·id (frij′id), *adj.* 1. very cold: *a frigid climate.* 2. cold in feeling or manner; stiff; chilling: *a frigid bow.* [< L, ult. < *frigus* cold] —fri·gid′i·ty, frig′id·ness, *n.* —frig′id·ly, *adv.*

Frigid Zone, region within the Arctic or the Antarctic Circle.

fri·jol (frē′hōl), **fri·jole** (frē′hōl; frē·hō′lē), *n.*, *pl.* fri·joles (frē′hōlz; frē·hō′lēz; *Sp.* frē·hō′-lās). *Am.* kind of bean much used for food in Mexico and SW United States. [< Sp.]

frill (fril), *n.* 1. a ruffle. 2. *Am.* thing added merely for show; useless ornament; affectation of dress, manner, speech, etc. 3. fringe of feathers, hair, etc., around the neck of a bird or animal. —*v.* decorate with a ruffle; adorn with ruffles. —frill′er, *n.* —frill′y, *adj.*

fringe (frinj), *n.*, *v.*, fringed, fring·ing. —*n.* 1. border or trimming made of threads, cords, etc., either loose or tied together in small bunches. 2. anything like this; border: *a fringe of hair hung over her forehead.* —*v.* 1. make a fringe for. 2. be a fringe for: *bushes fringed the road.* [< OF < L *fimbria*] —fringe′less, *adj.* —fringe′like′, *adj.* —fring′y, *adj.*

Fringes

frip·per·y (frip′ər·i), *n.*, *pl.* -per·ies. 1. cheap, showy clothes; gaudy ornaments. 2. a showing off; foolish display; pretended refinement. [< F *friperie*, ult. < *frepe* rag]

Fris., Frisian.

Fri·sian (frizh′ən), *adj.* of or having to do with Friesland, its people, or their language. —*n.* 1. native or inhabitant of Friesland or certain nearby islands. 2. language spoken in Friesland and certain nearby islands, a West Germanic dialect.

frisk (frisk), *v.* 1. run and jump about playfully; skip and dance joyously; frolic. 2. *Slang.* search (a person) for concealed weapons, stolen goods, etc., by running a hand quickly over his clothes. 3. *Slang.* steal from (a person) in this way. —*n.* a frolic. —*adj.* frisky. [orig. *adj.*, < F *frisque*] —frisk′er, *n.*

frisk·y (fris′ki), *adj.*, frisk·i·er, frisk·i·est. playful; lively. —frisk′i·ly, *adv.* —frisk′i·ness, *n.*

frit·ter[1] (frit′ər), *v.* 1. waste little by little. 2. cut or tear into small pieces; break into fragments. —*n.* a small piece; fragment. [< *fritters*, *n.*, small pieces, ? alter. of *fitters*] —frit′ter·er, *n.*

frit·ter[2] (frit′ər), *n.* a small cake of batter, sometimes containing fruit or other food, fried in fat. [< F *friture*, ult. < L *frigere* fry]

fri·vol·i·ty (fri·vol′ə·ti), *n.*, *pl.* -ties. 1. a being frivolous. 2. a frivolous act or thing.

friv·o·lous (friv′ə·ləs), *adj.* 1. lacking in seriousness or sense; silly. 2. of little worth or importance; trivial. [< L *frivolus*] —friv′o·lous·ly, *adv.* —friv′o·lous·ness, *n.* —Syn. 1. foolish. 2. trifling, unimportant, petty.

friz, frizz (friz), *v.*, frizzed, friz·zing, *n.*, *pl.* friz·zes. —*v.* 1. form into small, crisp curls; curl. 2. form into little tufts: *cloth with a frizzed nap.* —*n.* hair curled in small, crisp curls or a very close crimp. [appar. < F *friser*]

friz·zle[1] (friz′əl), *v.*, -zled, -zling. form into small, crisp curls; curl. [? akin to OE *frīs* curly] —friz′zler, *n.*

friz·zle[2] (friz′əl), *v.*, -zled, -zling. make a hissing, sputtering noise when cooking; sizzle.

friz·zly (friz′li), *adj.* full of small, crisp curls; curly.

friz·zy (friz′i), *adj.* frizzly. —friz′zi·ly, *adv.* —friz′zi·ness, *n.*

fro (frō), *adv.* 1. from; back. 2. to and fro, first one way and then back again; back and forth. [< Scand. *frā*; akin to FROM]

frock (frok), *n.* 1. gown; dress. 2. a loose outer garment. 3. robe worn by a clergyman. —*v.* clothe in a frock. [< OF *froc*] —frock′less, *adj.*

frock coat, a man's coat reaching about to the knees, and equally long in front and in back.

Froe·bel (frœ′bəl), *n.* Friedrich, 1782–1852, German educator who originated the kindergarten.

frog[1] (frog; frôg), *n.*, *v.*, frogged, frog·ging. —*n.* 1. a small, leaping animal with webbed feet, that lives in or near water. 2. animal like this. 3. *Am.* arrangement of a rail where a railroad track crosses or branches from another. 4. pad of horny substance in the middle of the bottom of a foot of a horse, donkey, etc. —*v.* hunt frogs. [OE *frogga*] —**frog'-like'**, *adj.*

frog² (frog; frôg), *n.* an ornamental fastening for a coat or dress. [? < Pg. *froco* < L *floccus* flock²]

frog·man (frog'man), *n., pl.* -men. person trained and equipped with aqualungs for underwater operations of various kinds. Most of the world's navies now have frogmen.

F, frogs on a cloak.

Frois·sart (froi'särt; *French* frwä·sär'), *n.* Jean, 1337?–1410?, French chronicler and poet.

frol·ic (frol'ik), *n., v.,* -icked, -ick·ing, *adj.* —*n.* 1. a gay prank; fun. 2. a merry game or party. [< *v.* or *adj.*] —*v.* play; have fun; make merry. [< *adj.*] —*adj.* full of fun; gay; merry. [< Du. *vrolijk* < MDu. *vro glad*] —**frol'ick·er,** *n.*

frol·ic·some (frol'ik·səm), *adj.* full of fun; gay; merry; playful. —**frol'ic·some·ly,** *adv.* —**frol'ic·some·ness,** *n.*

from (from; frum; *unstressed* frəm), *prep.* 1. out of: *a train from New York.* 2. out of the control or possession of: *take the book from her.* 3. starting at; beginning with: *from that time forward.* 4. caused by; because of; by reason of: *act from a sense of duty.* 5. as being unlike: *tell one tree from another.* [OE *from*]

frond (frond), *n. Bot.* 1. a divided leaf of a fern, palm, etc. 2. a leaflike part of a seaweed, lichen, etc. [< L *frons* leaf] —**frond'ed,** *adj.*

front (frunt), *n.* 1. the first part; foremost part. 2. part that faces forward. 3. part that faces a street or road: *the front of a house.* 4. part containing the main entrance. 5. thing fastened or worn on the front. 6. place where fighting is going on; line of battle. 7. the forces fighting for some political or social aim. 8. the united forces of a political or ideological movement, usually having diverse internal groups and elements. 9. land facing a street, river, etc. 10. manner of looking or behaving. 11. *Colloq.* an outward appearance of wealth, importance, etc. 12. *Am., Colloq.* person appointed to add respectability or prestige to an enterprise. 13. *Am., Colloq.* person or thing that serves as a cover for illicit or illegal activities. 14. *Meteorol.* the dividing surface between two dissimilar air masses. —*adj.* of, on, in, or at the front. —*v.* 1. have the front toward; face. 2. be in front of. 3. meet face to face; defy; oppose. [< L *frons*, lit., forehead]

front·age (frun'tij), *n.* 1. front of a building or of a lot. 2. length of this front. 3. direction that the front of a building or lot faces. 4. land facing a street, river, etc. 5. land between a building and a street, river, etc.

fron·tal (frun'tal), *adj.* 1. of, on, in, or at the front. 2. of the forehead. —*n.* bone of the forehead. —**fron'tal·ly,** *adv.*

fron·tier (frun·tir'; frun'tir; fron'tir), *n.* 1. *U.S.* the farthest part of a settled country, where the wilds begin. 2. *Esp. Brit.* part of a country next to another country. 3. an uncertain or undeveloped region: *the frontiers of science.* —*adj.* of or on the frontier. [< OF < *front* FRONT]

fron·tiers·man (frun·tirz'mən), *n., pl.* -men. man who lives on the frontier.

fron·tis·piece (frun'tis·pēs; fron'-), *n.* 1. a front part. 2. *Archit.* pediment over a door, gate, etc. 3. picture facing the title page of a book or of a division of a book. [< F < LL *frontispicium,* lit., looking at the forehead < L *frons* forehead + *specere* look]

front-page (frunt'pāj'), *adj.* suitable for the front page of a newspaper; important.

frost (frôst; frost), *n.* 1. freezing condition; act or process of freezing. 2. temperature below the point at which water freezes. 3. frozen dew or vapor. 4. coldness of manner or feeling. 5. *Slang.* failure. —*v.* 1. cover with frost. 2. cover with anything that suggests frost. 3. kill or injure by frost. [OE] —**frost'less,** *adj.* —**frost'like',** *adj.*

Frost (frôst; frost), *n.* Robert, born 1875, American poet.

frost·bite (frôst'bīt'; frost'-), *n., v.,* -bit, -bit·ten, -bit·ing. —*n.* injury to the body caused by severe cold. —*v.* injure by severe cold. —**frost-bit·ten** (frôst'bit'ən; frost'-), *adj.*

frost·ing (frôs'ting; fros'-), *n.* 1. mixture of sugar, eggs, water, etc., for covering a cake. 2. a dull finish on glass, metal, etc.

frost·y (frôs'ti; fros'-), *adj.,* frost·i·er, frost·i·est. 1. cold enough for frost; freezing. 2. covered with frost. 3. covered with anything like frost. 4. cold in manner or feeling; unfriendly. —**frost'i·ly,** *adv.* —**frost'i·ness,** *n.* —**frost'less,** *adj.*

froth (frôth; froth), *n.* 1. foam. 2. trivial notions, unimportant talk, etc. —*v.* 1. give out froth; foam. 2. cover with foam. 3. cause to foam. [ME *frothe;* ? < Scand. *frotha;* but cf. OE *āfrēothan,* v.] —**froth'er,** *n.* —Syn. *n.* 1. spume, lather, scum, suds.

froth·y (frôth'i; froth'i), *adj.,* froth·i·er, froth·i·est. 1. foamy. 2. trifling; unimportant. —**froth'i·ly,** *adv.* —**froth'i·ness,** *n.*

frou-frou (frü'frü'), *n.* a rustling. [< F]

fro·ward (frō'wərd; frō'ərd), *adj.* not easily managed; willful; contrary. [< *fro* + -*ward*] —**fro'ward·ly,** *adv.* —**fro'ward·ness,** *n.* —Syn. perverse, obstinate, refractory, untoward.

frown (froun), *n.* 1. a drawing together of the brows, usually in deep thought or in strong feeling. 2. any expression or show of disapproval. —*v.* 1. wrinkle the forehead in annoyance or disapproval. 2. look displeased or angry. 3. express by frowning. [< OF *froignier* < Celtic] —**frown'er,** *n.* —**frown'ing·ly,** *adv.* —Syn. *v.* 1, 2. scowl, lower, glower.

frowz·y, frows·y (frouz'i), *adj.,* frowz·i·er, frowz·i·est; frows·i·er, frows·i·est. 1. slovenly; untidy. 2. smelling bad. —**frowz'i·ly, frows'i·ly,** *adv.* —**frowz'i·ness, frows'i·ness,** *n.*

froze (frōz), *v.* pt. of freeze.

fro·zen (frō'zən), *adj.* 1. turned into ice; hardened by cold. 2. very cold. 3. killed or injured by frost. 4. covered or clogged with ice. 5. cold and unfeeling. 6. too frightened or stiff to move. 7. made temporarily impossible to sell or exchange: *frozen assets.* —*v.* pp. of freeze. —**fro'zen·ly,** *adv.* —**fro'zen·ness,** *n.*

fruc·ti·fy (fruk'tə·fī), *v.,* -fied, -fy·ing. 1. bear fruit. 2. make fruitful; fertilize. [< F < L, < *fructus* fruit + *facere* make] —**fruc'ti·fi·ca'-tion,** *n.*

fruc·tose (fruk'tōs), *n.* fruit sugar, $C_6H_{12}O_6$, a carbohydrate found in all sweet fruits and in honey.

fru·gal (frü'gəl), *adj.* 1. avoiding waste; saving: *a frugal housekeeper.* 2. costing little; barely sufficient: *a frugal meal.* [< L, < *frugi* economical] —**fru·gal'i·ty,** **fru'gal·ness,** *n.* —**fru'gal·ly,** *adv.* —Syn. 1. economical, sparing, thrifty.

fruit (früt), *n.* 1. product of a tree, bush, shrub, or vine that is good to eat. 2. *Bot.* part of a plant that contains the seeds. A fruit is the ripened ovary of a flower and the tissues connected with it. Pea pods, acorns, grains of wheat, etc., are fruits. 3. the useful product of plants: *the fruits of the earth.* 4. offspring. 5. product; result. —*v.* 1. have or produce fruit. 2. cause to produce fruit. [< OF < L *fructus*] —**fruit'like',** *adj.*

fruit·er·er (früt'ər·ər), *n.* dealer in fruit.

fruit fly, a small fly whose larvae feed on decaying fruits and vegetables.

fruit·ful (früt'fəl), *adj.* 1. producing much fruit. 2. producing much of anything. 3. having good results; bringing benefit or profit. —**fruit'-ful·ly,** *adv.* —**fruit'ful·ness,** *n.* —Syn. 2. productive, prolific, fertile.

fru·i·tion (frü·ish'ən), *n.* 1. condition of having results; fulfillment; attainment. 2. pleasure that comes from possession or use. 3. condition of producing fruit. [< LL, < *frui* enjoy]

fruit·less (früt'lis), *adj.* 1. having no results; useless; unsuccessful. 2. producing no fruit; barren. —**fruit'less·ly,** *adv.* —**fruit'less·ness,** *n.* —Syn. 1. ineffective, abortive, futile.

fruit sugar, fructose.

fruit·y (früt'i), *adj.,* fruit·i·er, fruit·i·est. tasting or smelling like fruit. —**fruit'i·ness,** *n.*

frump (frump), *n.* woman who is frumpish.
frump·ish (frump′ish), *adj.* shabby and out of style in dress.
frump·y (frump′i), *adj.*, **frump·i·er**, **frump·i·est**. frumpish. —**frump′i·ly**, *adv.* —**frump′i·ness**, *n.*
frus·trate (frus′trāt), *v.*, **-trat·ed**, **-trat·ing**. 1. bring to nothing; make useless or worthless; foil; defeat. 2. thwart; baffle. [< L, < *frustra* in vain] —**frus′trat·er**, *n.* —**frus·tra′tion**, *n.* —**frus·tra·tive** (frus′trə·tiv), *adj.* —Syn. 1. circumvent, outwit.
frus·tum (frus′təm), *n.*, *pl.* **-tums, -ta** (-tə). *Geom.* part of a conical solid left after the top has been cut off by a plane parallel to the base. [< L, piece]
fry[1] (frī), *v.*, **fried, fry·ing**, *n.*, *pl.* **fries.** —*v.* cook in hot fat. —*n.* 1. fried food; dish of fried meat, fish, etc. 2. *Am.* an outdoor social gathering at which food, usually fish, is fried and eaten. [< F < L *frigere*]
fry[2] (frī), *n.*, *pl.* **fry.** 1. a young fish. 2. small adult fish living together in large groups. 3. young creatures; offspring; children. [cf. Scand. *frjō seed*]
fry·er (frī′ər), *n.* 1. one who fries. 2. fowl (chicken, duck, etc.) intended for frying.
ft., 1. foot; feet. 2. fort.
fuch·sia (fū′shə), *n.* shrub with handsome pink, red, or purple flowers that droop from the stems. [< NL; named for L. *Fuchs*, botanist]
fud·dle (fud′əl), *v.*, **-dled, -dling.** 1. make stupid with drink; intoxicate. 2. confuse.
fudge (fuj), *n.*, *interj.*, *v.*, **fudged, fudg·ing.** —*n.* 1. a soft candy made of sugar, milk, butter, etc. 2. nonsense. —*interj.* nonsense! bosh! —*v.* 1. do or make in a perfunctory way. 2. talk nonsense. 3. fake.
fu·el (fū′əl), *n.*, *v.*, **-eled, -el·ing;** *esp. Brit.* **-elled, -el·ling.** —*n.* 1. thing that can be burned to make a fire. Coal and oil are fuels. 2. thing that keeps up or increases a feeling. —*v.* 1. supply with fuel. 2. get fuel. [< OF *feuaile*, ult. < L *focus* hearth] —**fu′el·er,** *esp. Brit.* **fu′el·ler,** *n.*
fuel injection, the spraying of gasoline or other fuel directly into the combustion chamber of an internal-combustion engine, without prior vaporization and mixing with air in a carburetor.
fu·gi·tive (fū′jə·tiv), *n.* person who is fleeing or who has fled. —*adj.* 1. fleeing; having fled; runaway. 2. lasting only a very short time; passing swiftly. 3. dealing with subjects of temporary interest. 4. roving; shifting. [< F < L *fugere* flee] —**fu′gi·tive·ly,** *adv.* —**fu′gi·tive·ness,** *n.*
fugue (fūg), *n. Music.* composition based on one or more short themes in which different voices or instruments repeat the same melody with slight variations. [< F < Ital. < L *fuga* flight] —**fugue′like′,** *adj.*
Füh·rer, Fueh·rer (fY′rər), *n. German.* 1. leader. 2. der Führer, Adolf Hitler.
Fu·ji·ya·ma (fū′ji·yä′mə), or **Fu·ji** (fū′ji), *n.* a beautiful mountain in S Japan, near Tokyo.
-ful, *suffix.* 1. full of, as in *cheerful.* 2. having; characterized by, as in *careful, thoughtful.* 3. having a tendency to, as in *harmful, mournful.* 4. enough to fill, as in *cupful, handful.* 5. other meanings, as in *manful, useful.* [see FULL, adj.]
ful·crum (ful′krəm), *n.*, *pl.* **-crums, -cra** (-krə). 1. support on which a lever turns or is supported. See the picture under lever. 2. a prop. [< L, bedpost, < *fulcire* to support]
ful·fill, ful·fil (fůl·fil′), *v.*, **-filled, -fill·ing.** 1. carry out (a promise, prophecy, etc.); cause to happen or take place. 2. do or perform (a duty); obey (a command, etc.). 3. satisfy (a requirement, condition, etc.); serve (a purpose). 4. finish; complete. [OE *fullfyllan*] —**ful·fill′er,** *n.* —**ful·fill′ment, ful·fil′ment,** *n.* —Syn. 1. accomplish, realize. 2. execute, discharge.
full (fůl), *n.* 1. the greatest size, amount, extent, volume, etc. 2. **in full,** a. to or for the complete amount. b. written or said with all the words; not abbreviated or shortened. —*v.* make or become full. —*adj.* 1. able to hold no more; filled:

a *full cup.* 2. complete; entire: *a full supply.* 3. of the greatest size, amount, extent, volume, etc.: *a full mile.* 4. more than enough to satisfy; well supplied; abundant. 5. well filled out; plump; round. 6. strong, sonorous, and distinct: *a full voice.* 7. made with wide folds or much cloth. —*adv.* 1. completely; entirely. 2. straight; directly: *the blow hit him full in the face.* [OE] —**full′ness,** *n.* —**ful′ly,** *adv.* —Syn. *adj.* 1. replete, sated. 2. whole. 4. ample, plentiful, copious.
full·back (fůl′bak′), *n. Football, etc.* player whose position is farthest behind the front line.
full-blood·ed (fůl′blud′id), *adj. Am.* 1. of pure race, breed, etc. 2. vigorous; hearty.
full dress, formal clothes worn in the evening or on important occasions.
full-dress (fůl′dres′), *adj.* 1. pertaining to full dress: *a full-dress dinner.* 2. complete; formal: *a full-dress conference, debate, etc.*
full·er (fůl′ər), *n.* person whose work is cleaning and thickening cloth. [< L *fullo* fuller]
fuller's earth, a claylike mixture used for removing grease from cloth and for purifying oil.
full-fash·ioned (fůl′fash′ənd), *adj.* knitted to fit the shape of the foot or leg.
full-grown (fůl′grōn′), *adj.* mature.
full house, a poker hand made up of three cards of one kind and two of another.
full moon, the moon seen as a whole circle.
ful·mi·nate (ful′mə·nāt), *v.*, **-nat·ed, -nat·ing,** *n.* —*v.* 1. lighten and thunder. 2. thunder forth in speech or writing. 3. denounce violently; censure strongly. 4. explode violently. —*n. Chem.* an unstable, explosive salt. [< L, < *fulmen* lightning] —**ful′mi·na′tion,** *n.* —**ful′mi·na′tor,** *n.*
ful·ness (fůl′nis), *n.* fullness.
ful·some (fůl′səm; fůl′-), *adj.* so much as to be disgusting; offensive. [< *full* + -*some*[1]; infl. in meaning by *foul*] —**ful′some·ly,** *adv.* —**ful′some·ness,** *n.* —Syn. excessive, immoderate.
Ful·ton (fůl′tən), *n.* Robert, 1765–1815, American inventor.
fu·ma·gil·lin (fū′mə·gil′in), *n.* an antibiotic derived from a fungus, used esp. against amoebic infections.
fum·ble (fum′bəl), *v.*, **-bled, -bling,** *n.* —*v.* 1. grope awkwardly. 2. handle awkwardly. 3. *Sports.* fail to hold (a ball). —*n.* 1. an awkward groping or handling. 2. *Sports.* failure to hold a ball. [cf. LG *fummeln*] —**fum′bler,** *n.* —**fum′bling,** *adj.*, *n.* —**fum′bling·ly,** *adv.*
fume (fūm), *v.*, **fumed, fum·ing,** *n.* —*v.* 1. give off fumes. 2. pass off in fumes. 3. make angry complaints; show anger or irritation. 4. treat with fumes. —*n.* 1. Often, **fumes.** vapor, gas, or smoke, esp. if harmful, strong, or odorous. 2. any smokelike or odorous exhalation. 3. fit of anger; angry or irritable mood. [< OF < L *fumus* smoke] —**fume′less,** *adj.* —**fum′er,** *n.* —**fum′ing·ly,** *adv.* —Syn. *v.* 1. smoke. 3. chafe, fret.
fu·mi·gate (fū′mə·gāt), *v.*, **-gat·ed, -gat·ing.** disinfect with fumes; expose to fumes. [< L *fumigatus* < *fumus* fume] —**fu′mi·ga′tion,** *n.* —**fu′mi·ga′tor,** *n. Am.*
fun (fun), *n.*, *v.*, **funned, fun·ning.** —*n.* 1. playfulness; merry play; amusement; joking. 2. for or in fun, playfully; as a joke. 3. **make fun of** or **poke fun at,** laugh at; ridicule. —*v. Colloq.* make fun; joke. [? orig. v., var. of obs. *fon* befool]
func·tion (fungk′shən), *n.* 1. proper work; normal action or use; purpose. 2. a formal public or social gathering for some purpose. 3. *Math.* quantity whose value depends on, or varies with, the value given to one or more related quantities. 4. thing, quality, or feature which depends on and varies with something else: *longevity is in part a function of health.* 5. *Gram.* role a linguistic form plays in communication. —*v.* work; be used; act. [< L *functio* < *fungi* perform] —**func′tion·less,** *adj.* —Syn. *n.* 1. capacity.
func·tion·al (fungk′shən·əl), *adj.* 1. having to do with a function or functions. 2. having a function; working; acting. 3. useful in many ways; adaptable. —**func′tion·al·ly,** *adv.*
func·tion·ar·y (fungk′shən·er′i), *n.*, *pl.* **-ar·ies.** person charged with a function or office.

function word, *Gram.* word whose function in a sentence is mainly to express relationships between other elements or to express grammatical meanings. Prepositions, conjunctions, and auxiliary verbs are considered the most important subgroups of function words.

fund (fund), *n.* **1.** sum of money set aside for a special purpose. **2.** stock or store ready for use; supply: *a fund of information.* **3.** funds, a. money ready to use. b. money. —*v.* **1.** set aside a sum of money to pay the interest on (a debt). **2.** change (a debt) from a short term to a long term. [< L *fundus* bottom, piece of land]

fun·da·men·tal (fun'də·men'təl), *adj.* **1.** of the foundation or basis; forming a foundation or basis; essential. **2.** *Music.* having to do with the lowest note of a chord. —*n.* **1.** principle, rule, law, etc., that forms a foundation or basis; essential part. **2.** *Music.* the lowest note of a chord. **3.** *Physics.* that component of a wave which has the greatest wave length. [< NL, < L *fundamentum* foundation, ult. < *fundus* bottom] —fun'da·men·tal'i·ty, *n.* —fun'da·men'tal·ly, *adv.* —Syn. *adj.* **1.** basic, indispensable.

fun·da·men·tal·ism (fun'də·men'təl·iz·əm), *n. Am.* **1.** the belief that the words of the Bible were inspired by God and should be believed and followed literally. **2.** movement in certain Protestant churches upholding this belief. —fun'da·men'tal·ist, *n., adj. Am.*

Fun·dy (fun'di), *n.* Bay of, a deep inlet of the Atlantic, in SE Canada.

fu·ner·al (fū'nər·əl; fūn'rəl), *n.* **1.** ceremonies performed when a dead person's body is buried or burned. **2.** procession taking a dead person's body to the place where it is buried or burned. —*adj.* of or suitable for a funeral. [< LL *funeralis* < L *funus* funeral, death]

fu·ne·re·al (fū·nir'i·əl), *adj.* **1.** of or suitable for a funeral. **2.** gloomy; dismal. —fu·ne're·al·ly, *adv.* —Syn. solemn, sad, mournful.

fun·gi·cide (fun'jə·sīd), *n.* any substance that destroys fungi. [< L *fungus* + *-cida* killer] —fun'gi·cid'al, *adj.*

fun·gous (fung'gəs), *adj.* **1.** of a fungus or fungi; like a fungus; spongy. **2.** caused by a fungus.

fun·gus (fung'gəs), *n., pl.* **fun·gi** (fun'jī), **fun·gus·es,** *adj.* —*n.* **1.** plant without flowers, leaves, or green coloring matter. Mushrooms, toadstools, molds, smuts, and mildews are fungi. **2.** something that grows or springs up rapidly like a mushroom. **3.** a diseased, spongy growth on the skin. —*adj.* fungous. [< L; prob. akin to Gk. *sphongos* sponge] —fun'gus·like', *adj.*

Fungi growing on a tree

funk (fungk), *Colloq.* —*n.* **1.** fear; panic. **2.** coward. —*v.* **1.** be afraid of. **2.** frighten. **3.** shrink from; shirk.

fun·nel (fun'əl), *n., v.,* -neled, -nel·ing; *esp. Brit.* -nelled, -nel·ling. —*n.* **1.** a small, tapering tube with a wide, cone-shaped mouth. **2.** anything shaped like a funnel. **3.** a round, metal chimney; smokestack. **4.** flue. —*v.* **1.** pass or feed through a funnel. **2.** converge. [< OF < LL < L, < *in-* in + *fundere* pour] —fun'nel·like', *adj.*

fun·ny (fun'i), *adj.,* -ni·er, -ni·est, *n., pl.* -nies. —*adj.* **1.** causing laughter; amusing. **2.** strange; queer; odd. **3.** *Am.* of or pertaining to the part of a newspaper containing comic strips. —*n.* funnies, *Am.* a. comic strips. b. section of a newspaper devoted to them. —fun'ni·ly, *adv.* —fun'ni·ness, *n.* —Syn. *adj.* **1.** comic, droll, witty, facetious.

funny bone, part of the elbow over which a nerve passes.

fur (fér), *n., v.,* furred, fur·ring. —*n.* **1.** the soft hair covering the skin of certain animals. **2.** skin with such hair on it. **3.** Usually, furs. garment made of fur. **4.** coating of foul or waste matter like fur. [< v.] —*v.* **1.** make, cover, trim, or line with fur. **2.** coat with foul or waste matter like fur. **3.** put furring on. [< OF *forrer* line, encase < *forre* sheath < Gmc.] —fur'less, *adj.*

fur·be·low (fér'bə·lō), *n.* bit of elaborate trimming. —*v.* trim in an elaborate way. [alter. of *falbala* < Rom.]

fur·bish (fér'bish), *v.* **1.** brighten by rubbing or scouring; polish. **2.** restore to good condition; make usable again. [< OF *forbir* polish < Gmc.] —fur'bish·er, *n.*

Fu·ries (fyūr'iz), *n.pl. Gk. and Roman Myth.* the three spirits of revenge.

fu·ri·ous (fyūr'i·əs), *adj.* **1.** intensely violent; raging. **2.** full of wild, fierce anger. **3.** of unrestrained energy, speed, etc.: *furious activity.* [< L, < *furia* fury] —fu'ri·ous·ly, *adv.* —fu'ri·ous·ness, *n.*

furl (férl), *v.* roll up; fold up: *furl a flag.* —*n.* **1.** act of furling. **2.** roll or coil of something furled. [< F *ferler* < AF *ferlier* < *fer* firm (< L *firmus*) + *lier* bind < L *ligare*] —furl'er, *n.*

fur·long (fér'lông; -long), *n.* measure of distance equal to one eighth of a mile. [OE *furlang* < *furh* furrow + *lang* long]

fur·lough (fér'lō), *n.* leave of absence, esp. for a soldier. —*v. Am.* give leave of absence to. [< Du. *verlof*]

fur·nace (fér'nis), *n.* **1.** an enclosed structure to make a very hot fire in. Furnaces are used to heat buildings. **2.** a very hot place. [< OF < L *fornax* < *fornus* oven] —fur'nace·like', *adj.*

fur·nish (fér'nish), *v.* **1.** supply; provide. The sun furnishes heat. **2.** supply (a room, house, etc.) with furniture, equipment, etc. [< OF *furnir* accomplish < Gmc.] —fur'nish·er, *n.*

fur·nish·ings (fér'nish·ingz), *n.pl.* **1.** furniture or equipment for a room, house, etc. **2.** accessories of dress; articles of clothing.

fur·ni·ture (fér'nə·chər), *n.* **1.** movable articles needed in a room, house, etc. **2.** articles needed; equipment. [< F *fourniture.* See FURNISH.]

fu·ror (fyūr'ôr), *n.* **1.** outburst of wild enthusiasm or excitement. **2.** craze; mania. **3.** madness; frenzy. [< F *fureur* < L, < *furere* rage]

furred (férd), *adj.* **1.** having fur. **2.** made, covered, trimmed, or lined with fur. **3.** wearing fur. **4.** with furring on it.

fur·ri·er (fér'i·ər), *n.* **1.** dealer in furs. **2.** person whose work is preparing furs or making and repairing fur coats, etc.

fur·ring (fér'ing), *n.* **1.** act of covering, trimming, or lining with fur. **2.** the fur used. **3.** a coating of foul or waste matter like fur. **4.** the nailing of thin strips of wood to beams, walls, etc. **5.** the strips so used.

fur·row (fér'ō), *n.* **1.** a long, narrow groove or track cut in the ground by a plow. **2.** any long, narrow groove or track. **3.** wrinkle. —*v.* **1.** plow. **2.** make furrows in. **3.** wrinkle. [OE *furh*] —fur'row·er, *n.* —fur'row·less, *adj.* —fur'row·like', *adj.* —fur'row·y, *adj.*

fur·ry (fér'i), *adj.,* -ri·er, -ri·est. **1.** of fur. **2.** covered with fur. **3.** looking or feeling like fur. —fur'ri·ness, *n.*

fur·ther (fér'thər), *compar. adj. and adv., superl.* **fur·thest** (fér'thist), *v.* —*adj.* **1.** farther; more distant: *on the further side.* **2.** more: *have you any further need of me?* —*adv.* **1.** at or to a greater distance: *seek no further for happiness.* **2.** to a greater extent: *inquire further into the matter.* **3.** also; besides: *say further.* —*v.* help forward; promote. [OE *furthra,* adj., *furthor,* adv., < *forth* forth] —fur'ther·er, *n.* ➤ See farther for usage note.

fur·ther·ance (fér'thər·əns), *n.* act of furthering; helping forward; promotion.

fur·ther·more (fér'thər·môr; -mōr), *adv.* moreover; also; besides.

fur·ther·most (fér'thər·mōst), *adj.* furthest.

fur·tive (fér'tiv), *adj.* **1.** done stealthily; secret: *a furtive glance.* **2.** sly; stealthy; shifty: *a furtive manner.* [< L, < *fur* thief] —fur'tive·ly, *adv.* —fur'tive·ness, *n.*

fu·ry (fyūr'i), *n., pl.* -ries. **1.** wild, fierce anger; rage. **2.** violence; fierceness. **3.** a raging or violent person. **4.** like fury, *Colloq.* violently; very rapidly. [< L *furia*] —Syn. **1.** frenzy, ire, wrath. **2.** vehemence.

furze (férz), *n.* a low, prickly, evergreen shrub

with yellow flowers, common on waste lands in Europe; gorse. [OE *fyrs*] —**furz′y**, adj.

fuse[1] (fūz), n. 1. *Elect*. part of a circuit that melts and breaks the connection when the current becomes dangerously strong. 2. a fuze (def. 1). [< Ital. < L *fusus* spindle] —**fuse′less**, adj. —**fuse′-like′**, adj.

fuse[2] (fūz), v., **fused, fus·ing. 1.** melt; melt together. Copper and zinc are fused to make brass. 2. blend; unite. [< L *fusus* poured, melted]

fu·see (fū·zē′), n. 1. a large-headed match that will burn in a wind. 2. a signal flare. Also, **fuzee.** [< F, spindle-ful, < unrecorded OF *fus* spindle < L *fusus*]

Furze

fu·se·lage (fū′zə·läzh; -lij; -sə-), n. framework of the body of an airplane that holds passengers, cargo, etc. [< F, < *fuselé* spindle-shaped. See FUSE[1].]

fu·sel oil (fū′zəl; -səl), an acrid, oily liquid that occurs in alcoholic liquors when they are not distilled enough.

fu·si·ble (fū′zə·bəl), adj. that can be fused or melted. —**fu′si·bil′i·ty, fu′si·ble·ness,** n. —**fu′si·bly,** adv.

fu·sil·ier, fu·sil·eer (fū′zə·lir′), n. formerly, a soldier armed with a light flintlock musket. [< F, < *fusil* musket]

fu·sil·lade (fū′zə·lād′), n., v., **-lad·ed, -lad·ing.** —n. 1. discharge of many firearms. 2. something that resembles a fusillade: *a fusillade of questions.* —v. attack or shoot down by a fusillade. [< F, < *fusiller* shoot < *fusil* musket]

fu·sion (fū′zhən), n. 1. a melting; melting together; fusing. 2. a blending; union. 3. a fused mass. 4. *Nuclear Physics.* the combining of two nuclei to create a nucleus of greater mass. The fusion of atomic nuclei releases tremendous amounts of energy which can be used, as in the hydrogen or fusion bomb.

fusion bomb, hydrogen bomb.

fu·sion·ist (fū′zhən·ist), n. person taking part in a union of political parties or factions. —**fu′-sion·ism,** n.

fuss (fus), n. 1. much bother about small matters; useless talk and worry. 2. person who fusses too much. —v. 1. make a fuss. 2. make nervous or worried; bother. —**fuss′er,** n. —**Syn.** n. 1. bustle, ado, commotion.

fuss·y (fus′i), adj., **fuss·i·er, fuss·i·est. 1.** inclined to fuss; hard to please; very particular. 2. much trimmed; elaborately made. 3. full of details; requiring much care. —**fuss′i·ly,** adv. —**fuss′i·ness,** n.

fus·tian (fus′chən), n. 1. a coarse, heavy cloth made of cotton and flax. 2. a thick cotton cloth like corduroy. 3. pompous, high-sounding language; would-be eloquence. —adj. 1. made of fustian. 2. pompous and high-sounding, but cheap. [< OF < Med.L < L *fustis* stick of wood]

fust·y (fus′ti), adj., **fust·i·er, fust·i·est. 1.** having a stale smell; musty; moldy; stuffy. 2. old-fashioned; out-of-date. [< *fust*, n., < OF *wine cask*, < L *fustis* cudgel] —**fust′i·ly,** adv. —**fust′-i·ness,** n.

fu·tile (fū′til), adj. 1. not successful; useless. 2. not important; trifling. [< L *futilis* pouring easily, worthless < *fundere* pour] —**fu′tile-ly,** adv. —**fu·til′i·ty, fu′tile·ness,** n. —**Syn.** 1. ineffectual, profitless, vain. 2. frivolous, idle, trivial.

fu·ture (fū′chər), n. 1. time to come; what is to come; what will be. 2. chance of success or prosperity. 3. *Gram.* a future tense or verb form. 4. **futures,** things bought or sold to be received or delivered at a future date. —adj. 1. that is to come; that will be; coming. 2. *Gram.* expressing or indicating time to come. *Shall go* or *will go* is the future tense of *go*. [< L *futurus,* future participle of *esse* be] —**fu′ture·less,** adj.

fu·tur·ism (fū′chər·iz·əm), n. movement in art, literature, music, etc., that opposes traditional methods and tries to express the life of the present and future in new ways. —**fu′tur·ist,** n.

fu·tur·i·ty (fū·tūr′ə·ti; -tyur′-), n., pl. **-ties.** 1. future. 2. a future state or event. 3. quality of being future.

fuze (fūz), n. 1. *Military.* a slow-burning wick or other device to detonate a shell, bomb, etc. 2. fuse[1].

fu·zee (fū·zē′), n. fusee.

fuzz (fuz), n. loose, light fibers or hairs; down. —v. 1. make fuzzy. 2. become fuzzy. 3. fly out in fuzz. [cf. Du. *voos* spongy]

fuzz·y (fuz′i), adj., **fuzz·i·er, fuzz·i·est.** 1. of fuzz. 2. like fuzz. 3. covered with fuzz. 4. blurred; indistinct. —**fuzz′i·ly,** adv. —**fuzz′i·ness,** n.

-fy, suffix. 1. make; cause to be; change into, as in *simplify, intensify.* 2. become, as in *solidify.* 3. other meanings, as in *modify, qualify.* [< F *-fier* < L *-ficare* < *facere* do, make]

G

G, g (jē), n., pl. **G's; g's.** 1. the seventh letter of the alphabet. 2. *Music.* the fifth note in the scale of C major.

G, German. Also, **Ger.**

g., 1. *Elect.* conductance. 2. gram.

Ga, *Chem.* gallium.

Ga., Georgia.

gab (gab), n., v., **gabbed, gab·bing.** *Colloq.* chatter; gabble.

gab·ar·dine, gab·er·dine (gab′ər·dēn; gab′ər·dēn′), n. a closely woven woolen or cotton cloth having small, diagonal ribs on its surface, used for raincoats, suits, etc. [< Sp. *gabardina*]

gab·ble (gab′əl), v., **-bled, -bling,** n. —v. 1. talk rapidly with little or no meaning; jabber. 2. make rapid, meaningless sounds: *the geese gabbled.* —n. rapid talk with little or no meaning. [< *gab,* var. of *gob* < Scotch Gaelic *gob* mouth] —**gab′bler,** n.

gab·by (gab′i), adj., **-bi·er, -bi·est.** loquacious.

ga·bi·on (gā′bi·ən), n. 1. cylinder of wicker filled with earth, used as a military defense. 2. a similar cylinder made of metal, etc., and filled with stones, used in building dams, supporting bridge foundations, etc. [< F < Ital. *gabbione,* ult. < L *cavea* cage] —**ga′bi·oned,** adj.

ga·ble (gā′bəl), n., v., **-bled, -bling.** *Archit.*

—n. 1. end of a ridged roof, with the three-cornered piece of wall that it covers. 2. an end wall with a gable. 3. a triangular ornament or canopy over a door, window, etc. —v. build or form as a gable. [< OF *gable* < Scand. *gafl*] —**ga′bled,** adj. —**ga′ble·like′,** adj.

GABLE

gable roof, roof that forms a gable at one or both ends.

Ga·bri·el (gā′bri·əl), n. archangel who acts as God's messenger.

ga·by (gā′bi), n., pl. **-bies.** *Colloq.* fool; simpleton.

gad[1] (gad), v., **gad·ded, gad·ding,** n. —v. move about restlessly; go about looking for pleasure or excitement. —n. a gadding. [? extended use of *gad*[2]] —**gad′der,** n.

gad[2] (gad), n. goad. [< Scand. *gaddr*]

Gad, gad (gad), n., interj. *Archaic.* word used as a mild oath; exclamation of surprise, etc.

gad·a·bout (gad′ə·bout′), n. *Colloq.* person who wanders about looking for pleasure or excitement; person fond of going from place to place.

gad·fly (gad′flī′), n., pl. **-flies.** 1. fly that stings cattle, horses, etc. 2. an irritating or annoying person. [< *gad²* + *fly*]

gadg·et (gaj'it), *n. Colloq.* a small mechanical device or contrivance; any ingenious device.

gad·o·lin·i·um (gad'ə·lin'i·əm), *n. Chem.* a rare metallic element, Gd.

Gael (gāl), *n.* 1. a Scottish Highlander. 2. Celt born or living in Scotland or the Isle of Man, or, occasionally, in Ireland.

Gael·ic (gāl'ik), *adj.* of or having to do with the Gaels or their language. —*n.* language of the Gaels.

gaff (gaf), *n.* 1. a strong hook or barbed spear for pulling large fish out of the water. 2. a sharp metal spur fastened to the leg of a gamecock. 3. *Naut.* spar or pole extending along the upper edge of a fore-and-aft sail. 4. **stand the gaff,** *Am., Slang.* hold up well under strain or punishment of any kind. —*v.* hook or pull (a fish) out of the water with a gaff. [< OF *gaffe* < Celtic]

gaf·fer (gaf'ər), *n.* an old man. [alter. of *godfather*]

gag (gag), *n., v.,* **gagged, gag·ging.** —*n.* 1. something thrust into a person's mouth to keep him from talking, crying out, etc. 2. anything used to silence a person; restraint or hindrance to free speech. 3. *Slang.* an amusing remark or trick; joke. —*v.* 1. put a gag into; keep from talking, crying out, etc., with a gag. 2. force to keep silent; restrain or hinder from free speech. 3. choke or strain in an effort to vomit. 4. cause to choke or strain in an effort to vomit. [prob. imit.] —**gag'ger,** *n.* —Syn. *v.* 2. silence, suppress.

gage¹ (gāj), *n.* 1. pledge to fight; challenge: *the knight threw down his gauntlet as a gage of battle.* 2. pledge; security. [< OF < Gmc. Doublet of WAGE.]

gage² (gāj), *n., v.,* **gaged, gag·ing. gauge.** —**gag'er,** *n.*

gai·e·ty (gā'ə·ti), *n., pl.* **-ties.** 1. cheerful liveliness; merriment. 2. gay entertainment. 3. bright appearance. Also, **gayety.**

gai·ly (gā'li), *adv.* 1. as if gay; happily; merrily. 2. brightly; showily. Also, **gayly.**

gain (gān), *v.* 1. get; obtain; secure. 2. get as an increase, addition, advantage, or profit; make a profit; benefit. 3. make progress; advance; improve. 4. be the victor in; win. 5. get to; arrive at. 6. **gain on,** come closer to; get nearer to. 7. **gain over,** persuade to join one's side. —*n.* 1. act of gaining or getting anything. 2. what is gained; increase; addition; advantage; profit. 3. getting wealth. 4. **gains,** profits; earnings; winnings. [< OF *gaaigner* < Gmc.] —**gain'a·ble,** *adj.* —Syn. *v.* 1. acquire, attain. —*n.* 2. benefit, acquisition.

gain·er (gān'ər), *n.* 1. person or thing that gains. 2. a fancy dive in which the diver turns a back somersault in the air.

gain·ful (gān'fəl), *adj.* bringing in money or advantage; profitable. —**gain'ful·ly,** *adv.* —**gain'ful·ness,** *n.*

gain·say (*v.* gān·sā'; *n.* gān'sā'), *v.,* **-said, -say·ing,** *n.* —*v.* deny; contradict; dispute. —*n.* contradiction. [< *gain-* against + *say*] —**gain·say'er,** *n.* —Syn. *v.* oppose. —Ant. *v.* affirm, assert, aver.

Gains·bor·ough (gānz'bėr'ō; *Brit.* gānz'brə, -brə), *n.* Thomas, 1727–1788, English painter.

gainst, 'gainst (genst; *esp. Brit.* gānst), *prep., conj. Poetic.* against.

gait (gāt), *n.* kind of steps used in going along; way of walking or running. [< Scand. *gata* way] —**gait'ed,** *adj.*

gai·ter (gā'tər), *n.* 1. a covering for the lower leg or ankle, made of cloth, leather, etc. 2. shoe with an elastic strip in each side. [< F *guêtre*]

gal., gallon; gallons.

ga·la (gā'lə; gal'ə), *n.* a festive occasion; festival. —*adj.* of festivity; for a festive occasion; with festivities. [< F < Ital. < OF *gale* merriment]

ga·lac·tic (gə·lak'tik), *adj.* 1. *Astron.* of or having to do with the Milky Way. 2. of milk; obtained from milk. [< Gk. *galaktikos* < *gala* milk]

Gal·a·had (gal'ə·had), *n.* Sir, noblest and purest knight of the Round Table, who found the Holy Grail.

gal·an·tine (gal'ən·tēn), *n.* veal, chicken, or other white meat boned, tied up, boiled, and then served cold with its own jelly. [< F]

Ga·lá·pa·gos Islands (gə·lä'pə·gəs; -gōs), group of islands in the Pacific, 600 miles west of and belonging to Ecuador.

Ga·la·tia (gə·lā'shə), *n.* an ancient country in C Asia Minor that later became a Roman province. —**Ga·la'tian,** *adj., n.*

Ga·la·tians (gə·lā'shənz), *n.pl.* book of the New Testament, written by the Apostle Paul.

gal·ax·y (gal'ək·si), *n., pl.* **-ax·ies.** 1. a brilliant or splendid group. 2. *Astron.* a so-called island universe, a portion of space in which stars are clustered relatively thickly. Our Milky Way is only one of over a million such galaxies. 3. **Galaxy,** Milky Way. [< LL *galaxias* < Gk., < *gala* milk]

gale¹ (gāl), *n.* 1. a very strong wind. 2. *Meteorol.* wind with a velocity of 25 to 75 miles per hour. 3. a noisy outburst: *gales of laughter.*

gale² (gāl), *n.* shrub with fragrant leaves that grows in marshy places. [OE *gagel*]

Ga·len (gā'lən), *n.* Claudius, 130?–200? A.D., famous Greek physician and medical writer.

ga·le·na (gə·lē'nə), *n.* a metallic, gray ore containing much lead sulfide, PbS. It is the most important source of lead. [< L]

Ga·li·cia (gə·lish'ə), *n.* region in C Europe, now divided between Poland and the Soviet Union.

Gal·i·le·an (gal'ə·lē'ən), *adj.* of or having to do with Galilee or its people. —*n.* 1. native or inhabitant of Galilee. 2. the Galilean, Jesus.

Gal·i·le·an (gal'ə·lē'ən), *adj.* of or having to do with Galileo.

Gal·i·lee (gal'ə·lē), *n.* 1. region in N Palestine that was a Roman province in the time of Christ. 2. **Sea of,** a small, fresh-water lake in NE Palestine.

Gal·i·le·o (gal'ə·lē'ō; -lā'ō), *n.* 1564–1642, Italian astronomer who was the first to use the telescope and prove that the earth goes round the sun. His full name was Galileo Galilei.

gal·i·ot (gal'i·ət), *n.* 1. a small, fast galley moved with oars and sails. 2. a single-masted Dutch cargo or fishing boat. [< OF *galiote,* dim. of *galie,* ult. < Med.Gk. *galea*]

gall¹ (gôl), *n.* 1. a bitter, yellow, brown, or greenish liquid secreted by the liver and stored in the gall bladder; bile of animals. 2. gall bladder. 3. anything very bitter or harsh. 4. bitterness; hate. 5. *U.S. Slang.* too great boldness; impudence. [OE *galla*]

gall² (gôl), *v.* 1. make or become sore by rubbing: *the rough strap galled the horse's skin.* 2. annoy; irritate. —*n.* 1. a sore spot on the skin caused by rubbing. 2. cause of annoyance or irritation. [extended use of *gall¹*]

gall³ (gôl), *n.* lump or ball that forms on the leaves, stems, or roots of plants where they have been injured by insects or fungi. [< F < L *galla*]

gal·lant (*adj.* 1–3 gal'ənt; *adj.* 4 gə·lant'; *n.* gal'ənt; *n.* gə·lant'), *adj.* 1. noble; brave; daring. 2. grand; fine; stately. 3. gay; showy. 4. very polite and attentive to women. —*n.* 1. a spirited or courageous man. 2. man who is gay or wears showy clothes; man of fashion. 3. man who is very polite and attentive to women. [< OF *galant,* ppr. of *galer* make a show. See GALA.] —**gal'lant·ly,** *adv.* —**gal'lant·ness,** *n.* —Syn. *adj.* 1. valiant, heroic. 4. chivalrous, courtly.

gal·lant·ry (gal'ən·tri), *n., pl.* **-ries.** 1. the conduct of a gallant. 2. noble spirit or conduct; dashing courage. 3. great politeness and attention to women. 4. a gallant act or speech. 5. gay appearance; showy display.

gall bladder, *Anat.* sac attached to the liver, in which excess gall or bile is stored until needed.

gal·le·on (gal'i·ən; gal'yən), *n. Naut.* a large, high ship, usually with three or four decks. [< Sp. *geleón* < *galea* GALLEY]

Galls on a leaf

gal·ler·y (gal′ər·i; gal′ri), *n.*, *pl.* **-ler·ies. 1.** a long, narrow platform or passage projecting from the wall of a building. **2.** a projecting upper floor in a church, theater, or hall with seats or room for part of the audience; a balcony. **3.** the highest floor of this kind in a theater. **4.** people who sit there. **5.** group of people watching or listening. **6.** a long, narrow room or passage; hall. **7.** *U.S.*, *S.* veranda. **8.** room or building where works of art are shown. **9.** collection of works of art. **10.** room or building where photographs are taken, shooting is practiced, etc. **11.** *Naut.* a balconylike platform or structure at the stern or quarters of old-time ships. [< Ital. *galleria*]

gal·ley (gal′i), *n.*, *pl.* **-leys. 1.** a long, narrow ship of former times having oars and sails. **2.** a large rowboat. **3.** kitchen of a ship. **4.** *Printing.* a long, narrow tray for holding type that has been set. **5.** galley proof. [< OF *galee*, ult. < Med.Gk. *galea*]

galley proof, *Printing.* proof printed from type in a galley.

galley slave, 1. person compelled or condemned to row a galley. **2.** drudge.

gall·fly (gôl′flī′), *n.*, *pl.* **-flies.** insect that causes galls on plants.

Gal·lic (gal′ik), *adj.* **1.** of or having to do with Gaul or its people. **2.** French.

gal·lic acid (gal′ik), *Chem.* acid obtained esp. from galls on plants, $C_7H_6O_5H_2O$.

Gal·li·cism, gal·li·cism (gal′ə·siz·əm), *n.* a French idiom or expression.

gal·li·na·ceous (gal′ə·nā′shəs), *adj.* belonging to a large group of birds that nest on the ground and fly only short distances. [< L, < *gallina* hen]

gall·ing (gôl′ing), *adj.* that galls; chafing.

gal·li·nule (gal′ə·nūl), *n.* any of certain long-toed wading birds of the rail family, as the moor hen of Europe.

Gal·lip·o·li (gə·lip′ə·li), *n.* peninsula in NW Turkey, forming the N shore of the Dardanelles.

gal·li·pot (gal′ə·pot), *n.* **1.** a small pot or jar of glazed earthenware used esp. by druggists to hold medicine, salve, etc. **2.** *Colloq.* druggist. [< *galley* + *pot*]

gal·li·um (gal′i·əm), *n. Chem.* a shining, white metal, Ga, with a low melting point. It is an element similar to mercury. [< NL, ? < L *gallus* cock, trans of *Lecoq* (de Boisbaudran), the discoverer]

gal·li·vant (gal′ə·vant), *v.* go about seeking pleasure; gad about. [? < *gallant*]

gall·nut (gôl′nut′), *n.* a nutlike gall on plants.

gal·lon (gal′ən), *n.* a measure for liquids, equal to 4 quarts. The U.S. gallon equals 231 cubic inches. The British gallon equals 277.274 cubic inches. [< OF *galen*]

gal·loon (gə·lün′), *n.* a narrow braid of gold, silver, or silk thread used in trimming uniforms, furniture, etc. [< F, < *galonner* dress the hair with ribbons]

gal·lop (gal′əp), *n.* **1.** the fastest gait of a horse or other four-footed animal. In a gallop, all four feet are off the ground together once in each stride. **2.** a ride at a gallop. **3.** rapid motion; rapid progress. —*v.* **1.** ride at a gallop. **2.** go at a gallop. **3.** cause to gallop. **4.** go very fast; hurry. [< F *galoper* < Gmc.] —**gal′lop·er,** *n.*

gal·lows (gal′ōz), *n.*, *pl.* **-lows·es** or **-lows. 1.** a wooden frame made of a crossbar on two upright posts, used for hanging criminals. **2.** any similar structure. **3.** hanging as a punishment. [OE *galga*]

gallows bird, *Colloq.* person who deserves to be hanged.

gall·stone (gôl′stōn′), *n.* a pebblelike mass that sometimes forms in the gall bladder or its duct.

ga·lore (gə·lôr′; -lōr′), *adv.* in abundance. [< Irish *go leōr*]

ga·losh (gə·losh′), *n.* Usually, **galoshes.** a rubber overshoe covering the ankle, worn in wet or snowy weather. Also, **golosh.** [< F *galoche*]

gals., gallons.

Gals·wor·thy (gôlz′wér′thi), *n.* John, 1867-1933, English author.

Gal·ton (gôl′tən), *n.* Sir Francis, 1822-1911, English scientist who studied heredity.

Gal·va·ni (gäl·vä′nē), *n.* Luigi, 1737-1798, Italian physicist.

gal·van·ic (gal·van′ik), *adj.* **1.** producing an electric current by chemical action. **2.** of or caused by an electric current. **3.** affecting or affected as if by galvanism; startling.

gal·va·nism (gal′və·niz·əm), *n.* **1.** electricity produced by chemical action. **2.** branch of physics dealing with this. **3.** use of such electricity for medical purposes. [for Luigi *Galvani*]

gal·va·nize (gal′və·nīz), *v.*, **-nized, -niz·ing. 1.** apply an electric current to. **2.** arouse suddenly; startle. **3.** cover (iron or steel) with a thin coating of zinc to prevent rust. —**gal′va·ni·za′tion,** *n.* —**gal′va·niz′er,** *n.*

galvanized iron, iron covered with a thin coating of zinc, which resists rust.

gal·va·nom·e·ter (gal′və·nom′ə·tər), *n.* instrument for measuring and determining the direction of an electric current. —**gal·va·no·met·ric** (gal′və·nə·met′rik; gal·van′ə-), *adj.* —**gal′va·nom′e·try,** *n.*

gal·va·no·scope (gal′və·nə·skōp; gal·van′ə-), *n.* instrument for detecting very small electric currents and showing their direction. —**gal·va·no·scop·ic** (gal′və·nə·skop′ik; gal·van′ə-), *adj.*

gam·bit (gam′bit), *n.* way of opening a game of chess by purposely sacrificing a pawn or a piece to gain some advantage. [< F < Pr. *cambi* an exchange]

gam·ble (gam′bəl), *v.*, **-bled, -bling,** *n.* —*v.* **1.** play games of chance for money. **2.** take a risk; take great risks in business, speculation, etc. **3.** bet; wager. **4.** lose or squander by gambling. —*n. Colloq.* a risky venture or undertaking. [prob. akin to *game*, v.] —**gam′bler,** *n.* —**gam′bling,** *n.*

gam·boge (gam·bōj′; -büzh′), *n.* gum resin from certain tropical trees, used as a yellow pigment and as a cathartic. [< NL *gambogium* < *Cambodia*, a district in Indo-China]

gam·bol (gam′bəl), *n.*, *v.*, **-boled, -bol·ing;** *esp. Brit.* **-bolled, -bol·ling.** —*n.* a running and jumping about in play; caper; frolic. —*v.* frisk about; run and jump about in play. [< F *gambade* < Ital., ult. < *gamba* leg]

gam·brel (gam′brəl), *n.* **1.** hock of a horse or other animal. **2.** *Am.* gambrel roof. [< OF *gamberel* < *gambe* leg < LL *gamba*]

Gambrel roof

gambrel roof, *Am.* roof having two slopes on each side. The lower slope is usually steeper than the upper one.

game[1] (gām), *n.*, *adj.*, **gam·er, gam·est,** *v.*, **gamed, gam·ing.** —*n.* **1.** way of playing; pastime; amusement. **2.** things needed to play a game: *this store sells games.* **3.** contest with certain rules. **4.** a single round in a game: *the winner won three games out of five.* **5.** number of points required to win. **6.** a particular manner of playing: *a betting game.* **7.** activity or undertaking that is carried on like a game: *the game of diplomacy.* **8.** plan; scheme: *we discovered his game.* **9.** what is hunted or pursued. **10.** wild animals, birds, or fish hunted or caught for sport or for food. **11.** flesh of wild animals or birds used for food. **12. make game of,** make fun of; laugh at; ridicule. **13. play the game,** *Colloq.* follow the rules; be a good sport. **14. the game is up,** the plan or scheme has failed. —*adj.* **1.** having to do with game, hunting, or fishing: *game laws protect wild life.* **2.** brave; plucky: *the losing team put up a game fight.* **3.** having spirit or will enough: *the explorer was game for any adventure.* —*v.* gamble. [OE *gamen* joy] —**game′ly,** *adv.* —**game′ness,** *n.*

game[2] (gām), *adj. Colloq.* lame; crippled; injured.

game bird, bird hunted for sport or food.

game·cock (gām′kok′), *n.* rooster bred and trained for fighting.

game fish, fish that fights to get away when hooked.

game of chance, game that depends on luck, not skill.

game·some (gām′səm), *adj.* full of play; sportive; ready to play. —**game′some·ly,** *adv.* —**game′some·ness,** *n.*

game·ster (gām′stər), *n.* gambler.

gam·ete (gam′ēt; gə·mēt′), *n. Biol.* a reproductive cell capable of uniting with another to form a fertilized cell that can develop into a new plant or animal. [< NL < Gk. *gamete* wife, *gametes* husband, ult. < *gamos* marriage] —**ga·met·ic** (gə·met′ik), *adj.*

ga·me·to·phyte (gə·mē′tə·fīt), *n.* part or structure producing gametes.

game warden, official whose duty it is to enforce the game laws in a certain district.

gam·in (gam′ən), *n.* a neglected boy left to roam about the streets. [< F]

gam·ing (gām′ing), *n.* the playing of games of chance for money; gambling.

gam·ma (gam′ə), *n.* **1.** the third letter of the Greek alphabet (Γ, γ). **2.** the third in any series or group.

gamma glob·u·lin (glob′yə·lin), a constituent of the human blood. Gamma globulin contains antibodies which are used against infantile paralysis and other diseases.

gamma rays, *Nuclear Physics.* penetrating electromagnetic radiations of very high frequency given off by atomic and other radioactive substances, that are like X rays, but have a shorter wave length. Lethal gamma rays are emitted by the nuclei of excited atoms in atomic explosions.

gam·mer (gam′ər), *n. Dial.* an old woman. [alter. of *godmother*]

gam·mon[1] (gam′ən), *n. Brit. Colloq.* nonsense; humbug. [cf. ME *gamen* game[1]]

gam·mon[2] (gam′ən), *n.* **1.** the lower end of a side of bacon. **2.** smoked or cured ham. [< OF *gambon* < *gambe* leg < LL *gamba*]

gam·mon[3] (gam′ən), *n.* **1.** the game of backgammon. **2.** in this game, a victory by throwing off all of one's men before the opponent throws off any.

gam·o·pet·al·ous (gam′ə·pet′əl·əs), *adj. Bot.* having the petals joined to form a tube-shaped corolla. [< Gk. *gamos* marriage + E *petal*]

gam·o·sep·al·ous (gam′ə·sep′əl·əs), *adj. Bot.* having the sepals joined together.

gam·ut (gam′ət), *n.* **1.** *Music.* **a.** the whole series of recognized musical notes. **b.** the major scale. **2.** the entire range of anything: *the gamut of feeling from hope to despair.* [contraction of Med.L *gamma ut* < *gamma* G, the lowest tone, + *ut,* later *do;* notes of the scale were named from syllables in a Latin hymn: *Ut queant laxis resonare fibris, Mira gestorum famuli tuorum, Solve polluti labi reatum, Sancte Iohannes*]

gam·y (gām′i), *adj.,* **gam·i·er, gam·i·est. 1.** having a strong taste or smell like the flesh of wild animals or birds; slightly tainted. **2.** abounding in game. **3.** brave; plucky. —**gam′i·ly,** *adv.* —**gam′i·ness,** *n.*

gan, 'gan (gan), *v. Archaic and Poetic.* pt. of *gin*[1].

gan·der (gan′dər), *n.* a male goose. [OE *gandra*]

Gan·dhi (gän′di; gan′-), *n.* Mohandas K., 1869–1948, Hindu political, social, and religious leader.

gang (gang), *n.* **1.** group of people acting or going around together. **2.** group of people working together under one foreman. **3.** set of similar tools or machines arranged to work together. —*v.* **1.** *Colloq.* a. form a gang. b. *Am.* attack in a gang. **2.** *Scot.* go; walk. [OE, a going]

Gan·ges (gan′jēz), *n.* river flowing across N India into the Bay of Bengal. It is regarded as sacred by the Hindus.

gan·gling (gang′gling), *adj.* awkwardly tall and slender; lank and loosely built. [appar. ult. < *gang,* v.]

gan·gli·on (gang′gli·ən), *n., pl.* **-gli·a** (-gli·ə), **-gli·ons. 1.** *Anat.* group of nerve cells forming a nerve center, esp. outside of the brain or spinal cord. **2.** center of activity, etc. [< LL < Gk.]

gang·plank (gang′plangk′), *n.* a movable bridge used in getting on and off a ship, etc.

gan·grene (gang′grēn; gang·grēn′), *n., v.,* **-grened, -gren·ing.** —*n.* decay of a part of a living person or animal when the blood supply is interfered with by injury, infection, freezing, etc. —*v.* cause or have gangrene in; decay. [< L < Gk. *gangraina*] —**gan·gre·nous** (gang′grə·nəs), *adj.*

gang·ster (gang′stər), *n. Am., Colloq.* member of a gang of criminals, roughs, etc.

gang·way (gang′wā′), *n.* **1.** passageway. **2.** passageway on a ship. **3.** gangplank. **4.** *Brit.* aisle in a theater, auditorium, etc. —*interj.* get out of the way! stand aside and make room!

gan·net (gan′it), *n.* a large, fish-eating sea bird somewhat like a pelican, but with long, pointed wings and a shorter tail. [OE *ganot*]

gan·oid (gan′oid), *adj.* of fishes, having hard scales of bone overlaid with enamel. —*n.* a ganoid fish. [< Gk. *ganos* brightness]

gant·let[1] (gônt′lit; gant′-; gänt′-), *n.* a former military punishment in which the offender had to run between two rows of men who struck him with clubs or other weapons as he passed. Also, **gauntlet.** [< Sw. *gatlopp* < *gata* lane + *lopp* course]

gant·let[2] (gônt′lit; gant′-; gänt′-), *n.* gauntlet[1].

Gan·y·mede (gan′ə·mēd), *n. Class. Myth.* a beautiful youth, cupbearer to the gods of Olympus.

gaol (jāl), *n. Brit.* jail. —**gaol′er,** *n.*

gap (gap), *n., v.,* **gapped, gap·ping.** —*n.* **1.** a broken place; opening. **2.** an empty part; unfilled space; blank. **3.** a wide difference of opinion, character, etc. **4.** a pass through mountains. —*v.* make a gap. [< Scand.; akin to GAPE]

gape (gāp; gap), *v.,* **gaped, gap·ing,** *n.* —*v.* **1.** open wide. **2.** open the mouth wide; yawn. **3.** stare with the mouth open. —*n.* **1.** a wide opening. **2.** act of opening the mouth wide; yawning. **3.** an open-mouthed stare. [< Scand. *gapa*]

gapes (gāps), *n.pl.* **1.** fit of yawning. **2.** disease of birds and poultry.

gar (gär), *n., pl.* **gars** or (*esp. collectively*) **gar.** *Am.* garfish. [for *garfish*]

G.A.R., Grand Army of the Republic.

ga·rage (gə·räzh′; -räj′), *n., v.,* **-raged, -raging.** —*n.* place where automobiles are kept; shop for repairing automobiles. —*v.* put or keep in a garage. [< F, < *garer* put in shelter]

Gar·and rifle (gar′ənd), a semiautomatic rifle used by the U.S. Army. [after J. C. *Garand,* the inventor]

garb (gärb), *n.* **1.** way one is dressed. **2.** clothing. **3.** outward covering, form, or appearance. —*v.* clothe. [< F < Ital. *garbo* grace]

gar·bage (gär′bij), *n.* waste animal or vegetable matter from a kitchen, store, etc.; scraps of food to be thrown away.

gar·ble (gär′bəl), *v.,* **-bled, -bling.** make unfair or misleading selections from (facts, statements, writings, etc.); omit parts of in order to misrepresent. [< Ital. < Ar. *gharbala* sift, prob. < LL *cribellare,* ult. < *cribrum* sieve] —**gar′bler,** *n.* —**Syn.** falsify, distort, misquote.

gar·çon (gär·sôN′), *n., pl.* **-çons** (-sôN′). *French.* **1.** a young man; boy. **2.** servant. **3.** waiter.

gar·den (gär′dən), *n.* **1.** piece of ground used for growing vegetables, herbs, flowers, or fruits. **2.** park or place where people go for amusements or to see things that are displayed. **3.** a fertile and delightful spot; well-cultivated region. —*v.* take care of a garden; make a garden; work in a garden. —*adj.* **1.** growing or grown in a garden; for a garden. **2.** common; ordinary. [< OF *gardin* < Gmc.] —**gar′den·er,** *n.* —**gar′den·like′,** *adj.*

gar·de·nia (gär·dē′nyə; -ni·ə), *n. Am.* **1.** a fragrant, roselike, white flower with waxy petals. **2.** shrub having these flowers. [< NL; named for A. *Garden,* botanist]

Gar·field (gär′fēld), *n.* James, 1831–1881, the 20th president of the United States, in 1881.

gar·fish (gär'fish'), n., pl. **-fish·es** or (esp. collectively) **-fish**. fish with a long, slender body and long, narrow jaws. [< gar (OE gār spear) + fish]

Gar·gan·tu·a (gär·gan'chù-ə), n. a good-natured giant in a satire by Rabelais. —**Gar·gan'tu·an**, adj.

gar·gle (gär'gəl), v., **-gled**, **-gling**, n. —v. wash or rinse (the throat) with a liquid kept in motion by the breath. —n. liquid used for gargling. [prob. imit.]

gar·goyle (gär'goil), n. spout for carrying off rain water, ending in a grotesque head that projects from the gutter of a building. [< OF gargouille. Cf. L gargulio gullet.] —**gar'goyled**, adj.

Gargoyle

Gar·i·bal·di (gar'ə·bôl'di), n. Giuseppe, 1807–1882, Italian patriot and general. —**Gar'i·bal'di·an**, adj., n.

gar·ish (gâr'ish), adj. unpleasantly bright; glaring; showy; gaudy. [ult. < obs. gaure stare] —**gar'ish·ly**, adv. —**gar'ish·ness**, n.

gar·land (gär'lənd), n. 1. wreath of flowers, leaves, etc. 2. book of short literary selections, esp. poems. —v. decorate with garlands. [< OF garlande]

gar·lic (gär'lik), n. 1. plant like an onion whose strong-smelling bulb is composed of small sections called cloves. 2. bulb or clove of this plant, used to season meats, salads, etc. [OE gārlēac < gār spear + lēac leek] —**gar'lick·y**, adj.

gar·ment (gär'mənt), n. 1. article of clothing. 2. an outer covering. —v. clothe. [< OF garnement < garnir fit out. See GARNISH.] —**gar'ment·less**, adj.

gar·ner (gär'nər), v. gather and store away. [< n.] —n. 1. storehouse for grain. 2. a store of anything. [< OF < L granarium < granum grain]

gar·net (gär'nit), n. 1. a hard, vitreous silicate mineral occurring in a number of varieties. A common deep-red, transparent variety is used as a gem. 2. a deep red. —adj. deep-red. [OF grenat < Med.L granatum < L, pomegranate] —**gar'net·like'**, adj.

gar·nish (gär'nish), n. 1. something laid on or around food as a decoration. 2. decoration; trimming. —v. 1. decorate (food). 2. decorate; trim. 3. Law. warn or notify by a garnishment. [< OF garnir provide, defend < Gmc.] —**gar'nish·er**, n. —Syn. v. 2. adorn.

gar·nish·ee (gär'nish·ē'), v., **-nish·eed**, **-nish·ee·ing**, n. Law. —v. 1. attach (money or property) by legal authority in payment of a debt. 2. notify (a person) not to hand over money or property belonging to the defendant in a lawsuit until the plaintiff's claims have been settled. —n. person served with a notice of garnishment.

gar·nish·ment (gär'nish·mənt), n. 1. decoration; trimming. 2. Law. a. a legal notice warning a person to hold in his possession property that belongs to the defendant in a lawsuit until the plaintiff's claims have been settled. b. summons to a third person to appear in court while a lawsuit between others is being heard.

gar·ni·ture (gär'nə·chər), n. decoration; trimming; garnish.

gar·ret (gar'it), n. space in a house just below a sloping roof; attic. [< OF garite < garir defend < Gmc.]

gar·ri·son (gar'ə·sən), n. 1. soldiers stationed in a fort, town, etc., to defend it. 2. place that has a garrison. —v. 1. station soldiers in (a fort, town, etc.) to defend it. 2. occupy (a fort, town, etc.) as a garrison. [< OF garison < garir. See GARRET.]

Gar·ri·son (gar'ə·sən), n. William Lloyd, 1805–1879, American editor and abolitionist.

gar·rote, gar·rotte, ga·rotte (gə·rōt', -rot'), n., v., **-rot·ed, -rot·ing; -rot·ted, -rot·ting**. —n. 1. a Spanish method of executing a person by strangling him with an iron collar. 2. the iron collar used for this. 3. a strangling and robbery; strangling. —v. 1. execute by garroting.

2. strangle and rob; strangle. [< Sp., stick for twisting cord] —**gar·rot'er, gar·rot'ter, ga·rot'ter**, n.

gar·ru·lous (gar'ə·ləs; -yə-), adj. 1. talking too much about trifles. 2. wordy. [< L, < garrire chatter] —**gar·ru·li·ty** (gə·rü'lə·ti), gar'ru·lous·ness, n. —**gar'ru·lous·ly**, adv. —Syn. 1. talkative, loquacious, prattling, babbling.

gar·ter (gär'tər), n. band or strap to hold up a stocking or sock. —v. fasten with a garter. [< OF gartier < garet bend of the knee]

garter snake, Am. a small, harmless, brownish or greenish snake with yellow stripes.

Gar·y (gâr'i), n. city in NW Indiana, on Lake Michigan.

gas (gas), n., pl. **gas·es**, n., gassed, gas·sing. —v. 1. Physics. any fluid substance that can expand without limit; not a solid or liquid. 2. any gas or mixture of gases except air. 3. any mixture of gases that can be burned, obtained from coal and other substances. 4. any gas used as an anesthetic. 5. an explosive mixture of firedamp with air. 6. substance used in warfare that poisons, suffocates, etc. 7. Am., Colloq. gasoline. 8. Am., Slang. empty or boasting talk. —v. 1. supply with gas. 2. treat with gas; use gas on. 3. give off gas. 4. attack with gas in warfare. 5. Colloq. supply with gasoline. 6. Am., Slang. talk idly. [alter. of Gk. chaos chaos; coined by J. B. van Helmont, physicist] —**gas'less**, adj.

Gas·con (gas'kən), n. 1. native of Gascony. Gascons were noted for their boastfulness. 2. gascon, boaster. —adj. 1. of Gascony or its people. 2. gascon, boastful.

gas·con·ade (gas'kən·ād'), n., v., **-ad·ed, -ad·ing**. —n. extravagant boasting. —v. boast extravagantly.

Gas·co·ny (gas'kə·ni), n. region in SW France.

gas·e·ous (gas'i·əs), adj. in the form of gas; of or like a gas. —**gas'e·ous·ness**, n.

gas fitter, person whose work is putting in and repairing gas pipes.

gash (gash), n. a long, deep cut or wound. [< v.] —v. make a long, deep cut or wound in. [earlier garsh < OF garser scarify]

gas·i·fy (gas'ə·fi), v., **-fied, -fy·ing**. change into a gas. —**gas'i·fi'a·ble**, adj. —**gas'i·fi·ca'tion**, n. —**gas'i·fi'er**, n.

gas jet, 1. a small nozzle of a gas fixture where gas comes out and is burned. 2. flame of gas.

gas·ket (gas'kit), n. 1. ring or strip of rubber, metal, plaited hemp, etc., packed around a piston, pipe joint, etc., to keep steam, gas, etc., from escaping. 2. Naut. cord or small rope used to secure a furled sail on a yard.

Gasket (def. 2)

gas mantle, a lacelike tube around a gas flame that glows and gives off light when heated.

gas mask, helmet or mask supplied with a filter containing chemicals to neutralize poisonous gases, etc.

gas·o·line, gas·o·lene (gas'ə·lēn; gas'ə·lēn'), n. Am. a colorless liquid that evaporates and burns very easily, made by distilling petroleum, used as a fuel, solvent, and cleansing agent.

gas·om·e·ter (gas·om'ə·tər), n. 1. container for holding and measuring gas. 2. tank in which gas is stored.

gasp (gasp; gäsp), n. a catching of the breath with open mouth, as if out of breath or surprised. —v. 1. catch the breath with difficulty; breathe with gasps. 2. utter with gasps. [< Scand. geispa yawn] —Syn. v. 1. pant, blow, puff.

gas station, place that sells gasoline and oil.

gas·sy (gas'i), adj., **-si·er, -si·est**. 1. full of gas; containing gas. 2. like gas.

gas·tric (gas'trik), adj. of or near the stomach. [< Gk. gaster stomach]

gastric juice, the digestive fluid secreted by glands in the lining of the stomach. It contains pepsin and other enzymes and hydrochloric acid.

gas·tri·tis (gas·trī'tis), n. inflammation of the stomach, esp. of its mucous membrane. —**gas·trit'ic** (gas·trit'ik), adj.

gas·tron·o·my (gas·tron′ə·mi), *n.* art or science of good eating. [< F < Gk., < *gaster* stomach + *nomos* law] —**gas·tro·nom·ic** (gas′-trə·nom′ik), **gas′tro·nom′i·cal**, *adj.* —**gas′tro·nom′i·cal·ly**, *adv.* —**gas·tron′o·mist**, *n.*

gas·tro·pod (gas′trə·pod), *n.* mollusk with a disklike organ of locomotion on the ventral surface of its body. —*adj.* of such mollusks. [< NL, < Gk. *gaster* stomach + *-podos* footed < *pous* foot]

gas·tru·la (gas′trü·lə), *n.*, *pl.* -lae (-lē). state in the development of all many-celled animals, when the embryo is usually saclike and composed of two layers of cells. [< NL, dim. of Gk. *gaster* stomach] —**gas′tru·lar**, *adj.*

gat[1] (gat), *v.* *Archaic.* pt. of get.

gat[2] (gat), *n.* *Am.*, *Slang.* a revolver or pistol. [for *Gatling gun*]

gate (gāt), *n.*, *v.*, **gat·ed**, **gat·ing**. —*n.* 1. a movable part or frame to close an opening in a wall or fence. 2. a movable barrier to close a road, bridge, etc. 3. fort or other structure at a gate. 4. an opening in a wall or fence where a gate is; gateway. 5. way to go in or out; way to get something. 6. door, valve, etc., to stop or control the flow of water in a pipe, dam, lock, etc. 7. number of people who pay to see a contest, exhibition, etc. 8. the total amount of money received from them. —*v.* *Brit.* punish by confinement to the grounds of a school. [OE *gatu*, pl. of *geat*] —**gate′less**, *adj.* —**gate′like′**, *adj.* —**gate′-man**, *n.*

gate crasher, person who attends parties, gatherings, etc., without an invitation; uninvited guest.

gate·way (gāt′wā′), *n.* 1. an opening in a wall or fence where a gate is. 2. way to go in or out; way to get to something.

gath·er (gath′ər), *v.* 1. bring into one place or group. 2. come together; assemble. 3. get together from various places or sources, or gradually: *gather sticks for a fire.* 4. form a mass; collect: *tears gathered in her eyes.* 5. pick and collect; take: *farmers gather their crops.* 6. get or gain little by little: *the train gathered speed.* 7. collect (oneself, one's strength, energies, thoughts, etc.) for an effort. 8. put together in the mind; conclude; infer. 9. pull together in folds; wrinkle: *she gathered her brows in a frown.* 10. pull together in little folds and stitch. 11. come to a head and form pus. —*n.* one of the little folds between stitches when cloth is gathered. [OE *gaderian* < *geador* together] —**gath′er·a·ble**, *adj.* —**gath′er·er**, *n.* —Syn. *v.* 1. muster. 4. accumulate. 5. harvest, garner. 8. deduce. —Ant. *v.* 1. scatter, separate.

gath·er·ing (gath′ər·ing), *n.* 1. act of one that gathers. 2. that which is gathered. 3. meeting; assembly; party; crowd. 4. *Med.* swelling that comes to a head and forms pus.

Gat·ling gun (gat′ling), *Am.* an early type of machine gun consisting of a revolving cluster of barrels. [for R. J. *Gatling*, the inventor]

gauche (gōsh), *adj.* awkward; clumsy; tactless. [< F, left] —**gauche′ly**, *adv.* —**gauche′ness**, *n.*

gau·che·rie (gō′shə·rē′), *n.* 1. awkwardness; tactlessness. 2. an awkward or tactless movement, act, etc.

Gau·cho (gou′chō), *n.*, *pl.* -chos. cowboy of mixed Spanish and Indian descent in the southern plains of South America. [< Sp.]

gaud (gôd), *n.* a cheap, showy ornament. [appar. < AF, < *gaudir* rejoice < L *gaudere*]

gaud·y (gôd′i), *adj.*, **gaud·i·er**, **gaud·i·est.** too bright and gay to be in good taste; showy but cheap. —**gaud′i·ly**, *adv.* —**gaud′i·ness**, *n.* —Syn. flashy, tawdry, garish.

gauge (gāj), *n.*, *v.*, **gauged**, **gaug·ing.** —*n.* 1. standard measure; scale of standard measurements; measure. 2. instrument for measuring. 3. means of estimating or judging. 4. size; capacity; extent. 5. distance between railroad rails or between the right and left wheels of a wagon, automobile, etc. —*v.* 1. measure accurately; find the size of with a gauge. 2. estimate; judge. Also, **gage.** [< OF *gauger*] —**gauge′a·ble**, *adj.*

gaug·er (gāj′ər), *n.* 1. person or thing that gauges. 2. official who measures the contents of barrels of taxable liquor. 3. collector of excise taxes. Also, **gager.**

Gau·guin (gō·gaṅ′), *n.* Paul, 1848–1903, French painter.

Gaul (gôl), *n.* 1. an ancient country in W Europe. It included France, Belgium, the Netherlands, and parts of Switzerland, Germany, and N Italy. 2. one of the Celtic inhabitants of ancient Gaul. 3. a Frenchman.

gaunt (gônt; gänt), *adj.* 1. very thin and bony; with hollow eyes and a starved look. 2. looking bare and gloomy; desolate; grim. —**gaunt′ly**, *adv.* —**gaunt′ness**, *n.* —Syn. 1. lean, spare, lank.

gaunt·let[1] (gônt′lit; gänt′-), *n.* 1. a stout, heavy glove, usually of leather covered with plates of iron or steel, that was part of a knight's armor. 2. a stout, heavy glove with a wide, flaring cuff. 3. the wide, flaring cuff. 4. throw down the gauntlet, challenge. Also, **gantlet.** [< OF *gantelet*, dim. of *gant* glove < Gmc.] —**gaunt′let·ed**, *adj.*

gaunt·let[2] (gônt′lit; gänt′-), *n.* gantlet[1].

Iron gauntlet

Gau·ta·ma (gô′tə·mə; gou′-), *n.* Buddha.

gauze (gôz), *n.* 1. a very thin, light cloth, easily seen through. 2. a thin haze. [< F *gaze*; named for *Gaza*, Palestine] —**gauze′like′**, *adj.*

gauz·y (gôz′i), *adj.*, **gauz·i·er**, **gauz·i·est.** like gauze; thin and light as gauze. —**gauz′i·ly**, *adv.* —**gauz′i·ness**, *n.*

gave (gāv), *v.* pt. of give.

gav·el (gav′əl), *n.* a small mallet used by a presiding officer to signal for attention or order. [OE *gafeluc* spear < Welsh]

ga·vi·al (gā′vi·əl), *n.* a large crocodile of India that has a long, slender snout. [< F < Hind. *ghariyāl*]

ga·votte, ga·vot (gə·vot′), *n.* 1. dance like a minuet but much more lively. 2. music for it. [< F < Pr. *gavoto* < *Gavots* Alpine people]

G.A.W., GAW, guaranteed annual wage.

Ga·wain (gä′win; -wān), *n.* knight of the Round Table and nephew of King Arthur.

gawk (gôk), *n.* an awkward person; clumsy fool. —*v.* *Colloq.* stare rudely or stupidly. [? < dial. *gaulick(-handed)* left(-handed)]

gawk·y (gôk′i), *adj.*, **gawk·i·er**, **gawk·i·est.** awkward; clumsy. —**gawk′i·ly**, *adv.* —**gawk′i·ness**, *n.*

gay (gā), *adj.*, **gay·er**, **gay·est.** 1. happy and full of fun; merry. 2. bright-colored; showy. 3. fond of pleasures. 4. dissipated; immoral. [< F *gai*] —**gay′ness**, *n.* —Syn. 1. blithe, jolly, jovial. 2. bright, brilliant, gaudy.

gay·e·ty (gā′ə·ti), *n.*, *pl.* -ties. gaiety.

gay·ly (gā′li), *adv.* gaily.

gaze (gāz), *v.*, **gazed**, **gaz·ing**, *n.* —*v.* look long and steadily. —*n.* a long, steady look. [cf. Scand. (dial. Norw.) *gasa*] —**gaz′er**, *n.*

ga·zelle (gə·zel′), *n.* a small, graceful antelope of Africa and Asia that has soft, lustrous eyes. [< F < Ar. *ghazāl*] —**ga·zelle′like′**, *adj.*

ga·zette (gə·zet′), *n.*, *v.*, **-zet·ted**, **-zet·ting.** —*n.* 1. a newspaper. 2. an official government journal containing lists of appointments, promotions, etc. —*v.* publish, list, or announce in a gazette. [< F < Ital. *gazzetta*, orig., coin; from price of paper]

gaz·et·teer (gaz′ə·tir′), *n.* 1. dictionary of geographical names. 2. writer for a gazette; newswriter. 3. official appointed to publish a gazette.

G clef, *Music.* the treble clef.

Gd, *Chem.* gadolinium.

Gdy·nia (gdēn′yä), *n.* seaport in N Poland.

Ge, *Chem.* germanium.

gear (gir), *n.* 1. wheel having teeth that fit into the teeth of another wheel of the same kind. 2. arrangement of fixed and moving parts for transmitting or changing motion; mechanism; machinery. 3. working order; adjustment: *his watch got out of gear and would not run.* 4. equipment needed for some purpose. 5. movable property; goods. —*v.* 1. connect by gears. 2. fit or work together; mesh. 3. provide with gear; equip. 4. provide with gearings. 5. connect by gearing. 6. put into gear. [appar. < Scand. *gervi, görvi*] —gear′less, *adj.*

gear·ing (gir′ing), *n.* set of gears, chains, etc., for transmitting motion or power; gears.

gear·shift (gir′shift′), *n.* device for connecting a motor, etc., to any of several sets of gears.

gear·wheel (gir′hwēl′), *n.* wheel having teeth that fit into the teeth of another wheel of the same kind; cogwheel.

geck·o (gek′ō), *n., pl.* geck·os, geck·oes. a small, harmless, insect-eating lizard with suction pads on its feet so that it can walk on ceilings, walls, etc. [< Malay *gĕkoq;* imit.]

Gecko (ab. 1 ft. long)

gee (jē), *interj., v.,* geed, gee·ing. —*interj.* 1. command to horses, oxen, etc., directing them to turn to the right. 2. exclamation or mild oath. —*v.* turn to the right.

geese (gēs), *n.* pl. of goose.

Ge·hen·na (gə·hen′ə), *n.* 1. *New Test.* hell. 2. *Old Test.* place of torment or misery.

Gei·ger counter (gī′gər), **Geiger-Mül·ler counter** (mul′ər; *Ger.* –mÿl′ər), device which detects and counts ionizing particles. It is used to measure radioactivity, test cosmic-ray particles, etc. [after H. *Geiger,* physicist]

Gei·gers (gī′gərz), *n. Colloq.* radioactive particles and radiation collectively.

gei·sha (gā′shə; gē′–), *n., pl.* –sha, –shas. a Japanese singing and dancing girl. [< Jap.]

gel (jel), *n., v.,* gelled, gel·ling. —*n.* a jellylike or solid material formed from a colloidal solution. —*v.* form a gel. Egg white gels when it is cooked. [for *gelatin*]

gel·a·tin (jel′ə·tən), **gel·a·tine** (–tən; –tēn), *n.* 1. an odorless, tasteless substance obtained by boiling animal tissues, bones, hoofs, etc. It dissolves easily in hot water and is used in making jellied desserts, camera film, glue, etc. 2. any of various vegetable substances having similar properties. 3. preparation or product in which gelatin is the essential constituent. [< F < Ital., < *gelata* jelly < L *gelare* freeze] —gel′a·tin-like′, *adj.*

ge·lat·i·nous (jə·lat′ə·nəs), *adj.* 1. jellylike. 2. of or containing gelatin. —ge·lat′i·nous·ly, *adv.* —ge·lat′i·nous·ness, *n.*

geld (geld), *v.,* geld·ed or gelt, geld·ing. remove the male glands of (a horse or other animal); castrate. [< Scand. *gelda* castrate]

geld·ing (gel′ding), *n.* a gelded horse or other animal.

gel·id (jel′id), *adj.* cold as ice; frosty. [< L, < *gelum* cold] —ge·lid′i·ty, gel′id·ness, *n.* —gel′id·ly, *adv.*

gem (jem), *n., v.,* gemmed, gem·ming. —*n.* 1. a precious stone; jewel. 2. person or thing that is very precious, beautiful, etc. 3. *Am.* a kind of muffin. 4. in printing, a very small size of type (4 point). —*v.* set or adorn with gems, or as if with gems. [< F < L *gemma* gem, bud] —gem′like′, *adj.*

gem·i·nate (jem′ə·nāt), *v.,* –nat·ed, –nat·ing. *adj.* —*v.* make or become double; combine in pairs. —*adj.* combined in a pair or pairs; coupled. [< L, < *geminus* twin] —gem′i·nate·ly, *adv.* —gem′i·na′tion, *n.*

Gem·i·ni (jem′ə·nī), *n.pl., gen.* Gem·i·no·rum (jem′ə·nô′rəm; –nō′–). 1. *Astron.* a northern constellation in the zodiac containing two bright stars. 2. the third sign of the zodiac; the Twins. 3. Castor and Pollux, the twin sons of Zeus.

gem·ma (jem′ə), *n., pl.* –mae (–mē). *Biol.* 1. a bud. 2. a budlike growth that can develop into a new plant or animal. [< L, bud]

gem·mate (jem′āt), *v.,* –mat·ed, –mat·ing. put forth buds; reproduce by budding.

gems·bok (gemz′bok′), *n.* a large antelope of South Africa, having long, straight horns and a long, tufted tail. [< Afrikaans < G, < *gemse* chamois + *bock* buck]

Gen., 1. General. 2. Genesis.

gen., 1. gender. 2. general. 3. genitive.

gen·darme (zhän′därm), *n., pl.* –darmes (–därmz). policeman with military training. [< F, < *gens d'armes* men of arms]

gen·der (jen′dər), *n.* 1. *Gram.* a. in many languages, the grouping of nouns into a series of classes, such as masculine, feminine, neuter, etc. b. one of such classes. 2. *Colloq.* sex. [< OF < L *genus* kind, sort]

gene (jēn), *n. Biol.* element of a germ cell transmitted from parent to offspring. Genes are carriers of hereditary traits. [< Gk. *genea* breed, kind]

ge·ne·al·o·gy (jē′ni·al′ə·ji; jen′i–; –ol′–), *n., pl.* –gies. 1. account of the descent of a person or family from an ancestor or ancestors. 2. descent of a person or family from an ancestor; pedigree; lineage. 3. the making or investigation of such accounts; study of pedigrees. [< L < Gk., ult. < *genea* generation + *–logos* treating of] —ge·ne·a·log·i·cal (jē′ni·ə·loj′ə·kəl; jen′i–), ge·ne·a·log′ic, *adj.* —ge·ne·a·log′i·cal·ly, *adv.* —ge′ne·al′o·gist, *n.*

gen·er·a (jen′ər·ə), *n.* pl. of genus.

gen·er·al (jen′ər·əl; jen′rəl), *adj.* 1. of all; for all; from all: *a government takes care of the general welfare.* 2. common to many or most; widespread: *there is a general interest in sports.* 3. not special; not limited to one kind, class, department, or use: *a general reader reads different kinds of books.* 4. not detailed; sufficient for practical purposes: *general instructions.* 5. indefinite; vague: *she referred to her trip in a general way.* 6. of or for all those forming a group: *"cat" is a general term for cats, lions, and tigers.* 7. in chief; of highest rank: *the postmaster general.* —*n.* 1. a general fact, idea, principle, or statement. 2. in the U.S. Army: a. officer ranking next below General of the Army and next above lieutenant general. b. any officer of the six highest ranks; officer ranking above a colonel. 3. head of a religious order. 4. in general, usually; for the most part. [< L *generalis* of a (whole) class < *genus* class, race] —gen′er·al·ness, *n.* —Syn. *adj.* 2. prevalent, ordinary, universal. —Ant. *adj.* 2. exceptional, rare. 3. specific, definite.

General Assembly, 1. *Am.* legislature of certain States of the United States. 2. the legislative body of the United Nations.

gen·er·a·lis·si·mo (jen′ər·ə·lis′ə·mō; jen′rəl–), *n., pl.* –mos. commander in chief of all or several armies in the field. [< Ital., superlative of *generale* general]

gen·er·al·i·ty (jen′ər·al′ə·ti), *n., pl.* –ties. 1. general quality or condition. 2. a general principle or rule. 3. the greater part; main body; mass. 4. a general statement; word or phrase not definite enough to have much meaning or value.

gen·er·al·ize (jen′ər·əl·īz; jen′rəl–), *v.,* –ized, –iz·ing. 1. make into one general statement; bring under a common heading, class, or law. 2. infer (a general rule) from particular facts. 3. state in a more general form; extend in application. 4. talk indefinitely or vaguely; use generalities. 5. make general; bring into general use or knowledge. 6. make general inferences. —gen′er·al·i·za′tion, *n.* —gen′er·al·iz′er, *n.*

gen·er·al·ly (jen′ər·ə·li; jen′rəl·i), *adv.* 1. in most cases; usually. 2. for the most part; widely. 3. in a general way; without giving details.

General of the Army, *U.S.* general of the highest rank.

gen·er·al·ship (jen′ər·əl·ship′; jen′rəl–), *n.* 1. ability as a general; skill in commanding an army. 2. skillful management; leadership. 3. rank, commission, authority, or term of office of a general.

general staff, *Mil.* group of high army officers who make plans for war or national defense.

gen·er·ate (jen′ər·āt), *v.,* –at·ed, –at·ing. 1. produce; cause to be: *friction generates heat.* 2.

produce (offspring). 3. *Math.* form (a line, surface, figure, or solid) by moving a point, line, etc. [< L, < *genus* race]

gen·er·a·tion (jen′ər·ā′shən), *n.* 1. all the people born about the same time. 2. time from the birth of one generation to the birth of the next generation; about 30 years. 3. one step or degree in the descent of a family. 4. production of offspring. 5. production: *generation of electricity.* 6. *Math.* the formation of a line, surface, or solid by moving a point, line, etc. 7. descent; genealogy. —**gen′er·a′tive,** *adj.*

gen·er·a·tor (jen′ər·ā′tər), *n.* 1. machine that changes mechanical energy into electrical energy; dynamo. 2. *Chem.* apparatus for producing gas or steam. 3. person or thing that generates.

gen·er·a·trix (jen′ər·ā′triks), *n., pl.* **gen·er·a·tri·ces** (jen′ər·ə·trī′sēz). *Math.* point, line, etc., whose motion produces a line, surface, figure, or solid.

ge·ner·ic (jə·ner′ik), *adj.* 1. having to do with or characteristic of a genus of plants or animals. 2. having to do with a class or group of similar things; inclusive. 3. applied to, or referring to, a group or class; general. —**ge·ner′i·cal·ly,** *adv.*

gen·er·os·i·ty (jen′ər·os′ə·ti), *n., pl.* **–ties.** 1. a being generous; willingness to share with others; unselfishness. 2. nobleness of mind; absence of meanness. 3. a generous act.

gen·er·ous (jen′ər·əs), *adj.* 1. willing to share with others; unselfish. 2. having or showing a noble mind; willing to forgive; not mean. 3. large; plentiful. 4. fertile: *generous fields.* 5. rich and strong: *a generous wine.* 6. *Archaic.* born of a good family. [< L *generosus* of noble birth < *genus* race, stock] —**gen′er·ous·ly,** *adv.* —**gen′er·ous·ness,** *n.* —**Syn.** 1. liberal, bountiful, lavish. 2. high-minded, magnanimous. 3. ample.

Gen·e·sis (jen′ə·sis), *n.* 1. the first book of the Old Testament, that gives an account of the creation of the world. 2. **genesis,** origin; creation. [< L < Gk.]

gen·et (jen′it), *n.* jennet.

ge·net·ic (jə·net′ik), *adj.* 1. having to do with origin and natural growth. 2. of or having to do with genetics. [< Gk. *genetikos* < *genesis* origin, creation] —**ge·net′i·cal·ly,** *adv.*

ge·net·ics (jə·net′iks), *n. Biol.* science dealing with the principles of heredity and variation in animals and plants. —**ge·net·i·cist** (jə·net′ə·sist), *n.*

Ge·ne·va (jə·nē′və), *n.* 1. city in SW Switzerland. 2. Lake of. Also, **Lake Leman.** a long, narrow lake in SW Switzerland. —**Ge·ne′van, Gen·e·vese** (jen′ə·vēz′; –vēs′), *adj., n.*

Geneva Convention, agreement between nations providing for the neutrality of the members and buildings of the medical departments on battlefields. It was first formulated at Geneva, Switzerland, in 1864.

Gen·ghis Khan (jeng′gis kän′), 1162–1227, Mongol conqueror of central Asia. Also, **Jenghis Khan, Jenghiz Khan.**

gen·ial (jēn′yəl), *adj.* 1. smiling and pleasant; cheerful and friendly: *a genial welcome.* 2. helping growth; pleasantly warming; comforting: *genial sunshine.* 3. pertaining to the production of offspring. [< L *genialis,* lit., belonging to the GENIUS] —**ge·ni·al·i·ty** (jē′ni·al′ə·ti), **gen′ial·ness,** *n.* —**gen′ial·ly,** *adv.* —**Syn.** 1. bland, cordial.

ge·nie (jē′ni), *n.* spirit; jinni. [< F *génie*]

gen·i·tal (jen′ə·təl), *adj.* having to do with reproduction or the sex organs. [< L *genitalis,* ult. < *gignere* beget]

gen·i·tals (jen′ə·təlz), *n.pl.* the external sex organs.

gen·i·tive (jen′ə·tiv), *Gram.* —*n.* 1. case in certain languages showing possession, source, origin, etc. 2. word or construction in this case. —*adj.* of this case; in this case; having to do with its forms or constructions. [< L *genitivus* of origin] —**gen·i·ti·val** (jen′ə·tī′vəl), *adj.* —**gen′·i·ti′val·ly,** *adv.*

gen·ius (jēn′yəs; jē′ni·əs), *n., pl.* **gen·ius·es** *for 1–4, 7,* **ge·ni·i** (jē′ni·ī) *for 5, 6, 8.* 1. very great natural power of mind. 2. person having

such power. 3. great natural ability of some special kind: *genius for acting.* 4. the special character or spirit of a person, nation, age, language, etc. 5. guardian spirit of a person, place, etc. 6. either of two spirits, one good and one evil, supposed to influence a person's fate. 7. person who powerfully influences another. 8. spirit; jinn. [< L, tutelary spirit, male generative power]

Gen·o·a (jen′ō·ə), *n.* seaport in NW Italy. —**Gen·o·ese** (jen′ō·ēz′; –ēs′), *adj., n.*

gen·o·cide (jen′ə·sīd), *n. Am.* systematic measures for the extermination of a cultural or racial group. [< Gk. *genos* race + E *–cide* killing < L *caedere* to kill; coined by R. Lemkin in 1944] —**gen·o·cid′al,** *adj.*

gen·re (zhän′rə), *n.* 1. kind; sort; style. 2. style or kind of painting, etc., that shows scenes from ordinary life. [< F < L *genus* kind]

gens (jenz), *n., pl.* **gen·tes** (jen′tēz). group of families in ancient Rome that claimed the same ancestor. [< L]

gen·teel (jen·tēl′), *adj.* 1. belonging or suited to polite society. 2. polite; well-bred; fashionable. [< F *gentil* < L *gentilis.* Doublet of GENTILE, GENTLE.] —**gen·teel′ly,** *adv.* —**gen·teel′ness,** *n.* —**Syn.** 2. refined, polished.

gen·tian (jen′shən), *n.* plant with funnel-shaped, usually blue flowers, stemless leaves, and bitter juice. [< L *gentiana;* said to be named for *Gentius,* king of Illyria (ancient country on the Adriatic)]

gen·tile, Gen·tile (jen′tīl), *n.* 1. person who is not a Jew. 2. heathen; pagan. 3. among Mormons, a person who is not a Mormon. —*adj.* 1. not Jewish. 2. heathen; pagan. 3. *Am.* among Mormons, of or having to do with those outside of the Mormon community. [< LL *gentilis* foreign < L, of a people, national. Doublet of GENTEEL, GENTLE.]

gen·til·i·ty (jen·til′ə·ti), *n., pl.* **–ties.** 1. gentle birth; membership in the aristocracy or upper class. 2. good manners. 3. refinement. 4. Usually, **gentilities.** pretended refinements.

gen·tle (jen′təl), *adj.* **–tler, –tlest,** *n., v.,* **–tled, –tling.** —*adj.* 1. not severe, rough, or violent; mild: *a gentle tap.* 2. soft; low: *a gentle sound.* 3. moderate: *a gentle wind.* 4. kindly; friendly: *a gentle disposition.* 5. easily handled or managed: *a gentle dog.* 6. of good family and social position; wellborn. 7. honorable; good; superior. 8. noble; gallant: *a gentle knight.* 9. refined; polite. —*n. Archaic.* person of good family. —*v. Colloq.* make mild or moderate; tame (a horse). [< OF < L *gentilis* of the (same) family, national < *gens* family, nation. Doublet of GENTEEL, GENTILE.] —**gen′tle·ness,** *n.* —**gen′tly,** *adv.* —**Syn.** *adj.* 4. tender, humane. 5. docile, tame. —**Ant.** *adj.* 1. rough, severe. 4. cruel, brutal. 5. wild.

gen·tle·folk (jen′təl·fōk′), **gen·tle·folks** (–fōks′), *n.pl.* people of good family and social position.

gen·tle·man (jen′təl·mən), *n., pl.* **–men.** 1. man of good family and social position. 2. man who is honorable and well-bred. 3. (as a polite term) any man. 4. valet or personal male servant: *a gentleman's gentleman.* —**gen′tle·man·like′,** *adj.* ≫ See man for usage note.

gen·tle·man·ly (jen′təl·mən·li), *adj.* like a gentleman; suitable for a gentleman; polite; well-bred. —**gen′tle·man·li·ness,** *n.*

gentleman's agreement, gentlemen's agreement, *Am.* agreement binding as a matter of honor, not legally.

gen·tle·wom·an (jen′təl·wùm′ən), *n., pl.* **–wom·en.** 1. woman of good family and social position. 2. a well-bred woman; lady. 3. formerly, a woman attendant of a lady of rank. —**gen′tle·wom′an·ly,** *adj.* —**gen′tle·wom′an·li·ness,** *n.*

gen·try (jen′tri), *n.* 1. people of good family and social position. The English gentry are next below the nobility. 2. people of any particular class. [alter. of *gentrice* < OF *genterise,* ult. < *gentil* GENTLE]

gen·u·flect (jen′yù·flekt), *v.* bend the knee as an act of reverence or worship. [< Med.L, < L *genu* knee + *flectere* bend] —**gen′u·flec′tor,** *n.*

gen·u·flec·tion, *esp. Brit.* **gen·u·flex·ion**

(jen'yu̇·flek'shən), *n.* a bending of the knee as an act of reverence or worship.

gen·u·ine (jen'yu̇·ən), *adj.* **1.** actually being what it seems or is claimed to be; real; true. **2.** without pretense; sincere; frank. [< L *genuinus*, native, ult. < *gignere* beget] —**gen'u·ine·ly**, *adv.* —**gen'u·ine·ness**, *n.* —**Syn. 1.** authentic. **2.** unaffected. —**Ant. 1.** false, sham, counterfeit.

ge·nus (jē'nəs), *n., pl.* **gen·er·a** (jen'ər·ə), **ge·nus·es. 1.** kind; sort; class. **2.** *Biol.* group of related animals or plants ranking below a family and above a species. The scientific name of an animal or plant consists of the genus written with a capital letter and the species written with a small letter. **3.** *Logic.* class or group of individuals divided into subordinate groups called species. [< L]

ge·o·cen·tric (jē'ō·sen'trik), **ge·o·cen·tri·cal** (-trə·kəl), *adj. Astron.* **1.** as viewed or measured from the earth's center. **2.** having or representing the earth as a center. [< *geo-* earth (< Gk. *ge*) + Gk. *kentron* center] —**ge'o·cen'tri·cal·ly**, *adv.*

ge·od·e·sy (ji·od'ə·si), **ge·o·det·ics** (jē'ə·det'iks), *n.* branch of applied mathematics dealing with the shape and dimensions of the earth, the determination of the shape and area of large tracts on its surface, variations in terrestrial gravity, and the exact position of geographical points. [< NL < Gk. *geodaisia* < *ge* earth + *daiein* divide] —**ge·o·des·ic** (jē'ə·des'ik; -dē'sik), **ge'o·des'i·cal**, *adj.* —**ge·od'e·sist**, *n.*

ge·o·det·ic (jē'ə·det'ik), *adj.* having to do with geodesy. —**ge'o·det'i·cal·ly**, *adv.*

ge·og·ra·phy (ji·og'rə·fi), *n., pl.* **-phies. 1.** study of the earth's surface, climate, continents, countries, peoples, industries, and products. **2.** the surface features of a place or region. **3.** textbook or treatise on geography. [< L < Gk., < *ge* earth + *graphein* describe] —**ge·og'ra·pher**, *n.* —**ge·o·graph·i·cal** (jē'ə·graf'ə·kəl), **ge'o·graph'ic**, *adj.* —**ge'o·graph'i·cal·ly**, *adv.*

geol., geology; geologic.

ge·ol·o·gy (ji·ol'ə·ji), *n., pl.* **-gies. 1.** science that deals with the earth's crust, the layers of which it is composed, and their history. **2.** features of the earth's crust in a place or region; rocks, rock formation, etc., of a particular area. [< NL, < Gk. *ge* earth + *-logos* treating of] —**ge·o·log·ic** (jē'ə·loj'ik), **ge'o·log'i·cal**, *adj.* —**ge'o·log'i·cal·ly**, *adv.* —**ge·ol'o·gist**, *n.*

geom., geometry; geometric.

geometrical progression, progression (def. 2).

ge·om·e·tri·cian (ji·om'ə·trish'ən; jē'əm·ə-), **ge·om·e·ter** (ji·om'ə·tər), *n.* person trained in geometry.

ge·om·e·trid (ji·om'ə·trid), *n.* any of a group of gray or greenish moths with slender bodies, whose larvae are called measuring worms or inchworms.

ge·om·e·try (ji·om'ə·tri), *n.* branch of mathematics that deals with lines, angles, surfaces, and solids. Geometry includes the definition, comparison, and measurement of squares, triangles, circles, cubes, cones, spheres, etc. [< L < Gk., < *ge* earth + *-metres* measurer] —**ge·o·met·ric** (jē'ə·met'rik), **ge'o·met'ri·cal**, *adj.* —**ge'o·met'ri·cal·ly**, *adv.*

ge·o·phys·ics (jē'ō·fiz'iks), *n.* science dealing with the relations between the features of the earth and the forces that produce them. —**ge·o·phys·i·cist** (jē'ō·fiz'ə·sist), *n.*

ge·o·po·lit·i·cal (jē'ō·pə·lit'ə·kəl), **ge·o·po·li·tic** (-pol'ə·tik), *adj.* pertaining to or involved in geopolitics. —**ge'o·po·lit'i·cal·ly**, *adv.* —**ge·o·pol·i·ti·cian** (jē'ō·pol'ə·tish'ən), *n.*

ge·o·pol·i·tics (jē'ō·pol'ə·tiks), *n.* study of government and its policies as affected by physical geography.

George (jôrj), *n.* **1.** Saint, died 303? A.D., Christian martyr, the patron saint of England. **2.** III, 1738–1820, king of England 1760–1820. **3.** V, 1865–1936, king of England 1910–1936. **4.** VI, 1895–1952, king of England 1936–1952.

Geor·gette (jôr·jet'), or **Georgette crepe,** *n.* a thin, fine, transparent silk cloth with a slightly wavy surface, used for dresses, etc. [from name of French modiste]

Geor·gia (jôr'jə), *n.* **1.** a Southern State of the U.S. *Capital:* Atlanta. *Abbrev.:* Ga. **2.** a Soviet republic in SE European Russia, between the Black and Caspian seas. —**Geor'gian**, *adj., n.*

ge·ot·ro·pism (ji·ot'rə·piz·əm), *n. Biol.* response to gravity. Positive geotropism is a tendency to move down into the earth. Negative geotropism is a tendency to move upward. [< *geo-* earth (< Gk. *ge*) + Gk. *tropikos* < *trope* turning] —**ge·o·trop·ic** (jē'ə·trop'ik), *adj.* —**ge'o·trop'i·cal·ly**, *adv.*

Ger., 1. Also, **G.** German. **2.** Germany. **3.** Also, **Gmc.** Germanic.

ger., gerund.

ge·ra·ni·um (jə·rā'ni·əm), *n.* **1.** a cultivated plant having large clusters of showy flowers or fragrant leaves. **2.** a wild plant having pink or purple flowers, deeply notched leaves, and long, pointed pods. [< L < Gk., < *geranos* crane; from resemblance of seed pod to crane's bill]

ger·fal·con (jér'fôl'kən; -fô'-), *n.* a large falcon of the arctic. Also, **gyrfalcon.** [< OF *gerfaucon* < Gmc.]

ger·i·at·rics (jer'i·at'riks), *n. Med.* science dealing with the study of old age and its diseases. [< Gk. *geras* old age + *iatreia* healing]

germ (jérm), *n.* **1.** a microscopic animal or plant that causes disease. **2.** the earliest form of a living thing; seed; bud. **3.** origin. [< F < L *germen* sprout] —**germ'less**, *adj.*

Ger·man (jér'mən), *n.* **1.** native or inhabitant of Germany. **2.** language of Germany, esp. that used in literature, on the radio, etc. See also High German and Low German. —*adj.* of Germany, its people, or their language.

ger·man (jér'mən), *adj.* **1.** having the same parents. Children of the same father and mother are brothers-german or sisters-german. **2.** related as a child of one's uncle or aunt. A cousin-german is a first cousin. [< OF < L *germanus*]

ger·mane (jér·mān'), *adj.* closely connected; to the point; pertinent. [var. of *german*]

Ger·man·ic (jér·man'ik), *adj.* **1.** German. **2.** Teutonic. —*n.* a branch of the Indo-European language family, customarily divided into East Germanic (Gothic), North Germanic (the Scandinavian languages), and West Germanic (English, Frisian, Dutch, German).

ger·ma·ni·um (jér·mā'ni·əm), *n. Chem.* a rare metallic element, Ge, with a grayish-white color. Its compounds resemble those of tin.

German measles, a contagious disease resembling measles, but much less serious.

German shepherd dog, police dog.

German silver, a white alloy of copper, zinc, and nickel, used for ornaments, utensils, etc.

Ger·ma·ny (jér'mə·ni), *n.* country in C Europe. Germany was divided after World War II into four zones occupied by the Soviet Union, Great Britain, France, and the United States.

germ cell, *Biol.* cell that can produce a new individual; egg or sperm cell.

ger·mi·cide (jér'mə·sid), *n.* any substance that kills germs, esp. disease germs. [< *germ* + *-cide* < L *-cida* killer < *caedere* to kill] —**ger'mi·cid'al**, *adj.*

ger·mi·nal (jér'mə·nəl), *adj.* **1.** of germs or germ cells. **2.** like that of germs or germ cells. **3.** in the earliest stage of development.

ger·mi·nant (jér'mə·nənt), *adj.* germinating.

ger·mi·nate (jér'mə·nāt), *v.,* **-nat·ed, -nat·ing.** start growing or developing; sprout. —**ger'mi·na'tion**, *n.* —**ger'mi·na'tor**, *n.*

germ warfare, the spreading of germs to produce disease among the enemy in time of war.

ger·on·tol·o·gy (jer'ən·tol'ə·ji), *n.* branch of science dealing with the phenomena and problems of old age. —**ge·ron·to·log·i·cal** (jér'ən·tə·loj'ə·kəl), *adj.* —**ger'on·tol'o·gist**, *n.*

ger·ry·man·der (ger'i·man'dər; jer'-), *Am.* —*n.* arrangement of the political divisions of a State, county, etc., made to give some one political party an unfair advantage in elections. —v. **1.** arrange the political divisions of (a State, county, etc.) to give one political party an unfair advantage in elections. **2.** manipulate unfairly. [< *Gerry* + (*sala*) *mander*; Gov. Gerry's party redistricted Mass. in 1812, and Essex Co. became roughly salamander-shaped]

ger·und (jer'ənd), *n. Gram.* a verb form used as a noun; verbal noun. [< LL *gerundium*, ult. < L *gerere* bear] —**ge·run·di·al** (jə·run'di·əl), *adj.* ▷ The English **gerund** ends in *-ing*. It has the same form as the present participle but differs in use. In "Watching him carefully was a job," *watching* is a gerund used as the subject of *was*; like a verb it can take an object (*him*) and can be modified by an adverb (*carefully*).

ge·run·dive (jə·run'div), *n. Gram.* **1.** a Latin verb form used as an adjective, frequently expressing the idea of necessity or duty. **2.** an analogous verbal adjective in other languages. —**ge·run·di·val** (jer'ən·di'vəl), *adj.* —**ge·run'dive·ly**, *adv.*

gest, geste (jest), *n. Archaic.* **1.** story or romance in verse. **2.** story; tale. **3.** deed; exploit. [< OF < L *gesta* deeds < *gerere* carry on, accomplish]

Ge·stalt psychology (gə·shtält'), ogy that emphasizes the fact that a whole may be something more than the sum of its parts, and that the parts of a whole are often modified by their relationships to it and to one another. [< G, configuration]

Ge·sta·po (gə·stä'pō; -shtä'-), *n.* an offical organization of secret police and detectives in Germany under Hitler. [< G *ge(heime) sta(ats) po(lizei)* secret state police]

ges·tate (jes'tāt), *v.,* -tat·ed, -tat·ing. **1.** carry (young) in the uterus from conception to birth. **2.** form and develop (a project, idea, etc.). [< L *gestatus* carried < *gestare* carry] —**ges·ta'tion,** *n.*

ges·tic·u·late (jes·tik'yə·lāt), *v.,* -lat·ed, -lat·ing. **1.** make or use gestures. **2.** make or use many vehement gestures. [< L *gesticulatus*, ult. < *gestus* gesture] —**ges·tic'u·la'tor,** *n.* —**ges·tic·u·la·to·ry** (jes·tik'yə·lə·tô'ri; -tō'-), **ges·tic'u·la'tive,** *adj.*

ges·tic·u·la·tion (jes·tik'yə·lā'shən), *n.* **1.** act of gesticulating. **2.** gesture.

ges·ture (jes'chər), *n., v.,* -tured, -tur·ing. —*n.* **1.** movement of the hands, arms, or any parts of the body, used instead of words or with words to help express an idea or feeling. **2.** the use of such movements. **3.** any action for effect or to impress others: *her refusal was merely a gesture; she really wanted to go.* —*v.* make or use gestures. [< Med.L *gestura* < L *gerere* to bear, conduct] —**ges'tur·er,** *n.* —**Syn.** *n.* **1.** gesticulation, flourish.

get (get), *v.,* got or (*Archaic*) gat, got or (*esp. U.S.*) got·ten, get·ting, *n.* —*v.* **1.** obtain by effort; gain; win: *get first prize.* **2.** attain; achieve: *get a reputation.* **3.** come (followed by an infinitive): *they never got to be good friends.* **4.** come to be; become: *get sick.* **5.** commit to memory; learn: *get one's lessons.* **6.** obtain by entreaty, insistence, etc.: *get permission.* **7.** receive: *get a gift.* **8.** receive as punishment or penalty: *get ten days in jail.* **9.** come to have; acquire: *get skill through practice.* **10.** catch or contract (a disease or illness). **11.** seek out and obtain or secure (something required). **12.** succeed in finding (a thing or a person). **13.** *U.S. Slang.* get into one's power. **14.** bring into a particular position, situation, or condition: *get a fire under control.* **15.** cause (a person or thing) to be (as specified): *get one's hair cut.* **16.** induce or cause to do something; persuade: *we got him to speak.* **17.** *Am.* succeed in making: *he got me nervous.* **18.** beget (now usually of animals). **19.** *Colloq.* with *have* and *had*, be obliged to: *we have got to die sometime.* **20.** come to or arrive in a place specified or implied: *his boat got in yesterday.* **21.** *Slang.* hit; strike. **22.** *Am., Colloq.* kill. **23.** puzzle; annoy. **24.** *Am., Slang.* understand (a person or idea). **25.** get across, *Colloq.* **a.** make clear or convincing. **b.** succeed. **26.** get along, **a.** go away. **b.** advance. **c.** *Am.* manage. **d.** *Am.* suc-

ceed; prosper. **e.** agree. **27.** get around, **a.** go from place to place. **b.** become widely known; spread. **c.** overcome. **d.** *Am.* deceive; trick. **28.** get away, **a.** go away. **b.** escape. **c.** start. **29.** get away with, *Am., Colloq.* **a.** get the advantage of. **b.** succeed in taking or doing something and getting off safely. **c.** eat. **30.** get back at, *Am., Slang.* get revenge. **31.** get behind, *Am.* support; endorse. **32.** get by, *Colloq.* **a.** pass. **b.** *Am.* not be noticed or caught. **33.** get down on, *Am.* develop a dislike for. **34.** get even, *Am.* retaliate. **35.** get into, *Am.* **a.** find out about. **b.** get control of. **36.** get off, **a.** *Am.* come down from or out of. **b.** take off. **c.** escape. **d.** help to escape. **e.** start. **f.** *Am.* put out; issue. **g.** *Am.* say or express (a joke or witticism). **h.** deliver (a speech). **37.** get on, **a.** go up on or into. **b.** put on. **c.** advance. **d.** manage. **e.** succeed. **f.** agree. **38.** get out, **a.** go out. **b.** take out. **c.** go away. **d.** escape. **e.** help to escape. **f.** *Am.* become known. **g.** publish. **h.** find out. **39.** get over, **a.** recover from. **b.** overcome. **c.** *Am., Colloq.* make clear or convincing. **d.** *Am., Colloq.* succeed. **40.** get there, *Am.* succeed. **41.** get through, *Am.* secure favorable action on. **42.** get together, *Colloq.* **a.** bring or come together; meet; assemble. **b.** *Am.* come to an agreement. **43.** get up, **a.** get out of bed, etc. **b.** stand up. **c.** prepare; arrange. **d.** dress up. **e.** *Am.* go ahead. —*n.* **1.** a getting. **2.** offspring of an animal. [< Scand. *geta*] —**get'ta·ble, get'a·ble,** *adj.* —**get'ter,** *n.* ▷ Get is increasingly used as an emphatic passive auxiliary: *He got thrown out.*

get·a·way (get'ə·wā'), *n. Colloq.* **1.** act of getting away. **2.** start of a race.

Geth·sem·a·ne (geth·sem'ə·nē), *n.* garden near Jerusalem, the scene of Jesus's agony, betrayal, and arrest. Matt. 26:36.

get-to·geth·er (get'tù·geth'ər), *n. Am., Colloq.* an informal social gathering or party.

Get·tys·burg (get'iz·bèrg), *n.* town in S Pennsylvania; Civil War battle, July 1, 2, and 3, 1863.

get-up (get'up'), *n. Colloq.* **1.** way a thing is put together; arrangement. **2.** dress; costume. **3.** *Am.* initiative; energy; ambition.

gew·gaw (gū'gô), *n.* a showy trifle; bauble.

gey·ser (gī'zər), *n.* spring that sends a column of hot water and steam into the air at intervals. [< Icelandic *Geysir*, name of a spring in Iceland, < *geysa* gush]

G.G., GG, *Colloq.* gamma globulin.

Gha·na (gä'nə), *n.* country in W Africa, member of the British Commonwealth of Nations. It includes most of the former British colony of the Gold Coast.

ghast·ly (gast'li; gäst'-), *adj.,* -li·er, -li·est, *adv.* —*adj.* **1.** horrible: *a ghastly wound.* **2.** like a dead person or ghost; deathly pale. **3.** *Colloq.* shocking: *a ghastly failure.* —*adv.* in a ghastly manner; deathly. [OE *gāstlic* < *gāst* ghost] —**ghast'li·ness,** *n.* —**Syn.** *adj.* **1.** frightful, hideous, grisly, gruesome. **2.** deathlike, pallid.

ghat (gôt), *n.* in India: **1.** a landing place. **2.** a mountain pass. [< Hind.]

Ghent (gent), *n.* city in NW Belgium.

gher·kin (gėr'kən), *n.* **1.** a small, prickly cucumber often used for pickles. **2.** a young, green cucumber used for pickles. [< earlier Du. *agurkje*, dim. of *agurk* < G < Slavic < Med.Gk., ult. < Pers. *angorah* watermelon]

ghet·to (get'ō), *n., pl.* -tos. **1.** part of a city where Jews are required to live. **2.** part of a city where many Jews live. [< Ital.]

ghost (gōst), *n.* **1.** spirit of a dead person. It is supposed to live in another world and appear to living people as a pale, dim, shadowy form. **2.** a faint image; slightest suggestion: *not a ghost of a chance.* **3.** give up the ghost, die. **4.** a ghost writer. **5.** *Television.* a secondary image resulting from the reflection of a transmitted signal. —*v. Am., Colloq.* be a ghost writer for. —*adj.* designating a habitation, town, etc., that is deserted: *a ghost town.* [OE *gāst*] —**ghost'like',** *adj., adv.* —**Syn.** *n.* **1.** specter.

ghost·ly (gōst'li), *adj.,* -li·er, -li·est. **1.** like a ghost; pale, dim, and shadowy. **2.** spiritual; religious. —**ghost'li·ness,** *n.*

ghost-write (gōst'rīt'), *v.,* -wrote, -writ·ten.

–writ·ing. *Am.* **1.** write (something) for an employer who is the ostensible author. **2.** write (a supposedly factual account) entirely from imagination.

ghost writer, *Am.* person who writes something for another who takes the credit.

ghoul (gül), *n.* **1.** a horrible demon in Oriental stories, believed to feed on corpses. **2.** person who robs graves or corpses. **3.** person who enjoys what is revolting, brutal, and horrible. [< Ar. *ghūl*] **—ghoul′ish,** *adj.* **—ghoul′ish·ly,** *adv.* **—ghoul′ish·ness,** *n.*

G.H.Q., *Mil.* General Headquarters.

G.I., GI (jē′ī′), *adj., n., pl.* **G.I.'s; GI's or GIs** (jē′īz′). **—adj. 1.** from government issue; from general issue; designating anything issued by the U.S. Army Quartermaster: *G.I. equipment.* **2.** *Colloq.* conforming to regulations; standard: *G.I. dress.* **3.** *Colloq.* of, characteristic of, or for enlisted army personnel: *a G.I. story, a G.I. obstacle course.* **—n.** *Colloq.* an enlisted soldier; serviceman. [< the initial letters of the phrase "Government Issue"]

gi·ant (jī′ənt), *n.* **1.** an imaginary being having human form, but larger and more powerful than a man. **2.** person or thing of unusual size, strength, importance, etc. **—adj.** like a giant; unusually big and strong; huge. [< OF < L < Gk. *gigas*]

gi·ant·ess (jī′ən·tis), *n.* a woman giant.

giaour (jour), *n.* in Mohammedan usage, a person who does not believe in the Mohammedan religion. [< Turk. < Pers. *gaur*]

gib·ber (jib′ər; gib′–), *v.* chatter senselessly; talk rapidly and indistinctly. **—n.** senseless chattering. **—Syn.** *v.* babble, prattle.

gib·ber·ish (jib′ər·ish; gib′–), *n.* senseless chatter; rapid, indistinct talk; jargon.

gib·bet (jib′it), *n., v.,* –bet·ed, –bet·ing. **—n. 1.** an upright post with a projecting arm at the top, from which the bodies of criminals were hung after execution. **2.** gallows. **—v. 1.** hang on a gibbet. **2.** hold up to public scorn or ridicule. **3.** put to death by hanging. [< OF *gibet*, dim. of *gibe* club]

gib·bon (gib′ən), *n.* a small, long-armed ape of SE Asia and the East Indies, that lives in trees. [< F]

Gib·bon (gib′ən), *n.* Edward, 1737–1794, English historian.

gib·bous (gib′əs), *adj.* **1.** curved out; humped. A gibbous moon is more than half full but less than full. **2.** hunchbacked. [< L *gibbus* a hump]

Gibbon
(ab. 30 in. tall)

gibe (jīb), *v.,* gibed, gib·ing, *n.* **—v.** jeer; scoff; sneer. **—n.** a sneering or sarcastic remark. Also, jibe. [? < OF *giber* handle roughly < *gibe* staff] **—gib′er,** *n.* **—Syn.** *v.* mock, taunt, ridicule.

gib·let (jib′lit), *n.* Usually, **giblets.** the heart, liver, or gizzard of a fowl. [< OF *gibelet* stew of game]

Gi·bral·tar (jə·brôl′tər), *n.* **1.** seaport and fortress on a high rock at the S tip of Spain. It is a British colony. **2.** Rock of, the large rock on which this fortress stands. **3.** Strait or strait between Africa and Europe, connecting the Mediterranean Sea with the Atlantic.

gid·dy (gid′ī), *adj.,* –di·er, –di·est, *v.,* –died, –dy·ing. **—adj. 1.** having a confused, whirling feeling in one's head; dizzy. **2.** likely to make dizzy; causing dizziness. **3.** rarely or never serious; flighty. **—v.** make or become giddy. [OE *gydig* mad, possessed (by an evil spirit) < *god* a god] **—gid′di·ly,** *adv.* **—gid′di·ness,** *n.* **—Syn.** *adj.* **1.** light-headed. **3.** frivolous, unstable.

Gid·e·on (gid′i·ən), *n.* **1.** hero of Israel who defeated the Midianites. Judges 6 and 7. **2.** *Am.* member of a Christian organization of American commercial travelers, founded in 1899.

gift (gift), *n.* **1.** thing given; present. **2.** act of

giving: *get a thing by gift.* **3.** power or right of giving: *the office is within his gift.* **4.** natural ability; special talent. **—v.** present with a gift or gifts; endow. [< Scand.; akin to *give*] **—Syn.** *n.* **1.** donation, contribution, offering. **4.** aptitude.

gift·ed (gif′tid), *adj.* having natural ability or special talent: *a gifted musician.*

gig (gig), *n.* **1.** a light, two-wheeled carriage drawn by one horse. **2.** a long, light ship's boat moved by oars or sails.

gi·gan·tic (jī·gan′tik), *adj.* like a giant; unusually big; huge; enormous. **—gi·gan′ti·cal·ly,** *adv.* **—gi·gan′tic·ness,** *n.* **—Syn.** immense, colossal, herculean.

gig·gle (gig′əl), *v.,* –gled, –gling, *n.* **—v.** laugh in a silly or undignified way. **—n.** a silly or undignified laugh. [< *giglet* laughing girl] **—gig′gler,** *n.* **—gig′gling·ly,** *adv.* **—gig′gly,** *adj.*

gig·o·lo (jig′ə·lō), *n., pl.* –los. man who is paid for being a dancing partner or escort for a woman. [< F]

Gi·la monster (hē′lə), *Am.* a large, poisonous lizard of Arizona and New Mexico, covered with beadlike, orange-and-black scales. [after *Gila* River, Arizona]

Gila monster (1½ ft. long)

Gil·bert (gil′bərt), *n.* Sir William Schwenck, 1836–1911, English humorist who wrote the words for most of the operas for which Sir Arthur Sullivan wrote the music. **—Gil·bert′i·an,** *adj.*

Gilbert and El·lice Islands (el′is), a British colony in the C Pacific which includes a large number of small islands near the equator.

gild¹ (gild), *v.,* gild·ed or gilt, gild·ing. **1.** cover with a thin layer of gold or similar material; make golden. **2.** make (a thing) look bright and pleasing. **3.** make (a thing) seem better than it is. [OE *gyldan* < *gold*] **—gild′a·ble,** *adj.* **—gild′ed,** *adj.* **—gild′er,** *n.* **—gild′ing,** *n.*

gild² (gild), *n.* guild. **—gilds·man** (gildz′mən), *n.*

gild·hall (gild′hôl′), *n.* guildhall.

gill¹ (gil), *n.* part of the body of a fish, tadpole, crab, etc., arranged for breathing in water. [< Scand. (Sw.) *gäl*] **—gilled,** *adj.* **—gill′-like′,** *adj.*

gill² (jil), *n.* measure for liquids; one fourth of a pint. [< OF *gille* wine measure]

gil·lie (gil′i), *n. Scot.* **1.** attendant of a hunter or fisherman. **2.** follower; servant. [< Scotch Gaelic *gille* lad]

gil·ly·flow·er (jil′i·flou′ər), *n.* any of various flowers that have a spicy fragrance. [< OF < L < Gk. *karyophyllon* clove tree < *karyon* clove + *phyllon* leaf]

gilt (gilt), *v.* pt. and pp. of **gild¹.** **—n.** a thin layer of gold or similar material with which a thing is gilded. **—adj.** gilded.

gilt-edged (gilt′ejd′), *adj.* **1.** having gilded edges. **2.** of the very best quality.

gim·bals (jim′bəlz; gim′–), *n.pl. Naut.* arrangement for keeping an object horizontal. A ship's compass is supported on gimbals. [ult. < OF *gemel* twin < L *gemellus*]

gim·crack (jim′krak), *n.* a showy, useless trifle. **—adj.** showy but useless.

gim·let (gim′lit), *n.* a small tool with a screw point, for boring holes. [< OF *guimbelet*]

gim·let-eyed (gim′lit·īd′), *adj.* having eyes that are sharp and piercing.

gim·mick (gim′ik), *n. U.S. Slang.* **1.** a secret device by which a magician is able to perform a trick. **2.** any tricky device.

Gimlet

gimp (gimp), *n.* a braidlike trimming made of silk, worsted, or cotton, sometimes stiffened with wire, used on garments, curtains, furniture, etc. [< F *guimpe* < Gmc. Doublet of GUIMPE.]

gin¹ (jin), *n.* a strong alcoholic drink, usually flavored with juniper berries. [short for *geneva* liquor]

gin² (jin), *n.*, *v.*, **ginned, gin·ning.** —*n.* 1. Am. machine for separating cotton from its seeds. 2. trap; snare. —*v.* 1. separate (cotton) from its seeds. 2. catch in a gin. [< OF *engin* ENGINE]

gin³ (jin), *n.* Cards. gin rummy.

gin⁴ (gin), *v.*, **gan, gun, gin·ning.** Archaic and Poetic. begin. [OE *onginnan*]

gin·ger (jin′jər), *n.* 1. spice made from the root of a tropical plant, used for flavoring and in medicine. 2. the root, often preserved in syrup or candied. 3. the plant. 4. Am., Colloq. liveliness; energy. [< LL < L < Gk. < Prakrit (an ancient lang. of India) *singabēra*] —**gin′ger·y,** *adj.*

ginger ale, a nonalcoholic, bubbling drink flavored with ginger.

ginger beer, an English drink similar to ginger ale, but made with fermenting ginger.

gin·ger·bread (jin′jər·bred′), *n.* 1. cake flavored with ginger and sweetened with molasses. 2. something showy and elaborate, but not in good taste. —*adj.* gaudy.

gin·ger·ly (jin′jər·li), *adv.* with extreme care or caution. —*adj.* extremely cautious. —**gin′ger·li·ness,** *n.*

gin·ger·snap (jin′jər·snap′), *n.* a thin, crisp cooky flavored with ginger.

ging·ham (ging′əm), *n.* a cotton cloth made from colored threads, usually in stripes, plaids, or checks. [< F < Malay *ginggang,* orig., striped]

gink·go (ging′kō; jing′kō), **ging·ko** (ging′kō), *n.*, *pl.* **-goes; -koes.** a large, ornamental tree of China and Japan with fan-shaped leaves and edible nuts. [< Jap.]

gin rummy (jin), Am., Cards. a kind of rummy in which players form sequences and matching combinations and lay down their hands when having ten or less points.

gin·seng (jin′seng), *n.* 1. a low plant with a thick, branched root. 2. this root, much used in medicine by the Chinese. [< Chinese *jên shên; jên* = man]

Giot·to (jot′ō), *n.* 1266?–1337?, the greatest Italian painter before the Renaissance.

Gip·sy, gip·sy (jip′si), *n.*, *pl.* **-sies,** *adj.* Esp. Brit. Gypsy. —**gip′sy·like′,** *adj.*

gipsy moth, gypsy moth.

gi·raffe (jə·raf′; -räf′), *n.* a large African mammal with a very long neck and legs and a spotted skin, the tallest of living animals. [< F < Ar. *zarāfah*]

gird (gérd), *v.*, **girt** or **gird·ed, gird·ing.** 1. put a belt or girdle around. 2. fasten with a belt or girdle. 3. surround; enclose. 4. get ready for action. 5. clothe; furnish. [OE *gyrdan*]

gird·er (gér′dər), *n.* a main supporting beam. A tall building or big bridge often has steel girders for its frame. [< *gird*]

gir·dle (gér′dəl), *n.*, *v.*, **-dled, -dling.** —*n.* 1. belt, sash, cord, etc., worn around the waist. 2. anything that surrounds or encloses. 3. support like a corset worn about the hips or waist. —*v.* 1. form a girdle around; encircle. 2. Am. kill (a tree) by cutting a ring around its trunk. 3. put a girdle on or around. [OE *gyrdel.* See GIRD.] —**gir′dle·like′,** *adj.* —**gir′dler,** *n.*

girl (gérl), *n.* 1. a female child. 2. a young, unmarried woman. 3. a female servant. 4. Colloq. sweetheart. 5. Colloq. woman of any age. [OE *gyrl-* in *gyrlgyden* virgin goddess] —**girl′ish,** *adj.* —**girl′ish·ly,** *adv.* —**girl′ish·ness,** *n.*

girl·hood (gérl′hud), *n.* 1. time or condition of being a girl. 2. girls as a group.

girl·ie (gér′li), *n.* Colloq. a little girl.

girl scout, Am. member of the Girl Scouts.

Girl Scouts, Am. organization for girls that seeks to develop health, character, and a knowledge of homemaking.

girt (gért), *v.* 1. pt. and pp. of gird. 2. put a girth around. 3. fasten with a girth.

girth (gérth), *n.* 1. the measure around anything: *man of large girth.* 2. strap or band that keeps a saddle, pack, etc., in place on a horse's back. 3. girdle. —*v.* 1. measure in girth. 2. fasten with a strap or band. 3. girdle. [< Scand. *gjörth* girdle; akin to GIRD]

gist (jist), *n.* the essential part; main idea; substance of a longer statement. [< OF, (it) consists (in), depends (on) < L *jacet* it lies] —Syn. essence, pith.

git·tern (git′ərn), *n.* an old musical instrument with wire strings, somewhat like a guitar. [< OF *guiterne*]

give (giv), *v.*, **gave, giv·en, giv·ing,** *n.* —*v.* 1. hand over as a present: *my brother gave me his watch.* 2. hand over; deliver: *please give me a drink, give a person into custody, give one's word.* 3. hand over in exchange for something: *I gave it to him for $5.* 4. let have; cause to have: *give me permission.* 5. propose; offer: *give a toast.* 6. furnish; provide: *give aid to the enemy.* 7. set forth; show: *the newspaper gave a long account.* 8. deal; administer: *give one a blow.* 9. communicate: *give advice.* 10. allot; award: *give a contract to a person.* 11. assign as a basis: *given these premises.* 12. attribute: *give credit to another.* 13. produce; deliver: *give a lecture, a play, etc.* 14. put forth; utter: *give a cry.* 15. cause; occasion: *give trouble.* 16. do; perform: *give battle.* 17. afford a passage or view: *a window that gives upon a court.* 18. make a gift. 19. yield to force or pressure. 20. **give away,** Colloq. a. give as a present. b. hand over (a bride) to a bridegroom. c. Am. betray a secret, esp. unintentionally; expose (a person). 21. **give back,** return. 22. **give out,** a. send out; put forth. b. distribute. c. make known. b. become used up or worn out. 23. **give up,** a. hand over; deliver; surrender. b. stop having or doing. c. stop trying. d. have no more hope for. e. devote entirely. —*n.* a yielding to force or pressure; elasticity. [< Scand. (Dan.) *give*] —**giv′er,** *n.*

give-and-take (giv′ən·tāk′), *n.* 1. an even or fair exchange; mutual concession. 2. good-natured banter; exchange of talk.

give·a·way (giv′ə·wā′), *n.* Am., Colloq. 1. an unintentional revelation; exposure; betrayal. 2. Also, **giveaway show** or **program.** a radio or television show in which the studio audience participates and receives prizes.

giv·en (giv′ən), *adj.* 1. stated; fixed; specified. 2. inclined; disposed. 3. assigned as a basis of calculating, reasoning, etc. 4. Math. known. —*v.* pp. of give.

given name, name given to a person in addition to his family name. *John* is the given name of John Smith.

giz·zard (giz′ərd), *n.* a bird's second stomach, where the food from the first stomach is ground up fine. [< OF, ult. < L *gigeria* cooked entrails of a fowl]

Gk., Greek. Also, **Gr.**

Gl, Chem. glucinum.

gla·brous (glā′brəs), *adj.* Bot., Zool. without hair or down; smooth. [< L *glaber* smooth]

gla·cé (gla·sā′), *adj.* 1. covered with sugar, frosting, or icing. 2. frozen. 3. finished with a glossy surface. [< F, pp. of *glacer* impart a gloss to]

gla·cial (glā′shəl), *adj.* 1. of ice or glaciers; having much ice or many glaciers. 2. relating to a glacial epoch or period. 3. made by the action of ice or glaciers. 4. very cold; icy. [< L, < *glacies* ice] —**gla′cial·ly,** *adv.*

gla·ci·ate (glā′shi·āt), *v.*, **-at·ed, -at·ing.** 1. cover with ice or glaciers. 2. act on by ice or glaciers. —**gla·ci·a·tion** (glā′shi·ā′shən; -shi-), *n.*

gla·cier (glā′shər), *n.* a large mass of ice formed from snow on high ground wherever winter snowfall exceeds slowly melting, which moves very slowly down a mountain or along a valley. [< F, ult. < L *glacies*] —**gla′ciered,** *adj.*

glad (glad), *adj.*, **glad·der, glad·dest.** 1. happy; pleased. 2. bringing joy; pleasant. 3. bright; gay. [OE *glæd* bright, shining] —**glad′ly,** *adv.* —**glad′ness,** *n.* —Syn. 1. delighted, gratified. 3. joyful, joyous, cheerful, merry. —Ant. 1. sad.

Giraffe
(ab. 18 ft. tall)

glad·den (glad'ən), v. make or become glad. —**glad'den·er,** n. —Syn. cheer, enliven, delight.

glade (glād), n. 1. an open space in a wood or forest. 2. Am. a marshy tract of low ground covered with grass. [prob. akin to glad]

glad hand, Am., Colloq. the hand extended in cordial greeting.

glad-hand·er (glad'hand'ər), n. Am., Colloq. person who makes a show of being friendly to all.

glad·i·a·tor (glad'i·ā'tər), n. 1. in ancient Rome, a slave, captive, or paid fighter who fought at the public shows. 2. a skilled contender in any field or cause. [< L, < gladius sword] —**glad·i·a·to·ri·al** (glad'i·ə·tō'ri·əl; -tō'-), adj.

glad·i·o·lus (glad'i·ō'ləs; glə·dī'-ə-), **glad·i·o·la** (-lə), n., pl. -li (-lī), -lus·es; -las. kind of iris with spikes of large, handsome flowers in various colors. [< L, dim. of gladius sword]

glad·some (glad'səm), adj. 1. glad; joyful; cheerful. 2. causing gladness. —**glad'some·ly,** adv. —**glad'some·ness,** n.

Gladiolus

Glad·stone (glad'stōn; -stən), n. 1. William Ewart, 1809–1898, British statesman. 2. Gladstone bag.

Gladstone bag, a traveling bag that opens flat into two equal compartments. [so named in compliment to W. E. Gladstone]

glair (glār), n. 1. the raw white of an egg or any similar viscous substance. 2. glaze or size made from it. [< OF glaire, ult. < L clarus clear] —**glair'y,** adj.

glaive (glāv), n. Archaic. sword; broadsword. [< OF < L gladius sword]

glam·or·ize (glam'ər·īz), v., -ized, -iz·ing. make (someone or something) glamorous.

glam·or·ous (glam'ər·əs), adj. full of glamour; fascinating. —**glam'or·ous·ly,** adv.

glam·our, glam·or (glam'ər), n. 1. mysterious fascination; alluring charm. 2. a magic spell or influence; enchantment. [alter. of grammar or its var. gramarye occult learning; orig., a spell] ➤ Glamor is rapidly gaining ground. The adjective should always be glamorous.

glance (glans; gläns), n., v., glanced, glanc·ing. —n. 1. a quick look. 2. flash of light; gleam. 3. a glancing off; deflected motion; swift, oblique movement. 4. a passing reference. —v. 1. direct in a quick look. 2. flash with light; gleam. 3. direct obliquely. 4. hit and go off at a slant. 5. make a short reference and go on to something else. [var. of ME glace(n) strike a glancing blow < OF glacier to slip] —Syn. n. 1. glimpse.

gland (gland), n. Anat. organ in the body by which certain substances are separated from the blood and changed into some secretion for use in the body, such as bile, or into a product to be discharged from the body, such as sweat. [< F glande, ult. < L glandula, dim. of glans acorn] —**gland'less,** adj. —**gland'like',** adj.

glan·ders (glan'dərz), n. a serious contagious disease of horses, mules, etc., accompanied by swellings beneath the lower jaw and a profuse discharge from the nostrils. [< OF glandre GLAND] —**glan'der·ous,** adj.

glan·du·lar (glan'jə·lər), **glan·du·lous** (-ləs), adj. of or like a gland; having glands.

glare[1] (glār), n., v., glared, glar·ing. —n. 1. a strong, bright light; light that shines so brightly that it hurts the eyes. 2. a fierce, angry stare. 3. too great brightness and showiness. —v. 1. give off a strong, bright light; shine so brightly as to hurt the eyes. 2. stare fiercely and angrily. 3. express by a fierce, angry stare. 4. be too bright and showy. [ME glaren. Cf. OE glæren glassy.]

glare[2] (glār), Am. —n. a bright, smooth surface. —adj. bright and smooth. [extended use of glare[1]]

glar·ing (glār'ing), adj. 1. very bright; dazzling. 2. staring fiercely and angrily. 3. too bright and showy. 4. conspicuous. —**glar'ing·ly,** adv. —**glar'ing·ness,** n. —Syn. 1. brilliant.

glar·y (glār'i), adj. glaring.

Glas·gow (glas'gō; -kō; gläs'-), n. the largest city and chief seaport in Scotland.

glass (glas; gläs), n. 1. a hard, brittle substance that is usually transparent, made by melting sand with soda, potash, lime, or other substances. 2. thing to drink from made of glass. 3. as much as a glass holds. 4. something made of glass. A windowpane, a mirror, a watch crystal, a telescope, or an hourglass is a glass. 5. things made of glass. 6. glasses, a pair of lenses to correct defective eyesight; eyeglasses; spectacles. b. field glasses; binoculars. —v. 1. put glass in; cover or protect with glass. 2. reflect. —adj. made of glass. [OE glæs]

glass blowing, art or process of shaping glass by blowing while it is still hot and soft. —**glass blower.**

glass·ful (glas'fùl; gläs'-), n., pl. -fuls. as much as a glass holds.

glass snake, Am. a legless, snakelike lizard of the S United States, whose tail breaks off very easily.

glass·ware (glas'wār; gläs'-), n. articles made of glass.

glass·y (glas'i; gläs'i), adj., glass·i·er, glass·i·est. 1. like glass; smooth; easily seen through. 2. having a fixed, stupid stare. —**glass'i·ly,** adv. —**glass'i·ness,** n.

glau·co·ma (glô·kō'mə), n. disease of the eye, characterized by hardening of the eyeball and gradual loss of sight. [< Gk. glaukoma. See GLAUCOUS.] —**glau·co·ma·tous** (glô·kō'mə·təs; -kom'ə-), adj.

glau·cous (glô'kəs), adj. 1. light bluish-green. 2. Bot. covered with whitish powder as plums and grapes are. [< L < Gk. glaukos gray]

glaze (glāz), v., glazed, glaz·ing, n. —v. 1. put glass in; cover with glass. 2. make a smooth, glassy surface or glossy coating on (china, food, etc.). 3. become smooth, glassy, or glossy. —n. 1. a smooth, glassy surface or glossy coating: the glaze on a china cup. 2. Am. a. a coating of smooth ice. b. an area covered with such a coating. [ME glase(n) < glas GLASS] —**glaz'er,** n. —**glaz'ing,** n. —**glaz'y,** adj. —**glaz'i·ness,** n.

gla·zier (glā'zhər), n. person whose work is putting glass in windows, picture frames, etc.

gleam (glēm), n. 1. flash or beam of light. 2. a short or faint light. 3. a faint show: a gleam of hope. —v. 1. flash or beam with light. 2. shine with a short or faint light. 3. appear suddenly. [OE glǣm]

glean (glēn), v. 1. gather (grain) left on a field by reapers. 2. gather little by little or slowly. [< OF < LL glennare < Celtic] —**glean'er,** n.

glebe (glēb), n. 1. Poetic. soil; earth; field. 2. portion of land assigned to a parish church or clergyman. [< L gleba]

glee (glē), n. 1. joy; delight; mirth. 2. song for three or more voices singing different parts, usually without instrumental accompaniment. [OE glēo] —Syn. 1. merriment, gaiety, jollity.

glee club, group organized for singing songs.

glee·ful (glē'fəl), adj. filled with glee; merry; joyous. —**glee'ful·ly,** adv. —**glee'ful·ness,** n. —Syn. gay, jolly, mirthful.

glee·man (glē'mən), n., pl. -men. Archaic. singer; minstrel.

glee·some (glē'səm), adj. gleeful. —**glee'some·ly,** adv. —**glee'some·ness,** n.

glen (glen), n. a small, narrow valley. [< Scotch Gaelic gle(a)nn] —**glen'like',** adj.

glen·gar·ry (glen·gar'i), n., pl. -ries. a Scottish cap with straight sides and a creased top, often having short ribbons at the back. [after Glengarry, valley in Scotland]

glib (glib), adj., glib·ber, glib·best. 1. speaking or spoken smoothly and easily. 2. speaking or spoken too smoothly and easily to be sincere: a glib excuse.

Glengarry

3. acting smoothly and easily. [short for *glibbery* slippery. Cf. Du. *glibberig*.] —**glib′ly**, *adv.* —**glib′ness**, *n.* —**Syn.** 1. fluent, voluble, smooth-tongued.

glide (glīd), *v.*, **glid·ed, glid·ing,** *n.* —*v.* 1. move along smoothly, evenly, and easily. 2. pass gradually, quietly, or imperceptibly. 3. of an airplane, come down slowly at a slant without using a motor. —*n.* 1. a smooth, even, easy movement. 2. of an airplane, act of gliding. 3. *Music.* a slur. 4. *Phonet.* sound made in passing from one speech sound to another. [OE *glīdan*] —**glid′ing·ly,** *adv.*

glid·er (glīd′ər), *n.* 1. aircraft resembling an airplane without a motor. Rising air currents keep it in the air. 2. person or thing that glides.

glim·mer (glim′ər), *n.* 1. a faint, unsteady light. 2. a vague idea; dim notion; faint glimpse. —*v.* 1. shine with a faint, unsteady light. 2. appear faintly or dimly. [cf. OE *gleomu* splendor] —**glim′mer·ing,** *n.* —**glim′mer·ing·ly,** *adv.*

glimpse (glimps), *n., v.,* **glimpsed, glimps·ing.** —*n.* 1. a short, quick view. 2. a short, faint appearance. —*v.* 1. catch a short, quick view of. 2. look quickly; glance. [akin to *glimmer*] —**glimps′er,** *n.*

glint (glint), *v., n.* gleam; flash. [cf. dial. Sw. *glinta*]

glis·ten (glis′ən), *v., n.* sparkle; glitter; shine. [OE *glisnian*] —**glis′ten·ing·ly,** *adv.*

glis·ter (glis′tər), *v., n.* Archaic. glisten; glitter; sparkle. [? < *glisten*]

glit·ter (glit′ər), *v.* 1. shine with a bright, sparkling light. 2. be bright and showy. —*n.* 1. a bright, sparkling light. 2. brightness; showiness. [cf. Scand. *glitra*] —**glit′ter·ing, glit′ter·y,** *adj.* —**glit′ter·ing·ly,** *adv.*

gloam·ing (glōm′ing), *n.* Poetic. evening twilight; dusk. [OE *glōmung* < *glōm* twilight]

gloat (glōt), *v.* gaze intently; ponder with pleasure; stare: *the miser gloated over his gold.* [cf. Scand. *glotta* smile scornfully] —**gloat′er,** *n.* —**gloat′ing·ly,** *adv.*

glob·al (glōb′əl), *adj.* 1. shaped like a globe. 2. world-wide. —**glob′al·ly,** *adv.*

globe (glōb), *n., v.,* **globed, glob·ing.** —*n.* 1. anything round like a ball; sphere. 2. earth; world. 3. sphere with a map of the earth or sky on it. 4. planet, eyeball, or anything rounded like a globe. —*v.* gather or form into a globe. [< F < L *globus*]

globe·fish (glōb′fish′), *n., pl.* **-fish·es** or (*esp. collectively*) **-fish.** fish that can make itself nearly ball-shaped by drawing in air.

globe·trot·ter (glōb′trot′ər), *n.* person who travels widely over the world for sightseeing. —**globe′trot′ting,** *n., adj.*

glo·bose (glō′bōs), *adj.* globular. —**glo′bose·ly,** *adv.* —**glo·bos·i·ty** (glō·bos′ə·ti), *n.*

glob·u·lar (glob′yə·lər), *adj.* 1. shaped like a globe or globule; spherical. 2. consisting of globules. —**glob·u·lar·i·ty** (glob′yə·lar′ə·ti), *n.* —**glob′u·lar·ly,** *adv.*

glob·ule (glob′ūl), *n.* a very small ball; tiny drop.

glock·en·spiel (glok′ən·spēl′), *n.* Music. instrument consisting of a series of small, tuned bells, metal bars, or tubes mounted in a frame and struck by two little hammers. [< G, < *glocke* bell + *spiel* play]

glom·er·ate (glom′ər·it), *adj.* clustered together; collected into a rounded mass. [< L, < *glomus* ball] —**glom·er·a·tion** (glom′ər·ā′shən), *n.*

gloom (glüm), *n.* 1. deep shadow; darkness; dimness. 2. low spirits; sadness. 3. a dejected or sad look. —*v.* 1. be or become dark, dim, or dismal. 2. be in low spirits; feel miserable. 3. look sad or dismal. [OE *glōm* twilight] —**Syn.** *n.* 1. obscurity, shade. 2. despondency, dejection, depression, melancholy.

gloom·y (glüm′i), *adj.,* **gloom·i·er, gloom·i·est.** 1. dark; dim. 2. in low spirits; sad; melancholy. 3. causing low spirits; discouraging; dismal. —**gloom′i·ly,** *adv.* —**gloom′i·ness,** *n.* —**Syn.** 1. shadowy, somber. 2. dejected, downhearted. —**Ant.** 2. happy.

glo·ri·a (glô′ri·ə; glō′-), *n.* 1. song of praise to God, or its musical setting. 2. Gloria, one of three songs of praise to God, beginning "Glory be to God on high," "Glory be to the Father," and "Glory be to Thee, O Lord." 3. halo. [< L]

glo·ri·fy (glô′rə·fī; glō′-), *v.,* **-fied, -fy·ing.** 1. give glory to; make glorious. 2. praise; honor; worship. 3. make more beautiful or splendid. 4. exalt to the glory of heaven. [< OF < L, < *gloria* glory + *facere* make] —**glo′ri·fi′a·ble,** *adj.* —**glo′ri·fi·ca′tion,** *n.* —**glo′ri·fi′er,** *n.*

glo·ri·ous (glô′ri·əs; glō′-), *adj.* 1. having or deserving glory; illustrious. 2. giving glory. 3. magnificent; splendid. —**glo′ri·ous·ly,** *adv.* —**glo′ri·ous·ness,** *n.* —**Syn.** 1. famous, renowned. 3. grand, brilliant.

glo·ry (glô′ri; glō′-), *n., pl.* **-ries,** *v.,* **-ried, -ry·ing.** —*n.* 1. great praise and honor; fame; renown. 2. that which brings praise and honor; source of pride and joy. 3. adoring praise and thanksgiving. 4. radiant beauty; brightness; magnificence; splendor. 5. condition of magnificence, splendor, or greatest prosperity. 6. splendor and bliss of heaven; heaven. 7. halo. —*v.* be proud; rejoice. [< OF < L *gloria*] —**Syn.** *n.* 1. distinction, eminence. —**Ant.** *n.* 1. dishonor.

gloss¹ (glôs; glos), *n.* 1. a smooth, shiny surface; luster. 2. an outward appearance or surface that covers wrong underneath. —*v.* 1. put a smooth, shiny surface on. 2. smooth over; make seem right: *gloss over a mistake.* [cf. Scand. *glossi* flame] —**gloss′er,** *n.* —**Syn.** *n.* 1. sheen, polish.

gloss² (glôs; glos), *n.* 1. explanation; interpretation; comment. 2. glossary. 3. translation inserted between the lines of a text printed in a foreign language. —*v.* 1. comment on; explain; annotate. 2. explain away. 3. make glosses. [< L < Gk. *glossa,* lit., tongue] —**gloss′er,** *n.*

glos·sar·i·al (glo·sãr′i·əl; glō′-), *adj.* of or like a glossary. —**glos·sar′i·al·ly,** *adv.*

glos·sa·ry (glos′ə·ri; glôs′-), *n., pl.* **-ries.** list of special, technical, or difficult words with explanations or comments: *glossary of Shakespeare's plays.* [< L, < *glossa* GLOSS²] —**glos′sa·rist,** *n.*

gloss·y (glôs′i; glos′i), *adj.,* **gloss·i·er, gloss·i·est.** smooth and shiny. —**gloss′i·ly,** *adv.* —**gloss′i·ness,** *n.* —**Syn.** lustrous, polished, sleek.

glot·tal (glot′əl), *adj.* 1. of the glottis. 2. *Phonet.* produced in the glottis. H in *hope* is a glottal sound.

glot·tis (glot′is), *n.* an opening at the upper part of the windpipe, between the vocal cords. [< NL < Gk., ult. < *glotta* tongue]

Glouces·ter·shire (glos′tər·shir; glôs′-), *n.* county in SW England.

glove (gluv), *n., v.,* **gloved, glov·ing.** —*n.* 1. a covering for the hand, usually with separate places for each of the four fingers and the thumb. 2. a boxing glove. 3. handle with gloves, treat gently. —*v.* 1. cover with a glove; provide with gloves. 2. serve as a glove for. [OE *glōf*] —**glove′less,** *adj.* —**glove′like′,** *adj.*

glov·er (gluv′ər), *n.* person who makes or sells gloves.

glow (glō), *n.* 1. shine from something that is red-hot or white-hot; similar shine. 2. brightness: *the glow of sunset.* 3. a warm feeling or color of the body: *the glow of health on his cheeks.* 4. an eager look on the face: *glow of interest or excitement.* —*v.* 1. shine as if red-hot or white-hot. 2. show a warm color; be red or bright. 3. be hot; burn. 4. be eager or animated. [OE *glōwan*] —**glow′ing,** *adj.* —**glow′ing·ly,** *adv.*

glow·er (glou′ər), *v.* 1. stare angrily; scowl. 2. *Scot.* gaze intently; stare. —*n.* an angry or sullen look. [? < obs. *glow,* v., stare] —**glow′er·ing·ly,** *adv.*

glow·worm (glō′wérm′), *n.* any insect larva or wormlike insect that glows in the dark.

gloze (glōz), *v.,* **glozed, gloz·ing.** 1. smooth over; explain away. 2. talk flatteringly. [< F *gloser* < OF *glose* GLOSS²]

glu·ci·num (glü·sī′nəm), **glu·cin·i·um** (-sin′i·əm), *n.* Chem. beryllium.

glu·cose (glü′kōs), n. 1. Chem. kind of sugar, C6H12O6, occurring in fruits. 2. syrup made from starch.

glue (glü), n., v., glued, glu·ing. —n. 1. substance used to stick things together, often made by boiling the hoofs, skins, and bones of animals in water. 2. any similar sticky substance. —v. 1. stick together with glue. 2. fasten tightly; attach firmly. [< OF gluz < LL glutis] —glue′like′, adj. —glu′er, n.

glue·y (glü′i), adj., glu·i·er, glu·i·est. 1. like glue; sticky. 2. smeared with glue.

glum (glum), adj., glum·mer, glum·mest. gloomy; dismal; sullen. —glum′ly, adv. —glum′ness, n.

glut (glut), v., glut·ted, glut·ting, n. —v. 1. fill full; feed or satisfy fully. 2. fill too full; supply too much for. —n. 1. a full supply; great quantity. 2. too great a supply. [< obs. glut, n., GLUTTON < OF]

glu·ten (glü′tən), n. a tough, sticky substance that remains in flour when the starch is taken out. [< L, glue] —glu·te·nous (glü′tə·nəs), adj.

glu·ti·nous (glü′tə·nəs), adj. sticky. —glu′ti·nous·ly, adv. —glu′ti·nous·ness, glu·ti·nos·i·ty (glü′tə·nos′ə·ti), n.

glut·ton (glut′ən), n. 1. a greedy eater; person who eats too much. 2. person who never seems to have enough of something. 3. wolverine. [< OF < L gluto]

glut·ton·ous (glut′ən·əs), adj. greedy about food; having the habit of eating too much. —glut′ton·ous·ly, adv. —glut′ton·ous·ness, n.

glut·ton·y (glut′ən·i), n., pl. -ton·ies. excess in eating.

glyc·er·in (glis′ər·in), **glyc·er·ine** (-in, -ēn), n. a colorless, syrupy, sweet liquid, C3H8O3, obtained from fats and oils, used in ointments, lotions, antifreeze solutions, and explosives.

glyc·er·ol (glis′ər·ōl; -ol), n. glycerin.

gly·co·gen (glī′kə·jən), n. a starchlike substance in the liver and other animal tissues that is changed into sugar as needed.

gm., gram; grams.

G-man (jē′man′), n., pl. -men. Am., Colloq. a special agent of the U.S. Department of Justice; agent of the FBI.

Gmc., Germanic. Also, Ger.

gnarl (närl), n. knot in wood; hard, rough lump. —gnarled, gnarl′y, adj.

gnash (nash), v. 1. strike or grind (the teeth) together; grind together. 2. bite by gnashing the teeth. [var. of gnast, appar. < Scand. gnastan gnashing]

gnat (nat), n. 1. any of various small, two-winged insects or flies. Most gnats are blood-sucking and make bites that itch. 2. Brit. mosquito. [OE gnætt] —gnat′like′, adj.

gnaw (nô), v., gnawed, gnawed or gnawn (nôn), gnaw·ing. 1. bite at and wear away. 2. make by biting. 3. wear away; consume; corrode. 4. torment. [OE gnagan] —gnaw′er, n. —gnaw′ing, adj. —gnaw′ing·ly, adv.

gneiss (nīs), n. Geol. rock like granite, but with flatter crystals in more nearly parallel layers. [< G] —gneiss′ic, adj.

gnome (nōm), n. dwarf supposed to live in the earth and guard precious treasures. [< F < NL gnomus] —gnom′ish, adj.

gno·mic (nō′mik; nom′ik), adj. aphoristic; sententious. —gno′mi·cal·ly, adv.

gno·mon (nō′mon), n. rod, pointer, or triangular piece on a sundial, etc., that shows the time of day by the length of its shadow. [< Gk., indicator, < gignoskein know]

Gnos·tic (nos′tik), n. believer in Gnosticism. —adj. Also, Gnos′ti·cal. of Gnosticism or Gnostics. [< Gk. gnostikos of knowledge < gignoskein know]

Gnos·ti·cism (nos′tə·siz·əm), n. the mystical religious and philosophical doctrine of pre-Christian and early Christian times.

gnu (nü; nü), n., pl. gnus or (esp. collectively) gnu. an African antelope with an oxlike head and a long tail; wildebeest. [< Kaffir nqu]

go (gō), v., went, gone, go·ing, n., pl. goes. —v. 1. move along: go straight home. 2. move away; leave (opposed to come or arrive). 3. be in motion; act; work; run: the clock goes. 4. get to be; become: go mad. 5. be habitually: be go hungry. 6. proceed; advance: go to New York. 7. be current, as coin or notes. 8. be known: go under an alias. 9. put oneself: don't go to any trouble for me. 10. extend; reach: his memory does not go back that far. 11. pass: time goes. 12. be given: first prize goes to you. 13. be sold. 14. tend; lead: this goes to show. 15. turn out; have a certain result: how did the game go? 16. have its place; belong: this book goes on the top shelf. 17. harmonize: these colors go well together. 18. have certain words; be said. 19. explode. 20. refer; appeal: go to court. 21. Am., Colloq. or Dial. yield or produce (a certain amount). 22. Am., Colloq. or Dial. put up with: I can't go tea. 23. Am., Colloq. carry authority; be done without any question: what he says goes. 24. stop being; be given up, used up, or lost: his eyesight is going. 25. die: his wife went first. 26. break down; give way. 27. as people or things go, considering how others are. 28. go about, a. be busy at; work on. b. move from place to place. c. turn around; change direction. 29. go around, a. move from place to place. b. be enough to give some to all. 30. go at, attack. 31. go back of, Am., Colloq. investigate. 32. go back on, Am., Colloq. fail (one); break (one's word). 33. go behind, investigate the real or hidden reasons for. 34. go by, a. pass. b. be guided by; follow. c. be controlled by. d. be known by. 35. go down, a. descend; decline; sink. b. be defeated; lose. c. Am. decline in health. 36. go for, Colloq. a. try to get. b. favor; support. c. be taken or considered as. d. attack. 37. go in for, Am., Colloq. try to do; take part in; spend time and energy at. 38. go into, a. be contained in. b. investigate. 39. go off, a. leave; depart. b. be fired; explode. c. take place; happen. 40. go on, a. go ahead; go forward. b. manage. c. behave. 41. go out, a. stop being; end. b. go to parties, etc. c. give sympathy. d. go on strike. 42. go over, Colloq. a. look at carefully. b. do again. c. read again. d. succeed. 43. go through, a. go to the end of; do all of. b. undergo; experience. c. search. d. Am. be accepted or approved. 44. go together, Am. keep steady company as lovers. 45. go under, a. be overwhelmed or sunk. b. Am. be ruined; fail. c. Am. die. 46. go up, a. ascend. b. increase. 47. go with, a. accompany. b. be in harmony with. 48. let go, a. allow to escape. b. give up one's hold. c. give up. d. fail to keep in good condition. 49. let oneself go, a. give way to one's feelings or desires. b. fail to keep oneself in good condition. —n. 1. act of going. 2. Colloq. spirit; energy. 3. Colloq. state of affairs; way that things are. 4. Colloq. fashion; style. 5. Colloq. try; attempt; chance. 6. something successful. 7. on the go, Colloq. always moving or acting. [OE gān] —go′er, n.

Go·a (gō′ə), n. a small Portuguese possession in India, S of Bombay.

goad (gōd), n. 1. Also, gad. a sharp-pointed stick for driving cattle, etc. 2. anything that drives or urges one on. —v. drive on; urge on; act as a goad to. [OE gād] —goad′like′, adj.

go-a·head (gō′ə·hed′), Am., Colloq. —n. action of going forward; ambition; spirit; authority to proceed. —adj. disposed to push ahead.

goal (gōl), n. 1. place where a race ends. 2. place to which players try to advance a ball, etc., in certain games. 3. act of advancing a ball, etc., to this place. 4. score or points won by advancing a ball, etc., to this place. 5. goalkeeper. 6. thing wanted. [ME gol] —goal′less, adj.

goal·keep·er (gōl′kēp′ər), **goal·ie** (gōl′i), n. player who tries to prevent the ball, etc., from reaching the goal in certain games.

goat (gōt), n., pl. goats or (esp. collectively) goat. 1. a cud-chewing mammal with hollow horns and long, usually straight hair, closely related to the sheep, but stronger, less timid, and more active. 2. Am. the Rocky Mountain goat. 3. Goat, Astron. Capricorn. 4. U.S. Slang.

person made to suffer for the mistakes of others; scapegoat. **5.** get one's goat, *Am., Slang.* make a person angry or annoyed; tease him. [OE *gāt*] —**goat'like'**, *adj.*

goat·ee (gō·tē'), *n. Am.* a pointed beard on a man's chin.

goat·herd (gōt'hėrd'), *n.* person who tends goats.

goat·skin (gōt'skin'), *n.* **1.** skin of a goat. **2.** leather made from it.

goat·suck·er (gōt'suk'ər), *n.* bird with a flat head, wide mouth, and long wings that flies at night and feeds on flying insects.

Goatee

gob¹ (gob), *n. Am., Slang.* sailor in the navy.

gob² (gob), *n. Colloq.* lump; mass. [appar. < OF *gobe*]

gob·bet (gob'it), *n.* lump; mass. [< OF *gobet,* dim. of *gobe* gob²]

gob·ble¹ (gob'əl), *v.,* –**bled,** –**bling. 1.** eat fast and greedily; swallow quickly in big pieces. **2.** gobble up, *Am., Colloq.* seize upon eagerly. [< *gob²*] —**gob'bler,** *n.* —Syn. **1.** gulp, bolt, devour.

gob·ble² (gob'əl), *v.,* –**bled,** –**bling,** *n.* —*v.* make the throaty sound that a turkey does. —*n.* this sound. [imit.]

gob·ble·dy·gook, gob·ble·de·gook (gob'əl·di·gúk'), *n. Am., Colloq.* speech or exposition that is obscured by excessive use of technical terminology, involved sentences, and big words.

gob·bler (gob'lər), *n.* a male turkey.

go·be·tween (gō'bi·twēn'), *n.* person who goes back and forth between others with messages, proposals, etc.; intermediary.

Go·bi (gō'bi), *n.* desert in E Asia.

gob·let (gob'lit), *n.* a drinking glass with a base and stem. [< OF *gobelet,* dim. of *gobel* cup]

gob·lin (gob'lən), *n.* a mischievous sprite or elf in the form of an ugly-looking dwarf. [< F *gobelin* < MHG *kobold* demon]

go·by (gō'bī'), *n. Colloq.* a going by; casting off; intentional neglect.

go·cart (gō'kärt'), *n.* **1.** a low seat on wheels to take a small child around on. **2.** a light carriage.

God (god), *n.* **1.** the maker and ruler of the world; Supreme Being. **2.** god, *a.* a being thought of as superior to nature and to human beings and considered worthy of worship. *b.* a male god. *c.* image of a god; idol. *d.* person or thing worshiped like a god; person intensely admired and respected. [OE]

god·child (god'chīld'), *n., pl.* –**chil·dren.** child for whom a grown-up person takes vows at its baptism.

god·daugh·ter (god'dô'tər), *n.* a female godchild.

god·dess (god'is), *n.* **1.** a female god. **2.** a very beautiful or charming woman. —**god'dess·hood,** **god'dess·ship,** *n.*

god·fa·ther (god'fä'thər), *n.* man who takes vows for a child when it is baptized.

God·giv·en (god'giv'ən), *adj.* **1.** given by God. **2.** very welcome and suitable.

God·head (god'hed), *n.* **1.** God. **2.** divine nature; divinity.

god·hood (god'húd), *n.* divine character; divinity.

Go·di·va (gə·dī'və), *n.* in English legend, the wife of an English nobleman, who rode naked through the town of Coventry to win relief for the people from a burdensome tax.

god·less (god'lis), *adj.* **1.** not believing in God; not religious. **2.** wicked; evil. —**god'less·ly,** *adv.* —**god'less·ness,** *n.* —Syn. **1.** ungodly, impious.

god·like (god'līk'), *adj.* **1.** like God or a god; divine. **2.** suitable for God or a god. —**god'like'·ness,** *n.*

god·ly (god'li), *adj.,* –**li·er,** –**li·est.** obeying God's laws; religious; pious; devout. —**god'li·ly,** *adv.* —**god'li·ness,** *n.*

god·moth·er (god'muth'ər), *n.* woman who takes vows for a child when it is baptized.

god·par·ent (god'pâr'ənt), *n.* godfather or godmother.

God's acre, a burial ground; cemetery.

god·send (god'send'), *n.* something unexpected and very welcome, as if sent from God.

god·ship (god'ship), *n.* character of a god; divinity.

god·son (god'sun'), *n.* a male godchild.

God·speed (god'spēd'), *n.* wish of success to a person starting on a journey.

Goeb·bels (gœb'əls), *n.* Paul Joseph, 1897–1945, propaganda leader of Nazi Germany.

Goe·ring (gœ'ring), *n.* Hermann, 1893–1946, German field marshal and a Nazi leader.

Goe·the (gœ'tə), *n.* Johann Wolfgang von, 1749–1832, German poet, prose writer, and dramatist.

go·get·ter (gō'get'ər), *n. Am., Slang.* an energetic person who gets what he seeks.

gog·gle (gog'əl), *n., v.,* –**gled,** –**gling,** *adj.* —*n.* Usually, **goggles.** large, close-fitting spectacles to protect the eyes from light, dust, etc. —*v.* **1.** roll one's eyes; stare with bulging eyes. **2.** roll; bulge. —*adj.* rolling; bulging: *a frog has goggle eyes.* [ME *gogel(en)*] —**gog'gle-eyed',** *adj.*

Gogh (gō; gôk), *n.* Vincent van, 1853–1890, Dutch painter.

go·ing (gō'ing), *n.* **1.** a going away. **2.** condition of the ground or road for walking, riding, etc. —*adj.* **1.** moving; acting; working; running. **2.** that goes; that can or will go.

going concern, *U.S.* company, store, etc., that is doing business.

goi·ter, goi·tre (goi'tər), *n.* **1.** disease of the thyroid gland, that often causes a large swelling in the neck. **2.** the swelling. [< F *goitre,* ult. < L *guttur* throat]

gold (gōld), *n.* **1.** a shiny, bright-yellow, precious metal, used for making coins and jewelry. Gold is a chemical element. *Symbol:* Au. **2.** coins made of gold. **3.** money in large sums; wealth; riches. **4.** a bright, beautiful, or precious thing or material: *a heart of gold.* —*adj.* **1.** made of gold. **2.** of or like gold. **3.** bright-yellow. [OE]

gold brick, *Am., Colloq.* anything that looks good at first, but turns out to be worthless.

gold-brick (gōld'brik'), *Am., Colloq.* —*v.* **1.** pretend illness to avoid duties. **2.** swindle. —*n.* Also, **gold'-brick'er.** person, esp. in the army or navy, who avoids duty or shirks work.

Gold Coast, region in W Africa, former British colony, now largely included in Ghana.

gold digger, *Am., Slang.* woman who tries by various schemes to get money from men.

gold dust, gold in a fine powder.

gold·en (gōl'dən), *adj.* **1.** made or consisting of gold. **2.** containing or yielding gold. **3.** shining like gold; bright-yellow. **4.** very good; most excellent; extremely favorable, valuable, or important. **5.** very happy and prosperous; flourishing. **6.** pertaining to the fiftieth year or event in a series: *a golden wedding anniversary.* —**gold'en·ly,** *adv.* —**gold'en·ness,** *n.*

Golden Fleece, *Gk. Legend.* a fleece of gold taken from a ram. It was guarded by a dragon until Jason and the Argonauts carried it away.

Golden Gate, entrance to San Francisco Bay.

golden mean, avoidance of extremes; safe, sensible way of doing things; moderation.

gold·en·rod (gōl'dən·rod'), *n.* plant that blooms in the autumn and has many small yellow flowers on tall, branching stalks.

golden rule, rule of conduct set forth by Jesus: "All things whatsoever ye would that men should do to you, do ye even so to them." Matt. 7:12.

gold-filled (gōld'fild'), *adj.* made of cheap metal covered with a layer of gold.

gold·finch (gōld'finch'), *n.* **1.** a small American songbird. The male is yellow marked with black. **2.** a European songbird with yellow on its wings.

gold·fish (gōld'fish'), *n., pl.* –**fish·es** or *(esp. collectively)* –**fish.** a small, reddish-golden fish. Goldfish are often kept in garden pools or glass bowls.

American goldfinch (5 in. long)

gold leaf, gold beaten into very thin sheets.

gold rush, *Am.* a sudden rush of people to a place where gold has just been found.

gold·smith (gōld'smith'), *n.* man whose work is making articles of gold.

Gold·smith (gōld'smith'), *n.* Oliver, 1728–1774, British poet, novelist, and dramatist.

gold standard, *Am.* use of gold as the standard of value for the money of a country. A nation's unit of money value is declared by the government to be equal and exchangeable for a certain amount of gold.

golf (golf; gôlf), *n.* an outdoor game played with a small, hard ball and a set of long-handled clubs having wooden or iron heads. The player tries to hit the ball into a series of holes with as few strokes as possible. —*v.* play this game. —**golf'er,** *n.*

Gol·go·tha (gol'gə·thə), *n.* 1. place of Christ's crucifixion; Calvary. 2. place of burial.

Go·li·ath (gə·lī'əth), *n.* in the Bible, a giant whom David killed with a stone from a sling.

go·losh (gə·losh'), *n.* galosh.

Go·mor·rah, Go·mor·rha (gə·môr'ə; -mor'–), *n.* in the Bible, a wicked city destroyed, together with Sodom, by fire from heaven. Gen. 18 and 19.

Gom·pers (gom'pərz), *n.* Samuel, 1850–1924, American labor leader.

gon·ad (gon'ad; gō'nad), *n. Anat.* organ in which reproductive cells develop. Ovaries and testes are gonads. [< NL < Gk. *gone* seed] —**gon'ad·al, go·na·di·al** (gō·nā'di·əl), **go·nad·ic** (gō·nad'ik), *adj.*

gon·do·la (gon'də·lə), *n.* 1. a long, narrow boat with a high peak at each end, used on the canals of Venice. 2. *Am.* a large, flat-bottomed river boat with pointed ends. 3. car that hangs under a dirigible and holds the motors, passengers, etc. [< dial. Ital., < *gondola* rock]

gondola car, *Am.* a freight car that has low sides and no top.

gon·do·lier (gon'də·lir'), *n.* man who rows or poles a gondola.

gone (gôn; gon), *adj.* 1. moved away; left. 2. lost: *a gone case.* 3. dead. 4. *Am.* used up. 5. failed; ruined. 6. weak; faint: *a gone feeling.* 7. far gone, much advanced; deeply involved. 8. gone on, *Colloq.* in love with. —*v.* pp. of go.

gon·er (gôn'ər; gon'–), *n. Colloq.* person or thing that is dead, ruined, past help, etc.

gon·fa·lon (gon'fə·lən), *n.* flag or banner hung from a crossbar instead of a pole, often having several streamers. [< Ital., ult. < OHG *gundfano,* lit., war banner]

gong (gông; gong), *n.* 1. a metal disk with a turned-up rim, that makes a loud noise when struck. 2. bell shaped like a shallow bowl or saucer. [< Malay] —**gong'like,** *adj.*

gon·or·rhe·a, gon·or·rhoe·a (gon'ə·rē'ə), *n. Pathol.* a contagious venereal disease that causes inflammation of the genital and urinary organs. [< LL < Gk., < *gonos* seed + *rhoia* flow] —**gon'or·rhe'al, gon'or·rhoe'al,** *adj.*

goo·ber (gü'bər), *n. Am., S., Colloq.* peanut. [< Bantu]

good (gud), *adj.,* bet·ter, best, *n., interj.* —*adj.* 1. having the right qualities; admirable; desirable: *a good book, a good game.* 2. as it ought to be; right; proper: *do what seems good to you.* 3. well-behaved: *a good boy.* 4. kind; friendly: *say a good word for me.* 5. doing right. 6. honorable; worthy: *my good friend.* 7. reliable; dependable: *good judgment.* 8. real; genuine. 9. agreeable; pleasant: *have a good time.* 10. beneficial; advantageous; useful: *drugs good for a fever.* 11. satisfying; full: *a good day.* 12. sufficient; thorough: *a good whipping.* 13. skillful; clever: *a good manager, be good at arithmetic.* 14. fairly great; more than a little: *a good while.* 15. as good as, almost the same as; almost; practically. 16. feel good, *Am., Colloq.* feel well or elated. 17. good for, a. able to do, live, or last. b. able to pay. c. worth. —*n.* 1. benefit; advantage; use: *work for the common good.* 2. that which is good: *find the good in people.* 3. a good

thing. 4. good people. 5. for good or for good and all, forever; finally; permanently. 6. make good, a. make up for; give or do in place of; pay for. b. carry out; fulfill. c. succeed in doing. d. *Am.* succeed. e. prove. —*interj.* that is good! [OE gōd] ▶ **good, well.** *Good* is an adjective, *well* is either an adjective or an adverb: *I feel good* and *I feel well* (adjectives) are both usual but have different connotations (*good* implying actual bodily sensation, *well* referring merely to a state, "not ill"). In uneducated usage *well* is rarely used, *good* taking its place (*he rowed good* for *he rowed well*).

Good Book, Bible.

good-by, good-bye (gud'bī'), *interj., n., pl.* -bys; -byes. farewell. [contraction of *God be with ye*] ▶ **good-by, good-bye.** Both are in use—and the hyphen is dropping out in informal use: *goodby, goodbye.*

good English, language that is effective for a particular communication, that is appropriate to the subject and situation, to the listener or reader, and to the speaker or writer.

good-for-noth·ing (gud'fər·nuth'ing), *adj.* worthless; useless. —*n.* person who is worthless or useless.

Good Friday, Friday before Easter, observed in commemoration of Christ's crucifixion.

good-heart·ed (gud'här'tid), *adj.* kind and generous. —**good'-heart'ed·ly,** *adv.* —**good'-heart'ed·ness,** *n.*

Good Hope, Cape of, cape near the SW tip of Africa.

good humor, a cheerful, pleasant disposition or mood.

good-hu·mored (gud'hū'mərd; -ū'–), *adj.* cheerful; pleasant. —**good'-hu'mored·ly,** *adv.* —**good'-hu'mored·ness,** *n.*

good·ish (gud'ish), *adj.* 1. pretty good. 2. *Esp. Brit.* fairly great; considerable.

good-look·ing (gud'lük'ing), *adj.* having a pleasing appearance; handsome.

good·ly (gud'li), *adj.,* -li·er, -li·est. 1. pleasant; excellent: *a goodly land.* 2. good-looking: *a goodly youth.* 3. considerable: *a goodly quantity.* —**good'li·ness,** *n.*

good·man (gud'mən), *n., pl.* -men. *Archaic.* 1. master of a household; husband. 2. title for a man ranking below a gentleman: *Goodman Brown.*

good nature, a pleasant or kindly disposition; cheerfulness; agreeableness.

good-na·tured (gud'nā'chərd), *adj.* pleasant; kindly; cheerful; agreeable. —**good'-na'tured·ly,** *adv.* —**good'-na'tured·ness,** *n.*

Good Neighbor Policy, a diplomatic policy, first sponsored by the United States in 1933, to encourage friendly relations and mutual defense among the nations of the Western Hemisphere.

good·ness (gud'nis), *n.* 1. quality or state of being good. 2. excellence; virtue. 3. kindness; friendliness. 4. valuable quality; best part. —*interj.* exclamation of surprise.

good night, form of farewell said at night.

goods (gudz), *n.pl.* 1. personal property; belongings. 2. thing or things for sale; wares. 3. *Am.* material for clothing; cloth. 4. *Am., Slang.* what is needed to do something. 5. *Brit.* freight.

Good Samaritan, person who is unselfish in helping others.

Good Shepherd, Jesus. John 10:11.

good-tem·pered (gud'tem'pərd), *adj.* easy to get along with. —**good'-tem'pered·ly,** *adv.*

good·wife (gud'wīf'), *n., pl.* -wives. *Archaic.* 1. mistress of a household. 2. title for a woman ranking below a lady: *Goodwife Brown.*

good will, 1. kindly or friendly feeling. 2. cheerful consent; willingness. 3. reputation and steady trade that a business has with its customers.

good·y¹ (gud'i), *n., pl.* good·ies, *adj., interj. Colloq.* —*n.* something very good to eat; piece of candy or cake. —*adj.* making too much of being good; weakly good. —*interj.* exclamation of pleasure. [< *good*]

good·y² (gŭd'ĭ), *n., pl.* **good·ies. 1.** an old woman of humble station. **2.** Goody, term of address for such a woman. [var. of *goodwife*]

goon (gün), *n. Am., Slang.* **1.** thug hired to disrupt labor disputes. **2.** a stupid person. [from semihuman characters in a comic strip of the 1930's]

goose (güs), *n., pl.* **geese** *for 1-4,* **goos·es** *for 5.* **1.** a wild or tame web-footed swimming bird, like a duck but larger and having a longer neck. **2.** a female goose. **3.** flesh of a goose used for food. **4.** a silly person. **5.** a tailor's smoothing iron that has a long, curved handle like a goose's neck. **6. the goose hangs high,** *Am.* all is well; prospects are good. [OE *gōs*]

Goose Bay, air base in Labrador, built in World War II and subsequently important in transatlantic air service.

goose·ber·ry (güs'ber'ĭ; güz'-), *n., pl.* **-ries. 1.** a small, sour berry somewhat like a currant but larger, used to make pies, tarts, jam, etc. **2.** the thorny bush that it grows on.

goose flesh or **pimples,** a rough condition of the skin caused by cold or fear.

goose·neck (güs'nek'), *n.* anything long and curved like a goose's neck, such as an iron hook, or a movable support for a lamp.

goose step, a marching step in which the leg is swung high with a straight, stiff knee.

goose-step (güs'step'), *v.,* **-stepped, -stepping.** march with a goose step.

G.O.P., *Am.* the "Grand Old Party" (the Republican Party in the United States).

go·pher (gō'fər), *n. Am.* **1.** *S., W.* a burrowing, ratlike rodent with large cheek pouches. **2.** ground squirrel. [? < early United States F, *gaufre,* lit., honeycomb; with ref. to burrowing]

Gopher (total length ab. 9 in.)

Gor·di·an knot (gôr'dĭ·ən). **cut the Gordian knot,** find and use a quick, easy way out of a difficulty. [with ref. to the knot tied by *Gordius,* king of Phrygia, and cut by Alexander the Great]

gore¹ (gōr; gôr), *n.* blood that is shed; thick blood; clotted blood. [OE *gor* dirt, dung]

gore² (gōr; gôr), *v.,* **gored, gor·ing.** wound with a horn or tusk: *the savage bull gored the farmer to death.* [ME *gorre(n)*]

gore³ (gōr; gôr), *n., v.,* **gored, gor·ing.** —*n.* a long, triangular piece of cloth put or made in a skirt, sail, etc., to give greater width or change the shape. —*v.* put or make a gore in. [OE *gāra* point < *gār* spear] —**gored,** *adj.* —**gor'ing,** *n.*

gorge (gôrj), *n., v.,* **gorged, gorg·ing.** —*n.* **1.** a deep, narrow valley, usually steep and rocky. **2.** mass stopping up a narrow passage: *an ice gorge blocked the river.* **3.** *Archaic.* throat; gullet. —*v.* **1.** eat greedily until full; stuff with food. **2.** fill full; stuff. [< OF, ult. < LL *gurges* throat, jaws < L, abyss, whirlpool] —**gorg'er,** *n.*

gor·geous (gôr'jəs), *adj.* richly colored; splendid: *a gorgeous sunset.* [< OF *gorgias* fashionable] —**gor'geous·ly,** *adv.* —**gor'geous·ness,** *n.* —Syn. magnificent.

gor·get (gôr'jĭt), *n.* piece of armor for the throat. [< OF *gorgete,* dim. of *gorge* GORGE]

G. gorget.

Gor·gon (gôr'gən), *n.* **1.** *Gk. Legend.* any of three horrible sisters who had snakes for hair and whose look turned the beholder to stone. **2.** gorgon, a very ugly or terrible woman. [< L < Gk., < *gorgos* terrible]

Gor·gon·zo·la (gôr'gən·zō'lə), *n.* a strong, white Italian cheese that looks and tastes much like Roquefort cheese.

go·ril·la (gə·rĭl'ə), *n. Am.* **1.** a very large manlike ape of Africa. **2.** *Slang.* a strong and brutal man. [< NL < Gk. < an African lang.] —**go·ril'la·like',** *adj.*

Gor·ki (gôr'kĭ), *n.* **1.** Maxim (*A. M. Pyeshkov*), 1868-1936, Russian writer. **2.** city in C European Russia, on the Volga River.

gor·mand (gôr'mənd), *n.* gourmand.

gor·mand·ize (gôr'mən·dīz), *v.,* **-ized, -iz·ing.** stuff oneself with food; eat very greedily; gorge. [orig. n., < F *gourmandise* gluttony] —**gor'mand·iz'er,** *n.*

gorse (gôrs), *n. Esp. Brit.* furze. [OE *gorst*] —**gors'y,** *adj.*

gor·y (gôr'ĭ; gōr'ĭ), *adj.,* **gor·i·er, gor·i·est.** bloody. —**gor'i·ly,** *adv.* —**gor'i·ness,** *n.*

gosh (gosh), *interj.* exclamation or mild oath.

gos·hawk (gos'hôk'), *n.* a powerful, short-winged hawk, formerly much used in falconry. [OE *gōshafoc* < *gōs* goose + *hafoc* hawk]

Go·shen (gō'shən), *n.* **1.** *Bible.* a fertile part of Egypt where the Israelites were permitted to live. **2.** land of plenty and comfort.

gos·ling (goz'lĭng), *n.* a young goose.

gos·pel (gos'pəl), *n.* **1.** the teachings of Jesus and the Apostles. **2.** Usually, Gospel. any one of the first four books of the New Testament, by Matthew, Mark, Luke, and John. **3.** Often, Gospel. part of one of these books read during a religious service. **4.** *Colloq.* anything earnestly believed or taken as a guide for action. **5.** the absolute truth. —*adj.* **1.** evangelical. **2.** of or pertaining to the gospel. [OE *gōdspel* good tidings (i.e., of the Nativity) < *gōd* good + *spel* spell²]

gos·sa·mer (gos'ə·mər), *n.* **1.** film or thread of cobweb. **2.** a very thin, light cloth. **3.** *Am.* a thin, light, waterproof cloth or coat. **4.** anything very light and thin. —*adj.* Also, **gos·sa·mer·y** (gos'ə·mər·ĭ). very light and thin; filmy. [ME *gossomer* goose summer, name for "Indian summer," the season for goose and cobwebs]

gos·sip (gos'ĭp), *n., v.,* **-siped, -sip·ing.** —*n.* **1.** idle talk, not always true, about other people and their affairs. **2.** person who gossips a good deal. —*v.* repeat what one knows, or the idle talk that one hears, about other people and their affairs. [OE *godsibb,* orig., godparent < *god* God + *sibb* relative] —**gos'sip·er,** *n.* —**gos'sip·ing,** *n.* —**gos'sip·ing·ly,** *adv.* —**gos'sip·y,** *adj.* —Syn. *n.* **1.** tattle, scandal.

gos·soon (go·sün'), *n.* **1.** boy. **2.** a male servant. [alter. of *garçon*]

got (got), *v.* pt. and pp. of **get.** ▶ Got is often redundant—and so is generally confined to colloquial usage—in expressions like *have you got a pencil?* and *I've got to study now. Have you a pencil?* and *I have to study now* mean just as much and sound more formal—but in free and easy speech the *got* adds a little emphasis, being more vigorous than *have.* Ordinarily, in writing, these constructions are confined to dialogue. See also **gotten.**

Gö·te·borg (yœ'tə·bôr'ĭ), **Goth·en·burg** (got'ən·bérg), *n.* seaport in SW Sweden.

Goth (goth), *n.* **1.** member of a Teutonic tribe that overran the Roman Empire in the third, fourth, and fifth centuries A.D. The Goths settled in S and E Europe. **2.** an uncivilized person; barbarian.

Goth·am (goth'əm; gō'thəm), *n. Am.* New York City.

Goth·ic (goth'ĭk), *n.* **1.** style of architecture using pointed arches and high, steep roofs, developed in W Europe during the Middle Ages from about 1150 to 1550. **2.** language of the Goths. **3.** *Am.* kind of type used in printing. —*adj.* **1.** of Gothic architecture. **2.** of the Goths or their language. **3.** uncivilized; crude; barbarous. **4.** medieval. —**Goth'i·cal·ly,** *adv.*

Got·land (got'lənd), *n.* a Swedish island in the Baltic between Sweden and Latvia.

got·ten (got'ən), *v.* pp. of **get.** ▶ Gotten was brought to America by the colonists of the seventeenth century, when it was the usual English form, and has remained in general American usage ever since, while in England the form has given way to *got.* Today both forms are used by Americans as the past participle, the choice between them depending largely on the meaning: *I've gotten* = I've acquired, I've become. *I've got* = I have.

gouge (gouj), *n., v.,* **gouged, goug·ing.** —*n.* **1.** chisel with a curved blade. **2.** groove or hole made by gouging. **3.** *Am., Colloq.* trick; cheat;

swindle. —*v.* **1.** cut with a gouge. **2.** dig out; force out. **3.** *Am., Colloq.* trick; cheat. [< F < LL *gulbia*] —**goug'er,** *n.*

gou·lash (gü'läsh), *n.* stew made of beef or veal and vegetables, usually highly seasoned. [< Hung. *gulyás (hús)* herdsman's (meat)]

Gou·nod (gü'nō), *n.* Charles François, 1818–1893, French composer.

gourd (gōrd; gôrd; gürd), *n.* **1.** the hard-shelled fruit of certain vines. **2.** cup, bowl, bottle, rattle, etc., made from a dried shell of this fruit. **3.** vine that gourds grow on. **4.** any plant of the family to which cucumbers, pumpkins, and muskmelons belong. [< F < OF *cohorde* < L *cucurbita*] —**gourd'like',** *adj.* —**gourd-shaped** (gōrd'-shāpt'; gôrd'–; gürd'–), *adj.*

gour·mand (gür'mənd), *n.* person who is fond of good eating. Also, **gormand.** [< F, gluttonous < *gourmet* gourmet]

gour·met (gür'mā), *n.* person who is expert in judging and choosing fine foods, wines, etc.; epicure. [< F < OF *groumet* wine tester]

gout (gout), *n.* **1.** a painful disease of the joints, often characterized by a painful swelling of the big toe. **2.** drop; splash; clot. [< OF < L *gutta* a drop, in Med.L, gout]

goût (gü), *n. French.* taste.

gout·y (gout'i), *adj.,* **gout·i·er, gout·i·est. 1.** diseased or swollen with gout. **2.** of gout; caused by gout. **3.** causing gout. **4.** like gout. —**gout'i·ly,** *adv.* —**gout'i·ness,** *n.*

Gov., Governor.

gov., **1.** government. **2.** governor.

gov·ern (guv'ərn), *v.* **1.** rule; control; manage. **2.** exercise a directing or restraining influence over; determine: *motives governing a person's decision.* **3.** hold back; restrain; check. **4.** be a rule or law for: *principles governing a case.* **5.** *Gram.* require (a word) to be in a certain case or mood; require (a certain case or mood). [< OF < L < Gk. *kybernaein* steer] —**gov'ern·a·ble,** *adj.* —Syn. **1.** direct, conduct. **3.** curb, bridle.

gov·ern·ance (guv'ər·nəns), *n.* rule; control.

gov·ern·ess (guv'ər·nis), *n.* woman who teaches children in a private house.

gov·ern·ment (guv'ərn·mənt; –ər–), *n.* **1.** act or fact of governing; rule; control. **2.** rule or authority over a country, state, district, etc.; direction of the affairs of state. **3.** person or persons ruling a country, state, district, etc.; administration. **4.** system of ruling: *republican government.* **5.** country, state, district, etc., ruled. **6.** *Gram.* the influence of one word in determining the case or mood of another. —**gov·ern·men·tal** (guv'ərn·men'təl; –ər–), *adj. Am.* —**gov'ern·men'tal·ly,** *adv.*

gov·er·nor (guv'ər·nər; guv'nər), *n.* **1.** *Am.* official elected as the executive head of a State of the United States. **2.** official appointed to govern a province, city, fort, etc. **3.** *Esp. Brit.* person who manages or directs a club, society, institution, etc. **4.** an automatic device that controls the supply of steam, gas, etc., and keeps a machine going at a certain speed. **5.** *Esp. Brit. Slang.* one's father, guardian, or employer.

governor general, *pl.* **governors general.** governor who has subordinate or deputy governors under him. —**gov'er·nor·gen'er·al·ship',** *n.*

gov·er·nor·ship (guv'ər·nər·ship'; guv'nər–), *n. Am.* position or term of office of governor.

govt., Govt., government.

gown (goun), *n.* **1.** a woman's dress. **2.** a loose outer garment worn to show position, profession, etc., as that of a judge. **3.** nightgown or dressing gown. —*v.* put a gown on; dress in a gown. [< OF < LL *gunna*]

gowns·man (gounz'mən), *n., pl.* **-men.** person who wears a gown to show his position, profession, etc.; judge, lawyer, clergyman, or member of a university.

Go·ya (gō'yə), *n.* Francisco, 1746–1828, Spanish painter and etcher.

Gr., 1. Grecian. **2.** Greece. **3.** Also, **Gk.** Greek.

gr., 1. grain. **2.** gram. **3.** gross.

grab (grab), *v.,* **grabbed, grab·bing,** *n.* —*v.* **1.**

seize suddenly; snatch. **2.** seize unscrupulously. —*n.* **1.** a snatching; a sudden seizing. **2.** that which is grabbed. **3.** a mechanical device for firmly holding something that is to be lifted. [cf. MDu. *grabben*] —**grab'ber,** *n.*

grace (grās), *n., v.,* **graced, grac·ing.** —*n.* **1.** beauty of form, movement, or manner; pleasing or agreeable quality. **2.** good will; favor. **3.** mercy; pardon. **4.** God's free and undeserved favor to and love for mankind. **5.** the condition of being influenced and favored by God. **6.** a short prayer of thanks before or after a meal. **7.** favor shown by granting a delay. **8.** allowance of time. **9.** virtue; merit; excellence. **10.** Usually, **Grace.** title used in speaking to or of a duke, duchess, or archbishop. **11.** *Music.* grace note. **12. Grace,** *Class. Myth.* one of the three sister goddesses controlling beauty and charm in people and in nature. —*v.* **1.** give or add grace to; set off with grace. **2.** do a favor or honor to. **3.** *Music.* add grace notes to. [< F < L *gratia* < *gratus* pleasing] —Syn. *n.* **1.** charm, ease, elegance. **2.** kindness. *-v.* **1.** adorn, decorate. **2.** honor.

grace·ful (grās'fəl), *adj.* having or showing grace; beautiful in form, movement, or manner. —**grace'ful·ly,** *adv.* —**grace'ful·ness,** *n.*

grace·less (grās'lis), *adj.* **1.** without grace. **2.** not caring for what is right or proper. —**grace'less·ly,** *adv.* —**grace'less·ness,** *n.*

grace note, *Music.* note not essential to the harmony or melody, added for embellishment.

gra·cious (grā'shəs), *adj.* **1.** pleasant; kindly; courteous. **2.** pleasant, kindly, and courteous to people of lower social position. **3.** merciful; kindly. —*interj.* exclamation of surprise. [< OF < L *gratiosus*] —**gra'cious·ly,** *adv.* —**gra'cious·ness,** **gra·ci·os·i·ty** (grā'shi·os'ə·ti), *n.*

grack·le (grak'əl), *n. Am.* kind of blackbird. [< L *graculus* jackdaw]

grad., graduate; graduated.

Grackle (1 ft. long)

gra·da·tion (grā·dā'shən), *n.* **1.** a change by steps or stages; gradual change. **2.** Usually, **gradations.** step, stage, or degree in a series. **3.** act or process of grading. [< L *gradatio.* See GRADE.] —**gra·da'tion·al,** *adj.* —**gra·da'tion·al·ly,** *adv.*

grade (grād), *n., v.,* **grad·ed, grad·ing.** —*n.* **1.** *Am.* any one division of a school arranged according to the pupils' progress. **2.** step or stage in a course or process. **3.** degree in a scale of rank, quality, value, etc. **4.** group of people or things having the same rank, quality, value, etc. **5.** **the grades,** *Am., Colloq.* grade school. **6.** *Am.* number or letter that shows how well one has done. **7.** *Am.* slope of a road, railroad track, etc. **8.** *Am.* amount of slope. **9.** **make the grade,** a. ascend a steep slope. b. *Am.* overcome difficulties. —*v.* **1.** *Am.* place in classes; arrange in grades; sort. **2.** be of a particular grade or quality. **3.** *Am.* give a grade to. **4.** *Am.* make more nearly level. **5.** change gradually; go through a series of stages or degrees. [< F < L *gradus* step, degree]

grade crossing, *Am.* place where a railroad crosses a street or another railroad on the same level.

grad·er (grād'ər), *n.* **1.** person or thing that grades. **2.** *Am.* person who is in a certain grade at school.

grade school, graded school, *Am.* elementary school; grammar school.

gra·di·ent (grā'di·ənt), *n.* **1.** rate at which a road, railroad track, etc., rises. **2.** the sloping part of a road, etc. **3.** rate at which temperature or pressure changes. **4.** rate of change of any variable. —*adj.* **1.** going up or down gradually. **2.** moving by taking steps; walking. **3.** adapted to walking. [< L *gradiens* walking. See GRADE.]

grad·u·al (graj'ü·əl), *adj.* by degrees too small to be separately noticed; little by little. —**grad'u·al·ly,** *adv.* —**grad'u·al·ness,** *n.*

grad·u·ate (v. graj'ú·āt; n., adj. graj'ú·it), v. –at·ed, –at·ing, n., adj. —v. 1. finish a course of study at a school, college, or university and receive a diploma or other document saying so. 2. give a diploma to for finishing a course of study. 3. mark with degrees for measuring. A thermometer is graduated. 4. arrange (anything) in regular steps, stages, or degrees. 5. change gradually. —n. 1. person who has graduated. 2. container marked with degrees for measuring. —adj. 1. that is a graduate: a graduate student. 2. of or for graduates. [< Med.L graduatus. See GRADE.] —grad'u·a'tor, n. ⟩ graduate. The idiom to be graduated from an institution has generally gone out of use except in formal and somewhat archaic writing, replaced by graduated from: He graduated from Yale in 1902.

grad·u·a·tion (graj'ú·ā'shən), n. 1. a graduating from a school, college, or university. 2. graduating exercises. 3. a marking with degrees for measuring. 4. mark or set of marks to show degrees for measuring. 5. arrangement in regular steps, stages, or degrees.

graft¹ (graft; gräft), v. 1. insert (a shoot, bud, etc.) from one tree or plant into a slit in another so that it will grow there permanently. 2. produce or improve (fruit, flower, etc.) by grafting. 3. do grafting on. 4. transfer (a piece of skin, bone, etc.) from one part of the body to another so that it will grow there permanently. —n. 1. shoot, bud, etc., used in grafting. 2. place on a tree or plant where the shoot, bud, etc., is grafted. 3. tree or plant that has had a shoot, bud, etc., grafted on it. 4. act of grafting. 5. piece of skin, bone, etc., transferred in grafting. [earlier graff < OF < L < Gk. grapheion stylus < graphein write; from similarity of shape] —graft'er, n. —graft'ing, n.

graft² (graft; gräft), Am. —n. 1. the taking of money dishonestly in connection with public business. 2. method of getting money dishonestly. 3. money dishonestly taken or obtained. —v. Colloq. make money dishonestly through one's job, esp. in political positions. —graft'er, n. Am.

gra·ham (grā'əm), adj. Am. made from unsifted whole wheat or whole-wheat flour. [for S. Graham, reformer of dietetics]

Grail (grāl), n. the Holy Grail. [< OF < Med.L gradale plate, or < VL cratale < crater bowl < Gk.]

grain (grān), n. 1. a single seed or seedlike fruit of wheat, oats, and similar cereal grasses. 2. seeds or seedlike fruits of such plants in the mass. 3. plants that these seeds or seedlike fruits grow on. 4. a tiny, hard particle of sand, salt, sugar, etc. 5. the smallest unit of weight. One pound avoirdupois equals 7000 grains; one pound troy equals 5760 grains. 6. the smallest possible amount; tiniest bit: grain of truth. 7. arrangement or direction of fibers in wood, layers in stone, etc. 8. little lines and other markings in wood, marble, etc. 9. the rough surface of leather. 10. texture. 11. natural character; disposition. —v. 1. form into grains. 2. paint in imitation of the grain in wood, marble, etc. 3. roughen the surface of (leather). 4. give a granular surface to. [< OF < L granum grain, seed] —grained (grānd), adj. —grain'er, n. —grain'less, adj. —grain'y, adj.

grain alcohol, ethyl alcohol, often made from grain.

grain elevator, Am. a building for storing grain.

gram, esp. Brit. **gramme** (gram), n. unit of weight in the metric system. Twenty-eight grams weigh about one ounce avoirdupois. [< F < LL < Gk. gramma small weight < graphein write]

–gram, word element. 1. something written; message, as in cablegram, telegram, monogram. [< Gk. –gramma something written, ult. < graphein write] 2. grams; of a gram, as in kilogram, milligram. [< Gk., < gramma small weight, ult. < graphein write]

gram., grammar; grammatical.

gram·mar (gram'ər), n. 1. scientific study and classification of the classes, forms, sounds, and uses of words of a particular language. 2. systematic study comparing the forms and con-

structions of two or more languages. 3. systematic study comparing present with past forms and usage. 4. a treatise or book on one of these subjects. 5. manner of speech or writing with reference to conformity to established usage. 6. statements about the use of words. 7. the elements of any subject: grammar of painting. [< OF < L < Gk. grammatike (techne) (art) of letters, ult. < graphein write]

gram·mar·i·an (grə·mãr'i·ən), n. expert in grammar.

grammar school, 1. Am. a public school in the United States having the grades between primary school and high school. 2. Brit. a secondary school.

gram·mat·i·cal (grə·mat'ə·kəl), adj. 1. according to correct use of words. 2. of grammar. —gram·mat'i·cal·ly, adv. —gram·mat'i·cal·ness, n.

gram·mo·lec·u·lar (gram'mə·lek'yə·lər), adj. of or having to do with a gram molecule.

gram molecule, gram-molecular weight, Chem. amount of an element or compound that equals its molecular weight expressed in grams.

gram·o·phone (gram'ə·fōn), n. Am. 1. phonograph. 2. Gramophone, Trademark. type of sound-recording machine. [inversion of phonograph]
gram < Gk. phone
speech + gramma a
writing < graphein
write]

gram·pus (gram'pəs), n. 1. a large, fierce dolphin; killer whale. 2. a small, toothed whale. [earlier grapays < OF < Med.L crassus piscis fat fish]

Grampus (15 to 20 ft. long)

Gra·na·da (grə·nä'də), n. city in S Spain.

gran·a·ry (gran'ə·ri; grān'–), n., pl. –ries. 1. place where grain is stored. 2. region having much grain. [< L, < granum grain]

grand (grand), adj. 1. large and of fine appearance: grand mountains. 2. fine; noble; dignified; stately; splendid: grand music, a grand old man. 3. highest or very high in rank; chief: grand jury. 4. great; important; main: the grand staircase. 5. complete; comprehensive: grand total. 6. Colloq. very satisfactory. 7. in names of relationship, in the second degree of ascent or descent: grandmother, grandson. —n. Am., Slang. a thousand dollars. [< OF < L grandis big] —grand'ly, adv. —grand'ness, n. —Syn. adj. 1. great, lofty. 2. majestic, imposing.

gran·dam (gran'dam), **gran·dame** (–dām), n. 1. grandmother. 2. old woman. [< AF graund dame. See GRAND, DAME.]

grand·aunt (grand'ant'; –änt'), n. great-aunt.

Grand Bank, shoal off SE Newfoundland. It is important for cod fishing.

Grand Canyon, Am. a deep gorge of the Colorado River, in N Arizona.

grand·child (grand'chīld'), n., pl. –chil·dren. child of one's son or daughter.

Grand Cou·lee Dam (kü'lē), a large dam on the Columbia River, in E Washington.

grand·daugh·ter (grand'dô'tər), n. daughter of one's son or daughter.

grand duchess, 1. wife or widow of a grand duke. 2. lady equal in rank to a grand duke. 3. princess of the ruling house of Russia before it became a republic in 1917.

grand duchy, territory under the rule of a grand duke or grand duchess.

grand duke, 1. prince who ranks just below a king. 2. prince of the ruling house of Russia before it became a republic in 1917.

gran·dee (gran·dē'), n. 1. a Spanish or Portuguese nobleman of the highest rank. 2. person of high rank or great importance. [< Sp., Pg. grande. See GRAND.]

gran·deur (gran'jər; –jŭr), n. greatness; majesty; nobility; dignity; splendor.

grand·fa·ther (grand'fä'тнər), n. 1. father of one's father or mother. 2. forefather. —grand'fa·ther·ly, adj.

gran·dil·o·quent (gran·dil′ə·kwənt), *adj.* using lofty or pompous words. [< L, < *grandis* grand + *loquens* speaking] —**gran·dil′o·quence,** *n.* —**gran·dil′o·quent·ly,** *adv.*

gran·di·ose (gran′di·ōs), *adj.* 1. grand in an imposing or impressive way. 2. grand in an affected or pompous way; trying to seem magnificent. [< F < Ital. *grandioso*] —**gran′di·ose·ly,** *adv.* —**gran·di·os·i·ty** (gran′di·os′ə·ti), *n.*

grand jury, jury chosen to investigate accusations and bring an indictment against the accused if there is enough evidence for trial before an ordinary jury.

Grand Lama, Dalai Lama.

grand·ma (grand′mä′; gram′mä′; gram′ə), *n. Colloq.* grandmother.

grand·moth·er (grand′muth′ər), *n.* 1. mother of one's father or mother. 2. ancestress. —**grand′moth′er·ly,** *adj.*

grand·neph·ew (grand′nef′ū; -nev′ū), *n.* son of one's nephew or niece.

grand·niece (grand′nēs′), *n.* daughter of one's nephew or niece.

Grand Old Party, *Am.* the Republican Party.

grand opera, a musical drama in which all the speeches are sung to the accompaniment of an orchestra.

grand·pa (grand′pä′; gram′pä′; gram′pə), *n. Colloq.* grandfather.

grand·par·ent (grand′pãr′ənt), *n.* grandfather or grandmother.

Grand Rapids, city in SW Michigan.

grand·sire (grand′sīr′), *n. Archaic.* 1. grandfather. 2. forefather. 3. an old man.

grand·son (grand′sun′), *n.* son of one's son or daughter.

grand·stand (grand′stand′), *n.* the principal seating place for people at an athletic field, race track, etc.

grand·un·cle (grand′ung′kəl), *n.* great-uncle.

grange (grānj), *n.* 1. farm. 2. *Esp. Brit.* farmhouse with barns, etc. 3. Grange, *Am.* a. organization of farmers for the improvement of their welfare. b. a local branch of this organization. [< OF < VL *granica* < L *granum* grain]

grang·er (grān′jər), *n.* 1. farmer. 2. Granger, *Am.* member of the Grange.

gran·ite (gran′it), *n.* a hard igneous rock made of grains of other rocks, chiefly quartz and feldspar. [< Ital. *granito* grained, ult. < L *granum* grain] —**gran′ite·like′,** *adj.* —**gra·nit·ic** (grə·nit′ik), *adj.*

gran·ny, gran·nie (gran′i), *n., pl.* -**nies.** *Colloq.* 1. grandmother. 2. an old woman. 3. a fussy person.

granny knot, knot differing from a square knot in having the ends crossed the wrong way.

grant (grant; gränt), *v.* 1. give what is asked; allow. 2. admit to be true; accept without proof; concede. 3. bestow or confer (a right, etc.) by formal act; transfer or convey (the ownership of property), esp. by deed or writing. —*n.* 1. thing granted, such as a privilege, right, sum of money, or tract of land. 2. act of granting. 3. **take for granted,** assume to be true; use as proved or agreed to. [< OF *granter,* var. of *creanter,* promise, authorize, ult. < L *credens* trusting] —**grant′a·ble,** *adj.* —**grant·ee′,** *n.* —**grant′er,** *Law* **grant·or** (gran′tər; gran·tôr′; grän-), *n.* —**Syn.** *v.* 1. gift, present, allowance.

Grant (grant), *n.* Ulysses Simpson, 1822–1885, American general, 18th president of the United States, 1869–1877.

gran·u·lar (gran′yə·lər), *adj.* 1. consisting of or containing grains or granules. 2. resembling grains or granules. —**gran·u·lar·i·ty** (gran′yə·lar′ə·ti), *n.* —**gran′u·lar·ly,** *adv.*

granular eyelids, eyelids roughened inside by disease.

gran·u·late (gran′yə·lāt), *v.,* -**lat·ed,** -**lat·ing.** 1. form into grains or granules. 2. roughen on the surface. 3. become granular; develop granulations. —**gran′u·lat′ed,** *adj.* —**gran′u·lat′or, gran′u·la′tor,** *n.* —**gran′u·la′tion,** *n.* —**gran′u·la′tive,** *adj.*

gran·ule (gran′ūl), *n.* 1. a small grain. 2. a small bit or spot like a grain. [< LL *granulum,* dim. of *granum* grain]

grape (grāp), *n.* 1. a small, round fruit that grows in bunches on a vine. 2. grapevine. 3. a dark, purplish red. 4. grapeshot. [< OF, bunch of grapes, < *graper* pick grapes < *grape* hook < Gmc.] —**grape′less,** *adj.* —**grape′like′,** *adj.*

grape·fruit (grāp′früt′), *n.* a pale-yellow citrus fruit like an orange, but larger and sourer.

grape·shot (grāp′shot′), *n.* cluster of small iron balls used as a charge for cannon.

grape sugar, sugar formed in all green plants, but esp. in grapes; dextrose.

grape·vine (grāp′vīn′), *n.* 1. vine that bears grapes. 2. *Am., Colloq.* a. way by which reports are mysteriously spread. b. a baseless report.

graph (graf; gräf), *n.* 1. line or diagram showing how one quantity depends on or changes with another. 2. any line or lines representing a series of relations. —*v.* draw (such a line or diagram); draw a line representing some change, equation, or function. [for *graphic formula.* See GRAPHIC.]

-graph, *word element.* 1. make a picture, draw, or write, as in *photograph.* 2. machine that makes a picture, draws, or writes, as in *seismograph.* 3. drawn or written, as in *autograph.* 4. something drawn or written, as in *lithograph.* [< Gk. *graphein* write]

graph·ic (graf′ik), **graph·i·cal** (-ə·kəl), *adj.* 1. lifelike; vivid. 2. of or about diagrams and their use. 3. shown by a graph. 4. of or about drawing, painting, engraving, or etching: *the graphic arts.* 5. of or used in handwriting: *graphic symbols.* 6. written; inscribed. [< L < Gk., < *graphein* write] —**graph′i·cal·ly, graph′ic·ly,** *adv.* —**graph′i·cal·ness,** *n.*

graph·ite (graf′īt), *n.* a soft, black form of carbon with a metallic luster, used for lead in pencils and for lubricating machinery. [< G *graphit* < Gk. *graphein* write] —**gra·phit·ic** (grə·fit′ik), *adj.*

grap·nel (grap′nəl), *n.* 1. instrument with one or more hooks for seizing and holding. 2. a small anchor with three or more hooks. [< OF *grapin* hook, dim. of *grape* hook]

grap·ple (grap′əl), *v.,* -**pled,** -**pling,** *n.* —*v.* 1. seize and hold fast; grip or hold firmly. 2. struggle; fight. 3. use a grapnel; search for with a grapnel. [< n.] —*n.* 1. a seizing and holding fast; firm grip or hold. 2. grapnel. [< OF *grapil* hook] —**grap′pler,** *n.* —**Syn.** *v.* 1. grasp, clinch. 2. wrestle, contend.

grappling iron, grapnel.

grasp (grasp; gräsp), *v.* 1. seize and hold fast by closing the fingers around. 2. understand. 3. **grasp at,** a. try to take hold of. b. accept eagerly. —*n.* 1. a seizing and holding tightly; clasp of the hand. 2. power of seizing and holding. 3. control; possession. 4. understanding. [ME *graspe(n);* akin to GROPE] —**grasp′a·ble,** *adj.* —**grasp′er,** *n.* —**Syn.** *v.* 1. grip, clutch, grab, snatch. 2. comprehend.

grasp·ing (gras′ping; gräs′-), *adj.* 1. eager to get all that one can; greedy. 2. that grasps. —**grasp′ing·ly,** *adv.* —**grasp′ing·ness,** *n.*

grass (gras; gräs), *n.* 1. any of various plants that cover fields, lawns, and pastures, and are eaten by horses, cows, and sheep. 2. such plants collectively. 3. land covered with grass; pasture. 4. plant that has jointed stems and long, narrow leaves. Wheat, corn, sugar cane, and bamboo are grasses. —*v.* 1. cover with grass. 2. feed on growing grass; graze. 3. lay on grass to bleach. [OE *græs;* akin to GREEN, GROW] —**grass′less,** *adj.* —**grass′like′,** *adj.*

grass·hop·per (gras′hop′ər; gräs′-), *n.* 1. insect with strong legs and wings for jumping. 2. *Mil.* a small airplane used for scouting and for directing fire from artillery units.

Grasshopper (2 to 3 in. long)

grass·land (gras′land′; gräs′-), *n.* land with grass on it, used for pasture.

grass roots, the ordinary citizens of a region or State taken all together: *Senator Tompkins is sure he will get support from the grass roots.*

grass widow, woman divorced or separated from her husband.

grass·y (gras′i; gräs′i), *adj.,* grass·i·er, grass·i·est. 1. covered with grass. 2. of or like grass. —grass′i·ness, *n.*

grate¹ (grāt), *n., v.,* grat·ed, grat·ing. —*n.* 1. framework of iron bars to hold a fire. 2. framework of bars over a window or opening; grating. —*v.* furnish with a grate or grating. [< Med.L < Ital. < LL *cratis,* L, hurdle] —grate′less, *adj.* —grate′like′, *adj.*

grate² (grāt), *v.,* grat·ed, grat·ing. 1. make (a grinding sound); sound harshly. 2. rub with a harsh sound: *the door grated on its old, rusty hinges.* 3. have an annoying or unpleasant effect: *his rude manners grate on me.* 4. wear down or grind off in small pieces: *grate cheese.* [< OF *grater* < Gmc.] —grat′er, *n.*

grate·ful (grāt′fəl), *adj.* 1. feeling gratitude; thankful. 2. pleasing; welcome. [< obs. *grate* agreeable (< L *gratus*) + *full*] —grate′ful·ly, *adv.* —grate′ful·ness, *n.*

grat·i·fy (grat′ə·fī), *v.,* -fied, -fy·ing. 1. give pleasure or satisfaction to; please. 2. satisfy; indulge. [< F < L, < *gratus* pleasing + *facere* make, do] —grat′i·fi·ca′tion, *n.* —grat′i·fi′er, *n.* —grat′i·fy′ing·ly, *adv.* —Syn. 1. delight.

grat·ing¹ (grāt′ing), *n.* framework of bars over a window or opening.

grat·ing² (grāt′ing), *adj.* harsh or unpleasant. —grat′ing·ly, *adv.*

grat·is (grat′is; grā′tis), *adv., adj.* free of charge. [< L, ult. < *gratia* favor]

grat·i·tude (grat′ə·tüd; -tūd), *n.* kindly feeling because of a favor received; thankfulness. [< LL, < *gratus* thankful]

gra·tu·i·tous (grə·tü′ə·təs; -tū′-), *adj.* 1. freely given or obtained; free. 2. without reason or cause. —gra·tu′i·tous·ly, *adv.* —gra·tu′i·tous·ness, *n.* —Syn. 2. unwarranted.

gra·tu·i·ty (grə·tü′ə·ti; -tū′-), *n., pl.* -ties. 1. present of money in return for service; tip. 2. present; gift. [< Med.L, gift, appar. < L *gratuitus* free]

gra·va·men (grə·vā′mən), *n., pl.* -vam·i·na (-vam′ə·nə). 1. grievance. 2. part of an accusation that weighs most heavily against the accused. [< L, ult. < *gravis* heavy]

grave¹ (grāv), *n.* 1. hole dug in the ground where a dead body is to be buried. 2. mound or monument over it. 3. any place that becomes the receptacle of what is dead: *a watery grave.* [OE *græf.* See GRAVE³.]

grave² (grāv), *adj., v.,* grav·er, grav·est, *n.* —*adj.* 1. important; weighty; momentous. 2. serious; threatening. 3. dignified; sober; solemn. 4. somber. 5. *Phonet.* a. low in pitch; not acute. b. having a particular accent (ˋ) that may indicate pitch, quality of sound (as in French *père*), or syllabic value (as in *beloved*). —*n.* the grave accent. [< F < L *gravis* serious] —grave′ly, *adv.* —grave′ness, *n.* —Syn. adj. 3. staid, sedate. —Ant. adj. 1. unimportant, trivial. 3. lively.

grave³ (grāv), *v.,* graved, graved or grav·en, grav·ing. 1. engrave; carve. 2. impress deeply; fix firmly. [OE *grafan*] —grav′er, *n.*

grave⁴ (grāv), *v.,* graved, grav·ing. clean (a ship's bottom) and cover with tar.

grave-clothes (grāv′klōz′; -klōthz′), *n.pl.* clothes in which a dead body is buried.

grav·el (grav′əl), *n., v.,* -eled, -el·ing; *esp. Brit.* -elled, -el·ling. —*n.* 1. pebbles and rock fragments coarser than sand. 2. *Pathol.* a. small, hard substances formed in the bladder and kidneys. b. disease causing them. —*v.* 1. lay or cover with gravel. 2. puzzle; perplex. [< OF *gravele,* dim. of *grave* sand, seashore < Celtic] —grav′el·ly, *adj.*

grav·en (grāv′ən), *adj.* 1. engraved; carved; sculptured. 2. deeply impressed; firmly fixed. —*v.* pp. of grave³.

graven image, 1. statue. 2. idol.

grave·stone (grāv′stōn′), *n.* stone that marks a grave.

grave·yard (grāv′yärd′), *n.* place for burying the dead; cemetery; burial ground.

graveyard shift, *Am., Colloq.* working hours between midnight and the morning shift.

grav·i·tate (grav′ə·tāt), *v.,* -tat·ed, -tat·ing. 1. move or tend to move by gravitation. 2. settle down; sink. 3. tend to go; be strongly attracted. [< NL, ult. < L *gravis* heavy]

grav·i·ta·tion (grav′ə·tā′shən), *n.* 1. *Physics.* a. force that attracts bodies toward one another. b. a moving or tendency to move caused by this force. 2. a natural tendency toward some point or object of influence: *gravitation of population to the cities.* —grav′i·ta′tion·al, *adj.* —grav′i·ta′tion·al·ly, *adv.*

grav·i·ty (grav′ə·ti), *n., pl.* -ties. 1. the natural force that causes objects to move or tend to move toward the center of the earth. Gravity causes objects to have weight. 2. the natural force that makes objects move or tend to move toward each other; gravitation. 3. heaviness; weight. 4. seriousness; solemnity; earnestness. 5. serious or critical character; importance. 6. lowness of pitch. [< L, < *gravis* heavy]

gra·vure (grə·vyŭr′; grā′vyər), *n.* 1. photogravure. 2. plate or print produced by photogravure. [< F, < *graver* engrave < Gmc.]

gra·vy (grā′vi), *n., pl.* -vies. 1. juice that comes out of meat in cooking. 2. sauce for meat, potatoes, etc., made from this juice. [ME *grave,* a mistaken writing of OF *grané* properly grained, seasoned, ult. < L *granum* grain]

gray (grā), *n.* 1. color made by mixing black and white. 2. gray cloth or clothing. 3. person dressed in gray. —*adj.* 1. having a color between black and white. 2. having gray hair. 3. old; ancient. 4. dark; gloomy; dismal. —*v.* make or become gray. Also, *esp. Brit.* **grey.** [OE *græg*] —gray′ly, *adv.* —gray′ness, *n.*

Gray (grā), *n.* Thomas, 1716–1771, English poet.

gray·beard (grā′bird′), *n.* old man. Also, *esp. Brit.* **greybeard.**

gray·hound (grā′hound′), *n.* greyhound.

gray·ish (grā′ish), *adj.* somewhat gray. Also, *esp. Brit.* **greyish.**

gray·lag (grā′lag′), *n.* a wild, gray goose that is common in Europe. Also, *esp. Brit.* **greylag.** [< *gray* + *lag;* because these birds migrate south at a very late date]

gray·ling (grā′ling), *n.* a fresh-water fish somewhat like a trout.

gray market, the buying and selling of products at prices considered exorbitant.

gray mar·ket·eer (mär′kə·tir′), one who deals in the gray market.

gray matter, 1. *Anat.* grayish tissue in the brain and spinal cord that contains nerve cells and some nerve fibers. 2. *Colloq.* intelligence; brains.

graze¹ (grāz), *v.,* grazed, graz·ing. 1. feed on growing grass. 2. put (cattle, sheep, etc.) to feed on growing grass or a pasture. 3. tend or look after (cattle, sheep, etc.) while they are grazing. [OE *grasian* < *græs* grass] —graz′er, *n.*

graze² (grāz), *v.,* grazed, graz·ing, *n.* —*v.* 1. touch lightly in passing; rub lightly (against). 2. scrape the skin from. —*n.* 1. a grazing. 2. a slight wound made by grazing. —graz′ing·ly, *adv.*

graz·ing (grāz′ing), *n.* growing grass that cattle, sheep, etc., feed on; pasture.

grease (*n.* grēs; *v.* grēs, grēz), *n., v.,* greased, greas·ing. —*n.* 1. soft animal fat. 2. any thick, oily substance. —*v.* 1. smear with grease; put grease on. 2. cause to run smoothly by grease. 3. *Slang.* give money as a bribe or tip. [< OF, ult. < L *crassus* fat] —grease′less, *adj.* —greas′er, *n.*

grease·wood (grēs′wŭd′), *n. Am.* a stiff, prickly shrub with narrow leaves, growing in alkaline regions in the western United States.

greas·y (grēs′i; grēz′i), *adj.,* greas·i·er, greas·i·est. 1. smeared with grease; having grease on it. 2. containing much grease. 3. like grease; smooth; slippery. —greas′i·ly, *adv.* —greas′i·ness, *n.*

great (grāt), *adj.* 1. big; large: *a great house,*

a great crowd. 2. more than usual; much: *great ignorance.* 3. important; remarkable; famous: *a great composer.* 4. most important; main; chief: *the great seal.* 5. noble; generous. 6. much in use; favorite: *that is a great habit of his.* 7. very much of a: *a great talker.* 8. *Am., Colloq.* very good; fine: *we had a great time at the party.* 9. of the next generation before or after. 10. *Archaic.* pregnant. [OE *grēat*] —**great′ly**, *adv.* —**great′ness**, *n.* —Syn. 1. immense, enormous. 3. renowned, eminent, distinguished. 5. magnanimous. 8. first-rate, excellent. —Ant. 1. small. 3. insignificant, obscure.

great-aunt (grāt′ant′; -änt′), *n.* aunt of one's father or mother; grandaunt.

Great Barrier Reef, reef in the S Pacific, off NE Australia.

Great Bear, *Astron.* the constellation Ursa Major.

Great Britain, England, Scotland, and Wales. It is the largest island of Europe.

great circle, any circle on the surface of a sphere having its plane passing through the center of the sphere.

great·coat (grāt′kōt′), *n. Esp. Brit.* a heavy overcoat.

Great Dane, one of a breed of large, powerful, short-haired dogs.

Great Divide, *Am.* the Rocky Mountains of N America.

Greater Antilles, Cuba, Haiti, Puerto Rico, and Jamaica, the largest islands in the West Indies.

great-heart·ed (grāt′här′tid), *adj.* 1. noble; generous. 2. brave; fearless. —**great′-heart′ed-ness,** *n.*

Great Lakes, *Am.* series of lakes between the United States and Canada; Lakes Ontario, Erie, Huron, Michigan, and Superior.

Great Plains, *Am.* a semiarid region just east of the Rocky Mountains in the United States and SW Canada.

great seal, the most important seal of a country or state, stamped on official documents as proof of approval by the government.

Great Slave Lake, lake in Northwest Territories, in NW Canada.

Great Smoky Mountains, or **Great Smokies,** part of the Appalachian Mountains in Tennessee and North Carolina.

great-un·cle (grāt′ung′kəl), *n.* uncle of one's father or mother; granduncle.

Great White Way, *Am.* brightly lighted theater district along Broadway, a street in New York City.

greave (grēv), *n.* armor for the leg below the knee. [< OF]

grebe (grēb), *n.* a diving bird like a loon, having feet not completely webbed and a pointed bill. [< F]

Gre·cian (grē′shən), *adj., n.* Greek.

Gre·co - Ro·man (grē′kō-rō′mən), *adj.* Greek and Roman.

Grebe (ab. 19 in. long)

Greece (grēs), *n.* country in S Europe, on the Mediterranean Sea.

greed (grēd), *n.* extreme or excessive desire, esp. for money. [OE *grǣd*] —**greed′less,** *adj.* —Syn. avidity, avarice, cupidity, covetousness.

greed·y (grēd′i), *adj.,* greed·i·er, greed·i·est. 1. wanting to get more than one's share; having a very great desire to possess something. 2. wanting to eat or drink a great deal in a hurry; piggish. [OE *grǣdig*] —**greed′i·ly,** *adv.* —**greed′i-ness,** *n.*

Greek (grēk), *adj.* of Greece, its people, or their language. —*n.* 1. native or inhabitant of Greece. 2. language of Greece. Ancient or classical Greek was the language until about 200 A.D.; modern Greek is the language since about 1500.

Greek Orthodox Church, 1. Christian church of the countries in communion or doctrinal agreement with the patriarch of Constantinople. 2. Also, **Greek Church.** part of this church that constitutes the established church in Greece.

Gree·ley (grē′li), *n.* Horace, 1811–1872, American journalist and politician.

green (grēn), *n.* 1. color of most growing plants, grass, and leaves. 2. green coloring matter, dye, paint, etc. 3. grassy land or a plot of grassy ground. 4. *Golf.* a putting green. 5. a grassy plot, as a town common. 6. greens, a. green leaves and branches used for decoration. b. leaves and stems of plants used for food. —*adj.* 1. having the color green. 2. covered with growing plants, grass, leaves, etc.: *green fields.* 3. characterized by growing grass, etc.: *a green Christmas.* 4. not dried, cured, seasoned, or otherwise prepared for use. 5. not ripe; not fully grown. 6. not trained or experienced; not mature in age, judgment, etc. 7. easily fooled; easy to trick or cheat. 8. having a pale, sickly color because of fear, jealousy, or sickness. —*v.* make or become green. [OE *grēne;* akin to GRASS, GROW] —**green′ish,** *adj.* —**green′ness,** *n.* —Syn. *adj.* 5. immature, unripe. 6. inexperienced, untrained, unsophisticated, callow. 7. gullible, ignorant. —Ant. *adj.* 2. sear, parched. 6. experienced. 7. clever, shrewd, astute.

green·back (grēn′bak′), *n. Am.* paper money having the back printed in green.

green·bri·er (grēn′brī′ər), *n.* a climbing smilax with prickly stems and green leaves.

green corn, *Am.* fresh, tender corn.

green·er·y (grēn′ər·i), *n., pl.* -er·ies. 1. green plants, grass, or leaves; verdure. 2. place where green plants are grown or kept.

green-eyed (grēn′īd′), *adj.* 1. having green eyes. 2. jealous.

green·gage (grēn′gāj′), *n.* a large plum with a light-green skin and pulp. [after Sir Wm. *Gage,* who introduced it into England]

green·gro·cer (grēn′grō′sər), *n. Brit.* person who sells fresh vegetables and fruit. —**green′-gro′cer·y,** *n.*

green·horn (grēn′hôrn′), *n. Colloq.* person without experience. [with ref. to the green horns of young oxen]

green·house (grēn′hous′), *n.* a building with a glass roof and glass sides kept warm for growing plants; hothouse.

green·ing (grēn′ing), *n.* apple with a yellowish-green skin when ripe.

Green·land (grēn′lənd), *n.* the largest island in the world, belonging to Denmark. It lies northeast of North America.

green light, *Am., Colloq.* official permission to proceed on a particular task or undertaking.

Green Mountains, part of the Appalachian Mountains extending through Vermont.

green·room (grēn′rüm′; -rùm′), *n.* room in old theaters for the use of actors and actresses when they are not on the stage.

green·sward (grēn′swôrd′), *n.* green grass.

green tea, tea whose leaves have been withered by steam.

green thumb, a remarkable ability to grow flowers, vegetables, etc., esp. as a hobby.

Green·wich (grin′ij; gren′-; -ich), *n.* borough in SE London, England. Longitude is measured east and west of Greenwich.

Green·wich Village (gren′ich), section of New York City, famous as a district where artists and writers live.

green·wood (grēn′wùd′), *n.* forest in spring and summer when the trees are green.

greet (grēt), *v.* 1. speak or write to in a friendly, polite way; address in welcome. 2. address; salute. 3. interchange greetings. 4. receive: *his speech was greeted with cheers.* 5. present itself to; meet. [OE *grētan*] —**greet′er,** *n.* —Syn. 1. welcome. 2. hail, accost.

greet·ing (grēt′ing), *n.* 1. act or words of a person who greets another; welcome. 2. greetings, friendly wishes, as on a special occasion.

gre·gar·i·ous (grə-gâr′i-əs), *adj.* 1. living in

flocks, herds, or other groups. 2. fond of being with others. 3. of or having to do with a flock or crowd. 4. *Bot.* growing in open clusters. [< L *gregarius < grex* flock] —**gre·gar′i·ous·ly**, *adv.* —**gre·gar′i·ous·ness**, *n.*

Gre·go·ri·an calendar (grə·gô′ri·ən; -gō′-), calendar now in use in the United States and most other countries, introduced by Pope Gregory XIII in 1582. It is a correction of the calendar of Julius Caesar.

Gregorian chant, vocal music having free rhythm and a limited scale, used in the Roman Catholic Church.

Greg·o·ry I (greg′ə·ri), Saint, 540?-604 A.D., pope 590-604 A.D.

Gregory XIII, 1502-1585, pope 1572-1585.

grem·lin (grem′lən), *n.* an imaginary elf that troubles the pilots of airplanes.

gre·nade (grə·nād′), *n.* 1. *Mil.* a small bomb, usually hurled by hand. 2. a round, glass bottle filled with chemicals that scatter as the glass breaks. Fire grenades are thrown on fires to put them out. [< F < Sp. *granada* pomegranate (lit., having grains) < L *granatus.* See GARNET.]

gren·a·dier (gren′ə·dir′), *n.* 1. originally, a soldier who threw grenades. 2. later, a very tall foot soldier. 3. now, a member of a special regiment of guards in the British army. [< F, < *grenade* GRENADE] —**gren′a·dier′i·al**, *adj.* —**gren′a·dier′ly**, *adv.*

gren·a·dine¹ (gren′ə·dēn; gren′ə·dēn′), *n.* thin, openwork fabric used for women's dresses. [< F, ? named for *Granada*, Spain]

gren·a·dine² (gren′ə·dēn′; gren′ə·dēn), *n.* syrup made from pomegranate or currant juice. [< F *grenadin.* See GRENADE.]

Gret·na Green (gret′nə), village in S Scotland where many runaway couples from England were married.

grew (grü), *v.* pt. of grow.

grew·some (grü′səm), *adj.* gruesome. —**grew′some·ness**, *n.*

grey (grā), *n., adj., v. Esp. Brit.* gray. —**grey′ly**, *adv.* —**grey′ness**, *n.*

grey·beard (grā′bird′), *n. Esp. Brit.* graybeard.

grey·hound (grā′hound′), *n.* one of a breed of tall, slender, swift dogs. Also, grayhound. [prob. < Scand. *greyhundr < grey* bitch + *hundr* dog]

grey·ish (grā′ish), *adj. Esp. Brit.* grayish.

grey·lag (grā′lag′), *n. Esp. Brit.* graylag.

grid (grid), *n.* 1. framework of parallel iron bars; grating; gridiron. 2. the lead plate in a storage battery. 3. *Radio.* electrode in a vacuum tube that controls the flow of current between the filament and the plate. [short for *gridiron*]

grid·dle (grid′əl), *n., v.,* -dled, -dling. —*n.* a heavy, flat plate of metal or soapstone, used for cooking griddlecakes, etc. —*v.* cook by means of a griddle. [< unrecorded OF *gredil;* cf. OF *grediller* singe. See GRILL.]

grid·dle·cake (grid′əl·kāk′), *n.* thin, flat cake of batter cooked on a griddle; pancake; flapjack.

grid·i·ron (grid′ī′ərn), *n.* 1. a cooking utensil consisting of a framework of parallel iron bars or wires, usually with a handle. 2. any framework or network that looks like a gridiron. 3. *Am.* a football field. [ME *gredire* GRIDDLE; final element assimilated to *iron*]

grid leak, *Radio.* a very high resistance placed in a vacuum tube to prevent the accumulation of electrons on the grid.

grief (grēf), *n.* 1. deep sadness caused by trouble or loss; heavy sorrow. 2. come to grief, have trouble; fail. 3. cause of sadness or sorrow. [< OF, < *grever* GRIEVE] —**grief′less**, *adj.* —Syn. 1. anguish, heartache, distress, melancholy.

Grieg (grēg), *n.* Edvard, 1843-1907, Norwegian musical composer.

griev·ance (grēv′əns), *n.* a real or imagined wrong; reason for being angry or annoyed; cause for complaint. —Syn. injustice, injury.

...**ieve** (grēv), *v.,* grieved, griev·ing. 1. feel ...ef; be very sad. 2. cause to feel grief; make ...ry sad; afflict. [< OF *grever,* ult. < L *gravis* ...avy] —**griev′er**, *n.* —**griev′ing·ly**, *adv.*

griev·ous (grēv′əs), *adj.* 1. hard to bear; causing great pain or suffering. 2. flagrant; atrocious. 3. causing grief. 4. full of grief; showing grief: *a grievous cry.* —**griev′ous·ly**, *adv.* —**griev′ous·ness**, *n.* —Syn. 1. distressing, oppressive, severe.

grif·fin, grif·fon (grif′ən), *n. Gk. Myth.* creature with the head and wings of an eagle, and the body of a lion. Also, gryphon. [< OF *grifon < L gryphus,* var. of *gryps* < Gk.]

grig (grig), *n. Dial.* 1. a small or young eel. 2. a cricket. 3. a grasshopper.

grill (gril), *n.* 1. a cooking utensil consisting of a framework of parallel iron bars for broiling meat, fish, etc.; gridiron. 2. dish of broiled meat, fish, etc. 3. restaurant or dining room that specializes in serving broiled meat and fish. —*v.* 1. broil. 2. torture with heat. 3. *Am.* question severely and persistently: *the detectives grilled the prisoner until he finally confessed.* [< F *gril,* ult. < LL *cratis* grate < L, hurdle] —**grill′er**, *n.*

grille (gril), *n.* an openwork metal structure or screen, used as a gate, door, or window. [< F < L *craticula < cratis* hurdle] —**grilled**, *adj.*

grill·room (gril′rüm′; -rum′), *n.* restaurant or dining room that specializes in serving broiled meat, fish, etc.

grilse (grils), *n., pl.* grilse. a young salmon that has returned from the sea to the river for the first time.

grim (grim), *adj.,* grim·mer, grim·mest. 1. without mercy; stern; harsh; fierce. 2. not yielding; not relenting. 3. looking stern, fierce, or harsh. 4. horrible; ghastly. [OE *grimm* fierce] —**grim′ly**, *adv.* —**grim′ness**, *n.* —Syn. 1. cruel, merciless. 2. relentless, unyielding. 3. hard, forbidding, severe. —Ant. 1. kind, tender.

gri·mace (grə·mās′; grim′is), *n., v.,* -maced, -mac·ing. —*n.* twisting of the face; ugly or funny smile. —*v.* make grimaces. [< F < Sp. *grimazo* panic] —**gri·mac′er**, *n.*

gri·mal·kin (grə·mal′kən; -môl′-), *n.* 1. cat. 2. an old female cat. 3. a spiteful old woman. [prob. < *gray + Malkin,* dim. of *Maud,* proper name]

grime (grīm), *n., v.,* grimed, grim·ing. —*n.* dirt rubbed deeply and firmly into a surface. —*v.* cover with grime; make very dirty. [? OE *grima* mask]

Grimm (grim), *n.* 1. Jakob, 1785-1863, German philologist and collector of fairy tales. 2. his brother, Wilhelm, 1786-1859, German philologist and collector of fairy tales.

grim·y (grīm′i), *adj.,* grim·i·er, grim·i·est. covered with grime; very dirty. —**grim′i·ly**, *adv.* —**grim′i·ness**, *n.*

grin (grin), *v.,* grinned, grin·ning, *n.* —*v.* 1. smile broadly. 2. show, make, or express by smiling broadly: *he grinned approval.* —*n.* a broad smile. [OE *grennian*] —**grin′ner**, *n.* —**grin′ning·ly**, *adv.*

grind (grīnd), *v.,* ground or (*Rare*) grind·ed, grind·ing, *n.* —*v.* 1. crush into bits or into powder. 2. crush by harshness or cruelty. 3. sharpen, smooth, or wear by rubbing on something rough. 4. rub harshly (on, into, against, or together): *grind one's heel into the earth, grind one's teeth in anger.* 5. work by turning a crank; produce by turning a crank: *grind a hand organ.* 6. *Colloq.* work or study long and hard. —*n.* 1. act of grinding. 2. *Colloq.* long, hard work or study. 3. *Am., Colloq.* person who works long and hard at his studies. [OE *grindan*] —**grind′ing·ly**, *adv.* —Syn. v. 1. pulverize, powder. 2. oppress, persecute. 4. grit, grate.

grind·er (grīn′dər), *n.* 1. person or thing that grinds. 2. man or machine that sharpens tools. 3. a back tooth for grinding food; molar.

grind·stone (grīnd′stōn′), *n.* 1. a flat, round stone set in a frame and turned by a crank, treadle, etc., used to sharpen tools, such as axes and knives, or to smooth and polish things. 2. have, keep, or put one's nose to the grindstone, work long and hard.

Grindstone

grin·go (gring′gō), n., pl., -gos. Am. among Spanish-Americans, an unfriendly term for a foreigner, esp. for an American or Englishman. [< Mex. Sp. < Sp., gibberish]

grip (grip), n., v., gripped (gript) or gript (gript), grip·ping. —n. 1. a firm hold; seizing and holding tight; tight grasp. 2. power of gripping. 3. thing for gripping something. 4. part to take hold of; handle. 5. special way of shaking hands. 6. Am. a small suitcase; handbag. 7. firm control. 8. mental grasp. 9. a sudden, sharp pain. 10. Am. grippe; influenza. 11. Am. in the theater, a stagehand. —v. 1. take a firm hold on; seize and hold tight. 2. get and keep the interest and attention of: an exciting story grips you. [OE gripe < grīpan to grasp] —grip′per, n. —grip′ping·ly, adv.

gripe (grīp), v., griped, grip·ing, n. —v. 1. clutch; pinch. 2. oppress; distress. 3. cause pain in the bowels. 4. U.S. Colloq. complain. 5. U.S. Colloq. bother; annoy. —n. 1. fast hold; gripping; clutch. 2. grasp; control. 3. U.S. Colloq. complaint. 4. gripes, pain in the bowels; colic. [OE grīpan]

grippe (grip), n. a contagious disease like a very severe cold with fever; influenza. [< F < Russ. khrip hoarseness] —grippe′like′, adj.

grip·sack (grip′sak′), n. Am. valise.

Gri·sel·da (gra-zel′da), n. heroine of an old romance famed for her patience.

gri·sette (gra-zet′), n. a French working girl. [< F, < gris gray; from usual color of their dresses]

gris·ly (griz′li), adj., -li·er, -li·est. frightful; horrible; ghastly. [OE grislic] —gris′li·ness, n.

grist (grist), n. 1. grain to be ground. 2. grain that has been ground; meal or flour. [OE grist < grindan grind]

gris·tle (gris′əl), n. cartilage. [OE]

gris·tly (gris′li), adj., -tli·er, -tli·est. of, containing, or like gristle.

grist mill, mill for grinding grain.

grit (grit), n., v., grit·ted, grit·ting. —n. 1. very fine gravel or sand. 2. a coarse sandstone. 3. Am., Slang. courage; pluck. —v. grate; grind: he gritted his teeth and plunged into the cold water. [OE grēot] —grit′less, adj.

grits (grits), n.pl. 1. coarsely ground corn, oats, etc., with the husks removed. 2. Am. coarse hominy. [OE gryttan, pl.]

grit·ty (grit′i), adj., -ti·er, -ti·est. 1. of or containing grit; like grit; sandy. 2. Am., Slang. courageous; plucky. —grit′ti·ly, adv. —grit′ti·ness, n.

griz·zled (griz′əld), adj. 1. grayish; gray. 2. gray-haired. [< grizzle gray hair, (adj.) gray < OF grisel, dim. of gris gray < Gmc.]

griz·zly (griz′li), adj., -zli·er, -zli·est, n., pl. -zlies. —adj. 1. grayish; gray. 2. gray-haired. —n. Am. grizzly bear.

grizzly bear, Am. a large, fierce, gray or brownish-gray bear of western North America.

groan (grōn), n. a deep-throated sound expressing grief, pain, or disapproval; short moan. —v. 1. give a groan or groans. 2. be loaded or overburdened. 3. express by groaning. 4. suffer greatly. [OE grānian] —groan′er, n. —groan′ing, n., adj. —groan′ing·ly, adv.

groat (grōt), n. 1. an old English silver coin worth fourpence. 2. a very small sum. [< MDu. groot, lit., thick (coin)]

groats (grōts), n.pl. hulled grain; hulled and crushed grain. [OE grotan, pl.]

gro·cer (grō′sər), n. person who sells food and household supplies. [< OF grossier, ult. < L grossus thick]

gro·cer·y (grō′sər·i; grōs′ri), n., pl. -cer·ies. 1. Am. store that sells food and household supplies. 2. groceries, food and household supplies sold by a grocer. 3. business of a grocer.

grog (grog), n. Esp. Brit. 1. drink made of rum or any other strong alcoholic liquor, diluted with water. 2. any strong alcoholic liquor. [short for grogram, nickname of Brit. Admiral Vernon, from his grogram cloak]

grog·ger·y (grog′ər·i), n., pl. -ger·ies. Esp. Brit. saloon.

grog·gy (grog′i), adj., -gi·er, -gi·est. 1. shaky; unsteady. 2. drunk; intoxicated. —grog′gi·ly, adv. —grog′gi·ness, n.

grog·ram (grog′rəm), n. a coarse cloth made of silk, wool, or combinations of these with mohair. [< F gros grain coarse grain]

grog·shop (grog′shop′), n. Esp. Brit. place where strong alcoholic drinks are sold.

groin (groin), n. 1. Anat. part of the body where the thigh joins the abdomen. 2. Archit. a curved line where two vaults of a roof cross. —v. Archit. build with groins. [ME grynde, infl. by loin]

grom·met (grom′it), n. 1. a metal eyelet. 2. Naut. ring of rope, used as an oarlock, to hold a sail on its stays, etc. [< obs. F gromette curb of bridle < gourmer curb]

Gro·my·ko (grō·mē′kō), n. Andrei Andreievich, born 1909, Russian diplomat.

groom (grüm), n. 1. man or boy who has charge of horses. 2. bridegroom. 3. any of several officers of the English royal household. 4. Archaic. manservant. —v. 1. feed and take care of (horses); rub down and brush. 2. take care of the appearance of; make neat and tidy. 3. Am. prepare (a person) to run for a position or political office. [ME grom(e) boy] —groom′er, n.

grooms·man (grümz′mən), n., pl. -men. man who attends the bridegroom at a wedding.

groove (grüv), n., v., grooved, groov·ing. —n. 1. a long, narrow channel or furrow, esp. one cut by a tool. 2. a fixed way of doing things. 3. in the groove. Slang. a. Music. playing or played smoothly and with great skill. b. in best form. —v. make a groove in. [OE grōf ditch] —groove′less, adj. —groove′like′, adj. —groov′er, n.

grope (grōp), v., groped, grop·ing. 1. feel about with the hands. 2. search blindly and uncertainly. 3. find by feeling about with the hands. [OE grāpian, akin to grīpan to grasp] —grop′er, n. —grop′ing·ly, adv.

gros·beak (grōs′bēk′), n. finch with a cone-shaped bill. [< F, < gros large + bec beak]

gros·grain (grō′grān′), n. a closely woven silk or rayon cloth with heavy cross threads and a dull finish. —adj. having heavy cross threads and a dull finish. [var. of grogram]

Red-breasted grosbeak (ab. 8 in. long)

gross (grōs), adj., n., pl. gross·es for 1, gross for 2. —adj. 1. with nothing taken out; whole; entire: gross receipts. 2. very bad: gross errors. 3. coarse; vulgar. 4. too big and fat; overfed. 5. thick; heavy; dense: the gross growth of a jungle. —n. 1. whole sum; total amount. 2. unit consisting of twelve dozen; 144. [< OF < L grossus thick] —gross′ly, adv. —gross′ness, n. —Syn. adj. 1. aggregate, total. 2. shameful, outrageous, glaring. 3. broad, indecent, low. 5. rank.

gross ton, 2240 pounds.

gro·tesque (grō-tesk′), adj. 1. odd or unnatural in shape, appearance, manner, etc.; fantastic; queer. 2. ridiculous; absurd. —n. 1. painting, sculpture, etc., combining designs, ornaments, figures of persons or animals, etc., in a fantastic or unnatural way. 2. any piece of such work. [< F < Ital. grottesco < grotta grotto] —gro·tesque′ly, adv. —gro·tesque′ness, n. —Syn. adj. 1. bizarre, strange.

grot·to (grot′ō), n., pl. -toes, -tos. 1. cave. 2. an artificial cave made for coolness or pleasure. [< Ital. grotta < L < Gk. kryptē. vault. Doublet of CRYPT.]

grouch (grouch), Am., Colloq. —v. be sulky or ill-tempered; complain. —n. 1. a sulky person. 2. a sulky, discontented feeling. [var. of obs. grutch < OF groucher murmur]

grouch·y (grouch′i), adj., grouch·i·er, grouch·i·est. Am., Colloq. sulky; sullen; discontented. —grouch′i·ly, adv. —grouch′i·ness, n.

ground¹ (ground), n. 1. the solid part of the earth's surface. 2. soil; dirt. 3. particular piece of land; land for some special purpose. 4. foundation for what is said, thought, claimed, or done; basis; reason. 5. underlying surface; background: *a blue pattern on a white ground.* 6. Often, **grounds.** land or area for some purpose or special use. 7. **grounds,** land, lawns, and gardens around a house. 8. **grounds,** small bits that sink to the bottom of a drink such as coffee or tea; dregs; sediment. 9. **grounds,** foundation; basis. 10. connection of an electrical conductor with the earth. 11. connection in a radio for the conductor that leads to the ground. 12. bottom (of an ocean, lake, etc.). 13. **cover ground,** a. go over a certain distance or area. b. travel. c. do a certain amount of work, etc. 14. **gain ground,** a. go forward; advance; progress. b. become more common or widespread. 15. **give ground,** retreat; yield. 16. **hold one's ground,** keep one's position; not retreat or yield. 17. **lose ground,** a. go backward; retreat; yield. b. become less common or widespread. 18. **shift one's ground,** change one's position; use a different defense or argument. 19. **stand one's ground,** keep one's position; refuse to retreat or yield. —*adj.* of, on, at, or near the ground; living or growing in, on, or close to the ground. —*v.* 1. put on the ground; cause to touch the ground. 2. *Naut.* run aground; hit the bottom or shore. 3. put on a firm foundation or basis; establish firmly. 4. have a foundation or basis. 5. instruct in the first principles or elements: *well grounded in grammar.* 6. furnish with a background. 7. connect (an electric wire or other conductor) with the earth. [OE *grund* bottom] —**Syn.** *n.* 2. loam, mold. 4. premise, motive.

ground² (ground), *v.* pt. and pp. of **grind.**

ground crew, *U.S. Air Force.* the nonflying personnel responsible for conditioning and maintenance of airplanes.

ground·er (groun′dər), *n.* baseball hit or thrown so as to bound or roll along the ground.

ground floor, *Am.* the most advantageous position in relation to a business deal, etc.

ground hog, *Am.* the woodchuck.

ground·less (ground′lis), *adj.* without foundation, basis, or reason. —**ground′less·ly,** *adv.* —**ground′less·ness,** *n.* —**Syn.** baseless.

ground·ling (ground′ling), *n.* 1. plant or animal that lives close to the ground. 2. fish that lives at the bottom of the water. 3. spectator or reader who has poor taste.

ground·nut (ground′nut′), *n. Am.* 1. any of various plants having edible underground parts, such as the peanut. 2. the edible tuber, pod, or the like, of such a plant.

ground pine, *Am.* a low, creeping evergreen, a kind of club moss, used for Christmas decorations and the like.

ground plan, 1. plan of a floor of a building. 2. first or fundamental plan.

ground·sel (ground′səl), *n.* plant with small heads of yellow flowers. [OE *g*(*r*)*undeswelge < grund* ground or *gund* pus + *swelgan* swallow¹]

ground·sill (ground′sil′), *n.* a horizontal timber used as a foundation; lowest part of a wooden framework; sill. [ME *gronsel.* See **GROUND¹, SILL.**]

ground squirrel, *Am.* any one of various burrowing rodents belonging to the squirrel family, esp. the chipmunk.

ground swell, broad, deep waves caused by a distant storm, earthquake, etc.

ground water, water from a spring or well.

ground wire, wire connecting electric wiring, a radio, etc., with the ground.

ground·work (ground′wérk′), *n.* foundation; basis.

ground zero, *Mil.* the exact point where a bomb strikes the ground or, in an atomic explosion, the area directly beneath the core of radiation.

group (grüp), *n.* 1. number of persons or things together. 2. number of persons or things belonging or classed together. 3. number of persons or things that act as a unit. 4. *Chem.* a radical. 5. . an air-force unit smaller than a wing and ger than a squadron, corresponding to an antry regiment. —*v.* 1. form into a group. 2.

put in a group. 3. arrange in groups. [< F < Ital. *gruppo*] —**Syn.** *n.* 1. cluster, aggregation, assemblage, crowd.

group·er (grüp′ər), *n., pl.* -ers or (*esp. collectively*) -er. a large food fish of warm seas. [< Pg. *garupa*]

grouse¹ (grous), *n., pl.* **grouse.** a game bird with feathered legs. The prairie chicken, sage hen, and ruffed grouse of the United States are different kinds. —**grouse′like′,** *adj.*

Ruffed grouse
(ab. 17 in. long)

grouse² (grous), *v.,* **groused, grous·ing,** *n. Slang.* —*v.* grumble; complain. —*n.* complaint. —**grous′er,** *n.*

grove (grōv), *n.* group of trees standing together; orchard. [OE *grāf*]

grov·el (gruv′əl; grov′-), *v.,* -eled, -el·ing; *esp. Brit.* -elled, -el·ling. 1. lie face downward; crawl at someone's feet; humble oneself. 2. enjoy low, mean, or contemptible things. [< *groveling,* orig. adv., <phrase *on grufe* prone <Scand. *ā grūfu*] —**grov′el·er,** *esp. Brit.* **grov′el·ler,** *n.* —**grov′el·ing·ly,** *esp. Brit.* **grov′el·ling·ly,** *adv.* —**Syn.** 1. creep, cringe, fawn.

grow (grō), *v.,* **grew, grown, grow·ing.** 1. become bigger by taking in food, as plants and animals do: *a tree growing only in the tropics.* 2. germinate; sprout. 3. exist; spring; arise: *the affair grew out of an indiscreet letter.* 4. become greater; increase: *his fame grew.* 5. **grow on** or **upon,** have an increasing effect or influence on: *the habit grew on me.* 6. become gradually attached or united by growth: *grow fast to the wall.* 7. become: *grow cold, grow rich.* 8. **grow up,** a. advance to or arrive at full growth. b. come into being; be produced; develop. 9. cause to grow; produce; raise: *grow corn.* 10. allow to grow: *grow a beard.* [OE *grōwan;* akin to **GRASS, GREEN**] —**grow′er,** *n.* —**Syn.** 4. expand, develop, flourish. 9. cultivate.

growl (groul), *v.* 1. make a deep, low, angry sound. 2. express by growling. —*n.* a deep, low, angry sound; deep, warning snarl. [prob. imit.] —**growl′er,** *n.* —**growl′ing·ly,** *adv.* —**Syn.** *v.* 1, 2. grumble.

grown (grōn), *adj.* 1. arrived at full growth. 2. covered with a growth. —*v.* pp. of **grow.**

grown-up (*adj.* grōn′up′; *n.* grōn′up′), *adj.* 1. adult. 2. characteristic of or for adults. —*n.* adult.

growth (grōth), *n.* 1. process of growing; development. 2. amount of growing or developing; increase. 3. what has grown or is growing: *a thick growth of bushes covered the ground.* 4. an unhealthy mass of tissue formed in or on the body, as a tumor. —**Syn.** 2. expansion, enlargement.

grub (grub), *n., v.,* **grubbed, grub·bing.** —*n.* 1. a wormlike form or larva of an insect, esp. the smooth, thick larva of a beetle. 2. drudge. 3. *Slang.* food. [< v.] —*v.* 1. dig. 2. root out of the ground; dig up. 3. drudge. [ME *grubbe*(*n*)] —**grub′ber,** *n.*

grub·by (grub′i), *adj.,* -bi·er, -bi·est. 1. dirty; grimy. 2. infested with grubs. —**grub′bi·ly,** *adv.* —**grub′bi·ness,** *n.*

grub·stake (grub′stāk′), *n., v.,* -staked, -stak·ing. *Am., W., Colloq.* —*n.* food, outfit, money, etc., supplied to a prospector on the condition of sharing in whatever he finds. —*v.* supply with a grubstake. —**grub′stak′er,** *n. Am., W., Colloq.*

grudge (gruj), *n., v.,* **grudged, grudg·ing.** —*n.* ill will; sullen feeling against; dislike of long standing. —*v.* 1. feel anger or dislike toward (a person) because of (something); envy the possession of. 2. give or let have unwillingly. [var. of obs. *grutch* < OF *groucher*] —**grudg′er,** *n.* —**grudg′ing·ly,** *adv.* —**Syn.** *n.* resentment, spite. —*v.* 1. envy, begrudge.

gru·el (grü′əl), *n., v.,* -eled, -el·ing; *esp. Brit.* -elled, -el·ling. —*n.* a thin, almost liquid food made by boiling oatmeal, etc., in water or milk. —*v.* subject to an exhausting or tiring experience. [< OF. ult. < Gmc.] —**gru·el·ing**, esp. Brit. **gru·el·ling** (grü′əl·ing), adj.

grue·some (grü′səm), adj. revolting in a ghastly way; horrible. Also, grewsome. [< grue to shudder. Cf. MDu., MLG gruwen.] —**grue′some·ly**, adv. —**grue′some·ness**, n.

gruff (gruf), adj. 1. deep and harsh; hoarse. 2. rough; rude; unfriendly; bad-tempered. [< Du. grof] —**gruff′ly**, adv. —**gruff′ness**, n. —Syn. 2. grumpy, brusque, impolite. —Ant. 2. courteous.

grum·ble (grum′bəl), v., -bled, -bling, n. —v. 1. mutter in discontent; complain in a bad-tempered way. 2. express by grumbling. 3. rumble. —n. 1. mutter of discontent; bad-tempered complaint. 2. rumble. [akin to OE grymettan roar, and GRIM] —**grum′bler**, n. —**grum′bling·ly**, adv. —Syn. v. 1, 2. growl, murmur.

grump·y (grump′i), adj., grump·i·er, grump·i·est. surly; ill-humored; gruff. —**grump′i·ly**, adv. —**grump′i·ness**, n.

grunt (grunt), n. 1. the deep, hoarse sound that a hog makes. 2. sound like this. 3. an edible sea fish that grunts when taken out of the water. —v. 1. make this sound. 2. say with this sound. [OE grunnettan < grunian grunt] —**grunt′er**, n. —**grunt′ing·ly**, adv.

Gru·yère (grı̇̈·yâr′; grü-), n. variety of firm, light-yellow cheese made from whole milk. [after Gruyère, district in Switzerland]

gryph·on (grif′ən), n. griffin.

Gua·dal·ca·nal (gwä′dəl·kə·nal′), n. one of the Solomon Islands in the Pacific. The Japanese were defeated here by U.S. armed forces, 1942–43.

Gua·de·loupe (gwä′də·lüp′), n. a French island in the West Indies.

Guam (gwäm), n. a U.S. island in the W Pacific, east of the Philippines.

gua·no (gwä′nō), n., pl. -nos. 1. manure of sea birds, found esp. on islands near Peru, used for fertilizing. 2. Am. fertilizer made from fish. [< Sp. < Kechua (Ind. lang. of Peru) huanu]

guar·an·tee (gar′ən·tē′), n., v., -teed, -tee·ing. —n. 1. a promise to pay or do something if another fails; pledge to replace goods if they are not as represented. 2. person who so promises. 3. one to whom such a pledge is made. —v. 1. stand back of; give a guarantee for; assure genuineness or permanence of. 2. undertake to secure for another. 3. make secure (against or from). 4. engage to do (something). [prob. var. of guaranty] —Syn. n. 1. warrant, security, surety.

guar·an·tor (gar′ən·tôr; -tər), n. person who makes or gives a guarantee.

guar·an·ty (gar′ən·ti), n., pl. -ties, v., -tied, -ty·ing. —n. 1. act or fact of giving security. 2. pledge or promise given as security; security. 3. person who acts as guarantee. —v. guarantee. [< OF guarantie < guarant warrant < Gmc. Doublet of WARRANTY.]

guard (gärd), v. 1. keep safe; watch over carefully; defend; protect. 2. keep in check; prevent from getting out; hold back. 3. act as a guard; take precautions (against); watch. —n. 1. somebody or something that guards. 2. anything that gives protection; contrivance or appliance to protect against injury, loss, etc. 3. careful watch. 4. defense; protection. 5. position of defense in boxing, fencing, or cricket. 6. person who opens and closes the doors or gates on a train. 7. Football. player at either side of the center. 8. Basketball. either of two players defending the goal. 9. guards, certain groups of soldiers in the British army. [< F garder, v., garde, n. < Gmc. Doublet of WARD.] —**guard′er**, n. —Syn. v. 1. shield. 3. safeguard, preserve. —n. 1. defender, protector, sentry, sentinel. 4. bulwark, shield.

guard·ed (gär′did), adj. 1. kept safe; carefully watched over; protected. 2. careful; cautious. —**guard′ed·ly**, adv. —**guard′ed·ness**, n. —Syn. 1. defended. 2. circumspect, reserved.

guard·house (gärd′hous′), n. Am., Mil. 1. a building used as a jail for soldiers. 2. a building occupied by soldiers on guard.

guard·i·an (gär′di·ən), n. 1. person appointed by law to take care of the affairs of someone who

cannot take care of them himself. 2. any person who takes care of somebody or something. —adj. protecting: a guardian angel. —**guard′i·an·ship′**, n. —Syn. n. 1. trustee, warden, keeper, guard. 2. protector, defender.

guards·man (gärdz′mən), n., pl. -men. 1. guard. 2. U.S. soldier who belongs to the National Guard.

Gua·te·ma·la (gwä′tə·mä′lə), n. 1. country in NW Central America. 2. Also, Guatemala City. its capital. —Gua′te·ma′lan, adj., n.

gua·va (gwä′və), n. 1. a tropical American tree or shrub with a yellowish, pear-shaped fruit. 2. the fruit, used for jelly, jam, etc. [< Sp. guayaba]

Guay·a·quil (gwī′ə·kēl′), n. seaport in W Ecuador.

gua·yu·le (gwä·ü′lā), n. Am. a small shrub growing in Mexico and Texas. Rubber is obtained from its juice. [< a Mexican lang.]

gu·ber·na·to·ri·al (gü′bər·nə·tô′ri·əl; -tô′-; gü′-), adj. Am. of or having to do with a governor. [< L gubernator, orig., pilot. See GOVERN.]

gudg·eon (guj′ən), n. 1. a small European fresh-water fish. It is easily caught and often used for bait. 2. minnow. 3. person easily fooled or cheated. —v. dupe; cheat. [< OF goujon, ult. < L gobius, a kind of fish < Gk. kobios]

guer·don (gėr′dən), n., v. Poetic. reward. [< OF, var. of werdon < Med.L < OHG widarlōn, infl. by L donum gift] —**guer′don·er**, n.

Guern·sey (gėrn′zi), n., pl. -seys. 1. any of a breed of dairy cattle resembling the Jersey, but somewhat larger. 2. a British island in the English Channel.

guer·ril·la, gue·ril·la (gə·ril′ə), n. fighter in a war carried on by independent bands which harass the enemy by sudden raids, plundering supplies, etc. —adj. of or by guerrillas. [< Sp., dim. of guerra war]

guess (ges), v. 1. form an opinion without really knowing: guess the height of a building. 2. get right by guessing: guess a riddle. 3. Esp. U.S. think; believe; suppose: I guess I can get there. —n. opinion formed without really knowing. [prob. < Scand. (Sw.) gissa] —**guess′er**, n. —**guess′ing·ly**, adv. —Syn. v. 1. estimate, suppose, surmise, conjecture. —n. estimate, supposition, surmise, conjecture. ≫ See calculate for usage note.

guess·work (ges′wėrk′), n. work, action, or results based on guessing; guessing.

guest (gest), n. 1. person who is received and entertained at one's home, club, etc.; person who is not a regular member; visitor. 2. person staying at a hotel, boarding house, etc. [< Scand. gestr. Cf. OE giest.] —**guest′less**, adj.

guf·faw (gu·fô′), n. a loud, coarse burst of laughter. —v. laugh loudly and coarsely.

Gui·a·na (gē·ä′nə; -an′ə), n. region in N South America, divided into British, Dutch, and French colonies.

guid·ance (gīd′əns), n. 1. a guiding; leadership; direction. 2. thing that guides.

guide (gīd), v., guid·ed, guid·ing, n. —v. 1. show the way; lead; conduct; direct. 2. manage; control. —n. 1. person who shows the way, leads, conducts, or directs. 2. mark, sign, etc. to direct the eye or mind. 3. guidebook. [< OF guider < Gmc.] —**guid′a·ble**, adj. —**guide′less**, adj. —**guid′er**, n. —Syn. v. 1. pilot, steer. 2. regulate, govern. —n. 1. leader, conductor, director, pilot.

guide·book (gīd′bu̇k′), n. book of directions and information, esp. one for travelers.

guided missile, Mil. projectile that can be guided accurately for great distances by means of transmitted electronic impulses.

guide·post (gīd′pōst′), n. post with signs and directions on it for travelers.

gui·don (gī′dən), n. 1. a small flag or streamer carried as a guide by soldiers, or used for signaling. 2. U.S. Army. flag, streamer, or pennant of a company, regiment, etc. 3. soldier who carries the guidon. [< F < Ital. guidone]

guild (gild), n. 1. society for mutual aid or for

āge, cãre, fär; ēqual, tėrm; īce; ōpen, ôrder; pu̇t, rüle, ūse; th, then; ə=a in about.

some common purpose: *the Ladies' Auxiliary Guild of the church.* 2. in the Middle Ages, a union of the men in one trade to keep standards high and to look out for the interests of their trade. Also, **gild.** [< Scand. *gildi*]

guil·der (gil′dər), *n.* 1. a silver coin or unit of money in the Netherlands. 2. coin formerly used in the Netherlands, Germany, or Austria. Also, **gulden.** [alter. of *gulden*]

guild·hall (gild′hôl′), *n.* 1. hall in which a guild meets. 2. *Brit.* a town hall; city hall. Also, **gildhall.**

guilds·man (gildz′mən), *n.*, *pl.* **-men.** member of a guild. Also, **gildsman.**

guile (gil), *n.* crafty deceit; craftiness; sly tricks. [< OF < Gmc. Doublet of WILE.] —Syn. cunning, wiliness, trickery. —Ant. honesty.

guile·ful (gil′fəl), *adj.* crafty and deceitful; sly and tricky. —**guile′ful·ly,** *adv.* —**guile′ful·ness,** *n.* —Syn. cunning, wily, artful.

guile·less (gil′lis), *adj.* without guile. —**guile′less·ly,** *adv.* —**guile′less·ness,** *n.* —Syn. sincere, honest, frank, candid.

guil·le·mot (gil′ə·mot), *n.* any of several arctic diving birds of the auk family with narrow bills. [< F, prob. < *Guillaume* William]

guil·lo·tine (*n.* gil′ə·tēn; *v.* gil′ə·tēn′), *n.*, *v.*, **-tined, -tin·ing.** —*n.* machine for beheading persons by means of a heavy blade that slides down between two grooved posts. —*v.* behead with this machine. [< F; named for J. I. *Guillotin,* physician and advocate of its use] —**guil′lo·tin′er,** *n.*

guilt (gilt), *n.* 1. fact or state of having done wrong; being guilty; being to blame. 2. guilty action or conduct. [OE *gylt* offense] —Syn. 1. guiltiness, culpability. 2. crime, wrongdoing.

guilt·less (gilt′lis), *adj.* not guilty; free from guilt; innocent. —**guilt′less·ly,** *adv.* —**guilt′less·ness,** *n.*

guilt·y (gil′ti), *adj.*, **guilt·i·er, guilt·i·est.** 1. having done wrong; deserving to be blamed and punished: *the jury pronounced the prisoner guilty of murder.* 2. knowing or showing that one has done wrong: *a guilty conscience.* 3. *Obs.* conscious. —**guilt′i·ly,** *adv.* —**guilt′i·ness,** *n.* —Syn. 1. culpable, sinful, criminal.

guimpe (gimp; gamp), *n.* blouse worn under a dress and showing at the neck or at the neck and arms. [< F < Gmc. Doublet of GIMP.]

guin·ea (gin′i), *n.* 1. amount equal to 21 shillings, used in England in stating prices, fees, etc. 2. a former English gold coin worth 21 shillings. 3. guinea fowl.

Guin·ea (gin′i), *n.* region along the coast of W Africa, divided into French, Portuguese, and Spanish colonies.

guinea fowl, a domestic fowl somewhat like a pheasant, having dark-gray feathers with small, white spots.

guinea hen, 1. guinea fowl. 2. a female guinea fowl.

guinea pig, 1. a short-eared, tailless animal like a big, fat, harmless rat, often used for laboratory experiments. 2. any person or thing serving as a subject for experiment or observation.

Guinea pig (ab. 6 in. long)

Guin·e·vere (gwin′ə·vir), **Guin·e·ver** (-vər), *n.* King Arthur's queen.

guise (gīz), *n.* 1. style of dress; garb: *the soldier went in the guise of a monk.* 2. external appearance; aspect; semblance. 3. assumed appearance; pretense: *under the guise of friendship.* [< OF < Gmc.]

gui·tar (gə·tär′), *n.* a musical instrument having six strings, played with the fingers. [< Sp. *guitarra* < Gk. *kithara* cithara. Doublet of CITHARA and ZITHER.] —**gui·tar′ist,** *n.* —**gui·tar′-like′,** *adj.*

gulch (gulch), *n. Am.* a deep, narrow ravine with steep sides, esp. one marking the course of a stream or torrent.

·den (gúl′dən), *n.*, *pl.* **-dens, -den.** guilder. Du., G, lit., golden (coin)]

gules (gūlz), *n.*, *adj. Heraldry.* red. [< OF *gueules* red fur neckpiece, ult. < *gole* throat < L *gula*]

gulf (gulf), *n.* 1. a large bay; arm of an ocean or sea extending into the land. 2. a very deep break or cut in the earth. 3. any wide separation: *a gulf between old friends.* 4. the Gulf, *Am.* the Gulf of Mexico. —*v.* engulf. [< F < Ital., ult. < Gk. *kolpos,* orig., bosom] —**gulf′like′,** *adj.*

Gulf Stream, *Am.* current of warm water flowing north from the Gulf of Mexico along the Atlantic coast to Newfoundland, where it turns northeast toward the British Isles.

gull[1] (gul), *n.* a graceful, gray-and-white bird with long wings, webbed feet, and a thick, strong beak, living on or near large bodies of water. [? < Welsh *gwylan*]

Gull (ab. 18 in. long)

gull[2] (gul), *v.* deceive; cheat. —*n.* person who is easily deceived or cheated.

Gul·lah (gul′ə), *n. Am.* 1. one of a group of Negroes living along the coast of South Carolina and Georgia and on the islands off the coast. 2. dialect of English spoken by the Gullahs.

gul·let (gul′it), *n.* 1. passage for food from the mouth to the stomach; esophagus. 2. throat. [< OF, ult. < L *gula* throat]

gul·li·ble (gul′ə·bəl), *adj.* easily deceived. —**gul′li·bil′i·ty,** *n.* —**gul′li·bly,** *adv.*

gul·ly (gul′i), *n.*, *pl.* **-lies,** *v.* **-lied, -ly·ing.** —*n.* a narrow gorge; ditch made by running water. —*v. Am.* erode (land) so as to form gullies. [? var. of *gullet*]

gulp (gulp), *v.* 1. swallow eagerly or greedily. 2. keep in; choke back. 3. gasp; choke. —*n.* 1. act of swallowing. 2. amount swallowed at one time; mouthful. [imit.] —**gulp′er,** *n.* —**gulp′ing·ly,** *adv.*

gum[1] (gum), *n.*, *v.*, **gummed, gum·ming.** —*n.* 1. a sticky juice, obtained from or given off by certain trees and plants, that hardens in the air and dissolves in water. Gum is used to make candy, medicine, and mucilage. 2. any similar secretion, such as resin. 3. preparation of such a substance for use in industry or the arts. 4. *Am.* chewing gum. 5. substance on the back of a stamp, the flap of an envelope, etc.; mucilage; glue. —*v.* 1. smear, stick together, or stiffen with gum. 2. give off gum; form gum. 3. *Am.* make or become sticky; clog with something sticky. [< OF < L < Gk. *kommi*] —**gum′like′,** *adj.* —**gum′mer,** *n.*

gum[2] (gum), *n.* Often, **gums.** flesh around the teeth. [OE *gōma* palate]

gum ammoniac, a natural mixture of gum and resin, used in medicine; ammoniac.

gum arabic, gum obtained from acacia trees, used in making candy, medicine, mucilage, etc.

gum·bo (gum′bō), *n.*, *pl.* **-bos.** *Am.* 1. the okra plant. 2. its sticky pods. 3. soup thickened with okra pods. 4. *W.* soil that contains much silt and becomes very sticky when wet. [of African origin]

gum·boil (gum′boil′), *n.* a small abscess on the gums.

gum·drop (gum′drop′), *n. Am.* a stiff, jellylike piece of candy made of gum arabic, gelatin, etc., sweetened and flavored.

gum·my (gum′i), *adj.*, **-mi·er, -mi·est.** 1. sticky like gum. 2. covered with gum. 3. giving off gum. —**gum′mi·ness,** *n.*

gump·tion (gump′shən), *n. Colloq.* 1. initiative; energy. 2. good judgment.

gum·shoe (gum′shü′), *n.*, *v.*, **-shoed, -shoe·ing.** *Am.* —*n.* 1. a rubber overshoe. 2. gumshoes, sneakers. 3. *Slang.* detective. —*v. Slang.* go around quietly and secretly.

gum tree, a sweet gum, tupelo, eucalyptus, or other tree that yields gum.

gun[1] (gun), *n.*, *v.*, **gunned, gun·ning.** —*n.* 1. rifle, cannon, or other weapon with a long metal tube for shooting bullets, shot, etc. 2. *Am.* pistol or revolver. **3.** anything resembling a gun in use or shape. **4.** the shooting of a gun as a signal or salute. —*v.* **1.** *Am.* shoot with a gun; hunt with a gun. **2.** *Slang.* open the throttle of (an airplane) wide; accelerate rapidly. [< OF *engan* engine, trap, snare, ult. < L *canna* reed] —**gun′less,** *adj.*

gun² (gun), *v.*, *Archaic* and *Poetic.* pp. of **gin⁴**.

gun·boat (gun′bōt′), *n. Am.* a small warship that can be used in shallow water.

gun·cot·ton (gun′kot′ən), *n.* explosive made by treating cotton with nitric and sulfuric acids.

gun·fire (gun′fīr′), *n.* the shooting of a gun or guns.

gun·lock (gun′lok′), *n.* part of a gun by which the charge is fired.

gun·man (gun′mən), *n., pl.* -men. *Am.* man who uses a gun to rob, kill, etc.

gun metal, 1. a dark-gray alloy used for chains, buckles, handles, etc. **2.** dark gray. **3.** kind of bronze formerly used for making guns. —**gun′-met′al,** *adj.*

gun·nel¹ (gun′əl), *n.* gunwale.

gun·nel² (gun′əl), *n.* a small N Atlantic fish resembling a perch.

gun·ner (gun′ər), *n.* **1.** man trained to fire artillery; soldier who handles and fires cannon. **2.** a navy officer in charge of a ship's guns. **3.** person who hunts with a gun.

gun·ner·y (gun′ər·i), *n.* **1.** art and science of constructing and managing big guns. **2.** use of guns; shooting of guns. **3.** guns collectively.

gun·ning (gun′ing), *n.* hunting with a gun.

gun·ny (gun′i), *n., pl.* -nies. **1.** a strong, coarse fabric used for sacks, bags, etc. **2.** Also, **gunny sack.** sack, bag, etc., made of this. [< Hind. *goni*]

gun·pow·der (gun′pou′dər), *n.* powder that explodes with force when brought into contact with fire, used esp. in gunnery.

gun·run·ning (gun′run′ing), *n.* the bringing of guns and ammunition into a country illegally. —**gun′run′ner,** *n.*

gun·shot (gun′shot′), *n.* **1.** shot fired from a gun. **2.** the shooting of a gun. **3.** distance that a gun will shoot.

gun·smith (gun′smith′), *n.* person whose work is making or repairing small guns.

gun·stock (gun′stok′), *n.* the wooden support to which the barrel of a gun is fastened.

Gun·ther (gun′tər), *n.* a Burgundian king, husband of Brunhild.

gun·wale (gun′əl), *n.* the upper edge of a ship's or boat's side. Also, **gunnel.**

gup·py (gup′i), *n., pl.* -pies. a very small, brightly colored, viviparous fish of tropical fresh water. [for R. J. L. *Guppy*]

gur·gle (gér′gəl), *v.,* -gled, -gling, *n.* —*v.* **1.** flow or run with a bubbling sound. **2.** make a bubbling sound. —*n.* a bubbling sound. [? imit.] —**gur′gling·ly,** *adv.*

gush (gush), *v.* **1.** rush out suddenly; pour out. **2.** *Colloq.* talk in a silly way about one's affections or enthusiasms. **3.** give forth suddenly or very freely. —*n.* **1.** rush of water or other liquid from an enclosed place. **2.** *Colloq.* silly, emotional talk. [prob. imit.] —**gush′ing,** *adj.* —**gush′ing·ly,** *adv.* —Syn. *v.* **1.** spurt, spout.

gush·er (gush′ər), *n.* **1.** *Esp. U.S.* an oil well that gives oil in large quantities without pumping. **2.** a gushy person.

gush·y (gush′i), *adj.,* gush·i·er, gush·i·est. showing silly feeling; effusive; sentimental. —**gush′i·ness,** *n.*

gus·set (gus′it), *n.* a triangular piece of material inserted to give greater strength or more room. [< OF *gousset* < *gousse* husk]

gust (gust), *n.* **1.** a sudden, violent rush of wind. **2.** a sudden burst of rain, smoke, sound, etc. **3.** outburst of anger, enthusiasm, etc. [< Scand. *gustr*]

gus·ta·to·ry (gus′tə·tô′ri; -tō′-), *adj.* of the sense of taste; having to do with tasting. [< L *gustatus,* pp. of *gustare* taste]

Gus·ta·vus V (gus·tā′vəs; -tä′-), born 1858, king of Sweden since 1907.

gus·to (gus′tō), *n., pl.* -tos. **1.** keen relish; hearty enjoyment. **2.** liking or taste. [< Ital., orig., taste < L *gustus*]

gust·y (gus′ti), *adj.,* gust·i·er, gust·i·est. **1.** coming in gusts; windy; stormy. **2.** marked by outbursts: *gusty laughter.* —**gust′i·ly,** *adv.* —**gust′i·ness,** *n.*

gut (gut), *n., v.,* gut·ted, gut·ting. —*n.* **1.** intestine. **2.** guts, a. *Slang.* pluck; courage; endurance. b. entrails; bowels. **3.** a tough string made from the intestines of a sheep, cat, etc., used for violin strings, tennis rackets, etc. —*v.* **1.** remove the entrails of; disembowel. **2.** plunder or destroy the inside of. [OE *guttas,* pl.] —**gut′ter,** *n.*

Gu·ten·berg (gü′tən·bérg), *n.* **Johann,** 1398?-1468, German printer, supposedly the first European to print from movable type.

gut·ta-per·cha (gut′ə·pér′chə), *n.* substance resembling rubber, obtained from the thick, milky juice of certain tropical trees, used in dentistry, etc. [< Malay]

gut·ter (gut′ər), *n.* **1.** channel along the side of a street or road to carry off water; low part of a street beside the sidewalk. **2.** channel or trough along the lower edge of a roof to carry off rain water. **3.** channel; groove. —*v.* **1.** form gutters in. **2.** flow or melt in streams. **3.** become channeled. [< OF *goutiere,* ult. < L *gutta* drop] —**gut′ter·like′,** *adj.* —**gut′ter·y,** *adj.*

gut·ter·snipe (gut′ər·snīp′), *n. Colloq.* **1.** gamin who lives in the streets. **2.** person without breeding or decency; mucker.

gut·tur·al (gut′ər·əl), *adj.* **1.** of the throat. **2.** formed in the throat; harsh. **3.** *Phonet.* formed between the back of the tongue and soft palate. The *g* in *go* is a guttural sound. —*n.* sound formed in this way. [< NL, < L *guttur* throat] —**gut′tur·al′i·ty,** *n.* —**gut′tur·al·ly,** *adv.* —**gut′tur·al·ness,** *n.*

guy¹ (gī), *n., v.,* guyed, guy·ing. —*n.* rope, chain, wire, etc., attached to something to steady or secure it. —*v.* steady or secure with a guy or guys. [< OF *guie* a guide, ult. < Gmc.]

guy² (gī), *n., v.,* guyed, guy·ing. —*n.* **1.** *Slang.* fellow; chap. **2.** a queer-looking person. —*v. Colloq.* make fun of; tease. [for *Guy* Fawkes]

guz·zle (guz′əl), *v.,* -zled, -zling. drink greedily; drink too much. —**guz′zler,** *n.*

gym (jim), *n.* gymnasium.

gym·na·si·um (jim·nā′zi·əm), *n., pl.* -si·ums, -si·a (-zi·ə). room, building, etc., fitted up for physical exercise or training and for indoor athletic sports. [< L < Gk. *gymnasion,* ult. < *gymnos* naked]

Gym·na·si·um (jim·nā′zi·əm; *Ger.* gim·nä′zi·üm), *n.* a German secondary school that prepares students for the universities.

gym·nast (jim′nast), *n.* expert in gymnastics. [< Gk., < *gymnazein* exercise. See GYMNASIUM.]

gym·nas·tic (jim·nas′tik), *adj.* having to do with bodily exercise or activities. —**gym·nas′ti·cal·ly,** *adv.*

gym·nas·tics (jim·nas′tiks), *n.* physical exercises for developing the muscles.

gym·no·sperm (jim′nə·spérm), *n. Bot.* any of a large group of plants having the seeds exposed, not enclosed in ovaries. The pine, fir, and spruce, which bear seeds on the surface of cone scales instead of in pods, are gymnosperms. [< NL < Gk., < *gymnos* naked + *sperma* seed]

gy·ne·col·o·gy, gy·nae·col·o·gy (gī′nə·kol′ə·ji; jī′nə-; jin′ə-), *n.* branch of medical science that deals with the functions and diseases peculiar to women. [< Gk. *gyne* woman + -LOGY] —**gy′ne·co·log′ic** (gī′nə·kə·loj′ik; jī′nə-; jin′ə-), **gy′nae·co·log′ic, gy′ne·co·log′i·cal, gy′nae·co·log′i·cal,** *adj.* —**gy′ne·col′o·gist, gy′nae·col′o·gist,** *n.*

gy·noe·ci·um (jī·nē′si·əm; jī-), *n., pl.* -ci·a (-si·ə). *Bot.* pistil or pistils of a flower. [< NL, < Gk. *gyne* woman + *oikion* house]

gyp (jip), *v.,* gypped, gyp·ping, *n. U.S. Slang.* —*v.* defraud or rob by some sharp practice; cheat; swindle. —*n.* **1.** a cheat or swindle. **2.** a swindler. [shortened from *gypsy*] —**gyp′per,** *n.*

gyp·soph·i·la (jĭp·sŏf′ə·lə), *n.* plant with many small, fragrant, white or pink flowers on delicate, branching stalks with few leaves.

gyp·sum (jĭp′səm), *n.* a hydrated calcium sulfate, CaSO₄·2H₂O, a mineral used for making plaster of Paris, fertilizer, etc. [< L < Gk. *gypsos*]

Gyp·sy (jĭp′sĭ), *n., pl.* **-sies,** *adj.* —*n.* **1.** person belonging to a wandering group of people having dark skin and black hair, who probably came from India originally. **2.** language of the Gypsies. **3.** gypsy, *U.S.* person who looks or lives like a Gypsy. —*adj.* **gypsy,** *a.* of the Gypsies. **b.** resembling a Gypsy or gypsy. Also, *esp. Brit.* **Gipsy, gipsy.** [ult. < *Egyptian*] —**gyp′sy·like′,** *adj.*

gypsy moth, a brownish or white moth whose larvae eat the leaves of trees. Also, **gipsy moth.**

gy·rate (jī′rāt; jī·rāt′), *v.,* **-rat·ed, -rat·ing. 1.** move in a circle or spiral. **2.** whirl; rotate. [< L, < *gyrus* circle < Gk. *gyros*] —**gy·ra′tion,** *n.*

—**gy·ra′tor,** *n.* —**gy·ra·to·ry** (jī′rə·tô′rĭ; -tō′-), *adj.*

gyr·fal·con (jẽr′fôl′kən; -fô′-), *n.* gerfalcon.

gy·ro·com·pass (jī′rō·kum′pəs), *n.* compass using a motor-driven gyroscope instead of a magnetic needle to point to the north. It points to the geographic North Pole instead of to the magnetic pole.

gy·ro·scope (jī′rə·skōp), *n.* a heavy wheel or disk mounted so that its axis can turn freely in one or more directions. A spinning gyroscope tends to resist change in the direction of its axis. —**gy·ro·scop·ic** (jī′rə·skŏp′ĭk), *adj.* —**gy′-ro·scop′i·cal·ly,** *adv.*

gy·ro·sta·bi·liz·er (jī′rō·stā′bə·līz′ər), *n.* device for stabilizing a seagoing vessel by counteracting its rolling motion.

gyve (jĭv), *n., v.,* **gyved, gyv·ing.** —*n.* Usually, **gyves.** shackle, esp. for the leg; fetter. —*v.* fetter; shackle.

H

H, h (āch), *n., pl.* **H's; h's.** the eighth letter of the alphabet.

H, 1. *Elect.* henry (unit of inductance). **2.** *Chem.* hydrogen.

h., H., 1. high. **2.** *Baseball.* hits. **3.** hour.

ha (hä), *interj.* **1.** exclamation of surprise, joy, triumph, etc. **2.** sound of a laugh.

Haa·kon VII (hô′kŭn), 1872–1957, king of Norway from 1905 to 1957.

Haar·lem (här′ləm), *n.* city in W Netherlands.

Hab·ak·kuk (hăb′ə·kuk; hə·băk′ək), *n.* **1.** a Hebrew prophet. **2.** book of the Old Testament.

Ha·ba·na (ä·vä′nä), *n.* Spanish name of Havana.

ha·be·as cor·pus (hā′bĭ·əs kôr′pəs), *Law.* writ requiring that a prisoner be brought before a judge or into court to decide whether he is being held lawfully. [L, you may have the person]

hab·er·dash·er (hăb′ər·dash′ər), *n.* **1.** *Am.* dealer in men's wear. **2.** dealer in small articles, such as needles, trimmings, etc.

hab·er·dash·er·y (hăb′ər·dash′ər·ĭ; -dash′rĭ), *n., pl.* **-er·ies. 1.** articles sold by a haberdasher. **2.** shop of a haberdasher.

hab·er·geon (hăb′ər·jən), *n.* **1.** a short hauberk. **2.** any hauberk. Also, **haubergeon.** [< OF *haubergeon,* dim. of *hauberc* HAUBERK]

ha·bil·i·ment (hə·bĭl′ə·mənt), *n.* **1.** habiliments, articles of clothing. **2.** dress; attire. [< OF, < *abiller* prepare, fit out, orig., reduce (a tree) to a trunk by stripping off the branches < *a-* (< L *ad*) + *bille* long stick < Celtic]

hab·it (hăb′ĭt), *n.* **1.** tendency to act in a certain way or to do a certain thing; usual way of acting: *habit of smoking.* **2.** the distinctive dress or costume worn by members of a religious order. **3.** a woman's riding suit. **4.** condition of body or mind. **5.** the characteristic form, mode of growth, etc., of an animal or plant. —*v.* put a habit on; dress. [< OF < L *habitus* < *habere* hold, live in, stay] —Syn. *n.* **1.** custom, practice, usage, use, wont.

hab·it·a·ble (hăb′ə·tə·bəl), *adj.* fit to live in. —**hab′it·a·bil′i·ty, hab′it·a·ble·ness,** *n.* —**hab′it·a·bly,** *adv.*

hab·it·ant (hăb′ə·tənt), *n.* inhabitant. [< F < L, ppr. of *habitare* live in]

hab·i·tat (hăb′ə·tat), *n.* **1.** place where an animal or plant naturally lives or grows. **2.** a dwelling place.

hab·i·ta·tion (hăb′ə·tā′shən), *n.* **1.** place to live in. **2.** an inhabiting. —Syn. **1.** home, dwelling, residence.

ha·bit·u·al (hə·bĭch′ū·əl), *adj.* **1.** done by ~~habit;~~ caused by habit: *a habitual smile.* **2.** being ~~do~~ing something by habit: *a habitual reader.* ~~of~~ten done, seen, or used: *ice and snow are a* ~~ha~~tual *sight in arctic regions.* —**ha·bit′u-** ~~al·ly,~~ *adv.* —**ha·bit′u·al·ness,** *n.* —Syn. **2.** regu-

lar, steady. **3.** customary, ordinary. ➤ **habitual** action. *Would* is the typical auxiliary verb for habitual action in the past, especially in formal English: *He would always go by the longer way.* Habitual action is also expressed by *used to* or by an adverb: *He used to go by the longer way. He usually went by the longer way.*

ha·bit·u·ate (hə·bĭch′ū·āt), *v.,* **-at·ed, -at·ing.** make used (to); accustom. —**ha·bit′u·a′tion,** *n.* —Syn. familiarize, naturalize, acclimate.

hab·i·tude (hăb′ə·tūd; -tŭd), *n.* **1.** characteristic condition of body or mind. **2.** custom.

ha·bit·u·é (hə·bĭch′ū·ā′), *n.* person who has the habit of going to any place frequently. [< F]

ha·ci·en·da (hä′sĭ·en′də), *n. Am.* a large ranch; landed estate; country house. [< Sp. < L *facienda* (things) to be done < *facere* do]

hack¹ (hak), *v.* **1.** cut roughly or unevenly; deal cutting blows. **2.** give short, dry coughs. —*n.* **1.** a rough cut. **2.** tool or instrument for hacking, such as an ax, pick, hoe, etc. **3.** a short, dry cough. [OE *haccian*] —**hack′er,** *n.*

hack² (hak), *n.* **1.** *U.S.* carriage for hire. **2.** *Colloq.* taxi. **3.** *Brit.* horse for hire. **4.** an old or worn-out horse. **5.** horse for ordinary riding. **6.** person hired to do routine literary work; drudge. —*v.* **1.** ride on horseback over roads. **2.** *Colloq.* drive a taxi. —*adj.* working or done merely for money. [short for *hackney*] —Syn. *adj.* hired, drudging.

hack·a·more (hak′ə·môr; -mōr), *n. Am.* a halter (def. 1).

hack·ber·ry (hak′ber′ĭ), *n., pl.* **-ries.** *Am.* **1.** tree related to the elm that has small, cherrylike fruit. **2.** the fruit.

hack·le¹ (hak′əl), *n., v.,* **-led, -ling.** —*n.* **1.** comb used in dressing flax, hemp, etc. **2.** one of the long, slender feathers on the neck of certain birds. **3.** the neck plumage of certain birds. **4.** a wingless artificial fly, used by fishermen. —*v.* comb (flax, hemp, etc.) with a hackle. [ME *hakell;* akin to HECKLE] —**hack′ler,** *n.*

hack·le² (hak′əl), *v.,* **-led, -ling.** cut roughly; hack; mangle. [< *hack¹*]

hack·ney (hak′nĭ), *n., pl.* **-neys,** *adj., v.,* **-neyed, -ney·ing.** —*n.* **1.** horse for ordinary riding. **2.** carriage for hire. —*adj.* hired. —*v.* use too often; make commonplace. [< OF *haquenee*]

hack·neyed (hak′nĭd), *adj.* used too often; commonplace. —Syn. trite, stale, banal.

hack·saw (hak′sô′), *n.* saw for cutting metal, consisting of a narrow, fine-toothed blade fixed in a frame.

had (had), *v.* pt. and pp. of **have.** ➤ **had better, had rather.** *Had better* is the usual idiom for giving advice or making an indirect command: *you had better take care of that cold. You'd better go. Had rather* and *would rather* are both used to express preference: *He would rather ski than eat. He had rather ski than eat.*

had·dock (had′ək), *n., pl.* **-docks** or (*esp. col-*

lectively) –dock. a food fish of the N Atlantic, somewhat like a cod, but smaller. [ME *haddok*]

Ha·des (hā′dēz), *n.* 1. *Gk. Myth.* a. home of the dead, below the earth. b. Pluto. 2. hades, *Colloq.* hell. [< Gk. *Haidēs*]

had·n't (had′ənt), had not.

Ha·dri·an (hā′dri·ən), *n.* 76–138 A.D., Roman emperor 117–138 A.D.

hadst (hadst), *v. Archaic.* 2nd pers. sing. pt. of have.

haem·a·tite (hem′ə·tīt; hē′mə-), *n.* hematite.

hae·mo·glo·bin (hē′mə·glō′bən; hem′ə-), *n.* hemoglobin.

hae·mo·phil·i·a (hē′mə·fil′i·ə; hem′ə-), *n.* hemophilia. —**hae·mo·phil·i·ac** (hē′mə·fil′i·ak; hem′ə-), *n.*

haem·or·rhage (hem′ə·rij; hem′rij), *n.* hemorrhage. —**haem·or·rhag·ic** (hem′ə·raj′ik), *n.*

haem·or·rhoids (hem′ə·roidz), *n.pl.* hemorrhoids.

haf·ni·um (haf′ni·əm; häf′-), *n. Chem.* a rare metallic element, Hf, somewhat like zirconium. [< *Hafnia*, L name for Copenhagen]

haft (haft; häft), *n.* handle (of a knife, sword, dagger, etc.). —*v.* furnish with a handle or hilt; set in a haft. [OE *hæft*]

hag (hag), *n.* 1. a very ugly old woman, esp. one who is vicious or malicious. 2. witch. [ME *hagge*, akin to OE *hægtesse* witch, fury] —**hag′gish**, *adj.* —**hag′like′**, *adj.*

Ha·gar (hā′gär; -gər), *n. Bible.* slave of Abraham's wife Sarah. Gen. 16.

hag·fish (hag′fish′), *n., pl.* **-fish·es** or (*esp. collectively*) **-fish.** a small salt-water fish shaped like an eel, that attaches itself to other fish by its round mouth and bores into them with its horny teeth.

Hag·ga·dah, Hag·ga·da (hə·gä′də), *n., pl.* **-doth** (-dōth). 1. story or legend in the Talmud that explains the law. 2. the legendary part of the Talmud. 3. religious rites for the first two nights of the Jewish Passover. —**hag·gad·ic** (hə·gad′ik; -gä′dik), **hag·gad·i·cal,** *adj.*

Hag·ga·i (hag′i·ī; hag′ī; -ā·ī), *n.* 1. a Hebrew prophet. 2. book of the Old Testament.

hag·gard (hag′ərd), *adj.* wild-looking from pain, fatigue, worry, hunger, etc. —**hag′gard·ly,** *adv.* —**hag′gard·ness,** *n.* —Syn. gaunt, care-worn, emaciated.

hag·gis (hag′is), *n. Scot.* heart, lungs, and liver of a sheep mixed with suet and oatmeal and boiled in the stomach of the animal.

hag·gle (hag′əl), *v.,* **-gled, -gling.** 1. dispute about a price or the terms of a bargain; wrangle. 2. mangle in cutting; hack. [< *hag* chop < Scand. *höggva*] —**hag′gler,** *n.*

hag·i·ol·o·gy (hag′i·ol′ə·ji; hā′ji-), *n., pl.* **-gies.** 1. literature that deals with the lives and legends of saints. 2. list of saints. [< Gk. *hagios* holy + -LOGY] —**hag·i·o·log·ic** (hag′i·ə·loj′ik; hā′ji-), **hag·i·o·log·i·cal,** *adj.* —**hag′i·ol′o·gist,** *n.*

hag·rid·den (hag′rid′ən), *adj.* worried or tor-mented, as if by witches.

Hague (hāg), *n.* The, the city in SW Netherlands; site of the World Court.

Hai·fa (hī′fə), *n.* seaport in NW Israel.

hail¹ (hāl), *v.* 1. shout in welcome to; greet; cheer. 2. greet as: *they hailed him leader.* 3. call loudly to; shout to. 4. hail from, come from. [< *n.*] —*n.* 1. greeting; cheer. 2. a loud call; shout. 3. within hail, near enough to hear a call or shout. —*interj. Poetic.* greetings! welcome! [< Scand. *heill* health] —**hail′er,** *n.* —Syn. *v.* 1. address, salute.

hail² (hāl), *n.* 1. small, roundish pieces of ice coming down from the clouds in a shower; frozen rain. 2. shower like hail: *a hail of bullets.* —*v.* 1. come down in hail. 2. pour down or upon in a shower like hail. [OE *hægel*]

hail·stone (hāl′stōn′), *n.* a small, roundish piece of ice coming down from the clouds.

hail·storm (hāl′stôrm′), *n.* storm with hail.

hair (hār), *n.* 1. a fine, threadlike growth from the skin of people and animals. 2. mass of such growths. 3. a fine, threadlike growth from the outer layer of plants. 4. a very narrow space; something very small; least degree. 5. split hairs, make too fine distinctions. [OE *hǣr*] —**hair′less,** *adj.* —**hair′less·ness,** *n.* —**hair′like′,** *adj.*

hair·breadth (hār′bredth′), *n., adj.* hairs-breadth.

hair·cloth (hār′klôth′; -kloth′), *n.* cloth made of horsehair or camel's hair, used to cover furniture, stiffen garments, etc.

hair·cut (hār′kut′), *n.* act or manner of cut-ting the hair. —**hair′cut′ter,** *n.*

hair·do (hār′dü′), *n., pl.* **-dos.** way of arrang-ing the hair.

hair·dress·er (hār′dres′ər), *n.* person whose work is taking care of people's hair or cutting it. —**hair′dress′ing,** *n., adj.*

hair·line (hār′līn′), *n.* a very thin line.

hair·pin (hār′pin′), *n.* pin, usually a U-shaped piece of wire, shell, or celluloid, used by women to keep the hair in place.

hair·rais·ing (hār′rāz′ing), *adj. Colloq.* mak-ing the hair stand on end; terrifying.

hair's-breadth, hairs-breadth (hārz′-bredth′), *n.* a very small space or distance. —*adj.* extremely narrow or close. Also, **hair′-breadth′.**

hair shirt, a rough shirt or girdle made of horsehair, worn as a penance.

hair·split·ting (hār′split′ing), *n., adj.* mak-ing too fine distinctions. —**hair′split′ter,** *n.*

hair·spring (hār′spring′), *n.* a fine, hairlike spring that regulates the motion of the balance wheel in a watch or clock.

hair trigger, trigger that operates by very slight pressure.

hair·y (hār′i), *adj.,* **hair·i·er, hair·i·est.** 1. cov-ered with hair; having much hair. 2. of or like hair. —**hair′i·ness,** *n.* —Syn. 1. shaggy, hirsute.

Hai·ti (hā′ti), *n.* 1. former name of Hispaniola. 2. republic in the western part of this island. —**Hai·ti·an** (hā′ti·ən; hā′shən), *adj., n.*

hake (hāk), *n., pl.* **hakes** or (*esp. collectively*) **hake.** a sea fish related to the cod. [? < Scand. (Norw.) *hakefisk*, lit., hook fish; from the hook-like growth under the lower jaw]

ha·kim¹ (hə·kēm′), *n.* in Moslem use, a physi-cian. [< Ar. *ḥakīm* wise man]

ha·kim² (hä′kim), *n.* in Moslem use, a ruler or judge. [< Ar. *ḥākim*]

hal·berd (hal′bərd), **hal·bert** (-bərt), *n.* weapon that is both a spear and a battle-ax, used in warfare in the 15th and 16th centuries. [< F *hallebarde* < Ital. *alabarda*]

hal·berd·ier (hal′bər·dir′), *n.* sol-dier armed with a halberd.

hal·cy·on (hal′si·ən), *adj.* calm; peaceful; happy. —*n. Archaic* or *Poetic.* bird that was supposed to calm the waves; kingfisher. [< L < Gk., var. of *alkyon* kingfisher]

hale¹ (hāl), *adj.,* **hal·er, hal·est.** strong and well; healthy. [OE *hāl*] —**hale′ness,** *n.* —Syn. sound, robust. —Ant. sickly.

hale² (hāl), *v.,* **haled, hal·ing.** 1. drag by force. 2. compel to go. [< OF *haler* < Gmc. Doublet of HAUL.]

Hale (hāl), *n.* Nathan, 1755–1776, American patriot hanged as a spy by the British.

half (haf; häf), *n., pl.* **halves,** *adj., adv.* —*n.* 1. one of two equal (or approximately equal) parts. 2. one of two equal periods in certain games. 3. a half-hour: *half past ten.* —*adj.* 1. forming a half; being or making half of. 2. not complete; being only part of: *a half truth.* —*adv.* 1. to half of the full amount or degree: *a glass half full of milk.* 2. partly: *half aloud.* 3. almost: *half dead from hunger.* 4. not half bad, fairly good. [OE] ⟩ **half.** The more formal idiom is *a half,* the informal *half a: He ran half a mile, half an hour* (informal). *He ran a half mile, a half hour* (formal).

Halberdier

half-and-half (haf′ənd·haf′; häf′ənd·häf′),

adj. 1. half one thing and half another. 2. not clearly one thing or the other. —*adv.* in two equal parts. —*n.* 1. U.S. mixture of milk and cream. 2. *Brit.* beverage of two mixed liquors.

half-back (haf'bak'; häf'-), *n. Football.* player whose position is behind the forward line.

half-baked (haf'bākt'; häf'-), *adj.* 1. not cooked enough. 2. *Colloq.* not fully worked out; incomplete. 3. *Colloq.* not experienced; showing poor judgment.

half-blood (haf'blud'; häf'-), *n.* 1. half-breed. 2. person related to another person through one parent only. —**half'-blood'ed**, *adj.*

half blood, relationship between persons who are related through one parent only.

half-breed (haf'brēd'; häf'-), *n.* person whose parents are of different races.

half brother, brother related through one parent only.

half-caste (haf'kast'; häf'käst'), *n.* half-breed.

half cock, 1. position of the hammer of a gun when it is pulled back halfway and locked. 2. go off at half cock, a. fire too soon. b. act or speak without sufficient thought or preparation.

half dollar, *Am.* a silver coin of the United States and Canada, worth 50 cents.

half eagle, *Am.* a former gold coin of the United States, worth $5.00.

half-heart·ed (haf'här'tid; häf'-), *adj.* lacking courage, interest, or enthusiasm. —**half'-heart'ed·ly**, *adv.* —**half'-heart'ed·ness**, *n.* —Syn. indifferent, perfunctory, lukewarm.

half hitch, an easily unfastened knot, formed by passing the end of a rope under and over its standing part and then inside the loop.

half-hour (haf'our'; häf'-), *n.* 1. thirty minutes. 2. the halfway point in an hour. —*adj.* of or lasting a half-hour. —**half'-hour'ly**, *adv.*

Half hitch

half-life (haf'līf'; häf'-), *n.* time in which half of the original radiant energy of an element is given off, used to measure radioactivity.

half-mast (haf'mast'; häf'mäst'), *n.* position halfway down from the top of a mast, staff, etc. —*v.* hang at half-mast.

half moon, 1. moon when only half of its surface appears bright. 2. something shaped like a half moon or crescent.

half nelson, *Wrestling.* hold accomplished by hooking one arm under an opponent's armpit and putting the hand on the back of his neck.

half note, *Music.* note held half as long as a whole note; minim.

Half note

half-pen·ny (hā'pə·ni; häp'ni), *n., pl.* **half-pen·nies** (hā'pə·niz; häp'niz), **half-pence** (hā'pəns), *adj.* —*n. Brit.* a bronze coin worth half a British penny. —*adj.* 1. worth only a halfpenny. 2. having little value.

half sister, sister related through one parent only.

half sole, sole of a shoe or boot from the toe to the instep.

half-sole (haf'sōl'; häf'-), *v.*, **-soled**, **-soling.** put a new half sole or half soles on (shoes, etc.).

half step, 1. *Music.* difference in pitch between two adjacent keys on a piano. 2. *U.S. Army.* a marching step of 15 inches in quick time, or of 18 inches in double time.

half-tone (haf'tōn'; häf'-), *n.* 1. process in photoengraving for making pictures for books and magazines. 2. picture made by this process. 3. *Painting.* tone between the highlight and deep shades.

half tone, *Music.* half step (def. 1).

half-track, half·track (haf'trak'; häf'-), *n.* 1. an endless-track mechanism for vehicles, driven by revolving inside wheels. 2. *U.S. Army.* motor vehicle that has wheels in front and [trac]ks in the rear for driving, used to [pull ar]tillery personnel and weapons.

[half]·way (haf'wā'; häf'-), *adv.* 1. half the [way. 2.] *halfway home.* 2. go or meet halfway, do

one's share to agree or be friendly (with). —*adj.* 1. midway: *a halfway house between two towns.* 2. not going far enough; incomplete.

half-wit (haf'wit'; häf'-), *n.* 1. a feeble-minded person. 2. a stupid, foolish person.

half-wit·ted (haf'wit'id; häf'-), *adj.* 1. feeble-minded. 2. very stupid; foolish. —**half'-wit'ted·ly**, *adv.* —**half'-wit'ted·ness**, *n.*

hal·i·but (hal'ə·bət; hol'-), *n., pl.* **-buts** or (*esp. collectively*) **-but.** a large flatfish much used for food, often weighing several hundred pounds. [ME *halybutte* < *haly* holy + *butte* flatfish; eaten on holy days]

hal·i·dom (hal'ə·dəm), **hal·i·dome** (-dōm), *n. Archaic.* 1. sanctuary. 2. a holy relic. [OE *hāligdōm.* See HOLY, -DOM.]

Hal·i·fax (hal'ə·faks), *n.* seaport in SE Canada, the capital of Nova Scotia.

hal·ite (hal'īt; hā'līt), *n.* a native rock salt. [< NL, < Gk. *hals* salt]

hal·i·to·sis (hal'ə·tō'sis), *n.* bad or offensive breath. [< NL, < L *halitus* breath]

hall (hôl), *n.* 1. *U.S.* way to go through a building; passageway. 2. passageway or room at the entrance of a building. 3. a large room for holding meetings, parties, banquets, etc. 4. a building for public business: *the town hall.* 5. a building of a school, college, or university. 6. *Brit.* residence of a landowner. [OE *heall*]

Hal·le (häl'ə), *n.* city in C Germany.

hal·le·lu·jah, hal·le·lu·iah (hal'ə·lü'yə), *interj.* praise ye the Lord! —*n.* a rendering of this. Also, **alleluia.** [< Heb. *hallēlū-yāh* praise ye Yah (Jehovah)]

hal·liard (hal'yərd), *n. Naut.* halyard.

hall·mark (hôl'märk'), *n.* 1. an official mark indicating standard of purity, put on gold and silver articles. 2. mark or sign of genuineness or good quality. —*v.* put a hallmark on. [from Goldsmiths' *Hall* in London, the seat of the Goldsmiths' Company, by whom the stamping was legally regulated]

hal·loo (hə·lü'), *interj., n., pl.* **-loos**, *v.*, **-looed**, **-loo·ing.** —*interj.* 1. shout to make hounds run faster. 2. call or shout to attract attention. —*n., v.* shout; call.

hal·low¹ (hal'ō), *v.* 1. make holy; make sacred. 2. honor as holy or sacred. [OE *hālgian* < *hālig* holy] —Syn. 1. consecrate, sanctify.

hal·low² (hə·lō'), *interj., n., v.* halloo.

hal·lowed (hal'ōd; in *worship, often* hal'ō·id), *adj.* 1. made holy; sacred; consecrated. 2. honored or observed as holy. —**hal'lowed·ness**, *n.*

Hal·low·een, Hal·low·e'en (hal'ō·ēn'; hol'-), *n.* evening of October 31, preceding All Saints' Day. [for *Allhallow-even*]

Hal·low·mas (hal'ō·məs; -mas), *n.* a former name of All Saints' Day.

hal·lu·ci·na·tion (hə·lü'sə·nā'shən), *n.* 1. apparent perception of an object or sound that is not really present. 2. the object or sound apparently perceived; illusion. [< LL, < *alucinari* wander (of the mind)]

hall·way (hôl'wā'), *n.* 1. *Am.* way to go through a building. 2. passageway or room at the entrance of a building. —Syn. 1. corridor, passage. 2. hall.

ha·lo (hā'lō), *n., pl.* **-los**, **-loes**, *v.*, **-loed**, **-loing.** —*n.* 1. ring of light around the sun, moon, or other shining body. 2. a golden circle of light represented about the head of a saint, etc. 3. glory or glamour that surrounds an idealized person or thing: *a halo of romance surrounds King Arthur and his knights.* —*v.* surround with a halo. [< L (def. 1) < Gk. *halos* disk, threshing floor (with ref. to circular path of the oxen)] —**ha'lo·like'**, *adj.*

Halo about the head of Joan of Arc

hal·o·gen (hal'ə·jən), *n. Chem.* any one of the elements iodine, bromine, chlorine, and fluorine, that combine directly with metals to form salts. [< Gk. *hals* salt + *gennaein* to produce]

Hals (häls), *n.* Frans, 1580?-1666, Dutch painter of portraits and everyday scenes.

halt¹ (hôlt), *v.* stop for a time, as in marching.

[< n.] —n. 1. a temporary stop. 2. **call a halt,** order a stop. [< F *halte* < G *halt* < *halten* to stop]

halt[2] (hôlt), v. 1. be in doubt; hesitate; waver: *speak in a halting manner.* 2. be faulty or imperfect: *a halting line of verse.* 3. *Archaic.* be lame. —*adj. Archaic.* lame. —*n. Archaic.* lameness. [OE *healt,* adj.] —**halt'ing·ly,** *adv.* —**halt'ing·ness,** *n.*

hal·ter (hôl'tər), n. 1. rope, strap, etc., for leading or tying an animal. 2. rope for hanging a person; noose. 3. death by hanging. 4. an abbreviated shirt for women which fastens behind the neck and across the back. —v. put a halter on; tie with a halter. [OE *hælftre*]

halve (hav; häv), v., **halved, halv·ing.** 1. share equally: *halve expenses on a trip.* 2. reduce to half: *halve the time of doing the work.* [< *half*]

halves (havz; hävz), n. 1. pl. of **half.** 2. **by halves,** a. partly. b. in a half-hearted way. 3. **go halves,** share equally.

hal·yard (hal'yərd), n. *Naut.* rope or tackle used on a ship to raise or lower a sail, yard, flag, etc. Also, **halliard.** [ME *hallyer* < HALE[2]]

ham (ham), n. 1. salted and smoked meat from the upper part of a hog's hind leg. 2. the upper part of an animal's hind leg, used for food. 3. Often, **hams.** back of the thigh; thigh and buttock. 4. part of the leg back of the knee. 5. *Am., Slang.* a poor actor or performer. 6. *Am., Slang.* an amateur radio operator. [OE *hamm*]

Ham (ham), n. *Bible.* the second son of Noah.

ham·a·dry·ad (ham'ə·drī'əd; -ad), n. *Gk. Myth.* a wood nymph supposed to live and die with the tree she dwelt in; dryad. [< L < Gk. *Hamadryas* < *hama* together (with) + *drys* tree]

ham·burg (ham'bėrg), n. *Am.* hamburger.

Ham·burg (ham'bėrg), n. city in NW Germany, on the Elbe River.

ham·burg·er (ham'bėr·gər), n. *Am.* 1. ground beef, usually shaped into round, flat cakes and fried or broiled. 2. *Colloq.* sandwich made with this meat. [< G, pertaining to *Hamburg*]

Hamburg steak, hamburg steak, *Am.* hamburger (def. 1).

Ham·il·ton (ham'əl·tən), n. 1. Alexander, 1757–1804, American statesman, the first secretary of the treasury. 2. city in SE Canada. 3. capital of Bermuda.

Ham·it·ic (ham·it'ik; hə·mit'-), *adj.* of or having to do with a group of languages in N and E Africa, including ancient Egyptian, Berber, Ethiopian, etc.

ham·let (ham'lit), n. a small village. [< OF *hamelet,* dim. of *hamel* village < Gmc.; akin to HOME]

Ham·let (ham'lit), n. 1. one of Shakespeare's greatest tragedies, first printed in 1603. 2. the principal character in this play.

Ham·mar·skjöld (ham'ər·shěld'), n. Dag, born 1905, Swedish statesman; Secretary General of the United Nations since April 10, 1953.

ham·mer (ham'ər), n. 1. tool with a metal head and a handle, used to drive nails and beat metal into shape. 2. anything shaped or used like a hammer: a. mallet or gavel used by an auctioneer. b. cock of a gun or pistol. —v. 1. drive, hit, or work with a hammer. 2. beat into shape with a hammer. 3. fasten by using a hammer. 4. hit again and again. 5. force by many efforts. 6. work out with much effort. [OE *hamor*] —**ham'mer·er,** n. —**ham'mer·less,** *adj.* —**ham'mer·like',** *adj.*

hammer and sickle, symbol of a sickle and hammer crossed, used on the flag of the Soviet Union since 1923. The two elements represent the farmer and the laborer.

ham·mer·head (ham'ər·hed'), n. a fierce shark whose wide head looks somewhat like a double-headed hammer.

hammer lock, *Wrestling.* a hold in which an opponent's arm is twisted and held behind his back.

ham·mock (ham'ək), n. a hanging bed or couch made of canvas, netted cord, etc. [< Sp. *hamaca* < Carib] —**ham'mock·like',** *adj.*

ham·per[1] (ham'pər), v. hold back; hinder. [ME *hampre(n)*] —**Syn.** restrain, restrict.

ham·per[2] (ham'pər), n. a large basket, usually with a cover. [var. of *hanaper* < OF, < *hanap* cup < Gmc.]

Hamp·ton Roads (hamp'tən), a southern extension of Chesapeake Bay.

ham·string (ham'string'), n., v., **-strung** or (*Rare*) **-stringed, -string·ing.** —n. 1. one of the tendons at the back of the knee in man. 2. the great tendon at the back of the hock of a four-footed animal. —v. 1. cripple by cutting the hamstring. 2. destroy activity, efficiency, etc., of.

Han·cock (han'kok), n. John, 1737–1793, American statesman, the first signer of the Declaration of Independence.

hand (hand), n. 1. the end part of an arm; part that a person grasps and holds things with. 2. anything resembling a hand in shape, appearance, or use. 3. a hired worker who uses his hands: *a farm hand.* 4. Often, **hands.** possession; control: *this is no longer in my hands.* 5. part or share in doing something: *he had no hand in the matter.* 6. side: *at her left hand stood two men.* 7. source: *she heard the story at second hand.* 8. style of handwriting: *he writes in a clear hand.* 9. a person's signature. 10. skill; ability. 11. person, with reference to action, skill, or ability: *she is a great hand at thinking up new games.* 12. round of applause or clapping: *the crowd gave the winner a big hand.* 13. promise of marriage. 14. measure used in giving the height of horses, etc.; breadth of a hand; 4 inches. 15. cards held by a player in one round of a card game. 16. one round of a card game. 17. player in a card game. 18. **at hand,** a. within reach; near; close. b. ready. 19. **bear or give a hand,** help. 20. **by hand,** by using the hands, not machinery. 21. **change hands,** pass from one person to another. 22. **hand in hand,** a. holding hands. b. together. 23. **in hand,** a. under control. b. in possession. c. going along; being done. 24. **lay hands on,** a. seize; take; get. b. arrest. c. attack; harm. d. bless by touching with the hands. 25. **on hand,** a. within reach; near; close. b. ready. c. *Am.* present. 26. **on the other hand,** considering the other side; from the opposite point of view. 27. **out of hand,** a. beyond control. b. at once. c. finished; done with. —v. 1. give with the hand; pass; pass along: *please hand me the butter.* 2. help with the hand: *the polite boy handed the lady into her car.* —*adj.* of, for, by, or in the hand. [OE] —**hand'less,** *adj.*

hand·bag (hand'bag'), n. 1. a woman's small bag for money, keys, cosmetics, etc. 2. a small traveling bag to hold clothes, etc.

hand·ball (hand'bôl'), n. 1. game played by hitting a small ball against a wall with the hand. 2. ball used in this game.

hand·bar·row (hand'bar'ō), n. frame with two handles at each end by which it is carried.

hand·bill (hand'bil'), n. a printed announcement to be handed out to people.

hand·book (hand'bŭk'), n. 1. a small book of reference; manual. 2. guidebook for tourists. 3. book for recording bets.

hand·breadth (hand'bredth'), n. breadth of a hand, used as a measure. It varies from 2½ to 4 inches. Also, **hand's-breadth.**

hand·cart (hand'kärt'), n. a small cart pulled or pushed by hand.

hand·cuff (hand'kuf'), n. Usually, **handcuffs.** device to keep a person from using his hands, usually one of a pair of metal clasps joined by a short chain and fastened around the wrists. —v. put handcuffs on.

Handcuffs and key

-handed, *suffix.* 1. having a hand or hands. 2. having a certain kind or number of hands, as in *left-handed.* 3. using a certain number of hands: *a two-handed stroke.*

Han·del (han'dəl), n. George Frederick, 1685–1759, German musical composer.

hand·ful (hand'fŭl), n., pl. **-fuls.** 1. as much

or as many as the hand can hold. 2. a small number or quantity. 3. *Colloq.* person or thing that is hard to manage.

hand·i·cap (han'di·kap), *n., v.,* –capped, –cap·ping. —*n.* 1. race, contest, game, etc., in which the better contestants are given certain disadvantages, or the poorer ones certain advantages, so that all have an equal chance to win. 2. disadvantage or advantage given. 3. something that puts a person at a disadvantage; hindrance. —*v.* 1. give a handicap to. 2. put at a disadvantage; hinder. [for *hand in cap;* appar. with ref. to an old game] —hand'i·cap'per, *n.*

hand·i·craft (han'di·kraft; –kräft), *n.* 1. skill with the hands. 2. trade or art requiring skill with the hands. [alter. of *handcraft,* patterned after *handiwork*] —hand'i·crafts'man, *n.* —hand'i·crafts'man·ship, *n.*

hand·i·work (han'di·wêrk'), *n.* 1. work done with the hands. 2. work that a person has done himself. 3. result of a person's action. [OE *handgeweorc* handwork]

hand·ker·chief (hang'kər·chif), *n.* 1. a soft, square piece of cloth used for wiping the nose, face, eyes, etc. 2. piece of cloth worn over the head or around the neck; kerchief.

han·dle (han'dəl), *n., v.,* –dled, –dling. —*n.* 1. part of a thing made to be held or grasped by the hand. 2. chance; opportunity; occasion: *a handle for gossip.* —*v.* 1. touch, feel, hold, or move with the hand; use the hands on. 2. manage; direct; control. 3. behave or act when handled: *this car handles easily.* 4. deal with; treat. 5. *Am.* deal in; trade in: *that store handles meat and groceries.* [OE, < *hand*] —han'dled, *adj.* —han'dle·less, *adj.*

handle bar. Often, **handle bars.** the bar, usually curved, in front of the rider, by which a bicycle, etc., is guided.

han·dler (han'dlər), *n.* 1. person or thing that handles. 2. person who helps to train a boxer or who acts as his second.

hand·made (hand'mād'), *adj.* made by hand, not by machinery; not machine-made.

hand·maid (hand'mād'), **hand·maid·en** (–mād'ən), *n.* 1. a female servant. 2. a female attendant.

hand organ, a large music box that is made to play tunes by turning a crank.

hand·out (hand'out'), *n. Am., Slang.* portion of food handed out.

hand·picked (hand'pikt'), *adj.* 1. picked by hand. 2. carefully selected. 3. unfairly selected.

hand·rail (hand'rāl'), *n.* railing used as a guard or support on a stairway, platform, etc.

hand·saw (hand'sô'), *n.* saw used with one hand.

hand's-breadth (handz'bredth'), *n.* handbreadth.

hand·sel (han'səl), *n.* gift made at New Year's or on entering a new job, house, etc. Also, hansel. [OE *handselen* giving of the hand (i.e., to confirm a bargain)]

hand·shake (hand'shāk'), *n.* a clasping and shaking each other's hands in friendship.

hand·some (han'səm), *adj.* –som·er, –som·est. 1. good-looking; pleasing in appearance. We usually say that a man is handsome, but that a woman is pretty or beautiful. 2. fairly large; considerable: *a handsome sum of money.* 3. generous: *a handsome gift.* [ME, easy to handle, ready at hand < *hand* + –*some*¹] —hand'some·ly, *adv.* —hand'some·ness, *n.*

hand·spike (hand'spīk'), *n.* bar used as a lever, esp. on a ship.

hand·spring (hand'spring'), *n.* spring or leap in which a person turns his heels over his head while balancing on one or both hands.

hand-to-hand (hand'tə·hand'), *adj.* close together; at close quarters.

hand-to-mouth (hand'tə·mouth'), *adj.* not providing for the future; not thrifty.

[han]d·work (hand'wêrk'), *n.* work done by [han]d, not by machinery.

[han]d·writ·ing (hand'rīt'ing), *n.* 1. writing [by] hand; writing with pen, pencil, etc. 2. manner or style of writing.

hand·y (han'di), *adj.,* hand·i·er, hand·i·est. 1. easy to reach or use; saving work; convenient. 2. skillful with the hands. 3. easy to handle or manage. —hand'i·ly, *adv.* —hand'i·ness, *n.*

handy man, man who does odd jobs.

Han·ford (han'fərd), *n.* community in S Washington, important industrial center for atomic research.

hang (hang), *v.,* **hung** or (*esp. for execution or suicide*) **hanged, hang·ing,** *n.* —*v.* 1. fasten or be fastened to something above. 2. fasten or be fastened so as to swing or turn freely: *hang a door on its hinges.* 3. put to death by hanging with a rope around the neck. 4. die by hanging. 5. cover or decorate with things that hang: *hang a window with curtains.* 6. bend down; droop: *he hung his head in shame.* 7. fasten in position. 8. attach (paper, etc.) to walls. 9. depend. 10. hold fast; cling. 11. be doubtful or undecided; hesitate; waver. 12. *Am.* keep (a jury) from making a decision or reaching a verdict. One member can hang a jury by refusing to agree with the others. 13. loiter; linger. 14. hover. 15. hang on, a. hold tightly (to). b. be unwilling to let go, stop, or leave. c. depend on. d. consider or listen to very carefully. 16. hang up, a. put on a hook, peg, etc. b. put a telephone receiver back in place. —*n.* 1. way that a thing hangs. 2. *Am., Colloq.* way of using or doing; idea; meaning. 3. a trifle: *not care a hang.* [OE *hangian*] —hang'a·ble, *adj.* ➤ hanged, hung. In formal English the principal parts of *hang* when referring to the death penalty are *hang, hanged, hanged,* the archaic forms kept alive by legal phrases such as "hanged by the neck until dead"; in other senses they are *hang, hung, hung:* murderers are *hanged,* pictures are *hung.* Informal usage does not keep this distinction.

hang·ar (hang'ər), *n.* 1. shed for airplanes or airships. 2. shed. [< F, ? < Gmc.]

hang·bird (hang'bêrd'), *n. Am.* any bird that builds a hanging nest, esp. the Baltimore oriole.

Hang·chow (hang'chou'), *n.* seaport in E China.

hang·dog (hang'dôg'; –dog'), *adj.* ashamed; sneaking; degraded.

hang·er (hang'ər), *n.* 1. person who hangs things: *a paper hanger.* 2. tool or machine that hangs things. 3. thing on which something else is hung: *a coat hanger.* 4. kind of short sword.

hang·er-on (hang'ər·on'; –ôn'), *n., pl.* hang·ers-on. 1. follower; dependent. 2. an undesirable follower. 3. person who often goes to a place.

hang·ing (hang'ing), *n.* 1. death by hanging with a rope around the neck. 2. Often, **hangings.** thing that hangs from a wall, bed, etc. Curtains and draperies are hangings. —*adj.* 1. deserving to be punished by hanging. 2. fastened to something above. 3. leaning over or down. 4. located on a height or steep slope. 5. directed downward; downcast.

hang·man (hang'mən), *n., pl.* –men. man who puts criminals to death by hanging them.

hang·nail (hang'nāl'), *n.* bit of skin that hangs partly loose near a fingernail.

hang·out (hang'out'), *n. Slang.* 1. place lived in or frequented. 2. a rendezvous, esp. for criminals.

hang·o·ver (hang'ō'vər), *n. Am.* 1. *Colloq.* something that remains from an earlier time or condition. 2. *Slang.* condition the morning after drinking too much alcoholic liquor.

hank (hangk), *n.* 1. coil; loop. 2. skein. [appar. < Scand. *hǫnk*]

han·ker (hang'kər), *v.* wish; crave. —hank'er·er, *n.* —han'ker·ing, *n.*

Han·kow (han'kou'), *n.* city in E China, on the Yangtze River.

Han·ni·bal (han'ə·bəl), *n.* 247–183? B.C., a Carthaginian general who invaded Italy.

Ha·noi (hä·noi'), *n.* capital of the northern zone of Viet Nam; formerly the capital of French Indo-China.

Han·o·ver (han'ō·vər; han'ə–), *n.* 1. city in NW Germany. 2. the English royal house from 1714 to 1901. —Han·o·ve·ri·an (han'ō·vir'i·ən; han'ə–), *adj., n.*

hanse (hans), *n.* medieval guild of a town. [< OF < OHG *hansa* band, MHG *hanse* merchants' guild]

Han·se·at·ic League (han'si·at'ik), a medieval league of towns in Germany and nearby countries for the promotion and protection of commerce.

han·sel (han'səl), *n.* handsel.

han·som (han'səm), *n.* a two-wheeled cab for two passengers, drawn by one horse, with the driver on a seat high up behind the cab. [from name of early designer of such cabs]

hap (hap), *n., v.,* **happed, hap·ping.** *Archaic.* —*n.* chance; luck. —*v.* happen. [< Scand. *happ*]

hap·haz·ard (*n.* hap'haz'ərd; *adj., adv.* hap'-haz'ərd), *n.* chance. —*adj.* random; not planned: *haphazard answers.* —*adv.* by chance; at random. —**hap'haz'ard·ly,** *adv.* —**hap'haz'-ard·ness,** *n.*

hap·less (hap'lis), *adj.* unlucky; unfortunate. —**hap'less·ly,** *adv.* —**hap'less·ness,** *n.*

hap·ly (hap'li), *adv. Archaic.* by chance.

hap·pen (hap'ən), *v.* 1. take place; occur: *nothing happens here.* 2. be or take place by chance: *accidents will happen.* 3. have the fortune; chance: *I happened to sit by Mary.* 4. be done (to): *something has happened to this lock.* 5. happen on, **a.** meet. **b.** find. [ME *happene(n)* < HAP]

hap·pen·ing (hap'ən·ing), *n.* thing that happens; event; occurrence.

hap·py (hap'i), *adj.,* **-pi·er, -pi·est.** 1. feeling or showing pleasure and joy; glad. 2. lucky; fortunate: *by a happy chance, I found the money.* 3. clever and fitting; apt; successful and suitable. [ME, < HAP] —**hap'pi·ly,** *adv.* —**hap'pi·ness,** *n.* —Syn. 1. pleased, contented, joyful, delighted. 2. favorable. 3. appropriate, felicitous.

hap·py-go-luck·y (hap'i·gō·luk'i), *adj.* taking things easily; trusting to luck. —*adv.* by mere chance.

Haps·burg (haps'bėrg), *n.* a German princely family, prominent since about 1100.

har·a·ki·ri (här'ə·kir'i; hä'rə-), **har·a·kar·i** (-kar'i; -kä'ri), *n.* suicide by ripping open the abdomen with a knife, the national form of honorable suicide in Japan. Also, **hari-kari.** [< Jap., belly cut]

ha·rangue (hə·rang'), *n., v.,* **-rangued, -rangu·ing.** —*n.* 1. a noisy speech. 2. a long, pompous speech. —*v.* 1. address in a harangue. 2. deliver a harangue. [< OF *arenge* < Gmc.] —**ha·rangu'er,** *n.*

har·ass (har'əs; hə·ras'), *v.* 1. trouble by repeated attacks; harry. 2. disturb; worry; torment. [< F *harasser* < OF *harer* set a dog on] —**har'ass·er,** *n.* —**har'ass·ing·ly,** *adv.* —**har'ass·ment,** *n.* —Syn. 2. plague, bother, pester.

Har·bin (här'bēn'; -bin), *n.* city in C Manchuria.

har·bin·ger (här'bin·jər), *n.* one that goes ahead to announce another's coming; forerunner. —*v.* announce beforehand; announce. [< OF *herbergere* provider of shelter (hence, one who goes ahead), ult. < *herberge* lodging < Gmc.]

har·bor, *esp. Brit.* **har·bour** (här'bər), *n.* 1. place of shelter for ships and boats. 2. any place of shelter. —*v.* 1. give shelter to; give a place to hide: *a dog that harbors fleas.* 2. keep or nourish in the mind: *harbor unkind thoughts.* [OE *herebeorg* lodgings < *here* army + *beorg* shelter] —**har'bor·er,** *esp. Brit.* **har'bour·er,** *n.* —**har'bor·less,** *esp. Brit.* **har'bour·less,** *adj.* —Syn. *n.* 2. refuge, retreat.

har·bor·age, *esp. Brit.* **har·bour·age** (här'bər·ij), *n.* 1. shelter for ships and boats. 2. any shelter.

harbor master, officer who has charge of a port and enforces the rules respecting it.

hard (härd), *adj.* 1. solid and firm to the touch; not soft. 2. firmly formed; tight: *a hard knot.* 3. needing much ability, effort, or time; difficult: *a hard problem.* 4. causing much pain, trouble, care, etc.; severe: *a hard illness.* 5. stern; unfeeling: *be hard on a person.* 6. not pleasant; harsh: *a hard face.* 7. *Am., Colloq.* bad; dis-

reputable. 8. stingy. 9. acting or done with energy, persistence, etc.: *a hard worker.* 10. containing mineral salts that interfere with the action of soap: *hard water.* 11. *U.S.* containing much alcohol: *hard liquor.* 12. *Phonet.* pronounced as an explosive sound, not as a fricative or an affricate. The *c* and *g* in *corn* and *get* are "hard"; in *city* and *gem* they are "soft." 13. **hard of hearing,** somewhat deaf. 14. **hard up,** *Colloq.* needing money or anything very badly. —*adv.* 1. so as to be hard, solid, or firm: *frozen hard.* 2. firmly; tightly: *hold hard.* 3. with difficulty: *breathe hard.* 4. so as to cause trouble, pain, care, etc.; harshly; severely: *taxes that bear hard upon us.* 5. with effort or energy: *try hard.* 6. close; near: *the house stands hard by the bridge.* 7. *Naut.* to the extreme limit; fully. [OE *heard*] —**hard'ness,** *n.* —Syn. *adj.* 1. rigid. 3. arduous, laborious, burdensome. 5. strict.

hard-bit·ten (härd'bit'ən), *adj.* stubborn; unyielding; dogged.

hard-boiled (härd'boild'), *adj.* 1. boiled until hard. 2. *Colloq.* not easily influenced by the feelings. 3. *Slang.* hard; rough; tough.

hard coal, anthracite.

hard core, the permanent or most persistent part of any thing or group; central or vital part. —**hard-core** (härd'kôr'; -kōr'), *adj.*

hard·en (här'dən), *v.* 1. make or become hard. 2. make or become capable of endurance. 3. make or become unfeeling or pitiless. 4. strengthen. —**hard'en·er,** *n.* —Syn. 1. solidify. 2. discipline, accustom, brace. 4. toughen.

hard goods, machinery, vehicles, appliances, and other heavy goods. —**hard-goods** (härd'-gŭdz), *adj.*

hard-head·ed (härd'hed'id), *adj.* 1. not easily excited or deceived. 2. stubborn; obstinate. —**hard'-head'ed·ly,** *adv.* —**hard'-head'ed·ness,** *n.* —Syn. 1. practical, shrewd.

hard-heart·ed (härd'här'tid), *adj.* without pity; cruel; unfeeling. —**hard'-heart'ed·ly,** *adv.* —**hard'-heart'ed·ness,** *n.*

hard-hit·ting (härd'hit'ing), *adj. Colloq.* vigorous; aggressive; powerful.

har·di·hood (här'di·hŭd), *n.* boldness; daring.

Har·ding (här'ding), *n.* Warren Gamaliel, 1865–1923, the 29th president of the United States, 1921–1923.

hard·ly (härd'li), *adv.* 1. only just; barely: *he had hardly reached there, when it began to snow.* 2. not quite: *hardly strong enough.* 3. almost not: *hardly ever.* 4. probably not: *he will hardly come now.* 5. with trouble or effort: *money hardly earned.* 6. harshly; severely: *deal hardly with a person.* ▶ **hardly.** In writing there is danger of falling into a concealed double negative when using *hardly.* In formal and informal English a sentence like "For the most part our college paper contains hardly nothing" should read "For the most part our college paper contains *hardly anything.*"

hard palate, the front, bony part of the roof of the mouth.

hard·pan (härd'pan'), *n.* 1. hard, firm, underlying earth. 2. *Am.* a solid foundation; hard, underlying reality.

hard-pressed (härd'prest'), *adj. Colloq.* under severe pressure; in difficulty.

hard·ship (härd'ship), *n.* something hard to bear; hard condition of living.

hard·tack (härd'tak'), *n.* a very hard, dry biscuit, eaten by sailors.

hard·top (härd'top'), *adj.* of a passenger car, having a nonfolding top but maximum window space. —*n.* a passenger car of this design.

hard·ware (härd'wār'), *n.* articles made from metal, as locks, hinges, screws, tools, etc.

hard·wood (härd'wŭd'), *n.* 1. any hard, compact wood. 2. in forestry, any tree that has broad leaves or does not have needles. 3. wood of such a tree, as the oak or maple.

har·dy (här'di), *adj.,* **-di·er, -di·est.** 1. able to bear hard treatment, fatigue, etc.; strong; robust. 2. able to withstand the cold of winter in the open air: *hardy plants.* 3. bold; daring. 4. too bold; rash. [< OF *hardi,* pp. of *hardir* **harden**

āge, cāre, fär; ēqual, tėrm; īce; ōpen, ôrder; pŭt, rüle, ūse; tн, then; ə=a in about.

< Gmc.] —har'di·ly, adv. —har'di·ness, n. —Syn. 1. hale, hearty. 3. courageous, intrepid.

Har·dy (här'di), n. Thomas, 1840–1928, English novelist and poet.

hare (hãr), n., pl. **hares** or (esp. collectively) **hare**. 1. a gnawing animal very much like a rabbit but larger, having long ears, long hind legs, a short tail, and a divided upper lip. 2. a rabbit. [OE hara] —hare'like', adj.

hare·bell (hãr'bel'), n. a slender plant with blue, bell-shaped flowers; bluebell.

hare·brained (hãr'brānd'), adj. giddy; heedless; reckless.

hare·lip (hãr'lip'), n. a congenital deformity caused when parts of the lip fail to grow together before birth. —hare'lipped', adj.

har·em (hãr'əm), n. 1. part of a Mohammedan house where the women live. 2. its occupants; the wives, female relatives, female servants, etc., of a Mohammedan household. [< Ar. harim forbidden]

har·i·cot (har'ə·kō), n. string bean. [< Mex. (Nahuatl) ayecotli]

har·i·kar·i (har'i·kar'i; hä'ri·kä'ri), n. hara-kiri.

hark (härk), v. 1. listen. 2. **hark back**, go back; turn back. [ME herkien]

hark·en (här'kən), v. hearken. [OE heorcnian] —hark'en·er, n.

Har·lem (här'ləm), n. part of New York City where many Negroes live.

har·le·quin (här'lə·kwin; -kin), n. 1. Often, **Harlequin**. character in comedy and pantomime who is usually masked, has a costume of varied colors, and carries a wooden sword. 2. a mischievous person; buffoon. —adj. varied in color; many-colored. [< F; OF var. of Herlequin < ME Herle King King Herla (mythical figure); modern meaning in French is from Ital. arlec-chino < F Harlequin]

har·lot (här'lət), n. prostitute. [< OF, vagabond]

har·lot·ry (här'lət·ri), n. prostitution.

harm (härm), n. 1. hurt; damage. 2. evil; wrong. —v. damage; injure; hurt. [OE hearm] —harm'er, n.

harm·ful (härm'fəl), adj. causing harm; injurious; hurtful. —harm'ful·ly, adv. —harm'ful·ness, n. —Syn. detrimental, deleterious, pernicious.

harm·less (härm'lis), adj. causing no harm; that would not harm anyone or anything. —harm'less·ly, adv. —harm'less·ness, n. —Syn. innocuous, inoffensive.

har·mon·ic (här·mon'ik), adj. 1. Music. having to do with harmony. 2. musical. 3. Physics. indicating a series of oscillations accompanying a fundamental frequency. —n. a fainter and higher tone heard along with the main tone; overtone. [< L < Gk. harmonikos harmonic, musical. See HARMONY.] —har·mon'i·cal·ly, adv.

har·mon·i·ca (här·mon'ə·kə), n. Am. a small, oblong musical instrument with metal reeds, played by the mouth; mouth organ.

Harmonica

har·mon·ics (här·mon'iks), n. science of musical sounds.

har·mo·ni·ous (här·mō'ni·əs), adj. 1. agreeing in feelings, ideas, or actions; getting along well together: play together in a harmonious group. 2. arranged so that the parts are orderly or pleasing; going well together: harmonious colors. 3. sweet-sounding; musical. —har·mo'ni·ous·ly, adv. —har·mo'ni·ous·ness, n. —Syn. 1. peaceable, cordial, amicable. 2. congruous, consonant, consistent. 3. melodious. —Ant. 1. antagonistic, unfriendly, hostile.

har·mo·ni·um (här·mō'ni·əm), n. a small organ with metal reeds.

har·mo·nize (här'mə·nīz), v., -nized, -niz·ing. ring into harmony or agreement. 2. be in ony or agreement: the colors in the room ionized. 3. Music. add tones to (a melody) to e successive chords. —har'mo·ni·za'tion, n. r'mo·niz'er, n.

har·mo·ny (här'mə·ni), n., pl. -nies. 1. agreement of feeling, ideas, or actions; getting along well together: work in perfect harmony. 2. an orderly or pleasing arrangement of parts; going well together: harmony of colors in a picture. 3. Music. a. sounding together of notes in a chord. b. study of chords and of relating them to successive chords. [< F < L < Gk. harmonia concord, a joining < harmos joint] —Syn. 1. unity, friendship, peace. 2. congruity.

har·ness (här'nis), n. 1. combination of leather straps, bands, and other pieces used to connect a horse or other animal to a carriage, wagon, plow, etc. 2. Archaic. armor for a knight, soldier, or horse. 3. **in harness**, in or at one's regular work. —v. 1. put harness on. 2. cause to produce power. 3. Archaic. put armor on. [< OF harneis < Scand.] —har'ness·er, n. —harness·less, adj. —har'ness·like', adj.

Har·old II (har'əld), 1022?–1066, the last Saxon king of England, defeated by William the Conqueror in 1066.

harp (härp), n. Music. instrument with strings set in a triangular frame, played by plucking the strings with the fingers. —v. 1. Music. play on a harp. 2. **harp on**, keep on tiresomely talking or writing about; refer continually to. [OE hearpe] —harp'er, n. —harp'ist, n. —harp'like', adj.

har·poon (här·pün'), n. a barbed spear with a rope tied to it, used for catching whales and other sea animals. —v. strike, catch, or kill with a harpoon. [(? < Du.) < F harpon < L harpe sickle, hook < Gk.] —har·poon'er, n. —harpoon'like', adj.

harp·si·chord (härp'sə·kôrd), n. Music. a stringed instrument like a piano, used from about 1550 to 1750. [< obs. F harpechorde < harpe harp (< Gmc.) + chorde CHORD[2]]

Har·py (här'pi), n., pl. -pies. 1. Gk. Legend. any of several filthy, greedy monsters having women's heads and birds' bodies, wings, and claws. 2. **harpy**, a very greedy person; person who preys upon others. [< L < Gk. harpyia, prob. akin to harpazein snatch]

har·que·bus (här'kwə·bəs), n. an old form of portable gun, used before muskets. Also, arquebus. [< F < Ital. < Du. haakbus, lit., hook gun]

har·ri·dan (har'ə·dən), n. a bad-tempered, disreputable old woman.

har·ri·er[1] (har'i·ər), n. 1. a small hound of the kind used to hunt hares. 2. a cross-country runner. [appar. < hare]

har·ri·er[2] (har'i·ər), n. 1. person who harries. 2. Am. hawk that preys on small animals.

Har·ri·man (har'ə·mən), n. W(illiam) Averell, born 1891, American political leader, governor of New York since 1954.

Har·ris (har'is), n. Joel Chandler, 1848–1908, American author.

Har·ris·burg (har'is·berg), n. capital of Pennsylvania, in the S part.

Har·ri·son (har'ə·sən), n. 1. Benjamin, 1833–1901, the 23rd president of the United States, 1889–1893. 2. his grandfather, William Henry, 1773–1841, American general and ninth president of the United States, in 1841.

har·row (har'ō), n. a heavy frame with iron teeth or upright disks, used on plowed fields for breaking up clods, covering seeds, etc. —v. 1. draw a harrow over (land, etc.). 2. hurt; wound. 3. arouse uncomfortable feelings in; distress; torment. [ME harwe] —har'row·er, n. —har'row·ing, adj. —har'row·ing·ly, adv.

har·ry (har'i), v., -ried, -ry·ing. 1. raid and rob with violence. 2. keep troubling; worry; torment. [OE hergian < here army]

harsh (härsh), adj. 1. rough to the touch, taste, eye, or ear; sharp and unpleasant. 2. without pity; cruel; severe. 3. rugged; bleak. [var. of ME harsk < Scand. (Dan.) harsk rancid] —harsh'ly, adv. —harsh'ness, n. —Syn. 1. grating, rasping, acrid, sour, inharmonious, discordant, strident, raucous. 2. unfeeling, unkind.

hart (härt), n., pl. **harts** or (esp. collectively) **hart**. 1. a male red deer after its fifth year. 2. a male deer; stag. [OE heorot]

Harte (härt), n. (Francis) Bret, 1839–1902, American writer of short stories.

har·te·beest (här′tə·bēst′; härt′bēst′), *n.*, *pl.* –beests or (*esp. collectively*) –beest. a large, swift African antelope with ringed, curved horns bent backward at the tips. [< Afrikaans, hart beast]

Hart·ford (härt′fərd), *n.* capital of Connecticut, in the C part.

harts·horn (härts′hôrn′), *n.* 1. ammonia dissolved in water. 2. smelling salts.

har·um-scar·um (hār′əm·skâr′əm), *adj.* reckless; rash. —*adv.* recklessly; wildly. —*n.* 1. a reckless person. 2. reckless behavior. [appar. < *hare* frighten + *scare*]

har·vest (här′vist), *n.* 1. a reaping and gathering in of grain and other food crops, usually in the late summer or early autumn. 2. time or season when grain, fruit, etc., are gathered in. 3. one season's yield of any natural product; crop. 4. result; consequences. —*v.* gather in and bring home for use. [OE *hærfest*]

har·vest·er (här′vis·tər), *n.* 1. person who works in a harvest field; reaper. 2. *Am.* machine for harvesting crops, esp. grain.

har·vest·man (här′vist·mən), *n.*, *pl.* –men. 1. man who harvests. 2. daddy-longlegs.

harvest moon, full moon at harvest time or about September 23.

Har·vey (här′vi), *n.* William, 1578–1657, English physician who discovered the circulation of the blood.

has (haz), *v.* 3rd pers. sing. pres. indic. of have.

has-been (haz′bin′), *n. Colloq.* person or thing whose best days are past.

hash (hash), *n.* 1. mixture of cooked meat, potatoes, etc., chopped into small pieces and fried or baked. 2. mixture; jumble. 3. mess; muddle. 4. *Am.*, *Colloq.* meal or meals. [< v.] —*v.* 1. chop into small pieces. 2. mess; muddle. [< F *hacher* < *hache* ax]

hash·ish, hash·eesh (hash′ēsh), *n.* the dried flowers, top leaves, and tender parts of Indian hemp, used in the Orient for its narcotic effect. [< Ar. *hashish* dried hemp leaves]

has·n't (haz′ənt), has not.

hasp (hasp; häsp), *n.* clasp or fastening for a door, window, trunk, box, etc., esp. one that fits over a staple or into a hole and is fastened by a peg, padlock, etc. [var. of OE *hæpse*]

has·sle (has′əl), *n.* struggle; contest. [appar. < Southern U.S. dial. *hassle* pant, breathe noisily (cf. E dial. *hussle*, same meaning), frequentative of E dial. *hoose* cough, wheeze; related to *wheeze*]

has·sock (has′ək), *n.* 1. a thick cushion to rest the feet on, sit on, or kneel on. 2. tuft or bunch of coarse grass. [OE *hassuc* coarse grass]

hast (hast), *v. Archaic.* 2nd pers. sing. pres. indic. of have.

haste (hāst), *n.*, *v.*, hast·ed, hast·ing. —*n.* 1. a trying to be quick; hurrying: *the king's business required haste.* 2. quickness without thought or care: *haste makes waste.* 3. in haste, a. in a hurry; quickly. b. without careful thought; rashly. 4. make haste, hurry; be quick. —*v. Poetic.* hasten. [< OF < Gmc.] —Syn. *n.* 1. speed.

has·ten (hās′ən), *v.* 1. cause to be quick; speed; hurry: *hasten everyone off to bed.* 2. be quick; go fast: *hasten to explain, hasten to a place.* —has′ten·er, *n.* —Syn. 1. quicken, accelerate.

hast·y (hās′ti), *adj.*, hast·i·er, hast·i·est. 1. hurried; quick: *a hasty visit.* 2. not well thought out; rash: *a hasty decision.* 3. easily angered; quick-tempered. —hast′i·ly, *adv.* —hast′i·ness, *n.*

hasty pudding, 1. *Am.* mush made of corn meal. 2. *Brit.* mush made of flour or oatmeal.

hat (hat), *n.*, *v.*, hat·ted, hat·ting. —*n.* 1. a covering for the head, usually with a brim. 2. pass the hat, ask for contributions; take up a collection. —*v.* cover or furnish with a hat. [OE *hætt*] —hat′less, *adj.* —hat′like′, *adj.*

hat·band (hat′band′), *n.* band around the crown of a hat, just above the brim.

hatch¹ (hach), *v.* 1. bring forth (young) from an egg or eggs. 2. keep (an egg or eggs) warm

until the young come out. 3. come out from the egg: *three chickens hatched today.* 4. arrange; plan. 5. plan secretly; plot. —*n.* 1. act of hatching. 2. the brood hatched. [ME *hacche(n)*] —hatch′er, *n.* —Syn. *v.* 5. scheme, contrive.

hatch² (hach), *n.* 1. an opening in a ship's deck through which the cargo is put in. 2. an opening in the floor or roof of a building, etc. 3. a trap door covering such an opening. [OE *hæcc*]

hatch³ (hach), *v.* draw, cut, or engrave fine parallel lines on. [< F *hacher* chop, hatch. See HASH.]

hatch·er·y (hach′ər·i; hach′ri), *n.*, *pl.* –er·ies. place for hatching eggs of fish, hens, etc.

hatch·et (hach′it), *n.* 1. a small ax with a short handle, for use with one hand. 2. tomahawk. 3. bury the hatchet, *Am.* make peace. [< OF *hachette*, dim. of *hache* ax. See HASH.] —hatch′et·like′, *adj.*

hatch·ing (hach′ing), *n.* fine, parallel lines drawn, cut, or engraved close together.

hatch·ment (hach′mənt), *n.* in heraldry, a square tablet bearing the coat of arms of a dead person, usually placed diagonally.

hatch·way (hach′wā′), *n.* 1. an opening in the deck of a ship to the lower part. 2. a similar opening in a floor, roof, etc.

hate (hāt), *v.*, hat·ed, hat·ing, *n.* —*v.* 1. dislike very strongly: *do good to them that hate you.* 2. dislike: *I hate to study.* —*n.* 1. a strong dislike. 2. object of hatred. [OE *hatian*] —hat′a·ble, hate′a·ble, *adj.* —hat′er, *n.* —Syn. *v.* 1. detest, abhor, loathe, despise.

hate·ful (hāt′fəl), *adj.* 1. causing hate; to be hated. 2. feeling hate; showing hate. —hate′ful·ly, *adv.* —hate′ful·ness, *n.* —Syn. 1. detestable, odious.

hath (hath), *v. Archaic.* 3rd pers. sing. pres. indic. of have.

ha·tred (hā′trid), *n.* very strong dislike; hate. —Syn. loathing, aversion, animosity, ill will.

hat·ter (hat′ər), *n.* person who makes or sells hats.

hau·ber·geon (hô′bər·jən), *n.* habergeon.

hau·berk (hô′bėrk), *n.* a long coat of mail. [< OF *hauberc* < Gmc., lit., neck cover]

Hauberk

haugh·ty (hô′ti), *adj.*, –ti·er, –ti·est. 1. too proud of oneself and too scornful of others: *a haughty man.* 2. showing pride and scorn: *a haughty smile.* 3. *Archaic.* exalted; noble. [< *haut* or *haught* < F *haut* < L *altus* high; form infl. by OG *hauh* high] —haugh′ti·ly, *adv.* —haugh′ti·ness, *n.* —Syn. 1. arrogant, disdainful, contemptuous.

haul (hôl), *v.* 1. pull or drag with force: *haul logs to a mill with horses.* 2. haul up, *Naut.* a. turn a ship nearer to the direction of the wind. b. change the course of (a ship). 3. change; shift: *the wind hauled around to the east.* —*n.* 1. act of hauling; hard pull. 2. load hauled. 3. *Am.* distance that a load is hauled. 4. amount won, taken, etc., at one time; catch: *a good haul of fish.* [< F *haler* < Gmc. Doublet of HALE².] —haul′er, *n.*

haul·age (hôl′ij), *n.* 1. act of hauling. 2. force used in hauling. 3. charge made for hauling.

haunch (hônch; hänch), *n.* 1. part of the body around the hip; the hip. 2. a hind quarter of an animal. 3. leg and loin of a deer, sheep, etc., used for food. [< OF *hanche* < Gmc.]

haunt (hônt; hänt), *v.* 1. go often to; visit frequently: *ghosts were supposed to haunt the old house.* 2. be often with; come often to: *memories of his youth haunted the old man.* 3. stay habitually. —*n.* 1. Often, haunts. place frequently gone to or often visited: *a swimming pool is a favorite haunt of boys in summer.* 2. *Dial.* ghost. [< OF *hanter* < OE *hāmettan* shelter (cf. HOME).] —haunt′er, *n.* —haunt′ing·ly, *adv.*

haunt·ed (hôn′tid; hän′–), *adj.* visited or frequented by ghosts.

haut·boy (hō′boi; ō′–), *n.* oboe. [< F, < *haut* high + *bois* wood; with ref. to its high notes]

hau·teur (hō·tėr′; ō–), *n.* haughtiness; haughty manner or spirit. [< F, < *haut* high < L *altus*]

Ha·van·a (hə·van′ə), *n.* 1. capital of Cuba, on the NW coast. Also, *Spanish* Habana. 2. cigar made from Cuban tobacco.

have (hav; *unstressed* həv, əv), *v.*, *pres.* 1 have, 2 have or (*Archaic*) hast, 3 has or (*Archaic*) hath, *pl.* have; *pt. and pp.* had; *ppr.* hav·ing. 1. hold; possess; own: *I have a house in the country.* 2. cause to: *have him shut the door.* 3. be obliged: *men have to eat.* 4. obtain; receive; take; get: *have a seat.* 5. show by action: *have the courage to.* 6. experience: *have fun.* 7. engage in; carry on; perform: *have a talk with him.* 8. allow; permit: *he won't have any noise while he is reading.* 9. maintain; assert: *they will have it so.* 10. keep; retain: *he has the directions in mind.* 11. know; understand: *he has no Latin.* 12. hold in the mind: *have an idea.* 13. be in a certain relation to: *she has three brothers.* 14. *Colloq.* hold an advantage over: *you have him there.* 15. become the father or mother of. 16. *Have* is used with past participles to express completed action (the perfect tense): *they have come.* 17. have it in for, *Colloq.* have a grudge against; try to get revenge on. 18. have it out, fight or argue until a question is settled. 19. have on, wear. 20. have to do with, a. be connected with; be related to. b. be a companion, partner, or friend of; associate with. [OE *habban*]

ha·ven (hā′vən), *n.* 1. harbor; port. 2. place of shelter and safety. —*v.* shelter in a haven. [OE *hæfen*] —**ha′ven·less**, *adj.*

have-not (hav′not′), *n. Colloq.* person or country that has little or no property or wealth.

have·n't (hav′ənt), have not.

hav·er·sack (hav′ėr·sak), *n.* bag used by soldiers and hikers to carry food. [< F < LG *habersack* oat sack]

hav·oc (hav′ək), *n.*, *v.*, –ocked, –ock·ing. —*n.* 1. very great destruction or injury. 2. play havoc with; injure severely; ruin; destroy. —*v.* devastate. [< AF var. of OF *havot* plundering, devastation, esp. in phrase *crier havot* cry havoc < Gmc.] —**hav′ock·er**, *n.* —**Syn.** *n.* 1. wreck, ruin.

Ha·vre (hä′vər; –vrə), *n.* Le Havre.

haw¹ (hô), *n.* 1. the red berry of the hawthorn. 2. the hawthorn. [OE *haga*]

haw² (hô), *interj.*, *n.* a stammering sound between words. —*v.* make this sound; stammer.

haw³ (hô), *interj.* word of command to horses, oxen, etc., directing them to turn to the left. —*v.* turn to the left.

Ha·wai·i (hə·wī′ē; –wä′yə), *n.* 1. the Hawaiian Islands. 2. the largest of the Hawaiian Islands. —**Ha·wai′ian**, *adj.*, *n.*

Hawaiian Islands, an island group in the N Pacific, a Territory of the United States. *Capital:* Honolulu.

hawk¹ (hôk), *n.* 1. bird of prey with a strong hooked beak, large curved claws, short rounded wings, and a long tail. 2. bird of prey like a hawk; buzzard or kite. —*v.* hunt with trained hawks. [OE *hafoc*] —**hawk′er**, *n.* —**hawk′ing**, *n.* —**hawk′ish**, **hawk′like′**, *adj.*

Red-tailed hawk (ab. 2 ft. long)

hawk² (hôk), *v.* 1. carry (goods) about for sale as a street peddler does. 2. spread (a report) around. [< *hawker* peddler, prob. < MLG *hoker*. See HUCKSTER.] —**hawk′er**, *n.*

hawk³ (hôk), *v.* clear the throat noisily. —*n.* a noisy effort to clear the throat. [prob. imit.]

hawk-eyed (hôk′īd′), *adj.* having sharp eyes like a hawk.

hawk moth, a large moth with a long body [and] narrow wings.

hawks·bill turtle (hôks′bil′), **hawk's-** [bill], or **hawksbill**, *n.* a sea turtle whose [shell] is shaped like a hawk's beak and whose [horn]y plates furnish tortoise shell.

hawse (hôz; hôs), *n.* 1. part of a ship's bow having holes for hawsers or cables to pass through. 2. one of these holes. 3. space between the bow of a ship at anchor and her anchors. [< Scand. *hāls*]

hawse-hole (hôz′hōl′; hôs′–), *n.* hole in a ship's bow for a hawser to pass through.

haw·ser (hô′zər; –sər), *n.* a large rope or small cable, esp. one used for mooring or towing ships. [appar. < AF *hauceour* < OF *haucier* hoist, ult. < L *altus* high]

haw·thorn (hô′thôrn), *n.* a thorny shrub or tree with clusters of white, red, or pink blossoms and small, red berries called haws.

Haw·thorne (hô′thôrn), *n.* Nathaniel, 1804–1864, American author of novels and stories.

hay (hā), *n.* grass, alfalfa, clover, etc., cut and dried for use as food for cattle, horses, etc. —*v.* cut and dry grass, alfalfa, clover, etc., for hay. [OE *hēg*; akin to HEW]

hay·cock (hā′kok′), *n. Esp. Brit.* a small pile of hay in a field.

Hay·dn (hī′dən; hā′–), *n.* Franz Joseph, 1732–1809, Austrian composer.

Hayes (hāz), *n.* Rutherford B., 1822–1893, the 19th president of the United States, 1877–1881.

hay fever, disease like a cold, caused by the pollen of ragweed and other plants.

hay·field (hā′fēld′), *n.* field where grass, alfalfa, clover, etc., is grown or cut for hay.

hay·loft (hā′lôft′; –loft′), *n.* place in a stable or barn where hay is stored.

hay·mak·er (hā′māk′ər), *n.* 1. one who makes hay, esp. one who tosses and spreads hay to dry. 2. apparatus for drying and curing hay. 3. *Am.* a swinging, upward blow in a fight with fists, often wild but usually of considerable force.

hay·mow (hā′mou′), *n.* 1. hayloft. 2. heap of hay stored in a barn.

hay·seed (hā′sēd′), *n.* 1. seed shaken out of hay. 2. *U.S. Slang.* person from the country; farmer.

hay·stack (hā′stak′), *esp. Brit.* **hay·rick** (–rik′), *n.* a large pile of hay outdoors.

hay·wire (hā′wīr′), *n. Am.* wire used to tie up bales of hay. —*adj. Slang.* 1. in a mess; in utter confusion. 2. crazy; insane.

haz·ard (haz′ərd), *n.* 1. risk; danger; peril: *at all hazards.* 2. chance. 3. any obstruction on a golf course. 4. a dice game. —*v.* 1. take a chance with; risk; venture. 2. expose to risk. [< OF *hasard* < Ar. *az-zahr* the die] —**haz′ard·a·ble**, *adj.* —**haz′ard·er**, *n.* —**haz′ard·less**, *adj.* —**Syn.** *n.* 1. jeopardy. —**Ant.** *n.* 1. security, safety.

haz·ard·ous (haz′ər·dəs), *adj.* dangerous; risky; perilous. —**haz′ard·ous·ly**, *adv.* —**haz′ard·ous·ness**, *n.*

haze¹ (hāz), *n.* 1. a small amount of mist, smoke, dust, etc., in the air. 2. vagueness of the mind; slight confusion. [cf. E dial. *haze* to drizzle, be foggy]

haze² (hāz), *v.*, hazed, haz·ing. *Am.* in schools, universities, etc., force (a fellow student, esp. a freshman) to do unnecessary or ridiculous tasks; bully. [< OF *haser* irritate, annoy] —**haz′er**, *n.* —**haz′ing**, *n.*

ha·zel (hā′zəl), *n.* 1. shrub or small tree whose light-brown nuts are good to eat. 2. a light brown. —*adj.* 1. light-brown. 2. of or pertaining to the hazel. [OE *hæsel*]

ha·zel·nut (hā′zəl·nut′), *n.* nut of the hazel.

Haz·litt (haz′lit), *n.* William, 1778–1830, English critic and essayist.

ha·zy (hā′zi), *adj.*, –zi·er, –zi·est. 1. full of haze; misty; smoky: *hazy air.* 2. rather confused; vague; obscure: *hazy ideas.* —**ha′zi·ly**, *adv.* —**ha′zi·ness**, *n.*

H-bomb (āch′bom′), *n.* the hydrogen bomb.

he (hē; *unstressed* ē, i), *pron.*, *nom.*, he; *poss.*, his, of him, of his; *obj.*, him; *pl.nom.*, they; *poss.*, theirs, their, of them, of theirs; *obj.*, them; *n.*, *pl.* he's. —*pron.* 1. boy, man, or male animal spoken about or mentioned before. 2. anyone: *he who hesitates is lost.* —*n.* boy; man; male animal. [OE *hē*]

He, *Chem.* helium.

head (hed), *n.*, *pl.* heads (1–7, 9–28), head (*def. 8*), *adj.*, *v.* —*n.* **1.** the top part of the human body where the eyes, ears, and mouth are. **2.** the corresponding part of an animal's body. **3.** the top part of anything: *head of a pin.* **4.** the foremost part or end of anything; the front: *the head of a column of troops.* **5.** chief person; leader. **6.** position of head; chief authority; leadership. **7.** person: *the crowned heads of England.* **8.** one or ones; individual or individuals: *ten head of cattle.* **9.** anything rounded like a head: *head of lettuce.* **10.** hair covering the head. **11.** *Bot.* cluster of flowers in which the flowers or florets grow close together from the main stem. **12.** part of a boil or pimple where pus is about to break through the skin. **13.** the striking part of a tool or implement. **14.** *Music.* piece of skin stretched tightly over the end of a drum, tambourine, etc. **15.** either end of a barrel. **16.** the side of a coin that bears the more important figure. **17.** the higher or more important end of anything: *head of a lake.* **18.** headland. **19.** mind; understanding; intelligence; intellect: *have a good head for mathematics.* **20.** topic; point: *he arranged his speech under four main heads.* **21.** a decisive point; crisis; conclusion: *his sudden refusal brought matters to a head.* **22.** headline. **23.** strength or force gained little by little: *the movement for old-age pensions has gathered head.* **24.** *Mach.* part containing or holding one or more cutting implements. **25.** pressure of water, steam, etc. **26.** body of water at a height above a particular level. **27.** source of a river or stream. **28.** foam; froth. **29. go to one's head, a.** affect one's mind. **b.** make one dizzy. **c.** make one conceited. **30. lose one's head,** get excited; lose one's self-control. **31. off or out of one's head,** *Colloq.* crazy; insane. **32. over one's head, a.** beyond one's power to understand. **b.** to a person higher in authority. **33. turn one's head, a.** affect the mind. **b.** make one dizzy. **c.** make one conceited. —*adj.* **1.** at the head, top, or front: *the head division of a parade.* **2.** coming from in front: *a head wind.* **3.** chief; leading; commanding; directing. —*v.* **1.** be or go at the head, top, or front of: *head a parade.* **2.** move or face (toward): *head a boat toward shore.* **3.** be the head or chief of: *head a business.* **4.** put a head on; furnish with a head. **5.** form a head; come to a head. **6. head off,** get in front of and turn back or aside. [OE *hēafod*] —Syn. *n.* **5.** commander, director. **6.** command, direction. —*v.* **3.** lead, command, direct.

head·ache (hed′āk′), *n.* **1.** pain in the head. **2.** *Am.*, *Slang.* thing, situation, etc., that is the cause of great bother, vexation, etc.

head·cheese (hed′chēz′), *n.* *Am.* a jellied loaf formed of parts of the head and feet of hogs cut up, cooked, and seasoned.

head·dress (hed′dres′), *n.* **1.** a covering or decoration for the head. **2.** way of wearing or arranging the hair.

head·ed (hed′id), *adj.* **1.** having a head. **2.** having a heading. **3.** shaped into a head.

–headed, *suffix.* **1.** having a certain kind of head, as in *long-headed.* **2.** having a specified number of heads, as in *two-headed.*

head·er (hed′ər), *n.* **1.** person, tool, or machine that puts on or takes off heads of grain, barrels, pins, nails, etc. **2.** *Am.* machine that harvests heads of grain. **3.** *Colloq.* a plunge or dive headfirst.

head·first (hed′fèrst′), *adv.* **1.** with the head first. **2.** hastily; rashly.

head·fore·most (hed′fôr′mōst; –fōr′–), *adv.* headfirst.

head·gear (hed′gir′), *n.* **1.** a covering for the head; hat, cap, etc. **2.** harness for an animal's head.

head·hunt·ing (hed′hun′ting), *n.* practice among some savage tribes of taking the heads of enemies as signs of victory, manhood, etc. —head′hunt′er, *n.*

head·ing (hed′ing), *n.* **1.** part forming the head, top, or front. **2.** something written or printed at the top of a page. **3.** title of a page, chapter, etc.; topic.

head·land (hed′lənd), *n.* point of land jutting out into water; cape.

head·less (hed′lis), *adj.* **1.** having no head. **2.** without a leader. **3.** without brains; stupid.

head·light (hed′līt′), *n.* **1.** *Am.* a bright light at the front of an automobile, streetcar, locomotive, etc. **2.** light at a masthead.

head·line (hed′līn′), *n.*, *v.*, –lined, –lin·ing. —*n.* **1.** *Am.* words printed at the top of an article in a newspaper, indicating what it is about. **2.** line at the top of a page giving the running title, page number, etc. —*v.* furnish with a headline.

head·long (hed′lông′; –long), *adv.*, *adj.* **1.** headfirst. **2.** with great haste and force. **3.** in too great a rush; without stopping to think. **4.** rash; rashly.

head·man (hed′man′; –mən), *n.*, *pl.* –men. chief; leader.

head·mas·ter (hed′mas′tər; –mäs′–), *n.* person in charge of a school, esp. of a private school; principal. —head′mas′ter·ship, *n.*

head·mis·tress (hed′mis′tris), *n.* a woman headmaster.

head·most (hed′mōst), *adj.* first; foremost.

head·on (hed′on′; –ôn′), *adj.* with the head or front first.

head·phone (hed′fōn′), *n.* a telephone or radio receiver held on the head, against the ears.

head·piece (hed′pēs′), *n.* **1.** piece of armor for the head; helmet. **2.** hat, cap, or other covering for the head. **3.** headphone. **4.** head; mind; intellect.

head·quar·ters (hed′kwôr′tərz), *n. pl. or sing.* **1.** place from which the chief or commanding officer of an army, police force, etc., sends out orders. **2.** center from which any organization is controlled and directed; main office.

head·set (hed′set′), *n.* headphone.

head·ship (hed′ship), *n.* position of head; chief authority. —Syn. leadership, command, direction.

heads·man (hedz′mən), *n.*, *pl.* –men. man who beheads condemned persons.

head·stall (hed′stôl′), *n.* part of a bridle or halter that fits around a horse's head.

head·stock (hed′stok′), *n.* part of a machine that contains the revolving or working parts.

Headstall

head·stone (hed′stōn′), *n.* **1.** stone set at the head of a grave. **2.** cornerstone.

head·stream (hed′strēm′), *n.* stream that is the source of a larger stream.

head·strong (hed′strông′; –strong′), *adj.* **1.** rashly or foolishly determined to have one's own way; hard to control or manage; obstinate. **2.** showing rash or foolish determination to have one's own way. —head′strong′ness, *n.* —Syn. **1.** willful, perverse, stubborn.

head·wait·er (hed′wāt′ər), *n.* man in charge of the waiters in a restaurant, hotel, etc.

head·wa·ters (hed′wô′tərz; –wot′ərz), *n.pl.* sources or upper parts of a river.

head·way (hed′wā′), *n.* **1.** motion forward: *the ship made headway against the tide.* **2.** progress with work, etc. **3.** a clear space overhead in a doorway or under an arch, bridge, etc.; clearance.

head wind, wind blowing straight against the front of a ship, etc.

head·work (hed′werk′), *n.* mental work; thought. —head′work′er, *n.*

head·y (hed′i), *adj.*, head·i·er, head·i·est. **1.** hasty; rash. **2.** apt to affect the head and make one dizzy; intoxicating. —head′i·ly, *adv.* —head′i·ness, *n.*

heal (hēl), *v.* **1.** make whole, sound, or well; bring back to health; cure (a disease or wound). **2.** become whole or sound; get well. **3.** get rid of (anything bad). [OE *hǣlan* < *hāl* whole] —heal′er, *n.* —heal′ing, *n.* —heal′ing·ly, *adv.*

health (helth), *n.* **1.** a being well; freedom from sickness. **2.** condition of body or mind: *in poor health.* **3.** a drink in honor of a person, with a wish for health and happiness: *drink a health to the bride.* [OE *hǣlth* < *hāl* whole]

health·ful (helth′fəl), *adj.* giving health; good for the health. —**health′ful·ly,** *adv.* —**health′ful·ness,** *n.* ➤ **healthful, healthy.** *Healthful* means "giving health"; *healthy* carries the same meaning in informal English but formal usage restricts it to "having health."

health·y (hel′thi), *adj.,* **health·i·er, health·i·est. 1.** having good health. **2.** showing good health: *a healthy appearance.* **3.** healthful. —**health′i·ly,** *adv.* —**health′i·ness,** *n.* —Syn. 1. hale, hearty, robust, strong, sound. 3. nourishing, salutary.

heap (hēp), *n.* **1.** pile of many things thrown or lying together: *a heap of sand.* **2.** *Colloq.* a large amount. —*v.* **1.** form into a heap; gather in heaps. **2.** give generously or in large amounts. **3.** fill full or more than full: *heap a plate with food.* [OE *hēap*] —**heap′er,** *n.* —Syn. *n.* 1. mass, stack, accumulation.

hear (hir), *v.,* **heard** (hėrd), **hear·ing,** *interj.* —*v.* **1.** perceive by the ear: *hear sounds.* **2.** be able to perceive by the ear: *he cannot hear well.* **3.** listen (often in the imperative). **4.** listen to: *hear a person's explanation.* **5.** listen to with favor: *hear my prayer.* **6.** give a chance to be heard; give a formal hearing to, as a judge, teacher, etc., does. **7.** find out by hearing: *hear news.* **8.** be told; receive news or information: *hear from a friend.* **9.** will not hear of it, will not listen to, think of, agree to, or allow it. —*interj.* **hear! hear!** *Esp. Brit.* shouts of approval; cheering. [OE *hēran*] —**hear′er,** *n.*

hear·ing (hir′ing), *n.* **1.** sense by which sound is perceived: *the old man's hearing is poor.* **2.** act or process of perceiving sound. **3.** a formal or official listening: *the judge gave both sides a hearing in court.* **4.** chance to be heard: *give us a hearing.* **5.** distance that a sound can be heard: *be within hearing.*

heark·en (härk′ən), *v.* **1.** listen; listen attentively. **2.** *Poetic.* listen to; give heed to; hear. Also, **harken.** [OE *hercnian, heorcnian*] —**heark′en·er,** *n.*

hear·say (hir′sā′), *n.* common talk; gossip.

hearse (hėrs), *n.* **1.** automobile, carriage, etc., for carrying a dead person to his grave. **2.** *Archaic.* bier; coffin; tomb. [< OF < L *hirpex* harrow; orig., a frame like a harrow]

heart (härt), *n.* **1.** a hollow, muscular organ that pumps the blood throughout the body by contracting and dilating. **2.** feelings; mind; soul: *a kind heart.* **3.** source of the emotions, esp. of love: *give one's heart.* **4.** person loved or praised: *group of stout hearts.* **5.** kindness; sympathy: *have no heart.* **6.** spirit; courage; enthusiasm: *take heart.* **7.** the innermost part; middle; center: *heart of the forest.* **8.** the main part; vital or most important part: *the very heart of the matter.* **9.** figure shaped somewhat like this ♥. **10.** *Cards.* **a.** a playing card with one or more red, heart-shaped figures. **b. hearts,** suit of playing cards with red designs like hearts on them. **c. hearts** (*sing. in use*), game in which the players try to get rid of cards of this suit. **11. after one's own heart,** just as one likes it; pleasing one perfectly. **12. at heart,** in one's deepest thoughts or feelings. **13. by heart, a.** by memory. **b.** from memory. **14. with all one's heart, a.** sincerely. **b.** gladly. [OE *heorte*]

heart·ache (härt′āk′), *n.* sorrow; grief.

heart·beat (härt′bēt′), *n.* pulsation of the heart, including one complete contraction and dilation.

heart·break (härt′brāk′), *n.* a crushing sorrow or grief. —**heart′break′er,** *n.* —**heart′break′ing,** *adj.* —**heart′break′ing·ly,** *adv.*

heart·bro·ken (härt′brō′kən), *adj.* crushed with sorrow or grief. —**heart′bro′ken·ly,** *adv.* —**heart′bro′ken·ness,** *n.*

heart·burn (härt′bėrn′), *n.* **1.** a burning feeling in the stomach, often rising to the chest and throat. **2.** Also, **heart′burn′ing.** envy; jealousy.

…rt·ed (härt′tid), *adj.* having a heart (of the … mentioned): *good-hearted.*

…rt·en (härt′ən), *v.* encourage; cheer up.

…rt·felt (härt′felt′), *adj.* sincere; genuine.

hearth (härth), *n.* **1.** floor of a fireplace. **2.** home; fireside. **3.** the lowest part of a blast furnace. [OE *heorth*]

hearth·stone (härth′stōn′), *n.* **1.** stone forming a hearth. **2.** home; fireside.

heart·i·ly (här′tə·li), *adv.* **1.** sincerely; genuinely. **2.** with enthusiasm; vigorously. **3.** with a good appetite. **4.** very; completely; thoroughly.

heart·less (härt′lis), *adj.* **1.** without kindness or sympathy. **2.** without courage, spirit, or enthusiasm. —**heart′less·ly,** *adv.* —**heart′less·ness,** *n.* —Syn. 1. unfeeling, cruel.

heart·rend·ing (härt′ren′ding), *adj.* causing mental anguish; very distressing. —**heart′rend′ing·ly,** *adv.*

heart·sick (härt′sik′), *adj.* sick at heart; very much depressed; very unhappy. —**heart′sick′ness,** *n.*

heart·sore (härt′sōr′; -sôr′), *adj.* feeling or showing grief; grieved.

heart·strik·en (härt′strik′ən), *adj.* struck to the heart with grief; shocked with fear; dismayed.

heart·strings (härt′stringz′), *n.pl.* deepest feelings; strongest affections.

heart·throb (härt′throb′), *n. Colloq.* **1.** a pleasant emotion. **2.** person who is the object of passionate affection.

heart-to-heart (härt′tə·härt′), *adj. Am.* without reserve; frank; sincere.

heart·wood (härt′wúd′), *n.* the hard, central wood of a tree.

heart·y (här′ti), *adj.* **heart·i·er, heart·i·est,** *n., pl.* **heart·ies.** —*adj.* **1.** warm and friendly; genuine; sincere: *a hearty welcome.* **2.** strong and well; vigorous: *the old man was still hale and hearty.* **3.** full of energy and enthusiasm; not restrained: *a loud, hearty laugh.* **4.** with plenty to eat; nourishing: *a hearty meal.* **5.** requiring or using much food: *a hearty eater.* **6.** fertile. —*n.* **1.** a fellow sailor; brave and good comrade. **2.** sailor. [< *heart*] —**heart′i·ness,** *n.* —Syn. *adj.* 1. cordial, genial. 2. hale, healthy, robust.

heat (hēt), *n.* **1.** hotness; high temperature. **2.** degree of hotness; temperature. **3.** sensation or perception of hotness or warmth. **4.** *Physics.* form of energy that consists of the motion of the molecules of a substance. The rate of motion determines the temperature. **5.** hot weather. **6.** warmth or intensity of feeling. **7.** the hottest point; most violent or active state. **8.** *Slang.* pressure; coercion; torture. **9.** *Slang.* a trailing or hunting down and investigating. **10.** *Sports.* one trial in a race. **11.** one operation of heating in a furnace or a forge. **12.** *Zool.* sexual excitement in female animals. —*v.* **1.** make hot or warm; become hot or warm. **2.** fill with strong feeling; excite; become excited. [OE *hǣtu;* akin to нот] —**heat′ed,** *adj.* —**heat′less,** *adj.* —Syn. *n.* 6. anger, violence, excitement, eagerness, ardor.

heat barrier, point of speed beyond which the wings and fuselage of a plane are made dangerously hot by friction with the atmosphere.

heat·ed·ly (hēt′id·li), *adv.* in a vigorous, angry, or excited manner.

heat·er (hēt′ər), *n.* stove, furnace, or other apparatus that gives heat or warmth.

heat exchanger, device by means of which heat is transferred from one medium to another in order that it may be utilized as a source of power, as in an atomic power plant, gas turbine, etc.

heath (hēth), *n.* **1.** *Brit.* open, waste land with heather or low bushes growing on it, but few or no trees. **2.** a low bush growing on such land. Heather is one kind of heath. **3.** one's native heath, place where one was born or brought up. [OE *hǣth*] —**heath′like′,** *adj.* —**heath′y,** *adj.*

hea·then (hē′thən), *n., pl.* **-thens, -then,** *adj.* —*n.* **1.** person who does not believe in the God of the Bible; person who is not a Christian, Jew, or Mohammedan. **2.** an irreligious or unenlightened person. —*adj.* **1.** of or having to do with the heathen. **2.** irreligious; unenlightened. [OE *hǣthen* < *hǣth* heath] —**hea′then·dom,** *n.* —**hea′then·ish,** *adj.* —**hea′then·ish·ly,** *adv.* —**hea′then·ish·ness,** *n.* —**hea′then·ism,** *n.* —**hea′then·ness,** *n.*

heath·er (heth′ər), *n.* a low, evergreen shrub with stalks of small, rosy-pink, bell-shaped flowers, covering many heaths of Scotland and N England. [? < *heath*] —**heath′er·y,** *adj.*

heat lightning, *Am.* flashes of light without any thunder, seen near the horizon, esp. on hot summer evenings.

heat·stroke (hēt′strōk′), *n.* collapse or sudden illness caused by too much heat.

heat wave, a long period of very hot weather.

heave (hēv), *v.*, **heaved** or (*esp. Naut.*) **hove, heav·ing,** *n.* —*v.* 1. lift with force or effort: *heave a heavy box into a wagon.* 2. lift and throw: *heave the anchor overboard.* 3. pull with force or effort; haul: *they heaved on the rope.* 4. give (a sigh, groan, etc.) with a deep, heavy breath. 5. rise and fall alternately: *waves heave in a storm.* 6. breathe hard; pant. 7. try to vomit; vomit. 8. rise; swell; bulge. 9. heave in sight, come into view. 10. heave to, stop a ship; stop. —*n.* 1. act or fact of heaving. 2. **heaves** (*sing. in use*), *Am.* disease of horses characterized by difficult breathing, coughing, and heaving of the flanks. [OE *hebban*] —**heav′er,** *n.*

heav·en (hev′ən), *n.* 1. in Christian use, the place where God and the angels live. 2. Heaven, God; Providence: *the will of Heaven.* 3. place or condition of greatest happiness. 4. Usually, **heavens.** the upper air; sky. [OE *heofon*]

heav·en·ly (hev′ən·li), *adj.* 1. of or in heaven; divine; holy: *our heavenly Father.* 2. like heaven; suitable for heaven: *a heavenly spot.* 3. of or in the heavens: *the moon and other heavenly bodies.* —**heav′en·li·ness,** *n.* —**Syn.** 2. blissful, beautiful, excellent.

heav·en·ward (hev′ən·wərd), *adv.* Also, **heav′en·wards.** toward heaven. —*adj.* directed toward heaven.

Heav·i·side layer (hev′i·sīd), the ionosphere's second layer, which reflects radio waves of frequencies produced in short-wave broadcasting.

heav·y (hev′i), *adj.*, **heav·i·er, heav·i·est,** *n.*, *pl.* **heav·ies,** *adv.* —*adj.* 1. hard to lift or carry; of great weight. 2. having much weight for its size or kind: *heavy metal, heavy silk.* 3. of great amount, force, or intensity; greater than usual; large: *a heavy vote, heavy sleep, heavy rain.* 4. being such in an unusual degree: *a heavy buyer, heavy smoker.* 5. hard to bear or endure: *heavy taxes.* 6. hard to deal with; trying or difficult in any way: *a heavy road, heavy slope, heavy food.* 7. weighted down; laden: *air heavy with moisture, eyes heavy with sleep.* 8. weary; sorrowful; gloomy. 9. grave; serious; sober; somber: *a heavy part in a play.* 10. cloudy: *a heavy sky.* 11. broad; thick; coarse: *a heavy line, heavy features.* 12. clumsy; sluggish; slow: *a heavy walk.* 13. ponderous; dull: *heavy reading.* 14. loud and deep: *the heavy roar of cannon.* 15. *Mil.* a. heavily armed or equipped. b. of large size: *heavy artillery.* 16. not risen enough: *heavy bread.* 17. not easily digested: *heavy food.* 18. *Chem.* among isotopes, indicating one possessing a greater atomic weight. 19. pregnant. —*n.* 1. a heavy person or thing. 2. *Colloq.* villain in a play. —*adv.* 1. in a heavy manner; heavily. 2. hang heavy, pass slowly and uninterestingly. [OE *hefig* < *hebban* heave] —**heav′i·ly,** *adv.* —**heav′i·ness,** *n.* —**Syn.** *adj.* 1. massive, ponderous. 6. hard. 8. depressed, sad. 12. lumbering.

heav·y-heart·ed (hev′i·här′tid), *adj.* sad; gloomy. —**heav′y-heart′ed·ness,** *n.*

heavy hydrogen, *Chem.* deuterium, D.

heavy water, water formed of oxygen and heavy hydrogen, D_2O, similar to ordinary water, but 1.1 times as heavy.

heav·y·weight (hev′i·wāt′), *n.* 1. person or thing of much more than average weight. 2. boxer or wrestler who weighs 175 pounds or more. 3. *Am., Colloq.* person who has much intelligence or importance.

Heb., 1. Hebrew. 2. Hebrews.

heb·dom·a·dal (heb·dom′ə·dəl), *adj.* weekly. [< LL, < L *hebdomas* seven, seven days < Gk.] —**heb·dom′a·dal·ly,** *adv.*

He·be (hē′bē), *n.* the Greek goddess of youth, the cupbearer to the gods before Ganymede was given that duty.

He·bra·ic (hi·brā′ik), *adj.* of or having to do with the Hebrews or their language or culture; Hebrew. —**He·bra′i·cal·ly,** *adv.*

He·bra·ism (hē′brā·iz·əm), *n.* 1. Hebrew usage or idiom. 2. Hebrew character, spirit, thought, or practice. —**He′bra·ist,** *n.* —**He′bra·is′tic,** *adj.*

He·brew (hē′brü), *n.* 1. Jew; Israelite. 2. the ancient language of the Jews, in which the Old Testament was recorded. 3. the present-day language of Israel. —*adj.* Jewish.

He·brews (hē′brüz), *n.* book of the New Testament.

Heb·ri·des (heb′rə·dēz), *n.pl.* group of Scotch islands off NW Scotland. —**Heb′ri·de′an,** *adj.*

Hec·a·te (hek′ə·tē), *n. Gk. Myth.* the goddess of the moon, earth, and infernal regions, later associated with magic and witchcraft. Also, **Hekate.**

hec·a·tomb (hek′ə·tōm; -tüm; -tom), *n.* 1. sacrifice of 100 oxen at one time. 2. any great slaughter. [< L < Gk. *hekatombe* sacrifice of 100 oxen < *hekaton* hundred + *bous* ox]

heck·le (hek′əl), *v.*, **-led, -ling.** harass and annoy by asking many bothersome questions, etc. Also, **hatchel.** [< *heckle,* n., ME *hekele*; akin to HACKLE¹] —**heck′ler,** *n.* —**heck′ling,** *n.*

hec·tare (hek′tār), *n.* measure of area in the metric system, equal to 100 ares, 10,000 square meters, or 2.471 acres. [< F < Gk. *hekaton* hundred + F *are* ARE²]

hec·tic (hek′tik), *adj.* 1. flushed. 2. feverish. 3. *Colloq.* very excited or exciting. 4. showing the signs of tuberculosis; consumptive. [< L < Gk. *hektikos* habitual, consumptive] —**hec′ti·cal·ly,** *adv.*

hecto-, *prefix.* hundred, as in *hectogram, hectoliter, hectometer.* [< Gk. *hekaton*]

hec·to·graph (hek′tə·graf; -gräf), *n.* 1. machine for making copies of a page of writing, a drawing, etc., in which the original is transferred to a gelatinous surface, and reproductions are made from this. 2. this process. —*v.* make copies of with a hectograph. [< *hecto-* hundred (< Gk. *hekaton*) + -GRAPH] —**hec′to·graph′ic,** *adj.*

Hec·tor (hek′tər), *n. Gk. Legend.* in the *Iliad,* a son of Priam, the bravest of the Trojans, who was killed by Achilles.

hec·tor (hek′tər), *n.* a bragging, bullying fellow. —*v.* 1. bluster; bully. 2. tease.

Hec·u·ba (hek′yü·bə), *n. Gk. Legend.* in the *Iliad,* the wife of Priam and mother of Hector.

he'd (hēd; *unstressed* ēd, id, hid), 1. he had. 2. he would.

hedge (hej), *n., v.*, **hedged, hedg·ing.** —*n.* 1. Also, **hedge·row** (hej′rō′). a thick row of bushes or small trees, planted as a fence or boundary. 2. any barrier or boundary. 3. act of hedging. —*v.* 1. put a hedge around. 2. enclose or separate with a hedge. 3. avoid giving a direct answer or taking a definite stand. 4. protect (a bet, etc.) by taking some offsetting risk. 5. hedge in, a. hem in; surround on all sides. b. keep from getting away or moving freely. [OE *hecg*] —**hedg′er,** *n.*

hedge·hog (hej′hog′; -hôg′), *n.* 1. *Am.* the porcupine. 2. any of a group of small European mammals that have spines on the back. 3. *Mil.* a. an X-shaped portable obstacle, usually laced with barbed wire. b. an area defended by pillboxes, mines, and lanes for machine-gun fire.

hedge-hop (hej′hop′), *v.*, **-hopped, -hop·ping.** fly an airplane very low. —**hedge′-hop′per,** *n.* —**hedge′-hop′ping,** *adj., n.*

He·djaz (he·jaz′; -jäz′), *n.* Hejaz.

he·don·ism (hē′dən·iz·əm), *n.* doctrine that pleasure or happiness is the highest good. [< Gk. *hedone* pleasure] —**he′don·ist,** *n., adj.* —**he′do·nis′tic,** *adj.* —**he′do·nis′ti·cal·ly,** *adv.*

heed (hēd), *v.* give careful attention to; take notice of. —*n.* careful attention. [OE *hēdan*] —**heed′er,** *n.* —**heed′ing·ly,** *adv.* —**Syn.** *v.* regard, note, consider, mind. —n. notice, regard.

heed·ful (hēd′fəl), adj. careful; attentive.
—heed′ful·ly, adv. —heed′ful·ness, n. —Syn. mindful, watchful. —Ant. neglectful.

heed·less (hēd′lis), adj. careless; thoughtless.
—heed′less·ly, adv. —heed′less·ness, n.

heel[1] (hēl), n. 1. the back part of a person's foot, below the ankle. 2. part of a stocking or shoe that covers the heel. 3. part of a shoe or boot that is under the heel or raises the heel. 4. part of the hind leg of an animal that corresponds to a person's heel. 5. anything shaped, used, or placed at an end like a heel, such as an end crust of bread, etc. 6. down at the heel or heels, a. with the heel of the shoe worn down. b. shabby. c. slovenly. 7. out at the heels, a. with the heel of the stocking or shoe worn through. b. shabby. c. slovenly. —v. 1. follow closely. 2. put a heel or heels on. [OE *hēla*] —heel′less, adj.

heel[2] (hēl), v. lean over to one side; tilt: *the ship heeled as it turned.* —n. act of heeling. [alter. of earlier *heeld* < OE *h(i) eldan* < *heald* inclined]

heel[3] (hēl), n. U.S. Colloq. a hateful or odious person. [special use of *heel*[1]]

heeled (hēld), adj. Am., Slang. provided with money.

heel·er (hēl′ər), n. 1. person who puts heels on shoes. 2. Am., Slang. follower or hanger-on of a political boss.

heft (heft), n. 1. Colloq. weight; heaviness. 2. Am., Colloq. the greater part; bulk. —v. 1. judge the weight or heaviness of by lifting. 2. lift; heave. [< *heave*]

heft·y (hef′ti), adj., heft·i·er, heft·i·est. Colloq. 1. weighty; heavy. 2. big and strong.

He·gel (hā′gəl), n. Georg Wilhelm Friedrich, 1770–1831, German philosopher. —He·ge·li·an (hā·gā′li·ən; hi·jē′–), adj.

he·gem·o·ny (hi·jem′ə·ni; hej′ə·mō′ni), n., pl. -nies. political domination, esp. the leadership or domination of one state in a group; leadership. [< Gk., < *hegemon* leader] —heg·e·mon·ic (hej′ə·mon′ik; hē′jə–), adj.

He·gi·ra (hi·jī′rə), n. 1. flight of Mohammed from Mecca to Medina in 622 A.D. 2. hegira, departure; flight. Also, Hejira.

Hei·del·berg (hī′dəl·bėrg), n. city in SW Germany.

heif·er (hef′ər), n. a young cow that has not had a calf. [OE *hēahfore*]

heigh (hā; hī), interj. sound used to attract attention, give encouragement, express surprise, etc.

height (hīt), n. 1. measurement from top to bottom; how high a thing is; elevation above ground, sea level, etc. 2. a fairly great distance up. 3. a high point or place; hill. 4. the highest part; top. 5. the highest point; greatest degree: *the height of folly.* [OE *hīehthu* < *hēah* high] ➤ height, heighth. Uneducated English usually has *heighth*, like *width* and *breadth* (and the original Old English form had *th*), but *height* is the only form current in formal and informal English.

height·en (hīt′ən), v. 1. make or become higher. 2. make or become stronger or greater; increase. —height′en·er, n.

heil (hīl), interj. German. hail!

Hei·ne (hī′nə), n. Heinrich, 1797–1856, German poet and prose writer.

hei·nous (hā′nəs), adj. very wicked; extremely offensive; hateful. [< OF *haïnos*, ult. < OF *haïr* hate < Gmc.] —hei′nous·ly, adv. —hei′nous·ness, n. —Syn. odious, infamous, atrocious.

heir (ār), n. 1. person who receives, or has the right to receive, someone's property or title after the death of its owner. 2. person who inherits anything. —v. inherit. [< OF < L *heres* heir] —heir′dom, heir′ship, n. —heir′less, adj.

heir apparent, pl. heirs apparent. person who will be heir if he lives longer than the one holding the property or title.

· · ·ess (ār′is), n. 1. a female heir. 2. woman inheriting great wealth.

· · · (ār′lim′), n. possession handed · · · generation to generation. [< *heir* + · · ·mplement]

heir presumptive, pl. heirs presumptive. person who will be heir unless a nearer relative is born.

He·jaz (he·jaz′; –jäz′), n. a former country in NW Arabia, now part of Saudi Arabia. Also, Hedjaz.

He·ji·ra (hi·jī′rə; hej′ə–), n. Hegira.

Hek·a·te (hek′ə·tē), n. Hecate.

held (held), v. pt. and pp. of hold[1].

Hel·e·na (hel′ə·nə), n. capital of Montana, in the W part.

Helen of Troy, Gk. Legend. the beautiful wife of King Menelaus of Sparta. Her abduction by Paris led to the Trojan War.

hel·i·cal (hel′ə·kəl), adj. having to do with, or having the form of, a helix; spiral. —hel′i·cal·ly, adv.

hel·i·ces (hel′ə·sēz), n. pl. of helix.

Hel·i·con (hel′ə·kon; –kən), n. Mount, Gk. Myth. mountain in S Greece, considered by ancient Greeks as sacred to the Muses. —Hel·i·co·ni·an (hel′ə·kō′ni·ən), adj.

hel·i·cop·ter (hel′ə·kop′tər; hē′lə–), n. a flying machine lifted from the ground and kept in the air by horizontal propellers. [< F, < Gk. *helix* spiral + *pteron* wing]

he·li·o·cen·tric (hē′li·ō·sen′trik), adj. 1. viewed or measured from the sun's center. 2. having or representing the sun as a center. [< Gk. *helios* sun + *kentron* center]

he·li·o·graph (hē′li·ə·graf′; –gräf′), n. device for signaling by means of a movable mirror that flashes beams of light to a distance. —v. communicate or signal by heliograph. —he·li·og·ra·pher (hē′li·og′rə·fər), n. —he′li·o·graph′ic, adj. —he′li·og′ra·phy, n.

He·li·os (hē′li·os), n. Gk. Myth. the sun god.

he·li·o·scope (hē′li·ə·skōp′), n. device for looking at the sun without injury to the eye. [< Gk. *helios* sun + –*skopion* means of viewing < *skopos* watcher]

he·li·o·trope (hē′li·ə·trōp′; hēl′yə–), n. 1. plant with clusters of small, fragrant purple or white flowers. 2. a pinkish purple. 3. bloodstone. —adj. pinkish-purple. [< L < Gk., < *helios* sun + –*tropos* turning]

he·li·ot·ro·pism (hē′li·ot′rə·piz·əm), n. an involuntary response to the sun's rays; tendency that makes a plant turn itself toward the light.

hel·i·port (hel′ə·pôrt; hē′lə–; –pōrt), n. airport designed esp. for helicopters.

he·li·um (hē′li·əm), n. Chem. a rare, very light, inert gaseous element, He, that will not burn, much used in balloons and dirigibles. [< NL, < Gk. *helios* sun]

he·lix (hē′liks), n., pl. hel·i·ces (hel′ə·sēz), he·lix·es. 1. spiral, as a screw thread or a watch spring. 2. a spiral ornament. 3. Anat. rim of the outer ear. [< L < Gk., a spiral]

Helixes as used for ornament

hell (hel), n. 1. in Christian use, a place where wicked persons are punished after death. 2. the powers of evil. 3. the persons in hell. 4. abode of the dead; Hades. 5. any place or state of wickedness, torment, or misery. [OE]

he'll (hēl), 1. he will. 2. he shall.

Hel·las (hel′əs), n. Greece.

hell·bend·er (hel′ben′dər), n. Am. a large salamander that is common in the Ohio River and its tributaries.

hell-bent (hel′bent′), adj. Am., Slang. recklessly determined.

hell·cat (hel′kat′), n. 1. a mean, spiteful woman. 2. witch.

hel·le·bore (hel′ə·bôr; –bōr), n. 1. any of several plants of the buttercup family with showy flowers that bloom before spring. 2. any of several tall plants of the lily family. [< L < Gk. *helleboros*]

Hel·lene (hel′ēn), n. Greek.

Hel·len·ic (he·len′ik; –lē′nik), adj. 1. Greek. 2. of Greek history, language, or culture from 776 B.C. to the death of Alexander the Great in 323 B.C.

Hel·len·ism (hel′ən·iz·əm), *n.* **1.** ancient Greek culture or ideals. **2.** adoption or imitation of Greek speech, ideals, or customs. **3.** idiom or expression peculiar to the Greek language. —**Hel′len·ist**, *n.* —**Hel′len·is′tic**, **Hel′len·is′ti·cal**, *adj.*

Hel·len·ize (hel′ən·īz), *v.,* **-ized, -iz·ing. 1.** make Greek in character. **2.** use or imitate the Greek language, ideals, or customs. —**Hel′len·i·za′tion**, *n.* —**Hel′len·iz′er**, *n.*

Hel·les·pont (hel′əs·pont), *n.* an ancient name of the Dardanelles.

hell·fire (hel′fīr′), *n.* fire of hell; punishment in hell.

hel·lion (hel′yən), *n. Colloq.* a mischievous, troublesome person.

hell·ish (hel′ish), *adj.* **1.** fit to have come from hell; devilish; fiendish. **2.** of hell. —**hell′ish·ly**, *adv.* —**hell′ish·ness**, *n.* —Syn. **1.** diabolical, infernal, wicked.

hel·lo (he·lō′; hə-), *interj., n., pl.* **-los,** *v.,* **-loed, -lo·ing.** —*interj.* **1.** exclamation to attract attention or express greeting (much used over the telephone). **2.** exclamation of surprise. —*n.* **1.** call of greeting or surprise. **2.** call to attract attention. —*v.* shout or call to attract attention or in greeting or surprise.

helm¹ (helm), *n.* **1.** handle or wheel by which a ship is steered. **2.** the entire steering apparatus. **3.** position of control or guidance. —*v.* steer. [OE *helma*] —**helm′less**, *adj.*

helm² (helm), *Archaic.* —*n.* helmet. —*v.* put a helmet on. [OE. See HELMET.]

hel·met (hel′mit), *n.* a covering, usually metal, which protects the head. [< OF. dim. of *helme* helm² < Gmc.] —**hel′met·ed**, *adj.*

hel·minth (hel′minth), *n.* an intestinal worm, such as the tapeworm, etc. [< Gk. *helmins*]

helms·man (helmz′mən), *n., pl.* **-men.** man who steers a ship.

Hel·ot, hel·ot (hel′ət; hē′lət), *n.* **1.** slave or serf in ancient Sparta. **2.** slave; serf. [< L < Gk. *Heilos,* prob. akin to Gk. *haliskesthai* be captured] —**hel′ot·ism**, *n.* —**hel′ot·ry**, *n.*

help (help), *v.,* helped or (*Archaic*) holp, helped or (*Archaic*) holp·en, help·ing, *n.* —*v.* **1.** provide with what is needed or useful: *help a person with one's strength.* **2.** aid; assist: *help someone with his work.* **3.** make better; relieve: *this will help your cough.* **4.** prevent; stop: *it can't be helped.* **5.** avoid; keep from: *he can't help yawning.* **6.** give food to; serve with food: *help her to some cake.* —*n.* **1.** thing done or given in helping; aid; assistance. **2.** person or thing that helps. **3.** *Am.* a hired helper or group of hired helpers. **4.** means of making better; remedy. **5.** means of preventing or stopping. **6.** portion of food served to a person at one time. [OE *helpan*] —**help′a·ble**, *adj.* —**help′er**, *n.* —Syn. *v.* **1.** support, uphold, back, abet. **3.** remedy, heal, alleviate, mitigate. ▶ See **can't** for usage note.

help·ful (help′fəl), *adj.* giving help; useful. —**help′ful·ly**, *adv.* —**help′ful·ness**, *n.* —Syn. serviceable, beneficial.

help·ing (help′ing), *n.* portion of food served to a person at one time.

help·less (help′lis), *adj.* **1.** not able to help oneself; weak. **2.** without help, protection, etc. —**help′less·ly**, *adv.* —**help′less·ness**, *n.*

help·mate (help′māt′), **help·meet** (-mēt′), *n.* companion and helper; wife or husband.

Hel·sin·ki (hel′sing·ki), *Swedish* **Hel·sing·fors** (hel′sing·fôrz; -fôrs), *n.* seaport and capital of Finland.

hel·ter-skel·ter (hel′tər·skel′tər), *adv.* with headlong, disorderly haste. —*n.* noisy and disorderly haste, confusion, etc. —*adj.* carelessly hurried; confused.

helve (helv), *n. Esp. Brit.* handle of an ax, hammer, etc. [OE *hielfe*]

Hel·ve·tia (hel·vē′shə), *n. Poetic.* Switzerland.

hem¹ (hem), *n., v.,* hemmed, hem·ming. —*n.* **1.** border or edge on a garment; edge made by

folding over the cloth and sewing it down. **2.** border; edge. —*v.* **1.** fold over and sew down the edge of (cloth). **2.** hem in, around, or about, a. surround on all sides. **b.** keep from getting away or moving freely. [OE *hemm*] —**hem′mer**, *n.*

hem² (hem), *interj., n., v.,* hemmed, hem·ming. —*interj., n.* sound like clearing the throat, used to attract attention or show doubt or hesitation. —*v.* **1.** make this sound. **2.** hesitate in speaking. [imit.]

hem·a·tite (hem′ə·tīt; hē′mə-), *n.* an important iron ore, Fe_2O_3, that is reddish-brown when powdered. Also, **haematite.** [< L < Gk. *haimatites* bloodlike < *haima* blood] —**hem·a·tit·ic** (hem′ə·tit′ik; hē′mə-), *adj.*

hemi-, *prefix.* half, as in *hemisphere.* [< Gk.]

Hem·ing·way (hem′ing·wā), *n.* Ernest, born 1898, American novelist and short-story writer.

he·mip·ter·ous (hi·mip′tər·əs), *adj.* belonging to a large group of insects including bedbugs, chinch bugs, lice, and aphids. [< Gk. *hemi-* half + *pteron* wing]

hem·i·sphere (hem′ə·sfir), *n.* **1.** half of a sphere or globe. **2.** half of the earth's surface. [< F < L < Gk., < *hemi-* half + *sphaira* sphere] —**hem·i·spher·i·cal** (hem′ə·sfer′ə·kəl), *adj.* —**hem·i·spher′i·cal·ly**, *adv.*

hem·i·stich (hem′ə·stik), *n.* **1.** half a line of verse. **2.** an incomplete line of verse. [< L < Gk., < *hemi-* half + *stichos* row] —**he·mis·ti·chal** (hi·mis′tə·kəl; hem′ə·stik·əl), *adj.*

hem·lock (hem′lok), *n.* **1.** *Esp. Brit.* a poisonous plant of the carrot family, with spotted stems, finely divided leaves, and small white flowers. **2.** poison made from it. **3.** *Am.* an evergreen tree of the pine family with small cones and drooping branches, whose bark is used in tanning. **4.** its wood. [OE *hymlice*]

he·mo·glo·bin (hē′mə·glō′bən; hem′ə-), *n.* the protein matter in the red corpuscles of the blood that carries oxygen from the lungs to the tissues, and carbon dioxide from the tissues to the lungs. Also, **haemoglobin.** [for *hematoglobulin,* ult. < Gk. *haima* blood + L *globulus,* dim. of *globus* globe]

he·mo·phil·i·a (hē′mə·fil′i·ə; hem′ə-), *n. Pathol.* an inherited condition in which the blood does not clot normally, resulting in excessive bleeding from the slightest cut. Also, **haemophilia.** [< NL, < Gk. *haima* blood + *philia* affection, tendency] —**he·mo·phil·i·ac** (hē′mə·fil′i·ak; hem′ə-), *n.*

hem·or·rhage (hem′ə·rij; hem′rij), *n.* discharge of blood, as a nosebleed. Also, **haemorrhage.** [< L < Gk. *haimorrhagia,* ult. < *haima* blood + *rhegnynai* break, burst] —**hem·or·rhag·ic** (hem′ə·raj′ik), *adj.*

hem·or·rhoids (hem′ə·roidz), *n.pl.* painful swellings formed by the dilation of blood vessels near the anus; piles. Also, **haemorrhoids.** [< L < Gk., ult. < *haima* blood + *-rhoos* flowing] —**hem·or·rhoi′dal**, *adj.*

hemp (hemp), *n.* **1.** a tall Asiatic plant whose tough fibers are made into heavy string, rope, coarse cloth, etc. **2.** the tough fibers of this plant. **3.** a hangman's rope. **4.** hashish or other drug obtained from some kinds of hemp. [OE *henep*] —**hemp′en**, *adj.*

hem·stitch (hem′stich′), *v.* hem along a line from which threads have been drawn out, gathering the cross threads into a series of little groups. —*n.* **1.** the stitch used. **2.** ornamental needlework made by hemstitching. —**hem′stitch′er**, *n.*

hen (hen), *n.* **1.** a female domestic fowl. **2.** female of other birds. [OE *henn*]

hen·bane (hen′bān′), *n.* a coarse, bad-smelling plant with sticky, hairy leaves and clusters of yellowish-brown flowers, poisonous to fowls.

hence (hens), *adv.* **1.** as a result of this; therefore: *it is very late, hence you must go to bed.* **2.** from now; from this time onward: *years hence.* **3.** from this source or origin. **4.** from a mile hence. —*interj.* go away! [ME *hennes* < OE *heonan* + *-s,* adv. end] ▶ Hence is a formal word for the less ——al conse-

quently, therefore; rare in current informal writing.

hence·forth (hens′fôrth′; –fôrth′), **hence·for·ward** (–fôr′wərd), *adv.* from this time on.

hench·man (hench′mən), *n., pl.* **–men.** a trusted attendant or follower. [ME *henxstman* < OE *hengest* horse + MAN; orig., a groom]

hen·e·quen, hen·e·quin (hen′ə·kin), *n.* 1. a yellow fiber from leaves of an agave of Yucatán, used for making binder twine, ropes, coarse fabrics, etc. 2. plant that yields this fiber. [< Sp. < native Yucatán word]

hen·house (hen′hous′), *n.* house for poultry.

hen·na (hen′ə), *n., adj., v.,* **–naed, –na·ing.** —*n.* 1. a dark, reddish-orange dye used on the hair. 2. tree of Asia and Africa from whose leaves this dye is made. —*adj.* reddish-brown. —*v.* dye or color with henna. [< Ar. *ḥinnā*]

hen·ner·y (hen′ər·i), *n., pl.* **–ner·ies.** place where fowls are kept.

hen·peck (hen′pek′), *v.* domineer over: *he was henpecked by his wife.* —**hen′pecked′,** *adj.*

Hen·ry (hen′ri), *n.* 1. O., 1862–1910, American writer of short stories. His real name was William Sydney Porter. 2. **Patrick,** 1736–1799, American patriot, orator, and statesman. 3. **II,** 1519–1559, king of France 1547–1559. 4. **VII,** 1457–1509, king of England 1485–1509. 5. **VIII,** 1491–1547, king of England 1509–1547. He made himself head of the Church of England.

hen·ry (hen′ri), *n., pl.* **–ries, –rys.** *Elect.* unit of inductance. When a current varying at the rate of one ampere per second induces an electromotive force of one volt, the circuit has an inductance of one henry. [after J. *Henry,* physicist]

hep (hep), *adj. Am., Slang.* having intimate knowledge; informed.

he·pat·ic (hi·pat′ik), *adj.* 1. of or having to do with the liver. 2. acting on the liver as a medicine. [< L < Gk., < *hepar* liver]

he·pat·i·ca (hi·pat′ə·kə), *n.* a low plant with delicate purple, pink, or white flowers that bloom early in the spring. [< NL, ult. < Gk. *hepar* liver; leaf thought to resemble the liver in shape]

hep·cat (hep′kat′), *n. Slang.* 1. performer in a swing band. 2. an informed admirer of swing music.

hep·ta·gon (hep′tə·gon), *n.* a plane figure having seven angles and seven sides. [< LL < Gk., < *hepta* seven + *gonia* angle] —**hep·tag·o·nal** (hep·tag′ə·nəl), *adj.*

Heptagon

hep·tam·e·ter (hep·tam′ə·tər), *n.* line of verse having seven feet. [< LL < Gk., < *hepta* seven + *metron* measure] —**hep·ta·met·ri·cal** (hep′tə·met′rə·kəl), *adj.*

her (hėr; *unstressed* hər, ėr), *pron.* the objective case of she: *I like her.* —*adj.* the possessive form of she; of her; belonging to her; done by her: *her look, her book, her work.* [OE *hire*]

her., heraldic; heraldry.

He·ra (hir′ə), *n. Gk. Myth.* goddess, wife of Zeus and queen of gods and men, identified by the Romans with Juno. Also, **Here.**

Her·a·cles, Her·a·kles (her′ə·klēz), *n.* Hercules. —**Her′a·cle′an, Her′a·kle′an,** *adj.*

her·ald (her′əld), *n.* 1. formerly, an officer who carried messages, made announcements, arranged and supervised tourneys and other public ceremonies, and regulated the use of armorial bearings. 2. person who carries messages and makes announcements; messenger. 3. forerunner; harbinger: *dawn is the herald of day.* —*v.* 1. bring news of; announce. 2. go before and announce the coming of. [< Med.L *heraldus* < Rom. < Gmc.] —Syn. *n.* 3. precursor.

he·ral·dic (he·ral′dik), *adj.* of or having to do with heraldry or heralds. —**he·ral′di·cal·ly,** *adv.*

her·ald·ry (her′əld·ri), *n., pl.* **–ries.** 1. science or art dealing with coats of arms; science of settling a person's right to use a coat of arms, of tracing family descent, of making up a coat of arms for a new country, etc. 2. a heraldic device. 3. coat of arms.

herb (ėrb, hėrb), *n.* 1. plant whose leaves or

stems are used for medicine, seasoning, food, or perfume. Sage, mint, and lavender are herbs. 2. a flowering plant whose stems live only one season. Herbs do not form woody tissue as shrubs and trees do, though their roots may live many years. Peonies, buttercups, corn, wheat, cabbage, lettuce, etc., are herbs. 3. herbage. [< OF < L *herba*] —**herb′less,** *adj.* —**herb′like′,** *adj.*

her·ba·ceous (hėr·bā′shəs), *adj.* 1. of an herb; like an herb; having stems that are soft and not woody. 2. like a leaf; green.

herb·age (ėr′bij; hėr′–), *n.* 1. herbs. 2. grass. 3. the green leaves and soft stems of plants.

herb·al (hėr′bəl; ėr′–), *adj.* of herbs. —*n.* book about herbs.

herb·al·ist (hėr′bəl·ist; ėr′–), *n.* 1. person who gathers or deals in herbs. 2. formerly, a botanist.

her·bar·i·um (hėr·bãr′i·əm), *n., pl.* **–bar·i·ums, –bar·i·a** (–bãr′i·ə). 1. collection of dried plants systematically arranged. 2. room or building where such a collection is kept.

Her·bert (hėr′bərt), *n.* **Victor,** 1859–1924, American composer of operettas, born in Ireland.

her·biv·o·rous (hėr·biv′ə·rəs), *adj.* feeding on grass or other plants. [< NL, < L *herba* herb + *vorare* devour]

her·cu·le·an, Her·cu·le·an (hėr·kū′li·ən; hėr′kyə·lē′ən), *adj.* 1. of great strength, courage, or size; very powerful. 2. requiring great strength, courage, or size; hard to do.

Her·cu·les (hėr′kyə·lēz), *n.* 1. *Class. Legend.* hero famous for his great strength. 2. a northern constellation. Also, **Heracles, Herakles.**

herd (hėrd), *n.* 1. number of animals together, esp. large animals: *a herd of cows, a herd of elephants.* 2. a large number of people. 3. the common people; rabble. —*v.* 1. join together; flock together. 2. form into a flock, herd, or group. 3. tend or take care of (cattle, sheep, etc.). [OE *heord*] —**herd′er,** *n.*

herds·man (hėrdz′mən), *n., pl.* **–men.** man who takes care of a herd.

here (hir), *adv.* 1. in this place; at this place: *place it here, here the speaker paused.* 2. to this place: *come here.* 3. at this time; now. 4. in this life. 5. (often used to call attention to some person or thing): *my friend here can help you.* 6. here and there, in this place and that; at intervals. 7. here's to!, a wish of health, happiness, or success to. 8. neither here nor there, off the subject; unimportant. —*n.* 1. this place. 2. this life. —*interj.* answer showing that one is present when the roll is called. [OE *hēr*]

here·a·bout (hir′ə·bout′), **here·a·bouts** (–bouts′), *adv.* about this place; around here; near here.

here·af·ter (hir·af′tər; –äf′–), *adv.* 1. after this; in the future. 2. in life after death. —*n.* 1. the future. 2. life after death.

here·at (hir·at′), *adv.* 1. when this happened; at this time. 2. because of this.

here·by (hir·bī′), *adv.* by this means; in this way.

he·red·i·ta·ble (hə·red′ə·tə·bəl), *adj.* that can be inherited. —**he·red′i·ta·bil′i·ty,** *n.* —**he·red′i·ta·bly,** *adv.*

he·red·i·tar·y (hə·red′ə·ter′i), *adj.* 1. coming by inheritance: *a hereditary title.* 2. holding a position by inheritance: *a hereditary ruler.* 3. transmitted or caused by heredity: *hereditary color blindness.* 4. having to do with inheritance or heredity. —**he·red′i·tar′i·ly,** *adv.* —**he·red′i·tar′i·ness,** *n.* —Syn. 3. inherited.

he·red·i·ty (hə·red′ə·ti), *n., pl.* **–ties.** *Biol.* 1. the fact that one generation of plants and animals produces the next. 2. the transmission of genetic physical or mental characteristics from parent to offspring. 3. qualities that have come to offspring from parents. 4. tendency of offspring to be like the parents. [< L *hereditas* < *heres* heir]

Her·e·ford (hėr′fərd; hėr′ə·fərd), *n.* one of a breed of beef cattle having a red body, white face, and white markings under the body.

here·in (hir·in′), *adv.* **1.** in this place. **2.** in this matter; in view of this.

here·in·af·ter (hir′in·af′tər; –äf′–), *adv.* afterward in this document, statement, etc.

here·in·be·fore (hir·in′bi·fôr′; –fōr′), *adv.* before in this document, statement, etc.

here·in·to (hir·in′tü), *adv.* **1.** into this place. **2.** into this matter.

here·of (hir·ov′; –uv′), *adv.* of this; about this.

here·on (hir·on′; –ôn′), *adv.* **1.** on this. **2.** immediately after this.

her·e·sy (her′ə·si), *n., pl.* **–sies. 1.** belief different from the accepted belief of a church, school, profession, etc. **2.** the holding of such a belief. [< OF < L < Gk. *hairesis* a taking, choosing < *haireein* take]

her·e·tic (her′ə·tik), *n.* person who holds a belief that is different from the accepted belief of his church, school, profession, etc. —*adj.* holding such a belief. —**Syn.** *n.* dissenter.

he·ret·i·cal (hə·ret′ə·kəl), *adj.* **1.** of or having to do with heresy or heretics. **2.** containing heresy; characterized by heresy. —**he·ret′i·cal·ly,** *adv.*

here·to (hir·tü′), *adv.* to this place, thing, etc.

here·to·fore (hir′tə·fôr′; –fōr′), *adv.* before this time; until now.

here·un·to (hir′un·tü′), *adv.* **1.** unto this. **2.** until this time.

here·up·on (hir′ə·pon′; –pôn′), *adv.* **1.** upon this. **2.** immediately after this.

here·with (hir·with′; –with′), *adv.* **1.** with this. **2.** by this means; in this way.

her·it·a·ble (her′ə·tə·bəl), *adj.* **1.** capable of being inherited. **2.** capable of inheriting. —**her′-it·a·bil′i·ty,** *n.* —**her′it·a·bly,** *adv.*

her·it·age (her′ə·tij), *n.* what is or may be handed on to a person from his ancestors; inheritance. [< OF, < *heriter* inherit < LL, ult. < L *heres* heir]

her·maph·ro·dite (hér·maf′rə·dīt), *n.* **1.** animal or plant having the reproductive organs of both sexes. **2.** person or thing that combines two opposite qualities. **3.** *Naut.* a hermaphrodite brig. —*adj.* of or like a hermaphrodite. [< L < Gk. *Hermaphroditos* Hermaphroditus, son of Hermes and Aphrodite, who became united in body with a nymph] —**her·maph′ro·dit·ic** (hér·maf′rə·dit′ik), *adj.* —**her·maph′ro·dit′i·cal·ly,** *adv.*

hermaphrodite brig, a two-masted ship, square-rigged forward and schooner-rigged aft.

Her·mes (hér′mēz), *n. Gk. Myth.* god who was the messenger of Zeus and the other gods, identified by the Romans with Mercury.

her·met·ic (hér·met′ik), **her·met·i·cal** (–ə·kəl), *adj.* airtight. [< Med.L *hermeticus* < *Hermes* Hermes] —**her·met′i·cal·ly,** *adv.*

Her·mi·o·ne (hér·mī′ə·nē), *n. Gk. Myth.* daughter of Menelaus and Helen of Troy.

her·mit (hér′mit), *n.* person who goes away from other people and lives by himself, esp. one who does so for religious reasons; anchorite. [< OF < LL < Gk. *eremites* < *eremia* desert < *eremos* solitary] —**her·mit′ic,** **her·mit′i·cal,** *adj.* —**her·mit′i·cal·ly,** *adv.* —**her′mit·like′,** *adj.*

her·mit·age (hér′mə·tij), *n.* **1.** home of a hermit. **2.** place to live away from other people.

hermit crab, a soft-bodied crab that lives in the empty shells of snails, whelks, etc.

her·ni·a (hér′ni·ə), *n., pl.* **–ni·as, –ni·ae** (–ni·ē). protrusion of a part of the intestine or some other organ through a break in its surrounding walls; rupture. [< L] —**her′ni·al,** *adj.*

he·ro (hir′ō), *n., pl.* **–roes. 1.** man or boy admired for his bravery, great deeds, or noble qualities. **2.** the most important male person in a story, play, poem, etc. [ult. < L < Gk. *heros*]

Her·od (her′əd), *n.* **1.** ("the Great") 73?–4 B.C., king of the Jews from 37? to 4 B.C. **2.** his son, Herod An·ti·pas (an′tə·pas), ruler of Galilee from 4 B.C. to 39 A.D.

He·rod·o·tus (hə·rod′ə·təs), *n.* 484?–425 B.C., Greek historian, called "the father of history."

he·ro·ic (hi·rō′ik), *adj.* Also, **he·ro′i·cal. 1.** like a hero, his deeds, or his qualities. **2.** of or about heroes and their deeds: *heroic poetry.* **3.** noble. **4.** unusually daring or bold. **5.** magniloquent; grand. **6.** unusually large; larger than life size. —*n.* **1.** a heroic poem. **2.** heroics, high-sounding language. **3.** heroics, words, feelings, or actions that seem grand or noble but are only for effect. **4.** Usually, heroics. heroic verse. —**he·ro′i·cal·ly,** *adv.* —**he·ro′i·cal·ness,** **he·ro′ic·ness,** *n.* —**Syn.** *adj.* **1.** brave, great.

heroic couplet, two successive lines of poetry in iambic pentameter that rhyme.

heroic verse, iambic pentameter couplets.

her·o·in (her′ō·in), *n.* **1.** a poisonous, habit-forming drug made from morphine. **2.** Heroin, a trademark for this drug.

her·o·ine (her′ō·in), *n.* **1.** woman or girl admired for her great deeds or noble qualities. **2.** the most important female person in a story, play, poem, etc. [< L < Gk., fem. of *heros* hero]

her·o·ism (her′ō·iz·əm), *n.* **1.** actions and qualities of a hero or heroine; great bravery; daring courage. **2.** a very brave act or quality. —**Syn. 1.** valor, gallantry, intrepidity.

her·on (her′ən), *n.* a wading bird with a long neck, long bill, and long legs. [< OF *hairon* < Gmc.]

her·on·ry (her′ən·ri), *n., pl.* **–ries.** place where many herons come in the breeding season.

her·pes (hér′pēz), *n.* **1.** disease of the skin or mucous membrane characterized by clusters of blisters. **2.** shingles (the disease). [< L < Gk., shingles, < *herpein* creep] —**her·pet·ic** (hér·pet′ik), *adj.*

her·pe·tol·o·gy (hér′pə·tol′ə·ji), *n.* branch of zoölogy dealing with reptiles. [< Gk. *herpeton* reptile (< *herpein* creep) + -LOGY] —**her·pe·to·log′i·cal** (hér′pə·tə·loj′ə·kəl), *adj.* —**her′pe·tol′o·gist,** *n.*

Herr (her), *n., pl.* **Her·ren** (her′ən). *German.* **1.** Mr.; Sir. **2.** gentleman.

Her·rick (her′ik), *n.* Robert, 1591–1674, English lyric poet.

her·ring (her′ing), *n., pl.* **–rings** or (*esp. collectively*) **–ring.** a small food fish of the N Atlantic. [OE *hǣring*]

her·ring·bone (her′ing·bōn′), *adj.* having a zigzag pattern or arrangement. —*n.* a zigzag pattern or arrangement.

hers (hérz), *pron.* **1.** of her; belonging to her. **2.** the one or ones belonging to her.

her·self (hér·self′), *pron.* **1.** the emphatic form of she or her: *she herself did it.* **2.** the reflexive form of her: *she hurt herself.* **3.** her real self: *in those fits she is not herself.*

hertz·i·an wave (hert′si·ən), an electromagnetic radiation, such as the wave used in communicating by radio, produced by irregular fluctuation of electricity in a conductor. [first investigated by H. R. Hertz, physicist]

Her·ze·go·vi·na (her′tsə·gō·vē′nə), *n.* region in W Yugoslavia, formerly a part of Austria-Hungary.

he's (hēz; *unstressed* ēz, iz, hiz), **1.** he is. **2.** he has.

hes·i·tan·cy (hez′ə·tən·si), **hes·i·tance** (hez′ə·təns), *n., pl.* **–cies; –tanc·es.** hesitation; doubt; indecision.

hes·i·tant (hez′ə·tənt), *adj.* hesitating; doubtful; undecided. —**hes′i·tant·ly,** *adv.*

hes·i·tate (hez′ə·tāt), *v.,* **–tat·ed, –tat·ing. 1.** fail to act promptly; hold back because one feels doubtful; be undecided; show that one has not yet made up one's mind. **2.** feel that perhaps one should not; not want: *I hesitated to ask you, because you were so busy.* **3.** stop for an instant; pause. **4.** speak with stops or pauses. [< L *haesitare* < *haerere* stick fast] —**hes′i·tat′er, hes′-i·ta′tor,** *n.* —**hes′i·tat′ing,** *adj.* —**hes′i·tat′ing·ly,** *adv.* —**Syn. 1.** doubt, waver, vacillate, falter. **4.** stammer, stutter.

hes·i·ta·tion (hez′ə·tā′shən), *n.* **1.** a hesitating; doubt; indecision; unwillingness; delay. **2.** a speaking with short stops or pauses.

Hes·per·i·des (hes·per'ə·dēz), n.pl. Gk. Myth. 1. the four nymphs who guarded the golden apples of Hera. 2. garden where these apples were kept.

Hes·per·us (hes'pər·əs), **Hes·per** (hes'pər), n. the evening star.

Hesse (hes; hes'ə), n. district in W Germany.

Hes·sian (hesh'ən), adj. of Hesse or its people. —n. 1. native or inhabitant of Hesse. 2. U.S. a German soldier hired by England to fight against the Americans during the American Revolution. 3. hireling; ruffian.

Hessian fly, Am. a small, two-winged insect whose larvae are very destructive to wheat.

hest (hest), n. Archaic. behest; command. [alter. of OE hǣs]

he·tae·ra (hi·tir'ə), n., pl. -tae·rae (-tir'ē). courtesan of ancient Greece. [< Gk. hetaira, fem., companion]

heter–, hetero–, word element. other; different, as in heterogeneous. [< Gk., < heteros]

het·er·o·dox (het'ər·ə·doks), adj. rejecting the regularly accepted beliefs or doctrines; differing from an acknowledged standard; not orthodox. [< LL < Gk., < heteros other + doxa opinion]

het·er·o·dox·y (het'ər·ə·dok'si), n., pl. -dox·ies. 1. rejection of regularly accepted beliefs or doctrines; departure from an acknowledged standard; opposite of orthodoxy. 2. belief, doctrine, or opinion not in agreement with what is regularly accepted.

het·er·o·dyne (het'ər·ə·dīn'), adj. having to do with the production of sounds by combining radio oscillations of slightly different frequencies.

het·er·o·ge·ne·ous (het'ər·ə·jē'ni·əs; -jēn'yəs), adj. 1. different in kind; unlike; not at all similar; varied. 2. made up of unlike elements or parts; miscellaneous. [< Med.L heterogeneus, ult. < Gk. heteros other + genos kind] —het·er·o·ge·ne·i·ty (het'ər·ə·jə·nē'ə·ti), het'er·o·ge'ne·ous·ness, n. —het'er·o·ge'ne·ous·ly, adv.

hew (hū), v., hewed, hewed or hewn (hūn), hew·ing. 1. cut with an ax, sword, etc. 2. cut into shape; form by cutting: hew stone for building. 3. cut down; fell with cutting blows. [OE hēawan] —hew'er, n.

hex (heks), Am., Colloq. —v. practice witchcraft on; bewitch. [< n.] —n. 1. witch. 2. a magic spell. [< G hexe witch]

hex·a·gon (hek'sə·gon), n. a plane figure having six angles and six sides. [< LL < Gk., ult. < hex six + gonia angle] —hex·ag·o·nal (heks·ag'ə·nəl), adj. —hex·ag'o·nal·ly, adv.

Hexagons

hex·a·gram (hek'sə·gram), n. a six-pointed star formed of two equilateral triangles.

hex·a·he·dron (hek'sə·hē'drən), n., pl. -drons, -dra (-drə). a solid figure having six faces. [< Gk., < hex six + hedra surface] —hex'a·he'dral, adj.

hex·am·e·ter (heks·am'ə·tər), adj. of poetry, consisting of six feet or measures. —n. poetry having six feet or measures in each line. [< Gk., < hex six + metron measure] —hex·a·met·ric (hek'sə·met'rik), hex'a·met'ri·cal, adj.

hex·a·pod (hek'sə·pod), n. a true insect; arthropod having six feet. —adj. having six feet. [< Gk., < hex six + pous foot] —hex·ap·o·dous (heks·ap'ə·dəs), adj.

hey (hā), interj. sound made to attract attention, to express surprise or other feeling, or to ask a question.

hey·day (hā'dā'), n. period of greatest strength, vigor, spirits, prosperity, etc.

Hez·e·ki·ah (hez'ə·kī'ə), n. king of Judah. II Kings 18–20.

Hf, Chem. hafnium.

HG, High German.

Hg, Chem. mercury.

hhd., hogshead.

hi (hī), interj. Colloq. hello! how are you?

H.I., Hawaiian Islands.

hi·a·tus (hī·ā'təs), n., pl. -tus·es, -tus. 1. an empty space; gap. 2. interruption of continuity: several hiatuses in the testimony. 3. a slight pause between two vowels that come together in successive syllables or words, as between the e's in preëminent. [< L, gap, < hiare gape]

hi·ber·nal (hī·bėr'nəl), adj. of winter; wintry.

hi·ber·nate (hī'bər·nāt), v., -nat·ed, -nat·ing. spend the winter in sleep or in an inactive condition, as bears and woodchucks do. [< L, < hibernus wintry] —hi'ber·na'tion, n.

Hi·ber·ni·a (hī·bėr'ni·ə), n. Poetic. Ireland. —Hi·ber'ni·an, n., adj.

hi·bis·cus (hə·bis'kəs; hī–), n. plant, shrub, or tree with large, showy, bell-shaped flowers. [< L]

hic·cup, hic·cough (hik'up; –əp), n. an involuntary catching of the breath. —v. catch the breath in this way.

hick (hik), Slang. —n. 1. farmer. 2. an unsophisticated person. —adj. of or like hicks.

hick·o·ry (hik'ə·ri; hik'ri), n., pl. -ries. Am. 1. a North American tree whose nuts are good to eat. 2. its tough, hard wood. [< Am.Ind.]

hi·dal·go (hi·dal'gō), n., pl. -gos. a Spanish nobleman of the second class, not so high in rank as a grandee. [< Sp., < OSp. hijo de algo son of property (orig., son of something)]

hid·den (hid'ən), adj. concealed; secret; mysterious; obscure. —v. pp. of hide[1]. —Syn. adj. covert, clandestine, occult, esoteric, latent.

hide[1] (hīd), v., hid (hid), hid·den or hid, hid·ing. 1. put or keep out of sight; conceal. 2. cover up; shut off from sight. 3. keep secret. 4. conceal oneself. 5. turn away in displeasure. [OE hȳdan] —hid'er, n. —Syn. 1. secrete. —Ant. 1. uncover.

hide[2] (hīd), n., v., hid·ed, hid·ing. —n. skin of an animal, either raw or tanned. —v. Colloq. beat; thrash. [OE hȳd]

hide-and-seek (hīd'and·sēk'), n. children's game in which some hide and others try to find them.

hide·bound (hīd'bound'), adj. 1. with the skin sticking close to the bones. 2. narrow-minded and stubborn.

hid·e·ous (hid'i·əs), adj. 1. very ugly; frightful: a hideous monster. 2. revolting to the moral sense: a hideous crime. [< OF hide fear, horror] —hid'e·ous·ly, adv. —hid'e·ous·ness, n. —Syn. 2. detestable, odious.

hide-out (hīd'out'), n. Am. place for hiding or being alone.

hid·ing[1] (hīd'ing), n. 1. concealment. 2. place to hide.

hid·ing[2] (hīd'ing), n. Colloq. a beating.

hie (hī), v., hied, hie·ing or hy·ing. hasten; go quickly. [OE hīgian]

hi·er·ar·chy (hī'ər·är'ki), n., pl. -chies. 1. government by priests. 2. body of church officials of different ranks, as archbishops, bishops, priests, etc. 3. any system of persons, etc., which has higher and lower ranks. [< Med.L < Gk., < hieros sacred + archos ruler] —hi'er·ar'chi·cal, adj. —hi'er·ar'chi·cal·ly, adv.

hi·er·at·ic (hī'ər·at'ik), **hi·er·at·i·cal** (–ə·kəl), adj. 1. having to do with the priestly caste; used by the priestly class; priestly. 2. designating or having to do with a form of Egyptian writing used by the early priests in their records. Hieratic writing is a simplified form of hieroglyphics. [< L < Gk., ult. < hieros sacred] —hi'er·at'i·cal·ly, adv.

hier·o·glyph·ic (hīr'ə·glif'ik), n. 1. picture or symbol of an object standing for a word, idea, or sound, used by ancient Egyptians, etc. 2. any writing that uses hieroglyphics. 3. a secret symbol. 4. hieroglyphics, letter or word that is hard to read. —adj. Also, hier'o·glyph'i·cal. 1. of or written in hieroglyphics. 2. symbolical. 3. hard to read. [< LL < Gk., < hieros sacred + glyphe carving] —hier'o·glyph'i·cal·ly, adv.

hi-fi (adj. hī'fī'; n. hī'fī'), Slang. —adj. high-fidelity. —n. high-fidelity reproduction, as of music, or the equipment for this.

hig·gle (hig'əl), v., -gled, -gling. dispute about prices in a petty way; haggle. [? akin to HAGGLE] —hig'gler, n.

hig·gle·dy-pig·gle·dy (hig'əl·di·pig'əl·di), adv. in jumbled confusion. —adj. jumbled; confused. —n. a jumble; confusion.

high (hī), *adj.* **1.** of more than usual height; tall: *a high building.* **2.** rising to a specified extent: *the mountain is 20,000 feet high.* **3.** far above the ground or some base: *an airplane high in the air.* **4.** extending to or down from a height: *a high leap.* **5.** above others in rank, quality, character, etc.: *high office.* **6.** greater, stronger, or better than average: *high temperature.* **7.** most important; chief; main: *the high altar.* **8.** extreme of its kind: *high crimes.* **9.** costly: *strawberries are high in winter.* **10.** not low in pitch; shrill; sharp: *a high voice.* **11.** advanced to its peak: *high summer.* **12.** slightly tainted: *game is often eaten after it has become high.* **13.** haughty: *a high manner.* **14.** *Colloq.* excited by alcoholic drinks. —*adv.* at or to a high point, place, rank, amount, degree, price, pitch, etc.: *the eagle flies high.* —*n.* **1.** something that is high. **2.** arrangement of gears to give the greatest speed. **3.** *Am., Meteorol.* region or area of high barometric pressure. **4.** on high, a. high above; up in the air. b. in heaven. [OE *hēah*] —**Syn.** *adj.* **1.** lofty, towering. **5.** eminent, elevated, exalted, noble.

high·ball (hī′bôl′), *n. Am.* whiskey, brandy, etc., mixed with soda water or ginger ale and served with ice in a tall glass.

high·born (hī′bôrn′), *adj.* of noble birth.

high·boy (hī′boi′), *n. Am.* a tall chest of drawers on legs.

high·bred (hī′bred′), *adj.* **1.** of superior breeding or stock. **2.** well-mannered; refined.

high·brow (hī′brou′), *Am., Colloq.* —*n.* person who claims to care a great deal about knowledge and culture. —*adj.* of or suitable for a highbrow.

High Church, in the Anglican Church, a party which lays great stress on church authority and ceremonial observances. —**High′-Church′,** *adj.* —**High Churchman.**

high comedy, comedy dealing with polite society and depending more on witty dialogue and well-drawn characters than on comic situations.

high·er-up (hī′ər-up′), *n. Am., Colloq.* one occupying a superior position.

high·fa·lu·tin, high·fa·lu·ting (hī′fə-lū′tən), *adj. Am., Slang.* pompous; bombastic.

high·fi·del·i·ty (hī′fə-del′ə-ti; -fī-), *adj. Electronics.* indicating reproduction of the full audio range of a transmitted signal with a minimum of distortion.

high·fli·er, high·fly·er (hī′flī′ər), *n.* **1.** person or thing that flies high. **2.** person who is extravagant or has pretentious ideas.

high·flown (hī′flōn′), *adj.* **1.** aspiring; extravagant. **2.** attempting to be elegant or eloquent: *high-flown compliments.*

high·fre·quen·cy (hī′frē′kwen·si), *adj. Electronics.* of a frequency having from 1.5 to 30 megacycles per second.

High German, the literary and official language of Germany, a development of the dialects of the highlands in central and southern Germany.

high·grade (hī′grād′), *adj.* superior.

high·hand·ed (hī′han′did), *adj.* bold; arbitrary; domineering; overbearing. —**high′-hand′ed·ly,** *adv.* —**high′-hand′ed·ness,** *n.* —**Syn.** tyrannical, autocratic.

high·hat (*v.* hī′hat′; *adj.* hī′hat′), *v.,* —**hatted,** —**hat·ting,** *adj. U.S. Slang* —*v.* treat as inferior; snub. —*adj.* **1.** stylish; grand. **2.** snobbish.

high jump, *Athletics.* contest or event in which the contestants try to jump as high as possible.

high·land (hī′lənd), *n.* **1.** country or region that is higher and hillier than the neighboring country. **2.** a mountain region.

High·land·er (hī′lən·dər), *n.* native or inhabitant of the Highlands of Scotland.

Highland fling, a lively dance of the Highlands of Scotland.

High·lands (hī′ləndz), *n.pl.* a mountainous region in N and W Scotland.

high·light (hī′līt′), *n., v.,* —**light·ed,** —**light·ing.** —*n.* Also, **high light. 1.** effect or representation of bright light. **2.** part of a painting,

photograph, etc., in which light is represented as falling with full force. **3.** the most conspicuous or interesting part, event, scene, etc. —*v.* **1.** cast a bright light on. **2.** make prominent.

high·ly (hī′li), *adv.* **1.** in a high degree; very. **2.** favorably. **3.** at a high price.

High Mass, a complete ritual of Mass with music. The priest chants the service, assisted by a deacon and subdeacon.

high-mind·ed (hī′mīn′did), *adj.* **1.** having or showing high principles and feelings. **2.** proud. —**high′-mind′ed·ly,** *adv.* —**high′-mind′ed·ness,** *n.* —**Syn. 1.** noble.

high·ness (hī′nis), *n.* **1.** a being high; height. **2.** Highness, title of honor given to members of royal families.

high-pitched (hī′picht′), *adj.* **1.** of high tone or sound; shrill. **2.** having a steep slope.

high-pres·sure (hī′presh′ər), *adj.,* *v.,* -sured, -sur·ing. *Am.* —*adj.* **1.** having or using more than the usual pressure. **2.** *Colloq.* using strong, vigorous methods. —*v. Colloq.* use strong, vigorous methods in selling, etc.

high priest, 1. a chief priest. **2.** head of the ancient Jewish priesthood.

high·road (hī′rōd′), *n.* **1.** a main road; highway. **2.** a direct and easy way.

high school, *Am.* school attended after the elementary school. —**high′-school′,** *adj.* ≫ **high school.** Capitalize only when referring to a particular school (some newspaper styles do not use capitals even then): *I graduated from high school at seventeen; I graduated from the Lincoln High School in 1951.*

high seas, the open ocean, outside the authority of any country.

high-sound·ing (hī′soun′ding), *adj.* having an imposing or pretentious sound.

high-spir·it·ed (hī′spir′it·id), *adj.* **1.** proud. **2.** courageous. **3.** spirited; fiery.

high spot, *Am.* **1.** an outstanding part or feature. **2.** hit the high spots, *Colloq.* go with great speed; mention briefly.

high-strung (hī′strung′), *adj.* very sensitive; easily excited; nervous.

hight (hīt), *v.* pp. of an archaic verb hight; named; called. [OE *heht,* preterit of *hātan* be called]

high-test (hī′test′), *adj.* **1.** passing very difficult requirements and tests. **2.** having a very low boiling point.

high tide, 1. the highest level of the tide. **2.** time when the tide is highest. **3.** the highest point.

high time, 1. time just before it is too late. **2.** *Am., Colloq.* a gay, jolly time at a party, etc.

high-toned (hī′tōnd′), *adj.* **1.** high in tone or pitch. **2.** *Am.* dignified. **3.** *Colloq.* fashionable; stylish.

high treason, treason against one's sovereign, state, or government.

high water, 1. highest level of water. **2.** high tide.

high-wa·ter mark (hī′wô′tər; -wot′ər), **1.** the highest level reached by a body of water. **2.** any highest point.

high·way (hī′wā′), *n.* **1.** a public road. **2.** a main road or route. **3.** a direct line or way to some end.

high·way·man (hī′wā′mən), *n., pl.* -men. man who robs travelers on the public road.

hi·jack (hī′jak′), *v. Am., Colloq.* rob or take by force, esp. goods, liquor, etc., being transported illegally. —**hi′jack′er,** *n. Am.*

hike (hīk), *v.,* hiked, hik·ing, *n. Colloq.* —*v.* **1.** take a long walk; tramp; march. **2.** move, draw, or raise with a jerk. —*n. Am.* **1.** a march or tramp. **2.** increase. —**hik′er,** *n.*

hi·lar·i·ous (hə·lār′i·əs; hī-), *adj.* very merry; noisily gay. —**hi·lar′i·ous·ly,** *adv.* —**hi·lar′i·ous·ness,** *n.* —**Syn.** rollicking, boisterous.

hi·lar·i·ty (hə·lar′ə·ti; hī-), *n.* great mirth; noisy gaiety. [< L, < *hilaris, hilarus* gay < Gk. *hilaros*]

hill (hil), *n.* **1.** a raised part on the earth's

surface, not so big as a mountain. 2. a little heap or pile: *an ant hill*. 3. a little heap of soil put over and around the roots of a plant or cluster of plants. 4. the plant or plants so surrounded. —*v.* 1. cover with soil in this way. 2. form into a heap. [OE *hyll*] —hill′er, *n.*

hill·bil·ly (hil′bil′i), *n., pl.* -lies. *Am., Colloq.* person who lives in the backwoods or a mountain region, esp. in the South.

hill·ock (hil′ək), *n.* a little hill. —hill′ock·y, *adj.*

hill·side (hil′sīd′), *n.* side of a hill.

hill·top (hil′top′), *n.* top of a hill.

hill·y (hil′i), *adj.,* hill·i·er, hill·i·est. 1. having many hills. 2. like a hill; steep. —hill′i·ness, *n.*

hilt (hilt), *n.* 1. handle of a sword, dagger, etc. 2. up to the hilt, completely. [OE] —hilt′ed, *adj.*

hi·lum (hī′ləm), *n., pl.* -la (-lə). *Bot.* mark or scar on a seed at the point of attachment to the seed vessel. [< L, trifle]

him (him; *unstressed* im), *pron.* the objective case of he: *take him home.*

Him·a·la·yas (him′ə·lā′əz), or **Himalaya Mountains,** *n.pl.* a mountain range extending for 1600 miles along the N border of India. —Him′a·la′yan, *adj.*

Himm·ler (him′lər), *n.* Heinrich, 1900–1945, head of the Gestapo in Nazi Germany.

him·self (him·self′; *unstressed* im·self′), *pron.* 1. the emphatic form of he or him: *he himself did it.* 2. the reflexive form of him: *he hurt himself.* 3. his real self: *he feels like himself again.*

hind[1] (hīnd), *adj.,* hind·er, hind·most or hind·er·most. back; rear. [see HINDER[2], BEHIND]

hind[2] (hīnd), *n., pl.* hinds or (*esp. collectively*) hind. a female deer, usually a female red deer after its third year. [OE]

hind[3] (hīnd), *n. Archaic or Brit. Dial.* 1. a farm worker. 2. peasant. [OE *hīne*, pl.]

Hind., Hindustani.

hind·brain (hīnd′brān′), *n. Anat.* the back part of the brain.

Hin·den·burg (hin′dən·bėrg), *n.* Paul von, 1847–1934, German general and field marshal, president of Germany, 1925–1934.

hin·der[1] (hin′dər), *v.* keep back; hold back; get in the way of; make difficult; stop; prevent. [OE *hindrian*] —hin′der·er, *n.* —hin′der·ing·ly, *adv.* —Syn. impede, encumber, retard, hamper.

hind·er[2] (hīn′dər), *adj.* hind; back; rear. [cf. OE *hinder* and *hindan* in back, behind]

Hin·di (hin′di), *n.* 1. an Indo-European vernacular language of N India. 2. form of Hindustani.

hind·most (hīnd′mōst), **hind·er·most** (hīn′dər·mōst), *adj.* furthest behind; last.

hind·quar·ter (hīnd′kwôr′tər), *n.* the hind leg and loin of a carcass of beef, lamb, etc.

hin·drance (hin′drəns), *n.* 1. person or thing that hinders; obstacle. 2. act of hindering.

hind·sight (hīnd′sīt′), *n. Am., Colloq.* ability to see, too late, what should have been done.

Hin·du, Hin·doo (hin′dū), *n., pl.* -dus; -doos; *adj.* —*n.* 1. member of a native race of India. 2. person who believes in Hinduism. —*adj.* having to do with the Hindus, their languages, or their religion.

Hin·du·ism, Hin·doo·ism (hin′dù·iz·əm), *n.* the religious and social system of the Hindus.

Hin·du·stan (hin′dú·stän′; -stan′), *n.* 1. India. 2. part of India north of the Deccan.

Hin·du·sta·ni, Hin·doo·sta·ni (hin′dù·stä′ni; -stan′i), *adj.* having to do with India, its people, or their languages. —*n.* the commonest language of India.

hinge (hinj), *n., v.,* hinged, hing·ing. —*n.* 1. joint on which a door, gate, cover, lid, etc., moves back and forth. 2. a natural joint doing similar work: *hinge of the knee.* 3. a critical point. —*v.* 1. furnish with hinges; attach by hinges. 2. hang or turn on a hinge. 3. depend. [OE *henge-*; akin to HANG] —hinged, *adj.*

hin·ny (hin′i), *n., pl.* -nies. a mulelike animal that is the offspring of a male horse and a female donkey. [< L *hinnus* < Gk. *innos*]

hint (hint), *n.* a slight sign; indirect suggestion. —*v.* 1. give a slight sign of; suggest indirectly. 2. hint at, give a hint of; suggest. [appar. < *hent*, v., seize, OE *hentan*] —hint′er, *n.* —hint′ing·ly, *adv.* —Syn. *n.* intimation, allusion, inkling, innuendo, insinuation.

hin·ter·land (hin′tər·land′), *n.* 1. land or district behind a coast; back country. 2. remote parts; background. [< G]

hip[1] (hip), *n.* 1. the projecting part on a person where the leg joins the body; joint formed by the upper thighbone and pelvis. 2. on the hip, at a disadvantage. [OE *hype*] —hip′like′, *adj.*

hip[2] (hip), *n.* pod containing the ripe seed of a rose bush. [OE *hēope*]

hipped (hipt), *adj. Am., Slang.* obsessed. [var. of *hypt* < *hyp,* n., for *hypochondria*]

Hip·poc·ra·tes (hi·pok′rə·tēz), *n.* 460?–357? B.C., Greek physician, called "the father of medicine." —Hip·po·crat·ic (hip′ə·krat′ik), *adj.*

Hippocratic oath, a famous oath describing the duties and obligations of a physician.

Hip·po·crene (hip′ə·krēn; hip′ə·krē′nē), *n. Gk. Myth.* fountain sacred to the Muses and regarded as a source of poetic inspiration.

hip·po·drome (hip′ə·drōm), *n.* 1. in ancient Greece and Rome, an oval track for horse races and chariot races, surrounded by tiers of seats for spectators. 2. arena or building for a circus, rodeo, etc. [< L < Gk., < *hippos* horse + *dromos* course]

hip·po·pot·a·mus (hip′ə·pot′ə·məs), *n., pl.* -mus·es, -mi (-mī). a huge, thick-skinned, hairless mammal found in and near the rivers of Africa. [< L < Gk., < *hippos* horse + *potamos* river]

hir·cine (hėr′sīn; -sin), *adj.* of goats; resembling a goat. [< L, < *hircus* goat]

Hippopotamus (ab. 13 ft. long)

hire (hīr), *v.,* hired, hir·ing, *n.* —*v.* 1. pay for the use of (a thing) or the work or services of (a person). 2. give the use of (a thing) or the work or services of (a person) in return for payment. [OE *hȳrian,* < n.] —*n.* 1. payment for such use or work. 2. a hiring. [OE *hȳr*] —hir′a·ble, hire′a·ble, *adj.* —hir′er, *n.* —Syn. *v.* 1, 2, lease, rent.

hire·ling (hīr′ling), *n.* person who works only for money, without interest or pride in the task. —*adj.* to be had for hire; mercenary.

Hir·o·hi·to (hir′ō·hē′tō), *n.* born 1901, emperor of Japan since 1926.

Hir·o·shi·ma (hir′ə·shē′mə), *n.* seaport in W Japan, largely destroyed by the first military use of the atomic bomb, Aug. 6, 1945.

hir·sute (hėr′sūt), *adj.* hairy. [< L *hirsutus*] —hir′sute·ness, *n.*

his (hiz; *unstressed* iz), *pron.* 1. of him; belonging to him: *this is his.* 2. the one or ones belonging to him: *the others are not his.* —*adj.* of him; belonging to him: *this is his book.* [OE, gen. of *hē* he]

His·pa·ni·a (his·pā′ni·ə; -nyə), *n. Poetic.* Spain. —His·pan·ic (his·pan′ik), *adj.*

His·pan·io·la (his′pən·yō′lə), *n.* the second largest island in the West Indies, divided into the Dominican Republic and the republic of Haiti. Former name, Haiti.

hiss (his), *v.* 1. make a sound like *ss.* Geese and snakes hiss. 2. show disapproval of or scorn for by hissing: *hiss poor acting.* 3. force or drive by hissing: *hiss him off the stage.* 4. say or show by hissing. —*n.* a sound like *ss.* [imit.] —hiss′er, *n.*

hist (hist), *interj.* be still! listen!

hist., historian; historical; history.

his·ta·mine (his′tə·mēn; -min), *n.* an amine, $C_5H_9N_3$, released by the body in allergic reactions. It lowers the blood pressure, stimulates contraction of the uterus, etc.

his·tol·o·gy (his·tol′ə·ji), *n.* science of the tissues of animals and plants; study of the structure, esp. the microscopic structure, of

organic tissues. [< Gk. *histos* web + -LOGY]
—his·to·log·i·cal (his'tə·loj'ə·kəl), his'to·log'ic,
adj. —his·tol'o·gist, *n.*

his·to·ri·an (his·tô'ri·ən; -tō'-), *n.* 1. person
who writes about history. 2. scholar who is an
authority on history.

his·tor·ic (his·tôr'ik; -tor'-), *adj.* 1. famous
or important in history. 2. historical.

his·tor·i·cal (his·tôr'ə·kəl; -tor'-), *adj.* 1. of
or having to do with history. 2. according to
history; based on history. 3. known to be real or
true; in history, not in legend. 4. historic. —his·
tor'i·cal·ly, *adv.* —his·tor'i·cal·ness, *n.*

historical present, *Gram.* the present tense
used in describing past events.

his·to·ri·og·ra·pher (his·tô'ri·og'rə·fər;
-tō'-), *n.* 1. historian. 2. the official historian of
a court, public institution, etc. —his·to'ri·og'·
ra·phy, *n.*

his·to·ry (his'tə·ri; his'tri), *n., pl.* -ries. 1.
statement of what has happened. 2. story of a
man or a nation; systematic written account. 3.
a known past: *this ship has a history.* 4. all past
events considered together; course of human
affairs. 5. a recording and explaining of past
events; study of such records. [< L < Gk. *his·
toria* inquiry, record, history. Doublet of STORY¹.]

his·tri·on·ic (his'tri·on'ik), *adj.* 1. having to
do with actors or acting. 2. theatrical; insincere.
[< L, < *histrio* actor < Etruscan (h)*ister*] —his'·
tri·on'i·cal·ly, *adv.*

his·tri·on·ics (his'tri·on'iks), *n.pl.* 1. dra·
matic representation; theatricals; dramatics. 2.
a theatrical or insincere manner, expression, etc.

hit (hit), *v.,* **hit, hit·ting,** *n.* —*v.* 1. come against
with force; give a blow to; strike; knock. 2. pro·
pel by a stroke: *hit the ball over the fence.* 3.
Am., Colloq. arrive at: *hit town.* 4. have a pain·
ful effect on; affect severely. 5. attack or criticize.
6. *Colloq.* of an engine, ignite the mixture in a
cylinder: *the car hits on all eight cylinders.* 7.
agree with; suit exactly. 8. **hit it off,** *Colloq.* get
along well together; agree. 9. **hit on** or **upon,** a.
come on; meet with; get to. b. find, esp. by acci·
dent; guess correctly. 10. **hit or miss,** by chance;
at random. —*n.* 1. a blow; stroke. 2. a getting
to what is aimed at. 3. attack or criticism. 4.
a successful attempt, performance, or produc·
tion: *the song was a hit.* 5. *Baseball.* ball so
struck that the batter can get to first base
safely, and perhaps further. [< Scand. *hitta*]
—hit'ter, *n.*

hitch (hich), *v.* 1. move or pull with a jerk;
move jerkily. 2. limp; hobble. 3. harness to a
cart or conveyance. 4. fasten with a hook, ring,
rope, strap, etc. 5. become fastened or caught;
catch. —*n.* 1. a short, sudden pull or jerk; jerky
movement. 2. limp; hobble. 3. a making fast;
catching hold. 4. a fastening; catch. 5. obstacle;
hindrance. 6. *Naut.* kind of knot used for tem·
porary fastening. [ME *hyche*(n)] —hitch'er, *n.*
—Syn. *v.* 4. attach, tie, hook, tether, harness.

hitch·hike (hich'hīk'), *v.,* -hiked, -hik·ing.
Am., Slang. travel by getting free rides from
passing automobiles. —hitch'hik'er, *n. Am.*

hith·er (hiŧẖ'ər), *adv.* to this place; toward
this place; here: *come hither.* —*adj.* on this side;
nearer. [OE *hider;* akin to HERE]

hith·er·to (hiŧẖ'ər·tü'), *adv.* up to this time;
until now.

hith·er·ward (hiŧẖ'ər·wərd), **hith·er·**
wards (-wərdz), *adv.* toward this place; hither.

Hit·ler (hit'lər), *n.* Adolf, 1889–1945, German
dictator, born in Austria, chancellor of Ger·
many from 1933 to 1945.

Hit·ler·ism (hit'lər·iz·əm), *n.* program and
teachings of the political party founded in Ger·
many by Hitler and others in 1919 and 1920.
—Hit·ler·ite (hit'lər·īt'), *n.*

Hit·tite (hit'īt), *n.* 1. member of an ancient
people in Asia Minor and Syria, existing from
about 2000 B.C. until about 1200 B.C. 2. language
of the Hittites. —*adj.* of or having to do with the
Hittites or their language.

hive (hīv), *n., v.,* **hived, hiv·ing.** —*n.* 1. house
or box for bees to live in. 2. a large number of
bees living together. 3. a busy, swarming place

full of people or animals. 4. a swarming crowd.
—*v.* put (bees) in a hive. [OE *hȳf*]

hives (hīvz), *n.* any of various diseases in which
the skin itches and shows patches of red.

H.M., His Majesty; Her Majesty.

H.M.S., His (Her) Majesty's Service; His (Her)
Majesty's Ship.

ho (hō), *interj.* 1. exclamation of scornful
laughter, joy, or surprise. 2. exclamation to at·
tract attention.

Ho, *Chem.* holmium.

hoar (hôr; hōr), *adj.* hoary. —*n.* 1. hoariness.
2. hoarfrost. [OE *hār*]

hoard (hôrd; hōrd), *n.* what is saved and stored
away; things stored. —*v.* save and store away.
[OE *hord*] —hoard'er, *n.* —Syn. *v.* treasure,
amass, accumulate.

hoard·ing (hôr'ding; hōr'-), *n. Brit.* 1. a tem·
porary board fence around a building that is
being put up or repaired. 2. billboard. [< *hoard*
fence, appar. < AF *hurdis,* ult. < Gmc.]

hoar·frost (hôr'frôst'; hōr'-; -frost'), *n.*
white frost.

hoar·hound (hôr'hound'; hōr'-), *n.* hore·
hound.

hoarse (hôrs; hōrs), *adj.,* **hoars·er, hoars·est.**
1. sounding rough and deep. 2. having a rough
voice. [OE *hās;* infl. by Scand. *hāss*] —hoarse'·
ly, *adv.* —hoarse'ness, *n.* —Syn. 1. harsh, husky.

hoar·y (hôr'i; hōr'i), *adj.,* **hoar·i·er, hoar·i·est.**
1. white or gray. 2. white or gray with age. 3.
old; ancient. —hoar'i·ness, *n.*

hoax (hōks), *n.* a mischievous trick, esp. a
made-up story. —*v.* play a mischievous trick on;
deceive in fun or to injure. (prob. alter. of *hocus*)
—hoax'er, *n.*

hob¹ (hob), *n.* 1. shelf at the back or side of a
fireplace. 2. peg at which quoits, etc., are thrown.

hob² (hob), *n.* 1. hobgoblin; elf. 2. *Am., Colloq.*
play hob or raise hob, cause trouble. [ME, for
Rob (*Robert* or *Robin*)]

Ho·bart (hō'bärt; -bərt), *n.* capital of Tas·
mania.

hob·ble (hob'əl), *v.,* -bled, -bling, *n.* —*v.* 1.
walk awkwardly; limp. 2. cause to walk awk·
wardly or limp. 3. move unsteadily. 4. tie the legs
of (a horse, etc.) together. 5. hinder. —*n.* 1. an
awkward walk; limp. 2. rope or strap used to
hobble a horse, etc. [ME *hobelen.* Cf. Du. *hob·
belen* to rock.] —hob'bler, *n.* —hob'bling, *adj.*

hob·ble·de·hoy (hob'əl·di·hoi'), *n.* 1. youth
between boyhood and manhood. 2. an awkward,
clumsy boy.

hob·by (hob'i), *n., pl.* -bies. 1. something a
person especially likes to work at or study apart
from his main business; any favorite pastime,
topic of conversation, etc. 2. hobbyhorse. [ME
hobyn small horse]

hob·by·horse (hob'i·hôrs'), *n.* 1. stick with a
horse's head, used as a toy horse by
children. 2. a rocking horse.

hob·gob·lin (hob'gob'lən), *n.* 1. gob·
lin; elf. 2. bogy. [< *hob²* + *goblin*]

hob·nail (hob'nāl'), *n.* a short nail
with a large head to protect the soles of Hobnails
heavy shoes. [< *hob* peg + *nail*] —hob'nailed',
adj.

hob·nob (hob'nob'), *v.,* -nobbed, -nob·bing.
1. associate intimately; talk together on familiar
terms. 2. drink together. [from drinking phrase
hob or *nob* give or take, ult. < OE *hæbbe* have +
næbbe not have]

ho·bo (hō'bō), *n., pl.* -bos, -boes. *Am.* a tramp
or vagrant.

Hob·son's choice (hob'sənz), choice of tak·
ing the thing offered or nothing. [from T. *Hob·
son,* who rented the horse nearest his stable door
or none]

Ho Chi Minh (hō' chē' min'), born 1892,
Indo-Chinese politician, leader of the Communist
Viet Minh since 1942.

hock (hok), *n.* joint in the hind leg of a horse,
cow, etc., above the fetlock joint. See the picture
under cannon bone. Also, hough. [OE *hōh*]

āge, cãre, fär; ẽqual, tẽrm; īce; ōpen, õrder; pūt, rūle, ūse; ŧẖ, then; ə=a in about.

hock[2] (hok), *n. Esp. Brit.* kind of white Rhine wine. [for *Hockamore*, alter. of *Hochheimer*]

hock[3] (hok), *v., n. Am., Slang.* pawn. [orig. n. Cf. Du. *hok* pen, jail.]

hock·ey (hok'i), *n.* game played by two teams on ice or on a field, where players hit a rubber disk or ball with curved sticks to drive it across a goal.

ho·cus (hō'kəs), *v.,* -cused, -cus·ing; *esp. Brit.* -cussed, -cus·sing. 1. play a trick on; hoax; cheat. 2. stupefy with drugs. 3. put drugs in (alcoholic drink). [short for *hocus-pocus*]

ho·cus-po·cus (hō'kəs-pō'kəs), *n., v.,* -cused, -cusing; *esp. Brit.* -cussed, -cus·sing. —*n.* 1. form of words used in conjuring. 2. sleight of hand; magic. 3. trickery; deception. —*v.* play tricks on; deceive. [sham Latin used by jugglers, etc.]

hod (hod), *n.* 1. trough or tray with a long handle, used for carrying bricks, mortar, etc., on the shoulder. 2. a coal scuttle. [cf. MDu. *hodde*]

hodge·podge (hoj'poj'), *n.* a disorderly mixture; mess; jumble. [var. of *hotchpot* < OF *hochepot* ragout]

hoe (hō), *n., v.,* hoed, hoe·ing. —*n.* tool with a small blade set across the end of a long handle, used to loosen soil and cut weeds. —*v.* 1. loosen, dig, or cut with a hoe. 2. use a hoe. [< OF *houe* < Gmc.] —hoe'like', *adj.*

hoe·cake (hō'kāk'), *n. Am., S.* kind of bread made of corn meal.

hog (hog; hôg), *n., v.,* hogged, hog·ging. —*n.* 1. pig. 2. a full-grown pig, raised for food. 3. *Colloq.* a selfish, greedy, or dirty person. —*v. Am., Slang.* take more than one's share of. [OE *hogg*]

Ho·garth (hō'gärth), *n.* William, 1697-1764, English painter and engraver.

hog·gish (hog'ish; hôg'-), *adj.* 1. like a hog; very selfish; greedy. 2. dirty; filthy. —hog'gish·ly, *adv.* —hog'gish·ness, *n.*

hog·nose snake (hog'nōz'; hôg'-), *Am.* a harmless North American snake with an up-turned snout.

hogs·head (hogz'hed; hôgz'-), *n.* 1. a large barrel that contains from 63 to 140 gallons. 2. a liquid measure, usually equal to 63 gallons.

hog·tie (hog'tī'; hôg'-), *v.,* -tied, -ty·ing. tie all four feet together.

hog·wash (hog'wosh'; -wôsh'; hôg'-), *n.* 1. swill. 2. worthless stuff; nonsense.

Hoh·en·zol·lern (hō'ən·zol'ərn), *n.* the family that included the kings of Prussia, 1701-1918, and the emperors of Germany, 1871-1918.

hoi·den (hoi'dən), *n., adj.* hoyden.

hoi pol·loi (hoi' pə·loi'), the masses. [< Gk.]

hoist (hoist), *v.* raise on high; lift up, often with ropes and pulleys. —*n.* 1. a hoisting; lift. 2. elevator or other apparatus for hoisting heavy loads. [earlier *hoise* < Du. *hijschen*] —hoist'er, *n.*

hoi·ty-toi·ty (hoi'ti·toi'ti), *interj.* exclamation showing surprise and some contempt. —*adj.* 1. giddy; flighty. 2. inclined to put on airs; haughty. —*n.* 1. flightiness. 2. haughtiness.

Hok·kai·do (ho·kī'dō), *n.* the second largest island in Japan.

ho·kum (hō'kəm), *n. Slang.* 1. sentimental matter introduced merely for effect. 2. humbug; nonsense; bunk. [? < *hocus*]

hold[1] (hōld), *v.,* held, held or (*Archaic*) hold·en, hold·ing, *n.* —*v.* 1. take in the hands or arms and keep: *hold a child.* 2. not let go. 3. keep from getting away. 4. keep a grasp. 5. keep in some position or condition: *please hold still.* 6. keep from falling; support. 7. keep from acting; keep back: *hold your breath.* 8. keep by force against an enemy; defend: *hold the fort.* 9. keep or have within itself; contain: *this theater holds 500 people.* 10. have and keep as one's own. 11. possess; occupy: *hold an office.* 12. have a property, right, title, etc.: *the vassal held directly from the king.* 13. have and take part in; carry on together. 14. keep or have in mind: *hold a belief.* 15. think; consider: *hold human life cheap.* 16. remain firm; adhere; cling: *hold to one's purpose.* 17. be true; be in force or effect: *the rule holds in all cases.* 18. keep on; continue:

the weather held warm. 19. decide legally: *the court holds him guilty.* 20. hold back, keep back; keep from acting. 21. hold down, a. keep down; keep under control. b. *Am., Slang.* have and keep: *hold down a job.* 22. hold forth, a. talk; preach. b. offer. 23. hold off, keep at a distance; keep from acting or attacking. 24. hold on, *Colloq.* a. keep one's hold. b. keep on; continue. c. stop! wait a minute! 25. hold out, a. continue; last. b. extend. c. keep resisting; not give in. d. offer. e. keep back; restrain. 26. hold over, a. keep for future action or consideration. b. *Am.* stay in office beyond the regular term. 27. hold up, a. keep from falling; support. b. show; display. c. continue; last; endure. d. stop. e. *Am.* stop by force and rob. —*n.* 1. act of holding: *release one's hold.* 2. thing to hold by, as a handle. 3. thing to hold something else with. 4. a controlling force or influence: *have a secret hold on a person.* 5. *Wrestling, etc.* way of holding one's opponent; grasp or grip. 6. sign for a pause in music. 7. *Archaic.* fort; stronghold. 8. prison. [OE *healdan*] —Syn. *v.* 6. bear. 15. regard.

hold[2] (hōld), *n.* interior of a ship below the deck. [var. of *hole*]

hold·back (hōld'bak'), *n.* 1. thing that holds back; restraint; hindrance. 2. device that enables a horse to hold back or to back a vehicle.

hold·er (hōl'dər), *n.* 1. person who holds something. 2. thing to hold something else with. 3. *Law.* one legally entitled to receive payment on, or negotiate, a note, bill, etc.

hold·fast (hōld'fast'; -fäst'), *n.* device used to hold things in place, as a catch, hook, etc.

hold·ing (hōl'ding), *n.* 1. land; piece of land. 2. **Often, holdings.** property in stocks or bonds.

holding action, 1. a military operation that seeks merely to prevent an enemy advance. 2. any undertaking that resembles this: *a holding action against inflation.*

holding company, company that owns stocks or bonds of other companies and often controls them.

hold·out (hōld'out'), *n.* refusal to compromise or come to an agreement on something, esp. in order to exact a higher price, better terms, etc.

hold·up (hōld'up'), *n.* 1. *Am., Colloq.* act of stopping by force and robbing. 2. a stopping. ▸ holdup. The verb is written as two words. See definition 27e of *hold.*

hole (hōl), *n., v.,* holed, hol·ing. —*n.* 1. an open place. 2. a hollow place. 3. place dug by an animal to live in. 4. a small, dark, dirty place. 5. dungeon. 6. *Colloq.* flaw; defect. 7. *Colloq.* position hard to get out of; embarrassing position. 8. *Sports.* a small place into which a ball, marble, or the like, is to be hit, rolled, or tossed. 9. *Golf.* part of a course leading from a tee to such a place. 10. pick holes, find fault with; criticize. —*v.* 1. make holes in. 2. hit or drive (a golf ball) into a hole. 3. hole out, hit a golf ball into a hole. 4. hole up, go into a hole for the winter. [OE *hol*] —hole'less, *adj.* —hole'y, *adj.*

hol·i·day (hol'ə·dā), *n.* 1. day when one does not work; day for pleasure and enjoyment. 2. **Often, holidays,** *Esp. Brit.* vacation. 3. Now usually, **holy day,** a religious festival. —*adj.* suited to a holiday; gay. [OE *hāligdæg* holy day]

ho·li·ness (hō'li·nis), *n.* 1. a being holy. 2. Holiness, title used in speaking to or of the Pope.

Hol·land (hol'ənd), *n.* the Netherlands, a small country in N Europe. —Hol'land·er, *n.*

Hol·lands (hol'əndz), or **Holland gin,** *n.* a strong gin made in Holland.

hol·low (hol'ō), *adj.* 1. having nothing, or only air, inside; empty; with a hole inside; not solid. A tube or pipe is hollow. 2. bowl-shaped; cup-shaped: *a hollow dish for vegetables.* 3. coming from something hollow; dull: *a hollow voice.* 4. not real or sincere; false; hollow *promises, hollow praise.* 5. deep and sunken: *hollow eyes and cheeks.* 6. hungry. —*n.* 1. a hollow place; hole: *a hollow in the road.* 2. valley: *Sleepy Hollow.* —*v.* 1. make hollow; bend or dig out to a hollow shape. 2. become hollow. —*adv. Colloq.* thoroughly. [OE *holh,* n.] —hol'low·ly, *adv.* —hol'low·ness, *n.* —Syn. *adj.* 1.

void, unfilled, vacant. 4. hypocritical, insincere. 5. concave, depressed. —**Ant.** *adj.* 1. filled, full, solid. 4. sincere, straightforward.

hol·ly (hol′ĭ), *n., pl.* -lies. 1. tree or shrub with shiny, sharp-pointed, green leaves and bright-red berries. 2. the leaves and berries used as Christmas decorations. [OE *holegn*]

hol·ly·hock (hol′ĭ·hok), *n.* a tall plant with clusters of large, showy flowers of various colors. [ME *holihoc* < *holi* holy + *hoc* mallow (OE *hocc*)]

Hol·ly·wood (hol′ĭ·wụd′), *n.* section of Los Angeles where many motion pictures are made.

Holmes (hōmz), *n.* 1. Oliver Wendell, 1809-1894, American author, humorist, and physician. 2. his son, **Oliver Wendell**, 1841-1935, an associate justice of the U.S. Supreme Court from 1902 to 1932. 3. **Sherlock**, detective in stories by A. Conan Doyle.

hol·mi·um (hōl′mĭ·əm), *n. Chem.* a rare metallic element, Ho, belonging to the yttrium group. [< NL; named for *Stockholm*]

holm oak (hōm), an evergreen oak of S Europe with leaves like those of the holly. [OE *holegn* holly + *āc* oak]

hol·o·caust (hol′ə·kôst), *n.* 1. an offering all of which is burned. 2. complete destruction by fire, esp. of animals or human beings. 3. great or wholesale destruction. [< L < Gk., < *holos* whole + *kaustos* burned] —**hol′o·caus′tal, hol′o·caus′tic**, *adj.*

hol·o·graph (hol′ə·graf; -gräf), *adj.* wholly written in the handwriting of the person in whose name it appears: *a holograph will.* —*n.* a holograph manuscript, letter, document, etc. [< LL < Gk., < *holos* whole + *graphe* writing] —**hol′o·graph′ic**, *adj.*

holp (hōlp), *v. Archaic.* pt. of **help**.

hol·pen (hōl′pən), *v. Archaic.* pp. of **help**.

Hol·stein (hōl′stīn; -stēn), **Holstein-Friesian** (-frē′zhən), *n.* any of a breed of large, black-and-white dairy cattle.

hol·ster (hōl′stər), *n.* a leather case for a pistol, attached to a belt or a horseman's saddle. [cf. Du. *holster*] —**hol′stered**, *adj.*

ho·ly (hō′lĭ), *adj.,* -li·er, -li·est, *n., pl.* -lies. —*adj.* 1. set apart or devoted to the service of God, the church, or religion: *a holy man.* 2. declared sacred by religious use and authority: *a holy day.* 3. like a saint; spiritually perfect; very good; pure in heart. 4. worthy of reverence. 5. religious: *holy rites.* —*n.* a holy place. [OE *hālig*] —**Syn.** *adj.* 2. hallowed, blessed. 3. devout, pious, pure, saintly.

Holy City, 1. city considered sacred by the adherents of any religion. Jerusalem, Rome, and Mecca are Holy Cities. 2. heaven.

Holy Communion, 1. a sharing in the Lord's Supper as a part of church worship; a receiving of the Holy Eucharist. 2. celebration of the Lord's Supper.

holy day, a religious festival, esp. one not occurring on Sunday, as Ash Wednesday, Good Friday, etc.

Holy Father, *Rom. Cath. Church.* a title of the Pope.

Holy Ghost, spirit of God; third person of the Trinity.

Holy Grail, cup or dish supposed to have been used by Christ at the Last Supper, in which one of His followers received the last drops of blood from Christ's body on the cross.

Holy Land, Palestine.

holy of holies, 1. the holiest place. 2. the inner shrine of the Jewish tabernacle and temple.

holy orders, 1. the rite or sacrament of ordination. 2. the rank or position of an ordained Christian minister or priest. 3. the three higher ranks or positions in the Roman Catholic and Anglican churches. Bishops, priests, and deacons are members of holy orders.

Holy Roman Empire, empire in western and central Europe regarded both as the continuation of the Roman Empire and as the temporal form of a universal dominion whose spiritual head was the Pope, begun in 962 A.D., or, according to some, in 800 A.D., and ended in 1806.

Holy Scriptures, the Bible; scripture (def. 2).

Holy See, 1. position or authority of the Pope. 2. the Pope's court.

Holy Spirit, Holy Ghost.

ho·ly·stone (hō′lĭ·stōn′), *n., v.,* -stoned, -ston·ing. —*n.* piece of soft sandstone used for scrubbing the wooden decks of ships. —*v.* scrub with a holystone.

Holy Week, week before Easter.

Holy Writ, the Bible; the Scriptures.

hom·age (hom′ij; om′-), *n.* 1. respect; reverence: *pay homage to a great leader.* 2. a formal acknowledgment by a vassal that he owed loyalty and service to his lord. 3. thing done or given to show such acknowledgment. [< OF, < *hom* man, vassal < L *homo*] —**Syn.** 1. deference.

hom·bre (ôm′brā), *n. Spanish.* man.

hom·burg (hom′bėrg), *n.* a man's soft felt hat with the crown dented in at the top.

home (hōm), *n., adj., adv., v.,* homed, hom·ing. —*n.* 1. place where a person or family lives; one's own house. 2. place where a person was born or brought up; one's own town or country. 3. place where an animal or plant lives; habitat. 4. place where a person can rest and be safe. 5. place where people who are homeless, poor, old, sick, blind, etc., may live. 6. place of existence after death. 7. family life. 8. *Sports, etc.* point to be hit; goal. 9. *Baseball.* home plate. 10. **at home, a.** in one's own home or country. **b.** in a friendly place or familiar condition; at ease; comfortable. **c.** ready to receive visitors. —*adj.* 1. having to do with one's own home or country. 2. reaching its goal; effective: *a home thrust.* —*adv.* 1. at, to, or toward one's own home or country: *go home.* 2. to the place where it belongs; to the thing aimed at: *strike home.* 3. to the heart or center; deep in: *drive a nail home.* 4. bring home, make clear, emphatic, or realistic. —*v.* 1. go home. 2. send or bring home. 3. have a home. 4. furnish with a home. [OE *hām*] —**home′like′**, *adj.* —**Syn.** *n.* 1. residence, dwelling, abode.

home·bred (hōm′bred′), *adj.* 1. native; domestic. 2. crude; unsophisticated.

home·brew (hōm′brū′), *n.* beer or other alcoholic liquor made at home.

home economics, *Am.* science and art that deals with the management of a household.

home·land (hōm′land′), *n.* one's native land.

home·less (hōm′lĭs), *adj.* having no home. —**home′less·ly**, *adv.* —**home′less·ness**, *n.*

home·ly (hōm′lĭ), *adj.,* -li·er, -li·est. 1. suited to home life; simple; everyday: *homely pleasures.* 2. of plain manners; unpretending: *a simple, homely man.* 3. lacking cultivation; rude. 4. *U.S.* not good-looking; ugly; plain. —**home′li·ness**, *n.*

home·made (hōm′mād′), *adj.* made at home.

ho·me·op·a·thy (hō′mĭ·op′ə·thĭ; hom′ĭ-), *n.* method of treating disease by drugs, given in very small doses, which would in large doses produce in a healthy person symptoms similar to those of the disease. Also, homoeopathy. [< Gk. *homoios* similar + -*PATHY*] —**ho·me·o·path** (hō′mĭ·ə·path; hom′ĭ-), **ho′me·op′a·thist**, *n.* —**ho′me·o·path′ic**, *adj.* —**ho′me·o·path′i·cal·ly**, *adv.*

home plate, *Am., Baseball.* block or slab beside which a player stands to bat the ball, and to which he must return, after hitting the ball and rounding the bases, in order to score.

hom·er (hōm′ər), *n.* 1. *Am., Baseball.* a home run. 2. a homing pigeon.

Ho·mer (hō′mər), *n.* about the 10th cent. B.C., the great epic poet of ancient Greece; author of the *Iliad* and the *Odyssey*.

Ho·mer·ic (hō·mer′ĭk), *adj.* 1. by Homer. 2. of or pertaining to Homer or his poems. 3. in the style of Homer. 4. of the time when Homer lived.

Homeric laughter, loud, hearty laughter.

home rule, local self-government.

home run, *Am., Baseball.* run made by a player on a hit that enables him, without aid from fielding errors of the opponents, to make the entire circuit of the bases without a stop.

home·sick (hōm′sik′), *adj.* longing for home. —**home′sick′ness,** *n.*

home·spun (hōm′spun′), *adj.* **1.** spun or made at home. **2.** not polished; plain; simple. —*n.* **1.** cloth made of yarn spun at home. **2.** a strong, loosely woven cloth similar to it.

home·stead (hōm′sted), *n. Am.* **1.** house with its land and other buildings; farm with its buildings. **2.** parcel of 160 acres of public land granted to a settler under certain conditions by the U.S. government. —**home′stead·er,** *n. Am.*

home stretch, 1. *Am.* part of a track over which the last part of a race is run. **2.** the last part.

home·ward (hōm′wərd), *adv.* Also, **home′wards.** toward home. —*adj.* being in the direction of home.

home·work (hōm′wėrk′), *n.* **1.** work done at home. **2.** lesson to be studied or prepared outside the classroom.

home·y (hōm′i), *adj.,* **hom·i·er, hom·i·est.** *Colloq.* like home; cozy and comfortable.

hom·i·cide[1] (hom′ə·sīd; hō′mə-), *n.* the killing of one human being by another. Intentional homicide is murder. [< OF < L, < *homo* man + -*cidium* act of killing] —**hom′i·cid′al,** *adj.* —**hom′i·cid′al·ly,** *adv.*

hom·i·cide[2] (hom′ə·sīd; hō′mə-), *n.* person who kills a human being. [< OF < L, < *homo* man + -*cida* killer]

hom·i·let·ics (hom′ə·let′iks), *n.* art of composing and preaching sermons. [< LL < Gk., affable, ult. < *homileein* associate with. See HOMILY.] —**hom′i·let′ic,** *adj.* —**hom′i·let′i·cal·ly,** *adv.*

hom·i·ly (hom′ə·li), *n., pl.* -**lies. 1.** sermon, usually on some part of the Bible. **2.** a serious moral talk or writing. [< OF < LL < Gk. *homilia* < *homilos* throng < *homou* together]

homing pigeon, pigeon trained to fly home from great distances carrying written messages.

hom·i·ny (hom′ə·ni), *n. Am.* corn hulled and coarsely ground or crushed, usually eaten boiled. [< Algonquian]

ho·mo (hō′mō), *n., pl.* **hom·i·nes** (hom′ə·nēz). man. [< L]

ho·moe·op·a·thy (hō′mi·op′ə·thi; hom′i-), *n.* homeopathy. —**ho·moe·o·path** (hō′mi·ə·path; hom′i-), **ho′moe·op′a·thist,** *n.* —**ho′moe·o·path′ic,** *adj.* —**ho′moe·o·path′i·cal·ly,** *adv.*

ho·mo·ge·ne·ous (hō′mə·jē′ni·əs; -jēn′yəs; hom′ə-), *adj.* **1.** of the same kind; similar. **2.** composed of similar elements or parts. [< Med.L < Gk., < *homos* the same + *genos* kind] —**ho·mo·ge·ne·i·ty** (hō′mə·jə·nē′ə·ti; hom′ə-), —**ho·mo·ge′ne·ous·ness,** *n.* —**ho′mo·ge′ne·ous·ly,** *adv.*

ho·mog·e·nize (hə·moj′ə·nīz), *v.,* -**nized,** -**niz·ing.** make homogeneous. In homogenized milk the fat is distributed evenly throughout and does not rise in the form of cream.

hom·o·graph (hom′ə·graf; -gräf; hō′mə-), *n.* word having the same spelling as another, but a different origin and meaning. *Mail,* meaning "letters," and *mail,* meaning "armor," are homographs. [< Gk., < *homos* the same + *graphe* writing] —**hom′o·graph′ic,** *adj.*

ho·mol·o·gous (hō·mol′ə·gəs), *adj.* **1.** corresponding in position, value, etc. **2.** *Biol.* corresponding in type of structure and in origin. The wing of a bird and the foreleg of a horse are homologous. [< Gk., agreeing, < *homos* same + *logos* reasoning, relation]

ho·mol·o·gy (hō·mol′ə·ji), *n., pl.* -**gies.** correspondence in position, proportion, value, structure, origin, etc.

hom·o·nym (hom′ə·nim), *n.* word having the same pronunciation as another, but a different meaning. *Meat* and *meet* are homonyms. [< L < Gk., < *homos* same + *onyma* (dial.) name] —**hom′o·nym′ic,** *adj.*

hom·o·phone (hom′ə·fōn; hō′mə-), *n.* **1.** letter or symbol having the same sound as another.

The letters *c* and *k* are homophones in the word *cork.* **2.** homonym. [< Gk., < *homos* same + *phone* sound]

ho·moph·o·ny (hō·mof′ə·ni; hom′ə·fō′ni), *n.* **1.** sameness of sound. **2.** music having one part or melody predominating. —**hom·o·phon·ic** (hom′ə·fon′ik; hō′mə-), **ho·moph·o·nous** (hō·mof′ə·nəs), *adj.*

ho·mop·ter·ous (hō·mop′tər·əs), *adj. Zool.* belonging to a group of insects (including the aphids and cicadas) with mouth parts adapted to sucking and wings of the same texture throughout. [< Gk. *homos* same + *pteron* wing]

Ho·mo sa·pi·ens (hō′mō sā′pi·enz), man; human being; the species including all existing races of mankind. [L, lit., man having sense]

ho·mo·sex·u·al (hō′mə·sek′shú·əl), *adj.* pertaining to or manifesting sexual feelings for one of the same sex. —*n.* a homosexual person. [< Gk. *homos* same + L *sexus* sex] —**ho′mo·sex′u·al′i·ty,** *n.*

ho·mun·cu·lus (hō·mung′kyə·ləs), *n., pl.* -**li** (-lī). a little man. [< L, dim. of *homo* man]

Hon., Honorable; Honorary.

Hon·du·ras (hon·dúr′əs; -dyúr′əs), *n.* country in N Central America. —**Hon·du′ran,** *adj., n.*

hone (hōn), *n., v.,* **honed, hon·ing.** —*n.* a fine-grained whetstone on which to sharpen cutting tools, esp. razors. —*v.* sharpen on a hone. [OE *hān* a stone]

hon·est (on′ist), *adj.* **1.** not lying, cheating, or stealing; fair and upright; truthful: *an honest man.* **2.** obtained by fair and upright means: *honest profits.* **3.** not hiding one's real nature; frank; open: *honest opposition.* **4.** not mixed with something of less value; genuine; pure: *honest goods.* **5.** *Archaic.* chaste; virtuous. [< OF < L *honestus* < *honos* honor] —**hon′est·ly,** *adv.* —**Syn. 1.** just, incorruptible. **3.** sincere, candid.

hon·es·ty (on′is·ti), *n.* **1.** fairness and uprightness. **2.** truthfulness. **3.** freedom from deceit or fraud. **4.** *Archaic.* chastity.

hon·ey (hun′i), *n., pl.* **hon·eys,** *adj., v.,* **hon·eyed** or **hon·ied, hon·ey·ing.** —*n.* **1.** a thick, sweet, yellow liquid, good to eat, that bees make out of the drops they collect from flowers. **2.** drop of sweet liquid, found in many flowers, that draws bees to them. **3.** sweetness. **4.** darling; dear. —*adj.* of or like honey; sweet; dear. —*v.* **1.** sweeten with or as with honey. **2.** talk sweetly; flatter. [OE *hunig*] —**hon′ey·like′,** *adj.*

hon·ey·bee (hun′i·bē′), *n.* bee that makes honey.

hon·ey·comb (hun′i·kōm′), *n.* **1.** structure of wax containing rows of six-sided cells formed by bees, in which to store honey, pollen, and their eggs. **2.** anything like this. —*adj.* like a honeycomb: *a honeycomb pattern.* —*v.* **1.** make like a honeycomb. **2.** pierce with many holes. **3.** permeate: *the city is honeycombed with crime.*

Honeycomb

hon·ey·dew (hun′i·dū; -dü′), *n.* **1.** a sweet substance on the leaves of certain plants in hot weather. **2.** a sweet substance on leaves and stems, secreted by tiny insects called aphids. **3.** a honeydew melon.

honeydew melon, a variety of melon with sweet, green flesh and a smooth, whitish skin.

hon·eyed (hun′id), *adj.* **1.** sweetened with honey. **2.** laden with honey. **3.** sweet as honey.

honey locust, *Am.* a thorny North American tree with long, divided leaves and large, flat pods containing sweet pulp.

hon·ey·moon (hun′i·mün′), *n.* **1.** vacation spent together by a newly married couple. **2.** the first month of marriage. —*v.* spend or have a honeymoon. —**hon′ey·moon′er,** *n.*

hon·ey·suck·le (hun′i·suk′əl), *n.* **1.** shrub or vine with small, fragrant flowers. **2.** any of various similar plants. —**hon′ey·suck′led,** *adj.*

Hong Kong, Hong·kong (hong′ kong′; hông′ kông′), *n.* a British colony in SE China.

honk (hongk; hôngk), *n. Am.* **1.** cry of the wild goose. **2.** any similar sound: *honk of a taxi.* —*v.* make such a sound. [imit.] —**honk′er,** *n.*

honk·y-tonk (hong′ki·tongk′; hông′ki·tôngk′), *n. Am., Slang.* a cheap saloon, cabaret, etc.

Hon·o·lu·lu (hon′ə·lü′lü), *n.* seaport and capital of the Hawaiian Islands.

hon·or (on′ər), *n.* **1.** glory; fame; renown. **2.** credit for acting well; good name. **3.** source of credit; cause of honor. **4.** a nice sense of what is right or proper; sticking to action that is right or that is usual and expected. **5.** great respect; high regard: *hold in honor.* **6.** act of respect: *funeral honors.* **7.** rank; dignity; distinction: *knighthood is an honor.* **8.** chastity; virtue. **9.** Honor, title used in speaking to or of a judge, mayor, etc. **10.** honors, a. special favors or courtesies. b. special mention, grade, or credit given to a student. c. ace, king, queen, jack, and ten of trumps, or the four aces in no-trump in the game of bridge. **11.** do the honors, act as host or hostess. —*v.* **1.** respect greatly; regard highly. **2.** show respect to. **3.** worship. **4.** confer dignity upon; be an honor to; favor: *be honored by a royal visit.* **5.** accept and pay (a bill, draft, note, etc.) when due. Also, *esp. Brit.* honour. [< OF < L *honos, honor*] —**hon′or·er,** *n.* —Syn. *n.* **4.** integrity, uprightness. **5.** deference, veneration, reverence. **7.** eminence, position.

hon·or·a·ble (on′ər·ə·bəl), *adj.* **1.** having or showing a sense of what is right and proper; honest; upright. **2.** causing honor; bringing honor to the one that has it. **3.** worthy of honor; to be respected; noble. **4.** Honorable, in the U.S., a widely used, but vague, title of respect before the names of certain officials and many others: *the Honorable Robert M. La Follette.* Also, *esp. Brit.* honourable. —**hon′or·a·ble·ness,** *n.* —**hon′or·a·bly,** *adv.*

hon·o·rar·i·um (on′ə·rãr′i·əm), *n., pl.* **-rar·i·ums, -rar·i·a** (-rãr′i·ə). fee for professional services on which no fixed price is set.

hon·or·ar·y (on′ər·er′i), *adj.* **1.** given or done as an honor. **2.** as an honor only; without pay or regular duties: *an honorary secretary.*

hon·or·if·ic (on′ər·if′ik), *adj.* **1.** doing or giving honor. **2.** showing respect or deference. —*n.* an honorific word or phrase. —**hon′or·if′i·cal·ly,** *adv.*

honor system, *Am.* system of trusting people in schools and other institutions to obey the rules and do their work without being watched or forced.

hon·our (on′ər), *n., v. Esp. Brit.* honor. —**hon′our·a·ble,** *adj.* —**hon′our·a·ble·ness,** *n.* —**hon′our·a·bly,** *adv.* —**hon′our·er,** *n.*

Hon·shu (hon′shü), *n.* the main island of Japan.

hooch (hüch), *n. Am., Slang.* alcoholic drink, esp. that which is made illegally. [for *hoochinoo,* alter. of *Hutsnuwa,* Alaskan Indians who made liquor]

hood (hud), *n.* **1.** a soft covering for the head and neck, either separate or as part of a cloak. **2.** anything like a hood in shape or use. **3.** *Am.* a metal covering over the engine of an automobile. **4.** in falconry, a cover for the head of a hawk. **5.** *Slang.* hoodlum. —*v.* cover with a hood. [OE *hōd*] —**hood′ed,** *adj.* —**hood′less,** *adj.* —**hood′like′,** *adj.*

Hood (hud), *n.* **1.** Mount, mountain in N Oregon. **2.** Robin, a legendary English outlaw.

-hood, *suffix.* **1.** state or condition of being, as in *boyhood, likelihood.* **2.** character or nature of, as in *manhood, sainthood.* **3.** group, body of, as in *priesthood, sisterhood.* [OE *-hād*]

hood·lum (hüd′ləm), *n. Am., Colloq.* a young rowdy; street ruffian. —**hood′lum·ism,** *n. Am.*

hoo·doo (hü′dü), *n., pl.* **-doos,** *v.,* **-dooed, -doo·ing.** *Am.* —*n.* **1.** voodoo. **2.** person or thing that brings bad luck. **3.** bad luck. —*v.* bring or cause bad luck to. [? var. of *voodoo*]

hood·wink (hud′wingk), *v.* **1.** mislead by a trick; deceive. **2.** blindfold. —**hood′wink·er,** *n.*

hoo·ey (hü′i), *Am., Slang.* —*n.* nonsense. —*interj.* exclamation of disgust or disapproval.

hoof (huf; hüf), *n., pl.* **hoofs** or (*Rare*) **hooves,** *v.* —*n.* **1.** a hard, horny covering on the feet of horses, cattle, sheep, pigs, and some other animals. **2.** the whole foot of such animals. **3.** on the hoof, alive; not killed and butchered. —*v. Colloq.* **1.** walk. **2.** dance. [OE *hōf*] —**hoofed,** *adj.* —**hoof′er,** *n.* —**hoof′like′,** *adj.*

hoof·beat (huf′bēt′; hüf′-), *n.* sound made by an animal's hoof.

hook (huk), *n.* **1.** piece of metal, wood, or other stiff material, curved or having a sharp angle for catching hold of something or for hanging things on. **2.** a curved piece of wire, usually with a barb at the end, for catching fish. **3.** trap; snare. **4.** anything curved or bent like a hook. **5.** a sharp bend. **6.** point of land. **7.** act of hooking. **8.** *Baseball.* a curve. **9.** *Golf.* a ball's path of flight curving to the left away from a right-handed player. **10.** *Boxing.* a short, swinging blow. **11.** *Music.* line on the stem of certain notes. **12.** by hook or by crook, in any way at all; by fair means or foul. **13.** on one's own hook, *Slang.* independently. —*v.* **1.** attach or fasten with a hook or hooks: *please hook my dress for me.* **2.** join; fit; be fastened: *this dress hooks up the back.* **3.** catch or take hold of with a hook. **4.** catch (fish) with a hook. **5.** give the form of a hook to. **6.** be curved or bent like a hook. **7.** catch by a trick. **8.** *Colloq.* steal. **9.** throw (a ball) so that it curves. **10.** *Golf.* hit a hook. **11.** *Boxing.* hit with a hook. **12.** hook up, a. attach or fasten with a hook or hooks. b. arrange and connect the parts of (a radio set, telephone, etc.). [OE *hōc*] —**hook′less,** *adj.* —**hook′like′,** *adj.*

hook·ah, hook·a (huk′ə), *n.* a tobacco pipe with a long tube by which the smoke is drawn through water. [< Ar. *huqqa* vase, pipe]

hooked (hukt), *adj.* **1.** curved or bent like a hook. **2.** having hooks. **3.** made with a hook. —**hook·ed·ness** (huk′id·nis), *n.*

Man smoking a hookah

hooked rug, *Am.* rug made by pulling yarn or strips of cloth through a piece of canvas, burlap, etc.

hook·up (huk′up′), *n.* **1.** arrangement and connection of the parts of a radio set, telephone, radio-broadcasting facilities, etc. **2.** an effecting of relationships: *a hookup between nations.*

hook·worm (huk′werm′), *n. Am.* **1.** worm that gets into the intestines and causes a disease characterized by weakness and apparent laziness. **2.** the disease.

hook·y (huk′i), *n.* play hooky, *Am.* run away; be absent without reason.

hoo·li·gan (hü′lə·gən), *n. Slang.* a street ruffian; hoodlum. —**hoo′li·gan·ism,** *n.*

hoop (hüp; hüp), *n.* **1.** ring or flat band in the form of a circle: *hoop for holding the staves of a barrel.* **2.** a circular frame formerly used to expand a woman's skirt. **3.** *Croquet.* arch or wicket. **4.** anything shaped like a hoop. —*v.* fasten together with hoops. [OE *hōp*] —**hooped,** *adj.* —**hoop′er,** *n.* —**hoop′like′,** *adj.*

hoop·la (hüp′lä′), *n. Am., Slang.* any meaningless, showy, or overexuberant activity to gain publicity, promote a product, etc.; ballyhoo.

hoo·poe (hü′pü), *n.* a bright-colored bird with a long, sharp bill and a fanlike crest on its head. [earlier *hoop* < F < L *upupa* (imit.)]

hoop skirt, a woman's skirt worn over a flexible hoop.

hoo·ray (hu·rā′), *interj., n., v.* hurrah.

hoose·gow (hüs′gou), *n. Am., Slang.* jail. [? < Sp. *juzgado* a court, in Mex.Sp., a jail]

Hoo·sier (hü′zhər), *n. Am.* native or inhabitant of Indiana.

Hoop skirt

hoot (hūt), *n.* 1. sound that an owl makes. 2. any similar sound. 3. shout to show disapproval or scorn. 4. thing of little value. —*v.* 1. make the sound that an owl makes or one like it. 2. make a shout to show disapproval or scorn. 3. show disapproval of, or scorn for, by hooting. 4. force or drive by hooting. 5. say or show by hooting. [ME *hute*(*n*); ? imit.] —**hoot′er,** *n.*

Hoo·ver (hü′vər), *n.* Herbert Clark, born 1874, the 31st president of the United States, 1929–1933.

Hoover Dam, dam on the Colorado River between Arizona and Nevada. Also, **Boulder Dam.**

hooves (húvz; hüvz), *n. Rare.* pl. of hoof.

hop[1] (hop), *v.,* **hopped, hop·ping,** *n.* —*v.* 1. spring, or move by springing, on one foot. 2. spring, or move by springing, with all feet at once: *many birds hop.* 3. jump over: *hop a ditch.* 4. *Colloq.* jump on (a train, car, etc.). 5. *Colloq.* fly across in an airplane; make a flight. 6. dance. 7. hop off, *Colloq.* rise from the ground in an airplane. —*n.* 1. a hopping; spring. 2. *Colloq.* flight in an airplane. 3. *Colloq.* a dancing party. 4. *Colloq.* dance. [OE *hoppian*]

hop[2] (hop), *n., v.,* **hopped, hop·ping.** —*n.* 1. vine having flower clusters that look like small, yellow pine cones. 2. hops, dried flower clusters of the hop vine, used to flavor beer and other malt drinks. —*v.* 1. pick hops. 2. flavor with hops. [< MDu. *hoppe*]

hope (hōp), *n., v.,* **hoped, hop·ing.** —*n.* 1. a feeling that what one desires will happen. 2. instance of such a desire. 3. person or thing that expectation centers in: *he is the hope of the family.* 4. thing hoped for. 5. ground for expectation: *no hope of recovery.* 6. *Archaic.* trust; reliance. —*v.* 1. wish and expect. 2. *Archaic.* trust; rely. [OE *hopa*] —**Syn.** *n.* 1. expectation, anticipation, optimism.

hope chest, *Am.* chest in which a young woman collects articles that will be useful after she marries.

hope·ful (hōp′fəl), *adj.* 1. feeling or showing hope. 2. causing hope; giving hope; likely to succeed. —*n.* boy or girl thought likely to succeed. —**hope′ful·ly,** *adv.* —**hope′ful·ness,** *n.*

hope·less (hōp′lis), *adj.* 1. feeling no hope. 2. giving no hope: *a hopeless illness.* —**hope′less·ly,** *adv.* —**hope′less·ness,** *n.*

Ho·pi (hō′pi), *n., pl.* **-pis.** *Am.* member of a tribe of Pueblo Indians living largely in stone-built towns in N Arizona.

hop·lite (hop′līt), *n.* a heavily armed foot soldier of ancient Greece. [< Gk., < *hopla* arms]

hop·per (hop′ər), *n.* 1. person or thing that hops. 2. grasshopper or other hopping insect. 3. container to hold something and feed it into another part, usually larger at the top than at the bottom.

hop·scotch (hop′skoch′), *n.* a children's game in which the players hop over the lines of a figure drawn on the ground.

Hor·ace (hôr′is; hor′-), *n.* 65–8 B.C., Roman poet and satirist. —**Ho·ra·tian** (hə·rā′shən; hō-), *adj.*

horde (hôrd; hōrd), *n., v.,* **hord·ed, hord·ing.** —*n.* 1. crowd; swarm. 2. a wandering tribe or troop. —*v.* gather in a horde. [< F < G < Polish < Turk. *urdū* camp]

hore·hound (hôr′hound′; hōr′-), *n.* 1. plant with woolly, whitish leaves and clusters of small, whitish flowers. 2. a bitter extract made from the leaves of this plant. 3. candy or cough medicine flavored with it. Also, **hoarhound.** [OE *hārhūne* < *hār* hoar + *hūne* name of a plant]

ho·ri·zon (hə·rī′zən), *n.* 1. line where the earth and sky seem to meet. 2. limit of one's thinking, experience, interest, or outlook. [< OF < L < Gk. *horizon* (*kyklos*) bounding (circle), ult. < *horos* limit]

hor·i·zon·tal (hôr′ə·zon′təl; hor′-), *adj.* 1. parallel to the horizon; at right angles to a vertical line. 2. flat; level. 3. placed, acting, or working wholly or mainly in a horizontal direction. 4. in commercial fields, etc., so organized as to include only one stage in production or one

group of people or crafts: *a horizontal union, horizontal trusts.* —*n.* a horizontal line, plane, direction, position, etc. —**hor′i·zon′tal·i·ty, hor′i·zon′tal·ness,** *n.* —**hor′i·zon′tal·ly,** *adv.*

hor·mone (hôr′mōn), *n.* 1. *Physiol.* substance formed in certain parts of the body that enters the blood stream and influences the activity of some organ, as adrenalin and insulin. 2. *Bot.* any similar substance produced in plants. [< Gk. *hormon* setting in motion) —**hor·mo′nal, hor·mon·ic** (hôr·mon′ik), *adj.*

horn (hôrn), *n.* 1. a hard growth, usually curved and pointed, on the heads of cattle, sheep, goats, and some other animals. 2. anything that sticks up on the head of an animal: *a snail's horns, an insect's horns.* 3. the substance or material of horns. 4. thing made, or formerly made, of horn. 5. container made by hollowing out a horn: *a drinking horn, a powder horn.* 6. *Music.* instrument sounded by blowing into the smaller end. 7. device sounded as a warning signal: *a foghorn.* 8. anything that projects like a horn or is shaped like a horn: *a saddle horn, the horn of an anvil.* 9. either pointed tip of a new or old moon, or of a crescent. 10. horns of a dilemma, two unpleasant choices, one of which must be taken. —*adj.* made of horn. —*v.* 1. hit or wound with horns; gore. 2. furnish with horns. 3. horn in, *U.S. Slang.* meddle; intrude. [OE] —**horned,** *adj.* —**horn′less,** *adj.* —**horn′like′,** *adj.*

Horn (hôrn), *n.* Cape on an island at the southern tip of South America.

horn·bill (hôrn′bil′), *n.* a large bird having a very large bill with a horn or horny lump on it.

horn·blende (hôrn′blend′), *n.* a common black, dark-green, or brown mineral found in granite and other rocks. [< G] —**horn·blen′dic,** *adj.*

horn·book (hôrn′bůk′), *n.* 1. page with the alphabet, etc., on it, covered with a sheet of transparent horn and fastened in a frame with a handle, formerly used in teaching children to read. 2. a primer.

horned toad, *Am.* a small lizard with a broad, flat body, short tail, and many spines.

hor·net (hôr′nit), *n.* a large wasp that can give a very painful sting. [OE *hyrnet*(*u*)]

horn of plenty, cornucopia.

horn·pipe (hôrn′pīp′), *n.* 1. a lively dance done by one person, formerly popular among sailors. 2. music for it. 3. a musical wind instrument of olden times, consisting of a wooden pipe with a bell-shaped end.

Hornet
(ab. 1 in. long)

horn·swog·gle (hôrn′swog′əl), *v.,* **-gled, -gling.** *Am., Slang.* hoax; cheat.

horn·y (hôr′ni), *adj.,* **horn·i·er, horn·i·est.** 1. made of horn or a substance like it. 2. hard like a horn: *hands horny from work.* 3. having a horn or horns. —**horn′i·ness,** *n.*

hor·o·loge (hôr′ə·lōj; -loj; hor′-), *n.* timepiece, as a clock, sundial, hourglass, etc. [< OF < L < Gk. *horologion* < *hora* hour + *logos* telling]

hor·ol·o·ger (hō·rol′ə·jər), **hor·ol·o·gist** (-jist), *n.* expert in horology.

hor·ol·o·gy (hō·rol′ə·ji), *n.* 1. science of measuring time. 2. art of making timepieces. —**hor·o·log·ic** (hôr′ə·loj′ik; hor′-), **hor′o·log′i·cal,** *adj.*

hor·o·scope (hôr′ə·skōp; hor′-), *n.* 1. appearance of the heavens with the relative position of the planets at the hour of a person's birth, regarded as influencing his life. 2. diagram of the heavens at given times, used in telling fortunes by the planets and the stars. [< F < L < Gk., *hora* hour + *skopos* watcher]

hor·ren·dous (hô·ren′dəs; ho-), *adj.* horrible; terrible; frightful. —**hor·ren′dous·ly,** *adv.*

hor·ri·ble (hôr′ə·bəl; hor′-), *adj.* 1. causing horror; terrible; dreadful; frightful; shocking. 2. *Colloq.* extremely unpleasant or amazing. [< OF < L, < *horrere* bristle] —**hor′ri·ble·ness,** *n.* —**hor′ri·bly,** *adv.* —**Syn.** 1. hideous, grim, horrid.

hor·rid (hôr′id; hor′-), *adj.* 1. terrible; frightful. 2. *Colloq.* very unpleasant. —**hor′rid·ly,** *adv.* —**hor′rid·ness,** *n.*

hor·ri·fy (hôr′ə·fī), *v.,* -fied, -fy·ing. 1. cause to feel horror. 2. *Colloq.* shock very much. —**hor′ri·fi·ca′tion,** *n.*

hor·ror (hôr′ər; hor′-), *n.* 1. a shivering, shaking fear and dislike; terror and disgust caused by something frightful or shocking. 2. a very strong dislike; very great disgust. 3. quality of causing horror. 4. cause of horror. [< L, < *horrere* bristle] —**Syn.** 1. dread. 2. loathing, abhorrence, aversion.

hor·ror-strick·en (hôr′ər·strik′ən; hor′-), **hor·ror-struck** (-struk′), *adj.* horrified.

hors d'oeu·vre (ôr′dérv′; *Fr.* ôr dœ′vrə), *pl.* **d'oeu·vres** (dérvz′; *Fr.* dœ′vrə). relish or light food served before the regular courses of a meal, as olives, celery, anchovies, etc. [F, apart from (the main) work]

horse (hôrs), *n., pl.* **hors·es** or (*esp.* collectively) **horse,** *v.,* **horsed, hors·ing,** *adj.* —*n.* 1. a four-legged animal with solid hoofs and flowing mane and tail, used from very early times to draw loads, carry riders, etc. 2. a full-grown male horse. 3. soldiers on horses; cavalry. 4. piece of gymnasium apparatus to jump or vault over. 5. frame with legs to support something. —*v.* 1. provide with a horse or horses. 2. put or go on horseback. 3. set or carry on a person's back; carry on one's own back. 4. *Colloq.* tease in a rough way. 5. *Colloq.* act boisterously. —*adj.* 1. having to do with horses. 2. on horses. [OE *hors*]

horse·back (hôrs′bak′), *n.* the back of a horse. —*adv.* on the back of a horse.

horse·car (hôrs′kär′), *n. Am.* 1. streetcar pulled by a horse or horses. 2. car used for transporting horses.

horse chestnut, 1. a shade tree with spreading branches, large leaves, clusters of showy white flowers, and glossy brown nuts. 2. the nut. 3. any tree or shrub of the same family as the horse chestnut.

horse·flesh (hôrs′flesh′), *n.* 1. horses. 2. meat from horses.

horse·fly (hôrs′flī′), *n., pl.* -**flies.** fly that bites horses.

horse·hair (hôrs′hãr′), *n.* 1. hair from the mane or tail of a horse. 2. a stiff fabric made of this hair.

Horsefly (somewhat over life size)

horse·hide (hôrs′hīd′), *n.* 1. hide of a horse. 2. leather made from this hide.

horse latitudes, two regions where there is often very calm weather, extending around the world at about 30° north and 30° south of the equator.

horse laugh, a loud, boisterous laugh.

horse·less (hôrs′lis), *adj.* 1. without a horse. 2. not requiring a horse; self-propelled: *automobiles were called horseless carriages.*

horse·man (hôrs′mən), *n., pl.* -**men.** 1. man who rides on horseback. 2. man skilled in riding or managing horses. —**horse′man·ship,** *n.*

horse pistol, a large pistol that used to be carried by horsemen.

horse·play (hôrs′plā′), *n.* rough, boisterous fun.

horse·pow·er (hôrs′pou′ər), *n.* unit for measuring the power of engines, motors, etc.; 1 horsepower = 550 foot-pounds per second.

horse·rad·ish (hôrs′rad′ish), *n.* 1. a tall plant with a white, hot-tasting root that is ground up and used as a relish with meat, oysters, etc. 2. relish made of this root.

horse sense, *Am., Colloq.* common sense; plain, practical good sense.

horse·shoe (hôrsh′shü′; hôrs′-), *n., v.,* -shoed, -shoe·ing. —*n.* 1. a U-shaped metal plate nailed to a horse's hoof to protect it. 2. thing shaped like a horseshoe. 3. **horseshoes** (*sing. in use*), game in which the players try to throw horseshoes over or near a stake. —*v.* put a horseshoe or horseshoes on. —**horse′sho′er,** *n.*

horseshoe crab, *Am.* a crablike sea animal with a body shaped like a horseshoe and a long, spiny tail; king crab.

horse·tail (hôrs′tāl′), *n.* a flowerless plant with hollow, jointed stems and scalelike leaves at each joint.

horse·whip (hôrs′hwip′), *n., v.,* -whipped, -whip·ping. —*n.* whip for driving or controlling horses. —*v.* beat with a horsewhip.

horse·wom·an (hôrs′wum′ən), *n., pl.* -wom·en. 1. woman who rides on horseback. 2. woman skilled in riding or managing horses.

hors·y (hôr′si), *adj.,* hors·i·er, hors·i·est. 1. having to do with horses. 2. fond of horses or horse racing. 3. dressing or talking like people who spend much time with horses. 4. *Slang.* large and awkward in appearance. —**hors′i·ness,** *n.*

hort., horticultural; horticulture.

hor·ta·tive (hôr′tə·tiv), *adj.* hortatory. —**hor′ta·tive·ly,** *adv.*

hor·ta·to·ry (hôr′tə·tô′ri; -tō′-), *adj.* serving to urge or encourage; giving advice; exhorting. [< LL, < L *hortari* exhort]

hor·ti·cul·ture (hôr′tə·kul′chər), *n.* 1. science of growing flowers, fruits, vegetables, etc. 2. cultivation of a garden. [< L *hortus* garden + *cultura* cultivation] —**hor′ti·cul′tur·al,** *adj.* —**hor′ti·cul′tur·ist,** *n.*

ho·san·na (hō·zan′ə), *interj.* shout of praise to the Lord. —*n.* a shout of "hosanna." [< LL < Gk. < Heb. *hōshī′āh nnā* save now, we pray]

hose (hōz), *n., pl.* **hose** or (*Archaic*) **ho·sen** (hō′zən), *v.,* hosed, hos·ing. —*n.* 1. stockings. 2. a close-fitting outer garment extending from the waist to the toes, formerly worn by men. 3. tube made of rubber, canvas, or other flexible material, used to carry water or other liquids for short distances. —*v.* put water on with a hose. [OE *hosa*]

Ho·se·a (hō·zē′ə; -zā′ə), *n.* 1. book of the Old Testament. 2. its author, a Hebrew prophet who lived in the eighth century B.C.

ho·sier (hō′zhər), *n.* person who makes or sells hosiery.

ho·sier·y (hō′zhər·i), *n.* 1. hose; stockings. 2. business of a hosier.

hos·pice (hos′pis), *n.* house where travelers can lodge. [< F < L *hospitium* < *hospes* guest, host]

hos·pi·ta·ble (hos′pi·tə·bəl; hos·pit′ə-), *adj.* 1. giving or liking to give a welcome, food and shelter, and friendly treatment to guests or strangers: *a hospitable family.* 2. willing and ready to entertain; favorably receptive: *hospitable to new ideas.* —**hos′pi·ta·ble·ness,** *n.* —**hos′pi·ta·bly,** *adv.*

hos·pi·tal (hos′pi·təl), *n.* 1. place where sick or injured people are cared for. 2. similar place for animals. [< OF < Med.L *hospitale* inn. See HOST¹.]

hos·pi·tal·i·ty (hos′pə·tal′ə·ti), *n., pl.* -ties. friendly, generous reception and treatment of guests or strangers. [< L *hospitalitas.* See HOST¹.]

hos·pi·tal·ize (hos′pi·təl·īz), *v.,* -ized, -iz·ing. put in a hospital. —**hos′pi·tal·i·za′tion,** *n.*

host¹ (hōst), *n.* 1. person who receives another at his house as his guest. 2. keeper of an inn or hotel. 3. plant or animal in or on which a parasite lives. [< OF < L *hospes* guest, host]

host² (hōst), *n.* 1. a large number; multitude. 2. army. [< OF < LL *hostis* army < L, enemy (orig., stranger)]

Host (hōst), *n. Eccles.* bread or wafer used in the Eucharist. [< OF *oiste* < L *hostia* animal sacrificed]

hos·tage (hos′tij), *n.* 1. person given up to another or held by an enemy as a pledge that certain promises, agreements, etc., will be carried out. 2. pledge; security. [< OF, ult. < L *hospes* guest] —**hos′tage·ship,** *n.*

hos·tel (hos′təl), *n.* a lodging place, esp. a supervised lodging place for young people on

āge, câre, fär; ēqual, tèrm; īce; ōpen, ôrder; pṳt, rṳle, ūse; th, then; ə=a in about.

bicycle trips, hikes, etc.; inn; hotel. [< OF, < oste HOST[1]. Doublet of HOTEL.] —hos'tel·er, n.

hos·tel·ry (hos'təl·ri), n., pl. -ries. inn; hotel.

host·ess (hōs'tis), n. 1. woman who receives another person as her guest. 2. woman paid to entertain or dance with guests, travelers, etc.

hos·tile (hos'təl; sometimes hos'tīl), adj. 1. of an enemy or enemies. 2. opposed; unfriendly; unfavorable. [< L, < hostis enemy] —hos'tile·ly, adv. —Syn. 2. inimical, antagonistic.

hos·til·i·ty (hos·til'ə·ti), n., pl. -ties. 1. feeling as an enemy does; being an enemy; unfriendliness. 2. state of being at war. 3. opposition; resistance. 4. hostilities, acts of war; warfare; fighting.

hos·tler (os'lər; hos'-), n. person who takes care of horses at an inn or stable. Also, ostler.

hot (hot), adj., hot·ter, hot·test, adv. —adj. 1. much warmer than the body; having much heat: a fire is hot. 2. having a relatively high temperature: the food is too hot to eat. 3. having a sensation of great bodily heat: a person hot with fever. 4. having a sharp, burning taste: pepper and mustard are hot. 5. Elect. actively conducting current: a hot wire. 6. Nuclear Physics. charged (with radioactivity); radioactive: the hot debris left by an atomic explosion. 7. full of any strong feeling: hot with rage. 8. thrilling; exciting: a hot singer. 9. Colloq. good; excellent: he's not so hot. 10. full of great interest or enthusiasm; very eager. 11. new; fresh: a hot scent. 12. following closely: in hot pursuit. 13. of swing music or jazz, played with variations from the score. 14. Slang. obtained illegally. —adv. in a hot manner. [OE hāt] —hot'ly, adv. —hot'ness, n. —Syn. adj. 1. scorching, scalding. 4. pungent, peppery. 7. passionate, violent, vehement, fiery. 10. ardent, fervent, fervid.

hot air, Am., Slang. empty talk or writing.

hot atom, Nuclear Physics. atom whose nucleus is radioactive.

hot·bed (hot'bed'), n. 1. bed of earth covered with glass and kept warm for growing plants. 2. place favorable to rapid growth.

hot·blood·ed (hot'blud'id), adj. 1. easily excited or angered. 2. rash; reckless. 3. passionate.

hot·box (hot'boks'), n. Am. an overheated bearing on a shaft or axle.

hot cake, Am. a griddle cake.

hot cross bun, bun marked with a cross, usually eaten during Lent or on Good Friday.

hot dog, Am., Slang. a hot frankfurter enclosed in a roll.

ho·tel (hō·tel'), n. house or large building that provides lodging, food, etc., to travelers and others. [< F hôtel < OF hostel. Doublet of HOSTEL.]

hot·foot (hot'fut'), Colloq. —adv. in great haste. —v. go in great haste; hurry.

hot·head (hot'hed'), n. a hot-headed person.

hot·head·ed (hot'hed'id), adj. 1. having a fiery temper. 2. impetuous; rash. —hot'-head'ed·ly, adv. —hot'-head'ed·ness, n.

hot·house (hot'hous'), n. greenhouse.

hot laboratory or **lab**, Nuclear Physics, Chem. laboratory exposed to radiations of more than one curie.

hot rod, Am., Slang. 1. a stripped-down flivver with a supercharged motor. 2. person, esp. an adolescent boy, who drives such an automobile.

hot-tem·pered (hot'tem'pərd), adj. easily angered.

Hot·ten·tot (hot'ən·tot), n. 1. member of a South African race having a dark, yellowish-brown complexion. 2. their language.

hot war, war involving actual fighting.

hou·dah (hou'də), n. howdah.

hough (hok), n. hock[1].

hound (hound), n. 1. dog of any of various breeds, most of which hunt by scent and have large, drooping ears and short hair. 2. any dog. 3. a contemptible person. 4. Slang. person who is very fond of something. 5. follow the hounds or ride to hounds, go hunting on horseback with hounds. —v. 1. hunt; chase. 2. urge (on). [OE hund]

hour (our), n. 1. 60 minutes; ¼ of a day. 2. one of the 12 points that measure time from noon to midnight and from midnight to noon. 3. time of day. Some clocks strike the hours and half-hours. 4. a particular or fixed time: the breakfast hour. 5. period in a classroom, often less than a full hour. 6. the present time: the man of the hour. 7. 15 degrees of longitude. 8. hours, a seven special times of the day set aside for prayer and worship, as in a monastery. b. prayers or services for these times. c. time for work, study, etc. d. usual time for going to bed and getting up. [< OF < L < Gk. hōra season, time, hour]

hour·glass (our'glas'; -gläs'), n. device for measuring time, requiring just an hour for its contents (sand or mercury) to go from the container on top to one on the bottom.

hou·ri (hûr'i; hou'ri), n., pl. -ris. a young, eternally beautiful girl of the Mohammedan paradise. [< F < Pers. hūr < Ar. hūr black-eyed]

hour·ly (our'li), adj. 1. done, happening, or counted every hour. 2. coming very often; frequent. —adv. 1. every hour; hour by hour. 2. very often; frequently.

Hourglass

house (n. hous; v. houz), n., pl. hous·es (houz'iz), v., housed, hous·ing. —n. 1. a building in which people live. 2. people living in a house; household. 3. abode; habitation. 4. a building to hold anything: greenhouse, warehouse. 5. assembly for making laws and considering questions of government; lawmaking body: the House of Representatives. 6. the building in which such an assembly meets. 7. place of business. 8. Am. a business firm. 9. place of entertainment; theater. 10. audience. 11. family regarded as consisting of ancestors, descendants, and kindred, esp. a noble or royal family. 12. bring down the house, Colloq. be loudly applauded. 13. keep house, manage a home and its affairs; do housework. 14. on the house, paid for by the owner of the business; free. —v. 1. put or receive into a house; provide with a house. 2. give shelter to; harbor; lodge. 3. place in a secure or protected position. [OE hūs] —house'less, adj.

house·boat (hous'bōt'), n. boat that can be used as a place to live in.

house·break·er (hous'brāk'ər), n. person who breaks into a house to steal or commit some other crime. —house'break'ing, n.

house·bro·ken (hous'brō'kən), **house-broke** (-brōk'), adj. of a dog, cat, etc., trained to live indoors.

house·coat (hous'kōt'), n. a light dress-like garment with a long skirt, for casual wear in one's home.

house·fly (hous'flī'), n., pl. -flies. a two-winged fly that lives around and in houses, feeding on food, garbage, and filth.

house·hold (hous'hōld'), n. 1. all the people living in a house; family; family and servants. 2. home and its affairs. 3. a royal household. —adj. of a household; having to do with a household; domestic: household expenses.

house·hold·er (hous'hōl'dər), n. 1. person who owns or lives in a house. 2. head of a family.

household word, very familiar word or phrase.

house·keep·er (hous'kēp'ər), n. 1. woman who manages a home and its affairs and does the housework. 2. woman who directs the servants that do the housework. —house'keep'ing, n.

house·maid (hous'mād'), n. woman servant who does housework.

House of Burgesses, Am. the lower house of the colonial legislature in Virginia or Maryland.

House of Commons, the lower, elective branch of the lawmaking body of Great Britain and Northern Ireland, or of Canada.

house of correction, place of confinement and reform for persons convicted of minor offenses and not regarded as confirmed criminals.

House of Delegates, *Am.* the lower branch of the legislature in Maryland, Virginia, and West Virginia.

House of Lords, the upper, nonelective branch of the lawmaking body of Great Britain and Northern Ireland, composed of nobles and clergymen of high rank.

House of Representatives, 1. *Am.* the lower branch of the lawmaking body of the United States. **2.** *Am.* the lower branch of the lawmaking body of certain states of the United States. **3.** the lower branch of the Parliament of Australia, or of the general assembly of New Zealand.

house party, entertainment of guests in a home for a few days.

house·top (hous′top′), *n.* top of a house; roof.

house·warm·ing (hous′wôr′ming), *n.* party given when a family moves into a house for the first time.

house·wife (hous′wīf′ *for 1;* huz′if *for 2*), *n., pl.* **–wives. 1.** woman who is the head of a household. **2.** a small case for needles, thread, etc. —**house′wife′ly,** *adj.* —**house′wife′li·ness,** *n.*

house·wif·er·y (hous′wīf′ər·i; –wīf′ri), *n.* work of a housewife; housekeeping.

house·work (hous′wėrk′), *n.* work to be done in housekeeping, such as washing, ironing, cleaning, sweeping, or cooking.

hous·ing[1] (houz′ing), *n.* **1.** act of sheltering; provision of houses as homes. **2.** houses. **3.** shelter; covering. **4.** frame or plate to hold part of a machine in place.

hous·ing[2] (houz′ing), *n.* an ornamental covering for a horse. [< *house* covering < OF *huche*]

Hous·ton (hūs′tən), *n.* **1.** Samuel, 1793–1863, American frontier soldier and hero, twice president of Texas before it became a State in 1845. **2.** city in SE Texas.

hove (hōv), *v. Esp. Naut.* pt. and pp. of **heave.**

hov·el (huv′əl; hov′–), *n., v.,* **–eled, –el·ing;** *esp. Brit.* **–elled, –el·ling.** —*n.* **1.** house that is small, mean, and unpleasant to live in. **2.** an open shed for sheltering cattle, tools, etc. —*v.* lodge in a hovel. [ME]

hov·er (huv′ər; hov′–), *v.* **1.** stay in or near one place in the air: *the two birds hovered over their nest.* **2.** wait near at hand. **3.** be in an uncertain condition; waver: *the sick man hovered between life and death.* —*n.* **1.** act of hovering. **2.** state of hovering. [ME *hover(en)* < *hoven* hover] —**hov′er·er,** *n.* —**hov′er·ing·ly,** *adv.*

how (hou), *adv.* **1.** in what way; by what means: *tell her how to do it.* **2.** to what degree, extent, etc.: *how long?* **3.** at what price: *how do you sell these apples?* **4.** in what state or condition: *tell me how Mrs. Jones is.* **5.** for what reason; why: *how is it you are late?* **6.** to what effect; with what meaning; by what name: *how do you mean?* **7.** what? —*n.* **1.** question beginning with "how." **2.** way or manner of doing: *she considered all the hows and wherefores.* [OE *hū*]

how·be·it (hou·bē′it), *adv.* nevertheless.

how·dah (hou′də), *n.* seat for persons riding on the back of an elephant. Also, **houdah.** [< Hind. < Ar. *haudaj*]

how·e′er (hou·ãr′), *conj., adv.* however.

How·ells (hou′əlz), *n.* William Dean, 1837–1920, American novelist and writer.

how·ev·er (hou·ev′ər), *adv.* **1.** to whatever degree or amount; no matter how. **2.** in whatever way; by whatever means. —*conj.* nevertheless; yet. ➤ **however. 1.** As a connective, *however* is more appropriate to the fully developed sentences of formal style, and is especially useful as a connective between sentences. We can read many pages of informal English without encountering *however,* its place being taken by the lighter *but,* even as a connective between sentences. **2.** As a simple adverb, *however* modifies an adjective or other adverb: *However hard we tried, the current swept us back.*

how·itz·er (hou′it·sər), *n.* a short cannon for firing shells in a high curve. [earlier *howitz* < Du. < G < Czech *houfnice* catapult]

howl (houl), *v.* **1.** give a long, loud, mournful cry. Dogs and wolves howl. **2.** give a long, loud cry of pain, rage, scorn, etc. **3.** yell; shout: *howl with laughter.* **4.** force or drive by howling. —*n.* **1.** a long, loud, mournful cry. **2.** a loud cry of pain, rage, etc. **3.** yell of scorn, amusement, etc. **4.** yell; shout. [ME *houle(n)*]

howl·er (houl′ər), *n.* **1.** person or thing that howls. **2.** *Colloq.* a ridiculous mistake; stupid blunder.

how·so·ev·er (hou′sō·ev′ər), *adv.* **1.** to whatever degree or amount. **2.** in whatever way.

hoy·den (hoi′dən), *n.* a boisterous, romping girl; tomboy. —*adj.* boisterous; rude. Also, **hoiden.** —**hoy′den·ish,** *adj.* —**hoy′den·ish·ly,** *adv.* —**hoy′den·ish·ness,** *n.*

Hoyle (hoil), *n.* **1.** book of rules and instructions for playing card games. **2. according to Hoyle,** according to the rules or customs; fair; correct.

HP, H.P., hp., or **h.p.,** horsepower.

H.Q., h.q., headquarters.

hr., *pl.* **hrs.** hour.

H.R., House of Representatives.

H.R.H., His (Her) Royal Highness.

ht., height.

hub (hub), *n.* **1.** the central part of a wheel. **2.** any center of interest, importance, activity, etc.

hub·bub (hub′ub), *n.* a noisy tumult; uproar.

huck·a·back (huk′ə·bak), *n.* a heavy, coarse, linen or cotton cloth with a rough surface, used for towels.

huck·le·ber·ry (huk′əl·ber′i), *n., pl.* **–ries.** *Am.* **1.** a small berry like a blueberry, but darker. **2.** shrub that it grows on.

huck·ster (huk′stər), *n.* Also, **huck·ster·er** (–stər·ər). **1.** peddler. **2.** person who sells small articles. **3.** *U.S. Colloq.* person who is in the advertising business. **4.** mean and unfair trader. —*v.* sell; peddle; haggle. [cf. MDu. *hokester.* See HAWK[2].]

hud·dle (hud′əl), *v.,* **–dled, –dling,** *n.* —*v.* **1.** crowd close: *the sheep huddled together in a corner.* **2.** nestle in a heap: *the cat huddled itself on the cushion.* **3.** *Football.* group together behind the line of scrimmage to receive signals. —*n.* **1.** a confused heap, mass, or crowd. **2.** slovenly hurry; confusion. **3.** *Football.* a grouping of players behind the line of scrimmage to receive signals. **4. go into a huddle,** *Colloq.* confer secretly.

Hud·son (hud′sən), *n.* **1.** Henry, died 1611, English navigator and explorer in America. **2.** river in E New York State, flowing into New York Bay.

Hudson Bay, a large bay in C Canada.

Hudson seal, a muskrat fur that is dyed and plucked to look like seal.

hue[1] (hū), *n.* **1.** color. **2.** that quality whereby one color (as red) differs from other colors (as blue, green, etc.). **3.** a particular color: *a greenish hue.* [OE *hiw*] —**hued,** *adj.*

hue[2] (hū), *n.* **1.** a shouting. **2. hue and cry,** shouts of alarm or protest. [< F *hu* < *huer* shout]

huff (huf), *n.* fit of anger or peevishness. —*v.* **1.** make angry; offend. **2.** *Dial.* puff; blow.

huff·y (huf′i), *adj.,* **huff·i·er, huff·i·est. 1.** offended. **2.** easily offended; touchy. —**huff′i·ly,** *adv.* —**huff′i·ness,** *n.*

hug (hug), *v.,* **hugged, hug·ging,** *n.* —*v.* **1.** put the arms around and hold close, esp. in affection. **2.** squeeze tightly with the arms, as a bear does. **3.** cling firmly or fondly to: *hug an opinion.* **4.** keep close to: *the boat hugged the shore.* —*n.* **1.** a tight clasp with the arms. **2.** a tight squeeze with the arms; grip in wrestling. [cf. Scand. *hugga* comfort]

huge (hūj), *adj.,* **hug·er, hug·est.** extremely large. [< OF *ahuge*] —**huge′ly,** *adv.* —**huge′ness,** *n.* —Syn. enormous, immense, gigantic.

hug·ger-mug·ger (hug′ər·mug′ər), *n.* confusion; disorder. —*adj.* **1.** confused; disorderly. **2.** secret. —*v.* **1.** keep secret. **2.** act secretly. —*adv.* in a confused, disorderly manner.

Hughes (hūz), *n.* **Charles Evans**, 1862–1948, American statesman, chief justice of the U.S. Supreme Court, 1930–1941.

Hu·go (hū′gō), *n.* **Victor**, 1802–1885, French poet, novelist, and dramatist.

Hu·gue·not (hū′gə·not), *n.* a French Protestant of the 16th and 17th centuries.

Huk (huk), *n.* one of a Communist group in the Philippines engaged in military and other violent activities against the government.

hu·la-hu·la (hū′lə·hū′lə), or **hula**, *n.* a native Hawaiian dance. [< Hawaiian]

hulk (hulk), *n.* 1. body of an old or worn-out ship. 2. ship used as a prison. 3. a big, clumsy ship. 4. a big, clumsy person or thing. [OE *hulc*, ? < Med.L < Gk. *holkas* merchant ship]

hulk·ing (hul′king), *adj.* big and clumsy.

hull[1] (hul), *n.* 1. the outer covering of a seed. 2. calyx of some fruits, such as the green frill of a strawberry. 3. any outer covering. —*v.* remove the hull or hulls from. [OE *hulu*] —**hull′er**, *n.*

hull[2] (hul), *n.* 1. body or frame of a ship, exclusive of masts, sails, or rigging. 2. the main body or frame of a seaplane, airship, etc. —*v.* strike or pierce the hull of (a ship) with a shell, torpedo, etc. [? same word as *hull*[1]]

hul·la·ba·loo (hul′ə·bə·lū′), *n.* uproar.

hul·lo (hə·lō′), *interj., n., pl.* **-los**, *v.*, **-loed**, **-lo·ing.** hello.

hum (hum), *v.*, **hummed**, **hum·ming**, *n.*, *interj.* —*v.* 1. make a continuous murmuring sound like that of a bee or of a spinning top: *the sewing machine hums busily.* 2. make a low sound like the letter *m*, in hesitation, embarrassment, dissatisfaction, etc. 3. sing with closed lips, not sounding words. 4. put or bring by humming: *hum a baby to sleep.* 5. *Colloq.* be busy and active: *make things hum.* —*n.* 1. a continuous murmuring sound: *the hum of the city street.* 2. a low sound like that of the letter *m*, used to express hesitation, disagreement, etc. 3. a singing with closed lips, not sounding words. —*interj.* a low sound like that of the letter *m*, used to express hesitation, disagreement, etc. [imit.] —**hum′mer**, *n.* —Syn. *v.* 1. drone, buzz, murmur.

hu·man (hū′mən), *adj.* 1. of a person; that a person has: *selfishness is a human weakness.* 2. being a person or persons; having the form or qualities of people: *men, women, and children are human beings.* 3. having or showing qualities (good or bad) natural to people: *he is more human than his brother.* 4. of people; having to do with people: *human affairs.* 5. having to do with people and what they can or cannot do: *beyond human power.* —*n.* a human being; person. [< OF < L *humanus*] —**hu′man·ness**, *n.*

hu·mane (hū·mān′), *adj.* 1. kind; merciful; not cruel or brutal. 2. tending to humanize and refine: *humane studies.* [var. of *human*] —**hu·mane′ly**, *adv.* —**hu·mane′ness**, *n.* —Syn. 1. tender, compassionate. —Ant. 1. brutal, cruel.

hu·man·ism (hū′mən·iz·əm), *n.* 1. any system of thought or action concerned with human interests. 2. study of the humanities. 3. Sometimes, **Humanism,** the principles or culture of the scholars of the Renaissance who pursued and spread the study, and a truer understanding of the literature, ideas, etc., of ancient Rome and Greece. —**hu′man·ist**, *n.* —**hu′man·is′tic**, *adj.*

hu·man·i·tar·i·an (hū·man′ə·tãr′i·ən), *adj.* helpful to humanity; philanthropic. —*n.* person who is devoted to the welfare of all human beings. [< *humanity*; patterned after *unitarian*, etc.] —**hu·man′i·tar′i·an·ism**, *n.*

hu·man·i·ty (hū·man′ə·ti), *n., pl.* **-ties.** 1. human beings taken as a group; people: *advances in science help all humanity.* 2. fact of being human; human character or quality. 3. fact of being humane; humane treatment; kindness: *treat animals with humanity.* 4. the humanities, a. the Latin and Greek languages and literatures. b. languages, literatures, art, etc. c. branches of learning concerned with man.

hu·man·ize (hū′mən·īz), *v.*, **-ized**, **-iz·ing.** 1. make human; give a human character or quality to. 2. make humane; cause to be kind or merciful. —**hu′man·i·za′tion**, *n.* —**hu′man·iz′er**, *n.*

hu·man·kind (hū′mən·kīnd′), *n.* human beings; people; human race; mankind.

hu·man·ly (hū′mən·li), *adv.* 1. in a human manner; by human means. 2. according to the feelings, knowledge, or experience of people.

hum·ble (hum′bəl), *adj.*, **-bler**, **-blest**, *v.*, **-bled**, **-bling.** —*adj.* 1. low in position or condition; not important or grand: *a humble place to live.* 2. having or showing a feeling that one is unimportant, weak, poor, etc.; modest in spirit. 3. deeply or courteously respectful: *in my humble opinion.* —*v.* make humble; make lower in position, condition, or pride. [< OF < L *humilis* low < *humus* earth] —**hum′ble·ness**, *n.* —**hum′bler**, *n.* —**hum′bly**, *adv.* —Syn. *adj.* 1. unpretentious.

hum·ble·bee (hum′bəl·bē′), *n.* bumblebee. [ME *humblebee*, ult. < *hum*]

humble pie. eat humble pie, be forced to do something very disagreeable and humiliating.

hum·bug (hum′bug′), *n., v.*, **-bugged**, **-bugging.** —*n.* 1. a cheat; sham. 2. quality of falseness, deception, etc. —*v.* deceive with a sham; cheat. —**hum′bug′ger**, *n.*

hum·bug·ger·y (hum′bug′ər·i), *n.* sham.

hum·drum (hum′drum′), *adj.* without variety; commonplace; dull. —*n.* humdrum routine.

hu·mer·us (hū′mər·əs), *n., pl.* **-mer·i** (-mər·ī). 1. *Anat.* the long bone in the upper part of the forelimb or arm, from the shoulder to the elbow. 2. the upper part of the forelimb or arm. [< L *umerus*] —**hu′mer·al**, *adj.*

hu·mid (hū′mid), *adj.* 1. moist; damp, esp. moist with aqueous vapor: *humid air.* 2. characterized by much moisture in the air: *a humid region.* [< L *umidus* < *umere* be moist] —**hu′mid·ly**, *adv.* —**hu′mid·ness**, *n.*

hu·mid·i·fy (hū·mid′ə·fī), *v.*, **-fied**, **-fy·ing.** make humid, moist, or damp. —**hu·mid′i·fi·ca′tion**, *n.* —**hu·mid′i·fi′er**, *n.*

hu·mid·i·ty (hū·mid′ə·ti), *n.* 1. moistness; dampness. 2. amount of moisture in the air.

hu·mi·dor (hū′mə·dôr), *n.* box, jar, etc., for keeping things, esp. tobacco, moist.

hu·mil·i·ate (hū·mil′i·āt), *v.*, **-at·ed**, **-at·ing.** lower the pride, dignity, or self-respect of: *John felt humiliated by his failure.* [< L, < *humilis* HUMBLE] —**hu·mil′i·at′ing·ly**, *adv.* —**hu·mil′i·a′tion**, *n.* —Syn. humble, mortify, chagrin.

hu·mil·i·ty (hū·mil′ə·ti), *n., pl.* **-ties.** 1. humbleness of mind; meekness. 2. Usually, **humilities,** act that shows a humble spirit. —Syn. 1. lowliness, modesty.

hu·mit (hū′mit), *n.* unit of measurement used in expressing humiture. If the temperature is 80° and relative humidity is 60%, the humiture is 70 humits. [< *humiture*]

hu·mi·ture (hū′mə·chər), *n.* a combined measurement of temperature and humidity, arrived at by adding degrees of temperature to percentage of relative humidity and dividing by two. [< *humi·(dity)* + *(tempera)ture*; coined by O. F. Hevener of New York in 1937]

hum·ming·bird (hum′ing·bėrd′), *n. Am.* a very small, brightly colored American bird with a long, narrow bill and narrow wings that make a humming sound.

Hummingbird (ab. 3 ¾ in. long)

hum·mock (hum′ək), *n.* 1. a very small, rounded hill; knoll; hillock. 2. bump or ridge in a field of ice. —**hum′mock·y**, *adj.*

hu·mor, *esp. Brit.* **hu·mour** (hū′mər; ū′-), *n.* 1. funny or amusing quality: *I see no humor in your tricks.* 2. ability to see or show the funny or amusing side of things. 3. speech, writing, etc., showing this ability. 4. state of mind; mood; disposition: *success puts you in good humor.* 5. fancy; whim. 6. in old physiology, any of various body fluids supposed to determine a person's health and disposition: blood, phlegm, choler (yellow bile), and melancholy (black bile). —*v.* 1. give in to the fancies or whims of (a person); indulge: *a sick person has to be humored.* 2. adapt oneself to; act so as to agree with. [< L *umor* fluid] —**hu′mor·less**, *esp. Brit.* **hu′mour·less**, *adj.*

hu·mor·esque (hū′mər·esk′), *n.* a light, playful, or humorous piece of music.

hu·mor·ist, *esp. Brit.* **hu·mour·ist** (hū′mər·ist; ū′-), *n.* 1. person with a strong sense of humor. 2. a humorous talker; writer of jokes and funny stories. —**hu′mor·is′tic**, *esp. Brit.* **hu′mour·is′tic**, *adj.*

hu·mor·ous, *esp. Brit.* **hu·mour·ous** (hū′mər·əs; ū′-), *adj.* full of humor; funny; amusing. —**hu′mor·ous·ly**, *esp. Brit.* **hu′mour·ous·ly**, *adv.* —**hu′mor·ous·ness**, *esp. Brit.* **hu′mour·ous·ness**, *n.*

hump (hump), *n.* 1. a rounded lump that sticks out. 2. mound. —*v.* 1. raise or bend up into a lump: *the cat humped her back when she saw the dog.* 2. *U.S. Slang.* exert (oneself). [cf. Du. *homp* lump] —**humped**, *adj.* —**hump′less**, *adj.*

hump·back (hump′bak′), *n.* 1. hunchback. 2. back having a hump on it. 3. *Am.* a large whale that has a humplike dorsal fin. —**hump′-backed′**, *adj.*

humph (humf), *interj.*, *n.* exclamation expressing doubt, disgust, contempt, etc.

Hum·phrey (hum′fri), *n.* George M(agoffin), born 1890, American banker, secretary of the treasury since 1953.

hump·y (hump′i), *adj.*, **hump·i·er**, **hump·i·est**. 1. full of humps. 2. humplike.

hu·mus (hū′məs), *n.* soil made from decayed leaves and other vegetable matter, containing valuable plant foods. [< L, earth]

Hun (hun), *n.* 1. member of a warlike, brutal Asiatic people who overran eastern and central Europe between about 375 and 453 A.D. 2. a barbarous, destructive person; vandal.

hunch (hunch), *v.* 1. hump. 2. draw, bend, or form into a hump: *he sat hunched up with his chin between his knees.* 3. move, push, or shove by jerks. —*n.* 1. a hump. 2. *Am.*, *Colloq.* a vague feeling or suspicion: *he had a hunch that it would rain.* 3. a thick slice or piece; chunk.

hunch·back (hunch′bak′), *n.* 1. person with a hump on his back; humpback. 2. back having a hump on it. —**hunch′backed′**, *adj.*

hun·dred (hun′drəd), *n.*, *pl.* **-dreds** or (*as after a numeral*) **-dred**, *adj.* —*n.* 1. a cardinal number, ten times ten. 2. symbol of this number; 100. 3. set of one hundred persons or things. 4. *Brit.* division of a county. —*adj.* ten times ten; 100. [OE] —**hun·dredth** (hun′drədth), *adj.*

hun·dred·fold (hun′drəd·fōld′), *adj.* 1. a hundred times as much or as many. 2. having one hundred parts. —*adv.* a hundred times as much or as many.

hun·dred·weight (hun′drəd·wāt′), *n.*, *pl.* **-weights** or (*as after a numeral*) **-weight**. measure of weight, equal to 100 pounds in the United States or 112 pounds in England.

hung (hung), *v.* pt. and pp. of **hang**. ▷ See **hang** for usage note.

Hung., 1. Hungarian. 2. Hungary.

Hun·gar·i·an (hung·gãr′i·ən), *adj.* of Hungary, its people, or their language. —*n.* 1. native or inhabitant of Hungary. 2. language of Hungary.

Hun·ga·ry (hung′gə·ri), *n.* country in C Europe, formerly a part of Austria-Hungary.

hun·ger (hung′gər), *n.* 1. an uncomfortable or painful feeling or weak condition caused by lack of food. 2. desire or need for food. 3. a strong desire: *a hunger for kindness.* —*v.* 1. feel hunger; be hungry. 2. starve. 3. have a strong desire. [OE *hungor*] —**hun′ger·ing·ly**, *adv.*

hunger strike, refusal to eat until certain demands are granted.

hun·gry (hung′gri), *adj.*, **-gri·er**, **-gri·est**. 1. feeling a desire or need for food. 2. showing hunger: *a hungry look.* 3. causing hunger. 4. having a strong desire or craving; eager: *hungry for books.* 5. not rich or fertile: *hungry soil.* —**hun′gri·ly**, *adv.* —**hun′gri·ness**, *n.* —Syn. 1. ravenous, famished, starved.

hunk (hungk), *n. Colloq.* a big lump or piece.

hunt (hunt), *v.* 1. chase or go after (wild animals, game birds, etc.) for food or sport. 2. search through (a region) in pursuit of game. 3. use (horses or dogs) in the chase. 4. drive (out, away); pursue. 5. try to find: *hunt a clue.* 6. look thoroughly; search carefully: *hunt through drawers.* —*n.* 1. act of hunting. 2. group of persons hunting together. 3. region hunted over with hounds. 4. attempt to find something; thorough look; careful search. [OE *huntian*] —Syn. *v.* 4. harry, persecute. 6. ransack.

hunt·er (hun′tər), *n.* 1. person who hunts. 2. horse or dog for hunting.

hunting ground, place or region for hunting.

hunting horn, horn used in a hunt.

hunt·ress (hun′tris), *n.* woman who hunts.

hunts·man (hunts′mən), *n.*, *pl.* **-men**. *Esp. Brit.* 1. hunter. 2. manager of a hunt.

hur·dle (hér′dəl), *n.*, *v.*, **-dled**, **-dling**. —*n.* 1. barrier for people or horses to jump over in a race. 2. hurdles, hurdle race, race in which the runners jump over hurdles. 3. obstacle; difficulty. 4. frame made of sticks used as a temporary fence. —*v.* 1. jump over. 2. overcome (an obstacle, difficulty, etc.). 3. enclose with a hurdle. [OE *hyrdel*] —**hur′dler**, *n.*

hur·dy-gur·dy (hér′di·gér′di), *n.*, *pl.* **-dies**. a barrel organ or street piano played by turning a handle. [? imit.]

hurl (hérl), *v.* 1. throw with much force. 2. fling forth (words, cries, etc.) violently; utter with vehemence. —*n.* a forcible or violent throw. [cf. LG *hurreln*] —**hurl′er**, *n.*

hurl·y-burl·y (hér′li·bér′li), *n.*, *pl.* **-burl·ies**. disorder and noise; tumult.

Hu·ron (hyūr′ən), *n. Am.* 1. Lake, the second largest of the five Great Lakes, between the United States and Canada. 2. member of a tribe of Iroquois Indians. —*adj.* of this tribe.

hur·rah (hə·rä′; -rô′), **hur·ray** (hə·rā′), *interj.*, *n.* shout of joy, approval, etc. —*v.* shout hurrahs; cheer. Also, **hooray**.

hur·ri·cane (hér′i·kān), *n.* 1. a tropical cyclone; storm with violent wind and rain; very heavy rain. 2. a sudden, violent outburst. [< Sp. *huracán* < Carib]

hurricane deck, an upper deck on a ship.

hur·ried (hér′id), *adj.* 1. forced to hurry. 2. done or made in a hurry; hasty. —**hur′ried·ly**, *adv.* —**hur′ried·ness**, *n.*

hur·ry (hér′i), *v.*, **-ried**, **-ry·ing**, *n.*, *pl.* **-ries**. —*v.* 1. drive, carry, send, or move quickly. 2. move or act with more than an easy or natural speed. 3. urge to act soon or too soon. 4. urge to great speed or to too great speed. 5. cause to go on or occur more quickly; hasten. —*n.* 1. a hurried movement or action. 2. eagerness to have quickly or do quickly. —**hur′ry·ing·ly**, *adv.* —Syn. *v.* 3. quicken, accelerate, expedite.

hur·ry-scur·ry, **hur·ry-skur·ry** (hér′i·skér′i), *n.*, *pl.* **-ries**, *adj.*, *adv.* —*n.* a hurrying and confusion. —*adj.* hurried and confused. —*adv.* with hurrying and confusion.

hurt (hért), *v.*, **hurt**, **hurt·ing**, *n.* —*v.* 1. cause pain, harm, or damage. 2. cause pain to; give a wound to; injure. 3. suffer pain. 4. have a bad effect on. —*n.* 1. pain; injury; wound. 2. a bad effect; damage; harm. [appar. < OF *hurter* strike < Gmc.] —**hurt′er**, *n.* —**hurt′less**, *adj.*

hurt·ful (hért′fəl), *adj.* causing hurt, harm, or damage; injurious. —**hurt′ful·ly**, *adv.* —**hurt′ful·ness**, *n.* —Syn. harmful, pernicious. —Ant. helpful, beneficial, salutary.

hur·tle (hér′təl), *v.*, **-tled**, **-tling**. 1. dash or drive violently; rush suddenly; come with a crash: *spears hurtled against shields.* 2. move with a clatter; rush noisily or violently: *the train hurtled past.* 3. dash or drive violently; fling. 4. dash against; collide with. [? < *hurt*]

hus·band (huz′bənd), *n.* man who has a wife; married man. —*v.* 1. marry. 2. manage carefully; be saving of: *husband one's resources.* [OE *hūsbonda* < *hūs* house + *bōnda* head of family < Scand. *bōndi*] —**hus′band·less**, *adj.*

hus·band·man (huz′bənd·mən), *n.*, *pl.* **-men**. farmer.

hus·band·ry (huz′bənd·ri), *n.* **1.** farming. **2.** management of one's affairs or resources. **3.** careful management.

hush (hush), *v.* **1.** stop making a noise; make or become silent or quiet. **2.** soothe; calm. **3.** hush up, keep from being told; stop discussion of. —*n.* a stopping of noise; silence; quiet. —*interj.* stop the noise! be silent! keep quiet! [< ME *hussht* silent]

hush money, money paid to keep a person from telling something.

husk (husk), *n.* **1.** the dry outer covering of certain seeds or fruits. An ear of corn has a husk. **2.** the dry or worthless outer covering of anything. —*v.* remove the husk from. [ME *huske*] —**husk′er,** *n.*

husking bee, *Am.* a gathering of neighbors and friends to husk corn.

husk·y¹ (hus′ki), *adj.*, **husk·i·er, husk·i·est,** *n., pl.* **husk·ies.** —*adj.* **1.** dry in the throat; hoarse; rough of voice. **2.** of, like, or having husks. **3.** *Am., Colloq.* big and strong. —*n. Am., Colloq.* a big, strong person. —**husk′i·ly,** *adv.* —**husk′i·ness,** *n.*

Husk·y, husk·y² (hus′ki), *n., pl.* **Husk·ies, husk·ies.** *Am.* an Eskimo dog.

Huss (hus), *n.* John, 1369?–1415, Bohemian religious reformer. —**Huss·ite** (hus′īt), *n.*

hus·sar (hù·zär′), *n.* a European light-armed cavalry soldier. [< Hung. < OSerbian < Ital. *corsaro* runner. See CORSAIR.]

hus·sy (huz′i; hus′–), *n., pl.* **–sies. 1.** a bad-mannered or pert girl. **2.** a worthless woman. [ME *huswif* < HOUSE + WIFE]

hus·tings (hus′tingz), *n. pl.* or *sing.* platform from which speeches are made in a political campaign. [< Scand. *hūsthing* council < *hūs* house + *thing* assembly]

hus·tle (hus′əl), *v.,* **–tled, –tling,** *n.* —*v.* **1.** hurry. **2.** force hurriedly or roughly. **3.** push or shove roughly; jostle rudely. **4.** *Am., Colloq.* work with tireless energy. —*n.* **1.** a hurry. **2.** a rough pushing; rude jostling. **3.** *Am., Colloq.* tireless energy. [< Du. *hutselen* shake] —**hus′tler,** *n.*

hut (hut), *n.* a small, roughly built house; small cabin. [< F < G *hütte*] —**hut′like′,** *adj.*

hutch (huch), *n.* **1.** pen for rabbits, etc. **2.** hut. **3.** box; chest; bin. —*v.* put in a hutch; hoard. [< OF < Med.L *hutica* chest]

Hux·ley (huks′li), *n.* Thomas Henry, 1825–1895, English biologist.

huz·za (hə·zä′), *interj., n., pl.* **–zas,** *v.,* **–zaed, –za·ing.** —*interj., n.* a loud shout of joy, encouragement, or applause; hurrah. —*v.* shout huzzas; cheer.

Hwang Ho, Hwang·ho (hwäng′hō′), *n.* river in China flowing from E Tibet into the Yellow Sea. Also, **Yellow River.**

hy·a·cinth (hī′ə·sinth), *n.* **1.** plant of the lily family that grows from a bulb and has a spike of small, fragrant, bell-shaped flowers. **2.** a reddish-orange gem, a variety of zircon. [< L < Gk. *hyakinthos* kind of flower]

hy·ae·na (hī·ē′nə), *n.* hyena.

hy·a·lu·ron·i·dase (hī′ə·lù·ron′ə·dās), *n.* enzyme that aids the circulation of body fluids.

hy·brid (hī′brid), *n.* **1.** offspring of two animals or plants of different species, varieties, etc. A loganberry is a hybrid between a raspberry and blackberry. **2.** anything of mixed origin. A word formed of parts from different languages is a hybrid. —*adj.* **1.** bred from two different species, varieties, etc. A mule is a hybrid animal. **2.** of mixed origin. [< L *hybrida,* var. of *ibrida* mongrel, hybrid] —**hy′brid·ism,** *n.*

hy·brid·ize (hī′brid·īz), *v.,* **–ized, –iz·ing. 1.** cause to produce hybrids. Botanists hybridize different kinds of plants to get new varieties. **2.** produce hybrids. —**hy′brid·i·za′tion,** *n.*

Hyde Park (hīd), **1.** park in London, England. **2.** village in SE New York State, birthplace of Franklin D. Roosevelt.

Hy·der·a·bad (hī′dər·ə·bad′; –bäd′; hī′drə–), *n.* **1.** a state in S India. **2.** its capital.

hy·dra (hī′drə), *n., pl.* **–dras, –drae** (–drē). **1.** any persistent evil. **2.** *Zool.* kind of fresh-water polyp, so called because when the body is cut into pieces, each piece forms a new individual. **3. Hydra,** *Gk. Legend.* a monstrous serpent having nine heads. [< L < Gk., water serpent]

hy·dran·gea (hī·drān′jə), *n.* shrub with opposite leaves and large, showy clusters of small white, pink, or blue flowers. [< NL, < Gk. *hydor* water + *angeion* vessel, capsule]

hy·drant (hī′drənt), *n. Am.* an upright street fixture from which water may be drawn to fight fires, wash the streets, etc. [< Gk. *hydor* water]

hy·drate (hī′drāt), *n., v.,* **–drat·ed, –drat·ing.** *Chem.* —*n.* compound produced when certain substances unite with water, represented in formulas as containing molecules of water. Washing soda ($Na_2CO_3 \cdot 10H_2O$) is a hydrate. —*v.* become or cause to become a hydrate; combine with water to form a hydrate. [< Gk. *hydor* water] —**hy·dra′tion,** *n.* —**hy′dra·tor,** *n.*

hy·drau·lic (hī·drô′lik), *adj.* **1.** having to do with water in motion. **2.** operated by water: *a hydraulic press.* **3.** hardening under water: *hydraulic cement.* [< L < Gk., ult. < *hydor* water + *aulos* pipe] —**hy·drau′li·cal·ly,** *adv.*

hy·drau·lics (hī·drô′liks), *n.* science treating of water and other liquids in motion, their uses in engineering, the laws of their actions, etc.

hy·dride (hī′drīd; –drid), **hy·drid** (–drid), *n. Chem.* compound of hydrogen with another element or radical.

hydro–, hydr–, *word element.* **1.** of or having to do with water, as in *hydrometer, hydrostatics.* **2.** combined with hydrogen, as in *hydrochloric, hydrosulfuric.* [< Gk., < *hydor* water]

hy·dro·car·bon (hī′drō·kär′bən), *n. Chem.* any of a class of compounds containing only hydrogen and carbon, as methane, benzene, and acetylene. Gasoline is a mixture of hydrocarbons.

hy·dro·chlo·ric acid (hī′drə·klô′rik; –klō′–), *Chem.* **a.** a colorless gas, HCl, with a strong, sharp odor. **b.** an aqueous solution of this.

hy·dro·cor·ti·sone (hī′drō·kôr′tə·zōn), *n.* an adrenal hormone similar to cortisone, used experimentally in treating arthritis. Also, Compound F.

hy·dro·cy·an·ic acid (hī′drō·sī·an′ik), prussic acid.

hy·dro·dy·nam·ics (hī′drō·dī·nam′iks; –di–), *n.* branch of physics dealing with the forces that water and other liquids exert, often called hydraulics. —**hy′dro·dy·nam′ic,** *adj.*

hy·dro·e·lec·tric (hī′drō·i·lek′trik), *adj.* of or pertaining to the production of electricity by water power. —**hy·dro·e·lec·tric·i·ty** (hī′drō·i·lek′tris′ə·ti), *n.*

hy·dro·flu·or·ic acid (hī′drō·flü·ôr′ik; –or′–), *Chem.* a colorless, corrosive, volatile liquid, HF, used for etching glass.

hy·dro·gen (hī′drə·jən), *n. Chem.* a very light, colorless gas, H, that burns easily and weighs less than any other known element. [< F, ult. < Gk. *hydor* water + *geinasthai* produce; form infl. by *–genes* born] —**hy·drog·e·nous** (hī·droj′ə·nəs), *adj.*

hy·dro·gen·ate (hī′drə·jən·āt; hī·droj′ən–), *v.,* **–at·ed, –at·ing.** combine with hydrogen; treat with hydrogen.

hy·dro·gen·a·tion (hī′drə·jən·ā′shən), *n.* **1.** combination with hydrogen. **2.** a method of producing hydrocarbons by pulverizing coal and combining it with hydrogen under very high pressure.

hydrogen bomb, bomb that uses the fusion of atoms to cause an explosion of tremendous force; fusion bomb; superatomic bomb. It will, supposedly, be many times more powerful than the atomic bomb. Also, **H-bomb.**

hy·dro·gen·ize (hī′drə·jən·īz; hī·droj′ən–), *v.,* **–ized, –iz·ing.** hydrogenate.

hydrogen peroxide, a colorless, unstable liquid, H_2O_2, often used in dilute solution as an antiseptic, bleaching agent, etc.

hy·drog·ra·phy (hī·drog′rə·fi), *n.* science of the measurement and description of seas, lakes, rivers, etc., with special reference to their use for navigation and commerce. —**hy·drog′ra·pher,** *n.* —**hy·dro·graph·ic** (hī′drə·graf′ik), *adj.*

hy·droid (hī′droid), *n. Zool.* a very simple form

Husk on an ear of corn

of hydrozoan that grows into branching colonies by budding; polyp. —*adj.* like a polyp.

hy·drol·y·sis (hī·drol′ə·sis), *n., pl.* -ses (-sēz). *Chem.* decomposition that changes a compound into other compounds by taking up the elements of water. [<**hy·dro·lyt·ic** (hī′drə·lit′ik), *adj.*

hy·dro·lyze (hī′drə·līz), *v.*, -lyzed, -lyz·ing. decompose by hydrolysis. —**hy′dro·lyz′a·ble**, *adj.* —**hy′dro·ly·za′tion**, *n.*

hy·drom·e·ter (hī·drom′ə·tər), *n. Physics.* a graduated instrument for finding the specific gravities of liquids. It is used to test the battery of an automobile. —**hy·dro·met·ric** (hī′drə·met′rik), **hy′dro·met′ri·cal**, *adj.* —**hy·drom′e·try**, *n.*

hy·drop·a·thy (hī·drop′ə·thi), *n.* treatment of disease by external or internal use of water; hydrotherapy; hydrotherapeutics. —**hy·dro·path·ic** (hī′drə·path′ik), **hy′dro·path′i·cal**, *adj.* —**hy·drop′a·thist**, *n.*

hy·dro·pho·bi·a (hī′drə·fō′bi·ə), *n.* **1.** an infectious disease of dogs and other flesh-eating mammals that causes convulsions, frothing at the mouth, and madness; rabies. **2.** a morbid dread of water. —**hy·dro·pho·bic** (hī′drə·fō′bik), *adj.*

hy·dro·phyte (hī′drə·fīt), *n.* any plant that can grow only in water or very wet soil.

hy·dro·plane (hī′drə·plān), *n., v.*, -planed, -plan·ing. —*n.* **1.** motorboat that glides on the surface of water. **2.** airplane provided with floats or with a boatlike underpart, enabling it to alight upon and ascend from water; seaplane. —*v.* ride in a hydroplane.

hy·dro·pon·ics (hī′drə·pon′iks), *n.* the growing of plants without soil. [<HYDRO- + L *ponere* to place] —**hy′dro·pon′ic**, *adj.*

hy·dro·sphere (hī′drə·sfir), *n.* **1.** water on the surface of the globe. **2.** water vapor in the atmosphere.

hy·dro·stat (hī′drə·stat), *n.* **1.** device for preventing injury to a steam boiler from low water. **2.** device for detecting the presence of water.

hy·dro·stat·ics (hī′drə·stat′iks), *n.* branch of physics that deals with the equilibrium and pressure of water and other liquids. —**hy′dro·stat′ic**, **hy′dro·stat′i·cal**, *adj.* —**hy′dro·stat′i·cal·ly**, *adv.*

hy·dro·ther·a·peu·tics (hī′drō·ther′ə·pū′tiks), *n.* hydropathy. —**hy′dro·ther′a·peu′tic**, *adj.*

hy·dro·ther·a·py (hī′drō·ther′ə·pi), *n.* hydropathy. —**hy·dro·the·rap·ic** (hī′drō·thə·rap′ik), *adj.*

hy·drot·ro·pism (hī·drot′rə·piz·əm), *n.* tropism in response to water.

hy·drous (hī′drəs), *adj.* **1.** containing water. **2.** *Chem.* containing water or its elements in some kind of union, as in hydrates or in hydroxides.

hy·drox·ide (hī·drok′sīd; -sid), **hy·drox·id** (-sid), *n. Chem.* any compound consisting of an element or radical combined with one or more hydroxyl radicals.

hy·drox·yl radical or **group** (hī·drok′səl), *Chem.* a univalent group or radical, OH, in all hydroxides.

hy·dro·zo·an (hī′drə·zō′ən), *n.* any of a group of invertebrate water animals including hydras, polyps, many jellyfishes, etc. [<NL *Hydrozoa*, genus name < Gk. *hydor* water + *zoion* animal]

hy·e·na (hī·ē′nə), *n.* a wolflike, flesh-eating mammal of Africa and Asia. Most hyenas are cowardly, but utter blood-curdling yells. Also, **hyaena**. [<L < Gk. *hyaina* < *hys* pig]

Hy·gei·a (hī·jē′ə), *n. Gk. Myth.* goddess of health.

hy·giene (hī′jēn; -ji·ēn), *n.* rules of health; science of keeping well. [<NL (*ars*) *hygieina* the healthful art < Gk., ult. <*hygies* healthy] —**hy·gien·ist** (hī′jēn·ist; -ji·en-), *n.*

Striped hyena (ab. 2 ft. high at the shoulder)

hy·gi·en·ic (hī′ji·en′ik; -jē′nik), *adj.* **1.** healthful; sanitary. **2.** having to do with health or hygiene. —**hy′gi·en′i·cal·ly**, *adv.*

hy·grom·e·ter (hī·grom′ə·tər), *n.* instrument for determining the amount of moisture in the air. [<Gk. *hygron* moisture (neut. of *hygros* wet) + -METER]

hy·grom·e·try (hī·grom′ə·tri), *n.* science of determining the amount of moisture in the air. —**hy·gro·met·ric** (hī′grə·met′rik), *adj.*

hy·gro·scope (hī′grə·skōp), *n.* instrument that shows the variations in the humidity of the air.

hy·gro·scop·ic (hī′grə·skop′ik), *adj.* **1.** pertaining to or perceptible by the hygroscope. **2.** absorbing or attracting moisture from the air. —**hy′gro·scop′i·cal·ly**, *adv.*

hy·ing (hī′ing), *v.* ppr. of hie.

hy·la (hī′lə), *n.* a tree toad. [< NL < Gk. *hyle* woods]

Hy·men (hī′mən), *n. Gk. Myth.* god of marriage.

hy·men (hī′mən), *n. Anat.* a fold of mucous membrane extending partly across the opening into the vagina. [< LL < Gk.]

hy·me·ne·al (hī′mə·nē′əl), *adj.* having to do with marriage. —*n.* a wedding song.

hy·me·nop·ter·ous (hī′mə·nop′tər·əs), *adj.* belonging to a group of insects including ants, bees, and wasps. [< Gk., < *hymen* membrane + *pteron* wing]

hymn (him), *n.* **1.** song in praise or honor of God. **2.** any song of praise. —*v.* praise or honor with a hymn. [< L < Gk. *hymnos*] —**hymn′like′**, *adj.*

hym·nal (him′nəl), *n.* Also, **hymn′book′**. book of hymns. —*adj.* of hymns.

hym·nol·o·gy (him·nol′ə·ji), *n.* **1.** study of hymns, their history, classification, etc. **2.** hymns. —**hym·no·log·ic** (him′nə·loj′ik), **hym′no·log′i·cal**, *adj.* —**hym·nol′o·gist**, *n.*

hy·oid (hī′oid), *n. Anat.* the U-shaped bone at the root of the tongue. [< NL < Gk. *hyoeides* U-shaped < Υ (upsilon) + *eidos* form]

hyper-, *prefix.* over; above; beyond; exceedingly; to excess, as in *hyperacidity, hypersensitive, hypertension.* [< Gk. *hyper*]

hy·per·a·cid·i·ty (hī′pər·ə·sid′ə·ti), *n.* excessive acidity. —**hy·per·ac·id** (hī′pər·as′id), *adj.*

hy·per·bo·la (hī·pėr′bə·lə), *n., pl.* -las. *Geom.* a curve formed when a cone is cut by a plane making a larger angle with the base than the side of the cone makes. [< NL < Gk. *hyperbole*, ult. < *hyper-* beyond + *ballein* throw]

Hyperbola

hy·per·bo·le (hī·pėr′bə·lē), *n.* exaggeration for effect. *Example:* Waves mountain high broke over the reef. [< L < Gk. See HYPERBOLA.]

hy·per·bol·ic (hī′pər·bol′ik), *adj.* **1.** of, like, or using hyperbole; exaggerated; exaggerating. **2.** of hyperbolas. —**hy′per·bol′i·cal·ly**, *adv.*

Hy·per·bo·re·an (hī′pər·bō′ri·ən; -bō′-), *n. Gk. Legend.* one of a group of people described as living in a land of perpetual sunshine and plenty beyond the north wind. —*adj.* hyperborean, of the far north; arctic; frigid.

hy·per·crit·i·cal (hī′pər·krit′ə·kəl), *adj.* too critical. —**hy′per·crit′i·cal·ly**, *adv.*

hy·per·sen·si·tive (hī′pər·sen′sə·tiv), *adj.* excessively sensitive. —**hy′per·sen′si·tive·ness**, **hy′per·sen′si·tiv′i·ty**, *n.*

hy·per·ten·sion (hī′pər·ten′shən), *n. Med.* an abnormally high blood pressure.

hy·per·ten·sive (hī′pər·ten′siv), *Med.* —*adj.* having or marked by rising, or unusually high, blood pressure. —*n.* a hypertensive person.

hy·per·tro·phy (hī·pėr′trə·fi), *n., pl.* -phies, *v.*, -phied, -phy·ing. *Pathol., Bot.* —*n.* enlargement of a part or organ; growing too big. —*v.* grow too big. [< NL, < Gk. *hyper-* over + *trophe* nourishment] —**hy·per·troph·ic** (hī′pər·trof′ik), *adj.*

hy·phen (hī′fən), *n.* mark (-) used to connect the parts of a compound word, or the parts of a

word divided at the end of a line, etc. —*v.* hy·phenate. [< LL < Gk., in one, hyphen, < *upo*- under + *hen* one] ≫ **hyphen.** The conclusion one comes to after serious consideration of current habits in the use of hyphens is well put by John Benbow in *Manuscript and Proof*, the stylebook of the Oxford University Press of New York: "If you take hyphens seriously you will surely go mad." The only consolation is that hyphening is more a publisher's worry than a writer's. A publisher may wish for uniformity in principle and may struggle to get it in printing particular words, though absolute consistency is impossible. But in a person's ordinary writing, he does not need to be too particular. For words in common use he can consult this dictionary.
It is obvious that use of hyphens should be appropriate to other traits of style, esp. to punctuation. In general, formal and conservative writers tend to use more hyphens, informal writers tend to use fewer, and those who follow an open punctuation often get along with almost no hyphens. The present style is to use rather few, writing the word pairs as two separate words or joined as one.
The following rules may help:
1. In certain types of compounds of a preposition and a root word a hyphen is necessary to avoid confusion, or for emphasis or appearance:
a. between a prefix ending with a vowel and a root word beginning with the same vowel; as in *re-enter.* Usage is divided on words made with *co-*, the more common ones now generally being written solid or with a dieresis, as in *coöperate, cooperate,* or *co-operate.*
b. to avoid confusion with another word; as in *re-cover—recover.*
c. between a prefix and a proper name; as in *anti-Nazi.*
d. when the prefix is stressed; as in *ex-husband, ex-wife, anti-aircraft.*
2. With modifiers preceding a noun:
a. occasionally some pairs of modifiers might be ambiguous without a hyphen: *a light yellow scarf* might be either a light scarf that was yellow or a scarf that was light yellow, so that *light-yellow* is safest for the latter meaning, and conservative writers would put *light, yellow scarf* for the first.
b. Usage is divided on hyphening noun phrases when used as modifiers, as in *seventeenth century philosophy.* Formal writers would usually write *seventeenth-century,* informal *seventeenth century.* This division applies to such expressions as the following: *a Seventh Avenue shop, summer vacation freedom.*
c. A hyphen is used to carry the force of a modifier over to a later noun ("suspension hyphen"): *The third-, fourth-, and fifth-grade rooms have been redecorated.*
3. A hyphen is conventionally used in certain group words:
a. in the compound numerals from twenty-one to ninety-nine, and in fractions: *one hundred sixty-two, three-sixteenths.*
b. in names of family relationships: (hyphened) *father-in-law, daughter-in-law, etc.*; (one word) *stepson, stepdaughter, stepmother;* (two words) *half brother, half sister.*
c. in compounds with *self-,* which are usually hyphened in dictionaries but are often found in print as two words: *self-government—self government. Selfhood, selfless* are written as one word. If words of this sort raise any question, consult this dictionary.
4. The question of compound and occasionally compounded words is more complex. Many compound words will be found written as two words, hyphened, or as one word. As a rule the form does not affect meaning: *tax payers, tax-payers,* and *taxpayers* all pay taxes. In the past, words that were becoming fused into compounds were required to pass through a probationary period with hyphens before being admitted as single words. *Baseball,* for instance, was hyphened for a time, and *football* and *basketball* until quite recently. There is less tendency to use hyphens now, except in quite formal writing, and compounds are now made immediately without hy-

phens if the word is really needed. A hyphen is less likely to be used when one of the elements has two or more syllables, as in *tenement house. Schoolbook* is usually written solid, *pocket book* is written solid, hyphened, or as two words; *reference book* would almost always be found as two separate words. ≫ See division for another usage note.

hy·phen·ate (hī′fən·āt), *v.*, -at·ed, -at·ing. connect by a hyphen; write or print with a hyphen. —**hy′phen·a′tion,** *n.*

hyp·no·sis (hip·nō′sis), *n., pl.* -ses (-sēz). state resembling deep sleep, but more active, in which a person has little will of his own and little feeling, and acts according to the suggestions of the person who brought about the hypnosis.

hyp·not·ic (hip·not′ik), *adj.* 1. of hypnosis. 2. easily hypnotized. 3. causing sleep. —*n.* 1. person who is hypnotized or easily hypnotized. 2. drug or other means of causing sleep. [< LL < Gk. *hypnotikos* putting to sleep < *hypnoein* put to sleep < *hypnos* sleep] —**hyp·not′i·cal·ly,** *adv.*

hyp·no·tism (hip′nə·tiz·əm), *n.* 1. the inducing of hypnosis. 2. science dealing with hypnosis. —**hyp′no·tist,** *n.*

hyp·no·tize (hip′nə·tīz), *v.*, -tized, -tiz·ing. 1. put into a hypnotic state; cause hypnosis. 2. *Colloq.* dominate the mind by suggestion. —**hyp′no·tiz′a·ble,** *adj.* —**hyp′no·ti·za′tion,** *n.* —**hyp′no·tiz′er,** *n.*

hy·po¹ (hī′pō), *n. Chem.* a colorless, crystalline salt used as a fixing agent in photography.

hy·po² (hī′pō), *n., pl.* -pos. *Colloq.* a hypodermic.

hypo-, *prefix.* under; beneath; below; less than; slightly; somewhat, as in *hypodermic.* [< Gk., < hypo]

hy·po·chlo·rite (hī′pə·klō′rīt; -klō′-), *n.* salt of hypochlorous acid.

hy·po·chlo·rous acid (hī′pə·klō′rəs; -klō′-), *Chem.* an acid, HClO, used as a bleach, disinfectant, etc.

hy·po·chon·dri·a (hī′pə·kon′dri·ə), *n.* 1. unnatural anxiety about one's health; imaginary illness. 2. low spirits without any real reason. [< LL, abdomen, < Gk., < *hypo*- under + *chondros* cartilage (of the breastbone); from the supposed seat of melancholy]

hy·po·chon·dri·ac (hī′pə·kon′dri·ak), *n.* person suffering from hypochondria. —*adj.* Also, hy·po·chon·dri·a·cal (hī′pō·kon·drī′ə·kəl). suffering from hypochondria. —**hy′po·chon·dri′a·cal·ly,** *adv.*

hy·po·cot·yl (hī′pə·kot′əl), *n. Bot.* part of the stem below the cotyledons in the embryo of a plant. —**hy′po·cot′y·lous,** *adj.*

hy·poc·ri·sy (hi·pok′rə·si), *n., pl.* -sies. 1. act or fact of putting on a false appearance of goodness or religion. 2. pretending to be what one is not. [< OF < LL < Gk. *hypokrisis* acting, dissimulation, ult. < *hypo*- under + *krinein* judge]

hyp·o·crite (hip′ə·krit), *n.* 1. person who puts on a false appearance of goodness or religion. 2. person who pretends to be what he is not. [< OF < L < Gk. *hypokrites* actor. See HYPOCRISY.] —**hyp′o·crit′i·cal,** *adj.* —**hyp′o·crit′i·cal·ly,** *adv.*

hy·po·der·mic (hī′pə·der′mik), *adj.* 1. under the skin. 2. injected under the skin: *a hypodermic needle.* —*n.* 1. dose of medicine injected under the skin. 2. syringe used to inject a dose of medicine under the skin. [< NL, < Gk. *hypo*- under + *derma* skin] —**hy′po·der′mi·cal·ly,** *adv.*

hy·po·phos·phite (hī′pə·fos′fīt), *n. Chem.* a salt of hypophosphorous acid.

hy·po·phos·phor·ic acid (hī′pō·fos·fôr′ik; -fôr′-), an acid, H₄P₂O₆, produced by the slow oxidation of phosphorus in moist air.

hy·po·phos·pho·rous acid (hī′pə·fos′fə·rəs), *adj. Chem.* an acid of phosphorus, H₃PO₂.

hy·po·sul·fite (hī′pə·sul′fīt), *n. Chem.* salt of hyposulfurous acid.

hy·po·sul·fur·ous acid (hī′pō·sul′fər·əs; -fyər-; -sul·fyûr′əs), acid, H₂S₂O₄, used as a reducing and bleaching agent.

hy·pot·e·nuse, hy·poth·e·nuse (hī·pot′ənŭs; -nūs), *n*. *Geom*. side of a right-angled triangle opposite the right angle. [< LL < Gk. *hypoteinousa* subtending < *hypo-* under + *teinein* stretch]

hy·poth·e·cate (hī·poth'ə·kāt), *v*., -cat·ed, -cat·ing. pledge to a creditor as security; mortgage. [< Med.L *hypothecatus* < L < Gk. *hypotheke* pledge < *hypo-* under + *tithenai* place] —hy·poth'e·ca'tion, *n*. —hy·poth'e·ca'tor, *n*.

hy·poth·e·sis (hī·poth'ə·sis), *n*., *pl*. -ses (-sēz). 1. something assumed because it seems likely to be a true explanation; theory. 2. proposition assumed as a basis for reasoning. 3. a mere guess. [< NL < Gk., < *hypo-* under + *thesis* a placing]

hy·poth·e·size (hī·poth'ə·sīz), *v*., -sized, -siz·ing. 1. make a hypothesis. 2. assume; suppose.

hy·po·thet·i·cal (hī'pə·thet'ə·kəl), **hy·po·thet·ic** (-ik), *adj*. 1. of or based on a hypothesis; assumed; supposed. 2. fond of making hypotheses: *a hypothetical scientist*. 3. in logic, conditional: *a hypothetical proposition*. 4. of a syllogism, having a hypothetical proposition for one of its premises. —hy'po·thet'i·cal·ly, *adv*.

hy·son (hī'sən), *n*. a Chinese green tea. [< Chinese *hsi-ch'un* blooming spring]

hys·sop (his'əp), *n*. 1. *Am*. a fragrant, bushy plant of the same family as mint, used for medicine, flavoring, etc. 2. *Bible*. a plant whose twigs were used in certain Jewish ceremonies. Psalms 51:7. [< L < Gk. *hyssopos* < Semitic]

hys·ter·ec·to·my (his'tər·ek'tə·mi), *n*., *pl*. -mies. removal of the uterus or a portion of it. [< Gk. *hystera* uterus + *ex-* out + *tomos* cutting]

hys·te·ri·a (his·tir'i·ə; -ter'-), *n*. 1. a nervous disorder that causes violent fits of laughing and crying, imaginary illnesses, or general lack of self-control. 2. senseless excitement. [< NL, < Gk. *hystera* uterus; because women are thought to be more often affected than men]

hys·ter·ic (his·ter'ik), *adj*. hysterical. —*n*. Usually, **hysterics**. fit of hysterical laughing and crying.

hys·ter·i·cal (his·ter'ə·kəl), *adj*. 1. unnaturally excited; showing an unnatural lack of control; unable to stop laughing, crying, etc. 2. suffering from hysteria. 3. of, characteristic of, or pertaining to hysteria. —hys·ter'i·cal·ly, *adv*.

I

X, 1 (ī), *n*., *pl*. **I's; i's.** 1. the ninth letter of the alphabet. 2. the Roman numeral for 1.

I (ī), *pron*., *nom*. I, *poss*. my or mine, *obj*. me; *pl*. *nom*. we, *poss*. ours or our, *obj*. us; *n*., *pl*. **I's.** —*pron*. the nominative case singular of the pronoun of the first person, used by a speaker or writer to denote himself. —*n*. the pronoun *I* used as a noun. [OE *ic*] ➤ The pronoun *I* is written with a capital simply because in the old manuscript hands a small *i* was likely to get lost or to get attached to a neighboring word, and a capital helped keep it a distinct word. There is no conceit implied. The widely circulated theory that *I* should not be the first word in a letter (sometimes even that it should not be the first word of a sentence) is unfounded. The best way to avoid conspicuous use of *I* is to keep it out of emphatic sentence positions, especially from the stressed beginning of a sentence. A subordinate clause or longish phrase put first will throw the stress off the *I*: *After a long struggle I decided to go*.

I, *Chem*. iodine.

I., 1. Island; Islands. 2. Isle; Isles.

Ia., Iowa.

-ial, *suffix*. form of -al, as in *adverbial, facial*, etc.

i·amb (ī'amb), *n*. an iambic foot or measure. [< L < Gk. *iambos*]

i·am·bic (ī·am'bik), *n*. 1. measure in poetry consisting of two syllables, an unaccented followed by an accented as in English poetry, or a short by a long (◡ —) as in Latin and Greek poetry. 2. Usually, **iambics**. verse of iambics. —*adj*. of or containing such measures. Much English poetry is iambic.

-ian, *suffix*. form of -an, as in *Bostonian, Episcopalian*, etc.

I·be·ri·a (ī·bir'i·ə), or **Iberian Peninsula**, *n*. peninsula in SW Europe, occupied by Spain and Portugal. —I·be'ri·an (ī·bir'i·ən), *adj*., *n*.

i·bex (ī'beks), *n*., *pl*. **i·bex·es**, **ib·i·ces** (ib'ə·sēz; ī'bə-), or (*esp. collectively*) **i·bex**. a wild goat of Europe, Asia, or Africa, the male of which has very large horns. [< L]

ibid., **ib.**, ibidem. ➤ ibid. is used in a footnote to refer to the work mentioned in the immediately preceding footnote.

i·bi·dem (i·bī'dem), *adv*. Latin. in the same place; in the same book, chapter, page, etc.

i·bis (ī'bis), *n*., *pl*. **i·bis·es** or (*esp. collectively*)

i·bis. a long-legged wading bird like a heron, regarded by ancient Egyptians as sacred. [< L < Gk. < Egyptian]

-ible, *suffix*. that can be ——ed, as in *impressible, perfectible, reducible*. [< OF < L -*ibilis*] ➤ See -able for usage note.

Ib·sen (ib'sən), *n*. Henrik, 1828-1906. Norwegian dramatist and poet.

-ic, *suffix*. 1. of or pertaining to, as in *atmospheric, Icelandic*. 2. having the nature of, as in *artistic, heroic*. 3. constituting or being, as in *bombastic, monolithic*. 4. characterized by; containing; made up of, as in *alcoholic, iambic*. 5. made by; caused by, as in *phonographic*. 6. like; like that of; characteristic of, as in *meteoric, sophomoric*. 7. *Chem*. -ic implies a smaller proportion of the element than -*ous* implies, as in *sulfuric*. [< F -*ique* or L -*icus* or Gk. -*ikos*]

-ical, *suffix*. 1. -ic, as in *geometrical, parasitical, hysterical*. 2. -ic specialized or differentiated in meaning, as in *economical*. 3. -ical sometimes equals -al added to nouns ending in -ic, as in *critical, musical*.

Ic·a·rus (ik'ə·rəs; ī'kə-), *n*. *Gk. Legend*. the son of Daedalus. Icarus and his father escaped from Crete by using wings that Daedalus had made. Icarus flew so high that the sun melted the wax by which his wings were attached. —I·car·i·an (i·kār'i·ən; ī-), *adj*.

ICBM, Intercontinental Ballistic Missile, a ballistic missile of great range (up to 5000 miles).

I.C.C., ICC, Interstate Commerce Commission.

ice (īs), *n*., *v*., iced, ic·ing, *adj*. —*n*. 1. water made solid by cold; frozen water. 2. layer or surface of ice. 3. something that looks or feels like ice. 4. a frozen dessert usually made of sweetened fruit juice. 5. icing. 6. *Slang*. diamonds. 7. **break the ice**, a. make a beginning. b. overcome first difficulties in talking or getting acquainted. 8. **on thin ice**, in a dangerous or difficult position. —*v*. 1. cool with ice; put ice in or around. 2. cover with ice. 3. turn to ice; freeze. 4. cover (cake) with icing. —*adj*. of ice; having to do with ice. [OE *īs*] —ice'less, *adj*. —ice'like', *adj*.

ice age, *Geol*. the glacial epoch.

ice·berg (īs'bėrg'), *n*. a large mass of ice floating in the sea. [< Dan. *isbjerg*, or Swed. *isberg*, or Du. *ijsberg*, lit., ice mountain]

ice·boat (īs'bōt'), *n*. 1. a triangular frame on runners, fitted with sails for sailing on ice. 2. icebreaker (def. 1).

ice·bound (īs'bound'), *adj*. 1. held fast by ice. 2. shut in or obstructed by ice.

ice·box (īs'boks'), *n*. *Am*. an insulated box in which to keep food, liquids, etc., cool with ice, etc.

Ibis (ab. 3½ ft. long)

āge, cāre, fär; ēqual, tèrm; īce; ōpen, ôrder; pùt, rüle, ūse; tħ, then; ə=a in about.

ice·break·er (īs′brāk′ər), *n. Am.* **1.** a strong boat used to break a channel through ice. **2.** machine **or** tool for cutting ice into small pieces.

ice·cap (īs′kap′), *n.* a permanent covering of ice over an area, sloping down on all sides from an elevated center.

ice cream, a frozen dessert made of cream or custard sweetened and flavored.

iced (īst), *adj.* **1.** cooled with ice; with ice in or around it. **2.** covered with icing.

ice field, a large sheet of ice floating in the sea.

Ice·land (īs′lənd), *n.* a large island in the N Atlantic, formerly a Danish possession, an independent republic since 1944. —**Ice·land·er** (īs′lan′dər; -lən-dər), *n.*

Ice·lan·dic (īs-lan′dik), *adj.* of or having to do with Iceland, its people, or their language. —*n.* the language of Iceland.

ice·man (īs′man′), *n., pl.* -**men** (-mēn′). *Am.* man who sells, delivers, or handles ice.

ice pack, 1. large area of masses of ice floating in the sea. **2.** bag containing ice for application to the body.

ice sheet, a broad, thick sheet of ice covering a very large area for a long time.

ice-skate (īs′skāt′), *v.,* -**skat·ed,** -**skat·ing.** skate on ice.

ice skates, a pair of metal runners, usually attached to shoes, for skating.

ich·neu·mon (ik-nū′mən; -nū′-), *n.* **1.** a small brown, weasellike animal of Egypt. **2.** the ichneumon fly. [< L < Gk., lit., searcher (supposedly for crocodile's eggs), ult. < *ichnos* track]

ich·neu·mon fly, insect that looks like a wasp but does not sting. Its larvae live as parasites in or on other insects, usually killing them.

ich·thy·ol·o·gy (ik′thi-ol′ə-ji), *n.* branch of zoölogy dealing with fishes. [< Gk. *ichthys* fish + -LOGY] —**ich·thy·o·log·ic** (ik′thi-ə-loj′ik), **ich·thy·o·log′i·cal,** *adj.* —**ich·thy·ol′o·gist,** *n.*

ich·thy·o·saur (ik′thi-ə-sôr′), **ich·thy·o·sau·rus** (ik′thi-ə-sô′rəs), *n., pl.* -**saurs;** -**sau·ri** (-sô′rī). an extinct fishlike marine reptile with four paddlelike flippers. [< NL, < Gk. *ichthys* fish + *sauros* lizard]

Ichthyosaur
(from 4 to 40 ft. long)

i·ci·cle (ī′si·kəl), *n.* a pointed, hanging stick of ice formed by the freezing of dripping water. [ME *isykle* < OE *is* ice + *gicel* icicle] —**i′ci·cled,** *adj.*

ic·ing (īs′ing), *n.* mixture of sugar with white of egg or other things, used to cover cakes.

i·con (ī′kon), *n., pl.* **i·cons, i·co·nes** (ī′kə-nēz). **1.** in the Eastern Church, a sacred picture or image of Christ, an angel, a saint, etc. **2.** picture; image. Also, **ikon, eikon.** [< L < Gk. *eikon*]

i·con·o·clast (ī·kon′ə·klast), *n.* **1.** person opposed to worshiping images. **2.** person who attacks cherished beliefs or institutions as wrong or foolish. [< Med.L < Med.Gk. *eikonoklastes* < Gk. *eikon* image + *klaein* to break] —**i·con′o·clas′tic,** *adj.* —**i·con′o·clas′ti·cal·ly,** *adv.*

-ics, *suffix.* **1.** facts, principles, science, as in *physics.* **2.** methods, system, activities, as in *athletics, politics, tactics.* ≯ Nouns formed with –ics were originally plural, denoting things pertaining to a particular subject, but are now chiefly singular in use (without dropping the –*s*), denoting the body of knowledge, facts, principles, etc., pertaining to a subject, and hence a science, study, or art, as *economics, linguistics, physics.* Some are singular or plural according to the context, as *acoustics, athletics, ethics: Ethics is a new course in the philosophy department. The young lawyer's ethics are above reproach.* Others can be construed either way. See the usage note under *politics.*

ic·tus (ik′təs), *n., pl.* -**tus·es,** -**tus. 1.** rhythmical or metrical stress. **2.** beat of the pulse. [< L, < *icere* to hit]

i·cy (ī′si), *adj.,* **i·ci·er, i·ci·est. 1.** like ice; very cold; slippery. **2.** having much ice; covered with ice. **3.** of ice. **4.** without warm feeling; cold and unfriendly. —**i′ci·ly,** *adv.* —**i′ci·ness,** *n.* —Syn. **1.** frosty, frigid.

id (id), *n. Psychoanalysis.* the preformed, primitive psychic force in the unconscious, which is the source of instinctive energy essential for propagation and self-preservation. [< G use of L *id* it]

I'd (īd), **1.** I should. **2.** I would. **3.** I had.

id., *idem.*

Ida., Id., Idaho.

I·da·ho (ī′də·hō), *n.* a Western State of the United States. *Capital:* Boise. *Abbrev.:* Ida. or Id. —**I′da·ho′an,** *adj., n.*

-ide, -id, *suffix.* compound of, as in *chloride, sulfide.* [< *oxide*]

i·de·a (ī·dē′ə), *n.* **1.** plan, picture, or belief of the mind. **2.** thought; fancy; opinion. ≯ **Idea** strictly means a "concept," something thought about something. It is frequently used as a substitute for *intention* and similar words in constructions that are usually wordy: *I got the idea that* [I thought] *every policeman was my enemy.* [< L < Gk., < *idein* see] —**i·de′a·less,** *adj.* —Syn. **1.** conception, concept. **2.** notion.

i·de·al (ī·dē′əl; ī·dēl′), *n.* perfect type; model to be imitated; what one would wish to be: *religion holds up high ideals for us to follow.* —*adj.* **1.** just as one would wish; perfect: *an ideal day for a picnic.* **2.** existing only in thought. A point without length, breadth, or thickness is an ideal object. **3.** not practical; visionary. **4.** having to do with ideas; representing an idea. —**i·de′al·ness,** *n.* —Syn. *adj.* **3.** unreal, fanciful. —Ant. *adj.* **1.** imperfect, faulty. **3.** practical, real, actual.

i·de·al·ism (ī·dē′əl·iz·əm), *n.* **1.** an acting according to one's ideals of what ought to be, regardless of circumstances or of the approval or disapproval of others. **2.** the cherishing of fine ideals. **3.** in art or literature, representing imagined types rather than an exact copy of any one person, instance, or situation. **4.** in philosophy, belief that all our knowledge is a knowledge of ideas and that it is impossible to know whether there really is a world of objects on which our ideas are based.

i·de·al·ist (ī·dē′əl·ist), *n.* **1.** person who acts according to his ideals; person who has fine ideals. **2.** person who neglects practical matters in following ideals. **3.** adherent of idealism in art or philosophy.

i·de·al·is·tic (ī·dē′əl·is′tik), *adj.* **1.** having high ideals and acting according to them. **2.** forgetting or neglecting practical matters in trying to follow out one's ideals; not practical. **3.** of idealism or idealists. —**i·de′al·is′ti·cal·ly,** *adv.*

i·de·al·ize (ī·dē′əl·īz), *v.,* -**ized,** -**iz·ing.** make ideal; think of or represent as perfect rather than as is actually the case: *Mary idealized her older sister and thought that everything she did was right.* —**i·de′al·i·za′tion,** *n.* —**i·de′al·iz′er,** *n.*

i·de·al·ly (ī·dē′əl·i), *adv.* **1.** according to an ideal; perfectly. **2.** in idea or theory.

i·dem (ī′dem; id′em), *pron., adj. Latin.* the same as previously given or mentioned.

i·den·ti·cal (ī·den′tə·kəl), *adj.* **1.** the same: *both events happened on the identical day.* **2.** exactly alike; identical: *identical houses.* [< Med.L *identicus* < L *idem* same] —**i·den′ti·cal·ly,** *adv.* —**i·den′ti·cal·ness,** *n.*

identical twin, one of twins, of the same sex, developing from a single fertilized ovum.

i·den·ti·fi·ca·tion (ī·den′tə·fə·kā′shən), *n.* **1.** an identifying or being identified. **2.** something used to identify a person or thing.

i·den·ti·fy (ī·den′tə·fī), *v.,* -**fied,** -**fy·ing. 1.** recognize as being, or show to be, a certain person or thing; prove to be the same: *identify handwriting.* **2.** make the same; treat as the same. **3.** connect closely; link; associate (*with*). —**i·den′ti·fi′a·ble,** *adj.* —**i·den′ti·fi′er,** *n.*

i·den·ti·ty (ī·den′tə·ti), *n., pl.* -**ties. 1.** individuality; who a person is; what a thing is: *the writer concealed his identity under an assumed name.* **2.** exact likeness; sameness: *the identity of the two crimes.* **3.** state or fact of being the same one: *establish the identity of a person seen today with one seen yesterday.*

id·e·o·graph (id′i·ə·graf′; -gräf′; ī′di-), **id-**

e·o·gram (-gram′), *n.* a graphic symbol that represents a thing or an idea without indicating a word for the thing or the idea, as Egyptian hieroglyphics and Chinese characters. [< Gk. *idea* idea + -GRAPH] —**id′e·o·graph′ic**, id′e·o·graph′i·cal, *adj.* —id′e·o·graph′i·cal·ly, *adv.*

i·de·ol·o·gy (ī′di·ol′ə·ji; id′i-), *n.*, *pl.* -gies. 1. set of doctrines; body of opinions. 2. fundamental doctrines and point of view. 3. the combined doctrines, assertions, and intentions of a social or political movement. —**i·de·o·log·ic** (ī′di·ə·loj′ik; id′i-), i′de·o·log′i·cal, *adj.* —i′de·o·log′i·cal·ly, *adv.* —i′de·ol′o·gist, *n.*

ides (īdz), *n.pl.* in the ancient Roman calendar, the 15th day of March, May, July, and October, and the 13th day of the other months. [< F < L *idus* < Etruscan]

id·i·o·cy (id′i·ə·si), *n.*, *pl.* -cies. 1. being an idiot. 2. very great stupidity or folly.

id·i·om (id′i·əm), *n.* 1. phrase or expression whose meaning cannot be understood from the ordinary meanings of the words in it. "How do you do?" and "I have caught cold" are English idioms. 2. dialect. 3. a people's way of expressing themselves. 4. individual manner of expression in music, art, etc. [< LL < Gk. *idioma*, ult. < *idios* one's own]

id·i·o·mat·ic (id′i·ə·mat′ik), **id·i·o·mat·i·cal** (-ə·kəl), *adj.* 1. using an idiom or idioms. 2. of or concerning idioms. 3. characteristic of a particular language. —**id′i·o·mat′i·cal·ly**, *adv.* —id′i·o·mat′i·cal·ness, *n.*

id·i·o·syn·cra·sy (id′i·ō·sing′krə·si; -sin′-), *n.*, *pl.* -sies. personal peculiarity. [< Gk., < *idios* one's own + *synkrasis* temperament < *syn* together + *kerannymi* mix] —**id·i·o·syn·crat·ic** (id′i·ō·sin·krat′ik), *adj.*

id·i·ot (id′i·ət), *n.* 1. person born with such slight mental capacities that he can never learn to read or count. 2. a very stupid or foolish person. 3. *Psychol.* the lowest grade of feeblemindedness, ranging in IQ from 0 to 25. [< L < Gk. *idiotes*, orig., private person < *idios* one's own]

id·i·ot·ic (id′i·ot′ik), *adj.* of or like an idiot; very stupid or foolish. —**id′i·ot′i·cal·ly**, *adv.*

i·dle (ī′dəl), *adj.*, i·dler, i·dlest, *v.*, i·dled, i·dling. —*adj.* 1. doing nothing; not busy; not working: *idle hands, money lying idle.* 2. not willing to do things; lazy. 3. useless; worthless: *idle pleasures.* 4. without any good reason, cause, or foundation: *idle fears.* —*v.* 1. be idle; do nothing. 2. waste (time); spend. 3. *Mach.* run slowly without transmitting power. [OE *īdel*] —**i′dle·ness**, *n.* —**i′dler**, *n.* —**i′dly**, *adv.* —Syn. *adj.* 1. inactive, unemployed. 2. indolent.

I·dle·wild (ī′dəl·wīld), *n.* a major international airport, near New York City.

i·dol (ī′dəl), *n.* 1. image or other object worshiped as a god. 2. *Bible.* a false god. 3. object of extreme devotion. 4. a fallacy. [< OF < L < Gk. *eidolon* image < *eidos* form]

i·dol·a·ter (ī·dol′ə·tər), *n.* 1. person who worships idols. 2. admirer; adorer; devotee.

i·dol·a·trous (ī·dol′ə·trəs), *adj.* 1. worshiping idols. 2. having to do with idolatry. 3. blindly adoring. —**i·dol′a·trous·ly**, *adv.* —i·dol′a·trous·ness, *n.*

i·dol·a·try (ī·dol′ə·tri), *n.*, *pl.* -tries. 1. worship of idols. 2. worship of a person or thing; extreme devotion. [< OF < L < Gk., < *eidolon* image + *latreia* service]

i·dol·ize (ī′dəl·īz), *v.*, -ized, -iz·ing. 1. worship as an idol. 2. love or admire very much; be extremely devoted to. —**i′dol·i·za′tion**, *n.*

i·dyl, i·dyll (ī′dəl), *n.* 1. a short description in poetry or prose of a simple and charming scene or event, esp. one connected with country life. 2. scene or event suitable for such a description. [< L < Gk. *eidyllion*, dim. of *eidos* form]

i·dyl·lic (ī·dil′ik), *adj.* suitable for an idyl; simple and charming. —**i·dyl′li·cal·ly**, *adv.*

Idol

i.e., that is; that is to say. ▶ i.e. is the abbreviation for Latin *id est*, "that is." It is not common now outside rather routine reference exposition, *that is* being ordinarily written.

if (if), *conj.* 1. supposing that; on condition that; in case that: *if you are going, leave now.* 2. whether: *I wonder if he will go.* 3. *Colloq.* although; even though: *if he is little, he is strong.* 4. as if, as it would be if. —*n.* condition; supposition. [OE *gif*] ▶ if. 1. *If* is a subordinating conjunction introducing a condition: *If the weather holds good, we shall stay another week.* 2. if and whether. In formal usage, *if* is used for conditions, and *whether*, usually with *or*, is used, though not consistently, in indirect questions (*He asked whether the mail had come*), in conditions, and in expressions of doubt (*We could not be sure whether the State was Republican or Democratic*).

if·fy (if′i), *adj. Colloq.* 1. full of ifs. 2. doubtful.

ig·loo, ig·lu (ig′lū), *n.*, *pl.* -loos; -lus. a dome-shaped hut used by Eskimos, often built of blocks of hard snow. [< Eskimo, house]

Ig·na·tius Loy·o·la (ig·nā′shəs loi·ō′lə), Saint, 1491–1556, Spanish monk who founded the Jesuit order.

ig·ne·ous (ig′ni·əs), *adj.* 1. of fire; pertaining to fire. 2. *Geol.* produced by fire, intense heat, or volcanic action. [< L, < *ignis* fire]

ig·nis fat·u·us (ig′nis fach′ū·əs), *pl.* ig·nes fat·u·i (ig′nēz fach′ū·ī). 1. a flitting phosphorescent light seen at night chiefly over marshy ground; will-o′-the-wisp. 2. something deluding or misleading.

ig·nite (ig·nīt′), *v.*, -nit·ed, -nit·ing. 1. set on fire. 2. *Chem.* make intensely hot; cause to glow with heat. 3. take fire; begin to burn. [< L, < *ignis* fire] —**ig·nit′a·ble, ig·nit′i·ble**, —**ig·nit′a·bil′i·ty, ig·nit′i·bil′i·ty**, *n.* —ig·nit′er, ig·ni′tor, *n.*

ig·ni·tion (ig·nish′ən), *n.* 1. a setting on fire. 2. a catching on fire. 3. apparatus for igniting the explosive vapor in the cylinders of an internal-combustion engine.

ig·no·ble (ig·nō′bəl), *adj.* 1. mean; base; without honor. 2. of low birth. [< L, < in- not + Old L *gnobilis* noble] —**ig′no·bil′i·ty, ig·no′ble·ness**, *n.* —**ig·no′bly**, *adv.* —Syn. 1. degraded, dishonorable, contemptible. —Ant. 1. noble.

ig·no·min·i·ous (ig′nə·min′i·əs), *adj.* 1. shameful; disgraceful; humiliating. 2. contemptible. —**ig′no·min′i·ous·ly**, *adv.* —ig′no·min′i·ous·ness, *n.*

ig·no·min·y (ig′nə·min′i), *n.*, *pl.* -min·ies. 1. loss of one's good name; public shame and disgrace; dishonor. 2. shameful action or conduct. [< L *ignominia* < in- not + *nomen* name]

ig·no·ra·mus (ig′nə·rā′məs; -ram′əs), *n.*, *pl.* -mus·es. an ignorant person. [< L, we do not know]

ig·no·rance (ig′nə·rəns), *n.* lack of knowledge; quality or condition of being ignorant.

ig·no·rant (ig′nə·rənt), *adj.* 1. knowing little or nothing; without knowledge. A person who has not had much chance to learn may be ignorant but not stupid. 2. uninformed; unaware: *he was ignorant of the fact that the town had been destroyed.* 3. showing lack of knowledge: *an ignorant remark.* [< L *ignorans* not knowing] —**ig′no·rant·ly**, *adv.* —Syn. 1. untaught, uneducated. 2. unknowing. —Ant. 1. learned.

ig·nore (ig·nôr′; -nōr′), *v.*, -nored, -nor·ing. pay no attention to; disregard. [< L *ignorare* not know] —**ig·nor′er**, *n.* —Syn. overlook, neglect.

Ig·o·rot (ig′ə·rōt′), **Ig·or·ro·te** (-rō′tē), *n.*, *pl.* -rot, -rots; -ro·te, -ro·tes. 1. member of a Malay tribe of the Philippine Islands. 2. their language.

i·gua·na (i·gwä′nə), *n.* a large climbing lizard found in tropical America. See picture on next page. [< Sp. < Carib] —**i·gua·ni·an** (i·gwä′ni·ən), *adj.*, *n.*

IHS, first three letters of the name of Jesus in Greek.

i·kon (ī′kon), *n.* icon.

Il, *Chem.* illinium.

Il Du·ce (ēl dṳ′chā). See duce (def. 2).

il·e·i·tis (ĭl′ĭ·ī′tĭs), *n.* inflammation of the ileum, due to infection, a tumor, or other cause and involving partial or complete blocking of the passage of food through the small intestine.

il·e·um (ĭl′ĭ·əm), *n. Anat.* the lowest part of the small intestine. [< LL, var. of *ilium,* sing. to L *ilia* loins, entrails] —**il·e·ac** (ĭl′ĭ·ak), *adj.*

i·lex (ī′lĕks), *n.* 1. holm oak. 2. holly. [< L]

il·i·ac (ĭl′ĭ·ak), *adj. Anat.* of or having to do with the ilium; near the ilium.

Il·i·ad (ĭl′ĭ·əd), *n.* a long Greek epic poem about the siege of Ilium, or Troy, supposedly written by Homer. —**Il·i·ad·ic** (ĭl′ĭ·ad′ĭk), *adj.*

Iguana (ab. 5 ft. long)

il·i·um (ĭl′ĭ·əm), *n., pl.* **il·i·a** (ĭl′ĭ·ə). *Anat.* the broad upper portion of the hipbone. [< NL < LL, sing. to L *ilia* flank, groin]

Il·i·um (ĭl′ĭ·əm), *n.* ancient Troy.

ilk (ĭlk), *adj. Archaic.* same. —*n.* 1. *Colloq.* family; kind; sort. 2. of that ilk, *Colloq.* a. of the same place or name. b. of that kind or sort. [OE *ilca* same]

ill (ĭl), *adj.,* worse, worst, *n., adv.* —*adj.* 1. having some disease; not well; sick. 2. bad; evil; harmful: *an ill deed.* 3. unfavorable; unfortunate: *an ill wind.* 4. unkind; harsh; cruel. 5. ill at ease, uncomfortable. —*n.* 1. sickness; disease. 2. an evil; a harm; a trouble. —*adv.* 1. badly; harmfully. 2. unfavorably; unfortunately. 3. in an unkind manner; harshly; cruelly. 4. with trouble or difficulty; scarcely. [< Scand. *illr*] ⮞ ill. See sick for usage note.

I'll (īl), 1. I shall. 2. I will.

Ill., Illinois.

ill., illustrated; illustration.

ill-ad·vised (ĭl′əd·vīzd′), *adj.* acting or done without enough consideration; unwise. —**ill·ad·vis·ed·ly** (ĭl′əd·vīz′ĭd·lĭ), *adv.*

ill-bred (ĭl′brĕd′), *adj.* badly brought up; rude.

ill breeding, bad manners; rudeness.

ill-con·sid·ered (ĭl′kən·sĭd′ərd), *adj.* unwise.

ill-dis·posed (ĭl′dĭs·pōzd′), *adj.* unfriendly.

il·le·gal (ĭ·lē′gəl), *adj.* not lawful; against the law; forbidden by law. —**il·le′gal·ly,** *adv.* —**il·le′gal·ness,** *n.* —**Syn.** unlawful, illicit.

il·le·gal·i·ty (ĭl′ē·gal′ə·tĭ), *n., pl.* -ties. 1. unlawfulness. 2. an illegal act.

il·leg·i·ble (ĭ·lĕj′ə·bəl), *adj.* very hard or impossible to read. —**il·leg′i·bil′i·ty, il·leg′i·ble·ness,** *n.* —**il·leg′i·bly,** *adv.*

il·le·git·i·mate (ĭl′ə·jĭt′ə·mĭt), *adj.* 1. born of parents who are not married to each other. 2. not according to the law or the rules. —**il′le·git′i·ma·cy, il′le·git′i·mate·ness,** *n.* —**il′le·git′i·mate·ly,** *adv.*

ill-fat·ed (ĭl′fāt′ĭd), *adj.* 1. sure to have a bad fate or end. 2. unlucky.

ill-fa·vored, *esp. Brit.* **ill-fa·voured** (ĭl′fā′vərd), *adj.* 1. ugly. 2. offensive. —**ill′-fa′vored·ly,** *esp. Brit.* **ill′-fa′voured·ly,** *adv.* —**ill′-fa′vored·ness,** *esp. Brit.* **ill′-fa′voured·ness,** *n.*

ill-found·ed (ĭl′foun′dĭd), *adj.* without a good reason or sound basis.

ill-got·ten (ĭl′got′ən), *adj.* acquired by evil or unfair means; dishonestly obtained.

ill health, poor health.

ill humor, *esp. Brit.* **ill humour,** cross, unpleasant temper or mood.

ill-hu·mored, *esp. Brit.* **ill-hu·moured** (ĭl′hū′mərd; -ū′-), *adj.* cross; unpleasant. —**ill′-hu′mored·ly,** *esp. Brit.* **ill′-hu′moured·ly,** *adv.* —**ill′-hu′mored·ness,** *esp. Brit.* **ill′-hu′moured·ness,** *n.*

il·lib·er·al (ĭ·lĭb′ər·əl), *adj.* 1. not liberal; narrow-minded; prejudiced. 2. stingy; miserly. 3. without liberal culture. —**il·lib′er·al′i·ty, il·lib′er·al·ness,** *n.* —**il·lib′er·al·ly,** *adv.*

il·lic·it (ĭ·lĭs′ĭt), *adj.* not permitted by law; forbidden. —**il·lic′it·ly,** *adv.* —**il·lic′it·ness,** *n.*

il·lim·it·a·ble (ĭ·lĭm′ĭt·ə·bəl), *adj.* limitless; boundless; infinite. —**il·lim′it·a·bil′i·ty, il·lim′it·a·ble·ness,** *n.* —**il·lim′it·a·bly,** *adv.*

il·lin·i·um (ĭ·lĭn′ĭ·əm), *n. Chem.* promethium. [< NL; named after *Illinois*]

Il·li·nois (ĭl′ə·noi′; -noiz′), *n.* 1. a Middle Western State of the United States. *Capital:* Springfield. *Abbrev.:* Ill. 2. *Am.* member of an American Indian tribe formerly living between the Mississippi and Wabash rivers. —*adj.* of this tribe. —**Il′li·nois′an,** *adj., n. Am.*

il·lit·er·a·cy (ĭ·lĭt′ər·ə·sĭ), *n., pl.* -cies. 1. inability to read or write. 2. lack of education. 3. error in speaking or writing, caused by ignorance.

il·lit·er·ate (ĭ·lĭt′ər·ĭt), *adj.* 1. unable to read or write. 2. lacking in education. 3. showing lack of culture. —*n.* an illiterate person. —**il·lit′er·ate·ly,** *adv.* —**il·lit′er·ate·ness,** *n.*

ill-judged (ĭl′jŭjd′), *adj.* unwise; rash.

ill-man·nered (ĭl′man′ərd), *adj.* having or showing bad manners; impolite; rude. —**ill′-man′nered·ly,** *adv.* —**ill′-man′nered·ness,** *n.*

ill nature, crossness; disagreeableness; spite. —**ill-na·tured** (ĭl′nā′chərd), *adj.* —**ill′-na′tured·ly,** *adv.* —**ill′-na′tured·ness,** *n.*

ill-ness (ĭl′nĭs), *n.* sickness; disease.

il·log·i·cal (ĭ·loj′ə·kəl), *adj.* not logical; not reasonable. —**il·log′i·cal′i·ty, il·log′i·cal·ness,** *n.* —**il·log′i·cal·ly,** *adv.* —**Syn.** unreasonable, irrational, unsound, fallacious.

ill-spent (ĭl′spĕnt′), *adj.* spent badly; wasted.

ill-starred (ĭl′stärd′), *adj.* unlucky; disastrous.

ill-suit·ed (ĭl′sūt′ĭd; -sūt′-), *adj.* unsuitable.

ill temper, bad temper or disposition; crossness. —**ill-tem·pered** (ĭl′tem′pərd), *adj.* —**ill′-tem′pered·ly,** *adv.* —**ill′-tem′pered·ness,** *n.*

ill-timed (ĭl′tīmd′), *adj.* inappropriate.

ill-treat (ĭl′trēt′), *v.* treat badly or cruelly; do harm to; abuse. —**ill′-treat′ment,** *n.*

il·lu·mi·nant (ĭ·lū′mə·nənt), *adj.* giving light. —*n.* something that gives light.

il·lu·mi·nate (ĭ·lū′mə·nāt), *v.,* -nat·ed, -nat·ing. 1. light up; make bright. 2. make clear; explain. 3. decorate with lights. 4. decorate with gold, colors, pictures, and designs: *some old books and manuscripts were illuminated.* 5. enlighten; inform; instruct. 6. make illustrious. [< L *illuminatus,* ult. < *in-* in + *lumen* light] —**il·lu′mi·nat′ing,** *adj.* —**il·lu′mi·nat′ing·ly,** *adv.* —**il·lu′mi·na′tive,** *adj.* —**il·lu′mi·na′tor,** *n.*

il·lu·mi·na·tion (ĭ·lū′mə·nā′shən), *n.* 1. a lighting up; a making bright. 2. amount of light; light. 3. a making clear; explanation. 4. decoration with lights. 5. decoration of books and letters with gold, colors, pictures, and designs. 6. enlightenment.

il·lu·mine (ĭ·lū′mən), *v.,* -mined, -min·ing. make or become bright; illuminate; light up. —**il·lu′mi·na·ble,** *adj.*

illus., illust., illustrated; illustration.

ill-use (*v.* ĭl′ūz′; *n.* ĭl′ūs′), *v.,* -used, -us·ing, *n.* —*v.* treat badly, cruelly, or unfairly. —*n.* Also, ill-us′age. bad, cruel, or unfair treatment.

il·lu·sion (ĭ·lū′zhən), *n.* 1. appearance which is not real; misleading appearance. 2. a false impression or perception. 3. a false idea, notion, or belief. 4. thing that deceives by giving a false impression or idea: *an optical illusion.* [< L *illusio* < *illudere* mock] —**il·lu′sion·al,** *adj.* ⮞ **Illusion, allusion** are sometimes confused. *Illusion* is "a misleading appearance," as in *an illusion of wealth; allusion* is a reference to something written or to someone or something: *He made allusions to recent events without recounting them.*

Optical illusion.

The verticals appear to converge and diverge under the influence of the crosspieces.

il·lu·sive (ĭ·lū′sĭv), *adj.* due to an illusion;

unreal; misleading; deceptive. —il·lu'sive·ly, adv. —il·lu'sive·ness, n. —Syn. delusive.

il·lu·so·ry (i·lü'sə·ri), adj. illusive. —il·lu'so·ri·ly, adv. —il·lu'so·ri·ness, n.

il·lus·trate (il'əs·trāt; i·lus'-), v., -trat·ed, -trat·ing. 1. make clear or explain by stories, examples, comparisons, etc. 2. provide with pictures, diagrams, maps, etc., that explain or decorate. [< L illustratus lighted up, ult. < in·lustrum purification] —il'lus·tra'tor, n. —Syn. 1. demonstrate, elucidate, exemplify.

il·lus·tra·tion (il'əs·trā'shən), n. 1. picture, diagram, map, etc., used to explain or decorate something. 2. story, example, comparison, etc., used to make clear or explain something. 3. act or process of illustrating.

il·lus·tra·tive (i·lus'trə·tiv; il'əs·trā'-), adj. illustrating; used to illustrate; helping to explain. —il·lus'tra·tive·ly, adv.

il·lus·tri·ous (i·lus'tri·əs), adj. very famous; outstanding. [< L illustris lighted up, bright] —il·lus'tri·ous·ly, adv. —il·lus'tri·ous·ness, n. —Syn. distinguished, renowned, eminent.

ill will, unkind or unfriendly feeling; dislike; hate. —ill'-willed', adj.

I'm (īm), I am.

im·age (im'ij), n., v., -aged, -ag·ing. —n. 1. likeness; picture; copy. 2. likeness made of stone, wood, etc.; statue. 3. picture in the mind; idea. Your memory or imagination forms images of people and things that you do not actually see. 4. description or figure of speech that helps the mind to form forceful or beautiful pictures. Poetry often contains images. 5. Physics. picture of an object produced by a mirror, lens, etc. —v. 1. form an image of. 2. reflect as a mirror does. 3. picture in one's mind; imagine. 4. symbolize. [< OF < L imago]

im·age·ry (im'ij·ri), n., pl. -ries. 1. pictures in the mind; things imagined. 2. descriptions and figures of speech that help the mind to form forceful or beautiful pictures. 3. images; statues. —im·a·ge·ri·al (im'ə·jir'i·əl), adj.

i·mag·i·na·ble (i·maj'ə·nə·bəl), adj. that can be imagined. —i·mag'i·na·ble·ness, n. —i·mag'i·na·bly, adv.

i·mag·i·nar·y (i·maj'ə·ner'i), adj. existing only in the imagination; not real: the equator is an imaginary line. —i·mag'i·nar'i·ly, adv. —i·mag'i·nar'i·ness, n.

i·mag·i·na·tion (i·maj'ə·nā'shən), n. 1. an imagining; power of forming pictures in the mind of things not present to the senses. 2. ability to create new things or ideas or to combine old ones in new forms. 3. creation of the mind; fancy. —i·mag'i·na'tion·al, adj.

i·mag·i·na·tive (i·maj'ə·nā'tiv; -nə·tiv), adj. 1. showing imagination. 2. able to imagine well; fond of imagining. 3. of imagination. 4. fanciful. —i·mag'i·na'tive·ly, adv. —i·mag'i·na'tive·ness, n. —Syn. 1, 2. inventive, creative.

i·mag·ine (i·maj'ən), v., -ined, -in·ing. 1. picture in one's mind; have an idea: we can hardly imagine life without electricity. 2. suppose: imagine this to be the case. 3. guess: I cannot imagine what you mean. 4. think; believe: she imagined someone was watching her. [< F < L, < imago image] —Syn. 2. assume, surmise. 3. conjecture. 4. fancy.

im·ag·ism (im'ij·iz·əm), n. theory or practice of the imagists.

im·ag·ist (im'ij·ist), n. poet who expresses his ideas and feelings by images or word pictures. Most imagists use free verse. —im·ag·is'tic, adj.

i·ma·go (i·mā'gō), n., pl. i·ma·gos, i·mag·i·nes (i·maj'ə·nēz). Zool. insect in the final adult, esp. winged, stage. [< L, image]

im·be·cile (im'bə·səl), n. 1. person of very weak mind: an imbecile is almost an idiot. 2. a very stupid or foolish person. —adj. 1. very weak in mind. 2. very stupid or foolish. [< F < L imbecillus weak < in- without + bacillus staff] —im'be·cile·ly, adv. —im'be·cil'i·ty, n.

im·bed (im·bed'), v., -bed·ded, -bed·ding. embed.

im·bibe (im·bīb'), v., -bibed, -bib·ing. 1. drink; drink in. 2. absorb. 3. take into one's mind. [< L, < in- in + bibere drink] —im·bib'er, n.

im·bri·cate (v. im'brə·kāt; adj. im'brə·kit, -kāt), v., -cat·ed, -cat·ing, adj. —v. overlap. —adj. overlapping. [< L imbricatus < imbrex hollow tile] —im'bri·cate·ly, adv. —im'bri·ca'tion, n. —im'bri·ca'tive, adj.

im·bro·glio (im·brōl'yō), n., pl. -glios. 1. a difficult situation. 2. a complicated disagreement. [< Ital.]

im·brue (im·brü'), v., -brued, -bru·ing. wet; stain, esp. with blood. [< OF embreuver give to drink, ult. < L bibere drink] —im·brue'ment, n.

im·bue (im·bū'), v., -bued, -bu·ing. 1. fill; inspire: he imbued his son's mind with the ambition to succeed. 2. fill with moisture or color. [< L imbuere] —im·bue'ment, n.

imit., imitative (def. 2).

im·i·ta·ble (im'ə·tə·bəl), adj. that can be imitated. —im'i·ta·bil'i·ty, n.

im·i·tate (im'ə·tāt), v., -tat·ed, -tat·ing. 1. try to be like; follow the example of: the little boy imitated his father. 2. make or do something like; copy: a parrot imitates the sounds it hears. 3. act like: John imitated a bear. 4. be like; look like; resemble: wood painted to imitate stone. [< L imitatus] —im'i·ta'tor, n. —Syn. 2. reproduce. 3. mimic, ape.

im·i·ta·tion (im'ə·tā'shən), n. 1. an imitating: we learn many things by imitation. 2. a copy: give us an imitation of a rooster crowing. —adj. not real: imitation pearls. —im'i·ta'tion·al, adj.

im·i·ta·tive (im'ə·tā'tiv), adj. 1. likely or inclined to imitate others: monkeys are imitative. 2. imitating; showing imitation. Bang and whiz are imitative words. 3. not real. —im'i·ta'tive·ly, adv. —im'i·ta'tive·ness, n.

im·mac·u·late (i·mak'yə·lit), adj. 1. without a spot or stain; absolutely clean. 2. without sin; pure. 3. having no faults, flaws, or errors. [< L, < in- not + macula spot] —im·mac'u·la·cy, im·mac'u·late·ness, n. —im·mac'u·late·ly, adv. —Syn. 1. spotless, stainless.

Immaculate Conception, Rom. Cath. Ch. doctrine that the Virgin Mary was conceived free of original sin.

im·ma·nence (im'ə·nəns), im·ma·nen·cy (-nən·si), n. state of being immanent.

im·ma·nent (im'ə·nənt), adj. dwelling within. [< L, < in- in + manere stay] —im'ma·nent·ly, adv.

Im·man·u·el (i·man'yū·əl), n. Christ. Also, Emmanuel.

im·ma·te·ri·al (im'ə·tir'i·əl), adj. 1. not important; insignificant. 2. not material; spiritual. —im'ma·te'ri·al·ly, adv. —im'ma·te'ri·al·ness, n. —Syn. 1. unimportant, unessential.

im·ma·ture (im'ə·chùr'; -tùr'; -tyùr'), adj. not mature; not ripe; not full-grown; not fully developed. —im'ma·ture'ly, adv. —im'ma·tur'i·ty, im'ma·ture'ness, n.

im·meas·ur·a·ble (i·mezh'ər·ə·bəl), adj. too vast to be measured; boundless; without limits. —im·meas'ur·a·bil'i·ty, im·meas'ur·a·ble·ness, n. —im·meas'ur·a·bly, adv.

im·me·di·a·cy (i·mē'di·ə·si), n. a being immediate.

im·me·di·ate (i·mē'di·it), adj. 1. coming at once; without delay: an immediate reply. 2. with nothing between: in immediate contact. 3. direct: the immediate result. 4. closest; nearest: my immediate neighbor. 5. close; near: the immediate neighborhood. 6. pertaining to the present: our immediate plans. [< LL immediatus, ult. < L in- not + medius in the middle] —im·me'di·ate·ness, n.

im·me·di·ate·ly (i·mē'di·it·li), adv. 1. at once; without delay. 2. with nothing between. 3. next. 4. directly.

im·me·mo·ri·al (im'ə·mô'ri·əl; -mō'-), adj. extending back beyond the bounds of memory; extremely old. —im'me·mo'ri·al·ly, adv.

im·mense (i·mens′), *adj.* **1.** very big; huge; vast. **2.** *Slang.* very good. [< L, < *in-* not + *mensus* measured] —**im·mense′ly**, *adv.* —**im·mense′ness**, *n.* —Syn. **1.** enormous.

im·men·si·ty (i·men′sə·ti), *n., pl.* –**ties. 1.** very great or boundless extent; vastness. **2.** infinite space or existence.

im·merse (i·mèrs′), *v.*, –**mersed**, –**mers·ing. 1.** plunge (something) into a liquid. **2.** baptize by dipping (a person) under water. **3.** involve deeply; absorb: *immersed in business affairs.* [< L *immersus* < *in-* in + *mergere* plunge] —**im·mer·sion** (i·mèr′shən; -zhən), *n.* —Syn. **1.** submerge, duck, dip. **3.** engross, occupy.

im·mi·grant (im′ə·grənt), *n.* person who comes into a foreign country or region to live: *Canada has many immigrants from Europe.* —*adj.* immigrating.

im·mi·grate (im′ə·grāt), *v.*, –**grat·ed**, –**grat·ing.** come into a foreign country or region to live. [< L, < *in-* into + *migrare* move] —**im′mi·gra′tor**, *n.* ▶ See **emigrate** for usage note.

im·mi·gra·tion (im′ə·grā′shən), *n.* **1.** a coming into a foreign country or region to live. **2.** immigrants: *the immigration of 1918.*

im·mi·nence (im′ə·nəns), **im·mi·nen·cy** (-nən·si), *n.* **1.** state or fact of being imminent. **2.** thing that is imminent; evil or danger about to occur.

im·mi·nent (im′ə·nənt), *adj.* **1.** likely to happen soon; about to occur. **2.** overhanging. [< L *imminens* overhanging] —**im′mi·nent·ly**, *adv.* —Syn. **1.** impending.

im·mis·ci·ble (i·mis′ə·bəl), *adj.* incapable of being mixed. —**im·mis′ci·bil′i·ty**, *n.* —**im·mis′ci·bly**, *adv.*

im·mo·bile (i·mō′bəl; -bēl), *adj.* **1.** not movable; firmly fixed. **2.** not moving; not changing; motionless. —**im·mo·bil·i·ty** (im′ō·bil′ə·ti), *n.*

im·mo·bi·lize (i·mō′bə·līz), *v.*, –**lized**, –**liz·ing.** make immobile. —**im·mo′bi·li·za′tion**, *n.*

im·mod·er·ate (i·mod′ər·it), *adj.* not moderate; too much; going too far; extreme; more than is right or proper. —**im·mod′er·ate·ly**, *adv.* —**im·mod′er·ate·ness**, *n.* —Syn. excessive, intemperate, exorbitant, inordinate.

im·mod·est (i·mod′ist), *adj.* **1.** bold and rude. **2.** indecent; improper. —**im·mod′est·ly**, *adv.* —Syn. **1.** forward, impudent. **2.** lewd, obscene.

im·mod·es·ty (i·mod′is·ti), *n.* **1.** lack of modesty; boldness and rudeness. **2.** lack of decency; improper behavior.

im·mo·late (im′ə·lāt), *v.*, –**lat·ed**, –**lat·ing. 1.** kill as a sacrifice. **2.** sacrifice. [< L *immolatus* sacrificed, orig., sprinkled with sacrificial meal < *in-* on + *mola* sacrificial meal] —**im′mo·la′tion**, *n.* —**im′mo·la′tor**, *n.*

im·mor·al (i·môr′əl; i·mor′-), *adj.* **1.** morally wrong; wicked. Lying and stealing are immoral. **2.** lewd; unchaste. —**im·mor′al·ly**, *adv.*

im·mo·ral·i·ty (im′ə·ral′ə·ti), *n., pl.* –**ties. 1.** wickedness; wrongdoing; vice. **2.** lewdness; unchastity. **3.** an immoral act.

im·mor·tal (i·môr′təl), *adj.* **1.** living forever; never dying; everlasting. **2.** perpetual; lasting; constant. **3.** remembered or famous forever. **4.** heavenly; divine. —*n.* **1.** an immortal being. **2.** Usually, **immortals.** one of the gods of ancient Greek and Roman mythology. **3.** person remembered or famous forever: *Shakespeare is one of the immortals.* —**im·mor′tal·ly**, *adv.* —Syn. *adj.* **1.** eternal, endless.

im·mor·tal·i·ty (im′ôr·tal′ə·ti), *n.* **1.** endless life; living forever. **2.** fame that lasts forever.

im·mor·tal·ize (i·môr′təl·īz), *v.*, –**ized**, –**iz·ing. 1.** make immortal. **2.** give everlasting fame to. —**im·mor′tal·i·za′tion**, *n.* —**im·mor′tal·iz′er**, *n.*

im·mov·a·ble (i·müv′ə·bəl), *adj.* **1.** that cannot be moved; firmly fixed. **2.** not moving; not changing position; motionless. **3.** firm; steadfast; unyielding. **4.** unfeeling; impassive. —*n.* **im·movables,** *Law.* land, buildings, and other property that cannot be carried from one place to another. —**im·mov′a·bil′i·ty**, **im·mov′a·ble·ness**, *n.* —**im·mov′a·bly**, *adv.* —Syn. *adj.* **1.** stationary. **3.** resolute.

im·mune (i·mūn′), *adj.* having immunity: **a.** exempt, as from taxes, laws, etc. **b.** protected against disease, as by inoculation. [< L *immunis*, orig., free from obligation]

im·mu·ni·ty (i·mū′nə·ti), *n., pl.* –**ties. 1.** resistance to disease, poison, etc. **2.** freedom or protection from obligation, service, or duty.

im·mu·nize (im′yu·nīz), *v.*, –**nized**, –**niz·ing.** give immunity to; make immune. —**im′mu·ni·za′tion**, *n.*

im·mu·nol·o·gy (im′yu·nol′ə·ji), *n.* science of the nature and causation of immunity from diseases. —**im·mu·no·log·ic** (i·mū′nə·loj′ik), **im·mu′no·log′i·cal**, *adj.* —**im′mu·nol′o·gist**, *n.*

im·mure (i·myūr′), *v.*, –**mured**, –**mur·ing. 1.** imprison. **2.** confine closely. [< Med.L, < L *in-* in + *murus* wall] —**im·mure′ment**, *n.*

im·mu·ta·ble (i·mū′tə·bəl), *adj.* never changing; unchangeable. —**im·mu′ta·bil′i·ty**, **im·mu′ta·ble·ness**, *n.* —**im·mu′ta·bly**, *adv.* —Syn. unalterable, permanent.

imp (imp), *n.* **1.** a young or small devil or demon. **2.** a mischievous child. [OE *impe* a shoot, graft, ult. < VL *imputus* < Gk. *emphytos* engrafted]

imp., **1.** imperative. **2.** imperfect. **3.** imperial. **4.** import.

im·pact (im′pakt), *n.* the striking (of one thing against another): *the impact of the two swords broke both of them.* [< L *impactus* struck against. See IMPINGE.] —**im·pac′tion**, *n.*

im·pact·ed (im·pak′tid), *adj.* of a tooth, pressed between the jawbone and another tooth.

im·pair (im·pâr′), *v.* make worse; damage; weaken. [< OF *empeirer*, ult. < L *in-* + *pejor* worse] —**im·pair′er**, *n.* —**im·pair′ment**, *n.* —Syn. harm, hurt, injure.

im·pale (im·pāl′), *v.*, –**paled**, –**pal·ing. 1.** pierce through with anything pointed; fasten upon anything pointed. **2.** torture or punish by thrusting upon a pointed stake. [< F, ult. < L *in-* on + *palus* stake] —**im·pale′ment**, *n.* —**im·pal′er**, *n.*

im·pal·pa·ble (im·pal′pə·bəl), *adj.* **1.** that cannot be perceived by the sense of touch: *sunbeams are impalpable.* **2.** very hard for the mind to grasp: *impalpable distinctions.* —**im·pal′pa·bil′i·ty**, *n.* —**im·pal′pa·bly**, *adv.*

im·pan·el (im·pan′əl), *v.*, –**eled**, –**el·ing;** *esp. Brit.* –**elled**, –**el·ling. 1.** put on a list for duty on a jury. **2.** select (a jury) from the list. Also, **empanel.** —**im·pan′el·ment**, *n.*

im·part (im·pärt′), *v.* **1.** give a share in; give: *rich furnishings that impart elegance to a room.* **2.** communicate; tell: *impart a secret.* [< L, < *in-* in + *pars* part] —**im′par·ta′tion**, **im·part′ment**, *n.* —**im·part′er**, *n.* —**im·part′i·ble**, *adj.* —Syn. **1.** bestow, convey. **2.** relate, reveal.

im·par·tial (im·pär′shəl), *adj.* showing no more favor to one side than to the other; fair; just. —**im·par′tial·ly**, *adv.* —**im·par′tial·ness**, *n.* —Syn. unbiased, unprejudiced.

im·par·ti·al·i·ty (im′pär·shi·al′ə·ti), *n.* fairness; justice.

im·pass·a·ble (im·pas′ə·bəl; -päs′-), *adj.* not passable; so that one cannot go through or across. —**im·pass′a·bil′i·ty**, **im·pass′a·ble·ness**, *n.* —**im·pass′a·bly**, *adv.*

im·passe (im·pas′, -päs′; im′pas, -päs), *n.* **1.** position from which there is no escape; deadlock. **2.** road or way closed at one end. [< F]

im·pas·si·ble (im·pas′ə·bəl), *adj.* **1.** unable to suffer or feel pain. **2.** that cannot be harmed. [< L *impassibilis*, ult. < *in-* not + *pati* suffer] —**im·pas′si·bil′i·ty**, **im·pas′si·ble·ness**, *n.* —**im·pas′si·bly**, *adv.*

im·pas·sioned (im·pash′ənd), *adj.* full of strong feeling; ardent; emotional. —**im·pas′sioned·ly**, *adv.* —**im·pas′sioned·ness**, *n.*

im·pas·sive (im·pas′iv), *adj.* **1.** without feeling or emotion; unmoved; indifferent. **2.** calm; serene. —**im·pas′sive·ly**, *adv.* —**im·pas′sive·ness**, *n.* —Syn. **1.** apathetic, passive.

im·pas·siv·i·ty (im′pa·siv′ə·ti), *n.* state of being impassive.

im·pa·tience (im·pā′shəns), *n.* **1.** lack of patience; being impatient. **2.** uneasiness and eagerness. **3.** unwillingness to bear delay, opposition, pain, bother, etc., calmly.

im·pa·tient (im·pā'shənt), adj. 1. not patient; not willing to bear delay, opposition, pain, bother, etc., calmly. 2. restless: *the horses were impatient to start in the race.* 3. showing lack of patience: *an impatient answer.* —im·pa'tient·ly, adv. —im·pa'tient·ness, n.

im·peach (im·pēch'), v. 1. call in question: *to impeach a person's honor or accuracy.* 2. charge with wrongdoing; accuse. 3. accuse (a public officer) of wrong conduct during office before a competent tribunal: *a judge may be impeached for taking a bribe.* [< OF *empechier* hinder, ult. < L *in-* on + *pedica* shackle] —im·peach'a·ble, adj. —im·peach'a·bil'i·ty, n. —im·peach'er, n. —im·peach'ment, n.

im·pec·ca·ble (im·pek'ə·bəl), adj. 1. faultless. 2. sinless. [< LL, < *in-* not + *peccare* sin] —im·pec'ca·bil'i·ty, n. —im·pec'ca·bly, adv.

im·pe·cu·ni·os·i·ty (im'pi·kū'ni·os'ə·ti), n. lack of money; pennilessness.

im·pe·cu·ni·ous (im'pi·kū'ni·əs), adj. having little or no money; penniless; poor. [< L, < *in-* not + *pecunia* money] —im'pe·cu'ni·ous·ly, adv. —im'pe·cu'ni·ous·ness, n.

im·ped·ance (im·pēd'əns), n. *Elect.* the apparent resistance in an alternating-current circuit, made up of two components, reactance and true or ohmic resistance.

im·pede (im·pēd'), v., -ped·ed, -ped·ing. hinder; obstruct. [< L *impedire* < *in-* on + *pes* foot] —im·ped'er, n. —im·ped'ing·ly, adv. —Syn. hamper, retard.

im·ped·i·ment (im·ped'ə·mənt), n. 1. hindrance. 2. defect in speech. —im·ped'i·men'tal, im·ped·i·men·ta·ry (im·ped'ə·men'tə·ri), adj.

im·ped·i·men·ta (im·ped'ə·men'tə), n.pl. 1. traveling equipment; baggage. 2. military supplies carried along with an army. 3. *Law.* obstacles; hindrances. [< L]

im·pel (im·pel'), v., -pelled, -pel·ling. 1. cause to move; drive forward; push along: *the wind impelled the boat to shore.* 2. drive; force; cause: *hunger impelled the lazy man to work.* [< L, < *in-* on + *pellere* push] —im·pel'ler, n.

im·pend (im·pend'), v. 1. be likely to happen soon; be near: *when war impends, wise men try to prevent it.* 2. hang; hang threateningly. [< L, < *in-* over + *pendere* hang]

im·pend·ing (im·pen'ding), adj. 1. likely to happen soon. 2. overhanging. —Syn. 1. imminent.

im·pen·e·tra·ble (im·pen'ə·trə·bəl), adj. 1. that cannot be entered, pierced, or passed. 2. not open to ideas, influences, etc. 3. impossible for the mind to understand; inscrutable. —im·pen'e·tra·bil'i·ty, im·pen'e·tra·ble·ness, n. —im·pen'e·tra·bly, adv.

im·pen·i·tent (im·pen'ə·tənt), adj. not penitent; feeling no sorrow or regret for having done wrong. —im·pen'i·tence, im·pen'i·ten·cy, im·pen'i·tent·ness, n. —im·pen'i·tent·ly, adv.

imper., imperative.

im·per·a·tive (im·per'ə·tiv), adj. 1. not to be avoided; urgent; necessary. 2. expressing a command; peremptory. 3. *Gram.* expressing command: *the imperative mood.* —n. 1. a command. 2. *Gram.* a. the imperative mood. b. a verb form in this mood. [< L, < *imperare* order] —im·per·a·ti·val (im·per'ə·tī'vəl), adj. —im·per'a·tive·ly, adv. —im·per'a·tive·ness, n. ▶ imperative. The imperative has the form of the infinitive: *Go! Please shut the door.*

im·pe·ra·tor (im'pə·rā'tər), n. 1. an absolute or supreme ruler. 2. emperor; commander. [< L, < *imperare* command] —im·per·a·to·ri·al (im·per'ə·tô'ri·əl; -tō'-), adj. —im·per·a·to'ri·al·ly, adv.

im·per·cep·ti·ble (im'pər·sep'tə·bəl), adj. 1. that cannot be perceived or felt. 2. very slight; gradual. —im'per·cep'ti·bil'i·ty, im'per·cep'ti·ble·ness, n. —im'per·cep'ti·bly, adv.

imperf., imperfect.

im·per·fect (im·pėr'fikt), adj. 1. not perfect; having some defect or fault. 2. not complete; lacking some part. 3. *Gram.* expressing continued or customary action in the past. 4. *Music.* diminished. —n. *Gram.* the imperfect tense or verb form. English has no imperfect, but such forms as *was studying* and *used to study* are like the imperfect in other languages. —im·per'fect·ly, adv. —im·per'fect·ness, n.

im·per·fec·tion (im'pər·fek'shən), n. 1. lack of perfection. 2. fault; defect.

im·per·fo·rate (im·pėr'fə·rit; -rāt), **im·per·fo·rat·ed** (-rāt'id), adj. 1. not pierced through with holes. 2. not separated from other stamps by perforations. —im·per'fo·ra'tion, n.

im·pe·ri·al (im·pir'i·əl), adj. 1. of or pertaining to an empire or its ruler. 2. of or having to do with the rule or authority of one country over other countries and colonies. 3. supreme; majestic; magnificent. 4. imperious; domineering. 5. of larger size or better quality. 6. according to the British standard of weights and measures. —n. 1. a small beard left growing beneath the lower lip. 2. size of paper, 23 by 31 inches (in England 22 by 30 inches). [< L, < *imperium* empire] —im·pe'ri·al·ly, adv. —im·pe'ri·al·ness, n.

imperial gallon, British gallon, equal to about 1¼ U.S. gallons.

im·pe·ri·al·ism (im·pir'i·əl·iz'əm), n. 1. policy of extending the rule or authority of one country over other countries and colonies. 2. an imperial system of government. —im·pe'ri·al·ist, n. —im·pe'ri·al·is'tic, adj. —im·pe'ri·al·is'ti·cal·ly, adv.

Man wearing an imperial

Imperial Valley, a flat irrigated region in S California.

im·per·il (im·per'əl), v., -iled, -il·ing; *esp. Brit.* -illed, -il·ling. put in danger. —im·per'il·ment, n. —Syn. endanger, jeopardize.

im·pe·ri·ous (im·pir'i·əs), adj. 1. haughty; domineering. 2. imperative; urgent. [< L *imperiosus* commanding. See IMPERATIVE.] —im·pe'ri·ous·ly, adv. —im·pe'ri·ous·ness, n. —Syn. 1. dictatorial, arrogant, overbearing.

im·per·ish·a·ble (im·per'ish·ə·bəl), adj. everlasting; not perishable; indestructible. —im·per'ish·a·bil'i·ty, im·per'ish·a·ble·ness, n. —im·per'ish·a·bly, adv.

im·per·ma·nent (im·pėr'mə·nənt), adj. temporary. —im·per'ma·nence, im·per'ma·nen·cy, n. —im·per'ma·nent·ly, adv.

im·per·me·a·ble (im·pėr'mi·ə·bəl), adj. 1. impassable. 2. impervious. —im·per'me·a·bil'i·ty, im·per'me·a·ble·ness, n. —im·per'me·a·bly, adv.

impers., impersonal.

im·per·son·al (im·pėr'sən·əl; -pėrs'nəl), adj. 1. referring to all or any persons, not to any special one: *"first come, first served" is an impersonal remark.* 2. having no existence as a person: *electricity is an impersonal force.* 3. *Gram.* of a verb, having nothing but an indefinite *it* for a subject. Example: *rained* in "It rained yesterday."

im·per·son·al·i·ty (im·pėr'sən·al'ə·ti), n., pl. -ties. 1. impersonal character. 2. impersonal thing, force, etc.

im·per·son·al·ly (im·pėr'sən·əl·i; -pėrs'nəl·i), adv. in an impersonal manner; without personal reference or connection.

im·per·son·ate (im·pėr'sən·āt), v., -at·ed, -at·ing. 1. act the part of: *impersonate Hamlet on the stage.* 2. pretend to be; mimic the voice, appearance, and manners of: *impersonate a well-known news commentator.* 3. personify; typify. —im·per'son·a'tion, n. —im·per'son·a'tor, n.

im·per·ti·nence (im·pėr'tə·nəns), **im·per·ti·nen·cy** (-nən·si), n., pl. -nenc·es; -cies. 1. impertinent quality. 2. impertinent act or speech. 3. lack of pertinence; irrelevance. —Syn. 1. impudence, insolence.

im·per·ti·nent (im·pėr'tə·nənt), adj. 1. saucy; impudent; insolent. 2. not pertinent; not to the point; out of place. —im·per'ti·nent·ly, adv. —Syn. 1. officious, presumptuous, uncivil, pert. 2. inappropriate, incongruous, irrelevant.

im·per·turb·a·ble (im'pər·tėr'bə·bəl), adj.

unexcitable; not easily excited; calm. —**im'per·turb'a·bil'i·ty,** **im'per·turb'a·ble·ness,** *n.* —im'per·turb'a·bly, *adv.*

im·per·vi·ous (im·pér'vi·əs), *adj.* **1.** not letting things pass through; not allowing passage. **2.** not open to argument, suggestions, etc. —imper'vi·ous·ly, *adv.* —imper'vi·ous·ness, *n.*

im·pe·ti·go (im'pə·tī'gō), *n.* an infectious skin disease causing pimples filled with pus. [< L, < *impetere* attack < *in-* + *petere* aim for]

im·pet·u·os·i·ty (im·pech'ū·os'ə·ti), *n., pl.* -ties. sudden or rash energy; ardor.

im·pet·u·ous (im·pech'ū·əs), *adj.* **1.** moving with great force or speed. **2.** acting hastily, rashly, or with sudden feeling. —im·pet'u·ous·ly, *adv.* —im·pet'u·ous·ness, *n.*

im·pe·tus (im'pə·təs), *n.* **1.** force with which a moving body tends to maintain its velocity and overcome resistance. **2.** a driving force; incentive. [< L, attack] —**Syn. 1.** momentum. **2.** stimulus, impulse.

im·pi·e·ty (im·pī'ə·ti), *n., pl.* -ties. **1.** lack of piety or reverence for God. **2.** lack of respect. **3.** an impious act.

im·pinge (im·pinj'), *v.,* -pinged, -ping·ing. **1.** hit; strike: *rays of light impinge on the eye.* **2.** encroach; infringe. [< L *impingere* < *in-* on + *pangere* strike] —im·pinge'ment, *n.* —im·ping'er, *n.*

im·pi·ous (im'pi·əs), *adj.* not pious; not having or not showing reverence for God; wicked; profane. —im'pi·ous·ly, *adv.* —im'pi·ous·ness, *n.*

imp·ish (imp'ish), *adj.* **1.** of or like an imp. **2.** mischievous. —imp'ish·ly, *adv.* —imp'ish·ness, *n.*

im·pla·ca·ble (im·plā'kə·bəl, -plak'ə-), *adj.* that cannot be placated, pacified, or appeased. —im·pla'ca·bil'i·ty, im·pla'ca·ble·ness, *n.* —im·pla'ca·bly, *adv.* —**Syn.** unforgiving, relentless, inexorable.

im·plant (im·plant', -plänt'), *v.* **1.** instill or fix deeply (a desire, opinion, etc.): *a good teacher implants high ideals in children.* **2.** plant in something. —im'plan·ta'tion, *n.* —im·plant'er, *n.*

im·ple·ment (*n.* im'plə·mənt; *v.* im'plə·ment), *n.* a useful article of equipment; tool; instrument; utensil, such as a plow, ax, shovel, broom, etc. —*v.* **1.** provide with implements or other means. **2.** provide the power and authority necessary to accomplish or put (something) into effect: *implement a directive or policy.* **3.** carry out; get done. [< LL *implementum,* lit., that which fills a need, ult. < *in-* in + *-plere* fill] —im'ple·men'tal, *adj.*

im·pli·cate (im'plə·kāt), *v.,* -cat·ed, -cat·ing. **1.** show to have a part or to be connected; involve: *the thief's confession implicated two other men.* **2.** imply. **3.** entangle. [< L, < *in-* in + *plicare* fold]

im·pli·ca·tion (im'plə·kā'shən), *n.* **1.** an implying or being implied: *admit a thing by implication.* **2.** indirect suggestion; hint: *no implication of dishonesty.* —im'pli·ca'tion·al, *adj.*

im·plic·it (im·plis'it), *adj.* **1.** without doubting, hesitating, or asking questions; absolute: *implicit obedience.* **2.** meant, but not clearly expressed or distinctly stated; implied: *implicit consent.* **3.** involved as a necessary part or condition. [< L *implicitus,* pp. of *implicare* IMPLICATE] —im·plic'it·ly, *adv.* —im·plic'it·ness, *n.* —**Syn. 1.** unquestioning, unreserved. **3.** tacit.

im·plied (im·plīd'), *adj.* involved, indicated, suggested, or understood without express statement. —im·pli·ed·ly (im·plī'id·li), *adv.*

im·plore (im·plôr'; -plōr'), *v.,* -plored, -plor·ing. **1.** beg earnestly for. **2.** beg (a person to do some act). [< L, < *in-* toward + *plorare* cry] —im'plo·ra'tion, *n.* —im·plor·a·to·ry (im·plôr'ə·tō'ri; im·plōr'ə·tō'ri), *adj.* —im·plor'er, *n.* —im·plor'ing·ly, *adv.* —im·plor'ing·ness, *n.* —**Syn. 1.** beseech, entreat.

im·ply (im·plī'), *v.,* -plied, -ply·ing. **1.** indicate without saying outright; express indirectly; suggest: *her smile implied that she had forgiven us.* **2.** involve as a necessary part or condition: *speech implies a speaker.* **3.** signify; mean. [< OF *emplier* involve, put (in). See IMPLICATE.] —**Syn.**

1. insinuate. > imply, infer. Strictly, a writer or speaker *implies* something in his words or manner; a reader or listener *infers* something from what he reads or hears.

im·po·lite (im'pə·līt'), *adj.* not polite; having or showing bad manners; rude; discourteous. —im'po·lite'ly, *adv.* —im'po·lite'ness, *n.* —**Syn.** disrespectful, uncivil.

im·pol·i·tic (im·pol'ə·tik), *adj.* not politic; not expedient; unwise. —im·pol'i·tic·ly, *adv.* —im·pol'i·tic·ness, *n.*

im·pon·der·a·ble (im·pon'dər·ə·bəl), *adj.* without weight that can be felt or measured. —*n.* something imponderable. —im·pon'der·a·bil'i·ty, im·pon'der·a·ble·ness, *n.* —im·pon'der·a·bly, *adv.*

im·port (*v.* im·pôrt', -pōrt', im'pôrt, -pōrt; *n.* im'pôrt, -pōrt), *v.* **1.** bring in from a foreign country for sale or use: *we import coffee from Brazil.* **2.** mean; signify: *tell me what your remark imports.* **3.** be of importance or consequence. —*n.* **1.** thing imported: *rubber is a useful import.* **2.** an importing; importation. **3.** meaning: *what is the import of your remark?* **4.** importance. [< L, < *in-* in + *portare* carry] —im·port'a·ble, *adj.* —im·port'a·bil'i·ty, *n.* —im·port'er, *n.*

im·por·tance (im·pôr'təns), *n.* quality or fact of being important; consequence; significance.

im·por·tant (im·pôr'tənt), *adj.* **1.** meaning much; worth noticing or considering; having value or significance. **2.** having social position or influence. **3.** acting or seeming important. [< F < Med.L *importans* being significant < L, bringing on or in. See IMPORT.] —im·por'tant·ly, *adv.* —**Syn. 1.** significant, momentous, weighty.

im·por·ta·tion (im'pôr·tā'shən; -pōr-), *n.* **1.** act of importing. **2.** something imported.

im·por·tu·nate (im·pôr'chə·nit), *adj.* asking repeatedly; annoyingly persistent. —im·por'tu·nate·ly, *adv.* —im·por'tu·nate·ness, *n.*

im·por·tune (im'pôr·tün'; -tün'; im·pôr'chən), *v.,* -tuned, -tun·ing. ask urgently or repeatedly; trouble with demands. [< MF < L *importunus* inconvenient] —im'por·tune'ly, *adv.* —im'por·tun'er, *n.*

im·por·tu·ni·ty (im'pôr·tü'nə·ti; -tū'-), *n., pl.* -ties. persistence in asking; act of demanding again and again.

im·pose (im·pōz'), *v.,* -posed, -pos·ing. **1.** put (a burden, tax, punishment, etc.) on. **2.** force or thrust one's or its authority or influence on another or others. **3.** force or thrust (oneself or one's company) on another or others. **4.** pass off (a thing upon a person) to deceive. **5.** arrange (pages of type) for printing. [< F, < *in-* on + *poser* put, place, POSE] —im·pos'a·ble, *adj.* —im·pos'er, *n.* —**Syn. 3.** obtrude, presume.

im·pos·ing (im·pōz'ing), *adj.* impressive because of size, appearance, dignity, etc.: *the Capitol is an imposing building.* —im·pos'ing·ly, *adv.* —im·pos'ing·ness, *n.* —**Syn.** commanding, stately, majestic.

im·po·si·tion (im'pə·zish'ən), *n.* **1.** act or fact of imposing. **2.** tax, duty, task, burden, etc. **3.** an unfair tax, etc. **4.** an imposing upon a person by taking advantage of his good nature. **5.** deception; fraud; trick.

im·pos·si·bil·i·ty (im·pos'ə·bil'ə·ti; im'pos-), *n., pl.* -ties. **1.** quality of being impossible. **2.** something impossible.

im·pos·si·ble (im·pos'ə·bəl), *adj.* **1.** that cannot be or happen: *the accident seemed impossible.* **2.** not possible to use; not to be done: *few things are impossible.* **3.** that cannot be true: *an impossible rumor.* **4.** not endurable; very objectionable: *an impossible person.* —im·pos'si·ble·ness, *n.* —im·pos'si·bly, *adv.* —**Syn. 2.** impracticable, unfeasible.

im·post (im'pōst), *n.* **1.** tax on goods brought into a country. **2.** tax; tribute. —*v.* fix duties on. [< OF, ult. < L *in-* on + *ponere* place, put]

im·pos·tor (im·pos'tər), *n.* **1.** person who assumes a false name or character. **2.** deceiver; cheat. [< LL, < L *imponere* impose. See IMPOST.]

im·pos·ture (im·pos'chər), *n.* deception; fraud.

im·po·tence (im′pə·təns), **im·po·ten·cy** (-tən·si), n. lack of power; condition or quality of being impotent.

im·po·tent (im′pə·tənt), adj. 1. not having power; helpless. 2. lacking in sexual power. —im′po·tent·ly, adv. —im′po·tent·ness, n. —Syn. 1. weak, feeble, infirm.

im·pound (im·pound′), v. 1. shut up in a pen or pound. 2. shut up; enclose; confine. 3. put in the custody of a law court: the court impounded the documents to use as evidence. —im·pound′-age, n. —im·pound′er, n.

im·pov·er·ish (im·pov′ər·ish; -pov′rish), v. 1. make very poor. 2. exhaust the strength, richness, or resources of. [< OF empoveriss-, ult. < L in- + pauper poor] —im·pov′er·ish·er, n. —im·pov′er·ish·ment, n.

im·pow·er (im·pou′ər), v. empower. —im·pow′er·ment, n.

im·prac·ti·ca·ble (im·prak′tə·kə·bəl), adj. 1. not working well in practice: impracticable suggestions. 2. that cannot be used: an impracticable road. —im·prac′ti·ca·bil′i·ty, im·prac′ti·ca·ble·ness, n. —im·prac′ti·ca·bly, adv.

im·prac·ti·cal (im·prak′tə·kəl), adj. not practical. —im·prac·ti·cal·i·ty (im·prak′tə·kal′ə·ti), n.

im·pre·cate (im′prə·kāt), v., -cat·ed, -cat·ing. call down (curses, evil, etc.). [< L imprecatus, ult. < in- on + prex prayer] —im′pre·ca′tion, n. —im′pre·ca′tor, n. —im·pre·ca·to·ry (im′prə·kə·tô′ri; -tō′-), adj.

im·preg·na·ble (im·preg′nə·bəl), adj. that cannot be overthrown by force; able to resist attack: an impregnable fortress, an impregnable argument. [< F, < in- not + prenable pregnable] —im·preg′na·bil′i·ty, im·preg′na·ble·ness, n. —im·preg′na·bly, adv.

im·preg·nate (im·preg′nāt), v., -nat·ed, -nat·ing. 1. make pregnant; fertilize. 2. fill (with); saturate. 3. inspire; imbue. [< LL impraegnatus made pregnant] —im′preg·na′tion, n. —im·preg′na·tor, n.

im·pre·sa·ri·o (im′prə·sä′ri·ō), n., pl. -sa·ri·os, Ital. -sa·ri (-sä′rē). organizer or manager of an opera or concert company. [< Ital., < impresa undertaking, ult. < L in- on + prehendere take] —im′pre·sa′ri·o·ship′, n.

im·pre·scrip·ti·ble (im′pri·skrip′tə·bəl), adj. existing independently of law or custom; not justly to be taken away or violated. —im′pre·scrip′ti·bil′i·ty, n. —im′pre·scrip′ti·bly, adv.

im·press[1] (v. im·pres′; n. im′pres), v., -pressed or (Archaic) -prest (-prest), -press·ing. —v. 1. have a strong effect on the mind or feelings of: a hero impresses us with his courage. 2. fix in the mind: she repeated the words to impress them in her memory. 3. mark by pressing or stamping; imprint. —n. 1. impression; mark; stamp. 2. act of impressing. [< L impressus < in- in + premere press] —im·press′er, n. —im·press′i·ble, adj. —im·press′i·bil′i·ty, n.

im·press[2] (im·pres′), v., -pressed or (Archaic) -prest, -press·ing. 1. seize by force for public use. 2. force (men) to serve in the navy or army. 3. bring in and use. [< in-² + press²] —im·press′ment, n.

im·pres·sion (im·presh′ən), n. 1. effect produced on a person: make a bad impression. 2. idea; notion: a vague impression. 3. something produced by pressure; mark, stamp, print, etc.: impression of a rabbit's feet in the snow. 4. the total number of copies of a book made at one time. 5. a printed copy.

im·pres·sion·a·ble (im·presh′ən·ə·bəl), adj. sensitive to impressions; easily impressed or influenced. —im·pres′sion·a·bil′i·ty, im·pres′sion·a·ble·ness, n.

im·pres·sion·ism (im·presh′ən·iz·əm), n. 1. method of painting or writing that gives general impressions without much attention to details. 2. method of composing music that expresses impressions and feelings by new and unusual means. —im·pres′sion·ist, n. —im·pres′sion·is′tic, adj.

im·pres·sive (im·pres′iv), adj. able to impress the mind, feelings, conscience, etc.: an impressive sermon. —im·pres′sive·ly, adv. —im·pres′sive·ness, n. —Syn. imposing, commanding, striking.

im·pri·ma·tur (im′pri·mā′tər; -prī-), n. 1. an official license to print or publish a book, etc., now usually works sanctioned by the Roman Catholic Church. 2. sanction; approval. [< NL, let it be printed. See IMPRESS.]

im·print (n. im′print; v. im·print′), n. 1. mark made by pressure; print: the imprint of a foot in the sand. 2. impression; mark: suffering left its imprint on her face. 3. a publisher's name, with the place and date of publication, on the title page or at the end of a book. —v. 1. mark by pressing or stamping; print: imprint a postmark on an envelope. 2. press or impress: a scene imprinted on my memory. —im·print′er, n.

im·pris·on (im·priz′ən), v. 1. put in prison; keep in prison. 2. confine closely; restrain. —im·pris′on·ment, n.

im·prob·a·ble (im·prob′ə·bəl), adj. not probable; not likely to happen; not likely to be true. —im·prob′a·bil′i·ty, im·prob′a·ble·ness, n. —im·prob′a·bly, adv.

im·promp·tu (im·promp′tū; -tū), adv., adj. without previous thought or preparation; offhand. —n. improvisation. [< L in promptu in readiness] —Syn. adj. extempore, improvised.

im·prop·er (im·prop′ər), adj. 1. not correct. 2. not suitable. 3. not decent. —im·prop′er·ly, adv. —im·prop′er·ness, n. —Syn. 2. inappropriate, unfit. 3. indecent, indecorous, unseemly.

improper fraction, fraction greater than 1. Examples: ½, ⅘.

im·pro·pri·e·ty (im′prə·prī′ə·ti), n., pl. -ties. 1. lack of propriety; quality of being improper. 2. improper conduct. 3. improper act, expression, etc.

im·prove (im·prüv′), v., -proved, -prov·ing. 1. make better. 2. become better: his health is improving. 3. Am. increase the value of (land or property). 4. use well; make good use of: improve your time by studying. 5. improve on, make better; do better than. [< AF emprouer < OF en- in + prou profit] —im·prov′a·ble, adj. —im·prov′a·bil′i·ty, im·prov′a·ble·ness, n. —im·prov′a·bly, adv. —im·prov′er, n. —im·prov′ing·ly, adv. —Syn. 1. ameliorate, promote. 3. develop. 4. utilize.

im·prove·ment (im·prüv′mənt), n. 1. a making or becoming better. 2. increase in value. 3. change or addition that increases value: a house with all the modern improvements. 4. better condition; thing that is better than another; advance. 5. good use.

im·prov·i·dent (im·prov′ə·dənt), adj. lacking foresight; not looking ahead; not careful in providing for the future; not thrifty. —im·prov′i·dence, n. —im·prov′i·dent·ly, adv. —Syn. shiftless, imprudent, wasteful.

im·pro·vise (im′prə·vīz), v., -vised, -vis·ing. 1. compose or utter (verse, music, etc.) without preparation. 2. prepare or provide offhand; extemporize. [< F < Ital. improvvisare, ult. < L in- not + pro- beforehand + videre see] —im·pro·vi·sa·tion (im′prə·vi·zā′shən; im′prov·ə-), n. —im′pro·vi·sa′tion·al, adj. —im′pro·vis′er, n.

im·pru·dence (im·prü′dəns), n. lack of prudence; imprudent behavior.

im·pru·dent (im·prü′dənt), adj. not prudent; rash; not discreet. —im·pru′dent·ly, adv. —im·pru′dent·ness, n. —Syn. indiscreet, ill-advised, heedless.

im·pu·dence (im′pyə·dəns), n. lack of shame or modesty; rude boldness.

im·pu·dent (im′pyə·dənt), adj. without shame or modesty; offensively impertinent; rudely bold. [< L, < in- not + pudere be modest] —im′pu·dent·ly, adv. —im′pu·dent·ness, n. —Syn. insolent, presumptuous. —Ant. modest, meek.

im·pugn (im·pūn′), v. call in question; attack by words or arguments; challenge as false. [< OF < L impugnare assault < in- against + pugnare fight] —im·pugn′a·ble, adj. —im·pug·na-

tion (im'pug·nā'shən), im·pugn'ment, n. —im·pugn'er, n.

im·pulse (im'puls), n. 1. a sudden, driving force or influence; push: *the impulse of hunger.* 2. effect of a sudden, driving force or influence. 3. a sudden inclination or tendency to act. 4. the stimulating force of desire or emotion: *an angry mob is influenced more by impulse than by reason.* 5. *Physiol.* a change in living matter that is transmitted, esp. by nerve cells, and influences action in the muscle, gland, or other nerve cells that it reaches. [< L *impulsus* < *impellere* IMPEL] —Syn. 1. thrust, impetus, drive.

im·pul·sion (im·pul'shən), n. 1. an impelling; driving force. 2. impulse. 3. impetus.

im·pul·sive (im·pul'siv), adj. 1. acting upon impulse; easily moved. 2. driving onward; impelling; pushing. —im·pul'sive·ly, adv. —im·pul'sive·ness, n. —Syn. 1. rash, hasty, impetuous.

im·pu·ni·ty (im·pū'nə·ti), n. freedom from punishment, injury, or other bad consequences. [< L *impunitas*, ult. < in- without + *poena* punishment]

im·pure (im·pyúr'), adj. 1. not pure; dirty. 2. immoral; corrupt. 3. mixed with something of lower value; adulterated. 4. not of one color, style, etc.; mixed. 5. forbidden by religion as unclean. —im·pure'ly, adv. —im·pure'ness, n. —Syn. 1. filthy, unclean.

im·pu·ri·ty (im·pyúr'ə·ti), n., pl. -ties. 1. lack of purity; being impure. 2. Often, impurities. impure thing or element; thing that makes something else impure.

im·pute (im·pūt'), v., -put·ed, -put·ing. consider as belonging; attribute; charge (a fault, etc.) to a person; blame. [< L, < in- in + *putare* reckon] —im·put'a·ble, adj. —im·pu·ta·tion (im'pyū·tā'shən), n. —im·put·a·tive (im·pūt'ə·tiv), adj. —im·put'a·tive·ly, adv. —im·put'a·tive·ness, n. —im·put'er, n.

in (in), prep. In expresses inclusion, situation, presence, existence, position, and action within limits of space, time, state, circumstances, etc. 1. inside; within: *in the box.* 2. into: *go in the house.* 3. with; by: *cover in an envelope.* 4. of; made of; using: *a dress in silk.* 5. from among; out of: *one in a hundred.* 6. because of; for: *act in self-defense.* 7. about; concerning: *a book in American history.* 8. at; during: *in the present time.* 9. while; when: *in crossing the street.* 10. in that, because. —adv. 1. in or into some place, position, condition, etc.: *come in.* 2. present, esp. in one's home or office: *he is not in today.* 3. in for, unable to avoid; sure to get or have. 4. in with, a. friendly with. b. partners with. —adj. that is in; being in. —n. 1. ins, people in office; political party in power. 2. ins and outs, a. turns and twists; nooks and corners. b. different parts; details. [OE] ► in, into, in to. *In* generally shows location (literal or figurative); *into* generally shows direction: *He was in the house. He came into the house.* However, *in* is often used for *into: He fell in the brook.* In to is the adverb *in* followed by the preposition *to: They went into the dining room. They went in to dinner.*

In, *Chem.* indium.

in-¹, *prefix.* not; the opposite of; the absence of, as in *inexpensive, inattention.* [< L; in- becomes *il-* before *l*, *im-* before *b*, *m*, and *p*, and *ir-* before *r*] ► in- or un- prefixed to many words gives them a negative meaning: *inconsiderate, incapable, uneven, unloved.* American and British usage differs in many words. If you are not sure whether a word takes *in-* or *un-* consult this dictionary.

in-², *prefix.* in; within; into; toward, as in *inborn, indoors, inland.* [OE]

in., inch; inches.

in·a·bil·i·ty (in'ə·bil'ə·ti), n. lack of ability, power, or means; fact or state of being unable.

in ab·sen·tia (in ab·sen'shə), *Latin.* while absent.

in·ac·ces·si·ble (in'ak·ses'ə·bəl), adj. 1. not accessible; that cannot be reached or entered. 2. hard to get at; hard to reach with. 3. that

cannot be obtained. —in'ac·ces'si·bil'i·ty, in'ac·ces'si·ble·ness, n. —in'ac·ces'si·bly, adv.

in·ac·cu·ra·cy (in·ak'yə·rə·si), n., pl. -cies. 1. lack of accuracy. 2. error; mistake.

in·ac·cu·rate (in·ak'yə·rit), adj. not exact; containing mistakes. —in·ac'cu·rate·ly, adv. —in·ac'cu·rate·ness, n. —Syn. inexact, erroneous, faulty.

in·ac·tion (in·ak'shən), n. absence of action; idleness.

in·ac·ti·vate (in·ak'tə·vāt), v., -vat·ed, -vat·ing. make inactive. —in·ac·ti·va·tion (in'ak·tə·vā'shən; in·ak'-), n.

in·ac·tive (in·ak'tiv), adj. not active; idle; sluggish. —in·ac'tive·ly, adv. —in·ac·tiv'i·ty, in·ac'tive·ness, n. —Syn. inert, passive, motionless.

in·ad·e·quate (in·ad'ə·kwit), adj. not adequate; not enough; not as much as is required. —in·ad'e·qua·cy, in·ad'e·quate·ness, n. —in·ad'e·quate·ly, adv.

in·ad·mis·si·ble (in'əd·mis'ə·bəl), adj. 1. not allowable; not to be admitted. —in'ad·mis'si·bil'i·ty, n. —in'ad·mis'si·bly, adv.

in·ad·vert·ence (in'əd·vér'təns), **in·ad·vert·en·cy** (-tən·si), n., pl. -enc·es, -cies. 1. lack of attention; carelessness. 2. oversight; mistake.

in·ad·vert·ent (in'əd·vér'tənt), adj. 1. not attentive; heedless; negligent. 2. not done on purpose; caused by oversight. —in'ad·vert'ent·ly, adv. —Syn. 1. thoughtless. 2. unintentional, accidental.

in·ad·vis·a·ble (in'əd·vīz'ə·bəl), adj. not advisable; unwise; not prudent. —in'ad·vis'a·bil'i·ty, in'ad·vis'a·ble·ness, n. —in'ad·vis'a·bly, adv.

in·al·ien·a·ble (in·āl'yən·ə·bəl; -āl'li·ən-), adj. that cannot be given away or taken away. —in·al'ien·a·bil'i·ty, n. —in·al'ien·a·bly, adv.

in·am·o·ra·ta (in·am'ə·rä'tə), n., pl. -tas. girl or woman with whom one is in love; sweetheart. [< Ital., ult. < L in- in + amor love]

in·ane (in·ān'), adj. 1. silly; senseless. 2. empty. [< L inanis] —in·ane'ly, adv. —in·ane'ness, n. —Syn. 1. foolish. 2. void.

in·an·i·mate (in·an'ə·mit), adj. 1. lifeless. 2. dull. —in·an'i·mate·ly, adv. —in·an'i·mate·ness, n.

in·a·ni·tion (in'ə·nish'ən), n. 1. emptiness. 2. weakness from lack of food. [< LL, < L inanire to empty]

in·an·i·ty (in·an'ə·ti), n., pl. -ties. 1. silliness; lack of sense. 2. a silly or senseless act, practice, remark, etc. 3. emptiness.

in·ap·pli·ca·ble (in·ap'lə·kə·bəl; in'ə·plik'ə·bəl), adj. not applicable; not appropriate; not suitable. —in·ap'pli·ca·bil'i·ty, in·ap'pli·ca·ble·ness, n. —in·ap'pli·ca·bly, adv. —Syn. unbecoming, unfitting.

in·ap·po·site (in·ap'ə·zit), adj. not pertinent; inappropriate. —in·ap'po·site·ly, adv.

in·ap·pre·ci·a·ble (in'ə·prē'shi·ə·bəl; -shə·bəl), adj. too small to be noticed or felt; very slight. —in'ap·pre'ci·a·bly, adv.

in·ap·pro·pri·ate (in'ə·prō'pri·it), adj. not suitable; not fitting. —in'ap·pro'pri·ate·ly, adv. —in'ap·pro'pri·ate·ness, n.

in·apt (in·apt'), adj. 1. not apt; not suitable; unfit. 2. unskilful; awkward. —in·apt'ly, adv. —in·apt'ness, n. —Syn. 1. inappropriate. 2. unhandy.

in·ap·ti·tude (in·ap'tə·tüd; -tūd), n. 1. unfitness. 2. lack of skill.

in·ar·tic·u·late (in'är·tik'yə·lit), adj. 1. not distinct; not like regular speech: *an inarticulate mutter or groan.* 2. unable to speak in words; dumb. 3. *Zool.* not jointed. 4. not hinged. —in'ar·tic'u·late·ly, adv. —in'ar·tic'u·late·ness, n.

in·ar·tis·tic (in'är·tis'tik), adj. not artistic; lacking good taste. —in'ar·tis'ti·cal·ly, adv.

in·as·much as (in'əz·much'), 1. because. 2. in so far as.

attention; negligence. —Syn. heedlessness, disregard.

in·at·ten·tive (in'ə·ten'tiv), *adj.* not attentive; careless; negligent. —**in'at·ten'tive·ly,** *adv.* —**in'at·ten'tive·ness,** *n.* —Syn. heedless, unmindful, preoccupied.

in·au·di·ble (in·ô'də·bəl), *adj.* that cannot be heard. —**in·au'di·bil'i·ty, in·au'di·ble·ness,** *n.* —**in·au'di·bly,** *adv.*

in·au·gu·ral (in·ô'gyə·rəl), *adj.* of or for an inauguration. —*n.* 1. *Am.* inaugural address. 2. inaugural ceremonies.

inaugural address, *Am.* speech made by a president of the United States, or a governor of a State, when he is inaugurated.

in·au·gu·rate (in·ô'gyə·rāt), *v.,* –rat·ed, –rat·ing. 1. install in office with a ceremony. 2. make a formal beginning of; begin. [< L, ult. < *in–* for + *augur* taker of omens] —**in·au'gu·ra'tor,** *n.*

in·au·gu·ra·tion (in·ô'gyə·rā'shən), *n.* 1. act or ceremony of installing a person in office. 2. formal beginning; beginning. 3. opening for public use with a ceremony or celebration.

in·aus·pi·cious (in'ôs·pish'əs), *adj.* unfavorable; unlucky. —**in'aus·pi'cious·ly,** *adv.* —**in'aus·pi'cious·ness,** *n.* —Syn. unpromising.

in·board (in'bôrd'; –bōrd'), *adv., adj.* inside the hull of a ship.

in·born (in'bôrn'), *adj.* born in a person; instinctive; natural. —Syn. innate, inbred, native.

in·bound (in'bound'), *adj.* inward bound.

in·bred (in'bred'), *adj.* 1. inborn; natural: *an inbred courtesy.* 2. bred for generations from ancestors closely related.

in·breed (in'brēd'), *v.,* –bred, –breed·ing. 1. breed from closely related animals or plants. 2. produce or develop within.

in·breed·ing (in'brēd'ing), *n.* breeding from closely related persons, animals, or plants.

inc., 1. inclosure. 2. including. 3. inclusive. 4. Also, **Inc.** incorporated. 5. increase.

In·ca (ing'kə), *n.* member of the race of South American Indians who ruled Peru before the Spanish conquest. —**In'can,** *n., adj.*

in·cal·cu·la·ble (in·kal'kyə·lə·bəl), *adj.* 1. too great in number to be counted; numerous. 2. not to be reckoned beforehand. 3. not to be relied on; uncertain. —**in·cal'cu·la·bil'i·ty, in·cal'cu·la·ble·ness,** *n.* —**in·cal'cu·la·bly,** *adv.*

in·can·desce (in'kən·des'), *v.,* –desced, –desc·ing. glow or cause to glow.

in·can·des·cence (in'kən·des'əns), *n.* red-hot or white-hot condition.

in·can·des·cent (in'kən·des'ənt), *adj.* 1. glowing with heat; red-hot or white-hot. 2. intensely bright; brilliant. 3. pertaining to or containing a material that gives light by incandescence: *an incandescent filament or lamp.* [< L *incandescens* beginning to glow < *in–* + *candere* be gleaming white] —**in'can·des'cent·ly,** *adv.*

in·can·ta·tion (in'kan·tā'shən), *n.* 1. set of words spoken as a magic charm or to cast a magic spell. 2. use of such words. [< L, ult. < *in–* against + *cantare* chant]

in·ca·pa·ble (in·kā'pə·bəl), *adj.* 1. without ordinary ability; not efficient; not competent: *incapable workers.* 2. incapable of, a. without the ability, power, or fitness for: *incapable of work.* b. not legally qualified for: *a foreigner is incapable of becoming president of the United States.* c. not susceptible to; not capable of receiving or admitting: *incapable of exact measurement.* —**in·ca'pa·bil'i·ty, in·ca'pa·ble·ness,** *n.* —**in·ca'pa·bly,** *adv.*

in·ca·pac·i·tate (in'kə·pas'ə·tāt), *v.,* –tat·ed, –tat·ing. 1. deprive of ability, power, or fitness; disable. 2. legally disqualify. —**in'ca·pac'i·ta'tion,** *n.*

in·ca·pac·i·ty (in'kə·pas'ə·ti), *n., pl.* –ties. 1. lack of ability, power, or fitness; disability. 2. legal disqualification. —Syn. 1. unfitness, inability.

in·car·cer·ate (in·kär'sər·āt), *v.,* –at·ed, –at·ing. imprison. [< LL, < L *in–* in + *carcer* jail] —**in·car'cer·a'tion,** *n.* —**in·car'cer·a'tor,** *n.*

in·car·na·dine (in·kär'nə·din; –dīn; –dēn),

adj., v., –dined, –din·ing, *n.* —*adj.* 1. blood-red. 2. flesh-colored. —*v.* make incarnadine. —*n.* a blood-red color. [< F < Ital. *incarnadino.* See INCARNATE.]

in·car·nate (*adj.* in·kär'nit, –nāt; *v.* in·kär'nāt), *adj., v.,* –nat·ed, –nat·ing. —*adj.* embodied in flesh, esp. in human form. —*v.* 1. make incarnate; embody. 2. put into an actual form; realize. 3. be the living embodiment of. [< L, < *in–* + *caro* flesh]

in·car·na·tion (in'kär·nā'shən), *n.* 1. a taking on of human form by a divine being. 2. embodiment. 3. person or thing that represents some quality or idea. 4. the Incarnation, *Theol.* the union of divine nature and human nature in the person of Jesus Christ.

in·case (in·kās'), *v.,* –cased, –cas·ing. 1. put into a case. 2. cover completely; enclose. Also, **encase.** —**in·case'ment,** *n.*

in·cau·tious (in·kô'shəs), *adj.* not cautious; heedless; reckless; rash. —**in·cau'tious·ly,** *adv.* —**in·cau'tious·ness,** *n.* —Syn. imprudent, unwary.

in·cen·di·ar·y (in·sen'di·er'i), *adj., n., pl.* –ar·ies. —*adj.* 1. having to do with the setting of property on fire maliciously. 2. causing fires; used to start a fire: *incendiary bombs.* 3. deliberately stirring up strife or rebellion: *incendiary speeches.* —*n.* 1. person who maliciously sets fire to property. 2. person who deliberately stirs up strife or rebellion. 3. *Mil.* shell or bomb containing chemical agents which cause fire. [< L, < *incendium* fire] —**in·cen·di·a·rism** (in·sen'di·ə·riz'əm), *n.*

in·cense[1] (in'sens), *n., v.,* –censed, –cens·ing. —*n.* 1. substance giving off a sweet smell when burned. 2. perfume or smoke from it. 3. something sweet like incense, such as the perfume of flowers, flattery, or praise. —*v.* burn or offer as incense. [< LL *incensus* < L *incendere* burn] —**in'cense·less,** *adj.*

in·cense[2] (in·sens'), *v.,* –censed, –cens·ing. make very angry; fill with rage. [< L *incensus* kindled] —**in·cense'ment,** *n.* —Syn. enrage, madden, provoke.

in·cen·tive (in·sen'tiv), *n.* motive; stimulus. —*adj.* inciting; encouraging. [< L *incentivus* striking up the tune < *in–* + *canere* sing] —Syn. *n.* spur, incitement.

in·cep·tion (in·sep'shən), *n.* a beginning; commencement. [< L *inceptio* < *incipere* begin < *in–* on + *capere* take] —**in·cep'tive,** *adj.* —Syn. origin.

in·cer·ti·tude (in·sér'tə·tüd; –tūd), *n.* uncertainty; doubt.

in·ces·sant (in·ses'ənt), *adj.* never stopping; continued or repeated without interruption. [< LL, < L *in–* not + *cessare* cease] —**in·ces'san·cy, in·ces'sant·ness,** *n.* —**in·ces'sant·ly,** *adv.* —Syn. ceaseless, continual, constant.

in·cest (in'sest), *n.* crime of sexual intercourse between persons so closely related that their marriage is prohibited by law. [< L *incestum* < *in–* not + *castus* chaste]

in·ces·tu·ous (in·ses'chü·əs), *adj.* 1. involving incest. 2. guilty of incest. —**in·ces'tu·ous·ly,** *adv.* —**in·ces'tu·ous·ness,** *n.*

inch (inch), *n.* 1. measure of length, $\frac{1}{12}$ of a foot. 2. the amount of rainfall, etc., that would cover a surface to the depth of one inch. 3. the smallest part, amount, or degree; very little bit. 4. **by inches** or **inch by inch,** slowly; little by little. —*v.* move slowly or little by little: *a worm inches along.* [< L *uncia,* orig., a twelfth. Doublet of OUNCE[1]]

inch·meal (inch'mēl'), *adv.* little by little; slowly. —*n.* **by inchmeal,** little by little; slowly.

in·cho·ate (in·kō'it), *adj.* just begun; in an early stage; incomplete; undeveloped. [< L *inchoatus* begun] —**in·cho'ate·ly,** *adv.* —**in·cho'ate·ness,** *n.*

inch·worm (inch'wérm'), *n. Am.* a measuring worm.

in·ci·dence (in'sə·dəns), *n.* 1. range of occurrence or influence; extent of effects; way of falling on or affecting: *in an epidemic the incidence* *of a disease is widespread.* **2.** a falling on; a striking. **3.** direction in which one thing falls on or strikes another, esp. the angle (angle of incidence) that a line or ray of light falling upon a surface makes with a line perpendicular to that surface.

in·ci·dent (in′sə·dənt), *n.* **1.** a happening; event. **2.** event that helps or adds to something else. **3.** a distinct piece of action in a story, play, or poem. —*adj.* **1.** liable to happen; belonging: *hardships incident to the life of an explorer.* **2.** falling or striking (upon): *rays of light incident upon a mirror.* [< L *incidens* happening < *in*- on + *cadere* to fall] —**Syn.** *n.* **1.** occurrence, episode. —*adj.* **1.** relating, accessory.

Angle of incidence.

Ray IC impinges on surface AB at point C, CD being the perpendicular and angle ICD the angle of incidence. The angle DCR is the angle of reflection.

in·ci·den·tal (in′sə·den′təl), *adj.* **1.** happening or likely to happen along with something else more important: *discomforts incidental to camping out.* **2.** occurring by chance. **3.** secondary. —*n.* something incidental. —**Syn.** *adj.* **2.** occasional, casual.

in·ci·den·tal·ly (in′sə·den′təl·i; -dent′li), *adv.* as an incident along with something else; accidentally.

in·cin·er·ate (in·sin′ər·āt), *v.,* -at·ed, -at·ing. burn to ashes. [< Med.L, < L *in*- into + *cinis* ashes] —**in·cin′er·a′tion,** *n.*

in·cin·er·a·tor (in·sin′ər·ā′tər), *n.* furnace or other arrangement for burning things.

in·cip·i·ent (in·sip′i·ənt), *adj.* just beginning; in an early stage. [< L *incipiens* beginning < *in*- on + *capere* take] —**in·cip′i·ence, in·cip′i·en·cy,** *n.* —**in·cip′i·ent·ly,** *adv.*

in·cise (in·sīz′), *v.,* -cised, -cis·ing. **1.** cut into. **2.** carve; engrave. [< F *inciser,* ult. < *in*- into + *caedere* cut] —**in·cised′,** *adj.*

in·ci·sion (in·sizh′ən), *n.* **1.** cut made in something; gash. **2.** act of incising. **3.** incisive quality.

in·ci·sive (in·sī′siv), *adj.* sharp; penetrating; piercing; keen: *an incisive criticism.* [< Med.L *incisivus* < L *incidere* INCISE] —**in·ci′sive·ly,** *adv.* —**in·ci′sive·ness,** *n.*

in·ci·sor (in·sī′zər), *n.* tooth adapted for cutting; one of the front teeth.

in·ci·ta·tion (in′sī·tā′shən; -si-), *n.* an inciting.

in·cite (in·sīt′), *v.,* -cit·ed, -cit·ing. move to action; urge on; stir up; rouse. [< L *incitare,* ult. < *in*- on + *ciere* cause to move] —**in·cite′ment,** *n.* —**in·cit′er,** *n.* —**in·cit′ing·ly,** *adv.* —**Syn.** impel, instigate, provoke, goad, spur.

in·ci·vil·i·ty (in′sə·vil′ə·ti), *n., pl.* -ties. **1.** rudeness; lack of courtesy; impoliteness. **2.** a rude or impolite act. —**Syn.** **1.** discourtesy, disrespect.

incl., **1.** inclosure. **2.** including. **3.** inclusive.

in·clem·en·cy (in·klem′ən·si), *n., pl.* -cies. severity; harshness: *the inclemency of the weather kept us at home.*

in·clem·ent (in·klem′ənt), *adj.* **1.** rough; stormy. **2.** severe; harsh. —**in·clem′ent·ly,** *adv.* —**Syn.** **1.** rigorous, boisterous. **2.** cruel.

in·cli·na·tion (in′klə·nā′shən), *n.* **1.** tendency: *an inclination to become fat.* **2.** preference; liking: *a strong inclination for sports.* **3.** a leaning; a bending; a bowing: *a nod is an inclination of the head.* **4.** slope; slant: *the inclination of a roof.* **5.** Geom. the angle between two lines or planes. —**in′cli·na′tion·al,** *adj.* —**Syn.** **1.** proneness. **2.** bias, predilection. **4.** declivity.

in·cline (*v.* in·klīn′; *n.* in′klīn, in·klīn′), *v.,* -clined, -clin·ing, *n.* —*v.* **1.** be favorable; be disposed; tend: *dogs incline toward meat as a food.* **2.** make favorable or willing; influence: *incline your hearts to obey God's laws.* **3.** slope; slant. **4.** lean; bend; bow. **5.** incline one's ear, listen favorably. —*n.* **1.** slope; slant. **2.** a sloping surface. [< L, < *in*- + *clinare* bend] —**in·clined′,** *adj.* —**in·clin′er,** *n.*

inclined plane, plank or other plane surface put at an oblique angle with a horizontal surface.

in·cli·nom·e·ter (in′klə·nom′ə·tər), *n.* instrument for measuring the angle that an aircraft makes with the horizontal.

in·close (in·klōz′), *v.,* -closed, -clos·ing. enclose. —**in·clos′er,** *n.*

in·clo·sure (in·klō′zhər), *n.* enclosure.

in·clude (in·klüd′), *v.,* -clud·ed, -clud·ing. **1.** put, hold, or enclose within limits. **2.** contain; comprise: *the farm includes 160 acres.* **3.** put in a total, a class, or the like; reckon in a count: *all on board the ship were lost, including the captain.* [< L *includere* < *in*- in + *claudere* shut] —**in·clud′i·ble, in·clud′a·ble,** *adj.* —**Syn.** **2.** comprehend, embrace.

in·clu·sion (in·klü′zhən), *n.* **1.** an including or being included. **2.** thing included.

in·clu·sive (in·klü′siv), *adj.* **1.** including in consideration; including; comprising: *read pages 10 to 20 inclusive.* **2.** including much; including everything concerned: *an inclusive list of expenses.* —**in·clu′sive·ly,** *adv.* —**in·clu′sive·ness,** *n.*

in·cog·ni·to (in·kog′nə·tō; in′kog·nē′tō), *adj., adv., n., pl.* -tos. —*adj., adv.* with one's name, character and rank, etc., concealed. —*n.* **1.** person who is incognito. **2.** a disguised state or condition. [< Ital. < L *incognitus* unknown, ult. < *in*- not + *cognoscere* come to know]

in·co·her·ence (in′kō·hir′əns), **in·co·her·en·cy** (-ən·si), *n., pl.* -ences; -cies. **1.** failure to stick together; looseness. **2.** lack of logical connection. **3.** disconnected thought or speech.

in·co·her·ent (in′kō·hir′ənt), *adj.* **1.** not sticking together. **2.** disconnected; confused. —**in′co·her′ent·ly,** *adv.* —**Syn.** **2.** inconsistent.

in·com·bus·ti·ble (in′kəm·bus′tə·bəl), *adj.* that cannot be burned; fireproof. —*n.* an incombustible substance. —**in′com·bus′ti·bil′i·ty,** in′com·bus′ti·ble·ness, *n.* —**in′com·bus′ti·bly,** *adv.*

in·come (in′kum), *n.* what comes in from property, business, labor, etc.; receipts. —**Syn.** revenue, proceeds, profit, salary.

income tax, government tax on a person's income.

in·com·ing (in′kum′ing), *adj.* coming in.

in·com·men·su·ra·ble (in′kə·men′shə·rə·bəl; -sər·ə-), *adj.* **1.** that cannot be compared because not measurable in the same units or by the same scale. **2.** having no common integral divisor except 1, as 8, 17, and 11. **3.** utterly disproportionate. —**in′com·men′su·ra·bil′i·ty,** in′com·men′su·ra·ble·ness, *n.* —**in′com·men′su·ra·bly,** *adv.*

in·com·men·su·rate (in′kə·men′shə·rit; -sə·rit), *adj.* **1.** not in proportion; not adequate. **2.** incommensurable. —**in′com·men′su·rate·ly,** *adv.* —**in′com·men′su·rate·ness,** *n.*

in·com·mode (in′kə·mōd′), *v.,* -mod·ed, -mod·ing. inconvenience; trouble. [< L, ult. < *in*- not + *commodus* convenient] —**Syn.** annoy.

in·com·mo·di·ous (in′kə·mō′di·əs), *adj.* **1.** not roomy enough. **2.** inconvenient; uncomfortable. —**in′com·mo′di·ous·ly,** *adv.* —**in′com·mo′di·ous·ness,** *n.*

in·com·mu·ni·ca·ble (in′kə·mū′nə·kə·bəl), *adj.* not capable of being communicated or told. —**in′com·mu′ni·ca·bil′i·ty,** in′com·mu′ni·ca·ble·ness, *n.* —**in′com·mu′ni·ca·bly,** *adv.*

in·com·mu·ni·ca·do (in′kə·mū′nə·kä′dō), *adj. Am.* deprived of communication with others. [< Sp.]

in·com·pa·ra·ble (in·kom′pə·rə·bəl; -prə-bəl), *adj.* **1.** without equal; matchless: *incomparable beauty.* **2.** not to be compared; unsuitable for comparison. —**in′com′pa·ra·bil′i·ty,** in·com′pa·ra·ble·ness, *n.* —**in·com′pa·ra·bly,** *adv.* —**Syn.** **1.** peerless, unequaled, unrivaled.

in·com·pat·i·bil·i·ty (in′kəm·pat′ə·bil′ə·ti), *n., pl.* -ties. **1.** lack of harmony. **2.** incompatible thing, quality, etc.

in·com·pat·i·ble (in′kəm·pat′ə·bəl), *adj.* **1.** not able to live or act together peaceably; opposed in character. **2.** inconsistent: *late hours* are *incompatible with health.* —in'com·pat'i-ble·ness, *n.* —in'com·pat'i·bly, *adv.*

in·com·pe·tence (in·kom′pə·təns), **in·com·pe·ten·cy** (-tən·si), *n.* 1. lack of ability, power, or fitness. 2. lack of legal qualification.

in·com·pe·tent (in·kom′pə·tənt), *adj.* 1. not competent; lacking ability, power, or fitness. 2. not legally qualified. —*n.* an incompetent person. —in'com'pe·tent·ly, *adv.* —Syn. *adj.* 1. incapable, unfit.

in·com·plete (in′kəm·plēt′), *adj.* not complete; lacking some part; unfinished. —in'com·plete'ly, *adv.* —in'com·plete'ness, in'com·ple'tion, *n.* —Syn. imperfect, deficient.

in·com·pre·hen·si·ble (in′kom·pri·hen′sə·bəl), *adj.* 1. impossible to understand. 2. *Archaic.* illimitable. —in'com·pre·hen'si·bil'i·ty, in'-com·pre·hen'si·ble·ness, *n.* —in'com·pre·hen'si·bly, *adv.*

in·com·press·i·ble (in′kəm·pres′ə·bəl), *adj.* not capable of being squeezed into a smaller size. —in'com·press'i·bil'i·ty, *n.*

in·con·ceiv·a·ble (in′kən·sēv′ə·bəl), *adj.* impossible to imagine; unthinkable; incredible. —in'con·ceiv'a·bil'i·ty, in'con·ceiv'a·ble·ness, *n.* —in'con·ceiv'a·bly, *adv.*

in·con·clu·sive (in′kən·klü′siv), *adj.* not decisive; not effective. —in'con·clu'sive·ly, *adv.* —in'con·clu'sive·ness, *n.*

in·con·gru·i·ty (in′kong·grü′ə·ti; —kon′-; —kən-), *n., pl.* —ties. 1. unfitness; inappropriateness; being out of place. 2. lack of agreement or harmony; inconsistency. 3. something that is incongruous.

in·con·gru·ous (in·kong′grü·əs), *adj.* 1. out of keeping; not appropriate; out of place. 2. lacking in agreement or harmony; not consistent. —in'con'gru·ous·ly, *adv.* —in'con'gru·ous·ness, *n.* —Syn. 1. inappropriate, unsuited. 2. inharmonious, inconsistent.

in·con·se·quent (in·kon′sə·kwent; —kwənt), *adj.* 1. not logical; not logically connected. 2. not to the point; off the subject. 3. apt to think or talk without logical connection. —in'con'se·quence, *n.* —in'con'se·quent·ly, *adv.*

in·con·se·quen·tial (in′kon·sə·kwen′shəl), *adj.* 1. unimportant; trifling. 2. inconsequent. —in'con·se·quen'ti·al'i·ty, *n.* —in'con·se·quen'tial·ly, *adv.*

in·con·sid·er·a·ble (in′kən·sid′ər·ə·bəl), *adj.* not worthy of consideration; not important. —in'con·sid'er·a·ble·ness, *n.* —in'con·sid'er·a·bly, *adv.* —Syn. unimportant, insignificant, petty.

in·con·sid·er·ate (in′kən·sid′ər·it), *adj.* 1. not thoughtful of the rights and feelings of others. 2. thoughtless; heedless. —in'con·sid'er·ate·ly, *adv.* —in'con·sid'er·ate·ness, in'con·sid'er·a'tion, *n.*

in·con·sist·en·cy (in′kən·sis′tən·si), *n., pl.* —cies. 1. lack of agreement or harmony; variance. 2. failure to keep to the same principles, course of action, etc.; changeableness. 3. thing, act, etc., that is inconsistent.

in·con·sist·ent (in′kən·sis′tənt), *adj.* 1. lacking in agreement or harmony; at variance. 2. lacking harmony between its different parts; not uniform. 3. failing to keep to the same principles, course of action, etc.; changeable. —in'con·sist'ent·ly, *adv.* —Syn. 1. discrepant, incongruous.

in·con·sol·a·ble (in′kən·sōl′ə·bəl), *adj.* not to be comforted. —in'con·sol'a·bil'i·ty, in'con·sol'a·ble·ness, *n.* —in'con·sol'a·bly, *adv.*

in·con·so·nant (in·kon′sə·nənt), *adj.* not harmonious; not in agreement or accord. —in'con'so·nance, *n.* —in'con'so·nant·ly, *adv.*

in·con·spic·u·ous (in′kən·spik′yü·əs), *adj.* attracting little or no attention. —in'con·spic'u·ous·ly, *adv.* —in'con·spic'u·ous·ness, *n.*

in·con·stan·cy (in·kon′stən·si), *n.* fickleness.

in·con·stant (in·kon′stənt), *adj.* not constant; changeable; fickle. —in'con'stant·ly, *adv.* —Syn. variable, capricious.

in·con·test·a·ble (in′kən·tes′tə·bəl), *adj.* not to be disputed; unquestionable. —in'con·test'-a·bil'i·ty, in'con·test'a·ble·ness, *n.* —in'con·test'a·bly, *adv.* —Syn. indisputable, undeniable, certain.

in·con·ti·nence (in·kon′tə·nəns), *n.* 1. lack of self-restraint. 2. lack of chastity.

in·con·ti·nent (in·kon′tə·nənt), *adj.* 1. without self-restraint. 2. not chaste; licentious. —in·con'ti·nent·ly, *adv.*

in·con·tro·vert·i·ble (in′kon·trə·vér′tə·bəl), *adj.* that cannot be disputed; unquestionable. —in'con·tro·vert'i·bil'i·ty, in'con·tro·vert'-i·ble·ness, *n.* —in'con·tro·vert'i·bly, *adv.*

in·con·ven·ience (in′kən·vēn′yəns), *n., v.,* -ienced, -ienc·ing. —*n.* 1. lack of convenience or ease; trouble; bother. 2. cause of trouble, difficulty, or bother. —*v.* cause trouble, difficulty, etc., to.

in·con·ven·ient (in′kən·vēn′yənt), *adj.* not convenient; troublesome; causing bother or discomfort. —in'con·ven'ient·ly, *adv.* —Syn. embarrassing, awkward.

in·con·vert·i·ble (in′kən·vér′tə·bəl), *adj.* incapable of being converted or exchanged. —in'con·vert'i·bil'i·ty, in'con·vert'i·ble·ness, *n.* —in'con·vert'i·bly, *adv.*

in·cor·po·rate (*v.* in·kôr′pə·rāt; *adj.* in·kôr′pə·rit), *v.,* -rat·ed, -rat·ing, *adj.* —*v.* 1. make (something) a part of something else; join or combine (something) with something else: *we will incorporate your suggestion in this new plan.* 2. form into a corporation: *incorporate a business.* 3. form a corporation. 4. unite or combine so as to form one body. 5. embody; give material form to: *incorporate one's thoughts in an article.* —*adj.* united; combined; incorporated. [< L, < *in-* into + *corpus* body] —in·cor'po·ra'tive, *adj.* —in·cor'po·ra'tor, *n.* —Syn. *v.* 1. merge, unite.

in·cor·po·ra·tion (in·kôr′pə·rā′shən), *n.* 1. an incorporating: *the incorporation of air bubbles in the glass spoiled it.* 2. a being incorporated: *incorporation gives a company the power to act as one person.*

in·cor·po·re·al (in′kôr·pô′ri·əl; —pō′-), *adj.* not made of any material substance; spiritual. —in'cor·po're·al·ly, *adv.* —Syn. immaterial, disembodied.

in·cor·rect (in′kə·rekt′), *adj.* 1. not correct; wrong; faulty. 2. not proper. —in'cor·rect'ly, *adv.* —in'cor·rect'ness, *n.* —Syn. 1. erroneous, inaccurate.

in·cor·ri·gi·ble (in·kôr′ə·jə·bəl; in·kor′-), *adj.* 1. so firmly fixed (in bad ways, a bad habit, etc.) that nothing else can be expected: *an incorrigible liar.* 2. so fixed that it cannot be changed or cured. —*n.* an incorrigible person. —in·cor'ri·gi·bil'i·ty, in·cor'ri·gi·ble·ness, *n.* —in·cor'ri·gi·bly, *adv.* —Syn. *adj.* 1. hardened.

in·cor·rupt·i·ble (in′kə·rup′tə·bəl), *adj.* 1. not to be corrupted; honest. 2. not capable of decay. —in'cor·rupt'i·bil'i·ty, in'cor·rupt'-i·ble·ness, *n.* —in'cor·rupt'i·bly, *adv.*

in·crease (*v.* in·krēs′; *n.* in′krēs), *v.,* -creased, -creas·ing. —*v.* 1. make greater or more numerous; make richer, more prosperous, or more powerful. 2. become greater; grow in numbers, esp. by propagation; advance in quality, success, power, etc. —*n.* 1. gain in size, numbers, etc.; growth; multiplication by propagation. 2. addition; result of increasing; increased product. 3. **on the increase,** increasing. 4. offspring. [< AF var. of OF *encreistre* < L, < *in-* in + *crescere* grow] —in'creas'a·ble, *adj.* —increas'er, *n.* —Syn. *v.* 1. enlarge, extend, augment. —*n.* 1, 2. enlargement, extension.

in·creas·ing·ly (in·krēs′ing·li), *adv.* more and more.

in·cred·i·ble (in·kred′ə·bəl), *adj.* seeming too extraordinary to be possible; unbelievable: *incredible bravery.* —in·cred'i·bil'i·ty, in·cred'i·ble·ness, *n.* —in·cred'i·bly, *adv.* ▸ **incredible, incredulous.** A story or situation is *incredible* (unbelievable); a person is *incredulous* (unbelieving).

in·cre·du·li·ty (in′krə·dü′lə·ti; —dū′-), *n.* lack of belief; doubt. —Syn. unbelief, distrust.

in·cred·u·lous (in·krej′ə·ləs), *adj.* 1. not ready to believe; not credulous; doubting. 2. showing a lack of belief. —in·cred′u·lous·ly, *adv.* —in·cred′u·lous·ness, *n.* ⊳ See **incredible** for usage note.

in·cre·ment (in′krə·mənt; ing′-), *n.* 1. increase; growth. 2. amount by which something increases. [< L *incrementum* < *increscere* IN-CREASE] —in′cre·men′tal, *adj.*

in·crim·i·nate (in·krim′ə·nāt), *v.*, -nat·ed, -nat·ing. accuse of a crime; show to be guilty: *in his confession the thief incriminated two others who helped him steal.* [< LL, < L *in*-against + *crimen* charge] —in·crim′i·na′tion, *n.* —in·crim′i·na′tor, *n.* —in·crim·i·na·to·ry (in·krim′ə·nə·tô′ri; -tō′-), *adj.*

in·crust (in·krust′), *v.* 1. cover with a crust or hard coating. 2. form a crust; form into a crust. Also, encrust. —in′crus·ta′tion, *n.*

in·cu·bate (in′kyə·bāt; ing′-), *v.*, -bat·ed, -bat·ing. 1. sit on (eggs) in order to hatch them. 2. brood. 3. keep (eggs, etc.) warm so that they will hatch or grow. [< L, < *in*- on + *cubare* lie] —in′cu·ba′tive, *adj.*

in·cu·ba·tion (in′kyə·bā′shən; ing′-), *n.* 1. an incubating or being incubated. 2. stage of a disease from the time of infection until the appearance of the first symptoms. —in′cu·ba′tion·al, *adj.*

in·cu·ba·tor (in′kyə·bā′tər; ing′-), *n.* 1. apparatus having a box or chamber for keeping eggs at a specific temperature so that they will hatch. 2. a similar apparatus for rearing children born prematurely. 3. apparatus in which bacterial cultures are developed.

in·cu·bus (in′kyə·bəs; ing′-), *n., pl.* -bi (-bī), -bus·es. 1. an evil spirit supposed to descend upon sleeping persons. 2. nightmare. 3. an oppressive or burdensome thing. [< Med.L (def. 1), LL (def. 2), < L, < *in*- on + *cubare* lie]

in·cul·cate (in·kul′kāt; in′kul·kāt), *v.*, -cat·ed, -cat·ing. impress by repetition; teach persistently. [< L *inculcatus*, orig., trampled in, ult. < *in*- in + *calx* heel] —in′cul·ca′tion, *n.* —in·cul′ca·tor, *n.*

in·cul·pate (in·kul′pāt; in′kul·pāt), *v.*, -pat·ed, -pat·ing. 1. blame; accuse. 2. involve in responsibility for wrongdoing; incriminate. [< LL, < L *in*- in + *culpa* blame] —in′cul·pa′tion, *n.*

in·cum·ben·cy (in·kum′bən·si), *n., pl.* -cies. a holding of an office, position, etc., and performance of its duties; term of office.

in·cum·bent (in·kum′bənt), *adj.* 1. lying, leaning, or pressing (on). 2. resting (on a person) as a duty: *it is incumbent on a judge to be just.* —*n.* person holding an office, position, church living, etc. [< L *incumbens* lying down on] —in·cum′bent·ly, *adv.*

in·cum·ber (in·kum′bər), *v.* encumber.

in·cum·brance (in·kum′brəns), *n.* encumbrance.

in·cu·nab·u·la (in′kyū·nab′yə·lə), *n.pl., sing.* -lum (-ləm). 1. earliest stages or first traces of anything; beginnings. 2. books printed before the year 1500. [< L, cradle] —in′cu·nab′u·lar, *adj.*

in·cur (in·kėr′), *v.*, -curred, -cur·ring. run or fall into (something unpleasant); bring (blame, punishment, danger, etc.) on oneself: *the hunter incurred great danger in killing the tiger.* [< L, < *in*- upon + *currere* run]

in·cur·a·ble (in·kyur′ə·bəl), *adj.* not capable of being cured or remedied. —*n.* person having an incurable disease. —in·cur′a·bil′i·ty, in·cur′a·ble·ness, *n.* —in·cur′a·bly, *adv.* —Syn. *adj.* fatal, hopeless.

in·cu·ri·ous (in·kyur′i·əs), *adj.* not curious; without curiosity. —in·cu·ri·os·i·ty (in′kyur·i·os′ə·ti), in·cu′ri·ous·ness, *n.* —in·cu′ri·ous·ly, *adv.*

in·cur·sion (in·kėr′zhən; -shən), *n.* invasion; raid; sudden attack. [< L *incursio* < *incurrere*. See INCUR.]

in·cur·sive (in·kėr′siv), *adj.* making incursions.

in·curve (*v.* in·kėrv′; *n.* in′kėrv′), *v.*, -curved, -curv·ing, *n.* —*v.* curve inward. —*n.* Baseball.

pitch that curves toward the batter. —in′cur·va′tion, *n.*

in·cus (ing′kəs), *n.* the middle one of a chain of three small bones in the middle ear of man and other animals. [< L, anvil]

Ind., 1. India. 2. Indian. 3. Indiana.

ind., 1. independent. 2. index. 3. indicative.

in·debt·ed (in·det′id), *adj.* in debt; obliged; owing money or gratitude. —in·debt′ed·ness, *n.*

in·de·cen·cy (in·dē′sən·si), *n., pl.* -cies. 1. lack of decency. 2. an indecent act or word.

in·de·cent (in·dē′sənt), *adj.* 1. not decent; in very bad taste; improper: *an indecent lack of gratitude to the man who saved his life.* 2. not modest; morally bad; obscene. —in·de′cent·ly, *adv.* —Syn. 1. unbecoming, unseemly. 2. coarse, disgusting.

in·de·ci·pher·a·ble (in′di·sī′fər·ə·bəl), *adj.* incapable of being deciphered; illegible. —in′de·ci′pher·a·bil′i·ty, *n.*

in·de·ci·sion (in′di·sizh′ən), *n.* lack of decision; tendency to delay or to hesitate. —Syn. hesitation, uncertainty.

in·de·ci·sive (in′di·sī′siv), *adj.* 1. having the habit of hesitating and putting off decisions. 2. not deciding or settling the matter. —in′de·ci′sive·ly, *adv.* —in′de·ci′sive·ness, *n.*

in·de·clin·a·ble (in′di·klīn′ə·bəl), *adj.* not changing its form for changes in grammatical use. *None* is an indeclinable pronoun. —in′de·clin′a·bly, *adv.*

in·de·co·rous (in·dek′ə·rəs; in′di·kô′rəs, -kō′-), *adj.* not suitable; improper. —in·dec′o·rous·ly, *adv.* —in·dec′o·rous·ness, *n.* —Syn. unseemly, rude.

in·de·co·rum (in′di·kô′rəm; -kō′-), *n.* 1. lack of decorum. 2. improper behavior, dress, etc.

in·deed (in·dēd′), *adv.* in fact; really; truly; surely. —*interj.* expression of surprise, incredulity, irony, or contempt.

indef., indefinite.

in·de·fat·i·ga·ble (in′di·fat′ə·gə·bəl), *adj.* tireless; untiring. —in′de·fat′i·ga·bil′i·ty, in′de·fat′i·ga·ble·ness, *n.* —in′de·fat′i·ga·bly, *adv.* —Syn. unflagging, unwearying, persistent.

in·de·fea·si·ble (in′di·fē′zə·bəl), *adj.* not to be annulled or made void. —in′de·fea′si·bil′i·ty, *n.* —in′de·fea′si·bly, *adv.*

in·de·fen·si·ble (in′di·fen′sə·bəl), *adj.* 1. that cannot be defended. 2. not justifiable. —in′de·fen′si·bil′i·ty, in′de·fen′si·ble·ness, *n.* —in′de·fen′si·bly, *adv.*

in·de·fin·a·ble (in′di·fīn′ə·bəl), *adj.* that cannot be defined. —in′de·fin′a·ble·ness, *n.* —in′de·fin′a·bly, *adv.*

in·def·i·nite (in·def′ə·nit), *adj.* 1. not clearly defined; not precise; vague. 2. not limited. 3. *Gram.* not specifying (person, time, etc.) precisely. *Some, many,* and *few* are often indefinite pronouns. —in·def′i·nite·ly, *adv.* —in·def′i·nite·ness, *n.* —Syn. 1. obscure, ambiguous, equivocal, inexact.

indefinite article, *Gram. a* or *an.*

in·de·his·cent (in′di·his′ənt), *adj. Bot.* not opening at maturity. —in′de·his′cence, *n.*

in·del·i·ble (in·del′ə·bəl), *adj.* 1. that cannot be erased or removed; permanent: *indelible ink, an indelible disgrace.* 2. making an indelible mark: *an indelible pencil.* [< L, < *in*- not + *delere* destroy] —in·del′i·bil′i·ty, in·del′i·ble·ness, *n.* —in·del′i·bly, *adv.* —Syn. 1. fixed, fast, ineffaceable.

in·del·i·ca·cy (in·del′ə·kə·si), *n., pl.* -cies. lack of delicacy; being indelicate.

in·del·i·cate (in·del′ə·kit), *adj.* 1. not delicate; coarse; crude. 2. improper; immodest. —in·del′i·cate·ly, *adv.* —in·del′i·cate·ness, *n.* —Syn. 2. vulgar.

in·dem·ni·fi·ca·tion (in·dem′nə·fə·kā′shən), *n.* 1. an indemnifying or being indemnified. 2. compensation; recompense.

in·dem·ni·fy (in·dem′nə·fī), *v.*, -fied, -fy·ing. 1. repay; make good; compensate for damage, loss, or expense incurred. 2. secure against damage or loss; insure. —in·dem′ni·fi′er, *n.* —Syn. 1. recompense, reimburse.

in·dem·ni·ty (in·dem'nə·ti), *n.*, *pl.* –ties. 1. payment for damage, loss, or expense incurred: *money demanded by a victorious nation at the end of a war as a condition of peace is an indemnity.* 2. security against damage or loss; insurance. [< LL, < L *indemnis* unhurt < in- not + *damnum* damage]

in·dent¹ (*v.* in·dent'; *n.* in'dent, in·dent'), *v.* 1. cut (an edge) so that it looks like a row of teeth; notch. 2. form deep notches or bays in. 3. form a notch or recess. 4. begin (a line) farther from the edge than the other lines. —*n.* 1. a notch. 2. an indenting. 3. an indenture. [< OF *endenter*, ult. < L *in-* in + *dens* tooth] —in·dent'er, *n.*

Indented molding

in·dent² (in·dent'), *v.* 1. make a dent in. 2. press in; stamp. [< in-² + dent]

in·den·ta·tion (in'den·tā'shən), *n.* 1. an indenting or being indented. 2. dent; notch; cut. 3. indention.

in·den·tion (in·den'shən), *n.* 1. a beginning of a line farther from the edge than the other lines. 2. blank space left by doing this. 3. indentation.

in·den·ture (in·den'chər), *n.*, *v.*, –tured, –tur·ing. —*n.* 1. written agreement. 2. contract by which a person is bound to serve someone else. 3. indentation. —*v.* bind by a contract for service. [< OF *endenteure* indentation]

in·de·pend·ence (in'di·pen'dəns), *n.* 1. freedom from the control, influence, support, or help of another. 2. enough to live on.

In·de·pend·ence (in'di·pen'dəns), *n.* city in W Missouri. It was one of the terminals of the Santa Fé Trail.

Independence Day, *Am.* the Fourth of July.

in·de·pend·en·cy (in'di·pen'dən·si), *n.*, *pl.* –cies. 1. independence. 2. an independent country.

in·de·pend·ent (in'di·pen'dənt), *adj.* 1. needing, wishing, or getting no help from others: *independent thinking.* 2. acting, working, or esp. voting by one's own ideas, not as the crowd does. 3. guiding, ruling, or governing oneself; not under another's rule. 4. not depending on others. 5. having an adequate private income. 6. not resulting from another thing; not controlled or influenced by something else; separate; distinct. —*n.* 1. person who is independent in thought or behavior. 2. person who votes without regard to party. —in'de·pend'ent·ly, *adv.* —Syn. *adj.* 6. free, uncontrolled.

in·de·scrib·a·ble (in'di·skrīb'ə·bəl), *adj.* that cannot be described; beyond description. —in'de·scrib·a·bil'i·ty, in'de·scrib'a·ble·ness, *n.* —in'de·scrib'a·bly, *adv.*

in·de·struct·i·ble (in'di·struk'tə·bəl), *adj.* that cannot be destroyed. —in'de·struct'i·bil'i·ty, in'de·struct'i·ble·ness, *n.* —in'de·struct'i·bly, *adv.*

in·de·ter·mi·na·ble (in'di·tér'mə·nə·bəl), *adj.* 1. not capable of being settled or decided. 2. not capable of being ascertained. —in'de·ter'mi·na·bly, *adv.*

in·de·ter·mi·nate (in'di·tér'mə·nit), *adj.* not determined; indefinite; vague. —in'de·ter'mi·nate·ly, *adv.* —in'de·ter'mi·nate·ness, *n.*

in·de·ter·mi·na·tion (in'di·tér'mə·nā'shən), *n.* 1. lack of determination. 2. an unsettled state.

in·dex (in'deks), *n.*, *pl.* –dex·es, –di·ces (–də·sēz), *v.* —*n.* 1. list of what is in a book, telling on what pages to find topics, names, etc., usually put at the end of the book and arranged in alphabetical order. 2. thing that points out or shows; sign. 3. Also, **index finger.** finger next to the thumb; forefinger. 4. pointer: *a dial or scale usually has an index.* 5. in printing, a sign (☞) used to point out a particular note, paragraph, etc. 6. number or formula expressing some property, ratio, etc., in science. 7. *Math.* an exponent. 8. **Index,** list of books that the Roman Catholic Church forbids its members to read. —*v.* 1. provide with an index; make an index of. 2. enter in an index. [< L, orig., that which points out]

In·di·a (in'di·ə), *n.* a country and peninsular subcontinent of Asia, S of the Himalayas, between the Bay of Bengal and the Arabian Sea, projecting into the Indian Ocean. Until Aug. 15, 1947, largely under British rule; now chiefly divided between the republic of India and Pakistan, both self-governing affiliated units of the British Commonwealth of Nations.

India ink, 1. a black pigment consisting of lampblack mixed with a binding material. 2. liquid ink prepared from this pigment.

In·di·a·man (in'di·ə·mən), *n.*, *pl.* –men. a ship in the trade with India.

In·di·an (in'di·ən), *n.* 1. *Am.* member of the so-called red race living in America before the Europeans came; an American Indian. 2. *Am.* any one of the languages of the American Indians. 3. native of India or the East Indies. —*adj.* 1. *Am.* of or having to do with American Indians. 2. of, living in, or belonging to India or the East Indies.

In·di·an·a (in'di·an'ə), *n.* a Middle Western State of the United States. *Capital:* Indianapolis. *Abbrev.:* Ind. —In·di·an·i·an (in'di·an'i·ən), *adj.*, *n.*

In·di·an·ap·o·lis (in'di·ən·ap'ə·lis), *n.* capital of Indiana, near the center of the State.

Indian club, a bottle-shaped wooden club swung for exercise.

Indian corn, *Am.* 1. grain that grows on large ears; maize. 2. plant that it grows on.

Indian file, *Am.* single file.

Indian giver, *Am.*, *Colloq.* person who takes back a gift after having bestowed it.

In·di·an·ize (in'di·ən·īz), *v.*, –ized, –iz·ing. 1. *Am.*, *Colloq.* make Indian in form, shape, or manner. 2. in India, replace British officials and personnel by Indians. —In'di·an·i·za'tion, *n.*

Indian corn (ears vary in length from 1 to 20 in.)

Indian Ocean, ocean S of Asia, E of Africa, and W of Australia.

Indian pipe, *Am.* a leafless plant with a solitary flower that looks like a tobacco pipe.

Indian pudding, *Am.* a baked pudding made with corn meal, molasses, milk, and suet.

Indian summer, *Am.* time of mild, dry, hazy weather in late autumn.

India paper, a thin, tough paper, used for Bibles, prayer books, etc.

India rubber, india rubber, substance of great elasticity derived from the coagulated, milky juice of various tropical plants; rubber.

indic., indicative.

in·di·cate (in'də·kāt), *v.*, –cat·ed, –cat·ing. 1. point out; point to: *the arrow on a sign indicates the right way to go.* 2. show; make known: *a thermometer indicates temperature.* 3. be a sign or hint of: *fever indicates sickness.* 4. give a sign or hint of. 5. state; express: *indicate one's intention.* 6. show to be needed as a remedy or treatment. [< L, < in- in + *dicare* proclaim] —Syn. 1. designate. 2. reveal, disclose. 3. signify, evidence.

in·di·ca·tion (in'də·kā'shən), *n.* 1. an indicating. 2. thing that indicates; sign. 3. amount or degree indicated.

in·dic·a·tive (in·dik'ə·tiv), *adj.* 1. pointing out; showing; being a sign (of); suggestive. 2. *Gram.* expressing or denoting a state, act, or happening as actual; asking a question of simple fact. In "I go" and "Did I go?" the verbs are in the indicative mood. —*n. Gram.* a. the indicative mood. b. a verb form in this mood. —in·dic'a·tive·ly, *adv.*

in·di·ca·tor (in'də·kā'tər), *n.* 1. person or thing that indicates. 2. pointer on the dial of an instrument that measures something. 3. a measuring or recording instrument. 4. *Chem.* substance used to indicate chemical conditions or changes, as litmus. —in·di·ca·to·ry (in'də·kə·tô'ri, –tō'-), *adj.*

in·di·ces (in'də·sēz), *n. pl.* of **index.**

in·dict (in·dīt'), v. 1. charge with an offense or crime; accuse. 2. find enough evidence against (an accused person) so that a trial is necessary. [< AF enditer INDITE] —in·dict'a·ble, adj. —in·dict'er, in·dict'or, n.

in·dict·ment (in·dīt'ment), n. 1. Law. a formal accusation, esp. the legal accusation presented by a grand jury. 2. accusation.

In·dies (in'dēz), n.pl. 1. East Indies, India, and Indo-China. 2. the East Indies. 3. the West Indies.

in·dif·fer·ence (in·dif'ər·əns; -dif'rəns), n. 1. lack of interest or attention. 2. lack of importance: where we ate was a matter of indifference. —Syn. 1. apathy, unconcern. 2. insignificance.

in·dif·fer·ent (in·dif'ər·ənt; -dif'rənt), adj. 1. having no feeling for or against: indifferent to an admirer. 2. impartial; neutral; without preference: an indifferent decision. 3. unimportant; not mattering much: the time for starting is indifferent to me. 4. neither good nor bad; just fair. 5. rather bad. 6. neutral in chemical, electrical, or magnetic quality. —Syn. 1. apathetic, unconcerned. 2. unbiased, disinterested, fair.

in·dif·fer·ent·ly (in·dif'ər·ənt·li; -dif'rənt-), adv. 1. with indifference. 2. without distinction; equally. 3. moderately; tolerably; passably. 4. poorly; badly.

in·di·gence (in'də·jəns), n. poverty.

in·dig·e·nous (in·dij'ə·nəs), adj. 1. originating in the region or country where found; native. 2. innate; inherent. [< L indigena native] —in·dig'e·nous·ly, adv. —in·dig'e·nous·ness, n. in·di·gen·i·ty (in'də·jen'ə·ti), n.

in·di·gent (in'də·jənt), adj. poor; needy. [< L indigens needing] —in'di·gent·ly, adv.

in·di·gest·i·ble (in'də·jes'tə·bəl; -dī-), adj. that cannot be digested; hard to digest. —in'di·gest'i·bil'i·ty, in'di·gest'i·ble·ness, n. —in'di·gest'i·bly, adv.

in·di·ges·tion (in'də·jes'chən; -dī-), n. inability to digest food; difficulty in digesting food.

in·dig·nant (in·dig'nənt), adj. angry at something unworthy, unjust, or mean. —in·dig'nant·ly, adv. —Syn. incensed, provoked.

in·dig·na·tion (in'dig·nā'shən), n. anger at something unworthy, unjust, or mean; righteous anger. [< L, ult. < in- not + dignus worthy]

in·dig·ni·ty (in·dig'nə·ti), n., pl. -ties. injury to dignity; an insult; slight.

in·di·go (in'də·gō), n., pl. -gos, -goes, adj. —n. 1. blue dyestuff that can be obtained from certain plants, but is now usually made artificially. 2. plant from which indigo is obtained. 3. a deep violet blue. —adj. deep violet-blue. [< Sp. < L < Gk. indikon, orig. adj., Indian]

indigo bunting or bird, Am. a small American finch, the male of which is a deep violet-blue.

in·di·rect (in'də·rekt'; -dī-), adj. 1. not direct; not straight: an indirect route. 2. not directly connected; secondary: an indirect consequence. 3. not straightforward and to the point: an indirect reply. 4. dishonest, deceitful: indirect methods. —in'di·rect'ly, adv. —in'di·rect'ness, n. —Syn. 1. circuitous, roundabout. 2. incidental.

indirect discourse, repetition of the substance of a person's speech without directly quoting it. Example: "He said that he would come," instead of "He said, 'I will come.' "

in·di·rec·tion (in'də·rek'shən; -dī-), n. 1. roundabout act, means, etc. 2. dishonesty; deceit.

indirect object, Gram. person or thing that is indirectly affected by the action of the verb. The indirect object usually comes before the direct object and shows to whom or for whom something is done. In "I gave John a book," John is the indirect object and book is the direct object.

indirect tax, tax paid by the consumer in the form of higher prices for the taxed goods.

in·dis·cern·i·ble (in'di·zėr'nə·bəl; -sėr'-), adj. imperceptible. —in'dis·cern'i·ble·ness, n. —in'dis·cern'i·bly, adv.

in·dis·creet (in'dis·krēt'), adj. not discreet; not wise and judicious; imprudent. —in'dis·creet'ly, adv. —in'dis·creet'ness, n. —Syn. unwise, foolish, rash.

in·dis·cre·tion (in'dis·kresh'ən), n. 1. lack of good judgment. 2. an indiscreet act.

in·dis·crim·i·nate (in'dis·krim'ə·nit), adj. 1. with no feeling for differences: an indiscriminate reader. 2. confused: an indiscriminate mass. —in'dis·crim'i·nate·ly, adv. —in'dis·crim'i·nate·ness, n.

in·dis·pen·sa·ble (in'dis·pen'sə·bəl), adj. absolutely necessary: air is indispensable to life. —n. an indispensable person or thing. —in'dis·pen'sa·bil'i·ty, in'dis·pen'sa·ble·ness, n. —in'dis·pen'sa·bly, adv.

in·dis·pose (in'dis·pōz'), v., -posed, -pos·ing. 1. make unwilling; make averse. 2. make slightly ill. 3. make unfit or unable.

in·dis·posed (in'dis·pōzd'), adj. 1. slightly ill. 2. unwilling; without inclination; averse. —Syn. 1. sick. 2. disinclined.

in·dis·po·si·tion (in'dis·pə·zish'ən), n. 1. disturbance of health; slight illness. 2. unwillingness; disinclination; aversion.

in·dis·put·a·ble (in'dis·pūt'ə·bəl; in·dis'pyə·tə-), adj. not to be disputed; undoubtedly true; unquestionable. —in'dis·put'a·bil'i·ty, in'dis·put'a·ble·ness, n. —in'dis·put'a·bly, adv. —Syn. undeniable, certain, positive.

in·dis·sol·u·ble (in'di·sol'yə·bəl), adj. not capable of being dissolved, undone, or destroyed; lasting; firm. —in'dis·sol'u·bil'i·ty, in'dis·sol'u·ble·ness, n. —in'dis·sol'u·bly, adv.

in·dis·tinct (in'dis·tingkt'), adj. not distinct; not clear to the eye, ear, or mind. —in'dis·tinct'ly, adv. —in'dis·tinct'ness, n. —Syn. undefined, confused, vague, obscure.

in·dis·tin·guish·a·ble (in'dis·ting'gwish·ə·bəl), adj. that cannot be distinguished. —in'dis·tin'guish·a·ble·ness, n. —in'dis·tin'guish·a·bly, adv.

in·dite (in·dīt'), v., -dit·ed, -dit·ing. put in words or writing; compose, as a letter, poem, etc. [< OF enditer < L in- in + dictare DICTATE, express in writing] —in·dite'ment, n. —in·dit'er, n.

in·di·um (in'di·əm), n. Chem. a metallic element, In, that is soft, white, malleable, and easily fusible. [< NL, < L indicum INDIGO]

in·di·vid·u·al (in'də·vij'ů·əl), n. 1. person. 2. one person, animal, or thing. —adj. 1. single; particular; separate: an individual question. 2. for one person only: individual saltcellars. 3. pertaining or peculiar to one person or thing: individual tastes. 4. marking off one person or thing specially: an individual style. [< Med.L, ult. < L in- not + dividuus divisible] ➤ See person for usage note.

in·di·vid·u·al·ism (in'də·vij'ů·əl·iz'əm), n. 1. theory that individual freedom is as important as the welfare of the community or group as a whole. 2. any ethical, economic, or political theory that emphasizes the importance of individuals. 3. each for himself; selfishness. 4. individuality.

in·di·vid·u·al·ist (in'də·vij'ů·əl·ist), n. 1. one who lives his own life for himself and does not try to coöperate with others. 2. supporter of individualism. —in'di·vid'u·al·is'tic, adj.

in·di·vid·u·al·i·ty (in'də·vij'ů·al'ə·ti), n., pl. -ties. 1. individual character; sum of the qualities that make a person himself, not someone else. 2. state of being individual; existence as an individual. 3. an individual person or thing.

in·di·vid·u·al·ize (in'də·vij'ů·əl·īz), v., -ized, -iz·ing. 1. make individual; give a distinctive character to. 2. consider as individuals; list one by one; specify. —in'di·vid'u·al·i·za'tion, n. —in'di·vid'u·al·iz'er, n.

in·di·vid·u·al·ly (in'də·vij'ů·əl·i), adv. 1. personally; one at a time; as individuals: the teacher helps us individually. 2. each from the other: people differ individually.

in·di·vis·i·ble (in'də·viz'ə·bəl), adj. 1. not capable of being divided. 2. not capable of being divided without a remainder. —in'di·vis'i·bil'i·ty, in'di·vis'i·ble·ness, n. —in'di·vis'i·bly, adv.

In·do-Chi·na (in'dō·chī'nə), n. 1. the southeastern peninsula of Asia, comprising part of Burma, Siam, the Malay Peninsula, and the area which formerly constituted French Indo-China. 2. countries in the E part of this peninsula; Laos, Cambodia, and Viet Nam.

In·do-Chi·nese (in'dō-chī-nēz'; -nēs'), *adj.* 1. of or having to do with Indo-China, the Mongoloid peoples living there, or their languages. 2. of or having to do with the family of languages comprising these languages and the Tibetan and Chinese groups of languages.

Indo-China (def. 1)

in·doc·tri·nate (in-dok'trə-nāt), *v.*, **-nat·ed**, **-nat·ing**. 1. teach a doctrine, belief, or principle to. 2. inculcate. [prob. < Med.L, < *in-* in + *doctrinare* teach < L *doctrina* DOCTRINE] **—in·doc'tri·na'tion,** *n.* **—in·doc'tri·na'tor,** *n.*

In·do-Eu·ro·pe·an (in'dō-yur'ə-pē'ən), *adj.* 1. of India and Europe. 2. of or having to do with a group of related languages spoken in India, western Asia, and Europe. English, German, Latin, Greek, Persian, and Sanskrit are some of the Indo-European languages. **—n.** this group of languages.

In·do-Ger·man·ic (in'dō-jėr-man'ik), *adj.* Indo-European.

in·do·lence (in'də-ləns), *n.* laziness; dislike of work; idleness.

in·do·lent (in'də-lənt), *adj.* lazy; disliking work. [< LL, < *in-* not + *dolere* be in pain] **—in'do·lent·ly,** *adv.* **—Syn.** idle, slothful, sluggish.

in·dom·i·ta·ble (in-dom'ə-tə-bəl), *adj.* unconquerable; unyielding. [< LL *indomitabilis*, ult. < L *in-* not + *domare* tame] **—in·dom'i·ta·ble·ness,** *n.* **—in·dom'i·ta·bly,** *adv.*

In·do·ne·sia (in'dō-nē'shə; -zhə), *n.* 1. Republic of, an autonomous republic in the Malay Archipelago, including Java, Sumatra, Madura, Borneo, Celebes, Bali, and other islands. It formerly belonged to the Netherlands, and was technically a member of the Netherlands Union from 1949 to 1954. 2. Malay Archipelago. **—In'do·ne'sian,** *adj., n.*

in·door (in'dôr'; -dōr'), *adj.* done, used, etc., in a house or building: *indoor tennis.*

in·doors (in'dôrz'; -dōrz'), *adv.* in or into a house or building.

in·dorse (in-dôrs'), *v.*, **-dorsed**, **-dors·ing.** endorse. **—in·dors'a·ble,** *adj.* **—in·dor·see',** *n.* **—in·dorse'ment,** *n.* **—in·dors'er,** *n.* **in·dor'sor,** *n.*

in·du·bi·ta·ble (in-dū'bə-tə-bəl; -dū'-), *adj.* not to be doubted; certain. **—in·du'bi·ta·ble·ness,** *n.* **—in·du'bi·ta·bly,** *adv.*

in·duce (in-dūs'; -dūs'), *v.*, **-duced**, **-duc·ing.** 1. lead on; influence; persuade: *advertising induces people to buy.* 2. cause; bring about: *some drugs induce sleep.* 3. produce (an electric current, electric charge, or magnetic change) without contact. 4. infer by reasoning from particular facts to a general rule or principle. [< L, < *in-* in + *ducere* lead] **—in·duc'er,** *n.* **—in·duc'i·ble,** *adj.* **—Syn.** 1. incite, impel.

in·duce·ment (in-dūs'mənt; -dūs'-), *n.* something that influences or persuades; incentive.

in·duct (in-dukt'), *v.* 1. bring in; introduce (into a place, seat, position, office, benefice, etc.). 2. put formally in possession of (an office, etc.): *Mr. Gage was inducted into the office of governor.* 3. *U.S.* enroll in military service: *I expect to be inducted next month.* 4. initiate. [< L *inductus*, pp. of *inducere.* See INDUCE.]

in·duct·ance (in-dukt'əns), *adj.* property of an electrical conductor or circuit that makes induction possible.

in·duc·tee (in-duk'tē), *n.* 1. person who is soon to be inducted. 2. person who is inducted, esp. one who is inducted into military service.

in·duc·tile (in-duk'təl), *adj.* not ductile. **—in'·duc·til'i·ty,** *n.*

in·duc·tion (in-duk'shən), *n.* 1. process by which an object having electrical or magnetic properties produces similar properties in a nearby object, usually without direct contact. 2. reasoning from particular facts to a general rule or principle. 3. conclusion reached in this way. 4. act of inducting; act or ceremony of installing a person in office.

induction coil, *Elect.* device in which an interrupted direct current in one coil produces an alternating current in a surrounding coil.

Magnetic induction

in·duc·tive (in-duk'tiv), *adj.* 1. of or using induction; reasoning by induction. 2. having to do with electrical or magnetic induction. **—in·duc'tive·ly,** *adv.* **—in·duc'tive·ness,** *n.*

in·duc·tiv·i·ty (in'duk-tiv'ə-ti), *n., pl.* **-ties.** *Elect.* inductive property; capacity for induction.

in·duc·tor (in-duk'tər), *n.* part of an electrical apparatus that works or is worked by induction.

in·due (in-dū'; -dū'), *v.*, **-dued**, **-du·ing.** endue.

in·dulge (in-dulj'), *v.*, **-dulged**, **-dulg·ing.** 1. yield to the wishes of; humor: *indulge a sick person.* 2. give way to: *indulge our desires.* 3. give way to one's pleasures; give oneself up to; allow oneself something desired: *indulge in tobacco.* [< L *indulgere*] **—in·dulg'er,** *n.* **—in·dulg'ing·ly,** *adv.* **—Syn.** 1. gratify, satisfy, pamper.

in·dul·gence (in-dul'jəns), *n.* 1. an indulging: *indulgence in rich food.* 2. thing indulged in. 3. favor; privilege. 4. in the Roman Catholic Church, remission of the punishment still due to sin after the guilt has been forgiven.

in·dul·gent (in-dul'jənt), *adj.* indulging; kind; almost too kind: *the indulgent mother bought her boy everything he wanted.* **—in·dul'gent·ly,** *adv.*

in·du·rate (v. in'dù-rāt, -dyù-; *adj.* in'dù·rit, -dyù-), *v.*, **-rat·ed**, **-rat·ing**, *adj.* **-v.** 1. harden. 2. make or become unfeeling. **—adj.** hardened; unfeeling. [< L, < *in-* + *durus* hard] **—in'du·ra'tion,** *n.* **—in'du·ra'tive,** *adj.*

In·dus (in'dəs), *n.* river flowing from NW India through Pakistan into the Arabian Sea.

in·dus·tri·al (in-dus'tri-əl), *adj.* 1. of or resulting from industry or productive labor. 2. having to do with or connected with the industries, trades, or manufactures: *industrial workers.* 3. manufacturing rather than agricultural or commercial: *an industrial community.* 4. of or having to do with the workers in industries: *industrial insurance.* **—in·dus'tri·al·ly,** *adv.*

in·dus·tri·al·ism (in-dus'tri-əl-iz'əm), *n.* system of social and economic organization in which large industries are very important and industrial activities or interests prevail.

in·dus·tri·al·ist (in-dus'tri-əl-ist), *n.* person who conducts or owns an industrial enterprise.

in·dus·tri·al·i·za·tion (in-dus'tri-əl-ə-zā'-shən), *n.* development of large industries as an important feature in a country or a social or economic system.

in·dus·tri·al·ize (in-dus'tri-əl-īz), *v.*, **-ized**, **-iz·ing.** 1. make industrial. 2. organize as an industry.

in·dus·tri·ous (in-dus'tri-əs), *adj.* hardworking. **—in·dus'tri·ous·ly,** *adv.* **—in·dus'tri·ous·ness,** *n.* **—Syn.** diligent, busy.

in·dus·try (in'dəs-tri), *n., pl.* **-tries.** 1. systematic work or labor. 2. steady effort. 3. any branch of business, trade, or manufacture: *the automobile industry.* 4. management and ownership of factories, mills, etc. [< L *industria*] **—Syn.** 2. diligence.

in·dwell (in-dwel'), *v.*, **-dwelt**, **-dwell·ing.** dwell in; dwelling within. **—in'dwell'er,** *n.*

-ine[1], *suffix.* of; like; like that of; characteristic

of; having the nature of; being, as in *crystalline,* *elephantine.* [< L *-inus*]

-ine², *suffix.* used esp. in the names of chemicals, as in *chlorine, aniline.* [< F < L *-ina*]

in·e·bri·ate (v. in·ē′bri·āt; n., adj. in·ē′bri·it), v., **-at·ed, -at·ing,** n., adj. —v. **1.** make drunk; intoxicate. **2.** intoxicate mentally; excite. —n. habitual drunkard; intoxicated person. —adj. intoxicated; drunk. [< L, < *in-* + *ebrius* drunk] —in·e′bri·a′tion, n.

in·e·bri·e·ty (in′i·brī′ə·ti), n. drunkenness.

in·ed·i·ble (in·ed′ə·bəl), adj. not fit to eat. —in·ed′i·bil′i·ty, n.

in·ef·fa·ble (in·ef′ə·bəl), adj. **1.** not to be expressed in words; too great to be described in words. **2.** that must not be spoken. [< L *ineffabilis,* ult. < *in-* not + *fari* speak] —in·ef′fa·bil′i·ty, in·ef′fa·ble·ness, n. —in·ef′fa·bly, adv.

in·ef·face·a·ble (in′ə·fās′ə·bəl), adj. that cannot be rubbed out or wiped out. —in′ef·face′a·bil′i·ty, n. —in′ef·face′a·bly, adv.

in·ef·fec·tive (in′ə·fek′tiv), adj. **1.** not effective; of little use. **2.** unfit for work; incapable. —in′ef·fec′tive·ly, adv. —in′ef·fec′tive·ness, n.

in·ef·fec·tu·al (in′ə·fek′chü·əl), adj. **1.** without effect; useless. **2.** not able to produce the effect wanted. —in′ef·fec′tu·al′i·ty, in′ef·fec′tu·al·ness, n. —in′ef·fec′tu·al·ly, adv. —Syn. **1.** ineffective, futile, vain.

in·ef·fi·ca·cious (in′ef·ə·kā′shəs), adj. not efficacious; not able to produce the effect wanted. —in′ef·fi·ca′cious·ly, adv. —in′ef·fi·ca′cious·ness, in·ef·fi·cac·i·ty (in′ef·ə·kas′ə·ti), n.

in·ef·fi·ca·cy (in·ef′ə·kə·si), n. lack of efficacy; inability to produce the effect wanted.

in·ef·fi·cien·cy (in′ə·fish′ən·si), n. lack of efficiency; inability to get things done.

in·ef·fi·cient (in′ə·fish′ənt), adj. **1.** not efficient; not able to produce, accomplish, or effect anything without waste of time, energy, etc. **2.** incapable; not able to get things done. —in′ef·fi′cient·ly, adv. —Syn. **1.** incompetent, ineffective.

in·e·las·tic (in′i·las′tik), adj. not elastic; stiff; inflexible; unyielding.

in·e·las·tic·i·ty (in′i·las·tis′ə·ti), n. lack of elasticity.

in·e·le·gance (in·el′ə·gəns), **in·e·le·gan·cy** (-gən·si), n., pl. **-gances;** **-cies. 1.** lack of elegance; lack of good taste. **2.** something that is not elegant or graceful.

in·e·le·gant (in·el′ə·gənt), adj. not elegant; not in good taste; crude; vulgar. —in·el′e·gant·ly, adv. —Syn. rough, unrefined.

in·e·li·gi·ble (in·el′ə·jə·bəl), adj. not suitable; not qualified. —n. person who is not suitable or not qualified. —in·el′i·gi·bil′i·ty, n. —in·el′i·gi·bly, adv.

in·e·luc·ta·ble (in′i·luk′tə·bəl), adj. that cannot be escaped. [< L *ineluctabilis* < *in-* not + *ex-* out of + *luctari* to struggle] —in′e·luc′ta·bil′i·ty, n. —in′e·luc′ta·bly, adv.

in·ept (in·ept′), adj. **1.** not suitable; out of place. **2.** absurd; foolish. [< L *ineptus* < *in-* not + *aptus* apt] —in·ept′ly, adv. —in·ept′ness, n.

in·ep·ti·tude (in·ep′tə·tüd; -tūd), n. **1.** unfitness; foolishness. **2.** a silly or inappropriate act or remark.

in·e·qual·i·ty (in′i·kwol′ə·ti), n., pl. **-ties. 1.** lack of equality; a being unequal in amount, size, value, rank, etc. **2.** lack of evenness, regularity, or uniformity. **3.** *Math.* expression showing that two quantities are unequal, like $a > b$ or $c < d$. —Syn. **1.** disparity. **2.** unevenness, variableness.

in·eq·ui·ta·ble (in·ek′wə·tə·bəl), adj. unfair; unjust. —in·eq′ui·ta·bly, adv.

in·eq·ui·ty (in·ek′wə·ti), n., pl. **-ties.** unfairness; injustice.

in·e·rad·i·ca·ble (in′i·rad′ə·kə·bəl), adj. that cannot be rooted out or got rid of. —in′e·rad′i·ca·ble·ness, n. —in′e·rad′i·ca·bly, adv.

in·ert (in·ėrt′), adj. **1.** having no power to move or act; lifeless. **2.** inactive; slow; sluggish. **3.** with few or no active properties. Helium and neon are inert gases. [< L *iners* idle, unskilled < *in-* without + *ars* art, skill] —in·ert′ly, adv. —in·ert′ness, n.

in·er·tia (in·ėr′shə), n. **1.** tendency to remain in the state one is in and not start changes. **2.** *Physics.* **a.** tendency of all objects and matter in the universe to stay still if still, or if moving, to go on moving in the same direction unless acted on by some outside force. **b.** a like property of other physical quantities. [< L, < *iners* INERT] —in·er′tial, adj.

in·es·cap·a·ble (in′əs·kāp′ə·bəl), adj. that cannot be escaped or avoided.

in·es·ti·ma·ble (in·es′tə·mə·bəl), adj. too good, great, valuable, etc., to be measured or estimated. —in·es′ti·ma·bly, adv. —Syn. invaluable, priceless.

in·ev·i·ta·ble (in·ev′ə·tə·bəl), adj. not avoidable; sure to happen; certain to come. —n. that which is inevitable. —in·ev′i·ta·bil′i·ty, in·ev′i·ta·ble·ness, n. —in·ev′i·ta·bly, adv.

in·ex·act (in′ig·zakt′), adj. not exact; not accurate. —in′ex·act′ly, adv. —in′ex·act′ness, n.

in·ex·cus·a·ble (in′iks·kūz′ə·bəl), adj. that ought not to be excused; that cannot be justified. —in′ex·cus′a·bil′i·ty, in′ex·cus′a·ble·ness, n. —in′ex·cus′a·bly, adv. —Syn. unpardonable, unjustifiable.

in·ex·haust·i·ble (in′ig·zôs′tə·bəl), adj. **1.** that cannot be exhausted; very abundant. **2.** tireless. —in′ex·haust′i·bil′i·ty, in′ex·haust′i·ble·ness, n. —in′ex·haust′i·bly, adv.

in·ex·o·ra·ble (in·ek′sər·ə·bəl), adj. relentless; unyielding; not influenced by prayers or entreaties. [< L, < *in-* not + *ex-* successfully + *orare* entreat] —in′ex·o·ra·bil′i·ty, in·ex′o·ra·ble·ness, n. —in·ex′o·ra·bly, adv. —Syn. unrelenting, implacable, immovable.

in·ex·pe·di·en·cy (in′iks·pē′di·ən·si), n. lack of expediency; being inexpedient.

in·ex·pe·di·ent (in′iks·pē′di·ənt), adj. not expedient; not practicable, suitable, or wise —in′ex·pe′di·ent·ly, adv. —Syn. inadvisable, unwise, unprofitable.

in·ex·pen·sive (in′iks·pen′siv), adj. not expensive; cheap; low-priced. —in′ex·pen′sive·ly, adv. —in′ex·pen′sive·ness, n.

in·ex·pe·ri·ence (in′iks·pir′i·əns), n. lack of experience; lack of practice; lack of skill or wisdom gained from experience. —in′ex·pe′ri·enced, adj.

in·ex·pert (in·eks′pėrt; in′iks·pėrt′), adj. unskilled. —in·ex·pert′ly, adv. —in·ex·pert′ness, n.

in·ex·pi·a·ble (in·eks′pi·ə·bəl), adj. that cannot be atoned for: *murder is an inexpiable crime.* —in·ex′pi·a·ble·ness, n. —in·ex′pi·a·bly, adv.

in·ex·pli·ca·ble (in·eks′pli·kə·bəl; in′iks·plik′ə·bəl), adj. impossible to explain or understand; mysterious. —in·ex′pli·ca·bil′i·ty, in·ex′pli·ca·ble·ness, n. —in·ex′pli·ca·bly, adv. —Syn. unaccountable.

in·ex·press·i·ble (in′iks·pres′ə·bəl), adj. that cannot be expressed; beyond expression. —in′ex·press′i·bil′i·ty, in′ex·press′i·ble·ness, n. —in′ex·press′i·bly, adv. —Syn. unutterable.

in·ex·pres·sive (in′iks·pres′iv), adj. not expressive; lacking in expression. —in′ex·pres′sive·ly, adv. —in′ex·pres′sive·ness, n.

in·ex·tin·guish·a·ble (in′iks·ting′gwish·ə·bəl), adj. that cannot be put out or stopped. —in′ex·tin′guish·a·bly, adv.

in ex·tre·mis (in iks·trē′mis), at the point of death. [< L, lit., amid the final things]

in·ex·tri·ca·ble (in·eks′tri·kə·bəl), adj. **1.** that one cannot get out of. **2.** that cannot be disentangled or solved. —in·ex′tri·ca·bil′i·ty, in·ex′tri·ca·ble·ness, n. —in·ex′tri·ca·bly, adv.

inf., **1.** Also, **Inf.** infantry. **2.** infinitive. **3.** information. **4.** infra (below).

in·fal·li·bil·i·ty (in·fal′ə·bil′ə·ti), n. absolute freedom from error.

in·fal·li·ble (in·fal′ə·bəl), adj. **1.** free from error; that cannot be mistaken. **2.** absolutely reliable; sure. **3.** in the Roman Catholic Church, incapable of error in explaining matters pertaining to faith or morals. —in·fal′li·ble·ness, n. —in·fal′li·bly, adv.

in·fa·mous (in'fə·məs), *adj.* **1.** shamefully bad; extremely wicked. **2.** having a very bad reputation; in public disgrace. —in'fa·mous·ly, *adv.* —in'fa·mous·ness, *n.* —Syn. 1. odious. 2. notorious, disreputable.

in·fa·my (in'fə·mi), *n., pl.* -mies. 1. very bad reputation; public disgrace. 2. shameful badness; extreme wickedness. [< L, < *in-* without + *fama* (good) reputation]

in·fan·cy (in'fən·si), *n., pl.* -cies. 1. condition or time of being an infant; babyhood. 2. early stage; beginning of development. 3. condition of being under legal age of responsibility (in common law, under 21).

in·fant (in'fənt), *n.* 1. baby; very young child. 2. person under the legal age of responsibility; a minor. 3. beginner. —*adj.* 1. of or for an infant. 2. in an early stage; just beginning to develop. [< L *infans*, orig., not speaking < *in-* not + *fari* speak] —in'fant·hood, *n.*

in·fan·ta (in·fan'tə), *n.* royal princess of Spain or Portugal. [< Sp., Pg., fem.]

in·fan·te (in·fan'tā), *n.* royal prince of Spain or Portugal, but not the heir to the throne. [< Sp., Pg.]

in·fan·ti·cide (in·fan'tə·sīd), *n.* the killing of a baby. [< L, < *infans* INFANT + *-cidium* act of killing < *caedere* kill] —in'fan'ti·cid'al, *adj.*

in·fan·tile (in'fən·tīl; -til), *adj.* 1. of an infant or infants; having to do with infants. 2. like an infant; babyish; childish. 3. in an early stage; just beginning to develop.

infantile paralysis, an acute infectious disease that destroys tissue in the brain and spinal cord, causing fever, paralysis of various muscles, and often death; poliomyelitis.

in·fan·ti·lism (in·fan'tə·liz·əm), *n.* abnormal persistence or appearance of childish traits in adults.

in·fan·tine (in'fən·tīn; -tin), *adj.* infantile; babyish; childish.

in·fan·try (in'fən·tri), *n., pl.* -tries. soldiers who fight on foot. [< F < Ital., < *infante, fante* foot soldier, orig., a youth. See INFANT.]

in·fan·try·man (in'fən·tri·mən), *n., pl.* -men. soldier who fights on foot.

in·fat·u·ate (*v.* in·fach'ū·āt; *adj., n.* in·fach'ū·it, -āt), *v.,* -at·ed, -at·ing, *adj.* —*v.* 1. make foolish. 2. inspire with a foolish or extreme passion. —*adj.* infatuated. —*n.* an infatuated person. [< L, < *in-* + *fatuus* foolish]

in·fat·u·at·ed (in·fach'ū·āt'id), *adj.* extremely adoring; foolishly in love. —in·fat'u·at'ed·ly, *adv.*

in·fat·u·a·tion (in·fach'ū·ā'shən), *n.* 1. an infatuating or being infatuated. 2. foolish love; unreasoning fondness.

in·fect (in·fekt'), *v.* 1. cause disease in by introducing germs: *dirt infects an open cut.* 2. influence in a bad way; contaminate: *one bad companion can infect a whole group of boys.* 3. influence by spreading from one to another: *the captain's courage infected his soldiers.* [< L *infectus* dyed, orig., put in < *in-* in + *facere* make] —in·fec'tor, *n.* —Syn. pollute.

in·fec·tion (in·fek'shən), *n.* 1. causing of disease in people, animals, and plants by the introduction of germs. 2. disease caused in this way. 3. influence, feeling, or idea spreading from one to another. 4. fact or state of being infected.

in·fec·tious (in·fek'shəs), *adj.* 1. spread by infection: *measles is an infectious disease.* 2. causing infection. 3. apt to spread. —in·fec'tious·ly, *adv.* —in·fec'tious·ness, *n.* —Syn. 3. contagious, catching.

in·fec·tive (in·fek'tiv), *adj.* infectious. —in·fec'tive·ness, *n.*/in·fec·tiv'i·ty, *n.*

in·fe·lic·i·tous (in'fə·lis'ə·təs), *adj.* 1. unsuitable; not appropriate. 2. unfortunate; unhappy. —in·fe·lic'i·tous·ly, *adv.*

in·fe·lic·i·ty (in'fə·lis'ə·ti), *n., pl.* -ties. 1. unsuitability; inappropriateness. 2. misfortune; unhappiness. 3. something unsuitable; inappropriate word, remark, etc.

in·fer (in·fėr'), *v.,* -ferred, -fer·ring. 1. find out by reasoning; conclude: *from the facts*

known we *infer* his innocence. 2. indicate; imply: *ragged clothing infers poverty.* 3. draw inferences. [< L, < *in-* in + *ferre* bring] —in·fer·a·ble (in·fėr'ə·bəl; in'fər-), *adj.* —in·fer'a·bly, *adv.* —in·fer'rer, *n.* —Syn. 1. deduce. ➤ See imply for usage note.

in·fer·ence (in'fər·əns), *n.* 1. process of inferring. 2. that which is inferred; conclusion.

in·fer·en·tial (in'fər·en'shəl), *adj.* having to do with inference; depending on inference. —in'fer·en'tial·ly, *adv.*

in·fe·ri·or (in·fir'i·ər), *adj.* 1. lower in position or rank: *a lieutenant is inferior to a captain.* 2. not so good; lower in quality; worse. 3. below average: *an inferior mind.* 4. inferior to, a. below; lower than. b. not so good or so great as; worse than. —*n.* 1. person who is lower in rank or station. 2. an inferior thing. [< L, compar. of *inferus,* adj., situated below] —in·fe'ri·or·ly, *adv.*

in·fe·ri·or·i·ty (in·fir'i·ôr'ə·ti; -or'-), *n.* inferior condition or quality.

inferiority complex, an abnormal or morbid feeling of being inferior to other people.

in·fer·nal (in·fėr'nəl), *adj.* 1. of hell; having to do with the lower world. 2. hellish; diabolical. 3. *Colloq.* abominable; outrageous. 4. of the lower world which the ancient Greeks and Romans thought was the abode of the dead. [< LL *infernalis,* ult. < L *inferus* below] —in·fer'nal'i·ty, *n.* —in·fer'nal·ly, *adv.*

infernal machine, an explosive apparatus for maliciously destroying life and property.

in·fer·no (in·fėr'nō), *n., pl.* -nos. 1. hell. 2. a hell-like place or thing. [< Ital.]

in·fer·tile (in·fėr'təl), *adj.* not fertile; sterile. —in·fer·til·i·ty (in'fėr·til'ə·ti), *n.*

in·fest (in·fest'), *v.* trouble or disturb frequently or in large numbers: *mosquitoes infest swamps.* [< L, attack, < *infestus* hostile] —in'fes·ta'tion, *n.* —in·fest'er, *n.* —Syn. overrun.

in·fi·del (in'fə·dəl), *n.* 1. person who does not believe in religion. 2. person who does not accept a particular faith: *Mohammedans call Christians infidels.* 3. person who does not accept Christianity. —*adj.* 1. not believing in religion. 2. not accepting a particular faith, esp. Christianity or Mohammedanism. [< L, < *in-* not + *fides* faith]

in·fi·del·i·ty (in'fə·del'ə·ti), *n., pl.* -ties. 1. lack of religious faith. 2. unbelief in Christianity. 3. unfaithfulness, esp. of husband or wife; disloyalty. 4. an unfaithful or disloyal act.

in·field (in'fēld'), *n. Am.* 1. a baseball diamond. 2. first, second, and third basemen and shortstop of a baseball team.

in·field·er (in'fēl'dər), *n. Am., Baseball.* an infield player.

in·fil·trate (in·fil'trāt), *v.,* -trat·ed, -trat·ing, *n.* —*v.* 1. pass into or through by, or as by, filtering: *enemy troops infiltrated the front lines.* 2. filter into or through; permeate. —*n.* that which infiltrates. —in'fil·tra'tion, *n.* —in·fil'tra·tive, *adj.*

infin., infinitive.

in·fi·nite (in'fə·nit), *adj.* 1. without limits or bounds; endless: *the infinite power of God.* 2. extremely great. —*n.* 1. that which is infinite. 2. the Infinite, God. [< L, < *in-* not + *finis* boundary] —in'fi·nite·ly, *adv.* —in'fi·nite·ness, *n.* —Syn. *adj.* 1. boundless, unlimited. 2. immeasurable, immense.

in·fin·i·tes·i·mal (in'fin·ə·tes'ə·məl), *adj.* so small as to be almost nothing. —*n.* an infinitesimal amount. [< NL *infinitesimus* the "nth" < L *infinitus* INFINITE] —in'fin·i·tes'i·mal·ly, *adv.*

in·fin·i·tive (in·fin'ə·tiv), *n. Gram.* a form of a verb not limited by person and number. *Examples:* Let him *go.* We want to *go* now. [< LL, < *infinitus* unrestricted, INFINITE] —in·fin'i·tive·ly, *adv.* ➤ **to and the infinitive.** *To* is the "sign of the infinitive" when the infinitive is used as a noun (Just *to hear* him talk is an inspiration) and usually when it is used to complete the meaning of a verb (They all tried to *get* in first). After some verbs (*can, may, shall,*

āge, cãre, fär; ēqual, tėrm; īce; ōpen, ôrder; pùt, rüle, ūse; tɧ, then; ə=a in about.

will, do, dare, make, help, need, . . .) no *to* is used (Do not make him *stop*). In short, clear, unemphatic series of infinitives in parallel constructions, the *to* is not repeated (*To sit* and *smoke* and *think* and *dream* was his idea of pleasure). The infinitive may be used as a subject (*To err* is human), object (he wanted *to go* fishing), adjective modifier (money *to burn*), adverbial modifier (They came *to play*), and with auxiliaries (He will *pass* this time). See also usage note under split infinitive.

in·fin·i·tude (in·fin′ə·tūd; -tūd), *n.* 1. a being infinite. 2. an infinite extent, amount, or number. 3. infinity.

in·fin·i·ty (in·fin′ə·ti), *n., pl.* -ties. 1. state of being infinite. 2. an infinite distance, space, time, or quantity. 3. an infinite extent, amount, or number.

in·firm (in·fêrm′), *adj.* 1. weak; feeble. 2. weak in will or character; not steadfast. 3. not firm; not stable. —in·firm′ly, *adv.* —in·firm′ness, *n.* —Syn. 1. shaky, decrepit.

in·fir·ma·ry (in·fêr′mə·ri), *n., pl.* -ries. 1. place for the care of the infirm, sick, or injured; hospital in a school or institution. 2. a hospital.

in·fir·mi·ty (in·fêr′mə·ti), *n., pl.* -ties. 1. weakness; feebleness. 2. sickness; illness. 3. moral weakness or failing.

in·fix (v. in·fiks′; n. in′fiks), *v.* 1. fix in; drive in. 2. fix in the mind or memory; impress. 3. *Gram.* insert an infix. —*n. Gram.* a formative element inserted within the body of a word.

infl., influenced.

in·flame (in·flām′), *v.,* -flamed, -flam·ing. 1. excite; make more violent. 2. become excited with intense feeling. 3. make unnaturally hot, red, sore, or swollen. 4. become red or hot from disease, etc. 5. set ablaze; set on fire. [< OF *enflamer* < L, ult. < *in-* in + *flamma* flame] —in·flam′er, *n.* —in·flam′ma·bly, *adv.* —Syn. 1. arouse, fire. 5. kindle.

in·flam·ma·ble (in·flam′ə·bəl), *adj.* 1. easily set on fire. 2. easily excited or aroused. —*n.* something inflammable. —in·flam′ma·bil′i·ty, in·flam′ma·ble·ness, *n.* —in·flam′ma·bly, *adv.*

in·flam·ma·tion (in′flə·mā′shən), *n.* 1. a diseased condition of some part of the body, marked by heat, redness, swelling, and pain. 2. an inflaming or being inflamed.

in·flam·ma·to·ry (in·flam′ə·tô′ri; -tō′-), *adj.* 1. tending to excite or arouse. 2. of, causing, or accompanied by inflammation.

in·flate (in·flāt′), *v.,* -flat·ed, -flat·ing. 1. blow out or swell with air or gas: *inflate a balloon.* 2. swell or puff out: *inflate with pride.* 3. increase (prices or currency) beyond the normal amount. [< L, < *in-* into + *flare* blow] —in·flat′a·ble, *adj.* —in·flat′er, *n.* —in·flat′or, *n.* —Syn. 1. distend, expand.

in·fla·tion (in·flā′shən), *n.* 1. a swelling (with air, gas, pride, etc.). 2. swollen state; too great expansion. 3. increase of the currency of a country by issuing much paper money. 4. a sharp and sudden rise of prices resulting from a too great expansion in paper money or bank credit.

in·fla·tion·ar·y (in·flā′shən·er′i), *adj.* of or having to do with inflation; tending to inflate.

in·fla·tion·ist (in·flā′shən·ist), *n. Am.* person who favors inflation.

in·flect (in·flekt′), *v.* 1. change the tone or pitch of (the voice). 2. *Gram.* vary the form of (a word) to show case, number, gender, person, tense, mood, comparison, etc. 3. bend; curve. [< L, < *in-* in + *flectere* bend] —in·flec′tive, *adj.* —in·flec′tor, *n.*

in·flec·tion, *esp. Brit.* **in·flex·ion** (in·flek′shən), *n.* 1. change in the tone or pitch of the voice. We usually end questions with a rising inflection. 2. *Gram.* variation in the form of a word to show case, number, gender, person, tense, mood, comparison, etc. 3. bend; curve. —in·flec′tion·al·ly, *esp. Brit.* in·flex′ion·al·ly, *adv.* —Syn. 1. modulation, intonation, accent.

in·flec·tion·al, *esp. Brit.* **in·flex·ion·al** (in·flek′shən·əl), *adj.* of, pertaining to, or exhibiting grammatical inflection.

in·flex·i·ble (in·flek′sə·bəl), *adj.* 1. firm; un-

yielding; steadfast. 2. that cannot be changed; unalterable. 3. not easily bent; stiff; rigid. —in·flex′i·bil′i·ty, in·flex′i·ble·ness, *n.* —in·flex′i·bly, *adv.* —Syn. 1. dogged, stubborn, obstinate. 3. unbending, firm.

in·flict (in·flikt′), *v.* 1. give or cause, as a blow, wound, pain, etc. 2. impose, as a burden, suffering, anything unwelcome, etc. [< L *inflictus* < *in-* on + *fligere* dash] —in·flict′er, in·flic′tor, *n.* —in·flic′tive, *adj.*

in·flic·tion (in·flik′shən), *n.* 1. act of inflicting. 2. something inflicted; pain; suffering; burden; punishment.

in·flo·res·cence (in′flô·res′əns; -flō-), *n.* 1. flowering stage. 2. *Bot.* a. arrangement of flowers on the stem or axis. b. a flower cluster. c. flowers collectively. [< NL *inflorescentia* < L *in-* in + *flos* flower] —in′flo·res′cent, *adj.*

in·flow (in′flō′), *n.* 1. a flowing in or into. 2. that which flows in.

in·flu·ence (in′flū·əns), *n., v.,* -enced, -enc·ing. —*n.* 1. power of persons or things to act on others. 2. power to produce an effect without using coercion: *a person may have influence by his ability, personality, position, or wealth.* 3. person or thing that has such power. —*v.* have power over; change the nature or behavior of: *the moon influences the tides.* [< Med.L *influentia,* orig., a flowing in, ult. < L *in-* in + *fluere* to flow] —in′flu·enc·er, *n.* —Syn. *v.* move, stir, sway, persuade.

in·flu·en·tial (in′flū·en′shəl), *adj.* 1. having much influence; having influence. 2. using influence; producing results. —in′flu·en′tial·ly, *adv.*

in·flu·en·za (in′flū·en′zə), *n.* an acute contagious disease, like a very bad cold in its symptoms, but much more dangerous and exhausting; flu. [< Ital., INFLUENCE] —in′flu·en′zal, *adj.*

in·flux (in′fluks), *n.* 1. a flowing in; steady flow. 2. the mouth of a stream. [< LL *influxus,* ult. < L *in-* in + *fluere* flow]

in·fold (in·fōld′), *v.* 1. fold in; wrap up: *infolded in a shawl.* 2. embrace; clasp. Also, enfold. —in·fold′er, *n.* —in·fold′ment, *n.*

in·form (in·fôrm′), *v.* 1. supply with knowledge, facts, or news; tell. 2. instruct; train. 3. make an accusation or complaint: *one thief informed against the others.* 4. animate. [< L, < *in-* + *forma* form] —in·form′ing·ly, *adv.* —Syn. 1. notify, acquaint.

in·for·mal (in·fôr′məl), *adj.* 1. not in the regular or prescribed manner. 2. done without ceremony. 3. used in everyday, common talk, but not used in formal talking or writing. —in·for′mal·ly, *adv.* —Syn. 2. unconventional, easy.

▷ Informal English is the typical language of an educated person going about his everyday affairs. It lies between the uncultivated level on one side and the more restricted formal level on the other. It is used not only for personal affairs, but for most public affairs—of business and politics, for example, except in strictly legal matters—for most newspaper and magazine articles, for the bulk of fiction and drama, for a good deal of poetry. In the last generation or so it has come to dominate English writing, partly in reaction against the more elaborate style of the nineteenth century. It has a long and honorable tradition. Informal usage is characteristic of the pamphleteers and popular storytellers of Elizabethan literature, of the plainer portions of the English Bible, especially of the direct narratives; of the works of such writers as Defoe and Fielding and to a large degree of Swift. Formal English is passed on chiefly through reading and so represents in many respects the usage and style of the preceding generation of writers; informal English lies closer to speech.

in·for·mal·i·ty (in′fôr·mal′ə·ti), *n., pl.* -ties. 1. lack of ceremony. 2. an informal act.

in·form·ant (in·fôr′mənt), *n.* 1. person who gives information to another. 2. person who speaks in his native language or dialect for the benefit of persons studying that language or dialect, or for purposes of transcription.

in·for·ma·tion (in′fər·mā′shən), *n.* 1. knowledge; facts; news: *a dictionary gives informa-*

tion about words. **2.** an informing: *a guidebook is for the information of travelers.* **3.** person or office whose duty it is to answer questions. **4.** accusation or complaint against a person. —**in′for·ma′tion·al,** *adj.*

in·form·a·tive (in·fôr′mə·tiv), *adj.* giving information; instructive.

in·form·er (in·fôr′mər), *n.* **1.** person who makes an accusation or complaint against others: *an informer told the police that the store was selling stolen goods.* **2.** informant.

in·frac·tion (in·frak′shən), *n.* a breaking of a law or obligation; violation. [< L *infractio* < *in-* in + *frangere* to break]

in·fra·red (in′frə·red′), *n.* the invisible part of the spectrum whose rays have wave lengths longer than those of the red part of the visible spectrum. —*adj.* pertaining to the infrared.

in·fre·quen·cy (in·frē′kwən·si), **in·fre·quence** (–kwəns), *n.* a being infrequent; scarcity; rarity.

in·fre·quent (in·frē′kwənt), *adj.* not frequent; occurring seldom or far apart. —**in·fre′quent·ly,** *adv.* —**Syn.** scarce, rare.

in·fringe (in·frinj′), *v.,* **–fringed, –fring·ing. 1.** violate: *infringe the food and drug law.* **2.** trespass; encroach: *infringe upon rights.* [< L, < *in-* in + *frangere* break] —**in·fringe′ment,** *n.* —**in·fring′er,** *n.* —**Syn. 1.** break. **2.** intrude.

in·fu·ri·ate (in·fyūr′i·āt), *v.,* **–at·ed, –at·ing.** put into a fury; make furious; enrage. [< Med. L, < L *in-* into + *furia* fury] —**in·fu·ri·ate·ly** (in·fyūr′i·it·li), *adv.* —**in·fu′ri·at′ing·ly,** *adv.* —**in·fu′ri·a′tion,** *n.*

in·fuse (in·fūz′), *v.,* **–fused, –fus·ing. 1.** introduce as by pouring: *the captain infused his own courage into his soldiers.* **2.** inspire: *infuse with courage.* **3.** steep or soak in a liquid to get something out. [< L *infusus* < *in-* in + *fundere* pour] —**in·fus′er,** *n.*

in·fu·si·ble (in·fū′zə·bəl), *adj.* that cannot be fused or melted. —**in·fu′si·bil′i·ty, in·fu′si·ble·ness,** *n.*

in·fu·sion (in·fū′zhən), *n.* **1.** act or process of infusing. **2.** something poured in or mingled; infused element. **3.** a liquid extract obtained by steeping or soaking.

in·fu·so·ri·an (in′fyū·sô′ri·ən; –sō′–), *n.* one of a group of one-celled animals that move by vibrating filaments.

-ing¹, *suffix.* **1.** action, result, product, material, etc., of some verb, as in *hard thinking, the art of painting.* **2.** action, result, product, material, etc., of some other part of speech, as in *lobstering, offing, shirting.* **3.** of one that ——s; of those that ——, as in *smoking habit, printing trade, drinking song.* [ME *-ing,* OE *-ing, -ung*]

-ing², *suffix.* **1.** element forming the present participle. **2.** that ——s, as in *seeing eye, lasting happiness, growing child.* [ME *-ing, -inge*]

in·gen·ious (in·jēn′yəs), *adj.* **1.** skillful in making; good at inventing. **2.** cleverly planned and made. [< L *ingenium* natural talent] —**in·gen′ious·ly,** *adv.* —**in·gen′ious·ness,** *n.* —**Syn. 1.** clever, inventive, resourceful.

in·gé·nue (an′zhə·nū), *n., pl.* **–nues. 1.** a simple, innocent girl or young woman, esp. as represented on the stage. **2.** actress who plays such a part. [< F, orig. adj., ingenuous]

in·ge·nu·i·ty (in′jə·nū′i·ti; –nū′–), *n., pl.* **–ties.** skill in planning, inventing, etc.; cleverness. [< L *ingenuitas* frankness < *ingenuus* ingenuous; infl. by association with *ingenious*]

in·gen·u·ous (in·jen′yū·əs), *adj.* **1.** frank; open; sincere. **2.** simple; natural; innocent. [< L *ingenuus,* orig., native, free born] —**in·gen′u·ous·ly,** *adv.* —**in·gen′u·ous·ness,** *n.* —**Syn. 1.** candid. **2.** naïve, guileless.

in·gest (in·jest′), *v.* take (food, etc.) into the body for digestion. [< L *ingestus* < *in-* in + *gerere* carry] —**in·ges′tion,** *n.* —**in·ges′tive,** *adj.*

in·gle·nook (ing′gəl·nůk′), *n.* corner by the fire.

in·glo·ri·ous (in·glô′ri·əs; –glō′–), *adj.* **1.** bringing no glory; shameful; disgraceful. **2.**

having no glory; not famous. —**in·glo′ri·ous·ly,** *adv.* —**in·glo′ri·ous·ness,** *n.* —**Syn. 1.** ignoble. **2.** humble, obscure.

in·go·ing (in′gō′ing), *adj.* entering.

in·got (ing′gət), *n.* mass of metal, such as gold, silver, or steel, cast into a convenient shape in a mold. [< OE *in-* in + *goten* poured]

in·graft (in·graft′; –gräft′), *v.* engraft. —**in·graft′ment,** *n.*

in·grained (in·grānd′; in′grānd′), *adj.* **1.** deeply and firmly fixed; thoroughly imbued: *ingrained honesty.* **2.** thorough; inveterate.

in·grate (in′grāt), *n.* an ungrateful person. [< L, < *in-* not + *gratus* thankful]

in·gra·ti·ate (in·grā′shi·āt), *v.,* **–at·ed, –at·ing.** bring (oneself) into favor: *ingratiate oneself by giving presents.* [< *in-²* + L *gratia* favor] —**in·gra′ti·at′ing·ly,** *adv.* —**in·gra′ti·a′tion,** *n.*

in·grat·i·tude (in·grat′ə·tūd; –tūd), *n.* lack of gratitude; being ungrateful.

in·gre·di·ent (in·grē′di·ənt), *n.* one of the parts of a mixture: *the ingredients of a cake.* [< L *ingrediens* entering < *in-* in + *gradi* go] —**Syn.** constituent, component.

In·gres (an′grə), *n.* Jean Auguste Dominique, 1780–1867, French painter.

in·gress (in′gres), *n.* **1.** a going in: *ingress to a field.* **2.** way in; entrance. **3.** right to go in. [< L *ingressus* < *ingredi.* See INGREDIENT.] —**in·gres′sion,** *n.* —**in·gres′sive,** *adj.* —**in·gres′sive·ness,** *n.*

in·grow·ing (in′grō′ing), *adj.* **1.** growing inward. **2.** growing into the flesh.

in·grown (in′grōn′), *adj.* **1.** grown within; grown inward. **2.** grown into the flesh.

in·gui·nal (ing′gwə·nəl), *adj.* of the groin; in or near the groin. [< L, < *inguen* groin]

in·gulf (in·gulf′), *v.* engulf.

in·hab·it (in·hab′it), *v.* live in (a place, region, house, cave, tree, etc.). [< L, < *in-* in + *habitare* dwell < *habere* have, dwell] —**in·hab′it·a·ble,** *adj.* —**in·hab′it·a·bil′i·ty,** *n.* —**in′hab·i·ta′tion,** *n.* —**in·hab′it·er,** *n.*

in·hab·it·ant (in·hab′ə·tənt), *n.* person or animal that lives in a place. —**Syn.** dweller.

in·hal·ant (in·hāl′ənt), *n.* **1.** medicine to be inhaled. **2.** apparatus for inhaling it.

in·hale (in·hāl′), *v.,* **–haled, –hal·ing.** draw into the lungs; breathe in (air, gas, fragrance, tobacco smoke, etc.). [< L, < *in-* in + *halare* breathe] —**in·ha·la·tion** (in′hə·lā′shən), *n.*

in·hal·er (in·hāl′ər), *n.* **1.** apparatus used in inhaling medicine. **2.** person who inhales.

in·har·mon·ic (in′här·mon′ik), **in·har·mon·i·cal** (–ə·kəl), *adj.* not harmonic; not musical.

in·har·mo·ni·ous (in′här·mō′ni·əs), *adj.* discordant; disagreeing. —**in′har·mo′ni·ous·ly,** *adv.* —**in′har·mo′ni·ous·ness,** *n.*

in·here (in·hir′), *v.,* **–hered, –her·ing.** exist; belong to as a quality or attribute: *greed inheres in human nature, power inheres in a ruler.* [< L, < *in-* in + *haerere* to stick]

in·her·ent (in·hir′ənt; –her′–), *adj.* belonging to (a person or thing) as a quality or attribute: *inherent modesty, inherent probability.* —**in·her′ence,** *n.* —**in·her′ent·ly,** *adv.* —**Syn.** intrinsic, existing, abiding.

in·her·it (in·her′it), *v.* **1.** receive as an heir: *the widow inherited the farm.* **2.** get or possess from one's ancestors: *she inherits her father's blue eyes.* [< OF *enheriter,* ult. < L *in-* + *heres* heir] —**in·her′i·tor,** *n.*

in·her·it·a·ble (in·her′ə·tə·bəl), *adj.* **1.** capable of being inherited. **2.** capable of inheriting; qualified to inherit. —**in·her′it·a·bil′i·ty,** **in·her′it·a·ble·ness,** *n.*

in·her·it·ance (in·her′ə·təns), *n.* **1.** act or process of inheriting: *he obtained his house by inheritance from an aunt.* **2.** right of inheriting. **3.** anything inherited: *good health is a fine inheritance.* —**Syn. 3.** heritage, legacy.

inheritance tax, *U.S., Law.* tax on inherited property.

in·hib·it (in·hib′it), *v.* **1.** hinder by obstruction or restriction; restrain: *the soldier's sense of duty inhibited his impulse to run away.* 2. prohibit; forbid. [< L *inhibitus* < *in-* in + *habere* hold] —in·hib'it·a·ble, *adj.* —in·hib'it·er, in·hib'i·tor, *n.* —in·hib'i·tive, *adj.* —Syn. 1. check, repress, stop. 2. interdict.

in·hi·bi·tion (in'i·bish'ən; in'hi-), *n.* 1. an inhibiting or being inhibited. 2. *Psychol.* idea, emotion, habit, or other inner force that restrains natural impulses. —in·hib·i·tive (in·hib'ə·tiv), in·hib·i·to·ry (in·hib'ə·tô'ri; -tō'-), *adj.*

in hoc sig·no vin·ces (in hok sig'nō vin'sēz), *Latin.* in this sign shalt thou conquer.

in·hos·pi·ta·ble (in·hos'pi·tə·bəl; in'hos·pit'ə·bəl), *adj.* 1. not hospitable. 2. providing no shelter; barren: *an inhospitable shore.* —in·hos'pi·ta·ble·ness, *n.* —in·hos'pi·ta·bly, *adv.* —Syn. 2. cheerless, uninviting.

in·hos·pi·tal·i·ty (in·hos'pə·tal'ə·ti), *n.* lack of hospitality; inhospitable behavior.

in·hu·man (in·hū'mən), *adj.* not human; not having the qualities natural to a human being. —in·hu'man·ly, *adv.* —in·hu'man·ness, *n.* —Syn. unfeeling, hardhearted, brutal, cruel, pitiless, merciless.

in·hu·mane (in'hū·mān'), *adj.* lacking in compassion, humanity, or kindness. —in'hu·mane'ly, *adv.* —Syn. cruel, brutal.

in·hu·man·i·ty (in'hū·man'ə·ti), *n., pl.* -ties. 1. inhuman quality; lack of feeling; cruelty; brutality. 2. an inhuman, cruel, or brutal act.

in·im·i·cal (in·im'ə·kəl), *adj.* 1. unfriendly; hostile. 2. adverse; unfavorable; harmful. [< LL, < L *inimicus* < *in-* not + *amicus* friendly] —in·im'i·cal·i·ty, n. —in·im'i·cal·ly, *adv.* —Syn. 1. antagonistic.

in·im·i·ta·ble (in·im'ə·tə·bəl), *adj.* that cannot be imitated or copied; matchless. —in·im'i·ta·bil'i·ty, in·im'i·ta·ble·ness, *n.* —in·im'i·ta·bly, *adv.*

in·iq·ui·tous (in·ik'wə·təs), *adj.* 1. very unjust. 2. wicked. —in·iq'ui·tous·ly, *adv.* —in·iq'ui·tous·ness, *n.*

in·iq·ui·ty (in·ik'wə·ti), *n., pl.* -ties. 1. very great injustice. 2. wickedness. 3. a wicked or unjust act. [< L *iniquitas*, ult. < *in-* not + *aequus* just]

i·ni·tial (i·nish'əl), *adj., n., v.,* -tialed, -tialing; *esp. Brit.* -tialled, -tial·ling. —*adj.* occurring at the beginning; first; earliest. —*n.* the first letter of a word. —*v.* mark or sign with initials. [< L *initialis*, ult. < *inire* begin < *in-* in + *ire* go]

i·ni·tial·ly (i·nish'əl·i), *adv.* at the beginning.

i·ni·ti·ate (*v.* i·nish'i·āt; *n., adj.* i·nish'i·it, -āt), *v.,* -at·ed, -at·ing, *n., adj.* —*v.* 1. be the first one to start; begin. 2. admit (a person) by special forms or ceremonies (into mysteries, secret knowledge, or a society). 3. introduce into the knowledge of some art or subject. —*n.* person who is initiated. —*adj.* initiated. [< L *initiatus*, ult. < *inire* begin. See INITIAL.] —Syn. *v.* 1. commence, originate. 2. install, induct. —i·ni'ti·a'tor, *n.*

i·ni·ti·a·tion (i·nish'i·ā'shən), *n.* 1. an initiating or being initiated. 2. formal admission into a group or society. 3. ceremonies by which one is admitted to a group or society.

initiation fee, *Am.* fee one pays upon being initiated into a society, club, etc.

i·ni·ti·a·tive (i·nish'i·ə·tiv; -i·ā'tiv), *n.* 1. active part in taking the first steps in any undertaking; the lead: *take the initiative in making acquaintances.* 2. readiness and ability to be the one to start a course of action: *a leader must have initiative.* 3. right to be the first to act, legislate, etc. 4. right of citizens outside the legislature to introduce or enact a new law by vote. —*adj.* that initiates; introductory. —i·ni'ti·a·tive·ly, *adv.*

i·ni·ti·a·to·ry (i·nish'i·ə·tô'ri, -tō'-), *adj.* 1. first; beginning; introductory. 2. of initiation. —i·ni'ti·a·to'ri·ly, *adv.*

in·ject (in·jekt'), *v.* 1. force (liquid) into (a passage, cavity, or tissue). 2. throw in: *inject a remark into the conversation.* [< L *injectus* < *in-*

in + *jacere* to throw] —in·jec'tion, *n.* —in·jec'tor, *n.*

in·ju·di·cious (in'ju·dish'əs), *adj.* showing lack of judgment; unwise; not prudent. —in'ju·di'cious·ly, *adv.* —in'ju·di'cious·ness, *n.*

in·junc·tion (in·jungk'shən), *n.* 1. command; order. 2. a formal order issued by a law court ordering a person or group to do, or refrain from doing, something. [< LL *injunctio* < L *injungere* ENJOIN]

in·jure (in'jər), *v.,* -jured, -jur·ing. 1. do damage to; harm; hurt. 2. do wrong to; be unfair to. [< *injury*] —in'jur·er, *n.*

in·ju·ri·ous (in·jûr'i·əs), *adj.* 1. causing injury; harmful. 2. wrongful; unfair; unjust. —in·ju'ri·ous·ly, *adv.* —in·ju'ri·ous·ness, *n.*

in·ju·ry (in'jər·i), *n., pl.* -ju·ries. 1. damage; harm; hurt. 2. wrong; unfairness. [< L *injuria* < *in-* not + *jus* right] —Syn. 2. injustice.

in·jus·tice (in·jus'tis), *n.* 1. lack of justice; being unjust. 2. an unjust act.

ink (ingk), *n.* liquid used for writing or printing. —*v.* put ink on; mark or stain with ink. [< OF *enque* < LL < Gk. *enkauston* < *en* in + *kaiein* burn] —ink'er, *n.* —ink'less, *adj.* —ink'like', *adj.*

ink·horn (ingk'hôrn'), *n.* a small container formerly used to hold ink, often made of horn. —*adj.* bookish; pedantic.

Inkhorn

ink·ling (ingk'ling), *n.* slight suggestion; vague notion; hint. [< OE *inca* doubt]

ink·stand (ingk'stand'), *n.* 1. stand to hold ink and pens. 2. container used to hold ink.

ink·well (ingk'wel'), *n.* container used to hold ink on a desk or table.

ink·y (ingk'i), *adj.,* ink·i·er, ink·i·est. 1. like ink; dark; black. 2. covered with ink; marked or stained with ink. 3. of ink. —ink'i·ness, *n.*

in·laid (in'lād'), *adj.* 1. set in the surface as a decoration or design. 2. decorated with a design or material set in the surface.

in·land (*adj.* in'lənd; *n., adv., also* in'land'), *adj.* 1. away from the coast or the border; situated in the interior: *an inland sea.* 2. domestic; not foreign: *inland trade.* —*n.* interior of a country; land away from the border or the coast. —*adv.* in or toward the interior.

in-law (in'lô'), *n. Colloq.* relative by marriage.

in·lay (in'lā'), *v.,* -laid, -lay·ing, *n.* —*v.* 1. set in the surface as a decoration or design: *inlay strips of gold.* 2. decorate with something set in the surface: *inlay a wooden box with silver.* —*n.* 1. an inlaid decoration, design, or material. 2. a shaped piece of gold, porcelain, etc., cemented in a tooth as a filling. —in'lay'er, *n.*

in·let (in'let), *n.* 1. a narrow strip of water extending from a larger body of water into the land or between islands. 2. entrance.

in lo·co pa·ren·tis (in lō'kō pə·ren'tis), *Latin.* in the place of a parent; as a parent.

in·ly (in'li), *adv. Poetic.* 1. inwardly. 2. thoroughly.

in·mate (in'māt), *n.* 1. person confined in a prison, asylum, hospital, etc. 2. occupant; inhabitant.

in me·di·as res (in mā'di·äs rās'; in mē'di·as rēz'), *Latin.* into the midst of things.

in me·mo·ri·am (in mə·mô'ri·əm; -mō'-), in memory (of); to the memory (of). [< L]

in·most (in'mōst), *adj.* 1. farthest in; deepest within: *inmost depths.* 2. most private; most secret: *inmost desire.*

inn (in), *n.* 1. a public house for lodging and caring for travelers, now largely superseded by hotels. 2. tavern. [OE, lodging] —inn'less, *adj.*

in·nate (i·nāt'; in'āt), *adj.* natural; inborn: *an innate talent for drawing.* [< L *innatus* < *in-* in + *nasci* be born] —in·nate'ly, *adv.* —in·nate'ness, *n.*

in·ner (in'ər), *adj.* 1. farther in; inside. 2. more private; more secret: *inner thoughts.* 3. of the mind or soul: *a person's inner life.* —**in'ner·ly,** *adv.* —**in'ner·ness,** *n.*

in·ner·most (in'ər·mōst), *adj.* farthest in; inmost: *the innermost parts.*

in·ning (in'ing), *n.* **1.** turn of one side in a game; chance to play. **2.** time a person or party is in power. [OE *innung* a taking in]

in·nings (in'ingz), *n. Esp. Brit.* an inning.

inn·keep·er (in'kēp'ər), *n.* person who owns, manages, or keeps an inn.

in·no·cence (in'ə·səns), **in·no·cen·cy** (-sən·si), *n.* **1.** freedom from sin, wrong, or guilt. **2.** simplicity.

in·no·cent (in'ə·sənt), *adj.* **1.** doing no wrong; free from sin or wrong; not guilty. **2.** without knowledge of evil: *a baby is innocent.* **3.** without evil effects; harmless: *innocent amusements.* **4.** simple; artless. —*n.* an innocent person. [< L, < *in-* not + *nocere* to harm] —**in'no·cent·ly,** *adv.* —**Syn.** *adj.* 1. pure, clean, guiltless. 4. naïve, guileless.

in·noc·u·ous (i·nok'yū·əs), *adj.* harmless. [< L, < *in-* not + *nocuus* hurtful < *nocere* to harm] —**in·noc'u·ous·ly,** *adv.* —**in·noc'u·ous·ness,** *n.*

in·no·vate (in'ə·vāt), *v.,* **-vat·ed, -vat·ing.** make changes; bring in something new or new ways of doing things. [< L, < *in-* + *novus* new] —**in'no·va'tive,** *adj.* —**in'no·va'tor,** *n.*

in·no·va·tion (in'ə·vā'shən), *n.* **1.** change made in the established way of doing things. **2.** making changes; bringing in new things or new ways of doing things. —**in'no·va'tion·al,** *adj.* —**in'no·va'tion·ist,** *n.*

in·nox·ious (i·nok'shəs), *adj.* harmless.

in·nu·en·do (in'yū·en'dō), *n., pl.* **-does. 1.** indirect hint or reference. **2.** indirect suggestion against somebody: *spread scandal by innuendo.* [< L, lit., by giving a nod to, < *in-* in + *-nuere* nod] —**Syn.** insinuation.

in·nu·mer·a·ble (i·nū'mər·ə·bəl; -nū'-), *adj.* too many to count; very many. —**in·nu'mer·a·ble·ness,** *n.* —**in·nu'mer·a·bly,** *adv.* —**Syn.** countless, myriad.

in·oc·u·late (in·ok'yə·lāt), *v.,* **-lat·ed, -lat·ing. 1.** infect (a person or animal) with germs that will cause a very mild form of a disease so that thereafter the individual will not take that disease. **2.** use disease germs to prevent or cure diseases. **3.** put bacteria, serums, etc., into: *inoculate soil with bacteria.* **4.** fill (a person's mind). [< L *inoculatus* engrafted < *in-* in + *oculus* bud, eye] —**in·oc'u·la'tion,** *n.* —**in·oc'u·la'tive,** *adj.* —**in·oc'u·la'tor,** *n.*

in·of·fen·sive (in'ə·fen'siv), *adj.* harmless; not arousing objections. —**in'of·fen'sive·ly,** *adv.* —**in'of·fen'sive·ness,** *n.*

in·op·er·a·tive (in·op'ər·ā'tiv; -op'rə·tiv), *adj.* without effect. —**in·op'er·a'tive·ness,** *n.*

in·op·por·tune (in'op·ər·tūn'; -tūn'), *adj.* not opportune; coming at a bad time; unsuitable. —**in'op·por·tune'ly,** *adv.* —**in'op·por·tune'ness,** *n.* —**Syn.** untimely, unseasonable.

in·or·di·nate (in·ôr'də·nit), *adj.* much too great; excessive; unrestrained. [< L, < *in-* not + *ordo* order] —**in·or·di·na·cy** (in·ôr'də·nə·si), **in·or'di·nate·ness,** *n.* —**in·or'di·nate·ly,** *adv.*

in·or·gan·ic (in'ôr·gan'ik), *adj.* **1.** not having the organized physical structure of animals and plants: *minerals are inorganic.* **2.** not produced by animal or plant activities. —**in'or·gan'i·cal·ly,** *adv.*

inorganic chemistry, branch of chemistry dealing with all compounds except the organic compounds.

in·put (in'pùt), *n.* **1.** what is put in or taken in. **2.** power supplied to a machine.

in·quest (in'kwest), *n.* a legal inquiry, esp. before a jury, to determine the cause of a death that may possibly have been the result of a crime. [< OF *enqueste,* ult. < L *inquirere* IN-QUIRE]

in·qui·e·tude (in·kwī'ə·tūd; -tūd), *n.* restlessness; uneasiness.

in·quire (in·kwīr'), *v.,* **-quired, -quir·ing. 1.** try to find out by questions; ask. **2.** make a

search for information, knowledge, or truth; make an examination of facts or principles. Also, **enquire.** [< L *inquirere* < *in-* into + *quaerere* ask] —**in·quir'er,** *n.* —**in·quir'ing·ly,** *adv.*

in·quir·y (in·kwīr'i; in'kwə·ri), *n., pl.* **-quir·ies. 1.** an inquiring; an asking. **2.** question. **3.** search for information, knowledge, or truth; examination of facts or principles.

in·qui·si·tion (in'kwə·zish'ən), *n.* **1.** a thorough investigation; searching inquiry. **2.** official investigation; judicial inquiry. **3.** the **Inquisition,** **a.** court appointed by the Roman Catholic Church to discover and suppress heresy and to punish heretics. **b.** activities of this court. —**in'qui·si'tion·al,** *adj.*

in·quis·i·tive (in·kwiz'ə·tiv), *adj.* **1.** asking many questions. **2.** too curious; prying into other people's affairs. —**in·quis'i·tive·ly,** *adv.* —**in·quis'i·tive·ness,** *n.* —**Syn.** 1. curious. —**Ant.** 1. uninterested.

in·quis·i·tor (in·kwiz'ə·tər), *n.* **1.** person who makes an inquisition; official investigator; judicial inquirer. **2.** **Inquisitor,** member of the Inquisition.

in·quis·i·to·ri·al (in·kwiz'ə·tô'ri·əl; -tō'-), *adj.* **1.** of or pertaining to an inquisitor or inquisition. **2.** making searching inquiry; thorough. **3.** unduly curious. —**in·quis'i·to'ri·al·ly,** *adv.* —**in·quis'i·to'ri·al·ness,** *n.*

in re (in rē'; rā'), *Latin.* concerning; in the matter of.

I.N.R.I., Jesus of Nazareth, King of the Jews. [for Latin *Iesus Nazarenus, Rex Iudaeorum*]

in·road (in'rōd), *n.* **1.** attack; raid. **2.** forcible encroachment: *inroads upon savings.*

in·rush (in'rush'), *n.* rushing in; inflow. —**in'rush'ing,** *n., adj.*

ins., **1.** inches. **2.** inspector. **3.** insurance.

in·sane (in·sān'), *adj.* **1.** not sane; mentally deranged. **2.** for insane people: *an insane asylum.* **3.** characteristic of an insane person. **4.** extremely foolish. —**in·sane'ly,** *adv.* —**in·sane'ness,** *n.* —**Syn.** 1. demented, lunatic, mad. 4. senseless, wild.

in·san·i·tar·y (in·san'ə·ter'i), *adj.* unhealthful. —**in·san'i·tar'i·ness,** *n.*

in·san·i·ty (in·san'ə·ti), *n., pl.* **-ties. 1.** state of being insane. **2.** extreme folly.

in·sa·ti·a·ble (in·sā'shə·bəl), *adj.* that cannot be satisfied. —**in·sa'tia·bil'i·ty, in·sa'tia·ble·ness,** *n.* —**in·sa'tia·bly,** *adv.* —**Syn.** unquenchable.

in·sa·ti·ate (in·sā'shi·it), *adj.* never satisfied. —**in·sa'ti·ate·ly,** *adv.* —**in·sa'ti·ate·ness,** *n.*

in·scribe (in·skrīb'), *v.,* **-scribed, -scrib·ing. 1.** write, engrave, or mark (words, letters, etc.) on paper, metal, stone, etc. **2.** mark or engrave (with words, letters, etc.). **3.** address or dedicate (a book, etc.) informally to a person. **4.** impress deeply: *my father's words are inscribed in my memory.* **5.** put in a list; enroll. **6.** *Geom.* draw (one figure) within another figure so that the inner touches the outer at as many points as possible. [< L, < *in-* on + *scribere* write] —**in·scrib'a·ble,** *adj.* —**in·scrib'er,** *n.*

in·scrip·tion (in·skrip'shən), *n.* **1.** something inscribed, as by writing or engraving. A monument or a coin has an inscription on it. **2.** informal dedication in a book, on a picture, etc. —**in·scrip'tion·al,** *adj.*

in·scru·ta·ble (in·skrü'tə·bəl), *adj.* that cannot be understood; so mysterious or obscure that one cannot make out its meaning. [< LL, < L *in-* not + *scrutari* examine, ransack < *scruta* trash] —**in·scru'ta·bil'i·ty, in·scru'ta·ble·ness,** *n.* —**in·scru'ta·bly,** *adv.* —**Syn.** unfathomable, incomprehensible.

in·sect (in'sekt), *n.* **1.** *Zool.* a small invertebrate animal with its body divided into three

FEELERS, HEAD, THORAX, WINGS, LEG, ABDOMEN
Parts of an insect

parts (head, thorax, and abdomen), with three pairs of legs, and usually two pairs of wings, as flies, mosquitoes, and beetles. **2.** any similar small animal with its body divided into several parts, with several pairs of legs, as spiders, centipedes, etc. [< L *insectum*, lit., divided < *in-* into + *secare* to cut] —**in'sect·like'**, *adj.*

in·sec·ti·cide (in·sek'tə·sīd), *n.* substance for killing insects. —**in·sec'ti·cid'al**, *adj.*

in·sec·tiv·o·rous (in'sek·tiv'ə·rəs), *adj.* **1.** insect-eating; feeding mainly on insects. **2.** of or belonging to a group of small mammals including moles, hedgehogs, etc. —**in·sec·ti·vore** (in·sek'tə·vôr; -vōr), *n.*

in·se·cure (in'si·kyūr'), *adj.* **1.** not secure; unsafe. **2.** liable to give way; not firm: *an insecure lock.* —**in'se·cure'ly**, *adv.* —**Syn. 1.** uncertain. **2.** unstable, shaky.

in·se·cu·ri·ty (in'si·kyūr'ə·ti), *n., pl.* -ties. **1.** lack of security. **2.** something insecure.

in·sem·i·nate (in·sem'ə·nāt), *v.*, -nat·ed, -nat·ing. **1.** sow; implant. **2.** impregnate. —**sem'i·na'tion**, *n.*

in·sen·sate (in·sen'sāt; -sit), *adj.* **1.** without sensation. **2.** unfeeling: *insensate cruelty.* **3.** senseless; stupid: *insensate folly.* —**in·sen'sate·ly**, *adv.* —**in·sen'sate·ness**, *n.*

in·sen·si·bil·i·ty (in·sen'sə·bil'ə·ti), *n., pl.* -ties. **1.** lack of feeling. **2.** lack of consciousness.

in·sen·si·ble (in·sen'sə·bəl), *adj.* **1.** not sensitive; not able to feel or observe: *a blind man is insensible to colors.* **2.** not aware: *insensible of the danger.* **3.** not able to feel anything; unconscious: *the man hit by the truck was insensible for hours.* **4.** not easily felt: *the room grew cold by insensible degrees.* —**in·sen'si·bly**, *adv.*

in·sen·si·tive (in·sen'sə·tiv), *adj.* **1.** not sensitive. **2.** slow to feel or notice. —**in·sen'si·tive·ness, in·sen'si·tiv'i·ty**, *n.*

in·sen·ti·ent (in·sen'shi·ənt; -shənt), *adj.* unable to feel; lifeless.

in·sep·a·ra·ble (in·sep'ə·rə·bəl; -sep'rə·bəl), *adj.* that cannot be separated. —*n.* inseparables, inseparable persons or things. —**in·sep'a·ra·bil'i·ty, in·sep'a·ra·ble·ness**, *n.* —**in·sep'a·ra·bly**, *adv.*

in·sert (*v.* in·sėrt'; *n.* in'sėrt), *v.* put in; set in: *insert a key into a lock or a letter into a word.* —*n.* something set in or to be set in: *an insert of several pages.* [< L, < *in-* in + *serere* entwine] —**in·sert'er**, *n.*

in·ser·tion (in·sėr'shən), *n.* **1.** an inserting: *the insertion of pictures in a book.* **2.** thing inserted. **3.** band of lace or embroidery to be sewed at each edge between parts of other material.

in·set (*v.* in·set'; in'set'; *n.* in'set'), *v.*, -set, -set·ting, *n.* —*v.* set in; insert. —*n.* **1.** something inserted. **2.** influx.

in·shore (in'shôr'; -shōr'), *adj.* near the shore. —*adv.* in toward the shore.

in·side (*n., adj.* in'sīd'; *adv., prep.* in'sīd'), *n.* **1.** side or surface that is within; inner part: *the inside of a house.* **2.** inward nature. **3.** Often, insides. *Colloq.* parts inside the body; stomach and bowels. —*adj.* **1.** being on the inside: *an inside seat.* **2.** *Slang.* done or known by those inside; private; secret: *the theft was an inside job.* **3.** *Slang.* working within a group or company as an emissary or spy: *an inside man.* —*adv.* **1.** on or to the inside; within. **2.** indoors: *go inside.* **3.** inside out, so that what should be inside is outside; with the inside showing. —*prep.* Often, **inside of,** in; within the limits of. —**Syn.** *adj.* **1.** internal, interior.

in·sid·er (in'sīd'ər), *n.* **1.** person who is inside some place, society, organizaton, etc. **2.** *Am., Colloq.* person who is so situated as to understand the actual conditions or facts of a case.

in·sid·i·ous (in·sid'i·əs), *adj.* **1.** crafty; tricky; treacherous. **2.** working secretly or subtly: *an insidious disease.* [< L, < *insidiae* ambush, ult. < *in-* in + *sedere* sit] —**in·sid'i·ous·ly**, *adv.* —**in·sid'i·ous·ness**, *n.* —**Syn. 1.** wily, sly.

in·sight (in'sīt'), *n.* **1.** a viewing of the inside or inner parts of (something) with understanding. **2.** wisdom and understanding in dealing with people or with facts.

in·sig·ni·a (in·sig'ni·ə), *n.pl., sing.* **in·sig·ne** (in·sig'nē). emblems, badges, or other distinguishing marks of a high position, military order, etc. [< L, pl. of *insigne* badge < *in-* on + *signum* mark]

in·sig·nif·i·cance (in'sig·nif'ə·kəns), *n.* **1.** unimportance. **2.** meaninglessness.

in·sig·nif·i·cant (in'sig·nif'ə·kənt), *adj.* **1.** having little use or importance. **2.** meaningless. —**in'sig·nif'i·cant·ly**, *adv.* —**Syn. 1.** petty, trifling.

in·sin·cere (in'sin·sir'), *adj.* not sincere; not honest or candid; deceitful. —**in'sin·cere'ly**, *adv.* —**Syn.** hypocritical.

in·sin·cer·i·ty (in'sin·ser'ə·ti), *n., pl.* -ties. lack of sincerity; hypocrisy.

in·sin·u·ate (in·sin'yū·āt), *v.*, -at·ed, -at·ing. **1.** push in or get in by an indirect, twisting way: *the spy insinuated himself into the confidence of important army officers.* **2.** suggest indirectly; hint. [< L, < *in-* in + *sinus* a curve] —**in·sin'u·at'ing·ly**, *adv.* —**in·sin'u·a'tive**, *adj.* —**in·sin'u·a'tor**, *n.*

in·sin·u·a·tion (in·sin'yū·ā'shən), *n.* **1.** an insinuating. **2.** indirect suggestion against someone. **3.** hint; suggestion. **4.** act or speech to gain favor.

in·sip·id (in·sip'id), *adj.* **1.** without much taste. **2.** uninteresting; colorless; weak. [< LL *insipidus* < L *in-* not + *sapidus* tasty] —**in·sip'id·ly**, *adv.* —**in·sip'id·ness**, *n.* —**Syn. 1.** flat. **2.** stupid, dull, vapid.

in·si·pid·i·ty (in'si·pid'ə·ti), *n., pl.* -ties. **1.** lack of flavor; lack of interest. **2.** something insipid.

in·sist (in·sist'), *v.* keep firmly to some demand, some statement, or some position. [< L, < *in-* on + *sistere* take a stand] —**in·sist'er**, *n.* —**Syn.** urge, persist, press.

in·sist·ent (in·sis'tənt), *adj.* **1.** insisting; continuing to make a strong, firm demand or statement. **2.** compelling attention or notice; pressing; urgent. —**in·sist'ence, in·sist'en·cy**, *n.* —**in·sist'ent·ly**, *adv.*

in·snare (in·snâr'), *v.*, -snared, -snar·ing. ensnare.

in·so·bri·e·ty (in'sə·brī'ə·ti), *n.* intemperance.

in·sole (in'sōl'), *n.* the inner sole of a shoe or boot.

in·so·lence (in'sə·ləns), *n.* bold rudeness; insulting behavior or speech.

in·so·lent (in'sə·lənt), *adj.* boldly rude; insulting. [< L *insolens*, orig., unusual < *in-* not + *solere* be wont] —**in'so·lent·ly**, *adv.* —**Syn.** arrogant, impudent.

in·sol·u·ble (in·sol'yə·bəl), *adj.* **1.** that cannot be dissolved. **2.** that cannot be solved. —**in·sol'u·bil'i·ty, in·sol'u·ble·ness**, *n.* —**in·sol'u·bly**, *adv.*

in·solv·a·ble (in·sol'və·bəl), *adj.* that cannot be solved.

in·sol·vent (in·sol'vənt), *adj.* **1.** not able to pay one's debts; bankrupt. **2.** pertaining to bankrupts. —*n.* an insolvent person. —**in·sol'ven·cy**, *n.*

in·som·ni·a (in·som'ni·ə), *n.* inability to sleep; sleeplessness. [< L, < *in-* not + *somnus* sleep] —**in·som'ni·ous**, *adj.*

in·so·much (in'sō·much'), *adv.* **1.** to such an extent or degree; so. **2.** inasmuch.

in·sou·ci·ance (in·sü'si·əns), *n.* freedom from care or anxiety; carefree feeling.

in·sou·ci·ant (in·sü'si·ənt), *adj.* free from care or anxiety. [< F] —**in·sou'ci·ant·ly**, *adv.*

in·spect (in·spekt'), *v.* **1.** look over carefully; examine. **2.** examine officially. [< L *inspectus* < *in-* upon + *specere* look]

in·spec·tion (in·spek'shən), *n.* **1.** an inspecting. **2.** formal or official examination. —**in·spec'tion·al**, *adj.*

in·spec·tor (in·spek'tər), *n.* **1.** person who inspects. **2.** police officer ranking next below a superintendent. —**in·spec'to·ral, in·spec·to·ri·al** (in'spek·tô'ri·al; -tō'-), *adj.* —**in·spec'tor·ship**, *n.*

in·spi·ra·tion (in'spə·rā'shən), *n.* **1.** influence of thought and strong feelings on actions, esp. on good actions: *get inspiration from a sermon.* 2. any influence that arouses effort to do well: *the captain was an inspiration to his men.* 3. idea that is inspired. 4. suggestion to another; act of causing something to be told or written by another. 5. divine influence directly and immediately exerted upon the mind or soul of man. 6. a breathing in; a drawing air into the lungs. —**in'spi·ra'tion·al**, *adj.* —**in'spi·ra'tion·al·ly**, *adv.*

in·spire (in·spīr'), *v.*, **-spired, -spir·ing.** 1. put thought, feeling, life, force, etc., into: *the speaker inspired the crowd.* 2. cause (thought or feeling): *the leader's courage inspired confidence in others.* 3. affect; influence: *his sly ways inspire me with distrust.* 4. arouse or influence by a divine force. 5. suggest; cause to be told or written: *his enemies inspired false stories about him.* 6. breathe in; breathe in air. [< L, < *in-* in + *spirare* breathe] —**in·spir'a·ble**, *adj.* —**in·spir'er**, *n.* —**in·spir'ing·ly**, *adv.*

in·spir·it (in·spir'it), *v.* put spirit into; encourage; hearten. —**in·spir'it·ing·ly**, *adv.*

in·spis·sate (in·spis'āt), *v.*, **-sat·ed, -sat·ing.** thicken, as by evaporation; condense. [< LL, < L *in-* + *spissus* thick] —**in'spis·sa'tion**, *n.* —**in'spis·sa'tor**, *n.*

inst., 1. installment. 2. instant. 3. Also, **Inst.** institute; institution. ➤ **inst.** Abbreviations such as *inst.* (of the current month: "Yours of the 18th inst. duly rec'd and contents noted") are not now used by businessmen who pay attention to the impression their correspondence will make on readers.

in·sta·bil·i·ty (in'stə·bil'ə·ti), *n.* lack of firmness; liability to give way or change.

in·stall (in·stôl'), *v.* 1. place (a person) in office with ceremonies. 2. establish in a place: *install oneself in an easy chair.* 3. put in position for use: *install a telephone.* [< Med.L, < *in-* in (< L) + *stallum* STALL (< Gmc.)] —**in·stal·la·tion** (in'stə·lā'shən), *n.* —**in·stall'er**, *n.*

in·stall·ment¹, in·stal·ment¹ (in·stôl'mənt), *n.* 1. part of a sum of money or of a debt to be paid at certain regular times. 2. any of several parts furnished or issued at successive times: *a serial story in a magazine in six installments.* [prob. < *install* pay periodically]

in·stall·ment², in·stal·ment² (in·stôl'mənt), *n.* installation.

installment plan, *Am.* system of paying for goods in installments.

in·stance (in'stəns), *n.*, *v.*, **-stanced, -stanc·ing.** —*n.* 1. example; case: *an instance of neglect.* 2. stage or step in an action; occasion: *in the first instance.* 3. request; suggestion; urging: *he came at our instance.* 4. for instance, for example. —*v.* 1. refer to as an example. 2. exemplify. [< OF < L *instantia* insistence < *instans* insistent. See INSTANT.]

in·stant (in'stənt), *n.* 1. particular moment: *stop talking this instant.* 2. moment of time: *he paused for an instant.* —*adj.* 1. immediate; without delay: *instant relief.* 2. pressing; urgent: *an instant need for action.* 3. of the present month; present. —*adv. Poetic.* at once. [< L *instans* insisting, standing near < *in-* in + *stare* stand]

in·stan·ta·ne·ous (in'stən·tā'ni·əs), *adj.* occurring, done, or made in an instant. —**in·stan·ta'ne·ous·ly**, *adv.* —**in'stan·ta'ne·ous·ness**, *n.*

in·stan·ter (in·stan'tər), *adv.* immediately. [< L, insistently]

in·stant·ly (in'stənt·li), *adv.* 1. in an instant; at once; immediately. 2. urgently.

in·state (in·stāt'), *v.*, **-stat·ed, -stat·ing.** install. —**in·state'ment**, *n.*

in·stead (in·sted'), *adv.* 1. in place (of): *instead of studying, she read a book.* 2. in one's or its place: *let him go instead.*

in·step (in'step), *n.* 1. the upper surface of the human foot between the toes and the ankle. 2. part of a shoe, stocking, etc., over the instep.

in·sti·gate (in'stə·gāt), *v.*, **-gat·ed, -gat·ing.** urge on; stir up: *foreign agents instigated a re-*

bellion. [< L *instigatus*] —**in'sti·ga'tion**, *n.* —**in'sti·ga'tive**, *adj.* —**in'sti·ga'tor**, *n.* —Syn. incite, provoke.

in·still, in·stil (in·stil'), *v.*, **-stilled, -still·ing.** 1. put in little by little; impart gradually: *reading good books instills a love of literature.* 2. put in drop by drop. [< L, < *in-* in + *stilla* a drop] —**in·stil·la·tion** (in'stə·lā'shən), *n.* —**in·still'er**, *n.* —**in·still'ment, in·stil'ment**, *n.*

in·stinct¹ (in'stingkt), *n.* 1. natural feeling, knowledge, or power, such as guides animals; unlearned tendency: *an instinct leads birds to fly.* 2. a natural bent, tendency, or gift; talent: *an instinct to govern.* [< L *instinctus*, n. < *instinguere* impel]

in·stinct² (in·stingkt'), *adj.* charged or filled with something: *the picture is instinct with life and beauty.* [< L *instinctus*, pp. See INSTINCT¹.]

in·stinc·tive (in·stingk'tiv), *adj.* of, caused, or done by instinct; born in an animal or person, not learned. —**in·stinc'tive·ly**, *adv.* —Syn. intuitive, natural, innate, inherent.

in·sti·tute (in'stə·tūt), *v.*, **-tut·ed, -tut·ing**, *n.* —*v.* 1. set up; establish; begin: *the Pilgrims instituted Thanksgiving.* 2. set in operation; initiate: *the police instituted an inquiry into the causes of the accident.* 3. establish in a position; inaugurate. —*n.* 1. an established principle, law, custom, organization, or society. 2. organization or society for some special purpose, as an art institute. [< L *institutus* < *in-* in + *statuere* establish] —**in'sti·tut'er, in'sti·tu'tor**, *n.* —Syn. v. 1. found, organize.

in·sti·tu·tion (in'stə·tū'shən; -tū'-), *n.* 1. organization or society for some public or social purpose, as a church, school, hospital, etc. 2. established law, custom, organization, or society: *giving presents on Christmas is an institution.* 3. setting up; establishing; beginning: *the institution of a savings bank in our city.* 4. *Colloq.* a familiar person or thing.

in·sti·tu·tion·al (in'stə·tū'shən·əl; -tū'-), *adj.* 1. of, like, or established by an institution. 2. *Advertising.* promoting reputation and establishing good will for a business rather than aiming at immediate sales. —**in'sti·tu'tion·al·ly**, *adv.*

in·struct (in·strukt'), *v.* 1. teach. 2. give directions or orders to. 3. inform. [< L *instructus* < *in-* on + *struere* to pile] —Syn. 1. train, educate, tutor, coach. 2. direct, order, command.

in·struc·tion (in·struk'shən), *n.* 1. a teaching; knowledge; education. 2. instructions, directions; orders. —**in·struc'tion·al**, *adj.*

in·struc·tive (in·struk'tiv), *adj.* useful for instruction; instructing: *an instructive experience.* —**in·struc'tive·ly**, *adv.* —**in·struc'tive·ness**, *n.*

in·struc·tor (in·struk'tər), *n.* 1. teacher. 2. *Am.* teacher ranking below an assistant professor in American colleges and universities. —**in·struc'tor·less**, *adj.* —**in·struc'tor·ship**, *n.*

in·stru·ment (in'strə·mənt), *n.* 1. thing with or by which something is done; a person so made use of; means. 2. tool or mechanical device: *a dentist's instruments.* 3. device for producing musical sounds: *stringed instruments.* 4. a formal legal document, such as a contract. [< L *instrumentum* < *instruere* arrange, INSTRUCT]

in·stru·men·tal (in'strə·men'təl), *adj.* 1. acting or serving as a means; useful; helpful. 2. *Music.* played on or written for instruments. 3. of an instrument; made by a device or tool. —**in'stru·men'tal·ly**, *adv.*

in·stru·men·tal·ist (in'strə·men'təl·ist), *n. Music.* person who plays on an instrument. —**in'stru·men'tal·is'tic**, *adj.*

in·stru·men·tal·i·ty (in'strə·men·tal'ə·ti), *n.*, *pl.* **-ties.** helpfulness as an instrument; agency; means.

in·stru·men·ta·tion (in'strə·men·tā'shən), *n.* 1. *Music.* arrangement or composition for instruments. 2. use of instruments.

instrument flying, directing an airplane by instruments only.

in·sub·or·di·nate (in'sə·bôr'də·nit), *adj.* resisting authority; disobedient; unruly. —*n.* one

āge, cāre, fär; ēqual, tėrm; īce; ōpen, ôrder; put, rūle, ūse; ŧH, then; ə=a in about.

who is insubordinate. —in′sub·or′di·nate·ly, adv. —Syn. adj. mutinous.

in·sub·or·di·na·tion (in′sə·bôr′də·nā′shən), n. resistance to authority; disobedience.

in·sub·stan·tial (in′səb·stan′shəl), adj. **1.** frail; flimsy; weak: a cobweb is very insubstantial. **2.** unreal; not actual; imaginary: ghosts are insubstantial. —in′sub·stan′ti·al′i·ty, n.

in·suf·fer·a·ble (in·suf′ər·ə·bəl; -suf′rə·bəl), adj. intolerable; unbearable: insufferable insolence. —in·suf′fer·a·ble·ness, n. —in·suf′fer·a·bly, adv.

in·suf·fi·cien·cy (in′sə·fish′ən·si), n. too small an amount; lack; deficiency.

in·suf·fi·cient (in′sə·fish′ənt), adj. not enough. —in′suf·fi′cient·ly, adv.

in·su·lar (in′sə·lər), adj. **1.** of or having to do with islands or islanders. **2.** living or situated on an island. **3.** forming an island. **4.** narrow-minded; prejudiced. [< L, < L insula island] —in′su·lar·ism, in·su·lar·i·ty (in′sə·lar′ə·ti), n. —in′su·lar·ly, adv.

in·su·late (in′sə·lāt), v., -lat·ed, -lat·ing. **1.** Physics. keep from losing or transferring electricity, heat, sound, etc. **2.** cover or surround (electric wire, etc.) with nonconducting material. **3.** set apart; separate from others; isolate. [< L insulatus formed into an island < insula island]

in·su·la·tion (in′sə·lā′shən), n. **1.** an insulating or being insulated. **2.** material used in insulating.

in·su·la·tor (in′sə·lā′tər), n. that which insulates; nonconductor.

in·su·lin (in′sə·lin), n. **1.** hormone secreted by the pancreas that enables the body to use sugar and other carbohydrates. **2.** Insulin, Trademark. extract containing this hormone, obtained from the pancreas of slaughtered animals, used in treating diabetes. [< L insula island (i.e., of the pancreas)]

Glass insulator for electric wires

in·sult (v. in·sult′; n. in′sult), v. treat with scorn, abuse, or great rudeness: the rebels insulted the flag by throwing mud on it. —n. an insulting speech or action. [< L insultare < in- on, at + salire to leap] —in·sult′er, n. —in·sult′ing, adj. —in·sult′ing·ly, adv.

in·su·per·a·ble (in·sü′pər·ə·bəl), adj. that cannot be passed over or overcome: an insuperable barrier. —in·su′per·a·bil′i·ty, in·su′per·a·ble·ness, n. —in·su′per·a·bly, adv. —Syn. insurmountable, impassable.

in·sup·port·a·ble (in′sə·pôr′tə·bəl; -pōr′-), adj. unbearable; unendurable; intolerable. —in′-sup·port′a·ble·ness, n. —in′sup·port′a·bly, adv.

in·sur·a·ble (in·shur′ə·bəl), adj. capable of being insured; fit to be insured. —in·sur′a·bil′-i·ty, n.

in·sur·ance (in·shur′əns), n. **1.** an insuring of property, person, or life: fire insurance, life insurance. **2.** the business of insuring property, life, etc. **3.** amount of money for which a person or thing is insured: he has $10,000 insurance, which his wife will receive when he dies. **4.** amount of money paid for insurance; premium: his insurance is $300 a year. Also, Brit. assurance.

in·sure (in·shur′), v., -sured, -sur·ing. **1.** make sure; ensure: check your work to insure its accuracy. **2.** make safe; protect; ensure: more care will insure you against making so many mistakes. **3.** arrange for money payment in case of loss of (property, profit, etc.) or accident or death to (a person): an insurance company will insure your life. **4.** make safe from financial loss by accident, death, etc., by paying money to an insurance company: was he insured at the time of the accident? **5.** issue an insurance policy. [var. of ensure < AF, < en- in + OF seur SURE]

in·sured (in·shurd′), n. person whose property, life, etc., are insured.

in·sur·er (in·shur′ər), n. **1.** person who insures. **2.** something that insures or protects.

in·sur·gence (in·sér′jəns), **in·sur·gen·cy** (-jən·si), n. a rising in revolt; rebellion.

in·sur·gent (in·sér′jənt), n. **1.** person who rises in revolt; rebel. **2.** U.S. rebel within a political party. —adj. rising in revolt; rebellious. [< L, < in- against + surgere rise]

in·sur·mount·a·ble (in′sər·moun′tə·bəl), adj. that cannot be overcome. —in′sur·mount′a·bly, adv.

in·sur·rec·tion (in′sə·rek′shən), n. an uprising against established authority; revolt. [< LL insurrectio < L insurgere. See INSURGENT.] —in′sur·rec′tion·al, adj. —in′sur·rec·tion·al·ly, adv. —in·sur·rec·tion·ar·y (in′sə·rek′shən·er′i), adj., n. —in′sur·rec′tion·ism, n. —in′sur·rec′tion·ist, n. —Syn. rebellion, revolution, riot.

in·sus·cep·ti·ble (in′sə·sep′tə·bəl), adj. not susceptible; not easily influenced. —in′sus·cep′-ti·bil′i·ty, n. —in′sus·cep′ti·bly, adv.

int., **1.** interest. **2.** international. **3.** intransitive.

in·tact (in·takt′), adj. with no part missing; untouched; uninjured; whole: dishes left intact after a fall. [< L intactus, ult. < in- not + tangere touch] —in·tact′ness, n.

in·tag·li·o (in·tal′yō; -täl′-), n., pl. in·tag·li·os, Ital. in·ta·gli (ēn·tä′lyē), v., -ioed, -io·ing. —n. **1.** process of engraving by making cuts in a surface. **2.** design engraved in this way. **3.** gem ornamented in this way. —v. engrave in intaglio. [< Ital., ult. < in- into + tagliare to cut]

in·take (in′tāk′), n. **1.** place where water, gas, etc., enters a channel, pipe, or other narrow opening. **2.** a taking in. **3.** amount or thing taken in.

in·tan·gi·ble (in·tan′jə·bəl), adj. **1.** not capable of being touched. **2.** not easily grasped by the mind. —n. something intangible. —in·tan′gi·bil′i·ty, in·tan′gi·ble·ness, n. —in·tan′gi·bly, adv. —Syn. adj. **1.** insubstantial.

in·te·ger (in′tə·jər), n. **1.** a whole number as distinguished from a fraction or mixed number. 1, 2, 3, 15, 106, etc., are integers. **2.** thing complete in itself; something whole. [< L, whole]

in·te·gral (in′tə·grəl), adj. **1.** necessary to the completeness of the whole; essential. **2.** entire; complete. **3.** having to do with whole numbers; not fractional. —n. a whole; a whole number. [< LL, < L integer whole] —in′te·gral′i·ty, n. —in′te·gral·ly, adv.

in·te·grate (in′tə·grāt), v., -grat·ed, -grat·ing. **1.** make into a whole; complete. **2.** bring together (parts) into a whole. **3.** indicate the total amount or mean value of. **4.** U.S. make all schools, parks, etc. available to white and Negro citizens on an equal basis. [< L, < integer whole] —in′te·gra′tion, n. —in′te·gra′tive, adj. —in′te·gra′tor, n.

in·teg·ri·ty (in·teg′rə·ti), n. **1.** honesty; sincerity; uprightness: a man of integrity. **2.** wholeness; completeness: defend the integrity of one's country. **3.** perfect condition; soundness. [< L integritas. See INTEGER.]

in·teg·u·ment (in·teg′yu·mənt), n. an outer covering, as a skin or a shell. [< L integumentum < in- on + tegere to cover]

in·tel·lect (in′tə·lekt), n. **1.** power of knowing; understanding. **2.** great intelligence; high mental ability: a man of intellect. **3.** person having high mental ability. [< L intellectus < intellegere. See INTELLIGENT.]

in·tel·lec·tu·al (in′tə·lek′chü·əl), adj. **1.** of the intellect: intellectual power. **2.** needing or using intelligence: an intellectual process. **3.** possessing or showing intelligence: an intellectual type of mind. **4.** directed or inclined toward things that involve the intellect: intellectual tastes. —n. person who is well informed, or chiefly concerned with things that involve the intellect. —in′tel·lec′tu·al′i·ty, in′tel·lec′tu·al·ness, n. —in′tel·lec′tu·al·ly, adv.

in·tel·lec·tu·al·ism (in′tə·lek′chü·əl·iz′əm), n. exercise of the intellect; devotion to intellectual pursuits. —in′tel·lec′tu·al·ist, n. —in′tel·lec′tu·al·is′tic, adj.

in·tel·li·gence (in·tel′ə·jəns), n. **1.** ability to learn and know; understanding; mind. **2.** knowledge; news; information. **3.** the obtaining or distributing of information, esp. secret information. **4.** group of persons engaged in obtaining secret information. **5.** Often, Intelligence. intelligent being or spirit. —**Syn. 1.** intellect, discernment, insight. **2.** tidings, notice.

in·tel·li·gence quo·tient, number used to measure a child's intelligence, obtained by dividing the mental age by the chronological age (up to 16 years).

in·tel·li·gence test, test used to measure mental development.

in·tel·li·gent (in·tel′ə·jənt), *adj.* having or showing intelligence; able to learn and know; quick at learning. [< L *intelligens* understanding < *inter-* between + *legere* choose] —**in·tel′li·gent·ly,** *adv.* —**Syn.** bright, clever.

in·tel·li·gent·si·a (in·tel′ə·jent′si·ə; -gent′-), *n.pl.* persons representing, or claiming to represent, the superior intelligence or enlightened opinion of a country; the intellectuals. [< Russ. < L *intelligentia.* See INTELLIGENT.] ▶ Intelligentsia often carries the suggestion of too great preoccupation with intellectual matters.

in·tel·li·gi·ble (in·tel′ə·jə·bəl), *adj.* capable of being understood; comprehensible. [< L, < *intelligere.* See INTELLIGENT.] —**in·tel′li·gi·bil′i·ty,** in·tel′li·gi·ble·ness, *n.* —**in·tel′li·gi·bly,** *adv.* —**Syn.** understandable, plain, clear.

in·tem·per·ance (in·tem′pər·əns; -prəns), *n.* **1.** lack of moderation or self-control; excess. **2.** the excessive use of intoxicating liquor.

in·tem·per·ate (in·tem′pər·it; -prit), *adj.* **1.** not moderate; lacking in self-control; excessive. **2.** drinking too much intoxicating liquor. **3.** not temperate; severe: *an intemperate winter.* —**in·tem′per·ate·ly,** *adv.* —**in·tem′per·ate·ness,** *n.* —**Syn. 1.** extreme, inordinate.

in·tend (in·tend′), *v.* **1.** have in mind as a purpose; mean; plan: *we intend to go home soon.* **2.** design; destine: *a book intended for beginners.* [< L, < *in-* toward + *tendere* stretch] —**in·tend′er,** *n.* —**Syn. 1.** contemplate, propose.

in·tend·an·cy (in·ten′dən·si), *n., pl.* -cies. position or work of an intendant.

in·tend·ant (in·ten′dənt), *n.* person in charge; director. [< F, ult. < L *intendere* attend to. See INTEND.]

in·tend·ed (in·ten′did), *adj.* **1.** meant; planned. **2.** prospective: *a woman's intended husband.* —*n. Colloq.* a prospective husband or wife.

in·tense (in·tens′), *adj.* **1.** very much; very great; very strong: *intense pain.* **2.** full of vigorous activity, strong feelings, etc.: *an intense life.* **3.** having or showing strong feelings: *an intense person.* [< L *intensus,* pp. of *intendere* strain. See INTEND.] —**in·tense′ly,** *adv.* —**in·tense′ness,** *n.*

in·ten·si·fy (in·ten′sə·fī), *v.,* -fied, -fy·ing. make or become intense or more intense; strengthen: *blowing on a fire intensifies the heat.* —**in·ten′si·fi·ca′tion,** *n.* —**in·ten′si·fi′er,** *n.* —**Syn.** heighten, aggravate, increase.

in·ten·si·ty (in·ten′sə·ti), *n., pl.* -ties. **1.** a being intense; great strength; extreme degree. **2.** great strength or violence of feeling. **3.** amount or degree of strength of electricity, heat, light, sound, etc., per unit of area, volume, etc.

in·ten·sive (in·ten′siv), *adj.* **1.** deep and thorough: *an intensive study.* **2.** *Gram.* giving force or emphasis; expressing intensity. In "He himself said it," *himself* is an intensive pronoun. **3.** increasing in intensity. —*n.* **1.** something that makes intense. **2.** *Gram.* intensive word, prefix, etc. —**in·ten′sive·ly,** *adv.* —**in·ten′sive·ness,** *n.*

in·tent¹ (in·tent′), *n.* **1.** purpose; intention. **2.** meaning; significance. **3.** to all intents and purposes, in almost every way; practically. [< OF *entent, entente* < L *intentus* INTEND]

in·tent² (in·tent′), *adj.* **1.** very attentive; having the eyes or thoughts earnestly fixed on something; earnest. **2.** earnestly engaged; much interested. [< L *intentus,* pp. of *intendere* to strain. See INTEND.] —**in·tent′ly,** *adv.* —**in·tent′ness,** *n.*

in·ten·tion (in·ten′shən), *n.* **1.** purpose; design; plan: *our intention is to travel next summer.* **2.** meaning. **3.** intentions, *Colloq.* purposes with respect to marrying. —**Syn. 1.** intent.

in·ten·tion·al (in·ten′shən·əl), *adj.* done on purpose; meant; intended. —**in·ten′tion·al·ly,** *adv.* —**Syn.** deliberate, premeditated, designed.

in·ter (in·tėr′), *v.,* -terred, -ter·ring. put (a dead body) into a grave or tomb; bury. [< OF *enterrer,* ult. < L *in-* in + *terra* earth]

inter-, *prefix.* **1.** together; one with the other, as in *intercommunicate, intermixture.* **2.** between, as in *interpose, interlay, interlude.* **3.** among a group, as in *interscholastic.* [< L, < *inter,* prep., adv., among, between, during]

in·ter·act (in′tər·akt′), *v.* act on each other. —**in′ter·ac′tion,** *n.* —**in′ter·ac′tive,** *adj.*

in·ter a·li·a (in′tər ā′li·ə), *Latin.* among other things.

in·ter·breed (in′tər·brēd′), *v.,* -bred, -breed·ing. breed by the mating of different kinds; breed by using different varieties or species of animals or plants.

in·ter·ca·lar·y (in·tėr′kə·ler′i), *adj.* inserted in a calendar: *February 29 is an intercalary day.*

in·ter·ca·late (in·tėr′kə·lāt), *v.,* -lat·ed, -lat·ing. **1.** put into the calendar. **2.** put in between; interpolate. [< L, < *inter-* between + *calare* proclaim] —**in·ter′ca·la′tion,** *n.*

in·ter·cede (in′tər·sēd′), *v.,* -ced·ed, -ced·ing. **1.** plead or beg in another's behalf: *Will interceded with the teacher for Dan.* **2.** interfere in order to bring about an agreement. [< L, < *inter-* between + *cedere* go] —**in′ter·ced′er,** *n.*

in·ter·cel·lu·lar (in′tər·sel′yə·lər), *adj.* situated between or among cells.

in·ter·cept (in′tər·sept′), *v.* **1.** take or seize on the way from one place to another: *intercept a letter.* **2.** cut off (light, water, etc.). **3.** check; stop: *intercept the flight of a criminal.* **4.** *Math.,* etc. mark off between two points or lines. [< L *interceptus* < *inter-* between + *capere* catch] —**in′ter·cep′tion,** *n.* —**in′ter·cep′tive,** *adj.* —**in′ter·cep′tor,** *n.*

The line intercepts the circle at A and B.

in·ter·ces·sion (in′tər·sesh′ən), *n.* act or fact of interceding. —**in′ter·ces′sion·al,** *adj.* —**in·ter·ces·sor** (in′tər·ses′ər; in′tər·ses′ər), *n.* —**in′ter·ces′so·ry,** *adj.*

in·ter·change (*v.* in′tər·chānj′; *n.* in′tər·chānj′), *v.,* -changed, -chang·ing, *n.* —*v.* **1.** put each of (two or more persons or things) in the place of the other. **2.** give and take; exchange: *interchange gifts.* **3.** cause to happen by turns; alternate: *interchange severity with indulgence.* **4.** change places. —*n.* **1.** a putting each of two or more persons or things in the other's place. **2.** a giving and taking; exchanging. **3.** alternate succession; alternation. **4.** one of several places, usually widely spaced, on certain modern highways where automobiles, etc., can enter or leave the highway and tolls are paid.

in·ter·change·a·ble (in′tər·chān′jə·bəl), *adj.* **1.** capable of being used in place of each other. **2.** able to change places. —**in′ter·change′a·bil′i·ty,** in′ter·change′a·ble·ness, *n.* —**in′ter·change′a·bly,** *adv.*

in·ter·col·le·gi·ate (in′tər·kə·lē′jit; -ji·it), *adj.* between colleges or universities.

in·ter·com (in′tər·kom′), *n. Slang.* telephone apparatus with which members of the crew of an airplane, tank, ship, etc., can talk to each other.

in·ter·com·mu·ni·cate (in′tər·kə·mū′nə·kāt), *v.,* -cat·ed, -cat·ing. communicate with each other. —**in′ter·com·mu′ni·ca′tion,** *n.*

in·ter·con·nect (in′tər·kə·nekt′), *v.* connect with each other. —**in′ter·con·nec′tion,** *n.*

in·ter·cos·tal (in′tər·kos′təl; -kôs′-), *adj.* between the ribs. —*n.* muscle, part, or space situated between the ribs. [< NL, < L *inter-* between + *costa* rib] —**in′ter·cos′tal·ly,** *adv.*

in·ter·course (in′tər·kôrs; -kōrs), *n.* **1.** communication; dealings between people; exchange of thoughts, services, feelings, etc. **2.** sexual connection.

in·ter·de·nom·i·na·tion·al (in′tər·di·nom′ə·nā′shən·əl; -nāsh′nəl), *adj.* between or involving different religious denominations.

in·ter·de·pend·ence (in′tər·di·pen′dəns), **in·ter·de·pend·en·cy** (-dən·si), *n.* dependence on each other; mutual dependence.

āge, cāre, fär; ēqual, tėrm; īce; ōpen, ôrder; pŭt, rüle, ūse; tₕ, then; ə=a in about.

in·ter·de·pend·ent (in'tər·di·pen'dənt), *adj.* dependent each upon the other. —**in'ter·de·pend'ent·ly,** *adv.*

in·ter·dict (*v.* in'tər·dikt'; *n.* in'tər·dikt), *v.* 1. prohibit; forbid. 2. restrain. 3. cut off from certain church privileges. —*n.* 1. prohibition based on authority; formal order forbidding something. 2. a cutting off from certain church privileges. [< L, < *inter-* between + *dicere* speak] —**in'ter·dic'tion,** *n.* —**in'ter·dic'tive,** *adj.* —**in'ter·dic'tor,** *n.* —**in'ter·dic'to·ry,** *adj.*

in·ter·est (in'tər·ist; -trist), *n.* 1. a feeling of wanting to know, see, do, own, share in, or take part in: *an interest in sports.* 2. power of arousing such a feeling: *a dull book lacks interest.* 3. share; part; portion: *buy a half interest in a business.* 4. thing in which a person has an interest, share, or part, as a business, pastime, etc. 5. group of people having the same business, activity, etc. 6. advantage; benefit. 7. regard for one's own advantage; self-interest. 8. power of influencing action. 9. **in the interest of,** for; to help. 10. money paid for the use of money: *the interest on the loan was 5 per cent.* 11. something extra given in return. —*v.* 1. arouse the attention, curiosity, concern, etc., of: *an exciting story interests you.* 2. cause (a person) to take a share or interest in: *the agent tried to interest us in buying a car.* [< L, it is of importance, it makes a difference < *inter-* between + *esse* be] —Syn. *v.* 1. engage, occupy, entertain. ➤ The noun *interest* has no antonym made from itself (*disinterest* not being a word in general use). It is necessary to resort to specific words like *boredom* or phrases like *lack of interest.*

in·ter·est·ed (in'tər·is·tid; -tris·tid; -tər·es'-tid), *adj.* 1. feeling or showing interest. 2. having an interest or share. 3. influenced by personal considerations; prejudiced. —**in'ter·est·ed·ly,** *adv.* —**in'ter·est·ed·ness,** *n.* ➤ *interested.* The adjective *interested* has two opposites: *uninterested,* which is merely its negative, and *disinterested,* which means "not motivated by personal interest, impartial," though informally the latter is sometimes used in the sense of *uninterested.*

in·ter·est·ing (in'tər·is·ting; -tris·ting; -tər·es'ting), *adj.* arousing interest; holding one's attention. —**in'ter·est·ing·ly,** *adv.* —**in'ter·est·ing·ness,** *n.*

in·ter·fere (in'tər·fir'), *v.,* -fered, -fer·ing. 1. come into opposition; clash: *come on Saturday if nothing interferes.* 2. disturb the affairs of others; meddle. 3. take part for a purpose: *the police interfered to stop the riot.* 4. interfere with, hinder. 5. *Am.,* *Football.* obstruct the action of an opposing player who is trying to tackle. 6. *Physics.* of waves, act one upon another. [< OF, < L *inter-* between + *ferire* to strike] —**in'ter·fer'er,** *n.* —**in'ter·fer'ing·ly,** *adv.* —Syn. 1. conflict. 3. intervene.

in·ter·fer·ence (in'tər·fir'əns), *n.* 1. an interfering. 2. *Physics.* the reciprocal action of waves by which they reinforce or neutralize one another. 3. *Radio.* a. interruption or scrambling of a desired signal by other signals. b. signals thus interfering. 4. *Am.,* *Football.* act of interfering with a player who is trying to tackle.

in·ter·fold (in'tər·fōld'), *v.* fold one within another; fold together.

in·ter·fuse (in'tər·fūz'), *v.,* -fused, -fus·ing. 1. be diffused through; permeate. 2. fuse together; blend. [< L *interfusus* < *inter-* between + *fundere* pour] —**in'ter·fu'sion,** *n.*

in·ter·im (in'tər·im), *n.* meantime; time between. —*adj.* for the meantime; temporary. [< L, in the meantime < *inter* between]

in·te·ri·or (in·tir'i·ər), *n.* 1. inside; inner surface or part. 2. part of a region or country away from the coast or border. 3. affairs within a country: *Department of the Interior.* —*adj.* 1. on the inside; inner. 2. away from the coast or border. 3. domestic. 4. private; secret. [< L, inner] —**in·te·ri·or·i·ty** (in·tir'i·ôr'ə·ti; -or'-), *n.* —**in·te'ri·or·ly,** *adv.*

in·terj., interjection.

in·ter·ject (in'tər·jekt'), *v.* throw in between other things; insert abruptly: *interject a witty remark.* [< L *interjectus* < *inter-* between + *jacere* throw] —**in'ter·jec'tor,** *n.*

in·ter·jec·tion (in'tər·jek'shən), *n.* 1. *Gram.* an exclamation regarded as a part of speech, as oh!, hurrah! 2. an interjecting. 3. something interjected; remark; exclamation. —**in'ter·jec'tion·al,** *adj.* —**in'ter·jec'tion·al·ly,** *adv.*

in·ter·lace (in'tər·lās'), *v.,* -laced, -lac·ing. 1. cross over and under each other; weave together; intertwine. 2. cross in an intricate manner. —**in'ter·lace'ment,** *n.*

in·ter·lard (in'tər·lärd'), *v.* give variety to; mix; intersperse. [< F, < L *inter-* between + *lardum* fat] —**in'ter·lard'ment,** *n.*

in·ter·lay (in'tər·lā'), *v.,* -laid, -lay·ing. 1. lay between. 2. diversify with something laid between.

in·ter·leave (in'tər·lēv'), *v.,* -leaved, -leav·ing. insert a leaf or leaves of paper between the pages.

in·ter·line[1] (in'tər·līn'), *v.,* -lined, -lin·ing. insert an extra lining between the outer cloth and the ordinary lining of (a garment).

in·ter·line[2] (in'tər·līn'), *v.,* -lined, -lin·ing. write, print, or mark between the lines.

in·ter·lin·e·ar (in'tər·lin'i·ər), *adj.* 1. inserted between the lines. 2. containing two different languages or versions in alternate lines.

in·ter·lin·ing (in'tər·līn'ing), *n.* an extra lining inserted between the outer cloth and the ordinary lining of a garment.

in·ter·link (in'tər·lingk'), *v.* link together.

in·ter·lock (in'tər·lok'), *v.* lock or join with one another. —**in'ter·lock'er,** *n.*

in·ter·loc·u·tor (in'tər·lok'yə·tər), *n.* 1. person who takes part in a conversation or dialogue. 2. *Am.* man in a minstrel show who asks the end man questions. [< L *interlocutus* < *inter-* between + *loqui* speak]

in·ter·loc·u·to·ry (in'tər·lok'yə·tô'ri; -tō'-), *adj.* 1. of or in conversation or dialogue. 2. made during a lawsuit or other action; not final.

in·ter·lop·er (in'tər·lōp'ər), *n.* intruder.

in·ter·lude (in'tər·lūd), *n.* 1. anything thought of as filling the time between two things; interval. 2. piece of music played between the parts of a song, church service, play, etc. 3. entertainment between the acts of a play. [< Med.L, < L *inter-* between + *ludus* play]

in·ter·mar·ry (in'tər·mar'i), *v.,* -ried, -ry·ing. 1. become connected by marriage. 2. marry within the family. —**in'ter·mar'riage,** *n.*

in·ter·med·dle (in'tər·med'əl), *v.,* -dled, -dling. meddle; interfere. —**in'ter·med'dler,** *n.*

in·ter·me·di·ar·y (in'tər·mē'di·er'i), *n.,* *pl.* -ar·ies. —*n.* person who acts for one person with another; go-between. —*adj.* 1. acting between. 2. being between; intermediate.

in·ter·me·di·ate (in'tər·mē'di·it), *adj.* being or occurring between: *gray is intermediate between black and white.* —*n.* 1. something in between. 2. mediator. [< Med.L, ult. < L *inter-* between + *medius* in the middle] —**in'ter·me'di·ate·ly,** *adv.* —**in'ter·me'di·ate·ness,** *n.* —Syn. *adj.* intervening.

in·ter·ment (in·tér'mənt), *n.* burial.

in·ter·mez·zo (in'tər·met'sō; -med'zō), *n.,* *pl.* -zos, -zi (-sē; -zē). 1. a short dramatic or musical entertainment between the acts of a play. 2. a short musical composition between the main divisions of an extended musical work. 3. an independent musical composition of similar character. [< Ital.]

in·ter·mi·na·ble (in·tér'mə·nə·bəl), *adj.* endless; so long as to seem endless. —**in·tér'mi·na·bly,** *adv.* —Syn. unending, limitless.

in·ter·min·gle (in'tər·ming'gəl), *v.,* -gled, -gling. mix together; mingle. —**in'ter·min'gle·ment,** *n.*

in·ter·mis·sion (in'tər·mish'ən), *n.* 1. time between periods of activity; pause. 2. stopping for a time; interruption: *rain without intermission.* —Syn. 1. interval.

in·ter·mit (in'tər·mit'), *v.,* -mit·ted, -mit·ting. stop for a time. [< L, < *inter-* between + *mittere* to leave] —**in'ter·mit'ter,** *n.* —**in'ter·mit'ting·ly,** *adv.*

in·ter·mit·tent (in′tər·mit′ənt), *adj.* 1. stopping and beginning again. 2. pausing at intervals. —in′ter·mit′tence, in′ter·mit′ten·cy, *n.* —in′ter·mit′tent·ly, *adv.*

in·ter·mix (in′tər·miks′), *v.* mix together; blend. —in′ter·mix′ture, *n.*

in·tern[1] (in·tėrn′), *v.* 1. confine within a country: *intern soldiers in a neutral country.* 2. force to stay in a certain place. [< F *interner* < L *internus* within] —in·tern′ment, *n.*

in·tern[2] (in′tėrn), *n.* Also, **interne.** *Am.* doctor acting as a resident assistant in a hospital. —*v.* act as an intern. [< F *interne.* See INTERN[1].] —in′tern·ship, *n. Am.*

in·ter·nal (in·tėr′nəl), *adj.* 1. inner; on the inside: *internal injuries.* 2. to be taken inside the body: *internal remedies.* 3. entirely inside; coming from within: *internal evidence.* 4. having to do with affairs within a country; domestic: *internal disturbances.* 5. of the mind; subjective: *thoughts are internal.* —*n.* 1. inner nature. 2. internals, inner organs. [< Med.L *internalis.* See INTERN[1].] —in′ter·nal′i·ty, *n.* —in·ter′nal·ly, *adv.*

internal-combustion engine, engine in which the pressure is produced by gas or vapor exploding inside the cylinder and against the piston.

in·ter·na·tion·al (in′tər·nash′ən·əl; -nash′nəl), *adj.* 1. between or among nations: *an international agreement.* 2. of or pertaining to different nations or their citizens. 3. having to do with the relations between nations: *international law.* —*n.* **International,** one of several international socialist or communist organizations. —in′ter·na′tion·al′i·ty, *n.* —in′ter·na′tion·al·ly, *adv.* **International Date Line,** date line (def. 1).

in·ter·na·tion·al·ism (in′tər·nash′ən·əl·iz′-əm; -nash′nəl-), *n.* principle of international coöperation for the good of all nations. —in′ter·na′tion·al·ist, *n.*

in·ter·na·tion·al·ize (in′tər·nash′ən·əl·iz; -nash′nəl-), *v.,* -ized, -iz·ing. make international; bring (territory) under the control of several nations. —in′ter·na′tion·al·i·za′tion, *n.*

in·terne (in′tėrn), *n. Am.* intern[2].

in·ter·ne·cine (in′tər·nē′sin; -sīn), *adj.* 1. destructive to both sides. 2. deadly; destructive. [< L *internecinus,* ult. < *inter-* between + *nex* slaughter]

in·tern·ee (in′tėr·nē′), *n.* person interned, as a prisoner of war, enemy alien, etc.

in·ter·pel·late (in′tėr·pel′āt; in·tėr′pə·lāt), *v.,* -lat·ed, -lat·ing. ask formally in a legislature for an explanation of official action or government policy. [< L *interpellatus* interrupted] —in′ter·pel·la′tion (in′tėr·pe·lā′shən; in·tėr′-pə-), *n.* —in′ter·pel·la′tor (in′tėr·pe·lā′tər; in·tėr′pə·lā′tər), *n.*

in·ter·pen·e·trate (in′tər·pen′ə·trāt), *v.,* -trat·ed, -trat·ing. 1. penetrate thoroughly; permeate. 2. penetrate each into the other. —in′ter·pen′e·tra′tion, *n.* —in′ter·pen′e·tra′tive, *adj.*

in·ter·phone (in′tėr·fōn′), *n.* intercom.

in·ter·plan·e·tar·y (in′tər·plan′ə·ter′i), *adj. Astron.* within the solar system, but not within the atmosphere of the sun or any planet.

in·ter·play (in′tər·plā′), *n.* action or influence on each other: *interplay of light and shadow.*

in·ter·po·late (in·tėr′pə·lāt), *v.,* -lat·ed, -lat·ing. 1. alter (a book, passage, etc.) by putting in new words or groups of words. 2. put in (new words, passages, etc.). 3. *Math.* insert (intermediate terms) in a series. [< L *interpolatus* refurbished] —in·tėr′po·lat′er, or in·tėr′po·la′tor, *n.* —in·tėr′po·la′tion, *n.* —in·tėr′po·la′tive, *adj.*

in·ter·pose (in′tər·pōz′), *v.,* -posed, -pos·ing. 1. put between; insert. 2. come between; be between. 3. interrupt. 4. interfere in order to help; intervene: *mother interposed in the dispute.* 5. put in as an interference or interruption. [< F, < *inter-* between + *poser* place, POSE] —in′ter·pos′er, *n.* —in′ter·pos′ing·ly, *adv.* —in·ter·po-

si·tion (in′tėr·pə·zish′ən), *n.* —Syn. 4. intercede, mediate.

in·ter·pret (in·tėr′prit), *v.* 1. explain the meaning of: *interpret a dream.* 2. bring out the meaning of: *interpret a part in a play.* 3. understand in a certain way: *interpret silence as consent.* 4. serve as an interpreter; translate. [< L *interpretari* < *interpres* mediary] —in·tėr′pret·a·ble, *adj.* —in·tėr′pret·a·bil′i·ty, *n.* —in·tėr′pre·tive, *adj.* —in·tėr′pre·tive·ly, *adv.* —Syn. 1. expound, elucidate, unfold.

in·ter·pre·ta·tion (in·tėr′prə·tā′shən), *n.* 1. an interpreting; explanation: *different interpretations of the same facts.* 2. bringing out the meaning of a dramatic part, music, etc. 3. translation. —in·tėr′pre·ta′tion·al, in·tėr′pre·ta′-tive, *adj.* —in·tėr′pre·ta′tive·ly, *adv.*

in·ter·pret·er (in·tėr′prə·tər), *n.* 1. person who interprets. 2. person whose business is translating from a foreign language.

in·ter·ra·cial (in′tər·rā′shəl), *adj.* between or involving different races.

in·ter·reg·num (in′tər·reg′nəm), *n., pl.* -nums, -na (-nə). 1. time between the end of one ruler's reign and the beginning of the next one. 2. any time during which a nation is without its usual ruler. 3. period of inactivity; pause. [< L, < *inter-* between + *regnum* reign] —in′ter·reg′nal, *adj.*

in·ter·re·late (in′tər·ri·lāt′), *v.,* -lat·ed, -lat·ing. connect closely with each other; bring into mutual relation. —in′ter·re·lat′ed, *adj.* —in′ter·re·la′tion, *n.* —in′ter·re·la′tion·ship, *n.*

in·ter·ro·gate (in·tėr′ə·gāt), *v.,* -gat·ed, -gat·ing. 1. question thoroughly; examine by asking questions: *interrogate a witness.* 2. ask a series of questions. [< L, < *inter-* between + *rogare* ask] —in·tėr′ro·gat′ing·ly, *adv.* —in·tėr′ro·ga′tor, *n.*

in·ter·ro·ga·tion (in·tėr′ə·gā′shən), *n.* 1. a questioning. The formal examination of a witness by asking questions is interrogation. 2. a question. —in·tėr′ro·ga′tion·al, *adj.*

interrogation mark or **point,** question mark (?).

in·ter·rog·a·tive (in′tə·rog′ə·tiv), *adj.* asking a question; having the form of a question. —*n. Gram.* a word used in asking a question. —in′ter·rog′a·tive·ly, *adv.*

in·ter·rog·a·to·ry (in′tə·rog′ə·tô′ri; -tō′-), *adj., n., pl.* -to·ries. —*adj.* questioning. —*n.* a formal question. —in′ter·rog·a·to′ri·ly, *adv.*

in·ter·rupt (in′tə·rupt′), *v.* 1. break in upon (talk, work, rest, a person speaking, etc.); hinder; stop. 2. make a break in: *interrupt the view.* 3. cause a break; break in: *do not interrupt the speech.* [< L *interruptus* < *inter-* between + *rumpere* break] —in′ter·rupt′er, *n.* —in′ter·rup′tive, *adj.*

in·ter·rup·tion (in′tə·rup′shən), *n.* 1. an interrupting. 2. a being interrupted. 3. thing that interrupts. 4. intermission.

in·ter·scho·las·tic (in′tər·skə·las′tik), *adj.* between schools: *interscholastic competition.*

in·ter·sect (in′tər·sekt′), *v.* 1. cut or divide by passing through or crossing. 2. cross each other. [< L, < *inter-* between + *secare* cut]

in·ter·sec·tion (in′tər·sek′shən), *n.* 1. an intersecting. 2. point or line where one thing crosses another. In the diagram there are two intersections where the line AB crosses the parallel lines. —in′ter·sec′tion·al, *adj.*

The line AB intersects the parallel lines.

in·ter·sperse (in′tər·spėrs′), *v.,* -spersed, -spers·ing. 1. vary with something put here and there: *grass interspersed with beds of flowers.* 2. scatter here and there among other things: *bushes were interspersed among trees.* [< L *interspersus* < *inter-* between + *spargere* scatter] —in′ter·sper′sion (in′tər·spėr′zhən; -shən), *n.*

in·ter·state (in′tər·stāt′; in′tər·stāt′), *adj.* between states: *interstate commerce.*

in·ter·stel·lar (in′tər·stel′ər; in′tər·stel′ər), *adj.* among or between the stars.

in·ter·stice (in·tėr′stis), *n.* a small or nar-raw space between things or parts; chink. [< LL *interstitium* < L *inter-* between + *stare* to stand] —in·ter·sti·tial (in'tər·stish'əl), *adj.* —in'ter·sti'tial·ly, *adv.*

in·ter·twine (in'tər·twīn'), *v.,* -twined, -twin·ing. twine, one with another. —in'ter·twine'ment, *n.* —in'ter·twin'ing·ly, *adv.*

in·ter·twist (in'tər·twist'), *v.* twist, one with another. —in'ter·twist'ing·ly, *adv.*

in·ter·ur·ban (in'tər·ér'bən; in'tər·ér'bən), *Am.* —*adj.* between cities or towns. —*n.* an interurban railroad.

in·ter·val (in'tər·vəl), *n.* **1.** time or space between: *an interval of a week.* **2.** at intervals, a. now and then. b. here and there. **3.** *Music.* the difference in pitch between two tones. [< L *tervallum,* orig., space between palisades < *inter-* between + *vallum* wall]

in·ter·vene (in'tər·vēn'), *v.,* -vened, -ven·ing. **1.** come between; be between: *a week intervenes between Christmas and New Year's.* **2.** come in to help settle a dispute: *the President intervened in the strike.* [< L, < *inter-* between + *venire* come] —in'ter·ven'er, in'ter·ve'nor, *n.* —Syn. **2.** mediate, intercede.

in·ter·ven·tion (in'tər·ven'shən), *n.* **1.** an intervening. **2.** interference by one nation in the affairs of another. —in'ter·ven'tion·al, *adj.* —in'ter·ven'tion·ist, *n.*

in·ter·view (in'tər·vū), *n.* **1.** a meeting to talk over something special: *an interview with a manager for a job.* **2.** *Am.* a. a meeting between a reporter and a person from whom information is sought for publication. b. newspaper or magazine article resulting from such a meeting. —*v.* have an interview with; meet and talk with. [< F *entrevue,* ult. < L *inter-* between + *videre* see] —in'ter·view'er, *n.*

in·ter·weave (in'tər·wēv'), *v.,* -wove or -weaved, -wo·ven or -wove or -weaved, -weav·ing. **1.** weave together. **2.** intermingle; connect closely. —in'ter·weave'ment, *n.* —in'ter·weav'er, *n.* —in'ter·wo'ven, *adj.*

in·tes·tate (in·tes'tāt, -tit), *adj.* **1.** having made no will. **2.** not disposed of by a will. —*n.* person who has died without making a will. [< L, < *in-* not + *testari* make a will < *testis* witness] —in·tes·ta·cy (in·tes'tə·si), *n.*

in·tes·ti·nal (in·tes'tə·nəl), *adj.* of or in the intestines. —in·tes'ti·nal·ly, *adv.*

in·tes·tine (in·tes'tən), *n. Anat.* **1.** part of the alimentary canal that extends from the stomach to the anus. **2.** a portion of this. The first, narrower and longer portion is the small intestine and the other the large intestine. —*adj.* within a country; internal: *intestine strife.* [< L *intestina,* neut. pl., internal, ult. < *in* in]

in·thrall, in·thral (in·thrôl'), *v.* enthrall. —in·thrall'ment, in·thral'ment, *n.*

in·throne (in·thrōn'), *v.,* -throned, -throning. enthrone.

in·ti·ma·cy (in'tə·mə·si), *n., pl.* -cies. **1.** a being intimate; close acquaintance. **2.** a familiar or intimate act. **3.** sexual relations. —Syn. **1.** closeness. **2.** familiarity.

in·ti·mate[1] (in'tə·mit), *adj.* **1.** very familiar; known very well; closely acquainted. **2.** close; thorough: *intimate knowledge of a matter.* **3.** very personal; most private. **4.** far within; inmost. **5.** maintaining illicit sexual relations. —*n.* a close friend. [< L *intimatus* (see INTIMATE[2]), confused with *intimus* inmost] —in'ti·mate·ly, *adv.* —in'ti·mate·ness, *n.*

in·ti·mate[2] (in'tə·māt), *v.,* -mat·ed, -mat·ing. **1.** suggest indirectly; hint. **2.** announce; notify. [< L *intimatus,* orig., made to sink in, ult. < L *intimus* inmost] —in'ti·mat'er, *n.*

in·ti·ma·tion (in'tə·mā'shən), *n.* **1.** indirect suggestion; hint. **2.** announcement; notice.

in·tim·i·date (in·tim'ə·dāt), *v.,* -dat·ed, -dat·ing. **1.** frighten; make afraid. **2.** influence or force by fear. [< Med.L, < L *in-* + *timidus* fearful] —in·tim'i·da'tion, *n.* —in·tim'i·da'tor, *n.*

in·ti·tle (in·tī'təl), *v.,* -tled, -tling. entitle.

in·to (in'tü; *unstressed* in'tù, -tə), *prep.* **1.** to the inside of; toward the inside; within: *go into*

the house. **2.** to the condition of; to the form of: *divided into ten rooms.* ▶ See in for usage note.

in·tol·er·a·ble (in·tol'ər·ə·bəl), *adj.* unbearable; too much, too painful, etc., to be endured. —in·tol'er·a·bil'i·ty, in·tol'er·a·ble·ness, *n.* —Syn. unendurable, insufferable.

in·tol·er·a·bly (in·tol'ər·ə·bli), *adv.* unbearably; beyond endurance.

in·tol·er·ance (in·tol'ər·əns), *n.* **1.** lack of tolerance; unwillingness to let others do and think as they choose, esp. in matters of religion. **2.** inability to endure; unwillingness to endure.

in·tol·er·ant (in·tol'ər·ənt), *adj.* **1.** not tolerant; unwilling to let others do and think as they choose, esp. in matters of religion. **2.** intolerant of, not able to endure; unwilling to endure. —in·tol'er·ant·ly, *adv.* —Syn. **1.** bigoted, narrow, dogmatic.

in·tomb (in·tüm'), *v.* entomb. —in·tomb'ment, *n.*

in·to·na·tion (in'tō·nā'shən; -tə-), *n.* **1.** act of intoning. **2.** pattern of modulation and inflection in connected speech.

in·tone (in·tōn'), *v.,* -toned, -ton·ing. **1.** read or recite in a singing voice; chant. **2.** utter with a particular tone. [< Med.L, ult. < L *in-* in + *tonus* tone] —in·ton'er, *n.*

in to·to (in tō'tō), *Latin.* completely.

in·tox·i·cant (in·tok'sə·kənt), *n.* any intoxicating agent, esp. alcoholic liquor. —*adj.* intoxicating.

in·tox·i·cate (in·tok'sə·kāt), *v.,* -cat·ed, -cat·ing. **1.** make drunk. **2.** excite beyond self-control. [< Med.L, ult. < L *in-* in + *toxicum* poison. See TOXIC.] —in·tox'i·cat'ed, *adj.* —in·tox'i·cat'ing·ly, *adv.* —in·tox'i·ca'tive, *adj.* —in·tox'i·ca'tor, *n.*

in·tox·i·ca·tion (in·tok'sə·kā'shən), *n.* **1.** drunkenness. **2.** great emotional excitement. **3.** *Pathol.* poisoning.

intra-, *prefix.* within; inside; on the inside. [< L *intra,* prep.; *adv.*]

in·trac·ta·ble (in·trak'tə·bəl), *adj.* hard to manage; stubborn. —in·trac'ta·bil'i·ty, in·trac'ta·ble·ness, *n.* —in·trac'ta·bly, *adv.* —Syn. unruly, perverse, headstrong.

in·tra·dos (in·trā'dos), *n. Archit.* the interior curve or surface of an arch or vault. [< F, < L *intra-* within + F *dos* back]

in·tra·mu·ral (in'trə·myùr'əl), *adj.* within the walls; inside. ▶ intramural. No hyphen. It means "within the walls," referring specifically to college activities carried on by groups from the same college; the opposite of *intercollegiate.*

intrans., intransitive.

in·tran·si·gence (in·tran'sə·jəns), in·tran·si·gen·cy (-jən·si), *n.* uncompromising hostility.

in·tran·si·gent (in·tran'sə·jənt), *adj.* unwilling to agree or compromise; irreconcilable. —*n.* person who is unwilling to agree or compromise. [< F < Sp., ult. < L *in-* not + *transigere* come to an agreement < *trans-* through + *agere* to drive] —in·tran'si·gent·ly, *adv.*

in·tran·si·tive (in·tran'sə·tiv), *Gram.* —*adj.* of verbs, not taking a direct object. —*n.* an intransitive verb. —in·tran'si·tive·ly, *adv.* —in·tran'si·tive·ness, *n.* ▶ See verb for usage note.

in·tra·state (in'trə·stāt'), *adj. Am.* within a state.

in·tra·ve·nous (in'trə·vē'nəs), *adj.* **1.** within a vein or the veins. **2.** into a vein. [< INTRA- + L *vena* vein] —in'tra·ve'nous·ly, *adv.*

in·treat (in·trēt'), *v.* entreat.

in·trench (in·trench'), *v.* entrench. —in·trench'er, *n.* —in·trench'ment, *n.*

in·trep·id (in·trep'id), *adj.* fearless; dauntless; very brave. [< L, < *in-* not + *trepidus* alarmed] —in·tre·pid'i·ty, *n.* —in·trep'id·ly, *adv.* —Syn. bold, courageous, daring, valiant.

in·tri·ca·cy (in'trə·kə·si), *n., pl.* -cies. **1.** a being intricate; complexity. **2.** complication; something involved; intricate proceeding.

in·tri·cate (in'trə·kit), *adj.* **1.** with many twists and turns; entangled; complicated: *an intricate knot.* **2.** very hard to understand; perplexing: *an intricate piece of machinery.* [< L *intricatus* entangled, ult. < *in-* in + *tricae* hindrances] —in′tri·cate·ly, *adv.* —in′tri·cate·ness, *n.* —Syn. 1. involved, complex.

in·trigue (n. in·trēg′, in′trēg; v. in·trēg′), *n.*, *v.*, -trigued, -tri·guing. —*n.* 1. underhand planning; plotting; secret scheming. 2. a crafty plot; secret scheme. 3. a secret love affair. —*v.* 1. carry on an underhand plan; scheme secretly; plot. 2. excite the curiosity and interest of. 3. have a secret love affair. [< F < Ital. < L *intricare* entangle. See INTRICATE.] —in·tri′guer, *n.* —in·tri′guing·ly, *adv.* —Syn. *n.* 1. conspiracy.

in·trin·sic (in·trin′sik), in·trin·si·cal (-sə-kəl), *adj.* belonging to a thing by its very nature; essential; inherent: *the intrinsic value of a dollar bill is only that of a piece of paper.* [< Med.L *intrinsecus* internal < L, inwardly] —in·trin′si·cal·ly, *adv.* —Syn. genuine.

in·tro·, in·trod·, introduction; introductory.

in·tro·duce (in′trə·dūs′; -dūs′), *v.*, -duced, -duc·ing. 1. bring in: *introduce a story into the conversation.* 2. put in; insert: *introduce a tube into the throat.* 3. bring into use, notice, knowledge, etc.: *introduce a new word.* 4. make known: *introduce a speaker.* 5. present formally: *introduce (one) to society.* 6. give an introduction to: *this book introduces us to biochemistry.* 7. bring forward: *introduce a question for debate.* 8. begin: *relative pronouns introduce adjective clauses.* [< L, < *intro-* in + *ducere* lead] —in′tro·duc′er, *n.* —in′tro·duc′i·ble, *adj.*

in·tro·duc·tion (in′trə·duk′shən), *n.* 1. an introducing: *the introduction of steel made tall buildings easy to build.* 2. a being introduced; introduction to strangers. 3. thing that introduces; first part of a book, speech, piece of music, etc., leading up to the main part. 4. first book for beginners. 5. thing introduced.

in·tro·duc·to·ry (in′trə·duk′tə·ri), in·tro·duc·tive (-tiv), *adj.* used to introduce; serving as an introduction; preliminary. —in′tro·duc′to·ri·ly, in′tro·duc′tive·ly, *adv.*

in·tro·spec·tion (in′trə·spek′shən), *n.* examination of one's own thoughts and feelings. [< L, < *intro-* into + *specere* to look] —in′tro·spec′tive, *adj.* —in′tro·spec′tive·ly, *adv.*

in·tro·ver·sion (in′trə·vėr′zhən; -shən), *n.* tendency to be more interested in one's own thoughts and feelings than in what is going on around one. —in·tro·ver·sive (in′trə·vėr′siv), *adj.*

in·tro·vert (v. in′trə·vėrt′; n., adj. in′trə·vėrt′), *v.* 1. turn (one's thoughts, etc.) upon oneself. 2. turn or bend inward. —*n.* person more interested in his own thoughts and feelings than in what is going on around him; person tending to think rather than act. —*adj.* characterized by introversion. [< L *intro-* within + *vertere* to turn]

in·trude (in·trüd′), *v.*, -trud·ed, -trud·ing. 1. thrust oneself in; come unasked and unwanted. 2. *Geol.* thrust in; force in. [< L, < *in-* in + *trudere* to thrust] —in·trud′er, *n.* —in·trud′ing·ly, *adv.* —Syn. 1. trespass.

in·tru·sion (in·trü′zhən), *n.* act of intruding.

in·tru·sive (in·trü′siv), *adj.* intruding. —in·tru′sive·ly, *adv.* —in·tru′sive·ness, *n.*

in·trust (in·trust′), *v.* entrust.

in·tu·i·tion (in′tü·ish′ən; -tyü-), *n.* 1. perception of truths, facts, etc., without reasoning. 2. something so perceived. [< LL *intuitio* a gazing at, ult. < *in-* at + *tueri* to look] —in′tu·i′tion·al, *adj.* —in′tu·i′tion·al·ly, *adv.*

in·tu·i·tive (in·tü′ə·tiv; -tū′-), *adj.* 1. perceiving by intuition. 2. acquired by intuition: *intuitive knowledge.* —in·tu′i·tive·ly, *adv.* —in·tu′i·tive·ness, *n.*

in·un·date (in′un·dāt; in·un′dāt), *v.*, -dat·ed, -dat·ing. overflow; flood. [< L, < *in-* onto < *undare* flow] —in′un·da′tion, *n.* —in′un·da′tor, *n.*

in·ure (in·yu̇r′), *v.*, -ured, -ur·ing. 1. toughen or harden; accustom; habituate; have effect; be useful. [< *in* + obs. *ure* use, n. < AF < L *opera* work] —in·ure′ment, *n.*

inv., 1. inventor; invented. 2. invoice.

in·vade (in·vād′), *v.*, -vad·ed, -vad·ing. 1. enter with force or as an enemy; attack: *soldiers invaded the country.* 2. enter as if to take possession: *tourists invaded the city.* 3. interfere with; encroach upon; violate: *invade the rights of others.* [< L, < *in-* in + *vadere* go, walk] —in·vad′er, *n.*

in·va·lid[1] (in′və·lid), *n.* a sick, weak person not able to get about and do things. —*adj.* 1. not well; weak and sick. 2. of or for an invalid or invalids. —*v.* 1. make weak or sick; disable. 2. remove from active service because of sickness or injury. [< L, < *in-* not + *validus* strong]

in·val·id[2] (in·val′id), *adj.* not valid; without force or effect. —in·va·lid·i·ty (in′və·lid′ə·ti), *n.* —in·val′id·ly, *adv.* —Syn. worthless.

in·val·i·date (in·val′ə·dāt), *v.*, -dat·ed, -dat·ing. make valueless; deprive of force or effect. —in·val′i·da′tion, *n.* —in·val′i·da′tor, *n.*

in·va·lid·ism (in′və·lid·iz′əm), *n.* condition of being an invalid; prolonged ill health.

in·val·u·a·ble (in·val′yü·ə·bəl), *adj.* very precious; valuable beyond measure. —in·val′u·a·ble·ness, *n.* —in·val′u·a·bly, *adv.* —Syn. priceless.

in·var·i·a·ble (in·vãr′i·ə·bəl), *adj.* always the same; unchangeable; unchanging. —in·var′i·a·bil′i·ty, in·var′i·a·ble·ness, *n.* —in·var′i·a·bly, *adv.* —Syn. uniform, constant.

in·va·sion (in·vā′zhən), *n.* 1. an invading; an attack. 2. interference; encroachment; violation. —in·va·sive (in·vā′siv), *adj.*

in·vec·tive (in·vek′tiv), *n.* violent attack in words; abusive language. —*adj.* inveighing; denouncing. [< LL *invectivus.* See INVEIGH.] —in·vec′tive·ly, *adv.* —in·vec′tive·ness, *n.*

in·veigh (in·vā′), *v.* make a violent attack in words. [< L, < *in-* against + *vehere* carry] —in·veigh′er, *n.*

in·vei·gle (in·vē′gəl; -vā′-), *v.*, -gled, -gling. lead by trickery; entice; allure. [ult. < F *aveugler* make blind < *aveugle* blind, ult. < L *ab-* away + *oculus* eye] —in·vei′gle·ment, *n.* —in·vei′gler, *n.* —Syn. ensnare, beguile, dupe.

in·vent (in·vent′), *v.* 1. make or think out (something new): *Bell invented the telephone.* 2. make up; think up: *invent an excuse.* [< L, < *in-* in + *venire* come] —in·vent′i·ble, *adj.* —in·ven′tor, in·vent′er, *n.*

in·ven·tion (in·ven′shən), *n.* 1. a making something new: *the invention of gunpowder.* 2. thing invented. 3. power of inventing. 4. a made-up story; false statement. —in·ven′tion·al, *adj.*

in·ven·tive (in·ven′tiv), *adj.* 1. good at inventing. 2. of invention. 3. showing power of inventing. —in·ven′tive·ly, *adv.* —in·ven′tive·ness, *n.*

in·ven·to·ry (in′vən·tô′ri; -tō′-), *n.*, *pl.* -to·ries, *v.*, -to·ried, -to·ry·ing. —*n.* 1. a detailed list of articles with their estimated value. 2. collection of articles that are or may be so listed; stock. —*v.* make a detailed list of; enter in a list. [< Med.L *inventorium.* See INVENT.] —in′ven·to′ri·al, *adj.* —in′ven·to′ri·al·ly, *adv.*

In·ver·ness (in′vər·nes′), or Inverness cape, *n.* overcoat with a long removable cape.

Inverness

in·verse (*adj.*, *n.* in·vėrs′, in′vėrs; *v.* in·vėrs′), *adj.*, *n.*, *v.*, -versed, -vers·ing. —*adj.* reversed in position, direction, or tendency; inverted: *DCBA is the inverse order of ABCD.* —*n.* 1. an inverted condition. 2. something reversed. 3. direct opposite: *evil is the inverse of good.* —*v.* invert. [< L *inversus,* pp. of *invertere* INVERT] —in·verse′ly, *adv.*

in·ver·sion (in·vėr′zhən; -shən), *n.* 1. an inverting or being inverted. 2. something inverted.

in·vert (*v.* in·vėrt′; *n.* in′vėrt), *v.* 1. turn upside down. 2. turn around or reverse in position, direction, order, etc. 3. *Music.* change by making the lower or lowest note an octave higher or the higher or highest note an octave lower. —*n.* one that is inverted. [< L, < *in-* + *vertere* to turn] —in·vert′er, *n.* —in·vert′i·ble, *adj.*

in·ver·te·brate (in·vér′te·brit; –brāt), *adj.* 1. *Zool.* without a backbone. 2. of or having to do with invertebrates. —*n.* animal without a backbone. All animals except fishes, amphibians, reptiles, birds, and mammals are invertebrates. —in·ver·te·bra·cy (in·vér′te·bre·si), in·ver′te·brate·ness, *n.*

in·vest (in·vest′), *v.* 1. use (money) to buy something that is expected to produce a profit, or income, or both: *people invest their money in stocks, bonds, lands, etc.* 2. invest money: *learn to invest wisely.* 3. loosely, lay out; spend: *invest large sums in books.* 4. clothe; cover; surround: *darkness invests the earth at night.* 5. give power, authority, or right to: *he invested his lawyer with complete power to act for him.* 6. install in office with a ceremony: *a king is invested in office by crowning him.* 7. *Mil.* surround with soldiers or ships; besiege: *the enemy invested the city and cut it off from our army.* [< L, < *in-* in + *vestis* clothing] —in·ves′tor, *n.*

in·ves·ti·gate (in·ves′te·gāt), *v.,* –gat·ed, –gat·ing. search into; examine closely: *scientists investigate nature.* [< L, < *in-* in + *vestigare* to track, trace] —in·ves′ti·ga′tive, in·ves·ti·ga·to·ry (in·ves′te·ge·tô′ri; –tō′–), *adj.* —in·ves′ti·ga′tor, *n.* —Syn. explore, scrutinize.

in·ves·ti·ga·tion (in·ves′te·gā′shen), *n.* careful search; detailed or careful examination.

in·ves·ti·ture (in·ves′te·cher), *n.* 1. a formal investing of a person with an office, dignity, power, right, etc. 2. clothing; covering.

in·vest·ment (in·vest′ment), *n.* 1. an investing; a laying out of money. 2. amount of money invested. 3. something that is expected to yield money as income or profit or both. 4. a surrounding with soldiers or ships; siege. 5. investiture.

in·vet·er·a·cy (in·vet′er·e·si), *n.* settled, fixed condition; habitualness.

in·vet·er·ate (in·vet′er·it), *adj.* 1. confirmed in a habit, practice, feeling, etc.; habitual: *an inveterate smoker.* 2. long and firmly established. [< L, < *in-* in + *veterascere* grow old < *vetus* old] —in·vet′er·ate·ly, *adv.* —in·vet′er·ate·ness, *n.* —Syn. 1. hardened, chronic.

in·vid·i·ous (in·vid′i·es), *adj.* likely to arouse ill will or resentment; giving offense because unfair or unjust. [< L, < *invidia* envy] —in·vid′i·ous·ly, *adv.* —in·vid′i·ous·ness, *n.* —Syn. hateful, odious, offensive.

in·vig·or·ate (in·vig′er·āt), *v.,* –at·ed, –at·ing. give vigor to; fill with life and energy. [< *vigor*] —in·vig′or·at′ing·ly, *adv.* —in·vig′or·a′tion, *n.* —in·vig′or·a′tive, *adj.* —in·vig′or·a·tive·ly, *adv.* —in·vig′or·a′tor, *n.* —Syn. brace, refresh, stimulate, animate.

in·vin·ci·ble (in·vin′se·bel), *adj.* not to be overcome; unconquerable. [< L, < *in-* not + *vincere* conquer] —in·vin′ci·bil′i·ty, in·vin′ci·ble·ness, *n.* —in·vin′ci·bly, *adv.*

in·vi·o·la·ble (in·vī′e·le·bel), *adj.* 1. that must not be violated or injured; sacred. 2. that cannot be violated or injured. —in·vi′o·la·bil′i·ty, in·vi′o·la·ble·ness, *n.* —in·vi′o·la·bly, *adv.*

in·vi·o·late (in·vī′e·lit; –lāt), *adj.* not violated; uninjured; unbroken; not profaned. —in·vi·o·la·cy (in·vī′e·le·si), in·vi′o·late·ness, *n.* —in·vi′o·late·ly, *adv.*

in·vis·i·ble (in·viz′e·bel), *adj.* 1. not visible; not capable of being seen: *germs are invisible to the naked eye.* 2. out of sight. 3. hidden: *invisible assets.* —*n.* 1. an invisible being or thing. 2. the invisible, the unseen world. —in·vis′i·bil′i·ty, in·vis′i·ble·ness, *n.* —in·vis′i·bly, *adv.*

in·vi·ta·tion (in′ve·tā′shen), *n.* 1. request to come to some place or to do something. 2. act of inviting. 3. attraction; inducement. —in′vi·ta′tion·al, *adj.*

in·vite (*v.* in·vīt′; *n.* in′vīt), *v.,* –vit·ed, –vit·ing, *n.* —*v.* 1. ask (someone) politely to come to some place or to do something. 2. make a polite request for: *he invited our opinion of his work.* 3. give occasion for: *the letter invites some question.* 4. attract; tempt. —*n. Colloq.* invitation.

[< L *invitare*] —in·vit′er, *n.* —Syn. *v.* 1. bid, request. 4. encourage, incite. ➤ Invite is ordinarily a verb. Its use as a noun (in′vīt) is colloquial or would-be humorous: *Did you get an invite?*

in·vit·ing (in·vīt′ing), *adj.* attractive; tempting. —in·vit′ing·ly, *adv.* —in·vit′ing·ness, *n.*

in·vo·ca·tion (in′ve·kā′shen), *n.* act of calling upon in prayer; appeal for help or protection.

in·voice (in′vois), *n.,* *v.,* –voiced, –voic·ing. —*n.* list of goods sent to a purchaser showing prices, amounts, shipping charges, etc. —*v.* make an invoice of; enter on an invoice. [earlier *invoyes,* pl. of *invoy,* var. of ENVOY]

in·voke (in·vōk′), *v.,* –voked, –vok·ing. 1. call on in prayer; appeal to for help or protection. 2. ask earnestly for; beg for. 3. call forth by magic. [< L, < *in-* on + *vocare* call] —in·vok′er, *n.*

in·vo·lu·cre (in′ve·lü′ker), *n.* circle of bracts around a flower cluster. [< F < L *involucrum* a cover < *involvere.* See INVOLVE.] —in′vo·lu′cral, *adj.*

INVOLUCRE

in·vol·un·tar·y (in·vol′en·ter′i), *adj.* 1. not voluntary; not done of one's own free will; unwilling: *an involuntary witness.* 2. not done on purpose; not intended: *an involuntary injury.* 3. not controlled by the will: *breathing is mainly involuntary.* —in·vol′un·tar′i·ly, *adv.* —in·vol′un·tar′i·ness, *n.* —Syn. 1. compulsory, forced. 2. unintentional, inadvertent. 3. automatic, instinctive.

in·vo·lute (in′ve·lüt), *adj.* 1. involved; intricate. 2. rolled up on itself; curved spirally. 3. *Bot.* rolled inward from the edge. 4. *Zool.* having the whorls closely wound, as a spiral shell. —*n.* something involved. [< L *involutus,* pp. of *involvere* INVOLVE] —in′vo·lut′ed·ly, *adv.*

in·vo·lu·tion (in′ve·lü′shen), *n.* 1. an involving. 2. a being involved; entanglement; complexity. 3. something involved; complication. —in′vo·lu′tion·al, *adj.*

in·volve (in·volv′), *v.,* –volved, –volv·ing. 1. have as a necessary part, condition, or result; affect; take in; include. 2. cause to be unpleasantly concerned; implicate; bring (into difficulty, danger, etc.). 3. entangle; complicate: *involved sentences are hard to understand.* 4. take up the attention of; occupy: *involved in working out a puzzle.* 5. wrap; infold; envelop: *the outcome of the war is involved in doubt.* [< L, < *in-* in + *volvere* to roll] —in·volve′ment, *n.* —in·volv′er, *n.* —Syn. 1. entail. 4. absorb. 5. surround.

in·vul·ner·a·ble (in·vul′ner·e·bel), *adj.* that cannot be wounded or injured; proof against attack. —in·vul′ner·a·bil′i·ty, in·vul′ner·a·ble·ness, *n.* —in·vul′ner·a·bly, *adv.*

in·ward (in′werd), *adv.* Also, in′wards. 1. toward the inside: *a passage leading inward.* 2. into the mind or soul: *turn your thoughts inward.* —*adj.* 1. placed within; internal: *the inward parts of the body.* 2. inland: *inward Australia.* 3. directed toward the inside: *an inward slant of the eyes.* 4. in the mind or soul: *inward peace.* —*n.* in·wards (in′erdz). parts inside the body.

in·ward·ly (in′werd·li), *adv.* 1. on the inside; within. 2. toward the inside. 3. in the mind or soul. 4. not aloud or openly.

in·ward·ness (in′werd·nis), *n.* 1. inner nature or meaning. 2. spirituality. 3. earnestness.

in·weave (in·wēv′), *v.,* –wove or –weaved, –woven or –wove or –weaved, –weav·ing. weave in.

in·wrap (in·rap′), *v.,* –wrapped, –wrap·ping. enwrap.

in·wrought (in·rôt′), *adj.* 1. having a decoration worked in. 2. worked in. 3. mixed together; closely blended. Also, enwrought.

I·o (ī′ō), *n. Gk. Myth.* maiden loved by Zeus, changed into a white heifer by Hera.

Io, *Chem.* ionium.

i·o·dide (ī′e·dīd; –did), **i·o·did** (–did), *n. Chem.* compound of iodine with another element or radical.

i·o·dine (ī′e·dīn, –din; *Chem.* ī′e·dēn), **i·o·din**

(–din), *n. Chem.* **1.** a nonmetallic element, I, consisting of blackish crystals that give off a dense, violet-colored vapor with an irritating odor, used in medicine, in making dyes, in photography, etc. **2.** a brown liquid, tincture of iodine, used as an antiseptic. [< F *iode* iodine < Gk. *iodes* rust-colored < *ios* rust]

i·o·do·form (ī·ō′də·fôrm; ī·od′–), *n. Chem.* a crystalline compound of iodine, CHI₃, used as an antiseptic.

i·on (ī′ən; ī′on), *n. Physics, Chem.* **1.** either of the two substances into which a compound is broken up by an electric current. **2.** an electrified atom or group of atoms. **3.** an electrically charged particle formed in a gas. [< Gk., neut. ppr. of *ienai* go] —**i·on·ic** (ī·on′ik), *adj.*

-ion, *suffix.* **1.** act of ———ing, as in *attraction.* **2.** condition or state of being ———ed, as in *adoption.* **3.** result of ———ing, as in *abbreviation.* [< F < L -io, -ionis]

I·o·ni·a (ī·ō′ni·ə), *n.* an ancient region on the W coast of Asia Minor, with nearby islands, colonized by the Greeks in very early times. —**I·o′ni·an,** *adj., n.*

Ionian Sea, part of the Mediterranean Sea between Greece and S Italy.

I·on·ic (ī·on′ik), *adj.* **1.** noting or pertaining to the order of Greek architecture having scrolls in the capitals of the columns. **2.** of Ionia or its people.

Ionic capital

i·o·ni·um (ī·ō′ni·əm), *n. Chem.* a radioactive element, Io, formed from disintegrating uranium.

i·on·ize (ī′ən·īz), *v.,* -ized, -izing. separate into ions; produce ions in. Acids, bases, and salts ionize in solution. —**i′on·i·za′tion,** *n.* —**i′on·iz′er,** *n.*

i·on·o·sphere (ī·on′ə·sfir), *n.* a region of ionized layers of air beginning 18 to 28 miles above the earth's surface.

i·o·ta (ī·ō′tə), *n.* **1.** the ninth letter of the Greek alphabet (I, ι). **2.** a very small quantity. —Syn. **2.** bit, jot.

I.O.U., I O U (ī′ō′ū′), **1.** I owe you. **2.** informal note showing a debt.

I·o·wa (ī′ə·wə), *n.* a Middle Western State of the United States. *Capital:* Des Moines. *Abbrev.:* Ia. —**I′o·wan,** *n.*

ip·e·cac (ip′ə·kak), **ip·e·cac·u·an·ha** (ip′ə·kak′yū·an′ə), *n. Am.* **1.** medicine made from the dried roots of a South American vine, used as an emetic or purgative. **2.** the dried roots. **3.** the vine. [< Pg. < Tupi *ipe-kaa-guéne* creeping plant causing nausea]

Iph·i·ge·ni·a (if′ə·jə·nī′ə), *n. Gk. Legend.* daughter of Agamemnon and Clytemnestra.

ip·se dix·it (ip′sē dik′sit), a dogmatic assertion. [< L, he himself said (it)]

ip·so fac·to (ip′sō fak′tō), *Latin.* by that very fact; by the fact itself.

IQ, I.Q., intelligence quotient.

Ir, *Chem.* iridium.

Ir., Ireland; Irish.

I·ran (i·rän′; ī–; ē·rän′), *n.* kingdom in SW Asia. Formerly called Persia. —**I·ra·ni·an** (i·rā′ni·ən; ī–), *adj., n.*

I·raq, I·rak (i·räk′; ē·räk′), *n.* country in SW Asia, N of Arabia. Formerly called Mesopotamia.

I·ra·qi (ē·rä′kē; i·rak′i), *n., pl.* -qis, *adj.* —*n.* native of Iraq or Iraqis. —*adj.* of or having to do with Iraq or its inhabitants.

i·ras·ci·ble (i·ras′ə·bəl), *adj.* **1.** easily made angry; irritable. **2.** showing anger. [< LL, < L *irasci* grow angry < *ira* anger] —**i·ras′ci·bil′i·ty,** **i·ras′ci·ble·ness,** *n.* —**i·ras′ci·bly,** *adv.*

i·rate (ī′rāt; ī·rāt′), *adj.* angry. [< L, < *ira* anger] —**i·rate′ly,** *adv.*

IRBM, Intermediate Range Ballistic Missile, a ballistic missile of great range (up to 1500 miles) but less than that of the ICBM.

ire (īr), *n.* anger; wrath. [< OF < L *ira*] —**ire′ful,** *adj.* —**ire′ful·ly,** *adv.* —**ire′ful·ness,** *n.* —**ire′less,** *adj.*

Ire., Ireland.

Ire·land (īr′lənd), *n.* **1.** one of the British Isles divided into the Republic of Ireland and Northern Ireland. **2.** Republic of, the Irish Republic.

ir·i·des·cence (ir′ə·des′əns), *n.* changing or play of colors, as in mother-of-pearl, opals, a peacock's feathers, etc. [< L *iris* rainbow < Gk.] —**ir′i·des′cent,** *adj.* —**ir′i·des′cent·ly,** *adv.*

i·rid·i·um (i·rid′i·əm), *n. Chem.* a rare metallic element, Ir, that resembles platinum and is twice as heavy as lead, used for the points of gold pens.

i·ris (ī′ris), *n., pl.* **i·ris·es,** **i·ri·des** (ir′ə·dēz; ī′rə–). **1.** *Bot.* **a.** a plant with sword-shaped leaves and large flowers with three upright petals and three drooping petallike sepals. **b.** the flower. **2.** *Anat.* the colored part around the pupil of the eye. **3.** Iris, *Gk. Myth.* goddess of the rainbow and messenger of the gods. **4.** rainbow. [< L < Gk., rainbow]

I·rish (ī′rish), *adj.* of or having to do with Ireland, its people, or their language. —*n.* **1.** (*pl. in use*) people of Ireland. **2.** the Celtic language spoken in part of Ireland; Gaelic. **3.** English as spoken by the Irish.

Irish Free State, former name of the Irish Republic.

I·rish·man (ī′rish·mən), *n., pl.* -men. man of Irish birth.

Irish potato, the common white potato.

Irish Republic, an independent republic in C and S Ireland. *Capital:* Dublin.

Irish Sea, part of the Atlantic between Ireland and England.

Irish setter, a hunting dog with long, silky, reddish-brown hair.

Irish stew, stew made of meat, potatoes, and onions.

Irish terrier, a small dog with brown wiry hair, somewhat like a small Airedale.

I·rish·wom·an (ī′rish·wùm′ən), *n., pl.* -wom·en. woman of Irish birth or Irish descent.

Irish terrier (ab. 18 in. high at the shoulder)

irk (ėrk), *v.* weary; disgust; annoy; trouble. [ME *irke(n)*]

irk·some (ėrk′səm), *adj.* tiresome; tedious. —**irk′some·ly,** *adv.* —**irk′some·ness,** *n.* —Syn. annoying.

Ir·kutsk (ir·kútsk′), *n.* city in S Soviet Union in Asia.

i·ron (ī′ərn), *n.* **1.** the commonest and most useful metal, from which tools, machinery, etc., are made. It is a chemical element, Fe. **2.** tool, instrument, or weapon made from this metal. **3.** great hardness and strength; firmness: *men of iron.* **4.** tool with a flat surface for smoothing cloth or pressing clothes. **5.** golf club with an iron or steel head. **6. irons,** chains or bands of iron; handcuffs; shackles. —*adj.* **1.** made of iron; pertaining to iron. **2.** like iron; hard or strong; unyielding: *an iron will.* **3.** harsh or cruel: *the iron hand of fate.* —*v.* **1.** smooth or press (cloth, etc.) with a heated iron. **2.** furnish or cover with iron. [OE *īren,* ? < Celtic] —**i′ron·like′,** *adj.*

i·ron·bound (ī′ərn·bound′), *adj.* **1.** bound with iron. **2.** hard; firm; rigid; unyielding. **3.** rocky.

i·ron·clad (ī′ərn·klad′), *adj.* **1.** protected with iron plates. **2.** very hard to change or get out of: *an ironclad agreement.* —*n.* warship protected with iron plates.

Iron Curtain, an imaginary wall separating Russia and the nations under Russian control or influence from the rest of the world, behind which strict censorship and secrecy are enforced.

i·ron·i·cal (ī·ron′ə·kəl), **i·ron·ic** (–ik), *adj.* **1.** expressing one thing and meaning the opposite: *"Speedy" would be an ironical name for a snail.* **2.** contrary to what would naturally be expected. —**i·ron′i·cal·ly,** *adv.* —**i·ron′i·cal·ness,** *n.*

ironing board, board covered with a smooth cloth, used for ironing clothes.

iron lung, device to give artificial respiration.

i·ron·mon·ger (ī′ərn·mung′gər; –mong′–), *n.*

Esp. Brit. dealer in ironware or hardware. —**i'ron·mon'ger·y**, *n.*

iron pyrites, mineral, FeS₂, that looks somewhat like gold; fool's gold.

i·ron·sides (ī'ərn·sīdz'), *n.pl.* (*sing. in use*) an armor-clad warship.

i·ron·ware (ī'ərn·wâr'), *n.* articles made of iron, such as pots, kettles, tools, etc.; hardware.

i·ron·wood (ī'ərn·wu̇d'), *n. Am.* **1.** any of various trees with hard heavy wood. **2.** the wood itself.

i·ron·work (ī'ərn·wėrk'), *n.* **1.** things made of iron. **2.** work in iron. —**i'ron·work'er,** *n.*

i·ron·works (ī'ərn·wėrks'), *n. pl. or sing.* place where iron is made or worked into iron articles.

i·ro·ny (ī'rə·ni), *n., pl.* **-nies. 1.** method of expression in which the ordinary meaning of the words is the opposite of the thought in the speaker's mind: *the boys called the very thin boy "Fatty" in irony.* **2.** event contrary to what would naturally be expected. [< L < Gk. *eironeia* dissimulation < *eiron* dissembler] —Syn. **1.** sarcasm, satire.

Ir·o·quois (ir'ə·kwoi), *n. sing.* and *pl. Am.* member of a powerful group of American Indian tribes called the Five Nations, formerly living mostly in New York State. —**Ir·o·quoi·an** (ir'ə·kwoi'ən), *adj. Am.*

ir·ra·di·ate (i·rā'di·āt), *v.,* **-at·ed, -at·ing,** *adj.* —*v.* **1.** shine upon; make bright; illuminate. **2.** shine. **3.** radiate; give out. **4.** treat with ultraviolet rays. —*adj.* bright. [< L, < *in-* + *radius* ray] —**ir·ra'di·a'tion,** *n.* —**ir·ra'di·a'tive,** *adj.* —**ir·ra'di·a'tor,** *n.*

ir·ra·tion·al (i·rash'ən·əl; i·rash'nəl), *adj.* **1.** not rational; unreasonable: *it is irrational to be afraid of the number 13.* **2.** unable to think and reason clearly. **3.** *Math.* that cannot be expressed by a whole number or a common fraction. √3 is an irrational number. —**ir·ra'tion·al'i·ty, ir·ra'tion·al·ness,** *n.* —**ir·ra'tion·al·ly,** *adv.* —Syn. **1.** illogical, unsound.

Ir·ra·wad·dy (ir'ə·wod'i), *n.* river in E Asia, flowing through Burma into the Bay of Bengal.

ir·re·claim·a·ble (ir'i·klām'ə·bəl), *adj.* that cannot be reclaimed. —**ir're·claim'a·bil'i·ty, ir're·claim'a·ble·ness,** *n.* —**ir're·claim'a·bly,** *adv.*

ir·rec·on·cil·a·ble (i·rek'ən·sīl'ə·bəl; i·rek'-ən·sil'-), *adj.* that cannot be reconciled; that cannot be made to agree; opposed. —*n.* person who persists in opposing. —**ir·rec'on·cil'a·bil'i-ty, ir·rec'on·cil'a·ble·ness,** *n.* —**ir·rec'on·cil'-a·bly,** *adv.*

ir·re·cov·er·a·ble (ir'i·kuv'ər·ə·bəl), *adj.* **1.** that cannot be regained or got back: *wasted time is irrecoverable.* **2.** that cannot be remedied: *irrecoverable sorrow.* —**ir're·cov'er·a·ble·ness,** *n.* —**ir're·cov'er·a·bly,** *adv.* —Syn. **1.** irretrievable.

ir·re·deem·a·ble (ir'i·dēm'ə·bəl), *adj.* **1.** that cannot be bought back. **2.** that cannot be exchanged for coin: *irredeemable paper money.* **3.** beyond remedy; hopeless. —**ir're·deem'a·bly,** *adv.*

ir·re·duc·i·ble (ir'i·düs'ə·bəl; -düs'-), *adj.* that cannot be reduced. —**ir're·duc'i·bil'i·ty, ir're·duc'i·ble·ness,** *n.* —**ir're·duc'i·bly,** *adv.*

ir·ref·ra·ga·ble (i·ref'rə·gə·bəl), *adj.* that cannot be refuted; unanswerable; undeniable. [< LL, < L *in-* not + *refragari* oppose] —**ir·ref'ra·ga·bil'i·ty,** *n.* —**ir·ref'ra·ga·bly,** *adv.*

ir·re·fut·a·ble (i·ref'yə·tə·bəl; ir'i·fūt'ə·bəl), *adj.* that cannot be refuted or disproved. —**ir·ref'u·ta·bil'i·ty,** *n.* —**ir·ref'u·ta·bly,** *adv.* —Syn. undeniable, unanswerable.

irreg., 1. irregular. **2.** irregularly.

ir·reg·u·lar (i·reg'yə·lər), *adj.* **1.** not regular; not according to rule; out of the usual order or natural way: *irregular breathing.* **2.** not even; not smooth; not straight; without symmetry: *an irregular pattern.* **3.** not according to law or morals: *irregular behavior.* **4.** *Mil.* not in the regular army. **5.** not accepted as a member of some established group: *an irregular doctor.* **6.** *Gram.* not inflected in the usual way. *Come* is an irregular verb. —*n.* one that is irregular.

—**ir·reg'u·lar·ly,** *adv.* —Syn. *adj.* **1.** unnatural, abnormal, erratic. **2.** uneven, variable. **3.** lawless.

ir·reg·u·lar·i·ty (i·reg'yə·lar'ə·ti), *n., pl.* **-ties. 1.** lack of regularity. **2.** something irregular.

ir·rel·e·vant (i·rel'ə·vənt), *adj.* not to the point; off the subject. —**ir·rel'e·vance, ir·rel'e·van·cy,** *n.* —**ir·rel'e·vant·ly,** *adv.*

ir·re·li·gion (ir'i·lij'ən), *n.* **1.** lack of religion. **2.** hostility to religion; disregard of religion. —**ir're·li'gion·ist,** *n.*

ir·re·li·gious (ir'i·lij'əs), *adj.* **1.** not religious; indifferent to religion. **2.** contrary to religious principles; impious. —**ir're·li'gious·ly,** *adv.* —**ir're·li'gious·ness,** *n.*

ir·re·me·di·a·ble (ir'i·mē'di·ə·bəl), *adj.* that cannot be remedied; incurable. —**ir're·me'di·a·ble·ness,** *n.* —**ir're·me'di·a·bly,** *adv.*

ir·re·mov·a·ble (ir'i·müv'ə·bəl), *adj.* that cannot be removed. —**ir're·mov'a·bil'i·ty,** *n.* —**ir're·mov'a·bly,** *adv.*

ir·rep·a·ra·ble (i·rep'ə·rə·bəl), *adj.* that cannot be repaired or made good. —**ir·rep'a·ra·bil'-i·ty, ir·rep'a·ra·ble·ness,** *n.* —**ir·rep'a·ra·bly,** *adv.*

ir·re·place·a·ble (ir'i·plās'ə·bəl), *adj.* not replaceable; impossible to replace with another.

ir·re·press·i·ble (ir'i·pres'ə·bəl), *adj.* that cannot be repressed or restrained. —**ir're·press'-i·bil'i·ty, ir're·press'i·ble·ness,** *n.* —**ir're·press'i·bly,** *adv.*

ir·re·proach·a·ble (ir'i·prōch'ə·bəl), *adj.* free from blame; faultless. —**ir're·proach'a·ble·ness,** *n.* —**ir're·proach'a·bly,** *adv.* —Syn. blameless.

ir·re·sist·i·ble (ir'i·zis'tə·bəl), *adj.* that cannot be resisted; too great to be withstood. —**ir're·sist'i·bil'i·ty, ir're·sist'i·ble·ness,** *n.* —**ir're·sist'i·bly,** *adv.*

ir·res·o·lute (i·rez'ə·lüt), *adj.* not resolute; unable to make up one's mind. —**ir·res'o·lute·ly,** *adv.* —**ir·res'o·lute·ness, ir·res'o·lu'tion,** *n.* —Syn. hesitating, doubtful, vacillating.

ir·re·spec·tive (ir'i·spek'tiv), *adj.* regardless: *any person, irrespective of age, may join the club.* —**ir're·spec'tive·ly,** *adv.*

ir·re·spon·si·ble (ir'i·spon'sə·bəl), *adj.* **1.** not responsible; that cannot be called to account: *a dictator is an irresponsible ruler.* **2.** without a sense of responsibility. —*n.* an irresponsible person. —**ir're·spon'si·bil'i·ty, ir're·spon'si·ble·ness,** *n.* —**ir're·spon'si·bly,** *adv.*

ir·re·triev·a·ble (ir'i·trēv'ə·bəl), *adj.* that cannot be retrieved or recovered; that cannot be recalled or restored to its former condition. —**ir're·triev'a·bil'i·ty, ir're·triev'a·ble·ness,** *n.* —**ir're·triev'a·bly,** *adv.*

ir·rev·er·ence (i·rev'ər·əns), *n.* **1.** lack of reverence; disrespect. **2.** act of showing irreverence.

ir·rev·er·ent (i·rev'ər·ənt), *adj.* not reverent; disrespectful. —**ir·rev'er·ent·ly,** *adv.*

ir·re·vers·i·ble (ir'i·vér'sə·bəl), *adj.* not capable of being reversed. —**ir're·vers'i·bil'i·ty, ir're·vers'i·ble·ness,** *n.* —**ir're·vers'i·bly,** *adv.*

ir·rev·o·ca·ble (i·rev'ə·kə·bəl), *adj.* not to be recalled, withdrawn, or annulled: *an irrevocable decision.* —**ir·rev'o·ca·bil'i·ty, ir·rev'o·ca·ble·ness,** *n.* —**ir·rev'o·ca·bly,** *adv.*

ir·ri·ga·ble (ir'i·gə·bəl), *adj.* that can be irrigated.

ir·ri·gate (ir'ə·gāt), *v.,* **-gat·ed, -gat·ing. 1.** supply (land) with water by using ditches. **2.** *Med.* supply (a wound, cavity in the body, etc.) with a continuous flow of some liquid. **3.** supply land, wounds, etc., thus. [< L, < *in-* + *rigare* wet] —**ir'ri·ga'tion,** *n.* —**ir'ri·ga'tion·al,** *adj.* —**ir'ri·ga'tor,** *n.*

ir·ri·ta·bil·i·ty (ir'ə·tə·bil'ə·ti), *n., pl.* **-ties. 1.** a being irritable; impatience. **2.** unnatural sensitiveness (of an organ or part of the body). **3.** *Biol.* property that living plant or animal tissue has of responding to a stimulus.

ir·ri·ta·ble (ir'ə·tə·bəl), *adj.* **1.** easily made angry; impatient. **2.** unnaturally sensitive or sore. **3.** *Biol.* able to respond to stimuli. —**ir'ri·ta·ble·ness,** *n.* —**ir'ri·ta·bly,** *adv.* —Syn. **1.** touchy, testy.

ir·ri·tant (ĭr′ə·tənt), *n*. thing that causes irritation. —*adj*. causing irritation. —ir′ri·tan·cy, *n*.

ir·ri·tate (ĭr′ə·tāt), *v*., -tat·ed, -tat·ing. 1. arouse to impatience or anger; provoke: *his foolish questions irritated me*. 2. make unnaturally sensitive or sore: *sunburn irritates the skin*. 3. *Biol*. stimulate (an organ, muscle, tissue, etc.) to perform some characteristic action or function. [< L *irritatus* enraged, provoked] —ir′ri·tat′ing, ir′ri·ta′tive, *adj*. —ir′ri·tat′ing·ly, *adv*. —ir′ri·ta′tion, *n*. —ir′ri·ta′tor, *n*. —Syn. 1. vex, annoy, exasperate.

ir·rup·tion (ĭ·rŭp′shən), *n*. a breaking or bursting in; violent invasion. [< L *irruptio*, ult. < *in-* in + *rumpere* break] —ir·rup′tive, *adj*.

Ir·ving (ėr′vĭng), *n*. Washington, 1783–1859, American writer, author of *Rip Van Winkle*.

is (ĭz), *v*. 1. 3rd pers. sing. pres. indic. of be. He is, she is, it is. 2. as is, as it is now; in its present condition. [OE]

is., Is., 1. island. 2. isle.

Isa., Is., Isaiah.

I·saac (ī′zək), *n*. son of Abraham and Sarah, and father of Jacob and Esau. Gen. 21:3.

Is·a·bel·la I (ĭz′ə·bĕl′ə), 1451–1504, queen of Castile and León, patron of Columbus.

I·sai·ah (ī·zā′ə; ī·zī′ə), **I·sai·as** (-əs), *n*. 1. the greatest of the Hebrew prophets. 2. book of the Old Testament.

Is·car·i·ot (ĭs·kar′ī·ət), *n*. 1. surname of Judas, who betrayed Christ for money. 2. a traitor.

-ise, *suffix*. variant of -ize. ➤ See -ize for usage note.

I·seult (ĭ·sŭlt′), *n*. Arthurian Legend. 1. the daughter of the King of Ireland and the wife of King Mark of Cornwall, loved by Tristram. 2. daughter of the ruler of Brittany, and Tristram's wife. Also, Isolde.

-ish, *suffix*. 1. somewhat, as in *oldish, sweetish*. 2. resembling; like, as in *a childish man*. 3. like that of; having the characteristics of, as in *a childish idea*. 4. of or pertaining to; belonging to, as in *British, Spanish, Turkish*. 5. tending to; inclined to, as in *bookish, thievish*. 6. near, but usually somewhat past, as in *fortyish*. [OE *-isc*]

Ish·ma·el (ĭsh′mi·əl), *n*. 1. son of Abraham and Hagar, driven into the wilderness by Sarah. Gen. 16. 2. outcast.

Ish·ma·el·ite (ĭsh′mi·əl·īt), *n*. 1. descendant of Ishmael. 2. outcast. —Ish′ma·el·it′ish, *adj*.

i·sin·glass (ī′zing·glas′; -gläs′), *n*. 1. kind of gelatin obtained from air bladders of sturgeon, cod, and similar fishes, used for making glue, clearing liquors, etc. 2. mica, esp. in thin semitransparent layers. [alter. of MDu. *huysenblas* sturgeon bladder; infl. by *glass*]

I·sis (ī′sĭs), *n*. the Egyptian goddess of fertility.

isl., 1. *pl*. isls. island. 2. isle.

Is·lam (ĭs′ləm; ĭs·läm′), *n*. 1. the Mohammedan religion. 2. Mohammedans as a group. 3. the countries under Mohammedan rule. —Is·lam′ic (ĭs·lam′ĭk; -lä′mĭk), Is·lam·it·ic (ĭs′ləm·ĭt′ĭk), *adj*. —Is·lam·ism (ĭs′ləm·ĭz·əm), Is·lam·ite (ĭs′ləm·īt), *n*., *adj*.

is·land (ī′lənd), *n*. 1. body of land surrounded by water. 2. something resembling this. 3. a safety platform in the middle of a busy street. 4. *Physiol., Anat*. a group of cells distinct from its neighbors in structure or function. 5. *Naut*. superstructure, esp. of a battleship or aircraft carrier. —*v*. make into an island. [OE *īgland* < *ig* island + *land* land; spelling infl. by *isle*] —is′land·less, *adj*. —is′land·like′, *adj*.

is·land·er (ī′lən·dər), *n*. native or inhabitant of an island.

isle (īl), **is·let** (ī′lĭt), *n*. a small island. [< OF < L *insula*]

ism (ĭz′əm), *n*. distinctive doctrine, theory, system, or practice. [see -ISM]

-ism, *suffix*. 1. action; practice, as in *baptism, criticism*. 2. doctrine; system; principle, as in *communism, socialism*. 3. quality; characteristic; state; condition, as in *heroism, paganism, Americanism*. 4. illustration; case; instance, as in

colloquialism, witticism. 5. *Med*. unhealthy condition caused by, as in *alcoholism, morphinism*. [< Gk. *-ismos, -isma*]

is·n't (ĭz′ənt), is not.

iso-, is-, *word element*. equal; alike, as in *isosceles, isometric, isotherm, isotope*. [< Gk., < *isos* equal]

i·so·bar (ī′sə·bär), *n*. 1. line on a weather map connecting places having the same average atmospheric pressure. 2. *Physics, Chem*. one of two or more kinds of atoms that have the same atomic weight, but in most cases different atomic numbers. [< Gk., < *isos* equal + *baros* weight] —i·so·bar·ic (ī′sə·bar′ĭk), *adj*.

i·soch·ro·nous (ī·sŏk′rə·nəs), *adj*. 1. equal in time. 2. performed in equal times. —i·soch′ro·nous·ly, *adv*.

i·so·gon·ic (ī′sə·gŏn′ĭk), *adj*. 1. having equal angles; having to do with equal angles. 2. having equal deviations of the magnetic needle from the true north. —*n*. line connecting points that have such equal deviations.

i·so·late (ī′sə·lāt; ĭs′ə-), *v*., -lat·ed, -lat·ing. 1. place apart; separate from others. 2. *Chem*. obtain (a substance) in a pure or uncombined form. 3. *Med*. keep apart or separate (an infected person) from other noninfected persons. [< *isolated* < F < Ital. *isolato* < L *insulatus*, ult. < *insula* island] —i′so·la′tion, *n*. —i′so·la′tor, *n*.

i·so·la·tion·ist (ī′sə·lā′shən·ĭst), *n*. *Am*. one who objects to his country's participation in international affairs. —i′so·la′tion·ism, *n*.

I·sol·de (ĭ·sŏl′də; ĭ·sōld′; ĭ·zŏl′də), *n*. Iseult.

i·so·mer (ī′sə·mər), *n*. *Chem*. an isomeric compound.

i·so·mer·ic (ī′sə·mer′ĭk), *adj*. *Chem*. composed of the same elements in the same proportions by weight, but differing in one or more properties because of the difference in arrangement of atoms. [< Gk., < *isos* equal + *meros* part] —i·som·er·ism (ī·sŏm′ər·ĭz·əm), *n*.

i·som·er·ous (ī·sŏm′ər·əs), *adj*. *Bot*. of a flower, having the same number of members in each whorl.

i·so·met·ric (ī′sə·met′rĭk), **i·so·met·ri·cal** (-rə·kəl), *adj*. pertaining to equality of measure; having equality of measure. —i′so·met′ri·cal·ly, *adv*.

i·so·mor·phic (ī′sə·môr′fĭk), *adj*. having similar appearance or structure, but different ancestry. —i′so·mor′phism, *n*.

i·so·ni·a·zid (ī′sō·nī′ə·zĭd), *n*. drug chemically related to nicotinic acid, used in the treatment of tuberculosis.

i·sos·ce·les (ī·sŏs′ə·lēz), *adj*. *Geom*. having two sides equal. [< LL < Gk., < *isos* equal + *skelos* leg]

Isosceles triangles

i·so·therm (ī′sə·thėrm), *n*. line connecting places having the same average temperature. [< *iso-* + Gk. *therme* heat] —i′so·ther′mal, *adj*. —i′so·ther′mal·ly, *adv*.

i·so·tope (ī′sə·tōp), *n*. *Chem*. any of two or more elements that have the same chemical properties and the same atomic number, but different atomic weights or radioactive behavior. Hydrogen and heavy hydrogen are isotopes. [< *iso-* + Gk. *topos* place] —i·so·top·ic (ī′sə·tŏp′ĭk), *adj*.

i·so·trop·ic (ī′sə·trŏp′ĭk), **i·sot·ro·pous** (ī·sŏt′rə·pəs), *adj*. *Physics*. having the same properties, such as conduction, in all directions.

Is·ra·el (ĭz′rĭ·əl), *n*. 1. name given to Jacob after he had wrestled with the angel. Gen. 32:28. 2. name given to his descendants; the Jews; the Hebrews. 3. ancient kingdom in N Palestine. 4. republic comprising a portion of Palestine, declared a Jewish state May 15, 1948. 5. the Christian church.

Is·rae·li (ĭz·rā′lĭ), *n., pl.* -lis, *adj*. —*n*. citizen or inhabitant of Israel. —*adj*. of or pertaining to Israel.

Is·ra·el·ite (ĭz′rĭ·əl·īt), *n*. Jew; Hebrew; descendant of Israel. —*adj*. of or pertaining to Israel or the Jews. —Is·ra·el·it·ic (ĭz′rĭ·əl·ĭt′ĭk), Is·ra·el·it·ish (ĭz′rĭ·əl·īt′ĭsh), *adj*.

Is·sei (ēs'sā'), *n., pl.* **–sei.** a first-generation Japanese living in the United States. [< Jap., first generation]

is·su·ance (ish'ú·əns), *n.* an issuing; issue.

is·sue (ish'ü), *v.,* **–sued, –su·ing,** *n.* —*v.* 1. send out; put forth: *the government issues stamps.* 2. come out; go out; proceed: *smoke issues from the chimney.* 3. put into public circulation; publish: *issue a bulletin.* 4. emerge. 5. result or end (in): *the game issued in a tie.* 6. result (from). 7. be born; be descended; be derived. —*n.* 1. something sent out; quantity (of bonds, stamps, copies of a magazine, etc.) sent out at one time. 2. a sending out; a putting forth: *issue of an order.* 3. a coming forth; a flowing out; a discharge: *an issue of blood.* 4. way out; outlet; exit. 5. that which comes out. 6. result; outcome: *the issue of the battle.* 7. point to be debated; problem: *the issues of a political campaign.* 8. child or children; offspring. 9. at issue, in question; to be considered or decided. 10. take issue, disagree. [< OF, ult. < L *ex–* out + *ire* go] —is'su·a·ble, *adj.* —is'su·er, *n.* —Syn. *v.* 2. emanate. 3. print. —*n.* 3. outflow. 6. conclusion, upshot.

–ist, *suffix.* 1. a person who does or makes, as in *theorist, tourist.* 2. one who knows about or has skill with, as in *biologist, flutist.* 3. one engaged in or busy with, as in *horticulturist, machinist.* 4. one who believes in; adherent of, as in *abolitionist, idealist.* [< Gk. *–istes*]

Is·tan·bul (is'tän·bül'; –tan–), *n.* a city in European Turkey. Formerly called **Constantinople.**

isth·mi·an (is'mi·ən), *adj.* 1. of or having to do with an isthmus. 2. **Isthmian,** a. of or having to do with the Isthmus of Panama. b. of or having to do with the Isthmus of Corinth in Greece.

isth·mus (is'məs), *n., pl.* **–mus·es, –mi** (–mī). 1. a narrow strip of land, having water on either side, connecting two larger bodies of land. 2. **Isthmus,** the Isthmus of Panama. [< L < Gk. *isthmos*]

it (it), *pron., nom.* it, *poss.* its or (*Obs. or Dial.*) it, *obj.* it; *pl. nom.* they, *poss.* their or theirs, *obj.* them; *n.* —*pron.* 1. thing, part, animal, or person spoken about. 2. subject of an impersonal verb: *it rains.* 3. apparent subject of a clause when the logical subject comes later: *it is hard to believe that he is dead.* 4. antecedent to any relative pronoun when separated by the predicate: *it was a blue car that passed.* 5. object without definite force: *he lorded it over us.* —*n. Games.* player who must perform a given task. [OE *hit*]

Ital., It., Italian; Italy.

ital., italic.

I·tal·ian (i·tal'yən), *adj.* of Italy, its people, or their language. —*n.* 1. native or inhabitant of Italy. 2. language of Italy.

i·tal·ic (i·tal'ik), *adj.* of or in type whose letters slant to the right: *these words are in italic type.* —*n.* 1. an italic type, letter, or number. 2. Often, **italics.** type whose letters slant to the right. [< L, < *Italia* Italy < Gk.] ▶ In manuscript, both longhand and typewritten, italics are shown by underlining.

i·tal·i·cize (i·tal'ə·sīz), *v.,* **–cized, –ciz·ing.** 1. print in type in which the letters slant to the right. 2. underline with a single line to indicate italics. 3. use italics.

It·a·ly (it'ə·li), *n.* country in S Europe on the Mediterranean, including Sicily and Sardinia.

itch (ich), *n.* 1. a tickly, prickling feeling in the skin that makes one want to scratch. 2. **the itch,** contagious disease of the skin caused by a tiny mite, accompanied by this feeling. 3. a restless, uneasy feeling, longing, or desire for anything. —*v.* 1. cause an itching feeling. 2. have an itching feeling. 3. have an uneasy desire. [OE *gyccan*] —itch'y, *adj.* —itch'i·ness, *n.*

–ite[1], *suffix.* person associated with, as in *Israelite, Canaanite, laborite.* [< Gk. *–ites*]

–ite[2], *suffix.* 1. salt of, as in *phosphite, sulfite, nitrite.* 2. new substances often receive names ending in *–ite,* as in *bakelite, dynamite.* [< Gk. *–ites*]

i·tem (ī'təm), *n.* 1. a separate thing or article:

the list contains twelve items. 2. piece of news; bit of information: *the interesting items in to-day's paper.* —*adv.* also; likewise. [< L, *adv.,* likewise]

i·tem·ize (ī'təm·īz), *v.,* **–ized, –iz·ing.** *Am.* give each item of; list by items: *itemize the cost of a house.* —i'tem·i·za'tion, *n.* —i'tem·iz'er, *n.*

it·er·ate (it'ər·āt), *v.,* **–at·ed, –at·ing.** repeat. [< L, < *iterum* again] —it'er·a'tion, *n.*

it·er·a·tive (it'ər·ā'tiv), *adj.* repeating; full of repetitions.

Ith·a·ca (ith'ə·kə), *n.* 1. a small island west of Greece, the home of Odysseus. 2. city in S New York.

i·tin·er·ant (ī·tin'ər·ənt; i·tin'–), *adj.* traveling from place to place. —*n.* person who travels from place to place. [< LL *itinerans* traveling < L *iter* journey] —i·tin'er·an·cy, i·tin'er·a·cy, *n.* —i·tin'er·ant·ly, *adv.*

i·tin·er·ar·y (ī·tin'ər·er'i; i·tin'–), *n., pl.* **–ar·ies,** *adj.* —*n.* 1. route of travel; plan of travel. 2. record of travel. 3. guidebook for travelers. —*adj.* 1. of traveling or routes of travel. 2. itinerant.

i·tin·er·ate (ī·tin'ər·āt; i·tin'–), *v.,* **–at·ed, –at·ing.** travel from place to place. —i·tin'er·a'tion, *n.*

–itis, *suffix.* inflammation of; inflammatory disease of, as in *appendicitis, bronchitis, tonsillitis.* [< Gk. *–itis,* fem. of *–ites*]

its (its), *pron., adj.* of it; belonging to it: *the dog wagged its tail.*

it's (its), 1. it is: *it's going to rain.* 2. it has: *it's rained over a week.*

it·self (it·self'), *pron.* 1. emphatic form of it: *the land itself is worth more than the old house.* 2. reflexive form of it: *the horse tripped and hurt itself.*

–ity, *suffix.* condition or quality of being; ——ness, as in *absurdity, brutality, cordiality, activity, hostility, sincerity.* [< F *–ité*]

I·van III (ī'vən; i·vän'), ("the Great") 1440–1505, grand duke of Muscovy, 1462–1505.

Ivan IV, ("the Terrible") 1530–1584, grand duke of Muscovy from 1533 to 1547, and czar of Russia, 1547–1584.

I've (īv), I have.

–ive, *suffix.* 1. of or pertaining to, as in *interrogative, inductive.* 2. tending to; likely to, as in *active, appreciative, imitative.* [< L *–ivus*]

i·vied (ī'vid), *adj.* covered or overgrown with ivy.

i·vo·ry (ī'və·ri; īv'ri), *n., pl.* **–ries,** *adj.* —*n.* 1. a hard white substance composing the tusks of elephants, walruses, etc. 2. substance like ivory. 3. any article made of ivory. 4. creamy white. 5. **ivories,** *Slang.* a. piano keys. b. dice. —*adj.* 1. made of ivory. 2. of or like ivory. 3. creamy-white. [< AF < L *eboreus* of ivory < *ebur* ivory < *Egyptian*] —i'vo·ry·like', *adj.*

ivory tower, *Am.* place or condition of withdrawal from the world of action into a world of ideas and dreams.

i·vy (ī'vi), *n., pl.* **i·vies.** 1. Also, **English ivy.** a climbing plant with smooth, shiny, evergreen leaves. 2. any of various other climbing plants that resemble this plant, as *American ivy, poison ivy,* etc. [OE *ifig*] —i'vy·like', *adj.*

I·wo Ji·ma (ē'wō jē'mə), a small island in the N Pacific, formerly held by the Japanese, captured by U.S. forces Feb.–Mar., 1945.

Ivy:
A, English ivy; B, poison ivy

I.W.W., Industrial Workers of the World.

–ize, *suffix.* 1. make, as in *legalize, centralize.* 2. become, as in *crystallize, materialize.* 3. engage in; be busy with; use, as in *apologize, theorize.* 4. treat with, as in *circularize, macadamize.* 5. other meanings, as in *alphabetize, criticize, memorize.* Also, **–ise.** [< Gk. *–izein*] ▶ –ize, –ise. English has many words ending in the sound of iz, some of which are spelled -ise and some -ize, and on many usage is divided. American usage, differing somewhat from British, prefers -ize, as in the following common verbs of this class: *apologize, characterize, realize, revolutionize, visualize; -ise* is the usual spelling in the following: *advertise, chastise, devise, exercise, super-*

vise, surmise. In general, follow American usage, and when that is divided, use whichever you are accustomed to.

Iz·mir (iz′mir; iz·mir′), *n.* seaport in W Turkey, on the Aegean Sea. Formerly, Smyrna.

iz·zard (iz′ərd), *n. Colloq.* the letter Z. [< F *isard*]

J

J, j (jā), *n., pl.* J's; j's. the tenth letter of the alphabet.

j., *Physics.* joule.

Ja., January. Also, Jan.

jab (jab), *v.,* **jabbed, jab·bing,** *n.* —*v.* thrust with something pointed; poke. —*n.* a sharp thrust or poke. [ME *jobbe(n);* prob. imit.]

jab·ber (jab′ər), *v.* talk very fast in a confused, senseless way; chatter. —*n.* rapid, unintelligible talk; chatter. [prob. imit.] —**jab′ber·er,** *n.* —**jab′ber·ing·ly,** *adv.* —Syn. *v.* babble.

ja·bot (zha·bō′; zhab′ō; jab′ō), *n.* ruffle or frill of lace, worn at the throat or down the front of a woman's dress or, formerly, on a man's shirt. [< F, orig., maw of a bird]

ja·cinth (jā′sinth; jas′inth), *n.* a reddish-orange gem. [< OF < L *hyacinthus* hyacinth]

jack (jak), *n.* 1. man; boy; fellow. 2. Jack or jack, sailor. 3. tool or machine for lifting or pushing up heavy weights a short distance. 4. *U.S.* playing card with a picture of a court page on it; knave. 5. a jackstone. 6. jacks, jackstones. 7. a small flag used on a ship to show nationality or as a signal. 8. *Am.* a male donkey. 9. *Am.* jack rabbit. 10. *Elect.* device to receive a plug. 11. *Naut.* a horizontal bar of iron at the head of a topgallant mast. —*v.* 1. lift or push up with a jack. 2. jack up, *Colloq.* a. raise (prices, wages, etc.). b. remind of one's duty. [orig. proper name < *Jackie,* var. of *Jankin,* dim. of *John*]

jack·al (jak′ôl; –əl), *n.* 1. a wild dog of Asia and Africa. 2. person who does drudgery for another. [< Turk. < Pers. *shaghāl*]

jack·a·napes (jak′ə·nāps), *n.* 1. a pert, presuming fellow. 2. monkey.

jack·ass (jak′as′; –ăs′), *n.* 1. a male donkey. 2. a very stupid person; fool.

jack·boot (jak′bút′), *n.* a large strong boot reaching above the knee.

Jackal (ab. 15 in. high at the shoulder)

jack·daw (jak′dô′), *n.* 1. a European crow. 2. *Am.* one of several kinds of American grackle.

jack·et (jak′it), *n.* 1. a short coat. 2. an outer covering, as the paper cover for a book or the skin of a potato. —*v.* put a jacket on; cover with a jacket. [< OF *jaquet,* dim. of *jaque* tunic < Sp. *jaco* < Ar.] —**jack′et·ed,** *adj.* —**jack′et·less,** *adj.* —**jack′et·like′,** *adj.*

jack-in-the-box (jak′in·thə·boks′), **jack-in-a-box** (–ə·boks′), *n.* a toy figure that springs up from a box when the lid is unfastened.

jack-in-the-pul·pit (jak′in·thə·púl′pit), *n. Am.* a plant with a greenish, petallike sheath arched over the flower stalk.

jack·knife (jak′nīf′), *n., pl.* **-knives.** *Am.* 1. a large strong pocketknife. 2. kind of dive in which the diver touches his feet with his hands before entering the water.

jack of all trades, person who can do many different kinds of work fairly well.

jack-o'-lan·tern (jak′ə·lan′tərn), *n.* 1. pumpkin hollowed out and cut to look like a face, used as a lantern at Halloween. 2. will-o'-the-wisp (def. 1).

jack pot, *Am.* stakes that accumulate in a poker game until some player wins with a pair of jacks or something better.

jack rabbit, *Am.* a large hare of W North America, having very long legs and ears.

jack·screw (jak′skrü′), *n.* tool or machine for lifting heavy weights short distances, operated by a screw.

Jack·son (jak′sən), *n.* 1. Andrew, 1767–1845, the seventh president of the United States, 1829–1837. 2. Thomas Jonathan ("*Stonewall Jackson*") 1824–1863, American Confederate general. 3. capital of Mississippi, in the C part.

Jack·so·ni·an (jak·sō′ni·ən), *Am.* —*adj.* of or like Andrew Jackson or his principles. —*n.* follower of Andrew Jackson.

Jack·son·ville (jak′sən·vil), *n.* city in NE Florida.

jack·stone (jak′stōn′), *n.* 1. pebble or piece of metal tossed up and caught in a child's game. 2. jackstones (*sing. in use*), game played with a set of these; jacks.

jack·straw (jak′strô′), *n.* 1. straw, strip of wood, bone, etc., used in a game. 2. jackstraws (*sing. in use*), game played with a set of these thrown down in a confused pile and picked up one at a time without moving any of the rest of the pile.

Ja·cob (jā′kəb), *n.* son of Isaac, and younger twin brother of Esau. Gen. 25–50.

Jac·o·be·an (jak′ə·bē′ən), *adj.* of King James I of England or the period of his reign, 1603–1625.

Jac·o·bin (jak′ə·bin), *n.* 1. member of a radical political club organized in 1789 during the French Revolution. 2. an extreme radical in politics. —**Jac′o·bin′ic,** **Jac′o·bin′i·cal,** *adj.* —**Jac′o·bin′i·cal·ly,** *adv.* —**Jac′o·bin·ism,** *n.*

Jac·o·bite (jak′ə·bīt), *n.* supporter of James II and his descendants in their claims to the English throne after the English Revolution in 1688. —**Jac·o·bit·ic** (jak′ə·bit′ik), **Jac′o·bit′i·cal,** *adj.*

Jacob's ladder, *Naut.* a rope ladder used on ships.

jade¹ (jād), *n.* 1. a hard stone, usually green, used for jewels and ornaments. 2. Also, jade green. sea green. [< F < Sp. (*piedra de*) *ijada* (stone of) colic (jade being supposed to cure this), ult. < L *ilia* flanks] —**jade′like′,** *adj.*

jade² (jād), *n., v.,* **jad·ed, jad·ing.** —*n.* 1. an inferior or worn-out horse. 2. (*used opprobriously or playfully*) woman. —*v.* 1. wear out; tire; weary. 2. dull by continual use; surfeit; satiate. —**jad′ish,** *adj.* —Syn. *v.* 1. exhaust, fatigue.

jad·ed (jād′id), *adj.* 1. weary. 2. satiated. —**jad′ed·ly,** *adv.* —**jad′ed·ness,** *n.*

jae·ger (jā′gər; jā′-), *n.* a sea bird like a gull, that pursues weaker birds and makes them disgorge their prey.

Jaf·fa (jaf′ə), *n.* seaport in W Israel.

jag¹ (jag), *n., v.,* **jagged, jag·ging.** —*n.* a sharp point sticking out; pointed projection. —*v.* 1. make notches in. 2. cut or tear unevenly.

jag² (jag), *n. U.S. Slang.* a fit of drunkenness.

jag·ged (jag′id), *adj.* with sharp points sticking out. —**jag′ged·ly,** *adv.* —**jag′ged·ness,** *n.* —Syn. notched, craggy.

Jaguar (total length ab. 6 ft.)

jag·uar (jag′wär; –yú·är), *n.* a fierce animal of tropical America, much like a leopard, but larger. [< Tupi-Guarani]

Jah·ve, Jah·veh (yä′vā), n. Yahweh.

Jail (jāl), n. 1. Also, Brit. **gaol.** prison for people awaiting trial or being punished for minor offenses. 2. break jail, escape from jail. —v. put in jail; keep in jail. [< OF jaiole, ult. < L cavea coop] —**jail′less,** adj. —**jail′like′,** adj.

Jail·bird (jāl′bėrd′), n. 1. prisoner in jail. 2. person who has been in jail many times.

Jail·break (jāl′brāk′), n. Colloq. escape from prison.

jail·er, jail·or (jāl′ər), n. keeper of a jail. Also, Brit. gaoler.

Ja·kar·ta (jə·kär′tə), n. seaport in NW Java, capital of Indonesia. Formerly, Batavia.

ja·lop·y (jə·lop′i), n., pl. -lop·ies. Am., Colloq. an old automobile or airplane in bad repair.

jam¹ (jam), v., jammed, jam·ming, n. —v. 1. press tightly; squeeze. 2. crush; bruise. 3. push; shove. 4. fill up; block up. 5. stick or catch so that it cannot be worked. 6. cause to stick or catch. 7. make (radio signals, etc.) unintelligible by sending out others of approximately the same frequency. 8. Slang. make a musical composition more lively by improvisations, etc. —n. 1. mass of people or things crowded together so that they cannot move freely: a traffic jam. 2. a jamming or being jammed. 3. Am., Colloq. a difficulty or tight spot. [? imit.] —Syn. v. 1. wedge, pack. 3. force, thrust, ram. 4. obstruct.

jam² (jam), n. fruit boiled with sugar until thick. [? special use of jam¹] —**jam′like′,** adj.

Ja·mai·ca (jə·mā′kə), n. 1. a British island in the West Indies, south of Cuba. 2. kind of rum made there. —**Ja·mai′can,** adj., n.

jamb, jambe (jam), n. the upright piece forming the side of a doorway, window, fireplace, etc. [< F jambe, orig., leg < LL gamba]

jam·bo·ree (jam′bə·rē′), n. Am., Slang. a noisy party; lively entertainment.

James (jāmz), n. 1. the name of two of Christ's disciples. 2. book of the New Testament. 3. Henry, 1843–1916, American novelist who lived in England. 4. Jesse, 1847–1882, American bandit and outlaw. 5. William, 1842–1910, American psychologist and philosopher, brother of Henry James. 6. river flowing from western Virginia into Chesapeake Bay.

James I, 1566–1625, king of England, 1603–1625.

James II, 1633–1701, king of England, 1685–1688. He was deposed by Parliament.

James·town (jāmz′toun′), n. a ruined village in SE Virginia; site of the first successful English settlement in North America, in 1607.

jam-packed, jam-packed (jam′pakt′). adj. Am., Colloq. filled to absolute capacity.

jam session, Slang. gathering at which musicians play music enlivened by improvisation.

Jan., January. Also, **Ja.**

jan·gle (jang′gəl), v., -gled, -gling, n. —v. 1. sound harshly. 2. cause to sound harshly. 3. quarrel; dispute. —n. 1. harsh sound. 2. quarrel; dispute. [< OF jangler] —**jan′gler,** n.

jan·i·tor (jan′ə·tər), n. 1. person hired to take care of a building, offices, etc. 2. doorkeeper. [< L, doorkeeper]

Jan·u·ar·y (jan′yū·er′i), n., pl. -ar·ies. the first month of the year. It has 31 days. [< L, < Janus Janus]

Ja·nus (jā′nəs), n. Roman god of gates and doors, and of beginnings and endings. He is represented with two faces, one looking forward and the other looking backward.

Jap (jap), adj., n. Colloq and Contemptuous. Japanese.

Jap., Japan; Japanese.

Ja·pan (jə·pan′), n. an island empire in the Pacific, east of Asia. Also, Japanese Nippon.

ja·pan (jə·pan′), n., v., -panned, -pan·ning. —n. 1. a hard, glossy varnish, used on wood or metal. 2. articles varnished and decorated in the Japanese manner. 3. liquid used to make paint dry faster. —v. put japan on.

Jap·a·nese (jap′ə·nēz′; -nēs′), adj., n., pl. -nese. —adj. of Japan, its people, or their language. —n. 1. native of Japan. 2. language of Japan.

Japanese beetle, a small green-and-brown beetle that eats fruits, leaves, and grasses.

jape (jāp), n., v., japed, jap·ing. 1. joke; jest. 2. trick. —**jap′er,** n.

ja·pon·i·ca (jə·pon′ə·kə), n. 1. camellia. 2. shrub with showy red, pink, or white flowers. [< NL, orig. fem. adj., Japanese]

jar¹ (jär), n. 1. a deep container made of glass, earthenware, etc., with a wide mouth. 2. amount that it holds. [< F jarre, ult. < Ar. jarrah]

jar² (jär), n., v., jarred, jar·ring. —n. 1. shake; rattle. 2. a harsh, grating noise. 3. a harsh, unpleasant effect; shock. 4. clash; quarrel. —v. 1. shake; rattle. 2. make a harsh, grating noise. 3. have a harsh, unpleasant effect on; shock. 4. clash; quarrel. [OE ceorran creak] —Syn. n. 3. jolt. -v. 2. scrape, grate, grind.

jar·di·niere (jär′də·nir′), n. an ornamental pot or stand for flowers or plants. [< F, < jardin garden]

jar·gon (jär′gən; -gon), n. 1. confused, meaningless talk or writing. 2. language that is not understood. 3. language of a special group, profession, etc. Doctors, actors, and sailors have jargons. 4. mixture of languages. 5. chatter. —v. 1. talk jargon. 2. chatter. [< OF, prob. ult. imit.] —Syn. n. 3. lingo, cant, argot, slang. ▶ jargon. 1. Applied to style, jargon is the name for verbal fuzziness of various sorts—wordiness, abstract for concrete words, big words, and the use of words that add nothing to the meaning of a statement. 2. In a linguistic sense, jargon means a dialect composed of two or more languages. Jargons involving English are used by non-English-speaking peoples in doing business with the English, as the Chinook jargon of the Pacific Northwest and the Chinese-English jargon, pidgin English.

jas·mine, jas·min (jas′mən; jaz′-), n. shrub or vine with clusters of fragrant flowers. There are yellow, white, and red jasmines. Also, jessamine. [< F jasmin < Ar. < Pers. yāsmīn]

Ja·son (jā′sən), n. Gk. Legend. Greek hero who led the expedition of the Argonauts and secured the Golden Fleece.

jas·per (jas′pər), n. 1. a colored quartz, usually red or brown. 2. a green precious stone of ancient times. [< OF jaspre, ult. < L < Gk. iaspis < Phoenician]

ja·to (jā′tō), n. Aeron. a unit consisting of one or more jet engines, used to provide auxiliary propulsion for speeding up the take-off of an airplane. [< j(et) + a(ssisted) + t(ake)-o(ff)]

jaun·dice (jôn′dis; jän′-), n., v., -diced, -dicing. —n. 1. disease that causes yellowness of the skin, eyes, and body fluids, and disturbed vision. 2. a disturbed or unnaturally sour mental outlook, due to envy, jealousy, etc. —v. 1. cause jaundice in. 2. prejudice the mind and judgment of, by envy, discontent, or jealousy; sour the temper of. [< OF jaunisse, ult. < L galbinus greenish-yellow]

jaunt (jônt; jänt), n. a short pleasure trip or excursion. —v. take such a trip.

jaun·ty (jôn′ti; jän′-), adj., -ti·er, -ti·est. 1. easy and lively; sprightly; carefree: jaunty steps. 2. smart; stylish: a jaunty little hat. [< F gentil GENTLE] —**jaun′ti·ly,** adv. —**jaun′ti·ness,** n. —Syn. 1. airy, gay.

Ja·va (jä′və; jav′ə), n. 1. a large island southeast of Asia. 2. Am. kind of coffee obtained from Java and nearby islands. 3. Am., Colloq. coffee.

Jav·a·nese (jav′ə·nēz′; -nēs′), adj., n., pl. -nese. —adj. of Java, its people, or their language. —n. 1. native of Java. 2. language of Java.

jave·lin (jav′lin; -ə·lin), n. a light spear thrown by hand. [< F javeline]

jaw (jô), n. 1. either of the two bones, or sets of bones, that form the framework of the mouth. 2. jaws, a. mouth with its jawbones and teeth. b. narrow entrance to a valley, mountain pass, channel, etc. 3. either of the parts in a tool or machine that grip and hold. 4. Slang. talk; gossip. —v. Slang. 1. talk; gossip. 2. find fault; scold. [? akin to chew; infl. by F joue cheek]

Jaw·bone (jô′bōn′), n. 1. bone of either jaw. 2. bone of the lower jaw.

Jay (jā), n. 1. a noisy American bird with blue feathers; bluejay. 2. a noisy European bird with a crest. 3. any of various birds of the same family as these two. 4. Slang. a silly, stupid person. [< OF]

Jay (jā), n. **John,** 1745–1829, the first chief justice of the U.S. Supreme Court, 1789–1795.

Jay·hawk·er (jā′hôk′ər), n. Am. native or inhabitant of Kansas.

Jay·walk (jā′wôk′), v. Am., Colloq. walk across a street without paying attention to traffic rules. —jay′walk′er, n. —jay′walk′ing, n.

European jay (ab. 1 ft. long)

Jazz (jaz), n. 1. Am. music with the accents falling at unusual places; syncopated music. 2. Slang. liveliness. —adj. of or like jazz: a jazz band. —v. 1. Am. play (music) as jazz. 2. Slang. make lively. [of American Negro orig.]

JCS, J.C.S., Joint Chiefs of Staff.

Je., June. Also, **Jun.**

Jeal·ous (jel′əs), adj. 1. fearful that a person one loves may love someone else better or may prefer someone else. One may be jealous of the person loved or of the rival. 2. full of envy; envious: he is jealous of John or of John's marks. 3. requiring complete loyalty or faithfulness: "The Lord thy God is a jealous God." 4. watchful in keeping or guarding something; careful: a city jealous of its rights. 5. close; watchful; suspicious: the dog was a jealous guardian of the child. [< OF gelos, ult. < L zelus ZEAL] —jeal′ous·ly, adv. —jeal′ous·ness, n. —Syn. 2. grudging, resentful.

Jeal·ous·y (jel′əs·i), n., pl. —ous·ies. jealous condition or feeling.

Jean (jēn), n. 1. a strong twilled cotton cloth, used for overalls, etc. 2. jeans, overalls; trousers. [prob. < F Gênes Genoa]

Jeanne d'Arc (zhän därk′), French. Joan of Arc.

Jeep (jēp), n. a small, but powerful, army general-purpose automobile with a four-wheel drive and a quarter-ton capacity. [back formation from "Jeepers creepers!" (the exclamation of Major General George Lynch, Chief of Infantry, U.S. Army, upon the occasion of his first ride in the prototype model of the vehicle, in November, 1939, at Fort Myers, Virginia; coined at the time by Mr. Charles H. Payne, his companion in, and designer of, the vehicle)]

Jeer (jir), v. make fun rudely or unkindly; mock; scoff. —n. a jeering remark; rude, sarcastic comment. —jeer′er, n. —jeer′ing·ly, adv.

Jef·fer·son (jef′ər·sən), n. **Thomas,** 1743–1826, American statesman, third president of the United States, 1801–1809. He drafted the Declaration of Independence. —Jef·fer·so·ni·an (jef′ər·sō′ni·ən), adj., n. Am.

Jefferson City, capital of Missouri.

Je·hol (jē′hōl′; rä′hō′), n. part of NE China.

Je·ho·vah (ji·hō′və), n. one of the names of God in the Old Testament.

Je·hu (jē′hū), n. Colloq. 1. a fast driver. 2. coachman.

Je·june (ji·jün′), adj. 1. lacking nourishing qualities. 2. flat and uninteresting; unsatisfying. [< L jejunus, orig., hungry] —je·june′ly, adv.

Je·ju·num (ji·jü′nəm), n. Anat. the middle portion of the small intestine, between the duodenum and the ileum. [< NL < L, neut., empty]

Jell (jel), v. Colloq. become jelly. [< jelly]

Jel·lied (jel′id), adj. 1. turned into jelly. 2. having the consistency of jelly. 2. spread with jelly.

Jel·ly (jel′i), n., pl. —lies, v., —lied, -ly·ing. —n. 1. a food, soft when hot, but somewhat firm and partly transparent when cold, made by boiling fruit juice and sugar together, cooking bones and meat juice, using gelatin, etc. 2. a jellylike

substance. —v. become jelly; turn into jelly. [< OF gelee, orig., frost, ult. < L gelare congeal]

Jel·ly·fish (jel′i·fish′), n., pl. —fish·es or (esp. collectively) —fish. any of a group of invertebrate sea animals with a body formed of a mass of jellylike tissue that is often transparent. Most jellyfish have long trailing tentacles that may bear stinging hairs or feelers.

Jen·ghis Khan, Jen·ghiz Khan (jeng′gis kän′; jen′-), Genghis Khan.

Jen·net (jen′it), n. a small Spanish horse. Also, genet.

Jen·ny (jen′i), n., pl. —nies. 1. spinning jenny. 2. female of certain animals. [orig. proper name, dim. of Jane, fem. of John]

Jeop·ard·ize (jep′ər·dīz), v., -ized, -iz·ing; -ard·ed, -ard·ing. risk; endanger; imperil: soldiers jeopardize their lives in war. —Syn. hazard.

Jeop·ard·y (jep′ər·di), n. 1. risk; danger; peril: his life was in jeopardy when the tree fell. 2. Law. condition of a person on trial for a criminal offense. [< OF jeu parti an even or divided game, ult. < L jocus play + pars part]

Jer., 1. Jeremiah. 2. Jersey.

Jer·bo·a (jər·bō′ə), n. a small, jumping, mouselike mammal of Asia and northern Africa. [< NL < Ar. yarbū′]

Jer·e·mi·ad (jer′ə·mī′ad), n. a mournful complaint; lamentation. [< F, < Jérémie Jeremiah (reputed author of Lamentations in the Bible)]

Jer·e·mi·ah (jer′ə·mī′ə), **Jer·e·mi·as** (-əs), n. 1. a Hebrew prophet who denounced and lamented the evils of his time. 2. book of the Old Testament.

Jerboa (total length ab. 15 in.)

Jer·i·cho (jer′ə·kō), n., pl. —chos. 1. an ancient city in Palestine. 2. an out-of-the-way place.

Jerk¹ (jėrk), n. 1. a sudden, sharp pull, twist, or start: get up with a jerk. 2. pull or twist of the muscles that one cannot control; twitch. 3. Slang. an unsophisticated or stupid person. —v. 1. pull or twist suddenly: jerk one's hand out of hot water. 2. throw with a movement that stops suddenly. 3. move with a jerk: the old wagon jerked along. 4. speak or say abruptly. [prob. imit.]

Jerk² (jėrk), v. preserve (meat) by cutting it into long thin slices and drying it in the sun. [< Am. Sp. charquear, v., < charquí < Kechua (Ind. lang. of Peru)]

Jer·kin (jėr′kən), n. a short coat or jacket, with or without sleeves.

Jerk·wa·ter (jėrk′wô′tər; -wot′ər), Am., Colloq. —n. train on a branch railway. —adj. 1. not on the main line. 2. insignificant.

Jerk·y (jėr′ki), adj., jerk·i·er, jerk·i·est. with sudden starts and stops; with jerks. —jerk′i·ly, adv. —jerk′i·ness, n.

Je·rome (jə·rōm′; esp. Brit. jer′əm), n. Saint, 340?–420 A.D., monk and scholar, author of the Latin translation of the Bible, the Vulgate.

Jer·ry-build (jer′i·bild′), v., -built, -building. build quickly and cheaply of poor materials.

Jer·sey (jėr′zi), n., pl. —seys. 1. one of a group of British islands, near the coast of France. 2. one of a breed of small, fawn-colored cattle that came from this island. 3. New Jersey.

jer·sey (jėr′zi), n., pl. —seys. 1. a close-fitting sweater that is pulled on over the head. 2. a woman's close-fitting knitted undergarment. 3. a machine-knitted cloth.

Jersey City, seaport in NE New Jersey, across the Hudson River from New York City.

Je·ru·sa·lem (jə·rü′sə·ləm), n. capital of Palestine, in the E part. It is a holy city to Jews, Christians, and Mohammedans. —Je·ru·sa·lem·ite′, adj., n.

Jerusalem artichoke, 1. kind of sunflower whose root is edible. 2. its root.

Jess (jes), *n.* a short strap fastened around a falcon's leg. [< OF *ges,* ult. < L *jacere* to throw]

Jes·sa·mine (jes′ə·min), *n.* jasmine.

Jest (jest), *n.* 1. joke. 2. act of poking fun; mockery. 3. thing to be mocked or laughed at. 4. in jest, in fun; not seriously. —*v.* 1. joke. 2. poke fun (at); make fun. 3. deride; banter. [< OF *geste,* orig., story, exploit, ult. < L *gerere* accomplish] —**jest′ing·ly,** *adv.*

Jest·er (jes′tər), *n.* 1. person who jests. 2. in the Middle Ages, a professional clown.

Je·su (jē′zū; -zü; -sū), *n. Poetic.* Jesus.

Jes·u·it (jezh′ū·it; jez′yů-), *n.* member of a Roman Catholic religious order called the Society of Jesus, founded by Saint Ignatius Loyola in 1534. —**Jes′u·it′ic, Jes′u·it′i·cal,** *adj.* —**Jes′-u·it′i·cal·ly,** *adv.*

Je·sus (jē′zəs), or **Jesus Christ,** *n.* founder of the Christian religion.

jet¹ (jet), *n., v.,* **jet·ted, jet·ting.** —*n.* 1. a stream of water, steam, etc., sent with force, esp. from a small opening. 2. liquid or gas that comes forth. 3. a spout or nozzle for sending out a jet. 4. a jet plane. —*v.* gush out; shoot forth in a jet or forceful stream. [< F, < *jeter* to throw]

jet² (jet), *n.* 1. a hard black mineral, glossy when polished, used for making beads, buttons, etc. 2. a deep glossy black. —*adj.* 1. made of jet. 2. deep glossy black. [< OF < L < Gk. *gagates* <*Gagai,* in Lycia]

jet-black (jet′blak′), *adj.* very black.

jet-lin·er (jet′lin′ər), *n.* a transport airplane driven by jet propulsion.

jet pilot, one who operates a jet plane.

jet plane, airplane driven by jet propulsion.

jet propulsion, propulsion in one direction by a jet of air, gas, etc., forced in the opposite direction. —**jet-pro·pelled** (jet′prə·peld′), *adj.*

jet·sam (jet′səm), *n.* 1. goods thrown overboard to lighten a ship in distress and often afterward washed ashore. 2. thing tossed aside as useless.

jet stream, a high-speed air current (up to 250 miles per hour or more) traveling from west to east at high altitudes (six to ten miles).

jet·ti·son (jet′ə·sən; -zən), *v.* 1. throw (goods) overboard to lighten a ship in distress. 2. throw away; discard. —*n.* 1. act of doing this. 2. goods thrown overboard; jetsam. [< AF *getteson,* ult. < L *jacere* throw]

jet·ty (jet′i), *n., pl.* **-ties.** 1. structure built out into the water to protect a harbor or influence the current; breakwater. 2. a landing place; pier. [< OF, < *jeter* throw, ult. < L *jacere*]

Jew (jü), *n.* 1. member of a people that formerly lived in Palestine, but now live in many countries. 2. person whose religion is Judaism; Hebrew. —*adj.* Jewish.

jew·el (jü′əl), *n., v.,* **-eled, -el·ing;** *esp. Brit.* **-elled, -el·ling.** —*n.* 1. a precious stone; gem. 2. a valuable ornament to be worn, set with precious stones. 3. person or thing that is very precious. 4. gem or some substitute used as a bearing in a watch. —*v.* set or adorn with jewels or with things like jewels. [< OF *juel,* ult. < L *jocus* joke, game] —**jew′el·like′,** *adj.*

jew·el·er, *esp. Brit.* **jew·el·ler** (jü′əl·ər), *n.* person who makes, sells, or repairs jewels, jeweled ornaments, watches, etc.

jew·el·ry, *esp. Brit.* **jew·el·ler·y** (jü′əl·ri), *n.* jewels.

Jew·ess (jü′is), *n.* Jewish woman or girl.

jew·fish (jü′fish′), *n., pl.* **-fish·es** or (*esp. collectively*) **-fish.** 1. giant sea bass. 2. any of various other large fishes of warm seas.

Jew·ish (jü′ish), *adj.* of, belonging to, or characteristic of the Jews. —*n.* Yiddish.

Jew·ry (jü′ri), *n., pl.* **-ries.** 1. Jews as a group; Jewish people. 2. district where Jews live; ghetto. 3. Judea.

jews'-harp, jew's-harp (jüz′härp′), *n.* a simple musical instrument, held between the teeth and played by striking the free end of a piece of metal with a finger.

Jez·e·bel (jez′ə·bəl; -bel), *n.* 1. the wicked wife of Ahab, king of Israel. II Kings 9:7–10, 30–37. 2. a shameless, immoral woman.

jg, j.g., junior grade.

jib¹ (jib), *n.* 1. *Naut.* a triangular sail in front of the foremast. 2. cut of one's jib, *Colloq.* one's outward appearance. [? < *jib²*]

jib² (jib), *v.,* **jibbed, jib·bing.** *Dial.* jibe¹.

jib³ (jib), *v.,* **jibbed, jib·bing.** *Esp. Brit.* move sidewise or backward instead of forward; refuse to go ahead. —**jib′ber,** *n.*

jib boom, *Naut.* spar extending out from a ship's bowsprit.

jibe¹ (jīb), *v.,* **jibed, jib·ing.** 1. shift (a sail) from one side of a ship to the other when sailing before the wind. 2. of a sail or boom, shift thus. 3. change the course of a ship so that the sails shift in this way. Also, jib. [< Du. *gijben*]

jibe² (jīb), *v.,* **jibed, jib·ing,** *n.* gibe. —**jib′er,** *n.*

jibe³ (jīb), *v.,* **jibed, jib·ing.** *U.S. Colloq.* be in harmony; agree.

jif·fy (jif′i), **jiff** (jif), *n., pl.* **jif·fies; jiffs.** *Colloq.* a very short time; moment.

jig¹ (jig), *n., v.,* **jigged, jig·ging.** —*n.* 1. a lively dance, often in triple time. 2. music for it. 3. **the jig is up,** *Slang.* there's no more chance. —*v.* 1. dance a jig. 2. move jerkily; jerk up and down or back and forth. [< OF *giguer* dance < *gigue* fiddle] —**jig′like′,** *adj.*

jig² (jig), *n.* 1. fishhook, or set of fishhooks, loaded with a bright metal or having a spoon-shaped piece of bone attached, for drawing through the water. 2. any of various mechanical contrivances or devices, esp. a guide in using a drill, file, etc. [var. of *gauge*]

jig·ger¹ (jig′ər), *n.* 1. *Naut.* a. a small set of ropes and pulleys used on a ship. b. a small sail. c. a jigger mast. 2. machine with a jerky motion. 3. *Colloq.* some device, article, or part that one cannot name more precisely; gadget; contraption. 4. jig used in fishing. 5. *Am.* a. a small glass used to measure liquor. b. the quantity it holds, usually 1½ oz. [< *jig²*]

jig·ger² (jig′ər), *n.* 1. a small flea; chigoe. 2. *Am.* chigger. [alter. of *chigoe*]

jigger mast, mast in the stern of a ship.

jig·gle (jig′əl), *v.,* **-gled, -gling,** *n.* —*v.* shake or jerk slightly. —*n.* a slight shake; light jerk; rocky motion. [< *jig¹*]

jig·saw (jig′sô′), *n.* a narrow saw mounted in a frame and worked with an up-and-down motion, used to cut curves or irregular lines. —*v.* cut with a jigsaw.

jigsaw puzzle, picture sawed into irregular pieces that can be fitted together again.

jill, Jill (jil), *n.* 1. woman; girl. 2. sweetheart; woman.

jilt (jilt), *v.* cast off (a lover or sweetheart) after giving encouragement. —*n.* woman who casts off a lover after encouraging him. —**jilt′er,** *n.*

Jim Crow (jim′ krō′), **Jim Crow·ism** (krō′iz·əm), *Am., Slang.* discrimination against Negroes.

jim·my (jim′i), *n., pl.* **-mies,** *v.,* **-mied, -my·ing.** —*n.* a short crowbar used esp. by burglars to force windows, doors, etc., open. —*v.* force open with a jimmy.

jim·son weed, Jim·son weed (jim′sən), *Am.* a coarse, bad-smelling weed with white flowers and poisonous, narcotic leaves. [alter. of *Jamestown* (Va.)]

jin·gle (jing′gəl), *n., v.,* **-gled, -gling.** —*n.* 1. sound like that of little bells, or of coins or keys striking together. 2. verse or music that has a jingling sound. —*v.* 1. make a jingling sound: *the sleigh bells jingle as we ride.* 2. cause to jingle: *jingle one's money.* 3. make jingling verse. [imit.] —**jin′gling·ly,** *adv.* —**jin′gly,** *adj.*

jin·go (jing′gō), *n., pl.* **-goes,** *adj.* —*n.* person who favors an aggressive foreign policy that might lead to war with other nations. —*adj.* of jingoes; like that of jingoes. —**jin′go·ism,** *n.* —**jin′go·ist,** *n.* —**jin′go·is′tic,** *adj.*

jinn (jin), *n.pl., sing.* **jin·ni** (ji·nē′). *Mohammedan Myth.* 1. spirits that can appear in human or animal form and do good or harm to people. 2.

(*sing.* in use with *pl.* **jinns**) one of these spirits; jinni. [< Ar.]

jin·rik·i·sha, jin·rick·sha (jin·rik'shə; -shō), *n.* a small, two-wheeled, hooded carriage pulled by one or more men, used in Japan, China, etc. Also, rick-shaw, ricksha. [< Jap., < *jin* man + *riki* strength + *sha* vehicle]

Jinrikisha

jinx (jingks), *Am.*, *Slang.* —*n.* person or thing that brings bad luck. —*v.* bring bad luck to. [< L *iynx* bird used in charms < Gk.]

jit·ney (jit'ni), *n.*, *pl.* -neys, *v.* -neyed, -ney-ing. *Am.*, *Slang.* —*n.* 1. automobile that carries passengers for a small fare. 2. a five-cent piece; nickel. —*v.* travel in or carry in a jitney.

jit·ter (jit'ər), *Am.*, *Slang.* —*n.* jitters, extreme nervousness. —*v.* act nervous.

jit·ter·bug (jit'ər·bug'), *n.*, *v.*, -bugged, -bug-ging. *Colloq.* —*n.* person who is extremely fond of swing music and excited by it to queer dance movements and gesticulations. —*v.* dance in such a way.

jit·ter·y (jit'ər·i), *adj.* *U.S. Slang.* nervous.

jiu·jit·su, jiu·jut·su (jü·jit'sü), *n.* jujitsu.

jive (jīv), *n.*, *v.*, jived, jiv·ing. *Slang.* —*n.* 1. swing music. 2. the jargon of technical terms associated with it. 3. the latest slang. —*v.* perform swing music.

jo (jō), *n.*, *pl.* joes. *Scot.* sweetheart. [var. of JOY]

Joan of Arc (jōn' əv ärk'), 1412–1431, French heroine who led armies against the invading English and saved the city of Orléans. She was condemned as a witch and burned to death. In 1920 she was made a saint. *French*, Jeanne d'Arc.

Job (job), *n.*, *adj.*, *v.*, jobbed, job·bing. —*n.* 1. piece of work. 2. definite piece of work done regularly for pay. 3. *Am.*, *Colloq.* work; employment. 4. anything one has to do. 5. *Colloq.* affair; matter. 6. on the job, *Slang.* tending to one's work or duty. —*adj.* done by the job; hired for a particular piece of work. —*v.* 1. buy (goods) from manufacturers in large quantities and sell to dealers in smaller lots. 2. let out (work) to different contractors, workmen, etc. —job'less, *adj.* —job'less·ness, *n.* ➤ Job is informal and colloquial for the formal *position: He got a job at Baker's.* It is shoptalk for something made, as an automobile, refrigerator, etc.: *a nice little job.*

Job (jōb), *n.* 1. a very patient man in the Bible who kept his faith in God in spite of many troubles. 2. book of the Old Testament.

job·ber (job'ər), *n.* 1. person who buys goods from manufacturers in large quantities and sells to retailers in smaller quantities. 2. person who works by the job; pieceworker.

job·ber·y (job'ər·i), *n.* dishonest management of public business for private gain.

job·hold·er (job'hōl'dər), *n.* 1. person regularly employed. 2. employee of the U.S. government.

job lot, quantity of goods bought or sold together, often containing several different kinds of things usually of inferior quality.

Jo·cas·ta (jō·kas'tə), *n.* in *Gk. Legend.* mother of Oedipus, who married him without knowing who he was.

jock·ey (jok'i), *n.*, *pl.* -eys, *v.*, -eyed, -ey·ing. —*n.* boy or man whose occupation is riding horses in races. —*v.* 1. ride (a horse) in a race. 2. trick; cheat. 3. maneuver to get advantage: *the crews were jockeying their boats to get into the best position for the race.* [orig. proper name, < Jack] —jock'ey·ship, *n.*

jo·cose (jō·kōs'), *adj.* jesting; humorous; playful. [< L, < *jocus* jest] —jo·cose'ly, *adv.* —jo·cose'ness, jo·cos·i·ty (jō·kos'ə·ti), *n.*

joc·u·lar (jok'yə·lər), *adj.* funny; joking. [< L, < *jocus* jest] —joc·u·lar·i·ty (jok'yə·lar'ə·ti), *n.* —joc'u·lar·ly, *adv.*

joc·und (jok'ənd; jō'kənd), *adj.* cheerful; merry; gay. [< var. of L *jucundus* pleasant < *juvare* please] —jo·cun·di·ty (jō·kun'də·ti), *n.* —joc'und·ly, *adv.* —Syn. blithe, joyous.

Jodh·purs (jod'pərz), *n.pl.* breeches for horse-back riding, loose above the knees and fitting closely below. [< *Jodhpur*, India]

Jo·el (jō'əl), *n.* 1. a Hebrew prophet of the fifth century B.C. 2. book of the Old Testament.

Jof·fre (zhôf'rə), *n.* Joseph Jacques Césaire, 1852–1931, French general in World War I.

jog¹ (jog), *v.*, jogged, jog·ging, *n.* —*v.* 1. shake with a push or jerk: *jog a person's elbow to get his attention.* 2. stir up (one's own or another person's memory). 3. move up and down with a jerking or shaking motion: *the old horse jogged along.* 4. go forward heavily and slowly. —*n.* 1. a shake, push, or nudge. 2. a hint or reminder: *give one's memory a jog.* 3. a slow walk or trot. [blend of *jot* jolt and *shog* shake] —jog'ger, *n.*

jog² (jog), *n.* *Am.*, *Colloq.* part that sticks out or in; unevenness in a line or a surface: *a jog in a wall.* [var. of JAG¹]

jog·gle¹ (jog'əl), *v.*, -gled, -gling, *n.* —*v.* 1. shake slightly. 2. move with a jerk. —*n.* a slight shake. [< *jog¹*]

jog·gle² (jog'əl), *n.*, *v.*, -gled, -gling. —*n.* projection on one of two joining surfaces, or notch on the other, to prevent slipping. —*v.* join or fasten with a joggle. [? < *jog²*]

jog trot, a slow, regular trot.

Jo·han·nes·burg (jō·han'is·bèrg; yō·hän'-), *n.* largest city in Union of South Africa, noted for its gold mines.

John (jon), *n.* 1. one of Christ's Apostles who may be the author of the Gospel of Saint John, the three epistles of John, and Revelation. 2. the fourth book of the New Testament. 3. John the Baptist. 4. 1167?–1216, king of England, 1199–1216. He signed the Magna Charta in 1215.

John Bull, 1. the typical Englishman. 2. the English nation.

John Doe, a fictitious name used in legal forms or proceedings for the name of an unknown person.

John Hancock, *Am.* a person's signature.

john·ny·cake (jon'i·kāk'), *n.* *Am.* kind of corn bread.

John·ny-jump-up (jon'i·jump'up'), *n.* *Am.* 1. a wild pansy. 2. violet.

John·son (jon'sən), *n.* 1. Andrew, 1808–1875, the 17th president of the United States, from 1865 to 1869. 2. Samuel, 1709–1784, English author, dictionary maker, and literary leader.

John·so·ni·an (jon·sō'ni·ən), *adj.* having a literary style like that of Samuel Johnson; pompous and ponderous.

Johns·town (jonz'toun), *n.* city in SW Pennsylvania. A serious flood occurred there in 1889.

John the Baptist, *Bible.* man who foretold the coming of Christ and baptized him. Matt. 3.

Jo·hore (jō·hôr'; -hōr'), *n.* a native state at the southern end of the Malay Peninsula.

joie de vi·vre (zhwä də vē'vrə), *French.* joy of living; enjoyment of life.

join (join), *v.* 1. bring or put together; connect; fasten: *join hands.* 2. come together; meet: *the two roads join here.* 3. meet and unite with: *the brook joins the river.* 4. make or become one; combine; unite: *join in marriage.* 5. take part with others: *join in a song.* 6. become a member of: *join a club.* 7. come into the company of: *I'll join you later.* 8. take or return to one's place in: *after a few days on shore the sailor joined his ship.* 9. adjoin: *his farm joins mine.* 10. join battle, begin to fight. —*n.* 1. place or line of joining; seam. 2. act or fact of joining. [< OF *joindre* < L *jungere*] —Syn. *v.* 1. link, couple.

join·er (join'ər), *n.* 1. person or thing that joins. 2. a skilled workman who makes woodwork and furniture. 3. *Am.*, *Colloq.* person who joins many clubs, societies, etc.

join·er·y (join'ər·i), *n.* 1. skill or trade of a joiner. 2. things made by a joiner.

joint (joint), *n.* 1. place at which two things or

parts are joined together. 2. the way parts are joined: *a perfect joint.* 3. in an animal, the parts where two bones move on one another. 4. one of the parts of which a jointed thing is made up: *the middle joint of the finger.* 5. *Zool., Bot.* part between two articulations or nodes. 6. out of joint, a. out of place at the joint. b. out of order; in bad condition. 7. *Bot.* part of the stem from which a leaf or branch grows. 8. piece of meat cut for cooking. 9. *Am., Slang.* a. a cheap, low place, often for the illegal sale of liquor. b. any place or establishment. —*v.* 1. connect by a joint or joints. 2. divide at the joints. —*adj.* 1. owned together; owned by, held by, or done by two or more persons: *joint efforts.* 2. sharing: *joint owners.* [< OF, < *joindre* JOIN] —**joint′less,** *adj.*

joint·ly (joint′li), *adv.* together; in common: *the two boys owned the newsstand jointly.*

joint-stock company, company or firm whose capital is owned in shares by stockholders, any of whom can sell some or all of his shares without the consent of the others.

join·ture (join′chər), *n. Law.* property given to a woman at the time of her marriage. [< F < L *junctura* a joining < *jungere* join. Doublet of JUNCTURE.]

joist (joist), *n.* one of the parallel pieces of timber to which the boards of a floor or ceiling are fastened. —*v.* provide with joists. [< OF *giste,* ult. < L *jacere* lie] —**joist′less,** *adj.*

joke (jōk), *n., v.,* **joked, jok·ing.** —*n.* 1. something said or done to make somebody laugh; something amusing: *this was a good joke on me.* 2. person or thing laughed at. —*v.* 1. make a joke; say or do something as a joke. 2. laugh at; make fun of; tease. [< L *jocus*] —**jok′ing·ly,** *adv.* —**Syn.** *n.* 1. jest, witticism.

jok·er (jōk′ər), *n.* 1. person who jokes. 2. *Am.* phrase or sentence hidden away in a law, contract, etc., to defeat its apparent purpose. 3. an extra playing card used in some games.

jol·li·fi·ca·tion (jol′ə·fə·kā′shən), *n.* gay entertainment; merrymaking.

jol·li·ty (jol′ə·ti), *n., pl.* -ties. fun; merriment; festivity; gaiety.

jol·ly (jol′i), *adj.,* -li·er, -li·est, *adv., v.,* -lied, -ly·ing. —*adj.* 1. full of fun; merry: *a jolly disposition.* 2. *Esp. Brit. Colloq.* pleasant; agreeable; delightful. 3. *Esp. Brit. Colloq.* big; large. —*adv. Esp. Brit. Colloq.* extremely; very. —*v.* 1. *Am.* flatter (a person) to make him feel good or agreeable. 2. *Colloq.* make fun of; kid. [< OF *joli,* ? < Gmc.] —**jol′li·ly,** *adv.* —**jol′li·ness,** *n.* —**Syn.** *adj.* 1. gay, joyful, mirthful, jovial.

jolly boat, a small boat carried on a ship.

Jolly Rog·er (roj′ər), a pirates' black flag with a skull and crossbones on it.

jolt (jōlt), *v.* 1. move with a shock or jerk; jar; shake up: *the wagon jolted us when the wheel went over a rock.* —*n.* jar; shock; jerk: *stop with a jolt.* —**jolt′er,** *n.* —**jolt′y,** *adj.*

Jo·nah (jō′nə), *n.* 1. *Am.* a Hebrew prophet who was thrown overboard during a storm, swallowed by a large fish, and later cast up on land. 2. book of the Old Testament. 3. person whose presence is supposed to bring bad luck.

Jon·a·than (jon′ə·thən), *n.* son of Saul, and a devoted friend of David. I Sam. 19:1–10.

Jones (jōnz), *n.* John Paul, 1747–1792, American naval commander in the American Revolution.

jon·gleur (jong′glər; *Fr.* zhôn·glœr′), *n.* a wandering minstrel or entertainer in the Middle Ages. [< F < OF *jogleor* juggler. See JUGGLE.]

jon·quil (jong′kwəl; jon′-), *n.* 1. plant of the narcissus family with yellow or white flowers and long slender leaves. 2. the flower. [< F < Sp. *junquillo,* ult. < L *juncus* reed]

Jon·son (jon′sən), *n.* Ben, 1573?–1637, English dramatist and poet.

Jor·dan (jôr′dən), *n.* 1. river in Palestine, flowing into the Dead Sea. 2. country in SW Asia, officially called the Hashemite Kingdom of Jordan. Formerly, **Transjordan.**

Jo·seph (jō′zəf), *n.* 1. the favorite son of Jacob. His jealous brothers sold him into slavery in Egypt, where he finally became governor. Gen. 37, 39–41. 2. the husband of Mary, the mother of Jesus.

Jo·se·phine (jō′zə·fēn), *n.* 1763–1814, first wife of Napoleon Bonaparte.

Joseph of Ar·i·ma·the·a (ar′ə·mə·thē′ə), a rich man who put the body of Jesus in his own tomb. 27:57–60.

josh (josh), *v. Am., Slang.* make good-natured fun of; tease playfully; banter. —*n.* a bantering remark. —**josh′er,** *n.*

Josh·u·a (josh′ū·ə), *n.* 1. successor of Moses. He led the children of Israel into the Promised Land. 2. book of the Old Testament.

joss (jos), *n.* image of a Chinese god; Chinese idol. [pidgin Eng. form of Pg. *deos* god < L *deus*]

joss house, a Chinese temple.

joss stick, a slender stick of dried fragrant paste, burned by the Chinese as incense.

jos·tle (jos′əl), *v.,* -tled, -tling, *n.* —*v.* crowd, strike, or push against; elbow roughly: *we were jostled by the big crowd at the entrance.* —*n.* a jostling; push; knock. Also, **justle.** [< *joust*] —**jos′tle·ment,** *n.* —**jos′tler,** *n.*

jot (jot), *n., v.,* **jot·ted, jot·ting.** —*n.* little bit; very small amount: *not care a jot.* —*v.* write briefly or in haste: *jot down the order.* [< L < Gk. *iota* iota] —**jot′ter,** *n.*

Jo·tun, Jo·tunn, Jö·tunn (yō′tun), *n. Norse Myth.* giant.

Jo·tun·heim, Jo·tunn·heim, Jö·tunn·heim (yō′tun·hām), *n. Norse Myth.* home of the giants.

joule (joul; jūl), *n. Physics.* a unit of work or energy, equal to ten million ergs. [for J. P. *Joule,* scientist]

jounce (jouns), *v.,* jounced, jounc·ing, *n.* —*v.* bounce; bump; jolt. —*n.* a jolting movement.

jour·nal (jér′nəl), *n.* 1. a daily record. 2. account of what happens or of what one thinks or notices, as a diary. 3. a ship's log. 4. newspaper; magazine. 5. *Bookkeeping.* book in which every item of business is written down so that the item can be entered under the proper account. 6. *Mach.* part of a shaft or axle that turns on a bearing. [< OF < LL *diurnalis.* Doublet of DIURNAL.]

jour·nal·ese (jér′nəl·ēz′; -ēs′), *n.* careless style of writing such as is sometimes used in newspapers.

jour·nal·ism (jér′nəl·iz·əm), *n.* 1. work of writing for, editing, managing, or producing a newspaper or magazine. 2. newspapers and magazines as a group.

jour·nal·ist (jér′nəl·ist), *n.* person engaged in journalism, as an editor or reporter. —**jour′nal·is′tic,** *adj.* —**jour′nal·is′ti·cal·ly,** *adv.*

jour·ney (jér′ni), *n., pl.* -neys, *v.,* -neyed, -ney·ing. —*n.* 1. travel; trip: *a journey around the world.* 2. distance traveled or that one can travel in a certain time. —*v.* take a trip; travel. [< OF *journee,* orig., a day, ult. < L *diurnus* of one day] —**Syn.** *n.* 1. excursion, tour, voyage.

jour·ney·man (jér′ni·mən), *n., pl.* -men. a qualified workman who has completed his apprenticeship, but has not become an employer or master workman.

joust (just; joust; jūst), *n.* 1. combat between two knights on horseback, armed with lances. 2. jousts, a tournament. —*v.* fight with lances on horseback. [< OF *jouster,* ult. < L *juxta* beside] —**joust′er,** *n.*

Jove (jōv), *n.* 1. the Roman god Jupiter. 2. by Jove, exclamation of surprise, pleasure, etc. —**Jo′vi·an,** *adj.*

jo·vi·al (jō′vi·əl), *adj.* good-hearted and full of fun; good-humored and merry. [< L *Jovialis* pertaining to Jupiter (those born under the planet's sign being supposedly cheerful)] —**jo′vi·al·ly,** *adv.* —**jo′vi·al·ness, jo·vi·al·i·ty** (jō′vi·al′ə·ti), *n.*

jowl¹ (joul; jōl), *n.* 1. part under the jaw; jaw. 2. cheek. [OE *ceafl*]

jowl² (joul; jōl), *n.* fold of flesh hanging from the jaw. [akin to OE *ceole* throat]

joy (joi), *n.* **1.** a strong feeling of pleasure; gladness; happiness. **2.** something that causes gladness or happiness: *"a thing of beauty is a joy forever."* **3.** expression of happiness; outward rejoicing. —*v.* be joyful. [< OF *joie* < L *gaudia* joys] —Syn. *n.* **1.** delight, rapture, bliss.

Joyce (jois), *n.* James, 1882–1941, Irish writer.

joy·ful (joi'fəl), *adj.* **1.** glad; happy: *a joyful heart.* **2.** causing joy: *joyful news.* **3.** showing joy: *a joyful look.* —joy'ful·ly, *adv.* —joy'fulness, *n.*

joy·less (joi'lis), *adj.* **1.** without joy; sad; dismal. **2.** not causing joy: *a joyless prospect.* —joy'less·ly, *adv.* —joy'less·ness, *n.*

joy·ous (joi'əs), *adj.* joyful; glad; gay. —joy'ous·ly, *adv.* —joy'ous·ness, *n.*

joy ride, *Am., Colloq.* ride in an automobile for pleasure, esp. when the car is driven recklessly or used without the owner's permission. —joy rider, *Am.* —joy riding, *Am.*

joy-ride (joi'rīd'), *v.,* -rode, -rid·den, -rid·ing. *Am., Colloq.* take a joy ride.

J.P., Justice of the Peace.

Jr., jr., Junior. Also, Jun.

ju·bi·lance (jü'bə·ləns), *n.* a rejoicing.

ju·bi·lant (jü'bə·lənt), *adj.* **1.** rejoicing; exulting. **2.** expressing or showing joy. [< L *jubilans* shouting with joy < *jubilum* wild shout] —ju'bi·lant·ly, *adv.* —Syn. **1.** joyful, exultant.

ju·bi·la·tion (jü'bə·lā'shən), *n.* **1.** a rejoicing. **2.** a joyful celebration.

ju·bi·lee (jü'bə·lē), *n.* **1.** time of rejoicing or great joy: *hold a jubilee over a victory.* **2.** rejoicing; great joy: *a day of jubilee.* **3.** 25th or 50th anniversary. [< OF < LL < Gk. *iobelaios* < Heb. *yōbēl,* orig., trumpet, ram('s horn)]

Ju·dah (jü'də), *n.* **1.** son of Jacob and ancestor of the tribe of Judah. **2.** the most powerful of the twelve tribes of Israel. **3.** an ancient Hebrew kingdom in S Palestine, consisting of the tribes of Judah and Benjamin.

Ju·da·ic (jü·dā'ik), **Ju·da·i·cal** (-ə·kəl), *adj.* of the Jews; Jewish.

Ju·da·ism (jü'di·iz·əm; -dā-), *n.* **1.** the religion of the Jews. **2.** the following of Jewish rules and customs.

Ju·das (jü'dəs), *n.* **1.** the disciple who betrayed Christ for money. **2.** an utter traitor; person treacherous enough to betray a friend. —Ju'das·like', *adj.*

Judas tree, tree that has red, pink, or purplish flowers before the leaves come out.

Jude (jüd), *n.* **1.** one of the twelve disciples chosen by Jesus as his Apostles. **2.** book of the New Testament. **3.** its author.

Ju·de·a, Ju·dae·a (jü·dē'ə), *n.* the southern part of Palestine when it was a province of the Roman Empire.

Ju·de·an, Ju·dae·an (jü·dē'ən), *adj.* **1.** of Judea. **2.** of the Jews. —*n.* a Jew.

judge (juj), *n., v.,* judged, judg·ing. —*n.* **1.** a government official appointed or elected to hear and decide cases in a law court. **2.** person chosen to settle a dispute or decide who wins. **3.** person qualified to form an opinion: *a good judge of cattle.* **4.** person who decides: *let me be the judge of that.* **5.** ruler in ancient Israel before the time of the kings. —*v.* **1.** hear and decide in a law court. **2.** settle (a dispute); decide who wins (a race, contest, etc.). **3.** form an opinion or estimate (of): *judge the merits of a book.* **4.** think; suppose; consider: *I judged the slight to be intentional.* **5.** criticize; condemn: *who can judge another?* [< OF < L *judex* < *ius* law + root of *dicere* say] —judge'less, *adj.* —judge'like', *adj.* —judg'er, *n.* —Syn. *v.* **4.** deem, regard.

judge advocate, officer who acts as a prosecutor at a court-martial.

Judg·es (juj'iz), *n.* book of the Old Testament dealing with the period in Hebrew history between Joshua and the birth of Samuel.

judge·ship (juj'ship), *n.* position, duties, or term of office of a judge.

judg·ment, *esp. Brit.* **judge·ment** (juj'mənt), *n.* **1.** act of judging: *hall of judgment.* **2.** decision, decree, or sentence given by a judge or court. **3.** certificate embodying such a decision. **4.** debt arising from a judge's decision. **5.** opinion: *it was a bad plan in his judgment.* **6.** ability to form opinions; good sense. **7.** criticism; condemnation. **8. the Judgment,** judgment day. —Syn. **5.** estimation, belief.

judgment day, day of God's final judgment of mankind at the end of the world.

ju·di·ca·to·ry (jü'də·kə·tô'ri; -tō'-), *adj., n., pl.* -to·ries. —*adj.* of the administration of justice: *a judicatory tribunal.* —*n.* **1.** administration of justice. **2.** court of justice. [< LL *judicatorius,* ult. < L *judex* judge]

ju·di·ca·ture (jü'də·kə·chər), *n.* **1.** administration of justice. **2.** position, duties, or authority of a judge. **3.** extent of jurisdiction of a judge or court. **4.** group of judges. **5.** court of justice.

ju·di·cial (jü·dish'əl), *adj.* **1.** of or having to do with courts, judges, or the administration of justice: *judicial proceedings.* **2.** ordered, permitted, or enforced by a judge or a court: *a judicial separation.* **3.** of or suitable for a judge: *a judicial mind considers both sides of a question.* [< L *judicialis,* ult. < *judex* judge] —ju·di'cial·ly, *adv.* —Syn. **3.** impartial, fair.

ju·di·ci·ar·y (jü·dish'i·er'i), *n., pl.* -ar·ies, *adj.* —*n.* **1.** branch of government that administers justice; system of courts of justice of a country. **2.** judges of a country, state, or city. —*adj.* of or having to do with courts, judges, and the administration of justice.

ju·di·cious (jü·dish'əs), *adj.* having, using, or showing good judgment; wise; sensible: *a judicious historian selects and considers facts carefully and critically.* [< F *judicieux,* ult. < L *judex* judge] —ju·di'cious·ly, *adv.* —ju·di'cious·ness, *n.* —Syn. discreet, prudent, astute.

Ju·dith (jü'dith), *n.* **1.** a Hebrew woman who saved her countrymen by killing an Assyrian general. **2.** book of the Apocrypha and of the Douay Version of the Bible that relates her story.

ju·do (jü'dō), *n.* jujitsu.

jug (jug), *n., v.,* jugged, jug·ging. —*n.* **1.** container for liquids, usually one with a spout or a narrow neck and a handle. **2.** *Slang.* jail. —*v.* **1.** put in a jug. **2.** *Slang.* jail. [prob. orig. proper name, alter. of *Joan,* fem. of *John*]

Jug·ger·naut (jug'ər·nôt), *n.* **1.** idol of the Hindu god Krishna, pulled around on a huge car. Devotees of the god are said to have thrown themselves under the wheels to be crushed to death. **2.** something to which a person blindly devotes himself or is cruelly sacrificed.

jug·gle (jug'əl), *v.,* -gled, -gling, *n.* —*v.* **1.** do tricks that require skill of hand or eye. **2.** do such tricks with: *juggle three balls in the air.* **3.** change by trickery: *juggle accounts to hide thefts.* —*n.* **1.** a juggling. **2.** trick; deception; fraud. [< OF *jogler* < L *joculari* to joke, ult. < *jocus* jest] —jug'gler, *n.*

jug·gler·y (jug'lər·i), *n., pl.* -gler·ies. **1.** sleight of hand. **2.** trickery; fraud.

Ju·go·slav, Ju·go·Slav (ü'gō·släv'; -slav'), *n., adj.* Yugoslav. —Ju'go·slav'ic, Ju'go·Slav'ic, *adj.*

Ju·go·sla·vi·a, Ju·go·Sla·vi·a (ü'gō·slä'vi·ə), *n.* Yugoslavia. —Ju'go·sla'vi·an, Ju'go·Sla'vi·an, *adj., n.*

jug·u·lar (jug'yə·lər; jü'gyə-), *Anat.* —*adj.* **1.** of the neck or throat. **2.** of the jugular vein. —*n.* jugular vein. [< NL, < L *jugulum* collarbone, dim. of *jugum* yoke]

jugular vein, one of the two large veins in the neck that return blood from the head to the heart.

juice (jüs), *n.* **1.** liquid in fruits, vegetables, and meats. **2.** liquid help to the body. The gastric juices of the stomach help to digest food. **3.** *Am., Slang.* electricity. **4.** *Slang.* gasoline. [< OF < L *jus* broth] —juice'less, *adj.*

juic·y (jüs'i), *adj.,* juic·i·er, juic·i·est. **1.** full of juice; having much juice. **2.** full of interest; lively. —juic'i·ly, *adv.* —juic'i·ness, *n.*

ju·jit·su, ju·jut·su (jü·jit'sü), *n.* Japanese method of wrestling or fighting without weapons

āge, cāre, fär; ēqual, tėrm; īce; ōpen, ôrder; pút, rüle, ūse; th, then; ə=a in about.

that uses the strength and weight of an opponent to his disadvantage. Also, **jiujitsu, jiujutsu, judo.** [< Jap., < *jū* soft + *jutsu* art]

ju·jube (jü'jüb), *n.* 1. lozenge or small tablet of gummy candy. 2. an edible datelike fruit of a shrub or tree, used to flavor this candy. [< F or < Med.L *jujuba*, ult. < Gk. *zizyphon*]

juke box (jük), *Am., Slang.* an automatic phonograph that plays one record for each nickel deposited in the slot.

juke joint (jük), *Am., Slang.* 1. tavern, roadhouse, etc., where music is furnished by a juke box. 2. any small building where liquor is sold.

Jul., July. Also, **Jy.**

ju·lep (jü'ləp), *n. Am.* drink made of whiskey or brandy, sugar, crushed ice, and fresh mint. [< F < Ar. < Pers. *gulāb*, orig., rose water]

Jul·ian (jül'yən), *adj.* of Julius Caesar.

Ju·li·an·a (jü'li·an'ə; –ä'nə), *n.* (in full, *Juliana Louise Emma Marie Wilhelmina*) born 1909, queen of the Netherlands since 1948.

Julian calendar, calendar in which the average length of a year was 365¼ days. It was introduced by Julius Caesar in 46 B.C.

ju·li·enne (jü'li·en'), *adj.* cut in thin strips or small pieces, as potatoes. —*n.* a clear soup containing vegetables cut into thin strips or small pieces.

Ju·li·et (jü'li·et; –ət), *n.* the young heroine of Shakespeare's play *Romeo and Juliet.*

Jul·ius Cae·sar (jül'yəs sē'zər). See Caesar.

Ju·ly (jù·lī'), *n., pl.* –lies. the seventh month of the year. It has 31 days. [after *Julius Caesar*]

jum·ble (jum'bəl), *v.* –bled, –bling, —*v.* mix; confuse: *things strangely jumbled together.* —*n.* a confused mixture. [? imit.] —**Syn.** *n.* medley, hodgepodge, muddle, mess.

jum·bo (jum'bō), *n., pl.* –bos, *adj. Am., Colloq.* —*n.* a big, clumsy person, animal, or thing. —*adj.* very big.

jump (jump), *v.* 1. spring from the ground; leap; bound: *jump up and down.* 2. leap over; skip; pass over: *jump a stream.* 3. cause to jump: *jump a horse over a fence.* 4. move suddenly and quickly: *I jumped from my bed.* 5. give a sudden start or jerk: *you made me jump.* 6. rise suddenly: *prices jumped.* 7. *Am.* in checkers, pass over and capture (an opponent's piece). 8. in contract bridge, raise (a partner's bid) by more than one trick. 9. *Slang.* evade by running away: *jump bail.* 10. *Am., Slang.* get aboard (a train) by jumping. 11. **jump a claim,** seize a piece of land claimed by another. 12. **jump at,** accept eagerly and quickly. 13. **jump off,** *Mil.* leave one's lines for an attack on the enemy. 14. **jump on,** *Slang.* blame; scold; criticize. 15. **jump the track,** leave the rails suddenly. —*n.* 1. spring from the ground; leap; bound. 2. thing to be jumped over. 3. distance jumped. 4. contest in jumping. 5. a sudden nervous start or jerk. 6. a sudden rise. 7. in checkers, move made to capture an opponent's piece. 8. **get or have the jump on,** *Am., Slang.* get or have an advantage over. [prob. imit.] —**Syn.** *v.* 2. vault, hop.

jump area, *Mil.* locality assigned for the landing of parachute troops, usually behind enemy lines.

jump·er¹ (jump'ər), *n.* one that jumps.

jump·er² (jump'ər), *n.* 1. a loose jacket. 2. a loose blouse reaching to the hips. 3. a one-piece dress without sleeves, worn over a blouse. 4. **jumpers,** rompers. [< *jump* short coat, ? alter. of F *juppe*, ult. < Ar. *jubbah* long open coat]

jumping bean, *Am.* seed of a Mexican plant containing a larva whose movements cause the seed to jump.

jumping jack, toy man or animal that can be made to jump by pulling a string.

jump·mas·ter (jump'mas'tər; –mäs'–), *n. Mil.* officer who controls the dropping of parachute troops and their equipment from an aircraft.

jump·y (jump'i), *adj.* jump·i·er, jump·i·est. 1. moving by jumps; making sudden, sharp jerks. 2. easily excited or frightened; nervous. —**jump'i·ness,** *n.*

Jun., 1. June. Also, **Je.** 2. Also, **Jr.** Junior.

Junc., Junction.

jun·co (jung'kō), *n., pl.* –cos. *Am.* any of several small North American finches often seen in flocks during the winter. [< Sp. < L *juncus* reed]

Junco (ab. 6 in. long)

junc·tion (jungk'shən), *n.* 1. a joining or being joined: *the junction of two armies.* 2. place where things join. 3. place where railroad lines meet or cross.

junc·ture (jungk'chər), *n.* 1. point of time. 2. state of affairs. 3. crisis. 4. joint. 5. a joining or being joined; junction. [< L *junctura.* Doublet of JOINTURE.]

June (jün), *n.* the sixth month of the year. It has 30 days. [< L *Junius,* a Roman gens]

Ju·neau (jü'nō), *n.* capital of Alaska, in the SE part.

June bug or **beetle,** *Am.* 1. a large brown beetle of the N United States that appears in June. 2. figeater.

Jung·frau (yung'frou'), *n.* mountain in the Alps of S Switzerland.

jun·gle (jung'gəl), *n.* 1. a wild land thickly overgrown with bushes, vines, trees, etc. 2. a tangled mass. 3. *U.S. Slang.* camp for tramps. [< Hind. *jangal* < Skt. *jangala* desert]

jun·ior (jün'yər), *adj.* 1. the younger: *John Parker, Junior, is the son of John Parker, Senior.* 2. of lower position, rank, or standing; of more recent appointment: *a junior officer, a junior partner.* 3. of or having to do with juniors in high school or college. 4. of later date; subsequent (to). —*n.* 1. a younger person. 2. person of lower position, rank, or standing; person of more recent appointment. 3. *Am.* student in the third year of high school or college. [< L, compar. of *juvenis* young]

junior college, school giving only the first two years of a regular four-year college course.

junior high school, *Am.* school consisting of grades 7, 8, and 9.

ju·ni·per (jü'nə·pər), *n. Am.* an evergreen shrub or tree with small berrylike cones. [< L *juniperus*]

junk¹ (jungk), *n.* 1. *Am.* old metal, paper, rags, etc. 2. *Slang.* rubbish; trash. —*v. Colloq.* throw away or discard as junk.

junk² (jungk), *n.* a Chinese sailing ship. [< Pg. *junco,* prob. ult. < Javanese *jong*]

Jun·ker, jun·ker (yung'kər), *n.* member of the aristocratic, formerly privileged class in Prussia. [< G]

jun·ket (jung'kit), *n.* 1. curdled milk, sweetened and flavored. 2. feast; picnic. 3. pleasure trip. 4. *Am.* trip taken by an American official at the expense of the government. —*v.* go on a junket. [prob. < dial. OF *jonquette* basket < *jonc* reed < L *juncus*] —**jun'ket·er,** *n. Am.*

junk·man (jungk'man'), *n., pl.* –men. *Am.* man who buys and sells old metal, paper, rags, etc.

Ju·no (jü'nō), *n., pl.* –nos. 1. *Roman Myth.* goddess of marriage, wife of Jupiter and queen of the gods, identified with the Greek goddess Hera. 2. a stately, majestic woman.

jun·ta (jun'tə), *n.* 1. a Spanish council for deliberation or administration. 2. junto. [< Sp., ult. < L *jungere* join]

jun·to (jun'tō), *n., pl.* –tos. a political faction; group of plotters or partisans. [alter. of *junta*]

Ju·pi·ter (jü'pə·tər), *n.* 1. *Roman Myth.* the ruler of the gods and men, identified with the Greek god Zeus. 2. the largest planet.

Ju·ra Mountains (jûr'ə), mountain range in France and Switzerland.

Ju·ras·sic (jù·ras'ik), *n.* 1. geological period when birds first appeared. 2. rocks of this period. —*adj.* of this period.

ju·rid·i·cal (jù·rid'ə·kəl), **ju·rid·ic** (–ik), *adj.* 1. having to do with the administration of justice. 2. of law; legal. [< L, ult. < *jus* law + *dicere* say] —**ju·rid'i·cal·ly,** *adv.*

Ju·ris·dic·tion (jŭr′is·dik′shən), *n.* **1.** right or power of administering law or justice. **2.** authority; power; control. **3.** extent of authority: *the judge ruled that the case was not within his jurisdiction.* [< L, ult. < *jus* law + *dicere* say] —ju′ris·dic′tion·al, *adj.* —ju′ris·dic′tion·al·ly, *adv.*

Ju·ris·pru·dence (jŭr′is·prū′dəns), *n.* **1.** science or philosophy of law. **2.** system of laws. **3.** branch of law: *medical jurisprudence.* [< L, < *jus* law + *prudentia* prudence] —ju·ris·pru·den·tial (jŭr′is·prū·den′shəl), *adj.*

Ju·rist (jŭr′ist), *n.* **1.** expert in law. **2.** a learned writer on law. [< Med.L *jurista* < L *jus* law]

Ju·ris·tic (jů·ris′tik), **ju·ris·ti·cal** (-tə·kəl), *adj.* of or having to do with jurists or jurisprudence; relating to law. —ju·ris′ti·cal·ly, *adv.*

Ju·ror (jŭr′ər), *n.* member of a jury.

Ju·ry¹ (jŭr′i), *n., pl.* **ju·ries. 1.** group of persons selected to hear evidence in a law court and sworn to give a decision in accordance with the evidence presented to them. See also **grand jury** and **petty jury. 2.** group of persons chosen to give a judgment or to decide a contest and award prizes. [< AF *jurie*, ult. < L *jurare* swear] —ju′ry·less, *adj.*

Ju·ry² (jŭr′i), *adj. Naut.* for temporary use on a ship; makeshift. [prob. ult. < OF *ajurie* help, ult. < L *ad-* + *juvare* aid]

Ju·ry·man (jŭr′i·mən), *n., pl.* -men. juror.

Just (just), *adj.* **1.** right; fair. **2.** righteous. **3.** deserved; merited: *a just reward.* **4.** having good grounds; well-founded: *just anger.* **5.** lawful: *a just claim.* **6.** in accordance with standards or requirements; proper: *just proportions.* **7.** true; correct: *a just description.* **8.** exact: *just weights.* —*adv.* **1.** exactly: *just a pound.* **2.** almost exactly: *I saw him just now.* **3.** a very little while ago: *he has just gone.* **4.** barely: *it just missed the mark.* **5.** only; merely: *just an ordinary man.* **6.** *Colloq.* quite; truly; positively: *the weather is just glorious.* [< L *justus* upright < *jus* right] —just′ly, *adv.* —just′ness, *n.* —Syn. *adj.* **1.** impartial, equitable. **2.** upright, honest. **3.** due, rightful. **6.** fitting. **8.** precise.

Jus·tice (jus′tis), *n.* **1.** just conduct; fair dealing: *have a sense of justice.* **2.** a being just; fairness; rightness; correctness: *uphold the justice of our cause.* **3.** rightfulness; lawfulness; well-founded reason: *complain with justice.* **4.** just treatment; deserved reward or punishment. **5.** exercise of power and authority to maintain what is just and right. **6.** administration of law; trial and judgment by process of law: *a court of justice.* **7.** judge: *the justices of the U.S. Supreme Court.* **8.** justice of the peace. **9.** bring a person to justice, do what is necessary in order that a person shall be legally punished for his crime or crimes. **10. do justice to,** a. treat fairly. b. show proper appreciation for. **11. do oneself justice,** do as well as one really can do. [< OF < L *justitia*] —jus′tice·ship, *n.*

Justice of the peace, a local magistrate who tries minor cases, administers oaths, performs civil marriages, etc.

Jus·ti·fi·a·ble (jus′tə·fī′ə·bəl), *adj.* capable of being justified; that can be shown to be just and right; defensible. —jus′ti·fi′a·bil′i·ty, jus′ti·fi′a·ble·ness, *n.* —jus′ti·fi′a·bly, *adv.*

Jus·ti·fi·ca·tion (jus′tə·fə·kā′shən), *n.* **1.** a justifying or being justified. **2.** fact or circumstance that justifies; good reason. **3.** *Theol.* a freeing or being freed from the guilt or penalty of sin.

Jus·ti·fy (jus′tə·fī), *v.,* -fied, -fy·ing. **1.** show to be just or right; give a good reason for: *the fine quality of the cloth justifies its high price.* **2.** clear of blame or guilt. **3.** make (lines of type) the right length by proper spacing. **4.** *Law.* show a satisfactory reason or excuse for something done. —jus′ti·fi′er, *n.* —Syn. **1.** uphold, defend. **2.** exonerate.

Jus·tin·i·an (jus·tin′i·ən), *n.* 483-565 A.D., emperor of the Eastern Roman Empire, 527-565 A.D.

Jus·tle (jus′əl), *v.,* -tled, -tling, *n.* jostle.

Jut (jut), *v.,* jut·ted, jut·ting, *n.* —*v.* stick out; project: *the pier juts out from the shore into the water.* —*n.* part that sticks out; projection. [var. of *jet¹*]

Jute (jüt), *n.* strong fiber used for making coarse sacks, burlap, rope, etc., obtained from two tropical plants. [< Bengali (lang. of Bengal) *jhōto* < Skt. *jūta* mat of hair] —jute′like′, *adj.*

Jute (jüt), *n.* member of a Germanic tribe. Some of the Jutes invaded and settled in SE Britain in the fifth century A.D. —Jut′ish, *adj.*

Jut·land (jut′lənd), *n.* peninsula of Denmark.

Ju·ve·nal (jü′və·nəl), *n.* 60-140? A.D., Roman satirical poet.

Ju·ve·nile (jü′və·nəl; -nīl), *adj.* **1.** young; youthful; childish. **2.** of or for young people: *juvenile books.* —*n.* **1.** a young person. **2.** book for young people. **3.** in the theater, a. a youthful male part. b. actor who plays youthful parts. [< L, < *juvenis* young] —ju′ve·nile·ly, *adv.* —ju′ve·nile·ness, ju·ve·nil·i·ty (jü′və·nil′ə·ti), *n.* —Syn. *adj.* **1.** immature, undeveloped.

Juvenile court, *Am.* law court where cases involving boys and girls are heard.

Jux·ta·pose (juks′tə·pōz′), *v.,* -posed, -pos·ing. put close together; place side by side. [< F, < L *juxta* beside + F *poser* place, POSE] —jux·ta·po·si·tion (juks′tə·pə·zish′ən), *n.*

Jy., July. Also, **Jul.**

K

K, k (kā), *n., pl.* K's; k's. the 11th letter of the alphabet.

K, *Chem.* potassium.

K., **1.** King; Kings. **2.** Knight.

k., **1.** karat. **2.** kilogram. **3.** knot.

Kaa·ba (kä′bə), *n.* the sacred shrine of the Mohammedans, a small structure, containing a black stone, in the great mosque at Mecca. Also, **Caaba.**

Ka·bul (kä′bul), *n.* capital of Afghanistan.

ka·di (kä′di; kä′-), *n., pl.* -dis. cadi.

Kaf·ir, Kaf·ir (kaf′ər), *n.* **1.** member of a Negroid race in South Africa. **2.** their language. **3.** kaffir, kafir, kaffir corn.

kafir corn, kafir corn, a sorghum grown for grain and forage in dry regions.

kaf·tan (kaf′tən; käf·tän′), *n.* caftan.

kai·ak (kī′ak), *n.* kayak.

Kai·ser, kai·ser (kī′zər), *n.* **1.** title of the rulers of Germany from 1871 to 1918. **2.** title of the rulers of Austria from 1804 to 1918. **3.** title of the rulers of the Holy Roman Empire from 962 A.D. to 1806. [< G, < Julius *Caesar*] —Kai′ser·ship, kai′ser·ship, *n.*

kale, kail (kāl), *n.* **1.** any of various kinds of cabbage that have loose leaves instead of a compact head. Kale looks somewhat like spinach. **2.** *Am., Slang.* money; cash. [var. of *cole*]

ka·lei·do·scope (kə·lī′də·skōp), *n.* **1.** tube containing bits of colored glass and two mirrors. As it is turned, it reflects continually changing patterns. **2.** anything that changes continually; a continually changing pattern. [< Gk. *kalos* pretty + *eidos* shape + E -*scope* instrument of viewing < Gk. *skopein* look at] —ka·lei·do·scop·ic (kə·lī′də·skop′ik), ka·lei′do·scop′i·cal, *adj.* —ka·lei′do·scop′i·cal·ly, *adv.*

kal·ends (kal′əndz), *n.pl.* calends.

Ka·le·va·la (kä′lä·vä′lä), *n.* the national epic poem of Finland.

Ka·li·nin (kä·lē′nin), *n.* Mikhail Ivanovich, 1875-1946, Russian political leader.

Ka·li·nin·grad (kə·lē′nin·grad), *n.* city in W Soviet Union, in East Prussia. Formerly, Königsberg.

Kal·muck, Kal·muk (kal′muk), *n.* **1.** member of a group of Mongol tribes living in W China and SE Soviet Union. **2.** their language.

kal·so·mine (kal′sə·mīn; -min), *n., v.,* -mined, -min·ing. calcimine.

Kam·chat·ka (kam·chat′kə), *n.* peninsula of NE Asia between the Sea of Okhotsk and Bering Sea.

Ka·nak·a (kə·nak′ə; kan′ə·kə), *n. Am.* **1.** native of Hawaii. **2.** native of any island in the S Pacific; South Sea islander. [< Hawaiian, man]

kan·ga·roo (kang′gə·rü′), *n., pl.* -roos or (*esp. collectively*) -roo. mammal of Australia and New Guinea having small forelegs and very strong hind legs, which give it great leaping power. The female kangaroo has a pouch in front in which she carries her young. [prob. < Australian lang.] —**kan′ga·roo′like′,** *adj.*

kangaroo rat, *Am.* a small, mouselike animal of the desert regions of the United States and Mexico.

Kans., Kan., Kansas.

Kan·sas (kan′zəs), *n.* **1.** a Middle Western State of the United States. *Capital:* Topeka. *Abbrev.:* Kans. or Kan. **2.** river flowing from NE Kansas into the Missouri River. —**Kan′san,** *adj., n. Am.*

Kansas City, 1. city in W Missouri, on the Missouri River. **2.** city in NE Kansas adjoining it.

Kant (kant; *Ger.* känt), *n.* Immanuel, 1724–1804, German philosopher. —**Kant·i·an** (kan′ti·ən), *adj., n.*

ka·o·lin, ka·o·line (kā′ə·lin), *n.* a fine white clay, used in making porcelain. [< F < Chinese *Kao-ling,* mountain in China]

ka·pok (kā′pok; kap′ək), *n.* the silky fibers around the seeds of a tropical tree, used for stuffing pillows and mattresses. [< Malay *kapoq*]

kap·pa (kap′ə), *n.* the tenth letter (K, κ) of the Greek alphabet.

Ka·ra·chi (kə·rä′chi), *n.* capital of Pakistan, in the W part.

kar·a·kul (kar′ə·kəl), *n.* **1.** variety of Russian or Asiatic sheep. **2.** caracul. [< *Kara Kul,* lake in Turkestan]

kar·at (kar′ət), *n.* carat.

Ka·re·li·a (kə·rē′li·ə; -rēl′yə), *n.* Soviet republic in NW Russia, next to Finland.

Kar·nak (kär′nak), *n.* village in Egypt on the Nile River. The N part of ancient Thebes was located there.

Kash·mir (kash·mir′; kash′mir), *n.* district in N India. Also, Cashmere. —**Kash·mir·i·an** (kash·mir′i·ən), *adj., n.*

Kat·man·du (kät′män·dü′), *n.* capital of Nepal.

Kat·te·gat (kat′ə·gat), *n.* arm of the North Sea between Denmark and Sweden.

ka·ty·did (kā′ti·did), *n. Am.* a large green insect somewhat like a grasshopper. The male makes a shrill noise sounding like "Katy did, Katy didn't."

Katydid (ab. 1¾ in. long from forehead to tips of folded wings)

Kau·nas (kou′näs), *n.* capital of Lithuania.

kau·ri, kau·ry (kou′ri), *n., pl.* -ris; -ries. **1.** a tall pine tree that grows in New Zealand. **2.** its wood. **3.** a resin obtained from it that is used in varnish. [< Maori]

kay·ak (kī′ak), *n.* an Eskimo canoe made of skins stretched over a light frame of wood or bone with an opening in the middle for a person. Also, **kaiak.** [< Eskimo]

Ka·zan (kä·zän′), *n.* city in E European Russia, near the Volga River.

kc., kilocycle; kilocycles.

K.C., 1. King's Counsel. **2.** Knights of Columbus.

ke·a (kā′ə; kē′ə), *n.* a large, greenish parrot of New Zealand, that kills sheep to feed upon their fat. [< Maori]

Keats (kēts), *n.* John, 1795–1821, English poet.

kedge (kej), *v.,* kedged, kedg·ing, *n.* —*v.* move (a ship, etc.) by pulling on a rope attached to an anchor that has been dropped some distance away. —*n.* Also, **kedge anchor.** a small anchor used in kedging a boat, etc.

keel (kēl), *n.* **1.** the main timber or steel piece that extends the whole length of the bottom of a ship or boat. **2.** *Poetic.* ship. **3.** part in an airplane or airship resembling a ship's keel. **4.** on an even keel, horizontal. —*v.* **1.** turn upside down; upset. **2.** keel over, **a.** turn over or upside down; upset. **b.** fall over suddenly. **c.** *Am., Colloq.* faint. [< Scand. *kjölr*]

keel·haul (kēl′hôl′), *v. Naut.* haul (a person) under the keel of a ship for punishment.

keel·son (kel′sən; kēl′-), *n.* beam or line of timbers or iron plates fastened along the top of a ship's keel to strengthen it. Also, **kelson.** [< keel]

keen[1] (kēn), *adj.* **1.** so shaped as to cut well: *a keen blade.* **2.** sharp; piercing; cutting: *keen wind, keen hunger, keen wit, keen pain.* **3.** strong; vivid. **4.** able to do its work quickly and accurately: *a keen mind, a keen sense of smell.* **5.** *Colloq.* full of enthusiasm; eager: *keen to go, keen about sailing.* [OE *cēne*] —**keen′ly,** *adv.* —**keen′ness,** *n.* —**Syn. 2.** acute, penetrating, biting, bitter. **4.** acute, penetrating. **5.** ardent.

keen[2] (kēn), *n.* a wailing lament for the dead. —*v.* wail; lament. [< Irish *caoine*] —**keen′er,** *n.*

keep (kēp), *v.,* kept, keep·ing, *n.* —*v.* **1.** have for a long time or forever: *keep a job.* **2.** have and not let go: *keep the interest of the public.* **3.** have and let nobody else have: *keep a secret.* **4.** have and take care of: *keep chickens.* **5.** take care of and protect: *may God keep you.* **6.** have; hold: *keep a thing in mind.* **7.** have in one's service: *keep servants.* **8.** hold back; prevent: *what is keeping her from coming?* **9.** hold oneself back; refrain: *she could not keep from laughing.* **10.** maintain in good condition; maintain: *keep a garden.* **11.** stay in good condition: *the butter kept in the icebox.* **12.** continue; remain; stay: *he kept indoors all day.* **13.** cause to continue in some stated place, condition, etc.: *keep a light burning.* **14.** do the right thing with; celebrate: *keep Christmas.* **15.** be faithful to: *keep a promise.* **16.** provide for; support: *he is not able to keep himself, much less a family.* **17.** have habitually for sale: *that store keeps canned goods.* **18.** keep books, make a record of all money received or spent. **19.** *Am.* of school, be in session. **20.** keep company, **a.** be together. **b.** *Colloq.* be sweethearts. **21.** keep tab or tabs, **a.** keep a record. **b.** *Colloq.* check. **22.** keep track of, *Colloq.* keep informed about. —*n.* **1.** food and a place to sleep: *he works for his keep.* **2.** the strongest part of a castle or fort. **3.** for keeps, **a.** for the winner to keep his winnings. **b.** *Am., Colloq.* forever. [OE *cēpan* observe] —**Syn.** *v.* **2.** retain. **3.** withhold, repress. **4.** raise. **5.** shield, guard. **8.** detain, restrain. **14.** observe, commemorate. **15.** fulfill. **17.** stock. —*n.* **1.** maintenance, support. **2.** stronghold.

keep·er (kēp′ər), *n.* **1.** person or thing that keeps: *a keeper of promises.* **2.** guard; watchman. **3.** guardian; protector. —**keep′er·less,** *adj.*

keep·ing (kēp′ing), *n.* **1.** care; charge; maintenance: *the keeping of the orphaned children was paid for by their uncle.* **2.** celebration; observance: *the keeping of Thanksgiving Day is an old American custom.* **3.** agreement; harmony: *a good man's actions are in keeping with his promises.* **4.** being kept for future use; preservation. —**Syn. 1.** support. **2.** commemoration.

keep·sake (kēp′sāk′), *n.* thing kept in memory of the giver. —**Syn.** remembrance, souvenir.

Ke·fau·ver (kē′fô·vèr), *n.* Estes, born 1903, American political leader, senator from Tennessee since 1948.

keg (keg), *n.* **1.** a small barrel, usually holding less than 10 gallons. **2.** 100 pounds of nails. [< Scand. *kaggi*]

Kei·jo (kā′jō), *n.* Japanese name of Seoul.

Kel·ler (kel′ər), *n.* Helen, born 1880, American writer. She was deaf, dumb, and blind from babyhood, but was taught to read and speak, and graduated from college.

kelp (kelp), *n.* **1.** a large, tough, brown seaweed that contains iodine. **2.** ashes of seaweed.

kel·pie, kel·py (kel′pi), *n., pl.* –pies. a water spirit, usually in the form of a horse, supposed to drown people or warn them of drowning.

kel·son (kel′sən), *n.* keelson.

Kelt (kelt), *n.* Celt. —**Kelt′ic,** *adj., n.*

kel·ter (kel′tər), *n. Brit. Dial.* kilter.

Ke·mal A·ta·türk (ke·mäl′ ä′tä·trk′; at′-ə·térk′), **Mustafa,** 1878–1938, president of Turkey, 1923–1938.

ken (ken), *n., v.,* **kenned** or **kent** (kent), **ken·ning.** —*n.* 1. range of sight. 2. range of knowledge: *what happens on Mars is beyond our ken.* [< v.] —*v. Scot.* know. [OE *cennan* make declaration < *cann* know, can¹]

Ken., Kentucky.

ken·nel (ken′əl), *n., v.,* –neled, –nel·ing; *esp. Brit.* –nelled, –nel·ling. —*n.* 1. house for a dog or dogs. 2. Often, **kennels.** place where dogs are bred. 3. pack of dogs. —*v.* 1. put or keep in a kennel. 2. take shelter or lodge in a kennel. [< OF *kenel*, ult. < L *canis* dog]

ke·no (kē′nō), *n. Am.* a gambling game somewhat like lotto.

Kent (kent), *n.* 1. county in SE England. 2. an early English kingdom.

Kent·ish (ken′tish), *adj.* of Kent or its people. —*n.* an Anglo-Saxon dialect spoken in the kingdom of Kent.

Ken·tuck·y (kən·tuk′i), *n.* 1. a Southern State of the United States. *Capital:* Frankfort. *Abbrev.:* Ky. or Ken. 2. river flowing from E Kentucky into the Ohio River. —**Ken·tuck′i·an,** *adj., n. Am.*

Ken·ya (ken′yə; kēn′yə), *n.* a British colony and protectorate in E Africa.

kep·i (kep′i), *n., pl.* kep·is. cap with a round flat top, worn by French soldiers. [< F, ult. < G *kappe* cap]

Kep·ler (kep′lər), *n.* **Johann,** 1571–1630, German astronomer.

kept (kept), *v.* pt. and pp. of **keep.**

ker·a·tin (ker′ə·tin), *n.* a complex protein, the chief constituent of horn, nails, hair, feathers, etc. [< Gk. *keras* horn]

kerb (kérb), *n. Brit.* curb of a pavement.

ker·chief (kér′chif), *n.* 1. piece of cloth worn over the head or around the neck. 2. handkerchief. [< OF, < *couvrir* COVER + *chief* head (< L *caput*)]

Ke·ren·ski (ke·ren′ski), *n.* **Alexander,** born 1881, one of the leaders of the Russian Revolution in March, 1917.

kerf (kérf), *n.* 1. cut made by saw, axe, etc. 2. something cut off. [OE *cyrf* < *ceorfan* carve]

ker·mis, ker·mess (kér′mis), *n.* 1. fair with games and merrymaking, held in Holland, Belgium, and adjacent regions. 2. any fair or entertainment, usually to raise money for charity. Also, **kirmess.** [< Du., < *kerk* church + *mis* Mass]

kern (kérn), *n.* part of a letter of type that projects beyond the body. [< F *carne* edge < L *cardo* hinge]

ker·nel (kér′nəl), *n.* 1. the softer part inside the hard shell of a nut or inside the stone of a fruit. 2. grain or seed like wheat or corn. 3. the central or most important part. [OE *cyrnel* < *corn* seed, grain] —**ker′nel·less,** *adj.*

ker·o·sene (ker′ə·sēn; ker′ə·sēn′), *n. Am.* a thin oil produced by distilling petroleum; coal oil. It is used in lamps and stoves. [< Gk. *keros* wax]

kes·trel (kes′trəl), *n.* a small European falcon. [prob. < OF *cresserelle,* ult. < L *crista* crest]

ketch (kech), *n.* 1. a fore-and-aft-rigged sailing ship with a large mainmast toward the bow and a smaller mast toward the stern. 2. formerly, a sturdy sailing vessel with two masts. [? < *catch*]

Kestrel (ab. 1 ft. long)

ketch·up (kech′əp), *n.* catchup.

ket·tle (ket′əl), *n.* 1. a metal container for boiling liquids, cooking fruit, etc. 2. teakettle. 3. kettle of fish, awkward state of affairs; mess; muddle. [< L *catillus,* dim. of *catinus* vessel]

ket·tle·drum (ket′əl·drum′), *n.* drum consisting of a hollow brass or copper hemisphere and a parchment top.

key¹ (kē), *n., pl.* keys, *adj., v.,* keyed, key·ing. —*n.* 1. instrument that locks and unlocks; thing that turns or opens: *key to a door.* 2. thing that explains or answers: *key to a puzzle.* 3. a book, etc., giving the answers to problems. 4. place that commands or gives control of a sea, a district, etc., because of its position: *Gibraltar is the key to the Mediterranean.* 5. an important or essential person, thing, etc. 6. pin, bolt, wedge, or other piece put in a hole or space to hold parts together. 7. device to turn a bolt or nut, as a key for a roller skate. 8. one of a set of parts pressed in playing a piano, in typewriting, and in operating other instruments. 9. scale or system of notes in music related to one another in a special way and based on a particular note: *key of B flat.* 10. tone of voice; style of thought or expression: *write in a melancholy key.* —*adj.* controlling; very important: *the key industries of a nation.* —*v.* 1. regulate the pitch of: *key a piano up to concert pitch.* 2. adjust; attune: *key a speech to an audience.* 3. fasten or adjust with a key. 4. lock. 5. key up, raise the courage or nerve of (to the point of doing something): *the coach keyed up the team for the big game.* [OE *cǣg*]

key² (kē), *n., pl.* keys. a low island; reef. [< Sp. < F *quai* < Celtic]

Key (kē), *n.* **Francis Scott,** 1779–1843, American lawyer, author of "The Star-Spangled Banner."

key·board (kē′bôrd′; –bōrd′), *n.* set of keys in a piano, organ, typewriter, etc.

keyed (kēd), *adj.* 1. having keys: *a keyed flute.* 2. set or pitched in a particular key. 3. fastened or strengthened with a key.

key·hole (kē′hōl′), *n.* opening in a lock through which a key is inserted to turn the lock.

key·note (kē′nōt′), *n., v.,* –not·ed, –not·ing. —*n.* 1. note on which a scale or system of tones in music is based. 2. main idea; guiding principle. —*v.* give the keynote speech of.

keynote speech, *Am.* speech, usually at a political gathering, that presents the principal issues in which those present are interested.

key signature, sharps or flats placed after the clef at the beginning of a staff of music to indicate the key.

KEYSTONE

key·stone (kē′stōn′), *n.* 1. middle stone at the top of an arch, holding the other stones or pieces in place. 2. part on which other associated parts depend; essential principle.

Key West, 1. island off the coast of SW Florida. 2. seaport on this island.

kg., kilogram; kilograms.

khak·i (kak′i; kä′ki), *adj., n., pl.* khak·is. —*adj.* 1. dull yellowish-brown. —*n.* 1. a dull, yellowish brown. 2. a stout twilled cloth of this color, used for soldiers' uniforms. 3. uniform or uniforms made of this cloth. [< Pers., orig., dusty < *khāk* dust]

kha·lif (kā′lif; kal′if), *n.* caliph.

khan¹ (kän; kan), *n.* 1. title of a ruler among Tartar or Mongol tribes, or of the emperor of China during the Middle Ages. 2. title of dignity in Iran, Afghanistan, India, etc. [< Turk.]

khan² (kän; kan), *n.* in Turkey and nearby countries, an inn without furnishings. [< Pers.]

Khar·kov (kär′kof; –kôf), *n.* city in the S Soviet Union.

Khar·toum, Khar·tum (kär·tüm′), *n.* capital of Sudan, on the Nile.

khe·dive (kə·dēv′), *n.* title of the Turkish viceroys who ruled Egypt between 1867 and 1914.

[< Turk. < Pers. *khidīv* ruler] —**khe·di′val,** khe·di·vi·al (kə·dē′vi·əl), *adj.*

Khru·shchev (krŭ′shef), *n.* Nikita S., born 1894, Soviet political leader.

Khu·fu (kŭ′fŭ), *n.* Cheops.

Khy·ber Pass (kī′bər), a mountain pass between Pakistan and Afghanistan.

kibe (kīb), *n.* a chapped or ulcerated sore, inflammation, or swelling on the heel caused by exposure to cold.

kib·butz (ki·bŭts′), *n., pl.* **kib·butz·im.** *Hebrew.* a collective farm in Israel.

kib·itz (kib′its), *v. Am., Slang.* look on as an outsider and offer unwanted advice. [< Yiddish < colloq. G *kiebitzen* look on at cards < *kiebitz* an annoying onlooker, appar. Austrian army slang use of G *kiebetz* plover]

kib·itz·er (kib′it·sər), *n. Am., Colloq.* 1. person watching a card game. 2. person watching a card game who insists on making suggestions to the players. 3. meddler. [< *kibitz*]

kick (kik), *v.* 1. strike out with the foot: *that horse kicks when anyone comes near him.* 2. strike with the foot: *the horse kicked the boy.* 3. drive, force, or move by kicking: *kick a ball.* 4. win by a kick: *kick a goal in football.* 5. spring back when fired: *this shotgun kicks.* 6. *Colloq.* complain; object; grumble. 7. **kick back,** *Colloq.* a. recoil suddenly and unexpectedly. b. return (a stolen item) to its owner. c. return a portion of money received as a fee. 8. **kick in,** *Slang.* a. die. b. *Am.* pay what is due or expected. 9. **kick off,** a. *Am.* put a football in play with a kick. b. *Slang.* die. 10. **kick up,** *Slang.* start; cause. —*n.* 1. act of kicking. 2. recoil of a gun. 3. *Am., Slang.* complaint. 4. *Am., Slang.* thrill. —**kick′er,** *n.*

kick·back (kik′bak′), *n. Am., Colloq.* 1. a restoring of stolen goods. 2. amount or portion returned, esp. as a fee.

kick·off (kik′ôf′; -of′), *n. Am.* kick that puts a football in play.

kick·shaw (kik′shô′), *n.* 1. delicacy. 2. trifle; trinket. [alter. of F *quelque chose* something]

kid¹ (kid), *n.* 1. a young goat. 2. its flesh, used as food. 3. its skin, used as fur. 4. leather made from the skin of young goats, used for gloves and shoes. 5. *Colloq.* child. [< Scand. (Dan.)]

kid² (kid), *v.,* **kid·ded, kid·ding.** *Slang.* 1. tease playfully; talk jokingly. 2. humbug; fool. [? < *kid¹* in sense of "treat as a child"] —**kid′der,** *n.*

Kidd (kid), *n.* William, 1645?–1701, British privateer and pirate, known as "Captain Kidd."

kid·nap (kid′nap), *v.,* **-naped, -nap·ing;** *esp. Brit.* **-napped, -nap·ping.** steal (a child); carry off (a person) by force; seize and hold (a person) against his will by force or by fraud. [< *kid¹* child + *nap* snatch away] —**kid′nap·er,** *esp. Brit.* **kid′nap·per,** *n.*

kid·ney (kid′ni), *n., pl.* **-neys.** 1. one of the pair of organs in the body that separate waste matter and water from the blood and pass them off through the bladder as urine. 2. kidney or kidneys of an animal, cooked for food. 3. nature; disposition. 4. kind; sort. [? < *kiden-,* of uncert. meaning + *ey* egg] —**kid′ney·like′,** *adj.*

kidney bean, 1. a kidney-shaped bean. 2. plant that it grows on. 3. the scarlet runner.

Kiel (kēl), *n.* seaport in NW Germany.

Kiel Canal, ship canal from the North Sea to the Baltic Sea.

Ki·ev (kē′ef), *n.* capital of the Ukraine, in the SW Soviet Union.

Ki·ku·yu (kik′ə·yŭ; ki·kŭ′-), *n.* one of the principal Negro tribes in Kenya.

Ki·lau·e·a (kē′lou·ā′ä), *n.* crater on the volcano Mauna Loa, in Hawaii.

Kil·i·man·ja·ro (kil′i·män·jä′rō), *n.* Mount, the highest mountain in Africa, in Tanganyika Territory.

kill¹ (kil), *v.* 1. put to death; cause the death of: *the blow killed him.* 2. cause death: *"Thou shalt not kill."* 3. put an end to; destroy: *kill odors, kill faith.* 4. *Am.* cancel (a word, paragraph, item, etc.). 5. defeat or veto (a legislative bill). 6. destroy or neutralize the active qualities of: *kill the law by overusing it.* 7. spoil the effect of: *one color may kill another near it.* 8. use up

(time). 9. overcome completely. —*n.* 1. act of killing. 2. animal killed. [ME *kyllen, cullen;* prob. akin to QUELL] —**Syn.** *v.* 1. assassinate, slay.

kill² (kil), *n. Am., Dial.* stream. [< Du. *kil*]

Kil·lar·ney (ki·lär′ni), *n.* 1. town in SW Republic of Ireland. 2. Lakes of, three beautiful lakes near there.

kill·deer (kil′dir′), **kill·dee** (-dē′), *n., pl.* **-deers** or (*esp. collectively*) **-deer; -dees** or (*esp. collectively*) **-dee.** *Am.* a small wading bird that has a loud, shrill cry, the commonest plover of North America. [imit. of its call]

kill·er (kil′ər), *n.* 1. person, animal, or thing that kills. 2. *Am., Slang.* criminal who recklessly or wantonly kills others.

killer whale, dolphin that kills and eats large fish, seals, and even whales.

kill·ing (kil′ing), *adj.* 1. deadly; destructive; fatal: *a killing frost.* 2. overpowering; exhausting: *ride at a killing pace.* 3. *Colloq.* irresistibly funny. —*n. Am., Colloq.* a sudden great financial success: *make a killing in stocks.*

kill-joy (kil′joi′), *n.* person who spoils other people's fun.

kiln (kil; kiln), *n.* furnace or oven for burning, baking, or drying something. —*v.* burn, bake, or dry in a kiln. [< L *culina* kitchen]

ki·lo (kē′lō; kil′ō), *n., pl.* **ki·los.** 1. kilogram. 2. kilometer.

kilo-, *prefix.* one thousand, as in *kilogram, kilometer, kilowatt.* [< F]

kil·o·cal·o·rie (kil′ə·kal′ə·ri), *n. Physics.* a large calorie. See **calorie.**

kil·o·cy·cle (kil′ə·sī′kəl), *n.* 1. 1000 cycles. 2. 1000 cycles per second.

kil·o·gram, *esp. Brit.* **kil·o·gramme** (kil′ə-gram), *n.* unit of mass and weight equal to 1000 grams, or 2.2046 pounds avoirdupois.

kil·o·gram-me·ter, *esp. Brit.* **kil·o·gram-me·tre** (kil′ə-gram-mē′tər), *n.* unit used in measuring work, equal to 7.2334 foot-pounds.

kil·o·li·ter, *esp. Brit.* **kil·o·li·tre** (kil′ə-lē′-tər), *n.* unit of capacity equal to 1000 liters, or one cubic meter; 264.17 U.S. gallons, or 1.308 cubic yards.

kil·o·me·ter, *esp. Brit.* **kil·o·me·tre** (kil′ə-mē′tər, kə·lom′ə·tər), *n.* distance equal to 1000 meters, or 3280.8 feet. —**kil·o·met·ric** (kil′ə-met′rik), **kil′o·met′ri·cal,** *adj.*

kil·o·watt (kil′ə-wot′), *n. Elect.* unit of power equal to 1000 watts.

kil·o·watt-hour (kil′ə·wot′our′), *n. Elect.* unit of energy equal to the work done by one kilowatt acting for one hour.

kilt (kilt), *n.* a pleated skirt reaching to the knees, worn by men in the Scottish Highlands. —*v. Scot.* tuck up; fasten up. [prob. < Scand. (Dan.) *kilte* tuck up] —**kilt′like′,** *adj.*

Man wearing a kilt

kil·ter (kil′tər), *n. Colloq.* good condition; order: *our radio is out of kilter.* Also, *Brit. Dial.* **kelter.**

Kim·ber·ley (kim′bər·li), *n.* city in the C part of the Union of South Africa. The world's largest diamond mines are near it.

ki·mo·no (kə·mō′nə), *n., pl.* **-nos.** 1. a loose outer garment held in place by a sash, worn by Japanese men and women. 2. a woman's loose dressing gown. [< Jap.]

kin (kin), *n.* 1. family or relatives; kindred. 2. family relationship; connection by birth or marriage: *what kin is she to you?* 3. of kin, related. —*adj.* related. [OE *cynn*] —**kin′less,** *adj.*

-kin, *suffix.* little, as in *lambkin.* [ME]

kind¹ (kīnd), *adj.* 1. friendly; doing good: *kind words.* 2. gentle: *be kind to animals.* 3. showing or characterized by kindness: *a kind master.* [OE (*ge*)*cynde* natural < (*ge*)*cynd* kind²] —**Syn.** 1. benevolent, charitable. 2. tender.

kind² (kīnd), *n.* 1. class; sort; variety: *many kinds of candy.* 2. natural group; race: *snakes belong to the serpent kind.* 3. **in kind,** a. in goods or produce, not in money. b. in something of the same sort. c. in characteristic quality: *difference in kind not merely in degree.* 4. **kind of,** *Colloq.*

nearly; almost; somewhat; rather. **5.** of a kind, **a.** of the same kind; alike. **b.** of a poor or mediocre quality: *two boxes and a plank make a table of a kind.* [OE (ge)cynd] —Syn. **1.** type, description. **2.** species, genus. ❯ **kind**, **sort**. *Kind* and *sort* are both singular nouns in form: *This kind of a person is a menace. This sort of thing shouldn't be allowed.* But *kind* and *sort* are so closely associated with the noun they stand before that they seem like adjectives, and colloquially the demonstrative adjectives used with them usually agree with the principal noun of the construction: *those sort of ideas; that sort of life.*

kin·der·gar·ten (kin′dər·gär′tən), *n.* school that educates children from 3 to 6 years old by games, toys, and pleasant occupations. [< G, < *kinder* children + *garten* garden] ❯ Kindergarten preserves the spelling of its German origin and is pronounced and spelled with *t*.

kin·der·gart·ner, **kin·der·gar·ten·er** (kin′dər·gärt′nər), *n.* **1.** child who goes to kindergarten. **2.** teacher in a kindergarten.

kind-heart·ed (kīnd′härt′tid), *adj.* having or showing a kind heart; kindly; sympathetic. —kind′-heart′ed·ly, *adv.* —kind′-heart′ed·ness, *n.*

kin·dle (kin′dəl), *v.,* -dled, -dling. **1.** set on fire; light. **2.** catch fire; begin to burn. **3.** arouse; stir up: *kindle suspicion.* **4.** become stirred up or aroused. **5.** light up; brighten: *the boy's face kindled as he told about the circus.* [prob. ult. < Scand. *kynda* kindle] —kin′dler, *n.* —Syn. **1, 2.** ignite. **3.** excite, awaken, stimulate.

kin·dling (kin′dling), *n.* small pieces of wood for starting a fire.

kind·ly (kīnd′li), *adj.,* -li·er, -li·est, *adv.* —*adj.* **1.** kind; friendly: *kindly faces.* **2.** pleasant; agreeable: *a kindly shower.* —*adv.* **1.** in a kind or friendly way. **2.** pleasantly; agreeably: *he does not take kindly to criticism.* **3.** cordially; heartily: *thank you kindly.* —kind′li·ness, *n.*

kind·ness (kīnd′nis), *n.* **1.** quality of being kind; kind nature. **2.** kind treatment. **3.** a kind act.

kin·dred (kin′drid), *n.* **1.** family or relatives. **2.** family relationship; connection by birth or marriage. **3.** likeness; resemblance. —*adj.* **1.** related: *kindred tribes.* **2.** like; similar: *we are studying about dew, frost, and kindred facts of nature.* [< *kin*] —Syn. *adj.* **1.** cognate, allied.

kine (kīn), *n.pl. Archaic* or *Dial.* cows; cattle.

kin·e·mat·ics (kin′ə·mat′iks), *n.* branch of physics that deals with the characteristics of different kinds of pure motion, that is, without reference to mass or to the causes of the motion. [< Gk. *kinema* motion < *kineein* move] —kin′e·mat′ic, kin′e·mat′i·cal, *adj.*

kin·e·mat·o·graph (kin′ə·mat′ə·graf; -gräf), *n.* cinematograph.

kin·e·scope (kin′ə·skōp), *n.* **1.** record on film of a television show or other entertainment that may be rebroadcast. **2.** Kinescope, *Trademark.* a cathode-ray tube that has a screen at one end on which images are reproduced.

kin·es·thet·ic (kin′əs·thet′ik), *adj.* of or having to do with muscular movement.

ki·net·ic (ki·net′ik), *adj.* **1.** of motion. **2.** caused by motion. [< Gk., < *kineein* move]

ki·net·ics (ki·net′iks), *n.* branch of physics that deals with the effects of forces in causing or changing the motion of objects.

kin·folk (kin′fōk′), **kin·folks** (-fōks′), *n.pl. Dial.* kinsfolk.

king (king), *n.* **1.** the male ruler of a nation; male sovereign, either with absolute or limited power. **2.** *Am., Colloq.* man supreme in a certain sphere: *a baseball king.* **3.** something best in its class. **4.** the chief piece in chess. **5.** piece that has moved entirely across the board in checkers. **6.** a playing card bearing a picture of a king. [OE *cyning*] —king′less, *adj.*

King (king), *n.* (William Lyon) McKenzie, 1874–1950, Canadian statesman and prime minister, 1921–1926, 1926–1930, and 1935–1948.

King Arthur, hero in a group of legends about the knights of the Round Table.

king·bird (king′bėrd′), *n. Am.* a quarrelsome bird that catches and eats insects as it flies.

king·bolt (king′bōlt′), *n.* a vertical bolt connecting the body of a wagon, etc., with the front axle, or the body of a railroad car with a set of wheels.

king crab, *Am.* horseshoe crab.

king·dom (king′dəm), *n.* **1.** country that is governed by a king or a queen. **2.** realm; domain; province: *the mind is the kingdom of thought.* **3.** one of the three divisions of the natural world; the animal kingdom, the vegetable kingdom, or the mineral kingdom.

king·fish (king′fish′), *n., pl.* -fish·es or (esp. collectively) -fish. **1.** *Am.* any of several large food fishes of the Atlantic or Pacific coast. **2.** *Colloq.* person having uncontested control in a group or community.

king·fish·er (king′fish′ər), *n.* a bright-colored bird with a large head and a strong beak. The American kingfishers eat fish; some of the European kinds eat insects.

King James Version, English translation of the Bible published in 1611, still widely used by English-speaking Protestants.

king·let (king′lit), *n.* a petty king; ruler over a small country.

king·ly (king′li), *adj.,* -li·er, -li·est, *adv.* —*adj.* **1.** of a king or kings; of royal rank. **2.** fit for a king: *a kingly crown.* **3.** like a king; royal; noble. —*adv.* as a king does. —king′li·ness, *n.* —Syn. *adj.* **3.** regal, majestic, august.

king·pin (king′pin′), *n.* **1.** pin in front or in the center in bowling games. **2.** *Am., Colloq.* the most important person or thing. **3.** kingbolt.

king post, a vertical post between the apex of a triangular roof truss and a tie beam.

Kings (kingz), *n.pl.* **1.** in the Protestant Old Testament, either of two books (I Kings or II Kings) containing the history of the reigns of the Hebrew kings after David. **2.** in the Roman Catholic Old Testament, one of four books that include I and II Samuel and I and II Kings.

king's English, correct English.

king's evil, scrofula, a disease that was supposed to be cured by the touch of a king.

king·ship (king′ship), *n.* **1.** position, rank, or dignity of a king. **2.** rule of a king; government by a king.

king-size (king′sīz′), *adj. Colloq.* large or long for its kind: *a king-size cigarette.*

king snake, *Am.* a large, harmless snake that lives in the southern United States. It eats mice and rats and is supposed to kill other snakes.

king's ransom, very large amount of money.

Kings·ton (king′stən), *n.* capital and chief seaport of Jamaica.

kink (kingk), *n.* **1.** a twist or curl in thread, rope, hair, etc. **2.** pain or stiffness in the muscles of the neck, back, etc.; crick. **3.** *Am., Colloq.* mental twist; queer idea; odd notion; eccentricity; whim. —*v.* form a kink; make kinks in. [prob. < Du., twist]

kin·ka·jou (king′kə·jü), *n.* a yellowish-brown mammal of Central and South America. It resembles a raccoon, but has a long prehensile tail. [< F *quincajou* < Tupi]

Kinkajou
(total length ab. 2½ ft.)

kink·y (kingk′i), *adj.,* kink·i·er, kink·i·est. full of kinks; twisted; curly. —kink′i·ly, *adv.* —kink′i·ness, *n.*

kins·folk (kinz′fōk′), **kins·folks** (-fōks′), *n.pl.* family; relatives; kin. Also, *Dial.* kinfolk, kinfolks.

kin·ship (kin′ship), *n.* **1.** family relationship. **2.** relationship. **3.** resemblance.

kins·man (kinz′mən), *n., pl.* -men. a male relative.

kins·wom·an (kinz′wum′ən), *n., pl.* -wom·en. a female relative.

ki·osk (kĭ·ŏsk'; kĭ'ŏsk), *n.* a small building with one or more sides open, used as a newsstand, a bandstand, or an opening to a subway. [< F < Turk. *kiûshk* pavilion]

Kio·to (kyō'tō), *n.* Kyoto.

kip (kĭp), *n.* hide of a young or undersized animal.

Kip·ling (kĭp'lĭng), *n.* Rudyard, 1865–1936, English writer of stories, novels, and poems.

kip·per (kĭp'ər), *v.* salt and dry or smoke (herring, salmon, etc.). —*n.* 1. herring, salmon, etc., that has been kippered. 2. male salmon or sea trout during or after the spawning season. [OE *cypera* (def. 2)]

Kir·ghiz (kĭr·gēz'), *n., pl.* -ghiz, -ghiz·es. 1. a member of a Mongolian people widely scattered over the western part of central Asia. 2. their language.

kirk (kėrk), *n. Scot.* church.

kir·mess (kėr'mĭs), *n.* kermis.

kir·tle (kėr'təl), *n. Archaic.* 1. skirt or dress. 2. a man's short coat. [OE *cyrtel*, prob. ult. < L *curtus* short] —**kir'tled,** *adj.*

kis·met (kĭz'mĕt; kĭs'–), *n.* fate; destiny. [< Turk. < Ar. *qismat*]

kiss (kĭs), *v.* 1. touch with the lips as a sign of love, greeting, or respect. 2. touch gently: *a soft wind kissed the treetops.* 3. put, bring, take, etc., by kissing: *kiss away tears.* —*n.* 1. a touch with the lips. 2. a gentle touch. 3. a fancy cake made of white of egg and powdered sugar. 4. a piece of candy of certain sorts. [OE *cyssan*] —**kiss'a·ble,** *adj.* —**kiss'er,** *n.*

kit (kĭt), *n.* 1. equipment that a soldier carries with him. 2. any person's equipment packed for traveling. 3. outfit of tools: *a shoemaker's kit.* 4. bag, case, knapsack, etc., for carrying such equipment or such an outfit. 5. *Colloq.* lot; set; collection. 6. a small wooden tub or pail. [prob. < MDu. *kitte*]

kitch·en (kĭch'ən), *n.* 1. room where food is cooked. 2. cooking department. [ult. < L *coquina* < *coquus* a cook]

kitch·en·ette, kitch·en·et (kĭch'ən·net'), *n. Am.* a very small, compactly arranged kitchen.

kitchen garden, garden where vegetables and fruit for a family are grown. —**kitchen gardener.**

kitchen police, 1. army duty of helping the cook prepare and serve the food, wash the dishes, and clean up the kitchen. 2. soldiers assigned to this duty.

kitch·en·ware (kĭch'ən·wâr'), *n.* kitchen utensils.

kite (kīt), *n., v.,* kit·ed, kit·ing. —*n.* 1. a light wooden frame covered with paper or cloth, flown in the air on the end of a long string. 2. hawk with long pointed wings. 3. any of the very high and light sails of a ship. 4. *Com.* a fictitious certificate, check, contract, etc., not representing any actual transaction, used for raising money or sustaining credit. —*v.* 1. *Colloq.* fly like a kite; move rapidly and easily. 2. *Com.* obtain money or credit through kites. [OE *cȳta*]

kith and kin (kĭth), 1. friends and relatives. 2. kin. [OE *cȳththth* acquaintance, ult. < *cunnan* know]

kit·ten (kĭt'ən), *n.* a young cat. [< var. of OF *cheton,* ult. < LL *cattus* cat]

kit·ten·ish (kĭt'ən·ish), *adj.* 1. like a kitten; playful. 2. coquettish. —**kit'ten·ish·ly,** *adv.* —**kit'ten·ish·ness,** *n.*

kit·ti·wake (kĭt'i·wāk), *n.* kind of sea gull. [imit. of its call]

kit·ty¹ (kĭt'i), *n., pl.* -ties. 1. kitten. 2. pet name for a cat. [ult. < *kitten*]

kit·ty² (kĭt'i), *n., pl.* -ties. 1. stakes in a poker game. 2. money pooled by the players in other games for some special purpose.

Kiu·shu (kyū'shū), *n.* Kyushu.

Ki·wa·nis (kĭ·wä'nĭs), *n. Am.* an international group of clubs of business and professional men, organized for civic service and higher ideals in business and professional life. —**Ki·wa·ni·an** (kĭ·wä'ni·ən), *n., adj.*

ki·wi (kē'wi), *n., pl.* -wis. apteryx. [< Maori]

K.K.K., KKK, Ku Klux Klan.

kl., kiloliter.

Klan (klăn), *n. Am.* Ku Klux Klan.

Klans·man (klănz'mən), *n., pl.* -men. *Am.* member of the Ku Klux Klan.

klep·to·ma·ni·a (klĕp'tə·mā'ni·ə), *n.* an insane impulse to steal. [< NL, < Gk. *kleptes* thief + *mania* madness] —**klep·to·ma·ni·ac** (klĕp'tə·mā'ni·ak), *n.*

klieg light (klēg), *Am.* a bright, hot arc light used in taking motion pictures. [after *Kliegl* brothers, the inventors]

Klon·dike (klŏn'dīk), *n.* region in NW Canada, along the Yukon River, famous for its gold fields.

km., 1. kilometer; kilometers. 2. kingdom.

knack (năk), *n.* 1. special skill; power to do something easily. 2. trick; habit. —**Syn.** 1. aptitude, facility.

knap·sack (năp'sak'), *n.* a canvas or leather bag for carrying clothes, equipment, etc., on the back. [< LG, < *knappen* eat + *sack* sack¹]

knave (nāv), *n.* 1. a tricky, dishonest person; rogue; rascal. 2. the jack, a playing card with a picture of a servant or soldier on it. 3. *Archaic.* a male servant; man of humble birth or position. [OE *cnafa* boy] —**Syn.** 1. scoundrel.

Knapsack

knav·er·y (nāv'ər·i; nāv'ri), *n., pl.* -er·ies. 1. behavior characteristic of a knave. 2. a tricky, dishonest act. 3. *Obs.* mischief.

knav·ish (nāv'ish), *adj.* tricky; dishonest. —**knav'ish·ly,** *adv.* —**knav'ish·ness,** *n.* —**Syn.** rascally, villainous, fraudulent.

knead (nēd), *v.* 1. mix (dough, clay, etc.) by pressing and squeezing, usually with one's hands: *a baker kneads dough.* 2. press and squeeze with the hands; massage. 3. make or shape by kneading. [OE *cnedan*] —**knead'er,** *n.*

knee (nē), *n., v.,* kneed, knee·ing. —*n.* 1. the joint between the thigh and the lower leg. 2. any joint corresponding to the human knee or elbow. 3. anything like a bent knee in shape or position. 4. part of a garment covering the knee. 5. bring to one's **knees,** force to yield. —*v.* strike or touch with the knee. [OE *cnēo*]

knee·cap (nē'kap'), *n.* a flat, movable bone at the front of the knee; patella; kneepan.

knee-deep (nē'dēp'), *adj.* so deep as to reach the knees.

kneel (nēl), *v.,* knelt (nelt) or kneeled, kneeling. 1. go down on one's knee or knees. 2. remain in this position. [OE *cnēowlian* < *cnēo* knee] —**kneel'er,** *n.*

knee·pad (nē'pad'), *n.* pad worn around the knee for protection.

knee·pan (nē'pan'), *n.* kneecap; the patella.

knell (nel), *n.* 1. sound of a bell rung slowly after a death or at a funeral. 2. warning sign of death, failure, etc. 3. a mournful sound. —*v.* 1. ring slowly. 2. give a warning sign of death, failure, etc. 3. make a mournful sound. [OE *cnyllan*]

knew (nū; nū), *v.* pt. of **know.**

Knick·er·bock·er (nik'ər·bok'ər), *n.* descendant of the early Dutch settlers of New York.

knick·ers (nik'ərz), or **knick·er·bock·ers** (nik'ər·bok'ərz), *n.pl.* short loose-fitting trousers gathered in at or just below the knee.

knick-knack (nik'nak'), *n.* a pleasing trifle; ornament; trinket. Also, **nicknack.** [varied reduplication of *knack*]

knife (nīf), *n., pl.* knives, *v.,* knifed, knif·ing. —*n.* 1. a cutting tool with a sharp-edged blade and handle. 2. a cutting blade in a tool or machine: *the knives of a lawn mower.* 3. under the knife, *Colloq.* undergoing a surgical operation. —*v.* 1. cut or stab with a knife. 2. *Am., Slang.* try to defeat in an underhand way. [OE *cnif*] —**knife'less,** *adj.* —**knife'like',** *adj.*

knight (nīt), *n.* 1. in the Middle Ages, a man raised to an honorable military rank and pledged to do good deeds. After serving as a page and squire, a man was made a knight by the king or a lord. 2. in modern times, a man raised to an honorable rank because of personal achievement or because he has won distinction in some way. A knight has the title *Sir* before his name. 3. man devoted to the service or protection of a lady. 4. *Am.* member of the Knights of Columbus, the Knights Templar, etc. 5. piece in the game of chess. —*v.* raise to the rank of knight. [OE *cniht boy*] —**knight′less,** *adj.*

knight·er·rant (nīt′er′ənt), *n., pl.* **knightser·rant.** knight traveling in search of adventure.

knight·er·rant·ry (nīt′er′ən·tri), *n., pl.* **knight·er·rant·ries.** 1. conduct or action characteristic of a knight-errant. 2. quixotic conduct or action.

knight·hood (nīt′hůd), *n.* 1. rank or dignity of a knight. 2. profession or occupation of a knight. 3. character or qualities of a knight. 4. knights as a group or class.

knight·ly (nīt′li), *adj.* of a knight; brave; generous; courteous; chivalrous. —*adv.* as a knight should do; bravely; generously; courteously. —**knight′li·ness,** *n.*

Knights of Columbus, a fraternal society of Roman Catholic men, founded in 1882.

Knight Templar, *pl.* **Knights Templars** *for 1;* **Knights Templar** *for 2.* 1. Templar (def. 1). 2. member of an order of Masons in the United States.

knit (nit), *v.,* **knit·ted** or **knit, knit·ting.** 1. make (cloth or article of clothing) by looping yarn or thread together with long needles: *mother is knitting a sweater.* 2. make an article or fabric by looping yarn or thread together: *she knits all day.* 3. form into cloth by looping stitches, not by weaving: *jersey is cloth knitted by machine.* 4. join closely and firmly together. 5. grow together; be joined closely and firmly: *a broken bone knits.* 6. draw (the brows) together in wrinkles. [OE *cnyttan < cnotta* knot] —**knit′ter,** *n.*

knit·ting (nit′ing), *n.* knitted work.

knitting needle, one of a pair of long needles used in knitting.

knives (nīvz), *n. pl.* of **knife.**

knob (nob), *n.* 1. a rounded lump. 2. handle of a door, drawer, etc. 3. a rounded hill or mountain. [cf. MLG *knobbe*] —**knobbed,** *adj.* —**knob′like′,** *adj.* —**Syn.** 1. knot, protuberance.

knob·by (nob′i), *adj.,* **-bi·er, -bi·est.** 1. covered with knobs. 2. rounded like a knob. —**knob′bi·ness,** *n.*

knock (nok), *v.* 1. hit: *he knocked him on the head.* 2. hit each other: *his knees knocked with fright.* 3. hit and cause to fall. 4. hit with a noise: *knock on a door.* 5. make a noise, esp. a rattling or pounding noise: *the engine is knocking.* 6. *Am., Slang.* criticise; find fault. 7. knock about, *Colloq.* wander from place to place. 8. knock down, a. sell (an article) to the highest bidder at an auction. b. take apart. c. strike down. 9. knock off, *Colloq.* a. take off; deduct. b. stop work. c. make quickly; do quickly. 10. knock out, hit so hard as to make helpless or unconscious. 11. knock together, make or put together hastily. —*n.* 1. hit. 2. hit with a noise. 3. act of knocking. 4. sound of knocking: *she did not hear the knock at the door.* 5. sound caused by loose parts: *a knock in the engine.* [OE *cnocian*] —**Syn.** *v.* 1. strike, rap, beat. 4. rap.

knock·a·bout (nok′ə·bout′), *n. Am.* a small, easily handled sailboat having one mast, a mainsail, and a jib, but no bowsprit. —*adj.* 1. suitable for rough use. 2. noisy; boisterous.

knock·er (nok′ər), *n.* 1. person or thing that knocks. 2. knob, ring, etc., fastened on a door for use in knocking.

knock-kneed (nok′nēd′), *adj.* having legs bent inward at the knees.

knock·out (nok′out′), *n.* 1. act of knocking out. 2. condition of being knocked out. 3. blow that knocks out. 4. *Am., Slang.* a very attractive person; overwhelming or striking thing. —*adj. Slang.* that knocks out: *a knockout blow.*

knoll (nōl), *n.* a small rounded hill; mound. [OE *cnoll*]

Knos·sos (nos′əs), *n.* the ancient capital of Crete. Also, **Cnossus.**

knot (not), *n., v.,* **knot·ted, knot·ting.** —*n.* 1. a fastening made by tying or twining together pieces of rope, cord, string, etc. 2. bow of ribbon, etc., worn as an ornament. 3. group; cluster: *a knot of people.* 4. a hard mass of wood formed where a branch grows out from a tree, which shows as a roundish, cross-grained piece in a board. 5. a hard lump: *a knot sometimes forms in a tired muscle.* 6. joint where leaves grow out on the stem of a plant. 7. *Naut.* a. unit of speed used on ships; one nautical mile per hour: *the ship averaged 12 knots.* b. nautical mile, 6080.27 feet. 8. difficulty; problem. 9. thing that unites closely or intricately. —*v.* 1. tie or twine together in a knot. 2. tangle in knots. 3. form (a fringe) by making knots. 4. form or knit knots in making fringes. 5. form into a hard lump. 6. unite closely or intricately. [OE *cnotta*] —**knot′less,** *adj.* —**knot′ted,** *adj.* —**Syn.** *n.* 3. company. 5. knob. 8. puzzle, perplexity. 9. bond, tie, link. —*v.* 2. snarl. 6. bind.

Knots: A, overhand; B, figure of eight; C, square; D, slip.

knot·hole (not′hōl′), *n.* hole in a board where a knot has fallen out.

knot·ty (not′i), *adj.,* **-ti·er, -ti·est.** 1. full of knots: *knotty wood.* 2. difficult; puzzling: *a knotty problem.* —**knot′ti·ness,** *n.*

knout (nout), *n.* whip formerly used in Russia to inflict punishment. —*v.* flog with a knout. [< F < Russ. *knut*]

know (nō), *v.,* **knew, known, know·ing.** *n.* —*v.* 1. be sure of; have true information about: *he knows the facts of the case.* 2. have firmly in the mind or memory: *know a lesson.* 3. be aware of; have seen or heard; have information about: *know a person's name.* 4. be sure; have information: *he does not have to guess; he knows.* 5. be acquainted with; be familiar with: *I know her.* 6. have an understanding of; have experience with; be skilled in: *he knows that subject.* 7. recognize; identify: *you would hardly know him nowadays.* 8. be able to tell apart from others; distinguish: *you will know his house by the red roof.* —*n.* in the know, *Colloq.* having inside information. [OE *cnāwan*] —**know′er,** *n.*

know·a·ble (nō′ə·bəl), *adj.* capable of being known. —**know′a·ble·ness,** *n.*

know-how (nō′hou′), *n. Am., Colloq.* ability to do something.

know·ing (nō′ing), *adj.* 1. having knowledge; well-informed. 2. clever; shrewd. 3. suggesting shrewd or secret understanding of matters: *a knowing look.* —**know′ing·ly,** *adv.* —**know′ingness,** *n.* —**Syn.** 2. sharp, cunning.

knowl·edge (nol′ij), *n.* 1. what one knows: *his knowledge of the subject is limited.* 2. all that is known or can be learned. 3. fact of knowing: *the knowledge of our victory caused great joy.* 4. act of knowing. 5. practical understanding. 6. a branch of learning: *all the knowledges and skills.*

knowl·edge·a·ble (nol′ij·ə·bəl), *adj. Colloq.* intelligent.

know-noth·ing (nō′nuth′ing), *n.* 1. an ignorant person. 2. Know-Nothing, *Am.* a. American political party prominent from 1853 to 1856. It aimed to keep control of the government in the hands of native-born citizens. b. member of this party.

Knox (noks), *n.* John, 1505?-1572, Scottish preacher and religious reformer.

Knox·ville (noks′vil), *n.* city in E Tennessee, on the Tennessee River.

knuck·le (nuk′əl), *n., v.,* **-led, -ling.** —*n.* 1. finger joint; joint between a finger and the rest of the hand. 2. knee or hock joint of an animal used as food: *boiled pigs′ knuckles.* 3. knuckles, pieces of metal worn over the knuckles as a weapon. —*v.* 1. put the knuckles on the ground in playing marbles. 2. **knuckle down,** a. submit; yield. b. *Am., Colloq.* apply oneself earnestly; work hard. 3. **knuckle under,** submit; yield. [cf. Du. *kneukel* < *knok* bone]

knurl (nérl), *n.* 1. knot; knob. 2. a small ridge, as on the edge of a coin or round nut. [? < *knur* knot. Cf. MDu. *knorre.*] —**knurled** (nérld), *adj.*

knurl·y (nér′lĭ), *adj.,* **knurl·i·er,** **knurl·i·est.** gnarled.

k.o., K.O., knockout.

ko·a·la (kō·ä′lə), *n.* a gray, furry animal of Australia that carries its young in a pouch. [< Australian lang.]

Ko·be (kō′bē; –bā), *n.* seaport in W Japan.

ko·dak (kō′dak), *n., v.,* –**daked,** –**dak·ing.** *Am.* —*n.* 1. a small camera with rolls of film on which photographs are taken. 2. **Kodak,** *Trademark.* a small camera made by the Eastman Kodak Company. —*v.* take photographs with a kodak. —**ko′dak·er,** *n.*

Koala   (2 ft. long)

Ko·di·ak (kō′di·ak), *n.* island in the N Pacific near Alaska.

Koh·i·noor (kō′ə·nŭr), *n.* a very large and famous diamond that is now one of the British crown jewels.

kohl·ra·bi (kōl′rä′bĭ), *n., pl.* –**bies.** vegetable that looks somewhat like a turnip, but is a kind of cabbage. [< G <Ital. *cavoli rape,* ult. <L *caulis* cabbage + *rapa* turnip]

ko·la (kō′lə), *n.* 1. kola nut. 2. stimulant or tonic made from kola nuts. Also, **cola.** [< African lang.]

kola nut, a bitter brownish nut of a tropical tree. It contains about 3 per cent of caffein.

ko·lin·sky (kə·lin′ski), *n.* 1. mink that lives in Asia. 2. its tawny fur. [< Russ. *kolinski,* adj., from *Kola,* section of Russia]

Kö·nigs·berg (kœ′niks·berk), *n.* Kaliningrad.

koo·doo (kü′dü), *n., pl.* –**doos.** kudu.

ko·peck, ko·pek (kō′pek), *n.* a Russian copper or bronze coin. 100 kopeks = 1 ruble. Also, **copek.** [< Russ. *kopeika*]

Ko·ran (kō·rän′; –ran′; kō–), *n.* the sacred book of the Mohammedans. It consists of reports of revelations to the prophet Mohammed. [< Ar. *qur′ān* a reading < *qara′a* to read]

Ko·re·a (kō·rē′ə; kō–), *n.* a country on a peninsula in E Asia. After World War II it was divided into two republics, North Korea and South Korea. In 1950 war broke out between North and South Korea; a cease-fire agreement was signed in 1953. Also, *Japanese* **Chosen.** —**Ko·re′an,** *adj., n.*

Kos·ci·us·ko (kos′i·us′kō), *n.* Thaddeus, 1746–1817, Polish general who served in the American army during the American Revolution.

ko·sher (kō′shər), *adj.* 1. right or clean according to Jewish ritualistic law. 2. *Am., Slang.* all right; fine; legitimate. —*v.* prepare (food) according to the Jewish law. —*n. Colloq.* food thus prepared. [< Heb. *kāshēr* proper]

kou·mis, kou·miss, kou·myss (kü′mis), *n.* kumiss.

kow·tow (kou′tou′), *ko·tow* (kō′–), *v.* 1. kneel and touch the ground with the forehead to show deep respect, submission, or worship. 2. show slavish respect or obedience. —*n.* act of kowtowing. [< Chinese *k′o-t′ou,* lit., knock (the) head] —**kow′tow′er, ko′tow′er,** *n.*

K.P., kitchen police.

Kr, *Chem.* krypton.

kraal (kräl), *n.* 1. village of South African natives, protected by a fence. 2. pen for cattle or sheep in South Africa. [< Afrikaans < Pg. *curral* corral]

Kras·no·dar (kräs′nō·där), *n.* city in S Soviet Union.

K-ra·tion (kā′rash′ən; –rā′shən), *n. U.S. Army.* one of the emergency field rations used when other rations are not available.

Kreis·ler (krīs′lər), *n.* Fritz, born 1875, Austrian violinist and composer, in the U.S.

Krem·lin (krem′lin), *n.* citadel of Moscow.

The chief offices of the Soviet government are in the Kremlin. [< F < Russ. *kreml* < Tatar]

Kril·i·um (kril′i·əm), *n. Trademark.* a soil conditioner obtainable in liquid, powder, or flake form, made by Monsanto Chemical Company. [< (sodium salt of hydrolyzed *polya*) cryl(onitrile)]

krim·mer (krim′ər), *n.* a gray fur resembling Persian lamb, made from lambskins from the Crimea. [< G, < *Krim* Crimea]

kris (krēs), *n.* creese.

Krish·na (krish′nə), *n.* one of the most important Hindu gods, one of the incarnations of Vishnu.

Kriss Krin·gle (kris′ kring′gəl), *Am.* Santa Claus. [< G *Christkindl, –del* Christ child, Christmas gift]

kro·na (krō′nə), *n., pl.* –**nor** (–nôr). a Swedish or Icelandic silver coin. [< Swed., Icel., crown]

kro·ne[1] (krō′ne), *n., pl.* –**ner** (–ner). a Danish or Norwegian silver coin. [< Dan., Norw., crown]

kro·ne[2] (krō′nə), *n., pl.* –**nen** (–nən). 1. former German gold coin, worth about $2.38. 2. former Austrian silver coin, worth about 20 cents. [< G, crown]

Kron·stadt (krōn′shtät), *n.* fortress and naval station in NW Soviet Union, near Leningrad.

Krupp (krup), *n.* Alfred, 1812–1887, German manufacturer of artillery, munitions, etc.

kryp·ton (krip′ton), *n. Chem.* a rare inert gas, Kr, one of the chemical elements. [< NL < Gk., neut. adj., hidden]

Kt., 1. Also, **kt.** karat. 2. Knight.

Kua·la Lum·pur (kwä′lə lüm′pür′), capital of the Malayan Union.

Ku·blai Khan (kü′blī kän′), 1216?–1294, Mongol emperor from 1259 to 1294. He was the first of the Mongol rulers of China.

ku·dos (kū′dos; kü′–), *n. Colloq.* glory; fame. [< Gk. *kydos*]

ku·du (kü′dü), *n.* a large, grayish-brown African antelope with white stripes. Also, **koodoo.**

Ku Klux Klan (kü′ kluks′ klan′; kü′), or **Ku-Klux, Ku·klux,** *n. Am.* 1. a secret society of white people in the southern United States formed after the Civil War to regain and maintain their control. 2. a secret society founded in 1915, opposed to Negroes, Jews, Catholics, and foreigners.

ku·lak (kü·läk′), *n.* a Russian farmer who had poorer peasants working for him or who opposed the Soviet government. [< Russ., lit., fist]

ku·miss (kü′mis), *n.* fermented mare's or camel's milk used as a drink by Asiatic nomads. Also, **koumis, koumiss,** or **koumyss.** [< Russ. < Tatar *kumiz*]

küm·mel (kim′əl), *n.* liqueur flavored with caraway seeds, anise, etc. [< G]

kum·quat (kum′kwot), *n.* 1. a yellow fruit somewhat like a small orange. It has a sour pulp and a sweet rind, and is used in preserves and candy. 2. tree that it grows on. Also, **cumquat.** [< Chinese (Cantonese dial.)]

Kun·ming (kun′ming′), *n.* city in S China.

Kuo·min·tang (kwō′min·tang′; –täng′), *n.* a Chinese nationalist party organized by Sun Yat-sen.

Kurd (kérd; kůrd), *n.* member of a nomadic and warlike Mohammedan people living chiefly in Kurdistan. —**Kurd′ish,** *adj.*

Kur·di·stan (kér′də·stan; kůr′di·stän′), *n.* an extensive plateau and mountainous region in SW Asia now divided between Turkey, Iran, and Iraq.

Ku·rile Islands, Ku·ril Islands (kůr′il; kü·rēl′), chain of 31 small islands N of Japan, returned to Russia after World War II.

Ku·wait (ků·wāt′), *n.* 1. a British protectorate in NE Arabia. 2. its capital.

kw., kilowatt.

K.W.H., kw-hr., kilowatt-hour.

Ky., Kentucky.

Kyo·to (kyō′tō), *n.* city in C Japan. It was formerly the capital. Also, **Kioto.**

Kyu·shu (kyü′shü), *n.* a large island at the SW end of the Japanese empire. Also, **Kiushu.**

AMERICAN ENGLISH GRAMMAR

Charles C. Fries and Aileen Traver Kitchin

All of us wish to speak and write "good English." For more than a century its teaching has been one of the major concerns of our educational system. To its study all pupils are required to give a large portion of their school time and it is the one required subject of the school curriculum that enjoys almost unanimous support from the general public and school authorities.

Nevertheless, in spite of this general agreement as to its importance, many of us do not understand what "good English" really is. Many of us would doubtless agree with the statement that "a sound knowledge of grammar is important to a person who desires to speak good English." But what do we mean by "knowledge of grammar"? And how is it linked to "good English"? In order to answer these questions we must first of all understand the meaning and purpose or grammar as a science.

THE RELATIONSHIP BETWEEN GRAMMAR AND USAGE

One of the chief purposes of a scientific study of the grammar of any language is to identify and describe the forms and patterns of the language as they are actually used in various situations and by various groups of speakers of the language. The "rules" and "laws" of scientific grammar are not rules and laws in the common sense of something that must be obeyed; rather they are general statements which attempt to describe the ways in which a particular language operates in order to fulfill its communicative function. They are based on careful observation of the language itself and are valid only in so far as they are accurate generalizations. They do not in any way determine or affect the way in which the language is used by its speakers; they are, on the contrary, entirely determined by this usage.

This may sound rather different from the grammar with which most of us are familiar, for we have learned not about the scientific grammar described above, but about the so-called "prescriptive" or "normative" grammar which seeks to impart skill in language (1) through the prescribing of rules for correct usage which are often based, not on what is actually in accepted use in the language, but on what some "authority" thinks should be used, and (2) through the analysis of sentences by a study of clauses, phrases, and parts of speech. It is the tendency of this type of grammar to attempt to fit the language to the rules, rather than the rules to the language. It is because of this tendency that we often encounter a great divergence between the language we actually use, and which we hear being used by educated people, and the language which the "rules of grammar" tell us we should use. In cases of this kind, the scientific grammarian will often insist that the rules are wrong, not the speaker.

For ordinary purposes, if we ignore the special differences that separate the speech of New England, the South, and the Middle West, we do have in the United States a set of language habits, broadly conceived, in which the major matters of the political, social, economic, educational, and religious life of this country are carried on. This set of language habits has thus achieved considerable prestige and therefore furnishes the English usage which it is the obligation of our schools to teach.

HOW OUR LANGUAGE OPERATES

Linguistic forms

Our language is made up of forms (all words are forms, and so also are such elements as "–ing" and "–s" which indicate inflection, plural number, and so forth), and these can be separated roughly into two classes:

The first class includes the words which stand for the things, the acts, the qualities, judgments, times, places, etc. of which we are conscious in the world about us, words like *cat, man, faith, honor; walk, sit, think; big, little, good, slow.* These words are classified, on the basis of the forms which each has, as nouns, verbs, and adjectives. Such words constitute the "lexicon" of the language and are said to have "lexical" meaning. Words such as *here, now,* and *slowly* may also be included in the lexicon, since, in a sense, they are labels for time, place, and manner.

The second class includes forms which do not in themselves stand for things, acts, etc., but which serve to show the relationship between the things, acts, etc. represented by the first class. This class includes words like *the, in, between, of, shall, might.* These words play an essential part in the mechanics or the grammar of our language. They are said to have "relational" or "grammatical" rather than "lexical" meaning and hence are called grammatical items.

In the sentence "The little boy is sitting on a big chair," the words *little, boy, sit, big, chair* belong to the first class and are part of the English lexicon, while *the, is, –ing, on,* and *a* are grammatical items (and are, except for "–ing," of the type called function words).

Relationships of Linguistic Forms

A study of the way these lexical and grammatical forms are used in English involves four chief matters:

A. The first matter to be considered is the kinds of utterances or sentences we make, which may be called the "sentence patterns" of English.

1. There are in English only three major sentence patterns: the statement or report ("John gave a kitten to his brother"), the question ("What did John give his brother?"), and the request or command ("Give the cat to John!").

2. There are many minor sentence patterns, among which are: conventionalized cries ("Ouch!"), answers to questions ("Where is John?" "Downtown."), calls ("Oh, John!"), and exclamations ("What a beautiful cat!").

B. The second matter to be considered is the means we use to indicate in a sentence the performer of the act, the thing affected by the act, and the one to or for whom the act is performed.

John/ gave/ his brother/ a cat.
His brother/ gave/ John/ a cat.

C. The third matter is the way in which we indicate "character," that is, the way in which we describe the things about which we speak.

John, *who is much older*, gave his *little* brother a *Persian* cat.

D. The fourth of the main points to be considered in a study of English is the means by which we state the variety of times, aspects, moods, and conditions under which an action is performed, that is, the various verb forms and verbal expressions which we have at our disposal to express different types of action.

John *gave* his brother a cat.
Tommy *is going to feed* the cat.
Tommy *feeds* the cat every morning.
John *has given* his brother a cat.
John *would give* his brother a cat, *if* he *could find* just the right kind.

Linguistic forms and English grammar

The study of English grammar is a study of the devices English uses to indicate relationships such as those stated above in paragraphs A, B, C, and D. For this purpose our language uses the following three important devices:

A. The Device of Word Order

In the earlier stages of English the relationships between the lexical items in an utterance were indicated to a large extent by the forms of words or inflections. A noun, for instance, had one form when it was used as the subject in a sentence, another form when it was used as direct object, and still another form when it was used as indirect object. As the language changed over the years, however, many of these inflectional forms were gradually lost and word-order patterns became progressively more significant as signals.

1. The Chief Positions of Noun and Verb in Statements.

a. Position before the verb. In the sentence "The boy killed the bear," notice that the starting point of the action, the performer of the act or subject, is indicated by the position of that noun *before* the verb. The fact that it is position primarily that signals the subject is illustrated by the following sentence in which, although the words are gibberish, we can easily pick out the subject of the sentence as "mirl" (we are aided here, of course, by the fact that *mirl*, like *boy*, has one of the chief formal characteristics of a noun in that it is preceded by *the*).

The mirl sooled the pogle.

In some sentences more than one noun precedes the verb but there are various signals which indicate which of the nouns is the subject.

The *boy's dog* is sitting on the chair.
In the *afternoon* the little *boy* played in the garden.
The older *boy*, a handsome *chap*, came to call.
The *boy* and his *sister* played in the garden.
The *bread, butter*, and *cheese* were on the table.
The *stone house* on the corner belongs to John's grandfather.

b. Position after the verb.
If a single noun follows the verb and if it refers to the *same* person or thing as the subject noun, it is an identifying noun:

John's brother is a *surgeon*.

If a single noun follows the verb and does not refer to the same person or thing as the subject noun, then it represents the end point of the action, the person or thing affected by the act, the direct object.

The boys crossed the *river*.

Sometimes two nouns follow the verb. In these instances there are also various signals which indicate which noun is "direct object" and which is "indirect object," or "object complement."

They call the *baby Corky*.
The children need *shoes* and *underwear*.
John gave his little *brother* an *apple*.

In this section we have seen how the order of words serves as a device to indicate the relationships discussed in paragraph B on page xxv above, namely, the performer of the act, the person or thing affected by the act, and the one to or for whom the act is performed. We have seen that in English statements, position before the verb is "subject" position, while position after the verb is "object" position, with the indirect object preceding the direct object.

2. The Chief Positions of a Noun and a Modifier.

a. Single-word modifiers. Single-word modifiers of a noun (such as adjectives, noun adjuncts) precede the words they modify, but word-group modifiers (phrases and clauses) follow the words they modify.

When a single word with the characteristics of an adjective (that is, inflection with –er or –est or use with *more* or *most* for comparison) precedes a noun, it is a modifier of that noun.

a *beautiful* view   a *prettier* girl

When two nouns are used together, often with a word like *the, a, these* before the first noun, the first noun modifies the second. In such cases there is no formal indication of the fact that the first noun is used as a modifier except its position before the second noun.

a *brick* wall   the *meat* bill
my *college* course   *school* spirit

In some constructions there are frequently two or even more modifiers for a single noun.

fair and *beautiful* children
an *easy, accurate* manner

When two or more modifiers are not leveled, the word-order pattern shows the direction of the modification.

in *reasonably good* health
high moral character

b. Word-group modifiers. In English there are also modifiers that are made up of groups of words. These word-group modifiers immediately follow the words they modify.

the cat *in the chair*
a trip *by air*
the community *where he lived*
the environment *in which they grew up*

Subordinate clauses are generally introduced by function words like *which, who, that*, but frequently these function words are omitted and then the position of the clause after the noun is all that indicates its function of modifying the noun. Position without function word is sufficient.

Any information *you can send me* will be appreciated.

B. The Uses of Function Words

A second important device for indicating relationships between the lexical items in our language is the use of function words. Some of the more important classes of function words are (a) prepositions (the function words that are used with nouns or pronouns), (b) auxiliaries (the function words that are used with verbs), (c) the words modifying adjectives that become function words of degree, and (d) conjunctions (words which have as one of their functions the signaling of relationship between clauses).

1. Function Words Used with Substantives.

The nine function words most frequently used with substantives are *at, by, for, from, in, of, on, to, with.* These nine occur in about 90 per cent of all constructions using function words with substantives. Other important function words are *about, after, against, before, between, near, over, since, through, under,* and *among.* There are also combinations such as *into, onto, without, within.* Such groups of words as *on account of, for the sake of,* and *in view of* operate frequently as single units and are considered a kind of compound preposition.

These function words bring substantives (primarily nouns) into several types of grammatical relationships. Only the most frequent are illustrated here. Through function words a noun is made to modify (a) another noun ("the cat *on* the chair is John's"), (b) a verb ("the cat is sitting *on* the chair"), (c) a verb and a noun simultaneously ("the little boy received a present *from* his brother"), (d) an adjective ("arithmetic was very difficult *for* John's little brother"), (e) the subject, although the modifying noun stands after the verb *to be* and the phrase functions as a predicate adjective ("but he is happy and *without* a care in the world").

2. Function Words Used with Verbs.

There are two types of function words used with verbs: (a) those that are used with verbal substantives or infinitives (the name of an action, as *run, walk, play*) and (b) those that are used with verbal adjectives, that is, present participles (*playing*) and past participles (*played*).

a. Function Words Used with the Infinitive.

(1) *To.* The function word *to* is frequently called the "sign" of the infinitive, and certainly in present-day English the infinitive is most often preceded by the word *to. To* brings the infinitive into several types of relationships, only a few of which are illustrated here: (a) as a verb or sentence modifier, expressing purpose ("the little boy is running *to see* his new cat"), (b) as object of such verbs as *want, wish, try,* etc. ("he wants *to pull* the cat's tail"), (c) with a substantive preceding, the whole expression serving as an object ("John wants him *to quit* pulling the cat's tail"), (d) as modifier of a noun ("John has a tendency *to preach* to his little brother"), (e) as a modifier of an adjective ("the cat was unable *to escape*").

(2) *Do.* While *do* still retains its lexical meaning of "perform" or "accomplish" in such expressions as "what is John going to *do* tonight?", it more frequently operates simply as a function word: (a) in questions ("*do* you know the name of John's little brother?") and (b) with negative

verbs ("I *don't* know his name"). Two other uses of *do* are (c) the emphatic *do* ("but I *do* like cats") and (d) as a substitute verb, referring to a previously used verb ("John likes cats better than I *do*").

(3) *Shall* and *will,* the so-called auxiliaries of the future tense. *Shall* and *will* are function words used to indicate that the action expressed takes place in the future. Actually, however, English has many different ways of expressing the future, as in "John leaves tomorrow" and "John is going to leave tomorrow." For a discussion of the problems in the use of *shall* and *will,* see their entries in the main list of this dictionary.

(4) *Be.* The function word *be* in its various forms used with *to* and an infinitive may express "plan" or "appointment," as in "he *is to leave*" and "he *was to leave.*" With *about* to and an infinitive, as in "he *is about to leave*" and "he *was about to leave,*" it expresses an immediate future. With *going* to and an infinitive, as in "he *is going to leave*" and "he *was going to leave,*" it expresses near future.

(5) *Have* + *to.* In the sentence "John has to leave tomorrow," the phrase *has to leave* expresses "obligation" or "necessity" for going somewhere. In such uses as this the verb *have* is said to be a function word of necessity.

(6) *Used* + *to,* for customary action. In a sentence such as "he *used to sit* there every sunny afternoon," the word *used* is said to be a function word expressing customary action in the past.

(7) *May, might, can, could, would, should, must, ought to* + the infinitive. These words, the so-called modal auxiliaries, are function words used primarily to express attitudes toward the action or state indicated by the infinitive (attitudes such as permission, obligation, possibility, and doubt: "Can I go to the movies this afternoon, Mother?", "You ought to drive slowly when it's slippery," "It may rain tomorrow," "His statement could be true, but I don't really believe it").

b. Function Words Used with Participles.

(1) *Be* in its various forms, with the present participle (the progressive form of the verb). This combination of the function word *be* and the present participle of a verb is used primarily in expressions with a definite time for the action ("I *am writing* a letter to John right now") as opposed to the habitual or general time of the simple tense form ("I *write* a letter to John every Sunday" and "the sun *rises* in the east"). At other times the participle after the verb *be* has more of the quality of an adjective than of an action ("John's departure *was exciting*").

(2) *Keep,* in its various forms, with the present participle, expresses continuous or repetitive action, as in "he *kept writing* furiously all morning" and "the two boys *kept singing* off key."

(3) *Be,* in its various forms, with the past participle, sometimes signals action and sometimes an adjectival quality. Observe the difference in "my knowledge of little boys is very *limited*" and "the kitten *was frightened* by the storm." To call both these verb phrases examples of the passive voice is somewhat misleading. Although the grammatical form of both is exactly the same, only the second one can really be called "passive"; the subject of the sentence is the "receiver" of the act only when an agent of the action is expressed either in the sentence or in the context. The term "passive," therefore, really applies to the meaning of the sentence rather than to the grammatical form of the verb.

(4) *Have*, in its various forms, with the past participle (the perfect tenses). *Have* + the past participle signals that an action has occurred and stands completed within a period of time considered to be the present, as in "what *have* you done today, my dear?" and "I *have washed* my hair and I *have* baked a pie." *Had* + the past participle indicates that an act occurred and was completed before some other time in the past, as in "I *had* just *washed* my hair when John came to call."

c. Function Words Used with Adjectives.

(1) *More* and *most*, function words of comparison. At earlier stages of the English language, adjectives were compared by the inflectional endings *-er* (comparative), *-est* (superlative), but for several centuries the function words *more* and *most* have been replacing the older inflectional forms. Today, many of the adjectives are still inflected for the comparative and superlative (*longer, longest; prettier, prettiest*), but most unfamiliar words, new words, and the more learned words are compared by the use of function words (*more beautiful, most beautiful*).

(2) When standing before an adjective, certain words serve simply to intensify or to tone down the adjective which they precede. Notice how the word *pretty* in "a pretty girl" means one thing, while in the expression "a pretty bad girl" it has lost the meaning it had previously and serves only to intensify the adjective *bad*. The intensifier that we use most frequently is the word *very*, as in "that was a *very* good play" and "he was a *very* able speaker." Other words commonly used to intensify or tone down adjectives are *stark* ("stark mad"), *dead* ("dead sure"), *precious* ("precious few"), and *good* ("a good long time"). Many such words end in *-ly*, as in "*practically* impossible," "*perfectly* able," "not *really* necessary," and "*entirely* alone."

d. Function Words Used with Word Groups. The particular function words with which we will be concerned here are those that join sentences and clauses, that is to say, word groups in which there are two essential elements: (a) a substantive and (b) a verb with inflection for tense (a finite verb). The most frequently used conjunctions are *and*, *that*, *which*, *if*, *who*, *as*, *what*, *when*, *while*, *where*, and *so*. Traditionally the conjunctions are classified into two groups, "coördinating" and "subordinating." But this classification is not particularly important. Each of these function words signals a particular relationship between the clauses which it joins, and what is important is the precise nature of the relationship. For example, it has frequently been said that the conjunction *and* can be used only in an "additive" sense. An examination of the actual usage of educated speakers of English, however, reveals that the function word *and* indicates much more than simple addition. As a matter of fact, when simple addition is meant between the word groups, *also* is frequently added to *and* to make that meaning perfectly clear.

> Her father has been out of work for several months, *and* he is *also* in very poor physical condition.

And is consistently found in the following uses:

(1) Adversative or contrasting use of *and*, as in "John is a blond *and* Tommy is a brunet."

(2) *And* can introduce a consequence or a result, as in "there was not enough milk, *and* Tommy gave his to the kitten."

(3) *And* can introduce the concluding clause of a condition, as in "give a child a kitten *and* he will entertain himself for hours."

e. Three Miscellaneous Function Words: it, there, and one.

The words *it* and *there* (unstressed) operate as "pattern filling" words in certain sentence types.

> *It* rains very frequently.
> Is *it* raining now?
> *There* was an old man at the gate.
> Was *there* anybody home?
> *One* (the function word as distinct from the numeral) appears very frequently with adjectives.
> (Of dresses) I like the two red *ones*.
> (Of books) One good *one* is "War and Peace."

C. The Uses of the Forms of Words

Of all the inflections that our language originally had, only six are left in present-day English. Of these six, only two are vigorously alive; the other four are dying.

1. The Two Major or Live Inflections.

a. The forms for number. The contrast of forms to signal plural and singular has, in English, practically disappeared in all parts of speech except nouns and pronouns. The *-s* ending is today the regular plural inflection for the vast majority of nouns. Among those nouns not forming the plural by adding *-s* (irregular plurals) are a few very common and much-used words from older English (*men, feet, teeth, children*). Also some foreign words still maintain the inflectional forms of the language from which they come (*data, alumni, phenomena*).

Since at the present time so few words in English other than nouns have any distinctive forms for number, agreement in number has nearly passed out of the language. The only possibilities for number concord in present-day English are (a) in the use of *this, that, these*, and *those* as modifiers of other words (*this book, these books*), (b) in the use of *am, is, are, was, were*, and of the present indicative third-person singular *-s* of other verbs (*I am, we are; he walks, they walk*), and (c) in the use of the third-person pronouns when they refer to substantives already mentioned ("I had a *book* but I lost *it*; I had two *books* but I lost *them*"). There are situations in present-day English where even the very few number-forms that still survive in verbs are not used in accord with the demand for a formal concord of number. A collective noun like *family* may be followed by a plural verb whenever the meaning stresses the individuals that make up the group rather than the group itself ("My family *are* all going out this evening, each one to a different place"). We often choose the form of the verb in accordance with the meaning of the word rather than in accordance with its form.

The indefinite pronouns (*none, any, everyone, everybody, nobody, anyone, anybody*) are much like collective words. *None* and *any* already occur consistently with both the singular and the plural forms of the verb. The others, although they are still immediately followed only by the singular form of the verb, frequently appear with a pronoun referring to them in the plural, as in "did *everyone* have *their* books?" There was a time in the language when the collective nouns were at this same stage of development, that is, they were always immediately followed by a singular form of the verb, but the pronoun referring to them would occur in the plural. Similarly, when a subject consists of two or more words joined by *and* which refer to things that are felt as a unit the verb frequently has a singular form, as in "the organization and work of this office is very complex."

b. The forms for tense. The forms of words which distinguish the past tense of the verb from the present tense provide the second most important use of inflection in modern English. Within the past-tense form there is now no distinction for number or for person except in the verb *to be* in which *was* is used with singulars (except second person) and *were* with plurals (I *walked*, we *walked*, but I *was*, we *were*).

The particular form which has become the pattern for the past tense in present-day English is the suffix which is regularly spelled *-ed* (*raised, saved, raced, walked, nodded, wanted*). In English these "regular" verbs comprise the great body of verbs in the language. In this regular pattern there is no difference in form between the past tense and the past participle (I *walked*, I have *walked*).

There are, however, several groups of verbs that have not yet adjusted themselves to the pattern of tense inflection in present-day English. Among these are such verbs as *bite, drive, freeze, fly, drink, sing, shine, strike, fight, find, be, go, do, sell, teach, think, bring*, and *spend*.

2. Four Minor Inflections, Remnants of Older Patterns.

While the inflections for number and tense are still vigorously alive in the language, the inflections for the so-called "possessive" and "objective" cases, for comparison of adjectives, and for person and mood in the verb are gradually dying out.

a. The genitive inflection. The term "genitive" is used here because this form is frequently used to indicate a relationship other than that of possession or ownership: *John's hat, the man's coat, John's teacher, the man's physician, in a month's time, three days' grace, in a woman's college.*

This genitive inflection of nouns has tended to be displaced by the use of the function word *of*, until, in present-day English, the proportion of inflected genitive forms to this use of *of* is very small indeed; for instance, *the king of England, the effect of heat on rubber, the color of that paint.*

(1) The genitive form of pronouns. Although the genitive inflections of nouns have been largely displaced by the use of the function word *of*, genitive inflections of pronouns still persist. Most pronouns have two genitive forms, one which is used before nouns in so-called "attributive" position ("This is *our* house"), and one which stands alone in so-called "absolute" position ("This house is *ours*"). Not all the pronouns have two forms for the attributive and absolute position. *His* remains unchanged in both positions ("*his* book; the book is *his*").

The genitive forms of the pronouns are used in combination with *self* (*myself, ourselves*), except for *themselves* and *himself*, which have the objective forms *them* and *him* rather than the genitive forms *their* and *his*.

b. The objective forms. Only six "objective" forms remain in present-day English: *me, us, her, him, them, whom.* These forms do not today constitute effective signals of relationships but usually simply accompany the signals of position. Thus *Who* did you call? occurs rather than *Whom* did you call? It's *me*, rather than It's *I*, is the frequent answer to the question Who's there?

c. The inflection for comparison. *More* and *most* occur more frequently than the inflectional forms *-er* and *-est* for the comparative and superlative of adjectives. The comparative form is not now restricted to use when two things only are being compared, with the superlative being used when more than two things are involved. Speakers of English now use the comparative form in definite statements of comparison with *than* ("John is *older than* all the other children") and use the superlative form in statements without *than* regardless of the number of people or things involved ("John is the *smartest*").

d. Forms for person and mood.

(1) Person. In discussions of grammar the term "person" refers to distinctions which indicate whether the subject of a verb is the one speaking (first person), the one spoken to (second person), or the one spoken of (third person). The pronouns which make this distinction in their forms are therefore called personal pronouns. *I* and *we* are first-person pronouns; *you* is a second-person pronoun; and *he, she, it*, and *they* are third-person pronouns. In older English, verbs as well as pronouns had person-forms. Such a person-form of the verb could be used in a sentence in which no subject was expressed. In present-day English all that is left of the person-forms of the verbs are the present singular forms *am* for the first person and *is* for the third person, and the *-s* ending to indicate the third-person singular present of other verbs, *walks, eats, reads.* With the loss of the older person-forms of the verb, we must look in present-day English to the subject itself to determine the person. Except in commands and requests, English verbs do not now stand alone with no subject expressed. If no noun is used as subject, one of the personal pronouns is used ("*They* live in the country, but *we* live in the city").

(2) Mood. The disappearance of the inflections for the "subjunctive" mood has been accompanied by greatly increased use of the function words known as modal auxiliaries, *may, might, should*, etc. ("I might go" and "he should come soon").

The verb *be* retains today more forms that are distinctly subjunctive than any other verb in present-day English.

> The president recommended that they *be* moved to another office.
>
> I asked that my request *be* granted.
>
> If their mother *were* well, the children could go to school.

Actually, however, in situations where such subjunctive forms could be used, they appear less than 20 per cent of the time.

It is evident that such a short study as this can only touch some of the intricacies of the English language, but even from this brief survey we can see that the mechanics of English have changed over the years. Of the three devices used to express grammatical relationships, word order, function words, and inflection, the last is now of much less importance than it formerly was. The first two devices, on the other hand, have become increasingly vigorous, taking over in many instances the functions of inflection. It should always be kept in mind that English, like all languages, is in a constant state of change and that, as has happened many times in the past, forms, use of words, and ways of expressing relationships which are now considered to be "good English" may very well become the "vulgar English" of the future.

PUNCTUATION

Albert H. Marckwardt

Speech is the primary or basic form of language. Writing is a secondary form which has developed only recently, relatively speaking, in the history of mankind. Speech communicates meaning in part by means of sounds of distinctive quality—the vowel of *pit* as distinct from that of *pet* or of *peat*. Speech also employs stress, intonation, or cadence, and pauses between utterances as an integral part of its communicative mechanism.

Most systems of writing are based almost wholly upon the phonetic quality of the speech sounds included in the language. But this is not enough. The four words *we, are, going,* and *now* may be uttered in that order as a plain statement of fact, as a question, or excitedly as an exclamation. In writing, as illustrated by the examples below, the pointing or punctuation is the only means even of suggesting these totally different meanings, clearly indicated in speech by stress and intonation:

> We are going now.
> We are going now?
> We are going now!

The relative length of pause between words may also have a considerable bearing upon meaning. Again the written language has developed certain mechanical ways of differentiating possibly confusing situations. Note the difference between:

> the English teaching-staff
> the English-teaching staff

In the former example, we may be referring to a staff which is of English, rather than French, German, or some other nationality; in the latter example, we mean the staff which teaches English, without reference to the nationality of its members.

Punctuation thus becomes in a sense an auxiliary to systems of writing, lending to the written word some of the color and body that pause, pitch, and stress add to the spoken.

The word *punctuation* goes back ultimately to Latin *punctus*, "a point," and we may say as well that the purpose of punctuation is to give point to what is written. Isolated words, in and by themselves, are not language. Rarely do they communicate meaning. By putting certain words together and by separating these words from other combinations, marks of punctuation are vital to communication. They might almost be called road markers along the highway of written thought; they guide the reader's mind from point to point in a passage of writing very much as road signs and speed limits channel and control the flow of automobile traffic. Too much punctuation, like needless starting and stopping on the road, can be irritating; too little punctuation, like an unmarked highway, can cause a reader to lose his way completely.

There are, of course, certain marks of punctuation which have no equivalents in the pauses, stresses, or intonation turns of spoken English. Among these are the apostrophe, quotation marks, and the hyphen in some of its uses. The chief use of these marks is often primarily mechanical, as with the hyphen when it is used to break a word at the end of a line or to form compound words (such as *forty-seven*). Another function is to indicate meanings which are in spoken English made clear by the syntax of the sentence, as when *you are* is combined into *you're*. A more detailed discussion of when and how these marks of punctuation should be used will be found below.

Punctuation That Terminates. It is impossible to speak or write ordinary English without using sentences, and it is impossible to speak or write a sentence without giving it an ending. In speech this ending is usually marked by a decided pause; in writing, by a punctuation mark calling for a full stop. A few writers, including Don Marquis's famous archy the cockroach, have sought to write without using punctuation at the close of a sentence, but in such cases these writers have then simply had to devise some means other than punctuation to indicate the end of a sentence. As illustrated below, archy may not have used terminal points, but he nevertheless found it necessary to separate his sentences (or units of language) by putting each one on a different line:

> "expression is the need of my soul
> i was once a vers libre bard
> but i died and my soul went into the
>   body of a cockroach
> it has given me a new outlook upon
>   life"

Most sentences, including this one, are declarations or statements of a fact or condition. Sentences of this kind are terminated by a period. Such sentences are usually grammatically complete, which means that they contain a subject-verb sequence (*John works.*). But we will do well to recall that meaning rather than grammatical analysis is the prime factor in determining what is a sentence. The affirmative replies below are punctuated with periods, indicating a full-stop termination:

> "Will you be home by bedtime?" asked John's mother.
> "Yes."
> "Will you have your homework done?"
> "Certainly."

The one-word replies here suggest, of course, "Yes, I will be home" and "Certainly I will have my homework done." Inasmuch as this is entirely clear from the one-word statements, these may be properly treated as sentences and closed with periods.

Sentences which ask questions are usually terminated by a question mark. Two examples of such sentences as this are provided by the mother's words above. Note, however, that the same meaning may be conveyed even when the sentences are rearranged as below:

> "You will be home by bedtime?"
> "You will have your homework done?"

Though normally this word-order pattern is associated with a declarative statement, a speaker may convert it into a question by selecting and employing the appropriate intonation pattern. The use of the question mark performs the same function for the written language. On the other hand, a sentence which is actually a command or request will often be put in question form as a matter of politeness:

Will you be sure to have these letters done by five.

Will you please close the door.

Although a question mark may be used with sentences of this kind, the intent is clearly not interrogative, and a period is more often used.

Sentences which are outright commands may be followed either by a period or an exclamation point, depending on the tone which the writer intends to suggest:

You must be home by five!

You must be home by five.

Both of these sentences convey the meaning of a direct order, but the latter one suggests by its punctuation the intonation pattern of a simple or factual statement rather than an emphatic tone of command.

Some sentences may be exclamations and are in this use followed by exclamation points:

What weather to have for our vacation!

Of all the marks of punctuation indicating a full stop, this one is probably the least used by most people. It is also the one most easily misused. When it is properly and sparingly employed, it conveys a sense of great emphasis, of what might almost be called visual shock; but if it is too often used, it will lose its effect. Before finally deciding to use an exclamation point, one should consider very carefully whether a particular sentence would not be more appropriately concluded by a period. In the jargon of many proofreaders, an exclamation point is called a "bang," and it is the mark of a good writer that he uses it in such a way as not to diminish by too frequent use the explosive force which this suggests.

Punctuation That Joins. Thus far we have dealt with sentences so simple in structure as to require little or no internal punctuation. However, when we begin to deal with two or more related thoughts, we may find ourselves writing compound sentences consisting of at least two main clauses, each of which is itself the grammatical equivalent of a sentence. Because punctuation is an effective way of showing the organization of words into groups, it is often employed as a link between clauses. Clauses may be thus joined in a sentence by a conjunction alone, by a comma alone, by a comma and a conjunction, by a semicolon, or by a semicolon with a conjunction. The kind of punctuation employed in linking separate clauses is dependent upon the closeness of relationship in idea between the compound members and upon the degree of separation which the writer wishes to suggest. Short, closely related clauses require little linking punctuation. Contrasted ideas should usually be separated by some pointing. If the clauses themselves contain a good deal of internal punctuation, a stronger linking element, usually a semicolon, is appropriate. In the illustrative examples below, the elements of linkage in each sentence have been placed in brackets:

He graduated on Friday [and] by Monday morning he was married.

I came [,] I saw [,] I conquered.

He sued for damages at once [, and] his lawyer assured him that his case was a good one.

The foreign minister protested that an apology was not enough [;] his country would insist on reparations.

Stirred by the speaker's tales of insults and injuries to their fellow country-

men abroad, the young men cried out for war [; but] in the little villages in the hills, their wives and mothers prayed for peace.

Because of the bad roads, we arrived much later than we had intended [;] consequently, there was almost no time left for swimming.

Probably most ordinary writing will require the use of no more linking than the first three of the methods here illustrated, especially if the writer is using open, fairly informal punctuation. The third method, comma and conjunction, is very widely employed. The semicolon is, however, one of the basic and most useful marks of punctuation, and may be used (indeed, some authorities have insisted that it must be used) between any main clauses not linked by a conjunction.

Punctuation That Introduces. We do not always begin a sentence or statement by immediately naming the principal person or thing it concerns. Sometimes we find it helpful to begin with a subordinate idea or bit of information, thus placing the principal statement in its proper frame of reference. When this is done, a comma is helpful in showing that the initial group of words is a logically related unit and in suggesting that it has some bearing upon what is to come. This is true even when the introductory element is no more than a single word. Although introductory phrases and clauses are not always punctuated, at least a comma is sometimes necessary to avoid ambiguity, as in the following:

True to his promise, the next day Charles returned the book.

Other examples of introductory punctuation follow:

Midway through one of the smaller rooms, still questing for an elusive presence, she caught sight of someone that she knew.

In those early days, after it became a custom for each family to prepare its own Christmas potion, the quality of the drink depended upon the wealth of the host.

Spring having come, robins are seen frequently.

Mr. Norris, I want to congratulate you on your splendid record.

Oh, he's somewhat of a nuisance.

Yes, now you have the correct answer.

After introductory clauses and phrases of a somewhat formal or extended nature, the colon is used. The colon also usually follows the salutation of a business letter.

Punctuation That Inserts. At times there may be inserted within a sentence certain clauses, phrases, or words which add useful but not absolutely essential information to the idea or statement as a whole. Because they do not affect the central meaning of the sentence which includes them, elements of this kind are termed nonrestrictive. In spoken English, these are marked by intonations and sometimes by pauses. In writing, they are set off from the rest of the sentence by punctuation. In the examples listed below, the nonrestrictive elements have been bracketed:

The king [, who feared a surprise attack,] insisted on mobilization.

John Jones [, a newspaper reporter,] was present.

The boxer [, bleeding,] struggled to his feet.

In these examples, commas have been used to set off the nonrestrictive elements; they are unquestionably the marks of punctuation used most frequently for this purpose. However, there are cases where dashes or parentheses may be used instead of commas. Dashes are most often found in fairly informal writing where the nonrestrictive element conveys information closely related to the word or words immediately preceding:

> The dogs—all eight of them—were at our throats.

Parentheses, on the other hand, are chiefly used where the information conveyed by the nonrestrictive element is related only slightly to the sentence as a whole:

> The prime minister (who was related to the royal family) did not appear for the ceremony.

Special caution must be exercised to place the commas, or whatever other marks of punctuation are used, at *both* extremities of the parenthetical expression.

One must be very careful, however, to distinguish between nonrestrictive elements such as these, which are set off by punctuation, and restrictive elements which establish some important condition or limitation to the meaning of the sentence of which they are a part. Restrictive clauses and phrases are not set off by punctuation. In the following sentences the restrictive elements have been bracketed:

> Dogs [who bite people] are not welcome here.
> The night [before Christmas] is called Christmas Eve.

The bracketed elements above have a definite bearing on the meaning of the entire sentences which include them. They could not be omitted from the sentences of which they are a part without changing the meaning considerably, if indeed the statements could then be said to have left any of the intended meaning at all.

Series Punctuation. When a number of coördinate items—words, phrases, or clauses—modify a single sentence-element, the members of such a series are indicated in the spoken language by the intonation. In writing it is equally necessary to mark the various items in a series. This function is regularly performed by the comma. Examples of punctuation between coördinate elements in series are bracketed below:

> The unceasing [,] shrill [,] nerve-shattering whine of the shells broke the soldier's will to fight.
> Life became for him an unending torture of bitterness [,] recrimination [,] and frustrated ambition.

If the last two in a series of coördinate elements are separated by a conjunction, a comma may or may not be used. In formal punctuation, as in the last example immediately above, the comma is used; in less formal punctuation, as illustrated below, no comma is used:

> The speech was long, dull and meaningless.

In the same way, a series of adjectives are regularly separated by commas, but only if they are really coördinate:

> He was an ambitious, successful young man.

Here *ambitious* and *successful* are coördinate, whereas neither is really coördinate with *young*, for both of them are felt as modifying not *man* alone, but the combination *young man.*

Punctuation That Unifies. It is often necessary to show that two or more words are being used as a unit in modifying another word or words in a sentence, or that a prefix is being attached to a particular word to give it another meaning. This is done, in most cases, through use of the hyphen. In the examples immediately following, the hyphen is used to form unit modifiers:

> A three-year-old child can seldom swim.
> The freedom-hating mercenaries swept into the city.

In the following example, the hyphen is used to unite a prefix and verb. Observe that without the hyphen in *re-dress* there would be the possibility of some confusion:

> If you will re-dress in more suitable clothes, we will see if we can't get him to redress the wrong done to you.

The hyphen is always used in uniting a prefix to a proper name:

> It is obvious that he must have pro-German sympathies, but for that reason alone, one can scarcely be certain that he is anti-French.

The apostrophe is used to indicate that letters have been omitted in combining two words into a single word:

> I couldn't [could not] be there.
> If we're [we are] not careful, we'll [we will] spend more than we earn.
> I'm [I am] not sure that I can keep the appointment.

Punctuation That Indicates Exact Speech. Exact and direct quotation of spoken or written words is usually indicated in writing by quotation marks around the quoted passage. When a paraphrase or summary of a speech or written selection is given, quotation marks are never used, except for those parts of the paraphrase or summary taken verbatim from the original. Quotations which are being cited within quotations are indicated by single rather than double quotation marks:

> The witness took the stand and said: "As I recall it, he said, 'I won't come with you.' Perhaps I am wrong. He may have said he didn't want to come with me."

If a quoted passage is so long that it is broken into paragraphs, quotation marks are put only at the beginning of each paragraph until the last one, which has them also at the end. Any interruptions within the quotation of such an extended passage are, of course, placed outside of quotation marks. It is also possible, when citing an extended passage from a book or other written material, to indicate clearly in the wording of the introduction that the material is being quoted and then to indent from six to ten spaces from either margin until the quotation has been completed. This is recommended only, however, for passages of considerable length. Quotation marks are not necessary where this block style is used.

Punctuation That Indicates Possession. The apostrophe is used to indicate the possessive or genitive form of all nouns and a few indefinite pronouns:

> It is man's duty to defend the right.
> That looks like a child's toy.
> One's instincts are not always the best guide.

In some styles of punctuation, words ending with an *s* or a sound close to it take only an apostrophe; in other styles, such words take an apostrophe and another *s* to form the possessive. For example:

> John Adams' house.

or

> John Adams's house.

However, plural forms ending in *s* take only the apostrophe:

> The cows' condition is deplorable.
> The countries' various resolutions were futile.

The apostrophe is frequently omitted in the names of organizations when the possessive case is implied, and in certain geographic designations:

> Citizens League
> Actors Equity Association
> Teachers College
> Pikes Peak

Punctuation for Special Purposes. Certain marks of punctuation have special uses which are not covered by any of the foregoing sections. Most of these uses are very well known, but mention should be made of them. The period, for example, indicates abbreviation:

> *Dr.* for *Doctor.*
> *Ave.* for *Avenue.*

These and most other common abbreviations will be found entered in the main body of this dictionary and may be used in all cases where abbreviation is proper.

Letters used alone, figures, and words used as examples of themselves all form their plurals by adding an apostrophe plus *s*:

> It is a well-known fact that the *e's* are the most frequently used of all the letters of the English alphabet.
> The *7's* and the *9's* are the figures he transcribes best.
> The *and's* and *but's* in his speech irritate me.

Quotation marks are widely used for titles of articles in periodicals, or for chapters or other divisions of a book, the title of the entire book or periodical being distinguished, as noted below, by being put in italic type.

In some written passages it is desirable, for the sake of emphasis or distinctness, to employ italic type. Titles, whether of books, publications, musical selections, or works of art, words from other languages, and words or letters spoken of as words or letters are generally italicized. (On this last point, observe the illustrative examples immediately preceding this paragraph.) In manuscript or typescript, italics are indicated by underlining:

> I suppose you have read War and Peace.
> It is a de facto, not a de jure government.

In written English it is often necessary to indicate that a word has been broken at the end of a line and carried over to the beginning of the next line. This may be done by placing a hyphen at the end of any syllable within the word to be broken unless (1) the word is extremely short (it is seldom desirable to break such words as *money*, *plenty*, or *early*) or (2) the break would leave a single letter hanging at the end or beginning of one of the two lines involved (never break such words as *emit*, *adore*, or *heady*). The points at which all words in this dictionary may be broken are indicated in their form of entry.

What Is "Good" Punctuation? Many rules have been formulated for the use of the various marks of punctuation, and people have thought that by simply memorizing these rules they might find a key to good writing. Unfortunately, as teachers of punctuation will be among the first to point out, this is not the case. By acting as a visual aid, punctuation can help one to comprehend a carefully thought out piece of writing, but it cannot supply meaning. If a written composition, be it a letter, set of directions, or a critical essay, seems to lack precision and directness, the writer will do well to consider first of all whether it is properly organized, not whether it is properly punctuated. Ordinarily, meaningful and well-organized writing is not hard to punctuate. One's style of punctuation is generally determined by the type and purpose of the writing. Compared to a sports story in the daily paper, a treatise on physics will be marked by more complex constructions, and accordingly, a greater amount of punctuation. This does not mean that one kind or style of punctuation is better than another. It simply indicates that the precise distinctions in thought and meaning which concern the scholar and scientist require more detailed, complex statement, and hence more detailed and complex punctuation, than the factual, comparatively simple story of a baseball game. The former type of writing is designed to compress a maximum amount of exact and complicated information within a limited space. The purpose of the latter is to provide a simple, easily readable account which will entertain and inform its readers. In both instances, the punctuation has the same function: to aid the writer in conveying his particular message to his readers. Punctuation that performs this function is "good" punctuation; when punctuation fails to realize this aim it is faulty.

A full explanation of each mark of punctuation dealt with in this preface will be found in the main alphabetical list under the entry on each mark. For information on rules of capitalization see the special note under that entry in the main body of the book.

WRITING AND EDITING: MANUSCRIPT TO PRINTED PAGE

Ethel M. Ryan and W. D. Halsey

The first and most obvious requirement of a publishable piece of writing is that it should have something to say which will be interesting or useful to its readers. A second requirement is that it should be prepared in a fashion which will enable the editor or typesetter to work with it. There can be no question that many articles, stories, and book-length manuscripts which were otherwise acceptable have failed to find a publisher simply because their authors neglected to meet this second requirement. An article which is scrawled in pencil on odd bits of paper may contain information fully as important as one which is neatly typed, but it has far less chance of ever appearing in print. Not only is it harder (and thus more expensive) to set such manuscript in type, but there is also the possibility that serious errors may creep into it through misreading of illegible characters. Good common sense will tell us that final manuscript should be as easy for the editor and typesetter to work with as possible.

Even though one may not be a professional writer, many of us today have occasion to work with editors and typesetters on material which will appear in print. It may be that one will have made a speech which is to be printed in a newspaper or magazine, written an article which is to appear in the publication of some society or group, prepared a feature article or news story for a company or school newspaper, or written a short piece of advertising copy for one's business. Regardless of the nature of the material, and whether one is a professional writer or amateur, it is desirable to prepare it and work on it according to the rules outlined below. These rules and principles apply to work by writers, editors, and typesetters all over the United States; their purpose is to produce good printed work.

How to Prepare a Manuscript

Typewritten Manuscript. It is standard practice today to type material which is to be submitted to a magazine or book publisher. In preparing final manuscript for this purpose, an author should pay careful attention to the following:

(1) Use a good quality of bond paper in one of the standard sizes (the most often used, and probably the best, size measures 8½ by 11 inches). A poor grade of paper, particularly one which permits the letters to show through, makes a manuscript hard to read and work on; paper cut in an odd size often makes a manuscript difficult to file.

(2) Use a black typewriter ribbon and change it for a new one as soon as it fails to produce letters which are sharp and clear on the page. More than one manuscript has been rejected with the notation that its typed characters were too faint to read.

(3) Make an original and two carbons in final typing. The original should always be sent to the publisher; the carbons safeguard the writer against possible loss of his manuscript in the mail or elsewhere.

(4) Type on one side of the paper only, use double-spacing between the lines, and leave a margin of at least one inch at the top, bottom, and each side of every page. If in any doubt as to the desirable margin, leave slightly more than one inch, but once the margin has been established, observe it consistently on every page thereafter to the end of the manuscript.

(5) The author should enter his name and complete address in the upper left-hand corner of the first page. Some authors repeat this information in the same place on every subsequent page, while others insert only their names or the title of their work; although this reduces the possibility of confusing pages from one manuscript with those from another, it is not absolutely necessary. The endorsement of the first page, however, is essential on any manuscript submitted for publication. Moreover, unless a publisher has specifically requested or already accepted a manuscript, it is desirable to enclose return postage.

(6) Some typewriters have slightly larger type than others and for this reason produce slightly fewer characters within a line of a given length than a machine using smaller type. A manuscript may be typed in either size, but it is important that a writer should not switch from one to the other within the same manuscript. If he does so he will make it difficult to estimate the number of pages which the manuscript will require in print.

(7) Manuscript pages should always be consecutively numbered. Do not number each chapter or section as a unit by itself; number the pages of a manuscript as a whole in one sequence through to the last page. The page numbers should be clearly typed or written (some writers use a number-stamping machine) in the top margin of each page.

(8) If a short section is being extracted from the work of another author, or if particular works are being cited as sources of information, specific credit should be given either in the body of the manuscript or in a footnote. If the quoted material is only a few words or one or two lines in length, it may be set off by quotation marks; if it is longer, it should be typed as a separate section in block form with an indention of at least six spaces at the beginning and end of each line in the block.

(9) Minor changes in manuscript may be typed or made in ink between the lines, but a page which is heavily marked should be retyped. The reason for adding and correcting material between the lines on manuscript is that the typesetter reads the copy line by line in setting, and material which is entered marginally makes his work enormously more difficult. This is, as the reader will note in a later part of this pref-

ace, exactly the reverse of work in proof, in which all corrections are made marginally. The following example will show how a manuscript should be corrected:

a publishable piece of writing is that it should have something to say which will be interesting or useful to its readers. A second requirement is that it should be prepared in a fashion which will enable the editor or typesetter to work with it. There can be no question that many articles, stories, and booklength manuscripts which were otherwise acceptable have failed to find a publisher simply because their authors neglected to meet this second requirement; an article which is scrawled in pencil on odd bits of paper may contain information fully as important and well presented as one which is neatly typed, but it has far less chance of ever appearing in print. Not only is it harder (and thus more expensive) to set such manuscript in type, there is also the possibility

(10) Particularly with book-length manuscripts, an editor will often suggest deletions, rewriting of certain sections, or other alterations. After these have been discussed and, where desirable, incorporated into the manuscript, the writer's work is sent to the copy editor. It is the copy editor's responsibility to read the manuscript for error in factual data, grammatical construction, sequence, punctuation, capitalization, and consistency. The copy editor in most publishing houses is guided in doing this by a style manual which gives the rules which that particular publisher wishes to observe in these matters, and the writer will usually find that consistent observance of these rules greatly improves his manuscript.

Handwritten Manuscript. Manuscripts in longhand are now confined almost entirely to classroom compositions or themes, and even here (particularly at the graduate level in universities) typing is usually preferable, and often required. However, in those cases where longhand manuscript is acceptable, the following rules should be observed:

(1) Write with a medium-pointed pen in black or dark blue ink. Take special pains to write legibly, and be sure that the letters are grouped so that each word may easily be read as a unit.

(2) Use paper which will take ink without blurring. Be sure it is heavy enough so that the writing will not show through the back. Standard theme paper with lines about one half inch apart is preferred in many schools and colleges.

(3) Leave a margin of at least one inch at each side of every page, write on only one side of each sheet, and number the pages consecutively in the top margin.

How to Work in Proof

An author will often see his work in print for the first time when the publisher or printer sends him what are called galley proofs. These are long sheets (usually covering the equivalent of two or three pages in a printed book) on which is made an inked impression from the slugs or pieces of type while they are in the trays, or galleys, in which they are stored until all copy has been set and all corrections made. In most cases, the printer will already have proofread the galleys and the amount of correction which the author will have to make may therefore be very slight. The rules which an author should follow in working on galleys are given below:

(1) Check for typographical errors and correct them where found. Other errors should, of course, also be corrected at this time, but a careful author does not submit final manuscript which contains very many errors. Authors should not at this stage make corrections which involve merely a reworking or polishing of language. It costs an author little or nothing to move his pen, but it can cost a publisher hundreds of dollars to make the changes thus called for. Typesetters and compositors do not charge for the correction of typographical errors, but an unreasonable number of additional changes (or "author's alterations") will, and quite justly, result in an increased charge for typesetting and composition.

(2) Answer all queries made on the proofs by the proofreader or editor. These will be found written in the margins next to the section of copy to which they apply. If the answer to a query is "no," and if the copy is correct as set, it is enough simply to cross out the query. If it is "yes," or if some additional comment is required, this should be written below the query and circled. If the query requires insertion or change in copy, this should be done in the fashion outlined in the example on page xxxviii.

(3) Each proof should be initialed in the upper right-hand corner by the author after he has finished checking it. This will inform the printer that the author has checked it and noted the corrections which should be made.

(4) All corrections should be made in ink, and great care should be taken to see that they are legibly written.

(5) Each correction should be made in the margin next to the line to which it applies. This is the exact reverse of the interlinear method of correction preferred for manuscripts, and it is extremely important that authors follow this preferred practice in marking galleys. The reason for it is that the compositor, in working on galleys, looks only at the margins of the proof; a change which is not clearly indicated there may well, for this reason, be overlooked.

Following is a list of the special symbols most often used by editors and proofreaders in marking proof sheets. Also shown is a galley proof in which these marks have been properly used to make corrections.

HOW TO CORRECT PROOF

It does not appear that the earliest printers had any method of correcting errors before the form was on the press. The learned correctors of the first two centuries of printing were not proofreaders in our sense; they were rather what we should term office editors. Their labors were chiefly to see that the proof corresponded to the copy, but that the printed page was correct in its latinity; that the words were there, and that the sense was right. They cared but little about orthography, bad letters, or purely printers' errors, and when the text seemed to them wrong they consulted fresh authorities or altered it on their own responsibility. Good proofs in the modern sense, were impossible until professional readers were employed, men who had first a printer's education, and then spent many years in the correction of proof. The orthography of English, which for the past century has undergone little change, was very fluctuating until after the publication of Johnson's Dictionary, and capitals, which have been used with considerable regularity for the past 80 years, were previously used on the miss or hit plan. The approach to regularity, so far as we have it, may be attributed to the growth of a class of professional proof readers, and it is to them that we owe the correctness of modern printing. More errors have been found in the Bible than in any other one work. For many generations it was frequently the case that Bibles were brought out stealthily, from fear of governmental interference. They were frequently printed from imperfect texts, and were often modified to meet the views of those who published them. The story is related that a certain woman in Germany, who was the wife of a printer, and had become disgusted with the continual assertions of the superiority of man over woman, which she had heard, hurried into the composing room while her husband was at supper and altered a sentence in the Bible, which he was printing, so that it read Narr instead of Herr, thus making the verse read "And he shall be thy fool" instead of "And he shall be thy lord." The word not was omitted by Barker, the king's printer in England in 1632, in printing the seventh commandment. He was fined £3,000 on this account.

PROOFREADERS' MARKS

∧	Make correction indicated in margin.
Stet	Retain crossed-out word or letter; let it stand.
• • • •	Retain words under which dots appear; write "Stet" in margin.
×	Appears battered; examine.
▬	Straighten lines.
⌄⌄⌄	Unevenly spaced; correct spacing.
∥	Line up; i.e., make lines even with other matter.
run in	Make no break in the reading; no ¶
no ¶	No paragraph; sometimes written "run in."
out see copy	Here is an omission; see copy.
¶	Make a paragraph here.
tr	Transpose words or letters as indicated.
ℐ	Take out matter indicated; dele.
℥	Take out character indicated and close up.
ȼ	Line drawn through a cap means lower case.
☉	Upside down; reverse.
⌒	Close up; no space.
#	Insert a space here.
⊥	Push down this space.
⌷	Indent line one em.
[	Move this to the left.
]	Move this to the right.

⌐⌐	Raise to proper position.
⌊⌋	Lower to proper position.
∥∥	Hair space letters.
w.f.	Wrong font; change to proper font.
Qu?	Is this right?
l.c.	Put in lower case (small letters).
s.c.	Put in small capitals.
Caps	Put in capitals.
C&sc	Put in caps and small caps.
rom.	Change to Roman.
ital.	Change to Italic.
≡	Under letter or word means caps.
═	Under letter or word, small caps.
—	Under letter or word means Italic.
∼∼∼	Under letter or word, bold face.
⸝/	Insert comma.
⸴/	Insert semicolon.
⸴/	Insert colon.
⊙	Insert period.
/?/	Insert interrogation mark.
(!)	Insert exclamation mark.
/=/	Insert hyphen.
⸜	Insert apostrophe.
⸢⸣	Insert quotation marks.
ℓ	Insert superior letter or figure.
⌃	Insert inferior letter or figure.
[/]	Insert brackets.
(/)	Insert parenthesis.
$\frac{\prime}{m}$	One-em dash.
$\frac{2}{m}$	Two-em parallel dash.

XXXIX

LETTER WRITING: BUSINESS AND PERSONAL

John A. Kouwenhoven

Letter writing is the one kind of writing in which all of us engage and which most directly concerns the personal welfare of each of us. One may never write a novel or a play, but one is virtually certain to write letters when seeking a job, when applying for entrance to a college, or when announcing a birth or a wedding. In business particularly, the ability to write a letter which is brief, neat, and to the point is one of the most valuable skills one can have.

The two most frequently used classifications for letters are (1) business letters and (2) personal letters. The chief rules of style and form for both of these classifications are covered below. Anyone who applies these rules will be able to write a satisfactory letter for almost any occasion if he will bear in mind that a letter builds in the mind of its reader, particularly if he is a person whom one has never met, a picture of its writer's personality and habits. A letter which is free of smudges and erasures, and in which the points to be covered have been well thought out and concisely stated, cannot help but convey a good impression of its writer. Some carelessness or untidiness may be forgiven in personal letters to one's friends and relatives (although it is surely more courteous to prepare a neat letter), but in business a poor letter may create in its reader's mind so unflattering an image of the writer as to defeat one's whole purpose in writing.

(1) *Addresses should be written clearly on the envelope.* The name and address of the person being written to should be centered on the envelope; the address (and often the name) of the person writing the letter may be placed in the upper left-hand corner of the envelope. Postal zone numbers, where obtainable, should be included after the name of the city. Instructions for special handling, such as "Air Mail" or "Special Delivery," should be noted on the envelope. It is helpful to the post office if the address of the recipient can be double spaced with the name of the State on the line below the name of the city. If the name of the State is abbreviated (this dictionary gives standard abbreviations, where these exist, for the names of the various States), the abbreviation should be clearly written. However, it is never wrong to write out the name of the State in full, and many people prefer to do so. If a line in the address is required in order to indicate an apartment number or particular department of a company, this should be indicated in the lower left-hand corner of the envelope:

return address ➤	R. N. Jackson 27 West Street Portsmouth 7 New Hampshire
special in-structions ➤	Air Mail
envelope address ➤	Mr. John L. Jones 970 West 4th Street New York 17 New York
additional address ➤	Apartment 3A

(2) *Use as good a grade of stationery as possible.* Good paper costs very little more than poor paper, and vastly improves the appearance of any letter. Printed letterheads are, of course, common on business stationery, and increasingly so on personal stationery, but a perfectly satisfactory letter may be written on plain paper of good quality. Many styles and sizes of stationery exist, but the standard ones are always easily obtainable and proper. Two standard business sizes are 8½ by 11 inches and 6 by 9 inches.

(3) *Typewritten letters: business and personal.* In business correspondence the typewritten letter is standard; in the United States, typed personal letters between friends or relatives are increasingly common, and usually welcome because of greater legibility. Longhand is perhaps preferable in the earlier stages of a friendship, and should probably always be used for invitations, acknowledgments, or other social correspondence of a formal nature. Letters expressing condolence, or otherwise concerning particularly deep sentiment or feeling, should also be written in longhand.

(4) *Margins should be generous and letters centered on the page.* Unless there is some particular reason for not doing so, it is customary to single space the heading, the inside address, and each separate paragraph of a typewritten letter. Two spaces should be left between the single-spaced paragraphs in the body of a letter. If a line in the inside address is so long as to spoil the appearance of the address as a whole, it may be made into two lines. If the line being broken deals with something which must be treated as a unit, the lower line may be indented two spaces:

> The Southern New England
> Commodity Shipping Co.
> 127 Worth Street
> Hartford 37, Connecticut

Note that the name of the State in the inside address is ordinarily written on the same line as the city, unlike the practice preferred for the envelope address. However, if this handling should produce an address which is out of balance, the State may be dropped to the next line:

> Mr. Joseph L. Jones
> Yazoo City
> Mississippi

A little care in the placement of the heading, the inside address, and the body of the copy will enable one to put even a very short letter on paper as large as 8½ by 11 inches in such a way as to create an effect which is pleasing to the eye; a letter which is cramped almost entirely in the upper half of the sheet suggests to its recipient that its writer either didn't know when he started how much he wanted to say, or that he was simply too lazy to try to make the letter attractive.

BUSINESS LETTERS

Most business letters written in the United States today use a modification of the block style.

This pattern for the arrangement of a letter forms, as the name suggests, "blocks" of typescript with no indention on the left. Because it enables a typist to begin a maximum number of lines flush with the left-hand margin, a minimum amount of time is lost in hitting the space bar or tabular key for indentions. In its most extreme form, every unit of the letter (heading, inside address, body paragraphs, etc.) is blocked to the left, but this arrangement, although extremely efficient from the mechanical point of view, tends to produce a letter too heavily weighted on the left to be attractive. For this reason, most companies today use a modification of this extreme style, which permits some indention.

In the pattern letters shown below, a modified block style is used. In the first one, which shows how to write a letter on a sheet which does not contain a printed letterhead, the heading is blocked in the upper right-hand portion of the sheet so as to align with the right-hand margin of the letter. Such a heading should be placed with some regard to the length of the letter as a whole, so that in a short letter the heading will be closer to the middle of the page than in a long letter, but in no case should the heading on a sheet which measures 8½ by 11 inches be more than about three inches or less than one and one half inches from the top of the page. When a sheet with printed letterhead is being used, only the date needs to be inserted. As shown in the second pattern letter below, this is usually put in from three to six lines below the letterhead and aligned with the right-hand margin.

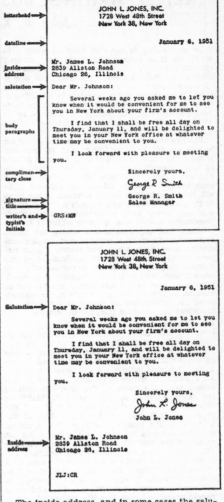

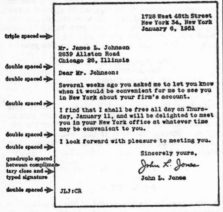

Any of the three letters on this page would be acceptable for all ordinary business purposes. The second one deviates further from the most extreme block style in that it uses indentions for the paragraphs in the main body of the letter.

Some firms, and many professional men, may use the salutation Dear Sir: or Dear Mr. Johnson: at the opening of the letter, and put the full inside address two to five lines below the signature flush with the left-hand margin, as shown in the third letter on this page. This type of letter, which may also be used as a formal personal letter, retains all the information required for the carbon copy in a business letter, but manages to have at the same time some of the appearance of a personal letter.

The inside address, and in some cases the salutation, should include any title (and sometimes the academic or honorary degree) which is held by the recipient of the letter. Where no other title applies or is called for, it is correct to use Mr., Mrs., or Miss (the last is used in letters to women whose marital status is unknown or who are known to be single, and to whom no academic or professional title may be applied). If it is not known whether the person being written to is a man or a woman, it is proper to use Mr. before the name. The abbreviations Mr. and Mrs. are always used, and the abbreviation Dr. is entirely permissible; it is perhaps safest to write out all other titles in full. Many doctors in fields other than medicine prefer the use of Mr. in the salutation, as do many professors and other people in the academic world. Where preferences of this kind are known, they should, of course, be followed; where no preference is known, it is safest to use a title.

Where a letter is being sent to a company or organization, and there is no need to specify a particular individual, the salutation (which is always followed in business letters by a colon) may read Gentlemen: or Dear Sirs:. If the points dealt with by the letter may be expected to concern a particular department of the company, this may be noted two lines below the inside address and two lines above the salutation:

> John L. Jones, Inc.
> 1728 West 48th Street
> New York 38, New York

double spaced ➤

> Attention: Personnel Department

double spaced ➤

> Gentlemen:

If some particular subject is involved, this may be noted as follows:

> John L. Jones, Inc.
> 1728 West 48th Street
> New York 38, New York
>
> Subject: Display Advertising
>
> Gentlemen:

The complimentary close in business letters has been vastly simplified from the elaborate forms which once prevailed. The two forms now most often used in the United States are probably *Sincerely yours* and *Yours truly*, both of which may be varied slightly, as with *Very truly yours* or *Yours sincerely*. Official correspondence, or correspondence with some distinguished person, may use *Respectfully yours* or *Very respectfully*. Only the first letter of the first word is capitalized in a complimentary close, and the phrase as a whole is always followed by a comma.

Signatures to business letters are usually placed immediately over the name in typescript, beneath which the title or position of the person signing the letter is also often indicated. The block style is entirely proper here, and is used in the examples below:

Sincerely yours,

John Smith

John Smith
Advertising Manager

Sincerely yours,

J. L. Jones, Inc.

John Smith

John Smith
Advertising Manager

The chief purpose of a business letter is to convey information of some sort to its recipient, but a business letter also provides, through its carbon copy or copies (some firms regularly make several carbon copies of certain kinds of correspondence), a record of the matters dealt with and decisions made, with the name and address of the person written to, the date of writing, and the name and position of the person writing. It is customary to show the initials of both writer and typist at the left-hand margin two lines below the signature. The initials of the writer are placed first: JS:mn, JS/mn, JS:MN, and JS/MN are four acceptable ways of doing this.

Although the various styles and conventions which have been covered above are acceptable for any kind of business use, it is probable that the "house style" of a particular company or organization will be found to require a slightly different handling of certain parts of a letter. The difference will not, in all probability, be very great; very few companies in the United States now follow a style of correspondence which is not based upon the same principles as have been used in preparing the patterns here shown. However, it is always advisable for a person just starting his employment with a particular company to familiarize himself with the particular style preferred by his employer, either by asking questions of those who know the style or by glancing over letters which have gone out under the letterhead of that company.

PERSONAL LETTERS

Many letters to one's friends and relatives constitute a kind of informal written conversation. To a great extent, therefore, the standards for spoken conversation may be applied to such letters. One may be extremely informal, and even casual, with a classmate or other close friend in one's own generation; with an older person, such as a teacher, one's letter, although still informal, would properly and naturally have a more respectful tone. A young man is perhaps equally anxious to please his fiancée and her mother, but he will hardly attempt to do so with the same kind of letter. Here, as in conversation, common sense and good taste are the best possible guides.

Personal letters between people who regularly write each other need no heading other than the date; letters between people who are not closely acquainted, or who write each other infrequently, should include the address in the heading. Not everyone keeps an address book, and failure to give one's address may make it impossible for an occasional correspondent to reply to one's letter.

The salutation in a personal letter may range from great informality (Dear Joe,) to comparative formality (Dear Mr. Jones:). The comma (or sometimes a dash) may be used with very informal salutations, while the colon is placed after those which are more formal. In cases which require great formality, as with an older person whom one knows only slightly, the form My dear Mr. Jones: is often used. The complimentary close, like the salutation, may range from the extreme informality of Yours, to the formality of Sincerely yours.

Many personal letters to editors of newspapers or the like are written as "open letters," which means that the writer will permit (and usually hopes for) their publication in a newspaper or some other medium of public information. Such letters are one means of drawing general attention to some matter of public interest. They should be well organized and written in a courteous, dignified manner, although if criticism of some public policy is the purpose of the letter it may (and should) be forthrightly expressed. The preferred form for addressing the editor of a particular paper may be determined by looking at the letter column of that paper.

One type of personal correspondence for which certain very definite rules exist is that known as social correspondence. An invitation to a party or to a wedding is a form of social correspondence, and the first (and possibly most important) rule for the recipient of such an invitation is that he should acknowledge it. The form of the acknowledgment may range from an informal note to a highly formal one cast in the third person. Examples of all of these are shown below.

Note that the formal acceptance follows the same arrangement as the note of invitation. If an engraved note of invitation is being used, it is desirable to seek and follow the advice of the engraver as to the style of type, the size and kind of stationery, and the arrangement of the lines.

Dear Mary,

My cousin Karen will be staying with us for a few days next week and I have planned a buffet supper for her on Thursday evening at seven o'clock so that she may meet my friends. I should be delighted if you could join us. I hope you will let me know that you can.

Yours,
Barbara

Mr. and Mrs. Jonathan L. Jones
request the pleasure
of the company of
(Miss Barbara L. Smith)
at a reception
in honor of
Miss Karen Newton,
on Friday, the twelfth of May
at eight o'clock in the evening

R. S. V. P.

Dear Barbara,

Thank you for your very kind invitation to the buffet supper you are giving next Thursday for your cousin. I shall be very happy indeed to come, and look forward with pleasure to meeting the cousin you have told me so much about.

Cordially yours,
Mary

Miss Barbara L. Smith accepts with pleasure the very kind invitation of Mr. and Mrs. Jonathan L. Jones to a reception in honor of Miss Karen Newton on Friday, the twelfth of May at eight o'clock in the evening.

SPECIAL FORMS OF ADDRESS

Listed below are various forms of address and salutation which may be used for letters to various public officials, religious dignitaries, and the like. The complimentary close which is used for these various letters may be any one of the various formal types: "Respectfully yours," "Very truly yours," or "Sincerely yours." A Catholic writing to a dignitary of the Roman Catholic Church will usually add "in Christ" if he uses either the first or third of the forms listed. Slight deviations from these forms are permissible if they do not alter the respectful tone of the letter; when in doubt it is desirable to follow without any change the forms here shown:

Dignitary Being Addressed	Inside Address	Salutation	Complimentary Close
President of the United States	The President The White House Washington 25, D.C.	Sir: (formal) My dear Mr. President: (less formal)	Very respectfully yours,
Member of the Cabinet	The Honorable (full name) Secretary of State Washington 25, D.C.	Sir: (formal) My dear Mr. Secretary: (less formal)	Very truly yours,
Senator of the United States (or of a State)	The Honorable (full name) United States (or State) Senate Washington 25, D.C. (or capital city and State)	Sir: (formal) My dear Senator (name): (less formal)	Very truly yours,
Congressman	The Honorable (full name) House of Representatives Washington 25, D.C.	Sir: (formal) My dear Mr. (name): (less formal)	Very truly yours,

Dignitary Being Addressed	Inside Address	Salutation	Complimentary Close
American Ambassador	The Honorable (full name) American Ambassador London, England	Sir: (formal) My dear Mr. Ambassador: (less formal)	Very truly yours,
Justice (or Chief Justice) of the Supreme Court of the United States (or of a State)	The Honorable (full name) Associate (or Chief) Justice of the United States (or State) Supreme Court Washington 25, D.C. (or city and State)	Sir: (formal) My dear Mr. Justice: (less formal)	Very truly yours,
Governor of a State	The Honorable (full name) Governor of (State) (capital city and State)	Sir: (formal) My dear Governor (name): (less formal)	Very truly yours,
Member of a State Legislature (except a State Senate)	The Honorable (full name) Member of Assembly (or other name of legislature) (capital city and State)	Sir: (formal) My dear Mr. (name): (less formal)	Very truly yours,
Judge (except of a Supreme Court)	The Honorable (full name) (name of court) (city and State)	Sir: (formal) My dear Judge (name): (less formal)	Very truly yours,
Mayor	The Honorable (full name) Mayor of (city) (city and State)	Sir: (formal) My dear Mr. Mayor: (less formal)	Very truly yours,
Foreign Ambassador or Minister	His Excellency (full name) Ambassador of (country) Washington, D.C.	My dear Mr. Ambassador:	Very truly yours,
American (or foreign) Consul	(full name), Esq. American (or other) Consul (city and State or country)	My dear Mr. Consul:	Very truly yours,
Cardinal of the Roman Catholic Church	His Eminence (first name) Cardinal (last name) Archbishop (or other title) of (city, etc.) (city and State)	Your Eminence:	Respectfully yours, (in Christ is usually added if the writer is a Catholic)
Bishop of the Roman Catholic Church	The Most Reverend (full name) Bishop of (diocese) (city and state)	Your Excellency:	Sincerely yours,
Bishop of the Methodist Church	Bishop (full name) (city and state)	Dear Bishop (name):	Sincerely yours,
Bishop of the Protestant Episcopal Church	The Right Reverend (full name) Bishop of (diocese) (city and state)	Dear Bishop (name):	Sincerely yours,
Monsignor of the Roman Catholic Church	The Right Reverend Msgr. (full name) (city and state)	Right Reverend Monsignor:	Sincerely yours,
Protestant Minister	Rev. (full name) (street address, city, and State)	My dear Mr. (surname):	Sincerely yours,
Roman Catholic Priest	The Reverend (full name) (street address, city, and State)	My dear Father (surname):	Sincerely yours,
Rabbi	Rabbi (full name) (street address, city, and State)	My dear Rabbi (surname):	Sincerely yours,

Note: Wherever full name is called for above, initials and last name may also be used.

COMPLETE PRONUNCIATION KEY

The pronunciation of each word is shown just after the word, in this way: **ab.bre.vi.ate** (ə.brē′vi.āt). The letters and signs used are pronounced as in the words below. The mark ′ is placed after a syllable with primary or strong accent, as in the example above. The mark ′ after a syllable shows a secondary or lighter accent, as in **ab.bre.vi.a.tion** (ə.brē′vi.ā′shən).

Some words, taken from foreign languages, are spoken with sounds that otherwise do not occur in English. Symbols for these sounds are given at the end of the table as "Foreign Sounds."

a	hat, cap	i	it, pin	s	say, yes
ā	age, face	ī	ice, five	sh	she, rush
ã	care, air			t	tell, it
ä	father, far	j	jam, enjoy	th	thin, both
		k	kind, seek	ŧħ	then, smooth
b	bad, rob	l	land, coal		
ch	child, much	m	me, am	u	cup, son
d	did, red	n	no, in	u̇	put, book
		ng	long, bring	ü	rule, move
e	let, best	o	hot, rock	ū	use, music
ē	equal, see	ō	open, go		
èr	term, learn	ô	order, all	v	very, save
		oi	oil, toy	w	will, woman
f	fat, if	ou	out, now	y	you, yet
g	go, bag	p	pet, cup	z	zero, breeze
h	he, how	r	run, try	zh	measure, seizure

ə occurs only in unaccented syllables and represents the sound of *a* in *a*bout, *e* in tak*e*n, *i* in penc*i*l, *o* in lem*o*n, and *u* in circ*u*s.

FOREIGN SOUNDS

Y as in French *lune,* German *süss.* Pronounce ē as in *equal* with the lips rounded for ü as in *rule.*

œ as in French *deux,* German *könig.* Pronounce ā as in *age* with the lips rounded for ō as in *open.*

N as in French *bon.* The N is not pronounced, but shows that the vowel before it is nasalized.

H as in German *ach,* Scottish *loch.* Pronounce k without closing the breath passage.